# THE ENCYCLOPEDIA OF COUNTRY MUSIC

**SECOND EDITION**

Edited by **PAUL KINGSBURY, MICHAEL McCALL,**
and **JOHN W. RUMBLE**

with the assistance of Michael Gray and Jay Orr

**FIRST EDITION**

Edited by **PAUL KINGSBURY**

with the assistance of Daniel Cooper, Laura Garrard,
and John W. Rumble

# THE ENCYCLOPEDIA OF COUNTRY MUSIC

## SECOND EDITION

THE ULTIMATE GUIDE
TO THE MUSIC

COMPILED BY THE STAFF OF THE

**COUNTRY MUSIC HALL OF FAME®
AND MUSEUM**

OXFORD
UNIVERSITY PRESS

# OXFORD

UNIVERSITY PRESS

Oxford University Press, Inc., publishes works that further
Oxford University's objective of excellence
in research, scholarship, and education.

Oxford New York
Auckland   Cape Town   Dar es Salaam   Hong Kong   Karachi
Kuala Lumpur   Madrid   Melbourne   Mexico City   Nairobi
New Delhi   Shanghai   Taipei   Toronto

With offices in
Argentina   Austria   Brazil   Chile   Czech Republic   France   Greece
Guatemala   Hungary   Italy   Japan   Poland   Portugal   Singapore
South Korea   Switzerland   Thailand   Turkey   Ukraine   Vietnam

Published by Oxford University Press, Inc.
198 Madison Avenue, New York, NY 10016
www.oup.com

Library of Congress Cataloging-in-Publication Data
The encyclopedia of country music: the ultimate guide to the music/compiled by the staff of the
Country Music Hall of Fame and Museum;  edited by Paul Kingsbury, Michael McCall, and John W. Rumble
with the assistance of Michael Gray and Jay Orr.—2nd ed.
p. cm.
ISBN 978-0-19-539563-1
1. Country music—Encyclopedias. I. Kingsbury, Paul. II. McCall, Michael. III. Rumble, John Woodruff.
IV. Gray, Michael. V. Orr, Jay. VI. Country Music Hall of Fame and Museum (Nashville, Tenn.)
ML102.C7E54 2012
781.64203—dc22
2010045104

1 3 5 7 9 8 6 4 2
Printed in the United States of America
on acid-free paper

# CONTENTS

## THE SOUND SEEN: COUNTRY ALBUM COVER ART

## APPENDICES

# FOREWORD

For me, country music has always been connected to family. I remember falling in love with music as my grandmother played the piano and my mother blew on the harmonica. I remember tagging along with my father to local hoedowns. I remember my older brother helping me learn my first chords on the guitar. I cherish those memories like I cherish my family photo albums.

Since moving to Nashville, I have looked at the country music community as family, too. The Country Music Hall of Fame and Museum is the keeper of that family history. The museum's vast collection, the largest and finest of its kind, is like a big family album for those of us who love country music.

That is why the Country Music Hall of Fame and Museum is so important to me. In country music, as in many things, it's crucial that we comprehend and hold onto what preceded us. We must collect, study, and cherish the music and musicians of the past, not just because they brought us to where we are now, but because their triumphs and trials tell an amazing American story. We need to know about their lives as much as we need to know their music. Every item the museum collects—every instrument, every article of clothing, every book, every film and video, every interview, every note of music—helps make that story clearer and more real to us.

But the museum's mission isn't just to collect; it also is to study, to translate, to exhibit—and to publish. The beautiful museum in downtown Nashville is only one way this great institution shares its collective knowledge with the public. This grand book is yet another important way that information reaches fans and researchers worldwide.

I've always considered the *Encyclopedia of Country Music* as the greatest of family albums. Here are the most important careers and stories, through the ages, and all together, complete with photos and well-researched details that compile the facts and statistics while adding context and perspective.

I'm proud to say this fine, immense book has been updated with a second edition. It brings the story of my country music family forward another generation.

**—VINCE GILL**

# INTRODUCTION

The first edition of this work, published by Oxford University Press in 1998, was compiled by the staff of the Country Music Hall of Fame and Museum and edited by Paul Kingsbury, with the assistance of Daniel Cooper, Laura Garrard, and John W. Rumble. This revised and updated edition builds on that pioneering effort. As Kingsbury noted in his introduction to the original edition, performers, broadcasters, record companies, and journalists have been debating what to call country music and how to define it ever since the music emerged as a commercial form in the 1920s. Because our diverse society has engendered many different kinds of music and because musicians typically borrow from each other, there have never been rigid boundaries among American musical styles, and performers have delighted in crossing these porous borders. Still, the advantage of hindsight brings country's evolution into focus.

After World War I, an economic depression led recording executives to seek new markets outside the realms of Tin Pan Alley pop tunes, John Philip Sousa marches, and operatic performances by the likes of Enrico Caruso. The advent of commercial radio broadcasting in 1920 gave this quest new urgency; after all, why pay for recordings when one could buy a radio set and be entertained for free? As a result, record companies began developing two overlapping streams of American vernacular music: blues and jazz, on the one hand, and what would come to be called country music on the other.

Although black and white musicians alike embraced these traditions and sometimes performed together, record catalogs often listed jazz and blues artists under the heading "Race Music," and record labels typically marketed black performers to African American audiences. Likewise, labels aimed recordings by white rural fiddlers, stringbands, ballad singers, and sacred quartets at white consumers. Pioneering artists of both races drew on many sources: fiddle tunes and folk songs brought from the British Isles and handed down through generations; American story songs recounting murders, train wrecks, and natural disasters; Tin Pan Alley songs penned for touring vaudeville performers and minstrel troupes and spread into the hinterlands by medicine shows and tent shows; African American folk music and the commercial styles it inspired, including blues, ragtime, and jazz; and gospel music disseminated through itinerant "singing school" teachers and traveling quartets sponsored by hymnal publishers. Much of this music was absorbed into rural folk tradition, especially in the South.

Record companies and music publishers devised various names for white, rural music, including "Old Familiar Tunes," "Old Time Melodies of the Sunny South," "Hill Country Songs and Ballads," and "Mountain Ballads and Old Time Songs." A more common name, used by businessmen and performers alike, was "Hillbilly"—a pejorative term to some, but claimed proudly by many a country entertainer. By the early 1940s, this had changed to "folk," and in 1949 *Billboard* magazine adopted the term "country and western," later switching to "country."

Whatever its stylistic variations, country music has been marked by simple melodies and direct, down-to-earth lyrics that deal realistically with everyday experiences, such as family, work, love won and lost, patriotism, death, and religion. Country professionals traditionally have come from working-class backgrounds and sung to audiences of similar origins, though the music has always claimed followers from every walk of life. Characteristically, country singers have taken an unpretentious approach to performing and developed close and lasting relationships with their fans.

Knowing that these qualities gave their music market potential, southern hillbilly musicians or their regional business allies took the lead in gaining the attention of northern recording company executives, who, by 1920, had held sessions with jazz and blues acts. Eck Robertson and Henry Gilliland, two southern fiddlers, walked uninvited into Victor's New York offices and recorded a number of sides on June 30 and July 1, 1922. The company eventually issued three 78s but did not record either musician again until 1929. Meanwhile, Atlanta merchant Polk Brockman persuaded New York–based Ralph Peer, then an OKeh executive stopping in Atlanta in search of blues singers, to record local fiddling champion Fiddlin' John Carson and thus give Brockman the means to boost his sales of record players. Issued in July 1923, Carson's "The Little Old Log Cabin in the Lane" b/w "The Old Hen Cackled and the Rooster's Going to Crow" was country's first commercially successful record. Within three years, Vernon Dalhart's Victor pairing of "The Wreck of the Old 97" and "The Prisoner's Song" became the genre's first million-selling disc. A Texan who had specialized in light-operatic recordings, Dalhart sang in a formal manner that some listeners (and, later, some scholars) considered stilted, but his precise diction made his performances accessible to a broad audience.

Then as now, Peer and his counterparts at other labels used sales as their yardstick, not purity or authenticity (however these qualities might be determined). Success prompted them to redouble their efforts in combing the South for recording talent. In towns with radio stations, they scheduled sessions with hillbilly radio artists—typically in local radio studios, hotels, or warehouses—and recorded their most popular numbers. Recording costs were low, and even minimal sales would cover the investment. Executives also relied on performers to recruit prospects. Peer, who switched from OKeh to Victor, found an ally in Ernest V. "Pop" Stoneman, a singer and instrumentalist who had a hit with "The Titanic" on OKeh and began selling well on Victor in 1926. Stoneman lined up several musicians for sessions Peer planned for Bristol, Tennessee, in the summer of 1927. There, Peer recorded Stoneman with various friends and family members, but two acts drawn by Peer's advertising soon exceeded Stoneman in fame and influence: the Carter Family and Jimmie Rodgers. Through hit recordings, personal appearances, and radio broadcasts, the Carters established country's domestic tradition emphasizing home and family, while Rodgers, though often paying homage to these themes, became the model for the male country singer—the rambling, world-wise troubadour who entertains listeners simply with his songs and his guitar.

By the early 1930s, the hillbilly field encompassed various styles—solo singing, family and duet harmony, Cajun music, and western swing, in addition to stringband music, whether old-timey or hot and jazzy. As the decades passed, new variants evolved: honky-tonk and bluegrass by the late 1940s; rockabilly in the 1950s; the pop-influenced Nashville Sound, the hard-edged sounds of Bakersfield, and the beginnings of country-rock in the 1960s; full-blown country-pop in the 1970s and early 1980s; and various hybrid styles since then. Along the way, businesspeople, fans, and music critics have voiced their own ideas about sounds and singers that qualify as country. In light of today's short, stylistically restrictive playlists, defining the genre by the music now played on country radio would be far too limiting, and this encyclopedia deliberately reflects country's diversity, present as well as past.

As the music itself has changed, country has long since proven its popularity beyond its original southern stronghold. It has become a major component of the U.S. music industry, with cable TV channels, satellite radio channels, Internet exposure, more than 2,000 full-time country radio stations, and artists whose album sales and concert-attendance figures rival those of rock stars. Therefore, while emphasizing performers, we have approached country music as both art and enterprise, and readers will find entries on important recording companies, music publishers, and other corporations, along with entries for radio and TV stations and programs, broadcasting personalities, promoters, songwriters, and musicians.

The opening of the Country Music Hall of Fame and Museum on Nashville's Music Row in April 1967 reflected the rapidly growing country music industry. It also demonstrated the foresight of its leaders in creating an institution that would document the music's history while advocating country's importance as a part of American culture. In addition to costumes and musical instruments needed for museum exhibits, staff began collecting books, recordings, and other resources for a library that has expanded steadily since then. In 2001 the museum moved to a 140,000-square-foot facility in downtown Nashville, where it has greatly expanded its school and public programs. Today the museum's Frist Library and Archive houses costumes, instruments, sound recordings, photos, clipping files, books and periodicals, musicians' union contracts, record producers' files, films and videotapes, song manuscripts and songbooks, and a large number of recorded interviews with country music veterans. These vast holdings comprise one of the world's largest and finest collections relating to a single form of popular music. Combined with staff expertise, these materials undergird the museum's exhibitions, programs, publications, and CD/DVD reissues while facilitating staff assistance to the academic community, print and broadcast journalists, broadcast producers, and documentary filmmakers. In 2011 the museum announced plans for an expansion of some 210,000 square feet.

Creating a one-volume reference work required that we limit the number of entries; updating also forced us to make many difficult choices. We have confined ourselves almost exclusively to the years since 1922, when country performers first began broadcasting on the new medium of radio and made their first recordings. Moreover, we have focused on country music in the United States, though we certainly acknowledge country's worldwide popularity and the country scenes that flourish in other nations. We have included those persons and entities that, in our judgment, have had the greatest influence on country music, even if certain individuals were also active outside the country field and did not consider themselves country. The march of time has given us new perspective on the original edition of the encyclopedia. Some subjects assigned entries then have faded in importance in the ensuing years. Those entries were deleted to make way for some ninety new entries and two new essays. Additionally, we have updated and revised all entries and appendices from the original edition. For several reasons, we eliminated the "representative recordings" listed in that edition. With the volatile state of the recording industry, the ready availability of information about recordings on the Internet, and the increasing popularity of digital formats such as iTunes, we felt that any attempt to point readers to particular recordings would be superfluous, if not downright futile.

As with the original volume, we enlisted both staff writers and nonstaff scholars, music journalists, and other experts to produce this new edition. They supplement the work of the 150 experts who contributed to the original edition. Authors for both editions relied on the museum's rich collections in helping to make this work what we believe to be the most accurate, authoritative, and accessible volume of its kind.

How to use this encyclopedia:

1. Entries are titled and alphabetized by the most commonly used name for that person or organization (e.g., the Big Bopper rather than J. P. Richardson, ASCAP rather than the American Society of Composers, Authors, and Publishers). Wherever possible, we have included full names for individuals and business enterprises within entry texts.
2. Cross-references to other entries are indicated within entry texts in small capitals.
3. See the appendices in the back for tables of record sales and major awards.
4. If you wish to find additional information, we encourage you to visit the Country Music Hall of Fame and Museum, and to visit our website at www.CountryMusicHallofFame.org

**—MICHAEL McCALL AND JOHN W. RUMBLE**

# ACKNOWLEDGMENTS

This encyclopedia has required the dedication of many people, all of whom deserve recognition for their significant contributions to this work. Our thanks go first of all to the writers who prepared entries and essays; they are experts, and they responded enthusiastically to the challenge to compile the most authoritative encyclopedia in the country field. We are grateful to the Board of Officers and Trustees and the hardworking staff of the Country Music Hall of Fame and Museum for aiding the production of this volume in innumerable ways. For farsighted guidance and support, thanks to former Director Bill Ivey and Director Kyle Young. Thanks in particular go to museum staff past and present who worked diligently to ensure the accuracy and relevance of each of the encyclopedia's entries, especially Michael Gray, Kent Henderson, Jay Orr, Bob Pinson, and Ronnie Pugh. Other staff members who made valuable contributions include Jonita Aadland, Sally Allen, Steve Betts, Mick Buck, Lauren Bufferd, Tim Davis, William P. Davis, Warren Denney, Chrissie Dickinson, Lauren Finney, Linda Gross, Elek Horvath, Bob Kramer, Tracy Landino, Mark Medley, Michael Manning, Becky Miley, Lee Rowe, Laura Seivert, Chris Skinker, Alan Stoker, Carolyn Tate, Tina Wright, and the staff of Hatch Show Print. For help in compiling our invaluable databases, thanks to John Knowles. For administrative assistance, thanks to LeAnn Bennett and Kelley Sallee Snead. Thanks also to Volunteer and Intern Coordinator Sandy Conatser and many energetic and dedicated interns and volunteers: Shannon Becker, David and Sallylou Cloyd, Kara Furlong, Cindy Gray, Amanda James, Rob Porter, Elizabeth Potts, Charley Stefl, and Charlotte Walker. Volunteer Nancy Kruh deserves special recognition for her editorial efforts. For contributions of incalculable value at every stage of producing the first edition, thanks to Daniel Cooper. Our gratitude and appreciation go to Laura Garrard, Ashley LaRoche, and John Gouge, each of whom, during their respective tenures, helped to manage this project on a daily basis and keep it running smoothly. Laura was particularly involved in assisting with editing the final manuscript for the original edition, and John shepherded the revised edition to completion. In producing the second edition, we are grateful to William P. and Marlys Davis for genealogical research, Gene McKay and Liz Naldrett at Inside Radio/M Street Corp., and Country Aircheck's Chuck Aly. As he has on many occasions, Les Leverett provided invaluable assistance with photographs. Finally, thanks to Mary Araneo, Casper Grathwohl, Richard Johnson, Ben Keene, Megan Kennedy, Soo Mee Kwon, Grace Labatt, Maribeth Anderson Payne, Jennifer Quigley, Max Sinsheimer, Jonathan Wiener, and Damon Zucca at Oxford University Press for their unstinting support of this project and their considerable editorial expertise.

**—PAUL KINGSBURY, MICHAEL McCALL, AND JOHN W. RUMBLE**

## Abbott Records

established in Hollywood, California, fall 1951

Hollywood-based Abbott Records was an important independent label in country music in the early 1950s. It was founded by Fabor Robison, primarily to promote the career of country singer Johnny Horton. The name Abbott came from Robison's partner, a drugstore owner who put up part of the funding. Though Horton had no major hits on Abbott, Robison soon found and recorded artists such as Jim Reeves, who had his first #1 hit, "Mexican Joe," on the label, and Mitchell Torok, whose record "Caribbean" was a #1 country hit in 1953. Many of Abbott's artists as well as studio musicians were drawn from Shreveport's KWKH and its *Louisiana Hayride* show. By 1954 Robison had turned most of his attention to a new label, Fabor Records. —*Stacey Wolfe*

## Nathan Abshire

b. Gueydan, Louisiana, June 27, 1913; d. May 13, 1981

Cajun accordionist Nathan Abshire learned much of his music from his parents and an uncle, all of whom played the accordion. He was also strongly influenced by pioneer Creole accordionist Amédé Ardoin, with whom he often played dances. Abshire began performing at age eight, when he appeared at a dance hall in Mermentau Cove. In the 1930s he recorded for Bluebird Records with the Rayne-Bo Ramblers, but the 1940s saw a decline in the popularity of the accordion in Cajun music, and Abshire's career suffered as a result.

In 1949 Abshire helped revive the popularity of the accordion with his hit recording of "Pine Grove Blues" on the O.T. label. He followed this with other, moderately successful recordings, such as "Pine Grove Boogie," "La Valse de Holly Beach," and "Shamrock Waltz," but was unable to duplicate the success of "Pine Grove Blues." Abshire's career enjoyed another upturn when he was discovered by folk music enthusiasts during the folk music revival of the 1960s and 1970s. One of the best-loved and most influential figures in Cajun music, he remained a favorite on the folk festival circuit until his death in 1981. —*Charlie Seemann*

## Accordion

The accordion is an instrument made of an airtight box in which a bellows pushes air through free reeds. A free reed is a tongue made of metal or wood, attached at one end over a close-fitting opening through which the free end vibrates when air passes over it. The period from 1818 to 1848 was the time of development of a whole new group of musical instruments, the free reed instruments, today represented by the accordion, the harmonium, and the harmonica. In the early nineteenth century, much experimentation was done in developing effective reed instruments. The single-row melodeon, the lap organ, and the Viennese Physharmonica were a few of the first experiments. One of the earliest popular accordions was the concertina, an instrument with an octagonally shaped body, a very complete chromatic scale of notes (divided between the two sides of the body), and double-action reeds (the tone is different according to whether the air is drawn or blown through the reeds). This instrument was perfected in 1844 by Charles Wheatstone of England. The first famed player of this instrument was the Italian Giulio Regondi, followed by the Englishman Richard Blagrove.

In the twentieth century, the accordion gained its greatest popularity in 1910, when various makers, notably Mariano Dallapé of Italy, began to make the reeds out of steel. Steel reeds have a steadier pitch and a much greater volume, thus giving them the bite and power to hold the attention of an audience. The popular types of accordion in this century are the single-row diatonic, a small rectangular instrument with one row of double-action reeds; the double row, larger with two rows of double-action or diatonic reeds; the triple row with three rows of double-action reeds; the triple row with a chromatic scale (a scale containing all the accidental, or sharp and flat, notes); and lastly the piano-key accordion, a large accordion with single-action reeds (reeds that make the same tone whether played by pushing or drawing air through them) and a piano-style keyboard. The piano-key accordion was first developed in Vienna and Paris and later adopted in Italy and Germany.

The accordion has been used in several styles of country music, particularly in the western songs of the singing cowboys, in Cajun music, and in conjunto music. Sally Ann Forrester even played the instrument briefly in Bill Monroe's Blue Grass Boys during the early 1940s. Probably the most famous accordionist in country music was Golden West Cowboys bandleader Pee Wee King. In the mid-1800s German settlers introduced the diatonic accordion to the Acadian population of southwestern Louisiana, and it soon became a key ingredient of the Cajun sound. Among its famous practitioners have been Joseph Falcon, Iry LeJeune, Lawrence Walker, Nathan Abshire, Octa Clark, and Clifton Chenier. More recently, Zachary Richard, Steve Riley, Wayne Toups, and this author's husband, Marc Savoy, have carried on the tradition of the accordion in Cajun music. Flaco Jimenez is a leading accordionist in the conjunto tradition. —*Ann Allen Savoy*

## ACE
established in Nashville, Tennessee, November 4, 1974; ended September 25, 1981

Following the October 14, 1974, *CMA Awards Show*, which saw Australian pop star OLIVIA NEWTON-JOHN win the Female Vocalist of the Year award, GEORGE JONES and TAMMY WYNETTE hosted a meeting of twenty-two other country artists at their home in Nashville. Artists attending included BILL ANDERSON, JIM ED BROWN, BRENDA LEE, BARBARA MANDRELL, DOLLY PARTON, CAL SMITH, HANK SNOW, MEL TILLIS, CONWAY TWITTY, PORTER WAGONER, DOTTIE WEST, and FARON YOUNG. A week later this group announced the formation of the Association of Country Entertainers (ACE), an organization restricted to country performers. Ostensibly, these Nashville-based artists united to look after the specific interests of entertainers and to bolster the CMA's efforts in promoting country music growth worldwide. They announced that they were primarily concerned about inadequate entertainer representation in the CMA's board of directors and problems with country radio's playlists. But owing to the timing of ACE's formation and public statements made ten days after their first meeting, many observers concluded that the organization's purpose was to protest the increasing acceptance of pop singers in the country community and that ACE was opposed to change. In fact, ACE convened a screening committee to determine the country credentials of prospective ACE members.

Two years later, on November 4, 1976, ACE presented a more carefully refined set of views during a press conference that focused on problems arising from short radio playlists and suggested a need for additional choice in country radio formats. ACE never had adequate funding to do its job, and the office closed in 1981.

The artists most active in ACE were all connected with the GRAND OLE OPRY. They included GRANDPA JONES, ERNEST TUBB, Vic Willis (of THE WILLIS BROTHERS), JEAN SHEPARD, HANK SNOW, LITTLE ROY WIGGINS, Patsy Stoneman, JUSTIN TUBB, DEL WOOD, Oscar Sullivan (LONZO & OSCAR), GEORGE MORGAN, WILMA LEE & STONEY COOPER, CONNIE SMITH, Barbara Mandrell, Charlie Louvin (who continued on the Opry after THE LOUVIN BROTHERS broke up), BILL CARLISLE, Jesse McReynolds (of JIM & JESSE), BILLY GRAMMER, and LITTLE JIMMY DICKENS. —*Paul W. Soelberg*

## ACM
established in Los Angeles, California, 1964

The stated mission of the Academy of Country Music, a trade organization formed by Tommy Wiggins, EDDIE MILLER, and Chris and Mickey Christensen, is "to enhance and promote the growth of country music." This mission was undertaken in 1964 by a combined membership of performers and fans. Many key figures in West Coast country, including TEX WILLIAMS, JOHNNY BOND, and CLIFFIE STONE, served as presidents; EDDIE DEAN and JIMMY WAKELY were also active in the organization, which focused on thirteen western states and California-based country artists for its first ten years.

Initially known as the Country & Western Music Academy and renamed the Academy of Country Music in 1974, the organization presented its first awards—for 1965 accomplishments—in 1966, one year before the Nashville-based CMA adopted a similar program. Among the winners, determined by membership vote, were BUCK OWENS, BONNIE OWENS, MERLE HAGGARD, and ROGER MILLER. Beginning in 1972, ACM's awards show was broadcast nationally on ABC. In 1979, longtime ACM executive director Bill Boyd and TV director Gene Weed—with the assistance of Dick Clark Productions—moved the highly rated program to NBC and later to CBS.

Following Boyd's death in 1995, Fran Boyd succeeded her husband until her retirement in 2002, when Bob Romeo took the reins and continued ACM's national expansion. The awards show moved from Los Angeles to Las Vegas in 2003. An associate membership program created in 2004 allowed fans to vote online for the Video of the Year Award, and beginning in 2008 they could vote for ACM's Entertainer of the Year Award following selection of nominees by the organization's professional members. —*Jonny Whiteside*

## Roy Acuff
b. Maynardville, Tennessee, September 15, 1903; d. November 23, 1992

Named the King of Country Music by baseball great Dizzy Dean, Roy Claxton Acuff emerged as a star during the early 1940s. He helped intensify the star system at the GRAND OLE OPRY and remained its leading personality until his death. In so doing, he formed an important bridge between country's rural STRINGBAND era and the modern era of star singers backed by fully amplified bands. In addition, he cofounded ACUFF-ROSE PUBLICATIONS with songwriter FRED ROSE, thus laying an important cornerstone of the Nashville music industry.

Although he helped bring country music to the city and to the world of big business, Acuff came from a rural, folk-based background. His father farmed while also serving as Maynardville's postmaster and as pastor of a local Baptist church. As a youth, Acuff soaked in music of all sorts: folk ballads and fiddle tunes learned from neighbors and kin, hymns learned from itinerant singing school instructors, recordings of early country artists, and even some of the classical vocal training pursued by his sister Sue after the family moved to Fountain City, a Knoxville suburb. But Acuff's real love at the time was sports; in high school he lettered in football, basketball, and baseball.

*Roy Acuff*

After graduation, Acuff turned down a scholarship to nearby Carson-Newman College and worked temporarily at a variety of jobs, including that of railroad "call boy," the one responsible for rounding up other workers as the need arose. He also played semiprofessional baseball and boxed informally. Early in 1929, major-league baseball scouts recruited Acuff for training camp, but his collapse during a game—an aftereffect of earlier sunstroke—prompted a nervous breakdown and sidelined him for most of 1930.

During his recuperation, Acuff began to practice his fiddle, and in 1932 he worked a MEDICINE SHOW tour of the Tennessee-Virginia mountains that fired his enthusiasm for show business. Next, he began playing square dances and other gatherings with various local musicians, including Lonnie Wilson and BEECHER "PETE" KIRBY, who would both become longtime members of his band. Radio broadcasts on Knoxville's WROL and WNOX widened his experience. It was a WROL announcer, in fact, who named Acuff's band the Crazy Tennesseans. His radio fame caught the attention of AMERICAN RECORD CORPORATION (ARC) producer W. R. CALAWAY, who brought the band to Chicago to cut their first twenty numbers in 1936. Follow-up sessions yielded recordings released on a series of department-store labels, budget priced for Depression-era buyers.

Acuff tried to gain a spot on the Grand Ole Opry, but the Opry's GEORGE D. HAY repeatedly refused his services until promoter J. L. FRANK intervened on Acuff's behalf. A 1937 guest shot produced no results, but another, on February 5, 1938, did the trick when Acuff's performance of the classic "The Great Speckled Bird" generated sacks of fan mail. J. L. Frank suggested a new band name, the Smoky Mountain Boys, and WSM executives HARRY STONE and DAVID STONE immediately put the singer at the center of a budding star system, pushing another Acuff trademark song, "Wabash Cannon Ball," equally hard. His clear, heartfelt vocals modernized the era's predominant stringband sound just enough to seem both innovative and traditional.

Early in the 1940s, Acuff zoomed to the top of his field with help from WSM's 50,000-watt transmitter, Opry promotion, and his status as headliner of the PRINCE ALBERT SHOW, the Opry's NBC network segment begun in October 1939. Fast-selling SONGBOOKS; hit records such as "Wreck on the Highway" and "Fireball Mail," for COLUMBIA RECORDS' OKeh label; mushrooming gate receipts on the road; and appearances in a series of films all boosted his income to the $200,000 mark in 1942. In that year he formed Acuff-Rose Publications—legally a partnership between Acuff's wife, Mildred, and FRED ROSE—a company that laid the foundation for country music publishing in Nashville while providing the Acuffs with their greatest source of wealth.

Acuff's star did not shine as brightly during the late 1940s. The rise of HONKY-TONK MUSIC, exemplified by the Opry's ERNEST TUBB, and a smoother, pop-oriented brand of country music personified by EDDY ARNOLD were eclipsing Acuff's OLD-TIME sound. But his music remained highly popular, and he remained an important star in country music's growing constellation of hit-making artists. Although he left the Opry during 1946–47 in a salary dispute, he returned to host the *Royal Crown Cola Show* segment. He also opened a recreational park near Clarksville, Tennessee; ran—unsuccessfully—for the governorship of Tennessee on the Republican ticket in 1948; and made his first international tour with an Opry troupe that performed at U.S. military bases in Europe in 1949. His subsequent travels outside the U.S. mainland included Alaska, Korea, Japan, the Caribbean, and the Mediterranean.

By the early 1950s, Acuff could easily have retired, but he remained active, recording for CAPITOL, DECCA, MGM, and, after 1957, HICKORY RECORDS, a label he formed with Fred Rose and WESLEY ROSE in 1953. His records charted occasionally during the 1950s, but his sales generally amounted to a small, if steady, 25,000 copies per release. Combined with falling road show receipts during the late '50s and early '60s, his modest sales prompted him temporarily to incorporate a snare drum and electric guitar into his band, but he ultimately dropped these experiments and returned to his standby all-acoustic sound. After he suffered serious injuries in a July 1965 car wreck that also nearly killed band member SHOT JACKSON, he began to speak of retiring from the road, though he would continue to make personal appearances for some time to come.

In 1971 Acuff received a substantial boost by participating in the famous *Will the Circle Be Unbroken* album project, which featured the NITTY GRITTY DIRT BAND and a number of country artists. This added to the exposure he'd gained on the college circuit during the 1960s folk music revival. Other testaments to his continuing popularity were the 1974 chart-making records "Back in the Country" and "Old Time Sunshine Song," composed by Acuff-Rose singer-songwriter EDDY RAVEN.

Although appearances on *HEE HAW* and TV specials also kept Acuff in the public eye, his primary showcase continued to be the Grand Ole Opry. The Roy Acuff Theater at OPRYLAND, the Roy Acuff Museum (housing his collection of instruments and other memorabilia), and his long-held role as the Opry's senior statesman gave him a status that no Opry star has surpassed.

Acuff was elected the first living member of THE COUNTRY MUSIC HALL OF FAME in 1962. —*John W. Rumble*

## Acuff-Rose Publications
established in 1942

As Nashville's first country music publishing company, Acuff-Rose Publications was a key player in the city's emergence as a music center beginning in the early 1940s. The company was organized in 1942 by GRAND OLE OPRY star ROY ACUFF and Nashville songwriter FRED ROSE. Acuff put up $25,000 he had saved from sales of SONGBOOKS, while Rose contributed his personal songwriting catalog as capital. As it turned out, Rose, who ran the firm, never had to touch Acuff's working capital, due to Acuff-Rose's earnings from early hits with BOB WILLS, Acuff, and BOB ATCHER. After the war, the company had continuing success with such artists as CURLY FOX & TEXAS RUBY, EDDY ARNOLD, and PAUL HOWARD, all of whom scored hits with Acuff-Rose material.

The firm's most significant connection, however, was with HANK WILLIAMS. He began publishing songs regularly through Acuff-Rose in 1946 and signed an exclusive writer's contract with the company in 1948. In addition, Rose steered Williams to a profitable recording contract with MGM, beginning in 1947. Besides Williams's own country hits, Rose and his son WESLEY ROSE, who came aboard in 1945 as general manager, secured numerous lucrative recordings of Williams's songs by pop acts. Other memorable Acuff-Rose copyrights of the late 1940s and early 1950s included "Tennessee Waltz," a country hit for PEE WEE KING and a pop smash for Patti Page, and "Chattanoogie Shoe Shine Boy," a dual-market chart-topper for RED FOLEY.

During these same years, Acuff-Rose pioneered in advocating songwriters' interests. In 1948 the Roses worked out the

"Nashville Plan" with BMI to secure performance ROYALTIES for songwriters. Acuff-Rose would pay writers a portion of its BMI earnings, for which BMI would reimburse the company. In 1953 Acuff and the Roses established HICKORY RECORDS as an outlet for rising songwriters and recording artists. (In 1959, the Acuff-Rose Artists Corporation, a booking agency, joined the complex.)

Wesley Rose ran the publishing firm successfully after his father died in 1954. From the late 1950s into the early 1970s, Acuff-Rose remained a power in the country and pop fields, helping to develop singers and songwriters such as THE EVERLY BROTHERS, MARTY ROBBINS, DON GIBSON, JOHN D. LOUDERMILK, ROY ORBISON, MICKEY NEWBURY, EDDY RAVEN, and DALLAS FRAZIER. (Earlier, Acuff-Rose had been responsible for bringing ace songwriters BOUDLEAUX AND FELICE BRYANT to Nashville.) Beginning in 1957, Acuff-Rose set up offices abroad. The company's development of new writers and artists waned after the early 1970s, but the firm's impressive catalog continued to generate hits, making it an attractive purchase by Gaylord Broadcasting in 1985, when Acuff-Rose became part of Gaylord's Opryland Music Group. JERRY BRADLEY ran this publishing operation until it was purchased by Sony/ATV Music Publishing in 2002. —*John W. Rumble*

## Kay Adams
b. Knox City, Texas, April 9, 1941

During the mid-1960s, Princetta Kay Adams recorded a series of concept albums in the hard-country style popularized by BAKERSFIELD legends BUCK OWENS and MERLE HAGGARD. *Wheels and Tears* (1966) is perhaps the best of Adams's records. A collection of truck-driving songs sung from a woman's point of view, it included the minor (but enduring) hit single "Little Pink Mack."

Raised in Vernon, Texas, Adams moved to Bakersfield in 1964. There she met producer CLIFFIE STONE, who signed her to the Tower label, a subsidiary of CAPITOL RECORDS. Adams's first single for Tower, "Honky-Tonk Heartache" (1964), earned her the 1965 ACM award for Most Promising Female Vocalist (Merle Haggard won Most Promising Male Vocalist honors the same year). Adams starred in a country music opera (*The Legend of Johnny Brown*, 1966) and appeared in the road shows of Owens and Haggard. She subsequently recorded for Capitol, Granite, Ovation, and Frontline. In 1996, after years of relative professional inactivity, Adams teamed up with Nashville neo-HONKY-TONK act BR549 to record "Mama Was a Rock (Daddy Was a Rolling Stone)" for *Rig Rock Deluxe*, a collection of truck-driving songs compiled by Jeremy Tepper of Diesel Only Records and Jake Guralnick for the Upstart label. —*Bill Friskics-Warren*

## Trace Adkins
b. Springhill, Louisiana, January 13, 1962

Tracy Darrell "Trace" Adkins, a six-and-a-half-foot-tall Louisiana HONKY-TONK singer with a rich baritone voice, earned his first #1 single and platinum album in 1997, the same year he was named Top New Male Artist by the ACM. Adkins began singing in the gospel quartet New Commitment while in high school and recorded two albums for an independent label. He played for Louisiana Tech University's football team and studied petroleum technology until a knee injury ended his sports career. Next, he

spent eight years as an oil derrick man and pipe fitter and joined a band that played clubs in Texas, Louisiana, New Mexico, and Mississippi.

Adkins moved to Nashville in 1992 to pursue music full time. CAPITOL RECORDS Nashville president SCOTT HENDRICKS signed him after seeing him perform at a Mount Juliet bar. In 1996, Hendricks produced the singer's platinum-selling debut album, *Dreamin' Out Loud*. Adkins penned his own debut single, the Top Twenty hit "There's a Girl in Texas," and followed with the Top Five record "Every Light in the House" and his first #1, "(This Ain't No) Thinkin' Thing." His second album, 1997's *Big Time*, was certified gold. Subsequent Top Ten singles led to his GRAND OLE OPRY induction in 2003. Adkins checked himself into a rehabilitation center for a drinking problem, but finished the year by releasing *Comin' On Strong*, which eventually went platinum.

Adkins heightened his rough-hewn image with his 2005 hit "Honky Tonk Badonkadonk," whose sensual video pushed album sales of *Songs About Me* above the 2 million mark; his role as co-headliner (with GRETCHEN WILSON) of 2006's *Redneck Revolution* tour; and his book *A Personal Stand: Observations and Opinions of a Freethinking Roughneck*, covering contemporary social and political issues.

In 2008 Adkins joined other contestants on the reality TV series *The Celebrity Apprentice*. Finishing second, he raised thousands of dollars for the Food Allergy & Anaphylaxis Network; this organization educates the public and funds research on food allergies, which had threatened his daughter Brianna's life. In that year, he notched his third #1 country single with "You're Gonna Miss This," which won ACM's Single of the Year award, and was honored with a star on Nashville's Music City Walk of Fame. He also released his tenth album, *X*, featuring "Muddy Water" and "Marry for Money." Adkins signed with Show Dog–Universal Records in January 2009 after fourteen years with Capitol. He released the album *Cowboys Back in Town* on Show Dog–Universal in August 2010. "Hillbilly Bone," a #1 duet with BLAKE SHELTON, earned Adkins the 2009 ACM Vocal Event of the Year award and the 2010 CMA Musical Event of the Year honor. —*Beverly Keel*

## AFM
established in New York, New York, November 6, 1896

The American Federation of Musicians (AFM) of the United States and Canada is the world's largest organization representing professional musicians. Through negotiating contracts, securing health care and pension benefits, and lobbying legislators, AFM works to put professional musicians "in the foreground of the cultural landscape." AFM was originally chartered in New York with Owen Miller as president. He resolved to improve musicians' wages, employment hours, and benefits. By 1906 AFM included Canada and organized more than 400 locals and represented some 45,000 members. As of 2011, membership stood at approximately 85,000 spread among 242 locals and concentrated heavily in New York City and Los Angeles, whose chapters each have some 8,000 members. Chicago's local counts some 3,200 members, and Canadian members total some 14,000, with the Toronto and Montreal locals accounting for 6,400 of these.

For more than half a century, only three presidents had headed the union: Joseph Weber, who served thirty-nine years; Frank Carothers (1914–15), and James C. Petrillo (1940–58). Petrillo called a strike against record labels, effective August 1, 1942, halting recordings. In September 1943, DECCA RECORDS became the first label to come to agreement with the union, establishing a performance trust fund to aid out-of-work musicians. A second strike, on January 1, 1948, was settled to the union's satisfaction on December 14, 1948. Ray Hair was voted AFM president in 2010.

AFM Los Angeles was chartered March 15, 1897; and AFM Chicago was chartered September 17, 1901. Nashville Local 257 was chartered December 11, 1902, with Joe Miles as president. GEORGE W. COOPER JR. held the 257-branch presidency the longest, serving successively from 1937 to 1973. HAROLD BRADLEY, elected in December 1990, was president until Dave Pomeroy assumed this role early in 2009. With its growth as a major recording center, AFM Nashville has become an important union branch, numbering some 2,500 members. —*Walt Trott*

## AFRS
established fall 1943

The Armed Forces Radio Service (AFRS) was a special program of the U.S. military created to boost the morale of U.S. servicemen overseas. The AFRS accomplished this by creating and distributing to troops 16-inch radio transcription discs providing timely information, education, and, importantly, entertainment. These transcriptions offered AFRS-produced fare, network radio broadcasts, and, starting in 1945, commercial recordings of current pop, jazz, Latin, classical, and country music. Among the important country music programs in the AFRS library are the AFRS-created *Melody Roundup* series of more than 2,000 fifteen-minute shows (originally distributed at the rate of four per week) and Nashville's long-running GRAND OLE OPRY, which was used for more than twenty-five years. Although AFRS was officially established in the fall of 1943 as a branch of the Special Services Division (SSD), in reality the SSD had already been providing the unique service one commonly associates with AFRS since summer 1942.

AFRS discs were heard on naval vessels (including submarines), in the field via mobile 50-watt suitcase units, at military hospitals abroad, and in the United States through closed-circuit broadcasts, shortwave and AFRS-developed station transmissions, and even on foreign station broadcasts via airtime provided gratis or on a lease basis. By 1945 more than 800 AFRS outlets were sharing a weekly mailing of 200 sets of discs from AFRS's primary production center, Los Angeles.

AFRS's entertainment programming emphasized music, but not to the exclusion of comedy, drama, and sports. And this philosophy continued into the television era as the AFRS became the AFRTS (Armed Forces Radio and Television Service). Since 1953, TV programs have been distributed to troops via film, videotape, and satellite. Meanwhile, AFRTS radio programming, which was originally distributed on 16-inch discs, was issued on 12-inch microgroove LPs beginning in the early 1960s and then on cassettes as of 1994. By the late 1990s, satellite radio and TV programming feeds to AFRTS made the need for older storage media almost inessential. —*Bob Pinson*

## AFTRA
established in New York, New York, 1937

The American Federation of Television and Radio Artists (AFTRA) is a national union representing television and radio artists, including announcers, actors, dancers, singers, and broadcasters. Chartered in 1937 with actor Eddie Cantor as president, today it is a 70,000-member organization, headquartered in New York City. As of 2011, Holter Graham is president of the New York chapter, which counts some 22,000 members; Stephen Burrow is executive director. The Los Angeles chapter, also chartered in 1937, boasts some 28,000 members. Ron Morgan (president) and Bill Thomas (executive director) lead AFTRA–L.A., dealing largely with TV, radio, and phonograph recordings. The Nashville chapter, founded in 1961, is 1,200 members strong and acts as local representative for the Screen Actors Guild in regard to locally produced motion pictures, commercials, and TV shows. Randall Himes has been executive director since 1986; CeCe DuBois is president as of 2011.

Country has a strong voice in the Nashville chapter. Past presidents Jim Ferguson and Louis Nunley still perform regularly. Nunley and ANITA KERR (both formerly of the ANITA KERR SINGERS) were among the local founding members. Ferguson and Nunley are past national vice presidents. "We are the only phonograph-driven local in the United States," Himes said in 1995. "We process more session reports than any other AFTRA local. We have jurisdiction for audio- and videotapes. . . . [O]ur blanket [license] fee is a contribution to the Performers Benefit Fund, which we instituted as part of our negotiations with the [GRAND OLE] OPRY." —*Walt Trott*

## Alabama
Jeffrey Alan Cook b. Fort Payne, Alabama, August 27, 1949
Teddy Wayne Gentry b. Fort Payne, Alabama, January 22, 1952
Mark Joel Herndon b. Springfield, Massachusetts, May 11, 1955
Randy Yeuell Owen b. Fort Payne, Alabama, December 13, 1949

Few bands have affected country music's commercial success as much as Alabama. Between 1980 and 1993, this family-based act took thirty-two recordings to the top of the *Billboard* country charts and sold millions of albums, substantially broadening country's audience while becoming one of the most popular acts in American musical history.

Unlike vocal groups the OAK RIDGE BOYS and THE STATLER BROTHERS, Alabama was a self-contained band—they handled the instruments as well as the vocals, an unprecedented phenomenon at the upper reaches of the country charts. Although session musicians contributed to Alabama's recordings, guitarist Randy Owen, bassist Teddy Gentry, drummer Mark Herndon, and guitarist Jeff Cook acquitted themselves as competent if not virtuosic players on the band's tours. By applying this rock & roll model to country music, Alabama paved the way for RESTLESS HEART, SHENANDOAH, and THE MAVERICKS.

Owen and Gentry are first cousins raised on farms outside Fort Payne, Alabama. Distant cousin Jeff Cook lived in town, and as teenagers the three formed a band called Wildcountry. In 1973 they quit their day jobs and played their blend of Allman Brothers–style southern rock and country-pop throughout the South, most notably at the Bowery in Myrtle Beach, South Carolina. In 1977 Wildcountry changed its name to Alabama, and in 1979 they hired rock & roller Herndon. Alabama recorded for the small labels GRT and MDJ in the late 1970s and even scored Top Forty country hits for MDJ with "I Wanna Come Over" in 1979 and "My Home's in Alabama" in 1980. This won the group an invitation to the "New Faces" show at Nashville's annual Country Radio Seminar, and their popular performance led to a contract with RCA RECORDS in April 1980.

Alabama's first RCA single, "Tennessee River," began a streak of twenty-one consecutive #1 country hits between 1980 and

*Alabama: (from left) Teddy Gentry, Jeff Cook, Randy Owen, and Mark Herndon*

1987, some of which crossed over to the pop charts. Among the more memorable singles were "Feels So Right," "Love in the First Degree" (both1981), and 1983's "The Closer You Get." (The latter also won a Grammy.) In addition, the albums *Feels So Right* (1981), *Mountain Music* (1982), *The Closer You Ge*t . . . (1983), *Roll On* (1984), *40 Hour Week* (1985), and *Greatest Hits* (1986) all went platinum and broke into the Top Thirty pop album charts.

From 1982 to 1997, Alabama sponsored the June Jam, a music festival in Fort Payne. With Alabama as the annual headliner, the June Jam drew as many as 60,000 fans at a time and raised millions for local charities.

Despite Alabama's immense commercial success, critics complained about vacuous songs and watered-down, middle-of-the-road arrangements that blurred the lines between country and pop and neglected country's musical roots. Nevertheless, fans helped the band notch Top Ten singles through the 1990s and continued to pack performance venues through Alabama's 2003 "farewell" tour, after which the act retired. Alabama also won scores of industry awards, including the CMA's Entertainer of the Year award for three consecutive years, 1982–84.

In 2005, the group was elected to THE COUNTRY MUSIC HALL OF FAME. Three years later Randy Owen issued the solo album *One on One* on BROKEN BOW RECORDS and published his memoir *Born Country: How Faith, Family, and Music Brought Me Home.* —Geoffrey Himes

## Jason Aldean
b. Macon, Georgia, February 28, 1977

With his edgy vocals and rocking country sound, Jason Aldean established himself as a hit maker of the late 2000s. His self-titled 2005 debut on the independent label BROKEN BOW RECORDS

*Jason Aldean*

went platinum and included his breakout #1 hit "Why" along with the Top Ten singles "Amarillo Sky" and "Hicktown." These achievements helped him become ACM's 2005 Top New Male Vocalist.

Born Jason Aldine Williams, Aldean was born to parents who divorced when he was young; he was raised by his mother in Georgia and spent summers with his father in Florida. His mother arranged his first performance at a VFW Hall in Macon at age fourteen, and his father later helped him book shows.

Aldean joined the house band at Nashville South, a Macon club, while in high school. After graduating, he toured the Deep South with his band. He attracted the interest of Warner/Chappell Music at an Atlanta showcase and moved to Nashville in 1998 as a songwriter before ultimately landing with Broken Bow.

His gold-selling second album *Relentless* (2007) featured two Top Ten hits ("Johnny Cash" and "Laugh Until We Cried"). His third album, *Wide Open* (2009), returned him to platinum sales with the consecutive #1 hits "She's Country," "Big Green Tractor," and "The Truth." In November 2010, Aldean released *My Kinda Party,* his fourth album, which sold nearly 200,000 copies in its first week, and included his first country rap excursion on "Dirt Road Anthem." —*Warren Denney*

## Pat Alger
b. LaGrange, Georgia, September 23, 1947

In the early 1990s, Patrick J. Alger emerged as one of Nashville's most perceptive songwriters by bringing a literary touch and insightful social commentary to the catchy song craft valued by MUSIC ROW. While he contributed significant hits to several artists, he made his biggest mark by cowriting four #1 hits and several other cuts for superstar GARTH BROOKS.

In 1973 Alger joined the Woodstock Mountain Revue, a group that included John Sebastian, Paul Butterfield, Eric Andersen, JIM ROONEY, BILL KEITH, and Happy & Artie Traum. He also recorded a duet album with Artie Traum, *From the Heart* (ROUNDER, 1980).

In 1980 Livingston Taylor recorded Alger's "First Time Love," a Top Ten adult-contemporary hit. Moving to Nashville the following year, Alger received a welcome reception, securing cuts by NANCI GRIFFITH ("Once in a Very Blue Moon," "Lone Star State of Mind"), DON WILLIAMS ("True Love"), TRISHA YEARWOOD ("Like We Never Had a Broken Heart"), and HAL KETCHUM ("Small Town Saturday Night"). KATHY MATTEA scored hits with Alger's "Goin' Gone," "She Came from Fort Worth," and "A Few Good Things Remain."

Alger also reconnected with Woodstock cohort Jim Rooney, a partner in Nashville-based Forerunner Music, a publishing company Rooney co-owned with Garth Brooks's producer, ALLEN REYNOLDS. This connection led to Brooks's enjoying chart-topping success with Alger's songs "Unanswered Prayers," "The Thunder Rolls," "What She's Doing Now," and "That Summer."

Alger was named ASCAP Songwriter of the Year in 1992, and from 1995 to 1997 he served as president of the NSAI board. Alger also has released two solo albums, *True Love and Other Stories* on SUGAR HILL and *Seeds* on LIBERTY. Alger was inducted into the NASHVILLE SONGWRITERS HALL OF FAME in 2010. —*Michael McCall*

## Gary Allan
b. Montebello, California, December 5, 1967

A distinctive, soulful singer, Gary Allan kept hard country sounds vital amid pop- and rock-influenced country hits of the 1990s and 2000s. He grew up playing honky-tonks with his father's band in California, later fronting his own group. Influenced by the music of BAKERSFIELD, Allan went gold with his debut album, *Used Heart for Sale* (DECCA, 1996).

*Smoke Rings in the Dark* (MCA, 1999), his third album, went platinum on the strength of two singles—the title track and the Top Five hit "Right Where I Need to Be." His first #1, "Man To Man," appeared on the follow-up platinum album, *Alright Guy,* in 2001.

The platinum *See If I Care* (2003) yielded two #1 hits—"Tough Little Boys" and "Nothing On but the Radio." *Tough All Over* (2005), reflecting the impact of his wife's suicide, topped *Billboard's* country album charts. During 2006, touring with supergroup RASCAL FLATTS exposed Allan to millions of new listeners while setting his straightforward style in bold relief. (That year, a *New York Times* concert reviewer praised him as "the anti-Rascal Flatts: one of country music's most stoic singers.") *Greatest Hits* and *Living Hard,* both released in 2007, went gold. His popular 2009 single "Today" was included on *Get Off on the Pain*, released in 2010. —*Warren Denney*

## Deborah Allen
b. Memphis, Tennessee, September 30, 1953

Deborah Allen (born Deborah Lynn Thurmond) was a successful Nashville songwriter before achieving popularity as a performer. In 1978 she began collaborating with Rafe VanHoy, creating hits for JOHN CONLEE, LEE GREENWOOD, JANIE FRICKE, and TANYA TUCKER. She and VanHoy married in 1982.

A former Memphis beauty queen, Allen moved to MUSIC CITY at age nineteen. After stints at OPRYLAND USA and as a backup singer for ROY ORBISON, she began recording duets with the deceased JIM REEVES in 1979. Allen added ethereal harmonies to Reeves's tracks, and three of these tunes, including "Don't Let Me Cross Over," became Top Ten country hits.

Allen's country-pop style, marked by a wall of sound and soulful singing, was showcased in her 1983 RCA hit "Baby I Lied." Three more chart successes followed in 1984. Allen cultivated a disarmingly open sexual image, posing in unclothed innocence and holding an apple on the jacket of her 1980 CAPITOL debut album, *Trouble in Paradise.* This trend continued with the Allen-in-bed cover photo of her 1984 RCA album *Let Me Be the First.* In 1987 Allen's RCA album *Telepathy* featured a Madonna-like image and a title tune by the pop star Prince.

In 1992 Allen re-emerged in the country field on the GIANT label, using her blended Memphis-Nashville style to good effect. She re-recorded her best-known songs for a CD release on CURB RECORDS in 2000. —*Mary A. Bufwack*

## Jules Verne Allen
b. Waxahachie, Texas, April 1, 1883; d. 1945

Jules Verne Allen was one of the few early singing cowboys who had actually been a working cowboy. His classic renditions of songs such as "'Long Side the Santa Fe Trail," "The Dying Cowboy," and "The Days of '49" are considered some of the finest examples of authentic traditional cowboy songs ever captured on record.

Allen began ranch work at age ten in his native Ellis County, Texas. He held various jobs, including horse wrangler, and eventually became an experienced all-around hand. He participated in trail drives from the Mexican border to railroad shipping centers in Montana. During this time he began playing guitar and performing cowboy songs for fellow ranch hands. After a World War I military stint, he returned to ranching and decided to try singing professionally. During the 1920s he began broadcasting over radio stations that eventually included WFAA in Dallas, KFI and KNX in Los Angeles, and WOAI and KTSA in San Antonio, calling himself "the Original Singing Cowboy," "Longhorn Luke," and "Shiftless." His San Antonio sponsor, the Longhorn Portland Cement Company, published a SONGBOOK titled *Cowboy Songs Sung by Longhorn Luke and His Cowboys.*

Allen began his brief recording career in 1928, cutting three songs, "Little Joe the Wrangler," "Jack O' Diamonds," and "Po' Mourner," for the Victor Talking Machine Company's Victor label. His six Victor and RCA VICTOR sessions of 1928–29 resulted in a total of twenty-four recorded performances. In 1933 the Naylor Company published *Cowboy Lore,* a book Allen compiled, including thirty-six cowboy songs and tidbits of information about ranch life. Though his recording contract was not renewed, Allen continued to perform on radio and appeared at rodeos for several years. —*Charlie Seemann*

## Red Allen
b. Pigeon Roost, Kentucky, February 12, 1930; d. April 3, 1993

A singer-guitarist with a high, mountain-flavored voice, Harley "Red" Allen was an influential figure in BLUEGRASS from the 1950s into the 1980s. His early career, centered around Dayton, Ohio, included small-label recordings, and radio and club appearances with mandolinist Frank Wakefield and banjo player Noah Crase. Allen teamed with THE OSBORNE BROTHERS in 1956, performing on the *WWVA JAMBOREE.* Before their partnership ended in 1958, they recorded sixteen sides for MGM RECORDS, among which "Once More" is considered a landmark in the development of sophisticated three-part vocal harmony in bluegrass.

In the 1960s Allen moved to Washington, D.C., often working and recording with Wakefield, including a 1963 performance at CARNEGIE HALL. His hard-driving style attracted young urban bluegrass enthusiasts DAVID GRISMAN, BILL KEITH, and Peter (Roberts) Kuykendall, who were members of Allen's Kentuckians before launching their own careers. In 1967 Allen worked with EARL SCRUGGS during LESTER FLATT's recuperation from surgery; from late 1968 until spring 1969 Allen performed and recorded in Lexington, Kentucky, with banjo player J. D. CROWE and mandolinist DOYLE LAWSON.

Before failing health forced his semiretirement in the 1980s, Allen recorded with his sons, Neal (d. 1974), Ronnie, Greg, and Harley (later a Nashville singer-songwriter), and with later versions of the Kentuckians. —*Frank and Marty Godbey*

## Rex Allen
b. Willcox, Arizona, December 31, 1920; d. December 17, 1999

The last and arguably best vocalist of the singing cowboys (although EDDIE DEAN and Ken Curtis could justifiably contend), Rex Elvie Allen possessed a voice of astonishing range and strength. He first worked as an entertainer during World War II before being called

to fill the singing cowboy slot at the *NATIONAL BARN DANCE* in 1945, following in the illustrious footsteps of GENE AUTRY and Eddie Dean. Allen remained in the cast into the late 1940s.

A trip to Hollywood followed, and the first of Allen's nineteen films for Republic, *The Arizona Cowboy,* was released in 1950; his last, *The Phantom Stallion* (1954), is considered the final singing cowboy movie, marking the end of an era in American music and film. He later starred in the television series *Frontier Doctor.* His resonant, authoritative speaking voice became familiar nationwide through a long association with Walt Disney as a narrator of more than fifty films and television shows, as well as hundreds of commercials. In his last years, living in semiretirement in his native Arizona, he helped found the Western Music Association and served as an elder statesman of the genre.

Allen's recording career began with the MERCURY label in Chicago in 1945, and, although his voice was best suited to western ballads, he occasionally appeared on the country charts, notably with "Crying in the Chapel" (1953) and "Don't Go Near the Indians" (1962).

Each of Rex Allen's three sons entered the entertainment business, and his eldest, Rex Jr. (born August 23, 1947), made a significant mark on the country charts in the 1970s and 1980s. Rex Jr. had six Top Ten hits on WARNER BROS. RECORDS in the late 1970s and is still active. In 1995 Rex Sr. and Rex Jr. teamed up for the Warner Western album *The Singing Cowboys.* —*Douglas B. Green*

## Rosalie Allen
b. Old Forge, Pennsylvania, June 27, 1924; d. September 23, 2003

Known as the Queen of the Yodelers, Rosalie Allen was born Julie Marlene Bedra, one of eleven children of Polish parents living in the coal fields of Pennsylvania.

Her story is a classic tale of the Depression. At age nine she worked and boarded in a restaurant and sent her earnings home. Fascinated with singing she heard on the radio, she defied her parents and hit the road with a hillbilly band at age thirteen, after winning a talent contest.

At nineteen Allen was gaining recognition for her elaborate yodeling. Her arrival in New York City in 1943 with DENVER DARLING's Swing Billies cowboy troupe marked the start of her solo career. With many male entertainers drafted, she became one of country music's female radio pioneers, finding popularity as a country disc jockey with her *Prairie Stars* show on New York's WOV (1944–56). She made the transition to TV with two early 1950s country programs. In addition, she owned New York City's first country record shop and wrote columns for fan magazines.

Allen made soundies (short films of performances) in the mid-1940s, and she also appeared in a 1949 feature film, *Village Barn.* She recorded with RCA VICTOR in the late 1940s; titles included "Guitar Polka (Old Monterey)," "Yodel Boogie," and "He Taught Me to Yodel." One of her biggest hits, however, was "Quicksilver," a 1950 duet with ELTON BRITT; like many Britt–Allen pairings, this recording did not feature yodeling. —*Mary A. Bufwack*

## Allen Brothers
Austin Ambrose Allen b. Sewanee, Tennessee, February 7, 1901; d. January 5, 1959
Lee William Allen b. Sewanee, Tennessee, June 1, 1906; d. February 24, 1981

One of country music's first successful BROTHER DUETS, the Allen Brothers melded Chattanooga-area folk music, blues, and vaudeville influences into a distinctive style that made them a highly influential OLD-TIME act. Unlike later brother acts, such as the BLUE SKY BOYS and the MONROE BROTHERS, who featured sentimental and gospel songs, the Allens preferred rowdy, double-entendre material, such as their biggest hit, "Salty Dog Blues." In fact, the Allens were so adept at performing white blues that in 1927 COLUMBIA RECORDS mistakenly released their "Laughin' and Cryin' Blues" in the "race" series instead of the "old-time" series. (Unamused, the Allens sued and promptly moved to the Victor Talking Machine Company's Victor label.)

The Allens toured widely, and between 1926 and 1934 they recorded for Columbia, RCA VICTOR, and ARC, making some eighty-nine sides, including hits such as "Roll Down the Line" (1930) and "Jake Walk Blues" (about the Jamaica Ginger poisoning scare, 1930). After 1934, on the heels of an unsuccessful stint in legitimate theater, both brothers left the business. Reissues of their work in the 1970s spurred new interest in their music, and Lee Allen made a brief comeback before his death in 1981. Austin died in 1959. —*Charles Wolfe*

## Shelly Lee Alley

b. Colorado County, Texas, July 6, 1894; d. June 1, 1964

Remembered as the writer of JIMMIE RODGERS's 1931 classic "Traveling Blues" and for his 1930s WESTERN SWING recordings, fiddler Shelly Lee Alley was a pop bandleader who switched to country at midcareer.

Alley led a military orchestra in San Antonio during World War I and then spent the 1920s fronting early radio and dance orchestras in the Dallas–Fort Worth area. After he made Rodgers's acquaintance and the latter recorded "Traveling Blues" (with Alley and brother Alvin providing twin fiddles) and "Gambling Barroom Blues," Alley began to concentrate on string music. He joined the original SWIFT JEWEL COWBOYS in Houston in 1933 and then took his own Cowboys to XEPN at Eagle Pass. The emergence of western swing in the mid-1930s provided Alley with an opportunity to combine his pop/jazz sensibilities with STRINGBAND instrumentation.

Alley recorded an odd mix of ballads ("My Precious Darling") and off-color blues ("She Just Wiggled Around") for the Vocalion, OKEH, and BLUEBIRD labels, using musicians such as CLIFF BRUNER and TED DAFFAN. Never attaining the level of success he believed his talent merited, he gave up performing after 1946. He wrote songs until his death, however, including MOON MULLICAN's "Broken Dreams" (1947) and BIFF COLLIE's and Little Marge's "Why Are You Blue?"(1950). Alley's "Traveling Blues" was revived by LEFTY FRIZZELL (1951) and later by MERLE HAGGARD. Alley's stepson is multi-instrumentalist western swing stalwart Clyde Brewer, who now leads the Houston-based River Road Boys, a band including Shelly Lee Alley Jr. on guitar. —*Kevin Coffey*

## Joe Allison

b. McKinney, Texas, October 3, 1924; d. August 2, 2002

As a radio personality, publishing and recording executive, and songwriter, Joe Marion Allison contributed greatly to country music from the late 1930s to the mid-1970s. After attending an Oklahoma junior college, he broke into radio as a country and pop announcer and manager for several Texas stations during the late 1940s, broadening his musical education during several tours

with TEX RITTER. In 1949 he moved to Nashville and became an influential disc jockey on WMAK.

Through the early 1950s Allison divided his time between Nashville and Pasadena, California, where for a time he succeeded TENNESSEE ERNIE FORD on KXLA. In Nashville Allison worked in TV and radio on WSM and WSIX. In 1953 he helped to found the COUNTRY MUSIC DISC JOCKEYS ASSOCIATION (CMDJA), forerunner of CMA. Late in the decade he moved to Hollywood to coproduce *Country America*, a country-pop TV show aired over the ABC network.

In the early 1960s, Allison held down two jobs: professional manager for the Hollywood-based publishing company CENTRAL SONGS and country recording chief for LIBERTY RECORDS, where he produced early recordings by HANK COCHRAN and WILLIE NELSON and helped to revive BOB WILLS's career. During these years, Allison began a long-running international radio show over the Armed Forces Radio Service (AFRS). He also wrote and produced a series of sales presentations for CMA, which helped convince advertisers and broadcasters to program country music and thus played a vital role in country radio's expansion. For his efforts he received CMA's Founding President's Award in 1964.

By 1967 Allison had become an independent producer and turned out hits such as "The Tips of My Fingers" and "Yesterday When I Was Young" with ROY CLARK and "Smoky the Bar" with HANK THOMPSON. Helming the country department for Paramount in Nashville (1970–72), Allison signed Tommy Overstreet and JOE STAMPLEY. Allison worked in a parallel capacity with CAPITOL RECORDS from 1972 to 1974, developing RED STEAGALL and producing *Tex Ritter: An American Legend*, the star's final LP.

Allison was also instrumental in launching both CMA and the COUNTRY MUSIC HALL OF FAME AND MUSEUM. He was a 1978 inductee into the NASHVILLE SONGWRITERS HALL OF FAME for numbers such as the FARON YOUNG hit "Live Fast, Love Hard, Die Young" and the JIM REEVES classic "He'll Have to Go." By the early 1980s Allison had retired from music to become an antiques dealer. —*John W. Rumble*

## American Federation of Musicians (*see* AFM)

## American Federation of Television and Radio Artists (*see* AFTRA)

## American Record Corporation

The New York–based American Record Corporation had a life span of ten years (1929–38). Founded in July 1929 (primarily through a merger of the Regal and Cameo label complexes), ARC, in turn, was bought by Consolidated Film Industries (CFI) in October 1930. As an autonomous subsidiary, ARC acquired the BRUNSWICK Record Corporation (BRC) division from Warner Brothers Pictures (December 1931) and purchased the Columbia Phonograph Company from Grigsby-Grunow (1934).

Via BRC came rights to the Vocalion and Melotone labels in addition to the Brunswick name itself. Vocalion and Brunswick label product was marketed under BRC's banner, but ARC disregarded such rights to the COLUMBIA RECORDS and OKEH RECORDS names, conveyed through Columbia Phonograph, and chose instead to market recordings on Melotone, Perfect, Banner (sold by W. T. Grant stores), Oriole (McCrory's), and Romeo (S. H. Kress). Each ARC release featured identical song couplings on the relevant labels. Sears, Roebuck also leased ARC/BRC-derived product for its Conqueror label from the early to late 1930s, but Conqueror's couplings often differed from those on the ARC/BRC labels.

During its heyday, ARC/BRC was a major marketer of recorded pop, blues, and country performances, competing successfully with RCA Victor Records, Decca Records, and others. Art Satherley and his protégé, Don Law, fulfilled A&R responsibilities for country and blues product, establishing an artist slate of such stalwarts as Roy Acuff, Gene Autry, Big Bill Broonzy, the Carlisle Brothers (Bill Carlisle), the Chuck Wagon Gang, Al Dexter, Red Foley, Blind Boy Fuller, Robert Johnson, the Light Crust Doughboys, Patsy Montana, The Prairie Ramblers, and Bob Wills, among others.

In December 1938, CFI sold its ARC/BRC subsidiary to the Columbia Broadcasting System, thus allowing CBS to acquire rights to the Columbia Records name as well as to OKeh. CBS then retired the ARC labels. In 1940, due to a licensing violation, Brunswick/Vocalion reverted to Warner Bros., which subsequently sold those label names and catalogs to Decca the following year. —*Bob Pinson*

## American Society of Composers, Authors and Publishers (*see* ASCAP)

## Americana

Americana emerged in the 1990s as a genre for artists who draw on a variety of roots-music styles or who prefer vintage sounds over contemporary trends. The music described as Americana often includes traditional country among its primary influences, but it can include echoes of bluegrass, blues, folk, rock, soul, western swing, and jazz.

Americana considers several iconoclasts among its pioneers, from country-rock purveyors Bob Dylan and Gram Parsons to groundbreaking acts Emmylou Harris, Joe Ely, Jason & The Scorchers, and Uncle Tupelo. The latter's 1990 album, *No Depression*—named for a Carter Family song—provided the title of a magazine that focused on music loosely fitting what was first described as alternative-country (or alt-country) and eventually became known as Americana.

In an effort to create a format for these category-defying musicians, San Francisco–based trade magazine *The Gavin Report* launched an Americana chart on January 20, 1995, to track the airplay of roots musicians ignored by country or adult-alternative (also known as AAA) radio stations. The chart's first week included artists Nanci Griffith, Jim Lauderdale, Nick Lowe, and The Mavericks.

In September 2000, a new trade group, the Americana Music Association, sponsored its first convention, held in Nashville. The inaugural Americana Honors and Awards program followed in 2002, with Lifetime Achievement awards given to T Bone Burnett, Emmylou Harris, and Billy Joe Shaver. In 2008 the annual gathering expanded to four days and by then was called the Americana Music Festival and Conference. Over the years, the awards program has featured such disparate artists as the Avett Brothers, Solomon Burke, Elvis Costello, Steve Earle, Patty Griffin, Levon Helm, Alison Krauss, Mavis Staples, and Neil Young.

Starting in 2010, the Grammy Awards introduced a Best Americana Album category. —*Michael McCall*

## Bill Anderson
b. Columbia, South Carolina, November 1, 1937

One of country music's most successful singer-songwriters, James William Anderson III recorded thirty-seven *Billboard* Top Ten singles between 1960 and 1978, and he has written country standards for more than fifty years. His breathy, conversational tenor earned him the nickname "Whisperin' Bill," a sobriquet bestowed by comedian Don Bowman.

While earning a degree in journalism, Anderson worked his way through the University of Georgia as DJ (WJJC–Commerce), sportswriter (*DeKalb New Era*), and performer. In 1957 he recorded "City Lights" for TNT Records in San Antonio, Texas. This honky-tonk song found its way to Columbia recording artist Ray Price, whose 1958 rendition became a #1 country hit.

Quickly signed to Decca Records, Anderson first recorded for the label in August 1958 and joined the Grand Ole Opry in July 1961. He wrote many of his #1 hits, including "Mama Sang a Song," "Still" (also a pop Top Ten), "I Get the Fever," and "My Life." He helped discover Connie Smith and wrote her #1 breakthrough, "Once a Day" (1964), plus five Top Ten followups. Others scoring substantial hits with Anderson tunes include Jim Reeves, Roger Miller, Hank Locklin, Kitty Wells, Porter Wagoner, and Cal Smith. His songs gave new life to the careers of Lefty Frizzell ("Saginaw, Michigan"), Charlie Louvin [The Louvin Brothers] ("I Don't Love You Anymore"), and Jean Shepard ("Slippin' Away"). His "Tip of My Fingers" made the Top Ten for himself (1960), Roy Clark (1963), Eddy Arnold (1966), and Steve Wariner (1992). Revivals of Anderson songs worked for Mickey Gilley ("City Lights," #1, 1974) and Conway Twitty ("I May Never Get to Heaven," #1, 1979).

*Bill Anderson*

Anderson's hit "Po' Folks" inspired both his band name and a restaurant chain, for which he was a longtime spokesperson. His duet partners have included JAN HOWARD ("For Loving You," #1) and Mary Lou Turner ("Sometimes," #1).

The tall, versatile entertainer hosted his own syndicated TV series (1965–73); a network game show (ABC's *The Better Sex*, 1977–78); a soap opera (ABC's *One Life to Live*, 1977–1980); and TNN's *Fandango* (1983–89). He cohosted TNN's long-running *The Opry Backstage* and starred in several low-budget, country-oriented films, such as *Las Vegas Hillbillies* (1966). He is the author of a 1989 autobiography and a 1993 memoir, the humorous *I Hope You're Living as High on the Hog as the Pig You Turned Out to Be*, and wrote a *Country Song Round-Up* magazine column for many years. He began hosting a SiriusXM Radio program, *Bill Anderson Visits with the Legends*, in 2006.

Anderson's last hit as an artist was "I Can't Wait Any Longer" (#4, 1978). After nearly twenty-five years at DECCA/MCA RECORDS, he left the label in 1982. His recordings have since appeared on the Southern Tracks, WARNER BROS., Varese Sarabande, CURB, Madacy, and TWI labels.

As a writer, however, Anderson began a resurgence in the late 1990s, coauthoring Vince Gill's 1995 hit "Which Bridge to Burn" with the younger singer.

In 1998 Anderson cowrote a pair of #1 hits, "Wish You Were Here," by Mark Wills, and the Grammy-nominated "Two Teardrops," by STEVE WARINER. Anderson's "Too Country," recorded by BRAD PAISLEY along with Anderson, BUCK OWENS, and GEORGE JONES, became CMA's 2001 Vocal Event of the Year. In 2002 KENNY CHESNEY, hit with the Anderson–DEAN DILLON masterpiece "A Lot of Things Different." Anderson and Jon Randall took 2005 CMA Song of the Year honors for their moving ballad "Whiskey Lullaby," recorded by Paisley and ALISON KRAUSS. Anderson won a Dove Award from the Gospel Music Association (GMA) for cowriting with Tia Sillers GMA's 2007 Country Recorded Song of the Year, "Jonah, Job, and Moses," sung by the OAK RIDGE BOYS; and he garnered his first ACM Song of the Year Award for "Give It Away," penned with BUDDY CANNON and JAMEY JOHNSON and recorded by GEORGE STRAIT. "Give It Away" was also CMA's 2007 Song of the Year. In addition, Anderson's work can be heard on releases by SUGARLAND, JOE NICHOLS, and SARA EVANS.

Bill Anderson was elected to THE COUNTRY MUSIC HALL OF FAME in 2001. —*Walt Trott*

## John Anderson
b. Orlando, Florida, December 13, 1954

John Anderson's voice and songwriting typify the NEW TRADITIONALISM with which he was first associated in the late 1970s and early 1980s. His distinctive vocals and songs have a modern quality while remaining firmly rooted in the HONKY-TONK MUSIC of the 1950s—most notably that of LEFTY FRIZZELL.

After playing with a rock band in high school, John David Anderson moved to Nashville in 1971. There he worked the Nashville club scene and signed as a writer with AL GALLICO. Anderson signed with WARNER BROS. RECORDS in 1977 but did not enjoy a Top Ten hit until early 1981, when his "1959" went to #7.

Anderson's early- to mid-eighties albums contained such solid material as his forthright rendition of BILLY JOE SHAVER's

"I'm Just an Old Chunk of Coal" (#4, 1981) and "I Just Came Home to Count the Memories" (#7, 1981), in addition to covers of honky-tonk standards such as Frizzell's "I Love You a Thousand Ways" (1983). Featuring hard-core country arrangements and highlighting Anderson's plaintive voice and distinctive phrasing, these albums were commercially and critically successful, placing Anderson alongside GEORGE STRAIT and RICKY SKAGGS as an effective purveyor of contemporary country music that remained traditional.

Anderson's biggest hit during these years was the 1983 novelty song "Swingin'." Cowritten by Lionel Delmore and Anderson, it became a chart-topping phenomenon, the CMA Single of the Year, and an enduring favorite on JUKEBOXES. That same year Anderson won CMA's Horizon award.

Anderson's career faded during the late 1980s as his singles found little success on country radio and his albums leaned toward R&B and southern rock. A brief tenure with MCA proved relatively unproductive, but in 1992 Anderson re-emerged with the impressive album *Seminole Wind*. Recorded for BNA Entertainment (RCA RECORDS), it spawned a hit title track (#2, 1992) and the memorable #1 "Straight Tequila Night." He recorded three more albums for BNA—*Solid Ground* (1993), *Country 'til I Die* (1995), and *Paradise* (1996)—before leaving the label. Subsequent record deals with MERCURY and EPIC did not restore his momentum, nor did a 2007 Warner Bros. album, *Easy Money*, produced by John Rich (BIG & RICH).

In 2009 Anderson reunited with *Seminole Wind* producer JAMES STROUD for *Bigger Hands*, released that year on Country Crossings, a division of Stroud's own Stroudivarious label. This album featured a powerful rendition of the topical Anderson-Rich composition "Shuttin' Detroit Down." —*Mark Fenster*

## Liz Anderson
b. Roseau, Minnesota, March 13, 1930

Best known for her songwriting, Elizabeth Jane Haaby Anderson penned, among many other tunes, the MERLE HAGGARD classics "(My Friends Are Gonna Be) Strangers" and "The Fugitive" (cowritten with her husband, Casey).

Anderson played mandolin at age eight and performed duets with her brother. She married Casey at age sixteen and had daughter LYNN ANDERSON at seventeen. The Andersons moved to California in 1951, and, though Liz wrote often, she didn't do so commercially until 1958. Booker-manager JACK McFADDEN was able to get Liz's songs to DEL REEVES and ROY DRUSKY. Her success with Haggard's "(My Friends Are Gonna Be) Strangers" (also a hit for Drusky) brought her a BMI award in 1965 and gained the attention of RCA RECORDS producer CHET ATKINS, who signed her to the label.

The Andersons soon moved to Nashville. Anderson's image as a sweet, domestic mother contrasted with her witty songwriting and performances. Top Ten hits included "The Game of Triangles" (1966, with BOBBY BARE and NORMA JEAN) and "Mama Spank" (1967). She sang about her husband as "Ekcedrin Headache #99," and her divorce songs "Go Now, Pay Later" and "So Much for Me, So Much for You" were unashamedly tough and spirited.

Five of Lynn Anderson's early hits were penned by Liz, and in 1968 the mother-daughter team had a #21 duet, "Mother May I." In the 1980s Liz and Casey cohosted a Nashville Network TV travel show, *Side by Side*. —*Mary A. Bufwack*

## Lynn Anderson
b. Grand Forks, North Dakota, September 26, 1947

Lynn (Rene) Anderson's 1970 hit "Rose Garden" helped usher in a decade in which women country performers achieved significant crossover success and national fame.

Raised in Sacramento, California (and an accomplished equestrienne since childhood), Anderson joined the Chart label after singing backup with her mother, singer-songwriter LIZ ANDERSON, on sessions for RCA RECORDS. Lynn had her first Top Ten record, "If I Kiss You (Will You Go Away)," in 1967, and she performed regularly on ABC-TV's *The Lawrence Welk Show* in 1967 and 1968.

In 1968 Lynn married GLENN SUTTON, the Grammy-winning songwriter who produced her hit records. Her 1970 COLUMBIA RECORDS rendition of "Rose Garden," a JOE SOUTH song, became her first country chart-topper. The record also hit #3 pop, earned Anderson a Grammy award, and propelled her toward recognition as CMA's 1971 Female Vocalist of the Year. Anderson's success was substantial, with nearly sixty chart singles and eighteen Top Ten hits.

As the decade progressed she stretched stylistically from the upbeat "What a Man My Man Is" to the poignant "I've Never Loved Anyone More." Anderson found additional popularity on TV and in her stage shows, typically featuring designer costuming. In 1977, the year she and Sutton divorced, she had her own TV special on the CBS network. In 1980, she updated her image with a skintight, white satin cowgirl outfit and was poised to be Columbia's answer to RCA's DOLLY PARTON and MCA's BARBARA MANDRELL.

However, Anderson married Louisiana oilman Harold Stream and retired to raise a family. She filed for divorce in 1982, citing physical abuse, and returned to performing. Custody litigation was no help to her career, though she released albums in 1983 and 1988. Her 1992 *Cowboy's Sweetheart* album and 2006's *Cowgirl* demonstrated her love of western music. She also released a BLUEGRASS album in 2004. —*Mary A. Bufwack*

## Pete Anderson
b. Detroit, Michigan, July 23, 1948

Pete Anderson gained notice as a country guitarist and producer when he joined forces with DWIGHT YOAKAM in the early 1980s. Moving to Los Angeles in 1976, Anderson at first worked in R&B and blues, producing the vocal group the Gliders and issuing singles under his own name. He made a living playing in country bars around Los Angeles, and it was at a gig at J. R.'s in Chatsworth that Yoakam first sat in with Anderson's band. The two started working together in 1981. Yoakam's *Guitars, Cadillacs, Etc., Etc.* EP was released on the tiny Oak label in 1984, and the following year Yoakam signed with WARNER BROS. RECORDS and began releasing a successful string of albums, all produced by Anderson. Anderson also coproduced the first two *A Town South of Bakersfield* compilations of young Los Angeles–based country performers.

Expanding beyond Yoakam's albums, Anderson became a busy L.A. producer—his work included the duet "Crying" by ROY ORBISON and K. D. LANG, which won a 1988 Grammy for Best Country Vocal Collaboration. He started Little Dog Records in 1994, releasing his own solo albums as well as albums by other country and rock artists.

More recent Anderson productions include albums by ROSIE FLORES, TANYA TUCKER, and MARK CHESNUTT. —*Todd Everett*

## The Andy Griffith Show

*The Andy Griffith Show*, a popular comedy about life in mythical Mayberry, North Carolina, premiered on CBS-TV in 1960. A spin-off from an episode of Danny Thomas's *Make Room for Daddy* that featured Griffith as a small-town sheriff, it garnered several Emmys during its eight-year run.

The program's peaceful, southern setting made it easy for Griffith and his producers to work traditional music into the script. Griffith, a North Carolina native, had a deep love of folk music and played his D-18 Martin guitar in many episodes. Professional musicians frequently guested on the show as well. Fiddler Curly Fox (of CURLY FOX & TEXAS RUBY), Salty Holmes, and the California-based Country Boys all appeared in the "Mayberry on Record" episode. The Country Boys—including CLARENCE AND ROLAND WHITE—made a second appearance later that year.

Proof of the show's impact on folk and BLUEGRASS was evident when THE DILLARDS succeeded the Country Boys as the program's occasional musical guests. Exposure as the Darling Family sent sales of The Dillards's ELEKTRA album *Back Porch Bluegrass* through the roof and helped bluegrass gain a crop of young, new fans. The show signed off in 1968, but it is still syndicated and appears often throughout the United States. —*Chris Skinker*

## ARC (*see* American Record Corporation)

## Arista Records
established in New York, New York, 1974

One of the first major labels to open a Nashville office during country's popularity boom in the late 1980s, Arista Records soon became one of the most successful. The company was founded by record executive Clive Davis in 1974, and it was Davis who named TIM DUBOIS head of Arista Nashville in 1989. The label found immediate success with its first album release, ALAN JACKSON's *Here in the Real World*.

DuBois focused on developing new artists, and by mid-1995 Arista had received gold, platinum, or multiplatinum certifications for seventeen of its approximately three dozen albums. The label's roster has included PAM TILLIS, BROOKS & DUNN, DIAMOND RIO, STEVE WARINER, BlackHawk, the Tractors, and BR549, among others. During its heyday, Arista launched two short-lived subsidiaries: Arista Texas, based in AUSTIN, with a roster including FREDDY FENDER and FLACO JIMENEZ; and Career Records, with former Arista artist LEE ROY PARNELL and singer-songwriter Brett James. Arista also acquired Christian label Reunion Records (sold to Zomba in 1996), which included Michael W. Smith and Kathy Troccoli on its roster.

During 1999–2000 the Bertelsmann Music Group (BMG) combined its Arista Nashville label with the RCA Nashville Labels Group (RCA RECORDS and BNA Entertainment) under the BMG umbrella. In 2004 SONY MUSIC and BMG merged their music properties into a joint venture named SONY BMG, and when Sony bought Bertelsmann's interest in the venture in 2008, Arista Nashville artists—including powerhouses Brooks & Dunn,

BRAD PAISLEY, Alan Jackson, and CARRIE UNDERWOOD—became part of newly named SONY MUSIC ENTERTAINMENT. Brooks & Dunn retired as a duo in 2010, and Jackson left in 2011 and signed with Capitol Nashville. —*Brian Mansfield*

## Aristocratic Pigs (*see* Fisher Hendley)

## Arkie the Arkansas Woodchopper
b. near Knob Noster, Missouri, March 2, 1907; d. June 23, 1981

After previously working at KMBC in Kansas City, Luther W. Ossenbrink joined the WLS *NATIONAL BARN DANCE* in 1929 as Arkie the Arkansas Woodchopper. Although he left the show a year or two before its demise on April 30, 1960, he was one of several *National Barn Dance* veterans who moved to WGN to work the *WGN Barn Dance* until that program folded in 1969. A fiddler, guitar player, singer, and square dance caller, he endeared himself to audiences with his ability (and sometimes inability) to maintain his composure while fellow musicians good-naturedly heckled him. His recordings of mostly cowboy songs between 1928 and 1941—for COLUMBIA, GENNETT, ARC, and OKEH—sold well but failed to establish him as a major recording artist.—*Wayne W. Daniel*

## Armed Forces Radio and Television Service (*see* AFRS)

## Eddy Arnold
b. Henderson, Tennessee, May 15, 1918; d. May 8, 2008

Perhaps more than any other artist, Eddy Arnold personified country music's adaptation to the modern, urban world and its transition from folk-based sounds, styles, and images to pop-influenced ones. He was also one of country music's most prolific hit makers, regularly placing songs high in the charts from the 1940s through the 1960s and scoring Top Ten hits as late as 1980.

Richard Edward Arnold came from a large farming family in Chester County, Tennessee. (Hence his later stage name, the "Tennessee Plowboy.") Early on, his mother helped him learn to play a borrowed Sears, Roebuck guitar, and he listened to records by GENE AUTRY, Bing Crosby, and JIMMIE RODGERS on a wind-up Victrola. He also sang at school near Jackson, Tennessee, and in church.

Arnold's father died when Eddy was eleven, and when creditors auctioned the family farm the Arnolds became sharecroppers during the Great Depression. Arnold's singing at candy pulls and barbecues for $1 a night supplemented the household's income while providing relief from daily toil. Understandably, he jumped at the chance to pursue music professionally. Beginning at age seventeen, he performed on radio and in beer joints in Jackson, Tennessee, while also working as an undertaker's driver. Next he moved on to radio work in Memphis and St. Louis.

Arnold's prospects brightened when he joined PEE WEE KING's Golden West Cowboys as a featured singer in 1940. With King, he worked the GRAND OLE OPRY and WSM's famous CAMEL CARAVAN tour of military bases in the United States and Central America. Striking out on his own in 1943, he broadcast on WSM

*Eddy Arnold*

daytime shows and eventually on the Opry. WSM station manager HARRY STONE and Chicago music publisher Fred Forster brought Arnold to the attention of RCA VICTOR RECORDS, and in December 1944 the singer recorded his first session for the company in WSM's studios. Meanwhile, he began to work show dates at churches and schools.

Arnold's early releases sold well, and he dominated *Billboard*'s country charts into the mid-1950s with hits such as "That's How Much I Love You" (1946), "I'll Hold You in My Heart (Till I Can Hold You in My Arms)" (1947), "Bouquet of Roses" (1948), and "Easy on the Eyes" (1952). Many of his hits crossed over into the pop market, setting the stage for later dual-market acts such as JIM REEVES and PATSY CLINE. With help from his manager, COLONEL TOM PARKER, Arnold became host of the Mutual Network's Purina-sponsored segment of the Opry and of Mutual's *Opry House Matinee*, a noontime show shared with ERNEST TUBB and broadcast from a Nashville theater. Syndicated radio shows Arnold recorded widened his exposure, as did the live CBS Network series *Hometown Reunion*, launched after Arnold left the Opry in 1948. In 1949 and 1950 Arnold appeared in the Columbia films *Feudin' Rhythm* and *Hoedown*, respectively. Soon his earnings from recordings and road shows—together with a lucrative publishing arrangement with HILL AND RANGE SONGS, INC.—enabled him to diversify his investments and build a fine home in Brentwood, Tennessee. He was determined never to be poor again, and he succeeded.

By the time he played the Sahara Hotel in Las Vegas in 1953—making him one of the first country stars to work the Vegas scene—Arnold was also pioneering on television. He guested on *The Milton Berle Show* in 1949 and hosted summer replacement series for Perry Como (1952) and Dinah Shore (1953). *Eddy Arnold Time*, a syndicated series made in Chicago, appeared in 1955, and ABC-TV's *The Eddy Arnold Show*, shot in Springfield, Missouri, followed in 1956.

During country music's late-1950s slump, Arnold's record sales flagged, and he considered retiring from music. In fact, he was on the verge of a new wave of popularity, as he traded his Tennessee Plowboy image for an uptown, sophisticated look. By the mid-1950s his somewhat plaintive singing style had already begun to mellow, and songs such as "I Really Don't Want to Know" (1954), recorded without the earlier trademark steel parts of LITTLE ROY WIGGINS, and a new version of "Cattle Call" (1955), recorded with an orchestra, anticipated the country-pop groove he would later establish with "Make the World Go Away" (1965) and other #1 records of the late 1960s. Now managed by Gerard Purcell, Arnold began to wear tuxedos and make personal appearances with orchestras. His nightclub and TV work increased markedly, and his discs charted abroad as well, paving the way for international tours.

In 1966 Arnold was elected to THE COUNTRY MUSIC HALL OF FAME, in 1967 he won the CMA's coveted Entertainer of the Year Award, and in 1984 he received the ACM's Pioneer Award. In 1970 RCA honored him for reaching the 60 million mark in lifetime record sales, a number that reportedly topped 80 million by 1985. In 1993 RCA released the album *Then and Now*, marking Arnold's fiftieth year with the label, an association interrupted only briefly from 1973 to 1975, when he recorded for MGM. He continued to tour heavily during the 1970s and beyond, until announcing his retirement from the stage on May 16, 1999, during a show at the Orleans Hotel in Las Vegas. He continued to record, however, and his hundredth album, *After All These Years*, was released in 2005 on RCA. The National Academy of Recording Arts and Sciences inducted his recording of "Make the World Go Away" into the Grammy Hall of Fame in 1999, and he received a Grammy Lifetime Achievement Award in 2005.

Soon after Arnold's death on May 8, 2008, RCA released "To Life," a song from *After All These Years* that distilled the singer's reflections on his remarkable personal journey. Peaking at #49, it marked the seventh decade in which he made *Billboard*'s country charts. —*John W. Rumble*

## Jimmy Arnold

b. Fries, Virginia, June 11, 1952; d. December 26, 1992

A tattooed mountain man whose outlaw ways often overshadowed his prodigious talent, James Edward Arnold was a BLUE-GRASS multi-instrumentalist whose most enduring legacy remains a Civil War concept album, *Southern Soul*.

The only son of a Pentecostal cotton mill hand, Arnold became a child prodigy on a Silvertone banjo ordered from a Sears catalog. At thirteen he recorded his first record, a cover of "Make Me a Pallet on the Floor," for Stark; at sixteen, his rendition of "Old Joe Clark" won first prize at the Old Time Fiddlers' Convention in GALAX, VIRGINIA, held annually near his native Fries. As a teen on the bluegrass festival circuit, Arnold fell under the spell of OLD-TIME fiddler TOMMY JARRELL, who taught him Civil War–era songs that Jarrell had learned from Confederate veterans. Stints with Cliff Waldron's the New Shades of Grass, CHARLIE MOORE's Dixie Partners, and KEITH WHITLEY's New Tradition established Arnold's reputation as a brilliant multi-instrumentalist—and notorious boozer—of the Washington, D.C., bluegrass scene. He spent the later 1970s as a fiddler with Judy Lynn in Las Vegas; during rambling forays into Texas, New Orleans, and Mexico he added harmonica and DOBRO, among other instruments, to his vast musical arsenal. In the early 1980s Arnold relocated to the Washington, D.C., area, where his encyclopedic grasp of southern styles—from Appalachian reels to WESTERN SWING to New Orleans blues—stunned audiences at shows that often included veteran fiddler Tex Logan.

Arnold recorded several solo instrumental albums on REBEL RECORDS in the 1970s, including his banjo tour de force, *Strictly Arnold* (1974), and made frequent sideman appearances, most notably as fiddler on dobro master Mike Auldridge's *Eight-String Swing* (SUGAR HILL, 1982). But Arnold's definitive work remains *Southern Soul* (Rebel, 1983), a Civil War concept album recorded near the Chancellorsville battlefield outside Fredericksburg, Virginia. Revealing himself a gifted singer and composer, Arnold weaved autobiographical fragments into a first-person song cycle about a Confederate soldier. The record featured original compositions, Civil War–era tunes such as "Lorena," Moore's "Rebel Soldier," and The Band's "The Night They Drove Old Dixie Down." Using extensive studio overdubs, Arnold provided most of the instrumental backup on the critically acclaimed album, which proved a commercial dud. Bouts with the law and the bottle sabotaged Arnold's later career, which was littered with unfinished projects—including tribute sessions to idols JIMMIE RODGERS, Leadbelly, and HANK WILLIAMS. Arnold was planning a comeback that included an East European tour when he died of heart failure at age forty. In 2006 Rebel Records issued *Riding with Ol' Mosby*, a retrospective combining previously available material with three newly released performances: "Wildwood Casket," "If," and "Travis Blues." —*Eddie Dean*

## Charline Arthur

b. Henrietta, Texas, September 2, 1929; d. November 27, 1987

Though none of her single releases—for BULLET RECORDS, RCA, Republic, or any number of smaller labels—ever made the *Billboard* charts, Charline Arthur, with her gutsy, blues-flavored vocal style and brassy stage presence, had more influence on her times than her commercial fortunes might suggest. Among her fans were ELVIS PRESLEY and PATSY CLINE.

Born Charline Highsmith to an impoverished Pentecostal preacher and his guitar-playing wife, Arthur began her career in the mid-1940s singing at radio station KPLT in Paris, Texas. In 1948 she married bass player Jack Arthur, who became her manager. In 1949 Bullet Records released her self-penned song "I've Got the Boogie Blues." When COLONEL TOM PARKER happened to hear Arthur singing at station KERM in Kermit, Texas (where she was also a DJ), he brought her to the attention of the influential New York music publishing firm HILL and RANGE. Hill and Range signed her as a songwriter in 1952 and in turn brought Arthur to RCA Records, which signed her in January 1953. She was produced at RCA first by STEVE SHOLES and later by CHET ATKINS, with whom the tempestuous singer claimed to have had a serious personality clash. Among the country boogie and HONKY-TONK songs she recorded for RCA were "Kiss the Baby Goodnight," "I'm Having a Party All by Myself," "Leave My Man Alone," and "Just Look, Don't Touch, He's Mine." In 1955 she was named runner-up to KITTY WELLS in *Country & Western Jamboree* magazine's annual "DJ Choice" poll.

After she left RCA in 1956, the temperamental performer ceased to be a presence in country music, although she did continue recording sporadically into the 1970s.

When Arthur died in rural Idaho in 1987 she'd been living for quite a few years on a modest $335-a-month disability pension. —*Bob Allen*

## Emry Arthur
b. Wayne County, Kentucky, ca. 1900; d. August 1966

As a vocalist, Emry Arthur cut more than eighty sides for Vocalion, Paramount, and DECCA RECORDS from January 1928 to January 1935. More than half were solos; on others he performed in duet with various partners and as part of his own Arthur's Sacred Singers group. Arthur played guitar and harmonica; one Vocalion release of his harmonica solos labeled him "The Jack Harmonica Player."

Arthur's music was rooted in the folk heritage of his southern Kentucky family. His father, Harry B. Arthur, was a locally known bass singer, and a brother, Henry (who assisted Emry on some cuts), played fiddle and steel guitar. Another relation, William Rexroat, led the locally based Cedar Crest Singers, who also recorded in January 1929 for Vocalion.

Although born in Kentucky, Arthur lived most of his life in Indianapolis, Indiana, where he died in 1966. —*Bob Pinson*

## ASCAP
established in New York, New York, February 1914

The American Society of Composers, Authors and Publishers—ASCAP—was America's first song-licensing firm and remains one of its largest. Founded in New York City in February 1914 and modeled on France's SACEM, ASCAP sought to enforce the provision of the 1909 Copyright Act requiring payment to songwriters and publishers for the public performance of their works. ASCAP collects license fees from music users (hotels, clubs, restaurants, broadcasters, and the Internet) on behalf of its members, to whom it distributes all income above operating expenses—half to writer members and half to publisher members. ASCAP license fees can vary widely: local radio stations pay less than broadcast networks, and a tavern pays less than a big-city hotel. Distribution is based on the number and kind of music performances logged by ASCAP's sophisticated survey formula. Performances of a song on radio stations that pay ASCAP a $25,000-per-year license will be worth five times as much as performances on a station that pays $5,000 per year.

ASCAP began with 170 writers and 22 publishers and has grown to a membership of more than 360,000 songwriters and publishers. ASCAP now licenses all kinds of music but in its early years concentrated on classical music and Tin Pan Alley pop. Within the country field, its biggest early writers were GENE AUTRY, FRED ROSE, and BOB WILLS. ASCAP still licenses such country standards as "Blue Eyes Crying in the Rain," "Cattle Call," and "Tumbling Tumbleweeds."

ASCAP came to Nashville in the 1950s with a branch office for Alabama and Tennessee headed by Asa W. Bush in the West End building. Juanita Jones led a Nashville branch office when it was established in 1963, the same year ASCAP gave its first country music awards. By that time various forces, including competition from rival BMI, had led ASCAP to open up its membership policies and broaden its logging procedures to include non-network as well as network broadcasts. Plans were announced for the first ASCAP building on MUSIC ROW in October 1968, about the time Ed Shea became southern regional director for ASCAP. This building, at the corner of Seventeenth and Division, opened in 1969 and was replaced by a newer, multistory complex at the same site in January 1992. Shea became national coordinator of public affairs for ASCAP in 1980–81, at which time CONNIE BRADLEY replaced him as southern regional director.

Through the 1980s, ASCAP strengthened its country music presence and began to compete on equal footing with BMI. In February 2010, ASCAP announced that its Nashville office would become a regional center serving all genres of music. At the same time, longtime record executive TIM DuBOIS became the Nashville office's vice president and managing executive. —*Ronnie Pugh*

## Clarence "Tom" Ashley
b. Bristol, Tennessee, September 29, 1895; d. June 2, 1967

A respected musician and comedian from eastern Tennessee, Clarence "Tom" Ashley recorded as a soloist and with various bands during the late 1920s and early 1930s; he successfully resumed his career during the urban folk revival of the early 1960s.

Although Ashley (born Clarence Earl McCurry) learned banjo and traditional ballads from his aunts at an early age, his musical education stemmed largely from itinerant musicians who lodged at his mother's boardinghouse. By 1913 he was an all-around entertainer, telling jokes, singing, and playing banjo and guitar with horse-drawn MEDICINE SHOWS throughout the Cumberland Mountains. Young ROY ACUFF reportedly served a brief apprenticeship under Ashley during the early 1930s.

Ashley first recorded for GENNETT in February 1928. Country record producers quickly recognized his abilities as a utility singer and musician. Victor Talking Machine Company producer RALPH PEER recruited him for four CAROLINA TARHEELS sessions in 1928–29. (Two April 1929 session were held shortly after Victor's purchase by the Radio Corporation of America, after which RCA formed RCA VICTOR RECORDS.) COLUMBIA recorded Ashley in 1929–30 as a soloist and with Byrd Moore & His Hot Shots. During the early 1930s he recorded for the AMERICAN RECORD CORPORATION labels. Ashley basically retired from entertaining by 1943, although he occasionally worked as a comedian with the CHARLIE MONROE and THE STANLEY BROTHERS shows.

After meeting OLD-TIME MUSIC enthusiasts RALPH RINZLER and Eugene Earle at the 1960 Union Grove Fiddlers' Convention, Ashley realized that many young folk musicians and collectors treasured his original recordings. He resumed singing and playing banjo; for his first recording session in nearly thirty years, Ashley recruited a guitarist neighbor, DOC WATSON, to accompany him. In 1961 Ashley, Watson, Clint Howard, and Fred Price formed a band to play at colleges, clubs, and folk festivals. —*Dave Samuelson*

## Ashley's Melody Makers

Ashley's Melody Makers, an Ozark stringband also known as Ashley's Melody Men, are important representatives of the Ozark STRINGBAND MUSIC tradition. The group played for local occasions in the Arkansas Ozarks, with a fluid lineup that changed slightly at almost every performance. Their leader was steel guitarist Hobart Ashley (1895–1969) of Marshall, Arkansas. Other members included Anson Fuller (1907–36), fiddle; Homer Treat (b. 1910), banjo; Vern Baker (1905–73), guitar; Hugh Ashley (1915–2008), guitar; and Gerald Ashley (b. 1917). The latter two were Hobart's sons. This band had three recording sessions: the first two in Memphis in October 1929 and June 1930, the last in Dallas in February 1932. They recorded mainly songs written by Hugh Ashley, who later wrote "One Step at a Time" for BRENDA LEE, "The Old Fiddler" for BILL MONROE, and "What Would You Do (If Jesus

Came to Your House)" for PORTER WAGONER, although the band did record the traditional song "Methodist Pie." —*W. K. McNeil*

## Jesse Ashlock
b. Walker County, Texas, February 22, 1915; d. August 9, 1976

Jesse Thedford Ashlock was already a well-known, revered WESTERN SWING fiddler by the time BOB WILLS & His Texas Playboys recorded his first songwriting efforts in 1941. Ashlock's "Please Don't Leave Me" and "My Life's Been a Pleasure" produced a double-sided smash for Wills and established him as an important songwriter as well as musician.

In 1930, at age fifteen, Ashlock was apprenticing behind Wills at Crystal Springs, west of Fort Worth. In addition to Wills, Ashlock idolized and emulated jazz violinist Joe Venuti. In 1932 Ashlock became a member of MILTON BROWN's seminal Musical Brownies. With CECIL BROWER, Ashlock formed the first significant twin fiddle team in western swing and helped pioneer the genre. By 1935 he was in Tulsa with Wills and, from then until the war—except for a brief stretch in Texas with Bill Boyd (BILL AND JIM BOYD), ROY NEWMAN, and in California with RAY WHITLEY— his hot fiddling was an important element in Wills's early sound.

Ashlock worked intermittently with Wills after World War II and recorded with Sam Nichols, PORKY FREEMAN, and others. He continued to score as a songwriter, penning Wills's classics "The Kind of Love I Can't Forget" (1946) and "Still Water Runs the Deepest" (1947). A capable vocalist, Ashlock also recorded under his own name for COLUMBIA in 1947. He drifted into obscurity until the western swing revival of the 1970s. Based in AUSTIN at his death, he guested with youngsters such as Alvin Crow and ASLEEP AT THE WHEEL and performed with the reconstituted Texas Playboys. —*Kevin Coffey*

## Ernie Ashworth
b. Huntsville, Alabama, December 15, 1928; d. March 2, 2009

Ernest Bert Ashworth made his mark as a songwriter and GRAND OLE OPRY performer in the 1950s and early 1960s. His first radio job was at his hometown station of WBHP in 1948; he moved up to Nashville two years later. WESLEY ROSE eventually signed him as an ACUFF-ROSE PUBLICATIONS songwriter and in 1955 placed him with MGM RECORDS, where he recorded as "Billy Worth" into 1957, with no chart impact. During this time Ashworth also wrote songs recorded by LITTLE JIMMY DICKENS, CARL SMITH, and JOHNNY HORTON. After a more successful stint with DECCA RECORDS (1960–62) that led to three Top Twenty hits, Ashworth signed with the Acuff-Rose–affiliated HICKORY RECORDS. Between 1957 and 1964 he commuted to Nashville from Huntsville, where he worked by day at the Redstone Arsenal defense plant. In 1963 he scored his first (and only) #1 hit with JOHN D. LOUDERMILK's "Talk Back Trembling Lips," which showcased his yearning tenor to great effect. The bouncy breakthrough record earned him Most Promising Artist awards from *Cashbox* and *Billboard* in 1963. Nevertheless, he hung on to his Huntsville day job until he joined the Grand Ole Opry in March 1964. The following year he appeared in the musical comedy film *The Farmer's Other Daughter*. Though he placed records on the charts through 1970, they came with decreasing frequency and impact. He continued to perform at the Grand Ole Opry for many years while owning radio station WSLV in Ardmore, Tennessee. —*Walt Trott*

## Asleep at the Wheel

Though known for their pivotal role in the WESTERN SWING revival, Asleep at the Wheel was the brainchild of two high school rock musicians: Ray Benson Siefert (b. March 16, 1951), known as Ray Benson, and Reuben "Lucky Oceans" Gosfield (b. April 22, 1951). They formed Asleep at the Wheel in about 1969, when they moved from the Philadelphia area to tiny Paw Paw, West Virginia, and played locally. The band's musicians came and went, but a young Virginia high school graduate named Chris O'Connell and singer-songwriter Leroy Preston stayed on. The group drew inspiration from both HONKY-TONK MUSIC and BOB WILLS–styled western swing.

A 1972 move to Berkeley, California, brought two years of playing bars and their meeting pianist Jim Haber, known professionally as "Floyd Domino." They signed with United Artists Records that year, but the group's debut LP wasn't successful. In 1974 they moved to AUSTIN, TEXAS, just as that city's music scene was gaining national attention. A 1974 LP for EPIC RECORDS fizzled. But after signing with CAPITOL RECORDS in 1975, the act had a hit single with "The Letter That Johnny Walker Read" and released the classic *Texas Gold* LP, which revealed their matured mix of country, R&B, and western swing. The band expanded with a full horn section and added big band swing to their sound, spreading western swing's appeal nationwide. In 1978 their Capitol LP cut of Count Basie's "One O'Clock Jump" won them a Grammy for Best Country Instrumental Performance.

Although the band has frequently changed labels, they have won seven additional Grammys to date and recorded a series of landmark albums, including the acclaimed 1993 all-star *Tribute to the Music of Bob Wills* featuring various former Texas Playboys; *Ride with Bob* (1999), another multiartist tribute, recorded with DIXIE CHICKS, DWIGHT YOAKAM, WILLIE NELSON, Manhattan Transfer, and others; *Asleep at the Wheel Remembers the Alamo* (2003); and *Reinventing the Wheel* (2006).

Benson, the only remaining original band member, has also branched out beyond the group. In 1991 he acted in the TV movie *Wild Texas Wind* with DOLLY PARTON and Gary Busey in addition to contributing original music. He released his first solo album, *Beyond Time*, in 2003 and has produced recordings by PAM TILLIS and SUZY BOGGUSS. *A Ride with Bob*, his original musical based on Wills's career, debuted in 2005.

Benson and his long-lived group still command a loyal following and tour widely, often with artists such as EMMYLOU HARRIS, BOB DYLAN, Willie Nelson, and GEORGE STRAIT. The band accompanied Nelson, MERLE HAGGARD, and RAY PRICE on their 2007 album *Last of the Breed* and its associated tour. —*Rich Kienzle*

## Association of Country Entertainers (*see* ACE)

## Asylum Records
established 1970; Nashville branch established 1992

Asylum Records began under the wing of ATLANTIC RECORDS in 1970, soon merged with ELEKTRA RECORDS under the Warner Music umbrella, and entered the country marketplace in 1992 with a strong commitment to artistic vision. With record producer KYLE LEHNING heading the Nashville operation in its early years, the label signed such critically acclaimed acts as GUY CLARK and EMMYLOU HARRIS.

Under entertainment mogul David Geffen, the label's founder, Asylum initially gained recognition with a roster including THE EAGLES, Jackson Browne, and Joni Mitchell as well as LINDA RONSTADT, who scored numerous country-pop crossover hits during the 1970s.

Asylum became Elektra's first country outlet in nearly a decade when the Nashville office opened in 1992. The label's penchant for art came with a price, however, because it earned only one Top Ten single—Brother Phelps's 1993 release "Let Go"—during its first three years in MUSIC CITY. Asylum's commercial fortunes later improved with the success of BRYAN WHITE and Kevin Sharp. Also in 1996, Joe Mansfield joined as co-president (with Kyle Lehning) and CEO, and the two remained until 1998.

Their successor, Evelyn Shriver, became the first female president of a major MUSIC ROW label. During her tenure the label issued GEORGE JONES's album *Cold Hard Truth* and *Trio II* by Emmylou Harris, DOLLY PARTON, and Linda Ronstadt. In 2000–2001, however, staff was radically cut, Shriver resigned, and Asylum was folded into Nashville's WARNER BROS. operation.

In 2003 the Warner Music Group and MIKE CURB launched the Asylum–CURB RECORDS imprint, which charted with artists including LeANN RIMES, HANK WILLIAMS JR., and WYNONNA, but soon abandoned this effort as sales fell short of expectations and Warner revived Asylum as an independently managed label focusing on urban music. —*Tom Roland*

## Bob Atcher

b. Hardin County, Kentucky, May 11, 1914; d. October 31, 1993

Robert Owen Atcher is best remembered through his hit recordings of the early 1940s and later appearances on Chicago's WLS *NATIONAL BARN DANCE*. Adept at folksongs, country material, and COWBOY MUSIC, he typically prefaced each song with a descriptive story while softly strumming chords on his guitar.

Early successes on Louisville radio brought Atcher to Chicago in 1932; he remained there for most of his career. In 1939 he began recording for Vocalion. His first hit was a cover of "I'm Thinking Tonight of My Blue Eyes," a parody punctuated by sobs and screams; other successes included "Cool Water" and "You Are My Sunshine." Many of Atcher's early records were duets with Loeta Applegate, billed as "Bonnie Blue Eyes."

In 1942 Atcher shared billing with popular bandleader Ben Bernie on CBS Radio's *Wrigley Spearmint Show*. He later hosted many Chicago-based network radio shows of his own, and in 1949 he joined the *National Barn Dance*. For years he remained one of Chicago's busiest performers. He eventually reduced his performing schedule, although he remained a *Barn Dance* regular through the show's 1960–71 tenure on WGN. From 1959 to 1975 he served as mayor of Schaumburg, Illinois.

Atcher's brother Randy (b. December 7, 1918, Tip Top, Kentucky; d. October 9, 2002) worked with Bob before World War II and then later developed a strong regional following of his own around Louisville. —*Dave Samuelson*

## Chet Atkins

b. Luttrell, Tennessee, June 20, 1924; d. June 30, 2001

No single country instrumentalist achieved the notoriety and respect that Chester Burton Atkins did. He influenced country, rock, and jazz musicians—from JERRY REED to George Harrison,

*Chet Atkins*

Duane Eddy, and Earl Klugh—for nearly half a century. Many hits he produced for RCA RECORDS are now classics.

Atkins grew up in the hills near a remote eastern Tennessee hamlet called Luttrell. James Atkins, his father, was an itinerant music teacher. His wife, Ida, Chester's mother, sang and played piano. After the Atkinses divorced, Ida Atkins remarried, in 1932, and Chester began to learn guitar and fiddle, often playing with his brother and sister and their stepfather, Willie Strevel. A 1936 asthma attack forced Chester to relocate to the improved climate at his father's Georgia farm, where, in the late 1930s, he first heard MERLE TRAVIS playing guitar over WLW in Cincinnati. Travis's thumb-and-finger picking style fascinated Atkins, who created his own thumb-and-two-finger variation.

After high school, Atkins landed a job at WNOX in Knoxville, fiddling for the team of singer BILL CARLISLE and comic ARCHIE CAMPBELL. WNOX executive Lowell Blanchard heard Chester's guitar playing and began featuring him on the *MID-DAY MERRY-GO-ROUND*, the station's popular daily barn dance show. Atkins broadened his repertoire through listening sessions in the station's music library. In 1945 he briefly joined WLW in Cincinnati; then in early 1946 he worked with JOHNNIE & JACK in Raleigh, North Carolina, before moving to Chicago, where RED FOLEY, leaving the WLS *NATIONAL BARN DANCE* to host the GRAND OLE OPRY's *Prince Albert Show*, hired Atkins and took him to Nashville. There he made his first solo recording, "Guitar Blues," for the local BULLET label.

Moving on to KWTO in Springfield, Missouri, Atkins received his nickname "Chet" from station producer SI SIMAN. Other officials there considered his style too polished for "hillbilly" music and eventually fired him. Meanwhile, however, Siman worked hard to interest record companies in Atkins, and RCA VICTOR's STEVE SHOLES signed him as a singer and guitarist in 1947. By 1948 Atkins returned to WNOX, working first with

HOMER & JETHRO and then joining Mother Maybelle Carter and the CARTER SISTERS as lead guitarist. They subsequently worked at KWTO before relocating to Nashville to join the Opry in 1950.

With FRED ROSE's help, Chet became one of Nashville's early "A-Team" of session musicians, recording with everyone from WADE RAY to HANK WILLIAMS and WEBB PIERCE. He also appeared on the Opry as a solo act. His first chart hit, a cover of the pop hit "Mister Sandman," came in 1955, followed by a hit guitar duet with HANK SNOW on "Silver Bell."

Through the 1950s, as Atkins became Sholes's trusted protégé, Atkins began organizing sessions, and if the New York–based Sholes couldn't come to Nashville, Atkins produced the records himself. In 1955 Sholes made him manager of RCA's new Nashville studio, which eventually led to an RCA vice-presidential position.

After rock & roll set back country record sales, Atkins's production skills came to the foreground. Intent on making country records appeal to pop and country audiences, he—along with OWEN BRADLEY at DECCA RECORDS, DON LAW at COLUMBIA RECORDS, and KEN NELSON at CAPITOL RECORDS—began to produce singers backed by neutral rhythm sections and to replace steel guitars and fiddles with vocal choruses and string arrangements. The result was soon known as THE NASHVILLE SOUND. Atkins transformed hard-country RCA artists JIM REEVES and DON GIBSON by producing crossover hits for both artists. Among the many acts Atkins produced successfully were EDDY ARNOLD, SKEETER DAVIS, BOBBY BARE, and FLOYD CRAMER. In 1965 Atkins took a major step forward by signing African American country singer CHARLEY PRIDE to RCA. In that same year Atkins enjoyed his own biggest hit single with "Yakety Axe," an adaptation of BOOTS RANDOLPH's hit "Yakety Sax."

Atkins produced a constant stream of solo RCA albums during these years. As he hired additional producers at RCA, he cut back his own production work to focus on recording and made albums with other fine RCA guitarists: Hank Snow, Jerry Reed, Merle Travis, and LES PAUL.

In 1973 Atkins was elected to THE COUNTRY MUSIC HALL OF FAME, and from 1967 to 1988 he won the CMA's Instrumentalist of the Year nine times. Relinquishing his RCA executive role in 1982, he left the label to record for Columbia in 1983, from this point concentrating mostly on jazz. Frequent collaborations with younger players, such as British rock guitarist Mark Knopfler, reflected his desire to remain contemporary. In 1993 Atkins received a Lifetime Achievement Award from the National Academy of Recording Arts and Sciences (NARAS), placing him among such musical greats as Louis Armstrong, RAY CHARLES, Leonard Bernstein, and Paul McCartney.

In 1997 Atkins won his fifteenth Grammy award, for his 1996 recording of "Jam Man." That same year he was diagnosed with brain cancer, and he lost his battle with the disease in 2001. —Rich Kienzle

## Rodney Atkins
b. Knoxville, Tennessee, March 28, 1969

Along with his signature ball cap and accessible persona, many of Rodney Allan Atkins's hits echo the sentiments of rural America. Although first signed to CURB RECORDS in 1997, he did not gain national attention until 2006 with *If You're Going Through Hell*. The album's title track, recorded in Atkins's home studio, topped the country charts and was followed by three more consecutive *Billboard* #1 hits: "Watching You," "These Are My People," and "Cleaning This Gun (Come on in Boy)."

As an orphaned infant, Atkins was returned twice to a Greenville, Tennessee, children's home by adoptive families overburdened by his health problems, but he was permanently adopted by Allan and Margaret Atkins of Cumberland Gap, Tennessee. As his health improved, he sang in church, played guitar, and began writing songs. While attending Tennessee Technological University in Cookeville, he regularly traveled to Nashville to perform and write, and eventually he caught the ears of music executives. His 2003 debut album, *Honesty*, earned him a Top Five hit with the single "Honesty (Write Me a List)."

Atkins again captured the country's #1 *Billboard* spot in 2009 with the title track from his album *It's America*, released that same year. —*Jeremy Rush*

## Atlantic Records
established in New York, New York, 1947

Atlantic Records began primarily as a jazz and R&B label; by the mid-1990s its Nashville branch epitomized the country music mainstream. TRACY LAWRENCE, NEAL MCCOY, and JOHN MICHAEL MONTGOMERY comprised the label's core, each with albums selling more than 1 million copies. The Atlantic group CONFEDERATE RAILROAD also sold more than 1 million.

Founded by Herb Abramson and Ahmet Ertegun, who were joined by Jerry Wexler in 1953, Atlantic occasionally flirted with country music, releasing singles by DOTTIE WEST and Dale Hawkins in 1962, for instance. Eventually the label became part of the Warner Music Group.

Atlantic first operated a Nashville office from 1972 to 1974 under the direction of Rick Sanjek; its roster then included WILLIE NELSON, JOHN PRINE, Doug Sahm, and HENSON CARGILL. Prompted by BILLY JOE ROYAL's success on the Atlantic America subsidiary between 1985 and 1988, Atlantic reopened Nashville offices in 1989 with RICK BLACKBURN and Nelson Larkin at the helm; Blackburn later became president of the division, continuing in that role until 1999, when Barry Coburn took the reins.

Under Blackburn, Atlantic succeeded with a combination of marketing savvy and a small, radio-friendly roster. Lawrence and McCoy both joined in 1991, Montgomery and Confederate Railroad in 1992. Besides these mega-sellers, other acts of the 1990s included Robin Lee, Girls Next Door, Mila Mason, and Matt King.

Atlantic closed its country division in 2001 and transferred most of its acts to WARNER BROS. RECORDS' Nashville division. The Atlantic Nashville division was resurrected in 2008 and soon gained success with the ZAC BROWN BAND. —*Brian Mansfield*

## Austin, Texas

Ever since the early 1970s, when WILLIE NELSON and others made Austin, Texas, a well-known music locale, the city's musical history has been a healthy reminder that country is not synonymous with Nashville. Long before it attained national attention as a country music center, Austin had several country music clubs, such as the Broken Spoke, the Split Rail, and the Skyline Club (where both HANK WILLIAMS and JOHNNY HORTON gave last performances). Threadgill's Bar, housed in a converted filling station on the north edge of town, was a bridge between the country music of the 1950s and the eclectic, youth-oriented COUNTRY-ROCK of the 1970s. Kenneth Threadgill, the proprietor, was a JIMMIE RODGERS–style yodeler who encouraged other people to sing. In the early 1960s Threadgill's became a microcosm of the later country scene when spillovers from the University of Texas folk music club (including Janis Joplin) began mixing their personas and repertoires with the older country styles that had long been present there.

In the late '60s the Vulcan Gas Company club became a meeting place for hippies and college students and such local rock bands as the Thirteenth Floor Elevators, Shiva's Headband, and others. When the Vulcan folded, the Armadillo World Headquarters, housed in a vacant armory building, replaced it in 1970 as the center of countercultural music activity. Musicians of varying stripes were already coming to Austin, and during the early 1970s remnants of the rock scene (and a few ex-folkies, such as JERRY JEFF WALKER), began to meld the disparate strains of country, BLUEGRASS, urban folk, blues, and rock. Two groups, Greezy Wheels and Freda & the Firedogs (the latter headed by pianist and blues singer Marcia Ball), were pioneers in this attempt at musical fusion, and they were soon joined by Doug Sahm, MICHAEL MARTIN MURPHEY, B. W. Stevenson, Steve Fromholz, Willis Alan Ramsey, and others. The Armadillo World Headquarters became the center of the emerging blend of rock and country music, though after February 1973 the Soap Creek Saloon also became an active arena for musicians. Many performers began adopting cowboy names and dress in order to establish identities that seemed consonant with the Texas Hill Country. Jim Franklin, who had already been painting armadillo posters for Shiva's Headband, and Kerry Awn, who created the Soap Creek calendars, contributed greatly to the imagery that surrounded Austin music with their depictions of longhorn steers, cactus, sagebrush, armadillos, and longneck beers.

As the Austin musical mix gained notoriety, observers were hard-pressed to find a name that sufficiently encompassed the emerging musical culture. The terms "redneck rock" and "cosmic cowboy music" were sometimes affixed to the city's varied styles. The most often-used term, "progressive country," was introduced in 1973 by Austin radio station KOKE-FM to describe the wide-ranging mixture of records played by its disc jockeys. A stockbroker and ardent music fan, Townsend Miller was also a strong contributor to the idea of Austin as a "musical colony." He began touting the city's music in a local newspaper column and in music magazines.

A thriving musical setting already existed, then, when Willie Nelson moved to the city in late 1971. He, Jerry Jeff Walker, Marcia Ball, ASLEEP AT THE WHEEL, Alvin Crow, KINKY FRIEDMAN, Steve Fromholz, and frequent visitor WAYLON JENNINGS made Austin's laid-back musical landscape famous throughout the nation. Nelson's giant outdoor festivals, held first at nearby Dripping Springs and later at other Texas locations, further heightened Austin's musical profile while also uniting musicians as diverse as LEON RUSSELL and ROY ACUFF.

Since 1987 Austin has hosted the annual South by Southwest Music and Media Conference, one of the nation's preeminent music industry gatherings. Nevertheless, Austin's prominence as a country music capital has declined since the 1980s, partly because the city never built a recording complex that could augment its numerous live-performance venues. With the notable exceptions of Willie Nelson and Jerry Jeff Walker, very few of the Austin musicians even had recording contracts during the highly publicized events of the 1970s. Music, however, is still extremely popular in Austin, and some notable country personalities, such as Walker, Asleep at the Wheel, JOE ELY, the Austin Lounge Lizards, JUNIOR BROWN, and JIMMIE DALE GILMORE still make the city their chief base of operations. —Bill C. Malone

## Austin City Limits
established in Austin, Texas, summer 1975; first aired fall 1976

*Austin City Limits* is a long-running, influential music series produced for public television in AUSTIN, TEXAS. The series was launched to help expose the city's "cosmic cowboy" progressive country music to the world at large. It was developed by Bill Arhos, then program director for KLRU-TV. After a pilot featuring WILLIE NELSON, the first program paired ASLEEP AT THE WHEEL with a reunion of the Texas Playboys, BOB WILLS's famous band.

The series has since featured a wide range of Austin artistry extending well beyond country, along with nationally known performers in the country-folk, roots-music, indie-rock, and singer-songwriter veins. Among the most significant artists to have appeared on the program are RAY CHARLES, ROY ORBISON, B. B. King, EMMYLOU HARRIS, and NEIL YOUNG. Among the artists more commonly associated with Austin, NANCI GRIFFITH, JIMMIE DALE GILMORE, and Stevie Ray Vaughan were featured on the show well before they had achieved national prominence.

"We try to come up with a mix or balance of original music that reflects a variety of styles that are uniquely American," explained Terry Lickona, who has been booking and producing the program since 1978.

*Austin City Limits* has long been a favorite with artists, both for the concert format that keeps the focus on music and for the enthusiasm of the Austin audience. GARTH BROOKS, ALAN JACKSON, and VINCE GILL are among the many musicians who were regular viewers of the series long before they were invited to appear on it. During his years on the Texas club circuit, LYLE LOVETT was such a regular in the audience that when he finally appeared as a performer, the program (as an insider joke) inserted a shot of him watching from the crowd.

Although *Austin City Limits* was once among the primary vehicles of television exposure for country artists, the boom in the music's popularity and the proliferation of cable TV programming has meant more competition among TV shows for top country talent. The series has responded by featuring a wider variety of performers, such as ROBBIE FULKS, the Avett Brothers, and St. Vincent. Country music continues to be an essential element in its programming, but in diminished concentration.

In 2002, producers launched the annual Austin City Limits Music Festival, three days of live outdoor concerts in a downtown park. Starting with the 2011 season, the program moved from the KRLU-TV studio on the University of Texas campus into the newly built Moody Theater in downtown Austin. —Don McLeese

## Gene Autry
b. Tioga, Texas, September 29, 1907; d. October 2, 1998

While he was unquestionably the best-selling country & western artist from the early days of the Depression through the close of World War II, Gene Autry was also much more. His status as a top box-office attraction in motion pictures brought his music to the

*Gene Autry*

attention of a vast audience otherwise unfamiliar with country music. In addition, his success as a singing cowboy launched an entire genre of movies and paved the way for successful rivals such as ROY ROGERS and TEX RITTER.

Orvon Grover Autry, grandson of a Baptist minister, was born in a farmhouse near Tioga, Texas, to Delbert and Elnora Autry. He first performed as a boy soprano in his grandfather's church choir. Subsequently he mastered a $12 Sears mail-order guitar, which he used to accompany his singing at local events. When the Autrys moved to Oklahoma, young Gene took a job as relief telegrapher for the St. Louis & Frisco Railroad, where he eventually met Jimmy Long, an older fellow railroader who also made music on the side and had ideas about cutting records. Inspired by Long (and possibly by a chance, encouraging encounter with humorist Will Rogers), nineteen-year-old Autry took a leave of absence from his job to make the rounds of New York City record companies, auditioning with his versions of Gene Austin and Al Jolson hits.

Befriended by fellow Oklahomans FRANKIE AND JOHNNY MARVIN, pop singers recording in New York, Autry made test records for EDISON and the Victor Talking Machine Company before returning home and gaining experience as a performer. He spent two years (1928–29) on Tulsa's KVOO, billed as "Oklahoma's Yodeling Cowboy" and singing JIMMIE RODGERS's hits before returning to New York in October 1929, days before the stock market crashed. He began recording with a vengeance, cutting masters for five different companies, each of which issued records on several labels for chain-store distribution. For two years he

recorded prolifically, covering Rodgers's hits and performing other songs in that style.

Stardom came the first time Autry broke away from the Rodgers mold, recording "That Silver-Haired Daddy of Mine" as a duet with Jimmy Long for the ARC family of labels and its A&R man ART SATHERLEY. Lilting and sentimental in the tradition of the turn-of-the-century parlor ballad, the recording became a major hit and propelled Autry to a radio career on Chicago's WLS, beginning with his first morning broadcast on December 1, 1931, on his own show, *Conqueror Record Time*. Urged by Satherley, Autry focused on western songs and attire, and recorded his first western songs in 1933. In addition, WLS announcer Anne Williams created skillful word-pictures building Autry's cowboy image, which was reinforced by his hit recordings of "The Last Roundup" and "Cowboy's Heaven."

In the summer of 1934 Gene and his wife, Ina (Jimmy Long's niece), and his friend Lester "SMILEY" BURNETTE, a musician-composer-comedian with the Autry radio troupe, drove to California, where the singing cowboy made a guest appearance in the Republic Pictures western movie *In Old Santa Fe*. His own series of films began the following year (with the science fiction serial *The Phantom Empire*), and by 1937 exhibitors voted Autry the #1 box-office attraction in westerns, a position he would earn many times in the years that followed.

Hit records, such as "Tumbling Tumbleweeds," "Mexicali Rose," "Take Me Back to My Boots and Saddle," "Gold Mine in the Sky," "South of the Border (Down Mexico Way)," "Back in the Saddle Again," and "Be Honest With Me," abounded. His smooth, relaxed baritone extended his appeal to devotees of mainstream pop music, while the down-home warmth of his vocal approach assured the country audience he never ceased to be one of them. The virtual antithesis of today's vocalists, he adhered to the melody line with a total absence of vocal gymnastics or bluesy embellishments, with his clear, straightforward delivery evoking sincerity and serenity.

His screen presence, as gentle and reassuring as his singing style, offered comfort and inspiration to a Depression-weary audience. Invariably cast as himself—that is, Gene Autry—a good-natured and unassuming country singer, he was no super-hero but, rather, a guileless young man who triumphed over all odds by virtue of his innate goodness. Charismatic and handsome astride his horse, Champion, Autry filled his movies with humor (Smiley Burnette was his usual comic sidekick), music, and a minimum of gunplay. In 1940 he was voted the fourth most popular Hollywood star, outpolling Tyrone Power and James Cagney.

The Wm. Wrigley Jr. Company sponsored the Autry CBS radio series *Melody Ranch* from 1940 through 1956, interrupted only during Autry's service in the Army Air Corps during World War II (he joined voluntarily on July 26, 1942, during a *Melody Ranch* broadcast and served as a transport plane pilot in the Pacific Theater for three years). The postwar years brought more million-selling records, including "Here Comes Santa Claus" (1947), "Rudolph, the Red-Nosed Reindeer" (1949), and "Peter Cottontail" and "Frosty the Snow Man" (both 1950). Autry produced his own feature films from 1947 through 1953 and, shrewdly perceiving the importance of the new medium (television), became the first major star to appear in his own filmed TV series. *The Gene Autry Show*, produced by Autry's Flying A Productions, was sponsored on CBS-TV by Wrigley from July 23, 1950, through August 7, 1956.

Fulfilling a lifelong fantasy, Autry became owner of the Los Angeles Angels (now Los Angeles Angels of Anaheim) baseball team in December 1960. Although he continued to perform sporadically during the next five years, he left the arena before country singers' personal appearances were termed "concerts" and before it became commonplace to attribute artistic genius to country or rock artists. Lavish praise for his talent and his impact on our popular culture was slow in coming, but he continues to be idolized by generations, including many country singers who patterned their lives after his and who cheered his 1969 induction into THE COUNTRY MUSIC HALL OF FAME. —*Jonathan Guyot Smith*

## Hoyt Axton
b. Duncan, Oklahoma, March 25, 1938; d. October 26, 1999

Singer-songwriter and movie actor Hoyt Wayne Axton came by his talent and ambition naturally. His mother, Mae Boren Axton (b. Bardwell, Texas, September 14, 1914; d. April 9, 1997) cowrote the early ELVIS PRESLEY hit "Heartbreak Hotel" and was long a fixture in Nashville's music community as a TV and radio personality, public relations person, journalist, and friend to the stars.

Hoyt Axton began his career as a country-flavored folksinger in the southern California coffeehouse scene. As a songwriter he first scored with "Greenback Dollar," an early 1960s hit for the Kingston Trio that became a folk standard. Another Axton original, "The Pusher," was a hit for the rock group Steppenwolf and was featured in the soundtrack of the 1969 film *Easy Rider*.

Axton recorded for several small labels beginning in 1961 but had no significant chart action until the mid-1970s. His biggest country record was his 1974 Top Ten hit "Boney Fingers" on A&M Records.

Axton flourished in the early 1970s, recording for A&M and MCA. His songs "Joy to the World" and "Never Been to Spain" were big pop hits for the rock group Three Dog Night. Axton also produced country-rockers Commander Cody & The Lost Planet Airmen's album *Tales from the Ozone*.

Forming his own Jeremiah label, he scored a hit with "Della and the Dealer" in 1979. He signed briefly with ELEKTRA RECORDS in the early 1980s, with disappointing results. He also appeared in films, most notably *The Black Stallion* (1979) and *Gremlins* (1984).

A comeback album, *Spin of the Wheel* (1990), proved to be his last major release. After he suffered a stroke in mid-decade, his health declined, and following several heart attacks he died October 26, 1999. —*Bob Allen*

THE LONESOME ACE
"WITHOUT A YODEL"
ELECTRICALLY RECORDED
1-A
Vocal
Guitar Acc.
Old Rub Alcohol Blues
Dock Boggs-Banjo and Singing
Acc. by Emry Arthur, Guitar
21404

## The Bailes Brothers

Kyle O. Bailes b. Kanawha County, West Virginia, May 7, 1915; d. March 3, 1996
John Jacob Bailes b. Kanawha County, West Virginia, June 24, 1918; d. December 21, 1989
Walter Butler Bailes b. Kanawha County, West Virginia, January 17, 1920; d. November 27, 2000
Homer Abraham Bailes Jr. b. Kanawha County, West Virginia, May 8, 1922

The Bailes Brothers carried the harmony duet tradition of the 1930s into the next two decades. Though there were four brothers, they usually worked in combinations of two. Reared in poverty by a proud, determined, widowed mother on the outskirts of Charleston, West Virginia, various brothers struggled to make it on radio stations in their home state but had little success until John and Walter worked at WSAZ–Huntington in 1942. Two years later ROY ACUFF helped them secure a spot on the GRAND OLE OPRY and a contract with COLUMBIA RECORDS. Their original songs, such as "Dust on the Bible" and "I Want to Be Loved," also helped further their popularity.

At the end of 1946 the brothers moved to KWKH in Shreveport, where they helped initiate the LOUISIANA HAYRIDE and supported the fledgling career of HANK WILLIAMS. By this time Homer had joined on fiddle and Kyle on bass. When Walter joined the ministry in 1947, Homer replaced him in the duo. The act broke up at the end of 1949, but John and Walter reformed as a gospel duo in 1953 and recorded for KING RECORDS. In later years various combinations of the brothers reunited for occasional recordings and appearances, especially Kyle and Walter, the latter releasing material on his Loyal and White Dove labels. At different times, Homer, John, and Walter recorded individually.
—Ivan M. Tribe

## DeFord Bailey

b. Smith County, Tennessee, December 14, 1899; d. July 2, 1982

A pioneer member of the GRAND OLE OPRY and the program's first black star, DeFord Bailey was one of the show's most popular early performers. Opry master of ceremonies GEORGE D. HAY dubbed him the "Harmonica Wizard" and reported that Bailey's "Pan American Blues"—a COUNTRY BLUES rendition of a fast-moving locomotive, the Pan American Express—inspired Hay's renaming of the show, first known simply as the *WSM Barn Dance*.

Bailey grew up hearing and playing what he called "black hillbilly music." A harmonica virtuoso, Bailey recorded in 1927 for COLUMBIA (unissued) and BRUNSWICK and in 1928 for the Victor Talking Machine Company's Victor label, in the first recording sessions held by a major label in Nashville. There, as almost always, he used the simple Hohner Marine Band harmonica. His "harp" classics included "Ice Water Blues," "Old Hen Cackle,"

"Fox Chase," "Lost John," "Muscle Shoals Blues," "Up Country Blues," "Evening Prayer Blues," and his train tunes. When he played the guitar and banjo, he did so in a unique left-handed, upside-down style.

The grandson of a skilled Smith County fiddler, Bailey moved to Nashville in 1918. His introduction to radio broadcasting came in 1925 on WDAD, Nashville's pioneer station. A few weeks later, with strong encouragement from harmonicist DR. HUMPHREY BATE, he came to WSM radio, and, except for a brief period in 1928–29 on WNOX in Knoxville, he was an Opry regular for nearly fifteen years.

One evening in 1927, following an NBC radio network broadcast of classical music over WSM, Hay introduced a live performance by Bailey by saying that although some believed there was "no place in the classics for realism," Hay and his performers would "present nothing but realism." Bailey's performance led Hay to remark that his rustic music program wasn't grand opera, but it could certainly be considered "grand opry." The term stuck, and WSM's *Barn Dance* had a new name.

Bailey performed virtually every Saturday night while frequently working weekday road shows throughout the South and Midwest with UNCLE DAVE MACON, the DELMORE BROTHERS,

*DeFord Bailey*

BILL MONROE, ROY ACUFF, and other WSM artists. Bailey was always well received by the white audiences they entertained, but, in this heyday of Jim Crow, he faced real hardships in finding accommodations and restaurants that would serve him.

Bailey was able to cope with the indignities of segregation, but his firing by WSM in 1941 was more devastating to him; although still extremely popular, he had become victim of a BMI-ASCAP performance rights licensing conflict that prevented his playing his most popular tunes on the air. Having previously shined shoes, operated a barbecue stand, and rented out rooms in his home for extra money, he now turned to these activities to provide for himself, his wife, and their three children. He never stopped playing his harp but rarely performed publicly for the next forty years. When he agreed to perform on the Opry in February 1974, it became the occasion for the first annual Old Timers Show.

Bailey was inducted into THE COUNTRY MUSIC HALL OF FAME in 2005. —*David C. Morton*

## Razzy Bailey
b. Hugley, Alabama, February 14, 1939

The musical style that took Erastus Michael "Razzy" Bailey to the top of the charts in the early 1980s reflects what he heard while growing up on his family's southern farm. The singings held in Bailey's house were country, but he also became fascinated with the rhythm & blues of black farmhands. These genres would later merge in Bailey's singing, guitar playing, and songwriting.

Bailey played with a country band after graduating from high school but later worked in sales during a musical dry spell. He formed a pop trio called Daily Bread in 1958 and recorded for MGM RECORDS in the early 1970s. In 1976 Bailey's song "9,999,999 Tears" provided a career jolt when DICKEY LEE took it to #3 on the country charts. After efforts on small labels, Bailey signed as an artist with RCA RECORDS, and his first RCA release, "What Time Do You Have to Be Back to Heaven," reached the Top Ten in 1978. That ignited an eleven-year chart run that peaked in 1980–82 with five #1 hits, including "Loving Up a Storm" and "She Left Love All Over Me." Bailey later recorded for MCA, Spectra, and SOA Records. —*Gerry Wood*

## Kenny Baker
b. Jenkins, Kentucky, June 26, 1926; July 8, 2011

For nearly twenty years, BLUEGRASS patriarch BILL MONROE introduced sideman Kenneth "Kenny" Baker as "the greatest fiddler in bluegrass music." Monroe wasn't exaggerating simply because Baker worked for him. Few musicians have had the impact on bluegrass that Baker has had. His jazzy, swinging arrangements of traditional numbers, smooth long-bow technique, and ability to write original tunes have made him a favorite on the bluegrass circuit for five decades.

A third-generation fiddler from the coal-mining town of Jenkins, Kentucky, Baker picked up the instrument at about age eight. After a stint in the navy during World War II, Baker returned to Jenkins and took a job with Consolidated Coal Company. He was playing local dances when DON GIBSON hired him in 1953. Bill Monroe first saw Baker with Gibson on Knoxville's *Tennessee Barn Dance* and promptly offered Baker a job.

In 1956 Baker joined Monroe's band. Two years later he and Bobby Hicks twin-fiddled on the Monroe instrumentals

"Scotland" and "Panhandle Country." Baker also cut a handful of sides with Austin Wood for the Sure label.

Raising a family, Baker returned to the mines, where income was steady. He rejoined Monroe's band in 1962–63, long enough to help bring singer Del McCoury (DEL MCCOURY BAND) and banjo player BILL KEITH into the fold. Baker left in June 1963 and rejoined for the final time in 1967.

That year Baker recorded the album *High Country* with Joe Greene for COUNTY RECORDS. Baker's first solo album, *Portrait of a Bluegrass Fiddler*, was released on County in 1968. His most popular recording is probably his tribute album to his boss, *Kenny Baker Plays Bill Monroe* (County, 1994).

Baker left Monroe in 1985 and joined forces with DOBRO player UNCLE JOSH GRAVES. He toured and recorded with Graves, banjo player Eddie Adcock, and mandolinist Jesse McReynolds (JIM & JESSE) as The Masters. Still touring and recording, Baker was inducted into the Bluegrass Hall of Fame in 1999. —*Chris Skinker*

## Bakersfield

Bakersfield, in California's Kern County, spawned and exported so much country music from the 1940s through the 1970s that, by the late 1960s, some observers called it "Nashville West." (BUCK OWENS countered: "We call Nashville Bakersfield East.") The seeds for this phenomenon were sown by the Depression-era tide of migrants from Oklahoma, Texas, and Arkansas into the agriculture- and oil-rich San Joaquin Valley.

By the time their Texas-born hero BOB WILLS settled in the San Fernando Valley in 1945, Bakersfield had dance halls such as the Beardsley Garden & Rhythm Rancho to host the era's WESTERN SWING bands and the huge crowds they drew. Radio station KGEE began broadcasts of BILL WOODS & the Orange Blossom Playboys in 1946, and the local scene perked up with the opening of "drinking-and-fighting" clubs, including the Corral and the Blackboard. It was in such places that the stripped-down, amped-up blend of western swing and HONKY-TONK MUSIC later dubbed the "Bakersfield sound" was honed in the 1950s. This harder-edged musical style contrasted with—and commercially rivaled—the smoother NASHVILLE SOUND, then in its ascendancy in the East. Bill Woods's band was a proving ground through which BILLY MIZE, Owens, and MERLE HAGGARD passed. Other key players on the scene were FERLIN HUSKY, TOMMY COLLINS, and the influential but underrated WYNN STEWART.

The 1950s was the era when the creative spark ignited Bakersfield. It wasn't until the mid-1960s, however, when Owens built his Bakersfield-based empire (radio stations, publishing companies, and the management of local talent, including Merle Haggard for a time), that the notion of Bakersfield as an upstart country music center spread. For all of Owens's local boosterism, he and his hometown's finest musicians still made the one-hundred-mile drive south to Hollywood to record. RED SIMPSON and a few other Bakersfield-based artists enjoyed hits well into the 1970s, but the hopes of "Nashville West" were never realized. Nevertheless, Rank & File and other Los Angeles–based alternative country bands of the 1980s viewed 1960s Bakersfield as the embodiment of a golden age. In tribute, producer PETE ANDERSON delivered two anthologies of these acts called *A Town South of Bakersfield Volumes I & II* in 1985 and 1988. A third volume, without Anderson's involvement, was released in 1992. The crowning glory of the 1980s Bakersfield consciousness was the

Dwight Yoakam–Buck Owens duet "Streets of Bakersfield," a #1 hit in 1988.

In the twenty-first century, Owens's Crystal Palace has provided both a memorial for the artist and a venue for younger performers. —*Mark Humphrey*

## Dewey Balfa
b. Grand Louis, Louisiana, March 20, 1927; d. June 17, 1992

Dewey Balfa and his brothers provided some of the best examples of traditional Cajun music ever recorded. Their unique style of toning down the accordion and featuring the fiddles and of taking the words of old ballads and putting them to dance hall–type arrangements, made their music richly varied and broad in scope.

Balfa and his eight brothers and sisters were born into the family of sharecropper Charles Balfa, and it was from their father and grandmother Marie Richard that Dewey and his brothers learned much of their music. In 1948 Dewey, Will, and Harry Balfa formed a band, the Musical Brothers, with accordionist Hadley Fontenot. They played at local dances and for many years hosted a live weekend radio program at Mouche's Lounge in Basile.

In 1964 Dewey Balfa performed at the Newport Folk Festival in Rhode Island; three years later he returned to the festival with brothers Will and Rodney (both of whom would die in a car wreck in 1979), along with daughter Nelda and Hadley Fontenot. The Balfas recorded for Swallow and other labels, and Dewey Balfa became known as a major ambassador of Cajun culture. —*Ann Allen Savoy*

## David Ball
b. Rock Hill, South Carolina, July 9, 1953

After years on the progressive-music fringe, David Ball found success in the mid-1990s with a solid brand of Texas honky-tonk music exemplified by his 1994 Warner Bros. album *Thinkin' Problem*.

During the 1970s, Ball joined forces with Walter Hyatt and Deschamps "Champ" Hood in an eclectic Austin-based trio, Uncle Walt's Band. Ball's initial attempt to enter the Nashville scene in the late 1980s failed. Signed to RCA Records in 1987, he released three singles, the most successful of which stalled at #46. After a hiatus, Ball found new life and a new sense of direction in the honky-tonk vein as both songwriter and musician. *Thinkin' Problem* was produced by Blake Chancey, and the rousing, honky-tonk title tune, which reached #2 on the *Billboard* country chart, was one of 1994's surprise hits. Unfortunately, Ball's equally strong follow-up album, *Starlite Lounge*, did not produce any hits to rival the impact of "Thinkin' Problem." A 1999 album, *Play*, fared even worse.

Ball came back strong in 2001 with the song "Riding with Private Malone," a #2 single. It appeared on the album *Amigo*, released on the independent Dualtone Records. Since then, Ball has continued to tour and to release hard-country albums on independent labels. —*Bob Allen*

## Ballads

In modern country, the term *ballad* is often used (rather vaguely) to refer to any slow, emotive love song, a usage borrowed from popular music of the big band era. In a more holistic sense, however, the term *ballad* refers to a specific song type that has been a staple of country music from its earliest days. In the folk music from which country grew, the ballad was a narrative song—one that told a story. Many ballads originated in England, Scotland, and Ireland, and ballads such as "Barbara Allen," "The House Carpenter," and "The Wexford Girl," often dealing with murder and romance, became as popular in America as in England. By the early nineteenth century Americans were developing their own native ballads, some circulated orally, others by broadsides (sheets of paper or small cards) and in cheap songsters, or songbooks. Studied and classified by scholar Malcolm Laws, these pieces are generally known as Laws ballads.

In the 1920s a new type of ballad emerged, one written by commercial songwriters for specific use on the first generation of country records and referred to by the record industry as the "event song." Many of these were first cousins to the older broadside ballads, which often dealt with recent historical or topical events. As early as 1924, with Ernest V. Stoneman's OKeh recording of "The Sinking of the Titanic" and Vernon Dalhart's rendition of the train song "The Wreck of the Old 97" for the Victor Talking Machine Company, pioneer country recording artists set the stage for this new style. When Dalhart's disc became country's first million-seller, labels scrambled to find and issue similar song material. The year 1925 was the high-water mark for such efforts, with Dalhart's recording of "The Death of Floyd Collins," about a spelunker trapped in a Kentucky sand cave, and "Little Mary Phagan," about a sensational murder in Georgia, selling more than 300,000 copies for Columbia Records. In fact, of the seven best-selling Columbia singles for 1925, only two did not feature an event song. These compositions ranged from "The Scopes Trial" to "The Santa Barbara Earthquake," both events that were still dominating the headlines. Songwriters who specialized in this material included Atlanta evangelist Rev. Andrew Jenkins, Memphis native Bob Miller, and then–Dalhart partner Carson Robison.

The commercial boom in event songs was short-lived, and within a couple of years other types of country songs were dominating the field. Through the 1920s and 1930s, companies and singers repeatedly tried to resurrect topical songs, with pieces such as "The Death of Jimmie Rodgers" (Gene Autry), "The Fate of Will Rogers and Wiley Post" (Bob Miller), and "Amelia Earhart's Last Flight" (Red River Dave). In the 1940s, folk-based murder ballads such as "The Hills of Roane County" (the Blue Sky Boys) and "Tragic Romance" (Grandpa Jones, The Morris Brothers, Cowboy Copas) achieved widespread popularity.

In the 1960s, amid the folk music revival, a new cycle of ballads began appearing on the charts. Sometimes called "saga songs," they included items such as "The Battle of New Orleans" (Jimmy Driftwood, Johnny Horton) and Marty Robbins's remarkable "El Paso." Lefty Frizzell's "The Long Black Veil" so successfully copied the folk ballad style that many assumed this commercially written number was a genuine traditional folksong.

Though most modern country songs are technically lyrics—highly subjective songs that express emotion—the older ballad forms and techniques continue to infuse and influence modern songwriters, as evidenced in Don Schlitz's "The Gambler," a monster hit for superstar Kenny Rogers. And many of the ballads themselves continue to survive in repertoires of bluegrass and tradition-leaning country singers. —*Charles Wolfe*

## A. V. Bamford
b. Havana, Cuba, April 5, 1909; d. July 8, 2003

Alfred Vincent Bamford was a major country music concert promoter during the 1950s. He came to the United States at age fourteen. Educated at a military school in Pennsylvania, the University of Alabama, and New York University, Bamford sold radio advertising and managed radio stations before entering the concert booking field in San Francisco in the late 1930s. He promoted shows for Benny Goodman, Tommy Dorsey, and then switched to country music in the late 1940s, when he worked for BOB WILLS. Promoter OSCAR DAVIS introduced Bamford to JIM DENNY, who represented GRAND OLE OPRY acts as head of Nashville radio station WSM's booking department (1946–1956), and Bamford soon became one of country music's top promoters. He was promoting HANK WILLIAMS's shows at the time of the singer's death, and he handled early dates for ELVIS PRESLEY. Bamford later owned and managed several country radio stations. —*Al Cunniff*

## Moe Bandy
b. Meridian, Mississippi, February 12, 1944

From the time he made his breakthrough record, "I Just Started Hatin' Cheatin' Songs Today," in 1974 and until he left COLUMBIA RECORDS in 1986, Marion Franklin Bandy Jr. seldom strayed from the Texas HONKY-TONK style on which he was nurtured. With smooth and crisply articulated vocals, performed to the accompaniment of fiddles and PEDAL STEEL GUITAR, Bandy thrived commercially at a time when most country musicians were experimenting with country-pop sounds and striving for crossover acceptance. His clean-cut, choirboy looks stood in dramatic contrast to the long string of songs about hurting, drinking, and cheating that he placed on the country charts.

Bandy grew up in San Antonio listening to the music of visiting country stars and to his father's band, the Mission City Playboys. His first commercial recording was the self-penned "Lonely Lady" on the Satin label in 1964. Ten years later, when Bandy was toiling as a sheet metal worker by day and playing music in local clubs at night, Nashville producer Ray Baker became his manager. Baker and Bandy independently produced a recording of "I Just Started Hatin' Cheatin' Songs Today" on the Footprint label and eventually got it released on the independent Atlanta label GRC, where it became a Top Twenty hit. After signing with Columbia in 1975, several hits followed, including "It Was Always So Easy to Find an Unhappy Woman" and "Bandy the Rodeo Clown," both written by WHITEY SHAFER, and "Hank Williams, You Wrote My Life," from the pen of PAUL CRAFT. In his post-Columbia years, Bandy often has ventured beyond the honky-tonk style and has found only indifferent success. His recordings with JOE STAMPLEY (1979–85), which exploited the stereotype of the southern "good ole boy," were marked generally by good humor and self-mockery. Since the 1990s, Bandy has appeared regularly from March to December in BRANSON, MISSOURI. —*Bill C. Malone*

## Banjo

Generically, banjos are plucked or strummed stringed instruments whose distinctive tone stems from the strings' being supported by a bridge that rests on a tightly stretched skin membrane.

American banjos are descendants of a broadly related family of lutes developed in West Africa from earlier Middle Eastern models. The slave trade brought banjo prototypes to the New World, where such powerful transforming forces as nineteenth-century BLACKFACE MINSTRELSY and mass manufacture changed the instrument and its associated playing styles many times over.

The family of banjos today includes four-string tenors (similar to the standard banjo but with a shorter neck and no fifth string), plectrums (so called because they are played with a plectrum, and in form identical to the standard banjo but with no fifth string), and six-string guitar-banjos. Most common now is the five-string banjo, on which the fifth string is a short string usually tuned to function as a high drone or chanterelle. Five-string banjos may be found in open-back folk or OLD-TIME MUSIC types using gut or steel strings and also in resonator-backed variations, almost always steel-strung. Banjos may be fretted or fretless, acoustic or electric, mass-manufactured or individually handcrafted.

The banjo is visually and aurally one of the most recognizable instruments associated with country music. To early recordings and broadcasts of country music the banjo brought not only its distinctive frailing or finger-picked sounds but also its African and minstrel connotations. In both the nineteenth-century minstrel show and the early twentieth-century country music show, banjo players typically played comedy roles and were often musically marginal, although they were significant symbolically and for their tonal contributions within an ensemble. Beginning in the 1940s, Pete Seeger's revival of the five-string banjo to accompany folk music began to introduce the instrument to new northern and urban audiences. At the same time, the emergent sound of BLUEGRASS music, built in large part around the stylistic breakthrough into a smooth three-finger picking style of Earl Scruggs (FLATT & SCRUGGS AND THE FOGGY MOUNTAIN BOYS), began to stimulate yet another renaissance for this ancient instrument. Today the banjo is enormously popular around the world, particularly the five-string form played in bluegrass and other genres of folk and country music. —*Thomas A. Adler*

## Bar X Cowboys

Founded in about 1932–33 by fiddler Ben Christian (1885–1956) and guitarist Lynn Henderson in Houston, the prolific and long-lived Bar X Cowboys were the city's first organized country dance band. More musically conservative than most WESTERN SWING bands, the Cowboys responded less to jazz and blues than their contemporaries, and their straightforward approach ensured their popularity, especially in German communities west of Houston. The band first recorded for DECCA RECORDS in 1937. It recorded for RCA VICTOR's BLUEBIRD imprint in the years 1940–41, by which time steel guitarist–composer TED DAFFAN had joined its lineup. Bandleader Ben Christian departed in 1940 to form another group, with his brother Elwood "Elmer" Christian (1892–1970) taking the helm of the Bar X Cowboys, although JERRY IRBY, who replaced guitarist-vocalist Chuck Keeshan in 1941, was the band's frontman until 1947. Irby's replacement, Paul Brown (1911–2001), bought the Bar X Cowboys from Elmer Christian in 1949 and kept a band going through the early 1950s. The group recorded for several small concerns after the war, including Globe, Macy's, Nucraft, and Eddie's, for which it covered the notorious "Cocain [sic] Blues" in 1948. —*Kevin Coffey*

## Bobby Bare
b. Lawrence County, near Ironton, Ohio, April 7, 1935

Innovative and smart, funny and laid back, Robert Joseph Bare has taken an eclectic musical approach identifying him as a story-teller, humorist, folkie, and country OUTLAW. His instinct for songs (longtime friend WAYLON JENNINGS described him as "the best songhound in the world") has led to associations with country songwriting legends, including KRIS KRISTOFFERSON, BILLY JOE SHAVER, MICKEY NEWBURY, BOB McDILL, TOM T. HALL, HARLAN HOWARD, and RODNEY CROWELL. Collaborations with the eccentric songwriter-author-cartoonist SHEL SILVERSTEIN are among Bare's most notable artistic achievements.

Born and raised on a hillside farm in southern Ohio, Bare moved to Springfield, Ohio, as a teenager and began his musical career there. Arriving in the Los Angeles area in December 1953, he befriended steel guitarist Speedy West (SPEEDY WEST & JIMMY BRYANT), songwriter Harlan Howard, and singer-songwriter WYNN STEWART.

Bare recorded briefly for CAPITOL and CHALLENGE in the mid-1950s and was signed to write songs for Opal Music. He had just been drafted into the army in November 1958 when he agreed to help a friend, Bill Parsons, record demos for a possible record deal. At the session, Bare sang an unfinished song, "All-American Boy," intending for Parsons to record it later. The acetates were copied at Cincinnati's Fraternity Records studio, and Fraternity decided to release the demo as it was. When Bare finished basic training several weeks later, the record was a pop hit, eventually rising to #2. Ironically, Parsons was credited as both singer and writer because of Bare's preexisting contracts with Challenge and Opal.

After military service, Bare kept recording for Fraternity until signing with CHET ATKINS and RCA RECORDS in early 1962. The following year, his version of the song "Detroit City"—by MEL TILLIS and Danny Dill (ANNIE LOU & DANNY DILL)—became his first Top Ten country hit, reached #16 pop, and earned him a

*Bobby Bare*

Grammy for Best Country & Western Recording. Subsequent hits with "500 Miles Away from Home," "Miller's Cave," and "Four Strong Winds" linked him to the folk music movement of the early 1960s. He moved to Nashville in 1964.

During the 1960s, along with his solo works, Bare recorded two RCA albums with SKEETER DAVIS, one with NORMA JEAN and LIZ ANDERSON, and another with the British country group the Hillsiders. He recorded for MERCURY in 1970–72 and then returned to RCA. In 1973 he cut his first album with Silverstein, *Lullabys, Legends and Lies*, which produced a #2 hit duet with his five-year-old son, Bobby Jr. ("Daddy, What If"), and his first #1 song, "Marie Laveau."

Bare has since recorded for COLUMBIA and EMI, and in the mid-1980s he hosted the critically acclaimed *Bobby Bare and Friends* TV show (1983–88) on TNN: THE NASHVILLE NETWORK. In 1998, he joined forces with Jennings, Tillis, and JERRY REED to record the ATLANTIC RECORDS album *Old Dogs*. He worked with Bobby Jr., now a rock recording artist, on the 2005 album *The Moon Was Blue*. —*Dale Vinicur*

## Max D. Barnes
b. Hardscratch, Iowa, July 24, 1936; d. January 11, 2004

Max Duane Barnes emerged in the 1980s as one of MUSIC ROW's leading songwriters, with concise, miniature dramas such as "Storms of Life" and "Chiseled in Stone." Raised in Nebraska, Barnes attended Omaha South High. Jobs as a farmhand, carpenter, and long-distance trucker instilled in him an abiding respect for the struggles of the working class. His music career began in earnest with his self-penned record "Ribbons of Steel," released on John Denny's JED label in 1971. After signing a writing contract with the Denny family's CEDARWOOD PUBLISHING COMPANY in 1972, Barnes moved to Nashville on May 1, 1973.

His first song to hit the charts came in 1979 with CONWAY TWITTY's recording of "Don't Take It Away." It was followed by another Twitty hit, "Redneckin', Love Makin' Night" (1981), written with Barnes's frequent cowriter Troy Seals. Other Barnes-Seals collaborations include "Who's Gonna Fill Their Shoes" (GEORGE JONES, 1985), "Storms of Life" (RANDY TRAVIS, 1985), "Ten Feet Away" (KEITH WHITLEY, 1986), and "I Won't Need You Anymore (Always and Forever)" (Travis, 1987). Barnes enjoyed particular success cowriting with VERN GOSDIN. Their compositions include "Do You Believe Me Now" (1987) and "Chiseled in Stone" (1988), the 1989 CMA Song of the Year. Barnes took CMA's Song of the Year award again in 1992 with "Look at Us," written with VINCE GILL. Barnes attributed his long run of success to a simple rule of thumb: "I try to write so there's no confusion. Country music is for ordinary people. That's what I am, and I don't ever want to get above that."

Barnes's son Max Troy Barnes (b. October 25, 1962) is a successful tunesmith in his own right. Among his hit songs are "Love, Me" (COLLIN RAYE, 1991), "Before You Kill Us All" (Randy Travis, 1994), and "How Your Love Makes Me Feel" (DIAMOND RIO, 1997). —*Kent Henderson*

## Bashful Brother Oswald
b. Sevier County, Tennessee, December 26, 1911; d. October 17, 2002

The shimmery cry of Bashful Brother Oswald's DOBRO was essential to the signature sound of ROY ACUFF's Smoky Mountain Boys for more than a half century. Oswald also sang high harmony with Acuff, frailed banjo, and did rube comedy, but his distinctive dobro parts on 1940s classics such as "The Wreck on the Highway" are Oswald's true legacy. His HAWAIIAN-style playing underlined the pathos of "The Precious Jewel" and similar Acuff performances. Oswald's presence on Acuff's radio programs, records, and stage shows helped save the dobro, a link between acoustic Hawaiian and electric steel guitars, from possible oblivion after World War II preempted production.

Oswald was born Beecher Ray Kirby, one of the eleven children of George Wesley Kirby, who provided for his brood by barbering, moonshining, and leading shape-note "singing schools." Beecher, who preferred the nickname Pete, left the Smoky Mountains in 1929 for Flint, Michigan, to join an uncle working at the Buick factory. The Depression kept Kirby off the assembly line, but in Flint he encountered Hawaiian guitarist Rudy Waikiki, whose playing he emulated. Kirby bought a metal National Hawaiian guitar, and by 1933 he was performing in Chicago-area bars, theaters, and burlesque houses by night while serving as a cook at the world's fair by day.

Back in Tennessee in 1936, Kirby toiled at a Knoxville bakery and occasionally filled in for dobro player Cell Summey (a.k.a. Cousin Jody) in Acuff's Knoxville-based Crazy Tennesseans. Acuff joined the GRAND OLE OPRY in February 1938, and when Summey and other members of the now-renamed Smoky Mountain Boys quit on New Year's Day 1939, Acuff sent for Kirby, who in turn recruited guitarist Lonnie Wilson and mandolinist Jess Easterday. Kirby first appeared on the Opry on January 7, 1939. Later that year, Acuff dubbed him Bashful Brother Oswald after singer-banjoist Rachel Veach joined Acuff's troupe. Many of Acuff's fans were scandalized by the presence of an unescorted female, but the ruse of a "brother" in the band as Veach's guardian stopped Acuff's negative mail.

Bashful Brother Oswald was the sole member of the 1939 Smoky Mountain Boys still accompanying Acuff when the bandleader died in 1992. Long a familiar presence (with Acuff guitarist Charlie Collins) at OPRYLAND USA, Oswald was inducted into the Grand Ole Opry on January 21, 1995. —*Mark Humphrey*

## Dr. Humphrey Bate
b. Castalian Springs, Sumner County, Tennessee, May 25, 1875;
    d. June 12, 1936

WSM announcer GEORGE D. HAY called Dr. Humphrey Bate "the Dean of the GRAND OLE OPRY," and for the first decade of the show it was Dr. Bate's colorful band, the Possum Hunters, that served as the program's musical anchor. Dr. Bate's group was also the first to play country music over Nashville radio (on station WDAD, in 1925) and the first to play the music on WSM. Dr. Bate was a close friend of Opry founder Hay and was responsible for getting numerous other pioneer performers, such as THE CROOK BROTHERS and DEFORD BAILEY, on the show.

Dr. Bate was a genuine country doctor, a graduate of Vanderbilt University who enjoyed classical music. At heart, though, he was a skilled harmonica player who had learned much of his repertoire on his father's middle Tennessee plantation; by World War I he was running two or three separate bands. Dr. Bate's groups were large by STRINGBAND MUSIC standards—often containing two fiddles, two guitars, a banjo, a harmonica, a cello, and a bowed bass. His repertoire, some of which he preserved on disc for BRUNSWICK RECORDS in 1928, included "Old Joe," "Greenback Dollar," and "Going Uptown" (the first sheet music published by

an Opry star). Key members of the Possum Hunters included fiddlers Oscar Stone and Bill Barret and banjoist Walter Liggett. Dr. Bate's records, only twelve sides, are considered to be among the finest and most complex in OLD-TIME MUSIC.

Dr. Bate died in 1936, though his band continued to play on the Opry. His son Buster performed on the show for a few years, and his daughter Alcyone Bate Beasley remained a singer on WSM throughout the 1950s. —*Charles Wolfe*

## Eddie Bayers
b. Patuxent, Maryland, January 28, 1949

One of the top studio drummers of country music's modern era, Edward Howard Bayers Jr. received his career break when he was employed by record producer JIM ED NORMAN to work on the soundtrack for the movie URBAN COWBOY. Bayers played on MICKEY GILLEY's "Stand By Me" and ANNE MURRAY's "Could I Have This Dance," both #1 hits from the film, and more recent credits include hits for BROOKS & DUNN, KENNY CHESNEY, SARA EVANS, ALAN JACKSON, MARTINA MCBRIDE, and GEORGE STRAIT. At one time Bayers was the drummer on the Top Eleven country albums and Top Thirteen country singles listed on *Billboard*'s popularity charts.

The son of a fighter pilot, Bayers grew up in such varied locations as a Maryland air force base (where he was born), San Diego, and North Africa. Originally a keyboard player, he shifted to drums once he became a fixture on the Nashville music scene in the mid-1970s.

In the mid-1980s Bayers nearly lost his place among the top session players when he suffered a broken left wrist. The injury kept him out of work for a year, and after his recovery several producers were reluctant to hire him, believing his skills had deteriorated.

Most of the industry disagreed. During the 1990s Bayers received ACM's Top Drummer Award eleven straight years, and at this writing he has been nominated as CMA's Musician of the Year nine times. —*Tom Roland*

## Bean Blossom
established in Bean Blossom, Indiana, June 1967

The granddaddy of BLUEGRASS festivals started when BILL MONROE staged his first weekend event in June 1967 at his music park in Bean Blossom, Indiana. In planning the festival, Monroe followed the lead of promoter CARLTON HANEY, who staged similar events in 1965 and 1966. Washington, D.C.–area DJ and promoter Don Owens and BILL CLIFTON had also organized one-day bluegrass events, in 1960 and 1961, respectively.

Prior to the founding of the Bean Blossom gathering, the local Brown County Jamboree had been entertaining the populace since 1931, generally featuring local talent in weekend shows. In 1951 Monroe purchased the Jamboree's property and hired his brother Birch as the Jamboree's manager. Bill Monroe booked many of his GRAND OLE OPRY peers, including ROY ACUFF, ERNEST TUBB, and KITTY WELLS, while providing a venue for older artists such as FIDDLIN' ARTHUR SMITH and CLAYTON MCMICHEN.

In the late 1970s Monroe expanded the event to ten days. Today, it runs for eight days each June, and the Bean Blossom site hosts numerous musical celebrations each year. Now named the

Bill Monroe Memorial Bean Blossom Bluegrass Festival, it remains the longest-running bluegrass festival in the United States and has inspired countless others. —*Chris Skinker*

## BeauSoleil

Since 1975, BeauSoleil has expanded the parameters of CAJUN MUSIC while honoring the genre's roots and reviving OLD-TIME material. Led by fiddler, vocalist, and songwriter Michael Doucet (b. Scott, Louisiana, February 14, 1951), BeauSoleil combines traditional Cajun and zydeco songs with rock, blues, jazz, country, BLUEGRASS, and Caribbean music. The group's passionate, adventurous approach brought the band two Grammy awards—for 1997's *L'Amour ou folie* and 2009's *Jazz Fest Live*. In 2005 the National Endowment for the Arts honored Doucet with a National Heritage Fellowship for his work with BeauSoleil.

Cajun/Creole music and culture were often scorned during the 1950s, when Doucet was growing up; by the mid-1970s, these rich musical traditions began to gain respect. Doucet, an accomplished fiddler, emerged as a pioneer in its new acceptance. In 1974 he formed the regionally oriented Bayou Drifter Band with singer/accordionist Zachary Richard. While Richard went on to blend Cajun music with rock and other musical styles, Doucet explored traditional sounds through informal apprenticeships with such venerable Cajun/Creole fiddlers as DENNIS MCGEE, Luderin Darbone (of THE HACKBERRY RAMBLERS), and Canray Fontenot. Will and DEWEY BALFA and HARRY CHOATES also influenced Doucet's fiddling, and BeauSoleil often records songs by these and other Louisiana music masters.

Doucet formed BeauSoleil in 1975 to celebrate this legacy while expressing his modernism in a popular rock band called Coteau, also known as "the Cajun Grateful Dead." When Coteau disbanded in 1977, Doucet channeled both approaches into BeauSoleil. Appearances on radio's *A PRAIRIE HOME COMPANION* and inclusion on the soundtracks of such films as 1987's *The Big Easy* spurred the band's rise to national and then global prominence.

Besides BeauSoleil, Michael Doucet has recorded with the Savoy-Doucet Band, Keith Richards, Richard Thompson, Mark Knopfler, Thomas Dolby, Wayne Toups, zydeco accordionist Nathan Williams, the Hackberry Ramblers, and MARY CHAPIN CARPENTER—whose work with the group won her a Grammy in 1992. In addition, Doucet has recorded several solo releases and a children's album.

BeauSoleil's prolific recordings reflect Michael Doucet's eclectic vision, ranging from acoustic, all-Cajun albums such as *Parlez-nous à Boire* to the rock-influenced productions *Bayou Boogie* and *Cajun Conja*, which also feature guest guitarist Sonny Landreth. Still active in 2010, BeauSoleil continues to champion the resurgent Cajun and Creole sounds, new and old, that have deeply influenced contemporary music during the past thirty-five years. —*Ben Sandmel*

## Jim Beck

b. Marshall, Texas, August 11, 1916; d. May 3, 1956

Jim Beck was a Dallas recording engineer who, but for a tragic accident, might well have changed the course of country music. As it was, his brief stint in the limelight, 1950–56, influenced a number of artists, including LEFTY FRIZZELL, RAY PRICE, BILLY WALKER, and others; indeed, any singer from the Southwest who came up in the 1950s knew of Beck's legendary Dallas studio and the hits produced there. When COLUMBIA RECORDS A&R man DON LAW began updating his company's roster in the early 1950s, he recorded more in Beck's studio than in Nashville or New York, and for a time it seemed that Dallas might emerge as country's top recording center.

By all accounts, Beck was something of a self-taught engineering genius who had built a working radio station in his bedroom by the time he was fourteen. During his World War II army years he gained more experience with broadcasting and recording techniques, and in 1945 he returned to Dallas and built his first recording studio. The army was his first main client, but to support his studio he became an announcer at KRLD, then developing into a powerful country station through the *BIG D JAMBOREE*. It was there that Beck learned to appreciate country music.

Beck eventually borrowed enough money to open a regular studio on Ross Avenue in Dallas, where he made the first demo recordings of Lefty Frizzell. These not only launched Frizzell's career (the singer would use the Beck studio to record most of his early hits) but also brought Beck to the attention of Law, who began to make Beck's operation the base for much of Columbia's country product. Word spread, as Beck also engineered for Nashville's BULLET label, SYD NATHAN's KING label as well as for IMPERIAL RECORDS and DECCA RECORDS. Artists using his studio ranged from Ray Price to Fats Domino, and from Sid King to classical pianist Gregor Sandor. Beck's contacts allowed him to make regular trips to New York to study the latest innovations in sound technology; often he would return to Dallas, reproduce these changes, and make improvements in them.

Beck's star was still rising when he died tragically in 1956; he had been cleaning his recording machine heads with carbon tetrachloride and had forgotten to open the windows for ventilation. The poison lodged in his system, and he died a few weeks later. —*Charles Wolfe*

## Barry Beckett

b. Birmingham, Alabama, February 4, 1943, d. June 10, 2009

After a lengthy stint as a member of the acclaimed rhythm section at FAME Recording Studios in Muscle Shoals, Alabama, keyboardist Barry Edward Beckett became a prominent Nashville-based producer, with credits ranging from BOB DYLAN, Etta James, and Bob Seger to ALABAMA, KENNY CHESNEY, and HANK WILLIAMS JR.

Beckett was playing in a lounge band in Pensacola, Florida, when he met "Papa Don" Schroeder, a local disc jockey. Schroeder brought Beckett to Muscle Shoals, where Beckett's first hit session was James and Bobby Purify's "I'm Your Puppet" (Bell Records, 1966). "About a year later," Beckett recalled, "[producer] Rick Hall was about to expand FAME Studios, and the musicians asked me if I'd like to come up and play with them full-time."

The FAME rhythm section, which then included Jimmy Johnson, David Hood, Roger Hawkins, Junior Lowe, and Beckett, played on hits including Wilson Pickett's "Land of 1,000 Dances," Aretha Franklin's "I Never Loved a Man," and Percy Sledge's "When a Man Loves a Woman." Later, Beckett, Johnson, Hawkins, and Hood opened their own Muscle Shoals Recording Studios, where they backed Paul Simon (*There Goes Rhymin' Simon*), Bob Dylan (*Slow Train Coming*), and Bob Seger (*Night Moves*).

After producing hits including Mary MacGregor's "Torn Between Two Lovers" (Ariola America, 1976) and the Sanford-Townsend Band's "Smoke from a Distant Fire" (Warner Bros., 1977), Beckett moved to Nashville in 1982, where he became country A&R director for WARNER BROS. RECORDS and coproduced HANK WILLIAMS JR. with JIM ED NORMAN.

After leaving Warner Bros., Beckett worked independently with ALABAMA, ASLEEP AT THE WHEEL, Kenny Chesney, JASON & THE SCORCHERS, DELBERT McCLINTON, NEAL McCOY, K. T. OSLIN, LEE ROY PARNELL, and EDDY RAVEN, among others. In the 1990s Beckett began producing rock acts, including Brendan Croker, Feargal Sharkey, and the Waterboys. Beckett continued playing sessions until health problems forced him to retire in 2005. —*Todd Everett*

## Bob Beckham
b. Stratford, Oklahoma, July 8, 1927

Robert Joseph Beckham began working in Nashville publishing circles as a song plugger for THE LOWERY MUSIC GROUP in 1961. After a stint with SHELBY SINGLETON Music, he joined COMBINE MUSIC PUBLISHING in 1964, becoming president in 1966. There he helped build the careers of DOLLY PARTON, KRIS KRISTOFFERSON, RAY STEVENS, JERRY REED, DENNIS LINDE, and TONY JOE WHITE, among others.

Beckham started in entertainment with a traveling show at age eight. He worked in movies (*Junior G Men, Star Maker*) in California but returned to Oklahoma in 1940, attending school before he became an army paratrooper at seventeen. After a post-war stint as an electrician, he worked in radio with Arthur Godfrey, enjoyed two Top Forty pop hits as a singer ("Just As Much As Ever," "Crazy Arms"), and toured with BRENDA LEE before settling in Nashville in 1959.

Through hard work and shrewd, pioneering deals for song exposure in commercials, he built Combine into a major publishing company before its 1986 sale to the SBK music publishing firm. In 1990 he established HoriPro Music, a part of Taiyo Music, Japan's biggest publisher. In 2001 Beckham became chairman of HoriPro Entertainment Group, and he served as president until 2006, when he retired. —*John Lomax III*

## Carl Belew
b. Salina, Oklahoma, April 21, 1931; d. October 31, 1990

Carl Robert Belew recorded for the FOUR STAR, RCA, DECCA, and Vocalion labels, achieving such hits as "Am I That Easy to Forget" (#9, 1959), "Hello Out There" (#8, 1962), and "Crystal Chandelier" (#12, 1965). But his greatest impact came as a songwriter. "Am I That Easy to Forget" was also a hit for SKEETER DAVIS and for JIM REEVES; other country chestnuts written by Belew include "Even the Bad Times Are Good," "I Can't Forget," "Lonely Street," "Stop the World (And Let Me Off)," "What's He Doing in My World," and "That's When I See the Blues (In Your Pretty Brown Eyes)."

Belew began playing guitar as an Oklahoma farm boy and migrated to the West Coast in the early 1950s. After stints on the California regional television programs *TOWN HALL PARTY* and *HOMETOWN JAMBOREE* in 1956, he joined the *LOUISIANA HAYRIDE* in 1957. He released his last single in 1974 and died of cancer in 1990. —*Walt Trott*

## Bellamy Brothers
Homer Howard Bellamy b. Darby, Florida, February 2, 1946
David Milton Bellamy b. Darby, Florida, September 16, 1950

The Bellamy Brothers first gained attention as a pop act with the smooth, upbeat multimarket hit "Let Your Love Flow," which peaked at #1 on the *Billboard Hot 100* charts in 1976. As the duo veered toward country in the late 1970s, they enjoyed another crossover hit, "If I Said You Have a Beautiful Body Would You Hold It Against Me," whose crafty title came from a line David Bellamy heard Groucho Marx use on his TV series *You Bet Your Life*.

The Bellamys grew up in west-central Florida, surrounded by cattle ranches and orange groves. Homer Bellamy, their father, was a musician who encouraged his sons to take up music. They were also influenced by ELVIS PRESLEY, BUDDY HOLLY, RICK NELSON, and THE EVERLY BROTHERS, by migrant Jamaican orange-pickers, and by the Beatles-led British Invasion of the 1960s.

The Bellamy Brothers first performed in 1958 with their father at the Rattlesnake Roundup in San Antonio, Florida. In the late 1960s they migrated to Atlanta, where they were influenced by the Allman Brothers and Frank Zappa. Eventually the brothers returned to the ranch, where David concentrated on songwriting. One night they came home late, and, rather than wake their parents, they spent the night in the adjoining bunkhouse. Howard woke up with a chicken snake in his sleeping bag. That gave David the idea for "Spiders and Snakes," a pop hit for Jim Stafford in 1974.

Encouraged, the Bellamys moved to Los Angeles. Stafford's manager, Phil Gernhard, helped them sign with CURB RECORDS, and "Let Your Love Flow," a WARNER BROS./Curb release, quickly became an international hit. The Bellamys' country career grew slowly until "Beautiful Body" hit #1 in 1979. Subsequent singles included "Redneck Girl" (1982) and the cultural explorations "Old Hippie" (1985) and "Kids of the Baby Boom" (1987).

The duo spent their most successful years on Curb, which they left in 1991 to join ATLANTIC RECORDS. They later recorded for their own Bellamy Brothers Records and for Blue Hat Records before rejoining Curb in 2002. —*Gerry Wood*

## Richard Bennett
b. Chicago, Illinois, July 22, 1951

Richard Bennett has made his mark as a session guitarist and as a producer. In both cases he has combined a strong respect for country's traditions with a knack for remaking those traditions afresh.

Born in Chicago, Bennett was reared in a household full of music. His mother sang light opera on the radio; his father was an amateur accordionist. At age eight, the family moved to Phoenix, where Richard took guitar lessons from Forrest Skaggs, former host of the *Arizona Hayride* barn dance. Through Skaggs's connections and those of session guitarist Al Casey, Bennett began playing guitar in Los Angeles recording sessions in 1968. Among the hundreds of pop and rock artists he backed on record through 1975 were Peggy Lee, Johnny Mathis, Barbra Streisand, Helen Reddy, Billy Joel, and Neil Diamond. He also served in Diamond's touring band for seventeen years.

In the early 1980s, Bennett traveled to Nashville to play sessions for BRENDA LEE, ROSANNE CASH, GEORGE STRAIT, and others.

In 1985, at STEVE EARLE's urging, Bennett moved to Nashville to coproduce and play lead guitar on Earle's landmark *Guitar Town* album. *Guitar Town* proved to be a watershed in Bennett's career, for his muscular guitar playing received notice in the press and in the Nashville music industry. Since then, Bennett has produced or coproduced records for JO-EL SONNIER, Marty Brown, EMMYLOU HARRIS, Phil Lee, Kim Richey, and MARTY STUART. He has continued to make appearances as a session guitarist and has been a member of Mark Knopfler's studio and road band since the mid-1990s. —*Paul Kingsbury*

## Ed Benson
b. Nashville, Tennessee, February 18, 1945

Edwin W. Benson Jr. became executive director of CMA in January 1992, following the retirement of JO WALKER-MEADOR. Benson had joined CMA in August 1979 as its first associate executive director. He also opened the first international office for CMA in London in 1982. (This office later closed.) He retired in 2008.

Benson is a native Nashvillian born into the prominent Benson musical family; his great-grandfather John T. Benson established the first gospel music publishing company in the city, in 1902. Later the family established Benson Publishing and Recordings. Ed Benson graduated from Vanderbilt in 1967 with a B.A. in business administration and worked for the Benson Company from 1970 to 1978. —*Don Cusic*

## Dierks Bentley
b. Phoenix, Arizona. November 20, 1975

One of the new century's most consistent country hit makers, as both performer and songwriter, Dierks Bentley has artfully balanced traditional HONKY-TONK MUSIC and BLUEGRASS with rock-influenced drive and romantic balladry. In so doing, he has won diverse fans, from stadiums to the stage of the GRAND OLE OPRY, whose cast he joined in October 2005.

After playing guitar in rock bands, Bentley moved to Nashville at age nineteen, struck by the potency of HANK WILLIAMS JR.'s records and envisioning a future for himself in country music.

*Dierks Bentley*

For nearly a decade he worked as a research assistant in TNN's video library, played in pickup bands, and soaked up bluegrass at Nashville's famous Station Inn.

Since signing with CAPITOL RECORDS Nashville, Bentley has released sonically diverse albums—including his 2003 self-titled debut, 2005's *Modern Day Drifter*, 2006's *Long Trip Alone*, and 2009's *Feel That Fire*—that have married contemporary lyrics with sounds that range from leathery, WAYLON JENNINGS–style honky-tonk ("Lot of Leavin' Left to Do") to seductive, CONWAY TWITTY–influenced ballads ("Come a Little Closer"), comic novelty ("What Was I Thinkin' "), and bluegrass-tinged footloose rambler rock ("Free and Easy (Down the Road I Go)"). At this writing, he has gained seven #1 singles, and he won CMA's 2005 Horizon Award. His 2010 album *Up on the Ridge* and an accompanying acoustic band tour spotlighted his bluegrass and roots music influences. —*Barry Mazor*

## Matraca Berg
b. Nashville, Tennessee, February 3, 1964

A respected performer, Matraca Maria Berg has found greater success writing songs for other artists. Country stars ranging from REBA McENTIRE ("The Last One to Know" 1987) to MARTINA McBRIDE ("Wild Angels" 1995) and DEANA CARTER ("Strawberry Wine" 1996) have topped the charts with Berg's material, and her songs have been covered by pop-rock vocalist LINDA RONSTADT nearly every contemporary female country singer, including PATTY LOVELESS, TRISHA YEARWOOD, SUZY BOGGUSS, DIXIE CHICKS, and GRETCHEN WILSON.

One of the few performer-songwriters to grow up in Nashville, Berg is the daughter of the late songwriter–session singer Icie Berg. From the time Matraca had her first #1 hit as a songwriter in 1982 (T. G. SHEPPARD and Karen Brooks's "Faking Love," cowritten with BOBBY BRADDOCK), she's been one of MUSIC CITY's most successful songwriters, ultimately winning CMA's Song of the Year Award in 1997 for "Strawberry Wine" (cowritten with Gary Harrison).

As an RCA recording artist, Berg has fared less well, at least commercially. Only two of her singles, "Baby, Walk On" and "The Things You Left Undone," have reached the Top Forty. Her album *Sunday Morning to Saturday Night* appeared on Rising Tide in 1997. Berg is married to Jeff Hanna of the NITTY GRITTY DIRT BAND. She was inducted into the NASHVILLE SONGWRITERS HALL OF FAME in 2008. —*Brian Mansfield*

## Byron Berline
b. Caldwell, Kansas, July 6, 1944

A fiddle virtuoso, Byron Berline has been a prominent figure in BLUEGRASS circles since the 1960s. Growing up on a Kansas farm near the Oklahoma border, he played fiddle by age five and won his first contest at ten while studying the great southwestern fiddlers, such as Benny Thomasson and ECK ROBERTSON.

While a student at the University of Oklahoma, Berline formed his first band, the Cleveland County Ramblers, and began learning to play bluegrass. In 1963 he joined THE DILLARDS, with whom he recorded *Pickin' and Fiddlin'* (1965) for ELEKTRA RECORDS. In 1967 he worked with BILL MONROE's Bluegrass Boys for a few months before enlisting in the U.S. Army.

Leaving the service in 1969, Berline became a sought-after session musician in Los Angeles, even recording with the Rolling Stones. He later played with the groups Hearts and Flowers, the Dillard and Clark Expedition, and, most notably, THE COUNTRY GAZETTE. His quintet California, with guitarist Dan Crary, won IBMA Instrumental Group of the Year honors in 1992, 1993, and 1994.

In April 1995, Berline moved to Guthrie, Oklahoma, and opened the Double Stop fiddle shop. He formed the Byron Berline Band the same year. Two years later, he founded the Oklahoma Bluegrass International Festival. Berline also can be heard on many film soundtracks, including *Basic Instinct*, *Blaze*, *Star Trek*, and *Stay Hungry*. —*Charlie Seemann*

## Hattie Louise "Tootsie" Bess (*see* Tootsie's Orchid Lounge)

## The Beverly Hill Billies

From their initial appearance on Los Angeles radio station KMPC on April 6, 1930, the Beverly Hill Billies became one of the most popular country music acts in Southern California, and they opened the door to wider acceptance of country music on the West Coast. They were the creation of KMPC station manager/announcer Glen "Mr. Tall-feller" Rice and announcer John McIntire. Beginning with that first broadcast, Rice informed the listening audience that a band of hillbillies had been found far back in the hills of Beverly, adding that he had persuaded them to ride in each night to perform on his radio station—a myth that many listeners accepted at face value.

Combining the talents of accordionist "Zeke Manners" (Leo Mannes), guitarist Tom "Pappy" Murray, vocalist "Ezra Longnecker" (Cyprian Paulette), and fiddler "Hank Skillet" (Henry Blaeholder), the Hill Billies quickly became a sensation, drawing huge crowds with their heart songs, striking solos, strong harmonies, and comedy routines. The group made its first recordings for BRUNSWICK on April 25, 1930, and continued to record for the label through September 1932. That month the Hill Billies left KMPC for rival station KTM. The group also appeared in several western movies with Charles Starrett, RAY WHITLEY, GENE AUTRY, and TEX RITTER.

Friction within the group and the appearance of two strong L.A.–area competitors, STUART HAMBLEN's Lucky Stars and the SONS OF THE PIONEERS, caused interest in the Hill Billies to wane, although they retained a following into the early 1940s. Other talents featured in the group were singer ELTON BRITT (Jimmy Baker), guitarist "Lem Giles" (Aleth Hansen), guitarist "Charlie Slater" (Charles Quirk), guitarist and singer Ashley Dees, and singers Hubert Walton, Marjorie Bauersfeld, Stuart Hamblen, and Lloyd Perryman.

In 1963 members of the group sued and won a settlement from the TV producers of CBS's *THE BEVERLY HILLBILLIES* for name infringement. —*Ken Griffis*

## *The Beverly Hillbillies*

CBS-TV's *The Beverly Hillbillies* is one of America's most successful situation comedies. Premiering in the fall of 1962, it exposed millions of Americans to BLUEGRASS music each week via its theme song, performed by FLATT & SCRUGGS AND THE FOGGY MOUNTAIN BOYS. Initially the duo was ambivalent about doing "The Ballad of Jed Clampett," because the word "hillbilly" had a derogatory connotation among country musicians. After viewing the pilot episode, however, Flatt & Scruggs decided to record the song for television broadcast, with western singer Jerry Scoggins on lead vocals. Then, at the suggestion of Scruggs's wife, Louise, Flatt & Scruggs recorded and released "The Ballad of Jed Clampett," with Flatt singing lead, as a COLUMBIA RECORDS single in 1962. The recording topped *Billboard*'s country charts, making it the first bluegrass hit to reach #1. Through 1968 Flatt & Scruggs made yearly appearances on the program; as the duo's popularity increased dramatically, banjo sales soared.

Singer-guitarist ROY CLARK made a handful of guest appearances after Flatt & Scruggs disbanded in 1969. As Cousin Roy, Clark wore an outrageous plaid suit and played a guitar full of hot licks. Superbly cast, the show's principals included actor-dancer Buddy Ebsen as widower Jed Clampett, Irene Ryan as Granny, Donna Douglas as Elly May, and Max Baer Jr. as the nitwit nephew Jethro. Raymond Bailey as banker Milburn Drysdale and Nancy Kulp as Drysdale's assistant Jane Hathaway provided excellent support. In 1971 the show ceased production, but it continues to air in syndication. —*Chris Skinker*

## Shelia Shipley Biddy
b. Scottsville, Kentucky, October 2, 1952

In 1994, Shelia Shipley Biddy became the first woman to run a major country record label when she became senior vice president/general manager of MCA RECORDS's newly revived DECCA label. There she furthered the careers of GARY ALLAN, MARK CHESNUTT, and LEE ANN WOMACK, among others, until the label was shuttered by the 1999 merger of Universal Music Group and PolyGram Label Group.

Opening Shipley Biddy Entertainment, she managed the careers of singers Jeff Carson and Danni Leigh (a former Decca artist). In 2003, she took over leadership of the independent label Vivaton, and when it folded, she joined Hallmark Direction Company, heading the management team for The Parks, Ray Scott, and Trent Willmon.

Biddy started her music career in 1976 as an administrative assistant at MONUMENT RECORDS. She later served at RCA RECORDS before joining MCA in 1984 as director of sales and marketing. She was named director of national promotion a year later and became senior vice president of national promotion in 1992, working with VINCE GILL, REBA MCENTIRE, WYNONNA, and GEORGE STRAIT. —*Beverly Keel*

## Big & Rich
Kenneth "Big Kenny" Alphin b. Culpeper, Virginia, November 1, 1963
John Rich b. Amarillo, Texas, January 7, 1974

Big & Rich shook up country music with a genre-bending sound blending contemporary country with rap, hard rock, and gospel testifying. Kenny Alphin and John Rich initially collaborated as songwriters and then launched a weekly musical event in Nashville, hosted by MuzikMafia, an organization they founded. Previously, Alphin recorded for Hollywood Records as Big Kenny; Rich had been in LONESTAR but left before the band's 1999 platinum breakthrough album. He recorded a solo album for BNA Entertainment (RCA RECORDS) that wasn't released until after Big & Rich's success.

Producer PAUL WORLEY signed Big & Rich to WARNER BROS. RECORDS, where the duo created a stir with their first singles, especially "Save a Horse (Ride a Cowboy)." The duo's 2004 debut album, *Horse of a Different Color,* went #1. Their first #1 single, "Lost in This Moment," took their third album, *Between Raising Hell and Amazing Grace,* to #1 in 2007.

Rich produced other acts, including JOHN ANDERSON and GRETCHEN WILSON (a MuzikMafia colleague). His 2009 solo album, *Son of a Preacher Man,* included the hit "Shuttin' Detroit Down." He also hosted the CMT series *Gone Country.* In 2006, Alphin began spearheading an ongoing charity and awareness program directed at the Darfur region of Sudan. —*Michael McCall*

## The Big Bopper (J. P. Richardson)
b. Sabine Pass, Texas, October 24, 1930; d. February 3, 1959

Jiles Perry Richardson Jr.—the Big Bopper—is remembered chiefly for perishing in the plane crash that took the lives of Ritchie Valens and BUDDY HOLLY; as a result, Richardson's accomplishments as a singer and country songwriter have often been overlooked.

A career DJ, Richardson joined KTRM in Beaumont, Texas, in 1949. He first recorded for J. D. MILLER in Crowley, Louisiana, although the tracks went unissued at the time. Then he recorded "Beggar to a King" (later a hit for HANK SNOW) and "Crazy Blues" for Mercury-Starday Records (1957).

In June 1958, as the partnership between MERCURY RECORDS and STARDAY RECORDS was dissolving, Richardson recorded "Chantilly Lace" for PAPPY DAILY's D RECORDS. The single was issued under the pseudonym "The Big Bopper" (a name Richardson used to host an R&B show on KTRM). After strong sales in Texas, Mercury leased it, and it rose to #6 on the pop charts. Richardson quit KTRM in December 1958 to work show dates; two months later, he was dead.

Richardson also wrote "Running Bear" for Johnny Preston as well as "White Lightnin'" and "Treasure of Love," both recorded by GEORGE JONES. —*Colin Escott*

## Big D Jamboree
established in Dallas, Texas, fall 1948

Not as long-lived or as fabled as many of country music's Saturday night barn dances, Dallas's *Big D Jamboree* was nevertheless an important regional broadcast that propelled several artists toward national prominence and proved a key venue for both touring acts and area talent.

Begun in 1946 as the *Texas State Barn Dance* by radio personality Uncle Gus Foster and Dallas club owner Slim McDonald—and using coproducer Ed McLemore's wrestling arena, the Sportatorium—the show was rechristened the *Lone Star Jamboree* when it began airing on WFAA radio, probably in late 1947. The show was renamed *Big D Jamboree* when it began airing on KRLD in the fall of 1948. Hosted and coproduced by KRLD's Johnny Hicks and its original host, KLIF disc jockey Big Al Turner (who would be replaced by John Harper), the *Jamboree* featured regional stars such as THE CALLAHAN BROTHERS, Riley Crabtree, and Gene O'Quin.

Over the next decade, on both radio and television, the *Jamboree* served as springboard for artists such as BILLY WALKER, HANK LOCKLIN, and SONNY JAMES, while also providing a valuable outlet for regionally based stars such as CHARLINE ARTHUR and for national touring acts. The LIGHT CRUST DOUGHBOYS, usually billed as the Country Gentlemen (not the famous BLUEGRASS group), served as house band for many years. Johnny Hicks left the show in 1959, but it continued in some form into the mid-1960s; its subsequent hosts included LAWTON WILLIAMS and former *Louisiana Hayride* host Horace Logan. In 1963 STARDAY RECORDS released an album of live recordings from the show, which enjoyed a brief but unsuccessful revival in about 1970. Three more albums of historic live recordings, including one featuring female performers and another highlighting males, were released on Dallas's Dragon Street Records between 2000 and 2002. —*Kevin Coffey*

## Big Machine Records
established Nashville, Tennessee, 2005

Big Machine Records launched in September 2005 under the leadership of veteran Nashville record industry executive SCOTT BORCHETTA and as a joint venture with Show Dog Records, a label started and directed by country star TOBY KEITH. Initially sharing staffs to cut costs, the two labels ended their partnership in March 2006.

Big Machine quickly established itself, signing TAYLOR SWIFT, whose pop crossover success led her to become the biggest-selling musical artist of 2009. The label and its subsidiaries developed new acts while forging deals with superstars GARTH BROOKS, MARTINA McBRIDE, REBA McENTIRE, RASCAL FLATTS, and TRISHA YEARWOOD.

In 2007, Borchetta founded Valory Music Group, a Big Machine subsidiary. Its roster included McEntire as well as pop star-turned-country artist Jewel and Justin Moore. In 2009, Big Machine partnered with New York–based Universal Republic Records to form another country music label, Republic Records Nashville. As of 2011, the Republic roster included McBride, newcomers The Band Perry, and Texas HONKY-TONK stylist Sunny Sweeney, who had been one of the first artists on Big Machine. —*Michael McCall*

## Binkley Brothers' Dixie Clodhoppers
Amos Binkley b. Cheatham County, Tennessee, March 30, 1895; d. October 6, 1985
Gale Binkley b. Cheatham County, Tennessee, May 7, 1896; d. April 1979

One of GEORGE D. HAY's famed "hoedown bands" that helped start the GRAND OLE OPRY, the Binkley Brothers brought to Nashville the clean, precise instrumental style of west-central Tennessee—the same area that later produced FIDDLIN' ARTHUR SMITH and HOWDY FORRESTER. Watchmakers and jewelry repairmen by day, Amos and Gale Binkley were featured on WSM and rival station WLAC from 1926 to 1938. Gale was a contest-winning fiddler; brother Amos was a banjoist. Their guitar player was Tom Andrews, and for much of their career their vocalist was Jack Jackson the Strolling Yodeler, a popular Nashville radio singer of the early 1930s.

In 1928 the Binkley Brothers earned a footnote in history by becoming the first artists to make commercial records in Nashville.

They recorded for the Victor Talking Machine Company's Victor label in the YMCA building, cutting "Watermelon Hanging on the Vine" and "Give Me Back My Fifteen Cents." These first sides were rejected, however. A few days later they joined forces with Jack Jackson and recorded a series of more successful sides, including a classic of OLD-TIME MUSIC, "I'll Rise When the Rooster Crows."

When the Binkleys quit the Opry in 1939, their place was taken by a new STRINGBAND called BILL MONROE and the Blue Grass Boys. —*Charles Wolfe*

## Clint Black

b. Long Branch, New Jersey, February 4, 1962

Clint Patrick Black shot to stardom by singing modern Texas HONKY-TONK MUSIC with a versatile, expressive baritone. He first drew attention on the Houston-Galveston club circuit, where he formed a songwriting partnership in 1986 with singer-songwriter Hayden Nicholas. Rock band ZZ Top's manager Bill Ham started working with Black in 1987 and landed him a recording contract with RCA RECORDS.

Black wrote ten songs—five with Nicholas—on his 1989 debut album, *Killin' Time*, and coproducers JAMES STROUD and MARK WRIGHT gave it an old-fashioned honky-tonk feel, albeit with crisp, state-of-the-art fidelity. The album topped the country album charts for twenty-eight weeks and yielded four consecutive #1 singles ("Better Man," "Killin' Time," "Nobody's Home," and "Walkin' Away"). *Killin' Time*'s success helped Black garner the 1989 CMA Horizon Award, and by 1994 the album had sold more than three million copies.

The Texan followed with 1990's *Put Yourself in My Shoes*, a double-platinum smash that produced two #1 singles: "Loving Blind" and "Where Are You Now." Black won the 1990 CMA Best

*Clint Black*

Male Vocalist Award and was inducted as a member of the GRAND OLE OPRY in 1991. That year, he married TV personality Lisa Hartman. Black continued to release platinum-selling albums through the 1990s, including 1992's *The Hard Way* (the first Black coproduced with Stroud), 1993's *No Time to Kill,* 1994's *One Emotion,* and 1997's *Nothin' but the Taillights.* He also released a 1994 holiday album, *Looking for Christmas,* and a 1996 *Greatest Hits* album. The latter was certified double-platinum in 1999.

By 1994, Black followed his wife into acting, appearing in the TV sitcom *Wings* and the film remake of *Maverick.* He had the starring role in the 1998 TV movie *Still Holding On: The Legend of Cadillac Jack* and appeared in the TV movie *Going Home* and the 2003 feature film *Anger Management.* In 2008 he was a contestant on the CBS reality show *Secret Talents of the Stars,* in which he competed as a standup comic. The following year he participated in the second season of NBC's *The Celebrity Apprentice,* coming in fifth after being eliminated in the eleventh week.

Black took over production of his albums with the late-1999 release of *D'Electrified,* an acoustic album that mixed cover songs, updates of old hits, and original material. It was the first of Black's albums not to go platinum and, as of 2011, the last to have gone gold. He and Hartman had a daughter, Lily Pearl, in May 2001. Black took three years off to focus on his family and to reassess his career. He left RCA to form his own label, Equity Music Group, and released two albums, *Spend My Time* (2004) and *Drinkin' Songs and Other Logic* (2005), before Equity closed in 2008. —*Geoffrey Himes*

## Black Artists in Country Music

When CHARLEY PRIDE first made the country charts in 1966, he was often asked how it felt to be a black man singing "white" music. His reply: "I'm not a black man singing white man's music. I'm an American singing American music." Although country music has been viewed as a white man's province, black influences in country have been profound, and black musicians have played prominent roles in its evolution.

Long before the music emerged as a commercial force in the 1920s, black-white American musical interchange was well under way, as described in the 1998 WARNER BROS. RECORDS boxed set *From Where I Stand: The Black Experience in Country Music,* 1998). Slave fiddlers were noted as early as the eighteenth century, and the banjo—later to become integral to OLD-TIME MUSIC and BLUEGRASS—was of African origin. Black spirituals, plantation work songs, and minstrel tunes all made their way into white folk and commercial traditions that nurtured early country music, just as ragtime, jazz, and blues would do in the late nineteenth and early twentieth centuries. Blues and STRINGBAND musicians of both races—especially in the South, where most black Americans lived—often shared songs and styles. Judging from the southern origins of recent black country acts, the region's importance to racial musical interchange is still strong.

Blacks have influenced white country musicians for decades. Two early examples are JIMMIE RODGERS, who absorbed music from black railroad workers and recorded with black musicians Clifford Gibson and Louis Armstrong, and JIMMIE DAVIS, who borrowed heavily from blues and recorded with black sideman Oscar Woods. During the 1920s, black Kentuckian ARNOLD SHULTZ, widely acknowledged as a major source of the modern thumb-style guitar, performed with BILL MONROE and ultimately inspired CHET ATKINS and MERLE TRAVIS through his influence on white guitarists Kennedy Jones and MOSE RAGER. Black string-bands continued to influence whites into the 1930s; Bo Chatman and His Mississippi Sheiks first popularized "Sittin' on Top of the World," later recorded by BOB WILLS and by Monroe. By far the most significant prewar black country star was the GRAND OLE OPRY's DEFORD BAILEY, a diminutive harmonica player whose song "Pan American Blues" inspired Opry founder GEORGE D. HAY's renaming of the show in 1927.

After World War II, rhythm & blues inspired many country acts, including KING RECORDS's MOON MULLICAN, who recorded with black drummer Calvin "Eagle Eye" Shields and worked closely with black producer HENRY GLOVER. BILL HALEY, ELVIS PRESLEY, JOHNNY CASH, and CARL PERKINS, among others, made R&B a building block for rock & roll. Black artist BIG AL DOWNING joined the ROCKABILLY trend, recording on his own and backing WANDA JACKSON.

In the early 1960s, R&B superstar RAY CHARLES broadened country's mainstream pop exposure through his gold albums *Modern Sounds in Country and Western Music* and its follow-up "Volume 2" release; both reinterpreted country standards such as DON GIBSON's "I Can't Stop Loving You" and TED DAFFAN's "Born to Lose." Esther Phillips, O. C. Smith, and other black singers followed Charles's lead by scoring major pop hits with country material.

The first black artist to emerge as a major modern country act was Charley Pride, of Sledge, Mississippi. At first, RCA RECORDS was cautious in marketing him to country's primarily white audience, but he went on to mass acceptance with sixty-seven chart records between 1966 and 1992 (fifty-two of them Top Ten). With a smooth-yet-hard-edged voice, Pride brought an honesty to stage and studio that made CMA's 1971 and 1972 Male Vocalist of the Year and Entertainer of the Year in 1971. Pride's success paved the way for other black country singers, such as LINDA MARTELL, who in 1969 became the first black female country singer to work the Opry.

Although Pride has been called the "Jackie Robinson of country music," no black country artist who followed him has yet reached his level of stardom. HONKY-TONK stylist STONEY EDWARDS, from Seminole, Oklahoma, had fifteen country chart singles between 1971 and 1980, but major success eluded him, as it did Ruby Falls and singer-songwriter O. B. MCCLINTON.

Black artists active in country music during the 1980s mainly crossed over from pop. Ray Charles hit with "I Didn't See a Thing" (a duet with GEORGE JONES) in 1983–84 and "Seven Spanish Angels" (a pairing with WILLIE NELSON) in 1984. Pop star Lionel Richie wrote the #1 country and pop hit "Lady" (1980) for KENNY ROGERS and hit #10 country himself with "Deep River Woman" (recorded with ALABAMA) in 1987. Pop hitmaker Dobie Gray also made a pop-to-country chart transition during the late 1980s.

Despite the links these artists forged with wider audiences, black singers attempting country careers fared poorly during the 1980s and '90s. Nisha Jackson, of Tyler, Texas, was signed to CAPITOL RECORDS after winning a TNN *You Can Be a Star* contest in 1987, but the label released only one recording and dropped her in 1990. CLEVE FRANCIS, a cardiologist from Jennings, Louisiana, caught LIBERTY RECORDS mogul JIMMY BOWEN's eye in 1991 and released three albums, but poor sales led to Francis's return to medicine four years later. Although the uncertain fortunes facing any artist doubtless played their part, Jackson explained black country singers' problems partly in terms of music executives' conservatism (if not racism) and failure to market black artists aggressively.

Early in 1995, however, Francis began to publicize survey data showing that some 17 percent to 24 percent of black adults over age eighteen were listening to country music, revealing an under-served market of some 5 million to 7 million listeners. Country music executives have used black artists to tap this potential since the late 1990s, with mixed results. Trini Triggs, of Natchitoches, Louisiana, issued a self-titled album on MCG/CURB in 1998 but failed to score hit singles. Six-foot-four-inch Cowboy Troy (Troy Coleman) of Victoria, Texas, fared somewhat better with a combination of country and rap he called "hick-hop." After working Dallas-area clubs and making two self-released albums, he released albums on RAYBAW/Warner Bros. in 2005 and 2007 (he left in 2008). He also cohosted *Nashville Star* (2006–07) and recorded with fellow MuzikMafia act BIG & RICH. To date, neither Rhonda Towns nor Miko Marks, both of whom released albums between 2005 and 2007, has gained traction in the marketplace. Pittsburgh native Rissi Palmer put two songs on the country charts in 2007–08, but neither broke the Top 40, and her self-titled album reached only #56 on *Billboard*'s Country Albums chart. Outside the commercial realm, a black stringband trio, Carolina Chocolate Drops, revived old-time music with a modern flair and drew attention from critics and fans.

Among recent country artists, former Hootie & the Blowfish frontman DARIUS RUCKER is the only black singer whose career has shown superstar potential. By August 2009, his 2008 Capitol album *Learn to Live* had gone platinum and yielded three #1 singles. In November 2009, Rucker was named CMA New Artist of the Year. His followup album, *Charleston, SC 1966*, was released in October 2010 and included his fourth country #1, "Come Back Song." —*John W. Rumble*

## Rick Blackburn
b. Cincinnati, Ohio, November 16, 1942

Rick Blackburn spent nearly two decades running Nashville divisions of major record companies, managing CBS Records' COLUMBIA and EPIC labels and, later, ATLANTIC RECORDS, during a period of extensive growth and change for the genre.

Blackburn's career began in 1964 when, after graduating from the University of Cincinnati, he worked in pop radio and record distribution. He moved to Chicago in 1965 to promote pop product for MERCURY RECORDS and then Epic Records a year later. Blackburn transferred to Epic's New York office in 1968 to become director of merchandising, formed the CBS-distributed Ode Records (with Herb Alpert and Lou Adler) in Los Angeles in 1970, and returned to New York as director of national sales and distribution. He moved to Nashville in 1974 as general manager of MONUMENT RECORDS. Two years later Blackburn accepted the position of vice president of marketing for CBS's Nashville division, and by 1980 he was vice president and general manager.

Under his leadership, CBS jumped from fourth to first in country market share. Mainstays such as RICKY SKAGGS, MERLE HAGGARD, ROSANNE CASH, EXILE, RICKY VAN SHELTON, CHET ATKINS, and VERN GOSDIN came aboard during his tenure. When Japanese conglomerate SONY MUSIC ENTERTAINMENT bought CBS in November 1987, Blackburn had already decided to leave the label to form Venture Entertainment, a publishing/management/production partnership with Blake Mevis.

On August 7, 1989, Atlantic opened its doors in Nashville, and Blackburn was named vice president of operations and head of the Nashville division. He used research and music testing to help the label launch four platinum acts: JOHN MICHAEL MONTGOMERY, TRACY LAWRENCE, NEAL MCCOY, and CONFEDERATE RAILROAD. Blackburn became chairman emeritus of Atlantic in 1999 and left the company when Atlantic closed its Nashville office in 2001 (the Atlantic Nashville label was revived in 2008). —*Michael Hight*

## Blackface Minstrelsy

In the 1830s Thomas D. Rice and George Washington Dixon established one of that century's most successful types of American popular theater when they masked their whiteness in blackface makeup and dressed, danced, sang, played, spoke, joked, and acted in stereotypical portrayals of American blacks. By so doing they were developing musical theater along racial lines, whereas class had figured prominently earlier in the century, principally in theater that featured the familiar country rube stereotype. Quickly the form grew in size, and by midcentury a typical minstrel show featured a team of blackface performers (four to six initially; dozens later in the century) who presented whole evenings of entertainment. By this time, too, minstrelsy had become essentially derogatory in its representation of blacks especially to northern, urban audiences.

Although minstrelsy's heyday was the nineteenth century, it enjoyed considerable popularity well into the middle of the twentieth century. Minstrelsy reached many parts of popular culture, not least of which was country music. In obvious ways, the hillbilly persona employed by many in country music (e.g., GRANDPA JONES, STRINGBEAN, ARCHIE CAMPBELL, even MINNIE PEARL) is a direct legacy of rube plays, which paralleled minstrel shows. Several songs from the minstrel tradition became barn dance staples, especially "Zip Coon" (known more widely as "Turkey in the Straw") and "Old Dan Tucker." Many early country stars gained valuable stage experience while performing (sometimes in blackface) in traveling MEDICINE SHOWS, which by convention included blackface performers. CLAYTON MCMICHEN of the Skillet Lickers frequently appeared in such shows. Both JIMMIE RODGERS and BOB WILLS were accomplished blackface entertainers, which gave them better reason to perform in blues-inflected styles. ROY ACUFF and BILL MONROE, like many other such artists, worked alongside blackface comics and may have appeared as such.

Minstrelsy's comedic style also affected country music. Blackface humor typically featured a patter of low-order puns and jokes from complementary comics (typically named Bones and Tambo), a device that has served country performance to the present. JAMUP AND HONEY, a popular early blackface Bones/Tambo duo, headlined one of the popular GRAND OLE OPRY tent shows in the early 1940s. A midcentury comedy duo, HOMER & JETHRO, even sported something like "fright wigs" (popular among minstrels a hundred years earlier), although they never performed in blackface.

The format of minstrelsy directly influenced early country music performance as well. The *Boone County Jamboree* (later named the *MIDWESTERN HAYRIDE*), broadcast by WLW–Cincinnati, often arrayed cast members in a semicircle onstage for the entire show, exactly as the minstrel show did; a "shout," featuring everyone, concluded the evening in lively fashion, much like the "walk around" ended a minstrel show. Lasses White, who organized minstrel shows for WSM from the 1920s, brought his craft to the Grand Ole Opry as its first blackface performer. By the mid-1930s the Opry had absorbed aspects of minstrelsy's

performance conventions, many of which are still in evidence today. Country music's most obvious link to minstrelsy in its more recent history is provided by the television show *HEE HAW*, whose structure, humor, characterization, and, in many ways, music were like those of a minstrel show in "rube-face."

Blackface entertainment was endemic during country music's birth as a commercial art form, so it is not surprising that many aspects of one genre would have migrated to the other. Minstrelsy, like country music, was also by, for, and about everyday people who occupied lower social echelons, one ostensibly about black people and the other about white. Arguably, both minstrelsy and country music were at their most expressive (and, in some ways, most popular) when they acknowledged that American culture, especially among common folk, has evolved from interaction among the nation's races. —*Dale Cockrell*

## Randy Blake (see *Suppertime Frolic*)

## Lowell Blanchard (see *Mid-Day Merry-Go-Round*)

## Frank Blevins
b. Smyth County, Virginia, February 25, 1911; d. July 27, 2001

The music of Walter Franklin Blevins not only embodies the traditions of Appalachian fiddling but also reflects the influences of technology and social change that helped shape country music in the years preceding World War II. Raised in Ashe County, North Carolina, Blevins learned to play violin as a child and formed a STRINGBAND in his teen-age years with his brother Edd on guitar and neighbor Fred Miller on banjo. Billed as Frank Blevins & His Tar Heel Rattlers, the trio traveled to Atlanta in 1927 and 1928 to record OLD-TIME mountain songs for COLUMBIA RECORDS.

After moving to Marion, Virginia, in 1929, Blevins became a protégé of folklorist Annabel Morris Buchanan and was twice champion fiddler at the annual White Top Folk Festival. At the 1933 festival, Frank and Edd Blevins teamed with banjoist Jack Reedy in a special program for visiting First Lady Eleanor Roosevelt, who awarded them top honors for best band performance.

The group expanded in 1934 with the addition of guitarist Corwin Matthews, dubbing themselves the Southern Buccaneers. Led by Frank Blevins's dynamic fiddling and singing, the Southern Buccaneers reigned as the foremost country stringband in south-western Virginia throughout the 1930s, with a diverse repertoire and frequent radio broadcasts. The death of Edd Blevins in 1944 signaled the end of Frank Blevins's professional fiddling career, though he continued to make music informally for another two decades. —*Marshall Wyatt*

## Blue Sky Boys
William A. Bolick b. Hickory, North Carolina, October 28, 1917; d. March 13, 2008
Earl A. Bolick b. Hickory, North Carolina, November 16, 1919; d. April 19, 1998

It is not enough to describe Bill and Earl Bolick as simply one of country music's many BROTHER DUETS. Their beautifully crafted vocal harmonies, tasteful mandolin and guitar accompaniment, and repertoire of mostly traditional BALLADS and gospel songs put them in a class by themselves. Their understated vocals, characterized by Earl's baritone lead and Bill's tenor harmony conveyed a pathos and sincerity that have rarely been equaled in country music, and their influence can still be heard in the singing of such modern duos as JIM & JESSE McReynolds, the Whitstein Brothers (Charles and Robert), and Skaggs and Rice (RICKY SKAGGS and TONY RICE).

The Bolicks began singing on radio in North Carolina in 1935, and in 1936 they began a recording career with RCA VICTOR that lasted (except for their military stint during World War II) until their retirement in 1951. They named themselves the Blue Sky Boys in tribute to the Blue Ridge Mountains ("the Land of the Sky"), which lay west of their North Carolina home. After military service, they resumed their career in 1946 on WGST in Atlanta but thereafter played on a series of radio stations and programs, including the *Louisiana Hayride* in Shreveport. On their postwar recordings and radio shows, they also employed a fiddler, most often Curly Parker, who sang the third part in their trios. In the 1960s they gave concerts at a few university campuses and BLUEGRASS festivals and recorded some highly praised albums for STARDAY and CAPITOL. Excellent collections assembled from home recordings or radio transcriptions also have been released on the COUNTY, ROUNDER, and Copper Creek labels.
—*Bill C. Malone*

## Bluebird Café

Founded in 1982 by Amy Kurland as a lunch and music spot in a strip mall, the Bluebird Café quickly evolved into the premier Nashville listening room for singer-songwriters. KATHY MATTEA, PAM TILLIS, TRISHA YEARWOOD, FAITH HILL, GARTH BROOKS, KENNY CHESNEY, DIERKS BENTLEY, and TAYLOR SWIFT played to the 120-capacity room before moving on to national stardom. Longer, and harder to catalog, is the list of songs first publicly performed there before becoming country and pop hits.

The club has hosted its own cable television series, *Live from the Bluebird*, on the Turner South Network; it has its own book, *The Bluebird Café Scrapbook*, published by HarperEntertainment; CBS-TV has featured it on the *Evening News with Katie Couric* and its *48 Hours* news program; and the feature film *The Thing Called Love*, directed by Peter Bogdanovich and starring the late River Phoenix, set several scenes in the venue.

The Bluebird is popular with songwriters because its staff demands quiet attention to performances and gives great care to sound quality. A popular format features in-the-round sessions, with three or four songwriters facing each other in the middle of the room and taking turns performing songs while surrounded by the audience. The arrangement creates intimacy between performers and the audience and encourages the easy sharing of original work. The practice dates from 1987, when DON SCHLITZ, PAUL OVERSTREET, Fred Knobloch, and THOM SCHUYLER pioneered the presentation. A year later, Pam Tillis, Ashley Cleveland, Karen Staley, and Tricia Walker countered with a popular women-in-the-round arrangement.

Kurland took Bluebird-style shows on the road to Florida, New York, and elsewhere. In 2008 she transferred ownership of the club to Nashville Songwriters Association International (NSAI), which continues to run the venue in the manner she established. —*Jay Orr*

## Bluebird Records
established in New York, April 1933

Bluebird Records was a budget-line subsidiary of RCA VICTOR RECORDS. From the early 1920s, nonclassical 78-rpm records had been marketed to sell for twenty to thirty-five cents, but RCA Victor tried to hold fast to a seventy-five cent retail price for all records on all of its imprints. As the Depression deepened, company executives had second thoughts and—after test-marketing lower prices on the Sunrise, Timely Tunes, Electradisk, and Bluebird labels—decided to sell Bluebird recordings at thirty-five cents. The first regular release appeared in April 1933—six months before England's DECCA RECORDS debuted its American imprint, also at thirty-five cents.

Bluebird's releases were a mix of dance bands, blues, and, early on, country reissues from the RCA Victor catalog. Soon after RCA noted the strong sales response to Bluebird's low prices, all RCA "race" and country products appeared solely on Bluebird. RCA had no staff for this label; RCA personnel in Camden, New Jersey, handled all Bluebird functions. The vast majority of Bluebird's country recordings were cut by remote recording units that ventured south four or five times annually. Country artists who contributed substantially to the label's sales were the BLUE SKY BOYS, the DELMORE BROTHERS, J. E. MAINER, WADE MAINER, Bill Boyd, (BILL AND JIM BOYD), the MONROE BROTHERS, the CARTER FAMILY, and ELTON BRITT.

Bluebird continued an aggressive release program until 1942, when an AFM recording strike—along with wartime shellac shortages and a government ban against increasing list pricing—caused RCA to begin phasing out the budget label. RCA Victor's use of the Bluebird label name was far from over, however. In 1953 RCA used the name for a budget line of classical 12-inch LPs, and in 1956 the company used it for a line of children's records. In 1970 Bluebird was once again revived as a label for a series of vintage music on long-playing records. Beginning in 2001, Bluebird was used exclusively for jazz releases, new and reissued. By the end of the decade the focus was on jazz reissues only. —*Brad McCuen*

## Bluegrass

Bluegrass is a traditionally oriented country music initially created as the STRINGBAND sound of BILL MONROE & His Blue Grass Boys, which became widely imitated and evolved into a distinctive musical genre. Singer, songwriter, and mandolin player Monroe (1911–96) formed his band in 1938, naming it in honor of his home state of Kentucky, the Blue Grass State. Monroe had intended simply to develop a sound that differentiated him from other performers, but he soon inspired admirers who patterned their music after his.

There has been considerable debate about what constitutes bluegrass, yet the music has certain recognizable characteristics. Its many varieties are all artistic descendants of Monroe's sound. Bluegrass combines elements of OLD-TIME MUSIC's mountain modal sound and BALLAD singing, square dance fiddling (with some WESTERN SWING influence), blues, gospel music, and Tin Pan Alley songwriting. It maintains a jazz-influenced performance format in which instrumental soloists take turns playing improvisational variations on the melody while at other times backing the vocals or instrumental solos. Bluegrass bands generally consist of a five-string banjo (played in a syncopated, finger-picking style), fiddle, mandolin, six-string guitar, and bass, with occasional use of resophonic slide guitar (DOBRO) or additional fiddles or guitars. Aside from occasional harmonica and electric bass, bluegrass is an acoustic stringband music. Vocalists typically play an instrument and sing in keys pitched to their upper ranges. These pitches, bluegrass singers' austere, tight-throated style, and the mournful themes that permeate many of the music's standard songs have caused bluegrass to be dubbed "the high lonesome sound." Close-harmony duets, trios, and quartets are often featured. As in most country music, the upbeats (second and fourth beats) are emphasized, but bluegrass has a distinctive timing that surges slightly ahead of or anticipates the main beat to create an energized effect (the opposite of jazz or blues, often played slightly behind the main beat, for drama).

The first Blue Grass Boys lineup contained fiddle, mandolin, guitar, and bass, and Monroe often stated that his sound was built around fiddling and a surging tempo. However, some critics hold that bluegrass was truly defined by the addition of syncopated banjo picking and that the 1946–48 edition of the Blue Grass Boys—combining Monroe with Earl Scruggs on banjo and Lester Flatt on guitar (who would soon form FLATT & SCRUGGS AND THE FOGGY MOUNTAIN BOYS), CHUBBY WISE on fiddle, and Joel Price or Bill's brother, Birch Monroe, on bass—was the first true bluegrass band and perhaps the finest.

The evolution of bluegrass into a genre started as early as 1946, when THE STANLEY BROTHERS began performing covers of Monroe material while retaining the feel of old-time mountain music. In 1948 Flatt and Scruggs founded their own band, emphasizing the banjo and smoother lead vocals while deemphasizing Monroe-style mandolin and modal melodic or harmonic lines. Bluegrass developed regional shadings in the 1950s, 1960s, and 1970s: JIMMY MARTIN, RED ALLEN, and others adopted elements of HONKY-TONK MUSIC while playing in midwestern bars catering to transplanted southern industrial workers; in Washington, D.C., a geographical and political meeting point for the nation, THE COUNTRY GENTLEMEN and the SELDOM SCENE mixed southern sensibilities and northern folk-pop influences; in Nashville, GRAND OLE OPRY bluegrassers such as THE OSBORNE BROTHERS and JIM & JESSE employed elements of mainstream country; and California saw both the traditionalism of the Hillmen or High Country and the adventurous eclecticism of THE DILLARDS.

Monroe did not name his music "bluegrass" (a term now written as one word). Although a 1950 SONGBOOK published by Bill Monroe Music, Inc., was titled *Bill Monroe's Blue Grass Country Songs*, until the mid- to late-1950s most Monroe-influenced performers referred to what they played simply as "country" or "hillbilly" music. But during this period disc jockeys and music historians recognized that Monroe's admirers were playing a distinctive style of roots-based acoustic music that differentiated it from country. They began using the word "bluegrass," a reference to the name of Monroe's band. There is also evidence that during this period fans of Flatt & Scruggs wished to hear songs the duo had performed with Monroe's group but, aware of frictions between the bands, did not mention Monroe's name but simply requested "some of those Blue Grass songs." Whatever the case, the term's late development bears witness that bluegrass, although traditionally rooted, is a modern commercial music. Thus the use of "bluegrass" as a generic label for mountain folk music is incorrect.

The market for bluegrass withered in the late 1950s due to the rise of rock & roll and electrified country, although individual bands, notably Flatt & Scruggs and the Osborne Brothers, prospered with their polished presentations and ability to appeal to crossover audiences. Bluegrass rebounded in the early 1960s, when it was embraced as a traditional music by the national folk music revival. The music also advanced with the development of bluegrass festivals as separate entities from country or folk shows that included only token bluegrass acts in their lineups.

Singer-promoter BILL CLIFTON staged an all-bluegrass program in Luray, Virginia, in July 1961, but many consider the three-day gathering at Fincastle, Virginia, on September 3–5, 1965, organized by country music promoter CARLTON L. HANEY with the assistance of folklorist RALPH RINZLER, the first full-fledged bluegrass festival. As festivals proliferated, they provided bands with increased bookings and record sales opportunities, reinforced the bluegrass community's sense of identity, and attracted many curious first-time listeners who became loyal fans. Bluegrass has also benefited from grassroots clubs that promote shows and from such publications as *Bluegrass Unlimited* (founded in 1966), which disseminate information about performers, new recordings, and upcoming events. Although bluegrass has largely functioned as a niche music supported by hobbyists, the International Bluegrass Music Association (IBMA), a trade organization founded in Owensboro, Kentucky, in 1985 and now headquartered in Nashville, Tennessee, has boosted the music's business activities and professional image.

Many of those who discovered bluegrass in the 1960s and 1970s were young, innovative musicians who mixed elements of jazz, pop, and rock with bluegrass to create what is broadly called "newgrass." Early practitioners were NEW GRASS REVIVAL, the New Deal String Band, and Breakfast Special—all of whom built on earlier experiments of the Osborne Brothers, the Country Gentlemen, and the Dillards. To some, the movement helped prevent bluegrass from ossifying into a museum piece. To others, newgrass was dissonant and thoroughly unrelated to the music established by Monroe. Time has softened these positions as the progressive banjo stylings of BILL KEITH, Tony Trischka, BÉLA FLECK, and others have become familiar to mainstream fans, and young experimentalists have gained respect for the considerable technical virtuosity of Monroe, Scruggs, and other bluegrass pioneers.

An overseas bluegrass boom began in the 1970s, most notably in Japan and Europe. Monroe-Stanley-styled bluegrass reemerged as a vital force in the 1980s with the popularity of the DEL McCOURY BAND, the JOHNSON MOUNTAIN BOYS, and other traditionally oriented acts, while the Nashville-influenced music of such groups as the Lonesome River Band represented another style of bluegrass. The most striking trend of the 1990s was the rise of popular female performer-bandleaders in this previously male-dominated music, notably ALISON KRAUSS (the most successful bluegrass performer, male or female, of modern times), LAURIE LEWIS, and LYNN MORRIS, and in the new century with RHONDA VINCENT, Dale Ann Bradley, Claire Lynch, and others.

Bluegrass gained another bump in popularity with the success of the 2000 movie *O BROTHER, WHERE ART THOU?*, which featured RALPH STANLEY (who also appeared onscreen) and Dan Tyminski of Krauss's band in the soundtrack, along with several bluegrass songs. The soundtrack and resulting tour spawned a CD and DVD, *Down from the Mountain*, which included bluegrass players and music among its eclectic folk mix. Besides Vincent and Bradley, other popular bluegrass acts to rise in the 2000s included Cherryholmes, Dailey & Vincent, and the Grascals, as well as a young cadre of newgrass players led by the innovative NICKEL CREEK. —*Richard D. Smith*

## The Bluegrass Alliance

In the late 1960s, the Louisville-based Bluegrass Alliance attracted young, urban audiences to BLUEGRASS through instrumental prowess and an innovative repertoire. The band's adaptations of pop and rock songs excited a new generation of bluegrass fans for whom "cabins" and "mountains" had little relevance.

The definitive unit—Dan Crary, guitar; Danny Jones, mandolin; Lonnie Peerce, fiddle; Buddy Spurlock, banjo; and Harry "Ebo Walker" Shelor, bass—showcased Crary's lead guitar, rare at the time, for bluegrass. The group's first non-regional performance of note was at Camp Springs, North Carolina, in 1969.

Recordings for American Heritage and appearances on the emerging festival circuit followed; by 1970, Crary, Jones, and Spurlock had left, replaced by TONY RICE, guitar; SAM BUSH, mandolin; and Courtney Johnson, banjo. In 1971, again at Camp Springs, Rice played the event with both the Alliance and J. D. CROWE & the New South, of which he became a key member.

Soon replacing Rice in the Alliance was Curtis Burch, who then joined Bush, Shelor, and Johnson in forming NEW GRASS REVIVAL in the fall of 1971. The Alliance continued, with Peerce filling empty slots from a seemingly endless list of talented young musicians, including future country star VINCE GILL. The Peerce-led Bluegrass Alliance was not active after the late 1970s. In 1998 Georgia-based banjo player Barry Palmer, as heir to the band name, re-formed the group, whose album *re-alliance* appeared in 2001. As of 2011, the band is still active. —*Frank and Marty Godbey*

## The Bluegrass Cardinals
Don Parmley b. Monticello, Kentucky, October 19, 1933
David Parmley b. Alameda, California, February 2, 1959

A popular BLUEGRASS outfit for a quarter-century, the Bluegrass Cardinals trace their origins to banjo player Don Parmley's move to Los Angeles in the 1950s. Parmley provided soundtrack banjo for *THE BEVERLY HILLBILLIES* television program (although FLATT & SCRUGGS AND THE FOGGY MOUNTAIN BOYS played the show's famous theme), and he also worked with the Golden State Boys, an early 1960s group that included Rex Gosdin, VERN GOSDIN, and CHRIS HILLMAN.

The Bluegrass Cardinals developed in the early 1970s when Parmley and mandolinist Randy Graham were playing together. Parmley's teenage son David sang and played bass, and the three worked local venues, including Disneyland. When David moved to guitar, the group added fiddler Dennis Fetchet and bassist Bill Bryson.

Promoting their first album, released on Briar, the Cardinals toured the East in 1976. The Parmleys and Graham relocated near Washington, D.C., a decision celebrated with the 1977 release of the ROUNDER RECORDS album *Welcome to Virginia*. Their instrumental skill, their vocals (Graham's intense tenor, David's rich lower lead, Don's harmony), and their ability to personalize material into a distinctive group sound made them bluegrass favorites. The band recorded a series of well-received albums for CMH and SUGAR HILL RECORDS and then formed their BGC label.

Among Cardinal alumni are fiddlers Warren Blair, Mike Hartgrove, and Tim Smith; mandolinists Herschel Sizemore, Larry Stephenson, and Norman Wright; and tenor-singing bass player Ernie Sykes. In 1992 David Parmley left the band, but the

Cardinals, led by Don Parmley, continued on the bluegrass circuit until January 1997. —*Frank and Marty Godbey*

## BMG (*see* RCA Victor/RCA Records)

## BMI (Broadcast Music, Inc.)
established in New York, New York, 1940

BMI (the well-known acronym for Broadcast Music, Inc.) is one of America's largest music-licensing firms. The for-profit company collects and distributes monies paid to the creators and publishers of music for public performance rights. For decades, BMI was the principal licenser of country music; today, it is one of three major such licensers, with ASCAP and, to a lesser degree, SESAC.

BMI was established with headquarters in New York City in 1940 by leaders of the national radio industry unhappy with that industry's stalled contract negotiations with ASCAP. Previously the only major U.S. licenser of musical public performance rights, ASCAP had proposed a 50 percent raise in radio's payment rates. Rather than agree to the new terms, the broadcasters created their own music licensing firm, BMI, and, since the previous ASCAP-radio contract had expired, ceased airing ASCAP tunes for most of 1941.

Late in 1941 the large radio stations and broadcast networks (NBC, CBS, and Mutual) settled with ASCAP, but BMI continued to grow because of its open-door policy toward writers and publishers of music that had not received much support from ASCAP: primarily country, blues, and R&B. Country music prospered during and after World War II; meanwhile, BMI grew to 6,300 licensees and 1,362 affiliated publishers by 1950. BMI's logging system, which took into account more local programming (as well as network shows) and record plays (in addition to live performances) was also beneficial to country writers and publishers. Also, more than a few country writers and publishers got a start in the business with monies BMI advanced in return for their affiliation.

BMI and ASCAP feuded in the courts and the trade press for much of BMI's first two decades, but all the while BMI established a strong position in fields of music where ASCAP had once stood alone: motion picture soundtracks, pop, jazz, even classical. Rock & roll proved a big boost to BMI's fortunes during and after the mid-1950s; its worth as music was yet another bone of contention with ASCAP.

Attorney Sydney M. Kaye was BMI's founder, organizer, and first president, though several persons were influential in its early growth—especially Carl Haverlin. Russell Sanjek, Robert Sour, George Marlo, Thea Zavin, and JUDGE BOB BURTON also contributed much. BMI has given country music awards since 1953, and its first Nashville offices were established in 1958 by FRANCES PRESTON, a former WSM receptionist. In 1963 BMI broke ground for what became the first MUSIC ROW office of any performance rights licensing firm. Preston became BMI's president and CEO in 1986, succeeding longtime president Edward Cramer. DEL BRYANT succeeded Preston in 2004. JODY WILLIAMS has been head of Nashville writer-publisher relations since becoming a BMI vice president in 2006.

Through its formative years, many of the best-known country publishers (ACUFF-ROSE PUBLICATIONS, CEDARWOOD PUBLISHING COMPANY, HILL AND RANGE SONGS, INC., Moss Rose, PAMPER

Music, and Tree Publishing Company) and most of country's important writers (Bill Anderson, Harlan Howard, Kris Kristofferson, Loretta Lynn, Roger Miller, Willie Nelson, Dolly Parton, Ernest Tubb, and Hank Williams, to name a select few) affiliated with BMI. The majority of country music's best-known standards are lodged within BMI's catalog, which numbers in the multimillions. In recent years, however, ASCAP has become an equal competitor in country and roots music. —*Ronnie Pugh*

## BNA Entertainment (*see* RCA Victor/RCA Records)

## Dock Boggs
b. West Norton, Virginia, February 7, 1898; d. February 7, 1971

Dock Boggs was perhaps the most emotionally deep and certainly the least musically tractable of all traditional country singers—"hillbilly" or "old-time" they called his music when he first recorded it in 1927. His professional career as an entertainer ended in the early 1930s with the onset of the Great Depression. Boggs went back to the coal mines of southwestern Virginia and eastern Kentucky, where he had worked since 1910 and where he would continue until 1954, when his age left him unable to find a job. In 1963 he was recorded again by Mike Seeger of The New Lost City Ramblers, eventually cutting three albums for the Folkways label and performing around the country on the festival circuit of the folk revival. Boggs's story can be seen as typical of many performers of traditional music, black or white—the sort of artists whose work, generally forgotten but somewhat persistent, was first collected on Harry Smith's landmark 1952 *Anthology of American Folk Music*. And yet Boggs's life and music raise the question of whether such categories as "traditional" and "folk" and even "country" are of any use at all when confronted with music as powerful and as strange as what Boggs left behind.

He was born Moran Lee Boggs, the youngest of ten children, in West Norton, Virginia, in 1898, and died on his birthday in nearby Needmore in 1971. Both spots were on the edges of Norton, a coal mining center and in 1927 the site of a mass audition of "mountain talent" held by Brunswick Records. Boggs's father, formerly a mountain farmer, was a blacksmith and also a singer who could read music; several of Boggs's siblings sang and played the banjo, the instrument that would become his. Many of his most striking performances—"Pretty Polly," "Country Blues," and others—were utterly traditional in origin. In this sense Boggs personified the folk strain of country music in both his life and his art. When, after passing the Brunswick audition, he traveled to New York to record, he had never been out of his home mountains.

Nevertheless, Boggs's "Country Blues"—a variant of "Hustlin' Gamblers" or "Darlin' Corey"—is no more traditional in Boggs's performance than Hank Williams's 1949 "Alone and Forsaken." Boggs is not frailing his banjo, but picking the strings and sliding the notes toward blues, into discord and disharmony. The old song, it seems, is being sung for the first time, or the last. It is the same with "Down South Blues" and "Sugar Baby," performances Boggs derived from records by northern, urban blues singers such as Sara Martin. The momentum of the playing seems to overtake the singer's cadence, and the result is an awful suspense. Get it over with, the banjo says in the murder fable "Pretty Polly." Not yet, the singer replies.

In this sense, Boggs is no traditionalist but, again, like Williams, a modernist—that is, a solitary individual who can no longer fall back on the comforts and assurances of an unquestioned religion; an immutable family; a stable, rural society; or a predictable economy—Boggs confronted the world directly and as it was, naked, with a music so strong, cruel, and unforgiving of its own sinfulness that it could repel any belief brought to it. —*Greil Marcus*

## Noel Boggs
b. Oklahoma City, Oklahoma, November 14, 1917; d. August 30, 1974

One of the smoothest and most influential western swing steel guitarists, Noel Edwin Boggs played and recorded with almost every major artist in the genre, from Bob Wills and Spade Cooley to Bill Boyd, (Bill and Jim Boyd), Tommy Duncan, and Hank Penny. Admired by his peers for his full tone and innovative tunings, Boggs was a supreme stylist.

His early experience was in Oklahoma, but he got his first big break in New Orleans, a job with Hank Penny's Radio Cowboys, an act based in Atlanta for several years, beginning in 1938. Boggs recorded with the group for Vocalion in 1939, his solo work indicating he was already moving away from the established Bob Dunn style of western swing steel and into new territory. By 1940 Boggs had returned to Oklahoma City, backing Jimmy Wakely, with whom he worked often throughout his career.

In 1944 Boggs joined Bob Wills & His Texas Playboys in California and quickly established himself as a star sideman, recording the classic "Texas Playboy Rag" in January 1945. Boggs was with Spade Cooley's large western swing group by 1946 and worked several stints with Cooley over the next decade, recording classics such as "Boggs Boogie" (1947). He also recorded with T. Texas Tyler, Wade Ray, and others and became a charter member of Tommy Duncan's Western All-Stars in 1948. During the mid-fifties Boggs led his own trio and signed with Columbia Records, releasing his signature "Steelin' Home" in 1954. He drifted into obscurity in the 1960s, unfortunately dying just as western swing was experiencing a revival. —*Kevin Coffey*

## Suzy Bogguss
b. Aledo, Illinois, December 30, 1956

Susan Kay Bogguss took an unusual route to her success in the 1990s. Bogguss majored in art at Illinois State University, planning to make jewelry. But exposed to art, drama, and music, she began performing. She eventually became an itinerant folk-country performer, living in a camper for five years and traveling from Massachusetts to Wyoming.

In 1984 Bogguss recorded an album to sell at performances. She landed in Nashville in 1985 and got a job singing in a restaurant near Music Row. She made demo tapes for songwriters and married one of them, Doug Crider, in 1986. After headlining at Dolly Parton's Dollywood theme park in Pigeon Forge, Tennessee, Bogguss signed with Capitol Records.

Bogguss's Capitol debut album, *Somewhere Between* (1989), sold modestly, as did the follow-up. But her third Capitol album, *Aces* (1991), was her breakthrough. The fine songs showcased the strength and versatility of her voice, and "Outbound Plane" and "Aces" were Top Ten hits. "Drive South," from her 1992 album *Voices in the Wind*, climbed to #2 on the *Billboard* charts, and that year she received CMA's Horizon Award.

Her 1994 album *Simpatico*, recorded with guitarist CHET ATKINS, covered material ranging from JIMMIE RODGERS to Elton John and was a critical success. Bogguss's *Give Me Some Wheels* (1996) followed a two-year break devoted to raising her son, and it failed to generate any hits. She left Capitol Records after the 1998 release of *Nobody Love, Nobody Gets Hurt*. She has continued to tour and to release albums independently, including a 2003 album of songs befitting its title, *Swing*, produced by ASLEEP AT THE WHEEL leader Ray Benson. —*Mary A. Bufwack*

## Bill and Earl Bolick (*see* Blue Sky Boys)

## Eddie Bond
b. Memphis, Tennessee, July 1, 1933

Edward James Bond was one of the few Memphis rockabillies born in the city. But being in the right place at the right time didn't translate into a successful recording career.

Bond led bands from 1952 (early band members included future Nashville session musicians JOHN HUGHEY and REGGIE YOUNG), and began recording country music in 1955 for Ekko Records. Switching to MERCURY RECORDS and to ROCKABILLY in 1956, the singer briefly was a hepcat contender with singles such as "Slip Slip Slippin' In," "Boppin' Bonnie," and "Rockin' Daddy." He continued to record prolifically for ever-smaller labels and started a parallel career as a DJ, concert promoter, club owner, and radio station owner.

Bond had a fascination with the career of lawman Buford Pusser from Finger, Tennessee, and eulogized him on several releases before the Pusser legend, such as it was, was enshrined in the 1973 movie *Walking Tall*; Bond contributed to the movie's soundtrack. In 1974 Bond ran unsuccessfully for sheriff of Shelby County, Tennessee, which includes Memphis. —*Colin Escott*

## Johnny Bond
b. Enville, Oklahoma, June 1, 1915; d. June 12, 1978

Laconic, humorous, and self-deprecating, Johnny Bond was one of the true gentlemen of western music as well as an important songwriter and musician. Raised in south-central Oklahoma, Cyrus Whitfield Bond moved in 1937 to Oklahoma City, where he formed a trio with JIMMY WAKELY and Scotty Harrell, known as the Bell Boys, after their sponsor, the Bell Clothing Company. Regional success followed, and in 1939 the group moved to Hollywood, where they appeared in a ROY ROGERS film, *Saga of Death Valley*. The trio landed a spot on GENE AUTRY's CBS *Melody Ranch* radio show in 1940 and stayed together until Wakely's solo career took off. Meanwhile, they pulled a clever musical scam, recording for DECCA as the Jimmy Wakely Trio and for COLUMBIA as Johnny Bond & the Cimarron Boys.

Although he composed hundreds of songs ("I Wonder Where You Are Tonight," "Love Gone Cold," "Your Old Love Letters," "Tomorrow Never Comes," "Those Gone and Left Me Blues," and many others, mostly in the country idiom), Bond is best remembered for his western classic "Cimarron," which he wrote in Oklahoma City as a theme song for the Bell Boys. As a recording artist he enjoyed moderate success, from his earliest recordings in 1941 through the 1950s, and even placed a few hits high on the charts during the late 1940s. In 1965 Bond's recording career

*Johnny Bond*

briefly revived on the STARDAY label with the novelty drinking song "10 Little Bottles," a number he first recorded for Columbia in 1951.

Whereas Wakely's career was meteoric, Bond's was steadier. He remained a mainstay of the *Melody Ranch* cast until the show's end in 1956, and his distinctive acoustic guitar runs became an Autry trademark on radio and on recordings. Bond had small parts in many films, recorded frequently, began a MUSIC PUBLISHING business with TEX RITTER, and spent nearly a decade as host and writer on the television show *TOWN HALL PARTY*. In his later years he wrote a brief autobiography and a biography of Ritter.

Bond was elected to THE COUNTRY MUSIC HALL OF FAME in 1999. —*Douglas B. Green*

## Bonnie Lou
b. Towanda, Illinois, October 27, 1924

Singer Mary Jo Kath was known throughout the tri-state area of Ohio, Kentucky, and Indiana simply as Bonnie Lou. The central Illinois native was playing both fiddle and guitar by age eleven and began working on her Swiss yodel. Kath started her professional radio career at Peoria radio station WMBD in 1939. In 1940 she moved to WJBC in Bloomington, Illinois, and upon high school graduation in 1942 she moved to KMBC in Kansas City. Billed as Sally Carson, she performed as a soloist and as a member of the Rhythm Rangers on the *Brush Creek Follies*.

In the spring of 1945 Kath moved to WLW in Cincinnati. Station executive Bill McCluskey changed her name to Bonnie Lou and added her to the *MIDWESTERN HAYRIDE* cast. There she won many fans both as a soloist and as a member of the Trailblazers. By 1953 she had her first chart single, "Seven Lonely Days," on KING RECORDS. The follow-up, "The Tennessee Wig

Walk," also broke into the country Top Ten. Bonnie Lou stayed with the *Hayride* until 1966.

WLW programmed a number of live shows from the 1950s through the mid-1970s. Bonnie Lou performed on several of these, including the station's morning variety program, *The Paul Dixon Show*, and Ruth Lyons's noontime program, *The 50–50 Club*. For the most part, Bonnie Lou has lived in retirement since the early 1980s, occasionally appearing on local television and commercials. *—Chris Skinker*

## Boone County Jamboree (see Midwestern Hayride)

## Boone Creek (see Ricky Skaggs)

## Scott Borchetta
b. Burbank, California, July 3, 1962

Scott Borchetta prospered as a record company promotion executive before launching his own label, BIG MACHINE RECORDS, in 2005. Finding quick success by signing fifteen-year-old TAYLOR SWIFT, Borchetta expanded his empire to include the labels Valory Music Group in 2007 and Republic Records Nashville in 2009, the latter in partnership with New York's Universal Republic Records.

A former rock musician and an auto-racing professional, Borchetta followed his father, veteran promotion executive Mike Borchetta, into the music business. Working at MCA Nashville in the 1980s and '90s, the younger Borchetta promoted the careers of VINCE GILL, REBA MCENTIRE, GEORGE STRAIT, and others.

*Scott Borchetta*

When California entertainment company DREAMWORKS opened a Nashville record label, Borchetta took the head promotion job, rising to label general manager. When DreamWorks Nashville merged with the Universal Music Group, Borchetta was named senior vice president of promotion and artist development for the company's Nashville division, including DreamWorks, MCA, and MERCURY RECORDS.

Borchetta resigned from Universal to launch Big Machine, initially in partnership with singer TOBY KEITH's new label, Show Dog Records. Within a year, Big Machine and Show Dog split, and Big Machine began finding success with JACK INGRAM, Swift, and veteran TRISHA YEARWOOD. By 2008, under Borchetta's guidance, Big Machine ranked among Nashville's most successful record companies. His companies continued to expand, signing McEntire in 2009 and RASCAL FLATTS and MARTINA MCBRIDE in 2010. *—Michael McCall*

## Border Radio

The term "border radio" refers to an American broadcasting industry that sprang up on Mexico's northern border in the early 1930s and flourished for half a century. High-powered transmitters on Mexican soil, beyond the reach of U.S. regulators, blanketed North America. Early on, hillbilly music proved to be one of the most effective means of pulling fan mail and moving merchandise; in turn, the border stations played a significant role in popularizing country music during its crucial pre– and post–World War II growth years.

Mexico accommodated these "outlaw" media folk, some of whom had been denied U.S. broadcasting licenses, because Canada and the United States had divided the long-range radio frequencies between themselves, allotting none to Mexico.

The first border station, XED, began broadcasting from Reynosa, Tamaulipas, in 1930. Owned for a time by Houston theater operator and philanthropist Will Horwitz, the station hosted occasional performances by Horwitz's friend JIMMIE RODGERS.

DR. JOHN R. BRINKLEY—who offered goat gland implants to impotent men—opened XER (later called XERA) in Villa Acuña, Coahuila, the following year. Brinkley also acquired XED, changing the name to XEAW. In 1939 he sold XEAW to Carr Collins, owner of CRAZY WATER CRYSTALS. According to Collins's son Jim, W. LEE "PAPPY" O'DANIEL was part owner of the station. The Mexican government confiscated XERA in 1941 and tried to confiscate XEAW shortly thereafter, but Collins moved his equipment north of the border.

Engineer Bill Branch and businessman C. M. Bres operated XEPN in Piedras Negras in the 1930s. Iowan Norman Baker, whose experimental cancer treatments made him a controversial figure, broadcast from his station XENT in Nuevo Laredo.

Border station power generally ranged from 50,000 to 500,000 watts, and some listeners claimed to enjoy broadcasts on dental work, bedsprings, and fence wire. American network programs were often lost in the ether when a Mexican border outlet was broadcasting near its frequency.

HANK THOMPSON, who grew up in Waco, Texas, in the 1930s, said the American-Mexican stations "were about the only ones where you could hear country music most all the time." Thompson and other listeners heard NOLAN "COWBOY SLIM" RINEHART, PATSY MONTANA, the CARTER FAMILY, the PICKARD FAMILY, Pappy O'Daniel's Hillbilly Boys, Roy "Lonesome Cowboy" Faulkner, SHELLY LEE ALLEY, and others. Performers broadcast live and via transcription disc, sometimes syndicating a show on several of the maverick stations.

Important postwar stations included XEG in Monterrey and XERF in Ciudad Acuña. WEBB PIERCE, JIM REEVES, and other stars appeared live in the studio with XERF DJ Paul Kallinger. In a colorful exaggeration that may hold a nugget of truth, Pierce said country music "might not have survived if it hadn't been for border radio."

Some border musicians, such as Dallas "Nevada Slim" Turner, filled several functions, such as singing cowboy, evangelist, and pitchman. "Only three things will sell on the border," said Turner, "health, sex, and religion." Many country music shows on *la frontera* radio combined all three.

In 1986, after years of waning influence, the border stations were dealt a crippling blow by an international broadcasting agreement between the United States and Mexico that allowed both Mexican and American broadcasters to use each other's clear-channel frequencies for low-powered stations in the evening. That meant that local broadcasts would drown out the signals of the border stations in many communities, effectively putting an end to the era of high-powered, far-ranging radio. —*Gene Fowler*

## Chris Bouchillon
b. Oconee County, South Carolina, August 21, 1983; d. September 18, 1968

One of the most enduring bits of country comedy is a spoken lyric that begins "If you want to get to heaven, let me tell you how to do it." Over the years it has been popularized by WOODY GUTHRIE, Curly Fox (of CURLY FOX & TEXAS RUBY), GRAND OLE OPRY star ROBERT LUNN, and many others. A rare example of a song that became a musical genre, it is usually called "The Talking Blues" or "The Original Talking Blues." Though its ultimate origins probably lie in nineteenth-century vaudeville, the artist who first made it famous was a bespectacled, pipe-smoking comedian named Christopher Allen Bouchillon (pronounced BUSH-alon).

The son of a mountain banjo player, Bouchillon grew up near an iron foundry in Greenville, South Carolina; as a teenager he performed with his brothers Uris and Charlie, recording briefly as the Greenville Trio. In 1926 Chris recorded his "Talking Blues" for COLUMBIA; A&R chief FRANK WALKER later claimed he told Bouchillon to talk through the song because he didn't like Bouchillon's singing voice. Friends, however, insisted that Bouchillon himself came up with the style after spending hours listening to African American performers in the area. Issued in February 1927, the disc sold almost 100,000 copies—a huge hit by 1920s standards. Several of his later recordings also became best-sellers: "Born in Hard Luck" did well, as did "My Fat Girl" and a singing effort, "Hannah" (later revived by a MEL TILLIS rewrite as "Honey [Open That Door]" and turned into a #1 hit by RICKY SKAGGS).

Bouchillon seemed uninterested in exploiting his hit records and did not tour or try radio. In later years, seemingly unaware of how influential his work had been, he operated a dry cleaning shop and lived in relative obscurity. —*Charles Wolfe*

## Rory Bourke
b. Cleveland, Ohio, July 14, 1942

Recently graduated from college, Rory Michael Bourke came to Nashville in 1964 for a sales and promotion position with MERCURY RECORDS. When ELVIS PRESLEY's recording of Bourke's

"Patch It Up" was the B-side of a Top Twenty single in 1970, Bourke decided to pursue songwriting full time. Mentored by music executive Don Gant and signed to Chappell Music in 1971, Bourke hit with "The Most Beautiful Girl," cowritten with NORRO WILSON and BILLY SHERRILL. The song topped the country and pop charts in 1973 for CHARLIE RICH, and Bourke was off to an award-winning career that has included ASCAP Writer of the Year honors in 1975, 1979, and 1983.

Bourke began a partnership with Charlie Black in 1979, and the two songwriters collaborated on several #1 hits for ANNE MURRAY, including "Shadows in the Moonlight" and "A Little Good News" (with Tommy Rocco). Bourke and Black also cowrote "Do You Love As Good As You Look" (with Jerry Gillespie) for the BELLAMY BROTHERS and K. T. OSLIN's "Come Next Monday" (with Oslin), both chart toppers. Other #1 hits written or cowritten by Bourke include GEORGE STRAIT's "You Look So Good in Love," and JANIE FRICKE's "Let's Stop Talking About It." The NASHVILLE SONGWRITERS HALL OF FAME inducted Bourke in 1989. —*Scott Anderson*

## Jimmy Bowen
b. Santa Rita, New Mexico, November 30, 1937

Few individuals have had as big an impact on the Nashville music industry as James Allen Bowen, an outspoken, controversial, and colorful maverick who relocated to MUSIC CITY from Los Angeles in 1977. Over his forty-year career, he was a DJ, pop artist, publishing employee, record label A&R head, record producer, and, finally, the Nashville boss of major labels including (in chronological order) MGM, MCA, ELEKTRA/ASYLUM, WARNER BROS., MCA (again), Universal, CAPITOL, and LIBERTY, as well as the short-lived Liberty subsidiary PATRIOT RECORDS.

*Jimmy Bowen*

While in Nashville, Bowen proved skilled at delegating tasks. He frequently produced two or more acts simultaneously, working with a personally trained corps of recording engineers. Often he directed the early recording stages from a mobile phone on his golf cart and then listened to the rough mixes at night before showing up at the studio to immerse himself in the final mixing process. He always seemed to be a central figure in the Music City rumor mill and was not above starting some of the rumors himself.

Bowen grew up in Dumas, Texas, and cut his teeth as a teenage DJ. By eighteen he was playing bass and singing with Buddy Knox & the Rhythm Orchids, a ROCKABILLY group that scored a pop smash with "Party Doll" (#1, 1957), sung by Knox, backed with "I'm Stickin' with You" (#14), sung by Bowen.

Bowen forsook performing in 1959 and moved to Los Angeles, where he had remarkable success as a producer with Frank Sinatra, Sammy Davis Jr., and Dean Martin. Bowen produced fifteen gold albums with Martin, including his best-known hit, "Everybody Loves Somebody" (#1 pop, 1964), and crafted legendary Sinatra records such as "Strangers in the Night" (#1 pop, 1966) and "That's Life" (#4 pop, 1967). He also started his own record label, A.M.O.S., working with, among others, KENNY ROGERS and future EAGLES Don Henley and Glenn Frey.

In 1977 Bowen moved to Nashville and apprenticed at a studio owned by Tompall Glaser (THE GLASER BROTHERS) and then known as "Hillbilly Central." Bowen spent about three years there, producing hits for MEL TILLIS along the way. Shortly afterward he began producing HANK WILLIAMS JR. and helped give Williams's career a more commercially successful direction.

During the 1980s Bowen's production whirlwind peaked, delivering hits for CONWAY TWITTY, GEORGE STRAIT, REBA MCENTIRE, JOHN ANDERSON, and WAYLON JENNINGS. Known for slashing artist rosters, he nevertheless endeared himself to many artists by coproducing their albums with them.

Bowen pushed to upgrade the sound quality of Nashville records, boasting that he "taught the hillbillies how to make a $40,000 album for $150,000." He advocated digital recording and began transferring MCA's country catalog to CD as early as 1984. A number of Bowen employees became leaders in the industry, including JIM ED NORMAN, TONY BROWN, Martha Sharp, Nick Hunter, and JAMES STROUD.

Bowen established the MCA Masters Series in 1986 and oversaw recordings of noncountry artists, primarily instrumentalists. He created his own label in 1988, Universal Records. When MCA terminated that venture, Bowen moved to Capitol, whose Nashville division was temporarily renamed Liberty Records. Bowen was instrumental in the rise of GARTH BROOKS, working closely with parent company EMI's New York corporate brass to prioritize the marketing of Brooks's multiplatinum second and third albums, No Fences and Ropin' the Wind.

Bowen long maintained better working relationships with corporate higher-ups on both coasts than many other Nashville label heads enjoyed. In 1994, however, his luck ran out. His relationship with Brooks soured, and he became entangled in disputes with EMI's New York leadership. Bowen's time on the golf course increased as he seemed to lose interest in the label, though he eventually coproduced DEANA CARTER's 1996 career-launching "Strawberry Wine." A bout with thyroid cancer also took its toll. In early 1995 he moved to Maui to recuperate and write his autobiography, Rough Mix, published by Simon & Schuster in 1997.

In about 2000, Bowen moved to the Phoenix area. Except for a MERLE HAGGARD album, Chicago Wind, coproduced with Mike Post, he has been inactive in the industry since then. —John Lomax III

## Boxcar Willie
b. Sterratt, Texas, September 1, 1931; d. April 12, 1999

Lecil Travis Martin was forty-four years old when he donned a hobo costume and turned down-home vocals and a shrill railroad whistle into a million-dollar telemarketing act as Boxcar Willie. After spending most of the 1950s as an air force C-5 pilot, he worked in TV in Nebraska for two years as Marty Martin, then spent the 1960s as an Idaho DJ. In 1970 he moved to Texas, working as a pilot, mechanic, and DJ. In the fall of 1975 in Fort Worth, he began performing in hobo garb as Boxcar Willie on the Grapevine Opry. In 1978 he toured the United Kingdom, taking the headlining role when a star bowed out. The Texan's booming vocals and hobo persona caught on with British audiences. Without a major label or a hit single, Boxcar Willie appeared at England's 1979 Wembley International Country Music Festival and was named Most Promising International Artist, though still largely unknown in the United States.

Shortly afterward he had four albums top the English country charts and became the British CMA's International Entertainer of the Year. His success transferred to the United States in 1980 with his King of the Road album for Main Street Records, which sold in the millions via TV advertising. He debuted at the GRAND OLE OPRY on June 19, 1980, and joined the cast on February 21, 1981. In 1986 he became one of the first artists to open a theater in BRANSON, MISSOURI, where he performed into the 1990s. —Walt Trott

## Boy Howdy (see Jeffrey Steele)

## Bill and Jim Boyd
Bill Boyd b. Fannin County, Texas, September 29, 1910; d. December 7, 1977
Jim Boyd b. Fannin County, Texas, September 28, 1914; d. March 11, 1993

Bill Boyd's Cowboy Ramblers are usually considered one of the four major WESTERN SWING bands of the prewar era, along with BOB WILLS & His Texas Playboys, MILTON BROWN & His Musical Brownies, and the LIGHT CRUST DOUGHBOYS. William Lemuel Boyd was known as the King of the Instrumentals for cutting classics such as "Under the Double Eagle" (1935), "New Spanish Two-Step" (1938), and "Lone Star Rag" (1949) during a prolific association with RCA VICTOR RECORDS. Brother Jim Boyd—who had a longer career than Bill's—served as his right-hand man for most of the Cowboy Ramblers' existence, which spanned two decades, from the early 1930s through the mid-1950s.

Bill Boyd was essentially a country singer-guitarist whose first incarnation of the Cowboy Ramblers, formed at Dallas's WRR in about 1932, focused on COWBOY MUSIC and OLD-TIME tunes. Under the influence of Fort Worth's Musical Brownies, Boyd gravitated toward western swing, sharing personnel such as fiddler Art Davis and banjoist Walker Kirkes with ROY NEWMAN's jazzy WRR STRINGBAND. Boyd's recording ensembles were rarely like his daily radio and road bands. For his BLUEBIRD (and later RCA VICTOR) recordings he borrowed jazz-minded men such as Knocky Parker and Marvin Montgomery from the Light Crust Doughboys, recording a far different repertoire and style than his live performances featured. In the early 1940s Boyd's repertoire leaned more toward originals or songs that Boyd partially owned; if these compositions did not always measure up to the material Boyd had played previously, they were nevertheless performed expertly.

In the early 1940s Boyd appeared in a series of western films. "Lone Star Rag" was his last hit, in 1949, and after leaving RCA in 1951 he recorded for TNT and for STARDAY RECORDS.

Arguably a better singer and musician than his brother, Jim Boyd played extensively with Roy Newman's band, worked the first of many stints with the Light Crust Doughboys in 1938–39, and led his own Men of the West, recording for RCA in 1949–51. Jim remained musically active until shortly before his death. —*Kevin Coffey*

## BR549

Gary Bennett b. Las Vegas, Nevada, October 9, 1964
Donald John Herron Jr. b. Steubenville, Ohio, September 23, 1962
Jay Michael McDowell b. Bedford, Indiana, June 11, 1969
Charles Lynn Mead b. Nevada, Missouri, December 22, 1960
Randall Edward Shaw Wilson b. Topeka, Kansas, July 10, 1960

From 1994 to 1996, BR549 stepped up from playing for tips in downtown Nashville to become one of the most talked-about acts in country music at the time. The hillbilly-boogie quintet's long run at Robert's Western World touched off a street-level industry buzz that landed the band on the cover of *Billboard* magazine before they had a record deal.

Originally, BR549 coalesced around Gary Bennett and Chuck Mead, a pair of singer-songwriter-guitarists who began working together in 1994. The group took its name (which initially had a dash between the "5" and the "4") from Junior Samples's used-car salesman routine on *HEE HAW*. BR549 went through various personnel changes before solidifying the best-known lineup, which included drummer "Hawk" Shaw Wilson, bassist "Smilin'" Jay McDowell, and multi-instrumentalist Don Herron. Their four-hour sets at Robert's, a combination bar and western wear store, had become standing-room-only affairs. Their high-energy mixture of classic country covers (WEBB PIERCE, FARON YOUNG, JOHNNY HORTON) and original tunes spearheaded a downtown Nashville music revival that made national news. In 1995 the band signed with ARISTA RECORDS Nashville. A *Live from Robert's* EP was released in April 1996, followed in September by a self-titled full-length album. The debut single from the latter album, a cover of the MOON MULLICAN hit "Cherokee Boogie," was nominated for a Grammy. The album crested just inside the Top Forty, but country radio's refusal to embrace the band's traditional sound limited their status to that of cult favorites who never achieved the platinum sales of major country acts of the 1990s.

BR549 released two more albums on Arista, one on SONY MUSIC ENTERTAINMENT–affiliated Lucky Dog Records, and two on Dualtone, a leading Nashville independent label. In 2002 Bennett and McDowell left the group, replaced by guitarist Chris Scruggs and bassist Geoff Firebaugh. Mark Miller eventually replaced Firebaugh. Meanwhile, Herron was hired for BOB DYLAN's road band. In recent years BR549 has been generally inactive as a group. Bennett released his first solo album in 2006, and Mead followed suit with his solo debut in 2009. —*Daniel Cooper*

## Bobby Braddock

b. Lakeland, Florida, August 5, 1940

One of Nashville's most admired songwriters, Robert Valentine Braddock moved to Nashville in 1964 and began work as MARTY ROBBINS's piano player in 1965. Braddock landed his first cut

*Bobby Braddock*

that year when Robbins recorded "While You're Dancing." Braddock signed with the city's TREE PUBLISHING COMPANY in 1966.

In the late 1960s Braddock parlayed his close association with producer BILLY SHERRILL into landmark hits by TAMMY WYNETTE and later GEORGE JONES. Braddock's major hits include "D-I-V-O-R-C-E" (Wynette, 1968), "Golden Ring" (Jones and Wynette, 1976), "He Stopped Loving Her Today" (Jones, 1980), "Time Marches On" (TRACY LAWRENCE, 1996), "I Wanna Talk about Me" (TOBY KEITH, 2002), and "People Are Crazy" (BILLY CURRINGTON, 2009). Other artists charting with Braddock tunes include JOHN ANDERSON, MARK CHESNUTT, LACY J. DALTON, JOHNNY PAYCHECK, T. G. SHEPPARD, TANYA TUCKER, and BLAKE SHELTON (whom Braddock produced).

In addition to songwriting, Braddock has recorded for the MGM, COLUMBIA, MERCURY, ELEKTRA, and RCA labels, with modest sales results. His offbeat sense of humor is perhaps best displayed on the RCA album *Hardpore Cornography*.

Braddock was elected to the NASHVILLE SONGWRITERS HALL OF FAME in 1981 and to THE COUNTRY MUSIC HALL OF FAME in 2011. In 2007, Louisiana State University published the first volume of Braddock's memoirs, *Down in Orburndale: A Songwriter's Youth in Old Florida*. —*Kent Henderson*

## Connie Bradley

b. Fayetteville, Tennessee, October 1, 1945

Connie Bradley accepted the post of ASCAP southern executive director in 1980. She eventually became the performing rights organization's senior vice president, making her one of MUSIC Row's top executives until transitioning to the role of strategic advisor in February 2010, when TIM DUBOIS took the helm of the ASCAP's Nashville-based southern operations.

Born Connie Darnell, Bradley grew up in Shelbyville, Tennessee, and worked for Nashville's WLAC-TV, Famous Music/DOT RECORDS, the Bill Hudson & Associates public relations firm, and RCA RECORDS before joining ASCAP in 1976. She has served on the boards of numerous music and community organizations and chaired CMA's board in 1989.

Bradley has won numerous awards, including Lady Executive of the Year (1985) from the National Women Executives, Community Salesperson of the Year (1992) from the Tennessee Association of Sales Professionals, and the Nashville Symphony's Harmony Award (2006). Bradley is the wife of former RCA Records executive JERRY BRADLEY and the daughter-in-law of the late country music pioneer OWEN BRADLEY. —*Don Cusic*

## Harold Bradley
b. Nashville, Tennessee, January 2, 1926

Harold Ray Bradley, considered the "Dean of Nashville Session Guitarists," grew up in Nashville, and he first set out to learn the tenor banjo. Older brother OWEN BRADLEY suggested that he switch to guitar to improve his prospects for work. Harold was playing amplified jazz guitar by 1943, and Owen got him a summer job playing lead guitar with ERNEST TUBB's Texas Troubadours. After service in the navy (1944–46), Harold returned to Nashville to study music and play in Owen's dance band. Harold's first country recording session came in 1946, when he recorded with PEE WEE KING's Golden West Cowboys in Chicago. As Nashville's recording activities increased, Harold's studio workload grew. His acoustic rhythm guitar opened RED FOLEY's massive 1950 crossover hit "Chattanoogie Shoe Shine Boy."

Over the years Harold Bradley played on hundreds of hit recordings, including EDDY ARNOLD's "Make the World Go Away," BRENDA LEE's "I'm Sorry," RAY PRICE's "Danny Boy," and PATSY CLINE's "Crazy." He also contributed to hits by pop artists such as Ray Anthony ("Do the Hokey Pokey"), Bobby Vinton ("Blue Velvet"), and Burl Ives ("Holly Jolly Christmas"). As a featured artist, Bradley made a trio of excellent albums in the early 1960s: *Bossa Nova Goes to Nashville*, *Misty Guitar*, and *Guitar for Lovers Only*.

Though he is a capable lead guitarist, Bradley's frequent studio specialty was rhythm work. On many sessions he was part of a

*Harold Bradley*

studio guitar triumvirate with lead specialists HANK GARLAND and GRADY MARTIN. Garland specialized in jazzy licks, Martin in funkier leads. After Garland's disabling 1961 accident, Bradley took Garland's place, and RAY EDENTON increasingly supplied rhythm guitar support. Bradley's rhythm playing wasn't always apparent when listening to recordings, although his parts were essential. Occasionally he did play lead parts that stood out. For example, he played the opening tenor banjo notes (the instrument was tuned like a guitar) on JOHNNY HORTON's 1959 hit "The Battle of New Orleans" and the beautiful lead guitar passages on ELVIS PRESLEY's "Indescribably Blue" (#33 pop, 1967). Moreover, he became the go-to player for the six-string electric bass guitar style known as "tic-tac."

After operating two small recording studios in town in the early 1950s, Harold and Owen opened the Bradley Film and Recording Studios on Sixteenth Avenue South in 1955. COLUMBIA RECORDS purchased this complex in 1962, and Owen and his son Jerry later opened Bradley's Barn east of Nashville in Mount Juliet, Tennessee.

In addition to his studio achievements, Harold Bradley was the first president of Nashville's chapter of the National Academy of Recording Arts and Sciences (NARAS). In the 1980s he toured with FLOYD CRAMER and served as bandleader for SLIM WHITMAN. He also produced Irish country singer Sandy Kelly and EDDY ARNOLD's later albums for RCA RECORDS. As president of Nashville's chapter of the American Federation of Musicians (AFM) from 1991 to 2008, Bradley helped establish a union presence in BRANSON, MISSOURI. Additionally, he served as AFM's international vice president from 1999 to 2010. Shortly before the announcement of his 2006 election to THE COUNTRY MUSIC HALL OF FAME, he received AFM's prestigious Lifetime Achievement Award. —*Rich Kienzle*

## Jerry Bradley
b. Nashville, Tennessee, January 30, 1940

As the son of famed Nashville recording pioneer OWEN BRADLEY, Jerry Bradley was groomed to succeed in the music business. After working as a publisher with his father's Forest Hills Music, he succeeded CHET ATKINS as head of RCA RECORDS' Nashville office in 1973. At the time, Atkins's influence still loomed large over RCA, and Bradley was eager to make his own mark. Seeing his opportunity in country's burgeoning OUTLAW movement, Bradley assembled an album package consisting of cuts by WAYLON JENNINGS; some by Jennings's wife, JESSI COLTER; and others by WILLIE NELSON and Tompall Glaser (THE GLASER BROTHERS), and released it in 1976 as *Wanted! The Outlaws*. It became country music's first album to be certified platinum (for sales of 1 million copies) and expanded Nashville executives' view of country's sales potential.

Bradley signed a number of significant country acts to RCA, including ALABAMA, RONNIE MILSAP, EDDIE RABBITT, and STEVE WARINER. He also supervised the careers of DOLLY PARTON, ELVIS PRESLEY, CHARLEY PRIDE, JERRY REED, and GARY STEWART, among others. Bradley was succeeded in 1982 as RCA Nashville chief by JOE GALANTE. In 1986, Bradley took the reins of the newly developed OPRYLAND MUSIC GROUP, which grew out of GAYLORD ENTERTAINMENT COMPANY's acquisition of the ACUFF-ROSE PUBLICATIONS catalogs. He left when SONY/ATV Music Publishing bought these catalogs in 2002. —*Chet Flippo*

# Owen Bradley
b. Westmoreland, Tennessee, October 21, 1915; d. January 7, 1998

William Owen Bradley produced the hits of more than a half dozen members of THE COUNTRY MUSIC HALL OF FAME. He built the first music business on MUSIC ROW and was an architect of THE NASHVILLE SOUND.

The Bradley family moved to Nashville when Owen was a boy. He was fascinated with music and learned harmonica, steel guitar, trombone, piano, vibraphone, and organ. He was working professionally as a musician by age fifteen.

By the late 1930s Bradley was leading his own band, which eventually included future pop stars Snooky Lanson and Kitty Kallen as vocalists. He broadcast on WLAC during 1937–40, then became a regular on WSM. DECCA RECORDS executive PAUL COHEN noted Bradley's studio skills during his recording visits to Nashville, and in 1947 he hired Bradley to lead the label's sessions there and head the company's local office.

In addition to those duties and cowriting songs such as ROY ACUFF's 1942 hit "Night Train to Memphis," Bradley found time for his own recording career. "Zeb's Mountain Boogie," issued by "Brad Brady and His Tennesseans," launched BULLET RECORDS in 1946. Bradley's group had additional hits on Coral in 1949 ("Blues Stay Away from Me") and in 1950 ("The Third Man Theme").

One of Bradley's first big production successes was RED FOLEY's 1950 million seller "Chattanoogie Shoe Shine Boy." In that same year BILL MONROE joined Decca, and Bradley soon began producing a string of BLUEGRASS classics. He started working with HONKY-TONK masters ERNEST TUBB and WEBB PIERCE in 1947 and 1952, respectively. He also supervised the session that yielded KITTY WELLS's 1952 blockbuster "It Wasn't God Who Made Honky-Tonk Angels," which made Wells a star and revolutionized the role of women in country music.

Owen and his brother HAROLD BRADLEY were among the first to build independent recording studios in Nashville. Paul Cohen

was contemplating relocating Decca's country headquarters to Dallas, but in 1955 Owen Bradley promised him a Nashville recording center, built in an old house at 804 Sixteenth Avenue South; the Bradleys later added an army Quonset hut film and recording studio behind it.

Ironically, the earliest hits from Bradley Studios weren't all Decca recordings. Rented to other labels, the studio became the birthplace of SONNY JAMES's "Young Love" and Gene Vincent's "Be-Bop-a-Lula" (both CAPITOL, 1956), MARTY ROBBINS's "Singing the Blues" (COLUMBIA, 1956), CONWAY TWITTY's "It's Only Make Believe" (MGM, 1958), Mark Dinning's "Teen Angel" (MGM, 1959), and JOHNNY HORTON's "The Battle of New Orleans" (Columbia, 1959), to mention but a few.

Named head of Decca's Nashville division in 1958, Bradley helped shape the evolution of the Nashville Sound. In addition to turning out hits by Decca's country acts, he produced a Grammy-winning record for folk star BURL IVES (1962) and attracted Dixieland clarinetist Pete Fountain and pop organist Lenny Dee to Nashville. Bradley himself scored pop hits for Decca in 1957 ("White Silver Sands") and 1958 ("Big Guitar").

Many of Bradley's finest Decca productions were with female vocalists. He produced numerous Top Ten hits with Kitty Wells, and his collaborations with PATSY CLINE remain the standard against which female country records are measured. Bradley produced twelve Top Ten pop hits by BRENDA LEE in the early 1960s, and he also produced the fifty-plus hits that made LORETTA LYNN a country legend.

By the early 1960s Bradley's facility was hosting some 700 sessions annually and had been joined by similar businesses in a district that would come to be known as Music Row. Columbia Records bought the operation in 1962 and built the label's Nashville headquarters around the Quonset Hut studio. Columbia continued to use it until 1982.

In 1965 Bradley converted a Mount Juliet, Tennessee, barn into another studio. "Bradley's Barn," as it was called, witnessed sessions by Gordon Lightfoot, Joan Baez, the Beau Brummels, and other pop acts. Meanwhile, Bradley continued to sign important artists to Decca, most notably Conway Twitty. Bradley was inducted into the Country Music Hall of Fame in 1974. He stepped down as a label head in 1976 (by which time Decca had been absorbed into MCA) to become an independent producer and develop his publishing firm, Forest Hills Music. He built yet another studio (on the same site) after the original Bradley's Barn was destroyed by fire in 1980.

Actress Sissy Spacek portrayed Loretta Lynn in the 1980 movie *Coal Miner's Daughter*; the soundtrack, produced by Bradley, received an Academy Award nomination. In 1985 Jessica Lange portrayed Patsy Cline in the film *Sweet Dreams*; again, Bradley produced the soundtrack. Canadian K. D. LANG came to Nashville in 1987 to record the million-selling album *Shadowland: The Owen Bradley Sessions*.

In the 1990s Bradley produced records for Marsha Thornton, Brenda Lee, and Pete Fountain and went into semiretirement. The Recording Academy gave him its Governors Award at a 1995 gala, and the reactivated Decca label saluted him with a 1996 compilation called *The Nashville Sound*.

Bradley fathered a musical dynasty. Son JERRY BRADLEY ran RCA's Nashville operations and, later, OPRYLAND MUSIC GROUP for lengthy periods. Grandson Clay Bradley has worked at Opryland Music Group, MCA, and BMI. Daughter Patsy retired from BMI; nephew Bobby is a studio engineer. Daughter-in-law CONNIE BRADLEY helmed Nashville's ASCAP office for three

*Owen Bradley*

decades. Younger brother Harold became a leading Nashville session guitarist and the president of the Nashville musicians' union from 1991 to early 2009.

When Owen Bradley died in 1998, his memorial service was held at THE RYMAN AUDITORIUM. His statue graces a small, namesake park at the head of Music Row. —*Robert K. Oermann*

## Branson, Missouri

The Ozark Mountains community of Branson, in southwestern Missouri, is one of America's most popular and distinctive resort and entertainment areas. Since the 1960s, the town has grown into a major live-performance center for the music industry, where stars of country, pop, and big band music perform to enthusiastic audiences from April through October. As of 2011, the city of 7,500 welcomes an estimated 7 million visitors annually, who attend live shows in some forty theaters. Country stars appearing regularly in Branson in recent years included MOE BANDY, MICKEY GILLEY, NEAL MCCOY, the OAK RIDGE BOYS, and BUCK TRENT.

Branson was a tourism center before the live-music boom. Tours of Marvel Cave (now part of the area's largest employer, the theme park Silver Dollar City) have brought visitors to Branson for more than a century. The region has flourished as a fishing and camping haven since the 1920s, and water sports are popular in the three lakes that surround the city.

The first live-performance attraction in Branson started in 1959 with a hillbilly jamboree called Baldknobbers (named for a turn-of-the-century Ozarks vigilante gang). Built in 1967, Presley's Jubilee was the first theater on 76 Country Boulevard, known locally as "The Strip."

In the early 1990s the town's booming popularity as a country music tourism destination caught the attention of the national media, which for a few years portrayed Branson as threatening Nashville's dominant position as a country music mecca. But soon it became clear that both cities carved distinctive niches as tourism centers, while Nashville held onto its role as country music's songwriting, MUSIC PUBLISHING, and recording capital. —*Janet E. Williams*

## Rod Brasfield
b. Smithville, Mississippi, August 22, 1910; d. September 12, 1958

From 1947 to 1958, Rodney Leon Brasfield was the premier comedian at the GRAND OLE OPRY and very likely in country music. He began his career as straight man for his brother Lawrence (known as "Boob") during several years with Bisbee's Dramatic Shows, one of many such troupes that traversed the South during the late 1800s and mid-1900s. Rod served one year in the army air corps during World War II but returned to Bisbee's because of a childhood back injury. Boob eventually wound up playing "Uncle Cyp" on Springfield, Missouri's *OZARK JUBILEE* television program (1955–60).

While working the road in the Southeast, Rod Brasfield was recruited by GEORGE D. HAY for the Grand Ole Opry in 1944. By this time Brasfield was playing both comic and straight parts, and he became an immediate hit with the show's stage and radio audiences, as well as in Opry TENT SHOWS. With his trademark baggy suit, button shoes, beat-up hat, rubbery face, and clacking false teeth, he could have the audience laughing before he spoke a word. Playing the drawling bumpkin to the hilt, he had a finely

*Rod Brasfield*

honed sense of timing and worked easily with host RED FOLEY on the Opry's NBC network segment beginning in 1947, when Brasfield replaced THE DUKE OF PADUCAH in this regard. Much of the show's comedy contrasted the tall, broad-shouldered Foley with the diminutive Brasfield, who skillfully milked running gags by deferentially addressing the singer as "Mr. Foley" and complaining good-naturedly about the sweltering summer heat in THE RYMAN AUDITORIUM.

Audiences instinctively sympathized with Brasfield's hapless character, a good ol' country boy who was constantly unlucky. Like MINNIE PEARL, with whom he frequently teamed from 1948 until his death, he often poked fun at country life—always with good humor. Reinforcing his small-town identity, he took his moniker, the Hohenwald Flash, from the name of a Tennessee town southwest of Nashville. Brasfield and Pearl's comic exchanges (in which they alternated in delivering punch lines—that is, neither was the straight man) were not only broadcast on the Opry radio show but also televised on a 1955–56 series of ABC network programs starring Opry acts. In addition, Brasfield did comedy routines with singer-comedienne June Carter. Brasfield's role as Andy Griffith's sidekick in the 1957 film *A Face in the Crowd* hinted at a film career that might have been. A victim of heart failure and a widely known drinking problem, Brasfield was elected to THE COUNTRY MUSIC HALL OF FAME in 1987. —*John W. Rumble*

## David Briggs
b. Killeen, Alabama, March 16, 1943

When David Paul Briggs moved to Nashville in 1964, at twenty-one, he had already established a significant career as a session musician. Briggs began working as a teenager at

Rick Hall's FAME Recording Studios in Muscle Shoals, Alabama, and helped shape classics such as Arthur Alexander's "You Better Move On" and Jimmy Hughes's "Steal Away." "The only reason I ended up playing piano in Muscle Shoals," Briggs has said, "was because nobody else there was good enough. I was the best of the worst."

Signed to DECCA RECORDS by OWEN BRADLEY as a singer-songwriter in 1962, Briggs had some success but returned to sessions because "I could get paid in two weeks," instead of waiting for twice-a-year artist royalty checks. In 1965 he played piano on ELVIS PRESLEY's recording of "Love Letters," beginning a twelve-year association with Presley. In 1969 Briggs opened Quadrafonic Studios in Nashville with Norbert Putnam.

Briggs has also excelled in production, arranging, publishing, jingle writing, and performing with Area Code 615. His session credits include recordings with ALABAMA, Bob Seger, HANK WILLIAMS JR., NEIL YOUNG, REBA MCENTIRE, LINDA RONSTADT, WILLIE NELSON, B. B. King, DOLLY PARTON, James Brown, ERNEST TUBB, ROY ORBISON, and MARTY ROBBINS, among many others.

In 1985 Briggs and Will Jennings established a publishing company, Willin' David Music, and published the Academy Award–winning "Up Where We Belong" and Steve Winwood's "Higher Love." Briggs has had his own studio on MUSIC ROW, House of David, since 1980. He also has served as musical director for several TV and radio specials. —*John Lomax III*

## Dr. John R. Brinkley
b. Beta, North Carolina, July 8, 1885; d. May 26, 1942

In the 1930s and early 1940s, John Romulus Brinkley owned a super-powered BORDER RADIO station that reached most of North America with hillbilly music and COWBOY MUSIC.

A 1915 graduate of Kansas City's Eclectic Medical Institute, Brinkley set up practice in Milford, Kansas, where he became rich and famous in the Roaring Twenties for pioneering a controversial rejuvenation operation in which he implanted slivers of billy goat sex glands into the human body. "A man is only as old as his glands," the diamond-studded, goateed physician told listeners of his Kansas radio station KFKB.

Medical and radio authorities drove Brinkley out of the Sunflower State, but not before he almost won the Kansas governorship in 1930, campaigning on the slogan "Let's pasture the goats on the statehouse lawn." Undaunted, the maverick medicine man moved to the Rio Grande badlands, establishing the second border radio station, XER (later XERA), broadcasting at more than 100,000 watts from Villa Acuña, Mexico, just across the border from Del Rio, Texas, in 1931. Among the performers who worked at his station were the CARTER FAMILY, from 1938 to 1942.

Brinkley moved his hospital to Del Rio in 1933 and switched his medical practice from goat glands to an equally controversial prostate treatment. His early advertising proved so effective, however, that listeners remembered him long after his death as "the Goat Gland Man." In the radio business, he pioneered the use of prerecorded programming through electrical transcription discs. He built a palatial Spanish Mission–style home in Del Rio (which still stands) that *Texas Centennial* magazine described in 1936 as "the showplace of the Southwest." Along with splashing fountains and colored lights that spelled his name, the grounds contained Galapagos turtles and other exotic sights.

A 1939 libel suit against the American Medical Association, which Brinkley lost, began the fall of his peculiar empire. Dissatisfied patients sued for malpractice, and the Mexican government confiscated his radio station. The IRS hit him for back taxes. Bankrupt, Brinkley was slated to stand trial for mail fraud when he died in San Antonio. But for decades afterward, radio fans chuckled at an old Texas joke that HANK THOMPSON sometimes told: "What's the fastest thing on four legs? A goat passing the Brinkley Hospital." —*Gene Fowler*

## Bristol, Tennessee-Virginia

A small city straddling the border of northeastern Tennessee and southwestern Virginia, Bristol has had an important impact on the history of country music. Since the 1920s its strategic location has placed it at the crossroads of several key musical traditions. In 1927 talent scout RALPH PEER set up temporary recording studios on State Street to record for the Victor Talking Machine Company (predecessor to RCA VICTOR) a series of recordings that included the first made by the CARTER FAMILY and JIMMIE RODGERS as well as important recordings by ERNEST V. STONEMAN and other artists from Tennessee, Virginia, West Virginia, and Kentucky.

Country acts had recorded successfully in Atlanta, New York, and other locations since 1922, and Peer's success with Stoneman's earlier records led him to schedule Stoneman for additional sessions in Bristol and enlist his help in recruiting new talent. But the success of the Bristol sessions dramatically boosted country music as a viable commercial commodity. From the first, Bristol's city fathers encouraged this activity, and in early 1928 an editorial in a local newspaper chronicled the local musicians who were recording. Peer returned to the town in the summer of 1928, and rival COLUMBIA RECORDS set up sessions in nearby Johnson City.

Further support for the music came in 1929, when local businessman W. A. Wilson opened radio station WOPI and began to feature live music. By the late 1940s a second station, WCYB, began broadcasting the new BLUEGRASS sounds of FLATT & SCRUGGS, THE STANLEY BROTHERS, and CARL STORY. Two important regional companies marketed the area's music: Jim Stanton's RICH-R-TONE RECORDS, which recorded the Stanley Brothers and WILMA LEE & STONEY COOPER in the late 1940s, and Joe Morrell's Shadow label, which recorded everything from traditional STRINGBAND MUSIC to rhythm and blues in the 1950s.

Bristol has continued to support and celebrate its musical heritage. In 1994, the Bristol Country Music Alliance formed to promote the region's musical history. Though the building where Ralph Peer made his first recordings no longer stands, a historical marker was dedicated on the site in July 2009. Nearby, East Tennessee State University has a traditional music program that has trained a number of young acoustic musicians. —*Charles Wolfe*

## Elton Britt
b. Zack, Arkansas, June 27, 1913; d. June 23, 1972

Elton Britt (real name James Elton Baker) was the first country musician to be awarded a gold record and one of music's finest yodelers. The youngest child of Martella and James Baker, he was what is now known as a "blue baby" and was plagued with heart trouble all his life. At age ten he started playing a Montgomery Ward mail-order guitar. Impressed with JIMMIE RODGERS, he taught himself to yodel by listening to the Singing Brakeman's records.

Breath control he learned as a swimmer enabled Britt to maintain an extremely long yodel. Recruited by THE BEVERLY HILL BILLIES, he joined the group and journeyed to Los Angeles in 1930. "Little Elton," as he was then billed, remained with the Hill Billies for several years, during which time he acquired the name Britt. He probably made his first commercial recordings with this band. Beginning in August 1933 he recorded for the AMERICAN RECORD CORPORATION as part of the Wenatchee Mountaineers, a band that included his brothers Vern and Arl. Elton's first success was "Chime Bells" in 1934 (he had a bigger hit with it in 1948), and by 1939 he had signed with RCA VICTOR. His RCA hits included "Someday" (1946), "Detour" (1946), "Candy Kisses" (1949), and "Quicksilver" (1950, a duet with ROSALIE ALLEN). But his biggest hit was his 1942 recording of "There's a Star Spangled Banner Waving Somewhere," which reportedly sold 4 million copies and earned Britt the aforementioned gold record, presented to him by RCA.

In the 1930s and 1940s Britt appeared in three movies, but they did little to advance his career. By the 1950s he entered into the first of many retirements, though he signed with ABC-Paramount at the close of the decade. He made a brief, unsuccessful run for president in 1960. Eight years later, again with RCA, he had his last Top Forty success with a seven-minute yodeling song, "The Jimmie Rodgers Blues." Shortly before starting a concert tour in 1972, Britt died of a heart attack. Although he recorded extensively, as of 2011 relatively little of Britt's work remains in print. —*W. K. McNeil*

## Broadcast Music, Inc. (*see* BMI)

## Broken Bow Records
established in Nashville, 1999

Broken Bow Records is an independent label founded in 1999 by businessman Benny Brown, the company's CEO. Early acts, such as the Great Divide, had relatively little success. Then, in 2001, the label signed former Atlantic artist CRAIG MORGAN, who notched a #6 single with "Almost Home" in 2002–03. During 2004–05, JOE DIFFIE, Sherrie Austin, and Lila McCann each gained chart-making singles, but all three left when sales proved weak. However, Morgan's second album, *My Kind of Livin*' (2004), yielded "That's What I Love about Sunday," the first #1 for artist and label alike. JASON ALDEAN followed in 2005 with a self-titled, platinum album featuring the Top Ten single "Hick Town." Subsequent Aldean #1's include "Why" and "She's Country." Morgan exited for BNA Entertainment (RCA RECORDS) in 2008, the year that Broken Bow released *One on One*, ALABAMA veteran Randy Owen's first solo album. Aldean continued as Broken Bow's leading artist. His 2009 album *Wide Open* went platinum by 2010, providing additional hit singles. Companion imprint Stoney Creek Records debuted in 2009. —*John W. Rumble*

## Garth Brooks
b. Luba, Oklahoma, February 7, 1962

Troyal Garth Brooks emerged in the 1990s to become one of the biggest-selling music acts of all time. He greatly heightened country music's media profile and helped move the genre into the

*Garth Brooks*

mainstream of American entertainment. In 2007, the RIAA named the Oklahoman the best-selling solo artist in American music history, citing sales of 123 million albums to that point. In 2009, emerging from retirement, Brooks announced he would perform fifteen concerts annually for five years at the 1,500-seat encore theater in Las Vegas. The first twenty concerts sold out at $125 a ticket in five hours.

Brooks was the sixth child of Troyal and Colleen Brooks. His mother appeared on the *OZARK JUBILEE* in the 1950s and recorded briefly for CAPITOL RECORDS. Brooks started performing while attending Oklahoma State University, concentrating on songs by James Taylor, Billy Joel, and Bob Seger while mixing in tunes by GEORGE STRAIT and other 1980s country stars.

His first trip to Nashville in 1985 ended in disappointment, and he returned to Oklahoma. Two years later, after marrying first wife Sandy Mahl, he came back to Nashville and found encouragement from MUSIC ROW executive Bob Doyle, who left a position at ASCAP to form a publishing company, with Brooks as his first client. Doyle and Pam Lewis teamed to manage Brooks, and JIM FOGLESONG oversaw his signing with Capitol Records in 1988.

The record label introduced Brooks to veteran producer ALLEN REYNOLDS, who had worked with KATHY MATTEA, DON WILLIAMS, and CRYSTAL GAYLE. Reynolds gently altered Brooks's singing, encouraging him to stop belting out ballads in a full-throated style similar to GARY MORRIS and suggesting he use a more relaxed, natural approach. The change brought out an intimate tone in Brooks's voice, which he used to great effect on his early hit ballads, "If Tomorrow Never Comes" and "The Dance." With his first album—*Garth Brooks*, his most traditional country effort to date—he also established his credentials as an evocative songwriter. He wrote or cowrote his first three hits, "Much Too Young (To Feel This Damn Old)," "If Tomorrow Never Comes," and "Not Counting You." He has continued to contribute songs throughout his recording career.

Sales of Brooks's first album initially were strong but not spectacular: It sold 500,000 copies in the first year. But after the release of "The Dance" in the spring of 1990, sales doubled within a month. His second album, *No Fences*, appeared in the summer of 1990; sparked by the popularity of the hit "Friends in Low Places," it sold more than 700,000 copies within ten days of its release. His third album, *Ropin' the Wind*, became the first album by a country singer to debut at #1 on the *Billboard* pop charts. By 1991 these three albums had sold a mind-boggling 30 million units. Brooks had reached sales levels unprecedented for a country music performer.

"Garthmania" was fueled not only by his radio hits but also by the athletic performer's explosive stage show. A fan of 1970s rock acts—Kiss, Kansas, and Queen among them—Brooks added an arena-rock flash to his performances, utilizing dramatic lighting effects while smashing guitars, swinging from ropes, dousing himself in water, and tearing across the stage while exhorting the crowd. His ticket sales rivaled those of tours by the Rolling Stones, U2, The Eagles, and the Grateful Dead.

By the mid-1990s Brooks settled into a winning musical formula: His albums repeatedly combined melodramatic ballads, high-speed COUNTRY-ROCK, the occasional WESTERN SWING or HONKY-TONK tune, and a cowboy song thrown in for its down-to-earth effect. He benefited from pushing boundaries with controversial songs: From the banned video of "The Thunder Rolls," a song that vividly discussed the horrors of domestic violence, to the gay rights statement in "We Shall Be Free," to the cheeky wordplay of "Papa Loved Mama" and "Bury the Hatchet," Brooks took chances, courted controversy, and gained media attention. Though album sales for *The Chase, In Pieces*, and *Fresh Horses* did not equal those of *No Fences* and *Ropin' the Wind*, Brooks still captured the public's attention while compiling remarkable sales numbers.

On August 7, 1997, Brooks performed in New York's Central Park before an audience estimated to be 250,000—and millions more via a live HBO broadcast. As the biggest star in Nashville, he wielded his power openly, negotiating new contracts and shaking up the executive staff at Capitol's country division. He delayed the release of his album *Sevens* until November 1997, after helping choose the label's new chief executive, Pat Quigley.

Before long, Brooks reached a crossroads. In 1998 he appeared at spring training with the San Diego Padres, the first of several years of participating in baseball training camps to raise awareness for his Teammates for Kids foundation. He released the successful *Double Live* album in late 1998 and his first *Greatest Hits* CD in 1999. That same year, he gambled on an unusual project under the name Chris Gaines. Designed to become a character in a movie about a conflicted rock & roller, Chris Gaines was introduced by Brooks in a rock album, *Garth Brooks in . . . The Life of Chris Gaines*. Described as a "pre-soundtrack," it sold 2 million copies, which was considered a disappointment. Eventually, the movie deal fell apart and the Gaines project ended.

In 2000, Brooks divorced wife, Sandy Mahl, and, three weeks later, said he would retire to raise his three daughters. He released the album *Scarecrow* in 2001. In 2005, he signed an exclusive deal with Wal-Mart to release *The Limited Series*, a six-CD box set. That December, he married singer TRISHA YEARWOOD. Wal-Mart released *The Lost Sessions* in 2006 and *The Ultimate Hits* in 2007, with a new single, "More than a Memory," debuting at #1.

In November 2007, Brooks performed nine sold-out shows in Kansas City. In January 2008, he made five sold-out appearances at Los Angeles's Staples Center. He announced his five-year Las Vegas commitment in October 2009. In December 2010, he performed nine sold-out shows in Nashville, donating proceeds to the city's ongoing relief effort from a devastating flood in May of that year. —*Michael McCall*

## Brooks & Dunn
Kix Brooks b. Shreveport, Louisiana, May 12, 1955
Ronnie Dunn b. Coleman, Texas, June 1, 1953

Kix Brooks had recorded an album for CAPITOL RECORDS and written hits for other country artists and Ronnie Dunn had won a national country talent competition when the two paired up. ARISTA RECORDS Nashville chief TIM DuBOIS urged them to join forces, resulting in the high-energy country duo Brooks & Dunn. The team released its first album, *Brand New Man*, in 1991. By October 2009, when they announced plans to retire as a duo, Brooks & Dunn had sold more than 26 million albums and scored twenty #1 *Billboard* hits. They also had won nineteen CMA awards (including fourteen in the vocal duo category), twenty-four ACM awards (including fifteen as the top vocal duo), and two Grammy awards.

Leon Eric "Kix" Brooks III gravitated to music at an early age. He grew up on the same Shreveport, Louisiana, street as Billie Jean Horton, who had been married to both HANK WILLIAMS and JOHNNY HORTON. Brooks's first paying performance was at age twelve with Horton's daughter, and he still lists Williams and Horton as key influences. Brooks worked the Louisiana club circuit before leaving for stretches in Alaska and Maine. He moved to Nashville in 1979 to pursue a country career, and record producer Don Gant nurtured his budding talents. Brooks recorded a single for independent label Avion but fared better as a writer, penning #1 hits "I'm Only in It for the Love" for JOHN CONLEE

*Brooks & Dunn: Kix Brooks (left) and Ronnie Dunn*

(1983) and "Modern Day Romance" for the Nitty Gritty Dirt Band (1985). In 1989 Capitol Records Nashville released Brooks's self-titled debut album. A single, "Sacred Ground," did not do well, but the song went on to become a hit in 1992 for McBride & The Ride.

After studying theology at Abilene Christian College in his native Texas, Ronnie Gene Dunn moved with his parents to Tulsa, Oklahoma, where he fronted the house band at Duke's Country, a popular nightclub. Dunn recorded for Churchill Records, owned by Oklahoma talent agent Jim Halsey, and released two singles in 1983–84. Victory in a country talent contest led to recording sessions with up-and-coming engineer-producer Scott Hendricks, who brought Dunn to DuBois's attention.

The Arista label chief introduced the two singers over lunch and suggested they write and record together. Pleased with the results, DuBois offered them a record deal as a duo. Their first album, *Brand New Man* (1991), sold 6 million copies and yielded the #1 hits "Brand New Man," "My Next Broken Heart," "Neon Moon," and "Boot Scootin' Boogie." The latter song inspired a country line dance that helped fuel a national country dance craze.

Under the guidance of producer-songwriter Don Cook, Brooks & Dunn's success continued with their second album, 1993's *Hard Workin' Man*, which sold 5 million units and generated the hits "We'll Burn That Bridge" (#2), "She Used to Be Mine" (#1), and "That Ain't No Way to Go" (#1). The duo's 1994 release, *Waitin' on Sundown*, sold 3 million copies and included chart-toppers "She's Not the Cheatin' Kind," "Little Miss Honky-Tonk," and "You're Gonna Miss Me When I'm Gone." Brooks & Dunn's fourth album, *Borderline*, released in 1996, featured a hit cover of the B. W. Stevenson hit "My Maria."

An outstanding singer, Dunn handled most of the lead vocals, with Brooks supplying harmonies. In concert, Brooks played the animated crowd rouser, sometimes leaving the stage during a number to dance with audience members. Five years into their career, in 1996, both the CMA and the ACM gave the act their highest prizes, Entertainer of the Year. Headlining arena tours and multiplatinum sales continued until 1999's *Tight Rope,* which only went gold, spurring some creative soul-searching during an extended break from the studio and the road.

Returning with 2001's *Steers & Stripes,* the duo took over production and came roaring back, with the #1s "Ain't Nothing 'Bout You," "Only in America," and "The Long Goodbye" showing new vigor. The follow-up, 2003's *Red Dirt Road*, drew the best reviews of their career, especially for the slice-of-life title song, yet another #1. With 2005's *Hillbilly Deluxe*, the partners brought in veteran record man Tony Brown to coproduce. They balanced back-to-their-roots hits such as "Play Something Country" with the award-winning spiritual song "Believe." Brown stayed on for 2007's *Cowboy Town,* an expansive and experimental album that found Brooks taking more lead vocals.

Afterward, the duo planned to take a break to work on solo efforts. But before the albums were released, Brooks & Dunn announced that they would split, amicably, after the September 2009 release of a two-CD compilation album, *#1s and Then Some . . .* , and a final tour, billed as "The Last Rodeo," that would eventually end in Nashville in September 2010. A CBS special aired in May 2010, with artists such as Kenny Chesney, George Strait, Taylor Swift, and Keith Urban paying tribute to the duo by singing their songs.

Since early 2006, Brooks has hosted *American Country Countdown,* a nationally syndicated radio program. Dunn signed a recording contract with Arista and released his first solo album in 2011. —*Jay Orr*

## Brother Duets

Brother vocal duets have thrived in country music since the early 1930s. Similar vocal timbres, common word pronunciations, familiarity with each other's singing style, and shared cultural origins help to explain siblings' ability to phrase and harmonize so well. With the appearance in 1925 of electrical microphones, which replaced acoustical horns in recording, the subtleties of harmony singing could at last be preserved on disc and disseminated through recordings and live or recorded radio broadcasts.

Brother teams also learned from and were inspired by the music of other duets who were not brothers. Thanks to the strong signal of Chicago station WLS, two National Barn Dance acts—Mac & Bob (Lester McFarland and Robert Gardner) and Karl & Harty (Karl Davis and Hartford Connecticut Taylor)—exerted a powerful musical influence, for their mandolin and guitar playing, close harmony, and a repertoire of old-time songs were broadcast far and wide in the 1920s and 1930s. The heyday of brother duet singing followed in the late '30s when The Monroe Brothers (Charlie and Bill), The Callahan Brothers (Bill and Joe), the Blue Sky Boys (Bill and Earl Bolick), The Delmore Brothers (Alton and Rabon), The Shelton Brothers (Bob and Joe), The Morris Brothers (Wiley and Zeke), The Dixon Brothers (Dorsey and Howard), and similar acts became prominent on radio and recordings. Although the mandolin was generally the preferred lead instrument, other instruments, such as Rabon Delmore's tenor guitar and Howard Dixon's Hawaiian guitar, also figured prominently in the music of these duos.

The Bailes Brothers (first as Walter and Johnnie and later as Johnnie and Homer) added their soulful sound to the genre in the 1940s. The number of brother duets has declined since that time, but the tradition has never disappeared. In fact, the quality and influence of this tradition probably reached its peak in the 1950s with the marvelous and highly influential singing of The Louvin Brothers (Charlie and Ira), the Wilburn Brothers (Doyle and Teddy), and The Everly Brothers (Don and Phil). The style could even be detected in the 1960s in the singing of the Beatles. The brother duet style continued into modern times with the singing of such performers as Jim & Jesse McReynolds, the Whitstein Brothers (Charles and Robert), and the Gibson Brothers (Eric and Leigh). Bluegrass act Dailey & Vincent referenced the influence of brotherly harmony by naming their 2009 album *Brothers from Different Mothers. —Bill C. Malone*

## Cecil Brower
b. Bellevue, Texas, November 28, 1914; d. November 21, 1965

One of the architects of western swing and the man who established its fundamental fiddle style, Cecil Lee Brower was a classically trained violinist with an ear cocked toward jazz and country when Milton Brown persuaded him to join his Musical Brownies in 1933. Brower left the Southern Melody Boys, with whom he and Kenneth Pitts played arranged duets and Brower had begun improvising choruses in the manner of jazz violinist Joe Venuti. With the Brownies, Brower teamed with Jesse Ashlock, forming the first identifiably western swing twin fiddle team.

Over the next few years Brower set the basic model for western swing fiddling, with a fluid style full of essential tricks of the trade, such as "rocking the bow." He was the fiddler on all of Brown's recordings from 1934 through 1936, successfully teaming with CLIFF BRUNER at the last of these sessions. After Brown's death in 1936 Brower worked for bandleader ROY NEWMAN in Dallas and also recorded with BOB WILLS and BILL BOYD during this time. After a period with pop bandleader Ted Fio Rito, Brower returned to Texas in 1939 and worked until World War II with the LIGHT CRUST DOUGHBOYS, reteaming with old cohort Kenneth Pitts.

Brower served in the coast guard, and after the war he worked with the HI FLYERS before leading his own Kilocycle Cowboys in Odessa from 1946 to 1949. Stints with LEON McAULIFFE and AL DEXTER followed; then Brower moved to Springfield, Missouri, to work with RED FOLEY on ABC-TV's *Jubilee, U.S.A.* (as the *OZARK JUBILEE* was then billed on the small screen.) He followed Foley to Nashville and became an in-demand session musician before joining JIMMY DEAN, with whom he was playing when he died from a bleeding ulcer after a show at CARNEGIE HALL. —*Kevin Coffey*

## Hylo Brown
b. River, Kentucky, April 20, 1922; d. January 17, 2003

Frank "Hylo" Brown Jr.—nicknamed for his broad vocal range—was one of the most admired BLUEGRASS voices of the mid- to late 1950s and early 1960s. Born in the Kentucky mountains and reared in an atmosphere of traditional music, young Frank Brown migrated with his family to Springfield, Ohio, during World War II. For some years thereafter he worked in a factory and performed on the local music scene, including radio programs at WPFB in nearby Middletown. In 1954 his composition "Lost to a Stranger" came to the attention of KEN NELSON, who signed him to a CAPITOL RECORDS contract. Most of Brown's recordings used acoustic, bluegrass-style accompaniment and were well received by fans of traditional sounds. He worked the *WWVA JAMBOREE* for a time and then became a featured opening act with the FLATT & SCRUGGS band. For three years Brown led his own bluegrass band, the highly regarded Timberliners (mandolinist Red Rector, fiddler Clarence "Tater" Tate, banjoist Jim Smoak, and bassist Joe Phillips), with whom he worked a series of TV shows for MARTHA WHITE FLOUR. The group appeared at the 1959 NEWPORT FOLK FESTIVAL, where they backed EARL SCRUGGS. Later Brown rejoined Flatt & Scruggs and afterward toured for many years as a solo act. He cut four albums for STARDAY RECORDS in the early 1960s and six more for the Rural Rhythm label later in the decade. Brown became increasingly inactive in his later years, following retirement to his native Kentucky. —*Ivan M. Tribe*

## Jim Ed Brown
b. Sparkman, Arkansas, April 1, 1934

James Edward Brown rose to fame with his sisters Bonnie and Maxine recording for RCA RECORDS as THE BROWNS trio from 1954 until 1967. Jim Ed's success was not limited to the trio, however. As a solo act for RCA, he began placing records on the charts in 1965 with "I Just Heard from a Memory Last Night." His Top Ten country hits include "Pop A Top" (1967), "Morning" (1970), "Southern Loving" (1973), "Sometime Sunshine" (1973), and "It's That Time of Night" (1974).

In 1976 he began recording duets with Helen Cornelius (b. Hannibal, Missouri, December 6, 1941). A year later they became CMA's Vocal Duo of the Year. Their best-known hits are "I Don't Want to Have to Marry You" (1976), "Saying Hello, Saying I Love You, Saying Goodbye" (1976), "Lying in Love with You" (1979), and "Fools" (1979). In addition to joining the GRAND OLE OPRY as a member of the Browns in 1963, Jim Ed hosted TNN's *You Can Be a Star* talent show in the 1980s. As of 2011, Brown was in his eighth year as host of the syndicated radio program *Country Music Greats Radio Show*. —*Stacey Wolfe*

## Junior Brown
b. Cottonwood, Arizona, June 12, 1952

Jamieson "Junior" Brown is an idiosyncratic, formidable musician who helped define the difference between AUSTIN's "alternative" approach to country music and Nashville's commercial mainstream in the 1990s. With his cowboy hat, deep baritone, bent sense of humor, and total command of 1940s–1970s country, Brown would seem to be a throwback to an earlier era. But his clever songwriting and virtuoso guitar work gave him an updated style of his own.

After performing in clubs in Albuquerque, New Mexico, Brown arrived in Austin in 1979, working as a lead guitarist and PEDAL STEEL GUITAR player in country bands. A regular gig at Austin's Continental Club with his own band, featuring his wife, Tanya Rae, on rhythm guitar, drew fervent crowds as he showed off his instrumental ability on the guit-steel, his double-necked invention combining electric guitar and steel guitar. His self-produced first album, *12 Shades of Brown*, led to a contract with CURB RECORDS, which re-released the first album along with the new *Guit with It* in 1993. In 1996, Brown won CMA's Music Video of the Year award for "My Wife Thinks You're Dead," from the album *Semi-Crazy*. Country radio never embraced his distinctive sound, and Brown moved from Curb to Telarc Records in 2004. His music has been popular on film soundtracks, and he provided the voice-over narration for the 2005 film remake of *The Dukes of Hazzard*. —*Rick Mitchell*

## Milton Brown
b. Stephenville, Texas, September 8, 1903; d. April 18, 1936

Widely regarded as an originator of WESTERN SWING, vocalist-bandleader Milton Brown was largely responsible for establishing the genre in the early 1930s. Though not as familiar to modern audiences as his contemporary BOB WILLS, Brown, along with his influential band the Musical Brownies, introduced many elements to western swing recordings: the 2/4 dance rhythm of New Orleans jazz, twin fiddles playing in harmony, slapped bass fiddle, jazz piano, and the first amplified instrument in country music, BOB DUNN's steel guitar. During a sensational three-and-a-half-year career, the Brownies became the Southwest's preeminent STRINGBAND, only to see their fortunes collapse when their leader died after an automobile accident.

Brown began singing in childhood in Stephensville. After moving to Fort Worth in 1918, he accompanied his father, a breakdown fiddler, at local house dances and formed a small vocal group in 1927, building a repertoire of popular standards. At a house dance in 1930, Brown met Wills and guitarist Herman Arnspiger. The three began playing on radio as the Aladdin Laddies and later as the original LIGHT CRUST DOUGHBOYS.

*Milton Brown (center) & His Musical Brownies*

In September 1932 Brown formed the Musical Brownies. Original personnel included Brown, vocals; younger brother Derwood on guitar; JESSE ASHLOCK, fiddle; Wanna Coffman, bass; and OCIE STOCKARD, tenor banjo. Shortly after, jazz pianist Fred "Papa" Calhoun joined, followed by swing fiddler CECIL BROWER. Other key additions included amplified steel guitarist Bob Dunn (1934) and fiddler CLIFF BRUNER (1935). The Brownies played a daily radio program on Fort Worth's KTAT (1932–35) and WBAP (1935–36) and barnstormed the state playing dances. Their regular Saturday night dances at the city's Crystal Springs Dancing Pavilion became de rigueur for their legion of fans.

Brown also introduced a new kind of singing to Texas country music. His style was smooth, rhythmic, sophisticated, and highly improvisatory, more jazzlike than country, and similar to those of jazz vocalists Cab Calloway and Jack Teagarden. Brown established recorded western swing's initial repertoire of jazz, blues, and pop songs, introducing to the genre such staples as "Right or Wrong," "Corrine Corrina," and "Sitting on Top of the World" through sessions for BLUEBIRD RECORDS (1934) and DECCA RECORDS (1935–36). The Brownies' April 4, 1934, Bluebird session is considered to have been history's first authentic western swing recording session.

On the morning of April 13, 1936, Brown was injured in an automobile accident that killed his passenger, a sixteen-year-old girl. Brown's untreated punctured lung resulted in pneumonia, which caused his death on April 18 at age thirty-two. The funeral drew an estimated 3,500 mourners. —*Cary Ginell*

## T. Graham Brown
b. Arabi, Georgia, October 30, 1954

Born Anthony Graham Brown, this Georgia-raised singer dabbled in southern beach music (in a duo called Dirk & Tony), soul music (in a band called Rack of Spam), and OUTLAW country (in an eight-piece ensemble called Reo Diamond) before reaching the country charts as a solo act.

Signing with CAPITOL RECORDS, Graham achieved eleven Top Ten hits between 1985 and 1990, including three #1s: "Hell and High Water" (1986), "Don't Go to Strangers" (1987), and "Darlene" (1988). Onstage, Brown infused his R&B-influenced country with an irrepressible extroversion. He took a long break from recording after his last Capitol album in 1991, although he continued to tour. His 1998 album, *Wine into Water,* and 2003's *Next Right*

*Thing* found him dealing with weightier subject matter while continuing to emphasize the soulful abilities of his strong voice. —*Bob Allen*

## Tony Brown
b. Greensboro, North Carolina, December 11, 1946

In an April 1996 cover story, the *Los Angeles Times Magazine* crowned Tony Brown, at the time the president of MCA RECORDS, the "King of Nashville," a description reflecting the enormous influence he held on MUSIC ROW in the 1990s as a producer, talent scout, and record executive.

The North Carolina native earned his reputation with discerning musical taste, a likable personality, a sense of civic responsibility, and keenly honed musical skills. As a producer, he has overseen gold and platinum albums by RODNEY CROWELL, VINCE GILL, PATTY LOVELESS, REBA MCENTIRE, GEORGE STRAIT, MARTY STUART, STEVE WARINER, WYNONNA, and many others. Brown's reputation also stems from his role as a progressive musical leader who has signed and produced such artistically ambitious talents as STEVE EARLE, JOE ELY, NANCI GRIFFITH, LYLE LOVETT, THE MAVERICKS, Allison Moorer, and KELLY WILLIS.

As a child Brown traveled in his family's singing group, appearing at churches of every denomination. In his early teens he began playing piano onstage, and after high school he worked with the renowned gospel group the Stamps Quartet, then led by J. D. Sumner, and later with the OAK RIDGE BOYS. Around the time the Oaks made the transition from gospel to country music, Brown left to join Voice, a gospel group placed on call to sing for and accompany ELVIS PRESLEY. From Voice, Brown graduated to a spot in the band backing the Sweet Inspirations, an opening act for Presley. When Glen D. Hardin left the main Presley band in 1975, Brown took another step up the ladder, joining Presley's "A-team," where he stayed until Presley's death in 1977.

Forced to look for another job, Brown parlayed a referral from pianist DAVID BRIGGS into a spot with EMMYLOU HARRIS's

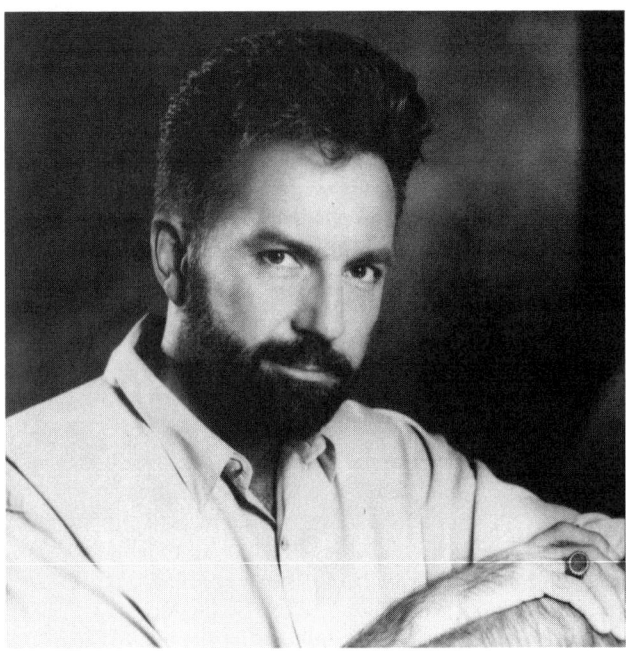

*Tony Brown*

highly regarded Hot Band. In so doing he again replaced the departing Hardin. Brown began to show his potential as a record company staffer at about this time. In 1978 he took a post with Free Flight Records, an RCA RECORDS pop venture. The label closed two years later, and Brown transferred to RCA's Nashville division, where he stayed long enough to help bring super group ALABAMA aboard. He then answered a highway call to join the Cherry Bombs, the touring band backing progressive country singer-songwriters Rodney Crowell and ROSANNE CASH.

In 1983 Brown returned to Nashville and RCA, this time adding friend and former bandmate Vince Gill to the company's roster. Brown's gospel credentials landed him a job as producer of three albums for Shirley Caesar, including *Sailin'*, a Grammy winner in 1985.

In 1984, record company iconoclast JIMMY BOWEN recruited Brown to join him at MCA as vice president of A&R. Brown learned from Bowen, but he also followed his own instincts. After Bowen's departure from MCA, Brown renegotiated his contract with the company and, in 1993, assumed the title of president, in partnership with another Bowen colleague, chairman BRUCE HINTON. MCA consistently proved itself one of Nashville's most successful labels under the Brown-Hinton executive team.

In 2002, Brown left MCA to launch UNIVERSAL RECORDS SOUTH with former ARISTA Nashville head TIM DuBOIS. There he signed Scooter Jennings, JOE NICHOLS, and others. In 2007, after leaving Universal Records South, he opened Tony Brown Enterprises. —*Jay Orr*

## Brown Radio Productions
established in Nashville, Tennessee, ca. 1945; ended ca. 1953

Brown Radio Productions and its companion firm, Monogram Radio Productions, constituted one of the earliest commercial recording enterprises in Nashville. Charles Brown and his brother Bill launched their operation in about 1945. Located on Fourth Avenue North, the Brown company first made its mark by handling midday shows starring ERNEST TUBB and EDDY ARNOLD. Sponsored by Purina, they were produced from a downtown Nashville theater and fed to the Mutual radio network via Nashville station WSM. Charles, a veteran of both the prominent Gardner Agency in St. Louis and a Nashville advertising firm, was aggressive in securing accounts, and the brothers were soon producing syndicated soap operas and musical programs using local radio talent, such as Arnold, THE DUKE OF PADUCAH, and others.

In about 1950 the Brown studio (a small affair located on the second floor of a downtown office building) began to host sessions held by RCA RECORDS. Over the next few years, major RCA country acts Arnold, HANK SNOW, and JOHNNIE & JACK recorded hits there, including "Lovebug Itch," "I'm Moving On," and "Poison Love," respectively.

By 1953 the Nashville company had faded, and the Browns sold their equipment to engineer Cliff Thomas, who began to hold RCA sessions in a building on Thirteenth Avenue North. Charles Brown eventually moved to Springfield, Missouri, then a rising radio syndication and TV production center, where he and his brother had started a branch office in 1950. There Charles wrote and produced *The Eddy Arnold Show* for Springfield's Crossroads TV Productions and ABC-TV. In 1956 Charles made the move from broadcasting to politics, eventually representing his district in the U.S. House of Representatives. —*John W. Rumble*

## The Browns
Ella Maxine Brown b. Campti, Louisiana, April 27, 1931
James Edward Brown b. Sparkman, Arkansas, April 1, 1934
Bonnie Marie Brown Ring b. Sparkman, Arkansas, July 31, 1937

Jim Ed, Maxine, and Bonnie Brown, known professionally as the Browns, were a highly successful vocal group of THE NASHVILLE SOUND era. Their smooth three-part harmonies, which have influenced acts ranging from the Beatles to THE WHITES, were centered around Jim Ed's rich baritone. Maxine's alto voice and Bonnie's breathy soprano added the spice.

The Brown siblings grew up in southwestern Arkansas, where they sang at church socials and school functions while still in their teens. Their first career break came in 1952, when Maxine entered Jim Ed in a talent contest staged at *Dutch O'Neal's Barnyard Frolic* on KLRA in Little Rock, Arkansas. Although Brown lost to a harmonica whiz, he was invited to join the cast. Maxine soon joined Jim Ed onstage to sing, and their career was launched. By 1954 the duo was a featured act on the *LOUISIANA HAYRIDE*, broadcast over Shreveport station KWKH. On March 15, 1954, they recorded "Looking Back to See" in the KWKH studios. Written by Maxine— with a little help from Jim Ed—the song was released on FABOR RECORDS. Three months later, the record debuted on the *Billboard* charts, topping out at #8. From Shreveport the duo moved to KWTO's *OZARK JUBILEE* in Springfield, Missouri.

In 1955 Bonnie joined the act, and the trio's recording of "Here Today and Gone Tomorrow" climbed to #7. That year they signed with RCA RECORDS. Over the next four years they enjoyed sizable hits, including "I Take the Chance" and "I Heard the Bluebirds Sing."

In 1959 the Browns recorded their signature song, "The Three Bells," at RCA's Nashville studio. At the time, the Browns had grown disillusioned with the music business and were thinking of quitting. As their swan song, they asked producer CHET ATKINS to let them try the number, earlier recorded by French pop

*The Browns: Bonnie, Jim Ed, and (below) Maxine*

star Edith Piaf. Within a month of its chart debut, their rendition sold more than half a million copies. Network television appearances on *The Ed Sullivan Show* and *American Bandstand* followed, pushing "The Three Bells," "Scarlet Ribbons (For Her Hair)" and "The Old Lamplighter" high on the country and pop charts. In 1963 the group joined the cast of the GRAND OLE OPRY.

The Browns disbanded in 1967: Maxine and Bonnie retired to Arkansas to raise their young families, while Jim Ed stayed in Nashville, pursued a solo career with RCA, and hosted a string of syndicated TV shows.

In the 1990s the Browns made a limited number of personal appearances, including guest spots at the Grand Ole Opry that brought standing ovations. In 2005, Maxine Brown published an autobiography, *Looking Back to See: A Country Music Memoir.* —*Chris Skinker*

## Brown's Ferry Four

Emerging in the 1940s, Brown's Ferry Four was, along with the CHUCK WAGON GANG, one of the first highly successful country gospel quartets. Although formal gospel quartet music had been popular since the World War I era, most of the time it was sung a cappella or with a piano, as in the case of the STAMPS-BAXTER Quartet or the Vaughan Quartet. But Brown's Ferry Four featured a guitar accompaniment and singers who were mainstream country singers.

Brown's Ferry Four began as a radio group playing over WLW–Cincinnati, in 1943. As World War II continued, a mainstay of the station, the Drifting Pioneers, was broken up by the draft. The Pioneers had always performed gospel songs, and WLW's program director, George Biggar, began searching for a replacement. By coincidence, the WLW roster at that time included a young MERLE TRAVIS (who had been a member of the Pioneers), GRANDPA JONES, and the DELMORE BROTHERS. Alton Delmore was interested; as a boy in Alabama he had learned to sing shape notes from paperback gospel SONGBOOKS. He talked his brother, Jones, and Travis into forming an impromptu quartet (they literally rehearsed in the studio hallway), promising to teach them enough shape note music to get by. They were accepted, and Alton named them after Brown's Ferry, near the Delmore home in northern Alabama (and after his bawdy hit song "Brown's Ferry Blues").

The group found itself doing a thirty-minute show each day, drawing material from Stamps-Baxter songbooks as well as black gospel records they hunted up in local used-records shops. As Grandpa Jones recalled, "We were amazed at the response we started getting from farmers and factory workers." Before long both Travis and Alton Delmore had to leave for military service, but the station—which owned the quartet's name—kept the broadcasts going with local singers such as Rome Johnson, Roy Lanham, and even Dollie Good of THE GIRLS OF THE GOLDEN WEST. The original group did not reunite until 1946, when SYD NATHAN recorded them for KING RECORDS; their first single, "Just a Little Talk with Jesus" paired with "Will the Circle Be Unbroken," was wildly successful, some forty-four similar sides followed between 1946 and 1952.

Travis soon had to exit the group, and both Jones and the Delmores left WLW. The recordings continued, though, with a stellar cast of replacements: RED FOLEY, Red & Lige Turner, CLYDE MOODY, and LOUIS INNIS. Often Jones and the Delmores contributed to these recordings. WLW kept a radio version of the quartet on the air through the 1950s.

In later years Grandpa Jones kept the memory of Brown's Ferry Four alive. He made a fine album, with Travis helping to re-create

the sound, for MONUMENT RECORDS in the 1960s, and instigated the *HEE HAW* Gospel Quartet on the popular TV show in 1975. Like the original Brown's Ferry group, the *Hee Haw* Quartet (also composed of mainstream country singers) delighted audiences throughout the nation. —*Charles Wolfe*

## Ed Bruce
b. Keiser, Arkansas, December 29, 1940

A multitalented performer, William Edwin Bruce Jr. has scored as a hit recording artist, songwriter, actor, and singer of commercials.

Bruce was raised in Memphis, where he recorded for SUN RECORDS in 1957–58. In the early 1960s he recorded on the Wand/Scepter label, and in 1966 he quit his job as a Memphis car salesman and moved to Nashville. His first *Billboard* chart record came in 1967 with "Walker's Woods" on the RCA label. He later recorded for MONUMENT; United Artists; EPIC; MCA; and then, beginning in 1984, for RCA again. He had a #1 record for MCA in 1981 with "You're the Best Break This Old Heart Ever Had."

As a songwriter, Bruce won his first BMI award for country airplay with "See the Big Man Cry," a 1965 Top Ten for Charlie Louvin (THE LOUVIN BROTHERS). Bruce also wrote or cowrote such hits as "The Man That Turned My Mama On" and "Texas (When I Die)," recorded by TANYA TUCKER, and "Mammas Don't Let Your Babies Grow Up to Be Cowboys," a 1978 #1 classic for WAYLON JENNINGS and WILLIE NELSON.

Bruce's distinctive voice has graced nationally broadcast commercials for John Deere, McDonald's, AC/Delco, and Ford Trucks. As an actor he has appeared in the CBS-TV miniseries *The Chisholms*, with James Garner in the *Maverick* TV series, in the feature film *Public Enemies,* and in the made-for-TV movies *The Last Days of Frank and Jesse James* and *Separated by Murder*. Besides acting and recording voice-overs, Bruce concentrated on gospel music after the turn of the twenty-first century. —*Gerry Wood*

## Albert E. Brumley
b. LeFlore County, Oklahoma, October 29, 1905; d. November 15, 1977

Even the most casual students of country and gospel music recognize the name and the songs of Albert Edward Brumley. Working from the tiny town of Powell, Missouri, Brumley produced an amazingly potent body of work that made him one of gospel's most influential songwriters. His masterpiece "I'll Fly Away" has been recorded more than 500 times by artists across the musical spectrum, and dozens of other Brumley songs also have become standards.

Brumley's star began to rise in the late 1920s, when he left his eastern Oklahoma farm to apprentice at the Hartford Music Company in nearby Hartford, Arkansas. This was a "convention" book publisher, in the mold of JAMES D. VAUGHAN and STAMPS-BAXTER, which published new gospel songs in seven-shape notation systems. After studying with several of Hartford's veteran writers, Brumley began to create his own songs. Between 1932 and 1945 he published—often in Hartford books—his best-known works. These included "I'll Fly Away" (1932), "Jesus Hold My Hand" (1933), "I'd Rather Be an Old-Time Christian" (1934), "I'll Meet You in the Morning" (1936), "Camping in Canaan's Land" (1937), "There's a Little Pine Log Cabin" (1937), "Turn Your Radio On" (1938), "Did You Ever Go Sailing" (1938), "I've Found a Hiding Place" (1939), "Rank Stranger to Me" (1942), and "If We Never Meet Again" (1945). Though gospel quartets turned these into standards, they were also featured on radio and records by groups such as Bill Monroe & the Blue Grass Quartet (the name Monroe used when performing gospel material), the Chuck Wagon Gang, the Brown's Ferry Four, Red Foley, and The Stanley Brothers.

Brumley began publishing songbooks to circulate his compositions even further; by 1937, *Albert E. Brumley's Book of Radio Favorites* had appeared. He purchased the Hartford Music Company in the late 1940s, primarily to regain copyright control of his classic songs. Brumley died in 1977, but his son Bob continues to run his publishing company. His son Tom Brumley, who died in 2009, was an influential steel guitarist best known for his work with Buck Owens. —*Charles Wolfe*

## Tom Brumley
b. Stella, Missouri, December 11, 1935; d. February 3, 2009

As a pedal steel guitar player in Buck Owens's band, Tom Brumley helped shape the Bakersfield Sound, which signaled a new direction in country music and later influenced the emerging country-rock movement. The son of gospel music composer Albert E. Brumley, Thomas R. Brumley joined Owens's group in 1963. Until 1969, the young steel player was an integral part of Owens's greatest period of success, adding his distinctive touch to #1 hits such as "I've Got a Tiger by the Tail" and "Buckaroo." Brumley's solo on 1964's "Together Again," featuring his articulate, high-pitched style, became a benchmark for generations of pedal steel players.

In 1969, Rick Nelson invited Brumley to play on a live album at the Troubadour in Los Angeles. What was supposed to be a four-show commitment for Brumley turned into a decade as a member of Nelson's Stone Canyon Band. Brumley was also a member of the Desert Rose Band from 1990 to 1993, and when he was not recording sessions for Dwight Yoakam, Merle Haggard, and others, he performed with his sons in Branson, Missouri. Tied with Ralph Mooney as ACM's Top Steel Guitar Player in 1966, Brumley was inducted into the Steel Guitar Hall of Fame in 1992. —*Scott Anderson and Robert Kramer*

## Cliff Bruner
b. Texas City, Texas, April 25, 1915; d. August 25, 2000

One of country music's most hard-driving fiddlers, Cliff Bruner enjoyed significant influence and popularity as a musician and bandleader during the 1930s and 1940s.

By age fourteen Bruner was hopping freight trains in search of musical opportunities. Although an instinctive, rurally reared musician, he was never enamored of country fiddling and became essentially a jazz player. Bruner was already a seasoned veteran when he joined Milton Brown's pioneering western swing band, the Musical Brownies, in Fort Worth in 1935. Teaming with the classically trained Cecil Brower to form the genre's classic twin fiddle duo, Bruner recorded forty-nine sides with Brown in March 1936.

Brown died soon after, and Bruner formed his Texas Wanderers in Houston in that same year. He moved to Beaumont, Texas, broadcasting on KDFM and gaining an enthusiastic following in the region. His band influenced Cajun music as well as country dance music with a lineup that included electric steel pioneer Bob Dunn, pianist Moon Mullican, electric mandolinist Leo Raley, and smooth vocalist Dickie McBride (of Laura Lee & Dickie McBride). Bruner signed with Decca Records in 1937,

and by decade's end he had waxed such seminal classics as Floyd Tillman's "It Makes No Difference Now"; Ted Daffan's "Truck Driver's Blues"; and his signature tune, "Jessie," an old Mexican polka.

In about 1939, Bruner experienced a religious conversion and temporarily gave up bandleading to work for Texas governor W. Lee "Pappy" O'Daniel and with Jimmie Davis in Louisiana. Bruner led a band in Chicago during 1942 before returning to the Beaumont–Port Arthur area. Often teamed with Moon Mullican and calling his band the Showboys, Bruner was one of the most popular bandleaders on the Texas-Louisiana Gulf Coast in the mid-1940s, recording for Mercury and Houston's Ayo label after his association with Decca ended. A family man, Bruner refused to tour far beyond his home base, which may account for his failure to hit nationally. After 1950, following his wife's death and the drowning of singer and right-hand man Buddy Duhon, Bruner played only part-time. In the late 1970s, though, his musical activities increased, and he remained active until shortly before his death. —*Kevin Coffey*

## Brunswick Records
established in Dubuque, Iowa, 1919; ended 1970s

A subsidiary of the piano and bowling equipment manufacturer Brunswick-Balke-Collender, Brunswick Records debuted in 1919 and made its first foray into country music in November 1924 with recordings by Bill Chitwood and Bud Landress. A month later, Brunswick acquired Vocalion Records, which included mid-1924 country product by Uncle Dave Macon, among others. In 1927 Vocalion's 5000 series for country material was launched, followed a year later by Brunswick's 100 country series. Following the lead of other major labels, Brunswick/Vocalion conducted field recording trips in the South from 1928 to 1930 as a means of capturing the region's vast array of ethnic sounds.

Consolidated Film Industries, parent of the American Record Corporation, acquired Brunswick/Vocalion in December 1931 and later secured Columbia Records/OKeh Records in August 1934. The entire record complex was subsequently bought by the Columbia Broadcasting System in February 1938, thus becoming the CBS subsidiary Columbia Recording Corporation. Rights to pre-1932 recordings by Brunswick/Vocalion were not included, though, and were later acquired by Decca Records, which also gained rights to the Brunswick label name. The Vocalion label name remained Columbia's until mid-1940, and it, too, became a Decca property in 1941, only to remain dormant until its revival in 1949. Meanwhile, Decca debuted a Brunswick 80000 reissue series in 1943 (which existed for more than a decade) and began the 54000 (LP) and 55000 (singles) series for newer product. The latter two Brunswick series ran from the late 1950s into the mid-1970s. —*Bob Pinson*

## Boudleaux and Felice Bryant
Diadorius Boudleaux Bryant b. Shellman, Georgia, February 13, 1920; d. June 25, 1987
Matilda Genevieve "Felice" (Scaduto) Bryant b. Milwaukee, Wisconsin, August 7, 1925; d. April 22, 2003

Husband and wife Boudleaux and Felice Bryant were among the first in Nashville to make a full-time career of songwriting. More importantly, they wrote some of the most memorable songs of the 1950s and 1960s, including many of The Everly Brothers'

*Felice and Boudleaux Bryant*

best-known hits. Many Bryant compositions have become enduring country, rock, or pop classics.

Diadorius Boudleaux Bryant grew up in Moultrie, Georgia, the son of a small-town lawyer and his wife. The name Boudleaux came from the elder Bryant, who named his son after a Frenchman who saved his life during World War I. A classical violin student from age six through seventeen, Boudleaux spent the 1937–38 season with the Atlanta Philharmonic. Afterward he made the leap to hillbilly fiddling when he joined HANK PENNY's Radio Cowboys, then performing at WSB in Atlanta. Boudleaux remained with Penny into 1940, long enough to appear on a few of Penny's records. He later worked with Gene Steele & His Sunny Southerners in Memphis over WMC before moving on to a touring jazz group. In the summer of 1945, while Boudleaux was performing at Milwaukee's Schroeder Hotel, he met Felice, then working there as an elevator operator. After a whirlwind courtship, they married in Newport, Kentucky, on September 5, 1945.

In contrast to Boudleaux, Felice wasn't a musician, though she had sung on radio as a child and later did some volunteer entertaining during World War II with a Milwaukee USO show. Her real passion was poetry. During the couple's first year together, they began putting his melodies together with her verses, and a songwriting team was born. Their break came in late 1948, when singer Rome Johnson passed their song "Country Boy" along to FRED ROSE of ACUFF-ROSE PUBLICATIONS in Nashville. Rose got the song to LITTLE JIMMY DICKENS, who scored a #7 hit with it on *Billboard*'s Best-Selling Retail Folk Records chart in the spring of 1949. The following year, Rose persuaded the Bryants to move to Nashville, where they concentrated on songwriting full time, with Dickens and CARL SMITH being their most dependable clients early on. Among the many tailor-made Bryant songs Dickens recorded are "I'm Little but I'm Loud," "Take Me As I Am," "Out Behind the Barn," and "Hole in My Pocket." Smith had big hits with "Hey, Joe," "Back Up, Buddy," and "It's a Lovely, Lovely World." Meanwhile, between 1951 and 1953, the prolific couple recorded four singles for MGM, the last three billing them as "Bud & Betty Bryant."

In 1957 the Bryants connected with their biggest outlet for their songs—the Everly Brothers. The Bryants supplied the Everlys' first hit, "Bye, Bye Love," and continued to be the Everlys' main source of material through the early sixties (a relationship facilitated by their publisher WESLEY ROSE, who was also the Everlys' manager). All told, the Bryants wrote twenty-nine songs

for the Everly Brothers, twelve of them hits, including "Wake Up, Little Susie," "All I Have to Do Is Dream," "Take a Message to Mary," and "Sleepless Nights," (the last also recorded by EMMYLOU HARRIS and PATTY LOVELESS). The diversity and quantity of the Bryants' total output are staggering. Among their hits for others are RED FOLEY's "Midnight" (co-written with Chet Atkins), EDDY ARNOLD's "How's the World Treating You" (also with Atkins), JIM REEVES's "Blue Boy," BOB LUMAN's "Let's Think About Living," and ROY ORBISON's "Love Hurts." (The latter became an international pop hit for British rock band Nazareth in 1975–76.) One of the Bryants' best-known songs is "Rocky Top." First popularized by THE OSBORNE BROTHERS in 1968, "Rocky Top" is now known as an official Tennessee state song and the fight song for the University of Tennessee's athletic teams. In the pop field, numerous acts have recorded the Bryants' "Have a Good Time" since Tony Bennett made it a 1952 hit.

During their career the Bryants had some 1,500 songs recorded by more than four hundred artists, amounting to sales of more than 250 million records. Along the way, they raised two sons, Dane and DEL BRYANT. Dane now works in Nashville real estate; Del is president and CEO of BMI. Both continue to supervise House of Bryant, the publishing firm their parents founded. Boudleaux and Felice Bryant were inducted into the NASHVILLE SONGWRITERS HALL OF FAME in 1972; they were elected to THE COUNTRY MUSIC HALL OF FAME in 1991. —*Paul Kingsbury*

## Del Bryant
b. Moultrie, Georgia, October 5, 1948

Del René Bryant has been president and CEO of BMI since August 2004. The elder son of legendary songwriters BOUDLEAUX AND FELICE BRYANT, he grew up in the Nashville music industry. After attending the University of Miami, serving in the air force reserves and pitching his parents' songs for a time, in 1972 he joined BMI's Nashville office. There he worked in the writer/publisher relations and performing rights departments and broadened his knowledge of country, pop, rock, and other musical fields. He relocated to BMI's New York headquarters in 1988 as vice president, performing rights, and was instrumental in modernizing BMI's

*Del Bryant*

royalty distribution system. Bryant became senior vice president, performing rights and writer/publisher relations in 1991, supervising staffs in New York, Los Angeles, Nashville, Atlanta, Miami, Puerto Rico, and London. Under his leadership, BMI has re-energized its television department, expanded its European outreach through its London office, established a Latin music division, and launched an urban music division. All of these efforts have advanced a writer affiliation strategy that has brought to BMI talents including Lady Gaga, TAYLOR SWIFT, Juanes, Kanye West, film composers Mike Post and Danny Elfman, Leiber & Stoller, WILLIE NELSON, and Lil Wayne, among many others. —*John W. Rumble*

## Jimmy Bryant (*see* Speedy West & Jimmy Bryant)

## Slim Bryant
b. Atlanta, Georgia, December 7, 1908; d. May 28, 2010

The writer of the JIMMIE RODGERS song "Mother, the Queen of My Heart," Thomas Hoyt Bryant had a long career in country music. After performing in Atlanta, he worked on radio stations in Cincinnati, Chicago (where he served two stints on the *NATIONAL BARN DANCE*), Louisville, Richmond, and Pittsburgh. In the last city, he also appeared on television. In 1950 the *Slim Bryant Show* was broadcast on NBC Radio, and in 1959–60 he performed on WTRF-TV in Wheeling, West Virginia.

From 1939 until the end of his performing career he led a band called the Wildcats (briefly known as the Georgia Wildcats). The group consisted of Bryant, guitar; his brother Raymond ("Loppy"), bass; Jerry Wallace (not the later star singer), banjo; and Kenny Newton, fiddle. First organized in Richmond, Virginia, as CLAYTON MCMICHEN's Georgia Wildcats, the five-man unit became a quartet when the famous fiddler left in 1939 for Louisville, where he formed a new band.

One of the highlights of Bryant's career was playing with Rodgers on two recording sessions, one of which included the first recording of "Mother, the Queen of My Heart." Bryant later recorded for Majestic, DECCA, and Lion, frequently waxing his own compositions. Of more than 200 original songs, the biggest hit was "Eeny Meeny Dixie Deeny."

Bryant supplemented his income with various enterprises, including a gift shop, a guitar studio, and writing radio theme songs and commercial jingles for Westinghouse, Chevrolet, U.S. Steel, and Alcoa Aluminum. In the 1980s he appeared at a few festivals, and into the 1990s he taught guitar in Pittsburgh. —*W. K. McNeil*

## Buck dancing; buck and wing (*see* Square Dancing)

## Steve Buckingham
b. Richmond, Virginia, February 24, 1949

Steve Buckingham is a versatile producer whose track record included hit singles in pop, R&B, Hispanic, and dance music before he became a leading country producer in the 1980s and '90s.

A guitarist who toured in rock bands, Buckingham began working sessions in Virginia and later in Atlanta, where he produced his first #1 hit: Alicia Bridges's disco smash "I Love the Night Life." Clive Davis of ARISTA RECORDS then hired him to oversee records by Melissa Manchester and Dionne Warwick.

In 1980 Buckingham moved to Nashville, and in 1986 he was appointed president of A&R for CBS Records (later renamed SONY MUSIC ENTERTAINMENT), where he remained for nine years. During his CBS/Sony tenure, he advanced the careers of MARY CHAPIN CARPENTER, DOLLY PARTON, RICKY VAN SHELTON, RICKY SKAGGS, and TAMMY WYNETTE.

In 1994 Buckingham formed Blue Eye Records with Parton and became the label's president. He produced the Parton–VINCE GILL duet "I Will Always Love You," which won CMA Vocal Event of the Year honors in 1996. In 2009 Buckingham left his post of senior vice president of A&R at the Welk Music Group, after eleven years of working with the company's SUGAR HILL and Vanguard labels. —*Beverly Keel*

## Buddy Lee Attractions (*see* Buddy Lee)

## Bug Music
established in Los Angeles, March 1975

One of the world's largest independent publishing administration companies, Bug Music has nurtured the careers of many of country music's more maverick songwriters and artists, including ROSANNE CASH, NANCI GRIFFITH, BUDDY AND JULIE MILLER, and JOHN PRINE.

Bug was founded in Los Angeles in March 1975 when music-industry veteran Dan Bourgoise, manager of pop star Del Shannon, tracked down a decade's worth of back ROYALTIES owed Shannon for such hits as "Runaway." A portion of those royalties funded the creation of Bug, which Bourgoise helmed until retiring in 2006, when he sold his majority interest to Spectrum Equity Partners and Crossroads Media. Fred Bourgoise, Dan's brother, joined Bug shortly after its creation and signed such trend-setting L.A. bands as the Blasters and Los Lobos.

The Bourgoises had a long-standing interest in country music (Dan Bourgoise signed ASLEEP AT THE WHEEL to the group's first record deal), and by the early 1980s Bug had established a presence in Nashville. A permanent Nashville office was opened in 1985, with Garry Velletri as the head. Since then, Bug's Nashville operation has grown into a thriving MUSIC ROW enterprise, a place where country producers and singers often look to find interesting, less mainstream material. The company established a London office in 1992, and in 1997 a New York office was opened, with Velletri relocating there to run it. The Nashville office has since been led, in succession, by Dave Durocher, John Allen, and, from early 2009 to August 2011. —*Daniel Cooper*

## Jim Bulleit
b. Corydon, Indiana, November 4, 1908; d. December 12, 1988

Jim Bulleit was a pioneer of the Nashville record industry, although he left the business just before the city became country music's epicenter.

Bulleit attended Illinois Wesleyan College in Bloomington and worked in radio in South Carolina and San Francisco before moving to Nashville in late 1943 to join the WSM announcing staff; later, he briefly ran the station's booking department. He cofounded BULLET RECORDS in 1946 and stayed until 1949. Subsequently he started Delta Records and bought and sold masters and copyrights in country and R&B.

At some point in 1950, Bulleit acquired part ownership of four LEFTY FRIZZELL copyrights, including "If You've Got the Money, I've Got the Time" and "I Love You a Thousand Ways," and, as a result, was embroiled in a publishing power struggle; ultimately he sold these copyrights to New York music publisher RALPH PEER. In early 1951 Bulleit joined KWKH in Shreveport to start a booking service for the *LOUISIANA HAYRIDE*, but he left in August 1951 and tried unsuccessfully to start his own jamboree in Spruce Pine, North Carolina. Back in Nashville, he launched J-B Records, and in 1953–54 owned a share of SUN RECORDS, which he sold prematurely for $1,200, shortly before the label's successes with ELVIS PRESLEY, JOHNNY CASH, and JERRY LEE LEWIS. Bulleit then left the music business and worked in several different occupations. In his retirement he started a candy brokerage business, which he operated until his death. —*Colin Escott*

## Bullet Records
established in Nashville, Tennessee, April 1946; ended 1956

Bullet Records was quite possibly the first independent label in Nashville and certainly the first to achieve a national profile. The company developed a diverse musical catalog, and its biggest sales success was Francis Craig's "Near You," the best-selling pop record of 1947.

The Bullet Recording and Transcription Company was incorporated in April 1946. The principals were JIM BULLEIT, an announcer at WSM; banker Orville Zickler; and C. V. Hitchcock, owner of the Hermitage Music Store and Volunteer Music Sales. Hitchcock couldn't get enough country records to service his clients' JUKEBOXES and tried to solve the problem by manufacturing his own. The first recordings were made during the 1945 Christmas season, and the first record—"Zeb's Mountain Boogie" by "Brad Brady," a pseudonym for OWEN BRADLEY, and Zeb Turner (ZEB AND ZEKE TURNER)—was issued the following May. Bradley was the de facto musical director.

Bullet recorded an eclectic mix of artists. PEE WEE KING, SHEB WOOLEY, MINNIE PEARL, CHET ATKINS, and RAY PRICE made their first recordings for the label, as did B. B. King. LEON PAYNE also cut the original version of "Lost Highway" for Bullet. Bullet recorded R&B sides by Wynonie Harris, Red Miller, and Cecil Gant that sold well, but everything was eclipsed by "Near You." Its success heightened Nashville's profile as a recording center and in 1949 enabled Bullet to incorporate Bullet Plastics, Nashville's first record-pressing plant, located near Berry Field airport. Bulleit himself was forced out that year as the company tried to become a major label, signing big-name acts such as Milton Berle and Bob Crosby. It limped into the 1950s under Hitchcock's ownership, continuing until 1956. In the early 1960s the imprint was revived by Red Wortham for a dozen or so releases. —*Colin Escott*

## Samantha Bumgarner
b. Jackson County, North Carolina October 31, 1878; d. December 24, 1960

Samantha Bumgarner was a link between Appalachian folk music traditions and the country music industry. The daughter of mountain fiddler Has Biddix, she began playing fiddle and banjo

in public in 1895. After winning local OLD-TIME fiddle competitions, she traveled from Sylva, North Carolina, to New York with fiddler Eva Davis to record for COLUMBIA RECORDS in 1924. Bumgarner was one of the first five-string-banjo players ever recorded.

Bumgarner appeared at the 1927 Georgia Old-Time Fiddlers Convention in Atlanta. Back in North Carolina, she became a yearly headliner at Bascom Lamar Lunsford's Mountain Dance and Folk Festival in Asheville from 1928 to 1959.

Folk enthusiasts of the 1950s "rediscovered" her as "Aunt Samanthy," and she was recorded for the 1955 Riverside Records LP *Banjo Songs of the Southern Mountains*. As of 2011 a few of her 1920s recordings are available on Internet websites and on CD compilations, including *North Carolina Banjo Collection* (ROUNDER, 1998) and *Hard Times Come Again No More: Early American Rural Songs Of Hard Times And Hardships Vol. 1* (Yazoo, 1998). —*Robert K. Oermann*

## Sonny Burgess
b. Newport, Arkansas, May 28, 1931

Sonny Burgess belongs to a small group of artists who embodied the energetic spirit of ROCKABILLY music created for SAM PHILLIPS's SUN RECORDS. Albert Burgess heard country music on Nashville's GRAND OLE OPRY but found himself more attracted to blues and R&B. After an unsuccessful audition for Phillips, Burgess returned to Memphis on May 2, 1956, with an expanded band called the Pacers. Phillips recorded them that day, creating the frenzied rockabilly classics "We Wanna Boogie" and "Red Headed Woman."

Later singles "Ain't Got a Thing" and "My Bucket's Got a Hole in It" continued the promise, but Burgess and the Pacers never achieved huge commercial success. So Burgess played for a short stretch in CONWAY TWITTY's road band and eventually became a traveling sales representative. With the Sun Rhythm Section—first-generation rock & roll musicians from the Memphis area—Burgess became active again in the mid-1980s. In 1992 he released *Tennessee Border*, produced by ex-Blaster Dave Alvin. Later, in 1996, he recorded a self-titled album with producer Garry Tallent, bassist of Bruce Springsteen's E Street Band. Springsteen contributed an original song, "Tiger Rose," to the album. Burgess has recorded several concert CDs and studio albums in the 2000s. —*Jay Orr*

## Johnny Burnette & the Rock 'n' Roll Trio
Johnny Burnette b. Memphis, Tennessee, March 25, 1934; d. August 1, 1964
Dorsey Burnette b. Memphis, Tennessee, December 28, 1932; d. August 19, 1979
Paul Burlison b. Brownsville, Tennessee, February 4, 1929; d. September 27, 2003

Between May 1956 and March 1957 Johnny Burnette & the Rock 'n' Roll Trio recorded seventeen tracks in three sessions, pioneered the use of distortion, and achieved a reputation as the wildest ROCKABILLY band of all.

In 1953 the Memphis-based trio of Johnny Burnette on vocals and guitar, brother Dorsey Burnette on bass, and Paul Burlison on lead guitar started playing straight country music—recording a country single for Von Records—but found the wilder they got, the more the audience reacted. In early 1956, as the Rock 'n' Roll Trio, the threesome auditioned for the *Ted Mack Amateur Hour* network television show in New York. After winning three weeks

*The Rock 'n' Roll Trio: (from left) Johnny Burnette, Dorsey Burnette, and Paul Burlison*

performed today, but Lester Alvin "Smiley" Burnette's highly successful work on film overshadowed his recorded music.

The son of two ordained ministers, Burnette was singing and playing piano, accordion, guitar, and two dozen more instruments at WDZ in Tuscola, Illinois, when promoter J. L. Frank urged Gene Autry to hire Burnette in December 1933. Six months later, Burnette and Autry went to Hollywood, where they made movies (together and apart) for the next twenty years.

A natural and often-inspired comedian, Burnette became singing cowboy Autry's sidekick "Frog Millhouse" at Republic Pictures and composed many of the songs used in their early films. By the late 1930s his screen popularity was such that he became the first sidekick ranked among the Top Ten western stars.

After 150 movies and two syndicated radio series, Burnette became jovial railroad engineer Charley Pratt on CBS-TV's *Petticoat Junction* in 1963. His classic compositions include "Ridin' Down the Canyon," "It's My Lazy Day," "Hominy Grits," and "Catfish, Take a Look at That Worm." —*Jonathan Guyot Smith*

## James Burton
b. Minden, Louisiana, August 21, 1939

At age fourteen, James Burton was the youngest staff musician on Shreveport's *Louisiana Hayride*. Within a few years—thanks to his work on Dale Hawkins's 1957 rock & roll classic "Susie-Q" and on hit singles by Rick Nelson—Burton was among the world's most influential guitarists. A highly regarded session player noted for the distinctive, steely tone he got from his 1953 Fender Telecaster, Burton helped popularize a Telecaster-based electric guitar sound that remains a part of country music.

"I was just trying to create my own identity, mixing blues and country together," Burton later explained, commenting on his famous tone and his technique of using fingerpicks with a flat pick instead of the conventional thumb pick.

In addition to working the *Hayride*, Burton played in local bands, including those led by Hawkins (with whom he cowrote and recorded "Susie-Q" at fifteen), Johnny Horton, and Bob Luman. Luman took Burton to Los Angeles to record, and it wasn't long before the young guitarist came to Rick Nelson's attention. Nelson invited Burton to meet his parents and soon thereafter was hired to play on the Nelson family TV show, *The Adventures of Ozzie & Harriet*.

With Nelson, Burton started playing second guitar to the lead parts Joe Maphis (Joe & Rose Lee Maphis) played on singles, including "Waitin' in School" and "Stood Up" (both 1957); his first session as lead guitarist included "Believe What You Say" (1958). During the 1960s he recorded with such varied acts as Merle Haggard, Buck Owens, Frank Sinatra, the Supremes, and Johnny Rivers.

Burton appeared in the house band on ABC-TV's *Shindig* and on numerous television and film soundtracks, including Elvis Presley's *Viva Las Vegas*. Later, Presley hired Burton to organize and lead a band for his 1969 debut at the International Hotel in Las Vegas; Burton remained with Presley's touring band until the singer's death in 1977. The guitarist also played on Gram Parsons's solo albums, and after Parsons's death, he joined Emmylou Harris's first Hot Band. Burton also recorded and toured for years with John Denver, Jerry Lee Lewis, and Elvis Costello.

in a row, they were offered a contract with Decca Records subsidiary Coral Records. The trio enjoyed two regional hits, "Tear It Up" and "The Train Kept a-Rollin'," and released a self-titled album in December 1956. Although hugely influential and revered by rockabilly collectors, the act didn't chart nationally. After their final recording session, Dorsey Burnette quit. He was replaced by Johnny Black, brother of bassist Bill Black, and this lineup appeared in the 1957 film *Rock, Rock, Rock*.

In 1957 the band broke up. Johnny and Dorsey moved to California and formed a songwriting partnership, with Rick Nelson recording two of their songs. As artists, Dorsey hit the pop charts twice in 1960 and enjoyed a run on the country charts between 1972 and 1977. Johnny was more successful, gaining four Top Twenty pop hits in 1960 and 1961; "You're Sixteen" peaked at #8 in December 1960. Johnny died in a boating accident in 1964, and Dorsey succumbed to a heart attack in 1979. Johnny's son, Rocky Burnette, had a Top Ten pop hit in 1980; Dorsey's son, Billy Burnette, achieved limited success as an artist in the rock and country fields.

Paul Burlison settled in Memphis, where he established a successful construction business. In the mid-1980s he fronted a band of Sun Records alumni dubbed the Sun Rhythm Section and recorded an album for Flying Fish Records. —*Rob Bowman*

## Smiley Burnette
b. Summum, Illinois, March 18, 1911; d. February 17, 1967

He had a vast and adoring country audience for more than thirty years, brought down the house whenever he guested on the Grand Ole Opry, and composed hundreds of songs, some still

Burton's solo albums include *Corn Pickin' and Slick Slidin'* for CAPITOL RECORDS (1967), *James Burton* on A&M (1971), and *The Spiritual Strings of James Burton*, which he released in 2010. He was inducted into the Rock and Roll Hall of Fame in 2001. In 2005 he started the James Burton International Guitar Festival in Shreveport, where he makes his home. —*Todd Everett*

## Judge Bob Burton
b. New York, New York, September 21, 1914; d. March 29, 1965

Judge Robert J. "Bob" Burton, a visionary BMI executive, was an early and powerful advocate for Nashville and country music. He was instrumental in formulating an important system of tracking musical performances that encompassed the many rural and small-town radio stations programming country performers and recordings. Previously these stations had not been included in any surveys on which royalty payments were based.

Close to many country artists, songwriters, and publishers, Burton was a founder of the CMA and a member of its first board of directors. He played a major role in raising money for building the COUNTRY MUSIC HALL OF FAME AND MUSEUM. He further demonstrated his belief in the importance and future of country music by the part he played in opening a BMI office in MUSIC CITY in 1958, years before most major New York or Los Angeles companies did so.

Raised in Larchmont, New York, Burton joined BMI in 1941, four years after earning a degree from Columbia University Law School. As BMI grew, Burton advanced rapidly, and he became the organization's president in 1964. Sadly, *Billboard*'s Country Music Man of the Year for 1964 didn't live long enough to witness the full impact of what he had done for Nashville and country music—indeed, for all forms of popular music—for he died in 1965 in a hotel fire in Vancouver, British Columbia. Today BMI honors the most performed country song of the year with the Robert J. Burton Award. —*Burt Korall*

## Buzz Busby
b. Eros, Louisiana, September 6, 1933; d. January 5, 2003

An energetic, eccentric singer and mandolinist, Buzz Busby (real name: Bernarr Graham Busbice) pioneered the supercharged style that defined the early Baltimore–Washington BLUEGRASS scene: taut vocals with edgy harmonies, and swooping, unconventional instrumental breaks driven by exaggerated guitar runs.

Busby learned both guitar and mandolin while growing up near Monroe, Louisiana; BILL MONROE was an early influence. In 1951 Busby moved to Washington to work for the FBI; he formed a band featuring Scotty Stoneman on fiddle and "COWBOY" JACK CLEMENT on guitar. In 1953 Busby left the FBI to pursue a career in music. After a brief period with MAC WISEMAN, Busby and Clement formed a comedy duo, Ham and Scram, which toured with the HAWKSHAW HAWKINS show (Pete Pike later replaced Clement). In 1954 Busby organized the Bayou Boys, whose members included such bluegrass notables as BILL HARRELL, Don Stover, Charlie Waller, Bill Emerson, and Carl Nelson.

In the fall of 1955, the Bayou Boys headed west for a nine-month stint on the LOUISIANA HAYRIDE in Shreveport. After returning to Washington, Busby recorded five STARDAY singles that many consider to be among the most intense bluegrass performances ever released. Escalating personal and legal problems

unraveled Busby's career during the early 1960s. He recorded sporadically for various labels into the mid-1980s, but with largely indifferent results.

His brother Wayne Busbice (b. Chatham, Louisiana, March 28, 1929) recorded country and ROCKABILLY music under the names Wayne Busby and Red McCoy. —*Dave Samuelson*

## Johnny Bush
b. Houston, Texas, February 17, 1935

With his early musical associations with both WILLIE NELSON and RAY PRICE, singer-songwriter John Bush Shin III was a minor but significant figure in 1960s and 1970s Texas HONKY-TONK MUSIC who grew into a respected elder statesman for traditional country music in his later years. With a vocal style reminiscent of Price's, Bush enjoyed modest chart success between 1969 and 1981 on Stop Records and RCA RECORDS as well as various independent labels. But his career was hampered by a neurological condition known as spasmodic dysphonia that affected his voice.

Bush began his professional career in San Antonio–area clubs in the early 1950s. An early band he joined as drummer included Nelson, then an aspiring artist. In the 1960s Bush became a member of the Record Men, one of Nelson's early road bands. Bush soon moved to join Price's band, the Cherokee Cowboys, for three years. In 1968 Bush recorded his own first Top Ten single, "Undo the Right," on the Stop label. His spirited rendition of "You Gave Me a Mountain," a MARTY ROBBINS original, reached #7 in 1969.

Nelson provided Bush his biggest career boost by recording his song "Whiskey River" and making it his theme song. As a single, "Whiskey River" only reached #12 in 1978 for Nelson, but he has featured it on several best-selling albums and positioned it prominently in his live shows for years.

A breakthrough in treatment restored the majority of Bush's vocal power and range in the 1990s. After a long hiatus, he returned to recording with 1994's *Time Changes Everything*, and he has continued to release independent albums regularly through the 2000s. —*Bob Allen*

## Sam Bush
b. Bowling Green, Kentucky, April 13, 1952

Fiddler-mandolinist Charles Samuel Bush ranks among the most influential acoustic musicians of his time. Known for fusing BLUEGRASS, rock, blues, and jazz, he helped found the groundbreaking band NEW GRASS REVIVAL, which he led from 1971 to 1989. He remains an in-demand session player and bandleader with a long-running solo career.

Bush began playing mandolin at age eleven and fiddle at thirteen. In 1969, after three consecutive wins in the junior division of the National Oldtime Fiddlers' Contest, Bush joined with banjoist Alan Munde and guitarist Wayne Stewart to record an instrumental album, *Poor Richard's Almanac*. The following year, Bush joined the Louisville-based BLUEGRASS ALLIANCE as mandolinist.

In 1971, leaving fiddler Lonnie Peerce to continue the Bluegrass Alliance with all new personnel, Bush, banjoist Courtney Johnson, guitarist Curtis Burch, and bassist Harry "Ebo Walker" Shelor, adopted a different name—New Grass Revival. Their penchant for long hair, casual clothing, and eclectic influences upset traditionalists but excited young musicians and fans. New Grass Revival became a rare all-acoustic band on a major country label when signing with EMI Records in 1986. After a self-titled debut album, the band switched to CAPITOL RECORDS and released *Hold to a Dream* and *Friday Night in America* before breaking up in 1989.

Bush released his first solo album, *Late as Usual*, on ROUNDER RECORDS in 1985. In 1989 he joined with acoustic music leaders JERRY DOUGLAS, MARK O'CONNOR, and Edgar Meyer to record under the group name Strength in Numbers. EMMYLOU HARRIS invited Bush to join her new band, the Nash Ramblers, who recorded the 1991 live album *At the Ryman*. He stayed until Harris dissolved the group in 1995. Since then, Bush has remained a sought-after solo performer and session musician. He joined the SUGAR HILL RECORDS roster as a solo artist in 1996 and released his sixth album, *Circles Around Me*, for the label in 2009.

A two-time cancer survivor, he serves as a role model for others afflicted by the disease. In 2009, the AMERICANA Music Association honored Bush with its Lifetime Achievement Award. —*Frank and Marty Godbey*

## Carl & Pearl Butler

Carl Roberts Butler b. Knoxville, Tennessee, June 2, 1927; d. September 4, 1992
Pearl Dee Jones b. Nashville, Tennessee, September 20, 1927; d. March 1, 1989

Carl & Pearl Butler's first charted duet became their greatest success: "Don't Let Me Cross Over," which spent eleven weeks at #1 on the country charts in 1962 and 1963. On the strength of this hit Pearl joined her husband on the GRAND OLE OPRY, where he had been a regular since 1958.

Carl Butler had been playing guitar in public since age twelve, when he entertained between square dance sets. Later he was featured on WROL and WNOX in Knoxville and WPTF in Raleigh, North Carolina. While in Knoxville he began amassing credits as a tunesmith with such songs as "My Tears Don't Show,"

*Pearl and Carl Butler*

"If Teardrops Were Pennies," "Guilty Conscience," "Hold Back the Dawn," and "Cryin' My Heart Out Over You." His songs were recorded through the years by ROY ACUFF, CARL SMITH, BILL MONROE, Rosemary Clooney, FLATT & SCRUGGS, and RICKY SKAGGS. Pearl Jones cowrote "Kisses Don't Lie," a Carl Smith hit.

Carl Butler kicked off his solo recording career in 1951 with CAPITOL RECORDS, switching to COLUMBIA RECORDS in 1953. His early recordings included "River of Tears" and "That's What It's Like to Be Lonesome," but "Honkytonkitis" became his first chart record (#25, 1961). Although Pearl often sang with her husband at shows, she resisted recording until "Don't Let Me Cross Over." In 1964 the couple had another *Billboard* Top Ten hit, "Too Late to Try Again" (#9), and a few months later they scored with "I'm Hanging Up the Phone" (#14). Their last chart entry, "We'll Sweep Out the Ashes in the Morning" (#63, 1969), was later recorded as a duet by GRAM PARSONS and EMMYLOU HARRIS.

In Knoxville the Butlers took in child performer DOLLY PARTON when she performed for Cas Walker's local TV show and later helped arrange for Parton's first appearance on the Opry in 1959. The Butlers appeared in the film *Second Fiddle to a Steel Guitar* (1967). —*Walt Trott*

## Larry Butler

b. Pensacola, Florida, March 26, 1942

The multitalented Larry Lee Butler has been the only Nashville producer to win the Grammy for Producer of the Year, Non-Classical, which is selected from all genres of popular music. (He won for the year 1980.)

A child prodigy, Butler began playing piano at age four. At age ten he sang with RED FOLEY, and as a preteen he hosted a local radio show and cohosted a TV show. Encouraged by music publisher BUDDY KILLEN, Butler moved to Nashville in 1963 and became a top session player, providing piano on BOBBY GOLDSBORO's "Honey" and CONWAY TWITTY's "Hello Darlin,'" among other hits.

Butler moved to Memphis in the late 1960s to work with producer CHIPS MOMAN. Butler recorded as a member of the pop group the Gentrys and as a solo artist, and he became Goldsboro's musical director and pianist. After returning to Nashville, Butler produced for CAPITOL RECORDS, then for COLUMBIA RECORDS, where he worked with JOHNNY CASH, becoming Cash's pianist, producer, studio manager, and musical director. Butler joined United Artists Records in 1973 as head of the Nashville division and signed DOTTIE WEST and CRYSTAL GAYLE. His biggest success there came when he produced KENNY ROGERS's hits "Lucille" and "The Gambler."

Leaving United Artists in 1983, Butler formed Larry Butler Productions and worked with MAC DAVIS, CHARLIE RICH, Debby Boone, Don McLean, JOHN DENVER, and BILLIE JO SPEARS. As a songwriter, Butler co-wrote with Moman "(Hey Won't You Play) Another Somebody Done Somebody Wrong Song," a #1 country and pop hit for B. J. THOMAS and a 1975 Grammy winner as Best Country Song. —*Gerry Wood*

## Kenny Buttrey

b. Nashville, Tennessee, April 1, 1945; d. September 12, 2004

One of Nashville's most influential drummers, Kenny Buttrey played on mainstream country sessions while anchoring rhythm sections on seminal rock and R&B recordings of the 1960s and '70s. Aaron Kenneth Buttrey was playing drums professionally by age eleven. In his teens he formed the MUSIC CITY show band the Escorts and recruited CHARLIE MCCOY, who helped Buttrey become established in the local studio scene. Buttrey's credits include Arthur Alexander's 1962 country-soul classic "Anna (Go to Him)" and Robert Knight's 1967 R&B-pop crossover hit "Everlasting Love."

With countercultural affinities and spontaneous arranging skills, Buttrey helped to spearhead a fusion of country and rock that continues to affect country music. He played on landmark albums by BOB DYLAN, including *Blonde on Blonde, John Wesley Harding*, and *Nashville Skyline*.

In 1969 Buttrey cofounded COUNTRY-ROCK band Area Code 615, a group of Nashville session luminaries that released two albums. When remnants of the band re-formed as Barefoot Jerry, Buttrey played on that group's 1971 debut, *Southern Delight*. He toured and recorded with NEIL YOUNG, appearing on landmark albums such as *After the Gold Rush* and *Harvest*. Buttrey's flash-free, fluid touch also graces recordings by Jimmy Buffett (including "Margaritaville"), KRIS KRISTOFFERSON, LINDA RONSTADT, and many others. —*Michael Gray*

## Billy Byrd
b. Nashville, Tennessee, February 17, 1920; d. August 7, 2001

William Lewis "Billy" Byrd is best known for having been ERNEST TUBB's longtime lead guitarist. A self-taught player enamored of jazz greats Stephane Grappelli and Django Reinhardt, Byrd gained his earliest professional experience in radio and club work with Nashville pop bands, but his earliest recordings were made with Herald Goodman's GRAND OLE OPRY group in 1938. After military service, Byrd worked at the Opry for PAUL HOWARD's Arkansas Cotton Pickers and WALLY FOWLER's Oak Ridge Quartet before moving to Shreveport in 1948 to work with Fowler alumnus Curley Kinsey and later with CURLEY WILLIAMS & HIS GEORGIA PEACH PICKERS. Upon returning to Nashville in about early 1949, Byrd backed Opry newcomers LITTLE JIMMY DICKENS and GEORGE MORGAN, and then joined Ernest Tubb's Texas Troubadours in mid-1949. For the next ten years Tubb relied on his electric lead guitarist not only for dependable instrumental support but also as one of his limo and bus drivers. Meanwhile, on hit after hit, Tubb immortalized Byrd with his oft-repeated aside of "Aw, Billy Byrd now," which introduced the guitarist's succinct, melodic solos. In 1955 Byrd and HANK GARLAND collaborated to design the Byrdland semi-hollow-body electric guitar for the Gibson company.

In 1959 Byrd made his first instrumental recordings (two albums) for WARNER BROS. RECORDS. After leaving Tubb that year, Byrd worked briefly in California for GORDON TERRY and then returned to Nashville for club work, TV shows, and more recording. Byrd briefly rejoined Ernest Tubb's band, not once but twice—in 1969–70 and 1973–74. After driving a cab for many years, he retired in Nashville. —*Ronnie Pugh*

## Jerry Byrd
b. Lima, Ohio, March 29, 1920; d. April 11, 2005

Gerald Lester Byrd ranks as one of country music's most influential steel guitar stylists. Inspired by a HAWAIIAN MUSIC troupe he saw in a traveling TENT SHOW, he played steel guitar on local Ohio

*Jerry Byrd*

radio programs and worked with the RENFRO VALLEY BARN DANCE while still in high school. This led to a full-time job with the show, where he backed stars RED FOLEY and Ernie Lee, blending Hawaiian sounds into country material. By this time Byrd had begun to experiment with slanted-bar left-hand techniques and alternate tunings, such as his trademark C6 tuning.

A case of pneumonia temporarily sidelined him, but Byrd returned to the Renfro Valley stage before moving to Detroit's WJR with Lee. After World War II, Byrd went to Nashville to play with ERNEST TUBB and then with Foley, both GRAND OLE OPRY stars at the time. Byrd's popularity as a studio musician increased steadily through his years at WLW's *MIDWESTERN HAYRIDE* in Cincinnati (1948–51), when he also worked sessions at the nearby E. T. HERZOG RECORDING STUDIO and at the KING RECORDS studio, backing local talent and visiting country and pop stars, including JIMMY WAKELY, Patti Page, and HANK WILLIAMS.

Byrd returned to Nashville to play in GEORGE MORGAN's band for three years while continuing to work sessions. After signing with MERCURY RECORDS in 1949, Byrd recorded "Steelin' the Blues" and other original hits for that label before making well-received albums for DECCA, RCA, and MONUMENT during the 1950s and 1960s. During these years he appeared on numerous Nashville-originated TV programs, including *Country Junction, The Bobby Lord Show*, and syndicated shows using Opry talent.

Despite the rise of the PEDAL STEEL GUITAR in the mid-1950s, Byrd stuck by his original nonpedal style, and his session work dwindled. In 1972 he moved to Hawaii and found acceptance in resort hotels, sometimes recording for small labels as well. Even after retiring, in the 1980s, he continued to teach young Hawaiian players their own native instrument until his death in 2005. "It's gone full circle," he said in 1988, "in that I'm putting it back where I got it from." —*John W. Rumble*

## Tracy Byrd
b. Vidor, Texas, December 17, 1966

Tracy Lynn Byrd emerged from the fertile southeastern Texas nightclub circuit in the 1990s to build a national career by bringing a Lone Star flavor to contemporary country hits. Signed to MCA RECORDS by TONY BROWN, Byrd released his self-titled debut album in 1993. Besides a #1 hit, "Holdin' Heaven," the album revealed an easy command of WESTERN SWING, HONKY-TONK MUSIC, and lonesome barstool ballads.

The follow-up album, *No Ordinary Man*, established Byrd as a star. Although weighted toward novelty numbers, including the hits "Watermelon Crawl" and "Lifestyles of the Not So Rich and Famous," the collection's most lasting song is the love ballad "The Keeper of the Stars." A popular wedding tune ever since, it was named CMA Song of the Year in 1995.

Byrd's third album, *Love Lessons*, didn't fare as well, with only the title song making the *Billboard* country Top Ten. The singer enjoyed three more Top Ten hits—"Big Love," a JOHNNY PAYCHECK cover retitled as "Don't Take Her She's All I Got," and "I'm from the Country"—before leaving MCA in 1999. Signing with RCA RECORDS, Byrd had four significant hits over three albums: "Put Your Hand in Mine" (#11) from *It's About Time*; "Just Let Me Be in Love" (#9) and "Ten Rounds with Jose Cuervo" (#1) from *Ten Rounds*; and "Drinkin' Bone" (#7) from *The Truth About Men*, his last RCA album, released in 2004. Byrd released *Different Things* on his own Blind Mule label in 2007. In 2010 he began an extended break from touring. —*Rick Mitchell*

## The Byrds
Harold Eugene Clark b. Tipton, Missouri, November 17, 1944; d. May 24, 1991
Michael Clarke (Michael Dick) b. New York, New York, June 3, 1946; d. December 19, 1993
David Van Cortlandt Crosby b. Los Angeles, California, August 14, 1941
Chris Hillman b. Los Angeles, California, December 4, 1944
Roger McGuinn (James Joseph McGuinn III) b. Chicago, Illinois, July 13, 1942

The Byrds were among the first successful purveyors of folk-rock in the mid-1960s and one of the 1960s rock acts most heavily influenced by country music. The original members came mostly from folk music backgrounds (CHRIS HILLMAN was steeped in BLUEGRASS as well), but cofounder Roger McGuinn had an eclectic vision for the Byrds that enveloped his own folk roots, the harmonic rock & roll of the Beatles, and American rock, along with any music that reflected the times.

Not long after BOB DYLAN's "Mr. Tambourine Man" gave the Los Angeles–based band their first hit record, in 1965, they began to reveal their interest in country. On their second album, *Turn! Turn! Turn!*, they recorded the country standard "Satisfied Mind" at Hillman's suggestion. And on their 1967 release *Younger Than Yesterday*, the song "Time Between" featured acclaimed bluegrass guitarist Clarence White (CLARENCE AND ROLAND WHITE) of the Kentucky Colonels and VERN GOSDIN on rhythm guitar.

But it was GRAM PARSONS who pointed the Byrds toward Nashville. Parsons and Hillman had struck up a friendship late in 1967. A few months later, when the Byrds needed to replace David Crosby, who had left the band, Hillman suggested Parsons. He joined the Byrds along with drummer Kevin Kelley, who replaced Michael Clarke. (Gene Clark had earlier departed the Byrds, though he returned briefly after Crosby's departure.)

McGuinn recalled Parsons as a forceful personality with a musical plan "to blend the Beatles and country; to really do something revolutionary. Gram thought we could win over the country audience. He figured, once they dig you, they never let go." The Byrds went country all the way. After deciding to cut their next record in Nashville, they got outfitted at NUDIE THE RODEO TAILOR's and, with help from COLUMBIA RECORDS, got booked onto the GRAND OLE OPRY. With several Nashville musicians onboard, they recorded several tracks in MUSIC CITY—including Parsons's evocative "Hickory Wind"—then played the Opry on March 15, 1968. The long-haired California boys drew a few hoots and suggestions that they get haircuts. The Byrds quieted the crowd with a straightforward rendition of MERLE HAGGARD's "Sing Me Back Home." Then, instead of performing an expected second Haggard song, Parsons pulled a switch and led the shocked band into "Hickory Wind," upsetting Opry producers.

Back in Los Angeles, the band finished the album, titled *Sweetheart of the Rodeo*. Though now considered a landmark in the meshing of country traditions with rock & roll sensibilities, *Sweetheart of the Rodeo* received mixed notices and was the poorest-selling Byrds album to that point. Disgruntled over a proposed South African tour, Parsons left, replaced by Clarence White. Hillman also soon left, as did Kelley, and Hillman and Parsons went on to form the Flying Burrito Brothers. Other musicians who joined the Byrds for varying lengths of time included Skip Battin, Gene Parsons, and John York. In all their numerous permutations, the Byrds continued to include country as part of their wide-ranging repertoire. McGuinn finally disbanded the group in early 1973. —*Ben Fong-Torres*

## Cackle Sisters (*see* DeZurik Sisters)

## Cajun Music

Cajun music is the music of French-speaking Cajun people of Louisiana and southeastern Texas. Originally descended from French Canadians who had been forced by the English to leave their homeland of Acadia (now Nova Scotia) in the mid-1700s, many Acadians settled in Louisiana, where there was already a sizable French-speaking population. There the Cajuns, as they came to be known, freely intermarried with French and Spanish colonials, African slaves, and Native Americans. Their music came to reflect their diverse heritage as well as a lingering melancholy rooted in their forced exile from their homeland. The related music developed by the region's black Creoles came to be known as *zydeco*.

As the music developed, the Cajuns added new songs reflecting their lives in the bayous and prairies of Louisiana to the body of old French folk songs and tunes they had brought with them. By the late 1700s the Cajuns were developing a distinctive style of twin fiddling based on their traditional dance tunes and incorporating elements of Anglo-American fiddling. In the mid-1800s German settlers introduced the diatonic accordion, which became a key ingredient of the Cajun sound. By 1900 a typical Cajun band included an accordion, a fiddle, perhaps a triangle, and later a guitar.

Scholars generally agree that the first commercial recordings of Cajun music were made in 1928, when accordionist JOSEPH FALCON and his wife, Cleoma, made their first discs for COLUMBIA RECORDS. Other companies, notably RCA VICTOR RECORDS and BRUNSWICK RECORDS, were not far behind. Quickly realizing the regional sales potential for French music in Cajun country, they recorded artists such as DENNIS McGEE, Amédé Ardoin, LEO SOILEAU, and the Walker Brothers.

Cajun music underwent significant changes in the 1920s and 1930s. As radio and records became popular, Cajun musicians were influenced by country music and WESTERN SWING. As bands such as THE HACKBERRY RAMBLERS and the Rayne-Bo Ramblers incorporated those sounds into their music, the accordion passed out of style, replaced by fiddles and steel guitars. After World War II the accordion enjoyed a resurgence, thanks primarily to accordion masters such as IRY LEJEUNE, LAWRENCE WALKER, and NATHAN ABSHIRE.

During the 1950s and 1960s Cajun music continued to draw on other forms of popular music, from HONKY-TONK to R&B. HANK WILLIAMS, in particular, had a profound impact on professionals such as D. L. MENARD, Aldus Roger, and Vin Bruce.

Cajun music remained essentially regional, although performers such as HARRY CHOATES, JIMMY C. NEWMAN, and DOUG KERSHAW placed hits on the mainstream country charts. The 1960s saw a revival of traditional Cajun music, as the folk music boom brought artists such as the Balfa Brothers (DEWEY BALFA) to the attention of audiences at venues such as the NEWPORT FOLK FESTIVAL and renewed interest in older forms among younger Cajun musicians. Mark Savoy (MARK & ANN SAVOY), MICHAEL DOUCET, JO-EL SONNIER, Zachary Richard, Wayne Toups, Paul Daigle, Bruce Daigrepont, and Steve Riley were among those inspired to play Cajun music ranging from the highly traditional to the deliberately commercial and contemporary. Cajun musicians were regularly invited to perform at folk festivals around the nation, while the general Cajun cultural and linguistic revival of the 1970s and 1980s also energized the Cajun music scene.

Cajun and zydeco music have evolved and changed greatly since the 1800s; they have been repeatedly modified by the introduction of new instruments—from the accordion to the electric guitar—and by popular musical influences from country to rock & roll and reggae. Still, Cajun music remains a popular and vital tradition, reflecting, as it always has, the culture, lives, and times of the Cajun people. —*Charlie Seemann*

## W. R. Calaway
b. Boone, North Carolina, date unknown; d. 1949

From 1928 to 1938 William Ronald "Bill" Calaway was active as an A&R man connected with various country and blues artists' recording careers, including those of ROY ACUFF, THE CALLAHAN BROTHERS, BILL CARLISLE and his brother Cliff, David Miller, JOHN McGHEE & FRANK WELLING, Charley Patton, and Walter Roland, to name a few.

Working with GENNETT RECORDS (1928–30) and the AMERICAN RECORD CORPORATION (1930–38), Calaway served as a recruiter-auditioner-producer of talent, often benefiting on the side by acquiring full or part ownership of publishing rights and writer's copyrights of certain songs. Thus he frequently received writer's credit on songs that his artists recorded. From 1930 to 1938, from addresses in Huntington, West Virginia (1930), New Richmond, Ohio (1931–32), New York City (1931), and Orlando, Florida (1935 on), Calaway registered approximately 180 song copyrights in which he shared. Among these songs are CLIFF CARLISLE's "Don't Marry the Wrong Woman," Ramblin' Red Lowery's "Take Me Back to Tennessee," the Callahan Brothers' "She's My Curly Headed Baby," and Roy Acuff's "Steel Guitar Blues."

He reportedly died in an automobile accident in 1949. —*Bob Pinson*

## The Callahan Brothers

Walter Tommie "Joe" Callahan b. Madison County, North Carolina, January 27, 1910; d. September 10, 1971
Homer C. "Bill" Callahan b. Madison County, North Carolina, March 27, 1912; d. September 12, 2002

During the 1930s the Callahan Brothers ranked as one of country music's leading harmony duos (see BROTHER DUETS) and the main act of this kind represented on AMERICAN RECORD CORPORATION labels. Natives of Asheville, North Carolina, in the Appalachian highlands, Homer and Walter—sometimes known as Bill and Joe—may have been a little less skilled than some of their competitors on BLUEBIRD RECORDS, but their heavier blues influences and a knack for duet yodeling distinguished them from their rivals.

The brothers began their professional careers at WWNC–Asheville in 1933 and first recorded in 1934. By 1935 their discs had received sufficient attention to take them to WHAS–Louisville and then to radio jobs in Wheeling, West Virginia; Cincinnati; Tulsa; and Springfield, Missouri. Their repertory ranged from blues numbers such as "Gonna Quit My Rowdy Ways" and sentimental mountain songs such as "Little Poplar Log House" to sacred numbers and even risqué tidbits typified by "She Came Rollin' Down the Mountain." "She's My Curly Headed Baby" was probably their best-known song.

By 1941 the Callahans had moved to Texas, where they spent their remaining show business years alternating between KWFT–Wichita Falls and KRLD–Dallas. In that same year they switched to DECCA RECORDS for one session and also cut numerous radio programs for Sellers Transcriptions. In 1945 they were featured in the film *Springtime in Texas*, which starred JIMMY WAKELY. Their final recordings in 1951, with COLUMBIA RECORDS, displayed a more modern sound. Walter Callahan later returned to North Carolina. Homer Callahan played bass and performed comedy in the Dallas area for many years on a part-time basis while earning his living as a photographer. —*Ivan M. Tribe*

## Camel Caravan

began June 1941; ended December 1942

The WSM Camel Caravan played a significant role in popularizing country music. In 1941, with World War II raging in Europe and mobilization under way in the United States, the R. J. Reynolds Tobacco Company began sponsoring groups of entertainers to tour U.S. military bases, mostly in the States. Named for Camel Cigarettes, one of R. J. Reynolds's most popular brands, Camel Caravan shows were intended to boost R. J. Reynolds's sales as well as troop morale. (Presumably, distributing free cigarettes, sometimes shot into audiences with slingshots, would stimulate demand for Camels.)

The most important Camel Caravan unit was organized by Nashville-based promoter J. L. FRANK, who assembled a team of WSM country and pop talent. Central to this group were PEE WEE KING's Golden West Cowboys, then including EDDY ARNOLD as lead vocalist, and featured comedienne MINNIE PEARL. Also in King's band were fiddler REDD STEWART, singer San Antonio Rose, and bassist JOE ZINKAN. Kay Carlisle, a young pop vocalist; a trio of female pop singers (Mary Dinwiddie, Evelyn Wilson, and Alcyone Bate Beasley, daughter of GRAND OLE OPRY pioneer DR. HUMPHREY BATE); dancer Dollie Dearman; and four dancers called the Camelettes enlarged the troupe, while Opry singer Ford

Rush served as MC. The tour began in the summer of 1941 and concluded in December 1942. Although the group made occasional rest stops back in Nashville, most of this period was spent on the road at U.S. military installations, especially in the South. The 75,000-mile itinerary included shows in thirty-two states, the Canal Zone, Panama, and Guatemala. —*John W. Rumble*

## Camp Creek Boys

The Camp Creek Boys were a loose aggregation of OLD-TIME musicians from the Round Peak area of North Carolina, a region famous for its hard-driving style of traditional mountain fiddle and banjo music and its wealth of great musicians. The group was started by banjo player Kyle Creed in the early 1960s and included a number of musicians as personnel changed over the years. The original band included Creed on banjo, Paul Sutphin on guitar, Ronald Collins on guitar, Vernon Clifton on mandolin, and Fred Cockerham and Earnest East on fiddles. Eventually, fiddler Benton Flippen would play with the group, as would guitarist Larry Flippen and mandolin player Hoyle Jones. A later incarnation of the band included the BLUEGRASS banjo of Bobby Patterson, with Pete Lissman on guitar and Dave Freeman on mandolin. —*Charlie Seemann*

## Archie Campbell

b. Bulls Gap, Tennessee, November 7, 1914; d. August 29, 1987

Archie James Campbell was a popular country comedian before he joined *HEE HAW* in 1969, but that hit TV show made him a household name.

After two years at North Carolina's Mars Hill College, Campbell traveled the South as a musician and sign painter before

*Archie Campbell*

he landed a job at Knoxville's WNOX in 1936. There he sang on a daily program, the *Mid-Day Merry-Go-Round*, with Roy Acuff & His Crazy Tennesseans. In 1936 announcer Lowell Blanchard came to WNOX to beef up country programming, and he saw a need for comedy. Under his tutelage Campbell developed a character named Grandpappy, who was a hit with listeners.

Campbell later had his own shows at Bristol's WOPI and at Chattanooga's WDOD before spending two years in the navy in World War II. He then rejoined the *Mid-Day Merry-Go-Round*. In 1949, however, he went to WNOX's rival station WROL for a program called *Country Playhouse*, which became the city's first country music television show.

In 1958 Campbell won a spot on the Grand Ole Opry as a comedian on the *Prince Albert Show*, the Opry's NBC network segment, replacing the recently deceased Rod Brasfield. There Campbell shed his Grandpappy character and worked in everyday clothes. In addition to radio, Campbell played road shows and made comedy records for the RCA label (1959–62), including "Trouble in the Amen Corner"; "The Cockfight"; and "Rinderceller," a spoonerism version of the fairy tale Cinderella. Spoonerisms—transpositions of word sounds—became his trademark. In 1962 he signed with Starday Records (1962–65) but returned in 1966 to RCA, where he had modest hits revealing his singing abilities in duets with Lorene Mann: "Dark End of the Street" (1968), "Tell It Like It Is" (1968), and "My Special Prayer" (1969). In 1976 Elektra Records released his album *Archie Campbell*.

In 1969 Campbell was hired as a writer-comedian for *Hee Haw*, which first aired in June of that year, and he won a CMA award as Comedian of the Year that fall. The routines and characters he developed—such as the lecherous country doctor who ogled Nurse Goodbody—had been inspired by earlier skits he and Lowell Blanchard had created in Knoxville. In 1987 Campbell died of complications following a heart attack. —*Loyal Jones*

## Cecil Campbell
b. Danbury, North Carolina, March 22, 1911; d. June 18, 1989

Steel guitar pioneer Cecil Robert Campbell was born into a farming family. After working in local musical groups, he turned professional at twenty-one at WSJS–Winston-Salem and broadcast over a number of radio stations during the 1930s, mostly in the South but also ranging into Pennsylvania and New York. An excellent showman with a quick wit, he became known for his rapid-fire comedy as well as his musicianship. With the primary exception of a 1938–39 stint at WSB in Atlanta, he was based at WBT–Charlotte from the mid-1930s into the 1950s, working on the station's popular *Briarhopper Time* as well as on the *Dixie Jamboree*, *Carolina Hayride*, and *Carolina Calling*, all carried by regional CBS networks.

During the mid-1930s Campbell was a key member of Dick Hartman's Tennessee Ramblers, recording with that group for RCA's Bluebird imprint. Later Campbell took over the group name and recorded as the Tennessee Ramblers and under his own name for Bluebird, Super Disc, and RCA Victor between 1939 and 1951. He later recorded for MGM (1960) and Starday (1965). Other credits include several musical performances in films with Gene Autry, Tex Ritter, Roy Acuff, and Charles Starrett during the late 1930s and early 1940s. Like many steel players, Campbell made the switch from acoustic dobro to electric steel guitar and composed numerous instrumentals,

the best known including "Hawaiian Skies" and "Beaty Steel Blues." Following TV work in Charlotte during the late 1950s, Campbell went into real estate in 1958 and remained active in this field into the 1970s, all the while keeping a hand in recording and publishing with his own Winston Records (not to be confused with Slim Willet's label of the same name). —*John W. Rumble*

## Glen Campbell
b. Delight, Arkansas, April 22, 1936

A gifted singer and accomplished guitarist, Glen Travis Campbell is best known for his string of pop and country hits released in the 1960s and 1970s—"Gentle on My Mind" (1967), "By the Time I Get to Phoenix" (1967), "Wichita Lineman" (1968), "Galveston" (1969), "Rhinestone Cowboy" (1975), and "Southern Nights" (1977), to cite only a few.

At his peak, Campbell hosted *The Glen Campbell Goodtime Hour*, a CBS-TV musical variety show, from 1968 to 1972. He also starred in several feature films, including *True Grit* (1969) with John Wayne.

The seventh son in a sharecropper's family of twelve children, Campbell was born into hard times. From an early age he set himself apart with his proficiency on guitar, and by the time he was a teenager he was playing in his uncle's western swing band.

By his early twenties, Campbell had moved to the West Coast. From October 1960 to May 1961 he toured as lead guitarist for the Champs, two years after they hit with "Tequila." His first pop hit came in 1961 with "Turn Around, Look at Me" on Crest Records. In 1962 he played guitar and sang on "Kentucky Means Paradise," a single by the Green River Boys. It was the first of

*Glen Campbell*

Campbell's efforts to hit the country charts, though he remained an unknown and the group released only one album, *Big Bluegrass Special.*

In 1962 he signed with CAPITOL RECORDS, but for several years he recorded without success. Indeed, between 1962 and 1967 Campbell was in much more demand as a session guitarist and vocalist than as an artist. During the 1960s he worked with such notables as RICK NELSON, Frank Sinatra, Bobby Darin, Dean Martin, MERLE HAGGARD, the Mamas & the Papas, and the Beach Boys. In 1964 he toured briefly with the Beach Boys as Brian Wilson's replacement. During these years Campbell also poured his instrumental prowess into his own records, recording several guitar-dominated albums, including two with TUT TAYLOR and THE DILLARDS in an ensemble billed as the Folkswingers.

Campbell's breakthrough came with JOHN HARTFORD's modern hobo song "Gentle on My Mind" in 1967. Though it reached only #30 on the country charts and #39 on the pop charts, the song struck a chord with listeners. In 1990, in a testament to its copious radio airplay, BMI named the song its fourth-most-played song to date.

Campbell scored his first country Top Five in 1967 with "By the Time I Get to Phoenix." In 1968 he gained his first Top Five pop hit with "Wichita Lineman." Between 1967 and 1980 Campbell effortlessly straddled country and pop, racking up thirty Top Twenty country hits and nineteen Top Forty pop records, including the crossover smashes "Galveston," "Country Boy," "Southern Nights," and his signature, "Rhinestone Cowboy."

During the 1980s Campbell recorded for WARNER BROS. RECORDS and ATLANTIC RECORDS and continued to have occasional Top Ten country hits. He lost ground, however, due to alcohol and cocaine problems, three divorces, and a much-publicized, tempestuous engagement to TANYA TUCKER in 1980.

In 1987 Campbell was signed to MCA's country division by record producer JIMMY BOWEN, with whom he'd worked extensively on the West Coast in the 1960s. At MCA Campbell had Top Ten hits with "The Hand That Rocks the Cradle" (with STEVE WARINER), "Still Within the Sound of My Voice," and "She's Gone, Gone, Gone." In 1990 he returned to Capitol, but he has logged no big hits since then.

By the late 1990s Campbell largely abandoned his wild ways and became a devout Christian, though in 2003 he was arrested for drunk driving following a hit-and-run collision, which he attributed to drinking while taking prescription drugs. In 1994 Villard Books published his memoirs, *Rhinestone Cowboy: An Autobiography,* coauthored with Tom Carter.

Campbell was elected to THE COUNTRY MUSIC HALL OF FAME in 2005. In 2011 Campbell announced a farewell album and tour following a diagnosis of Alzheimer's Disease. —*Bob Allen*

## Buddy Cannon
b. Lexington, Tennessee, April 20, 1947

Murray Franklin Cannon has distinguished himself as a musician, songwriter, and record executive. He emerged as one of the most successful producers on MUSIC ROW in the 1990s and 2000s by overseeing, initially with NORRO WILSON, a string of hit-filled, million-selling albums for KENNY CHESNEY. Cannon played bass with BOB LUMAN in the early 1970s before joining MEL TILLIS's band and going to work for his music publishing company. Tillis had a #1 hit in 1978 with Cannon's "I Believe in You." As director of A&R for MERCURY RECORDS for six years, Cannon played a

key role in recruiting stars such as SHANIA TWAIN, BILLY RAY CYRUS, and SAMMY KERSHAW. He produced several hits for Kershaw, including the #1 "She Don't Know She's Beautiful." Cannon left a post at Polydor/Nashville in 1995 to pursue independent production. Among his many clients have been SARA EVANS, JAMEY JOHNSON, GEORGE JONES, REBA McENTIRE, JOHN MICHAEL MONTGOMERY, and JOE NICHOLS. Cannon demonstrated great writing skill on hits such as the VERN GOSDIN classic "Set 'Em Up Joe" and GEORGE STRAIT's "I've Come to Expect It from You" and "Give It Away," which was named 2007 Song of the Year at the CMA Awards. —*Jay Orr*

## Judy Canova
b. Starke, Florida, November 20, 1913; d. August 5, 1983

For a number of years, Juliette "Judy" Canova was the nation's preeminent hillbilly comedienne. With her brother Leon and sister Diane, she started professionally in a family group, "Anne, Judy, and Zeke, the Three Georgia Crackers." Judy had sung on radio at age twelve, and after her father's death her mother had encouraged the children's theatrical ambitions. They hit New York City in the early 1930s with an act that included hillbilly costumes, comedy, dance routines, songs, yodels, and hog calls. They began a Broadway career in 1934 in *Calling All Stars,* and in 1939 they became one of country's first acts to appear on television. On radio and records the Canovas' songs were merry and cornball, with titles such as "Me and My Still."

*Scatterbrain* (1940) was Judy's first in a fifteen-year string of feature films that showcased her characters' guileless country simplicity triumphing over sophisticated urban corruption. Other titles included *Joan of Ozark* (1942) and *Singin' in the Corn* (1946). She became the Republic studio's top moneymaking female, surpassed at the box office only by cowboy stars such as ROY ROGERS.

From 1943 to 1955, her hit radio program, *The Judy Canova Show,* ran nationally on CBS and later on NBC. Forming her own production company to gain further financial control of the profits from her work, she became a millionaire. Her fine recordings during these years captured her gifted singing, a unique blend of jazz phrasing, country yodeling, and gymnastic vocal leaps.

By the time her radio show ended, Canova was a TV star, and over the years she appeared on dozens of shows, from *The Colgate Comedy Hour* to *Alfred Hitchcock Presents* to *Love Boat.* She also performed in Las Vegas and in Broadway shows, touring in *No, No Nanette* in 1971. She continued to act in films, too, including 1960's *The Adventures of Huckleberry Finn* and 1976's *Cannonball.* —*Mary A. Bufwack*

## Capitol Records
established in Hollywood, California, April 8, 1942

When Capitol Records was formed by pop lyricist-singer Johnny Mercer, music store owner Glenn Wallichs, and Paramount Pictures executive and songwriter George "Buddy" DeSylva, three major record companies dominated popular music (including country): COLUMBIA, RCA, and DECCA. In less than a decade, Capitol became a major label to reckon with. From the 1940s through the 1960s, Capitol recorded nearly all West Coast country artists of note, and it played a major role in popularizing the BAKERSFIELD sound.

Named Liberty at its April 1942 formation, the label was renamed Capitol on June 4, 1942, to avoid a conflict with Liberty Music Shops in New York. Scoring two quick Top Ten pop hits with Johnny Mercer's "Strip Polka" and Freddie Slack's "Cow-Cow Boogie" by September 1942, the label soon signed an impressive array of pop artists, including Nat King Cole, Peggy Lee, Les Paul & Mary Ford, and (in 1954) Frank Sinatra. In the early 1940s Capitol became the first record company ever to service radio stations with free records to encourage airplay. In 1949 it became the first label to release records in all three speeds: 78 rpm, 33-1/3 rpm, and 45 rpm.

Initially located above Wallichs's Music City store at Hollywood's Sunset & Vine, Capitol had a West Coast orientation that became a boon to California country music. Starting with the signing of Tex Ritter in 1942, executives proved astute in assessing country talent. Under the direction of A&R man Lee Gillette and assistant Cliffie Stone, the label signed Merle Travis, Tex Williams, Hank Thompson, Jimmy Wakely, and Tennessee Ernie Ford.

When Ken Nelson took over as country A&R man in 1951, he ushered in such talents as Faron Young, Ferlin Husky, Jean Shepard, Sonny James, Wanda Jackson, The Louvin Brothers, Gene Vincent, and Rose Maddox (of the Maddox Brothers & Rose). Nelson was particularly adept at mining the talent pool of Bakersfield, signing Tommy Collins, Buck Owens, Merle Haggard, and Wynn Stewart.

Meanwhile, behind the scenes, corporate changes had taken place. On January 1, 1955, British conglomerate EMI announced its purchase of a controlling interest in Capitol for $8.5 million; Capitol president Glenn Wallichs became a director of EMI. On April 6, 1956, the company's famous cylindrical office building, Capitol Towers, opened in Hollywood.

Following Nelson's retirement in 1976, Capitol's country division increasingly developed a Nashville orientation. After the brief tenure of A&R man Marvin Hughes, Kelso Herston ran the label's Music City office in the mid- to late-1960s. Frank Jones was Nashville chief from 1973 to 1978. Owing to the departures of Merle Haggard and Buck Owens in the 1970s, Capitol's country division was no longer the industry power it had been, but during that decade the label continued to sign commercial acts, such as Anne Murray, Freddie Hart, Gene Watson, and Mel McDaniel. In the 1980s, under Jim Foglesong's leadership (1984–89), Capitol hit with T. Graham Brown, Sawyer Brown, and Tanya Tucker and scored its biggest country coup in 1989 by signing Garth Brooks, who became one of the modern era's biggest-selling recording artists.

Jimmy Bowen took over the Nashville division in late 1989 and helped maximize Brooks's commercial potential through canny efforts spearheaded by marketing specialist Joe Mansfield. From 1992 to 1995 the Nashville division was known as Liberty Records. Following Bowen's departure in the spring of 1995, record producer and engineer Scott Hendricks took the reins of the division and had the name changed back to Capitol Nashville; the most commercially successful new artists to emerge during his tenure were Deana Carter (signed and initially produced by Bowen) and Trace Adkins.

In November 1997, reportedly at the insistence of Garth Brooks, Hendricks was replaced as the Nashville division head by Patrick Quigley, a transfer from EMI's New York office whose previous experience consisted principally of marketing beer. On Quigley's watch, the label released Brooks's long-delayed *Sevens* and followed with his *Double Live* but faltered when Brooks's

experimental pop album . . . *In the Life of Chris Gaines* fell short of sales expectations. Moreover, Carter's sales dropped precipitously, though Quigley did temporarily reinvigorate Steve Wariner's career.

Former Arista Records executive Mike Dungan, who replaced Quigley in July 2000, helped push Adkins and Keith Urban (initially signed to EMI's Australian branch by 1991) to country's front ranks, while Dierks Bentley gained his first Capitol hit in 2003. Luke Bryan, Eric Church, Lady Antebellum, Little Big Town, and Darius Rucker all joined the roster by the end of 2008. —*Paul Kingsbury*

## Captain Stubby & the Buccaneers
Captain Stubby b. near Galveston, Indiana, November 24, 1918; d. May 24, 2004

Captain Stubby & the Buccaneers are best remembered for their stint on Chicago radio station WLS (ca. 1949–60), where their eclectic mix of novelty, gospel, and uptown country music was a feature of the National Barn Dance. They had previously worked at WDAN in Danville, Illinois, and WLW in Cincinnati. When the group joined WLS, it consisted of Tom C. Fouts (a.k.a. Captain Stubby), washboard and other novelty instruments; Dwight "Tiny" Stokes, string bass; Jerry Richards, clarinet; Sonny Fleming, guitar; and Tony Walberg, accordion. Pete Kaye joined the band as accordionist following the death of Walberg. Ralph "Rusty" Gill later replaced Fleming, who left the act. The group recorded for Decca, Mercury, Majestic, and Columbia. —*Wayne W. Daniel*

## Henson Cargill
b. Oklahoma City, Oklahoma, February 5, 1941; d. March 24, 2007

Ex-deputy sheriff Henson Cargill was a fitting choice for "Skip a Rope" (#1, 1968), a near million-seller. The song is interesting not only for its provocative message but also for a successful fusion of country and pop music elements.

The son of a trial lawyer and grandson of an Oklahoma City mayor, Cargill attended Colorado State University. He had long nurtured an interest in music, playing guitar from an early age. After college he joined the Kimberleys, touring the Pacific Northwest, and later performed on the Las Vegas nightclub circuit. In 1966 he met producer Don Law in Nashville. Law got Cargill signed to Monument Records and produced "Skip a Rope," his first and only #1 country hit. He scored only two more: "Row, Row, Row" (#11, 1968) and "None of My Business" (#8, 1969), both for Monument. Between 1971 and 1972 he recorded for Mega Records. He then signed with Atlantic Records in 1973 but was left in the lurch when Atlantic closed its Nashville doors. He did, however, chart with two more songs, "Silence on the Line" (1979) and "Have a Good Day" (1980) on the Copper Mountain label. —*Walt Trott*

## Bill Carlisle
b. Wakefield, Kentucky, December 19, 1908; d. March 17, 2003

William Toliver "Bill" Carlisle enjoyed a long and productive musical career that began in the 1920s and extended into the twenty-first century. Among country's first generation of professionals, Bill and his older brother, Clifford Raymond "Cliff" Carlisle (b. Mount Eden, Kentucky, March 6, 1904; d. April 2, 1983),

*The Carlisles: (from left) Tommy Bishop, Bill Carlisle, Tillman Franks (manager), and Betty Amos*

were among the genre's most prolific recording artists of the 1930s. In addition, they penned some of country music's most enduring songs, including Cliff's "I Believe I'm Entitled to You" and "Shanghai Rooster Yodel" and Bill's "Rattlesnake Daddy," "No Help Wanted," and "Too Old to Cut the Mustard." Bill also wrote the gospel song "Gone Home," a staple of his own repertoire and a favorite of the HEE HAW Gospel Quartet.

The brothers were born into a musical family and began singing and playing instruments as children. Bill accompanied his vocals on guitar; Cliff, fascinated with Hawaiian guitar players he heard on record and in person, achieved a similar sound by putting a nut under the strings of his own guitar, and he would eventually help to popularize the DOBRO as a hillbilly instrument.

Cliff began performing publicly at age sixteen, playing locally at social gatherings and talent contests with a cousin, Lillian Truax, until Truax's marriage ended the act. Next, Cliff teamed with construction worker Wilbur Ball, who played guitar, sang tenor harmony, and joined Cliff on harmony yodels as they worked vaudeville and TENT SHOW circuits during the 1920s and early 1930s. In about 1930, Carlisle and Ball broadcast over Louisville, Kentucky, radio station WHAS and began backing each other in the recording studio, first for the GENNETT and Champion labels. Carlisle's numbers typically followed patterns established by JIMMIE RODGERS, and in 1931 Carlisle and Ball backed Rodgers on several sides.

In that same year, Cliff signed with the AMERICAN RECORD CORPORATION. From October 1931 until September 1933, working with various partners including Ball, FRED KIRBY, and brother Bill, Cliff made dozens of records for the label, including sentimental tunes, songs of prisoners and hobos, love songs, and rowdy, risqué numbers such as "Shanghai Rooster Yodel" and "Tom Cat Blues." Bill also backed Cliff on sessions for BLUEBIRD and DECCA between 1936 and 1939, as did Cliff's son, billed as "Sonny Boy Tommy." Recording success helped Cliff gain radio exposure on powerful stations WBT–Charlotte, WLS– Chicago, and WLW–Cincinnati.

Bill began performing with Cliff over a Louisville, Kentucky, radio station on the *Carlisle Family Saturday Night Barn Dance*, a show that featured their father and other family members. In about 1934 Cliff asked Bill to become his musical partner, and for the next decade and a half they were one of the more popular

country music BROTHER DUETS on the air and on disc. Their work on several southeastern radio stations included approximately thirteen years at Knoxville's WNOX, where they starred on the daily *MID-DAY MERRY-GO-ROUND* and the Saturday night *Tennessee Barn Dance*. Through the years, Bill also recorded as a featured artist for a variety of labels, including BLUEBIRD, RCA VICTOR, MERCURY, KING, and HICKORY. The Carlisle Brothers' largest output as a duet was for Decca Records, for which they recorded from 1938 to 1940. However, perhaps their biggest hit, "Rainbow at Midnight" (1946), appeared on King.

In the late 1940s Cliff and Bill again followed separate paths, and thereafter Cliff's profile as an entertainer shrank in proportion to the expansion of Bill's. With a newly formed group called the Carlisles, Bill achieved his greatest fame on Mercury Records during the early 1950s, with signature novelty hits including "Too Old to Cut the Mustard," "No Help Wanted," "Is Zat You Myrtle," and "Knothole," many of which he wrote or cowrote. (Hilariously funny, Bill had earlier created a comic alter ego named Hotshot Elmer, whose antics paved the way for fans' acceptance of Bill's later novelties.) His last novelty hit was "What Kinda Deal Is This," a #4 chart-maker of 1965–66.

After stints at WNOX, Atlanta's *WSB Barn Dance*, and the *LOUISIANA HAYRIDE*, Bill joined the GRAND OLE OPRY in 1953. There he delighted fans not only with his music and comic banter but also with sudden, midsong jumps that earned him the name "Jumping Bill." (These vertical flights had originated when, working with Cliff, Bill jumped over a chair to escape from his brother during mock onstage fights.) A comic showman even as he worked the Opry in his nineties, he typically approached center stage with the help of a walker, which he would fold up and carry under his arm as he exited without assistance. Elected to THE COUNTRY MUSIC HALL OF FAME in 2002, Bill Carlisle continued to perform until shortly before his death in 2003. —*Wayne W. Daniel*

## Cliff Carlisle (*see Bill Carlisle*)

## Carnegie Hall
Opened 1892

Country music was first heard in New York City's Carnegie Hall when DENVER DARLING performed country songs as one of several artists during a 1945 concert. The September 18–19, 1947, two-night appearance by a troupe of country performers led by ERNEST TUBB has come to be known as the genre's breakthrough at that venue. Tubb headlined a GRAND OLE OPRY show that included MINNIE PEARL, Radio Dot & Smoky Swann, and MC GEORGE D. HAY, with prominent New York DJ and performer ROSALIE ALLEN also appearing. Though press reaction was scanty and mixed, both shows were well attended. T. TEXAS TYLER appeared at Carnegie on April 25, 1948, on the strength of his hit "Deck of Cards," and the SONS OF THE PIONEERS played there in June 1951. On December 29, 1961, the Grand Ole Opry presented a Carnegie show to benefit the Musicians Aid Society, which assisted unemployed local musicians. A sellout crowd of 2,700 saw PATSY CLINE, GRANDPA JONES, JIM REEVES, BILL MONROE, FARON YOUNG, MARTY ROBBINS, the JORDANAIRES, and Minnie Pearl. A year later, on December 8, 1962, FLATT & SCRUGGS, along with MERLE TRAVIS, enjoyed another full house, as did BUCK OWENS for his March 25, 1966, appearance; both shows were recorded for live concert albums. Since then, country musicians including JOHNNY CASH, DOTTIE WEST, and REBA MCENTIRE have held successful concerts at this prestigious international venue. —*Don Roy*

## Carolina Cotton
b. Cash, Arkansas, October 20, 1926; d. June 10, 1997

From 1944 to 1954, Carolina Cotton came to symbolize the yodeling cowgirl and the spirit of rural youth in B-westerns and country music movies. Born Helen Hagstrom in the tiny community of Cash, Arkansas, the youngster moved in early childhood to California with her family. The Hagstroms enrolled their daughter in dancing classes, and she began working on radio in San Francisco with Dude Martin, who gave her the southern-sounding name of Carolina Cotton. In 1944 she landed a small role in the Republic film *Sing, Neighbor Sing*, with ROY ACUFF. From there, Cotton appeared in a string of movies, mostly at Columbia Studios, with Ken Curtis, Charles Starrett, EDDY ARNOLD, GENE AUTRY, and others. She had sessions for KING RECORDS, Crystal, Mastertone, and MGM RECORDS, some of the latter with backing by BOB WILLS & His Texas Playboys. An excellent yodeler, her signature song became "Three Miles South of Cash in Arkansas."

Through much of the 1950s she had the Armed Forces Radio Service (AFRS) program *Carolina Calls* and became a favorite with GIs, touring extensively in Korea and elsewhere. Later she opted for a teaching career and spent her last years teaching elementary school in BAKERSFIELD, California. Appearances at western film festivals found her a continued favorite with fans until her death from cancer. —*Ivan M. Tribe*

## Carolina Tarheels
Doctor Coble "Dock" Walsh b. Wilkes County, North Carolina, July 23, 1901; d. May 1967
Garley Foster b. Wilkes County, North Carolina, January 10, 1905; d. October 1968
Clarence Earl McCurry ("Tom Ashley") b. Bristol, Tennessee, September 29, 1895; d. June 2, 1967

The Carolina Tarheels were among the best OLD-TIME southern STRINGBANDS of the 1920s and 1930s. Although the group's personnel varied, the central figure was Dock Walsh, a banjo player who made his first solo recordings in 1925. Walsh teamed briefly with guitarist and harmonica player Gwen Foster, with whom he formed a short-lived quartet that recorded for the Victor label (later RCA Victor) in 1927. Walsh then established a lasting partnership with Garley Foster (no relation to Gwen), who played guitar and harmonica and was a talented whistler often billed as "the human bird." In 1929 they were joined for some recording sessions by guitarist and banjo player CLARENCE "TOM" ASHLEY. In 1962 Walsh and Foster were "rediscovered" and recorded an LP for Folk Legacy. —*Charlie Seemann*

## Carolwood Records (*see* Lyric Street Records)

## Mary Chapin Carpenter
b. Princeton, New Jersey, February 21, 1958

Among the folkie singer-songwriters who came to Nashville in the 1980s believing they could translate their quirky, personal songs into country stardom, Mary Chapin Carpenter was one of the few who succeeded. She did it by mixing catchy, COUNTRY-ROCK dance numbers with confessional ballads and story songs. The result: five platinum albums, 1989's ACM Top New Female Vocalist award, two trophies as CMA Female Vocalist of the Year (1992 and 1993), and five Grammys.

For a singer who found acceptance among country fans, Carpenter had an atypical background. The daughter of a *Life* magazine executive, she grew up in Princeton, spent two years in Tokyo, and graduated from Brown University with a degree in American Civilization. In Washington, D.C., where she performed at local coffeehouses, local guitarist John Jennings recorded her songs in his basement studio.

Carpenter was ready to sign with independent label ROUNDER RECORDS when COLUMBIA RECORDS' Nashville office asked to hear her tape and released it as the album *Hometown Girl* in 1987. Although it was enthusiastically reviewed, it failed to penetrate country radio. Carpenter had more luck with *State of the Heart* (1989), which established her pattern of including uptempo songs such as Top Twenty country hits "How Do" and "Never Had It So Good" amid more reflective album cuts.

Carpenter's breakthrough came in 1991 with her self-penned "Down at the Twist & Shout" (from her album *Shooting Straight in the Dark*), expressing her joy in dancing to BEAUSOLEIL at a Bethesda, Maryland, nightclub. She convinced the CAJUN band to back her on the song, which became a #2 country hit and won a Grammy for Best Country Vocal Performance, Female. (She would receive this award three more times, for recordings eligible in 1992, 1993, and 1994.) Carpenter reached new heights with *Come On Come On* (1992), which sold 3 million copies and yielded seven Top Twenty country singles. Among these were "I Feel Lucky" (cowritten by Carpenter and DON SCHLITZ), "Passionate Kisses," and "Not Too Much to Ask" (a duet with JOE DIFFIE).

Carpenter resisted many of country's standard formulas. She continued to record in the D.C. area with Jennings and mainly used local musicians. She also avoided the expensive hairdos and costumes favored by most country divas and retained her low-key collegiate look. Carpenter remained outspoken as well, supporting the Country Music AIDS Awareness Campaign in Nashville and allying herself with other causes. "Stones in the Road," a Carpenter original recorded earlier by Joan Baez, became the title track for Carpenter's #1 1994 album. "Shut Up and Kiss Me," the only boisterous cut on *Stones in the Road*, became her first #1 single.

"Almost Home," in 1999, was her twenty-first and last Top Forty country single. Shunning categories, Carpenter had never

*Mary Chapin Carpenter*

considered herself a country singer, but she continued to place her albums on the country charts, even as her CDs moved in the folk-pop direction of her friends and collaborators ROSANNE CASH and Shawn Colvin. Even her two albums on the pop-rock imprint Zoe Records, 2007's *The Calling* and 2010's *The Age of Miracles*, landed in the country Top Ten. —*Geoffrey Himes*

## Jerry Carrigan
b. Florence, Alabama, September 13, 1943

Jerry Carrigan's R&B-inspired drumming was a mainstay of Nashville recordings from the 1960s to the 1990s. His work can be heard on WAYLON JENNINGS's "Only Daddy That'll Walk the Line," GEORGE JONES's "He Stopped Loving Her Today," JERRY REED's "When You're Hot, You're Hot," CHARLIE RICH's "Behind Closed Doors," and KENNY ROGERS's "The Gambler." Carrigan played on sessions with JOHNNY CASH, JOHN DENVER, DOLLY PARTON, JOHNNY PAYCHECK, ELVIS PRESLEY, CHARLEY PRIDE, and TAMMY WYNETTE, among many more.

Carrigan worked his first recording session at age thirteen as a member of Little Joe Allen and the Offbeats. Prior to arriving in Nashville in 1964, Carrigan helped lay the groundwork for the Muscle Shoals Sound, which garnered international attention and made the Alabama city—and Fame Studios—a recording Mecca for R&B, rock, and pop artists, including Arthur Alexander, Jimmy Hughes, Tommy Roe, and the Tams.

By the mid-1970s Carrigan had become a first-call, Nashville-based session drummer, not only for country sessions but for recording dates with Joan Baez, Al Hirt, Tom Jones, Henry Mancini, Johnny Mathis, and Andy Williams. From 1981 to 1990, Carrigan toured internationally backing JOHN DENVER. Carrigan remains active today both as a performer and a session musician. —*Jeremy Rush*

## Johnny Carroll
b. Cleburne, Texas, October 23, 1937; d. February 18, 1995

John Lewis Carrell was best known as a ROCKABILLY performer and for appearing in the 1956 rock & roll cult film *Rock, Baby, Rock It*. His group, the Moonlighters, later renamed the Hot Rocks, appeared on KCLE–Cleburne, Texas, as early as 1952. Three commercially unsuccessful but musically significant 1956 singles for DECCA RECORDS—"Hot Rock," "Wild, Wild Woman," and "Rock & Roll Ruby"—established his reputation and are considered rockabilly classics. (Legend has it that the label misspelled Carrell's last name, and he decided to stick with it.) Subsequent recordings on Phillips International, WARNER BROS., and other labels were less successful. In the early 1970s Carroll and Judy Lindsey formed the Judy & Johnny Band, performing in the North Texas area, and he released three solo albums between 1977 and 1985. He commanded a faithful following in Europe and later appeared there to enthusiastic audiences. —*William P. Davis*

## Fiddlin' John Carson
b. Fannin County, Georgia, March 23, ca. 1868; d. December 11, 1949

A pioneering country performer on record and radio in the genre's commercial infancy, John William Carson was the first folk-based southern artist to sell a large number of records,

spurring record companies and performers alike to record hill-billy music.

Carson spent his early life in northern Georgia working at several jobs—farming, railroading, horse jockeying, and moonshining. Early on, he distinguished himself as a fiddler and became acquainted with Bob Taylor, fiddler and three-time governor of Tennessee. Carson played in the campaigns of many politicians, including Georgia Senator Tom Watson and Georgia governors Eugene and Herman Talmadge.

In 1900 Carson moved to Atlanta to work in a cotton mill, but a 1913 strike pointed him toward fiddling and singing on the streets. Carson became well known in Atlanta, partly through performing for crowds gathered in connection with the case of Leo Frank, who was falsely accused of murdering Mary Phagan; Carson knew the young girl personally and composed at least four songs about her, one dealing with Frank's lynching.

Of the fiddlers who participated in a series of Georgia fiddlers' contests beginning in 1913, Carson received the most press coverage. His defeat by Lowe Stokes in one of these competitions inspired Stephen Vincent Benét's poem "The Mountain Whippoorwill." From September 9, 1922, Carson was a featured performer on station WSB; as such he was one of the earliest country artists on radio. On June 14, 1923, he cut his first sides in Atlanta for OKEH RECORDS A&R man RALPH PEER, marking Carson as one of the first country acts to be commercially recorded in the South. His first released single, pairing the minstrel song "The Little Old Log Cabin in the Lane" and a fiddle instrumental called "The Old Hen Cackled and the Rooster's Going to Crow," did not immediately impress Peer. But when OKeh's first pressing of 500 copies (issued without an assigned release number) quickly sold out, Peer and other recording executives recognized that hill-billy music could reach an untapped market. Thus country music was launched as a commercial genre.

Through the 1920s Carson continued to record for OKeh—solo, with his daughter Rosa Lee, and with a band called the

*Fiddlin' John Carson and daughter Moonshine Kate*

Virginia Reelers. Some recordings mixed "moonshiner comedy" with music, and in these Rosa Lee played the role of Moonshine Kate. Carson recorded 123 different songs and fiddle tunes, many of them more than once, thereby providing early texts of prominent folksongs. After a hiatus during the Great Depression, he made a final session for RCA Victor's Bluebird label in 1934. His primitive style was already out of favor, and thereafter Carson received little attention outside Georgia. There, however, he remained a well-known showman, comedian, and political campaigner, winning a sinecure as elevator operator in the state capitol. —*Gene Wiggins*

## Jenny Lou Carson
b. Decatur, Illinois, January 13, 1915; d. December 16, 1978

From membership in The Three Little Maids, a prominent 1930s sister act on Chicago radio station WLS, Lucille Overstake went on to individual fame as singing-songwriting cowgirl Jenny Lou Carson.

As teenagers, the Three Little Maids became regulars at WLS, on weekday programs and on the Saturday night *National Barn Dance* Evelyn Overstake's was the distinctive low voice on their records, but Lucille's guitar was their only accompaniment. Under the pseudonym Lucille Lee, she also recorded suggestive records with jazzy, swinging instrumentation provided by The Prairie Ramblers, identified on disc as the Sweet Violet Boys; her vocals on titles such as "Chiselin' Daddy" are among her finest.

Adopting the name Jenny Lou Carson in the early 1940s, she continued to record, but it's really her songs that are memorable. Her songwriting credits include such classics as "Jealous Heart," a #2 hit for Tex Ritter in 1944. Most famous is "Let Me Go Lover," a #1 hit for Hank Snow in 1954 and later recorded by Teresa Brewer and Patti Page. Eddy Arnold recorded many of Carson's songs, including the 1949 #1 hit "Don't Rob Another Man's Castle." Her World War II patriotic tunes were also numerous. —*Mary A. Bufwack*

## Martha Carson
b. Neon, Kentucky, May 19, 1921; d. December 16, 2004

Martha Carson, born Irene Ethel Amburgey, rose to prominence in the late 1940s and early 1950s as a powerful singer of uptempo country gospel songs. Born in the coal-mining country of eastern Kentucky, she was the middle sister of a trio who first sang on Lexington, Kentucky's WLAP as the Sunshine Sisters in 1938. Renfro Valley's John Lair invited Irene and sisters Bertha and Opal (later known as Jean Chapel) to join Atlanta's *WSB Barn Dance* as the Hoot Owl Holler Girls—inspired by his Coon Creek Girls (in which the Amburgeys substituted briefly). Lair also gave the Amburgeys quaint stage names as Hoot Owl Holler Girls: Minnie (Bertha), Marthie (Irene), and Mattie (Opal).

When her sisters married and departed, Marthie began blending her big, rawboned alto in harmony with James Roberts, son of Fiddlin' Doc Roberts. She played guitar, and he mandolin, and together Martha and James recorded country gospel for Capitol Records (as James & Martha Carson) and were known at WSB as the Barn Dance Sweethearts. They were married on June 8, 1939. After moving to WNOX in Knoxville, however, personal problems ended their marriage and their act in 1951. In the early 1950s Martha Carson reunited with her sisters to record for Capitol (as the Amber Sisters) and King Records.

*Martha Carson*

While with WNOX's *Mid-Day Merry-Go-Round* (where she toured and recorded for a time with Bill Carlisle and his band, Carson recorded what would become her signature song, "Satisfied," for Capitol on November 5, 1951. Although the rousing gospel number was not a chart hit, it proved immensely popular and became her springboard to the Grand Ole Opry, which she joined on April 26, 1952. In Nashville she met and wed promoter X. Cosse (1953), who encouraged her to leave Capitol and sign with RCA Records. Cosse also attempted to glamorize the statuesque redhead and steer her music toward big-band pop gospel, which she recorded with some success in the pop market. At about this time the couple moved to New York, and Carson increasingly played the northeastern supper-club circuit and appeared on TV series hosted by Steve Allen, Tennessee Ernie Ford, and Arthur Godfrey. She also recorded some proto–rock & roll material. After a few years playing Las Vegas supper clubs and California's *Town Hall Party* TV show and a brief return to the New York area, Carson opted for semiretirement and released only a few more records on the Decca, Cadence, and Sims labels.

A gifted writer, she composed "I Can't Wait," a #5, 1953 single for Faron Young; "I'm Gonna Walk and Talk with My Lord," a hit by pop stylist Johnnie Ray; and "I Can't Stand Up Alone," a successful cut for R&B singer Clyde McPhatter. Carson's dynamic performing style influenced Elvis Presley, Brenda Lee, and Connie Smith. —*Walt Trott*

## Carlene Carter
b. Madison, Tennessee, September 26, 1955

She's the daughter of Carl Smith and June Carter; her stepfather was Johnny Cash; her stepmother was Goldie Hill. Still, Rebecca Carlene Smith, better known as Carlene Carter, didn't take a predictable path to a country career. She had her own rock band, the Yellow Submarines, at twelve; studied music theory at Nashville's Belmont College (dropping out to record her first album); and cites LINDA RONSTADT as an early inspiration.

Nevertheless, Carter hadn't ignored country music. She took guitar lessons from grandmother Maybelle Carter and performed as a child during Cash's sets. She married aspiring country singer Jack Routh in 1974, and made her recording debut (billed as "Carlene Routh") guesting on Cash's 1974 album *The Junkie and the Juicehead Minus Me*. She also included country songs on her earliest albums.

Carter's self-titled debut album (WARNER BROS., 1977)—recorded in England with Graham Parker's group, the Rumour—had a decided rock flavor. But it was her third album, *Musical Shapes*, that marked her artistic breakthrough. Produced by her third husband, English musician Nick Lowe, this album (like its two predecessors) combined Carter originals with canny outside choices; Rockpile, a band led by Lowe and Dave Edmunds, backed her in the studio. Beginning in 1988, Howie Epstein, bassist for Tom Petty and the Heartbreakers, produced several of her albums.

Carter began recording for GIANT RECORDS in 1993; in 1996 the label released *Hindsight—20/20*, a career retrospective. Though her recordings were consistently interesting and her writing above average, her singles rarely charted well. "I Fell in Love," "Come on Back" (both 1990), and "Every Little Thing" (1993) fared best, all reaching #3.

In 1995 Carter and her father, Carl Smith, recorded a duet remake of Smith's 1954 hit "Loose Talk" for her *Little Acts of Treason* album. In 1996 she toured with fellow country star progeny LORRIE MORGAN and PAM TILLIS.

For a number of years Carter struggled with personal problems, including (all in 2003) the deaths of her longtime companion Epstein, her half-sister, Rosie Nix, and June and Johnny Cash. In 2008, tempered by these adversities, Carter released *Stronger* on Yep Roc Records. Produced by John McFee of the Doobie Brothers, the album showcases Carter's original songs. —*Todd Everett*

*Deana Carter*

## Deana Carter
b. Nashville, Tennessee, January 4, 1966

Deana Carter's 1996 debut album, the breezy *Did I Shave My Legs for This?*, was propelled to multiplatinum status by her #1 debut single, "Strawberry Wine." Written by MATRACA BERG and Gary Harrison, the steamy yet sweetly nostalgic song, with its mature theme of lost innocence, was a bit risky for country radio but proved wildly successful. Carter's follow-up single, "We Danced Anyway," also went to #1.

A fan of adult contemporary pop music, Carter was also influenced by her father, famed session guitarist Fred Carter Jr. She studied rehabilitation therapy in college and worked briefly as a physical therapist. In 1994, Carter recorded *Did I Shave My Legs for This?* for LIBERTY RECORDS, with JIMMY BOWEN producing; it was released in Europe though not in the United States.

SCOTT HENDRICKS, who replaced Bowen in 1995, hired producer Chris Farren to remake the album. When finally released under the same title for CAPITOL RECORDS in 1996, only two Bowen-produced tunes remained. "Strawberry Wine," re-recorded from the original album, won CMA's Single of the Year and Song of the Year awards in 1997. (That year, Carter also sang the haunting "Once Upon a December" in the animated film *Anastasia*.) A followup album, *Everything's Gonna Be Alright*, did not meet expectations, and she later left the label.

ARISTA RECORDS issued Carter's *I'm Just a Girl* in 2003 but dropped her soon afterward. Seeking greater artistic freedom, she released the self-produced *The Story of My Life* on Vanguard in 2005. Two years later Vanguard released *The Chain*, a tribute to her father. This album showcases Deana dueting with the likes of JESSI COLTER, GEORGE JONES, KRIS KRISTOFFERSON, WILLIE NELSON, DOLLY PARTON, and others. Fred Carter played on many of these artists' records, and his musicianship can also be heard throughout this collection. —*Stephen L. Betts*

## Wilf Carter
b. Guysboro, Nova Scotia, Canada, December 18, 1904; d. December 5, 1996

Wilf Carter, known to American fans as Montana Slim, is a legend in Canada, where his popularity once rivaled that of fellow Canadian HANK SNOW.

Carter's father, a Baptist minister, frowned on his son's singing ambitions, but, as Carter put it, he "couldn't stop me even

*Carlene Carter*

*Wilf Carter*

though he wore out more than a dozen slippers on the seat of my pants." Carter left his Nova Scotia home at an early age to seek adventure in Alberta and the Canadian West, where he became a cowboy and rodeo performer. There he also pursued his career as a musician and singer, broadcasting on radio station CFCN in Calgary, Alberta, in the early 1930s. He simultaneously launched a recording career with RCA VICTOR, a relationship that would last more than fifty years. Shortly thereafter, while performing on CBS Radio in New York, he adopted the name Montana Slim for his United States appearances. Like many country singers of his day, Carter was inspired by JIMMIE RODGERS. He became one of COWBOY MUSIC's most accomplished yodelers, incorporating a strong Swiss influence evident in his renditions of "Little Old Log Shack I Can Always Call My Home," "My Little Yoho Lady," and "Streamlined Yodel Song," among others. He created what he called "the three-in-one-yodel," which can be heard in recordings such as "My Swiss Moonlight Lullaby."

Carter's repertoire included many cowboy numbers, such as "Pete Knight's Last Ride," "Old Alberta Plains," and "The Fate of Old Strawberry Roan." He wrote more than 500 songs and enjoyed one of the longest careers in the business. In addition, he was an important figure in the transition from traditional cowboy music to the composed, romanticized songs of the popular singing cowboys.
—*Charlie Seemann*

## Carter Family

A. P. Carter b. Maces Spring, Virginia, December 15, 1891; d. November 7, 1960
Sara Dougherty Carter b. Flat Woods, Virginia, July 21, 1898; d. January 8, 1979
Maybelle Addington Carter b. Nickelsville, Virginia, May 10, 1909;
    d. October 23, 1978

Many regard the Carter Family as "the first family of country music." Not only were they key players at the famed BRISTOL sessions—where producer RALPH PEER first recorded them and produced JIMMIE RODGERS's first recordings—but they also were one of the genre's dominant acts during its first two decades as a commercial art form. Their recordings and radio broadcasts widely exposed a type of harmony singing used by country performers for years.

Maybelle Carter crafted the "Carter lick" on the guitar and watched it become one of country's best-known picking styles. In addition, the group popularized dozens of songs that became country standards; served as a platform for two of the most creative and talented women in the music, Sara and her cousin Maybelle; produced a slew of hit records between 1927 and 1941; and explored a wide variety of song genres, from blues and gospel to traditional BALLADS and nineteenth-century parlor songs. In A. P. the Carters had one of the most skilled song doctors in country music history. In spite of these advantages, however, the Carters never enjoyed spectacular financial success rivaling that of Jimmie Rodgers or GENE AUTRY. They never really crossed over to the huge mainstream audiences of network radio, Hollywood films, and big-time vaudeville. Instead, they kept returning to their beloved Clinch Valley, disgusted or puzzled by the show business world.

Alvin Pleasant Delaney Carter (A. P.) grew up on a farm in hilly Scott County, Virginia, near the Virginia-Tennessee border. His father was also a well-respected banjo player, and his mother sang folk ballads. An uncle, Flanders Bays, ran singing schools for local churches and taught A. P. to read the shape note SONG-BOOKS (many of which provided gospel material for the Carter repertoire). By 1915, after extensive traveling, A. P. returned home to start selling fruit trees; at about this time he met Sara Dougherty. (According to family legend she was sitting under a tree, playing her autoharp and singing "Engine 143.") After a courtship, the couple married on June 18, 1915. For the next several years they entertained informally in the neighborhood, often at churches. Unlike many older mountain singers, who often sang unaccompanied, the Carters backed their vocals with their guitar and autoharp; occasionally A. P. even played the fiddle. In early 1927 the pair auditioned for the BRUNSWICK RECORDS in nearby Norton; the company wanted to develop A. P. as a fiddler, but he believed his real talent was singing and passed on the offer.

Also in 1927, Sara and A. P. were joined by Sara's younger cousin Maybelle Addington. As a girl of twelve, Maybelle had begun playing the guitar, then a relatively new instrument in the mountains. Influenced by black guitarist Lesley Riddle, who also helped A. P. rework older songs and compose new ones, Addington came up with her own style of picking the melody on the bass strings while the fingers kept rhythm by downstroking the higher ones—the

*The Carter Family: (from left) Maybelle, A. P., and Sara*

"thumb brush" technique. In March 1926 Maybelle married A. P.'s brother Ezra and later joined the group as a guitarist and part-time singer. In late July 1927 they traveled to Bristol, which straddles the Tennessee-Virginia border, to make their first records for Victor Talking Machine Company producer Ralph Peer. Their first recording was "Bury Me Under the Weeping Willow" (Victor 21074), an old folk lyric that A. P. had modified. They would record many more songs for the company and its successor, RCA VICTOR, over the next eight years. These included best-sellers such as "The Storms Are on the Ocean" (1927), "Keep on the Sunny Side" (their theme song), "Wildwood Flower," "John Hardy Was a Desperate Little Man," "Anchored in Love" (all 1928), "I'm Thinking Tonight of My Blue Eyes," "Wabash Cannonball" (both 1929), and "Worried Man Blues" (1930). Their sparse but elegant arrangements helped make these songs country classics. All told, they recorded more than 300 sides for Victor, RCA Victor, and for the AMERICAN RECORD CORPORATION, the Sears custom label CONQUEROR RECORDS, and DECCA RECORDS. Sara and Maybelle typically did most of the singing and picking, with A. P. occasionally joining in on harmony. A. P. found their songs, arranged them, and booked the group's show dates.

During the height of their popularity, the Carters were often separated for various reasons. In 1931 Maybelle and her husband lived as far away as Washington, D.C., where Ezra's work took them; for a time A. P. was in Detroit working in auto plants. In early 1932 Sara left A. P., returning only for record sessions or important concerts.

In 1939 Sara remarried, to one of A. P.'s cousins. By the mid-1930s the Carters landed decent radio contracts, and late in the decade they found a lucrative job at the Texas BORDER RADIO station XERA in Del Rio; this station broadcast from across the Mexican border, using a much more powerful signal than American stations were allowed to use, and helped spread the Carter sound throughout the United States. By now the family act involved its children: Sara's daughter, Janette, and Maybelle's girls, Helen, June, and Anita. In 1943 the group broke up for good, even though A. P., Sara, and Maybelle were at the peak of their performing careers. A. P. returned to Maces Spring to open a general store, and Sara moved to California with her husband. By 1942 Maybelle started her own career featuring her daughters, working at Charlotte radio station WBT before moving to other radio outlets. They settled in Nashville in 1950.

In 1952 A. P. and Sara briefly reunited and made a series of records for the independent label Acme. In 1967 Sara and Maybelle made a reunion LP issued on COLUMBIA RECORDS. —*Charles Wolfe*

## Carter Sisters

Helen Myrl Carter b. Maces Spring, Virginia, September 12, 1927; d. June 2, 1998
Valerie June Carter b. Maces Spring, Virginia, June 23, 1929; d. May 15, 2003
Ina Anita Carter b. Maces Spring, Virginia, March 31, 1933; d. July 29, 1999

Helen, June, and Anita Carter were born to Maybelle Addington Carter and Ezra Carter. A member of the famous CARTER FAMILY—with her cousin Sara Dougherty Carter and brother-in-law A. P. Carter—Maybelle eventually brought her children into the group, thus beginning the sisters' influential careers as family members and as solo performers.

In 1938, while the Carter Family was broadcasting on BORDER RADIO in Texas, Anita became the first sister to join the act; June

and Helen followed in 1939. The trio of girls also recorded their own border radio shows.

After Sara left the group in 1943, Maybelle retired briefly, but she was soon back on the airwaves in Virginia at WRVA–Richmond, with her teenage girls as full-time musicians. Maybelle played guitar; Helen, the most capable instrumentalist, played accordion as well as guitar; June, the best comedienne and liveliest performer, was on autoharp; and Anita, the soprano and best singer, handled the bass (sometimes standing on her head to play). Their material was a combination of Carter Family songs and popular tunes of the day. By 1947 they were top stars at WRVA's *OLD DOMINION BARN DANCE*, and soon moved up to WNOX–Knoxville's *Tennessee Barn Dance*. CHET ATKINS joined the band there in 1949, later moving with them briefly to KWTO in Springfield, Missouri.

Mother Maybelle & the Carter Sisters became GRAND OLE OPRY members in 1950. Though they maintained an old-fashioned image, in 1956–57 they opened for ELVIS PRESLEY, and in 1961 they joined JOHNNY CASH's road show. Maybelle and her daughters found a new audience in the 1960s with the folk revival. Anita also performed as a solo act, and her mid-1960s albums of folksongs rivaled those of Joan Baez. (In 1951 Anita and HANK SNOW had enjoyed a twin-sided duet hit single pairing "Bluebird Island" with "Down the Trail of Achin' Hearts.")

In 1969 the Carters became regulars on Johnny Cash's ABC network TV series, for which June was especially well prepared, having studied at the Actors' Studio in New York and appeared on television in the 1950s. An excellent comic, she and HOMER & JETHRO had a Top Ten hit with "Baby It's Cold Outside" in 1949, and June and MERLE KILGORE had penned Cash's 1963 #1 tune "Ring of Fire." Her greatest recording success came with Cash on a series of strong, folk-country hit duets including the Grammy-winners "Jackson" (1967) and "If I Were a Carpenter" (1970). The couple married in 1968, and in 1975 June released her mountain-flavored LP *Appalachian Pride*, produced by Cash. The Carter Sisters continued to perform together, and in 1988, with June's daughter CARLENE CARTER, they recorded *Wildwood Flower* for MERCURY.

The multitalented June was also a touching and philosophical writer; her autobiography, *Among My Klediments*, appeared in 1979, and she published a memoir, *From the Heart*, in 1987. She displayed her acting talents as a cast member on the TV series *Dr. Quinn, Medicine Woman* and as Mrs. "Mama" Dewey Sr. in Robert Duvall's 1997 film *The Apostle*. Her album *Press On* (1999) won a Grammy, and her 2003 album *Wildwood Flower*—produced by her son, John Carter Cash—resulted in two additional Grammys. —*Mary A. Bufwack*

## Claude Casey

b. Enoree, South Carolina, September 13, 1912; d. June 24, 1999

Singer and bandleader Jesse Claude Casey rose to regional prominence in the Southeast from the mid-1930s to the mid-1950s. During the late 1930s he fronted the Pine State Playboys, specializing in love songs that earned him the monikers "The Lady Killer" and "The Boy with the Golden Voice." Casey made three sessions for RCA VICTOR's BLUEBIRD label with this group between 1938 and 1941 and then three sessions under his own name for the RCA Victor label during 1945–46.

In 1941 Casey began a twelve-year stint on Charlotte, North Carolina's 50,000-watt WBT. In addition to daytime radio shows such as the popular *Briarhopper Time*, Casey appeared on regional network originations, including *Carolina Hayride* and *The Dixie Jamboree*, both weekly barn dances. For the latter, he also served as writer and MC. Between 1946 and 1953 he made three sessions for MGM RECORDS and continued to write tunes on his own or with ACUFF-ROSE PUBLICATIONS songwriter–promotion man Mel Foree. Casey also had minor musical roles in several films, among them *Swing Your Partner* (1943), *Square Dance Jubilee* (1949), and *Buster and Billie* (1973).

Following his WBT years Casey moved on to radio and TV work in the Carolinas and Georgia, both in sales and on the air. In 1961 he began his own successful radio operation, WJES, in Johnston, South Carolina, where he spent his last years. —*John W. Rumble*

# Johnny Cash
b. Kingsland, Arkansas, February 26, 1932; d. September 12, 2003

Beginning with his mid-1950s recordings for SUN RECORDS, John R. "Johnny" Cash established an international profile as an ambassador of American roots music. From humble beginnings he reached superstar status by the late-1960s and continued to hew his own artistic path into the twenty-first century. With extensive hit singles and albums on the country and pop charts, he helped broaden country's scope—and its audience—by boldly exploring diverse lyric themes and song types. A creative songwriter and an astute selector of others' material, he mined folk and rock sources for his huge repertory, and his music consistently appealed to both country and rock fans. Cash was honored for his enormous contributions through election to THE COUNTRY MUSIC HALL OF FAME (1980) and the Rock and Roll Hall of Fame (1992) and as a recipient of the Grammy Legend Award (1991). Surviving personal and professional problems, he reached a new generation of listeners after 1994 and was hailed as an American cultural hero by the time he died.

Cash grew up in a government resettlement colony for struggling farmers in Dyess, Arkansas, where he worked the cotton fields with his family and absorbed gospel music in church. The tragic death of his older brother Jack at age fourteen dramatically affected John's life and often colored the tone of his music.

Listening to a battery-operated radio, Cash heard local country shows from Memphis, the CARTER FAMILY on BORDER RADIO, and a host of GRAND OLE OPRY singers. He gained performing experience in high school assemblies and on KLCN in Blytheville, Arkansas. After working briefly in Pontiac, Michigan, he joined the U.S. Air Force and served in Germany for four years, during which he wrote the future Sun Records classics "Folsom Prison Blues" and "Hey Porter." In 1954, his military stint over, Cash settled in Memphis, married Vivian Liberto, and became an appliance salesman. Seeking a musical career, he teamed with mechanics Luther Perkins (electric guitar) and Marshall Grant (upright bass) to perform gospel songs in churches and on local radio.

In the wake of ELVIS PRESLEY's 1954 breakthrough at Sun, Cash and his minimalist band auditioned for Sun owner-producer SAM PHILLIPS. Beginning with the double-sided hit "Cry! Cry! Cry!" b/w "Hey Porter" in 1955, Cash became one of the label's most promising young artists. Country hits "I Walk the Line," "Ballad of a Teenage Queen," and "Guess Things Happen That Way" crossed over to the pop charts and made Cash a dominant new country singer of 1956–58. He joined the Grand Ole Opry on July 7, 1956. Within a few years he left for California to pursue an acting career—without much success, initially. The style Cash set

early on—his deep baritone voice fronting a stark rhythmic background punctuated by Perkins's simple but effective lead and fill parts—changed little over the years. In fact, the addition of drummer W. S. Holland in 1960 reinforced the singer's trademark rhythm-based sound.

Cash left Sun and signed with COLUMBIA RECORDS in mid-1958. Hit singles such as "Don't Take Your Guns to Town" (1959) and "Ring of Fire" (1963) followed, but increasingly Cash focused on concept albums, including *Ride This Train* (1960); *Blood, Sweat and Tears* (1962), celebrating the American working man; *Bitter Tears: Ballads of the American Indian* (1964); and *Ballads of the True West* (1965). Producer DON LAW encouraged Cash to connect with the burgeoning folk music audience of the day, and the adventuresome artist did just that, recording cowboy songs, gospel material, songs of social conscience and protest, and adaptations of folk songs. Appearing at the 1964 NEWPORT FOLK FESTIVAL, where he began a friendship with BOB DYLAN, Cash continued to widen his appeal and deepen his creative wellsprings. His efforts did not always please music industry gatekeepers, however. In 1964, when his recording of "The Ballad of Ira Hayes" (about the tragic end suffered by a Native American World War II hero) initially received what Cash considered a lukewarm reception from radio, he took out a full-page ad in *Billboard* demanding of programmers, "Where are your guts?"

During the 1960s, Cash's amphetamine addiction worsened, straining his relationships with his four daughters and wrecking his marriage. In 1965 he was arrested for carrying a large quantity of pills across the Mexican border at El Paso. But with the help of June Carter (of the CARTER SISTERS), with whom he recorded several hit duets and whom he married on March 1, 1968, he controlled his addiction for a time, though it would resurface periodically.

*Johnny Cash*

On January 13, 1968, Cash recorded his masterful live album at California's Folsom Prison. The project yielded a new, chart-topping version of "Folsom Prison Blues," a #4 country hit for him in 1956. This album and his 1969 live recording at San Quentin Prison pushed his career to new heights. Taken from the San Quentin album, "A Boy Named Sue" (#1 country, #2 pop) became his biggest-selling single and 1969's CMA Single of the Year, while *Johnny Cash at San Quentin* won CMA Album of the Year honors. The CMA also named Cash its 1969 Male Vocalist of the Year and Entertainer of the Year.

From 1969 through 1971 Cash hosted a prime-time ABC-TV variety program that showcased his status as a national icon while featuring an eclectic mix of guest performers from various genres. A live cut from this show, "Sunday Morning Coming Down" (written by KRIS KRISTOFFERSON), became a #1 country hit in 1971. Cash recorded and broadcast the work of new songwriters drawn to country from folk and rock music backgrounds. His popularity helped his younger brother Tommy (b. 1940) establish a singing career that boasted several hits, including "Six White Horses" (1969).

Into the 1970s and beyond, Cash continued to make U.S. and overseas tours with his impressive road troupe—which embraced at various times Mother Maybelle Carter (CARTER FAMILY), the Carter Sisters, and THE STATLER BROTHERS. He also continued to pursue acting. His credits included the film *Gospel Road: A Story of Jesus* (1973), featuring June as Mary Magdalene. (Deeply religious, Cash published *Man in White: A Novel About the Apostle Paul* in 1986.) Cash appeared in *A Gunfight* (1971), starring Kirk Douglas; the made-for-TV movies *Thaddeus Rose and Eddie* (1978, with June) and *The Pride of Jesse Hallam* (1981); and as guest star in several TV series.

As the years progressed, Cash's hits grew more infrequent. But with old friends WAYLON JENNINGS, WILLIE NELSON, and Kris Kristofferson, Cash topped the charts with the title cut of the 1985 album *Highwayman*, leading to a series of concert tours.

After leaving Columbia in 1986, Cash recorded for MERCURY until 1992, with minimal success. His recording career seemed over until producer Rick Rubin's American label released the widely praised *American Recordings* (1994), a Grammy-winning album Cash made with only his acoustic guitar for accompaniment. The thirteen songs—some his own, some adaptations of folk pieces, and some from songwriters such as Tom Waits, Nick Lowe, and Loudon Wainwright—included searing explorations of loss and sorrow. His 1996 American album *Unchained*, featuring Cash backed by Tom Petty & the Heartbreakers and a similar mix of material, won a Grammy for Best Country Album. In 1997 (with Patrick Carr) Cash also published *Cash: The Autobiography*, adding to the experiences he shared in his 1975 autobiography *Man in Black*.

The year 1997 brought tragedy as well as triumph, for Cash's health declined. Eventually diagnosed with degenerative nerve disease associated with diabetes, he was hospitalized in 1998 with acute pneumonia. Understandably, his albums *American III: Solitary Man* (2000) and *American IV: The Man Comes Around* (2002), both of which resulted in Grammys for Cash, were darker than his earlier American releases. His Grammy-winning video of the Nine Inch Nails song "Hurt," a song Cash recorded for *American IV*, revealed a man reviewing his own shortcomings and facing his own mortality.

Cash continued to win critical acclaim and popular acceptance following his death in 2003. A hugely successful 2005 film, *Walk the Line*, portrayed Cash's life, focusing on his youth and his relationship with June; the movie sparked even broader interest in his work and legend. *American V: A Hundred Highways* appeared posthumously on July 4, 2006—a date particularly appropriate for an artist so quintessentially American—and the album quickly debuted at #1 in *Billboard*'s Top 200 album chart.

*American VI: Ain't No Grave* was released in 2010. —*Fred Danker*

# Rosanne Cash
b. Memphis, Tennessee, May 24, 1955

The daughter of American music icon JOHNNY CASH, singer-songwriter Rosanne Cash faced the unenviable challenge of forging an artistic identity in the shadow of her larger-than-life father. That she has done so with candor, grace, and commercial success—including eleven #1 country singles—makes her musical legacy all the more impressive.

Cash's parents divorced while she was still a young girl; her mother, Vivian Liberto, raised her in Southern California. After high school, Cash moved to Nashville and began working with her father's show—primarily in the wardrobe department but occasionally performing as well. She moved to London in 1976 but soon returned to the United States to study acting. Her self-titled debut album for the German Ariola label was never released in the United States, but it helped secure Cash a COLUMBIA recording contract. At this time she began a long-term musical and romantic partnership with RODNEY CROWELL, whom she married in 1979.

Produced by Crowell, Cash's debut Columbia album, *Right or Wrong*, featured three Top Forty singles. But it was her second Columbia album, *Seven Year Ache*, that broke through commercially,

*Rosanne Cash*

yielding the #1 singles "Seven Year Ache" (1981), "My Baby Thinks He's a Train" (1981), and "Blue Moon with Heartache" (1981–82). After hastily recording *Somewhere in the Stars* during her first pregnancy, Cash followed with the new-wave-influenced *Rhythm & Romance,* which earned her two more #1 hits and a 1985 Grammy for Best Country Vocal Performance, Female. She then returned to her country roots with *King's Record Shop,* which charted four more #1 hits, among them covers of JOHN HIATT's "The Way We Make a Broken Heart" (1987) and her father's "Tennessee Flat Top Box" (1987–88). A newly recorded cover of the Beatles' "I Don't Want to Spoil the Party" also topped the charts.

Cash's music and personal life then took a dramatic turn, with the dark, introspective *Interiors* (1990) chronicling her painful divorce from Crowell in 1992. Although it sold relatively poorly, the album was one of the most affecting and ambitious of her career.

In 1995, now living in Manhattan, Cash married producer-songwriter-guitarist John Leventhal. Signing with CAPITOL RECORDS, she released the minimalist *10 Song Demo* in 1996. That year, she published *Bodies of Water,* a short-story collection. In 1998 Cash and Leventhal began another album, but vocal problems kept her from singing for more than two years. Meanwhile, she wrote a children's book and edited a collection of short fiction by songwriters. Her voice recovered, she released *Rules of Travel* (2003), featuring a moving duet with her father. *Black Cadillac* (2006) reflected the loss of her father, mother, and stepmother, June Carter (all in 2003). Author of a regular *New York Times* column on songwriting, Cash released *The List* on Manhattan Records in 2009. The album is based on a list of essential country songs her father made for her when she was eighteen. Her well-received memoir, *Composed,* was published by Penguin Group in August 2010. —*Bill Friskics-Warren*

## Pete Cassell
b. Cobb County, near Atlanta, Georgia, August 27, 1917; d. July 29, 1954

A popular radio performer of the 1940s and early 1950s, Peter Webster Cassell delivered soulful interpretations of "Where the Old Red River Flows," "Freight Train Blues," "One Step More," and other country standards. Because of his smooth, expressive voice, critics have compared Cassell favorably with JIM REEVES, GEORGE MORGAN, RED FOLEY, and EDDY ARNOLD.

When he was three days old, Cassell was robbed of his sight when a physician erred in applying medicine to his eyes. As a result, he attended special schools, including the Georgia Academy for the Blind in Macon. Cassell showed an early interest in music, especially country and gospel, and by the time he entered high school he had learned to play piano and guitar. Except for some lessons at the Academy for the Blind, he was self-taught.

In 1937 Cassell made his professional debut on radio station WDOD in Chattanooga, Tennessee. He soon returned to Atlanta to work at WAGA and WSB, where he reigned as one of the most popular artists on the *WSB Barn Dance* during the 1940s. He later worked on WWVA in Wheeling, West Virginia (where he hosted his own show as well as appearing on the WWVA JAMBOREE); on WARL in Arlington, Virginia; and on CONNIE B. GAY's *Town & Country Time* radio and TV programs.

Cassell recorded some twenty-five sides on the DECCA, Majestic, and MERCURY labels. —*Wayne W. Daniel*

## Castle Recording Studio
established 1946; ended 1955

As Nashville's first major professional recording service, the Castle Recording Studio was crucial to Nashville's growth as a recording center during the decade after World War II. Officially named Castle Recording Laboratories, the operation was organized shortly after war's end by three WSM radio engineers: Aaron Shelton, Carl Jenkins, and George Reynolds. Although Castle took its name from the WSM logo "Air Castle of the South," WSM executives tolerated rather than encouraged the enterprise.

At first the three entrepreneurs used WSM studios in the old National Life Building at Seventh Avenue North and Union Street, with signals transferred via telephone line to their lathe at WSM's backup transmitter site at Fifteenth Avenue South and Weston. As their workload increased, the Castle engineers rented space on the mezzanine level of the Tulane Hotel on Church Street between Seventh and Eighth Avenue North. Equipment eventually included a mixing board the engineers designed themselves, an up-to-date Scully lathe, and Ampex tape recorders.

Castle cut master discs for all major labels except RCA RECORDS, which had an exclusive contract with the National Association of Broadcast Employees and Technicians (NABET) to provide engineers. Independent labels using Castle's services included Cincinnati's KING RECORDS and Nashville's own DOT and BULLET labels. In addition, Castle recorded radio shows for regional networks (some issued on its own label) and local advertising jingles. Castle-recorded hits such as RED FOLEY's crossover smash "Chattanoogie Shoeshine Boy" and HANK WILLIAMS's "You Win Again" helped put Nashville on the map as a hit-making music hub. From a technical standpoint, Castle engineers helped chart new territory by putting more "level" on their recordings (i.e., cutting grooves more deeply) than most New York or Chicago engineers, thus giving the resulting commercial discs a hotter, more exciting sound.

By 1956, when the Tulane Hotel was razed, Castle had closed because of a WSM policy change that forced employees to choose between sideline enterprises and continuing employment with WSM. The Castle engineers had established twenty-five-year service records and elected to stay with WSM's radio and television operations, but by then they had helped Nashville earn its MUSIC CITY moniker in the entertainment trade press. —*John W. Rumble*

## Cedarwood Publishing Company
established in Nashville, Tennessee, 1953

Cedarwood Publishing Company was a top country music publisher of its day and one of the first music publishers to locate on MUSIC ROW. WSM talent booking manager JIM DENNY and country artist WEBB PIERCE each put up $200 to start Cedarwood in 1953. Pierce was one of country music's hottest artists, and the firm quickly thrived on the strength of his hits.

Cedarwood soon became the focus of controversy. Denny was promoting his own shows on the side, and it was rumored that as WSM's booking department boss he favored GRAND OLE OPRY acts who recorded Cedarwood songs. When WSM, owner of the Opry, asked Denny and other WSM staffers to drop their involvement in outside businesses, Denny left WSM in September 1956.

Immediately forming the Jim Denny Artist Bureau, he secured agreements to book many of the acts he had represented at the

Opry. During his years at the Opry, Denny had built solid relationships with performers, TV producers, DJs, and record label A&R men, and those connections paid off. Both Cedarwood and the Denny Artist Bureau flourished.

Denny's strong ties to talent fueled the publishing company's success. His bureau's contract to provide acts for the PHILIP MORRIS COUNTRY MUSIC SHOW (1957–58) attracted even more country performers to Denny. The relationship was mutually beneficial: Denny offered TV and concert exposure as well as strong record label connections; in return, acts often recorded songs Denny published. Stars who recorded many Cedarwood tunes included Webb Pierce, CARL SMITH (who also shared music publishing interests with Denny), HANK SNOW, KITTY WELLS, and dozens of others.

Through the years Cedarwood staff writers MEL TILLIS, CARL PERKINS, WAYNE WALKER, Danny Dill (ANNIE LOU & DANNY DILL), MARIJOHN WILKIN, JOHN D. LOUDERMILK, and others wrote hits such as "Detroit City," "Ruby, Don't Take Your Love to Town," "The Long Black Veil," "Tobacco Road," "Teddy Bear," "I Ain't Never," "Waterloo," "Are You Sincere," "Daddy Sang Bass," and many more. At the time of Denny's death in August 1963, Cedarwood boasted a catalog of more than 2,200 songs and a staff of approximately a dozen songwriters. Denny's sons Bill and John subsequently managed Cedarwood until Mel Tillis purchased the company in 1983 for nearly $3 million. Tillis later sold the song catalog to PolyGram Music. Following PolyGram's merger with MCA–affiliated publishing interests in the newly named Universal Music Group in 1998, PolyGram Music became part of Universal Music Publishing. —*Al Cunniff*

## Central Songs
established ca. 1946; sold to Capitol Records, 1969

An important country publishing firm, Central Songs was active from the late 1940s into the mid-1960s. The company was formed as Century Songs in Chicago in about 1946, organized by LEE GILLETTE, KEN NELSON, and CLIFFIE STONE. Gillette, who had played in pop bands with Nelson, was then head of country recording for CAPITOL RECORDS, while Stone played bass on the label's West Coast sessions and helped produce rising Capitol talent such as MERLE TRAVIS. Nelson assumed Gillette's role in 1951 when Gillette took over Capitol's transcription department. By this point Central shifted headquarters to Los Angeles and changed its name to "Central" to avoid conflict with other "Century" music firms.

While Nelson handled accounting behind the scenes, Stone served as president, signing writers and placing songs with record producers—including Nelson, of course. Central's first country chartmakers were "The Gods Were Angry with Me" (1948–49), penned by "Foreman" Bill and Ruth "Roma" Mackintosh, and several 1949–50 hits written and recorded by Capitol powerhouse TENNESSEE ERNIE FORD with assistance from Stone. During the 1950s the company published hits composed by TOMMY COLLINS ("You Better Not Do That"), Jack Rhodes ("Conscience I'm Guilty"), Audrey and JOE ALLISON ("He'll Have to Go"), and Hazel Houser ("My Baby's Gone"). By 1959 Central also was publishing songs composed by Capitol star BUCK OWENS, who wrote and recorded hits such as "Under Your Spell Again" (with Rhodes) and "Foolin' Around" (with HARLAN HOWARD) over the next few years. During Central's early 1960s heyday, achieved under

Joe Allison's leadership, singer-songwriter NED MILLER, among others, supplied additional hit tunes.

Gradually, however, the proliferation of new publishers eroded Central's position; many of these—including Owens's Blue Book Music—were artist owned, making it increasingly difficult to secure recordings and thus attract writers. What's more, Gillette and Nelson were ready to retire, while Stone had attractive—and ultimately successful—options in publishing. In 1969 the partners sold Central to Capitol Records. Through this corporate connection, the catalog today resides with the international conglomerate EMI. —*John W. Rumble*

## Curly Chalker
b. Enterprise, Alabama, October 22, 1931; d. April 30, 1998

The sophisticated chordal steel guitar style of Curly Chalker graced many enduring country records of the 1950s, 1960s, and 1970s and added a touch of class to the bucolic set of HEE HAW. The youngest of ten children, Harold Lee Chalker was raised on an Alabama farm. Beginning with an Electromuse lap steel, he emulated notable steel players of the 1940s: JERRY BYRD, ROY WIGGINS, NOEL BOGGS, and JOAQUIN MURPHEY.

Chalker started working in Cincinnati clubs at age thirteen. By 1950 he was in Paris, Texas, where he soon began touring with LEFTY FRIZZELL. The instrumentalist made his recording debut on Frizzell's "Always Late (With Your Kisses)" (1951), followed by further recordings with Frizzell and with HANK THOMPSON, whose "Wild Side of Life" (1952) featured Chalker and whose band Chalker joined.

After an army stint (1952–54), Chalker worked with Bill Wimberley's band in Wichita, Kansas, and on the OZARK JUBILEE before playing Las Vegas venues with groups led by WADE RAY and HANK PENNY (1959–62). Chalker rejoined Thompson in 1963 and then moved in the late 1960s to Nashville. There he distinguished himself on sessions with DON GIBSON, Sue Thompson, CARL SMITH, WEBB PIERCE, and RAY PRICE, for whom he played "For the Good Times" (1970). In 1973 Chalker became the staff PEDAL STEEL GUITAR player with *Hee Haw*.

Accomplished on trumpet and jazz guitar, Chalker executed jazz-based bar-quivering techniques, fast and fluid chordal runs, and sudden volume changes that sometimes surprised even the artists he accompanied. Once, while entertaining at a truck drivers' convention, DICK CURLESS missed his cue to sing after a jaw-dropping Chalker solo. "Folks," Curless said, temporarily stopping the performance, "I'm really sorry, but Curly Chalker just played such a hell of a solo I plumb forgot what I was doing." Chalker was inducted into the Steel Guitar Hall of Fame in 1985. —*Mark Humphrey*

## Challenge Records
established Los Angeles, California, March 1957; ended 1976

Challenge Records enjoyed substantial success from the late 1950s into the early 1970s. The independent label was founded in Los Angeles in March 1957 by GENE AUTRY and Joe Johnson, a recording entrepreneur and music publisher then managing Golden West Melodies and Western Music, Autry's principal publishing firms. Difficulties with major labels in securing recordings of their copyrights led the partners to establish their own record operation, although profits from pop star Johnnie Ray's COLUMBIA rendition of "Just Walking in the Rain" did provide the capital to start Challenge.

Originally, Autry and Johnson had called the label "Champion," after the name of Autry's famous horse, but DECCA RECORDS already owned the title. Thus, Johnson said, they named the company "Challenge," issuing a challenge to those who denied the partners permission to use their first choice.

Early on, Challenge's country artists included WYNN STEWART (chart years: 1959–64) and JAN HOWARD (1960). JEANNIE SEELY, JUSTIN TUBB, BOBBY BARE, Johnny and Jonie Mosby, and Bobby Austin recorded briefly for the label but did not chart. Challenge also leased AL DOWNING's "Down on the Farm," now a ROCKA-BILLY cult classic, from a small Texas label. In the beginning, though, Challenge made a bigger mark with pop acts such as the Champs and JERRY WALLACE.

Autry soon sold his 56 percent controlling interest in Challenge to Johnson and sales manager John Thompson. Johnson moved Challenge's headquarters to Nashville in 1972. By this time he had secured major-label distribution through the Decca label (soon folded into MCA RECORDS) and turned out chart-making records with artists such as Jerry Wallace (now primarily a country act), Marie Owens, GEORGE MORGAN, CARL BELEW, and BONNIE GUITAR. By 1976, however, personal financial problems plagued Johnson, and he eventually struck an administration deal with TREE PUBLISHING COMPANY (now Sony/ATV Tree), which today leases Challenge masters to various labels. —*John W. Rumble*

## Lightnin' Chance

b. Como, Mississippi, December 21, 1925; d. April 11, 2005

Onetime GRAND OLE OPRY staff musician Floyd Taylor Chance was a stand-up acoustic bass player on the road and in the recording studio for artists ranging from MARTHA CARSON to MARTY ROBBINS. His specialty was providing a foundation for harmony while adding tonal color. "I played with tone as much as possible," Chance said. "Back then there were no electrified amplifiers [for basses], but you could achieve varied effects, offering a greater variety of tones. . . . It's all in the wrist movement, really."

Chance's father, Jody, a Dixieland banjoist, first gave him a four-string Martin guitar. In school Chance played clarinet, saxophone, and bass horn. While making touchdowns on the football field he earned the nickname "Lightnin'."

During World War II, the U.S. Naval Conservatory provided Chance with advanced musical training while he served with the Fourth Fleet Band, entertaining the troops in battle zones. Discharged, Chance moved to Memphis, playing in EDDIE HILL's band (1947–51) and performing on WMPS radio and WMC-TV. Chance's first recordings were in SAM PHILLIPS's Memphis studio, which later housed SUN RECORDS.

In Nashville, Chance played on HANK WILLIAMS's last session (September 23, 1952), which yielded three #1 records of 1953: "Your Cheatin' Heart," "Kaw-Liga," and "Take These Chains from My Heart." Other million sellers reflecting Chance's bass work include CONWAY TWITTY's "It's Only Make Believe," FARON YOUNG's "Hello Walls," and THE EVERLY BROTHERS' rockabilly classics "Bye Bye Love" and "Bird Dog."

Noting the JORDANAIRES' vocal chart relating to the tones of the diatonic scale, Chance, CHARLIE MCCOY, and other players helped adapt it so that studio instrumentalists who did not read music might follow along. It became the Nashville Number System.

In 1952 Chance joined an Opry touring contingent that played New York City's Astor Hotel. During the 1960s he opened the Nashville office for Chappell Music publishing and worked on Nashville's WLAC-TV. He later played on RALPH EMERY's early-morning WSM-TV program until 1988, when Chance retired. —*Walt Trott*

## Blake Chancey

b. Nashville, Tennessee, September 11, 1962

Blake Allen Chancey is an award-winning record producer, former record label executive, and current Chief Creative Officer and Partner of RPM Music Group. The son of accomplished record producer and label executive Ron Chancey, the younger Chancey soon became a sound engineer. After completing the music business program at Middle Tennessee State University, Chancey furthered his career by joining the COMBINE MUSIC PUBLISHING staff under the leadership of legendary publisher BOB BECKHAM.

Chancey came into his own in the early 1990s as an A&R executive and record producer at SONY MUSIC, where he signed DIXIE CHICKS, MONTGOMERY GENTRY, and MARY CHAPIN CARPENTER. During his tenure at Sony he produced albums by BILLY RAY CYRUS, Dixie Chicks, WAYLON JENNINGS, LITTLE BIG TOWN, and many other acts. The critical and commercial success of the Dixie Chicks albums *Wide Open Spaces* and *Fly*, both of which won Grammys for Best Country Album, made him especially visible. In addition, Chancey received two CMA awards and two ACM awards for his production work on these multiplatinum collections.

Chancey has remained an in-demand record producer and publisher, producing such artists as Montgomery Gentry, GRETCHEN WILSON, the Lost Trailers, KELLIE PICKLER, and Jeff Bates. —*LeAnn Bennett*

## Jean Chapel

b. Neon, Kentucky, March 6, 1925; d. August 12, 1995

During her long, colorful career, Opal Jean "Jean Chapel" Amburgey performed in a variety of styles under several billings while leaving a significant songwriting legacy. With sisters Bertha and Irene, Chapel performed on Kentucky and West Virginia radio as the Sunshine Sisters beginning in 1938. In 1940 they joined the COON CREEK GIRLS at Kentucky's *RENFRO VALLEY BARN DANCE*. Chapel played banjo, fiddle, bass, and guitar.

At Atlanta's *WSB Barn Dance* in the 1940s they were dubbed the Hoot Owl Holler Girls—Mattie (Jean), Marthie (Irene), and Minnie" (Bertha). Irene married James Roberts and they became "James & MARTHA CARSON."

Jean married Floyd "Salty" Holmes, of PRAIRIE RAMBLERS fame. They were billed as Salty and Mattie on MGM RECORDS, and on WLW's televised *MIDWESTERN HAYRIDE* in Cincinnati, WLS's *NATIONAL BARN DANCE* in Chicago, and the GRAND OLE OPRY's earliest syndicated TV programs. During this period she wrote and sang "Don't Sell Daddy Any More Whiskey" (1950), best known via MOLLY O'DAY's recording of it. By 1954 Chapel had penned more than 300 songs, gaining recordings by Rosemary Clooney, Milton Berle, and WILMA LEE COOPER, among others.

In the early 1950s the sister trio reunited to record for CAPITOL (as the Amber Sisters) and KING. As a solo, Chapel was "Opal Jean" on HICKORY RECORDS. She became "Jean Chapel" in 1956 when she signed with SUN to sing ROCKABILLY. Next on RCA VICTOR, she toured in Alan Freed's famed rock & roll road show.

In the 1960s Chapel recorded for the Smash, London, and CHALLENGE labels and continued songwriting. Artists who recorded her songs included GEORGE JONES, HANK SNOW, PATSY CLINE, RED FOLEY, and SONNY JAMES. EDDY ARNOLD hit #1 with Chapel's "Lonely Again" in 1967, the same year "Lay Some Happiness on Me" became a pop hit for Dean Martin. "To Get to You," recorded by JERRY WALLACE, was nominated for 1972's CMA Song of the Year.

In the 1970s and 1980s Chapel entertained as "Opal Jean Cologne." Daughter Lana Chapel also became a Nashville singer-songwriter, as did younger brother Don Chapel, TAMMY WYNETTE's second husband. —*Robert K. Oermann*

## Leon Chappelear
b. Tyler, Texas, August 1, 1909; d. October 22, 1962

An associate of JIMMIE DAVIS for many years, guitarist-vocalist-bandleader Horace Leon Chappelear began a two-decade recording career in 1932 as a soloist of country and cowboy fare for Starr Piano's Champion label. Along with THE SHELTON BROTHERS, Chappelear was part of the Lone Star Cowboys, a Texas string trio that recorded the classics "Just Because" and "Deep Elm Blues" for RCA VICTOR in 1933. He supplied excellent blues guitar backings for several Davis recordings that year as well.

After Davis established himself as a star at DECCA RECORDS in the mid-1930s, he brought Chappelear to the label. Calling his band Leon's Lone Star Cowboys, Chappelear recorded several dozen WESTERN SWING sides from 1935 through 1937. After World War II, Davis also helped secure Chappelear a CAPITOL RECORDS contract. Under the name Leon Chappel, Chappelear recorded several memorable HONKY-TONK numbers for the label, including "True Blue Poppa," later revived by fellow Texan FRANKIE MILLER on STARDAY RECORDS. In 1962 Chappelear ended his life by gunshot. —*Kevin Coffey*

## Ray Charles
b. Albany, Georgia, September 23, 1930; d. June 11, 2004

Best known for gospel-driven R&B classics such as "What'd I Say" and "Georgia on My Mind" and highly respected for a series of jazz piano recordings, Ray Charles Robinson also had a major impact on country music. His 1962 album *Modern Sounds in Country and Western Music* was a landmark recording, bringing untold numbers of new fans to country. He repeatedly worked country into the unique mix of R&B, gospel, and jazz that made him one of the most important figures in American popular music.

Completely blind since age seven, Charles first heard country as a child in Greenville, Florida, by way of GRAND OLE OPRY broadcasts. "I felt it was the closest music, really, to the blues—they'd make them steel guitars cry and whine, and it really attracted me," he later recalled. Early in his performing career he played piano in a country band, and among the now legendary R&B recordings he made for the ATLANTIC label was a version of HANK SNOW's "I'm Movin' On" (1959).

*Ray Charles*

After he left Atlantic to accept a lucrative offer from ABC-Paramount, Charles struck gold. In 1960, "Georgia on My Mind" became his first #1 pop hit; then, after a couple more jazz outings, he released the pivotal *Modern Sounds in Country and Western Music*. The album melded his swinging, big-band R&B sound with classic country tunes such as "You Win Again," "Half as Much," and "Hey, Good Lookin'" (all associated with HANK WILLIAMS), and DON GIBSON's "I Can't Stop Loving You."

Although Charles thought of *Modern Sounds* as a concept album and didn't intend it to produce any singles, his hand was forced when the actor Tab Hunter covered "I Can't Stop Loving You." Charles agreed to release the song as a single, and it rocketed to #1 on the pop charts, selling more than a million copies. After another hit ("You Don't Know Me") from the album, Charles cut *Modern Sounds in Country and Western Music, Volume Two*, which included the Top Ten hits "You Are My Sunshine" and "Take These Chains from My Heart."

Although he'd proven his point—that good music is good music and that country music need not be confined to country audiences—Charles didn't quit recording country material; later hits included "Crying Time" in 1966 and "Don't Change on Me," from the album *Love Country Style*, in 1971. Through much of the 1980s Charles recorded country for the COLUMBIA label, including *Friendship* (1984), an album of duets with such stars as HANK WILLIAMS JR., MERLE HAGGARD, and WILLIE NELSON. His duet with Nelson on "Seven Spanish Angels" hit #1 on the country charts. *Ray*, a 2004 autobiographical film, starred Jamie Foxx, whose performance won him the Academy Award for Best Actor. During 2006–07, the COUNTRY MUSIC HALL OF FAME AND MUSEUM presented a biographical exhibition on Charles's remarkable career, with special emphasis on his contributions to country music's growth and cultural stature. —*Ben Fong-Torres*

## Hugh Cherry

b. Louisville, Kentucky, October 7, 1922; d. October 15, 1998

One of Nashville's first postwar hillbilly disc jockeys, Hugh Cherry perfected a smooth, straightforward presentation and mood-driven programming style that made him a major figure in country music. As a child he saw performances by both JIMMIE RODGERS and the CARTER FAMILY; as a soldier, he was among the forces that liberated Dachau. In 1946 Cherry began broadcasting at tiny WKAY in Glasgow, Kentucky, and then moved to WKLO in Louisville. PEE WEE KING befriended and mentored him, offering advice and access to a cache of country music SONGBOOKS and clippings from periodicals.

Arriving at Nashville's WKDA in 1949, the restless, intense Cherry developed an urbane style that established him as a popular radio personality who showcased artists such as HANK WILLIAMS, UNCLE DAVE MACON, and GRANDPA JONES. At Memphis's WMPS in 1950–51, he won fervent listeners, including JOHNNY CASH, CARL PERKINS, and ELVIS PRESLEY. In 1951 he returned to Nashville to broadcast over WMAK. There he played important roles in convincing GRAND OLE OPRY officials to hire FARON YOUNG and landing Pat Boone his first recording contract. During 1955–57 Cherry worked at Cincinnati superstation WLW.

Discouraged by rock & roll's impact, Cherry turned to television news at Nashville's WSIX and covered the Civil Rights movement—starting at Little Rock—for four years. He relocated to California in 1959 and soon had a nightly radio show on KFOX in Long Beach, often airing rarely broadcast folk and hillbilly recordings that influenced listeners such as GRAM PARSONS and David Crosby. Cherry also wrote liner notes for numerous country albums and scripted and narrated several radio and television documentaries about the genre. —*Jonny Whiteside*

## Kenny Chesney

b. Knoxville, Tennessee, March 26, 1968

Kenneth Arnold "Kenny" Chesney became one of his era's most reliable hit makers and in-demand concert acts through perseverance, steady touring, and a predilection for catchy songs that mixed escapism and nostalgia. With beach-bum anthems such as "When the Sun Goes Down" (2005), he brought an island flavor to country radio, whereas other hits mixed contemporary country and classic-rock influences.

Chesney turned professional at a later age than most modern country artists, and his career misfired before it caught momentum—marking his story as one of struggle and determination. Once he finally broke through to stardom, he built an enduring career and became a consistent winner of country music's most coveted annual prizes; as of 2011, he had been named CMA Entertainer of the Year four times (2004, 2006, 2007, 2008) and ACM Entertainer of the Year four times (2005–2008).

Growing up in Luttrell, Tennessee—hometown of COUNTRY MUSIC HALL OF FAME member CHET ATKINS—Chesney concentrated on sports, not music. He played football and baseball at Gibbs High School, and he didn't start singing and playing guitar until after he began studying advertising at East Tennessee State University, where he participated in the ETSU Bluegrass Program. While a college student, he began performing in small nightclubs and restaurants around Johnson City. He recorded his first album independently in BRISTOL, TENNESSEE-VIRGINIA, and sold more than a thousand copies at club dates.

After graduation in December 1990, Chesney moved to Nashville to pursue music, performing regularly in the city's Lower Broad tourist district. He gained an audition with OPRYLAND Music Group and, that day, signed a writer's contract.

Capricorn Records founder Phil Walden signed Chesney in 1993, shortly after the label opened a Nashville office. Chesney's debut album, *In My Wildest Dreams,* sold only 10,000 copies, and Capricorn closed its Nashville division in 1994. Chesney left Capricorn for BNA Entertainment, an RCA imprint. His 1995 album, *All I Need to Know,* included two Top Ten singles, but in the midst of country music's early 1990s sales explosion, Chesney's standing remained unimpressive.

With *Me and You* (1996), Chesney's career started to come to life. The title track and the single "When I Close My Eyes" reached #2 on the charts. The album also included the song "Back Where I Come From"; although not released as a single, it became a staple of Chesney's concerts and one of his most requested tunes. He took another small step forward with *I Will Stand* (1997), which featured his first #1 hit, "She's Got It All," and another fan favorite, "That's Why I'm Here," a powerful song about an alcoholic starting rehabilitation.

At this point, Chesney remained a mid-level artist, but his standing ratcheted up with *Everywhere We Go* (1999). The album included two #1 hits, "How Forever Feels" and "You Had Me from Hello," a song inspired by a line spoken in the movie *Jerry Maguire* by actress Renée Zellweger. A third single, "She Thinks My Tractor's Sexy," stalled at #11 but soon became one of the singer's signature tunes. A *Greatest Hits* collection, released in 2000, reclaimed two songs from his past, "Back Where I Come From" and "The Tin Man," and raised their profile among his fans.

Chesney's career exploded as the new century turned, and he became one of country's best-selling artists for the next decade. His winning streak continued with *No Shoes, No Shirt, No Problems*, which recast him from a sensitive country singer to a beach-loving extrovert and life of the party. He also began celebrating his second home in the Virgin Islands and his attachment

*Kenny Chesney*

to the laid-back island lifestyle. The album yielded five Top Ten singles, including the #1 hit "The Good Stuff." The title song and the upbeat country-rockers "Young" and "Big Star" injected energy into Chesney's rambunctious concerts, and he grew into one of country music's biggest ticket sellers. The album would sell more than 4 million copies, doubling the sales of any of his previous releases.

After a holiday collection that heightened his island-loving image, *All I Want for Christmas Is a Real Good Tan*, Chesney released *When the Sun Goes Down*, another blockbuster. It debuted at #1 on the *Billboard* 200 chart, which ranks albums of all genres, by selling 550,000 copies during its first week. The album featured six Top Ten hits, including five singles that went to #1 or #2. *When the Sun Goes Down* became CMA's 2004 Album of the Year, and that year the singer won his first CMA Entertainer of the Year award.

Chesney would release two albums in 2005: *Be As You Are: Songs from an Old Blue Chair*, an acoustic side project without any single releases, and *The Road and the Radio*, which had a more somber side, represented by the title cut, as well as rocking hit singles "Summertime," "Living in Fast Forward," and "Beer in Mexico"—all #1s. On May 9, 2005, Chesney married actress Renée Zellweger, but the two jointly announced their divorce four months later, with Chesney citing rigors of the road and his busy career as primary reasons.

The popular concert performer released his first live album, *Live: Live Those Songs Again*, in 2006, followed in 2007 by *Just Who I Am: Poets & Pirates*, his eighth consecutive platinum album. The collection included three #1 singles and the #2 "Shiftwork," a duet with George Strait.

The 2008 album *Lucky Old Sun* included Chesney's most pronounced reggae song, "Everybody Wants to Go to Heaven," recorded in Jamaica with members of the Wailers, as well as a cover of Mac McAnally's "Down the Road." Both songs topped the country charts. Chesney released *Hemingway's Whiskey* in September 2010. It debuted at #1 on the *Billboard* 200 and sold 183,000 copies within its first week on the market. As one of America's most popular entertainers, Chesney continued to sell out stadiums, arenas, and amphitheaters on his 2011 tour. —*Michael McCall*

## Jerry Chesnut
b. Loyall, Kentucky, May 7, 1931

A severe back injury Jerry Donald Chesnut suffered in his twenties proved to be a blessing in disguise, inadvertently leading to one of country music's most successful songwriting careers. Chesnut was raised in the coal-mining camps of Harlan County, Kentucky. After serving in the U.S. Air Force during the Korean War, he settled in northeastern Florida, where he performed on radio and worked as a railroad conductor.

Chesnut moved to Nashville in 1958 to pursue music, long going unnoticed. He spent most of 1965 recuperating from back surgery, a decade after first hurting his back while lifting a cow. Physically restricted, he spent hours each day analyzing country radio, gaining insight into commercial songs and improving his original material. Chesnut achieved his first success with Del Reeves's 1967 hit "A Dime at a Time" and soon provided Reeves with "Looking at the World Through a Windshield" and "Good Time Charlie's."

Often writing alone at dawn, Chesnut turned out classics including "A Good Year for the Roses" (George Jones), "Another Place Another Time" (Jerry Lee Lewis), "T-R-O-U-B-L-E" (Elvis Presley, Travis Tritt), "It's Four in the Morning" (Faron Young), and "Holding on to Nothin'" (Porter Wagoner and Dolly Parton). Chesnut was inducted into the Nashville Songwriters Hall of Fame in 1996. —*Michael Gray*

## Mark Chesnutt
b. Beaumont, Texas, September 6, 1963

Mark Nelson Chesnutt rode country's second wave of New Traditionalism in the late 1980s and early 1990s. His music reflects the mix of sounds he heard growing up along the Texas-Louisiana border: honky-tonk music, Outlaw-country, Cajun music and zydeco, R&B, and a touch of western swing.

Chesnutt dropped out of high school to play drums in a rock band. By the time he released his first album (on the independent Axbar label) at twenty-six, he'd already logged ten years playing in clubs. He was signed to MCA Records after a regional promotion rep heard the single "Too Cold at Home," which Chesnutt had recorded for Houston's independent Cherry label. The mournful barstool ballad became the title track to his debut album, a Top Five hit, and an instant country classic. While love ballads are Chesnutt's forte, he's also adept at uptempo ditties, such as "Blame It on Texas," "Old Flames Have New Names," and "Bubba Shot the Jukebox"—all early 1990s hits—and covers of vintage songs by Don Gibson, Ray Price, Charlie Rich, and other veterans. Chesnutt's second album, *Longnecks & Short Stories*, featured a duet with his hero George Jones on "Talkin' to Hank." "It Sure Is Monday" (1993) and "Gonna Get a Life" (1995) showed his flair for Cajun-country.

*Mark Chesnutt*

Winner of CMA's 1993 Horizon Award, Chesnutt released *What a Way to Live* (1994) on MCA's revived Decca imprint and gained additional hits, including "It's a Little Too Late" (1996–97). But when Decca folded and he shifted back to MCA, he did not regain his momentum, and the label eventually dropped him. Since 2000 he has released albums on Columbia, Vivation, Lofton Creek, and Time Life/Saguaro. —*Rick Mitchell*

## Lew Childre
b. Opp, Alabama, November 1, 1901; d. December 3, 1961

"Doctor Lew" Childre, as he is fondly remembered, was one of the great one-man shows in country music. He was among the last country stars to come up through the medicine show and vaudeville circuits, and he was a master of classic nineteenth-century and early twentieth-century entertaining skills. He could buck-dance, sing, play the acoustic Hawaiian steel guitar, do hundreds of vintage jokes and comedy routines, ad lib commercials, recite poetry, and improvise dialog. Though many fans remember Childre for his days on the Grand Ole Opry in the late 1940s and 1950s (when he often teamed with a young Stringbean), he had earlier enjoyed a long and influential career. Over the years Childre did comedy for many of the greats, including Wiley Walker (Wiley & Gene), Floyd Tillman, Curly Fox, Bill Monroe, and Bill Boyd ( Bill and Jim Boyd).

Growing up in Opp, Alabama, near the Florida line, young Childre embarrassed his father, a local judge, by buck-dancing on street corners for tips. He finished college in 1923 but couldn't resist the lure of show business and joined the Milt Tolbert tent show as a pop singer. Childre later formed his own group, a jazz band called the Alabama Cotton Pickers. He preferred to work in traveling tent shows in the 1930s, yet he did record a number of sides—first for Gennett in 1930 and again for the American Record Corporation in 1934. His most popular releases were "Fishing Blues," "Hang Out the Front Door Key," and "Riding on the Elevated Railway."

Eventually Childre managed to translate his tent-circuit showmanship to radio, having popular programs over WWL (New Orleans), XERA (Villa Acuña, Coahuila, Mexico), WWVA (Wheeling), and WAGA (Atlanta). He joined the Opry in 1945 but also recorded several series of syndicated radio shows. In later years he invented a number of fishing lures that earned impressive royalties. He died in 1961, shortly after completing an album for Starday Records. —*Charles Wolfe*

## Harry Choates
b. Rayne, Louisiana, December 26, 1922; d. July 17, 1951

In his brief life, fiddler Harry Henry Choates immortalized the traditional Cajun song "Jolie Blonde (Pretty Blonde)" with his best-selling 1946 recording titled "Jole Blon." Unfortunately, a longtime battle with alcoholism took this talented musician's life before he reached age thirty.

Choates's childhood was rocky. His father died when he was nine years old, and as a boy he moved frequently, living off kindly friends and relatives and tips he made playing fiddle in bars. Soon he also mastered the guitar, mandolin, and accordion. By his early teens he became a professional musician—and a heavy drinker.

After his father's death, Choates spent a lot of time in Basile, Louisiana, where he played guitar in fiddle master Leo Soileau's band in the late 1930s. A great innovator in Cajun music, Soileau mentored Choates, who learned many of Soileau's stage tricks and songs, including "Jolie Blonde." Choates also played in other popular bands of the time, including those of Happy Fats, whom he joined in December 1939, and Shelly Lee Alley, whom he joined in summer 1940.

Never a dependable band member, Choates eventually formed his own Rhythm Boys, with bassist B. D. Williams, banjoist-vocalist Joe Manuel, guitarist Ed Pursley, steel guitarist "Papa Cairo" Lamperez, and pianist Johnnie Mae Smirle. The band worked for Basile music mogul Quincy Davis, who had a habit of taking in musicians, feeding them, and hiring them out seven nights a week—plus radio shows and matinees—for a meager ten dollars a week. The musicians rarely complained, since for most it was better than picking cotton.

Choates spent much of his life in Texas and was proficient in jazz and western swing, though he specialized in Cajun. French was not his native language; he learned just enough to sing the Cajun songs he loved. In April 1946 Choates made his epochal recording of "Jole Blon" (backed with "Basile Waltz") for Houston's Gold Star Records; in January 1947 it entered *Billboard*'s national country charts, peaking at #4. So popular was the tune that Moon Mullican, Roy Acuff, and others rushed in with cover versions. Between 1946 and 1950 Choates toured extensively throughout Texas and Louisiana, and he recorded several more sessions for Gold Star before moving to Macy's Records in early 1950.

The brilliant young musician had a sad end. A 1945 marriage to Helen Daenen ended in divorce, but not before the couple had two children. On July 14, 1951, Choates was arrested in Austin, Texas, for chronic failure to pay child support. Deprived of alcohol in jail, he suffered withdrawal symptoms and went into delirium tremens. When he died three days later, the official cause of death was cirrhosis of the liver, though rumors of a jailhouse beating still persist. Choates was only twenty-eight, but in just six years he had taken Cajun music to national popularity, recorded its biggest hit to date, and left behind beautiful recordings of "Allons à Lafayette," "Lawtell Waltz," "Poor Hobo," and "Opelousas Waltz" that still live today. —*Ann Allen Savoy*

## Chuck Wagon Gang
David Parker "Dad" Carter b. Milltown, Kentucky, September 25, 1889; d. April 28, 1963
Effie Juanita "Anna" Carter b. Shannon, Texas, February 15, 1917; d. March 5, 2004
Rosa Lola Lee "Rose" Carter b. Snyder, Oklahoma, December 31, 1914; d. May 13, 1997
Ernest Ray "Jim" Carter b. Tioga, Texas, August 10, 1910; d. February 2, 1971

Of all the gospel groups flourishing during the Depression and early war years, the Chuck Wagon Gang had the closest relationship to country music in both style and song material. The original ensemble, composed of Dad Carter and three of his children—Anna, Rose, and Jim—began singing in Lubbock, Texas, in 1935 and by 1936 had inaugurated their popular radio show on WBAP-KGKO in Fort Worth. There they assumed the name of a cowboy act, the Chuck Wagon Gang, which had already been on local radio, as well as the sponsorship of a local flour concern, Bewley Mills. Their first recordings for the American

*The Chuck Wagon Gang, 1959: (from left) Ronnie Crittenden, Rose Carter-Karnes, Howard Gordon, Anna Carter-Gordon, and Howard Welborn*

RECORD CORPORATION, in 1936, included both secular and religious material; they did not turn to the exclusive recording of gospel songs until April 1940.

The Chuck Wagon Gang became a radio institution in the Southwest, singing songs that came directly from shape-note hymnals and using a vocal style strongly influenced by gospel publishing house quartets. Generally accompanied only by a chorded guitar (played at first by Jim), the group produced a style of four-part harmony that was cherished by their many fans because of its warmth and predictability. Rose's high soprano lead and Anna's rich alto harmony were supported by Dad's baritone and Jim's bass.

Greater national exposure came in the 1950s, when radio evangelist J. Bazzel Mull began featuring and selling their records on his widely syndicated radio show, *Mull's Singing Convention*, and after 1966, when the group moved to Nashville. Although the act has experienced numerous personnel changes—beginning with Jim's retirement in 1951, Dad's departure in 1955, and, most significantly, Rose's retirement in 1966—the Chuck Wagon Gang style has remained intact, and the group has enjoyed one of the longest careers in American entertainment. They also introduced many of ALBERT E. BRUMLEY's gospel compositions to a wide public, and, with the release of *Favorite Country Hymns* (COLUMBIA, 1950), the Chuck Wagon Gang became the first gospel group to release an album of songs.

Inducted into the GMA Gospel Music Hall of Fame in 1998, the ensemble released an album, *70th Anniversary*, in 2006, featuring duets with country stars, including GEORGE JONES, the JORDANAIRES, and RICKY SKAGGS. The Chuck Wagon Gang continues to tour and record, with current members Dave Emery, Penny Greene, Stan Hill, and Julie Hudson. —*Bill C. Malone*

## Guy Clark
b. Monahans, Texas, November 6, 1941

One of Nashville's most influential and respected songwriters, Guy Clark began his career in the 1960s as a guitar-picking folksinger, playing clubs in Houston and AUSTIN alongside TOWNES VAN ZANDT, K. T. OSLIN, and JERRY JEFF WALKER. In the late 1960s, Clark moved to San Francisco, then back to Houston, and then to Southern California, where he built DOBROS at the Dopyera Brothers' guitar factory in Long Beach. After eight months in Los Angeles, where he signed a songwriting contract with RCA's Sunbury Music, Clark moved to Nashville in 1971 with his wife, Susanna, an accomplished painter and songwriter ("Easy from Now On," among others).

The son of an attorney, Clark grew up in Monahans, in West Texas, and in Rockport, near the Texas Gulf Coast. These two locales have provided memories and inspiration for his songs "Desperados Waitin' for a Train" (Jerry Jeff Walker, 1973), "Texas 1947" (JOHNNY CASH, 1975), and "Blowin' Like a Bandit" (ASLEEP AT THE WHEEL, 1987).

Clark's recording career began in 1975 with his classic collection *Old No. 1* and has included the notable albums *Texas Cookin'* (1976), *Dublin Blues* (1995), *Workbench Songs* (2006), and *Sometimes the Song Writes You* (2009), the latter two featuring songs cowritten with other writers. Although these and other albums have earned extensive critical praise, Clark has enjoyed greater commercial success with songs covered by other artists. His songwriting breakthrough came in 1973 with Jerry Jeff Walker's recording of "L.A. Freeway." Clark hit #1 in 1982 via RICKY SKAGGS's recording of "Heartbroke" and in 1988 with RODNEY CROWELL's "She's Crazy for Leavin'," which Clark and Crowell cowrote. Other Clark hits have included "New Cut Road" (BOBBY BARE, 1982), "Oklahoma Borderline" (VINCE GILL, 1985), "The Carpenter" (JOHN CONLEE, 1986), and "Baby I'm Yours" (STEVE WARINER, 1988).

Clark was elected to the NASHVILLE SONGWRITERS HALL OF FAME in 2004. —*Jack Bernhardt*

## Roy Clark
b. Meherrin, Virginia, April 15, 1933

Roy Linwood Clark's country music credentials range from touring with GRANDPA JONES as a teenager, to hosting *HEE HAW* for the show's twenty-five-year run, to pioneering in the development of BRANSON, MISSOURI, as a prime country music tourist destination. Yet in a career managed for many years by JIM HALSEY, he positioned himself as an all-around entertainer who could host *The Tonight Show* (which he did, several times) and could win crowds in Las Vegas showrooms as easily as he could perform on the GRAND OLE OPRY. A singer, instrumentalist, actor, and comic, Clark was one of the first country musicians to perform with a symphony orchestra and to tour in the Soviet Union.

Clark's father, Hester, moved the family around (Virginia, West Virginia, the District of Columbia, even New York City) seeking work during the Depression and World War II. Hester Clark was also a semiprofessional musician, playing guitar, fiddle, and banjo, instruments that Roy would master. Roy's mother, Lillian, played piano, and his brother and sister played mandolin and guitar. By 1949 Roy had made his television debut (on the Dumont Network's District of Columbia affiliate), toured with Grandpa Jones, and played for two weeks on a bill headed by

Hank Williams. Clark eventually signed on with singer Jimmy Dean, who was hosting daily television and radio programs in the Washington, D.C., area.

In 1957, Clark—fired by Dean for chronic lateness—appeared on Arthur Godfrey's nationally televised *Talent Scouts* program. Before long, Dean's manager, Connie B. Gay, arranged a regular spot on an ABC television series headlined by another client, George Hamilton IV.

Clark continued working in the D.C. area until 1960, when he was recruited by Wanda Jackson. Clark joined her at the Golden Nugget Hotel in Las Vegas, performing a twenty-minute opening set and then joining her backing group as guitarist. Jackson's manager, Jim Halsey, brought Clark to Capitol Records. His first Capitol album, *The Lightning Fingers of Roy Clark*, was released in 1962. In 1963 his first hit single—a version of Bill Anderson's "Tips of My Fingers"—reached #10 on *Billboard*'s country chart and went to #45 pop. Clark never duplicated that success on Capitol, though the label allowed him to record a wide array of albums, including a jazz album with guitarist Barney Kessel and saxophonist Plas Johnson.

In 1967 Clark moved to the Dot label, which resulted in a string of hits, including "Yesterday When I Was Young" (1969), "I Never Picked Cotton" (1970), "Come Live with Me" (1973), and "If I Had to Do It All Over Again" (1976). His albums included duet efforts with banjo player Buck Trent and blues artist Clarence "Gatemouth" Brown. Leaving Dot (by 1974 it had been absorbed by ABC), Clark recorded throughout the 1980s on the MCA, Churchill, Songbird, Silver Dollar, and Hallmark labels but largely concentrated on live performances and his *Hee Haw* work, begun in 1969.

In 1983 Clark opened his Roy Clark Celebrity Theater in Branson. He joined the Grand Ole Opry as a member on August 22,

1987, and was inducted into The Country Music Hall of Fame in 2009. —*Todd Everett*

## Terri Clark
b. Montréal, Québec, August 5, 1968

Raised in Calgary, Alberta, Terri Clark (born Terri Sauson) moved to Nashville in 1987 and landed a gig at the famed Tootsie's Orchid Lounge. A four-song demo brought her to the attention of singer-songwriter-producer Keith Stegall, who signed her to Mercury Records Nashville.

Clark's debut single, "Better Things to Do," reached #3 on the *Billboard* charts. Follow-up Top Ten hits included "When Boy Meets Girl" and "If I Were You." Her self-titled first album, released in 1995, sold a million copies. Clark's next two albums, *Just the Same* (1996) and *How I Feel* (1998), also went platinum, thanks to the hits "Poor Poor Pitiful Me," "Emotional Girl," "Now That I Found You," and "You're Easy on the Eyes." Her fourth album, *Fearless,* fell from favor with country radio, but she regained her footing with 2003's *Pain to Kill*, which included the hits "I Just Wanna Be Mad" and "I Wanna Do It All." Clark's #1 "Girls Lie Too" (2004), from the album *Greatest Hits 1994–2004*, was her last major hit as of 2011. She signed with BNA (RCA Records) in 2007, but two singles failed to chart highly, and she left the label in 2008. —*Janet E. Williams*

## Al Clauser
b. Manitoa, Illinois, February 23, 1911; d. March 3, 1989

As the leader of Al Clauser & His Oklahoma Outlaws, Henry Alfred Clauser became a popular western swing bandleader-guitarist-songwriter in the 1930s. He started his musical career in Illinois, where he claimed to have used the actual term "western swing" as early as 1928. Later his band broadcast their radio show from WHO in Des Moines, Iowa, and by 1938 the program was carried by 272 Mutual network stations. In 1937 Gene Autry used Clauser's band in the movie *Rootin' Tootin' Rhythm*, and that year they also recorded twelve sides for the American Record Corporation.

In 1942 Clauser moved the band to Tulsa, Oklahoma, where it grew to nine members and competed with Johnnie Lee Wills and Leon McAuliffe for dance crowds. Broadcasting daily over station KTUL, the Clauser outfit introduced twelve-year-old Clara Ann Fowler, who became known professionally as Patti Page; she made her first recording with them (as Al Clauser & the Oklahomans) in Tulsa for the Okla label. Clauser disbanded the group in the 1950s and worked for KTUL-TV in Tulsa. —*Guy Logsdon*

## Joe Clay
b. Harvey, Louisiana, September 9, 1938

Never a best-selling artist, Joe Clay enjoys high regard among rockabilly enthusiasts for recording some of the finest examples of the style ever waxed. The Cajun raver's reputation rests on nine songs he cut in just over a month. Claiborne Joseph Cheramie was living in Harvey, Louisiana, when he was discovered by a New Orleans–based disc jockey, who knew that the RCA subsidiary Vik Records was looking for talent. Clay landed a recording

*Roy Clark*

session for the company on the strength of a demo tape he made at a local radio station. He recorded on April 24, 1956, at Bill Quinn's Gold Star studio in Houston. Two songs, "Duck Tail" and "Sixteen Chicks," were released by Vik and helped Clay gain bookings on the LOUISIANA HAYRIDE in Shreveport.

In May, Clay went to New York for a guest spot on *The Ed Sullivan Show*—several months before ELVIS PRESLEY appeared on the CBS network television program—and to record with a band that included fiery guitarist Mickey Baker and two drummers. Again Vik released two songs, "Get on the Right Track" and "Cracker Jack," but neither established Clay as a star.

After leaving a thirty-year job as a school bus driver in Gretna, Louisiana, Clay released a comeback album, *The Legend Is Now*, in 2004. His 1950s work is available on CD, and he continues to perform as leader of the C. J. Cheramie Trio in southern Louisiana. As Joe Clay, he occasionally tours America and Europe.
—*Jay Orr*

## "Cowboy" Jack Clement
b. Whitehaven, Tennessee, April 5, 1931

Born and raised in suburban Memphis, Jack Henderson Clement became one of the most highly regarded—and colorful—producers, songwriters, and entrepreneurs in country music history. Following a stint in the marines (1948–52), Clement played BLUEGRASS up and down the eastern seaboard with BUZZ BUSBY and Scotty Stoneman in a band called Buzz and Jack & the Bayou Boys. In 1954 Clement returned to Memphis, where he joined SUN RECORDS as producer and engineer; from 1956 to 1959 he mixed recording sessions for ROY ORBISON, CARL PERKINS, JOHNNY CASH, CHARLIE RICH, and JERRY LEE LEWIS. An accomplished songwriter, Clement penned "Guess Things Happen That Way"

*"Cowboy" Jack Clement*

and "Ballad of a Teenage Queen" (both 1958 hits for Cash) and went on to write hits for JIM REEVES ("I Know One," 1960), CHARLEY PRIDE ("Just Between You and Me," 1966–67), BOBBY BARE ("Miller's Cave," 1964), and other top artists.

Fired in 1959 by Sun owner SAM PHILLIPS over what Clement described as a misunderstanding, Clement moved to Nashville in 1960 to work as a songwriter and producer for CHET ATKINS at RCA VICTOR but soon relocated to Beaumont, Texas, where he and producer Bill Hall opened Gulf Coast Recording Studios. There Clement met GEORGE JONES and suggested he cut DICKEY LEE's "She Thinks I Still Care," a #1 hit for Jones in 1962. Jones hit #3 with Clement's "A Girl I Used to Know" that same year.

In 1965 Clement moved back to Nashville and began his lengthy association with Charley Pride. Clement financed a demo session and passed the tape to Atkins, who signed Pride to RCA. Clement produced or coproduced Pride's first thirteen albums for RCA.

During the early 1970s Clement established the JMI label, expanded his publishing company, and opened three Nashville recording studios. He produced the 1975 OUTLAW classic *Dreaming My Dreams* for WAYLON JENNINGS and hosted recording sessions for MERLE HAGGARD, Ivory Joe Hunter, RAY STEVENS, WANDA JACKSON, MICKEY NEWBURY, and DON WILLIAMS. Williams was a member of Clement's songwriting stable, as were BOB McDILL ("Amanda") and ALLEN REYNOLDS ("Dreaming My Dreams with You"). During this time, artists ranging from TAMMY WYNETTE to Eric Clapton to Perry Como to ELVIS PRESLEY recorded material from Clement's vast publishing catalog.

Clement had cut several sides for Sun in the 1950s, and his album debut, *All I Want to Do in Life* (1978), included "When I Dream," a song CRYSTAL GAYLE took to #3 in 1979. During the 1980s Clement produced records for Cash as well as portions of U2's 1988 tribute album to American roots music, *Rattle and Hum*.

Still active as performer, writer, studio owner, record producer, and filmmaker, Clement released the album *Guess Things Happen That Way* in 2004. His *Cowboy Jack's Home Movies* was named best documentary at the 2005 Nashville Film Festival. In 2007 Clement released the DVD *Shakespeare Was a Big George Jones Fan*, a documentary made up largely of home movies. —*Bill Friskics-Warren*

## Vassar Clements
b. Kinards, South Carolina, April 25, 1928; d. August 16, 2005

Vassar Carlton Clements was one of America's foremost fiddle virtuosos. His mastery of many styles—from BLUEGRASS and country to rock and jazz—led to work with artists ranging from BILL MONROE and EARL SCRUGGS to the Band, THE BYRDS, the Grateful Dead, the NITTY GRITTY DIRT BAND, and Bonnie Raitt.

Clements grew up in a musical family in Kissimmee, Florida, and could play his stepfather's fiddle by age five. Legendary Florida bluegrass fiddler CHUBBY WISE, a family friend, was a great influence. In 1949 Clements joined Bill Monroe's Blue Grass Boys, and he performed with the band on and off until 1956. From 1958 to 1961 he worked with JIM & JESSE (McReynolds), recording for STARDAY.

Clements all but left professional music for several years until 1967, when he resumed performing full time with bluegrass pioneer JIMMY MARTIN and with country singer FARON YOUNG. In 1971 Clements formed a lasting association with JOHN HARTFORD. Clements's career received a major boost in 1972 when he appeared on the Nitty Gritty Dirt Band's landmark *Will the Circle Be Unbroken* album. As he broadened his musical horizons, Clements worked with the progressive Earl Scruggs Revue and became one of Nashville's most in-demand session musicians, known for his rich tone and authoritative style. In 1974 he collaborated with guitarist David Bromberg on the classic *Hillbilly Jazz* double album.

While touring and working sessions, Clements made records of his own. His highly acclaimed *Grass Routes* (ROUNDER, 1991) showcased him at the top of his bluegrass form. In 2004 he joined forces with the Dirt Band, Earl Scruggs, JERRY DOUGLAS, and RANDY SCRUGGS on a Grammy-winning version of "Earl's Breakdown."
—*Charlie Seemann*

## Zeke Clements
b. Warrior, Alabama, September 6, 1911; d. June 4, 1994

One of the most versatile yet unheralded figures in country music, Marlon R. "Zeke" Clements starred on radio and films in the 1930s and 1940s and composed some of that era's best-known songs. A native of northern Alabama, he came from a family that included other early recording artists, such as Stanley Clements. Though he enjoyed fiddle tunes and Sacred Harp singing, Zeke began his career by specializing in yodeling and COWBOY MUSIC, billing himself as the Alabama Cowboy and the Dixie Yodeler. Working on Chicago radio station WLS in 1929, he then moved to Philadelphia. He eventually arrived in Nashville, where he joined WSM as a member of Ken Hackney's Bronco Busters, the first western act on the station. For a time he also teamed with Texas Ruby Owens (CURLY FOX & TEXAS RUBY), moving on to WHAS in Louisville and WHO in Des Moines.

While appearing on the *HOLLYWOOD BARN DANCE* in 1937, Clements answered an ad from the Walt Disney studio for a cowboy singer who could both read musical scores and yodel. The job was for the soundtrack to *Snow White and the Seven Dwarfs*, and Clements became the voice for the cartoon character Bashful in that classic. This led to appearances in B-grade westerns, often as the sidekick for Charles Starrett. By 1939, after Clements and Texas Ruby ended their professional partnership, he returned to WSM, where he became a leading GRAND OLE OPRY soloist and successful songwriter. His "Smoke on the Water," a strongly worded World War II song pledging revenge on Japan, became a major hit for RED FOLEY in 1944. EDDY ARNOLD had hits with Clements's "Just a Little Lovin' (Will Go a Long Way)" (1948), "Why Should I Cry?" (1950), and "Somebody's Been Beatin' My Time" (1951). During this period, Clements also founded his own record company, for which he recorded such acts as PAUL HOWARD, the John Daniel Quartet, and himself. By the 1950s he was a seasoned veteran, headlining TV variety shows in New Orleans, Birmingham, Atlanta, and Nashville. He died in Nashville.
—*Charles Wolfe*

## Bill Clifton
b. Riderwood, Maryland, April 5, 1931

Singer-guitarist Bill Clifton played a major role in popularizing BLUEGRASS abroad and in highlighting the music's traditional roots. William August Marburg—he changed his last name to counter family objections to his pursuit of a career in music—was raised on a farm in Maryland's Baltimore County and played with the Dixie Mountain Boys while pursuing a graduate business degree at the University of Virginia in Charlottesville. With Bill Wiltshire (fiddle), Curly Lambert (mandolin), Johnny Clark

(banjo), and Jack Cassidy (bass), the band made its first records for the Blue Ridge label in 1954. "Flower Blooming in the Wildwood" became a regional hit and led to a second session in 1955 while Clifton was in the U.S. Marines, just before Blue Ridge folded.

Clifton's 1955 SONGBOOK *150 Old-Time Folk and Gospel Songs* included many traditional songs taken from early country records favored by Clifton. It was the first such collection directed to bluegrass performers and wielded a major influence. Discharged from military service in 1956, he resumed performing and recorded successful titles for MERCURY, including "Gathering Flowers from the Hillside," "Little Whitewashed Chimney," and "Mary Dear."

Clifton organized the first bluegrass festival at Oak Leaf Park in Luray, Virginia, on July 4, 1961, bringing JIM & JESSE, THE STANLEY BROTHERS, BILL MONROE, THE COUNTRY GENTLEMEN, and himself together for an all-day show that (along with the NEWPORT FOLK FESTIVALS) provided a model for CARLTON HANEY's seminal Roanoke bluegrass festival in 1965. Clifton moved to England in 1963 and spent the 1960s and 1970s overseas, returning to the United States in 1978. In recent years he has made occasional concert appearances and records for his own Elf label. He was inducted into the IBMA Hall of Fame in 2008.
—*Dick Spottswood*

## Patsy Cline
b. Winchester, Virginia, September 8, 1932; d. March 5, 1963

Popular in her time, Patsy Cline has achieved iconic status since her tragic death at age thirty in 1963. Cline is invariably invoked as a standard for female vocalists, and she has inspired scores of singers, including K. D. LANG, LORETTA LYNN, REBA MCENTIRE, LINDA RONSTADT, TRISHA YEARWOOD, and WYNONNA. Her unique, crying style and impeccable vocals have established her reputation as the quintessential torch singer.

Cline's short life reads like the heart-torn lyrics of many of the ballads she recorded. Born Virginia Patterson Hensley in Winchester, Virginia, in the midst of the Depression, she demonstrated musical proclivity at an early age—a talent inherited from her father, an accomplished amateur singer. Cline later confessed that he sexually abused her as a child. The family moved nineteen times around Virginia before "Ginny," as she was known in her youth, reached fifteen. A perpetual outsider, Cline dropped out of school at age fifteen to support her family after her father deserted them. They settled in Winchester, the Shenandoah Valley town with which she would grow to have a love-hate relationship.

Haunted by early experiences, the teenage Cline directed herself toward a singing career with unbending single-mindedness. She sang in juke joints in the Winchester area and did a nightclub cabaret act à la Helen Morgan, the tear-stained pop chanteuse of the 1920s said to be one of Cline's primary influences (along with Kay Starr, Kate Smith, and CHARLINE ARTHUR). Cline also appeared in amateur musicals, talent shows, and on local radio station WINC.

By age twenty Cline connected with local country bandleader Bill Peer, an association that intensified her desire for country music stardom. She adopted the name Patsy after her middle name, Patterson, and possibly in a nod to singer Patsy Montana, whose feisty cowgirl persona anticipated both Cline's spunk and early stage costuming. Cline married her first husband, Gerald Cline, on March 7, 1953, but she found the relationship unfulfilling, and they divorced four years later.

*Patsy Cline*

During this period Cline made inroads into the thriving Washington, D.C., country music scene, masterminded by country music's "media magician," CONNIE B. GAY. Beginning in the fall of 1954, Gay spotlighted Cline as a soloist on his *Town & Country* TV broadcasts, which included JIMMY DEAN as host, ROY CLARK, GEORGE HAMILTON IV, BILLY GRAMMER, Dale Turner, and Mary Klick. Through her Washington connections Cline landed her first recording contract in September 1954, with BILL MCCALL's Pasadena, California–based FOUR STAR RECORDS, an association that lasted six years and became the single greatest hindrance to her career. Cline alleged that McCall swindled her out of royalties and gave her substandard material to record.

Cline's debut single, the country weeper "A Church, a Courtroom and Then Goodbye," sold poorly when released in July 1955 on the DECCA label's Coral subsidiary (by lease arrangement between McCall and Decca A&R man PAUL COHEN). Cohen turned production over to his protégé and eventual successor, OWEN BRADLEY, who became Cline's guiding light for the duration of her recording career.

Cline's first four singles flopped, but the "hillbilly with oomph" act she developed on TV and in personal appearances earned her regional fame. Her recording stalemate ended when she made her national TV debut on the *Arthur Godfrey's Talent Scouts* show on January 21, 1957, singing "Walkin' After Midnight," which hit #2 country and #12 pop. Cline rode high on the hit for the next year, working show dates and performing regularly on Godfrey's weekly CBS broadcast *Arthur Godfrey and Friends* and on ABC's *Country Music Jubilee*, but there were no follow-up hits. Her September 1957 marriage to second husband Charlie Dick resulted in a tumultuous relationship glamorized in *Sweet Dreams*, the 1985 biographical film starring Jessica Lange as Cline. By the end of 1957 Cline had retreated into semiretirement.

After giving birth to a daughter (Julia) in August 1958, Cline moved to Nashville and signed with manager RANDY HUGHES,

who attempted to revive her career by booking one-nighters across the country and helping her ride out her Four Star contract. Back to working $50 gigs, she was at her nadir when the GRAND OLE OPRY belatedly made her a member on January 9, 1960. That summer she signed with Decca, and Bradley directed her toward becoming a leading exponent of the emergent NASHVILLE SOUND, beginning with her recording of the HARLAN HOWARD–HANK COCHRAN song "I Fall to Pieces." Cline initially resisted Bradley's lush arrangements, which featured backings by the JORDANAIRES, but ultimately accepted his guidance.

Cline gave birth to a son (Randy) in January 1961 and survived a near-fatal car accident in June as "Pieces" slowly started its climb up the charts, reaching #1 country in August and peaking at #12 in *Billdoard*'s pop rankings. Cline maintained her chart momentum with the crossover hits "Crazy" and "She's Got You" and with albums such as *Patsy Cline Showcase* and *Sentimentally Yours*. Other highlights included appearances at CARNEGIE HALL and the Hollywood Bowl and on Dick Clark's *American Bandstand*. Cline joined The Johnny Cash Show as the touring group's star female vocalist in January 1962, and over the next fourteen months she played numerous dates with Cash's "family," which included DON GIBSON, GEORGE JONES, CARL PERKINS, JUNE CARTER, BARBARA MANDRELL, GORDON TERRY, and Johnny Western.

Cline related premonitions of her death to close friends LORETTA LYNN, DOTTIE WEST, and JUNE CARTER as early as September 1962. Her last public performance was a benefit in Kansas City, March 3, 1963. Returning home, she was killed in a plane crash that also took the lives of pilot Randy Hughes and fellow Opry stars COWBOY COPAS and HAWKSHAW HAWKINS. Cline's singles "Leavin' on Your Mind," "Sweet Dreams (Of You)," and "Faded Love" charted Top Ten after she died. Numerous new or reissue recordings have appeared since her death, and she has remained one of the MCA label's most consistent sellers. The subject of both *Sweet Dreams* and the hit 1990s play *Always . . . Patsy Cline*, she was elected to THE COUNTRY MUSIC HALL OF FAME in 1973. —*Margaret Jones*

## Clogging

Clogging is a form of percussive rhythmic dance performed on toes and heels, to music with duple or 6/8 time. The elemental clogging step (called a "basic") consists of a double toe (two-tap movement) followed by a transfer of weight to the opposite foot. Although sometimes referred to as "square dance in overdrive" and often performed to similar music, clogging did not descend directly from square dancing but, rather, from several kinds of European step-dancing.

English clogging (rendered by industrial workers in their wooden-soled clogs and eventually perfected in Northern England music halls) and jig-influenced Irish step-dancing, or "shoe music," immigrated to North America during the eighteenth and nineteenth centuries. This melded dance form, which eventually incorporated sliding movements from Cherokee ceremonial dances and syncopation from African-descended slave dances, became a popular feature in vaudeville and traveling minstrel shows and later at folk music festivals.

According to clogging authority Ira Bernstein, the American dance now known as clogging got its name in 1939, when Sam Queen's Soco Gap Dancers were asked to perform at the White House for the Roosevelts and the king and queen of England, who likened the distinctive performance to the clog dancing performed in her own country.

In the 1940s and 1950s American clogging benefited from the growing popularity of square dances, where showing off clogging steps became a popular diversion during breaks between dance sets. In 1968 the National Clogging and Hoe-Down Council organized to standardize steps. Other institutions and activities followed, including the U.S. National Clogging Competition, the National Clogging Hall of Fame, the National Cloggers Association, and numerous conventions, workshops, and championships offering trophies and cash prizes. Clogging is performed to country, BLUE-GRASS, and even rock & roll music—anything with a steady beat—often with directions called out by a "cuer." Cloggers wear leather shoes with two metal taps sandwiched together, called "jingle taps." In performance (called "precision clogging"), dancers usually form a line, and, although encouraged to improvise, they follow certain choreographed formation steps.

Although many consider "buck dancing" a subgenre of contemporary clogging, there are distinctive differences. According to traditional dance expert Jackie Christian, clogging (which evolved primarily in the southern Appalachians) has English and Scots-Irish roots and is danced with an erect upper body, on the toes, with an emphasis on "down" rhythms. Buck dancing, on the other hand, has African-based roots and is performed flat-footed, lower to the floor than clogging, with more fluid body movements and an emphasis on the "up" rhythms (the sixteenth notes between eighth notes). —*Patricia Hall*

## Jerry Clower
b. Liberty, Mississippi, September 28, 1926; d. August 24, 1998

A successful country comedian, Howard Gerald "Jerry" Clower got into show business at age nine, he said, when he joined a 4-H club to get out of a class. Four years later, he won a 4-H district competition, but it would be thirty more years before he became a professional entertainer.

While in the U.S. Navy, Clower was asked to tell humorous southern stories; later, after becoming a fertilizer field representative with Mississippi Chemical Company, he used his humor as part of his sales technique. Clower became so well known for his comic routines that a friend suggested he record an album. The resulting *Jerry Clower from Yazoo City Mississippi Talkin'* was released on the Lemon label in 1970 and advertised only by word of mouth. It sold more than 8,000 copies and brought Clower to the attention of MCA RECORDS, which signed him in 1971. His album enjoyed a long run on the *Billboard* charts and was followed by several other strong-selling LPs, including *Clower Power* and *The Mouth of Mississippi*, leading to Clower's joining the GRAND OLE OPRY in 1973.

In addition to performing, Clower hosted the nationally syndicated radio show *Country Crossroads* and the syndicated TV program *Nashville on the Road*. Clower is also the subject of a documentary film, *Ain't God Good*.

Clower's routines are based on people he knew growing up in Amite County, Mississippi. He wrote three books based on this material, among them *Stories from Home* (1992). In addition to his comedy, the deeply religious Clower served as a Baptist deacon and an active member of the Gideon Bible Society. He identified Christianity as the greatest influence on his life and was a passionate advocate of education, family life, and racial equality and integration. —*W. K. McNeil*

## CMA
established in Nashville, Tennessee, November 1958

The Country Music Association (CMA) was organized in 1958 amid the rise of rock & roll and the expansion of TV broadcasting, which temporarily threatened country record sales, road show receipts, and radio shows. Country publishers, disc jockeys and broadcasting executives, artists, recording executives, songwriters, managers, and talent agents joined forces to heighten public awareness of country music while convincing broadcasters and advertisers of the music's selling power.

A move to reform the five-year-old Country Music Disc Jockeys Association (CMDJA) led to the new, more active, and more comprehensive organization. CMDJA dissolved itself in the summer of 1958, and a caretaker CMA committee took charge pending CMA's formal organization at Nashville's annual DJ CONVENTION the following November. With CONNIE B. GAY and WESLEY ROSE respectively serving as founding president and founding board chairman, HARRY STONE became CMA's first executive director.

Stone resigned a year later due to CMA's lack of funds, and it was not until 1962 that the board appointed CMA secretary JO WALKER-MEADOR as executive director, a role she filled until ED BENSON took over in January 1992. When Benson became seriously ill in 2003, Tammy Genovese served temporarily in his place, and after Benson announced his impending retirement in 2005 she served as chief operating officer (2006) and chief executive officer (2007) until resigning in December 2009. Concert promoter STEVE MOORE, a longtime CMA board member, served as interim CEO until his appointment as CEO in 2010.

Early on, CMA boosted the number of full-time country radio stations (a mere eighty-one in 1961) through demographic research, advertising sales kits, and special presentations to broadcasters' and advertisers' conventions. Combined with radio's increasing market segmentation along stylistic lines, CMA's efforts pushed country stations past the 600 mark by 1970 and to more than 2,000 in 2011. CMA membership has risen from 233 in 1958 to more than 6,000 organizational and individual members in forty-one countries, while CMA's market research has grown ever more sophisticated.

In 1961 CMA created THE COUNTRY MUSIC HALL OF FAME. Plaques were displayed at the Tennessee State Museum in downtown Nashville until the COUNTRY MUSIC HALL OF FAME AND MUSEUM opened on MUSIC ROW on April 1, 1967. CMA spearheaded the building's funding drive and also contributed greatly to the museum's expanded downtown facility, which opened in May 2001.

In 1967 CMA held its first awards show, in Nashville. The program was first televised in 1968, as part of the NBC *Kraft Music Hall* series, and has consistently drawn high ratings ever since.

In the late 1950s, CMA established Country Music Week, held in Nashville each fall. Building on the Disc Jockey Convention, CMA added seminars, talent showcases, and awards ceremonies staged by music trade publications and performance rights organizations. One spinoff was Country Radio Broadcasters (CRB), which has held annual conventions in Nashville since 1969. In 1972 CMA and WSM organized the first International Country Music Fan Fair, later called the CMA MUSIC FESTIVAL.

In the new century, CMA continues to advance country's development worldwide while serving as a unifying force within the country music industry. —*John W. Rumble*

## CMA Music Festival
established in Nashville, Tennessee, 1972

The CMA Music Festival, held each June, is the most celebrated uniting of country music fans and entertainers in the world and has been since its earlier days, when it was known as the International Country Music Fan Fair. The four-day event has attracted more than 100,000 fans each summer since moving to downtown Nashville in 2001 from its previous location, the Tennessee State Fairgrounds.

According to the Country Music Association (CMA), the 2009 gathering averaged 56,000 ticket buyers each day, with many others enjoying free events at the festival and at venues around town. That same year, more than 200 country artists performed, offering more than seventy hours of live music and more than thirty hours of autograph signings. A portion of the proceeds from the event is donated to Nashville public schools to support music education.

The festival began because so many fans attended the annual country music DJ CONVENTION, now known as Country Radio Seminar (CRS), that CMA leaders wanted to relieve the congestion by giving fans their own event. Along with radio station WSM, the association launched Fan Fair in April 1972 at Nashville's Municipal Auditorium. More than 5,000 fans attended the first year; this figure doubled in 1973. In 1982, to accommodate ticket demand, Fan Fair moved to the Tennessee State Fairgrounds. For many years, ticket sales were capped at 24,000, which filled the fairgrounds, and the event regularly sold out.

Once again, larger audiences led to another move, this time in 2001 to downtown Nashville, where several stages could be used, including Riverfront Park and the football stadium where the NFL's Tennessee Titans play. Three years later the CMA assumed full sponsorship, changed the name to CMA Music Festival, and put more emphasis on live concert performances—although autograph sessions still occur daily at the Nashville Convention Center, at private fan-club parties, and at other venues. Some devotees protested removing "fan" from the festival's title and lamented how the downtown location lacked the intimate feel of the old Fan Fair. But with time the CMA Music Festival received an enthusiastic response from attendees for its expanded live music opportunities. In 2004, ABC-TV started presenting an annual prime-time special, *CMA Music Festival: Country's Night to Rock,* spotlighting the festival. *—Janet E. Williams*

## CMF (*see* Country Music Hall of Fame and Museum)

## CMT
established in Nashville, Tennessee, March 6, 1983

Founded in 1983 as CMTV and spending its first sixteen years as a twenty-four-hour-a-day video channel, CMT has evolved into a multifaceted television network that blends country music programs with country-lifestyle programs, reality shows, and reruns of scripted series that previously had run on other networks. CMT is part of MTV Networks, a subsidiary of Viacom, which bought the music channel in 1999.

Glenn D. Daniels, a broadcasting veteran, launched CMTV on March 6, 1983, from headquarters in Hendersonville, Tennessee; the network's name changed to CMT (Country Music Television) after a copyright infringement suit brought by music channel MTV.

In 1991, GAYLORD ENTERTAINMENT COMPANY bought CMT for $30 million. The network remained an all-video channel while another Gaylord network, TNN, mixed videos with talk shows, live-music programs, and lifestyle programming. In the 1990s, BILLY RAY CYRUS, TRAVIS TRITT, SHANIA TWAIN, and other artists credited CMT for helping to establish their careers. In an interview with the trade magazine *Gavin Report*, DWIGHT YOAKAM stated that "the biggest change in country music has to do with CMT's impact on the marketing of country music and its artists."

On October 19, 1992, CMT International was launched in Europe; on October 4, 1994, it became available in the Asia-Pacific region, and on April 1, 1995, in Latin America. The network closed its international telecasts in 1998, citing lost revenue. In 1997, Gaylord sold CMT and TNN to Westinghouse, owners of the CBS television network. Viacom, owners of MTV and VH1 networks, bought CBS from Westinghouse. Viacom soon broadened CMT beyond music videos to match the more episodic programming it had given MTV and VH1.

When Viacom changed the name and format of TNN, CMT became the most watched country music channel in America. In May 2006, Viacom renamed VH1 Country network to CMT Pure Country, keeping its all-video format. The network's website, CMT.com, actively reports on country music and related issues, as well as providing programming information. As of 2011, CMT was available in more than 92 million homes. *—Bob Paxman*

## Eddie Cochran
b. Oklahoma City, Oklahoma, October 3, 1938; d. April 17, 1960

Though he died tragically at an early age, rock & roll singer and guitarist Eddie Cochran ensured his place in pop music history when he cowrote the classic "Summertime Blues" with partner Jerry Capehart.

Raised in Albert Lea, Minnesota, Edward Ray Cochran was living in the Bell Gardens suburb of Los Angeles by the time he reached his teens. In 1954 he performed and recorded as one of a country duo, the Cochran Brothers, with future songwriting great HANK COCHRAN (not related).

Eddie Cochran made his national chart debut with a remake of "Sittin' in the Balcony," originally recorded by Johnny Dee (songwriter JOHN D. LOUDERMILK). Cochran's breakthrough came in late 1958, when his recording of "Summertime Blues" became a Top Ten pop hit. Cochran appeared in several rock & roll–oriented films but had only modest success on the pop charts after "Summertime Blues." While in England, where he enjoyed great popularity and was touring for a second time with fellow rock & roller Gene Vincent, Cochran died in a car crash on April 17, 1960, near Chippenham, Wiltshire.

Rock groups Blue Cheer and the Who had hits with "Summertime Blues" in 1968 and 1970, respectively, and ALAN JACKSON's version of the song, with accompanying water skiing video, was a #1 country hit in 1994. Cochran was inducted into the Rock and Roll Hall of Fame in 1987. *—Jay Orr*

## Hank Cochran
b. Isola, Mississippi, August 2, 1935; d. July 15, 2010

Along with HARLAN HOWARD, BILL ANDERSON, and DALLAS FRAZIER, Hank Cochran helped define country songwriting in the 1960s. He also continued to be a creative force in Nashville into the 1990s.

Garland Perry "Hank" Cochran spent part of his childhood in a Memphis orphanage. He dropped out of school and eventually moved to California, where he joined future ROCKABILLY star EDDIE COCHRAN (no relation) in the Cochran Brothers. They appeared on TV's *Town Hall Party* and briefly backed LEFTY FRIZZELL.

After publishing songs with Nashville's PAMPER MUSIC while in California, Cochran moved to MUSIC CITY in 1959 to write and plug songs for Pamper for $50 a week. SKEETS MCDONALD recorded his "Where You Go I'll Follow" that year, and other stars scored Cochran-penned hits in the 1960s: PATSY CLINE ("She's Got You," "I Fall to Pieces"), EDDY ARNOLD ("Make the World Go Away," "I Want to Go with You"), GEORGE JONES ("You Comb Her Hair"), BURL IVES ("A Little Bitty Tear"), JIM REEVES ("I'd Fight the World"), and RAY PRICE ("Don't You Ever Get Tired of Hurting Me"). Cochran wrote most of his big hits solo, but at times he has cowritten with such notables as HARLAN HOWARD, WILLIE NELSON, and, since the 1980s, DEAN DILLON.

In 1962 Ives's recording of Cochran's "Funny Way of Laughing" won a Grammy award, and in 1966 JEANNIE SEELY's version of his "Don't Touch Me" did, too. Cochran and Seely were married from 1969 to 1979; she saluted him with the 1967 album *Thanks, Hank!*

Over the years, Cochran made several records himself. In addition to Cochran Brothers efforts on Ekko, he recorded for LIBERTY, RCA, Gaylord, MONUMENT, CAPITOL, and ELEKTRA, among other labels. His biggest hit as a singer was 1962's "Sally Was a Good Old Girl." He sometimes harmonized with good friend Nelson, who featured him in the 1980 film *Honeysuckle Rose*.

Cochran's 1970s hits included "It's Not Love (But It's Not Bad)" for MERLE HAGGARD and "Why Can't He Be You" for LORETTA LYNN. MICKEY GILLEY's "That's All That Matters to Me," VERN GOSDIN's "What Would Your Memories Do," and GEORGE STRAIT's "The Chair" and "Ocean Front Property" were among Cochran's 1980s achievements.

*Hank Cochran*

In the 1990s LORRIE MORGAN and Etta James both revived "Don't Touch Me." Cochran entered the NASHVILLE SONGWRITERS HALL OF FAME in 1974. For many years he helmed the publishing firm Co-Heart Music Group, and he recorded a 1997 duet album with Billy Don Burns. In 2002 Cochran released the album *Livin' for a Song: A Songwriter's Autobiography.* —*Robert K. Oermann*

## David Allan Coe
b. Akron, Ohio, September 6, 1939

A genuine country music eccentric, David Allan Coe is an accomplished singer-songwriter, gifted mimic, and effective performer whose personal excesses have often obscured his talents and undermined his career.

Coe arrived in Nashville in 1967 after frequent periods of incarceration, including a stint in the Ohio State Penitentiary. His claim to have spent time on Death Row for killing another inmate has been debunked and was the first of many outlandish "image" ploys that marked his career.

Though he recorded for SHELBY SINGLETON's Plantation label, Coe first achieved recognition as a songwriter, providing a #1 hit for TANYA TUCKER in 1973 with "Would You Lay with Me (In a Field of Stone)." After signing with the COLUMBIA label in 1973, he adopted the stage persona of the Mysterious Rhinestone Cowboy (complete with mask) and attached himself to the country's burgeoning progressive sounds, later known as music of the OUTLAW movement. Despite significant recording success—"You Never Even Called Me by My Name" (1975, written by Steve Goodman), "Longhaired Redneck" (1976), and "Willie, Waylon and Me" (1976)—Coe's career stalled in the late 1970s.

GLEN CAMPBELL's 1976 hit "Like a Rhinestone Cowboy" undercut Coe's image, and he suffered from his own penchant for peppering his shows with obscenities and graphic sexual allusions. After providing JOHNNY PAYCHECK with a #1 song, "Take This Job and Shove It" (1977), Coe drifted from commercial success until an eighties comeback.

For a while, Coe's outlaw image attracted more attention than his music. He claimed to sport more than 300 tattoos, to follow a polygamist lifestyle with as many as seven concurrent wives, and to enjoy an affiliation with the Outlaws motorcycle gang. He also released sexually explicit albums and a pornographic novel. It wasn't until 1983 that he gained another Top Ten hit with "The Ride" (written by Gary Gentry), followed by the #2 hit "Mona Lisa Lost Her Smile" and the #11 chart-maker "She Used to Love Me a Lot."

In the 2000s, Coe collaborated with members of the heavy metal band Pantera and with Hank Williams III and toured with Kid Rock. Images aside, Coe's recorded legacy is substantial, revealing a songwriter of lyrical sensitivity ("Jody Like a Melody") and a singer of masculine bravado ("Jack Daniel's, If You Please"). —*Stephen R. Tucker*

## Paul Cohen
b. Chicago, Illinois, November 10, 1908; d. April 1, 1970

Chicago-born Paul E. Cohen, longtime DECCA RECORDS executive, was one of the men chiefly responsible for Nashville's emergence as country music's recording capital.

Cohen first worked for COLUMBIA RECORDS in the late 1920s, but in 1934 he joined Decca's newly formed American operation,

*Paul Cohen*

organized by brothers JACK KAPP and DAVE KAPP—old Chicago friends of Cohen's. Cohen moved to Cincinnati to become Decca's midwestern branch manager in 1935, scouting and signing new talent in addition to marketing records. During World War II he gradually took over Decca's hillbilly production work from Dave Kapp, and in the mid-1940s he moved to New York to head that department of the company.

With two of Decca's main country stars at Nashville's GRAND OLE OPRY—ERNEST TUBB and RED FOLEY—in August 1947 Cohen began regular recording of his country roster in the CASTLE RECORDING STUDIO's new facility in downtown Nashville's Tulane Hotel. At WSM, musicians Beasley Smith and OWEN BRADLEY helped Cohen schedule his intense, two- to three-week Nashville visits by lining up stars and musicians, and working out musical arrangements (many of them created during recording sessions). Cohen is remembered for an energetic production style—as much cheerleader as executive—and a knack for finding new artists and matching them with songs, often published by his own companies. KITTY WELLS, WEBB PIERCE, BRENDA LEE, PATSY CLINE, and BOBBY HELMS were all signed to Decca during Cohen's tenure, while Tubb, Foley, JIMMIE DAVIS, and other established label mates enjoyed continued success.

Cohen left Decca's country department early in 1958 (replaced by Owen Bradley some weeks later), first to handle pop production for Decca's Coral subsidiary and then to launch his own company, Todd Records. In addition to signing country acts such as PEE WEE KING and Dub Dickerson, the label enjoyed a pop hit, Joe Henderson's "Snap Your Fingers." In 1964 Cohen rejoined his old boss, Dave Kapp, as head of Kapp Records' country division in Nashville. In four years at Kapp, Cohen signed and produced Hugh X. Lewis, CAL SMITH, MEL TILLIS, and BILLY EDD WHEELER, among others. Cohen's last major executive position was as head

of ABC's Nashville office (1968–69), a position he left after being diagnosed with cancer.

As CMA president, Cohen was on hand when the COUNTRY MUSIC HALL OF FAME AND MUSEUM opened in 1967. He died in Bryan, Texas, on April 1, 1970. In an unprecedented gesture, Nashville's MUSIC ROW offices closed for a memorial service a week later (April 7). His posthumous election to THE COUNTRY MUSIC HALL OF FAME in 1976 was a lasting testimony to his memory and importance. —*Ronnie Pugh*

## Nudie Cohn (*see* Nudie the Rodeo Tailor)

## Ben Colder (*see* Sheb Wooley)

## M. M. Cole (*see* M. M. Cole Publishing, under M)

## Biff Collie
b. Little Rock, Arkansas, November 25, 1926; d. February 19, 1992

Hiram Abiff "Biff" Collie was a pioneer country disc jockey, show promoter, and trade reporter. Born in Little Rock, Collie was raised in San Antonio and first worked in radio there at KMAC, in 1943. After military service, he returned to Texas radio work and in 1948 became Houston's first and most popular country disc jockey at KNUZ, later promoting big shows at Cook's Hoedown Club. He made his first recordings for Houston's Macy's Records and later recorded for COLUMBIA, Specialty, and STARDAY (early 1950s), but his only charted record came in 1972 as "Billy Bob Bowman" for United Artists. At Columbia he recorded with "Little Marge" Tillman, first wife of FLOYD TILLMAN, who in 1953 became Collie's first wife. (After a divorce, Collie married Shirley Caddell.)

Collie emceed the PHILIP MORRIS COUNTRY MUSIC SHOW (1957–58) and then moved to Southern California, ultimately becoming one of the many outstanding DJs on KFOX in Long Beach, where he stayed until 1969. Just as he had taken one song-writer's wife, so another songwriter—WILLIE NELSON—took his wife, in 1962, when Shirley Caddell Collie became the second Mrs. Nelson. By this time Biff Collie had found an auxiliary career as trade paper reporter; later he started a radio reporting service. During the 1970s and 1980s he produced and hosted several network or syndicated radio programs.

Elected to the Country Music DJ Hall of Fame in 1978, Collie was a guiding force behind ROPE and briefly operated his own station, Brentwood, Tennessee's, WWCR (1985–86). —*Ronnie Pugh*

## Tom Collins
b. Lenoir City, Tennessee, May 30, 1942

Producer and publisher Bernie Tom Collins has received seven Grammy Award nominations and three CMA awards as Producer of the Year. Some of those honors came from his production work with BARBARA MANDRELL, RONNIE MILSAP, SYLVIA, STEVE WARINER, MARIE OSMOND, and flutist James Galway.

Collins grew up in Lenoir City, Tennessee, and attended the University of Tennessee at Knoxville. An interest in dentistry was outweighed by his fascination with music. He moved to Nashville in 1970 when he was hired by Jack D. Johnson and CHARLEY PRIDE at Pi-Gem Music.

In 1982 Collins established his own publishing company, Tom Collins Music, which received BMI's 1983 Robert J. Burton Award for Most Performed Song of the Year: Dennis Morgan and Kye Fleming's "Nobody," recorded by RCA artist Sylvia. Collins's growing catalogs soon made him one of Nashville's most successful independent publishers. In 1991 he acquired the valuable catalog of hit songwriter TOM T. HALL. Collins sold Tom Collins Music, Collins Court Music, and Hallnote Music to ACUFF-ROSE PUBLICATIONS in 1999; today these catalogs are part of music publishing giant SONY/ATV Music Publishing. —*Gerry Wood*

## Tommy Collins
b. near Oklahoma City, Oklahoma, September 28, 1930; d. March 14, 2000

Hailed by his friend MERLE HAGGARD's 1980 song "Leonard," Leonard Raymond Sipes, better known as Tommy Collins, was one of the first recording artists to set the standard for country music's BAKERSFIELD sound. His intellectual, humorous songwriting influenced writers including Haggard and ROGER MILLER (who once told Collins, "I got my attitude for songwriting from you"). Beginning with FERLIN HUSKY and FARON YOUNG in the early 1950s, Collins's songs have been recorded by some of country music's brightest stars.

While attending college near Oklahoma City, Leonard Sipes worked as a DJ and performer on local radio station KLPR and, in 1951, recorded four sides with the small Morgan label out of Fresno, California. He arrived in Bakersfield in 1952, having traveled there with WANDA JACKSON and her family on their vacation, and was immediately befriended by performer–disc jockey Ferlin Husky). It was Husky who renamed Sipes "Tommy Collins" when a musician ordered a Tom Collins drink during a recording session.

By 1953, Collins was writing for CENTRAL SONGS music publishing firm and recording for CAPITOL RECORDS, assisted on sessions by Husky and BUCK OWENS. Top Ten Collins hits, including

*Tommy Collins*

"You Better Not Do That," "Whatcha Gonna Do Now," "Untied," and "It Tickles," significantly influenced the lively, guitar-driven sound widely associated with Bakersfield.

In 1957, preparing to enter the ministry, Collins enrolled at the Golden Gate Theological Seminary at Berkeley, California. A few years later, however, he began to miss professional music. After hearing Merle Haggard on radio, Collins sought out Haggard, and the two became friends while fishing together on the Kern River and contributing to each other's recording sessions. In 1964 Haggard cut Collins's "Sam Hill," and he later cut more Collins originals, including "Carolyn" and "The Roots of My Raising."

Collins began recording for COLUMBIA RECORDS in 1966, turning out hits such as "If You Can't Bite, Don't Growl." He made a 1972 album for STARDAY RECORDS, moved to Nashville in 1976, and continued to write professionally into the 1990s. Faron Young's 1954 hit "If You Ain't Lovin' (You Ain't Livin')," a Collins composition, went to #1 for GEORGE STRAIT in 1988. Collins was elected to the NASHVILLE SONGWRITERS HALL OF FAME in 1999. —*Dale Vinicur*

## Collins Kids
Lawrence "Larry" Albert Collins b. Tulsa, Oklahoma, October 4, 1944
Lawrencine "Lorrie" May Collins b. Tulsa, Oklahoma, May 7, 1942

Regulars on the *TOWN HALL PARTY* TV program, brother-sister team Lorrie and Larry Collins were stars of the late 1950s West Coast country scene. Although their records failed to chart, they exemplify California ROCKABILLY, and these vintage COLUMBIA releases are greatly admired today.

At age eight Lorrie won a Tulsa talent contest hosted by LEON MCAULIFFE, who encouraged her parents to move to Southern California to give her greater professional exposure. Lorrie appeared on several local programs, and Larry won a talent contest on disc jockey Squeakin' Deacon Moore's local country radio show. The duo joined the *Town Hall Party* cast in February 1954 and won audiences with colorful costumes and energetic performances. Larry was an outstanding double-neck guitarist, trained by JOE MAPHIS, while Lorrie handled lead vocals. Appearances on the *Ozark Jubilee*, the *Steve Allen Show*, and the GRAND OLE OPRY extended their influence. In 1958 Lorrie began dating RICK NELSON, but the relationship proved to be short-lived.

The Collins Kids also toured with JOHNNY CASH's road show, where Lorrie met Cash's manager, Stu Carnall; the two married in 1959. Lorrie and Larry dissolved their act in 1961 after Lorrie's first child was born. Larry continued to record solo, though without chart success. As a songwriter, however, he scored with country hits "Delta Dawn" (TANYA TUCKER) and "You're the Reason God Made Oklahoma" (DAVID FRIZZELL with SHELLY WEST) to his credit. Several reissue albums have appeared, and the siblings reunite for occasional performances. —*William P. Davis*

## Jessi Colter
b. Phoenix, Arizona, May 25, 1943

With her religious upbringing and refined manner, singer-songwriter Jessi Colter seemed an unlikely participant in the OUTLAW movement that transformed country music in the 1970s. Yet the hazel-eyed beauty's tremulous voice disguised the fact that she was no more obedient to MUSIC ROW convention than the rowdy "Willie, Waylon, and the boys."

Profoundly influenced by her mother—an ordained Pentecostal minister—Colter joined the church choir at age six and became its pianist five years later. She was discovered in Phoenix by celebrated rock & roll guitarist Duane Eddy, who produced her first recording on the Jamie label. Released under Colter's real name, Mirriam Johnson, in 1961, the single "Lonesome Road" revealed a style aptly described on the picture sleeve as a mixture of "church music with western music . . . and overtones of the blues." In 1962 she married Eddy, and they eventually settled in California.

After the couple divorced in 1968, she returned to Phoenix and took her stage name from her great-great uncle Jesse Colter, a member of the notorious James Gang. There she met rising star Waylon Jennings, who not only became her second husband, in 1969, but also proved instrumental in nurturing her career in Nashville.

*A Country Star Is Born* (RCA, 1970), her Jennings-produced debut album, proved to be mistitled, for Colter's vocal and songwriting talents came to fruition five years later at Capitol Records. Spearheaded by the Grammy-nominated "I'm Not Lisa," a #1 crossover lament, *I'm Jessi Colter* was certified gold. It was followed into the pop album charts by *Jessi* (1976), and Colter scored hit singles with two other original compositions: "What's Happened to Blue Eyes" (#5, 1975) and "It's Morning" (#11, 1976).

Colter has not revisited the Top Forty as a solo artist since 1976. Nevertheless, her presence on RCA's platinum 1976 collection *Wanted! The Outlaws*, as well as Waylon & Jessi duets such as the self-penned "Storms Never Last" (#17, 1981), have maintained her profile in country circles. After Jennings's death in 2002, Colter largely withdrew from public view, but in 2006 she released *Out of the Ashes*, her first solo album in two decades. —*Pete Loesch*

# Columbia Records
established in Washington, D.C., 1889

Columbia Records began as a distributor for Edison phonographs and supplies. In the early 1890s the company began to produce its own machines and cylinder records. It entered the disc record market in 1902 and gradually abandoned cylinder production over the next decade. Columbia's first "race" records (aimed toward the African American market) came out in 1921. In September 1924 the company brought the blind minstrel Ernest Thompson, the North Carolina fiddle-and-banjo team of Samantha Bumgarner & Eva Davis, and North Georgia's Gid Tanner and Riley Puckett to New York to make the company's first country records.

Under the direction of vice president and A&R man Frank Walker, who also made many field recording trips to the South, Columbia introduced the 14000-D series in 1923, exclusively for African American music. Early in 1925 a 15000-D series was added for white country music. Its prominent artists included Gid Tanner's Skillet Lickers (with Puckett), Charlie Poole, Smith's Sacred Singers, Vernon Dalhart, and Darby & Tarlton.

In 1926, shortly before Walker left the company, Columbia acquired the General Phonograph Corporation and its OKeh Records label, which continued to operate independent of Columbia. OKeh country artists included Fiddlin' John Carson, Narmour & Smith, and Frank Hutchison. The label went into eclipse in 1932, when Columbia's 15000-D series was also terminated.

Consolidated Film Industries, which owned the American Record Corporation (ARC) and bought Brunswick Records in December 1931, purchased Columbia/Okeh in 1934. Columbia-label releases were then gradually limited to classical and ethnic material. ARC released country and "race" items on a series of low-priced labels, including Banner, Melotone, Oriole, Perfect,

Romeo, Vocalion, and Conqueror, a Sears, Roebuck label. The series' major country artists included Roy Acuff, Gene Autry, Bill Carlisle (and his older brother Cliff), The Prairie Ramblers (with Patsy Montana), and Bob Wills.

When the Columbia Broadcasting System (CBS) purchased the Brunswick-ARC group of labels in 1938, only the Vocalion and Conqueror labels remained. (Art Satherley, an ARC employee at the time of the purchase, continued as the head of A&R for the hillbilly and race divisions of the newly launched Columbia Records until 1952.) In 1940 Vocalion was discontinued as the old OKeh label was revived. Conqueror was dropped in 1942. OKeh was dropped again in 1945 as country music began to appear once again on Columbia, for the first time since 1932.

In 1945 the Columbia roster still included Autry, Acuff, and Wills. New additions in the postwar years included Bill Monroe, Molly O'Day, and The Bailes Brothers. By the early 1950s Columbia's impressive stable included Carl Smith, Lefty Frizzell, The Stanley Brothers, Marty Robbins, Ray Price, Wilma Lee & Stoney Cooper, Little Jimmy Dickens, Flatt & Scruggs, and George Morgan.

In June 1948 Columbia introduced the modern long-play (LP) record, primarily to present uninterrupted versions of classical and other longer works. When twelve-inch LPs began to dominate the market in the mid-1950s, Columbia produced albums by all its major country artists, as it has continued to do in the compact disc and digital eras.

Don Law headed country A&R for Columbia from 1952 to 1967, assisted by Frank Jones (who later served as country marketing director). Law was succeeded briefly by Bob Johnston and Ron Bledsoe (ca. 1971–77). During 1978–79, operating from Nashville, Rick Blackburn supervised marketing while Billy Sherrill oversaw A&R, each reporting to New York superiors. Blackburn ran the Nashville office from 1980 to 1987, followed by Roy Wunsch (1988–93) and Allen Butler (1993–2003), whose tenure saw the creation of Lucky Dog Records and the relaunching of Monument Records under the Sony Music Entertainment umbrella. From the 1960s into the 2000s this series of executives enjoyed the successes of such notable artists as Johnny Cash, Willie Nelson, Janie Fricke, Rosanne Cash, Rodney Crowell, Mary Chapin Carpenter, Doug Stone, Joe Diffie, Collin Raye, Patty Loveless, and *Gretchen Wilson*.

Prior to 1961, the Columbia Broadcasting System (CBS) distributed Columbia recordings outside North America through an arrangement with music conglomerate EMI. In 1961, CBS formed CBS Records to handle releases overseas as well as in the United States and Canada. By 1968, the CBS Record Group included the Columbia, Epic, Date, and CBS Masterworks imprints.

In March 1968, the Columbia Broadcasting System established a fifty-fifty joint venture with Japan's Sony, Inc., named CBS/Sony Records (and renamed CBS Sony, Inc. in 1973). In November 1987, CBS sold its half of the joint venture to Sony, which renamed the label group as Sony Music Entertainment in the early 1990s.

In 2004 Sony merged its music division with Bertelsmann AG's BMG label to form Sony BMG, with former DMZ Records chief John Grady overseeing Columbia Nashville, Epic Nashville, Lucky Dog, and Monument. Meanwhile, Joe Galante continued to run the Nashville operations of RCA, BNA Entertainment, and Arista under the Sony BMG arrangement. Two years later Grady left, and Galante took charge of the entire label complex. Sony bought Bertelsmann's interest in Sony BMG in October 2008, and Sony has used the name Sony Music Entertainment for the combined label group. Galante helmed Sony Music Nashville until May 2010, when he surrendered the reins to former music publisher GARY OVERTON.

At this writing, the Sony Nashville group boasts a powerful set of rosters spanning the musical spectrum. Country acts include Arista's BRAD PAISLEY and CARRIE UNDERWOOD; BNA's KENNY CHESNEY and KELLIE PICKLER; Columbia Nashville's MIRANDA LAMBERT; and RCA Nashville's SARA EVANS. —*Dick Spottswood*

## Combine Music Publishing
established in Baltimore, Maryland, 1958; sold 1986

Organized by FRED FOSTER, in conjunction with his creation of MONUMENT RECORDS, Combine Music became a leading Nashville publishing house and a prototype of what today is called a "boutique" publisher. Foster, a record salesman and promotion man working out of Baltimore, established Monument in 1958, then Combine, seeking to own and develop the songs he recorded.

Foster moved his companies to MUSIC CITY in 1960, eventually locating his studios downtown. Building on Monument's success with ROY ORBISON in the early 1960s, Combine made greater strides after BOB BECKHAM was hired in 1964. Under Beckham, the firm nurtured such talents as DOLLY PARTON, KRIS KRISTOFFERSON, LARRY GATLIN, RAY STEVENS, JERRY REED, DENNIS LINDE, TONY JOE WHITE, BOB DIPIERO, Bob Morrison, John Scott Sherrill, and Johnny MacRae. Combine peaked in the early 1970s via Kristofferson songs such as "Me and Bobby McGee" (cowritten with Foster), "Help Me Make It Through the Night," and "Sunday Morning Coming Down" and ELVIS PRESLEY's version of Linde's "Burning Love," all smashes that became pop-country standards.

Cash flow and legal problems surrounding Monument's bankruptcy led to Combine's acquisition by the SBK publishing operation of New York City in 1986; today the Combine copyrights belong to EMI Music. —*John Lomax III*

## Comedy

From its beginnings as a commercial art form in the 1920s, comedy has been a part of country performance. Humor was already a centerpiece of vaudeville and BLACKFACE MINSTRELSY, from which country entertainers drew heavily; successful country entertainers such as UNCLE DAVE MACON, Whitey Ford (THE DUKE OF PADUCAH), and James "Goober" Buchanan were seasoned vaudeville veterans. Penetrating remote rural areas, MEDICINE SHOWS offered comedy and music to lure prospective customers. ROY ACUFF was one of many country musicians who worked medicine show tours that included blackface and unsophisticated rube characters.

Radio barn dance programs and road troupes required variety, and comedy became essential to both. JOHN LAIR, at Chicago's WLS beginning in 1928, and Lowell Blanchard, at Knoxville's WNOX from 1936, began writing scripts that borrowed from minstrel, vaudeville, and medicine show routines as well as from traditional folk humor. These scripts were performed by entertainers such as LULU BELLE and SCOTTY and the COON CREEK GIRLS at WLS and ARCHIE CAMPBELL (as Grandpappy), BILL CARLISLE (as Hotshot Elmer), and HOMER & JETHRO at WNOX. JAMUP and HONEY, whose WSM heyday spanned the 1940s, was the best-known blackface act of its day. Programs featuring these entertainers followed the format and content of early minstrel and vaudeville shows, usually with a straight man and one or more comedians.

Early on, most traveling country bands included a comedian, usually the bass player. Often performers assumed this role by necessity, as in the cases of Dave Sutherland and Chick Stripling, comedian for several BLUEGRASS bands. Some musicians worked in street clothing until comedy time and then donned outlandish costumes and put on makeup to play their comic parts. Other entertainers, such as SNUFFY JENKINS, GRANDPA JONES, and Old Joe Clark, dressed in character throughout their shows. Many comedians—Lazy Jim Day with his "singing news," Homer & Jethro, and LONZO & OSCAR—featured comic songs.

By the mid-1940s star comedians emerged: MINNIE PEARL, ROD BRASFIELD, and the Duke of Paducah at the GRAND OLE OPRY; Pat Buttram, SMILEY BURNETTE, and GEORGE GOBEL at the NATIONAL BARN DANCE; Archie Campbell, Bill Carlisle, and Homer & Jethro at the MID-DAY MERRY-GO-ROUND; and Crazy Elmer and Lazy Jim Day at the WWVA JAMBOREE. The Opry's Uncle Dave Macon embodied in a single individual what most country shows wanted to present: musical artistry, comedy, sentiment, and religion, all delivered with outstanding humor and showmanship.

Country humor reached its peak with the syndicated TV series *HEE HAW*, produced for twenty-three years beginning in 1969. The show was simple, rural, and corny, characteristics that would seem to guarantee failure in the modern age, but audiences loved it. *Hee Haw* helped make celebrities of hosts BUCK OWENS and ROY CLARK, along with a cast including seasoned comedians Grandpa Jones, Minnie Pearl, Archie Campbell, Roni Stoneman, JUNIOR SAMPLES, George "Goober" Lindsey, STRINGBEAN, and Lulu Roman.

With the deaths of Archie Campbell, Minnie Pearl, Grandpa Jones, and JERRY CLOWER, few veteran country comedians remain. But even though the genre has waned, MIKE SNIDER has made jokes and humorous anecdotes part of his Grand Ole Opry act, and many bluegrass bands do the same. The *RENFRO VALLEY BARN DANCE* still features comedians, as it always has, including Pete Stamper, Betty Lou York, Bun Wilson, and Old Joe Clark, until his death in 1998. Comedy clubs offer new venues for stand-up comics, and some of them—such as James Gregory, JEFF FOXWORTHY (famous for his "You might be a redneck" routines), and Cledus T. Judd—perform country-oriented routines. In 2000, Foxworthy teamed with Bill Engvall, Larry the Cable Guy, and Ron White for the first Blue Collar Comedy Tour, which led to a live album in 2001 and their DVD *Blue Collar Comedy: The Movie* in 2003. Some observers have attributed the decline in country comedy to the increasing sophistication of the music's audiences. Though fans value the music, they may be uneasy with the old rural-oriented humor. Nevertheless, many country entertainers continue to inject humor into their shows because they know that making audiences laugh helps them forget their problems, if only temporarily. —*Loyal Jones*

## Confederate Railroad
Danny Shirley b. Chattanooga, Tennessee, August 12, 1956
Chris McDaniel b. Rock Springs, Georgia, February 4, 1965
Wayne Secrest b. Alton, Illinois, April 29, 1950
Gates Nichols b. New York City, New York, May 26, 1944
Mark DuFresne b. Green Bay, Wisconsin, August 6, 1953
Jimmy Dormire b. Ann Arbor, Michigan, March 8, 1960

Covering the same turf as HANK WILLIAMS JR. and TRAVIS TRITT, Confederate Railroad pulls its audience from fans who favor both country and southern rock. ATLANTIC RECORDS originally signed singer Danny Shirley as a solo artist. Shirley had released a series of singles on independent Amor Records (1984–88), and the Danny Shirley Band was well known in the Chattanooga-Atlanta region, having backed JOHNNY PAYCHECK and DAVID ALLAN COE as well as performed on their own. Shirley and Atlantic changed the group's name to Confederate Railroad and billed Shirley's album as a band effort.

The group's first single, "She Took It Like a Man," was a #37 *Billboard* chart maker; the second, "Jesus and Mama," gave them their first Top Five hit. "Queen of Memphis," from the same album, reached #2. Confederate Railroad's sense of campy redneck humor brought them additional attention: the video for "Trashy Women" featured band members in drag.

The band's self-titled debut album (1992) sold more than 2 million copies; its follow-up, *Notorious* (1994), also topped the 1 million mark on the strength of singles, including "Daddy Never Was the Cadillac Kind" and "Elvis & Andy," an homage to ELVIS PRESLEY and Andy Griffith. The act won ACM's Best New Vocal Group award for 1992 and toured with Lynyrd Skynyrd and the MARSHALL TUCKER BAND in 1993. Guitarist Jimmy Dormire replaced Michael Lamb in January 1995, shortly before the release of *When and Where*. *Keep on Rockin'* (1998) failed to meet expectations, and McDaniel later exited, replaced by Cody McCarver. Leaving Atlantic, the band signed with Audium for the 2001 release *Unleashed*. Shanachie Records issued *Cheap Thrills* in 2007. —*Brian Mansfield*

## Conjunto Music

Conjunto, the button accordion–based music of South Texas, emerged as the popular music of the Texas-Mexican working class in the late nineteenth and early twentieth centuries. As such it represented the interests and aspirations of the *gente pobre*—the poorest people in Texas-Mexican society. Throughout its history, conjunto has been alternately despised as "low-class" or treasured as an expression of Texas-Mexican life.

From the late nineteenth century to 1935, conjunto strongly reflected its roots in the music of German and Czech immigrants, who brought the diatonic button accordion to Mexico and Texas. The earliest music consisted of polkas along with other popular salon dances—schottisches, mazurkas, waltzes, redowas. The Mexican *corrido* was also prominent. The accordion was played solo or with other instruments on an ad hoc basis.

From 1935 through World War II, more emphasis was placed on Mexican and Latin American song forms such as the huapango, bolero, and ranchera (country song). During this period the twelve-string guitarlike bajo sexto became the standard accompaniment to the accordion.

Following World War II the conjunto ensemble took its current form—three-row diatonic button accordion, bajo sexto, electric bass, and drum kit. Influences from dances including the Colombian *cumbia*, the tango, and the chachacha were introduced, along with elements of rock, blues, and country-western music.

Although conjunto is considered simple, happy, dance music whose lyrics focus on love and romance, there are many songs of political and social oppression, of discrimination and racism, of longing for a former homeland, of backbreaking labor, and, recently, of the social impact of the international drug trade. This last has given rise to the conjunto-based narco-corrido.

Major early figures in conjunto include accordionist Narciso Martinez, "El Huracán del Valle" (the Hurricane of the Valley).

Martinez and his musical partner, Santiago Almeida, established the accordion and bajo sexto as the basic constituents in the conjunto style. Almeida was the first to play the bajo sexto as a solo, melody-line instrument. Martinez concentrated on the right-hand lead of the accordion, disregarding the bass chord accompaniment and thus moving the music away from its Germanic roots.

Other important early figures in conjunto music are Pedro Ayala, "El Monarca del Acordeón" (the Monarch of the Accordion); Santiago Jimenez Sr., "El Flaco" (the Skinny One); and Bruno Villareal, "El Azote del Valle" (the Scourge of the Valley). Virtually blind since birth, Villareal said in a 1986 interview: "It's not been so beautiful our life—more a life of suffering, but, oh, well—I never saw anything else I could do but be a musician. I couldn't do ordinary work because of my blindness. My entire life was suffering. Like people say, only he who carries the burden knows its weight."

Major conjunto figures in the years following World War II include Valerio Longoria and Tony de la Rosa. Both are widely known for their inclusion of the drum kit, for the replacement of the acoustic upright bass (the tololoche) with the electric bass, for the use of amplification and PA systems, and for performing more vocal music. Longoria introduced the bolero to conjunto, while de la Rosa slowed the basic tempo of conjunto polkas, thus allowing for greater melodic emphasis; more complex fingering techniques; and a smoother, gliding dance form, *el tacuachito*, which replaced the European-influenced *baile de brinquito* (the hopping dance).

Many contemporary conjunto players, including Nick Villareal, Esteban Jordan, and FLACO JIMENEZ have performed hybrid music. Santiago Jimenez Jr. is a contemporary player who strives to maintain the conjunto style of the past, basing his playing largely on his father's style. Always a regional music, conjunto has begun to have a national and international following and is now crossing over into other Texas music forms (*orquesta*, *tejana*, *la onda chicana*) and into other national forms (rock, country, and western). Bands such as Los Bravos del Norte and Los Tigres del Norte, both Grammy-winning groups, have increased conjunto's visibility while retaining its working-class roots. —*David Romtvedt*

## John Conlee
b. Versailles, Kentucky, August 11, 1946

John Conlee achieved star status with a high-in-the-throat delivery and songs that voiced the everyday concerns of aging baby boomers. Stylistically, he drifted from neo-HONKY-TONK in his early years to a more pop-oriented country sound.

John Wayne Conlee came by his country credentials honestly, growing up on a farm near Versailles, Kentucky, a short distance from Lexington. After high school he earned a mortician's license and practiced for six years before putting his gift for gab to good use as a radio announcer. That line of work brought him to Nashville in 1971, where he served as an announcer at WLAC-FM.

By 1976 Conlee had a recording contract with ABC/Dot. An early release of "Backside of Thirty" failed to chart, but the bittersweet honky-tonk charm of "Rose Colored Glasses," cowritten by Conlee and framed by Bud Logan's lush production, gave the singer a #5 hit in 1978.

His first #1, "Lady Lay Down," topped the charts early in 1979, and a rereleased "Backside of Thirty" soon matched the feat. Conlee's hottest streak came during 1983–84, when he scored four consecutive #1s: "Common Man," "I'm Only in It for the Love," "In My Eyes," and "As Long as I'm Rockin' with You."

Listeners identified with his "regular Joe" looks, comforting voice, and songs about ordinary people in everyday situations. When Conlee pledged enduring faithfulness in "As Long as I'm Rockin' with You," "Old School," or "In My Eyes," he gained the credibility of a teddy bear.

A GRAND OLE OPRY cast member since 1981, Conlee continues to make appearances on the show. True to his agrarian roots, he has served as honorary chairman of the Family Farm Defense Fund and on the board of Farm Aid. He lives now on a Nashville-area farm. —*Jay Orr*

## Earl Thomas Conley
b. Portsmouth, Ohio, October 17, 1941

Merging a hard country sound with rock & roll energy, Earl Thomas Conley released four #1 singles from one album, a series of hit records that made him a strong presence in country music during the 1980s.

When Conley's father lost his railroad job, the family, with eight children, dipped to the poverty level in their small town of Portsmouth, situated across the Ohio River from Kentucky in a valley among hills known as the "Little Smokies." Conley's hometown later inspired his song "Smokey Mountain Memories" (cowritten with Dick Heard), a #13 hit for MEL STREET in 1975.

Conley credits schoolteacher John Brandel as a motivational influence. Following military service, Conley settled in Xenia, Ohio, and worked for the Pennsylvania Railroad. He also toiled in a Portsmouth steel mill before moving, in 1971, to Huntsville, Alabama, where he had met studio owner Nelson Larkin. Conley played clubs by night and gained valuable studio experience.

Conley moved from Huntsville to Nashville in 1973. Two years later he hit the charts as an artist on GRT Records. In 1976 CONWAY TWITTY took Conley's composition "This Time I've Hurt Her More Than She Loves Me" to #1.

After a brief stay at WARNER BROS. RECORDS, Conley moved to Sunbird Records, where he enjoyed his first #1 hit as a singer, "Fire and Smoke," in 1981. RCA RECORDS promptly signed him, and he accumulated seventeen #1 singles over the next eight years, including "Holding Her and Loving You," "Once in a Blue Moon," and "Nobody Falls Like a Fool." His Top Ten songs also included duets with Anita Pointer, EMMYLOU HARRIS, and KEITH WHITLEY. Conley coproduced his albums with Larkin, who also had moved to Nashville from Huntsville. —*Gerry Wood*

## Conqueror Records
established in Chicago, Illinois, 1928; ended 1942

The Conqueror label was in evidence from 1928 to 1942, and releases numbered almost three thousand. As a Sears, Roebuck–owned, Chicago-based label (along with CHALLENGE, Silvertone, and Supertone), Conqueror and its sister labels leased all of their material from other labels for mail-order catalog sales and were not in the recording business per se.

The Plaza group of labels, headed by Banner, provided initial product for Conqueror releases before becoming part of the evolving AMERICAN RECORD CORPORATION (ARC). In turn, ARC was bought by COLUMBIA in 1938. ARC/Columbia continued the leasing process with Conqueror thereafter. Thus, except for a minute block of GENNETT RECORDS matrices, rights to Conqueror-released material by ROY ACUFF, the CARTER FAMILY, BOB WILLS, and others

reside today with SONY MUSIC ENTERTAINMENT, whose predecessor, Sony Music, purchased Columbia in November 1987. —*Bob Pinson*

## Don Cook
b. San Antonio, Texas, May 25, 1949

A renowned producer, songwriter, and publishing executive, Don Cook rose through the ranks to become Chief Creative Officer of Sony/ATV Tree Publishing in 1998. He coproduced superduo BROOKS & DUNN's albums from 1991 to 1999 and cowrote several of their hits while also producing and writing for other top country performers.

Growing up in a desolate area near San Antonio, Texas, Cook found little to do but dream and write. His taste was formed by his father's love for big-band music, his mother's love for country, and his own affinity for rock & roll. After graduating from the University of Texas with a degree in English, he moved to MUSIC CITY, where he started crafting commercial jingles and performing at OPRYLAND USA. He toured the Soviet Union with the Opryland Country Music USA Tour in 1974. Soon after, Don Gant of ACUFF-ROSE PUBLICATIONS offered Cook his first writing deal. In 1976 he switched to TREE PUBLISHING, predecessor to Sony/ATV Tree, where he produced many of his own song demos and earned a reputation as a top-notch song-and-sound man.

There, Cook penned hits such as "Who's Lonely Now" (HIGHWAY 101), "Lady Lay Down" (JOHN CONLEE), and the Brooks & Dunn #1s "Brand New Man," "My Next Broken Heart," "That Ain't No Way to Go," "Only in America," and "It's Getting Better All the Time." After 1990 Cook concentrated largely on producing. Besides Brooks & Dunn, Cook has produced ALABAMA, THE MAVERICKS, SHENANDOAH, CONWAY TWITTY, MARTY STUART, and Wade Hayes, among other acts.

Cook left Sony/ATV in 2004 to focus on his family and on songwriting. In 2009 he signed with Skyline Music Publishing. —*Michael Hight*

## Spade Cooley
b. Grand, Oklahoma, December 17, 1910; d. November 23, 1969

The fiddler-bandleader who first popularized the term "WESTERN SWING" and advanced country music presentation with a natty, uniform-clad band and lush, melodic sound, Donnell Clyde "Spade" Cooley was a major force in World War II–era West Coast country.

An accomplished fiddler by his teens, he cut his teeth working with Oklahoma dance bands until hard times blew the Cooley family west, first to Oregon and then to Modesto, California, in 1931. Several years later, "with nothing but my fiddle and three cents in my pocket," as he put it, Cooley jumped a freight train to Los Angeles and was hired as a film set stand-in by ROY ROGERS. Cooley also picked up local musical jobs with Rogers, STUART HAMBLEN, Cal Shrum, and, later, JIMMY WAKELY.

When promoter FOREMAN PHILLIPS plucked the fiddler away from Wakely in 1942 and made him a bandleader at the Venice Pier Ballroom, Cooley's popularity soared. Throughout 1942–44 Cooley's large swing outfit (featuring players such as singer-guitarist SMOKEY ROGERS, steel guitarist JOAQUIN MURPHEY or steel player NOEL BOGGS, and vocalists TEX WILLIAMS and Deuce Spriggins) regularly drew thousands of dancers and stirred up a good-natured publicity feud between Cooley and BOB WILLS,

*Spade Cooley*

who had just moved to the San Fernando Valley. Cooley's band definitely swung, but their sound was fuller and richer, with an almost orchestral approach more refined than Wills's hot fiddle-band style; Tex Williams's urbane crooning provided additional elegance. It was a formula for success, and Cooley continued to pack the Pier, The Riverside Rancho, and the Santa Monica Ballroom.

Signed to OKeh Records, a subsidiary of Columbia Records, Cooley's band first recorded in December 1944 and immediately scored a double-sided hit with "Shame on You" (which spent nine weeks at #1) and "A Pair of Broken Hearts" (which entered the Top Ten). With his releases upgraded to the Columbia red label, Cooley scored more hits during 1946–47 ("Detour," "Crazy 'Cause I Love You") and, despite the departure of Tex Williams, remained one of the West Coast's top acts. When Cooley broke away from Columbia and signed with RCA Victor in 1947, he also began to appear regularly on Phillips's top-rated *Hoffman Hayride* KTLA television show as well as in a series of B-grade western movies.

Just as Cooley moved to Decca Records in 1951, western swing's popularity began to subside, and the hot-tempered, hard-drinking fiddler began a gradual psychological nosedive that culminated in the tragic, vicious torture-murder of his wife, Ella Mae, at his Kern County ranch in April 1961. In one of country music's most high-profile scandals, he testified that "rockets ran through my brain when Ella Mae told me of her desire to join a 'free love cult.'" Convicted of first-degree murder in August, largely on the gruesome eyewitness account of his fourteen-year-old daughter, Melody (whom Cooley branded "a liar"), he was sentenced to life in Vacaville Prison. In November 1969, on a seventy-two-hour furlough, Cooley performed three songs at a police benefit in Oakland, California. After the audience of almost 3,000 gave him a standing ovation, he strolled offstage, suffered a massive heart attack, and died on the spot, ending one of the most dramatic and tragic sagas in popular music history. —*Jonny Whiteside*

## Coon Creek Girls

Lily May Ledford b. Powell County, Kentucky, March 17, 1917; d. July 14, 1985
Charlotte "Rosie" Ledford b. Powell County, Kentucky, August 16, 1915;
   d. July 24, 1976
Esther "Violet" Koehler b. Wilton, Wisconsin, February 6, 1916; d. October 4, 1973
Evelyn "Daisy" Lange b. St. Henry, Ohio, July 7, 1919; d. February 10, 2002
Minnie "Susie" Ledford b. Powell County, Kentucky, October 10, 1923;
   d. July 22, 1987

A pioneering all-woman STRINGBAND, the Coon Creek Girls was organized and named by JOHN LAIR in 1937 around the talents of Lily May Ledford, a regular on his previous shows at WLS in Chicago. The act was enthusiastically received over WLW and WCKY in the Cincinnati area, as part of Lair's RENFRO VALLEY BARN DANCE, then broadcasting from Cincinnati's Music Hall. Playing off Lily's name, the other band members all received stage names from flowers: her older sister Charlotte became "Rosie," Esther Koehler became "Violet," and Evelyn Lange became "Daisy."

An OLD-TIME band with fiddle and banjo (Lily), guitar (Rosie), mandolin (Violet), and bass (Daisy), the Coon Creek Girls harmonized in vocal duets, trios, and quartets, playing folk songs and other numbers the women learned growing up or from Lair and fellow performers. In 1938 the group recorded nine numbers for Vocalion. In 1939, at the invitation of Eleanor Roosevelt, they performed their music and comedy routines at the White House for the Roosevelts and the king and queen of England.

When Lair's show moved to Renfro Valley, Kentucky, in 1939, Koehler and Lange went with THE CALLAHAN BROTHERS to KVOO in Tulsa and then to KRLD in Dallas. As a result, younger sister Minnie Ledford, who became "Black-Eyed Susie," joined sisters Lily and Daisy in the band, and the three Ledfords recorded several sides for the Renfro Valley label during their tenure with that barn dance. From Renfro Valley, the Coon Creek Girls went to the OLD DOMINION BARN DANCE in Richmond, Virginia, and were part of SUNSHINE SUE's New York Broadway show. By 1957, the Coon Creek Girls had ended the act so that they could raise families, but in 1968 RALPH RINZLER persuaded them to play at the NEWPORT FOLK FESTIVAL and the Smithsonian Institution's American Folklife Festival in 1972. In the 1970s Mike Seeger convinced Lily May to revive her career at college concerts and folk festivals. In 1983 she recorded an LP, *Banjo Picking Girl*, for the Greenhays label. —*Loyal Jones*

## Carol Lee Cooper (*see* Wilma Lee & Stoney Cooper)

## George Cooper Jr.

b. Nashville, Tennessee, December 20, 1897; d. July 17, 1974

Local 257 of the AMERICAN FEDERATION OF MUSICIANS was almost inactive and penniless when George Wesley Cooper Jr. became its president, in 1937. Founded in Nashville in 1902, the chapter had fallen on lean times during the Depression and had declined in membership to a total of seventy-five.

Many believe that the growth of Nashville's music industry might have been impossible without Cooper's leadership during the next thirty-six years. He led the fight against musical exams for union membership, allowing hillbilly, blues, and rock musicians who couldn't read music to join. He also pioneered "demo rates," recording studio payments to musicians for demo sessions that were lower than union-scale rates for master sessions. Demo rates permitted song publishing companies to thrive and encouraged musical experimentation. He raised union scale at the GRAND OLE OPRY and for master sessions and encouraged cooperation rather than confrontation at recording dates.

Cooper was a horn player and bassist who joined the AFM in 1918, when he was performing in a traveling circus band. He returned to Nashville to play for silent pictures and vaudeville and then joined the staff band at radio station WSM.

His early tenure at the union was marked by the national musicians' strike of 1942–44, which eventually resulted in session players' sharing in profits based on the number of records on which they performed, the "special payments fund."

Cooper retired in 1973. He was succeeded by Johnny DeGeorge (1973–86), Jay Collins (1986–91), HAROLD BRADLEY (1991–2008), and David Pomeroy (since 2009). —*Robert K. Oermann*

## Wilma Lee & Stoney Cooper

Wilma Leigh Leary Cooper b. Valley Head, West Virginia, February 7, 1921;
    d. September 13, 2011
Dale Troy "Stoney" Cooper b. Harman, West Virginia, October 16, 1918; d. March
    22, 1977

The duo of Wilma Lee & Stoney Cooper was one of country music's premier husband-wife teams for some three decades. Their career grew from the Leary Family Singers, for whom young Stoney had worked as a fiddler prior to his marriage to one of the group's members, Wilma Leigh Leary, on June 9, 1941. The Coopers worked at radio station WMMN in Fairmont, West Virginia, and on other stations in Arkansas, Nebraska, Illinois, and North Carolina before settling in for ten years at the *WWVA JAMBOREE* in 1947.

After a brief stint with RICH-R-TONE RECORDS in 1947, the duo signed with COLUMBIA and recorded most of their trademark numbers on that label, including "Thirty Pieces of Silver," "Legend of the Dogwood Tree," "Sunny Side of the Mountain," and

*Wilma Lee & Stoney Cooper with daughter Carol Lee*

"Walking My Lord up Calvary Hill." Like ROY ACUFF's Smoky Mountain Boys, the Coopers' band, the Clinch Mountain Clan, favored an acoustical sound highlighted by DOBRO, fiddle, and mandolin. In 1955 the pair switched to HICKORY RECORDS, where they registered their biggest chart-makers, including "Cheated Too," "Come Walk with Me," "Big Midnight Special," and "There's a Big Wheel." The first of these helped bring them to the GRAND OLE OPRY in 1957, where they were regulars for some twenty years. The Coopers vanished from *Billboard*'s country charts after 1961, but continued as a force for traditionalism in country music. Their later recordings appeared on the DECCA, Skylite, Power Pak, STARDAY, and ROUNDER labels.

Ill health plagued Stoney's last years, and after his death Wilma Lee Cooper veered somewhat more in the direction of BLUEGRASS, continuing at the Opry as a solo act until a stroke forced her retirement in 2001. Her recordings have been released on Rounder and REBEL RECORDS and rereleased on Varese Vintage. Daughter Carol Lee Cooper (b. March 21, 1942) has forged an independent career at the Grand Ole Opry since 1975 with a vocal background quartet known as the Carol Lee Singers, formed in 1973. —*Ivan M. Tribe*

## Cowboy Copas

b. Blue Creek, Ohio, July 15, 1913; d. March 5, 1963

Lloyd Estel "Cowboy" Copas's strong tenor voice, careful phrasing, and flat-top guitar picking gave his recordings a distinctive sound in an era dominated by instantly identifiable singers. He began performing at fairs and talent contests with his brother, Marion, when both were teenagers, and he was still a teenager when he teamed with local fiddler Lester Vernon Storer

*Cowboy Copas*

(known professionally as Natchee the Indian) and acquired the alliterative stage name Cowboy. To heighten this image, he claimed that he was born on a ranch in Oklahoma, a locale considered more colorful than his family's Ohio corn and tobacco farm. Copas never professed to be a cowboy singer, however, and recorded virtually nothing with a western motif. In fact, his music occupied a middle ground between HONKY-TONK and the country-pop sounds of smooth vocalists such as EDDY ARNOLD and GEORGE MORGAN.

In the early 1940s Copas worked at WLW in Cincinnati and signed with locally based KING RECORDS. He recorded "Filipino Baby" in 1944 during his first session for the label. When it was finally released in the summer of 1946, it became a #4 hit that boosted King's fortunes and propelled Copas to the GRAND OLE OPRY. In 1946 he joined PEE WEE KING's Golden West Cowboys, with whom he worked briefly as a guitarist and featured vocalist before going solo. "Tragic Romance," "Signed, Sealed and Delivered," "Tennessee Waltz," "Tennessee Moon," "The Strange Little Girl," and "Copy Cat" (a duet with his sixteen-year-old daughter, Kathy) were among his hits between 1948 and 1952. Copas's voice seemed best suited to lilting and melodious love songs, resulting in announcer GRANT TURNER's dubbing him "Waltz King of the Grand Ole Opry."

Like many country artists, Copas's career was temporarily muffled by the rock revolution, but he enjoyed a renaissance after signing with STARDAY Records in 1959. His album *Unforgettable* highlighted "Alabam," consisting of verses found in several lyrical folksongs. Released as a single in 1960, it became a #1 hit. Thereafter, Copas was consistently on the charts and recorded prolifically until, returning from a Kansas City benefit show in a plane piloted by Copas's son-in-law, RANDY HUGHES, Copas, Hughes, PATSY CLINE, and HAWKSHAW HAWKINS were killed in a crash near Camden, Tennessee. The final Copas single, with the too-prophetic title "Goodbye Kisses" (coauthored by Copas and LEFTY FRIZZELL a few weeks before the accident), was a posthumous hit. —*Jonathan Guyot Smith*

## Helen Cornelius (*see* Jim Ed Brown)

## Country Blues

In country music as in pop, the term "blues" today is used rather casually to describe a number of songs that have little in common with the classic, well-defined African American blues styles of the 1920s and 1930s. There was a time, however, in prewar country music, when white country singers created a number of subgenres based on legitimate forms of blues. Some of these singers, including major figures such as JIMMIE RODGERS, influenced later performers and songwriters, both in singing style and in song form.

Country's fascination with blues dates to at least as early as 1924, when OKEH RECORDS issued the first country disc bearing the name "blues," HENRY WHITTER's "Lonesome Road Blues," with its famous verse "I'm going down the road feeling bad." A few months later, UNCLE DAVE MACON, who had learned much of his music from blacks around middle Tennessee, cut "Hill Billie Blues," a reworking of W. C. Handy's "Hesitation Blues."

Few of these recordings actually sounded much like the distinctive Delta blues or Texas blues of black performers Charley Patton or Blind Lemon Jefferson, respectively. But in 1926 FRANK HUTCHISON, a West Virginia singer, began recording with a slide guitar, crafting pieces such as "Worried Blues" and "The Train

That Carried the Girl from Town." In 1927 the team of DARBY & TARLTON, who had listened intently to black singers in Georgia and South Carolina, recorded the two-sided hit "Columbus Stockade Blues" and "Birmingham Jail." These recordings, too, featured a slide guitar and closely resembled those made by black country blues singers of the day. Country act FLEMING & TOWNSEND, from western Tennessee, incorporated Memphis blues into a string of records for RCA Victor and the AMERICAN RECORD CORPORATION.

Appalachian coal miners and factory workers created a different type of "mountain blues," based on eerie modal chord patterns and a high, lonesome, keening style. Foremost among these singers was DOCK BOGGS, from Norton, Virginia, and Kentuckian B. F. Shelton. The Shepherd Family, miners from the Appalachia, Virginia area, adapted the style to STRINGBAND MUSIC, though they recorded fewer than twenty sides.

A third style involved the famous "blue yodel" of Jimmie Rodgers, first defined in his November 1927 recording "Blue Yodel #1 (T for Texas)." Though Rodgers often used the classic three-line blues stanza in his songs, his regular, almost bouncy tempo and fluid falsetto shared little with black styles. Two of Rodgers's emulators were Cliff Carlisle (brother of BILL CARLISLE) and the young GENE AUTRY, both of whom achieved great fame in the 1930s and who eventually moved into mainstream country. Cliff and Bill Carlisle also developed a form of off-color "hokum blues" of the sort popularized by Georgia Tom (Thomas A. Dorsey) and others. This style influenced the young BOB WILLS, who borrowed pieces such as "Eagle Riding Papa" from Dorsey. In the 1930s groups such as MILTON BROWN's Musical Brownies adapted blues (and even early jazz) to their WESTERN SWING sounds. —*Charles Wolfe*

## The Country Gazette

Byron Berline b. Caldwell, Kansas, July 6, 1944
Kenny Wertz b. Washington, D.C., February 4, 1942
Roger Bush b. Hollywood, California, September 16, 1940
Alan Munde b. Norman, Oklahoma, November 4, 1946
Roland White b. Madawaska, Maine, April 23, 1938
Herb Pedersen b. Berkeley, California, April 27, 1944

Los Angeles–based, the Country Gazette evolved from the Doug Dillard Expedition. Touring as members of the Flying Burrito Brothers, fiddler BYRON BERLINE, singer-guitarist Kenny Wertz, and bassist Roger Bush would perform a short BLUEGRASS set at each show. After the Burritos disbanded in early 1972, this core group decided to stay together. Calling themselves the Country Gazette, they added banjo player Alan Munde, formerly with JIMMY MARTIN's band. The new group landed a record deal with United Artists. Bringing singer and multi-instrumentalist HERB PEDERSEN aboard, Country Gazette released *A Traitor in Our Midst*, produced by Jim Dickson, who had found earlier success with THE BYRDS, THE DILLARDS, and the Flying Burrito Brothers.

In 1973 mandolin player ROLAND WHITE joined the Gazette, and Berline moved on to work sessions with musicians such as Elton John and Rod Stewart. White and Munde became the foundation of the band as other members came and went. The Gazette made several trips to Europe and were especially popular in England. The act dissolved briefly in 1982 after releasing *America's Bluegrass Band* on Flying Fish Records. They regrouped in 1983 but permanently called it a day four years later. White joined forces with one of bluegrass music's premier outfits, the NASHVILLE BLUEGRASS BAND, remaining with that organization through the

1990s before forming the Roland White Band. Munde developed a series of instructional materials and encouraged musicians to develop their bluegrass skills. —*Chris Skinker*

## The Country Gentlemen

Organized in Arlington, Virginia, the Country Gentlemen played their first official date on July 4, 1957. Although such musicians as Bill Emerson, Pete Kuykendall, Ed Ferris, Jimmy Gaudreau, JERRY DOUGLAS, DOYLE LAWSON, Bill Yates, and RICKY SKAGGS have played with the group during its long history, the performers most closely identified with it—the "Classic Country Gentlemen" who were elected to the IBMA Hall of Fame in 1996—are the late Charlie Waller, the late John Duffey, Eddie Adcock, and Tom Gray.

In the late 1950s, the Country Gentlemen were one of several bands who helped give BLUEGRASS its name and reputation through their popularization of sounds borrowed from BILL MONROE and other pioneers of the genre. On one hand, the Country Gentlemen played hyper-bluegrass, in that they accentuated the stylistic trademarks first introduced by Monroe and his musicians. Waller repeatedly played dynamic guitar runs; Duffey and Adcock played pyrotechnical instrumental breaks on mandolin and banjo, respectively; and Duffey soared into high, sometimes strident harmonies that competed favorably with Monroe's.

But while respecting tradition, the Country Gentlemen were one of the most important early innovative bands in bluegrass, taking the genre into new arenas of repertoire and stylistic performance while steadfastly using acoustic instruments. Although the Gentlemen could play hard-driving bluegrass reminiscent of Monroe or THE STANLEY BROTHERS, they were also at home with blues and jazz, a 1920s pop song such as "Heartaches," or a movie soundtrack melody such as "Theme from Exodus." On these and other numbers, Eddie Adcock's banjo improvisations forecast the "newgrass" departures of the 1970s.

Just as the Country Gentlemen were strongly influenced by the folk revival, their Folkways albums introduced them to listeners who had not earlier patronized bluegrass. "Handsome Molly" and "Poor Ellen Smith," among others, displayed their knowledge of early recorded country music, but these selections seemed to target folk music fans. The Country Gentlemen, in turn, influenced the folk community's acceptance and perception of bluegrass, and they became one of the earliest bluegrass bands to bridge the gap between the folk and bluegrass audiences.

The Country Gentlemen's modern, eclectic repertoire—encompassing pop, folk, rock, country, vintage bluegrass, BOB DYLAN songs, and, of course, newly composed songs—earned them one of the broadest constituencies any bluegrass band has ever enjoyed. While partisans of traditional bluegrass generally remained loyal to them, the band built an even larger following among middle-class professionals, a body of fans who have remained one of the core elements of the bluegrass fan base.

The act's appeal went well beyond musicianship; they were also first-class entertainers. Comedy sometimes meant little more than madcap stage antics, playing their instruments behind their backs, or Waller's imitations of HANK SNOW or MAC WISEMAN. But their humor often seemed spontaneous, especially when Duffey directed his barbs at fans who bought no records but instead taped their shows. Moreover, the group constantly refreshed its repertoire, though it will always be identified with such songs as "Two Little Boys," "Bringing Mary Home," "New Freedom Bell," "Legend of the Rebel Soldier,"

"This Morning at Nine," and other classics they introduced to the bluegrass canon.

As members came and went, the Gentlemen gave rise to several offshoot groups, including the SELDOM SCENE, Emerson & Waldron, and DOYLE LAWSON & QUICKSILVER. Despite numerous personnel changes, however, Waller's distinctive vocals provided continuity until his death in 2004. The Country Gentlemen continue today, with Waller's son Randy as guitarist and lead singer. —*Bill C. Malone*

## Country Music Association (*see* CMA)

## Country Music Disc Jockeys Association (*see* DJ Convention)

## Country Music Foundation (*see* Country Music Hall of Fame and Museum)

## The Country Music Hall of Fame
established by the Country Music Association in 1961

Membership in the Country Music Hall of Fame, the highest honor a country music professional can receive, is extended to performers, songwriters, broadcasters, musicians, and executives in recognition of their contributions to the development of country music. The Country Music Hall of Fame honor was created in 1961 by the Country Music Association (CMA); the first inductees were HANK WILLIAMS, JIMMIE RODGERS, and FRED ROSE. ROY ACUFF, the first living artist to join the Hall of Fame, was elected in 1962.

Over the Hall of Fame's history, the number of new members inducted each year has varied from one to twelve (no nominee was inducted in 1963, no candidate having received sufficient votes). The election procedure is as follows. A small CMA nominating committee drafts slates of candidates for each category; categories have been defined variously over the years. Award recipients are determined through a two-stage balloting process; the first round of voting narrows each category to five candidates; the second round selects winners. The large select committee of electors that votes on Hall of Fame membership is composed of CMA members who have participated in the country music industry for at least ten years. New Hall of Fame members receive special recognition in ceremonies at the COUNTRY MUSIC HALL OF FAME AND MUSEUM.

Bas-relief portraits cast in bronze honoring each Hall of Fame member were originally displayed at the Tennessee State Museum in downtown Nashville until the Country Music Hall of Fame and Museum opened its own building in April 1967; in this barn-roofed facility at the head of MUSIC ROW, the bronze plaques comprised a special exhibit. Today the plaques are displayed in a magnificent, seventy-foot-high rotunda at the museum's enlarged downtown Nashville facility, which opened in May 2001. —*Bill Ivey*

## Country Music Hall of Fame and Museum
established in Nashville, Tennessee, April 1, 1967

The Country Music Hall of Fame and Museum is one of the world's largest and most active popular music research centers and the world's largest repository of country music artifacts.

Early in the 1960s, as CMA's campaign to publicize country music was shifting into high gear, CMA leaders determined that a new organization was needed to operate a country music museum and to carry out research and educational activities beyond CMA's scope as a trade organization. Toward this end, the nonprofit Country Music Foundation (CMF) was chartered by the state of Tennessee in 1964 to collect, preserve, and publicize information and artifacts relating to the history of country music. Through CMF, industry leaders raised money to build the Country Music Hall of Fame and Museum, which opened on April 1, 1967. Located at the head of MUSIC ROW, the museum was erected on the site of a small Nashville city park. At this point, artifacts began to be displayed and a small library was begun in a loft above one of the museum's galleries.

Early in the 1970s the basement of the museum building was partially completed, and library expansion began, embracing not only recordings but also books and periodicals, sheet music and SONGBOOKS, photographs, business documents, and other materials. At the outset, CMA staff had run the museum, but by 1972 the museum (already governed by its own independent board of directors) acquired its own small staff, which has steadily increased to some seventy-five full-time professionals.

Building expansions took place in 1974, 1977, and 1984 to store and display the museum's growing collection of costumes, films, historic cars, musical instruments, and other artifacts. An education department was created to conduct ongoing programs with Middle Tennessee schools, an oral history program was begun, and a publications department was launched to handle books as well as the *Journal of Country Music*. The museum also began to reissue historic recordings (and, later, DVDs) on its own label and to provide consulting services for other labels.

To become more accessible to local and nonlocal audiences, in May 2001 the museum moved to a new, 130,000-square-foot facility in the heart of downtown Nashville's growing arts and entertainment district. In addition to state-of-the-art exhibits, the new museum offers a wide array of interactive programs for schoolchildren, families, and adults. Many of the museum's exhibits, books, and reissue recordings have won national recognition, including Grammys for the ten-CD compilation *The Complete Hank Williams* (1998) and the pioneering *Night Train to Nashville: Music City Rhythm & Blues, 1945–1970* (2004). Programs staged at Washington, D.C.'s John F. Kennedy Center for the Performing Arts and at the White House have further increased the museum's visibility as a world-class arts institution. The museum also owns Nashville's HATCH SHOW PRINT, a historic show business letterpress printing firm opened in 1879. In partnership with the MIKE CURB Family Foundation, the museum operates Studio B—an RCA RECORDS Nashville recording studio from 1957 to 1977—as a historic site and as a learning laboratory for students at Nashville's Belmont University.

In 2010 the Museum announced plans to integrate a 210,000-square-foot-expansion into a campus embracing a massive new Nashville convention center and a newly built hotel managed by Omni Hotels & Resorts. —*John W. Rumble*

## Country Radio Broadcasters (*see* CRB/CRS)

## Country Radio Seminar (*see* CRB/CRS)

## Country-Rock

The term "country-rock" generally refers to a blend of country and rock music that emerged in the late 1960s. Country-rock has been a source of controversy, mainly about whether the introduction of rock into country and country into rock was diluting or strengthening either music. With hindsight the Beatles can be seen to have performed country-rock many times with original material such as "I Don't Want to Spoil the Party" (1964), the groundbreaking *Rubber Soul* (1965) album, and a cover of BUCK OWENS's "Act Naturally" (1965). Certainly Lennon and McCartney's harmonies echo those of THE EVERLY BROTHERS, and George Harrison's guitar hero was CHET ATKINS as much as Chuck Berry.

Where the Beatles went, others followed. THE BYRDS, even before their lineup embraced GRAM PARSONS, were performing country material, with bassist CHRIS HILLMAN leading the way on a cover of the country standard "A Satisfied Mind" (1965). When Parsons joined in early 1968 after leaving his pioneering International Submarine Band, the Byrds recorded the seminal country-rock album, *Sweetheart of the Rodeo*.

In the early 1970s, country-rock proliferated. POCO, RICK NELSON's Stone Canyon Band, and the players behind LINDA RONSTADT all embraced country instrumentation, such as PEDAL STEEL GUITAR and banjo, as did such unlikely peers as the Grateful Dead and Rolling Stones. Ex-Byrds once again led the way, with Gene Clark using Doug Dillard's (THE DILLARDS) banjo to punctuate Dillard & Clark, and Gram Parsons and Chris Hillman relying on Sneaky Pete Kleinow's pedal steel in their FLYING BURRITO BROTHERS band.

These 1960s–1970s trends began to affect mainstream country, as WAYLON JENNINGS, in particular, sported long, shaggy hair; stressed a heavy, driving beat; and rebelled against his record label's production techniques. For recording, he insisted on using his road band—not exclusively session musicians—as well as a full drum kit, and he refused to limit sessions to RCA studios. Allied alongside him were WILLIE NELSON, Tompall Glaser (THE GLASER BROTHERS), and BOBBY BARE, and collectively their efforts kick-started country's rock-influenced OUTLAW movement. By the mid-1970s, THE EAGLES' smooth hybrid of rock & roll and country was garnering them a string of platinum albums, making them country-rock's greatest commercial success. Their selling sound opened the door for country-rock bands in mainstream country in the 1980s, as ALABAMA, the CHARLIE DANIELS Band, HANK WILLIAMS JR., and others enjoyed widespread country radio airplay. At the same time, young bands such as Green on Red, the Long Ryders, and JASON & THE SCORCHERS wedded the energy of punk rock with country licks and harmonies; in the process they sparked a brief musical movement dubbed "cowpunk."

Since then, country-rock has proliferated in many guises, ranging from the West Texas rave-ups of JOE ELY to the loose groove of the Tractors to the rock adventures of STEVE EARLE. In the mid-1990s, the alternative country movement coalesced around UNCLE TUPELO. Spinoff bands Wilco and Son-Volt further extended the possible combinations of country and rock and inspired a small but far-flung subculture built around the magazine *No Depression*, which began on the Internet and, in 2008, became a web-only entity.

By the new century, rock asserted such a pervasive influence on the majority of successful, mainstream country acts that the term "country-rock" has become nearly meaningless in modern times. —*Sid Griffin*

## County Records
established in New York, New York, 1963

County Records was an outgrowth of collector Dave Freeman's love of OLD-TIME MUSIC and traditional BLUEGRASS. In the early 1960s he compiled several LP sets of reissue anthologies, beginning with *A Collection of Mountain Fiddle Music* (County 501) and *A Collection of Mountain Ballads* (County 502). These were followed by County's first live recordings in 1964–65. County Sales, Freeman's mail-order record service, began in 1965 as a means of making his own and similar releases broadly available. Freeman also issued a regular newsletter that reviewed new recordings. County Sales is still a thriving business with an active mail-order website.

In 1978, Dave Freeman and Barry Poss founded SUGAR HILL RECORDS, which concentrated on contemporary bluegrass. Later, Poss bought out Freeman's share of Sugar Hill, and the label continues today as a subsidiary of the Welk Music Group. In 1979 Freeman acquired REBEL RECORDS from its founder, Dick Freeland. Rebel's primary artists, the SELDOM SCENE, RALPH STANLEY, and THE COUNTRY GENTLEMEN, continued to record for the label. When Gary Reid came to work for County/Rebel in 1983, he and Freeman focused on promising young bluegrass bands and developed an impressive catalog, with groups such as Lost & Found, the Virginia Squires, IIIRD TYME OUT, and RHONDA VINCENT. Today Rebel continues to flourish under Dave and son Mark's direction, with a catalog including Junior Sisk, Paul Williams, Kenny and Amanda Smith, and the Steep Canyon Rangers. —*Dick Spottswood*

## Farris Coursey
b. Mt. Pleasant, Tennessee, May 28, 1911; d. January 13, 1968

Farris H. Coursey worked as a Nashville session musician and WSM staff drummer for thirty years. As a young man, he performed in OWEN BRADLEY's big band. He joined WSM radio as a staff drummer in 1937 and later worked in WSM-TV's *Waking Crew* staff band.

During a historic November 7, 1949, CASTLE RECORDING STUDIO session with RED FOLEY for "Chattanoogie Shoe Shine Boy," producer PAUL COHEN and arranger Bradley wondered how to re-create the sound of a rhythmic shoeshiner's rag when Coursey started slapping his thigh, creating a catchy solution. Others benefiting from Coursey's creativity include HANK WILLIAMS in his last studio session (September 23, 1952), on "Kaw-Liga," and newcomer BOBBY HELMS, whose "Fräulein" (recorded November 15, 1956) charted fifty-two weeks. Coursey died of a heart attack. —*Walt Trott*

## Cousin Emmy
b. Lamb, Kentucky, 1903; d. April 11, 1980

Cousin Emmy was a boisterous, loudmouthed, dynamic entertainer best known for her banjo frailing, her jokes, and her platinum blond hair; during the 1930s and 1940s she became one of the best-loved and most popular figures on radio. In later years she became known as the person who taught GRANDPA JONES how to frail the banjo and as a figure on the folk revival circuit

linking the modern commercial industry and the older traditional folk music of rural Kentucky. The fact that she made relatively few phonograph records has caused many modern fans to underestimate her influence and importance.

Coming from a family of tobacco sharecroppers in the southern Kentucky barrens, Cynthia May Carver taught herself to read by looking at Sears catalogs and then joined two of her cousins, Noble "Bozo" Carver and Warner Carver, who had organized a local STRINGBAND that recorded for Paramount in the 1920s. Soon she was performing with them over WHB–Kansas City, and by 1935 she had returned to WHAS in Louisville. During the following decade she organized her own troupe—becoming one of the first women performers to do so—and swept through radio stations from West Virginia (where she met Grandpa Jones) to St. Louis. During the late 1940s, folklorist Alan Lomax heard her and got her a deal with DECCA RECORDS, where she cut what would become her most famous song, "Ruby," later re-popularized by THE OSBORNE BROTHERS.

As live radio declined in the 1950s, Cousin Emmy took her showmanship and talent to the West Coast, performing for a time at Disneyland and appearing in the 1955 film *The Second Greatest Sex*. In the 1960s she was discovered by a young stringband then riding the crest of the folk revival, THE NEW LOST CITY RAMBLERS. She toured with them and made her only LP with them for Folkways in 1968. She also appeared with THE STANLEY BROTHERS on an episode of Pete Seeger's TV series *Rainbow Quest*, which has become popular on home video. —*Charles Wolfe*

## Cousin Wilbur Wesbrooks
b. Gibson County, Tennessee, March 5, 1911; d. August 13, 1984

Bill E. "Cousin Wilbur" Wesbrooks was a comedian and bass player who was an important figure in a number of country careers and whose own work ranged from rural TENT SHOWS to television. He began performing as a singer on radio at WTJS in Jackson, Tennessee, and by 1936 he had organized a band that included a young EDDY ARNOLD and fiddler Speedy McNatt.

Coming to Nashville in 1940, he got a job as a bass player with BILL MONROE's band and played on the first Blue Grass Boys recording session (for RCA VICTOR) later that year. By 1945 he had his own GRAND OLE OPRY troupe, Cousin Wilbur & the Tennessee Mountain Boys, which traveled widely. In 1947 he married fellow entertainer Blondie Brooks, who became his performing partner. The 1950s saw them working on the *WWVA JAMBOREE* in Wheeling, West Virginia, and on their own television show in Asheville, North Carolina. In later years they often toured military bases and were active in various country reunion efforts. In 1979 Wesbrooks penned a fascinating and underappreciated autobiography, *Everybody's Cousin*. —*Stacey Wolfe*

## Cowboy Music

There are two types of cowboy music—traditional cowboy songs and the western songs of Hollywood and New York's Tin Pan Alley. Traditional cowboy music can be loosely described as any music working cowboys sing or play; but, more precisely, traditional cowboy music has focused on the cowboy, with setting, action, plot, and terminology based on working cowboys' experiences and attitudes. In contrast, the popular western song is usually a romanticized vision of the West that does not accurately reflect the working cowboy's life or language.

America's preoccupation with the cowboy image grew out of post–Civil War trail drives (1865–90), when millions of Texas longhorn cattle were herded north to market. Soon after the drives began, journalists and dime novelists started romanticizing the men who worked with horses and cattle. Although some cowboys may have sung to cattle while night herding, generally cowboys sang, hummed, or whistled more as a distraction from nighttime fears than to let cattle know a human was nearby. Cowboy music, like poetry and storytelling, was really for entertainment in the cow camp or bunkhouse. In the nineteenth century, the fiddle was the cowboy's popular instrument, followed by the banjo. The guitar and the harmonica were instruments imposed on the singing cowboy image by Hollywood.

Our popular conception of the cowboy came from those who trail-herded cattle north out of Texas. Their songs are generally considered the primary body of authentic traditional cowboy songs, even though Hispanics, Hawaiians, and Native Americans also had genuine cowboy songs of their own. Trail drive cowboys were mostly southerners who migrated to Texas seeking a new life and carrying strong English-Scottish traditions, and the traditional cowboy songs they sang were largely folk reconstructions of songs they brought with them.

Most scholars identify the oldest cowboy-themed song as "The Old Chisholm Trail," a variant of the English folksong "A Dainty Duck," which dates to 1640. Possibly the best-known traditional cowboy song is "Bury Me Not on the Lone Prairie," a folk reworking of Edwin Hubbell Chapin's 1839 poem "The Ocean-Buried." "Streets of Laredo" (also known as "The Cowboy's Lament") is a re-composition of the British broadside "The Unfortunate Rake," which dates to as early as 1790. Although many have claimed to have written such reconstructed songs, the identities of most cowboy balladeers have been lost.

New Mexico cowboy N. Howard "Jack" Thorp was the first known collector of cowboy songs. In 1889 he traveled on horseback from New Mexico to Texas and into Indian Territory, swapping songs as he rode from cow camp to cow camp, and in 1908 he paid the News Print Shop in Estancia, New Mexico, to print a small paperbound book titled *Songs of the Cowboys* (twenty-three song lyrics with no music). Thorp included some of his own songs, such as "Little Joe, the Wrangler," composed in 1898 while trail-herding cattle from New Mexico to Texas.

The most popular and influential cowboy song collection appeared two years later—*Cowboy Songs and Other Frontier Ballads*, collected by a non-cowboy Texan, John A. Lomax. His work was expanded and reissued in 1916 and 1938, with numerous reprintings between each new edition, and it remains in print.

The cowboy image changed radically, as did cowboy music, when Hollywood created versions of both. Even in the days of silent movies, filmmakers depicted cowboys as singers, posting lyrics onscreen to assist the audience in singing along with the actors. During the same period, Tin Pan Alley songwriters started penning material about cowboys and the West. When talking movies were introduced in 1927, Hollywood and Tin Pan Alley combined their creative talents and introduced idyllic images and songs that working cowboys scorned. Even so, the public loved onscreen western stars, and Hollywood's singing cowboys had their heyday in the 1930s.

Identifying the first cowboy or western recording artist is virtually impossible, for documentation of cylinder recordings is scarce, but as the flat, 78-rpm disc became popular, more information was preserved. The first hit cowboy song was CARL T. SPRAGUE's version of "When the Work's All Done This Fall," recorded August 5, 1925; reportedly it sold 900,000 copies. First recorded by FIDDLIN' JOHN CARSON under the title "Dixie Cowboy" in August 1924, the song had been recorded by at least twenty-nine additional artists by 1941, making it that period's most recorded traditional cowboy song. Numerous performers recorded cowboy songs in the 1920s and 1930s, including VERNON DALHART, JULES VERNE ALLEN, GEORGE RENEAU, ERNEST V. STONEMAN, OTTO GRAY, Harry "HAYWIRE MAC" McClintock, Marc Williams, BRADLEY KINCAID, CARSON ROBISON, PATSY MONTANA, GENE AUTRY, and many more.

After 1920, commercial radio broadcasting played a major role in popularizing cowboy material. By the 1930s there were hundreds of small stations across the nation, and each had local entertainers, many of whom claimed to be cowboy singers. From the 1930s through the 1950s, far-reaching Mexican BORDER RADIO stations broadcast hillbilly (country) and cowboy singers, such as Jules Verne Allen, COWBOY SLIM RINEHART, and Dallas "Nevada Slim" Turner, but the *NATIONAL BARN DANCE* on Chicago station WLS had the greatest impact on cowboy music.

One of its early stars, Gene Autry, set the pattern for Hollywood's singing cowboys. In 1934 he and his sidekick, SMILEY BURNETTE, traveled to Hollywood to appear in the Ken Maynard movie *In Old Santa Fe*. The following year Republic Pictures launched the singing cowboy film genre, with Autry starring in *Tumbling Tumbleweeds*. Though Ken Maynard is considered to be the first cowboy star to sing in a sound movie, Autry was the first singing cowboy star, followed in short order by Dick Foran, TEX RITTER, ROY ROGERS, and a host of others.

The 1930s also saw the proliferation of cowboy SONGBOOKS published by M. M. Cole, BOB MILLER, Joe Davis, RALPH PEER's Southern Music, and others who paid staff writers to churn out songs about cowboys and the West. When a recording artist, movie star, or radio personality gained fame, a publisher would pay the celebrity to use his or her name and photographs, and the publisher would issue a series of songbooks. Often the songs had never been sung by anyone (and remain unsung). The cowboy's commercial allure was so strong that even non-singing movie cowboys had songbooks published and their names added as songwriters (e.g., *Tom Mix Western Songs*, published by M. M. Cole, 1935).

In 1949, with the *Hopalong Cassidy* series leading the way, television introduced a new generation to westerns but had a limited impact on cowboy music, even though hit makers Gene Autry and Roy Rogers and DALE EVANS had their own TV shows. Some theme songs of TV westerns, such as Johnny Western's "Paladin," did enjoy popularity, but Rogers and Evans's closing song, "Happy Trails," and Autry's "Back in the Saddle Again" are the only ones to endure as western standards.

As rock & roll music gained popularity and public tastes changed, traditional cowboy music's fan base shrank to a small number of hard-core followers. The word "western" was removed from the "country & western" rubric; the music became simply "country," although many stars still wore western costumes. Western songs still fascinated certain country stars; MARTY ROBBINS, for example, wrote and recorded many western numbers, including his dramatic "El Paso." From the late 1970s RIDERS IN THE SKY have reacquainted country fans with western songs, both vintage and freshly composed.

In 1985 the first annual Cowboy Poetry Gathering in Elko, Nevada, marked a resurgence of traditional cowboy music, and similar gatherings throughout the West continue to create an audience for the genre. In this respect, MICHAEL MARTIN MURPHEY has had a powerful impact. He persuaded WARNER BROS. RECORDS to create its Warner Western division, with his collection *Cowboy Songs* as the imprint's first release. Though the division did not endure, Warner Western did sign cowboy or western singers such as RED STEAGALL, DON EDWARDS, the SONS OF THE SAN JOAQUIN, and Herb Jeffries, along with cowboy poet Waddie Mitchell, while reissuing western songs previously recorded by other stars. Murphey also attracted new fans to cowboy music through the long-running WestFest events, particularly an annual show at Copper Mountain, Colorado.

The animated film *Toy Story* (1995) and its sequels, which featured the character Woody, a cowboy doll, further spread cowboy music to mass audiences. (*Toy Story 2* [1999] also featured Jessie the Yodeling Cowgirl.) In the second film's soundtrack, Riders in the Sky perform the theme music for *Woody's Round-up*, the character's television show, and their album by this title received a Grammy as 1999's best musical album for children. Today, numerous self-produced albums of genuine working cowboys and cowgirls singing both traditional and contemporary songs are available, along with albums by non-cowboy vocalists who enjoy singing about the West. —*Guy Logsdon*

## Bill Cox
b. Kanawha County, West Virginia, August 4, 1897; d. December 10, 1968

A prolific recording artist for GENNETT (1929–31) and the AMERICAN RECORD CORPORATION and COLUMBIA labels (1933–40), William Jennings Cox was influenced as a youngster by his harmonica-playing, ballad-singing mother and as an adult by the recordings of VERNON DALHART, RILEY PUCKETT, JIMMIE RODGERS, and others. Cox learned to play harmonica and guitar during his youth and did some rudimentary songwriting at age sixteen.

While working periodically at an ax factory and a hotel, Cox began to ponder a musical career and performed at parties, picnics, and church functions. Walter Fredericks, owner of Charleston, West Virginia, radio station WOBU (later WCHS), became aware of Cox's music, hired him in 1928 to perform daily, and instigated his first recording session.

Nicknamed the Dixie Songbird, Cox was noted for several topical/social commentary songs: "NRA Blues" (1933), "Trial of Bruno Richard Hauptman" (1935), and "Franklin D. Roosevelt's Back Again" (1936), among others. Dueting with Cliff Hobbs, he made the first known recordings of "Sally Let Your Bangs Hang Down" (1936), "Oozlin' Daddy Blues" (1936), "Sparkling Brown Eyes" (1937, Cox's most successful composition), "Filipino Baby" (1937), and "Don't Make Me Go to Bed (And I'll Be Good)" (1937).

In 1965, a folklorist found a poverty-stricken Cox living in a Charleston slum. This led to one last recording effort—an album of seventeen songs released in 1966 on Kanawha Records. —*Bob Pinson*

## The Cox Family
Willard Lawrence Cox b. Cotton Valley, Louisiana, June 9, 1937
Evelyn Marie Cox Hobbs b. Springhill, Louisiana, June 20, 1959
Sidney Lawrence Cox b. Homer, Louisiana, July 21, 1965
Marla Suzanne Cox Ratcliff b. Springhill, Louisiana, June 5, 1967

In the 1990s, the Cox Family combined kindred harmonies and original songs to emerge as a well-received BLUEGRASS act. In 1972 oil refinery worker and fiddler Willard Cox formed a family group with his children. From an early age, each child learned an instrument: eldest sister Lynn took up the bass; Evelyn, the guitar; Suzanne, the mandolin; and Sidney, the DOBRO, banjo, and guitar. Together they developed their much-admired vocal harmonies. Early on, the group included sister Lynn and mother Marie.

"Broken Engagement" was the family's first, do-it-yourself record, in 1974, released on their own label with a run of about 1,000 copies (it appears in its original form on their 1995 album *Beyond the City*, along with an updated version). At a Perrin, Texas, music festival in 1988 they met ALISON KRAUSS. Mutual admiration led Krauss to record several of Sidney's songs, including "I've Got That Old Feeling," which appeared on her 1990 album of the same name. (In interviews, Krauss has cited Suzanne Cox as one of her chief vocal influences.) At Krauss's urging, ROUNDER RECORDS signed the Coxes in 1993, and Krauss produced their debut, *Everybody's Reaching Out for Someone*, and the follow-up albums *Beyond the City* and *Just When We're Thinking It's Over*. The latter, released in 1996, was the group's first album for ASYLUM RECORDS. In addition, Krauss produced and collaborated vocally with the Coxes on a jointly released Grammy-winning bluegrass gospel album, *I Know Who Holds Tomorrow* (Rounder, 1994).

The Coxes appeared in the 2000 hit film *O BROTHER, WHERE ART THOU?* as well as on the movie's soundtrack album, in the follow-up *Down from the Mountain* concert and documentary, and on the Down from the Mountain concert tour. Popular at bluegrass festivals nationwide, the Cox Family received widespread acclaim for their blend of bluegrass, gospel, country, and pop music and a repertoire that ranged from traditional songs such as "I'll Be All Smiles Tonight" and "Little Birdie" to bluegrass remakes of pop hits such as "Runaway," "Blue Bayou," and "That's the Way Love Is." In addition, Suzanne Cox has become a successful harmony vocalist in Nashville, backing DOLLY PARTON, RANDY TRAVIS, and many others. The group had stopped performing by the time of Marie's death from cancer in February 2009. —*Stephen L. Betts*

## Billy "Crash" Craddock
b. Greensboro, North Carolina, June 16, 1939

William Wayne "Crash" Craddock (the nickname came from his exploits as a high school running back) was one of country music's most consistent hit makers of the 1970s. Early in his career, in the mid-1950s, he emulated ELVIS PRESLEY, released a few unsuccessful singles on minor regional labels and Colonial Records, and played with his brother Ronald in a rock band called the Four Rebels. After a decade on the periphery of show business, he recorded a country cover of Dawn's #1 pop hit "Knock Three Times," for the Cartwheel label. Craddock's record was a #3 country hit in 1971, and from there he went on to achieve more than a dozen Top Ten releases, including #1 songs "Rub It In" and "Ruby, Baby," both released on the ABC label in 1974. He regularly released hits for Cartwheel, ABC/DOT, and CAPITOL throughout the 1970s—on ABC/Dot Craddock scored with "Easy as Pie" (#2, 1975) and "Broken Down in Tiny Pieces" (#1, 1976)—but his career declined in the early 1980s as subsequent affiliations with CeeCee (a self-owned company) and ATLANTIC RECORDS yielded no commercially significant recordings.

Craddock's career personified the shifting tastes of contemporary audiences. He was only marginally a country artist (like his model, Elvis), yet he was far too old-fashioned to appeal to rock audiences of the post-Woodstock era. Thus his Elvis-derived style—replete with spangled jumpsuits, copious displays of chest hair, masculine athleticism, and a Vegas-inspired version of ROCKABILLY music—made him popular until tastes changed and neotraditionalists RICKY SKAGGS, RANDY TRAVIS, and GEORGE STRAIT emerged. Still, Craddock continues to perform, and in 1996 Razor & Tie Music released the hits compilation *Crash's Smashes.* —*Stephen R. Tucker*

## Paul Craft
b. Memphis, Tennessee, August 12, 1938

One of Nashville's most understated and wry songwriters, Paul Charles Craft has composed a number of songs that have been pivotal in the success of country artists.

Born in Memphis, with a formative period in his youth spent in Richmond, Virginia (where he attended the OLD DOMINION BARN DANCE), Craft has lived mostly in Memphis and Nashville. He owned a Memphis music store (1966–70) before notching his first songwriting success—when JACK GREENE cut his song "Making Up Your Mind" in 1971. A warm, mellow-voiced singer, Craft signed as a vocalist with Truth Records in 1974; among the songs he cut was an early version of his humorous "It's Me Again, Margaret," covered by RAY STEVENS in 1985. Craft moved to Nashville in 1976 and signed with RCA RECORDS. The label released four Craft singles, including "Lean on Jesus Before He Leans on You" (#55, 1977) and "Brother Jukebox" (1978). The latter became a #1 hit for MARK CHESNUTT in 1991.

Hit songs began to mount through the 1970s, with "Keep Me from Blowing Away" (LINDA RONSTADT, 1974), "Hank Williams, You Wrote My Life" (MOE BANDY, 1975) and "Dropkick Me, Jesus (Through the Goal Posts of Life)" (BOBBY BARE, 1976). Craft's long list of compositions also includes "Come As You Were" (JERRY LEE LEWIS, 1983; T. GRAHAM BROWN, 1988), and "Teardrops Will Kiss the Morning Dew" (THE OSBORNE BROTHERS, 1973; ALISON KRAUSS, 1995).

In addition, Craft is a successful music publisher. His Writers Night Music firm published DON SCHLITZ's first hit, "The Gambler." In 2008 Craft rereleased his 1986 album, *Warnings,* on his self-named label. —*Don Rhodes*

## Floyd Cramer
b. Shreveport, Louisiana, October 27, 1933; d. December 31, 1997

When the piano became an integral part of Nashville arrangements in the early 1960s, the player who shouldered the load was Floyd Cramer. He popularized the "slip-note" technique but deserves to be just as famous for his unerring taste and his understanding of what not to play.

Cramer grew up in the small sawmill town of Huttig, Arkansas. He learned piano by ear, and, after finishing high school in 1951, he moved to Shreveport and found a job on the LOUISIANA HAYRIDE. He arrived just as LEFTY FRIZZELL's records were popularizing what Cramer termed "a plinking, HONKY-TONK-type piano." He played in that style on JIM REEVES's "Mexican Joe" and made his first solo recording for ABBOTT RECORDS in 1953.

Aside from OWEN BRADLEY, there were virtually no studio pianists in Nashville when Cramer visited in 1952 with T. TOMMY CUTRER. After a year or two of commuting, Cramer talked to CHET ATKINS about becoming a session pianist and left Shreveport

*Floyd Cramer*

in January 1955. "By 1956 and '57, I was in day and night doing sessions," he said. One of the few records on which he played something other than piano was JIMMY DEAN's "Big Bad John" (he created the pickax sound effects by attaching a microphone stand's iron counter-weight to a coat hanger, suspending the hanger from the stand's horizontal arm, and hitting the weight with a hammer).

In 1958 Atkins signed Cramer to RCA VICTOR as an instrumental artist; his fourth single, "Last Date," was his first hit and featured the slip-note style. Earlier, Cramer had worked on the HANK LOCKLIN session that had produced "Please Help Me, I'm Falling"; the composer, DON ROBERTSON, had sent a demo on which he played piano, sliding up into a note from the one beneath, and that was the technique Cramer incorporated into his style and made his signature. "It's been done for a long time on the guitar by people like Maybelle Carter," Cramer said, "and by lots of people on the steel guitar. Half-tones are very common, but the style I use mainly is a whole-tone slur which gives more of a lonesome, cowboy sound."

Atkins suggested that Cramer write "Last Date" to showcase the slip-note style. It was a bigger pop than country hit, climbing to #2 in 1960; the only record keeping it from #1 was ELVIS PRESLEY's "Are You Lonesome Tonight," another record Cramer had played on. In 1962 Cramer released two more Top Ten pop hits: "On the Rebound" and "San Antonio Rose." By the mid-1960s, he was established as an album act, recording prolifically for RCA. In addition, he recorded and toured widely with Atkins and saxophone master BOOTS RANDOLPH in the 1960s and '70s and joined them as a member of country's Million Dollar Band. Cramer continued to do occasional concerts and to record television-marketed albums until sidelined by cancer, which eventually took his life.

Cramer was named ACM's top keyboardist each year from 1969 through 1974. In 2003, he was inducted into both

THE COUNTRY MUSIC HALL OF FAME and the Rock and Roll Hall of Fame. —*Colin Escott*

## Crazy Water Crystals

A popular Depression-era nostrum that claimed to relieve conditions "caused or made worse by a sluggish system," Crazy Water Crystals sponsored country radio performers in several regions of the United States and Canada.

Produced in Mineral Wells, Texas, the crystals acted primarily as a laxative and were obtained by evaporation of the town's famed "Crazy" water, named for an alleged cure of two insane ladies in the early 1880s. Company owner Carr P. Collins, a political adviser to W. LEE "PAPPY" O'DANIEL, made the product familiar to radio listeners in the 1930s. When WSM's GRAND OLE OPRY was divided into fifteen-minute segments in 1934 and sold to sponsors, the first company to sign up was Crazy Water Crystals.

The *Crazy Water Barn Dance* on WBT in Charlotte, North Carolina, advertised the crystals, along with shows on thirteen other stations in the Carolinas and Georgia. The Crazy Hickory Nuts, the Crazy Mountaineers, and other groups adopted the "Crazy" theme. BLUEGRASS pioneer BILL MONROE played for Crazy Crystals–sponsored programs, as did J. E. MAINER, WADE MAINER, LEW CHILDRE, and Zeke Morris (THE MORRIS BROTHERS). Earl and Bill Bolick (the BLUE SKY BOYS) and Homer "Pappy" Sherrill performed for the company as the Crazy Blue Ridge Hillbillies.

In 1935 HANK SNOW made $10 a week singing cowboy songs for a Crazy Water Crystals show on CHNS in Halifax, Nova Scotia. Colonel Jack and Shorty's Hillbillies recorded transcriptions for the company in New York, performing their theme "Hot Time in the Old Town Tonight," along with tunes such as "Pop Goes the Weasel" and "Hand Me Down My Walking Cane."

In its home state, the company broadcast from the lobby of Mineral Wells's Crazy Hotel. Picked up by NBC in 1932, the Crazy Water Crystal programs were reportedly the first regular commercial broadcast of the NBC network originating outside the NBC studio. These Texas shows featured big band sounds as well as country musicians and comedians. Bassist Jim Boyd (BILL AND JIM BOYD), who later joined the LIGHT CRUST DOUGHBOYS, played with the Crazy Gang.

A typical regional Crazy broadcast in its home area, the *Saturday Night Stampede* of 1936 aired live from Ranger Junior College on Fort Worth's WBAP. Western song scholar and performer JULES VERNE ALLEN appeared on the *Stampede*, singing "Cowboy's Lament" and "Santa Fe Trail." Ranger's American Legion Tickville Band favored Crazy fans with lively renditions of "Washington and Lee" and "Smile, Darn You, Smile."

Changing health care trends—along with the Federal Drug Administration's anti-Crazy campaign and the product's high price—caused sales to decline dramatically in the 1940s, and the company's sponsorship of radio shows faded accordingly. —*Gene Fowler*

## CRB/CRS

CRB established 1969

The founding of Country Radio Broadcasters (CRB) reflected the growing professionalization of country broadcasting in the late 1960s. The Country Music Disc Jockeys Association, created in 1953, had been a loosely organized group based around the free-wheeling annual DJ CONVENTION. With the rise of CMA after 1958, increasingly sophisticated demographic research, and the segmentation of radio formats along stylistic lines, country broadcasters launched the nonprofit educational organization CRB in 1969 to focus more closely on country radio.

CRB's Country Radio Seminar (CRS), held early each year in Nashville, unites some 1,000 radio delegates with professionals from other parts of the industry. Staging numerous panels, CRS typically concludes with a New Faces of Country Music dinner featuring performances by prominent new artists selected by radio delegate attendees. CRS also includes the CRB Spring Town Meeting, an event providing opportunities for songwriters, artists, and executives who cannot attend CRS to interact with CRS radio station personnel. Toward this same end, CRS holds an annual Fall Forum in Nashville during Country Music Week as well as regional seminars and an online forum on CRB's website. CRB also presents various awards and serves as trustee of the Country Music Disc Jockey and Radio Hall of Fame. —*John W. Rumble*

## Crockett Mountaineers (Crockett's Kentucky Mountaineers; Crockett Family)

The Crockett Mountaineers, led by John "Dad" Crockett (b. West Virginia, April 28, 1877; d. January 1972) and including his five sons, was one of the earliest professional groups to play STRINGBAND MUSIC on the West Coast. Originally from West Virginia, the Crocketts eventually moved to California in 1919. The OLD-TIME act featured Dad (fiddle and banjo), John H. "Johnny" Jr. (banjo and guitar), Alan (harmony fiddle), George (fiddle), Clarence (guitar and harmonica), and Albert (tenor guitar and bass fiddle). Dad, Johnny, and Clarence did most of the singing. The band performed on a number of California radio stations in the 1920s and 1930s, including KNJ, KMJ, and KHJ. They traveled nationally as well as on the West Coast, eventually recording for BRUNSWICK and Crown and publishing two song folios. Alan left in fall 1938 to join THE PRAIRIE RAMBLERS, and the group disbanded after Clarence's death in the 1940s. —*Charlie Seemann*

## Crook & Chase

Lorianne Crook b. Wichita, Kansas, February 19, 1957
Charlie Chase b. Rogersville, Tennessee, October 19, 1952

Lorianne Lynee Crook is one of country music's most identifiable broadcast personalities. In 1983, television producer Jim Owens asked her to join Charlie Chase in cohosting the nationally syndicated *This Week in Country Music*, which ran through 1990. Previously she had worked as a news reporter for KAUZ in Wichita Falls, Texas, in 1980 and as host of *PM Magazine* at Nashville's WKRN in 1981. From 1986 to 1993 Crook teamed with Chase for TNN's popular *Crook & Chase*, a weeknight series combining entertainment, news, and celebrity interviews. Crook shared executive producer duties with her husband, Jim Owens, who produced her TV shows and whom she married in 1985. *Weekend with Crook & Chase*, a thirty-minute, syndicated weekly series, ran from 1987 to 1992. From 1988 to 1993 Crook produced and hosted TNN's *Celebrities Offstage*, an ongoing series of interview specials. From October 18, 1993, through December 1995, Crook and Chase hosted TNN's prime-time weeknight show

*Music City Tonight*, which replaced Ralph Emery's ten-year-old *Nashville Now* show. The duo also cohosted *The Nashville Record Review*, a four-hour weekly radio countdown of the week's Top Forty country hits, launched in 1988 and syndicated for many years.

Charles Wayne Chase's trademark deep voice is also familiar to country music listeners. He started in radio in his hometown and then worked at stations in Kingsport and Knoxville, Tennessee, before moving to Nashville in the early 1970s. From 1974 to 1983 Chase was a popular WSM radio personality. WSM-TV (renamed WSMV) produced a live daytime show, *Channel 4 Magazine*, which Chase hosted in 1982–83. Beginning in 1983 Chase shared hosting duties with Crook on various Jim Owens–produced TV series. Chase also hosted and produced *Funny Business with Charlie Chase* (1989–93), a TNN show devoted to playing practical jokes on country music headliners.

In January 1996 Crook and Chase began a new syndicated TV series produced in Hollywood. Owens later moved the operation back to Nashville, and the broadcasters hosted a daytime syndicated TV program before returning to TNN in September 1997. They remained on TNN until that network folded, in 2000. In January 2008 *Crook & Chase*, still produced by Owens, returned to the air on the RFD television network, which also carries *Lorianne Crook's Celebrity Kitchen*. A joint autobiography (written with Mickey Herskowitz), *Crook and Chase: Our Lives, the Music, and the Stars*, was published in 1995. —*Bob Paxman*

## The Crook Brothers

Matthew Crook b. Scottsboro, Tennessee, 1896; d. unknown
Herman Crook b. Scottsboro, Tennessee, December 2, 1898; d. June 10, 1988
Lewis Crook b. Castalian Springs, Tennessee, May 30, 1909; d. April 12, 1997

On July 24, 1926, the Crook Brothers Band first appeared on WSM's *Barn Dance*, an eight-month-old radio program on Nashville's WSM that would later become celebrated as the GRAND OLE OPRY. Various incarnations of this outstanding STRINGBAND would perform on the show nearly every Saturday night for the next sixty-two years.

The original group featured the twin harmonicas of brothers Matthew and Herman Crook, who hailed from the hill country south of Nashville that has produced many outstanding mouth organists. The Crooks performed at local functions and house parties as youngsters; in late 1925 they played regularly on Nashville's first station, WDAD, though they continued to make their living by day as "twist rollers" with the American Tobacco Company. Soon they began appearing at WSM and WLAC as well. In 1928 the band—consisting of Herman and Matthew on harmonicas, Tom J. Givans on banjo, George Miles on guitar, and Hick Burnett on guitar—recorded four instrumentals in Nashville for RALPH PEER of the Victor Talking Machine Company. These were the last recordings the group made until a joint album with SAM AND KIRK McGEE, released in 1962 on STARDAY.

In 1929, at a fiddlers' contest at Walter Hill High School in Murfreesboro, Tennessee, DR. HUMPHREY BATE introduced the Crooks to another musical Crook, banjo-playing Lewis Crook (no relation), who joined the band in the fall of 1929. Though Matthew left music to join the police force in 1930, the band continued under the same name without him, with Herman and Lewis remaining the only constant members. In the late 1950s the Crook Brothers were combined with the remaining members of Dr. Humphrey Bate's Possum Hunters and accompanied square dancers on the Opry. Herman Crook would occasionally play a harmonica solo on the show as well. The group's long run ended in 1988 with the death of this quiet, courtly mouth organist, who had lived the history of country music's preeminent showcase from its beginning. —*Kim Field*

## J. D. Crowe

b. Lexington, Kentucky, August 27, 1937

Although a "second generation" BLUEGRASS performer, banjo guru James Dee Crowe has credentials that begin in the 1950s, when the music was in its infancy. Captivated by EARL SCRUGGS's banjo artistry, Crowe studied FLATT & SCRUGGS's frequent performances in Crowe's hometown.

In his teens, Crowe played part-time in bands headed by Esco Hankins, Curley Parker & Pee Wee Lambert, MAC WISEMAN, and JIMMY MARTIN. Full-time employment with Martin in 1956 included work on the *LOUISIANA HAYRIDE* and recording twenty-four sides for DECCA RECORDS. Leaving Martin in 1960, Crowe returned in 1963 to record four more titles and in 1966 for five instrumentals.

Experience with Martin taught Crowe about professional musicianship and the inner workings of the music business, knowledge he used in building his own bands and passed along to his musicians. Eventually a road-weary Crowe based his Kentucky Mountain Boys near home. By 1969 he had attracted RED ALLEN (guitar), DOYLE LAWSON (mandolin), and Bobby Slone (fiddle and bass) to the band. A lengthy Holiday Inn engagement drew listeners from great distances and led to regular appearances on the emerging bluegrass festival circuit.

In 1970 Lawson switched to guitar when Larry Rice came to play mandolin; Rice's brother, guitarist TONY RICE, of THE BLUEGRASS ALLIANCE, joined in September 1971, when Lawson went to THE COUNTRY GENTLEMEN. Crowe's band, already leaning away from bluegrass tradition, developed a more contemporary flavor, with material drawn from COUNTRY-ROCK pioneer GRAM PARSONS and folk balladeer Gordon Lightfoot. With this new sound came a new name—the New South.

Mandolinist RICKY SKAGGS replaced Larry Rice in 1974, and the release of the group's self-titled album on ROUNDER RECORDS in 1975 was a watershed event. Characterized by smooth vocal harmonies and meticulous instrumentation, the influential 1975 lineup only lasted through the summer, when Rice, Skaggs, and DOBRO player JERRY DOUGLAS, who had joined for the summer, all left.

Through the remainder of the decade, though, the New South was a magnet for young musicians. Gene Johnson (later of DIAMOND RIO), Jimmy Gaudreau, and the late KEITH WHITLEY passed through the band, each contributing to stylistic changes.

Crowe retreated from the music business in the late 1980s, limiting himself to reunion concerts and selected recording opportunities, including six Bluegrass Album Band recordings produced by Tony Rice.

In 1992 Crowe formed a new band, striving for the sound of his forward-looking 1975 band, and re-entered the bluegrass mainstream. In 1994 and 2004 he was IBMA's Instrumental Performer of the Year, Banjo. Crowe was inducted into the IBMA Hall of Fame in 2003. —*Frank* and *Marty Godbey*

## Rodney Crowell
b. Houston, Texas, August 7, 1950

Arriving in Nashville in 1972, Rodney Crowell had a musical background embracing the classic HONKY-TONK he learned as drummer in his father's band and the influence of the Beatles and other pop acts. With a circle of friends including progressive Texas songwriters GUY CLARK and TOWNES VAN ZANDT, Crowell parlayed his eclecticism into an endearing songwriting and performing style that blended honky-tonk poetics with rock & roll spunk, earning him widespread respect as one of country music's most versatile artists.

In 1975 Crowell joined EMMYLOU HARRIS's Hot Band as guitarist, songwriter, and arranger. During this time, he developed his production skills while contributing "'Til I Gain Control Again," "Bluebird Wine," and other songs to Harris's repertoire.

In 1977 Crowell left Harris and began working on his first album, *Ain't Livin' Long Like This* (WARNER BROS., 1978). He also assembled his legendary road band, the Cherry Bombs, which included a young VINCE GILL and future producers RICHARD BENNETT, EMORY GORDY JR., and TONY BROWN. Released the following year, the album sold modestly, but it boosted Crowell's writing reputation when three of its songs became hits for other artists: the title track for WAYLON JENNINGS, "Leaving Louisiana in the Broad Daylight" for the OAK RIDGE BOYS, and "An American Dream" for the NITTY GRITTY DIRT BAND.

Throughout the 1980s Crowell penned hits for artists such as rocker Bob Seger, who took Crowell's "Shame on the Moon" to #2 on *Billboard's* pop chart in 1983. Crowell also produced albums for ROSANNE CASH, to whom he was married from 1979 to 1992. His own recordings had limited success until his benchmark *Diamonds and Dirt* (COLUMBIA, 1988). Produced by Crowell and Tony Brown, it was the first country album to yield five #1 singles: "It's Such a Small World," "She's Crazy for Leavin'," "I Couldn't Leave You if I Tried," "Above and Beyond," and "After All This Time," which also won Crowell a 1989 Grammy for Best Country Song.

Crowell continued to write and record, hitting with "Lovin' All Night" and "What Kind of Love" in 1992. He also produced albums

*Rodney Crowell*

by Guy Clark and JIM LAUDERDALE, among others. In 1997 Crowell joined STEUART SMITH, MICHAEL RHODES, and Vince Santoro in the COUNTRY-ROCK band the Cicadas. From 1994 to 2001, however, he dropped road work to focus on his daughters following his divorce from Cash. (He later remarried.) Crowell has found acceptance among both country and AMERICANA audiences with albums including *The Houston Kid* (2001), *Fate's Right Hand* (2003), *The Notorious Cherry Bombs* (2004), *The Outsider* (2005), and *Sex and Gasoline* (2008). In 2009, WYNONNA's rendition of his "Sing: Chapter 1" reached #4 on *Billboard's* Dance Club Songs chart. His memoir, *Chinaberry Sidewalks*, was issued in January 2011 by Knopf Publishing. —*Jack Bernhardt*

## Simon Crum (*see* Ferlin Husky)

## Jerry Crutchfield
b. Paducah, Kentucky, August 10, 1934

Jerry Crutchfield has distinguished himself as a Nashville performer, studio singer and musician, songwriter, record producer, music publisher, and corporate executive.

While attending Kentucky's Murray State University, Crutchfield made his first foray to MUSIC CITY in the mid-1950s as part of the Escorts, a group signed by RCA RECORDS. However, sparked by country artists' interest in his material, Crutchfield decided to focus on songwriting rather than singing.

After college, Nashville's TREE PUBLISHING agreed to handle his songs and convinced him to work for the company. He stayed there for more than a year, learning the music-publishing business. Meanwhile, artists such as TAMMY WYNETTE, ELVIS PRESLEY, and BRENDA LEE recorded his tunes.

Later Crutchfield joined the staff of DECCA RECORDS' publishing arm, which subsequently merged with MCA RECORDS' publishing operation. In 1971 he fulfilled his first producing assignment for a major label, supervising COLUMBIA's BARBARA FAIRCHILD; the singer soon topped the charts with "Teddy Bear Song" and hit #2 with Crutchfield's "Kid Stuff." Crutchfield's contributions to singer-songwriter Dave Loggins's 1974 hit "Please Come to Boston" advanced his reputation as one of Nashville's most effective producers. Crutchfield has since produced gold and platinum albums for Wynette, LEE GREENWOOD, TRACY BYRD, ANNE MURRAY, DOTTIE WEST, LARRY GATLIN, GLEN CAMPBELL, and TANYA TUCKER.

Crutchfield was executive vice president/general manager with CAPITOL/LIBERTY RECORDS from 1989 to 1992. He briefly returned to MCA Records as president and built MCA Music (now Universal Music Publishing) by developing writers such as Loggins, DON SCHLITZ, Gary Burr, and Mark Nesler. Crutchfield sold his publishing companies, whose catalogs include hits by GEORGE STRAIT, TIM MCGRAW, and MARTINA MCBRIDE, to EverGreen Copyrights in 2006 but continued to work with EverGreen in developing the companies' catalogs. (German-based BMG Rights Management acquired EverGreen in 2010.)

Crutchfield's brother Jan is also a respected songwriter; his credits include the country standard "Statue of a Fool." —*Janet E. Williams*

## Manuel Cuevas (*see* Manuel)

## Cumberland Ridge Runners

Hugh Ballard Cross b. Oliver Springs, Tennessee, October 19, 1904; d. ca. 1970
Karl Victor Davis b. Mt. Vernon, Kentucky, December 17, 1905; d. May 30, 1979
Clyde Julian "Red" Foley b. Berea, Kentucky, June 17, 1910; d. September 19, 1968
Doctor Howard "Doc" Hopkins b. Harlan County, Kentucky, January 26, 1899; d. January 3, 1988
John Lee Lair b. Renfro Valley, Kentucky, July 1, 1894; d. November 12, 1985
Homer Edgar "Slim" Miller b. Lizton, Indiana, March 8, 1898; d. August 27, 1962
Linda Parker b. Covington, Kentucky, January 18, 1912; d. August 12, 1935
Hartford Connecticut "Harty" Taylor b. Mt. Vernon, Kentucky, April 11, 1905; d. October 18, 1963

In 1930 JOHN LAIR put the Cumberland Ridge Runners on the radio at WLS in Chicago, where they appeared on the Saturday night NATIONAL BARN DANCE broadcast and were the featured act on weekday programs *Home Folks* and *Coon Creek Social*. Lair carefully crafted the act's image, and, according to WLS publicity, the group's programs were like a "chapter out of the past, suggesting the days of the long rifles and coonskin caps of pioneer Kentucky. Many of their songs have come straight out of the hills." The STRINGBAND offered listeners a variety of instrumentals as well as vocal solos, duets, and trios on such numbers as "Chicken Reel," "Treasures Untold," and "River of Jordan." The original members were Lair (jug, group manager), Harty Taylor (vocals, guitar), Gene Ruppe (fiddle), DOC HOPKINS (vocals, banjo), and Karl Davis (vocals, mandolin). Hugh Cross, RED FOLEY, and Slim Miller later replaced Ruppe and Hopkins. Karl Davis and Harty Taylor formed their own act, KARL & HARTY, in the BROTHER DUET style. LINDA PARKER, known as the Sunbonnet Girl, added her straightforward renditions of sentimental OLD-TIME songs such as "Bury Me Beneath the Weeping Willow," "Give My Love to Nell," and "I'll Be All Smiles Tonight."

In 1935 Linda Parker died unexpectedly. Other members of the troupe eventually went separate ways, thereby closing the book on the act. —*Wayne W. Daniel*

## Mike Curb

b. Savannah, Georgia, December 24, 1944

Mike Curb is the founder and president of CURB RECORDS, one of America's most successful independent record labels. Experienced in many musical genres, he is a noted producer, recording artist, and songwriter, having penned more than 400 songs recorded by artists ranging from Solomon Burke and ANNE MURRAY to Andy Williams and HANK WILLIAMS JR. Some fifty films—including *The Wild Angels, City Slickers, Legally Blonde 2,* and *Evan Almighty*—have showcased his songs or soundtracks.

As a teenager in California, Curb formed the Mike Curb Congregation, a vocal group whose Top 40 pop single "Burning Bridges" (which Curb cowrote) was featured in the 1970 film *Kelly's Heroes*. The act appeared regularly on *The Glen Campbell Goodtime Hour*, opened in Las Vegas for major artists, and recorded hits such as "The Candy Man" with Sammy Davis Jr. and "All for the Love of Sunshine" (another Curb cowrite) with Hank Williams Jr.

By 1964, while a student at California State University, Northridge, Curb formed Sidewalk Records (later renamed Curb) and recorded "You Meet the Nicest People on a Honda," which Honda used to advertise motorcycles nationwide. Soundtracks he produced for movies advanced the label's fortunes, as did recordings by rockers Davie Allan & the Arrows and the Stone Poneys (featuring LINDA RONSTADT).

*Mike Curb*

After Curb merged his label with MGM RECORDS in 1969, he became MGM's president, overseeing hits by the likes of DON GIBSON, Donny and MARIE OSMOND, Lou Rawls, MEL TILLIS, RAY STEVENS, KENNY ROGERS, EDDY ARNOLD, and Hank Williams Jr. Curb also supervised MGM's jazz-oriented Verve label. In 1972 *Billboard* magazine named him Producer of the Year.

Curb sold his interest in MGM to PolyGram in 1974 and subsequently formed the Warner/Curb imprint, which scored hits with the Four Seasons, Shaun Cassidy, the BELLAMY BROTHERS, EXILE, and Debby Boone.

Curb served as State Chairman of Ronald Reagan's 1976 presidential bid, Lieutenant Governor of California from 1979–1983, National Co-Chairman of Reagan's 1980 campaign, and Chair of the Republican National Finance Committee during 1983–84.

In 1986 Curb refocused on his music ventures, and moved with his family to Nashville in 1992. In addition to running Curb Records, he later became chairman and partner of gospel label Word Entertainment.

Active in auto racing, Curb founded the Curb Museum for Music and Motorsports in Kannapolis, North Carolina. He is also a noted philanthropist. The Mike Curb Family Foundation has generously supported Belmont University's Mike Curb College of Entertainment and Music Business; Vanderbilt University's Curb Center for Arts, Enterprise, and Public Policy; similar centers at Baylor University, California State Northridge, Claremont College, Daytona State College, Fisk University, and Honolulu State College; as well as the Curb Center for Free Enterprise in Los Angeles. Moreover, his foundation has preserved Nashville's Historic RCA

Studio B and Historic Quonset Hut Studio; established the Curb/ Stout Patriots Theatre at Fort Campbell, Kentucky; and assisted numerous other organizations, including the COUNTRY MUSIC HALL OF FAME AND MUSEUM, the American Heart Association, the Nashville Symphony, the Nashville Public Library, and Junior Achievement Centers in both Nashville and Los Angeles.

Curb has been honored in both the Hollywood Walk of Fame and the Music City Walk of Fame. He has been elected to the Georgia Music Hall of Fame, the West Coast Stock Car Hall of Fame, and the National Business Hall of Fame. —*Don Cusic*

## Curb Records
established in Los Angeles, 1964

Through more than four decades songwriter and producer MIKE CURB built his record company into one of country music's most important independent labels. Curb's roster included one of country's biggest-selling artists, TIM MCGRAW, and as of 2011 still boasted established female acts LEANN RIMES, JO DEE MESSINA, and Wynonna.

Curb was a student at California State University, Northridge, when he founded his empire in 1964. Initially called Sidewalk Records, the label's name soon changed to Curb to avoid conflict with another firm. Early releases were primarily motion picture soundtracks that Curb composed for major film studios. During the same period, Curb launched his own group, the Mike Curb Congregation, whose albums won international fame. The act recorded Curb's original "All for the Love of Sunshine" with HANK WILLIAMS JR. and topped the country charts in 1970.

In 1969 Curb merged his company with MGM RECORDS and was named president. In this role he produced a series of hits, including "The Candy Man" (Sammy Davis Jr.) and "I'm Leaving It All Up to You" (Donny & MARIE OSMOND).

After MGM was sold in 1974, Curb continued to run his publishing company and a new label partnership with WARNER BROS./ REPRISE RECORDS known as Warner/Curb Records. Through the 1970s and 1980s he was involved in several co-ventures with other labels, including RCA RECORDS and MCA RECORDS. These arrangements allowed Curb to build his own catalog of master recordings by concentrating on writing and producing while letting his partners handle distribution, marketing, and radio promotion.

Over the years Curb Records evolved into a full-service record company. Mike Curb had maintained a Nashville office, but in 1992 he decided to move his headquarters to MUSIC CITY and left the L.A. operation as a satellite office. By 1996 the Curb Group was operating three labels: Curb, MCG/Curb, and Curb/Universal. In addition to Hank Williams Jr., McGraw, Rimes, and Messina, by the late 1990s their combined rosters included Wynonna, HAL KETCHUM, MERLE HAGGARD, LYLE LOVETT, JUNIOR BROWN, EDDY ARNOLD, and SAWYER BROWN. In the new century, Trick Pony, Heidi Newfield, and Rodney Atkins lengthened Curb's list of hit makers. In addition to contemporary releases, Curb's reissues and compilations now total more than 500 albums. —*Calvin Gilbert*

## Dick Curless
b. Fort Fairfield, Maine, March 17, 1932; d. May 25, 1995

Richard William Curless, nicknamed the Baron of Country Music after his 1966 recording "The Baron," was a regional favorite in the Northeast for his wide-ranging repertoire and his smooth, sonorous baritone. Curless's family moved to Massachusetts from Maine when he was eight. He grew up in Gilbertville, and in 1948 he landed his own fifteen-minute radio slot as the Tumbleweed Kid in Ware, Massachusetts. In 1952 he was drafted and shipped out to Korea, where he served as Rice Paddy Ranger, a GI-DJ for the AFRS (Armed Forces Radio Service), through 1954. His own record, "China Nights," became a hit in the Far Eastern Theater.

Back home in 1957, he won an *Arthur Godfrey's Talent Scouts* contest singing "Nine Pound Hammer." In 1965 Curless released the hard-driving "A Tombstone Every Mile" on his own Allagash label; the trucker's song eventually became a #5 hit after being picked up by CAPITOL's Tower subsidiary label. He followed with twenty-one more country chart hits, including "Six Times a Day" (#12, 1965) and "Big Wheel Cannonball" (#27, 1970). In the 1960s he toured with BUCK OWENS's All-American Show, and in 1968 he was heard on the *Killers Three* movie soundtrack. He died shortly after recording his final album, *Traveling Through* (ROUNDER, 1995). —*Walt Trott*

## Billy Currington
b. Savannah Georgia, November 19, 1973

Billy Currington began hitting the country Top Ten in 2003 with a pop- and R&B-inspired brand of country. His breakthrough hit, "Walk a Little Straighter," drew on his own experiences with an alcoholic stepfather. Currington wrote the song's chorus when he was only twelve years old.

Raised in Rincon, Georgia, near Savannah, William Matthew Currington continued writing songs as a teenager, drawing on country music, gospel, soul, and blues. In high school he auditioned unsuccessfully for a stage show in Nashville's OPRYLAND USA theme park, but eventually settled in MUSIC CITY to pursue his dream while working at jobs ranging from concrete worker to personal trainer. He met producer Carson Chamberlain, and the two began writing and recording demos that helped the singer land a deal with MERCURY RECORDS Nashville, which issued his self-titled debut album in 2003.

Currington's "Must Be Doin' Somethin' Right" topped *Billboard's* country charts in 2005, as "Good Directions" (from the same album, *Doin' Somethin' Right*) did in 2007. Other Currington hits include "I Got a Feelin'" (2004), "Don't" (2009), and "People are Crazy" (2009), another #1. The latter two are featured on his 2008 release *Little Bit of Everything*, which also included another #1, "That's How Country Boys Roll." He rode the momentum of those hits into his 2010 album, *Enjoy Yourself*, which kicked off with the #1 hit "Pretty Good at Drinkin' Beer."—*Jeremy Rush*

## Sonny Curtis
b. Meadow, Texas, May 9, 1937

Throughout his career as a songwriter, singer, and musician, Sonny Curtis has helped shape the sound of American music. Citing BLUEGRASS as his earliest musical influence, he began performing at age fourteen, playing with numerous young musicians around Lubbock, Texas, among them WAYLON JENNINGS and BUDDY HOLLY. Curtis played on Holly's first commercial recordings and wrote his "Rock Around with Ollie Vee."

After Curtis finished high school, his song "Someday" was recorded by WEBB PIERCE, whose version reached #12 on *Billboard's* country chart in 1957. Curtis joined SLIM WHITMAN's band in 1956, and Dot Records released his first solo recordings in 1958. As a member of the Crickets (post-Holly), he backed the Everly Brothers on a tour of England. Drafted into the army in 1960, he wrote the Everlys' "Walk Right Back" during basic training.

Other Curtis-penned hits have included Bobby Fuller's "I Fought the Law" (1966) and Keith Whitley's "I'm No Stranger to the Rain" (1989). He also wrote and performed the TV theme "Love Is All Around" for *The Mary Tyler Moore Show*. After recording for a variety of record labels through the 1960s and 1970s, he released three albums for Elektra Records in the early 1980s and scored a Top Twenty hit with "Good Ol' Girls" in 1981.

In addition to writing, Curtis has continued to tour internationally. He was featured in 1994 along with Eric Clapton, Mark Knopfler, and Keith Richards in a television special celebrating the fortieth anniversary of the Fender Stratocaster guitar. Curtis participated in the 1996 Decca album *Not Fade Away (Remembering Buddy Holly)* as a member of the Crickets.

Curtis was inducted into the Nashville Songwriters Hall of Fame in 1991. —*Janet E. Williams*

## T. Tommy Cutrer
b. Osyka, Mississippi, June 29, 1924; d. October 11, 1998

Thomas Clinton Cutrer was one of country broadcasting's best-known personalities—and one of its busiest. Cutrer (pronounced Cut-*trair*) announced both national programs (ABC-TV's *Johnny Cash Show*) and regional broadcasts (*Nashville Scene, Music City USA*); recorded for Mercury, Dot, and RCA; and worked as a promoter and restaurateur (Kentucky Fried Chicken franchises). In a bid for Congress in 1976 he lost to Albert Gore Jr., but he was elected in 1978 to the Tennessee State Senate. Serving as Transportation Committee chairman indirectly led to work on behalf of the national AFL/CIO.

McComb, Mississippi, radio station WSKB hired Cutrer at age eighteen. He moved on to WDSU–New Orleans; WJDX–Jackson, Mississippi; KARK–Little Rock; WMC–Memphis; and WREC–Memphis, where he worked with studio engineer Sam Phillips (who later founded Sun Records). After stints at WSLI in Jackson, Mississippi, and KWYZ and KNUZ in Houston, Cutrer landed at KCIJ in Shreveport. A drummer, he played in honky-tonks and inherited Webb Pierce's band (including Jimmy Day, Floyd Cramer, and Lloyd Ellis) when Pierce joined the Grand Ole Opry in 1952. Cutrer's own drumming halted when he lost a leg in a 1953 car crash; at the time he was moving to Nashville to work for WSM. During his ten years at WSM, Cutrer announced at the Opry and handled the all-night show *Opry Star Spotlight*. He augmented his pay doing commercials, including many in the syndicated Flatt & Scruggs TV shows sponsored by Martha White Flour.

In 1964 Cutrer left WSM to buy his own station, WJQS, in Jackson, Mississippi. He was inducted into the Country Disc Jockey Hall of Fame in 1980. —*Walt Trott*

## Billy Ray Cyrus
b. Flatwoods, Kentucky, August 25, 1961

In the 1990s Billy Ray Cyrus proved the increasing importance of country dance clubs. In early 1992 his debut album, *Some Gave All*, went #1 country and topped *Billboard's* Hot 200 pop album chart, boosted by its catchy, guitar-driven, #1 country single (#4 pop), "Achy Breaky Heart." By year's end the single went platinum, while album sales topped 5 million units.

Cyrus was no overnight success, however. At age twenty he dropped out of Kentucky's Georgetown College and began playing Flatwoods-area nightclubs. After two years of trying to break into the Los Angeles rock scene, he returned to Flatwoods in 1986, formed the band Sly Dog, and began to alternate nightclub gigs with trips to Nashville. In 1989 manager Jack McFadden agreed to handle Cyrus. Harold Shedd signed him to Mercury Records in 1990, and in 1991 Cyrus and Sly Dog completed *Some Gave All*. For many months, Mercury executives pondered how to market the rock-influenced record to country fans. Initially they offered the album's debut single, "Achy Breaky Heart," only to country dance clubs, along with a dance contest and instructional dance video. Next, the song's music video premiered in March 1992 on TNN and CMT, where Cyrus's good looks and dance moves helped sell the number and increased radio exposure. By the time *Some Gave All* was finally released, demand was skyrocketing.

Cyrus's white-hot popularity cooled after 1992, though he continued to make the country Top Ten during 1992–93 with "Could've Been Me," "She's Not Cryin' Anymore," and other hits. He went five years without a Top Ten until 1998–99's "Busy Man." Album sales also dropped off after his second and third albums, *It Won't Be the Last* and *Storm in the Heartland,* respectively.

The singer's fortunes revived as he switched briefly to Monument Records and scored a Top Twenty single in 2000 with "You Won't Be Lonely Now," from his album *Southern Rain*. New Door Records issued *I Wanna Be Your Joe* in 2006, when Cyrus also began appearing on the Disney Channel's popular *Hannah Montana* series, starring his daughter, Miley Cyrus (b. November 23, 1992). Disney released his *Home at Last* in 2007, and Miley's popularity—and her vocal contributions on "Ready, Set, Don't Go"—helped push the song to #4 and the album to #3 in *Billboard's* country charts. Father and daughter also appeared in 2009's *Hannah Montana: The Movie*. Miley's top-selling soundtrack album conveniently publicized her father's *Back to Tennessee* (2009), released on Disney/Lyric Street. In 2010 Cyrus joined a rock band, Brother Clyde, as lead singer; the group released an album in August of that year. —*Paul Kingsbury*

# The Look of Country
## The Colorful History of Country Music Costuming

## HOLLY GEORGE-WARREN

Perhaps more than any other form of American music, country music has been closely identified with visual style. From the music's earliest popular entertainers—including JIMMIE RODGERS and the CARTER FAMILY—to contemporary superstars such as BRAD PAISLEY and CARRIE UNDERWOOD, fashion has played a key role in defining the public personas of country artists. During country's first decade or so as a commercial music form, a link was forged between many a performer's music and his or her geographical and cultural roots in the rural Southeast. Entertainers' typical attire ranged from work clothes such as overalls to Sunday-go-to-meeting best. By the late 1930s, with the greater dissemination of American popular culture via movies, radio, and recordings, the heroic look of the cowboy—reinforced and popularized by B-western and singing-cowboy idols—became de rigueur among country artists and remains a major component of the country image today.

Back in the 1920s and 1930s, the Carter Family dressed as their audiences would for church. This was only fitting, since many of the Carters' early performances took place in church halls and schoolhouses in rural Virginia and Tennessee. The Singing Brakeman, Jimmie Rodgers, also typically gussied himself up in a crisp white linen suit with matching boater but also drew on his background as a railroad worker to create a look (railroad cap and canvas railman garb) that gave credence to his moniker. For one publicity shot, Rodgers dressed like a cowboy, down to his chaps, neckerchief, and Stetson—a signpost of what was to come. Popular at about this time were traveling vaudeville and minstrel shows, which usually featured a backwoods rube character or family dressed like denizens of Dogpatch in the *Li'l Abner* comic strip. Patched britches and gingham dresses, worn-out straw hats, pigtails and blackened front teeth, corncob pipes—these exaggerated clichés defined hayseed style, the look that predominated during the early years of the WLS *National Barn Dance*, the GRAND OLE OPRY, and other radio barn dance programs. Like his counterparts at WLS, Opry founder GEORGE D. HAY required his performers to forgo Sunday suits for hillbilly clothes.

Things began to change, though, in the mid-1930s, when western-attired singers such as GENE AUTRY and PATSY MONTANA, stars of the *National Barn Dance*, and the Los Angeles–based Sons of the Pioneers began hitting with buckaroo-themed songs, including Autry's "The Last Roundup" and Montana's "I Wanna Be a Cowboy's Sweetheart." Building on precedents established earlier by OTTO GRAY and a handful of others, these stars pushed the trend toward heroic-looking western wear, which helped country performers overcome negative hillbilly stereotypes. After all, who wouldn't prefer the image of a dashing buckaroo to that of a backwoods clodhopper? Autry, who grew up in rural Texas and Oklahoma, was a natural in his wide-brimmed Stetson, western shirt with neckerchief, and cowboy boots. Likewise, Montana's cowgirl outfits, which included a western hat, bolero vest, neck scarf, and fringed split skirt, influenced generations of female country performers, as did her contemporaries THE GIRLS OF THE GOLDEN WEST and LOUISE MASSEY & THE WESTERNERS. Later in his career, when he starred on his own TV show, Autry dropped fancy cowboy duds and dressed in a casual, workaday western style like that of cattle-punching cowpokes. This practical clothing style can be traced to the mid-1800s, when cowboys developed functional garb to cope with the necessities of life on the range. The prototypical denim jeans, Levi's, were "invented" in 1849 when Levi Strauss, of a New York tailoring family, joined the California Gold Rush, intending to finance his venture by selling bolts of canvas to make into tents. Instead, he found customers needing britches, so he fashioned the durable fabric into trousers. By 1860 his indigo-dyed pants with copper rivets were a smashing success among miners, though the majority of cowboys didn't begin wearing them until the early twentieth century.

Cowboy boots and Stetson hats—a roughrider's essential accoutrements—also date from the mid-1800s. Cowboy boots with high heels, high tops, and stitching on the toes derived from British cavalry boots in the 1860s and gradually evolved over forty years. Designed to fit easily into stirrups without sliding out, boots with tall leather tops protected cowpunchers' legs and feet from such hazards as snakebite and stinging nettles. By 1920, with rodeos and dude ranches commonplace out West and with westerns popular on the silver screen, fancier boot styles, with colorful inlaid designs, variation of toe styles, and intricate stitching, began to appear. When he became a sensation, Autry ordered custom boots from Lucchese, Olsen-Stelzer, and other specialty leathercraft companies that created one-of-a-kind handmade boots in a variety of shades; this footwear featured intricate hand tooling and inlays of arrows, bald eagles, flowers, butterflies, suits of cards, and other designs on the boot fronts.

Cowboy hats developed from a prototype designed by John B. Stetson, a Philadelphia milliner who ventured to Colorado during the Gold Rush in 1865. Fashioning a broad-brimmed, high-crowned creation from beaver and rabbit hide that he boiled and turned into felt, Stetson crafted a waterproof derivative of the sombreros that Mexican vaqueros had been wearing for years. After selling his sample to a Westerner for the then-hefty sum of five dollars, Stetson rushed back to Philadelphia and began sending his "Boss of the Plains" headgear to the frontier market. Dimensions for crown height and brim width varied, evolving into the ten-gallon hat (so called for its high crown and volume) as matinee idols, hit recording artists, and rodeo stars chose individual looks with which they became identified. The first hats were taupe or beige, but by the time of B-western talkies, white and black hats—which came to signify good and evil—had become popular. Cowboy hats and boots graced the Grand Ole Opry stage at least as early as western singer Zeke Clements's 1934–36 stint with the long-running radio program. In 1937 Pee Wee King's flashy Golden West Cowboys joined the show and took stylish western wear to new heights there.

Cowboy shirts and western suits assumed greater importance beginning in the 1930s. By this time, casual western clothes had already been catching on among country performers and, of course, the singing cowboys of Hollywood movies. Moreover, the western shirt had distinctive styling developed specifically for the working cowboy and rodeo rider. Front and back yokes and bib fronts, for example, provided extra warmth and padding; snaps (which first appeared on mass-produced shirts in the 1940s) substituted for buttons to prevent rodeo injuries. "If your shirt got snagged on the pommel of your saddle, the snaps would pop open and not hang you there like buttons would," explained western-wear manufacturer Jack Weil, who established Rockmount in 1946 after eleven years in the business at Miller and Company. Other design elements found in the West made their way into cowboy clothes: fringe and buckskin, inspired by the garments of various Indian tribes; the fancy embroidery of Mexican vaqueros' jackets; and the intricate beadwork found on Plains Indians' attire.

Eventually the opulent merged with the ordinary in the work of a few tailors who specialized in western wear. One of the first, Philadelphia-based Ben the Rodeo Tailor (or Rodeo Ben, for short), gained a batch of clients among B-western, rodeo, and singing-cowboy stars who wanted unique, customized looks. Born on April 10, 1893, Rodeo Ben opened his first shop, billed "the East's most western store," in 1930. With a retail business in front and custom tailoring in back, Ben attracted Ken Maynard and Gene Autry, among others, with kaleidoscopic fabrics (including gabardine, flannel, and twill), fine embroidery (from Indian heads to bluebirds), and high-quality designs. When Roy Rogers became his client a few years after Autry (Rogers's Republic Films predecessor), the tailor vowed never to design similar outfits for the two. Rodeo Ben is credited with being the first to put metal glove snaps instead of buttons on cowboy shirts, in 1933, for his rodeo customers; he began using mother-of-pearl snaps for Autry's and Rogers's shirts.

Just outside Los Angeles, amid the San Fernando Valley's ranches and western movie sets, was the Turk of Hollywood shop, opened in 1923 by Nathan Turk, born May 10, 1895, in Poland. By the 1930s, Turk's Sherman Oaks operation was catering to rodeo riders as well as to the film industry. Soon Turk won Autry and Rogers's business. Turk specialized in ornate costumes for Pasadena's annual Rose Bowl parade, and his designs became more and more spectacular. West Coast–based artists the Maddox Brothers & Rose and western swing bandleader Spade Cooley had discovered Turk's beautifully embroidered garments by the 1940s. Ernest Tubb and Hank Snow became clients in 1944 and 1946, respectively. By then, the genre's nomenclature had changed from hillbilly to country & western, while the western look took hold among country artists. As vintage-clothing collector MARTY STUART has remarked, "Western wear and country music—there was a marriage there and it made perfect sense."

Perhaps more responsible than anyone else for country's embrace of fancy cowboy clothes was the loquacious, North Hollywood-based tailor NUDIE. Born in Kiev, Ukraine, on December 15, 1902, and raised in Brooklyn, Nudie Cohn landed in Los Angeles in 1940 and opened a dry-cleaning and tailoring establishment. In 1947 he began creating custom western wear when his first major West Coast client, TEX WILLIAMS, outfitted his band in Nudie's custom-made western suits. Though Nudie's measurements for this initial order were way off, Williams loved the suits anyway and began spreading the word. Nudie set up at the popular nightclub RIVERSIDE RANCHO, where Williams regularly performed, and customers began ordering custom clothes from the tailor. To meet the demand, Nudie's Rodeo Tailors opened at 11000 Victory Boulevard in 1950. There, he tried to top each outfit with the next, embellishing the cowboy look with detailed embroidered designs, fringe, and, by late 1951, rhinestones. "My impression of an entertainer is that he should wear a flashy outfit," Nudie once said, "to be fair to the public." Autry and Rogers began commissioning Nudie to design spectacular outfits for their public appearances. Said Rogers of his sparkly Nudie suits, "When I came through the gates and the lights hit me, I lit up like a Christmas tree."

LITTLE JIMMY DICKENS was the first entertainer to wear a Nudie suit onstage at the Grand Ole Opry, in 1949. Soon after, western wear became so popular in Nashville that AUDREY WILLIAMS and HANK WILLIAMS, both satisfied Nudie customers, opened Hank and Audrey's Corral there in 1951; Hank's trademark white suit dotted with black musical notes was a Nudie. By the late 1950s, rhinestones had become synonymous with country music. "Back in those days," says Marty Stuart, "they wore rhinestones as if they were badges on a uniform." Nudie's specialty lay in designing ensembles featuring an artist's unique trademark, such as PORTER WAGONER's wagon wheel–covered costumes, and embroidered details from hit songs such as WEBB PIERCE's "In the Jailhouse Now" and GEORGE JONES's "White Lightnin.'" Appearing next to their shimmering cowboy-suited counterparts, female country artists dressed in rhinestone-studded or appliquéd-and-fringed cowgirl suits (the favorite look of Audrey Williams, DALE EVANS, and the young PATSY CLINE) or colorful tiered-and-trimmed gauze frocks inspired by Mexican fiesta dresses and Navajo Indian skirts (favored by Mother Maybelle and the CARTER SISTERS).

Beginning in the mid-1960s, Nudie employed English-born embroidery artisan Rose Clements (b. Rose Grossman in London, August 13, 1919; d. June 13, 2003), who brought special machines with her when she moved from Britain to California. Her intricate and original designs required great skill and encompassed Swiss, chain, and satin stitches. Nudie also hired expert leatherworkers, who created fancy, custom cowboy boots that often matched his outfits.

To meet the demand, Nudie eventually employed twenty-one tailors, one of whom, MANUEL Cuevas, soon became a star in his own right. Born on April 23, 1933 (or 1934), in Coalcoman, Mexico, Manuel (who, following Nudie's example, uses only his first name) learned to sew from an older brother and apprenticed with a tailor before moving to Los Angeles. He joined Nudie in the 1950s, just in time for western wear's eye-popping peak, when the shop's clientele included the aforementioned artists plus HANK SNOW (bullfrogs and lily pads on one suit), FARON YOUNG, COWBOY COPAS, MERLE TRAVIS, RAY PRICE, JOHNNY CASH (black, of course), and JIMMY C. NEWMAN (a Cajun motif).

"That's when I discovered what I wanted to do with my life," Manuel said. "I dressed artists in rhinestones, fringe, and embroidery, and brought all this craftsmanship into clothing for entertainers." Manuel, who was married to and divorced from Nudie's daughter and eventually branched out on his own in the 1970s, became the link to the next generation of flashy western wearers.

By the late 1960s, country's look had become more sophisticated as its music became sweetened via THE NASHVILLE SOUND. Cocktail dresses and tuxedos came into vogue. Gradually, gleaming cowboy clothes became less popular in Nashville, though BAKERSFIELD-based BUCK OWENS began wearing his own distinctive Nudie suits featuring short bolero jackets sparkling with luminous rhinestones and metallic embroidery.

In the early 1970s, polyester leisure suits proliferated until the OUTLAW movement spearheaded by WAYLON JENNINGS and WILLIE NELSON ushered in the down-home-meets-counterculture style, with bandannas worn on the head rather than around the neck. Scuffed cowboy boots—or tennis shoes—peeked out from under faded, patched jeans, and simple cowboy shirts were often made of denim. A segment of the long-haired audience who became the Outlaws' fans stuck with flash, however.

Beginning in the late 1960s, members of the Rolling Stones and THE BYRDS began buying from Nudie, culminating in the unforgetable Nudie suits designed by Manuel for GRAM PARSONS and his FLYING BURRITO BROTHERS. The embodiment of Parsons's musical goal—taking traditional country to the rock & roll audience—his most famous suit featured white flared hip-hugger pants festooned with flames on each leg and a short fitted jacket embroidered with naked women, marijuana leaves, pills, and a large cross on the jacket's back. Other country-rock artists who embraced the western look included NEW RIDERS OF THE PURPLE SAGE, Commander Cody, and western swing practitioners ASLEEP AT THE WHEEL. Traditionalist cowboy band RIDERS IN THE SKY always dressed the part as well and would later commission eye-catching suits from Manuel. Into the 1980s, cowpunks—artists playing country-tinged, high-energy music outside the mainstream of both rock & roll and country—wore western garb, including Rank & File, Lone Justice, and, before she evolved into a pop chanteuse, K. D. LANG.

It wasn't until the late 1970s and early 1980s that the decorative cowboy look began returning to mainstream country music in a big way. Two quite different trends in the music—URBAN COWBOY and NEW TRADITIONALISM—ushered in western wear's resurgence. The former tended toward the polyester, mass-market look popularized by the 1980 film *Urban Cowboy*, starring John Travolta. The clean-cut New Traditionalist look, established largely by GEORGE STRAIT in the early 1980s, called for top-quality cowboy boots and hats, along with jeans and western shirts. That clothing style has pervaded country music since the 1990s and has been worn by ALAN JACKSON, Brad Paisley, TIM McGRAW, and nearly every best-selling young male star. Paisley, who sported a white Stetson for many years, insisted on wearing a cowboy hat when, in 1999, record execs advised against it: "There was a little bit of negative stigma attached to it," according to Paisley, "because they'd had so many cookie-cutter, wannabe people just throw them on." He stuck to his guns, though, since to Paisley a cowboy hat was a visual calling card to fans that he is a link in the chain of country music.

GARTH BROOKS took the western traditionalist look a step further with his trademark style—oversized hat, snug, crisp jeans, and busy-print cowboy shirt with oversized yoke—which became prevalent among the boot-scooting set. BROOKS & DUNN parlayed their flamboyant image into their own retail line of western ready-to-wear manufactured by Panhandle Slim. Donning a straw cowboy hat, but favoring puka shells over a bolo tie, KENNY CHESNEY preferred his jeans tight and his shirts skimpy—a kind of Key West cowboy style increasingly popular among younger country performers. KEITH URBAN spearheaded the hatless look, and with his blond tresses and earring he illustrates today's "rockist" approach some country singers have taken toward their repertoire and their wardrobes. Conversely, in the 2000s, such rock artists as Mike Mills of R.E.M., Jack White of the White Stripes, Jeff Tweedy of Wilco, and Beck began sporting decorative western suits designed by Manuel.

As for female country stars, by the late 1970s the dominant look was high glitz, a style ushered in by DOLLY PARTON. Parton wore relatively conservative dresses at first, but with her bubbly personality and hourglass figure she was never as reserved as the demurely attired KITTY WELLS, who had risen to stardom in the 1950s wearing full-skirted gingham dresses (accessorized with an old-fashioned bonnet in one early promo shot). As Parton evolved from Porter Wagoner's duet partner, a country-lass bombshell busting out of denim and lace, to solo superstar, her look rivaled that of a Las Vegas showgirl, with sparkly and sheer fabrics that clung to every curve. Other stars followed suit, with LORETTA LYNN and TAMMY WYNETTE abandoning ladylike gowns, down-homey denim, and polyester pantsuits for glitzy tulle and sequin-studded Bob Mackie ensembles. In the late 1980s, former rodeo cowgirl REBA McENTIRE also began indulging in a lavish, Hollywood-style wardrobe for personal appearances—changing into and out of as many as ten different outfits in a single concert.

As country became more like rock, its dress code did too. By the mid-1990s, the hottest new country queens were almost indistinguishable from their pop-diva sisters, in both their vocal styles and their stage looks. SHANIA TWAIN made a splash with sexy midriff-baring tops, miniskirts, glittering halter tops, hot pants, and skin-tight catsuits, in short, dressing as if she were a rock star. Of course, TANYA TUCKER had blazed the country-coquette-meets-rock-star trail back in the 1970s with her second-skin leather jumpsuits, modeled after those of ELVIS PRESLEY. The members of DIXIE CHICKS, who started their career emulating Dale Evans, became fashionistas with the addition of vocalist Natalie Maines and via cutting-edge ensembles designed by Todd Oldham. Tomboy style, á la distressed jeans and tank tops, found favor among such artists as midwesterner GRETCHEN WILSON and Texan MIRANDA LAMBERT. Carrie Underwood and FAITH HILL, following in the footsteps of TRISHA YEARWOOD, impersonated the girl next door, dressing up for awards shows but most often looking like they do their shopping at the mall.

The New Traditionalist look of the 1980s, which modeled itself on the golden years of western wear, still has its followers, however. Los Angeles–based DWIGHT YOAKAM made a large contribution to the revival of classic western styling when he sought out Manuel. "I asked him about what I used to call the Buck Owens jacket," said Yoakam, "and he started making them for me." Yoakam and Manuel began a creative partnership that resulted in the singer's signature western style: low-slung cowboy hat, with fancy embroidered bolero or suede-fringed jacket over skin-tight, concho-studded jeans or leather pants, and cowboy boots. "Manuel makes reality from ideas I have in my head," Yoakam affirmed. In more recent years, Yoakam sometimes has sported a 1940s-style Western-cut suit, frequently created by North Hollywood–based tailor Jaime, who got his start working for Nudie and Manuel.

In Nashville, where Manuel moved his shop in October 1989, his foremost client is Marty Stuart, who, in the late 1980s, began collecting classic designs by Manuel, Nudie, and Turk after borrowing a classic western jacket from veteran singer CARL SMITH. "I thought, 'If I got some of those and put them on a band, it might make our videos jump a little better and give us an identity,'" Stuart recalled. "Nashville never wore them anymore, so I called everyone who ever wore rhinestones" to inquire about buying their old show clothes. Stuart's magnificent collection was showcased in the 2008–09 traveling exhibition *Sparkle & Twang*, as was Manuel's work in the 2004–05 exhibition *Star-Spangled Couture*, which traveled from Nashville's Frist Center for the Visual Arts to Fort Worth's National Cowgirl Museum and Hall of Fame. The exhibition included fifty lavish jackets embroidered with symbols of each of the fifty United States.

Manuel and Stuart have collaborated on an array of resplendent pieces, many featuring Stuart's trademark horseshoes and hearts. Stuart also frequents Jaime's shop and Ranch Dressing, the Nashville boutique owned by designer Katy K (née Kattelman), who began making imaginatively embroidered cowboy shirts and jackets in New York in the 1980s. Encouraged by Manuel, Katy K moved her distinctive line of western wear—along with her collection of vintage pieces by Turk, Nudie, and Rodeo Ben—to MUSIC CITY and opened her Ranch Dressing shop in November 1994.

One of the most beautiful objects in Stuart's *Sparkle & Twang* exhibition was an elaborately detailed, exquisitely embroidered wall hanging. He had commissioned it from Rose Clements, the English artist responsible for many of Nudie and Manuel's most intricate embroidery designs. Asked about the origin of his obsession with western wear and its accoutrements, Stuart explained, "I thought about those old suits people used to wear when I was a kid, when country was colorful, happy, and carefree. I think that's what those clothes represent. A tremendous amount of integrity and labor goes into their art. They are truly pieces of art."

# D

## D Records
established in Houston, Texas, 1958

Formed by HAROLD "PAPPY" DAILY after he and DON PIERCE, his partner in STARDAY RECORDS, parted in 1958, D Records has continued in some form into the twenty-first century, still operated by the Daily family.

Pierce kept the Starday name, but Daily managed, at least initially, to hold on to some of its roster, including EDDIE NOACK, James O'Gwynn, and Glenn Barber. Intended originally as an experimental label—material was issued in hopes that it would hit and be leased to a major label, as proved the case with THE BIG BOPPER's "Chantilly Lace"—D issued a varied, uneven flow of material, from country classics like Noack's "Have Blues Will Travel" to custom issues of questionable quality. Between 1976 and 1979 GEORGE STRAIT and the Ace in the Hole Band had three singles released on D Records. Into the twenty-first century, the label has continued as an affiliate of its parent firm, the music publisher Glad Music Company, releasing recordings by steel guitar greats HERB REMINGTON and JIMMY DAY as well as albums by young, aspiring singers. —*Kevin Coffey*

## Da Costa Woltz's Southern Broadcasters

This remarkable STRINGBAND consisted of fiddler Ben Jarrell (father of TOMMY JARRELL) and banjo players Da Costa Woltz and Frank Jenkins, whose homes were in the Mount Airy–Round Peak area of western North Carolina. The group seems to have existed only for purposes of an extended session for GENNETT RECORDS in Richmond, Indiana, where they journeyed for the session in April 1927.

Leader Woltz had visions of radio work (hence the band's name) and other public appearances for the band, but these never materialized. A fourth member, Price Goodson, was only twelve and was featured on only a few solos. Jenkins performed solos on fiddle and banjo; the remainder of the eighteen sides consisted of old songs and breakdowns by the band, forcefully led by Jarrell's singing and fiddling.

Gennett issued the records on its own imprint as well as a variety of inexpensive, poorly distributed labels, including Champion, Challenge (not the same firm as GENE AUTRY's CHALLENGE RECORDS), and Herwin. Good copies of these discs are rare today, though an LP featuring some of the band's 1927 recordings was issued in 1972. —*Dick Spottswood*

## Ted Daffan
b. Beauregard Parish, Louisiana, September 21, 1912; d. October 6, 1996

Theron Eugene Daffan, who helped usher in the modern era of country songwriting, was also one of the best-selling bandleaders of the 1940s.

Uninterested in a music career until he fell in love with HAWAIIAN MUSIC at age twenty, Daffan quickly began learning the steel guitar. At twenty-one he was not only teaching guitar but also leading his Blue Islanders on Houston radio. His introduction to country music came via the Blue Ridge Playboys, a fledgling local WESTERN SWING band including fiddler LEON SELPH and guitarist FLOYD TILLMAN, in 1934. Daffan was with the group

*Ted Daffan*

until sidelined by ill health. In 1936 he teamed with vocalist JERRY IRBY and first recorded the following year with SHELLY LEE ALLEY; selections included Daffan's first composition, "I'm Still in Love with You." Soon he joined the popular BAR X COWBOYS, but concentrated on songwriting in hopes of getting his own label deal.

Daffan's big break came when CLIFF BRUNER recorded a number of his songs at his 1939 DECCA sessions, including the seminal trucker's song "Truck Driver's Blues," which sold more than 100,000 copies. The hit led to a COLUMBIA recording contract for Daffan, who began recording solo in 1940, though he remained with the Bar X Cowboys until mid-1941. Daffan's band, the Texans, featured lead guitarist Buddy Buller and accordionists Harry Sorensen and Freddy Courtney. Daffan's emphasis on these instruments proved distinctive and influential. He immediately produced the major hits "Worried Mind" and "I'm a Fool to Care" and was already one of Columbia's top acts when he followed these with the two-sided million-seller "Born to Lose" b/w "No Letter Today," recorded in Hollywood in 1942. These original songs established Daffan as a major star, and he worked the competitive West Coast dance circuit from 1944 to 1946. Although he subsequently returned to Texas, the hits kept coming, including the HONKY-TONK– themed "Heading Down the Wrong Highway" to "I've Got Five Dollars and It's Saturday Night." By the early 1950s, his career was in eclipse, and he returned to Houston and disbanded the Texans. In 1955 Daffan started his own label, Daffan Records, which he revived intermittently until 1971, but his main source of income became new hit versions of his classic songs, such as Joe Barry's 1961 revival of "I'm a Fool to Care" and especially RAY CHARLES's early-1960s covers of "Born to Lose," "No Letter Today," and "Worried Mind." —Kevin Coffey

## Pappy Daily

b. Yoakum, Texas, February 8, 1902; d. December 5, 1987

Almost a caricature of an old-time record man, Harold Westcott Daily was blunt, cigar-chomping, and very much a hands-on operator who knew every facet of the business but made a point of emphasizing his lack of musical knowledge. Based in Houston, he was able to tap into a pool of talent that most labels ignored. He made the first commercial recordings by GEORGE JONES, WEBB PIERCE, HANK LOCKLIN, ROGER MILLER, THE BIG BOPPER, and WILLIE NELSON. Even GEORGE STRAIT made early recordings for Daily's D RECORDS.

After serving in the marines during World War I, Daily joined the Southern Pacific Railroad as a bookkeeper and stayed until 1932. Then he started the South Coast Amusement Company, selling and servicing amusement machines. South Coast branched into JUKEBOXES and then records. In 1949 Daily began recording local acts, selling the masters to FOUR STAR RECORDS, a label he distributed. Among the artists he uncovered were Pierce and Locklin (the latter bestowing the affectionate nickname "Pappy"). Seeing little return from the Four Star arrangement, Daily launched STARDAY RECORDS with Jack Starnes Jr. in June 1953.

Daily's distribution companies, H. W. Daily, Inc., and Big State, dominated record wholesaling in Texas, although he sold them to his sons in 1957 shortly after Starday entered into a pact with MERCURY RECORDS. After Mercury and Starday split, Daily started D Records, which is still in business at this writing. He shunted virtually all the promising artists he discovered to major labels, forging a particularly close alliance with Art Talmadge, who was first at Mercury, then United Artists, and then Musicor

*Pappy Daily (standing) with George Jones*

(a label in which both Talmadge and Daily had ownership stakes). Daily also will be remembered as George Jones's producer from 1953 until 1971. Their relationship ended acrimoniously when Jones bought his way out of his Musicor contract to join TAMMY WYNETTE at EPIC RECORDS. —Colin Escott

## Vernon Dalhart

b. Jefferson, Texas, April 6, 1883; d. September 14, 1948

Vernon Dalhart was one of the most productive and versatile figures of the early recording industry. By chance, he slipped into the role of a singer of hillbilly songs and became by far the most prolific recorder of such material in the 1920s. Born Marion Try Slaughter, he derived his professional name from two Texas towns where he worked as a cattle puncher in his teens before studying voice at the Dallas Conservatory of Music. By 1910 he was pursuing his career in New York, where he filled roles in opera and operetta productions. His first recording, "Can't You Heah Me Callin', Caroline?" (EDISON, 1917), revealed his skill with dialect songs, and for some years he was busy making records for Edison, COLUMBIA, and other labels, a journeyman studio artist handling every kind of repertoire required by the popular disc market, from "coon song" to HAWAIIAN.

His 1924 Victor recording of "The Wreck of the Old '97," coupled with "The Prisoner's Song," became country music's first million-seller and redirected the course of his career. Over the next nine years he devoted himself primarily to hillbilly songs, of which he recorded several hundred, routinely cutting the same material for half a dozen or more different companies. Since many of these recordings would then be released on subsidiary labels, a collection of all his distinct issues would run into thousands, though this near-domination of the hillbilly disc market was

*Vernon Dalhart*

somewhat masked by an extensive use of pseudonyms, such as Al Craver (Columbia) and Tobe Little (OKeh).

A typical Dalhart recording featured a studio violinist, his own harmonica and sometimes Jew's harp, and the guitar of CARSON ROBISON, Dalhart's regular partner from 1924 to 1928, who also frequently sang a tenor part and wrote much of Dalhart's material. They were joined in trio performances by singer and violinist Adelyne Hood. Dalhart drew on minstrel-stage repertoire such as "Golden Slippers" and cowboy songs such as "Bury Me Not on the Lone Prairie," which he had learned in his youth in Texas, but his richest vein of song was topical compositions such as "The Death of Floyd Collins," "The John T. Scopes Trial" (about the Dayton, Tennessee, court case over the teaching of evolution), "Little Marian Parker," "Farm Relief Song," and other pieces inspired by news stories of the day.

Although Dalhart is regarded by most scholars as peripheral to the stylistic development of country music, his recordings undoubtedly circulated widely in the South and disseminated songs that were taken up by professional and amateur country performers. He is perhaps more important, however, for conveying a flavor of southern song to audiences unaccustomed to it, without the distractions of bucolic humor or impenetrable accent. As the veteran producer RALPH PEER wrote in *Variety* in 1955, "Dalhart had the peculiar ability to adapt hillbilly music to suit the taste of the non-hillbilly population. . . . He was a professional substitute for a real hillbilly." In this respect Dalhart may be seen as a kind of role model for BRADLEY KINCAID as well as for more obviously dependent figures, such as FRANK LUTHER.

Dalhart's recording career virtually ended with the Depression—after 1933 there was just one final session for BLUEBIRD, in 1939—and by 1942 he was reduced to working as a factory night watchman. For a few years he offered his services as a voice teacher, though the thousands of recordings that could have furnished his credentials had long passed out of circulation, and the musical idiom to which he had made so singular a contribution had left him far behind. —*Tony Russell*

## Lacy J. Dalton
b. Bloomsburg, Pennsylvania, October 13, 1946

Lacy J. Dalton—born Jill Byrem—differed from her female country music counterparts thanks to a gritty attitude and a sensuous barroom voice. She also has been  a successful songwriter who has often written about working-class trials and triumphs. Dalton was named ACM's Most Promising New Female Vocalist of 1979, but her career predated the 1990s era of strong, independent women, and she never realized the commercial potential her talents demonstrated.

Recording as Jill Croston, she released a 1978 album sent by a friend to COLUMBIA RECORDS. BILLY SHERRILL signed her to the label and suggested the name Lacy J. Dalton. Early hits included "Hard Times" (#7, 1980); "Takin' It Easy" (#2, 1981); "Everybody Makes Mistakes (#5, 1981); and her signature song, the Nashville songwriters' anthem "16th Avenue" (#7, 1982).

The last of Dalton's seven Columbia albums, *Highway Diner*, was released in 1986. A contract dispute and personal problems kept her from recording until 1988, when JIMMY BOWEN signed her to Universal. Her Universal debut, 1989's *Survivor*, featured KRIS KRISTOFFERSON's "The Heart" (#13, 1989) and the self-penned "Walking Wounded" and "Hard Luck Ace." She next recorded *Lacy J.* for CAPITOL and scored a minor hit with "Black Coffee" (#15, 1990) but lost the momentum she had earlier enjoyed.

In the new century, Dalton has found acceptance among audiences abroad. In 2004 she coproduced her first independent label CD, *The Last Wild Place*, on Song Dog Records. She released the album *Here's to Hank*, featuring covers of Hank Williams's songs, in 2010. —*Jack Bernhardt*

## Dance (*see* separate entries for Line Dancing, Square Dancing, and Clogging)

## Charlie Daniels
b. Wilmington, North Carolina, October 28, 1936

Instrumentalist, bandleader, and songwriter Charlie Daniels has been a major presence in country music since the late 1960s, adding southern rock elements to country's sound and image while openly voicing his conservative social and political views.

The son of a Tarheel State lumberman, Charles Edward Daniels taught himself guitar by age fifteen and began learning the rudiments of rock, BLUEGRASS, jazz, and country music that would undergird his career. After several years playing in rock bands, he enjoyed some success as a songwriter when ELVIS PRESLEY recorded his "It Hurts Me" in 1964. Urged by BOB DYLAN's producer BOB JOHNSTON, Daniels moved to Nashville in 1967 and began working as a session guitarist. He contributed to Dylan's *Nashville Skyline* and to albums by Ringo Starr, Leonard Cohen, and MARTY ROBBINS, among others.

Daniels released his self-titled debut album in 1970 on CAPITOL RECORDS, and the next year he assembled the Charlie Daniels Band. *Te John, Grease & Wolfman* (1972), named for the band members' nicknames, was the first of five albums on the Kama Sutra label. Reflecting the influence of the Allman Brothers, the album exemplifies the style that Daniels would develop as a prominent exponent of southern rock.

*Honey in the Rock* (1973) included "Uneasy Rider," a talking blues tale of confrontation between a long-haired, peace-loving hippie and a bar full of antagonistic honky-tonkers. A Top Ten pop hit, it began Daniels's tradition of recording successful topical numbers. He later revised the song as "Uneasy Rider '88," changing the scene of action from a honky-tonk to a gay bar.

*Fire on the Mountain* (Kama Sutra, 1974; EPIC, 1980) is perhaps Daniels's best album, featuring several concert favorites, including the redneck anthems "Long Haired Country Boy" and "The South's Gonna Do It," along with a hard-driving cover of the bluegrass classic "Orange Blossom Special."

Daniels's greatest success came with *Million Mile Reflections* (1979). Although musically similar to his earlier work, it featured "The Devil Went Down to Georgia," a rousing story song based on the South's fiddle contest tradition and the oft-told tale of gambling one's soul. Daniels's only #1 country hit, it also went #3 pop and earned Daniels a Grammy and a CMA award for Single of the Year. Both the single and the album sold 1 million copies. The Charlie Daniels Band was named the CMA's Instrumental Group of the Year for 1979 and 1980.

Daniels has continued writing conservative topical songs that deal scathingly with such issues as crime, farm foreclosures, homelessness, and immigration; examples include "In America" (1980), "American Farmer" (1985), "Simple Man" (1989–90), and "America, I Believe in You" (1993). He further championed his opinions through his 2003 book *Ain't No Rag: Freedom, Family and the Flag* and through the Soap Box Articles section of his website.

Daniels's 1994 Sparrow collection *The Door* was honored with a Dove award for Best Gospel Album. In 2005 he released *Songs from the Longleaf Pines: A Gospel Bluegrass Collection* on Koch/BlueHat. He joined the GRAND OLE OPRY in January 2008. Daniels lives on his ranch in Mount Juliet, Tennessee. Even with a mild stroke suffered in 2010, he continues to record and tour.
—*Jack Bernhardt*

## Darby & Tarlton

Tom Darby b. Columbus, Georgia, 1891; d. August 20, 1971
Jimmie Tarlton b. Cheraw, South Carolina, May 8, 1892; d. November 29, 1979

Tom Darby and Jimmie Tarlton were among the earliest white country musicians to incorporate blues in a substantial way. With Darby's soulful singing and Tarlton's remarkable work on what was then called the HAWAIIAN guitar, they made an impressive series of records in the late 1920s and early 1930s, including several that became country standards. Their eclectic repertoire ranged from traditional BALLADS to vaudeville pieces and from parlor songs to blues. Their loose, improvisational style, vastly different from the quiet precision of later duets such as the BLUE SKY BOYS, linked them more closely to African American country blues than to other OLD-TIME styles.

The son of Orange County, South Carolina, sharecroppers, Tarlton was learning to play slide guitar from local blacks by the time he was twelve. At seventeen he left home and began playing for tips in bars and on street corners. In 1922 he met famed Hawaiian guitarist Frank Ferrara, who helped him improve his slide bar technique. Returning to Georgia in 1927, Tarlton met another skilled guitarist, Tom Darby, of Cherokee ancestry. A cousin of RILEY PUCKETT, Darby was a solid blues musician. The pair joined forces, and soon they attracted the attention of COLUMBIA RECORDS talent scout FRANK WALKER.

Their second Columbia session, in November 1927, produced their career record—the two-sided hit "Columbus Stockade Blues" b/w "Birmingham Jail." Sales topping 200,000 made it one of Columbia's best-selling discs of the day and helped the songs become country classics. Both songs had genuine folk roots, but they had been reworked by the singers; in later years, Tarlton would claim he had written "Birmingham Jail" in 1925, when he was actually incarcerated there; whatever the case, the number helped him secure a pardon.

Between 1927 and 1933 Darby & Tarlton recorded some sixty songs for three major labels, but they never duplicated their initial success. By 1935 both had essentially retired from the professional circuit. During the 1960s historians and folk music buffs rediscovered them, and Tarlton made a comeback of sorts, working several major festivals and recording a new solo LP.
—*Charles Wolfe*

## Denver Darling

b. Whopock, Illinois, April 6, 1909; d. April 27, 1981

Remembered mainly as a songwriter, Denver Darling was a successful country performer and recording artist during the 1940s. After playing guitar and singing locally, he landed his first

*Charlie Daniels*

professional job in 1929 broadcasting on WBOW in Terre Haute, Indiana, and moved on to other radio stations, mostly in the Midwest. Briefly he worked the NATIONAL BARN DANCE in a trio with George "Shug" Fisher and Hugh Cross.

Moving to New York City in September 1937, Darling initially appeared on WOR and at THE VILLAGE BARN in Greenwich Village. He quickly landed his own WNEW radio show and eventually led bands, including the Trail Blazers, the Texas Cowhands, and the Georgie Porgie Boys. In 1941 he made the first of several recording sessions for DECCA, later recording for Deluxe (mostly under the pseudonym Tex Grande) and MGM. Following the bombing of Pearl Harbor he recorded FRED ROSE's "Cowards over Pearl Harbor," the first of several successful topical songs Darling popularized during World War II. (His 1945 recording of "Juke Joint Mama" may have inspired Jerry Lieber and Mike Stoller's "Kansas City.") Jazz cornetist Wild Bill Davison backed Darling on this and additional discs.

In about 1945, in collaboration with Vaughn Horton and Milton Gabler, Darling wrote his most famous song: "Choo Choo Ch' Boogie." Although he never recorded it, several artists did, including the enormously popular Louis Jordan & His Tympany Five. BILL HALEY resurrected the number in 1950, and ASLEEP AT THE WHEEL revived it again in the 1970s.

Darling appeared at the First Annual Clef Award Presentation in CARNEGIE HALL, thereby becoming in 1945 the first country artist to perform in the prestigious venue. Within two years, however, he quit performing due to persistent throat problems and a desire to raise his family in small-town surroundings. Retiring to Jewett, Illinois, he lived the life of a gentleman farmer. He kept writing songs but never again achieved the popularity he attained during the 1940s. —W. K. McNeil

## Johnny Darrell
b. Hopewell, Alabama, July 23, 1940; d. October 7, 1997

During his heyday, Johnny Darrell practically made a career of releasing lyrically adventurous country singles that then became standards through other singers' versions. Among the landmark tunes he helped introduce were CURLY PUTMAN's "Green Green Grass of Home" (1965), MEL TILLIS's "Ruby, Don't Take Your Love to Town" (1967), and DALLAS FRAZIER's "The Son of Hickory Holler's Tramp" (1967). Darrell once described his career as "big, but unfortunately not many ever realized it."

Born in Alabama, Darrell grew up in Marietta, Georgia, an Atlanta suburb. When he was thirteen he bought a guitar, though he didn't dream of a career in music. In the army he sang in the base clubs, but as the self-deprecating singer put it, "If I remember correctly, they threw me out every time I sang."

In 1964 Darrell moved to Nashville, where he managed the Holiday Inn near MUSIC ROW. There he got to know producer Kelso Herston of United Artists, whose office was next door. Herston heard Darrell sing and signed him. "Green Green Grass of Home" was Darrell's first United Artists single, and "Ruby, Don't Take Your Love to Town," which encountered radio resistance, nevertheless became his first Top Ten hit. Darrell's biggest hit was "With Pen in Hand," which went to #3 in 1968.

During the 1970s Darrell became associated with the OUTLAW movement, but by then his career was in decline. After a period of inactivity and poor health, the determined singer returned to recording and songwriting in the late 1980s. —Daniel Cooper

## Dave & Sugar
Dave Rowland b. Sanger, California, January 26, 1942
Vicki Hackeman b. Louisville, Kentucky, August 4, 1950
Jackie Frantz b. Sidney, Ohio, October 8, 1950

The pop-country vocal group Dave & Sugar enjoyed a string of hit records in the 1970s, beginning with "Queen of the Silver Dollar" (1975–76) and including the #1s "The Door Is Always Open" (1976), "Tear Time" (1978), and "Golden Tears" (1979). Between 1976 and 1979 they notched ten consecutive Top Ten songs with their smooth, tight harmonies and mellow pop sound.

Formed in 1975 by Dave Rowland, original members included Vicki Hackeman and Jackie Frantz. In 1977 Frantz was replaced by Sue Powell; Vicki Hackeman left in 1979. Afterward a series of women performed with the group, including Melissa Dean, Lisa Alvey, Jamie Kaye, and Cindy Smith.

Rowland's background included stints as trumpeter in the 75th Army band, as a member of the Stamps Quartet while they toured with ELVIS PRESLEY, and as a member of THE FOUR GUYS. Rowland then formed a vocal group to back RCA artist CHARLEY PRIDE, who steered them to a recording deal with the label.

After their RCA contract expired in 1981, ELEKTRA released a pair of Dave & Sugar albums, and Rowland released the 1982 solo album Sugar Free, also on Elektra. Later he resumed his earlier trio approach, performing as Dave Rowland & Sugar with two female singers. —Don Cusic

## Gail Davies
b. Broken Bow, Oklahoma, June 5, 1948

Versatile singer-songwriter Patricia Gail Dickerson is an often-overlooked figure among the West Coast transplants who counteracted Nashville's crossover excesses in the early 1980s URBAN COWBOY era. As an artist and one of the first women in country music to produce her own recordings, Davies has exerted an influence well beyond that decade. Oddly, while most of her hits were written by others, it was her pen that propelled Ava Barber ("Bucket to the South," 1978) and Jann Browne ("Tell Me Why," 1989) to their loftiest chart positions.

Davies drew musical inspiration from her father, a country singer who worked Texas and Oklahoma clubs in the 1940s. At age five, when her parents separated, she moved from Oklahoma to the Seattle area with her mother (who would marry Darby Alan Davies) and two brothers. Graduating in 1966, she headed for Los Angeles and spent most of the next decade on the road with a rock band. The cumulative toll on her voice prompted a return to her roots.

In 1976 Davies relocated to Nashville. Her self-titled debut LP appeared on CBS/Lifesong Records two years later. Spiced with three revivals of country oldies, the album featured such enduring originals as the autobiographical "Grandma's Song" and "Someone Is Looking for Someone Like You" (1979)—her first significant hit. Though not a strong seller, Gail Davies earned the artist a WARNER BROS. deal and total control in the studio. Her four albums for the label (1980–83) yielded several hit singles that deftly explored BLUEGRASS ("Blue Heartache"); traditional country ("I'll Be There" and "It's a Lovely, Lovely World"); soul ("'Round the Clock Lovin'"); and even jazz ("Singin' the Blues").

Then, despite Davies's consistently excellent output for RCA, MCA, and CAPITOL, she encountered stubborn resistance—perhaps attributable to antifeminism on MUSIC ROW and a turbulent personal life. More likely, her increasingly rock-oriented RCA recordings (including a 1986 LP by her experimental band Wild Choir) alienated the notoriously conservative gatekeepers of country radio.

Following three years as a LIBERTY RECORDS staff producer, Davies formed her own label, Little Chickadee Productions. Subsequent album releases have included 1995's *Eclectic*, 1999's *Love Ain't Easy*, and 2003's *The Songwriter Sessions*.

Davies shared in IBMA's 2002 Vocal Event of the Year Award for *Clinch Mountain Sweethearts*, a multiartist album of duets with RALPH STANLEY. She received an AMERICANA Music Association award nomination for producing *Caught in the Webb* (Audium/Koch, 2002), a multiartist tribute to WEBB PIERCE. —*Pete Loesch*

## Danny Davis
b. Dorchester, Massachusetts, May 29, 1925; d. June 12, 2008

A trumpet player with a pop music background, Danny Davis (born George Nowlan) arrived in Nashville in 1968 to become production assistant to RCA's CHET ATKINS as well as a staff producer. Davis soon formed a band called the Nashville Brass, which blended swing music with country and found success on disc and onstage.

A soloist with the Massachusetts All State Symphony Orchestra at age fourteen, Davis later worked with drummer Gene Krupa. Davis then did stints with big bands led by Art Mooney, Freddy Martin, and Bob Crosby, respectively.

As a New York–based producer, Davis had sometimes used Nashville studios, as he did with Connie Francis for MGM RECORDS during 1962–65. After moving to Nashville he produced RCA artists, including WAYLON JENNINGS, WILLIE NELSON, DOTTIE WEST, and DON GIBSON.

Big band experience and the 1960s success of Herb Alpert & the Tijuana Brass gave Davis the idea for founding the Nashville Brass, in 1968. That year he released the band's first RCA album, *The Nashville Brass Featuring Danny Davis Play the Nashville Sound*. The follow-up, *The Nashville Brass Featuring Danny Davis Play More Nashville Sounds*, won the group a 1968 Grammy for Best Country Instrumental Performance.

Davis and his band were named the CMA's Instrumental Group of the Year from 1969 through 1974. The group became a popular touring attraction, often appearing with symphonies and playing Las Vegas engagements. They also appeared on such TV programs as *The Red Skelton Show* and *The Ed Sullivan Show*. —*Gerry Wood*

## Jimmie Davis
b. Beech Springs (near Quitman), Louisiana, September 11, 1899; d. November 5, 2000

Jimmie Davis rose to prominence in the 1930s with a smooth vocal approach that helped popularize country music far beyond its original rural southern audience. In many ways, his music was a harbinger of EDDY ARNOLD's broadly accessible style. Davis's best-selling songs—particularly "Nobody's Darling but Mine" and "You Are My Sunshine"—not only made him wealthy and well known but also carried him to the governorship of Louisiana.

One of eleven children born to a sharecropping couple in Beech Springs, Louisiana, James Houston Davis began his singing

*Jimmie Davis*

career in the Glee Club of Louisiana College in Pineville. At the same time he sang in a local quartet, the Wildcat Four and also participated in street singing. As a graduate student at Louisiana State University in Baton Rouge, he sang in the Glee Club and as a tenor in a quartet, the Tiger Four. Soon after, he began to sing regularly at KWKH in Shreveport.

In about September 1927, Davis accepted a teaching position at Dodd College, a Baptist junior college for women, but he resigned in 1928 and began working as a clerk at the Shreveport Criminal Court. This lasted until 1938 and helped usher him into politics.

Davis's recording career developed noticeably during this ten-year period. After recording a couple of piano-accompanied records for KWKH in 1928, he made sixty-eight sides for RCA VICTOR RECORDS from 1929 to 1933, proving himself an able JIMMIE RODGERS imitator and an enthusiastic singer of risqué blues such as "Organ Grinder's Blues" and "Tom Cat and Pussy Blues." In 1934 he began recording for the newly formed DECCA RECORDS. His first release, "Nobody's Darling but Mine," became his first substantial hit. Although risqué songs remained in his repertoire for a time, Davis soon focused on WESTERN SWING, recording briefly with MILTON BROWN's Brownies.

From 1938 to 1942 Davis served as the public safety commissioner of Shreveport. In this period he established a hugely successful campaign style in which he followed a brief speech with songs backed by a hillbilly band. During these years he put many of his musicians on the payroll as Shreveport policemen, including Charles Mitchell, MOON MULLICAN, CLIFF BRUNER, and BUDDY JONES.

Between 1942 and 1947 Davis appeared in five Hollywood motion pictures: *Strictly in the Groove* (1942); *Riding Through Nevada* (1943); *Frontier Fury* (1943); *Cyclone Prairie Ramblers* (1944); and his own life story, *Louisiana* (1947).

Davis was elected as the public service commissioner of Louisiana in 1942 and as Democratic governor of Louisiana in 1943. (His four-year term as governor began early in 1944.) On both occasions he exploited his reputed authorship of "You Are My Sunshine," which had become nationally known in 1941 through recordings by GENE AUTRY and Bing Crosby. (Davis's own Decca recording was released in 1940; prior to his purchase of the song, it was credited to Paul Rice of THE RICE BROTHERS, who previously may have bought the copyright himself.) After his term as governor, Davis began singing full time and tended toward a gospel style, as represented by "Suppertime," a hit in the early 1950s. Since serving as Louisiana's governor for a second term, from 1960 to 1964 (elected largely on a segregationist platform), he recorded for Decca and afterward for a handful of small labels.

After the death of his first wife, Alvern, in 1967, he married Anna Carter Gordon, a member of the CHUCK WAGON GANG gospel group, in 1969. Davis was elected to THE COUNTRY MUSIC HALL OF FAME in 1972, the year after he lost the election for his third-term governorship. Even in his nineties, Davis was continuously involved in performing. In the spring of 1992 he appeared on CBS-TV's special celebrating the Country Music Hall of Fame's twenty-fifth anniversary. —*Toru Mitsui*

## Mac Davis
b. Lubbock, Texas, January 21, 1942

A major pop-country crossover star during the 1970s and 1980s, Mac Davis initially made his mark as a songwriter, penning such compositions as ELVIS PRESLEY's "In the Ghetto," "Memories," and "Don't Cry Daddy"; BOBBY GOLDSBORO's "Watching Scotty Grow"; the oft-recorded "I Believe in Music"; and Davis's own 1972 hit "Baby Don't Get Hooked on Me."

Scott "Mac" Davis spent most of his early years in Atlanta; he played in a rock & roll band and worked for a couple of record labels as a regional manager. After his songwriting success with Presley and other artists during 1968–69, Davis signed with COLUMBIA RECORDS. His first chart single, "Whoever Finds This, I Love You," appeared in 1970; two years later his recording career took off with the #1 pop hit "Baby Don't Get Hooked on Me."

Though most of Davis's pop hits received country airplay, he didn't make major inroads in country radio until "It's Hard to Be Humble," recorded for Casablanca Records, cracked the country Top Ten in 1980. Subsequent hits included "Texas in My Rear View Mirror" (#9, 1980) and "Hooked on Music" (#2, 1981), but his country career soon waned. Davis recorded briefly for MCA, and he cowrote and recorded the duet "Wait 'Til I Get You Home" with DOLLY PARTON for her 1989 *White Limozeen* album, the title cut of which Davis and Parton also cowrote.

Davis parlayed his musical success into film and television work (he hosted his own TV variety show from 1974 to 1976). He has also appeared on Broadway in the title role of *The Will Rogers Follies*.

Davis was the ACM Entertainer of the Year in 1974 and was elected to the NASHVILLE SONGWRITERS HALL OF FAME in 2000. —*Chet Flippo*

## Oscar Davis
b. Providence, Rhode Island, May 20, 1902; d. April 5, 1975

Oscar William Davis, the Baron of the Box Office, was one of the most active early country music promoters. In addition, he managed several famous country artists during a long-lived career.

A World War I veteran, Davis studied law at the American University in Paris and later at Boston University, but he eventually followed his father into the theater business. Though he was an actor, a singer, and a violinist as a young man, Davis also showed a flair for promoting dance marathons; walkathons; and, after about 1937, hillbilly music. At first he teamed with Birmingham promoter-performer "Happy" Hal Burns, later going solo. To plug his shows, Davis used saturation radio ads—typically recording them with a rapid-fire delivery marked by his tag line, "Don't you dare miss it!" He supplemented these with eye-catching newspaper ads and hyped his shows through such gimmicks as yodeling and fiddling contests and onstage weddings.

By the early 1940s his National Hillbilly Jamborees, held in such southern cities as Little Rock, Dallas, Memphis, and Atlanta, were drawing large crowds and six-figure box office receipts over the course of a summer. Most of these cities broadcast Burns's *Garrett Snuff Varieties* acts; therefore, Davis's large shows often featured Burns along with big-name performers such as ROY ACUFF, ERNEST TUBB, LULU BELLE & SCOTTY, and the HOOSIER HOT SHOTS.

Davis later expanded his endeavors and managed artists including CURLY FOX, Ernest Tubb, MINNIE PEARL, HANK WILLIAMS, GEORGE MORGAN, and RAY PRICE—many of whom enjoyed their peak years under Davis's tutelage. Although most eventually complained that Davis spent too much money on promotion, none denied that his techniques helped to draw huge crowds.

A stroke slowed Davis in the 1960s, but he remained active until his death, working at different times for talent booking agents JIM DENNY, CONNIE B. GAY, and BUDDY LEE. —*Ronnie Pugh*

## Skeeter Davis
b. Dry Ridge, Kentucky, December 30, 1931; September 19, 2004

Few artists have traversed the perilous line between country and pop as disarmingly as Mary Frances Penick—a product, fittingly, of the border state of Kentucky. Under the aegis of NASHVILLE SOUND mastermind CHET ATKINS, she amassed a sizable following in both camps during her 1960s heyday. Yet the musical legacy of the outspoken singer has been obscured by a series of personal tragedies and controversies.

Born at the onset of the Depression, Skeeter (a nickname bestowed by her grandfather) learned early on to harmonize with singers she heard on the GRAND OLE OPRY. In high school, she and her best friend, Betty Jack Davis (no relation), formed a vocal duo called the Davis Sisters. Radio and television exposure eventually landed them on RCA RECORDS in 1952. But as their smashing label debut ("I Forgot More Than You'll Ever Know") began its six-month run on the country charts in 1953, Skeeter and Betty Jack were involved in a car accident that fatally injured the latter.

Devastated, Skeeter nonetheless persevered in her career. Although she and Betty Jack's sister Georgia were unable to duplicate the original Davis Sisters' success, Skeeter ultimately established herself as a solo act with such Top Ten hits as "Set Him Free" (1959), the "answer" song "(I Can't Help You) I'm Falling Too" (1960), and "My Last Date (With You)" (1961). On these as well as most of her early 1960s releases, producer Atkins "double-tracked" the artist's plaintive voice to re-create the feel of her Davis Sisters work. The subsequent addition of uptown embellishments resulted in a string of crossover hits highlighted by the blockbuster "The End of the World" (1962) and the Gerry Goffin/Carole King composition "I Can't Stay Mad at You" (1963).

Meanwhile, Davis joined the Opry in 1959 and wed Nashville media celebrity RALPH EMERY one year later. As would be

*Skeeter Davis*

chronicled in their respective autobiographies, the stormy relationship lasted only until 1964—not much longer than her earlier marriage to Kenneth Depew. Later, in 1973, the deeply religious singer became embroiled in a well-publicized dispute with Opry management over her broadcast support for some "Jesus people" who had been arrested at a local shopping mall. She was suspended for more than a year.

Though hitless since the early 1970s, Davis continued to perform regularly, and her wide-ranging album catalog remains of considerable interest to collectors. *She Sings, They Play* (1985), a charming collaboration with the revered rock band NRBQ, led to her third marriage, in 1987—to the group's bassist, Joey Spampinato. Her autobiography, *Bus Fare to Kentucky,* was published in 1993. Davis died of breast cancer in 2004. —*Pete Loesch*

## Jimmy Day
b. Tuscaloosa, Alabama, January 9, 1934; d. January 22, 1999

A PEDAL STEEL GUITAR innovator specializing in hard-core HONKY-TONK and WESTERN SWING, Jimmy Day idolized SHOT JACKSON, LITTLE ROY WIGGINS, and JERRY BYRD as well as West Coast pedal steel pioneer SPEEDY WEST and western swing master HERB REMINGTON. As a teenager, Day landed a job playing (non-pedal) steel on Shreveport's *LOUISIANA HAYRIDE*, remaining there into the 1950s and backing many *Hayride* performers whose careers blossomed in that decade, including HANK WILLIAMS, FARON YOUNG, JOHNNY HORTON, ELVIS PRESLEY, and JIM REEVES.

Day eventually became a regular member of Reeves's mid-1950s touring band and changed to a pedal steel. When Reeves moved to Nashville, Day came along in late December 1955. In January 1956 RAY PRICE asked him to join his Cherokee Cowboys; except for two brief absences, Day remained with them until 1962. He quickly placed his imprint on Price's sound, beginning with solos and fills on Price's 1956 smash "Crazy Arms." Day's sensitive way of modulating from one chord to another also created rich tonal colors on Price's "Heartaches by the Number," "City Lights," and "Invitation to the Blues" and on CHARLIE WALKER's 1958 hit "Pick Me Up on Your Way Down."

In 1962 Day left Price to work with former Cherokee Cowboy WILLIE NELSON, whose hit recording of "Touch Me" had launched Nelson's solo career. Day also made two solo LPs for Philips in 1962 and 1963. In the mid-1960s, Day worked on his own with both Price and Nelson. The steel player kept working with Nelson when the singer moved to AUSTIN, TEXAS; Day can be heard on Nelson's 1973 *Shotgun Willie* LP. In addition, Day recorded a solo LP for DeWitt Scott's Mid-Land label.

Day was inducted into the International Steel Guitar Hall of Fame in 1982. He continued to perform around Texas and play selected dates with Price into the 1990s. —*Rich Kienzle*

## De Luxe Records
established in Linden, New Jersey, 1944

The small, independent De Luxe label, founded by the Braun family in Linden, New Jersey, issued pop, R&B, jazz, country, and gospel recordings; country artists included the ROUSE BROTHERS, BUDDY STARCHER, THE SHELTON BROTHERS, DENVER DARLING, Lost John Miller, LOUIS INNIS, ARTHUR Q. SMITH, and Tex Atchison. SYD NATHAN, founder of KING RECORDS, purchased a portion of De Luxe in 1947. The Brauns operated the label under Nathan's control from 1947 to 1949, when the office moved to Cincinnati, King's headquarters. Nathan issued De luxe masters on the King label, bought the Brauns' remaining interest in 1951, and revived De Luxe in the 1950s. De Luxe masters passed to STARDAY-KING in 1968 and now reside with GML, owner of Gusto Records. —*Don Roy*

## Billy Dean
b. Quincy, Florida, April 2, 1962

William Harold "Billy" Dean began scoring hits at the start of the 1990s country boom; amid a flood of male hat acts, he found his niche as a sensitive singer-songwriter. Dean was a steady presence on country radio through the decade, attaining eleven Top Ten hits over a fourteen-year period.

A Florida native, Dean moved to Nashville at nineteen, competing in national talent competitions and recording advertising jingles. Near the end of the 1980s, he signed with EMI Music as a songwriter and provided songs for the OAK RIDGE BOYS, Shelly West, and RANDY TRAVIS, who recorded "Somewhere in My Broken Heart," a song that Dean cowrote with Richard Leigh.

Dean's songwriting success led to a contract with SBK/LIBERTY RECORDS and his first album, *Young Man,* released in 1990. His first single, "Only Here for a Little While," went to #3. Since Travis never released "Somewhere in My Broken Heart," Dean made it his second single, also reaching #3. Dean's achievements did not go unnoticed by the industry. He won the 1991 ACM Top New

Male Vocalist award, and "Somewhere in My Broken Heart" won Song of the Year honors.

Dean's self-titled second album, released in 1991, included another hit single, "Billy the Kid" (#4). In 1992, his third album *Fire in the Dark* revealed stronger pop sensibilities, including a remake of Dave Mason's 1977 hit, "We Just Disagree," another Top Ten. His third album, *Men'll Be Boys,* failed to get a single into the Top Twenty, so Dean took a hiatus to concentrate on songwriting. During his break, Liberty folded into CAPITOLNashville, which released Dean's fourth album, 1996's *It's What I Do,* resulting in two Top Ten hits.

Dean didn't achieve another major hit until 2004, after he left Capitol for ASYLUM/CURB RECORDS and reached #8 with "Let Them Be Little," his last Top Ten hit as of early 2010. He has continued to tour. —*Calvin Gilbert*

## Eddie Dean
b. Posey, Texas, July 9, 1907; d. March 4, 1999

Although Eddie Dean didn't gain the notoriety of first-tier singing cowboys, he is remembered for a voice that matched that of any big-screen western star. Texas-born Edgar Glosup changed his last name to Dean and journeyed to Chicago in 1926, seeking a career as a singer. From there he moved to Shenandoah, Iowa, in 1927 and then to Yankton, South Dakota, in 1929. Dean and his brother Jimmy (not the artist of "Big Bad John" fame) spent 1930–32 at radio station WIBW in Topeka, Kansas, before returning to Chicago, where they performed on the NATIONAL BARN DANCE for three years and recorded for the AMERICAN RECORD CORPORATION and later for DECCA.

In 1937 Dean moved to Los Angeles, where he gradually landed small parts in films starring ROY ROGERS, GENE AUTRY, Don "Red" Barry, and William Boyd (Hopalong Cassidy). Dean's roles ranged from villain to vocalist. Beginning in 1944, he starred in his own western film series, including *Harmony Trail* and *Song of Old Wyoming.* Over the next four years he also starred in twenty western films. Dean wrote many of his film songs, including his trademark "On the Banks of the Sunny San Juan," a song he recorded for Decca. In 1948 his song "One Has My Name (The Other Has My Heart)" became a hit for him and an even bigger hit for his friend JIMMY WAKELY (JERRY LEE LEWIS revived the song in 1969). In 1955 Dean wrote and recorded his hit "I Dreamed of a Hillbilly Heaven." TEX RITTER's 1961 recording of that song became a major hit in the country and pop fields.

Throughout the years Eddie Dean toured steadily and appeared frequently on radio and on television. He was featured on JUDY CANOVA's network radio show and frequently guested on the *TOWN HALL PARTY* radio and television series in the 1950s. He also worked *Western Ranch Party,* a syndicated TV show that used many *Town Hall Party* cast members. In later years he performed primarily in nightclubs, balancing his repertoire between country music and the western songs for which he was best known. In 1993 he was inducted into the Cowboy Hall of Fame. —*Laurence Zwisohn*

## Jimmy Dean
b. Olton, Texas, August 10, 1928; d. June 13, 2010

Jimmy Dean's cornflake charm and fresh-faced good looks epitomized the country TV star of the 1950s. Though Dean was able to parlay his specialty, the dramatic narration, into a string of hit

*Jimmy Dean*

records in the 1960s, he gained his biggest success as a television personality.

Born Jimmy Ray Dean in a poor, rural West Texas family, Dean first entertained fellow servicemen at Bolling Air Force Base near Washington, D.C. Upon his discharge in 1948 he formed his group, the Texas Wildcats. Under the tutelage of Washington, D.C., country music impresario CONNIE B. GAY, Dean honed his act as an all-around entertainer via live appearances on WARL radio and WMAL-TV as well as in the then-thriving D.C. country music club scene. Popular locally and in syndication, Gay's *Town and Country Time* shows helped Dean build his audience.

In 1952, FRED FOSTER, eventual founder of MONUMENT RECORDS, first saw Dean perform at Washington's Covered Wagon club. Then breaking into the business with local music publisher Ben Adelman, Foster told Adelman, "He may not be the greatest singer in the world, but he communicates with the audience like you cannot believe." Foster and Adelman arranged for West Coast label FOUR STAR RECORDS to issue Dean's recording of "Bumming Around," a #5 country hit of 1953.

Although this was Dean's only chart-making country disc of the 1950s, he flourished as the star of Gay's televised *Town and Country Time,* a program filled with music, comedy, hoedown fiddling, and square dancing. Dean served as MC, sang, and played accordion, backed by the Texas Wildcats; other regulars included singer Mary Klick and fiddler Buck Ryan. ROY CLARK, PATSY CLINE, BILLY GRAMMER, and GEORGE HAMILTON IV also made frequent appearances. By 1956 the series was airing in fifty markets, including Spokane, Tulsa, Houston, Los Angeles, and Detroit as well as Washington, D.C. In 1957, Dean graduated to CBS-TV with *The Jimmy Dean Show,* again featuring his band, George Hamilton IV, and guests. The program originated from Washington, D.C., during daytime hours and on Saturday nights during the summer of 1957. CBS then purchased Dean's contract from Gay and moved the show to New York City as a weekday series that ran from September 1958 to June 1959.

On records, Dean found a niche reciting dramatic stories, including "Big Bad John," a massive self-penned hit on Columbia Records in 1961. (The song inspired a 1988 motion picture starring Dean, Ned Beatty, and Bo Hopkins.) With its hammer sound effects and lean production, the recording exemplified Nashville's early 1960s creativity and topped *Billboard*'s country and pop charts alike. "Big Bad John" was also one of the earliest country performances to win a Grammy, for Best Country & Western Recording. Dean followed with five more Top Thirty crossover hits in 1962, three of them spoken narratives: "Dear Ivan," "The Cajun Queen," "To a Sleeping Beauty," "Little Black Book," and "P.T. 109," which recounted President John F. Kennedy's World War II exploits.

Dean's string of hits and proven on-camera charisma brought him back to network television from 1963 to 1966 on ABC. His new version of *The Jimmy Dean Show* increased national exposure for himself and numerous guest artists, including country talents such as Eddy Arnold, Homer & Jethro, and Molly Bee as well as a parade of pop acts. The Jim Henson Muppet dog Rowlf was a continuing character, and semi-regulars included Ron Martin, a humorous, accident-prone singer; Lud & Lester, a folksy, Lum & Abner–style team; and the Jubilee Four gospel quartet. The Chuck Cassey Singers, wearing Stetson hats and playing guitars, added vocal support. In its final season, the show made special originations from Nashville's Ryman Auditorium—then home of the Grand Ole Opry—Miami Beach, and Carnegie Hall.

After topping the country charts in 1965 with "The First Thing Ev'ry Morning (and the Last Thing Ev'ry Night)," a song he cowrote with Ruth Roberts, Dean switched from Columbia to RCA Victor. He charted consistently from 1966 to 1972, though he didn't replicate his early 1960s recording success. His final Top Ten country disc was 1976's "I.O.U." (on the Casino label), a narrative tribute to his mother.

Nevertheless, Dean's career progressed apace as he played top venues such as the Hollywood Bowl and Las Vegas showrooms. In the late 1960s he appeared regularly on the NBC-TV series *Daniel Boone*, in the role of Boone's friend Josh Clements, a fur trapper. Dean also appeared with the likes of Lee Majors, Dennis Weaver, and Mark Hamill in a number of televised Movies of the Week, and in 1971 he made his feature film debut in Sean Connery's James Bond movie *Diamonds Are Forever*, playing the reclusive millionaire Willard Whyte. Additionally, Dean became a popular guest host for network talk show stars Johnny Carson, Mike Douglas, Merv Griffin, Dinah Shore, and Joey Bishop. Ads for his Jimmy Dean Meat Company—which he eventually sold to Consolidated Foods (later Sara Lee Corporation)—further established him as a household name. Dean and wife Donna Meade Dean cowrote his autobiography, *Thirty Years of Sausage, Fifty Years of Ham*, published by Penguin Books in 2004. He was elected to The Country Music Hall of Fame in 2010, shortly before his death. —*Margaret Jones*

## Decca Records
established in New York, New York, July 1934

Decca Records was one of country music's most influential labels. In 1934, with initial capital from English stockbroker Edward Lewis (who owned the British corporation Decca Records, founded in 1929), Brunswick Records executive Jack Kapp established Decca Records in the United States. His younger

brother Dave Kapp became A&R director for the hillbilly music division. Although Decca used its own recording studios in New York and Chicago, Dave Kapp made many expeditions across America to find new artists and record them on site. From 1934 he signed a wealth of talent, including Stuart Hamblen (the first Decca country act to record: August 3, 1934), Jimmie Davis, the Sons of the Pioneers, Milton Brown, Rex Griffin, the Carter Family, Ernest Tubb, and Red Foley.

In the late 1940s the hillbilly division was renamed country & western. By this time Dave Kapp had turned his duties over to Paul Cohen, Decca's Cincinnati branch manager. Cohen was the industry's first producer to record country artists in Nashville on a regular basis, beginning in earnest by mid-1947.

During Cohen's tenure, Jack Kapp died (1949), and in 1952 Decca gained controlling interest in Universal Pictures. With assistance from Owen Bradley, a Nashville bandleader and arranger who began working with Cohen in 1947, Cohen signed and produced many new acts, including Bill Monroe, Webb Pierce, Kitty Wells, Bobby Helms, and Brenda Lee. Cohen also made a distribution deal with Four Star Records to release recordings by Patsy Cline (1955–60).

In 1958 Cohen became head of Decca's Coral Records subsidiary and relinquished his position to Bradley, whose recently built Music Row studios had been hosting Decca sessions since 1955. A gifted musician, Bradley helped develop a pop-oriented country style known as The Nashville Sound. His formula was most successful for Patsy Cline (signed in 1960) and Brenda Lee (who joined as a pop act in 1956). Bradley and his assistant, Harry Silverstein, nurtured the existing roster while bringing Bill Anderson, Loretta Lynn, The Osborne Brothers, and Conway Twitty aboard.

In June 1962 Music Corporation of American (MCA) purchased a majority of Decca's stock, and Decca officially became a division of MCA on January 1, 1966. On March 1, 1973, Decca (and other labels MCA had acquired) ceased to exist, and MCA Records was launched. In 1994, MCA briefly reactivated Decca as a country music label, first signing Dawn Sears and adding artists such as Mark Chesnutt, Lee Ann Womack, Gary Allan, and Rhett Akins. Except for Sears, who left, these artists eventually moved to MCA Nashville. By 1999 MCA parent company Seagram merged MCA with PolyGram to form the Universal Music Group and Decca Nashville was shuttered, though Universal kept using the Decca name for classical releases. Universal resumed issuing records on Decca in 2008, but this operation has no ties to the company's Nashville office.

Along with numerous Decca artists, two Decca A&R men have been inducted into The Country Music Hall of Fame— Owen Bradley (1974) and Paul Cohen (1976). —*Don Roy*

## Delmore Brothers
Alton Delmore b. Elkmont, Alabama, December 25, 1908; d. June 8, 1964
Rabon Delmore b. Elkmont, Alabama, December 3, 1916; d. December 4, 1952

The Delmore Brothers were perhaps the most musically sophisticated, most creative, and most technically proficient of the many great Brother Duets of the 1930s. Their soft, pliant harmony; dazzling guitar work; love of blues; and well-crafted songs have endeared them to generations of fans, and Delmore hits such as "Brown's Ferry Blues," "Gonna Lay Down My Old Guitar," and "Blues Stay Away from Me" became country standards. Nevertheless, the Delmores never won fame and fortune.

*The Delmore Brothers: Alton (left) and Rabon*

Hailing from the red clay hills of northern Alabama, the brothers grew up in a gospel music tradition of shape note SONGBOOKS and temporary singing schools that taught congregational singing; their mother, Mollie, composed such songs, and some of Alton's first efforts were gospel songs cowritten with her. The brothers soon developed a style based around the new microphone and radio technology—which let their soft voices be heard—and first built their reputation by singing at local fiddling contests. After an early record for COLUMBIA in 1931 ("Got the Kansas City Blues"), they joined the GRAND OLE OPRY in 1933. That year they began recording for RCA VICTOR's new budget label, BLUEBIRD, and Alton began writing songs in earnest. They soon drew buckets of fan mail, and by 1936 the Opry identified them as one of the show's most popular acts.

For several years they toured and recorded with fellow Opry star UNCLE DAVE MACON, and in 1936 they teamed with FIDDLIN' ARTHUR SMITH. With Smith they cut classic tunes such as "There's More Pretty Girls Than One" and "Beautiful Brown Eyes." On their own, they recorded pieces such as "Southern Moon" and "When It's Time for the Whippoorwill to Sing."

Disagreements with the Opry management over bookings led the brothers to leave the show in 1938; it proved to be a mistake, and while their records continued to sell (they switched to DECCA in 1940), they had a hard time establishing a new radio base. The next few years saw them moving restlessly to Raleigh, North Carolina, and then to Birmingham, until finally landing at Cincinnati's powerhouse station, WLW.

Here they resurrected their career. In 1943 Alton organized the gospel quartet the BROWN'S FERRY FOUR with MERLE TRAVIS and GRANDPA JONES; one of country's first successful gospel quartets, it excelled on radio and on records. The Delmores signed with the locally based KING RECORDS and increasingly spiced their songs with blues and boogie influences. Often working with harmonica ace WAYNE RANEY, they produced pieces such as "Hillbilly Boogie," "Freight Train Boogie," and "Blues Stay Away from Me."

Still, the brothers seemed unable to capitalize on these hits. During the late 1940s they moved to Memphis; to Chattanooga; to Jackson, Mississippi; to Athens, Alabama; to Covington, Kentucky; to Fort Smith, Arkansas; to Del Rio, Texas; and finally to Houston, where they dissolved the act. Alton wanted to try his hand at full-time songwriting (he had been responsible for most of the duet's original numbers), and Rabon was diagnosed with lung cancer, which took his life in 1952. Alton continued to record with independent labels but eventually dropped out of music, bitter and disillusioned. He derived satisfaction from seeing some of the 1,000 songs he wrote recorded by a wide variety of modern artists, and he completed most of a remarkable autobiography published posthumously as *Truth Is Stranger Than Publicity.*

The Delmore Brothers were elected to THE COUNTRY MUSIC HALL OF FAME in 2001. —*Charles Wolfe*

## Iris DeMent
b. Paragould, Arkansas, January 5, 1961

Singer-songwriter Iris Luella DeMent has won critical acclaim—though not massive commercial success—combining a spare folk and OLD-TIME country musical style with incisive, heartfelt, largely autobiographical lyrics. The youngest of fourteen children in a religious home filled with music, DeMent grew up in California, where she sang gospel music and absorbed country and folk sounds.

At seventeen, DeMent moved to Kansas City to attend college and began performing at local writers' nights. She moved to Nashville in 1990 and backed EMMYLOU HARRIS and others as a studio vocalist. In 1992 Philo Records, a division of ROUNDER, released her critically acclaimed debut, the JIM ROONEY–produced *Infamous Angel.* WARNER BROS. signed her in 1993 and rereleased the album, followed by 1994's *My Life.* Both feature original, predominantly acoustic material, alongside faithful remakes of songs from the CARTER FAMILY and LEFTY FRIZZELL. DeMent's 1996 Warner Bros. album, the rock-influenced *The Way I Should,* featured songs with a more political edge and included "Trouble," a rollicking duet with DELBERT MCCLINTON. She recorded duets with JOHN PRINE for his 1999 album *In Spite of Ourselves,* a collection of country duet hits revisited by Prine and various vocal partners. DeMent has also dueted with Harris and with STEVE EARLE and has sung on albums by numerous other artists.

In 1994 DeMent contributed the track "Big City" to the MERLE HAGGARD tribute album *Tulare Dust,* leading to cowriting and joint stage appearances. Her songs have been featured on the television series *Northern Exposure* and *MTV Unplugged.* A frequent guest on *A PRAIRIE HOME COMPANION,* she portrayed the character Rose Gentry in the 2000 film *Songcatcher* and sang on the soundtrack. In 2004 DeMent returned to her roots with *Lifeline,* an album of gospel songs. —*Stephen L. Betts*

## Jim Denny
b. Buffalo Valley, Tennessee, February 28, 1911; d. August 27, 1963

James Rae Denny (he changed his last name to Denny) was a longtime manager of the GRAND OLE OPRY Artists Service who went on to become one of the most successful talent agents and song publishers in country music history. His skill as a promoter and developer of talent played a vital role in the growth of country music in the 1950s and early 1960s.

*Jim Denny*

Born in the poor Buffalo Valley region of Tennessee, Denny moved to Nashville and found work at age sixteen as a mailroom clerk for the National Life and Accident Insurance Company, owner of radio station WSM and the Grand Ole Opry. While rising through the ranks of the insurance company's accounting division, Denny found himself increasingly drawn to side jobs backstage at the Opry. In the late 1940s he eventually took over as director of WSM's Artists Service, or booking department, while also serving as house manager for the Opry.

During his tenure at the Opry, Denny dealt with dozens of major country music acts, record label executives, and top show promoters such as A. V. Bamford, Dub Albritten, Jim Halsey, Oscar Davis, X. Cosse, and others.

Denny formed Cedarwood Publishing Company in early 1953 with Webb Pierce (Carl Smith later acquired an interest as well). Over the next decade Cedarwood's staff of writers churned out hit after hit, including "Detroit City," "Tobacco Road," and others. In 1955 Denny was voted Country and Western Man of the Year by *Billboard* magazine, but he challenged WSM management's decree that employees choose between their WSM positions and their outside businesses, and he was fired from the station in September 1956. Denny then formed the Jim Denny Artist Bureau and signed most of the Opry's top acts. Three months later, in what was then called country's largest individual package sale to date, he signed an agreement with Philip Morris Tobacco Company to provide the talent for the Philip Morris Country Music Show. This show simultaneously made a fortune for Denny's talent agency and helped boost the popularity of country music across America. Denny's company booked most of the top country acts of the day, including Pierce, Smith, Minnie

Pearl, Red Sovine, Hank Snow, Goldie Hill, The Duke of Paducah, Moon Mullican, and many more. By 1963 the Denny Artist Bureau was booking nearly 4,000 country shows annually.

Denny was a hard-nosed businessman whose charismatic personality and devotion to his acts and songs earned him respect and devotion—sometimes tinged with fear—from artists, writers, and others with whom he did business. He and Pierce, who quit the Opry a few months after Denny was fired, prospered from their investment in Cedarwood and branched out to acquire several radio stations.

At the time of Denny's death, Cedarwood and the Jim Denny Artist Bureau were outstanding in their respective fields. Lucky Moeller quickly took over the artist bureau, but without Denny's guiding force it withered away within a few years. Denny's sons Bill and John managed Cedarwood until its sale to Mel Tillis in 1983. Jim Denny was elected to The Country Music Hall of Fame in 1966. —*Al Cunniff*

## John Denver
b. Roswell, New Mexico, December 31, 1943; d. October 12, 1997

John Denver became a country star in the 1970s by accident, just as most of his career seemed to come together by happenstance. Henry John Deutschendorf Jr. was raised in a U.S. Air Force family that moved frequently. His acoustic guitar—a gift from his grandmother—became a constant in his nomadic life, and he began studying folk music of the late 1950s and early 1960s. He made his breakthrough as a performer at Leadbetter's in Los Angeles. Club owner Randy Sparks, founder of the folk music group the New Christy Minstrels, hired Denver as a regular. After performing in Sparks's road band, the Back Porch Majority, Denver got word that the popular Chad Mitchell Trio was auditioning for a replacement for Mitchell on the road. Denver got the job and was well received, especially when performing his own material. Peter, Paul & Mary made Denver's composition "Leaving on a Jet Plane" a #1 pop hit in 1969.

After leaving the Chad Mitchell Trio, Denver settled in Aspen, Colorado, where he serenaded the ski crowd. On a tour stop in Washington, D.C., Denver attracted the attention of influential manager Jerry Weintraub, who took Denver to broader audiences. Denver signed with RCA Records, and in 1971 his million-selling "Take Me Home, Country Roads" became a #2 pop hit.

Though "Country Roads" received some country airplay, country music audiences encountered Denver primarily though such 1974–75 crossover hits as "Annie's Song," "Back Home Again," and "Thank God I'm a Country Boy." In retrospect, it's difficult to explain why Denver suddenly became a country favorite and just as suddenly fell out of favor. In any case, CMA's selection of Denver as its 1975 Entertainer of the Year was controversial, for many in the Nashville music industry did not consider him a country artist. During the nationally televised awards ceremony that year, after proclaiming Denver as the winner, performer Charlie Rich took out his cigarette lighter and ignited the official announcement envelope.

Denver never repeated his mid-1970s recording success, though he did have a Top Ten country hit in 1981 with "Some Days Are Diamonds (Some Days Are Stone)." Among his other activities, he starred with George Burns in the 1977 movie *Oh, God* and was well known for his longtime work on behalf of the environment and various humanitarian causes. Denver's last years were marked by personal problems, including two arrests for drunken driving. He was killed at age fifty-three when the home-built, single-engine plane he was piloting crashed into California's Monterey Bay. A pilot for more than twenty years, Denver was testing the Long EZ model on a planned one-hour flight when its engine quit. —*Chet Flippo*

## Desert Rose Band
Chris Hillman b. Los Angeles, California, December 4, 1944
Herb Pedersen b. Berkeley, California, April 27, 1944
John Jorgenson b. Madison, Wisconsin, July 6, 1956

One of the foremost exponents of the West Coast country sound in the 1980s was the Desert Rose Band. The group was the commercial culmination of CHRIS HILLMAN's decades around the fringes of country, beginning with California BLUEGRASS groups (the Scottsville Squirrel Barkers, the Hillmen) in the early 1960s and extending into pioneering COUNTRY-ROCK bands (THE BYRDS, Flying Burrito Brothers) in the late 1960s and early 1970s. By 1984 Hillman, who had played bass with the Byrds and writes his songs on guitar, was again playing bluegrass mandolin and singing country classics on a solo album, *Desert Rose* (SUGAR HILL, 1984). On it he was accompanied by (among others) veteran session vocalist and picker HERB PEDERSEN (guitar, banjo). Hillman and Pedersen assisted Dan Fogelberg on his *High Country Snows* album (1985) and, joined by veteran bassist Bill Bryson and young guitar wizard JOHN JORGENSON, opened for Fogelberg on his tour later that year. This was the nucleus of the Desert Rose Band, filled out by PEDAL STEEL GUITAR ace J. D. MANESS (formerly of BUCK OWENS's Buckaroos) and drummer Steve Duncan (longtime house drummer at North Hollywood's Palomino Club).

Building their sound around the tight vocal harmonies of Hillman and Pedersen, Jorgenson's twangy guitar hooks, and Hillman's songs, the Desert Rose Band was, in Hillman's words, "a highly evolved Burrito Brothers." Signed to CURB RECORDS, the Desert Rose Band enjoyed eight Top Ten hits from September 1987 through September 1990, including two #1s in 1988, "He's Back and I'm Blue" and "I Still Believe in You." A six-month hiatus (1990–91) that Hillman used to write songs may have signaled the beginning of the end for the group, which never regained its momentum afterward and soon lost Maness (in 1990), Duncan (1992), and founding member Jorgenson (1992). Outflanked by younger, hungrier bands in the early 1990s, Desert Rose quietly faded in 1994 after its belated validation of Chris Hillman's commitment to country music.

Pedersen and Hillman, however, continued to collaborate for specific projects, and the group reunited for show dates in 2008, 2010, and 2011. —*Mark Humphrey*

## Ott Devine
b. Gadsden, Alabama, May 1, 1910; d. January 30, 1994

Ottis Edward Devine was a prominent radio executive at Nashville radio station WSM from the 1940s through the 1960s. After high school in Anniston, Alabama, he worked as announcer at WJBY in Gadsden, Alabama; WRGA in Rome, Georgia; and WDOD in Chattanooga before signing on as a WSM staff announcer in 1935. He shifted into the program department in 1942 and, along with program director JACK STAPP, supervised WSM-originated programs such as *Sunday Down South* and *Wormwood Forest*, fed to

regional networks and to the NBC, CBS, and Mutual radio networks. By the late 1950s Devine replaced Stapp as program director and took on the additional role of GRAND OLE OPRY manager when D KILPATRICK relinquished this position in 1959. Devine signed many new acts during the 1960s, including LORETTA LYNN, ROY DRUSKY, BILL ANDERSON, JAN HOWARD, BOBBY BARE, JIM & JESSE McReynolds, CONNIE SMITH, DOTTIE WEST, and JACK GREENE. Devine retired from WSM in 1968. —*John W. Rumble*

## Al Dexter
b. Troup, Texas, May 4, 1905; d. January 28, 1984

Clarence Albert Poindexter, better known as Al Dexter, was one of country music's biggest stars of the 1940s. He released a string of huge hits, beginning in 1943 with the million-seller "Pistol Packin' Mama," which also became one of the first important country crossovers when Dexter's recording reached #1 on the pop charts that year. Dexter's music is hard to categorize, falling somewhere along an indistinct line between WESTERN SWING and HONKY-TONK, and, as Nick Tosches pointed out, his reputation has likely suffered as a result.

Stardom came relatively late to Dexter, who was almost forty by the time COLUMBIA RECORDS issued "Pistol Packin' Mama" on its OKEH imprint. He began playing music as a youth, graduating from banjo and harmonica to mandolin and guitar, but the beginning of his professional career is uncertain. Dexter was performing and running his own Round-Up club in Longview, Texas, by the mid-1930s, but AMERICAN RECORD CORPORATION executive DON LAW signed him in New Orleans in 1936. Supposedly unable to convince any local country dance musicians to take him seriously, Dexter, who at one point led an all-black band for similar

*Al Dexter*

reasons, had to pick up a trio of San Antonio musicians for his first recordings. The Nite Owls would also record under their own name for Vocalion and work on Dexter's sessions through 1938. Early electric guitarist Bob Symons was a band member.

Dexter's first release was the seminal "Honky-Tonk Blues," and many of his later 1930s recordings retained a hard-edged, proto–honky-tonk approach. Dexter began playing lead guitar and mandolin in 1939 and started calling his band the Troopers. (It included novelty musician Aubrey Gass, of postwar "Dear John" fame.) By the early 1940s Dexter's music was becoming decidedly smoother. His watershed 1942 Hollywood sessions for Columbia featured studio musicians such as accordionist Paul Sells and trumpeter Holly Hollinger and arrangements that, on paper, seemed ill suited for material such as "Pistol Packin' Mama." It all worked wonderfully in the studio, however, and more hits followed: "Too Late to Worry, Too Blue to Cry" and "So Long Pal" (1944), "I'm Losing My Mind Over You" (1945), and "Guitar Polka" (1946). Dexter's star began to fade by decade's end, and he relocated to Texas, opening his own club in Dallas. By the 1960s, Dexter—who also recorded for KING, DECCA, CAPITOL, Ekko, and Aldex—had essentially retired from music. —*Kevin Coffey*

## DeZurik Sisters

Mary Jane DeZurik b. Royalton, Minnesota, February 1, 1917; d. September 3, 1981
Carolyn DeZurik b. Royalton, Minnesota, December 24, 1918; d. March 16, 2009

A popular singing duo, sisters Carolyn and Mary Jane DeZurik combined European Swiss-style yodeling with African American–influenced JIMMIE RODGERS vocal runs. Warbling, tweeting, and whistling their way through multiple octaves, often imitating animal sounds and bird calls, the DeZurik Sisters eventually earned spots on both the WLS *National Barn Dance* and WSM's GRAND OLE OPRY. They were among the first female performers to gain recognition on country music's most popular radio shows.

Born in Royalton, Minnesota, to a Dutch dairy farming family, Mary Jane and Carolyn were two of seven siblings. With Carolyn playing guitar, the sisters were hired in 1936 by the Chicago-based *National Barn Dance*, which billed the fresh-faced duo as trick yodelers. In 1941 Carolyn and Mary Jane (by this time, married to fellow *Barn Dance* performers Rusty Gill and Augie Klein, respectively) appeared on WLW–Cincinnati's *Boone County Jamboree* (soon renamed the *MIDWESTERN HAYRIDE*). By mid-decade the DeZurik Sisters were amazing millions with their distinctive chicken yodel as part of the Ralston Purina–sponsored portion of the Grand Ole Opry, where they performed as the Cackle Sisters.

After years of shuttling between Nashville and Chicago to broadcast over WLS and WSM, Mary Jane DeZurik retired in 1948, and younger sister Lorraine took her place for a time. (Occasionally, sister Eva DeZurik also would stand in if one sister could not appear.) The Cackle Sisters continued performing on the Opry into the early 1950s, their precision yodeling style becoming even more intricate.

Despite a near twenty-year career, the DeZurik sisters recorded only six commercial 78-rpm sides (all in 1938) for the AMERICAN RECORD CORPORATION. However, many of their live performances are preserved on radio transcriptions of Ralston Purina programs. The sisters' inventive vocalizing, spirited performance style, and willingness to experiment all inspired later female country yodelers. —*Patricia Hall*

## Diamond Rio

Gene Johnson b. Jamestown, New York, August 10, 1949
Jimmy Olander b. Minneapolis, Minnesota, August 26, 1961
Brian Prout b. Troy, New York, December 4, 1955
Marty Roe b. Lebanon, Ohio, December 28, 1960
Dan Truman b. St. George, Utah, August 29, 1956
Dana Williams b. Dayton, Ohio, May 22, 1961

In Nashville, where groups have often followed the southern gospel model of vocal harmonizers fronting anonymous musicians, Diamond Rio is something of an anomaly: a band of six excellent musicians who play on their albums as well as on the road. Their music embraces facile picking, old-fashioned virtues (as in "Mama Don't Forget to Pray for Me"), and broad puns ("This Romeo Ain't Got Julie Yet"). Although the act's principal inspiration remains BLUEGRASS, members draw on styles ranging from pop to jazz to traditional country.

Diamond Rio evolved from the Tennessee River Boys bluegrass band, which once featured TY HERNDON. Marty Roe sings lead vocals, and both guitarist Jimmy Olander and keyboardist Dan Truman play in the group. Drummer Brian Prout previously worked in Heartbreak Mountain (which also included SHENANDOAH's Marty Raybon). Bassist-vocalist Dana Williams and Gene Johnson, who plays fiddle and mandolin and sings backing vocals, complete the act, which became Diamond Rio after signing with ARISTA RECORDS.

The band's first single, "Meet in the Middle," was a charming tale of young, rural love that hit #1 in 1991, and Diamond Rio, combining musical talent and accessible songs, quickly became one of country's premier groups. The act won ACM's Top Vocal Group award in 1991 and 1992; CMA named Diamond Rio its Vocal Group of the Year from 1992 to 1994. Diamond Rio's self-titled debut album was certified platinum; the next two, *Close to the Edge* and *Love a Little Stronger*, both went gold. Hit singles of the 1990s included "Mirror Mirror," "Norma Jean Riley," "In a Week or Two," "Love a Little Stronger," "Unbelievable," and the 1997 chart-topper "How Your Love Makes Me Feel." That year the act again captured CMA's Vocal Group of the Year award, and in 1998 the band joined the GRAND OLE OPRY.

The #1 hit "One More Day" (2000–01), which comforted listeners amid the 2001 terrorist attacks, recharged Diamond Rio's career. In 2002–03 the band notched two more #1 singles: "Beautiful Mess" and "I Believe." Subsequent singles sold modestly, and the band left Arista in 2006. Word Records released a Christmas album in 2007, followed by *The Reason*, the group's first contemporary Christian album, in 2009. —*Brian Mansfield*

## Hazel Dickens

b. Mercer County, West Virginia, June 1, 1935; d. April 22, 2011

The eighth of eleven children in a family that often went hungry, Hazel Jane Dickens spent her childhood in poverty. One of the family's few possessions was a radio, on which Hazel listened to UNCLE DAVE MACON, the CARTER FAMILY, and WILMA LEE & STONEY COOPER.

In 1954 Dickens moved to Baltimore. There she attended "pickin' parties" where musicians played BLUEGRASS and OLD-TIME country and where she first sang publicly. Through her brother Robert she met Mike Seeger, and she began performing with him in a band that included her brothers Robert and Arnold. Next, she played bass and sang with several bands, including the

Pike County Boys and THE GREENBRIAR BOYS, before taking a break from professional music.

In the early 1960s Dickens met Alice Gerrard, a classically trained singer enthusiastic about traditional country music, and the two began singing and writing together. They built up an extensive repertoire of original material and songs learned from Library of Congress files and old-time musicians the duo taped at folk festivals. The pair then began touring festivals, and between 1965 and 1976 they recorded four albums that featured both women trading lead and harmony vocals. Although they acquired a devoted following, the act broke up in 1976.

After parting with Gerrard, Dickens won acclaim for her songwriting, particularly after four of her songs were included on the soundtrack of the award-winning film *Harlan County, U.S.A.*, a 1976 documentary about striking Kentucky coal miners. The soundtrack to *Babies and Banners: Story of the Women's Brigade* (1979), a movie exploring the role of women in the 1936–37 sit-down strike within the General Motors plant at Flint, Michigan, also featured her music. In 1980 her first solo album, *Hard Hitting Songs for Hard Hit People*, appeared on ROUNDER RECORDS. Subsequent albums followed in 1983 and 1987, and she became a popular figure at U.S. folk festivals and on worldwide tours. In 1994 Dickens received IBMA's Distinguished Achievement Award, given for her contributions to bluegrass.

The National Endowment for the Arts presented Dickens with a prestigious National Heritage Fellowship in 2001. In that year, she contributed to the soundtrack to *Songcatcher*, a film about a female music scholar who journeys through Appalachia. The soundtrack also features DOLLY PARTON, PATTY LOVELESS, and other female artists. —*W. K. McNeil*

## Little Jimmy Dickens

b. Bolt, West Virginia, December 19, 1920

James Cecil Dickens burst onto the country scene at the end of the 1940s with a string of humorous novelty songs typified by "Take an Old Cold 'Tater (And Wait)" (1949), "Country Boy" (1949), and "A-Sleeping at the Foot of the Bed" (1950). His small physical stature (four feet, eleven inches), big voice, and brassy style have made him a longtime favorite with country fans.

Born into a large West Virginia family, Dickens gained early experience on local radio station WJLS with performers such as Mel Steele, MOLLY O'DAY, and Johnnie Bailes (THE BAILES BROTHERS). Through the 1940s he had his own radio programs in Fairmont, West Virginia; Indianapolis; Cincinnati; Topeka, Kansas; and Saginaw, Michigan. ROY ACUFF first heard him in Cincinnati in 1947 and brought him to the attention of GRAND OLE OPRY officials and COLUMBIA RECORDS. After guest appearances Dickens joined the Opry on September 25, 1948, having signed with Columbia on September 16. Dickens became an instant success for both, beginning in early 1949.

At the Opry, HANK WILLIAMS gave Dickens the nickname Tater, from the Dickens hit "Take an Old Cold 'Tater (And Wait)." Shortly after joining the show, Dickens took over PAUL HOWARD's band, which included crack guitarists R. M. "Jabbo" Arrington and GRADY MARTIN (later Jimmy "Spider" Wilson and Howard Rhoton) and bassist BOB MOORE. Named the Country Boys, Dickens's band became known for its topflight musicianship and for its pioneering twin lead guitar sound. Later Dickens hired young steel guitarist BUDDY EMMONS and guitarist Thumbs Carllile.

*Little Jimmy Dickens*

In the late 1950s Dickens cut some ROCKABILLY records, including "Salty Boogie," "Blackeyed Joe's," and "I Got a Hole in My Pocket" (later a hit for RICKY VAN SHELTON). Additional well-known Dickens novelty numbers include "Hillbilly Fever," "Bessie the Heifer," "Hot Diggity Dog," and "Cold Feet." He also performed romantic ballads, such as "I've Just Got to See You Once More" and "My Heart's Bouquet," but his novelty hits overshadowed them.

Following his #9 hit with BOUDLEAUX AND FELICE BRYANT's "Out Behind the Barn" in 1954, Dickens failed to chart until "The Violet and a Rose" in 1962. In 1957 he left the Opry to tour with the PHILIP MORRIS COUNTRY MUSIC SHOW, but he returned in 1975. His biggest hit came in 1965 with a new novelty song, "May the Bird of Paradise Fly Up Your Nose," which peaked at #1 country and #15 pop. Thereafter, his singles regularly charted until 1972. He moved to DECCA RECORDS in 1967 and United Artists in 1971. Of his later songs, "Country Music Lover" in 1967 had the highest chart ranking (#23), but the sentimental recitation "Raggedy Ann" has probably retained the longest popularity with his fans.

A superb showman, Dickens remains an enduring Grand Ole Opry favorite. He was elected to THE COUNTRY MUSIC HALL OF FAME in 1983. —*Ivan M. Tribe*

## Joe Diffie

b. Tulsa, Oklahoma, December 28, 1958

In the early 1990s, Joe Logan Diffie was a flag-waver for traditional country music, but in 1993 he became a major proponent of the high-energy "turbo tonk" sound that mixed country with a heavy dose of rock.

Diffie's traditional bent came naturally, because his father favored hard country acts and the family often sang country and gospel songs. Early on, Diffie joined rock, gospel, and BLUEGRASS groups before performing solo, working industrial jobs to support himself.

In 1986 Diffie moved to Nashville, worked at Gibson Guitars, and began singing on songwriters' demos and writing his own material. Diffie was signed to EPIC RECORDS by BOB MONTGOMERY; his 1990 debut single, "Home," topped multiple industry popularity charts. At times Diffie embodied GEORGE JONES or BUCK OWENS in his early singles, including the ballads "Is It Cold in Here" and "Ships That Don't Come In" and the HONKY-TONK efforts "If the Devil Danced (In Empty Pockets)" and "New Way (To Light Up an Old Flame)."

But with 1993's *Honky Tonk Attitude*, Diffie launched a string of seminovelty hits that melded rock guitar parts with honky-tonk elements. "Prop Me Up Beside the Jukebox (If I Die)," "John Deere Green," "Pickup Man" (#1, 1994), and "Third Rock from the Sun" received mixed critical reaction but fueled his commercial success. *Life's So Funny* (1995) and *Twice Upon a Time* (1997), however, failed to catch fire, and Diffie dropped longtime manager and producer Johnny Slate. Working with producer DON COOK, Diffie released a 1998 greatest-hits package that yielded the Top Five hit "Texas Size Heartache." The title track to Diffie's final Epic album, *A Night to Remember* (1999), reached #6, and "It's Always Somethin'" climbed to #5 on *Billboard*'s country singles chart.

In 2001 parent company SONY MUSIC moved Diffie from Epic to Sony's MONUMENT imprint. The title track to *In Another World*, his only Monument album, was a #10 country single. A lone album for BROKEN BOW RECORDS sold disappointingly. However, his song "My Give a Damn's Busted" became a 2005 smash for JO DEE MESSINA. In 2008 Diffie began releasing his early demo recordings through his website. ROUNDER RECORDS released his 2010 acoustic collection, *Homecoming: The Bluegrass Album*. —Tom Roland

## Annie Lou & Danny Dill

Annie Lou Stockard Dill b. Skull Bone, Tennessee, July 27, 1925; d. January 4, 1982
Horace Eldred "Danny" Dill b. Dollar Hill, Tennessee, September 19, 1924; d. October 23, 2008

Annie Lou & Danny, as they were known professionally, were a duet act on the GRAND OLE OPRY between 1946 and the mid-1950s. After their joint career, Danny Dill became one of the CEDARWOOD PUBLISHING COMPANY's leading songwriters.

Annie Lou Stockard was singing with her twin sisters on radio in Jackson, Tennessee, when she met and in 1945 married another radio singer, Horace Dill—later dubbed Danny by early touring partner THE DUKE OF PADUCAH. Their music resembled that of LULU BELLE & SCOTTY. The couple joined the Grand Ole Opry in January 1946 and first recorded for BULLET in 1949. Besides their Nashville radio work, they toured with the Duke of Paducah, EDDY ARNOLD, ERNEST TUBB, GEORGE MORGAN, and other Opry stars until their act and marriage broke up in the 1960s.

Danny Dill recorded solo for ABC and Cub and turned to songwriting, his first hit being "If You Saw Her Through My Eyes" for CARL SMITH (1954). His later hits included "Long Black Veil" (cowritten with MARIJOHN WILKIN, 1959) for LEFTY FRIZZELL and "Detroit City" (cowritten with MEL TILLIS, 1963) for BOBBY BARE.

Annie Lou never remarried, and she died in 1982. Danny performed in songwriter showcases for many years and played the part of an old man in STEVE WARINER's 1992 video "The Tips of My Fingers." —Ronnie Pugh

## The Dillards

Douglas Flint Dillard b. East St. Louis, Illinois, March 6, 1937
Rodney Adean Dillard b. East St. Louis, Illinois, May 18, 1942
Mitchell Jayne b. Hammond, Indiana, July 5, 1930; d. August 2, 2010
Roy Dean Webb b. Independence, Missouri, March 28, 1937

A leading progressive BLUEGRASS band, the Dillards modernized and popularized the genre through innovative albums and appearances on CBS-TV's *THE ANDY GRIFFITH SHOW*. As Briscoe Darling's four boys, they never uttered a word on camera but played like the dickens. As a result, they became one of the best-selling and most popular groups in folk and bluegrass.

Raised in Salem, Missouri, brothers Rodney (guitar) and Doug Dillard (banjo) grew up in a musical family. In 1962, with bassist Mitch Jayne and mandolin player Dean Webb, they moved to Los Angeles, where an ELEKTRA RECORDS producer heard them at the Ash Grove club and quickly signed them. Shortly thereafter they debuted on Griffith's hit TV series. Their first album, *Back Porch Bluegrass* (1963), featured "The Old Home Place" and "Dooley," songs that became bluegrass standards. In 1964 they released *Live . . . Almost*; recorded at the folk club Mecca, the album highlights the group's homespun comedy in addition to their tight picking. Selections range from the original "There Is a Time" and the traditional "Pretty Polly" to a cover of BOB DYLAN's "Walking Down the Line," apparently the first Dylan song recorded by a bluegrass outfit. For *Pickin' and Fiddlin'* (1965), the Dillards teamed with prominent bluegrass fiddler BYRON BERLINE.

Influenced by West Coast rock musicians, the Dillards began experimenting in the recording studio. The masterful *Wheatstraw Suite* (1968) showcases high-tech vocals by banjoist HERB PEDERSEN, who had replaced Doug Dillard. (Doug joined forces with Gene Clark—formerly with THE BYRDS—before launching a solo career.) Vocal tracks were doubled and tripled to give the performances a fuller sound. Orchestral arrangements, drums, and PEDAL STEEL GUITAR puzzled traditionalists, but the album—and 1970's *Copperfields*—won new young listeners for bluegrass. Billy Ray Latham had replaced Pederson (who left in 1972 to join Berline's COUNTRY GAZETTE) by the time a tour with Elton John boosted sales for *Roots and Branches* (Anthem, 1972). The COUNTRY-ROCK album *Tribute to the American Duck* appeared on Poppy in 1973.

The years 1974–79 witnessed various projects reflecting changing personnel—including the four original members—and reunion recordings and albums continued into the 1990s. Over the years, Rodney and Doug have formed their own bands while repeatedly joining forces to tour and record, as a duo and as the Dillards.

Influential NITTY GRITTY DIRT BAND cofounder John McEuen paid tribute to original Dillards in his 2006 documentary film *A Night in the Ozarks: An Audio Lithograph*. In 2008, Arlo Guthrie released *Arlo Guthrie and the Dillards,* which featured Doug and Rodney on covers of WOODY GUTHRIE tunes.

The Dillards were elected to the IBMA Hall of Fame in 2009. —Chris Skinker

## Dean Dillon

b. Lake City, Tennessee, March 26, 1955

During the 1980s, Dean Dillon became one of country music's most prominent songwriters, thanks in part to his association with GEORGE STRAIT. Dillon and Frank Dycus penned Strait's first hit single, "Unwound" (#6, 1981), whose simple chord progressions and soulful lyrical twists matched Strait's affinity for traditional country. Since then, Strait has cut more than fifty Dillon compositions, including "Marina Del Rey," "The Chair," "Ocean Front Property," "Easy Come, Easy Go," "If I Know Me," and "I've Come to Expect It From You."

Growing up, Dillon seemed destined for a musical career. He started performing publicly by age nine and wrote his first song by age eleven. He was a regular on Knoxville's *The Kathy Hill Show* in his teens.

Pursuing a singing career, Dillon hitchhiked to Nashville in 1976. Music publisher TOM COLLINS signed him as a writer, and Dillon notched his first Top 5 hit with "Lying in Love with You" (JIM ED BROWN and Helen Cornelius). Dillon released several chart singles on RCA, teamed with GARY STEWART for two albums, and later recorded for ATLANTIC and CAPITOL.

In 1981, however, Dillon began his association with Strait, and songwriting became Dillon's primary path. In addition to his many Strait classics, Dillon's songwriting credits include GEORGE JONES's "Tennessee Whiskey," VERN GOSDIN's "Set 'Em Up Joe," and KEITH WHITLEY's "Homecoming '63." More recently, Dillon cowrote the KENNY CHESNEY hit "A Lot of Things Different" (2002–03) with BILL ANDERSON and TOBY KEITH's 2006 smash "A Little Too Late." Strait's 2008 album *Troubadour* includes a Dillon-Strait duet, "West Texas Town," cowritten by Dillon and ROBERT EARL KEEN JR., and Dillon cowrote two songs with Strait and his son Bubba for the 2009 album *Twang*, including the hit "Living for the Night."

Dillon was elected to the NASHVILLE SONGWRITERS HALL OF FAME in 2002. —*Tom Roland*

## Bob DiPiero
b. Youngstown, Ohio, March 3, 1951

After three decades, Bob DiPiero has remained at the top of the country songwriting profession. His dozens of hits include numerous #1s, ranging from the OAK RIDGE BOYS' "American Made" (1983) to TIM MCGRAW's "Southern Voice" (2010).

Also regarded for his guitar skills and humorous storytelling, Robert John DiPiero put himself through college playing rock shows. He earned a music degree from Youngstown State University before moving to Nashville in 1978.

His first songwriting success came in 1980 with REBA MCENTIRE's "I Can See Forever in Your Eyes." His next hit, "American Made," reached a wider audience as a national ad jingle for Miller beer. DiPiero's "Wink" (a #1 hit recorded by NEAL MCCOY) was BMI's most performed country song of 1995. He also has topped the charts with McEntire's "Little Rock," SHENANDOAH's "The Church on Cumberland Road," JOHN ANDERSON's "Money in the Bank," and GEORGE STRAIT's "Blue Clear Sky," among others. He also penned "Cleopatra, Queen of Denial" and additional hits for former spouse PAM TILLIS.

With his own short-lived band, Billy Hill, he reached the Top Thirty with "Too Much Month at the End of the Money" in 1989. DiPiero entered the NASHVILLE SONGWRITERS HALL OF FAME in 2007. He starred in the GAC series *The Hitmen of Music Row.* —*Michael Gray*

## Dixie Chicks
Martha "Martie" Erwin Maguire b. York, Pennsylvania, October 12, 1969
Emily Erwin Robison b. Pittsfield, Massachusetts, August 16, 1972
Natalie Maines b. Lubbock, Texas, October 14, 1974

Dixie Chicks may be known as much for the controversies they have stirred as for their many artistic and commercial achievements. From 1998 to 2003, their feistiness and musicianship challenged stereotypes for women in country, while multiplatinum album sales, Grammy awards, and multiple CMA and ACM honors spoke to their wide acceptance. But a politically charged remark in 2003 instantly knocked them off country radio, while talk radio derided them as pariahs or paraded them as unlikely poster girls for dissent.

Sisters Martie and Emily Erwin (who later adopted their married names) emerged as child prodigies on the Texas BLUEGRASS scene, playing fiddle and banjo, respectively. Originally calling themselves Dixie Chickens in 1989, after a song by Little Feat, they leaned toward a humorously nostalgic western style. Robin Lynn Macy sang lead on the group's first two independent albums—by then they had shortened the name to Dixie Chicks—while Laura Lynch assumed the frontwoman role on the third, and Macy left the group.

Seeking a new sound and image, the sisters split with Lynch and brought in Natalie Maines, daughter of renowned Texas steel guitarist Lloyd Maines, as their third lead singer. Maines initially cared little for 1990s country, but her entrée contemporized the trio and landed them a contract with SONY MUSIC's MONUMENT label. Their debut, *Wide Open Spaces* (1998), quickly sold 6 million copies, eventually topping 12 million. "There's Your Trouble," a single from the album, earned the group a Grammy, and the title cut was CMA's 1998 Single of the Year. The follow-up album, *Fly* (1999), which sold 2 million by year's end and later surpassed 10 million, resulted in the band's second pair of Grammys for Best Country Performance by a Duo or Group (the #2 hit "Ready to Run") and Best Country Album. Nevertheless, some critics regarded them as a manufactured, country version of the Spice Girls.

Such opinions paled beside objections to "Goodbye Earl" (1999–2000), which gleefully celebrated the murder of a battering husband. Maines claimed Sony had a bigger problem with "Sin Wagon," because of its reference to "mattress dancing." These playfully defiant anthems roused audiences when the trio appeared on a prestigious, all-female Lilith Fair tour.

*Dixie Chicks: (from left) Martie Maguire, Natalie Maines, and Emily Robison*

During their five-year love affair with country radio, the act enjoyed fourteen Top Ten singles, six of which reached #1. The band exchanged lawsuits with Sony in 2002 over money matters, declaring themselves free agents. During the estrangement, they recorded an album they considered releasing independently but ultimately issued on Monument. Although *Home* was more acoustically based than its predecessors, it was mainstream enough to sell a commanding 6 million copies.

It might have sold more, if not for a history-making casual remark Maines made on a London stage in March 2003, shortly before the United States invaded Iraq. "Just so you know, we're ashamed the president of the United States is from Texas," she told the crowd. Their hit single "Travelin' Soldier" (#1, 2002)—ironically, about the fallout of the Vietnam War—instantly disappeared from the airwaves, with some broadcasters hosting CD-smashing rallies. The Grammy-winning "Long Time Gone" as well as their cover of Stevie Nicks's "Landslide" reached #2 in 2002, but 2003 saw only two modest chart entries. The aggressively patriotic Toby Keith drew cheers on tour by showing a doctored photo of Maines cozying up to Saddam Hussein. Their tenure as mainstream country superstars was over—even before they defiantly posed nude for the cover of *Entertainment Weekly* with pro and con slogans stenciled onto their bodies.

"We've been called communists and domestic terrorists," Martie Maguire told the magazine, dismissing such accusations as ridiculous. Emily Robison doubted they would have faced the attacks in another form of music. "No matter what people say," she insisted, "I feel really patriotic. And strong."

Predictably, country radio ignored their return in 2006—though it didn't help that their comeback single was the boldly unrepentant "Not Ready to Make Nice," from *Taking the Long Way*. Airplay or no airplay, both single and album took home all-category Grammys for Song of the Year and Album of the Year, respectively. And even with heavy erosion among their country fan base, their more Americana-influenced sound picked up converts from the rock audience, and their Rick Rubin-produced CD became one of the year's best-sellers.

Subsequently, a long layoff led to breakup rumors. When Maguire and Robison reemerged in early 2010, they did so as the Court Yard Hounds, featuring Robison as primary singer/songwriter, with ruminative songs inspired by her divorce from country singer Charlie Robison.

Like Maines, Robison expressed fatigue with the political dust-ups that had eclipsed their music: "When the Chicks do regroup," she predicted, "it'll be because it's gonna be so much fun and so awesome and everyone wants to be there." —*Chris Willman*

## The Dixon Brothers

Dorsey Murdock Dixon b. Darlington, South Carolina, October 14, 1897; d. April 17, 1968
Howard Briten Dixon b. Darlington, South Carolina, June 19, 1903; d. March 24, 1961

Although the Dixon Brothers built influential careers as country musicians and introduced songs valued by fans and folklorists, they never made music their full-time profession. Instead, they remained cotton mill workers until Howard's death in 1961 and Dorsey's retirement. The Dixons sang in a rough but affecting style that suggested country-gospel singing, and Dorsey played finger-style guitar while Howard played Hawaiian-style steel guitar (inspired by seeing Jimmie Tarlton of Darby & Tarlton

play the instrument). Their material embraced a wide variety of songs, mostly written or arranged by Dorsey, that span most of country music's principal themes. These include humorous songs ("The Intoxicated Rat"), religious numbers ("I'm Not Turning Backward"), moralistic songs ("Wreck on the Highway," made famous by Roy Acuff), topical pieces ("Down with the Old Canoe," about the sinking of the *Titanic*), and social commentaries that graphically document or recall their experiences as cotton mill workers ("Weave Room Blues," "Spinning Room Blues"). The Dixons recorded a total of fifty-five released sides for Bluebird from 1936 to 1938. Fortunately for modern fans of old-time country music, Dorsey Dixon made a few concert appearances in the 1960s and was recorded (with his sister Nancy) in 1962 by Eugene Earle and Archie Green for an album that appeared on the independent Testament label. —*Bill C. Malone*

## DJ Convention

began November 22, 1952

Since 1952 the annual fall festival once known as the DJ Convention has honored the Grand Ole Opry while consolidating Nashville's role in the country music industry. Now popularly called Country Music Week or CMA Week, the event originally commemorated the birth of the Grand Ole Opry and was first organized by radio station WSM, using Acuff-Rose Publications' DJ list.

The first event took place on November 22, 1952, and involved some one hundred DJs who were welcomed by WSM and treated to a Grand Ole Opry show. The 1953 celebration extended over two days, with record companies and publishers hosting receptions and BMI giving its first country music awards for broadcast airplay. Additionally, DJs organized the Country Music Disc Jockeys Association (CMDJA), precursor to CMA. By 1958 attendance had grown to 2,000 DJs; entertainers were making special appearances; and several trade magazines were bestowing awards. In addition to formal and informal parties, there were now panels on industry issues such as merchandising and radio programming. In that year, CMDJA disbanded, and CMA was organized at the fall DJ Convention. Since then, CMA has made the event an ongoing project. In 1963 CMA began a successful push to have state governors proclaim October as Country Music Month, and the festival was shifted from November to October to avoid winter weather. By then attendance had reached 3,500, and ASCAP held its first country awards ceremony. (SESAC followed suit in 1964, and NSAI in 1970.)

In 1969 the first Country Radio Broadcasters (CRB/CRS) seminar was held, and CRB soon established its own board of directors. This annual event is now held early in the year, the distinction symbolizing the rise of tightly formatted radio and the declining power of once-freewheeling DJs vis-à-vis station program directors and radio consultants. In 1972 CMA organized the first Fan Fair (now called the CMA Music Festival) to relieve the congestion of the fall gathering and to give artists and fans a special early-summer event at which to meet each other. —*John W. Rumble*

## Dobro

Properly called a resophonic guitar, "Dobro" was originally a brand name for an instrument with metal resonating chambers. Generally played Hawaiian-style (positioned with strings facing up, tuned to an open chord, and noted using a metal bar), the dobro is valued for its bluesy, insinuating sound, its versatility in producing sustained slides or crisp arpeggios, and as an acoustic alternative to the electrified PEDAL STEEL GUITAR.

John and Rudy Dopyera perfected resophonic instruments in 1926 while attempting to mechanically amplify guitars in the days before electric instruments and multimicrophone sound systems. Built into their guitars' tops were one large or three small metal resonators similar in shape to record player speaker cones. Many variations followed, including metal- and wood-bodied instruments and cones of various designs and manufacture. In 1927 the Dopyeras joined with three partners to found the National Guitar Company. Of Czechoslovakian descent, the Dopyera brothers (five in all) called their creation the Dobro, using a Slavic word for "good" that also referenced their name and relation.

In 1929 the Dopyeras left National and formed the Dobro Company. (The two entities eventually merged, and in 1987 the Gibson Guitar Company acquired rights to the Dobro brand name.) The Dopyeras built resophonic mandolins, banjos, and ukuleles as well. Resophonic guitars became popular with blues musicians (who played them slide-style or by standard finger fretting) and Hawaiian music bands. By the late 1920s the dobro had begun to affect country music. Cliff Carlisle (BILL CARLISLE's brother and sometime duet partner) played on JIMMIE RODGERS sessions in the late 1920s and early 1930s, while ROY ACUFF featured dobro players in his band—notably Beecher "BASHFUL BROTHER OSWALD" Kirby, whose GRAND OLE OPRY appearances maintained interest in the dobro after electric guitars virtually supplanted resophonic instruments. George Edward "Speedy" Krise performed with MOLLY O'DAY in the late 1940s, and Ray Atkins and HAROLD "SHOT" JACKSON worked with JOHNNIE & JACK in the 1950s.

The dobro experienced a renaissance in the late 1950s thanks to UNCLE JOSH GRAVES. Hired by FLATT & SCRUGGS to play bass, Graves quickly switched to the dobro. His brilliant vocabulary of lead and backup lines and his dynamic three-finger picking inspired a new generation of BLUEGRASS and acoustic country musicians, notably Mike Auldridge, known for his work with the SELDOM SCENE, and JERRY DOUGLAS, who became Nashville's most active dobro session player and a featured musician with ALISON KRAUSS & UNION STATION. Other respected contemporary dobro players include TUT TAYLOR (with his trademark single-plectrum picking style), ROB ICKES, Randy Kohrs, Phil Leadbetter, Sally Van Meter, Cindy Cashdollar, and Gene Wooten (d. 2001). —*Richard D. Smith*

## Jimmie Dolan
b. Gardena, California, October 29, 1916; d. July 31, 1994

Jimmie Lee Dolan, best known as Ramblin' Jimmie Dolan, was a California recording artist, club singer, and disc jockey, most active between 1945 and 1955. Dolan learned to play guitar at fourteen through mail-order instruction and first sang on radio at KWK in St. Louis. After service as a naval radio operator in World War II, he returned to California and started a recording career with West Coast independents Colonial, Modern, and Crystal Records. He joined the CAPITOL roster in 1949; during his six-year tenure there, Dolan's best-remembered releases were his 1950 covers of MOON MULLICAN's "I'll Sail My Ship Alone" and Arkie Shibley's "Hot Rod Race."

As his nickname suggests, good-timing, fun-loving songs such as 1952's "Rack Up the Balls, Boys" and 1953's "Playin' Dominoes and Shootin' Dice" were his specialty. He was also a popular country DJ on California stations in the 1950s. With the coming of rock & roll, however, Dolan sank into obscurity, though he was cited as an active freelance musician and member of the Los Angeles Local 47 of the American Federation of Musicians (AFM) in his obituaries nearly forty years later. —*Ronnie Pugh*

## Dot Records
established in Gallatin, Tennessee, 1950

Dot Records was an independent label that initially focused on pop product but eventually became a major presence in country music. Randy Wood, owner of Randy's Record Shop in Gallatin, Tennessee, started Dot Records to augment his growing mail-order business. The label's first release was "Boogie Beat Rag" (1950) by the Tennessee Drifters, a teenage band from Nashville's East High School. Dot's biggest-selling artist by far was pop singer Pat Boone. His cover of the R&B hit "Two Hearts" in 1955 was the first of his fifty-nine chart records for the label.

MAC WISEMAN (a Dot artist from 1951 to 1961) was one of Dot's first country acts. The singer had several Top Ten country hits, among them "Ballad of Davy Crockett" (#10, 1955) and "Jimmy Brown the Newsboy" (#5, 1959). In the late 1950s Wiseman also served as Dot's A&R country director. Other Dot artists of the decade included fiddler TOMMY JACKSON (1952–55), JIMMY C. NEWMAN (1954–57), COWBOY COPAS (1957), and LEROY VAN DYKE (1956–58).

Wood moved the company to Hollywood in 1957 and later sold it to Paramount Pictures. ABC Records merged its country roster with Dot's in 1974 to create ABC/Dot. Among the label's 1970s hit makers were ROY CLARK (1968–77), BARBARA MANDRELL (1975–77), DON WILLIAMS (1974–77), JOE STAMPLEY (1971–75), Tommy Overstreet (1969–78), and DONNA FARGO (1972–76). In 1977 MCA RECORDS purchased ABC/Dot and, except for a brief period in the late 1980s, retired the Dot name. —*Don Roy*

## Michael Doucet (*see* BeauSoleil)

## Jerry Douglas
b. Warren, Ohio, May 28, 1956

Just as BILL MONROE and EARL SCRUGGS respectively transformed the roles of the mandolin and the banjo in American vernacular music, DOBRO player Jerry Douglas has redefined an instrument once associated primarily with vintage country acts and BLUEGRASS bands. Through innovative playing techniques and recordings with artists ranging from RICKY SKAGGS and THE WHITES to T. Bone Burnett, Elvis Costello, Paul Simon, and James Taylor, Douglas has widened the dobro's stylistic possibilities and extended its influence.

The son of a steelworker who played bluegrass on the side, Gerald Calvin Douglas was eight when he first heard both BASHFUL BROTHER OSWALD and UNCLE JOSH GRAVES in a FLATT & SCRUGGS concert. Smitten by their sound, Douglas acquired his first dobro in 1966 and began playing with his father's band. He joined THE COUNTRY GENTLEMEN in 1973, and in 1974 he joined J. D. CROWE's New South. Ricky Skaggs was also in Crowe's band at the time, and in 1976 Douglas and Skaggs formed Boone Creek. Two years later Douglas rejoined the Gentlemen and soon recorded his first solo album, *Fluxology* (ROUNDER, 1979), a title taken from his nickname, "Flux."

In 1979 Douglas joined Buck White in his family band while the Whites were touring as the opening act for EMMYLOU HARRIS. Douglas played on Harris's largely acoustic *Roses in the Snow* (1980) and became a recognized player in country's emerging traditionalist vanguard via recordings with Harris, Skaggs, and the Whites. Through his flashy, aggressive contributions to hits by Skaggs ("Don't Get Above Your Raising," 1981) and the Whites ("Hangin' Around" 1982), Douglas gave the dobro a voice in a mainstream country scene that honored the past even as it eagerly absorbed rock influences. Douglas retired from the Whites' road band in 1985 and began to concentrate on Nashville session work, appearing on recordings by JOHNNY CASH and RAY CHARLES, among many others. Meanwhile, Douglas continued his series of solo and multiartist albums released on Rounder, MCA, SUGAR HILL, and Koch, including *Glide* (2008) and *Jerry Christmas* (2009), both on Koch. He also contributed to the stellar *O BROTHER, WHERE ART THOU?* soundtrack. Behind the glass, he has produced albums by the DEL McCOURY BAND, NASHVILLE BLUEGRASS BAND, and Jesse Winchester.

For more than a decade, Douglas has been a featured member of ALISON KRAUSS & UNION STATION, performing on a string of best-selling albums and touring widely; he also tours with his own Jerry Douglas Band. A 2004 recipient of a National Endowment for the Arts National Heritage Fellowship, Douglas has received multiple Grammy awards and a host of honors from the IBMA. He was CMA's Musician of the Year in 2002, 2005, and 2007. —*Mark Humphrey*

## Big Al Downing

b. Centralia, Oklahoma, January 9, 1940; d. July 4, 2005

One of country music's best-selling African American artists, Downing eschewed classifying his music, also recording rock & roll, R&B, and disco, but always returning to country. Early influences included ERNEST TUBB, HANK WILLIAMS, and PORTER WAGONER, heard on WSM's GRAND OLE OPRY, and recordings by Fats Domino and other R&B and gospel artists heard over WLAC–Nashville.

Downing found his first piano, missing several keys, on a junk heap while returning from cutting hay. A 1956 trip to Coffeyville, Kansas, to appear on a WTTP-AM talent contest launched his professional career. Downing won playing "Blueberry Hill." Bobby Poe heard him on radio, and together they formed the biracial Poe Kats. Downing's 1958 ROCKABILLY release "Down on the Farm," on White Rock, was picked up by CHALLENGE and barely missed the charts, but it became a rock & roll classic.

That same year, WANDA JACKSON invited Downing to join her band. He appeared on several Jackson recordings, including her biggest hit, "Let's Have a Party." Backing Jackson on the road, the band opened for MARTY ROBBINS, BOBBY BARE, RED SOVINE, DON GIBSON, and others.

After the Jackson tour, Downing moved to Washington, D.C., for several years and then to the Boston area, where he recorded on several labels in a Fats Domino–influenced style. His band, the Chartbusters, charted with two rock releases in 1964. A soul duet with Little Esther Phillips charted in 1963, and a disco record charted in 1975.

A 1978 move to WARNER BROS. brought Downing back to his country roots. A release of "Mr. Jones" that year, followed by "Touch Me (I'll Be Your Fool Once More)," led to a string of fifteen country chart records over the next decade and appearances on *NASHVILLE NOW*, the GRAND OLE OPRY, and *HEE HAW*. He continued to perform, especially in Europe, until sidelined by leukemia, which took his life on July 4, 2005. Several Downing CDs appeared on Eagle, Hayden's Ferry, Crazy Music, and Albe Music between 1998 and 2008. —*William P. Davis*

## Pete Drake

b. Augusta, Georgia, October 8, 1932; d. July 29, 1988

As a producer, musician, and publisher of music from traditional country to rock and as a steel guitar innovator, Roddis Franklin "Pete" Drake made a lasting mark on country music.

Drake's father was a Pentecostal preacher, and his brothers Jack and Bill performed as the Drake Brothers. Jack later spent twenty-four years playing bass for ERNEST TUBB.

When eighteen-year-old Pete drove to Nashville to visit his brothers, he heard steel guitar maestro JERRY BYRD playing on the GRAND OLE OPRY. The sliding steel sound inspired Drake to buy a $38 steel guitar in an Atlanta pawnshop.

In the 1950s, Drake organized an Atlanta band including, at various points, future stars JACK GREENE, JERRY REED, ROGER MILLER, JOE SOUTH, and DOUG KERSHAW. Drake moved to Nashville in 1959 and later worked the road with DON GIBSON and MARTY ROBBINS. While playing on the Opry with CARL & PEARL BUTLER, Drake tested his innovative steel solos. Impressed, Opry star ROY DRUSKY booked him for a session that resulted in the hit single "Anymore" (#3, 1960).

As word spread about Nashville's new steel player, producers scheduled Drake for twenty-four sessions the next month, igniting

*Pete Drake*

the career of one of country music's most prolific and commercial studio musicians. In his heyday, *Billboard*'s weekly popularity charts often included multiple recordings reflecting his work. During the mid-1960s he began using his "talking" steel guitar technique (built on techniques pioneered by Alvino Rey). Put simply, Drake formed and amplified his words via a tube running from his mouth to the instrument.

Drake's influence and visibility went far beyond country music. As a producer he worked with Ringo Starr, the first Beatle to record in the United States, and also produced B. J. THOMAS, the Four Freshmen, Bobby Vinton, LEON RUSSELL, Tracy Nelson, Ernest Tubb, SLIM WHITMAN, BOXCAR WILLIE, the OAK RIDGE BOYS, and BILLIE JO SPEARS. Drake's steel guitar stylings graced the hit records of artists including BOB DYLAN, Joan Baez, George Harrison, and ELVIS PRESLEY, as well as his own recordings made for the Smash label. Five Presley movie tracks also featured Drake's "talking" steel guitar. As a music publisher Drake helped ED BRUCE, DAVID ALLAN COE, and DOTTIE WEST reach new heights. His label Stop Records released recordings by JOHNNY BUSH and others during the 1960s and early 1970s.

The Nashville Entertainment Association presented Pete Drake with its coveted Masters Award on May 7, 1987. In that year he was also inducted into the International Steel Guitar Hall of Fame. —*Gerry Wood and Robert Kramer*

## DreamWorks Records

After David Geffen's independent ASYLUM RECORDS hit pay dirt with multiartist country tribute album *Common Thread: The Songs of the Eagles* (1993), Geffen set up shop in Nashville through DreamWorks Records, an affiliate of his movie studio DreamWorks SKG (co-owned with Steven Spielberg and Jeffrey Katzenberg).

*Common Thread* executive producer JAMES STROUD took the reins when the DreamWorks Nashville office opened in 1997 and signed RANDY TRAVIS as the label's first act. Stroud steered the firm through its eight-year history. Despite the film connection, 1998's *Prince of Egypt Nashville* was the only significant soundtrack to emanate from DreamWorks in MUSIC CITY. Nevertheless, the label introduced Jessica Andrews, Jimmy Wayne, Emerson Drive, and DARRYL WORLEY. Stroud's largest prize was TOBY KEITH, who left MERCURY RECORDS in 1999. Keith's album *How Do You Like Me Now?!* established the swagger that soon made him one of country's most popular acts.

The young label ended when Mercury's parent company, the Universal Music Group, absorbed DreamWorks in 2004. In September 2005 Keith formed his own Show Dog Nashville imprint, and the remaining DreamWorks acts scattered elsewhere. So did DreamWorks promotion manager SCOTT BORCHETTA, who soon formed BIG MACHINE RECORDS. —*Tom Roland*

## The Drifting Cowboys

Although there were several bands called Drifting Cowboys, the name is indelibly associated with HANK WILLIAMS. He appears to have used it from the time he assembled his first bands in Montgomery, Alabama, in 1937 or 1938. It highlighted his fascination with Hollywood's western films, also reflected in Williams's preference for cowboy hats and boots. Over a fifteen-year period there were hundreds of Drifting Cowboys.

During the 1930s, most Drifting Cowboys played no more than a few shows with Williams, who was not then considered a plum employer. Two of the most famous Drifting Cowboys, Don Helms and Sammy Pruett, joined Williams as early as 1944. Helms played steel guitar, and Pruett played lead guitar. They left within a year, and by the time Williams signed with Sterling Records in 1946, his band comprised R. D. Norred on steel guitar, Joe Pennington (born Penney) on guitar, Lum York on bass, and Winston "Red" Todd on guitar. Williams's Cowboys seldom recorded with him until 1950; session musicians were used, although the Drifting Cowboys were label-credited.

Several months after Williams went to Shreveport in August 1948, to join the *LOUISIANA HAYRIDE*, he formed another band that comprised York, guitarist Bob McNett, Tony Francini on fiddle, steel guitarist Felton Pruett, and guitarist Clent Holmes. He left them in Shreveport after being offered a slot on the GRAND OLE OPRY in June 1949, although McNett was brought into the Nashville group. Helms also returned and provided high, whining steel parts essential to Williams's signature sound. Fiddle player Jerry Rivers and bassist Hillous Butrum rounded out the band. McNett left in 1950 to be replaced by Sammy Pruett, and Butrum left that year to be replaced by Howard Watts, a.k.a. Cedric Rainwater. Williams disbanded the group shortly before he underwent surgery in December 1951 and worked with pickup bands thereafter. Various Drifting Cowboys, almost always under the leadership of Helms and Rivers, re-formed at times to work independently and to back RAY PRICE, HANK WILLIAMS JR., and JETT WILLIAMS. Helms (b. New Brockton, Alabama, February 18, 1927; d. August 11, 2008) went on to launch the Wil-Helm booking agency with the WILBURN BROTHERS and to record with artists including PATSY CLINE, BRENDA LEE, LORETTA LYNN, and RODNEY CROWELL, among many others. —*Colin Escott*

## Jimmy Driftwood
b. near Mountain View, Arkansas, June 20, 1907; d. July 12, 1998

Mostly known as a songwriter, James Corbett Morris was born into a family locally noted as musicians and singers. Morris's first professional experience, however, was in education. He worked as a teacher, principal, and school superintendent, having studied at John Brown University, Arkansas State Teachers College (both in Arkansas), and the University of Southern Mississippi. At the same time, he wrote songs, frequently setting original lyrics to traditional melodies. For several years he also tried to become a country recording artist, but he found no success until the folk song revival of the late 1950s.

While trying to break into the folksinger market, he adopted the name "Driftwood." (This was either a deliberate substitution by recording studio personnel or a misunderstanding of the word "Richwood," the last name Jimmy had been using, borrowed from a community in his native Stone County.) He also started playing a primitive-looking guitar made during the late 1940s by two Mountain View, Arkansas, craftsmen.

In the late 1950s, Driftwood briefly joined the GRAND OLE OPRY, but he is better known as a songwriter. Although he recorded both numbers, the most successful versions of his songs were 1959 hits by JOHNNY HORTON ("Battle of New Orleans") and EDDY ARNOLD ("Tennessee Stud"). In the late 1960s and early 1970s, Driftwood worked for the Ozark Folk Center, a complex that was the brainchild of John Opitz, a representative of the

Arkansas Office of Economic Opportunity. The center opened in 1973 and continues today. —*W. K. McNeil*

## Roy Drusky
b. Atlanta, Georgia, June 22, 1930; d. September 23, 2004

Country music has always had its crooners, whose smooth voices are devoid of any twang. With his full, mellow baritone, Roy Frank Drusky Jr. is one of the best examples. According to Drusky, music did not enter his mind until he joined the U.S. Navy and met some fellow sailors who enjoyed performing. His interest piqued, Drusky purchased a guitar and taught himself to play. After his discharge he enrolled at Emory University in his home-town of Atlanta to study veterinary medicine. To make extra money he formed the Southern Ranch Boys, began to perform around the area, and soon had his own fifteen-minute radio show on WEAS in Decatur, Georgia.

Choosing music over animal husbandry, Drusky began a recording career with STARDAY RECORDS in 1953 and moved to COLUMBIA RECORDS in 1956. Failing to hit the charts on either label, Drusky took a disc jockey position at KEVE in Minneapolis. During that tenure, his songwriting ability began to be noticed. FARON YOUNG recorded the Drusky composition "Alone with You," and the ballad spent thirteen weeks at #1 on the country charts. Young had two more notable hits with Drusky songs: "That's the Way It's Gotta Be" (#11, 1959) and "Country Girl" (#1, 1959).

In the fall of 1958, OWEN BRADLEY signed Drusky to DECCA RECORDS, and he joined the cast of the GRAND OLE OPRY in June 1959. He cowrote his first two hits, "Another" (#2, 1960) and "Anymore" (#3, 1960). After three years with Decca, Drusky moved to MERCURY RECORDS, where he stepped out of character and recorded the novelty tune "Peel Me a Nanner" (#8, 1963). In 1965 "Yes Mr. Peters," a cheating-song duet with Priscilla Mitchell (JERRY REED's wife), became his only #1 hit. Drusky continued to place records on the charts until 1977, racking up a total of forty-two chart-making discs over a seventeen-year period. —*Don Roy*

## Tim DuBois
b. Grove, Oklahoma, May 4, 1948

As the first president of ARISTA RECORDS's Nashville division, founded in 1989, Tim DuBois built his roster from scratch, begin-ning with ALAN JACKSON and quickly adding BROOKS & DUNN. Under DuBois's guidance, the label's roster grew to include DIAMOND RIO, BRAD PAISLEY, LEE ROY PARNELL, PAM TILLIS, and BlackHawk, among others.

After finishing his master's degree at Oklahoma State, DuBois moved to Texas to work as a staff auditor for Arthur Andersen & Co. and then as a senior financial analyst at the Federal Reserve Bank of Dallas. He briefly taught accounting before moving to Nashville in 1977 to further his songwriting career. By 1982 he had written three #1 hits, including ALABAMA's "Love in the First Degree" and JERRY REED's "She Got the Goldmine (I Got the Shaft)," while also working with local music publishers and teaching at local universities. DuBois convinced Los Angeles–based manage-ment firm Fitzgerald-Hartley to open a Nashville office; then in 1985 he became a partner with the firm, personally managing RESTLESS HEART, a group he helped assemble and later produced.

When VINCE GILL became a Fitzgerald-Hartley client, DuBois and Gill became occasional writing partners. Their collaboration produced Gill's #1 hit "When I Call Your Name," Song of the Year for both the CMA and the ACM in 1992.

Arista tapped DuBois to start its Nashville division in 1989. DuBois continued to produce, overseeing albums for EXILE, DIAMOND RIO, STEVE WARINER, and BlackHawk. In 1991 DuBois encouraged singer-songwriters Kix Brooks and Ronnie Dunn to write and record together and then offered them a record deal. Brooks & Dunn went on to a stellar career lasting into 2010. DuBois also urged Henry Paul, Dave Robbins, and Van Stephenson to form BlackHawk, which scored six Top Ten country singles during 1994–96.

In 1993 DuBois founded the AUSTIN, TEXAS–based offshoot Arista Texas to tap indigenous music of the Lone Star State. He founded a second Arista country label, Career Records, in 1995, and moved Parnell over to it as flagship artist. DuBois restruc-tured Arista Texas in 1997, signing singer-songwriters ROBERT EARL KEEN, Jeff Black, and Abra Moore to the renamed Arista Austin division and grouping Spanish-speaking artists in sister label Arista Latin. (Both labels were short-lived.)

In 2002 DuBois and veteran Nashville record executive TONY BROWN launched UNIVERSAL RECORDS SOUTH as a joint ven-ture with New York–based Universal Music Group. The part-ners found success with JOE NICHOLS, PHIL VASSAR, and other artists before selling their interest to Universal in 2006. A part-ner with Marc Dottore in Dottore-DuBois Artist Management, DuBois joined the Vanderbilt University faculty in 2008 as a professor in the Owen School of Management. In 2010 he became head of ASCAP's Nashville-based southern regional office. —*Jay Orr*

## Dave Dudley
b. Spencer, Wisconsin, May 3, 1928; d. December 22, 2003

Beginning in the early 1960s, Dave Dudley spearheaded the trucking-song phenomenon. Between 1963 and 1980 he hit the *Billboard* charts consistently with numbers including "Truck Drivin' Son-of-a-Gun" (#3, 1965), "There Ain't No Easy Run" (#10, 1968), and "Me and Ole C.B." (#12, 1976). Born David Darwin Pedruska, Dudley learned guitar as a child growing up in Wisconsin. His real love was baseball, however, and after high school he played on semipro teams. An arm injury retired him from the sport and turned his attention toward music. Impressing a DJ friend, Dudley landed his own radio show and band.

Just as his career was gaining momentum, Dudley was struck by a car after a performance in Minneapolis in 1960. Following a six-month recovery, he returned to the music scene, charting in 1961 with "Maybe I Do" on Vee Records. In 1963 he recorded the truck-ers' anthem "Six Days on the Road," an Earl Greene–Earl "Peanut" Montgomery song passed along to him by JIMMY C. NEWMAN. Released on the independent Golden Wing label, it took the nation by storm as a #2 country hit and a #32 pop record. MERCURY RECORDS signed Dudley later that year, and he continued his string of workingman's songs, including "Last Day in the Mines" (#7, 1964), "Viet Nam Blues" (#12, 1966), "The Pool Shark" (#1, 1970), and "If It Feels Good Do It" (#14, 1971). In 1980, the last year he charted, a German pop group called Truck Stop recorded a tribute to Dudley ("I Want to Hear More Dave Dudley"). Later he had an active career in several European countries. —*Don Roy*

## Arlie Duff

b. Jack's Branch, Texas, March 28, 1924; d. July 4, 1996

If there ever were a country music anthem, it would have to be "You All Come," written by Arleigh "Arlie" Elton Duff. (Although later recorded as "Y'all Come" by other artists, STARDAY originally released the record as "You All Come.") Duff grew up in the Big Thicket area of southeastern Texas. He was teaching school in 1953 when, after hearing LEFTY FRIZZELL on the radio, he wondered if he could write a country song. Inspired by an elderly family friend who kept repeating "Y'all come" seventeen times as she was leaving Duff's house, Duff wrote the number in twenty minutes. He met JACK STARNES of Starday Records, who shortly thereafter recorded and released Duff's version, a #7 country hit in 1954. Other artists who popularized it included Bing Crosby, BILL MONROE, and PORTER WAGONER.

Known as the Singing School Teacher, Duff toured nationally, appeared on the GRAND OLE OPRY and the *LOUISIANA HAYRIDE*, and briefly joined the *OZARK JUBILEE* ABC-TV show. He recorded for DECCA in the mid-1950s, without chart success, and then left the road to raise a family and work as a radio announcer in Colorado Springs. In 1963 he returned to Texas and worked on radio in AUSTIN for several years. In 1983 Eakin Press of Austin published his autobiography. He moved to Woodbury, Connecticut, in June 1985 and passed away while playing golf in Waterbury, Connecticut, on July 4, 1996. —*Don Roy*

## The Duke of Paducah

b. DeSoto, Missouri, May 12, 1901; d. June 20, 1986

Benjamin Francis "Whitey" Ford was a leading country comedian from the late 1930s to the mid-1950s. He had only a third-grade education and often called himself a graduate of the "University of Hard Knocks." Following four years in the U.S. Navy (1918–22), he joined a Dixieland jazz group as a banjoist, working in Arkansas and Missouri. Based in Chicago, beginning around 1929, Ford performed on WLS and eventually toured with GENE AUTRY.

In the mid-1930s, while broadcasting over St. Louis station KWK, Ford acquired his Duke of Paducah stage moniker, earlier invented by humorist Irvin S. Cobb. (Ford's nickname "Whitey" came from his blond hair.) By then he had developed his comic rube character, begun to compile an enormous library of jokes, and adopted his famous tag line, "I'm goin' back to the wagon, boys, these shoes are killin' me!" In 1937 Ford teamed with RED FOLEY and JOHN LAIR to organize THE *RENFRO VALLEY BARN DANCE*.

During the late 1930s and early '40s, Ford starred with LOUISE MASSEY & THE WESTERNERS on the NBC network radio show *Plantation Party* out of Cincinnati and Chicago before moving in 1942 to star on the GRAND OLE OPRY's NBC network segment, a role he would maintain until replaced in 1947 by ROD BRASFIELD, whom he helped to recruit. Subsequently Ford made several series of popular radio shows, some of them fed to CBS and others recorded and syndicated widely.

Ford kept working at the Opry and touring, even heading a troupe billed as the Rock and Roll Revue during the mid-1950s. Beginning in 1958 he hosted *Country Junction,* a Nashville television show that aired on WLAC-TV for a number of years. Eventually many of his jokes found their way to *HEE HAW*, whose producers bought his joke library. The remainder of his

*Whitey Ford, a.k.a. The Duke of Paducah*

substantial collection of American humor was acquired by Emory University shortly before his death. Four months after his passing, he was elected to THE COUNTRY MUSIC HALL OF FAME. —*John W. Rumble*

## Glen Duncan

b. Columbus, Indiana, May 26, 1955

Glen Carlton Duncan, BLUEGRASS fiddle player–tenor singer since 1975 and busy session player since moving to Nashville in 1983, worked on the road with major bluegrass acts BILL MONROE, JIM & JESSE, LARRY SPARKS, and THE OSBORNE BROTHERS and toured with country stars REBA MCENTIRE and BARBARA MANDRELL.

Duncan's style incorporates bluesy elements from bluegrass fiddle masters KENNY BAKER, BENNY MARTIN, and Bobby Hicks as well as melodic and swing-oriented influences of mainstream country musicians. His adaptability and technique make him a valuable session musician who has appeared on recordings by McEntire, Monroe, DOLLY PARTON, and THE STATLER BROTHERS, among many others.

With Larry Cordle, Duncan formed the bluegrass act Lonesome Standard Time in 1990, but they disbanded in 1995 when the successful group began to interfere with Duncan's recording sessions and Cordle's songwriting. (Cordle later reorganized the band.) In 1997 Duncan was a founding member of the ROUNDER RECORDS part-time supergroup *Longview*.

With EARL SCRUGGS and other musicians, Duncan shared a 2001 Grammy for Best Country Instrumental Performance, and in 2003 he performed with Scruggs as part of Scruggs's Family and Friends tour.—*Frank and Marty Godbey*

## Johnny Duncan
b. Dublin, Texas, October 5, 1938; d. August 14, 2006

Johnny Duncan is best remembered for a series of sensual 1970s hits, including "Thinkin' of a Rendezvous." A cousin of DAN SEALS and Jim Seals (of Seals & Crofts), John Richard Duncan grew up on a Texas farm near Stephenville, where his mother taught him to play guitar.

Influenced by MERLE TRAVIS, LES PAUL, and CHET ATKINS, Duncan wanted to become a professional guitarist, but as a teenager he began to consider a singing career. After college he moved to Clovis, New Mexico, in 1959, and worked with producer Norman Petty for three years. Following a brief stint as a DJ in the Southwest, Duncan moved to Nashville in 1964.

There Duncan worked as a DJ at WAGG in nearby Franklin, Tennessee, and at a series of other jobs. Performing on WSM-TV shows emceed by RALPH EMERY and BOBBY LORD, he caught the eye of COLUMBIA RECORDS executive DON LAW, who signed him in 1966. In 1967 Duncan scored his first chart single, "Hard Luck Joe." Atkins recorded his song "Summer Sunday."

A straight-ahead country singer, Duncan topped the charts with "Rendezvous" (1976), "It Couldn't Have Been Any Better" (1977), and "She Can Put Her Shoes Under My Bed (Anytime)" (1978). JANIE FRICKE provided harmony vocals on three of his hits and joined Duncan for two duets—"Come a Little Bit Closer" and "He's Out of My Life."

Following a divorce, Duncan left the music business in the early 1980s and returned to Texas to raise his three daughters. He remarried and recorded for several small labels during the 1980s and 1990s. Attempting a career comeback, Duncan released an album in 2004. Two years later he planned a fall tour but died of a heart attack on August 14, 2006. —*Gerry Wood*

## Tommy Duncan
b. Hillsboro, Texas, January 11, 1911; d. July 23, 1967

Although he had a notable career as a solo artist, Tommy Duncan's name remains inseparable from that of BOB WILLS. Duncan's warm, bluesy vocal style was one of the keys to Wills's success and a cornerstone of the Texas Playboys' sound. Duncan was also an underrated songwriter who wrote or cowrote some of the most enduring songs in the Wills repertoire, including "Time Changes Everything," "Bubbles in My Beer," and "Misery."

One of the most influential singers in country music, Thomas Elmer Duncan began—as did so many of his contemporaries—as a devotee of JIMMIE RODGERS. Duncan was singing Rodgers songs at a Fort Worth root beer stand before replacing MILTON BROWN in the LIGHT CRUST DOUGHBOYS in 1932. Duncan quickly adapted to the Doughboys' varied repertoire, but he remained in obvious thrall to Rodgers and jazzy minstrel/yodeler EMMETT MILLER.

Duncan left the Doughboys with Wills in 1933, and over the next fifteen years in Tulsa and on the West Coast (with two years lost to war service) Duncan became Wills's chief vocalist and right-hand man, maturing into an instantly recognizable WESTERN SWING crooner. Classic vocals include "Right or Wrong" (1936), "The Waltz You Saved for Me" (1938), "New San Antonio Rose" (1940), "Roly Poly" (1945), and many others.

An artist in his own right, Duncan parted with Wills in 1948 to form his Western All-Stars. He scored with Rodgers's "Gambling Polka Dot Blues" for CAPITOL in 1949 and went on to record

*Tommy Duncan*

excellent sessions for Intro, Coral, and other labels. His career in western swing faded, however, until he reteamed with Wills in 1960. "Heart to Heart Talk" proved a best-seller that year, and the three albums the pair cut for LIBERTY remained in print for years. Duncan and Wills split again in 1962, and Duncan continued to perform as a solo act until his death from a heart attack at fifty-six. —*Kevin Coffey*

## Mike Dungan
b. Cincinnati, Ohio, March 15, 1954

Mike Dungan accepted the top executive post at CAPITOL Nashville in 2000 shortly before the departure of GARTH BROOKS. Under Dungan's leadership, Capitol rebuilt its roster, focusing on developing new talent and reviving the careers of a few veteran acts.

Dungan began his music business career in 1979 as a pop promotion representative in the Midwest for RCA RECORDS. After working in sales and marketing for RCA and ARISTA RECORDS, he moved to Nashville in 1990 as head of sales and marketing for Arista's new country division. There he helped develop the careers of BROOKS & DUNN, DIAMOND RIO, ALAN JACKSON, and PAM TILLIS. Dungan became general manager of Arista Nashville in 1998, the year he signed BRAD PAISLEY to the label.

After his appointment as Capitol Nashville's president and chief executive officer, Dungan developed KEITH URBAN into a solo superstar and helped lift TRACE ADKINS and Chris Cagle to greater career heights. He signed LITTLE BIG TOWN after its initial success on an independent label and brought Hootie & the Blowfish singer DARIUS RUCKER into country music. Dungan also launched the careers of DIERKS BENTLEY, Luke Bryan, Eric Church, and LADY ANTEBELLUM. —*Michael McCall*

*Mike Dungan*

## Bob Dunn
b. Braggs, Oklahoma, February 5, 1908; d. May 27, 1971

Robert Lee Dunn's electric amplification of his steel guitar, on joining MILTON BROWN's Musical Brownies in Fort Worth in late 1934, signaled an important change in the course of country music. His January 1935 recordings with Brown were the first country discs featuring an electric string instrument, and the impact was immediate and irrevocable. Dunn, who also played trombone, aspired to be a jazz musician, and he approached the steel like a jazz horn, blaring jagged yet sophisticated, swinging phrases. In the 1930s and early '40s, his playing style helped define WESTERN SWING, especially in the Southwest.

Dunn's first love was HAWAIIAN MUSIC, but he quickly moved beyond it. He was playing professionally by 1927, and before joining Brown he had played in a variety of vaudeville groups, jazz ensembles, and STRINGBANDS. Dunn made more than ninety recordings with the Brownies before Milton Brown's death in April 1936, including his classic signature tune, "Taking Off" (1935), and then resumed a nomadic lifestyle. He played and recorded with such acts as ROY NEWMAN & HIS BOYS (1937), THE SHELTON BROTHERS (1939), and extensively—and influentially—with former Brownie CLIFF BRUNER's Texas Wanderers. Recording with Bruner intermittently between 1937 and 1940, Dunn cut such classics as "It Makes No Difference Now" and "I'll Keep On Loving You," on which he took a searing solo. Dunn also formed his own band, THE VAGABONDS, and completed several jazz-filled sessions for DECCA RECORDS.

Dunn served in the U.S. Navy during World War II and then settled in Houston and opened a music store in 1950. He taught music there extensively, but—with the exception of the occasional local gig—his playing career basically ended by the early 1950s. He retired in 1970 and died of lung cancer within weeks of selling his store. His influence, however, reverberates into the twenty-first century in the sounds of countless steel players. —*Kevin Coffey*

## Holly Dunn
b. San Antonio, Texas, August 22, 1957

Singer-songwriter Holly Suzette Dunn emerged in the mid-1980s and is known for her clear soprano vocals and folk-tinged country style.

The daughter of a Church of Christ preacher and a landscape painter, Dunn started performing in the 1970s with the Freedom Folk Singers. She graduated from Abilene Christian College in 1979 with a degree in advertising and public relations and then moved to Nashville, where her brother, Chris Waters, was already established as a songwriter and record producer. For six years she worked as a receptionist, demo singer, and staff writer, penning LOUISE MANDRELL's 1984 Top Ten single "I'm Not Through Loving You Yet" as well as other hits.

In 1984 Dunn signed with MTM Records (MTM MUSIC GROUP), earning her first Top Ten single in 1986 with "Daddy's Hands," a song she wrote as a Father's Day gift. When MTM folded in 1989, Dunn signed with WARNER BROS. RECORDS; there she released four albums, including her two-volume greatest-hits package, *Milestones*, which included the #1"You Really Had Me Going" (1990).

In 1995 Dunn moved to River North's Nashville division, recording two albums before accepting a one-year position as morning drive show cohost at WWWW-FM radio in Detroit. In 1998 she returned to Nashville to concentrate on songwriting.

Dunn's honors include ACM's 1986 Top New Female Vocalist award, CMA's 1987 Horizon Award, and BMI's 1988 Country Songwriter of the Year award. She joined the GRAND OLE OPRY on October 14, 1989.

In 2003, Dunn retired from music to pursue her interest in art, painting subjects from the American Southwest. —*Marjie McGraw*

## Hal Durham
b. McMinnville, Tennessee, August 5, 1931; d. March 28, 2009

Through thirty years as announcer, radio executive, and general manager of the GRAND OLE OPRY, Harold L. "Hal" Durham helped bring the Opry forward from its AM radio days into the modern age of satellite TV—at the same time preserving the traditions and integrity of the show.

Durham started in radio at WROL in Knoxville while attending the University of Tennessee. He graduated in 1956 with a degree in journalism, intending to be a sportswriter, but found work as an announcer at WSB in Atlanta and then as program director for a small station in McMinnville, Tennessee, in 1960. He moved to WSM in 1964 and over the next decade progressed from Opry announcer to chief announcer to program director of WSM-AM.

In early 1974, E. W. "BUD" WENDELL, WSM vice president and general manager of the Opry, appointed Durham manager of the Opry, and at that point Durham stopped announcing. He succeeded Wendell as general manager in 1978.

Durham made constant adjustments to keep the Opry relevant to current country music. He allowed a full set of drums on the stage at the new Grand Ole Opry House (previously drummers had been limited to a snare and a cymbal). He relaxed the required number of Saturday night appearances for Opry cast members, and as a result he was able to sign such superstars as GARTH BROOKS, REBA MCENTIRE, VINCE GILL, and ALAN JACKSON to Opry membership. When he brought the Opry to television audiences, first through specials on the Public Broadcasting System and later with a *Grand Ole Opry Live* segment on TNN: THE NASHVILLE NETWORK, he insisted on an as-is, "look-in" format with no changes in the longstanding radio program.

In 1993 Durham turned over Opry management to Bob Whittaker and became president of the Grand Ole Opry group, which then included the Opry, Opryland Productions, and THE RYMAN AUDITORIUM. He retired in 1996. —*Walter Carter*

## Bob Dylan's Nashville Recording Sessions

When Bob Dylan (b. Robert Allen Zimmerman, Duluth, Minnesota, May 24, 1941) recorded *Blonde on Blonde* in Nashville in 1966, he not only made one of rock's finest albums but also opened the city's doors wider for rock musicians who followed him. Local recording studios had already hosted many rock singers in the 1950s and 1960s, but most of those artists—including THE EVERLY BROTHERS, ELVIS PRESLEY, ROY ORBISON, and

*Bob Dylan*

BRENDA LEE—had strong country music ties. Dylan's Nashville success beckoned rockers of all stripes.

*Blonde on Blonde* was recorded at COLUMBIA's studio, in the heart of MUSIC ROW. Work had originally begun on the project at the company's New York studios, with an exhaustive number of hours being spent and precious little to show for the effort. Columbia producer BOB JOHNSTON first invited Nashville session man CHARLIE MCCOY, then playing a New York gig, to assist on a session. After meeting McCoy, Dylan followed Johnston's suggestion to try a change of scenery.

From February to March 1966, the Nashville-based Johnston assembled some of the Row's top studio professionals: McCoy, HARGUS "PIG" ROBBINS, JERRY KENNEDY, HENRY STRZELECKI, KENNY BUTTREY, Bill Aikens, JOE SOUTH, Wayne Moss, and (uncredited on the album) Mac Gayden. Robbie Robertson of the Band and keyboardist Al Kooper also played on the sessions. They logged more than forty hours in the studio, then an enormously long period by Nashville standards. But the record's artistic and commercial acceptance more than justified the expense: Dylan's two-disc set climbed to #9 on *Billboard*'s country album charts and yielded three singles that made the pop charts: "I Want You," "Just Like a Woman," and "Rainy Day Women #12 & 35" (a #2 hit). Shortly after completing the album, Dylan crashed his motorcycle in Woodstock, New York. For nearly two years he avoided the limelight.

With his second Nashville album, *John Wesley Harding*—in stark contrast to his previous efforts—Dylan made a sharp turn back to his earthier days. Gone were the familiar heavy Hammond B-3 organ and such creative touches as Salvation Army–styled horns. In fall 1967 Dylan and Johnston brought McCoy and Buttrey into Nashville's Columbia studio. (PETE DRAKE's steel guitar can also be heard on two tracks.) They cut a scaled-back, acoustically dominated album, which peaked at #2 country. Among the songs cut and mixed during the six-hour session were "All Along the Watchtower," "The Ballad of Frankie Lee and Judas Priest," and "I'll Be Your Baby Tonight."

Dylan began his next Nashville project, *Nashville Skyline*, in February 1968, intending to record what he thought was a straight country record. Session personnel included keyboardist Bob Wilson and multi-instrumentalists CHARLIE DANIELS and Norman Blake. Friend and Columbia Records label mate JOHNNY CASH (who won a Grammy for the album's liner notes) sang a duet with Dylan on the selection "Girl from the North Country." Reported to have had only four songs ready for the sessions, Dylan is said to have written the remaining seven in his Nashville hotel room. The album went #3 country but failed to yield any country chart singles, though "Lay Lady Lay" was a #7 pop hit.

Dylan returned in 1969 and 1970 to record a portion of his covers album, *Self Portrait*, using many of the same musicians as on *Nashville Skyline,* and adding guitarist Fred Carter Jr. and fiddler Doug Kershaw on several cuts.

Money couldn't buy the publicity Dylan's Nashville sessions garnered, and soon numerous rock artists followed his path to MUSIC CITY. —*Chris Skinker*

## The Eagles

Bernie Leadon b. Minneapolis, Minnesota, July 19, 1947
Glenn Frey b. Detroit, Michigan, November 6, 1948
Randy Meisner b. Scottsbluff, Nebraska, March 8, 1946
Don Henley b. Gilmer, Texas, July 22, 1947
Don Felder b. Gainesville, Florida, September 21, 1947
Joe Walsh b. Wichita, Kansas, November 20, 1947
Timothy B. Schmit b. Sacramento, California, October 30, 1947

Formed in 1971 to back singer LINDA RONSTADT on tour, the Eagles capitalized on groundwork laid by others with their easy-listening COUNTRY-ROCK. Glenn Frey had sung backup on Bob Seger's "Ramblin' Gamblin' Man"; Bernie Leadon had been in pioneering country-rock groups Hearts & Flowers, Dillard & Clark, and the Flying Burrito Brothers; Don Henley had been in Shiloh; and Randy Meisner had been in POCO and RICK NELSON's Stone Canyon Band.

The Eagles became one of rock's most popular acts and the most successful country-rock act to date. On ASYLUM RECORDS they enjoyed many hit singles, and each album went platinum. Their self-titled debut from June 1972 yielded three Top Forty pop singles: "Take It Easy," "Witchy Woman," and "Peaceful Easy Feeling," smoothly harmonized recordings that defined the band's style for some time. Their second album, *Desperado*, told the story of the Old West's demise, but while *Desperado* has stood the test of time artistically, sales did not match their debut. Bill Szymczyk produced the third album, *On the Border*, on which slide guitarist Don Felder provided more of a rock sound. In 1974–75 the group notched its first #1 pop hit with the acoustic ballad "Best of My Love." The same team made *One of These Nights* in 1975, a #1 pop album for five weeks. The new direction proved too much for BLUEGRASS fan Bernie Leadon, and he was replaced by hard-rock guitarist Joe Walsh.

The Eagles hit their commercial stride with 1977's *Hotel California*. Singles "New Kid in Town" and the title track topped *Billboard*'s pop charts. Randy Meisner left in late 1977, replaced by Poco's Timothy B. Schmit, who had previously replaced Meisner in Poco.

*The Long Run* (1979) reached #1 and remained there for nine weeks. *Eagles Live* followed in 1980. The band then dissolved, having been largely inactive that year. Henley and Frey, in particular, went on to strong solo success.

*The Eagles: (from left) Glenn Frey,*
*Don Felder, Don Henley, Joe Walsh,*
*and Timothy B. Schmidt*

In 1993 the smash-hit, multiartist country tribute album *Common Thread: The Songs of the Eagles* underscored the group's strong influence on 1990s country. The band reunited for a successful tour in 1994 and released *Hell Freezes Over*, an album of live tracks and studio material. They were elected to the Rock and Roll Hall of Fame in 1998, and, though Felder left in 2001 amid internal legal wrangles, the act kept touring on occasion. In 2007 the Eagles released *Long Road Out of Eden* on their own label and toured North America and Europe during 2008–09 to support the album. —*Sid Griffin*

## Jim Eanes
b. Mountain Valley, Virginia, December 6, 1923; d. November 21, 1995

Although he frequently recorded in a country setting, Homer Robert Eanes Jr. (a.k.a. Jim Eanes) is better known as one of BLUEGRASS music's great baritone leads.

After a prewar apprenticeship with ROY HALL & HIS BLUE RIDGE ENTERTAINERS, Eanes worked with the Blue Mountain Boys, FLATT & SCRUGGS, and BILL MONROE before launching a solo career in 1949. Settling in Martinsville, Virginia, in February 1951, Eanes organized the Shenandoah Valley Boys for appearances on the WWVA JAMBOREE. Regional bluegrass hits on the RICH-R-TONE and Blue Ridge labels led to a DECCA contract in January 1952. Decca issued fourteen singles during the next four years; many were country sides using Nashville session musicians, but several were bluegrass and featured Hubert Davis on banjo, such as "Plunkin' Rag," "Possum Hollow," and "Ridin' the Waves."

Disbanding his group in 1955, Eanes became a disc jockey on WHEE, Martinsville, Virginia; he remained with the station for eleven years. When STARDAY RECORDS offered him a contract in 1956, Eanes assembled a new Shenandoah Valley Boys with banjo player Allen Shelton, fiddler Roy Russell, and bassist Arnold Terry. Considered one of bluegrass music's classic bands, this group continued into 1964 with minor personnel changes.

In 1967 Eanes briefly fronted the Shenandoah Cut-Ups on the *WWVA Jamboree*. He continued recording bluegrass and country music for various labels into the early 1990s.

His compositions include "Baby Blue Eyes," "Your Old Standby," "Wiggle Worm Wiggle," and "I Wouldn't Change You If I Could." —*Dave Samuelson*

## Steve Earle
b. Fort Monroe, Virginia, January 17, 1955

Steve Earle rose to stardom in the mid-1980s with a smart, gritty, new traditionalist brand of COUNTRY-ROCK that crossed over to pop radio. With sharply observed songs such as "Guitar Town," "Someday," and "Good Ol' Boy (Gettin' Tough)," he raised the artistic stakes in Nashville. But Earle foundered into the gray area between pop and country and then into a grayer period in his personal life. He went to prison on a drug charge, only to reemerge in 1995 clean, sober, and artistically recharged.

Raised outside San Antonio, Stephen F. Earle dropped out of high school in 1973 and began working the coffeehouse circuit, emulating idols TOWNES VAN ZANDT and GUY CLARK. He arrived in Nashville in the mid-1970s and was soon churning out songs for other artists. He issued some ROCKABILLY-tinged singles on an independent label and then signed with EPIC, which put out several singles but declined to release an album. Earle then signed

*Steve Earle*

with MCA and in 1986 became a critical darling and cultural phenomenon with *Guitar Town*. But after the less successful *Exit O* (1987), he veered toward rock with *Copperhead Road* in 1989. As an MCA pop artist handled from Los Angeles, he disappeared from country radio. *The Hard Way* and *Shut Up and Die Like an Aviator* completed his transition to loud, metallic arena rock.

Earle's always-turbulent personal life caught up with him after MCA dropped him in 1991. Following numerous Nashville arrests for cocaine and heroin possession he was finally jailed, though he was soon transferred to a rehabilitation center. Meanwhile, MUSIC ROW, previously turned off by Earle's irascible personality and hard-to-categorize music, rediscovered one of its most original artists. His publisher, Warner/Chappell Music, issued an industry-only disc called *Uncut Gems*, in hopes that country stars might cover some of the tunes Earle had penned during his song peddling days.

Post-rehab, Earle launched a comeback. With the folksy *Train A Comin'* (Winter Harvest, 1995) Earle returned to his troubadour roots, finally recording songs he'd written in the 1970s as well as dark, ominous songs he'd penned while strung out and pursuing a new record deal in Nashville. By 1998 he had formed his own E-Squared label, released two rock records, *I Feel Alright* and *El Corazon*, and contributed a song to the soundtrack of the Susan Sarandon–Sean Penn film *Dead Man Walking* (1995). An album made with DEL MCCOURY followed in 1999. Two years later Earle released *Transcendental Blues* on E-Squared and contributed to *Poet: A Tribute to Townes Van Zandt*. Earle has strongly opposed American intervention in Iraq and Afghanistan; 2002's *Jerusalem* featured his controversial "John Walker's Blues," about a young American reviled as a traitor for serving with the Taliban. Earle's anti-war *The Revolution Starts . . . Now* (Artemis/E-Squared, 2004) won a Grammy for Best Contemporary Folk Album. In 2006 he signed with New West Records, which released the Grammy-winning *Washington Square Serenade* in 2007, not long after he moved to New York City. The label released *Townes*, on which Earle covers Townes Van Zandt songs, in May 2009.

In addition to his musical accomplishments, Earle is a radio host, playwright, essayist, short story writer, and actor. He married singer Allison Moorer in 2005. —*Mark Schone*

## East Texas Serenaders

This influential STRINGBAND comprised a variety of musicians who came from the area around Mineola, Lindale, and Garden Valley, Texas. Its core cadre of performers included left-handed fiddler Daniel Huggins Williams (b. September 13, 1900; d. June 1974), guitarist Cloet Hammons (b. May 4, 1899; d. July 1982), cello player Henry Bogan, and banjoist John Munnerlyn. The group evolved from an earlier fiddle band headed by Will Hammons (Cloet's father), which played at house parties and other social functions after 1910. The Serenaders, who actually did go from house to house giving unexpected performances at night, stayed close to home and never played any farther away than Dallas, about a hundred miles distant. In fact, their only regular gig, at the Ashby Cafe in Tyler, lasted only a few months.

Although they made a number of prized recordings, from 1927 to 1930 and in 1937, they never gave up their day jobs and instead lived out their lives as farmers and craftsmen. Nevertheless, their influence has extended far beyond East Texas and beyond their own time because of their superb recordings for BRUNSWICK (1928–30) and DECCA (1937). Williams was a much-admired fiddler whose work affected musicians such as Buddy Brady, Red Hayes, and JOHNNY GIMBLE, who learned techniques and tunes from him. Because of their wide-ranging repertoire, which included ragtime, blues, waltzes, and breakdowns, the Serenaders pointed the way toward WESTERN SWING. —*Bill C. Malone*

## Ray Edenton
b. Mineral, Virginia, November 3, 1926

Ray Quarles Edenton was one of those Nashville studio musicians whose rhythm playing seldom stood out on records but whose subtle skills made him an essential contributor to hundreds of hits from the 1950s through the 1970s. As a boy he began performing on radio programs in Virginia and Maryland before World War II and after returning from the army in 1946. Edenton then served as bassist with guitarist JOE MAPHIS in the Korn Krackers at the WRVA *OLD DOMINION BARN DANCE* in Richmond. In 1949 Edenton began working at WNOX in Knoxville.

After a two-year convalescence from tuberculosis, Edenton moved to Nashville in 1952 and started playing acoustic rhythm guitar on the GRAND OLE OPRY. His first sessions came in 1953. Since few Nashville artists were recording with drums, Edenton's style, emulating a snare drum, impressed many producers. One of the first hits reflecting his efforts was the KITTY WELLS–RED FOLEY hit duet "One By One." Though he rarely soloed, Edenton did play the memorable electric guitar lead on MARTY ROBBINS's 1956 hit "Singin' the Blues."

The arrival of rock & roll briefly reduced Edenton's studio work. However, along with CHET ATKINS and HANK GARLAND, he became an integral part of THE EVERLY BROTHERS' recorded sound. Edenton joined Don Everly in playing the hard-strummed acoustic rhythm guitar on crossover hits such as "Wake Up Little Susie" and "Bye Bye Love." His contributions to the duo's records increased his session calls, and after Garland's disabling 1961 accident, Edenton became part of the triumvirate of Nashville

guitar players who worked countless recording dates together. Garland had specialized in jazz leads, a role that HAROLD BRADLEY resumed after Garland's accident. GRADY MARTIN played funkier solos, and Edenton moved into Bradley's former spot handling rhythm guitar chores. Edenton's rhythm playing, though nuanced, long made him a key member of Nashville's studio A-team. He retired in 1991. —*Rich Kienzle*

## Edison Records
established in West Orange, New Jersey, April 24, 1878; ended November 1, 1929

Although initially established as the Edison Speaking Phonograph Company in 1878, Thomas Alva Edison's firm began in earnest in 1888, when the inventor belatedly began to exploit his 1877 creation in partnership with businessman Jesse Lippincott and his North American Phonograph Company.

The earliest phonographs, aimed at the business community, could both record and reproduce sound. In 1889 and 1890, German manufacturers made tiny machines for talking dolls; U.S. companies built larger phonographs for amusement arcades and public exhibitions. The 1890s saw a slowly developing market for home phonograph entertainment, which ultimately proved to be the primary direction the industry would take.

Edison preferred the cylinder medium, even as disc records became dominant after 1900. He continued to manufacture cylinders until leaving the business in 1929, two years before his death. He did make disc records and phonographs in 1912 and thereafter, but they were of an unconventional design incompatible with competing media.

Edison made some country records in the 1920s. He encountered some fiddlers (Allen Sisson, Jasper Bisbee, and John Baltzell) through his friendship with industrialist Henry Ford, who sponsored a number of fiddle contests. VERNON DALHART's influential "Wreck of the Old 97" was first recorded for Edison, though it was the singer's re-recording for the Victor Talking Machine Company that became a best-seller. ERNEST V. STONEMAN and fellow musicians from GALAX, VIRGINIA, recorded frequently for Edison between 1926 and 1928. —*Dick Spottswood*

## Don Edwards
b. Boonton, New Jersey, March 20, 1939

Singer-songwriter Don Edwards, whose voice is often compared to that of MARTY ROBBINS, is one of the most popular contemporary performers of COWBOY and WESTERN SWING music. Growing up in New Jersey, he was enthralled by the cowboy mystique, and in 1958 he moved to Texas, where he sang at Six Flags Over Texas (1960–1964) and made his first recording, "The Young Ranger." A well-known Houston-area performer, he eventually released several albums on his own SevenShoux label, one of which, *Chant of the Wanderer*, won a Western Heritage Wrangler Award from the Cowboy Hall of Fame in 1991. Edwards has also penned a number of fine western songs, including "The Chant of the Night Songs" and "Horses" (both 1986).

Edwards was one of the first artists signed to the Warner Western label, which released three of his albums through 1996. Subsequently he has recorded for Shanachie (1997–2004) and Western Jubilee (since 2006). He has also appeared on television programs such as *Austin City Limits*, acted in films (*The Ghost Whisperer*), and has become a mainstay of the cowboy poetry and music scene, appearing at gatherings and festivals throughout the West. In 2005 he was elected to the Western Music Association Hall of Fame, and in 2008 he received a Lifetime Achievement Award from the American Cowboy Culture Association. —*Charlie Seemann*

## John Edwards
b. Sydney, Australia, July 22, 1932; d. December 24, 1960

Although he never set foot outside Australia, John Kenneth Fielder Edwards assembled one of the world's finest collections of early country and folk music. In so doing, he contributed significantly to the preservation and presentation of American vernacular music, particularly to that branch he designated as "Golden Age hillbilly recordings."

Raised in an educated professional family, Edwards moved against the grain of musical taste expected in Australian formal society. At age thirteen he heard CARTER FAMILY songs on a New South Wales radio station. A year later he began playing the guitar as well as seeking OLD-TIME songs and STRINGBAND instrumentals from the American South, then available on the Australian Regal Zonophone label. In 1948 Edwards started work in Sydney's Transport Department as a tram roster officer. He amassed an enormous 78-rpm disc library, initially by purchase in Australia and later by indefatigable correspondence with collectors and performers in the United States. Enthralled by Appalachian song lore rooted 10,000 miles from his home, he transcended global barriers by writing regularly for discographical journals in New Zealand, England, and America. Essentially he took country music seriously, although he found it difficult to accept Nashville's growth from bedrock tradition to pop-media success. Listening to his beloved music, Edwards sensed its links to other facets of expressive culture: JIMMIE RODGERS to Geoffrey Chaucer, BUELL KAZEE to John Donne, DORSEY DIXON to Herman Melville.

In a note written in late 1958, Edwards left instructions that in the event of his death his collection of more than 2,000 discs, reel-to-reel tapes, SONGBOOKS, photographs, and letters was to be sent to his American friend Eugene Earle "to be used for the furtherance of serious study, recognition, appreciation, and preservation of genuine country and hillbilly music." After Edwards's death in an auto accident, Eugene Earle, Ed Kahn, Archie Green, and friends formed the John Edwards Memorial Foundation (now Forum) to preserve his vast trove of recordings and related materials. Initially housed at the University of California, Los Angeles, since 1986 those materials have formed part of the Southern Folklife Collection of the University of North Carolina at Chapel Hill. —*Archie Green*

## Stoney Edwards
b. near Seminole, Oklahoma, December 24, 1929; d. April 5, 1997

During the 1970s, Frenchy "Stoney" Edwards was second only to CHARLEY PRIDE in commercial prominence as an African American star in country music. Born into a large, dysfunctional family in rural Depression-era Oklahoma, Edwards was forced into the role of caretaker for three younger siblings after his parents abandoned their children; he never attended school and never learned to read or write. Because of his mixed-race background

*Stoney Edwards*

(African American, Irish, and Native American), Edwards experienced constant discrimination. Yet he found he could gain a measure of social acceptance by performing country music. His first exposure to the music involved witnessing his bootlegger uncles' STRINGBAND MUSIC; on radio he listened to BOB WILLS out of Tulsa ("every day at twelve o'clock") and the GRAND OLE OPRY from Nashville. Edwards not only began to perform country music for those who would listen but also began to compose his own country songs.

In the early 1950s Edwards moved to Richmond, California, where he married and began a long stint as a manual laborer, performing only occasionally. In the late 1960s, unable to continue as a laborer because of a near-fatal work-related accident, Edwards focused on music. He wrote new songs and began to perform again. In 1970, while appearing at a benefit concert for Wills, who had suffered a recent stroke, Edwards was discovered by a local lawyer, who encouraged Edwards to make a demo. CAPITOL RECORDS, recognizing his singing and songwriting talents and noting Charley Pride's emergence as a country music star, signed Edwards to a recording contract. Five albums and a dozen chart singles for the label ensued, including "She's My Rock" (1972), later a #1 hit for GEORGE JONES, and "Hank and Lefty Raised My Country Soul" (1973), a tribute to country greats HANK WILLIAMS and LEFTY FRIZZELL. After his run with Capitol ended in 1977, Edwards went on to record for JMI, Music America, and Boot. —*Ted Olson*

## Elektra Records
established in New York, New York, 1950

An eclectic folk and rock label founded by Jac Holzman and Paul Rickholt in 1950, Elektra opened a Nashville office in 1973. The company's success with pop acts including the Doors, Bread, and Carly Simon helped fund the MUSIC CITY operation; after several years of instability in the organization, JIMMY BOWEN took charge of the Nashville office late in 1978.

By then the label had already established a country track record. In 1976 EDDIE RABBITT launched his string of thirty-four Top Tens (seventeen of them #1 records), including three crossover smashes, the biggest being 1981's "I Love a Rainy Night." In 1979 HANK WILLIAMS JR. made his big breakthrough with "Family Tradition," coproduced by Bowen. MEL TILLIS, signed in 1979, contributed seven Top Tens, most notably "Southern Rains" (#1). CONWAY TWITTY came aboard in 1981, racking up three #1s, including "Slow Hand," a cover of the Pointer Sisters' pop hit. Those four artists contributed the bulk of Elektra's country Top Tens and virtually all of the label's #1 country hits.

VERN GOSDIN made a comeback at Elektra between 1976 and 1979, while JERRY LEE LEWIS delivered his last major hits, including 1981's "Thirty Nine and Holding." Elektra also issued MELBA MONTGOMERY's #1 hit "No Charge" (1974), released Rabbitt and CRYSTAL GAYLE's pop crossover duet hit "You and I" (1982), and enjoyed moderate success with EDDY RAVEN, THE GLASER BROTHERS, THE WHITES, and Stella Parton.

Elektra's country division was folded into the WARNER BROS. Nashville operation in 1983, with Bowen taking over; many acts were dropped, but Hank Williams Jr. and Conway Twitty remained.

Eventually Elektra was made a subsidiary of ATLANTIC RECORDS and then shuttered in 2004. Atlantic revived it in June 2009, and the label is active again, though not in the country field. —*John Lomax III*

## Joe Ely
b. Amarillo, Texas, February 9, 1947

Nationally, Earle R. "Joe" Ely is far from a household name, but he is the uncrowned king of Texas roadhouse rock & roll. His career is proof that it's possible to maintain a regional musical identity despite the homogenization of the mass media.

In the early 1970s, Ely joined fellow singer-songwriters JIMMIE DALE GILMORE and BUTCH HANCOCK to form the critically acclaimed country-folk group THE FLATLANDERS. Based in Lubbock, Texas, the band recorded an album for SHELBY SINGLETON's Plantation label in Nashville in 1972. (The album was later released on ROUNDER RECORDS in 1990.) In 1974, Ely organized his own band with lead guitarist Jesse Taylor and PEDAL STEEL GUITAR player Lloyd Maines. Signed by MCA Nashville, Ely and his band brought a distinctively Texas approach to COUNTRY-ROCK and opened tours for acts ranging from MERLE HAGGARD to the Clash. Ely's self-titled 1977 album was a critical success, and *Rolling Stone* listed *Honky Tonk Masquerade* (1978), featuring songs by Hancock and Gilmore as well as Ely, as one of the decade's best albums.

MCA dropped Ely in 1984 following the critical and commercial failure of *Hi-Res*, a venture into techno-pop. He did not record again until 1987 (for HIGHTONE), but Ely's reputation grew, especially after AUSTIN guitar-slinger David Grissom joined Ely's tight, exciting rock & roll act.

In 1991, MCA vice president TONY BROWN re-signed Ely, saying the singer could record "real" rock & roll without the pressure to cut a hit. *Love and Danger* featured two gems penned by fellow Texan ROBERT EARL KEEN: "Whenever Kindness Fails" and "The Road Goes on Forever." 1995's *Letter to Laredo* was an ambitious acoustic affair in which flamenco guitar meets DOBRO and accordion to create gypsy-cowboy border music. *Twistin' in*

*Joe Ely*

*the Wind* (1998) and *Live at Antone's* (2000) preceded MCA "best of" releases in 2000 and 2004. *Streets of Sin* appeared on Rounder in 2003. During 2007–08 Ely released three albums on the Rack 'Em label.

Ely reunited with the Flatlanders for albums in 2002, 2004, and 2009. Like this group, Ely has enjoyed the support of the AMERICANA community, receiving the Americana Music Association's Lifetime Achievement Award for Performance in 2007. As of 2010 he had reunited with his hard-rocking band of the late 1980s and early 1990s, featuring David Grissom on guitar, Jimmy Pettit on bass, and Davis McLarty on drums. —*Rick Mitchell*

## Ralph Emery
b. McEwen, Tennessee, March 10, 1933

Walter Ralph Emery is the most famous radio and TV personality in country music history. From 1972 to 1991 he hosted the live, weekday *Ralph Emery Show*, aired over WSM-TV to Nashville-area audiences. He hosted the enormously popular TNN prime-time talk show *NASHVILLE NOW* from 1983 to 1993. He also hosted the syndicated *Pop Goes the Country* (1974–80) and the TBS network's *Nashville Alive* (1981–82) and served briefly as a GRAND OLE OPRY announcer.

Once dubbed "the Johnny Carson of Cable," Emery displayed a relaxed, low-key informality that endeared him to audiences and on-air guests. A longtime friend of many stars, he has been a comfortable and reassuring presence for country artists and fans across the nation.

*Ralph Emery*

For all his poise and confidence, Emery had a troubled early life. Happy times with grandparents punctuated turmoil resulting from an alcoholic father, a cold stepfather, and a mother who suffered a nervous breakdown after years of struggling to feed her family.

After his parents divorced, Emery worked at various odd jobs and studied broadcasting under Nashville broadcasting legend John R (John Richbourg) before landing a string of postings at low-wattage stations, including WTPR in Paris, Tennessee; WNAH in Nashville; and WAGG in nearby Franklin, Tennessee. Experience at Nashville's WSIX and WSIX-TV, WLCS radio in Baton Rouge, and Nashville radio station WMAK preceded a weeknight graveyard slot—10 p.m. to 3 a.m.—on Music City's 50,000-watt WSM, home of the Grand Ole Opry. Emery, who began at WSM in 1957, turned an oft-dreaded job into an art form with his open-house policy. Established and aspiring recording artists would often drop by his *Opry Star Spotlight* show to chat, drink coffee, and play their latest records.

Emery made a few recordings himself, though he has always acknowledged his limited singing talents. "Hello Fool," a sequel of sorts to the Faron Young hit "Hello Walls," became a #4 country hit on Liberty Records in 1961. In the 1960s Emery also appeared in several B-movies, including *The Road to Nashville*, *Country Music on Broadway*, and *The Girl from Tobacco Road*.

A self-described workaholic whose four marriages include a brief union with singer Skeeter Davis (1960–64), Emery scaled back somewhat in the 1990s, though he still made radio appearances and hosted occasional TV specials produced through his own company. In 1991 his autobiography (written with Tom Carter), *Memories*, became a national best-seller and led to a second memoir, *More Memories* (1993). *The View from Nashville* and *50 Years Down a Country Road* followed in 1998 and 2000, respectively.

In 2005 Emery launched a weekly webcast titled *The Nashville Show*, featuring puppet Shotgun Red as cohost. Two years later he was back on television with his *Ralph Emery Live* interview show, carried by the RFD cable network. Emery has also offered his immense collection of past interviews for sale as a set of forty-six audio CDs and two DVDs.

"I've always tried to bring respect to country music," Emery has said. In bringing dignity to his craft for more than fifty years, he has done just that. Emery was honored with election to The Country Music Hall of Fame in 2007. —*Bob Allen*

## Buddy Emmons
b. Mishawaka, Indiana, January 27, 1937

After Little Jimmy Dickens brought him to Nashville in 1955, Buddy Gene Emmons became one of country music's busiest and most influential steel guitarists. On recordings, he has backed artists ranging from Linda Ronstadt and Ray Charles to a host of country stars, and he has graced the road bands of acclaimed acts, including Dickens, Ernest Tubb, Ray Price, Roger Miller, and The Everly Brothers. A musical pioneer, Emmons was one of the first session men to play pedal steel guitar—and one of the first to design his own signature model.

Raised in South Bend, Indiana, Emmons first encountered the steel guitar when he and his father heard Hank Williams's steel player, Don Helms, on the Grand Ole Opry. Emmons's parents soon bought him a steel, and he was working locally by age fourteen. At sixteen he headed to Calumet City, Illinois, to play honky-tonks and strip joints. He moved to Kennett, Missouri, where Carl Smith heard him and then recommended him to Webb Pierce. When a job with Pierce didn't materialize, Emmons moved to Detroit. There he sat in with Little Jimmy Dickens for a night, and when Dickens offered him a job, Emmons moved to Nashville.

Known for his clearly articulated playing and strong-but-smooth approach, Emmons contributed greatly to landmark records such as Faron Young's "Sweet Dreams" (1956) and Ray Price's "Night Life" (1963), which features Emmons's jazz-inflected, bluesy intro and solo. For Price's 1963 single "You Took Her Off My Hands (Now Please Take Her Off My Mind)" Emmons added F-sharp and E-flat "chromatic" strings to the E-9th tuning, thus facilitating what he called a "scale sound." (These strings are now included in standard ten-string steel tuning.) A longtime jazz lover, Emmons recorded his *Steel Guitar Jazz* in New York in 1963 with a group of respected jazz players. All the while Emmons was experimenting with pedal steel design, having collaborated with Shot Jackson in a venture called Sho-Bud Guitars that preceded Emmons's marketing of his own namesake model.

Emmons worked the road with the Everlys for most of the 1990s. He continued to record until an injury to his right thumb and wrist (due to repetitive motion) temporarily sidelined him early in the new century. After recovering, he limited his session work to selected artists and continued to appear at steel guitar shows. He was elected to the Steel Guitar Hall of Fame in 1981. —*Daniel Cooper and Robert Kramer*

## Melvin Endsley
b. Drasco, Arkansas, January 30, 1934; d. August 16, 2004

Blending country and pop themes with simple, catchy melodies, Melvin Endsley became one of the most commercially astute songwriters of the 1950s. His biggest hit was "Singing the Blues," although he wrote several other hits and was a recording artist, albeit an unsuccessful one, for twenty years.

Endsley contracted polio when he was three, which left him with a withered right arm and confined to a wheelchair for life. He became interested in music in the Memphis Crippled Childrens' Hospital (inspired by local broadcasts by WAYNE RANEY and the DELMORE BROTHERS) and began writing songs after he returned to Arkansas. He wrote "Singing the Blues" in 1954, and in July 1955 he took it to Nashville. Backstage at the GRAND OLE OPRY, he pitched the song to MARTY ROBBINS. After Robbins's recording became a crossover hit in 1956, Endsley became an in-demand songwriter. "Love Me to Pieces" was recorded by Jill Corey and JANIS MARTIN; Robbins and Guy Mitchell had hits with "Knee Deep in the Blues"; Andy Williams covered "I Like Your Kind of Love," and THE BROWNS covered "I'd Just Be Fool Enough," the latter two first recorded by Endsley himself for RCA during his two-year stint (1957–58) with the label.

Endsley also recorded for MGM (1959), HICKORY (1960–61), and intermittently for his own Mel-Ark label. His last major hit was STONEWALL JACKSON's "Why I'm Walkin'" (1960). —Colin Escott

## Epic Records
established in New York, New York, 1953; Nashville office established in 1963

Formed in 1953 as a COLUMBIA subsidiary, Epic Records established a Nashville beachhead in 1963. Always a "weak sister" to Columbia, Epic never had a distinct identity on MUSIC ROW, and although the label counted prominent executives including BILLY SHERRILL, George Richey, and BOB MONTGOMERY, it never had a truly independent staff. Nevertheless, Epic made important contributions to Nashville and country music.

Epic's earliest notable country act was DAVID HOUSTON (1963–76), who achieved virtually all his success with the company. JIM & JESSE (1964–70) recorded some of their finest BLUEGRASS work for the label. CHARLIE WALKER scored two Top Tens between 1964 and 1971, but Epic didn't hit its stride until CHARLIE RICH (1968–81), Tommy Cash (1969–73), and TAMMY WYNETTE (1966–93) joined Houston and Walker in giving the label a consistent chart presence.

Along with Wynette and Rich, Epic's stalwarts of the 1970s were GEORGE JONES (1971–90), JOHNNY PAYCHECK (1968–83), JODY MILLER (1970–1979), BOB LUMAN (1968–77), and JOE STAMPLEY (1975–86). The label also tried to engineer country-crossover hits for pop acts Bobby Vinton, Tom Jones, and Engelbert Humperdinck, with moderate success.

During the late 1970s and 1980s, Epic's new stars included MICKEY GILLEY (1978–87), CHARLY McCLAIN (1976–88), RONNIE McDOWELL (1979–86), JOHNNY RODRIGUEZ (1978–86), and, especially, the million-selling CHARLIE DANIELS Band (1976–91), an act signed out of New York.

Other Epic hit makers of the 1980s were MERLE HAGGARD (1981–90), EXILE (1983–89), and RICKY SKAGGS (1981–92). But the company failed commercially with STEVE EARLE (1983–85), Pam Rose (1980), Russell Smith (1989), ASLEEP AT THE WHEEL

(1987–88), LINDA DAVIS (1988–89), JIM LAUDERDALE (1988), and SHELBY LYNNE (1988–1992). HONKY-TONK master GENE WATSON (1985–87) fared only moderately well, and veterans BILLY SWAN (1981–83), WAYLON JENNINGS (1990–91), and CONNIE SMITH (1985) stayed only briefly.

In the 1990s Epic found star power with acts such as PATTY LOVELESS, JOE DIFFIE, DOUG STONE, and COLLIN RAYE. In addition to Loveless, principal hit makers of the new century included GRETCHEN WILSON and MIRANDA LAMBERT. Epic's ownership had passed to SONY MUSIC in 1988 (along with Columbia), and to Sony BMG in 2004. Sony BMG shuttered Epic and combined it with Columbia in May 2006. —Robert K. Oermann

## Esmereldy
b. Memphis, Tennessee, June 1, 1913; d. March 29, 1999

Known as "The Streamlined Hillbilly," blond Esmereldy became a country headliner of the 1940s as a radio, disc, and film personality.

Born Laverne Eloise Sherrill, she was raised in Memphis, where she began her radio career at age eight on WMC. She moved to New York, married pop singer Harry Boersma, and sang with Zeke Manners, ELTON BRITT (both formerly of THE BEVERLY HILL BILLIES), and Jones & Hare (the Happiness Boys). In 1941 and 1944 Esmereldy became one of the earliest country acts to make "soundies," film shorts that were the precursors of music videos.

Instrumental in popularizing country music in New York, she became a pioneering female country disc jockey when she hosted her own show on WNBC during World War II. She was also a regular on NBC's Mirth & Madness radio program and an early country act on New York television. Esmereldy's first records appeared in the Musicraft label's "Authentic Hillbilly Ballads" series in 1947. She scored a Top Ten hit with 1948's comedic "Slap 'Er Down Agin', Paw," billed as "Esmereldy and Her Novelty Band." She also recorded for MGM.

In the 1950s she returned to Memphis to appear on WHBQ's daily Tennessee Jamboree (carried on the Mutual Radio Network) and her own DJ show.

Daughter Amy Holland became a pop recording artist in the 1980s. —Robert K. Oermann

## John Esposito (see Warner Bros./Reprise Records)

## Milton Estes
b. Arthur, Tennessee, May 9, 1914; d. August 23, 1963

Milton Esco Estes came to the GRAND OLE OPRY in 1937 as a featured performer with PEE WEE KING's Golden West Cowboys. An accomplished musician (guitar, bass, mandolin, piano) and superb master of ceremonies, he left King in 1941 to lead STAMPS-BAXTER's Lone Star Quartet at radio stations throughout the South. By 1946 Estes had returned to WSM and the Opry as the Old Flour Peddler and formed a band called the Musical Millers to promote MARTHA WHITE FLOUR. Band members included frontman Jimmy Selph and sidemen Oral "Curly" Rhodes, TOMMY JACKSON, Clell "Cousin Jody" Summey, and DALE POTTER. Estes worked as many as twenty-six live WSM radio shows weekly, including the weekday *Noontime Neighbors* with OWEN BRADLEY's orchestra. Estes also appeared on the Opry's NBC radio segment and became a familiar voice, calling Opry square dances.

Among the recordings Estes made for DECCA between 1947 and 1950 were "Whoa Sailor" b/w "Too Many Women" and "House of Gold" b/w "Thirty Pieces of Silver." With JOE ALLISON, he cowrote the BLUEGRASS classic "20-20 Vision."

Estes left country music in 1951, but the Martha White jingle "How Many Biscuits Can You Eat This Mornin'" and the company slogan "Goodness, Gracious, It's Good," begun by Estes and still used today, may be his most memorable contributions to the music's history. —*Dennis M. Estes and Micki Estes*

## Dale Evans
b. Uvalde, Texas, October 31, 1912; d. February 7, 2001

The most popular woman in western films was Dale Evans. She also wrote her husband's (ROY ROGERS's) theme song, "Happy Trails," a song that has become an icon of American culture. Known as the Queen of the West, the singer, actress, songwriter, and author was one of the first women to bring national attention to western music.

Texas-born Frances Octavia Smith (Dale's given name) grew up in Osceola, Arkansas. During her high school years her family moved to Memphis, Tennessee, where she worked as a secretary. Her boss overheard her singing at her desk and arranged for her to appear on a radio program the company sponsored. Before long she was employed full time as a Memphis radio vocalist. A few years later, station WHAS in Louisville, Kentucky, hired her and changed her name to Dale Evans.

In 1938 she moved to Chicago and became the vocalist with Anson Weeks's orchestra. After touring with his band for a year, Evans returned to Chicago, where she sang on WBBM, the CBS

radio affiliate, for two years. At this point in her career she wasn't singing western songs. Instead, she was singing pop music and jazz on radio and in some of the city's finer supper clubs.

An offer of a Hollywood screen test resulted in a short contract with Twentieth Century-Fox. After leaving Fox, Evans became the vocalist on NBC radio's top-rated *Edgar Bergen/Charlie McCarthy* program during the 1942 season. Republic Pictures began starring her in musicals before casting her as Roy Rogers's leading lady in his 1944 film *The Cowboy and the Señorita.*

The unique chemistry between the two led to Evans's being featured in Rogers's next nineteen films. In December 1947, a little more than a year after the death of his first wife, Rogers and Evans were married. Starting with Evans's son from a teenage marriage and Rogers's three children from his first marriage, the couple began building a large family. Their daughter Robin suffered from Down syndrome and died just before her second birthday. Evans expressed the impact Robin's life had on their family in her best-selling book *Angel Unaware.* Evans went on to write more than twenty books about her religious faith. Following Robin's death, Rogers and Evans added to their family by adopting four children from a variety of backgrounds; they became the parents of nine children, their faith sustaining them through the accidental deaths of son Sandy and daughter Debbie.

Moving from films to television, the couple starred in *The Roy Rogers Show* on NBC for seven years. The series became a Sunday night family viewing tradition. Each episode ended with Rogers and Evans singing "Happy Trails," which Evans had written especially for Rogers. Among the other songs Evans penned are "Aha San Antone" and "The Bible Tells Me So."

Beloved by millions worldwide, Dale Evans died on February 7, 2001. —*Laurence Zwisohn*

## Sara Evans
b. Booneville, Missouri, February 5, 1971

In the 2000s, Sara Lynn Evans emerged as one of contemporary country's most popular female artists, producing radio-friendly hits such as "No Place That Far," which she cowrote, and "As If."

One of seven children, Evans began performing with her family's BLUEGRASS band at age four. Though she cut short an initial foray into the Nashville recording industry to move to Oregon with her husband, she continued to play regionally, opening for WILLIE NELSON and TIM MCGRAW, and eventually returned to Nashville, where she caught the attention of songwriter HARLAN HOWARD. Her first album for RCA Nashville, *Three Chords and the Truth* (1997), was produced by PETE ANDERSON and, not surprisingly, presented Evans as a HONKY-TONK traditionalist; though well-received by critics, none of its singles broke the country Top Forty. On her second album, 1998's *No Place That Far,* Evans consciously pursued a softer, more pop-oriented sound criticized by admirers of her earlier work. The change proved popular with radio, however, and the title track, featuring VINCE GILL on harmony, became her first #1 hit.

With her third album Evans solidified her position as a major star. *Born to Fly* (2000) maintained her pop style, though the album's chart-topping title track emphasized her bluegrass background. The album yielded three Top Ten hits and was certified double platinum. Her next two albums, *Restless* (2003) and *Real Fine Place* (2005), confirmed Evans's ability to deliver both pop and roots-based material, with the twangy romp "Suds in

*Dale Evans*

*Sara Evans*

the Bucket" and the pop ballad "A Real Fine Place to Start" both becoming #1 hits.

Perhaps hampered by turmoil in her personal life, Evans enjoyed only moderate success on the charts for the next several years. Her sixth studio album, *Stronger*, was released in March 2011 on RCA Records. —*Diane Pecknold*

## The Everly Brothers
Isaac Donald Everly b. Brownie, Kentucky, February 1, 1937
Philip Everly b. Chicago, Illinois, January 19, 1939

In purely commercial terms, the Everly Brothers were one of popular music's most successful acts between 1957 and 1962. Only ELVIS PRESLEY, Pat Boone, and possibly RICK NELSON outsold them. In a sense, though, they were more important to Nashville. They were the city's first consistently successful rock & roll act. Their management and their songs came from Nashville, and they recorded there with local session musicians. In other words, they extended Nashville's sense of what was commercially possible.

In artistic terms, the Everlys took the country BROTHER DUET tradition one step farther. They added Bo Diddley riffs, teenage anxieties, and sharkskin suits, but—for all that—the core of their sound remained country brother harmony. That link was underscored on their album *Songs Our Daddy Taught Us.*

The Everlys' father, Ike, was an accomplished fingerstyle guitarist—a contemporary of MERLE TRAVIS—who went to Chicago trying to sustain a career in country radio and ended up in Iowa. He brought his family to Nashville in 1955, possibly hoping that his boys could find the success that had eluded him. Don made inroads as a songwriter ("Thou Shalt Not Steal" for KITTY WELLS, two songs for JUSTIN TUBB, and another for ANITA CARTER), but a contract with COLUMBIA RECORDS in 1955 yielded just one undistinguished single.

By the time the brothers signed with Cadence Records in March 1957 (a deal midwifed by WESLEY ROSE of ACUFF-ROSE PUBLICATIONS), they were singing teenage playlets crafted by BOUDLEAUX AND FELICE BRYANT overlaid with R&B rhythm patterns. The Everlys scored a string of hits, including "Bye Bye Love," "Wake Up Little Susie," "All I Have to Do Is Dream," "Bird Dog," and others. When they switched to WARNER BROS. RECORDS in 1960, they were, at first, even more successful, gaining hits with "Cathy's Clown," "Ebony Eyes," "Walk Right Back," and "So Sad." Their records were among the most immaculately crafted and

*The Everly Brothers: Phil (left) and Don*

innovative of the era, a testimony to the brothers' musical vision and to the skills of versatile Nashville session players.

The brothers' career downturn is often blamed on the Beatles (whose own harmonies drew on the duo's). But the Everlys' appeal was beginning to wane well before the Beatles appeared. They broke with Wesley Rose in 1961, moved to California, and began making singles that were probably too experimental for the time. A reduced touring schedule brought on by a joint enlistment in the marines, the loss of access to the Bryants' songs owing to the rift with Acuff-Rose, and Don's subsequent overreliance on prescription drugs probably figured in their decline, too.

In 1968 they issued *Roots*, a daring COUNTRY-ROCK record that failed to find them a new market. In 1970 they switched to RCA, but they split angrily from each other in July 1973. Don returned to Nashville; Phil stayed in Los Angeles. They reunited in September 1983, and they still tour. An annual festival staged in Central City, Kentucky, reissue recordings, and a stage play, *Bye Bye Love: The Everly Brothers Musical,* also kept them before the public.

In 1986 the Everlys were inducted into the Rock and Roll Hall of Fame, and they received a 1997 Grammy Lifetime Achievement Award. In 2001 the brothers were elected to both the NASHVILLE SONGWRITERS HALL OF FAME and THE COUNTRY MUSIC HALL OF FAME. —*Colin Escott*

## Skip Ewing
b. Redlands, California, March 6, 1964

Donald Ralph Ewing has earned a reputation as an in-demand songwriter while also issuing several albums as a singer. Already penning songs in his teens, he moved to Nashville after high school, landed a performing job at OPRYLAND USA, and signed with

Nashville music publishing company ACUFF-ROSE. GEORGE JONES was the first artist to record a Skip Ewing composition, titled "One Hell of a Song."

In 1988 Ewing scored three Top Ten hits—"The Gospel According to Luke," "I Don't Have Far to Fall," and "Burnin' a Hole in My Heart"—all from his debut MCA release, *The Coast of Colorado*. When his recording career quieted in the 1990s, Ewing's writing prowess brought him recognition for hits such as "Love, Me" (COLLIN RAYE, 1992), "If I Didn't Have You" (RANDY TRAVIS, 1993), and "You Had Me from Hello" (KENNY CHESNEY, 1999). BRYAN WHITE, in particular, did well with Ewing's material, including the #1 hits "Someone Else's Star" and "Rebecca Lynn," and the #4 hit "I'm Not Supposed to Love You Anymore."

After ending his stint with MCA in 1990, Ewing recorded for CAPITOL and LIBERTY from 1991 to 1993. By 1997 he had signed with the GAYLORD ENTERTAINMENT, Christian music label Word Nashville, which issued one Ewing album that year.

Ewing found continued writing success in the new century. With Donny Kees, he penned the 2003 DIAMOND RIO smash "I Believe." —*Michael Hight*

## Exile

J. P. Pennington b. Berea, Kentucky, January 22, 1949
Steve Goetzman b. Louisville, Kentucky, September 1, 1950
Marlon Hargis b. Somerset, Kentucky, May 13, 1949
Les Taylor b. Oneida, Kentucky, December 27, 1948
Sonny LeMaire b. Fort Lee, Virginia, September 16, 1946
Paul Martin b. Winchester, Kentucky, December 22, 1962
Lee Carroll b. Glasgow, Kentucky, January 27, 1953
Mark Jones b. Harlan, Kentucky, July 18, 1954

After a 1978 worldwide pop hit "Kiss You All Over," Exile appeared to live up to its name, seeming to fade quickly into obscurity. But the band refashioned itself with a different sound, adapting rhythmic elements of pop and R&B into an engaging, hook-oriented style of country music. From 1983 to 1992 they had ten #1 country hits.

J. P. Pennington, son of Lily May Ledford of the original COON CREEK GIRLS, formed the Exiles in high school in Richmond, Kentucky, in 1963 (they became Exile in 1973). In 1967 they toured with Dick Clark's Caravan of Stars. In 1978, after several albums for independent labels, their WARNER/CURB release "Kiss You All Over" topped *Billboard*'s pop charts for four weeks and sold more than 5 million copies. In 1980 Mark Gray (keyboards) joined for a two-year stint.

Unable to follow up, Exile quit touring, but the success of two Pennington-Gray tunes, "The Closer You Get" and "Take Me Down"—both hits for ALABAMA—inspired the act to try country music. In 1983 their second single on EPIC, "Woke Up in Love," became their first #1. During their 1980s run on the country charts, the band comprised Pennington (lead vocals, lead guitar), Les Taylor (guitar, vocals), Sonny LeMaire (bass, vocals), Marlon Hargis (keyboards), and Steve Goetzman (drums). Lee Carroll replaced Hargis on keyboards in 1985. Paul Martin replaced Pennington on lead vocals, and Mark Jones joined on acoustic guitar and vocals in 1989.

By the end of the 1980s, three members had departed, and a reconstituted act had to audition again for a record deal. Exile signed with ARISTA RECORDS and hit with "Keep It in the Middle of the Road" (#17, 1989), featuring Martin on lead vocals. They eventually returned to the country Top Five with "Yet," this time showcasing LeMaire as lead vocalist. At the end of 1993, after thirty years and more than twenty group members, Exile disbanded. LeMaire, Goetzman, Martin, Jones, and Carroll reunited for a 1995 album, *Latest and Greatest*. After disbanding again, Pennington and Taylor led another regrouping in December 1995. Taylor left in late 2006, but the entire original lineup reunited in October 2008 and resumed touring. The band released a five-song EP in 2011. —*Walter Carter*

# F·F·F

# Fabor Records
established in Malibu, California, October 1953; ended 1965

In August 1953, after JIM REEVES's success with "Mexican Joe" on ABBOTT RECORDS, FABOR ROBISON bought out all other interests in that label and, in October, launched his eponymous Fabor Records from his house/studio complex in Malibu, California. THE BROWNS were among his earliest signings.

Fabor Records went through several quiescent periods when Robison was out of the music business. In 1957 he concluded a deal that gave DOT RECORDS first refusal on all Fabor masters. Dot acquired BONNIE GUITAR's "Dark Moon" and NED MILLER's "From a Jack to a King" in this way. Soon after launching a rock & roll imprint, Radio Records, in 1958, Robison sold his music publishing and certain masters to Jamie/Guyden Records, and, when "From a Jack to a King" was reissued successfully on Fabor in 1962, it was via Jamie. Robison exited the business completely in 1965 and sold all remaining masters to the SHELBY SINGLETON Corporation. —*Colin Escott*

# Barbara Fairchild
b. Lafe, Arkansas, November 12, 1950

Barbara Fairchild, best known for her 1972–73 chart-topping hit "Teddy Bear Song," has enjoyed success as a songwriter and singer in country and gospel music.

During her teens Fairchild appeared on local TV and radio in St. Louis; she made her first record at fifteen. At seventeen she journeyed to Nashville. There she met producer-publisher JERRY CRUTCHFIELD, who heard potential in one of her songs and encouraged her to write more. Fairchild returned with fifteen songs; Crutchfield became her producer and manager and signed her to MCA Music Publishing as a songwriter.

After two unsuccessful Kapp Records singles, Crutchfield took Fairchild to BILLY SHERRILL, who signed her to COLUMBIA RECORDS. She first charted in 1969 with "Love Is a Gentle Thing," but her big break came three years later with "Teddy Bear Song" and two similar Top Ten hits: "Kid Stuff" and "Baby Doll" (both 1973).

Besides cowriting several of her own hits (though not "Teddy Bear Song"), Fairchild penned songs recorded by LORETTA LYNN and LIZ ANDERSON. Fairchild left Columbia in 1978. In 1990 she joined and recorded with a gospel group, Heirloom, and released her first gospel solo album, *The Light*, in 1991 on Benson Records. Eventually she opened the Barbara Fairchild Theater in BRANSON, MISSOURI, and, after the venue closed, started the Barbara Fairchild Diner in Branson, where she and husband Roy Morris

perform. She continued recording gospel albums for the Daywind label and making personal appearances. —*Gerry Wood*

# Joseph Falcon
b. Rayne, Louisiana, September 28, 1900; d. November 29, 1965

Accordion player Joseph Falcon and his wife, Cleoma Breaux, made the first commercial CAJUN MUSIC recordings in 1928, when they cut "Allons à Lafayette" and "The Waltz That Carried Me to My Grave" for COLUMBIA. The regional popularity of these performances led record companies to seek out other Cajun musicians.

Falcon began to learn the accordion at age seven, playing and singing traditional Cajun songs. Backed by Cleoma on guitar, he was in demand for local dances well before recording for Columbia. Joseph and Cleoma were often joined by Falcon's cousin Ulysses on fiddle. Cleoma, herself from a well-known musical family, recorded for Columbia with her brothers Amadie and Ophy Breaux in 1929. After recording for Columbia, the Falcons recorded for BLUEBIRD (1934) and for DECCA (1934, 1936–37).

Joseph Falcon's career suffered with the accordion's declining popularity, and he refused to record again, although he continued to play for dances with his Silver Bell Band. In 1963 a live performance was privately recorded at the Triangle Dance Hall in Scott, Louisiana, for Arhoolie Records. He died two years later in Crowley, Louisiana. —*Charlie Seemann*

# Fan Fair (see CMA Music Festival)

# Donna Fargo
b. Mount Airy, North Carolina, November 10, 1945

An important crossover artist in the early 1970s, Donna Fargo began her string of hits with her chart-topping, self-penned signature tune, "Happiest Girl in the Whole U.S.A.," followed by the #1 hits "Funny Face" and "Superman," also original compositions. Raised on her father's North Carolina tobacco farm, Yvonne Vaughn moved to a Los Angeles suburb after college and taught high school English courses. She met local record producer Stan Silver (whom she married in 1969), learned to play the guitar, and began writing songs.

Through publisher Don Sessions and disc jockey BIFF COLLIE, she met Floyd Ramsey, owner of Phoenix-based Ramco Records, for whom she recorded her first single, "Would You Believe," using the stage name Donna Fargo. After a second Ramco single she moved to Los Angeles–based CHALLENGE RECORDS for "Daddy." The Silvers financed the Nashville session (produced by Silver) that generated "Happiest Girl." Picked up by DOT RECORDS, it won a Grammy and became the CMA's 1972 Single of the Year. It was also the first of thirty-eight Fargo singles—six of them #1s—to make *Billboard*'s country chart on the Dot, ABC/Dot, WARNER BROS., RCA, COLUMBIA, MERCURY, and Cleveland International labels between 1972 and 1991. Fargo composed and published most of her hit material. The syndicated *Donna Fargo Show* television variety series aired during the 1978–79 season. Fargo was stricken with multiple sclerosis in 1979, and, although the disease is currently in remission, it caused a serious setback in her performing and recording career. —*Todd Everett*

## Charlie Feathers
b. Holly Springs, Mississippi, June 12, 1932; d. August 29, 1998

Charlie Feathers was a pioneer of the SUN RECORDS Memphis ROCKABILLY sound popularized by ELVIS PRESLEY in the mid-1950s. The extent and significance of Feathers's contributions are a matter of some debate, though; Feathers saw himself as Presley's mentor and main vocal coach, but his peers and most historians consider him a more peripheral figure. It is a matter of record that Feathers cowrote (with Stan Kesler) the 1955 Presley hit "I Forgot to Remember to Forget" and had a hand in writing some 200 other songs, mainly in the rockabilly vein. Although commercial success eluded Feathers, he wrote, recorded, and performed rockabilly material with passion into the 1990s. His fierce dedication and eccentric vocal style made him a cult figure among rockabilly fans and music journalists. He was also an accomplished country singer with an unvarnished rural style.

Feathers grew up in a sharecropping family in north central Mississippi, where he was strongly influenced by both country and blues performers. After working as an oil field laborer, Feathers settled in Memphis at age eighteen. He claimed to have been a creative force at SAM PHILLIPS's Sun studio since the early 1950s, although this assertion is unsubstantiated. Phillips did record Feathers for the Flip label, releasing a country single—"I've Been Deceived," backed with "Peepin' Eyes"—in 1955. After other sessions for Phillips with minimal results, Feathers went to a rival Memphis label, Meteor, and cut the rockabilly classics "Tongue Tied Jill" and "Get With It" in 1956. His next records of note, "Bottle for the Baby" and "One Hand Loose," appeared on Cincinnati's KING label. None of these—or many ensuing records—were hits, but they established Feathers as a rockabilly hero. —*Ben Sandmel*

## Freddy Fender
b. San Benito, Texas, June 4, 1937; d. October 14, 2006

Baldemar G. Huerta adopted the stage name Freddy Fender in the late 1950s as he transitioned from Spanish-speaking CONJUNTO MUSIC to ROCKABILLY-tinged rock & roll. Early on he used his birth name when recording on the Mission label (Spain). Thereafter billed as El Bebop Kid, the former migrant worker and marine achieved early success with the regional hit "Holy One" (1959), followed by the even more popular, self-penned "Wasted Days and Wasted Nights" (1959). The latter recording gained

national exposure when it was transferred from the San Antonio–based Duncan label to IMPERIAL RECORDS of Los Angeles in 1960.

Just as Fender's career was ascending, a marijuana possession conviction led to five years at the Louisiana State Penitentiary. While in prison, he cut recordings for Goldband. Released early in 1963 (thanks, in part, to Louisiana Governor JIMMIE DAVIS, himself a country music star), Fender moved to New Orleans and performed regularly at Bourbon Street nightclub Papa Joe's. In Louisiana he absorbed the emerging "swamp-pop" sound, an amalgam of CAJUN-inflected country and rhythm & blues, and met Cajun music entrepreneur Huey P. Meaux.

After five unproductive years back in Texas, Fender became reacquainted with Meaux, who had moved to Houston. Meaux persuaded a reluctant Fender to record "Before the Next Teardrop Falls," a love song that became one of the surprise hits of the 1970s. Released on Meaux's Crazy Cajun label in late 1974 and picked up for national distribution by ABC/DOT RECORDS in 1975, the recording topped *Billboard*'s country and pop charts and became CMA's 1975 Single of the Year. Not the least of its virtues was Fender's insertion of a verse in Spanish. In 1975–76, Fender enjoyed several hits: a rereleased "Wasted Days" that went #1 country and #8 pop, a version of Doris Day's pop standard "Secret Love," and his rendition of Ivory Joe Hunter's "Since I Met You Baby," among others. To each song, Fender brought an emotional power and ethnic appeal that attracted a mass audience. During this period, he also received numerous nominations and awards and made dozens of television appearances.

Subsequently, Fender's career declined rapidly, due in part to marital, drug, and alcohol problems. Later affiliations with Meaux's Starflite label and WARNER BROS. yielded little success. In the mid-1980s he pursued acting and appeared in the 1988 Robert Redford film *The Milagro Beanfield War*.

Early in the 1990s Fender returned to the limelight when teaming with Doug Sahm, Augie Myers, and FLACO JIMENEZ to form the all-star Tex-Mex country group Texas Tornados. After several albums, Fender resumed solo work. Health problems plagued him, however, and after a kidney transplant (2002) and a liver transplant (2004), he succumbed to lung cancer in October 2006. —*Stephen R. Tucker*

## Bob Ferguson
b. Willow Springs, Missouri, December 30, 1927; d. July 22, 2001

An RCA RECORDS staff producer in Nashville during the 1960s and early 1970s, Robert B. Ferguson played a prominent role in the careers of RCA artists, including CONNIE SMITH, PORTER WAGONER, and DOLLY PARTON. A successful songwriter as well, he penned Wagoner's "The Carroll County Accident" and, most significantly, FERLIN HUSKY's million-selling 1960 smash "Wings of a Dove."

A lifelong scholar and volunteer anthropologist, Ferguson attended Southwest Missouri State University and Washington State University in Pullman, Washington. At Washington State he worked as an announcer for the college station, KWSC, and organized a country band called the KWSC Ramblers. From 1955 to 1960 he produced movies for the Tennessee Game & Fish Commission. The success of "Wings of a Dove" made his music career, and Ferguson himself recorded a few numbers under the stage name Eli Possumtrot.

As an RCA producer, Ferguson was noteworthy for his relatively light touch on such landmark records as Connie Smith's "Once a Day." Though he often recorded his artists with lush string and choral arrangements typical of THE NASHVILLE SOUND, he also knew when to back away from them. Smith, Wagoner, and especially Parton all benefited from Ferguson's sensitive approach, especially evident on Dolly's spare and remarkably undated early RCA sides. After Ferguson left RCA, family ties and his non-music industry work led him to the reservation of the Mississippi Band of Choctaw Indians near Philadelphia, Mississippi. He served as tribal historian and helped found the Choctaw Museum of the Southern Indian while also remaining involved in local media. —*Daniel Cooper*

## Fiddle

The fiddle has always been one of the principal instruments in country music. Recorded country music began when Texas fiddler A. C. "ECK" ROBERTSON cut a number of sides for the Victor Talking Machine Company in New York in 1922. Beginning in 1923, sales of recordings by another fiddler, JOHN CARSON of Atlanta, led to the active exploitation of white southern rural music by the phonograph industry. Fiddlers such as Clark Kessinger (see THE KESSINGER BROTHERS) from West Virginia, CLAYTON MCMICHEN from Georgia, Charlie Bowman and FIDDLIN' ARTHUR SMITH from Tennessee, and DOC ROBERTS from Kentucky recorded extensively during country music's first two decades and influenced many fiddlers in succeeding generations.

The fiddle lies at the heart of many country music styles. BOB WILLS and MILTON BROWN built WESTERN SWING around the fiddle. Although fiddlers were rare in mainstream jazz, many young fiddlers in Texas and Oklahoma in the 1930s and 1940s eagerly listened to and took musical ideas from jazz violinists Joe Venuti, Stuff Smith, and Stephane Grappelli. CECIL BROWER, J. R. Chatwell, Hugh Farr (see SONS OF THE PIONEERS), CLIFF BRUNER, Joe Holley, JOHNNY GIMBLE, and many others learned how to make traditional fiddle tunes swing and how to take hot choruses on new songs such as "Stay All Night, Stay a Little Longer," "Take Me Back to Tulsa," "Fat Boy Rag," and "San Antonio Rose."

BILL MONROE likewise put the fiddle at the center of the BLUEGRASS sound. Monroe was greatly influenced by the music of his uncle, Pendleton Vandiver, who was a master OLD-TIME fiddler from Kentucky. Monroe not only recorded many tunes that he learned from his Uncle Pen but also wrote dozens of new tunes in the fiddle tune mold. Many Monroe compositions, such as "Jerusalem Ridge," "Big Mon," "Wheel Hoss," and "Brown County Breakdown," have become staples of the current bluegrass fiddler's repertoire. Most of the musicians who defined bluegrass fiddle style, including CHUBBY WISE, TOMMY MAGNESS, Bobby Hicks, Merle "Red" Taylor, BENNY MARTIN, Richard Greene, VASSAR CLEMENTS, and KENNY BAKER, toured or recorded as members of Monroe's Blue Grass Boys. Other fiddlers, such as Paul Warren, Clarence "Tater" Tate, Jimmy Buchanan, Scott Stoneman (see THE STONEMAN FAMILY), Stuart Duncan, Blaine Sprouse, Jason Carter, Aubrey Haynie, Michael Cleveland, and ALISON KRAUSS, also affected bluegrass music, and some of these players continue to affect the style as working musicians.

Over the years, mainstream country artists such as HANK WILLIAMS, ROY ACUFF, HANK SNOW, RAY PRICE, BUCK OWENS, PORTER WAGONER, MERLE HAGGARD, EMMYLOU HARRIS, and RICKY SKAGGS (an expert fiddler himself) have featured fiddlers prominently in their touring bands and on their recordings. Fiddlers such as DALE POTTER, TOMMY JACKSON, Tommy Vaden, HOWDY FORRESTER, and Tommy Williams played on the road and in recording sessions with a variety of country singers. MARK O'CONNOR, a prodigiously talented multi-instrumentalist who is best known as a fiddler, dominated the CMA's Instrumentalist of the Year competition throughout the 1990s.

Fiddling had existed in the United States for nearly three centuries prior to the beginning of country music as a commercial popular music genre, and it has its roots in European dance music traditions. The word "fiddle," in several variant spellings, has been used to designate various bowed stringed instruments since the twelfth century, and when the violin emerged in the middle of the sixteenth century, it acquired the name "fiddle" as an informal appellation. In its early years the violin was used primarily as a dance instrument, and it has maintained this function in a wide range of folk music traditions throughout Europe and North America. Early violinists playing for dancers probably performed a preexisting body of dance music; the "modern" fiddle tune repertoire is rooted in the body of tunes and tune types that crystallized throughout the British Isles and Ireland, and in places settled by people from these areas, in the mid- to late eighteenth century. Nevertheless, only a minority of the tunes current among American fiddlers can be traced directly to Old World antecedents, and it is probably incorrect to view American fiddling in terms of an imported tradition that developed its own characteristics in the New World. Rather, independent development of local styles and repertoires seems to have occurred more or less simultaneously in many different parts of the English-speaking world, including various regions of the United States.

Fiddle tunes typically consist of two distinct melodic sections, each of which is played twice in an AABB pattern for one complete execution of the tune. The tune is then repeated several times in a performance, sometimes with variations. In the context of a bluegrass or western swing band, players of other instruments will also take turns at playing the melody or in improvising solos based on it.

Country fiddling reflects a considerable amount of cultural synthesis. For example, the sliding into and out of notes—one of the distinguishing features of southern fiddling—is generally thought to be a stylistic trait derived from African American music. Popular fiddlers such as Fiddlin' Arthur Smith and Chubby Wise brought this bluesy trait to commercial country music. The CAJUN music of French Louisiana has long had a tangential but persistent relationship to mainstream country music, with fiddling being perhaps the most distinctive Cajun music element that has influenced country. Aspects of the repertoire and style of the German, Czech, and Hispanic communities in the Southwest have been incorporated into the fiddling of that region and, by extension, into regional commercial country styles. —*Paul F. Wells*

## Field Recording

In the first two decades of country music's commercial history, field recording was one of the basic methods used to find new talent and to record musicians of proven merit. Recording company talent scouts (known as artists and repertoire, or A&R, men), accompanied by engineers who transported and operated the recording equipment, traveled to various cities in the South, such as Atlanta, New Orleans, Memphis, and San Antonio, and recorded entertainers on location. The A&R men sometimes ran newspaper ads searching for potential talent, but they also acted on tips provided by other musicians or by local informants. Recording sessions were held in hotel rooms, radio stations, warehouses, or other rented spaces, and sometimes even in musicians' homes.

Country music's first field session came in June 1923 when RALPH PEER, talent scout for the OKEH company, discovered and recorded FIDDLIN' JOHN CARSON in Atlanta. Much more significant, though, were the sessions Peer supervised for the Victor Talking Machine Company in July and August 1927 in BRISTOL, TENNESSEE, where such historic figures as the CARTER FAMILY, JIMMIE RODGERS, and Alfred Karnes made their first recordings. In the years that followed, men such as FRANK WALKER, ART SATHERLEY, ELI OBERSTEIN, and DAVE KAPP conducted similar recording sessions that brought comparable talent to country music.

As important as these country music field sessions have been, they were not the first on-site explorations of American folk music. Field recording actually began with the private expeditions of collectors who looked for folk music in the southern Appalachians and other rural areas in the early years of the twentieth century. These first collections, however, were generally made with pen and paper, and they concentrated on songs and not the singers. The most significant early field recordings were conducted by John Lomax, whose findings were published in 1910 as *Cowboy Songs and Other Frontier Ballads*, and Cecil Sharp, whose collection of mountain ballads was first published in 1917 as *English Folk Songs from the Southern Appalachians*. In the 1920s Robert Winslow Gordon, who in 1928 became the first curator of the Archive of Folk Song in the Library of Congress, began collecting BALLADS and songs with a primitive wire recorder. —*Bill C. Malone*

## The Flatlanders

For decades, the Flatlanders lived up to the title of their 1990 release, *More a Legend Than a Band*. The group formed in 1970 when childhood friends Butch Hancock, JIMMIE DALE GILMORE, and JOE ELY began rooming together in their hometown of Lubbock, Texas. Each had experienced the counterculture in AUSTIN and on the coasts, and, on returning, they discovered they shared an affection for traditional country, contemporary folk, rock, and blues. Other members of the group included Steve Wesson, who played the musical saw and autoharp, and fiddler Tommy Hancock (no relation to Butch).

Together, the Flatlanders merged the lyrical sophistication of BOB DYLAN with the traditional country music of JIMMIE RODGERS and HANK WILLIAMS. In 1972 the Flatlanders traveled to Nashville to record for SHELBY SINGLETON's Plantation label. Singleton released a single, "Dallas" (later rerecorded separately by Ely and Gilmore), to radio with minimal response. Their initial album, titled *Jimmie Dale and the Flatlanders*, appeared on eight-track tape only. The Flatlanders played a few gigs and went their separate ways in 1973. In 1980, after Ely and Hancock's solo work received favorable notice, Plantation issued the first album on vinyl LP with the title *One More Road*. Gilmore's successful solo career launched in 1988, prompting ROUNDER RECORDS to release the first album, with additional tracks, in 1990 under the title *More a Legend Than a Band*.

Often working together on their respective independent albums, the trio reunited for a few concerts in the 1990s, which led them to contribute a song to the soundtrack of the 1998 Robert Redford film *The Horse Whisperer*. They released a reunion album, *Now Again*, on New West in 2002 and began touring regularly as a band. As of 2011, the Flatlanders had released two additional studio albums and a live set captured in 1972, also on New West. Their legend has continued to grow, but it's fair to say they are more of a band than they used to be. —*Rick Mitchell*

## Lester Flatt & the Nashville Grass

After dissolving his partnership with EARL SCRUGGS in late February 1969, Lester Flatt remained on the GRAND OLE OPRY featuring the traditional BLUEGRASS sound with which he felt most comfortable. Retaining longtime FLATT & SCRUGGS band members UNCLE JOSH GRAVES, E. P. "Jake" Tullock, and Paul Warren, he recruited banjo player Vic Jordan and mandolinist ROLAND WHITE from BILL MONROE's Blue Grass Boys. Critics and fans hailed Flatt's early recordings on Nugget and RCA VICTOR—particularly three duet albums with MAC WISEMAN—as a return to form.

Because Flatt was contractually prevented from using the Foggy Mountain Boys name, the advertising agency handling the MARTHA WHITE Foods account promoted a "name the band" contest. The Nashville Grass was selected from more than 20,000 entries. Flatt initially disliked the name, a punning reference to DANNY DAVIS's Nashville Brass. However, his resistance faded when it proved popular among fans. (Indeed, other bluegrass bands adopted similar "grass" monikers.)

The Nashville Grass lineup began turning over in 1972, but Flatt carefully maintained his trademark sound. MARTY STUART—not yet fourteen years old—joined as lead guitarist in September of that year. When White left the band in March 1973, Flatt persuaded his retired tenor singer, Curly Seckler, to replace him; Seckler played guitar, and Stuart switched to mandolin.

Troubled by lingering problems resulting from a 1967 heart attack, Flatt underwent open heart surgery in June 1975. Although his health continued to deteriorate, he kept the band on the road until shortly before his death on May 11, 1979. Seckler helmed the Nashville Grass until retiring from full-time touring in 1994, primarily in partnership with Flatt sound-alike Willis Spears. —*Dave Samuelson*

## Flatt & Scruggs and the Foggy Mountain Boys
Lester Raymond Flatt b. Duncan's Chapel, Tennessee, June 19, 1914; d. May 11, 1979
Earl Eugene Scruggs b. Flint Hill, North Carolina, January 6, 1924

For two decades, Flatt & Scruggs and the Foggy Mountain Boys led the way in popularizing BLUEGRASS music. Their sound became widely recognized in the 1960s through their heavy touring schedule, their popular syndicated TV show, and their recording of "The Ballad of Jed Clampett," the theme for CBS-TV's *THE BEVERLY HILLBILLIES*.

Both Flatt and Scruggs grew up in farm homes rich with musical traditions, and both worked in textile mills before becoming full-time musicians. Flatt, who left school at age twelve and married at seventeen, began his radio career in 1939 and played in several bands, including that of CHARLIE MONROE & His Kentucky Pardners, with whom, in 1943, he sang tenor and played guitar and mandolin. In 1945 Flatt became guitarist and lead singer in Bill Monroe's Blue Grass Boys.

Scruggs, who remained close to home through the war years to help his widowed mother, won recognition as a banjo prodigy from an early age. By his teens, he had developed a distinctive, three-finger banjo picking style that enabled him to play a broad variety of music with speed and clarity.

The two met in late 1945 when Scruggs joined Monroe's band, and both became part of what proved to be Monroe's most influential lineup. Along with fiddler Chubby Wise and bassist Cedric Rainwater (Howard Watts), Flatt and Scruggs played a crucial role in developing the sound that later came to be known as "bluegrass"—a name taken from Monroe's band. In addition to Monroe's high-tenor vocals and fiery mandolin playing, this sound featured Flatt's warm lead singing and solid rhythm guitar, Wise's fiddle, and Scruggs's banjo, which he used as a lead instrument, particularly on faster songs and instrumental numbers. This novel sound attracted considerable attention to their Grand Ole Opry performances and Columbia recordings.

Early in 1948, Flatt and Scruggs left Monroe's outfit. Later that spring they formed their own group, the Foggy Mountain Boys. Early band members included guitarist-vocalists Jim Eanes and Mac Wiseman along with fiddler Jim Shumate and bassist Rainwater. By year's end they were playing at WCYB in Bristol, Tennessee, and recording for Mercury. Afterward they worked at a number of other radio stations in the Southeast. In 1950 they signed with Columbia, their label for the rest of their joint career.

In 1949 mandolinist-tenor singer Curly Seckler joined the band. He remained for most years until 1962, although for several periods he was replaced by others, most notably Everett Lilly (see The Lilly Brothers). A number of outstanding fiddlers also played with the Foggy Mountain Boys early on; in 1954 master fiddler Paul Warren came aboard and remained with the band

until the act dissolved. Several bassists worked with the group before 1953, when English P. "Cousin Jake" Tullock joined. He, too, stayed until the end. However, the Flatt & Scruggs sound took its definitive form in 1955 with the addition of Uncle Josh Graves's resonator guitar, or dobro. With this instrument Flat & Scruggs departed significantly from Monroe's sound, although, like him, they maintained a purely acoustic approach. In 1953 Martha White Flour began sponsoring Flatt & Scruggs's daily early morning radio shows over Nashville radio station WSM and continued to support them for the rest of their career. Two years later they joined the Grand Ole Opry.

During the late 1950s and early 1960s their television shows were seen by millions of viewers in the Southeast. Their recordings, including gospel songs such as "Cabin on the Hill," began hitting the country charts. Meanwhile, their banjo-sparked acoustic sound found favor with young listeners in the folk music revival. Appearances at the Newport Folk Festival and on TV brought them national acclaim (*New York Times* music critic Robert Shelton compared Scruggs to Paganini), paving the way for a series of folk-oriented albums. An appearance at the Hollywood folk club The Ash Grove caught the ear of the producer of *The Beverly Hillbillies* and led to the recording of "The Ballad of Jed Clampett," the band's only single to reach #1 on the country charts.

The group's popularity grew steadily in the 1960s. And despite health problems for both partners (especially Flatt) later in the decade, Flatt & Scruggs continued to broadcast, record, and tour widely. Highlights from these years included sensational appearances in Japan and at San Francisco's Avalon Ballroom—during the peak of its hippie light-show years—and another soundtrack success when their 1949 recording of "Foggy Mountain Breakdown" was used in the movie *Bonnie and Clyde*, a major hit of 1967. Musical and business differences brought the act to an end in early 1969. Both men continued to perform,

*Flatt & Scruggs and the Foggy Mountain Boys: (from left) Burkett "Uncle Josh" Graves, Earl Scruggs, Paul Warren, E. P. "Cousin Jake" Tullock, and Lester Flatt*

Scruggs with his sons in the EARL SCRUGGS REVUE and Flatt with LESTER FLATT & THE NASHVILLE GRASS. In 1985 the duo of Flatt & Scruggs was elected to THE COUNTRY MUSIC HALL OF FAME. —Neil V. Rosenberg

## Béla Fleck
b. New York, New York, July 10, 1958

Named after composer Béla Bartok, banjo virtuoso Béla Anton Leos Fleck picked up his primary instrument at fifteen upon hearing FLATT & SCRUGGS's theme song to THE BEVERLY HILLBILLIES. Like his hero Earl Scruggs, Fleck would expand the language of the banjo, rewriting the rules and assumptions for the instrument as a solo artist, as a member of NEW GRASS REVIVAL, and as the leader of the Flecktones.

Two years after his grandfather gave him his first banjo, the teen-age musician witnessed keyboardist Chick Corea in concert at New York's Beacon Theater with the jazz supergroup Return to Forever. Fleck, who had mostly played BLUEGRASS and folk up to that point, has cited that evening as a musical milestone that changed his entire approach to playing the banjo: "I sat there in the audience, loving every minute of it and going, 'All of those notes they're playing have got to be on the banjo somewhere. I just have to find them.'" Fleck would go on to master a single-note style on the instrument.

Fleck launched his recording career in the late 1970s, contrib-uting to a pair of releases as a member of the Boston-based Tasty Licks. He moved to Kentucky and joined Spectrum, with whom he recorded two albums on ROUNDER RECORDS. After releasing one solo effort, 1979's Crossing the Tracks, he joined New Grass Revival in 1981 and moved to Nashville. Throughout the 1980s he made solo albums and worked with New Grass Revival until 1989, when he formed the jazz-based, highly improvisational Flecktones, with bassist Victor Wooten, Wooten's brother Roy "Future Man" Wooten, and Howard Levy, who left the band in 1993. (Future Man is the inventor of the synth-ax drumitar, a guitar-shaped electronic instrument on which percussive sounds are created via pressure-sensitive finger pads.)

Since 1995 Fleck has won multiple Grammy awards, including Best Country Instrumental Performance, Best Pop Instrumental, Best Instrumental Composition, Best Contemporary Jazz Album, Best Classical Crossover Album, Best Instrumental Arrangement, and Best Pop Instrumental Album. By late 2009 Sascha Paladino (Fleck's brother) had filmed two Fleck documentaries featuring Fleck and bassist Edgar Meyer shaping their repertoire on tour, in addition to the documentary Throw Down Your Heart, which explores the banjo's origins by capturing Fleck's on-location collab-orations with African musicians. In 2009 Fleck released an album by the same title, part of his Tales from the Acoustic Planet series. —Michael Gray

## Fleming & Townsend

Guitarist Reece Fleming and multi-instrumentalist Respers Townsend recorded seventy-six sides for RCA VICTOR, the AMERICAN RECORD CORPORATION, and DECCA from 1930 to 1937. Biographically, however, little is known about them beyond their Memphis, Tennessee, residency in 1930 when they cut their first songs.

Influential as a harmony-singing duet, Fleming & Townsend also pioneered the art of duet yodeling. This vocal technique and their cowriting on songs such as "I'm Blue and Lonesome," "She's Always on My Mind," "Just One Little Kiss," "She's Just That Kind," and others directly influenced the repertoire and vocal style of THE CALLAHAN BROTHERS, a highly successful recording and performing duo from 1934 to 1951. —Bob Pinson

## Rosie Flores
b. San Antonio, Texas, September 10, 1956

A prolific and creative singer-songwriter, Rosalie Durango Flores has been a key figure in the alternative-country movement that began on the West Coast in the 1980s, picked up steam in AUSTIN, TEXAS, in the 1990s, and continues into the present. After her family moved to Southern California, she formed (or joined) bands reflecting ROCKABILLY, surf music, blues, COUNTRY-ROCK, and punk influences. She returned to her hard-country roots on her self-titled 1987 debut album—produced by PETE ANDERSON for WARNER BROS.—but her music proved at once too edgy and too traditional for country radio, and the label dropped her.

Migrating between Texas and California, she recorded three albums for West Coast indie HIGHTONE RECORDS between 1992 and 1995. The last, Rockabilly Filly, highlighted her duets with rockabilly queens WANDA JACKSON and JANIS MARTIN and led to a national tour with Jackson. In 1997 ROUNDER RECORDS rereleased her Warner Bros. material and six new tracks on Honky Tonk Reprise, while Austin's Watermelon Records issued A Little Bit of Heartache, a joint effort with rockabilly veteran Ray Campi. Flores recorded the live album Dance Hall Dreams (Rounder, 1999) at an informal San Antonio venue called the Cibolo Creek Country Club.

In the new century Flores settled in Nashville but changed labels frequently. Speed of Sound (Eminent, 2001) again featured original songs and rockabilly covers; the more intimate Single Rose, released on her own Durango Rose label in 2004, was a solo acous-tic live set showcasing her expressive voice and confident guitar playing. Bandera Highway, on HighTone, also appeared in 2004. In 2009 Flores released Girl of the Century on Bloodshot Records. She continues to play venues ranging from folk and country festivals to blues clubs and rock & roll bars. —Rick Mitchell

## The Flying Burrito Brothers (see Gram Parsons)

## Jim Foglesong
b. Lundale, West Virginia, July 26, 1922

As a producer and record label executive, James Staton Foglesong advanced the careers of many major country acts while inspiring both artists and fellow executives with his high ethical standards. Born into a musical family, he grew up in Charleston, West Virginia, where he performed on radio during high school. Early on, he sang gospel songs, pop tunes, and light classics while soak-ing up country music from his family, from local radio shows, and from fellow servicemen during World War II.

A graduate of the Eastman School of Music in Rochester, New York, Foglesong moved in 1951 to New York City, where COLUMBIA RECORDS hired him as a musical assistant. He also sang with Fred Waring's Pennsylvanians, the Robert Shaw Chorale, and the New York Philharmonic Orchestra. He gained further vocal experience backing pop stars on network television

*Jim Foglesong*

and recording with pop acts (Rosemary Clooney) and teen idols (Neil Sedaka). Foglesong then returned to Columbia and helped form EPIC RECORDS, for which he produced Roy Hamilton and Bobby Vinton. Along the way, Foglesong studied the techniques of famed producers such as Mitch Miller and DAVE KAPP.

As a producer for Columbia and, starting in 1963, for RCA RECORDS, Foglesong worked with Julie Andrews, Ed Ames, and Robert Goulet and was among the earliest out-of-town pop producers who cut records in Nashville. In 1970 he moved from New York to Nashville as A&R chief for DOT RECORDS. With the success of ROY CLARK, DONNA FARGO, and other country acts, Foglesong became president of Dot in 1973. Serving as president of ABC-Dot after the American Broadcasting Corporation bought Dot in 1974, he continued his winning streak with JOHN CONLEE, FREDDY FENDER, BARBARA MANDRELL, the OAK RIDGE BOYS, and DON WILLIAMS.

When MCA RECORDS purchased ABC's labels in 1979, Foglesong presided over MCA's Nashville operation for five years, a period when REBA MCENTIRE, GEORGE STRAIT, and GENE WATSON joined the roster. Helming CAPITOL Nashville from 1984 to 1989, he oversaw the careers of MEL MCDANIEL and DAN SEALS—already on the label—as well as newly signed acts, including SUZY BOGGUSS, GARTH BROOKS, MARIE OSMOND, SAWYER BROWN, and TANYA TUCKER.

Honored by the Nashville Entertainment Association with its Master Award for bringing Nashville international prestige, Foglesong has received Leadership Music's Bridge Award for his role in uniting the city's music and business communities and Leadership Music's Dale Franklin Award for exemplifying "the highest quality of leadership." Foglesong is also a former CMA chairman and board member. He has remained active as a consultant, an independent producer, and a board member of the COUNTRY MUSIC HALL OF FAME AND MUSEUM. Since 1991 he has taught

music business courses at Vanderbilt University, and he has directed the music business program at Nashville's Trevecca Nazarene University since 1999. In 2009 Trevecca made him a Distinguished Professor, only the third such honor in the school's century-plus history. Jim Foglesong was elected to THE COUNTRY MUSIC HALL OF FAME in 1992. —*Gerry Wood*

## Red Foley

b. Blue Lick, Kentucky, June 17, 1910; d. September 19, 1968

Clyde Julian "Red" Foley contributed greatly to the rise of the country music industry following World War II. Emerging as a star in Chicago, he later played major roles in the expansion of Nashville and Springfield, Missouri, as country music centers. During the course of his career he recorded some of the genre's most durable sacred and secular performances.

Nicknamed for his red hair, Foley grew up around Berea, Kentucky. At his father's general store he learned to play harmonica and guitar while absorbing songs and styles from his father and other local musicians, black and white. Voice lessons improved his natural singing talent. After high school he briefly attended Kentucky's Georgetown College, where he continued his formal musical studies.

In 1931, however, WLS–Chicago executive JOHN LAIR recruited young Foley with an offer of $60 a week, and in short order he was winning crowds at the NATIONAL BARN DANCE. He played bass and guitar and sang in Lair's CUMBERLAND RIDGE RUNNERS, performed duets with LULU BELLE (Wiseman), and ultimately took solo spots as well.

Next, Foley joined forces with Lair, THE DUKE OF PADUCAH, and Chicago advertising executive Freeman Keyes to launch the

*Red Foley*

RENFRO VALLEY BARN DANCE, broadcasting from Cincinnati via WLW before shifting headquarters to Renfro Valley, Kentucky, and eventually airing over Louisville's WHAS. Foley didn't stay long, though, and went on to star on network radio shows such as *Avalon Time* and *Plantation Party* at WLW before returning to the *National Barn Dance* in 1940.

During the 1930s Foley had recorded for the AMERICAN RECORD CORPORATION (ARC) with the Cumberland Ridge Runners, but his recording career took off when DECCA signed him in 1941. Soon he hit with "Old Shep," a song he had written years earlier about his own German shepherd, Hoover, and which he had recorded earlier for ARC.

Other hits followed, and Foley was a hot property when he came to Nashville early in 1946 to host the *Prince Albert Show*, the GRAND OLE OPRY's NBC network segment, in the process replacing ROY ACUFF, who temporarily left the Opry in a salary dispute. The change personified the rise of smooth-voiced, solo country vocalists and the waning of the STRINGBAND era.

Along with HANK WILLIAMS and other artists, Foley became a focus of Nashville's nascent recording industry, and in 1947 Decca executive Paul Cohen began making frequent trips to record Foley, ERNEST TUBB, and other country talent there. Among the many hits Foley cut in Nashville were the boogie tune "Tennessee Saturday Night"; "Sugarfoot Rag"; the inspiring gospel song "Peace in the Valley"; and the crossover smash "Chattanoogie Shoe Shine Boy," a #1 country and pop hit of 1950.

Amid growing personal problems, in 1953 Foley quit his leading role on the *Prince Albert Show*, although he kept touring as an Opry act for a time. In 1954, executive SI SIMAN persuaded him to become headliner for KWTO–Springfield's *OZARK JUBILEE* on ABC radio. Early in 1955 Foley began hosting the program's ABC-TV incarnation, which ran until 1960 under various titles.

After working on the 1962–63 ABC television show *Mr. Smith Goes to Washington*, starring Fess Parker as Eugene Smith and featuring Foley as Smith's Uncle Cooter, a homespun philosopher, Foley moved back to Nashville and continued touring until his death. He had already lived to enjoy election to THE COUNTRY MUSIC HALL OF FAME, in 1967. —*John W. Rumble*

## Tennessee Ernie Ford
b. Bristol, Tennessee, February 13, 1919; d. Reston, Virginia, October 17, 1991

Ernest Jennings "Tennessee Ernie" Ford, a resonant-voiced baritone and master of good-natured corn, rose to great popularity during the 1950s and 1960s and is best remembered for his exuberant 1955 cover of MERLE TRAVIS's "Sixteen Tons."

As a child Ford was musically inclined, singing in school choirs and playing trombone in the school band. He was working at BRISTOL, TENNESSEE, radio station WOPI by 1937 and went on to study at the Cincinnati Conservatory of Music before joining the U.S. Air Force. Discharged in 1946 and living in San Bernardino, California, Ford soon landed an announcer's job with Pasadena's KXLA. His comical Tennessee Ernie character ("bless your little pea-pickin' hearts . . . ") caught the ear of disc jockey–TV host CLIFFIE STONE, who made Ford a regular cast member of L.A.'s *Hometown Jamboree* country television and radio shows.

Signed to CAPITOL RECORDS in 1948 by LEE GILLETTE, Ford began cutting typically hot California country-boogie and novelty records that were driven as much by his big, warm voice as by the guitar stylings of Merle Travis and the idiosyncratic steel wizardry of SPEEDY WEST. Most of Ford's early releases made the country

*Tennessee Ernie Ford*

Top Ten. He first guested on the GRAND OLE OPRY in 1950, and in 1953 he became the first country singer to appear at London's prestigious Palladium. Soon NBC hired him to MC the television game show the *Kollege of Musical Knowledge* (1954) and also to host his own weekday program.

But it was "Sixteen Tons," with sales totaling 4 million copies, that cemented Ford's place as one of America's top entertainers. Due partly to this hit, the Ford Motor Company recruited Ford to host a prime-time NBC variety program, *The Ford Show* (1956–61), and the daytime *The Tennessee Ernie Ford Show* (1961–65). He also made numerous guest appearances on *I Love Lucy* and other TV series and became a fixture on television for the next decade.

Ford's first spiritual album, *Hymns*, was certified gold in 1959; by 1963 it was the biggest-selling album in Capitol's catalog. He ultimately recorded eighty-one sacred LPs.

Ford remained active through the 1970s with many TV specials and guest appearances. He participated in a 1973 *Hometown Jamboree* reunion at Los Angeles's Palladium and recorded for Capitol until 1977. Inducted into THE COUNTRY MUSIC HALL OF FAME in 1990, Ford fell at a White House dinner in September 1991 and remained hospitalized until his death from liver disease the following month. —*Jonny Whiteside*

## Forester Sisters
Kathy Forester Adkins b. Fort Oglethorpe, Georgia, January 4, 1955
Karen June Forester b. Fort Oglethorpe, Georgia, September 22, 1956
Kimatha ("Kim") Joy Forester b. Fort Oglethorpe, Georgia, November 4, 1960
Christy Forester Smith b. Fort Oglethorpe, Georgia, December 21, 1962

The Forester Sisters enjoyed a steady stream of hits from 1986 to 1991. After "I Fell in Love Again Last Night," "Just in Case," and "Mama's Never Seen Those Eyes"—all from their self-titled debut album—reached #1, they became ACM's 1986 Vocal Group of the Year. By the end of 1991 their albums had yielded fifteen Top Ten singles, five of them #1 hits.

Kathy, June, Kim, and Christy Forester grew up on church singing, which greatly influenced the harmonies they brought to country music. While they were performing in clubs around Chattanooga, Tennessee, a demo tape ended up at WARNER BROS. RECORDS, which invited them to a Nashville showcase and signed them. Tightly crafted and naturally blended harmonies complemented Kathy and Kim's lead singing, and a spunky attitude imparted a strong female perspective to hits such as "Lyin' in His Arms Again," "Leave It Alone," and "Don't You." Controversial radio host Rush Limbaugh used the sassy track "Men," from 1991's *Talkin' 'Bout Men*, as the theme song for a segment of his show featuring unsympathetic critiques of feminism.

After this album the Foresters' hits fell off, though they continued to record occasionally through the 1990s. As of 2011 they were semiretired. —*Jack Bernhardt*

## Howdy Forrester
b. Vernon, Tennessee, March 31, 1922; d. August 1, 1987

Howard Wilson "Howdy" Forrester was central to developing the modern Texas fiddle style, a tradition continued by fiddlers such as MARK O'CONNOR and BYRON BERLINE. He came by his talent naturally: his father and a grandfather both fiddled, and his Uncle Bob Forrester was a champion contest fiddler. At age eleven Howdy contracted rheumatic fever, and during an extended convalescence he taught himself to play tunes on his father's fiddle by listening to his mother sing. (His father had been killed in an auto crash six years earlier.)

In 1935 Howdy's family moved to Nashville. After working local square dances with his brothers, he graduated to professional status with Curt Poulton's THE VAGABONDS on the GRAND OLE OPRY in 1938 and 1939. Next he moved to Tulsa, Oklahoma, station KVOO in 1939 to join the Tennessee Valley Boys, a band led by former Vagabond Herald Goodman, founder of KVOO's *Saddle Mountain Roundup* show In 1940 Forrester switched to Dallas station KRLD and then returned to Nashville during 1941–42 for a stint with BILL MONROE's Blue Grass Boys. (Forrester's wife, Wilene "Sally Ann" Russell, played accordion for Monroe while Howdy served in the U.S. Navy during World War II.)

His military stint over, Howdy went back to KRLD from 1946 to 1949, teaming with Robert "Georgia Slim" Rutland. There they joined Benny Thomasson, Red Franklin, and others in perfecting what came to be called the Texas fiddle style, an intricate, exciting approach emphasizing continuous melodic variations through long bow strokes, varied accents, and double stops (playing two strings together in harmony). After playing briefly with Opry star COWBOY COPAS in 1950, Forrester joined ROY ACUFF's Smoky Mountain Boys in 1951 and remained a pillar of that group until 1964, when he joined the Acuff-Rose Artists Corporation (ARAC), then the booking operation of the ACUFF-ROSE PUBLICATIONS empire. In 1965 he became ARAC's president, a position he held until his death, while still making occasional tours and working the Opry with Acuff.

Over the years, Forrester recorded principally with Acuff's band but also cut a few sides for MERCURY with Georgia Slim in the late 1940s and later made solo albums for MGM (1957), United Artists (1963), Stoneway (1970s), and COUNTY (1983).

In 1987 he received the prestigious Fiddler Trophy at the Grand Masters Fiddle Contest held at the OPRYLAND theme park in Nashville, an award honoring his lifetime influence and achievements. —*John W. Rumble*

## Fred Foster
b. Rutherford County, North Carolina, July 26, 1931

As founder of MONUMENT RECORDS and COMBINE MUSIC, Fred Luther Foster played a pivotal role in the careers of ROY ORBISON, DOLLY PARTON, and KRIS KRISTOFFERSON, among many other singular talents. All of Orbison's classic hits of the early 1960s were produced by Foster and released on Monument; Parton was signed to both Monument and Combine before joining PORTER WAGONER's troupe; and Kristofferson was with Combine when he wrote some of his best-known tunes (including "Me and Bobby McGee," on which Foster shares writer's credit). In addition, Foster bankrolled many of Nashville's independent pop and R&B enterprises of the 1960s and 1970s, ultimately generating one of MUSIC CITY's most complex and interesting legacies.

The youngest of eight children, Foster started writing songs while working in the food service industry in Washington, D.C. There he met JIMMY DEAN, whose career he helped push. Foster later worked for MERCURY RECORDS, for ABC-Paramount, and for an independent pop record distributor in Baltimore. In early 1958, with virtually no capital, Foster started Monument Records, which he named for the Washington Monument. Later that year, BILLY GRAMMER's "Gotta Travel On," recorded in Nashville, became Monument's first hit.

In 1960, with songwriter BOUDLEAUX BRYANT's help, Foster moved to Nashville. Orbison's first Monument smash, "Only the Lonely (Know How I Feel)," was released that year. In 1963 Foster launched Sound Stage 7, Nashville's most prominent soul music–oriented label of the 1960s, and two years later he signed Parton, in whom he presciently saw enormous pop-country crossover potential, to Monument. Foster's enterprises thrived into the early 1970s, but by March 1983 he had filed for Chapter 11 bankruptcy. Combine was sold in 1986, and the Monument masters were bought by CBS Special Projects a year later. Among those who had made a bid for both companies was Parton, who, in 1981, had summed up the feelings of many who worked with Foster when she said, "Fred believed in me when nobody else did."

Despite the setback, Foster remained active in music publishing and recording. For Audium Records he produced RAY PRICE's *Time* (2002), and for LOST HIGHWAY RECORDS he produced WILLIE NELSON's *You Don't Know Me: The Songs of Cindy Walker* (2006) and *Last of the Breed* (2007), featuring Price, Nelson, and MERLE HAGGARD. —*Daniel Cooper*

## Jerry Foster and Bill Rice
Jerry Foster b. Tallapoosa, Missouri, November 19, 1935
Bill Rice b. Datto, Arkansas, April 19, 1939

The songwriting team of Jerry Foster and Bill Rice penned a phenomenal run of hits that stretched from the late 1960s to the mid-1980s. MICKEY GILLEY, JERRY LEE LEWIS, JOHNNY PAYCHECK, CHARLEY PRIDE, and CONWAY TWITTY were among the artists who vaulted well-crafted Foster and Rice ballads such as "The Easy Part's Over," "Someone to Give My Love To," and "Here Comes the Hurt Again" into the upper reaches of the country charts.

Foster and Rice met in 1961 while working the same Missouri club circuit. Earlier, Foster had recorded for Houston's Backbeat label, while Rice first tasted success when ELVIS PRESLEY recorded his "Girl Next Door Went A'Walking" for the 1960 album *Elvis is Back!* The duo moved to Nashville in 1967. With Foster supplying most of the lyrics and Rice concentrating on melodies and arrangements, they scored their first hit in 1968 when Charley Pride's recording of "The Day the World Stood Still" climbed to #4.

The hits kept coming, and in 1972 Foster and Rice received ten ASCAP songwriting awards. They broke their own record in 1974, snagging eleven more ASCAP honors. Foster and Rice were inducted into the NASHVILLE SONGWRITERS HALL OF FAME in 1994. —*Mick Buck*

## Radney Foster (*see* Foster & Lloyd)

## Stephen Foster
b. Lawrenceville, Pennsylvania, July 4, 1826; d. January 13, 1864

Stephen Collins Foster, one of America's first great songsmiths, had an enduring impact on country music. The son of a local politician, Foster followed his brothers into business when he was twenty, but he had already evinced a strong interest in music, which eventually became his principal pursuit. He wrote 189 songs in the last eighteen years of his short life. For many songs he was poorly paid; some (including "Old Folks at Home") he allowed to be published without his name for fear they would stigmatize his more serious efforts. An unhappy marriage and poor health plagued him until he died, penniless, from the consequences of excessive drinking. Many of his sentimental ballads ("Jeanie with the Light Brown Hair," "Beautiful Dreamer") endure; but his deepest mark was on the minstrel stage (see BLACKFACE MINSTRELSY), which he enriched with such favorites as "Oh! Susanna," "Camptown Races," "Old Folks at Home," "My Old Kentucky Home, Good Night," "Old Black Joe," and "Massa's in de Cold Ground." All of the latter were recorded by country music's first generation of recording artists (1924–30), a fact that attests to Foster's impact on the music of rural America long after his death. Recordings of Foster compositions by MARTY ROBBINS, ROY ORBISON ("Beautiful Dreamer"), THE BYRDS, PETER ROWAN ("Susanna"), the NITTY GRITTY DIRT BAND ("Swanee"—an alternate title for "Old Folks at Home"), and other country musicians further attest to Foster's influence. A Grammy-winning 2004 tribute album, *Beautiful Dreamer: The Songs of Stephen Foster*, featured several country music performers, including DAVID BALL, SUZY BOGGUSS, BR549, ALISON KRAUSS, Raul Malo, and JOHN PRINE. —*Norm Cohen*

## Foster & Lloyd
Radney Foster b. Del Rio, Texas, July 20, 1959
John William "Bill" Lloyd III b. Fort Hood, Texas, December 6, 1955

Radney Foster and Bill Lloyd each brought rock influences to country music. Both had been rock & roll buffs, with Lloyd especially influenced by the Beatles. Consequently, they featured a rock beat, jangly guitars, and an uptempo attitude—a combination that brought a fresh, youthful style to country and won new fans for the genre.

Foster gained a Nashville toehold as a songwriter; with similar ambitions, Lloyd quit college to move to MUSIC CITY in the early 1980s. The two musicians met in 1985, and at MTM MUSIC GROUP they began writing songs together, including the 1986 SWEETHEARTS OF THE RODEO hit "Since I Found You."

In 1987 Foster & Lloyd released their self-titled debut album on RCA. Their first single, "Crazy Over You," borrowing from ROCKABILLY and THE EVERLY BROTHERS, became a #4 country hit, and "Sure Thing" peaked at #8. The duo's second album, *Faster & Llouder* (1989), also blended rock with country. Foster & Lloyd pleased critics and younger fans, but not so much traditional country listeners. The act broke up in February 1991.

Foster signed with ARISTA RECORDS in 1992. His first album, *Del Rio, Texas, 1959*, reflected stronger country influences than his previous duo did and contained two Top Ten singles, "Just Call Me Lonesome" and "Nobody Wins." Two additional albums sold disappointingly as Foster ventured back toward rock and pop, but after shifting to Dualtone Records he hewed closer to country again with *Are You Ready for the Big Show* (2001), the first of several albums he made for the independent label. In 2009, Foster released the spiritually moving *Revival* on his own Devil's River label.

Lloyd, whose rock-oriented *Feeling the Elephant* appeared in 1987, continued as a studio guitarist—contributing to albums by STEVE EARLE, RICKY VAN SHELTON, and Al Kooper—and a sideman with Marshall Crenshaw and Cheap Trick. Lloyd's solo albums include *Set to Pop* (1994), *Standing on the Shoulders of Giants* (1999), and *Back to Even* (2004). He has also penned songs for TRISHA YEARWOOD, SARA EVANS, and MARTINA MCBRIDE, among many others. Foster & Lloyd reunited for a new album, *It's Already Tomorrow*, and tour in 2011. —*Bob Paxman*

## The Four Guys
"Harold" Brent Burkett b. Steubenville, Ohio, July 28, 1939; d. October 13, 2007
Laddie Cain b. Houston, Texas, November 22, 1951
John Frost b. Eagleville, Tennessee, December 3, 1949
Samuel Wellington b. Steubenville, Ohio, March 20, 1939

The Four Guys, a harmony quartet, came to the GRAND OLE OPRY in 1967. The group formed in the late 1950s, with an original lineup comprising bass singer Sam Wellington, baritone Brent Burkett, Berl Lyons (all from Steubenville), and Richard Garratt of McKeesport, Pennsylvania. Later they landed a vocal backup spot on the *WWVA JAMBOREE* in Wheeling, West Virginia. On New Year's Day 1967 the Four Guys arrived in Nashville. "We were very lucky that first year. Songwriter Bill Brock took an interest and asked OTT DEVINE [then the Opry's manager] to listen to us . . . and we became the first [modern] group to join the Opry without a hit record," said group cofounder Sam Wellington. The act became members on April 22, 1967. Through the years the group's lineup changed. Ex-gospel singer Gary Buck, a tenor, came aboard when Lyons left. After Buck and Garratt departed, baritone John Frost and tenor Laddie Cain joined. Early on, the act opened for HANK WILLIAMS JR. and toured with the CHARLEY PRIDE Show.

Although the Four Guys recorded for the MERCURY, RCA, Collage, and JNB labels, the group logged only three singles at the lower end of the charts. ("We just didn't get the promotion," noted Wellington.) Owning and operating the Harmony House dinner theater in Nashville between 1975 and 1984, the act eventually left the Opry and disbanded in 1999. —*Walt Trott*

## Four Star Records
established in 1945

Founded in 1945 by Dick Nelson as a sister label to his successful R&B imprint Gilt Edge, Four Star initially developed a scattershot roster ranging from pop musician Ted Fio Rito to country artist T. TEXAS TYLER. Operating from a combination office/pressing plant located at 467 Larchmont Avenue in Pasadena, California, the label was on the brink of receivership when Bill McCall, a hard-nosed entrepreneur with no music business background, invested $5,000 and gained controlling interest in the company. DON PIERCE, another industry novice, also joined the operation, and shortly thereafter Tyler's recordings of "Remember Me," "Filipino Baby," and "Deck of Cards" became Four Star's first substantive hits and led the company to concentrate on hillbilly releases.

Among the label's early acts were the MADDOX BROTHERS & ROSE (ca. 1947–52), FERLIN HUSKY (1949–51), WEBB PIERCE (1950), and SLIM WILLET (1952). PATSY CLINE was signed to Four Star from 1954 to 1960 (though her recordings appeared on Coral and DECCA as the result of a licensing agreement), and Four Star singer-songwriter CARL BELEW (1955) introduced the standards "Lonely Street," "Stop the World and Let Me Off," and "Am I That Easy to Forget?"

Although Four Star's roster was impressive, most acts left the label as soon as possible because, as Webb Pierce said, "He [McCall] thought it was a sin to pay anybody." Notorious for exploiting his artists, McCall regularly failed to pay or release from contractual obligation any Four Star act—unless compelled to do so by circumstance (such as union intervention or threats of physical harm). McCall's contractual stipulation that Cline record only songs from the Four Star publishing catalog is generally perceived as having hobbled the singer's early career.

In 1948 Four Star pioneered the use of semi-flexible vinylite, squeezing songs from several artists onto ten-inch discs and making them available for broadcast—a forerunner of the twelve-inch LP. Don Pierce sold his interest in Four Star in 1953 to become a principal in STARDAY RECORDS; shortly thereafter McCall himself relocated to Nashville to concentrate on publishing. GENE AUTRY and Joe Johnson bought Four Star Records in 1961 and subsequently leased the masters to Pickwick for several years. Four Star closed in the 1980s, with its catalog and assets sold to pay creditors. —*Jonny Whiteside*

## Wally Fowler
b. near Adairsville, Georgia, February 15, 1917; d. June 3, 1994

A GRAND OLE OPRY star in the mid-1940s, John Wallace "Wally" Fowler founded the group that became the OAK RIDGE BOYS. As the originator of the monthly "All Night Sing" gospel show at Nashville's RYMAN AUDITORIUM, he was an important figure in gospel music history.

Fowler joined the John Daniel Quartet, a gospel act, in 1935 as baritone singer and comedian, and the Daniel group joined the Opry in 1940. Fowler left Daniel in 1943 for a solo spot on WNOX's MID-DAY MERRY-GO-ROUND in Knoxville, Tennessee. At this point he began to find songwriting success, penning JIMMY WAKELY's #2 hit "I'm Sending You Red Roses" (1944) and composing EDDY ARNOLD's first single release, "Mommy, Please Stay Home with Me" (1945). With his own Georgia Clodhoppers, Fowler recorded two original tunes for a CAPITOL RECORDS single

in 1945: "Propaganda Papa" and "Mother's Prayer." CHET ATKINS, then a fellow WNOX cast member, made his recording debut as lead guitarist on the session.

Fowler joined the Opry on September 15, 1945. He recorded again for Capitol in 1946 and made the cover of *Billboard*. He also opened his own song-publishing company, Wallace Fowler Publications. By 1947, however, his Oak Ridge Quartet (a gospel unit made up of the Clodhoppers) had gained such a following that he turned to promoting gospel music. On Friday, November 5, 1948, he booked several gospel acts into the Ryman Auditorium for the first of many all-night singing programs. Broadcast in part over WSM, for a time they were to gospel music what the Opry was to country. Fowler became one of the biggest gospel promoters of the 1950s, but as his son-in-law, gospel musician Larry McCoy, observed, "Wally was a visionary, but not a very adept businessman." He sold his interest in the Oak Ridge Quartet (twice—he was legally enjoined from using the group name in 1965) and assembled several country groups.

Fowler drowned accidentally while fishing on Dale Hollow Lake near Nashville, apparently slipping off the bank. His fall may have been precipitated by a heart attack, but his family did not request an autopsy. —*Walter Carter*

## Curly Fox & Texas Ruby
Arnim LeRoy Fox b. Graysville, Tennessee, November 9, 1910;
 d. November 10, 1995
Ruby Agnes Owens b. Decatur, Texas, June 4, 1909; d. March 29, 1963

Curly Fox & Texas Ruby were a popular husband-wife team at Cincinnati radio station WLW's *Boone County Jamboree* (forerunner of the *MIDWESTERN HAYRIDE*) and on the GRAND OLE OPRY. A flamboyant showman on the fiddle, Fox influenced many younger players, while Texas Ruby had a husky contralto voice that may well have influenced PATSY CLINE.

Fox's father played fiddle, and Curly was also influenced by area musicians Tom Douglas and Ab Ferguson as well as by black railroad workers. Early on, Curly and friends Jimmy Brown and Bob Douglas toured with White Owl's Medicine Show (see MEDICINE SHOWS).

Working with the Roane County Ramblers, Fox made his first recordings in 1929 for COLUMBIA RECORDS. He left that group in 1932 to play Atlanta station WSB as Curly Fox & the Tennessee Firecrackers. He also recorded with THE SHELTON BROTHERS for the DECCA label. CLAYTON MCMICHEN got Fox into a fiddle contest circuit (sponsored by promoter Larry Sunbrock) that took him to Fort Worth, Texas, where he teamed with Ruby Owens, the younger sister of TEX OWENS and an established performer. (She had worked with ZEKE CLEMENTS at the Grand Ole Opry and at WHO in Des Moines, Iowa.) By 1936 the duo joined the Opry, where they stayed until 1938. Moving on to the *Boone County Jamboree* from 1940 to 1944, they returned to the Opry from 1944 to 1948. They were married on July 1, 1939, during a stint in Arkansas.

In 1945 and 1946 they recorded for Columbia, with Ruby singing on numbers such as "Blue Love" and "Don't Let That Man Get You Down." Fox's instrumental recordings of the classic fiddle tunes "Fire on the Mountain," "Listen to the Mockingbird," and "Black Mountain Rag" were genuine hits of day, although popularity charts did not reflect their success. Fox's KING RECORDS version of "Black Mountain Rag," released in 1948, played a major role in popularizing the tune.

*Curly Fox & Texas Ruby*

Stylishly attired and crisp in performance, Curly Fox & Texas Ruby commanded a wide following. In the 1940s they toured with WSM's leading tent show unit, played Constitution Hall and CARNEGIE HALL, and worked the LOUISIANA HAYRIDE. By 1948 the William Morris Agency signed them to WNBC-TV in New York, followed by seven years on KPRC-TV in Houston, Texas. In August 1962 they returned to the Opry.

Texas Ruby died in a trailer fire on March 29, 1963, while Curly was playing the *Friday Night Frolics* at WSM. Fox moved back to Graysville, Tennessee, in 1975, and retired from music in 1991. He died in 1995 and is buried on a hill overlooking the town of his birth. —*Tom Morgan*

## Jeff Foxworthy
b. Hapeville, Georgia, September 6, 1958

After years as one of the biggest draws on the U.S. comedy club circuit, Jeff Foxworthy became a household name with the six-word setup "You might be a redneck if . . ." Those words also provided the title for a 1994 WARNER BROS. album that sold more than 3 million copies; *Games Rednecks Play* (1995) also went multiplatinum. Four more albums followed through 2004.

Foxworthy grew up in an Atlanta suburb, graduated from Georgia Tech in 1979, and worked as a computer engineer for IBM. In 1984 he became a stand-up comic, eventually performing as many as 500 shows annually and winning Best Standup Comic honors at the 1990 American Comedy Awards. Foxworthy used his trademark phrase as the basis for a series of books that sold a combined total of more than 2 million copies through 1998 and published a number of additional titles, including an autobiography, *No Shirt, No Shoes . . . No Problem!*

In January 2000 Foxworthy teamed with fellow comedians Bill Engvall, Larry the Cable Guy, and Ron White to launch the Blue Collar Comedy Tour, which resulted in an album, TV specials, movies, and a satellite radio series as well as several short-lived TV series.

*The Jeff Foxworthy Show* premiered on ABC-TV in 1995, lasting one season. The program returned on NBC-TV in 1996 for another brief run. He became host of the game show *Are You Smarter Than a 5th Grader* in 2007 and has hosted *The Foxworthy Countdown*, a nationally syndicated radio program, since 1999. —*Calvin Gilbert*

## Cleve Francis
b. Jennings, Louisiana, April 22, 1945

Cleveland Francis Jr. sought acceptance as a country artist, but the media never overlooked the fact that he was a black cardiologist. Francis left his successful practice in Alexandria, Virginia, to pursue a country music career. When LIBERTY RECORDS president JIMMY BOWEN signed him to a recording contract, Francis became the first black to join a major label's country roster in many a year.

The oldest of six children born to Louisiana sharecroppers, Francis grew up listening to gospel, country, and CAJUN MUSIC. He played a guitar made from a cigar box and window screen wire until his mother bought him a Sears, Roebuck Silvertone model. Francis sang in church and at school functions, social gatherings, and clubs before making some independent albums.

Eventually Miami's Playback Records signed him, long after he had become a cardiologist. To promote his 1990 Playback single, "Love Light," Francis invested $25,000 in a music video, featured prominently on CMT. The video, especially his smooth vocals, caught Bowen's attention, and Francis rerecorded the song for his 1991 Liberty album *Tourist in Paradise*. "Love Light," "You Do My Heart Good," and "How Can I Hold You" resulted in modest chart success. Nevertheless, after the meager sales of *Tourist in Paradise* and the follow-up albums *Walkin'* (1993) and *You've Got Me Now* (1994), the label dropped him. Francis resumed his cardiology practice, but he made his GRAND OLE OPRY debut in 1996 and continues to perform, mostly around Washington, D.C. In 2006 he released *Story Time Live at the Birchmere*, recorded at that noted Alexandria venue. —*Calvin Gilbert*

## J. L. Frank
b. Limestone County, Alabama, April 15, 1900; d. May 4, 1952

Known as the Flo Ziegfeld of Country Music, Joseph Lee "J. L." Frank was the first major promoter and manager on the Nashville country music scene. He grew up in Giles County, Tennessee, near the Alabama border, and worked in Birmingham steel mills as a young man before moving to the coal mines of Illinois. At twenty-three, Frank headed for Chicago, where he eventually became a booking agent for radio stars Fibber McGee & Molly, GENE AUTRY, and other entertainers.

During the mid-1930s Frank based his operations in Louisville, Kentucky, for a time, promoting Autry briefly before Autry's move to Hollywood. Other acts then under Frank's wing were fiddler CLAYTON MCMICHEN and Frankie More & His Log Cabin Boys, then including Frank's son-in-law, PEE WEE KING. In mid-decade King struck out on his own, and Frank promoted

*J. L. Frank*

GEORGE JONES, and GEORGE STRAIT as well as pop diva Barbra Streisand and rock acts Dire Straits, Sting, and Billy Joel. Franklin was named ACM's best steel guitarist from 1994 through 1998, and he received eighteen CMA Musician of the Year nominations between 1989 and 2010.

A PEDAL STEEL GUITAR prodigy by age nine, Franklin drew inspiration from virtuosos PETE DRAKE and LLOYD GREEN. His studio career began when he played on Gallery's 1972 pop hit "Nice to Be with You." After high school, Franklin moved to Nashville, where he worked sessions and joined BARBARA MANDRELL's road band. He later backed DOTTIE WEST, JERRY REED, and MEL TILLIS on tour. In 1986 he returned to session work, with a hiatus in 1992 for a world tour with Dire Straits.

Franklin's combination of traditional country playing with rock, jazz, and fusion sounds keeps him in demand among artists and producers. He is the master of the pick-blocking technique; instead of muting strings with his hand, Franklin mutes them with his picks, thus allowing him to play effortlessly, even at fast tempos.

Franklin has also brought the resophonic guitarlike sound of the hybrid Pedobro (patented by his father) to albums, including RANDY TRAVIS's *Forever and Ever, Amen*; Franklin played his own baritone steel (a standard steel tuned down an octave) on albums by LEE ANN WOMACK and Andy Griggs.

In 2008, after the passing of JOHN HUGHEY, Franklin joined the Time Jumpers, regularly playing WESTERN SWING at Nashville's Station Inn. He is a member of The Players, a band composed of Nashville's top session musicians who play jazz fusion and rock. Franklin's live performing and accessibility to fans and musicians have helped make him the foremost pedal steel player of his generation. —*Jonita Aadland and Robert Kramer*

him in the Knoxville area. In 1937 Frank helped King & His Golden West Cowboys land a slot in the GRAND OLE OPRY lineup. By this time Frank had met ROY ACUFF around Knoxville, and in 1938 the promoter helped him follow King to the show. It was Frank who suggested that Acuff change his band's name from Crazy Tennesseans to the nobler-sounding Smoky Mountain Boys.

Frank's determination and sense of show business flair were instrumental in boosting Opry acts from solo gigs at small-town theaters and schools to sellout PACKAGE SHOWS he staged at big-city auditoriums. In addition to Autry, King, and Acuff, artists Frank assisted included EDDY ARNOLD, MINNIE PEARL, and ERNEST TUBB. Opry veteran Alton Delmore (the DELMORE BROTHERS) described Frank as "a clean-cut, neat fellow, handsome, with a little mustache and a big Texas hat. . . . He always had his heart in his work, and he always had a good word for the down-and-out musician. . . . He was an excellent promoter and he knew just what he wanted and he always got it." Frank's death, at the peak of his career, was widely mourned in the country music industry. Frank was elected to THE COUNTRY MUSIC HALL OF FAME in 1967. —*John W. Rumble*

## Paul Franklin

b. Detroit, Michigan, May 31, 1954

Highly versatile and inventive, steel guitarist Paul V. Franklin has been one of Nashville's top session musicians since the late 1980s, backing country stars BROOKS & DUNN, ALAN JACKSON,

## Tillman Franks

b. Stamps, Arkansas, September 29, 1920; d. October 26, 2006

Tillman Franks rose from sideman to manager during his many years in country music. In the late 1940s Franks worked on the Shreveport, Louisiana, police force while ingratiating himself with the city's burgeoning country music community. He was soon playing bass for several acts on KWKH's *LOUISIANA HAYRIDE*. He tailored "whiskey-and-devil" songs for THE BAILES BROTHERS, wrote "How Far Is Heaven" for KITTY WELLS (1949), and brought Elmer Laird's "Poison Love" to JOHNNIE & JACK (1950).

Later Franks toured with the *Hayride*'s WEBB PIERCE, joining a band that included FLOYD CRAMER, FARON YOUNG, JIMMY DAY, and the WILBURN BROTHERS. In addition, Franks successfully managed Pierce, the Carlisles (see BILL CARLISLE), CLAUDE KING, SLIM WHITMAN, and JOHNNY HORTON, with whom he cowrote the classics "Honky Tonk Man," "When It's Springtime in Alaska," and "Sink the Bismarck." Franks operated KWKH's booking department between September 1957 and August 1960. He was injured in the Texas car crash that took Horton's life in November 1960.

A group Franks dubbed the Tillman Franks Singers hit the charts in the mid-1960s with two STARDAY recordings, at about the time he began a long managerial association with Shreveport-area native DAVID HOUSTON. Franks continued to work from a Shreveport office until shortly before his death. He published his autobiography, *I Was There When It Happened*, in 2000. —*Ronnie Pugh*

## Dallas Frazier
b. Spiro, Oklahoma, October 27, 1939

One of country music's most successful, prolific, and influential songwriters, Dallas J. Frazier began his entertainment career at age twelve by winning a singing contest hosted by FERLIN HUSKY in BAKERSFIELD, California. By age fourteen Frazier had recorded his original song "Ain't You Had No Bringin' Up at All" on CAPITOL RECORDS. During the years 1954–58, Frazier appeared regularly on CLIFFIE STONE's HOMETOWN JAMBOREE TV show in Los Angeles, and when the Hollywood Argyles' 1960 recording of Frazier's "Alley Oop" hit #1 on the pop charts, the young songwriter was on his way to a long and distinguished career.

Frazier arrived in Nashville in 1963 as a staff writer for Ferlin Husky's music publishing company. Then, in 1965, while writing for JIM REEVES's Acclaim Music, he penned "Mohair Sam" for CHARLIE RICH. For Blue Crest Music, owned by former Reeves song plugger Ray Baker, and for ACUFF-ROSE PUBLICATIONS, Frazier began reeling off hit after hit, including JACK GREENE's classic "There Goes My Everything," which won 1967 CMA Song of the Year honors. In the late 1960s Frazier, frequently writing with A. L. "DOODLE" OWENS, had songs recorded by CONNIE SMITH ("Ain't Had No Lovin'," 1966), GEORGE JONES ("If My Heart Had Windows," 1967), JOHNNY DARRELL and O. C. SMITH ("The Son of Hickory Holler's Tramp," 1968), CHARLEY PRIDE ("I'm So Afraid of Losing You Again," 1969), and BRENDA LEE ("Johnny One Time," 1969). Jones paid homage to Frazier's skills with his 1968 Musicor album Sings the Songs of Dallas Frazier. Frazier also wrote TANYA TUCKER's first #1 hit, "What's Your Mama's Name" (1973). This tremendous run of success earned Frazier induction into the NASHVILLE SONGWRITERS HALL OF FAME in 1976.

Hits continued to flow from Frazier's pen and catalog, inspiring new generations of artists and songwriters. "Fourteen Carat Mind" was a smash for GENE WATSON in 1981. "Elvira," written and recorded by Frazier in 1966, was cut by RODNEY CROWELL in 1978 and later covered by the OAK RIDGE BOYS; their million-selling version earned CMA's Single of the Year Award in 1981.

In 1990 Frazier retired from songwriting to focus on his Christian ministry. In 2008 he returned to writing songs and the occasional public performance. —Kent Henderson

## Porky Freeman
b. Vera Cruz, Missouri, June 29, 1916; d. July 8, 2001

Quilla Hugh "Porky" Freeman claimed to have been the first artist to play the eight-beats-to-the-bar, boogie woogie style of music on the guitar. "Back in 1935," Freeman recalled to this author, "I got the idea of playing boogie woogie on the guitar. It amazed everybody, so we included it whenever we played the blues. I didn't realize at the time that this style of music was to become the standard of rock music as we know it today." In 1943 "Porky's Boogie Woogie on the Strings" was recorded on the Morris Lee label and again as "Boogie Woogie on the Strings," issued in the spring of 1944 on the ARA label; the latter proved to be an extremely popular recording.

Freeman started out in Springfield, Missouri, as a staff musician at radio station KWTO and worked Slim Wilson's radio show at KGBX before joining THE WEAVER BROTHERS & ELVIRY troupe. A move to Fort Worth, Texas, resulted in an association with the ROY NEWMAN and Bill Boyd bands (see BILL AND JIM BOYD). Upon arriving in Hollywood, Freeman worked throughout Southern California, settling down with Red Murrell's band at one of western music's favorite watering holes, L.A.'s Four Aces Club. At that time Murrell's outfit included JACK GUTHRIE, MERLE TRAVIS, Red Egner, BILLY HUGHES, JIMMIE DOLAN, and Bill "Slumber" Nichols.

In the late 1940s and into the 1950s, Freeman appeared with numerous acts in the Los Angeles area, most notably TEXAS JIM LEWIS. Meanwhile, Freeman recorded for the FOUR STAR label while providing solos and background fills on a number of hit recordings—"Oklahoma Hills" (JACK GUTHRIE), "Remember Me" (T. TEXAS TYLER), and "Love Song in 32 Bars" (JOHNNY BOND), as well as guitar on recordings by MERLE TRAVIS, Curt Massey, STUART HAMBLEN, SHEB WOOLEY, and JESSE ASHLOCK, to name a few. An electric guitar pioneer, Freeman registered several guitar patents. —Ken Griffis

## Janie Fricke
b. South Whitney, Indiana, December 19, 1947

Building on a career as a background vocalist and jingle singer, Janie Fricke became a successful solo artist, charting hits from 1977 through the 1980s. She had nine #1 country singles (two were duets), and she was CMA Female Vocalist of the Year in 1982 and 1983.

Growing up on a 400-acre farm, Fricke sang in church and, while in high school, at local shows. At Indiana University in the mid-1960s, her performances showed the influence of Joan Baez and Judy Collins. Between her sophomore and junior years she sang radio station jingles in Memphis.

After post-graduation stays in Dallas, Los Angeles, and again in Memphis, Fricke moved to Nashville in 1975 and became one of the town's most requested background and jingle singers, contributing vocals to national ad campaigns by Coors Beer, McDonald's, Ford, Pizza Hut, United Airlines, and Red Lobster. She also sang backup with artists including ELVIS PRESLEY, DOLLY PARTON, TANYA TUCKER, CHARLEY PRIDE, and RONNIE MILSAP. Her work with JOHNNY DUNCAN caught the attention of BILLY SHERRILL, Duncan's producer at COLUMBIA RECORDS.

Signed to Columbia in 1977, Fricke recorded hit duets with Duncan and CHARLIE RICH and had her first solo #1 record in 1982 with "Don't Worry 'Bout Me Baby." That was followed by a second consecutive #1 hit, "It Ain't Easy Bein' Easy." During 1983–85 she notched five more #1s, including "He's a Heartache (Looking for a Place to Happen)," "Tell Me a Lie," "Let's Stop Talkin' about It," "Your Heart's Not in It," and "A Place to Fall Apart" (with MERLE HAGGARD). Her success fell off after her final chart-topping record, "Always Have, Always Will," in 1986. —Gerry Wood

## Kinky Friedman
b. Chicago, Illinois, October 31, 1944

One of country music's most acerbic and iconoclastic performers, Richard F. "Kinky" Friedman grew up in AUSTIN, where his father taught at the University of Texas. After graduation, the younger Friedman spent three years in Borneo with the Peace Corps.

He formed a COUNTRY-ROCK band, the Texas Jewboys, in 1971. Rebuffed by record companies in Los Angeles, Friedman relocated to Nashville. There he recorded Sold American for the Vanguard label. The album generated instant notoriety with its mix of caustic but somber ballads, such as the title song, "Ride 'Em Jewboy," and satirical bombshells such as "Get Your Biscuits in the Oven (and Your Buns in the Bed)." A critical success, the project failed commercially.

In 1974 Friedman released *Kinky Friedman* on ABC, with similar results. After touring with BOB DYLAN in 1975–76, Friedman's *Lasso From El Paso* appeared on the EPIC label. In each case he demonstrated a knack for ribald social commentary and a mocking ethnocentrism ("They Ain't Making Jews Like Jesus Anymore") as well as a talent for writing songs of remarkable melodic and emotional delicacy ("Popeye the Sailor"). In 1983 Friedman released the eloquent *Under the Double Ego*, showcasing the memorable "Marilyn and Joe" and "People Who Read People Magazine." His recent albums include *Mayhem Aforethought* (2005).

Friedman has published a series of mystery novels about a wise-cracking Jewish former country music star from Texas known as the "Kinkster." In 1986 Friedman ran unsuccessfully as a Republican for justice of the peace in Kerr County, Texas. Sporting his trademark cigar, he made an unsuccessful bid for the Texas governorship in 2006, running as an independent, and he campaigned for the 2010 Democratic gubernatorial nomination. —*Stephen R. Tucker*

## David Frizzell

b. El Dorado, Arkansas, September 26, 1941

Lewey David Frizzell, a younger brother of LEFTY FRIZZELL, first topped the charts in 1981 with "You're the Reason God Made Oklahoma," a duet he recorded with Shelly West, DOTTIE WEST's daughter. At the time, Frizzell and West appeared to be fast-rising young stars of the URBAN COWBOY era. But in Frizzell's case, his triumphs were the result of more than twenty years' worth of hard work and career perseverance.

Like his brother Lefty, David Frizzell grew up around the oil fields of the Southwest. But in 1956 his family moved to California, near where Lefty, already a star, was living, and Lefty soon started taking his adolescent brother out on the road. David made his first full-fledged tour with Lefty as "Little David (Rock & Roll Sensation)," and in 1959 he recorded a couple of singles for COLUMBIA, Lefty's label.

David's rock & roll career got sidetracked when he joined the U.S. Air Force in 1960, but after his discharge he made a go of it in the West Coast country music scene. He eventually re-signed with Columbia, and in 1970 he recorded a version of "L.A. International Airport" that preceded Susan Raye's hit version. Soon thereafter BUCK OWENS made Frizzell a member of his road troupe, featuring him on his syndicated TV show and bringing him to CAPITOL RECORDS in 1973. But it wasn't until "You're the Reason God Made Oklahoma" was picked up by WARNER BROS. and featured in the 1980 Clint Eastwood movie *Any Which Way You Can* that David Frizzell's career took off. A string of duets with West ensued, as did "I'm Gonna Hire a Wino to Decorate Our Home," a #1 solo hit for Frizzell in 1982. His last Top Forty hit was in 1984, though he has continued to be involved in the country music business. —*Daniel Cooper*

## Lefty Frizzell

b. Corsicana, Texas, March 31, 1928; d. July 19, 1975

Described by MERLE HAGGARD as "the most unique thing that ever happened to country music," William Orville "Lefty" Frizzell was certainly one of the most influential performers in country music history. A supreme vocal stylist, he introduced an intimate, vowel-bending style of singing that has been internalized by countless younger stars in the years since Frizzell burst to stardom in 1950. Besides Haggard, such major acts as GEORGE JONES, ROY ORBISON, GEORGE STRAIT, KEITH WHITLEY, and RANDY TRAVIS have all paid him homage.

The son of an oil field worker, Frizzell grew up in and around the oil towns of Arkansas, East Texas, and Louisiana. Captivated by the yodel of JIMMIE RODGERS, he decided by the time he was twelve years old that he, too, wanted to be a professional singer. He performed in public for the first time during a school program, and he picked up the lifelong nickname of Lefty by decking a schoolmate with his left hand.

Living in Greenville, Texas, during World War II, Frizzell performed on KPLT in nearby Paris. During that time he met Alice Harper, whom he married in March 1945. After moving to Roswell, New Mexico, in 1946, Frizzell made regular appearances on Roswell's KGFL and with the house band at the Cactus Garden. But disaster struck in July 1947 when Frizzell was charged with statutory rape. Convicted the following month, he served six months in the county jail, during which time he wrote numerous songs to his wife, including "I Love You a Thousand Ways."

Several months after his release in 1948, Frizzell traveled to Shreveport, Louisiana, for a failed audition with the *LOUISIANA HAYRIDE*. After a time in El Dorado, Arkansas, he returned to southeastern New Mexico, and from there moved to Big Spring, Texas, where he sang at the Ace of Clubs.

In early 1950, while working in Big Spring, Frizzell made a trip to Dallas to "audition" at JIM BECK's recording studio. Beck showed little interest in Frizzell as a singer but was impressed with one of Frizzell's original songs, "If You've Got the Money I've Got the Time," which was only half written when Frizzell arrived in Dallas. Beck recorded Frizzell singing a demo of the lively HONKY-TONK number and took it to Nashville, hoping to interest COLUMBIA executive DON LAW in the song as a vehicle for

*Lefty Frizzell*

LITTLE JIMMY DICKENS. Instead, Law took an immediate interest in Frizzell's voice. In June 1950 Frizzell signed with Columbia, and his first session for the label was held at the Beck studio the following month. The two songs chosen for the first single were "If You've Got the Money I've Got the Time" and "I Love You a Thousand Ways." Released near the end of that summer, both sides of the record eventually hit #1 on the charts.

From that point forward, Frizzell's star rose with phenomenal speed. The year 1951 saw the release of several of his most memorable records, including the double-sided sensation "Always Late (With Your Kisses)" b/w "Mom and Dad's Waltz." Kicked off by CURLY CHALKER's ascending steel guitar intro, which leads into Frizzell's multisyllabic delivery of the words "always late," the former hit remains perhaps the definitive example of Frizzell's revolutionary vocal technique. "Always Late" spent twelve weeks at #1, and in October 1951 it was one of four songs that Frizzell placed in the *Billboard* Top Ten simultaneously. In April of that year he toured for a week with HANK WILLIAMS, and in July he became a member of the GRAND OLE OPRY.

However, Frizzell's life had been in turmoil throughout this period. He drank heavily, and in August 1951 he was arrested backstage at the Opry and charged with contributory delinquency; the charge stemmed from a liaison in Arkansas during his tour with Williams. (Frizzell was never prosecuted.) Frizzell also signed a succession of ill-considered, conflicting contracts, including one in January 1951 that designated JACK STARNES JR. as his manager. That contract led to a major lawsuit filed by Starnes against Frizzell in June 1952. It was settled out of court a year later.

Frizzell's extended stay at the top of the charts (thirteen Top Ten hits in roughly two years' time) was over by 1953, but he remained a popular star on the road. In 1954 he embarked on a grueling three-month tour backed by musicians from the *Louisiana Hayride*. The tour bankrolled a Frizzell family relocation to Southern California, and they ultimately settled in Northridge. While in California, Frizzell became a regular on the television program *Town Hall Party* (he had previously made a succession of sellout appearances on *Hometown Jamboree*), starred in the first country concert ever held at the Hollywood Bowl (August 6, 1955), and was given a star in the Hollywood Walk of Fame. But without full-time managerial care, Frizzell's career went into decline. From early 1955 to late 1958 he failed to score a chart hit of any kind. (The rock & roll crisis that so affected the country industry during these years had less to do with Frizzell's troubles than did his basic lack of career direction.) But as the decade neared a close, Frizzell scored a pair of back-to-back hits with "Cigarettes and Coffee Blues" and his original, classic version of "The Long Black Veil."

In 1962 the Frizzells moved to Nashville, eventually settling north of the city, in Hendersonville. The following year Frizzell recorded the last #1 record of his career, "Saginaw, Michigan." It topped the charts early in 1964 and was nominated for a Grammy. Then Frizzell's career again went into decline. His main advocate, producer Don Law, retired from Columbia in 1967, and in 1972 Frizzell was dropped from the label. He was quickly signed by ABC Records, however, and in December of that year he recorded the first of his ABC sessions.

By that time Frizzell had befriended songwriter WHITEY SHAFER, with whom he began cowriting. Their collaborations included "That's the Way Love Goes" and "I Never Go Around Mirrors," two of the most well-known songs in Frizzell's catalog. (The former was a #1 hit for JOHNNY RODRIGUEZ in 1973–74 and for Merle Haggard in 1984.) Frizzell's own versions of the two

songs appeared on his 1973 ABC album *The Legendary Lefty Frizzell*, which was followed a year later by *The Classic Style of Lefty Frizzell*. Though applauded by critics in the years since, the two albums went largely unnoticed when released.

By early 1975 Frizzell was telling friends and family that he wanted to get off the road and concentrate on songwriting. His pet project was a gospel album for which he and his songwriter friends would write new material. The project never came to pass.

A heavy drinker all his adult life, Frizzell also suffered from high blood pressure. In the early hours of July 19, 1975, he was felled by a stroke. He died that night. In 1982, Frizzell was elected to THE COUNTRY MUSIC HALL OF FAME. —*Daniel Cooper*

## Fruit Jar Drinkers

The Fruit Jar Drinkers were one of the GRAND OLE OPRY's original hoedown bands, and one of the most dynamic. During the 1930s, as the Opry was beginning to consolidate its position in country music, the Fruit Jar Drinkers were often chosen to sign off the radio broadcasts, and they were one of the first Opry groups to tour beyond Nashville.

The band's leader and founder was George Wilkerson (b. Stevenson, Alabama, July 8, 1895; d. March 5, 1954), a fiddler who had lived in Nashville since he was thirteen and who as an adult worked in a West Nashville lumberyard. By late 1927 he had formed a STRINGBAND with mandolin player Tommy Leffew (b. June 3, 1905; d. July 1, 1971), banjoist Claude Lampley (b. Bon Aqua, Tennessee, February 10, 1896; d. May 30, 1975), and guitarist Howard Ragsdale (b. Lyles, Tennessee, February 9, 1908; d. December 1966). All the band members lived and worked in West Nashville.

Though the Fruit Jar Drinkers soon became Opry regulars, they were the only one of the regular hoedown bands that did not record in their prime. (A studio band formed by UNCLE DAVE MACON recorded for Vocalion under the name Fruit Jar Drinkers, but it had no connection to Wilkerson's band.) A handful of home recordings dating from the mid-1930s, as well as air checks from the 1940s, show the band as a fast, driving ensemble propelled by Wilkerson's fine fiddling and Ragsdale's tenorlike banjo.

Throughout the 1930s and 1940s the Fruit Jar Drinkers continued to play the OLD-TIME stringband style; even after Wilkerson's death in 1953, the group, with varying personnel, kept going, often playing for Opry square dancers through the mid-1970s. —*Charles Wolfe*

## Robbie Fulks
b. York, Pennsylvania, March, 25, 1963

Robert William Fulks III spent his youth in Pennsylvania, Virginia, and North Carolina before joining midwestern BLUEGRASS band The Special Consensus as vocalist and guitarist in the early 1980s. Next he taught guitar at Chicago's Old Town School of Folk Music. As a solo artist, Fulks first received national attention when two of his singles appeared on compilations of alternative country music released on the Chicago-based Bloodshot label. Fulks's debut album, *Country Love Songs* (Bloodshot, 1996), included one of those singles, "She Took a Lot of Pills (and Died)," and established him as one of the finest, if iconoclastic, traditionalists working in alternative-country circles.

Fulks sometimes evokes the BAKERSFIELD style of BUCK OWENS, as on the Owens tribute "The Buck Stops Here" and "Rock Bottom, Pop. 1," which boast the PEDAL STEEL GUITAR playing of original Buckaroo TOM BRUMLEY. Backed by Missouri band the Skeletons, Fulks also assays tortured 1950s HONKY-TONK à la WEBB PIERCE and GEORGE JONES, but always with a distinctly contemporary edge.

After one album on Geffen Records, in 2000 Fulks released a collection of previously unissued tracks on his own Boondoggle Records (distributed by Bloodshot). *Couples in Trouble*, a non-country effort, as well as *13 Hillbilly Giants*, consisting of covers of country songs, appeared in 2001. With *Georgia Hard* (2005), recorded for Yep Roc, Fulks again explored his country roots. *Revenge!* (Yep Roc, 2007) featured both live concert performances and newly recorded material. *Rap of the Dead 2007* appeared on Boondoggle in 2008. —*Bill Friskics-Warren*

## Garth Fundis
b. Lawrence, Kansas, September 20, 1949

Respected for his work with DON WILLIAMS, KEITH WHITLEY, and TRISHA YEARWOOD, among others, Garth M. Fundis worked his way up from second engineer to producer, studio owner, RCA executive, and record label chief. He has been associated with dozens of country hits, many of them reaching #1.

Fundis began his Nashville career in 1971 at Sound Emporium—the studio he now owns—as a gofer and second engineer to the legendary JACK CLEMENT. He then became a staff engineer there before building and operating Clements's Jack's Tracks Recording Studios. Fundis engineered and sang harmony on Don Williams's records until 1978, when Williams invited Fundis to become his coproducer. They collaborated on a long series of Williams's laid-back country hits, including "Tulsa Time," "I Believe in You" (and CMA's 1981 Album of the Year by the same name), "Good Ole Boys Like Me," and "Lord I Hope This Day Is Good."

Fundis succeeded Blake Mevis as Keith Whitley's Nashville producer and helped the young traditional singer break through to stardom in 1988, beginning with the hits "Don't Close Your Eyes," "When You Say Nothing at All," and "I'm No Stranger to the Rain" (CMA's Single of the Year for 1989). In 1991 Fundis assembled unreleased material for Whitley's posthumous album *Kentucky Bluebird*.

In early 1990, Fundis heard demo singer Trisha Yearwood at a Nashville nightclub and began a collaboration that yielded a string of quality albums and hits such as "She's in Love with the Boy,"

"Walkaway Joe," "The Song Remembers When," "Thinkin' About You," and "Believe Me Baby (I Lied)."

Fundis joined the RCA Label Group Nashville (see RCA RECORDS) in 1993 as vice president of A&R. He signed Jon Randall, a veteran of EMMYLOU HARRIS's Nash Ramblers, and former GARTH BROOKS guitarist Ty England before leaving the company in April 1995. At the invitation of industry veterans Herb Alpert and Jerry Moss, Fundis opened the Nashville office of their new label, Almo Sounds. There he signed Paul Jefferson and enlisted Fleetwood Mac member Billy Burnette, son of ROCKA-BILLY original DORSEY BURNETTE, and Bekka Bramlett, daughter of Delaney and Bonnie Bramlett, as a duo, Bekka & Billy.

By 2000 Almo Sounds closed its Nashville office, and Fundis returned to independent production. Since then he has worked with Yearwood, SUGARLAND, and other acts. He was board chairman for NARAS from 2001 to 2003 and has served as trustee and president of the Recording Academy's Nashville chapter. —*Jay Orr*

## J. B. Fusilier
b. Oberlin, Louisiana, April 17, 1901; d. August 1976

From the mid-1930s to the mid-1960s, Jean Batiste Fusilier was a leading fiddle pioneer of CAJUN MUSIC. The height of his success was in the Cajun STRINGBAND era, from 1935 to 1942. He is credited with writing the popular Cajun hit "Chère Te Te," and he recorded early stylized versions for many later fiddle standards, such as "Lake Arthur Stomp" and "Lake Arthur Waltz." His greatest Cajun hit was "Ma Cher Bassett," written for one of his wives, Regina Fontenot.

Initially Fusilier was the fiddler in Miller's Merrymakers, led by Beethoven Miller. But Fusilier's talent quickly had him leading the band, and when Miller left the group the act's name changed to J. B. Fusilier & His Merrymakers.

Live radio broadcasts propelled Fusilier's huge success. His early band, including Miller on drums, Preston Manual on guitar, and Atlas Frugé on steel, would work live radio shows during the day and then play dances at night. After World War II the band was composed of J.B. on accordion, Manual on guitar, Norris "T-Boy" Courville on drums, and Elius Soileau on fiddle.

Fusilier suffered a setback in 1955 when he was hit by a car while changing a tire in the fog on Highway 190 in Eunice, Louisiana. The legendary accordionist IRY LEJEUNE, with him at the time of the accident, was killed by the same car.

Fusilier died at age seventy-five, having made music his lifelong priority. —*Ann Allen Savoy*

# The Folk and Popular Roots of Country Music

## NORM COHEN

Just as there are many substyles of country music, so, too, the precursors to the music are many. Today's commercial country music did not evolve from a single strain of rural folk music but was a melding of a number of earlier musical types, including folk music, minstrel songs, jazz, ragtime, and the sentimental songs of Tin Pan Alley. The most well-known component of early country music, of course, was the folk music of the largely rural southern United States, much of which can be traced to the folk music of the British Isles.

Because a handful of folklorists were first among the few scholars to pay serious attention to country music, the strong link between early country (i.e., hillbilly) music and traditional folk music was long ago established. (In this article I use the term "hillbilly" nonpejoratively to refer to recorded country music of the period 1924–41. It is a term that was widely used in the industry at the time, though with varying degrees of deprecation.) John and Alan Lomax, in brochure notes to early LP reissues of 78-rpm recordings from the 1920s and 1930s, and D. K. Wilgus, Archie Green, Ed Kahn, and other folklorists, in the pages of the *Journal of American Folklore, Western Folklore*, and other scholarly publications, argued persuasively that early hillbilly recording acts in the years 1923–26 were folk musicians who learned their music orally from family and friends, as do any traditional folk artists. Pioneering scholars further argued that these performers' repertoires were rich in Anglo-American folk ballads, songs, and fiddle tunes of the nineteenth century—even including a small but significant handful of older material of Anglo-Celtic origin. In support of their thesis, they pointed to early recordings of British BALLADS (e. g., "Barbara Allen" by VERNON DALHART, "Pretty Polly" by DOCK BOGGS, and "Knoxville Girl" by MAC & BOB), English or Irish fiddle tunes (numerous recordings of "Soldier's Joy," "Leather Breeches," or "Devil's Dream"), and traditional American ballads from the nineteenth century ("Omie Wise" by G. B. Grayson & HENRY WHITTER, "When the Work's All Done This Fall" by CARL T. SPRAGUE, and "John Henry" by almost everyone). Wilgus, Green, and other scholars following their example expended considerable efforts in the 1950s, 1960s, and 1970s locating the hillbilly artists who had made the recordings of the 1920s and 1930s to document their careers and establish how traditional folk music became the basis for a commercially successful idiom.

In a general way, two standard patterns emerged, though many musicians fell between these two idealized extremes. On the one hand, record company A&R men ("artists and repertoire" men, the early term for producers), sought out well-known (and, incidentally, older) regional artists who, while not full-time professionals, had nevertheless established local reputations as popular performers at fiddlers' conventions, political rallies, and other social events. These musicians—FIDDLIN' JOHN CARSON, GID TANNER, Uncle Am Stuart, and Uncle Bunt Stephens among them—were happy to entertain on records as they did in person, but in most cases did not give up their day jobs. At the other extreme were a younger generation of artists—JIMMIE RODGERS, the CARTER FAMILY, CLAYTON MCMICHEN, BOB WILLS, and others—who cherished fervent aspirations of turning pro. These were the acts that provided the impetus for the changes in the styles of country music between the 1920s and 1940s. And, as the industry developed, the contributions of the "part-timers" diminished and their places were taken by those who made music their careers. In barest outline, this synopsis accounts for the emergence of a professional country music industry out of the casual efforts of semiprofessional folk artists—a transformation that took place in the late 1920s and early 1930s.

## THE LESS-WELL-KNOWN WELLSPRINGS OF COUNTRY

In addition to traditional British-American folk music, other important strains of American popular music affected the music we have come to know as country—namely, the American commercial musical traditions of the late nineteenth and early twentieth centuries, such as minstrel shows, vaudeville, rag-time, blues, jazz, Tin Pan Alley sentimental balladry, and hymnody and gospel music, both African American and Anglo-American. These tributary streams are evident not only in the recordings by early hillbilly musicians (which are our most extensive, most durable, and certainly most tangible documentation) but also in the fragmentary gleanings from reports of live concerts, radio broadcasts, fiddlers' conventions, and other public events featuring country music. (It is ironic that phonograph records, which are our primary sources of information, were justifiably regarded by most early hillbilly musicians as only of secondary or tertiary importance in terms of income potential.)

## THE MINSTREL STAGE

If we ignore the problem of the origins of minstrel music—a problem that in the past engendered some mean-spirited (if not outright racist) denigrations of the contributions of African American entertainers to the genre—the fact remains that the minstrel stage was the first important commercial entertainment medium in the United States to have demonstrable influence on our folk culture. BLACKFACE MINSTRELSY has shaped folk and commercial entertainment in both form and content, in areas musical and nonmusical.

Musically, minstrel traditions are most visible in the songs and tunes created for the minstrel stage that long outlived that form of presentation: songs by STEPHEN FOSTER ("My Old Kentucky Home," "Old Black Joe"), Daniel D. Emmett ("Old Dan Tucker," "De Blue Tail Fly," "Jawbone," and possibly "Dixie," whose authorship has been strongly contested), B. R. Hanby ("Darling Nellie Gray"), Sam DeVere ("Carve Dat Possum"), and others. In the twentieth century these titles came to be associated with country music entertainers such as UNCLE DAVE MACON, SAM AND KIRK MCGEE, GRANDPA JONES, and STRINGBEAN; a number of them are still current in repertoires of BLUEGRASS musicians. Some of the most racially offensive songs mercifully have been stripped of their lyrics, surviving in hillbilly/country music only as instrumental pieces (e. g., "Turkey in the Straw," published in 1834 as "Zip Coon").

From a nonmusical standpoint, mistrelsy heavily influenced performance style. The three stock minstrel show figures—Mr. Interlocutor, the pompous master of ceremonies who played the straight man, and Mr. Tambo and Mr. Bones, the tambourine- and bone- or castanet-playing virtuosi who excelled at humorous repartee—can be found in the comedy routines of innumerable country and bluegrass acts. (ARCHIE CAMPBELL's longtime favorite routine, "That's Good, That's Bad," was a minstrel show standard.) The very essence of the minstrel show—namely, the interspersion of musical with nonmusical entertainment—became part and parcel of live country music shows for much of the twentieth century. A recent manifestation of the minstrel show format was the widely popular *HEE HAW*, a network and, later, nationally syndicated television series that combined country music with humor. Furthermore, a case has been made (though it is not indisputable) for the role of the minstrel stage in making the banjo and certain styles of banjo playing traditional in the southern mountains.

Finally, the defining minstrel technique of blacking one's face with burnt cork to emulate—nay, caricature—the facial features of African American slaves became so taken for granted (even African American minstrel entertainers after the Reconstruction were obliged to use burnt cork!) that performers such as Al Jolson and Eddie Cantor continued the practice onstage well into the twentieth century. School and community groups routinely staged minstrel shows into the 1930s, and in more rural settings, "blacking up" survived in traveling musical troupes such as TENT SHOWS and MEDICINE SHOWS—entertainment media in which many early country music stars (Jimmie Rodgers, GENE AUTRY, Bob Wills, and ROY ACUFF among them) gained early experience.

## TIN PAN ALLEY

In the late 1880s, the sheet music–publishing business became centralized on New York's 28th Street. Out of this cluster of publishers, dubbed "Tin Pan Alley" by a newspaper reporter, came most of America's popular music for more than four decades. Since a major product of this pop music industry during the 1880s and 1890s was the sentimental ballad, it has sometimes been convenient to use the terms "Tin Pan Alley music" and "sentimental songs" interchangeably, notwithstanding the lack of perfect congruity between these rubrics. Among the titles that were long current in hillbilly repertoires and also were frequently encountered by folk-song collectors "in the field" were "When You and I Were Young, Maggie" (written by Johnson and Butterfield, 1866; recorded, for example, by Fiddlin' John Carson), "Little Rosewood Casket" (Goullaud and White, 1870; BRADLEY KINCAID), "Little Old Log Cabin in the Lane" (WILL HAYS, 1871; Carson), "Silver Threads Among the Gold" (Rexford and Danks, 1873; RILEY PUCKETT), "In the Baggage Coach Ahead" (Davis, 1896; GEORGE RENEAU), "The Letter Edged in Black" (Nevada, 1897; Vernon Dalhart), "Lightning Express" (Helf and Moran, 1898; BLUE SKY BOYS), and "Down By the Old Mill Stream" (Taylor, 1910; Cliff Carlisle [see BILL CARLISLE]). (Though only one recording artist has been noted for each of these songs; many others could also be cited.) Many of these compositions actually predate the geographic "Tin Pan Alley," but they came from the same urbane professional songwriting tradition. Also important in this period were novelty songs—in particular "coon songs" composed in pseudo-Negro dialect. Most of these portrayed the African American in a deprecatory light, though a few (e.g., "Golden Slippers") were fairly neutral.

The principal media of dissemination of Tin Pan Alley's products were at first the song sheet and the stage show. The successor to the minstrel show (though it began in the 1860s) was "variety," renamed in 1871 with the French term "vaudeville." Tony Pastor (not to be confused with the 1920s–1950s orchestra leader of the same name) is generally credited with launching variety/vaudeville on the stage, and he vigorously laundered his productions to make them acceptable to women and children. Pastor also was the first to send vaudeville troupes on tour. In the 1920s, vaudeville shows in many southern and midwestern cities, such as Nashville, Cincinnati, and Birmingham, occasionally included hillbilly acts and thus increased opportunities for the blending of popular and folk repertoires.

## RAGTIME

As the dance craze of the early 1900s seized the nation's attention, instrumental and dance music began to supplement the sentimental ballads and songs of the Victorian era. The term "ragtime" is used in two different senses. Some writers apply it narrowly to the highly formal creations of classically oriented composers, such as Scott Joplin, James Scott, and Joseph Lamb; others use it more broadly to encompass a much larger body of popular compositions, instrumental or vocal, with certain kinds of syncopation. In any case, it now seems clear that there was an earlier style of syncopated, or ragtime, music that existed on a folk level, which professional composers drew on and formalized. Few formal rags entered hillbilly tradition—"Dill Pickles" (recorded by THE KESSINGER BROTHERS ), "Black and White Rag" (Bill Boyd's Cowboy Ramblers [see BILL AND JIM BOYD]), "St. Louis Tickle" (Lowe Stokes & RILEY PUCKETT), and a few cakewalks were the principal ones. It seems, rather, that the ragtime influence entered folk/country music via the older African American folk ragtime tradition and expressed itself in pieces such as "Beaumont Rag" (Bob Wills, Bill Boyd), "East Tennessee Blues" (Al Hopkins & His Buckle Busters [see THE HILL BILLIES]), and "Ragtime Annie" (W. LEE O'DANIEL & HIS LIGHT CRUST DOUGHBOYS). Other sheet music standards with ragtime elements or precursors that entered hillbilly tradition included Kerry Mills's "At a Georgia Camp Meeting" (recorded by the LEAKE COUNTY REVELERS) and Irving Berlin's "Alexander's Ragtime Band" (Clayton McMichen's Georgia Wildcats).

## JAZZ

While its roots are older, jazz emerged in the 1910s as a style with major exposure and impact, to a large extent replacing ragtime as the most popular music in America. Many hillbilly musicians of the 1920s—notably younger ones, such as McMichen, Lowe Stokes, and Hoke Rice (see THE RICE BROTHERS), all of North Georgia—were fascinated by jazz and persevered in incorporating it into their recorded repertoires, though with mixed success. Important early examples include "Farewell Blues," "House of David Blues," "Take Me to the Land of Jazz," "Tiger Rag," and "Twelfth Street Rag." In the Southwest, this association was even stronger, with WESTERN SWING pioneers MILTON BROWN and Bob Wills regularly listening to, and borrowing from, jazz and blues hits of the day.

## BLUES

Commercial recordings of country blues began in 1924. There is ample evidence that early hillbilly performers listened to the records of such black musicians as Blind Lemon Jefferson (e.g., listen to Larry

Hensley's remarkable 1934 recording "Match Box Blues," reissued on CD in 1993), Blind Blake, the Mississippi Sheiks, and others. Still earlier were recordings of pop blues compositions by such writers as W. C. Handy, who created a formal style of blues out of folk tradition, much as did Scott Joplin with ragtime. Several of Handy's compositions subsequently became hillbilly and/or early western swing standards ("Hesitating Blues" and "Beale Street Blues" were both recorded by CHARLIE POOLE & THE NORTH CAROLINA RAMBLERS; "St. Louis Blues" by Milton Brown and Bob Wills), as did other blues of the 1920s, including "Corrine" (recorded by Wills and Milton Brown, probably learned from Cab Calloway), "Sittin' on Top of the World" (by Wills, Brown, BILL MONROE, and others, learned from the Mississippi Sheiks), and "(Steel) Guitar Rag" (originated by bluesman Sylvester Weaver and later popularized by Bob Wills's band).

## GOSPEL MUSIC AND HYMNODY

Even though some ninety years of recorded country music have witnessed the steady erosion of the barriers between country and pop in both musical style and lyrical content, one persistent difference is the extent to which country artists still incorporate religious songs into their performances and recordings. The distinction between a folk tradition and a more formal one is often difficult to discern in the sphere of religious music, yet there are many standard pieces in the early hillbilly repertoire that are unmistakably identified with sheet music or early concert-type recordings. Among them are "The Old Rugged Cross" (recorded by the Light Crust Doughboys, Mac & Bob, and others), "Shall We Gather at the River" (Uncle Dave Macon), "Sweet Bye and Bye" (SID HARKREADER & Grady Moore), and "Church in the Wildwood" (Carter Family, CHUCK WAGON GANG).

## THE EARLY INFLUENCE OF POPULAR RECORDINGS

Because hillbilly music was largely (though not exclusively) an aural/oral tradition, it is not surprising that recordings influenced pioneering hillbilly musicians far more than sheet music did. Wind-up cylinder and disc-playing machines found their way into many homes in the rural and small-town South early in the twentieth century. We also have the word of several artists who bought and listened to early records. Charlie Poole was captivated by the banjo playing of the oft-recorded turn-of-the-century virtuosi Fred Van Eps and Vess L. Ossman; Clayton McMichen doted on classical violinist Fritz Kreisler; Jimmie Rodgers learned "Bill Bailey" from an early pop recording; and Dorsey Dixon (see THE DIXON BROTHERS) learned "The Preacher and the Bear" in the same manner. Nonprofessional singers, too, absorbed songs and styles from the early records they played on their wind-up machines.

On the other hand, pianos and sheet music were not unfamiliar in rural southern homes. So the mere occurrence of a hillbilly recording of a song that had been recorded previously by popular entertainers does not necessarily prove that the song was learned from the early recording, if sheet music were also available. But in some cases, particularly if the vocal nuances of a hillbilly recording are strikingly reminiscent of an earlier pop recording, we can confidently assert a direct aural influence. Examples would be "Moving Day" (compare Arthur Collins's version with the later Charlie Poole rendition); "Ticklish Reuben," written and popularized by Cal Stewart ("Uncle Josh") and recorded by many hillbilly singers; and "Sleep, Baby, Sleep" (recorded by Jimmie Rodgers at his first session), with its ubiquitous yodel on both hillbilly recordings and earlier pop ones. Directly or indirectly, the numerous pop recordings of "Listen to the Mocking Bird" must have left their mark on (ARTHUR "GUITAR BOOGIE" SMITH, CURLY FOX, and others), since there is nothing in sheet-music sources to suggest the elaborate bird imitations that have become a standard part of the piece.

In certain instances, we can reasonably assume an influence by a phonograph recording simply on the grounds that the recording was much more popular and widespread than the sheet music for the same song. This would seem to be the case for Uncle Josh's "Monkey on a String" (covered by Charlie Poole) and "I'm Old but Awfully Tough" (the latter has been recorded by traditional folk artists but not commercially by hillbilly musicians), "Whistling Rufus," and various "laughing" and "crying" novelty records. On the other hand, while numerous pop recordings of the dialog "Arkansas Traveler" may have prompted hillbilly artists such as Gid Tanner & Riley Puckett, EARL JOHNSON & His Clodhoppers, J. W. Day, Clayton McMichen & Dan Hornsby, and the Tennessee Ramblers to record this humorous sketch, the textual variations suggest that the piece was known from other sources—probably oral tradition. With pre–World War I pieces such as "Casey Jones" and "The Bully" that were equally popular in sheet music and on record, it is difficult to assert the priority of disc influence. But by the 1920s, the influence of records had, in general, come to outweigh that of sheet music so preponderantly that an aural source can in most instances be assumed. Wendell Hall's "It Ain't Gonna Rain No Mo'" is a case in point. It must have been his recordings rather than the sheet music that inspired so many early folk and hillbilly singers (including Gid Tanner, The Tune Wranglers, and Hank Penny) to cover it.

As we have seen, along with the many songs derived from pieces like "Barbara Allen," "John Henry," and "Devil's Dream," there are just as many in the repertoires of early country/hillbilly musicians similar to "Letter Edged in Black" and "My Old Kentucky Home" whose paternities have indisputable genetic markers that still smell of the printer's ink or the turntable's wax. As country music became a commercially viable product, songs and ballads of regional interest gave way to lyrics with national appeal; local dialects and accents yielded to more homogeneous singing styles; and rustic instruments (banjo, mandolin, dulcimer, even fiddle) were supplemented if not replaced by various guitars, basses, pianos, and percussion instruments. As the 1930s wore on, most hillbilly artists who strove to establish professional careers with their musical skills exhausted their supply of old standards learned in childhood, from friends and relatives, or from early 78s and cylinders played on family phonographs and gramophones. Naturally, performers turned to composing their own material or to using songs crafted by professional tunesmiths. In the decades after World War II, such newly minted songs have become predominant in country music.

# G · G · G · G · G · G

## GAC

During the early twenty-first century, cable network Great American Country (GAC) became a significant media force, available in as many as 56 million North American homes via cable and satellite.

GAC launched December 31, 1995, as a venture of Jones Radio Network of Centennial, Colorado, a satellite provider of syndicated music programming. GAC went live with GARTH BROOKS's video "The Thunder Rolls." It built most of its programming around music videos, whereas its chief competitor, CMT, followed its corporate sibling, MTV, into reality and lifestyle shows, even as music-video viewing migrated heavily to the Internet.

Most cable providers would carry only one country music network, and growth was a challenge. In October 2004, Jones sold GAC to E.W. Scripps Company of Knoxville, Tennessee. Operating out of MUSIC ROW studios and a facility north of Nashville, hosts, including WSM radio's Bill Cody, have largely maintained a format of interviewing country stars and introducing MUSIC VIDEOS. In 2007 GAC premiered its first reality series, *The Hit Men of Music Row*, which followed top songwriters BOB DIPIERO, Tony Mullins, JEFFREY STEELE, and CRAIG WISEMAN. In 2009 the network renamed its long-running news show from *Country Music Across America*—hosted by Storme Warren—to *Headline Country*. —*Craig Havighurst*

## Joe Galante
b. Queens, New York, December 18, 1949

Joe Galante is one of country music's most successful and influential record executives. Under his leadership, RCA RECORDS became *Billboard*'s Country Label of the Year for more than a decade on the strength of acts including ALABAMA, THE JUDDS, CLINT BLACK, KEITH WHITLEY, and K. T. OSLIN. In the process, Galante applied pop promotion techniques to country music and greatly expanded its commercial horizons.

The son of working-class Italian immigrants, Galante graduated from Fordham University with a finance and marketing degree in 1971 and eventually joined RCA in New York as a budget analyst. He soon moved into product management and was transferred to Nashville in 1973 to become manager of administration. Though some found his direct, outspoken ways abrasive, he learned about country music and Nashville's southern customs from RCA executives CHET ATKINS and JERRY BRADLEY, and from RCA artists WAYLON JENNINGS, RONNIE MILSAP, and DOLLY PARTON.

In 1977 Galante was named director of Nashville operations, and he rapidly ascended to vice president of promotion and then

to vice president of marketing. In 1982 he succeeded Bradley as head of RCA Nashville, becoming the youngest person to lead a major Nashville label and one of the first to rise primarily through marketing instead of following the usual A&R route. Fiercely competitive, he boosted sales by cutting the roster and securing funds from corporate headquarters so that the Nashville division could market its own artists and recordings. RCA became the top country label during the 1980s, a track record that helped lead Germany's Bertelsmann Music Group (BMG) to purchase RCA in 1986.

Galante established a reputation for his aggressive, relentless approach to finance, marketing, and merchandising, but he also developed artists including Alabama, the Judds, and Keith Whitley. In 1988 Galante signed LORRIE MORGAN, and he

*Joe Galante*

confounded critics by signing K. T. Oslin, a mature singer-songwriter, who went on to win a Grammy. In addition, he brought CLINT BLACK, EARL THOMAS CONLEY, and RESTLESS HEART aboard. Over the years, Galante's RCA roster also has included VINCE GILL, KENNY ROGERS, JOHN ANDERSON, AARON TIPPIN, and JUICE NEWTON.

In 1990 Galante moved to New York to become president of RCA Records U.S. In this role he signed successful acts including the Dave Matthews Band and the hip-hop group Wu-Tang Clan, but he was unable to reverse the label's sagging national fortunes.

In late 1994 Galante returned to Nashville as chairman of BMG's RCA Label Group Nashville, which now included the BNA (RCA RECORDS) label, established as an RCA sister label in 1991. During his absence, the Label Group lost dominance to MCA and ARISTA, but Galante quickly regained momentum with KENNY CHESNEY, SARA EVANS, and MARTINA MCBRIDE, among others. BROOKS & DUNN, ALAN JACKSON, and BRAD PAISLEY came into the fold when BMG combined its Arista Nashville operations with the RCA Label Group during 1999–2000. In this arrangement, RCA, BNA, and Arista shared the same core marketing team.

Along with John Grady, Galante helmed the Nashville division of Sony BMG, created in 2004 as a joint venture between SONY MUSIC and BMG. Grady handled COLUMBIA, EPIC, Lucky Dog, and MONUMENT, while Galante oversaw the RCA, BNA and Arista labels until Grady's departure in 2006, after which Galante ran all of Sony BMG's Nashville operations. Following Sony's 2008 purchase of BMG's interest in the undertaking, Galante became chairman of Sony Music Entertainment Nashville until he decided to leave the company in 2010. In addition to aforementioned artists, Sony Music's various rosters include CARRIE UNDERWOOD, MIRANDA LAMBERT, and KELLIE PICKLER. —*Beverly Keel*

## Galax, Virginia

On the second weekend every August, thousands of OLD-TIME MUSIC and BLUEGRASS enthusiasts make the pilgrimage to Galax, a small textile town in the Blue Ridge Mountains, for the annual Old Fiddlers' Convention. Nestled between Carroll and Grayson Counties in southwestern Virginia, the Galax area was home to such early country music stalwarts as HENRY WHITTER and ERNEST V. STONEMAN, and it boasts a rich, centuries-old heritage of STRINGBAND music.

The earliest-known fiddle contest in the nation took place near Richmond in 1736, and the tradition remained strong in Appalachian communities. The first Galax convention was held in 1935 to raise money for local Moose Lodge #733; the winning fiddle tune was a rendition of "The Old Hen Cackled," and Galax's own Bog Trotters took honors as Most Entertaining Band. Through the years, contestants have included Stoneman; claw-hammer banjoist Wade Ward; MEDICINE-SHOW performer CLARENCE "TOM" ASHLEY; fiddler Benton Flippen; and bluegrass multi-instrumentalist JIMMY ARNOLD. One of the largest on the old-time festival circuit, the multiday event now features more than a dozen competitive categories embracing fiddlers and other musicians, thousands of dollars in prizes, and contestants from around the world. However, the basic rules remain as if etched in stone: only nonelectrified string instruments are allowed, and contestants must perform only folk and mountain songs in the public domain. —*Eddie Dean*

## Al Gallico
b. Brooklyn, New York, June 5, 1919; d. May 15, 2008

Al Gallico was one of country music's foremost independent publishers during the 1960s and 1970s; his firms handled such famous copyrights as "Almost Persuaded," "Stand By Your Man," and "The Most Beautiful Girl." Gallico also copublished "The Happiest Girl (In the Whole U.S.A.)," written and recorded by DONNA FARGO.

After working as an errand boy at G. Schirmer in New York in 1938, Gallico landed a job in 1939 at Leeds Music, and in 1953 he became general manager of pop publisher Shapiro-Bernstein. In 1961 he set up Shapiro-Bernstein's Painted Desert Music in Nashville, commuting monthly while singer-songwriter MERLE KILGORE oversaw the Nashville operation. A huge hit with Kilgore's "Wolverton Mountain" (recorded by CLAUDE KING) prompted Gallico to establish Al Gallico Music in 1963. Kilgore signed as a writer and ran the Nashville office. Affiliated companies eventually included Algee (a partnership with BILLY SHERRILL, whose songwriting and producing careers Gallico helped to launch), Altam (jointly owned by Gallico, Sherrill, and TAMMY WYNETTE), Flagship, Galleon, Starship, L&G, and Easy Listening.

In addition to Kilgore and Sherrill, other writers whose songs Gallico published over the years included GLENN SUTTON, NORRO WILSON, George Richey, and Earl Montgomery. Gallico's connections with producers such as Sherrill helped Gallico get songs recorded, as did his working to secure recording contracts for singer-songwriters such as DAVID HOUSTON, JOE STAMPLEY (whom Gallico managed), JOHN ANDERSON, Becky Hobbs, and BIG AL DOWNING.

In 1986 Gallico sold Al Gallico Music, Algee, and Easy Listening to Columbia Pictures; these interests now reside with EMI. He later sold Galleon and Altam to MCA's music publishing arm while retaining L&G and Mainstay, which includes several standards by the rock group the Zombies. —*Beverly Keel*

## Byron Gallimore
b. Puryear, Tennessee, March 23, 1950

With a Grammy award for his work on FAITH HILL's album *Breathe* and multiple CMA and ACM trophies, Byron Gallimore is one of country music's most commercially successful producers.

For a time, Gallimore's list of his pop-leaning hits—such as Hill's "This Kiss," TIM MCGRAW's "Please Remember Me," PHIL VASSAR's "Carlene," and SUGARLAND's "All I Want to Do"—earned him a reputation for pushing country's stylistic boundaries. But his contribution to LEE ANN WOMACK's 2005 traditionalist album *There's More Where That Came From* proved his ability to tailor songs and sonic foundations to the needs of stylistically varied artists.

In some ways, Gallimore was groomed for that kind of insight. Born in the West Tennessee town of Puryear, he first worked professionally playing with cover bands in local bars, where matching songs to audiences is paramount. Gallimore moved to Nashville in the 1980s after earning a $10,000 prize as the winner of the Music City Song Festival. He wrote a couple of hits, CHARLEY PRIDE's "Ev'ry Heart Should Have One" and the FORESTER SISTERS' "Love Will," but discovered that he preferred producing demos to crafting songs.

In the early 1990s Gallimore was shopping a then-unknown singer named JO DEE MESSINA when he also heard a struggling Tim McGraw and got a foot in the door as a producer by enlisting established hit maker JAMES STROUD to coproduce. In short order, Gallimore's name appeared in the credits for McGraw's first #1 record, "Don't Take the Girl," and Messina's breakthrough hit, "Heads Carolina, Tails California." His association with those artists helped him build a resume that would soon include hits by Faith Hill, BROOKS & DUNN, TERRI CLARK, Jessica Andrews, and others.

In 2006, Gallimore and McGraw cofounded StyleSonic Records, releasing the *Flicka* soundtrack and introducing the Kentucky-bred duo Halfway to Hazard. —*Tom Roland*

## Al Gannaway
b. April 3, 1920; d. August 27, 2008

Albert C. Gannaway was the first TV/movie producer to capture on film the live performances of many top country music acts of the mid-1950s. Gannaway worked as a TV and motion picture writer and producer in the 1940s and 1950s. In 1954, when country music's popularity was mounting, his Flamingo Films enterprise secured the cooperation of the GRAND OLE OPRY to make 16-mm black-and-white films of ROY ACUFF, ERNEST TUBB, CARL SMITH, and LITTLE JIMMY DICKENS performing onstage (though not during Opry radio broadcasts), sometimes at a Vanderbilt University auditorium. The shows, offered for TV syndication in thirty-minute packages as *Stars of the Grand Ole Opry*, were sponsored by the Pillsbury Flour Company in many parts of the nation. The success of the Gannaway-Opry pairing led to an additional ninety-two half-hour shows, featuring more than 1,000 performances by Opry stars shot in 35-mm Technicolor. Half-hour shows were packaged for TV syndication, and full-length two-hour movie versions were marketed under the names *Country Music Caravan*, *Country Music Jubilee*, and *Country Music Jamboree*. Gannaway worked with Opry booking department head JIM DENNY, WSM program director JACK STAPP, producer OWEN BRADLEY, and talent agent HUBERT LONG in coordinating the filming, most of which took place at Bradley's MUSIC ROW recording and film studios. Gannaway went on to direct a dozen or so low-budget feature films, including *Buffalo Gun*, *Hidden Guns*, and *Daniel Boone, Trailblazer*. Casts featured MARTY ROBBINS, WEBB PIERCE, FARON YOUNG, CARL SMITH, and other country stars. Gannaway's TV shows have been widely packaged for the home video market. —*Al Cunniff*

## Hank Garland
b. Cowpens, South Carolina, November 11, 1930; d. December 27, 2004

Of Nashville's "A-Team" of studio guitarists in the 1950s, few could match Hank Garland's versatility. At home on country, pop, or ROCKABILLY recordings, he was earning acclaim for his jazz skills when a near-fatal auto accident ended his musical career.

Walter Louis Garland, influenced as a child by the guitar playing of Maybelle Carter (CARTER FAMILY), became a guitar prodigy by age fifteen, playing with bands around Spartanburg. In 1945 GRAND OLE OPRY artist PAUL HOWARD, leader of the WESTERN SWING–oriented Arkansas Cotton Pickers, heard Garland while touring South Carolina and hired him. Child labor laws forced Garland to quit the Cotton Pickers and rejoin in 1946 at age sixteen, but he soon left Howard to become COWBOY COPAS's lead guitarist. Nashville guitarists BILLY BYRD and HAROLD BRADLEY taught him the rudiments of jazz, and in 1949 PAUL COHEN signed Garland to DECCA. Though his vocal records weren't successful,

*Hank Garland*

he recorded notable instrumentals, including "Sugarfoot Rag." With lyrics by Vaughn Horton, RED FOLEY recorded a hit version of this song in 1950, and Garland soloed behind him. Garland also worked in EDDY ARNOLD's touring band.

By the early 1950s Garland had become a fixture in Nashville studios, and in 1954 he and Byrd designed the Byrdland electric guitar for Gibson. Garland also recorded with everyone from THE EVERLY BROTHERS to pop star Patti Page. He created the memorable opening guitar figures on PATSY CLINE's "I Fall to Pieces" and the leads on ELVIS PRESLEY's "A Fool Such As I" and "Little Sister." After Presley's discharge from the army, Garland appeared with the singer at his 1961 Honolulu "Farewell Concert."

Meanwhile, Garland's jazz skills were growing. He and other like-minded session players frequently played jazz in jam sessions at Nashville's Carousel Club. In 1960 Garland recorded *Jazz Winds from a New Direction* for COLUMBIA RECORDS while continuing his session work. Then a September 1961 auto accident near Nashville left him comatose. Though he regained consciousness, his physical and motor skills were impaired. He struggled to regain his abilities but could never resume an active role in music. Even so, he appeared at an Opry old-timers show in 1975. The 2007 feature film *Crazy* was based on Garland's life but took extensive liberties with the facts. —*Rich Kienzle*

## Sonny Garrish
b. Fairplay, Maryland, May 14, 1943

Steel guitar great Bruce Franklin "Sonny" Garrish started in MUSIC CITY in the mid-1960s as a member of BILL ANDERSON's touring and TV show band, eventually turning to studio sessions exclusively. Over the years Garrish has graced recordings by THE KENDALLS, REBA MCENTIRE, TIM MCGRAW, TRACY LAWRENCE,

KENNY CHESNEY, TOBY KEITH, and many others. A studio work-horse, he has played on hits such as GEORGE STRAIT's "Unwound," THE JUDDS' "Mama He's Crazy," and MICHAEL MARTIN MURPHEY's "What's Forever For." He has also backed numerous gospel acts, and his pop credits include sessions with Dean Martin, Doris Day, and B. B. King.

Garrish was playing and singing by age seven. After learning HAWAIIAN lap steel, he bought records to learn PEDAL STEEL GUITAR licks in the late 1950s. Playing in a WESTERN SWING band at a Fairfax, Virginia, club that hosted Nashville acts allowed him to jam with the bands of RAY PRICE, FARON YOUNG, JOHNNY PAYCHECK, and others. Bill Anderson convinced Garrish to move to Nashville in 1966.

Garrish has helped keep the pedal steel relevant to pop trends and influences by adding a chorus effect to his steel sound and by replicating keyboard parts on his instrument. Often Garrish has doubled his steel parts by recording harmony over his original part. Mastering this technique has helped him remain busy in the twenty-first century. —*Michael Hight* and *Bob Kramer*

## The Gatlin Brothers
Larry Gatlin b. Seminole, Texas, May 2, 1948
Steve Gatlin b. Olney, Texas, April 4, 1951
Rudy Gatlin b. Olney, Texas, August 20, 1952

The words "blood harmony" aptly describe the tight-knit vocals of lead singer Larry Wayne Gatlin and his brothers Steve Daryl Gatlin and Rudy Michael Gatlin. With Larry's soaring melodies and the solid harmonies of Steve and Rudy, the brothers enjoyed a career that brought them #1 records, a Grammy award, and three ACM awards. In addition to the Gatlins' hits, Larry penned songs recorded by ELVIS PRESLEY, HANK SNOW, DOTTIE WEST, Barbra Streisand, CHARLIE RICH, the Carpenters, Judy Collins, Tom Jones, ANNE MURRAY, and JOHNNY CASH.

Raised in a musical family, the Gatlin Brothers were joined by their sister LaDonna, who sang on several Gatlin albums through 1976. The siblings grew up on the gospel harmonies of the Blackwood Brothers and the Statesmen Quartet. The brothers first performed in public when Larry was six, and they later sang on Abilene radio and television shows.

After studying English and law at the University of Houston, Larry worked various jobs and sang with the gospel group the Imperials. While touring with that group in 1972, he met DOTTIE WEST in Las Vegas. He later sent her a tape containing eight original songs, and West sent him an airplane ticket to Nashville. A few months later he moved to MUSIC CITY. In 1973 Larry and Rita Coolidge sang backup for KRIS KRISTOFFERSON's #1 record "Why Me," while Larry first charted with his self-penned MONUMENT RECORDS single "Sweet Becky Walker."

Before joining Larry, Steve and Rudy performed with Young Country (as did LaDonna and husband Tim Johnson), providing background vocals for TAMMY WYNETTE. Larry's career with his brothers featured smooth country stylings and went through several name incarnations (including Larry Gatlin; Larry Gatlin with Family and Friends; and Larry Gatlin & the Gatlin Brothers). "Broken Lady" (1973–74), their first Top Ten, won Larry a 1973 Grammy for Best Country Song, and the act first reached #1 in 1977–78 with "I Just Wish You Were Someone I Love." Switching from Monument to COLUMBIA, they again hit #1 with "All the Gold in California" (1979) and "Houston (Means I'm One Day Closer to You)" (1983).

Drug addiction led Larry to a California treatment center, where he made a recovery in 1984. The trio's chart performance slipped in 1985, though they scored three Top Ten hits between 1986 and 1988. In 1989–90 the Gatlins moved to Universal Records and then to CAPITOL RECORDS, but success eluded them. Late in 1992 the brothers began a farewell tour before settling into their own theater in Myrtle Beach, South Carolina. Larry has also played dramatic roles on Broadway. He published his memoir, *All the Gold in California,* in 1998.

In 2004 the Gatlins released an album of family gospel favorites on Dualtone. The autobiographical *Pilgrimage* appeared on CURB RECORDS in 2009. —*Gerry Wood*

## Connie B. Gay
b. Lizard Lick, North Carolina, August 22, 1914; d. December 4, 1989

Dubbed country music's Media Magician, Connie Barriot Gay was one of country's leading entrepreneurs of the 1950s, playing a seminal role in transforming what was still called "hillbilly" music into a modern entertainment industry from his base in the Washington, D.C., area.

One of the first to use the term "country music," Gay began his broadcasting career on the Farm Security Administration's *National Farm and Home Hour* radio program. Later, at WARL in Arlington, Virginia, Gay helped introduced country music to Washington, D.C., listeners, nurturing a vibrant, profitable music scene beginning in 1946 and continuing through the 1950s. His activities spanned TV and radio as well as blockbuster live stage shows, using the all-purpose moniker Town & Country.

Gay's early stable of talent included the Wheeler Brothers, CLYDE MOODY, and the Radio Ranchmen, with guitarist BILLY GRAMMER, GRANDPA JONES and Ramona Jones, HANK PENNY,

*Connie B. Gay*

and a then-unknown JIMMY DEAN. As his manager, Gay developed Dean into a TV star and host of the locally popular *Town & Country Time* show—also syndicated nationally—and the short-lived CBS television effort *The Jimmy Dean Show* (1957–59), until Dean and Gay split in 1959. In his heyday Gay's steady roster of talent also included PATSY CLINE (who made her TV debut on Gay's *Town & Country* shows), ROY CLARK, and GEORGE HAMILTON IV. In 1958 Gay became CMA's founding president, and several years later he helped launch the COUNTRY MUSIC HALL OF FAME AND MUSEUM. He was elected to THE COUNTRY MUSIC HALL OF FAME in 1980. —*Margaret Jones*

## Crystal Gayle
b. Paintsville, Kentucky, January 9, 1951

LORETTA LYNN's youngest sister bears no vocal and little physical resemblance to Lynn, but Crystal Gayle—CMA Female Vocalist of the Year for 1977 and 1978—was encouraged by Loretta, who suggested the stage name "Crystal" after the Krystal hamburger chain.

Born Brenda Gail Webb, the youngest of the Webb children, she grew up in Wabash, Indiana, after the family moved there from eastern Kentucky. Gayle began touring with Lynn after high school and signed with Lynn's record label, DECCA RECORDS. Gayle's first recording was a Lynn composition titled "I've Cried the Blue Right Out of My Eyes." The song charted in 1970 but failed to crack the country Top Twenty. Believing that she was being treated as a superstar's little sister, Gayle eventually signed with United Artists Records. There she teamed with producer ALLEN REYNOLDS, who guided her to a more pop-country approach, and she gained the first of eighteen #1 hits with "I'll Get Over You." Gayle consciously sang with a diction-perfect, almost operetta-like style.

In 1977 Gayle's single "Don't It Make My Brown Eyes Blue" was a country (#1) and pop (#2) hit, and she won Female Vocalist awards from both the CMA and the ACM. Her 1978 album *When I Dream* yielded the chart-topping "Talking in Your Sleep" and "Why Have You Left the One You Left Me For," and she repeated

as CMA's Female Vocalist of the Year. She switched labels to COLUMBIA in 1979 and scored with "Half the Way," "It's Like We Never Said Goodbye," and other songs. More #1 hits followed on ELEKTRA and WARNER BROS. between 1982 and 1987.

Gayle last charted in 1990, but she has continued to record specialty projects, including gospel material, a Hoagy Carmichael tribute, a children's album, an album of standards, and live concert albums. She remains a touring star, her trademark ankle-length hair nearly as famous as her hit songs. —*Chet Flippo*

## Gaylord Entertainment Company
established in Nashville, Tennessee, October 24, 1991

Gaylord Entertainment Company (GEC) has participated significantly in the growth of country music through its entertainment divisions. Gaylord owns and operates the Opryland Resort and Convention Center; the Wildhorse Saloon; radio station WSM-AM, home of the GRAND OLE OPRY since 1925; THE RYMAN AUDITORIUM; and the General Jackson Showboat, all located in Nashville. For most of the 1980s and 1990s Gaylord owned and operated TNN: THE NASHVILLE NETWORK and CMT (Country Music Television) and, until its closing in 1997, the OPRYLAND USA theme park. From 1985 until its sale to Sony/ATV Music Publishing in 2002, Gaylord also owned the ACUFF-ROSE music publishing catalogs, operating them as part of the Opryland Music Group. Gaylord owned WSM-FM from 1983 to 2003, when this radio operation was acquired by the giant Cumulus radio group.

Gaylord Broadcasting Company bought the Opryland properties from American General Corporation in July 1983. The purchase resulted in the creation of Opryland USA, Inc. On July 15, 1984, Gaylord Syndicom was launched as a division of Opryland USA to develop television shows for broadcast syndication. Gaylord Entertainment Company was officially created on October 24, 1991, when the new corporation offered its stock to the public. Opryland USA, Inc. became the cornerstone of GEC, ably guided by E. W. "BUD" WENDELL until his retirement in 1997. As of 2011, officers are Colin V. Reed, chairman and CEO, and David C. Kloeppel, president and chief operating officer.

In 1997 Gaylord sold CMT and TNN to CBS-Westinghouse and closed Opryland USA for redevelopment into the Opry Mills shopping and entertainment complex. —*Bob Paxman*

## The Geezinslaws
Samuel Morris Allred b. Austin, Texas, May 5, 1938
Raymond Dewayne Smith b. Bertram, Texas, September 19, 1946

The Geezinslaws have perfected the art of country parody over a lengthy career. The Texas-based act represents the alter egos of Sammy Allred and Dewayne Smith (also known as Son), who are not related but who have performed together since the 1950s. Their irreverent humor often involves putting a twist on well-known songs. Examples include "Help, I'm White and I Can't Get Down" and "Play It Backwards." Although they never enjoyed huge record sales, the Geezinslaws became cult favorites through television and video. Early on, they appeared on the *Ed Sullivan Show*; later they were regulars on TNN's *Nashville Now* and other TNN programs. Their video for "Help, I'm White and I Can't Get Down," nominated for several awards, was a long-running clip on CMT. From 1990 to 1993 they received nominations for

*Crystal Gayle*

Comedian of the Year from the TNN/*Music City News* Country Awards. The act won the National Association of Record Merchandisers (NARM) Independent Country Album of the Year in 1993, for *Feelin' Good, Gittin' Up, Gittin' Down*. As of 2011 they were still performing. —*Bob Paxman*

## Gennett Records
established in Richmond, Indiana, 1919; ended 1934

Gennett Records was formed as a subsidiary of the Starr Piano Company of Richmond, Indiana, which had marketed vertically cut Starr records as early as 1915. When the Gennett label (named after the family who owned Starr) appeared on some lateral-cut releases in 1919, the Victor Talking Machine Company sued, contending that the Gennett product was in violation of jointly owned Victor/COLUMBIA patents. A decision in Starr's favor enabled Gennett, OKEH, BRUNSWICK, and a host of smaller labels to compete for customers with conventionally produced discs.

Gennett's earliest records were made in New York. Studios in its Richmond factory went into operation in 1921. A few fiddlers, notably the Tweedy Brothers and William Houchens, recorded some early versions of traditional dance tunes there. When Gennett contracted with Sears, Roebuck to produce records for its budget Challenge and Silvertone labels (the former not to be confused with GENE AUTRY'S CHALLENGE RECORDS), the record company took a serious interest in country music, which Sears marketed via catalog sales to its rural customers. In 1928 Supertone replaced Sears's Silvertone label; in 1929 Sears issued some Gennett masters on CONQUEROR.

All were low-priced labels, which usually disguised performer identities with pseudonyms. Together with Champion, Gennett's own discount label, these labels were responsible for hundreds of country releases in the late 1920s. Artists such as BRADLEY KINCAID, ARKIE THE ARKANSAS WOODCHOPPER, and others associated with Chicago radio station WLS (owned by Sears early on) were prominently featured, but Gennett also recruited regional performers from nearby rural Kentucky, such as FIDDLIN' DOC ROBERTS, Asa Martin, and Taylor's Kentucky Boys. Other contacts brought musicians such as the Red Fox Chasers (North Carolina), Fiddlin' Sam Long (Arkansas), and DA COSTA WOLTZ'S SOUTHERN BROADCASTERS (North Carolina) from farther away.

In 1930 the Sears agreement was terminated, as was the Gennett label itself, except for a profitable sound-effects series. However, the company kept Champion and a new Superior label active, recording Autry, Cliff Carlisle (see BILL CARLISLE), the Tobacco Tags, LEW CHILDRE, and numerous STRINGBANDS before ceasing commercial record production in 1934.

DECCA purchased the Champion name and selected masters in 1935, mixing items from the original catalog with new releases for a few months. The label was permanently retired early in 1936. Producer Joe Davis revived the Gennett name briefly during World War II, when he made temporary use of the Richmond factory for pressing. The Starr Piano Company finally closed in 1952. —*Dick Spottswood*

## Bobbie Gentry
b. Chickasaw County, Mississippi, July 27, 1944

Best known as the writer and performer of the 1967 crossover smash "Ode to Billie Joe," Bobbie Gentry began writing songs at age seven. She was born Roberta Streeter and taught herself to play piano on her grandmother's upright. Her family moved to California when Gentry was thirteen, and she went on to study philosophy at UCLA and music at the Los Angeles Conservatory.

Working as a secretary, nightclub singer, and Las Vegas dancer, Gentry was finally able to cut "Ode to Billie Joe" as her first recording for CAPITOL. The record had a sparse and haunting sound, with Gentry's bluesy voice and guitar accompanied by strings. It held the #1 slot on the pop charts for four weeks and also made the country Top Twenty. Gentry won three Grammys, ACM named her its Top New Female Vocalist of 1967, and CMA chose her to cohost its first awards show, also in 1967. Gentry subsequently recorded several successful duets with GLEN CAMPBELL, including "Let It Be Me" (1969).

A prolific writer, Gentry's material typically displayed her characteristic drawling phrasing, Delta-tinged melodies, and vivid southern imagery. She further explored the seamy side of life in songs such as "Fancy" (1969–70), also a 1991 hit for REBA MCENTIRE.

Having produced many of her own records, Gentry went on to produce a Las Vegas nightclub revue. Television tried to tap her talent, but her 1974 program *The Bobbie Gentry Show* (also known as *Bobbie Gentry's Happiness*) on CBS aired only four episodes. "Ode to Billie Joe" inspired a TV movie by the same title in 1976.

Following a short-lived marriage to singer Jim Stafford, Gentry gradually retired from show business. —*Mary A. Bufwack*

## The Georgia Yellow Hammers
George Oscar "Uncle Bud" Landress b. Gwinnett County, Georgia, May 2, 1881; d. May 14, 1966
William Hewlett "Bill" Chitwood b. Resaca, Georgia, June 30, 1888; d. March 3, 1961
Charles Ernest "C. E." Moody b. Calhoun County, Georgia, October 8, 1891; d. June 1977
Phil Reeve b. 1896; d. 1949

A STRINGBAND active in Calhoun County in rural North Georgia during the mid- and late-1920s, the Georgia Yellow Hammers were distinguished from similar OLD-TIME groups by their strong singing and original songs. Their primary personnel included Uncle Bud Landress (banjo, fiddle, vocals), Bill Chitwood (fiddle, vocals), Phil Reeve (guitar, vocal), and C. E. Moody (ukulele, banjo, guitar, vocals). Moody was a particularly gifted songwriter who earlier had composed "Kneel at the Cross," "Drifting Too Far from the Shore," and other gospel songs. In addition to original numbers, the group recorded comedy skits, gospel quartets, sentimental songs, blues, pop songs, and fiddle breakdowns. Their most successful recording was "Picture on the Wall" b/w "My Carolina Girl" (1927), which sold in excess of 100,000 copies for the Victor Talking Machine Company. Primarily a studio group, they recorded in various combinations from 1924 to 1929 for Victor and other companies, using a number of different names. Among these were Bill Chitwood & His Georgia Mountaineers and the Turkey Mountain Singers. Occasional personnel on their sessions included African American musician Andrew Baxter (fiddle), Clyde Evans (guitar, vocal), Melvin Dupree (guitar), and Elias Meadows (vocals). —*John Lilly*

## Giant Records
established 1989; Nashville office established 1991; ended 2001

Small company, big presence. That was JAMES STROUD's goal when he became president of Giant Records' new Nashville operation in 1991. A successful independent producer, Stroud was hired by music mogul Irving Azoff, who founded the label as a joint venture with Warner Bros. in 1989.

Giant's first country release came in April 1992 with Dennis Robbins's "Home Sweet Home," but it wasn't until 1993 that the Nashville operation hit pay dirt with Carlene Carter's #3 single "Every Little Thing" and Clay Walker's Stroud-produced "What's It to You," a #1 country record. Meanwhile, the label found success with *Common Thread: The Songs of the Eagles* (1993), a triple-platinum tribute album featuring The Eagles covers by the likes of Alan Jackson, Lorrie Morgan, and Diamond Rio.

Wanting to keep the roster small but manageable, Stroud pursued something of a "boutique" approach. Giant offered acts that tested the boundaries of the country format—Carter, Mark Collie, Deborah Allen—along with mainstream country artists such as Doug Supernaw. In 1997 Doug Johnson replaced Stroud, who had moved to Dreamworks Records. Giant never attained the stature its name implied, and Warner Bros. closed and absorbed the label in 2001. —*Tom Roland*

## Terri Gibbs

b. Miami, Florida, June 15, 1954

In 1981 Terri Gibbs was the first artist to win CMA's Horizon Award for up-and-coming performers. The previous year she had won ACM's Best New Female Vocalist award.

Born Teresa Fay Gibbs, she lost her sight as a newborn in an incubator accident. After graduating high school in Augusta, Georgia, the bluesy-timbred alto and keyboard player began making independently produced records and appearing on local country music shows. Her early group, the Terri Gibbs Trio, included guitarist Warren Glowers, later a studio player and touring sideman with Ronnie Milsap.

In about 1979, Nashville songwriter-producer Ed Penney heard one of Gibbs's demonstration tapes and eventually tracked her to an Augusta restaurant where she had a regular gig. After Penney persuaded MCA Nashville chief Jim Foglesong to hear Gibbs perform, Foglesong signed her to the label. Penney cowrote and produced Gibbs's debut single, "Somebody's Knockin'" (#8, 1980), as well as her album by the same title.

Gibbs recorded three more albums for MCA—*I'm a Lady* (1981), *Some Days It Rains All Night Long* (1982), and *Over Easy* (1983)—but failed to crack the Top Ten singles charts again. Gibbs left MCA and made one Warner Bros. album, *Old Friends* (1985), with similar results. She then returned to her religious roots, recording Contemporary Christian albums for the Horizon, Canaan, and Morning Gate labels between 1987 and 1990 before scaling back to focus on her family. She released her fifth Christian album in December 2010. —*Don Rhodes*

## Don Gibson

b. Shelby, North Carolina, April 3, 1928; d. November 17, 2003

The title of Don Gibson's 1960 song "(I'd Be) A Legend in My Time" aptly describes his career. He wrote at least three of country music's most famous songs, helped to define the sound and studio style of modern country, and released more than seventy charted records between 1956 and 1980. "I consider myself a songwriter who sings rather than a singer who writes songs," Gibson once said, and as late as 1986 he estimated he had as many as 150 to 175 "working songs"— still performed enough to

*Don Gibson*

earn him regular royalties. As a singer, however, between 1949 and 1985 he recorded more than 500 titles for labels including Mercury, Columbia, MGM, RCA, Hickory, Hickory/MGM, ABC/Hickory.

Donald Eugene Gibson got his start with a local band called the Sons of the Soil on radio station WOHS in his native Shelby, North Carolina. In 1949 he made his first recording with them, a Mercury side called "Automatic Mama." By 1952 he had moved to Knoxville's WNOX and signed with Columbia. His recordings for this label were not commercially successful, but he was discovering he had a knack for songwriting. By 1955 Gibson had written his first masterpiece, "Sweet Dreams," later a hit for Gibson, Faron Young, and Patsy Cline. It won him a songwriter's contract with Acuff-Rose Publications and a record deal with MGM. Then, in 1957, while living in a trailer park north of Knoxville, he wrote his other two career songs on the same day: "Oh Lonesome Me" and "I Can't Stop Lovin' You." (The latter would eventually be recorded more than 700 times by singers in many music genres and sell more than 30 million records worldwide.)

In 1957 Gibson recorded "Oh Lonesome Me" for RCA in Nashville. He and producer Chet Atkins decided to abandon steel guitar and fiddle and use a new sound featuring only guitars, a piano, a drummer, an upright bass, and background singers. It became one of the first examples of The Nashville Sound and won Gibson a #1 hit; it also earned him Grand Ole Opry membership in 1958 and launched a long series of RCA hits, including "Blue Blue Day" (1958), "Just One Time" (1960), "Sea of Heartbreak" (1961), and "Rings of Gold" (1969, with Dottie West). These accomplishments were even more remarkable because Gibson achieved them while dealing with personal problems, including drug abuse. By 1967 he had married Bobbi Patterson, moved to Nashville, and once again concentrated on his first love, songwriting. Between 1970 and 1980 he charted more than forty times, scoring such Top Ten hits as "Country Green," the #1 "Woman (Sensuous Woman)," "Touch the Morning," and "One Day at a Time." He was inducted into the NASHVILLE SONGWRITERS HALL OF FAME in 1973 and THE COUNTRY MUSIC HALL OF FAME in 2001. —*Stacey Wolfe*

## Steve Gibson
b. Peoria, Illinois, July 31, 1952

During his years in Nashville, session guitarist–producer Steven D. Gibson has played on some 14,000 recording sessions. He has also produced records for MICHAEL JOHNSON, AARON TIPPIN, McBRIDE & THE RIDE, and MICHAEL MARTIN MURPHEY.

Gibson's parents owned Golden Voice Recording Studio in Pekin, Illinois, and they encouraged Steve to develop his talents there. By age twelve he was earning money playing guitar, and at fourteen he made his first record. The young picker gained steady session and production experience in Peoria before moving to Nashville in 1972. After working on jingles, Gibson got his big break playing on friend Dave Loggins's 1974 pop hit "Please Come to Boston"; soon after came sessions with Nashville-recorded pop acts such as Dr. Hook and England Dan & John Ford Coley. Since then Gibson has contributed to hits by ALABAMA, CLINT BLACK, GEORGE JONES, REBA McENTIRE, RONNIE MILSAP, JOHN MICHAEL MONTGOMERY, LORRIE MORGAN, ROY ORBISON, ELVIS PRESLEY, KENNY ROGERS, GEORGE STRAIT, RANDY TRAVIS, TAMMY WYNETTE, WYNONNA, and many others.

In 2002, Gibson served as a consultant to GRAND OLE OPRY officials in upgrading the show's broadcasting and archiving technology as well as improving Opry House acoustics. He subsequently became music director for the program. —*Michael Hight*

## Vince Gill
b. Norman, Oklahoma, April 12, 1957

With an aching tenor, award-winning songwriting skills, and virtuoso guitar chops that rival those of any Nashville session player, Vince Gill is one of the most awarded and instantly recognizable stars of his era. His easygoing demeanor, accessibility, and penchant for charitable causes have also made him one of MUSIC CITY's best-liked insiders. However, Gill was no overnight success, having spent years paying dues before achieving stardom. Since his 1989 breakthrough album, *When I Call Your Name*, he has reigned as a commercial and critical force. He's racked up a room full of awards, including, at this writing, twenty Grammys and eighteen CMA awards (two of which were for Entertainer of the Year).

Vincent Grant Gill was born and raised in Norman, Oklahoma. Through his federal appellate court judge father, Gill received his introduction to what would become the two greatest passions of his life—music and golf. A talented athlete who at one time considered a career as a professional golfer, Gill also proved a precocious BLUEGRASS student. He learned banjo from his dad and soon became proficient on a number of stringed instruments, including guitar. In high school he played with Mountain Smoke, an ensemble that went on to work an ill-fated opening gig for the theatrical rock band KISS.

Playing a progressive form of bluegrass, Gill began to perform in a series of bands. After high school he joined THE BLUEGRASS

*Vince Gill*

ALLIANCE, and he briefly relocated to Kentucky in 1975. While there he also played in the band Boone Creek with future country/bluegrass star RICKY SKAGGS.

In 1976 Gill moved to Los Angeles, where he played with bluegrass fiddler BYRON BERLINE in Sundance. After several years he joined the country-pop act PURE PRAIRIE LEAGUE and recorded three albums with the group. His stint with the outfit led to Gill's singing lead on the band's 1980 pop hit "Let Me Love You Tonight."

Gill married Janis Oliver on April 12, 1980, and their only child, Jenny, was born May 5, 1982. In the mid-1980s Janis and her sister Kristine formed the duo SWEETHEARTS OF THE RODEO, and for a time Janis's commercial success outshone that of her husband.

After leaving Pure Prairie League, Gill hooked up with then-married singer-songwriters ROSANNE CASH and RODNEY CROWELL, two musicians on the leading edge of progressive country. Gill became a respected guitarist in Crowell's backing band, the Cherry Bombs, an outfit that included, at different times, future powerhouse country producers EMORY GORDY JR. and RICHARD BENNETT. Playing extensive live dates with the band, Gill also began to refine his songwriting skills.

In the Cherry Bombs, Gill worked with TONY BROWN, the man who would become the key figure in Gill's eventual solo breakthrough. (A keyboardist who backed, among others, ELVIS PRESLEY, Brown subsequently became a top producer and Nashville-based record label honcho.)

In 1983 Brown had become, for the second time, an A&R man at RCA; he signed Gill. Shortly thereafter, Brown left the label to work at MCA. At RCA, Gill recorded three releases.

His six-song debut LP, *Turn Me Loose* (1984), was followed by *The Things That Matter* (1985) and *The Way Back Home* (1987). During his RCA tenure Gill charted several singles, including the Top Ten 1985 entries "Oklahoma Borderline" and a duet with Rosanne Cash, "If It Weren't for Him." Nevertheless, Gill languished as a solo artist, unable to establish himself as a bona fide star.

Meanwhile, Gill logged a long tour of duty as a session player, recording with the likes of REBA MCENTIRE, EMMYLOU HARRIS, Rosanne Cash, and Bonnie Raitt. He recorded with the English rock band Dire Straits and was invited by singer-guitarist Mark Knopfler to join the band. Gill declined and continued to pursue a solo career.

After leaving RCA, Gill signed on with his old pal Brown at MCA. The music, chemistry, and timing coincided at last. With Brown as producer, Gill's MCA debut album, *When I Call Your Name* (1989), eventually sold 2 million copies. The title track, a mournful PEDAL-STEEL-GUITAR–and-piano ballad with plaintive harmonies from singer PATTY LOVELESS, spotlighted Gill's wistful tenor and rocketed him to solo stardom.

Gill's hit-album streak continued, making him a top concert draw. He followed his MCA debut with *Pocket Full of Gold* (1991), which yielded hit singles such as the country-rocking "Liza Jane" and the tender love ballad "Look at Us." His next collection, *I Still Believe in You* (1992), continued to feature the winning Gill formula—ballads that highlighted his sensitive vocals, and sprightly country-pop rockers, such as "One More Last Chance," that showcased his impressive guitar skills. His 1994 album *When Love Finds You* produced six singles, including "Go Rest High on That Mountain." Gill composed this inspiring song reflecting over the deaths of singer KEITH WHITLEY and Gill's half-brother Bob Cohen, who had died about two years prior. "Go Rest High on That Mountain" earned Gill a 1996 CMA award for Song of the Year.

Although Gill's mix of pop, country, and rock influences are evident on all of his recordings, the release of *High Lonesome Sound* (1996) included some older influences. While many of the tracks were recorded in the contemporary adult country-pop vein, the title track featured a return to his newgrass roots (with harmony vocals by bluegrass-country star ALISON KRAUSS). Also in 1996, Gill's wife Janis filed for divorce.

*The Key*, released in 1998, took him even deeper into traditional country music, chronicling the death of his father and the breakup of his first marriage. He married pop singer Amy Grant and, that same year, released the album *Let's Make Sure We Kiss Goodbye*, which was heavy on love songs. Although his radio play and sales started to dip, his albums remained critically acclaimed, including 2003's *Next Big Thing* and 2006's four-CD set of original material, *These Days*, with each CD exploring a specific type of song, including traditional country, contemporary country, ballad, and bluegrass. In 2004 he participated in an album reuniting him with Crowell on the group album *The Notorious Cherry Bombs*.

Gill seems to have taken all of his career lows and highs in his laid-back stride. A photo of the man is just as likely to show him with a golf club in his hand as a guitar. But don't let the mellow demeanor fool you; Gill gets a lot done. On the personal front, he has long been an active participant in charitable causes, so much so that his friend Rodney Crowell has nicknamed him "Benefit." Gill also proved an amiable TV presence, hosting the CMA Awards from 1992 to 2003. In June 2011 he was elected to his tenth consecutive term as president of the COUNTRY MUSIC HALL OF FAME AND MUSEUM. Gill was elected to THE COUNTRY MUSIC HALL OF FAME in 2007. —*Chrissie Dickinson*

## Lee Gillette
b. Indianapolis, Indiana, October 30, 1912; d. August 20, 1981

Aside from cofounder Johnny Mercer, Lee Gillette was CAPITOL RECORDS's first A&R man. His pioneering work in country and pop music established the label's musical identity for its first twenty years.

Leland James Gillette grew up in the Chicago pop music scene, singing and playing drums. He often worked with teenage friend KEN NELSON, who had gained experience in song publishing during the 1920s and 1930s. As a drummer, Gillette visited Hollywood and met record store owner Glenn Wallichs. In 1944 Wallichs, cofounder of the two-year-old Capitol label, hired Gillette as head of country A&R. Gillette signed some of Capitol's greatest postwar country acts—among them were JACK GUTHRIE, MERLE TRAVIS, JIMMY WAKELY, TEX WILLIAMS, and TENNESSEE ERNIE FORD—and produced hits with all of them until he moved to pop A&R in 1950. Ken Nelson soon took over country recording duties, though Gillette continued to produce Ford, whose crossover appeal kept growing. As co-owner of CENTRAL SONGS publishing company with CLIFFIE STONE and Ken Nelson, Gillette helped to organize the National Academy of Recording Arts and Sciences (NARAS).

After Nat King Cole's death, in 1965, Gillette was devastated over the loss of his friend and took early retirement from Capitol to travel and occasionally produce independently. He died three weeks after suffering a serious fall at his California home in August 1981. —*Rich Kienzle*

## Mickey Gilley
b. Natchez, Mississippi, March 9, 1936

Mickey Leroy Gilley comes from a famous family. His first cousin Jimmy Swaggart became a controversial TV evangelist, and another first cousin, JERRY LEE LEWIS, became a rock & roll pioneer and later a country star. Gilley made his mark remaking vintage country and pop ballads and opening massive nightclubs in Pasadena, Texas, and later in BRANSON, MISSOURI, and Dallas, Texas.

*Mickey Gilley*

In 1970, millionaire Sherwood Cryer talked Gilley into becoming partners in a Pasadena, Texas nightclub they named GILLEY'S. Up to then, Gilley had recorded briefly for DOT RECORDS and had lived in Louisiana and Mississippi before moving to Pasadena. In 1974 he recorded a single on his own Astro label, pairing the 1964 PATSY CLINE hit "She Called Me Baby (All Night Long)" and the 1949 GEORGE MORGAN classic "Room Full of Roses." When the latter started getting airplay, Hugh Hefner's Playboy Records rereleased the disc, and "Room Full of Roses" became Gilley's first #1 country hit in 1974.

Sixteen more #1 recordings followed for Playboy and later for EPIC RECORDS, including "I Overlooked an Orchid" (1974), "Don't the Girls All Get Prettier at Closing Time" (1976), "True Love Ways," "Stand by Me," and "That's All That Matters" (all in 1980), and a duet with CHARLY McCLAIN, "Paradise Tonight" (1983).

After becoming ACM's Top New Male Vocalist of 1974, Gilley experienced his biggest year of accolades in 1976, winning four ACM awards: Entertainer of the Year, Top Male Vocalist, Single of the Year ("Bring It on Home to Me"), and Album of the Year (*Gilley's Smoking*).

Gilley parted acrimoniously from Cryer in the late 1980s; a Houston court awarded Gilley $17 million in damages from Cryer in July 1988, and the club closed in 1989. Soon, however, Gilley was back in business—this time launching the Mickey Gilley Theater in Branson on April 27, 1990. Its success led to the opening of the adjacent Gilley's Texas Cafe in 1992 and the founding of another Gilley's Texas Cafe in Myrtle Beach, South Carolina, in 1995. In 2003 the star opened a new Gilley's nightclub serving the Dallas–Fort Worth metropolitan area.

In his spare time Gilley acted on the TV series *Murder, She Wrote*; *Fantasy Island*; *CHiPs*; *The Fall Guy*; and *The Dukes of Hazzard*. —*Don Rhodes*

## Gilley's
### established in Pasadena, Texas, 1971

In its late-1970s to early-1980s heyday, Gilley's nightclub symbolized country music's growing mass appeal. Singer MICKEY GILLEY and manager Sherwood Cryer opened Gilley's in 1971 on the site of a former nightclub known as Shelley's. Catering to the young, well-paid, and restless workers in the oil refinery Houston suburb of Pasadena, Gilley's began as a local bar and dance hall with a capacity of 750 persons. Extensive expansion followed, and, prior to the opening of Billy Bob's in Fort Worth, Gilley's was the world's largest honky-tonk, encompassing more than 48,000 square feet and accommodating 5,000 people on its parquet dance floor. Attractions included not only Mickey Gilley and other country stars, but also a shooting gallery, pool tables, a sledgehammer strength test, and a mechanical bull that customers could ride.

Aaron Latham's article in *Esquire* magazine (September 12, 1978) introduced the Gilley's cultural phenomenon to the non-country populace. The hit movie *Urban Cowboy*, filmed largely in and around Gilley's and starring John Travolta and Debra Winger, followed in 1980.

The club, its mechanical bull, and Hollywood's romanticized version of the venue's country music milieu rose to fantastic, if short-lived, popularity. Modeled on this idealized Gilley's, smaller cowboy-themed nightclubs opened in such disparate places as New York City and Washington, D.C., during the early 1980s.

When the URBAN COWBOY fad ended in the mid-1980s, the business failed, Gilley's closed (in 1989), acrimonious lawsuits followed, and the building mysteriously burned down.

The new, 91,000-square-foot Gilley's Dallas opened in 2003. The facility embraces seven venues, hosts a variety of themed events, and features performances by acts in many musical genres. —*Bob Millard*

## Jimmie Dale Gilmore
### b. Amarillo, Texas, May 6, 1945

Jimmie Dale Gilmore is one of contemporary country's most original and affecting stylists. His tenor voice is ethereal yet twangy, and his songwriting reflects the blend of eastern philosophy and traditional country he's pursued since the late 1960s.

Gilmore was raised in Tulia, Texas; early musical influences included his father's HONKY-TONK band, HANK WILLIAMS, THE MADDOX BROTHERS & ROSE, and LEFTY FRIZZELL, with a heavy dose of rock radio. Moving to Lubbock, Gilmore learned guitar at sixteen and began performing mainstream country, strongly influenced by Lubbock artist Terry Allen and country-tinged songwriters, including TOWNES VAN ZANDT. Soon Gilmore himself began penning signature numbers, such as "Treat Me Like a Saturday Night," "Tonight I Think I'm Gonna Go Downtown," and "Dallas."

In 1970 Gilmore formed THE FLATLANDERS with Tony Pearson, Steve Wesson, and fellow singer-songwriters JOE ELY and BUTCH HANCOCK. This visionary aggregation combined roots-revival instrumentation (including a musical saw) with substantial, creative lyrics. The group recorded a fine album in 1972 that was hopelessly at odds with current trends and then disbanded. Gilmore spent the next fifteen years pursuing such interests as Buddhism, meditation, and Hindu cosmology. Joe Ely's renditions of his songs kept Gilmore's name in circulation, however, and in 1988–89 Gilmore recorded two progressive-country albums for HIGHTONE. In 1991 *After Awhile*, focusing on his own compositions, further established his spiritual, "sagebrush soul" style.

Subsequent ELEKTRA albums *Spinning Around the Sun* and *Braver Newer World* were both nominated for Grammy awards. Additional Gilmore albums appeared in 2000 (ROUNDER) and 2004 (HighTone), and in 2005 Rounder issued *Come on Back*, a collection of songs his father loved. Gilmore has recorded with WILLIE NELSON, THE HACKBERRY RAMBLERS, and Mudhoney. Gilmore, Ely, and Hancock, whose Flatlanders reunion appearances draw enthusiastic crowds, are now widely embraced by AMERICANA audiences. The trio released *Now Again* (2002), *Wheels of Fortune* (2004), and *Hills and Valleys* (2009), all on New West Records. Branching into cinema, Gilmore appeared in the 1998 feature film *The Big Lebowski* and has contributed to several motion picture soundtracks. —*Ben Sandmel*

## Johnny Gimble
### b. Tyler, Texas, May 30, 1926

One of country music's best-known fiddlers, Johnny Gimble is most recognized as a WESTERN SWING fiddler and electric mandolinist, though he has recorded in almost every style and context.

By age fourteen John Paul Gimble was playing fiddle around Tyler, Texas, alongside his brothers in the Rose City Swingsters. Inspired by western swing fiddle legends CLIFF BRUNER and

*Johnny Gimble*

J. R. Chatwell, Gimble himself would become a highly influential stylist. By 1943 he was playing banjo in JIMMIE DAVIS's gubernatorial campaign band. After World War II Gimble formed the Blues Rustlers with his brothers in Goose Creek, Texas, before joining Buck Roberts's Rhythmairs in 1948. Gimble made his recording debut with Roberts, introducing a Gimble trademark: scat singing in unison with his fiddle.

Recruited by BOB WILLS, Gimble joined the Texas Playboys in California in early 1949 and stayed until 1951, often playing intricate duets with fellow mandolinist TINY MOORE. Afterward, Gimble worked in Dallas with AL DEXTER and Dewey Groom while playing numerous sessions at JIM BECK's recording studios with MARTY ROBBINS, RAY PRICE, and others. In 1955 Gimble moved to Waco, where he played local TV shows and barbered for a living. He returned to Tyler in 1958. Although Gimble occasionally worked RED FOLEY's *Jubilee, U.S.A* (*OZARK JUBILEE*) in Springfield, his career really took off after moving to Nashville in the late 1960s. Contributing to thousands of recordings by others, Gimble also recorded under his own name with his Bosque Bandits, which included son Dick Gimble on bass.

Johnny Gimble returned to Texas in the 1980s, touring and recording with WILLIE NELSON; he appeared in the Nelson film *Honeysuckle Rose* (1980) and played the part of Bob Wills in Clint Eastwood's *Honky Tonk Man* (1982). Gimble has since proved a tireless champion of Texas swing. Known for his five-string fiddle, he still appears occasionally with the Wills-revival group Playboys II, an act he co-led with steel guitarist HERB REMINGTON for more than a decade, and he currently fronts Johnny Gimble & Texas Swing, whose recent recordings include *Just for Fun* (Tejas, 2006). He also backed RAY PRICE, WILLIE NELSON, and MERLE HAGGARD on their 2007 album *Last of the Breed*. As of 2011 Gimble has won CMA's Musician of the Year award five times and ACM's Best Fiddle Player award nine times. He was featured on two Grammy-winning instrumental albums by ASLEEP AT THE WHEEL in 1993

and 1995. In 2010, Gimble released *Celebrating with Friends,* an album featuring duets with Asleep at the Wheel's Ray Benson (who produced), VINCE GILL, Merle Haggard, and Willie Nelson, among other artists. —*Kevin Coffey*

## The Girls of the Golden West
Mildred Fern Goad ("Millie Good") b. Mount Carmel, Illinois, April 11, 1913; d. May 2, 1993
Dorothy Lavern Goad ("Dollie Good") b. Mount Carmel, Illinois, December 11, 1915; d. November 12, 1967

Probably the only country music duo named after a grand opera (Puccini, 1910), the Girls of the Golden West were also the first nationally successful all-woman act in country. To say they were a female version of the BLUE SKY BOYS is accurate but incomplete; they did sing a lot of sentimental songs in close harmony, but they also specialized in western songs and perfected the skills of harmonizing while yodeling and singing falsetto. They set the stage for later groups such as SWEETHEARTS OF THE RODEO and THE JUDDS, but there was nothing quite like them before, nor has there been anything like them since.

For decades the WLS publicity machine claimed that Millie and Dollie were from Muleshoe, Texas, and that their last name was Good. Good was actually a stage name, and the sisters were born in Illinois and grew up around St. Louis and in downstate Illinois. Though their mother was a singer of traditional BALLADS, the sisters found their harmony by accident; Millie explained, "When I hear a note, I automatically hear the harmony to it." Soon they found work on St. Louis radio stations and then on BORDER RADIO station XER. By the time they came to WLS and the *NATIONAL BARN DANCE* in 1933, they were using their new name and wearing stylish cowgirl costumes their mother made for them.

In 1933 the sisters began recording for BLUEBIRD, gaining hits such as "Old Chisholm Trail," "Cowboy Jack," and "My Love Is a Rider." Their biggest hit was a 1938 side cut for the AMERICAN RECORD CORPORATION, "There's a Silver Moon on the Golden Gate." Needing material voicing a female perspective, they began writing their own songs, and getting others from fellow WLS performers PATSY MONTANA and Lucille Overstake (later known as JENNY LOU CARSON). Devoted fans followed the sisters onstage and on radio and showered them with gifts when both married in the late 1930s: Dollie to PRAIRIE RAMBLERS fiddler Tex Atchison and Millie to announcer-promoter Bill McCluskey. By 1945 the Girls had relocated to WLW in Cincinnati, and they retired in about 1949. In 1963 they reunited for a series of albums on the Bluebonnet label. Dollie passed away in 1967; Millie died in 1993. —*Charles Wolfe*

## The Glaser Brothers
Thomas Paul Glaser b. Spalding, Nebraska, September 3, 1933
James William Glaser b. Spalding, Nebraska, December 16, 1937
Charles Glaser b. Spalding, Nebraska, February 27, 1936

Best known to country audiences today for Tompall Glaser's contribution to RCA's epochal *Wanted! The Outlaws* album (1976), the Glaser Brothers were prominent country performers of the 1960s and 1970s. After the brothers appeared on Arthur Godfrey's network television show in 1957, MARTY ROBBINS hired them to sing harmony in his concerts and, in 1959, signed them to his

Robbins Records label. That prompted a move from Nebraska to Nashville, where they worked recording sessions and toured with Robbins and JOHNNY CASH. Producer OWEN BRADLEY later recorded the trio as a folk music act for DECCA RECORDS. Signing with MGM RECORDS in 1966, they had modest chart hits with producer JACK CLEMENT and were named CMA Vocal Group of the Year in 1970. In 1971, "Rings" became their first single to hit the Top Ten.

The brothers eventually made a more substantial mark in Nashville with their publishing company (JOHN HARTFORD's "Gentle on My Mind" was an early signing), songwriting (Jim Glaser cowrote the Gary Puckett pop smash "Woman, Woman"), management careers, and historic recording studio. That studio, at 916 Nineteenth Avenue South, became known as Hillbilly Central, serving as clubhouse of sorts for Tompall and a recording center for the Glasers, WAYLON JENNINGS, BOBBY BARE, KRIS KRISTOFFERSON, KINKY FRIEDMAN & His Texas Jewboys (who were managed by Chuck Glaser), BILLY JOE SHAVER, and any number of self-proclaimed OUTLAWS.

As a performing group, the Glaser Brothers (sometimes billed as "Tompall & The Glaser Brothers") broke up in 1973, reunited in 1980, scored a #2 hit with Kristofferson's "Lovin' Her Was Easier (Than Anything I'll Ever Do Again)" in 1981, and finally retired in 1982. Chuck Glaser was sidelined by a stroke in 1975 but recovered within two years. Jim Glaser, who had recorded as a solo act in the 1960s and 1970s with little success, enjoyed a brief run of hits during the 1980s, including the 1984 chart-topper "You're Gettin' to Me Again." —*Chet Flippo*

## Lonnie Glosson
b. Judsonia, Arkansas, February 14, 1908; d. March 2, 2001

A talented harmonica player, guitarist, singer, and songwriter, Lonnie Glosson was one of the most popular country music disc jockeys of the late 1940s.

Taught the rudiments of the harmonica by his mother, Glosson hoboed throughout the South and Midwest before beginning his musical career in 1925 at KMOX–St. Louis. He later joined Chicago's WLS *NATIONAL BARN DANCE* and appeared on WJJD–Chicago's *SUPPERTIME FROLIC*. Paramount's Broadway label issued Glosson's first recordings in 1932, and his 1936 ARC recording of "Arkansas Hard Luck Blues" was an early example of the "talking blues" style later adopted by WOODY GUTHRIE and BOB DYLAN.

Glosson moved to California in 1934 to work for a Los Angeles radio station but soon moved to Kentucky to MC the *RENFRO VALLEY BARN DANCE*. In 1936 Glosson and WAYNE RANEY began a long musical partnership, fueled by the younger Raney's long-standing admiration for Glosson's harmonica style; in 1938 the two harmonica players teamed up briefly for a regular program at KARK in Little Rock. During the late 1940s the duo had a nationally syndicated radio program broadcast from WCKY in Cincinnati, and they also backed the DELMORE BROTHERS on several recordings for KING RECORDS, including the chart-topping "Blues Stay Away from Me" (1949–50). In addition, Glosson recorded for DECCA and MERCURY during this period. In 1949 he became one of the first country performers to work in Atlanta television when he hosted a program for WSB-TV.

After parting company with Raney in 1960, Glosson remained active into his nineties as a solo performer in the United States and Europe, delving into gospel music and often performing in schools. —*Kim Field*

## Henry Glover
b. Hot Springs, Arkansas, May 21, 1921; d. April 7, 1991

Henry Bernard Glover was country music's first major African American executive. He received extensive formal musical education during high school in Hot Springs and at Huntsville's Alabama A&M, where he graduated in 1943. For a time he pursued a master's program in political science at Detroit's Wayne State University, but he dropped out to work with bands led by Buddy Johnson, Tiny Bradshaw, and Lucky Millinder. While with Millinder, in about 1945, he began to produce Bull Moose Jackson, then Millinder's vocalist, as a separate act for Cincinnati-based KING RECORDS.

Glover wrote and produced several hits for Jackson, including "I Love You, Yes I Do" in 1947, and King owner SYD NATHAN signed Glover as a producer and songwriter in 1948. Soon Nathan and Glover organized a publishing company, Jay & Cee. In addition to R&B acts such as Bill Doggett and Little Willie John, Glover produced sessions with King's country roster, then including GRANDPA JONES, HAWKSHAW HAWKINS, JIMMIE OSBORNE, and COWBOY COPAS. Glover wrote "Blues Stay Away from Me" (based on his own "Boardinghouse Blues") with the DELMORE BROTHERS and produced their 1949 hit recording of the number. In blending country and R&B sounds, however, Glover found his most consistent success with country star MOON MULLICAN, with whom Glover cowrote "I'll Sail My Ship Alone," "Rocket to the Moon," "Southern Hospitality," and other songs, many of them derived from contemporary R&B hits. Glover continued to pen R&B hits as well, including the 1956 RAY CHARLES classic "Drown in My Own Tears."

Glover left King in about 1959 and eventually moved to Roulette Records, where he worked with Joey Dee ("Peppermint Twist"), Sarah Vaughan, and other artists. He rejoined the STARDAY-King organization in about 1968 and managed the New York office of LIN Broadcasting's music division after LIN purchased Starday. When LIN divested itself of its music holdings early in the 1970s, Glover pursued independent production. His credits include *The Muddy Waters Woodstock Album*, winner of a 1975 Grammy; Paul Butterfield's album *Put It in Your Ear* (1975); and the soundtrack for the Martin Scorsese film *The Last Waltz* (1978), documenting a 1976 concert by the Band. In 1986 Glover was placed on the National Academy of Recording Arts and Sciences (NARAS) Honor Roll of A&R Producers. —*John W. Rumble*

## George Gobel
b. Chicago, Illinois, May 20, 1919; d. February 24, 1991

George Leslie Gobel was a child star of the WLS *NATIONAL BARN DANCE* who grew up to become a popular TV comedian. While in grade school, he began singing in his church choir, and, because of his exceptional voice, he frequently was assigned solo parts.

In 1932, when he was thirteen, Gobel was hired to perform on the *National Barn Dance* and other WLS programs. Billed as the Little Cowboy, he sang a variety of popular songs, including the latest hits from the cowboy genre. Except for brief stints at radio stations WMAQ–Chicago (where he filled the juvenile role on the Tom Mix serial, *Tom Mix Ralston Straight Shooters*), WDOD–Chattanooga, Tennessee, and KMOX–St. Louis, he was a fixture at WLS for ten years. In 1933 he recorded four sides for the AMERICAN RECORD COMPANY, all released on the CONQUEROR label.

In the fall of 1942 Gobel was inducted into the U.S. Army's Flying Cadets in a ceremony held on the *National Barn Dance* stage. After World War II he returned to Chicago, where he worked as a stand-up comic. In the 1950s, while living in Los Angeles, he became one of television's most popular comedians, appearing on such programs as *The Colgate Comedy Hour*, *The Spike Jones Show*, and *Who Said That?* From 1957 to 1959 he had his own network program, *The George Gobel Show*. His signature expression, "Well, I'll be a dirty bird," entered the popular language of the era. The latter years of Gobel's career found him making guest appearances on television shows, performing in several movies, and entertaining in supper clubs nationwide. —*Wayne W. Daniel*

## Bobby Goldsboro
b. Marianna, Florida, January 18, 1941

Successfully bridging pop and country audiences, Bobby Goldsboro first hit the pop Top Ten in 1964 with "See the Funny Little Clown" and then exploded to the #1 spot on both the pop and country charts in 1968 with "Honey."

During a two-year stint at Auburn University, Goldsboro and his group, the Webs, played at parties. In 1962 they received an offer to go on the road with ROY ORBISON, who later collaborated with Goldsboro on a number of songs. Signed to United Artists, Goldsboro charted pop with "See the Funny Little Clown" and other self-penned songs, including "Little Things" and "Voodoo Woman" (both 1965). He toured with the Beatles in England and with the Rolling Stones on that group's first American tour.

Goldsboro's career soared with "Honey." Written by Bobby Russell, the song spent five weeks atop *Billboard*'s pop chart and three at #1 on the country chart. "Watching Scotty Grow" (1970–71), a wistful song of parenting, became another pop-country crossover hit. The singer-songwriter appeared often on network TV and starred in his own self-titled syndicated TV show from 1972 to 1975.

A shrewd businessman as well as entertainer, Goldsboro founded House of Gold Music, Inc., which, among other successes, published "Behind Closed Doors," the Kenny O'Dell–authored CHARLIE RICH hit that won CMA Song of the Year honors in 1973. Among those recording Goldsboro-written songs have been Al Hirt, Vikki Carr, and DOLLY PARTON. More than seventy artists have recorded his song "With Pen in Hand."

Goldsboro retired from the stage in the 1980s and began to focus on producing children's audiobooks and TV series. —*Gerry Wood*

## Randy Goodman (*see* Lyric Street Records)

## Emory Gordy Jr.
b. Atlanta, Georgia, December 25, 1944

A veteran musician and record producer, Emory Gordy Jr. began playing bass at age eighteen and got his big break in 1964, when he started working with JOE SOUTH in backing Tommy Roe. South asked Gordy to play on a session, and Gordy eventually recorded with BILLY JOE ROYAL, MAC DAVIS, and others. Gordy also cowrote the 1969 Classics IV hit "Traces."

Gordy moved to Los Angeles in 1970, joined Neil Diamond's band in 1971, and soon established a reputation as a recording and stage musician. In the studio, he backed ELVIS PRESLEY and contributed to GRAM PARSONS's *Grievous Angel*, in addition to touring with Presley and producing Debbie Reynolds and Liberace. In 1975 Gordy joined EMMYLOU HARRIS's Hot Band while continuing to record with Diamond, Tom Petty, and the BELLAMY BROTHERS. Gordy toured and recorded with JOHN DENVER and also worked in the Cherry Bombs, a band that backed RODNEY CROWELL and ROSANNE CASH and included VINCE GILL, TONY BROWN, and RICHARD BENNETT.

In 1984 Gordy began working in A&R with Brown at MCA Nashville; there Gordy met PATTY LOVELESS, whom he married in 1989. During his MCA tenure he coproduced STEVE EARLE's *Guitar Town* (1986) and *Exit O* (1987) as well as the Grammy-winning 1988 BILL MONROE album *Southern Flavor*. He also was ACM's 1986 Bass Player of the Year. Gordy joined Rising Tide as senior vice president of A&R in 1996 and helmed recordings by DELBERT McCLINTON, the NITTY GRITTY DIRT BAND, and MATRACA BERG, among others. Rising Tide ceased operations in March 1998.

After Loveless left MCA and underwent vocal cord surgery, Gordy helped put her back on track by producing *Only What I Feel* (EPIC,1993) and subsequent Epic albums, including *When Fallen Angels Fly*, CMA's 1995 Album of the Year. Gordy has continued to guide her studio efforts, including her 2009 Saguaro Road release *Mountain Soul II.* —*Beverly Keel*

## Vern Gosdin
b. Woodland, Alabama, August 5, 1934; d. April 28, 2009

After an early career in BLUEGRASS, Vernon Gosdin became one of his generation's finest hard-country singers. TAMMY WYNETTE once called him "the only other singer who can hold a candle to GEORGE JONES."

*Vern Gosdin*

Growing up in rural Alabama, Gosdin and his brother Rex formed a harmony duo modeled on THE LOUVIN BROTHERS and the BLUE SKY BOYS. The Gosdins also sang in a quartet with their brother Ray and fiddle champion Chuck Reeves. In the early 1960s Vern and Rex eventually reunited in Los Angeles, where they joined a bluegrass band, the Golden State Boys—renamed the Hillmen after its mandolinist, CHRIS HILLMAN. After one album, Hillman joined COUNTRY-ROCK pioneers THE BYRDS. The Gosdins shared a manager with that band; when Gene Clark left the Byrds in 1967, his first album was titled *Gene Clark with the Gosdin Brothers*. That same year the Gosdins had their own Top Forty country single, "Hangin' On," on Bakersfield International Records.

Vern and Rex later took day jobs in Atlanta, but in 1976 Vern convinced his West Coast pal EMMYLOU HARRIS to fly to Nashville for a demo session. A remake of "Hangin' On" and a new song, "Yesterday's Gone," convinced ELEKTRA to sign Gosdin as a solo artist, and with Harris singing harmony the songs became country hits. Gosdin also hit with "Till the End," featuring session vocalist JANIE FRICKE. From Elektra, Gosdin moved successively to Ovation Records, AMI—where he notched a Top Ten hit with "Today My World Slipped Away"—and Compleat. There he began a songwriting partnership with MAX D. BARNES that yielded the Top Ten hits "If You're Gonna Do Me Wrong (Do It Right)" and "Slow Burnin' Memory." Gosdin's Compleat years also included "Way Down Deep" (#5, 1983) and 1984's "I Can Tell by the Way You Dance," his first #1 record.

After Compleat folded, Gosdin signed with COLUMBIA in 1987, quickly scoring with the Gosdin-Barnes gems "Do You Believe Me Now" (#4, 1987–88) and "Chiseled in Stone" (#6, 1988), the latter becoming CMA's 1989 Song of the Year. With HANK COCHRAN, Gosdin coauthored such Gosdin hits as "Is It Raining at Your House," "This Ain't My First Rodeo," and the 1988 chart-topper "Set 'Em Up Joe," a tribute to HONKY-TONK pioneer ERNEST TUBB.

Gosdin's hits fell off sharply after 1991. A series of strokes curtailed his career and eventually ended the life of the man many called "The Voice." —*Geoffrey Himes*

## Billy Grammer
b. Benton, Illinois, August 28, 1925; d. August 10, 2011

"Gotta Travel On" put singer Billy Wayne Grammer on the musical map. Adapted from a 150-year-old British folk tune, the October 1958 release landed him on a trio of charts: country (#5), pop (#4), and R&B (#14). In addition, the million-selling record was the first hit for MONUMENT RECORDS and its founder, producer FRED FOSTER, who had helped craft the song's lyrics. A 1961 Grammer release, "Bonaparte's Retreat" b/w "The Kissing Tree," is estimated to have sold 500,000 units.

The eldest of thirteen children, Grammer began playing guitar at age five, and soon he was playing locally with fiddler father Arch Grammer. Billy made his radio debut on WJPF–Herrin, Illinois, in 1940. After military service in World War II, he worked for CONNIE B. GAY at WARL–Arlington, Virginia. There Grammer performed on JIMMY DEAN's CBS-TV show (1957–58). Grammer joined the GRAND OLE OPRY in 1959, remaining until he lost his eyesight.

He designed the Grammer Flat Top Guitar, donating his first model to the COUNTRY MUSIC HALL OF FAME AND MUSEUM in 1969. With partners, he manufactured the guitar from 1965 to 1970. The agile guitarist's sophisticated licks garnered numerous

studio sessions with artists such as EDDY ARNOLD, Louis Armstrong, and Patti Page and inspired other guitarists, including ROY CLARK. In 1965 Grammer had his own syndicated TV series.

Deeply religious, Grammer delivered the invocation for the Grand Ole Opry House opening on March 16, 1974. —*Walt Trott*

## Grand Ole Opry
established in Nashville, Tennessee, November 28, 1925

The longest-lived radio show in the United States, the Grand Ole Opry is also one of the most important radio programs in broadcasting history. Its popularity as America's leading country music radio show from 1945 through 1965 made possible Nashville's emergence as the undisputed center of the country music industry. Throughout its storied history, the Opry has featured a host of notable country performers.

The Grand Ole Opry's evolution is closely intertwined with that of its parent station, Nashville's WSM, broadcasting outlet of the National Life and Accident Insurance Company. Within weeks of WSM's inaugural broadcast, on October 5, 1925, owners hired star radio announcer GEORGE D. HAY away from WLS–Chicago, which had launched its own radio barn dance in 1924 (see NATIONAL BARN DANCE). Joining WSM as "radio director" on November 9, Hay quickly began increasing the number of local folk music performers in the station's programming, some of whom had appeared on WSM before he arrived. The epiphany that sparked the Grand Ole Opry came on the Saturday evening of November 28, 1925, when seventy-seven-year-old UNCLE JIMMY THOMPSON played his fiddle tunes on the air. His performance prompted a flood of favorable mail, telegrams, and telephone calls, and Hay moved to make the Saturday-night show a fixture in the station's lineup.

Initially the program featured an informal aggregation of local, mostly amateur performers. Among the most popular regulars were Thompson, UNCLE DAVE MACON, DEFORD BAILEY, and DR. HUMPHREY BATE. The show also featured a number of STRING-BANDS (colorfully named by Hay), including the GULLY JUMPERS, the FRUIT JAR DRINKERS, and the BINKLEY BROTHERS' DIXIE CLODHOPPERS. For his part, Hay wore an old-fashioned costume and created his persona as the Solemn Old Judge.

Early on, the *WSM Barn Dance*, as it was first known, was broadcast from WSM's Studio A on the fifth floor of the National Life building in downtown Nashville. As audiences expanded,

*Ad for the Purina segment of the Grand Ole Opry*

the show moved to more spacious surroundings. In about 1928 the Opry moved to the newly built, larger Studio B, which accommodated a studio audience of about 200.

In 1928 HARRY STONE joined WSM as a staff announcer and soon proved himself so capable that he assumed supervisory duties, rising to the position of station manager in 1932. Hay was relegated to announcing the Opry, writing press releases, and briefly helping to run WSM's Artist Service, which was created in 1933 to book WSM pop and country acts for personal appearances. Under Stone's direction, WSM librarian and Opry stage manager VITO PELLETTIERI divided the program into distinct, sponsored segments in 1934, a format the show retains to this day.

Stone, with the help of his brother DAVID STONE (who took over Artist Service duties), moved the Opry away from the hoedown stringbands and fiddlers that Hay preferred and increasingly cultivated a star system that followed Hollywood's example by focusing attention on individual, professional performers. During Harry Stone's tenure with the Opry (1930–50), he ushered in such key figures as THE VAGABONDS, the DELMORE BROTHERS, PEE WEE KING, ROY ACUFF, BILL MONROE, MINNIE PEARL, EDDY ARNOLD, ERNEST TUBB, HANK WILLIAMS, and HANK SNOW. During Stone's years, the Opry moved to WSM's Studio C in February 1934, the Hillsboro Theater in October 1934, the Dixie Tabernacle on Fatherland Street in East Nashville in June 1936, the War Memorial Auditorium in downtown Nashville in July 1939, and THE RYMAN AUDITORIUM in June 1943.

Through the efforts of Stone and WSM program director JACK STAPP, the NBC radio network began featuring a half hour of the Opry in October 1939. Sponsored by Prince Albert Smoking Tobacco, the segment became known as the *Prince Albert Show*. With its network affiliation, the Opry became the nation's most-listened-to country radio program, soon outdistancing WLS's *National Barn Dance*, which lost its network connection in 1946. In 1940 the Opry was the subject of a Republic Pictures movie titled *Grand Ole Opry* and featuring cast members Roy Acuff, Uncle Dave Macon, and Judge Hay.

In 1948 the Opry began a Friday night show, initially broadcast from Studio C and called the *Friday Night Frolics*. In 1963 this Friday program moved to the Ryman and became known as the *Friday Night Opry*, virtually identical to the Saturday night show.

Through the early 1950s the Opry solidified its position as America's most popular country radio program, weathering the 1950 departure of Harry Stone and the 1952 dismissal and subsequent death of star attraction Hank Williams. Other executive changes included the departures of JIM DENNY, WSM Artist Service chief (from 1946) and Opry manager (1951–56), and Jack Stapp, who left to run Nashville radio station WKDA in 1957.

In the late 1950s the Opry was buffeted by two major forces it failed to accommodate: television and rock & roll. Special shows using Opry talent aired briefly on a regular basis on ABC-TV in 1955 and 1956, and Opry stars were also featured in separate programs filmed and syndicated by AL GANNAWAY, but the Opry itself did not gain regular TV exposure until 1985. Meanwhile, despite inviting ELVIS PRESLEY to appear on the show in October 1954, Opry officials failed to sign him, allowing him to slip away to the *LOUISIANA HAYRIDE*. Afterward the Opry made only token efforts in signing a few rock & roll performers, such as THE EVERLY BROTHERS. Partly as a result of such shortsightedness—together with the rise of TV ownership, which kept viewers at home—the Opry's attendance plummeted in the late 1950s. The program suffered further in the early 1960s when some of its biggest stars, including PATSY CLINE and JIM REEVES, died in travel accidents.

In December 1964 management dismissed twelve cast members for making too few required appearances; only half of these eventually returned. During the 1960s and through the 1970s, fewer and fewer stars of real consequence joined the cast because of the show's low wages and the diminishing power of the live radio show to build careers in an industry dominated by stations that broadcast recordings. The Opry's managers during these years were D KILPATRICK (1956–59), OTT DEVINE (1959–68), and E. W. "BUD" WENDELL (1968–74).

Attendance rebounded for a time with the show's March 1974 move from the Ryman Auditorium to the opulent new Grand Ole Opry House at OPRYLAND. The March 16 opening ceremonies included an appearance by President Richard Nixon.

During his tenure as Opry manager (1974–93), HAL DURHAM relaxed the required number of appearances for cast members. This allowed an infusion of young, in-demand artists into the roster, among them RANDY TRAVIS, REBA McENTIRE, CLINT BLACK, ALAN JACKSON, GARTH BROOKS, and VINCE GILL. Other rising stars have come on board under managers Bob Whittaker (1993–99) and Pete Fisher (1999–), including TRACE ADKINS, DIERKS BENTLEY, MARTINA McBRIDE, ALISON KRAUSS, BRAD PAISLEY, JOSH TURNER, and CARRIE UNDERWOOD, among others. Unfortunately, most of these dynamic performers rarely make more than a half dozen appearances a year because the Opry pays artists at musicians' union scale—less than 1 percent of what stars earn for a single concert on the road.

In 1983 the Opry was purchased as part of the Opryland properties by Gaylord Broadcasting (see GAYLORD ENTERTAINMENT COMPANY). In 1985 TNN began televising a half-hour segment of the Opry—the show's first regular television exposure in thirty years. The program switched to CMT in 2001 (increasing to an hour) and then to GAC in 2003. As of 2010, SiriusXM Satellite Radio and wsmonline.com carried the show live. In 1999 the Opry began returning to the Ryman Auditorium—its most historic venue—in winter months. An 80th anniversary performance at New York's CARNEGIE HALL in 2005 drew further attention to the show, as did Opry members' participation in a multiday country music festival presented by the Kennedy Center for the Performing Arts in 2006.

Despite the occasional star-studded half-hour segment, the exciting performances of veterans (CONNIE SMITH, RIDERS IN THE SKY) as well as more recently added members (DEL McCOURY, BLAKE SHELTON), and headline-grabbing concerts, many observers believe these bright spots are overshadowed by aging acts who no longer have hit records. And yet somehow the Opry has endured, even after the May 2010 deluge of devastating flooding in Nashville that damaged the Opry House and forced the program to use other venues for several months. In spite of it all, the Opry is still broadcast live over WSM at 650 on the AM dial as well as online and on SiriusXM Satellite Radio, and it is still entertaining audiences in-house and around the world with folksy, family-oriented music and comedy. Whatever its shortcomings as a business enterprise, the Opry remains, for artists and fans alike, one of country music's most cherished institutions. —*Paul Kingsbury*

## Uncle Josh Graves

b. Tellico Plains, Tennessee, September 27, 1928; September 30, 2006

When Burkett H. "Uncle Josh" Graves joined FLATT & SCRUGGS in 1955, his bluesy DOBRO style added a new dimension to their music. Graves began his professional career in Gatlinburg in 1942 as bass player for the Pierce Brothers. In 1943 he joined Knoxville-based Esco Hankins, with whom Graves later made his professional recording debut on KING RECORDS.

Graves worked with MAC WISEMAN and WILMA LEE & STONEY COOPER before signing on with Flatt & Scruggs. Graves quickly switched to dobro, combining the guitar styles of Cliff Carlisle (see BILL CARLISLE) and blues artist Blind Boy Fuller with Scruggs's three-finger banjo roll. Graves also shared comedic duties with Cousin Jake Tullock. Although Tullock eventually left, Graves stayed on, recording hundreds of sides with Flatt & Scruggs for COLUMBIA RECORDS. After the group disbanded in 1969, Graves worked with LESTER FLATT & THE NASHVILLE GRASS from 1971 through 1974 before joining the EARL SCRUGGS REVUE.

The first of several Graves solo albums, *Alone At Last*, appeared on EPIC in 1974. He also recorded albums with KENNY BAKER and later toured with the fiddle virtuoso for some two decades. In 1989 Graves and Baker, along with banjo player Eddie Adcock and mandolinist Jesse McReynolds (see JIM & JESSE), recorded and toured as the Masters, winning IBMA's 1990 Recorded Performance award for their album *Saturday Night Fish Fry*. Graves shared this same honor in 1995 for his contribution to the multiartist *The Great Dobro Sessions*. He was elected to the IBMA Hall of Fame in 1997. Despite his declining health, he kept touring and recording, releasing *Memories of Foggy Mountain* on OMH in 2002. Few dobro players today fail to cite Graves as a major influence. —*Chris Skinker*

## Claude Gray
b. Henderson, Texas, January 25, 1932

Born a few miles from JIM REEVES in rural East Texas, Claude N. Gray refined a style that resembled Reeves's. The smooth-singing Gray scored several sizable hits in the early 1960s.

Gray left the U.S. Navy in 1954; attended college; and worked as a field rep for a haulage company before joining the on-air staff at radio station KOCA in Kilgore, Texas, in 1958. He moved to WDAI–Meridian, Mississippi, in 1959. Gray first recorded for Minor Records in 1958 and then for D RECORDS in 1959 and 1960. His second D release was WILLIE NELSON's song "Family Bible." It became the first hit for both men, though Nelson had sold the song to Gray, session musician Paul Buskirk, and Gray's manager, Walt Breeland. In August 1960 Gray signed with MERCURY RECORDS and immediately notched two Top Five hits, "I'll Just Have a Cup of Coffee (Then I'll Go)" and ROGER MILLER's composition "My Ears Should Burn (When Fools Are Talked About)."

Gray left Mercury in 1967 and recorded for DECCA until 1971. Later he recorded for several smaller companies and last charted in 1986 with a cover of Neil Diamond's "Sweet Caroline" on Country International. Based in Longview, Texas, as of 2011, he still toured occasionally. —*Colin Escott*

## Otto Gray
b. South Dakota, March 2, 1884; d. November 8, 1967

Otto Gray & His Oklahoma Cowboy Band were the nation's most popular western stage act during the late 1920s and early 1930s, touring widely on the Loew's, RKO, and Fox theater circuits. They were equally popular as radio and recording artists. NBC fed the band's radio shows to 150 stations, and the group recorded for OKeh, GENNETT, Vocalion, and BRUNSWICK's Melotone label. Equipped with elaborate stage sets, they were possibly the first touring group to use large, custom-made Cadillacs for transportation. The band started as the Billy McGinty Cowboy Band in Ripley, Oklahoma, in 1921. As their popularity and engagements increased, McGinty withdrew, turning over leadership to Gray, who changed the group's name and expanded its membership, which included Whitey Ford (THE DUKE OF PADUCAH) for a time. The troupe's radio appearances started in 1925 over KFRU (now KVOO in Tulsa, Oklahoma). Their stage program included COWBOY MUSIC, folk songs, and popular songs as well as trick roping, whip popping, dog tricks, and trick musical instrument playing. Otto Gray was the first western artist featured on the cover of *Billboard*, and Gray's band appeared in the 1929 movie short *Otto Gray and His Oklahoma Cowboys*. The group broke up by 1936. —*Guy Logsdon*

## G. B. Grayson (*see* Henry Whitter)

## Grayson & Whitter (*see* Henry Whitter)

## Charles Grean
b. New York, New York, October 1, 1913; d. December 20, 2003

As a key assistant to A&R representative STEVE SHOLES, Charles Randolph Grean (pronounced GREE-ahn) advanced Sholes's effort to bring RCA VICTOR to the forefront of recorded country music in the late 1940s. Grean collected repertoire, played bass on sessions, wrote musical arrangements, and produced acts including WILF CARTER, the SONS OF THE PIONEERS, ELTON BRITT, JOHNNIE & JACK, TEXAS JIM ROBERTSON, and ROY ROGERS. In 1947 he and Sholes coproduced three EDDY ARNOLD sessions that resulted in six Top Ten hits, including four #1s.

Before joining Sholes in 1946, Grean led New York society bands and worked as bandleader Glenn Miller's copyist. In 1950 Grean rose to head RCA's pop department. He cowrote several Eddy Arnold hits with Cy Coben and, alone, penned "The Thing," a 1950 novelty hit for pop singer Phil Harris. Grean also wrote the pop-country crossover hit "He'll Have to Stay"—the 1960 answer to JIM REEVES's 1959–60 crossover smash "He'll Have to Go"—for West Coast country singer Jeanne Black.

For forty years after leaving RCA in 1952, Grean maintained a periodic association with Arnold. Grean was a partner in the management group that briefly directed Arnold's career after the star split with manager TOM PARKER in 1953, and, as late as 1978, Grean produced Arnold's minor hit "I'm the South." Grean occasionally conducted Arnold's road band from the 1970s into the 1990s. —*Michael Streissguth*

## Lloyd Green
b. Leaf, Mississippi, October 4, 1937

Along with BUD ISAACS, BUDDY EMMONS, JIMMY DAY, and a handful of others, Lloyd Lamar Green revolutionized the steel guitar in the 1950s by utilizing pedals. He is known in MUSIC Row circles as "Mr. Nashville Sound" for his ability to play exactly what the singer and song require while turning many a recording into a standard. Praised for dramatic melodic runs as well as

*Lloyd Green*

innovative rhythmic and harmonic effects, Green also played on THE BYRDS' landmark COUNTRY-ROCK album *Sweetheart of the Rodeo* (1968), thereby influencing generations of players beyond the country mainstream.

Green started playing HAWAIIAN steel guitar at age seven, and by age ten he was playing pop music professionally around Mobile, Alabama. Bud Isaacs's seminal PEDAL STEEL work on WEBB PIERCE's "Slowly" turned Green toward country music at age sixteen, and the young picker immediately modified his own instrument, attaching a Model T Ford gas pedal.

In 1956, after attending the University of Southern Mississippi, Green arrived in Nashville, where he first played with HAWKSHAW HAWKINS. Green then joined FARON YOUNG's band and later worked with FERLIN HUSKY. After briefly leaving the music business, Green settled in Nashville for good in 1963. His studio career took off with WARNER MACK's 1965 #1 hit "The Bridge Washed Out," featuring Green's innovative style of playing staccato chords and single notes in fast, syncopated patterns with a bright tone. Between 1965 and 1985 Green played on more than 100 chart-topping country hits by TAMMY WYNETTE ("D-I-V-O-R-C-E"), CHARLEY PRIDE ("Is Anybody Goin' to San Antone"), FREDDIE HART ("Easy Lovin'"), DON WILLIAMS ("Some Broken Hearts Never Mend"), and many others.

As in-house arranger for LITTLE DARLIN' RECORDS in the late 1960s, Green made several Little Darlin' releases of his own and provided the "left field" licks for JOHNNY PAYCHECK's remarkable Little Darlin' sides. In 1973, Green scored a Top Forty hit on MONUMENT RECORDS with an instrumental version of "I Can See Clearly Now."

After the mid-1980s Green became far less active in the studio, but in the new century he made something of a comeback with his album *Lloyd Green, Revisited* (LG, 2003) and his memorable playing on ALAN JACKSON's #1 hit "Remember When" (2003–04). Elected to the Steel Guitar Hall of Fame in 1988, Green remains one of the most influential steel guitarists of all time. —*Daniel Cooper* and *Bob Kramer*

## Pat Green
b. San Antonio, Texas, April 5, 1972

When singer-songwriter Patrick Craven "Pat" Green signed with Universal Records in 2001, he had already released five independent-label albums and built a strong Texas fan base. As a student at Texas Tech in Lubbock, Green played local clubs and developed a raucous, crowd-pleasing stage show. In 1995, Texas PEDAL STEEL GUITAR player and producer Lloyd Maines began producing Green's earliest releases. Green's first album, *Dancehall Dreamer,* featured guest appearances by JACK INGRAM and Maines's daughter Natalie, of DIXIE CHICKS.

*Three Days*, a 2001 Universal Republic release, contained two *Billboard* chart singles; one of these, "Carry On," became a hit video on CMT and won Green new fans nationwide. The title track from his 2003 album *Wave on Wave* climbed to #3, while the album was eventually certified gold. In 2006, Green signed with BNA (see RCA RECORDS), and his album *Cannonball* included the #13 single "Feels Just Like It Should." The #12 single "Let Me" was the highest-charting hit from his 2009 album *What I'm For.* Green left BNA shortly afterward. —*Michael Manning*

## The Greenbriar Boys
John Herald (John Whittier Sirabian) b. New York, New York, September 6, 1939; d. July 18, 2005
Ralph Rinzler b. Passaic, New Jersey, July 20, 1934; d. July 2, 1994
Frank Wakefield b. Emory Gap, Tennessee, June 26, 1934
Bob Yellin b. New York, New York, June 10, 1936

One of the first professional BLUEGRASS bands to emerge from the northern folk music revival, the Greenbriar Boys coalesced from lower Manhattan picking sessions in 1958. The original band included guitarist/lead vocalist John Herald, banjo player/tenor Bob Yellin, and mandolinist/baritone Eric Weissberg. When Weissberg joined the Tarriers in November 1959, RALPH RINZLER replaced him.

In 1960 and 1961 the group won the OLD-TIME band competition in Union Grove, North Carolina. A fall 1961 tour with folksinger Joan Baez led to a Vanguard recording contract. The band's first full-length album was released in March 1962; Rinzler's detailed notes explained bluegrass music to first-time listeners.

The Greenbriar Boys primarily performed at urban folk music venues, featuring an eclectic repertoire considerably broader than their southern counterparts. When Rinzler left in early 1964, Herald and Yellin replaced him with Frank Wakefield, an established mandolinist with unorthodox ideas. With Wakefield aboard, the group extended its instrumental solos, mirroring changes in rock and jazz at the time. "Different Drum," a Michael Nesmith song from the band's only album with Wakefield, was successfully covered by LINDA RONSTADT and the Stone Poneys.

The Greenbriar Boys disbanded in 1966, although Wakefield continued using the name for two more years. During the late 1990s Herald, Yellin, and Weissberg occasionally reunited for festival appearances. —*Dave Samuelson*

## Jack Greene
b. Maryville, Tennessee, January 7, 1930

Jack Henry Greene graduated from ERNEST TUBB's Texas Troubadours to become an award-winning solo star. Starting in radio at WGAP–Maryville (1947), Greene was initially a singer-guitarist who played bass and drums in various groups, both in Tennessee and in Georgia. For a time he owned a downtown Atlanta club, the Covered Wagon, while working by day for a glassmaker. In 1961 Greene was working the *Dixie Jubilee* in East Point (an Atlanta suburb) when Ernest Tubb saw Greene play and hired him six months later. For the next five years Greene was the Texas Troubadours' "big-eared singing drummer," as Tubb liked to call him.

Greene's version of "The Last Letter," released on the Texas Troubadours' first album, was popular enough for DECCA RECORDS to issue it as a single and offer Greene his own recording contract in 1964. Greene's chart-topping 1966 release of the DALLAS FRAZIER song "There Goes My Everything" made him a star, and in May 1967 Tubb persuaded Greene to leave the band and build his own career.

Between then and 1969 Greene scored seven more Top Five country hits, including "All the Time," "You Are My Treasure," "What Locks the Door," and the majestic "Statue of a Fool." At the first CMA Awards ceremony, in 1967, Greene won Single of the Year (for "There Goes My Everything") and Male Vocalist of the Year. From 1969 through the mid-1970s Decca paired him with JEANNIE SEELY on a series of successful duets, including "Wish I Didn't Have to Miss You." Greene joined the GRAND OLE OPRY in 1967 and remains in the cast. —*Ronnie Pugh*

## Lee Greenwood
b. South Gate, California, October 27, 1942

Melvin Lee Greenwood's road to Nashville led him to #1 hits, a 1984 Grammy award, honors as CMA Male Vocalist of the Year in 1983 and 1984, and visits with United States presidents.

Greenwood formed his first band in high school in Sacramento, California. After graduation, he moved to Reno and toured the Nevada casino lounge circuit as a bandleader, performer, arranger, and songwriter, sometimes working as a blackjack dealer by day and playing sax and piano by night. Along the way Greenwood survived a band reorganization that forced him to assemble a new group; this act signed a record contract, but a planned album was shelved after the label was sold, and Greenwood, still under contract, wound up working in a fast-food restaurant.

Greenwood later returned to casino performing. Larry McFadden, of MEL TILLIS's organization, heard the husky-voiced singer in Reno, became Greenwood's manager, and arranged Nashville demo sessions with producer JERRY CRUTCHFIELD, then head of MCA Music Publishing. The result was Greenwood's first MCA RECORDS chart-maker, "It Turns Me Inside Out" (1981–82).

A polished contemporary country performer, Greenwood toured widely on the strength of twenty-one Top Ten hits (1982–1991), including his first #1, "Somebody's Gonna Love You" (1983), and "God Bless the USA," which earned recognition as CMA's 1985 Song of the Year. Other chart-toppers included 1983's "Dixie Road" and 1985's "Going, Going, Gone." Meanwhile, Ronald Reagan and George H. W. Bush used "God Bless the USA" during their presidential campaigns, as George W. Bush would later do.

From 1996 to 2001 Greenwood performed at his own theater in Sevierville, Tennessee, but after the September 11, 2001, terrorist attacks engendered a wave of patriotism, his new version of "God Bless the USA" went to #16 and he began touring again. —*Gerry Wood*

## Rex Griffin
b. Gadsden, Alabama, August 12, 1912; d. October 7, 1958

Though little remembered today, Alsie "Rex" Griffin was a popular and influential singer-songwriter who left a strong impression on HANK WILLIAMS, ERNEST TUBB, and HANK PENNY. A fan of JIMMIE RODGERS, Griffin performed in Rodgers's blue yodeling style, first around Gadsden in 1930. While Griffin was working in a Birmingham group, the Smokey Mountaineers, a WAPI announcer first called him Rex, since fan mail usually misspelled Alsie. Rex later became his legal name.

Griffin made thirty-six recordings for DECCA between 1935 and 1939, the most popular being "Everybody's Tryin' to Be My Baby" (later adapted, and adopted, by CARL PERKINS), "My Hillbilly Baby," and his masterful "The Last Letter." At his final Decca recording session (September 25, 1939) he cut "Lovesick Blues." Hank Williams's huge hit version ten years later was a close copy. In the late 1930s Griffin wrote but never recorded (though many others did) the popular "Won't You Ride in My Little Red Wagon."

In 1941 Griffin moved to KRLD in Dallas, Texas, to star on Gus Foster's *Texas Roundup* program. When Foster left the show, Griffin became its leader. After World War II Griffin worked Chicago nightclubs and then opened his own with Johnny Barfield near Columbus, Georgia. In 1946 Griffin made eight recordings for SYD NATHAN's KING, De Luxe, and Federal labels. Griffin continued to write songs until his death, though his performing was curtailed by diabetes, alcoholism, and tuberculosis. The best known of Griffin's later songs was 1955's "Just Call Me Lonesome," a big hit for EDDY ARNOLD. Griffin drifted between Gadsden (where a sister lived) and New Orleans for most of his later life. He died in a New Orleans charity hospital in 1958 and was buried in Gadsden. In 1970 Griffin was elected to the NASHVILLE SONGWRITERS HALL OF FAME. —*Ronnie Pugh*

## Nanci Griffith
b. Seguin, Texas, July 6, 1953

With influences ranging from folksinger Carolyn Hester to novelist Carson McCullers and greater acceptance at clubs and colleges than at country radio, Nanci Griffith proved to be alternative country when alt-country wasn't cool (see AMERICANA). In the mid-1980s neither labels nor radio knew what to make of her high, breathy voice and hard-to-classify songs. In the 1990s, however, she emerged as a role model in the burgeoning roots-music movement.

Griffith grew up in AUSTIN, TEXAS, where her parents encouraged her interest in music, literature, and theater; by age fourteen she was singing in local coffeehouses. After college she taught kindergarten, but she quit in 1977 to become a full-time musician. By 1982 she had recorded two obscure albums.

In 1985 Griffith arrived in Nashville, where she cut her groundbreaking *Once in a Very Blue Moon* with producer JIM ROONEY for the Philo label. The album gave many listeners their first exposure to songs by LYLE LOVETT and ROBERT EARL KEEN JR. and showcased Griffith's gift for evocative literary detail. As her audience grew, MCA Nashville signed her in 1986 to a roster that included offbeat singer-songwriters Lovett and STEVE EARLE.

Like those Texas troubadours, though, Griffith drew mostly blank stares from mainstream country radio programmers, despite her strong material. In 1986 KATHY MATTEA rode Griffith's signature song "Love at the Five and Dime" to the Top Five—a mixed triumph, since Griffith's own version never charted—just as SUZY BOGGUSS, not Griffith, later hit with Griffith's "Outbound Plane" in 1992. In frustration, MCA shuffled her to its Los Angeles pop division. The records that resulted, especially 1989's *Storms*, sounded uncomfortable.

Griffith signed with ELEKTRA in 1992 and returned to her folk roots with 1993's *Other Voices, Other Rooms*, a collection of material penned by songwriters including JOHN PRINE and TOWNES VAN ZANDT. The album won a 1993 Grammy for Best Contemporary Folk Album. Her startlingly personal 1995 album *Flyer* found her collaborating with members of U2, R.E.M., and other college-radio favorites. *Blue Roses from the Moons*, released in 1997, showcased past and present members of her band, the Blue Moon Orchestra, as well as guests DARIUS RUCKER, then of Hootie & the Blowfish, and the Crickets. Since then she has released albums on Damian Music, Elektra, MCA, New Door, and ROUNDER. Her nineteenth album, *The Loving Kind* (Rounder, 2009), is based on the struggles of an interracial couple. —*Jim Ridley*

## David Grisman
b. Hackensack, New Jersey, March 23, 1945

Mandolinist, composer, and producer David Jay Grisman was part of an early wave of talented New York City–area BLUEGRASS musicians and later became a pioneer of the jazz- and bluegrass-influenced genre known as "new acoustic" music. Introduced to the mandolin in 1960 by folklorist-musician RALPH RINZLER, Grisman was heavily influenced by the playing of BILL MONROE and Frank Wakefield. Grisman performed in the New York Ramblers (bluegrass contest winners at the 1964 Union Grove, North Carolina, fiddlers convention) and the Even Dozen Jug Band (with such future folk-pop stars as Maria Muldaur and John Sebastian). In 1963 he produced his first album, by bluegrass veterans RED ALLEN, Frank Wakefield, and the Kentuckians, for Folkways. Grisman and friend Jerry Garcia (the Grateful Dead rock singer-guitarist, who also played banjo) attracted new fans to bluegrass in 1973 as members of the band Old & In The Way.

Grisman later melded jazz, swing, Latin, and Jewish klezmer sounds with bluegrass to create the distinctive new acoustic style referred to as "dawg music" (after the canine nickname given him by Garcia). He formed the David Grisman Quintet in 1976 and founded the Acoustic Disc label in 1990. Grisman's eclectic tastes have led to collaborations with a broad range of talents, including fiddlers Stephane Grappelli, Svend Asmussen, VASSAR CLEMENTS, Richard Greene, and MARK O'CONNOR, mandolinists Jethro Burns (HOMER & JETHRO) and Andy Statman, and guitarists Jerry Garcia, John Carlini, TONY RICE, and Martin Taylor. But his frequent returns to traditional bluegrass and his widely admired mandolin playing, noted for its inventiveness, bright tone, and jaunty syncopations, have maintained his specific influence within country music. —*Richard D. Smith*

## Bonnie Guitar
b. Seattle, Washington, March 25, 1923

Chiefly known for the haunting, melancholic original of the 1957 Top Ten pop crossover hit "Dark Moon," Bonnie Guitar (born Buckingham) should be better remembered as one of the first women on the recording studio and production scene.

After performing in and around Seattle, Guitar moved to Los Angeles to work as a guitarist for FABOR ROBISON on mid-1950s sessions for his FABOR and ABBOTT labels and as a Fabor artist. She sang and played lead guitar on the demo of NED MILLER's "Dark Moon" and persuaded Robison to issue her version by foregoing royalties. Robison had an agreement with DOT RECORDS, and Dot not only picked up Guitar's original but covered "Dark Moon" with pop singer Gale Storm. Both were hits.

Leaving Robison, Guitar went back to Seattle and started the Dolphin label (soon renamed Dolton) in partnership with a refrigerator salesman, Bob Reisdorf, and a local record distributor, Lou Lavinthal. They scored pop hits with the Fleetwoods ("Come Softly to Me," "Mr. Blue") and the Ventures; Guitar herself had a minor pop hit on the label in 1959 with "Candy Apple Red." Dolton was later sold to LIBERTY, now owned by EMI.

Following a brief recording stint with RCA (1961–1962) Guitar re-signed with Dot in 1965 and consistently hit the country charts through the late 1960s; among the songs was a minor hit in 1969 recorded with BUDDY KILLEN (as Bonnie & Buddy), "A Truer Love You'll Never Find Than Mine." During the late 1960s, she also handled A&R work on the West Coast for Dot and ABC-Paramount. She later recorded for several other labels, including Paramount, COLUMBIA, MCA, FOUR STAR, and Playback. —*Colin Escott*

## Guitar

After Delta blues, country music was the first style of popular music based on the guitar, and the prominent guitar lines in the music of JIMMIE RODGERS and the CARTER FAMILY helped the guitar become the dominant stringed instrument of the twentieth century.

By 1800 the guitar had evolved in Europe from a lute-like instrument with paired strings into its present form with six single strings. It was refined in America into two major styles: the flat-top, perfected by 1850 by C. F. Martin of Nazareth, Pennsylvania; and the arch-top (carved in the manner of a violin), developed by Orville Gibson of Kalamazoo, Michigan, in the 1890s.

For decades the guitar was predominantly a refined parlor instrument overshadowed in American popular music by (chronologically) the lute, minstrel banjo, mandolin, and tenor banjo. By the late 1920s, however, many players found the guitar stylistically more versatile than the banjo. As a solo or ensemble instrument, the guitar could be strummed, "finger-picked" in a variety of patterns, or picked with a plectrum for solos and instrumental fills. Often, early blues and hillbilly musicians played cheaply built, inexpensive guitars whose loud, percussive tone characterized many prewar blues and country recordings. Others, such as Jimmie Rodgers and Maybelle Carter (Carter Family)—who played a Martin and a Gibson, respectively—chose top-quality instruments with richer sounds. Along with pop artist Nick Lucas and jazz players Eddie Lang and Lonnie Johnson, these and other country stars helped bring the guitar into prominence.

In 1932, the Rickenbacker company introduced a solid-body lap steel guitar with an electric pickup that was initially used in HAWAIIAN MUSIC and later country and pop. In 1949, however, Leo Fender of Fullerton, California, introduced an electric guitar with a solid wood body—an instrument with greater sustain and a sharper tone than traditional arched-top models. West Coast country guitarists including MERLE TRAVIS, Jimmy Bryant (SPEEDY WEST & JIMMY BRYANT), Bill Carson (with HANK THOMPSON),

Eldon Shamblin (with Bob Wills), and Don Rich (with Buck Owens) led the way in adopting the brilliant, piercing Fender sound. For years Nashville session players such as Chet Atkins, Hank Garland, and Harold Bradley preferred the warm tones of Gibson and Gretsch arch-top electrics, but the "hot" Fender telecaster style—as played by James Burton, Jerry Reed, Reggie Young, Albert Lee, Ray Flacke, Vince Gill, and Brent Mason—eventually prevailed as country's signature guitar sound. To reach larger audiences, today's country music incorporates the sounds of pop and rock music, provided by Nashville session guitarists such as Brent Rowan, Ilya Toshinsky, and Tom Bukovac. Brad Paisley and Keith Urban, both top-selling country artists, are also virtuoso guitarists. —*Walter Carter*

## Gully Jumpers

Paul Warmack b. Whites Creek, Tennessee, August 16, 1889; d. July 2, 1954
C. B. Arrington b. Cheatham County, Tennessee, 1893; d. unknown
William Roy Hardison b. Maury County, Tennessee, July 19, 1896;
    d. February 1966
Burt Hutcherson b. Bethel, Tennessee, 1893; d. July 10, 1980

One of the original hoedown bands that anchored the early Grand Ole Opry, the Gully Jumpers joined the show in 1927 and continued in various forms until the 1970s. The members all came from rural communities around Nashville; bandleader Paul Warmack, a mandolinist, guitarist, and vocalist, hailed from Goodlettsville and was a mechanic by trade. Fiddler Charlie Arrington, described by Opry founder George D. Hay as "an Irishman with quick wit," had a farm north of Nashville, in Joelton. (In the late 1930s Arrington played and recorded with Uncle Dave Macon.) Banjoist Roy Hardison was also a mechanic, and guitarist Bert Hutcherson was a woodworker.

In 1928 the Gully Jumpers appeared on the Opry more frequently than any other stringband, and, as the Early Birds, Warmack and Hutcherson had a separate morning show on WSM. The band recorded for the Victor Talking Machine Company at that company's first Nashville session in 1928, leaving behind masterpieces such as "Stone Rag," "Robertson County," and "The Little Red Caboose Behind the Train." —*Charles Wolfe*

## Hardrock Gunter

b. Birmingham, Alabama, February 27, 1925

A singer, songwriter, guitarist, booking agent, artist manager, DJ, and ultimately insurance agent, Sidney Louie "Hardrock" Gunter Jr. is perhaps best known as the author of "Birmingham Bounce." Released by Gunter on the tiny Bama label in 1950, the song was covered by Red Foley on Decca and became a crossover smash. Though Gunter's records—some of which fell into the pre-Elvis Presley transitional mode between country swing and rockabilly—went largely unnoticed when released, they have attracted considerable interest among rock & roll historians and collectors in the decades since.

Born and raised in Birmingham, Gunter fell under the spell of local swing hero Hank Penny. Gunter formed the Hoot Owl Ramblers when he was thirteen and then joined Happy Wilson in the Golden River Boys, who had a radio show on WAPI in Birmingham. Several band members, including Gunter, served in the army during World War II, but the group re-formed after the war and recorded for the Vulcan label in 1948. Gunter eventually went solo, becoming an active booking agent and appearing on local television station WABT in 1949.

With the success of "Birmingham Bounce," Decca signed Gunter in January 1951. But that same month he was called back into the army. Discharged in late 1952, he spent most of the remainder of the decade with the *WWVA Jamboree* in Wheeling, West Virginia. He continued to record his idiosyncratic records, two of which appeared on the Sun label. In 1963 he quit the *Jamboree* and relocated to Golden, Colorado, where he established himself in the insurance business. He still made the occasional record, the last of any note being a 1972 tribute album to Hank Williams, whom Gunter had known while both were coming up in the music business. In 2003 he moved to Arizona. —*Daniel Cooper*

## Jack Guthrie

b. Olive, Oklahoma, November 13, 1915; d. January 15, 1948

In his short career, Leon Jerry Guthrie developed a distinctive style of singing and yodeling influenced by his idol, Jimmie Rodgers. From his love of horses and his days as a rodeo rough stock rider, Guthrie developed a western persona. A talented singer-songwriter who played fiddle, guitar, bass, and other instruments, he was nevertheless undisciplined as a youth and as an entertainer.

In 1937 his cousin and good friend Woody Guthrie moved to Los Angeles, where Jack was living. Even with different musical styles, the two became a musical team, landing the *Oke & Woody Show* on KFVD–Hollywood. During the fall of that year Woody wrote "Oklahoma Hills," which they performed during their shows. Each cousin had different ambitions, and they soon went their separate ways.

In 1944 Capitol Records recorded Jack Guthrie singing "Oklahoma Hills." Released in 1945, it quickly became a #1 country hit. When Woody heard "Oklahoma Hills" on a jukebox, he called Capitol and claimed it as his song. Jack's position was that had he not recorded it, the song would have remained dormant among Woody's many songs. Furthermore, Jack maintained he had made modifications that improved the song. Eventually they decided to share the copyright.

Jack Guthrie served a short military stint in 1945–46, and when discharged he resumed playing western dances up and down the West Coast and recording for Capitol hits such as "Oakie Boogie." He was diagnosed with tuberculosis in 1946 but continued making personal appearances. In 1947 his friend Ernest Tubb arranged for Guthrie to appear in the movie *Hollywood Barn Dance*. His last recording session was similar to the final Jimmie Rodgers session, for a cot had to be set up in the studio so Guthrie could rest between takes. He died a few weeks later at a V.A. hospital in Livermore, California. —*Guy Logsdon*

## Woody Guthrie

b. Okemah, Oklahoma, July 14, 1912; d. October 3, 1967

Folksinger, artist, novelist, and prolific songwriter Woodrow Wilson Guthrie was a major influence in the folksong revival of the 1950s and 1960s. Through his early impact on Bob Dylan, Guthrie became a legendary figure in urban folk music. During the 1930s and 1940s Guthrie wrote more than a thousand songs, including such enduring standards as "Oklahoma Hills," "Philadelphia Lawyer," "So Long, It's Been Good to Know You,"

*Woody Guthrie*

and "This Land Is Your Land." Believing that songs could change social conditions, he produced a diverse catalog including children's songs, love songs, cowboy and hobo material, Dust Bowl songs, and social protest songs about peace and war, unions and bosses, and the problems of migrant farm workers.

Guthrie's parents were prosperous until Huntington's disease altered his mother's behavior and tore the family apart. When he was fourteen, she was committed to an insane asylum, and his father was taken to Pampa, Texas, to recuperate from severe burns. In his autobiographical novel *Bound for Glory*, Woody recounted how those tribulations taught him compassion and shaped his constant desire to travel.

In 1929 he joined his father in Pampa, and there he experienced the privations of the Dust Bowl. In 1937 Woody moved to California. There, driven by a desire to become a country singer, he teamed with his cousin JACK GUTHRIE on radio station KFVD–Hollywood. When Jack left, Maxine "Lefty Lou" Crissman became his partner on the *Woody and Lefty Lou Show*.

Guthrie became acquainted with socialist sympathizers, and in late 1939 he moved to New York City and involved himself in the social protest song movement. He recorded for the Library of Congress and for RCA VICTOR but he made his greatest number of recordings for Folkways Records. His album *Dust Bowl Ballads* (RCA, 1940), has sold consistently through the years in various reissue formats, and his Library of Congress recordings, released by ELEKTRA RECORDS in 1964, played a major role in the folk music revival.

Guthrie was hospitalized with Huntington's disease for the last fifteen years of his life. In 1966 the U.S. Department of the Interior honored him for his "Bonneville Power/Columbia River" songs by naming a substation after him. He was posthumously inducted into the NASHVILLE SONGWRITERS HALL OF FAME in 1977, and he was posthumously inducted into the Rock & Roll Hall of Fame in 1998. His influence continues to grow among songwriters and singers in folk, country, and rock & roll music. His son is the folk-rock artist Arlo Guthrie. —*Guy Logsdon*

# The Gospel Truth

## Christianity and Country Music

### BILL C. MALONE

Country music is the product of a society permeated with the culture of evangelical Protestant Christianity. The "Christ-haunted" South, as novelist Flannery O'Connor described it, consequently engendered a style of rural music that was distinctly different from that of the North, and that style has endured as one of the central components of commercial country music.

Religion has inspired much of the lyric content of country music while also contributing directly to its performance style. Many songs speak explicitly about God and spiritual matters, while others exhibit the shaping force of religion through their concern with guilt, shame, and retribution or through their advocacy of a tradition-based, religion-centered morality. Religious inspiration, though, has extended far beyond lyric content; it has also influenced the way country entertainers sing. Folklorist Alan Lomax may be correct in arguing that the repressive doctrine of southern Calvinism inhibited the free expression of emotionalism and consequently encouraged a tight or pinched-throat style of singing. But we should not forget that southern white folk also learned vocal mannerisms from their black neighbors and that both of these groups were encouraged to sing in a freewheeling, open-throated manner by the Pentecostal evangelists who swept through the South in the decades around the turn of the twentieth century.

Before the dawn of country recording and radio broadcasting in the 1920s, the public performance of vocal music in the rural South was most often done in religious settings. Plain working folk did occasionally have "musicals" in their homes, where they joined their neighbors in singing old ballads or hymns, but more often they sang at the outdoor camp meetings that began in the upper South in the early 1800s. They continued to do so in the worship services of evangelical churches or as participants in singing conventions—monthly religious sessions generally described as "all-day singings with dinner on the grounds." Not only did congregations receive community-sanctioned encouragement to sing, they also learned harmony and other vocal techniques by listening to each other or by practicing the rudiments of singing found in most of the "shape-note" SONGBOOKS that circulated widely in rural and small-town churches and at conventions.

Using symbols to indicate the pitch of musical notes, the shape-note system flourished in the rural South after 1800, when itinerant music teachers popularized the method at their multiday singing schools. After the Civil War, the shape-note method became the basis of a flourishing music-publishing business in the South, led notably by the Ruebush-Kiefer Company in Singer's Glen, Virginia, and by A. J. Showalter's company in Dalton, Georgia. While sending their books and music teachers throughout the South, these firms also circulated hundreds of original songs along with the new "gospel" songs that emerged after 1875 in the wake of the great revival campaigns that toured the nation. Although originating for the most part in the northern United States, these revivals, ironically, were the sources of many of the songs, such as "Softly and Tenderly," "The Unclouded Day," and "The Old Rugged Cross," that became greatly beloved by both the southern people and commercial country entertainers.

Thus, gospel music was already a pervasive force when country music began its commercial evolution in the 1920s. By 1916, working from his base in Lawrenceburg, Tennessee, music publisher JAMES D. VAUGHAN was sending his quartets far and wide before country entertainers began making public appearances or giving radio performances. Vaughan viewed gospel music through the lens of an evangelistic missionary (he was a devout member of the Church of the Nazarene), but as an astute businessman he also knew that his published songs could gain new audiences through the new media of radio and phonograph recordings, and he established his own radio station and record label. His pioneering fusion of gospel music and commerce was followed by other publishing houses, such as STAMPS-BAXTER, Hartford, and Trio, each of which employed traveling quartets as salesmen for their paperback gospel songbooks. Although gospel and country musicians professed to have dramatically different goals, their respective arts evolved commercially in a parallel interrelationship. Indeed, gospel and country have never ceased to influence each other.

Songs from paperback hymnals, from performances by gospel quartets, or from the older tradition of nineteenth-century hymnody began to appear on country recordings or radio broadcasts virtually from their beginning. Most artists, such as UNCLE DAVE MACON, BRADLEY KINCAID, and the CARTER FAMILY, usually performed older songs, but a few, such as BLIND ALFRED REED, ANDREW JENKINS, and Charles E. Moody (of THE GEORGIA YELLOW HAMMERS), inaugurated a tradition that still endures in country music: the writing of religious songs with strong moralistic content. Jenkins's "God Put a Rainbow in the Cloud" and Moody's "Drifting Too Far from the Shore," for example, became standards in the repertories of both country and gospel singers.

Probably the most important link between the shape-note gospel tradition and country music was a family of singers from Texas known as the CHUCK WAGON GANG. Ernest "Dad" Carter and his three children (Anna, Rose, and Jim) sang many types of OLD-TIME MUSIC when they began their career in Lubbock in 1935, and they didn't find their niche as gospel singers until after 1936, when they moved to Fort Worth and acquired the name of the Chuck Wagon Gang.

Despite their new moniker, the Carters were not cowboy singers. They had a decidedly rural sound and performed usually with only guitar accompaniment, but their style came directly from shape-note and gospel quartet sources. Appearing each weekday on a Fort Worth radio station, and recording for the COLUMBIA label, the Chuck Wagon Gang became household words in working-class homes throughout the Southwest. Unlike many of the gospel quartets of their day, they were never employed by a shape-note publishing house. Nevertheless, the Chuck Wagon Gang probably circulated the songs of Stamps-Baxter and other publishers more widely than did any other singing group, and they were instrumental in introducing the songs of ALBERT E. BRUMLEY to the country audience. Brumley claimed that he never explicitly wrote a "country" song, but such items as "I'll Fly Away," "I'll Meet You in the Morning," and "If We Never Meet Again" became standards in country repertoires largely through the performances of the Chuck Wagon Gang. Still other Brumley originals, such as "Rank Strangers to Me," "I'd Rather Live by the Side of the Road," and "Did You Ever Go Sailing," eventually became perennial favorites among BLUEGRASS entertainers.

Religious songs appeared so prominently in the repertoires of pre–World War II country singers that some of these numbers became permanently identified with particular acts. The Carter Family, for instance, used "Keep on the Sunny Side" as the theme for their broadcasts on the Mexican BORDER RADIO station XERA. The MONROE BROTHERS (Charlie and Bill) featured a wide variety of material but were most closely identified with "What Would You Give in Exchange for Your Soul?" ROY ACUFF similarly performed a broad spectrum of country items but was hired by WSM and the GRAND OLE OPRY on the strength of audience response to one song, his version of a rather mysterious religious composition titled "The Great Speckled Bird."

Despite the prominence of religious songs in early country repertoires, their peak came after World War II, during the late 1940s and early 1950s. In a sense, the popularity of sacred material reflects efforts made by transplanted rural people to preserve elements of their older culture in a newly emerging urban-industrial society while also using their religious traditions to explain and cope with new and sometimes-frightening problems.

Southern fundamentalism has never been more prominently displayed than in the music of entertainers such as the THE BAILES BROTHERS and THE LOUVIN BROTHERS. The Louvin Brothers, preeminently, employed their clear and searing tenor harmonies and the fine writing of Ira Louvin on songs including "The Family Who Prays," "Born Again," and "Insured Beyond the Grave," which describe a world of declining values and moral collapse that could only be redeemed by spiritual rebirth. Other songs, such as the Bailes Brothers' "Dust on the Bible" and "When Heaven Comes Down," the Louvins' "The Great Atomic Power," WILMA LEE & STONEY COOPER's "That's What's the Matter with This World," Roy Acuff's "This World Can't Stand Long," and MOLLY O'DAY's "Matthew 24," found prophetic meaning in the social instability and political events of the day and spoke of the imminent Second Coming of Christ. Recordings of this period even included a handful of powerful and rare performances made by Rev. Claude Ely, "the Gospel Ranger," at a Pentecostal revival in eastern Kentucky. In terms of gospel themes, country music has never since been so close to its folk roots or as clearly linked to its southern origins.

Other religious country songs of the era were not nearly as explicit in their doctrinal evocations but were probably appealing because of the heightened religious awareness that accompanied America's postwar affluence and the nation's ideological conflict with the avowedly atheistic rulers of Soviet Union. Recordings such as STUART HAMBLEN's "It's No Secret," RED FOLEY's "Peace in the Valley" and "Just a Closer Walk with Thee," MARTHA CARSON's "Satisfied," JIMMIE DAVIS's "Someone to Care," and HANK WILLIAMS's "I Saw the Light" promised spiritual assurance without apocalyptic portent and denominational identification.

To be sure, ELVIS PRESLEY loved gospel music and identified with the Blackwood Brothers, the Stamps Quartet, the JORDANAIRES, and similar groups. Yet in general the performance of religious material in mainstream country music has declined significantly since the 1960s. THE STATLER BROTHERS and the OAK RIDGE BOYS did come to country music from backgrounds in the gospel field, but they achieved immense popularity after they veered sharply away from full-time gospel careers. The decline of religious music among country performers has been a consequence perhaps of the country industry's growing affluence and middle-class pretensions and is a mark of its efforts to embrace a larger and non-regional constituency. Gospel songs, however, have never disappeared completely, as any observer of a WILLIE NELSON concert would readily know. Periodically, such songs have made their way to the charts, as did FERLIN HUSKY's version of "Wings of a Dove" in1960–61, JOHNNY CASH's rendition of "Daddy Sang Bass" in 1968–69, and KRIS KRISTOFFERSON's "Why Me?" in 1973. Albums devoted solely to gospel songs, such as MERLE HAGGARD's *Land of Many Churches* and EMMYLOU HARRIS's *Angel Band*, also appear occasionally but without the frequency once common in country music.

Although the proportion of religious music has declined in mainstream country performance, fans of spiritually oriented material need not despair. Bluegrass musicians still sing gospel songs that reflect country's traditional roots, while a newly defined genre of "positive country" singers (so called because they claim to be resisting the seamy and defeatist themes sometimes found in mainstream country) stress songs that combine the style of contemporary country-pop with Christian themes. Some bluegrass groups, such as THE LEWIS FAMILY, Jerry and Tammy Sullivan, and the Forbes Family, have sung religious songs exclusively, while other bluegrass acts, such as the venerable RALPH STANLEY and the Cherryholmes family band, showcased religious material along with secular numbers.

Stanley made the bluegrass world conscious of the a cappella performance of gospel hymns, many of them drawn from the repertoires of Old Regular Baptists in his corner of Appalachia, while his younger colleagues, NASHVILLE BLUEGRASS BAND and DOYLE LAWSON & QUICKSILVER, dipped into the African American song bag for songs earlier identified with sister Rosetta Tharpe and the Fairfield Four. PAUL OVERSTREET, RICKY VAN SHELTON, and other "positive country singers" generally favor modern styles of religious music and target listeners who tune in the broadcasts of contemporary Christian radio stations.

In the new century, mainstream country has increasingly referenced religious themes. JOSH TURNER's "Long Black Train" warned listeners to resist the Devil's temptations, while Buddy Jewel's "Help Pour Out the Rain (Lacey's Song)" voiced a father's efforts to explain his wife's death to their daughter. The evocative ending to RANDY TRAVIS's "Three Wooden Crosses" reminded hearers that God sometimes works in mysterious ways, while in JOHN MICHAEL MONTGOMERY's "The Little Girl," a young child recognizes a picture of Jesus because she had seen Him in her house "the night my parents died."

Religious music may be less important today in the country field than it was, say, forty years ago, but the profession of religious faith remains a defining trait of many country entertainers. Some country singers, such as Molly O'Day, have totally abandoned mainstream country songs after their conversions, but most, such as MARTY STUART, Ricky Skaggs, and GLEN CAMPBELL, have chosen to "witness for Christ" while maintaining their usual touring schedules. Stuart Hamblen's conversion in a Billy Graham crusade in Los Angeles in the early 1950s may have been the first well-publicized example of a country singer's acceptance of Christ, but it has been emulated many times since. Johnny Cash, for instance, became closely identified with Graham and participated in the famous evangelist's revivals.

Cash and many of his country colleagues—such as CONNIE SMITH, BILLY GRAMMER, BILLY WALKER, and Kris Kristofferson—made public avowals of religious commitment in the 1960s when Pentecostal evangelist Jimmie Rodgers Snow (the son of country singer HANK SNOW) began his ministry among country musicians in Nashville. The religious confessional, issued often in the form of an autobiography, has become a familiar element of country music's compendium of self-definition and a form of moral legitimization demanded by many country fans. It is tempting to interpret this kind of religious posturing as little more than an attempt to gain favor with audiences or to assert country music's moral superiority, but it is also the lingering evidence of the music's origins and of its enduring linkage to Protestant evangelical tradition.

## The Hackberry Ramblers

For seven decades after forming in 1933, the Hackberry Ramblers filled dance floors with a distinctive blend of CAJUN MUSIC and WESTERN SWING. The group remained active until 2005, still featuring its cofounders: fiddler Luderin Darbone (b. Evangeline, Louisiana, January 14, 1913; d. November 21, 2008) and Edwin Duhon (b. near Lafayette, Louisiana, June 11, 1910; d. February 26, 2006), who played accordion and, later, electric guitar.

Live radio broadcasts, beginning in 1933 from Lake Charles, Louisiana, established the band in local dance halls, many of which lacked electricity. To boost their acoustic STRINGBAND sound, Darbone powered a primitive PA system with his idling 1931 Ford. Amplification encouraged soloing and expanded the band's innovative Cajun-country synthesis, which influenced such seminal Cajun musicians as HARRY CHOATES and Michael Doucet (see BEAUSOLEIL).

In 1935 the Hackberry Ramblers signed with RCA VICTOR's BLUEBIRD subsidiary. Their diverse, prolific repertoire included the first recording of "Jolie Blonde" (Lennis Sonnier, vocal) in 1936, the blues standard "Sitting on Top of the World" (Floyd Rainwater, vocal) in 1935, and the country hit "Wondering" (Joe Werner, vocal) in 1936. From 1936 to 1939 Bluebird issued the group's recordings sung in English under the pseudonym Riverside Ramblers while releasing Cajun French recordings as the Hackberry Ramblers.

In the 1940s the Hackberry Ramblers evolved into a large western swing ensemble—including drummer Crawford Vincent (b. Gueydan, Louisiana, October 4, 1921; d. August 12, 2005) and played a regular Saturday gig at the Silver Star Club in Sulphur, Louisiana, from 1946 to 1956. With the 1960s slump in both Cajun music and western swing, the band considered retiring, but they recorded for Chris Strachwitz's Arhoolie label in 1963. Adding electric and steel guitarist Glen Croker (b. Lake Charles, Louisiana, February 29, 1934; d. August 23, 2011) changed the Ramblers' sound to a HONKY-TONK style; over the years, other personnel included bassist Johnny Faulk (b. Cameron Parish, Louisiana, March 24, 1925; d. October 17, 2004), rhythm guitarist Johnny Farque (b. Big Lake, Louisiana, April 23, 1920; d. April 24, 1997), and Ben Sandmel (b. Nashville, Tennessee, June 8, 1952) as drummer-producer.

In the 1990s appearances at festivals in the United States and abroad widened the band's reputation, as did its Grammy-nominated 1997 album *Deep Water*, featuring guest appearances by Marcia Ball, RODNEY CROWELL, Michael Doucet, and JIMMIE DALE GILMORE. In 2002, Darbone and Duhon received a National Heritage Fellowship from the National Endowment for the Arts. The hour-long documentary *Make 'Em Dance: The Hackberry Ramblers Story* aired on PBS in 2004. —*Ben Sandmel*

## Hadacol Caravan

The Hadacol Caravan was the last large-scale MEDICINE SHOW. Hadacol was a foul-tasting patent medicine developed in 1945 by a Louisiana politician, Dudley J. LeBlanc. He believed in music as an advertising tool and, in 1950, decided to promote Hadacol using a troupe of entertainers. He toured the South, giving free admission to anyone with a Hadacol box top. The stars of the first caravan were ROY ACUFF, Connee Boswell, George Burns & Gracie Allen, Chico Marx, and Mickey Rooney.

In 1951 LeBlanc became more ambitious—partly out of natural grandiosity, partly out of a desire to use the show as a platform for his bid for the Louisiana governorship, and partly to create a smoke screen around Hadacol's financial picture in order to sell the company. He hired HANK WILLIAMS as the principal act, supplemented by MINNIE PEARL, Candy Candido, and Cesar Romero. On some dates there were guests such as Bob Hope, Milton Berle, Jack Benny, and Jimmy Durante. The Caravan began in LeBlanc's hometown of Lafayette, Louisiana, on August 14 and was scheduled to end on October 2, but it closed down in Dallas on September 17 when LeBlanc sold the corporation to the Tobey-Maltz Foundation. The shows were hugely successful, and financially they were probably the high-water mark of Williams's career. —*Colin Escott*

## Merle Haggard
b. Bakersfield, California, April 6, 1937

Merle Ronald Haggard remains, with the arguable exception of HANK WILLIAMS, the single most influential singer-songwriter in country music history. Haggard is certainly one of the genre's most versatile artists. Stylistically, he has mined HONKY-TONK, blues, jazz, pop, and folk, and his repertory ranges widely: aching ballads ("Today I Started Loving You Again," "Silver Wings"); sly, frisky narratives ("Old Man from the Mountain," "It's Been a Great Afternoon"); semiautobiographical reflections ("Mama Tried," "Hungry Eyes"); political commentaries ("Under the Bridge," "Rainbow Stew"); proletarian homages ("Workin' Man Blues," "White Line Fever"); as well as drinking songs that are JUKEBOX, cover-band, and closing-time standards ("Swinging Doors," "The Bottle Let Me Down," "I Think I'll Just Stay Here and Drink"). His acolytes are legion and include many of country music's brightest and lesser lights as well as thousands of nightclub musicians.

Haggard was born poor, though not desperately so, in Depression-era BAKERSFIELD to Jim and Flossie Haggard, migrants from Oklahoma. Jim, a railroad carpenter, died of a stroke in 1946, forcing Flossie to find work as a bookkeeper. Flossie was a fundamentalist Christian and a stern, somewhat overprotective mother.

*Merle Haggard*

Not surprisingly, Merle grew quickly from rambunctious to rake-hell. By his twenty-first birthday he had run away regularly from home, been placed in two separate reform schools (from which he escaped a half dozen times), worked as a laborer, played guitar and sung informally, begun a family, and performed sporadically at Southern California clubs and on radio in Springfield, Missouri. He also spent time in local jails for theft and writing bad checks.

Haggard's woebegone criminal career culminated in 1957 when, drunk and confused, he was caught burglarizing a Bakersfield roadhouse. After an attempted escape from county jail, he was sent to San Quentin, where he got drunk on prison home brew and landed briefly in solitary confinement. Paroled in 1960, he worked a fitful series of odd jobs before snagging a regular gig playing bass for Wynn Stewart in Las Vegas.

Another Bakersfield mainstay, Fuzzy Owen, signed Haggard to his tiny Tally Records in 1962. After recording five singles there—the fourth, "(My Friends Are Gonna Be) Strangers," entered *Billboard*'s Top Ten (1965)—Haggard signed with Capitol. He moved to MCA in 1976, to Epic in 1981, and to Curb in 1990. (Since making several early-1990s Curb albums, he has recorded for various labels.)

Haggard's first album, *Strangers*, appeared in 1965. Dozens of feature albums have followed as well as repackagings, reissues, compilations, promotional and movie-soundtrack albums, and albums in which Haggard has participated—with the likes of Willie Nelson, Porter Wagoner, Johnny Paycheck, Bob Wills, Dean Martin, Ray Charles, and Clint Eastwood. Along with hardcore country, Haggard recorded two gospel albums in 2001, released a 2004 album of pop standards, and collaborated with Alison Krauss and others on 2007's *The Bluegrass Sessions*. As of 2011 he has had thirty-eight #1 hits, virtually all self-penned. (He often shares writing credits as gestures of financial and personal largess.) He has written some 400 songs, among them "Today I Started Loving You Again," which has been recorded by some 400 other artists. What's more, Haggard plays a commendable fiddle and a to-be-reckoned-with lead guitar. In addition to his own videos, he is featured on Gretchen Wilson's "Politically Uncorrect" (2005) and on a 2008 video collection in the Country Music Hall of Fame and Museum's *Legendary Performances* series.

He has entertained U.S. presidents Richard Nixon and Ronald Reagan (who, as California's governor, had pardoned Haggard for his criminal convictions) and played Washington, D.C.'s prestigious Kennedy Center, but everyday folk are his core audiences, including those who saw him on the 2003 Electric Barnyard tour he made with Marty Stuart, targeting small American towns. Haggard has toured with Bob Dylan (2005–06) and with fellow country veterans Ray Price and Willie Nelson, with whom he released the 2007 album *Last of the Breed*.

Haggard has won numerous CMA and ACM awards, including both organizations' 1970 Entertainer of the Year honors, been nominated for scores of others, was elected to the Nashville Songwriters Hall of Fame in 1977, and won Country Music Hall of Fame membership in 1994. In 1984 he won a Grammy in the Best Country Vocal Performance, Male, category for "That's the Way Love Goes," and in 2009 he received ACM's Poets Award for his many contributions to country music's canon. He received the prestigious Kennedy Center honor for artistic achievement in 2010. Even so, he has remained famously independent (he once walked out on an imminent appearance on network TV's *Ed Sullivan Show*), and he has kept himself at arm's length from musical Nashville's sociopolitical vortex. He currently lives near Redding, in northern California, well away from music industry power centers.

There is no such thing as a typical Merle Haggard concert. On any given night, he might divert from chart and fan favorites and play long sets of songs by Jimmie Rodgers, Lefty Frizzell, or Bob Wills, his most lasting musical influences. Additionally, Haggard takes great pride in his band members' musicianship, and their importance transcends that of mere sidemen. Ranging from three to ten persons over the years, The Strangers incorporate such atypical country instruments as trombones, trumpets, and saxophones; have included long-respected players such as Roy Nichols, Norm Hamlet, Biff Adam, and Clint Strong; and have garnered eight awards as ACM's Touring Band of the Year.

Ironically, Haggard is inextricably linked with a casual ditty that shifted attention from his soaring musicianship to his politics. "Okie from Muskogee" (Capitol, 1969), a #1 song for four weeks and the ACM and CMA 1970 Single of the Year, is a seemingly belligerent and defensive screen of traditional American-heartland values that appeared at the height of the fractious decade of the Vietnam War. Haggard's retellings of the song's intent are manifold and contradictory. In 1974 he told a Michigan newspaper reporter, "Son, the only place I don't smoke is Muskogee." A dozen years later, however, he told the Birmingham *Post-Herald* that "Okie" was "a patriotic song that went to the top of the charts at a time when patriotism wasn't really that popular." Although he has frequently bemoaned the public's perception of him as a political animal, he followed "Okie" with the truly angry "The Fightin' Side of Me" (Capitol, 1970) and, in 1988, a sentimental reaction to flag burning, "Me and Crippled Soldiers." In any case, his political views have been unpredictable, as his criticism of the Iraq War reveals.

Nor has Haggard's personal life been without drama. His business acumen is notoriously erratic, and he has been married five times. As of August 2011 he had six children, four by his first wife, Leona Hobbs, and two by his present wife, Theresa Lane. From 1965 to 1978 Haggard was married to singer Bonnie Owens (1932–2006), with whom he recorded a duet album, *Just Between the Two of Us* (Capitol, 1966) and who was a longtime member of Haggard's musical company even after their divorce. He was also married for a time to singer Leona Williams, who wrote his #1 hit "You Take Me for Granted" and cowrote (with Haggard) his chart-topping "Someday When Things Are Good."
—*Bryan Di Salvatore*

## Rob Hajacos
b. Richmond, Virginia, December 20, 1956

Even though Robert Hajacos played second fiddle to top session man MARK O'CONNOR through much of the 1980s, Hajacos became one of Nashville's busiest fiddle players beginning in the 1990s. His credits include albums by GARTH BROOKS, REBA MCENTIRE, Neil Diamond, PAM TILLIS, ALAN JACKSON, SHANIA TWAIN, BROOKS & DUNN, and MARK CHESNUTT. Hajacos has also graced albums by hitmakers KENNY CHESNEY, SUGARLAND, and TAYLOR SWIFT.

Hajacos's father was a professional fiddler who had a regular spot on the OLD DOMINION BARN DANCE, where Rob often hung out backstage. He didn't take his instrument seriously until junior high, when he joined the school orchestra and began classical training. Hajacos also played country music with his dad through high school but moved to Nashville in 1976 with a goal of playing alongside MEL TILLIS. Hajacos had a road gig with LITTLE JIMMY DICKENS, investigated studio work, and realized his dream when he toured with Tillis from 1982 to 1983. Since then he has focused on sessions and has performed in regular backing groups on country television programs. —*Michael Hight*

## Bill Haley
b. Highland Park, Michigan, July 6, 1925; d. February 9, 1981

Rock & roll historians have tended to emphasize ELVIS PRESLEY at the expense of Bill Haley, but the fact remains that Haley was scoring hits with what was identifiably rock & roll before Presley first set foot in a studio.

Like Presley, William Clifton Haley was a country musician before he developed his brand of rock & roll. Raised in Wilmington, Delaware, he played in accordion-led East Coast country bands and was a yodeling champion. Although he worked with VOGUE RECORDS' cowboy act, the Down Homers, his first records were made with the Four Aces of Western Swing (based in Chester, Pennsylvania) in 1948. Haley began introducing R&B into his music, experimenting constantly between 1951 and his first big hit, "Crazy, Man, Crazy," for Essex Records, in 1953.

Switching to DECCA RECORDS in 1954, Haley spearheaded the as-yet-unnamed music with a series of classic recordings, such as "(We're Gonna) Rock Around the Clock," "Shake, Rattle, and Roll," and "See You Later, Alligator." It was "Rock Around the Clock" that established Haley as a star. Cut in April 1954, the record languished until it appeared on the soundtrack of the 1955 teen rebellion film *Blackboard Jungle*. On June 19, 1955, it went #1 pop, and at year's end *Billboard* named it the best-selling single of 1955.

His downfall was swift; it was exacerbated by Presley's rise but was as much due to Haley's own lapse into self-parody and his tendency to draw too many substandard songs from his own publishing companies. Though he continued to place songs on the pop charts through the 1950s, the hits never broke the Top Twenty after 1956. His last chart-making record (until the 1974 reissue of "Rock Around the Clock") was 1960's "Skokiaan (South African Song)," which only reached #70. But even though Haley's star quickly set in the United States, he remained a revered figure in Britain and Europe and a big draw overseas until his death. —*Colin Escott*

## Roy Hall & His Blue Ridge Entertainers
Roy Davis Hall b. Waynesville, North Carolina, January 6, 1907; d. May 16, 1943

Roy Hall & His Blue Ridge Entertainers helped set the stage for BLUEGRASS with their uptempo brand of STRINGBAND MUSIC. A product of the Carolina textile mills, Hall initially recorded for BLUEBIRD with sibling Jay Hugh as the Hall Brothers in 1937 and 1938. In the fall of 1938, Roy formed the Blue Ridge Entertainers and played daily radio shows at WAIR in Winston-Salem and then at WDBJ in Roanoke, where his career peaked. Fiddler TOMMY MAGNESS and steel guitarist Bill Brown dominated the group's instrumental sound. After an eight-side session for Vocalion in 1938, Hall returned to Bluebird in 1940 and 1941. He died in an automobile crash. —*Ivan M. Tribe*

## Tom T. Hall
b. Olive Hill, Kentucky, May 25, 1936

In the late 1960s and early 1970s, Tom T. Hall, along with a handful of other songwriters, including KRIS KRISTOFFERSON, BILLY JOE SHAVER, and JAMES TALLEY, imbued country music with a new level of lyric and thematic sophistication and social consciousness without violating the music's inherent rusticity and simplicity of form.

Known as "The Storyteller," Hall also flourished as a recording artist for MERCURY RECORDS from the late 1960s through the early 1980s with his original, poignant, often-sardonic musical slices of life. "Ballad of Forty Dollars" (1968), "Homecoming" (1969), "A Week in a Country Jail" (1969), "The Year That Clayton Delaney Died" (1971), "(Old Dogs, Children and) Watermelon Wine" (1972), "I Love" (1973), and "Faster Horses" (1976) were all Top Five country hits.

Hall was born into near poverty in rural Kentucky. He worked as a DJ, led a BLUEGRASS band, served in the army in Germany,

*Tom T. Hall*

and briefly attended college on the GI Bill before moving to Nashville to write songs in the early 1960s. His breakthrough was "Harper Valley PTA." Recorded by JEANNIE C. RILEY, it became a million-selling hit in 1968, reaching #1 on *Billboard*'s country and pop charts. Other hits Hall crafted for fellow artists include "(Margie's at) The Lincoln Park Inn" (BOBBY BARE, 1969), "The Pool Shark" (DAVE DUDLEY, 1970), and "I'm Not Ready Yet" (GEORGE JONES, 1980). As Hall's success grew, he increasingly returned to his hardscrabble country roots for inspiration—even after his royalties had made him a millionaire and he was ensconced in Fox Hollow, his elegant Franklin, Tennessee, estate.

Hall is also a prolific author; his books include *How I Write Songs, Why You Can* (1976), *The Storyteller's Nashville* (1979), *The Laughing Man of Woodmont Coves* (1982), *The Acts of Life* (1986), *Spring Hill, Tennessee* (1990), and *What a Book!* (1996). Fascinated with American literature, he befriended noted authors William Styron and Kurt Vonnegut. Hall joined the GRAND OLE OPRY in 1971. For several years in the early 1980s, he hosted *Pop Goes the Country*, a Nashville-produced syndicated TV show, and he has been involved in numerous additional programs and productions.

In 1996, after a long absence from recording, he released *Songs from Sopchoppy*, a Mercury album of wry, laid-back recordings, including Hall's self-penned "Little Bitty." The song became a #1 hit for ALAN JACKSON that same year. Since the late 1990s Hall and his wife, Miss Dixie (Iris Lawrence), have been ardent supporters of aspiring and veteran bluegrass musicians, while also recording their own bluegrass songs and writing for numerous bluegrass bands. For their efforts they received an IBMA Distinguished Achievement Award in 2004. Hall was elected to the NASHVILLE SONGWRITERS HALL OF FAME in 1978 and to THE COUNTRY MUSIC HALL OF FAME in 2008. —*Bob Allen*

## Wendell Hall
b. St. George, Kansas, August 23, 1896; d. April 2, 1969

Wendell Woods Hall's professional career began in vaudeville as a singing xylophonist, but his most enduring contribution to America's music was his first recorded song, "It Ain't Gonna Rain No Mo'," cut for GENNETT RECORDS, the Victor Talking Machine Company, and EDISON RECORDS within weeks in October 1923. At one time, the song's country flavor led some observers to identify it as the first commercial hillbilly recording. Though copyrighted by Hall, parts of the song were traditional well before 1923, and Hall probably based his composition on fragments heard in his youth. Very likely he was aware of the piece's folk roots, because in 1926 he wrote to Robert W. Gordon, a leading authority on American folk music, suggesting that they collaborate to produce commercialized hit songs out of material Gordon had collected.

"It Ain't Gonna Rain" enjoyed great popularity, reportedly selling sheet music copies in the millions. This and some of Hall's other recordings also helped popularize the ukulele. The number's success on wax prompted several sequels: "It Ain't Gonna Rain No Mo'—2nd Installation," "It Ain't Gonna Rain No Mo'—Part 2," and others. "It Ain't Gonna Rain No Mo'" was among the early recordings of both FIDDLIN' JOHN CARSON and GID TANNER, and it has often been collected from both white and black folk-singers. Between 1923 and 1933 Hall, known as the "Red Headed Music Maker," made close to eighty recordings. He continued to write songs into the 1960s, even as he moved from a career in radio to one as an advertising executive. —*Norm Cohen*

## Jim Halsey
b. Independence, Kansas, October 7, 1930

James Albert Halsey has been one of country music's most influential business figures as a manager to stars, including ROY CLARK, HANK THOMPSON, and the OAK RIDGE BOYS, and as a promoter and booker of major concerts in the United States and abroad. Halsey also pioneered the placement of country acts on television, an emphasis that continued throughout his long career.

Beginning as a promoter while a teenager at Independence Junior College in his hometown, Halsey had founded his agency by 1951, the year he started representing rising country star Hank Thompson. Halsey achieved such milestones as booking some of the earliest country acts as headliners in Las Vegas in 1956–57; booking Roy Clark in 1963 as the first country music guest host on *The Tonight Show*; and arranging one of the earliest country headliners tours of the Soviet Union, with Clark and the Oak Ridge Boys in 1976. MERLE TRAVIS once joked that the circumspect and low-keyed Halsey would "use a pencil to write out a bomb threat," but his management and booking efforts have advanced the careers of such stellar names as THE JUDDS, MERLE HAGGARD, MEL TILLIS, LEE GREENWOOD, MINNIE PEARL, TAMMY WYNETTE, DWIGHT YOAKAM, CLINT BLACK, and many others.

On February 1, 1990, the booking division of the Jim Halsey Company merged with the long-established William Morris Agency, with Halsey continuing as consultant. Halsey founded Oklahoma City University's Music and Entertainment Business program and directed it from 1995 to 1999; later he established his own online school. Active in numerous professional organizations, he has published and lectured nationally and internationally on music business issues. —*Thomas Goldsmith*

## Stuart Hamblen
b. Kellyville, Texas, October 20, 1908; d. March 8, 1989

Singer-songwriter Carl Stuart Hamblen left a lasting impression on country and pop music through original songs, including "Texas Plains," "This Ole House," "It Is No Secret," "My Mary," and "Remember Me (I'm the One Who Loves You)."

Born to an itinerant preacher, James Henry Hamblen, and his wife, Ernestine, Stuart graduated from McMurray Teachers College in Abilene but chose a life in music instead. He first appeared on radio in 1925. RCA VICTOR RECORDS recorded him in June 1929, releasing "The Boy in Blue," "Drifting Back to Dixie," "When the Moon Shines Down on the Mountain," and "The Big Rock Candy Mountains #2," all Hamblen compositions.

In late 1929 Stuart appeared on KFI–Los Angeles as Cowboy Joe, possibly the earliest cowboy act on Los Angeles radio. The next year he joined the popular act THE BEVERLY HILL BILLIES, but he soon assembled his own band, which briefly included PATSY MONTANA. In 1932 Hamblen began his *Lucky Stars* program over KFWB–Los Angeles, and for the next twenty years he ranked among Los Angeles radio's most popular western performers.

In 1934 Hamblen became the first West Coast artist signed by DECCA RECORDS, for whom he recorded in August 1934 and February 1935 with his newly named band, Covered Wagon Jubilee. After a ten-year hiatus Hamblen's recording career began anew for the ARA label, followed by lengthier contracts with COLUMBIA (1949–53; 1960–62), RCA (1954–57), and Coral (1958–59).

*Stuart Hamblen*

Between 1949 and 1955 he scored four Top Ten country hits: "(I Won't Go Huntin', Jake) But I'll Go Chasin' Women," "(Remember Me) I'm the One Who Loves You," "It's No Secret," and "This Ole House," the last a pop hit for both Hamblen and Rosemary Clooney. Gospel singer George Beverley Shea made "It's No Secret" a worldwide standard through his work with evangelist the Reverend Billy Graham.

Hamblen widened his reputation by composing additional love ballads, religious songs, western tunes, country songs, patriotic material, and children's songs. A devout Christian following a conversion by the Rev. Billy Graham, Hamblen ran unsuccessfully for the U.S. presidency in 1952 on the Prohibition Party ticket. After 1952, he syndicated the popular *Cowboy Church of the Air* series, carried by selected radio stations into the 1970s.

For his many accomplishments in radio and the recording industry, the Hollywood Chamber of Commerce honored Hamblen in 1976 by placing his star in its Hollywood Walk of Fame. —*Ken Griffis*

## George Hamilton IV
b. Winston-Salem, North Carolina, July 19, 1937

Although George Hege Hamilton IV began his career as a teen idol with the pop hit "A Rose and a Baby Ruth," he was one of the first pop singers to switch to country music, and he broadened country's appeal with his recordings and extensive tours.

In 1956, as a freshman at the University of North Carolina, Hamilton recorded JOHN D. LOUDERMILK's "A Rose and a Baby Ruth" for the small Colonial label. ABC-Paramount bought the master, and the million-seller thrust Hamilton into national TV appearances and tours with pop stars BUDDY HOLLY and THE EVERLY BROTHERS.

In the late 1950s, Hamilton was a regular on CONNIE B. GAY's *Town & Country Time* broadcasts in Washington, D.C., starring JIMMY DEAN and featuring PATSY CLINE. Hamilton also fronted his own brief ABC-TV program in 1959. Hamilton moved to Nashville and began recording country music for RCA RECORDS in 1960. He joined the GRAND OLE OPRY in that same year. "Abilene" was a #1 country (and Top Twenty pop) hit for him in 1963, and other hit singles followed. In the mid-1960s singer-songwriter Gordon Lightfoot introduced Hamilton into Canadian folk music circles, and Hamilton recorded such hits as Lightfoot's "Early Morning Rain."

Since the mid-1970s, Hamilton has recorded folk/country/gospel albums on various labels; some have featured his son, George Hamilton V. Also in the 1970s, George IV hosted country television variety series in both Canada and the United Kingdom and he made a pioneering tour behind the Iron Curtain. Hamilton's continuing popularity overseas, especially in the UK, has earned him the title of International Ambassador of Country Music. An Opry regular, he still tours widely, focusing heavily on gospel music. —*Dale Vinicur*

## Butch Hancock
b. Lubbock, Texas, July 12, 1945

George Norman "Butch" Hancock is a West Texas singer-songwriter steeped in the tradition of WOODY GUTHRIE and BOB DYLAN. Hancock's songs have been popularized by boyhood buddies JOE ELY and JIMMIE DALE GILMORE—with whom he teamed in the early 1970s in THE FLATLANDERS—and others, including EMMYLOU HARRIS and JERRY JEFF WALKER. Among the best known of Hancock's hundreds of songs are the oft-recorded "If You Were a Bluebird," "West Texas Waltz," and "My Mind's Got a Mind of Its Own."

A free-spirited photographer and architect as well as a musician, Hancock long confined his own recording to self-released albums and cassettes. Selections were subsequently compiled for early-1990s SUGAR HILL CDs—*Own & Own* and *Own the Way Over Here*—and in 1995 the label issued his newly recorded *Eats Away the Night*. His prolific songwriting is additionally documented through the *No 2 Alike* fourteen-cassette subscription series, drawn from 1990 recordings of a week's engagement at AUSTIN's Cactus Café, during which Hancock never repeated a song.

Subsequently, Hancock, Ely, and Gilmore helped each other make individual albums while also reassembling for occasional personal appearances. Their 2002 Flatlanders reunion album, *Now Again,* prompted more regular tours and, as of 2011, two additional studio albums. —*Don McLeese*

## Carlton Haney
b. Rockingham County, North Carolina, September 19, 1928; d. March 16, 2011

Carlton L. Haney was a major figure in the growth of country and BLUEGRASS music from the 1950s to the 1980s. Best known as a founder of bluegrass music festivals, Haney also promoted country music package shows and helped to build the careers of artists ranging from BILL MONROE, RENO & SMILEY, and THE OSBORNE BROTHERS to PORTER WAGONER, LORETTA LYNN, MERLE HAGGARD, and CONWAY TWITTY.

Haney began his country music career as a booking agent for Monroe in 1953. For a decade, starting in 1955, Haney managed Reno & Smiley and the OLD DOMINION BARN DANCE in Richmond, Virginia. In 1964 Haney rented a coliseum in Winston-Salem, North Carolina, and began to promote country package shows, featuring artists such as RAY PRICE, Wagoner, and KITTY WELLS. This led to an eight-year series of Country Shindig shows in thirty-seven southeastern and northeastern cities.

In 1965, Haney and RALPH RINZLER, a member of THE GREENBRIAR BOYS (and, earlier, Bill Monroe's manager), conceived plans for a multiday outdoor bluegrass festival, modeled on the NEWPORT FOLK FESTIVAL and centered on musicians who had apprenticed with Monroe. Originally produced by Haney at Fincastle, Virginia, during Labor Day weekend (1965), the festival drew about 1,000 diehard fans. Haney served as MC. When the festival moved to Berryville, Virginia, and, later, Camp Springs, North Carolina, it grew and became a prototype for hundreds of such events now held throughout the United States. Haney was elected to the IBMA Hall of Fame in 1998. —*Fred Bartenstein*

## Happy Fats
b. Rayne, Louisiana, January 15, 1915; d. February 23, 1988

Leroy LeBlanc, better known as Happy Fats, led one of the most prolific CAJUN dance bands from the 1930s into the 1950s. Perhaps better than any other group, Happy Fats & His Rayne-Bo Ramblers showed the deep effect that WESTERN SWING had on Cajun musicians.

The Rayne-Bo Ramblers began recording as a traditional Cajun fiddle band in 1935, but as the decade progressed LeBlanc added instruments such as steel guitar and piano, played in the manner of western swing bands. Of particular importance was the impact of CLIFF BRUNER's Texas Wanderers, who were based in Texas but toured in Louisiana and blasted their radio shows eastward. By 1940, when LeBlanc was broadcasting on Lafayette, Louisiana, station KVOL, his BLUEBIRD sessions were as weighted toward western swing as they were to Cajun music, and his band included the soon-to-be-legendary fiddler HARRY CHOATES, then under Bruner's spell. After World War II, LeBlanc continued in this dual Cajun/western swing mode. By the end of the 1940s he had joined forces with fiddler Doc Guidry, recording for J. D. MILLER's Feature label as Happy, Doc & all the Boys and for DE LUXE. LeBlanc stayed active in later years, gaining some unfortunate notoriety for his segregationist recordings on Miller's Rebel Records (not the Maryland-based independent) in the 1960s. —*Kevin Coffey*

## Sid Harkreader
b. Gladeville, Tennessee, February 26, 1898; d. March 19, 1988

Best known today as UNCLE DAVE MACON's first partner, Sidney J. Harkreader was a distinctive fiddler and guitarist who had a long and varied career on and off the GRAND OLE OPRY. A native of the great Cedar Glades east of Nashville, Harkreader determined as a young man to make a living with his music—a daring plan for a country musician in the 1920s. In about 1923 he began performing with Macon, sometimes billed as Macon's "son." Harkreader backed Macon on many of his 1924–25 recordings as well as on several later ones. By 1926 Harkreader was leading his own troupe of Charleston dancers for the Loew's vaudeville

circuit; he also began recording for the Paramount and Broadway labels, first with guitarist Grady Moore and then with singer-guitarist Blythe Poteet.

By 1935 Harkreader was back on the Opry—this time with a full STRINGBAND, Sid Harkreader and Company, that included mandolinist Mack McGar and one-armed banjo player Emory Martin. By now Harkreader was known for two signature pieces: "Mocking Bird Breakdown" and "Old Joe." Trying to keep current, he organized his Round-Up Gang, a western band, but by 1940 he had decided to retire from music and open a restaurant in downtown Nashville. In later years he would return to the Opry, though, appearing with several of the hoedown bands, such as the GULLY JUMPERS. —*Charles Wolfe*

## Buddy Harman
b. Nashville, Tennessee, December 23, 1928; d. August 21, 2008

Nashville's first full-time studio session drummer, Murrey M. Harman played on an estimated 18,000 sessions during his career, backing stars ranging from THE EVERLY BROTHERS ("Bye Bye Love"), BRENDA LEE ("Rockin' Around the Christmas Tree"), ROY ORBISON ("Oh, Pretty Woman"), and ELVIS PRESLEY ("Little Sister") to JOHNNY CASH ("Ring of Fire"), Simon & Garfunkel ("The Boxer"), and many more.

Harman's parents had their own part-time band in Nashville, with his mother on drums, and jazz drummers Gene Krupa and Buddy Rich inspired the young musician to turn professional. After performing in high school and navy bands, he dropped out

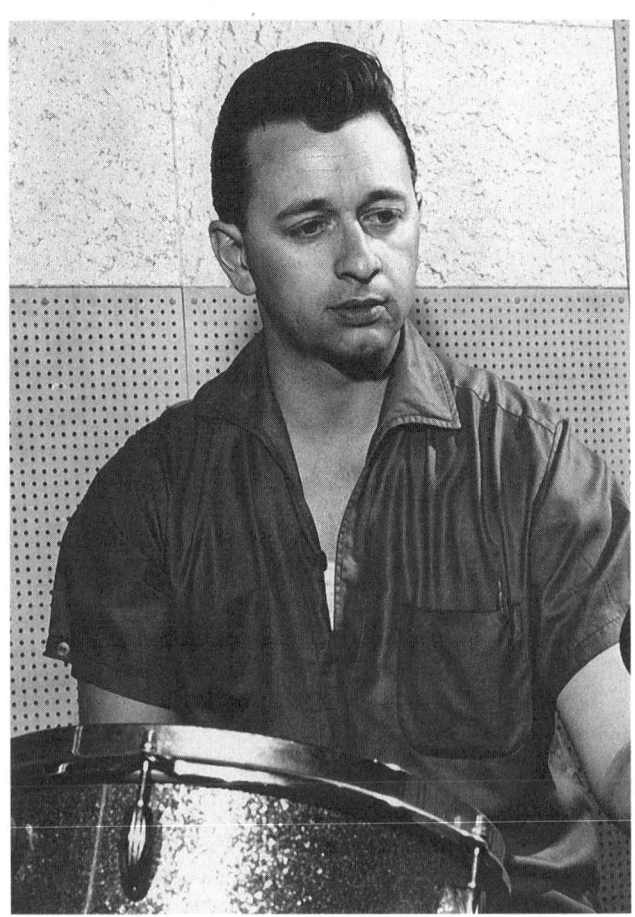

*Buddy Harman*

of college to study for three years at Chicago's Roy Knapp School of Percussion. In 1952 he returned to Nashville to play with area groups.

Harman gradually worked his way into Nashville's emerging recording scene and took up full-time studio work in about 1955. Initially country producers allowed him little leeway, but his solid, tasteful playing on sessions with artists such as MARTHA CARSON, the Everlys, MOON MULLICAN, and RAY PRICE helped to expand the role of drums in country music. By the mid-1960s, Harman was working some 600 sessions a year. This number declined by the late 1970s, as the influx of new players from other cities and Nashville's growing recording activity reduced the dominance he had once enjoyed. Harman remained active in the studio, however, and toured as a member of the Nashville Superpickers in the early 1980s. For many years he served as a business agent for the Nashville local of the AMERICAN FEDERATION OF MUSICIANS (AFM). —John W. Rumble

## Harmonica

The harmonica is based on the principle of the free reed, an Asian invention that dates back 3,000 years in which a tongue made of metal or wood is attached at one end over a close-fitting opening through which the free end vibrates when air passes over it. In 1821 a German named Christian Buschmann patented an instrument called the aura that had steel reeds placed in small channels. In 1825 a man named Richter devised a mouth organ with reed plates mounted on either side of a wooden comb that enabled both draw and blow notes. It was Richter's design and diatonic tuning scheme that became the basis for the harmonica as we know it.

The mouth organ proved immediately popular. The German harmonica manufacturer Matthias Hohner was the first to adopt mass-production techniques and to import mouth organs to the United States, successes that enabled his firm to attain a worldwide monopoly. By the middle of the nineteenth century the inexpensive and portable harmonica was commonly displayed on the shelves of general stores throughout America, especially in the South, where it was commonly known as the "French harp." Several regions settled largely by German immigrants—notably Texas, Illinois, and the Carolinas—became known for the high caliber of their harmonicists. The mouth organ's uncanny ability for mimicry led performers in rural America to perfect "talking" harmonica showpieces and startlingly realistic re-creations of fox chases and speeding locomotives. DeFORD BAILEY ("The Harmonica Wizard"), who performed on the GRAND OLE OPRY from 1926 until 1941, excelled at such showpieces.

Although the harmonica has been used successfully in every form of music, it is usually identified with the blues and with country music. HENRY WHITTER recorded several harmonica solos in 1923 that rank as some of the earliest recordings of country music. The Tennessee hill country around Nashville produced many first-rate harmonica players, including DR. HUMPHREY BATE, Herman Crook of THE CROOK BROTHERS, and DeFord Bailey. LONNIE GLOSSON and WAYNE RANEY reportedly helped stimulate mail-order sales of more than 5 million harmonicas during the 1940s and 1950s, when they hosted a nationally syndicated radio program. Jimmie Riddle and ONIE WHEELER were also prominent hillbilly mouth harpists.

By the mid-1960s the harmonica was rarely heard in country music, but all that changed with the arrival in Nashville of CHARLIE McCOY, a phenomenal player whose harmonica has been heard on thousands of recordings. The mouth organ work of Don Brooks and Mickey Raphael, members of the bands of WAYLON JENNINGS and WILLIE NELSON, respectively, built on McCoy's accomplishments, as did that of Terry McMillan (d. February 2, 2007). The fine playing of harmonicists such as Kirk "Jellyroll" Johnson is ensuring the instrument a prominent role in country music for the foreseeable future. —Kim Field

## Bill Harrell
b. Marion, Virginia, September 14, 1934; d. June 24, 2009

BLUEGRASS guitarist-singer William Harrell became active in the Washington, D.C., area in the late 1950s. Bill Harrell & the Virginians' recordings were included on STARDAY RECORDS singles and anthologies, and United Artists Records issued the group's first album in 1963. Appearing semi-regularly on The Jimmy Dean Show on ABC-TV in the early 1960s as Buck Ryan & Smitty Irvin, the band recorded an album for MONUMENT RECORDS in 1965.

Harrell and banjo great Don Reno (see RENO & SMILEY) formed a partnership in 1966, with prolific recordings (eventually for CMH Records) and live performances in the style Reno had established with his former partner, Red Smiley. In 1978 Harrell reactivated the Virginians, returned to performing and recording in his own style, and led the act for more than twenty years. He received an IBMA Distinguished Achievement Award in 2008. —Frank and Marty Godbey

## Kelly Harrell
b. Wythe County, Virginia, September 13, 1889; d. July 9, 1942

Like country music pioneers CHARLIE POOLE, Dave McCarn, HENRY WHITTER, and THE DIXON BROTHERS, Crockett Kelly Harrell left a job in the textile mills to try his luck as a full-time musician. The aspiring singer eventually failed to make his living in music, but along the way he made more than forty excellent records, including several definitive interpretations of traditional songs and several that became country standards. Ironically, he never recorded his most famous song, "Away Out on the Mountain"; JIMMIE RODGERS made it a hit, with Harrell receiving thousands of dollars in royalties. As a result, Harrell was one of the first country songwriters to make a considerable profit from his compositions.

As a young man in Fries, Virginia, he met OLD-TIME fiddler HENRY WHITTER. Whitter had gone north and talked record companies into recording him, and Harrell decided to follow suit—in spite of the fact that he couldn't play the guitar or banjo. In January 1925 he recorded four songs for the Victor Talking Machine Company in New York (predecessor to RCA VICTOR), including versions of "New River Train" and the traditional murder ballad "The Butcher's Boy." These sold well enough that a year later Victor asked him to rerecord them using the new electrical recording process. Soon Harrell organized his own backup band, the Virginia String Band, consisting of Posey Rorer on fiddle, R. D. Hundley on banjo, and Alfred Steagel on guitar. Over the next three years the act recorded numbers such as "My Name Is John Johanna," "Charles Guiteau," and "Row Us over the Tide." Some of these stayed in print through the 1950s, when they were included in Harry Smith's famous 1952 Anthology of American Folk Music.

Harrell's record royalties were impressive in their day, but when the Depression curtailed record sales and record companies began to pressure him to learn an instrument, he lost interest and returned to the mills. Plagued by asthma, he collapsed at work one day in 1942 and died on the way to the hospital. —*Stacey Wolfe*

# Emmylou Harris
b. Birmingham, Alabama, April 2, 1947

A country singer by way of folk music and COUNTRY-ROCK, Emmylou Harris has consistently taken her music beyond the conventional parameters of country, BLUEGRASS, and ROCKA-BILLY and paid heartfelt tributes to pop, rock, folk, gospel, and blues—all while remaining country at the core. Well before the NEW TRADITIONALISM of the 1980s, Harris was already stretching boundaries—and succeeding on her own terms, introducing traditional country to a wider audience while helping to redefine country music itself.

Harris has had seven #1 and twenty other Top Ten country hits. In addition to numerous gold albums, *Trio*, her 1987 album with DOLLY PARTON and LINDA RONSTADT, sold more than 1 million copies in its first year. (*Trio 2* followed in 1999.) Harris has received multiple Grammys, been named CMA Female Vocalist of the Year, and was inducted into the GRAND OLE OPRY in 1992.

Born in Birmingham, Alabama, and raised in Woodbridge, Virginia, Harris was considered an "oddball" in high school, she said, "because she kept her nose buried in her books." Seeking acceptance, she sang at parties, won a local beauty contest, and tried out to be a majorette. She ended up playing alto sax in the marching band.

At the University of North Carolina in Greensboro, she studied drama but soon turned to music, singing in a folk duo at a local club. Her first love, she said, was folk and country blues, because of their "intense emphasis on lyrics." She transferred briefly to Boston University and then moved to New York, where she sang in Greenwich Village and developed an appreciation for country music through fellow performers JERRY JEFF WALKER and David Bromberg.

Harris made a record (a disaster) for the Jubilee label, was married briefly, and had a daughter. In Nashville, with her marriage ended, she worked odd jobs, including a stint as a singing waitress.

*Emmylou Harris*

Barely able to pay her rent, Harris moved with her baby to Maryland in 1970 to live with her parents. There she began singing again, mostly at folk clubs in and around nearby Washington, D.C.

While performing in the back room of Clyde's, a singles bar in Georgetown, Harris was discovered by two members of the Flying Burrito Brothers, who for a time thought of adding her as a Burrito Sister. That didn't happen, but CHRIS HILLMAN of the Burritos told GRAM PARSONS—who had just left the band—about Harris.

Harris and Parsons clicked instantly. Possessed of a silvery, high-lonesome voice, Harris was an instinctive duet singer, and she soared with Parsons on two albums, helping him realize his dreams of a fusion of country and rock & roll. In later years, Harris would also record moving duets with such artists as ROY ORBISON ("That Lovin' You Feelin' Again," 1980) and DON WILLIAMS ("If I Needed You," 1981), among others.

Parsons died in 1973, and in 1975 Harris released her first major label solo album, *Pieces of the Sky*, on WARNER BROS./REPRISE. It included a version of THE LOUVIN BROTHERS' "If I Could Only Win Your Love" that became her first Top Ten country hit. Harris's first #1 hit, "Together Again" (from *Elite Hotel*, 1976), came from the pen of BUCK OWENS. But throughout, Harris made it a point to perform songs by Parsons and to talk about his legacy. "I wanted to carry on with what I thought he would have wanted me to do," she said, "bringing certain elements of folk music, with its emphasis on the lyric, trying eclectic things, but always coming back to that electric country blues."

A musicologist at heart, Harris found and employed a succession of excellent writers and musicians who brought new sounds and sensibilities to country music. These included RODNEY CROWELL (who wrote some of her material and anchored the initial version of her famous Hot Band), RICKY SKAGGS (who reflected Harris's devotion to bluegrass, most notably in *Roses in the Snow*, 1980), VINCE GILL (who appeared on several albums, including *The Ballad of Sally Rose*, 1985), EMORY GORDY JR., and BUDDY MILLER. Others who gained exposure through Harris included THE WHITES and steel guitarist Hank DeVito. Producer and A&R executive TONY BROWN, the Hot Band's pianist in the late 1970s, credits her for widening his own understanding of country music.

Harris's producers have included Brian Ahern, who worked on her early Warner Bros. albums and whom she married in 1977 (they divorced in 1984), and songwriter Paul Kennerley, who became her producer in 1985. She and Kennerley were married from 1985 to 1993.

Through the years, the constant in Harris's career has been adventurousness, whether it's to tackle a Chuck Berry or a Bruce Springsteen composition, to record her acoustic live *At the Ryman* album (1992), or to venture into the alternative arena with producer Daniel Lanois, as she did for her acclaimed 1995 album *Wrecking Ball*. As Harris herself has said, she's "always tried to fight against categories." With 2000's *Red Dirt Girl* and 2003's *Stumble into Grace*, both made for Nonesuch Records, she began to stress her own songwriting. In 2000 Harris contributed to the Grammy-winning 2000 film soundtrack *O BROTHER, WHERE ART THOU?* and to the related documentary and concert film *Down from the Mountain*. A duet album with British guitarist Mark Knopfler, *All the Roadrunning*, appeared in 2006, with a live album, *Real Live Roadrunning*, coming in the same year. A pioneering icon of the AMERICANA movement, in 2008 Harris released the Brian Ahern–produced Nonesuch album

*All I Intended to Be*, which recounts her fascinating musical journey and features appearances by Parton, Gill, and other previous musical partners.

Harris served on the board of the COUNTRY MUSIC HALL OF FAME AND MUSEUM for many years and is now a Trustee Emeritus. She also has involved herself in causes such as animal rescue and landmine removal. Harris was elected to THE COUNTRY MUSIC HALL OF FAME in 2008. —*Ben Fong-Torres*

## Freddie Hart
b. Loachapoka, Alabama, December 21, 1926

Freddie Hart's self-penned "Easy Loving"—a song he took to the top of the country charts in1971—was CMA's Song of the Year in 1971 and 1972 and the highlight of Hart's career. He never quite achieved the level of stardom such an honor might suggest, although his tenure in country music was long and successful.

Born Frederick Segrest in a family of fifteen children, Hart had a troubled childhood, running away from home at age seven and then being sent to a Civilian Conservation Corps camp at twelve. He joined the U.S. Marine Corps in 1942 when he was only fifteen and served in the Pacific Theater. He entertained at a number of NCO clubs and after his discharge worked in Texas and Hempstead, New York, as a laborer. In 1949 he came to Nashville, where he met HANK WILLIAMS. Hart had his first song recorded in 1952, when GEORGE MORGAN cut "Every Little Thing Rolled into One." Hart moved to Phoenix and met LEFTY FRIZZELL, touring with him until 1953; Hart then became a regular on *TOWN HALL PARTY* in Los Angeles until 1956.

Hart first recorded for CAPITOL RECORDS, then COLUMBIA and Kapp Records before returning to Capitol in 1970. His early-1954 song "Loose Talk" caught the attention of CARL SMITH, who covered it and had a #1 hit later that year. Another songwriting success for Hart was "Skid Row Joe," which went to #3 for PORTER WAGONER in 1966. Hart had a number of chart singles, but none was a major smash until his "Easy Loving" in 1971. He followed with a five-year string of hit singles (most of which he wrote), including "My Hang-Up Is You," "Bless Your Heart," "Got the All Overs for You (All Over Me)," "Super Kind of Woman," "Trip to Heaven," "Hang in There Girl," and "The First Time," all on Capitol. On all of these recordings, his breathy, yearning delivery intensified lyrics that typically put women on a pedestal. Hart continued releasing singles throughout the 1970s; in 1980 he moved to Sunbird and then to El Dorado and Fifth Street. Although he had chart records, he did not repeat his early 1970s achievements. —*Don Cusic*

## John Hartford
b. New York, New York, December 30, 1937; d. June 4, 2001

After making his mark as an innovative singer-songwriter, lanky banjo player John Cowan Harford (CHET ATKINS added a "t" to John's last name when he signed with RCA VICTOR) reversed his progressive musical direction to pursue the acoustic music he preferred.

Raised in St. Louis, Hartford was fascinated by country musicians he heard on radio, particularly FLATT & SCRUGGS. By the early 1960s he had learned banjo, guitar, fiddle, and mandolin and was playing with central Missouri and Illinois BLUEGRASS bands. In 1965 he moved to Nashville and became a late-night disc jockey

on WSIX. Chuck Glaser of the THE GLASER BROTHERS heard Hartford's songs, signed him to a publishing contract, and arranged an RCA record deal. Hartford's 1966 album debut, *John Hartford Looks at Life*, revealed a highly original talent; his introspective lyrics would influence a generation of Nashville songwriters. "Gentle on My Mind," a Grammy-winning love song from Hartford's second album, became a modest hit in 1967, and GLEN CAMPBELL's lush version landed on both pop and country charts. Over the years Hartford's composition has become one of American music's most recorded and broadcast songs.

Moving to California in 1968, Hartford became a writer-performer on CBS-TV's *The Smothers Brothers Comedy Hour* and *The Glen Campbell Goodtime Hour*. But within two years, Hartford grew dissatisfied with both Los Angeles and his commercial direction, returned to Nashville, and recruited bluegrass veterans VASSAR CLEMENTS, TUT TAYLOR, and Norman Blake to record the acoustic album *Aereo Plain*. Released on WARNER BROS. in 1971, it found an immediate audience among sharp, young bluegrass musicians, who best appreciated Hartford's unorthodox lyrics and rhythmic ideas.

After 1975 Hartford largely worked club, concert, and festival dates without a band; his first unaccompanied album, *Mark Twang* (Flying Fish, 1976), won a Grammy for Best Ethnic or Traditional Recording. He also recorded and toured with his son, Jamie, and with various configurations of the John Hartford String Band. He won a 2001 Grammy for his contributions to the *O BROTHER, WHERE ART THOU?*, soundtrack and he was part of the follow-up *Down from the Mountain* concert film and tour.

When not performing, Hartford pursued a second vocation as a riverboat pilot. He also published two books and did voice-overs for film and television documentaries, most notably Ken Burns's acclaimed PBS series *The Civil War*. At the time of his death Hartford was preparing a manuscript on the life and music of fiddler Ed Haley. Hartford was elected to the IBMA Hall of Fame in 2010. —*Dave Samuelson*

## Hatch Show Print
established 1879 in Nashville, Tennessee

Located at 316 Broadway in downtown Nashville, Hatch Show Print is believed to be the oldest active poster print shop in America. For years its most famous client was the GRAND OLE OPRY, and to this day the shop's evocative, archaic handiwork is favored by music industry art directors and others seeking the visual warmth of woodblock print. Through the years, artists ranging from the prewar blues queen Bessie Smith to ERNEST TUBB to EMMYLOU HARRIS (the cover of her 1992 *At the Ryman* album) have seen their music advertised in the bold, minimalist Hatch style. Recent clients include Bruce Springsteen, BOB DYLAN, Pizza Hut, Nike, and CNN.

Hatch was founded in 1879 by brothers Charles R. and Herbert H. Hatch of Wisconsin. Their first shop opened at the corner of what is now Fifth Avenue North and Deaderick Street in Nashville, and their first known job was a six-by-nine-inch "dodger" advertising an April 1879 appearance by the Rev. Henry Ward Beecher at the Grand Opera House. As the shop's fame grew, all manner of clients came its way—from circuses to BLACKFACE MINSTREL shows to Negro League baseball promoters. Charles's son William took over the business in 1921 and moved it three years later to 116 Fourth Avenue North. By 1938 Hatch was routinely printing the Opry's posters, which, along with those of Hatch's other clients, could be seen on barns and storefronts throughout the South. The business went into decline, however, when Will Hatch died in 1952. After various ownership changes, Hatch Show Print was successfully revived in 1987 by the COUNTRY MUSIC HALL OF FAME AND MUSEUM, which moved it to its current location in 1992 and operates the enterprise as a working business and historic site.

As evidence of the shop's ongoing impact, *Hatch Show Print: The History of a Great American Poster Shop* (Chronicle Books, 2001), coauthored by museum staff members Jim Sherraden, Elek Horvath, and Paul Kingsbury, won prestigious design and book awards from *Communication Arts* magazine. October 2008 marked the opening of *American Letterpress: The Art of Hatch Show Print*, an exhibit at Seattle's Experience Music Project museum. Supported by the Wallace Foundation and the Smithsonian Institution, in July 2009 the exhibit began a travel schedule including an additional thirteen museums over four years. —*Daniel Cooper*

## Hawaiian Music

Musicians from the Hawaiian Islands toured the United States before World War I, but the Hawaiian steel guitar was not in evidence until 1909. In that year, exotic dancer Toots Paka's troupe brought guitarist Joseph Kekuku to New York, where he and the group made several EDISON cylinders. According to popular accounts, Kekuku "invented" the instrument when a comb fell from his pocket and slid along his guitar neck.

Other surviving Hawaiian recordings show no further evidence of the steel guitar until Walter Kolomoku's appearance with the Hawaiian Quintette at New York's Winter Garden in a play that ran through the 1912–13 season. The Quintette recorded extensively for Victor in April 1913, and these recordings established Hawaiian music as a major genre on the mainland. Polynesian artists and their American counterparts recorded prolifically through World War I and beyond.

In those years, Hawaiian guitar style merged to an extent with African American blues slide guitar style. In 1921 Sam Moore recorded his "Laughing Rag" on his octo-chorda (presumably an eight-string Hawaiian guitar). Louisville, Kentucky, blues guitarist Sylvester Weaver's 1923 "Guitar Rag" was even more influential—thirteen years later it became LEON MCAULIFFE's signature piece, "Steel Guitar Rag," and his boss BOB WILLS's first major hit.

In the 1920s Hawaiian (or slide) guitars found a place in recorded country music. RILEY PUCKETT recorded a solo called "Darkey's Wail" in 1926. Jimmie Tarlton featured the instrument in duets with his partner Tom Darby (see DARBY & TARLTON), and even Maybelle Carter featured the instrument on CARTER FAMILY records from 1928 to 1930.

The amplified steel guitar was first recorded in 1933 by Noelani's Hawaiian Orchestra. By 1934, influential guitarists Sol Hoopii and Sam Koki were playing amplified instruments. Late that year, BOB DUNN brought one to MILTON BROWN's Musical Brownies; their January 1935 records with Dunn's aggressive solos redefined the sound of WESTERN SWING, especially after Leon McAuliffe followed Dunn's example and introduced the electric steel guitar with Bob Wills's Texas Playboys a few months later.

Back east, ROY ACUFF adopted the string bass and steel for his own music, though he almost always used a non-amplified steel guitar (or DOBRO). Acuff's 1937 "Steel Guitar Chimes" featured

Clell Summey (Cousin Jody) playing his version of the Hawaiian standard "Maui Chimes." Prominent dobro players, including Cliff Carlisle (see BILL CARLISLE) and CECIL CAMPBELL, also added Hawaiian elements to various acts. The postwar era witnessed the technological evolution of the electric steel guitar, and PEDAL STEEL players such as BUD ISAACS, PETE DRAKE, Johnny Sibert, HERB REMINGTON, LLOYD GREEN, and BUDDY EMMONS developed modern styles far removed from the Hawaiian sound, as did JERRY DOUGLAS and other acoustic dobro players. —*Dick Spottswood*

## Hawkshaw Hawkins
b. Huntington, West Virginia, December 22, 1921; d. March 5, 1963

One of country's best HONKY-TONK singers, the tall (six feet, six inches), deep-voiced Hawkshaw Hawkins was billed as "eleven and a half yards of personality." As a youth, Harold Franklin Hawkins traded five trapped rabbits for his first guitar, and a short time later, at age fifteen, he won a talent contest on radio station WSAZ in Huntington, West Virginia. In addition to the fifteen-dollar prize, Hawkins landed his first radio job there. He later moved to WCHS in Charleston, West Virginia, and occasionally teamed with Clarence "Sherlock" Jack. In 1941 Hawkins briefly worked in a traveling show for a Lawrence, Massachusetts, radio station and in a Baltimore shipyard before entering the military, serving in the Pacific Theater during World War II. While in the Philippines, he performed on Manila radio station WJUM.

Returning to civilian life, Hawkins joined the *WWVA JAMBOREE* and remained there until 1954; during this time he also had a CBS network radio program. He developed a large following due to his showmanship and recordings featuring his rich, smooth, honky-tonk vocals. Especially popular were his colorful

*Hawkshaw Hawkins*

summer shows, which included trained horse acts, roping exhibitions, and Australian bullwhip tricks.

Hawkins made most of his hits for KING RECORDS. First came 1948's "Pan American" and "Dog House Boogie." The following year he scored with "I Wasted a Nickel." In 1951 he had two Top Ten hits, "I Love You a Thousand Ways" and "I'm Waiting Just for You." His version of "Slow Poke" peaked at #7 in 1952.

On the strength of these successes, Hawkins joined the GRAND OLE OPRY in 1955. It was not until four years later, though, that he made another hit: "Soldier's Joy"—a pseudo–Revolutionary War song set to a traditional fiddle tune. The record, his only COLUMBIA hit, reached #15 on *Billboard*'s country charts. On November 26, 1960, he married fellow Opry star JEAN SHEPARD; the ceremony was conducted on an auditorium stage in Wichita, Kansas. In 1963 his King recording of JUSTIN TUBB's song "Lonesome 7-7203" turned out to be Hawkins's biggest hit. Tragically, he never lived to see it reach #1.

In 1963, Hawkins, along with PATSY CLINE, COWBOY COPAS, and pilot RANDY HUGHES, who was Copas's son-in-law and Cline's personal manager, were flying to Nashville from Kansas City. They had performed in a concert benefiting the family of a DJ who had lost his life in a car wreck. Their plane came down in a blinding thunderstorm and crashed in the hills near Camden, Tennessee, killing all aboard. Ironically, Hawkins feared flying and seldom traveled by air. —*W. K. McNeil*

## George D. Hay
b. Attica, Indiana, November 9, 1895; d. May 8, 1968

Founder of WSM's GRAND OLE OPRY, George Dewey Hay was a visionary and colorfully romantic figure who played a vital role in commercializing and promoting country music.

Following military service, Hay worked as a newspaper reporter for the Memphis *Commercial Appeal*. One of his assignments was the city court beat, from which he developed a series of popular humorous columns called "Howdy, Judge," based on the dialog between the judge and those charged with petty crimes. The success of these columns (later collected in book form) won him the sobriquet "The Solemn Ole Judge," though he was still in

*George D. Hay*

his twenties and had no legal training. When the newspaper established its own radio station, WMC, in January 1923, Hay soon became late-night station announcer and radio editor.

Hay had a flair for the job and brought to it a sense of showmanship and style. He chanted the station's call letters, artfully scripted his shows, and blew an imitation steamboat whistle (dubbed "Hushpuckena") to announce the start of the evening's programs. (All of these skills he would later bring to WSM.) His following grew so rapidly that in May 1924 he was hired to work at WLS in Chicago, where, among other duties, he announced for the show that would soon become the NATIONAL BARN DANCE.

In the fall of 1924 Hay won *Radio Digest* magazine's poll as the nation's most popular announcer. As a result, he was offered the position of "radio director" for the newly opened WSM in Nashville, and on November 9, 1925, he began work at the station. Hay told a friend shortly after arriving that he wanted to re-create the kind of barn dance he had worked on at WLS. (He later wrote that he had also been inspired by rural musicians he'd observed in Arkansas, and he was probably influenced by the wide variety of entertainment available in Memphis.) Hay was happy to see that performers such as DR. HUMPHREY BATE and UNCLE DAVE MACON had already made occasional WSM appearances.

In late November 1925 Hay invited a seventy-eight-year-old fiddler from Laguardo, Tennessee, UNCLE JIMMY THOMPSON, to play on the air. Astounded at the calls and telegrams that poured in, Hay announced a month later that due to the audience interest, WSM would feature "an hour or two" of OLD-TIME tunes on a weekly basis.

Hay bombarded local newspapers with a steady stream of press releases trumpeting the values of this kind of down-to-earth "folk music." He soon began to augment this image by rechristening his STRINGBANDS with colorful names (for instance, Dr. Bate's Augmented String Orchestra became the Possum Hunters) and by encouraging musicians to dress in overalls and straw hats. He eventually helped launch WSM's booking department, and by 1933 some of the bands were touring theaters as distant as Iowa. It was Hay, too, who redubbed the program—first called the *WSM Barn Dance*—the Grand Ole Opry in 1927.

Though Hay was the show's figurehead, publicist, and announcer, he began to lose influence with the station's owners in the 1930s. He lacked managerial skills, and by 1928 a series of professional managers began to take over many of his duties. To compound problems, Hay suffered a nervous breakdown in the late 1930s, prompting sick leaves as long as eighteen months. By the spring of 1938, however, he was back at work and participating in two key Opry developments: the show's half-hour contribution to the NBC network, beginning in 1939, and the 1940 Hollywood film *Grand Ole Opry*, whose cast included Hay, THE WEAVER BROTHERS & ELVIRY, ROY ACUFF, and Uncle Dave Macon. Hay also contributed folksy articles to *Rural Radio*, a magazine published by WSM during 1938–39.

Throughout the 1940s Hay remained as a major announcer with the show, often traveling with Opry road troupes. In September 1947 he made one of his last appearances with an Opry unit, at New York City's CARNEGIE HALL. In 1945 he wrote a fascinating little book called *A Story of the Grand Ole Opry*, and in 1953 he became an editor of the early country music newspaper *Pickin' and Singin' News*. In the 1960s he attempted two syndicated radio shows devoted to reminiscing about the Opry. Upset at the direction of the Opry and its virtual neglect of him, he left Nashville by the end of the 1950s and settled in Virginia Beach, Virginia, where he died in 1968 and where he is buried. —*Charles Wolfe*

## Will Hays
b. Louisville, Kentucky, July 19, 1837; d. July 23, 1907

William Shakespeare Hays was one of America's most popular songwriters of the late nineteenth century. Although he wrote some 350 songs and at least as many poems (some of which were set to music), he never pursued music full time. He was a riverboat pilot on the Ohio and Mississippi Rivers at various periods of his life (at least two steamboats were named for him) and served as river editor of the Louisville *Courier-Journal* from 1868 to 1898.

His songs were immensely popular in his day, but Hays could not have anticipated how some would endure. Several of his compositions—often mistakenly identified and collected as folksongs by scholars in the early twentieth century—moved into the hinterlands to become the possession of everyday working people. They became part of country music's repertoire when the first country recordings and radio broadcasts were made in the 1920s. Hays's "Little Old Log Cabin in the Lane" was on one side of FIDDLIN' JOHN CARSON's seminal first record in 1923, and other Hays songs, including "We Parted by the River Side," "You've Been a Friend to Me," "I'll Remember You, Love, in My Prayers," and "Nobody's Darling on Earth," also found their way onto country recordings. His "Jimmie Brown the Paper Boy," adapted by the CARTER FAMILY as "Jimmie Brown the Newsboy" and prominently recorded by FLATT & SCRUGGS and by MAC WISEMAN, has become a BLUEGRASS standard and Hays's most recorded composition. His biggest hit song, "Molly Darling," was a Top Ten country record for EDDY ARNOLD in 1948. —*Bill C. Malone*

## Haywire Mac
b. Knoxville, Tennessee, October 8, 1882; d. April 24, 1957

Alternately employed as cowboy, railroader, union organizer, songwriter, seaman, recording artist, and radio performer, Harry Kirby "Haywire Mac" McClintock was one of the most colorful personalities in American music. At age fourteen he left home for the life of a hobo, an experience that later contributed to his writing the classic hobo song "Hallelujah, I'm a Bum." After two years rambling around the country, he shipped out to the Philippines, where he worked as a mule packer for American troops, and then to China, where he assisted journalists covering the Boxer Rebellion. Later travel and trades took him to Australia, Africa, South America, and finally to the West Coast of the United States.

Throughout his checkered career, McClintock learned and sang songs. His original compositions include "Big Rock Candy Mountain" and numerous union songs written and performed while a member of the Industrial Workers of the World. In 1925 he had his own radio show on San Francisco station KFRC, performing solo as well as with his Haywire Orchestry. Three years later he began his recording career, eventually turning out forty-one sides for Victor Talking Machine Company (later RCA VICTOR) and several sides for other labels. He is best known for his recordings of hobo songs, railroad songs, and COWBOY MUSIC. McClintock continued to write and perform until his retirement in 1955. He died in San Francisco in 1957. —*Charlie Seemann*

## Jimmy Heap
b. Taylor, Texas, March 3, 1922; d. December 4, 1977

James Arthur Heap was a guitarist, songwriter, and HONKY-TONK bandleader (the Melody Masters), best known for early recordings of songs others turned into country standards.

Jimmy Heap's recorded output was large. He made thirty-two sides with IMPERIAL RECORDS (1948–52), including the original version of the HANK THOMPSON classic "The Wild Side of Life," cowritten by Heap's pianist, Arlie Carter. On CAPITOL (1951–55), Heap released thirty sides, among them the first big version of EDDIE MILLER's "Release Me" (1953) and an early cut of "Conscience I'm Guilty" (1955), later a HANK SNOW hit. Heap later recorded for the Big Band, Fame, and Winston labels.

When "Release Me" hit, Heap was booked on national tours, though normally he stayed close to his hometown of Taylor. He was killed in a boating accident at age fifty-five. —*Ronnie Pugh*

## Bobby Hebb
b. Nashville, Tennessee, July 26, 1938; d. August 3, 2010

One of the most intriguing examples of African American participation in country music is that of Bobby Hebb, who performed on the GRAND OLE OPRY in the 1950s and then went on to greater fame as the author and singer of the 1966 soul-pop smash "Sunny."

Hebb grew up near the Nashville neighborhood that became MUSIC ROW. His parents, both blind, were musicians, and Hebb absorbed heavy doses of gospel, classical, jazz, blues, and country. "It was very important that one understood more than one culture of music," he said. He also learned to tap-dance and play spoons, and while still a child he found work in nightclubs, fraternity houses, and at black-tie parties. Then, in 1950 ("the year that television came to Nashville," as Hebb put it), he landed a spot on a WSM-TV variety show hosted by OWEN BRADLEY. ROY ACUFF saw Hebb on TV and hired him.

Hebb worked on the Opry with Acuff from roughly 1950 to 1955, and in 1960 he recorded his own version of the Acuff hit "Night Train to Memphis." From there, Hebb's career moved toward R&B, but after "Sunny" made him an international star, he deliberately followed with a soul version of the country chestnut "A Satisfied Mind" in 1966. The song had multiple meanings for Hebb, but among them was his wish to tell his friends from the old days on the Opry, "Thanks, fellas." At an Opry appearance shortly after his move back to Nashville from Massachusetts (where he had been living for many years) in 2004, BMI presented him with an award commemorating 6 million performances of "Sunny," a song recorded by legions of artists. For his 2005 release *That's All I Wanna Know* (Tuition) he recorded a new arrangement of "A Satisfied Mind" and drew further inspiration from his Opry years with a rendition of HANK WILLIAMS's "Cold, Cold Heart." In 2009 Hebb retired from performing. He died of lung cancer the following year. —*Daniel Cooper*

## *Hee Haw*
established 1969; ended 1994

*Hee Haw* is considered the most successful country TV show of all time. It is also one of history's longest-lasting syndicated television programs.

Hee Haw *cast, 1970*

Created by Frank Peppiatt and John Aylesworth and produced by Sam Lovullo, all of whom had worked together on *The Jonathan Winters Show*, *Hee Haw* originated in 1969 as a country imitation of the comedy series *Laugh-In*, aping the earlier show's "black out" sketches and one-liners with hick/cornball versions. Stock rube vaudeville characters and hillbilly stereotypes from *Li'l Abner* and *Tobacco Road* were cast, as well as animated barnyard animals.

*Hee Haw* ranked among television's twenty most highly rated programs when CBS dropped it in 1971 in a move to de-countrify the network's programming. *Hee Haw* went immediately into syndication and thrived for nearly twenty-five years. More than 600 episodes were produced.

The initial hosts were BUCK OWENS and ROY CLARK. Owens left in 1986 and was not replaced. Key to the show's success were regulars ARCHIE CAMPBELL (who also wrote gags), GRANDPA JONES, Roni Stoneman, KENNY PRICE, STRINGBEAN, MINNIE PEARL, Gordie Tapp, and George Lindsey (who played "Goober" on *THE ANDY GRIFFITH SHOW*), all of whom had established careers when the series began.

But *Hee Haw* introduced equally talented and memorable characters who were less well known, including Lulu Roman, Gailard Sartain, JUNIOR SAMPLES (whose used-car-salesman phone number, BR5-49, later titled the country band of this name), Don Harron, Grady Nutt, the Hager Twins, and MIKE SNIDER.

Among the show's female cast, some of whom came to be known as the "Hee Haw Honeys," were Cathy Baker, Gunilla Hutton, Lisa Todd, Marianne Gordon Rogers, Misty Rowe, Linda Thompson, Irlene Mandrell, and Mackenzie Colt. Barbi Benton was a regular for five years. *Hee Haw Honeys* aired as a spinoff series in syndication, 1978–79.

Production values were first-rate, and the music segments were, too. George Richey, and then CHARLIE McCOY, led the house band, which featured the Nashville Edition singers. Virtually every legendary country star of the era guested at one time or another.

Controversy erupted in 1991 when the show was redesigned and many regulars were fired. A more modern *Hee Haw* broadcast on TNN bombed. The show died during the 1993–94 season, and TNN aired vintage *Hee Haw* programs thereafter.

In 1994, several former cast members reunited for a *Hee Haw Live* stage production at OPRYLAND. —*Robert K. Oermann*

## Bobby Helms
b. Bloomington, Indiana, August 15, 1933; d. June 19, 1997

Rock & roll opened the door for country singers who could adapt to the challenges of teen-age music. Bobby Lee Helms was one of the first to show the way, with a series of hits that were neither pop nor country but drew from both. The productions, all from Nashville, revealed that the country music industry adapted well to the new music.

Helms grew up with country music (his father hosted the *Monroe County Jamboree* in Bloomington). He made his first recordings for Nashville-based Speed Records in 1955 and was brought to Nashville by ERNEST TUBB the following year. Helms's voice worked the same tenor range as WEBB PIERCE's, and Helms's style was, in some regards, an update of Pierce's sound. Signed to DECCA RECORDS, Helms recorded "Fraulein"—a song written by LAWTON WILLIAMS for Tubb eight years earlier—during his second session, in November 1956. It was a #1 country hit in September 1957, broke into the pop Top Forty, and spent a total of fifty-two weeks on the country charts. He followed it with "My Special Angel," a country #1 in December 1957 as well as a pop Top Ten. He finished 1957 with "Jingle Bell Rock," soon to be a pop and country seasonal classic and an eventual million-seller. The latter two hits made Helms's connection to pop music explicit. After leaving Decca in 1962, he continued to record for a plethora of labels but with diminishing regularity and chart impact. His fame is wedded forever to his three 1957 hits. —*Colin Escott*

## Don Helms (*see* The Drifting Cowboys, Hank Williams)

## Fisher Hendley
b. Anson County, North Carolina, 1891; d. October 27, 1963

A noted southern contest winner with a drop-thumb, frailing, picking style on the five-string banjo, Fisher Hendley developed a career as a flashy instrumentalist, master of ceremonies, bandleader, and impresario. Shunning hillbilly stereotypes, he long demonstrated county music's debt to vaudeville and BLACKFACE MINSTRELSY.

Born into to a farming family in the musically rich North Carolina piedmont, he attended Trinity College (now Duke University), where his glee club tours included minstrel performances. After working in a World War I munitions plant, Hendley co-owned an Albemarle garage, recorded (unsuccessfully) for OKEH in 1925, and met fellow musicians at fiddlers conventions. By the mid-1920s he fronted a loosely organized group called the Albemarle Novelty Amusement Company and then made a brief solo vaudeville foray before assembling a minstrel troupe *cum* STRINGBAND. With HENRY WHITTER and Marshall Small, Hendley recorded for RCA VICTOR in 1930.

During the Depression, Hendley continued to organize fiddlers conventions and make personal appearances, including performances at New York City radio stations and nightclubs.

He made a session there for Vocalion in 1933. In 1934–35 he broadcast over WBT–Charlotte. Then in late 1935 he moved to Greeneville, South Carolina's WFBC, where he formed his Aristocratic Pigs, a name adapted from a meat-packing company that sponsored him. Sporting theater makeup and custom-made tuxedos, the band's image contributed strongly to its regional success. The act recorded two dozen additional sides for Vocalion in Columbia, South Carolina (1938), where Hendley and his band were popular on WIS into the mid-1940s. In 1949 he retired to Florida. —*Bob Pinson* and *John W. Rumble*

## Scott Hendricks
b. Clinton, Oklahoma, July 26, 1956

Scott Hendricks has been a highly successful producer, having worked with Trace Adkins, Brooks & Dunn, Alan Jackson, and Restless Heart. Hendricks served as president and CEO of Capitol Nashville Records (1995–97) and president of Virgin Records' Nashville division (1998–2001), and as of early 2011 he was senior vice president of A&R for Warner Bros./Reprise Nashville. He has produced or coproduced more than thirty #1 country hits, including "I'll Still Be Loving You," "I Swear," "That Rock Won't Roll," "Don't Rock the Jukebox," and "Neon Moon," along with numerous platinum albums.

While attending Oklahoma State University, Hendricks met Tim DuBois, soon to become a producer, and Greg Jennings, who became part of the group Restless Heart. After graduation all three moved to Nashville. Hendricks arrived in 1978 and began engineering at The Glaser Brothers studio and Bullet Recording before going independent in 1985. He then worked with producers including Jim Ed Norman, Barry Beckett, and Jerry Crutchfield.

Hendricks himself began producing in 1985, when he and DuBois began a successful run with Restless Heart. Hendricks quickly established himself as one of Nashville's top independent producers, having as many as seven #1 hits in a single year. Since 1991 he has produced Alan Jackson, Brooks & Dunn, Faith Hill, John Michael Montgomery, Steve Wariner, Suzy Bogguss, Deana Carter, and Blake Shelton. —*Beverly Keel*

## Ty Herndon
b. Butler, Alabama, May 2, 1962

A highly publicized arrest threatened Boyd Tyrone "Ty" Herndon's career at its outset. Shortly after his debut Epic single, "What Mattered Most," reached #1, Herndon was charged with indecent exposure after allegedly masturbating in front of a Fort Worth male policeman in June 1995. Herndon was also charged with drug possession.

Herndon pleaded guilty to possession, and authorities dropped the indecency charge. But the incident raised questions that had rarely been addressed in country music. Herndon's associates insisted he was not gay, and the event became merely a difficult hitch in an apparently promising career. Six Top Ten singles followed; along with two successive gold albums, they showed that country's audience was more tolerant than many believed. In 1996 Herndon won the fan-voted TNN Music City News Male Star of Tomorrow Award.

A precocious musician, Herndon left his Alabama home at seventeen for Nashville's Opryland theme park, where he performed intermittently for ten years. He attended that city's Belmont University, and in 1983 he became a winner on the syndicated television program *Star Search*. Herndon was featured on *Nashville Now*, sang jingles for Dodge and Pepsi, and became a model. But when record labels ignored him, he moved to Dallas to play local clubs.

Herndon eventually signed with Epic Records and released *What Mattered Most*—and its chart-topping title cut—in 1995. The title track of *Living in a Moment* (1996) also hit #1, as did his 1998 single "It Must Be Love." *Steam* (1999) sold disappointingly, however, and Herndon left Epic following a 2002 *Greatest Hits* collection. Christmas albums appeared on independent labels in 2003 and 2007. On Titan/Pyramid, he released *Right About Now* in 2007 and the gospel album *Journey On* in 2010. —*Tom Roland*

## E. T. Herzog Recording Studio
established in Cincinnati, Ohio, 1945; ended 1951

The E. T. Herzog Recording Studio, located at 811 Race Street in Cincinnati, Ohio, was one of the first independent commercial studios to record country music. Opened in 1945 by Earl T. Herzog (b. January 26, 1908; d. December 6, 1986), a moonlighting engineer from Cincinnati radio station WLW, the studio was used to record some of the earliest releases on King Records. Because of the availability of talented musicians working on WLW as well as Herzog's cooperative attitude and technical expertise, the studio also attracted artists from Nashville, including Hank Williams, who cut eight songs there in two sessions (1948–49). Though the Race Street studio closed in 1951, Herzog remained active, working in various other studios until his death. —*Jon Hartley Fox*

## The Hi Flyers

Cary Ginell has written that the Hi Flyers "best reflected the transition Texas stringbands went through during the turbulent 1930s"—from a traditional stringband to a jazzy dance band in the course of a few years.

Not the first Texas stringband to feature jazz improvisation, as has been claimed, the group was reportedly formed by Fort Worth radio personality Zack Hurt at KFJZ in 1929 as the High Fliers. The original group included Kentucky fiddler Clifford Gross and featured mainly breakdowns, waltzes, and pop tunes. By 1932, guitarist Elmer Scarborough had taken over the band, its name now streamlined to Hi Flyers. Inspired by Milton Brown's forays into string jazz, Scarborough and band members such as fiddler Pat Trotter and guitarist Willie Wells began to change the group's orientation. Several key band members left to form the Sons of the West in Amarillo in 1936, but by the time of the Hi Flyers' first sessions for Vocalion in 1937 the act could boast a lineup including hot steel guitarist Billy Briggs, versatile fiddler Darrell Kirkpatrick, and jazz pianist Landon Beaver.

Relocated to Eagle Pass for a time in 1937–38, the band broke up briefly before Scarborough revived it at Oklahoma City's KOMA in 1939. Featuring the vocals of Buster Ferguson and the forward-looking electric guitar of Sheldon Bennett, with former pianist Beaver returning for studio sessions, the group's recordings from 1939 to 1941 show it pointing not only toward the smoother sound of postwar Western swing but also toward the lyrical themes of postwar, beer-joint honky-tonk.

Scarborough disbanded the Hi Flyers as World War II dawned and re-formed it in Fort Worth in 1945, but by the end of 1946 the Hi Flyers were history. —*Kevin Coffey*

## John Hiatt
b. Indianapolis, Indiana, August 20, 1952

Raised in Indianapolis, John Hiatt moved in 1970 to Nashville, where he made his mark as a young songwriter at TREE PUBLISHING. Hiatt's acerbic songs have since appeared on records by artists ranging from EARL THOMAS CONLEY and SUZY BOGGUSS to the Neville Brothers to Iggy Pop. ROSANNE CASH scaled the country charts with Hiatt's "The Way We Make a Broken Heart" (1987), and Bonnie Raitt reached the #1 spot on *Billboard's* all-genre Hot 100 Singles Chart with his "Thing Called Love" (1989). Hiatt nonetheless had marginal success as a performer until 1987, when *Bring the Family* brought him critical and popular acclaim, including Best Male Vocalist honors in *Rolling Stone's* 1987 Critics Poll.

A pair of mid-1970s EPIC albums failed to generate much interest, and Hiatt moved to Los Angeles to record two albums for MCA; both drew comparisons to the music of fellow angry young men Graham Parker and Elvis Costello. Hiatt then cut three albums for Geffen, including 1983's excellent *Riding with the King*, before his wife's suicide and his own substance abuse nearly proved his undoing.

After remarrying and getting his life back on track, Hiatt enlisted Ry Cooder, Jim Keltner, and Nick Lowe to help make *Bring the Family*, which effortlessly fused country, rock, and R&B and brimmed with newfound affirmation and insight. He also re-established himself in Nashville and has continued to make gritty, soulful records, even though none has had more than a modest commercial impact. As testimony to his songwriting talent, in 1993 Rhino Records released *Love Gets Strange: The Songs of John Hiatt*, a collection of Hiatt originals recorded by other artists. Hiatt's 1997 release on CAPITOL, *Little Head*, reflected his continuing blend of rock & roll and country. Since 2000, he has released two studio albums on Vanguard and four on New West Records, including 2010's *The Open Road*. —*Bill Friskics-Warren*

## Hickory Records
established 1953; ended 1985

Hickory Records, a companion enterprise of ACUFF-ROSE PUBLICATIONS, was created in 1953 as a partnership among Acuff-Rose principals ROY ACUFF, FRED ROSE, and Rose's son WESLEY ROSE. Beginning shipments early in 1954, Hickory immediately provided a recording outlet for Acuff-Rose copyrights while allowing Fred Rose—also an aggressive talent scout—to record artists he believed the major labels had neglected.

In early 1954 Hickory scored its first country chart hit, "Good Deal, Lucille," with AL TERRY. The label remained fairly active during the 1960s but tapered off in the '70s, when its product was distributed for a time by the larger ABC organization. Hickory was virtually defunct by the time the GAYLORD ENTERTAINMENT COMPANY bought the Acuff-Rose publishing and recording properties in 1985 and merged Acuff-Rose into the Opryland Music Group. Other Hickory or ABC-Hickory artists, noted here with years of chart activity, include Rusty & Doug (see DOUG KERSHAW)

(1955–61), WILMA LEE & STONEY COOPER (1956–61), ERNIE ASHWORTH (1960–70), Roy Acuff (1958–59, 1965, 1974), DON GIBSON (1969–79), Don Everly of THE EVERLY BROTHERS (1976–77), and MICKEY NEWBURY (1977–80). —*John W. Rumble*

## HighTone Records
established 1983

Founded by record industry veterans Bruce Bromberg and Larry Sloven, the Oakland, California–based independent label HighTone Records took its name from the HANK WILLIAMS song "Mind Your Own Business," which includes the line "Mindin' other people's business seems to be hightone." The company first made its mark with Seattle bluesman Robert Cray. In 1987, after selling Cray's contract to PolyGram, Bromberg and Sloven ventured into country music with releases by AUSTIN-based singer-songwriter JOE ELY and BAKERSFIELD-based Bobby Durham.

Despite modest country radio exposure, HighTone released albums by JIMMIE DALE GILMORE, GARY STEWART, ROSIE FLORES, DALE WATSON, BUDDY MILLER, and MARTY BROWN. *Tulare Dust: A Songwriters' Tribute to Merle Haggard* (1994) featured IRIS DEMENT, DWIGHT YOAKAM, LUCINDA WILLIAMS, and others performing Haggard compositions.

"We've tried to make records that have something to say in a unique and compelling way," Bromberg told one writer, and his catalog suggests the company frequently succeeded. The 2006 five-CD set *American Music: The HighTone Records Story*, included many of the label's most significant recordings. HighTone closed in 2008 and sold its extensive catalog to Shout! Factory, which has released various reissues and compilations. —*Jay Orr*

## Highway 101
Paulette Carlson b. Northfield, Minnesota, October 11, 1953
Scott "Cactus" Moser b. Montrose, Colorado, May 3, 1957
Curtis Stone b. North Hollywood, California, April 3, 1950
Jack Daniels b. Choctaw, Oklahoma, October 27, 1949
Nikki Nelson b. San Diego, California, January 3, 1969

In the late 1980s, Highway 101 brought to country music a distinctive contemporary sound and style that blended California with Nashville and showcased the husky vocals of lead singer Paulette Carlson. Carlson played in country bar bands in Minnesota before moving to Nashville in 1978. There she wrote songs for the OAK RIDGE BOYS' publishing companies (Silverline/Goldline) and sang backup for GAIL DAVIES. After an unproductive stint as an RCA artist (1983–84), Carlson left Nashville.

However, NITTY GRITTY DIRT BAND manager Chuck Morris soon built Highway 101 around her, enlisting California COUNTRY-ROCK musicians Cactus Moser (drums, vocals), Curtis Stone (bass, vocals), and guitarist Jack Daniels. (Stone's father was West Coast country kingpin CLIFFIE STONE.) The band's casual-flash look combined a roots-music feel with show-business sensibilities. Carlson wore prairie skirts, boots, buckskin, and hats; the men, western shirts, embroidered jackets, and jeans. The act's WARNER BROS. debut single, "The Bed You Made for Me" (written by Carlson), reached #4 in 1987. Nine straight Top Tens followed during 1987–90, among them "Whiskey, If You Were a Woman" and "Somewhere Tonight," the first of four #1 hits. Highway 101 became CMA Vocal Group of the Year in 1988 and 1989.

Carlson left the band in 1991. She gave birth to a daughter and pursued a solo career, coproducing a highly personal album, *Love Goes On*, for which she penned seven of its ten songs.

Nikki Nelson was recruited to Highway 101 to replace Carlson. "Bing Bang Boom" and several minor hits ensued, but Daniels also left the act. After switching to LIBERTY, Highway 101 released the 1993 album *New Frontier*. In 1996 Carlson, Stone, and Daniels returned for *Reunited*, an Intersound/Willow Tree Records project. Curtis Stone and Cactus Moser later re-formed Highway 101 with vocalist Chrislynn Lee and guitarist Charlie White and recorded *Big Sky* for FreeFalls Entertainment in 2000. Various personnel changes ensued—including Nelson's return as lead vocalist in 2006—and the group has remained active. —*Mary A. Bufwack*

## The Highwaymen (*see* separate entries for Johnny Cash, Waylon Jennings, Kris Kristofferson, and Willie Nelson)

## Eddie Hill
b. Delano, Tennessee, July 21, 1921; d. January 18, 1994

Singer, songwriter, musician, television host, and DJ, Smilin' Eddie Hill was a jack-of-all-trades who performed with JOHNNIE & JACK and THE LOUVIN BROTHERS; for many years he was a mainstay as a radio announcer at WSM–Nashville, and hosting the station's all-night show helped him win numerous DJ polls. In 1975 he and GRANT TURNER were the first living inductees into the Country Disc Jockey Hall of Fame.

At an early age, James Edward Hill was inspired by his banjo-picking granddad and fiddling father. At seventeen Hill won a talent contest in Chattanooga, leading to his first major radio stint: WROL–Knoxville. Switching to WNOX, he performed on the popular MID-DAY MERRY-GO-ROUND with Buster Moore and Claude Boone before moving to WKRC–Cincinnati.

In 1943 he teamed with Johnnie Wright after Wright's partner, Jack Anglin, was drafted into the army. When Anglin mustered out in 1946, the trio worked briefly together at WPTF–Raleigh. Hill next moved to WMPS–Memphis, hooking up with a new duo, the Louvin Brothers.

Hill shared a session in 1947 with Johnnie & Jack at Apollo Records, a New York R&B label. He also recorded for MERCURY, DECCA, and RCA VICTOR, with minimal impact. During a March 1950 RCA session, however, he and bass player ERNIE NEWTON hit on a Latin rhythm for "Poison Love" that helped launch Johnnie & Jack to stardom. Hill's guitar and baritone enhanced other Johnnie & Jack sessions. He also sang trios with them on the GRAND OLE OPRY and played rhythm guitar on numerous Decca sessions for KITTY WELLS. His song "Someday You'll Call My Name" was a Top Ten single for JIMMY WAKELY (1949). From the mid-1950s, Hill served as a popular host on WLAC-TV in Nashville. In 1968 he suffered a stroke that left him partially paralyzed. Health problems sidelined him until his death, in 1994. —*Walt Trott*

## Faith Hill
b. Ridgeland, Mississippi, September 21, 1967

Faith Hill (born Audrey Faith Perry) has blended covergirl glamour with an earthy, friendly, girl-next-door appeal and a

*Faith Hill*

soulful voice to become one of the music industry's biggest country-pop stars. As of July 2011 she had achieved twenty-two Top Ten singles (including nine #1s), and three of her albums (*Breathe, Cry,* and *Fireflies*) have been #1 on the *Billboard* country and all-genre charts simultaneously. She also has won five Grammy Awards, three CMA awards, and twelve ACM awards, and she has starred in several of her own network TV specials.

Adopted less than one week after her birth, Hill grew up in the tiny community of Star, Mississippi. She made her first public appearance singing in church at age three. Moving to Nashville at nineteen in 1987, she landed a job selling T-shirts at Fan Fair (now called the CMA MUSIC FESTIVAL). A stint as receptionist for GARY MORRIS's music publishing company followed, leading to work as a demo singer. Top tunesmith Gary Burr fell in love with Hill's voice and asked her to sing with him during a performance at the BLUEBIRD CAFÉ. She was signed to WARNER BROS. RECORDS almost immediately.

She wasted no time establishing herself. Her 1993 introductory single, "Wild One," stayed #1 on the *Billboard* country singles chart for four weeks and propelled her debut album, *Take Me As I Am*, to selling more than 3 million units. Hill's follow-up singles, "Piece of My Heart" and "Take Me As I Am," also reached #1 and #2 on the charts, respectively.

Nonstop touring as an opening act for REBA MCENTIRE and BROOKS & DUNN took a toll on her voice, and she underwent vocal cord treatment in 1995. She recovered to release her second album, *It Matters to Me*, later that year. It did even better than her debut, selling more than 4 million copies and putting five singles in the country Top Ten.

In 1996, while on tour with fellow star TIM MCGRAW, the two became involved romantically; they married on October 6 of that year. In 1997 the husband-wife team recorded the chart-topping

"It's Your Love" for CURB RECORDS (then McGraw's label), thereby earning CMA's Vocal Event of the Year award.

Her third album, *Faith,* appeared in 1998. The single "This Kiss," a #1 country hit, also became her first Top Ten pop hit, fueling album sales that eventually exceeded 6 million. *Breathe,* her 1999 release, fared even better, with four Top Ten country singles (the #1s "Breathe" and "The Way You Love Me" also were Top Ten pop hits) and eventual sales of more than 8 million. At that time, Hill was one of America's biggest musical stars of any genre.

Her next album, 2002's *Cry,* was aimed even more aggressively at pop success. But country radio pulled back, and the album's highest-charting single, the title cut "Cry," stalled at #12 on the country charts while barely breaking the pop Top Forty. No other singles got higher than #26 on the country charts, and Hill's album sales, while still topping 2 million, dimmed, compared to her previous two efforts.

Hill took time off before returning with the decidedly back-to-her-roots album *Fireflies.* Country radio welcomed her back, making the album's first single, 2005's "Mississippi Girl," her first #1 hit in more than four years. Three more singles—"Like We Never Loved at All," "The Lucky One," and "Sunshine and Summertime"—also climbed into the country Top Ten, and album sales topped 2 million units. Hill released the career compilation *The Hits* in 2007 and a Christmas album, *Joy to the World,* in 2008. She's also branched out beyond country music, costarring in the 2004 film *The Stepford Wives* alongside Nicole Kidman and Bette Midler. In 2007 Hill started singing the opening theme for each episode of NBC's *Sunday Night Football,* a position she still held as of the 2011 season. She also launched her own line of fragrances, Faith Hill Parfums, in 2009. —*Janet E. Williams*

## Goldie Hill
b. Coy City, Karnes County, Texas, January 11, 1933; d. February 24, 2005

Known as "The Golden Hillbilly," Argolda Voncile "Goldie" Hill was country music's glamour girl of the 1950s and a popular DECCA recording artist.

The baby sister of musical brothers who practically raised her in San Antonio's hillbilly venues, "Golda" Hill began singing in her teens, and with brother TOMMY HILL she joined WEBB PIERCE's band at Shreveport's LOUISIANA HAYRIDE in about April 1952. On a Pierce recording trip to Nashville in July 1952, Goldie auditioned for Decca's PAUL COHEN and signed a contract on the spot, cutting "Why Talk to My Heart" (an answer to RAY PRICE's "Talk to Your Heart") and three other songs. Answer songs would always be her forte—"I Let the Stars Get in My Eyes" (1952), "I'm Yvonne" (1953), and "I'm Yesterday's Girl" (1953) were among her musical ripostes.

At about this same time, Hill moved to Nashville, where she worked the GRAND OLE OPRY and costarred briefly in a radio series, *Country Tune Parade,* with ERNEST TUBB (1954). In 1954–55 she recorded two popular duets with JUSTIN TUBB, "Looking Back to See" and "Sure Fire Kisses," and one with RED SOVINE, "Are You Mine."

Hill joined the traveling PHILIP MORRIS COUNTRY MUSIC SHOW at the beginning of 1957 but left the show to marry its star, CARL SMITH, on September 19 of that year. She did no further touring, staying home to raise three children on their Tennessee farm, although she recorded for Decca until 1964 and, briefly, for EPIC after that. Hill died of cancer in 2005. —*Ronnie Pugh*

## Tommy Hill
b. near Coy City, Texas, April 27, 1929; d. March 21, 2002

John Thomas Hill was the consummate journeyman in the country music industry. He was a songwriter, featured artist, session musician, engineer, record label owner, and A&R man. He played on and produced hundreds of sessions and wrote hundreds of songs, two of them classics: "Slowly" and "Teddy Bear."

Hill grew up near JIMMIE RODGERS's Blue Yodeler's Paradise in Kerrville, Texas, and it was Rodgers who inspired him to enter the music business. Hill worked with BIG BILL LISTER around San Antonio, and then Hill and his brother Ken joined SMILEY BURNETTE in California. Returning to Texas, Tommy joined WEBB PIERCE's band in Shreveport and showed him "Slowly"; Pierce's recording of it spent seventeen weeks at #1 in 1954. Hill also wrote "I Let the Stars Get in My Eyes" for his sister, GOLDIE HILL. Eventually moving to Nashville, Tommy worked as a front man for JIM REEVES and as a featured act on the PHILIP MORRIS COUNTRY MUSIC SHOW, but he couldn't get a solo recording career off the ground. In October 1959, after cutting a single for STARDAY RECORDS, Hill joined Don Pierce's maverick enterprise and later built a studio for him, which opened in 1960. Hill stayed until Starday was sold in 1968 and then joined a short-lived MGM subsidiary, Blue Valley Records. With PETE DRAKE, he then formed Stop Records, one of the more successful Nashville independents.

Hill took some of the Stop assets and started Gusto Records in 1972. He brought in Moe Lytle as a partner two years later, and Lytle later bought Starday-KING RECORDS. Hill continued to produce for Starday and penned the label's biggest hit, RED SOVINE's "Teddy Bear" (#1, 1976). After selling his interest in the company, Hill continued to work for Gusto until 1982. He retained the old Starday Studio and later worked on King and Starday tape restoration for Gusto until his death. —*Colin Escott*

## Hill and Range Songs, Inc.
established in New York, New York, December 9, 1944; sold to Chappell & Co., 1975

Between 1945 and 1955, a single corporation and its many affiliated companies published a large proportion of that decade's new country hits—Hill and Range Songs, Inc., the empire of the brothers Aberbach.

Joachim Jean Aberbach (known as "Jean," b. Vienna, Austria, August 12, 1910; d. May 24, 1992) and brother Julian J. (b. Vienna, Austria, February 8, 1909; d. May 17, 2002) had worked for various Berlin and Paris publishing offices before Jean moved to New York City in 1936 and joined the music publishing firm of Chappell & Co. Julian followed his brother to New York three years later. They found the field of hillbilly publishing relatively wide open, and eventually they bought out the remaining 50 percent share of Biltmore Music, a company they had co-owned with a Chicago transcription firm. By 1945 they had renamed the company Hill and Range Songs, Inc., with Julian running the company's offices from Hollywood. Jean remained with Chappell Music until 1948, when he was fired for not bringing his employer the Hill and Range copyright "Bouquet of Roses," a massive 1948 crossover hit for EDDY ARNOLD. Thereafter, both brothers focused on growing the Hill and Range enterprise.

Operating mostly with advance monies from BMI for their first two big hits, "Shame on You" and "Detour," they adopted an astoundingly successful strategy—luring singing stars into their fold with generous bonuses and advances and setting up subsidiary companies. Stars would co-own their respective companies with Hill and Range, which managed these firms. One by one many major country singers fell into line—BOB WILLS, ERNEST TUBB, EDDY ARNOLD, RED FOLEY, and, later, LEFTY FRIZZELL, HANK SNOW, LEON PAYNE, and JOHNNY CASH. Hill and Range employed several talented staff writers as well, such as Cy Coben, Jack Rollins, Steve and Ed Nelson, and Ben Weisman.

Not surprisingly, the list of Hill and Range hits became massive and includes (besides "Bouquet of Roses") "Candy Kisses," "Letters Have No Arms," "Faded Love," "I'm Moving On," "There Stands the Glass," "I Really Don't Want to Know," "Mexican Joe," "These Hands," and "I Walk the Line," to name a select few. The Aberbachs further enlarged their country catalog by buying older companies, but the brothers never limited themselves to country music, particularly after they established offices in New York City's Brill Building in 1953. From the thirty-plus publishers in the Aberbach Group came gospel classics ("Peace in the Valley"), pop standards ("Spanish Harlem"), and kiddie favorites ("Frosty the Snow Man," "Peter Cottontail," "Suzy Snowflake"). Signing ELVIS PRESLEY in 1955 was the brothers' biggest coup. In exchange for an unspecified amount of cash and services, which helped convince RCA RECORDS to buy Presley's SUN RECORDS contract, Hill and Range took control of his publishing; thereafter, most of what Presley recorded came from Hill and Range demos.

Demands of Presley's career and the growth of Nashville-based publishers cut into Hill and Range's country dominance after the 1950s. In 1975 the brothers sold their company to Chappell, Jean's early employer, though they retained a 25 percent share. —*Ronnie Pugh*

## The Hill Billies

Albert Green Hopkins b. Gap Creek, North Carolina, June 5, 1889; d. October 21, 1932
Alonzo Elvis "Tony" Alderman b. River Hill, Virginia, September 10, 1900; d. October 25, 1983
John Rector birthplace and birth date unknown; d. August 28, 1985
Joe Hopkins birthplace, birth date, and death date unknown
later: Charlie Bowman b. Gray Station, Tennessee, July 30, 1889; d. May 20, 1962

The first band to use the name Hill Billies on phonograph records—thereby contributing to the rapid acceptance of the term for the new commercial genre—was organized at GALAX, VIRGINIA, in the spring of 1924. The act made its first successful recordings in January 1925, in New York, for the OKEH label. After the group recorded six selections, A&R man RALPH PEER asked the quartet their name, and bandleader Al Hopkins replied, "We're nothing but a bunch of hillbillies from North Carolina and Virginia. Call us anything." Peer at once dubbed them the Hill Billies—an appellation not all band members felt comfortable with initially, because of the frequent pejorative connotation the term had. The act left OKeh later in 1925 to record for the jointly owned BRUNSWICK and Vocalion labels, using simultaneously the names Hill Billies and Buckle Busters. The band's repertoire consisted largely of OLD-TIME fiddle tunes (often played on twin fiddles by Tony Alderman and Charlie Bowman), with relatively little jazz and blues influence. Although Al Hopkins's piano playing was not unique in country music at that time, it was certainly not common, and it contributed to the group's distinctive sound, which was fleshed out by the banjo of John Rector and the guitar of Joe Hopkins. In addition to their recordings, the ensemble appeared frequently at fiddle conventions and county fairs and on radio. The band's promising career was abruptly terminated when

Al Hopkins, their able leader and promoter, died in an automobile accident. —*Norm Cohen*

## Donna Hilley
b. Birmingham, Alabama, June 30, 1946

A top executive with Sony/ATV Tree, a leading country publisher, Donna Hilley was one of the most successful and prominent women in the country music industry for more than thirty years. In addition to guiding Sony/ATV Tree to its frequent position as *Billboard*'s country music publisher of the year, Hilley expanded the company into such areas as film, television, Broadway, and commercials. She negotiated the company's acquisition of more than sixty songwriting catalogs, including those of CONWAY TWITTY, MERLE HAGGARD, JIM REEVES, and BUCK OWENS. Developing such copyrights as "He Stopped Loving Her Today," "Heartbreak Hotel," and "Crazy" she worked with acts including ROGER MILLER, BROOKS & DUNN, and TRAVIS TRITT. She also served on the boards of CMA, ASCAP, and the Music Publishers Association of the United States.

After moving to Nashville, Hilley accepted a job at radio station WKDA, which was run by JACK STAPP, cofounder of TREE PUBLISHING. After eight years at WKDA, she spent another eight years with a public relations firm before joining Tree in 1973. She was named vice president and COO in 1978, and she negotiated the sale of Tree to CBS (now Sony Music Publishing) in 1989. In 1994 Hilley was named president and chief executive officer of the publishing giant, known as Sony/ATV following Sony Music's creation of a joint venture with ATV Publishing in 1995. Slowed by health issues, she announced her retirement from Sony/ATV in December 2005, handing the reins to Troy Tomlinson on January 1, 2006. —*Beverly Keel*

## Chris Hillman
b. Los Angeles, California, December 4, 1944

Best known as a member of three influential groups—THE BYRDS, the Flying Burrito Brothers, and the DESERT ROSE BAND—Chris Hillman is a pioneer of what has come to be called California COUNTRY-ROCK. He is a singer and songwriter and a musician adept at guitar, bass, and the mandolin, his main instrument.

Hillman attended high school in North San Diego County and was strongly influenced by the music of LEFTY FRIZZELL and BILL MONROE. He met banjoist Kenny Wertz, who introduced him to guitarist-singer and songwriter Larry Murray. As the Scottsville Squirrel Barkers, they cut an album in one frantic, three-hour, early-1960s session. Not long after, Hillman joined the Golden State Boys, a band that included VERN GOSDIN, Rex Gosdin, and banjoist Don Parmley; they changed their name to the Hillmen and recorded one album before breaking up. Their producer, Jim Dickson, was also producing THE BYRDS and hired Hillman as their bass player.

Hillman's best-known compositions for the Byrds were "Time Between" and "So You Want to Be a Rock and Roll Star," the latter cowritten with band member Roger McGuinn. It was Hillman who started the Byrds along the path to country, he says, before CLARENCE WHITE and GRAM PARSONS joined the group. Later, with Parsons, Hillman formed the Flying Burrito Brothers; Hillman played guitar, and he and Parsons cowrote such songs as "Sin City," "Wheels," and "Devil in Disguise (Christine's Tune)."

Subsequent bands that Hillman recorded with included Manassas (with Stephen Stills, ATLANTIC, 1972–73); the Souther, Hillman, Furay Band (with John David Souther and Richie Furay, ASYLUM, 1974–75); and McGuinn, Clark, and Hillman (with Roger McGuinn and Gene Clark, CAPITOL, 1979–80). Hillman also recorded two solo albums for Asylum (*Slippin' Away*, 1976; and *Clear Sailin'*, 1977).

In 1982 Hillman recorded the BLUEGRASS-flavored *Desert Rose* album for SUGAR HILL RECORDS, which led to the formation of the Desert Rose Band and his post–Desert Rose Band solo albums for Sugar Hill. These have included 1996's *Bakersfield Bound* with HERB PEDERSEN, three albums Hillman and Pedersen made with bluegrass buddies Larry Rice and TONY RICE, and the solo album *Like a Hurricane* (1998). Hillman has subsequently recorded for Back Porch, Narada, and Sovereign Artists. He received an AMERICANA Music Association Lifetime Achievement Award in 2004. —*Todd Everett*

## Bruce Hinton

b. Tell City, Indiana, November 17, 1936

After moving from Los Angeles to Nashville in 1984, Bruce Hinton quietly built the administrative foundation for the rise to dominance of MCA's country music division, with an artist roster that would come to include REBA MCENTIRE, VINCE GILL, GEORGE STRAIT, WYNONNA, and GEORGE JONES, among others.

Hinton's first record company job, in 1960, put him in the New York warehouse of WARNER BROS./REPRISE RECORDS. He became national promotion manager for Warner/Reprise before jumping in 1965 to COLUMBIA RECORDS, where he served as western promotion manager and then director of custom label distribution in New York.

In 1967, the soft-spoken Hinton joined JIMMY BOWEN, a former colleague at Warner Bros., in Amos Productions, whose clients included singer–actor KENNY ROGERS, the act First Edition, Kim Carnes, and Mason Williams. Hinton later formed L.A.–based Hinton/Svendsen Promotions, evidently the first national independent promotion company in country music. The million-selling *Urban Cowboy* soundtrack (1980) was among the company's successful projects. TAMMY WYNETTE, CONWAY TWITTY, MICKEY GILLEY, and ANNE MURRAY eventually joined the Hinton/Svendsen client roster.

At the same time, Hinton founded Hin/Jen Productions with producer JIM ED NORMAN. In 1980 Hinton promoted two Norman-produced singles, by Mickey Gilley, which hit the Top Five within the same week of July 1980: "True Love Ways" and "Stand by Me."

Hinton moved to Nashville in 1984 to join Bowen again, this time as senior vice president and general manager at MCA. When Bowen left MCA for CAPITOL Nashville, in 1989, Hinton stepped in as president. Working with TONY BROWN, executive vice president and head of A&R, Hinton trimmed the MCA roster from forty-six to twenty, allowing the label to undertake a more focused approach to marketing, promotion, and publicity for each new release. Hinton assumed the title of chairman in 1993, when Brown became MCA's president. Hinton sustained MCA's status as a first-rate label in the country market until 2002, when LUKE LEWIS became chairman of Nashville operations for Universal Music Group labels MCA, MERCURY, and LOST HIGHWAY. Hinton then assumed the title of Chairman Emeritus. —*Jay Orr*

## John Hobbs

b. Long Beach, California, May 9, 1950

Though he came up through the L.A. studio system, keyboardist John Nolan Hobbs emerged as a major player in Nashville, contributing to classic country recordings, writing hit songs, and producing top-shelf stars. Through guitarist Larry Carlton, Hobbs in 1969 met KENNY ROGERS and joined his group, the First Edition. Hobbs widened his studio contacts, including influential producer JIMMY BOWEN, while working on records and TV and film scoring.

From 1984–95 Hobbs served as musical director for the annual ACM Awards, and he has won ten ACM trophies as top keyboardist. In 1984 he began commuting to Nashville, often to work with Bowen, and he moved there in 1994. Among his many country credits are GEORGE STRAIT's "Does Fort Worth Ever Cross Your Mind" (1984), REBA MCENTIRE's "Whoever's in New England" (1986), DEANA CARTER's "Strawberry Wine" (1996), SHANIA TWAIN's "You're Still the One" (1998), and KENNY CHESNEY's many hits.

In addition to cowriting hit songs for COLLIN RAYE and VINCE GILL, Hobbs produced recordings for Raye, and he won a 2007 Grammy for coproducing Gill's *These Days*. Gill's band leader since 2000, Hobbs also appears frequently with an all-star musicians' group, the Players. —*Jay Orr*

## Adolph Hofner

b. Moulton, Texas, June 8, 1916; d. June 2, 2000

Of German-Czech heritage and reared in musically, ethnically diverse central Texas, bandleader-vocalist-guitarist Adolph Hofner began his career playing HAWAIIAN MUSIC with brother Emil ("Bash," 1918–2002), a steel guitarist, in San Antonio in the early 1930s. The Hofners were soon converted by the WESTERN SWING of MILTON BROWN & His Musical Brownies. Adolph chose Brown and Bing Crosby as his vocal models, while Bash chose Brown's steel guitarist, BOB DUNN. One of the Hofners' early musical cohorts was future songwriting legend FLOYD TILLMAN.

By 1935 the Hofners had joined with JIMMIE REVARD to form the Oklahoma Playboys, a prolific, popular group that signed with BLUEBIRD in 1936. Adolph was recording as a solo act for Bluebird by April 1938. His first sessions were ad hoc affairs, a mix of swing numbers and Crosbyesque ballads. Adolph also worked with Tom Dickey's Show Boys, with whom he cut a hit version of Tillman's "It Makes No Difference Now" in October 1938. In 1939 Hofner formed his first working band, establishing from the beginning a distinctive split emphasis between swing and Czech music. Hofner had a sizable hit with "Maria Elina" (sic) for Bluebird in 1940, and by 1941 he was recording for OKEH with a band that boasted the influential swing fiddler J. R. Chatwell.

Hofner made California his base of operations at the close of World War II and went by the name of Dolph Hofner because his first name was deemed too close to Hitler's; he returned to San Antonio in 1946. Over the next half century, he became a legendary fixture in central Texas dance halls with his Pearl Wranglers, recording for IMPERIAL, COLUMBIA, and DECCA before beginning a two-decade association with Sarg Records. —*Kevin Coffey*

## Buddy Holly
b. Lubbock, Texas, September 7, 1936; d. February 3, 1959

For all that he accomplished in life, Charles Hardin Holley is chiefly famous for dying. The manner of his death and its untimeliness became a metaphor for the toll of the rock & roll lifestyle, and the timing of his death is often seen as marking the symbolic end of 1950s rock & roll. These views, enshrined in Don McLean's "American Pie," have tended to obscure both Holly's origins in country music and his brief, incendiary career.

Holly and a high-school friend, BOB MONTGOMERY, performed around their hometown of Lubbock, Texas, from about 1950 and broadcast over KDAV from 1953. They were introducing elements of R&B into their work before ELVIS PRESLEY, but it was Presley's influence in particular that galvanized Holly. Working as a solo act, he appeared as a local added attraction on several country package shows, and Eddie Crandall, then MARTY ROBBINS's manager, helped him develop an affiliation with prominent booker and publisher JIM DENNY. Denny placed him with DECCA RECORDS; the first session was held in January 1956. Holly was one of many ROCKABILLY acts sucked in and spat out by Decca during this period, and, after two releases, he was dropped.

Holly had more success with Norman Petty, who ran a maverick studio–music publishing operation in Clovis, New Mexico. A successful lounge act, Petty nevertheless saw the uniqueness in Holly and started recording him in February 1957. The first record, "That'll Be the Day," was offered around as recorded by "the Crickets" to sidestep the fact that Holly had previously recorded it for Decca, although Petty and music publisher Murray Deutch eventually placed the Crickets on Decca's BRUNSWICK

subsidiary and placed Holly (renamed from Holley) on Decca's Coral subsidiary as a solo act.

The records that Holly made for Coral/Brunswick were among the most innovative from rock & roll's formative years. He soon got out from under his debt to Presley and was a triple threat, in that he wrote the songs, sang them, and played lead guitar. "That'll Be the Day" went to #1 on the pop charts. There were seven more hits before Holly died; they ran the gamut from ballads such as "True Love Ways" to flat-out rockers such as "Oh, Boy!" Holly was, in many respects, the most accomplished all-around performer in early rock & roll.

In August 1958 he married Maria Elena Santiago and moved to New York. In that year he split with Petty and the Crickets. His career was on a downswing when he agreed to go on the Winter Dance Party Tour and subsequently lost his life in an airplane crash near Mason City, Iowa. Also killed were singers Ritchie Valens and THE BIG BOPPER, who, at the last minute, took the seat on the plane given up by Holly's bass player on this tour, WAYLON JENNINGS. —*Colin Escott*

## *Hollywood Barn Dance* Radio Program
established in Los Angeles, California, ca. 1932
CBS West Coast Network broadcast began December 4, 1943; network
    broadcast ended 1948

One of the earliest regularly scheduled live remote broadcasts of hillbilly and folk programming (as opposed to studio-originated shows), the *Hollywood Barn Dance* was a weekly outlet for western and country performers on the West Coast. Originally broadcast from a dance hall at the corner of Hollywood Boulevard and Orange Avenue (near Grauman's Chinese Theatre), the program, with its live audience, was a model for postwar shows such as CLIFFIE STONE's *HOMETOWN JAMBOREE* and Bill Wagnon's *TOWN HALL PARTY* (both of which graduated from radio to television).

Featuring the likes of EDDIE DEAN and JIMMY WAKELY, the *Barn Dance* had relocated to CBS's Fairfax Avenue studio by December 4, 1943, and moved to Santa Monica's Western Palisades Ballroom in January 1946. From these two locations folksy broadcaster Cottonseed Clark (Clark Fulks) and FOY WILLING (with his group, Riders of the Purple Sage) hosted the show, fed via station KNX to CBS's West Coast Network. Other regulars included Johnny Bond (as comedian) and singers Sally Foster, CAROLINA COTTON, and Kirby Grant. Frequent name guests included Bob Hope and ROY ROGERS.

Though important as a Tinsel Town focal point for country music and showcase for up-and-coming talent, the *Barn Dance*—faced with intense competition from *Hometown Jamboree* and *Town Hall Party*—was unable to make the switch to the small screen. —*Jonny Whiteside*

## Homer & Jethro
Henry Doyle "Homer" Haynes b. Knoxville, Tennessee, July 27, 1920; d. August
    7, 1971
Kenneth C. "Jethro" Burns b. Conasauga, Tennessee, March 10, 1920; d.
    February 4, 1989

*Buddy Holly*

Famous for their song satires, dry comic delivery, and instrumental virtuosity, Homer & Jethro became one of country music's most successful comedy acts. The team leaped beyond

*Homer & Jethro*

That Hound Dog in the Window" was an enormous hit, rising to #2 on *Billboard*'s country charts. Their most successful record was "The Battle of Kookamonga," which transformed JIMMIE DRIFTWOOD's saga of the Battle of New Orleans into a rowdy story about Boy Scouts raiding a nearby Girl Scout camp. The hit landed on both country and pop charts, and it won a 1959 Grammy in the Best Comedy Performance, Musical category.

Following the success of their classic 1960 live album *Homer & Jethro at the Country Club*, the team largely abandoned single releases to concentrate on albums. Their professional profile soared as on-air spokesmen for two highly successful Kellogg's Corn Flakes ad campaigns and as frequent guests on network TV variety shows.

When Haynes died suddenly while preparing for an August 1971 fair date, Burns's career took a different turn. Gifted young BLUEGRASS mandolinists sought him out for ideas, techniques, and inspiration, and Burns began playing folk clubs and festivals as a jazz instrumentalist. He briefly revived his comedy act with multi-instrumentalist Ken Eidson and then toured for five years with Chicago singer-songwriter Steve Goodman. Despite a lengthy battle with prostate cancer, Burns continued to perform until his death. Homer & Jethro were elected to THE COUNTRY MUSIC HALL OF FAME in 2001. —*Dave Samuelson*

conventional country venues of rural schoolhouses, TENT SHOWS, county fairs, and PACKAGE SHOWS to high-visibility bookings on network television variety shows and in Las Vegas showrooms and swank urban nightclubs.

Guitarist Henry "Junior" Haynes and mandolinist Kenneth "Dude" Burns joined forces in 1936, when radio impresario Lowell Blanchard pulled the youngsters from two separate bands auditioning for his MID-DAY MERRY-GO-ROUND on WNOX–Knoxville. As members of the String Dusters, Haynes and Burns handled country tunes, hoedowns, and contemporary pop tunes with ease. For comic relief, Junior & Dude satirized the deadly serious close-harmony duets of the era by wailing hillbilly versions of sophisticated pop standards. When Blanchard forgot their nicknames during a 1936 broadcast, he introduced the team as Homer & Jethro, and the amused teenagers quickly adopted the names.

The String Dusters disbanded in 1938, but Haynes and Burns continued as a duet, eventually joining the RENFRO VALLEY BARN DANCE. After serving in World War II, they resumed their act with a Saturday morning show on WLW–Cincinnati. Their musicianship impressed KING RECORDS owner SYD NATHAN, who recruited them for the label's house band in early 1946. Initially playing on numerous sessions for others, Homer & Jethro soon recorded a hillbilly version of Frank Sinatra's chart-topping "Five Minutes More" for King. The record's regional success prompted similar releases.

Veteran producer STEVE SHOLES signed the team to RCA VICTOR in spring 1949. Recognizing the limited potential of their act, Sholes encouraged them to write song parodies. Their first two attempts—"Baby, It's Cold Outside" and "Tennessee Border No. 2"—became best-sellers.

In 1950 Haynes and Burns joined WLS in Chicago; they frequently appeared on the NATIONAL BARN DANCE and Don McNeill's *The Breakfast Club*. Their 1953 parody "(How Much Is)

## Hometown Jamboree
established in El Monte, California, December 18, 1949; ended September 12, 1959

*Hometown Jamboree* was a popular TV variety show in Southern California that was broadcast from the American Legion Stadium, 11151 Valley Boulevard, El Monte, California. It was produced by CLIFFIE STONE, in association with promoter STEVE STEBBINS, under the umbrella of their newly formed AMERICANA Corporation.

In effect, the program was a continuation of Stone's *Dinner Bell Roundup* radio show, which was heard in the mid- to late-1940s over station KXLA in Pasadena. *Dinner Bell Roundup* featured a cast of West Coast performers, including MERLE TRAVIS, BILLY LIEBERT, TENNESSEE ERNIE FORD, Eddie Kirk, WESLEY TUTTLE, Harold Hensley, Herman the Hermit (Cliffie Stone's father, comedian Herman Snyder), Judy Hayden, and Tex Atchison.

In 1949 Cliffie Stone took most of the *Dinner Bell Roundup* cast to inaugurate *Hometown Jamboree*, which was televised over KLAC-TV (now KCOP-TV) in Los Angeles each Saturday night, from 7 p.m. to 8 p.m. A dance followed from 9 p.m. until 1 a.m., with the portion from 10 p.m. to 11 p.m. broadcast locally over KXLA. In 1953 the TV broadcast moved to KTLA-TV.

To augment the cast for *Hometown Jamboree*, Stone added several new members—vocalists Molly Bee, Bucky Tibbs, FERLIN HUSKY, Gene O'Quin, DALLAS FRAZIER, Jonie O'Brien, Harry Rodcay, and Jonell & Glennell McQuaid. Staff musicians included, at various times, pianists Les Taylor, Vic Davis, and MERRILL MOORE; drummers Johnny Powers and Roy Harte; guitarists Billy Strange, "Talkin'" Charlie Aldrich, and Jimmy Bryant; Bryant's frequent recording partner, steel guitarist SPEEDY WEST; and bassist Al Williams. EDDY ARNOLD, LEFTY FRIZZELL, JOHNNY HORTON, JIM REEVES, BOB WILLS, and THE EVERLY BROTHERS appeared as guest artists, as did GRANDPA JONES, the MADDOX BROTHERS & ROSE, PEE WEE KING, PATSY MONTANA, RED FOLEY, and T. TEXAS TYLER.

In 1954 the *Jamboree* moved for one year to the Valley Gardens Arena in Sun Valley, California, before returning to El Monte.

In 1957 the show moved to the Valley Garden Arena in North Hollywood and finally to KTLA's studios before signing off for the last time on September 12, 1959. —*Ken Griffis*

## Honky-Tonk Music

"Honky-tonk" is a term that is now used to describe a style of country music whose beat, rhythm, and mood evoke the ambience and flavor of the working-class beer and dancing clubs where the style was born. Neither the origin nor the precise meaning of the term has been sufficiently determined, although singer and folklorist Oscar Brand has speculated that it may have referred to clubs where Tonk pianos were used (a brand made and merchandised in the late nineteenth century by a New York firm, William Tonk and Sons). The term was being used to describe black dives by the 1890s but does not seem to have been widely applied to white clubs until the 1930s.

A similar imprecision clouds our understanding of exactly what a honky-tonk is, because the name has been applied to giant dance halls such as Billy Bob's in Fort Worth, the now-defunct GILLEY's club in Pasadena, Texas, and even Gilley's Dallas as well as to small clubs that scarcely have room for a dance floor. Today's large institutions typically have numerous pinball machines, pool tables, mechanical bulls, and other diversions (Billy Bob's even has a small rodeo arena), while little clubs might have only a bar, a few tables, and a JUKEBOX.

Whatever the size or style of the club, the linkage between the honky-tonk and country music appears to have begun in Texas in the years immediately following the repeal of prohibition. Country musicians began playing in the numerous beer joints that opened up in "wet" counties in the state, particularly in the rough oil field towns of East Texas, where money was available to Depression-starved patrons. One veteran of the East Texas dance hall scene, AL DEXTER, recorded in 1936 the first song in country music to bear "honky-tonk" in its title: "Honky Tonk Blues" (not the one later recorded by HANK WILLIAMS). Rowdy honky-tonks encouraged louder music, the electrification of instruments, strong dance beats, and lyrics that reflected honky-tonk life itself and the changing lives of country people. In this social milieu, where musicians adapted to new conditions and not-always-receptive audiences, country music lost much of the rustic or pastoral tone that had defined it during its early commercial existence. In 1943 Al Dexter evoked the rough environment from which honky-tonk music emerged in his wartime hit "Pistol Packin' Mama," a song inspired by an incident he had observed in an East Texas dance hall during the mid-1930s. Honky-tonks were not always dangerous, but enough violence occurred in them, or immediately outside their walls, that many musicians recalled them as "skull orchards."

By World War II the honky-tonk had become an escapist haven for many transplanted rural southerners, whose lives were being transformed by the new experiences of city life and industrial labor and who sought emotional release and camaraderie through drinking and dancing (and sometimes fighting). They also sought a musical style that would preserve their older values and social relationships while addressing the newer realities that were altering their lives. Although "honky-tonking" became a Saturday night diversion for working people throughout the South and was a pastime often enjoyed by wives as well as husbands, the honky-tonk was essentially a masculine retreat—a respite from the pressures of work and the responsibilities of home or simply a place to aggressively assert one's manhood. The woman who went there alone generally was not respected, even if her affections were desired. Women, however, were central preoccupations of honky-tonk song lyrics, either as "honky-tonk angels" or as the persons whose attentions were being sought or lost.

Honky-tonk songs have dealt with virtually every theme or issue found in country music, although religion, if treated at all, generally serves as an explanation or antidote for guilt. Rollicking or happy-go-lucky songs have abounded in the honky-tonk tradition and are often used as nothing more than backdrops for dancing. Honky-tonk numbers have spoken often about drinking, cheating, marital instability, and divorce, but such lyrics are not uniformly somber, as songs such as "Divorce Me C.O.D." and "If You've Got the Money, I've Got the Time" attest. Nevertheless, the "cry in your beer" theme has been a powerful ingredient of this repertory, and although observers might differ about the effects of such material—whether it is psychologically damaging or merely cathartic—emotionally wrenching items such as GEORGE JONES's "The Grand Tour" and GARY STEWART's "Drinking Thing" probably come closer than any other kind of songs to embodying the essence of honky-tonk music.

Honky-tonk vocal and instrumental styles have also varied widely. Worlds of difference, for example, separate the laid-back, understated vocal of Leon Seago's 1940 version of "Born to Lose" (performed with TED DAFFAN's Texans), the tenor wail of WEBB PIERCE's 1953 recording of "There Stands the Glass," and the soaring passion conveyed by GENE WATSON's 1979 rendition of "Farewell Party." The singers who popularized styles heard most often today on honky-tonk recordings—LEFTY FRIZZELL, ERNEST TUBB, Hank Williams, and George Jones—also projected dissimilar sounds, although each could interpret the message of a song in a very personal way.

Honky-tonk's instrumental sounds have also changed dramatically since the late 1930s, when Ernest Tubb, one of the genre's founding fathers, was performing with only an acoustic rhythm guitar. The adoption of drums, the introduction of the bass guitar, the development of the PEDAL STEEL GUITAR (first widely heard on Webb Pierce's recordings in the early 1950s), and the embracing of electrical amplification all resulted in the full-bodied ensemble sound that now defines honky-tonk instrumentation. Many musicians contributed to honky-tonk's evolution, but RAY PRICE's Cherokee Cowboys made crucial and enduring innovations in the 1950s with their heavily bowed fiddles, walking bass lines, and shuffle dance beat, while the sidemen associated with BUCK OWENS, WYNN STEWART, MERLE HAGGARD, and other California stylists popularized an even more aggressive electric sound in the 1960s, combining the beat and themes of honky-tonk with the energy of ROCKABILLY.

The honky-tonk sound still appears in the music of such entertainers as ALAN JACKSON, DAVID BALL, TOBY KEITH, and JAMEY JOHNSON, but it continues to reflect the social and musical contexts in which it exists. Modern honky-tonkers pay homage to and draw inspiration from veterans of the genre, but they also borrow ideas from jazz, rock, blues, and other styles that continue to win currency in modern America. This ability to be simultaneously eclectic and distinctive suggests that honky-tonk music is an organic reflection of a similarly dichotomous working-class culture, while its lyrics about everyday problems and dreams indicate that it honestly represents the changing lives of working people more than any other form of country music. —*Bill C. Malone*

## Hoosier Hot Shots

Frank Delaney Kettering b. Monmouth, Illinois, January 1, 1909; d. June 1973
Kenny "Rudy" Trietsch b. Arcadia, Indiana, September 13, 1903;
    d. September 17, 1987
Paul "Hezzie" Trietsch b. Arcadia, Indiana, April 11, 1905; d. April 27, 1980
Charles Otto "Gabe" Ward b. Knightstown, Indiana, November 26, 1904;
    d. January 14, 1992

The Hoosier Hot Shots' specialty was comic novelty songs—"I Like Bananas (Because They Have No Bones)," "From the Indies to the Andes in His Undies," and "When There's Tears in the Eyes of a Potato"—accompanied by a conglomeration of unorthodox instruments, such as the washboard and the tin whistle. They made their name on the WLS NATIONAL BARN DANCE, after joining in 1933.

Prior to their affiliation with WLS, the nucleus of the group, Kenny Trietsch, his brother Hezzie, and Gabe Ward had spent twelve years on the vaudeville circuit and two years in radio at WOWO in Fort Wayne, Indiana. Much of their repertoire appeared on records, of which they made more than a hundred for the AMERICAN RECORD CORPORATION, Vocalion, OKEH, and DECCA. The band reached the record charts with "She Broke My Heart in Three Places" (#3 country, #21 pop, 1944), "Someday (You'll Want Me to Want You)" (#3 country, #12 pop, 1946), and "Sioux City Sue" (#2 country, 1946). Onstage, on disc, and on the air, the Hot Shots introduced most of their numbers with the question "Are you ready, Hezzie?" The question became part of American vernacular speech during the 1930s and 1940s.

The band—including Gil Taylor, the replacement for Frank Kettering, who left the group in 1944—departed WLS and the National Barn Dance in the mid-1940s and settled on the West Coast, where they appeared in more than twenty movies and worked the Nevada nightclub circuit. With some personnel changes (Nate Harrison and Gil Hartman on bass and Keith Milheim on drums), the group continued to record, making an LP for DOT in 1963 and albums for Tops and Golden Tone, also in the 1960s. They went on to play a Fan Fair Reunion Show in June 1975.

Of the original members, Gabe Ward stayed active the longest, touring in the 1970s as a solo act and in a foursome with Hartman, Emil Staub, and Roy Wade. —Wayne W. Daniel

## Doc Hopkins

B. Harlan County, Kentucky, January 26, 1899; d. January 3, 1988

A fixture on Chicago radio during the 1930s and 1940s, Howard "Doc" Hopkins was a smooth-voiced balladeer with a storehouse of traditional material.

Raised on a farm near Mount Vernon, Kentucky, Hopkins learned to play guitar, banjo, and mandolin in his youth. Hopkins served in France with the American Expeditionary Forces during World War I; he also served in the U.S. Marine Corps after the war. Except for a brief tour with a Kentucky MEDICINE SHOW, Hopkins did not perform professionally until 1929, when he formed the Krazy Kats with Mount Vernon natives Karl Davis and Harty Taylor (later of KARL & HARTY). After a year on WHAS–Louisville, the band moved to Chicago to become the core of the CUMBERLAND RIDGE RUNNERS on the WLS NATIONAL BARN DANCE.

Hopkins soon left to pursue a solo career, and he made his first records for Paramount in December 1931. By 1935 he was featured on WJJD's SUPPERTIME FROLIC; he recorded for the AMERICAN RECORD CORPORATION in 1936 and for DECCA in 1941. In 1942 Hopkins returned to WLS, where he had a morning wake-up show in addition to making regular National Barn Dance appearances and numerous radio transcription recordings for M. M. COLE.

Retiring from show business in 1949, Hopkins worked as a machinist, first in Chicago and later in Los Angeles. He returned to Chicago in 1968. During the 1960s and 1970s Hopkins appeared at various folk festivals and also recorded an album for David Wylie's Birch label. —Dave Samuelson

## Hal Horton

b. Montclair, New Jersey, 1893; d. November 28, 1948

Hal Horton, popular Dallas disc jockey and show promoter, first acted onstage with his parents at age ten. He worked as a sideshow barker throughout the nation and entered broadcasting in Davenport, Iowa. From Mexican BORDER RADIO stations Horton came to Dallas in 1936; there an auto dealer sponsored his first hillbilly record programs on WRR.

In the early 1940s Horton launched the KRLD Hillbilly Hit Parade, a 10:30 p.m. program on which he played and ranked records and interviewed country stars. Later he added the Cornbread Matinee and in 1947 announced the Mutual Network's prerecorded Checkerboard Jamboree series, which featured EDDY ARNOLD. Horton cofounded Metro Music, publisher of HANK THOMPSON's earliest songs and Tommy Dilbeck's biggest hits for Arnold.

Horton made two records for Sonora in 1946. Plagued by a heart ailment in the last years of his life, he did his final broadcast from a back porch home studio two weeks before he died. —Ronnie Pugh

## Johnny Horton

b. Los Angeles, California, April 30, 1925; d. November 5, 1960

There were two hallmarks of Johnny Horton's style. The first was his amiability, which, by all accounts, reflected his sanguine nature; the second was his malleability, reflecting the fact that Horton was not a recording artist with a commanding vision of how his music should sound.

Born in Los Angeles to parents who shuttled between East Texas and California, John Gale Horton flirted with several lines of work before he won a talent contest in 1950 and decided to try singing for a living. He entered talent contests in California and was signed to a management contract by FABOR ROBISON, who placed him with Cormac Records in 1951. Cormac folded later that year, and Robison started ABBOTT RECORDS to record Horton. Early in 1952, shortly after his first marriage, to Donna Cook, Horton moved to Shreveport, Louisiana, to become a regular on the LOUISIANA HAYRIDE. In June, Robison sold Horton's recording contract to MERCURY RECORDS.

Horton's Mercury recordings made little impact. After a divorce, his first wife returned to Los Angeles, and on September 26, 1953, he married the widow of HANK WILLIAMS, Billie Jean Jones. Horton and Robison subsequently parted company, and Horton probably quit the music business for a while. Early in 1955, TILLMAN FRANKS began managing him, and Horton reoriented himself toward ROCKABILLY music. He left Mercury

*Johnny Horton*

*Roy Horton*

and signed with COLUMBIA RECORDS in Nashville. At his first Columbia session he recorded the seminal "Honky Tonk Man," a #9 hit of 1956.

For a short period Horton found success with rockabilly, but his career soon went cold again. He rebounded in late 1958 with the pseudo-folky "When It's Springtime in Alaska," a #1 country hit. The follow-up, "The Battle of New Orleans," topped both the country and the pop charts. Subsequent records in a similar vein, such as "Johnny Reb," "Sink the Bismarck," and "Johnny Freedom," all achieved varying degrees of success and gave Horton a reputation for saga songs. His last hit during his lifetime was "North to Alaska," the theme song to a John Wayne movie.

A firm believer in spiritualism, Horton had strong premonitions that he would die young. Paradoxically, he accepted his fate but tried to avoid it. He apparently tried to cancel what became his last show in AUSTIN, TEXAS, on November 4, 1960. While driving back to Shreveport, he was killed in a head-on collision on a bridge near Milano, Texas. —*Colin Escott*

## Roy Horton
b. near Broad Top, Pennsylvania, November 5, 1914; d. September 23, 2003

For some forty years Roy Horton was an important executive with RALPH PEER's music publishing companies. One of eleven children, Horton grew up in the Allegheny Mountains of western Pennsylvania, where he was born near Broad Top. He and older brother Vaughn (George Vaughn Horton, b. Broad Top, Pennsylvania, June 6, 1911; d. February 29, 1988) turned from coal mining, their father's occupation, to making music—first on radio in Pennsylvania and later in New York City, with club work along the East Coast. Roy played bass behind RED RIVER DAVE McEnery at the 1939 New York World's Fair. Roy also backed various artists on a good many New York recording sessions,

some of which were secured for him by Vaughn in his capacity as R&B-specialty producer for New York companies (Continental, National, Majestic, MGM, London, and Varsity, among others).

With three other men plus a female duo called the Beaver Valley Sweethearts, the Hortons formed the Pinetoppers, an act that popularized on Coral Records one of Vaughn's biggest songwriting hits—"Mockin' Bird Hill," in 1951. Vaughn did well with his country songwriting, penning "Hillbilly Fever," "'Til the End of the World," "Address Unknown," and "Sugarfoot Rag." Roy's talents turned toward music publishing.

In the 1940s Roy began his long association with Peer-Southern Music, promoting the classic repertoires of such artists as JIMMIE RODGERS, the CARTER FAMILY, FLOYD TILLMAN, TED DAFFAN, JIMMIE DAVIS, and BILL MONROE. Though headquartered in New York, Horton served the Nashville-based Country Music Association (CMA) and the COUNTRY MUSIC HALL OF FAME AND MUSEUM from their inceptions. As CMA board chairman in March 1967, he participated in the ribbon-cutting for the museum. Roy Horton was elected to THE COUNTRY MUSIC HALL OF FAME in 1982. —*Ronnie Pugh*

## Vaughn Horton (*see* Roy Horton)

## Hot Rize
Peter Wernick b. New York, New York, February 25, 1946
Tim O'Brien b. Wheeling, West Virginia, March 16, 1954
Nick Forster b. Beirut, Lebanon, May 16, 1955
Charles Sawtelle b. Austin, Texas, September 20, 1946; d. March 20, 1999

From its formation in 1978 until its end in 1990, Hot Rize ranked among the most popular acts in BLUEGRASS. Its forte was mixing traditional songs from the pre-1955 era with originals from various band members. The group's name was derived from the special "Hot Rize" ingredient in MARTHA WHITE FLOUR, a long-time sponsor of FLATT & SCRUGGS on the GRAND OLE OPRY.

Based in Colorado, Hot Rize evolved from the interaction of regional Colorado musicians Pete Wernick, Charles Sawtelle, and TIM O'BRIEN. A fourth member, Nick Forster, completed the lineup. Initial engagements were mainly in Colorado, but the band's impressive showmanship soon led to national tours.

Quality original material was a big plus for the group. O'Brien's "Walk the Way the Wind Blows," which was recorded by Hot Rize, was a major hit for KATHY MATTEA in 1986. Even bluegrass patriarch RALPH STANLEY recorded the O'Brien-Forster ballad "Footsteps So Near."

Eagerly anticipated at each Hot Rize performance was the appearance of the band's alter-ego persona, the traditional country band Red Knuckles & the Trailblazers. The latter group mixed genuine respect for country music with a lighthearted spoof to create a thoroughly entertaining package. The Trailblazers consisted of Red Knuckles (O'Brien) on lead vocals and flat-top guitar, Waldo Otto (Wernick) on steel guitar, Wendell Mercantile (Forster) on electric guitar, and Slade (Sawtelle) on electric bass.

Counting Red Knuckles & the Trailblazers recordings, Hot Rize released nine albums, including a French release. Their domestic releases were evenly split between Chicago's Flying Fish label and SUGAR HILL RECORDS. *Untold Stories* and *Take It Home* are fan favorites.

Ironically, in 1990, after Hot Rize disbanded, the group received IBMA's Entertainer of the Year award. The following year, the song "Colleen Malone," from the group's final Sugar Hill album, won IBMA's Song of the Year. Hot Rize ceased performing so that members could pursue individual careers. Wernick conducts music camps for aspiring banjo players and has served as president of IBMA. O'Brien maintains a high profile as an acoustic music/bluegrass personality. Forster hosts the nationally syndicated radio show *E-Town*. Sawtelle died of leukemia in 1999. —*Gary B. Reid*

## Gerry House
b. Independence, Kentucky, March 28, 1948

Gerry House blended a career as one of the nation's top country disc jockeys with an impressive string of hits as a country songwriter. For nearly three decades, House worked the morning shift at WSIX in Nashville, where his humor-filled *The House Foundation* show propelled the station to top ratings and earned him numerous industry awards.

After graduating from Eastern Kentucky University in 1970, House worked for an Ithaca, New York, radio station for one year before moving to a DJ position in Tallahassee, Florida, for one year, and then to a Jacksonville, Florida, station for more than two years. House joined WSIX-AM in 1975 and switched to WSIX-FM in 1981. After a stint with WSM, House jumped to the Los Angeles radio market in 1986 but returned to WSIX after two years. In the early 1990s he hosted two syndicated radio programs, *Saturday Night House Party* and *America's Number Ones*. He also has contributed country programs to BBC Radio 2 and released the MCA comedy albums *Cheater's Telethon* (1990) and *Bull* (1991).

As a songwriter, House had his first cut, "Old Time Lovin'" by the OAK RIDGE BOYS, in 1977. He cowrote such hits as REBA MCENTIRE's "Little Rock," GEORGE STRAIT's "The Big One," and

Pam TILLIS's "The River and the Highway." Frequent collaborators included MARK COLLIE, DON SCHLITZ, and BOB DIPIERO.

Elected to the Country Music Disc Jockey Hall of Fame in 2009, House retired in December 2010, shortly after the National Association of Broadcasters announced that he would be inducted into NAB's Hall of Fame in 2011. —*Beverly Keel*

## David Houston
b. Bossier City, Louisiana, December 9, 1938; d. November 30, 1993

David Houston had one of the widest vocal ranges of any country performer. His ability to slide from a warm baritone to a lofty tenor garnered him sixty charted singles during the 1960s and 1970s. Growing up in Bossier City, outside Shreveport, Houston claimed ancestry from both Robert E. Lee and Sam Houston. Music was an integral part of his life, and he was playing guitar by age five. Encouraged by his godfather, Gene Austin, who had been a popular singer during the 1920s and 1930s ("Ramona," "My Blue Heaven"), Houston learned to sing and perform. While still in his teens, he became a regular on the *LOUISIANA HAYRIDE* and recorded for RCA VICTOR RECORDS.

It wasn't until 1963, however, that Houston began to taste real success. He signed with EPIC RECORDS and had a #2 country hit with "Mountain of Love." Then, in 1966, he recorded the #1 hit "Almost Persuaded." Capturing his trademark frothy vocal style, it remained at the top of the charts for nine weeks and earned him a 1966 Grammy for Best Country Male Vocal Performance. Other hits followed in rapid succession: "A Loser's Cathedral" (#3, 1967), "You Mean the World to Me" (#1, 1967), and "Have a Little Faith" (#1, 1968).

Recording for Epic gave Houston the chance to record duets with two top female talents. He and TAMMY WYNETTE cut "My Elusive Dreams" (#1, 1967) and "It's All Over" (#11, 1968). Two years later, he began making hits with BARBARA MANDRELL, including "After Closing Time" (#6, 1970) and "I Love You, I Love You" (#6, 1973).

In 1972 Houston joined the GRAND OLE OPRY, where he remained a member until his death. In later years, he recorded for various labels, including Gusto-STARDAY, ELEKTRA, and Derrick. —*Don Roy*

## Harlan Howard
b. Detroit, Michigan, September 8, 1927; d. March 3, 2002

After arriving in Nashville in June 1960, Harlan Perry Howard came to represent the archetype of the professional MUSIC CITY songwriter. Among the thousands of songs he wrote or cowrote are such country standards as "Pick Me Up on Your Way Down," "Heartaches by the Number," "I Fall to Pieces," and "I've Got a Tiger by the Tail." Howard continued to pen hits into the 1990s, scoring with such songs as PATTY LOVELESS's "Blame It on Your Heart." Also a popular raconteur, Howard was routinely described as the "dean" of country songwriters.

Though Howard's family roots are in Kentucky, he was a native of Detroit. His first music idol was ERNEST TUBB, whose songwriting inspired Howard as much as his singing did. Howard spent four years in military service, worked a variety of mostly factory jobs, and moved to Los Angeles in 1955. Determined to make it as a country songwriter, he drove a forklift by day while spending his free time pitching his tunes to Hollywood

*Harlan Howard*

song publishers. "Looking back," he said, "I was probably just a country bumpkin running up and down with a guitar and a handful of lyrics."

Nevertheless, Howard befriended such fellow West Coast up-and-comers as BOBBY BARE, WYNN STEWART, and BUCK OWENS. He also met singer Lula Grace Smith (née Johnson), whom he married on May 11, 1957, and who would later attain country stardom as JAN HOWARD. (The two would divorce in August 1967.) His prolific writing and relentless song plugging began to pay off as singers such as SKEETS MCDONALD ("You Oughta See Grandma Rock," 1956) recorded Howard's material. Howard's big break came when CHARLIE WALKER, at RAY PRICE's suggestion, recorded Howard's "Pick Me Up on Your Way Down," a #2 country smash in 1958. Price himself soon followed with Howard's "Heartaches by the Number," likewise a #2 hit. When Guy Mitchell covered "Heartaches" for the pop market and took it to #1, Howard felt confident enough to pull up stakes and move to Nashville.

There Howard initially wrote for PAMPER MUSIC, which was partly owned by Price and was the songwriting home of WILLIE NELSON and HANK COCHRAN. In 1961 Howard and Cochran hit as the cowriters of PATSY CLINE's "I Fall to Pieces." Besides succeeding in the country field, Howard's songs proved readily adaptable to R&B. RAY CHARLES had a #4 pop hit in 1963 with Howard's "Busted," and in 1969 soul singer Joe Simon sold 1 million copies of Howard's "The Chokin' Kind." Howard cut a handful of albums himself during the 1960s, for labels such as CAPITOL, MONUMENT, and RCA VICTOR, but he never seriously pursued a career as an artist.

In 1974 MELBA MONTGOMERY hit #1 with Howard's "No Charge." The song became a gospel standard, and Howard often cited it as possibly his favorite among the songs he wrote. But shortly thereafter, Howard took a seven-year hiatus from songwriting. Returning to the field in the early 1980s, he continued to augment his impressive record with such hits as CONWAY TWITTY's "I Don't Know a Thing About Love (The Moon Song)" and

THE JUDDS' "Why Not Me" He formed a publishing company, Harlan Howard Songs, in 1990, which his widow, Melanie, has continued to operate since his death. (The songwriter had dabbled as a publisher in the mid-1960s with a firm called Wilderness Music, which he eventually sold to TREE PUBLISHING COMPANY). Though health problems slowed him down, he remained a major force in Nashville into the 1990s, and in 1997 he was elected to THE COUNTRY MUSIC HALL OF FAME. —*Daniel Cooper*

## Jan Howard
b. West Plains, Missouri, March 13, 1930

GRAND OLE OPRY star Jan Howard is best known for her hit duets with BILL ANDERSON and as the former wife of songwriter HARLAN HOWARD.

Born Lula Grace Johnson, she married for the first time at age sixteen, was the mother of three at age twenty-one, and was divorced at twenty-four. After moving to Los Angeles in 1953, she met singer WYNN STEWART, who in turn introduced her to his friend Harlan Howard. Then twice divorced, she married Howard in a civil ceremony in Las Vegas on May 10, 1957, and Howard quickly recruited her to sing demos intended for female stars. One of these demos, "Mommy for a Day," cowritten with BUCK OWENS, was targeted for KITTY WELLS. When a record executive heard her demo, he signed her to CHALLENGE RECORDS. Her first release for the label was "Yankee Go Home" (1959), a duet with Stewart; it was also her first appearance as Jan Howard. Her first record to make the charts was a solo effort, "The One You Slip Around With" (#13, 1960), which earned her the Jukebox Operators of America's Most Promising Country Female honor.

After a brief, unsuccessful stint on CAPITOL RECORDS, Howard signed with DECCA in 1964, and the following year she began working with Bill Anderson on his syndicated television show and on the road. Between 1967 and 1971 Anderson and Howard placed four duets in the country Top Five, including the #1 hit "For Loving You" (1967). Earlier, Howard scored two solo hits: "Evil on Your Mind" (#5, 1966) and "Bad Seed" (#10, 1966).

Following a divorce from Harlan Howard, Jan began writing songs, including "Love Is a Sometimes Thing" (collaborating with Anderson). Ironically, she cut a mother's tribute tune, "My Son" (#15, 1968), weeks before son Jim died in Vietnam. (Tragically, son David committed suicide four years later.) In 1971 Howard was invited to join the Grand Ole Opry. She has since cut back on performing, except to play the Opry. Her autobiography, *Sunshine & Shadow*, was published by Richardson & Steirman in1987. —*Walt Trott*

## Paul Howard
b. Midland, Arkansas, July 10, 1908; d. June 18, 1984

In some ways a forgotten pioneer, Paul Jack Howard is little remembered as the man who brought WESTERN SWING to the GRAND OLE OPRY and to the Southeast. He drifted in and out of music until 1940, when he joined the Opry as a solo singer. He was entranced by the BOB WILLS sound coming out of Texas, however, and began building a swing band that grew, at times, to nine or ten pieces. (Alumni of his band include guitarists HANK GARLAND and GRADY MARTIN.) One of the first to use drums on the Opry, he had previously skirted the longtime Opry ban on drums by using two basses to provide the dance-oriented rhythm.

Paul Howard & His Arkansas Cotton Pickers recorded for the COLUMBIA and KING labels in the band's 1940s heyday.

With the relative lack of attention western swing received in the Southeast, Howard eventually lost heart, and he left the Opry in 1949 to perform steadily in Texas, Louisiana, and Arkansas. He is credited for penning the WESLEY TUTTLE hit "With Tears in My Eyes," but after the rock era largely relegated western swing to the age of the dinosaur, he continued working on a smaller scale and leading a band out of Shreveport well into his sixties. He spent his last years in Little Rock, occasionally performing gospel and BLUEGRASS. —*Douglas B. Green*

## Dann Huff
b. Nashville, Tennessee, November 15, 1960

A gifted guitarist, Dann Huff emerged as one of country's most successful producers in the late 1990s and 2000s on the strength of an open-minded, nontraditional musical vision that fueled his work. Acts he guided ranged from rock group Megadeth and pop icon Michael Jackson to country acts FAITH HILL, RASCAL FLATTS, and KEITH URBAN.

Huff is the son of contemporary Christian arranger Ronn Huff, and he grew up around Nashville-area studios. He began playing guitar at age nine, and his tastes and sensibilities initially leaned towards rock & roll and R&B. Still in his teens, he played guitar on demo recordings and helped found Christian

*Dann Huff*

band Whiteheart. In 1982, Huff moved to Los Angeles and graced recordings by Jackson, Whitney Houston, and many others while organizing rock band Giant. Next, Huff returned to Nashville to work sessions for artists including SHANIA TWAIN, whose then husband, Robert "Mutt" Lange, encouraged him to try his hand at production. ("You are a producer in guitarist's clothes," Lange told him.) Huff's first major client was Hill, for whom he produced the multiplatinum 1999 album *Breathe*.

A slew of successes followed, and Huff became known for an unabashedly pop-leaning production style that was sometimes as displeasing to music critics as it was beloved by country radio programmers. "Critically," Huff said in a 2001 interview, "I'm to be avoided like the plague," yet LONESTAR, Urban, CARRIE UNDERWOOD, SHeDAISY, Rascal Flatts, MARTINA McBRIDE, and numerous others scored significant Huff-produced hits. In 2007, Huff was named ACM's producer of the year, and in 2009, Huff albums featuring McBride, Rascal Flatts, and Urban topped the *Billboard* country chart for three consecutive weeks. —*Peter Cooper*

## Leon Huff
b. Whitesboro, Texas, November 3, 1912; d. May 8, 1952

Nicknamed "The Texas Songbird," the honey-voiced Leon Huff lived up to the billing. Perhaps even more than MILTON BROWN or TOMMY DUNCAN, whom he replaced in the LIGHT CRUST DOUGHBOYS, Huff embodied the smoothness and versatility associated with WESTERN SWING's great vocalists.

Like Duncan, Huff venerated JIMMIE RODGERS and featured his songs often, displaying a distinct feel for blues. With the Doughboys from 1933 to 1935, Huff rendered classic vocals on Vocalion sides such as "My Mary" and "Prairie Lullaby." When boss W. LEE O'DANIEL was fired by the Burrus Mill Company (makers of Light Crust Flour) in 1935 and started his own flour mill and band, Huff left with him. Huff worked with O'Daniel for the next five years, dominating the Hillbilly Boys' on-record personality and excelling on Rodgers-like numbers such as "Dirty Hangover Blues." When O'Daniel won the Texas governorship, Huff followed him to AUSTIN, but the two parted angrily during O'Daniel's 1940 reelection bid. Huff sang for O'Daniel's opponent before leading his own band over San Antonio's WOAI. He guested on steel guitarist Charles Mitchell's 1941 BLUEBIRD classic "If It's Wrong to Love You" and then joined BOB WILLS after Tommy Duncan enlisted in the army in 1942. Huff recorded with Wills later that year, including the enduring "Ten Years," and, when Duncan returned, joined JOHNNIE LEE WILLS & His Boys. Huff would sing with the younger Wills for the rest of his life, recording for DECCA, BULLET, and RCA VICTOR. Huff sang Wills's 1950 hit "Peter Cottontail" and remained in top form until his untimely death. —*Kevin Coffey*

## Billy Hughes
b. Sallisaw, Oklahoma, September 14, 1908; d. May 6, 1995

Everette Ishmael "Billy" Hughes, although a fine fiddler heard on many recordings, was best known as a songwriter who penned hundreds of songs throughout his life. Many were placed with HILL AND RANGE SONGS, including "Tennessee Saturday Night," a #1 hit for RED FOLEY in 1948–49. Others who recorded his compositions included ROSALIE ALLEN, EDDY ARNOLD, SPADE COOLEY, TEX WILLIAMS, and ERNEST TUBB.

Hughes first came to prominence in "Pop" Moore's band in Oklahoma City, where Hughes also played and sang with JOHNNY BOND. In about 1938 Hughes moved to Southern California, finding success at a club called Murphy's in Los Angeles. His band, the Pals of the Pecos, included stellar musicians such as steel guitarist Curly Cochran and singer Johnny Tyler. Hughes started the Fargo label to record this band. His own records on FOUR STAR, KING, Mutual, and other labels showcase his exceptional WESTERN SWING and blues vocals. His compositions on these recordings, such as "Rose of the Alamo," "Take Your Hands Off of It," "Atomic Sermon," and "Stop That Stuff," ranged from ballad to novelty. Hughes also played fiddle and wrote for JACK GUTHRIE and sang on some of LUKE WILLS's recordings. —*Steve Hathaway*

## Marvin Hughes
b. Nashville, Tennessee, June 15, 1911; d. December 2, 1986

Marvin Hammond Hughes was a pianist who played a number of behind-the-scenes roles in Nashville from the 1940s into the 1960s. Hughes's first professional gig came in 1928 for Forrest Sanders's big band in Tennessee. Hughes subsequently appeared in New York and Chicago clubs as a blues soloist. He toured with the bands of Slatz Randall, Bob Crosby, and Ben Pollack and worked with Snooky Lanson of *Your Hit Parade* fame. Back in Nashville, Hughes performed on radio station WLAC before joining WSM's staff band. In 1958 he succeeded OWEN BRADLEY as WSM's music director, a position he held until 1964. During his WSM tenure he played keyboards at the GRAND OLE OPRY and frequently moonlighted as a session musician, playing piano on MARTHA CARSON's signature song, "Satisfied" (1951), and THE LOUVIN BROTHERS' "When I Stop Dreaming" (1955) and vibes on JIM REEVES's "He'll Have to Go" (1959).

After leaving WSM he served briefly as Nashville A&R chief for CAPITOL RECORDS. The World War II veteran produced air force recruiting programs for radio (*Country Music Time*) and was president of Larrick Music, a music publishing firm. In addition, he had been a member of the Nashville Symphony. Hughes is also credited with helping to introduce the NASHVILLE NUMBER SYSTEM of chord charts to MUSIC CITY. In 1963 he became the second husband of Kathy Copas Hughes, widow of RANDY HUGHES and daughter of COWBOY COPAS. —*Walt Trott*

## Randy Hughes
b. Gum, Tennessee, September 11, 1928; d. March 5, 1963

Ramsey Dorris Hughes is best remembered as PATSY CLINE's manager and pilot of the plane that crashed near Camden, Tennessee, and took both their lives—and those of COWBOY COPAS and HAWKSHAW HAWKINS—on March 5, 1963. But Hughes filled other roles as well. A rhythm guitarist, he worked the GRAND OLE OPRY as a sideman from age fifteen and frequently worked the road with MOON MULLICAN, MARTHA CARSON, and GEORGE MORGAN, among other stars. In 1951 and 1952 Hughes cut a string of sexually suggestive records on the TENNESSEE label, including "Birthday Cake," "Tattooed Lady," and "Not Big Enough" b/w "Tappin' That Thing." In 1952, while fronting Cowboy Copas's band, Hughes met and married Copas's daughter, Kathaloma (Kathy). By the late 1950s Hughes was working with FERLIN HUSKY, who introduced him to artist manager HUBERT LONG. Under Long's tutelage Hughes became acquainted

with Patsy Cline, whom he began managing in late 1959. At the time, Cline's career was at a standstill, both professionally and financially. Hughes believed he could change things for the better and increase both their earnings. He succeeded on both counts while also starting a music publishing company, working as a stockbroker for Jack M. Bass & Sons, running his own small insurance firm, playing guitar on most of Cline's recording sessions after 1959, and obtaining his pilot's license. —*Don Roy*

## John Hughey
b. Elaine, Arkansas, December 27, 1933; d. November 18, 2007

Playing the upper register of the fretboard with precise intonation, PEDAL STEEL GUITAR player John Hughey created the unmistakable "crying steel" heard on CONWAY TWITTY's "Hello Darlin'," VINCE GILL's "Look at Us," and numerous other country standards. Greatly admired by other steel players, Hughey was a master of the "bar shiver" technique, in which the player rapidly moves the tone bar back and forth.

He formed a band with schoolmate Harold Jenkins in the early 1950s and secured a radio show on KFFA in Helena, Arkansas. When Jenkins went into the army, Hughey toured regionally with several acts, but in 1968 he reunited with his former partner, who had adopted the stage name Conway Twitty.

From 1968 to 1988, Hughey was a member of Twitty's band and added his signature sound to the multitude of #1 hits Twitty amassed during that period. From 1990 to 2002, Hughey played for Vince Gill. Hughey was an in-demand session player for many artists, including RAY PRICE and WILLIE NELSON, and was inducted to the International Steel Guitar Hall of Fame in 1996. At the time of his death, he was a member of the Nashville WESTERN SWING band the Time Jumpers. —*Scott Anderson* and *Robert Kramer*

## Junior Huskey
b. Knoxville, Tennessee, July 21, 1928; d. September 8, 1971

Roy Madison Huskey Jr., known as Junior Huskey, was one of Nashville's early first-call session bassists. He performed with CHET ATKINS as a teenager and went on to play with DON GIBSON, THE EVERLY BROTHERS, and CARL SMITH. Huskey appeared weekly on the GRAND OLE OPRY and can be seen on the AL GANNAWAY–produced *Stars of the Grand Ole Opry* television shows, filmed and syndicated during the 1950s and later reissued for the retail market. Huskey contributed to numerous albums and hit singles of the 1950s and 1960s, including those of LORETTA LYNN, GEORGE JONES, and TAMMY WYNETTE. In August 1971 he appeared on the NITTY GRITTY DIRT BAND's landmark *Will the Circle Be Unbroken* album. When he died of a heart attack a month later, the album was dedicated to his memory. His son, ROY HUSKEY JR., followed in his footsteps as a noted country bassist. —*Jonita Aadland*

## Roy Huskey Jr.
b. Nashville, Tennessee, December 17, 1956; d. September 6, 1997

Roy Milton Huskey, known as Roy Huskey Jr., specialized in playing the upright, acoustic bass and for most of his career was widely acknowledged as the best in Nashville on his chosen instrument.

The son of one of Nashville's early first-call session bassists, JUNIOR HUSKEY, Roy Jr. started playing at age twelve and worked his first professional gig at age fourteen on the GRAND OLE OPRY with DEL WOOD. His first job on the road was with ROY ACUFF, at age sixteen. A regular on recording sessions in Nashville beginning in the 1980s, he was also a member of EMMYLOU HARRIS's Nash Ramblers during the early 1990s. His is the thumping bass heard on Harris's Grammy-winning *At the Ryman* album, and he can be heard on recordings by artists ranging from STEVE EARLE, NANCI GRIFFITH, and GILLIAN WELCH to ALAN JACKSON, GARTH BROOKS, and BILLY RAY CYRUS. He died of cancer in 1997.
—*Michael Hight* and *Jonita Aadland*

## Ferlin Husky

b. Cantwell, Missouri, December 3, 1925; d. March 17, 2011

During his lengthy career, Ferlin Eugene Husky established a reputation as one of country music's finest entertainers. Born in Cantwell, Missouri, he grew up on a farm. He was named Ferland after one of his father's friends, but his birth certificate nevertheless read "Ferlin," and the spelling stuck. An uncle taught him guitar before age ten; tuning the family radio to KMOX–St. Louis, he heard smooth-singing favorites RED FOLEY, GENE AUTRY, and Bing Crosby. Husky met a veteran of the Merchant Marines while working in St. Louis in the early 1940s, and after Pearl Harbor he rushed to enlist. On D-Day he served as a volunteer gunner on a troop ship off the beach at Cherbourg, France.

After the war Husky sang in St. Louis honky-tonks and then headed for California in the late 1940s and started performing with other musicians. Former Autry sidekick SMILEY BURNETTE recruited him for a multistate tour and persuaded Husky to adopt the name Terry Preston. Subsequently, Husky returned to California and hooked up with Ole Rasmussen, SMOKEY ROGERS, and others prominent on the club circuit. Through regular performances on CLIFFIE STONE's *HOMETOWN JAMBOREE* radio and TV series, Husky won audiences with his singing, comedy, and impersonations.

Next, Husky became a disc jockey on BAKERSFIELD radio station KBIS. Here he developed his comic alter-ego, Simon Crum, based on the popular radio characters Lum & Abner and on Simon Crump, a friend and neighbor from his youth. Hilarious dialog between Husky and "Simon" boosted sponsors' sales and helped prove country music's advertising power.

At Bakersfield's Rainbow Gardens club, Husky headlined family-friendly shows and hosted children's talent contests. At one such event he met twelve-year-old DALLAS FRAZIER; Husky soon steered him to CAPITOL RECORDS. Additionally, Husky mentored TOMMY COLLINS (born Leonard Sipes), also recommending him to the label. Husky played guitar on Collins's early recordings and renamed him when someone ordered a Tom Collins drink during a session.

By 1950 Husky was recording for independent FOUR STAR RECORDS and writing songs for Four Star Music. With help from Cliffie Stone (a Capitol producer), Husky moved up to Capitol in early 1953, using his Terry Preston moniker until producer KEN NELSON advised him to record under his real name.

Husky's first Capitol success was JEAN SHEPARD's 1953 blockbuster "A Dear John Letter," on which Shepard sang choruses punctuating Husky's recitation as a soldier whose sweetheart has decided to marry his brother. With the Korean War still under way, the recording shot to #1 and crossed over to #16 pop. Capitalizing on their success, the duo toured widely—after Husky was officially named guardian for Shepard, not yet twenty-one. Later in 1953 they notched a #4 country hit with the answer song "Forgive Me John." The year 1955 brought Husky three solo Top Tens: "I Feel Better All Over (More than Anywhere's Else)," "Little Tom," and "Cuzz Yore So Sweet," his first hit as Simon Crum.

In 1956 Husky rerecorded a song he had earlier released on Capitol as Terry Preston—Smokey Rogers's "Gone." Preparing for the session, held at OWEN BRADLEY's Nashville studio, Ken Nelson asked JORDANAIRES leader Gordon Stoker to recruit a soprano vocalist; Stoker asked Millie Kirkham to assist. Combined with echo and sparse instrumental support, the background singers heightened the drama of Husky's soaring vocal on a recording widely regarded as the first example of THE NASHVILLE SOUND production approach. A #1 country hit, "Gone" peaked at #4 pop.

Husky had worked the televised version of Springfield, Missouri's *Ozark Jubilee* in 1955 and then moved to the GRAND OLE OPRY. "Gone" propelled him to network television appearances on *Arthur Godfrey's Talent Scouts*—including spots as guest host—*Kraft Television Theater*, *The Ed Sullivan Show*, and eventually talk shows hosted by Steve Allen, Johnny Carson, and Merv Griffin. Husky had to give up his Opry slot, but TV exposure introduced him to millions of viewers.

He struck pay dirt again with "Wings of a Dove," a gospel classic penned by RCA Nashville producer BOB FERGUSON. During 1960–61, this upbeat recording became a huge crossover hit, reaching #1 country and #12 pop. Through 1972, Husky charted regularly on Capitol. He switched to ABC in 1973 and had his last chart-making single in 1975. His fifty-one charting country sides include his Simon Crum hit "Country Music Is Here to Stay"

*Ferlin Husky*

(#2, 1958–59). In 2005 he released the Heart of Texas album *The Way It Was (Is the Way It Is)*.

Recording success landed Husky featured roles in a number of movies. These included *Mr. Rock & Roll* (1957), *Country Music Holiday* (1958), and *The Las Vegas Hillbillys* (1966).

But Husky made his most lasting impression as a live performer, touring widely in the United States and abroad. "There were a lot of years when nobody in the business could follow Ferlin Husky," MERLE HAGGARD attested. "He was the big live act of the day. A great entertainer."

Husky was honored with a star on the Hollywood Walk of Fame in 1960 and was elected to THE COUNTRY MUSIC HALL OF FAME in 2010. —*John W. Rumble* and *Don Roy*

## Frank Hutchison

b. Raleigh County, West Virginia, March 20, 1897; d. November 9, 1945

Frank Hutchison displayed some of the most pronounced African American musical influences among white country artists of the 1920s, both in the bluesy quality of his bottleneck-style guitar playing and in his choice of traditional folk-blues material. Raised in the coal camps of Logan County, West Virginia, he spent much of his youth absorbing the guitar styles of black railroad hands and other workers and learning to play slide guitar using a pocket knife. At twenty he married; subsequently he had two daughters and toiled in the mines and at other jobs to support his family. For several years from the mid-1920s, Hutchison made his living as a musician, primarily in West Virginia and neighboring states.

In 1926 Hutchison began a three-year stint with OKEH RECORDS, recording thirty-two sides, including such significant songs as "Coney Isle" (later known as "Alabam"), "The Train That Carried My Girl from Town," "Stackalee," and "Worried Blues." He also waxed guitar tunes, including "Cannon Ball Blues" and "Logan County Blues." At his last session, in September 1929, Hutchison appeared on six sides in the "OKeh Medicine Show" series that also featured FIDDLIN' JOHN CARSON, NARMOUR & SMITH, and EMMETT MILLER.

The Great Depression ended Hutchison's recording career and curtailed his show business activity. At various later times he resided in Chesapeake, Ohio, where he worked occasionally as a showboat entertainer, and in Lake, West Virginia, where he ran a general store and post office. After his store was destroyed in a fire in 1942, he moved first to Columbus, Ohio, and then to Dayton, where he died of cancer. —*Ivan M. Tribe*

## IBMA
established in Owensboro, Kentucky, 1985

Headquartered in Nashville, Tennessee, since 2003, the International Bluegrass Music Association is the genre's principal trade association, with thousands of members involved in every corner of the industry.

Several dozen founders with broad experience in BLUEGRASS created the organization in 1985, hiring Art Menius as its first executive director and charging the association with two broad goals: "promotion of the bluegrass music industry and unity within it" and "coordination of the industry's public image and recognition." Subsequent mission statements added an emphasis on enhancing members' professionalism. First headquartered in Owensboro, Kentucky, IBMA held its initial trade show and presented its first awards in 1986. By 1990, when Dan Hays replaced Menius, the group had pushed annual revenues over the $100,000 mark, created an emergency trust fund for industry professionals, established an annual festival (Fan Fest) to raise money for the fund, helped create a bluegrass Grammy award, and improved the association's awards show production.

The 1990s saw further growth, as the IBMA boosted and benefited from the popularity of artists such as ALISON KRAUSS and DEL MCCOURY, both of whom featured prominently among its award winners. By mid-decade, membership surpassed 2,500, and the burgeoning annual World of Bluegrass—an umbrella title for the trade show, awards show, and Fan Fest—was moved to Louisville, Kentucky, in 1997. IBMA offered its first advanced training program for industry participants, Leadership Bluegrass, in 2000, and three years later moved its offices to Nashville. The World of Bluegrass moved there in 2005. —*Jon Weisberger*

## Rob Ickes
b. Millbrae, California, May 26, 1967

DOBRO player and educator Rob Ickes is a founding member of the BLUEGRASS band Blue Highway and one of the resophonic guitar's most inventive performers.

Ickes grew up in a musical family from the San Francisco Bay area. He gave up the fiddle for the dobro after hearing the SELDOM SCENE's Mike Auldridge. Moving to Nashville in 1992, young Ickes was tapped for *The Great Dobro Sessions*, an all-star project that won the 1994 Grammy for Best Bluegrass Album. Around this time, Ickes formed Blue Highway with five musicians from the Kingsport, Tennessee, area. The band's first album, *It's A Long, Long Road*, won IBMA's Album of the Year award for 1996, and that year Ickes earned his first of twelve IBMA Dobro Player of the Year awards (through 2010).

Ickes's first album as a featured artist, *Hard Times*, came in 1997, and four solo CDs that followed ranged from newgrass to jazz standards. He formed a progressive acoustic trio called Three Ring Circle and played scores of sessions for artists including MERLE HAGGARD, ALISON KRAUSS, DOLLY PARTON, WILLIE NELSON, and David Lee Roth. In 2007 Ickes launched the ResoSummit, an annual four-day dobro camp in Nashville. —*Craig Havighurst*

## IFCO (International Fan Club Organization)
established in Wild Horse, Colorado, 1965

Most country music fan clubs were not formed until the 1960s. The proliferation of these clubs and the success of Nashville's annual Fan Fair convention (now called the CMA MUSIC FESTIVAL) can be attributed in large part to the International Fan Club Organization created and run by three sisters: Loudilla Maxine Johnson (b. Forgan, Oklahoma, September 16, 1938), Loretta Irene Johnson (b. Forgan, Oklahoma, November 29, 1941; d. April 13, 2009), and Velma Kay Johnson (b. Alamosa, California, June 26, 1944).

In 1963 the Johnsons started the Loretta Lynn Fan Club at their family ranch in Wild Horse, Colorado, following a two-year correspondence between Lynn and Loretta Johnson. As word spread about Lynn's growing career and her fan club, fans of other singers began asking Lynn how to start fan clubs for their favorite artists. IFCO, which began with seventy-five fan clubs its first year, 1965, now unites and advises some 130 such clubs, supporting everyone from virtual unknowns to superstars, in country and other musical genres. The Johnson sisters served as co-presidents of both the Loretta Lynn Fan Club (until Lynn disbanded it in 1996) and IFCO.

In 1968 IFCO staged its first showcase concert to spotlight entertainers in Nashville during the DJ CONVENTION, four years before Fan Fair began, in April 1972. After years of staging concerts at the Tennessee State Fairgrounds during Fan Fair, the event was moved in 1995 to THE RYMAN AUDITORIUM. Through the years IFCO's showcase, now called the IFCO Fun Fest Show, has benefited various charities. The Fun Fest was not held in 2009 due to Loretta Johnson's death, but resumed in 2010.

Today IFCO has its own popular online website. "A fan club is the best promotional tool an artist can have," Loudilla Johnson has said. "It provides a kind of support an artist cannot buy." —*Don Rhodes*

## Imperial Records
established in Los Angeles, California, January 1946

Businessman Lew Chudd started Imperial Records and issued mostly ethnic (primarily Mexican) records until 1947. Instead of recording, he generally released masters that artists sent him.

The label issued material by various country acts, including JIMMY HEAP (1949–51), CHARLINE ARTHUR (1950), ZEKE CLEMENTS (1950), SLIM WHITMAN (1951–70), MITCHELL TOROK (1953), MERLE KILGORE (1954–56), BOB LUMAN (1957), and FREDDY FENDER (1960). By the time RICK NELSON (1957–62) signed, Imperial was in full swing. LIBERTY RECORDS absorbed it in 1963, and the Imperial name was retired in 1970. The masters are currently owned by CAPITOL, part of EMI's Capitol Music Group. —*Don Roy*

## Red Ingle
b. Toledo, Ohio, November 7, 1906; d. September 7, 1965

A former big-band sideman and Spike Jones comedian, Ernest Jansen "Red" Ingle successfully fused country music with outrageous satire. His first CAPITOL record, "Tim-Tayshun," became an unexpected #1 pop and #2 country hit during 1947 and inspired a brief flurry of ersatz hillbilly records by Jo Stafford, Johnny Mercer, Dorothy Shay, Arthur Godfrey, and other pop artists.

A violin prodigy as a child, Ingle took up the saxophone as a youth and landed jobs with dance bands around Toledo, Ohio. In 1927 he served two brief stints with the Jean Goldkette Orchestra, which then included jazz greats Bix Beiderbecke and Frankie Trumbauer. From 1931 to 1941 Ingle sang and played alto sax with Ted Weems.

In April 1943 former Weems bandmate Joseph "Country" Washburne recruited him for Spike Jones & His City Slickers. Ingle spent more than three years as the novelty band's principal comedian; his showcase number "Chloe" gave Jones a Top Five pop hit in 1945.

Signing a Capitol contract in March 1947, Ingle cut two sides as leader of "The Natural Seven," a recording band organized by Washburne and featuring NOEL BOGGS, Herman (the Hermit) Snyder (CLIFFIE STONE's father), Art Wenzel, and City Slickers alumni. The band's unorthodox hillbilly arrangement of the pop standard "Temptation" featured vocals by Ingle and Cinderella G. Stump, a pseudonym for pop singer Jo Stafford. The record's popularity led Ingle to assemble a road troupe, with Karen Tedder replacing Stafford. Other successful novelties followed, most notably "Them Durn Fool Things," "Nowhere," and "Cigareetes, Whuskey and Wild, Wild Women." Ingle showcases his violin skill on "Pagan Ninny's Keep 'Er Goin' Stomp," which turns a classical virtuoso piece into a fiddle breakdown. A 1948 musician's union recording strike prevented Ingle from appearing on his final hit, "Serutan Yob," a satire of Nat King Cole's "Nature Boy."

After disbanding his troupe in 1952, Ingle briefly toured with orchestra leaders Ted Weems and Eddy Howard before retiring from music. —*Dave Samuelson*

## Jack Ingram
b. Houston, Texas, November 15, 1970

Jack Ingram built a following as a concert act, especially in Texas, before enjoying success on country radio. After short stints with several major record companies—WARNER BROS., Rising Tide, and two SONY MUSIC labels—Ingram signed with BIG MACHINE RECORDS in 2005. His first #1 single, "Wherever You Are," also gave Big Machine its first #1—and came eight years after Ingram's first national single release.

Ingram began performing in Texas in 1992 and released a self-titled album that year. His 1995 album *Live at Adair's* sold in large figures for an independent release and was picked up by Warner Bros. for distribution. His 1997 Rising Tide album, *Livin' or Dyin'*, was produced by singer-songwriters STEVE EARLE and Ray Kennedy.

Ingram's reputation as an engaging live performer is underscored by the release of five live albums between 1995 and 2006. Fittingly, his first chart-topper came from the album *Live—Wherever You Are*, which combined studio and concert tracks.

Follow-up hits included "Love You," "Measure of a Man," and "Lips of an Angel," a cover of a rock hit by the band Hinder. Ingram was named ACM's Top New Male Vocalist in 2008. His 2009 Big Machine release, *Big Dreams & High Hopes,* included the Top Ten single "Barefoot and Crazy." —*Michael McCall*

## Imprint Records (*see* Roy Wunsch)

## Louis Innis
b. Seymour, Indiana, January 21, 1919; d. August 20, 1982

Singer and rhythm guitarist Louis Todd Innis was a key member of the Cincinnati-based String Dusters, a top-notch group consisting of steel guitarist JERRY BYRD, fiddler TOMMY JACKSON, and guitarists ZEB AND ZEKE TURNER. During the late 1940s and early 1950s, Innis was as well known as any of them. Besides recording for MERCURY and KING, he hosted radio shows at Cincinnati's WLW in addition to weekday TV shows in Cincinnati, Columbus, and Dayton.

The Indiana native turned pro in his teens, first playing fair dates. He broke into radio in Chattanooga in the mid-1930s and worked on Atlanta's *WSB Barn Dance* in the 1940s. In mid-decade he joined HANK PENNY's Radio Cowboys on WLW and began playing sessions for the Cincinnati-based King label. Chosen by GRAND OLE OPRY network host RED FOLEY for his new band, the Cumberland Valley Boys, in 1946, Innis moved to Nashville and stayed with Foley into 1948. In 1947 Innis first made his own feature recordings for Sterling (the label then introducing HANK WILLIAMS) and played early Nashville sessions behind Foley, Williams, and others. Innis joined Mercury in about 1948, when, lured by the prospect of higher income, he, Jackson, Byrd, and the Turners left Nashville for Cincinnati to perform on WLW's *MIDWESTERN HAYRIDE* and numerous other WLW radio and TV programs.

The String Dusters' vocal recordings typically featured Innis—and Innis's original songs. None really became hits, though the Innis-penned "Good Night, Cincinnati, Good Morning, Tennessee" (also recorded by COWBOY COPAS) is probably the best remembered. Studio skills brought Innis plenty of session work—including Hank Williams's breakthrough hit "Lovesick Blues"—and at one point King founder SYD NATHAN hired Innis as an A&R man. As his own producer, though, Innis probably hurt his long-term prospects through his fondness for novelty material. All told, he released sixteen Mercury sides (1949–52) and twenty-plus King-De Luxe sides (1953–55).

Although Innis would return to King intermittently over the years, he moved to Nashville by 1957, when he signed with TREE PUBLISHING. There his duties evidently included producing demo sessions. Later he performed similar functions for GRADY MARTIN's and FLOYD CRAMER's Craymart publishing firm. By the mid-1970s Innis was also working for DOLLY PARTON's Owepar publishing company, but his principal role was coordinator of album product for STARDAY-KING, where he was employed by 1969.

Until his death he continued in this position with Starday-King's successors: Lin Broadcasting, the Freddie Bienstock publishing group, and Gusto Records. —*Ronnie Pugh*

## International Fan Club Organization (*see* IFCO)

## Jerry Irby
b. New Braunfels, Texas, October 20, 1917; d. December 1983

A singer-songwriter who bridged WESTERN SWING and HONKY-TONK in a career that spanned more than forty-five years, Gerald F. Irby never quite attained the stardom he seemed poised for in the late 1940s.

Irby arrived in Houston, guitar in hand, in 1933 and teamed briefly with songwriter/steel guitarist TED DAFFAN in 1936. Irby's first band, the Serenaders, was not successful. He subsequently recorded with the Texas Wanderers (1939) and Bill Mounce (1941) before joining the BAR X COWBOYS in 1941. Irby recorded as the group's vocalist—and sang with THE MODERN MOUNTAINEERS—for BLUEBIRD in October of that year.

Irby remained with the Cowboys until 1947 but began recording under his own name in 1945, scoring a considerable hit with his "[Driving] Nails in My Coffin" for the Gulf label. He later recorded for Globe, MERCURY, Cireco, and IMPERIAL and formed his Texas Ranchers in mid-1947. He signed with MGM late that year and quickly had a sizable hit, "Roses Have Thorns." His songs were also hits for others, notably "Driving Nails in My Coffin" (FLOYD TILLMAN, ERNEST TUBB, 1946) and "Keeper of My Heart" (BOB WILLS, 1947). Irby opened his Texas Corral nightclub in 1948.

Irby's career was in a tailspin by the early 1950s. Several come-back attempts failed, although he did have a local hit when he teamed with Daffan to cut "Tangled Mind" in 1956. In the 1970s Irby switched to gospel music, reworking his old songs and recording several albums before his death. —*Kevin Coffey*

## Bud Isaacs
b. Bedford, Indiana, March 26, 1928

Although explored on the West Coast by the SPADE COOLEY band's JOAQUIN MURPHEY and SPEEDY WEST as early as 1947, the PEDAL STEEL GUITAR didn't become a fixture of Nashville-produced country until after Bud Isaacs played it on WEBB PIERCE's 1954 hit "Slowly." This watershed suddenly made pedals de rigueur for country steel guitarists. Rarely has a single performance by a side-man resulted in such a sweeping stylistic overhaul.

Isaacs grew up hearing JERRY BYRD on Cincinnati radio station WLW and learning six-string HAWAIIAN guitar. Isaacs debuted on radio at WIBC–Indianapolis, and by age sixteen he was playing the short-lived but pioneering four-pedal Gibson Electraharp. He used it at WOAI in San Antonio, where he got his first professional break in 1944. For most of the next decade, Isaacs followed the peripatetic sideman's life from Arizona to Lansing, Michigan, where LITTLE JIMMY DICKENS hired him. Isaacs's association with Dickens would lead to staff work on the GRAND OLE OPRY (1950–54), a regular spot in RED FOLEY's band at the *OZARK JUBILEE* (1954–57), and a return to the Opry staff band in the late 1950s and early 1960s.

"I began to realize how important it was to have a sound of your own," Isaacs told John Haggard in a 1976 *Guitar Player*

*Bud Isaacs*

interview. "Everybody in Nashville was trying to create his own thing; get tagged for it." Isaacs was tagged when Webb Pierce used him on his November 1953 recording of TOMMY HILL's original song "Slowly," which Pierce had previously recorded twice but shelved because he was dissatisfied with the performances.

The issued version became the nation's top country hit for seventeen weeks early in 1954. Isaacs's "moving tone," played on a double-neck, two-pedal steel with a knee lever built by West Coast innovator Paul Bigsby, was prominent on the hit and elicited "laundry bags stuffed with mail," Isaacs recalled, from fans and fellow players inquiring about his unique sound. Pierce, then at the peak of his popularity, made Isaacs's sound a feature of many subsequent hits, despite the fact that Isaacs only worked the one session with him.

In addition to extensive sideman chores in the 1950s, Isaacs enjoyed a solo career on RCA VICTOR (1954–60), which issued such instrumentals as "Hot Mocking Bird" and the steel guitar standard "Bud's Bounce." He later recorded for the Jabs and Midland labels. In 1956 Isaacs worked with Gibson in designing its Multiharp pedal steel, which debuted in 1957. With his wife, singer Geri Mapes, Isaacs performed for many years as the Golden West Singers; he is now retired. He was inducted into the Steel Guitar Hall of Fame in 1984. —*Mark Humphrey*

## Burl Ives
b. Hunt, Illinois, June 14, 1909; d. April 14, 1995

Burl Icle Ivanhoe Ives was the best-known folksinger of the 1940s and 1950s. The son of struggling Illinois tenant farmers, he showed interest and talent in singing and acting during his school years and considered both as careers. In 1929 he left college to hobo around the nation playing banjo and, later, guitar and learning songs everywhere. Arriving in New York in 1933, he struggled for years to make a living until success came with his CBS radio program, *The Wayfaring Stranger* (1940–42). His recording career began in 1941 with an album of folksongs for Columbia (though he had auditioned in 1929 for Gennett). In the mid-1940s a series of folksong albums on the Decca and Asch labels made his name almost synonymous with "folksinger"; he popularized such songs as "Foggy Foggy Dew," "The Erie Canal," "Blue-Tail Fly," and "Big Rock Candy Mountain," sung simply to unadorned guitar accompaniment—performances that came to define folk music for many in the late 1940s. He continued to record folk and country music through the 1950s to the 1970s for Decca (mostly in Nashville between 1952 and 1972), putting several songs in *Billboard*'s country Top Ten ("Wild Side of Life," "A Little Bitty Tear," "Funny Way of Laughin'," "Call Me Mr. In-Between"), but gradually the focus of his career shifted to stage, screen, and television. Today he is perhaps better remembered as the narrator and singer of the annual holiday TV staple *Rudolph the Red-Nosed Reindeer* and as Big Daddy in the 1958 film version of *Cat on a Hot Tin Roof*, a role he originated on Broadway. —*Norm Cohen*

## Bill Ivey

b. Detroit, Michigan, September 6, 1944

William James Ivey became the director of the Country Music Foundation (CMF) in 1971. At the University of Michigan and Indiana University, he earned degrees in history, folklore, and ethnomusicology. Initially appointed as librarian, Ivey was quickly promoted to the directorship. During his tenure the organization increased fourfold in budget and staff while expanding The Country Music Hall of Fame and Museum and its renowned collections. By the time CMF acquired and relaunched Hatch Show Print in 1991–92, CMF had emerged as the nation's premier popular music research organization.

Founding editor of the *Journal of Country Music* (1972–75), Ivey has written numerous articles on country, folk, and popular music; in 2008 the University of California Press published his *Arts, Inc.: How Greed and Neglect Have Destroyed Our Cultural Rights*. In addition, he has been writer, producer, or executive producer for several country music television programs and has assembled and annotated a number of pioneering record reissue projects. Ivey is a past national president of the National Academy of Recording Arts and Sciences (NARAS), past national chairman of the NARAS Board of Trustees, and past president of the American Folklore Society. He was also instrumental in the Country Music Hall of Fame and Museum's relocation to its current downtown Nashville site. In December 1997 President Clinton selected Ivey to chair the National Endowment for the Arts, based in Washington, D.C. Ivey became director of the Curb Center for Art, Enterprise, and Public Policy at Vanderbilt University in 2002. —*Paul Kingsbury*

# Alan Jackson
b. Newnan, Georgia, October 17, 1958

A modern country superstar, Alan Eugene Jackson has built an enduring career while holding fast to country traditions in an era when many of his contemporaries have embraced pop and rock influences. A member of country's vaunted "class of '89"—which included CLINT BLACK, GARTH BROOKS, and TRAVIS TRITT—the lanky Jackson gained a reputation for a no-frills concert style and a laid-back image that enhanced his standing among fans.

As of early 2011, Jackson had achieved twenty-six #1 *Billboard* hits, including a 2010 duet with the ZAC BROWN BAND on "As She's Walking Away," and placed twenty-four more in the Top Ten. He's won twelve CMA awards, including three as Entertainer of the Year, and fourteen ACM awards. He received a 2002 Grammy for Best Country Song for "Where Were You (When the World Stopped Turning)," which he wrote and recorded. His album sales have topped 50 million and are still climbing.

Jackson didn't aspire to a musical career until age twenty. Encouraged by his father, a mechanic, at age fifteen Jackson spent a year rebuilding a vintage Thunderbird, and after high school he went into the used-car business.

Jackson met his wife, Denise, when he was seventeen and married at eighteen. Three years later he began playing cover tunes with local country bands. A fan of GEORGE JONES, MERLE HAGGARD, and HANK WILLIAMS, Jackson also started writing songs. In 1985 he moved to Nashville. Denise Jackson, a flight attendant at the time, ran into singer GLEN CAMPBELL at an airport and asked for advice for her husband. Campbell referred her to his Nashville office, where Jackson received some tips on how to break into the business.

Jackson worked in the mailroom at TNN and began singing on songwriters' demos while continuing to write. His dedication paid off when he landed a songwriting deal with Campbell's KayTeeKay Music publishing firm.

After recording his own demos with producer KEITH STEGALL, Jackson became the first country artist signed to ARISTA RECORDS, in June 1989. His debut album, *Here in the Real World*, was coproduced by Stegall and SCOTT HENDRICKS. His first single, "Blue Blooded Woman," failed to make the Top Forty, but the next, "Here in the Real World" (which Jackson cowrote with Mark Irwin), hit #3 on the charts. Three other singles from that album reached the Top Ten: "Wanted" (#3), "Chasin' That Neon Rainbow" (#2), and "I'd Love You All Over Again" (#1). In 1990 Jackson was named ACM's Top New Male Vocalist.

His second album, *Don't Rock the Jukebox*, featured the #1 hit title track and sold more than four million units. His 1993 smash "Chattahoochee," from his third album, *A Lot About Livin' (And a Little 'bout Love)*, made Jackson a superstar. Supported by a

memorable video, "Chattahoochee" led the album's sales past the 6 million mark. Other Jackson hits have included a #1 he cowrote with RANDY TRAVIS, "She's Got the Rhythm (And I Got the Blues)," as well as "Livin' on Love," "Gone Country," "I Don't Even Know Your Name," "Little Bitty," "Between the Devil and Me," "Where I Come From," "Drive (For Daddy Gene)," "Remember When," "Small Town Southern Man," and many others.

In 1999, Jackson released a covers album, *Under the Influence*, which became a million-seller and showcased the #1 hit "It Must Be Love," a cover of a previous hit by DON WILLIAMS. That same year, at the CMA Awards, Jackson protested the show's production decision to limit George Jones to a ninety-second performance. Jones pulled out of the show, and Jackson, interrupting his live performance of one of his own songs, launched into the Jones hit "Choices" without warning the producers.

After the terrorist attacks of September 11, 2001, Jackson wrote and recorded "Where Were You (When the World Stopped Turning)," introducing the song at the 2001 CMA Awards. The song topped the charts, and Jackson received national attention for the anthem.

In 2006 Jackson took another commercial gamble with the release of an OLD-TIME gospel album, *Precious Memories*. Despite a lack of airplay, the album went to #1 on the *Billboard* country album charts and sold more than a million units. The same year, he worked with ALISON KRAUSS as his producer on the album *Like Red on a Rose*, with Krauss choosing and arranging the material. A stylistic departure, it didn't sell as well as Jackson's previous albums.

In addition to success as an artist, Jackson has penned hits for other singers. Randy Travis, whom Jackson befriended before

*Alan Jackson*

either was a star, recorded four Jackson tunes (three of which Travis cowrote), including the singles "Forever Together" and "Better Class of Losers." CLAY WALKER reached #1 with Jackson's "If I Could Make a Livin'," and FAITH HILL did well with Jackson's "I Can't Do That Anymore." Underscoring the commercial value of Jackson's songwriting, the publishing firm Warner Chappell in December 1994 acquired Jackson's catalog for a reported $13 million and made arrangements to copublish future Jackson songs.

Jackson also has participated on numerous collaborative projects. He teamed with idol George Jones for "A Good Year for the Roses" on *George Jones: The Bradley Barn Sessions,* and paid homage to Merle Haggard with "Trying Not to Love You" for the Haggard tribute album *Mama's Hungry Eyes.* Jackson sang on comedian JEFF FOXWORTHY's 1996 hit "Redneck Games," with GEORGE STRAIT on the provocative "Murder on Music Row," with Jeannie Kendall on her recording of "Timeless and True Love," and with Jimmy Buffett on the #1 hit "It's Five O'Clock Somewhere."

Over the years, Jackson has been sponsored by Ford Trucks, Fruit of the Loom, NAPA Auto Parts, and Cracker Barrel Old Country Stores, which released "The Alan Jackson Collection" in 2009, featuring a special-release CD; an array of clothing, toys, and food; and a customized wooden rocking chair.

Jackson's wife, Denise, whom he married in December 1979, has written two best-selling books about her commitment to Christianity: *It's All about Him: Finding the Love of My Life* and *The Road Home.* The couple has three daughters: Mattie, Ali, and Dani.

Jackson has been a member of the GRAND OLE OPRY since 1991. In 2011, Jackson left his longtime label, Arista Records, and signed with CAPITOL RECORDS Nashville. —*Janet E. Williams*

## Carl Jackson
b. Louisville, Mississippi, September 18, 1953

Multi-instrumentalist Carl Jackson, best known for his banjo skills, is an accomplished recording artist, songwriter, session musician, and record producer who was performing with his father's and uncle's BLUEGRASS band by age eleven.

Jackson first appeared on the GRAND OLE OPRY at fourteen while playing with JIM & JESSE's Virginia Boys. During his five years in the band, Jackson backed numerous other Opry performers before joining the Sullivan Family gospel group. In 1972, Jackson joined GLEN CAMPBELL's band, staying until 1984. Jackson began recording his own albums in 1971. They include *Banjo Player* (1973) and *Old Friends* (1978) for CAPITOL and *Banjo Man—A Tribute to Earl Scruggs* (1980), *Song of the South* (1982), *Banjo Hits* (1983), and (with John Starling) *Spring Training* (1991) for SUGAR HILL. The last received a Grammy for Best Bluegrass Recording. COLUMBIA released four Jackson singles during the mid-1980s.

As a songwriter, Jackson's hits include PAM TILLIS's "Put Yourself in My Place" (1991) and VINCE GILL's "No Future in the Past" (1993). RICKY SKAGGS's recording of "Little Mountain Church House" for the NITTY GRITTY DIRT BAND's *Will the Circle Be Unbroken, Volume II* album earned Jackson and cowriter Jim Rushing 1990's IBMA Song of the Year Award. In addition, GARTH BROOKS, PATTY LOVELESS, DIAMOND RIO, RHONDA VINCENT, and TRISHA YEARWOOD have recorded Jackson's compositions. Jackson is also an in-demand session musician and vocalist who

has contributed to albums by ALABAMA, JOE DIFFIE, STEVE EARLE, EMMYLOU HARRIS, and ROGER MILLER.

Jackson's production credits include Bobbie Cryner's critically acclaimed, self-titled debut album on EPIC and a multiartist tribute to GRAM PARSONS released in 2000 by Shell Point/Echo Music. Additionally, Jackson produced the Grammy-winning *Livin', Lovin', Losin': Songs of the Louvin Brothers* (UNIVERSAL RECORDS SOUTH, 2003), a collection including a Jackson performance with frequent collaborators Larry Cordle and Jerry Salley and Jackson duets with LINDA RONSTADT and MERLE HAGGARD. Jackson played guitar, sang, and produced most of the harmony vocals for Haggard's *The Bluegrass Sessions* (McCoury Music/Hag, 2007). —*Kent Henderson*

## Shot Jackson
b. Wilmington, North Carolina, September 4, 1920; d. January 24, 1991

As a sideman and session player Harold Bradley Jackson worked for both the king and the queen of country music: ROY ACUFF and KITTY WELLS. He also made many recordings on his own, but he was better known for innovative instrument designs, notably the Sho-Bud steel guitar, created in collaboration with BUDDY EMMONS, and the Sho-Bro, Jackson's seven-stringed DOBRO.

Jackson's stage name came from Buckshot, a family nickname. He first played Spanish guitar but soon mastered dobro and steel. In 1937 he joined George Smith's Rhythm Ramblers on WMBA–Jacksonville, Florida.

COUSIN WILBUR (Bill Wesbrooks) hired Jackson in 1944 for his GRAND OLE OPRY band. During 1945–46 Jackson served in the U.S. Navy. Returning, he played electric steel for THE BAILES BROTHERS and recorded with them for KING RECORDS (1946) and for COLUMBIA RECORDS (1947). Jackson also backed them as headliners of the first KWKH *LOUISIANA HAYRIDE* broadcast, on April 3, 1948.

*Shot Jackson*

At KWKH Jackson met Johnnie Wright and Jack Anglin (JOHNNIE & JACK) and Johnnie's wife, Kitty Wells; in 1949 he went to Atlanta with them to record for RCA VICTOR RECORDS. Jackson's steel guitar touches were heard on the first #1 hits for both Wells ("It Wasn't God Who Made Honky Tonk Angels," 1952) and Johnnie & Jack ("Oh Baby Mine," 1954). During 1950 Jackson also recorded with WEBB PIERCE and on his own for Pacemaker Records.

After playing a landmark country show in New York City's Palace Theatre with Wells and Acuff in November 1955, Jackson joined Acuff's Smoky Mountain Boys. In 1962 he left to manage, tour, and record with MELBA MONTGOMERY. Briefly reunited with Acuff, he was sidelined for many months recuperating from a near-fatal car crash suffered by Acuff's band in July 1965. In that year Jackson opened a shop in downtown Nashville to build and repair instruments, continuing until 1983, when ill health prompted his retirement. A member of the Steel Guitar Players Hall of Fame (inducted 1986), Jackson died in 1991. — *Walt Trott*

## Stonewall Jackson

b. Emerson, North Carolina, November 6, 1932

Stonewall Jackson has been a hard country singer for more than fifty years. His father, Waymond, claiming to be a descendant, had planned to name him after Confederate general Thomas "Stonewall" Jackson, but he died shortly before Stonewall's birth. Nearly destitute, Stonewall's mother moved the family to a brother-in-law's Georgia farm. After she remarried, her new husband physically abused the boy, and at fifteen he ran away to join the U.S. Army, lying about his age. The truth surfaced and he was discharged. Later serving in the U.S. Navy, Jackson returned to

*Stonewall Jackson*

Georgia in 1954 to work as a sharecropper, saving some $350 to finance a move to Nashville.

His career had a storybook start. In the second week of November 1956, Jackson drove his pickup into MUSIC CITY and walked uninvited into the office of ACUFF-ROSE PUBLICATIONS. Impressed by his singing and songwriting, WESLEY ROSE arranged an audition with the GRAND OLE OPRY's GEORGE D. HAY and D KILPATRICK, who added Jackson to the cast that weekend without benefit of a label deal or a hit record.

ERNEST TUBB took the singer under his wing, buying his first stage clothes, having Jackson open his show, and steering him to COLUMBIA RECORDS. Jackson's first hit was "Life to Go" (1958–59), written by GEORGE JONES, with whom he was then touring. Next, "Waterloo" became a 1959 crossover hit (#1 country, #4 pop), generating bookings on network TV programs such as Dick Clark's *American Bandstand*.

Other Jackson hits include "A Wound Time Can't Erase" (#3, 1962), "B.J. the D.J." (#1, 1964), "Don't Be Angry" (#4), and "I Washed My Hands in Muddy Water" (#8, 1965). He's also known for his 1966 pro–Vietnam War song "The Minute Men (Are Turning in Their Graves)" and for his 1971 rendition of the Lobo pop hit "Me and You and a Dog Named Boo," Jackson's last Top Ten. He left Columbia in 1973 for MGM RECORDS and logged his final chart record, "Herman Schwartz," that year.

After Pete Fisher became Grand Ole Opry manager in 1998, Jackson's scheduled appearances declined in number, and in 2007 the performer sued Fisher and GAYLORD ENTERTAINMENT, which owns the show, for age discrimination—though many older cast members continued to appear. The suit was settled privately in 2008, by which time Jackson, absent from the Opry for several months during the dispute, had resumed performing on the program. Today Jackson and his Minutemen band maintain a limited touring schedule. His autobiography, *From the Bottom Up*, was published by L. C. Parsons in 1991. — *Walt Trott*

## Tommy Jackson

b. Birmingham, Alabama, March 31, 1926; d. December 9, 1979

Tommy Jackson is generally considered one of the finest commercial country fiddle players of all time. He did for country fiddle playing what EARL SCRUGGS did for the banjo in BLUEGRASS: he set a precedent. On recordings by artists such as HANK WILLIAMS and WEBB PIERCE, Jackson popularized the playing of simple double-stop (playing two strings at once in harmony) restatements of the melody. In addition, he developed an influential single-string style that he introduced on RAY PRICE's massive 1956 hit "Crazy Arms." Nashville's first regular session fiddler, he played on thousands of recordings, utilizing fiddle styles ranging from bluegrass to WESTERN SWING.

Born Thomas Lee Jackson Jr. in Birmingham, Alabama, he and his family moved to Nashville when he was about a year old. As a youngster he played for tips in bars and on street corners before gaining experience in the early 1940s with the GRAND OLE OPRY bands of CURLEY WILLIAMS and PAUL HOWARD. Following service with the Army Air Corps in World War II, Jackson returned to civilian life in April 1946. He toured briefly with THE DUKE OF PADUCAH, ANNIE LOU & DANNY DILL, and THE YORK BROTHERS and then moved up to the bands of Opry stars MILTON ESTES and, later, RED FOLEY, who headlined the Opry's NBC network segment. While with Foley, Jackson worked sessions with Foley's band, the Cumberland Valley Boys, which also included JERRY

BYRD, LOUIS INNIS, and ZEKE TURNER. As independent session men, they called themselves the Pleasant Valley Boys.

In 1948, Cincinnati's WLW recruited Jackson and his cohorts for the MIDWESTERN HAYRIDE and other programs. While there they also worked sessions at KING RECORDS and the E. T. HERZOG RECORDING STUDIO. Returning to Nashville by the early 1950s, Jackson was probably Nashville's most in-demand session fiddler through the 1960s. As a featured artist he recorded numerous traditional hoedowns (twelve sides for MERCURY, twelve for DECCA, and nearly one hundred for DOT), all of which are prized by collectors and many of which remain definitive renditions of the tunes involved. Some of Jackson's best solo and backup work can be heard on virtually every Ray Price recording from 1955 to 1966. —Eddie Stubbs

## Wanda Jackson

b. Maud, Oklahoma, October 20, 1937

There have been several women singers, such as BRENDA LEE and even Patti Page, who have crossed easily between country and pop, but to date none has done so with quite the eruptive quality of Wanda Lavonne Jackson. Her unbridled sensuality ran contrary to expectations for female country singers, but it shouldn't distract from her singing and songwriting talent.

Jackson began performing on KLPR–Oklahoma City, in 1953, and sang with TOMMY COLLINS before working on and off with HANK THOMPSON in 1954. She made her first recordings for DECCA in March of that year in a deal Thompson facilitated. A duet with Thompson sideman Billy Gray, "You Can't Have My Love," cracked the country Top Ten. After graduating high school in June 1955, she joined the OZARK JUBILEE and worked road shows with ELVIS PRESLEY, whom she dated.

In June 1956 she switched to CAPITOL RECORDS. On her second session, she cut the original version of "Silver Threads and

*Wanda Jackson*

Golden Needles" and the ROCKABILLY classic "Hot Dog (That Made Him Mad)," underscoring how her recordings veered precipitously between country and rock & roll. Her bands were legendarily hot. She employed a mixed-race rock band including Bobby Poe, BIG AL DOWNING, and Vernon Sandusky; after she took up residency in Las Vegas in 1960, she hired ROY CLARK, then playing bars in the D.C. area, to be her guitarist and opening act.

Jackson scored a surprise hit in Japan in 1958 with "Fujiyama Mama," and, in 1960, had a late-blooming rock & roll hit in the United States with "Let's Have a Party," an album cut from two years earlier and a cover of a 1957 Elvis track. Shortly before, she had decided to revert to country music and scored Top Ten country hits in 1961 with "Right or Wrong" and "In the Middle of a Heartache." Twenty-six other country chart-makers followed over the next thirteen years. She also wrote BUCK OWENS's Top Ten country hit "(Let's Stop) Kickin' Our Hearts Around."

Jackson began recording in Nashville in 1960 but decided not to move there. In 1973 she became a born-again Christian, and for many years played religious and secular shows in the United States and toured overseas with a rockabilly show. She has recorded both sacred and secular albums, the latter including 2003's *Heart Trouble*. Jackson was elected to the Rock and Roll Hall of Fame in January 2009. In January 2011, she released a new album, *The Party Ain't Over*, produced by rocker Jack White and issued on White's Nashville-based label, Third Man Records. —Colin Escott

## Sonny James

b. Hackleburg, Alabama, May 1, 1929

Sonny James has enjoyed one of country music's most successful careers. Between 1953 and 1983 he scored seventy-two chart records, forty-three of which reached the Top Ten and twenty-three of which went to #1. According to *Billboard* statistics, between 1960 and 1979 he spent fifty-seven weeks at #1—more than any other country artist of the era. Known as the Southern Gentleman for his congenial personality and gracious manner, James has had his greatest success singing romantic ballads about the joys and trials of love.

James Hugh Loden was born into a family of professional entertainers. By age four Sonny (a family nickname) was performing with his parents and sister as the Loden Family, who soon had their own radio show in Birmingham. By his teens Sonny had mastered both the guitar and the fiddle and won several fiddle championships. He gained additional experience with his family on several southern radio stations and made solo appearances in the 1950s on Shreveport's LOUISIANA HAYRIDE and Dallas's BIG D JAMBOREE.

After military service, he signed with CAPITOL RECORDS, in 1952. Producer KEN NELSON suggested that James Loden adopt the stage name Sonny James (to keep it simple for the DJs and the record-buying public). James had several chart singles during the early 1950s, but "Young Love," written by Ric Cartey and Carole Joyner and released in 1956, was James's breakthrough hit. One of 1957's top songs, it reached #1 on both the country and pop charts. As a result, James frequently hosted the OZARK JUBILEE, broadcast weekly on ABC-TV from Springfield, Missouri, and often appeared on popular network variety programs such as *The Ed Sullivan Show*.

Following his initial success James spent several years searching for another hit while recording for NRC (1960), RCA VICTOR

*Sonny James*

(1961–62), and DOT (1962). Re-signing with Capitol in 1963, he bounced back with "The Minute You're Gone" (#9) and became a fixture on the country charts for the next decade. Between 1967 and 1971 James had sixteen consecutive #1 hits, including "Need You" (1967), "Heaven Says Hello" (1968), "Running Bear" (1969), and "Here Comes Honey Again" (1971). He received numerous awards, including being named #1 Country Male Artist of the Decade by *Record World* and #1 Artist by *Billboard* (1969).

In the 1970s James switched to COLUMBIA RECORDS and continued his string of hits with eleven Top Tens. In 1973 he produced MARIE OSMOND's "Paper Roses," a million-selling crossover record that went #1 country and #4 pop. He left Columbia in 1979 for MONUMENT and in 1981 moved on to Dimension Records, for whom he scored his last chart record in 1983 with "A Free Roamin' Mind."

James was elected to THE COUNTRY MUSIC HALL OF FAME in 2006. —*Don Roy*

### Jamup and Honey (Lasses and Honey)

Lee Roy "Lasses" White b. Wills Point, Texas, August 28, 1888;
    d. December 16, 1949
Lee Davis "Honey" Wilds b. Betton, Texas, August 23, 1902; d. March 29, 1982

This famed GRAND OLE OPRY blackface comedy team dates from 1932, when Nashville radio station WSM hired veteran comedian Lee Roy "Lasses" White to start a minstrel show. He came to Nashville with Lee Davis "Honey" Wilds, who had worked with him for a number of years.

White was one of the last avatars of vaudeville's longstanding blackface comedy tradition, which originated in BLACKFACE MINSTRELSY. Born in rural Wills Point, Texas, he was a protégé of the legendary George "Honey Boy" Evans and became known for a 1912 hit song called "Nigger Blues." By 1920 White had his own troupe and was recording sketches for COLUMBIA. Opry founder

GEORGE D. HAY, fond of the tradition White's act represented, hired White to reproduce it on WSM. Song parodies and *Amos 'n' Andy*–style dialog made the act immensely popular, and by 1934 the two comedians were Opry regulars.

In the mid-1930s White moved to Hollywood to become a character actor in cowboy films. In about 1939 Wilds left the Opry to tour as half of the Honey and Alexander duo, but late that year he returned to WSM. There he continued the blackface tradition with the act Jamup and Honey, which included a series of other partners, such as Tom Woods and Bunny Biggs. In 1940 Wilds became one of the first Opry acts to take a TENT SHOW on the road. By the early 1950s he was working at Knoxville radio station WNOX. —*Charles Wolfe*

### Tommy Jarrell

b. Surry County, North Carolina, March 1, 1901; d. January 28, 1985

Though he made his living as a moonshiner and a road grader, Thomas Jefferson Jarrell made a name for himself as a quintessential OLD-TIME fiddler. Raised in the Round Peak area of the Blue Ridge Mountains, he was one of eleven children of Ben Jarrell, who was the fiddler for DA COSTA WOLTZ's SOUTHERN BROADCASTERS, a STRINGBAND that recorded for GENNETT in 1927. At age fourteen Tommy bought his first fiddle with money won from gambling. Following his father's example, Jarrell mastered the Round Peak bowing style—an intricate wrist-and-elbow technique more frenzied than the long, smooth strokes favored by modern fiddlers.

Jarrell performed at house frolics and country dances for most of his life. It wasn't until the mid-1960s, after retiring from his job with the North Carolina Highway Department, that he attended his first music festival. During the next two decades Jarrell became a beloved figure on the festival circuit and nurtured an entire generation of young musicians, including JIMMY ARNOLD. A recipient of the 1982 National Heritage Fellowship Award, Jarrell was also the subject of Les Blank's documentary film *Sprout Wings and Fly*, which took its title from lyrics of Jarrell's signature tune, "Drunken Hiccups." —*Eddie Dean*

### John Barlow Jarvis

b. Pasadena, California, January 2, 1954

Regarded as a top Nashville session keyboard player, John Barlow Jarvis is also a hit songwriter. He shared writing credit with PAUL OVERSTREET and Naomi Judd on THE JUDDS' hit "Love Can Build a Bridge," which won a 1991 Grammy for Best Country Song. He collaborated with VINCE GILL on "I Still Believe in You," which won the same award for 1992, along with top song honors from ACM (1992) and CMA (1993). Other writing credits include cuts by THE HIGHWAYMEN, OLIVIA NEWTON-JOHN, and STEVE WARINER.

Jarvis came to Nashville in 1982 after a stint in Rod Stewart's band and several years working Los Angeles recording sessions. In the late 1980s he made four albums for the MCA RECORDS Master Series of recordings by Nashville musicians, which chronicle his virtuosity on piano and related keyboards. *Time* magazine ranked one of these, *Whatever Works*, as one of the ten best records of 1988. In 1989 James Taylor picked Jarvis to be a member of his fall touring group. By 1990 Jarvis was doing sessions steadily, contributing to albums by Gill, BROOKS & DUNN, MARY CHAPIN

CARPENTER, REBA MCENTIRE, DOLLY PARTON, and GEORGE STRAIT.

After LIBERTY issued Jarvis's *Balancing Act* in 1993, a decade passed before Jarvis released *View from a Southern Front Porch*. On this album he showcased original compositions while spanning stride, celtic, jazz, country, classical, and BLUEGRASS stylings. —*Michael Hight*

## Jason & the Scorchers

Jason Ringenberg b. Kewanee, Illinois, November 22, 1958
Warner Hodges b. Wurzburg, Germany, June 4, 1959
Jeff Johnson b. Nashville, Tennessee, December 31, 1959
Kenny Ames b. Pittsburgh, Pennsylvania, June 8, 1967
Perry Baggs b. Nashville, Tennessee, March 22, 1962

Wedding traditional country music with the confrontational energy and attitude of punk rock, Jason Ringenberg, son of an Illinois pig farmer, in 1981 formed a pioneering rock & roll band—Jason & the Nashville Scorchers, with guitarist Warner Hodges, bassist Jeff Johnson, and drummer Perry Baggs. One of Nashville's most dynamic live bands, the Scorchers recorded a four-song EP, *Reckless Country Soul*—including raved-up versions of HANK WILLIAMS and JIMMIE RODGERS standards—during December 1981. Another EP, 1983's *Fervor*, drew passionate critical acclaim and landed the act (now known simply as Jason & the Scorchers) a record deal with EMI.

In 1985 the Scorchers released the full-length album *Lost & Found*. Commercial success eluded them, however, and, after two more albums and some personnel changes, the band dissolved in 1989. Ringenberg courted the country mainstream on a 1991 solo album, *One Foot in the Honky Tonk*, for LIBERTY, but country radio didn't embrace his raw and rowdy vocal style.

At Johnson's urging, the Scorchers' original lineup reunited and resumed touring in mid-1993. Mammoth Records released *A Blazing Grace* in 1995, followed by a reissue of *Reckless Country Soul* (including six rediscovered tracks), and another studio album, *Clear Impetuous Morning*, in 1996. A new wave of acts indebted to the Scorchers and inspired by a similar mix of country and punk sensibilities emerged in the mid-1990s. Bassist Kenny Ames replaced the departed Johnson in 1998, and the band continued to impress fans, critics, and music industry insiders.

After Baggs left in 2003, the group played the occasional show while Ringenberg won a fan base of children, touring and recording as Farmer Jason. In 2008, Al Collins assumed bass duties, and the band toured Europe with Swedish drummer Pontus Snibb. That year the group received an AMERICANA Music Association Lifetime Achievement Award for Performance, prompting the 2010 album *Halcyon Times*. —*Jay Orr*

## JEMF (John Edwards Memorial Foundation, now Forum)

established in Los Angeles, California, 1961

Following JOHN EDWARDS's death on Christmas Eve 1960, in Australia, his mother, Irene, carried out her son's wishes by transferring his massive collection of 78-rpm discs, reel-to-reel tapes, photographs, letters, and ephemera to Eugene Earle in New Jersey. Long aware of John's affection for OLD-TIME MUSIC, Earle and colleagues Archie Green, Ed Kahn, Fred Hoeptner, and D. K. Wilgus chartered the John Edwards Memorial Foundation in California

in 1961. An educational nonprofit corporation, it pioneered the preservation and presentation of folk and vernacular American music in its varied manifestations. From its inception, the foundation brought together record collectors, ballad scholars, and country music artists and executives. From 1969 to 1985, Norm Cohen edited the influential *JEMF Quarterly* (seventy-eight issues); in these years he set superb analytic and aesthetic standards for treating sound recordings in their complex cultural roles. In foundation endeavors, enthusiastic volunteers and occasional staff members such as Ken Griffis, JOHN HARTFORD, Barry Hansen, Chris Strachwitz, Paul Wells, and Peter Tamony joined hands in housekeeping, fundraising, LP album issues, creating radio programs, and archive-building. From 1964 to 1983 UCLA's Folklore and Mythology Center housed the foundation. In 1986 the University of North Carolina's Southern Folklife Collection (Wilson Library, Chapel Hill) absorbed JEMF's holdings. —*Archie Green*

## Rev. Andrew Jenkins

b. Jenkinsburg, Georgia, November 26, 1885; d. April 25, 1957

The Reverend Andrew Jenkins was a blind preacher, musician, and writer of approximately 800 songs, including the gospel standard "God Put a Rainbow in the Cloud." During the 1920s and 1930s he was best known for his event songs, including "The Death of Floyd Collins," "The Wreck of the Royal Palm," "Frank Du Pree" [sic], and "Ben Dewberry's Final Run."

Blind most of his life, Rev. Jenkins pretended to be a preacher as a child, delivering sermons to his playmates from tree stumps and front porches. He also discovered at an early age that he could play any musical instrument he wanted to. The adult Jenkins became a real-life evangelist and parlayed his musical talents into a parallel career as a radio, stage, and recording artist.

On August 14, 1922, Rev. Jenkins and his two stepdaughters, Mary Lee Eskew and Irene Eskew Spain, made their debut on Atlanta's new radio station, WSB, in a program of sacred songs and secular ballads that included original compositions by Rev. Jenkins. The Jenkins Family was heard regularly on WSB during the ensuing decade. Radio exposure brought them to the attention of recording company executives, and from 1925 until 1934 the Jenkins Family, under various artist credits, recorded some one hundred sides for the OKEH and BLUEBIRD labels. —*Wayne W. Daniel*

## Snuffy Jenkins

b. Harris, North Carolina, October 27, 1908; d. April 30, 1990

Known primarily throughout South Carolina through his long musical partnership with fiddler Homer "Pappy" Sherrill, DeWitt "Snuffy" Jenkins was an important influence on such first-generation BLUEGRASS banjo players as EARL SCRUGGS, DON RENO, and RALPH STANLEY.

As a youth Jenkins learned banjo from pioneering three-finger stylists Rex Brooks and Smith Hammett. Forming a STRINGBAND with his brother Verl, Jenkins began his radio career in 1934 over WBT in Charlotte. In 1937 he worked with J. E. MAINER's Mountaineers on WIS–Columbia, South Carolina. When Mainer left, announcer Byron Parker fronted the renamed WIS Hillbillies; Sherrill joined the group in 1939. As a self-contained show band, the WIS Hillbillies—later called the Hired Hands—entertained South Carolinians with MEDICINE SHOW skits, comedy rooted in BLACKFACE MINSTRELSY, and outstanding musicianship.

Jenkins contributed broad, baggy-pants gags as well as banjo, guitar, and washboard specialties. He also worked South Carolina with FISHER HENDLEY's Aristocratic Pigs.

In 1956 Jenkins recorded several banjo instrumentals for OLD-TIME MUSIC enthusiast Mike Seeger; four appeared on the Folkways collection *American Banjo Tunes & Songs in Scruggs Style,* the first album devoted to bluegrass music. Sherrill and Jenkins made relatively few recordings during their prime, but later albums on Folk Lyric and ROUNDER fortunately preserve much of their repertoire.
—*Dave Samuelson*

## John Jennings (*see* Mary Chapin Carpenter)

## Waylon Jennings
b. Littlefield, Texas, June 15, 1937; d. February 13, 2002

In his 1996 autobiography, *Waylon* (Warner Books), Waylon Arnold Jennings graphically traced his journey from hardscrabble poverty in West Texas to teenage bassist for BUDDY HOLLY to Nashville rebel to OUTLAW star to cocaine addict to redemption.

Jennings escaped what he considered the futureless world of Littlefield, Texas, by working in radio in Lubbock and by picking up the guitar. Holly tapped him to play bass in Holly's new band on a midwestern tour in late 1958 and early 1959. While Jennings and others rode the bus one night, Holly, THE BIG BOPPER (J. P. Richardson), and singer Ritchie Valens took an ill-fated flight that claimed their lives. After the plane crashed, Jennings's musical world tumbled around him. Holly had been his mentor, producing his first record ("Jole Blon," BRUNSWICK, 1958), and Jennings felt responsible; according to Jennings, his last words to Holly had been "I hope your ole plane crashes," in a joking response to Holly's "I hope your damned bus freezes up again."

It took Jennings years to regain some career equilibrium. He went back to radio in West Texas and began performing again, ending up at J.D.'s, a bar in Phoenix, Arizona. Jennings became a local celebrity, and when performer BOBBY BARE passed through Phoenix and heard him, he called his producer, CHET ATKINS, at RCA in Nashville, about the raw young singer. Jennings had already cut some country-folk material for fledgling A&M Records in Los Angeles, but A&M demurred to Atkins, who signed Jennings to RCA in 1965.

Jennings moved to MUSIC CITY, and by sheer chance he became roommates with JOHNNY CASH; their legends as hell-raisers were

soon cemented. Jennings starred in the 1966 movie *Nashville Rebel* and scored Top Ten hits such as "The Chokin' Kind" (#8, 1967) and "Only Daddy That'll Walk the Line" (#2, 1968). His 1969 collaboration with the Kimberlys on "MacArthur Park" won a Grammy. But Jennings chafed under what he considered RCA's tight rein. When Atkins turned him over to staff producer DANNY DAVIS, Jennings once brandished a pistol in the studio to protest what he felt was Davis's bullying approach. For his part, Davis found Jennings's drug-induced, erratic behavior unmanageable and counterproductive.

Although he kept charting hits such as "Brown Eyed Handsome Man" (#3, 1969–70), by the early 1970s Jennings was finding country's mainstream too limiting. He hired hard-nosed New York manager Neil Reshen, who put Jennings into such high-profile venues as rock-retro Max's Kansas City nightclub in New York. In the studio Jennings stayed true to his musical instincts and recorded a gallery of landmark recordings, most notably the 1973 albums *Lonesome, On'ry and Mean* and *Honky Tonk Heroes.* He also staged an alternative show at the 1973 DJ CONVENTION in Nashville, with his buddy WILLIE NELSON, SAMMI SMITH, and Troy Seals joining him in an Outlaw program.

Jennings was dubbed an Outlaw for demanding and, with help from Reshen, getting what rock groups had enjoyed for years—the right to choose their own material, studios, and session musicians. (Nelson won his own independence from RCA by exiting the label, moving back to Texas, and recording there.) To Jennings, it was a simple matter of artistic freedom. RCA ultimately gave him that freedom—paying the performer's session and touring costs, despite the fact that by 1976 his account with the company was $1 million in the red due to less-than-spectacular sales.

Jennings won CMA's Male Vocalist of the Year Award in 1975, but what finally won the battle for Jennings and the Outlaws was the ultimate weapon: sales. *Wanted! The Outlaws*, an RCA package of recordings by Jennings, Nelson, Jennings's wife, JESSI COLTER, and Tompall Glaser (see THE GLASER BROTHERS), was released in January 1976. The album flew out of record stores and soon became the first album in country music history to be certified platinum. The Jennings-Nelson performance "Good Hearted Woman" became a major crossover hit in 1976, as did Jennings's "Luckenbach, Texas (Back to the Basics of Love)" the following year. *The Outlaws* became CMA's 1976 Album of the Year, and Jennings and Nelson, CMA's 1976 Duo of the Year, also won Single of the Year honors for "Good Hearted Woman." Their 1978 hit "Mammas Don't Let Your Babies Grow Up to be Cowboys" won a Grammy. Forever linked as "Waylon and Willie" whether recording separately or together, they began selling records in numbers previously associated with rock albums, and Nashville recording gradually moved away from a producer-dominated order to one in which the artist shares power.

Hit records led to Jennings's role as narrator on the popular TV series *The Dukes of Hazzard* (1979–85). Though his face was never shown onscreen, he also sang his self-penned "Good Ol' Boys," the show's theme song, as The Balladeer.

Sadly, Jennings's excesses also paralleled those of the rock world, and a $1,500-a-day cocaine habit eroded his success. He eventually overcame his addiction and returned to a scaled-down career, including stints on MCA and EPIC during the late 1980s and early 1990s. A high school dropout, he became something of a role model by earning his GED, or high school equivalency diploma, to set a good example for his young son.

In 1998 Jennings formed the group The Old Dogs with Bobby Bare, JERRY REED, and MEL TILLIS and recorded an eponymous double album of SHEL SILVERSTEIN songs. The next year Jennings organized the larger Waymore Blues Band and made selective

*Waylon Jennings*

appearances into 2001. In 2000 he recorded what proved to be his final album, *Never Say Die: Live*, at THE RYMAN AUDITORIUM. Jennings was elected to THE COUNTRY MUSIC HALL OF FAME in 2001 and died of complications related to diabetes in 2002. —*Chet Flippo*

## Jesse James & All the Boys
William Howard "Jesse" James b. Mississippi, December 5, 1916;
d. April 16, 1972

Long before AUSTIN became the center for progressive country in the 1970s, the Texas capital had a vibrant country music scene. The area's dominant band from the mid-1940s through the mid-1950s was the slick WESTERN SWING group Jesse James & All the Boys.

Airing over KTBC radio (and later on TV) and recording for Blue Bonnet and FOUR STAR RECORDS, the band included a slew of accomplished musicians, such as classically trained violinists Joe Castle and the exciting Roddy Bristol (who had come to Texas with PAUL HOWARD), steel guitarists Lefty Nason and Jimmy Grabowske, clarinetist-vocalist Hub Sutter, and others. The band's recorded output was of uniformly high quality, but the group never gained more than regional recognition. In addition to its own recordings, the band backed comedian Cactus Pryor on his Four Star releases. James disbanded the group in the mid-1950s. —*Kevin Coffey*

## Jim & Jesse
James Monroe McReynolds b. Carfax, Virginia, February 13, 1927;
d. December 31, 2002
Jesse Lester McReynolds b. Carfax, Virginia, July 9, 1929

First-generation BLUEGRASS performers Jim and Jesse McReynolds stretched musical boundaries while maintaining their traditional roots. They recorded and sang everything from OLD-TIME MUSIC and contemporary country material to gospel numbers, folk songs, and rock & roll hits.

The brothers' vocal harmonies—featuring Jim's soaring tenor—together with Jesse's innovative cross-picking and split-string mandolin techniques, earned them wide respect. Their band, the Virginia Boys, consistently showcased some of the genre's finest players, such as VASSAR CLEMENTS, banjoist Allen Shelton, and fiddlers Jim Buchanan and Jim Brock.

Raised in musically rich Appalachian Virginia, Jim and Jesse McReynolds began performing locally as the McReynolds Brothers before moving to various southeastern and midwestern radio stations. They first recorded as the Virginia Trio for Kentucky Records in 1951. By the time of their first CAPITOL sessions (1952), Jesse was experimenting with his cross-picking style, which uses a flat pick to simulate a three-finger banjo roll. At this point, they took the name Jim & Jesse and the Virginia Boys.

In the 1950s they appeared on radio barn dances including the *WDVA Barn Dance* in Danville, Virginia; the *MID-DAY MERRY-GO-ROUND* on WNOX in Knoxville; the *WWVA JAMBOREE* in Wheeling, West Virginia; and the *Suwannee River Jamboree* on WNER in Live Oak, Florida. They also launched their own local television shows in Florida, Georgia, and Alabama, which were picked up by sponsor MARTHA WHITE Foods in 1960 and expanded into additional markets.

In late 1960 Jim & Jesse began recording for EPIC, and their first two albums, *Bluegrass Special* and *Bluegrass Classics*, crystallized their style. In 1964, the year they joined the GRAND OLE OPRY, "Cotton Mill Man" became the duo's first chart record; "Diesel

*Jim (left) & Jesse McReynolds*

on My Tail," their most successful single, reached #18 in 1967. Their 1965 album *Berry Pickin' in the Country* honored rocker Chuck Berry, and Jesse played on the Doors album *The Soft Parade* (1969). From the mid-1960s into the 1970s Jim & Jesse had a popular syndicated TV program; on this show, as on their Epic recordings, they included electric guitars and steel guitars.

In the early 1970s the brothers formed Old Dominion Records, and in 1999 Pinecastle Records gave their Old Dominion sides new life in a boxed set. From the mid-1970s Jim & Jesse released many of their recordings on their own Double J label. Their 2001 album *Our Kind of Country* (Pinecastle) showcased songs earlier made famous by BUCK OWENS and RAY PRICE.

Jim & Jesse were elected to the IBMA Hall of Fame in 1993, and in 1997 they received the prestigious National Heritage Fellowship Award from the National Endowment for the Arts.

Since Jim's death in 2002, Jesse McReynolds & the Virginia Boys have continued to tour, make Opry appearances, and record. In 2010 McReynolds released an album devoted to the music of Grateful Dead member Jerry Garcia. —*Dale Vinicur*

## Jim Owens Productions (*see* Crook & Chase)

## Flaco Jimenez
b. San Antonio , Texas, March 11, 1939

Leonardo "Flaco" Jimenez belongs to what has been called the First Family of Texas CONJUNTO MUSIC. His father, Santiago "El Flaco" Jimenez Sr., who left Leonardo his nickname (*flaco* means "skinny" in Spanish), was a conjunto accordion pioneer. Flaco's brother, Santiago Jimenez Jr., is a traditionalist who performs in his father's style.

Known for his fast, flashy, hard-driving playing, Flaco Jimenez has pioneered in popularizing conjunto music outside of its traditional audience. He has performed with musicians such as Ry Cooder, LINDA RONSTADT, EMMYLOU HARRIS, DWIGHT YOAKAM, and BUCK OWENS. Touring North America, Europe, and Japan, Jimenez has brought conjunto to the world. With the Texas Tornados (formed in 1990), he created a music that combined conjunto's Hispanic roots with Anglo-American country music and rock & roll.

In 1990 the Texas Tornados received a Grammy for their single "Soy de San Luis," written by Jimenez's father. Flaco also received Grammys for his recording *Ay Te Dejo en San Antonio* (1986) and the albums *Flaco Jimenez* (1994) and *Said and Done* (1998). As part of Los Super Seven he won a second 1998 Grammy for the group's self-titled album. He has also contributed to many movie soundtracks and assisted the Hohner company in creating his signature series of accordions. —*David Romtvedt*

## John Edwards Memorial Foundation (*see* JEMF)

## Johnnie & Jack

Johnnie Robert Wright b. Mount Juliet, Tennessee, May 13, 1914; d. September 27, 2011
Jack Anglin b. Franklin, Tennessee, May 13, 1916; d. March 7, 1963

Johnnie & Jack helped carry the BROTHER DUET style into the 1940s and 1950s, though they were not brothers but brothers-in-law. They also pioneered the use of Latin rhythms in country music and played a crucial role in the career of KITTY WELLS.

Prior to teaming with Wright, Jack Anglin performed with brothers Jim Anglin (b. March 23, 1913; d. January 21, 1987) and Van Buren "Red" Anglin (b. April 20, 1910; d. August 23, 1975); the trio first recorded in 1937 for the AMERICAN RECORD CORPORATION as the Anglin Twins & Red.

Johnnie Wright first worked with Jack Anglin in 1938 as fundraising entertainment for flood victims. In June 1938 Jack Anglin married Wright's sister Louise, then singing with Johnnie and his wife, Muriel (a.k.a. Kitty Wells), as Johnnie Wright & the Harmony Girls on WSIX–Nashville. Johnnie and Muriel wed October 30, 1937. An unseen partner in the Johnnie & Jack act was Jack's elder brother, Jim, a gifted songwriter who penned "Beneath That Lonely Mound of Clay" and "Stuck Up Blues" (both sold to ROY ACUFF), "One by One," and "Ashes of Love."

With their Tennessee Hillbillies band (featuring Muriel), Johnnie & Jack moved from station to station, engaging sponsors and working show dates. Temporary bases included WBIG–Greensboro, North Carolina; WCHS–Charleston, West Virginia; and WNOX–Knoxville. World War II gasoline rationing prompted a touring halt. Anglin was drafted and sent overseas. EDDIE HILL convinced Wright to regroup in 1943. While at WNOX they briefly hired young fiddler CHET ATKINS, later a world-class guitarist. Discharged in February 1946, Anglin reunited with Wright at WPTF–Raleigh, North Carolina.

In 1947 Johnnie & Jack first recorded for the KING and Apollo labels. That year WSM offered the singers a regular spot on the GRAND OLE OPRY, contingent on dropping "hillbillies" from their band name, so the band was renamed the Tennessee Mountain Boys. They left WSM for KWKH–Shreveport, on New Year's Day 1948, and on April 3, 1948, they were in the cast of the first LOUISIANA HAYRIDE broadcast.

In 1949 the duo signed with RCA VICTOR; they enjoyed their greatest success in the 1950s. They injected a Latin beat into country via their breakthrough single, "Poison Love" (#4, 1951), followed by "Cryin' Heart Blues" (#5), which boasted a distinctive

*Johnnie & Jack: Johnnie Wright (left) and Jack Anglin*

calypso rhythm. Next, they adapted R&B to a country beat with covers of the Four Knights' pop million-seller "(Oh, Baby Mine) I Get So Lonely" (#1, 1954) and the Spaniels' "Goodnight, Sweetheart, Goodnight" (#3, 1954).

After "Poison Love" hit, the group was invited back to the Opry. When chart performance dipped after their #7 hit "Stop the World (And Let Me Off)" (1958), the act moved to DECCA (in 1961). Their first chart record for the label, "Slow Poison" (#17, 1962), was issued as Johnny & Jack. Wright took the misprint as a cue and afterward used this spelling.

Tragedy struck in 1963. Anglin died in a one-car crash on the day of services for plane-wreck victims PATSY CLINE, COWBOY COPAS, HAWKSHAW HAWKINS, and RANDY HUGHES. Afterward Wright continued as a solo recording act and scored a #1 single in 1965 with "Hello Vietnam." For many years he continued to tour with the Kitty Wells–Johnny Wright Family Show, which sometimes included son Bobby Wright. —*Walt Trott*

## Earl Johnson

b. Gwinnett County, Georgia, August 24, 1886; d. May 24, 1965

North Georgia fiddler Earl Johnson played in a supercharged breakneck style that excited live audiences and record buyers. Beginning his career in a family band, Johnson first won fame as a second fiddler for FIDDLIN' JOHN CARSON's Virginia Reelers, who recorded extensively for OKEH in the late 1920s. Johnson soon had his own OKeh contract, recording popular sides such as "Ain't Nobody's Business," "Shortenin' Bread," and "Bully of the Town" with his own Clodhoppers band. The Clodhoppers generally included the fine guitarist Byrd Moore as well as banjoist Emmett Bankston and guitarist Lee Henderson. In the 1930s Johnson recreated some of his best sides for RCA VICTOR. After his recording days, he remained active in local fiddling contests and became one of the first in his area to master the new BLUEGRASS banjo stylings of EARL SCRUGGS. —*Charles Wolfe*

## Jamey Johnson

b. Enterprise, Alabama, July 14, 1975

As a writer of #1 hits for GEORGE STRAIT and TRACE ADKINS, Jamey Johnson might have pursued a career as a Nashville songwriter.

*Jamey Johnson*

Instead, this singer with a Hell's Angel beard chose a path closer to that of his OUTLAW-country hero WAYLON JENNINGS.

Johnson grew up in Montgomery, Alabama. After two years of college, he served eight years in the Marine Corps Reserves while gigging with country bands around Montgomery. Moving to Nashville in 2000, he honed his craft singing on other song-writers' demos.

By 2005 Johnson had landed a songwriting contract and a record deal. He scored his first hit that year with the title track from his BNA (see RCA RECORDS) album *The Dollar*. Though dropped by BNA and divorced by his wife, he won ACM's 2006 Song of the Year award for cowriting George Strait's chart-topper "Give It Away."

Johnson's self-financed album, *That Lonesome Song,* was rere-leased by MERCURY Nashville in 2008. Drenched in PEDAL STEEL GUITAR, its throwback Outlaw sound—coupled with Johnson's bleakly insightful lyrics and gruff-yet-tender baritone—gained widespread critical acclaim, a gold record, and several Grammy nominations. The album also supplied his first Top Ten single, "In Color," a poignant ballad that earned Johnson CMA and ACM Song of the Year honors, in 2009. —*Mick Buck*

## Michael Johnson
b. Alamosa, Colorado, August 8, 1944

This talented singer, guitarist, and songwriter had a long track record in folk and pop when he started making country records in 1985. Michael J. Johnson brought a high level of musicianship and a literary approach to songwriting when country was emerging out of the doldrums to scale new heights.

Much earlier, Chuck Berry and Charlie Byrd influenced Johnson's guitar playing, as did classical styles Johnson learned in Barcelona studying with Graciano Tarragó. Johnson performed for a year with the folksy Chad Mitchell Trio, spent time as an actor, and by 1971 began working with producers Peter Yarrow and Phil Ramone on *There is a Breeze*, Johnson's ATLANTIC RECORDS debut. Two albums for the independent Sanskrit label followed. In 1978 Johnson began a partnership with Nashville producers STEVE GIBSON and BRENT MAHER that resulted in the tuneful pop hits "Bluer Than Blue" (1978) and "This Night Won't Last Forever" (1979), both on EMI America.

When Johnson came back to MUSIC CITY in the mid-1980s, he turned to Maher and guitarist DON POTTER, both part of THE JUDDS' hit sound. Now on RCA, Johnson's first foray into country produced "I Love You by Heart," a Top Ten duet with SYLVIA. His country album debut, *Wings* (1986), featured an acoustic-based sound and netted two #1 singles, "Give Me Wings," written by DON SCHLITZ and Kye Fleming, and "The Moon Is Still Over Her Shoulder," by Hugh Prestwood. *That's That* (1988) produced the Top Ten hits "Crying Shame," "I Will Whisper Your Name," and the title track. Johnson elected to leave RCA and was temporarily sidelined by a skin disorder, but he returned to disc for Atlantic in 1992 with a fine self-titled album. Despite its artistic merits, the collection failed to dent the charts. Johnson has continued to tour and record, releasing the AMERICANA-styled *Departure* for Vanguard in 1995 and a career retrospective, *Then and Now*, for Intersound in 1997. He released *Live at the Bluebird Café* on American Originals in 2002. —*Thomas Goldsmith*

## Johnson Mountain Boys
Dudley Dale Connell b. Olney, Maryland, February 18, 1956
Edward Lawrence Stubbs b. Bethesda, Maryland, November 25, 1961
David Wallace McLaughlin b. Washington, D.C., February 13, 1958
Richard Dean Underwood b. Washington, D.C., July 14, 1956
Larry Palmer Robbins b. Dickerson, Maryland, April 25, 1945
Richard Thomas Adams Jr. b. Gettysburg, Pennsylvania, November 17, 1958
Marshall Wilborn b. Austin, Texas, March 12, 1952
Hugh Clark "Earl" Yager b. Gordonsville, Virginia, November 2, 1953

In the late 1970s and early 1980s the Johnson Mountain Boys spearheaded a resurgence of interest in and respect for traditional BLUEGRASS music. Formed in 1975 as a tradition-oriented duet, the act quickly grew into a five-piece ensemble. One of the most popular incarnations of the band featured guitarist and lead and tenor vocalist Dudley Connell, fiddler Eddie Stubbs, banjoist Richard Underwood, mandolinist David McLaughlin, and bassist Larry Robbins. (In 1986 Marshall Wilborn took over for Robbins and Tom Adams replaced Underwood; Earl Yager joined on bass in 1989.) The band's self-titled debut release for ROUNDER RECORDS in 1981 met with critical acclaim and helped to establish the group on the bluegrass circuit as one of the genre's top bands.

Greater Washington, D.C., was the act's stomping ground, and career highlights included performances at the White House, Madison Square Garden, the Kennedy Center, the GRAND OLE OPRY, and CARNEGIE HALL as well as appearances in England and Africa. In 1988 the band bade an emotional and much-publicized farewell to music, citing a grueling schedule and marginal economic gains as the chief reasons. In 1989, however, the act returned to making festival and concert appearances on an abbreviated schedule before disbanding in late 1996. Of the group's nine Rounder albums, *At the Old Schoolhouse* (1989) and *Blue Diamond* (1993) were nominated for Grammys in the Best Bluegrass Recording category.

Eddie Stubbs, featured on his own radio show over WAMU–Washington, D.C., from 1990 to 2007, backed KITTY WELLS for a year beginning in early 1995 while becoming a popular radio host and Grand Ole Opry announcer at Nashville's WSM. There he remains a staunch advocate for historic and tradition-minded country acts. Dudley Connell joined SELDOM SCENE in 1996 and has worked for the Smithsonian Institution and the National Council for the Traditional Arts. Tom Adams has played in bluegrass bands led by Dale Ann Bradley, Bill Emerson, LYNN MORRIS, and RHONDA VINCENT; in 2009 he joined Michael Cleveland & Flamekeeper. McLaughlin has also performed with several bands. Wilborn helped organize the Lynn Morris Band and became a member of Michael Cleveland & Flamekeeper in 2007. —*Gary B. Reid*

## Bob Johnston

b. Hillsboro, Texas, May 14, 1932

For a brief period during the late 1960s, producer Don William "Bob" Johnston ran the Nashville A&R division of COLUMBIA RECORDS. Though his executive tenure was relatively short, his impact on MUSIC CITY's creative direction was huge. He produced BOB DYLAN's 1960s Nashville recordings as well as JOHNNY CASH's *Live at Folsom Prison* and *Live at San Quentin* LPs. His success with these and other artists proved instrumental in bringing pop acts such as Simon & Garfunkel to Nashville to record.

Johnston was born in Hillsboro, Texas, but was raised in Fort Worth. His grandmother was a songwriter, as was his mother, Diane Johnston, whose credits include ASLEEP AT THE WHEEL's "Miles and Miles of Texas." By the late 1950s Johnston himself was writing songs, working for publishing companies, recording as a solo artist, and producing such acts as the Jaguars, a rock & roll band that included CHARLIE DANIELS. Johnston often traveled to Nashville to produce song demos, which eventually led to A&R work for Kapp Records in New York. From Kapp, Johnston moved to Columbia's New York office, where in 1965 he scored his first major A&R success producing Patti Page's "Hush, Hush, Sweet Charlotte"—for which the basic tracks (but not the strings or vocal, according to Johnston) were recorded in Nashville.

In 1965 Johnston produced most of Bob Dylan's *Highway 61 Revisited* in New York. On the cut "Desolation Row" from that album, Nashville session pro CHARLIE McCOY played acoustic guitar. After this experience, Dylan elected to record his next album, *Blonde on Blonde* (1966), in Nashville. Johnston produced the record, as he would Dylan's *John Wesley Harding*, *Nashville Skyline*, and *Self Portrait*, all of which were cut in Music City (*Self Portrait* partially so).

In early 1967 Columbia chose Johnston as the label's director of country A&R, taking over from DON LAW, who had reached mandatory retirement age. Among his first moves, Johnston gave Johnny Cash the green light to record live at Folsom Prison. He also worked with FLATT & SCRUGGS, producing, for instance, their album *Changin' Times*.

In early 1968 BILLY SHERRILL succeeded Johnston as the head of country A&R for Columbia and its affiliated EPIC label. Johnston retained the title of executive producer at large and continued to work with some of Columbia's star country acts. Among these was MARTY ROBBINS, whose 1970 hit "My Woman, My Woman, My Wife" Johnston produced.

By the mid-1970s Johnson had returned to working as an independent producer. His profile was in decline, though he continued to play a behind-the-scenes role in such projects as Cheryl Lynn's 1979 disco smash "Got to Be Real" and WILLIE NELSON's *Who'll Buy My Memories: The IRS Tapes* (1991). Johnston was also heavily involved in the production of CARL PERKINS's 1996 album *Go Cat Go!* —*Daniel Cooper*

## Ann Jones

b. Hutchinson, Kansas, ca. 1920

Billed as the "Kate Smith of the West," husky Ann Jones recorded prolifically for the CAPITOL and KING labels during the post–World War II years and achieved prominence as a radio broadcaster, songwriter, and bandleader.

Born Ann Matthews in Kansas, she moved west as a child, singing in a duo with sister Frances in Enid, Oklahoma, and Anaheim, California. She married in 1937 and temporarily retired, starring on an all-girl softball team during the war years. She returned to music in 1947 on the West Coast, scoring her biggest hit in 1949 with "Give Me a Hundred Reasons" on Capitol. She wrote all of her material, making her one of country's trailblazing female singer-songwriters.

Jones hosted her own *Ranch Roundup* TV show on KTTV in Hollywood and worked radio shows elsewhere in California, North Carolina, and West Virginia. By 1952 Jones was active on KVAN in Vancouver, Washington. In about 1955 she formed the all-female swing band the Western Sweethearts in the Pacific Northwest. Billed as "the queens of WESTERN SWING," the group toured internationally and remained together for twenty years.

Jones was an active participant in the early DJ CONVENTIONS in Nashville, when women in radio were rare. She remained a touring attraction into the 1970s. —*Robert K. Oermann*

## Buddy Jones

b. Asheville, North Carolina, December 25, 1906; d. October 20, 1956

Oscar Bergan Riley, better known as Buddy Jones, is best remembered for recording raucous, off-color tales of wild women and beer joints throughout most of his career, but the prurience of those recordings has often obscured his role as a progenitor of HONKY-TONK. By grafting WESTERN SWING elements and a roadhouse mentality onto a JIMMIE RODGERS–inspired blues and ballad tradition, he helped pave the way for postwar honky-tonkers.

Taught guitar by his stepfather, Joe Jones, around Port Arthur, Texas, Buddy also absorbed Gulf Coast blues that gave his style a tougher edge than those of most Rodgers devotees. He settled in Shreveport in the late 1920s, joining the Pelican Wildcats, a trio that would record for COLUMBIA in 1931. He also backed up-and-coming JIMMIE DAVIS on several sessions for RCA VICTOR. As Davis began to tone down his own material, he secured a DECCA contract for Jones to record the same racy mix from which he was shying.

Initially Jones sang duets with Davis, such as the fine "Red River Blues" (1935), but soon he was recording on his own, easing from talking blues to Rodgers remakes before turning toward a largely original repertoire in the late 1930s. Usually accompanied by his steel-playing brother Buster, who also wrote or cowrote much of the material, Jones began producing JUKEBOX hits such as "She's Selling What She Used to Give Away" and "The Roughest Gal in Town." His recordings began leaning toward western swing, featuring musicians such as MOON MULLICAN, CLIFF BRUNER, and Leo Raley, but retained a decidedly country feel. His last sessions, in 1941, were more mainstream than before but hardly tame. A Shreveport traffic cop from the mid-1930s until his death, Jones performed only part-time after World War II. —*Kevin Coffey*

## Frank Jones
b. Toronto, Ontario, Canada, March 4, 1928; d. February 3, 2005

Music executive Frank Jones led organizations ranging from record and publishing companies to civic groups. He grew up in Ontario, Canada, where he was performing in his own band by age fifteen. By 1949 he had careers in radio broadcasting and talent booking. During the 1950s Jones began working for Columbia Records' Canadian counterpart in sales and promotions and eventually as head of A&R. Don Law, executive producer of Columbia's U.S. country music division, requested that Jones join Nashville's A&R staff in 1961. During Jones's tenure at the label, he and Law produced Johnny Cash, Marty Robbins, and Ray Price, championing these artists' insistence on pursuing their own musical goals. Jones later served as marketing director for all of Columbia's Nashville record releases and subsequently presided over the Nashville operations of Capitol (1973–78), Inergi (1979), Warner Bros. (1980–83), and Mercury (1983–85).

Jones served as a CMA board member as well as president and board chairman of the Country Music Hall of Fame and Museum. Jones received many honors, including the 1970 CMA President's Award for Outstanding Contributions to that organization and *Billboard*'s 1972 Record Executive of the Year award. He was elected to the Canadian Country Music Hall of Fame in 1993. —*Don Roy*

## George Jones
b. Saratoga, Texas, September 12, 1931

The unique vocal gifts of George Glenn Jones have made him one of the most important artists in country music history. A singer who can soar from a deep growl to dizzying heights, he is the undisputed successor of earlier natural geniuses such as Hank Williams and Lefty Frizzell.

*George Jones*

Jones's career has spanned more than fifty years, yet it is more than longevity or the purity of his hard-country instincts that has made him an iconic and influential figure. Indeed, Jones is one of country's last links to its rural past—a time and place before cable and satellite TV, FM rock radio, shopping malls, and cell phones, when life still revolved around the local church, the roadside honky-tonk, and Saturday night Grand Ole Opry broadcasts. The fact that Jones himself has changed little and at times seems genuinely bewildered by his own talent and success has only enhanced his credibility. Like Hank Williams, Jones has emerged—quite unintentionally—as an archetype of an era that has passed yet still exists in his life and music. And, like Williams, he earned his stature by living his songs. His humble origins, his painful divorces, his legendary drinking and drugging, and his many financial, legal, and emotional problems have repeatedly confirmed his sincerity and intensified his powerful mystique.

Born in a log cabin in the remote Big Thicket region of East Texas, Jones suffered the rages of an alcoholic father and took refuge in music. As a child he sang for tips on the streets of Beaumont, where he moved with his parents into a government-subsidized housing project. Roy Acuff, Williams, and Frizzell (whom he most resembles as a vocalist) comprised Jones's youthful musical models.

In the late 1940s Jones sang with a friend on radio station KTXJ in Jasper, Texas. Performing with husband-wife team Eddie & Pearl on Beaumont's KRIC, he met his idol Hank Williams, who dropped by to sing a song and promote a local show date.

In 1950 Jones married Dorothy Bonvillion, but they divorced just over a year later. In her petition Bonvillion cited Jones's "violent temper" and claimed he was "addicted to the drinking of alcoholic beverages," problems that would often resurface in Jones's life. After several incarcerations for failing to support Dorothy and their daughter, Jones joined the U.S. Marine Corps.

In January 1954, back in civilian clothes, Jones cut his first record, a prophetically titled original called "No Money in This Deal." The session took place in the crude home studio of Houston businessman Jack Starnes, an original partner in the regional Starday label. Starnes's partner, local jukebox operator Pappy Daily, served as Jones's producer and manager, roles he would play until 1970.

"Why Baby Why," Jones's first Top Five hit, which he cowrote, appeared on Starday in 1955. When he moved on to Mercury Records and began recording in Nashville shortly thereafter, the hits kept coming: "Color of the Blues," "White Lightning" (his first #1, 1959), "Who Shot Sam," "The Window Up Above" (also written by Jones), and "Tender Years" are early classics from Jones's vast recorded catalog.

In 1954 Jones married his second wife, Shirley Ann Corley, after a two-week courtship. They divorced in 1968.

In the 1960s Jones steadily recorded hits for the United Artists and Musicor labels, though his style began to mellow from the jittery honky-tonk of "Why Baby Why" and the handful of rockabilly sides he reluctantly cut in 1956 under the pseudonym Thumper Jones. High points of this era included "She Thinks I Still Care," "The Race Is On," "Walk Through This World with Me," and "A Good Year for the Roses," all Top Five chart-makers.

In 1971 Jones signed with Epic Records and began working with producer Billy Sherrill, who would coax out of the temperamental, often-hard-drinking Jones some of his best vocal performances. "A Picture of Me (Without You)" (1972), "The Grand Tour"

(1974), "The Door" (1974–75), and "Bartender's Blues" (1978) are just a few commercial and aesthetic peaks of the Jones-Sherrill collaboration.

In 1969 Jones married singer TAMMY WYNETTE, already a solo star on Sherrill's roster. Under Sherrill's direction, the two singers recorded hit duets such as "We're Gonna Hold On," "Golden Ring," "Near You," and "Two Story House," forging an indelible image as musical soul mates that transcended their divorce in 1975.

Following their breakup, the late 1970s and early 1980s were dark times for Jones. Due to alcohol and cocaine addiction, he was arrested and hospitalized numerous times. He missed dozens of performances (thus earning the nickname No Show Jones) and became ensnared in legal and financial problems. His health grew precarious, his weight plummeting to ninety-seven pounds.

In the midst of adversity, however, Jones recorded "He Stopped Loving Her Today," a mournful ballad that hit #1 in 1980 and propelled him toward honors as CMA's Male Vocalist of the Year in 1980 and 1981. Additionally, the recording earned Jones a 1980 Grammy for Best Male Country Vocal Performance.

In 1983 Jones's marriage to his fourth wife, Nancy Sepulvado, marked the beginning of his sometimes-erratic rehabilitation. In 1990 he signed with MCA; he recorded seven albums for the label over the next eight years. Jones was inducted into THE COUNTRY MUSIC HALL OF FAME in 1992, and his autobiography, *I Lived to Tell It All* (Villard Books, 1996), was a hardcover best-seller. He won CMA's Music Video of the Year award for "Who's Gonna Fill Their Shoes" in 1986; claimed CMA's 1993 Vocal Event of the Year award for "I Don't Need Your Rockin' Chair" (showcasing multiple artists); and guested on PATTY LOVELESS's "You Don't Seem to Miss Me," CMA's Vocal Event winner for 1998. Jones later appeared on BRAD PAISLEY's "Too Country" (also featuring BUCK OWENS and BILL ANDERSON), 2001's CMA Vocal Event of the Year.

By the 1990s, though, Jones's radio exposure was waning, for country stations favored younger rock- or pop-leaning artists in reaching for the youthful audiences advertisers covet. MCA dropped him, despite collective album sales of some 1.5 million units. Undaunted, Jones signed with ASYLUM in 1998 and released *Cold Hard Truth* in 1999, the same year he suffered serious injuries after driving while impaired and wrecking his car. The album quickly sold more than 500,000 units.

With "Choices," a selection from this album, Jones seemed to take responsibility for his problems. The Top Thirty recording won Jones another Grammy and was nominated for CMA Single of the Year, but *CMA Awards Show* producers would not let him perform the entire song, and Jones refused to appear. On the broadcast, ALAN JACKSON voiced his admiration for Jones by interrupting one of his own songs and launching into "Choices," earning a standing ovation intended for both artists.

In the 1990s and beyond, Jones has recorded chart-making duets with RANDY TRAVIS, SAMMY KERSHAW, Chad Brock, HANK WILLIAMS JR., GARTH BROOKS, and Shooter Jennings. Since 2000 he has also charted occasional solo singles while continuing to release new and previously recorded material on albums including *The Rock: Stone Cold Country 2001* (BNA/Bandit, 2001); *Hits I Missed . . . And One I Didn't* (Bandit, 2005); *Kickin' Out the Footlights . . . Again* (Bandit, 2005), recorded with MERLE HAGGARD; and *Burn Your Playhouse Down* (Bandit, 2008), featuring duets with the Rolling Stones' Keith Richards, Dire Straits singer-guitarist Mark Knopfler, and a number of leading country stars.

One of country music's most revered entertainers, Jones received the prestigious Kennedy Center Honors for lifetime achievement in 2008. —*Bob Allen*

## Grandpa Jones
b. Niagara, Kentucky, October 20, 1913; d. February 19, 1998

Best known for his exuberant banjo playing, novelty songs including "Rattler" and "Mountain Dew," and infectious verbal comedy on *HEE HAW*, Grandpa Jones was one of country music's most dedicated champions of OLD-TIME MUSIC. Not only did he keep clawhammer banjo playing alive during times when it had fallen into disfavor with most professional musicians, but he also helped to keep current the songs of pioneers such as JIMMIE RODGERS, BRADLEY KINCAID, LULU BELLE & SCOTTY, and the DELMORE BROTHERS. In addition, Jones helped maintain the venerable southern gospel quartet tradition in groups such as the BROWN'S FERRY FOUR and the *Hee Haw* Gospel Quartet. Though not an acoustic purist in the strict sense—he often used an electric guitar onstage and on his records—his devotion to "keeping it country" won fans nationwide for seven decades as well as a longtime tenure on the GRAND OLE OPRY and election to THE COUNTRY MUSIC HALL OF FAME in 1978.

The youngest of ten children born to a tobacco-farming couple, Louis Marshall Jones grew up in northwestern Kentucky. By his high school years, the family was living in Akron, Ohio, and young Marshall (as he was called then) was copying Jimmie Rodgers material and appearing on local station WJW as "The Young Singer of Old Songs." After a stint on the popular *Lum and Abner* network radio series (as part of the show's STRINGBAND), he and friend Joe Troyan ("Harmonica Joe") met influential country singer Bradley Kincaid. In 1935 they were working with Kincaid over WBZ–Boston when Kincaid gave Jones the nickname Grandpa because he sounded old and grouchy on their early-morning show. Kincaid had him outfitted with a vaudeville costume—including a fake mustache—and at age twenty-two Marshall Jones became Grandpa Jones.

By 1937 Jones struck out on his own, playing stations in West Virginia and Cincinnati. Along the way he met boisterous entertainer COUSIN EMMY, who taught him how to play clawhammer banjo—which he soon incorporated into his act. At WLW–Cincinnati he joined forces with the Delmore Brothers and

*Grandpa Jones*

MERLE TRAVIS to form the Brown's Ferry Four, one of country music's earliest and most popular gospel quartets. In the fall of 1943 Jones and Travis made their first recordings, for a new, locally based label to be called KING RECORDS; their disc, released under the pseudonym the Shepherd Brothers, was King's first release. Through the 1950s Jones recorded regularly for King, racking up hits such as "It's Raining Here This Morning," "Eight More Miles to Louisville," and "Mountain Dew."

In October 1946 Jones married Ramona Riggins, a talented fiddler and singer he had met at WLW, and the two moved to Nashville, where Jones began playing the Grand Ole Opry. Throughout the 1950s the couple entertained troops in Korea; made brief stays at Arlington and Richmond, Virginia, and Washington, D.C.; and recorded for RCA VICTOR and DECCA.

By 1959 they had settled permanently on the Opry, and a few years later they started a family that would include Mark, Alisa, and Marsha (a fourth child, Eloise, came from Jones's earlier marriage in West Virginia). In the early 1960s Jones began recording for FRED FOSTER's new MONUMENT label, producing a series of albums that Jones considered his best work. On Monument, Jones notched two of his biggest hits, a version of Jimmie Rodgers's "T for Texas" (1962–63) and the recitation "The Christmas Guest" (1969). In 1969 Jones joined the cast of *Hee Haw*, where he perfected his comedy with routines such as "What's for Supper?" and worked with MINNIE PEARL, his pal STRINGBEAN, and other greats.

In 1976 Jones and his wife began a series of albums for CMH that included remakes of many of his early hits and gave their talented children a chance to perform with their parents. In 1984 Jones wrote (with Charles Wolfe) a detailed autobiography, *Everybody's Grandpa*; he celebrated his fiftieth anniversary on the Opry in 1997. Jones had a severe stroke moments after his second-show Opry performance on January 3, 1998; he died the following February 19. —*Charles Wolfe*

## Jordanaires

Hugh Gordon Stoker b. Gleason, Tennessee, August 3, 1924
Culley Holt b. McAlester, Oklahoma, July 2, 1925; d. June 26, 1980
Neal Matthews Jr. b. Nashville, Tennessee, October 26, 1929; d. April 21, 2000
Hoyt Hawkins b. Paducah, Kentucky, March 31, 1927; d. October 23, 1982
Hugh Jarrett b. Nashville, Tennessee, October 11, 1929; d. May 31, 2008
Bill Matthews b. LaFollette, Tennessee, September 19, 1923; d. February 10, 2003
Monty Matthews b. Pulaski, Kentucky, August 25, 1927; d. March 5, 2005
Bob Money b. Mount Vernon, Missouri, May 4, 1929; died February 10, 2005
Bob Hubbard b. Chaffee, Missouri, July 3, 1928
Ray Walker b. Centerville, Mississippi, March 16, 1934
Duane West b. Salisbury, Maryland, April 28, 1941; d. June 23, 2002
Louis Nunley b. Sikeston, Missouri, October 15, 1931
Curtis Young b. January 9, 1943

Best known as Nashville's premier background vocal group and as key architects of THE NASHVILLE SOUND, the Jordanaires established themselves as a prominent gospel quartet well before they won fame for studio work. When young ELVIS PRESLEY, who loved gospel singing, asked the group to back him on his recording of "Hound Dog" in 1956, he wanted the best. With the Jordanaires, he was getting just that.

The Jordanaires began in Springfield, Missouri, in 1948, formed by two young evangelists, brothers Bill and Monty Matthews. Other original members included bass singer Culley Holt and baritone Bob Hubbard. A year later Gordon Stoker joined as pianist, fresh from a stint as pianist with WSM's John

Daniel Quartet, and switched to first tenor when Bill Matthews left in 1952 due to illness. Stoker recruited Neal Matthews (no relation) as second tenor. Monty Matthews soon returned to Missouri, and pianist Hoyt Hawkins became the group's baritone. Hugh Jarrett replaced Holt in 1954.

Meanwhile, the Jordanaires had signed with DECCA in 1949 and by1951 moved briefly to RCA RECORDS. Early on, they won a reputation for spirituals such as "Joshua Fit the Battle of Jericho," "Noah," and "Dry Bones." By March 1951 they began recording both sacred and secular material for CAPITOL and also sang background on records by mainstream country artists, including RED FOLEY ("Just a Closer Walk with Thee") and HANK SNOW. The Jordanaires had been regulars on the GRAND OLE OPRY since 1949 and they widened their appeal through appearances on EDDY ARNOLD's 1955 syndicated TV show.

Nonetheless, as Neal Matthews recalled, the Elvis recording "opened the doors for us." From the late 1950s well into the 1970s, the quartet often did four sessions a day, six days a week; when Elvis asked them to rejoin him in Las Vegas, they had to refuse: they had too much studio work in Nashville.

The Jordanaires maintained high standards through various personnel changes. In 1958, when Ray Walker replaced Jarrett as bass singer, the quartet stabilized for the next quarter-century. Hawkins developed health problems in 1982, and Duane West stepped into his shoes; in turn, Louis Nunley, formerly with the ANITA KERR SINGERS, replaced West in 1999. Curtis Young came on board after Matthews died in 2000.

The Jordanaires also appeared on military-recruiting shows and did dozens of commercials, first as staff members of WSM, later for nationally advertised products. Though they continued to work primarily in Nashville recording studios, British trade magazines have voted them the fourth-biggest vocal group in the world, behind the Beatles, the Rolling Stones, and the Beach Boys. They continued to make personal appearances into the twenty-first century. —*Charles Wolfe*

*The Jordanaires: (from left) Gordon Stoker, Neal Matthews Jr., Ray Walker, and Hoyt Hawkins*

## John Jorgenson

b. Madison, Wisconsin, July 6, 1956

Best known as a guitarist and musical director, John Jorgenson was a member of the popular COUNTRY-ROCK act the DESERT ROSE BAND and has played on recordings by country artists such as PAM TILLIS, HANK WILLIAMS JR., and MARTY STUART. But Jorgenson is proficient on many instruments and comfortable in a variety of styles, ranging from classical to jazz, BLUEGRASS, punk, and ROCKABILLY.

Jorgenson's father was an orchestral conductor and teacher at the University of Redlands (California); his mother taught piano. John began learning piano at age five, adding clarinet, ukulele, and guitar by age twelve. Later he performed in various symphonies and all-state orchestras and worked at Disneyland in bluegrass bands. In 1982, guitarist Jeff Ross drew him into the Southern California rockabilly scene.

Through his bluegrass connections, Jorgenson met ROSE MADDOX, with whom he wound up working for several years, and Bill Bryson. Bryson introduced him to CHRIS HILLMAN, with whom Jorgensen would help form the Desert Rose Band. In the meantime, Jorgenson had a band called the Cheatin' Hearts with former Flying Burrito Brothers steel guitarist Sneaky Pete Kleinow, future Desert Rose Band drummer Bryson, and single-named female singer Kittra (who later married renowned MUSIC ROW bassist BOB MOORE).

In 1988 Jorgenson began intensive studio work, eventually recording with Bonnie Raitt, CARLENE CARTER, Roger McGuinn, JOHN PRINE, and others. In 1990, guitarists Jorgenson, Will Ray, and Jerry Donahue formed the Hellecasters and recorded three acclaimed albums. Jorgenson won ACM's Guitarist of the Year award three times (1990–92) and was musical director of the *Hot Country Nights* television series (November 1991–March 1992) and Delta Burke's ABC sitcom *Delta* (1992–93). In 1994 Jorgenson joined Elton John's band for recording and six years of concerts, alternating with continuing session work. Today Jorgenson performs "gypsy jazz" with the John Jorgenson Quintet and fronts an electric band, John Jorgenson and Friends. —*Todd Everett*

## Cledus "T." Judd

b. Crowe Springs, Georgia, December 18, 1964

Former hairdresser Barry Poole, a.k.a. Cledus "T." Judd (the "T.," he says, stands for "Trouble," not "Tubby"), has established a reputation as a country music parodist whose humor lies somewhere between that of RAY STEVENS and "Weird Al" Yankovic. After winning an amateur contest at an Atlanta nightclub with his own "Farm Boy Rap," Judd moved to Nashville and tuned in to the radio, mining popular country hits as targets for his parodies. The first, a takeoff on TIM MCGRAW's "Indian Outlaw," was "Indian In-Laws," followed by "Gone Funky" and "Stinkin' Problem," spoofing ALAN JACKSON and DAVID BALL, respectively. Ball and other artists appeared in Judd's music videos, aired regularly on CMT. Following his debut Judd opened shows for BILLY RAY CYRUS and later toured with other country stars.

A quartet of albums for Razor & Tie included a DEANA CARTER takeoff, *Did I Shave My Back for This?* (1998). Four MONUMENT albums followed between 2000 and 2004, succeeded by a DIXIE CHICKS sendup, *Original Dixie Hick* (Audium, 2003). Highlights since then include *Bipolar & Proud* (Koch, 2004), a Ray Stevens tribute album on CURB, and *Polyrically Uncorrect* (E1, 2009), the latter featuring "Merger on Music Row," "Garth Must Be Busy," and "Waitin' on Obama." —*Stephen L. Betts*

## The Judds

Naomi Judd (Diana Ellen Judd) b. Ashland, Kentucky, January 11, 1946
Wynonna Judd (Christina Claire Ciminella) b. Ashland, Kentucky, May 30, 1964

With solid harmonies and Wynonna Judd's vocal power, this mother-daughter team became country's top vocal duet from 1984 until dissolving their act at the end of 1991. Their success helped to give a fresh, more acoustic direction to country music at the time.

The daughter of an Ashland, Kentucky, service station owner, Diana Ellen Judd was an imaginative child. Living in Los Angeles as the wife of a rising marketing executive and the mother of two daughters, Christina and Ashley, she dreamed of being a star. Her husband discovered he was not Christina's biological father, and the marriage ended in divorce in 1972. Diana rebounded by assuming a gypsy lifestyle in the wealthy New Age community of Marin County, California. While there, she and her elder daughter changed their names to Naomi and Wynonna, respectively

After attending several nursing schools across the United States, Naomi finished her nursing degree in 1977 in Hollywood. Her restored 1957 Chevy was rented for the movie *More American Graffiti*, and Naomi landed jobs as crowd scene extras for herself and Wynonna, plus a secretarial slot on the production staff. The film stint financed a move to Franklin, Tennessee, just south of Nashville.

While Naomi worked as a nurse, Wynonna was developing her astounding vocal talent. Naomi canvassed Nashville's MUSIC ROW, hoping to sell the concept she had developed for the mother-daughter duo. While few decision makers appreciated them, the pair became semi-regulars on RALPH EMERY's early-morning Nashville television show.

Their break came when Naomi gave a homemade demo tape to a patient in the hospital where she was working—the daughter of record producer BRENT MAHER. Maher paired them with talented guitarist/arranger DON POTTER to create an acoustic country sound that led to their "discovery." Dick Whitehouse at CURB RECORDS in Los Angeles heard the duo's potential and arranged an in-office audition at RCA RECORDS headquarters in Nashville that floored executives. The unusual audition became a key element in the Judds' self-described Cinderella story.

*The Judds: Wynonna (left) and Naomi*

RCA signed the duo, and their first release, "Had a Dream (For the Heart)," found favor with country radio, reaching #17 on *Billboard*'s country singles charts (1983–84). Their second single, the Grammy-winning "Mama He's Crazy," established the mother-daughter dialog that would focus their image; it became the first of eight straight #1 singles, including 1985 CMA Single of the Year "Why Not Me" (also a Grammy winner), "Have Mercy," and "Grandpa (Tell Me 'Bout the Good Old Days)," which earned the act a third Grammy. In 1988 "Give a Little Love" (#2) yielded a fourth.

Altogether, the Judds scored twenty Top Ten singles, fourteen of which were #1s, and dominated the competition for CMA Vocal Group and Vocal Duo of the year from 1985 through 1991, when mother Naomi retired from the act due to a chronic hepatitis infection. The retirement, in characteristic flair, was announced on a rainy day in a tearful press conference at the old RCA building. It was followed by a top-grossing 124-show farewell tour built around their *Love Can Build a Bridge* album, which was the only Judds album not to produce a #1 single, although it generated another Grammy.

Following her retirement from the duo, Naomi published her autobiography, *Love Can Build a Bridge* (Villard Books, 1993). She also tried her hand at acting again, with a prominent speaking role opposite Reba McEntire and Kenny Rogers in one of the last *Gambler* made-for-TV movies. The Judds eventually fired longtime manager Ken Stilts, and Naomi became the functional director of Wynonna's solo career, which got under way with a televised, pay-per-view concert in Murfreesboro, Tennessee, about a year after the duet act ended (see Wynonna). In addition, Naomi has been a spokesperson for the American Liver Foundation (recounting her recovery from hepatitis); worked as a motivational speaker; published the best-selling *Naomi's Breakthrough Guide: 20 Choices to Transform Your Life* (Simon & Schuster, 2003); served as a judge on *Star Search* (2003–04) and *Can You Duet* (2008–09); and hosted her own Sunday-morning TV talk show, *Naomi's New Morning* (2003–07).

As early as an appearance during halftime at the 1994 Super Bowl, mother and daughter have periodically reunited for live performances. Landmark joint appearances have included New Year's Eve concerts, their 2000 "Power to Change" tour of some thirty dates—which resulted in the 2000 Mercury/Curb album *Reunion Live*—the Kennedy Center's 2006 country music festival, the 2009 CMA Music Festival, and a 2011 reunion tour chronicled on an Oprah Winfrey Network TV series. —*Bob Millard*

## Jug Bands

Jug bands have their roots in African American music. The earliest known were from Louisville, where they were a popular feature during each Kentucky Derby season at Churchill Downs and private parties. A Louisville jug band performed in New York and Chicago during 1914–16. Other jug bands made records under various names from 1924 to 1927 and in 1931, including "My Good Gal's Gone Blues" with Jimmie Rodgers.

In the 1920s, Memphis groups followed the Louisville model. Guitarist Will Shade's loose-knit, rural-sounding Memphis Jug Band recorded extensively for Victor (later RCA Victor) from 1927 to 1930 with varying personnel. Gus Cannon's Jug Stompers did likewise from 1928 to 1930. Each contributed to the Memphis blues legacy.

Jugs and washboards became popular with country bands as they performed stage and radio comedy in the 1930s. The Shelton Brothers' popular 1933 recording (as the Lone Star Cowboys) of the "Crawdad Song" used a jug. The Prairie Ramblers' 1935 "Jug Rag" reflected the group's Kentucky origins and earlier familiarity with Louisville jug music; likewise, Kentuckian John Lair sometimes played a jug with the Cumberland Ridge Runners. Roy Acuff's band often did comedy jug routines. In 1953 the Acuff jug band made its only recording, Johnnie Masters's uproarious "Sixteen Chickens and a Tambourine." —*Dick Spottswood*

## Jukeboxes

"Jukebox" is the name applied colloquially to coin-operated record-playing machines that were once omnipresent in dance halls, cafés, honky-tonks, bowling alleys, skating rinks, and other recreational venues in the United States. Coin-operated music machines date from the turn of the twentieth century, but they were not called "jukeboxes" until the late 1920s and early 1930s, when they became identified with juke joints in Florida and Georgia. These were small black clubs where drinking and dancing were common, and the word "juke" itself may have been a term of African extraction that survived in the coastal South (whether it referred to dancing or sexual intercourse is unclear).

During Prohibition, speakeasies used jukeboxes because those illegal establishments needed music but could not always afford bands. The repeal of Prohibition in 1933, though, engendered even greater numbers of jukeboxes as dance halls and honky-tonks proliferated. In 1934 the Rudolph Wurlitzer Manufacturing Company, a major manufacturer of various music machines since the nineteenth century, introduced its first jukebox, the P-10. Although it met with intense competition from companies such as Mills, Seeburg, and Rock-ola, Wurlitzer dominated jukebox distribution until about 1950. In the early 1950s Seeburg made giant strides, first by introducing a machine that could play 45-rpm records and later through a model that offered 200 selections. All of these brands played major roles in country music's expansion and the rise of rock & roll.

Jukeboxes did more than play music. They served as centerpieces for social interaction and as symbols of America's capitalistic exuberance and technological know-how. New models introduced each year—particularly after 1946, when the Wurlitzer 1015 hit the market—not only played greater numbers of records; they also became increasingly sophisticated in design, providing visual as well as auditory entertainment. Led by the innovative Paul Fuller, Wurlitzer specialized in beautiful jukeboxes with Art Deco designs, brightly colored chrome-and-plastic exteriors, fluorescent illumination, and openly displayed record-changing mechanisms. The jukebox became a central focus for musical and social experience and a ready reminder to displaced country folk of American ingenuity and success.

Jukeboxes made crucial contributions to country music's expansion, especially during the World War II years, when uprooted military personnel and lonely civilians sought diversion through playing records. Some 400,000 of these machines were in operation by 1941. Their proliferation symbolized country music's growth while helping to fuel that growth. Jukebox distribution, along with the volume of records operators ordered, reflected the music's success as it moved north and west during and after the war. The earliest popularity charts found in *Billboard* magazine, for example, were compilations of the most popular songs heard on jukeboxes. With the country music boom of the 1940s and early 1950s, some distributors, such as SYD NATHAN in Cincinnati and PAPPY DAILY in Houston, launched their own important enterprises, initially with used recordings but soon centered on their own newly recorded material. Jukeboxes have been so intimately intertwined with country music's history that it's no wonder country singers have often celebrated them in song. ALAN JACKSON's "Don't Rock the Jukebox," MARK CHESNUTT's "Brother Jukebox," and JOE DIFFIE's "Prop Me Up Beside the Jukebox (If I Die)," pay simultaneous tribute to country music and to the marvelous machine that did so much to introduce it to a receptive world. —*Bill C. Malone*

## Kieran Kane (*see* The O'Kanes)

## Dave Kapp
b. Chicago, Illinois, August 7, 1904; d. March 1, 1976

The man most responsible for building DECCA RECORDS' early hillbilly catalog was David Kapp, younger brother of label founder JACK KAPP. Together the two owned and ran a Chicago music store from 1921 to 1931. Joining Decca in 1935 (its second year), Dave Kapp and a company engineer traveled several times per year into the South to find and record hillbilly talent. Under Kapp's supervision, MILTON BROWN, CLIFF BRUNER, REX GRIFFIN, ERNEST TUBB, and others made their most important recordings.

Kapp left Decca in 1951 and headed RCA VICTOR's pop department for two years. Then, in 1954, he founded Kapp Records. Years later Kapp added a country roster—BOB WILLS, MEL TILLIS, and CAL SMITH became the label's best-known artists in this field.

Also a writer ("160 Acres") and publisher (Garland Music), Kapp served as president of the Recording Industry Association of America (RIAA) during 1966–67. He sold Kapp Records to MCA in 1967. —*Ronnie Pugh*

## Jack Kapp
b. Chicago, Illinois, 1901; d. March 25, 1949

Jacob "Jack" Kapp, cofounder of American DECCA RECORDS, helped revitalize the U.S. popular music industry in the depths of the Depression with Decca's thirty-five-cent, 78-rpm records at a time when most companies retailed their discs for seventy-five cents.

Kapp worked in his hometown of Chicago as a mail clerk for COLUMBIA RECORDS, later taking a production job for BRUNSWICK. A proven talent and song scout, Kapp left Brunswick in 1934 to cofound Decca Records in partnership with Edward R. Lewis and his English branch of Decca (established in 1929). Kapp took some of Brunswick's leading pop acts with him, including Bing Crosby, Guy Lombardo, and the Mills Brothers.

Decca corporate policy, as dictated by Kapp, stressed clear pronunciation of lyrics, simple melodies, and repetitive use of a song's title on the company's recordings. Kapp's genius for teaming his talent in various duet combinations also became a Decca trademark. Its cheaper product (discounted further to JUKEBOX operators) helped Decca corner some 36 percent of the U.S. record market by 1940.

In its March 7, 1949, issue, a laudatory *Life* magazine editorial (later read into the *Congressional Record*) heralded Kapp as "living proof that no man in America is destined by circumstances to spend his life behind a large and immovable eight ball." Only weeks later, Kapp died of a cerebral hemorrhage. —*Ronnie Pugh*

## Karl & Harty
Karl Victor Davis b. Mount Vernon, Kentucky, December 17, 1905; d. May 30, 1979
Hartford Connecticut "Harty" Taylor b. Mount Vernon, Kentucky, April 11, 1905;
    d. October 18, 1963

Popular figures on Chicago country music radio during the 1930s and 1940s, Karl Davis and Harty Taylor probably are better known today through Davis's compositions than through their own recordings. Modeling themselves after Lester McFarland and Robert Gardner (MAC & BOB), they favored sentimental material with gentle, understated harmonies. Taylor strummed guitar and sang lead, while Davis played mandolin and harmonized.

In 1929 DOC HOPKINS recruited Davis and Taylor for the Krazy Kats, a STRINGBAND that mixed folk songs with current pop tunes. After a year on WHAS–Louisville, the band moved to Chicago to become the core of the CUMBERLAND RIDGE RUNNERS on WLS's *NATIONAL BARN DANCE*. Davis and Taylor originally were billed as the Renfro Valley Boys; they recorded under that name for Paramount in February 1932. However, radio listeners best knew them as Karl & Harty. In March 1934 the duo began recording for the AMERICAN RECORD CORPORATION labels. "I'm Just Here to Get My Baby out of Jail" was their first hit; later successes included "The Prisoner's Dream" and Davis's most enduring song, "Kentucky," recorded by THE LOUVIN BROTHERS, THE EVERLY BROTHERS, and THE OSBORNE BROTHERS, among others.

Karl & Harty joined WJJD–Chicago's popular *SUPPERTIME FROLIC* in 1937, but returned to WLS in December 1947. At odds with the HONKY-TONK sound that dominated much of postwar country music, they amiably dissolved their partnership in 1951. Davis continued writing songs: "The Country Hall of Fame" was a Top Ten hit for HANK LOCKLIN in 1967. —*Dave Samuelson*

## Buell Kazee
b. Magoffin County, Kentucky, August 29, 1900; d. August 31, 1976

Buell Kazee was a singer of traditional BALLADS who made his mark in the late 1920s and then again during the folk revival in the 1960s. Reared in the mountains of eastern Kentucky, in a community where almost everybody sang ballads or hymns and where banjo players were plentiful, he started playing banjo when he was five years old but decided in his teens to become a Baptist preacher.

Kazee's interest in formal folksinging began during his studies at Kentucky's Georgetown College, when he realized that the ballads he was reading in English literature classes were still being sung in his native state. Between 1927 and 1929 he made nearly sixty recordings for the BRUNSWICK label, of which one of the most memorable (certainly the most often reissued) was an old British ballad titled "Lady Gay," a version of the British folksong "The Wife of Usher's Well." Kazee's formal musical training put an overlay of polish and professionalism on his native folksinging style, resulting in a clear, high tenor and exceptionally careful diction. Years later he recalled that Brunswick's producers would not let him sing in his "good" (concert) voice but preferred his "bad" (hillbilly) voice. His banjo playing was in the "frailing" style characteristic of eastern Kentucky—but with a few unusual features, such as occasionally brushing upward across the strings with his thumb. In the 1960s and 1970s Kazee enjoyed a second round of musical exposure on college campuses and at folk festivals across the nation. —*Norm Cohen*

## Robert Earl Keen
b. Houston, Texas, January 11, 1956

Robert Earl Keen Jr. has carved his own niche as a link between western underground COWBOY MUSIC and alternative country. He is one in the Lone Star line of singing storytellers reaching back to the cowboy poets and balladeers of the late nineteenth century. "I listened to MARTY ROBBINS's *Gunfighter* album over and over when I was about four years old," he says. "The thing that's appealing to me is that there's always a real story going on in those songs, like 'Little Joe the Wrangler' or the one about tying the knot in the Devil's tail. Being as how I'm not much of a singer, I always try to tell the best story I can."

In the 1980s and 1990s, Keen recorded for SUGAR HILL, Philo/ROUNDER, Rosetta, and ARISTA Texas. His song "The Road Goes on Forever" was covered by JOE ELY and by the Highwaymen, who made it the title track of their third album. Keen is a fun-loving performer who sometimes leads audiences in drunken sing-alongs about the joys of eating barbecue, but he's also a serious songwriter with an almost frightening ability to empathize with the losers, boozers, and psychopaths who populate his songs. He clearly identifies with the drunken oil rig worker in "Corpus Christi Bay," the itchy-fingered gunslinger in "Whenever Kindness Fails," and the dysfunctional relatives in the hilarious happy-holiday snapshot "Merry Christmas from the Family."

The son of a West Texas oilman and a Houston attorney, Keen grew up listening to his parents' folk and country records. He skipped his high school prom to see WILLIE NELSON play a Pasadena club. Attending Texas A&M University, he started setting his original poems to music, sometimes assisted by college buddy LYLE LOVETT. The two arrived in Nashville at about the same time in the 1980s. Lovett was signed by MCA RECORDS; except for a 1984 album with Philo (*No Kinda Dancer*), Keen mostly languished in a series of dead-end day jobs.

Taking a cue from his longtime hero Willie Nelson, Keen returned to Texas and found success as a performer, especially in venues west of the Mississippi River. His following in California and the mountain states rivals that in his home state, where he is now regarded as the spiritual godfather to successive generations of Texas and "red-dirt" singer-songwriters, including PAT GREEN, JACK INGRAM, and Cody Canada. In the 2000s Keen has recorded principally for LOST HIGHWAY, his efforts including the 2009 album *Rose Hotel*. —*Rick Mitchell*

## Garrison Keillor (see *A Prairie Home Companion*)

## Bill Keith
b. Boston, Massachusetts, December 20, 1939

Influenced by Appalachian musicians Don Stover and THE LILLY BROTHERS, who played at Boston's Hillbilly Ranch, banjo innovator William Bradford Keith became fascinated with BLUEGRASS music in the late 1950s.

In the early 1960s Keith joined his Amherst College roommate, JIM ROONEY, to play folk and bluegrass shows, often with Joe Val, Herb Hooven, and Herb Applin. Keith eventually developed a banjo style that enabled him to play fiddle tunes in a melodic, note-for-note fashion, an outgrowth of a "bluegrass roll" in the EARL SCRUGGS style. The first recorded examples of Keith's playing in his melodic style appeared on Keith & Rooney's Prestige/Folklore album, *Livin' on the Mountain*, in 1962.

Keith recorded and performed with RED ALLEN and Frank Wakefield prior to a brief stint with BILL MONROE's Blue Grass Boys in the spring of 1963. (Monroe dubbed him Brad Keith; there was already a Bill in the band.) With the Allen and Wakefield album *Bluegrass* on Folkways Records and Monroe's performances and recordings featuring Keith's banjo, his style spread rapidly.

After less than a year with Monroe, Keith joined Jim Kweskin's Jug Band. By the early 1970s he had temporarily focused on the PEDAL STEEL GUITAR, moved to Woodstock, New York, and worked with Jonathan Edwards, later playing with Judy Collins. During the 1970s and 1980s, touring in the United States and overseas with Jim Rooney, Keith built a large following while also playing banjo in the Woodstock Mountains Revue. By 1990 he and Rooney joined former musical buddies Eric Weissberg and Kenny Kosek in the New Blue Velvet Band.

Keith is known today for his instructional books and workshops and his ability to communicate music theory, in terms of the five-string banjo, to students at all levels. Owner of the Beacon Banjo Company, manufacturer of Keith Tuners (devices that permit rapid, accurate pitch changes while playing), Keith continues to perform a wide range of music. —*Frank and Marty Godbey*

## Toby Keith
b. Clinton, Oklahoma, July 8, 1961

A six-foot-four former oilfield worker and semipro football player, Toby Keith (born Toby Keith Covel) not only has delivered country songs with swagger but also has brought similar bravado to his business decisions. Brashly outspoken, Keith has assumed more control of his career along the way to becoming one of his generation's most successful hit-makers and songwriters.

As of 2010, Keith had achieved nineteen #1 *Billboard* country singles. Twelve of his first thirteen studio albums reached the Top Ten country sales chart; seven went to #1. Keith was named CMA Vocalist of the Year in 2001 and has won seven ACM awards, including Entertainer of the Year in 2002 and 2003. He had also starred in two movies, *Broken Bridges* (2006) and *Beer for My Horses* (2008), the latter named for his #1 duet with WILLIE NELSON.

Keith spent nine years as a regional act working out of Oklahoma City before signing with MERCURY RECORDS in 1993. His self-titled debut album featured four Top Five hits: "Should've

*Toby Keith*

Been a Cowboy," "He Ain't Worth Missing," "A Little Less Talk and a Lot More Action," and "Wish I Didn't Know Now."

From there, Keith tried on different personas: *Boomtown* (1994) focused on working-class themes and contained the #1 hit "Who's That Man" (1994); *Blue Moon* (1996) went for romantic ballads, netting the #1 hit "Me Too." *Dream Walkin'* (1997) had a sophisticated feel and included a Grammy-nominated collaboration with Sting, "I'm So Happy I Can't Stop Crying."

But Keith butted heads with Mercury over creative control, and in 1998 he departed for the newly established DREAMWORKS Nashville label. He immediately started recording songs with a more distinctive, in-your-face approach, starting with a 2000 #1 hit, "How Do You Like Me Now?"

He also improved his game, achieving nine #1 hits from 2001 to 2004, from "You Shouldn't Kiss Me Like This" through "Whiskey Girl." Among them were bold novelties, such as "I Wanna Talk About Me" and "Who's Your Daddy?," as well as the controversial "Courtesy of the Red, White & Blue (The Angry American)," written in response to the September 11, 2001, terrorist attacks on the United States. The song's aggressive call to arms and the line "We'll put a boot in your ass/ It's the American way" drew a chorus of comments, pro and con, from inside and outside of country music. In particular, DIXIE CHICKS lead singer Natalie Maines (who whipped up her own controversy by criticizing President George W. Bush and the Iraq war) called even more attention to the song by branding it "ignorant." Keith responded during subsequent interviews but later called an end to what the media portrayed as a public feud.

Keith founded his own independent label, Show Dog Nashville, in 2005 and continued to score Top Ten hits, still occasionally reaching #1, although not as consistently as in the previous five years. In 2009 Show Dog Nashville and UNIVERSAL RECORDS SOUTH merged to form Show Dog–Universal Music, with Keith serving as principal of the company. In October 2010 Keith issued a new album, *Bullets in the Gun*. —*Calvin Gilbert*

## The Kendalls

Royce Kuykendall b. St. Louis, Missouri, September 25, 1934; d. May 22, 1998
Jeannie Kuykendall b. St. Louis, Missouri, November 30, 1954

Just when it appeared that close harmony singing was nearing extinction in country music, the father-daughter duo of Royce and Jeannie Kendall brought it back into prominence. The duo's thirty-seven *Billboard* charts singles from 1970 through 1989 usually dealt with the theme of adultery. The idea of a father and daughter singing such suggestive lyrics to one another was a little too much for many industry sophisticates to bear, but fans loved the Kendalls' hard-country, unabashed approach.

After early 1970s releases for the Stop and DOT labels, they signed with Chicago-based Ovation Records and enjoyed their greatest success there. Jeannie's high-pitched vocals drove uptempo songs such as 1977's "Heaven's Just a Sin Away" and 1978's "Sweet Desire" to #1. Her delivery on ballads such as "Pittsburgh Stealers" and "Just Like Real People" was equally effective. Daddy Royce's rich baritone was the grounding rod for Jeannie's electric performances. All told, the duo cracked *Billboard*'s Top Ten eleven times. In 1981 they released their first single for MERCURY RECORDS, "Teach Me to Cheat," which climbed to #7. Consistently hitting through the early 1980s, their 1984 release "Thank God for the Radio" topped *Billboard*'s country rankings during its twenty-three-week chart run.

Beginning in the latter half of the 1980s, their career began to ebb as they moved from Mercury to MCA/CURB, EPIC, and then STEP ONE. After recording for Lonesome Dove (1994–95) and for American Harvest (1996), the duo signed with ROUNDER RECORDS. They were touring in 1998 when Royce had a stroke on May 20. He died two days later. Jeannie has since pursued a solo career, releasing a self-titled 2003 Rounder album featuring duets with ALAN JACKSON, ALISON KRAUSS, RICKY SKAGGS, and other top names. *All the Girls I Am* followed on Golden/CBuJ Entertainment in 2005. —*Chris Skinker*

## Jerry Kennedy

b. Shreveport, Louisiana, August 10, 1940

During his long career, Jerry Glenn Kennedy produced hit-making acts including ROGER MILLER, THE STATLER BROTHERS, TOM T. HALL, JOHNNY RODRIGUEZ, and REBA MCENTIRE; played guitar on hundreds of sessions (including the DOBRO lead on "Harper Valley P.T.A." for JEANNIE C. RILEY); and ran the country music division of MERCURY RECORDS from 1969 to 1984.

Kennedy learned guitar from TILLMAN FRANKS and then played guitar for FARON YOUNG and JOHNNY HORTON and performed on Shreveport's *LOUISIANA HAYRIDE*. Kennedy moved to Nashville in 1961 and became SHELBY SINGLETON's assistant at Mercury Records. In 1965 Kennedy was promoted to A&R manager at the label and in 1969 became a Mercury vice president in charge of country music, including the label's Nashville operation. An easy-going but effective producer, Kennedy helped Roger Miller win eleven Grammys in 1964 and 1965, guided rocker JERRY LEE LEWIS to country stardom, and helped Singleton record R&B acts

*Jerry Kennedy*

Brook Benton, Ruth Brown, and Clyde McPhatter. Kennedy also worked as a session guitarist for TAMMY WYNETTE, Patti Page, ROY ROGERS, KRIS KRISTOFFERSON, GLEN CAMPBELL, BRENDA LEE, Faron Young, and Clint Eastwood. Kennedy played on BOB DYLAN's *Nashville Skyline* and ROY ORBISON's "Oh, Pretty Woman."

In 1984 Kennedy left Mercury and established his own independent firm, JK Productions, which produced the Statler Brothers and other acts. Kennedy is now retired. —*Don Cusic*

## Kentucky Colonels (*see* Clarence and Roland White)

## The Kentucky HeadHunters

Richard Young b. Glasgow, Kentucky, January 27, 1955
Fred Young b. Glasgow, Kentucky, July 8, 1958
Greg Martin b. Louisville, Kentucky, March 31, 1954
Doug Phelps b. Leachville, Arkansas, February 16, 1960
Ricky Lee Phelps b. Paragould, Arkansas, October 8, 1953
Mark Orr b. Charlotte, Michigan, November 16, 1949
Anthony Kenney b. Glasgow Kentucky, October 8, 1953

This Edmonton, Kentucky–based COUNTRY-ROCK band had fleeting commercial success and wielded considerable influence in the late 1980s and early 1990s. To many people's surprise, the group was CMA's Vocal Group of the Year in 1990 and 1991 and won a 1990 Grammy for Best Country Performance by a Duo or Group with Vocal.

The HeadHunters' ragged, hard-driving style contrasted sharply with the more conventional sounds of country bands such as ALABAMA and EXILE, which had flourished in the country charts during the 1980s. The irony of the HeadHunters' making it big in country after scuffling around the southern rock scene for years was not lost on the members themselves. "I don't know how it happened," said founding member Richard Young. "I'm just sure as hell glad it did."

The HeadHunters' original members were brothers Richard Young (rhythm guitar) and Fred Young (drums); the Youngs' first cousin Greg Martin (lead guitar); and two Arkansas-born brothers, unrelated to the rest: Doug Phelps (bass) and Ricky Lee Phelps (vocals). The act evolved out of Itchy Brother, an earlier southern rock band that enjoyed regional popularity from 1968 into the

early 1970s. In late 1980 three Itchy Brother survivors, the Young brothers and Martin, joined with the Phelps brothers to form the Kentucky HeadHunters. In 1989 they recorded a demo cassette that landed them a contract with MERCURY RECORDS. Mercury Nashville's head of A&R, HAROLD SHEDD (Alabama's producer for many years), liked their tape so much that Mercury released its eight recordings as-is adding two new tracks to complete their debut album, *Pickin' on Nashville*. The collection included their only Top Ten country hit, a cover of DON GIBSON's "Oh Lonesome Me."

In 1992 the Phelpses left the band and began recording on their own as Brother Phelps. They were replaced in the HeadHunters by two other Itchy Brother alumni: the Youngs' cousin Anthony Kenney (bass) and Mark Orr (lead vocals). In 1994 the band recorded *That'll Work*, a blues album, with former Chuck Berry pianist Johnnie Johnson. In 1996, with the breakup of Brother Phelps, Doug Phelps rejoined the HeadHunters as lead vocalist, replacing Orr. Though the HeadHunters had ceased to be a presence on the country scene by the mid-1990s, they are still touring and have released albums on BNA (see RCA RECORDS), Audium, CBuJ, and Mercury. —*Bob Allen*

## Anita Kerr/Anita Kerr Singers

Anita Kerr b. Memphis, Tennessee, October 13, 1927
Dottie Dillard b. Springfield, Missouri, August 3, 1923
Louis Nunley b. Sikeston, Missouri, October 15, 1931
Gil Wright b. Nashville, Tennessee, July 3, 1929

Anita Kerr was one of the most influential vocal and instrumental arrangers in the early evolution of THE NASHVILLE SOUND. Her group, the Anita Kerr Singers, became a staple on countless recordings, helping to broaden country music's market in the wake of the commercial threat posed by rock & roll.

Born Anita Jean Grilli to an Italian family who ran a Memphis grocery store, Kerr started piano lessons at age four. Later she played pipe organ and prepared vocal arrangements for the St. Thomas Church choir in Memphis. By age fourteen she was leading the Grilli Sisters vocal group. They performed on her mother's radio show, and Kerr herself became a singer, pianist, and organist on Memphis radio station WREC.

In 1948 Kerr moved to Nashville and started a singing group for WSM's *Sunday Down South* radio show. Her big break was supplying backup on RED FOLEY's 1950 crossover hit "Our Lady of Fatima." She became a regular on the GRAND OLE OPRY's *Prince Albert Show* and led an eight-voice group, the Anita Kerr Singers, for DECCA RECORDS recording sessions. In June 1956 the ensemble was invited to appear on *Arthur Godfrey's Talent Scouts* (CBS-TV), necessarily shrinking down to a quartet: Kerr, Dottie Dillard, Louis Nunley, and Gil Wright.

By the late 1950s Kerr was supplying vocals for many labels. She assisted on hits such as Decca artist BOBBY HELMS's "My Special Angel" (#1 country; #7 pop, 1957) and RCA VICTOR star JIM REEVES's "He'll Have to Go" (#1 country; #2 pop, 1959).

Starting in 1961, Kerr became CHET ATKINS's recording assistant at RCA sessions, working as vocal group leader, arranger, and occasional producer for Reeves, EDDY ARNOLD, HANK SNOW, WILLIE NELSON, FLOYD CRAMER, and others on the RCA roster. She also recorded sides of her own as Anita & th' So-And-So's.

Tired of technical record-producing tasks—for which she received scant credit—Kerr resigned in 1963. Her later, non-country career was launched by a move to California, where she

*The Anita Kerr Singers: (from left) Gil Wright, Kerr, Dottie Dillard, and Louis Nunley*

wrote soundtracks for Rod McKuen's poetry readings and cut albums with her group. In about 1970 Kerr and her husband, Alex Grob, moved to his native Switzerland, where they opened their own recording studio in 1975. There, Kerr has continued to compose, arrange, and write musical scores for feature films. —*Steve Eng*

## Doug Kershaw
b. Tiel Ridge, Louisiana, January 24, 1936

CAJUN fiddler Doug Kershaw, along with HARRY CHOATES, JIMMY C. NEWMAN, and JO-EL SONNIER, is one of a handful of Cajun musicians who enjoyed success in mainstream country music. Douglas James Kershaw began his career as a child, performing with his mother, Mama Rita, a fiddler, guitarist, and singer. In 1948 he formed the Continental Playboys with his brothers Russell·Lee ("Rusty") and Nelson ("Pee Wee"); he worked at station KPLC–Lake Charles in 1953. Doug and singer-guitarist Rusty then began performing as a duo and soon hooked up with Crowley, Louisiana, record producer J. D. MILLER's Feature label. As Rusty & Doug they recorded a number of country songs for Feature before making the pilgrimage to Nashville, where they began recording for the HICKORY label with Doug's composition "So Lovely, Baby" (#14, 1955).

The Kershaws performed in the close vocal harmony style popularized by THE EVERLY BROTHERS, and their career began to flourish. In 1955 they appeared on the *LOUISIANA HAYRIDE* before moving on to the *WWVA JAMBOREE* in Wheeling, West Virginia. In September 1957 their song "Love Me to Pieces" rose to #14, and that November they joined the GRAND OLE OPRY. In 1958 they

notched a #22 single with BOUDLEAUX BRYANT's "Hey Sheriff" before their career was short-circuited when they were both drafted.

After finishing their military stints, Rusty & Doug returned to the recording studio to cut some hard-hitting Cajun-flavored songs, including "Louisiana Man," a #10 country hit of 1962, and "Diggy Diggy Lo," which went to #14 later that year. The brothers split up after 1964, and Doug went on to win fame as the "Cajun Hippie," whose outrageous stage antics and driving performance style made him a favorite of the musical counterculture during the 1970s and helped popularize Cajun music to mass audiences. Since then he has continued to tour and has released numerous albums, including the French-language collection *Two Step Fever* (Era, 2000). —*Charlie Seemann*

## Sammy Kershaw
b. Kaplan, Louisiana, February 24, 1958

Hard-country singing came naturally to Sammy Kershaw, a cousin of legendary CAJUN fiddler DOUG KERSHAW. Sammy had his share of tough times, losing his father early on and working various day jobs and playing roadhouses at night to help his mother support the family. In the late 1980s, burned out from traveling and chasing his dream, Kershaw struggled with alcohol and drug abuse and quit the business, working at Walmart for a time. In 1990, however, he signed with MERCURY RECORDS, which released his debut album, *Don't Go Near the Water*, in 1991. An immediate hit from the album, "Cadillac Style," went to #3 and led to a series of regional commercials for the Cadillac division of General Motors. Like his debut, Kershaw's sophomore album, *Haunted Heart* (1993), went gold, but it proved more contemporary with its southern-rock feel. The collection boasted the #1 hit "She Don't Know She's Beautiful" (1993) as well as three more Top Ten singles: the title track (1993), "Queen of My Double Wide Trailer" (1993), and "I Can't Reach Her Anymore" (1994).

With *Feelin' Good Train* (1994), Kershaw further distanced himself from early comparisons to GEORGE JONES, though the album included a duet with Jones, "Never Bit a Bullet Like This Before." Indeed, the album confirmed Kershaw's stature as an interpreter of COUNTRY-ROCK—what he calls "southern-fried rock & roll"—particularly with "National Working Woman's Holiday" and his version of the Amazing Rhythm Aces' "Third Rate Romance," both #2 singles of 1994.

Kershaw's chart success faded in the late 1990s, and Mercury dropped him in 2000. He married sometime–duet partner LORRIE MORGAN in 2001, but the union proved tumultuous and ended in divorce in 2007. Meanwhile, Kershaw released an album on Audium in 2003 and gained attention with his collection *Honky Tonk Boots* (Category 5, 2006). In 2007 he ran unsuccessfully for lieutenant governor of Louisiana. —*Bob Paxman*

## Stan Kesler
b. Abbeville, Mississippi, August 11, 1928

Stan Kesler enjoyed a varied career as a Memphis songwriter, session musician, engineer, and producer. Growing up, Kesler played mandolin and guitar and learned steel guitar while serving in the U.S. Marines. Discharged in 1947, he moved to Memphis, where he played radio and club gigs with a number of WESTERN SWING and country bands, including Clyde Leoppard & the Snearly Ranch Boys. Leoppard auditioned successfully for SAM PHILLIPS's

Sun Records in September 1954, initially recording "Lonely Sweetheart" and "Split Personality." Inspired by Hank Williams, Kesler had penned both sides of the Leoppard single. Impressed, Phillips subsequently recorded a number of Kesler's songs with Sun artists, including Smokey Joe Baugh, Warren Smith, Barbara Pittman, the Miller Sisters, and Elvis Presley, who cut the best known of Kesler's compositions, "I'm Left, You're Right, She's Gone" and "I Forgot to Remember to Forget," in 1954 and 1955, respectively.

By late 1954 a Sun house country band had gelled, consisting of Kesler on steel guitar, Quinton Claunch on guitar, Bill Cantrell on fiddle, Wayne Deal or Marcus Van Storey on bass, and Clyde Leoppard or Johnny Bernero on drums. In late 1956 Kesler began playing bass, which eventually became his primary instrument. He founded his first label, Crystal Records, in 1957 and later followed with Penn and XL. On XL Kesler produced nine pop hits for Sam the Sham & the Pharaohs, including "Wooly Bully" (1965), as well as seminal blues recordings by Willie Cobb and the Binghampton Blues Boys.

Kesler later nurtured another recording group, the Dixie Flyers, at the Sounds of Memphis Studio, until they relocated to Miami. In 1983 Kesler, Paul Burlison, D.J. Fontana, Smoochy Smith, and Marcus Van Storey formed the Sun Rhythm Section, performing regularly on the road and recording one album for Flying Fish Records. Kesler continued to engineer at Phillips Recording in Memphis into the twenty-first century. —*Rob Bowman*

## The Kessinger Brothers
Clark W. Kessinger b. South Hills, West Virginia, July 27, 1896; d. June 4, 1975
Luches Kessinger b. Kanawha County, West Virginia, August 21, 1906;
    d. May 6, 1944

Legendary West Virginia fiddler Clark Kessinger was playing the fiddle in a local saloon, making ten to fifteen dollars a night, when he was only seven years old. By age ten, he was playing for nearby country dances. Kessinger's great-grandfather and great-uncle were both OLD-TIME fiddlers, and he was influenced by other fiddlers around Charleston, West Virginia, such as Ed Haley, Bob and Abe Glenn, and George Dillon.

After serving in the U.S. Navy during World War I he began playing in 1919 with his cousin, Luches "Luke" Kessinger, who accompanied him on guitar. In February 1928 they began recording for the Brunswick label as the Kessinger Brothers, eventually waxing more than seventy sides for the company through September 1930. They also performed on Charleston radio station WCHS. After Luches's death, Clark played little until he was rediscovered in 1964, when he recorded for Ken Davidson's Folk Promotions (later Kanawha) label and began appearing at fiddle contests and folk festivals. In 1971 Kessinger suffered a stroke that effectively ended his fiddling career. He died in 1975. —*Charlie Seemann*

## Hal Ketchum
b. Greenwich, New York, April 9, 1953

Hal Michael Ketchum blew onto the country scene in 1991 with his first hit single, "Small Town Saturday Night." A thoughtful songwriter with a literary eye for detail and a knack for simplicity, he's a male version of Mary Chapin Carpenter: folk-tinged, intellectual, and honest. Combined with the sex appeal of his long, salt-and-pepper mane and massive eyebrows, these qualities brought Ketchum popular and critical success.

Raised near Vermont, Hal Michael Ketchum had a banjo-playing father. A young fan of Buck Owens, he played drums in an R&B band at age fifteen. After moves to Florida (at seventeen) and Texas, a local dance hall became his proving ground as a songwriter and performer while he earned his living as a carpenter. In 1986 he moved to Nashville and concentrated on songwriting. He released a collection of ten original songs, *Threadbare Alibis*, on the independent Watermelon Records in 1989.

The album helped Ketchum land a publishing deal and ultimately a contract with Curb Records. Instantly embraced by fans and country radio, Ketchum followed his breakthrough single with signature hits "I Know Where Love Lives" (#13, 1991), "Past the Point of Rescue" (#2, 1992), "Sure Love" (#3, 1992–93), "Hearts Are Gonna Roll" (#2, 1993), and "Mama Knows the Highway" (#8, 1993).

Ketchum's albums have been marked by his ability to write and find catchy ditties and place them alongside more artistically revealing songs. In 1994 he joined the Grand Ole Opry. Between 1998 and 2008 he released five albums of new material, though his hits faded after 1995's "Stay Forever." —*Clark Parsons*

## Merle Kilgore
b. Chickasha, Oklahoma, August 9, 1934; d. February 6, 2005

As a teenager in Shreveport, Louisiana, Wyatt Merle Kilgore carried Hank Williams's guitar up the staircase to the KWKH studios. Later he became Hank Williams Jr.'s opening act and then vice president of Hank Williams Jr. Enterprises. In between he was a songwriter, song plugger, performer, DJ, and radio program director. He worked with almost every major country act of the 1950s and 1960s while becoming a beloved raconteur.

Kilgore grew up in Shreveport and hung around KWKH and the *Louisiana Hayride*. His first job as a DJ was with KENT–Shreveport, in 1950. After leaving Louisiana Tech in 1953, he moved to Monroe, Louisiana, to work for American Optical.

*Merle Kilgore*

He worked as a DJ, sang at various stations around Monroe, and starred on KFAZ-TV as "The Tall Texan." Webb Pierce, originally from Monroe, spotted him on one of his trips home, landed Kilgore a contract with Los Angeles–based Imperial Records, and covered Kilgore's "More and More," making it a #1 country hit.

Recording for Imperial for the next five years, Kilgore lagged just behind every trend, from rockabilly to folk. He even cut a teenage pop session in New Orleans with Fats Domino's producer, Dave Bartholomew. For most of that time, Kilgore worked at KCIJ–Shreveport. In 1959 Kilgore recorded for Jim Branch's Jim Records, and one of his songs, "Dear Mama," was leased to Starday and charted at #12. It was followed by "Love Has Made You Beautiful," Kilgore's only Top Ten hit as a performer. Meanwhile, he scored a #10 country hit as the writer of Johnny Horton's "Johnny Reb."

Kilgore moved to Nashville on December 31, 1961, to work for Al Gallico at Shapiro-Bernstein Music and later for Gallico's own publishing operation. Kilgore placed one of his songs, "Wolverton Mountain," with Claude King, and later Kilgore and June Carter wrote "Love's Burning Ring of Fire," first recorded by Anita Carter and later potently revived by Johnny Cash as "Ring of Fire." Kilgore continued to record for various labels and gained modest chart records for Columbia, Elektra, and Warner Bros. between 1967 and 1985. He made several forays into movie acting (*Nevada Smith*, *Country Music on Broadway*, and *Five Card Stud*), and for twenty-one years he was the opening act for Hank Williams Jr. He later managed Hank Jr. from an office in Paris, Tennessee, commuting between there and Nashville. Kilgore was elected to the Nashville Songwriters Hall of Fame in 1998. —*Colin Escott*

## Buddy Killen
b. Lexington, Alabama, November 13, 1932; d. November 1, 2006

Buddy Killen was affiliated with Tree Publishing Company for more than thirty-six years, first as an employee, then as

*Buddy Killen*

part owner, and finally as sole owner of the publishing giant. During this time he also served as a musician, songwriter, and producer.

William D. "Buddy" Killen grew up in Florence, Alabama, where his family had a restaurant. After high school, he moved to Nashville in 1950 at the invitation of country singer Autry Inman. There Killen joined the blackface comedy act Jamup and Honey as a bass player.

In 1953 Killen played bass for three months with the comedy group Cousin Jody, Mart & Bart on the *WWVA Jamboree* in Wheeling, West Virginia. When the trio split, Killen returned to Nashville, where Jack Stapp hired him at $35 a week to handle Tree's day-to-day activities of signing songwriters and pitching songs to artists and producers.

In 1957 Stapp bought out two of Tree's original owners and gave Killen 30 percent of the company and the title of vice president. Killen continued to write songs, penning the pop hit "Forever," while producing records for soul singer Joe Tex, Ronnie McDowell, Exile, and others. In 1974 Killen became Tree's president and COO and remained its driving force, while Stapp kept the titles of board chairman and CEO.

In 1980 Jack Stapp died and Killen purchased Stapp's interest. In 1989 he sold the company to Sony Music Publishing for $40 million. In 1994 he published his autobiography, *By the Seat of My Pants*, written with Tom Carter. Killen remained actively involved in several business ventures and charities until his death. —*Don Cusic*

## D Kilpatrick
b. Charlotte, North Carolina, July 18, 1919; d. May 21, 2008

Walter David "D" Kilpatrick was a notable music executive from the late 1940s to the late 1960s. After high school, service with the U.S. Marine Corps, and sales experience in the auto parts field, he broke into the record business as a salesman with the Capitol Records distributorship in Charlotte, North Carolina, servicing retailers and jukebox operators in parts of North Carolina and South Carolina. This prepared him for three years as Atlanta branch manager, beginning in early 1948. There he recruited and produced James and Martha Carson and the Statesmen for the label. In 1950 Kilpatrick became the first salaried country producer to be based in Nashville. In this role, using various studios around the nation, he recorded artists including Hank Thompson, Carl Butler, Jimmie Skinner, Tex Ritter, and Bob Atcher.

In 1951 Kilpatrick shifted to the Mercury label's country A&R slot. Although he remained heavily involved in southeastern sales and promotion, he concentrated on recording Jerry Byrd, the Carlisles (see Bill Carlisle), Johnny Horton, Jimmy Dean, Benny Martin, Ernie Lee, and Carl Story. In 1956 Kilpatrick became manager of WSM's Grand Ole Opry and its associated booking operation and brought in new blood, such as Rusty & Doug (see Doug Kershaw), Wilma Lee & Stoney Cooper, Porter Wagoner, and The Everly Brothers. Two years later Kilpatrick helped found the Country Music Association (CMA). He left the Opry in mid-1959 to form Acuff-Rose Artists Corporation (ARAC)—a booking agency—with Roy Acuff and Wesley Rose. A companion firm to Acuff-Rose Publications and Hickory Records, ARAC promoted not only Opry acts but also pop stars such as Roy Orbison and Mark Dinning. Next, Kilpatrick served as southern district regional sales manager for Warner Bros. Records (1962–64), South and Southwest distribution and promotion manager for Philips Records (1964–65), and Mercury's national sales and promotion chief (1965–66). A number of smaller musical ventures followed, until Kilpatrick left the music industry to run a custom drapery and fabrics business. —*John W. Rumble*

## Bradley Kincaid
b. Point Leavell, Kentucky, July 13, 1895; d. September 23, 1989

One of country music's earliest stars, Bradley Kincaid built bridges from folk music to commercial country on radio and on records. He was an early pillar of the WLS NATIONAL BARN DANCE, and he increased his fame through his own WLS shows.

After his first performance of "Barbara Allen" and similar folk songs, he received bushels of mail, and fans sent the Kentucky Mountain Boy 300,000 letters during his WLS years (1926–29). His warm tenor voice, rustic songs, and simple guitar accompaniment (on his "Hound Dog Guitar," for which his father had traded a dog) especially appealed to rural and small-town audiences. Kincaid was evidently the first country radio star to publish a SONGBOOK, *Favorite Mountain Ballads and Old Time Songs* (1928), selling 110,000 copies (through six printings) for fifty cents each on the air and at performances. He made regular trips through the Appalachians to collect songs but also included popular sentimental numbers in twelve additional songbooks. Total sales probably amounted to half a million.

Kincaid's mail kept coming as he moved from station to station, staying a year or so at each: WLW–Cincinnati; KDKA–Pittsburgh; WGY–Schenectady, New York; WEAF–New York City, and the NBC Red Network; WBZ–Boston; WTIC–Hartford; back to WGY; and then WHAM–Rochester. From these strategic bases, broadcasts and personal appearances heightened his songbook sales. During many of these years, Kincaid teamed with GRANDPA JONES and "Harmonica" Joe Troyan. Kincaid worked at WLW (and WKRC) in Cincinnati from 1941 to 1944; in 1946 he joined WSM's GRAND OLE OPRY, remaining until 1950. Subsequently he bought into radio station WWSO in Springfield, Ohio, and operated a music store.

*Bradley Kincaid*

Kincaid recorded more than a hundred songs released on more than thirty different labels, including GENNETT, BRUNSWICK, BULLET, BLUEBIRD, DECCA, and CAPITOL. Scotty Wiseman (LULU BELLE & SCOTTY), DOC HOPKINS, MAC WISEMAN, EDDY ARNOLD, BILL MONROE, and Grandpa and Ramona Jones all acknowledged Kincaid's influence. —*Loyal Jones*

## Claude King
b. near Keithville, Louisiana, February 5, 1923

Despite a career that spanned more than forty years, Claude King remains identified with just one song, "Wolverton Mountain," and, by implication, the early 1960s NASHVILLE SOUND it epitomized.

King worked semiprofessionally in music before World War II, and in 1947 he moved to Little Rock to work with Buddy Attaway and TILLMAN FRANKS. They made their first recording there for President Records. Back in Shreveport in 1948, King worked in construction, played occasionally on the *LOUISIANA HAYRIDE*, and recorded for Pacemaker, Specialty, and Dee-Jay.

King and JOHNNY HORTON were fellow hunters, and, after Horton's death, Tillman Franks, who had been the late singer's manager, groomed King as his replacement. King was signed to COLUMBIA RECORDS in Nashville, and after two Top Ten hits with songs based on movies, "Big River, Big Man" and "The Comancheros," King recorded MERLE KILGORE's "Wolverton Mountain," which peaked at #1 country and #6 pop in 1962.

Although King charted another twenty-seven records over the next fifteen years, nothing ever eclipsed "Wolverton Mountain." He stayed in Shreveport, recording for several small labels after Columbia and slowly scaled back his touring to the point where he had virtually retired by the mid-1980s. —*Colin Escott*

## Nelson King
b. Portsmouth, Ohio, April 1, 1914; d. March 16, 1974

The role of the radio disc jockey within country music grew dramatically following World War II, but few DJs would come to wield more power than Nelson King, who ruled the airwaves at WCKY in Cincinnati, Ohio, from 1946 until 1961. King was voted America's top country music DJ for eight consecutive years in nationwide polls conducted by *Billboard*, at a time when WCKY, a 50,000-watt giant, was considered one of country music's premier radio outlets.

King worked at a number of radio stations in West Virginia, Kentucky, and Ohio before the war, but earned his greatest fame at WCKY, where he hosted the *Jamboree* program and was active in various commercial ventures (for a time serving as a producer for Cincinnati-based KING RECORDS). He is listed as a cowriter on several country songs, most notably HANK WILLIAMS's "There'll Be No Teardrops Tonight," but those credits were likely more about securing airplay than actual collaboration.

King also made at least two recordings as an artist, "Deck of Cards" (1947) and "The Story of Our Lady of Fatima" (1950), both released on King Records. King left WCKY in 1961 and, except for a brief comeback at Covington, Kentucky, station WCLU (1968–70), worked outside the music business until his death. —*Jon Hartley Fox*

## Pee Wee King
b. Milwaukee, Wisconsin, February 18, 1914; d. March 7, 2000

Pee Wee King was an unlikely candidate for country music stardom. Yet as a songwriter, bandleader, recording artist, and television entertainer, he broke new ground in the genre, and he helped to bring waltzes, polkas, and COWBOY MUSIC into mainstream country during ten productive years at the GRAND OLE OPRY and his even more substantive post-Opry career.

Born Julius Frank Anthony Kuczynski into a working-class Polish-German family, he grew up in Wisconsin's polka-and-waltz culture. He made his musical debut at age fifteen when he played the accordion in his father's polka band. The teenager changed his name to King (after then-popular polka performer Wayne King) and formed his own high school band, Frankie King & the King's Jesters. In 1933 he joined WJRN–Racine's *Badger State Barn Dance* and soon snagged his own featured show.

King's lucky break came in the spring of 1934 when he met promoter J. L. FRANK. Later that year, King moved with Frank to Louisville, Kentucky, to back GENE AUTRY for a time, joined Frankie More's Log Cabin Boys as accordionist on Louisville station WHAS, and in 1936 married Frank's stepdaughter, Lydia.

In 1936 King was in Knoxville performing on WNOX. Next, in 1937, he formed the Golden West Cowboys and moved to Nashville to begin a decade at the Grand Ole Opry. In 1941–42 he and his band were featured with WSM's CAMEL CARAVAN unit, a touring company that presented some 175 shows at military installations in the United States and Central America. At various times his group included EDDY ARNOLD, REDD STEWART, ERNEST TUBB, COWBOY COPAS, and MINNIE PEARL.

After joining the Opry in June 1937, King helped introduce an array of new instruments and sounds to that program's stage, including the trumpet, drums, and the electric guitar. In addition, he dressed his band members in spiffy western outfits designed by the Hollywood tailor NUDIE. His nattily attired Golden West

*Pee Wee King*

Cowboys generally produced a smooth and danceable sound during their 1940s heyday; in the 1950s they even branched out briefly into mild ROCKABILLY.

King is credited with more than 400 songs, including some of the most popular songs in American musical history, most notably the hugely successful "Tennessee Waltz," penned with Redd Stewart. Patti Page's 1950 version reached #1 on the pop charts and within six months sold almost 5 million copies. It became an official Tennessee state song in 1965 and has been recorded by scores of additional artists. King's own recording career included more than twenty albums and 157 singles, most of them issued during his seventeen-year association with RCA VICTOR. His massive 1951 hit "Slow Poke" made him one of the earliest country musicians to cross over into the pop field.

King became a pioneer television performer in 1947, when he returned to Louisville to work on WAVE radio and television. In the 1950s and 1960s his regional and national TV shows originated from Louisville, Cincinnati, Cleveland, and Chicago.

King appeared in four movies: *Gold Mine in the Sky* with Gene Autry in 1938; *Flame of the West* with Johnny Mack Brown in 1945; and *Ridin' the Outlaw Trail* (1951) and *The Rough, Tough West* (1955) with Charles Starrett. In 1967 King released his own production, *Country-Western Hoedown*, with disappointing artistic and financial results. King and his writing partner Redd Stewart were elected to the NASHVILLE SONGWRITERS HALL OF FAME in 1970. King was elected to THE COUNTRY MUSIC HALL OF FAME in 1974. —*Wade Hall*

## King Records
established in Cincinnati, Ohio, November 1943

Perhaps more than any other record label, King was shaped by its founder, SYD NATHAN. Under his direction, it became a highly vertical company, controlling as much as possible of the process that took music from composition to the consumer. At its peak, the King organization had its own studio, printing press, design operation, and pressing plant as well as a wholly owned sales and distribution network. With that infrastructure Nathan hoped to solve problems endemic to independent labels.

King started in Cincinnati in November 1943 with two records by MERLE TRAVIS and GRANDPA JONES that were pressed in minimal quantities. It was relaunched a year later with $25,000 raised from family members. At first King was a country label. Several radio barn dances were on King's doorstep in Cincinnati, and many rural Kentuckians and Tennesseans worked in local factories, giving Nathan both a pool of talent and a ready-made market. King stayed exclusively in country music for two years and ultimately scored many major hits with COWBOY COPAS, MOON MULLICAN, the DELMORE BROTHERS, and others.

Nathan entered the R&B market to give his distribution company more to sell and then found the climate of this market better suited for independents. His country releases slowly atrophied, and by the 1960s King's small country roster consisted mostly of a few BLUEGRASS acts. One of the label's few mainstream country artists was HAWKSHAW HAWKINS, who re-signed in 1962 and scored a #1 hit with "Lonesome 7-7203" the following year. It's worth noting, though, that King advanced R&B's influence on country music through black producer HENRY GLOVER, who sometimes recorded Moon Mullican's R&B-style discs using black musicians.

King began limping in the early 1960s, and, when Nathan closed out his distribution system in 1965, the label was almost entirely dependent on soul star James Brown. Nathan died in March 1968, and in October King was sold to STARDAY RECORDS just as Starday was about to be sold to Lin Broadcasting. In July 1971, shortly before Lin sold King-Starday, it sold James Brown's contract and catalog to Polydor. King-Starday then went to Tennessee Recording and Publishing, which retained the music publishing and, in 1975, sold the masters to their current owner, GML, Inc., of Nashville. —*Colin Escott*

## Beecher "Pete" Kirby (*see* Bashful Brother Oswald)

## Fred Kirby
b. Charlotte, North Carolina, July 19, 1910; d. April 22, 1996

Frederick Austin Kirby was one of several prominent country singers who emerged on radio around Charlotte, North Carolina, in the 1930s. He entered professional broadcasting on WIS in Columbia, South Carolina, in 1931, but "really hit the big time," as he phrased it, when he switched to WBT–Charlotte soon thereafter. During the 1930s he teamed first with Bob Phillips and then Cliff Carlisle (see BILL CARLISLE) on *Briarhopper Time* and the *Crazy Barn Dance*, modeling his musical style on that of the late JIMMIE RODGERS. (Unlike Rodgers, however, Kirby typically dressed in cowboy garb.)

While with Phillips, Kirby worked at stations WIP and WFIL in Philadelphia. During the late 1930s and early 1940s he joined forces with western singer Don White for appearances on WLW's *Boone County Jamboree* in Cincinnati and the WLS NATIONAL BARN DANCE in Chicago. After parting ways with White early in the 1940s, Kirby moved to St. Louis, where his success entertaining at World War II bond rallies earned him the name Victory Cowboy.

In mid-decade Kirby returned to WBT to work *Briarhopper Time*, the *Dixie Jamboree*, and *Carolina Hayride*, and he hosted his own disc jockey programs between 1945 and 1950. Kirby recorded for BLUEBIRD (1936–37), DECCA (1938), Sonora (1946–47), MGM (1949), and COLUMBIA (1950) in addition to writing songs such as "Atomic Power," a 1946 chart-maker for the Buchanan Brothers. For more than two decades, running into the 1980s, Kirby was a featured western entertainer at the Tweetsie Railroad in Blowing Rock, North Carolina, where he sang and helped reenact life in the Old West. —*John W. Rumble*

## Alison Krauss (& Union Station)
b. Decatur, Illinois, July 23, 1971

From her beginnings as a young, contest-winning BLUEGRASS fiddler, Alison Krauss has become one of the world's most recognized musicians. She holds twenty-six Grammys as of 2010 as well as multiple trophies from CMA, ACM, IBMA, the AMERICANA Music Association, and other organizations. Since the late 1980s she has won vast new audiences for country music in general and bluegrass in particular while extending her artistic range to the folk, pop, and classical fields.

Krauss grew up in the college town of Champaign, Illinois, and at age twelve she joined a local folk-bluegrass band including John Pennell and Nelson Mandrell, who have since supplied her with many songs. Three years later ROUNDER RECORDS signed her, hoping she would develop into a fiddle virtuoso in the MARK O'CONNOR mode. But her debut album, 1987's *Too Late to Cry*, revealed her pure, aching soprano, and her vocals would soon surpass her fiddling. Backed by her handpicked quartet of stellar young pickers, Union Station, she started making albums that topped the bluegrass charts. They also helped to transform and reinvigorate a style dominated by mostly male singers and

*Alison Krauss & Union Station: (from left) Jerry Douglas, Barry Bales, Krauss, Ron Block, and Dan Tyminski*

pickers playing fast, flashy solos to one embracing female vocalists delivering intensely personal lyrics framed by artfully crafted STRINGBAND arrangements.

The follow-up, 1989's *Two Highways*, was credited to Alison Krauss & Union Station and defined her style. The album reflected the brokenhearted subject matter of mainstream country but with lyrics that shared the detail and irony of modern folk music; likewise, the melodies had the sweet accessibility of modern country-pop but were set in acoustic string arrangements uncluttered by drums. These two projects included hot-picking instrumentals, but 1990's *I've Got That Old Feeling* stressed contemporary, personal songwriting, including four numbers by THE COX FAMILY's Sidney Cox. Krauss also produced and arranged three albums for the Louisiana bluegrass gospel group. Since then she has produced the bluegrass act NICKEL CREEK, REBA MCENTIRE's 2002 single "Sweet Music Man," ALAN JACKSON's album *Like Red on a Rose*, and others.

In 1992 Krauss released *Every Time We Say Goodbye*, with selections penned by Pennell, Cox, and Union Station members Ron Block and Dan Tyminski. (Barry Bales and featured DOBRO player JERRY DOUGLAS complete the band.) On July 3, 1993, the twenty-one-year-old Krauss became the first bluegrass artist to join the GRAND OLE OPRY since THE OSBORNE BROTHERS' and JIM & JESSE's 1964 inductions. *I Know Who Holds Tomorrow*, recorded with the Cox Family, appeared in 1994.

In 1995 Rounder released *Now That I've Found You: A Collection*. It included three new songs, one each from her first five albums, and four of her guest appearances on other artists' albums. (Over the years performers ranging from Yo-Yo Ma to RALPH STANLEY have featured her, and she has worked recording sessions behind the Chieftains, Kenny Loggins, Michael McDonald, Maura O'Connell, and many more.) For an album on a small label, the anthology defied conventional wisdom and sold more than 2 million copies. The project pointed her toward two Grammy awards (for singles from the album) and four CMA awards: Female Vocalist of the Year, the Horizon Award, Single of the Year (with Union Station, "When You Say Nothing at All"), and Vocal Event of the Year (with SHENANDOAH, "Somewhere in the Vicinity of the Heart"). She also won her second IBMA Entertainer of the Year award, the first coming in 1991.

With her ace backing group, Krauss widened her artistic and commercial reputation in the new century. She contributed to the soundtrack of the hit film *O BROTHER, WHERE ART THOU?* (2000) as well as to *Down from the Mountain* (LOST HIGHWAY, 2001)—a follow-up album and DVD of live concert performances—and to related tours. Her soundtrack duet with GILLIAN WELCH on "I'll Fly Away" became IBMA's 2001 Gospel Recorded Performance of the Year. Krauss recorded two tracks (one with rock musician Sting) for the 2003 film *Cold Mountain* and has contributed to other films and television series. *Alison Krauss & Union Station Live* (2003) took two Grammys as well as IBMA's Album of the Year honors, while "How's the World Treating You," a duet with James Taylor for the tribute album *Livin', Lovin', Losin': Songs of the Louvin Brothers*, also won a 2003 Grammy. The following year, Krauss and BRAD PAISLEY garnered ACM's Video of the Year and Vocal Event of the Year prizes for their duet "Whiskey Lullaby." *Raising Sand* (Rounder, 2007), recorded with former Led Zeppelin singer Robert Plant, led to six Grammy Awards, one for 2007 and five for 2008. The album was also CMA's Vocal Event of the Year for 2008. At this writing Krauss remains one of America's most talented, creative, and respected musicians. —*Geoffrey Himes*

*Kris Kristofferson*

# Kris Kristofferson

b. Brownsville, Texas, June 22, 1936

Few singer-songwriters have exerted more influence on country music or have been as successful within and beyond the limits of MUSIC ROW as Kris Kristofferson. Since the 1960s, Kristofferson has excelled as a recording artist and Hollywood actor, and he has helped set standards for country music songwriting that continue to guide and inspire tunesmiths worldwide.

A Rhodes Scholar and son of a U.S. Air Force major general, Kristofferson served as an army captain and helicopter pilot before turning to music. In 1965, two weeks before he was scheduled to begin teaching English literature at West Point, he resigned his commission to take up songwriting in Nashville, signing first with Buckhorn Music and later with COMBINE MUSIC PUBLISHING. For years he paid his dues with part-time jobs, including a stint as janitor at the COLUMBIA studios while BOB DYLAN was recording *Blonde on Blonde*.

Inspired by the Romantic poets, Greenwich Village folk-poet troubadours, and songwriter friend MICKEY NEWBURY, Kristofferson developed a songwriting style that reflected the sense of alienation and loss that characterized the 1960s while also celebrating the decade's insistence on freedom, honesty, and sexual candor. Kristofferson's profile heightened when ROGER MILLER recorded his "Me and Bobby McGee" (#12, 1969) and RAY PRICE scored a #1 hit and earned a Grammy in 1970 with Kristofferson's "For the Good Times." In that same year, JOHNNY CASH hit #1 with Kristofferson's moody hangover anthem "Sunday Morning Coming Down," later named CMA's Song of the Year. SAMMI SMITH's recording of "Help Me Make It Through the Night," unusual for the times in its open embrace of a one-night stand, topped the country charts in 1971, garnered CMA's 1971 Single of the Year Award, and earned Kristofferson a Grammy for Best Country Song. Also in 1971, a version of "Me and Bobby McGee" recorded by rock singer Janis Joplin (with whom Kristofferson had been romantically involved) became a million-selling pop hit.

Kristofferson's literary, sensuous approach to writing helped open the doors of the generally conservative Nashville establishment and made the city inviting to artists intent on exploring the issues and tensions of the times. "Hearing Kristofferson's 'Me and Bobby McGee' on the radio and knowing it came out of Nashville made Nashville seem a lot more accessible to me," said GUY CLARK, a celebrated songwriter who moved from Los Angeles to MUSIC CITY in 1971.

Kristofferson's own recording career has met with uneven success. While he's popular as a live performer, his gruff, gravelly voice has rarely been a hit with radio programmers. Still, he managed to earn #1 singles as a solo artist with the gospel-flavored "Why Me" (1973) and with "Highwayman" (1985), the signature song of the Highwaymen, a superstar quartet that also included WAYLON JENNINGS, WILLIE NELSON, and Johnny Cash. From the mid-1980s to the late 1990s, Kristofferson put recording on the back burner, but in the new century his album releases have become more frequent.

Kristofferson was married to pop singer Rita Coolidge from 1973 to 1980. They recorded several albums together and earned two Grammys for Best Country Vocal Performance by a Duo or Group: 1973's "From the Bottle to the Bottom" and "Lover Please," their 1975 cover of Clyde McPhatter's 1962 R&B hit written by BILLY SWAN, a member of Kristofferson's band, the Borderlords.

Kristofferson has appeared in numerous films and made-for-TV movies, including *Pat Garrett and Billy the Kid* (1973), *A Star Is Born* (1976), and (with Willie Nelson) *Songwriter* (1984), for which he received an Oscar nomination for Best Original Song Score. Now one of American music's most respected artists, Kristofferson continues to act, write songs, record, and tour occasionally as a solo act. Rock musicians demonstrated the breadth of his influence with the 2002 album *Don't Let the Bastards Get You Down: A Tribute to Kris Kristofferson*. He is an activist who speaks out on social justice and human rights issues, and the American Veteran Awards named him Veteran of the Year in 2002. In 2003 he received the Spirit of AMERICANA Free Speech Award from the Americana Music Association. A member of the NASHVILLE SONGWRITERS HALL OF FAME (elected 1977), Kris Kristofferson was elected to THE COUNTRY MUSIC HALL OF FAME in 2004.
—*Jack Bernhardt*

## Sleepy LaBeef
b. Smackover, Arkansas, July 20, 1935

A one-man melting pot of roots-music styles, Sleepy LaBeef is regarded as one of rock & roll's great live performers. Whether playing ROCKABILLY, straight-ahead country, R&B, or gospel, this towering (six-foot, six-inch) singer-guitarist invests nearly every performance with rare conviction and soulfulness.

Born Thomas Paulsley LaBeff (from LaBoeuf), he grew up in Arkansas but moved to Houston as a young man. With a strong gospel music background, he performed on the *Houston Jamboree*, and PAPPY DAILY eventually recorded him for STARDAY in 1957. Other records appeared on the tiny Wayside, Gulf, and Finn labels. Though none hit, they are generally revered by rockabilly fans and collectors.

Signed to COLUMBIA RECORDS in 1964, LaBeef moved to Nashville but again had no measurable success (though he did play the monster in the low-budget film *The Monster and the Stripper*). By the 1970s he was recording for SHELBY SINGLETON's Plantation label and then later for Singleton's version of SUN RECORDS. A 1977 residency at Alan's Fifth Wheel Lounge in Amesbury, Massachusetts, sparked laudatory articles (most notably by music historian Peter Guralnick), while the late 1970s rockabilly revival further enlarged LaBeef's visibility. In 1981 his *It Ain't What You Eat (It's the Way You Chew It)* was released on ROUNDER RECORDS, the label for which he recorded a series of critically heralded albums into the late 1990s. *Tomorrow Never Comes* (M.C., 2000) showcased guest vocals by Maria Muldaur. Since then, compilations of previously unissued tracks have enhanced his status as a rockabilly stalwart. LaBeef continues to work the road as he always has, with each performance offering fresh takes on some of the 6,000+ tunes he is said to have at his command. —*Daniel Cooper*

## Lady Antebellum
Dave Haywood, b. Augusta, Georgia, July 5, 1982
Charles Kelley, b. Augusta, Georgia, September 11, 1981
Hillary Scott, b. Nashville, Tennessee, April 1, 1986

The vocal trio Lady Antebellum grew out of a chance meeting in a Nashville nightclub, when Hillary Scott, the daughter of country singer Linda Davis, recognized Charles Kelley from his MySpace page and introduced herself. Kelley and his childhood friend, Dave Haywood, had already moved to Nashville to write songs together. In 2006 the trio became Lady Antebellum, choosing the name to evoke their southern heritage. Scott and Kelley share lead vocals, with multi-instrumentalist Haywood helping with harmonies. Together, they create a contemporary, soaring sound that blends Fleetwood Mac-style vocal dynamics with songs that explore the push-and-pull of modern relationships.

*Lady Antebellum: (from left) Charles Kelley, Hillary Scott, and Dave Haywood*

Success came quickly. The trio's first single on CAPITOL Nashville, "Love Don't Live Here," reached #3 on the country charts in 2008. "Run to You" (2009), launched a succession of #1 hits, including "Need You Now" and "American Honey." Lady Antebellum's self-titled debut album and its follow-up, *Need You Now,* together had sold more than five million units by spring 2011. The act has won 2008 awards from CMA for New Artist of the Year and from ACM for Top New Duo or Group; a 2009 Grammy for Best Country Performance by Duo or Group with Vocals; 2009 ACM Awards for Top Vocal Group of the Year, Song of the Year, and Single of the Year; 2009 CMA Awards for Vocal Group of the Year and Best Country Song (for "Run to You"); and 2010 CMA awards for Vocal Group of the Year and Single of the Year (for "Need You Now"). Lady Antebellum also swept the 2010 Grammy Awards, taking five honors, including Record of the Year and Song of the Year for "Need You Now." —*Michael McCall*

## John Lair
b. Renfro Valley, Kentucky, July 1, 1894; d. November 12, 1985

Few individuals in country music have filled as many roles as John Lee Lair, a composer, collector, talent scout, radio producer, and performer best known for founding Kentucky's RENFRO VALLEY BARN DANCE. Lair brought a wealth of experience to country radio, which he entered full time in the late 1920s at Chicago's WLS. After graduating from high school in Mount Vernon, Kentucky, he served as principal of Renfro Valley's high school, helped to write and produce the show *Atta Boy* in a special services unit during World War I, performed in a sketch from this show included in Broadway's Ziegfeld Follies, and wound up in

Chicago as claims manager for an insurance company. There he began performing on the WLS *National Barn Dance*, recruiting fellow Kentuckians such as Karl Davis and Harty Taylor (Karl & Harty) for the Cumberland Ridge Runners, in which Lair played the jug. Eventually Lair became WLS's music director and scoured the nation for folk and popular tunes, thus beginning what became one of America's largest private music libraries.

Fearing that the cowboy music trend of the 1930s was taking country music too far from its folk roots—and seeking independence from Chicago's powerful labor unions—Lair decided to found his own, more tradition-oriented *Renfro Valley Barn Dance* in Cincinnati in 1937, using many former WLS performers. In 1939 he realized his dream of bringing his show back home by building a 1,000-seat barn to stage the *Barn Dance* in Renfro Valley. Other programs Lair originated from the area included the *Sunday Morning Gatherin'* (which, like the barn dance, still runs today) and remote-location broadcasts of coon hunts, country breakfasts, and fish fries—all examples of his commitment to authentic broadcasts of community life and music.

By the mid-1950s Lair had lost his network outlet, though he continued to publish the *Renfro Valley Bugle* and operate his pioneer museum, general store, and other attractions. In 1968 he sold his operation to Nashville musical entrepreneur Hal Smith, but, with other partners, he bought it back again four years later. The show continues under new management, attracting thousands of visitors each year. Its theme song is still the one Lair wrote for it, "Take Me Back to Renfro Valley." —*John W. Rumble*

## Charlie Lamb
b. Knoxville, Tennessee, June 21, 1921

Charles Stacy Lamb worked for years behind the scenes in Nashville as a journalist, publisher (*Music Reporter*), and all-around promoter of country music. He started his career in Knoxville as a carnival barker, a copyboy for the *Knoxville Journal*, and a copywriter for radio station WKGN. In 1949 he ran the artists bureau at Knoxville's WROL, booking Molly O'Day and Carl Story. Lamb moved to Nashville in 1951 to write a column and sell ads for *Cash Box*. Having promoted records for Mercury Records, he formed his own agency, promoting notables such as Kitty Wells and Elvis Presley.

Convinced that Nashville's growth as a music center warranted a locally based trade journal, he founded *Country Music Reporter* in September 1956, which became simply *Music Reporter* in March 1957 and continued publication into 1964. His innovative touches in that magazine included expanding singles charts to fifty and, later, one hundred listings—in the process creating what some called the "one big chart" embracing records from pop, country, and R&B—using a "bullet" to denote hot sales or radio activity, and introducing an album chart for country records.

As a manager his clients included Ed Bruce and Connie Smith. In 1965 Lamb received a Grammy nomination for his liner notes to *Father & Son—Hank Williams Sr. & Jr.* released by MGM Records. In the 1960s Lamb turned performer and comic, delighting audiences at music-industry banquets and other events with his nonsensical "double-talk" routines. He guested on network TV's *Candid Camera*, acted in commercials and films such as *Ernest Goes to Jail* (1990), and won an *America's Funniest People* TV competition (1992). A member of founding boards for CMA and the Gospel Music Association, he was the first president of NARAS's Nashville chapter. Today he is semiretired. —*Walt Trott*

## Miranda Lambert
b. Lindale, Texas, November 10, 1983

With her first album, Miranda Lambert was hailed as an artist whose success signaled a rapprochement between mainstream and alternative country.

Only nineteen when she began competing in the inaugural season of *Nashville Star* in 2003, Lambert had already appeared in local and regional contests. Though she finished third on the show, she garnered a contract with Epic Nashville, and *Kerosene* (2005) debuted at #1. None of its singles made the country Top Ten, but the album went platinum, gained critical acclaim, and earned Lambert a 2007 ACM award for Top New Female Vocalist. She further developed *Kerosene*'s combination of pop balladry and raw, rocking style on *Crazy Ex-Girlfriend* (Columbia, 2007), which also topped the country album charts, yielded her first Top Ten hit, "Gunpowder & Lead," and won a 2008 ACM award for Album of the Year.

*Revolution* (2009) included several country chart-makers and her first Top 40 hit on *Billboard*'s all-genre Hot 100 charts. The album led to three 2009 ACM Awards: Album of the Year, Top Female Vocalist of the Year, and Video of the Year ("White Liar"). Her tradition-leaning smash "The House that Built Me" became her first #1 hit and further established her stardom by winning awards as CMA's 2010 Song of the Year and Video of the Year. On that same *CMA Awards* show, the association named Lambert its Female Vocalist of the Year and *Revolution* its Album of the Year.

Lambert's pedigree as a TV contestant, her commercial success, and her marketable good looks might have branded her as the kind of slick Nashville confection that critics often dismiss. But her songwriting talent, twangy Texas vocals, and self-identification with iconoclasts, from the Outlaws to contemporary alternative-country performers, endeared her to mainstream radio and the alternative press alike. —*Diane Pecknold*

*Miranda Lambert*

## Cristy Lane

b. Peoria, Illinois, January 8, 1940

Cristy Lane made her reputation through television marketing, promoting her 1980 cornerstone performance, "One Day at a Time." Her blend of religious, patriotic, and heartache music appealed to an audience that followed her to BRANSON, MISSOURI, where she became a featured performer.

Born Eleanor Johnston, Lane was the shy child among twelve in her midwestern family. She married Lee Stoller in 1959 and had three children by 1964. Stoller changed her name to Cristy Lane and pressed her to perform in public. It was a trying time for Lane; she attempted suicide in 1968, yet by 1969 she was touring outposts in Vietnam. Another suicide attempt followed.

Stoller and Lane moved to Nashville in 1972 and started their own label, promoting and selling Lane's singles themselves. Her Top Ten hits in the late 1970s, including "Let Me Down Easy," resulted in her winning ACM's Top New Female Vocalist award for 1979.

In 1980 Lane's recording of the MARIJOHN WILKIN–KRIS KRISTOFFERSON composition "One Day at a Time" became a #1 hit for United Artists. An album and autobiography, both likewise titled *One Day at a Time*, were sold through mail order and marketed on television and in supermarket tabloids. Lee Stoller's 1982 conviction under federal racketeering statutes did little to slow them down. After his release from prison he and Lane helped establish Branson as a country music tourist center. In the 2000s they have continued to sell her music via the Internet.
—*Mary A. Bufwack*

## Red Lane

b. Bogalusa, Louisiana, February 2, 1939

Red Lane, born Hollis Rudolph DeLaughter, is one of MUSIC ROW's most respected songwriters. After polishing his guitar skills in the U.S. Air Force, Lane was introduced in 1964 to JUSTIN TUBB, who arranged for BUDDY KILLEN to hear Lane's songs. Killen signed Lane to TREE PUBLISHING as an exclusive songwriter and encouraged Tubb to hire him as a guitar player so that Lane could move to Nashville. In short order Lane's songs were being recorded, beginning with "My Friend on the Right" (FARON YOUNG, 1964). Lane's list of hits grew to include "'Til I Get It Right" (TAMMY WYNETTE, 1973), "My Own Kind of Hat" (MERLE HAGGARD, 1979), "Miss Emily's Picture" (JOHN CONLEE, 1981), and "New Looks from an Old Lover" (B. J. Thomas, 1983).

Lane's guitar prowess led to his fronting DOTTIE WEST's road band, the Heartaches, and a stint in Merle Haggard's Strangers during the 1980s. Haggard recorded more than twenty of Lane's songs; on most of those recordings Lane played guitar. In the early 1970s Lane released four chart singles on RCA. He was inducted into the NASHVILLE SONGWRITERS HALL OF FAME in 1993. —*Kent Henderson*

## k. d. lang

b. Consort, Alberta, Canada, November 2, 1961

Critically heralded, k. d. lang released a series of country albums as distinctive as any produced during the artistically rich late 1980s, yet she never saw her acclaim translate into mainstream country success.

Kathryn Dawn Lang was classically trained and in college when she discovered country music. While attending Alberta's Red Deer College in 1982, she landed a role in a theater production based on PATSY CLINE's career. Hearing Cline's music changed her life. lang and her band, the reclines, became a sensation in Canada with the release of their 1984 album *A Truly Western Experience*. It included an homage to Cline, but most of the tunes were lang's own. Her show featured her band's HONKY-TONK sound and lang's powerful and expressive voice, while showcasing lang in square-dance dresses and western shirts as she whirled about the stage.

Signed to Sire Records, lang released *Angel with a Lariat* (1987), which made her a favorite among Nashville artists and music executives. But despite good sales, radio would not play her debut single, a remake of LYNN ANDERSON's "Rose Garden." lang's 1987 duet with ROY ORBISON on "Crying" won a Grammy yet didn't reach the Top Forty. For her 1988 album *Shadowland*, lang teamed with legendary producer OWEN BRADLEY, and KITTY WELLS, BRENDA LEE, and LORETTA LYNN joined her on the collection's "Honky-Tonk Angels' Medley." *Shadowland* went gold but, again, garnered little radio support; "I'm Down to My Last Cigarette" reached only #21 on the charts.

Her 1989 gold album *Absolute Torch and Twang* included original tunes and reinterpretations of country chestnuts. A popular and critical success, it won the 1989 Grammy for Best Female Country Performance.

With her 1992 pop-cabaret album *Ingenue*, lang moved away from country, though not necessarily for good. In 1994 she wrote and scored the soundtrack for *Even Cowgirls Get the Blues*, dipping again into her country vocabulary. Since then she has continued to explore jazz, pop, country, folk, and Latin music while developing her songwriting and producing skills.
—*Mary A. Bufwack*

## Jim Lauderdale

b. Troutman, North Carolina, April 11, 1957

James Russell Lauderdale has won recognition in the country, BLUEGRASS, and AMERICANA fields as a Nashville-based songwriter and performer. GEORGE STRAIT, VINCE GILL, and PATTY LOVELESS have recorded his songs, and MARK CHESNUTT notched a #1 in 1995 with "Gonna Get a Life," cowritten by Lauderdale and Nashville veteran Frank Dycus. Lauderdale's style of country applies the progressive mindset of GRAM PARSONS to the musical legacies of Memphis, BAKERSFIELD, Nashville, and Appalachia.

A precocious minister's kid raised in Due West, South Carolina, Lauderdale spent his teen years obsessed with bluegrass. Pursuing a performing career, he stopped in New York and Nashville before moving to Los Angeles, where he landed a cut on the second *Town South of Bakersfield* compilation, an anthology of Southern California's alternative country scene. Beginning with his first major-label singles on EPIC in 1988, Lauderdale's albums have won critical praise, though not mass acceptance. They include the RODNEY CROWELL–John Leventhal coproduction *Planet of Love* on Reprise (1991) and equally fine efforts for ATLANTIC, Upstart, BNA (RCA RECORDS), and RCA (1994–99). His 2002 Dualtone album *Lost in the Lonesome Pines*, recorded with RALPH STANLEY, won a Grammy for Best Bluegrass Album. Lauderdale won the same honor in 2007 for his solo album *The Bluegrass Diaries* on Yep Roc Records. His broad and adventurous tastes have led to recordings with Donna the Buffalo, Grateful Dead lyricist

Robert Hunter, and Lauderdale hero GEORGE JONES, whose role Lauderdale played in a 2001 stage musical about the life of TAMMY WYNETTE. In 2009 Lauderdale released *Could We Get Any Closer* on the Skycrunch label.

In 2002, Lauderdale won Artist of the Year and Song of the Year honors at the Americana Music Association's first awards show. He went on to become a recurring host of the Americana Music Awards starting in 2003. —*Mark Schone*

## Shorty Lavender
b. Old Fort, North Carolina, August 19, 1932; d. March 1, 1982

Grover C. "Shorty" Lavender gained early musical experience as a fiddler with RAY PRICE's Cherokee Cowboys. Lavender joined the WILBURN BROTHERS for their TV series, launched in 1963, and was a session player for artists such as WEBB PIERCE. HUBERT LONG hired Lavender as a talent agent, and he booked early dates for BILL ANDERSON and TAMMY WYNETTE. After Long died, in 1972, Lavender started a booking agency in partnership with Wynette (whom he managed) and GEORGE JONES. In 1975 Lavender merged with Dick Blake as Lavender/Blake, adding acts such as RONNIE MILSAP and THE STATLER BROTHERS. After 1978 Lavender ran his own agency. The Nashville Association of Talent Directors voted him 1981 Man of the Year. —*Walt Trott*

## Don Law
b. London, England, February 24, 1902; d. December 20, 1982

As the head of COLUMBIA RECORDS' country music division through most of the 1950s and 1960s, Don Law was one of the most important and successful producers in the annals of country music. Among the top-selling artists he worked with at Columbia were CARL SMITH, LEFTY FRIZZELL, RAY PRICE, JOHNNY HORTON, and JOHNNY CASH, to name but a few. Prior to that, as the protégé of record industry pioneer ART SATHERLEY, Law had been instrumental in bringing to Columbia and its affiliated labels such major pre–World War II talents as BOB WILLS and AL DEXTER (not to mention blues legend Robert Johnson, whose landmark recordings Law produced). Popular with most of his acts, Law was, as Price once put it, a producer who "let an artist be an artist."

An Englishman by birth, Law sang with the London Choral Society as a young man. After various jobs overseas, he immigrated to the United States in 1924, eventually landing in Dallas, Texas, where he worked as a bookkeeper for BRUNSWICK RECORDS. When the AMERICAN RECORD CORPORATION bought Brunswick in 1931, Law met ARC executive Satherley. When Columbia merged with ARC, both men wound up working for Columbia.

In 1942 Law was called to Columbia's New York office to oversee the children's music division, but his time in that position didn't last long. At some point after World War II (apparently in 1945, though the evidence is unclear), Columbia divided its country division in two, putting Law in charge of all territory east of El Paso and making Satherley responsible for everything west of it. "Right off the bat we got LITTLE JIMMY DICKENS, Carl Smith, and Lefty Frizzell," Law later remarked. He found Frizzell in 1950 through the JIM BECK studio in Dallas, where Law often recorded such artists as Frizzell, Price, BILLY WALKER, and MARTY ROBBINS. Though Law also utilized the Nashville studios, he always maintained close ties with Texas. It was only after Beck

*Don Law*

died, in 1956, that Law focused his attention on MUSIC CITY. By that point he was sole head of the country division at Columbia, Satherley having retired in 1952.

Along with CHET ATKINS at RCA, OWEN BRADLEY at DECCA, and KEN NELSON at CAPITOL, Law was instrumental in reestablishing country's commercial viability during the so-called NASHVILLE SOUND era (ca. 1957–72). Like Atkins and Bradley, Law headed a country division that amassed numerous country-pop crossover hits during the late 1950s and early 1960s. But unlike those two, he and his frequent coproducer FRANK JONES (and the session leaders to whom Law sometimes delegated the hands-on production duties) did not rely so much on the strings and smooth vocals commonly associated with the Nashville Sound. Rather, Columbia churned out such musically diverse crossover hits as Marty Robbins's "El Paso" and "Don't Worry," JOHNNY HORTON's "The Battle of New Orleans" and "North to Alaska," STONEWALL JACKSON's "Waterloo," and JIMMY DEAN's "Big Bad John." In February 1962, in the wake of this success, Columbia bought OWEN BRADLEY's Nashville recording studio on Sixteenth Avenue South and opened a permanent office there.

As successful as he was, Law nevertheless fell victim to the changes sweeping through American music in the late 1960s. In March 1967 he was forced to take mandatory retirement from Columbia. Law's place at the helm of the Nashville office was taken by BOB JOHNSTON, who had produced BOB DYLAN's *Blonde on Blonde* sessions in Music City the year before. Some of the Columbia artists, notably Ray Price, were allowed to continue working with Law as an independent producer. Calling his company Don Law Productions, he also scored an immediate crossover hit as an independent with HENSON CARGILL's "Skip a Rope," released on MONUMENT. But by the 1970s Law's role in the business was rapidly diminishing, and by the end of the decade he was fully retired. He died in 1982 in a suburb of Galveston, Texas. Law was elected to THE COUNTRY MUSIC HALL OF FAME in 2001. —*Daniel Cooper*

## Tracy Lawrence
b. Atlanta, Texas, January 27, 1968

Building on his #1 debut single for ATLANTIC, "Sticks and Stones" (1991–92), Tracy Lawrence established himself as a popular country singer in the 1990s, despite being shot in a Nashville holdup shortly before the release of his first album. Subsequent hits— "Today's Lonely Fool," "Runnin' Behind," and "Somebody Paints the Wall"—helped him become ACM's Top New Male Vocalist of 1992.

In 1994, however, Lawrence fired a handgun during a dispute with teenagers in nearby Wilson County, Tennessee. Admitting to overreacting, he cited his earlier experience at gunpoint for prompting his use of a weapon. The case was later dismissed.

Into 1997 Lawrence continued to win fans and critics with hits including "Alibis," "Can't Break It to My Heart," and "Time Marches On" (all #1) and the #2 hit "If the World Had a Front Porch." He also assumed his own career management, opened a music publishing company, and began coproducing his albums and producing other artists.

In 1998 Lawrence was convicted of spousal abuse, and Atlantic suspended him temporarily. Although "Lessons Learned," the title track from a 1999 album, became a #40 pop chart-maker of 1999–2000, other singles fared poorly. After Atlantic's Nashville operation closed in 2000, Lawrence was moved to WARNER BROS., where he cut one unsuccessful album. He fared better with *Strong*, his only DREAMWORKS album, which yielded "Paint Me a Birmingham," a #4 hit of 2004.

After a 2005 greatest-hits compilation for MERCURY, in 2006 Lawrence and his brother, Laney, formed Rocky Comfort Records, a joint venture with CO5 Nashville. "Find Out Who Your Friends Are," the first single from Tracy's 2006 album *For the Love*, climbed to #1 in mid-2007. An alternate version from the album, with guest vocalists TIM MCGRAW and KENNY CHESNEY, won CMA's 2007 Musical Event of the Year honors. In 2009 Lawrence released *The Rock*, an album of Christian music. —*Janet E. Williams*

## Doyle Lawson & Quicksilver
b. Ford Town, Tennessee, April 20, 1944

Following successful stints with J. D. CROWE (1966–71) and THE COUNTRY GENTLEMEN (1972–79), mandolinist Doyle Lawson assembled his own band, Quicksilver, in 1979, recruiting veteran BLUEGRASS performers Terry Baucom (banjo), Lou Reid Pirtle (bass), and Jimmy Haley (guitar). The band quickly established a reputation for precise harmony singing, hard-driving instrumental work, and vibrant new material as well as an a cappella gospel singing style based on quartet singing from both black and white southern gospel traditions.

As the band's success and influence spread in the 1980s, other groups began to emulate Lawson's approach, to the extent that, when his entire band left in 1986, he was able to hire immediate replacements. The membership stabilized in the late 1980s with Russell Moore (guitar), Scott Vestal (banjo), and Ray Deaton (electric bass). Each was an accomplished instrumentalist but,

more important to the overall structure of Lawson's sound, also a highly skilled vocalist.

Eventually these musicians also went on to other ventures, but by the late 1980s Lawson's style was being copied on such a wide scale that finding replacements posed few problems. As new members came and went, Quicksilver functioned as a training ground for emerging bluegrass acts. (Jamie Dailey, for example, went on to stardom as half of Dailey & Vincent.) Meanwhile, Lawson continued to inspire dozens of younger mandolin players.

Since the mid-1990s, Lawson has released a steady stream of secular and sacred albums on SUGAR HILL and then on ROUNDER RECORDS, remained in demand on the bluegrass circuit, and broadened his audience through his group's commitment to gospel music and Christian life. As of 2010, the IBMA had named Lawson's band Vocal Group of the Year from 2001–2007 and honored him with its Gospel Recorded Performance of the Year award in 1996, 2000, 2005, 2006, and 2007. In recognition of his lengthy and productive career, he received a prestigious National Heritage Fellowship from the National Endowment for the Arts in 2006. —*Frank and Marty Godbey*

## Zora Layman
b. Hutchinson, Kansas, March 12, 1900; d. November 2, 1981

Zora Layman was one of the first female artists to gain substantial sales with a country record, and her husband, FRANK LUTHER, was among the most popular and prolific country recording artists of the early 1930s. Nevertheless, major labels then viewed hillbilly music as a minor part of the music industry, and Layman was too busy and multifaceted to think of becoming a country star.

A classically trained violinist and vocalist, Layman recorded with her husband and Len Stokes as the Frank Luther Trio beginning in 1932, turning out an impressive number of successful records for RCA VICTOR, the AMERICAN RECORD CORPORATION, and DECCA. Composer BOB MILLER concocted a spunky answer to their hit "Seven Years with the Wrong Woman" for Layman to perform solo. Recorded in 1933, "Seven Years with the Wrong Man" delivered the woman's viewpoint in vivid terms, describing a bad marriage as "like living in hell" and advising women that they may "find more real friendship in owning a dog."

When Layman first delivered her plaintively sincere rendition of "Seven Years" on ETHEL PARK RICHARDSON's NBC series *Hillbilly Heart-Throbs*, switchboards were swamped with enthusiastic responses, and the tall, quiet contralto had a major hit. Subsequent Layman recordings included "Answer to Twenty-one Years," "Hooray, I'm Single Again," and the moving "Cowboy's Best Friend," written by Frank Luther for Zora to sing on horseback at rodeos staged in Madison Square Garden. —*Jonathan Guyot Smith*

## Leake County Revelers
Will Gilmer b. Leake County, Mississippi, February 27, 1897; d. 1960
Oscar Mosley b. Mississippi, 1885; d. 1930s
Jim Wolverton b. Mississippi, April 19, 1895; d. December 1969
Dallas Jones b. December 17, 1889; d. January 1985

One of the best-selling country records of the 1920s was "Wednesday Night Waltz," a 1927 COLUMBIA release by Sebastopol, Mississippi's Leake County Revelers. Unlike fast-paced Georgia STRINGBANDS, the Revelers preferred slower tempos and intricate waltzes of the rural nineteenth-century South. Powered by the smooth, flowing fiddle style of Will Gilmer, the band was discovered in 1926 by famed talent scout H. C. Spier and released some forty-four selections for Columbia before their breakup in the early 1930s. Other favorites included "Monkey in a Dog Cart" and "Crow Black Chicken," with Oscar Mosley playing mandolin, Jim Wolverton on banjo, and Dallas Jones on guitar. —*Charles Wolfe*

## Chris LeDoux
b. Biloxi, Mississippi, October 2, 1948; d. March 9, 2005

Chris LeDoux, the Singing Bronc Rider, was an authentic cowboy who kept country music's western traditions vital from the 1970s until his death. He was born in Mississippi and learned to ride on his grandfather's farm in Michigan. Eventually his family moved to Texas, where he developed an interest in music as well as rodeo and participated in saddle bronc and bull riding, later specializing in bareback-bronc riding. In 1976 he was World Champion Bareback Bronc Rider.

LeDoux established his own company, Lucky Man Music, in Mount Juliet, Tennessee, just outside Nashville, and spent almost twenty years recording and marketing his own records to fans in the rodeo and cowboy subculture. Between 1973 and 1991 he released more than twenty-four albums, including *Wild and Wooly*, *Rodeo Songs*, and *Old Cowboy Heroes*, and received a major boost when GARTH BROOKS, in the hit "Much Too Young to Feel This Damned Old" from his 1989 debut album, sang of listening to "a worn-out tape of Chris LeDoux." CAPITOL RECORDS, Brooks's label, soon signed LeDoux to a major contract, eventually reissued almost all of LeDoux's Lucky Man catalog on CD, and had him record *Western Underground*, his first album for the label.

On his second Capitol album, *Whatcha Gonna Do with a Cowboy*, his benefactor, Garth Brooks, joined him for a duet of the title cut, which produced a hit single. LeDoux was a prolific songwriter, and his repertoire ranged from traditional cowboy songs to his own compositions about rodeo life to contemporary cowboy and western songs by other writers. Although LeDoux performed many of his numbers in typical country style, his songs are an authentic window on the life of the modern-day rodeo cowboy. His career sales reached almost 6 million records before his death from liver disease and cancer of the bile duct. —*Charlie Seemann*

## Albert Lee
b. Herefordshire, England, December 21, 1943

The high-velocity sounds Albert Lee pioneered in EMMYLOU HARRIS's Hot Band in the late 1970s have informed the propulsive drive of many country lead guitar solos of the 1980s and beyond.

The first wave of American rock & roll to wash ashore in England, along with the skiffle sounds of Scotland-born Lonnie Donegan, nurtured Lee's penchant for American country music. Acquiring his first guitar in 1958, he promptly learned all of Cliff Gallup's solos from Gene Vincent's records.

Lee first distinguished himself in the London-based R&B band Chris Farlowe & the Thunderbirds (1964–67). By 1968 he was backing visiting country stars (CONNIE SMITH, BOBBY BARE) in a band called Country Fever. In 1969 he began working with a group that evolved into Head, Hands & Feet. Two years later, the band's self-titled debut album for Island Records featured Lee's theme song, "Country Boy" (a 1985 #1 *Billboard* hit for RICKY SKAGGS).

Following a 1973 tour with the Crickets, Lee joined the Los Angeles COUNTRY-ROCK fraternity in 1974, first working with Don Everly (THE EVERLY BROTHERS) and later replacing JAMES BURTON in Harris's Hot Band. From 1976 to 1978 his combination of breathtaking speed and tasteful discrimination helped turn her albums *Luxury Liner*, *Quarter Moon in a Ten Cent Town*, and *Blue Kentucky Girl* into classics. "My style came together when I played with Emmylou," Lee told *Country Guitar*'s Askold Buk. "I think I put an English rock edge to the country idiom."

In addition to recording many albums of his own, Lee has toured or recorded with (among others) Eric Clapton, the Everly Brothers—for whom Lee long acted as musical director—JOHN PRINE, RODNEY CROWELL, and CARLENE CARTER. Harris, who has called Lee's playing "hard and metallic but clear and lyrical," reenlisted him into her Hot Band for its 1995 twentieth anniversary tour. Lee won a 2001 Grammy for his contribution to "Foggy Mountain Breakdown," from the album *Earl Scruggs and Friends*. He won a second Grammy for his work on "Cluster Pluck," from BRAD PAISLEY's 2008 album *Play*. —*Mark Humphrey*

## Brenda Lee
b. Atlanta, Georgia, December 11, 1944

Brenda Lee is one of American music's most versatile singers, and her commercial success (as measured by cumulative record sales) is probably second only to that of ELVIS PRESLEY among pop artists who have recorded heavily in Nashville. A professional singer by age six and a recording artist by twelve, she has fashioned a career of uncommon durability that spans more than fifty years. In so doing, she has transcended the musical boundaries of pop and country to earn the accolades and respect of fans and peers worldwide.

Born Brenda Mae Tarpley, she grew up in the Atlanta area. Her talent blossomed early, for by age three she was able to sing songs after hearing them but twice. When she was five, her older sister entered her in a school talent contest, where she won first prize for belting out "Take Me Out to the Ball Game." Listeners were amazed at the big sound coming from such a little girl, and this performance led to regular stints on local radio and television shows.

When Lee was nine, her father died following a construction accident. Her mother remarried, and the family relocated first to Cincinnati and then to Augusta, Georgia. Soon Lee was a star on local television, and her show's producer rechristened her Brenda Lee.

With the help of a local DJ, Lee met RED FOLEY in February 1956. Foley was so impressed with Lee's talent that shortly thereafter, her family moved to Springfield, Missouri, so that Lee could become a regular on Foley's OZARK JUBILEE ABC telecast. This led to appearances on network TV shows hosted by Perry Como, Ed Sullivan, and Steve Allen. Dub Allbritten, Foley's manager, became Lee's personal manager in 1956 and held that position throughout her formative years.

Lee signed with DECCA RECORDS in May 1956 and two months later had her first recording session, supervised by PAUL COHEN with the assistance of OWEN BRADLEY. Her third single, the foot-stomping, hand-clapping "One Step at a Time," produced in

*Brenda Lee*

New York by Milt Gabler, became her first chart record (#15 country, #43 pop, 1957). It marked her only appearance on the country charts for the next eleven years.

Bradley took over as Lee's sole producer in 1958 and oversaw all of her Nashville sessions through 1968. Except for the rock & roll number "Dynamite" (which gave her the enduring nickname Little Miss Dynamite), chart hits eluded her at first. However, Allbritten discovered that her records were selling in Europe and scheduled a tour of France in February 1959. This was the beginning of Lee's international stardom. The following years would find her performing in South America, Australia, Japan, and Europe. During the 1960s she recorded in several languages.

Lee launched her string of pop hits in 1959 with the rocking "Sweet Nothin's" (#4 pop). Owen Bradley changed gears for her follow-up, the heartache ballad "I'm Sorry" (#1 pop). The recording's use of strings not only bridged the gap between country and pop but also became a hallmark of Lee's sound through the 1960s.

Lee soon became one of the best-selling female singers of the decade. She could rock with the best of them, but as her voice matured she concentrated on heartfelt standards and newly written ballads. Between 1960 and 1973 she charted fifty pop singles, including "I Want to Be Wanted" (#1, 1960), "Fool #1" (#3, 1961), "Break It to Me Gently" (#4, 1962), "All Alone Am I" (#3, 1962), "Too Many Rivers" (#13, 1965), "Coming on Strong" (#11, 1966), and the Christmas classic "Rockin' Around the Christmas Tree" (#14, 1960).

During the 1970s Lee began experiencing health problems. Along with damaged vocal cords, she had several serious abdominal operations, requiring her to take time off from touring. Even so, Lee notched four country chart records between 1969 and 1972. After teaming again with Owen Bradley, she broke into the country Top Ten in 1973 with "Nobody Wins" (#5), and for the next twelve years she enjoyed a run of country hits, including

"Big Four Poster Bed" (#4, 1974), "He's My Rock" (#8, 1975), and "Broken Trust" (#9, 1980).

In the 1980s Lee served as a television host for WILLIE NELSON's Farm Aid benefit concert and as guest host on TNN's prime-time talk show *NASHVILLE NOW*. She has starred in musical theater productions at OPRYLAND USA and has served on the boards of both CMA and the Recording Academy (which gives Grammy Awards). In addition, she recorded for WARNER BROS. RECORDS in the early 1990s and has continued to maintain a regular touring schedule. A strong supporter of Nashville's music community, she has also devoted her energies to the American Cancer Society, organizations seeking cures for multiple sclerosis and cerebral palsy, and the March of Dimes. With Robert K. Oermann and Julie Clay, she published her autobiography, *Little Miss Dynamite: The Life and Times of Brenda Lee*, in 2002. The legendary artist received a Grammy Lifetime Achievement Award in 2009, having already been inducted into THE COUNTRY MUSIC HALL OF FAME in 1997 and the Rock and Roll Hall of Fame in 2002. —*Don Roy*

## Buddy Lee
b. Brooklyn, New York, October 7, 1932; d. February 13, 1998

Buddy "Buddy Lee" Lioce rose from humble beginnings to establish one of country music's most successful booking agencies: Buddy Lee Attractions. Since opening its doors in Nashville in 1964, the agency has booked such artists as GARTH BROOKS, MARK CHESNUTT, DIXIE CHICKS, EMMYLOU HARRIS, WAYLON JENNINGS, TRACY LAWRENCE, MARTINA MCBRIDE, and WILLIE NELSON.

Growing up in an Italian neighborhood in New York, Lee worked in a restaurant and even tended bar at the tender, and illegal, age of fourteen. At age eighteen, weighing 230 pounds, he began a fourteen-year wrestling career. "I learned how to advertise and promote an event by listening and watching various wrestling promoters," he once said.

In 1955 Lee moved to Columbia, South Carolina, where for the next eight years he promoted and booked Fats Domino, Jackie Wilson, RAY CHARLES, and Little Stevie Wonder, among others. Invited to a country music show, Lee was impressed by FARON YOUNG, but not by the meager audience of 800 in a 3,285-seat venue. Lee began to handle country talent, however, and managed to sell out venues from the Carolinas to Maine. In 1963 he moved to Boston, where he promoted a show by HANK WILLIAMS JR. The following year, Audrey Williams, Hank Williams Jr.'s mother, asked Lee to move to Nashville to represent her son. "It's the best move I ever made," Lee remarked, noting that it led to the start of Aud-Lee Attractions, and, in 1964, Buddy Lee Attractions. Lee launched the affiliated Mainstage Productions, which stages live events across the United States, in 1982.

Lee served as the firm's CEO until his death in 1998, and longtime Buddy Lee Attractions executive Tony Conway (b. August 3, 1953) took over as CEO and president until leaving the firm in 2010. —*Gerry Wood*

## Dickey Lee
b. Memphis, Tennessee, September 21, 1936

Royden Dickey Lee kicked off his recording career in earnest in 1962, when he had his first big pop hit, "Patches," on Smash Records. After that, his major chart success came in the 1970s on

RCA RECORDS with ephemeral pop-flavored country hits, many of which were cover versions of songs that had already scaled the pop charts. "Never Ending Song of Love" (a Top Ten hit in 1971), "Rocky" (a #1 in 1975), and "9,999,999 Tears" (a RAZZY BAILEY composition that Lee took to #3 in 1976) are a few of Lee's better-known country hits.

Memphis disc jockey Dewey Phillips discovered Lee, who had released one single, "Stay True Baby," on Tampa Records and introduced the young Memphian to SAM PHILLIPS and his local SUN RECORDS label. In 1957 Lee recorded for Sun and forged a friendship with engineer-producer-songwriter JACK CLEMENT, with whom he would often work in coming years. Lee and his friend ALLEN REYNOLDS followed Clement to Beaumont, Texas, where they became part of a recording studio crew that also included BOB MCDILL. After a solid run through most of the 1970s with RCA, Lee signed with MERCURY in 1979, but his several years on that label produced no hits. Subsequently he continued to pen songs and work occasional package shows.

Lee's greatest claim to fame may be his original composition "She Thinks I Still Care," which has become a country classic. GEORGE JONES had a #1 hit with the song in 1962, and ANNE MURRAY took it to the top of the charts again in 1974 as "He Thinks I Still Care." Lee was inducted into the Nashville Songwriters Hall of Fame in 1995. —*Bob Allen*

## Johnny Lee
b. Texas City, Texas, July 3, 1946

Johnny Lee rose to fame in 1980 with the success of the movie *URBAN COWBOY*. Reared on a dairy farm south of Houston and schooled in 1960s rock bands, John Lee Hamm didn't have to travel far to join the house band at GILLEY's nightclub in the late 1970s. The connection with singer–club owner MICKEY GILLEY swept Lee into a deal to package the soundtrack for *Urban Cowboy*. Though Lee had had a few chart records between 1975 and 1978, the movie shifted his career into high gear. Overnight the strapping, bearded singer became a star, launched by the movie's theme song, "Looking for Love," a #1 country hit and a #5 pop chart-maker.

In the wake of that success, Lee toured incessantly as Gilley's opening act and scored a string of #1 and Top Ten hits through 1985, including "One in a Million"; "Pickin' Up Strangers"; "Prisoner of Hope"; "Bet Your Heart on Me"; "Cherokee Fiddle"; "Hey Bartender"; and a duet with Lane Brody, "The Yellow Rose."

Lee entered a widely publicized Hollywood marriage to Charlene Tilton, a petite blond actress who starred on TV's popular series *Dallas*. They married in 1982, and the tabloids had a field day with them for a time. They divorced in 1984, when Lee had his last #1 single, "You Could've Heard a Heart Break." His last chart hits came in 1989–90. —*Bob Millard*

## Kyle Lehning
b. Cairo, Illinois, April 18, 1949

If he had done nothing but produce the albums of RANDY TRAVIS, Kyle Lehning would merit a special place in country music history. But he has been a guiding force for several best-selling acts.

After earning a bachelor's degree in music at Millikin University in Decatur, Illinois, Lehning moved to Nashville in 1971, aspiring to be a session keyboard player. He gained early experience in sound engineering at THE GLASER BROTHERS studio, and by 1975 he had worked on records for WAYLON JENNINGS, WILLIE NELSON, KENNY ROGERS, and SHEL SILVERSTEIN. In 1976 Lehning began producing the pop act England Dan & John Ford Coley. Lehning's first single with them, "I'd Really Love to See You Tonight," sold more than 1 million copies, and he produced the successful duo through 1979. Afterward half of the group, DAN SEALS, kept working with Lehning, and together they amassed some two-dozen country chart records between 1983 and 1992, including eleven #1 hits and another five Top Tens.

Lehning began working with hard-country singer Randy Travis in 1985 for a series of singles that developed into Travis's first WARNER BROS. album, *Storms of Life*. That multimillion-selling collection signaled a strong return for hard-country sounds in the late 1980s, and its commercial and artistic success led to a long and prosperous association between the two men that has persisted through Travis's Warner Bros. releases and subsequent recordings for DREAMWORKS and Word-CURB/Warner. Meanwhile, Lehning kept producing other country artists, including RONNIE MILSAP, ANNE MURRAY, GEORGE JONES, and NEAL MCCOY. In February 1992 Lehning became executive vice president and general manager of the Nashville branch of ASYLUM RECORDS, and eventually he produced singers including Mandy Barnett and BRYAN WHITE. In 1996 Lehning was joined at the helm of Asylum by marketing specialist Joe Mansfield, who assumed the role of co-president/CEO. Lehning and Mansfield left Asylum in 1998, but Lehning has continued to produce independently. In 2003 Travis's "Three Wooden Crosses," a Lehning production, became ACM's Single of the Year and CMA Song of the Year. —*Paul Kingsbury*

## Iry Lejeune
b. Point Noir, Church Point, Louisiana, October 28, 1928; d. October 8, 1954

One of CAJUN MUSIC's finest traditional accordionists and singers, Ira "Iry" Lejeune is known for his exceptional instrumental work and searing, heartfelt vocals. He grew up in a remote farming region that was an enclave of OLD-TIME Cajun music and learned to play from his uncle Angelais Lejeune, also a popular musician, who recorded for BRUNSWICK in 1929. Iry was also influenced by Amédé Ardoin and Amadie Breaux.

Iry was almost completely blind, and music seemed his only viable career choice. He made his first recordings for the Opera label in Houston in 1948, releasing "Love Bridge Waltz" and "Evangeline Special." Though he later recorded for Folk-Star, he cut most of his performances for Goldband. Among the most popular of his classic recordings were "Lacassine Special," "Convict Waltz," and "Grande Bosco."

Lejeune's brief career came to a tragic end in 1954. He was traveling home from a dance with fellow musician J. B. FUSILIER when their car had a blowout. While fixing the flat tire, both men were struck by a passing car. Lejeune was killed and Fusilier was seriously injured. —*Charlie Seemann*

## Jerry Lee Lewis
b. Ferriday, Louisiana, September 29, 1935

Nicknamed the Killer, pianist and singer Jerry Lee Lewis may be the wildest performer in the history of American popular music. His greatest gift may be his assimilation of sundry forms into a

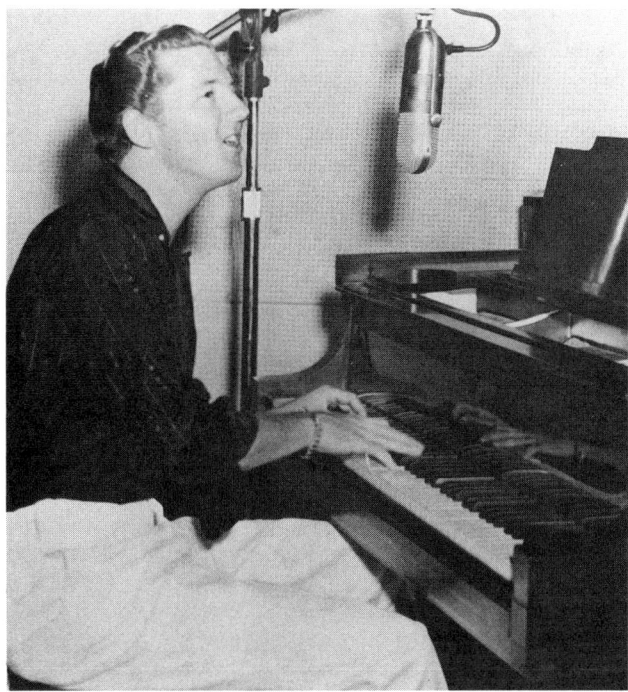

*Jerry Lee Lewis*

unique mixture that both respects and scrambles various musical elements. Lewis's ferocious early recordings, such as "Whole Lotta Shakin' Going On" and "Great Balls of Fire," routinely became hits on the pop, country, and R&B charts simultaneously, so great was Lewis's reach—and his ambition.

Lewis learned piano early on; his public debut was at a 1949 Ford dealership opening, and by 1950 he hosted a show on WANT–Natchez. Enrolling in Southwestern Bible Institute in Waxahachie, Texas, that same year, he was soon expelled, in part for slipping boogie-woogie riffs into hymns.

Lewis's blend of the sacred and the profane intrigued Sun Records owner Sam Phillips, who signed Lewis in late 1956. Lewis moved to Memphis, accompanied Carl Perkins, and soon cut records of his own. "Whole Lotta Shakin' Going On" (1957) made the Killer a star. His pumping piano and a frankly sexual arrogance in his singing appealed to teenagers and led many parents to call for banning his music from the airwaves. Wild televised performances on *American Bandstand* and the *Steve Allen Show* brought Lewis before millions, many of whom snatched up his next hit, "Great Balls of Fire," backed with his energetic rendition of Hank Williams's "You Win Again."

On December 12, 1957, Lewis secretly married Myra Gale Brown, the thirteen-year-old daughter of his cousin (and bass player) J. W. Brown. The marriage became public during a 1958 British tour, and the ensuing scandal ended the tour after only three dates. Much of Lewis's audience abandoned him, and a decade passed before he scored another Top Ten hit.

Lewis moved from Sun to Smash, a Mercury affiliate, in 1963, but his records did not match his Sun peaks. Even so, his live performances lost none of their manic energy, and his 1964 album *The Greatest Live Show on Earth* lived up to its title. In 1968 Lewis turned to hard-edged country, and with "Another Place, Another Time" (#4, 1968) the hits returned—initially on Smash and from 1970 forward on Mercury. From 1968 to early 1972 Lewis enjoyed sixteen Top Ten singles, including four #1s and such memorable performances as "What's Made Milwaukee Famous (Has Made a Loser Out of Me)" (#2, 1968). By mid-1972, however, this formula

was waning. Except for two rock & roll albums (*The Session* and *Southern Roots*, both 1973) and the 1977 hit single "Middle Age Crazy," his final Mercury years were unproductive. Lewis signed with Elektra in 1978 and made several spirited albums, including an especially strong eponymous collection released in 1979. The singles "Over the Rainbow" (1980) and "Thirty Nine and Holding" (1981) returned him to the country Top Ten. Next came a brief stint with MCA, followed by a long silence in the studio.

Lewis's life has been as bumpy as his career. Two teenage marriages proved short-lived. His thirteen-year marriage to Myra Gale Brown sabotaged his rock & roll success, and in the 1980s two more brief marriages ended tragically: one in a drowning, the other in a drug overdose. As of 2010, Lewis had been married and divorced six times.

In 1989 Lewis rerecorded his Sun hits for the soundtrack to the biographical film *Great Balls of Fire*. He recorded the 1995 Sire album *Young Blood* onstage. Since then, new releases, box sets, and other compilations have kept his music before the public. Lewis has never stopped touring, and in February 2005 he received a Grammy Lifetime Achievement Award. In 2006 he released *Last Man Standing: The Duets*, featuring new pairings with the likes of Mick Jagger, George Jones, B. B. King, and Willie Nelson. The album went gold and in 2007 inspired a DVD showcasing concert footage of Lewis with numerous guests, a PBS tribute special, and a multiday Rock & Roll Hall of Fame conference in his honor. Lewis toured Europe and the UK in 2008, and in 2009 he released "Mean Old Man," a single written by Kris Kristofferson, for Internet download. An album on Shangri-La music followed. —*Jimmy Guterman*

## Laurie Lewis
b. Long Beach, California, September 28, 1950

Fiddler, singer, and songwriter Laurie Lewis has focused her extraordinary musical abilities within bluegrass music, a style she has helped to reinvigorate. Introduced to the violin by her family at age twelve, she heard The Dillards in 1965 and became a bluegrass convert. She performed as bass player in the group The Phantom of the Opry in 1973 and as fiddler in the Good Ol' Persons String Band from 1975 to 1977. She then formed the Grant Street String Band.

Living in the San Francisco Bay Area, Lewis worked as a side musician for many performers and ran a violin repair shop. Her first album with the Grant Street String Band appeared in 1983, and her first solo album followed in 1986; she recorded albums for Flying Fish in 1989 and 1990. Lewis's fiddle virtuosity, touching vocals, and original songs brought critical acclaim. Kathy Mattea recorded her "Love Chooses You."

A leader among women bluegrass performers, Lewis recorded a 1989 album with the all-female band Blue Rose and made 1991's *Together* with Kathy Kallick, a Good Ol' Persons band member and frequent songwriting partner. Lewis has also given bluegrass more freedom through her smooth melodies and thoughtful songs, exemplified by her album *True Stories* (Rounder, 1993), which artfully combined new and old acoustic music. The IBMA named her Female Vocalist of the Year in 1992 and 1994. Although Lewis recorded prolifically for Rounder in the late 1990s, her output slowed in the new century. Recently, however, she has released a number of albums, including 2004's *Guest House* (with longtime band mate Tom Rozum on mandolin and vocals), 2006's

*The Golden West* (as Laurie Lewis & the Right Hands), and 2008's *Live* (with the Right Hands). —*Mary A. Bufwack*

## Luke Lewis
b. Philadelphia, Pennsylvania, January 2, 1947

Luke Lewis steadily climbed the career ladder at record companies until he headed a conglomeration of several of country music's largest and most historic record labels. Once there, he settled in for a long reign while shepherding some of country music's most remarkable success stories. As chairman of the Universal Music Group Nashville, Lewis oversees the long-running MCA Nashville and MERCURY Nashville labels. He also helped to found the adventurous record label LOST HIGHWAY, and works with the catalogs of such historic imprints as DECCA, MGM, and PolyGram.

His accomplishments include developing the career of topselling artist SHANIA TWAIN, launching the million-selling group SUGARLAND, and shepherding the Grammy-winning, multiplatinum soundtrack of *O BROTHER, WHERE ART THOU?* He helped JOHNNY CASH earn his first solo platinum album with *American IV: The Man Comes Around* and won Grammys as the executive producer of two HANK WILLIAMS collections: *Timeless* and *The Complete Hank Williams*.

After working as a journalist in the U.S. Army, Lewis took a job with CBS Records (SONY MUSIC ENTERTAINMENT), spending thirteen years in marketing, promotion, and sales. Lewis joined MCA Records in Los Angeles as vice president of sales and marketing in 1988. Two years later, he became vice president of Uni Distribution.

In 1992, Lewis took over leadership of Mercury Nashville. In 2002, Universal Music Group consolidated its Nashville divisions, and Lewis became chairman of MCA Nashville, Mercury Nashville, and Lost Highway Records.

*Luke Lewis*

At Universal, Lewis has guided the established careers of COUNTRY MUSIC HALL OF FAME members VINCE GILL, REBA MCENTIRE, WILLIE NELSON, and GEORGE STRAIT. He has also worked with veterans GARY ALLAN, LYLE LOVETT, and LEE ANN WOMACK, and he has helped launch BILLY CURRINGTON, Julianne Hough, JAMEY JOHNSON, Ashton Shepherd, JOSH TURNER, and Holly Williams as recording artists. —*Michael McCall*

## Texas Jim Lewis
b. Meigs, Georgia, October 15, 1909; d. January 23, 1990

Raised in a musical family, Texas Jim Lewis launched his long and varied career in 1928 with a Texas MEDICINE SHOW. After radio work with a trio at WTAW in College Station, Texas, in 1929 and a stint at KPRC–Houston, Lewis landed at WJR in Detroit by 1933. Here he formed his Lone Star Rangers, later called Lone Star Cowboys. Next, Lewis's trail led to New York City's VILLAGE BARN (1935–37) and to Hollywood (1940s) after vaudeville tours took him coast to coast and to England. In Hollywood, Lewis and his band appeared in B-western films starring the likes of GENE AUTRY and EDDIE DEAN. As "Sheriff Tex" he hosted children's TV shows in Seattle and Tacoma, Washington, and then Vancouver, British Columbia, in the 1950s. During Seattle's 1962 World's Fair, Lewis fronted a country dance band at a downtown nightclub and worked other local venues with a WESTERN SWING band into the early 1970s.

During 1937–1952 Lewis's recordings for Vocalion, DECCA, Exclusive, Magnolia, and Coral showcased western and western swing sounds, often with novelty overtones from his "hootin' nanny," a homemade contraption that made noises similar to those popularized by the HOOSIER HOT SHOTS. IMPERIAL RECORDS issued his "Sheriff Tex" children's songs in the late 1950s. Cowriter of the 1946 JACK GUTHRIE hit "I'm Telling You," Lewis was also the first to record "The Covered Wagon Rolled Right Along" (1940) and "Squaws Along the Yukon" (1944), the latter a 1958 hit for HANK THOMPSON. —*Bob Pinson*

## The Lewis Family
Roy "Pop" Lewis Sr. b. Pickens, South Carolina, September 22, 1905; d. March 23, 2004
Roy "Little Roy" Lewis Jr. b. Lincoln County, Georgia, February 24, 1942
Wallace Lewis b. Lincoln County, Georgia, July 6, 1928; d. May 16, 2007
Omega "Miggie" Lewis b. Richmond County, Georgia, May 22, 1926
Polly Lewis Copsey b. Lincoln County, Georgia, January 23, 1937
Janis Lewis Phillips b. Lincoln County, Georgia, February 13, 1939
Travis Lewis b. Greenwood, South Carolina, December 26, 1958
Lewis Phillips b. Washington, Georgia, April 5, 1972

Long considered the First Family of Bluegrass Gospel, the Lewis Family was one of the few groups to headline BLUEGRASS and gospel shows alike. Their performances featured crisp harmonies and a lively, humorous stage show led by Little Roy Lewis, whose comedic talents equaled his instrumental skills. The act included father "Pop" Lewis on bass; sons Little Roy (banjo, guitar) and Wallace (lead guitar); daughters Miggie, Polly (piano), and Janis (bass); and at various points Wallace's son Travis and Janis's son Lewis. Pauline "Mom" Lewis (June 20, 1900–February 8, 2003) staffed the family's retail records table at festivals for more than forty years.

Roy Lewis Sr. and Pauline Lewis married on October 25, 1925. The family became serious about performing in the late 1940s and early 1950s, when the act was known as the Lewis Brothers, featuring Wallace, Little Roy, Talmadge, and Esley. The latter two dropped out eventually (Esley in the 1950s, Talmadge in 1972), and the Lewis daughters gradually joined, along with their father.

In about 1951, the family made their first two singles on the Sullivan label. Next, they worked with entrepreneur DON PIERCE, then living in California, to release some singles on the Hollywood imprint. Shortly after Pierce started STARDAY RECORDS' Nashville operation in 1957, he collected the Lewis Family's singles and released them on the album *Singing Time Down South*. Numerous Starday albums followed in the 1960s, before the act signed with the Christian music label Canaan Records in 1970. The group moved to River Song in the mid-1980s and to Day Wind Records in 1995.

Meanwhile, in 1954 the Lewis Family had started a weekly television program on WJBF in Augusta, Georgia. Broadcast live for the first ten years, the show continued until 1992. At one point it was syndicated to several stations around the nation.

The group was elected to the Gospel Music Hall of Fame in 2005 and inducted into the IBMA Hall of Fame in 2006. The Lewis Family Homecoming & Bluegrass Festival was held annually in their hometown of Lincolnton, Georgia, from 1988 until the group's retirement in November 2009. Two family groups have since emerged: The Little Roy and Lizzy Show includes Lizzy Long, while the Lewis Tradition features Janis Lewis Phillips; her son, Lewis Phillips; her brother, Travis Lewis; and Travis's son, Jameson Lewis. —*Don Rhodes*

## Liberty Records
established in Los Angeles, 1955

Liberty Records has played an important part in country music through the label's forty-three-year evolution. The label was founded by Simon "Si" Waronker, a musician contractor for the 20th Century-Fox music department. He soon added Al Bennett as vice president and head of A&R. Liberty released several country singles during the early years (KEN CURTIS, 1955, and WILLIE NELSON, 1958), but it wasn't until 1959 that songwriter and broadcaster JOE ALLISON was asked to establish a country division.

One of the first artists Allison signed was WARREN SMITH (1960–64), whose first release, "I Don't Believe I'll Fall in Love Today," reached #5 on the country charts in 1960. Other acts added that same year included BOB WILLS & HIS TEXAS PLAYBOYS (1960–63), Ray Sanders (1960–63), and FLOYD TILLMAN (1960–61). Though the earliest Liberty country records were made in Hollywood, Allison preferred recording in Nashville and made periodic trips to do so.

By 1962 Liberty had aggressively expanded its country roster. Country disc jockey RALPH EMERY (1961–63) recorded "Hello Fool" (#4, 1961) as an answer song to FARON YOUNG's recording of "Hello Walls." Willie Nelson released his first successful record ("Touch Me," #7) in 1962, and his first album, titled . . . *And Then I Wrote.*

Throughout the 1960s, a variety of artists passed through Liberty's doors: HANK COCHRAN (1962), Molly Bee (1962–63), Shirley Collie (1961–63), the CARTER SISTERS (1962–64), TEX WILLIAMS (1963–64), and JERRY WALLACE (1967–1970). By the early 1970s, Liberty had been purchased by United Artists Records and its name retired. EMI/CAPITOL RECORDS purchased the UA catalog in 1979 and reactivated the Liberty name between 1980 and 1984, primarily as a country label. The roster included KENNY ROGERS, DOTTIE WEST, MICHAEL MARTIN MURPHEY, and DAN SEALS. The most recent incarnation came in January 1992, when

JIMMY BOWEN renamed Capitol's Nashville division Liberty. Shortly after SCOTT HENDRICKS succeeded Bowen as Liberty's new chief in May 1995, he announced that he had changed Liberty back to Capitol Nashville. —*Don Roy*

## Billy Liebert
b. Detroit, Michigan, April 18, 1925; d. April 13, 2001

Conductor, arranger, composer, and performing musician William E. Liebert was playing the accordion in bands appearing in the Greater Detroit area at age fourteen. At age sixteen he was teaching the accordion. TEXAS JIM LEWIS, who had a long and colorful career in western music, took Liebert under his wing in early 1942, covering the eastern and midwestern states on a "four-a-day" theater tour. In late 1942 Liebert continued his association with the newly expanded Texas Jim Lewis WESTERN SWING band, appearing at BERT "FOREMAN" PHILLIPS's numerous ballrooms in and around Los Angeles.

Shortly after his discharge from the navy in 1946, Liebert worked his first recording session, accompanying TEX RITTER. Over the next thirty-five years Liebert provided accordion and piano backing, arrangements, and musical direction for numerous recording artists—JOHNNY CASH, MERLE HAGGARD, TENNESSEE ERNIE FORD, MERLE TRAVIS, Kay Starr, Mel Tormé, the SONS OF THE PIONEERS, and ROY ROGERS, to name but a few. Liebert's other credits include acting as a musical director and arranger for CBS radio and TV from 1954 to 1969 and as a musical director and performer on CLIFFIE STONE's *HOMETOWN JAMBOREE*. In 1966 and again in 1967 the Academy of Country Music (ACM) honored Liebert with its Best Country Piano Player award. He was a member of the Sons of the Pioneers from 1973 to 1981. In 1972 Liebert composed, arranged, and conducted the John Wayne album *America, Why I Love Her*, which won the Freedom Foundation's George Washington Award. —*Ken Griffis*

## Light Crust Doughboys

Although they didn't originate WESTERN SWING, the Light Crust Doughboys became one of its most important exponents. The band's alumni are a who's who of the genre, and the group has continued into the 2000s.

The act originated in 1930, when the Burrus Mill & Elevator Company of Fort Worth, Texas, began sponsoring a STRINGBAND to promote its Light Crust Flour on radio. Comprising MILTON BROWN, BOB WILLS, Derwood Brown, and Herman Arnspiger, the group's popularity soared when mill general manager W. LEE "PAPPY" O'DANIEL moved them from tiny KFJZ to 50,000-watt WBAP and took over the band's announcing. The band recorded as the Fort Worth Doughboys for RCA VICTOR in 1932, but the Brown brothers left later that year, and Wills in 1933. Undaunted, O'Daniel secured a recording contract with Vocalion, hired such key replacements as vocalist LEON HUFF and fiddlers Clifford Gross and Kenneth Pitts, and wrote standards for the act, including "Beautiful Texas." The latter was a huge hit in 1934, as was Huff's rendering of STUART HAMBLEN's "My Mary."

Although O'Daniel was fired from Burrus in 1935, late that year the Doughboys received a boost when jazz-minded guitarist-vocalist DICK REINHART, bassist Bert Dodson, and tenor banjoist Marvin Montgomery came over from Dallas's Wanderers. Also arriving was pioneering electric guitarist Zeke Campbell.

The Doughboys appeared in two films with Gene Autry in 1936 and then hit a deep musical groove with the addition of jazz pianist Knocky Parker in 1937. Over the next few years, under announcer Parker Willson, the group produced some of the era's most sophisticated and forward-looking western swing, including classics such as "Gin Mill Blues" and Montgomery's notorious "Pussy, Pussy, Pussy" (1938). Important members in the late 1930s included vocalist-guitarist Jim Boyd (Bill and Jim Boyd) and fiddlers Buck Buchanan and Cecil Brower. The Doughboys broke up during World War II, but they regrouped in 1946 and recorded for King. Only Marvin (soon "Smokey") Montgomery, who would become the band's leader in 1948, remained from the prewar group, but the level of musicianship stayed high. The Doughboys served pseudonymously as a house band for the Big D Jamboree throughout the 1950s and have continued in various incarnations to the present, though their official association with Burrus eventually ended. Since 1990 they have focused increasingly on gospel music and contributed to a 2002 Grammy-winning tribute album honoring gospel great James Blackwood. After Montgomery died, on June 6, 2001, Art Greenhaw became the group's leader. —Kevin Coffey

## The Lilly Brothers

Mitchell Burt Lilly b. Clear Creek, West Virginia, December 15, 1921;
   d. September 18, 2005
Charles Everett Lilly b. Clear Creek, West Virginia, July 1, 1924

The Lilly Brothers are widely credited—together with Don Stover (1928–1996) and Tex Logan (1927–)—with introducing bluegrass music to New England. Natives of the West Virginia mountains, Everett and Burt (or B.) Lilly grew up performing in the harmony duet style with mandolin and guitar accompaniment. From 1940 onward, they plied their trade on local radio stations and in 1945 went to WNOX–Knoxville, with Lynn Davis and Molly O'Day. In 1948 they worked on the WWVA Jamboree in Wheeling, West Virginia, with Red Belcher and made their first recordings on the tiny Page label. Then Everett spent a year and a half as sideman with Flatt & Scruggs. In 1952 the brothers, along with Stover on banjo and Logan on fiddle, went to Boston, where they first worked on WCOP's Hayloft Jamboree.

The Lilly Brothers and Stover also made almost nightly appearances at a nightclub called Hillbilly Ranch, where they attained a following from the intellectual crowd as well as homesick country folk. The brothers initially recorded for Event and then for Folkways, Prestige, County, and the Japanese label Towa. They also introduced bluegrass at college concerts and folk festivals, spreading its popularity in the Northeast. In 1970 Everett lost a son in an automobile wreck and returned to West Virginia. Thereafter, the brothers played only a few concerts yearly. By the 1990s, even these had dwindled to one or two a year. In 2002 the Lilly Brothers and Don Stover were inducted into the IBMA Hall of Fame. After B. Lilly's death in 2005, Everett continued to perform with his Lilly Mountaineers. —Ivan M. Tribe

## Dennis Linde

b. Abilene, Texas, March 18, 1943; d. December 22, 2006

Dennis Linde's knack for imaginative lyrics made him one of the most successful country songwriters of his generation. Linde tallied fourteen BMI Million-Air songs and was selected to the

Nashville Songwriters Hall of Fame in 2001. BMI's Country Songwriter of the Year in 1993, Linde penned over 250 recorded songs, virtually all created without cowriters.

Linde's family moved from Texas to Miami before settling in St. Louis. His grandmother gave him a guitar at age fourteen; before long, he was playing in local bands, covering rock, pop, and R&B hits. He began writing songs when his driver's license was suspended and soon caught the ear of Combine Music chief Bob Beckham in Nashville. In 1970 Linde notched his first cuts—by Roger Miller, Roy Drusky, and Don Cherry. Linde's stature increased dramatically after Elvis Presley hit with the tunesmith's "Burning Love" in 1972.

During the 1970s Linde recorded four critically acclaimed rock albums. He also released an album as coleader of the rock band Jubal.

Linde then became a consistent, compelling hit country writer through a series of fascinating, quirky songs: "Queen of My Double-Wide Trailer," "John Deere Green," "Janie Baker's Love Slave," "Callin' Baton Rouge," "Bubba Shot the Jukebox," "It Sure Is Monday," "Walkin' a Broken Heart," and the controversial Dixie Chicks hit "Goodbye Earl."

His death resulted from a rare lung disease. —John Lomax III

## Line Dancing

Country line dancing is a dance form in which rows of western-garbed dancers kick, stomp, bend, shuffle, dip, turn, strut, and swivel their way through choreographed routines. Similar to many folk and ethnic traditional dances, country line dancing has existed for decades as a dance style requiring no partner. Fueled by the popularity of disco and by John Travolta's performances in the films Saturday Night Fever (1977) and Urban Cowboy (1980), line dancing came into its own in the 1980s. In 1992 Melanie Greenwood choreographed a music video for Billy Ray Cyrus's recording "Achy Breaky Heart," and even more Americans caught line dance fever.

By 1993 line dancing was proliferating in nightspots across the United States. Also quick to emerge were cable television shows, contests, workshops, trade and popular magazines, and instructional videos devoted to line dancing, and even exercise instructors adopted it as a beneficial aerobics workout.

Line dances are choreographed with repeated sequences of patterned foot and body movements. Schottische, polka, and cha-cha-cha comprise some of the basic steps of standard and regional versions of line dances, such as "Tush Push," "Cowboy Hustle," "Cowboy Boogie," "Tennessee Stroll," and "Cowboy Hip Hop." In some cases, hit songs such as Cyrus's "Achy Breaky Heart" and "Boot Scootin' Boogie" by Brooks & Dunn have inspired line dances of their own. By the early twenty-first century the trend had diminished, but by then line dancing had again proven the importance of dance in country music. —Patricia Hall

## Big Bill Lister

b. Karnes County, Texas, January 5, 1923; d. December 1, 2009

Weldon E. Lister was a journeyman country singer who never had the one hit that might have earned him some ongoing attention. His latter-day recognition revolves around his role in the Hank Williams Sr.–Hank Williams Jr. duet on "There's a Tear in My Beer."

Lister grew up in the Hill Country around Brady, Texas, idolizing JIMMIE RODGERS. He began performing in 1938 and became a staple of San Antonio–area radio for almost a decade. In 1950 he went to Nashville and landed a contract with CAPITOL RECORDS and a place on Hank Williams's shows starting in March 1951. In early 1952 Lister returned to San Antonio, worked the *BIG D JAMBOREE* in Dallas for several years, and then retired from the music business in the mid-1950s.

Williams wrote two songs for Lister, one of which was "There's a Tear in My Beer." Lister held on to the acetate demo, and, after his retirement, rediscovered it. He notified Hank Jr.'s management and in July 1988 gave the acetate to the performer. That September, Hank Jr. overdubbed himself onto the recording and released it with an accompanying video that featured father and son. Hank Jr. freely acknowledged Lister's role in the song's revival and introduced him on TNN's *NASHVILLE NOW* in August 1989. —*Colin Escott*

## Little Big Town

Karen Fairchild, b. Griffith, Indiana, September 28, 1969
Kimberly Roads Schlapman, b. Cornelia, Georgia, October 15, 1968
Phillip Sweet, b. Cherokee Village, Arkansas, March 18, 1974
Jimi Westbrook, b. Sumiton, Alabama, October 20, 1971

Little Big Town found success by adding contemporary flourishes to country's vocal group tradition. The four members—Karen Fairchild, Kimberly Roads Schlapman, Phillip Sweet, and Jimi Westbrook—all sing lead, but their soaring, four-part harmonies provide the act's signature sound.

Fairchild and Schlapman first sang together at Samford University in Birmingham, Alabama, where they also met Westbrook. The two women moved to Nashville in the mid-1990s and formed a duo, recruiting Westbrook in 1998. Sweet joined in 1999.

Little Big Town signed with MERCURY RECORDS in 1999, but no releases followed. The group joined MONUMENT RECORDS in 2002, but a self-titled album drew scant attention. In 2005, the quartet struck pay dirt after releasing *The Road to Here* on an independent label, Equity Music Group. The album sold more than a million copies and featured two Top Ten singles, "Boondocks" and "Bring It on Home."

Fairchild and Westbrook married secretly in May 2006, announcing their nuptials a month later. *A Place to Land* appeared in 2007 on Equity. When the label foundered, Little Big Town signed with CAPITOL RECORDS and rereleased the album in 2008 with three additional tracks. The entire group has backed John Mellencamp on several songs; "A Ride Back Home," a Mellencamp-Fairchild duet, appeared in 2009. The group's 2010 album, *The Reason Why*, included "Little White Church," a Top Ten country hit. —*Michael McCall*

## Little Darlin' Records

established in New York, New York, 1966

During its brief existence, Little Darlin' Records produced some of the most exciting, distinctive country records of its era. The label's primary artist was JOHNNY PAYCHECK, but others affiliated with Little Darlin' included BOBBY HELMS and JEANNIE C. RILEY (pre-"Harper Valley P.T.A."). At a time when the major labels in Nashville were, for the most part, still immersed in the pop-styled NASHVILLE SOUND, the independent Little Darlin' fashioned a hard-country product that favored LLOYD GREEN's dynamic steel guitar over soft strings. As label chief Aubrey Mayhew described it, when a Little Darlin' record was put on the turntable it "would jump right out of the radio at you."

Little Darlin' was the brainchild of Paycheck and Mayhew, his manager-producer. In 1965 Paycheck had recorded for Hilltop, a subsidiary of New York's Pickwick label, for which Mayhew worked. But when Pickwick refused to promote Paycheck, Mayhew quit his job and he and Paycheck started their own label. Little Darlin' was established in New York, apparently in early 1966, but soon moved to Nashville. Paycheck's first Little Darlin' single, "The Lovin' Machine," became his first Top Ten hit.

Paycheck was the only Little Darlin' act to enjoy significant success on the label; after he and Mayhew had a falling out, Mayhew dissolved the company in about 1969. He revived it briefly in 1979 and issued a few overdubbed items from Paycheck's catalog, but since then Little Darlin' has been inactive. Mayhew died in March 2009. —*Daniel Cooper*

## Little Texas

Del Anthony Gray b. Hamilton, Ohio, May 8, 1968
Porter Carleton Howell b. Longview, Texas, June 21, 1964
Dwayne Keith O'Brien b. Ada, Oklahoma, June 30, 1963
Duane Carlisle Propes b. Longview, Texas, December 17, 1966
Jeffrey Howard Huskins b. Arlington, Texas, April 26, 1966
Timothy Ray Rushlow b. Arlington, Texas, October 6, 1966
Brady Seals b. Hamilton, Ohio, March 29, 1969

With its pop-rock brand of country music, Little Texas attracted young, formerly non-country listeners. Influenced by RESTLESS HEART, EXILE, and THE EAGLES, the photogenic group had a rock & roll appearance and harmonies as tight as their jeans.

Bassist Duane Propes and lead guitarist Porter Howell, friends from Longview, Texas, were students at Nashville's Belmont University when they formed a band with lead vocalist Tim Rushlow and guitarist Dwayne O'Brien. The men met drummer Del Gray and keyboardist Brady Seals (a cousin of DAN SEALS) on a Massachusetts fair date. In 1988 WARNER BROS. RECORDS signed the group to a development deal, but after their first project failed to produce a signature sound the label sent them on a cross-country tour to develop a musical identity. Three years later they returned as a cohesive band and recorded *First Time for Everything*, which yielded "Some Guys Have All the Love" (#8, 1991) and the 1992 Top Five hit "You and Forever and Me."

"What Might Have Been," from *Big Time* (1993), established Little Texas as a hit-making act, as did "God Blessed Texas" (#4, 1993) and "My Love" (#1, 1994). The band became ACM's Vocal Group of the Year in 1994. Jeff Huskins replaced Seals after Seals left in mid-1994 to pursue a solo career.

Hits continued with the albums *Kick a Little* and *Greatest Hits*, including "Kick a Little" (#5, 1994), "Amy's Back in Austin" (#4, 1995), and "Life Goes On" (#5, 1995), pushing album sales past the 5 million mark. A self-titled fifth album appeared in April 1997, but disappointing sales led to the group's breakup later that year. Gray, Howell, O'Brien, and Propes reunited Little Texas in 2004 with Steven Troy as lead singer. Howell sang lead after Troy exited. In 2007 the band released two albums on the independent

Montage Music Group label and continued to tour as a four-piece group as of early 2011. —*Marjie McGraw*

## Hank Locklin
b. McLellan, Florida, February 15, 1918; d. March 8, 2009

Lawrence Hankins Locklin was a straightforward tenor singer who enjoyed big hits with "Send Me the Pillow You Dream On" and "Please Help Me, I'm Falling" in THE NASHVILLE SOUND era.

Locklin recalled being paid two dollars for one of his first professional gigs in a Florida roadhouse, while his expenses totaled five dollars. He fared better in 1942, with a regular stint on radio station WCOA in Pensacola. Later he was also a regular on the *BIG D JAMBOREE* on KRLD–Dallas.

In 1949 he joined Shreveport's *LOUISIANA HAYRIDE*. In that year he also scored his first Top Ten single, "The Same Sweet Girl," for FOUR STAR RECORDS. "Let Me Be the One" (1953) became his first #1 hit. After signing with RCA RECORDS, Locklin had quick success with "Why, Baby, Why" (#9, 1956), a cover of GEORGE JONES's record, followed by a pop-country crossover original, "Geisha Girl" (#4, 1957).

Locklin's self-penned "Send Me the Pillow You Dream On" (#5, 1958) was a substantial country hit and received pop airplay as well. (Dean Martin and Johnny Tillotson both later recorded his song.) Locklin's 1958 follow-up was "It's a Little More Like Heaven" (#3).

He scored his biggest success via his composition "Please Help Me, I'm Falling" (#1, 1960), which also hit #8 on the pop charts. Locklin joined the GRAND OLE OPRY in 1960. During nineteen years with RCA he recorded tribute albums to EDDY ARNOLD, HANK WILLIAMS, and ROY ACUFF. In the 1970s he hosted TV shows in Houston and Dallas and was honorary mayor of McLellan, Florida, where he bought a ranch on property where he had picked cotton as a youth. Locklin lived in Brewton, Alabama, from 1984 until his death. —*Walt Trott*

## Larrie Londin
b. Norfolk, Virginia, October 15, 1943; d. August 24, 1992

Drummer Larrie Londin spent the bulk of his career in Nashville playing on thousands of sessions and dozens of #1 hits and platinum albums. Through his twenty-three years in MUSIC CITY, he pounded out the beat for top country artists such as CHET ATKINS, JERRY REED, DOLLY PARTON, HANK WILLIAMS JR., MERLE HAGGARD, and WAYLON JENNINGS, as well as pop artists including B. B. King, Johnny Mathis, LINDA RONSTADT, Journey, and many more.

Londin (born Ralph Gallant) grew up in Miami, Florida, where he had a passion for boxing. As an unofficial bodyguard for a drummer friend, Londin soon became interested in drums himself and, while still a minor, migrated to Detroit with a band called the Headliners. That band was hired by Motown Records to back artists such as the Supremes, the Temptations, and Marvin Gaye in the studio.

At the urging of fellow instrumental virtuoso Chet Atkins, Londin moved to Nashville in 1969, introducing a somewhat unorthodox and impressive playing style to the normally tranquil country scene. Early country gigs included tours with Jerry Reed and GLEN CAMPBELL.

Londin snagged a house job at the Carousel Club in Printers Alley and began the studio tenure that earned him the Nashville NARAS chapter's Most Valuable Player Award from 1978 to 1980. He also took to the road with ELVIS PRESLEY (1976–77), RODNEY CROWELL and ROSANNE CASH, and THE EVERLY BROTHERS. Londin was no stranger to TV, either—he played *The Tonight Show* and variety programs hosted by Ed Sullivan, Dinah Shore, and Merv Griffin. Londin was honored as ACM's Drummer of the Year (1984 and 1986) and as *Modern Drummer* magazine's Country Drummer (1985–86).

While conducting a drum clinic in Texas, in 1992, Londin collapsed into a diabetic coma, resulting in his death two months later. —*Michael Hight*

## Lone Pine & Betty Cody
Lone Pine (Harold John Breau) b. Pea Cove, Maine, June 5, 1916; d. Maine, March 26, 1977
Betty Cody (Rita M. Coté Breau) b. Sherbrooke, Québec, Canada, August 17, 1921

Known professionally as Lone Pine & Betty Cody, the husband-wife team of Harold John and Rita M. Coté Breau enjoyed marked success during the 1950s, both individually and as a duo. Reportedly dubbed "Lone Pine" by Penobscot Indian playmates, Breau formed his Lone Pine Mountaineers band in the mid-1930s after winning several amateur contests in Bangor, Maine. By the late 1930s he was performing on Bangor radio station WABI. Almost concurrently, Rita Coté, then living in Auburn, Maine, had begun singing at age fifteen with a local country band on radio station WCOU in nearby Lewiston.

After meeting at a radio studio in 1938, Harold and Rita were married on June 29, 1940. As Lone Pine and Betty Cody, they became Maine radio stalwarts in the 1940s and achieved greater success in Canada's Maritime Provinces via radio broadcasts on

*Hank Locklin*

St. John, New Brunswick, station CFBC during the early 1950s. Their popularity led RCA RECORDS' Canadian division to sign them in 1950. Their first single, a solo by Lone Pine titled "Prince Edward Island Is Heaven to Me," sold well enough to warrant release by RCA in the United States a year later, in December 1951. Betty succeeded with "Tom-Tom Yodel" in early 1952, and they scored as a duet with "Trail of the Lonesome Pine" that spring. With all of their Canadian recordings also selling well in the United States, RCA's New York studios became the focal points for their sessions from July 1952 to September 1954. Their July 1952 rendering of "I Heard the Bluebirds Sing" sold fairly well and preceded THE BROWNS' hit by five years.

From their Canadian triumphs in 1950–52, their trail led to the *WWVA JAMBOREE* in Wheeling, West Virginia (1953–54), to Prince Edward Island, Schenectady, and Bangor (1955) and, in the late 1950s, to Winnipeg, Manitoba, where their marriage unraveled. Betty and their younger children returned to Maine, while their oldest son, Lenny, remained with his father. Lenny Breau would grow to prominence in jazz guitar circles in the 1970s and 1980s before being murdered on August 12, 1984, in Los Angeles. Lone Pine returned to Maine during the 1960s, where he remained musically active and remarried. By the early 1970s Betty was singing again in Maine on a part-time basis. She remarried in 1979. —*Bob Pinson*

## Lone Star Playboys

For several years after World War II, the Lone Star Playboys were one of the most important western dance bands in Texas. Perhaps best known as an early backing band for HANK THOMPSON, the Playboys also introduced the dancehall classic "Westphalia Waltz." The Playboys first formed in Waco in 1937, disbanded with the United States' entry into the war, and did not really hit their stride until reuniting in late 1943. In 1945 fiddler Cotton Collins replaced original member Ed Booker and played with the band during 1945–48, 1949–50, and 1951–53. Collins brought with him an unnamed German waltz he'd picked up during the war. Christened "Westphalia Waltz," the song became an immediate hit when it became the second release on Blue Bonnet Records, Herb Rippa's fledgling Dallas label, in 1947.

Spearheaded by tenor banjoist-leader Vince Incardona (in 1937–39 and 1943 and beyond), the Playboys owned their central Texas circuit over the next few years. Steel guitarist Lefty Nason, later one of the architects of Hank Thompson's sound, joined in 1947. Nason's "Steel Guitar Bounce" (Blue Bonnet) from 1949 stands as the highlight of the Playboys' recorded output. Swing legend JOHNNY GIMBLE joined the Playboys on mandolin and fiddle during 1948.

The Playboys' popularity declined (as did WESTERN SWING's) after their return from a 1949 West Coast tour with Thompson, but the band remained a Waco-area attraction into 1953. After Bluebonnet, the group recorded for Everstate and, under the name of bassist Charlie Adams, for IMPERIAL (1947–51). Adams left the group in 1951 and enjoyed several years of moderate success as a solo act, recording for DECCA and COLUMBIA and scoring a minor hit with "Hey Liberace!" in 1953.

Other members over the years included Sammy Incardona, bass (1937–41); Morris Booker, mandolin (1937–41, 1943–53); Hamlet Booker, guitar and vocals (1937–41, 1943–53); Pee Wee Truehitt, bass (1943–47); BILLY WALKER, guitar and vocals (ca. 1950); and Johnny Manson, fiddle (1949–50). —*Kevin Coffey*

## Lonesome Pine Fiddlers

Ezra Cline b. Baisden, West Virginia, January 13, 1907; d. July 11, 1984
Curly Ray Cline b. Gilbert, West Virginia, January 10, 1923; d. August 19, 1997
Charlie Cline b. Gilbert, West Virginia, June 6, 1931; d. November 20, 2004
Paul Williams b. Wytheville, Virginia, March 30, 1935
Melvin Ray Goins b. Bramwell, West Virginia, December 30, 1933
Ray Elwood Goins b. Bramwell, West Virginia, January 3, 1936; d. July 2, 2007

The Lonesome Pine Fiddlers were one of BLUEGRASS music's classic early bands. Long headquartered in West Virginia, the act was founded by bassist Ezra Cline in about 1937 and initially included Ezra's nephew Curly Ray Cline and kinsman Ireland "Lazy Ned" Cline as well as Gordon Jennings. Early on, the group's music embraced OLD-TIME and country sounds. The band stopped working during World War II—in which Ned was killed in action—but later the Fiddlers resumed regular radio shows on WHIS–Bluefield, with multi-instrumentalist Charlie Cline, also Ezra's nephew, coming aboard. After fiddler Ray Morgan, guitarist Bobby Osborne (THE OSBORNE BROTHERS), and banjo player Larry Richardson joined in 1949, the Fiddlers focused on bluegrass. Their 1950 Cozy Records material included "Pain in My Heart," now a bluegrass standard. Several excellent musicians, including Paul Williams and Ray and Melvin Goins, worked with the group into the mid-1960s.

In the early1950s, the Fiddlers became the first bluegrass act signed by RCA VICTOR RECORDS, for which they recorded "Dirty Dishes Blues" and "Brown Eyed Darling." They also recorded for STARDAY in the 1960s. The group popularized bluegrass at WJR in Detroit in the 1950s and hosted TV shows in Huntington, West Virginia, and Bristol, Virginia, during the late 1950s and early 1960s. The act disbanded in the late 1960s, but former members have distinguished themselves with other bands. The group was elected to the IBMA Hall of Fame in 2009. —*Gary B. Reid*

## Lonestar

Dean Sams b. Garland, Texas, August 3, 1966
John Rich b. Amarillo, Texas, January 7, 1974
Richie McDonald b. Lubbock, Texas, February 6, 1962
Michael Britt b. Fort Worth, Texas, June 15, 1966
Keech Rainwater b. Plano, Texas, January 24, 1963

Lonestar had its origins in 1992, when keyboardist Dean Sams and vocalist Richie McDonald met at an audition in Dallas for Nashville's OPRYLAND theme park. After moving to MUSIC CITY, the two invited vocalist John Rich and guitarist Michael Britt to join their band; later they added drummer Keech Rainwater, who had previously worked with Britt in Canyon, a 1980s country group.

With all members boasting Texas origins, Lonestar's music naturally bears hints of traditional country and dancehall swing, but the band also works folk-rock and emotional ballads into its overall sound. *Lonestar*, the act's debut album for BNA (see RCA RECORDS) in 1995, featured four original compositions by various members of the band. The album produced a hit single, "Tequila Talkin'," which reached #8 on *Billboard*'s country charts. The follow-up, "No News," became the first of nine #1 records Lonestar enjoyed between 1996 and 2004. Others included "Come Cryin' To Me" (1997), "Amazed"—a massive crossover hit of 1999—"What About Now" (2000), "Tell Her" (2000–01), "I'm Already There" (2001), "My Front Porch Looking In" (2003), and "Mr. Mom" (2004). In 1996 Lonestar won ACM's 1995 Best New Vocal Group or Duo, and the act was named 2001 Vocal Group of the Year by the CMA and the ACM.

John Rich departed in 1998, making McDonald the sole lead vocalist; the group gained greater success by focusing on McDonald's strengths as a dramatic balladeer. By time McDonald left at the end of 2007 the group's sales had slid and BNA had dropped the act. With Cody Collins singing lead, Lonestar pressed on, releasing a Co5 Records album titled *The Future* in 2008.
—*Bob Paxman*

## Hubert Long
b. Poteet, Texas, December 3, 1923; d. September 7, 1972

Hubert Long was one of the most influential country music executives of his day. As a leader in the industry and through his roles as talent promoter and music publisher, he helped to spread country music worldwide.

Long grew up in Freer, Texas, and relocated to Corpus Christi, where he worked in the record department of a dime store. After boosting record sales, he moved to San Antonio to work for DECCA RECORDS. When his Decca boss went to RCA VICTOR RECORDS, Long followed. At RCA he met COLONEL TOM PARKER, who hired him to do publicity work for EDDY ARNOLD.

In the early 1950s Long staked out the *LOUISIANA HAYRIDE* and signed *Hayride* stars WEBB PIERCE and FARON YOUNG to management contracts. In 1952 he established the Hubert Long Agency to expand his talent bookings, and in 1955 Long set up one of Nashville's first independent talent agencies, Stable of Stars. Throughout the following years he became involved in all aspects of the industry, including advertising, music publishing, and real estate, while continuing in artist management and booking. His Moss Rose company published early hits by CONNIE SMITH ("Once A Day") and BILL ANDERSON ("I Love You Drops") and administered the copyrights of smaller companies, such as

MARIJOHN WILKIN's Buckhorn Music ("One Day at a Time"). Long's booking clients included CHARLIE WALKER, TAMMY WYNETTE, MEL TILLIS, and other leading talents. Long was a founding board member of the Country Music Association (CMA) and the COUNTRY MUSIC HALL OF FAME AND MUSEUM, and he served as CMA president in the late 1960s. He was elected posthumously to THE COUNTRY MUSIC HALL OF FAME in 1979.
—*Don Roy*

## Lonzo & Oscar
Rollin Sullivan (Oscar) b. Edmonton, Kentucky, January 19, 1919
Lloyd Leslie George, a.k.a. Ken Marvin (Lonzo #1) b. Haleyville, Alabama, June 27, 1924; d. October 16, 1991
John Y. Sullivan (Lonzo #2) b. Edmonton, Kentucky, July 7, 1917; d. June 5, 1967
Dave Hooten (Lonzo #3) b. St. Claire, Missouri, February 4, 1935
Cleo C. Hogan Sr. (Lonzo #4) b. Park City, Kentucky, 1925; d. April 3, 1998
Billy Hinson (Lonzo #5, Oscar #2) b. Murfreesboro, Tennessee, December 12, 1937
Ron Ryan (Lonzo #6) b. Murfreesboro, Tennessee, October 17, 1948

The musical comedy duo of Lonzo & Oscar was a longtime fixture at the GRAND OLE OPRY. Over nearly a half-century, several men in succession played the role of Lonzo, while Rollin Sullivan held down the part of Oscar into July 1999.

The act's beginnings can be traced to the late 1930s, when Kentucky-born brothers Johnny and Rollin Sullivan toured as a duo and made their professional radio debut on WTJS in Jackson, Tennessee. In 1942 Rollin joined PAUL HOWARD's Arkansas Cotton Pickers at WSM's Grand Ole Opry, playing electric mandolin. Johnny went into the service during World War II.

From 1945 to 1947 the Sullivan brothers and Lloyd George worked as sidemen for EDDY ARNOLD at WSM and on record. While touring with Arnold, Rollin Sullivan and Lloyd George provided comic relief with an act they called Ichabod & Oscar. It was Arnold who changed George's moniker to Lonzo.

*Hubert Long*

*Lonzo & Oscar: Lloyd "Lonzo" George (left) and Rollin "Oscar" Sullivan*

In late 1947 Lonzo & Oscar left Arnold to become Opry stars in their own right. The following year they scored their biggest hit with "I'm My Own Grandpa" for RCA Victor. In 1950, when George left for a solo career under the name Ken Marvin, John Sullivan rejoined his brother, continuing the Lonzo & Oscar tradition of parody songs. The Sullivans often performed with Cousin Jody (Clell Summey), a toothless, hayseed alumnus of the Pee Wee King and Roy Acuff troupes. For the next seventeen years, the act held forth at the Opry with such bizarre numbers as "Did You Have to Bring That Up (While I Was Eatin')," and "There's a Hole in the Bottom of the Sea." The duo charted again with "Country Music Time" (Starday, 1961) and the noncomedic "Traces of Life" (GRC, 1974).

Following John Sullivan's death in 1967, Rollin engaged another Lonzo, Dave Hooten, who stayed until the duo left the Opry in 1985. Sullivan returned to Kentucky and teamed with broadcaster Cleo C. Hogan Sr. until illness forced Hogan's retirement in late 1997. Subsequently, Billy Hinson filled the role of Lonzo before buying the rights to the Lonzo & Oscar name from Sullivan in July 1999. Switching to the Oscar role, Hinson recruited Ron Ryan as Lonzo. —*Walt Trott*

## Bobby Lord
b. Sanford, Florida, January 6, 1934; d. February 16, 2008

Singer Bobby Lord's career began on television, and he continued to use the media effectively throughout the 1950s and 1960s. While a freshman at the University of Tampa, he had his own local program on WSUN-TV, the *Bobby Lord Homefolks Show*. In 1955, following appearances on several network programs, he joined ABC-TV's Ozark Jubilee, where he spent five years as a cast member and occasional fill-in MC for host Red Foley. After the *Jubilee* ended, Lord moved to the Grand Ole Opry from 1960 to 1969. In 1963 he began *The Bobby Lord Show*, produced by WSM-TV and syndicated by 1965. "Without Your Love," a #10 country Columbia release of 1956, marked Lord's chart debut. During the next fifteen years he charted an additional eight times, on either Hickory or Mercury, most successfully with "You and Me Against the World" (#15, 1970). In the 1980s, he hosted TNN's series *Country Sportsman*, later called *Celebrity Outdoors*. —*William P. Davis*

## Lost Highway Records
established in Nashville, Tennessee, January, 2001

In the new century, Lost Highway Records became known for releasing roots-oriented albums that burst through contemporary country's stylistic parameters, won critical acclaim, and occasionally sold in impressive numbers.

Mercury Records chairman Luke Lewis announced the opening of the imprint in 2001 as a coventure between Universal Music Group sister labels Mercury and Island/Def Jam, touting Lost Highway as a Music Row center for music that existed outside the mainstream. Lost Highway's first release, the soundtrack to the George Clooney film O Brother, Where Art Thou?, sold more than 8 million copies and won a 2001 Grammy for Album of the Year, despite minimal exposure on country radio. That soundtrack featured music by roots luminaries such as Alison Krauss, Gillian Welch, Emmylou Harris, and John Hartford. Subsequent Lost Highway releases included albums

by country legends Johnny Cash and Willie Nelson and by British alternative rocker Morrissey, but much of the Lost Highway catalog has focused on music that can be roughly categorized as Americana. Key artists have included Lucinda Williams, Ryan Adams, Hayes Carll, and Lyle Lovett. —*Peter Cooper*

## John D. Loudermilk
b. Durham, North Carolina, March 31, 1934

Though he started his career as an entertainer on Durham, North Carolina, radio and television stations, John D. Loudermilk achieved his greatest fame as one of Nashville's most successful songwriters, supplying numerous hits to country and pop artists. Loudermilk's compositions have repeatedly found favor with the public, beginning with George Hamilton IV's "A Rose and a Baby Ruth" in 1956 and continuing through Neal McCoy's 1996 country cover of "Then You Can Tell Me Goodbye" (a Top Ten pop hit in 1967 for the Casinos and a #1 country hit for Eddy Arnold in 1968).

Loudermilk's father was a carpenter, and country stars The Louvin Brothers, Ira and Charlie (real name Loudermilk), were his cousins. John D. Loudermilk received his musical training in a Salvation Army Band, where he learned to play trumpet, flugelhorn, saxophone, trombone, and bass drum. By age thirteen he had a daily, half-hour radio show on Durham's WTIK as Johnny Dee, and later, while working as an art director at Durham's first television station (WTVD-TV), he played stand-up bass on the live *Noon Show*. Loudermilk wrote "A Rose and a Baby Ruth," and the song first charted for Hamilton in late 1956. Loudermilk, as Johnny Dee, hit the pop charts himself early the following year with another original, "Sittin' in the Balcony." A week later,

*John D. Loudermilk*

however, EDDIE COCHRAN's recording of the same song became the rock & roller's first pop hit, climbing to #18, while Loudermilk's stalled at #38.

STONEWALL JACKSON scored his first #1 country record (and a #4 pop hit) in 1959 with Loudermilk's "Waterloo" (cowritten with MARIJOHN WILKIN), which featured a bass drum beat inspired by Loudermilk's Salvation Army Band years. Signed to ACUFF-ROSE PUBLICATIONS as a writer after a stint writing for CEDARWOOD, Loudermilk continued to record, registering modest pop hits in 1961 and 1962 for RCA. From 1963 to 1967 he moved to the label's country division, where he worked briefly as assistant to CHET ATKINS. Loudermilk's only Grammy came in 1967, for the liner notes to his album *Suburban Attitudes in Country Verse*. In 1971 he recorded for WARNER BROS.

Loudermilk's songwriting success far outstripped his performing career, however. THE EVERLY BROTHERS had a #8 pop hit in 1961 with "Ebony Eyes" (#25 country), the same year Sue Thompson went to #5 pop with "Sad Movies (Make Me Cry)" and Bobby Vee reached #33 pop with "Stayin' In." In 1963 George Hamilton IV scored again with "Abilene," a #15 pop record and a #1 country disc (to be recycled by SONNY JAMES, in 1977, as a #24 country chart-maker); also in 1963, ERNIE ASHWORTH gained a country #1 with Loudermilk's "Talk Back Trembling Lips."

Early the following year, Johnny Tillotson's MGM rendition of "Talk Back Trembling Lips" became a #7 pop single. Later in 1964, the Nashville Teens, a British rock group, found pop success with Loudermilk's dark rocker "Tobacco Road," and JOHNNY CASH landed a country Top Ten with the writer's "Bad News."

Once the rock era took hold in the mid-1960s, Loudermilk had more success as a country writer, though the Casinos' #6 pop smash "Then You Can Tell Me Goodbye" came in 1967. On the country side that year, George Hamilton IV went to #6 with "Break My Mind" (a #13 country charter for VERN GOSDIN in 1978), and GLEN CAMPBELL went to #1 country with "I Wanna Live."

Paul Revere & the Raiders scored their only #1 pop hit—and their last Top Ten—in 1971, with Loudermilk's "Indian Reservation (The Lament of the Cherokee Indian)." Lines from the song would show up later (with Loudermilk's permission) in TIM MCGRAW's 1994 country hit "Indian Outlaw."

Loudermilk was inducted into the NASHVILLE SONGWRITERS HALL OF FAME in 1976. *—Jay Orr*

## Louisiana Hayride
established 1948; ended early 1980s

The *Louisiana Hayride*, a popular and influential live country radio show, was first broadcast from Shreveport's Municipal Auditorium over the 50,000-watt, clear-channel station KWKH on April 3, 1948. The original cast included Harmie Smith, Hoot & Curley, Pappy Covington, Tex Grimsley, JOHNNIE & JACK with KITTY WELLS, and THE BAILES BROTHERS. Horace Logan served as producer and MC.

Several men played key roles in launching the *Hayride*: KWKH commercial manager Dean Upson (a veteran of THE VAGABONDS), who secured sponsors and recruited talent; Johnnie and Kyle Bailes, who served as announcer and booking agent, respectively (as well as performing with a third brother, Homer); Logan, who had worked at KWKH before World War II; and station manager Henry Clay, the authority on all matters—especially the show's finances. Beginning with HANK WILLIAMS's first appearance in August 1948, the show became a proving ground for future stars, eventually acquiring the nickname "Cradle of the Stars." Among those who followed Williams to Shreveport were Jim Ed & Maxine Brown (of THE BROWNS), JOHNNY HORTON, DAVID HOUSTON, SONNY JAMES, GEORGE JONES, Rusty & Doug (see DOUG KERSHAW), MERLE KILGORE, CLAUDE KING, the MADDOX BROTHERS & ROSE, and PATSY MONTANA. Other prominent *Hayride* artists included JIMMY C. NEWMAN, WEBB PIERCE, JIM REEVES (who began as a KWKH announcer), RED SOVINE, T. TEXAS TYLER, BILLY WALKER, the WILBURN BROTHERS, and FARON YOUNG. Like Williams, many of the aforementioned acts moved on to Nashville, and many of these joined the GRAND OLE OPRY.

The Maddoxes pointed the way toward ROCKABILLY, which the *Hayride* nurtured, primarily through ELVIS PRESLEY's tenure on the show from October to December 1954. Following Elvis, such rockabilly luminaries as JOHNNY CASH and BOB LUMAN, among many others, also made frequent appearances.

Though the *Hayride* was creatively successful, it was never a major financial success for KWKH or its parent company, the *Shreveport Times* (owned by the Ewing family). A regional network was established in 1950, and affiliation with the CBS radio network began in 1953. CBS broadcast the first thirty minutes of the program on every third Saturday through 1957, after which it

Louisiana Hayride *cast*

switched to every fifth Saturday. CBS dropped the *Hayride* in 1958, however, signaling a steady decline in the program's fortunes. In 1960 Henry Clay decided to discontinue the *Hayride* as a live weekly broadcast. Taped replays and periodic package shows (featuring mostly non-Shreveport–based acts) continued into the early 1970s. Local businessman David Kent attempted to revive a relocated *Hayride* (in neighboring Bossier Parish) in 1973 and renamed the show *Hayride, USA*. Kent's program ended in the early 1980s. Sporadic attempts to resuscitate the program have followed.

Competition from television and college football, rising production costs, and the rise of rock & roll all helped foster the *Hayride*'s demise. Still, the show's legacy is rich and venerable. Besides major stars, the *Hayride* encouraged offstage talent—music businessmen such as booking agent and recording executive JIM BULLEIT, promoter TILLMAN FRANKS (also a fine songwriter), record producer and promotion man SHELBY SINGLETON, booking agent and publisher HUBERT LONG, and producer JERRY KENNEDY (who began as a teenage guitarist). Significant instrumentalists among *Hayride* alumni include pianist FLOYD CRAMER, drummer D. J. Fontana, steel guitarists SHOT JACKSON and JIMMY DAY, and guitarists JAMES BURTON, Fred Carter Jr., and Charlie Waller. Announcers Frank Page, Ray Bartlett, Norm Bale, and Jeff Dale, among others, also contributed to the program's success, which has been explored in the Louisiana Public Television documentary *The Last Hayride*. —Stephen R. Tucker

*The Louvin Brothers: Ira (left) and Charlie*

## The Louvin Brothers

Ira Lonnie Loudermilk b. Section, Alabama, April 21, 1924; d. June 20, 1965
Charlie Elzer Loudermilk b. Section, Alabama, July 7, 1927; d. January 26, 2011

In country music's long tradition of duet singing, Ira and Charlie Louvin were the link between the DELMORE BROTHERS and THE EVERLY BROTHERS. More important, the Louvin Brothers' stratospheric vocal interplay made them one of country music's most influential harmony duets, touching artists ranging from EMMYLOU HARRIS to the cowpunk band Rank & File.

First cousins of singer-songwriter JOHN D. LOUDERMILK, Ira and Charlie grew up in a poor farm family in northeastern Alabama, mostly in Henegar. Ira mastered the mandolin, and Charlie picked guitar. They first performed as the Radio Twins in 1942, worked in Chattanooga in 1943, and changed their stage name to the Louvin Brothers in 1947 while broadcasting over WROL in Knoxville. After broadcasting in Memphis, they debuted on the GRAND OLE OPRY on January 29, 1955.

The Louvins recorded for Apollo in 1947, DECCA in 1949, and THE MGM in 1951 and 1952. They did not find commercial success, however, until they began recording for CAPITOL on September 30, 1952, an affiliation that would continue until the act broke up in August 1963. Although the duo's biggest Capitol hits were released in 1955 and 1956—during the early days of rock & roll—their musical style was already defiantly anachronistic. Their high, lonesome harmonies, punctuated by Ira's stirring mandolin solos, were closer to country music of the 1930s than the HONKY-TONK or country-pop of the mid-1950s. Moreover, their first three Top Ten singles, "When I Stop Dreaming," the chart-topping "I Don't Believe You've Met My Baby," and "Hoping That You're Hoping," didn't include drums, though their backing typically included electric guitar. They mixed gospel and secular forms, often focusing on the traditional themes of family, love, and obligation that link the two.

In the late 1950s a changing market and Ira's erratic, tempestuous behavior contributed to the brothers' sinking commercial fortunes. Capitol producer KEN NELSON made several attempts to update the duo's sound—including an ill-fated series of recordings without Ira's trademark mandolin—but 1959's "My Baby's Gone" was their last Top Ten hit. Increasing personal tensions led to the pair's 1963 breakup, after which each brother embarked on a separate career. Ira's 1964 album *The Unforgettable Ira Louvin*, recorded with electric mandolin and electric guitar, turned out to be his only solo LP; he died in a Missouri car crash on June 20, 1965. Charlie's solo career began with two Top Ten hits ("I Don't Love You Anymore" and "See the Big Man Cry"), but through the 1970s and 1980s he was best known as a fixture on weekly Opry broadcasts.

COUNTRY-ROCK pioneer GRAM PARSONS introduced the Louvins' songs to the rock world, in several instances as duets with Emmylou Harris. Harris, in turn, reintroduced the Louvins' material to country audiences when her 1975 version of their song "If I Could Only Win Your Love" became her first Top Ten country hit.

In 1996 Watermelon Records released Charlie's album *The Longest Train*, on which he was joined by guest performers such as BARRY AND HOLLY TASHIAN and JIM LAUDERDALE. *Livin', Lovin', Losin': Songs of the Louvin Brothers* (2003), a tribute album produced by CARL JACKSON and showcasing many top singers in folk, country, and rock, won a Grammy for Best Country Album. In 2007 Charlie released a Grammy-nominated self-titled album on the Tompkins Square label featuring GEORGE JONES, Elvis Costello, and TOM T. HALL, among others. *Steps to Heaven*, consisting of traditional gospel numbers, followed in 2008, as did *Charlie Louvin Sings Murder Ballads and Disaster Songs*. An album of war-related songs titled *The Battle Rages On* appeared in November 2010. His final recording, "Back When We Were Young" b/w "Alabama," was released that same month. In June 2010 Charlie Louvin was diagnosed with pancreatic cancer, which claimed his life on January 26, 2011.

The Louvin Brothers were elected to THE COUNTRY MUSIC HALL OF FAME in 2001. —*Jimmy Guterman*

## Patty Loveless
b. Pikeville, Kentucky, January 4, 1957

Patty Loveless has garnered immense artistic respect and has built an enduring career on consistently sensitive song choices and a skillful balance of modern and traditional country vocal stylings.

Like her distant cousin LORETTA LYNN, Patricia Ramey was a coal miner's daughter; she was born in the small Appalachian town of Pikeville, Kentucky, where her father died of black lung disease in 1979. Patty regularly listened to the GRAND OLE OPRY and sang with her brother Roger. In 1971, at age fourteen, she and Roger showed her songs to PORTER WAGONER, who encouraged Patty but counseled her to finish high school. Two years later she joined the WILBURN BROTHERS' touring show and signed with their publishing firm, Sure-Fire Music.

In 1976 she married the Wilburns' drummer, Terry Lovelace, and moved with him to Kings Mountain, North Carolina, where they played in Charlotte-area rock bands. In 1985, after recovering from a bout with alcoholism, she moved to Nashville to resume a country music career. Her marriage to Lovelace dissolved later that year, although she kept the name with a slight change of spelling. Assisted by her brother Roger, now her manager, Loveless landed a recording contract with A&R man TONY BROWN at MCA RECORDS. Although it began as a singles deal, she cut her self-titled first album in 1987.

Her first Top Ten hit was a cover of GEORGE JONES's "If My Heart Had Windows" (1988), which suggested a long-standing affinity for hard country that lay beneath the rock influences she later displayed. The hit also helped her gain Grand Ole Opry membership on June 11, 1988. Other Top Tens came from such varied sources as STEVE EARLE ("A Little Bit in Love," 1988), COUNTRY-ROCK band Lone Justice ("Don't Toss Us Away," 1989), and the transplanted Greek songwriter Kostas ("Timber, I'm Falling in Love," 1989).

A series of momentous life changes began with her February 1989 marriage to producer/bass player EMORY GORDY JR. In 1990 she ended her management contract with her brother and left MCA Records for SONY MUSIC's EPIC label in 1992. That fall she had laser surgery on her vocal cords, from which she fully recovered.

Gordy produced her first Epic album, *Only What I Feel*, as well as her subsequent Epic projects. A critical and commercial success, it became her first platinum album, and its sales were duplicated by the follow-up, *When Fallen Angels Fly*, the CMA's 1995 Album of the Year. In 1996 *The Trouble with the Truth* helped her win Female Vocalist of the Year awards from both the CMA and the ACM. Among her best-known hit singles are "Chains" (1990), "Blame It on Your Heart" (1993), "How Can I Help You Say Goodbye" (1994), "You Can Feel Bad" (1995), and "Lonely Too Long" (1996). "You Don't Seem to Miss Me," a 1997 hit duet with George Jones, became CMA's Vocal Event of the Year.

Although her singles chart performance slipped after 1997, she extended her artistic range with 2001's *Mountain Soul*, an acoustic album celebrating her heritage of gospel, BLUEGRASS, and traditional country material. She shared childhood memories in *Bluegrass & White Snow: A Mountain Christmas* (2002). Other notable efforts include *Sleepless Nights* (2008), a collection of country classics issued on Saguaro Road Records following her final Epic album in 2005; the title cut featured VINCE GILL on harmony, a role she has filled at times on his recordings. Saguaro Road released *Mountain Soul II* in 2009. —*Paul Kingsbury*

## Lyle Lovett
b. Klein, Texas, November 1, 1957

Lyle Pearce Lovett's eclectic music incorporates folk, jazz, and pop, yet it remains unmistakably country-rooted. Marked by dry wit, dark humor, and unforgettable characters, his lyrics are exceptionally vivid and memorable.

Lovett grew up in a town outside Houston that was founded by his great-great-grandfather. Early on he was influenced by Texas singer-songwriters he heard in folk clubs, and by the late 1970s he was composing songs and performing onstage. After graduating from Texas A & M University, Lovett made a tape of his tunes; fellow Texan GUY CLARK liked the result and began playing the tape for friends in Nashville.

MCA offered a recording contract. *Lyle Lovett* appeared in 1986 and spawned the Top Ten hit "Cowboy Man" along with Top Twenty singles including "God Will" and "Why I Don't Know." Critics grouped him with NANCI GRIFFITH, STEVE EARLE, K. D. LANG, and DWIGHT YOAKAM as "cutting edge" artists who were transforming the country idiom. *Pontiac*, Lovett's second album, yielded the Top Twenty hits "Give Back My Heart" (1987) and "She's No Lady" (1988). *Lyle Lovett & His Large Band* (1989) was half folk-country and half devoted to his bluesy, brassy road combo. Lovett's version of TAMMY WYNETTE's "Stand By Your Man" attracted particular attention, and the album won a 1989 Grammy.

As an actor, Lovett debuted in Robert Altman's *The Player* (1992). The gospel- and R&B-influenced album *Joshua Judges*

*Patty Loveless*

*Lyle Lovett*

*Ruth* soon followed. Though country radio virtually ignored it (and many subsequent albums), exposure on adult alternative radio and VH1 helped it go gold. While filming *The Player*, Lovett met actress Julia Roberts; the two soon married, but they divorced in 1995. *The Road to Ensenada*, which won a 1996 Grammy as Best Country Album and featured guests Jackson Browne, Shawn Colvin, Randy Newman, and CHRIS HILLMAN, pleased both country and pop audiences. Highlights of Lovett's subsequent efforts include a 1999 live album, *Live in Texas*; his soundtrack to the Altman film *Dr. T and the Women* (2000); a 2004 tour with singer-songwriter pals JOHN HIATT, Guy Clark, and JOE ELY; and LOST HIGHWAY albums such as *Natural Forces* (2009), which features songs written or cowritten by Lovett, DAVID BALL, TOWNES VAN ZANDT, and other Texas tunesmiths. —*Robert K. Oermann*

## The Lowery Music Group
established in Atlanta, Georgia, 1952

The Lowery Group of Music Publishing Companies was one of America's most significant music publishing houses outside Nashville, New York, Chicago, and the West Coast. Beginning as a two-person operation in a small back office of an Atlanta radio station, the Lowery Group progressed through quarters in the basement of founder Bill Lowery's home and space in an abandoned school building to a spacious office and studio complex in a suburban office park. From its first hit, the 1953 country gospel song "I Have But One Goal," the Lowery Group quickly diversified to encompass country, R&B, rock, and pop music, eventually building a catalog of more than 6,000 songs.

Despite phenomenal success in other genres, the Lowery Group never turned its back on country music. Over the years the proportion of its catalog devoted to country music has been as high as 60 percent. Country hits published by the Lowery Group include SONNY JAMES's "Young Love" (written by Ric Cartey and

Carole Joyner), PORTER WAGONER's "Misery Loves Company" (JERRY REED), LEROY VAN DYKE's "Walk On By" (Kendall Hayes), JOHN CONLEE's "Common Man" (Sammy Johns), and CONWAY TWITTY's "Desperado Love" (Michael Garvin and Sammy Johns). During the late 1960s JOE SOUTH was responsible for a raft of pop and country hits for the firm, writing and recording such songs as "(I Never Promised You a) Rose Garden," "Games People Play," and "These Are Not My People." The first was a 1967 #1 country hit for LYNN ANDERSON, and the latter two were big country hits for FREDDY WELLER.

Bill Lowery (October 21, 1924–June 8, 2004), a native of Leesville, Louisiana, came to Atlanta to manage a new radio station, WQXI. His previous experience had included management and announcing at several radio stations. Later, Lowery took a job at WGST, where he became a country music disc jockey known as Uncle Eb Brown, a rube character who attracted a host of aspiring young country performers to his broadcasts. The congenial Lowery not only gave them airtime but also began sharing advice, encouraging their songwriting efforts, introducing them to recording executives, and otherwise guiding and promoting their careers.

From these informal interactions the Lowery Music Group was born, and the world became acquainted with such Lowery protégés as Joe South, Jerry Reed, ROY DRUSKY, RAY STEVENS, BILL ANDERSON, EMORY GORDY JR., Gene Vincent, and MAC DAVIS, among many others. Lowery also owned the prominent Southern Tracks recording studio. He sold his publishing firms to Sony/ATV Music Publishing in 1999. —*Wayne W. Daniel*

## Lulu Belle & Scotty
Lulu Belle (Wiseman) Stamey b. Boone, North Carolina, December 24, 1913;
  d. February 8, 1999
Scott Greene Wiseman b. Ingalls, North Carolina, November 8, 1909;
  d. January 31, 1981

Known as the Hayloft Sweethearts and the Sweethearts of Country Music, Lulu Belle & Scotty starred for nearly twenty-five years on the NATIONAL BARN DANCE, the seminal country music radio program broadcast weekly by powerful Chicago station WLS from 1924 to 1960. With Scotty on banjo and Lulu Belle on guitar, the duo performed Appalachian folk songs, gospel tunes, novelty pieces, sentimental Tin Pan Alley favorites, and mainstream country and pop songs in close vocal harmonies, blending their music with folksy patter and cornball comedy routines. They eventually became the longest-lasting and perhaps best-loved husband-wife duet in country music.

"Lulu Belle" was the name given eighteen-year-old Myrtle Eleanor Cooper in 1932 by JOHN LAIR, artistic director of the *National Barn Dance*, when she joined the cast. In this persona she represented the Appalachian girlfriend of RED FOLEY (nicknamed "Burrhead"), then a member of Lair's CUMBERLAND RIDGE RUNNERS. Her rambunctious behavior (such as blowing huge bubbles with her bubble gum), her honest renditions of folk songs she had learned from her mother, and her comic duets with Foley endeared her to audiences, and she rapidly became one of the show's most popular performers. In 1936 readers of *Radio Guide* magazine voted her "National Radio Queen," the most popular woman on radio.

Scott grew up in a Blue Ridge Mountain community rich in traditional culture. He spent his early years collecting folk songs from his family and neighbors—and becoming proficient on

*Lulu Belle & Scotty*

banjo, guitar, and harmonica. His love for Appalachian folk music was strengthened further when he came under the influence of BASCOM LAMAR LUNSFORD and BRADLEY KINCAID, who had become one of WLS's biggest artists in the late 1920s. Scott joined the WLS staff in 1933, modeling himself closely on Kincaid. He performed as a solo act for a few months, singing folk songs as well as original compositions that evoked his mountain upbringing, but in 1934 he was paired onstage with Lulu Belle, whom he married on December 13 of that year. Except for a brief stay at Cincinnati's WLW (ca. 1938–40), the duo made WLS their radio home into the late 1950s.

Scott was a prolific songwriter. Some of his original songs became country classics, including "Brown Mountain Light," and "Remember Me." Scott's "Have I Told You Lately That I Love You?" has been recorded by innumerable pop and country artists. He was elected into the NASHVILLE SONGWRITERS HALL OF FAME in 1971.

Though their record sales were never spectacular, radio broadcasts, personal appearances, and seven Hollywood films disseminated Lulu Belle & Scotty's comic "battles of the sexes," elegant harmony singing, winning songs, and superb musicianship, earning them a secure position in country music history. —*William E. Lightfoot*

## Bob Luman
b. Nacogdoches, Texas, April 15, 1937; d. December 27, 1978

Bobby Glynn Luman grew up trying to decide whether to seek a career in baseball or country music. But when ELVIS PRESLEY played Kilgore, Texas, one evening in May 1955, Luman made his decision: He wanted to play Presley's brand of ROCKABILLY music. "That was the last time I ever tried to sing like LEFTY FRIZZELL," Luman told author Paul Hemphill.

Winning a Future Farmers of America Talent contest judged by JOHNNY HORTON paved the way for an invitation from the *LOUISIANA HAYRIDE* to replace a departing JOHNNY CASH. An invitation to join the Pittsburgh Pirates at spring training arrived at about the same time. Luman chose music.

IMPERIAL RECORDS signed Luman in early 1957. His backup group, assembled in Shreveport, consisted of JAMES BURTON on guitar, James Kirkland on bass, and Bruce White on drums. The first session produced a rockabilly classic, "Red Cadillac and a Black Mustache." Luman next traveled to California to appear in the film *Carnival Rock*. While there he became a regular on the *TOWN HALL PARTY* television program. RICK NELSON heard Luman's crack band at this time and hired them away.

Luman left Imperial and, after a brief stint with CAPITOL RECORDS, signed with WARNER BROS., but he was disappointed at the lack of progress in his career. During a performance at the Showboat Hotel in Las Vegas, Luman announced that he intended to ask the Pirates for another tryout. In the audience that night were THE EVERLY BROTHERS, also on Warner Bros., who suggested that Luman try recording a BOUDLEAUX BRYANT song they had turned down, "Let's Think About Living." It became Luman's top career single, charting #7 pop and #9 country in 1960. Luman soon was drafted into the army, however, and was unable to follow up on his success.

He moved to Nashville in 1964 and joined the GRAND OLE OPRY in a long-lasting but not always comfortable association with the program. Senior cast member ROY ACUFF once caustically remarked, "That boy can't decide if he's colored or white."

Between 1964 and his death in 1978, Luman placed thirty-eight singles on the country charts for the HICKORY, EPIC, and Polydor labels, but only four of them were Top Ten records. The highest-charting of these was "Lonely Women Make Good Lovers," a #4 hit of 1972. —*William P. Davis*

## Robert Lunn
b. Franklin, Tennessee, November 28, 1912; d. March 8, 1966

Robert Rainey Lunn was an early GRAND OLE OPRY comedian who built a career on variations of a genre called the talking blues. Growing up in Franklin, southwest of Nashville, he knew SAM and KIRK MCGEE, and as a youth he took his impersonations and left-handed guitar stylings to the vaudeville stage. After traveling widely, during which time he heard the kind of spoken songs pioneered by South Carolinian CHRIS BOUCHILLON, Lunn moved his act to radio, appearing on WCHS in Charleston, West Virginia, and KWTO in Springfield, Missouri. Thrown out of work during the Depression, he returned to Tennessee and finally found a job as a bellboy at Nashville's Hermitage Hotel.

Lunn began performing on the hotel's in-house radio station that piped music into guests' rooms, and soon he was invited to appear on the Opry. GEORGE D. HAY, the show's master of ceremonies, found his patter delightful and dubbed him the Original Talking Blues Man. Lunn began building on verses he knew, often creating new topical or personalized verses, until he finally had a repertoire of some one hundred verses. Sacks of fan mail poured in, and throughout the early 1940s Lunn traveled with Opry TENT SHOWS, especially those of ROY ACUFF. Oddly, Lunn never got around to recording his song "Talking Blues" until 1947, when he made a version for MERCURY. He retired from the Opry in 1958, shortly after cutting his first LP for STARDAY. —*Charles Wolfe*

## Bascom Lamar Lunsford
b. Mars Hill, North Carolina, March 21, 1882; d. September 4, 1973

Bascom Lamar Lunsford is best known as the originator of Asheville, North Carolina's Mountain Dance and Folk Festival—the first folk festival of its kind—in 1928. An avid collector and performer, he strongly influenced the folk revival of the late 1950s and early 1960s.

Raised in the Blue Ridge Mountains, Lunsford graduated from Rutherford College in 1909 and studied law at Trinity College (now Duke University), passing the bar exam in 1913. In addition to setting up a law practice, he pursued various occupations, including teaching at Rutherford College, auctioneering, newspaper work, and a position with the United States Justice Department. But he was always most committed to preserving the music of his native region.

A fiddler, banjoist, and singer, Lunsford recorded more than 300 songs, tunes, dance calls, and tales for the archives of Columbia University and the Library of Congress from his "memory collection" of traditional lore he had learned over the years. With Lamar Stringfield, he published *30 and 1 Folk Songs from the Southern Mountains* (Carl Fischer, 1929). Commercially, Lunsford recorded twenty-two sides for OKEH, BRUNSWICK, and COLUMBIA and four LPs for the Library of Congress, Folkways, Riverside, and ROUNDER. His best-known composition is "Mountain Dew," which he recorded for Brunswick in 1928 and later sold for twenty-five dollars to Scott Wiseman of LULU BELLE & SCOTTY, who recorded the song in 1939 for Vocalion. (Wiseman repaid Lunsford by arranging for Lunsford to receive a 50 percent royalty during his lifetime.)

Lunsford assisted Sarah Gertrude Knott in establishing the National Folk Festival, and in addition to the Asheville festival he organized other folk festivals at the North Carolina State Fair, the Cherokee Indian Fair, and the University of North Carolina, as well as gatherings in Kentucky, Virginia, and South Carolina. In 1939, at the request of President and Mrs. Franklin D. Roosevelt, he took a group of musicians and dancers to the White House to entertain the king and queen of England. Lunsford continued to organize, manage, and perform at the Asheville Mountain Dance and Folk Festival until he suffered a stroke in 1965. Afterward he continued to attend the festival until his death. —*Loyal Jones*

## Frank Luther
b. Lakin, Kansas, August 4, 1899; d. November 16, 1980

Frank Luther recorded prolifically with CARSON ROBISON and as a solo act during the early years of commercial country music before moving exclusively into the children's recording field after World War II.

Born Francis Luther Crow on a ranch near Lakin, he finished high school in BAKERSFIELD, California, and served as a minister, church choir director, and evangelistic singer. He first performed professionally with the De Rezske Singers and the Revelers Male Quartet and started recording country music in June 1928, when he replaced VERNON DALHART as Carson Robison's recording partner. Probably their best-selling records were some of the one hundred sides they recorded for the Victor Talking Machine Company (later RCA VICTOR RECORDS) as Bud & Joe Billings and Billings & Robison, many accompanied by a small orchestra. One of the best known was their joint composition "Barnacle Bill the Sailor," a popular novelty song.

Luther was the lead singer and soloist for most of the Carson Robison Trio records. He also sang duets with Robison under such pseudonyms as the Black Brothers, Jimson Brothers, Jones Brothers, and Harper Brothers, and he recorded solos as Jimmie Black, Harry Black, Lazy Larry, Weary Willie, Jeff Calhoun, Frank Evans, Francis Evans, Pete Wiggins, and Frank Tuttle, among other names.

Luther was an expert at varying his singing style, and he recorded more than 400 sides of vocal choruses with dance orchestras at the same time he was waxing country numbers.

After parting professionally with Robison in April 1932, Luther continued recording for RCA Victor for a time with his wife, ZORA LAYMAN, whom he had married in 1926, and with Leonard Stokes, as the Bud Billings Trio. They also recorded for the AMERICAN RECORD CORPORATION (ARC) labels as the Frank Luther Trio and the Buddy Spencer Trio. RAY WHITLEY later joined them, in January 1934.

During this time Luther also recorded more than 130 songs for radio broadcast, made several movie shorts, and was active in live radio. From 1933 to 1935 he was a regular guest on ETHEL PARK RICHARDSON's folk music radio programs on New York City station WOR and the NBC network. A noted songwriter, he published the book *Americans and Their Songs* through Harper Brothers in 1942.

In August 1934 Luther became one of the first performers to sign with DECCA RECORDS. He cut eight of the first ten records in the label's 5000 "hillbilly" series and continued with Decca throughout the remainder of his career. He made a majority of his later recordings for the children's market, becoming a leader in this field. (He had started recording children's songs for ARC in 1932 on the Playtime label.) After World War II he ran his own children's record label, LUTHERecords. In the 1950s Luther became a Decca executive in charge of children's and educational records. He remained active into the 1970s, as a composer and record producer. —*Bob Olson*

## Loretta Lynn
b. Butcher Holler, Kentucky, April 14, 1935

Loretta Lynn's life story reads more like fiction than fact. A poorly educated woman from the coal-mining hills of eastern Kentucky, married at age thirteen and a mother at fourteen, she became one of country music's most popular performers and broke ground for numerous female singers who followed her.

Loretta Webb was born in a one-room log cabin and was the second of eight children. At thirteen she attended a pie social, bringing a pie she had baked using salt instead of sugar. The highest bidder not only won the pie but also got to meet the girl who had baked it. Doolittle "Mooney" Lynn had just returned home from the army. A month after they had first met, still three months short of her fourteenth birthday, Loretta and Mooney married.

A year later, the couple moved to Washington State, where Mooney had heard job opportunities were better. It was the first time Loretta had been away from home. Mooney found work while Loretta, still a child herself, became pregnant with their first child. By the time she was eighteen, she had four children.

Loretta had grown up listening to country music and often sang around the house. Mooney bought her a guitar so she could play as she sang. Later he helped arrange an engagement at the local Grange hall, bragging that his wife could sing better than

*Loretta Lynn*

anyone except KITTY WELLS. Soon Loretta was performing with a local band and within months formed a band of her own.

Lynn came to the attention of Zero Records, a small firm in nearby Vancouver, Canada. The label signed her in February 1960 and sent her to Los Angeles to cut four songs. After the session she and Mooney stayed until the records were pressed and then mailed them to country radio stations. Loretta and Mooney then hit the road for Nashville, stopping at stations along the way to promote her rendition of "I'm a Honky Tonk Girl." The record began getting airplay and reached #14 on the country music charts in 1960. On the strength of this hit Lynn gained a first appearance on the GRAND OLE OPRY, on September 17, 1960.

One of Lynn's first stops in MUSIC CITY was the office of the WILBURN BROTHERS. Teddy and Doyle Wilburn were a top country vocal duo whose enterprises included a music publishing company, a booking agency, a syndicated television program, and a touring show. Recognizing her talent, Doyle Wilburn made her a part of the Wilburns' road show and a regular on their television series. He eventually secured Lynn's release from Zero Records and persuaded DECCA RECORDS, for which the Wilburns recorded, to sign her. (Later, Lynn's desire to assume full control of her career led to conflicts with the Wilburns. A lawsuit settled matters, and eventually they resumed their friendship.)

Two years after she recorded "I'm a Honky Tonk Girl," Lynn began scoring with additional hits, including "Success," "Before I'm Over You," and "Blue Kentucky Girl." But it wasn't until she wrote and recorded "You Ain't Woman Enough" and "Don't Come Home a-Drinkin' (with Lovin' on Your Mind)" that Lynn's music took a new direction. Her songs became more assertive, and the country girl from the Kentucky hills, who was raising a family of six, spoke more boldly and forcefully than many would have expected. Still, the humor of songs such as "Fist City" and "Your Squaw Is on the Warpath" kept her from alienating her audience.

Lynn was CMA's Female Vocalist of the Year in 1967, 1972, and 1973. What's more, she began appearing on television variety programs and talk shows that had rarely featured country music performers. By the end of the 1960s, Lynn's brother, Jay Lee Webb, and her sisters Peggy Sue and CRYSTAL GAYLE had also become country recording artists.

In 1970 Lynn's self-penned signature song, "Coal Miner's Daughter," became one of her biggest hits. She had made three albums of duets with ERNEST TUBB before recording her first song with CONWAY TWITTY that same year. "After the Fire Is Gone" topped the charts in 1971 and launched one of the most successful duets in country music history. Lynn and Twitty were CMA's Vocal Duo of the Year from 1972 through 1975. Among their many hits were "Lead Me On," "Louisiana Woman, Mississippi Man," and "Feelins'." In 1972 Lynn became the first woman to receive CMA's Entertainer of the Year Award.

Lynn's autobiography, *Coal Miner's Daughter* (1976), became a best seller and inspired a 1980 hit movie starring Sissy Spacek. Meanwhile, the singer continued to notch hits such as "Out of My Head and Back in My Bed," "I've Got a Picture of Us on My Mind," and the aptly titled "We've Come a Long Way, Baby." "I Lie" (1982) was her fifty-first Top Ten hit, with sixteen #1s between 1966 and 1978.

In 1988 Lynn was elected to THE COUNTRY MUSIC HALL OF FAME. Following her husband's death in 1996, she returned to solo recording after a hiatus of more than ten years. Audium Records released her album *Still Country* in 2000. She published her second autobiography, *Still Woman Enough*, in 2002, and in 2003 she received the prestigious Kennedy Center Honors for her lifetime contributions to the arts. Her strong-selling 2004 album *Van Lear Rose*, produced by singer-guitarist Jack White of the rock act the White Stripes, introduced her singing and songwriting skills to new audiences and won a Grammy for Best Country Album. It also took Album of the Year honors at the 2004 AMERICANA Awards, at which Lynn was also named Artist of the Year. By 2009 she began rerecording her hits (with John Carter Cash serving as producer) while also recording new material.
—Laurence Zwisohn

## Shelby Lynne
b. Quantico, Virginia, October 22, 1968

Like LYLE LOVETT and K. D. LANG before her, Shelby Lynne is a singer whose talent is too broad for the narrow confines of country music as dictated by the constraints of radio. Raised in Jackson, Alabama, Shelby Lynn Moorer had wanted to form a singing duo with her mother, but tragedy struck when Lynne was seventeen: Her father took the life of her mother and then took his own.

Lynne and her sister, Allison (who later pursued her own singing career), moved to Nashville in 1990, and, after an appearance on TNN's *Nashville Now*, Lynne found herself working with producer BILLY SHERRILL and singing a duet with GEORGE JONES. Signed to EPIC RECORDS, she released three albums whose singles mostly stalled between the Top Sixty and the Top Thirty. Nevertheless, she was ACM's Top New Female Vocalist of 1990. Her fourth album, *Temptation,* released on Morgan Creek Records in 1993, was a swing tribute to BOB WILLS and demonstrated Lynne's versatility, as did *Restless* (Magnatone, 1995), which blended country, BLUEGRASS, big band pop, and blues.

After a fallow period, Lynne returned to recording with the acclaimed 2000 Island Records release *I Am Shelby Lynne*, a confident, roots-based album that secured her a 2000 Grammy as Best New Artist—despite her decade in the business. *Love, Shelby* (2001) was smoother, but she found her footing again with *Identity Crisis* (CAPITOL/EMI, 2003). After *Suit Yourself* (2005) came 2008's *Just a Little Lovin'*, a tribute to pop singer Dusty Springfield produced by legendary rocker Phil Ramone and released by

Lost Highway Records. She recorded 2010's *Tears, Lies and Alibis* for her own Everso Records. Lynne proved her acting skills in the role of Johnny Cash's mother in the 2005 biopic *Walk the Line. —Clark Parsons*

## Lyric Street Records
established in Nashville, Tennessee, 1997

When Lyric Street Records opened in 1997, country music had just experienced a six-year historic boom in record sales. By the time the label started its second decade, the music business had undergone a drastic downturn; by then, Lyric Street stood as one of Nashville's few successful start-ups in the Internet age.

The launch of Lyric Street Records marked the entry of the Walt Disney Company into the Nashville market, expanding on the success of the Disney Music Group, a subsidiary based in California. To run its Nashville operation, Disney recruited Randy Goodman, a former general manager at RCA Records who had worked hand-in-hand with veteran record executive Joe Galante in Nashville and in New York.

Lyric Street began with a mix of newcomers (Kevin Denney, Sonya Isaacs, Rascal Flatts, SHeDAISY) and veterans (John Berry, Aaron Tippin, Lari White). The label's success was fueled by developing acts, as SHeDAISY jumped from the gate with three Top Ten singles and a million-selling album. In 2000, Rascal Flatts started its fast climb with its own string of Top Ten hits.

Over time, SHeDAISY lost momentum but continued as a presence on the contemporary country scene. Rascal Flatts flourished, becoming one of the hottest country acts of the new century. The band—Jay DeMarcus, Gary LeVox, and Joe Don Rooney—saw its self-titled first album reach #3 on the *Billboard* country album charts. Each subsequent studio album through 2009's *Unstoppable* spent weeks at #1, and each has sold in the multimillions. The 2004 album *Feels So Good* and the 2006 album *Me and My Gang* sold more than 5 million copies apiece and ranked among that period's best sellers in any genre.

Bucky Covington and Josh Gracin, two finalists from the *American Idol* TV talent series, would enjoy success with Lyric Street as well. In 2008, Lyric Street launched a subsidiary imprint, Carolwood Records, but announced the label would close in November 2009. Carolwood acts Love and Theft and Trent Tomlinson transferred to Lyric Street. The Nashville label also handled Disney album releases for country star Billy Ray Cyrus and worked in the country market for his daughter, Disney actress and pop recording artist Miley Cyrus. In April 2010 the label announced a phased closure, with a few acts remaining in the Disney Music Group. Subsequently, Rascal Flatts signed with Big Machine Records. —*Michael McCall*

# Extra! Read All About It!

## The Literature of Country Music

### NOLAN PORTERFIELD

Country music fans aren't known for being particularly bookish. "I only read when I want to think," says a gravelly voice overheard in a dim Nashville bar, "and that ain't often." Reading what was written about country music for many years—well into the 1960s—didn't require (or provoke) much thought. For decades after "hillbilly" music emerged in the 1920s, what got into print was mostly sarcasm in urban newspapers and popular magazines, fanzine puffery, and occasional three-paragraph artist "profiles" that filled space in song-lyric magazines such as *Country Song Roundup* and *Cowboy Songs*. Serious commentary and historical accuracy were conspicuously absent.

In 1935 Carrie Rodgers wrote the first "life story" of a country star, *My Husband, Jimmie Rodgers*; Ruth Sheldon's *Hubbin' It: The Life of Bob Wills* followed three years later. Both were privately published, highly romanticized, and less than reliable, appealing not so much to a general audience as to those who were already committed fans of America's Blue Yodeler and the King of Western Swing. Their historical value, however, is such that they are still consulted by scholars and still available, more than seventy-five years later, in reprinted editions from the Country Music Foundation Press.

By the 1960s, country music was outgrowing its cornbread-and-coondog image and reaching a broader, more diverse audience. As the Denim Chic crowd, hip academics, and the national media began tuning in, serious writers and scholars turned their attention to pickers 'n' singers past and present, producing at first a small trickle of books and articles that in recent years has become a steady stream. A groundbreaking event was the 1965 "Hillbilly Issue" of the *Journal of American Folklore*, devoted entirely to the history and sources of country music, with articles by such pioneering scholars as Archie Green, Norman Cohen, L. Mayne Smith, Ed Kahn, and D. K. Wilgus. A year later came *The Country Music Story* by *New York Times* writer Robert Shelton, the first of many illustrated histories. Now out of print, *The Country Music Story* was an important work, despite errors and omissions, and it remains valuable for its many rare photographs.

The one book every fan and student of country music should own first appeared in 1968. Bill C. Malone's *Country Music U.S.A.* immediately established itself as the definitive history, well written, thoroughly researched, and exhaustively documented. This is the book that took country music from the realm of mere popular culture and made it intellectually respectable; the publication of revised and expanded editions in 1985, 2002, and 2010 further confirmed it as the most comprehensive and authoritative work on the subject yet available. Other useful histories include *Country Roots* (1976) by Douglas B. Green ("Ranger Doug" of Riders in the Sky) and *The Illustrated History of Country Music* (1979). Green's book is no longer in print, but an updated edition of The *Illustrated History of Country Music* was published in 1995. The Country Music Foundation's whopping *Country: The Music and the Musicians* (595 pages in its original 1988 edition, covering the subject from its beginnings) features a wealth of photographs and incisive essays by the cream of country music writers and scholars, as does its successor, the Foundation-produced *Will the Circle Be Broken: Country Music in America* (2006). Both are intriguingly written and serve as valuable sourcebooks.

With increasing scholarly interest in country music came the need for basic reference works—indexes, directories, encyclopedias, and the like. A pioneering effort was *A History and Encyclopedia of Country, Western, and Gospel Music*, privately printed by Linnell Gentry in 1961 and updated in 1969. Unfortunately, Gentry's book is long out of print and is available in few libraries.

In pursuit of the "Big Picture" in the 1970s and 1980s there came a spate of books and would-be "encyclopedias," many of which were well intended but error laden and more glitter than gold. These included Irwin Stambler and Grelun Landon's *Encyclopedia of Folk, Country & Western Music*; *The Harmony Illustrated Encyclopedia of Country Music* by Fred Dellar, Roy Thompson, and Douglas B. Green; and Barry McCloud's *Definitive Country: The Ultimate Encyclopedia of Country Music and Its Performers*, all now dated or out of print. Still available is *Country Music* magazine's *Comprehensive Country Music Encyclopedia*, which is well illustrated and more reliable than most. Each of these and similar reference works is strong in certain areas and weak in others, and anyone in search of comprehensiveness and accuracy would do well to consult as many as possible.

The earliest periodicals dealing with country music were fan-club newsletters and cheaply printed (sometimes mimeographed) little magazines, such as *Country and Western Spotlight* and *Disc Collector*, which circulated among record collectors interested mostly in old-time artists and obscure recording data. In 1965 the John Edwards Memorial Foundation began issuing a newsletter that soon evolved into the more substantial *JEMF Quarterly*, an early forum for country music scholarship.

It was joined in 1971 by two other important periodicals, the *Journal of Country Music*, published by the Country Music Foundation, and Tony Russell's *Old Time Music*, which was edited and printed in England, attesting to the international appeal of American country music, since it was devoted almost entirely to vintage artists on this side of the Atlantic. The following year there appeared *Country Music* magazine, a newsstand slick aimed at a more popular audience. Regrettably, all four have ceased publication, *JEMF Quarterly* in 1985, *Old Time Music* in 1989, *Country Music* in 2003, and the *Journal of Country Music* in 2007. Shamefully, country music scholars are left without a regular outlet for news and views on the subject. Back issues of these departed publications, however, offer a rich reference treasure for those who kept subscription copies or have access to the few libraries that acquired them.

It has been said that we live in the age of biography. Certainly the lives of country artists, old and new, have gotten their share of scrutiny in the past thirty years or so. By interesting coincidence, the subjects of the two earliest books back in the 1930s—Bob Wills and Jimmie Rodgers—were the first to get serious scholarly attention. Charles Townsend's 1976 biography of Wills, *San Antonio Rose*, is a landmark work that at once solidified Wills's reputation and broke new ground in detailing his life and career. On the downside, Townsend's objectivity was sometimes clouded by his reverence for his subject, leading to distortions and exaggerations that later scholars have sought to correct. Nevertheless, *San Antonio Rose* remains an important work and ought to be in every country fan's library. It is still available in paperback, issued in 1986. My own contribution to the genre, *Jimmie Rodgers: The Life and Times of America's Blue Yodeler* (originally published in 1979), took considerable inspiration from Townsend's pioneering effort and was aimed at producing an accurate and detailed account for a general audience. Whether I succeeded is for the reader to decide, but that book also remains in print, with a new introduction, published in 2007. Rodgers's reputation was further burnished in 2009 with the publication of Barry Mazor's *Meeting Jimmie Rodgers*, which diligently chronicles Rodgers's influence on everyone from the young GENE AUTRY to BOB DYLAN, Odetta, and the Blasters. Jocelyn Neal, a musicologist at the University of North Carolina, in *The Songs of Jimmie Rodgers*, offers in-depth analysis of three of the best-known Rodgers songs and commentary on sixteen more. This volume provides a welcome addition to our understanding of Rodgers's genius and is a good read as well.

Jimmie Rodgers also makes a few walk-on appearances in the invaluable *Will You Miss Me When I'm Gone? The Carter Family & Their Legacy in American Music* (2002), by Mark Zwonitzer with Charles Hirshberg. It's a thorough, engrossing, and well-written account of one of country music's First Families, but it is also flawed by the absence of an index or citation of any sources, a serious impediment to readers and scholars alike.

At least three other country music "immortals"— HANK WILLIAMS, LEFTY FRIZZELL, and ERNEST TUBB—have been well served by their biographers. There are many books dealing with the tragedy and glory of Hank Williams, but the two that clearly stand out are *Sing a Sad Song* by Roger Williams (no relation) and, especially, Colin Escott's *Hank Williams: The Biography*. Roger Williams's book established a solid reputation when it appeared back in the 1970s, but the addition of an excellent discography by Bob Pinson in a 1981 reissue gave it a permanent place on any country music bookshelf. Fourteen years later, Escott, whose work is always knowledgeable and interesting, sought to unearth new material and reinvigorate the Hank Williams legend, and his biography is a testament to his success. Lefty Frizzell's story waited a long time for a writer to do it justice but finally found one in Daniel Cooper, whose *Lefty Frizzell* is among the most solid, engaging, and entertaining country biographies. Ronnie Pugh, a long-time expert on Ernest Tubb, put all his research into definitive book form; *Ernest Tubb: The Texas Troubadour* is a volume every country fan should have.

Holly George-Warren's superb *Public Cowboy No. 1: The Life and Times of Gene Autry* (2007) is the definitive account of the singing cowboy whose movies and TV shows reached millions of all ages for decades. A valuable supplement to George-Warren's book is the late Johnny Bond's *Thirty Years on the Road with Gene Autry: Recollections*. Almost all of the warbling shoot-'em-up heroes get detailed attention in *Singing in the Saddle*, by Douglas B. Green (2003).

Another important historical figure who finally received the attention he deserved is Milton Brown. In *Milton Brown and the Founding of Western Swing*, Cary Ginell chronicles Brown's role as the innovator whose jazzy style and repertoire, pre–Bob Wills, was the original force behind western swing. Ginell is obviously a partisan, but his case is well documented and his book a welcome corrective to the extravagant claims made for Wills. Also historically important to country music, if less influential, was the career of DeFord Bailey, for years a popular member of the Grand Ole Opry and the only prominent black professional in country music prior to Charley Pride. His story is set down honestly and sympathetically in *DeFord Bailey: A Black Star in Early Country Music* (1991), by David C. Morton, in collaboration with Charles K. Wolfe. Other useful, appealing biographies of historical figures include Elizabeth Schlappi's *Roy Acuff* (one of the more evenhanded fan-written biographies, available in a new edition since 1993); Gene Wiggins's story of Fiddlin' John Carson, *Fiddlin' Georgia Crazy*; and Ivan Tribe's *The Stoneman Family*, the history of one of country music's founding families.

Since the 1970s, biographies of contemporary stars—mostly glitzy rip-offs—have been pouring from the presses. Among the few worthy of attention are Joe Nick Patoski's *Willie Nelson: An Epic Life*; Margaret Jones's *Patsy: The Life and Times of Patsy Cline*; Bob Allen's *George Jones: The Saga of an American Singer*; Steve Eng's *A Satisfied Mind: The Country Music Life of Porter Wagoner*; Jonny Whiteside's *Ramblin' Rose: The Life and Career of Rose Maddox*; Diane Diekman's *Live Fast, Love Hard: The Faron Young Story*; Michael Streissguth's *Eddy Arnold*: *Pioneer of the Nashville Sound*, *Johnny Cash: The Biography*, and *Always Been There: Rosanne Cash, the List, and the Spirit of Southern Music*; and Alanna Nash's *The Colonel: The Extraordinary Story of Colonel Tom Parker and Elvis Presley*.

Although Elvis belongs to rock & roll, every fan should know about his country roots. Books about the King would fill a small library, but there are only two that reach the level of serious biography: Peter Guralnick's excellent *Last Train to Memphis* and *Careless Love*, together chronicling the influential performer's career.

Then there's Country Music Bizarro, the parallel literary universe where the stars of today write books about their own lives, or pretend to, and turn them into best-sellers. To the casual reader, a biography and an autobiography are pretty much the same thing. Each is the story of someone's life, and who cares who tells it, right? But, as Mark Twain almost said, the difference between biography and autobiography is the difference between lightning and the lightning bug. When celebrities sit down to write about their troubled-life-and-times—or, more often, make a tape for an "as told to" coauthor—the result is often an exercise in ego-tripping, self-justification, revenge on ex-spouses, and shallow pontificating on the Meaning of Life. But these are the country music books the public knows best—in recent decades bookstores and best seller lists across the nation have been flooded with "as told to" autobiographies of wildly varying quality by the likes of Hank Williams Jr., Willie Nelson, Waylon Jennings, Merle Haggard, Charley Pride, Gene Autry, Reba McEntire, Naomi Judd, and others.

In many respects the first of them was the best—Loretta Lynn's *Coal Miner's Daughter* (1976), a literary sleeper and source for the hit movie of the same name, one of the finest country music films yet made. Credit coauthor George Vecsey for much of the book's success, but he wisely preserved Lynn's artless candor and her feisty (if sometimes irritating) voice. *Coal Miner's Daughter* records a vital slice of country music history as well as capturing the inner life of its subject. Published more than thirty years ago, it has recently been reissued by Da Capo Press.

Equally valuable for many of the same reasons and also back in print is the 1977 autobiography of Alton Delmore of the Delmore Brothers, *Truth Is Stranger Than Publicity*. As a relic of an earlier time, the Delmore book is less trendy than *Coal Miner's Daughter* and unlikely to spawn a movie of any kind, but it is both an honest, illuminating record of human experience and a rare source of information about the country music business in its first three decades. It includes notes, commentary, and discography by the ubiquitous country music scholar Charles K. Wolfe, who was largely responsible for unearthing Delmore's unpublished and forgotten manuscript. The authentic voice and experiences of another country music mainstay were preserved in *The Hank Snow Story*.

A few country celebrities have had the talent and courage to go it alone and write about themselves without the crutch of a coauthor. Their books tend to be a cut above the rest; see, for example, Tom T. Hall's *A Storyteller's Nashville*, Skeeter Davis's *Bus Fare to Kentucky*, Dolly Parton's *Dolly*, Bill Anderson's *Whisperin' Bill*, and even Johnny Cash's book-length sermon *Man in Black* ("'God's Superstar' tells his own story in his own words"). *Cash: An Autobiography* (1997) covers some of the same ground but adds interesting new dimensions, never-before-published photos, and the graceful prose of coauthor Patrick Carr. Among "as told to" collaborators, the most prolific and probably the best is journalist Tom Carter, who has wielded the pen for Reba McEntire, George Jones, Glen Campbell, Ronnie Milsap, and Ralph Emery. (Emery's *Memories* is valuable reading; forget the sequel, *More Memories*).

Country music books of a general nature aimed at a national audience can be traced back to journalist Paul Hemphill's *The Nashville Sound*, a lively anecdotal account of the Music City scene in the late 1960s. It was reissued in paperback in 1975 and again in 2005. The most engrossing of all efforts to catch the scope and flavor of country music is Nick Tosches's eccentric, irreverent *Country: The Twisted Roots of Rock 'N' Roll* (originally subtitled *The Biggest Music in America* when first published in 1977), full of obscure detail, written with wit and great precision. Briefly available in a revised 1985 paperback, *Country* is now back in print in paperback, updated with a couple of appendices. Covering the general ground in another fashion, *The Country Reader* presents some of the best writing and photos that appeared in the *Journal of Country Music*. Subject and author indexes to twenty-five years of *JCM* are an added bonus. Like Tosches's book, it belongs in the library of anyone interested in country music.

Regional styles and subgenres are the subjects of several important books, such as Charles K. Wolfe's *Tennessee Strings*, *Kentucky Country*, and *The Devil's Box: Masters of Southern Fiddling*. Wolfe was one of country music's preeminent scholars and the most prolific; any work with his name on it deserves serious attention. Bill Malone and David Stricklin's *Southern Music, American Music*, which examines the role of the South as a source of musical styles, is a valuable treatise as well, and so are his *Don't Get Above Your Raisin': Country Music and the Southern Working Class* and *Singing Cowboys and Musical Mountaineers: Southern Culture and the Roots of Country Music*. Barry Jean Ancelet and Elmore Morgan Jr.'s *Cajun and Creole Music Makers* is an essential work on that subject. *Ye Yaille, Chere!: Traditional Cajun Dance Music*, by Raymond Francois, includes 247 transcribed songs. Neil Rosenberg's *Bluegrass: A History* has just about everything one needs to know about the development of that rich and pervasive musical form; if further analysis interests you, go to *Bluegrass Breakdown* by Robert Cantwell, a subjective and more theoretical approach, and *The Music of Bill Monroe*, by Neil Rosenberg and Charles K. Wolfe. Western swing is covered by the Townsend and Ginell books cited earlier, while another vital phenomenon of the Southwest's early music scene is chronicled in *Border Radio* by Gene Fowler and Bill Crawford. Also valuable as an account of an especially fertile region is Joe Carr and Alan Munde's *Prairie Nights to Neon Lights: The Story of Country Music in West Texas*. Until the focus shifted to Nashville, Atlanta could lay claim to being country music's capital; for an account of that city's key role in the early years, see Wayne W. Daniel's excellent *Pickin' on Peachtree*. Michael Ann Williams's *Staging Tradition: John Lair and Sarah Gertrude Knott* (2006) is the best book on Lair's Renfro Valley Barn Dance, encompassing as well Lair and Knott's diverse attitudes about "keeping it country." Also useful is Pete Stamper's earlier *It All Happened in Renfro Valley*.

The role—and plight—of women in country music is narrated at length by Mary Bufwack and Robert Oermann in *Finding Her Voice: The Saga of Women in Country Music*, the first comprehensive study of this much-neglected topic. Bulging with biographical information and social commentary, *Finding Her Voice* is both exhaustive and exhausting, but it stands as an important reference work, with a large and valuable bibliography. It is now available in a second edition, with the subtitle changed to *Women in Country Music 1800–2000*. A more specialized aspect of the subject can be found in Kristine M. McCusker's *Lonesome Cowgirls and Honky-Tonk Angels: The Women of Barn Dance Radio* (2008).

In 2007, Diane Pecknold published *The Selling Sound: The Rise of the Country Music Industry*, an important and unique work that surveys the growth of the industry in the context of evolving media amid changing economic and social conditions. Pecknold systematically examines the roles that fans have played in the maturing of country as a business.

As an enduring institution, the Grand Ole Opry has inspired a veritable horde of pseudo-histories, picture books, and souvenir programs, but until recently few were of much lasting value, except as curiosities out of the past. Jack Hurst's 1975 *Nashville's Grand Ole Opry*, now out of print, was an elephantine picture book redeemed by its lucid prose and "official" photos from Opry files. Next came Chet Hagan's detailed but not very reliable popular account, *Grand Ole Opry* (1989), and then *The Grand Ole Opry History of Country Music* (1995) by Paul Kingsbury, which is accurate, well written, and beautifully packaged. But for a history of the Opry's early years, 1925–1940, nothing surpasses Charles K. Wolfe's *A Good Natured Riot: The Birth of the Grand Ole Opry*. With the possible exception of Wolfe's book, you won't find much about the dark side of the Opry—personal or commercial—in any of these books, and, as with country music "encyclopedias," a serious reader may need them all.

More recently, serious scholars have moved from history and genre to sociocultural issues in country music, producing highly evolved academic studies such as Cecelia Tichi's *High Lonesome: The American Culture of Country Music* (1994) and Curtis Ellison's *Country Music Culture: From Hard Times to Heaven* (1995). Tichi traces various country & western themes and motifs through other American art forms—poetry, novels, paintings, etc.—to argue that country music is the force behind our national culture. Unfortunately, her knowledge of country music is rather slight, and her conclusion is not radically different from ideas set forth in more restrained fashion by Malone and Stricklin in *Southern Music, American Music*, but her analyses are provocative. Like Tichi, Ellison ranges far and wide through intellectual jungle and plain, using institutions, traditions, interviews, and song texts to explore the interplay between country music and a broad flow of social and cultural currents. *Country Music Culture* shows a firm grasp of the subject and is written with grace and authority.

The issue of "authenticity" seems to be a hot topic these days. It is dealt with at length in the late Richard Peterson's *Creating Country Music: Fabricating Authenticity* (1997), although Peterson's view is that of an academic sociologist. Perhaps more accessible is *The Nashville Sound: Authenticity, Commercialization and Country Music* (1998), by Joli Jensen.

Focusing more narrowly on country song texts, Dorothy Horstman's *Sing Your Heart Out, Country Boy* tells the stories behind hundreds of favorite country songs and how they were written. Addressed to a rather popular audience, it has proved no less compelling to scholars over the years since it first appeared in 1975. Reissued in 1996 in a new, expanded edition, *Sing Your Heart Out* contains an extensive discography and bibliography.

Perhaps the most serious impediment to country music research and scholarship for years was the lack of a truly comprehensive discography, on the order of Brian Rust's jazz and dance band discographies. That lacuna began to be filled—magnificently—in 2004 when Oxford University Press published Tony Russell's 1,183-page *Country Music Records: A Discography, 1921–1942*, the product of some thirty years of research and labor.

When all else is said and done—picture books, artists' biographies, social studies, lyrical analyses—the songs themselves remain. Where does one go to find out how country songs ranked as hits through the years and where to find them? Start with Joel Whitburn's *Hot Country Songs* (2008), which has every song that reached *Billboard*'s country charts between 1944 and 2008, with separate listings for titles and artists and a bundle of fascinating statistical trivia. Most impressive of all is the Country Music Foundation's *Country on Compact Disc* (1993), containing reviews and rankings for more than 2,000 CDs, arranged alphabetically by artists (with a special section on various-artists' compilations). In addition to separate listings of the highest-ranked CDs by artist, album title, and record company, there's an especially useful appendix of *Billboard*'s #1 country hits from 1944 to 1992, showing which songs were issued on CD and the discs they're found on. The imposing list of contributors includes many of the people who've written seriously about country music in the past thirty years. This guide will be a standard reference work for a long time to come.

## SIXTY BOOKS TOWARD A COUNTRY MUSIC LIBRARY

Although many bad books have been written about country music, the number of good ones runs into the dozens. Almost every book about country music—even the trashiest—is interesting in one way or another and adds something to our knowledge of the subject. Nonetheless, distinctions have to be made. I have the presumption to offer the following list as a thorough yet manageable survey of the publications that anyone who follows country music, for fun, knowledge, or profit, should know about. The list is admittedly subjective and to some degree arbitrary. A few historically important works are conspicuously absent because they are no longer readily available; others, old and new, fell by the wayside only in the interests of some reasonable limit to the list. Finally, the inclusion of certain entries will no doubt be the source of lasting—but, one hopes, profitable—dispute.

## GENERAL WORKS

The Editors of *Country Music* Magazine. *The Comprehensive Country Music Encyclopedia.* New York: Times Books, 1994.

Country Music Foundation. *Country: The Music and the Musicians from the Beginnings to the '90s,* rev. ed. Edited by Paul Kingsbury and Alan Axelrod. New York: Abbeville Press, 1994.

Horstman, Dorothy. *Sing Your Heart Out, Country Boy,* 3rd ed. Nashville: Country Music Foundation Press, 1996.

Kingsbury, Paul, ed. *The Country Reader: Twenty-five Years of the Journal of Country Music.* Nashville: Country Music Foundation Press and Vanderbilt University Press, 1996.

Kingsbury, Paul, and Alanna Nash, eds. *Will the Circle Be Unbroken: Country Music in America.* New York and other cities: DK Publishing, 2006.

Malone, Bill C. *Country Music U.S.A.,* 3rd rev. ed. Austin: University of Texas Press, 2010.

Tosches, Nick. *Country: The Twisted Roots of Rock 'N' Roll,* 3rd ed. New York: Da Capo Press, 1996.

## REFERENCE WORKS

Jones, Loyal. *Country Music Humorists and Comedians.* Urbana: University of Illinois Press, 2008.

Meade, Guthrie T., Jr., Dick Spottswood, and Douglas S. Meade. *Country Music Sources: A Biblio-Discography of Commercially Recorded Traditional Music.* Chapel Hill: The Southern Folklife Collection, University of North Carolina at Chapel Hill Library, in association with the John Edwards Memorial Forum, 2002.

Russell, Tony. *Country Music Originals: The Legends and the Lost.* New York: Oxford University Press, 2007.

Russell, Tony, with editorial research by Bob Pinson, assisted by the staff of the Country Music Hall of Fame and Museum. *Country Music Records: A Discography, 1921–1942.* New York: Oxford University Press, 2004.

## AUTOBIOGRAPHY

Cash, Johnny, with Patrick Carr. *Cash: The Autobiography.* San Francisco: Harper, 1997.

Delmore, Alton. *Truth Is Stranger Than Publicity,* rev. ed. Nashville: Country Music Foundation Press, 1995.

Emery, Ralph, with Tom Carter. *Memories: The Autobiography of Ralph Emery.* New York: Macmillan Publishing, 1991.

Jennings, Waylon, with Lenny Kaye. *Waylon: An Autobiography.* New York: Warner Books, 1996.

Lee, Brenda, with Robert K. Oermann and Julie Clay. *Little Miss Dynamite: The Life and Times of Brenda Lee.* New York: Hyperion, 2002.

Parton, Dolly. *Dolly: My Life and Other Unfinished Business.* New York: HarperCollins, 1994.

Stanley, Dr. Ralph, with Eddie Dean. *Man of Constant Sorrow: My Life and Times.* New York: Gotham Books, 2009.

Snow, Hank, with Jack Ownbey and Bob Burris. *The Hank Snow Story.* Urbana: University of Illinois Press, 1994.

## BIOGRAPHY

Allen, Bob. *George Jones: The Saga of an American Singer.* Garden City, NY: Doubleday & Co., 1984; rev., updated, and republished as *George Jones: The Life and Times of a Honky Tonk Legend.* New York: Birch Lane Press, 1994.

Bond, Johnny. *Thirty Years on the Road with Gene Autry: Recollections*. Burbank, CA: Riverwood Press and the Beverly and Jim Rogers Museum of Lone Pine Film History, 2007.

Cooper, Daniel. *Lefty Frizzell: The Honky-Tonk Life of Country Music's Greatest Singer*. New York: Little, Brown and Company, 1995.

Escott, Colin, with George Merritt and William MacEwen. *Hank Williams: The Biography*. New York: Little, Brown and Company, 1994.

George-Warren, Holly. *Public Cowboy No. 1: The Life and Times of Gene Autry*. New York: Oxford University Press, 2007.

Ginell, Cary. *Milton Brown and the Founding of Western Swing*. Urbana: University of Illinois Press, 1994.

Guralnick, Peter. *Last Train to Memphis: The Rise of Elvis Presley*. Boston: Little, Brown and Company, 1994.

——. *Careless Love: The Unmaking of Elvis Presley*. Boston: Little, Brown and Company, 1999.

Hemphill, Paul. *Lovesick Blues: The Life of Hank Williams*. New York: Viking, 2005.

Jones, Louis M. "Grandpa," with Charles K. Wolfe. *Everybody's Grandpa: Fifty Years Behind the Mike*. Knoxville: University of Tennessee Press, 1984.

Jones, Margaret. *Patsy: The Life and Times of Patsy Cline*. New York: HarperCollins, 1994; Boston: Da Capo Press, 2007.

Patoski, Joe Nick. *Willie Nelson: An Epic Life*. Boston: Little, Brown and Company, 2008.

Porterfield, Nolan. *Jimmie Rodgers: The Life and Times of America's Blue Yodeler*. Urbana: University of Illinois Press, 1979; rev. ed. 1992, with new introduction. Jackson: University Press of Mississippi, 2007.

Pugh, Ronnie. *Ernest Tubb: The Texas Troubadour*. Durham, NC: Duke University Press, 1996.

Schlappi, Elizabeth. *Roy Acuff: The Smoky Mountain Boy*, 2nd ed. Gretna, LA: Pelican, 1993.

Sheldon, Ruth. *Bob Wills: Hubbin' It*, rev. ed. Nashville: Country Music Foundation Press, 1995.

Smith, Richard D. *Can't You Hear Me Callin': The Life of Bill Monroe, Father of Bluegrass*. Boston: Little, Brown and Company, 2000.

Streissguth, Michael. *Eddy Arnold: Pioneer of the Nashville Sound*. New York: Schirmer Books, 1997.

——. *Johnny Cash: The Biography*. Boston: Da Capo Press, 2006.

Townsend, Charles R. *San Antonio Rose: The Life and Music of Bob Wills*. Urbana: University of Illinois Press, 1976.

Whiteside, Jonny. *Ramblin' Rose: The Life and Career of Rose Maddox*. Nashville: Country Music Foundation Press and Vanderbilt University Press, 1997.

Zwonitzer, Mark, with Charles Hirshberg. *Will You Miss Me When I'm Gone? The Carter Family & Their Legacy in American Music*. New York: Simon & Schuster, 2002.

## REGIONS, TYPES, AND SPECIAL STUDIES

Ancelet, Barry Jean, and Elemore Morgan Jr. *Cajun and Creole Music Makers: Musiciens cadiens et créoles*. Jackson: University Press of Mississippi, 1999.

Bufwack, Mary A., and Robert K. Oermann. *Finding Her Voice: Women in Country Music, 1800–2000*. Nashville: Country Music Foundation Press and Vanderbilt University Press, 2003.

Fowler, Gene, and Bill Crawford. *Border Radio: Quacks, Yodelers, Pitchmen, Psychics, and Other Amazing Broadcasters of the American Airwaves*, rev. ed. Austin: University of Texas Press, 2002.

Havighurst, Craig. *Air Castle of the South: WSM and the Making of Music City*. Urbana: University of Illinois Press, 2007.

Hemphill, Paul. *The Nashville Sound: Bright Lights and Country Music*. New York: Simon & Schuster, 1970; rev. ed. Atlanta: Everthemore Books, 2005.

Huber, Patrick. *Linthead Stomp: The Creation of Country Music in the Piedmont South*. Chapel Hill: University of North Carolina Press, 2008.

Kienzle, Rich. *Southwest Shuffle: Pioneers of Honky-Tonk, Western Swing, and Country Jazz*. New York: Routledge, 2003.

Malone, Bill C., and David Stricklin. *Southern Music, American Music*, rev. ed. Lexington: The University Press of Kentucky, 2003.

Mazor, Barry. *Meeting Jimmie Rodgers: How America's Original Roots Music Hero Changed the Pop Sounds of a Century.* New York: Oxford University Press, 2009.

McCusker, Kristine M, and Diane Pecknold, eds. *A Boy Named Sue: Gender and Country Music.* Jackson: University Press of Mississippi, 2004.

Rosenberg, Neil V. *Bluegrass: A History*, Twentieth Anniversary ed. Urbana: University of Illinois Press, 2005.

Williams, Michael Ann. *Staging Tradition: John Lair and Sarah Gertrude Knott.* Urbana: University of Illinois Press, 2006.

Wolfe, Charles K. *The Devil's Box: Masters of Southern Fiddling.* Nashville: Country Music Foundation Press and Vanderbilt University Press, 1997.

——. *A Good-Natured Riot: The Birth of the Grand Ole Opry.* Nashville: Country Music Foundation Press and Vanderbilt University Press, 1999.

## SCHOLARLY ANALYSES

Ellison, Curtis. *Country Music Culture: From Hard Times to Heaven.* Jackson: University Press of Mississippi, 1995.

Fox, Aaron A. *Real Country: Music and Language in Working Class Culture.* Durham, NC: Duke University Press, 2004.

Neal, Jocelyn R. *The Songs of Jimmie Rodgers: A Legacy in Country Music.* Bloomington and Indianapolis: Indiana University Press, 2009.

Malone, Bill C. *Don't Get Above Your Raisin': Country Music and the Southern Working Class.* Urbana: University of Illinois Press, 2002.

Pecknold, Diane. *The Selling Sound: The Rise of the Country Music Industry.* Durham, NC: Duke University Press, 2007.

## RECORD GUIDES

Cantwell, David, and Bill Friskics-Warren. *Heartaches by the Number: Country Music's 500 Greatest Singles.* Nashville: Vanderbilt University Press, 2002.

Bogdanov, Vladimir, Chris Woodstra, and Stephen Thomas Erlewine, eds. *All Music Guide to Country: The Definitive Guide to Country Music*, 2nd ed. San Francisco: Backbeat Books, 2003.

## M. M. Cole Publishing
established in Chicago, Illinois, February 1930

Born ca. 1893, company founder Morris M. Cole was raised in New York City but moved to Chicago as a young man; there he became a sundries salesman. Soon he invested with a brother-in-law in a near-bankrupt music store, and afterward he started his own wholesale firm, Illinois Music Jobber.

By February 1930 Cole had sold his jobbing business and formed M. M. Cole Publishing, the Chicago company that became his most successful endeavor and one to which he devoted himself until his death on August 19, 1958.

M. M. Cole's product line, which benefited greatly from sales in major mail-order retailers' catalogs, ran the gamut from musical instruction publications to sheet music to SONGBOOKS. The latter were often associated with country stars, including GENE AUTRY, Cliff Carlisle (see BILL CARLISLE), and RED FOLEY. Other songbooks featured songs of multiple performers on particular barn dance radio shows. The company also printed generic folios of folk songs, such as *Play and Sing: America's Greatest Collection of Old Time Songs and Mountain Ballads* (1930), possibly Cole's first effort. The firm's music licensing agreements were with SESAC until 1940, when M. M. Cole, along with subsidiaries Calumet Music and others, became some of the first song publishers to affiliate with the newly formed BMI.

As an accessory to the firm's publishing interests, the M. M. Cole transcription library was active in the 1940s. This service provided fresh Cole-recorded product for radio use via subscription, and its artists included such Chicago-based talent as REX ALLEN, Rusty Gill, and Judy Martin.

In January 1965 ABC-Paramount purchased the M. M. Cole catalog of song copyrights, including such standards as "That Silver Haired Daddy of Mine," "Mexicali Rose," and "Old Shep." MCA's publishing arm acquired the bulk of the Cole catalog through purchasing ABC-Paramount in January 1979. At this writing the copyrights are administered by the Universal Music Group, successor to MCA. —*Bob Pinson*

## Mac & Bob
Lester "Mac" McFarland b. Gray, Kentucky, February 2, 1902; d. July 24, 1984
Robert A. Gardner b. Oliver Springs, Tennessee, December 16, 1897;
     d. September 30, 1978

Stylistically, Mac & Bob reflect country music's roots in nineteenth-century popular song. Their repertoire featured primarily sentimental and sacred material; their vocals were precise and clearly enunciated, with none of the modality, syncopation, or blues inflections favored by many of their contemporaries. Not surprisingly,

the duo was popular with older listeners, who remembered hearing such music in the parlors of a bygone America.

Both blind from birth, Lester McFarland and Robert Gardner met in 1915 while attending the Kentucky School for the Blind in Louisville. A musical prodigy, McFarland played piano, mandolin, cornet, trombone, and other instruments; he taught Gardner how to play guitar. They formed their professional partnership in 1922; Gardner played guitar and sang lead, while McFarland played mandolin and sang tenor.

By 1925 they were appearing on WNOX–Knoxville, and their popularity led to a BRUNSWICK recording contract in 1926. "When the Roses Bloom Again" was a significant hit. Later successes included "I'm Tying the Leaves So They Won't Come Down," "Twenty-one Years," and "'Tis Sweet to Be Remembered." The team also recorded gospel numbers for Brunswick as members of the Smoky Mountain Sacred Singers and the Old Southern Sacred Singers.

In 1931 the duo moved to Chicago, where they were featured on the WLS *NATIONAL BARN DANCE* as Mac & Bob. In the late 1930s they worked on KDKA–Pittsburgh and KMA–Shenandoah, Iowa, before returning to WLS in 1939. The musical partners dissolved their act in 1950, when Gardner decided to devote his time to a Chicago religious mission. McFarland continued at WLS, first with KARL & HARTY and then as a soloist. He left broadcasting in 1953 to work in Chicago State Hospital's recreation department. The two men reunited for special occasions, including a 1964 WGN-TV appearance honoring the *National Barn Dance*'s fortieth anniversary. —*Dave Samuelson*

## Bill Mack
b. Shamrock, Texas, June 4, 1929

A country broadcaster since the late 1940s, Bill Mack, a.k.a. The Midnight Cowboy, also enjoyed success as a singer, songwriter, and producer. Early STARDAY recordings, especially "Kitty Cat" and "The Cat Just Got in Town," represent Texas ROCKABILLY at its best. Later country recordings for several labels, including Starday, HICKORY, MGM, and United Artists, garnered moderate attention. Mack has been more successful as a songwriter. His "Drinking Champagne" was a hit twice—for CAL SMITH in 1968 and for GEORGE STRAIT in 1990. LEANN RIMES's recording of "Blue," originally written and recorded by Mack in 1959, was a 1996 sensation.

Mack's far-reaching, midnight-to-morning trucking show, launched in 1969 over powerful Fort Worth, Texas, station WBAP, gave him his nickname, "The Midnight Cowboy," and provided some of country radio's most creative programming, including diverse playlists, a variety of guests, trucker call-ins, and nationwide information on weather and road conditions. Eventually the program

(*The Bill Mack Show*) moved to XM Satellite Radio's Open Road channel and then to SiriusXM's Willie's Place channel. Mack resigned from SiriusXM in 2011. Mack also hosts the two-hour gospel music program *Sunday Social* on Willie's Place. His syndicated country music inspirational program *Country Crossroads*, begun in 1969, is now heard on more than 800 stations, and he has been hosting *Country Crossroads* on FamilyNet cable television since 1993. In 2004 he published *Bill Mack's Memories from the Trenches of Broadcasting*. —*William P. Davis*

## Warner Mack
b. Nashville, Tennessee, April 2, 1935

Country traditionalist singer-songwriter Warner McPherson appeared regularly on the charts through the 1960s and early 1970s. He became Warner Mack when his nickname was inadvertently used in place of his last name on a record label. He grew up in Vicksburg, Mississippi, and began performing while still in high school. After gaining experience in clubs and radio, he moved on to the *Louisiana Hayride* and the *Ozark Jubilee*. During this time he recorded one of his own compositions, "Is It Wrong (For Loving You)," for the Decca label. The pop-sounding release not only reached #9 in 1958 and remained on the country charts for nine months but also became a hit for two other artists: Webb Pierce (#11, 1960) and Sonny James (#1, 1974). On November 29, 1964, in a snowstorm near Princeton, Indiana, Mack was involved in a serious car accident that set his career back several months.

After a six-year career lull, Mack bounced back with "Sittin' in an All Nite Cafe" (#4, 1965) and followed with his biggest hit, "The Bridge Washed Out" (#1, 1965). He continued to chart regularly into 1974, though with considerably diminished impact after 1970. He also wrote Ricky Van Shelton's 1995 Top Ten single "After the Lights Go Down." —*Don Roy*

## Uncle Dave Macon
b. Smart Station, Warren County, Tennessee, October 7, 1870; d. March 22, 1952

Nicknamed the Dixie Dewdrop by Grand Ole Opry founder George D. Hay, David Harrison Macon, with his chin whiskers, gold teeth, gates-ajar collar, and open-backed Gibson banjo, was the first substantial star of the Grand Ole Opry and one of the most colorful personalities in the history of American entertainment. He was an influential bridge between the folk and vaudeville music of the nineteenth century and the more modern music of the phonograph record, the radio, and motion pictures. He was a supremely skilled banjo player (modern historians have identified at least nineteen different picking styles on his records), a strong singer, a skilled songwriter, an outrageous comedian, and a dedicated preserver of vintage songs and styles. Above all, he was a master showman, bringing to country music a professionalism and polish that helped to establish it as a viable commercial art form.

Born into a well-to-do family in Warren County, in the central Tennessee hills, Macon began learning local folk songs by the time he was nine. In 1884, following financial reversals after the Civil War, the Macons moved to Nashville, where they ran a hotel on Broadway. By coincidence, the hotel was headquarters for many touring vaudeville performers, and the teenaged Dave Macon watched them as they rehearsed in the basement. He was especially entranced with the various trick banjo players then in vogue,

especially one named Joel Davidson. Soon young Macon had talked his mother into buying him a banjo, and he began to absorb as much as he could from these vaudevillians. But after his father was stabbed and killed in front of the hotel, the family broke up and returned to the country. Dave stayed with his mother, who ran a stagecoach rest stop at Readyville. In charge of watering the horses, young Macon also built a stage on the barn and entertained passengers with his banjo.

Growing up away from Nashville, Macon suppressed any hopes he may have had for a show business career. He married a local girl, inherited a large farm, and opened a freight line between Murfreesboro and Woodbury, Tennessee. But in the 1920s, when a rival company began to compete with trucks, Macon abandoned his faithful mules and thought about retiring (he was over fifty). Then one day when Macon was performing for customers in a Nashville barber shop, he was spotted by a talent scout for the Loew's vaudeville theater chain. Impressed, he offered Macon a job, and, accompanied by local fiddler Sid Harkreader, Macon opened in Birmingham and created a sensation. The tour extended as far north as Boston, and soon Macon established a wide reputation. In July 1924 he went to New York to record for Vocalion. The results were several best-sellers, including "Keep My Skillet Good and Greasy" (a Macon favorite throughout his career), and "Hill Billie Blues."

Macon joined the cast of the WSM *Barn Dance* in 1925—he was one of the first two regulars, along with Uncle Jimmy Thompson—and until The Vagabonds arrived in 1931 Macon was the show's most famous entertainer. Throughout the 1920s, though, he appeared sporadically, finding more money in touring and making records.

From 1924 through 1938, Macon recorded more than 180 songs for almost every major label. He also recorded and performed often with his son Dorris, the remarkable flat-top guitarist Sam McGee, and McGee's brother Kirk. In the 1930s Macon worked

*Uncle Dave Macon*

for a time with the DELMORE BROTHERS as well as with young ROY ACUFF and BILL MONROE. A sharp dresser with a keen sense of humor, Macon frequently delighted his colleagues with his offstage antics. He was a highlight of the 1940 Republic film *Grand Ole Opry*, in which he sang and danced around his banjo to "Take Me Back to My Carolina Home." Other popular Macon favorites include "Bully of the Town," "Late Last Night When Willie Came Home," "(She Was Always) Chewing Gum," "Rock About My Saro Jane" (which he had learned from black stevedores on the Cumberland River in the l880s), "Buddy, Won't You Roll Down the Line," and "Sail Away, Ladies." His signature hymn was "How Beautiful Heaven Must Be," which is carved on his monument near Woodbury, Tennessee.

Though his banjo playing began to suffer in the 1940s, Macon's comedy and singing helped carry him through Opry shows and tours. He was still in the lineup in 1952 when he became ill; he passed away in March of that year. Macon was elected to THE COUNTRY MUSIC HALL OF FAME in 1966. Uncle Dave Macon Days, an annual festival in his honor, has been held in Murfreesboro, Tennessee, since 1978. —*Charles Wolfe*

## Maddox Brothers & Rose

Clifton R. E. Maddox b. Boaz, Alabama, 1912; d. 1949
John Calvin Maddox b. Boaz, Alabama, November 3, 1915; d. July 3, 1968
Fred Roscoe Maddox b. Boaz, Alabama, July 2, 1919; d. October 29, 1992
Kenneth Chalmer (Don) Maddox b. Boaz, Alabama, December 7, 1922
Roselea Arbana Maddox b. Boaz, Alabama, August 15, 1925; d. April 15, 1998
Henry Ford Maddox b. Boaz, Alabama, March 19, 1928; d. June 1974

Touted as the Most Colorful Hillbilly Band in America, the California-based Maddox Brothers & Rose were one of the post-war era's most hard-charging, forward-looking country bands. A family of sharecroppers driven by hard times from their Alabama home in the spring of 1933, they spent three weeks hitchhiking and jumping boxcars to reach California. After four years of migrant farm labor, seventeen-year-old Fred Maddox formed a family band and persuaded a Modesto businessman to sponsor them on local station KTRB—agreeing to the stipulation that the band have a "girl singer."

In 1937, dubbed the Alabama Outlaws and fronted by eleven-year-old Rose (and managed by their strict mother, Lula Maddox), the family hit the airwaves and quickly garnered thousands of fan letters. Renamed the Maddox Brothers & Rose by year's end, the band built an avid following with their mix of southern folk music, contemporary western song, and roguish, black-influenced boogie. In 1939 they took first place in a hillbilly band competition at the California State Fair, winning a two-year contract for programs broadcast from Sacramento station KFBK over the McClatchy Broadcasting network.

After war broke out and the brothers shipped overseas, Rose, at Lula's behest, entered into a short-lived marriage that produced a son, Donnie, but the union broke up before the child was born. In December 1945, the band (now working without firstborn Cliff due to a mother-son rift) returned to the airwaves at Stockton's KGDM and soon were recording for FOUR STAR RECORDS. They hired rodeo tailor NATHAN TURK (who supplied wardrobe for Western stars GENE AUTRY and ROY ROGERS) to create some of the most elaborate and striking costumes worn by a country music act to date. The Maddoxes' unorthodox, high-volume HONKY-TONK MUSIC was matched by their legendary show-and-dance presentation—a fast-paced blend of gags, magic tricks, jokes, and pantomime; each member had a special stage nickname ("Cal the

*Maddox Brothers & Rose*

Laughing Cowboy," "Friendly Henry, the Workin' Girl's Friend"). Records such as "Alimony," "Single Girl," and "Hangover Blues" established Rose as an independent, almost protofeminist figure, and by the time the family guested on the GRAND OLE OPRY in February 1949, she was possibly the leading national female star in country music.

In 1950, disgusted with the abysmal financial arrangements at Four Star (the group was never paid by owner Bill McCall), the Maddoxes were freed of their contract through union intervention. They promptly answered Uncle ART SATHERLEY's call to sign with COLUMBIA. Although Rose was so popular that by the mid-1950s Columbia held three separate contracts on her (one with her brothers, one as a single, and one as a short-lived duet act with her sister-in-law), Satherley's retirement (in 1952), succeeding-producer DON LAW's desire to tone down their sound, and Rose's ambition to cut more pop-slanted records worked against the group. They split up in late 1956 after Rose, with Cal accompanying, made a spectacular return to the Grand Ole Opry in September, as a member. After changing into a risqué, bare-midriff cowgirl suit, Rose hid until her name was called, then appeared to a tumultuous reception to sing "Tall Men." Tensions between California-based and Tennessee-based performers ultimately led to her dismissal (at ROY ACUFF's request) in March 1957.

By 1959 Rose had married club owner Jim Brogdon and had landed a seven-year contract with CAPITOL that produced her biggest chart successes: "Sing a Little Song of Heartache" (#3, 1962–63) and, with BUCK OWENS, "Loose Talk" (#4, 1961). At BILL MONROE's invitation, she also became the first woman to record a BLUEGRASS album (one of five Capitol LPs). However, by 1965 Capitol had dropped her, and her marriage broke up. She cut an album (*Rosie*) at STARDAY in 1967 and continued to record for a variety of independents, but she never regained a high national profile. Nonetheless, Rose's work with her brothers defined California's freewheeling country music style, and she was one of country's most influential performers. —*Jonny Whiteside*

## Tommy Magness
b. Mineral Bluff, Georgia, October 21, 1916; d. October 5, 1971

Thomas Magness fiddled with both the King of Country Music, ROY ACUFF, and the Father of Bluegrass, BILL MONROE. At age sixteen Magness played on WWNC–Asheville, North Carolina. After working at WBT–Charlotte he joined ROY HALL on WDBJ–Roanoke, Virginia, in 1938.

Magness composed the classic fiddle tune "Natural Bridge Blues." In October 1940 he recorded "Mule Skinner Blues" with Monroe, and in January 1947 he cut "Wabash Cannonball" with Acuff in Hollywood, where Magness also made four films with the GRAND OLE OPRY star. Magness recorded the fiddle tune "Black Mountain Rag" with Acuff's Smoky Mountain Boys in January 1949. Although Magness copyrighted his arrangement of the tune, it had been recorded previously by others (including CURLY FOX). Still, it became one of Magness's signature numbers. Other acts Magness worked with include CLYDE MOODY and RENO & SMILEY. In addition, Magness was featured on the Opry and the *RENFRO VALLEY BARN DANCE.* — *Walt Trott*

## Brent Maher
b. Great Bend, Kansas, August 14, 1942

One of the top record producers of the 1980s, Brent Maher produced THE JUDDS and helped place them with RCA RECORDS. In addition, he helped pen Judds hits including "Why Not Me," "Girls Night Out," "Rockin' with the Rhythm of the Rain," and "Born to Be Blue." Through the years, his songs have been recorded by DOTTIE WEST ("A Lesson in Leavin'"), TANYA TUCKER ("Some Kind of Trouble"), KENNY ROGERS, Tina Turner, the FORESTER SISTERS, JO DEE MESSINA, SHELBY LYNNE, and CARL PERKINS. Maher has also written music for television.

In Nashville, Maher apprenticed with MONUMENT RECORDS engineer BILL PORTER and then worked on the West Coast, engineering the initial album for Sly & the Family Stone as well as records for Ike & Tina Turner ("Proud Mary"), the Fifth Dimension ("Aquarius"), and Gladys Knight. Additional engineering credits include one of Duke Ellington's last albums.

Maher returned to MUSIC CITY in 1974 as chief engineer at Creative Workshop, where he contributed to albums by OLIVIA NEWTON-JOHN, LARRY GATLIN, LEON RUSSELL, and ELVIS PRESLEY. In 1978 Maher moved up to coproduce MICHAEL JOHNSON's big pop hit "Bluer Than Blue." Maher's daughter, treated in a Nashville-area hospital by nurse Naomi Judd, introduced her father to the Judds' music via a homemade tape; Maher subsequently brought the act to the attention of JOE GALANTE at RCA Records. Since the Judds' dissolution, Maher has produced Shelby Lynne, KATHY MATTEA, Jo Dee Messina, NICKEL CREEK, and Kenny Rogers.

In 1995 Maher cofounded the Nashville-based label Magnatone Records and served as the label's president until 1996. He owns the Moraine Music Group, a music production and publishing company, which found success with Canadian singer-songwriter Johnny Reid in 2009, when the video for the Reid-Maher song "A Woman Like You" won CMT Canada's 2009

Video of the Year award and Reid took home four additional trophies. —*Bob Millard*

## J. E. Mainer
b. Buncombe County, North Carolina, July 20, 1898; d. June 12, 1971

J. E. Mainer's Mountaineers were the leading Appalachian STRING-BAND of the middle and late 1930s. Joseph Emmett Mainer came from a western North Carolina mountain family and went to work in the cotton mills at an early age. In the early 1920s he settled in Concord, North Carolina, where he organized a band built around his own fiddle for local entertainment. By 1932 this endeavor landed him work at Charlotte radio station WBT under the sponsorship of CRAZY WATER CRYSTALS. In 1935 the Mountaineers included his brother WADE MAINER on banjo, with Zeke Morris and John Love on guitars.

The original band soon split up, but Mainer hired new musicians, most notably SNUFFY JENKINS, George Morris, and Leonard Stokes. Mainer continued to record for BLUEBIRD until 1939 and worked at various southern radio stations. After World War II Mainer became an early artist with KING RECORDS. His prominence faded during the 1950s, but the folk revival renewed interest in his music. He recorded again for King and the Arhoolie, Blue Jay, and Rural Rhythm labels. Mainer continued playing festivals and concerts until his death. —*Ivan M. Tribe*

## Wade Mainer
b. Buncombe County, North Carolina, April 21, 1907; d. September 12, 2011

Wade E. Mainer left his brother J. E.'s original Mainer's Mountaineers in 1936 to forge his own musical career. Wade's band, the Sons of the Mountaineers, worked on radio in Charlotte, Raleigh, Asheville, and Knoxville and turned out numerous BLUEBIRD recordings in a style that could best be labeled as proto-BLUEGRASS. Mainer's own unique two-finger banjo style was supplemented by the work of other musicians, who included at various times Tiny Dodson, Jay Hugh Hall, Steve Ledford, CLYDE MOODY, Zeke Morris, Homer Sherrill, and Jack and Curly Shelton. Through 1941 the Sons of the Mountaineers had nearly ninety numbers released on disc and had entertained at the Roosevelt White House.

Mainer revived his career after World War II, again working on radio and recording for KING. As his style became increasingly dated, he moved to Michigan in 1953 and went to work for General Motors in Flint. For some years thereafter he and his wife, Julia, sang only in churches. After retirement in 1973, Wade and Julia began performing at folk and bluegrass festivals and recorded several new albums for Old Homestead, a firm that also reissued many of his earlier sides. At eighty he won a National Heritage Fellowship, and he released albums as late as 1993. He remained semi-active in the early twenty-first century. —*Ivan M. Tribe*

## Mandolin

Derived from lutes of Renaissance Italy, the mandolin came into its present form as a short-necked instrument with eight paired strings in early eighteenth-century Naples, and it has endured as an important instrument in Italian popular music. Minor composers of the time wrote music for the mandolin; later opera composers, such as Handel, Mozart, and Verdi, scored occasional passages for the instrument when atmospheric touches were needed. Otherwise the mandolin was regarded as a minor-league instrument with limited possibilities.

In the United States, mandolin orchestras, with mandolas, mando-cellos, and even an occasional mando-bass, were a popular feature of community life in many areas during the early twentieth century. A few early recordings were made by soloists Valentine Abt and Samuel Siegel. Giovanni Vicari and Giovanni Gioviale recorded some virtuoso pieces for Italian catalogs in the 1920s. Russian-born Dave Apollon headed a crack mandolin ensemble that toured the vaudeville circuit and made two memorable records for BRUNSWICK in 1932.

Luthier Orville Gibson introduced the flat-backed, scroll-bodied mandolin in 1898. When designer Lloyd Loar introduced his improvement of this design, the Gibson F-series mandolin, in 1923, the model's improved tone and greater volume enhanced the mandolin's appeal, as did BILL MONROE's distinctive use of the F-5 model in the 1940s and beyond.

Earlier, blind minstrels Lester McFarland and Robert Gardner (MAC & BOB) had formed a popular duo whose songs were spread via broadcasts from WLS in Chicago and their popular records. Their singing and mandolin/guitar accompaniments inspired a host of BROTHER DUETS in the 1930s, notably the BLUE SKY BOYS and the MONROE BROTHERS.

Bill Monroe became country music's first mandolin virtuoso and brought the instrument into new prominence when he joined the GRAND OLE OPRY in 1939 and featured it on his records, beginning in 1940. Combined with his group's instrumental and vocal blend, his mandolin prowess helped define the genre that later became known as BLUEGRASS.

Some important stylists in the 1940s, such as Paul Buskirk, Ernest Ferguson, TINY MOORE, Jethro Burns (HOMER & JETHRO), and Red Rector, developed individual approaches of their own. By 1950, however, the Monroe bluegrass model dominated; even unique performers such as Jesse McReynolds (JIM & JESSE) and BUZZ BUSBY drew on Monroe's example, as have mandolinists such as Bobby Osborne (THE OSBORNE BROTHERS), John Duffey (THE COUNTRY GENTLEMEN, SELDOM SCENE), DOYLE LAWSON, DAVID GRISMAN, Ronnie McCoury of the DEL McCOURY BAND, Butch Baldassari, NICKEL CREEK veteran Chris Thile, and ADAM STEFFEY. —*Dick Spottswood*

## Barbara Mandrell
b. Houston, Texas, December 15, 1948

Few entertainers have been as gifted or as hard-working as Barbara Mandrell. A seasoned professional by age fourteen, she was a hit recording artist at twenty-one and went on to star on network television. A talented singer and actress, she also earned fame as a dynamic stage performer, an accomplished dancer, and a musician adept at PEDAL STEEL GUITAR, banjo, saxophone, accordion, bass, and mandolin.

Born in Houston, Barbara Ann Mandrell was the eldest child of country guitarist Irby Mandrell and his wife, Mary, who taught Barbara to play accordion and read music. After the Mandrells moved to southern California, ten-year-old Barbara took steel guitar lessons while learning saxophone in school. Country veteran JOE MAPHIS spotted the "Princess of the Steel" at a 1960 music trade convention and recruited her for his Las Vegas act. Back in Los Angeles, Mandrell performed on *TOWN HALL PARTY*.

*Barbara Mandrell*

Additional Vegas work led to a national tour headlined by JOHNNY CASH, GEORGE JONES, and PATSY CLINE and, later, recordings for the BAKERSFIELD-based Mosrite label.

At fourteen, Mandrell joined the Mandrell Family Band and began playing military bases in the United States and in Asia. Barbara fell in love with the band's first drummer, Ken Dudney, who eventually left to become a Navy pilot. The couple married in 1967, and Mandrell temporarily retired from music. When Dudney shipped out, however, she visited her family, who had relocated to Tennessee. There she asked her father to manage her career, and she reentered show business. Signing with COLUMBIA RECORDS, Mandrell first charted in 1969 with a cover of Otis Redding's soul classic "I've Been Loving You Too Long (To Stop Now)." "After Closing Time," a duet with DAVID HOUSTON, rose to #6 in 1970, and in 1972 she notched her first Top Ten solo hit with "Tonight My Baby's Coming Home." That same year she joined the GRAND OLE OPRY. The sexually frank "The Midnight Oil," pioneering for a female artist, reached #7 in 1973.

Moving to ABC/DOT (and later ABC), she recorded other soulful performances, such as "Standing Room Only" (1975–76) and "Married, but Not to Each Other" (1977), both Top Ten hits. Two #1s followed: 1978's "Sleeping Single in a Double Bed" and 1979's "If Loving You Is Wrong (I Don't Want to Be Right)." Mandrell switched to MCA RECORDS in 1979 and continued her string of Top Tens into the late 1980s with songs including "Fooled by a Feeling," "Years," "Crackers," and "The Best of Strangers." George Jones guested on her chart-topping signature number, "I Was Country When Country Wasn't Cool."

Amid a shower of industry accolades, CMA recognized Mandrell's success by naming her its Female Vocalist of the Year in 1979 and 1981. In 1980 and 1981 she won the prestigious CMA Entertainer of the Year award, the first artist to do so in successive years.

From 1980 to 1982 she joined sisters Louise and Irlene in hosting NBC–TV's weekly program *Barbara Mandrell and the Mandrell Sisters*. Offering music and comedy, the series reached millions of viewers; featured Barbara's talents as singer, instrumentalist, and dancer; and showcased dozens of country artists. Each broadcast closed with a gospel number, and in 1982 Mandrell released the Grammy-winning *He Set My Life to Music*. Teaming with gospel singer Bobby Jones on "I'm So Glad I'm Standing Here Today," she won a second Grammy in 1983.

Although voice problems forced Mandrell to end her TV series, she bounced back in 1983 with *The Lady Is a Champ*, a Las Vegas show and HBO television special. A 1984 car crash left her with multiple injuries requiring a long recuperation, but recovery brought more hit records, tours, TV acting roles, and a best-selling autobiography, *Get to the Heart: My Story* (1990).

In 1997 Mandrell announced her retirement. That October her final concert was filmed for a TNN concert special. The BNA label (see RCA RECORDS) honored her in 2006 with the album *She Was Country When Country Wasn't Cool: A Tribute to Barbara Mandrell*, featuring many of the decade's top artists. Mandrell was elected to THE COUNTRY MUSIC HALL OF FAME in 2009. —*Robert K. Oermann*

## Louise Mandrell
b. Corpus Christi, Texas, July 13, 1954

Louise Mandrell, a younger sister of country star BARBARA MANDRELL, was one of the original members of Barbara's band the Do-Rites when Louise was fifteen years old. Louise later went on to modest success as a solo artist, with several country Top Ten singles in the mid-1980s. During 1980–82 she and sister Irlene were featured on the NBC television series *Barbara Mandrell and the Mandrell Sisters*. Louise also appeared on other musical and dramatic TV programs.

Noted for her showmanship, Louise Mandrell is proficient on many instruments, including bass, fiddle, piano, banjo, guitar, and horn. She is also a dancer as well as a singer. After performing in her sister's band, she began pursuing her own career in 1974, initially working as a backup vocalist for other acts. Signed by EPIC RECORDS in 1977, she had little success on the label. She fared better on RCA, beginning in 1982, hitting the Top Ten with such songs as "Save Me" (1983) and "I Wanna Say Yes" (1985). She toured into the late 1990s and then performed at her own theater in Pigeon Forge, Tennessee, from 1997 to 2005. —*Mary A. Bufwack*

## Jay Dee Maness
b. Loma Linda, California, January 4, 1945

Firmly grounded in the West Coast school of PEDAL STEEL GUITAR playing, with a strong overlay of Nashville's commercial steel tradition, Jay Dee Maness has a knack for landing in the middle of ground-shifting country recordings (the 1968 proto-COUNTRY-ROCK album *Sweetheart of the Rodeo* recorded by THE BYRDS), television (*The Dukes of Hazzard* soundtrack, HEE HAW's first-year house band), and movies (the URBAN COWBOY soundtrack).

Maness's forceful, driving style—showcasing fast double-stop passages and single-string lines balanced by a fat-toned bluesy ballad style—can be heard on hit songs by RAY STEVENS ("Misty"), ANNE MURRAY ("Could I Have This Dance"), and Eric Clapton ("Tears in Heaven") and on albums by DWIGHT YOAKAM (*Guitars, Cadillacs, Etc., Etc.*) and Bonnie Raitt (*Nick of Time*).

It can also be found in performances and recordings with BUCK OWENS (he played on Owens's #1 hit "Johnny B. Goode"), the country-rock group DESERT ROSE BAND (Maness was a founding member), VINCE GILL, and many other country, pop, and rock performers.

Never straying far from his California roots, Maness has evolved into one of the premier first-call Los Angeles studio instrumentalists for recordings, television themes, movie source (or background) tracks, and jingles. —*Elek Horvath* and *Robert Kramer*

## Manuel
b. Coalcoman, Michoacan, Mexico, April 23, 1933

Manuel Arturo José Cuevas Martinez has been designing clothes for country performers since the 1950s. Having apprenticed with western couturiers NATHAN TURK and NUDIE, he is a living link to the rhinestone-cowboy tradition pioneered in the 1930s and 1940s. Manuel's eye-catching designs for such artists as MARTY STUART and DWIGHT YOAKAM have helped to popularize ornate western wear among a new generation of country artists and fans.

One of eleven children, Manuel was making his own clothes by age eight and soon after began a tailoring apprenticeship and created costumes for the local theater. "My dream was to own my own shop where I made everything—from all the accessories to the clothing," he has said.

His dream took him to Los Angeles in about 1953, where, after briefly working with Nathan Turk, he found a steady job with celebrity tailor Sy Devore. There, Manuel fitted movie stars Dean Martin and Frank Sinatra for tuxedos and other formal wear. On a recommendation from embroidery artist Viola Grae, Nudie hired the young designer away from Devore in 1958. Soon Manuel began to create original designs. In 1964 he became Nudie's son-in-law, marrying Barbara Cohn, with whom he had a daughter, Morelia, in 1968. In the 1960s Manuel designed costumes for movie westerns and TV shows such as *Bonanza*. He also collaborated with GRAM PARSONS in creating the Flying Burrito Brother's outrageous white Nudie suit decorated with pills, naked ladies, and marijuana leaves. After Manuel's marriage ended in 1972, he opened a by-appointment-only shop on Lankershim Boulevard in North Hollywood in 1974.

Inspired by Manuel's earlier designs for BUCK OWENS, Dwight Yoakam became a client just as his career was taking off in 1985. When he wore Manuel's turquoise rhinestone–studded bolero jacket on the cover of his 1987 album *Hillbilly Deluxe*, WARNER BROS. RECORDS received a reported three thousand requests for information on obtaining the garment. In the early 1990s Manuel and Yoakam created a line of similar jackets called DY Ranchwear. Another longtime client is Marty Stuart, who commissioned an extensive wardrobe including rhinestone-studded jackets lavishly embroidered with dice, hearts, and horseshoes. In 1989 Manuel moved his shop from Los Angeles to Nashville's Broadway, near MUSIC ROW, where his star clients include ALAN JACKSON, WYNONNA, BOB DYLAN, and R.E.M.'s Mike Mills. His children, Morelia, Manny, and Jesse (the latter two from later marriages), have joined him in the family business. He has also mentored young western-wear designers such as Katy K, whom he advised to move from New York to Nashville. In 1996 Manuel introduced his ready-to-wear Manuel Collection of western shirts, dresses, and jackets. From 2004 to 2005, his work was featured in *Star-Spangled Couture*, a traveling exhibition including garments designed for Dylan, Yoakam, Stuart, JOHNNY CASH, and others, as well as fifty lavishly embroidered jackets, one for each of the fifty states. —*Holly George-Warren*

## Joe & Rose Lee Maphis

Otis Wilson "Joe" Maphis b. Suffolk, Virginia, May 12, 1921; d. June 27, 1986
Rose Lee (Schetrompf) Maphis b. Hagerstown, Maryland, December 29, 1922

The husband-wife team of Joe & Rose Lee Maphis enjoyed their greatest success as performers in the heyday of live country music programs on radio and television. Joe began radio work while still a teenager, moving from local stations in Virginia to the *Boone County Jamboree* on WLW in Cincinnati and the NATIONAL BARN DANCE on WLS in Chicago. After serving in the army in World War II, he became a charter member of the OLD DOMINION BARN DANCE over WRVA in Richmond, Virginia. Rose Lee followed a similar path, performing in St. Louis and in Blytheville, Arkansas, before moving to WRVA in 1948. It was there that she and Joe met. In 1951 Joe and Rose Lee relocated to Los Angeles to work in the then new medium of television, doing live broadcasts nearly four hours a day, six days a week. They were married in February 1952. The following year they joined the cast of TOWN HALL PARTY on KTTV.

Although his proficiency on a variety of instruments earned him the title King of the Strings, Joe had his greatest impact as a guitarist. His 1955 COLUMBIA recording of "Fire on the Strings" (a reworking of the fiddle tune "Fire on the Mountain") proved that he was among the first to adapt fiddle tunes to the guitar. A leading Hollywood session guitarist, he played on the soundtracks of the films *Thunder Road* and *God's Little Acre* as well as supplying background music for a number of 1950s and 1960s TV series. He also performed on pop and rock records by RICK NELSON, the Four Preps, WANDA JACKSON, and Tommy Sands, and his twangy sound influenced the surf music of the 1960s. Moreover, as a role model for CLARENCE WHITE, Joe influenced the guitar's development as a lead instrument in BLUEGRASS.

*Joe & Rose Lee Maphis*

Joe and Rose Lee also contributed as songwriters, with "Dim Lights, Thick Smoke (And Loud, Loud Music)" (Joe & Rose Lee Maphis, 1953; VERN GOSDIN, 1985) and "Love Is the Look You're Looking For" (CONNIE SMITH, 1972) being their most successful compositions. The Maphises recorded both as a duo and as solo artists for the COLUMBIA, CAPITOL, STARDAY, Chart, and CMH labels. Joe's 1981 instrumental double album *The Joe Maphis Flat-Picking Spectacular* was nominated for a Grammy. —*Paul F. Wells*

## Marshall Tucker Band

The Marshall Tucker Band combined elements of several southern musical styles (especially country, rock, blues, and soul) into an original musical blend that has strongly influenced contemporary country musicians such as HANK WILLIAMS JR., TRAVIS TRITT, and the ZAC BROWN BAND.

Formed in 1970 by six friends from Spartanburg, South Carolina, and named after a Spartanburg piano tuner, the Marshall Tucker Band included Toy Caldwell (b. November 13, 1947; d. February 25, 1993), lead and steel guitarist, lead vocalist, and chief songwriter; his brother Tommy Caldwell (b. November 9, 1949, d. April 28, 1980), bassist and background vocalist; George McCorkle (b. October 11, 1946; d. June 29, 2007), rhythm guitarist; Doug Gray (b. May 22, 1948), lead and background vocalist and percussionist; Paul Riddle (b. ca. 1953), drummer; and Jerry Eubanks (b. March 19, 1950), flutist, saxophonist, and background vocalist. The group gained a national fan base through constant touring and through commercially and artistically successful albums, especially the seven made for Macon, Georgia–based Capricorn Records between 1973 and 1978. The act subsequently recorded five albums for WARNER BROS. RECORDS.

The Marshall Tucker Band suffered a significant blow in 1980 when Tommy Caldwell died in an automobile accident; he was replaced by Franklin Wilkie. Although Toy Caldwell left in 1985, the group continued, signing with MERCURY RECORDS in 1987, recording for Cabin Fever in the early 1990s, and releasing albums on Ramblin' Records since 2003. Doug Gray has provided continuity through additional personnel changes. Both oldie and country radio stations continue to air classic Marshall Tucker hits, including "Fire on the Mountain" and "Heard It in a Love Song." —*Ted Olson*

## Linda Martell

b. Lexington County, South Carolina, June 4, 1941

The first black female vocalist to perform at the GRAND OLE OPRY was five-foot-four-inch South Carolina native Linda Martell, who was born Thelma Bynem. She grew up around Leesville, South Carolina, as one of five children. Her father was a minister, and she started singing in a church choir at age five.

"I also grew up singing country," Martell said. "My father, Clarence Bynem, loved country music. My three brothers were all musicians. We started out doing gospel at St. Mark Baptist Church in Leesville. I also started singing with a pop band in Columbia, South Carolina, when I was twelve and worked with them all around the Columbia area until I was nineteen." As a teenager, she began performing with a racially integrated R&B group, the Anglos, recording singles on the Fire and Vee-Jay labels. In addition, she sang backup at recording sessions in Atlanta and Muscle Shoals.

Nashville businessman Duke Rayner heard about Martell's outstanding voice and tracked her down. He talked her into flying to Nashville for a demo session and then took the tape to SHELBY SINGLETON, who signed her to Plantation Records. Martell made her first guest appearance on the Opry in August 1969, within a week after her Plantation Records single, "Color Him Father" (a country version of the Winstons' soul hit), was released. It went to #22 on the *Billboard* charts and was included in her album *Color Me Country*. Soon afterward she appeared on television in 1970 on *The BILL ANDERSON Show* and *HEE HAW*. Her second single, "Before the Next Teardrop Falls" (recorded well before FREDDY FENDER's 1975 hit), went to #33. Martell also made another charting single ("Bad Case of the Blues") and eleven more Opry appearances.

Although her recording career ended in 1974, she continued to perform, based in Florida, Tennessee, California, and New York before moving back to Leesville in 1992 and singing throughout South Carolina with a rhythm & blues band called Eazzy. —*Don Rhodes*

## Martha White Flour
established 1899

One of the South's most recognized brand names, Martha White Flour is linked to country music through its longtime sponsorship of the GRAND OLE OPRY and fifteen-year association with BLUEGRASS pioneers FLATT & SCRUGGS AND THE FOGGY MOUNTAIN BOYS.

Royal Flour Mill Company launched Martha White Flour in 1899; the brand was named after the original owner's young daughter. In 1941 the Nashville-based mill, officially called Royal, Barry-Carter Mills, was purchased by Cohen E. Williams and his sons, Cohen T. and Joe Williams. The younger Cohen became president of the company, which he eventually renamed Martha White Foods after its flagship product. The firm started sponsoring an Opry segment in 1945, and in 1946 Williams started sponsoring an early-morning WSM show with a western-style ensemble featuring a female singer billed as "Martha White."

In June 1953 Williams recruited Flatt & Scruggs to helm the wake-up show, although certain WSM executives feared repercussions from the musicians' former employer, BILL MONROE. Listeners immediately responded to the Foggy Mountain Boys' driving music and Flatt's warm personality. After Flatt & Scruggs were firmly established as the flour's on-air spokesmen, Williams demanded that WSM allow the band on the Martha White portion of the Opry. He threatened to pull his advertising from the station, and Flatt & Scruggs became Opry members in 1955.

Martha White's association with the Opry and Flatt & Scruggs proved mutually beneficial. Williams publicly credited the band for helping build Martha White Foods into a multimillion-dollar business; at the same time, Flatt & Scruggs's corporate relationship with Martha White helped them become one of the best-known acts in country music. The band rarely played a concert without performing the catchy "Bake Right with Martha White" theme. In the late 1950s and early 1960s the company sponsored bluegrass acts in other parts of the South, most notably HYLO BROWN and JIM & JESSE. In 2001 the company began sponsoring high-profile bluegrass artist RHONDA VINCENT.

Williams sold his company to Beatrice Foods in 1974 but remained as chairman until his retirement ten years later. He died May 29, 1988, at age eighty-one. —*Dave Samuelson*

## Benny Martin
b. Sparta, Tennessee, May 8, 1928; d. March 13, 2001

Although influential fiddler Benjamin Edward Martin sometimes fronted his own act, he is best known as a fiddle-and-guitar-playing sideman and session player for some of country music's greatest names. As a teenager, Martin played with Big Jeff & the Radio Playboys on station WLAC–Nashville in 1944. He also performed with ROBERT LUNN, CURLY FOX, and MILTON ESTES & His Musical Millers on WSM's GRAND OLE OPRY. In 1946 Martin cut his first record, "Me and My Fiddle," for Pioneer Records.

Impressed, BILL MONROE made him a Blue Grass Boy in 1948. Martin next replaced TOMMY MAGNESS in ROY ACUFF's Smoky Mountain Boys in 1949 and also recorded with Acuff. FLATT & SCRUGGS engaged Martin to play with the Foggy Mountain Boys at WNOX–Knoxville, on the MID-DAY MERRY-GO-ROUND, and, later, on WSM's *Martha White Biscuit Time* show. His fiddling can be heard on thirteen early Flatt & Scruggs sides. In 1953 MGM RECORDS released two Benny Martin singles, including vocals.

Martin joined the KITTY WELLS–JOHNNIE & JACK troupe in February 1954, remaining through fall of 1955. During that period MERCURY RECORDS released twenty-one Martin sides, including "Ice Cold Love" and "Coming Attractions." He also worked solo on the Opry.

On recording sessions, Martin restricted himself to providing fiddle, rhythm guitar, and backup vocals, but he also played auto-harp, bass, banjo, mandolin, ukelele, and viola. Occasionally he furnished compositions, notably "I'm in Love with You" and "Each Day" for Wells and "Weary Moments" for Johnnie & Jack.

RCA recorded Martin in 1957. A year later he cut sides for DECCA RECORDS—and introduced his invention, an eight-string fiddle. In 1960 STARDAY RECORDS signed Martin, releasing his first album, titled *Benny Martin: Country Music's Sensational Entertainer*, in 1961. A Starday single, "Rosebuds and You" (1963) charted, as did a single for MONUMENT, "A Soldier's Prayer in Viet Nam" (recorded with DON RENO), in 1966. Other musicians Martin recorded with include JOHN HARTFORD, UNCLE JOSH GRAVES, and JOE MAPHIS. Martin continued to work BLUEGRASS festivals and record for various labels until his health failed. By the 1990s he was rarely active; he died in 2001. —*Walt Trott*

## Grady Martin
b. Chapel Hill, Tennessee, January 17, 1929; d. December 3, 2001

Grady Martin was a legendary member of Nashville's original "A-Team" of studio musicians. Whether playing the fiddle or the guitar—electric, acoustic, or six-string electric bass—his versatility and creativity helped to make hits of many records from the 1950s through the 1970s.

Thomas Grady Martin was fifteen when he became the fiddler for Nashville's Big Jeff & the Radio Playboys. In 1946 Martin briefly joined PAUL HOWARD's WESTERN SWING–oriented Arkansas Cotton Pickers as half of Howard's "twin guitar" ensemble, along with Robert "Jabbo" Arrington. After Howard left the GRAND OLE OPRY, Opry newcomer LITTLE JIMMY DICKENS hired several former Cotton Pickers as his original Country Boys band. Martin backed Dickens in the studio but seldom toured with him.

Off the road, Martin began working recording sessions, also leading RED FOLEY's band on ABC-TV's *OZARK JUBILEE*. Paying service to a strong business relationship with DECCA A&R man PAUL COHEN and his successor, OWEN BRADLEY, Martin began to record instrumental singles and albums for Decca, including a country-jazz instrumental album as part of Decca's *Country and Western Dance-O-Rama* series. Martin made many more Decca recordings playing lead guitar for the Nashville pop band the Slew Foot Five.

Martin's role as studio guitarist yielded numerous memorable moments. It was he who played the throbbing leads on JOHNNY HORTON's 1956 hit "Honky Tonk Man" and the exquisite acoustic guitar fills on MARTY ROBBINS's 1959 crossover smash "El Paso" and LEFTY FRIZZELL's 1964 hit "Saginaw Michigan." One of his most famous sessions involved an accidental preamplifier malfunction in mid-take, when Martin played the distorted "fuzz" guitar solo on Robbins's 1960 hit "Don't Worry." Though studio musicians in those days rarely received credit for their work, Martin's efforts didn't go unnoticed. Producers often designated him "session leader," which meant that he directed the impromptu arrangements that became a trademark of Nashville recording and often became the de facto producer. COLUMBIA A&R man DON LAW used Martin in this capacity for years.

Martin continued to play sessions through the 1970s, working extensively with CONWAY TWITTY and LORETTA LYNN, and producing the country-rock band Brush Arbor. His signature lead parts helped to make a hit of JEANNE PRUETT's 1973 "Satin Sheets." Martin eventually returned to performing, first with JERRY REED and then with WILLIE NELSON's band, with whom he worked from 1980 to 1994. In 1983 Martin became the first recipient of the Nashville Music Association's prestigious Masters Award. —*Rich Kienzle*

## Janis Martin
b. Sutherlin, Virginia, March 27, 1940; d. September 3, 2007

Combining a spunky, boisterous vocal style with bold stage moves that drew comparisons to ELVIS PRESLEY, Janice Darlene Martin was an acclaimed female ROCKABILLY artist of the late 1950s.

Martin was singing and playing guitar by age six and working radio in Danville, Virginia, at age eleven. In 1953 she joined the cast of WRVA's *OLD DOMINION BARN DANCE* in Richmond, Virginia. Three years later Martin recorded a demo tape of "Will You, Willyum," written by two WRVA staff announcers. The tape reached RCA VICTOR executive STEVE SHOLES (who had recently signed Presley), and he brought Martin to Nashville to record under the direction of CHET ATKINS in March 1956.

Released as her first single, "Will You, Willyum" (backed with "Drugstore Rock and Roll") sold well, and Martin was soon in demand for appearances throughout the nation. RCA obtained Presley's permission to bill her as the Female Elvis, and catchy rockabilly recordings such as "My Boy Elvis," "Love Me to Pieces," "Love and Kisses," and "Ooby Dooby" heightened her profile. She appeared on the *Tonight Show*, *American Bandstand*, the *OZARK JUBILEE*, and the GRAND OLE OPRY. RCA booked her on the label's multiartist European tour in 1957. Back home, Martin formed her own band, the Marteens, and toured widely in the United States and Canada.

In 1958 Martin's success was cut short when she became pregnant, having secretly married her childhood sweetheart when she was fifteen. Her teen idol image was tarnished, and RCA soon dropped her. In 1960 she recorded four sides for the small Palette label, but family life took precedence and she retired.

Over the years Martin made attempts at revitalizing her career and remained popular among European rockabilly fans. In 1995 she appeared on ROSIE FLORES's *Rockabilly Filly* album for HIGHTONE. Martin died of cancer in 2007. —*Jonita Aadland*

## Jimmy Martin
b. Sneedville, Tennessee, August 10, 1927; d. May 14, 2005

BLUEGRASS great James Henry Martin was one of country music's most colorful characters, whose manic energy and knack for self-promotion matched his outstanding musical gifts. His professional break came in 1949, when he joined BILL MONROE's Blue Grass Boys. Martin was the first lead singer to record with Monroe on DECCA, and their renditions of "Uncle Pen," "On and On," and "The Little Girl and the Dreadful Snake"—among numerous other songs—have become classics. Few singers before or after Martin have complemented Monroe's voice so well. Martin worked local radio in Kingsport and Morristown, Tennessee, before joining with Monroe to play on and off with his band through 1955.

Meanwhile, Martin also pursued other projects. In 1951 he and Bobby Osborne recorded a handful of sides for Cincinnati's KING RECORDS. Martin and company made brief stops at WNOX's *MID-DAY MERRY-GO-ROUND* in Knoxville and WCYB–Bristol before settling temporarily in Detroit. In 1954 Martin and THE OSBORNE BROTHERS recorded six RCA sides, including "20/20 Vision" and "Save It! Save It!" Although popular in the Detroit area, Martin and the Osbornes parted ways about a year later. Martin landed a DECCA contract and recorded 139 sides over the next eighteen years, including the bluegrass standards "Rock Hearts," "Sophronie," "Hold Whatcha Got," "Widow Maker," "Tennessee," and "The Sunny Side of the Mountain."

Martin's powerful vocals, rock-solid rhythm guitar, and musical leadership yielded many influential recordings. Dozens of musicians honed their musical skills under his tutelage, including J. D. CROWE, Paul Williams, Alan Munde, Gloria Belle, and Bill Emerson. In the late 1950s and 1960s Martin was a featured act on both the *LOUISIANA HAYRIDE* in Shreveport and the

*Jimmy Martin*

*WWVA Jamboree* in Wheeling, West Virginia. After 1965 he was popular on the bluegrass festival circuit, but he restricted his appearances in later years. The self-styled King of Bluegrass was often abrasive, but there was no denying his achievements. He was inducted into the IBMA Hall of Fame in 1995. Martin died of cancer on May 14, 2005. —*Chris Skinner*

## Frankie and Johnny Marvin

Frank James Marvin b. Butler, Oklahoma, January 27, 1904; d. January 1985
John Senator Marvin b. Butler, Oklahoma, July 11, 1897; d. December 20, 1944

A side of Gene Autry not often recognized was his loyalty to old friends. Two of his closest associates were brothers Frankie and Johnny Marvin, who were popular vaudeville entertainers when young Autry, full of ambition but green as grass, showed up at their New York apartment in the late 1920s. They befriended their fellow Oklahoman, tutored him in the ways of show business, and sent him home for seasoning. When he became a film star a few years later, Autry sent for both brothers and integrated them into his growing organization.

John Senator Marvin was born in Butler, Oklahoma, in 1897; Frank James Marvin was born there in 1904. Johnny pursued a successful musical career in New York as a songwriter and radio performer, the Lonesome Singer of the Air; Frankie soon followed, working steadily as a steel guitarist, ukulele player, and comedian. Autry brought them to Hollywood when the Depression slowed their careers. Johnny became a producer for Autry's *Melody Ranch* network radio series, wrote songs, and helped run Autry's music publishing companies; Frankie became the steel guitarist in Autry's band, where his playing became a consistently recognizable component of the Autry sound. —*Douglas B. Green*

## Brent Mason

b. Vanwert, Ohio, July 13, 1959

Brent Mason was born into a guitar-playing family and taught himself the thumb-and-finger-picking style of Jerry Reed and Chet Atkins as a youngster. Perhaps best known for his electric guitar work on Alan Jackson's records ("Chattahoochee"), Mason has also graced albums by other country acts, including Brooks & Dunn, Trisha Yearwood, George Strait, and Toby Keith.

During and after high school, Mason played lounges and bowling alleys before corresponding with Nashville pedal steel guitar player Paul Franklin. Mason moved to Nashville in 1981 and quickly landed a regular gig at the Stagecoach Lounge. Atkins saw him there and invited him to play on his 1985 LP *Stay Tuned*, which featured George Benson, Earl Klugh, Larry Carlton, and other guitar virtuosos.

Since then, Mason has been an in-demand session player. He was CMA's Best Country Instrumentalist for 1997 and 1998, and he has collected numerous Top Guitarist trophies from ACM. With other guitarists, he won a 2008 Grammy for "Cluster Pluck," a track from Brad Paisley's 2008 album *Play*. As a songwriter, Mason has gained recordings of "Hurry Sundown" (McBride & the Ride) and "Who Needs It" (Clinton Gregory). Mercury issued *Hot Wired*, Mason's first solo album, in 1997, but he soon left the label, preferring lucrative studio work to touring. He released the side project *Smokin' Section* with his brother, Randy, in 2006. —*Michael Hight*

## Louise Massey & the Westerners

Victoria Louise Massey b. Midland, Texas, August 10, 1902; d. June 20, 1983
D. Curtis Massey b. Midland, Texas, May 3, 1910; d. October 20, 1991
Allen Massey b. Texas, December 12, 1907; d. March 3, 1983
Milt Mabie b. Independence, Iowa; June 27, 1900; d. September 29, 1973
Larry Wellington b. Oxnard, California, February 15, 1903; d. May 5, 1973

A classy western ensemble, Louise Massey & the Westerners achieved pop-crossover success, recorded abundantly throughout the 1930s and 1940s, starred on network radio, and were accomplished in Mexican, polka, cowboy, ragtime, and swing genres.

Louise, Curt, and Allen Massey were children of old-time fiddler and rancher Henry Massey, who formed an amateur family band in New Mexico. Louise married bassist Milt Mabie in 1919, and the act went professional. They toured the United States on the Chautauqua circuit in 1928; then Henry retired.

Adding accordionist Larry Wellington, the Massey children moved on. A five-year stint on KMBC in Kansas City—including CBS network exposure—led to fame on WLS's *National Barn Dance* in Chicago, beginning in 1933. Three years later the act hit New York, starring on NBC's *Log Cabin Dude Ranch* show and headlining at the Waldorf-Astoria, the Rainbow Room, and other midtown venues. The group also filmed several musical shorts and appeared in the 1938 Tex Ritter feature *Where the Buffalo Roam*. Returning to Chicago in 1939, the Massey band starred on NBC's *Plantation Party*.

The group recorded more than a hundred sides for the American Record Corporation (ARC) and Columbia from 1933 to 1942. Members doubled on several instruments. They also were bilingual, and so they were among the first recording acts to popularize Latin American material in the United States. The instrumental "Beer and Skittles" and Curt's "The Honey Song," hits of the early 1940s, sold steadily for years. Louise's self-composed ballad "When the White Azaleas Start Blooming" became a big hit in 1934, and her 1947 smash "My Adobe Hacienda" was one of the first country-pop crossover successes.

Louise and Mabie eventually retired to Roswell, New Mexico. Curt settled in Hollywood and became the musical director/theme composer for the hit 1960s TV series *The Beverly Hillbillies* and *Petticoat Junction*. —*Robert K. Oermann*

## Kathy Mattea

b. Cross Lanes, West Virginia, June 21, 1959

With her folk sensibilities and eclectic repertoire, Kathy Mattea opened doors for folk-influenced artists such as Mary Chapin Carpenter and Lyle Lovett, who followed her in commercial country music. Mattea was raised on the folk-pop repertoires of Buffy St. Marie, Joni Mitchell, and James Taylor, along with folk classics sung around Girl Scout campfires. She developed her voice through classical training and church singing and then joined a bluegrass band during her brief college career at West Virginia University in the mid-1970s. Falling in love with the bandleader, she quit school to move with him to Nashville in 1978.

When the relationship dissolved, Mattea decided to pursue her musical ambitions. Taking jobs as a typesetter's apprentice, a waitress, and a tour guide at the Country Music Hall of Fame and Museum, she found a home in Nashville's circle of songwriters. She became a rising star of the Music Row demo session scene while building a club act from little-known folk songs, novelty tunes, and the best of her friends' compositions.

*Kathy Mattea*

Signing with MERCURY in 1983, Mattea struggled until she cut a sweet yet earthy song written by contemporary folkie NANCI GRIFFITH, "Love at the Five and Dime," a #3 country hit in 1986 that defined Mattea for radio. A string of Top Tens followed, including the chart-topping "Goin' Gone" (1987–88) and "Eighteen Wheels and a Dozen Roses" (1988), both from her 1987 album *Untasted Honey*. The latter song became CMA's 1988 Single of the Year, and back-to-back CMA Female Vocalist of the Year honors in 1989 and 1990 confirmed her status in country music.

While "Eighteen Wheels and a Dozen Roses" remains her biggest chart hit, she became closely identified with left-of-center releases and songs of conscience, such as the 1990 Grammy-winning "Where've You Been," penned by her husband, Jon Vezner, and Don Henry. She won a 1993 Grammy for *Good News*, a Christmas album, as well. After a decade of records with producer ALLEN REYNOLDS, she worked with producer Josh Leo for *Walking Away a Winner* (1994) and in 1996 coproduced *Love Travels* with Ben Wisch.

After *The Innocent Years* (2000), her final Mercury album, sold disappointingly, Mattea switched to Narada Records for 2002's *Roses*. The 2005 collection *Right Out of Nowhere* reflected her separation from—and reconciliation with—Vezner and the deaths of her father (2003) and mother (2005). A social activist and early supporter of AIDS awareness, Mattea explored the harsh realities faced by coal miners and their families in *Coal* (2008), issued on her own Captain Potato label. "If you say my name over and over again," she explained, "and you speed up—and somewhere in there you have a beer or two—it will turn into 'Captain Potato.'" —*Bob Millard*

## The Mavericks
Raul Malo b. Miami, Florida, August 7, 1965
Robert Earl Reynolds b. Kansas City, Missouri, April 30, 1962
Paul Wylie Deakin b. Miami, Florida, September 2, 1959
Nicholas James "Nick" Kane b. Jerusalem, Georgia, August 21, 1954

A musically eclectic, self-contained group who played their own instruments and wrote many of their own songs, the Mavericks combined rock & roll exuberance, pop song craft, and

HONKY-TONK panache. In so doing, they corralled fans of many genres and suggested a future for country music free from both stern traditionalism and a rehash of 1970s COUNTRY-ROCK.

The Mavericks originated in Miami, where bassist Robert Reynolds had long played ELVIS PRESLEY and HANK WILLIAMS covers. Reynolds introduced his friend Paul Deakin—a drummer for various punk, new wave, and funk bands—to hard country and recruited Raul Malo, a lifelong Elvis Presley fan who had never sung in a band, as bassist. In 1990 the trio started playing Miami rock clubs. When Reynolds switched to bass and Malo began singing, people took notice. In 1990 the group released an independently produced, thirteen-song album, which, along with reports of the band's incendiary live shows, interested MUSIC Row label scouts.

Following a May 1991 showcase, MCA Nashville signed the band. Adding David Lee Holt on lead guitar, the Mavericks entered a Miami studio with producer Steve Fishell. The result was 1992's *From Hell to Paradise*, a mix of gently crooned ballads, revved-up standards, and five-minute protest songs of staggering ambition. (The astonishing title track detailed the flight of Malo's family from Castro's Cuba in 1959.) Although excellent, the album yielded only one charting single—a 90-mph cover of "Hey, Good Lookin'" that barely made the Top Seventy-five.

By 1994 the group had a new lead guitarist, Nick Kane, and a new approach. Sprawling social anthems gave way to tightly crafted three-minute tracks. The lush, retro sound of *What a Crying Shame* (courtesy of producer DON COOK) and irresistible operatic melodies propelled it to platinum status.

The Mavericks burnished their sound to a lounge-lizard gloss on 1995's *Music for All Occasions*, which drew mixed reviews. Nevertheless, it yielded two hit singles, and their live show remained a top draw, fueled by the piano-pounding antics of Jerry Dale McFadden and a repertoire that ranged from "Guantanamera" to Bob Marley songs. *Trampoline* followed in 1998, but the Mavericks soon disbanded, releasing a greatest-hits album in 1999. With Eddie Perez replacing Nick Kane, the group reunited for a self-titled 2003 album and 2004's *Live in Austin*, both released on Sanctuary Records. Since then Malo has pursued a solo career. —*Jim Ridley*

## MCA Records
established in Universal City, California, March 1, 1973

MCA Records accrued a lengthy history as a major force in country music and the recording industry in general. After several mergers, the historic label became part of the Universal Music Group by 1996 and is now owned by the French firm Vivendi Universal. As of 2011, only MCA Nashville and a Universal unit in the Philippines were still using the MCA brand.

Founded in 1925 by Jules Stein, the Music Corporation of America began as a talent booking agency in New York. Over the years MCA expanded to include music publishing, film, television, distribution, theme parks, and concert facilities.

MCA's recording endeavors began in 1962 with the purchase of DECCA RECORDS (which included the Coral, BRUNSWICK, and Vocalion labels). In 1967 MCA formed the UNI label and acquired Kapp Records (with a country roster that included MEL TILLIS, CAL SMITH, BILLY EDD WHEELER, BOB WILLS, and LEROY VAN DYKE). In 1973 MCA retired these various record labels and gathered all artists under the newly launched MCA label, headquartered in Universal City, California. OWEN BRADLEY, having run Decca's

Nashville operation since 1958, remained in charge of MCA's Nashville offices into 1976.

During the 1970s, MCA stars included MERLE HAGGARD, BRENDA LEE, LORETTA LYNN, JEANNE PRUETT, Cal Smith, CONWAY TWITTY, Mel Tillis, and TANYA TUCKER. Between 1976 and 1979 Chick Dougherty, Eddie Kilroy, and JIMMY BOWEN took turns presiding over the Nashville office. In 1979 MCA purchased ABC/DOT RECORDS to beef up the country division, and in so doing acquired the contracts of ROY CLARK, JOHN CONLEE, BARBARA MANDRELL, the OAK RIDGE BOYS, and DON WILLIAMS. That same year ABC/Dot president JIM FOGLESONG became head of MCA's Nashville operations.

In 1984 BRUCE HINTON replaced Foglesong as senior vice president/general manager and Bowen was named president of MCA Nashville. Artists signed during the 1980s included ED BRUCE, VINCE GILL, LEE GREENWOOD, PATTY LOVELESS, REBA McENTIRE, GEORGE STRAIT, MARTY STUART, STEVE WARINER, and GENE WATSON. In December 1988 Bowen left MCA to create Universal Records, Hinton was promoted to president, and producer TONY BROWN was named executive vice president and head of A&R.

In late 1990, Matsushita Electric Industrial (Japan's largest electronics company) purchased MCA. In 1993 Hinton was promoted to chairman and Brown to president. The following year, MCA reactivated the Decca label in Nashville, with MARK WRIGHT and Shelia Shipley in charge. In 1995 Matsushita sold 80 percent of MCA to the Seagram Company, a Montreal-based distiller, and the next year changed the name of MCA Music Entertainment Group to the Universal Music Group (UMG).

When Seagram acquired PolyGram in 1998, Decca's Nashville operation was shuttered, and artists GARY ALLAN, MARK CHESNUTT, and LEE ANN WOMACK shifted to MCA. In 2000 the French corporation Vivendi bought Seagram, including its UMG arm. In 2002 UMG consolidated its Nashville divisions under the leadership of LUKE LEWIS. Hinton and Brown departed MCA as Lewis became chairman of MCA Nashville, MERCURY Nashville, and LOST HIGHWAY RECORDS. Along with Allan and Womack, as of 2011 the MCA Nashville roster included Vince Gill, Ashton Shepherd, George Strait, JOSH TURNER, and Holly Williams. —*Don Roy*

## Mac McAnally
b. Red Bay, Alabama, July 15, 1957

Lyman "Mac" McAnally Jr. hails from the same Memphis/Mobile/New Orleans triangle of the Deep South that has produced Jimmy Buffett, TONY JOE WHITE, Steve Forbert, and Jesse Winchester—singer-songwriters who employ country music, rhythm & blues, and folk-rock interchangeably to tell their stories. McAnally is better known as a songwriter and session musician than as a recording artist, but industry insiders have long recognized him as one of the South's most gifted troubadours.

Raised in northern Mississippi, McAnally was performing by age thirteen; by nineteen he was a session guitarist in Muscle Shoals, Alabama. After hours, he recorded his 1977 debut album, *Mac McAnally*, which included a Top Forty pop single, "It's a Crazy World."

As of 2011, McAnally had recorded nine more albums for eight different labels, most recently (at press time) *Down by the River*, released on TOBY KEITH's Show Dog Records in 2009. (McAnally remained with the label after it merged with UNIVERSAL RECORDS SOUTH to become Show Dog–Universal Music). Despite

modest sales, his albums have fascinated critics and fellow musicians, who appreciate his insinuating melodies and understated narratives.

As an artist, his biggest solo chart success came with 1990's "Back Where I Come From," a #14 country single from his album *Simple Life*, which also featured McAnally's "Down the Road." In 2008 KENNY CHESNEY recorded "Down the Road" as a duet with McAnally, and the song topped the country charts in February 2009.

McAnally's compositions have been recorded by Jimmy Buffett ("It's My Job"), ALABAMA ("Old Flame"), SHENANDOAH ("Two Dozen Roses"), RANDY TRAVIS ("Written in Stone"), RICKY VAN SHELTON ("Crime of Passion"), and SAWYER BROWN ("Thank God for You"), among others. McAnally was elected to the NASHVILLE SONGWRITERS HALL OF FAME in 2007.

As a producer, he's worked with Buffett, CHRIS LEDOUX, Little Feat, RESTLESS HEART, Sawyer Brown, and RICKY SKAGGS. As a guitarist, he has played on albums by GEORGE JONES, DOLLY PARTON, TRISHA YEARWOOD, LINDA RONSTADT, HANK WILLIAMS JR., Buffett, and many more. McAnally was CMA's Musician of the Year in 2008, 2009, and 2010. —*Geoffrey Himes*

## Leon McAuliffe
b. Houston, Texas, January 3, 1917; d. August 20, 1988

William Leon McAuliffe was BOB WILLS's most famous steel guitarist and a popular WESTERN SWING bandleader in his own right. In 1933 he became the steel guitarist for the LIGHT CRUST DOUGHBOYS—only a month or two after Wills left the group. In March 1935 McAuliffe made the most important move of his career, joining Bob Wills & His Texas Playboys, who would eventually become the world's most famous western dance band. In 1936 McAuliffe recorded "Steel Guitar Rag" with the Wills band, and the instrumental number—adapted from a blues recording by Sylvester Weaver—is now seen as a seminal moment in the history of the steel guitar. In addition, the uninhibited Wills introduced the recording in a way that gave McAuliffe special attention. Wills hollered "Leon" and told him to "take it away." "Calling me by name on our recordings, as Bob did it, made me famous," McAuliffe later stated.

In 1942 McAuliffe left Wills and entered the U.S. Army Air Corps as a flight instructor. After the war McAuliffe formed his own western swing outfit, the Cimarron Boys, in Tulsa, where in 1950 he also opened his own nightclub, the Cimarron Ballroom. Handling vocals as well as steel for his act, he was quite successful, and recorded numerous sides for Majestic, COLUMBIA, STARDAY, DOT, CAPITOL, and his own Cimarron label (sometimes spelling his name "McAuliff"). His biggest-selling record was a 1949 steel guitar instrumental for Columbia, "Panhandle Rag."

McAuliffe broke up his band in the 1960s and devoted his time to real estate interests and his radio station in Rogers, Arkansas. In 1973 Bob Wills revived McAuliffe's musical career when the aging bandleader asked McAuliffe to join what proved to be Wills's final recording session. After Wills's death, Betty Wills permitted McAuliffe to lead an ensemble called Bob Wills's Original Texas Playboys, which made several albums and played concerts in the United States and Europe.

Because the steel guitarist left his most enduring mark on American music as a member of Wills's early band, McAuliffe's name is still linked to that of the King of Western Swing. —*Charles R. Townsend*

## Laura Lee & Dickie McBride

Dickie McBride b. New Baden, Texas, January 22, 1914; d. June 1971
Laura Lee Owens McBride b. Kansas City, Missouri, 1920; d. January 25, 1989

Although they worked as a duo from the mid-1940s, both Laura Lee and Dickie McBride are probably better known for their separate careers—Laura Lee for her stints with BOB WILLS's Texas Playboys and Dickie McBride for his days with CLIFF BRUNER's Texas Wanderers and with his own Village Boys.

The daughter of singer TEX OWENS and the niece of Texas Ruby (who performed with CURLY FOX), Laura Lee Owens began singing with her sister while still in her teens on Kansas City's *Brush Creek Follies.* After an early marriage to the Texas Rangers' guitarist Herb Kratoska and a stint with the Oklahoma Wranglers, she joined Bob Wills's Texas Playboys at the end of 1943. She became Wills's first female vocalist and was best known for the yodeling on her signature tune, "Betcha My Heart." She married Wills's guitarist Cameron Hill, and when Hill entered the army in 1945, she relocated to Houston, where she would meet and later marry McBride.

Dickie McBride, who idolized WESTERN SWING pioneer MILTON BROWN and pop crooner Perry Como, joined the band of Brown alumnus Cliff Bruner—the Texas Wanderers—in Houston during 1936. McBride's smooth vocals were prominent on Bruner's 1937–38 DECCA sides, including the FLOYD TILLMAN–penned, seminal HONKY-TONK hit "It Makes No Difference Now." When Bruner left, McBride continued to record for Decca with the Texas Wanderers and also under his own name. McBride and fiddler Grady Hester formed the Village Boys in 1940; after Hester's departure, the band became McBride's. The Village Boys disbanded in 1943; McBride picked up the pieces and formed his Music Macs.

Following their marriage, the McBrides worked mostly outside Houston; they made tours with Bob Wills and worked in California in 1948–50. Although they usually recorded as a team— for Decca, MGM, and several smaller labels—they continued to record separately on independent labels, such as Daffan, Ayo, and Freedom. As popular radio, TV, and dance performers in Houston throughout the 1950s they performed and recorded sporadically until just before Dickie McBride's death in 1971, after which Laura Lee became more active. She performed and recorded through the 1980s until her death in 1989. —*Kevin Coffey*

## Martina McBride

b. Sharon, Kansas, July 29, 1966

An enormously powerful voice, several defiantly female-centered message songs, and a stylishly modern haircut helped separate Martina Mariea Schiff McBride from the many long-haired brunette singers who flooded Nashville in the early 1990s. Once established, McBride built an enduring career that has included several awards, most of them recognizing her as one of the leading female country vocalists of her time.

McBride began singing country classics at age eight in a family band, the Schiffters, led by her father, Daryl Schiff. After high school she moved to Wichita, where she sang in local rock bands. In 1988 she married audio engineer John McBride, and the couple moved to Nashville the following year. John was hired as sound man for GARTH BROOKS's 1991 tour, and Martina ran the T-shirt booth. She signed with RCA RECORDS and, in 1992, released her tradition-leaning debut, *The Time Has Come,* which received a lukewarm reception at country radio.

For 1993's *The Way That I Am*, McBride adopted a more contemporary sound and look. The first single, "My Baby Loves Me," fought its way to #2. However, the third single, "Independence Day"—an anthem about a woman rising up against domestic abuse—connected with fans. It won 1995 CMA Song of the Year honors for songwriter Gretchen Peters and marked McBride as a bold new artist.

The singer enjoyed her first #1 hit with the title track of 1995's *Wild Angels,* her second consecutive million-selling album. Another message song, "A Broken Wing," from her 1997 album *Evolution,* became her second #1. "Valentine," a duet with pianist Jim Brickman, climbed to #3 on *Billboard*'s adult contemporary chart and rose to #4 in the trade magazine's country rankings. *Evolution* featured five Top Ten hits and sold more than 3 million units, both landmarks for McBride at the time.

With her next album, 1999's *Emotion,* McBride won her first industry award when the CMA named her Female Vocalist of the Year. She has since won the same CMA award three more times, from 2002 to 2004; she's also been named ACM's Top Female Vocalist three consecutive times, from 2001 to 2003.

After a *Greatest Hits* album in 2001, McBride has mostly focused on pop-country albums that follow a well-established pattern, mixing inspiring message songs with upbeat, female-oriented tunes and emotional ballads that showcase her extensive vocal range. The singer did step out with a 2005 tribute to classic country, *Timeless,* in which she covered songs by MERLE HAGGARD ("Today I Started Loving You Again"), LORETTA LYNN ("You Ain't Woman Enough"), HANK WILLIAMS ("You Win Again"), TAMMY WYNETTE ("'Til I Can Make It on my Own"), and others. The album sold a surprising 1 million units and revealed McBride as a potent interpreter of traditional country music.

McBride has coproduced her albums since 1993, with the exception of 2006's *Wake Up Laughing,* on which she took a solo producer credit—a rarity for a female country star. In 2011, McBride left RCA Records and signed with Republic Nashville, a label associated with BIG MACHINE RECORDS. —*Jim Ridley*

*Martina McBride*

## McCall, Bill (*see* Four Star Records)

## C. W. McCall
b. Audubon, Iowa, November 15, 1928

In 1975 the nation struggled with an energy crisis, the speed limit was set at 55 mph, citizens' band radio became a national craze, and C. W. McCall's "Convoy"—an ode to the defiant American trucker—enjoyed a six-week run at the top of *Billboard*'s country charts and also hit #1 pop.

As an advertising executive, McCall (William Fries) did the voice-over for a fictitious bread truck driver named C. W. McCall, which in turn inspired his stage name. On his albums McCall alternated between the narrative style of "Convoy" and other trucking/highway songs, and lethargic ballad crooning reminiscent of Leonard Cohen. McCall had a #2 hit in 1977 with "Roses for Mama," but in 1978 he left the music business, returning to the studio only occasionally thereafter. An environmentalist, he served as mayor of Ouray, Colorado, during the 1980s. —*Jack Bernhardt*

## Darrell McCall
b. New Jasper, Ohio, April 30, 1940

Anyone who loves the traditional country shuffles and sounds of FARON YOUNG or RAY PRICE during the late 1950s and early 1960s will probably admire the music of Darrell McCall. His intense and soulful hard-core HONKY-TONK style has amassed a loyal and dedicated following in both the United States and Europe.

McCall came up through the ranks the old-fashioned way— serving at least one apprenticeship as a frontman and harmony vocalist for a major star. McCall did this effectively for more than a dozen years in the bands of Faron Young, Ray Price, CARL SMITH, Charlie Louvin (THE LOUVIN BROTHERS), and HANK WILLIAMS JR. Though McCall had been recording during much of this period for CAPITOL, STARDAY, Philips, and Wayside, with some occasional chart success ("A Stranger Was Here" reached the Top Twenty in 1963), it wasn't until Hank Jr. recorded McCall's "Eleven Roses" in 1972 (#1) that McCall was able to embark on a successful solo career.

While with ATLANTIC RECORDS, McCall released "There's Still a Lot of Love in San Antone" (#48, 1974) before moving to COLUMBIA, where he had several chart records, including "Dreams of a Dreamer" and "Lily Dale," a duet with WILLIE NELSON. McCall released an album apiece on Hillside, STEP ONE, and BGM in the 1980s, a trio of albums on Artap in the 1990s, and *Old Memories and Wine* on Heart of Texas Records in 2005. Especially popular with singers and musicians, he continues to work the Texas and Oklahoma dance-hall circuit, where he has been an attraction for years. —*Eddie Stubbs*

## Charly McClain
b. Jackson, Tennessee, March 26, 1956

Charlotte Denise McClain mixed her country heritage with a contemporary feel to become a star of the URBAN COWBOY era. Raised in Memphis, she grew up with a rich variety of rock, country, jazz, and blues sounds but was most attracted to country.

At age nine, McClain recorded school songs to play for her father, who was hospitalized with tuberculosis, and began singing with her brother's band at age twelve. She was a regular on the Memphis country music showcase the *Mid-South Jamboree* from 1973 to 1975.

EPIC RECORDS signed McClain in 1976. Her first chart single, "Lay Down," and her debut album, *Here's Charly McClain*, appeared that year. Within two years she had hit the Top Ten, and in early 1981 "Who's Cheatin' Who" became her first #1. McClain's hit-making career peaked in 1985 with her #1 smash "Radio Heart" and a couple of Top Ten duets with her actor husband, Wayne Massey. She had earlier recorded duets with MICKEY GILLEY, including "Paradise Tonight," which topped the charts in 1983. Her last chart record stalled at #65 in 1989.

In addition to recording and touring, McClain appeared on such television shows as *Austin City Limits*, *Solid Gold*, and the ABC-TV series *Hart to Hart*. —*Gerry Wood*

## Delbert McClinton
b. Lubbock, Texas, November 4, 1940

A roadhouse veteran and prolific songwriter, Delbert McClinton blurs the lines between country, blues, and R&B. For example, he won a Grammy for a rock duet with Bonnie Raitt, "Good Man, Good Woman," and EMMYLOU HARRIS scored a #1 country hit with his "Two More Bottles of Wine."

McClinton began performing at seventeen on Lubbock's *Big V Jamboree*. In the late 1950s, with his band the Straitjackets, he backed blues legends Lightnin' Hopkins, Howlin' Wolf, and Big Joe Turner when they visited Fort Worth's famous Jack's Place nightclub. In 1960 McClinton's first single, a cover of Sonny Boy Williamson's "Wake Up Baby," was the first record by a white artist aired on Fort Worth radio station KNOK.

In a style he learned and adapted from Jimmy Reed, McClinton mastered the harmonica, contributing to Bruce Channel's #1 pop hit "Hey! Baby" (1962). Touring with Channel in the United Kingdom, McClinton shared his stylings with John Lennon, an influence clearly evident on the Beatles' chart-topping "Love Me Do" (1964).

In 1964–65 McClinton teamed with Ronnie Kelly as the Ron-Dels. In the early 1970s McClinton and fellow Texan Glen Clark recorded two albums as Delbert and Glen, and the Blues Brothers included the duo's "B Movie Box Car Blues" on their debut album.

McClinton signed as a solo artist with ABC Records in 1975, relocated briefly to Nashville, and won critical acclaim for *Victim of Life's Circumstances*, *Love Rustler*, and *Genuine Cowhide*. He moved to Capricorn in 1978, but the company folded just as his second album for the label, *Keeper of the Flame*, began to sell. A first album for CAPITOL, *The Jealous Kind*, included the 1980–81 pop hit "Giving It Up for Your Love." McClinton's 1989 album *Live from Austin* secured his first Grammy nomination, and he won his first Grammy, with Raitt, in 1991.

In 1989 McClinton moved back to Nashville, where he recorded critically acclaimed albums for CURB. He recorded an album for Rising Tide featuring guest appearances by Mavis Staples, LYLE LOVETT, JOHN PRINE, and other stars. In 2001 New West Records began issuing new McClinton studio albums. *Nothing Personal* (2001) and *The Cost of Living* (2005) both won Grammys for Best Contemporary Blues Album. —*Jay Orr*

## O. B. McClinton
b. Senatobia, Mississippi, April 25, 1940; d. Sept. 23, 1987

Active as a country performer during the 1970s and 1980s, Obie Burnett McClinton was one of the few black artists to land multiple songs on the country charts. Earlier, during the 1960s, he had distinguished himself as a songwriter in Memphis.

*O. B. McClinton*

McClinton grew up in the segregated South, working in the cotton fields. He enjoyed listening to the GRAND OLE OPRY as well as to the blues and ROCKABILLY records aired by WLAC in Nashville and WHBQ in Memphis, respectively. TENNESSEE ERNIE FORD's "Sixteen Tons" was a favorite of his.

McClinton graduated from Rust College in Holly Springs, Mississippi, served in the U.S. Air Force, and worked as a DJ at WDIA in Memphis. As a songwriter he provided material for soul artists such as Otis Redding and James Carr.

Influenced by MERLE HAGGARD, HANK WILLIAMS, and CHARLEY PRIDE, McClinton was signed as a country artist to Stax Records (but placed on the affiliated label Enterprise) in 1971. His most successful singles were "Don't Let the Green Grass Fool You" (1972–73) and "My Whole World Is Falling Down" (1973), both of which broke into the lower reaches of the country Top Forty. He also recorded albums for Enterprise, including *O. B. McClinton: Country* and *Obie from Senatobie*, and then later recorded for MERCURY, EPIC, and smaller labels. He died of cancer in 1987. —*Gerry Wood*

## Del McCoury Band
b. Bakersville, North Carolina, February 1, 1939

BLUEGRASS star Delano Floyd McCoury is one of the few current bandleaders who worked with BILL MONROE. Monroe encouraged McCoury to apply his piercing tenor voice to lead vocals, and McCoury would make it the centerpiece of his own sound, driven by his solid rhythm guitar work and notable for first-rate instrumental solos and a diverse repertoire embracing bluegrass standards, newly written songs, and covers such as Richard Thompson's "1952 Vincent Black Lightning" and the Lovin' Spoonful's "Nashville Cats."

McCoury grew up in southeastern Pennsylvania, where his father was a lumberman. Mother Hazel often entertained her family with her guitar playing and mountain-style singing. Inspired by a FLATT & SCRUGGS recording, Del played banjo with Jack Cooke's Virginia Mountain Boys at Baltimore-area gigs.

By 1963 McCoury had joined Monroe's Blue Grass Boys on banjo, but he soon became lead singer and guitarist. In 1964 McCoury moved to California, where he worked with the Golden State Boys before returning to Pennsylvania and forming the Dixie Pals. In 1968 he released his first album, *Del McCoury Sings Bluegrass*, for Arhoolie Records. Other albums followed in the 1970s on ROUNDER, REBEL, and Revonah.

McCoury's recording slowed in the 1980s, but he kept enlarging his following on the bluegrass festival circuit. In 1981 son Ronnie (mandolin) joined the band, followed by son Rob (banjo) in 1989. Del relocated to Nashville in 1992 and added fiddler Jason Carter and bassist Mike Bub.

McCoury won the International Bluegrass Music Association (IBMA) Male Vocalist of the Year award in 1990 and won again in 1991, 1992, and 1996. As of 2010 the band had been named IBMA Entertainer of the Year nine times, while taking home the Album of the Year award in 1994 and garnering Instrumental Group honors in 1996 and 1997. *Ronnie and Rob McCoury* was IBMA's Instrumental Album of the Year in 1996, and both Carter and Bub have received top honors on their respective instruments. (Alan Bartram replaced Bub in 2005.)

The title track to the group's landmark *Cold Hard Facts* (1996) ruled the bluegrass charts for months, and the album became a Top Five AMERICANA chart-maker. Albums such as *Family* (1999) and *Del & the Boys* (2001), both on RICKY SKAGGS's Ceili Music label, also attracted new listeners, as did exposure on late-night TV talk shows, McCoury's musically eclectic DelFest annual festival, and appearances with jam bands Phish and Leftover Salmon.

In 2003 the Del McCoury Band joined the GRAND OLE OPRY and released the act's first album on the McCoury Music label, *It's Just the Night*, which became IBMA's Album of the Year. The label has also issued the Grammy-winning *The Company We Keep* (2005), the gospel collection *The Promised Land* (2006), the fifty-song album *Celebrating 50 Years of Del McCoury* (2009), and *Family Circle* (2009)—all by the band—as well bluegrass albums by MERLE HAGGARD and LARRY SPARKS. —*Chris Skinker*

*The Del McCoury Band: (from left) Ronnie McCoury, Mike Bub, Del McCoury, Jason Carter, and Rob McCoury*

## Charlie McCoy
b. Oak Hill, West Virginia, March 28, 1941

Nashville studio legend Charlie McCoy has graced the recordings of artists ranging from ELVIS PRESLEY and BOB DYLAN to WAYLON JENNINGS and LORETTA LYNN. McCoy's trademark harmonica style, distinguished by its speed, precision, clarity, and unerring phrasing, was radically different from the down-home approach of his predecessors and reestablished the mouth organ as a voice in country music.

Born in Oak Hill, West Virginia, McCoy grew up in Miami, Florida, where he began playing harmonica at age eight. In his teens he worked as backup player at country and rock & roll show dates statewide. At one performance he met rising country star MEL TILLIS, who encouraged him to come to Nashville. Already enrolled in music theory and voice classes, McCoy made one trip to check out job prospects, but he returned home to sharpen his arranging and conducting skills.

Young McCoy moved to MUSIC CITY in 1960 and recorded several sides as a rock & roll singer and guitarist for the Cadence and MONUMENT labels. Through Tillis, he met booking agent-music publisher JIM DENNY, who used him on song demos. McCoy's playing caught the ear of RCA record producer CHET ATKINS, who enlisted him for a 1961 Ann-Margret session that yielded "I Just Don't Understand," a Top Twenty pop hit. Session calls mushroomed after ROY ORBISON's Monument rendition of "Candy Man," featuring McCoy's harmonica backup, became a #25 pop record that same year.

Since then McCoy has worked thousands of sessions, often as many as 400 in a year. His tasteful harmonica can be heard on "500 Miles Away from Home" (BOBBY BARE), "Old Dogs, Children, and Watermelon Wine" (TOM T. HALL), "Only Daddy That'll Walk the Line" (Waylon Jennings), "He Stopped Loving Her Today"

*Charlie McCoy*

(GEORGE JONES), "Take This Job and Shove It," (JOHNNY PAYCHECK), and dozens of other hits. Likewise, EDDY ARNOLD, ROY CLARK, PATSY CLINE, MERLE HAGGARD, BRENDA LEE, WILLIE NELSON, CHARLEY PRIDE, and TAMMY WYNETTE relied on McCoy's talents. For his efforts McCoy received CMA's Instrumentalist of the Year award in 1972 and 1973. Playing harmonica, bass, guitar, keyboards, percussion, trumpet, saxophone, and tuba, McCoy also assisted recording artists across the musical spectrum, including LEON RUSSELL, Joe Simon, Paul Simon, Nancy Sinatra, and STEVE YOUNG, among many more.

As a featured artist, McCoy has made several dozen albums for Monument and other labels. *The Real McCoy*, which won a 1972 Grammy for Best Country Instrumental Performance, contained "I Started Loving You Again," a #16 country single of 1972. He was also a key member of Area Code 615, an early COUNTRY-ROCK band. Backed in the studio by the band Barefoot Jerry, he notched a #11 single, "Boogie Woogie," in 1974.

McCoy has reached vast television audiences. He was a frequent musician and featured artist on *Nashville Now*, the *CMA Awards*, *Midnight Special*, and *The Johnny Cash Show*. McCoy was *HEE HAW's* music director for eighteen years and filled the same role for numerous TV specials. Regular tours of the United States, Europe, and Japan have let millions enjoy this gifted musician in person.

Charlie McCoy was elected to THE COUNTRY MUSIC HALL OF FAME in 2009. —*Kim Field*

## Neal McCoy
b. Jacksonville, Texas, July 30, 1958

Neal McCoy has survived music industry hurdles to sustain a lengthy country music career. The son of Irish and Filipino parents, he was born Hubert Neal McGaughey Jr. When he began singing in East Texas clubs, he changed his stage name to McGoy (the phonetic spelling of his surname) and later McCoy.

Early on, McCoy was influenced by country, gospel, big band music, and R&B. In 1981 JANIE FRICKE heard him sing at a Dallas talent show, which led to six years of opening shows for CHARLEY PRIDE. After recording for the independent 16th Avenue Records, in 1991 he released his debut ATLANTIC collection, *At This Moment*, the title cut a cover of an R&B-tinged pop hit by Billy Vera. This album and its follow-up, *Where Forever Begins* (1992), included several moderately successful chart singles.

*No Doubt About It* (1994) netted McCoy his first two #1s—the title track and "Wink." Three singles from *You Gotta Love That* (1995) reached #3, including the title cut. *Neal McCoy* (1996) contained the #4 hit "Then You Can Tell Me Goodbye," a 1967 Casinos pop smash penned by JOHN D. LOUDERMILK. The #5 hit "The Shake" (1997), from his *Greatest Hits* collection, marked McCoy's first effort with producer KYLE LEHNING, but it was also the singer's last 1990s hit. Although *No Doubt About It* and *You Gotta Love That* both went platinum, McCoy's recording career faltered in the early 2000s as he shifted unsuccessfully to GIANT RECORDS and then to WARNER BROS. In 2005 he and manager Karen Kane formed 903 Music. *That's Life*, his first album for the independent label, debuted in the country Top Ten and yielded a Top Ten country single, "Billy's Got His Beer Goggles On." The firm signed DARRYL WORLEY but folded in 2007 due to cash flow problems and the failure to gain further radio success. McCoy still tours extensively and has won recognition for his work with USO. —*Calvin Gilbert*

## Frank and James McCravy

Recording almost 200 sides for several labels between 1925 and 1935, brothers Frank and James McCravy were quite successful with a repertoire heavily anchored in gospel music. Their material reflected their concurrent evangelistic work in the South and led record companies to promote them as an authentic country act despite their rather refined, formal musical approach.

Natives of Laurens, South Carolina, the McCravys both attended Furman University and began establishing their baritone/tenor duet style at about this time. Since they emphasized careful diction, it's not surprising that the brothers trekked north to record all of their material in a more formal way, using New York studios and musicians. James, however, would occasionally play guitar; he may have played violin as well. —*Bob Pinson*

## Mindy McCready
b. Fort Myers, Florida, November 30, 1975

Malinda Gayle McCready made a brief splash in country music with a cocky musical persona, a penchant for skin-tight clothes and bare midriffs, and three Top Ten hits during 1996–97: "Ten Thousand Angels," the chart-topping "Guys Do It All the Time," and "A Girl's Gotta Do (What a Girl's Gotta Do)." Her humorous approach to male chauvinism won her an immediate fan base of women.

McCready took private vocal lessons and attended summer school so she could graduate from high school at sixteen and pursue music full time. In 1994 she took tapes of her karaoke vocals to Nashville and gave herself a year to land a recording contract. Producer NORRO WILSON heard the tapes, and he and producer David Malloy took McCready into the studio. Fifty-one weeks after arriving in MUSIC CITY, McCready signed with BNA (part of the RCA Label Group), and her debut album, *Ten Thousand Angels* (1996), was quickly certified platinum. In 1997 she became the youngest country artist ever elected to CMA's Board of Directors.

McCready soon lost focus, however, and clashes with RCA executives led to her departure after two more albums. She signed with CAPITOL in 2000, but the label dropped her after one album. Personal troubles beset her starting in 2004. In 2010 she released *I'm Still Here* on Linus Entertainment and began appearing on the VH1 TV reality series *Celebrity Rehab with Dr. Drew.* —*Marjie McGraw*

## Brad McCuen
b. New York, New York, May 17, 1921; d. July 9, 2002

A respected music industry veteran, Brad McCuen worked for RCA RECORDS in sales and production from 1948 until 1969, at which point he left and founded Mega Records. While at RCA he advanced the careers of DON GIBSON, EDDY ARNOLD, and HANK SNOW, among others, and as a field man in the Southeast he was among the first to alert RCA to the impact ELVIS PRESLEY was having on the region in 1954. In the 1960s McCuen produced RCA's Vintage line, one of the industry's earliest, and best, record reissue series. As head of Mega he oversaw, most notably, the release of SAMMI SMITH's 1970–71 smash "Help Me Make It Through the Night." McCuen was a longtime member of the COUNTRY MUSIC HALL OF FAME AND MUSEUM's Board of Officers and Trustees. Middle Tennessee State University's Center for Popular Music acquired his 30,000-piece record collection and business papers in 1997. —*Daniel Cooper*

## Mel McDaniel
b. Checotah, Oklahoma, September 6, 1942; d. March 31, 2011

Mel McDaniel was the quintessential journeyman honky-tonker, a burly purveyor of mainstream good-time country music. Inspired to pursue a singing career by ELVIS PRESLEY, McDaniel worked nightclubs in Oklahoma to help support his mother after his parents' divorce. Following two unsuccessful years in Nashville (1969–71), he moved near his father, in Alaska, and sang for oil field workers during the pipeline construction boom of the 1970s.

CAPITOL RECORDS signed him in 1976; he broke into the Top Twenty in 1977 and scored his first Top Ten hit, "Louisiana Saturday Night," in 1981. McDaniel cited 1950s ROCKABILLY and country artists as influences, but primarily his hits were JUKEBOX picks for a keg party, including "Big Ole Brew," "Let It Roll (Let It Rock)," "Stand Up," and "Baby's Got Her Blue Jeans On." Even so, he never stooped to smarmy romance or formulaic wordplay ditties, and most of his music could be symbolized by his 1988 hit "Real Good Feel Good Song" (ironically his last entry in the Top Ten).

McDaniel wrote songs cut by a number of artists, including HOYT AXTON, CONWAY TWITTY, KENNY ROGERS, and JOHNNY RODRIGUEZ. Among McDaniel's best-known compositions is "The Grandest Lady of Them All," a tribute to the GRAND OLE OPRY, cowritten with Bob Morrison. McDaniel joined the Opry cast on January 11, 1986.

In 1996, a near-fatal fall into the orchestra pit at a Louisiana concert kept him off the road for a decade. In June 2009 he suffered a heart attack and never resumed touring. —*Bob Millard*

## Bob McDill
b. Beaumont, Texas, April 5, 1944

With an artist's spirit and a keen sense of observation, songwriter Robert Lee McDill has captured character, emotion, and circumstance in hit after hit.

First influenced by his mother's piano playing and family gospel singing, McDill obtained his first guitar at fourteen and began to play in bands and folk groups. While attending Lamar University (1962–66) in Beaumont, he joined a folk group known as the Newcomers and met ALLEN REYNOLDS, who—along with DICKEY LEE, JACK CLEMENT, and Bill Hall—was operating Beaumont's Gulf Coast Recording Studios. Impressed with McDill's talent and potential, Reynolds arranged for pop star Perry Como to record McDill's "The Happy Man" (1967) during McDill's two-year stint in the U.S. Navy. The following year Sam the Sham & the Pharaohs' recording of "Black Sheep" became McDill's second hit song.

After military service, McDill moved to Memphis. When Clement purchased the local publishing company Il Gatto, he hired McDill, Reynolds, and Lee and shifted operations to Nashville in 1970, a move that introduced McDill to singer-songwriter DON WILLIAMS and producer GARTH FUNDIS. Writing for Clement's Jack Music, McDill began to focus on country music and, with the exceptions of the albums *Short Stories* (JMI, 1972) and *Signatures* (RCA, 1988), put his performing ambitions to rest.

McDill found country writing success with JOHNNY RUSSELL's 1973 recording of "Catfish John" (written with Reynolds). Also in 1973, Russell's hit "Rednecks, White Socks, and Blue Ribbon Beer" became a *Billboard* Top Five hit for McDill. He has since scored some thirty *Billboard* #1s, including RONNIE MILSAP's "Nobody Likes Sad Songs" (1979), WAYLON JENNINGS's "Amanda" (1979), MEL McDANIEL's "Baby's Got Her Blue Jeans On" (1984), DAN SEALS's "Everything That Glitters (Is Not Gold)" (1986), KEITH WHITLEY's "Don't Close Your Eyes" (1988), ALABAMA's "Song of the South," and ALAN JACKSON's "Gone Country" 1994. Don Williams's #2 hit "Good Ole Boys Like Me" (1980) demonstrated McDill's literary bent, southern regional identity, closeness to nature, and sense of family. The prolific McDill has also penned hits recorded by artists as diverse as RAY CHARLES, Joe Cocker, EARL THOMAS CONLEY, LEFTY FRIZZELL, ANNE MURRAY, THE OSBORNE BROTHERS, and JEAN SHEPARD, to mention only a few.

McDill's many awards include his 1985 induction into the NASHVILLE SONGWRITERS HALL OF FAME. In the new century, McDill retired from songwriting. —*Kent Henderson*

## Skeets McDonald
b. Greenway, Arkansas, October 1, 1915; d. March 31, 1968

Enos William "Skeets" McDonald is best known for his #1 1952 hit "Don't Let the Stars Get in Your Eyes" and his long tenure with *TOWN HALL PARTY*. He grew up in Rector, Arkansas, and got his nickname as a youngster after being attacked by a swarm of mosquitoes. After high school, he worked in auto plants around Detroit and in 1935 started playing on WEXL in Royal Oak, Michigan, in a band called the Lonesome Cowboys. Following military service in World War II he returned to Detroit and made his first recordings for Fortune Records in 1950, including the risqué "Tattooed Lady." He then recorded for London and MERCURY (as Skeets Saunders) before moving to the West Coast in February 1951.

CLIFFIE STONE signed McDonald to appear on his *HOMETOWN JAMBOREE* television show on KXLA–Pasadena, and he joined the CAPITOL RECORDS roster in April 1951. His only charted Capitol hit was his cover of the Perry Como hit "Don't Let the Stars Get in Your Eyes" in late 1952, but he recorded prolifically for the company until 1958 and appeared regularly on *Town Hall Party*. McDonald was slightly more successful on COLUMBIA, scoring four hits, including the Top Ten "Call Me Mr. Brown" in 1963. His last recording was for Uni Records in 1967. —*Colin Escott*

## Ronnie McDowell
b. Fountain Head, Tennessee, March 26, 1950

Ronald Dean McDowell shot to fame with his 1977 sound-alike tribute to ELVIS PRESLEY, "The King Is Gone." Snapped up by grieving Presley fans, the Scorpion Records release quickly became a Top Twenty country and pop hit. McDowell, long a Presley fan himself, had had earlier releases on Chart and Scorpion and wrote songs recorded by ROY DRUSKY and BILLY WALKER. But "The King Is Gone," cowritten with Lee Morgan, launched a career that produced fifteen Top Ten country hits.

A smooth singer with a flair for ROCKABILLY-flavored country-pop, McDowell has sometimes recorded shallow songs and novelty material, but fans kept him in the charts into 1991. He moved to EPIC in 1979, recording hits including the #1s "Older Women" and "You're Gonna Ruin My Bad Reputation." Moving to CURB/MCA in 1986 and to Curb in 1987, McDowell made

additional chart records, most notably a rocked-out 1987 remake of CONWAY TWITTY's massive 1958 hit "It's Only Make Believe," with Twitty providing a guest vocal.

A favorite of Priscilla Presley, McDowell has provided Elvis's singing voice for several biographical TV movies and for the 1990 ABC television series *Elvis*. He also led a 1993 touring package that included notable Presley sidemen such as Scotty Moore, D. J. Fontana, and the JORDANAIRES. Recording success played out, however, ending with "Unchained Melody" in 1990–91. In 2002 McDowell released two Curb albums—*Country* and a collection of beach music recorded with Bill Pinkney's Original Drifters. *Live at Church Street Station* (Acrobat, 2006) and *Lost in Dirty Dancing* (Curb, 2009), followed. —*Thomas Goldsmith*

## Red River Dave McEnery (*see* Red River Dave)

## Reba McEntire
b. McAlester, Oklahoma, March 28, 1955

Reba Nell McEntire ranks as the most successful female country performer of her generation, and she has been cited as a role model by nearly every successful female country singer to follow in her wake. She has achieved more than fifty Top Ten singles and more #1 country albums than any other female artist.

McEntire has won the ACM Female Vocalist of the Year award seven times and has been named CMA Female Vocalist of the Year four consecutive times, both records as of 2011. She was CMA's Entertainer of the Year in 1986 and ACM's Entertainer of the Year in 1994. In addition, she has won two Grammy awards.

But her success as a recording artist represents only part of her story. In 1988, she founded Starstruck Entertainment, a multi-dimensional corporation encompassing booking, management,

*Reba McEntire*

music publishing, a recording studio, and transportation services. She has starred in films, in her own hit TV comedy series (*Reba*) from 2001 to 2007, and on Broadway in the title role of a hit Broadway musical (a 2001 revival of *Annie Get Your Gun*).

McEntire grew up in Chockie, Oklahoma, on an eight-thousand-acre cattle ranch, traveling regularly to rodeos with her father, champion calf roper Clark McEntire. Her mother, Jackie, was a powerful singer and a strong influence. By the time Reba reached high school, she and her siblings Pake and Susie performed as the Singing McEntires. In 1974 she sang the national anthem at the National Rodeo finals in Oklahoma City. Cowboy singer RED STEAGALL heard her and financed a recording session, leading MERCURY RECORDS to sign her in 1975. The following June, she married Charlie Battles, a rodeo star ten years her senior, and she continued to compete in rodeos as a barrel racer while earning her degree from Southeastern Oklahoma State University.

McEntire began releasing singles in 1976, hitting stages dressed in cowgirl clothes and showing off her big voice, with its distinctive accent and emotion-rich phrasing. Her first Mercury album, released in 1977, didn't sell well. But in 1978 McEntire hit the Top Twenty with "Three Sheets in the Wind," a duet with Jacky Ward, and the following year with a remake of "Sweet Dreams," a song associated with one of her idols, PATSY CLINE. In 1980, McEntire entered the Top Ten with "(You Lift Me) Up to Heaven" and realized her first #1s in 1982–83 with "Can't Even Get the Blues" and "You're the First Time I've Thought About Leaving."

Shifting to MCA RECORDS in 1983, McEntire took more control of her career. Her back-to-basics album *My Kind of Country* contained the #1 hits "How Blue" and "Somebody Should Leave." She won her first CMA Female Vocalist of the Year award in 1984, and in 1986 she joined the GRAND OLE OPRY cast. Her video for her hit "Whoever's in New England" sparked an interest in acting, and her videos began to utilize powerful story lines, as in her portrayal of a waitress-wife-mother who goes back to school to get her degree in 1992's video of "Is There Life out There" (which led to a 1994 TV movie based on the same concept). McEntire's film-acting career began in 1990 with *Tremors* and continued with roles in *Luck of the Draw: The Gambler Returns* (1991), *The Man from Left Field* (1992), *North* (1994), *The Little Rascals* (1994), *Buffalo Girls* (1995), *Forever Love* (1998), *Secret of Giving* (2001), and *One Night at McCool's* (2001). Her best-selling autobiography, *Reba: My Story*, was published in 1994.

With her 1987 divorce from Battles, McEntire moved to Nashville and began building her business enterprises. She married Narvel Blackstock, a former steel guitarist who eventually assumed management of her career. Amid her climb to international success, McEntire encountered unimaginable tragedy: In March 1991, seven members of her band, her road manager, and the pilot and copilot of a chartered private jet were killed when the plane hit a mountainside during takeoff. The private jet was one of two booked by McEntire to take her team from a private corporate concert in San Diego to a public performance in Fort Wayne, Indiana. McEntire, Blackstock, and two other band members were booked on the other flight. The singer took an extended break from touring and recorded the 1992 album *For My Broken Heart*, one of her biggest sellers.

McEntire has always claimed the female country audience as her first concern, addressing their lives and troubles. "I'm trying to sing songs for women, to say for them what they can't say for themselves," she told the *Chicago Tribune*'s Jack Hurst. "But I'm trying to do it for the eighties and nineties." She also insisted on

higher production values for country concerts, creating elaborate stages complemented by video screens comparable to the flashiest high-tech rock and pop concerts.

When the TV series *Reba* ended after six seasons, McEntire refocused her energies and talents on recording and touring—with outstanding results. In November 2008, she left MCA Records after twenty-five years and signed with Valory Music Group, a subsidiary of BIG MACHINE RECORDS. Her next album, *Keep on Loving You*, was released on the joint Starstruck/Valory label in August 2009 and debuted at #1 on both the *Billboard* country chart and the all-genre *Billboard 200* album chart. In January 2010 her rendition of "Consider Me Gone" became her first #1 in five years, suggesting that McEntire still had plenty to offer as she entered her fifth decade as an entertainer. The song "Turn on the Radio," from her 2010 album *All the Women I Am*, gave her another chart-topper later that year.

With her election to THE COUNTRY MUSIC HALL OF FAME in 2011, McEntire achieved the rare feat of still placing hits on the country charts at the time of her induction. —*Mary A. Bufwack*

## Jack McFadden
b. Sikeston, Missouri, January 9, 1927; d. June 16, 1998

Jack McFadden's career as manager of country music performers began with, and will forever be associated with, the career of BUCK OWENS. A former movie theater and radio station manager, McFadden got his start as a booking agent in California for the MADDOX BROTHERS & ROSE shortly after World War II. He went on to book and promote other artists on the West Coast, including HANK WILLIAMS and TOMMY COLLINS. In 1963 McFadden made a quantum leap in income and prestige when he was hired by Owens, just as Owens's career was hitting a peak that would last through that decade. In 1965, with Owens, McFadden formed the BAKERSFIELD-based OMAC firm (Owens-McFadden Artists Corporation), which booked live appearances for Owens and an entire stable of West Coast talent that included, at one time or another, MERLE HAGGARD, Rose Maddox (see Maddox Brothers and Rose), and WYNN STEWART. In that capacity McFadden was one of the most important figures in California's country music scene, and he was one of the founding members of the Academy of Country Music (ACM), the West Coast's version of the Country Music Association (CMA). In 1983 he moved his operations to Nashville and established McFadden Artists Corporation as a major MUSIC CITY management firm with its own office building on Eighteenth Avenue South in the MUSIC ROW area. McFadden managed BILLY RAY CYRUS, RHONDA VINCENT, STEVE WARINER, KEITH WHITLEY, and LORRIE MORGAN. He died from liver cirrhosis at age seventy-one. —*Mark Fenster*

## Dennis McGee
b. Bayou Marron, Louisiana, January 26, 1893; d. October 3, 1989

Dennis McGee recorded the largest body of early CAJUN fiddle tunes committed to disc between the years 1929 and 1930. His work provides insights into original versions of these tunes and the early Acadian fiddle style and establishes a baseline for assessing how tunes are learned through aural traditions.

As an orphan in southwestern Louisiana, McGee was passed from household to household, mistreated and used as a servant by family members who took him in. Finally he found a happy home with his uncle Theodore McGee, who bought him a fiddle and nurtured his musical talent. In the late 1920s, Dennis performed at dances, entered local talent contests, played with various area musicians, and finally recorded, chosen from among other competitors at a music contest in Opelousas.

McGee recorded fiddle duets (the pre-accordion Cajun music) with two famed *segoneurs*, or second-fiddle players. One was his brother-in-law, Sady Courville of Eunice; the second was Ernest Frugé from Grand Marais. Courville's style was based on chording, whereas Frugé's approach involved more complex noting and bow rocking. Both styles complemented McGee's fiddle work in recordings for Vocalion (1929) and BRUNSWICK (1930).

In addition to these early fiddle pairings, McGee played second fiddle on recordings by accordionists Angelas LeJeune (from Church Point, Louisiana), and Amédé Ardoin. McGee's friendship with Ardoin, a legendary black Louisiana musician, produced eleven released sides for the COLUMBIA, Brunswick, and BLUEBIRD labels (1929–34). McGee's intense, rocking, second-fiddle style combined with Ardoin's syncopations and triplets to produce excellent examples of early Cajun accordion–fiddle duets.

McGee and friend Angelas LeJeune joined forces with Ernest Frugé on six interesting sides for Brunswick, including "Perrodin Two-Step" and "Valse de Pointe Noire," in September 1929. McGee and LeJeune also performed together in accordion contests and traveled throughout southwestern Louisiana, playing in dancehalls. McGee recorded two of his most influential early tunes, "Madame Young donnez-moi votre plus jolie blonde" (later to become "Allons danser Colinda") and the haunting "Mon cher bébé creole" with Sady Courville for Vocalion in March 1929, at McGee's first recording session.

After several years McGee retired from the dancehall scene and supported his family of twelve children through tenant farming, barbering, and various odd jobs. In later life he resumed his musical career, touring throughout the United States with his old friend Sady Courville. —*Ann Allen Savoy*

## Sam and Kirk McGee

Sam Fleming McGee b. Williamson County, Tennessee, May 1, 1894;
    d. August 21, 1975
Kirk McGee b. Williamson County, Tennessee, November 4, 1899;
    d. October 24, 1983

Though folk music fans remember them primarily as accompanists for UNCLE DAVE MACON, Sam and Kirk McGee had a career that extended from the early days of the GRAND OLE OPRY to the show's move from THE RYMAN AUDITORIUM to OPRYLAND in 1974. In fact, one of their acoustic guitar duets helped to inspire visiting journalist Garrison Keillor (covering the move for *The New Yorker*) to create his radio show *A PRAIRIE HOME COMPANION*.

The McGees' music was much more eclectic than that of most early Opry performers. Sam learned guitar tunings and slide techniques from black railroad workers near his family home; Kirk adapted the blues records of Papa Charley Jackson and others to a STRINGBAND format and sported a singing style derived partly from his tenure at church-based singing schools. Both brothers liked early jazz, and Sam adapted ragtime tunes (learned from piano rolls) to the guitar.

It was Sam who first tested the waters, playing guitar and banjo for the already famed Macon. While with Macon at a 1926

recording session, Sam made several guitar solos, including his famous "Buck Dancer's Choice" and "Franklin Blues." The discs were among country's first serious guitar solos, helping to launch a tradition that would continue through RILEY PUCKETT to CHET ATKINS and beyond. In the early 1930s the McGees teamed with Dickson County's FIDDLIN' ARTHUR SMITH to form the Dixieliners, by most accounts the hottest string band the early Opry ever had. Unfortunately, this band never recorded in its prime (BLUEBIRD recordings under the same name featured Smith and the DELMORE BROTHERS).

Even as other veteran Opry groups broke up, Sam and Kirk kept at it until the late 1950s, when they were discovered by folk revival fans. The McGees made a comeback of sorts, recording albums for Folkways and STARDAY and appearing at a number of festivals. Sam recorded several solo albums for Arhoolie and for MBA, a company he partly owned. In their later years, both Kirk and Sam hosted a procession of young instrumentalists anxious to learn from two masters.

Sam was killed in a farming accident in 1975; Kirk died in 1983. —*Charles Wolfe*

## John McGhee & Frank Welling

John Leftridge McGhee b. Griffithsville, West Virginia, April 9, 1882;
    d. May 9, 1945
Benjamin Franklin Welling b. Lawrence County, Ohio, February 16, 1898;
    d. January 23, 1957

John McGhee & Frank Welling recorded more than 200 sides between 1927 and 1933, for labels including BRUNSWICK, GENNETT, Melotone, Paramount, and various subsidiaries. Sacred material featuring McGhee's strong bass vocals and harmonica, coupled with Welling's lead singing and steel guitar, comprised their main fare, augmented by sentimental and humorous songs. Welling also performed some of the earliest recitations in recorded country music. Based in Huntington, West Virginia, in their duet days, Welling relocated to WCHS–Charleston, West Virginia, in 1937 and spent the rest of his life as a radio announcer, creating the character of Uncle Si. —*Ivan M. Tribe*

## Tim McGraw

b. Delhi, Louisiana, May 1, 1967

Tim McGraw initially achieved recognition by mixing uptempo novelty songs with sensitive ballads. He quickly expanded into a multifaceted career built on savvy song selection, dynamic concerts, and a talent for film acting. He also coproduced several albums for singer JO DEE MESSINA and the debut album of the country duo Halfway to Hazard.

Samuel Timothy McGraw grew up as Tim Smith, believing he was the son of his stepfather, Horace Smith, a long-distance trucker. He didn't realize his biological father was famous baseball pitcher Tug McGraw (1944–2004) until he was twelve.

In 1989 young McGraw moved to Nashville. In 1991, he sent a demo tape to Tug McGraw; Tug had a friend send it to CURB RECORDS, where Tim landed a deal. His self-titled debut album yielded three insignificant chart singles. His second album, however, 1994's *Not a Moment Too Soon*, rocketed him to stardom.

The album's first single, "Indian Outlaw," drew complaints from Native American groups, but it became McGraw's first

*Tim McGraw*

Top Ten country record. The next release, the emotional ballad "Don't Take the Girl," gave McGraw his first #1 hit. Ultimately, *Not a Moment Too Soon* reached #1 on *Billboard*'s all-genre sales chart, was named *Billboard*'s best-selling country album of 1994, and became ACM's 1994 Album of the Year. As of 2010 *Not a Moment Too Soon* had sold more than 6 million units.

McGraw's third album, 1995's *All I Want*, yielded five Top Ten country hits, including the #1 singles "I Like It, I Love It" and "She Never Lets It Go to Her Heart." On October 6, 1996, McGraw married singer FAITH HILL; their first duet, "It's Your Love," hit #1 on the country charts in July 1997 and won CMA's 1997 Vocal Event of the Year award. The song was the first single from the album *Everywhere*, a collection that included six hits in all, four of them #1s, and sold more than 4 million copies. McGraw's *Everywhere* was CMA's Album of the Year for 1998.

The singer's hot streak continued with 1999's *A Place in the Sun*, which debuted at #1 on the country and pop album charts. The album included five Top Ten hits, including four #1s ("Please Remember Me," "Something Like That," "My Best Friend," "My Next Thirty Years"). In 1999, McGraw repeated as the winner of CMA's Album of the Year; he won ACM's Top Male Vocalist awards for 1998 and 1999 and claimed CMA's Male Vocalist of the Year honors for 1999.

Coinciding with the release of McGraw's first *Greatest Hits* album in 2000, he and his wife launched the Soul2Soul Tour, which became the year's leading country music tour. McGraw's next studio album, 2001's *Set This Circus Down*, picked up where he had left off. It featured four #1 singles, "Grown Men Don't Cry," "Angry All the Time," "The Cowboy in Me," and "Unbroken." On his 2002 album, *Tim McGraw and the Dancehall Doctors*, he recorded with backing from his longtime touring band, today a rarity in country music. The album contained four Top Five hits, two of them #1s, "Real Good Man" and "Watch the

Wind Blow By." Two songs from the album were featured in the film *Black Cloud*, which marked McGraw's acting debut. In this same year, he had a critically lauded supporting role in a hit movie, *Friday Night Lights*.

Since 2004 McGraw has balanced recording and concert tours with film roles. He's continued to score massive hits, including "Live Like You Were Dying." *Billboard*'s most-played country song of 2004, the number won awards as single and song of the year from both the CMA and the ACM. It also earned McGraw a Grammy for 2004's Best Male Country Vocal Performance, while cowriters Tim Nichols and CRAIG WISEMAN snagged the Grammy for the year's Best Country Song. Also in 2004, McGraw guested on the pop hit "Over and Over" with rap star Nelly. In 2006, Taylor Swift scored her first hit with a song titled "Tim McGraw," a paean to an ex-boyfriend that used their shared love for a McGraw hit as a touchstone. McGraw's recording output began to slow, but he still enjoyed success, for each of the albums *Let It Go* (2007) and *Southern Voice* (2009) featured a #1 hit.

As an actor, McGraw followed his *Friday Night Lights* success with major roles in the films *Flicka*, *The Kingdom*, *Four Christmases*, *The Blind Side*, and *Country Strong*. —*Marjie McGraw*

## Clayton McMichen
b. Allatoona, Georgia, January 26, 1900; d. January 4, 1970

One of early country music's most influential stars, Clayton "Pappy" McMichen learned to fiddle at age eleven from uncles and from his father, a trained North Georgia musician who played fiddle tunes at local square dances and Viennese waltzes at uptown hotel society dances. In 1913 the family moved to Atlanta, where young

*Clayton McMichen*

Clayton became an automobile mechanic. He soon entered his first fiddlers' contest and took third prize. In about 1918 he assembled the Hometown Boys, who made their radio debut on the newly opened WSB in 1922. In 1926 McMichen joined GID TANNER, RILEY PUCKETT, and Fate Norris to record for COLUMBIA RECORDS as the SKILLET LICKERS, but concurrently and subsequently McMichen organized a succession of other bands, the best known being the Georgia Wildcats.

Dominated by Tanner and Puckett, the Skillet Lickers were heavily oriented toward traditional fiddle tunes, banjo songs, and BALLADS; McMichen, considerably younger than his cohorts and more attuned to jazz and contemporary pop, led his own bands in more modern directions. (McMichen also penned a number of pieces his bands recorded, the most successful of which was "Peach Pickin' Time in Georgia," subsequently recorded by JIMMIE RODGERS in 1932, with McMichen playing violin backup.)

Nevertheless, his skills as an OLD-TIME breakdown fiddler were seldom matched, and, together with Lowe Stokes, McMichen provided dynamic lead fiddling on all the Skillet Lickers' recordings between 1926 and 1931. The Skillet Lickers soon split, and McMichen's Wildcats played old-timey music, pop, and jazz throughout the eastern United States until the late 1930s, also recording for DECCA from 1937 to 1939. Additionally, McMichen began organizing and winning numerous fiddle contests. He settled in Louisville, Kentucky, in 1939 and created a larger dance band, while Wildcat stalwart SLIM BRYANT continued with a smaller group, briefly using the Georgia Wildcats name before dropping "Georgia." In 1945, no longer recording, McMichen's group became a Dixieland jazz band and for a decade played six days each week on Louisville radio stations. In the 1960s, the national revival in old-time music provided new venues for McMichen on college campuses and at folk festivals.

While most of country music's first generation of recording stars were farmers or tradesmen first and musicians second, McMichen stood out in his highly professional approach. He watched in frustration as Tanner and FIDDLIN' JOHN CARSON—players "Mac" considered less musically gifted—captured the limelight, and he kept struggling to raise country's image and standards. Embittered, McMichen stood before college crowds at the NEWPORT FOLK FESTIVAL and mocked their enthusiasm for the Skillet Lickers' older, traditional music—a genre he still held in contempt. Ironically, the music of the Skillet Lickers is still widely accessible, while the Georgia Wildcats' recordings were out of print for many years.

McMichen remained active until shortly before his death in 1970. MAC WISEMAN and MERLE TRAVIS honored the pioneering musician with their 1982 double-LP album *The Clayton McMichen Story.* —*Norm Cohen*

## Medicine Shows

Early in the nineteenth century, rural Americans, often without a resident physician within easy traveling distance, patronized purveyors of various elixirs, ointments, herbs, and tonics. These medicinal salesmen traveled by wagon from town to town, urging people to purchase remedies for their ills. Without the watchful eye of today's governmental regulatory agencies, the potions often lacked any demonstrable efficacy, but the "doctor" was miles away by the time his disenchanted customers might have come to such a conclusion. To attract large audiences of potential buyers, the dispenser of remedies would host free shows featuring musicians, comedians, dancers, jugglers, acrobats, short dramatic performances, and testimonials from confederates before launching into his pitch. These medicine shows flourished into the early twentieth century, languishing by World War I as a result of both improved medical care and competing forms of entertainment. In the rural Southeast, traveling medicine shows were still common into the 1930s, rare by the 1950s, and virtually extinct by the mid-1970s.

Many early country music performers (and African American entertainers in other fields) traveled with one or more medicine shows, and their experience affected their own musical styles and repertoires. Medicine show music was invariably secular and lighthearted and often comical or bawdy. Among the country musicians who worked medicine shows early in their careers were UNCLE DAVE MACON, CLARENCE "TOM" ASHLEY, DOC HOPKINS, LEW CHILDRE, JIMMIE RODGERS, ROY ACUFF, GENE AUTRY, and HANK WILLIAMS. In 1929 both COLUMBIA and OKEH issued recordings of rural comedy skits parodying the still-familiar medicine show (Columbia 15482-D: "Kickapoo Medicine Show"; OKeh 45380, 45391, and 45413: "The Medicine Show, Acts 1–6"). Microgroove recordings by veteran medicine show entertainers Harmonica Frank Floyd and Tom Ashley recreated typical medicine show musical humor, as did stage shows by RAMBLIN' TOMMY SCOTT. —*Norm Cohen*

## D. L. Menard

b. Erath, Louisiana, April 14, 1932

D. L. Menard, known as the Cajun Hank Williams, has given CAJUN MUSIC some of its most beloved songs. His "Porte d'en arrière" ("The Back Door") has remained a regional favorite since it was first released on the Swallow label in 1962.

Doris Leon Menard began his musical career as a teenage guitarist and vocalist in accordionist Elias Badeaux's band, Badeaux & the Louisiana Aces, in about 1949. This group made the first recording of "The Back Door," with Menard on guitar and vocals.

HANK WILLIAMS was the major influence on Menard's music. In a 1951 meeting in a Louisiana nightclub, Williams encouraged Menard to record his own songs, telling the aspiring songwriter that if music is truly one's own, it is valuable. In addition, Williams's insight that keeping music simple lets everyday people relate to it strongly affected Menard's writing.

Since then, Menard has penned many beautiful songs, such as "Under the Green Oak Tree," "I Can't Forget You," "She Didn't Know I Was Married," and "Rebecca Ann." His music has attracted such country musicians as RICKY SKAGGS, Buck White (of THE WHITES), and JERRY DOUGLAS, all of whom appeared with him on his 1985 ROUNDER release *Cajun Saturday Night*.

When not touring internationally, Menard has made his living building chairs. In his native town of Erath, living with some of his seven children, he runs a small, home-based chair factory, working with his wife, Louella, who puts hemp seats on ladder-back frames. Grandchildren are usually present as Menard and wife work on chairs or cook huge pots of food in their rocking-chair-filled kitchen.

In 1994 Menard received a prestigious National Heritage Fellowship from the National Endowment for the Arts. —*Ann Allen Savoy*

## Mercury Records
established in Chicago, Illinois, 1945

Mercury Records has evolved from a feisty independent record company into a leading country music label and subsidiary of one of the world's largest entertainment conglomerates.

Mercury was founded by record-pressing plant owner Irving Green, artist manager Berle Adams, and talent scout Art Talmadge. With a growing national economy and pent-up demand for recordings, Mercury used its efficient pressing capacity and aggressive promotion to compete head to head with major labels. Country music was an early label concentration—along with R&B, jazz, and classical music—but Mercury's country commitment blossomed in 1948 when MURRAY NASH assumed responsibilities as country A&R man. Operating from Knoxville, Nash signed FLATT & SCRUGGS, the Carlisles (see BILL CARLISLE), and CARL STORY, among others. In 1951 Mercury pop singer Patti Page had a huge hit with "Tennessee Waltz," written by RCA VICTOR artist PEE WEE KING and King band member REDD STEWART.

D KILPATRICK handled the country A&R position from 1951 to 1955 and added JOHNNY HORTON and THE STANLEY BROTHERS to the roster. In 1957, to bolster its country music presence, Mercury joined with STARDAY RECORDS of Houston to form Mercury/Starday. Although the merger lasted only a year and a half, it gave Mercury several artists, including GEORGE JONES.

In 1961 Dutch firm Philips Electronics purchased Mercury; the following year Philips expanded into three labels: Mercury, Smash, and Philips. Mercury became a mainstay in country music after SHELBY SINGLETON was appointed head of the Nashville office in 1961. With the aid of JERRY KENNEDY, he began producing hits by LEROY VAN DYKE, FARON YOUNG, ROY DRUSKY, and DAVE DUDLEY. Two of the company's top stars, ROGER MILLER and JERRY LEE LEWIS, were signed to Smash Records before joining Mercury in 1970.

As the 1970s began, Kennedy had already taken over country A&R duties and opened Mercury's Nashville studio. New talent during his tenure included TOM T. HALL, THE STATLER BROTHERS, JOHNNY RODRIGUEZ, and REBA MCENTIRE. In 1971 Dutch conglomerate PolyGram took over the Mercury labels and acquired MGM and Polydor.

During the 1980s, under the direction of FRANK JONES (1983–85) and Steve Popovich (1986–87), the label signed KATHY MATTEA and veteran performer JOHNNY CASH. With Paul Lucks (1987–93) and A&R chief HAROLD SHEDD (1988–94) supervising the Nashville office, Mercury released recordings by THE KENTUCKY HEADHUNTERS, SAMMY KERSHAW, and BILLY RAY CYRUS. In 1992 LUKE LEWIS took charge of the MUSIC CITY office, enjoying continued success with SHANIA TWAIN and TERRI CLARK.

The Universal Music Group bought PolyGram in 1998, and in 2002 UMG Nashville was formed, consolidating the labels MCA Nashville, Mercury Nashville, and LOST HIGHWAY RECORDS under Lewis's management. As of early 2011, the Mercury Nashville roster included, among others, Laura Bell Bundy, Easton Corbin, BILLY CURRINGTON, Julianne Hough, JAMEY JOHNSON, SUGARLAND, Shania Twain, and Holly Williams. —Don Roy

## MerleFest
established 1988

From its modest start as a two-day concert held in the spring of 1988 to memorialize guitarist Merle Watson (1949–1985) and to raise funds for a garden in his honor at Wilkes Community College in Wilkesboro, North Carolina, MerleFest has become one of America's most popular, diverse, and vibrant roots-music festivals.

Since the beginning, MerleFest has been figuratively—and, to some extent, literally—presided over by Watson's father, DOC WATSON, with whom Merle performed for many years. Doc's wide-ranging fan base and musical friendships set the tone for the gathering, which quickly became a favorite with BLUEGRASS and OLD-TIME country musicians, both traditional and adventurous. Among those who joined Doc Watson at the initial event were EARL SCRUGGS, MARTY STUART, JOHN HARTFORD, and NEWGRASS REVIVAL.

Over the years, MerleFest has grown to nearly a full week of concerts and workshops on multiple stages, along with a prominent songwriting contest named for country musician and songwriter Chris Austin (1963–1991). While bluegrass, old-time, and other country musicians continue to have a strong presence, Wilkesboro festival's growing identity as an AMERICANA showcase has led to an even more varied roster of artists, who perform for audiences numbering in the tens of thousands. —Jon Weisberger

## Jo Dee Messina
b. Framingham, Massachusetts, August 25, 1970

Massachusetts native Jo Dee Marie Messina established herself in the late 1990s and early 2000s with several uptempo country radio hits about women taking control of their lives and relationships. By 2009, though, Messina struggled to regain her standing after business and personal problems stalled her momentum.

In her teens, Messina led a family country band before moving to Nashville in 1990. While performing on a radio show in Kentucky, she met Nashville record producer BYRON GALLIMORE. Through Gallimore, Messina befriended country star TIM MCGRAW, and McGraw introduced her to his label, CURB RECORDS, which signed the young singer. Gallimore and McGraw coproduced Messina's first four studio albums. (Messina and BRENT MAHER coproduced her 2002 holiday album, A Joyful Noise).

Her self-titled debut album (1996) netted the #2 hit "Heads Carolina, Tails California." But I'm Alright (1998) provided her triumphant moment, with three consecutive #1s—"Bye-Bye," "I'm Alright," and "Stand Beside Me"—and a cover of DOTTIE WEST's "Lesson in Leavin'" that reached #2. The album Burn (2000) continued her success, with two #1s ("That's the Way" and a duet with McGraw, "Bring on the Rain") and two more Top Tens ("Burn," "Downtime").

In 2003, Curb Records decided to hold her fourth album in favor of a Greatest Hits package. Two years later, "My Give a Damn's Busted" launched the delayed album, Delicious Surprise, with a #1 hit, but as of this writing none of her subsequent singles has broken the Top Twenty. In 2004 Messina underwent treatment of alcoholism, and in 2007 she married businessman Chris Deffenbaugh. In 2010, Messina issued a trilogy of EPs: Unmistakable: Love; Unmistakable: Drive; and Unmistakable: Inspiration. —Calvin Gilbert

## MGM Records
established in New York, New York, March 1947

Loew's, Inc., parent company of MGM film studios (Metro-Goldwyn-Mayer, established in 1924), decided in 1945 to issue soundtracks from its musicals. In August of that year, veteran recording executive FRANK WALKER was hired to start MGM Records, and by the company's launch in March 1947 it was a full-line record firm headquartered in New York with a plant in New Jersey. Walker stayed until 1956.

Throughout its existence, the core of the business was soundtracks such as *Gone With the Wind*, *Brigadoon*, and *Gigi*. Walker signed pop acts including Jimmy Dorsey and Kate Smith, some R&B acts such as Billy Eckstine, and country artists such as HANK WILLIAMS and BOB WILLS, while his successor, Arnold Maxin, signed Connie Francis, the Animals, ROY ORBISON, Herman's Hermits, CONWAY TWITTY, and others. Even with those acquisitions, and the purchase of Verve Records in 1960, MGM never rose above quasi–major label status. It opened a Nashville office in 1965 under JIM VIENNEAU.

With wavering commitment from the parent corporation, there were several presidents after Maxin, including MIKE CURB (then twenty-five years old) and JIMMY BOWEN. Polydor Records eventually bought the non-movie repertoire of MGM Records in April 1972 and ceased using the MGM trademark in 1976; by then MGM artists were transferred to Polydor (now Universal), which manages MGM's nonsoundtrack catalog. WARNER BROS-Rhino manages MGM movie soundtracks. —*Colin Escott*

## Mid-Day Merry-Go-Round
established in Knoxville, Tennessee, 1936; ended 1962

From the mid-1930s into the 1950s, WNOX, Tennessee's oldest station and eighth in age nationwide, was known as a stepping-stone to the GRAND OLE OPRY because of the many Opry stars recruited from WNOX stages. The popular noontime *Mid-Day Merry-Go-Round* was the station's most prominent and longest-running country music program.

The acquisition of WNOX by E. W. Scripps Company (Scripps-Howard) in 1935 brought a new staff and increased the station's broadcasting power. Richard Westergaard became station manager and hired Lowell Blanchard (b. Palmer, Illinois, November 15, 1910; d. February 19, 1968), a young announcer just graduated from the University of Illinois. Blanchard began his twenty-eight-year WNOX career in late January 1936. He immediately began polishing acts, creating new gimmicks and comic materials, and developing a professional cast.

The *Mid-Day Merry-Go-Round*, launched soon after Blanchard arrived, was essentially a variety show with an experimental flavor. It catered to a largely rural audience, but the show did not present folk music or mainstream country music exclusively. Some of its headliners—the Stringdusters (HOMER & JETHRO) and the Dixieland Swingsters, for example—played a mixture of country and jazz, the latter including Dixieland and swing.

On WNOX country shows, comedy was king. Programs were laced with jokes, many masterminded by Blanchard himself. The station's country-comedy format helped to develop some of the most popular rural comedians of the twentieth century, including Homer & Jethro and ARCHIE CAMPBELL.

An abbreviated list of performers at WNOX between 1936 and 1962 includes ROY ACUFF, CHET ATKINS, BILL CARLISLE, DON GIBSON, EDDIE HILL, JOHNNIE & JACK, PEE WEE KING, THE LILLY BROTHERS, BENNY MARTIN, JIMMY MARTIN, Lost John Miller, CHARLIE MONROE, ARTHUR Q. SMITH, and the Tennessee Ramblers. After World War II, WNOX country shows reached their peak popularity as the Saturday night *Tennessee Barn Dance*

and weekday *Mid-Day Merry-Go-Round* attracted a constant stream of first-rate talent.

Ultimately, however, WNOX, with its relatively small 10,000-watt transmitter, could not compete with 50,000-watt radio giants such as WSM and WLW—or with television. In late 1954 the Federal Communications Commission ruled that WNOX could not have a television affiliate, further weakening the station's role in supporting country music in Knoxville. During the next five years, the *Mid-Day Merry-Go-Round* and *Tennessee Barn Dance* gradually died out. Without WSM's wattage, Nashville's central location, and local recording studios, music publishers, and strong talent bookers, WNOX could not turn Knoxville into a music center to rival the Tennessee capital. In 1962 the station changed its format to rock & roll. —*Willie Smyth*

## Midnite Jamboree (*see* Ernest Tubb)

## Midwestern Hayride
established in Cincinnati, 1938; ended 1972

The *Midwestern Hayride* was one of America's foremost and longest-running barn dance shows. After JOHN LAIR organized the RENFRO VALLEY BARN DANCE in Cincinnati in 1937 and broadcast it over WLW, the station launched its own barn dance, the *Boone County Jamboree*, the following year. Executive George Biggar was imported from Chicago's WLS, and, together with booker-agent-manager Bill McCluskey, another WLS veteran, Biggar built the show around talent such as HANK PENNY, CURLY FOX & TEXAS RUBY, HOMER & JETHRO, BRADLEY KINCAID, and Hugh Cross. LULU BELLE & SCOTTY, already major stars, moved from WLS for a time, and THE GIRLS OF THE GOLDEN WEST came for a longer stay.

By 1945 the show became the *Midwestern Hayride*, a name more appropriate to the broad area covered by WLW's 50,000-watt signal. At this point station managers deliberately began to feature polished, pop-influenced country acts to widen the program's appeal, but 1940s talent remained diverse and included Ernie Lee, KENNY ROBERTS, the DEZURIK SISTERS, and BONNIE LOU (Sally Carson). During the late 1940s and early 1950s, WLW singers and prominent instrumentalists such as LOUIS INNIS, TOMMY JACKSON, ZEB AND ZEKE TURNER, and JERRY BYRD helped sustain a local recording industry.

WLW began telecasting the *Hayride* in 1948. From this point TV became the program's primary outlet, and the show's radio broadcasts grew sporadic and ultimately ended. In the 1950s network slots broadened the *Hayride*'s TV presence. The program was a summer replacement show on NBC in 1950, 1951, 1952, 1954, 1955, and 1959 and an NBC fill-in during 1957 and 1958. The *Hayride* also gained network exposure during non-evening hours in the regular season. By 1966 it was syndicated on forty-one TV stations nationwide plus five stations run by AVCO Broadcasting, then WLW's owner.

Through the 1950s and 1960s the *Hayride* remained a variety show with a country flavor, featuring barn dance sets with wagon wheels, fences, and front porches and offering everything from solo and duet singing to comedy and square dancing. Performers including KENNY PRICE, Bonnie Lou, Bobby Bobo, and the Lucky Pennies sang both their own recordings and hits by bigger-name artists.

The *Hayride* held on amid the rise of rock and the proliferation of alternative TV programming, but its popularity was waning by the late 1960s. A revamped show featuring more name guests, background voices, and electric bass, together with new host HENSON CARGILL (followed by Kenny Price), who replaced long-time MC Dean Richards, failed to rally the *Hayride*'s fortunes, and the program left the airwaves in 1972. —*John W. Rumble*

## Bob Miller
b. Memphis, Tennessee, September 20, 1895; d. August 26, 1955

Bob Miller was one of country music's first full-time professional songwriters. As a native southerner who had been immersed in music for most of his life, he was highly conscious of regional grassroots musical traditions. He led a dance band for several years on the Mississippi River steamer *Idlewild* and played often at the Dreamland nightclub in Memphis. There he also established the Beale Street Music Shop, where he wrote jazz and blues tunes. In 1922 he moved to New York as an arranger for the Irving Berlin Publishing Company but soon began trying his hand, quite successfully, at writing country songs. In the years that followed Miller penned such country standards as "Twenty-one Years," "Seven Years with the Wrong Woman," "Eleven Cent Cotton and Forty Cent Meat," "When the White Azaleas Start Blooming," and "Rocking Alone in an Old Rocking Chair." In 1933 he joined ASCAP and opened his own music publishing firm. One of his many topical songs, which dealt with the death of Huey Long, was written a few years before the Louisiana politician was assassinated. Miller's greatest success, though, came during World War II, when he published, arranged, and wrote the melody for ELTON BRITT's enormous patriotic hit "There's a Star Spangled Banner Waving Somewhere." Miller also worked as an A&R man for the COLUMBIA and OKEH labels, managing the hillbilly and race divisions and recording many country artists, from the late 1920s until June 1, 1932. As music publisher, he nurtured artists and songwriters into the 1950s. —*Bill C. Malone*

## Buddy and Julie Miller
Steven Paul "Buddy" Miller b. Fairborn, Ohio, September 6, 1952
Julie Anne Miller b. Dallas, Texas, July 12, 1956

A critically acclaimed husband-wife duo who perform separately and together, Buddy and Julie Miller have found wide acceptance in the AMERICANA field. They met in 1976 in AUSTIN, TEXAS, where they played in the COUNTRY-ROCK band Partners in Crime, and married in 1981. Throughout the 1980s, the Millers were active in New York and Los Angeles, Buddy playing lead guitar and singing with JIM LAUDERDALE, Julie releasing four albums of contemporary Christian music.

Moving to Nashville in 1993, Buddy made inroads as session guitarist and songwriter and built a studio in the couple's home, where he recorded his solo debut, the hard-country album *Your Love and Other Lies* (HIGHTONE, 1995). Two of its songs landed on the mainstream country albums of BROOKS & DUNN and George Ducas. Meanwhile, jazz singer Jimmy Scott and EMMYLOU HARRIS both cut Julie's "All My Tears (Be Washed Away)," Harris for her influential *Wrecking Ball* album (1995). In 1997 Julie released her secular debut, *Blue Pony*—a beguiling mix of folk, blues, Appalachian, and Celtic music set to a rock backbeat. Buddy, then playing guitar with Harris and STEVE EARLE, released his second

HighTone album, *Poison Love*, with Harris contributing backing vocals. Earle assisted on Miller's home-recorded *Cruel Moon* (1999). Highlights of the Millers' subsequent output include *Buddy & Julie Miller* (HighTone, 2001) and Buddy's spiritually focused *Universal United House of Prayer* (New West, 2004).

The Millers won four AMERICANA Music Association awards in 2009: Buddy as Artist of the Year, the couple as Duo/Group of the Year, their album *Written in Chalk* as Album of the Year, and Julie's song "Chalk" (recorded by Buddy and Patty Griffin) as Song of the Year. —*Bill Friskics-Warren*

## Eddie Miller
b. Camargo, Oklahoma, December 10, 1919; d. April 11, 1977

Eddie Miller will forever be known as writer of the country-pop standard "Release Me," though he was a prolific tunesmith whose credits include such Top Ten hits as "There She Goes" (CARL SMITH, 1955), "After Loving You" (EDDY ARNOLD, 1962), and "Thanks a Lot" (ERNEST TUBB, 1963). He also was a music industry activist, having founded the Academy of Country Music (ACM) and cofounded the Nashville Songwriters Association International (NSAI).

Miller was born in southwestern Oklahoma and raised on WESTERN SWING. He formed his own swing outfit, Eddie Miller & His Oklahomans, but had to disband temporarily during World War II, when he worked on the Katy Line railroad in Texas. He later re-formed the Oklahomans and recorded for the Dallas-based Bluebonnet label ca. 1947–48. At some point after the war he moved to Los Angeles and signed with FOUR STAR as both artist and songwriter. On a club date in San Francisco, reportedly in late 1946, Miller overheard a woman say to the man she was with, "If you would release me, we'd get along all right." He went home and wrote "Release Me," which he recorded for Four Star in 1949. The song went largely unnoticed, however, until Jimmy Heap recorded it for CAPITOL RECORDS in 1953. Both RAY PRICE and KITTY WELLS covered it, and all three versions hit the Top Ten in 1954. By the 1970s, more than 200 versions of "Release Me" had been recorded, including the Top Ten pop renditions of Esther Phillips (1962) and Engelbert Humperdinck (1967). After turning to religion, Miller himself, by then living near Nashville, retooled the standard as "Please Release Me from My Sins."

Miller's wife, Barbara, also wrote songs, and his daughter, Pam, had a brief career as a singer. —*Daniel Cooper*

## Emmett Miller
b. Macon, Georgia, February 2, 1900; d. March 29, 1962

For most of his career, Emmett Dewey Miller worked in minstrel shows and in vaudeville as a blackface comedian, specializing in *Amos & Andy* types of dialog and in what the 1920s press described as "vocal contortions." Although Miller never considered himself a country singer, his yodeling and falsetto singing strongly influenced a number of early country vocalists. The blue yodels of JIMMIE RODGERS bear an uncanny resemblance to Miller's yodels, and there is circumstantial evidence that Rodgers heard Miller early in his own career. THE CALLAHAN BROTHERS learned the arrangement for their biggest hit, "St. Louis Blues," from Miller's rendition of the song. BOB WILLS was so fascinated with Miller that he copied down most of Miller's recorded songs—and skits—and recorded a Miller favorite, "I Ain't Got Nobody."

Miller's masterpiece, "Lovesick Blues," which he recorded in 1925 and again in 1928, was known by both REX GRIFFIN and HANK WILLIAMS. Miller was also the first to record country standards such as "Anytime" and "Right or Wrong." Later, artists as diverse as MERLE HAGGARD and Leon Redbone made albums paying homage to Miller's music and its enduring influence in country music.

Miller began his professional career in his late teens by joining Neil O'Brien's minstrel show, which evolved into the Dan Fitch Minstrels; here he did blackface comedy, perfected a comic walk and dialect, and sang in the show's quartet, the Kings of Harmony. Here, too, Miller learned classic minstrel stagecraft and showmanship. When the troupe hit New York, critics were ecstatic over Miller, and soon he was working solo spots featuring what he called "blues singing." After a stint in Asheville, North Carolina, as a soloist, he joined the granddaddy of touring minstrel troupes, the Al G. Field show, and won fame throughout the eastern United States. He recorded for OKEH RECORDS in 1924–25 and in 1928–30, with some thirty issued sides.

Miller played nightclubs in the 1930s and 1940s; cut an additional four sides for BLUEBIRD RECORDS in 1936; made a final minstrel tour, called "Dixieana," in 1949; and even appeared briefly in the 1951 film *Yes Sir, Mister Bones*. —*Charles Wolfe*

## Frankie Miller
b. Victoria, Texas, December 17, 1930

Best known for his 1959 smash "Blackland Farmer" and subsequent hits such as "Family Man" (1959) and "Baby Rocked Her Dolly" (1960), Frank Miller Jr. was hailed in those days as a throwback—a "pure country" singer when such vocalists seemed to be disappearing.

Miller had been recording for almost a decade before "Blackland Farmer" hit. Taught guitar by his brother Norman, he left Victoria College after his sophomore year to pursue a career in the clubs along his native Gulf Coast. A big break came in 1950, when he filled in for vacationing HANK LOCKLIN on Houston's KLEE; Locklin helped secure Miller a recording contract with the Gilt-Edge label, and during 1951 Miller released a series of excellent, mostly self-penned songs, including "I'm Getting Rid of You" and "I Don't Know." Then Miller was drafted, just as he seemed poised for greater success. He earned a Bronze Star in Korea and snared a COLUMBIA contract on returning in 1954. His solid recordings unfortunately coincided with the first wave of rock & roll and went nowhere, despite their occasional but undeniable ROCKABILLY tinge. Miller toured constantly and appeared regularly on such programs as the LOUISIANA HAYRIDE and BIG D JAMBOREE before landing a record deal with STARDAY on the strength of "Blackland Farmer" at the end of 1958. He spent the next few years turning out strong material for that label and United Artists, but he grew tired of the touring grind and retired by the end of the 1960s. He began performing and recording again on a limited basis around the turn of the millennium. —*Kevin Coffey*

## J. D. Miller
b. Iota, Louisiana, May 5, 1922; d. March 23, 1996

Beginning in 1946, producer-songwriter Joseph Delton "J. D." Miller (a.k.a. Jay Miller) operated an independent recording studio in Crowley, Louisiana, that exerted an influence far out of proportion to its size. He produced scores of CAJUN, country, ROCKABILLY, and blues artists, and his MTE studio was used for some recording on Paul Simon's *Graceland* LP. Yet for all Miller's achievements as a producer, his most famous contribution to country music may have been as a songwriter, for in 1952 it was Miller who wrote KITTY WELLS's first #1 hit, "It Wasn't God Who Made Honky Tonk Angels," a song he had originally released on his Feature Records label on a recording by Alice "Al" Montgomery.

Initially drawn to the cowboy style of GENE AUTRY, Miller didn't pay attention to Cajun music until he moved to Crowley in 1937. Playing in a variety of bands, he was influenced most strongly by WESTERN SWING star CLIFF BRUNER. Miller quit performing when he got married, however, and joined his father in the family music store, M&S Music (for Miller and Son). In 1946 he set up shop as a record company, using a small studio behind the music store. He put Cajun acts such as HAPPY FATS and Doc Guidry on his Fais Do Do label and country acts on his Feature imprint; among the artists who made their recording debuts on Feature were DOUG KERSHAW and JIMMY C. NEWMAN (who cowrote his first national hit, "Cry, Cry, Darling," with Miller). Miller also managed LEFTY FRIZZELL briefly in 1952, the year "It Wasn't God Who Made Honky Tonk Angels" soared to #1. Miller then signed a writer's contract with ACUFF-ROSE PUBLICATIONS, but by the mid-1950s he was focusing on recording rockabilly and blues artists, most notably Slim Harpo. Miller died in Lafayette, Louisiana, following quadruple cardiac bypass surgery. —*Daniel Cooper*

## Ned Miller
b. Raines, Utah, April 12, 1925

Singer-songwriter Ned Miller wrote and recorded a handful of classic country hits during a career spanning fewer than fourteen years. Henry Ned Miller grew up in Salt Lake City and began writing songs as a teen. In the mid-1950s, after working as a pipe-fitter, he moved to California. There he sought out independent record producer FABOR ROBISON, who signed him to a recording contract in 1956. Miller's first release on the Fabor label was the self-penned "From a Jack to a King," which did not chart. However, in 1957 DOT RECORDS artist BONNIE GUITAR scored her first hit with Miller's "Dark Moon" (#14 country, #6 pop).

After several unsuccessful outings for both CAPITOL and Jackpot Records, Miller's luck began to change when his original recording of "From a Jack to a King" was reissued and became a 1963 crossover hit (#2 country, #6 pop). He followed with "Invisible Tears" (#13 country, 1964) and "Do What You Do Do Well" (#7 country, 1965). In 1965 SONNY JAMES took Miller's "Behind the Tear" to the top of the country charts. Miller continued to record until 1970 and then retired to Arizona. In 1989 RICKY VAN SHELTON's recording of "From a Jack to a King" became a #1 country hit. —*Don Roy*

## Roger Miller
b. Fort Worth, Texas, January 2, 1936; d. October 25, 1992

One of the most multifaceted talents country music has ever known, Roger Dean Miller left a musical legacy of astonishing depth and range. A struggling HONKY-TONK singer and songwriter when he first hit Nashville in 1957, he blossomed into a country-pop superstar in the 1960s with self-penned crossover hits such as

*Roger Miller*

"Dang Me" and "King of the Road." In 1965–66 he won eleven Grammys. Two decades later, he received a 1985 Tony Award for his score for *Big River*, a Broadway musical based on Mark Twain's *The Adventures of Huckleberry Finn*. In between such career triumphs, Miller kept friends and fans in constant stitches as his extemporaneous wit proved almost as famous as his music.

Born in Fort Worth, Texas, Miller was sent to live with an uncle in Erick, Oklahoma ("population 1,500, and that includes rakes and tractors," he liked to joke), when he was three years old. He grew up in Erick, working the family farm and dreaming of a different life. As a teenager enamored of BOB WILLS and HANK WILLIAMS, Miller would drift from town to town in Texas and Oklahoma, trying to land nightclub gigs as a country singer. Drafted during the Korean War, Miller was sent to Fort McPherson in Atlanta, where he played fiddle in a U.S. Army Special Services outfit called the Circle A Wranglers. While stationed there he met BILL ANDERSON, and the two young, would-be country stars embarked on a lifelong friendship.

After his discharge, Miller headed to Nashville. While working as a bellhop, he wormed his way into the local music community. He was first hired to play fiddle in MINNIE PEARL's road band; then, in about the spring of 1957, he struck up a friendship with GEORGE JONES. Impressed with Miller's songwriting, Jones introduced him to PAPPY DAILY and DON PIERCE of STARDAY RECORDS (then operating as MERCURY-STARDAY). Miller's first single, "My Pillow" b/w "Poor Little John," was released on Starday in the fall of 1957. In the meantime, Jones and Miller had cowritten some songs, including "Tall, Tall Trees," which Jones released in 1957 to little response but which ALAN JACKSON would take to #1 nearly forty years later.

After a brief return to the Southwest, Miller was hired in 1958 to front RAY PRICE's Cherokee Cowboys. From that position he suggested that Price cover "Invitation to the Blues," a song Miller had written that was starting to take off in REX ALLEN's version. Released as the B-side of Price's 1958 smash "City Lights,"

"Invitation to the Blues" rose to #3 on the charts, giving Miller his first major success in the business.

Signed to TREE PUBLISHING as a staff writer in 1958, Miller began to see his tunes recorded by such stars as ERNEST TUBB, JIM REEVES, and FARON YOUNG. (Miller also served for a time as Young's drummer.) Though he had continued to record for Starday and then for DECCA, he had no success as an artist until he signed with RCA in 1960. His first RCA single, "You Don't Want My Love," became his first Top Forty hit. It was followed a year later by his first Top Ten hit, "When Two Worlds Collide," which he had written with his friend Bill Anderson.

Miller's RCA career never quite panned out, though, and by 1963 he was ready to quit Nashville to pursue an acting career in Los Angeles. He had made guest appearances on *The Jimmy Dean Show* and *The Tonight Show*, and his humor had been well received. Late that year, when his RCA contract ran out, he was picked up by Smash Records, in part because a Smash executive had liked Miller's TV routines. An agreement was struck whereby Miller would cut a single and an additional album's worth of material for $100 per side, thereby raising the money he would need to finance his move to Los Angeles. Not only did the recordings pay for the move, they also made Roger Miller a star, for out of those off-the-cuff 1964 sessions came "Dang Me."

A #1 smash on the country charts, "Dang Me" was also a Top Ten pop hit, as were four more of the singles he released during his first two years on Smash. The most famous was "King of the Road," a million-seller. Miller's success was all the more astounding for having arrived during the British Invasion. With his exceptional wordplay and jazz-like delivery, he was able to compete with the Beatles and the Rolling Stones on the pop charts. While he is often remembered as a novelty specialist due to mid-1960s crossover hits such as "Chug-a-Lug" and "Kansas City Star," he was capable of great soulfulness, as on the Top Five country hit "Husbands and Wives," also a Top Thirty pop record. Writing and recording fame led to his own NBC network TV show, aired in the fall of 1966.

By 1968, fearing his own songwriting well had run dry, Miller turned to the work of other imaginative young Nashville writers, such as KRIS KRISTOFFERSON, whose "Me and Bobby McGee" was recorded first by Miller. He continued to record into the 1970s, and in 1974 he provided soundtrack music for the Walt Disney movie *Robin Hood*. Still, Miller became less of a force on radio as the decade progressed. He apparently didn't mind, for he was content to live a quieter life with his third wife, Mary Arnold (formerly a singer with KENNY ROGERS and the First Edition), and their children. And so he would have done had he not been talked into writing the score for *Big River*.

Opening on Broadway in 1985, *Big River* was, in Miller's own eyes, the crowning achievement of his career. Rejuvenated by its success, he stayed active through the remainder of the decade. In 1991, though, he left the road when he learned he had cancer. He fought the disease for a year, but died on October 25, 1992. Three years later he was inducted posthumously into THE COUNTRY MUSIC HALL OF FAME. —*Daniel Cooper*

## The Miller Brothers

An enduring and highly popular WESTERN SWING band, the Miller Brothers (based in Wichita Falls, Texas) never scored any chart hits yet constantly finished high in trade polls of the 1950s, just behind HANK THOMPSON and BOB WILLS.

The group was originally formed in the late 1930s by the Gibbs brothers, Leon, Sam, and Nat, who adopted the pseudonym Miller to keep from getting fired from their day jobs. Fiddler Leon fronted the band, which broadcast over radio station KWFT. Drafted during World War II, the brothers returned to form a new Miller Brothers act in partnership with trumpeter Lee Cochran (who also adopted the Miller moniker). In 1947 the band recorded a fascinating combination of straight country dance titles and pure big-band music, coupled on singles by the local Delta label.

By 1953 the Millers had broadened their territory from North Texas and Oklahoma to include most of the western states. Touring and recording with former Texas Playboys vocalist TOMMY DUNCAN that year further widened their popularity. In the 1950s the band recorded a mix of swing instrumentals and vocal numbers for FOUR STAR with singers Billy Thompson and Jimmy McGraw, and soon their tours reached Puerto Rico and Canada.

Sam Gibbs left the group in 1953 (Nat Gibbs had left earlier) to concentrate on his work in a booking agency, which, in addition to the Millers, would boast such clients as Bob Wills. The Millers' Four Star association ended by 1960; by then both Leon Gibbs and Lee Cochran had left to join Sam in the booking agency. In about 1959 the Miller Brothers' name was sold to fiddler Bobby Rhodes, steel guitarist Bill Jourdan, and bassist Jimmy McGraw, who kept the act going into the early 1960s. (An interesting footnote: the Millers' longtime pianist Madge Suttee is perhaps best remembered for the distinctive playing she contributed to LEFTY FRIZZELL's early 1950s hits.) —*Kevin Coffey*

# Ronnie Milsap
b. Robbinsville, North Carolina, January 16, 1943

Ronnie Milsap's command of country, country-pop, rock & roll, rhythm & blues, funk, pop, and classical music has made the singer-keyboardist a formidable entertainer who defies pigeonholing. Nevertheless, he's one of country's most successful artists, with six Grammy awards for Best Male Country Vocal Performance, four CMA awards, and thirty-five #1 *Billboard* hits. An exemplar of the sometimes-bland country-pop sound of the late 1970s and early 1980s, the energetic and versatile performer kept scoring hits into the youth-driven country boom of the late 1980s and early 1990s.

Born blind into an Appalachian family named Millsaps, he went to live with grandparents at age one. According to his 1990 autobiography, *It Was Almost Like a Song*, his mother regarded his blindness as divine punishment and asked his father to take young Ronnie away. At age six, having heard gospel music at church and hillbilly music via radio, he entered the State School for the Blind in Raleigh, North Carolina. Despite harsh treatment, he blossomed musically, learning the school's classical techniques while absorbing pop styles available on radio.

Graduating in 1962, Milsap pursued music at Young Harris Junior College (he finished in 1964), and he released his debut single, "Total Disaster," in 1963 on Atlanta's Princess Records. He chose music over law school, and he was recording R&B-tinged pop for New York's famed Scepter label by 1965; that year he enjoyed a minor hit with "Never Had It So Good." A 1968 move to Memphis led him to CHIPS MOMAN's hot American Studio and a regular gig at "the jumping nightclub—T. J.'s." Milsap played piano and sang on ELVIS PRESLEY's "Kentucky Rain" (1970) and recorded briefly for Moman's Chips label; he then cut LPs for WARNER BROS. and Reprise in 1971–72.

*Ronnie Milsap*

Milsap moved to Nashville in 1972, performed at an industry hangout, the King of the Road, and began a long association with RCA RECORDS in 1973. Assisted by publisher-producer TOM COLLINS, Milsap started charting with country fare including "I Hate You" and "That Girl Who Waits on Tables" (1973) and won a 1974 Grammy for his #1 rendition of KRIS KRISTOFFERSON's "Please Don't Tell Me How the Story Ends." Despite Milsap's varied output, the #1 hits "Pure Love" (1974) and "Daydreams About Night Things" (1975) positioned him as a purveyor of positive, uptempo love songs. Hits continued in 1976 (when Milsap also joined the GRAND OLE OPRY) with "What Goes On When the Sun Goes Down" and the Grammy-winning "(I'm a) Stand By My Woman Man." The singer cracked the pop charts in 1977–78 with "It Was Almost Like a Song" and other #1 hits. CMA's Male Vocalist of the Year in 1974, 1976, and 1977, he was the organization's 1977 Entertainer of the Year.

Milsap logged forty-two Top Tens between 1976 and 1991, including "Back on My Mind Again" (1978–79), "I Wouldn't Have Missed It for the World" (1981–82), and 1981's "(There's) No Gettin' Over Me" (another Grammy winner). The 1985 single "Lost in the Fifties Tonight (In the Still of the Night)"—reinterpreting the 1956 Five Satins hit—displayed Milsap's R&B roots and secured his fourth and fifth Grammys.

Milsap established his Ronnie Milsap Foundation for visually challenged persons in 1985 and maintained a grueling schedule of recording, television appearances, and touring. He built his own studio and organized a publishing firm with business associate Rob Galbraith. And the hits kept coming. "Snap Your Fingers" (1987) reprised the 1962 Joe Henderson R&B hit, and a 1987 Milsap–KENNY ROGERS duet, "Make No Mistake, She's Mine," earned a Grammy for these two champions of country-pop. Milsap followed the dance-pop of "Button off My Shirt" (1988) with the hillbilly-hearted album *Stranger Things Have Happened* (1989).

Even as country radio embraced line-dance fodder, Milsap notched hits through 1992, but he signed with LIBERTY RECORDS and released *True Believer* (1993), with only modest success. In 1995 he opened his Ronnie Milsap Theatre in Myrtle Beach, South Carolina, having previously opened a restaurant in Gatlinburg, Tennessee. (Both later closed.) Singles released in 2000 and 2004 garnered little attention.

By contrast, *Just for a Thrill* (Image Entertainment, 2004), a collection of standards, showed another side of Milsap, and in 2006 he renewed his RCA association with the KEITH STEGALL–produced *My Life*. A 2007 tour with GEORGE STRAIT and TAYLOR SWIFT kept Milsap's name before the public, as did CD reissues of his RCA albums. In 2009 the EMI Christian Music Group released his two-CD set *Then Sings My Soul: 24 Favorite Hymns and Gospel Songs*. —*Thomas Goldsmith*

## Minstrel Shows (*see* Blackface Minstrelsy)

## Billy Mize
b. Arkansas City, Kansas, April 29, 1929

A stylish and popular radio and television personality in Los Angeles and BAKERSFIELD in the 1950s and 1960s, William Robert Mize became best known as the MC of several well-known West Coast country music variety programs, including his own *Chuck Wagon Show* (with singing, recording, and songwriting partner Cliff Crofford), *Cousin Herb Henson's Trading Post* show, and GENE AUTRY's *Melody Ranch*. Mize received ACM's award for Top TV Personality of 1966. He also worked as a WESTERN SWING steel guitarist and vocalist, appearing on *TOWN HALL PARTY*, and as a songwriter ("Who'll Buy the Wine"). Buddy Mize, Billy's brother, is a songwriter best known for the 1977 VERN GOSDIN hit "Hangin' On." —*Dale Vinicur*

## The Modern Mountaineers

Though short-lived, the influential and prolific Modern Mountaineers provided an early training ground for several important country musicians. The group formed in Houston in late 1936 as the Georgia Fliers, led by tenor banjoist Johnny Thames and managed by Johnny's brother Roy Thames. Broadcasting over Houston's KTRH, the band featured the Fats Waller–inspired piano and vocals of Smokey Wood, the hot jazz fiddle of J. R. Chatwell, and the saxophone of Hal Hebert. Prior to recording for BLUEBIRD in March 1937, the group became the Modern Mountaineers.

Their first session produced several hits, including the slyly obscene "Everybody's Truckin'." Wood was soon fired, and by the band's September 1937 session it had moved to Shreveport and added Waco fiddler Jimmy Thomason, fiddler-guitarist Buddy Ray, and others. The struggling act limped back into Houston in late 1937 and disbanded.

By 1940, Johnny and Roy Thames had taken over the Texas Wanderers (following CLIFF BRUNER's departure) and were contracted to DECCA, but they revived the Modern Mountaineers name for Bluebird sessions in February 1940 and April 1941. Musicians included pianist MOON MULLICAN, who cut the original version of his "Pipeliner's Blues" with the group. The band's last session, in October 1941, was an ad hoc affair led by Johnny Thames, with BAR X COWBOY singer JERRY IRBY on vocals. —*Kevin Coffey*

## Lucky Moeller
b. Okarche, Oklahoma, February 12, 1912; d. June 15, 1992

Walter Ernest "Lucky" Moeller was a prominent country music booking agent and promoter in the early 1960s, chiefly through his association with successful performer WEBB PIERCE and talent agent JIM DENNY. Moeller was a banker turned Oklahoma ballroom owner when he began promoting concerts for BOB WILLS in the mid-1940s. Moeller moved to Nashville in 1954 to help manage Pierce's career but three years later moved to Springfield, Missouri, to work with the *OZARK JUBILEE* and manage artists for the *Jubilee* owners' Top Talent Agency. He returned to Nashville in 1957 to work for the Jim Denny Artist Bureau, which represented most of the top country acts of the 1950s and early 1960s. After Denny's death in 1963 Moeller took over the agency, changing its name to Denny-Moeller Talent and then in 1965 to Moeller Talent. Soon after Moeller suffered a severe stroke in November 1974, Moeller moved the agency back to his hometown of Okarche; less than a year later, it closed. Son Larry Moeller, who had left his father's business in 1973, went on to form his own Nashville talent agency, at one time handling WAYLON JENNINGS, WILLIE NELSON, and SAMMI SMITH. Later he moved to AUSTIN, TEXAS, focusing exclusively on Willie Nelson for many years. —*Al Cunniff*

## Chips Moman
b. LaGrange, Georgia, ca. 1936

Lincoln Wayne Moman (called "Chips" for his skill as a poker player) rose to prominence as an R&B and pop record producer in Memphis during the 1960s. During the 1970s and 1980s he became a successful country producer as well.

While still in his teens, Moman worked as a road musician for Gene Vincent, WARREN SMITH, and JOHNNY BURNETTE & THE ROCK 'N' ROLL TRIO (which included Johnny's brother Dorsey), and then, with introductions from the Burnettes, as a session guitarist at L.A.'s Gold Star studio. At age twenty-one he began working with Jim Stewart and his newly founded Satellite Records, soon to become better known as Stax Records. At Stax, Moman functioned as Stewart's right-hand man, in-house producer, and chief songwriter until the men had a falling out in 1962. With a $3,000 settlement from Stewart, Moman started American Sound Studio in Memphis in 1964 while continuing to do session guitar work in Memphis and in Muscle Shoals, Alabama.

In 1965 Moman began producing pop hits at American for such acts as the Gentrys, Sandy Posey, Merilee Rush ("Angel of the Morning"), B. J. THOMAS, and Neil Diamond. Between 1968 and 1970 Moman produced more than one hundred charting pop singles, with help from the American studio band he assembled: REGGIE YOUNG (guitar), Bobby Wood and Bobby Emmons (keyboards), Tommy Cogbill and Mike Leech (bass), and Gene Chrisman (drums). In January and February 1969 Moman produced comeback hits for ELVIS PRESLEY—"In the Ghetto," "Suspicious Minds," and "Kentucky Rain"—at American Sound Studio.

Meanwhile, Moman wrote R&B standards in the 1960s with Dan Penn ("Do Right Woman," "Dark End of the Street") and 1970s country hits as well: B. J. Thomas's "(Hey Won't You Play) Another Somebody Done Somebody Wrong Song" and WAYLON JENNINGS's "Luckenbach, Texas (Back to the Basics of Love)."

In 1972 Moman closed American Sound Studio and moved to Atlanta. In 1975 he moved to Nashville. In the 1970s and 1980s he produced hit albums for Waylon Jennings (*Ol' Waylon*), WILLIE NELSON (*Always on My Mind*), Nelson and MERLE HAGGARD (*Pancho and Lefty*), and a pair of albums for the quartet of Jennings, Nelson, JOHNNY CASH, and KRIS KRISTOFFERSON (*Highwayman* and *Highwayman 2*). In 1985 Moman produced another all-star aggregation, the album *Class of '55: Memphis Rock & Roll Homecoming* (MERCURY, 1986), featuring Cash, JERRY LEE LEWIS, ROY ORBISON, and CARL PERKINS. Between 1986 and 1990, Moman ran Three Alarm Studio in Memphis. Since moving to Nashville in 1990 and back to the town of his birth, LaGrange, Georgia, in 1994, Moman has kept a low profile in the music business. —*Paul Kingsbury*

## Charlie Monk
b. Noma, Florida, October 29, 1938

A former disc jockey in Alabama and at WMTS–Murfreesboro, Tennessee, Charles Franklin Monk has spent the bulk of his career in music publishing after serving as an ASCAP associate director from 1970 to 1977. He headed CBS Songs in Nashville from 1977 to 1982, opened his own firm shortly afterward, and worked for Opryland Music Group as creative services director from 1988 until 1993.

As a music publisher he advanced the early careers of RANDY TRAVIS, KENNY CHESNEY, and AARON TIPPIN. Monk originated the Country Radio Seminar (see CRS/CRB) in 1969 with Tom McEntee, and Monk is widely known as longtime host of the Country Radio Seminar's New Faces Show. He received the Country Radio Broadcasters (CRB) President's Award in 2007 for service to that organization. Having previously hosted syndicated radio shows, he hosts the *Charlie Monk Show* on SiriusXM Satellite Radio and continues to run the Monk Family Music Group. —*Bob Millard*

## Bill Monroe
b. Rosine, Kentucky, September 13, 1911; d. September 9, 1996

No individual is so closely identified with an American musical style as is Bill Monroe, who excelled as a singer, songwriter, bandleader, showman, and instrumentalist. For more than half a century he shaped BLUEGRASS with his forceful mandolin playing; high, tight-throated singing; and mastery of his band, the Blue Grass Boys. In so doing he gave older country sounds new life; redefined the mandolin as a lead instrument in country, pop, and rock; and set standards for musicians as diverse as the THE EVERLY BROTHERS, ELVIS PRESLEY, GEORGE JONES, and rock star Jerry Garcia.

William Smith Monroe was the youngest of eight children born to James Buchanan "Buck" Monroe, a prosperous farmer who also ran timber and mining operations, and Melissa Monroe, who kept house and helped pass along dance steps and folk songs to her children. Other musical influences of Bill's youth include the OLD-TIME fiddling of his uncle Pendleton "Uncle Pen" Vandiver and the bluesy guitar playing of ARNOLD SHULTZ, a black musician with whom Bill and Uncle Pen sometimes worked local dances.

Monroe lost both his parents by age sixteen, and subsequently he followed some of his brothers to the Chicago area, where he labored in a Sinclair Oil refinery, performed as a square dancer on Chicago's WLS *NATIONAL BARN DANCE*, and sang and played

mandolin with brothers Charlie (guitar) and Birch (fiddle) on local radio. Birch soon left the trio, and Bill and Charlie pursued music full time as the MONROE BROTHERS, first gaining exposure on stations in Iowa and Nebraska.

The Monroes hit their stride after moving in 1935 to the Carolinas, where they based themselves mainly at Charlotte's 50,000-watt WBT. Their popularity grew rapidly, and they distinguished themselves by their hard-driving tempos and piercing harmony and Bill's aggressive mandolin solos. In 1936 RCA VICTOR producer ELI OBERSTEIN recorded them for the first time. Early releases such as "What Would You Give in Exchange for Your Soul" sold well, and before long the Monroes won a sizable regional audience, with help from live and recorded radio shows. The headstrong brothers feuded, however, and the act broke up in 1938. Bill would record two more sessions for RCA with his new band, the Blue Grass Boys, named for Kentucky, the Bluegrass State.

After rehearsing his group and working Carolina radio, Monroe headed for Nashville to audition for the GRAND OLE OPRY. WSM's GEORGE D. HAY, HARRY STONE, and DAVID STONE, impressed with Monroe's talent and star power, hired him in October 1939 on the strength of his performance of his trademark "Mule Skinner Blues," formerly a hit for JIMMIE RODGERS. WSM's 50,000-watt transmitter and guest spots on the Opry's NBC network segment quickly made Monroe's name a household word. By 1943 he was grossing some $200,000 a year from show dates, many of them staged as part of his own Opry TENT SHOW.

No one was yet calling Monroe's style "bluegrass" (this would not happen until the mid-1950s), but many of its basic elements were already present, including its pulsing drive and the intensity of Monroe's high-pitched vocals. During World War II he added the banjo, first played by STRINGBEAN (Dave Akeman), and experimented briefly with the accordion and harmonica, which complemented the basic mandolin-guitar-fiddle-bass combination Monroe would always retain. In 1945 he added the revolutionary three-finger banjo picking of EARL SCRUGGS, which provided bluegrass with its final building block. Monroe's late-1940s recordings for COLUMBIA, made with Scruggs, fiddler CHUBBY WISE, and LESTER FLATT, his singer-guitarist at the time, are now regarded as definitive.

In 1948 Scruggs and Flatt left and formed the highly successful FLATT & SCRUGGS AND THE FOGGY MOUNTAIN BOYS, and by the early 1950s several bands were playing variations of the bluegrass style, including THE STANLEY BROTHERS, JIM & JESSE McReynolds, and RENO & SMILEY. Monroe made his band sound higher, bluer, and more lonesome than ever, with help from singer-guitarist JIMMY MARTIN and other expert sidemen, some of whom (including Martin) later fronted bluegrass bands of their own. As ever, Monroe's repertoire included both sacred and secular material as well as both songs and instrumentals, and he composed much of his material himself or with members of his band. Over the years, Monroe originals such as "Uncle Pen," "Raw Hide," "Blue Moon of Kentucky," "Jerusalem Ridge," "I Want the Lord to Protect My Soul," and dozens of others have formed the basis of the bluegrass canon for professionals and amateurs alike.

Through the 1950s and beyond, Monroe's acoustic sound provided an alternative to HONKY-TONK, country-pop, and ROCKA-BILLY (though he did much to inspire the latter). By 1963 he began to attract the urban folk music audience, with help from folklorist and sometime manager RALPH RINZLER, who promoted Monroe as the Father of Bluegrass to audiences who thought the style

## Charlie Monroe
b. Ohio County, Kentucky, July 4, 1903; d. September 27, 1975

After the dissolution of the MONROE BROTHERS in mid-1938, Charles Pendleton Monroe carried on his musical career with a band initially called the Boys but later known as the Kentucky Pardners. At first Monroe used twin mandolins and a guitar for his basic sound in 1938 and 1939 BLUEBIRD sessions, but he later expanded the group to include fiddle, electric lead guitar, and harmonica, giving him a unique blend of OLD-TIME MUSIC and just a touch of modernization. Although the Pardners' radio work took them to Wheeling and Louisville, they achieved their greatest following in the Carolina Piedmont and in southern Appalachia. Monroe continued recording with RCA VICTOR through 1951, cutting some sixty-two solo sides, including the classic train song "Bringing in the Georgia Mail."

In 1952 and 1956 Monroe recorded some eight numbers for DECCA (among them "Old Kentucky Bound"), after which he retired to a farm in western Kentucky. During his inactive years he cut two albums with BLUEGRASS accompaniment for the Rem label. In 1972 he emerged from retirement, began working the bluegrass festival circuit, and recorded for STARDAY. Cancer curtailed his comeback and ended his life in September 1975. —*Ivan M. Tribe*

## Monroe Brothers
Bill Monroe b. Rosine, Kentucky, September 13, 1911; d. September 9, 1996
Charlie Monroe b. Ohio County, Kentucky, July 4, 1903; d. September 27, 1975

Before they started their separate careers, Bill and Charlie Monroe were a BROTHER DUET in the 1930s. Though fans sometimes regard this period as a rehearsal for the brothers' later contributions, the Monroe Brothers were one of the best-selling and most influential acts of the decade and would have secured their place in history for this alone.

The first incarnation of the Monroe Brothers included Charlie (on guitar), older brother Birch (on fiddle), and young Bill (on mandolin). In 1929 Bill had just moved to join his brothers in Whiting, Indiana, where they worked in oil refineries and appeared as square dancers on the WLS *NATIONAL BARN DANCE*. The trio soon received a sponsorship offer from Texas Crystals (a patent medicine company); Birch dropped out at this point, leaving Charlie and Bill to work radio stations in Shenandoah, Iowa, in 1934, and later Omaha, Nebraska, and then in the Carolinas. The Monroes' radio programs and stage shows in places such as Spartanburg and Charlotte drew even more attention from fans and a new sponsor, CRAZY WATER CRYSTALS, which supported numerous country radio acts from Texas to Pennsylvania.

Radio fame led to a contract with RCA VICTOR's BLUEBIRD RECORDS in 1936. The brothers' first release became their career record: "What Would You Give in Exchange for Your Soul," a song they had learned in a shape-note singing school years earlier. Bluebird would later claim that this song "outsold any song ever put on record by an OLD-TIME group." Subsequent recording sessions eventually encompassed some sixty sides within three years. Many would become standards: "Drifting Too Far from the Shore" (1936), "New River Train" (1936), "Roll in My Sweet Baby's Arms" (1936), "Roll on Buddy" (1937), "He Will Set Your Fields on Fire" (1937), "Little Joe" (1938), and "A Beautiful Life" (1938). The Monroes recorded many of the sides at breakneck speed, with

*Bill Monroe*

began with Flatt & Scruggs. The year 1965 saw the first bluegrass festival that made Monroe the centerpiece, and in 1967 he launched his own annual festival at BEAN BLOSSOM, Indiana, where he had long run a country music park. By 1970, when he won election to THE COUNTRY MUSIC HALL OF FAME, he had become the acknowledged patriarch of the bluegrass movement, a cult figure to hordes of fans for whom the music was a virtual religion.

During the last twenty-five years of his life Monroe propagated the Gospel of Bluegrass to worldwide audiences, appearing in all fifty states and in Canada, Japan, England, Ireland, Holland, Switzerland, and Israel. His venues ranged from rural festivals to urban performing arts centers and the White House. He recorded as well, and his career total topped more than 500 selections, most of them made for MCA (formerly DECCA).

In 1982 the National Endowment for the Arts gave Monroe its prestigious Heritage Award, and in 1988 he won a Grammy for his album *Southern Flavor*—the first bluegrass Grammy ever bestowed. Inducted into the IBMA Hall of Fame in 1991 and the Rock and Roll Hall of Fame in 1997, Monroe in 1993 received a Grammy Lifetime Achievement Award, an honor that placed him in the company of Louis Armstrong, CHET ATKINS, RAY CHARLES, and other legends. Although bluegrass constitutes a small part of country music's annual sales, such honors speak to the enormous influence Monroe exerted among musicians in many fields.

A stroke suffered in April 1996 ended Monroe's career as a touring artist and hastened his death on September 9 of that year. Memorial services at THE RYMAN AUDITORIUM in Nashville, and later in Monroe's native Rosine, Kentucky, where he is buried, united hundreds of friends and fellow musicians, who continue to nurture his legacy as one of country music's great historical personalities. —*John W. Rumble*

Charlie singing lead and playing muscular rhythm guitar and Bill singing tenor and executing powerful, fiddle-derived mandolin lead parts.

During their peak years, the Monroes toured widely through the Carolinas, often working for Crazy Water Crystals with announcer Byron Parker, nicknamed the Old Hired Hand. It was a turbulent time, however, since each brother had a strong temper, and the breaking point finally came in 1938. In later years, especially during a series of mid-1950s recordings for DECCA, Bill and Charlie occasionally reunited in a vain attempt to recapture some of their earlier magic. —*Charles Wolfe*

## Patsy Montana
b. Hope, Arkansas, October 30, 1908; d. May 3, 1996

Patsy Montana's 1935 recording of her polka-tempoed composition "I Wanna Be a Cowboy's Sweetheart" was the first record by a female solo country artist to become a runaway hit. With her energetic voice, sparkling yodeling, and eye-catching cowgirl outfits, Montana presented a cheerful image to Depression-era America. The lyrics of her great hit spoke of independence, love, and the kind of freedom cowboys had come to symbolize.

Montana was born Ruby Blevins into a struggling family of ten boys. At seventeen she added an "e" to her first name to make it more sophisticated, and a year later she left for California. A skilled guitarist and fiddler, she won a talent contest in 1931 singing JIMMIE RODGERS songs and landed a job on Los Angeles–area radio as Rubye Blevins, the Yodeling Cowgirl from San Antone. Adopting the name Patsy Montana, she also joined with two other female western singers and, as the Montana Cowgirls, worked radio station KMIC with singer-songwriter STUART HAMBLEN and cowboy star Monty Montana.

When the Montana Cowgirls disbanded, Patsy Montana moved back to Arkansas. Then a brief booking on KWKH in

*Patsy Montana*

Shreveport, Louisiana, brought her to the attention of RCA VICTOR recording artist JIMMIE DAVIS. Montana backed Davis in the studio on fiddle and vocals and cut her own RCA sides in 1932. A trip with her brothers Kenneth and Claude to the Century of Progress Exposition in Chicago in 1933 included an audition with WLS for a vocalist slot with the Kentucky Ramblers, a hot, swing-influenced STRINGBAND. That year Montana joined the Kentucky Ramblers, who became THE PRAIRIE RAMBLERS to accommodate their new western image.

Extensive road performances and radio appearances established a reputation for Montana and the band, and even after her marriage to Paul Rose, in 1934, she remained with the group. In 1935 producer ART SATHERLEY took them to New York to record for the AMERICAN RECORD CORPORATION. This led to the historic recording session that yielded "I Wanna Be a Cowboy's Sweetheart."

Montana's cowgirl image and material became her stock in trade, with many recordings following. Her exuberant yodeling and sunny singing were backed by sizzling instrumental work on songs such as 1940's "Swing Time Cowgirl."

From 1940, Montana was a solo act. She made a brief appearance in GENE AUTRY's 1939 film *Colorado Sunset*, but generally she worked on the road. She had her own network radio show during 1946 and 1947, and in 1948 she starred on the *LOUISIANA HAYRIDE*. Montana continued to book appearances and record until her death. She was elected to THE COUNTRY MUSIC HALL OF FAME in 1996. —*Mary A. Bufwack*

## Bob Montgomery
b. Lampasas, Texas, May 12, 1937

Bobby LaRoy Montgomery entered show business singing in a duo with BUDDY HOLLY in Lubbock, Texas, when both were in their early teens. Montgomery went on to become a successful songwriter, record producer, and music executive in Nashville, playing important roles in the careers of BOBBY GOLDSBORO, JOE DIFFIE, and COLLIN RAYE.

Montgomery and Holly performed locally (their business card read "Buddy and Bob, Western and Bop") and recorded several song demos. Montgomery followed Holly to Norman Petty's studio in Clovis, New Mexico, where Montgomery signed on as an engineer and received writer credits on Holly's songs "Wishing," "Love's Made a Fool of You," and "Heartbeat." Montgomery recorded a single for DECCA RECORDS' Coral subsidiary, then moved to Nashville in 1959 to concentrate on songwriting.

As a writer, Montgomery's early credits include "After Awhile" for JIM REEVES, "Back in Baby's Arms" for PATSY CLINE, and "Two of a Kind" for Sue Thompson. But his best-known early copyright is "Misty Blue," a country hit for Wilma Burgess (Decca, 1966), EDDY ARNOLD (RCA VICTOR, 1967) and BILLIE JO SPEARS (United Artists, 1976), and a pop hit for Dorothy Moore (Malaco, 1976).

Montgomery's first production credit was MEL TILLIS's "Stateside" (first released on Ric and rereleased on Kapp, 1966). Later, as head of A&R for United Artists Records in Nashville, Montgomery was responsible for hits by JOHNNY DARRELL, DEL REEVES, and Bobby Goldsboro. Montgomery and Goldsboro formed the House of Gold publishing company, which handled "Behind Closed Doors," "Wind Beneath My Wings," and other lucrative copyrights. Montgomery moved to TREE PUBLISHING

Company and worked there until Tree was sold to Sony Music Publishing; he then joined Epic Records as head of Nashville A&R, signing artists including Joe Diffie, Doug Stone, and Collin Raye.

In 1992 Montgomery and his wife, Cathy, formed an independent publishing company, Noosa Heads Music, which published the Tim McGraw hits "Down on the Farm" and "Maybe We Should Just Sleep on It." Montgomery retired in the 2000s and moved to Australia. —*Todd Everett*

## John Michael Montgomery
b. Danville, Kentucky, January 20, 1965

John Michael Montgomery joined Nashville's "hat act" stampede of the early 1990s with a string of top hits that balanced tender ballads with uptempo tongue-twisters. He won CMA's Horizon Award in 1994, and two of his songs, "I Swear" and "Sold (The Grundy County Auction Incident)," were cited by *Billboard* magazine as the most-played songs on country radio, in 1994 and 1995, respectively.

Montgomery began performing as a child in a family band led by his father, Harold Montgomery, and as a teen formed a group with his brother Eddie (later of the country music duo Montgomery Gentry). In 1991 Atlantic Records signed John Michael Montgomery as a solo artist after a label executive saw him perform in Lexington, Kentucky.

From 1992 through 1995, Montgomery ranked among country music's biggest sellers. His debut album, *Life's a Dance,* included his first #1, the ballad "I Love the Way You Love Me," 1993's ACM Song of the Year. The album went on to sell more than 3 million units.

*Kickin' It Up*, from 1994, did even better, selling more than 4 million, thanks to the hugely popular #1 "I Swear," 1994's CMA Single of the Year. "I Swear" also became ACM's Single Record of the Year and Song of the Year. Montgomery's self-titled third album continued his hot streak, also selling 4 million units. It contained the #1 "Sold (The Grundy County Auction Incident)".

In 1996, vocal cord issues caused a hiatus in Montgomery's career, and he never recovered his momentum. *What I Do Best* (1996) went platinum, and two more albums would go gold, but he didn't have another #1 hit until 2000's "The Little Girl." He left Atlantic in 2001 and signed with Warner Bros., where he had one successful hit, the title cut from his 2004 album, *Letters from Home*, which reached #2.

For several years afterward, Montgomery battled health and personal issues, including a DUI conviction in 2006. He entered a rehabilitation facility in 2008 for an undisclosed substance-abuse problem. He reemerged later that year with *Time Flies,* an album released on his own Stringtown Records label. —*Marjie McGraw*

## Melba Montgomery
b. Iron City, Tennessee, October 14, 1938

Her note-bending, heavily accented phrasing and her unmistakably country delivery make Melba Joyce Montgomery perhaps the closest stylistic equivalent to George Jones among female country singers. She and Jones recorded a series of highly regarded duets during the 1960s, and Montgomery is also known for the

1974 crossover hit "No Charge" as well as for her accomplished songwriting.

Raised near Florence, Alabama, Montgomery initially came to Nashville after winning the Grand Ole Opry's 1958 Pet Milk Amateur Contest. She toured as a member of Roy Acuff's troupe from 1958 to 1962 and then went solo.

Montgomery recorded solo for United Artists, Musicor, Nugget, Capitol, and other labels throughout the 1960s but achieved her biggest early hits as the duet partner of Gene Pitney ("Baby Ain't That Fine," 1966), Charlie Louvin ("Something to Brag About," 1970), and, unforgettably, George Jones. Montgomery wrote the #3 Jones–Montgomery duet "We Must Have Been Out of Our Minds" (1963) as well as many of their other 1963–68 efforts.

Solo success eluded Montgomery until she recorded the Harlan Howard recitation "No Charge," a celebration of motherhood, for Elektra. Her delivery was so emotion-packed that musicians at the session reportedly wept. The song hit #1 on Mother's Day 1974. Montgomery continued to record throughout the 1970s and sporadically into the 1980s. She reemerged as a songwriter in the 1990s, when a new generation of country stars began recording her collaborations with Carl Jackson, Jim Lauderdale, and others. With Lauderdale, she penned the George Strait hit "What Do You Say to That" (1999). —*Robert K. Oermann*

## Montgomery Gentry
Eddie Montgomery b. Danville, Kentucky, September 30, 1963
Troy Gentry b. Lexington, Kentucky, April 5, 1967

Eddie Montgomery and Troy Gentry, who form the powerhouse country duo Montgomery Gentry, have built a sustained career by wedding southern rock sounds to country themes of blue-collar values, small-town pride, religious faith, and patriotism.

Early on, Montgomery worked with his younger brother, John Michael Montgomery and Gentry in a group called Young Country; then he joined John Michael's band when the latter got

*Montgomery Gentry: Troy Gentry (left) and Eddie Montgomery*

a record deal. Gentry went solo, too, but eventually reunited with Eddie.

Montgomery Gentry's debut COLUMBIA Nashville release, 1999's *Tattoos and Scars*, produced the Top Five hit "Lonely and Gone" while helping them garner ACM's Top New Vocal Duet or Group award for 1999 and take home honors as CMA's 2000 Vocal Duo of the Year. The title track from *My Town* (2002), a #5 hit, became a barroom anthem and solidified their status as working-class champions.

"If You Ever Stop Loving Me," their first chart-topper, came from their 2004 album *You Do Your Thing*, a collection that produced "Something to Be Proud Of," another #1 hit celebrating family loyalty and a strong work ethic.

Controversy struck in 2006 when Gentry made national news for illegally killing a bear in captivity in Minnesota and tagging it as if caught in the wild. Under a plea agreement, he paid a substantial fine and received probation.

The incident did not seem to affect the duo's popularity. *Back When I Knew It All* (2008), recorded in Memphis, yielded two #1 hits—the title track and "Roll with Me." *For Our Heroes*, a Cracker Barrel Restaurants release, appeared in 2009. The duo left Columbia Records in September 2010; three months later, Montgomery underwent surgery for prostate cancer. The partners were back on tour in 2011. —*Warren Denney*

## Montgomery Ward Records
established 1933; ended 1941

The Montgomery Ward retail chain inaugurated its own budget record label in 1933, following the demise of Paramount's Broadway Records, which Ward had offered through mail-order catalog sales, much as competitor Sears, Roebuck had offered material on its Supertone, Challenge, and Silvertone labels in the 1920s and would continue to do on CONQUEROR until 1942.

Montgomery Ward's primary arrangement was with RCA VICTOR, which initially attempted to duplicate popular Broadway issues with matching titles from its own catalog. Thereafter, material from sessions recorded for RCA's budget BLUEBIRD imprint was frequently issued on the Montgomery Ward label until 1941, when the arrangement terminated. DECCA RECORDS supplied titles from its own catalog and older GENNETT/Champion matrices in 1935; most of Decca's own CARTER FAMILY titles also appeared on Montgomery Ward during 1937–39. Additionally, the label used a few Varsity Records selections during 1939–40. —*Dick Spottswood*

## Monument Records
established in Washington, D.C., March 1958

The Monument Records label was launched in 1958 by FRED FOSTER, an ex-promo man for several record companies and independent distributors. It was named for the Washington Monument. "When I was flying back, I'd see the monument and know I was almost home," said Foster. A local DJ, Buddy Deane, and the owners of a local record distributorship were minority stockholders. The label's first hit, BILLY GRAMMER's "Gotta Travel On," was issued in October 1958.

ROY ORBISON had been recording with only moderate success when Foster acquired him from RCA in 1959, in a deal facilitated by WESLEY ROSE of ACUFF-ROSE PUBLICATIONS.

Orbison's third Monument single, "Only the Lonely," peaked at #2 on the pop charts in 1960. In that year both Foster and Orbison relocated to Nashville. Subsequent Orbison hits included "Running Scared," "Crying," "In Dreams," and "Oh, Pretty Woman," all recorded in Nashville. Orbison recorded virtually all of his biggest hits for Monument between 1959 and 1965.

Foster expanded his music business interests to include a studio purchased from SUN RECORDS in 1963, COMBINE MUSIC (co-owned with BOB BECKHAM), and an R&B subsidiary, Sound-Stage 7 Records (a joint venture with DJ John "John R." Richbourg), which charted hits with Roscoe Shelton and Joe Simon.

After Orbison, Foster concentrated on country music, signing HENSON CARGILL, GRANDPA JONES, WILLIE NELSON, DOLLY PARTON, BOOTS RANDOLPH, JEANNIE SEELY, BILLY WALKER, and TONY JOE WHITE. The most successful artists after Orbison, though, were LARRY GATLIN, KRIS KRISTOFFERSON, and BILLY SWAN, who scored a #1 hit in 1974 with "I Can Help."

Monument ran into financial problems in 1981, and in August 1982 Foster relinquished the presidency to Bob Fead, who ran the label from the West Coast. The company's problems worsened, and it went into Chapter 11 bankruptcy in March 1983 with debts of $7.3 million. In 1985 Foster also lost his controlling 70 percent interest in Combine Music and all Monument real estate. On April 21, 1987, Monument assets were acquired by CBS Special Products for $810,000.

Ten years later, in October 1997, SONY MUSIC (owners of CBS Special Products) reactivated Monument as an imprint of Sony's Nashville division. DIXIE CHICKS, recording for Monument, became one of Sony's most successful acts. As of 2010, Monument again was dormant, with its catalog handled by Sony Legacy Recordings. —*Colin Escott*

## C. E. Moody (*see* The Georgia Yellow Hammers)

## Clyde Moody
b. Cherokee, North Carolina, September 19, 1915; d. April 7, 1989

Clyde Leonard Moody carved out a career that earned him renown among fans of OLD-TIME MUSIC, BLUEGRASS, and newer country styles. Of partial Native American descent, Clyde performed locally with Jay Hugh Hall before both joined WADE MAINER's Sons of the Mountaineers. Moody worked several recording sessions with Mainer, one with Mainer's brother J. E. MAINER, and another with Jay Hall and Steve Ledford as the Happy Go Lucky Boys. In 1940 Moody joined BILL MONROE's act and recorded with him for BLUEBIRD, introducing the blues-based song "Six White Horses" to the bluegrass idiom. After four years with Monroe, Moody became a solo vocalist at the GRAND OLE OPRY in 1944, exemplifying the country crooning style typically identified with EDDY ARNOLD.

After brief stints with BULLET and COLUMBIA, Moody signed with KING RECORDS and scored a major success in 1946 with "Shenandoah Waltz," a number he wrote with fiddler CHUBBY WISE. Three chart-making hits followed (1948, 1950). Later Moody worked on CONNIE B. GAY's Washington, D.C.–area radio and television programs and then on various radio and TV stations in the Carolinas. Moody left King in the early 1950s and signed with DECCA but never had another hit. He subsequently recorded with STARDAY, Wango, Old Homestead, Black Rose, and Longhorn and appeared as a frequent vocalist at various bluegrass festivals and concerts until his death. —*Ivan M. Tribe*

# The Sound Seen

## Country Album Cover Art

## PAUL KINGSBURY

Almost from its beginnings, commercial country music has been as concerned with its look as with its sound. In the 1920s, for example, GRAND OLE OPRY founder GEORGE D. HAY instructed the program's performers to dress in down-home clothes rather than their Sunday best to make the music seem more authentically rural. Likewise, JIMMIE RODGERS appeared in publicity photos dressed alternately in cowboy gear and railroad man's clothes to underscore the adventurous nature of his music. This preoccupation with appearances also has extended to country music recordings, often with dazzling results.

To illustrate the history of country album art, we have chosen seventy-eight colorful covers from the COUNTRY MUSIC HALL OF FAME AND MUSEUM's Frist Library and Archive, which encompasses more than 250,000 recordings. Country album covers are fascinating to pore over because they offer a window into how national record companies perceived country music and its audience. Because we have assembled these more or less chronologically, we can see how country album cover art has reflected the times.

In the 1940s, 78-rpm albums consisted of three or four sleeved 10-inch records in a stamp album–like booklet—hence the name "album." The covers often featured cartoon illustrations, sometimes combined with photos in images that suggested country music's essential simplicity, gaiety, and high spirits. The first ten covers displayed here are of 78-rpm albums.

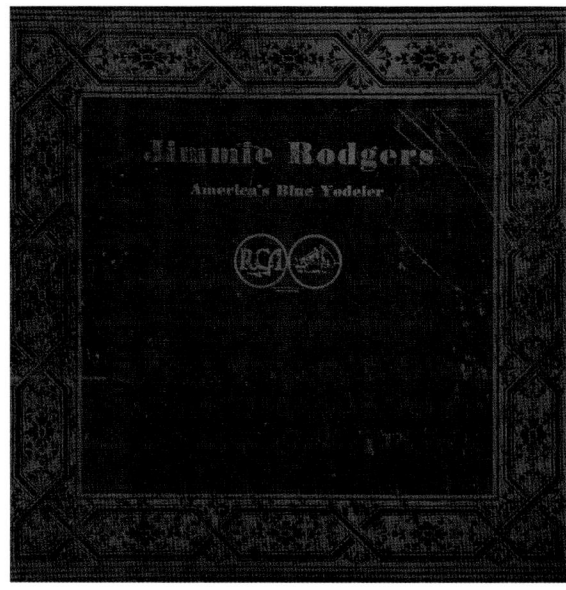

During the 1950s and 1960s, album images started reflecting the genre's increasing mainstream acceptance. Classy color portrait photography became the dominant theme, resulting in a more dignified depiction of the artists. On occasion, record companies still included rural imagery or colorful country costumes to show that the music was country. At other times, the labels wanted a more uptown look; to convey the sophistication of Jim Reeves's music, the cover for *A Touch of Velvet* featured the singer in a smart red dinner jacket.

In the 1960s, illustrations were still employed but tended toward greater sophistication than in the past. For instance, Columbia Records hired Tom Allen to paint a series of album covers for its star bluegrass act, Flatt & Scruggs, after Allen created an illustration to accompany Alan Lomax's famous profile of the duo in *Esquire* magazine in October 1959. Stretching out more, Smash Records chose to emphasize the wackiness of Roger Miller's songs with a head-rolling cartoon worthy of Monty Python on Miller's *Roger and Out* album in 1964.

As record company profits rose in the 1960s and 1970s, the labels committed more money to album art, and country stars began asserting more influence on the creative process. This artistic empowerment led to album art more accurately reflecting the performer's vision. Porter Wagoner used his growing commercial clout to arrange a striking series of album covers, including *The Cold Hard Facts of Life* and the Grammy-winning cover for *Confessions of a Broken Man*, both of which left no doubt as to the seriousness of the albums' content. In a similar vein, on the cover of Moe Bandy's *I Just Started Hating Cheating Songs Today* the singer sits forlornly in a bar, brandishing a broken bottle. Sometimes this tableau approach could go too far, as when Mack Vickery posed in front of a jail cell full of fetching women on the *Live! At the Alabama Women's Prison* album.

As country moved from the 1970s into the 1980s, record firms increasingly zeroed in on the artist's persona. Thus, Tanya Tucker was frequently depicted as a sexy nymphet, Hank Williams Jr. and Mickey Gilley as good-timin' hell-raisers, Outlaws Waylon Jennings and Willie Nelson as genuine desperadoes, Conway Twitty as a debonair man about town (with a prestardom Naomi Judd on one cover), the glamorous mother-and-daughter duo The Judds as virtual twins, and so on. To subtly communicate a traditional, hard-country sound, Randy Travis was shown in front of an old country store on the cover of *Storms of Life*, and Reba McEntire wore her rodeo belt while standing in front of a wide-open vista of the Rocky Mountains, with an American flag proudly waving in the background, for the Norman Rockwell-esque cover of *My Kind of Country*.

In contrast, edgier artists expressed their progressive leanings with covers that were out of the ordinary. In the 1980s, such unconventional talents as LYLE LOVETT and MARY CHAPIN CARPENTER used black-and-white, slightly out-of-focus images by photographer Peter Nash to cast themselves in a different light than other country singers. COLUMBIA RECORDS art director Bill Johnson won a 1987 Grammy for ROSANNE CASH's *King's Record Shop* album, showing Cash in front of a real, antique-looking record shop in Louisville, Kentucky (owned by PEE WEE KING's brother Gene), with no mention of Cash's name on the front cover.

In the 1990s, country album art became as attractive and as carefully constructed as anything from the realms of rock & roll or pop music. Key costume and rural motifs (hats, boots, the outdoors) remained, but they were employed with a more nuanced touch. By the 1990s, album art usually maintained a delicate equilibrium between rusticity and elegance, so as to attract the widest possible audience without alienating hard-core country fans. In the first decade of the twenty-first century, that delicate balance can be seen in how some acts—for example, TIM MCGRAW and the DIXIE CHICKS—opted for concept covers that did away with images of the artists. SUGARLAND proved to be the rare act that established a reputation for conceptual-art covers that relegated photos to the back cover or inside pages.

The new century brought new challenges to art directors as well. Just as photography and the music industry underwent striking changes, so did album covers. Whereas photos had always been shot on film, the digital age brought a revolution in photography, in which film became all but obsolete. The new methods sacrificed warmth and texture but made images much faster to produce and easier to manipulate and to share. With the advent of the Internet and digital music stores like iTunes and Amazon, cover images had to suit various forms of media and packaging.

Nonetheless, photo images of artists remain the most popular type of album cover, whatever the format. From full-body shots, as used on JASON ALDEAN's *Wide Open*, to extreme close-ups such as JOSH TURNER's *Haywire*, country album art continues to evolve while drawing on long-proven themes.

Regardless of what these commercial artworks tell us about record companies' views of the country audience over the years, one truth still stands clear: country recordings are as much a feast for the eye as they are for the ear.

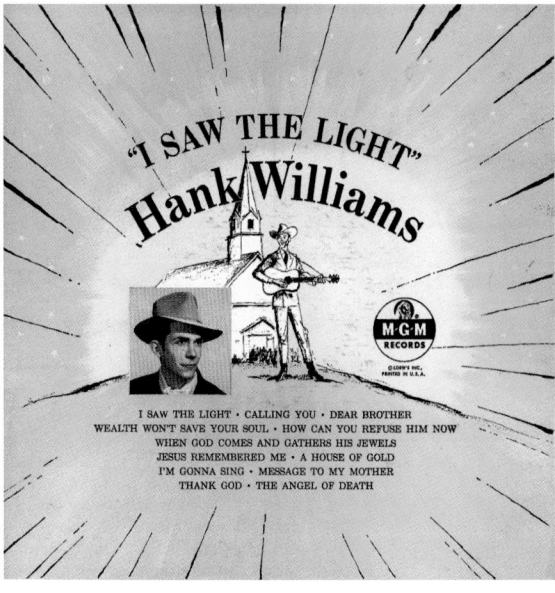

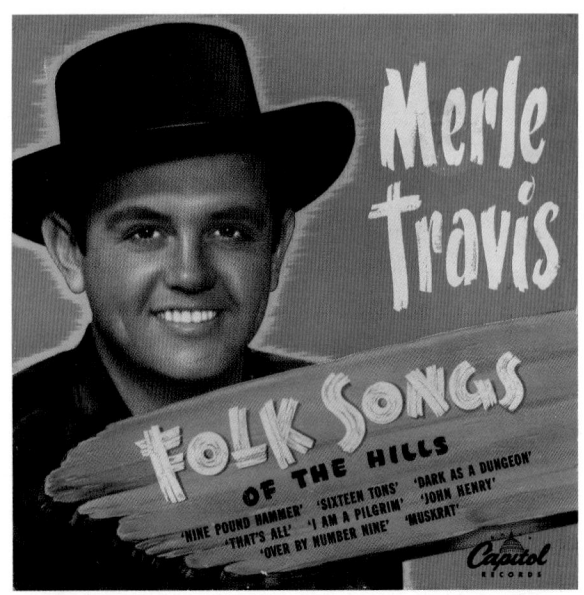

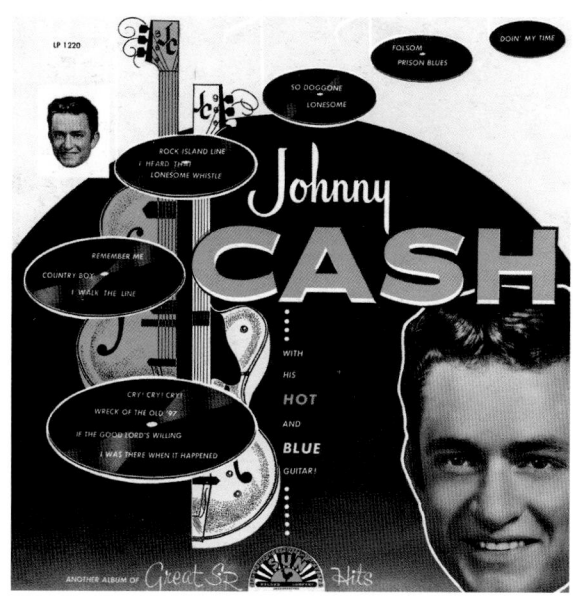

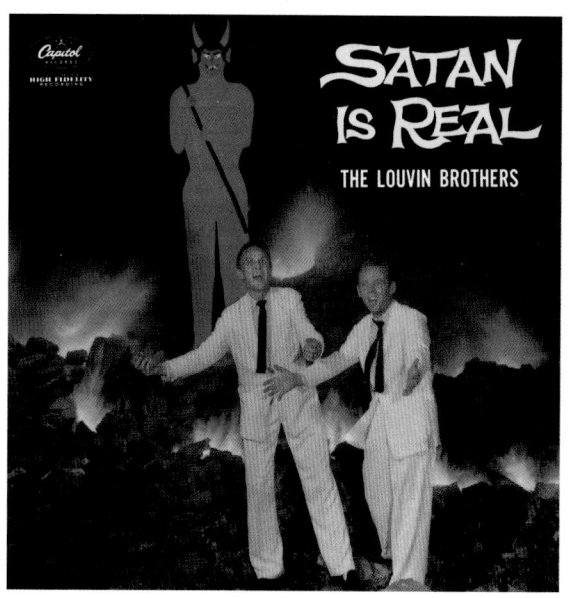

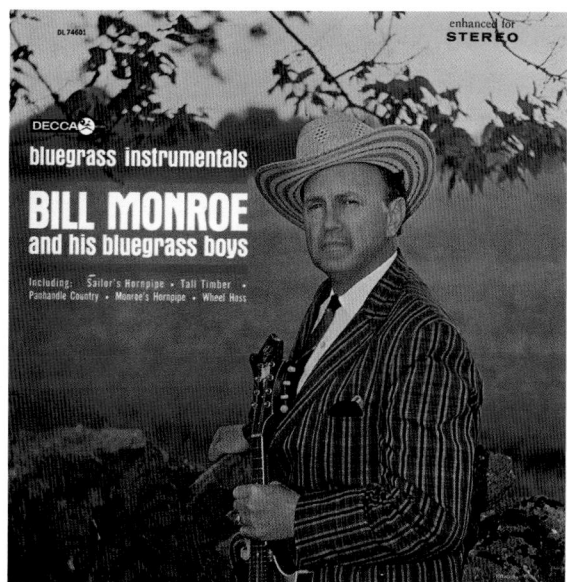

THE SONGS AND INSTRUMENTAL HITS MOST REQUESTED AT BUCK'S APPEARANCES ALL OVER THE COUNTRY

**BUCK OWENS · ON THE BANDSTAND**

SAW MILL · RELEASE ME · SALLY WAS A GOOD OLD GIRL · ORANGE BLOSSOM SPECIAL ·
I CAN'T STOP (My Lovin' You) · ONE WAY LOVE · SWEETHEARTS IN HEAVEN · TOUCH ME
· KICKIN' OUR HEARTS AROUND · KING OF FOOLS · COTTON FIELDS · DIGGY LIGGY LO

**GUNFIGHTER BALLADS**
AND TRAIL SONGS

**MARTY ROBBINS**

Big Iron · Cool Water · Billy the Kid
A Hundred and Sixty Acres · They're
Hanging Me Tonight · The Master's Call
The Strawberry Roan · Running Gun
El Paso · In the Valley · Utah Carol
The Little Green Valley

COLUMBIA

CHET ATKINS AT HOME

RCA VICTOR
LPM-1544

NIGHT LIFE · RAY PRICE

LSP-2487 · LIVING STEREO

a touch of Velvet · Jim Reeves

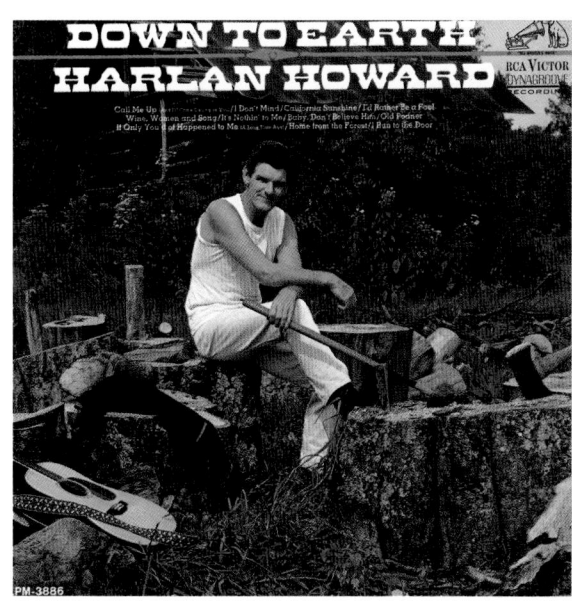

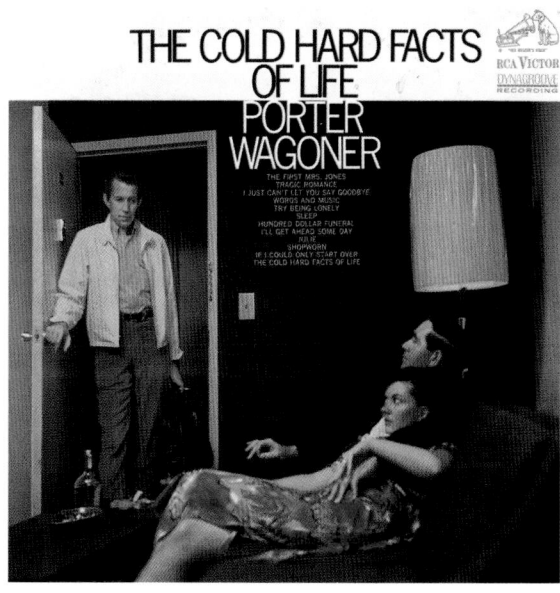

Confessions of a Broken Man
PORTER WAGONER

SKID ROW JOE
MY LAST TWO TENS
MAY YOU NEVER BE ALONE
JUST CAME TO SMELL THE FLOWERS
I'VE BEEN DOWN THAT ROAD BEFORE
MEN WITH BROKEN HEARTS
MY TEARS ARE OVERDUE
TAKE ME BACK AND TRY ME ONE MORE TIME
HOW FAR DOWN CAN I GO?
THY BURDENS ARE GREATER THAN MINE
I'M A LONG WAY FROM HOME
CONFESSIONS OF A BROKEN MAN

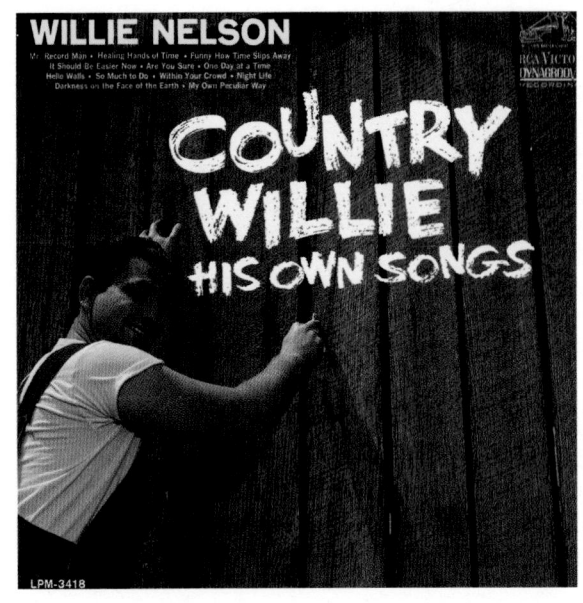

WILLIE NELSON

Mr. Record Man • Healing Hands of Time • Funny How Time Slips Away
It Should Be Easier Now • Are You Sure • One Day at a Time
Hello Walls • So Much to Do • Within Your Crowd • Night Life
Darkness on the Face of the Earth • My Own Peculiar Way

COUNTRY WILLIE HIS OWN SONGS

LPM-3418

LEAVIN' TOWN
WAYLON JENNINGS

RCA VICTOR
DYNAGROOVE
RECORDING

FOLK COUNTRY

Anita, You're Dreaming / Leavin' Town
Baby, Don't Be Looking in My Mind
Doesn't Anybody Know My Name
Falling for You / But That's Alright
Time to Bum Again / For Lovin' Me
If You Really Want Me to I'll Go
You're Gonna Wonder About Me
I Wonder Just Where I Went Wrong
Time Will Tell the Story

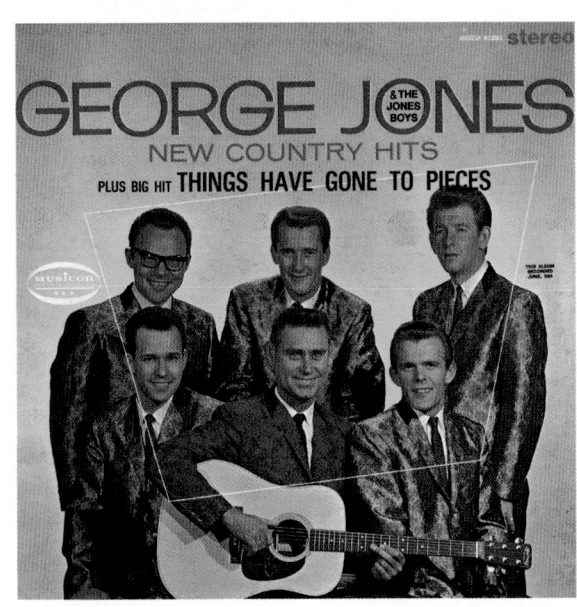

stereo

GEORGE JONES & THE JONES BOYS
NEW COUNTRY HITS
PLUS BIG HIT THINGS HAVE GONE TO PIECES

musicor

YOUR SQUAW IS ON THE WARPATH
LORETTA LYNN

YOUR SQUAW IS ON THE WARPATH
LIVING MY LIFETIME FOR YOU
BARKEY • SNEAKIN' IN
YOU'VE JUST STEPPED IN
TAKING THE PLACE OF MY MAN
KAW-LIGA
LET ME GO, YOU'RE HURTIN' ME
HARPER VALLEY P.T.A.
I WALK ALONE
HE'S SOMEWHERE BETWEEN YOU AND ME

DECCA

Lester Flatt & Earl Scruggs
The Story of Bonnie & Clyde

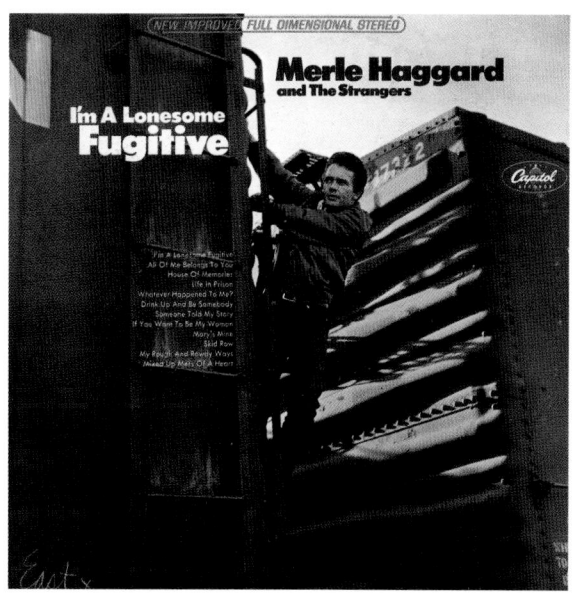

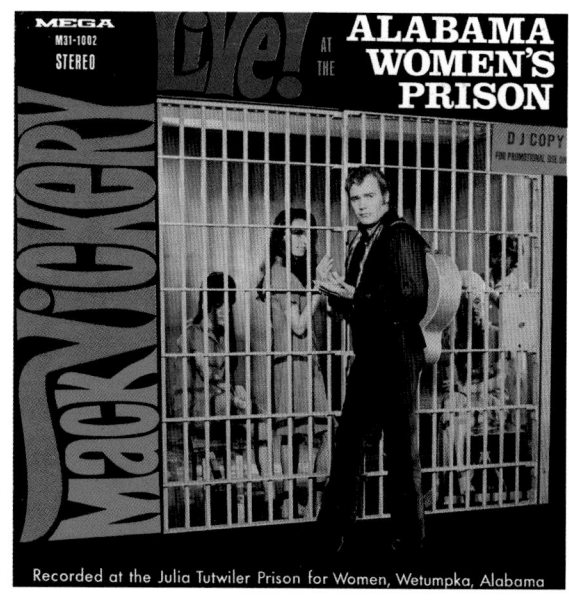

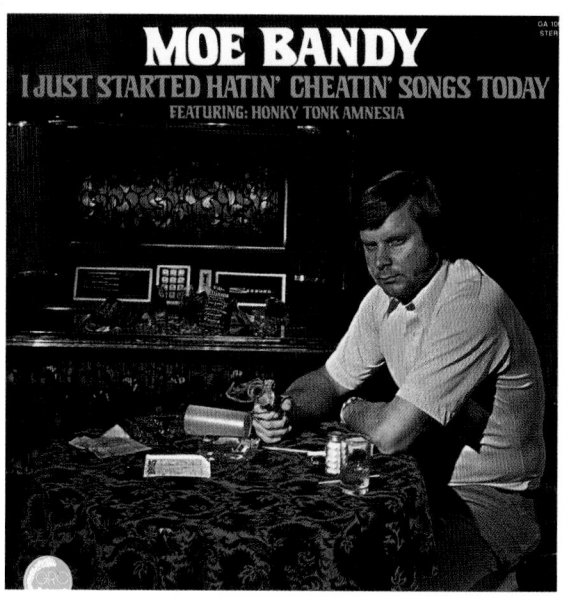

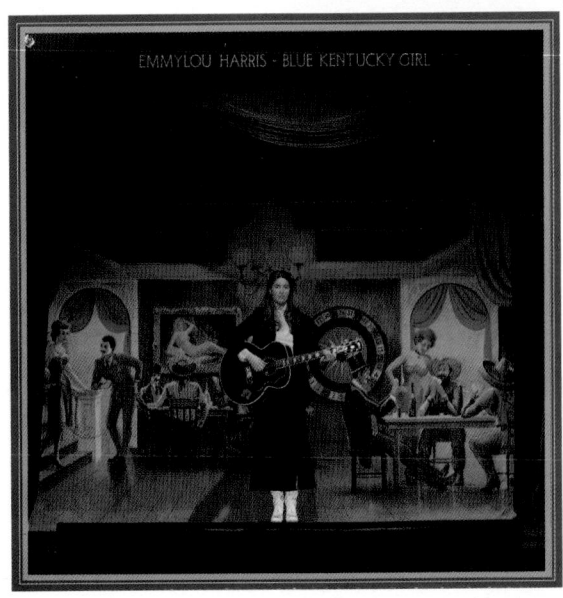

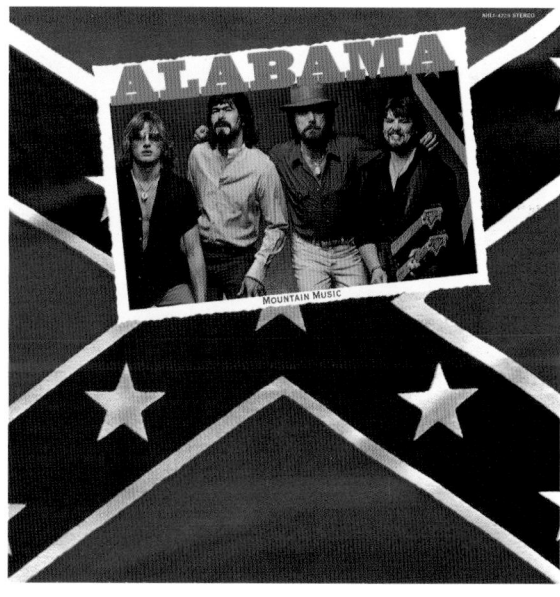

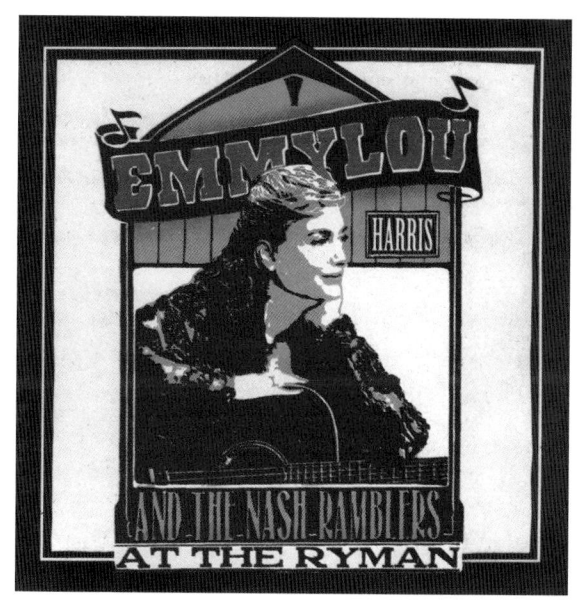

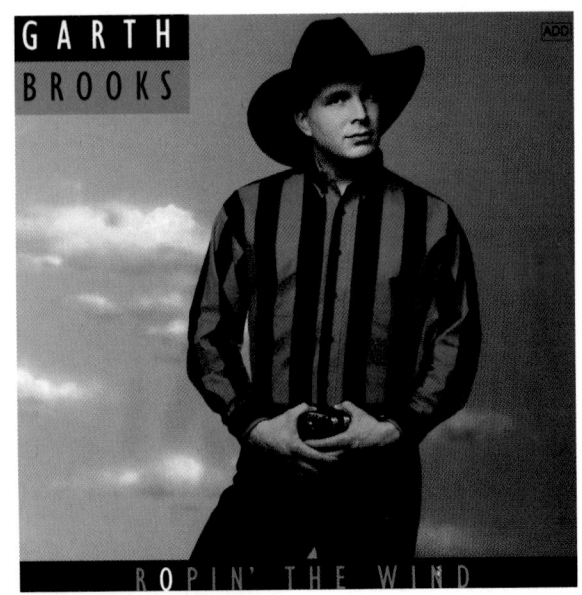

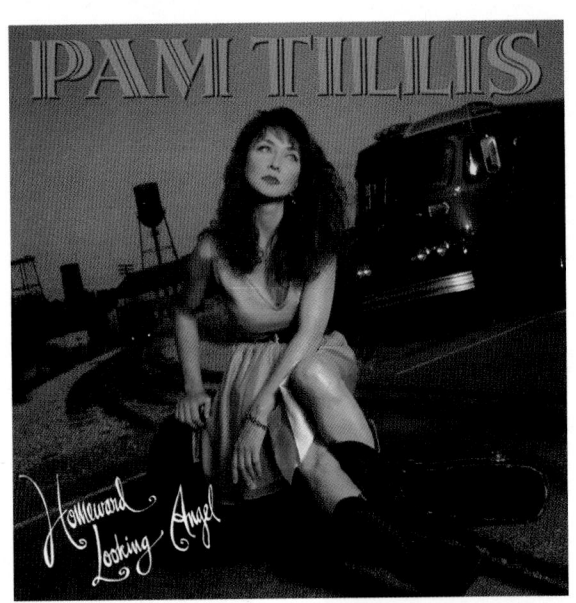

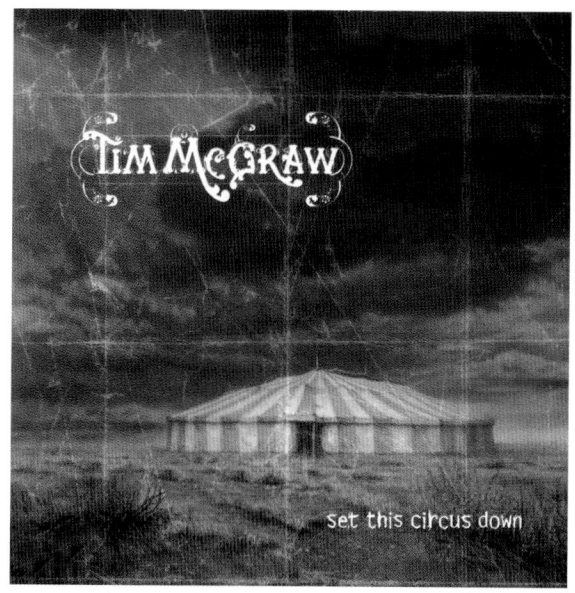

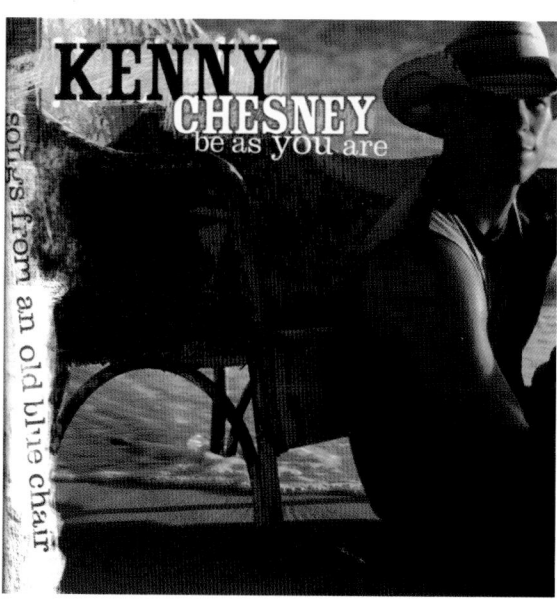

## Ralph Mooney
b. Duncan, Oklahoma, September 16, 1928; d. March 20, 2011

One of the formative influences behind the BAKERSFIELD sound, Ralph Eugene Mooney is known for his powerful PEDAL STEEL GUITAR technique, technical innovations, and timely associations with some of the icons of country music. An occasional songwriter, he cowrote the country classic "Crazy Arms" (with Chuck Seals), RAY PRICE's first #1 record (1956).

Performing and recording with Bakersfield stalwarts WYNN STEWART, BUCK OWENS, and MERLE HAGGARD, Mooney pioneered the West Coast, or California, style of pedal steel guitar playing—a bright, animated sound filled with fast-rolling arpeggios interlaced with chicken-pickin' and blues licks, signature takeoff intros, and solo work. The sound was augmented by technical changes he made in the high-end range of the instrument (such as the introduction of a G-sharp string), readily heard on hits by Stewart ("Wishful Thinking"), Owens ("Under Your Spell Again"), and Haggard ("Swinging Doors").

Mooney, however, may be best remembered for his work with WAYLON JENNINGS from 1970 to the early 1990s. Central to the rough-hewn OUTLAW sound that propelled Jennings to stardom, Mooney's clear, clean, resolutely country steel guitar licks kept Jennings squarely in the hard-country tradition.

Mooney was inducted into the Steel Guitar Hall of Fame in 1983. —*Elek Horvath and Robert Kramer*

## Bob Moore
b. Nashville, Tennessee, November 30, 1932

At fifteen, bassist Bobby L. Moore began working with the GRAND OLE OPRY comedy team JAMUP AND HONEY. In 1948 he joined PAUL HOWARD's Arkansas Cotton Pickers, also with the Opry, before backing JIMMY DICKENS and CURLY FOX & TEXAS RUBY on tour. Although Moore set out only to play country bass, he became an accomplished jazz player in OWEN BRADLEY's Nashville-based big band in the 1950s. Part of MUSIC CITY's "A-Team" of first-call studio musicians, Moore was one of Nashville's busiest session bassists from the 1950s on. He contributed to numerous #1 country hits, notably BOBBY HELMS's "Fraulein" (1956), MARTY ROBBINS's "El Paso" (1959), ROGER MILLER's "King of the Road" (1964), LORETTA LYNN's "Coal Miner's Daughter" (1969), and CONWAY TWITTY's "Hello Darlin'" (1969), generally playing string bass. He also played on ELVIS PRESLEY's "It's Now or Never" and PATSY CLINE's "Crazy."

As a studio orchestra leader Moore scored a pop instrumental hit via BOUDLEAUX BRYANT's "Mexico" (#7, 1961) and recorded "The Theme from My Three Sons," both for MONUMENT RECORDS. In addition, he organized and led sessions for ROY ORBISON and other Monument acts.

From 1983 to 1985 Moore was a sideman for JERRY LEE LEWIS. A hand injury prompted Moore to retire from music in the late 1980s. —*Walt Trott*

## Charlie Moore
b. Piedmont, South Carolina, February 13, 1935; d. December 24, 1979

Leader of the Dixie Partners from 1957 until his death, Charlie Moore was one of BLUEGRASS music's finest balladeers. Although his early 1960s KING RECORDS efforts with Bill Napier brought

him considerable notice, Moore's easygoing, warm baritone was not widely appreciated until much later.

Learning guitar as a youth, Charles Benjamin Moore Jr. launched his professional career in 1956 as part of COUSIN WILBUR WESBROOKS's show in Asheville, North Carolina. Back in his native state, Moore organized his first Dixie Partners lineup in 1957 and soon landed a weekly television show in Spartanburg, South Carolina. In 1960 he brought in THE STANLEY BROTHERS sideman Bill Napier as a full partner.

While based at WJHG-TV in Panama City, Florida, Moore and Napier signed with the King label. They made nine albums over the next four years, though most were hastily produced and failed to capture the band's essence. The two men eventually returned to Spartanburg and continued their partnership until late 1966; Moore soon quit performing for DJ work in Fountain City, South Carolina.

Encouraged by the rise of bluegrass festivals, Moore organized a new Dixie Partners in 1970 and began recording for several independent labels. He also sharpened his songwriting skills; his best-known composition, "Legend of the Rebel Soldier," reshaped an Irish BALLAD into a poignant narrative about a dying Confederate soldier.

By the mid-1970s Moore was a fixture on bluegrass circuits. His albums' overseas popularity led to a European tour in 1976. But by the time of his second tour three years later he was clearly in poor health, primarily due to advanced alcoholism. In late November 1979 Moore entered a Richmond, Virginia, hospital to relieve problems stemming from an earlier hernia operation. Complications led to his death a month later. —*Dave Samuelson*

## Merrill Moore
b. Algona, Iowa, September 26, 1923; d. June 14, 2000

Merrill Moore was known for his piano-driven country boogie recordings. He had an assured touch and impeccable taste, although he had no hits.

Born in rural Iowa, Moore weaned himself on the classic boogie-woogie records of Freddie Slack, Albert Ammons, and similar artists. Moore moved to San Diego in 1948, and in 1950 he started a residency at the Buckaroo Club. He began recording for CAPITOL RECORDS in 1952, and his music remained a sophisticated blend of boogie-woogie and WESTERN SWING. His vocal timbre resembled that of BILL HALEY, but his phrasing was rooted in the jazz leanings of western swing vocalists.

Moore never scored a charted hit, but some of his records apparently sold well. He toured rarely, though, confining himself to nightclubs on the West Coast and to session work for Capitol. In the late 1960s he was briefly a cause célèbre in England when Bill Haley fans embraced him. Moore toured there in 1970.

Moore continued to record for Capitol until 1958, closing out with a supper-club jazz set. He recorded again in England for B&C Records in 1970 and worked West Coast nightclubs into the mid-1990s. He died in 2000 after a long struggle with cancer. —*Colin Escott*

## Steve Moore
b. Pasadena, Texas, March 13, 1954

Steve Moore, a veteran concert promoter, is chief executive officer of the Country Music Association (CMA). Moore gained experience in a number of music-related businesses—among them Pace

Concerts—prior to moving to Nashville in 1985, when he opened Starwood Amphitheatre for Pace. He established Moore Entertainment in 1992, later selling this business to TBA Entertainment. In 2005, Moore was made senior vice president of AEG Live, a major provider of sporting events and live entertainment. In this role, Moore became executive producer of CMT on Tour, a yearly tour that spotlighted artists including TRACE ADKINS, JASON ALDEAN, JAMEY JOHNSON, BRAD PAISLEY, SUGARLAND, and KEITH URBAN. A CMA board member since 1989, Moore became president of the trade association in 2008, board chairman in 2009, and, after former CEO Tammy Genovese resigned in December 2009, interim CEO. In August 2010 Moore was named CEO. —*John W. Rumble*

## Tiny Moore
b. Hamilton County, Texas, May 12, 1920; d. December 15, 1987

Billie "Tiny" Moore popularized the electric mandolin as a jazz instrument in WESTERN SWING while a member of BOB WILLS's Texas Playboys. Others had played the instrument in western swing before Moore, but because he gained national exposure with Wills's band, Moore became the musician most associated with the mandolin in that musical genre.

Growing up in Port Arthur, Texas, Moore became a passionate jazz fan, and playing for the freewheeling Wills gave Moore's instincts free rein. A fixture with the Playboys from 1946 to the early 1950s, he married one of the McKinney Sisters (Dean and Evelyn McKinney), a vocal duo in the Wills troupe. The marriage continued until Moore died. After leaving the Playboys, Moore played in various bands near his home in Sacramento, where he and his wife owned a music store. In the 1970s he traveled and recorded with MERLE HAGGARD. At various times Moore also performed with the rock group Commander Cody & His Lost Planet Airmen. A highlight of his life came in 1979 when he and mandolinist Jethro Burns (HOMER & JETHRO), backed by various swing musicians, recorded *Tiny Moore and Jethro Burns: Back to Back*, an album that called attention to Moore's jazz mandolin style. —*Charles R. Townsend*

## Craig Morgan
b. Kingston Springs, Tennessee, July 17, 1964

Craig Morgan Greer developed a penchant for songs about family, country, and faith early on. At age ten he sang "The Star Spangled Banner" on a field trip to Nashville. Afterward, a lady approached him and said, "Son, someday you're going to be a famous singer." The lady was MINNIE PEARL, and her words ultimately proved true. After working various jobs, Morgan served in the army for ten years, leaving in 1996 to pursue a musical career.

Singing demos led to a deal with ATLANTIC RECORDS and Morgan's self-titled album (2000). Three singles had little success, and the label closed its Nashville office later that year. Next, Morgan signed with BROKEN BOW RECORDS for which he recorded the #6 hit "Almost Home" (2002–03), from *I Love It.*

Morgan developed his favorite themes on subsequent Broken Bow albums. *My Kind of Livin'* (2005) contained "That's What I Love About Sunday," his first #1 hit, and the #2 hit "Redneck Yacht Club." *Little Bit of Life*'s title track reached #7 in 2007.

In 2008 Morgan joined the GRAND OLE OPRY and signed with the BNA label (see RCA RECORDS). *That's Why*, his first BNA album, produced the Top Ten hits "Love Remembers" and "Bonfire." Morgan parted with BNA Records in February 2011. —*Michael Manning*

## George Morgan
b. Waverly, Tennessee, June 28, 1924; d. July 7, 1975

A fixture on the GRAND OLE OPRY for much of the period 1948–75, George Thomas Morgan possessed one of the smoothest tenor voices in country music.

Born about fifty miles west of Nashville, Morgan soon moved with his family to Barberton, Ohio. At age eleven he learned to play guitar, and he made early appearances on radio in Ohio at WAKR–Akron and WWST–Wooster. His career gathered momentum on the *WWVA JAMBOREE* in the 1940s. In September 1948 EDDY ARNOLD decided to leave the Grand Ole Opry. Morgan, whose singing style was similar, joined the cast on September 25, 1948, without benefit of a hit record. COLUMBIA RECORDS had signed Morgan just days before, on September 14, but due to the 1948 musicians union strike he didn't record until January 16, 1949.

Cut during that first session, his composition "Candy Kisses" launched his recording career with a bang, eventually reaching #1 on the country charts. On April 30, 1949, Morgan accounted for half of *Billboard*'s Country Top Ten. In addition to his three chart singles—"Candy Kisses" (#2), "Rainbow in My Heart" (#8), and "Please, Don't Let Me Love You" (#9)—the list included covers of "Candy Kisses" by ELTON BRITT (#8) and RED FOLEY (#10).

That first year proved to be Morgan's best on the charts, with six singles ultimately breaking the Top Ten in 1949. Of these, "Room Full of Roses" (#4, 1949) was Morgan's only record to make the pop charts (#25).

Morgan left the Opry in 1956 to host a TV show at Nashville station WLAC but returned to the Opry in 1959 and remained a

*George Morgan*

popular presence there until his death. After seventeen years with Columbia, Morgan exited the label in 1965, moving to STARDAY and Stop Records. In 1971 he shifted to DECCA/MCA, where he scored his biggest chart record in years with "Red Rose from the Blue Side of Town" (#21, 1974). His last recordings were made for FOUR STAR.

In 1973 Morgan watched proudly when his youngest daughter, LORRIE MORGAN, made her Opry debut. Sadly, George Morgan died not long after his fifty-first birthday, from complications following open-heart surgery. Through the wonders of electronics, a posthumous father-daughter duet, "I'm Completely Satisfied with You," charted briefly in 1979.

Morgan was elected posthumously to THE COUNTRY MUSIC HALL OF FAME in 1998. —*Walt Trott*

## Lorrie Morgan
b. Nashville, Tennessee, June 27, 1959

One of the top female country stars of the 1990s, Loretta Lynn Morgan has fashioned a persona and an approach to music that combines glamour with attention to the concerns of everyday life. Her delivery is often dramatic and torrid yet has a disarming directness.

The fifth child of GRAND OLE OPRY star GEORGE MORGAN, she grew up watching her father's performances from backstage. Morgan made her Opry debut at age thirteen and was working nightclubs when she was fifteen. She became an Opry member in 1984.

After recording for four record labels (COLUMBIA, FOUR STAR, ABC/HICKORY, and MCA) with little success, Morgan was signed to RCA in 1987. A year earlier she had married KEITH WHITLEY, her second husband, and in 1989 Morgan was touring Alaska to promote what would become her breakthrough RCA single, "Dear Me," when Whitley died from acute alcohol poisoning. "Dear Me" was followed by three other Top Ten singles from her platinum debut album, *Leave the Light On*, including the #1 hit

*Lorrie Morgan*

"Five Minutes." In addition, Morgan added new vocals to an older Whitley recording of "'Til a Tear Becomes a Rose," creating a duet performance that was recognized as CMA's Vocal Event of the Year in 1990.

*Something in Red* (1991) was an even stronger album, becoming Morgan's second million-selling collection. Highlights included uptempo numbers such as "We Both Walk," the emotionally urgent "Something in Red," and a powerful remake of GEORGE JONES's "A Picture of Me (Without You)." After a switch from RCA to the companion BNA (RCA RECORDS) label, her album *Watch Me* was released in 1992. It featured "What Part of No," which became another #1 hit.

In 1993 Morgan made her acting debut in the TNN movie *Proudheart*, a slice-of-life story of a working-class mother. In 1995 she appeared in a second film, *The Stranger Beside Me*.

"I Didn't Know My Own Strength" (1995), an anthem of independence, could be read as a description of Morgan's feelings about her personal life. Six marriages (including her marriage to Tennessee businessman Randy White, in 2010) and numerous high-profile romances (including Dallas Cowboys quarterback Troy Aikman and U.S. Senator and actor Fred Thompson) have made for a tumultuous love life. She addressed these issues in her 1997 autobiography, *Forever Yours, Faithfully: My Love Story*, published by Ballantine Books. The book preceded her marriage to singer SAMMY KERSHAW, which lasted from 2001 to 2007.

Morgan left BNA in 2000 and returned to RCA in 2001 for an album of duets with Kershaw titled *I Finally Found Someone*. In 2008 she filed for bankruptcy. In 2009 she released her tenth studio album, *Moment in Time*, on JAMES STROUD's Stroudavarious Records; it featured Morgan covering country standards. —*Mary A. Bufwack*

## Gary Morris
b. Fort Worth, Texas, December 7, 1948

In the 1980s, ruggedly handsome Gary Gwynn Morris transformed himself from country balladeer to television and Broadway star. Morris had a strong, classically influenced voice, and in 1982 he launched a string of hits embracing romance and vulnerability, including "Velvet Chains," "The Love She Found in Me," "The Wind Beneath My Wings," "Baby, Bye Bye," "I'll Never Stop Loving You," and "Leave Me Lonely."

From the country charts Morris leaped to TV soap opera appearances and the Broadway stage, singing the male lead in New York productions of *La Bohème* (1984 with LINDA RONSTADT) and *Les Misérables* (1988). But musical theater roles accentuated his tendency to hold notes beyond a length appropriate for most country tunes, and by the late 1980s country disc jockeys were ribbing him for oversinging.

By late 1987 Morris's record sales were suffering, partly due to fans' perception that he preferred TV and opera to country music. Though the title cut from his adventurous acoustic album called *Plain Brown Wrapper* went to #9 that year, he couldn't shake his image as an artist conflicted. After racking up five #1s and eleven more Top Ten hits between 1980 and 1987, Morris moved back to a touring cast of *Les Misérables*, performances in BRANSON, MISSOURI, and other comfortable theater gigs. (In 1997, he did produce the ATLANTIC RECORDS debut of Matt King.)

Morris's greatest contribution to American popular music may well have been "The Wind Beneath My Wings," a Top Five country hit for him in 1983—well before it became a multimillion-selling

#1 pop hit and a Grammy winner for Bette Midler in 1989. Today he runs a fly fishing and hunting retreat in southern Colorado. —*Bob Millard*

## Lynn Morris
b. Lamesa, Texas, October 8, 1948

Widely admired for her sensitive interpretations of traditional and contemporary material, in the 1990s Lynn Morris became a leading woman performer in BLUEGRASS music, a style historically dominated by men.

After studying guitar under legendary jazz guitarist Johnny Smith while in college in Colorado, she discovered the banjo, worked in a folk duo, and later joined City Limits, a Denver-based bluegrass band.

Experience with USO touring groups and the all-female band Cherokee Rose followed; by 1982 Morris was in State College, Pennsylvania, working in Whetstone Run, which later included her future husband, singer-bassist Marshall Wilborn. When the band folded in 1986, Morris performed with several bands, including LAURIE LEWIS & Grant Street, while Wilborn worked with the JOHNSON MOUNTAIN BOYS and JIMMY MARTIN.

During the 1988 festival season, the couple organized the Lynn Morris Band. Adept at clawhammer and three-finger-style banjo and guitar, Morris established her tradition-based sound with her clear, well-placed voice, and over the years personnel included such talents as David McLaughlin (guitar, mandolin), Tom Adams (banjo), and young Ron Stewart (fiddle, banjo). Five albums for ROUNDER (1990–2003) further established her reputation. Morris was IBMA's Female Vocalist of the Year for 1996, 1998, and 1999. In 2003 she suffered a stroke that kept her off the road and out of the recording studio. She received IBMA's 2010 Distinguished Achievement  Award and perseveres with her recovery. —*Frank* and *Marty Godbey*

## Philip Morris (*see* Philip Morris Country Music Show, under P)

## The Morris Brothers
Wiley Andrew Morris b. Old Fort, North Carolina, February 1, 1919; d. September 22, 1990
Zeke Edward Morris b. Old Fort, North Carolina, May 9, 1916; d. August 5, 1999

A spirited duo from western North Carolina, the Morris Brothers had considerable impact on the first generation of BLUEGRASS musicians. Though they were not a bluegrass act, they influenced modern bluegrass performance styles and vocal harmonies, and they contributed songs to the music's repertoire.

After performing locally with his older brother George, Zeke Morris turned pro with J. E. MAINER's Mountaineers; Morris played guitar and sang on the band's August 1935 BLUEBIRD sessions, which included the classic "Maple on the Hill." In early 1936 WADE MAINER and Zeke left to perform as a duo; when Wiley Morris joined them in 1937, Zeke switched to mandolin.

In late 1937 Wiley and Zeke Morris hired fiddler Homer Sherrill; for the next year they performed as the Smiling Rangers over WPTF–Raleigh. During 1938–39 the brothers recorded thirty-four titles for Bluebird, including such future bluegrass standards as "Let Me Be Your Salty Dog," "Don't Say Goodbye if You Love

Me," and "One Little Word." From 1939 to 1944 the Morrises were based at WWNC in Asheville; at various times their band featured bluegrass banjo pioneers Hoke Jenkins, Don Reno (RENO & SMILEY), and EARL SCRUGGS.

The brothers dissolved their partnership in 1944, shortly after moving to WIRL in Knoxville. Zeke moved to WJHL in Johnson City, Tennessee, where he formed a band including Red Smiley (Reno & Smiley), Red Rector, and Fred Smith. In November 1945 ELI OBERSTEIN reunited the brothers for an RCA VICTOR session that included benchmark renditions of "Tragic Romance," "Grave Upon the Green Hillside," "Somebody Loves You, Darling," and the retitled "Salty Dog Blues."

The Morrises retired from music in the late 1940s, although they made occasional festival appearances until 1983. In 1972 the Morris Brothers and Homer Sherrill recorded an album for ROUNDER, *Wiley, Zeke and Homer.* —*Dave Samuelson*

## MTM Music Group
established in Nashville, Tennessee, October 1984; ended December 1988

A short-lived subsidiary of actress Mary Tyler Moore's MTM Enterprises, Inc., television production company (which began in 1969 in Hollywood), the MTM Music Group opened as a record label, music publisher, and management company in Nashville in October 1984. The label's chairman and chief executive officer was Alan Bernard, formerly vice president of special projects for MTM Enterprises. Howard Stark served as president; Tommy West, as senior vice president.

The firm began releasing records in April 1985, distributed via CAPITOL/EMI. MTM Records was fairly successful in launching several country acts, among them HOLLY DUNN, S-K-O, PAUL OVERSTREET, Becky Hobbs, Judy Rodman, and the Girls Next Door. The label was also home to alternative rock band In Pursuit and R&B act the Voltage Brothers. The firm's twenty staff songwriters included Dunn, Hobbs, Rodman, Larry Boone, Hugh Prestwood, Radney Foster, and Bill Lloyd (soon to form FOSTER & LLOYD).

Following the July 1988 sale of MTM Enterprises to Great Britain's Television South PLC (TVS) for a reported $325 million, the MTM Music Group was soon up for sale as well. In December 1988 Howard Stark purchased the firm, and it ceased to exist as a record company and publishing house. Ownership of the MTM publishing catalog then passed to BMG Music Publishing, which sold it to Universal Music Group in 2007. MTM copyrights are now controlled by Universal Music Publishing. —*Paul Kingsbury*

## Moon Mullican
b. Corrigan, Texas, March 29, 1909; d. January 1, 1967

Aubrey Wilson Mullican, King of the Hillbilly Piano Players, was much more than his moniker implied. Just as comfortable with jazz, blues, or mainstream pop, he was pivotal in bringing boogie into country music. His work widened the range of possibilities for aspiring young pianists such as JERRY LEE LEWIS and FLOYD CRAMER.

Mullican's father bought a pump organ in 1917 to help his children learn religious music, but young Aubrey Mullican left home in 1925 to play pop music in bars. He had already acquired the nickname "Moon," which may have stood for "Moonshine" or alluded to his already-balding pate. By the late 1930s he was

*Moon Mullican*

working with LEON "PAPPY" SELPH's Blue Ridge Playboys and CLIFF BRUNER's Texas Wanderers as well as leading his own groups in Texas and Illinois. He recorded prolifically as a sideman with Bruner (singing on the seminal "Truck Driver's Blues"), BUDDY JONES, and others, making more than one hundred recordings between August 1939 and May 1940. In 1939 he appeared with the Texas Wanderers in the movie *Village Barn Dance*.

In the early 1940s Mullican worked with JIMMIE DAVIS at KWKH in Shreveport before organizing the Showboys with Cliff Bruner at KLAC–Port Arthur, Texas, in 1943. He left to work with Davis's gubernatorial campaign for a few months but rejoined Bruner soon after. In 1945 Mullican formed his own band, keeping the name Showboys and recording an unissued session for Houston's Gulf Records in 1946. In that same year he described his music as "Texas Socko" or "East Texas Sock"—played in 2/4 time and heavily accenting the second beats of each measure—and said he'd developed his style in Houston a decade earlier.

In 1946 Mullican signed with KING RECORDS; he soon recorded "New Pretty Blonde," a nonsense version of the recent CAJUN hit "Jole Blon," which became his first hit. Working with African American producer HENRY GLOVER over the next few years, Mullican struck pay dirt with both boogie numbers and sentimental songs. Among his hits were "Sweeter Than the Flowers" and "I'll Sail My Ship Alone" as well as country versions of the pop hits "Mona Lisa" and "Goodnight Irene."

Mullican briefly owned several nightclubs in the late 1940s and by 1950 was working in the oil boom town of Odessa, Texas, appearing on station KECK. He gave up his own band when HANK WILLIAMS brought him to the GRAND OLE OPRY in June 1951. He and Williams later collaborated on "Jambalaya," a reworking of Papa Cairo's contemporary Cajun hit "Big Texas." It became one of Williams's biggest hits, but Mullican's recording was less successful.

In 1955 Mullican left Nashville and returned to East Texas. He remained with King until 1956, but his last major hit, "Cherokee Boogie," had come in 1951. He subsequently recorded for Coral, STARDAY, and Hallway Records and had his last charted record, "Ragged but Right," on Starday in 1961.

Mullican's health began failing in the early 1960s. He had a heart attack onstage in Kansas City in 1962 and a fatal one shortly after midnight on New Year's Day 1967. —*Colin Escott*

## Joaquin Murphey
b. Hollywood, California, December 30, 1923; d. October 25, 1999

Joaquin Murphey was one of WESTERN SWING's most creative and original musicians, an influential steel guitarist best known for his recordings with SPADE COOLEY and TEX WILLIAMS.

Earl Murphey was an unknown when he dazzled Cooley and his band during a successful audition in 1943. (It was Cooley who nicknamed him "Joaquin," for California's San Joaquin Valley.) Murphey began recording with Cooley in November 1944 and played on the fiddler's hits "Shame on You" and "Crazy 'Cause I Love You," quickly winning fame for his sophisticated, acrobatic solos and innovative tunings. His masterful harmonic progressions and single-string work were all the more remarkable because he used a lap steel—not a pedal model. Murphey left Cooley in 1946 to work with Andy Parker & the Plainsmen; the steel guitarist also recorded with T. TEXAS TYLER, EDDIE DEAN, and others before joining Tex Williams's Western Caravan in the winter of 1947–48. Murphey returned to Cooley's band in 1953 and then worked in a quartet with fiddler Buddy Ray in 1956. By 1960, however, he had begun to slip into obscurity, as western swing faded and different, often less sophisticated steel guitar styles prevailed. DeWitt Scott coaxed him to record again in 1976, but Murphey quit playing for a number of years. He was inducted into the Steel Guitar Hall of Fame in 1980. —*Kevin Coffey*

## Michael Martin Murphey
b. Oak Cliff, Texas, March 14, 1945

Michael Martin Murphey first won fame as part of the AUSTIN, TEXAS, music scene in the early 1970s. Later he recorded mainstream country music albums, although he never lived in Nashville and maintained close ties to the West. By the end of the 1980s he had begun performing western music, and since then he has recorded numerous albums of COWBOY and western songs.

Growing up in Dallas, Murphey wanted to be a Baptist minister, prompting his enrolling in North Texas State University and studying Greek. At age twenty he moved to Los Angeles, where he studied creative writing at UCLA and penned songs for Screen Gems, including "What Am I Doing Hanging Around" for the Monkees. He formed the Lewis & Clark Expedition with Boomer Castleman (Murphey used the name Travis Lewis, while Castleman was Boomer Clarke); the duo notched their first pop chart single, "I Feel Good (I Feel Bad)," in 1967.

In 1971 Murphey joined Austin's alternative-music scene and began playing clubs. He recorded two albums for A&M as Michael Murphey, *Geronimo's Cadillac* (1972) and *Cosmic Cowboy Souvenirs* (1973), which featured the underground anthems "Geronimo's Cadillac" and "Cosmic Cowboy."

Moving to Colorado in 1974, he recorded *Michael Murphey* (1974) and *Blue Sky, Night Thunder* (1974) for EPIC RECORDS; the latter yielded the 1975 self-penned pop hits "Wildfire" (#3) and "Carolina in the Pines" (#21). Murphey moved to Taos, New Mexico, in 1979 and made the Epic albums *Swans Against the Sun* (1975) and *Flowing Free Forever* (1976). Next he signed with the LIBERTY label, where he recorded three mainstream country albums, *Michael Martin Murphey* (1982), *Tonight We Ride* (1985), and *Americana* (1987), all produced by JIM ED NORMAN. Murphey's eponymous Liberty album included the #1 country hit (#19 pop) "What's Forever For," while *Tonight We Ride* included a remake of "Carolina in the Pines" that became a #9 country hit in 1986.

Murphey later signed with WARNER BROS. RECORDS, and his interest in cowboys led him to organize the first West Fest (1986) in Copper Mountain, Colorado, and to record an album, *Cowboy Songs* (1990), featuring a number of cowboy standards. This inspired the formation of Warner Western, a Warner Bros. imprint devoted to western music. Murphey recorded several albums for the label, including *Sagebrush Symphony* (1995) and *The Horse Legends* (1997). In 1998 he formed his own label, WestFest/Real West Productions, and released albums showcasing both traditional and original western songs. Since 2004 his albums have appeared on Smith, ACME, and Rural Rhythm, the last offering his *Buckaroo Blue Grass* in 2009. —*Don Cusic*

## Roger Murrah
b. Athens, Alabama, November 20, 1946

Roger Murrah is a successful song publisher and songwriter whose work has been featured on country radio since the 1980s.

He began playing piano and writing songs in his teens. By the mid-1960s he fronted a regional band in Alabama. While in the army, he became a staff writer with Rick Hall's Florence Alabama Music Enterprises (FAME) in 1968.

Working at a Huntsville recording studio, Murrah met BOBBY BARE, who signed him to his publishing company. Murrah moved to Nashville in 1972 and soon entered the country charts with WYNN STEWART's "It's Raining in Seattle."

Murrah hit his stride by 1980, scoring his first #1 with MEL TILLIS's "Southern Rains," followed by Al Jarreau's international pop smash "We're in This Love Together." Other Murrah hits include "Life's Highway," "High Cotton," "Don't Rock the Jukebox," "Ozark Mountain Jubilee," and "Goodbye Time." He also cowrote WAYLON JENNINGS's autobiographical concept album, *A Man Called Hoss*.

In 1990 he started Murrah Music Corporation, which delivered a number of major hits. In 2009 BUG MUSIC acquired a portion of the company; Murrah served as senior vice president, Nashville, from early 2009 to August 2011. He was inducted into the NASHVILLE SONGWRITERS HALL OF FAME in 2005. —*Michael Gray*

## Anne Murray
b. Springhill, Nova Scotia, June 20, 1945

Anne Murray's discriminating musical choices and tastefully produced recordings, buoyed by a Canadian-accented alto perfectly suited for smooth pop-country material, made her one of the most successful female crossover artists of her time.

Morna Anne Murray grew up in the coal mining region of Nova Scotia, singing for fun while earning her college degree in physical education. The high school physical education teacher

*Anne Murray*

had to be coaxed into singing part time on a Canadian television show, *Sing-Along Jubilee*, in the late 1960s. In 1968, while she was still teaching, the program's musical director, Brian Ahern, produced her first album in Toronto, which led to her signing by CAPITOL/Canada and the eventual release of her first border-crossing hit, "Snowbird," a Top Ten country chart-maker in 1970. A pop hit in Great Britain and the United States, this record set the pace for her future success.

Murray received national exposure as a regular on *The Glen Campbell Goodtime Hour*, but she was unwilling to live in Los Angeles or deal with demanding network executives. In 1972–73 she scored her second major crossover record, establishing Kenny Loggins's "Danny's Song" (a country and pop Top Ten) as another signature song. "Love Song" (#5 country, #12 pop; 1973–74) won a Grammy for Best Country Vocal Performance, Female, further proving her mastery of the medium-tempo country-pop ballad.

In 1974 Murray paired the Beatles' "You Won't See Me" with a distaff version of the GEORGE JONES standard "She Thinks I Still Care." Capitol shipped the 45-rpm disc to both country and pop stations and netted Murray her first country #1 as well as another pop Top Ten.

Refined yet comfortably down-home, Murray toured extensively until 1975, when she married and decided to start a family with husband Bill Langsdroth. For the next couple of years she put her entertainment career on the back burner (and producer Ahern moved on to begin a long-running, fruitful collaboration with EMMYLOU HARRIS). In 1978 Murray came back strong with THE EVERLY BROTHERS chestnut "Walk Right Back," astutely picking a familiar song by artists who had earlier bridged pop and country. She later successfully reprised the Monkees' "Daydream Believer" and Bruce Channel's "Hey! Baby" A long string of hits and awards followed, with Grammys for Best Pop Vocal Performance, Female ("You Needed Me," 1978), and Best Country

Vocal Performance, Female ("Could I Have This Dance, 1980; "A Little Good News," 1983), and, with Dave Loggins, the 1985 CMA Vocal Duo of the Year award. Meanwhile, her vocals influenced other female singers, including KATHY MATTEA.

Murray maintained her Canadian residence, business headquarters, and self-directed management, which may help explain why country and pop fans never identified her exclusively with either genre. She was never a favorite of CMA or ACM voters, despite recording nine chart-topping country hits between 1979 and 1986, including "I Just Fall in Love Again," "Shadows in the Moonlight," and "Just Another Woman in Love." After notching twenty-five country Top Tens between 1970 and 1990, she gained her final country chart record in 1991.

Murray continued to record, work TV specials, and tour well into the 2000s. In 2008 she released two albums, *Anne Murray Duets: Friends & Legends*—which included duets with fellow Canadians Celine Dion, K. D. LANG, and SHANIA TWAIN—and *Anne Murray's Christmas Album*. In 2009 she published her autobiography, *All of Me*, written with Michael Posner. —*Bob Millard*

## Music City USA

The term "Music City USA" first reflected the proud tradition of live programming established by Nashville radio station WSM. From the mid-1930s to the late-1950s WSM originated numerous pop and country network shows, including *Magnolia Blossoms*, *Sunday Down South*, and the *Prince Albert Show*, the Grand Ole Opry's NBC network segment. Even non-network shows blanketed the nation because of Nashville's central location and the station's 50,000-watt, clear-channel transmitter. Nashville also boasted stars who rose through the WSM ranks, such as Metropolitan Opera veteran Joseph McPherson and pop singers Dinah Shore and Snooky Lanson.

It was on RED FOLEY's NBC radio show in 1950 that WSM announcer David Cobb coined the phrase "Music City" in a moment of serendipity. By 1953 music trade publications were using it to describe Nashville's bustling recording activity and the hits it yielded. Most sessions were country, but, as in radio, Nashville recording embraced pop, gospel, and R&B as well. In fact, pop bandleader Francis Craig's smash hit "Near You" (1947) helped alert musicians and executives to Nashville's potential as a recording center. Although country hits prevailed, variety continued; by 1979 nearly half of Nashville sessions were pop, rock, R&B, gospel, or disco. The city's musicians union chapter helped attract creative studio players by relaxing the requirement that they be able to read music.

By 1961 the Nashville music industry had a firm institutional base. Following the launching of ACUFF-ROSE PUBLICATIONS in 1942, the number of music publishers had grown to more than one hundred. Additionally, there were some 1,100 professional musicians, 200 songwriters, twelve talent agencies, fifteen recording studios, and 1,600 artists and sidemen. Nashville's musical ranks included the trade association CMA, promoters, radio syndicators, jingle companies, arrangers, record pressing firms, and performance rights licensing organizations. By 1963 most major labels had built offices in the city. Nashville entrepreneurs were also producing syndicated TV shows, building a solid audience base for TNN: THE NASHVILLE NETWORK and CMT in the 1980s and 1990s.

By 1998 Nashville boasted some ninety record companies, twenty-four talent agencies, 104 video and film production companies, nearly 300 music publishers, 174 recording studios,

and a host of other musical enterprises, with tourism—much of it music-based—adding to the music industry's economic impact. Small wonder that the Nashville Chamber of Commerce adopted the Music City logo for its promotional campaigns.

The introduction of SoundScan electronic retail monitoring revealed that country music artists sold 80.3 million albums in 1992, heightening Nashville's profile as country's primary production center. Since then, new digital recording and downloading technologies have freed artists from reliance on large corporations based in major music hubs, and the rise of the Internet has made it possible for artists to use their own websites to reach record buyers directly and to enhance sales through social networking. On the other hand, consolidation in the recording industry has fostered the rise of independent labels with Nashville offices run by professionals who had been let go by major labels; in turn, these newer independents have given rising talent a shot at success and perpetuated Nashville's reputation as a city of dreams for aspiring musicians.

In music publishing, Nashville's long-powerful independent music publishers have been absorbed by major conglomerates, but conglomerates have fueled their expansion by forming copublishing ventures with prominent songwriters and artist-writers, expanding economic opportunities for both.

Consolidation has also affected Nashville's broadcasting landscape. WSM-FM, owned by the giant Cumulus group since 2008, uses a short playlist typical in country radio; and with the rise of FM after 1970, WSM-AM is no longer the force it once was in the country music world. Nevertheless, WSM-AM still brings the Opry to millions of fans worldwide through its terrestrial, satellite, and online broadcasts. In 2009 the station began its *Music City Roots* series, featuring a wide array of country and AMERICANA artists. The Nashville office of SiriusXM Satellite Radio originates additional programs. Viacom bought TNN in 1997, soon dropped "The Nashville Network" from its name, and ended country programming in 2000. Viacom's CMT, though, has held its own, and it has been joined by GAC (Great American Country)—likewise airing news, videos, and interviews—as well as RFD-TV, whose Nashville-based programming office offers current and vintage musical shows and various lifestyle programs targeting rural Americans.

Nashville's music infrastructure has remained strong, embracing not only recording and broadcasting companies and performance rights organizations but also professional organizations (AFTRA/SAG, AFM, NSAI) and trade associations (CMA and IBMA, the latter moving to town in 2003). The city hosts annual conventions of CMA, the Gospel Music Association, IBMA (since 2005), and the Americana Music Association (since 2000). All four associations typically hold their annual awards shows here, adding to the live music presented at the CMA MUSIC FESTIVAL, NSAI's Tin Pan South songwriting festival, and regular performances at local venues ranging from honky-tonks to the prestigious Ford Theater of the COUNTRY MUSIC HALL OF FAME AND MUSEUM (opened 2001) and the Schermerhorn Symphony Center (opened 2006). —*John W. Rumble*

## Music Publishing

Generally speaking, music publishers became more important within the country music industry after World War II, even as they were becoming less powerful within American popular music as a whole. Country publishing bucked the general trend mainly because its development was slow. The big publishers who dominated much of American music before 1940 largely ignored country, considering it unworthy of their attention. Many prewar country songs were published only if they were recorded, and even many recorded tunes never got published at all. Early recorded country music consisted heavily of folk songs or older pop material, and new country songs were published by a handful of established companies, such as Chicago's M. M. Cole. More commonly, freshly written country music was published not by these older firms, which were based where hillbilly performers congregated for radio work, but by companies launched by country record producers. These savvy businessmen realized the profitability of country compositions, even if many recording artists and songwriters did not.

Record producers Eli Oberstein, Dave Kapp, W. R. Calaway, Art Satherley, and, most successfully, Ralph Peer all formed publishing companies. Only a few prewar writers and artists controlled their own publishing or even exploited the growing appeal of songbooks, hawked over the air and sometimes featuring only song lyrics and artist photos. Carson Robison, Asher Sizemore, Bradley Kincaid, Gene Autry, and Roy Acuff were among the first to do so.

Three factors spurred the proliferation of country publishing companies and their rising importance within the music industry: the birth of BMI in 1940; the surge in country music's national popularity during and after World War II; and the increasing business sophistication of country songwriters. As Nashville grew as a country recording center, it also became home to new music publishing ventures: Acuff-Rose (1942), launched by Roy Acuff and Fred Rose; Tree (1951), co-owned by WSM executive Jack Stapp; Cedarwood (1953), created by WSM executive Jim Denny; and Moss-Rose, started by talent manager Hubert Long. There were many others, but these came to the fore as major players by the early 1960s and ultimately challenged the immediate postwar strength of the Aberbach Brothers' Los Angeles and New York–based Hill and Range Songs, founded in the mid-1940s. As singers gravitated to Nashville seeking record contracts, so did songwriters intent on pitching their songs to the city's growing cadre of singers and publishers. Of course, some country artists continued to write and/or publish their own material. However, songwriters such as Danny Dill, Marijohn Wilkin, Cindy Walker, Harlan Howard, Boudleaux and Felice Bryant, Bob McDill, Jerry Chesnut, Curly Putman, and John D. Loudermilk, who made writing rather than performing their principal activity, became Music Row players along with their publishers. Artists and record producers often beat a path to their doors for new material.

Music publishers, finally established as power centers within the country music industry, handled song administration and exploitation, as publishers had always done, developing the value of copyrights via recordings, radio, TV, and other avenues of exposure. Even the best publishers today usually keep relatively small staffs of regular writers under contract, because so many well-known writers, no less than artists, have launched their own companies. And one reason why so many artist-writers do so, besides the desire to keep more of their songs' income, is that overhead is so low, with only three basic tasks to perform: song administration (securing copyrights, seeing that licenses are issued and monies are collected, and paying outside cowriters or copublishers), song plugging (working with artists and producers to get songs recorded), and creative work (signing new writers, pairing cowriters, and editing their songs).

Now that the sale of printed music (sheet music and songbooks) is relatively negligible, the monies shared by publishers and their writers consist mostly of mechanical and performance royalties and synchronization fees. Saving the larger matter of mechanical and performance royalties for a separate entry, synchronization fees (or "synch" fees) are paid for the use of music in synchronization with visual images. This covers songs used in motion pictures, television commercials, and videos made for the retail market, but not songs from live or recorded TV performances, which come under performance royalties. Fees paid by these users to publishers for synch licenses vary widely, based on length of a license, length of the song used, and size of the potential broadcast audience. Some motion picture uses of songs (usually granted in perpetuity) pay as much as $200,000; for local, short-term television use of part of a song, the cost may be as low as $1,000. One-year national use of a song in a TV commercial, though, is even more profitable than movies and might bring a publisher as much as $500,000 in synch fees.

The advent of digital technology and the Internet has markedly affected music publishing. As declining CD sales cut into mechanical royalties, music publishing companies have sought to maximize earnings for themselves and their songwriters by securing royalties for music sold, downloaded, or played through computers, MP3 players, and cell phones. —*Ronnie Pugh*

## Music Row (see *The Center of Music City: Nashville's Music Row*, page 370)

## Music Videos

After MTV debuted in 1981, popular music changed dramatically. Videos presented a powerful new promotional and marketing tool for introducing new artists, new songs, and new sounds. The rise of cable TV created a vast need for programmable content, and music videos rapidly became a popular phenomenon, especially with young viewers.

For the music industry, the format offered more than an alternative to radio for airing songs; it also married those songs to carefully created images of artists, helping fans tie a hit song to a face and helping new artists establish an identity with audiences. Successful videos proved to have an immediate effect on sales and trends. As a result, the music industry entered a new era.

Because country music tends toward a more conservative approach than rock or pop music, the reach of country videos wasn't as quick or as pervasive as in those fields. Nonetheless, video played a role in shaping the youth movement country music experienced in the 1980s, as photogenic artists like Rodney Crowell, The Judds, Reba McEntire, George Strait, Randy Travis, and Dwight Yoakam used videos as a means of introducing themselves and their songs to the mass market. All of them experienced sales in numbers that were rare prior to videos and video channels.

The first two primary outlets for country music videos, TNN: The Nashville Network and CMT (Country Music Television), launched within a week of each other in March 1983. At the time, both networks presented a down-home, just-folks aesthetic markedly different than that of MTV. TNN and CMT also were more guarded about sexual and violent content.

Nashville's major labels began producing promotional clips as early as 1981. But once the two country cable networks began drawing viewers, the number and quality of videos grew. Still, the medium didn't really take off until TNN increased its video programming in 1990 from three to thirty-one hours per week and purchased competitor CMT the next year. By 1995 the two networks were adding more than 200 videos per year to their play lists; by then, it became rare for a new single not to have a companion video.

Nashville's homegrown production companies, such as Scene Three and Deaton-Flanigen, became leaders in country videos. But the amount of work and the search for fresh ideas also brought video directors and producers from the coasts to MUSIC CITY. Bud Schaetzle, for example, directed several clips for GARTH BROOKS, including the controversial "The Thunder Rolls," which was banned from TNN and CMT because of its violent content about an abusive husband and a vengeful wife.

As the new medium grew, notable videos included HANK WILLIAMS JR.'s 1989 computer-generated duet with his father, "A Tear in My Beer." Stars such as BILLY RAY CYRUS and SHANIA TWAIN could point to hit videos as key to their sudden, immense success. But those aren't isolated cases: During the 1990s and beyond, nearly every superstar has benefited from memorable video clips, including BROOKS & DUNN, KENNY CHESNEY, DIXIE CHICKS, FAITH HILL, ALAN JACKSON, TOBY KEITH, TIM MCGRAW, BRAD PAISLEY, and KEITH URBAN.

Nevertheless, music videos became less significant in the new century. In 2000, TNN's new owner, Viacom, changed its format away from country programming, eventually giving the network a new name, Spike TV. Viacom also modified CMT, shifting from its down-home style and eventually removing its music-video focus in favor of reality and scripted programming. A new network, GAC (Great American Country), filled some of the gap. GAC started programming country videos in 1995 and kept gaining viewers through the 2000s, especially after being purchased by Scripps Networks in 2004. Not only was television exposure more limited, but the impact of the Internet revolution and the Great Recession dramatically reduced the promotion budgets of record companies. But thanks to how clips are used on artists' websites, YouTube, and such online music outlets as AOL and Yahoo, videos remain a part of the creative and promotional plans of country artists and their business allies. —*Mark Schone*

## Weldon Myrick
b. Jayton, Texas, April 10, 1939

Weldon Myrick is a hard-working, top-of-the-line, Nashville session PEDAL STEEL GUITAR player. An original member of BILL ANDERSON's Po Boys Band, Myrick was the session leader and steel guitarist behind the early RCA hit recordings of CONNIE SMITH and a GRAND OLE OPRY staff band member from 1966 to 1998. He has worked with BUDDY HOLLY (cowriting Holly's song "It's Not My Fault" in 1956) and ELVIS PRESLEY (the album *Today* in 1975), among many other artists.

A highly commercial stylist, Myrick creates a clean, in-the-pocket groove using his pedals to raise and lower string pitch in counterpoint harmony while picking breakneck double- and triple-stop passages. Memorable examples can be found on hits by Connie Smith ("Once a Day"), JEANNIE C. RILEY ("Harper Valley P.T.A."), CAL SMITH ("Country Bumpkin"), and GEORGE STRAIT ("Right or Wrong"). Myrick also contributed to the Nashville super-picker album *Area Code 615*; J. J. Cale's debut album, *Naturally*; and LINDA RONSTADT's 1970 pop hit "Long, Long Time."

Myrick has performed on country television shows and on the soundtracks for Robert Altman's landmark film *Nashville*, the Oscar-winning *Tender Mercies*, and all three *Smokey and the Bandit* comedies. Myrick was elected to the Steel Guitar Hall of Fame in 1997. —*Elek Horvath and Robert Kramer*

# Country Music as Music

## BILL EVANS

**W**here is the "country" in country music? This is a question posed by each new generation of musicians and listeners. Although the answer has changed over the years, country music has exhibited some remarkable continuities through a succession of numerous historical substyles. The sound, the instruments, and the technology used to make country music have changed greatly since the 1920s. Nevertheless, core assumptions related to melody, harmony, meter, song form, ensemble approach, and vocal style have helped to define country as a unique musical type, even in the face of recent stylistic trends that increasingly incorporate elements from other popular musical styles into the country music sound.

## HISTORICAL BACKGROUND

By the time of country music's first commercial recordings in the 1920s, three centuries of musical exchange had already occurred between Americans of European ancestry and those of African ancestry. This interaction was made possible in part by a general compatibility of West African and West European traditional musical systems. Cultural attitudes regarding the basic elements of music—scale types, rhythm, song forms, general instrument and ensemble types, and performance styles and contexts—were largely held in common by musicians of both continents, with different outcomes arising from the relative emphasis placed on these shared musical ingredients.

The results of this interchange have distinguished the American music scene from the early nineteenth century forward through a procession of folk and popular music styles, including religious camp meeting songs, ballad and story songs, fiddle and banjo traditions, minstrelsy, spirituals, ragtime, blues, gospel, and early jazz. Along with more recently imported sounds, such as the fiddle and accordion traditions of Irish and German immigrants, a wealth of musical styles and resources helped shape early country music in the first decades of the twentieth century.

America's legacy of European and African heritage has influenced country music in ways that are often taken for granted. Such fundamental characteristics as the predominance of stringed instruments in country ensembles and the ubiquity of song forms built around repetitive verse/chorus structures as well as country music's approach toward harmony and improvisation all reflect certain underlying attitudes toward music making that have been developing for centuries.

## MELODY

As in other genres of American vernacular music, a country song consists of a lyric matched to a sequence of musical notes (a *melody*). The melody is supported by a progression of chords (or *harmony*) played by an accompanying instrument or group of instruments.

Common to both West European and West African traditional music is an understanding of melody as a series of brief phrases related to one another through repetition, elaboration, or variation and that are joined together to form a song. Melodies from the BALLAD and fiddling traditions of the British Isles were enhanced on American soil by African performance styles, which placed high value on rhythmic vitality and melodic variation, often achieved through bent and/or sliding note choices not usually employed by the West European major and minor scale modes.

Like its traditional and popular predecessors, most country music is vocal music. Therefore, step-wise motion (in which a melody has an abundance of consecutive notes that are adjacent to each other in a scale) and a limited melodic range of an octave or less tend to characterize most country melodies. Of course, exceptions to this generalized rule abound, as in PATSY CLINE's performance of the WILLIE NELSON song "Crazy," a classic in part because of its leaping melody.

## HARMONY

One of country music's most distinctive musical features is the straightforward and sturdy way in which harmony is commonly employed to support a melody. The vast majority of country songs are harmonized with major rather than minor chords. However, a few notable exceptions, such as MERLE TRAVIS's "Sixteen Tons," are memorable in part because of their minor key settings.

Modulation, in which a song moves to a new key, was relatively rare in the first decades of country music history. JOHNNY CASH's 1956 recording of "I Walk the Line" is one remarkable exception, with stanzas sung in the successive keys of F, B-flat, and E-flat before returning once again to B-flat and F. Another example is BOB WILLS's "San Antonio Rose," in which the song's distinctive chorus is set in a different key from its verses. Modulation has become much more common in recent years, where, as in rock and pop styles, it functions as a dramatic device intended to bring a sense of intensity, climax, or finality to an arrangement. In this case, modulation usually shifts the key center up one scale step to the next pitch (as in SHANIA TWAIN's "Any Man of Mine").

The three-chord stereotype of country harmony, in which a song accompaniment is constructed exclusively from chords built on the first, fourth, and fifth notes of the scale, has become something of a signifying cliché for outsiders. As in the blues, often nothing more is really needed in the way of chords for many country pieces, as this famous JIMMIE DAVIS hit proves (in the key of C major, the I, IV, and V chords would be played as C, F, and G major chords):

I
You are my sunshine, my only sunshine

IV                     I
You make me happy when skies are gray,

IV                     I
You'll never know dear how much I love you

V          I
Please don't take my sunshine away.

The thousands of possible melodic and harmonic combinations that have sprung from this seemingly restrictive three-chord palette point to a central tenet of country creativity: to create the maximum emotional effect in the most direct way possible with the most basic of musical means. Nevertheless, country musicians have also employed more complex harmonies since the music's earliest years. Blues and ragtime songs learned by early twentieth-century folk musicians instilled new harmonic ideas, which by the 1920s had become part of the natural resources of early country performers as geographically dispersed as the North Carolina STRINGBAND musician CHARLIE POOLE (as in "Don't Let Your Deal Go Down") and WESTERN SWING bandleader MILTON BROWN (as in his version of W. C. Handy's blues standard "St. Louis Blues"). In this regard, JIMMIE RODGERS, who was greatly influenced by Tin Pan Alley, vaudeville, and early blues and jazz performances, recorded some of the most complex pieces, harmonically speaking, in country music history.

Basic chord progressions can be made more complex by grafting passing and substitute chords onto the basic I-IV-V framework. Western swing musicians became most adept at this skill, utilizing the harmonic formulas of swing-era jazz to create fast-moving extended choral harmonies in support of the free-wheeling improvisational flights of lead instrumentalists.

Although HANK WILLIAMS's classic "I'm So Lonesome I Could Cry" sounds just fine with an accompaniment that uses only the I, IV, and V chords, most modern performances involve a more complex progression originally implied in part by the moving bass line in the first verse of Williams's earliest recording of the piece (transposed here to the key of C with passing chords in parentheses):

```
    C       (C/B)      (Am)    (C/G)
Hear that lonesome whippoorwill

         C       (Am)    (Gm)    (C7)
He sounds too blue to fly

      F       (Dm)     C     (Am)
The midnight train is whining low

        C       G       C
I'm so lonesome I could cry
```

Harmonic embellishments of this kind became increasingly common in country music during the 1940s. However, many of the most distinctive hits of the past three decades maintain a clear relationship to an underlying I-IV-V harmonic foundation in spite of their more complex surface harmonies. REBA MCENTIRE's "Somebody Should Leave" and GARTH BROOKS's "Friends in Low Places" are examples of modern songs in which harmonically elaborate verses suggestive of pop music styles contrast with straightforward choruses that bring the listener firmly back to a country sensibility. In such ways, modern composers blend the traditional with the innovative, introducing new sounds and musical possibilities to the genre.

## METER, TEMPO, AND RHYTHM

Melodies and their accompanying chord progressions are organized in time within a recurring cycle of evenly spaced beats called *meter*. *Tempo* refers to the speed at which a song is performed. *Rhythm* is a much broader musical concept. This term may refer to the metrical arrangement of individual melody notes (as in the rhythm of a melody), to the relative stress given to each beat in a metrical cycle (as in the rhythm of a piece or style), or even to the ways in which the various instruments work together in an ensemble (as in a band's overall sense of rhythm). Another legacy of the shared European and African heritage of American folk and popular music is the prevalence of metrical cycles made up of either two (duple) or three (triple) beats. Duple meters of two- and four-beat cycles predominate in country music. Nevertheless, the waltz, which by definition is performed in triple meter, has developed into something of a sentimental staple, surviving in country music past its diminishing popularity in other American genres. Country waltzes come in a wide variety of tempos, from quite fast (as in MARTY ROBBINS's "El Paso") to decidedly slow (as in JIM REEVES's "He'll Have to Go").

Shifts in meter within a single piece are extremely rare but not altogether unknown (for example, MAC WISEMAN's "'Tis Sweet to Be Remembered" has verses in duple meter with waltz-time choruses). Occasionally a composition is sturdy enough to take on an entirely new identity when performed in a different meter, as ELVIS PRESLEY accomplished early in his career with his cover version of "Blue Moon of Kentucky." In this case, Presley transformed the original waltz time of this 1946 BILL MONROE hit into a brisk and rocking duple meter.

As with other forms of American popular music, the speed at which country music is performed is often a function of its historical association with a particular dance style. Of even greater importance is the need to establish a tempo that enables the lyric content of a song to be easily understood. As a result, country tempos tend to occupy a sensible, broad middle ground between the very fast and the very slow. One exception to this rule occurs with country instrumentals, which are often virtuosic displays of musical prowess taken at extremely fast tempos (as in FLATT & SCRUGGS's banjo showpiece "Foggy Mountain Breakdown").

In addition, each substyle of country music (HONKY-TONK, western swing, BLUEGRASS) tends to exhibit a degree of internal consistency in regard to a more specific range of acceptable tempos. With the exception of country ballad and heart songs, which are almost always performed at slow tempos, a typical honky-tonk song (such as RAY PRICE's "Crazy Arms") will usually be performed in a medium-fast tempo that is slower than a standard western swing song (such as Bob Wills's "Take Me Back to Tulsa"), which itself is slower in tempo than a fast bluegrass favorite (such as THE OSBORNE BROTHERS' "Rocky Top").

An even more important signifier of country music substyle is the unique approach each substyle takes to rhythm and accent. MAYBELLE CARTER helped to introduce to country music in the 1920s an accompanimental guitar technique derived from African American sources in which a bass note struck on the main beat(s) of a measure is followed by a chord brushed across the higher strings on the weaker off beat(s). This separation of main and weak beats in terms of musical role has characterized every subsequent country music style to this day. Some styles, such as western swing and bluegrass, place greater emphasis or accent on the weaker beats of a measure, while other styles, such as honky-tonk and much of rock-influenced modern country, tend either to smooth out these differences or to place greater stress on the main beats of each metrical cycle.

## FORM

The form that has served as a template for the songs of many American genres has its roots in the ballad traditions of the British Isles. It consists of a four-line stanza matched to four melodic phrases of nearly equal length, which are often assembled in such a way that melodic material from the last two phrases brings to a resolution similar material presented in the song's first two lines. Combined with a chorus or refrain of one to four phrases, this is the archetypal song structure of country music.

In reality, a wide variety of song forms are used, with much of this variation being the result of ingenious idiosyncratic extensions on the basic four-line format (as in Jimmie Rodgers's six-line stanza form in "Waiting for a Train"). Three-line blues forms with their own variations have always been common, as have more extended forms (such as Hank Williams's version of "Lovesick Blues") that reflect the enduring legacies of earlier ragtime and classic blues styles. Country instrumentals come in all of these formal varieties but are characteristically multisectional, with contrasting melodic content extending across two or more sections (as in the popular fiddle breakdown "Orange Blossom Special," which consists of three distinct sections).

The *turnaround* is a formal device common in country music. This is a brief phrase attached to the end of a verse or chorus that brings a sense of completion to a particular section of a tune. Its trademark is a I-V-I chord progression, over which an instrumentalist will play a variation on a set of standardized melodic phrases that have come to be closely associated with the turnaround itself. Turnarounds may also be sung, most memorably in the form of the country yodel, as popularized in different eras by Jimmie Rodgers, Hank Williams, and their admirers.

Some formal devices represent more recent borrowings from other popular styles. One example is the *bridge*, which is a short section of contrasting melodic material usually presented just before a song's climax. As appropriated by modern country songwriters, the lyric content of this penultimate section often provides resolution to a song's lyric or reveals its core sentiment (as in Garth Brooks's "Unanswered Prayers").

Short *instrumental interludes*, consisting of a brief melody that may or may not be related to the melody of the actual song itself, have provided a special element to some country songs for several decades. Like the turnaround, interludes provide an element of musical continuity to a country song, often serving as the introduction and/or ending of a piece. They can be so distinctive as to be a marker of the tune itself (as in the guitar part that opens and closes BOBBY BARE's "Detroit City") or be so memorable that they become virtually synonymous with a song's performer (as is the sonorous, eight-note introduction to Johnny Cash's "Folsom Prison Blues").

## ENSEMBLE APPROACH

It is no historical coincidence that the solo singer accompanied by a guitar occupies a space of great importance in country music. As a social role, the musician-as-storyteller can be traced back many centuries to medieval European minstrel and West African griot traditions. From such roots have emerged on American soil a panoply of styles and genres as disparate as the American broadside ballad, the nineteenth-century parlor song, and rural blues, as well as the twentieth- and twenty-first-century country song.

In this light, country music history can be traced in large part as the development of various ensemble styles, in which each successive stylistic innovation presents a new set of musical solutions to the central task of supporting a lead singer (or, as an extension of this principle, multiple singers or one or more lead instrumentalists). While particular instruments, such as the acoustic guitar, fiddle, PEDAL STEEL GUITAR, and banjo, have come to be viewed as closely associated with country music, it is the ways in which these and other instruments are played and how they relate to one another in an ensemble that is ultimately responsible for this genre's sound.

Many of the late-nineteenth-century and early-twentieth-century southern folk music traditions that were the historical precursors of early country music often involved unaccompanied performances in which one or more singers or an instrumentalist performed without the harmonic and rhythmic support of an instrument or group of instruments. By the early decades of the twentieth century, most musicians had incorporated some concept of instrumental accompaniment into their performance practices.

However, different ideas about ensembles, their instrumental makeup, and their sound were developed at varying points in time across widely dispersed southern regions. The spread of national radio programming into rural and small-town locales, along with the growth of the early country recording industry, helped to nationalize regional approaches to country music throughout the 1920s and early 1930s. Early country styles became somewhat more standardized as amateur musicians learned songs and instrumental styles presented on radio and on 78-rpm recordings by such artists as the CARTER FAMILY, Jimmie Rodgers, GENE AUTRY, and UNCLE DAVE MACON.

From these circumstances, a relatively stable model of the country ensemble has emerged whose underlying structural functions have remained more or less consistent to the present day. Central to this concept is a musical division of labor that assigns to each instrument a distinct musical function. Instruments are grouped into two main categories: those that primarily supply rhythmic and harmonic support (sometimes collectively referred to as the *rhythm section*) and those that also are capable of executing solos (called *lead instruments*).

Regardless of whether they may be featured in a lead capacity, all instruments spend most of their time in the service of the rhythm section. While the bass and drums are almost always exclusively associated with this supportive role, most other instruments divide their time between the two categories.

Stylistic innovations have often come from a talented instrumentalist who develops a new performance technique, thus expanding that instrument's potential as a lead instrument within the country band. In this manner, the piano, the resophonic guitar (DOBRO), the accordion, the mandolin, the lead guitar, the banjo, and even brass instruments, among others, have at various points in country music history helped to fuel the development of new country music sounds and styles.

Ensemble integrity is valued above individual virtuosity in country music. Behind this aesthetic imperative is a concept of musical arrangement in which each instrument maintains its individual voice within the ensemble. To accomplish this result, an instrument is assigned a different rhythmic role, so that its peculiar timbre is experienced as an identifiable ingredient in a total ensemble sound. Bluegrass music has developed this approach to a notable extent, with each instrument accenting different beats and subdivisions of the metrical cycle in precisely executed traditional playing styles.

Another way in which an individual instrument can maintain its identity within the country ensemble is through an accompanimental technique known as *backup*. Backup involves a lead instrumentalist performing a second melody behind a lead singer or other player, offering in effect a second musical point of interest, which ideally should complement and not overpower a lead singer or instrumental passage. Backup is a highly articulated skill in country music. As it is expressed in western swing, honky-tonk, bluegrass, and many modern styles, the exchange of backup opportunities among the various lead instruments creates constantly shifting musical patterns that add great variety to the ensemble sound while also giving lead instrumentalists additional opportunities to display their talents.

## VOCAL STYLES

Vocal styles are without doubt country's most significant distinguishing characteristic. While the solo male or female singer is the most ubiquitous presence, group singing in duet, trio, and quartet configurations has been cultivated to a higher degree in country music than in any other American genre, with the possible exceptions of rhythm & blues and gospel music. A wide variety of singing styles has been welcomed under the country music umbrella throughout its history. Much of this variety is the result not only of the music's deep historical roots but also of its close relationship with other twentieth-century American folk and popular music traditions.

Early country singing styles reveal a dichotomy reflecting the differing assumptions held by musicians of European and of African ancestry regarding vocal style and performance technique. Nowhere is this more evident than in the different approaches to singing taken by the two biggest names of early country music history, the Carter Family and Jimmie Rodgers.

Like the balladeers of the British Isles, the Carter Family is remembered for a plaintive, emotionally detached vocal style designed to draw the listener away from the singer and into the song's lyric. Operating within a musical climate of such overall restraint, emotion and meaning are conveyed by the subtlest of musical means, where a modest ornamental vocal turn or sigh or a slightly bent or delayed note can transmit a world of meaning to listeners who share the performer's worldview.

In contrast, Jimmie Rodgers's vocals were significantly influenced by both the African American musicians and the vaudeville and musical theater entertainers he encountered as a youth growing up in Mississippi. While he never adopted as declamatory a style as did many of the early African American Delta bluesmen, Rodgers's singing expresses a wide range of human emotions through an easygoing, conversational style that engages the listener through its unadulterated accessibility, sincerity, and openness.

Although there is much common ground between these two approaches, for many years country vocalists felt compelled to follow either one or the other of these artistic paths. It is no small accomplishment that artists such as Hank Williams, LEFTY FRIZZELL, and DOLLY PARTON, among others, managed to bridge this gap with singing styles that combine the best of both attitudes, managing to be both plaintive and conversational at the same time.

In recent years, country vocalists have often too easily worn their musical influences on their sleeves, openly borrowing techniques from many different singers. However, unique stylists such as Willie Nelson, EMMYLOU HARRIS, and ALISON KRAUSS have continued to emerge in the modern era, each providing fresh variations on established formulas. Today, pop, rock, rhythm & blues, and soul singers such as James Taylor, LINDA RONSTADT, THE EAGLES, Sam Cooke, and Otis Redding may be as much an influence on new singers as Patsy Cline and GEORGE JONES.

## CONCLUSION

So where is the "country" in country music? To borrow a well-worn advertising phrase, it might be more a state of mind than any specific set of particular musical characteristics. Country musicians seem to share certain assumptions about melody, harmony, form, and performance that together help to shape ideas about the nature of the country sound, its boundaries, and its possibilities. This musical roadmap will change as each succeeding generation introduces new ideas, which are either accepted or rejected as part of the country music landscape. As long as innovative musicians continue to look backward as well as forward in the ongoing process of musical creation, country music will continue to maintain its identity.

Betty Records
P.O. Box 125    Bellaire, Texas
GLAD MUSIC
BMI
5703
Time: 2:07
(1129)

MAN WITH THE BLUES
(Willie Nelson)
WILLIE NELSON

## Narmour & Smith

Will T. Narmour b. Carroll County, Mississippi, May 22, 1889; d. March 24, 1961
Shell W. Smith b. Carroll County, Mississippi, November 26, 1895; d. September 1968

Willie Narmour (fiddle) and Shell Smith (guitar) were one of the most popular instrumental duos on records in the late 1920s. According to blues singer and guitarist Mississippi John Hurt, they won a local fiddle contest for which the prize was an opportunity to record for OKeh. Narmour was a neighbor of Hurt's and recommended him to producer Tom Rockwell. The three musicians journeyed from their Avalon, Mississippi, homes to record in Memphis in February 1928. Hurt saw only one coupling released from his session, but the six Narmour & Smith duets were all issued and sold well.

Their 1929 "Carroll County Blues" was a major success and became a standard among southern fiddlers. Narmour & Smith made their last recordings for OKeh in 1930. They traveled to Atlanta in 1934 to rerecord most of the OKeh titles for Bluebird but did not record again after this effort.
—*Dick Spottswood*

## Murray Nash

b. Campbell, Nebraska, March 5, 1918; d. April 17, 2000

Robert Murray Nash was an important business figure in country music from the mid-1940s to the mid-1950s.

During the 1940s, while based in Knoxville, Tennessee, and working in southeastern distribution for RCA Records, he helped sign Cliff Carlisle (see Bill Carlisle ), Charlie Monroe, and Pee Wee King to the label. In 1948, still living in Knoxville, Nash took over the country department of the recently founded Mercury Records. In 1951 Nashville publisher Fred Rose hired Nash for Acuff-Rose Publications, where he promoted Acuff-Rose songs to record distributors and DJs. His wide respect among DJs assisted him in working with WSM to stage the first DJ Convention in 1952. In addition, Nash assisted in launching Acuff-Rose's Hickory Records.

Shortly before Fred Rose's death in 1954, professional and personality conflicts with Wesley Rose led to Nash's departure. In 1955 Nash formed Murray Nash Associates, his own advertising, publicity, promotion, recording, and publishing firm, which he left in 1958. Subsequently Nash became a postal worker while still running his own publishing company and recording service.
—*John W. Rumble*

## Nashville Bluegrass Band

Alan O'Bryant b. Reidsville, North Carolina, December 26, 1955
Mike Compton b. Meridian, Mississippi, February 29, 1956
Pat Enright b. Huntington, Indiana, April 22, 1945
Mark Hembree b. Chicago, Illinois, September 11, 1955
Stuart Duncan b. Quantico, Virginia, April 14, 1964
Roland White b. Wadawaska, Maine, April 23, 1938
Gene Libbea b. Pasadena, California, March 22, 1953
Dennis Crouch b. St. Louis, Missouri, January 19, 1967
Andy Todd, b. Murfreesboro, Tennessee, August 11, 1970

Emphasizing tight harmony vocals, well-selected songs, and stellar instrumental work, Nashville Bluegrass Band (NBB) has become one of the genre's leading acts. Collectively and individually, its members have received numerous IBMA awards, including Entertainer of the Year (1992, 1993) and Vocal Group of the Year (1990–93), as well as wins in IBMA's song, vocal event, album, instrumental album, recorded event, and fiddle categories. The band won Grammys for Best Bluegrass Album in 1993 and 1995.

At the same time, stage and studio work with artists ranging from Lyle Lovett and Mary Chapin Carpenter to Bernadette Peters and the Nashville Chamber Orchestra, together with NBB members' participation in the hit film O Brother, Where Art Thou? (2000), its multiplatinum soundtrack album, and the follow-up Down from the Mountain concert recording and tour series, has widened the genre's popularity. The band's appearances at Carnegie Hall, Wolf Trap, the White House, and prominent folk venues have helped bring bluegrass to new audiences, as have concerts in dozens of countries worldwide.

In addition, NBB features vocal interpretations of gospel songs and black spirituals. They have recorded and appeared with the famous black gospel act the Fairfield Four, one of the nation's oldest a cappella, jubilee-style groups.

NBB formed in 1984 to back Minnie Pearl and other artists on a package tour and subsequently released three well-received albums for Rounder Records. Initially the act included Pat Enright on guitar, Alan O'Bryant on banjo, Mike Compton on mandolin, and Mark Hembree on bass. Compton's strong Bill Monroe–influenced mandolin style gave the ensemble a decidedly traditional feel, as did the early addition of ace fiddler Stuart Duncan.

On July 21, 1988, NBB's tour bus was involved in an auto accident outside Roanoke, Virginia, that seriously injured Hembree. Compton and Hembree subsequently left the band and were replaced by Roland White and Gene Libbea, respectively. In 2000, Compton rejoined, filling the shoes of the departing White, and Dennis Crouch succeeded Libbea. Andy Todd took over bass duties from Crouch in 2005.

NBB began recording for SUGAR HILL RECORDS in 1998. As of 2011 the act continues to record and tour, even as individual members pursue session work, record producing, songwriting, and other projects. —Gary B. Reid

## The Nashville Network (*see* TNN)

## *Nashville Now*
established 1983; ended 1993

*Nashville Now* holds a major distinction not only for country music but also for cable television. Premiering March 7, 1983, on TNN: THE NASHVILLE NETWORK, *Nashville Now* was the first live, prime-time talk show on cable, launching in the 8 p.m. to 9:30 p.m. (Central Standard Time) slot. RALPH EMERY, a well-known radio and TV personality in Nashville, hosted the weeknight program, which featured celebrity guests from country music and other fields. Like most TV talk shows, *Nashville Now* included an in-house band, led by veteran musician Jerry Whitehurst. *Nashville Now* became TNN's flagship program and helped introduce fans to country's up-and-coming new talent. In particular, LORRIE MORGAN, who appeared frequently during the show's early days, credits *Nashville Now* with helping her land a recording contract. Other stars, such as RANDY TRAVIS and K. T. OSLIN, received their first national exposure through the program. *Nashville Now* first originated from the Stagedoor Lounge in the OPRYLAND Hotel and then moved to the Gaslight Studio at the Opryland complex. The final live telecast from Nashville aired September 24, 1993. *Nashville Now* concluded its TNN run with a week of programs from San Antonio's Fiesta Texas theme park, October 11–15, 1993. —Bob Paxman

## Nashville Number System

Since the early 1960s, the Nashville Number System has been the musical shorthand by which many players and singers communicate in the studio and onstage. For centuries, instrumentalists, composers, and theorists had substituted Roman numerals for chord letters, allowing their values to apply in any key. In the Baroque period, J.S. Bach and others used the "figured bass" method of harmony writing—underscoring the melodic notes with single bass notes and a set of Arabic numerals denoting scale-degree intervals to be played above them. Until the mid-twentieth century, however, no one had devised a system whereby an entire song could be quickly transcribed on a single page and understood with only a rudimentary background in music theory.

As a time-saving measure, JORDANAIRES member Neal Matthews Jr. began using numbers to map out vocal parts for the group's busy schedule of recording sessions and live appearances around 1957. Rather than adopt the shape notes commonly used by gospel quartets in the 1930s and 1940s or even Roman numerals, Matthews used regular numbers as his foundation. A few years later, studio musician CHARLIE McCOY applied Matthews's technique to create rhythm section chord charts, combining his own symbols and markings with formal notation standards. McCoy's sophisticated adaptation was quickly embraced by other Nashville session players, who previously had used no charts

but, rather, had memorized songs before recording. While fully developed today, the system still retains its informal quality; one musician's chart-writing techniques may not mirror those of a studio colleague—a badge of individuality characteristic of the system itself. —John Gouge

## Nashville Songwriters Association International (*see* NSAI)

## Nashville Songwriters Hall of Fame
established 1970

The Nashville Songwriters Hall of Fame honors the contributions and legacies of its members, who are elected by the Nashville Songwriters Hall of Fame Foundation. Election remains one of America's highest songwriting achievements.

Both the hall of fame and the foundation were launched by the nonprofit Nashville Songwriters Association (NSA), chartered in 1968 and later known as Nashville Songwriters Association International (NSAI). In 1970, the association's board voted to create the Nashville Songwriters Association Hall of Fame, now known as the Nashville Songwriters Hall of Fame. A credentials committee chose the initial twenty-one members, who were inducted in October 1970 at the association's first annual banquet and awards ceremony.

NSA added "International" to its name in 1976, and in 1977 NSAI opened a hall of fame in the lower level of its offices at 25 Music Square West to house member artifacts. In 1986 the International Songwriters Foundation was established to administer the hall of fame and a planned library, archives, and museum.

The foundation changed its name to the Nashville Songwriters Foundation in 1992 and in 2006 to the Nashville Songwriters Hall of Fame Foundation. As of 2010 the Nashville Songwriters Hall of Fame included more than 170 members. —John W. Rumble

## The Nashville Sound

The Nashville Sound is a term that denotes a style of country music and an era in which that style was especially influential. The term has also been more generally applied in describing the relaxed, improvisational feel of any recording produced within the informal, good-humored atmosphere that pervades Nashville recording studios. The term has been employed to convey the notion of a special mystique surrounding record making in Nashville and in this sense has been an important tool in marketing Nashville as a uniquely creative music center.

The term first appeared in *Music Reporter* in 1958. In November 1960 *Time* magazine published a profile of country music, focusing on the career of JIM REEVES. The *Time* article used "Nashville Sound" as a subheadline and as a term delineating "the essence of C&W," arguing that the absence of written arrangements in Nashville recording sessions imbued country recordings with spontaneous artistry. Quoting DON LAW, then staff producer and head of country recording for COLUMBIA RECORDS, *Time* indicated that New York and Los Angeles "let their sound become stereotyped. They write down their arrangements and even read and play the notes."

In 1960 Nashville's morning newspaper, the *Tennessean*, used the term, and it appeared in *Broadcasting* magazine the next year.

In 1962 *Music Reporter* described a "Magical Nashville Sound" in a headline. By that year the term had become a staple of news accounts describing country music and the Nashville recording scene.

Through the 1960s the Nashville Sound referred to the special atmosphere that could be found in Nashville studios. In 1970, when journalist Paul Hemphill published his examination of the country music business, he titled the book *The Nashville Sound: Bright Lights and Country Music* and stressed the term's magical connotation: "Even Bob Dylan and Buffy Sainte-Marie occasionally come to town in search of what is vaguely called 'the Nashville Sound.'"

By the mid-1970s scholars and journalists writing about country music began to employ the term in a different fashion, using it to define a specific substyle of country music and also as an identifying label for a phase in the evolution of Nashville recording.

Deliberately aimed at broadening country's adult listenership, Nashville Sound recordings are frequently cited as one of the country music's key responses to the popularity of youth-oriented rock & roll in the mid-1950s, which temporarily cut into mainstream country's sales. The Nashville Sound often featured pop-sounding singers such as Eddy Arnold, Jim Reeves, and Patsy Cline and displayed several distinctive musical characteristics, including string and horn sections and background choruses (most frequently groups such as the Jordanaires and the Anita Kerr Singers). Just as significantly, the Nashville Sound tended to exclude the fiddle and banjo, instruments identified with country music's hillbilly heritage. Taken together, the stylistic elements of the Nashville Sound often produced records that sounded more pop than country, and, in fact, many became dual-market hits.

Nashville Sound recordings present an audible stylistic consistency among tracks cut by various artists produced for different labels. This remarkable continuity derives from both distinctive vocal and instrumental settings and the unique approach to record making that evolved in Nashville in the late 1950s. First, Nashville Sound recordings were typically produced by in-house, full-time producers employed by record labels. It was not uncommon for a single producer, such as Chet Atkins or Owen Bradley, to supervise the work of as many as twenty or more artists or to spend twelve hours or more each day in the studio producing several different acts. The artistic authority of a handful of staff producers imposed similar elements on a wide variety of recordings.

In a similar fashion, a small number of accompanying musicians performed on a large percentage of recordings. Almost all Nashville recording sessions ran on the same schedule: four three-hour sessions per day, with the first beginning at 10 a.m. and the last at 10 p.m. and successive sessions separated by a one-hour break. In-demand session players sped from studio to studio with instruments stuffed in the trunks of inconspicuous cars to discourage theft, munching sandwiches and downing soft drinks on the fly. It was a demanding life, with the first note sounded in the morning and the last echoing away at 1 a.m.

Leading Nashville Sound studio musicians (sometimes referred to as the A-Team) included drummer Buddy Harman; guitarists Ray Edenton, Grady Martin, Hank Garland, and Harold Bradley; bassists Bob Moore and Henry Strzelecki; pianists Floyd Cramer and Hargus "Pig" Robbins; and steel guitarists Pete Drake, Lloyd Green, John Hughey, Weldon Myrick, and Hal Rugg. The Jordanaires and the Anita Kerr Singers provided vocal support, while string and horn players were frequently drawn from the Nashville Symphony.

The 1960 *Time* account was accurate: Nashville sidemen did not employ formally written arrangements but developed on-the-spot "head" arrangements in the course of a recording session—often using their own simplified Nashville Number System to jot down chord progressions. This informal approach to arranging executed by a crack team of players who worked together every day, combined with the talented artistic leadership of a handful of producers, provided background instrumentation of remarkable quality and consistency for thousands of country recordings, ranging from a rock & roll stylistic approach to straight country to country-pop.

As a historical era within the history of country music, the Nashville Sound is closely associated with the period from roughly 1957 to 1970. Examples of the style can be found as early as 1957 with Ferlin Husky's "Gone" and Jim Reeves's "Four Walls." The first use of the term "Nashville Sound" in print coincides closely with these early musical efforts. Other representative recordings include Jim Reeves, "He'll Have to Go" (1959; Chet Atkins, producer), Patsy Cline, "Crazy" (1961; Owen Bradley, producer), and Eddy Arnold, "Make the World Go Away" (1965; Atkins, producer). Many Nashville Sound recordings climbed high on both country and pop charts published by the music trade press.

By the mid-1970s the notion of staff producers handling a large stable of artists was falling out of favor. As Willie Nelson, Waylon Jennings, and the other Outlaws pushed country back toward its hard-edged roots, they demanded—and received—freedom to record in studios of their choosing; selecting their own, often independent, producers; and frequently coproducing their recordings. Nevertheless, important elements of the Nashville Sound remain, including its reliance on a relatively small number of top studio players and a cooperative, relaxed approach to recording that continues to set Nashville apart among music centers worldwide. —*Bill Ivey*

## Syd Nathan
b. Cincinnati, Ohio, April 27, 1903; d. March 5, 1968

Perhaps more than any record company executive in country music history, Syd Nathan fit the stereotype of "the record man" that arose with the new independent labels of the 1940s and 1950s. The founder and president of King Records was a cigar-chomping tyrant—loud, abrasive, argumentative, crude, and willing to take huge risks but always looking for an edge. He was also a genius of sorts who built King into one of the largest and most important independent record firms of the postwar era, changing both the music and the music business in the process.

When Nathan started King in 1943, he had behind him a string of failed business ventures impressive mostly for their variety. After dropping out of high school (extremely poor vision convinced him school was futile), he worked in a pawnshop, promoted wrestling matches, ran a shooting gallery, and operated a photo-finishing outfit. The turning point came when he began selling used records and realized there was a demand not being met by the major labels.

By concentrating on "the music of the little people" (by which he meant, basically, blacks and southern whites), Nathan built a substantial empire. At its peak, his business complex included a half-dozen different labels, publishing companies, a pressing plant, mastering and printing facilities, a national distribution network with thirty-two branch offices, and even his own trucking fleet. His operation would serve, in varying degrees, as a blueprint for scores of subsequent independent labels.

Nathan's other main contributions were recognizing that the lines between white and black musical styles were arbitrary and artificial and encouraging his writers, artists, musicians, and staff to blur those lines whenever possible. In this respect, he anticipated (and helped to create) rock & roll and all that would follow. For his contributions to the careers of BLUEGRASS acts, including RENO & SMILEY and THE STANLEY BROTHERS, Nathan was elected to the IBMA Hall of Fame in 2006. —*Jon Hartley Fox*

## National Barn Dance
established in Chicago, Illinois, April 19, 1924; ended April 30, 1960

The *National Barn Dance* was one of the most popular and influential radio barn dances and was the first such program to have an extended life on the air. It began on Saturday night, April 19, 1924, broadcast over Chicago's WLS, a station then owned by Sears, Roebuck and Company.

The show was the brainchild of WLS executive Edgar L. Bill, and one of its early announcers was GEORGE D. HAY, who would later become famous for organizing and announcing the GRAND OLE OPRY. The first *Barn Dance* program featured OLD-TIME fiddler Tommy Dandurand, who, with square dance caller Tom Owen, recreated the sounds of the old-fashioned country barn dance. Because of listeners' voluminous and enthusiastic response to the initial broadcast, the *Barn Dance* became a regular Saturday-night feature, aimed deliberately at both rural and urban listeners. Early on, the program's diverse roster balanced sentimental pop singers such as tenor Henry Burr and contralto Grace Wilson with more rustic acts, such as folk balladeer BRADLEY KINCAID and, by the mid-1930s, the husband-wife team LULU BELLE & SCOTTY.

By October 1, 1928, when Sears sold WLS to *The Prairie Farmer*, a midwestern farm periodical, the *Barn Dance*'s Saturday-night broadcast time had expanded to almost five and a half hours (7:35 p.m. to 1 a.m.). The following year, the program moved to *The Prairie Farmer*'s new office building on Chicago's Washington Boulevard. As Burridge D. Butler, publisher of *The Prairie Farmer*, extended his noted paternalistic management style to the operation of WLS, the *Barn Dance* became even more folksy, family oriented, and morally wholesome than ever.

In 1931 WLS became a 50,000-watt powerhouse that reached much of the central United States and southern Canada. When the demand for seats by listeners wanting to watch the weekly broadcast outgrew the studio's capacity, the show was moved from Studio A at *The Prairie Farmer*'s office building to Chicago's Eighth Street Theater, its home from March 19, 1932, to August 31, 1957.

The success of the *Barn Dance* as a radio and stage production led to the sponsorship, beginning September 30, 1933, of a program segment on the NBC Blue Network by Miles Laboratories, makers of the then relatively unknown Alka-Seltzer antacid. In 1938–40, the show suffered a setback when many of its top stars left temporarily for WLW–Cincinnati's *Boone County Jamboree* (later renamed the *MIDWESTERN HAYRIDE*). But when Miles Laboratories dropped its sponsorship in 1946 due to high, union-driven production costs, Alka-Seltzer was a household word, as were the names of many performers who at one time or another were cast members, including GENE AUTRY, GEORGE GOBEL, PATSY MONTANA, RED FOLEY, the HOOSIER HOT SHOTS, and comedian Pat Buttram.

Following Alka-Seltzer's withdrawal, the *Barn Dance* was without network exposure until 1949, when it went on the ABC network for a brief run, with the Phillips Petroleum Company as its sponsor. In 1960 *The Prairie Farmer* sold WLS to American Broadcasting–Paramount Theaters, which changed the station's musical format to rock & roll, thereby sounding the death knell of the homespun program.

On March 11, 1961, a similar radio program featuring many former *National Barn Dance* artists was launched on Chicago's WGN as the *New WGN Barn Dance*. This show, which began broadcasting on WGN-TV in 1963, went off the air in 1969. —*Wayne Daniel*

## Ken Nelson
b. Caledonia, Minnesota, January 19, 1911; d. January 6, 2008

As the A&R man who helmed the country division of CAPITOL RECORDS for many years, Kenneth F. Nelson played a major part in country music's post–World War II expansion. Noted as an artist-friendly producer, he brought a host of notable talents—including BUCK OWENS and MERLE HAGGARD—to the fore, showcasing them on record with a singularly crisp production style that helped define the BAKERSFIELD sound and West Coast country in general.

Nelson began his musical career in Chicago in a variety of capacities. He eventually applied for a job at Chicago radio station WJJD, where he wound up as music director and, due to an avid interest in classical music, became the top announcer for broadcasts by the Chicago Symphony Orchestra. He involved himself with country music after the station put him in charge of its *Suppertime Frolic* hillbilly show, which required that he audition performers as well as schedule them for the program. Scouting talent all over the Midwest and the Southeast, Nelson cemented his connection to country music.

*Ken Nelson*

Called to Hollywood by Capitol Records, Nelson first headed the label's transcription department. In 1951 he took over LEE GILLETTE's position as chief country A&R man when Gillette—an old friend of Nelson's from Chicago days—moved to pop A&R. In December of that year Nelson held a session with HANK THOMPSON that included the #1 smash "The Wild Side of Life," a success that set the pattern for Nelson's hit-making career at Capitol. Often working closely with CLIFFIE STONE, Nelson brought to Capitol and recorded FERLIN HUSKY, JEAN SHEPARD, TOMMY COLLINS, WANDA JACKSON, WYNN STEWART, and JERRY REED. Nelson, Gillette, and Stone also founded CENTRAL SONGS, a publishing company that quickly grew to dominate the West Coast country songwriting industry. (The partners sold the firm to Capitol in 1969.)

In the mid-1950s Nelson was among the powerful country music figures who embraced rock & roll early on, signing Gene Vincent after meeting the singer at Nashville's 1957 DJ CONVENTION. By then dividing his time between Nashville and Hollywood, Nelson continued to bring name talent to Capitol's roster and earned a reputation as one of the best producers in the business. Comfortable taking a laissez-faire approach in the studio, he was ideally suited to work with artists such as Owens and Haggard—those with strong, distinct artistic visions of their own. Nelson continued to produce Haggard well into the 1970s, even after Nelson had stepped aside as head of Capitol's country division. Also active in the Country Music Association (CMA), he remained involved in recording until his retirement in 1976.

Nelson was elected to THE COUNTRY MUSIC HALL OF FAME in 2001. He published his autobiography, *My First 90 Years Plus 3*, in 2007. —*Jonny Whiteside*

## Rick Nelson
b. Teaneck, New Jersey, May 8, 1940; d. December 31, 1985

Best known as a rock & roll teen idol, Rick Nelson also enjoyed brief periods of country music success.

Eric Hilliard Nelson was born into a show business family. Dad Ozzie led a big band and mom Harriet Hilliard was the band's female singer. Rick gained national attention on his parents' weekly network radio show, *The Adventures of Ozzie and Harriet*, and later on the program's incarnation on ABC-TV.

As a teenager, Rick admired ELVIS PRESLEY, CARL PERKINS, and JOHNNY CASH. When Rick wanted to record, Ozzie showed Los Angeles labels a film clip of Rick singing and landed his son a singles deal with Verve Records. Guitarist MERLE TRAVIS assisted on a March 1957 session that yielded "I'm Walkin'" b/w "A Teenager's Romance." Boosted by an *Ozzie and Harriet* TV episode titled "Ricky the Drummer," the disc quickly sold 500,000 copies, pushed the two songs to #17 and #2, respectively, on *Billboard*'s pop chart, and led to a hefty contract with IMPERIAL RECORDS.

Many consider Nelson's Imperial sides some of the best rock & roll ever recorded, thanks in no small part to Nelson's lead guitarist, JAMES BURTON. While signed with Imperial, from 1957 to 1962, Nelson placed thirty songs on *Billboard*'s pop chart, including two #1s, "Poor Little Fool" (1958) and "Travelin' Man" (1961). "Poor Little Fool," "Stood Up," "Believe What You Say," and a cover of HANK WILLIAMS's "My Bucket's Got a Hole In It" also made *Billboard*'s country Top Ten in 1958.

Nelson signed with DECCA in 1963, but his hits soon dried up, and the British Invasion of the mid-1960s deepened his

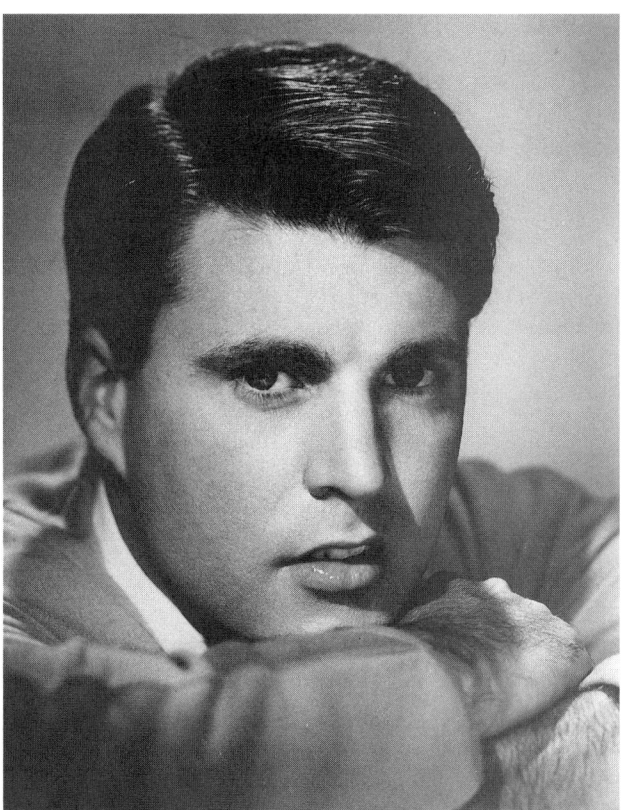

*Rick Nelson*

professional slump. His recordings of "Bright Lights and Country Music" (1966) and "Country Fever" (1967) went largely unnoticed.

Two years later, inspired by BOB DYLAN's *Nashville Skyline* album, Nelson formed his Stone Canyon Band, which included BUCK OWENS pedal steel veteran TOM BRUMLEY and Randy Meisner, a future member of THE EAGLES. Nelson launched his new COUNTRY-ROCK approach with a critically acclaimed live recording, *In Concert at the Troubadour*. He returned to the pop charts with a cover of Dylan's "She Belongs to Me" (1969–70). His self-penned "Garden Party," voicing his frustration with his identity as a onetime teen idol/oldies artist, went #6 pop and #44 country in 1972, and for the next few years he enjoyed a limited comeback. In the 1980s, however, Nelson switched from the country-rock sound he helped to forge to a rawer, ROCKABILLY sound, complete with stand-up bass. "Garden Party" notwithstanding, his live shows consisted primarily of his 1950s and early 1960s hits.

Nelson's career ended tragically on New Year's Eve 1985. He and band mates were en route to a show date in Dallas when their rickety DC-3 airplane experienced heater problems and went down in flames just outside DeKalb, Texas. Nelson, his fiancée, Helen Blair, and his entire band perished. Although it was rumored that Nelson was free-basing cocaine and contributed to the in-flight explosion, FAA findings cleared his name. Nelson was inducted into the Rock and Roll Hall of Fame in 1986. —*Chris Skinker*

## Tracy Nelson
b. Madison, Wisconsin, December 27, 1944

Tracy Nelson recorded blues, R&B, and rock in Chicago and San Francisco before adding country music to the mix when she and her band, Mother Earth, cut the album *Make a Joyful Noise* in Nashville. After renting a house while recording, Nelson stayed in Nashville and delved more deeply into country music on 1969's *Mother Earth Presents Tracy Nelson Country*. The solo album featured ELVIS PRESLEY sidemen D. J. Fontana and Scotty Moore—who was also coproducer, with PETE DRAKE—and Nashville session players. Nelson belted out originals and country hits ("I Fall to Pieces," "Stand by Your Man") in her power-packed voice, a bluesy instrument markedly different from predecessors PATSY CLINE and TAMMY WYNETTE.

In 1974 Nelson's duet with WILLIE NELSON on "After the Fire Is Gone" earned a Grammy nomination, and she periodically returned to country music in the following years. In 1993 Nelson ended a thirteen-year break from recording by signing with ROUNDER RECORDS. A 1998 album, *Sing It*, with veteran artists Marcia Ball and Irma Thomas, landed Nelson a second Grammy nomination. Her 2007 album, *You'll Never Be a Stranger at My Door*, was billed as a return to country music and included covers of country classics "I Still Miss Someone" and "Four Walls."
—*Michael McCall*

## Willie Nelson
b. Abbott, Texas, April 30, 1933

Willie Hugh Nelson is one of country music's most versatile, enduring, and influential talents. His success as a recording artist—between 1962 and 1993 he scored twenty-one #1 hits and charted every year—has been outstripped only by his boundless energy as a performer and songwriter. Since the mid-1950s his

*Willie Nelson*

vast recorded output has embraced country, pop, jazz, WESTERN SWING, gospel, and reggae, and his many collaborators have ranged from WEBB PIERCE, JOHNNY PAYCHECK, and KENNY CHESNEY to Bonnie Raitt, Elvis Costello, Paul Simon, Al Green, and Wynton Marsalis.

Growing up in central Texas, Nelson had many influences: GRAND OLE OPRY stars, local HONKY-TONK bands, BOB WILLS & the Texas Playboys, and even German American polka bands Nelson played in as a youth. After a brief stint in the U.S. Air Force, Nelson married Martha Mathews in 1952. He performed in various Texas bands and worked as a DJ at stations in Texas and Vancouver, Washington, where, in the mid-1950s, he made his earliest self-released recordings.

Back in Texas in the late 1950s, Nelson toiled at various day jobs and played in rowdy, Houston-area honky-tonks. He had begun writing songs as a boy, and by the 1950s he was turning out fully realized masterpieces such as "Night Life" (eventually recorded by dozens of artists, including Ray Price and Frank Sinatra) and "Family Bible."

In 1960 Nelson relocated to Nashville. There he met songwriter HANK COCHRAN, who connected him with HAL SMITH's PAMPER MUSIC publishing house. Nelson soon blossomed as one of MUSIC CITY's most gifted and prolific tunesmiths. "Crazy" (PATSY CLINE), "Funny How Time Slips Away" (BILLY WALKER), and "Hello Walls" (FARON YOUNG) are a few of his best-known 1960s songwriting hits. In 1963 Nelson married his second wife, Shirley Collie (formerly married to broadcaster BIFF COLLIE).

Nelson signed with LIBERTY RECORDS in 1962, and his first two singles—"Touch Me" and "Willingly" (a duet with Shirley Collie)—reached the country Top Ten that year. In November 1964 he joined the Grand Ole Opry. Nevertheless, despite numerous single and album releases on Liberty and then on RCA RECORDS, Nelson failed to reenter the Top Ten until 1975. His wiry baritone and pop vocal phrasing—singing slightly ahead of or behind the beat—sometimes strayed beyond the conventions of 1960s mainstream country and may have limited his radio airplay.

In 1970, with his second marriage ending and his house destroyed by fire, Nelson moved back to Texas. He was already popular there, and AUSTIN's looser, more progressive atmosphere provided a milieu in which his music could evolve and flourish.

An iconoclast and something of a gypsy, the former door-to-door salesman has always been a brilliant, unabashed self-promoter. With earnestness, foresight, and a dash of calculation, Nelson developed a hippie troubadour persona, replete with long braided hair, earrings, and worn-out denim, and began courting the youthful audience that had already boosted southern rock from a grassroots phenomenon to a national craze. Allying himself with longtime friend and fellow musician WAYLON JENNINGS, Nelson laid groundwork for country music's mid-1970s OUTLAW movement.

In 1973 Jerry Wexler signed Nelson to the fledgling country division of ATLANTIC RECORDS. Nelson recorded a pair of vivid and arrestingly sparse concept albums, *Shotgun Willie* and *Phases and Stages*, as well as a gospel album, *The Troublemaker*. Though singles from these LPs saw little chart action, the albums sold respectably, and critical reception was warm.

On July 4, 1973, Nelson held his first annual Willie Nelson Picnic in Dripping Springs, Texas. With its star-studded cast of stylistically diverse artists, the festival united socially conservative country music fans with new, young converts from the counterculture and evolved into a national media event.

One of Nelson's many creative high-water marks was *The Red Headed Stranger*, a 1975 concept album recorded in a small Texas studio on a shoestring budget. Some executives at COLUMBIA RECORDS, Nelson's label at this time, balked at releasing it, considering its raw minimalism typical of a mere demo record. Yet it proved to be his commercial breakthrough, the first of many hit albums Nelson enjoyed during the 1970s and 1980s. Moreover, it yielded his first #1 single, "Blue Eyes Crying in the Rain," a Grammy-winning, ethereal version of a 1945 FRED ROSE song.

Nelson marked another milestone with *Wanted! The Outlaws* (1976). Released by RCA, Nelson's former label, this album cleverly repackaged existing recordings by Nelson and Jennings as well as performances by Tompall Glaser (THE GLASER BROTHERS) and Jennings's wife, singer JESSI COLTER. *The Outlaws* became country music's first LP to be certified platinum (indicating sales of 1 million copies) by the Record Industry Association of American (RIAA) and helped raise the profiles of both Jennings and Nelson; indeed, they were often paired in the public imagination as Waylon & Willie (the title of one of their LPs). Often working together onstage, the two performers notched #1 duets with CMA Single of the Year "Good Hearted Woman" (1975) and the Grammy-winning "Mammas Don't Let Your Babies Grow Up to Be Cowboys" (1978).

Though Nelson has since made many fine recordings, the 1970s and 1980s constituted his commercial zenith. As always, he assimilated and interpreted many popular styles within the steadfast dimensions of his own gritty but fluid baritone and his bedrock musical instincts. For example, his 1977 album *To Lefty From Willie* saluted country star LEFTY FRIZZELL and Nelson's own Texas honky-tonk roots. Reliably unpredictable, Nelson followed with *Stardust* (1978), an inspired collection of pop standards that eventually sold in the millions. Excelling as both songwriter and singer, he took home Grammys for Best Country Song in 1980 ("On the Road Again") and for Best Country Vocal Performance in 1978 ("Georgia on My Mind") and 1982 ("Always on My Mind")—the latter also winning CMA's 1982 single and album trophies. A #1 duet with pop star Julio Iglesias, "To All the Girls I've Loved Before," led to 1984 CMA Vocal Duo honors. Nelson teamed with Waylon Jennings, JOHNNY CASH, and KRIS KRISTOFFERSON for the hit album *Highwayman* (1985), its chart-topping title track, and a well-publicized national tour.

In the late 1970s Nelson began venturing into feature films and proved a competent actor. He played a supporting role with Robert Redford in *The Electric Horseman* (1979) and went on to play the lead in *Honeysuckle Rose* (1980), *The Songwriter* (1984) (with Kristofferson), and *Red-Headed Stranger* (1987). For his role in the western *Barbarosa* (1982), with actor Gary Busey, Nelson earned accolades from the *New York Times*. Nelson has continued to appear in films, TV movies, and various television series.

Nelson's immense creativity and ambition have sometimes wreaked havoc with his personal life. He and his third wife, Connie Koepke, whom he married in 1971, divorced in 1988. Nelson married Ann-Marie D'Angelo in 1991. By the early 1990s he was millions of dollars in debt to the Internal Revenue Service (he has since erased his tax burden), and in 1992 his son Billy took his own life.

But Nelson's passion for music making has yet to diminish. In his sixties and seventies he has kept recording and performing with the energy of a man half his age. Though his chart singles waned after 1990, accolades still came his way. A member of the NASHVILLE SONGWRITERS HALL OF FAME since 1973, he was elected to THE COUNTRY MUSIC HALL OF FAME in 1993, and in 1998 he received the prestigious Kennedy Center Honors for lifetime achievement. His 2002 hit duet with LEE ANN WOMACK, "Mendocino County Line," was CMA's Vocal Event of the Year and won a Grammy for Best Country Vocal Collaboration.

Well into his seventies, Nelson showed no signs of slowing down, whether working solo or with other artists, in the studio or on tour. Dueting with TOBY KEITH, Nelson logged a #1 record with "Beer for My Horses" in 2002–03. In 2006 LOST HIGHWAY RECORDS released Nelson's *You Don't Know Me: The Songs of Cindy Walker*. The label followed in 2007 with *Last of the Breed*, featuring Nelson, RAY PRICE, and MERLE HAGGARD and including the Grammy-winning Nelson–Price duet "Lost Highway." With ASLEEP AT THE WHEEL Nelson released *Willie and the Wheel* in 2009. In the following year came *Country Music,* an album on which Nelson recorded older country, folk, and blues songs, most from the pre-rock era.

Offstage, Nelson remains involved in Texas and national politics, and he continues to devote time to animal welfare, disaster relief, bio-fuel development, and the annual Farm Aid benefit for struggling farmers. The author of several books, he is the subject of Joe Nick Patoski's biography *Willie Nelson: An Epic Life* (Little, Brown, 2008). —*Bob Allen*

## New Grass Revival

Sam Bush b. Bowling Green, Kentucky, April 15, 1952
Courtney Johnson b. Barren County, Kentucky, December 20, 1939;
 d. June 7, 1996
Curtis Burch b. Montgomery, Alabama, January 24, 1945
Harry "Ebo Walker" Shelor b. Louisville, Kentucky, October 19, 1941
John Cowan b. Evansville, Indiana, August 24, 1952
Béla Fleck b. New York, New York, July 10, 1959
Pat Flynn b. Los Angeles, California, May 17, 1952

New Grass Revival grew out of Louisville, Kentucky's THE BLUEGRASS ALLIANCE in 1971, when SAM BUSH (mandolin), Harry "Ebo Walker" Shelor (bass), Courtney Johnson (banjo), and Curtis Burch (guitar) decided to take their music in a different direction. Influenced by rhythm & blues and rock & roll as much as by BLUEGRASS or country music, they blended elements from these sources into "Newgrass," a musical style in which bluegrass instruments, often electrified, were combined with rock & roll's heavy rhythm and unbridled emotionalism.

New Grass Revival's music stretched beyond bluegrass and OLD-TIME traditions but remained connected to these earlier styles. Bush's fiddling retained the flavor that had won fiddling competitions, and Johnson's banjo work still reflected the roots of three-finger-style picking.

In performance, the extended rocklike jams on the band's STARDAY RECORDS 1972 debut album (*Arrival of the New Grass Revival*) supplanted the typical sixteen-bar instrumental break. In 1973, rock-influenced electric bassist John Cowan replaced Ebo Walker and became the band's solo vocalist; his powerful tenor, combined with Bush's intense mandolin and fiddle playing, resulted in highly charged performances.

In 1981 Johnson and Burch left, and were replaced by BÉLA FLECK (banjo) and Pat Flynn (guitar). Fleck's abilities and interests were well suited to the instrumental jam approach; long a student of jazz performance, he added lines and phrasings akin to bebop. Flynn, a studio musician with limited road experience, possessed the skill and direction necessary to complement the other members.

New Grass Revival reached its widest appeal during the 1980s. After many releases on the Flying Fish and SUGAR HILL labels, the band signed with CAPITOL RECORDS in 1986, recording four albums. "Callin' Baton Rouge" in 1989 became the act's only Top Forty single. The group reprised the song with GARTH BROOKS on his 1993 album *The Chase*. But New Grass Revival didn't fit the prevalent "hot young country" mold, and its members parted company—with the label and with each other—in 1990. In the new century New Grass Revival alumni have occasionally appeared together in varying combinations, in performance and on each others' recordings. —*Frank and Marty Godbey*

## The New Lost City Ramblers

Mike Seeger b. New York, New York, August 15, 1933; d. August 7, 2009
John Cohen b. New York, New York, August 2, 1932
Tom Paley b. New York, New York, March 19, 1928
Tracy Schwarz b. New York, New York, November 13, 1938

Founded in 1958 by Mike Seeger, John Cohen, and Tom Paley, the New Lost City Ramblers (NLCR) were the first of the folk revival STRINGBANDS to introduce northern urban audiences to the OLD-TIME MUSIC of the rural South. From their base in Washington, D.C., and with a repertoire drawn from 78-rpm recordings, field recordings made by the Library of Congress and others in the 1920s and 1930s, and their own southern song-hunting trips, the Ramblers helped to ignite an interest in old-time music that spread throughout cities and college campuses, where the folk revival was in full swing. They also helped to bring traditional southern musicians such as DOCK BOGGS, COUSIN EMMY, and ECK ROBERTSON to northern folk festivals.

The band's appeal derived in part from its academic approach to the music, a welcomed departure from the commercialized representations of the Kingston Trio and other popular performers of the folk revival. Recording engineer Seeger, son of musicologist Charles Seeger and half-brother of banjoist Pete Seeger, was steeped in folk music traditions from an early age. Yale-educated Cohen, a documentary filmmaker, was an active member of the New York City folk scene, while Paley, a mathematician, played in Boston folk clubs. Tracy Schwarz, another New York folkie, replaced Paley in 1963 and brought a wider range of old-time, BLUEGRASS, CAJUN, and BALLAD influences to the band.

The NLCR's first sixteen albums on the Folkways label served as sources of inspiration and repertoire for old-time stringbands that followed. Although the Ramblers performed only a few concerts each year, their influence can be heard today at folk concerts and square dances and at fiddlers' conventions throughout the United States. —*Jack Bernhardt*

## New Riders of the Purple Sage

A pioneering country-rock group, the New Riders of the Purple Sage based their name on FOY WILLING's earlier Riders of the Purple Sage. The newer band grew out of late-1960s jam sessions between its founder, songwriter-guitarist John "Marmaduke" Dawson, and the Grateful Dead's Jerry Garcia, then experimenting with PEDAL STEEL GUITAR. The jams soon coalesced into a working group, and the New Riders became the Grateful Dead's popular opening act. By the early 1970s, the New Riders were recording for COLUMBIA RECORDS and had branched out on their own.

The New Riders' classic lineup included Dawson, guitarist Dave Nelson, pedal steel guitarist Buddy Cage, drummer Spencer Dryden (formerly with Jefferson Airplane), and a series of bassists including Skip Battin and Stephen Love. The group's early albums helped engender the COUNTRY-ROCK explosion of the mid-1970s. Hits included "Louisiana Lady," "Henry," "Dead Flowers," and the signature PETER ROWAN–penned anthem "The Adventures of Panama Red," from the band's gold album of the same name. By the time the band signed with MCA RECORDS in 1976, however, it had begun to lose momentum and direction.

By 1982, only Dawson remained from the group's heyday, but key additions included multi-instrumentalist Rusty Gauthier, and the New Riders continued to tour and record, releasing in 1994 a live album made during a 1993 tour of Japan. Though the band called it quits in 1997, a reconstituted lineup including Cage and Nelson has been active since 2005. —*Kevin Coffey*

## New Traditionalism

The term "new traditionalism" was coined in the mid-1980s to describe the phenomenon of young country artists (including RICKY SKAGGS, GEORGE STRAIT, and RANDY TRAVIS) who were deliberately returning to older country styles, such as HONKY-TONK and BLUEGRASS, and adapting them to the modern commercial environment. Yet such a movement was nothing new for country music. During country's commercial infancy, the 1920s, musicians tended to perform familiar traditional material, and some of their songs and styles even had Old World origins. Even so, country performers also welcomed new ideas, frequently adopting more recently created songs from the realms of blues, ragtime, jazz, and Tin Pan Alley. Resistance to change or insistence on stylistic purity was as likely to come from recording directors, radio station executives, or advertisers as from the artists themselves. Occasionally a singer such as BRADLEY KINCAID held his material up as more authentic and more morally edifying than other forms of country music, while BILL MONROE developed his distinctive STRINGBAND sound and high-lonesome singing as examples of country music "as she should be sung and played" (to use his famous phrase). But conscious, organized campaigns to block innovation or to build conservative alternatives to pop styles have been rare. Few in country music dramatically resisted the smooth, pop-leaning sounds of VERNON DALHART, GENE AUTRY, BOB WILLS, RED FOLEY, EDDY ARNOLD, or JIM REEVES. Many tradition-minded artists, in fact, often borrowed elements introduced by these country-pop performers, and entertainers with widely divergent styles typically worked together on show dates, radio, and, eventually, television.

Largely in the wake of ELVIS PRESLEY's great impact, an increasing number of country fans, musicians, and collectors began to grumble about the weakening or disappearance of roots-based country music. The complaints grew stronger with the emergence of country-pop in the 1960s and the country industry's intensifying quest for crossover records. Those who worried about country's identity viewed artists like RAY PRICE, whose honky-tonk hits contrasted sharply with the dominant pop sounds of the late 1950s and 1960s, as saviors of country music purity (although Price seems never to have viewed himself this way and eventually embraced country-pop).

Not until the 1980s do we find a conscious campaign to bolster the forces of tradition. Ricky Skaggs, for example, sought to build a tradition-based but commercial sound centered on the bluegrass idiom he had grown up with while also restoring a tone of moral purity within the country music industry. Although his overall style synthesized bluegrass, honky-tonk, and WESTERN SWING and appealed broadly to fans of OLD-TIME country music, it also incorporated electric instruments, borrowed from contemporary rock music, and clearly reflected his years as frontman for EMMYLOU HARRIS's Hot Band. Other singers were not so self-conscious in their attachments to tradition or as concerned about country's moral image as Skaggs, but they nevertheless became identified with the new traditionalist movement. George Strait (whose debut came in 1981, with "Unwound") drew from western swing, while JOHN ANDERSON drew from both LEFTY FRIZZELL and ROCKABILLY music. Once it became clear that hard-core country sounds still could be commercial, major record labels began recruiting young, attractive singers who could perform creditably in styles that seemed to be tradition-based. Consequently, REBA MCENTIRE (who was only marginally traditional, but attractive and immensely talented) and Randy Travis (who was musically capable, handsome, and traditional) became new stars of the movement in the mid-1980s. Since their commercial success paralleled, and largely prompted, country music's recovery from its post–URBAN COWBOY era sales slump, they encouraged an even greater preoccupation with traditional styles among both musicians and recording executives. Some young artists openly asserted their traditionalism; for instance, DWIGHT YOAKAM and MARTY STUART proudly flaunted their "hillbilly" credentials and stressed their identification with older performers. Other singers who emerged in the 1980s and 1990s also have been identified as neotraditionalists, including KEITH WHITLEY, PATTY LOVELESS, IRIS DEMENT, MARK CHESNUTT, and ALAN JACKSON. Few, however, are unabashed, uncompromising hard-core stylists. Most of them like much of the youth-oriented music of the 1970s and 1980s. Stuart, for example, speaks with reverence about such bluegrass mentors as FLATT & SCRUGGS but also performs with passion music borrowed from rockabilly, southern rock, and soul sources.

In the new century, the remarkable success of the *O BROTHER, WHERE ART THOU?* soundtrack inspired a widespread interest in old songs and acoustic styles. Stringband music has also found new fans among young people, a movement that traces its origins to such musicians as the NEW LOST CITY RAMBLERS and DOC WATSON. In country music, tradition is clearly a relative term, encompassing a broad range of stylistic preferences. —*Bill C. Malone*

## Mickey Newbury

b. Houston, Texas, May 19, 1940; d. September 28, 2002

Like his friend KRIS KRISTOFFERSON, Milton Sims "Mickey" Newbury Jr. was among the first Nashville singer-songwriters who helped broaden the scope of mainstream country writing in the late 1960s. Among his best-known compositions, his semipsychedelic "Just Dropped In (To See What Condition My Condition Was In)" helped launch KENNY ROGERS & the First Edition to stardom in 1968, while "An American Trilogy," his musical montage of "Dixie," "Battle Hymn of the Republic," and "All My Trials," became a staple in the concerts of ELVIS PRESLEY after Newbury himself took it to #26 on the pop charts in 1971–72.

The cultural melting pot of fast-growing Houston provided a varied and rich creative environment for young Newbury, who absorbed the influences of country, R&B, and jazz—all genres he would later tuck into his soulful lyrics and gentle melodies. His father and uncles leaned toward the country sounds of ERNEST TUBB and JIMMIE RODGERS, but in the mid-1950s Newbury discovered R&B vocal groups such as the Flamingos and the Penguins. His first band, in which Newbury sang tenor harmony, performed such songs as "Annie Had a Baby" and "Earth Angel," and his later heartfelt ballads—many sad and dark—emphasized blues more than country.

During his senior year in high school, Newbury began writing songs. He spent the years 1959 to 1963 in the U.S. Air Force and then took his songs to Nashville, where WESLEY ROSE of ACUFF-ROSE PUBLICATIONS signed him to a writer's contract. Besides "Just Dropped In," Newbury composed "Here Comes the Rain, Baby," a crossover chart maker for EDDY ARNOLD in 1968. DOTTIE WEST and DON GIBSON charted as a duo with Newbury's "Sweet Memories"—a song later recorded by WILLIE NELSON—and ROGER MILLER also recorded Newbury material. Moreover, Newbury's writing inspired not only Kristofferson but also younger songwriters, such as Larry Gatlin (see THE GATLIN BROTHERS) and TOWNES VAN ZANDT.

As a performer, Newbury recorded for MERCURY, RCA, ELEKTRA, and other labels, but his only notable chart success was "An American Trilogy," released on Elektra in 1971. Though his delicately crafted records never cracked the country Top Fifty, his significance as a songwriter has remained undiminished. —*Gerry Wood*

## Jimmy C. Newman

b. High Point, Louisiana, August 29, 1927

One of the few CAJUN artists to enjoy major success in mainstream country music, Jimmy Yves Newman grew up on a farm about ten miles from Mamou, Louisiana, in the heart of Cajun country. In his youth he was mostly influenced by country music stars—JIMMIE RODGERS, the CARTER FAMILY, BOB WILLS—and movie cowboys ROY ROGERS and GENE AUTRY. It wasn't until Newman began his professional career in 1946 with Cajun fiddler Chuck Guillory that he began to learn Cajun music and came to admire Cajun artists such as IRY LEJEUNE and HARRY CHOATES. As a member of Guillory's Rhythm Boys, Newman sang mostly hillbilly songs in English, along with a few Cajun songs in French.

In 1951 he made his first solo recordings for the Feature label, including Cajun-country songs such as "Wondering" and "I Made a Big Mistake." In the early 1950s he also became a regular on the *LOUISIANA HAYRIDE* and gained a #4 country hit in 1954 with "Cry, Cry, Darling" on Gallatin, Tennessee's DOT label. Newman joined the GRAND OLE OPRY in 1956. The next year he had his biggest hit to date, "A Fallen Star" (#2 country, #23 pop). During this time WSM announcer T. TOMMY CUTRER gave Newman the middle name "Cajun," and the "C" stuck.

Newman moved to MGM RECORDS and then to DECCA, where he enjoyed hits including "Alligator Man" (1961), "Bayou Talk" (1962), "Artificial Rose" (1965), and "Blue Lonely Winter" (1967–68). He scored his last chart record in 1970. In 1974 he recorded *Jimmy Newman Sings Cajun* for the regional La Louisianne label in Lafayette, Louisiana. One cut from that album, "Lache Pas La Patate," sold more than 200,000 copies in French-speaking Canada. An Opry mainstay, he continues to include strong elements of the Cajun sound—the accordion and fiddle—in his music. Newman was inducted into the Cajun Music Hall of Fame in 2004. —*Charlie Seemann*

# Roy Newman
b. Santa Anna, Texas, November 12, 1899; d. February 23, 1981

Leader of one of the jazziest WESTERN SWING bands, Roy Newman began his career in the 1920s as a staff guitarist and pianist at Dallas radio station WRR. He switched primarily to piano in midcareer, with MILTON BROWN's pioneering pianist Fred "Papa" Calhoun as his model. Newman formed the Wanderers in the early 1930s with multi-instrumentalist-vocalist DICK REINHART and bassist-vocalist Bert Dodson but split with the group in about 1934 to form his own band around the Rhythm Aces, a group including guitarist Jim Boyd (see BILL AND JIM BOYD), jazz fiddler Thurman Neal, fiddler Art Davis, and tenor banjoist Walker Kirkes. Roy Newman & His Boys shared time—and often personnel—with BILL BOYD's Cowboy Ramblers on WRR's *Noon Hour Varieties* and landed a Vocalion recording contract within weeks of forming. Newman based his style on that of Milton Brown, but with even greater jazz emphasis, typically featuring tunes such as "Tiger Rag" and "Weary Blues." Vaudeville clarinetist Holly Horton and bluesy vocalist Earl Brown were important 1935 additions. Newman's 1935 sessions also featured the early electric guitar work of Jim Boyd.

By 1937 Newman's band included fiddler CECIL BROWER and steel guitarist BOB DUNN, both former Milton Brown stalwarts. Although Boyd left in 1938, Newman added guitarist-vocalist Gene Sullivan (later of WILEY & GENE) and replaced Brower with another excellent fiddler, Carroll Hubbard, from W. LEE O'DANIEL's group. Newman made his last recordings in 1939 and gave up his band in 1941, but his unusual repertoire and the impeccable musicianship of his ensembles had already made him one of western swing's most important early bandleaders. —*Kevin Coffey*

# The Newman Brothers
Henry J. "Hank" Newman b. Cochran, Georgia, April 3, 1905; d. July 25, 1978
Marion Alonzo "Slim" Newman b. Cochran, Georgia, June 18, 1910; d. October 1, 1982
Robert "Bob" Newman b. Cochran, Georgia, October 16, 1915; d. October 8, 1979

The Newman Brothers, also known as the Georgia Crackers, were the Midwest's answer to the SONS OF THE PIONEERS. Hank and Slim migrated northward from rural Georgia and broadcast on radio in Ohio and Pennsylvania, cutting a session for Vocalion in 1934 with a sound akin to those of VERNON DALHART and CARSON ROBISON. After Bob joined in 1935, the Newmans worked as a harmony trio. Usually based at WHKC–Columbus, Ohio, they performed in three Charles Starrett films and recorded for RCA VICTOR in the late 1940s. From 1950 through 1952 Bob recorded twenty-five solo sides for KING RECORDS. —*Ivan M. Tribe*

# Newport Folk Festival

In 1959 producers George Wein and Albert Grossman created a folk music festival at Newport, Rhode Island, already renowned as the site of an annual jazz festival. That summer and in the following year, they brought in the big names of the folk revival (the Kingston Trio, Odetta, Oscar Brand, Jean Ritchie, Pete Seeger, and others), but these events were financial failures. The matter would have ended there except for Pete Seeger; his wife, Toshi; his sister, Peggy; and Peggy's husband-to-be, Ewan MacColl, who proposed the establishment of a nonprofit foundation as the festival's basis, with minimum payment to all performers, so well-known performers could underwrite lesser-known traditional artists. With that premise, the Newport Folk Foundation was established and ran the festival through the 1960s.

The 1963 gathering attracted 40,000—a great improvement over the earlier festivals—and in 1965 attendance was twice as large. Then, in 1971, in response to complaints of Newport's denizens who objected to the crowds, noise, and disruptions, the festival was canceled and was not held again until it was revived in 1985. While Newport featured some of the best-known artists of the folk revival, it also served to launch national careers for others, such as Joan Baez, who made her initial Newport appearance in 1959 as an officially unscheduled guest singer invited by folksinger Bob Gibson. More importantly, in its heyday Newport offered a stage on which country, BLUEGRASS, and traditional folk artists were as welcome as the stars of the folk revival. Newport provided the first exposure of many northern college students to bluegrass music, starting with the appearance of EARL SCRUGGS (backed by HYLO BROWN & the Timberliners) and THE STANLEY BROTHERS, both at the first 1959 event, followed by other eminent bands in later years, including BILL MONROE, FLATT & SCRUGGS, JIM & JESSE, and the Kentucky Colonels. On the other hand, Newport and similar events alerted bluegrass musicians, whose performances had been confined principally to the southeastern United States, to potential audiences in other regions. Moreover, bluegrass and mainstream country musicians (including ROY ACUFF and JOHNNY CASH), seeing the interest in traditional folk material, modified their own repertoires accordingly, dusting off older numbers or even devoting entire albums to folk themes. —*Norm Cohen*

# Ernie Newton
b. Hartford, Connecticut, November 7, 1909; d. October 17, 1976

Ernest Newton was one the most frequently used stand-up acoustic bass players in Nashville recording sessions from 1946 through the late 1950s. Orphaned at five, Newton ran away at fifteen and performed in BLACKFACE MINSTREL shows. He performed at WLS in Chicago with Bob Gardner (see MAC & BOB) in 1933, recorded with the Hilltoppers (1935), and then joined LES PAUL's Trio. RED FOLEY engaged Newton for the GRAND OLE OPRY when Foley moved to Nashville in 1946 to host the NBC *Prince Albert Show* portion of the Opry. Newton was the first bassist in Nashville to use a drumhead mounted on his bass for rhythmic effect. (Between plucking the strings, Newton would hit the drumhead with a brush held in his right hand.) Newton's touch enhanced classics such as Foley's "Chattanoogie Shoe Shine Boy," HANK SNOW's "I'm Moving On," and JOHNNIE & JACK's "Poison Love." On this last, Newton used maracas to create a Latin beat that the duo used effectively on other recordings. During the 1960s Newton left music to become a golf pro. —*Walt Trott*

# Juice Newton
b. Lakehurst Naval Base, New Jersey, February 18, 1952

During the early 1980s, when many country acts consciously tailored their recordings for potential pop radio airplay, Judy Kay "Juice" Newton bridged the two formats naturally with her

COUNTRY-ROCK sound. Newton hits such as "Angel of the Morning," "Queen of Hearts," and "Break It to Me Gently" were among the era's major successes.

Nicknamed "Juice" as a child in Virginia Beach, she eventually adopted it as her legal name. Her brother's R&B records and a $120 España guitar her mother gave her pointed her toward a musical career. After high school, she enrolled in California's Foothill College; there she met Otha Young, a guitar-playing songwriter who became her musical partner until his death in August 2009. Their first group, Dixie Peach, eventually became Juice Newton & Silver Spur, recording for RCA in 1975.

Later signed to CAPITOL as a solo artist, Newton languished until 1981, when her remake of the 1968 Merrilee Rush hit "Angel of the Morning" became a Top Five pop single and also cracked the country charts. She quickly followed with the cross-format smashes "Queen of Hearts," "The Sweetest Thing (I've Ever Known)" (written by Young), "Love's Been a Little Bit Hard on Me," and the Grammy-winning "Break It to Me Gently."

Though her pop success proved short-lived, Newton, back on RCA, extended her run on the country charts with such mid-1980s #1 singles as "You Make Me Want to Make You Mine," "Hurt," and "Both to Each Other (Friends and Lovers)," a duet with EDDIE RABBITT.

Following her final RCA album, *Ain't Gonna Cry* (1989), she turned to performing pop material in concert and did not record a full album of new songs until *American Girl* (Renaissance, 1999). Since then she has continued to tour, occasionally recording new material. —*Tom Roland*

## Olivia Newton-John
b. Cambridge, England, September 26, 1948

Though far better known as a million-selling pop singer and a star of films including *Grease* (1978) and *Xanadu* (1980), Olivia Newton-John was a successful and controversial country star of the mid-1970s.

As a child she moved with her family to Australia, where her father became master of Ormond College in Melbourne. At age sixteen she won a trip to England in a talent contest. With Australian singer Pat Carroll she appeared as Pat & Olivia on BBC-TV and in cabarets for two years.

In 1971 Newton-John released her first single—BOB DYLAN's "If Not for You"—which became an international hit on the Uni label. She toured Europe with the Cliff Richard Show and was voted Best British Girl Singer in 1971 and 1972 by the readers of *Record Mirror*.

Newton-John first hit the U.S. country charts in 1973 with the Grammy-winning Top Ten single "Let Me Be There" (MCA). During 1974–75 she followed with the crossover hits "If You Love Me (Let Me Know)," "I Honestly Love You," and "Have You Never Been Mellow." Nevertheless, her selection as (CMA's 1974 Female Vocalist of the Year angered many in Nashville and incited a public debate about the merits of the era's country-pop trends.

Her country-chart presence waned after 1976, but she easily transitioned to soft-rock success as movie stardom helped her score ten Top Ten pop hits between 1978 and 1984. After overcoming breast cancer in 1993, she returned to recording and has since released several albums on various labels, with proceeds typically supporting charities in which she is actively involved. —*Gerry Wood*

## Joe Nichols
b. Rogers, Arkansas, November 26, 1976

Joe Edward Nichols began climbing the country charts in 2002 with his smooth, baritone voice and hard-country aesthetic. His breakthrough came after collaborating with producer and session guitarist BRENT ROWAN on Nichols's UNIVERSAL RECORDS SOUTH debut, *Man with a Memory*. "The Impossible," the album's first single, became a #3 *Billboard* hit, succeeded by the chart-topping "Brokenheartsville." The following year, Nichols took home CMA's Horizon Award.

Despite this newcomer accolade, Nichols had been writing songs since age fourteen and recording since the mid-1990s. He released his self-titled debut on Intersound at age nineteen. His HONKY-TONK style sprang partly from his truck-driving father, who also played bass and sang in local clubs. Other influences included MERLE HAGGARD, RANDY TRAVIS, and HANK WILLIAMS JR.

In 2004–2005 Nichols notched two Top Ten hits—"If Nobody Believed in You" and "What's a Guy Gotta Do," from 2004's *Revelation*. His third album, *III* (2005), included the crowd-pleasing "Tequila Makes Her Clothes Fall Off," another #1. Other Top Ten singles by Nichols include "Size Matters (Someday)" (2006) and "I'll Wait for You" (2007). After *Real Things* (2007) he released *Old Things New* (2009), featuring the #1 hit "Gimmie That Girl." A greatest hits package followed in 2011. —*Jeremy Rush*

## Roy Nichols
b. Chandler, Arizona, October 21, 1932; d. July 3, 2001

One of country music's most admired and distinctive guitar stylists, Roy Nichols and his angular, elegant melodic explorations helped redefine "takeoff," or lead, country guitar from the late 1940s forward. For many years a member of MERLE HAGGARD's backup band, the Strangers—both live and on record—Nichols and his crackling, moody Fender Telecaster also helped create the famous BAKERSFIELD sound.

Arriving in Fresno, California, in 1934, Nichols was accompanying his fiddle-playing father at local dances by age eleven. At fourteen he worked with acts such as Curley Roberts & the Rangers and Elwin Cross, and at one point he led his own band. In 1948 Nichols's already impressive abilities earned him a prestigious job as guitarist for MADDOX BROTHERS & ROSE, then California's top hillbilly band. (Fred Maddox was named the sixteen-year-old Nichols's guardian.) For the next two years Nichols recorded and toured extensively with the Maddoxes. Fired by their mother, Lula Maddox, during an engagement in Las Vegas, he returned to California and broadcast with Smiley Maxedon on KNGS–Hanford.

In 1953 Nichols toured with LEFTY FRIZZELL and played on some of Frizzell's classic JIMMIE RODGERS tribute recordings. Two years later Nichols moved to Bakersfield, where he joined Cousin Herb Henson's daily show on KERO–TV. Nichols soon found himself working with WYNN STEWART, and in 1960 he moved to Las Vegas to back Stewart at the singer's Nashville Nevada club. Nichols then joined Haggard's Strangers in 1965, thus beginning an artistic alliance that deeply influenced the overall tone of contemporary country.

Road-weary, Nichols finally left the Strangers in March 1987, though he continued to make sporadic appearances with Fred and Rose Maddox into the early 1990s. Nichols suffered a debilitating stroke in 1996 and died in 2001. —*Jonny Whiteside*

## Nickel Creek

Christopher Scott Thile b. Oceanside, California, February 20, 1981
Sara Ullrika Watkins b. Vista, California, June 8, 1981
Sean Charles Watkins b. Vista, California, February 18, 1977

Nickel Creek fused BLUEGRASS with elements of pop and rock, thereby introducing younger audiences to progressive acoustic music. The Southern California trio, comprising mandolinist Chris Thile and the Watkins siblings, Sean (guitar) and Sara (fiddle), were preteens when they joined forces in 1989. The young musicians spent their first decade together on the bluegrass festival circuit, maturing musically at a rapid pace.

Nickel Creek's first major release came in 2000 with a self-titled debut album on SUGAR HILL RECORDS. Produced by ALISON KRAUSS, the gold-selling collection featured buoyant instrumentals and harmonious ballads, such as their first single, "When You Come Back Down." In 2001, they were IBMA's Instrumental Group of

*Nickel Creek: (from left) Sara Watkins, Chris Thile, and Sean Watkins*

the Year. *This Side* (2002) added elements of indie rock and won a Grammy for Best Contemporary Folk Album. *Why Should the Fire Die?* (2005) delved even further into the pop/rock world but retained the band's signature mastery of their acoustic instruments.

In 2006 the act announced plans for an indefinite hiatus, and they completed their Farewell (for Now) tour in late 2007. All three members went on to pursue solo efforts as well as projects with other bands, and Thile became one of the most acclaimed mandolin players of his generation. —*Scott Anderson*

## Nitty Gritty Dirt Band

Jeff Hanna b. Detroit, Michigan, July 11, 1947
Jimmie Fadden b. Long Beach, California, March 9, 1948
John McEuen b. Oakland, California, December 19, 1945
Jim Ibbottson b. Philadelphia, Pennsylvania, January 21, 1947
Bob Carpenter b. Philadelphia, Pennsylvania, December 26, 1946

Originating in Southern California as a jug band during the 1960s folk movement, Nitty Gritty Dirt Band (NGDB) quickly evolved into one of America's first successful COUNTRY-ROCK groups. With 1972's historic *Will the Circle Be Unbroken* album, a three-disc set on United Artists, the band introduced veterans ROY ACUFF, VASSAR CLEMENTS, JIMMY MARTIN, Mother Maybelle Carter (see CARTER FAMILY), DOC WATSON, MERLE TRAVIS, and EARL SCRUGGS to youthful, rock-oriented audiences. A 1989 sequel on MCA RECORDS featured guests CHRIS HILLMAN, RICKY SKAGGS, various members of the JOHNNY CASH and Scruggs families, NEW GRASS REVIVAL, and others.

More than forty years after their first gig—May 13, 1966, at the Paradox Club in Orange County, California—NGDB continues, headed by founding members Jeff Hanna (vocals, guitar) and Jimmie Fadden (drums, harmonica, vocals). The original lineup also included Les Thompson, Bruce Kunkel, Ralph Barr, and singer-guitarist Jackson Browne. Browne left before the band's first album (*The Nitty Gritty Dirt Band*, LIBERTY RECORDS, 1967), but the group recorded his compositions, including "Buy for Me the Rain"

*Nitty Gritty Dirt Band: (from left) Jimmie Fadden, Jeff Hanna, Jimmy Ibbotson, John McEuen, and Les Thompson*

(their first pop hit) and "Jamaica Say You Will." The act was also among the first to record songs by Kenny Loggins ("House at Pooh Corner," 1970), Michael Nesmith, RODNEY CROWELL, JOHN HIATT, and DON SCHLITZ.

The group's lineup has changed frequently. Singer-songwriter and guitarist Jim Ibbotson joined in 1969, left in 1975, then returned in 1982 and stayed until retiring in 2004. John McEuen (whose brother William managed the group for many years) is another longstanding member, joining before the recording of the debut album in 1967. He left in 1986, replaced by Bernie Leadon, formerly of THE EAGLES, who stayed until 1988. McEuen rejoined the band in 2001. Pianist Bob Carpenter joined in 1977. Since 2005, the group has consisted of Hanna, Fadden, McEuen, and Carpenter.

Recording for WARNER BROS., Nitty Gritty Dirt Band enjoyed a string of hits on country radio between 1984 and 1990. Their Top Five singles included "Long Hard Road (the Sharecropper's Dream)," "High Horse," "Modern Day Romance," "Fishin' in the Dark," and "I've Been Lookin'." Subsequently the band has recorded for MCA, CAPITOL, Liberty (Capitol), Rising Tide, DREAMWORKS, Dualtone, and for their own label, NGDB.

Jeff Hanna married country singer-songwriter MATRACA BERG on December 5, 1994. In 2002 Capitol issued a thirtieth-anniversary edition of their landmark *Will the Circle Be Unbroken* album and a new collection, *Will the Circle Be Unbroken: Vol. III*, with Jimmy Martin, Earl Scruggs, and Doc Watson from the first album, Johnny Cash from the second album, as well as added guests including VINCE GILL, ALISON KRAUSS, DEL McCOURY, WILLIE NELSON, Tom Petty, and DWIGHT YOAKAM. —*Todd Everett*

## Hoyle Nix
b. Azel, Texas, March 22, 1918; d. August 21, 1985

West Texas fiddler, bandleader, and exponent of the BOB WILLS sound, Hoyle Nix helped keep WESTERN SWING alive on the Texas dancehall circuit for almost forty years. A longtime resident of Big Spring, Texas, Nix and his younger brother Ben (1920–94) formed the West Texas Cowboys in 1946. The band's first recordings were made for the Dallas-based Star Talent label in 1949. "Big Ball's in Cowtown," the first Star Talent release and a Hoyle Nix folk-derived rewrite, proved to be an enduring standard. He also recorded for Queen, Caprock, Bo-Kay, Stampede, Winston, and Oil Patch. Stampede was his own label, named after his Big Spring dance hall. By the early 1960s Nix's two sons, Larry (b. 1940) and Jody (b. 1952), had become regular members of the band. Throughout his career Nix readily acknowledged the influence of Bob Wills. The two first worked together in 1952 and became lifelong friends. Wills showed his respect for Nix by inviting Hoyle and Jody to participate on his own swan song, the 1974 album *For the Last Time*. After Nix's death Jody took over leadership of his father's band, ensuring that another generation of Texans would be dancing to the music of a Nix fiddle. —*Joe W. Specht*

## Eddie Noack
b. Houston, Texas, April 29, 1930; d. February 5, 1978

Singer-songwriter D. Armona "Eddie" Noack is best remembered as the composer of the inspirational classic "These Hands," although his disturbing 1968 recording of LEON PAYNE's "Psycho" on the K-Ark label has long been a cult favorite, covered by, among others, rock singer Elvis Costello.

Noack had already earned a degree in journalism and English from the University of Houston when he embarked on a music career. In 1947 he performed on radio for the first time, in Baytown, Texas. Two years later he recorded his first single, "Gentlemen Prefer Blondes," for the Gold Star label. Noack's big break came in 1956, when RCA released HANK SNOW's recording of "These Hands." This #5 country hit finally brought Noack recognition. Written the previous year, when Noack was in the army, it was originally meant as a statement for the workingman, not a testimony of faith.

Throughout the 1950s, Noack continued to drift from label to label without substantial success, though he did sign with PAPPY DAILY's D RECORDS in 1958 and score a moderate hit with "Have Blues—Will Travel." He also recorded a few ROCKABILLY tunes under the pseudonym Tommy Wood. During the 1960s he relocated to Nashville, where he worked for both LEFTY FRIZZELL's and Daily's publishing companies. Also during this time, GEORGE JONES (then produced by Daily) recorded several of Noack's songs as album cuts: "No Blues Is Good News," "For Better or for Worse (But Not for Long)," and "Barbara Joy."

Noack died of an apparent cerebral hemorrhage in 1978. —*Don Roy*

## Norma Jean
b. near Welliston, Oklahoma, January 30, 1938

Norma Jean Beasler was a popular recording artist and television star of the 1960s. Her cheerful, sisterlike smile and uncompromising, woman-oriented songs (written by others) created an enduring image of likable femininity.

A farmer's daughter, she moved with her family to Oklahoma City. Her aunt taught her to play guitar, and while still in school she had three weekly radio spots on KLPR. Her chief influence was KITTY WELLS. After working with WESTERN SWING bands, in 1958 Norma Jean joined the *OZARK JUBILEE* (ABC-TV), where she had met PORTER WAGONER during an early guest appearance.

In 1960 she moved to Nashville, soon joining Wagoner's syndicated TV show as Pretty Miss Norma Jean. In 1959 she began recording (unsuccessfully) for COLUMBIA; she moved to RCA in 1963. Her first hit, "Let's Go All the Way" (#11, 1964), became her best-known song. Of her twenty-two chart records, her highest was "The Game of Triangles" (#5, 1966), recorded with BOBBY BARE and LIZ ANDERSON. Porter Wagoner functioned as de facto producer on most of her recordings. Though he and Norma Jean occasionally sang live duets, they never recorded as a duo. She was a member of the GRAND OLE OPRY cast from 1965 through 1969.

She left Wagoner's show in 1967 (and was replaced by DOLLY PARTON) to marry Harold "Jody" Taylor, whom she later divorced. She had her last RCA chart record in 1971 and left the label in 1973. After her return to Oklahoma, her musical activity ebbed for two decades. In 2005 she released the album *The Loneliest Star in Texas*. Overcoming alcoholism through devotion to Christianity, with husband Al Martin she founded BRANSON, MISSOURI's interdenominational Cowboy Church, where she performs gospel music. —*Steve Eng*

## Jim Ed Norman
b. Fort Myers, Florida, October 16, 1948

Jim Ed Norman is regarded as a music business visionary with a strong sense of community responsibility. He played a major role in the resurgence of traditional country music in the late 1980s by

*Jim Ed Norman*

nurturing the careers of RANDY TRAVIS, DWIGHT YOAKAM, and TRAVIS TRITT, and later oversaw the work of artists including FAITH HILL and BLAKE SHELTON. As founding president of Leadership Music he contributed greatly to Nashville's business community.

Norman's preacher father played trumpet; his mother played piano. A keyboard player himself, Norman went to North Texas State University to become a music teacher. Fellow student Don Henley asked him to join a band, Shiloh, which moved to Los Angeles and recorded an album before breaking up. Henley subsequently formed THE EAGLES. Though not a member, Norman arranged and conducted strings for the group and played on numerous Eagles classics.

In California, Norman also arranged music for pop acts LINDA RONSTADT, Kim Carnes, Bob Seger, and America. In 1977 Norman produced "Right Time of the Night," a Top Ten pop hit for Jennifer Warnes. He also began a long association with ANNE MURRAY that yielded nine albums, four Grammys, CMA's 1984 Single of the Year ("A Little Good News"), and CMA Album of the Year awards.

In 1980 Norman opened Jensing/Jensong, a publishing and production company in Los Angeles and Nashville, while continuing to rack up production credits with CRYSTAL GAYLE, HANK WILLIAMS JR., JOHNNY LEE, MICKEY GILLEY, and MICHAEL MARTIN MURPHEY.

Norman joined WARNER BROS./REPRISE RECORDS in Nashville in 1983 as vice president of A&R, and in 1984, when company chief JIMMY BOWEN moved to MCA, Norman became Warner's executive vice president. He became president in 1989, although he remained involved in signing and producing talent.

In the late 1980s, due to the success of Travis, Yoakam, Tritt, and other Warner/Reprise artists, Norman possessed the leverage to establish a progressive, noncountry division in Nashville. He did this for artists such as Take 6, Beth Nielsen Chapman (both of whom he produced), and BÉLA FLECK & THE FLECKTONES. In 1989, Norman formed a gospel and contemporary Christian

label, Warner Alliance, and in 1992 he started Warner Western, aimed at audiences of western-themed music. Norman established Warner Resound in 1996 to release Christian and pop recordings.

Norman made important contributions outside the music field. For his efforts he received Time/Warner's Andrew Heiskell Community Service Award in 1990, the Anti-Defamation League's Johnny Cash Americanism Award in 1993, and Leadership Music's Bridge Award in 1996, for improving relations between Nashville's music and business communities. He left Warner/Reprise in 2004. —*Jay Orr*

## NSAI
### established 1968

The Nashville Songwriters Association International (NSAI) is a trade association embracing professional and aspiring songwriters from the United States and other nations, working in many musical genres. It is dedicated to winning recognition for songwriters, advancing their rights to compensation, teaching songwriters about the writing process, and educating them about the music industry.

NSAI traces its origins to November 1967, when songwriter EDDIE MILLER, who had been especially active on the West Coast, encouraged songwriters Buddy Mize and Bill Brock to launch a writers' organization in Nashville. The following month, the Nashville Songwriters Association held its initial organizational meeting, attended by some forty writers, including LIZ ANDERSON and her husband, Casey; BOUDLEAUX AND FELICE BRYANT; KRIS KRISTOFFERSON; and MARIJOHN WILKIN. Within a year, NSA received a charter from the state of Tennessee as a nonprofit institution, and in 1970 the board established the Nashville Songwriters Association Hall of Fame (now the NASHVILLE SONGWRITERS HALL OF FAME). NSA added "International" to its name in April 1976. Today NSAI continues to lobby for intellectual-property protection, sponsors Nashville's annual Tin Pan South songwriters' festival, conducts numerous songwriting workshops in the United States and abroad, and operates the BLUEBIRD CAFÉ, a listening room featuring in-the-round songwriters' performances. —*John W. Rumble*

## Nudie the Rodeo Tailor
### b. Kiev, Ukraine, December 15, 1902; d. May 9, 1984

Nudie Cohn brought flash and sparkle to the western-wear costumes that became synonymous with country music from the 1940s through the 1960s. From GENE AUTRY and HANK WILLIAMS to ELVIS PRESLEY and GRAM PARSONS, the Brooklyn-bred Jewish tailor outfitted popular music's biggest stars with unique and often outrageous custom designs.

The son of a boot maker, he was born Nutya Kotlyrenko. The young Ukrainian emigrated to New York City at age eleven (the name Nudie was an Ellis Island corruption of his real name) and first worked as a shoeshine boy on the streets of Brooklyn. After a stint as a boxer, Nudie moved in 1918 to Hollywood to get into the movies. Working sporadically as a negative cutter and an extra, he eventually hitchhiked back east in 1932, on the way meeting his future wife, Helen Barbara "Bobbie" Kruger (1913–2006), in a Mankato, Minnesota, boardinghouse. The couple eventually returned to New York, where Nudie worked as a tailor's apprentice

*Nudie*

and later made G-strings and pasties for New York City burlesque dancers.

In 1940 the Cohns moved to Los Angeles and set up a small tailoring shop in their garage. Nudie's big break came in 1947, when western singer TEX WILLIAMS fronted the money for a new sewing machine and commissioned ten costumes for his band. Williams spread the word, and soon business boomed, permitting Nudie, in 1950, to open Nudie's Rodeo Tailors at 11000 Victory Boulevard in North Hollywood. Catering to western film stars and musicians, Nudie stumbled on his signature design when he

dreamed up a rhinestone-accented shirt for LEFTY FRIZZELL in late 1951.

Nudie specialized in designing embroidered motifs symbolic of the star's name or repertoire: thus, jail cells for WEBB PIERCE, wagon wheels for PORTER WAGONER, and husky dogs for FERLIN HUSKY. In 1963 the successful business moved into a larger space at 5015 North Lankershim, which became a North Hollywood hangout for movie stars and musicians.

Beginning in the mid-1960s Nudie employed embroidery artisan Rose Clements (b. Rose Grossman, London, August 13, 1919; d. June 13, 2003), who brought special machines with her when she moved from Britain to California. Her intricate and original designs required a great amount of skill and encompassed Swiss, chain, and satin stitches.

Nudie's designs first crossed over to rock & rollers when COLONEL TOM PARKER commissioned a $2,500 gold lamé suit for Elvis Presley in 1957. In 1968 COUNTRY-ROCK pioneer Gram Parsons became a regular client, outfitting himself and his fellow Flying Burrito Brothers. Nudie's top tailor, MANUEL, actually did the work (which for Parsons included embroidered marijuana leaves and naked women); Manuel would later strike out on his own. Nudie suits became de rigueur among California (and British) rockers, and Nudie himself was featured the cover of *Rolling Stone's* issue for June 28, 1969.

Nudie's personality was as flamboyant as his designs. He spun around town in an extravagantly appointed El Dorado Cadillac convertible, complete with hundreds of silver dollars embedded in the dashboard and door panels, hand-tooled leather interior, pistol door handles, and steer horns mounted on the front. Curiously, the gregarious designer almost always wore two different cowboy boots (rarely a matching pair) with his lavishly decorated suits and ten-gallon hat. An amateur mandolin player, he recorded one album, which he released himself and sold in his store. The liner notes featured extensive photos of Nudie arm-in-arm with his celebrity clients; these pictures also covered the walls of his shop.

After suffering deteriorating health in the early 1980s, Nudie died of kidney failure at eighty-one. DALE EVANS delivered the eulogy at his star-studded funeral. Bobbie Cohn continued to run the shop, which also stocked belts, saddles, boots, hats, and ready-to-(western)-wear, until 1994, when she retired and closed it down. In 1997 the Autry National Center of the American West purchased Nudie's remaining business records and personal effects; the COUNTRY MUSIC HALL OF FAME AND MUSEUM has Nudie's personal sewing machine. Today Nudie suits are valuable collector's items, some worth tens of thousands of dollars. MARTY STUART is foremost among several individuals who have amassed significant collections of Nudie's extraordinary clothing.
—*Holly George-Warren*

# The Center of Music City

Nashville's Music Row

## JOHN LOMAX III

A unique section of Nashville, Music Row is arguably the world's most concentrated and creative music center. This less-than-two-square-mile area houses the music industry's major components: offices of most of the world's largest recording companies and music-publishing houses, regional or national headquarters of the nation's three performance rights organizations (ASCAP, BMI, SESAC), and most of the other trappings—recording studios, booking agencies, artist managers, video production companies, and PR firms—that make Nashville a world music capital along with New York, Los Angeles, and London.

Music Row studios have yielded GARTH BROOKS's multiplatinum albums; a stream of hits by REBA MCENTIRE and by VINCE GILL; BRENDA LEE's worldwide favorites; all of PATSY CLINE's recordings; most of THE EVERLY BROTHERS' classics; SHANIA TWAIN's multiplatinum *The Woman in Me* and TAYLOR SWIFT's *Fearless*, memorable sides by GEORGE JONES and by JOHNNY CASH; four BOB DYLAN albums; most of ROY ORBISON's enduring standards; and many of ELVIS PRESLEY's biggest-selling records. Strangely, the neighborhood has never been a popular location for live music. Rather, the OPRYLAND area; the Broadway, Second Avenue, and Fourth Avenue corridors—all downtown; and the West End Avenue/Elliston Place section have typically supported many of Nashville's performance venues. All the other elements of the industry, though, and even specialized branches of major Nashville banks can be found in Music Row.

Less than two miles from downtown, Music Row consists of Sixteenth, Seventeenth, Eighteenth, and Nineteenth Avenues South and cross streets McGavock, Roy Acuff Place, Chet Atkins Place, Grand (Music Square South between Sixteenth and Seventeenth Avenues South), Horton, Edgehill, Hawkins, South Street, and portions of Division and Demonbreun. It is bounded on the south by Wedgewood, on the north by McGavock, on the east by Music Square East (known as Sixteenth after passing Grand), and on the west by Twentieth Avenue South. Just over a mile long and less than a half mile wide, the district could fit inside a portion of New York's Central Park.

Though surrounded by more than a half million Nashville residents, Music Row retains much of the charm of a small town or a college campus. And despite its low-rise glass-and-steel office structures, most built during the 1970s and 1980s, the area still has a neighborhood flavor, thanks to its tree-lined streets and the many older two-story houses that remain, most restored and refurbished into small, homey offices.

No one is sure when the name "Music Row" was coined or who coined it. The area was developed before 1900 as a neighborhood of majestic homes for the wealthy. Ninety-odd years ago some of Nashville's most prominent citizens lived there: doctors, college presidents, architects, leading merchants. The northern end of the district then featured opulent two- and three-story Victorian mansions set back from the street, each enclosed inside wrought iron fences. Brick sidewalks were laid in a herringbone pattern, and magnolia trees dotted the yards. Smaller cottages lined the southern end of Belmont Boulevard, as Sixteenth Avenue South was then known, before all area streets were numbered, during the years 1901–08.

Ward-Belmont College, a "finishing school" for young women, presided over the district from its hillside location on Belcourt Street (now Wedgewood). The classically styled building, modeled after a similar structure in Venice, was built in 1850 by wealthy and socially prominent Adelicia Acklen, dubbed "Music Row's first superstar" by Nashville historian Libby Fryer.

Fryer, born in 1922, lived on the northwestern corner of the Division-Demonbreun-Music Square East intersection, in a house that later served variously as a funeral parlor and a museum for cars of dead celebrities and now the location of Dan McGuinness Pub. In 1928, when Fryer's family moved to the suburb of Green Hills, many believed that the neighborhood was deteriorating—the once-palatial home next door had become a boardinghouse. Soot from the soft coal everyone burned, smoke from the train station six blocks distant, and effluvia from passing streetcars were constant nuisances.

Indeed, the first half of the twentieth century represented one long, slow decline for the area that would become Music Row. Various economic reversals, capped by the Great Depression, decimated the fortunes of many residents, and the rush to suburbia following World War II further tarnished the neighborhood's luster. By 1955 Music Row was a blue-collar backwater, filled with decaying homes, rooming houses, duplexes, and a few small retail businesses.

In the postwar years, however, music came to the rescue. Though records were made in WSM radio studios as early as December 1944, parking and other problems hampered downtown locations as sites for music enterprises. Music Row was born when OWEN BRADLEY and brother HAROLD BRADLEY opened a studio at 804 Sixteenth Avenue South, in a house they renovated. The pair had previously operated film or recording facilities at Second Avenue South and Lindsley Avenue and in a low-ceilinged room behind a jewelry store on Twenty-first Avenue South, but the Sixteenth Avenue South enterprise proved to be the one that flourished.

Since the late 1940s Owen Bradley had organized recording sessions for PAUL COHEN, country recording chief for DECCA RECORDS, but Cohen eventually told the Bradleys he was going to take his business to JIM BECK's Dallas studio. As Harold remembered, "Owen asked him, 'What if we built a studio here?'" Cohen liked the idea, offered to be a silent partner (though he never contributed the funds he promised), and committed to schedule a hundred Decca sessions per year to help establish the enterprise.

As it happened, land on Sixteenth Avenue South had been rezoned for commercial use, and it was cheaper than downtown property. The Bradleys bought the house for $7,500 late in 1954 and soon removed the first floor to create a high-ceilinged studio. They built a room behind the control room and plastered it in; this eventually became an echo chamber. The facility opened in 1955, and by late 1956 it was producing such landmark crossover hits as FERLIN HUSKY's "Gone." The brothers spent another $7,500 to install a surplus army Quonset hut in back, initially for use as a film studio and later for making records. Appropriately, it became known as the "Quonset Hut." After they replaced the original tile floor with wood, installed burlap insulation and mood lighting, and developed isolation booths for better sound separation, the improved sound gave the Hut a reputation for near-magical properties, and it far outstripped the original studio in popularity and hits.

When the Bradleys launched their Sixteenth Avenue operation, the only vernacular music on Music Row took place at at tent revivals held on the empty lot at Sixteenth and Division (today the site of Owen Bradley Park). There were a couple of gas stations farther down Division, while Piggly Wiggly, Tillman's, and H. G. Hill's groceries, Seligman's five- and ten-cent store, Goodman's Bakery, and Foxall's Pharmacy were clustered around the intersection of Sixteenth and Grand. It was still a blue-collar neighborhood. Streetcars were gone (the steel rails ripped up for the war effort), traffic was light, and city buses ran through the area. The Belmont Apartments stood next to Bradley Studios, and the district's main church was just down Sixteenth at Grand Avenue. The district was also racially diverse, with black families living primarily on South Street, Hawkins, and Grand, while Villa Place, parallel to Sixteenth Avenue and a block east, was racially mixed, as it is today. "It was a vibrant neighborhood," remembered long-time resident Ludwig Reinheimer, whose family lived at 804 Sixteenth Avenue South before the Bradley purchase. "It was safe, the streets were lit, we used to walk everywhere after dinner. Kids were on the streets until eight or nine o'clock. Black and white kids played together."

The Bradley Studios opened at a propitious time. In the prosperous postwar decade, record labels increasingly found it cheaper and more convenient to record country artists in Nashville rather than in Chicago, New York, or Hollywood, the traditional centers of the entertainment industry. Decca's Paul Cohen had led the way in using WSM's studios and the CASTLE RECORDING STUDIO in the Tulane Hotel, and the label's success with artists including ERNEST TUBB, RED FOLEY, KITTY WELLS, and WEBB PIERCE, some of whom were selling to a general audience, soon convinced Decca's competitors to follow suit. Thus, when the Bradleys opened their doors, Cohen's counterparts, DON LAW (COLUMBIA) and KEN NELSON (CAPITOL), also began scheduling sessions there, respectively gaining crossover hits such as MARTY ROBBINS's "Singing the Blues" and SONNY JAMES's "Young Love."

In 1957 RCA became the first major label to open a studio on Music Row, with CHET ATKINS heading the operation. That November, RCA established its Nashville headquarters, and a new studio, in a building leased long-term from its builder, local businessman and landowner Dan Maddox. The facility stood a block west of and around the corner from the Bradley Studios, at Seventeenth Avenue South and Hawkins (now Roy Acuff Place). RCA had used other Nashville studios for several years, but now it made sense to locate in an area where the industry had already established a beachhead.

In those days, doing business on the Row was loose and informal. Often, Owen Bradley explained, he would decide to do a session in the morning: "We could usually find the pickers in time to go in and cut that afternoon"—a practice unheard of today, when top players are sometimes booked months in advance.

Music Row's emergence as an international center took time. In 1960 "Record Row," as it was then called, consisted principally of the Bradley Film & Recording Studios and RCA's offices. WSM and the GRAND OLE OPRY were still located downtown, as were TREE MUSIC PUBLISHING, CEDARWOOD, and MOSS ROSE—the respective music-publishing companies of JACK STAPP, JIM DENNY, and HUBERT LONG—and Denny and Long's talent agencies. ACUFF-ROSE PUBLICATIONS, along with its affiliated HICKORY RECORDS and Acuff-Rose Artists Corporation, a booking agency, were headquartered on Franklin Road, several miles southeast of Music Row. DON PIERCE ran STARDAY RECORDS from Madison, Tennessee, a Nashville suburb, and HAL SMITH helmed his booking agency and his publishing house, PAMPER MUSIC, from Goodlettsville, some twenty miles northwest of Nashville.

The major labels' long-term interest in Music Row was strengthened early in 1962 when Columbia Records paid some $300,000 for the Bradleys' Quonset Hut and surrounding property. The deal included a two-year noncompetition clause; but when this time had passed, the Bradleys opened a new studio, Bradley's Barn, in rural Mount Juliet, some twenty miles east of Nashville. By 1963 the trade magazine *Broadcasting* estimated that half of all U.S. recordings were being made in the city.

At this point the industry shifted into high gear. Most other businesses opened just north of Columbia Records. As of 1965 this part of Record Row included several labels (RCA, Columbia, Decca, Capitol, MERCURY, ABC-Paramount), music publishers (Cedarwood, HILL & RANGE, Tree, AL GALLICO, Moss-Rose, New Keys); talent agencies (Wil-Helm, Hubert Long), and performing rights organizations (BMI, SESAC). In 1967 the COUNTRY MUSIC HALL OF FAME AND MUSEUM opened on the former site of Rose Park, at the northern end of Sixteenth Avenue, and was soon attracting tourists in the hundreds of thousands. Industry giant ATLANTIC RECORDS, known heretofore primarily for its hit-making black artists, opened its first Nashville office in 1972.

In 1973 Sixteenth and Seventeenth avenues were converted to one-way thoroughfares, which maximized the use of the narrow streets. But there were still no tall buildings in the area—only four blocks of two- and three-story houses with a couple of two- or three-story office complexes. The largest building on the Row was then the RCA complex, a half-block-long split-level structure on Seventeenth Avenue South, built on parcels owned by Dan Maddox and by Owen and Harold Bradley (with Chet Atkins). There were still few traffic lights, drivers parked on both sides of the streets, and most of the labels leased space, with the principal exception of MCA, which had built a two-story structure on Sixteenth (later to become Music Square East).

Music Row's first two high-rise office buildings appeared in the mid-1970s, both proving to be ill-fated efforts for their visionary creators. The dark, octagonal building known as the United Artists Tower (50 Music Square West) was originally intended by Gordon Stoker and Neal Matthews as headquarters for the JORDANAIRES and was to be called the City Executive Building. However, escalating costs and other problems forced them to sell. United Artists Records became the biggest early tenant and thus the building's namesake when it opened in 1975. For many years it was the home of *Music City News* magazine and other tenants, including recording studios. Across Music Square West, a five-story building long housed the Nashville offices of *Billboard* magazine as well as a major recording studio. This structure was created as the FOUR STAR building. Label owner Joe Johnson envisioned recording, mastering, and pressing facilities so that a song could be written on one floor, recorded on another, and emerge as a finished record from a basement manufacturing plant. Four Star went bankrupt after the building's completion, and the space was converted into general offices. (Later the edifice was known as the FISI Building, for a financial services firm located there, and today cable TV channel GAC makes the building its home.) These experiences gave pause to developers—only one major new building was constructed on the Row between 1975 and 1988.

The fate of Music Row has always been tied to the success of larger corporate entities with Nashville offices. As the fortunes of those companies and the profits generated by Nashville have ebbed and flowed, so has corporate support for their respective "hillbilly" divisions. As long as country remained a consistent—and relatively small—profit center, relationships remained static. Corporate headquarters sent down budgets; Nashville offices sent back more money at year's end and added new masters to the labels' catalogs. But during the early 1990s, country music's gross revenues quadrupled—from $500 million in 1989 to more than $2 billion in 1994—largely due to Nashville's efforts. This caught the attention of those who ran international conglomerates based in Germany (Bertelsmann Music Group, then owners of RCA and ARISTA), England (Thorn-EMI, owners of CAPITOL), the Netherlands (PolyGram, then owners of Mercury), Japan (SONY), and Canada (Seagram, then owners of MCA). These corporate giants started looking for ways to maximize their country-generated income streams.

As a result, bigger buildings sprouted all over the Row, some built by companies heretofore content to rent space in buildings belonging to others. Music Row's next expansion came between 1988 and 1995. In November 1989 Opryland Music Group, by now owner of the prestigious Acuff-Rose catalogs, set up shop in a brand-new brick edifice on Music Square West. In 1990 BMG erected a four-story complex on Music Circle North to house its growing family of labels and its publishing operation. Mercury took over major offices on Music Square West in 1992, and Sony Music, having bought Columbia and EPIC, renovated and enlarged the venerable Columbia building (the site where it all began). CURB RECORDS had maintained a Nashville office for a number of years, but in 1993 it moved its headquarters from California to Music Square East. One year later MCA and WARNER BROS. each opened huge new offices on Music Square East. Meanwhile, publishing giants Warner-Chappell and EMI Music acquired and enlarged existing buildings on Music Square East, and down the street PolyGram Music bought and expanded Welk Music and its office. Sony/ATV/Tree Music also rebuilt in the 1990s after Sony acquired Tree Publishing in 1989.

ASCAP (having moved by 1972 from West End Avenue to Music Row at Music Square West and Division Street) and BMI completed ambitious expansions at their existing locations in 1992 and 1995, respectively. BMI thereafter moved its national administrative functions to town, quickly growing from thirty-three to more than 400 employees housed in a six-story building behind BMI's original office on Music Square East. SESAC moved into sparkling new quarters in a two-story steel-and-glass office farther down Sixteenth Avenue South in 1996. That same year also saw the completion of Reba McEntire's multimillion-dollar Starstruck headquarters, the largest building on the Row devoted to a single artist's enterprises. CMA completed a new building in 1991, at the corner of Music Circle North and Music Circle East; six years later, NARAS moved to the next overflow expansion area, in the 2000 block of Wedgewood Avenue, which runs perpendicular to Sixteenth and Seventeenth Avenues South.

Although Capitol Records left the Row in 1991 for a West End Avenue high-rise, in 1996 the label bought property on Music Square West and built a huge structure planned for its headquarters, ironically on the same spot where the company first had rented space. In early 1998, however, following executive changes, Capitol put the building up for sale without ever moving into it.

The twenty-first century has not been kind to the music business generally or to Nashville label offices. Diminished sales inevitably led to consolidation and staff downsizing. By 1998 five of the six major multinational recording conglomerates owned buildings on Music Row: Warner Bros. (also home to Reprise and Christian label Warner Alliance), Mercury, BMG (parent to RCA, Arista, and BNA), MCA, and Sony (whose labels then included Columbia, Epic, MONUMENT, and Lucky Dog). In 2004 Sony merged its music division with BMG's and sold Sony's building at 34 Music Square East to music magnate MIKE CURB. The Sony-BMG companies settled into the space formerly known as the RCA Label Group "campus" in 2005. In 2008 Sony took over BMG imprints RCA, Arista Nashville, and BNA to become Sony Music Nashville.

By 2010 only two of the four remaining behemoths—Warner Bros. (home to Atlantic, Reprise and Christian label Word) and Sony Music Nashville, housed just off the Row at 18th & Edgehill—had Music Row addresses. Universal (Mercury, MCA Nashville, LOST HIGHWAY) shifted its headquarters to a new downtown building overlooking THE RYMAN AUDITORIUM in 2008. Industry giant EMI's Nashville office remained "off-Row" on West End at Murphy Road, its location since JIMMY BOWEN moved it there in 1991.

In 1997 film industry giants Disney and DREAMWORKS SKG established Nashville recording operations, anticipating synergy between their West Coast film divisions and their Music Row offices.

Both Disney's LYRIC STREET label and DREAMWORKS RECORDS began releasing country product in 1998. Lyric Street opened in a renovated house on Nineteenth Avenue South but moved in 2003 to the Gulch area at 1100 Demonbreun. Disney closed the label in 2010. DreamWorks remained on the Row in a lovely restored two-story office at 1516 Sixteenth Avenue South until Universal purchased the company in 2005.

Former DreamWorks executive SCOTT BORCHETTA wound up heading his own BIG MACHINE RECORDS as well as Show Dog Records, owned by former DreamWorks superstar TOBY KEITH; both labels were initially housed and staffed in a small restored home on Sixteenth Avenue South. Keith soon moved Show Dog to separate, off-Row offices, however, and merged his label with UNIVERSAL RECORDS SOUTH in 2010. Meanwhile, Big Machine launched Taylor Swift—today one of the music industry's biggest-selling and most-awarded artists. The label opened a second imprint, the Valory Music Company, in 2008 and then partnered with New York's REPUBLIC RECORDS to establish Republic Nashville in 2009.

In the organizational sector, the International Bluegrass Music Association (IBMA) moved its headquarters from Kentucky to Music Circle South in 2003, and Nashville Songwriters Association International (NSAI) departed midtown for more spacious quarters in the Music Mill Building (Eighteenth Avenue South and Roy Acuff Place) in 2005. The American Federation of Musicians (AFM) Local 257 and the Nashville office of American Federation of Television & Radio Artists (AFTRA), both longtime Row denizens, continue in their respective Music Circle North and Seventeenth Avenue South locations.

In the new century, the Row's most dramatic growth has occurred where Music Square East and Music Square West converge with Division and Demonbreun. That intersection, now named BUDDY KILLEN Circle, for the late music publisher, features a roundabout and Alan LeQuire's stunning and controversial *Musica*, an enormous, multifigure nude sculpture embodying the spirit of creativity. The work stands across the street from Owen Bradley Park and is overlooked by a ten-story building.

The Demonbreun corridor from the roundabout down the hill to Interstate 40 received a makeover as souvenir shops gave way to trendy bars, boutiques, coffee shops, and a bank. The Row's nearest high-rise condo, rhythm [sic], was completed near the interstate in 2009.

Joy Ford's Country International Records office at 23 Music Circle East and Division became a nationally publicized battleground in 2008 when the city attempted to seize the property through eminent domain. Ford had rebuffed offers from an out-of-state developer who planned a new high-rise office/retail/condo project. Advocates for Lionstone, the developer, characterized the site as a "blighted area"—startling news to successful nearby businesses, including the ASCAP and BMI offices. Washington, D.C.'s Institute for Justice took up Ford's cause, leading to a compromise: Ford traded an area in the back of her parcel for a larger piece of property fronting on Division. The Recession of 2008 undermined the real estate market, and as of 2011 Lionstone had yet to break ground.

Hard times (and earlier storm damage) drove businesses out of the UA Tower, virtually empty as of July 2011. The recession also slowed encroachments on the Row made by Vanderbilt and Belmont universities, which had begun to buy up property. By contrast, new music industry offices, restaurants, and retail shops were built one block off the Row at the intersection of Edgehill and Villa Place, formerly the site of White Way Cleaners.

By the late 1990s many landlords had emerged, but, surprisingly, none had become the dominant propertyholder on the Row. As of 2011 many parties owned pieces of valuable frontage on at least one major artery, including an array of past and present industry figures, such as the Bradley family, the Atkins estate, RAY STEVENS (who began acquiring Row property in 1969), Mike Curb, Dale Morris (manager of KENNY CHESNEY and MARTINA MCBRIDE), Garth Brooks, Dane and DEL BRYANT (sons of famed songwriters BOUDLEAUX and FELICE BRYANT) Pam Lewis (Brooks's original comanager), Warner Bros., BRAD PAISLEY, Reba McEntire, CRYSTAL GAYLE, songwriter CRAIG WISEMAN, and Barbara Orbison, widow of the late singer.

As the twenty-first century advances, Music Row is coping with an extended downturn as the entire music industry faces huge new challenges. But the denizens of what is perhaps the world's most creative neighborhood may well be able to develop new business models that will keep Nashville the hub of country—and Christian—music and to continue its evolution as Music City USA.

# O Brother, Where Art Thou?
initial motion picture release December 22, 2000

Tapping into Homer's *Odyssey*, brothers Joel and Ethan Coen made the theme of their film the age-old hero's journey, a quest filled with dangers as he struggles to get home. They borrowed their title from Preston Sturgis's 1941 satirical film *Sullivan's Travels*, in which a pretentious Hollywood director wants to make a movie (titled *O Brother, Where Art Thou?*) for a downtrodden audience about which he knows nothing. With their own sweet, episodic, Depression-era saga, the Coens riveted a broad and diverse audience with a visually lyrical depiction of the Deep South—a valentine to the rich, original music of the region.

The Coens' *O Brother* (2000) proved to be a phenomenon, spawning a country music–dominated, T Bone Burnett–produced soundtrack on LOST HIGHWAY RECORDS that has sold more than 8 million copies in the United States and more than 1 million more internationally and was still selling 1,500 to 2,000 copies a week as of 2009. The film and album soundtrack sparked an acoustic, roots-music revival that set the stage for hit country albums—including DIXIE CHICKS' *Home* and PATTY LOVELESS's *Mountain Soul*—a 2000 documentary and concert film featuring artists from the soundtrack, and a star-studded follow-up tour series that packed auditoriums in more than fifty cities. The concert film and tours were central to the acceptance of RALPH STANLEY, a prominent contributor to the soundtrack, as a roots music icon.

The powerful latter-day impact of the film's 1930s music is largely attributable to its dramatic placement in lively, down-home contexts—at local radio stations, at political rallies, in railroad boxcars—and in bits of phantasmagoria: in a creek populated by "sireen" temptresses and at a Klan rally featuring choreography worthy of Broadway and Hollywood legend Busby Berkeley. The hit country video "I Am a Man of Constant Sorrow" was credited to the film's fictitious (and lip-synching) "Soggy Bottom Boys" (with actor George Clooney playing the lead singer), reemphasizing *O Brother*'s use of context to reach and build on country's core audience. (Dan Tyminski, of Union Station, actually provided Clooney's lead vocals.)

Still, in the hands of skilled interpreters, the music's power did not depend on the film alone. While many of the movie's off-screen performers were featured in the *Down from the Mountain* film—a trio of EMMYLOU HARRIS, ALISON KRAUSS, and GILLIAN WELCH; gospel's Fairfield Four; the young Peasall Sisters; Ralph Stanley; and, in one of his final appearances, JOHN HARTFORD—the rambunctious Soggy Bottom Boys were not. Here, the presentation stresses a decorum and even a solemnity at odds with the original movie and with country music's less refined aspects.

The *O Brother* soundtrack won 2001's Grammy for Album of the Year, while Ralph Stanley took Grammy honors for Best Male Country Vocal. On- and off-screen performers' concert hall credibility also gave the emerging AMERICANA music market a claim on the soundtrack's success, and many of the artists would become Americana stalwarts. The *O Brother* phenomenon's reach was further revealed when Dan Tyminksi won Male Vocalist of the Year and the soundtrack won Album of the Year at the 2001 IBMA Awards. —*Barry Mazor*

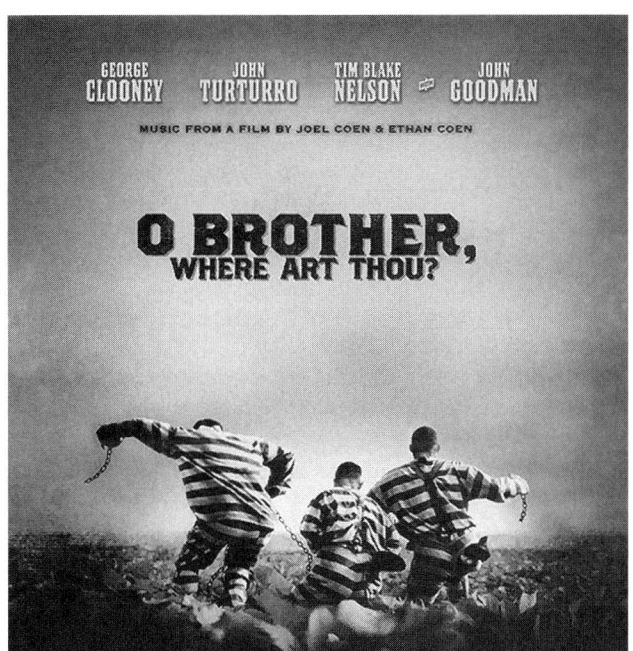

O Brother, Where Art Thou? *soundtrack*

# Oak Ridge Boys
Duane Allen b. Taylortown, Texas, April 29, 1943
Richard Sterban b. Camden, New Jersey, April 24, 1943
Joe Bonsall b. Philadelphia, Pennsylvania, May 18, 1948
William Lee Golden b. Brewton, Alabama, January 12, 1939
Steve Sanders b. Richland, Georgia, September 17, 1952; d. June 10, 1998

By injecting gospel-based, four-part harmonies and exciting live shows into country music, the Oak Ridge Boys helped pave the way for the many vocal groups that followed them. From 1977 to 1987—with a lineup of Duane Allen, lead; William Lee Golden, baritone; Richard Sterban, bass; and Joe Bonsall, tenor—they notched twenty-six Top Ten hits (including fifteen #1s), sold millions of records, won numerous industry awards, filled top-tier performance venues, and crossed into the pop charts with "Elvira" and "Bobbie Sue."

*The Oak Ridge Boys: (from left) William Lee Golden, Joe Bonsall, Richard Sterban, and Duane Allen*

Prior to 1977 the Oaks had been a gospel act for more than thirty years. They began in 1945 as the Oak Ridge Quartet, a gospel ensemble within WALLY FOWLER's country group, the Georgia Clodhoppers. The original quartet consisted of Fowler, lead; Curly Kinsey, bass; Lon "Deacon" Freeman, baritone; and Johnny New, tenor. They joined the GRAND OLE OPRY in September 1945.

In 1962 they changed their name to the Oak Ridge Boys. Golden joined the group in 1965, Allen in 1966, Sterban in 1972, and Bonsall in 1973. By then they had won a dozen of gospel music's Dove Awards as well as a Grammy. They signed with COLUMBIA RECORDS to broaden their audience, but three albums of "message" music produced two singles that didn't make the country charts and left them ostracized from gospel yet still unknown in country.

Fighting the prevailing industry view that there was room for only one gospel-rooted vocal quartet in country music (THE STATLER BROTHERS), the Oaks signed with ABC/Dot (later absorbed by MCA) and hit with their next single, "Y'All Come Back Saloon" in 1977. Although Allen sang most lead parts, all four singers were featured on hits. For example, in 1981 Sterban's thundering bass vocals on DALLAS FRAZIER's "Elvira" helped make the composition a #5 pop single as well as a #1 country hit. Other Oaks #1s of the late 1970s and 1980s included the moving story song "I'll Be True to You," the RODNEY CROWELL–penned "Leaving Louisiana in the Broad Day Light," the patriotic "American Made," and the love song "Make My Life with You."

In 1987 William Lee Golden was replaced by Steve Sanders, a former child star in gospel music and, at the time, the rhythm guitarist in the Oaks' band. Sanders sang lead on two subsequent hits, "Gonna Take a Lot of River" (1988) and "Beyond Those Years" (1989), but the group's chart performance soon tapered off. They left MCA for a brief tenure with RCA (1990–92) but couldn't reignite their record sales there, on CAPITOL (1995), or on Platinum (1999). In January 1996 Golden returned, replacing Sanders, who resigned from the group, and the Oaks continued their tradition of first-rate live performances. In 2000 they signed with Spring Hill Records and subsequently made gospel, patriotic, BLUEGRASS, Christmas, and mainstream country albums,

with the last including *Front Row Seats* (2006) and *The Boys Are Back* (2009). —*Walter Carter*

## Eli Oberstein
b. New York, December 13, 1901; d. June 12, 1960

A protégé of pioneer A&R man RALPH PEER, Eli Oberstein was responsible for recording most of the country acts for RCA VICTOR's budget BLUEBIRD imprint between 1933 and 1939. Indeed, Oberstein helped to pioneer the idea of cut-rate labels, first with Bluebird and later with his own labels, such as Varsity, Royale, and Rondo. While with Bluebird, he often recorded in temporary field studios and frequently made as many as twenty or more masters in a single day. Traveling widely, he oversaw classic recordings by artists such as J. E. MAINER, the MONROE BROTHERS, the BLUE SKY BOYS, MILTON BROWN, and dozens of others. During this time Oberstein also recorded many blues artists as well as jazz and dance bands; historians also give him credit for helping to create the style of big bands such as Tommy Dorsey and Larry Clinton. —*Charles Wolfe*

## Tim O'Brien
b. Wheeling, West Virginia, March 16, 1954

Blending BLUEGRASS, folk, country, rock & roll, soul, blues, and gospel, Timothy Page O'Brien has helped to modernize country music's STRINGBAND tradition for more than thirty years. Growing up in Wheeling, West Virginia, he learned guitar early on and followed artists based at Wheeling's WWVA and contemporary pop stars such as the Beatles. DOC WATSON's music turned O'Brien to bluegrass and traditional country, and the young singer eventually mastered the fiddle, mandolin, and bouzouki as well.

After playing in bands based in Wheeling and Boulder, Colorado, in 1978 O'Brien helped organize the innovative bluegrass group HOT RIZE, which stayed together until 1990, when they received IBMA's Entertainer of the Year honors. Along the way, O'Brien wrote hits such as "Untold Stories" for the band and for KATHY MATTEA, with whom he dueted on the 1990 Top Ten single "Battle Hymn of Love."

This hit landed O'Brien an RCA solo contract, but when RCA left his recordings unreleased he formed a new group, the Oh Boys. Subsequent releases on SUGAR HILL and other labels have included both solo albums and albums recorded with his sister, Mollie, a respected blues and folk singer. Tim was IBMA's Male Vocalist of the Year in 1993 and 2006. His album *Fiddler's Green* won a 2005 Grammy for Best Traditional Folk Album. He also spearheaded the project *Always Lift Him Up: A Tribute to Blind Alfred Reed* (Proper American, 2007), featuring artists associated with West Virginia, where Reed spent most of his life. To honor his father, who died in 2009, Tim released the Howdy Skies album *Chicken & Egg* in July 2010. The following month, he and fellow Hot Rize members reunited for their first tour in more than a decade. O'Brien has appeared frequently on network radio and television, and as a solo artist he continues to record and tour actively in the United States and abroad. *—John W. Rumble*

## Mark O'Connor
b. Seattle, Washington, August 5, 1961

Mark O'Connor rose from child prodigy to respected Nashville session player before pursuing a solo career filled with critically acclaimed albums embracing jazz, swing, country, BLUEGRASS, and classical music.

He began fiddling at age eleven and soon won the twelve-and-under division of the National Old Time Fiddlers' Contest. The young musician learned at the feet of Texas fiddling legend Benny Thomasson, who had moved to southwestern Washington. By his high school years, O'Connor had won fiddle competitions nationwide and recorded four ROUNDER albums. After graduation he began working with rock-fusion pioneers the Dixie Dregs and jazz greats DAVID GRISMAN and Stephane Grappelli.

At CHET ATKINS's suggestion, O'Connor moved to Nashville in 1982 and began to forge a studio career playing fiddle, guitar, and mandolin behind the likes of RANDY TRAVIS, CLINT BLACK, and RICKY VAN SHELTON. WARNER BROS. provided O'Connor a major label opportunity, and he balanced studio sessions with three solo albums. By 1990 he tired of studio gigs and focused on solo work. His album *New Nashville Cats*, a musical homage to MUSIC CITY's session players, won a 1991 Grammy. O'Connor also honored his major influences with 1994's *Heroes*, which found him performing with Grappelli, Jean-Luc Ponty, and Pinchas Zukerman.

O'Connor's classical work included a CARNEGIE HALL appearance with Isaac Stern and Itzhak Perlman and guest solo performance with the Boston Pops orchestra. In 1990 the Santa Fe Chamber Music Festival commissioned him to write his *Fiddle Concerto for Violin and Orchestra*, which later appeared on Warner Bros. *Appalachia Waltz*, his Sony project with classical cellist Yo Yo Ma and Nashville bassist Edgar Meyer, was one of the top-selling classical recordings of 1996; the three musicians released the Grammy-winning *Appalachian Journey* in 2000. Since then O'Connor has continued to compose while issuing albums on Sony and on his own Omac label.

At this writing, O'Connor is a six-time winner of CMA's Instrumentalist of the Year Award; ACM has named him Fiddle Player of the Year eight times. As an educator, he leads seminars at numerous universities and music institutions, also offering an annual fiddle camp in Tennessee and an annual strings conference in San Diego. *—Calvin Gilbert*

## W. Lee "Pappy" O'Daniel
b. Malta, Ohio, March 11, 1890; d. May 12, 1969

One of the most important men in the history of WESTERN SWING, Wilbert Lee "Pass the Biscuits, Pappy" O'Daniel never sang, never played an instrument, and couldn't even read music. Nevertheless, he became famous for founding western swing's LIGHT CRUST DOUGHBOYS and for riding their success into a career in Texas politics.

Born in Ohio, O'Daniel grew up on a farm in Kansas. In 1925 he moved to Fort Worth, Texas, and became sales manager for the Burrus Mill and Elevator Company, makers of Light Crust Flour. In 1930 the firm began sponsoring a radio program featuring a STRINGBAND consisting of singer MILTON BROWN, fiddler BOB WILLS, and guitarist Herman Arnspiger. Dubbed the Light Crust Doughboys, the trio became a huge success. After Brown and Wills left, O'Daniel added other musicians, acting as their announcer. He also wrote poetry and composed lyrics for songs, including the country standards "Beautiful Texas" and "Put Me in Your Pocket." In 1935 he formed his own company, Hillbilly Flour. Fronting a new band, the Hillbilly Boys, he was elected Texas governor in 1938 and was reelected in 1940. In 1941 he became a U.S. senator, winning a special election by defeating Congressman Lyndon B. Johnson. After a nonproductive term in the Senate, during which time no O'Daniel proposal received more than four votes, O'Daniel retired. He ran for President of the United States in 1952 and, in 1956 and 1958, made two halfhearted tries for the governorship of Texas, running a poor third in both elections. *—Cary Ginell*

## Molly O'Day
b. McVeigh, Kentucky, July 9, 1923; d. December 5, 1987

Lois LaVerne Williamson, better known as Molly O'Day, was perhaps the most widely admired traditional female country singer of the 1940s. Her expressive voice had a penetrating quality on sentimental and sacred songs that was virtually unequaled. She first worked on radio with her brother Skeets and Johnnie Bailes (see THE BAILES BROTHERS) at WCHS–Charleston, West Virginia, in 1939, under the stage name Mountain Fern. The next year they worked at WJLS–Beckley and WHIS–Bluefield, where she took the name Dixie Lee; in 1941 she married guitarist Lynn Davis (1914–2000). Thereafter, she and Davis performed together, and in 1942 she became "Molly O'Day." They subsequently worked for successive periods of several months in Birmingham; Louisville and Renfro Valley, Kentucky; and Dallas, meeting a young HANK WILLIAMS during their Alabama stay.

In May 1945 the couple came to WNOX in Knoxville and became stars of the *MID-DAY MERRY-GO-ROUND*. When Nashville-based FRED ROSE heard O'Day's rendition of "Tramp on the Street," he persuaded ART SATHERLEY to sign her to COLUMBIA RECORDS. In a related move, Rose recruited Hank Williams for ACUFF-ROSE PUBLICATIONS, in part because his songs seemed ideal for O'Day to record. Though she subsequently recorded five Williams compositions, her biggest numbers, such as "Tramp on the Street,"

*Molly O'Day*

"At the First Fall of Snow," "Matthew 24," and "Don't Sell Daddy Any More Whiskey," came from other writers.

Professional musicianship proved emotionally stressful for O'Day, and in 1950 she and her husband both had religious conversion experiences. Their last Columbia recording session took place the following year. Lynn Davis became a Church of God minister-evangelist, and his wife assisted him in his work. From the mid-1960s they lived in Huntington, West Virginia. O'Day steadfastly refused offers to perform publicly, though she recorded gospel albums for Rem (1962) and GRS (1968). From 1974 until 1987 O'Day and Davis disc-jockeyed a gospel program on Huntington radio station WEMM-FM. Davis continued the program for a number of years following O'Day's death from cancer in 1987. —*Ivan M. Tribe*

## Jamie O'Hara (*see* The O'Kanes)

## The O'Kanes
Jamie O'Hara b. Toledo, Ohio, August 8, 1950
Kieran Kane b. Queens, New York, October 7, 1949

With spare acoustic arrangements and BROTHER DUET–style harmonies, the O'Kanes briefly established themselves as a duo with a difference. Songwriters Jamie O'Hara and Kieran Kane joined forces in 1986, cowriting most of their recorded output and creating a signature sound featuring mandolin, fiddle, accordion, guitar, and banjo.

Kane played the northeastern BLUEGRASS and folk circuit and worked as a Los Angeles songwriter-guitarist before moving to Nashville in 1978. An eponymous 1982 album on ELEKTRA RECORDS charted two Top Twenty country singles. As a writer he

scored with JOHN CONLEE's #1 hit "As Long as I'm Rockin' with You" (1984).

After a knee injury refocused his ambitions from pro football to music, O'Hara moved to Nashville in 1975 and became a staff writer for TREE PUBLISHING. By the mid-1980s his cuts included RONNIE MCDOWELL's "Older Women" and THE JUDDS' "Grandpa (Tell Me 'Bout the Good Old Days)," which won a 1986 Grammy for Best Country Song.

Kane and O'Hara began writing together in 1985. In 1986 they signed with COLUMBIA RECORDS, and their simple studio work tapes became the O'Kanes' self-titled 1986 debut album. In 1987 they hit #1 with "Can't Stop My Heart from Loving You" and gained three additional Top Tens: "Oh Darlin'," "Daddies Need to Grow Up Too," and "Just Lovin' You." Their second album, *Tired of Runnin'*, yielded "One True Love" (#4, 1988) and "Blue Love" (#10, 1988). The partners disbanded in 1989 to resume their solo writing and recording careers; their Columbia album *Imagine That* appeared in 1990. In 1994 Kane and fellow musicians KEVIN WELCH, Tammy Rogers, and Harry Stinson founded Dead Reckoning Records. The label's first release was Kane's *Dead Rekoning* (sic, 1995). —*Marjie McGraw*

## OKeh Records
established in New York, New York, 1918; ended 1960s

The OKeh label (pronounced "okay") grew out of founder Otto Heineman's phonograph accessory business, with an assist from Germany's Lindström company, from whom OKeh leased Odeon and Fonotipia masters. The first vertically cut OKeh records were issued in 1918; lateral discs appeared the following year.

In 1920 Harlem singer Mamie Smith made the first blues records for OKeh; their success engendered immediate competition from other labels. In 1923 OKeh made the first field trip to the South, to record dance bands and blues singers in Atlanta. A local distributor, Polk Brockman, persuaded producer RALPH PEER to record two sides by colorful local personality and WSB radio star FIDDLIN' JOHN CARSON. Peer did so reluctantly, but the record realized surprising sales and is viewed today as the one that launched the country music industry. HENRY WHITTER, ROBA STANLEY, ERNEST V. STONEMAN, and KELLY HARRELL soon began recording for OKeh, as did local artists recruited on subsequent trips to Atlanta, Asheville, Dallas, and St. Louis.

In 1926 COLUMBIA purchased OKeh, which was then able to produce electrically made recordings using Columbia's Western Electric process. In the late 1920s, offerings by NARMOUR & SMITH, FRANK HUTCHISON, and EMMETT MILLER were added to the catalog.

OKeh went into eclipse in 1932, following the sale of its bankrupt parent company, Columbia, to the AMERICAN RECORD CORPORATION (ARC). In turn, the Columbia Broadcasting System (CBS) purchased ARC in 1938. ARC briefly revived OKeh during 1934–35. Following CBS's relaunching of Columbia Records, OKeh replaced Columbia's low-priced Vocalion imprint in 1940. Columbia's country artists, including GENE AUTRY, BOB WILLS, and ROY ACUFF, all appeared on OKeh through 1945, when OKeh was discontinued again and country acts appeared once more on Columbia.

Columbia revived OKeh briefly in the early 1950s, primarily as a rhythm & blues label, though it also released some country material briefly in 1953. It was revived once more in the 1960s for R&B releases and a few LP reissues. —*Dick Spottswood*

## Old Crow Medicine Show

Chris "Critter" Fuqua b. Austin, Texas, March 16, 1978
Kevin Hayes b. Malden, Massachusetts, December 27, 1964
Morgan Jahnig b. Chattanooga, Tennessee, November 29, 1978
Gill Landry b. Lake Charles, Louisiana, December 10, 1975
Kech Secor b. Denville, New Jersey, May 14, 1978
Willie Watson b. Elmira, New York, September 23, 1979

A popular STRINGBAND, Old Crow Medicine Show fuses OLD-TIME, BLUEGRASS, folk, and blues with a contemporary bent. While the group does play traditional standards, the majority of its recorded material is original, performed on fiddle (Secor, Fuqua), guitar (Watson, Landry, Secor), banjo (Watson, Landry), harmonica (Secor), and guitjo (Hayes)—a six-string banjo with a guitar neck. The band formed in 1998 in Ithaca, New York, and was playing a street corner in Boone, North Carolina, in 2000, when DOC WATSON invited them to play his annual MERLEFEST.

Based in Nashville since 2000, the group recorded two independent albums before signing with Nettwerk in 2003. The act's 2004 label debut, *O.C.M.S.*, featured its signature song, "Wagon Wheel," which vocalist and fiddler Ketch Secor wrote using the chorus of an unfinished BOB DYLAN song. *Big Iron World* (2006) and *Tennessee Pusher* (2008) followed. All three albums topped *Billboard's* bluegrass charts, and each appeared on the country charts as well, with *Pusher* reaching #7. In high-energy live shows, the band often showcases reworked versions of tunes from across the musical spectrum. Since 2008, founding member Chris "Critter" Fuqua has not performed live with the group. Nettwerk released a concert DVD, *Live at the Orange Peel and Tennessee Theater,* in 2009. —*Scott Anderson*

## *Old Dominion Barn Dance*

established in Richmond, Virginia, September 1946; ended 1957

This well-known Saturday-night country showcase was broadcast live on radio station WRVA, from the Lyric Theater at Ninth and Broad Streets in Richmond, Virginia. The show began in 1946 and ran into 1957.

WRVA, which debuted in 1925, was owned by Larus and Brothers Tobacco Company, makers of Edgeworth Pipe Tobacco and Domino Cigarettes. Some of the station's significant early bands were the Domino Hillbillies, the Tobacco Tags, and HOYT "SLIM" BRYANT & His Wildcats. The *Old Dominion Barn Dance* began when C. T. Lucy, general manager of WRVA, secured the lease to the Lyric Theater to stage the live show he envisioned. The program was built around the Workman family: SUNSHINE SUE; her husband, John Workman; and his brother Sam, known professionally as Sunshine Sue & the Smiling Rangers.

With Sunshine Sue as hostess, the show drew large crowds to see CHET ATKINS, WILMA LEE & STONEY COOPER, GRANDPA JONES and wife Ramona, Bonnie Lou & Buster Moore, Benny Kissinger and Curley Collins, and JOE MAPHIS. Mary Klick and Rose Lee (later Maphis) appeared as the Saddle Sweethearts, while humor was provided by country comedians Chick Stripling, Quincy Snodgrass, and others. The program's bluegrass artists, including the Farm Hands, Charlie Bailey, RENO & SMILEY, MAC WISEMAN, FLATT & SCRUGGS, and THE STANLEY BROTHERS, were exceptionally good. WRVA broadcast at 50,000 watts, so the program enjoyed a wide listening audience. In the mid-1950s it was carried nationally on the CBS Radio Network's weekly *Saturday Night Country Style* series, which alternated broadcasts from various radio barn dances, such as WNOX's *Tennessee Barn Dance* and the *WWVA JAMBOREE*.

The demise of the *Old Dominion Barn Dance* resulted from the rise of rock & roll and its negative impact on much of the country music industry, together with the spread of television, which competed for audiences' attention. By 1955 and 1956, attendance had fallen sharply. With the show losing money, WRVA management reluctantly closed it down in 1957.

Several months later, however, promoter CARLTON HANEY created the *New Dominion Barn Dance*. Broadcast over WRVA from the same theater and featuring more BLUEGRASS acts, it lasted until 1964. —*Walter V. Saunders*

## Old-Time Music

The term "old-time music" generally refers to the styles and repertoires that dominated commercial country music's earliest years, roughly 1923 to 1935, though these styles have continued into the twenty-first century. Old-time music was rooted in the folk traditions of the British Isles, Africa, and continental Europe. It evolved along with various folk dances, included BALLADS and other folk-song types, and was played with acoustic instruments, including the fiddle, guitar, and banjo. Since the late nineteenth century, commercial influences from BLACKFACE MINSTRELSY, vaudeville, gospel, and other vernacular music forms had affected old-time music. Old-time music existed throughout the United States by the nineteenth century, but by the 1920s it was most closely associated with the South.

The phrase apparently originated with the era's record companies and music publishers, who weren't sure what to call the music. "Country" was seldom used at this point, and record companies described it as "old-time music," "old-time singing," "songs from Dixie," or "old familiar tunes." In the 1920s "old" or "old-time" connoted older, respectable music, in contrast to contemporary jazz and its questionable morality.

Old-time music embraced a number of styles during the 1920s and 1930s. One was STRINGBAND music, either in bands (such as the SKILLET LICKERS) or as fiddle-guitar duets (such as THE KESSINGER BROTHERS). The CARTER FAMILY and duets such as the DELMORE BROTHERS represented harmony singing, while JIMMIE RODGERS and Cliff Carlisle (older brother of BILL CARLISLE) embodied blues and related yodeling. BRADLEY KINCAID and UNCLE DAVE MACON upheld a solo singing tradition in which artists rendered traditional material to various instrumental accompaniment. Subregional forms, including CAJUN, German-Czech, Polish, and Bohemian music, added further diversity.

Throughout the 1930s and 1940s, as other styles of country music developed, the old-time styles were often eclipsed. Exceptions were the popular stringbands of J. E. MAINER in the 1930s, and in the 1940s radio stars such as GRANDPA JONES, STRINGBEAN, and DOC & CHICKIE WILLIAMS. In the 1960s the legendary STONEMAN FAMILY had a successful syndicated TV show that kept older sounds alive in the heart of Nashville.

Starting with the folk music revival of the late 1950s and early 1960s, a number of more modern artists successfully revived many of the old-time styles, often supported by local and state folklore societies and various music publications. In the stringband tradition, THE NEW LOST CITY RAMBLERS influenced thousands with their faithful re-creations of earlier stringbands during the 1960s. The next decade saw the rise of groups such as the Highwoods String Band, the Hotmud Family, and the

RED CLAY RAMBLERS. Veteran artists, including TOMMY JARRELL and WADE MAINER, found new audiences and recorded widely. Upholding older singing traditions were the remarkable duo of HAZEL DICKENS and Alice Gerrard and, in the 1990s, the Whitstein Brothers.

Solo singers included the veteran Roy Harper as well as TNN star David Holt. A new generation of young fiddlers, including Brad Leftwich, Bruce Molsky, Greg Hooven, and Chirps Smith, carried that music into the 1990s. That same decade saw a third generation of new stringbands, such as the Freight Hoppers. In the new century, stringbands, including OLD CROW MEDICINE SHOW and the Carolina Chocolate Drops (a black group), the harmony team of GILLIAN WELCH and David Rawlings, and other acts proved that old-time styles were still alive and well.

Players have traditionally learned old-time styles by ear at jam sessions and festivals, though nonprofit, community-based folk music schools such as Chicago's Old Town School of Folk Music offer instruction. A number of newer schools have opened since the movie *O BROTHER, WHERE ART THOU?* increased popular interest in older, folk-based sounds. —*Charles Wolfe*

## Opryland USA
opened in Nashville, Tennessee, May 27, 1972

Opryland USA—renamed the Gaylord Opryland Resort and Convention Center in 2001—is a Nashville-based conglomerate owned by the GAYLORD ENTERTAINMENT COMPANY. It encompasses the Opryland Hotel, the GRAND OLE OPRY, radio station WSM-AM, the Opry House theater (home of the Opry), other smaller theaters, the *General Jackson* showboat, the Springhouse Links golf course, and THE RYMAN AUDITORIUM and Wildhorse Saloon in downtown Nashville. From 1972 to 1997 the complex included the Opryland amusement park, and from 1983 to 1997 TNN: THE NASHVILLE NETWORK and later the Country Music Television (CMT) cable network were additional components. After Gaylord bought the ACUFF-ROSE music publishing catalogs in 1985, the conglomerate included the Opryland Music Group, until its sale to Sony/ATV Music Publishing in 2002. WSM-FM's facilities were part of the complex from the mid-1980s until the station was purchased by Cumulus Broadcasting in 2003.

The National Life and Accident Insurance Company (the parent organization of WSM and the Grand Ole Opry) created the Opryland amusement park as a new home for the Opry and as a source of revenue. Plans for the park were announced on October 18, 1968; groundbreaking followed on June 30, 1970, and the facility opened on May 27, 1972. Built on sixty-five acres of land several miles up the Cumberland River from downtown Nashville, the facility cost $66 million. The Grand Ole Opry moved to the new Opry House on March 16, 1974. The Opryland Hotel, with 614 rooms, opened adjacent to the park in 1977.

In the early 1980s Texas-based American General Insurance bought National Life, but, with the exception of WSM-TV, American General sold all of National Life's entertainment holdings to Gaylord Broadcasting of Oklahoma City in 1983. In addition to expanding park rides and launching the *General Jackson*, Gaylord featured veteran and aspiring stars at the Opry House and in three additional theaters. By the 1990s the park was rechristened "Opryland Theme Park," with "Opryland USA" identifying the destination and embracing Gaylord's various Nashville properties. The park closed December 31, 1997. Opry Mills, a retail entertainment complex mixing shops, theaters, and restaurants, has occupied the park site since 2000, though the mall is not owned by Gaylord and has leased the Opry name. Nashville's extensive flooding in May 2010 forced Opry Mills to close until repairs could be made. —*Bob Millard*

## Roy Orbison
b. Vernon, Texas April 23, 1936; d. December 6, 1988

Although his background was in country music, Roy Kelton Orbison produced perhaps the most completely realized pop records of the early 1960s. They were symphonic in their composition and execution, and at their best they conveyed a sense of longing, as if Orbison himself was the lonely man who populated his work.

Orbison grew up in Wink, Texas, and his father was an oil rigger in Jal, New Mexico. A nearsighted child, Roy turned to music early. He was performing on local radio at age ten, and his first group, the Wink Westerners, played country music on local radio and television. Studying in Odessa in 1955, Orbison assembled the Teen Kings band and, touched by the furor attending ELVIS PRESLEY's early Texas tours, plunged into rock & roll.

The Teen Kings' first single, "Ooby Dooby," issued on Je-Wel Records, caught the ear of SUN RECORDS founder SAM PHILLIPS, who brought Orbison to Memphis to recut it. For two years Orbison tried hard to rock & roll at Phillips's behest, but nothing except the remake of "Ooby Dooby" charted. Shortly after writing "Claudette" for THE EVERLY BROTHERS in 1958, Orbison bought his way off Sun and signed with RCA in Nashville. Two undistinguished pop singles followed, and after a year Orbison was dropped. Orbison's music publisher, WESLEY ROSE, helped him sign with MONUMENT RECORDS in 1959, and 1960's "Only the

*Roy Orbison*

Lonely" defined the classic Orbison style. Between 1960 and 1965 he became a master of the pop single. "Running Scared," "Crying," "In Dreams," "Blue Bayou," and "It's Over" were among his hits, all written by Orbison, some cowritten with Joe Melson or Bill Dees. All featured his hypnotic tenor voice, and most reflected song structures that ventured far from standard formulas, though the biggest hit, "Oh, Pretty Woman," cowritten with Dees, was rooted in 1950s rock & roll. Orbison had moved to Nashville in 1960, and all his hits were recorded there with the same musicians who played on country sessions. One crucial difference, however, was that Monument's FRED FOSTER would not push for the industry norm of recording four songs in a three-hour session but settled instead for one song—if it was the one.

Until his death, Orbison enjoyed worldwide success, especially in Europe and Australia. At home his career went off the rails almost immediately after "Oh, Pretty Woman." His next two Monument singles sold poorly, and in July 1965 he signed with MGM RECORDS, where this pattern continued.

In addition, Orbison's personal life was touched by tragedy in the late 1960s. He had married his high school sweetheart, Claudette Frady, in 1957, but she died in a motorcycle accident in June 1966. In September 1968, two of their sons died in a house fire while Orbison was on tour in England. In March 1969 he married a seventeen-year-old German, Barbara Wellhonen.

After leaving MGM in 1973 Orbison went through a succession of contracts, including a short, artistically arid return to Monument in 1976. A 1980 Grammy for "That Loving You Feeling Again"—a #6 country duet with EMMYLOU HARRIS—and the movie *Blue Velvet* (1986), which used "In Dreams" to haunting effect, hastened his comeback, as did Bruce Springsteen's honorific speech at Orbison's 1987 induction into the Rock and Roll Hall of Fame. Orbison was elected to the NASHVILLE SONGWRITERS HALL OF FAME that same year. TV appearances, including the 1988 special *Roy Orbison and Friends: A Black and White Night*, acquainted younger generations with his work. His duet with K. D. LANG on "Crying" won a 1988 Grammy for Best Country Collaboration with Vocals. The Grammy-winning *The Traveling Wilburys, Vol. 1* (Wilbury, 1988), of which Orbison was a part, climbed to #3 on the pop album charts. His rehabilitation was completed when "You Got It," from his Virgin Records solo album *Mystery Girl*, reached #9 pop in 1989, and the album posthumously reached #5. His widow, an astute businesswoman, has extended his legacy with various projects, including the boxed set *The Soul of Rock and Roll* (Legacy/Monument/Orbison, 2008). —*Colin Escott*

## Oriole Records (*see* American Record Corporation)

## Jimmie Osborne
b. Winchester, Kentucky, April 8, 1923; d. December 26, 1957

James Osborne Jr., a singer-songwriter billed as the Kentucky Folk Singer, was one of the more traditional country music artists to emerge following World War II. His original songs addressed patriotic themes, lost love, and the religious life, but his best-known numbers were topical pieces.

In about 1939 Osborne began his career at radio station WLAP in Lexington, Kentucky. During the war he worked in defense plants and performed on weekends. At war's end he returned to WLAP and then followed with stints on stations in Asheville, North Carolina, and Texarkana, Arkansas.

In 1947 Osborne moved to KWKH in Shreveport, Louisiana, and later became a regular on the *LOUISIANA HAYRIDE*, subsequently joining THE BAILES BROTHERS' act as a featured vocalist. During this period he guested on ERNEST TUBB's segment of the GRAND OLE OPRY and signed with KING RECORDS. His initial release, "My Heart Echoes," made the country Top Ten in 1948.

Osborne returned to Kentucky and landed a job on WLEX–Lexington. He had his biggest hit in 1949, "The Death of Little Kathy Fiscus," an event BALLAD recounting the true-life tragedy of a child who died April 8, 1949, after falling into a deep well-pipe in San Marino, California. The song reached #7 on *Billboard*'s country charts; Osborne donated half of his royalties to the Kathy Fiscus memorial fund.

"God Please Protect America," a Korean War song that peaked at #9 in 1950, was Osborne's final chart hit. Other relatively successful songs from that period include the traditional "Hills of Roan County" and his own "Tears of St. Ann." During the early 1950s he appeared on Chicago's WLS *NATIONAL BARN DANCE* and on WLW's *MIDWESTERN HAYRIDE* in Cincinnati.

In 1952 Osborne moved to Louisville, Kentucky, where he opened a record store and hosted a popular DJ show on WKLO; he later switched to a smaller station, WGRC. Osborne continued recording through May 1955, but by this time he was recording other writers' songs and never had another hit. Finally, apparently despondent over marital problems and his waning career, he took his own life at age thirty-four. —*Walter V. Saunders*

## The Osborne Brothers
Robert Van "Bobby" Osborne Jr. b. Hyden, Kentucky, December 7, 1931
Sonny Roland Osborne b. Hyden, Kentucky, October 29, 1937

Sporting exquisite three-part harmonies and progressive musical ideas, the Osborne Brothers were one of the few BLUEGRASS acts to crack contemporary country radio playlists during the 1960s.

Bobby and Sonny Osborne were living in Dayton, Ohio, when they formed their professional partnership in August 1953. Both were seasoned professionals: Bob played guitar and mandolin with the LONESOME PINE FIDDLERS, JIMMY MARTIN, and THE STANLEY BROTHERS before serving in Korea; teenaged banjoist Sonny toured with BILL MONROE for two summers.

After working with Jimmy Martin in Detroit and Charlie Bailey in Wheeling, the brothers returned to Dayton in December 1955. Recruiting singer-guitarist RED ALLEN and fiddler Art Stamper, they played area clubs as the Osborne Brothers & Red Allen. Publisher-producer WESLEY ROSE signed them to MGM RECORDS, and "Ruby," driven by Bobby's keening tenor voice and a twin-banjo arrangement, became a bluegrass hit. On Dusty Owens's "Once More" (1958), Bobby sang lead, pitched higher than the two harmony parts, and the resulting #13 country single established the band's unmistakable trademark sound.

When Allen left in April 1958, the Osbornes replaced him with a succession of singer-guitarists, most notably Benny Birchfield and Dale Sledd. Doyle Wilburn, of the WILBURN BROTHERS, helped the Osbornes land a DECCA (later MCA) contract in 1963 and secure GRAND OLE OPRY membership the following year. The band also changed its musical direction; breaking ranks with bluegrass traditionalists, the Osbornes added steel guitars, a piano, and drums to their records. "Up This Hill and Down" (1966) appealed to country radio programmers leery of playing bluegrass discs. The brothers also benefited from a string of BOUDLEAUX

*The Osborne Brothers: Bobby (left) and Sonny*

AND FELICE BRYANT–penned hits, particularly "Rocky Top" (1968), "Tennessee Hound Dog" (1969), and "Georgia Pineywoods" (1971). In 1971 CMA named them Vocal Group of the Year; two years later they became the first bluegrass band to perform at the White House.

Eventually becoming dissatisfied with the demand for hit singles and the grueling road schedule needed to support them, the Osbornes left MCA in 1976 and returned to a more traditional, acoustic bluegrass sound. The move revitalized their music, and, together with festival appearances, a series of critically acclaimed albums for CMH, RCA, SUGAR HILL, and Pinecastle widened their reputation as one of America's premier bluegrass bands.

Following Sonny's retirement in 2005 due to a shoulder injury, Bobby formed the Rocky Top X-Press. He continued to work the Opry and recorded several albums for ROUNDER, including *Try a Little Kindness* (2006), *Bluegrass Melodies* (2007), and *Bluegrass & Beyond* (2009). —*Dave Samuelson*

## K. T. Oslin
b. Crossett, Arkansas, May 15, 1941

Kay Toinette Oslin came late and didn't stay long, but she left a repertoire of impassioned story songs speaking to her generation of women with a humor and poignancy unmatched since LORETTA LYNN at her peak.

Only five when her mother, a onetime big band singer, was widowed, Oslin was moved repeatedly before landing in Houston. Bitten by the show business bug, she took ballet at age eleven and majored in drama at a Texas junior college. She became a contemporary folksinger, teaming with GUY CLARK for a time, and then worked her way to New York City, where she first danced on Broadway in a *West Side Story* revival. She recorded jingles, sang backup vocals, toured colleges as a solo act, and became a Manhattan maven.

Oslin was nearly forty when she began making forays into Nashville as a songwriter. In the mid-1980s DOTTIE WEST recorded one of her tunes, and in 1985 GAIL DAVIES hit with Oslin's "Round the Clock Lovin'." Nevertheless, Oslin's material seemed too advanced for its time, and an ELEKTRA RECORDS deal fizzled in 1981. She returned in 1986 to tell with wit and passion the stories of women on the leading edge of the baby boom generation—whom she forever gave identity as "'80's Ladies" (#7, 1987).

From 1987 to 1991, with RCA hits such as "Do Ya'," "I'll Always Come Back," "Hold Me," "Hey Bobby," and "Come Next Monday," Oslin wove little plays into songs that did not always use formulas preferred by country radio. Her videos were also highly imaginative: "80's Ladies" was practically a feature film in miniature, "Come Next Monday" a high-budget farce. Along the way she picked up Grammys, ACM trophies, and CMA awards while recording a handful of gold and platinum albums. Most women are cashiered from country radio before the age at which Oslin began, but by writing her own sophisticated music and controlling her own themes and image, for a time she was the grand diva of country music speaking to her cohorts as no one had done before.

A noteworthy part in the Sandra Bullock–River Phoenix film *The Thing Called Love* (1993) reminded Oslin of her love of acting. Tiring of the road, in the mid-1990s she pulled back from music to pursue additional TV and film roles. In 2001, though, she released *Live Close By, Visit Often*, a BNA (see RCA RECORDS) album produced by Raul Malo. —*Bob Millard*

## Marie Osmond
b. Ogden, Utah, October 13, 1959

Olive Marie Osmond began her show business career at age three, when she appeared with her brothers on Andy Williams's network TV show. At age thirteen she enjoyed her first chart record—the crossover smash "Paper Roses" (MGM, 1973). Arranged and produced by SONNY JAMES, "Paper Roses" spent two weeks at #1 on the country charts, inaugurating a country career that later saw Osmond share in CMA's 1986 Vocal Duo of the Year award on the strength of her chart-topping duet with DAN SEALS, "Meet Me in Montana."

At age fourteen Marie began touring with the Osmond Brothers, and as a teenager she cohosted with brother Donny a musical TV variety series, *Donny & Marie*. The siblings' duet version of "I'm Leaving It (All) Up to You" (1974) hit the country Top Twenty and peaked at #4 pop, but their duet rendition of "Make the World Go Away" (1975) failed to make an impression in either format.

When the TV series ended, Marie briefly moved to New York to further her acting career, wrote a health and fitness book, and collaborated on an exercise video and two handbooks for expectant mothers. She made little additional headway as a recording artist until 1985, when "Meet Me in Montana" hit #1 on the country charts and opened a new chapter in her career as a contemporary country singer. Released later that year, "There's No Stopping Your Heart" also went to #1, as did a 1986 duet with Paul Davis, "You're Still New to Me."

Osmond gained her most recent country chart single in 1995. In the 1990s she worked in touring musicals and starred as Anna in a Broadway production of *The King and I*. She heads the Osmond Foundation for charitable work. —*Gerry Wood*

## Outlaws

Although hard-living, independent-minded artists such as HANK WILLIAMS and GEORGE JONES have long populated country music, the term "Outlaw" specifically described an amorphous group of dissident country musicians of the 1970s. It was probably first used in 1973 by Nashville publicist Hazel Smith, when asked by a North Carolina radio station to identify the music then produced by WILLIE NELSON, WAYLON JENNINGS, Tompall Glaser (see THE GLASER BROTHERS), and their comrades. Recalling Jennings's 1972 hit "Ladies Love Outlaws," Smith decided that the appellation and the image fit. But it wasn't until RCA released the million-selling 1976 album *Wanted! The Outlaws* that "Outlaw" became widely used to designate a type of country music. Michael Bane's 1978 book *The Outlaws: Revolution in Country Music,* which profiled the phenomenon and candidly summarized the careers of KRIS KRISTOFFERSON, Nelson, Jennings, Glaser, and JESSI COLTER (Jennings's wife), heightened the word's popularity.

Until 1976 the most common term was "progressive country," originally used to characterize the format of radio station KOKE-FM in AUSTIN, TEXAS. Jan Reid's *The Improbable Rise of Redneck Rock* (1974) was an early attempt to coin another term, and some music critics used "cosmic cowboy music," alluding to a 1973 MICHAEL MARTIN MURPHEY song title.

"Outlaw" seemed appropriate for musicians who had openly criticized the Nashville recording industry and the pop-oriented NASHVILLE SOUND of the 1960s. Most wanted to produce their own records and select their own backup musicians—often their road bands. The Outlaws adopted the dress, hairstyles, and lifestyles of rock musicians, including an open identification with drug use. Experimentation marked their actions, whether presenting sexually candid lyrics, performing at outdoor rock-styled festivals, hiring agents from New York, or recording outside Nashville, as Nelson did following his return to Texas.

The Outlaw persona, however, was fraught with irony. DAVID ALLAN COE, an ex-convict and motorcycle gang member, was the only Outlaw who actually had approximated true outlawry in his personal life. Moreover, Outlaw performers were gaining national commercial success at the very time they were projecting an image as industry outsiders. Indeed, *Wanted! The Outlaws* was a Nashville marketing effort from start to finish—a repackaging of old recordings from Nelson, Jennings, Colter, and Glaser that was conceived and executed by RCA executive JERRY BRADLEY.

Although the 1970s Outlaw phenomenon greatly enlarged country music's audience—especially among youthful fans—it was short-lived. By 1978 Nelson was recording pop standards; Jennings and Glaser openly split, reportedly over money; Kristofferson was pursuing a Hollywood acting career; Coe's outrageous behavior was becoming tiresome; and a hedonistic, drug-oriented lifestyle was creating legal and health problems for many Outlaw performers. Jennings effectively summarized the situation in his 1978 hit "Don't You Think This Outlaw Bit's Done Got Out of Hand."

Even so, "Outlaw" has retained its currency in the twenty-first century. In 2004 SiriusXM Satellite Radio launched its Outlaw Country channel, described as "a sanctuary for the freaks, misfits, rebels, and renegades of country music." In 2004 and 2005 CMT broadcast *CMT Outlaws,* multiartist concerts featuring 1970s Outlaws such as Jessi Colter and David Allan Coe, iconic hard-country veterans such as MERLE HAGGARD and BILLY JOE SHAVER, and newer acts who draw inspiration from these predecessors, including BIG & RICH, MONTGOMERY GENTRY, GRETCHEN WILSON, and TOBY KEITH. —*Stephen R. Tucker*

## Paul Overstreet
b. Antioch, Mississippi, March 17, 1955

Singer-songwriter Paul Overstreet overcame alcoholism and triumphed as a songwriter before adopting a God- and family-oriented emphasis as a solo recording artist.

Inspired as a child by the HANK WILLIAMS bio movie *Your Cheatin' Heart,* Overstreet moved to Nashville from Mississippi in 1973. Encouraged by members of DOLLY PARTON's family, he formed a group and spent several years working the road. His marriage in May 1975 to Parton's younger sister Freida ended in divorce in November 1976.

Overstreet didn't win his fight with alcohol until 1985, but he started having significant songwriting hits in 1982 with GEORGE JONES's recording of "Same Ole Me." Also in 1982, Overstreet released a self-titled RCA solo album that failed to catch fire. But by the mid-1980s his positive, innovative approach to hard-country songwriting produced a long string of hits, most notably the 1986 and 1987 CMA and ACM Songs of the Year, "On the Other Hand" and "Forever and Ever, Amen," both written with DON SCHLITZ and recorded by RANDY TRAVIS.

In 1986 Overstreet, a moving hard-country singer, recorded one album with the songwriting trio SKO (Schuyler, Knobloch & Overstreet) before resuming solo work. He recorded the 1987 #1 hit "I Won't Take Less Than Your Love" with TANYA TUCKER and Paul Davis. Top Ten Overstreet hits extolling the joys of home and family included 1990's "Richest Man on Earth" (#3) and the chart-topping "Daddy's Come Around," both marketed jointly by RCA and the Christian music Word label.

Overstreet was BMI's Songwriter of the Year from 1987 to 1991. He has won two Grammys—for "Forever and Ever, Amen" and THE JUDDS' 1990-91 hit "Love Can Build a Bridge"—as well as several Dove Awards for his gospel recordings. He was elected to the NASHVILLE SONGWRITERS HALL OF FAME in 2003.

In 1999 Overstreet launched Scarlet Moon Records and recorded his own album of hit songs previously recorded by others. In 2001 he released *Living by the Book,* an album of self-written Christian songs. With cowriter Rory Lee Feek, Overstreet scored a secular hit when BLAKE SHELTON took their song "Some Beach" to #1 in 2004. Today Overstreet continues to enjoy his large family and his evangelical and charitable work. —*Thomas Goldsmith*

## Gary Overton (*see* Sony Music Entertainment)

## Fuzzy Owen
b. Conway, Arkansas, April 30, 1929

One of the pioneers of the BAKERSFIELD, California, country music community, Charles Lee "Fuzzy" Owen cofounded Tally Records, the label that first recorded MERLE HAGGARD. Since the early 1960s, Owen has been instrumental in Haggard's recordings, and he has influenced Haggard's songwriting through advice and example. When Haggard signed with CAPITOL, Owen became his manager and helped Haggard transform himself from a virtual unknown to an American musical legend.

Growing up in Arkansas, Owen played steel guitar around Hot Springs and Little Rock, performing on radio shows before he moved to Bakersfield in 1949 to join his cousin Lewis Talley in a band. In August 1951 Owen entered the army, but after his discharge in 1952 he returned to Bakersfield, where he performed at the Blackboard and then at the Clover Club. This led to a regular job on Cousin Herb Henson's local TV show.

Owen cowrote "A Dear John Letter" with Lewis Talley and Billy Barton and recorded it with BONNIE OWENS for the Mar-Vel label; covered by Capitol artists FERLIN HUSKY and JEAN SHEPARD, the song became a huge crossover hit in 1953. Owen and Talley then established a Bakersfield studio and the Tally Records label. Owen recorded several self-penned songs for Tally, including "Arkie's Got Her Shoes On" and "You're Everything I Wish that She Could Be," with little commercial impact. As a writer, though, Owen scored again with "The Same Old Me," a #1 hit for RAY PRICE in 1959. When the Owen-Talley partnership was dissolved, Owen kept the label and its associated music publishing company.

Owen met Merle Haggard while both were performing at Bakersfield's Lucky Spot nightclub in about 1960, just after Haggard was released from San Quentin State Prison. Haggard recorded several songs for Tally (including Owen's "Singing My Heart Out") and later signed with Capitol. Owen began to focus on Haggard's career and became the singer's full-time manager in 1962.

Since then Owen has played an active role in Haggard's studio recordings, live concerts, and career guidance. Their longtime association has helped build Haggard's legendary status but has overshadowed Owen's success as a songwriter and musician as well as his own important influence in the development of the Bakersfield sound. —Don Cusic

## Bonnie Owens
b. Blanchard, Oklahoma, October 1, 1932; d. April 24, 2006

Bonnie Owens was the major female artist to emerge from BAKERSFIELD, California, as it became a center for West Coast country music in the 1950s. A sharecropper's daughter, Bonnie Maureen Campbell met BUCK OWENS when she was fifteen, after the family moved to Mesa, Arizona. There she joined his band, Mac & the Skillet Lickers, on radio station KTYL. The two married in 1948, and in 1951 they moved to Bakersfield, where Buck worked local clubs. Bonnie also sang in area clubs, sometimes doubling as a waitress. The couple had two sons but soon separated; they divorced in 1953.

From the mid-1950s into the early 1960s, Bonnie worked the local KERO-TV show Cousin Herb's Trading Post Gang, whose regulars included steel guitarist FUZZY OWEN and guitarist Lewis Talley. Her first recording was a Mar-Vel Records duet with Owen, "A Dear John Letter," which preceded the 1953 JEAN SHEPARD–FERLIN HUSKY crossover smash. Owen and Talley, who had cowritten this hit, formed the Tally label and signed Bonnie, who notched two Top Thirty singles in 1963–64 before recording "Just Between the Two of Us" with recently signed MERLE HAGGARD. This 1964 hit became the title cut for a successful duet album on CAPITOL after Capitol purchased both artists' contracts.

The singing partners married in 1965, and in the late 1960s Owens recorded solo albums in addition to contributing to Haggard's studio offerings. As a songwriter, her best-known composition is "Today, I Started Loving You Again," cowritten with Haggard.

Owens continued working with Haggard until 1991, even after their 1978 divorce. In 1994 she rejoined his show and kept making music, until Alzheimer's forced her retirement in the late 1990s. —Don Cusic

## Buck Owens
b. Sherman, Texas, August 12, 1929; d. March 25, 2006

Singer, songwriter, and guitarist Alvis Edgar Owens Jr. ruled country music for a period in the mid-1960s, producing a clear, twangy, danceable sound that he repeated across dozens of hit singles. Though he would later become a fixture on television through the success of HEE HAW, Owens is best remembered by fans and by younger stars he has influenced for timeless hits such as "Act Naturally" (#1, 1963) and "My Heart Skips a Beat" (#1, 1964).

His early life followed the classic Depression-era Dust Bowl story. Sharecroppers from North Texas near the Oklahoma border, his family moved west to Arizona in 1937, barely making ends meet. Having experienced poverty, Owens began playing the honky-tonks of Phoenix and Mesa, Arizona, to make money, learn a trade, and avoid back-breaking farm labor.

Young Owens's diverse musical influences reflected the popular music of the time and places in which he matured, along with the styles he had to master as a working dancehall musician in the Southwest. He listened to STRINGBAND and COWBOY music on Mexican border radio stations (see BORDER RADIO) and learned to synthesize WESTERN SWING, rhythm & blues, and the emerging genre of HONKY-TONK. In 1947 he met Bonnie Campbell, with whom he worked in a group called Mac & the Skillet Lickers; the two married in 1948.

In 1951 Buck and his wife, BONNIE OWENS, moved to BAKERSFIELD, California, where many Dust Bowl refugees had ended their trip west in fertile farm fields and a burgeoning oil industry. From 1951 to 1958 Buck played at the Blackboard, the center of Bakersfield's vibrant music scene. As lead guitar player and singer for the house band, led by BILL WOODS, Buck worked marathon shifts and played anything to get folks dancing, including country, R&B, ROCKABILLY, polkas, and even rhumbas and sambas.

He also took advantage of Bakersfield's proximity to Los Angeles to work sessions at CAPITOL studios, establishing himself as a session guitarist for artists such as TOMMY COLLINS and Gene Vincent. Owens made a few singles for local labels and even recorded a rockabilly single, "Hot Dog," for Pep Records in 1956, released under the name Corky Jones to preserve his country credibility. Producer KEN NELSON signed Owens to Capitol in 1957, and two years later "Second Fiddle" became Owens's first chart record.

While living in the Seattle area in the late 1950s, Owens struck up a musical relationship and personal friendship with a young fiddler, DON RICH. Their partnership was crucial in Owens's career, and Rich stayed with Owens as musician, guitarist, tenor harmony singer, and leader of his band, the Buckaroos, until his death in 1974.

Owens's first #1 hit was "Act Naturally" in 1963, later covered by the Beatles. Following with a series of equally incisive singles that seemed literally to jump out of AM transistor radios, Owens repeatedly topped the country charts with numbers such as "Love's Gonna Live Here" (1963), "Together Again" (1964), "I've Got a Tiger By the Tail" (1965), "Think of Me" (1966), and "Sam's Place" (1967), most of which he wrote or cowrote.

Unlike most artists during the heyday of THE NASHVILLE SOUND, Owens typically recorded with his road band, giving his records a distinctive sound and a live feel. From 1963 to 1967, the peak of Owens's recording career, Owens and Rich were joined by PEDAL STEEL GUITAR player TOM BRUMLEY, drummer Willie Cantu, and bassist Doyle Holly on all of Owens's records (and on the Buckaroos' own marginally successful releases on Capitol). While Nelson nominally produced his sessions, Owens shaped

*Buck Owens and the Buckaroos: (from left) Don Rich, Jerry Wiggins, Owens, Doyle Holly, and Tom Brumley*

the band's sound and songs. Bolstered by Owens's desire to keep the same winning formulas, these factors helped create his signature style, based on simple storylines, infectious choruses, piercing electric guitar leads and fills, an insistent rhythm supplied by placing drums forward in the mix, and high-pitched two-part harmonies featuring Owens and Rich. Owens was ACM's first Male Vocalist of the Year (1965), and he and his Buckaroos were ACM's top touring band from 1965 to 1968 as well as CMA's top instrumental group for 1967 and 1968.

The savvy performer controlled his business interests as well as his music. Early on, Owens established Blue Book, a music publishing company that handled his copyrights and those of other Bakersfield writers, such as MERLE HAGGARD. Owens also invested in radio stations throughout the Southwest and with his manager, JACK MCFADDEN, organized his own management and booking agency, which handled a number of artists.

After many career highlights, including shows at CARNEGIE HALL and the Fillmore in San Francisco, Owens's recording career faded commercially and artistically in the 1970s, though he kept busy with his business interests and with *Hee Haw*. He was coaxed out of retirement in 1988 by DWIGHT YOAKAM, who helped him return to the top of the charts with the duet "Streets of Bakersfield." Two new albums followed—*Hot Dog!* (1988) and *Act Naturally* (1989), the latter including a duet with Ringo Starr on the title track—though neither was especially memorable. Owens's classic songs are available in collections and rereleases and live on in the countless cover versions with which younger artists pay tribute to his music.

Owens was elected to THE COUNTRY MUSIC HALL OF FAME and the NASHVILLE SONGWRITERS HALL OF FAME in 1996, the year he opened his lavish Crystal Palace venue in Bakersfield. He died on March 25, 2006. —*Mark Fenster*

Among the enduring numbers he and Frazier wrote are "All I Have to Offer You (Is Me)" and "(I'm So) Afraid of Losing You Again," both #1 hits for CHARLEY PRIDE. Frazier eventually dropped out of the music business for a long spell, but Owens remained active into the late 1990s.

Born and raised in Waco, Texas, Owens drew inspiration from a pair of movies he saw while growing up; one was about the classical composer Frederic Chopin, the other about American pop composer George Gershwin. As a teenager, Owens hung around local radio stations, paying particular attention to fast-rising star HANK THOMPSON. Owens later played bass with Dallas-based country singer Charlie Adams, and during the mid-1950s he performed regularly on a television program hosted by JOHNNY GIMBLE. Owens also recorded a pair of obscure, pop-oriented singles for the MGM and Back Beat labels, respectively.

At RAY PRICE's suggestion, Owens moved to Nashville in 1965. Signed to Forest Hills Music, he enjoyed only modest success at first. But shifting to HILL AND RANGE gave Owens indirect access to ELVIS PRESLEY, and in 1969 two Owens-Frazier songs appeared on Presley's *From Elvis in Memphis* comeback LP. Owens and Frazier also cowrote BRENDA LEE's "Johnny One Time" and STONEY EDWARDS's "Hank and Lefty Raised My Country Soul." In addition, Owens and WHITEY SHAFER collaborated on MOE BANDY's first three chart singles.

Owens's successful run continued with GEORGE JONES's "Wine Colored Roses" (#10, 1986) and DOUG STONE's "Fourteen Minutes Old" (#6, 1990). But during the early 1990s Owens suffered heart and kidney problems so severe he was told he had no more than two or three months to live. Miraculously, he survived and picked up his writing again. In 1997, two years before his death, his "Show Me a Woman" (cowritten with Doug Johnson) appeared on JOE DIFFIE's album *Twice Upon a Time*. —*Daniel Cooper*

## Doodle Owens
b. Waco, Texas, November 28, 1930; d. October 4, 1999

Like his friend and frequent cowriter DALLAS FRAZIER, A. L. "Doodle" Owens arrived in Nashville during the mid-1960s and established himself as a premier hard-country songwriter.

## Tex Owens
b. Killeen, Texas, June 15, 1892; d. September 9, 1962

Best known for having written the classic western song "Cattle Call," Doie Hensley Owens also was the father of LAURA LEE MCBRIDE

(Bob Wills's first female vocalist) and the brother of Texas Ruby, who, with Zeke clements (ca.1936–38) and with her husband, Curly Fox (1940s), was a member of the Grand Ole Opry. Owens was a self-taught singer-guitar player; on guitar he plucked basic open chords with his fingers, and he sang in a pleasant western style. He wrote cowboy songs and sentimental songs about mother and love.

The oldest of thirteen children in a Texas sharecropping family, Owens worked on ranches at age fifteen before joining a minstrel show (see Blackface Minstrelsy). He eventually held many jobs, including town marshal in Bridgeport, Oklahoma. In 1932 he landed his own radio program as the Texas Ranger and became a member of the *Brush Creek Follies* at KMBC–Kansas City, Missouri, where he broadcast for eleven years. Owens had no band of his own but often appeared with KMBC's Prairie Pioneers and the Texas Rangers. In 1934 Owens recorded "The Dude Ranch Party" (with the Texas Rangers) and "Cattle Call" for Decca Records, along with three other self-penned songs. In 1936 he recorded for RCA Victor, but the label did not issue the sides. After leaving Kansas City, Owens broadcast over WLW–Cincinnati, KOMA–Oklahoma City, and KHJ–Hollywood. In 1960 he and his wife moved back to Texas. —*Guy Logsdon*

*Red Foley appearing on the* Ozark Jubilee

## Ozark Jubilee
established in Springfield, Missouri, 1953

Broadcast from Springfield, Missouri, from 1955 to 1960, the *Ozark Jubilee* was the most successful country music network television show of its time. The program helped prove the commercial viability of the music as televised entertainment, and it helped make stars of performers such as Porter Wagoner and Brenda Lee.

The show's popularity was all the more remarkable in that the *Ozark Jubilee* began in 1955, while rock & roll was first exploding and after two ABC-TV country shows had already failed (*Hayloft Hoedown*, 1948; and *ABC Barn Dance*, 1949). Still, by 1954 more than half of all American households had a TV set. Fearing that television would undermine its long-running country radio success (156 live shows per week), Springfield radio station KWTO decided to enter the country TV market. KWTO founder Ralph Foster—with colleagues John Mahaffey and Lester E. Cox—encouraged their partner, E. E. "Si" Siman, to spearhead the effort. (Siman had already helped place Chet Atkins and Wagoner with RCA Records.)

In 1953 KWTO had launched the *Ozark Jubilee* on local radio, and then, in 1954, on ABC radio, broadcasting from the Jewell Theater at 216 South Jefferson Street. At this point Siman recruited longtime Grand Ole Opry star Red Foley, who by then had fallen out with Opry management, for the *Jubilee*. Siman then went to New York City, where ABC-TV accepted his program idea.

The first show aired on January 22, 1955, and it was a regular Saturday-night feature for almost five years (except for some Thursday spots in 1956). The televised segment usually lasted one hour, though live in Springfield, it was a two-and-a-half-hour affair. Siman brought special cameras into the theater and hired Don Richardson as a scriptwriter, making the program more progressive than a mere live concert television show. Foley became its perpetual star host.

Other acts began heading to Springfield, including Jean Shepard, Hawkshaw Hawkins, and Webb Pierce (once-a-month host, 1955–56). Missouri-based acts included Wagoner and the Foggy River Boys. The "Junior Jubilee" youngsters' segment featured the square-dancing Tadpoles and an eleven-year-old singer from Georgia, Brenda Lee. Eventually Wagoner, and then Lee, left for Nashville, but numerous other *Jubilee* acts prospered, becoming national favorites. Among these were Bobby Lord, Marvin Rainwater, Wanda Jackson, Billy Walker, and Norma Jean.

As a result of the *Jubilee*'s success, ABC-TV launched three other country music TV programs: the Cleveland, Ohio–based *Pee Wee King Show* (1955); a series of specials showcasing Grand Ole Opry talent and sponsored by Purina (1955–56); and another Siman production broadcast from Springfield, *The Eddy Arnold Show* (1956), which also featured Chet Atkins.

The *Ozark Jubilee* changed its name to *Country Music Jubilee* (1957) and then to *Jubilee U.S.A.* (1958). Due in part to Foley's Internal Revenue Service tax trial, which scared off sponsors (although Foley eventually won the case), the show closed on September 24, 1960. Then Siman pioneered the color-telecast *Five Star Jubilee* (NBC-TV, 1961), built around Tex Ritter, Carl Smith, Jimmy Wakely, Rex Allen, and Nashville pop star Snooky Lanson. Ralph Emery and then wife Skeeter Davis appeared, as did eleven-year-old Barbara Mandrell. According to historian Reta Spears-Stewart, Foley closed the last show (September 22, 1961) saying: "We'll have to do this again someday." —*Steve Eng*

## Package Shows

Beginning in the 1940s, "package show" was the term used to describe a touring country music stage show featuring several performers. Prior to 1940, groups of country entertainers appeared on the vaudeville circuit, and radio station booking offices sent troupes to local schoolhouses, courthouses, and theaters. But the term "package shows" best applies to big-city shows that emerged during World War II. Promoters and booking agents, such as OSCAR DAVIS and J. L. FRANK, began to offer shows combining several stars from radio programs such as the GRAND OLE OPRY and sometimes drawing talent from several radio barn dances. Meanwhile, Frank organized WSM's CAMEL CARAVAN for the R. J. Reynolds Tobacco Company to stage free shows for servicemen stationed in the United States and Central America.

During the late-1950s crisis caused by rock & roll and the spread of television, when record sales and gate receipts dropped for many country artists, country entertainers often formed units of up to half a dozen acts that could collectively draw sufficient crowds to generate profits. Assisted by bookers and talent buyers, such units remained popular into the 1970s, when the growing popularity of superstars such as KENNY ROGERS and WILLIE NELSON began to make it possible for one or two acts to carry a show date by themselves. Although corporate sponsors have sometimes assembled large troupes, a star-and-opening-act format generally prevails today. —*John W. Rumble*

## Brad Paisley
b. Glen Dale, West Virginia, October 28, 1972

Brad Paisley brought a keen sense of humor and a dose of backwoods sentimentality to his triple-threat talents as a songwriter, vocalist, and guitarist. His creativity and genial personality made him one of country's most consistent stars at the outset of the twenty-first century.

By age thirteen, Paisley appeared regularly on *Jamboree USA,* a Saturday-night broadcast on radio station WWVA in Wheeling, West Virginia. As a teenager, he opened concerts for ROY CLARK, LITTLE JIMMY DICKENS, and GEORGE JONES at Wheeling's Capital Music Hall. Paisley started college at West Liberty State College in West Virginia but transferred to Nashville's Belmont University on an ASCAP scholarship. After graduation, he landed a songwriting contract with EMI Music Publishing. His early credits included "Another You," a Top Five hit for David Kersh.

Signed to ARISTA RECORDS, Paisley released *Who Needs Pictures* (1999), containing the poignant #12 title track and the equally moving #1 hits "He Didn't Have to Be" (1999) and "We Danced" (2000). The album also included the humorous "Me Neither" (#18), establishing a pattern of balancing clever, funny tunes with sentimental fare. Indeed, the only #1 from the 2001 album *Part II* was the tongue-in-cheek "I'm Gonna Miss Her (The Fishin' Song)," featuring an award-winning video costarring actress Kimberly Williams, who the singer wed in 2003. The collection yielded three more Top Ten songs: "Two People Fell in Love," "Wrapped Around," and "I Wish You'd Stay."

*Mud on the Tires* (2003) established Paisley as a top country star. His first #1 *Billboard* country album, it reached #8 on the all-genre *Billboard* 200 chart. Of its four Top Five songs, only the title cut reached #1, but the witty "Celebrity" and the award-winning ALISON KRAUSS duet, "Whiskey Lullaby," had more career impact. *Time Well Wasted* (2005) did even better, debuting at #1 country and #2 on the *Billboard* 200. The album produced four #1 hits: a DOLLY PARTON duet, "When I Get Where I'm Going," She's Everything," "The World," and "Waitin' on a Woman." A #4 comedic song, "Alcohol," proved to be a concert favorite.

*Brad Paisley*

By 2007's *5th Gear,* Paisley's golden touch was set. Another #1 country album, it reached #3 on the *Billboard* 200 and launched four #1 singles: "Ticks," "Letter to Me," "Online," and "I'm Still a Guy." As had become a pattern, it included an instrumental, a gospel song, and duets with contemporary stars and country legends. Long a Grammy nominee, Paisley finally won two: with "Throttleneck" (Best Country Instrumental Performance) in 2007 and "Letter to Me" (Best Male Country Vocal Performance) in 2008. Paisley released *Play: The Guitar Album* in 2008, highlighting his flashy, inventive instrumental work. It featured "Start a Band," a #1 duet with KEITH URBAN, and won Paisley another Best Country Instrumental Grammy for "Cluster Pluck," shared with seven guest guitarists.

In 2008, Paisley began co-hosting the televised CMA Awards with Carrie Underwood, a job they continued to hold, as of this writing, through the 2010 awards. Paisley's 2009 album, *American Saturday Night,* provided another career boost. It featured two #1 hits, "Then" and "Water," and two #2s, the title song and "Welcome to the Future." That led to Paisley's becoming CMA's Entertainer of the Year in 2010, giving him a total of fourteen CMA awards and fourteen ACM awards.

*Hits Alive,* a 2010 double-disc collection of past hits, and the following year's album of original material, *This Is Country Music,* further secured his standing among the primary country music figures of his time. *—Michael McCall*

## Pamper Music
established in Goodlettsville, Tennessee, January 1, 1959; sold, April 1969

During its decade of independent existence, Pamper Music developed one of country music's most heralded song catalogs and helped launch the songwriting careers of HANK COCHRAN, HARLAN HOWARD, and WILLIE NELSON.

The firm was founded by principal owners HAL SMITH, RAY PRICE, and Claude Caviness. Smith served as general manager of Pamper, whose Tennessee offices were located at 119 Two Mile Pike in Goodlettsville, twenty miles northwest of Nashville. Caviness, who owned the tiny Pep Records, ran Pamper's West Coast office, at 9652 Winchell Street, Pico Rivers, California. (Smith and Price purchased his interest in Pamper for six figures in 1965).

Cochran (1960–69), Howard (1962–64), and Nelson (1961–69) wrote many of their classic hits during their Pamper tenures, with Cochran also manning the position of writer relations manager. Ray Pennington, Chuck Howard, Don Rollins, and Fred Carter Jr. also contributed to the wealth and depth of the Pamper catalog. Standards published by the firm include "Crazy" (PATSY CLINE, 1961), "Heartaches by the Number" (Ray Price, 1959), "I Fall to Pieces" (Cline, 1961), "Hello Walls" (FARON YOUNG, 1961), and "Make the World Go Away" (EDDY ARNOLD, 1965). TREE PUBLISHING purchased Pamper in April 1969, and the acquisition helped to ensure Tree's status as a dominant force in country music publishing. *—Kent Henderson*

## Colonel Tom Parker
b. Breda, Netherlands, June 26, 1909; d. January 21, 1997

Colonel Tom Parker served as ELVIS PRESLEY's manager from November 1955 until the singer's death in August 1977. Although critics have charged him with exploiting and eroding Presley's

*Colonel Tom Parker*

talent, it can also be argued that without Parker, Presley might well have remained an obscure ROCKABILLY figure with no national impact.

Born Andreas Cornelis van Kuijk, the fifth of nine children of a Dutch stable manager and his wife, Parker reinvented himself after a second trip to America in 1929 (his first brief U.S. sojourn took place in 1926); he never returned to his homeland. In June 1929 he enlisted in the U.S. Army and was stationed in Hawaii with the 64th Coast Artillery and in Florida with the 13th Coast Artillery, serving four years. During his service, he took the name Thomas A. Parker (Thomas R. Parker was the name of an officer he met in Honolulu). After his discharge, he claimed a Huntington, West Virginia, birthplace and began working with the Royal American Shows traveling carnival as palm reader, sideshow barker, and advance man. He married Marie Mott in 1935 and settled in Tampa, Florida, where he became the field agent for the local Humane Society.

While keeping this job, Parker began booking tours for musical acts, including pop singer Gene Austin, cowboy star Tom Mix, and GRAND OLE OPRY stars ERNEST TUBB, ROY ACUFF, and JAMUP AND HONEY. Parker got to know singer EDDY ARNOLD while doing advance promotion for a Jamup and Honey TENT-SHOW tour in Florida, and in the fall of 1945 Parker began managing the rising singer, a job he would hold until September 1953. With Parker's guidance, Arnold became the hottest star in country music, with his own radio shows, movie roles, and a string of #1 records. Along the way, in October 1948, Louisiana governor JIMMIE DAVIS gave Parker an honorary colonel's commission, thus completing his new identity. Thereafter he was known as Colonel Parker.

In 1954 Parker began a booking and business partnership with HANK SNOW that brought Elvis Presley into his purview when Presley appeared as an incendiary opening act for Snow and other country stars in 1955. Parker quickly attached himself to Presley, and on August 15, 1955, Parker bought a controlling interest in

Presley's management contract from Memphis DJ Bob Neal for $2,500. Parker then engineered a complicated deal among HILL AND RANGE SONGS, INC., RCA RECORDS, and SUN RECORDS to buy out Presley's contract from Sun and sign him to RCA for $35,000—a sum considered astronomical at the time. (Hill and Range supplied an additional $5,000 to strengthen ties with the artist.) Presley signed with RCA in November 1955, Neal's management contract expired in March 1956, and within weeks Presley became the biggest star in popular music. Parker devoted himself almost exclusively to Presley from that moment on, arranging important TV and concert appearances as well as movie roles.

For his exclusive management services, Parker exacted a high price. In addition to his basic management fee of 25 percent, Parker received a third of Elvis's concert proceeds after 1972 and half of his record income after 1973. There was, in addition, the toll Parker may well have taken on Presley's creative career by shunting him into limiting arrangements with Hill and Range as his main song suppliers and with producer Hal Wallis on a series of musical movies that rarely rose above the level of pleasant formula. These arrangements, as well as Presley's grueling schedule as a Las Vegas performer, were almost certainly fueled by Parker's gambling habit, which kept Parker millions in debt.

Following Presley's death, Parker quietly removed himself from the music business, easing into retirement with a $2 million buyout from RCA Records in 1983 for his "right, title, and interest" in all Presley-related contracts. In his later years he split time between homes in Las Vegas and Madison, Tennessee. Among the younger stars he encouraged was GEORGE STRAIT, whom Parker urged to consider a movie career. —*Paul Kingsbury*

## Linda Parker
b. Covington, Indiana, January 18, 1912; d. August 12, 1935

A featured member of WLS's *NATIONAL BARN DANCE*, Linda Parker is generally considered the first woman to begin a successful solo career in country music. Her popularity helped open doors for other women in the field, most notably PATSY MONTANA.

Genevieve Elizabeth Muenich was an only child raised by working-class parents in Hammond, Indiana. She became interested in music after hearing pop singer Ruth Etting on Chicago radio. Dropping out of high school at age sixteen, Muenich sang at area parks and roadhouses; by late 1929 she was featured on WWAE–Hammond. In 1930 she moved to Chicago, where she landed a regular fifteen-minute show on WAAF as Jeanne Munich, the Red-Headed Bluebird.

Despite her lack of experience in folk or country music, promoter JOHN LAIR was impressed by Muenich's personality and talent; in spring 1932 he hired her for his CUMBERLAND RIDGE RUNNERS troupe on WLS. To avoid confusion with her WAAF audience, Lair molded her new persona as Linda Parker, the Sunbonnet Girl from the hills of Kentucky. As Parker she sang ballads and sentimental songs, using the same natural phrasing that reflected her stylistic debt to Etting. Despite her radio success, Parker made only two records during her lifetime; both were issued on Sears, Roebuck's CONQUEROR label.

Parker was stricken with acute appendicitis during an August 3, 1935, show in Elkhart, Indiana. She was rushed to a Mishawaka hospital, where she died nine days later from peritonitis. —*Dave Samuelson*

## Lee Roy Parnell
b. Abilene, Texas, December 21, 1956

Singer Lee Roy Parnell has brought a warm R&B sensibility to boogie and country tunes. Additionally, he has written songs recorded by JO-EL SONNIER, COLLIN RAYE, and SWEETHEARTS OF THE RODEO, and his soulful slide guitar can be heard on hits by MARY CHAPIN CARPENTER and PATTY LOVELESS.

Parnell's early influences ranged from BOB WILLS to the Allman Brothers and Muddy Waters. Based in AUSTIN, TEXAS, Parnell hit the road at age nineteen and made an unsuccessful run at Nashville before returning in 1987 and landing a publishing deal with Welk Music.

TIM DUBOIS signed Parnell to ARISTA Nashville, but the artist's eponymous 1990 debut album yielded no hit singles. *Love Without Mercy* (1992), however, produced the Top Ten title cut as well as the #2 hits "What Kind of Fool Do You Think I Am" and "Tender Moment." Parnell followed with "On the Road" (1993) and "I'm Holding My Own" (1994), both Top Ten singles. As the flagship artist for Career Records, Arista's short-lived sister label, Parnell released *We All Get Lucky Sometimes* in 1995 and the commercially disappointing *Every Night's A Saturday Night* in 1997. He returned to Arista when Career folded. Subsequently, Parnell has recorded for Vanguard and UNIVERSAL RECORDS SOUTH. —*Clark Parsons*

## Gram Parsons
b. Winter Haven, Florida, November 5, 1946; d. September 19, 1973

Every few years, a country or rock singer or band—among them Elvis Costello, Lone Justice, JIM LAUDERDALE, THE KENTUCKY HEADHUNTERS, and the Jayhawks—will point to Gram Parsons,

*Gram Parsons*

who never had a hit in more than ten years of recording, as a major influence. At least one will call Parsons the Father of Country-Rock.

Parsons wasn't the first to conceive COUNTRY-ROCK, but he was perhaps the most passionate about bringing country music into the increasingly prominent rock & roll world of the 1960s. Born Ingram Cecil Connor III, Parsons was raised in Waycross, Georgia, where he got his first musical ideas from ELVIS PRESLEY and other SUN RECORDS artists. After Parsons's father committed suicide in 1958, his family moved to his mother's hometown, Winter Haven, Florida, where she married Robert Parsons, a salesman.

At home, Parsons listened to music ranging from pop to R&B and jazz. In school he sang with a rock band as well as a folk group, playing guitar and singing with a thin but emotional voice. He rediscovered country during a brief stay at Harvard in 1965, when he also got into LSD and the Beatles. Saying the best country music was "white soul music," he formed the International Submarine Band, which, after Parsons moved to Los Angeles in 1966, made an album (*Safe at Home*) including songs by JOHNNY CASH and MERLE HAGGARD. Parsons himself wrote songs about love, about not being understood, about the constant need to move on.

He joined THE BYRDS in late 1967 and helped take them into country music. By the following spring he had left and cofounded THE FLYING BURRITO BROTHERS with CHRIS HILLMAN, his band mate from the Byrds. Other original members of the Burritos included bassist Chris Ethridge, who'd played briefly with Parsons in the International Submarine Band, and PEDAL STEEL GUITAR ace "Sneaky" Pete Kleinow. In an early description of the Burritos, Parsons told *Melody Maker* that the band was "basically a Southern soul group playing country and gospel-oriented music with a steel guitar."

The Burritos lived up to Parsons's promise of a blend of roots music with a rock & roll attitude. A strong first album earned excellent reviews, especially for songs such as "Sin City" and "Hot Burrito #1," but sales were disappointing. After a train tour wiped out much of the band's promotion budget, the album sank, and a second effort, *Burrito Deluxe*, didn't do any better, despite a superb rendition of the Rolling Stones' "Wild Horses," which Parsons's buddies Mick Jagger and Keith Richards sent him before they recorded it. After an appearance at the Stones' disastrous Altamont rock festival in late 1969, Parsons left the Flying Burrito Brothers.

In late 1971 Parsons heard about EMMYLOU HARRIS, who was singing in Washington, D.C.–area folk clubs. He convinced her to join him for an album featuring backup by several musicians who regularly worked with Parsons's idol, Elvis Presley. Parsons's and Harris's voices blended exquisitely. The album, *GP*, earned generally good reviews but didn't sell.

After a haphazard tour and another recording session, which resulted in the album *Grievous Angel*, Parsons was found dead of a mixture of alcohol and heroin in a motel room in the desert town of Joshua Tree, California, where he had often visited.

It was in death that Parsons gained his greatest notoriety. Saying they were fulfilling a pact, Parsons's friend and road manager, Phil Kaufman, and another friend spirited Parsons's casket away from a local airport, where it awaited shipment to Parsons's stepfather in Louisiana. Kaufman and his friend drove Parsons's body to Joshua Tree National Monument, where Kaufman tried to set the body on fire. Kaufman was later arrested, and Parsons's remains wound up in a cemetery in New Orleans.

A number of tribute albums have appeared since his death, and Parsons's boundary-crossing musical approach has made him a patron saint of the AMERICANA movement. —*Ben Fong-Torres*

## Dolly Parton
b. Locust Ridge, Tennessee, January 19, 1946

With their strong feminine stance in the 1960s and 1970s, Dolly Parton, LORETTA LYNN, and TAMMY WYNETTE revolutionized the world of country music for women performers. Expanding into the pop field, Parton landed on the cover of *Rolling Stone*, gained pop hits, and starred in Hollywood movies. She eventually returned to country music, recording contemporary country albums for COLUMBIA RECORDS—including one produced by RICKY SKAGGS—and BLUEGRASS albums for roots label SUGAR HILL RECORDS. With the #1 "When I Get Where I'm Goin'," a 2005 duet with BRAD PAISLEY, she had scored chart-topping hits in four consecutive decades.

Dolly Rebecca Parton came from deep Appalachia, where music was an integral part of life for those who, like the Partons, struggled to make a hard living. Her mother was a singer who taught Dolly church music along with the Elizabethan ballads her ancestors had brought to America. Dolly's grandfather was a fiddling preacher who wrote "Singing His Praise," a song recorded by KITTY WELLS. Several of Dolly's eleven siblings have been active in music, and some worked for a time in her family band.

Parton's childhood figured strongly in her desire to escape her circumstances and in the many straightforward, unromantic songs she wrote about life in Appalachia. For example, "Coat of Many Colors" (#4, 1971) frankly recounted her response to the humiliation she had suffered when classmates made fun of her patchwork, homemade coat.

*Dolly Parton*

Early on, Parton was encouraged by her uncle Bill Owens, who bought her a guitar and landed her a stint on a television variety show in nearby Knoxville by the time she was ten years old. Nashville soon took note of her, and she made her first guest appearance on the GRAND OLE OPRY at age thirteen in 1959. She also recorded a single for a small Louisiana label and one for MERCURY RECORDS in Nashville in 1962.

After graduating from high school in 1964, she packed her bags for Nashville. Her first day in town, she met her future husband, contractor Carl Dean, in a laundromat. Her musical career progressed apace; she cowrote (with her uncle) two Top Ten hits for BILL PHILLIPS in 1966. FRED FOSTER signed her to MONUMENT RECORDS, and in 1967 her song "Dumb Blonde"—which attacked female stereotypes—became her first Top Thirty country hit.

That year, Parton's pivotal career moment came when she joined PORTER WAGONER on the road and on TV as the replacement for the Opry star's previous duet partner, NORMA JEAN. As a team, the traditional-singing, flashily dressed Wagoner and the personable Parton became immediate audience favorites. Her hourglass figure, eye-catching outfits, and angelic voice played off perfectly against Wagoner's cornpone humor and old-fashioned country sensibility. RCA RECORDS signed Parton as Wagoner's duet partner and as a solo recording artist. The singers became CMA's Vocal Duo of the Year for 1970 and 1971. She became increasingly successful in her own right, too, and her fame began to eclipse Wagoner's.

Parton's first solo #1 hit was her composition "Joshua" (1971). Between 1973 and 1975, she had five consecutive #1s, four of them solo recordings: "Jolene," "I Will Always Love You," "Please Don't Stop Loving Me," (with Wagoner), "Love Is Like a Butterfly," and "The Bargain Store." She left Wagoner's TV show during its 1974–75 season, with "I Will Always Love You" her personal farewell to the singer. Under contractual obligations, he continued to produce her records until 1976, but she was soon on her own; though Wagoner brought legal action against her, the two artists later settled their disputes.

In retrospect, the early to mid-1970s was the most creatively fertile period of Parton's country music career. She was voted CMA's Female Vocalist of the Year in both 1975 and 1976. Additionally, 1973 yielded what many observers regard as her creative highpoint, *My Tennessee Mountain Home,* a bittersweet look backward at an existence she was determined to leave. The album cover is a picture of her family's Sevierville cabin; the songs, especially the title cut, are a matter-of-fact tribute to a people and a way of life that is vanishing. "I wanted to be free," she told *Rolling Stone* in 1977. "I had my songs to sing, I had an ambition, and it burned inside me. It was something I knew would take me out of the mountains. I knew I could see worlds beyond the Smoky Mountains."

By the mid-1970s, Parton secured West Coast management in her quest for broader audiences. Her first album after declaring her independence from Wagoner was 1977's *New Harvest, First Gathering,* which yielded the #11 single "Light of a Clear Blue Morning." That same year brought *Here You Come Again,* a glitzy—and successful—attempt at a country-pop crossover. The title song became her first pop Top Ten hit, and she won a Grammy for Best Country Vocal Performance by a Female for the album, her first million-seller. CMA named her Entertainer of the Year in 1978, and it seemed as if Parton could preserve the best of both worlds.

Parton's country career became more erratic as she grew into a household name and a constant presence on TV talk shows, music

and comedy specials, and made-for-TV movies as well as in sitcoms, including a 2002 role as "Aunt Dolly" in the Disney Channel hit *Hannah Montana.* She starred in a brief syndicated half-hour series of her own, *Dolly!,* in 1976–77; then she hosted an hourlong, ABC network variety series, also titled *Dolly,* in 1987–88. Her movie career bounced from stellar (*9 to 5*) to forgettable (*Rhinestone,* which tried to make Sylvester Stallone a believable country singer).

Her recording triumphs included 1987's *Trio* album with EMMYLOU HARRIS and LINDA RONSTADT (which won CMA's Vocal Event of the Year and a Grammy for Best Country Performance by a Duo or Group with Vocal) and her 1993 *Honky Tonk Angels* collaboration with Loretta Lynn and Tammy Wynette. In 1992 singer Whitney Houston's recording of Parton's "I Will Always Love You" became a #1 pop hit, partly due to its inclusion in the soundtrack for the movie *Bodyguard.* Since Parton also published this song, it became especially lucrative for her. Parton also has demonstrated her business acumen in several ventures, most notably her popular Dollywood theme park near Sevierville, which opened in 1985. Through Dollywood, Parton has contributed to her home county's economy and to scholarships, libraries, and health care for local residents as well as to book programs for prekindergarten children in the United States, Canada, and Great Britain.

In 1996 Parton and VINCE GILL won CMA's Vocal Event of the Year award for their duet recording of "I Will Always Love You." She reunited with Harris and Ronstadt for *Trio II* in 1999, which included their Grammy-winning cover of Neil Young's "After the Gold Rush." Parton also won Grammys for Best Bluegrass Album, for *The Grass Is Blue* (1999), and for Best Female Country Vocal Performance, for "Shine," from her 2001 album *Little Sparrow.*

In 2007 Parton launched Dolly Records and as of 2010 had released her albums *Backwoods Barbie* (2008) and the CD/DVD set *Live in London.* She also contributed to the score of the 2009 Broadway production *9 to 5: The Musical.*

As of July 2011, Parton has won eight Grammy Awards, nine CMA Awards, and nine ACM Awards. Parton was inducted into the NASHVILLE SONGWRITERS HALL OF FAME in 1986, THE COUNTRY MUSIC HALL OF FAME in 1999, and the national Songwriters Hall of Fame in 2001. She was given the National Medal of Arts in 2005, the Kennedy Center Honors in 2006, and a Grammy Lifetime Achievement Award in 2011. —*Chet Flippo*

## Les Paul & Mary Ford

Les Paul b. Waukesha, Wisconsin, June 9, 1915; d. August 13, 2009
Mary Ford b. Pasadena, California, July 7, 1924; d. September 30, 1977

One of pop music's most imaginative acts during the early 1950s, Les Paul & Mary Ford were rooted in country and western music. While their many hits often featured layers of vocal and guitar overdubs, the couple also recorded relaxed, unadorned covers of country hits and standards.

Born Lester William Polsfuss, Les Paul turned pro in 1932, playing guitar, harmonica, and jug with Joe Wolverton as the Ozark Apple Knockers on KMOX–St. Louis and WBBM–Chicago. In the mid-1930s he worked Chicago radio as "Rhubarb Red." Inspired by Belgian guitarist Django Reinhardt, Paul began playing more jazz; he also experimented with amplifying his guitar. Between 1937 and 1941 he led the Les Paul Trio with singer-guitarist Jimmy Atkins (CHET ATKINS's half brother) and bassist ERNIE NEWTON.

Moving to Los Angeles in 1943, Paul met Iris "Colleen" Summers, a popular western vocalist on KXLA's *Dinner Bell Round-Up*. Early in their romance, the couple maintained separate careers: Paul with Bing Crosby and the Andrews Sisters; Summers with Art Wenzel, GENE AUTRY, and JIMMY WAKELY. When they began recording together in 1949, Paul gave Summers the name "Mary Ford" to avoid conflicts with her established western music audience.

With their multitracked vocals and crisp electric guitar leads, Les Paul & Mary Ford generated numerous hits for CAPITOL RECORDS during the 1950s, most notably the enduring "How High the Moon" and "Vaya con Dios." During these years Paul also made significant contributions to electric guitar and tape recording technologies.

Like other popular artists, Paul and Ford were affected by the rise of rock & roll in the mid-1950s; a jump to COLUMBIA in 1958 failed to rekindle flagging record sales. In 1962 they abandoned their trademark sound for a contemporary Nashville approach that proved musically and commercially unsuccessful. Paul & Ford's professional partnership ended with their 1963 separation and eventual divorce; both later retired from public performance.

In 1976 Paul and Chet Atkins released *Chester & Lester*, an album of guitar duets; it won a Grammy for Best Country Instrumental Performance. A follow-up album, *Guitar Monsters*, appeared in 1978.

After recovering from a heart attack, Paul resumed public appearances in 1984 with a weekly stint at Fat Tuesdays, a lower-Manhattan jazz club, holding forth for more than a decade; subsequently he performed at New York's Iridium club until shortly before his death.

Paul's reemergence brought renewed acclaim for his musical and technical achievements. He was elected to the Rock and Roll Hall of Fame in1988. In 1991 Capitol issued a four-CD retrospective covering his years on the label; William Morrow & Company published Mary Alice Shaughnessy's biography *Les Paul: An American Original* in 1992. *Les Paul & Friends: American Made World Played* (Capitol, 2005), showcasing collaborations with electric guitarists (and fans), including Keith Richards, Buddy Guy, Jeff Beck, and Eric Clapton, earned Paul two additional Grammys. In 2008, the Rock and Roll Hall of Fame staged a multiday celebration of his life, featuring a live performance by Paul. He died of a heart attack in August 2009 at age ninety-four.
—*Dave Samuelson*

## Johnny Paycheck
b. Greenfield, Ohio, May 31, 1938; d. February 19, 2003

In 1977 "Take This Job and Shove It" made Johnny Paycheck a country superstar seemingly overnight. Yet by the time that blue-collar anthem hit the airwaves, Paycheck had been through twenty years of career ups and downs. He had worked as a frontman for some of country music's top talents, and he had recorded some of the most vigorous, fascinating HONKY-TONK MUSIC ever produced. He had also cowritten such country classics as "Apartment #9" and "Touch My Heart."

Born Donald Eugene Lytle, he received his first guitar at age six and began entering talent contests by age nine. He left home while still a teenager, traveling throughout Ohio and nearby states before enlisting in the U.S. Navy. Court-martialed in 1956 for slugging a superior officer, he spent two years in military prison.

*Johnny Paycheck*

Upon his release he took to the highway again, eventually landing in Nashville.

Adopting the professional name Donny Young, he signed as a songwriter with TREE PUBLISHING and as a singer with DECCA RECORDS. He also began a succession of jobs as bass player, frontman, and harmony vocalist for such stars as GEORGE JONES, PORTER WAGONER, FARON YOUNG, and RAY PRICE, and he recorded for MERCURY in 1962. The aspiring artist then came to the attention of industry veteran Aubrey Mayhew, who managed his career, changed his name to Johnny Paycheck, and recorded him for Hilltop Records in New York. The label released Paycheck's first Top Thirty country single, "A-11," in 1965.

Early in 1966 Paycheck and Mayhew started LITTLE DARLIN' RECORDS and moved their operations to Nashville. Paycheck's Little Darlin' catalog stands as one of the most musically audacious of its era, typified by such hits as "The Lovin' Machine" and such nonhits as "(Pardon Me) I've Got Someone to Kill." Unfortunately, Paycheck's health and personal well-being were in decline throughout this same period. By 1970 he and Mayhew had fallen out, and Paycheck had been reduced to living on skid row in Los Angeles.

Tracked down by industry insider Nick Hunter, Paycheck moved to Denver to dry out and eventually hooked up with producer-executive BILLY SHERRILL, who signed him to EPIC RECORDS. In 1971 Paycheck's Epic debut, a cover of the Freddie North R&B classic "She's All I Got," became a #2 country hit and was nominated for a Grammy. Paycheck stayed with Epic into 1982, marketed first as a love balladeer and later as a so-called OUTLAW.

Along the way he scored such memorable hits as "Someone to Give My Love To"; "Slide Off of Your Satin Sheets"; and his career record, "Take This Job and Shove It."

Paycheck's personal life remained tumultuous, however. He had drug problems and legal problems, and on December 19, 1985, he shot a man (not fatally) during a barroom confrontation in Hillsboro, Ohio. Sent to prison in February 1989, he was released in 1991. Completely straight, he picked up the pieces of his career and resumed performing, and he became a member of the GRAND OLE OPRY in November 1997. He died in 2003 after a long illness. The following year, a multiartist tribute album appeared on SUGAR HILL RECORDS. —*Daniel Cooper*

## Leon Payne
b. Alba, Texas, June 15, 1917; d. September 11, 1969

Leon Payne's reputation as a leading country songwriter has generally obscured his considerable talents as a vocalist. After graduating from the State School for the Blind in Austin, Texas, in 1935, Payne became a country singer, and by 1941 he was broadcasting over WRR in Dallas. He recorded for BLUEBIRD that April as a solo artist and as a guest vocalist with Bill Boyd's seminal WESTERN SWING band, the Cowboy Ramblers (see BILL AND JIM BOYD). In 1947, while living in Mineola, Texas, Payne recorded for Nashville's BULLET label (with brother-in-law Jack Rhodes's band), and his first release, "Lifetime to Regret," became a hit that eventually (1949) earned him a contract with CAPITOL RECORDS. The hit also brought his writing skills to the attention of other artists, and his stature increased when HANK WILLIAMS recorded his "Lost Highway" (1949) and "They'll Never Take Her Love from Me" (1950).

Payne's smooth tenor voice and finely crafted compositions, which numbered in the hundreds by the late 1940s, made him a popular regional performer. Based in Houston from 1948 to 1952, he moved to San Antonio, where he remained until his death. He also appeared regularly on the *LOUISIANA HAYRIDE* and the GRAND OLE OPRY.

Payne, who sometimes played electric lead guitar and trombone in addition to rhythm guitar, followed his stint at Capitol with stays at DECCA, STARDAY (where he tackled rock & roll under the pseudonym Rock Rogers), and several smaller labels. In 1968 EDDIE NOACK recorded Payne's stark and disturbing murder ballad "Psycho," which has since become a cult classic. "I Love You Because," though, is Payne's most universally admired song. Written for his wife, Myrtie, the number was a hit for Payne himself in 1949 and has since entered the repertoire of virtually everyone who has ever tried to sing a country song, including ELVIS PRESLEY. —*Bill C. Malone*

## Rufus Payne (*see* Tee-Tot, Hank Williams)

## Minnie Pearl
b. Centerville, Tennessee, October 25, 1912; d. March 4, 1996

Minnie Pearl was the undisputed queen of country comedy, known for her hopelessly styleless knee-length country dresses, her straw hat decorated with colorful plastic flowers and $1.98 price tag, and her cheerful shout of "How-dee! I'm just so proud to be here!" For fifty years she performed as a member of the GRAND OLE OPRY.

*Minnie Pearl*

She was born Sarah Ophelia Colley, the youngest of five daughters of a prosperous lumber magnate and his homemaker wife, who lost their fortune in the Great Depression. An aspiring actress, twenty-two-year-old Ophelia (as she was then called) settled for a job as an itinerant community theater director for the Wayne P. Sewell Producing Company, traveling to southern country towns and staging plays owned by the firm. While on the road in northern Alabama she met an elderly woman whose amusing country talk and mannerisms inspired Ophelia Colley to create a comic character eventually known as Minnie Pearl.

In April 1939 Colley made her first professional appearance as Minnie Pearl at a women's club function at the Highland Park Hotel in Aiken, South Carolina. In the fall of 1940 a performance at a banker's convention in Centerville brought her to the attention of WSM executives in Nashville. On November 30, 1940, she made her debut on the Grand Ole Opry. Less than a week later, more than 300 cards, telegrams, and letters addressed to Minnie Pearl flooded the WSM offices. On December 7, 1940, the name Minnie Pearl appeared among the Opry cast listing for the first time in the weekly radio guide of the Nashville *Tennessean*, slotted in the 8:45 p.m. segment.

With the help of her sister Virginia and coaching from the Opry's GEORGE D. HAY, Colley gradually developed a fully fledged comedic character and jokes to go with it. Minnie Pearl became the quintessential small-town spinster, preoccupied with chasing men and gossiping about her family and neighbors in the mythical town of Grinder's Switch—Brother, Uncle Nabob, and sometime-boyfriend Hezzie. In the spring of 1942 she graduated into the elite cast of the *Prince Albert Show*, the half hour of the Opry broadcast over the NBC radio network. Soon she added a distinctive new touch to her act: the big "How-DEE!" At the request of the William Esty advertising agency, which had the sponsor's account, she went from a wallflower's shy "Howdy" to a shouted "How-DEE!" that called for an audience response. It quickly became one of her trademarks.

On February 23, 1947, she married Henry Cannon (b. Franklin, Tennessee, August 11, 1917; d. November 7, 1997), a former Army Air Corps pilot and a partner in the charter airplane service Capitol Airways. Before long, he left Capitol Airways and set up his own charter service specializing in the country music business, flying a Beechcraft single-engine plane. Clients included EDDY ARNOLD and his then-manager TOM PARKER, HANK WILLIAMS, CARL SMITH, WEBB PIERCE, and eventually ELVIS PRESLEY. Client number one was Minnie Pearl, who soon became known in Nashville society circles as Sarah Cannon. Henry Cannon became her manager as well.

From 1948 to 1958 Minnie worked the Grand Ole Opry with veteran comedian ROD BRASFIELD, performing double comedy, meaning that neither one always played the straight man. Depending on how they felt, one or the other might take the punch line. Their partnership ended with Brasfield's death in 1958.

Following a May 1, 1957, appearance on NBC-TV's top-rated *This Is Your Life,* hosted by Ralph Edwards, Minnie Pearl began making many more appearances on NBC-TV shows hosted by TENNESSEE ERNIE FORD and Dinah Shore as well as *The Tonight Show.* In the 1960s she branched out to *The Carol Burnett Show* and *The Jonathan Winters Show,* whose producer, Sam Lovullo, recruited her for *HEE HAW's* cast in 1969. There she reached a wider audience than ever in her various continuing roles as a teacher in a one-room schoolhouse, a house mother in a girls' dormitory, editor of the *Grinder's Switch Gazette,* and the tough-to-get-along-with passenger in the "Driving Miss Minnie" segments. In the 1980s she began appearing each Friday night on TNN's *NASHVILLE NOW,* joking with host RALPH EMERY for the "Let Minnie Steal Your Joke" segment. She continued to play the Grand Ole Opry as well, frequently teaming in later years with ROY ACUFF.

In her entire career, she had a half dozen albums and about twice as many singles scattered among the BULLET, KING, RCA, Everest, and STARDAY labels. Most of her records were monologs. When she did sing, she exaggerated the flaws in her voice. She had only one hit, "Giddyup Go—Answer," a maudlin recitation that "answered" a similarly maudlin recitation by RED SOVINE. It did not reflect her comedic style, though it became a #10 hit in 1966.

After surviving breast cancer in 1990, she lent her name to Nashville's Sarah Cannon Cancer Center and Sarah Cannon Research Institute.

She performed her last show in Joliet, Illinois, on June 15, 1991; two days later she suffered a stroke that left her virtually bedridden in a Nashville nursing home for close to five years. When she died following a final series of strokes in 1996, all of Nashville, and indeed the world, mourned her passing. —*Paul Kingsbury*

## Pedal Steel Guitar

For more than seventy years, pedal steel guitar has been identified with country music. In 1939 Alvino Rey, a pop steel player, teamed with machinist John Moore to design a new type of electric steel guitar—one different from the nonpedal, solid-bodied, "lap" steels that had been popular for nearly a decade. The Gibson Guitar Company introduced this model as the "Electraharp," its pedals and mechanical system able to alter string pitches to create smoothly voiced and modulated chords.

The first country musician to explore the pedal steel was California-based SPEEDY WEST, who approached patternmaker Paul Bigsby to build a three-neck, four-pedal model that West acquired in February 1948. West first recorded with this instrument on Eddie Kirk's 1949 rendition of "Candy Kisses." From 1950 through 1956 West played on hundreds of country and pop recordings. BUD ISAACS, another Bigsby customer, pioneered the instrument in Nashville, and his solo on WEBB PIERCE's "Slowly" (#1, 1954) inspired steel guitarists nationwide to acquire pedal steels or to adapt their nonpedal instruments to alter string pitches with homemade mechanisms.

In 1955 BUDDY EMMONS, who played a Bigsby pedal steel in LITTLE JIMMY DICKENS's band and later worked sessions with many artists, joined SHOT JACKSON to build the first Sho-Bud pedal guitar. Fender began making pedal steels in 1957, designed with assistance from Speedy West. Sho-Bud models, however, became an early favorite among country players due to their quality and the company's Nashville roots. Pedal steel designs gradually stabilized (though many players had their own variations). Most had two eight-string necks, four or more pedals, and two or three knee levers. Many players tuned one neck to E9 for commercial country accompaniment and one to C6 for WESTERN SWING or jazz.

In Nashville other pedal steel greats emerged, including PETE DRAKE, skilled at playing commercial accompaniment behind singers. Others have included LLOYD GREEN, HAL RUGG, WELDON MYRICK, JOHN HUGHEY, Buddy Charleton, CURLY CHALKER, Doug Jernigan, and SONNY GARRISH. In California, RALPH MOONEY, renowned for his work with WYNN STEWART, BUCK OWENS, and MERLE HAGGARD, epitomized the high-pitched BAKERSFIELD style, later employing it with WAYLON JENNINGS. Other important West Coast players include TOM BRUMLEY and JAY DEE MANESS. Current Nashville session players include PAUL FRANKLIN, Tommy White, Mike Johnson, Bruce Bouton, and Dan Dugmore. Maness and Greg Leisz are today's first-call L.A. steel men.

Many companies have manufactured steels, including MSA, launched by Texas player Maurice Anderson; Franklin; Zumsteel; Sho-Pro; and Emmons, founded by Buddy Emmons after he and Shot Jackson dissolved their partnership. The Emmons model set the benchmark for pedal steel makers, just as Emmons became the world's foremost pedal steel guitarist. —*Rich Kienzle*

## Herb Pedersen
b. Berkeley, California, April 27, 1944

As a studio musician, banjo player, and harmony singer, multi-instrumentalist Herb Pedersen played a leading role in the evolution of COUNTRY-ROCK in the 1970s and 1980s. Pedersen honed his musical skills on the San Francisco Bay Area BLUEGRASS circuit. After a short Nashville stint in the early 1960s, he returned to California in 1963, joining DAVID GRISMAN in the Smokey Grass Boys. In 1964 he joined VERN GOSDIN and brother Ray Gosdin to play banjo. When EARL SCRUGGS had hip surgery in 1967, he asked Pedersen to take his place on road bookings. Pedersen recorded two influential albums with THE DILLARDS, *Wheatstraw Suite* (1968) and *Copperfields* (1970), having replaced Doug Dillard on banjo.

Pedersen made two albums of his own for EPIC RECORDS: *Southwest* (1975) and *Sandman* (1976). Meanwhile, as a studio musician, he worked with EMMYLOU HARRIS, LINDA RONSTADT, the Flying Burrito Brothers, GRAM PARSONS, JOHN PRINE, KRIS KRISTOFFERSON, and the Doobie Brothers.

In the mid-1980s Pedersen formed the DESERT ROSE BAND with longtime friend CHRIS HILLMAN and guitarist JOHN JORGENSON and recorded seven Top Ten hits for MCA/CURB. After disbanding in 1993, Pedersen returned to bluegrass in 1995, organizing the Laurel Canyon Ramblers with former Kentucky Colonels member Billy Ray Lathum. Subsequent projects have included several albums with Hillman and *Old & In the Gray* (Acoustic Disc, 2002), which reunited musicians who recorded the landmark 1975 bluegrass album *Old & In the Way*; on the 2002 album, Pedersen replaced the deceased Jerry Garcia. Today, Pedersen continues to make personal appearances and work studio sessions. —*Chris Skinker*

## Hap Peebles
b. Anthony, Kansas, January 4, 1913; d. January 8, 1993

Hap Peebles set high standards for show promoters during the 1950s and 1960s. His accomplishments helped country music weather the rock & roll crisis and paved the way for its later success.

The Dean of Country Music Promoters was born Harry Alexander Peebles and raised in Anthony, Kansas. In 1931, while working as a newspaper reporter for the *Anthony Republican*, he began to bring shows and sporting events to the town's new auditorium. Peebles expanded into booking major country acts in 1945, and for a time he managed BOB WILLS. A leader in providing country music to state and local fairs, Peebles founded the Harry Peebles Agency in Wichita and became the Midwest's most important country promoter. Moreover, he was one of the first to pair country and rock & roll acts on the same bill. A founder of CMA, he also helped organize the International Country Music Talent Buyers Association in 1971 and served as its first president. Peebles received numerous awards and honors over the years, including CMA's first Talent Buyer and Promoter of the Year award. —*Don Roy*

## Ralph Peer
b. Kansas City, Missouri, May 22, 1892; d. January 19, 1960

Ralph Sylvester Peer was the most prominent early businessman in country music. Moreover, his impact on the larger popular music industry—as a pioneer in recording, music publishing, and artist management—is incalculable. Among the country music figures he steered to success are JIMMIE RODGERS and the CARTER FAMILY, both of whom Peer discovered, recorded, and managed.

Peer was born in 1892 in Kansas City, Missouri. His father, a store owner in the Kansas City suburb of Independence, Missouri, sold records and gramophones, among other wares. At age eighteen Peer joined the COLUMBIA Phonograph Company. In 1919 New York's OKEH RECORDS hired him to assist company production director Fred Hagar. Neither the country music nor "race music" industries yet existed. According to Peer, OKeh's records were manufactured by a button company. "The business then was vocalists making records of 'Silver Threads Among the Gold' and 'Home Sweet Home,'" Peer said in 1959 in one of several interviews with Lillian Borgeson (the tapes, from which all subsequent quotes have been taken with permission, are held at the Southern Folklife Collection of the University of North Carolina, Chapel Hill).

The first moneymaking country record, FIDDLIN' JOHN CARSON's "The Little Old Log Cabin in the Lane" b/w "The Old

*Ralph Peer*

Hen Cackled and the Rooster's Going to Crow," was an accidental success, as was the first race music best-seller three years earlier (Hagar and Peer's production of Mamie Smith's "Crazy Blues"). In June 1923 Peer traveled to Atlanta, looking for a rival to Columbia's race music star, Bessie Smith. (FIELD RECORDING, then a major method of obtaining hillbilly and race material, was a Peer innovation.) Associates persuaded Peer to record Carson, whose music he considered "terrible," but he quickly capitalized on Carson's unexpected sales and recorded a flood of music by THE HILL BILLIES, ERNEST V. STONEMAN, VERNON DALHART, and other first-generation country stars. Peer claimed to have supplied country music with the name it wore until after World War II— "hillbilly." He took credit, too, for the industry's use of the name "race music."

Peer resigned from OKeh in 1925. In 1926 he approached the Victor Talking Machine Company's Victor label, then eager to expand its hillbilly business, with a novel plan. "This was a business of recording new copyrights," he recalled. "I would be willing to go to work for nothing, with the understanding that there would be no objection if I controlled these copyrights." It was a new way of running the record business, of infusing it with a built-in artistic dynamism. "I insisted on new material," said Peer. "I wouldn't let [artists] record the old stuff, like 'Home Sweet Home.' Painful experience had shown us it just wouldn't sell."

The first stop on Peer's midsummer 1927 recording trip for Victor was BRISTOL, TENNESSEE-VIRGINIA, a small southern Appalachian city. Jimmie Rodgers, a semiprofessional singer—of blues, primarily—turned up during the last days of the two-week session. Peer later said (inaccurately) that Rodgers "only knew, I think, two chords, on guitar," but he shrewdly perceived that Rodgers "was an individualist; he had his own style." Peer also responded eagerly to the Carter Family and took charge of both acts' careers. Peer managed Rodgers until his death in 1933.

Even though hillbilly and race music brought him success, Peer allowed, "I was always trying to get away from hillbilly and into the legitimate music field." By the 1930s he was publishing songs by Hoagy Carmichael, Johnny Mercer, and jazz composer-arranger Don Redman. Peer explained that he was unconsciously attempting "to take the profits out of the hillbilly and race business and spend that money trying to get established as a pop publisher." He'd founded Southern Music Publishing Company with $1,000 in 1928 and quickly sold it to Victor. Buying it back in 1932, he remained Southern's sole owner until he died.

During and after the Depression he founded a half-dozen branches overseas and started a classical music arm, Serious Music. He claimed to have conceived the idea of a rival publishers' group to ASCAP five years before BMI came into being in 1940; when it did, Peer founded Peer International, a BMI affiliate, as a companion firm to ASCAP-affiliated Southern Music. At Peer's death Peer International was the nation's biggest BMI publisher; Southern was among ASCAP's Top Twenty.

Peer died in Hollywood, California, in 1960 and was elected to The Country Music Hall of Fame in 1984. Today his company is known as peermusic, managed by his son, Ralph Peer II. —Tony Scherman

## Vito Pellettieri
b. Nashville, Tennessee, November 30, 1889; d. April 14, 1977

To Grand Ole Opry performers, Vito Pellettieri's name was synonymous with the show for nearly thirty years. As a stage manager and father figure, he became a source of stability and continuity for entertainers and staff alike.

Well before he graduated from high school, he began a twenty-eight-year career as a bandleader, playing dances and parties throughout much of the Southeast, Midwest, and Southwest. A grueling schedule led to a nervous breakdown in 1921, but after recovering he formed another band with his wife, Kathryn, and began to work at Nashville radio stations WCBQ, WLAC, and WSM.

Early in the 1930s, following Pellettieri's second nervous breakdown, WSM station manager Harry Stone hired him as music librarian; in this role he maintained the files of sheet music used by WSM performers, helped work out musical arrangements, kept logbooks of WSM programs, and verified that all songs broadcast were covered under performance rights licenses. In 1934 Stone assigned him to assist George D. Hay with the Grand Ole Opry, and Pellettieri reluctantly complied. "The performers would come anytime during the evening, do four numbers, and then leave," he recalled. "Some showed up drunk, and some wouldn't even come at all." To bring order out of chaos, Pellettieri brought unruly musicians in line and scheduled them for distinct Opry segments that Stone began to sell to advertisers. Today the Opry retains essentially the same format that Pellettieri helped to shape in the mid-1930s. —John W. Rumble

## Hank Penny
b. Birmingham, Alabama, September 18, 1918; d. April 17, 1992

As a bandleader, guitarist, and singer, Herbert Clayton "Hank" Penny was an early exponent of western swing. Though based initially in the Southeast, Penny freely admitted to the southwestern influence of Milton Brown and Bob Wills, apparent from Penny's earliest recordings.

He first worked professionally in 1936 as a member of "Happy" Hal Burns & His Tune Wranglers. Penny recognized the importance

of high-quality musicianship, and in forming his own group he surrounded himself with top-notch players. In 1937 he organized his own band, the Radio Cowboys. In 1938 Penny and his group signed with Atlanta radio station WSB, where their music gained national attention. With the addition in 1939 of two highly skilled performers, Noel Boggs (steel guitar) and Boudleaux Bryant (fiddle), the music of the Radio Cowboys measured up to the lofty standards Wills and Brown had set for western swing.

Penny first recorded for the American Record Corporation in 1938, and in 1939 he recorded "Won't You Ride in My Little Red Wagon," a Rex Griffin song that became a Penny trademark. In the early 1940s, Penny moved on to Cincinnati, Ohio, where he formed the Plantation Boys, appeared on the Boone County Jamboree/Midwestern Hayride, and began recording for the King label. In 1945 Penny departed for Los Angeles, forming a group as part of Foreman Phillips's organization. Following the war, he fronted several more bands, made appearances in a number of western movies, and contributed comedy to the Dude Martin and Spade Cooley bands. In the 1950s Penny recorded for the RCA Victor and Decca labels. Penny also opened the Palomino Club in North Hollywood, California, a showcase for country music for some thirty years. Among his five wives were notable entertainers Sue Thompson and Shari Nona. —Ken Griffis

## Carl Perkins
b. Tiptonville, Tennessee, April 9, 1932; d. January 19, 1998

A great Sun Records star, guitarist, singer, and songwriter Carl Lee Perkins personified rockabilly with his first big hit, "Blue Suede Shoes." Its whiplash guitar, stop-and-start beats, and teen lingo made it a crossover smash (#1 country, #2 pop) for Perkins in 1956; Elvis Presley recorded the song shortly after Perkins (Perkins's version entered Billboard's pop chart on March 3; Presley's, on April 7). Pee Wee King's band also cut a version that spring.

*Carl Perkins*

As with many of Sun's rockabilly acts, Perkins's childhood musical influences were a mixture of the hillbilly music he heard on the radio (especially GRAND OLE OPRY broadcasts) and the blues he heard from black sharecroppers while working in the fields himself. With older brother Clayton (on bass) and younger brother Jay (on guitar), he formed the Perkins Brothers, who focused on uptempo HONKY-TONK MUSIC.

Perkins first approached Sun Records in October 1954 after hearing Presley on the radio and identifying a kindred spirit. Perkins's first single, "Movie Magg" b/w "Turn Around," recorded in October 1954 (and released on Flip, a Sun subsidiary), showcased his range: a sprightly hillbilly number on the A side, a HANK WILLIAMS–derived honky-tonk weeper on the B side.

Throughout 1955 Perkins and his band, anchored by W. S. Holland on drums, performed frequently and developed new material. That December he recorded his third single, "Blue Suede Shoes" b/w "Honey Don't," which made him a star. He continued to record strong material for Sun, such as "Boppin' the Blues" and "Dixie Fried," archetypal rockabilly performances that were both country Top Tens. These and other hits spread his influence; together with Scotty Moore, Presley's guitar player, Perkins helped define rockabilly guitar.

On March 21, 1956, en route to a taping of *The Perry Como Show* in New York, the Chrysler Imperial carrying Perkins and his band collided with a poultry truck outside Dover, Delaware. The mishap killed the truck driver and sent all three Perkins brothers to the hospital. One month later, Perkins fulfilled his *Como Show* engagement.

Perkins recorded for Sun until December 1957; by then he had become disenchanted with the label as he perceived resources and attention being lavished on JOHNNY CASH and JERRY LEE LEWIS (who started at Sun supporting Perkins on "Matchbox"). Also, the pop market was turning toward sounds more uptown than those provided by Perkins's voice and music.

Perkins followed Cash to COLUMBIA in early 1958, but he recorded few songs of the quality of his Sun sides. He landed at DECCA in 1963 for a brief time, the high point being the fiery rocker "Big Bad Blues." Perkins recorded "Big Bad Blues" in London on May 22, 1964, with the Nashville Teens; during his London stay he met the Beatles and attended their recording of "Matchbox," the first of several Beatles covers of his songs.

Perkins's recordings in the 1960s and 1970s were infrequent, characterized by "event" sets, such as his collaboration with NRBQ. From 1965 to 1975 Perkins performed as part of Johnny Cash's road show and supplied the Man in Black with "Daddy Sang Bass" (#1, 1968). Through the 1980s Perkins was involved in many retrospective projects, among them a 1985 cable TV special in which he was supported by high-profile disciples such as George Harrison and Eric Clapton, and *Class of '55* (America/ Smash, 1986), an album with Cash, Lewis, and ROY ORBISON. At the same time, his songs were frequently covered by popular country performers such as THE JUDDS.

Perkins continued to record into the 1990s, having been elected to the Rock and Roll Hall of Fame in 1987. He died in 1998 of complications resulting from a series of strokes. —*Jimmy Guterman*

## Ben Peters
b. Greenville, Mississippi, June 20, 1933; d. May 25, 2005

Nashville-based songwriter Ben Peters crafted some of the biggest crossover hits of the 1970s, including FREDDY FENDER's "Before the Next Teardrop Falls." His songs have been recorded by artists as diverse as RAY CHARLES, Dean Martin, and ALAN JACKSON.

Born into poverty in the Mississippi Delta, Peters left home in his early teens to play in bands. After attending the University of Southern Mississippi and serving in the U.S. Navy, he moved to Nashville in 1966 and recorded several singles for LIBERTY and CAPITOL before concentrating solely on songwriting. In 1967, EDDY ARNOLD's recording of "Turn the World Around" gave Peters his first #1 hit. In 1971 "Kiss an Angel Good Mornin'" became the first of numerous hits Peters wrote for CHARLEY PRIDE, and it netted the tunesmith a Grammy for Best Country Song.

Although written in 1967 and recorded numerous times, major hit status eluded the Ben Peters–Vivian Keith composition "Before the Next Teardrop Falls" until 1975, when Freddy Fender's version topped the country and pop charts. Other #1 hits composed by Peters include JOHNNY RODRIGUEZ's "Love Put a Song in My Heart" (1975) and KENNY ROGERS's "Daytime Friends" (1977). Peters was inducted into the NASHVILLE SONGWRITERS HALL OF FAME in 1980. —*Mick Buck*

## Philip Morris Country Music Show
established January 1957; ended April 1958

Conceived as a promotional vehicle for the Philip Morris Tobacco Company, the Philip Morris Country Music Show provided a great boost to country music's popularity in 1957–58, when television and rock & roll were threatening country touring.

In 1956 Philip Morris approached JIM DENNY, formerly head of the GRAND OLE OPRY's booking department and now head of his own agency, with the concept of a Philip Morris– sponsored free road show featuring country's top acts. The extravaganza was to bring country music to southeastern audiences, with stars traveling in a bus provided and equipped by Philip Morris.

When Denny left the Opry in September 1956 (amid controversy relating to his outside interests, including concert promotion) and formed the Jim Denny Artists Bureau, Philip Morris decided to continue dealing with Denny and contracted with his bureau to provide the talent for the troupe. When the deal was announced in December 1956 it was called "the largest individual package sale in country music history."

The Philip Morris Country Music Show premiered in Richmond, Virginia, in January 1957 and then moved on to capacity houses in West Virginia, Kentucky, Tennessee, Mississippi, and Louisiana. The cast for the initial series of concerts included CARL SMITH, GOLDIE HILL, RED SOVINE, Ronnie Self, GORDON TERRY, Bun Wilson, and Carl Smith's band, the Tunesmiths. The lineup eventually included more than twenty top country music names.

Originally designed as a thirteen-week southeastern tour, the show expanded into a sixteen-month traveling country music festival that played before 4 million people coast-to-coast. It also spun off a weekly CBS network radio program, which debuted in October 1957.

The Philip Morris Country Music Show's impact on country music over that sixteen-month period was significant. The troupe brought country into new areas and played before many individuals who had not yet experienced the music. In addition to free concerts and radio broadcasts, artists gave special performances at veterans' hospitals, military bases, and industrial sites. The tour concluded in April 1958. —*Al Cunniff*

## Bill Phillips
b. Canton, North Carolina, January 28, 1938; d. August 23, 2010

Bill Clarence Phillips enjoyed his greatest success as a country performer during the mid-1960s. His best-known recording, "Put It Off Until Tomorrow," is remembered not only for his performance of the song, but also for the role it played in DOLLY PARTON's career. Young Parton cowrote the Phillips hit, and she provided the uncredited—but distinctive—vocal harmony on his recording.

Phillips grew up in North Carolina. In high school, he played guitar and sang in local groups around Canton and Asheville. Moving to Miami, he performed on station WMIL's *Ole South Jamboree* as well as on his own television show (1956–57).

In 1957 MEL TILLIS invited Phillips to Nashville, where he signed with CEDARWOOD PUBLISHING and eventually COLUMBIA RECORDS. In 1958 WEBB PIERCE charted with Phillips's "Falling Back to You" (#10). The next year Phillips's own record of "Sawmill" went to #27. He shifted to DECCA RECORDS and reached the Top Ten twice in 1966 with songs written by Parton and her uncle Bill Owens. The first was "Put It Off Until Tomorrow" (#6); the second, "The Company You Keep" (#8).

Phillips appeared on syndicated television shows fronted by BILL ANDERSON, PORTER WAGONER, and the WILBURN BROTHERS, and he was a regular on the KITTY WELLS–Johnny Wright Family Show, with which Phillips toured for many years.

In addition to some minor movie roles (*Road to Nashville, Second Fiddle to a Steel Guitar, The Sugarland Express*), Phillips was a guest on Parton's *Dolly* TV show in 1988. —*Steve Eng*

## Foreman Phillips
Birthplace unknown; b. August 20, 1897; d. April 15, 1968

Disc jockey, personal manager, and show promoter Bert "Foreman" Phillips was a major figure on the California country music scene between 1942 and 1952. Serving the vast audience that had migrated from the Dust Bowl of the Southwest to the humming wartime factories of Southern California, Phillips assembled a stable of talent, including SPADE COOLEY, JIMMY WAKELY, and TEX WILLIAMS. Together with top names from the GRAND OLE OPRY and other country radio shows, these locally based acts held forth at Phillips's legendary war-era "swing shift" dances staged at the Venice Pier Ballroom, beginning in the summer of 1942, between and concurrently at other nearby venues, such as the Santa Monica Ballroom, the Town Hall Ballroom in Compton, and the Plantation in Culver City. These all-night affairs routinely drew such huge crowds (an average of 5,000 to 7,000 people per show) that a *Time* magazine correspondent attending a Cooley dance worried that the pier itself would collapse.

Hailing from Texas, Phillips began his career as a radio ad salesman and in the early 1940s became a popular country DJ at KRKD in Los Angeles with his *Western Hit Parade* program. Later broadcasting over KXLA, he continued on radio into the 1950s. By the early 1950s Phillips was producing his own weekday KABK-TV program, the *Foreman Phillips Show*—hosted by WESLEY TUTTLE and Tuttle's wife, Marilyn. Phillips continued to promote dances as late as 1956, but he never again attained the spectacular success he enjoyed with his wartime dance extravaganzas. Eventually he retired to northern California. —*Jonny Whiteside*

## Sam Phillips
b. Florence, Alabama, January 5, 1923; d. July 30, 2003

One of American music's most important nonperformers, producer Samuel Cornelius Phillips founded SUN RECORDS and introduced the world to JOHNNY CASH, Howlin' Wolf, B. B. King, JERRY LEE LEWIS, ROY ORBISON, CARL PERKINS, ELVIS PRESLEY, CHARLIE RICH, and many others. In so doing, he strongly influenced many of the directions popular music has taken through the years in the wake of those artists' inspired work.

A blues fan from the Florence–Muscle Shoals region of Alabama, Phillips became involved in radio when he was young and wound up at WREC in Memphis in 1945. In October 1949 he decided to supplement his income as a WREC disc jockey and leased a building at 706 Union Avenue, where he would open his Memphis Recording Service studio. From the beginning, in January 1950, he balanced creative concerns with the need to cover the $150 monthly rent, so early on he focused on for-hire recording rather than the untamed music he loved.

Phillips tired of the wedding and bar mitzvah circuit and began documenting the city's rough-and-tumble blues scene. In August 1950 he started the short-lived Phillips label, but he soon found a calling in recording blues performers and turning the masters over to R&B labels such as RPM and Chess. Phillips often had to stop these artists from trying to smooth their sounds for white producers, insisting—as he did throughout his career—that direct, unfussy presentation was all that mattered. After Howlin' Wolf moved to Chicago, where he would record directly for Chess, Phillips began another label, Sun Records, and scored many regional and national R&B hits with the likes of Rufus Thomas and Little Junior's Blue Flames.

By early 1954 Phillips was delivering his message of straightforward, soulful performance to country artists as well as blues

*Sam Phillips*

singers, and he helped develop ROCKABILLY out of this country-blues mix. For Phillips, wild rockabilly and straight-ahead country were part of the same continuum; in either category, he wanted to establish a mood the second a song began and then for it to intensify and ignite.

His method reached its apotheosis in 1954 and 1955, when Phillips discovered and shepherded Elvis Presley. Phillips sold Presley's contract to RCA in 1955 for a reported $35,000, which he used to sustain a label whose cash flow was never as solid as its musical grounding. By the early 1960s Phillips supervised fewer and fewer of Sun's day-to-day recordings and made a fortune as an early investor in the Holiday Inn hotel chain. On July 1, 1969, he sold the Sun label to SHELBY SINGLETON and effectively retired, resurfacing only for rare public appearances and production assignments (he assisted on the 1979 JOHN PRINE album *Pink Cadillac* because his sons Knox and Jerry Phillips were producing it).

As Phillips told journalist David Halberstam, "I have one real gift and that gift is to look another person in the eye and be able to tell if he has anything to contribute, and if he does, I have the additional gift to free him from whatever is restraining him." More than merely creating a sound, Phillips initiated a sensibility.

Phillips was elected to THE COUNTRY MUSIC HALL OF FAME in 2001. —*Jimmy Guterman*

## Stu Phillips
b. Montreal, Quebec, Canada, January 19, 1933

Stu Phillips was a best-selling Canadian recording artist and genial television host for the Canadian Broadcasting Company (CBC) before joining the GRAND OLE OPRY in June 1967. He briefly enjoyed modest success on RCA RECORDS and also hosted the early 1970s syndicated variety show *Music Place*. An American citizen since 1998, he has toured extensively overseas. Today much of his music explores Christian themes; still an Opry performer, he serves as a minister in the Episcopal Church. —*Walt Trott*

## Piano

Pianos have been an integral part of country music from its beginnings. Even when amateur fiddlers, banjoists, and guitarists were playing at dances, piano was often included for its strong, percussive rhythm. During country's early commercial years, RALPH PEER recorded Virginia's Shelor Family String Band, which included piano, at the famous BRISTOL sessions where he first recorded JIMMIE RODGERS and the CARTER FAMILY.

In Texas, jazz piano became an essential part of WESTERN SWING. One of the first musicians MILTON BROWN hired upon forming his Musical Brownies in 1932 was pianist Fred "Papa" Calhoun. Al Stricklin later filled the same role with BOB WILLS & HIS TEXAS PLAYBOYS in Tulsa, while MOON MULLICAN made his name with CLIFF BRUNER's band and other Houston-area swing units. Mullican became the first singer-pianist to become a country star, after signing with KING RECORDS in 1946 and having a major hit with "New Pretty Blonde" in 1947, which led to his joining the GRAND OLE OPRY in 1949 and subsequent hits. On the West Coast, pianists were common in most country and western swing bands. In the early 1950s, San Diego pianist MERRILL MOORE accompanied his own vocals on his country boogie recordings for CAPITOL. In JIM BECK's Dallas studio, pianist

Madge Suttee helped to establish LEFTY FRIZZELL's influential HONKY-TONK sound of the early 1950s.

In Nashville, DEL WOOD's ebullient 1951 ragtime piano instrumental hit "Down Yonder" made her an Opry stalwart. In the early 1950s, veteran pop pianist and bandleader OWEN BRADLEY played on various country records, and publisher FRED ROSE occasionally played the instrument on certain HANK WILLIAMS recordings. Other early Nashville session pianists included local pop musicians MARVIN HUGHES and Papa John Gordy. FLOYD CRAMER, a teenage pianist on the *LOUISIANA HAYRIDE*, later became a Nashville studio musician; in this capacity and on his own recordings, he popularized the slip-note technique developed by songwriter DON ROBERTSON, which featured whole-tone grace notes reminiscent of a PEDAL STEEL GUITAR. It made Cramer as identified with the piano as CHET ATKINS was with the guitar.

JERRY LEE LEWIS's profound effect on country piano, derived from his love of black boogie-woogie and blues, was strong in his early ROCKABILLY days and in his later country career. CHARLIE RICH's piano always reflected the influence of modern jazz. Even such a traditionalist as ROY ACUFF routinely used piano with the Smoky Mountain Boys, while pop-leaning JIM REEVES would cancel shows if his pianist wasn't provided a decent instrument. RONNIE MILSAP, MICKEY GILLEY, GARY STEWART, and PHIL VASSAR have all used piano as their primary accompaniment. Today, electronic keyboards and synthesizers are increasingly used in country recording, yet acoustic piano remains a mainstay. —*Rich Kienzle*

## Pickard Family

One of country music's first professional singing groups and one of the first to appear on national network radio, the Pickard Family was founded by patriarch Obed "Dad" Pickard, a pioneering GRAND OLE OPRY star. Born on July 22, 1874, he became proficient on most stringed instruments as a boy. From 1900 to 1925, he made his home in Ashland City, Tennessee, worked as a traveling salesman, and raised four children: Ruth, Bubb, Charlie, and Ann. In 1926 Obed began working on the Opry as a soloist—dubbed the One-Man Orchestra by MC GEORGE D. HAY—and made his first records for COLUMBIA.

By 1928 Obed brought his family into the act, which auditioned for Henry Ford while visiting Detroit. This led to a forty-week contract with NBC to star in a sort of minstrel show called *The Cabin Door*. A similar job followed the next year, but in 1931, when wife Leila May Pickard became ill, the Pickards returned to Tennessee and to a second stint on the Opry. By 1933 they were off again, to stations in Chicago, Philadelphia, New York, New Orleans, and eventually Mexican BORDER RADIO outlet XERA. Their relatively slim number of recordings, for Plaza, BRUNSWICK, and the AMERICAN RECORD CORPORATION, consisted mostly of familiar folk songs.

In later years the family relocated to California, where Obed appeared on television; after his death in 1954, the family continued to work, even recording an album for Verve. —*Charles Wolfe*

## Kellie Pickler
b. Albemarle, North Carolina, June 28, 1986

North Carolinian Kellie Pickler parlayed a sixth-place finish on the 2006 season of *American Idol* into a recording contract with 19 Recordings/BNA (RCA RECORDS). Known on *Idol* for her southern twang and ditzy charm, she established herself as a successful singer-songwriter.

Raised primarily by her paternal grandparents, Pickler overcame a difficult upbringing—her mother abandoned her at age two, and her father was in and out of prison. The former waitress and beauty pageant hopeful drew on these experiences when writing songs for her debut album, *Small Town Girl*, released in October 2006. The collection contained five songs cowritten by Pickler, including Top Twenty hits "Red High Heels" and "I Wonder," the latter of which addressed her mother's desertion. *Small Town Girl* was certified gold in 2007.

Pickler's self-titled follow-up, released in September 2008, featured five more songs she cowrote. These include the Top Ten hit "Best Days of Your Life," which she penned with TAYLOR SWIFT. —*Tina Wright*

## Pie Plant Pete
b. Ridgeway, Illinois, July 9, 1906; d. February 7, 1988

Claud J. Moye, "Pie Plant Pete," entered show business in 1928 following a successful audition for a spot on the WLS NATIONAL BARN DANCE. He reputedly received his unusual nickname from a WLS announcer who heard him order pie plant pie (better known as rhubarb pie) for dessert in a restaurant. The following Saturday night the announcer introduced him to the *Barn Dance* audience by his new moniker.

Pie Plant Pete sang novelty and mountain songs and played, simultaneously, a guitar and a harmonica suspended in a wire frame. WLS announcers dubbed this combination of instruments a "two-cylinder cob crusher." After leaving WLS, he appeared on radio and television stations in Cleveland, Syracuse, Fort Wayne, Boston, Rochester, Detroit, and other cities. He recorded for GENNETT in the late 1920s and early 1930s, for DECCA and the AMERICAN RECORD CORPORATION in the mid-1930s, and for Process Records in the 1940s. Eventually he left the music business and formed an advertising agency. —*Wayne W. Daniel*

## Don Pierce
b. Ballard, Washington, October 10, 1915; d. April 3, 2005

Neither a musician nor a skilled A&R man, Don Pierce was one of the foremost marketers in country music. After assuming sole control of STARDAY RECORDS in 1958, he showed how music that the major labels ignored (BLUEGRASS, OLD-TIME) could be successfully marketed on LP.

After discharge from the navy in 1945, Donald Frederick Picht bought a stake in FOUR STAR RECORDS and rose to the position of sales manager. During that time he learned much about country music, and, after leaving Four Star in 1953, he joined the fledgling Starday label. As the only full-time partner, he was made president, and he moved to Nashville in 1957 when Starday was temporarily in partnership with MERCURY.

When Pierce took the helm of Starday in 1958, he reoriented the company toward acts that major labels considered marginal and marketed his catalog on LP using splashily colorful jackets. Utilizing his background in business management, he skillfully exploited the catalog and built his assets to the point that his share of Starday, bought for $333 in 1953, was worth $2 million when he sold it to Lin Broadcasting in 1968. Pierce then became

a successful real estate developer, primarily in Hendersonville, Tennessee. —*Colin Escott*

## Webb Pierce
b. West Monroe, Louisiana, August 8, 1921; d. February 24, 1991

One of the foremost country stars of the 1950s, Webb Pierce garnered thirteen #1 singles in those years—more than any of is illustrious contemporaries. His loud, nasal, high-pitched, and sometimes slightly off-key delivery marked him as one of the music's most distinctive singers in an era of great individualists. A successful investor for much of his life, Pierce spent freely to heighten his image, and he is perhaps as well remembered today for his silver-dollar-studded cars and flashy NUDIE suits as for his hit records.

Born Webb Michael (or Mike) Pierce in West Monroe, Louisiana, five years earlier than his publicists generally claimed, he grew up with the music of JIMMIE RODGERS, GENE AUTRY, regional WESTERN SWING bands, and the bands of his native state. He first sang professionally on KMLB–Monroe, but after a brief army stint during World War II he moved to Shreveport in 1944 and did early-morning shows on KTBS. For six years he worked for Shreveport's Sears, Roebuck store in the men's furnishings department while striving for a break in his singing career. Finally he moved to Shreveport's 50,000-watt KWKH and its Saturday night barn dance, the *LOUISIANA HAYRIDE*. Building a band with FLOYD CRAMER (piano), TILLMAN FRANKS (manager and bass), JIMMY DAY (steel guitar), Teddy and Doyle Wilburn (see WILBURN BROTHERS), and FARON YOUNG (guitars, extra vocalists), and Tex Grimsley (fiddle), Pierce soon became the show's hottest act.

With *Hayride* producer Horace Logan, Pierce formed Pacemaker Records, which featured several *Hayride* acts in addition to Pierce himself, who was also recording for California's FOUR STAR RECORDS. In late 1951 Pierce moved up to DECCA;

*Webb Pierce*

he scored his first big hit in 1952 with a version of the 1937 CAJUN favorite "Wondering," thus inspiring his nickname and band name, the Wondering Boy(s).

Following with two more #1s, "That Heart Belongs to Me" and BILLY WALLACE's HONKY-TONK anthem "Back Street Affair," Pierce joined the GRAND OLE OPRY in mid-1952. "It's Been So Long" and "There Stands the Glass" (the latter banned in some radio markets), both 1953 hits, established him as country's leading honky-tonk star in the wake of HANK WILLIAMS's death. Through 1955 Pierce consistently topped the charts with "Slowly" (featuring BUD ISAACS's pioneering PEDAL STEEL GUITAR work), "Even Tho," "More and More," "In the Jailhouse Now," "I Don't Care," "Love, Love, Love," and "Why Baby Why." By mid-decade Pierce's concert fee had risen to $1,250 per show, and advance orders for his new singles often reached 200,000 copies.

Pierce closely allied himself with Opry executive JIM DENNY, jointly launching CEDARWOOD MUSIC in 1953 and later buying radio stations. But after September 1956, when WSM fired Denny because these and other outside interests conflicted with his Opry role, Pierce soon left, too. Confident that he had outgrown the program, he was eager to work lucrative Saturday-night concerts instead of working Opry spots for union scale. Already he had been featured regularly on ABC-TV's OZARK JUBILEE out of Springfield, Missouri, and on syndicated television shows produced by AL GANNAWAY. Though the rock & roll tide of 1956–59 slowed his record success, Pierce drew on Cedarwood's growing stable of talented songwriters (DANNY DILL, WAYNE WALKER, MARIJOHN WILKIN, and especially MEL TILLIS), and in the late 1950s he recorded the memorable hits "I'm Tired," "Honky Tonk Song," "Tupelo County Jail," and "I Ain't Never" (all by Tillis).

After "Honky Tonk Song" (#1, 1957), Pierce gained Top Ten records until 1964. But he had no more #1s, even though he charted regularly into 1972. Shortly thereafter he left Decca/MCA, and recorded in the mid-1970s for SHELBY SINGLETON's Plantation Records. By then Pierce was better known for his expensive home and its guitar-shaped swimming pool—a regular stop on bus tours of Nashville—than for new hit records, and soon privacy-loving neighbors went to court and put an end to these intrusions.

In the 1980s WILLIE NELSON asked Pierce to sing with him on a remake of "In the Jailhouse Now" (1982). It was Pierce's ninety-sixth and last charted record, although young traditionalist RICKY SKAGGS revived two Pierce hits in that decade: "I Don't Care" (1982) and "I'm Tired" (1987).

Pierce died of pancreatic cancer on February 24, 1991. Posthumous reissues and a multiartist tribute album, *Caught in the Webb* (Audium/Koch, 2002), have somewhat revived his reputation, and even those irritated by his often-abrasive personality recognize his substantial commercial achievements.

Pierce was elected to THE COUNTRY MUSIC HALL OF FAME in 2001. —*Ronnie Pugh*

## Ray Pillow

b. Lynchburg, Virginia, July 4, 1937

Ray Pillow's dark good looks, outgoing personality, and pleasing baritone marked him as a real comer in the business during the mid-1960s. He had a CAPITOL RECORDS contract (signed 1963), tour sponsorship from MARTHA WHITE FLOUR, and a moderately successful single, "Thank You Ma'am" (#17), to welcome in the 1966 New Year. Soon a hit duet with JEAN SHEPARD, "I'll Take the Dog" (#9, 1966), led to GRAND OLE OPRY membership (April 30, 1966).

Fortunately, Pillow was prepared for the long dry spell that followed. (He charted into 1981 on various labels but had no more hits.) A U.S. Navy veteran, he had graduated from Lynchburg College with a business degree. Off-campus, Pillow had honed his talents playing in bands. Despite narrowly losing a WSM Pet Milk talent contest, he had moved his family to Nashville in 1963. Pillow and manager Joe Taylor started a booking agency in 1964, and Pillow established Sycamore Valley Music, a publishing house. Later, Pillow was instrumental in bringing LEE GREENWOOD to Nashville and signed him to his publishing company. As of 2011 Pillow was still working the Grand Ole Opry. —*Walt Trott*

## Poco

Richie Furay b. Yellow Springs, Ohio, May 9, 1944
Jim Messina b. Harlingen, Texas, December 5, 1947
Rusty Young b. Long Beach, California, February 23, 1946
George Grantham b. Cordell, Oklahoma, November 20, 1947
Randy Meisner b. Scottsbluff, Nebraska, March 8, 1946

Based in Los Angeles, Poco was formed in 1968 by rhythm guitarist Richie Furay and lead guitarist Jim Messina—two former members of legendary rock band Buffalo Springfield—together with PEDAL STEEL GUITAR player Rusty Young. Along with THE BYRDS, the Flying Burrito Brothers, Michael Nesmith, Dillard & Clark, and BOB DYLAN, Poco helped pioneer the synthesis of country and rock, combining such numbers as DALLAS FRAZIER's "Honky-Tonk Downstairs" (rendered with a strong satirical edge) with original material such as "You Better Think Twice" (a minor pop chart-maker on EPIC RECORDS in 1971).

Poco proved to be resilient despite personnel changes: Randy Meisner (later a member of THE EAGLES) departed in 1969, leaving a spot for bassist Timothy B. Schmit; Messina left in 1970 and was replaced by Paul Cotton; and Furay exited in 1973. Schmit (who also joined the Eagles) and drummer George Grantham quit in 1977, and Charlie Harrison, Kim Bullard, and Steve Chapman came aboard. Young stayed until 1984.

Commercially, Poco barely dented the country charts but gained moderate success on the pop charts, especially as the group moved toward a middle-of-the-road pop sound. In addition to "You Better Think Twice," their charted pop singles include "C'mon" (Epic, 1971), "Indian Summer" (ABC, 1977), "Crazy Love" (their highest at #17; ABC, 1978), "Heart of the Night" (MCA, 1978), and "Shoot for the Moon" (ATLANTIC, 1982). Artistic high points include the albums *Crazy Eyes* (1973), *Legend* (1978), and *Blue and Gray* (1981). Throughout the years, the band produced consistently fine music. Their influence on more popular bands, especially the Eagles, was substantial. Young, Furay, Messina, Grantham, and Meisner reunited in 1989 to make a successful RCA album called *Legacy*; they charted with pop singles "Call It Love" and "Nothin' to Hide." Various incarnations of the band performed and recorded into the twenty-first century. —*Stephen R. Tucker*

## Charlie Poole & the North Carolina Ramblers

b. Randolph County, North Carolina, March 22, 1892; d. May 21, 1931

The August 1927 COLUMBIA RECORDS *Old Familiar Tunes* catalog describes Charlie Poole as "unquestionably the best-known banjo picker and singer in the Carolinas." Indeed, Poole and his North

*Charlie Poole*

Carolina Ramblers had already sold more than 250,000 records since 1925, and they would double that figure by the time of their final release in January 1932.

Charles Cleveland Poole grew up in the cotton mill villages of the North Carolina Piedmont. Early on, he learned to play banjo in a three-finger roll derived from classical banjo playing. Poole's natural wanderlust led him as far as Montana and Canada before 1920.

With Posey Rorer, a fiddler from Franklin County, Virginia, Poole formed the North Carolina Ramblers. He eventually married Rorer's sister and settled in Spray, North Carolina. Tired of cotton mill work, Poole and Rorer quit their jobs in 1925 to record OLD-TIME MUSIC. Spray guitarist Norman Woodlieff joined them for a successful Columbia audition on July 27, 1925, resulting in two releases. "Don't Let Your Deal Go Down Blues" b/w "Can I Sleep in Your Barn Tonight Mister?" was a hit, selling more than 102,000 copies. The second release sold another 65,000 copies, though the band received only seventy-five dollars for recording both discs. Poole became a full-time musician, recording more than seventy sides for Columbia, BRUNSWICK, and Paramount between 1925 and 1931. Some were songs still performed today, including "White House Blues," "There'll Come a Time," "If I Lose," "Sweet Sunny South," and "Budded Rose."

During the group's five-year recording career, Rorer was replaced first by Lonnie Austin and then Odell Smith, while West Virginian Roy Harvey replaced Woodlieff. Poole chose superb sidemen, and each of the Ramblers was among the best on his instrument. Both Rorer and Harvey also had solo careers.

Poole's forceful and colorful personality made him a legend in his region. Even today his escapades circulate as folk tales in the Blue Ridge Mountains. In 1931 he was invited to play backup in a Hollywood western movie, but by then hard living and hard drinking had caught up with him, and he died at age thirty-nine. A 2005 Sony BMG reissue boxed set has kept his music alive, as has a Grammy-winning two-disc Loudon Wainwright III tribute album issued on Second Story Sound Records in 2009. —*Kinney Rorer*

## Bill Porter
b. St. Louis, Missouri, June 15, 1931; d. July 7, 2010

Billy Rhodes Porter was an important recording engineer on the Nashville scene from 1959 to 1966. He grew up in Nashville, spent five years as a television repairman, and moved on to Nashville's WLAC-TV as an audio engineer and cameraman.

In 1959 Porter became chief engineer for RCA VICTOR's Nashville studio, then under the direction of CHET ATKINS. There Porter recorded numerous hits for RCA country stars, including THE BROWNS ("The Three Bells"), JIM REEVES ("He'll Have to Go"), SKEETER DAVIS ("The End of the World"), and HANK LOCKLIN ("Please Help Me I'm Falling"). Porter also recorded RCA pop artists, such as Al Hirt ("Java," 1964). His sessions with acts on independent labels included THE EVERLY BROTHERS (Cadence, WARNER BROS.), ROY ORBISON (MONUMENT), Johnny Tillotson (Cadence), and other country and pop singers. After a brief stint with COLUMBIA's Nashville studio, in 1964 Porter became manager of Nashville's Monument Records studio, where he continued his work with Orbison on tunes such as "It's Over" and "Oh, Pretty Woman" and with Joe Tex on R&B hits such as "Hold What You've Got." Technology was then limited to three-track machines, with mixing taking place as songs were recorded. Nevertheless, Porter's choice of microphones, skillful microphone placement, and sensitivity to blends of voices and instruments produced clean, ambient recordings that remain hallmarks of THE NASHVILLE SOUND.

From 1966 to 1973 Porter ran his own studio in Las Vegas, also becoming audio engineer for ELVIS PRESLEY and other Vegas acts. From 1970 to 1977 he was the house mixing engineer for Presley's live Vegas shows as well as his road shows. Subsequently he taught at the University of Colorado at Denver, supervised audio for Jimmy Swaggart Ministries, and worked with several electronics firms. A 1992 recipient of *Mix* magazine's TEC Award for lifetime technical excellence and achievement, Porter developed one of the nation's first college-level courses in studio engineering, at the University of Miami. He taught for many years at Webster University in St. Louis prior to retiring. —*John W. Rumble*

# Dale Potter

b. Puxico, Missouri, April 28, 1929; d. March 14, 1996

One of the most outstanding fiddle players in country music history, Allen Dale Potter pioneered a use of double stops (playing two strings at once in harmony) that has been widely imitated by such pros as BUDDY SPICHER, VASSAR CLEMENTS, Bobby Hicks, and Scott Stoneman (THE STONEMAN FAMILY).

As a youngster, Potter listened to BOB WILLS & His Texas Playboys on the radio. The young musician thought that Wills's group had just one fiddle (instead of multiple fiddles, as he later discovered) and sought to duplicate the sound. After moving to Nashville in 1948, he began recording with HANK WILLIAMS ("Mind Your Own Business"), LITTLE JIMMY DICKENS, WEBB PIERCE, COWBOY COPAS, and CARL SMITH. Potter toured heavily with Copas and Smith as well as with GEORGE JONES, HYLO BROWN, MAC WISEMAN, and many others. Potter's twin fiddle work on record with TOMMY JACKSON is some of country music's best. One of Potter's finest moments on disc occurred at age twenty-three performing "Fiddle Patch" and "Fiddle Sticks" with the Country All-Stars, an RCA recording act that included CHET ATKINS and HOMER & JETHRO.

Potter left Nashville in the early 1960s and took a job with singer Judy Lynn in Las Vegas. In the 1970s he headed his own group in Hawaii, and in the 1980s and early 1990s he worked occasionally at BLUEGRASS festivals.

Potter died in 1996 following a bout with cancer and a massive stroke. —*Eddie Stubbs*

# Don Potter

b. Glens Falls, New York, September 4, 1946

Donald L. Potter's musical arrangements and guitar licks have created distinctive sounds for THE JUDDS, jazz trumpeter Chuck Mangione, and 1970s pop singer Dan Hill. Potter signed separate rock, folk, and country recording contracts with CBS Records in the 1960s and 1970s, but he found more success as the featured soloist and coarranger for Mangione's group, with whom he recorded thirteen albums. In the late 1970s and early 1980s Potter recorded two solo projects for Mirror Records, released two Myrrh gospel albums, and arranged and played lead guitar on seven Hill albums, including *Longer Fuse*, which included the worldwide million-selling pop hit "Sometimes When We Touch."

In 1983 producer BRENT MAHER hired Potter to play acoustic guitar on the demo recording that ultimately landed the Judds a deal with RCA RECORDS' Nashville division. By using the acoustic guitar as a lead instrument, Potter helped the duo create its trademark sound. He continued to serve as session guitarist, arranger, bandleader, and coproducer for all of the Judds' albums. He also cowrote their 1991 Top Ten single "One Hundred and Two."

When WYNONNA (Judd) became a solo artist in 1992, Potter continued his role as coproducer (with TONY BROWN), arranger, and session guitarist on her first three albums. In 1997 Potter left Nashville to enter the ministry. —*Marjie McGraw*

# Fiddlin' Cowan Powers

b. Russell County, Virginia, October 1877; d. early 1950s

A farmer and leatherworker from southwestern Virginia, James Cowan Powers won early regional fame as a contest fiddler; his family-based style highlighted double stops (playing two strings simultaneously in harmony) and remarkable bowing dexterity. After his wife died in 1916, Powers organized a STRING-BAND with his four children and hit the road. One of country music's first professional stringbands, the act was soon making a regular five-state circuit through Appalachia, finding especially receptive audiences in the coal towns of Kentucky and West Virginia. In August 1924 the group traveled to Camden, New Jersey, to record for Victor Records (predecessor to RCA VICTOR)—the first commercial recordings of a mountain stringband that had been performing together outside of the studio. The records were commercially successful and were used in Victor's early advertising for OLD-TIME MUSIC. Later the group recorded for EDISON and OKEH. As his children grew up and pursued their own lives, Powers returned to work as a fiddle soloist. He was still active and playing for THE STANLEY BROTHERS when he died onstage at a concert in Saltville, Virginia, in the early 1950s. —*Charles Wolfe*

# A Prairie Home Companion

established July 6, 1974

*A Prairie Home Companion*, syndicated over National Public Radio and available overseas on America One and via the Armed Forces Networks in Europe and the Far East, attracts millions of listeners with its blend of humor, music, stories, and poems. Humorist Garrison Keillor hosted the original program, which aired live on Saturday evenings from July 6, 1974, to June 13, 1987. His inspiration for the show came from listening to the GRAND OLE OPRY while in a Nashville hotel room. He had been sent there by *The New Yorker* in March 1974 to cover the Opry's move from THE RYMAN AUDITORIUM to OPRYLAND.

Each episode of *A Prairie Home Companion* revolved around the fictitious town of Lake Wobegon, Minnesota, and its citizens. Lake Wobegon was the location for Keillor's stories as well as the centerpiece for imaginary commercial sponsors, including Powdermilk Biscuits and Jack's Fountain Lounge. A native of Anoka, Minnesota, Keillor based his tales around actual people, and his combination of realism and invention kept the humor homespun yet contemporary.

In May 1980 the program began regular live broadcasts via satellite from Minneapolis. In that same year it received a George Peabody Award for excellence in broadcasting. Keillor won a 1987 Grammy for his recording *Lake Wobegon Days*, in the category of Best Spoken Word. During its last year, 1987, the show was televised by The Disney Channel. Among the guests on the farewell telecast was legendary guitarist CHET ATKINS, a longtime admirer of Keillor.

In November 1989 Keillor began his New York *American Radio Company of the Air*, a series produced by Minnesota Public Radio, which had produced the original *A Prairie Home Companion* in its beginnings. In 1992 the newer show moved back to Minnesota, and in 1993 it reclaimed the name of *A Prairie Home Companion*. Today approximately half the shows are produced in St. Paul, with the remainder being produced in various other locations and sponsored by local public radio stations. The series features a variety of music, including Celtic, jazz, BLUE-GRASS, gospel, and OLD-TIME. Country performers have included KATHY MATTEA, WILLIE NELSON, NICKEL CREEK, and the RED CLAY RAMBLERS. —*Bob Paxman*

## The Prairie Ramblers

Charles Gilbert "Chick" Hurt b. Willowshade, Kentucky, May 11, 1901; d. October 9, 1967

Jack Taylor b. Summershade, Kentucky, December 7, 1901; d. August 4, 1962

Floyd "Salty" Holmes b. Glasgow, Kentucky, March 6, 1909; d. January 1, 1970

Shelby David "Tex" Atchison b. Rosine, Kentucky, February 5, 1912; d. August 4, 1982

Mainstays of WLS's NATIONAL BARN DANCE, the Prairie Ramblers put a modern spin on Kentucky STRINGBAND music. The band's smooth, propulsive sound influenced a generation of midwestern and southeastern musicians during the 1930s, most notably BILL MONROE.

Initially called the Kentucky Ramblers, the act launched its professional career in 1932 over WOC–Davenport, Iowa; Ronald Reagan was its announcer. The original members were mandola and tenor banjo player Chick Hurt, bassist Jack Taylor, guitar and harmonica player Salty Holmes, and fiddler Tex Atchison.

Moving to Chicago in January 1933, the group changed its name to reflect WLS's parent company, *The Prairie Farmer*. Besides performing as a featured act, the Ramblers backed GENE AUTRY on his *National Barn Dance* broadcasts. WLS later hired Arkansas singer PATSY MONTANA to enhance the band's appeal on road shows. In 1934 Montana and the Ramblers moved to WOR–New York; in January 1935 they began recording for the AMERICAN RECORD CORPORATION. The Ramblers (without Montana) cut risqué novelties under the name "The Sweet Violet Boys," partly to take advantage of the burgeoning JUKEBOX industry, then a principal market for recordings.

When the band returned to WLS in 1935, it offered a full western sound. Country/swing fiddler Alan Crockett replaced Atchison in 1938; Ralph "Rusty" Gill replaced Holmes in 1942. WADE RAY joined in about 1947 following Crockett's death. After the Ramblers moved to WLW–Cincinnati, in March 1949, fiddler-guitarist Wally Moore replaced Ray. Moore remained with the group when it returned to Chicago in the summer of 1950.

In early 1956 Hurt and Taylor hired an accordionist as a front-man and reemerged as Stan Wolowic and the Polka Chips. From July 1956 to September 1957 this band had its own weekly ABC-TV series, *Polka Time*; the group also recorded for ABC Paramount and CAPITOL. Hurt and Taylor dissolved the act in 1960 following a dispute with Wolowic. —*Dave Samuelson*

## Elvis Presley

b. Tupelo, Mississippi, January 8, 1935; d. August 16, 1977

Elvis Aron Presley was indisputably the most influential performer in the history of rock & roll, and his life and career have been more thoroughly dissected than any other artist in popular music. The analysis continues at least partly because of the aura of mystery that even now surrounds him. He never gave an in-depth interview, possibly because of astute media handling but more likely because he found it impossible to account for all that had happened to him.

The one factor usually overlooked in discussions of Elvis Presley is that he came from the country market and, in a sense, had a more powerful and lasting impact on country music than preeminent country stars such as HANK WILLIAMS and JIMMIE RODGERS. Until Presley's arrival, country music had been considered regional, and only a few artists, such as EDDY ARNOLD, had shaken off this stigma. Presley opened the door for other country

*Elvis Presley*

singers, including MARTY ROBBINS, SONNY JAMES, and JOHNNY CASH, to bring their music to a broader market. The consensus around Nashville in the mid- to late 1950s was that Elvis Presley was disastrous for country music, that he had in fact almost killed it; in truth, he was very good for a younger generation of country musicians, giving them potential access to wider media exposure than their predecessors had enjoyed.

Presley, who was born in Tupelo, Mississippi, but who lived in Memphis from November 1948, developed a true catholicity of taste. The generally accepted notion that he fused country and R&B is essentially true, but he also embraced black and white gospel, mainstream pop, light opera, and more. Memphis was a good place to hear these genres, and by the time Elvis first went to SUN RECORDS to cut a commercial record in July 1954, he had more or less found his style. He succeeded in the country market surprisingly quickly. The music of established country artists such as WEBB PIERCE and CARL SMITH was adult in content and execution. Presley gave younger country fans something of their own. Much of its verve came from R&B, but it was marketed as country, and the best exposure he received in 1954 and 1955 was on the LOUISIANA HAYRIDE and on country radio stations.

Presley was already beginning to break out of the country market when his Sun contract was sold to RCA VICTOR in November 1955, a deal masterminded by his new manager, COLONEL TOM PARKER. Parker persuaded RCA to pay an unprecedented $35,000 for Presley, a singer of virtually untested appeal outside country music. (Music publisher HILL AND RANGE supplied another $5,000, thereby cementing a relationship with the singer.) RCA, though, was able to catapult him into the national marketplace via television and concentrated promotion. By April 1, 1956, his first RCA single, "Heartbreak Hotel," had sold 1 million copies. In a way that BILL HALEY never could, Presley became both a figurehead for rock & roll and a lightning rod for everyone who despised it. In his dress, his stage moves, and his few stage-managed interviews, he projected an image that was at once threatening and vulnerable.

Presley's diverse musical sensibilities and innate conservatism quickly became apparent in his career direction. He wanted to do movies, Christmas albums, gospel albums, and pop ballads. Perhaps he, too, saw rock & roll as something that might blow over, and he wanted a broad-based career in case it did. A stint in the army from March 1958 until March 1960 smoothed his transition. He had made four movies before he enlisted (*Love Me Tender*, *Loving You*, *Jailhouse Rock*, and *King Creole*), and movies rather than concerts or television became the medium by which Elvis met his public during the 1960s. There were twenty-seven of them in ten years, most of them frothy and inconsequential. *G.I. Blues* was followed by two quasi-serious dramatic roles in *Flaming Star* and *Wild in the Country*. When the latter two flopped, the pattern was reestablished with *Blue Hawaii*, which was a box-office smash. In succession came *Follow That Dream*; *Kid Galahad*; *Girls! Girls! Girls!*; *It Happened at the World's Fair*; *Fun in Acapulco*; *Kissin' Cousins*; *Viva Las Vegas*; *Roustabout*; *Girl Happy*; *Tickle Me*; *Harum Scarum*; *Frankie and Johnny*; *Paradise, Hawaiian Style*; *Spinout*; *Easy Come, Easy Go*; *Double Trouble*; *Clambake*; *Stay Away, Joe*; *Speedway*; *Live a Little, Love a Little*; *Charro!*; *The Trouble with Girls*; and *Change of Habit*.

By the late 1960s Presley's career was in serious trouble. The movies and the accompanying soundtracks had almost destroyed his reputation. He hadn't appeared live since March 1961, and it must have been with some trepidation that he made a live appearance at the NBC studios in Burbank in June 1968 for the taping of a television special that did much to restore his credibility. Apparently reinvigorated, Presley put more effort into song choice and returned to the upper reaches of the charts with "If I Can Dream," "In the Ghetto," and "Suspicious Minds." Some have attributed his return to the concert stage to his marriage to Priscilla Beaulieu on May 1, 1967, although financial pressures and a desire to escape from the stagnant pattern he had established were probably more important.

Presley began performing again in Las Vegas in July 1969, and his two remaining movies were of performances (*Elvis: That's the Way It Is* and *Elvis on Tour*). He continued performing live until his death eight years later. For an artist of his stature, he seemed to encounter problems in acquiring the best new material, and many of his 1970s recordings were of older songs ("The Wonder of You," "You Don't Have to Say You Love Me," "Promised Land"). It also became clear that Presley was starting to suffer from debilitating medical problems, most of them, it was later revealed, stemming from prescription drug abuse. Several posthumous biographies recounted an almost impossible level of drug ingestion. Priscilla divorced him on October 11, 1973, and the last years of his life were tragic indeed as he wrestled with failing health and a career that once again appeared to stultify him. Presley was elected to THE COUNTRY MUSIC HALL OF FAME in 1998. —*Colin Escott*

# Frances Preston
b. Nashville, Tennessee, August 27, 1934

Called "one of the true powerhouses in the pop music business" by *Fortune* magazine, Frances Williams Preston could have ended up a schoolteacher. A summer job while a student at the George Peabody School for Teachers in Nashville changed all that. She briefly worked at the National Life and Accident Insurance Company and then at National Life's subsidiary, Nashville radio station WSM, beginning as a receptionist.

Because of her contacts and all-around ability, JUDGE BOB BURTON hired Preston in 1958 to open a BMI southern regional office in Nashville. Quickly she led BMI to a position of

*Frances Preston*

preeminence in the South, signing and assisting countless country writers and publishers along with those rooted in other styles of popular music. Behind the scenes she played a major role in building Nashville's status as a music center.

In 1964, the year the BMI Building went up on MUSIC ROW, Preston became a vice president of BMI. She moved to BMI's New York office in 1985, becoming senior vice president for performing rights and president and CEO the following year. Before her retirement in 2004, she was responsible for the company's growth in a variety of areas, including domestic licensing, foreign performing rights, legislation for fair compensation for writers, publishers' interests, and copyright protection.

Nationally prominent in business and political circles, Preston long served on the CMA board and the board of the COUNTRY MUSIC HALL OF FAME AND MUSEUM. She was a member of several important national bodies, including President Jimmy Carter's Panama Canal Study Committee, the commission for the White House Record Library, and Vice President Albert Gore Jr.'s National Information Infrastructure Advisory Council. She has also served as president of the T. J. Martell Foundation for Leukemia, Cancer, and AIDS Research.

Preston was elected to THE COUNTRY MUSIC HALL OF FAME in 1992. —*Burt Korall*

# Kenny Price
b. Florence, Kentucky, May 27, 1931; d. August 4, 1987

Rotund singer Kenny Price, known as the Round Mound of Sound, is best known as a longtime cast member of *HEE HAW*, where he sang in the show's gospel quartet and contributed solo numbers and comedy routines.

Price was raised on a farm near Covington, Kentucky, and at fourteen he landed a spot singing on station WZIP in Cincinnati.

Following two years of military service in Korea, he appeared on Buddy Ross's *Hometowners* TV show on WLW in Cincinnati and also became a regular on the MIDWESTERN HAYRIDE.

He first hit the country charts in 1966 with "Walking on New Grass," a #7 hit on Boone Records. In 1969 he signed with RCA RECORDS and scored his biggest hit for that label with the #8 "Sheriff of Boone County," released in 1970. In later years he recorded for the MRC, Dimension, and Broadway labels. —*Walt Trott*

# Ray Price
b. near Perryville, Texas, January 12, 1926

When Noble Ray Price was elected to THE COUNTRY MUSIC HALL OF FAME in 1996, many noted that the honor was long overdue. Such feelings weren't based so much on the longevity of his career or on his many major hits, for in those regards Price was no different from many other deserving artists awaiting induction. More importantly, Price has been one of country's great innovators. He changed the sound of country music from the late 1950s forward by developing a rhythmic brand of HONKY-TONK that has been hugely influential ever since. As steel guitarist Don Helms, a veteran of HANK WILLIAMS's Drifting Cowboys, once put it, "Ray Price created an era."

Born near Perryville in East Texas, Price moved with his mother to Dallas after she and his father split up. Four years old at the time, he would spend most of his childhood moving between his mother's Dallas home and his father's farm. After serving in the U.S. Marines during World War II, Price enrolled at North Texas Agricultural College, intent on becoming a veterinarian. But while in school he started singing at a place called Roy's House Café. He eventually made his way to JIM BECK's Dallas recording studio, and Beck hooked him up with Nashville's BULLET RECORDS. Price made one single for Bullet in early 1950.

His Bullet release wasn't successful, but Price began singing on various Dallas-area programs, including the *BIG D JAMBOREE*. He caught the attention of Troy Martin of the Peer-Southern publishing firm, and on Martin's strong recommendation COLUMBIA RECORDS signed Price in March 1951. His first Columbia release was "If You're Ever Lonely, Darling," written by LEFTY FRIZZELL.

Price had little success on Columbia until an introduction to Hank Williams in the fall of 1951 changed his fortunes. Williams took Price with him on the road and the two cowrote a song, "Weary Blues (From Waiting)," that Price recorded. Though not a major hit, Price's rendition did fairly well, and in January 1952 he moved to Nashville to join the GRAND OLE OPRY. There he roomed with Williams and used the Drifting Cowboys as his backup band. Many of Price's recordings from this period show him self-consciously adopting Williams's style. Gradually, though, Price allowed his natural voice more sway on such early hits as the 1954 double-sider "I'll Be There (If You Ever Want Me)" b/w "Release Me."

The pivotal record of Price's career, however, was "Crazy Arms," recorded March 1, 1956. Introduced by TOMMY JACKSON's searing fiddle ("I whistled the sound I wanted Tommy to play," Price recalled) and driven by BUDDY KILLEN's pulsing bass line, "Crazy Arms" introduced a novel, modernist intensity to what was still an essentially classic honky-tonk sound. The record spent twenty weeks at #1 and established Price as a full-fledged star. For the next several years he continued to tinker with his sound, most importantly emphasizing a shuffle rhythm less evident on

*Ray Price*

"Crazy Arms." The 4/4 shuffle, which many artists soon adopted, became known in country circles as the "Ray Price beat."

Meanwhile, Price assisted many young musicians and songwriters. WILLIE NELSON, ROGER MILLER, and JOHNNY PAYCHECK all passed through his band, the Cherokee Cowboys, while Nelson, HARLAN HOWARD, and HANK COCHRAN wrote for the publishing company of which Price was part owner, PAMPER MUSIC. Price's 1959 rendition of Howard's "Heartaches by the Number" helped establish Howard in Nashville, and Price's 1958 smash "City Lights" did the same for its writer, BILL ANDERSON.

Yet as dominant a hard-country artist as Price had become, by the early 1960s he had begun to take a more pop-oriented approach, culminating in his 1967 hit "Danny Boy." Recorded with full orchestration, the single alienated many of Price's established fans, even as it drew new ones from a different direction. Three years later, both sets of fans embraced Price's "For the Good Times." Penned by KRIS KRISTOFFERSON, the song was a #1 country hit in 1970 and went to #11 pop. That year, Price won the ACM's top honors for both Single and Album of the Year. In 1971 his *I Won't Mention It Again* was CMA's Album of the Year.

Price's long association with Columbia ended in 1974, as did his years of chart success. Disgruntled with Nashville, he had already moved back to Texas. Subsequent recordings for Myrrh, ABC/DOT, MONUMENT, and various other labels were often musically unsatisfying, though a 1980 duet album with Willie Nelson showcased Price again in fine form. Through the late 1980s Price recorded for the Nashville independent STEP ONE, and in 1992 he returned to Columbia for an album that went undeservedly unnoticed. Nevertheless, by the mid-1990s, yet another generation of young country acts—many of them stars of the burgeoning hillbilly music underground—were trumpeting Price's work. To this day, the 4/4 shuffle is so deeply embedded in country music as to be second nature to many.

Price continues to record and tours whenever he likes. In 2002 he released the solo album *Time* (Audium/Koch), followed by a duet album with Willie Nelson, *Run That By Me One Time* (LOST HIGHWAY, 2003). "Lost Highway," a Nelson-Price duet from the 2007 Lost Highway release *Last of the Breed* (an album also featuring MERLE HAGGARD), won a Grammy for Best Country Collaboration with Vocals. —*Daniel Cooper*

## Charley Pride
b. Sledge, Mississippi, March 18, 1938

Although Charley Pride is country music's only black superstar, he would be a legend no matter what his ethnicity. With a masculine, southern-accented baritone voice, Pride was able during his remarkably long hit-making heyday (1966–89) to drive even forgettable songs into the Top Ten, if not the #1 position. Given a great song, it typically spent multiple weeks atop the charts.

Pride's background reads like a classic blues singer's story. The son of a stern sharecropper father, Charley Frank Pride (named "Charl" but spelled "Charley" on his birth certificate) was born on a forty-acre Mississippi farm fifty miles south of Memphis. Pride picked cotton to buy his first guitar, a ten-dollar Sears, Roebuck model, when he was fourteen. Pride's father was morally opposed to the culture and lyrics of blues and was an eager GRAND OLE OPRY fan. So instead of following B. B. King's Memphis radio show, Charley Pride was musically schooled on the likes of ERNEST TUBB, HANK WILLIAMS, and ROY ACUFF.

At age sixteen Pride left home to play baseball in the Negro American League. After two years with teams in Memphis and other cities he entered the army for two years. He married Rozene Cohran, an ambitious and determined Memphis woman who still oversees the couple's business interests. Mustering out of the service in 1958, the young man was intent on a big-league baseball career. Pride played briefly in the Pioneer League and then worked

*Charley Pride*

at a smelting plant in Helena, Montana, where he played for the plant ball team. He tried out with the California Angels in the early 1960s, but by then he had injured his throwing arm.

In 1962 RED SOVINE and RED FOLEY discovered Pride in Helena; they eventually helped him come to Nashville, where he hooked up with producer JACK CLEMENT. In 1965 Clement's demo recordings of Pride caught CHET ATKINS's ear at RCA RECORDS. At a Los Angeles meeting of RCA officials, Atkins played the sides for top label executives and gained their consent to sign the remarkable singer before he revealed Pride's color; Pride's first RCA recording session took place in August 1965, and his first single, "The Snakes Crawl at Night," appeared in January 1966. Pride's race was likewise shielded from country radio through three single releases until the third, "Just Between You and Me," reached the country Top Ten. His gold-selling first album, *Country Charley Pride*, was the first indication many fans had that he was black.

In clubs, Pride handled curious fans by allowing stage-side gawking before clearing the floor to give dancers room. He also put audiences at ease by referring to his "permanent tan." He was determined that talent was what counted, and his work spoke volumes. Between his chart debut in 1966 and 1989, he had sixty-seven chart records, including an astonishing fifty-two Top Tens and twenty-nine #1 country hits. Among these were such enduring classics as "Is Anybody Goin' to San Antone" (1970), "Kiss an Angel Good Mornin'" (1971), and 1969's "All I Have to Offer You (Is Me)."

He was not, however, the Jackie Robinson of country music, as he has been portrayed. Robinson opened the doors to black baseball players, and the most talented among them rushed in behind him. Although Pride established himself once and for all, to date no other black country singer has even approached his commercial achievements.

In addition to being a talented singer and entertainer, Pride is an astute, conservative businessman. He made his home in North Dallas, Texas, becoming an important real estate and banking investor in that community as well as setting up a booking and management company, Chardon, which introduced JANIE FRICKE, DAVE & SUGAR, and NEAL MCCOY to stardom. He was a partner in Pi-Gem song publishing with producer TOM COLLINS, all the while cranking out hit after hit and running hard as a nonstop touring artist, both in the United States and overseas.

Pride was named CMA's Entertainer of the Year in 1971 and CMA Male Vocalist of the Year in 1971 and 1972. His album *Charley Pride Sings Heart Songs* won a 1972 Grammy for Best Country Vocal Performance, Male. Although invited to join the Grand Ole Opry in 1968, Pride initially declined; he became a cast member in 1993. In 1994 William Morrow & Company published his autobiography, *The Charley Pride Story*, penned with Jim Henderson. Pride received a star in the Hollywood Walk of Fame in 1999 and was elected to THE COUNTRY MUSIC HALL OF FAME in 2000. A Lifetime Achievement Award from the Mississippi Arts Commission followed in 2008. —*Bob Millard*

## *Prince Albert Show* (*see* Grand Ole Opry)

## John Prine
b. Maywood, Illinois, October 10, 1946

John E. Prine has cited BOB DYLAN, HANK WILLIAMS, and ROGER MILLER as his three main influences. Like Dylan, Prine is a midwesterner who plays an acoustic guitar and overcomes his limited, nasal voice with lyrics that make you sit up and notice. Like Williams, Prine sings about common folks in their own terse vernacular. Like Miller, Prine twists those stories until they yield an absurdist humor.

Though they lived outside Chicago, Prine's parents were from Paradise, Kentucky, and John's childhood summers there profoundly affected the subject matter and sound of his songs, marked by the vocal drawl, HONKY-TONK two-step, and twangy strum of country music. In the summer of 1971 Steve Goodman, Prine's pal on the Chicago folk-coffeehouse circuit, dragged KRIS KRISTOFFERSON to hear Prine, who was still a mailman at the time. Impressed, Kristofferson invited Prine to the Bitter End in New York to play for Jerry Wexler of ATLANTIC RECORDS.

Wexler offered Prine a contract the next day, and by year's end Prine's self-titled debut album, recorded with ELVIS PRESLEY's rhythm section and boasting effusive liner notes by Kristofferson, was in the stores. The collection included such future standards as "Hello in There" (a poignant look at old age, soon recorded by Bette Midler), "Angel from Montgomery" (the private thoughts of an Alabama housewife, soon recorded by Bonnie Raitt), "Paradise" (an understated story of strip mining in Kentucky), and "Sam Stone" (a devastating portrait of a drug-addicted Vietnam veteran).

Before long, Prine moved away from topical material toward quirky vignettes about unlucky misfits stuck in prison on Christmas, in a bungalow too near the highway, or in a silent marriage. After four albums for Atlantic, he recorded some of his finest songs on *Bruised Orange* for ASYLUM in 1978. Following a third Asylum album, Prine and his manager, Al Bunetta, formed their own label, Oh Boy Records, so Prine could take his time writing and recording his songs just the way he wanted. Prine released only six studio albums between 1981 and 2005, including 1999's *In Spite of Ourselves*, which featured covers of classic country songs recorded as duets with female singers. With MAC WISEMAN he released another covers album, *Standard Songs for Average People*, in 2007. Each was greeted by hosannas from the music press.

Meanwhile, Prine had moved to Nashville in the early 1980s and enjoyed modest success writing for such artists as TAMMY WYNETTE ("Unwed Fathers") and DON WILLIAMS ("Love Is on a Roll"). Prine won Grammys for Best Contemporary Folk Recording for his 1991 album *The Missing Years* and his 2005 album *Fair & Square*. In 2003 he was inducted into the NASHVILLE SONGWRITERS HALL OF FAME and received an AMERICANA Music Association (AMA) Lifetime Achievement Award for songwriting. Prine was also AMA's 2005 Artist of the Year. —*Geoffrey Himes*

## Jeanne Pruett
b. Pell City, Alabama, January 30, 1937

Born Norma Jean Bowman, Jeanne Pruett acquired her stage name through marriage to guitarist Jack Pruett. The two moved to Nashville in 1956, and Jack held a job in MARTY ROBBINS's road band. Jeanne made her first recordings for RCA in 1963. She signed with DECCA RECORDS in 1969 and enjoyed moderate success with her self-composed song "Hold to My Unchanging Love" in 1971. She also scored as a staff writer for Marty Robbins Enterprises in 1972 when Robbins hit the Top Ten with her song "Love Me."

Her career-making hit came in 1973 when Pruett's producer Walter Haynes remembered a sultry ballad called "Satin Sheets,"

written by John Volinkaty, and urged Pruett to record it, even though Opry stars BILL ANDERSON and JAN HOWARD had previously recorded the song as a duet. In an unusual promotion gimmick for her single, Pruett personally cut 1,600 pieces of pink satin sheets and mailed them to everyone on the CMA's membership list. The effort caught the attention of radio station program directors, and the record hit #1 on May 26, 1973. In the wake of the single's success, she joined the GRAND OLE OPRY cast on July 21, 1973.

Among Pruett's other Top Ten hits are "I'm Your Woman" (1973), "Back to Back" (1979), and "Temporarily Yours" (1980). She also published *Feedin' Friends*, a cookbook series. Pruett retired from touring in 2006. —*Don Rhodes*

## Riley Puckett
b. near Alpharetta, Georgia, May 7, 1894; d. July 13, 1946

A founding member of the seminal OLD-TIME group known as the SKILLET LICKERS, vocalist-guitarist George Riley Puckett was the principal reason for this STRINGBAND's popularity. Nearly blinded shortly after birth through a faulty eye treatment, Puckett learned to play guitar and banjo in his teens. From then on he made his living playing music, first at dances, parties, and on street corners, and later on radio, at fiddlers' conventions, and on records.

He made his first recordings in 1924 in the company of GID TANNER, his musical associate for many years. Puckett's repertoire was astonishingly varied, ranging from older British BALLADS to sentimental songs of the late 1800s and contemporary hits of the 1930s. He was featured on more than 200 issued recordings (among them some of the best-selling hits of COLUMBIA's 15000-D hillbilly series), apart from his work with the Skillet Lickers; on at least one occasion he was the uncredited accompanist of a black blues singer. Puckett's idiosyncratic guitar backup was unmistakable on record, and his syncopated bass runs (which were sometimes disparaged by a few of the fiddlers he accompanied) were widely emulated in the 1960s by young guitarists of the urban folk song revival.

Puckett died in an Atlanta hospital of blood poisoning at age fifty-two. —*Norm Cohen*

## Pure Prairie League

Among the successful COUNTRY-ROCK bands to emerge from the shadow of THE BYRDS and Buffalo Springfield, Pure Prairie League is remembered for a handful of singles and constantly changing personnel, including, at times, singer-songwriters Craig Fuller, VINCE GILL, and Gary Burr.

Named after a women's temperance organization in the 1939 Errol Flynn film *Dodge City*, the band was formed in Cincinnati, its membership (Fuller, singer-guitarist George Powell, bassist Jim Lanham, steel guitarist John Call, and drummer Tom McGrail) all from the Ohio River valley. McGrail, who had conceived the group's name, was replaced by Jim Caughlin prior to their first album, *Pure Prairie League* (RCA, 1971). Original lead singer and chief composer Fuller left the ensemble after their second album, *Bustin' Out* (RCA, 1972), to serve two years working in a Kentucky hospital as a conscientious objector to the Vietnam War. In his absence, RCA dropped the act, but the group continued staging as many as 275 shows a year, many of them on college campuses.

FM airplay of "Amie," a concert favorite from *Bustin' Out*, led to an edited version that became a Top Thirty pop hit in 1975. RCA re-signed the band, with only Powell and Call remaining from the original lineup.

The group's 1979 RCA album *Can't Hold Back* marked twenty-two-year-old Vince Gill's debut with the act. Gill sang lead on the band's highest-charting single, "Let Me Love You Tonight" (#10 pop, 1980), on Casablanca Records. Though the outfit's last charted record was 1981's "You're Mine Tonight," Pure Prairie League continued to tour with several more personnel changes, including brief periods with SWEETHEARTS OF THE RODEO (Kristine Arnold and Janis Gill) on backing vocals. Songwriter Gary Burr served as lead singer from 1982 to 1985. Fuller rejoined in 1985, briefly sharing leads with Burr. After the act dissolved in 1987, Fuller joined the rock band Little Feat from 1988 until September 1993, when he left to concentrate on songwriting. —*Todd Everett*

## Curly Putman
b. Princeton, Alabama, November 20, 1930

Songwriter Claude Putman Jr. is responsible for many memorable songs, including "He Stopped Loving Her Today," a massive hit for GEORGE JONES, which Putman cowrote with BOBBY BRADDOCK and which won CMA's Song of the Year award in both 1980 and 1981.

Putman and Braddock also cowrote the chart-topping "D-I-V-O-R-C-E" (TAMMY WYNETTE, 1968). Additional hits written or cowritten by Putman include "My Elusive Dreams" (with which DAVID HOUSTON and Wynette scored a #11 duet hit in 1967), TANYA TUCKER's "Blood Red and Goin' Down" (#1, 1973), and "Dumb Blonde" (DOLLY PARTON's first chart single, 1967). Putman's "Green, Green Grass of Home," initially cut by JOHNNY DARRELL, has been recorded by dozens of artists; PORTER WAGONER made it a #4 country hit in 1965, and Tom Jones made it an international pop hit in 1966–67.

*Curly Putman*

After serving in the U.S. Navy, Putman worked as a sawmill hand and as a shoe salesman and played steel guitar in country bands in Huntsville, Alabama. A meeting with BUDDY KILLEN landed Putman a job with TREE PUBLISHING COMPANY as a song plugger, and before long he connected as a songwriter. As an artist, he had minor chart action for the Cherokee and ABC labels in the 1960s.

Putman was elected to the NASHVILLE SONGWRITERS HALL OF FAME in 1996. —*Bob Allen*

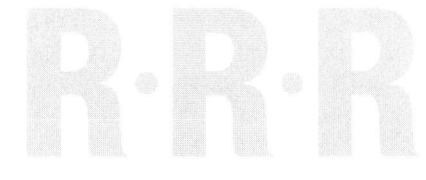

## Eddie Rabbitt
b. Brooklyn, New York, November 27, 1941; d. May 7, 1998

Edward Thomas Rabbitt brought a smooth, broad-based approach to country music as both songwriter and singer. Raised in New Jersey, Rabbitt touched audiences with slightly husky, understated vocals and workmanlike songs that bridged the gap between country and pop. In part, his achievements flowed from the combination of his East Orange upbringing and his parents' Irish roots.

A scoutmaster with a hillbilly alter ego inspired a twelve-year-old Rabbitt to play guitar and sing country music. By the mid-1960s Rabbitt began to play professionally and recorded for the 20th Century-Fox and COLUMBIA labels before testing the Nashville market in 1968. His first songwriting success came with "Working My Way Up from the Bottom," recorded by ROY DRUSKY. A songwriting deal with ACUFF-ROSE Publications resulted in cuts by GEORGE MORGAN and others. But the turning point came in 1970 when ELVIS PRESLEY hit with Rabbitt's distinctive country-pop tune "Kentucky Rain." With its backwoods imagery and complex chord changes, the song captured Rabbitt's far-reaching appeal.

Rabbitt started his country recording career for ELEKTRA in 1974 (when he also scored a #1 as a writer with RONNIE MILSAP's "Pure Love"). By 1976 he had released his first #1, "Drinkin' My Baby (Off My Mind)." That ode launched a hit-crafting mode—often in partnership with Even Stevens—that made Rabbitt a standout during an era when pop-leaning country ruled. Other #1s included 1978's "I Just Want to Love You"; "Every Which Way but Loose," from the 1978 movie starring Clint Eastwood; the Dylanesque "Drivin' My Life Away" and "I Love a Rainy Night" (both 1980 and the latter a #1 pop tune); "Step by Step" and "Someone Could Lose a Heart Tonight" (both 1981); and 1982's "You and I," a duet with CRYSTAL GAYLE. Additional Top Ten hits came on WARNER BROS. in 1983 and 1984 with "You Can't Run from Love" and "B-B-B-Burnin' Up With Love," respectively.

After a move to RCA and 1986's successful Rabbitt–JUICE NEWTON duet "Both To Each Other (Friends & Lovers)," Rabbitt topped the charts again in 1988 with the energetic "I Wanna Dance with You" and "The Wanderer," the latter a remake of Dion's 1961 pop hit. Although Rabbitt's eclectic 1990 *Jersey Boy* LP touched his customary bases of pop, R&B, rock, and country, its lone #1 single was "On Second Thought."

As a new generation of hit singers and songwriters led by GARTH BROOKS emerged, Rabbitt continued to tour nationally and internationally, but he made little further impact in the youth-dominated worlds of radio and recording.

His death was due to cancer. —*Thomas Goldsmith*

## Mose Rager
b. Smallhous, Kentucky, April 2, 1911; d. May 14, 1986

Moses "Mose" Rager, along with his coal-mining buddy Ike Everly, was a crucial link in the musical chain that connected African American folk musicians, including ARNOLD SHULTZ, with influential guitarists MERLE TRAVIS and CHET ATKINS. In the early 1930s Rager and Everly passed on to Travis a rich tradition of chords, runs, rolls, and songs (rags, blues, gospel) and a deep appreciation of black music. Rager and Everly also showed Travis a guitar-playing technique they had assimilated from white Kentucky musician Kennedy Jones, who had learned the style directly from Shultz in the early 1920s. Deriving ultimately from southeastern ragtime-based instrumental methods, this style became widely known in the 1950s and 1960s as "Travis-picking," a technique in which a guitarist, using only the thumb and fore-finger (sometimes adding the middle finger), plays melody, harmony, rhythm, and bass simultaneously. The style became enormously popular among country music guitarists during the 1950s, influencing numerous musicians, most notably Chet Atkins.

At various points in the late 1940s Rager worked as a sideman for GRANDPA JONES and CURLY FOX & TEXAS RUBY (with whom he appeared on a few recordings, "Black Mountain Rag" perhaps the best among them), but the guitarist returned to Muhlenberg County in 1950, where he worked as a heavy-equipment operator until his retirement in 1973. Travis readily acknowledged Rager as his mentor, commenting frequently on his "magnetism," once writing that Rager "was a Pied Piper—the kind of guy who could pick up a guitar, walk down the street, and have the whole town following him." —*William E. Lightfoot*

## Marvin Rainwater
b. Wichita, Kansas, July 2, 1925

Marvin Karlton Percy, known as Marvin Rainwater, was a maverick performer whose work, though broadly country, distilled many influences and perhaps covered too many bases to find a niche. He wrote and performed one classic country hit, "Gonna Find Me a Bluebird" (1957), and had a #1 hit in England in 1958 with a rock & roll song, "Whole Lotta Woman." He also recorded the original version of "The Pale Faced Indian," later a pop hit (as "Indian Reservation") for Don Fardon and Paul Revere & the Raiders.

One-quarter Cherokee, Rainwater grew up in Kansas studying classical piano. After World War II he launched his country music career in the Washington, D. C., area with ROY CLARK as his guitarist. In 1955 he appeared on *Arthur Godfrey's Talent Scouts* TV show, signed with MGM RECORDS, and joined the *OZARK JUBILEE*, remaining a cast member until 1957. He scored both country and rock & roll hits but found a permanent home in neither field; playing up his part-Indian lineage made him hard to market. After leaving MGM in 1961, Rainwater recorded for many labels, including his own Brave Records. He gained a hit in Scandinavia in 1981 with "Henryetta, Oklahoma." —*Colin Escott*

## Boots Randolph
b. Paducah, Kentucky, June 3, 1927; d. July 3, 2007

As a key contributor to THE NASHVILLE SOUND, saxophonist Homer Louis Randolph III helped broaden country music's appeal in the late 1950s and 1960s.

His breakthrough number, "Yakety Sax" (#35 pop, 1963), was a collaborative instrumental he worked up with guitarist James "Spider" Rich, cleverly blending country, jazz, blues, and gospel styles. Randolph originally recorded it for RCA, but his later MONUMENT version provided the hit. (As "Yakety Axe," the song was a #4 hit for RCA artist-producer CHET ATKINS in 1965).

Randolph began playing saxophone in high school. In Indiana and Illinois he performed in local bands until Kenneth "Jethro" Burns (see HOMER & JETHRO) caught his act and recommended him to Atkins, Burns's brother-in-law. After hearing Randolph's tape of "Chicken Reel," Atkins invited the young musician to Nashville.

Producer OWEN BRADLEY also admired Randolph's talent, and the instrumentalist quickly became a session regular, playing on 250 to 300 studio dates annually for nearly every name artist in Nashville throughout the 1960s. Randolph can be heard on hits including BRENDA LEE's "Rockin' Around the Christmas Tree," ROY ORBISON's "Oh, Pretty Woman," ELVIS PRESLEY's "Return to Sender," and dozens more as well as on soundtracks for eight Presley films. As a featured artist, Randolph released more than forty albums and charted with 1960s singles, including the haunting "The Shadow of Your Smile."

In the 1960s and 1970s Randolph toured widely with Atkins and FLOYD CRAMER. He was also a member of *HEE HAW's* Million Dollar Band and a frequent guest on network TV programs. From 1977 to 1994 he had his own club in downtown Nashville's Printers Alley. Later he owned a club with DANNY DAVIS on Music Valley Drive, which lasted until late 1997. —*Walt Trott*

## Wayne Raney
b. Wolf Bayou, Arkansas, August 17, 1920; d. January 23, 1993

A disc jockey, singer, instrumentalist, recording artist, songwriter, producer, and studio owner, Wayne Raney taught himself the mouth organ as a five-year-old after hearing a blind hobo playing in the street. At age thirteen Raney had his own program on Mexican BORDER RADIO station XEPN.

In 1936 Raney met his idol, guitarist and harmonica player LONNIE GLOSSON, and the pair began a twenty-five-year, on-again, off-again partnership highlighted by a long stint at Cincinnati's WCKY beginning in 1941. Some 230 stations eventually carried their syndicated radio show, and they reportedly sold more than 5 million harmonicas through the mail.

In 1945, while working at WMC–Memphis, Glosson and Raney began recording and touring with the DELMORE BROTHERS. Several of the Delmores' trailblazing country boogie records for KING

RECORDS, including their hit "Blues Stay Away from Me," featured the duo's twin harmonica playing.

Raney scored a #1 hit and a guest spot on the GRAND OLE OPRY with his composition "Why Don't You Haul Off and Love Me" (King, 1949). In 1950 he recorded four sides for London Records as Lonesome Willie Evans. After Rabon Delmore's death in 1952, Raney appeared regularly on KOVR–Stockton's *California Hayride* (1953–54). He briefly joined LEFTY FRIZZELL's band in about 1953, supplying harmonica and harmony vocals and cowriting with Frizzell before joining Wheeling, West Virginia's *WWVA JAMBOREE*. Raney flirted briefly with ROCKABILLY for DECCA before beginning another five-year stint at WCKY. In 1958 he began devoting more time to business interests, starting his own studio and founding the Rimrock label. His last recordings were released on STARDAY in 1964. In 1976 he launched Wayne Raney Cassette Duplication. During this period he also played his harmonica on *HEE HAW*, his last performance coming in 1979. In the 1980s, having already sold his studio and pressing plant to Stax Records, he retired from show business. —*Kim Field*

## Rascal Flatts
Jay DeMarcus, b. Columbus, Ohio, April 26, 1971
Gary LeVox, b. Columbus, Ohio, July 10, 1970
Joe Don Rooney, b. Baxter Springs, Kansas, September 13, 1975

Sporting a spiky-haired image and contemporary pop influences, the trio Rascal Flatts emerged as one of country music's most successful acts during an era of industry change and turmoil.

Gary Wayne Vernon Jr. who adopted LeVox ("the voice") as his stage name, and Stanley Wayne "Jay" DeMarcus Jr. are second cousins who played music together as kids. DeMarcus recorded two albums with Christian rockers East to West for Benson Records in 1993 and 1995. Shortly after the act broke up in 1997, DeMarcus became bandleader for country singer Chely Wright and met Joe Don Rooney, a guitarist for Wright.

LeVox had been working for the Ohio Department of Mental Retardation before moving to Nashville in 1997 and singing regularly in Printers Alley downtown. DeMarcus joined LeVox's band when not on the road with Wright. One night, LeVox's regular guitarist didn't show, so Rooney substituted. The three musicians detected a special chemistry and formed a trio in 1998. The next year, they signed with LYRIC STREET RECORDS, a new Nashville imprint started by the Disney Music Group.

The group's debut single, "Prayin' for Daylight," reached #3 on the *Billboard* country charts in 2000, and the act won ACM's 2000 New Vocal Duo/Group honors. Three more Top Ten singles from their self titled debut album followed. One of them, "I'm Movin' On," was named ACM's Song of the Year for 2002, the same year Rascal Flatts claimed CMA's Horizon Award. The act was ACM's Top Vocal Group for the years 2002–08 and CMA's Vocal Group of the Year from 2003 to 2008.

As on *Rascal Flatts*, the group worked with producers Mark Bright and Marty on *Melt* (2002). The album included the band's first #1 hit, "These Days," and a second with "Mayberry." From 2004's *Feels Like Today*, the single "Bless the Broken Road" camped longer at #1 than any of their previous hits and gained airplay on adult-contemporary radio stations. "Fast Cars and Freedom" became the trio's fourth #1. Radio stations began playing a hidden track, "Skin (Sarabeth)," about a high school cancer patient whose boyfriend shaves his head in sympathy for her. Lyric Street released it nationally, and it became a #2 hit.

*Rascal Flatts: (from left) Jay DeMarcus, Gary LeVox, and Joe Don Rooney*

With *Me and My Gang* (2006), Rascal Flatts changed producers to DANN HUFF. The single "What Hurts the Most" continued the band's multiformat success, reaching #1 on the country and adult-contemporary charts and landing in the Top Ten of the all-genre *Billboard Hot 100*. The collection spent fifteen weeks as America's best-selling album and placed second for the year behind the soundtrack album *High School Musical*.

Both 2007's *Still Feels Good* and 2009's *Unstoppable* furthered the group's winning streak, with the single "Here Comes Goodbye" becoming the act's tenth #1 hit, in April 2009. In April 2010 Lyric Street closed; the trio signed with BIG MACHINE RECORDS in July, and the album *Nothing Like This* was released in November 2010. In 2011, the trio accepted an invitation to join the cast of the Grand Ole Opry. —*Michael McCall*

## Leon Rausch
b. Springfield, Missouri, October 2, 1927

Active since the 1950s, Edgar Leon Rausch ranks among WESTERN SWING's great vocal stylists.

He spent his early career with local bands in Missouri. His mid-1950s recording debut—an excellent "Lost Highway"—was with Waco, Texas–based Clyde Chesser's Village Boys, and by 1958 he was singing with BOB WILLS & His Texas Playboys. When Wills reteamed with TOMMY DUNCAN a year later, Rausch's singing opportunities decreased, but the early 1960s found him touring and recording with JOHNNIE LEE WILLS, with whom he first recorded what became his signature tune, "Milk Cow Blues," for the Sims label.

When Bob Wills gave up bandleading in 1965, Rausch took over the Texas Playboys, appearing and recording with Wills in that capacity during 1965 and 1966. Later in the decade Rausch was leading his own Texas Panthers. Rausch reunited with Bob Wills for Wills's final album, *For the Last Time*, in 1973 and then joined the reorganized Texas Playboys from 1976 to 1986.

Since then, arguably singing better than ever, Rausch has worked with the JOHNNY GIMBLE–HERB REMINGTON–led Playboys II and recorded prolifically with Tom Morrell and his Time-Warp Top Hands. Rausch has also continued to lead his own bands and record for small labels, offering a three-CD Bob Wills tribute album (Sims, 1997) and making the particularly fine

Southland albums *The Rausch Touch* (1985), *Deep in the Heart of Texas* (1997), and the Cindy Walker tribute, *Close to You* (1998). In 2010, the veteran singer took a starring role in the well-received album, *It's a Good Day!: Asleep at the Wheel and Leon Rausch* —*Kevin Coffey*

## Eddy Raven
b. August 19, 1944, Lafayette, Louisiana

Edward Garvin Futch, better known as Eddy Raven, parlayed his soulful singing, artful songwriting, and CAJUN heritage into country music stardom.

Starting on radio in Georgia as a teen, Raven returned with his family to the musically fertile Lafayette area in the late 1950s. Singer-songwriter Bobby Charles recorded one of his songs, and by 1962 Raven had cut his own single for Cosmos. In the 1960s he worked with R&B/blues acts, including the Boogie Kings and Johnny and Edgar Winter, and recorded his first LP in 1969. Encouraged by JIMMY C. NEWMAN, he moved to Nashville in 1970.

Raven signed with the powerful ACUFF-ROSE PUBLICATIONS and soon gained recordings of his songs by ROY ORBISON, CONNIE SMITH, DON GIBSON ("Country Green"), and ROY ACUFF ("Back in the Country"). The OAK RIDGE BOYS' rendition of Raven's "Thank God for Kids" went to #3 in 1982–83.

Raven recorded for ABC, ABC/DOT, MONUMENT, and Dimension before breaking into the Top Twenty in 1981 with the wistful #13 ELEKTRA hit "I Should've Called." With a relaxed Caribbean-flavored groove, the number set the pattern for "Who Do You Know in California" (#11, 1981–82) and the chart-topping "I Got Mexico" (1984), the first of thirteen straight Top Tens he made for RCA. Other RCA #1s include "Shine, Shine, Shine" (1987) and "Joe Knows How to Live" (1988).

Dissatisfied with his RCA sales, Raven moved in 1989 to the Universal label. Two more #1s resulted—"In a Letter to You" and "Bayou Boys" (both 1989)—but subsequent CAPITOL releases stopped charting in 1991. After an unproductive stint with Intersound later in the 1990s, Raven and Texas businessman Larry Bennett launched Row Music Group in 2001, releasing albums that year by Raven, GENE WATSON, and Ricky Lynn Gregg. By 2006 Raven had released two more albums on the label, and he continues to tour actively. —*Thomas Goldsmith*

## Wade Ray
b. Griffin, Indiana, April 6, 1918; d. November 18, 1998

WESTERN SWING fiddler and vocalist Lyman Wade Ray grew up in Arkansas and started playing fiddle at age three. As a child he toured vaudeville theater circuits as the World's Youngest Violin Player. In 1934 he joined Pappy Cheshire's National Champion Hillbillies in St. Louis, staying with them until 1942, when a two-year army stint interrupted his career.

In about 1947, after returning to Cheshire's Hillbillies for a time, he replaced fiddler Alan Crockett in THE PRAIRIE RAMBLERS at Chicago's WLS *NATIONAL BARN DANCE*. When WLS dropped the Ramblers, Ray and his friend REX ALLEN, a fellow *Barn Dance* star, moved to Los Angeles in January 1949. By midyear Ray was fronting his own swing band. He recorded for the tiny Cowtown label, recorded briefly for CAPITOL, and in 1951 signed with RCA VICTOR. His best-known RCA singles were the ballads "Walk Softly" and "The Things I Might Have Been."

From 1956 into the early 1960s, Ray led bands in Las Vegas. He later worked with both the SONS OF THE PIONEERS and with ROY ROGERS until moving to Nashville in 1964. There Ray recorded fiddle instrumentals for RCA and became a regular on ERNEST TUBB's syndicated TV show. After spending a year with RAY PRICE's Cherokee Cowboys in 1964, Ray became WILLIE NELSON's touring bass player. From 1967 to 1970 Wade managed Kentucky's RENFRO VALLEY BARN DANCE. Then, back in Nashville, he became an artists' representative for Fender Musical Instruments.

In 1979 Ray and his wife, Gracie, moved to St. Louis; they later retired to Sparta, Illinois. —*Rich Kienzle*

## Collin Raye
b. DeQueen, Arkansas, August 22, 1959

Collin Raye made recordings in three different incarnations before his blend of uptempo rockers and emotional ballads made him a country star in the 1990s.

Born Floyd Collin Wray, the son of ROCKABILLY singer Lois Wray, Collin and his brother Scott formed the Wray Brothers and recorded for independent Oregon labels. In 1986–87, calling himself Bubba Wray, his group, the Wrays, charted two singles with MERCURY. During this time Raye played primarily in the Pacific Northwest as well as in the casinos of Reno, Nevada. He signed with EPIC RECORDS Nashville in 1990 and later moved from Reno to Greenville, Texas, where he continued to live to be with his children.

The handsome, smooth-singing artist made his reputation with love songs, which some listeners dismissed as lightweight. Others, however, inscribed the lyrics of "Love, Me" (1991), Raye's first #1 hit, on tombstones. "In This Life" (#1, 1992) became a popular wedding song. Similar hits included "That Was a River," "Little Rock," and "One Boy, One Girl." Raye's entertaining skills, honed as a Reno cover act, led him to perform energetic, rock-tinged songs as well, including "I Want You Bad (and That Ain't Good)," "That's My Story," and "My Kind of Girl." He also charted successfully with songs of social commentary, including "Not That Different" (#3, 1996) and "I Think About You" (#3, 1996), the video for the latter becoming ACM's Video of the Year. Each of his first four albums, *All I Can Be, In My Life, Extremes,* and *I Think About You,* sold more than 1 million copies.

Raye's *The Walls Came Down* (1998) included three Top Tens, including the #1 hit "I Can Still Feel You." With *Tracks* (2000), produced by DANN HUFF, the singer tried to regain his slipping momentum, but 2002's *Can't Back Down* proved to be his final Epic project. He signed with independent Infinity Records, but the label folded before he could release an album. Another independent, Aspirion Records, issued *Twenty Years and Change* in 2005. Other albums include *Never Going Back* (Time-Life Records, 2009). —*Brian Mansfield*

## RCA Victor/RCA Records
established 1929

RCA Victor Records has a long and distinguished history of involvement in country music. Its roots extend to 1901, when the Victor Talking Machine Company, predecessor to RCA, was organized.

In 1922 Victor held what is now considered the first country recording session, with southern fiddlers ECK ROBERTSON and Henry Gilliland. Another benchmark was VERNON DALHART's 1924 recording of "The Prisoner's Song" b/w "Wreck of the Old 97," country's first million-selling disc.

During the late 1920s A&R man RALPH PEER developed Victor's country catalog by recording performers in New York and making annual recording trips to southern cities. In a 1927 trip to BRISTOL, TENNESSEE, he supervised the first recordings of JIMMIE RODGERS and the CARTER FAMILY. Trips by Peer and, later, ELI OBERSTEIN continued after 1929, when the Radio Corporation of America (RCA) bought Victor and involved talent as diverse as JIMMIE DAVIS, the ALLEN BROTHERS, and the Stamps Quartet. During the Great Depression RCA featured these artists on its budget-priced BLUEBIRD label.

After 1940 RCA shared in a dramatic expansion of the music industry sparked by the economic recovery associated with World War II. By the late 1940s STEVE SHOLES supervised country recording for the company, whose foremost country artist was EDDY ARNOLD. In 1950 Sholes began to record frequently in Nashville, using a succession of local studios. Helping him organize sessions was CHET ATKINS, who assisted in cutting discs by HANK SNOW, PEE WEE KING, GRANDPA JONES, and others.

During the mid-1950s Sholes responded to the challenge of rock & roll by signing ELVIS PRESLEY. Presley's success helped Sholes convince RCA to commission a new studio in Nashville in 1957, the first established there by a major label. (RCA rented the facility from local developer Dan Maddox.) By now Atkins was RCA's man in MUSIC CITY, and in this studio he recorded such successful singers as Arnold, DON GIBSON, JIM REEVES, and BOBBY BARE, often framing them country-pop backgrounds. Together with OWEN BRADLEY's studio, the RCA studio provided the birthplace of THE NASHVILLE SOUND.

During the 1970s and early 1980s RCA often featured country-pop artists such as KENNY ROGERS and RONNIE MILSAP, dropping more traditional acts such as PORTER WAGONER and Hank Snow. However, RCA played a major part in the OUTLAW movement of the mid-1970s, a reaction against label-controlled studios and the sometimes-formulaic arrangements of the Nashville Sound era. JERRY BRADLEY, who took over RCA's Nashville operation in 1974, oversaw country's first certified platinum album—titled *Wanted! The Outlaws*—by assembling recordings by WILLIE NELSON, WAYLON JENNINGS, JESSI COLTER, and Tompall Glaser (THE GLASER BROTHERS).

During the 1980s RCA coped with a mid-decade sales crisis by developing established acts such as ALABAMA and by signing new artists such as THE JUDDS, VINCE GILL, KEITH WHITLEY, and CLINT BLACK, most of whom took traditionalist approaches to their music. These acts were supervised by new Nashville chief JOE GALANTE, who assumed this role in 1982. With a strong background in marketing, Galante established a track record that made RCA an attractive purchase by the German corporation Bertelsmann AG in 1986.

After a long run of market leadership, however, RCA slipped behind other labels active in country music in the early 1990s, particularly when Galante left for New York to serve as the label's chief national executive from 1990 to 1994. During his absence, Tom Weston ran the operation from 1990 to 1992, succeeded by THOM SCHUYLER, who became VP/director of operations and senior VP of A&R in 1992.

By 1991 RCA had established a companion label, BNA Entertainment, to overcome radio's practice of limiting the number of selections that it would play from any one label. JOHN ANDERSON, the first artist signed, enjoyed a second run of chart success before switching to MERCURY in 1997. Schuyler signed both KENNY CHESNEY and LONESTAR to BNA, boosted LORRIE MORGAN's career by moving her to BNA from RCA, and released MARTINA McBRIDE's first RCA solo album. In 1994 BNA and RCA were consolidated under the RCA Labels Group umbrella, sharing a core marketing group.

Also in 1994, Galante returned to lead the entire Nashville operation, which signed new talent, such as SARA EVANS (RCA), and continued to hone marketing expertise with new technology enabling users to monitor airplay of particular records on individual radio stations. During 1999–2000 BMG merged its ARISTA unit with the RCA Label Group, thus bringing BROOKS & DUNN, ALAN JACKSON, and BRAD PAISLEY aboard. In short order, the same core marketing team served RCA, BNA, and Arista artists.

In 2004 BMG formed a joint venture with SONY MUSIC ENTERTAINMENT and created Sony BMG. Galante ran RCA, BNA and Arista, with executive John Grady supervising Sony's COLUMBIA, EPIC, Lucky Dog, and MONUMENT labels. After Grady exited in 2006, Galante was responsible for all of Sony BMG's Nashville endeavors. He became chairman of Sony Music Nashville in 2008, after Sony bought BMG's interest in the joint venture. Galante left the conglomerate in May 2010, at which point Gary Overton took the helm. As of February 2011, Sony Music Nashville's various rosters included CARRIE UNDERWOOD, MIRANDA LAMBERT, KELLIE PICKLER, and Chris Young, in addition to Chesney, Evans, and Paisley. —*John W. Rumble*

## Rebel Records
established in Mount Rainier, Maryland, 1959

As a premier independent BLUEGRASS label, Rebel Records helped establish the Washington, D.C., bluegrass scene. It remains a haven for many of the music's most important acts. Rebel was founded in 1959 by Charles R. Freeland and two fellow bluegrass enthusiasts in the Mount Rainier, Maryland, suburb of Washington, then a country music hotbed for rural migrants who had settled there after World War II. Though its initial releases featured local country performers, Rebel soon focused on bluegrass at a time when major labels gave the music relatively little attention. Along with the folk revival, Rebel spurred bluegrass's commercial comeback in the 1960s. By the 1970s Rebel boasted such successful acts as THE COUNTRY GENTLEMEN, the SELDOM SCENE, and RALPH STANLEY. In 1979 Freeland sold Rebel to Dave Freeman, the founder of the OLD-TIME MUSIC reissue and mail-order label County Sales. Now based in Charlottesville, Virginia, Rebel has been the label for such traditionalists as LARRY SPARKS, DEL MCCOURY, and Dave Evans, and has featured such enduring mainstream bluegrass groups as Lost & Found, the Lonesome River Band, and Blue Highway. In the 2000s, Rebel has released albums of new or previously recorded music by the Steep Canyon Rangers, Paul Williams, J. D. CROWE, MAC WISEMAN, Bill Emerson, and Jimmy Gaudreau. —*Eddie Dean*

## Red Clay Ramblers

In 1972 the Red Clay Ramblers formed in Chapel Hill, North Carolina, to play traditional STRINGBAND music, and they quickly developed a distinctive sound derived from the diverse influences of early jazz, gospel, country, BLUEGRASS, Tin Pan Alley pop, Irish music, and more. Banjo player Tommy Thompson, fiddler Bill Hicks,

and guitarist-mandolinist Jim Watson were the group's founding members; pianist Mike Craver joined in 1973.

The Ramblers released their first album, a collaboration with fiddler Al McCanless, on Folkways in 1974, and in January 1975 went to New York to appear for seven months in an off-Broadway musical about Jesse James called *Diamond Studs*—cowritten by playwright and future band member Bland Simpson. During the show's run the Ramblers met cast member Jack Herrick, a multi-instrumentalist who joined the band and expanded the group's repertoire with trumpet, pennywhistle, and bouzouki.

The Ramblers have recorded for the Flying Fish and SUGAR HILL labels as well as issuing albums on their own label. Michelle Shocked and avant-garde musician Eugene Chadbourne have both enlisted them for recording projects, and the group has distinguished itself with work for theater and film, including the score for playwright Sam Shepard's off-Broadway play *A Lie of the Mind* (1985) and the soundtrack to his feature film directorial debut, *Far North* (1988). The band also provided the musical score for the 1998 film *Paradise Falls*.

In addition, the Ramblers served as the pit band for a pre-Broadway run of ROGER MILLER's *Big River* (1985). Thompson, Herrick, and Simpson composed music and lyrics for the stage musical *Lone Star Love: The Merry Wives of Windsor, Texas* (1984), and Thompson and Herrick wrote a score for *Ear Rings*, a play based on author Lee Smith's 1983 novel *Oral History*. The band appeared in several Broadway productions of *Fool Moon* (beginning in 1993), and they collaborated on *Kudzu* (1998), a musical based on Doug Marlette's popular newspaper cartoon strip. The Ramblers also have contributed music for two original ballets, *Ramblin' Suite* (2002) and *Carolina Jamboree* (2005).

Thompson, the last original member, left the group in 1994 (he died of an Alzheimer's-related illness on January 24, 2003). The current lineup includes Herrick (b. Teaneck, New Jersey, September 19, 1947), Buckner (b. Titusville, Florida, November 10, 1952), Simpson (b. Durham, North Carolina, October 16, 1948), and Chris Frank (b. Omaha, Nebraska, April 2, 1952). —*Jay Orr*

## Red River Dave
b. San Antonio, Texas, December 15, 1914; d. January 15, 2002

A veteran western entertainer whose career spanned seven decades, Red River Dave is best known as a prolific composer of topical, patriotic, and sentimental ballads.

A native of San Antonio, David McEnery toured the rodeo circuits as a youth, winning Texas championships at rope twirling and yodeling. With interest in singing cowboys on the rise, McEnery began his broadcasting career in San Antonio and on BORDER RADIO before moving east in the mid-1930s. After performing on stations in Virginia and Florida, he landed a regular slot on WOR–New York in 1938; the Mutual Radio Network fed his program to its nationwide affiliates. Encouraged by songwriter-publisher BOB MILLER, McEnery began writing and recording topical songs; "Amelia Earhart's Last Flight" became a country-folk standard. In May 1939 he sang on an experimental television broadcast at the New York World's Fair.

Returning to Texas after World War II, McEnery recorded for numerous postwar labels, appeared in several low-budget westerns, and began performing over WOAI–San Antonio. He also cut transcriptions for Mexican border stations. McEnery was a popular San Antonio television personality through the 1950s and 1960s. In 1967 he largely retired from music to concentrate on his real estate business, although he continued producing self-accompanied topical singles on his own labels. He returned to music in the late 1970s in Nashville; he then moved to California, where he occasionally performed at Knott's Berry Farm near Anaheim. —*Dave Samuelson*

## Blind Alfred Reed
b. Floyd, Virginia, June 15, 1880; d. January 17, 1956

Although he was born in Virginia, Alfred Reed spent most of his life in West Virginia, mainly near the towns of Princeton, Pipestem, and Hinton. Neither of his parents was musically inclined, but he learned to play fiddle, guitar, banjo, and mandolin at an early age. Although blind from birth, these abilities, combined with his singing and songwriting, enabled him to earn a living for himself, his wife, Nettie, and their six children. He gave music lessons to youngsters, but the greater portion of his earnings came from performing at dances, meetings, and churches and occasionally from playing on street corners and in city parks for tips.

Although he performed in an archaic style, Reed won local popularity by effectively accompanying his strong baritone voice with his own fiddling. He learned songs from oral tradition, SONGBOOKS, and the radio in addition to writing his own material. In fact, one of his original compositions led to a two-year recording career.

On May 24, 1927, a passenger train and a freight train on the Virginian Railway collided head-on at Ingleside, West Virginia, killing two and injuring twenty-nine. After hearing radio reports of the accident, Reed composed "The Wreck of the Virginian," a song that became well-known in his section of the state. Soon RALPH PEER, a talent scout and producer for the Victor Talking Machine Company, contacted Reed. A friend drove the blind singer to BRISTOL, TENNESSEE, where, on July 28, 1927, he recorded his train-wreck BALLAD and three religious songs, accompanied only by his own guitar or fiddle. All four sides were issued and sold well locally; reportedly, his 78s sold as soon as they reached the stores.

Reed's next session took place in Camden, New Jersey, on December 19, 1927. Accompanied by his guitar-playing son, Arville, and fiddler Fred Pendleton, he recorded six songs, including "Always Lift Him Up and Never Knock Him Down," his home community's favorite Reed song, and a critique of the popular flapper hairstyles, "Why Do You Bob Your Hair, Girls?" Nearly two years later, on December 3–4, 1929, Alfred and Arvill Reed made their last recording session, in New York City. Twelve songs were waxed and ten were released, including "Beware," Alfred's version of a German folk song first published in the 1860s, and a second recording of "Why Do You Bob Your Hair, Girls?"

Although the Great Depression ended Reed's recording career, he continued to perform for several years thereafter in the Princeton area, by himself, with Arville and Pendleton, and with another locally known blind musician, Richard Harold (who himself cut four sides in 1928 for the COLUMBIA label). By the late 1930s Reed was playing in public infrequently, primarily because of local laws restricting street musicians, but he continued to compose songs, writing them in Braille.

*Always Lift Him Up: A Tribute to Blind Alfred Reed* (Proper American, 2007) features performances of Reed's songs by artists associated with West Virginia, his home state. —*W. K. McNeil*

## Jerry Reed
b. Atlanta, Georgia, March 20, 1937; d. September 1, 2008

A successful recording artist, songwriter, and movie star, Jerry Reed Hubbard brought something highly individual and hot to country music, beginning with his 1967 chart-maker "Guitar Man," an infectious sound marked by syncopated, complex fingerstyle guitar and plenty of Deep South attitude. "If you wasn't wearing that black robe, I'd take you out back of this courthouse and I'd try a little bit of Your Honor on! You understand that, you hillbilly?" That's Reed blustering away at a city judge during the fade of his 1971 Grammy winner "When You're Hot, You're Hot."

During his lifetime, Reed influenced singer-guitarists such as STEVE WARINER, prominent studio guitar players such as BRENT MASON, and even CHET ATKINS, who did several Reed tunes on his own albums. Still widely emulated, Reed combined complex independent lines in the guitar's bass and treble ranges and also used rippling combinations of fretted and open strings. His composition "The Claw" remains a standard many players seek to master. "His playing had the complexity of classical music," said scholar-guitarist John Knowles, "but the rhythmic sense that comes from country, rock, and gospel."

Yet Reed's electric mix of picking and grinning caught fire only after years spent paying his dues. Beginning guitar at age nine, Reed appeared on shows with FARON YOUNG and ERNEST TUBB by his early teens. CAPITOL RECORDS producer KEN NELSON signed Reed at age seventeen, but ten single releases brought little success. Atlanta music publisher Bill Lowery (THE LOWERY MUSIC GROUP) encouraged Reed to write songs, and he scored tunes recorded by Gene Vincent and by BRENDA LEE ("That's All You Gotta Do," a #6 pop hit). Switching to COLUMBIA yielded the minor 1962 pop hits "Goodnight Irene" and "Hully Gully Guitar."

After military service, Reed moved to Nashville in 1962 with his wife, Priscilla (who had her own #1 record as ROY DRUSKY's duet partner on 1965's "Yes, Mr. Peters"). Reed started playing sessions, appearing on chart-makers by BOBBY BARE and others, and penning hits such as PORTER WAGONER's 1962 #1 "Misery Loves Company." A move to RCA in 1964 brought Reed together with his idol, producer-picker-executive Chet Atkins, who had already been encouraging Reed's picking.

Attempts to cast Reed in a standard country mold failed, and by 1966 Atkins was telling Reed simply to be himself on record, to let fly with his funky, down-home wit and hard-earned guitar mastery. ELVIS PRESLEY recorded Reed's "Guitar Man" and "U.S. Male,"

*Jerry Reed*

with Reed on guitar, as well as tunes from Reed's more reflective side as a writer. Artists ranging from JOHNNY CASH to Engelbert Humperdinck also cut Reed's songs.

"Guitar Man" set the tone for raucous numbers such as "Tupelo Mississippi Flash" (1967–68), "Alabama Wild Man" (1968), and "Are You from Dixie" (1969). In turn, these paved the way for two landmark Reed hits. The highly rhythmic "Amos Moses," a story set in the Louisiana bayou country, became a 1970 country hit and #8 pop song, while "When You're Hot, You're Hot" was a country chart-topper of 1971. In addition, he and Atkins earned a 1970 Grammy for their instrumental album *Me and Jerry*.

Meanwhile, Reed's regular appearances on CBS's *Glen Campbell Goodtime Hour* led to his wisecracking country boy role in the 1975 Burt Reynolds vehicle *W. W. and the Dixie Dance Kings*. Mostly playing to his own wilder side, Reed appeared in Reynolds's *Gator* (1976), *Smokey and the Bandit* (1977), *High-Ballin'* (1978), *Hot Stuff* (1979), *Concrete Cowboys* (a 1979 TV movie that resulted in a brief 1981 CBS series starring Reed), *Smokey and the Bandit II* (1980), *Smokey and the Bandit III* (1983), and *Survivors* (1983).

As Reed's film career prospered, however, his records lost steam. After 1973's #1 hit "Lord, Mr. Ford," he posted only two Top Ten hits—1977's *Smokey* theme, "East Bound and Down," and 1978's tender "(I Love You) What Can I Say"—until his pair of 1982 novelty hits, "She Got the Goldmine (I Got the Shaft)" and "The Bird." Reed and WAYLON JENNINGS joined forces for a 1983 hit remake of the Sam and Dave oldie "Hold On, I'm Comin'," but by 1984 Reed was off RCA.

In 1985 Reed produced, directed, and starred in the music-business action flick *What Comes Around*, with dismal box-office results. In 1988 he coproduced, starred in, and wrote songs for the Vietnam action movie *BAT 21*, with Gene Hackman. *Nashville 99*, Reed's 1976–77 police action TV series, was short-lived.

Reed kept a relatively low profile after 1990, although he continued to tour and make occasional television appearances into the 2000s. He reunited with Atkins in 1992 for the CBS album *Sneakin' Around*, and in 1998 Reed appeared in Adam Sandler's comic film *The Water Boy*.

*Bloom*, a 2005 album by American guitarist Eric Johnson, included the track "Tribute to Jerry Reed." Darrell Toney & Friends (an act including prominent Nashville session players) released the tribute album *Jerry Reed . . . Revisited* in 2006. Elected to the NASHVILLE SONGWRITERS HALL OF FAME in 2005, Reed died in 2008, of complications resulting from emphysema. —*Thomas Goldsmith*

## Ola Belle Reed
b. Lansing, North Carolina, August 17, 1916; d. August 16, 2002

Folksinger, banjo and guitar player, and songwriter Ola Belle Reed was a prominent figure in OLD-TIME MUSIC. One of thirteen children of Arthur Campbell, a schoolteacher and bandleader, she grew up on old-time music and learned to play the guitar early on, later teaching her brother Alec Campbell to play the instrument. The family moved to Maryland in the 1930s. During World War II, Alec was a member of GRANDPA JONES & His Munich Mountaineers, who broadcast in Germany following the Nazi surrender.

Reed first worked professionally in the North Carolina Ridge Runners. After the war, she and Campbell organized the New River Boys, a STRINGBAND named after the river that flowed by their childhood home, and gained radio audiences from stations in Havre de Grace, Maryland, and Coatesville, Pennsylvania. They also broadcast over WBMO–Baltimore and recorded radio shows for syndication. Their wide-ranging repertoire included many of their estimated 200 original songs, which often dealt with Appalachian life. "High on a Mountain," Reed's most famous composition, has been recorded by DEL MCCOURY, TIM O'BRIEN, and MARTY STUART.

In 1951, Campbell, Reed, and Ola Belle's husband, singer-guitarist Bud Reed, established one of the nation's most active country music parks—the New River Ranch near Rising Sun, Maryland. In 1958, turning New River's management over to others, they became the "house band" at nearby Sunset Park in West Grove, Pennsylvania, where they remained for more than two decades and performed on a regular Sunday radio show. In addition, they ran a successful store in Oxford, Pennsylvania, specializing in mail-order sales of country and gospel records; Campbell bought airtime from major radio stations and advertised during remote broadcasts from an in-store studio. For a brief period in the early 1960s they were featured on station WWVA in Wheeling, West Virginia. Reed often appeared on the folk festival circuit, and in the 1970s her albums appeared on ROUNDER and Folkways.

Reed received an NEA National Heritage Fellowship in 1986. Not long afterward she suffered a stroke that kept her from performing, but until her death in 2002 she still welcomed visitors who stopped by to make music at her home. —*W. K. McNeil*

## Del Reeves
b. Sparta, North Carolina, July 14, 1932; d. January 1, 2007

Franklin Delano Reeves made his biggest impact recording uptempo trucker tunes such as "Girl on the Billboard" (#1, 1965), "The Belles of Southern Bell" (#4, 1965), and "Looking at the World Through a Windshield" (#5, 1968), but he also delighted GRAND OLE OPRY fans with humorous impressions of other country singers.

The youngest of eleven children, Reeves sang on local radio at age twelve. After attending Appalachian State College in Boone, North Carolina, he served four years in the U.S. Air Force. While stationed in California, he appeared on television and made his first recordings for CAPITOL in 1957–58. With his wife, Ellen Schiell, he coauthored "Sing a Little Song of Heartache," a #3 hit for Capitol artist ROSE MADDOX in 1962–63.

Reeves recorded for DECCA in 1961–62 and moved to Nashville in 1962 at the urging of songwriter HANK COCHRAN. After short stints with Reprise (1963) and COLUMBIA (1964), Reeves began a fourteen-year association with United Artists Records in 1965 that led to his biggest hits and Grand Ole Opry membership (1966). He appeared in eight movies, notably *Sam Whiskey* (1969), and hosted the *Del Reeves Country Carnival* TV series (1970–73). Leaving United Artists in 1978, he moved on to Koala and Playback, but his recording success had already faded after 1971. His last chart-maker came in 1986. Later he nurtured the career of singer BILLY RAY CYRUS. —*Walt Trott*

## Goebel Reeves
b. Sherman, Texas, October 9, 1899; d. January 26, 1959

Goebel Leon Reeves, known as the Texas Drifter, was a genuine hobo who sang hobo and cowboy songs to his own guitar accompaniment. Noted for his distinctive yodel, which included a trill, and for his charismatic recitations, he made popular recordings, including "Big Rock Candy Mountain," "Hobo's Lullaby," "Railroad Boomer," and "Little Joe, the Wrangler."

Reeves spent his childhood in Sherman, Texas, where his mother taught music and his father was a salesman and state legislator. During sessions the family lived in AUSTIN, where Goebel became a legislative page, learned guitar and trumpet, and first encountered hobos and their songs. After serving in World War I, he entered into the first of several short-lived marriages. He worked as a railroad machinist but soon adopted an itinerant lifestyle.

In 1925 Reeves teamed with JIMMIE RODGERS, guitarist Lucien "Piggy" Parks, and others to tour midwestern and southern states. Following a stint as a merchant seaman, in June 1929 he began broadcasting on KRLD–Dallas and recording for OKEH. Subsequently he recorded for GENNETT, BRUNSWICK, and other labels, sometimes under pseudonyms such as George Riley.

Eventually, famed radio announcer Graham McNamee heard Reeves singing in a New York restaurant, and an NBC contract led to appearances on network programs, including *The Rudy Vallee Show*. Thereafter Reeves worked the Balaban and Katz and Paramount Publix vaudeville circuits but tired of urban audiences, who found his songs comical. Returning to Dallas, he began a ten-year odyssey to local radio stations in southern and western states. Still under contract to NBC, he appeared at the 1933 Chicago World's Fair and later on the GRAND OLE OPRY and the *NATIONAL BARN DANCE*.

By the advent of World War II, Reeves had retired from active entertaining. He died from a heart condition at the Long Beach, California, Veterans Hospital. —*Fred Hoeptner*

## Jim Reeves

b. Panola County, Texas, August 20, 1923; d. July 31, 1964

Jim Reeves stands as one of country music's most distinctive singers. His smooth, warm baritone was a major component of THE NASHVILLE SOUND, a sophisticated, pop-influenced style that emerged during the late 1950s and early 1960s and pushed country music to new commercial heights.

James Travis Reeves was the youngest of nine children, and his older brothers were forced to leave school to help support the family after their father died, when Jim was still a baby. Fascinated by music as a boy, by age twelve he was singing and playing guitar at local dances and broadcasting with a band on Shreveport, Louisiana, radio station KRMD.

After high school in Carthage, Texas, Reeves won a baseball scholarship to the University of Texas at Austin, quit to volunteer for military service in World War II, and became a welder after failing his physical. He continued to play baseball in the minor leagues in several states while working as a salesman between seasons. By 1947, however, a leg injury ended his baseball career, so he landed announcer's jobs on several East Texas radio stations that allowed him to advertise local personal appearances.

Although Reeves first recorded for Macy's Records in Houston, in about 1949, his recording career began in earnest when he signed with ABBOTT RECORDS in 1952. Early success with "Mexican Joe" helped him move up to 50,000-watt KWKH in Shreveport, where he served as an announcer and performed on the LOUISIANA HAYRIDE. From there he graduated to the GRAND OLE OPRY, joining in October 1955 on the strength of early hits on the RCA label, for which he began recording the previous May. At first Reeves generally took a hard-country approach in the

*Jim Reeves*

studio, but "Four Walls," a #1 country and #11 pop hit, marked his transition to pop-tinged love ballads sung close to the microphone in an intimate, low register. In so doing, he continued a pattern set by EDDY ARNOLD and RED FOLEY and helped make crossover success a continuing trend for country singers. Between 1957 and 1958 Reeves fronted his own pop radio show, fed from WSM to the ABC Network. At about this time Reeves also began to reshape his image, shifting from cowboy outfits to sport coats and slacks and even tuxedos on occasion.

A demanding perfectionist in the studio, Reeves worked closely with RCA producer CHET ATKINS in choosing material, and their efforts paid off. Hits such as "Blue Boy," "Billy Bayou," "Home," and "Am I Losing You" solidified his stardom while demonstrating his versatility. In 1959–60 he scored his biggest hit, "He'll Have to Go," which topped the country charts and went #2 pop in the bargain. As CMA began to push country-pop sounds in converting radio stations to all-country formats, Reeves became a natural with stations that followed the emerging Nashville Sound trend. Soon he became an international star, making a 1962 tour to South Africa and later trips to England, Ireland, and Europe. Even if fans couldn't understand the lyrics, one journalist wrote, "The resonant purr from the honeyed larynx of Jim Reeves [had] an almost hypnotic effect."

Although Reeves was killed in a plane crash in 1964, his recordings have continued to sell. Posthumous hits helped him win election to THE COUNTRY MUSIC HALL OF FAME in 1967, and he charted as late as 1983. —*John W. Rumble*

## Mike Reid

b. Altoona, Pennsylvania, May 24, 1947

Mike Reid is the only former All-Pro NFL football player and NCAA All-American to be elected to the NASHVILLE SONGWRITERS HALL OF FAME (2005). Born into a working-class family, Reid won the

Maxwell Award as the outstanding college football player in 1969 as a two-time All-American at Penn State University. He then became a star defensive tackle for the Cincinnati Bengals while also performing with the city's symphony orchestra as a classical pianist. He quit football in 1975 to devote himself to music.

Reid became an ATV publishing staff songwriter in 1980 and moved to Nashville. In 1982 he signed with RONNIE MILSAP's publishing firm, eventually writing eleven hits for Milsap, including "Inside," "In Love," and "Lost in the Fifties Tonight (in the Still of the Night)." Milsap's recording of Reid's "Stranger in My House" won the songwriter a 1983 Grammy for Best Country Song. Reid also penned hits for THE JUDDS ("Born to Be Blue"), LORRIE MORGAN ("He Talks to Me"), DON WILLIAMS ("One Good Well"), and CONWAY TWITTY ("Fallin' for You for Years"). Reid was ASCAP's Country Songwriter of the Year in 1985.

The 1988 Top Ten hit "Old Folks," a Milsap–Reid duet, featured the tunesmith's gospel-tinged baritone and led to a COLUMBIA recording contract. Reid's first solo release, 1990's "Walk on Faith," went to #1, and three Top Twenty chart-makers followed in 1991–92. But Reid was a soul singer in his early forties, and when country turned toward young honky-tonkers, his subsequent singles fared less well.

As a songwriter, though, Reid's reputation grew as Bonnie Raitt took his wistful "I Can't Make You Love Me" to the pop Top Twenty and country stars such as Tim McGraw ("Everywhere") topped the charts with his material. Reid has also composed theatrical/operatic works, including *A House Divided* (1991), *Tales of Appalachia* (1995), and *The Ballad of Little Jo* (1997), which won a Richard Rodgers Development Award from the American Academy of Arts and Letters. —*Robert K. Oermann*

## Dick Reinhart
b. Tishomingo, Oklahoma, February 17, 1907; d. December 3, 1948

Richard "Dick" Reinhart ranks among the best WESTERN SWING vocalists. Displaying the versatility typically associated with the genre, Reinhart was an especially fine blues singer, having learned directly from black bluesmen in Dallas's Deep Ellum district. He was also a gifted songwriter ("Fort Worth Jail," "A Broken Heart for a Souvenir") and instrumentalist, playing guitar, mandolin, banjo, and bass.

He was living in Dallas by the late 1920s, and as 1929 recordings sessions reveal, he was already a formidable vocalist. His western ballads for BRUNSWICK hinted at the black influences that were explicit in his falsetto jazz vocal on the Three Virginians' "June Tenth Blues" for OKEH. Later, Reinhart formed the Wanderers with ROY NEWMAN and Bert Dodson, recording for BLUEBIRD in 1935 before joining the LIGHT CRUST DOUGHBOYS late that year; with this group he shared vocal duties with Dodson until the latter's departure. Classic Reinhart performances with the Doughboys included "Ding Dong Daddy" (1936) and "Sittin' on Top of the World" (1938). He departed in 1938 to join the Universal Cowboys, completing a session for Vocalion in 1939 before obtaining his own contract in 1940. He moved to Oklahoma for the first of several stints with JIMMY WAKELY, with whom he headed to the West Coast, where he also worked with GENE AUTRY. Reinhart became more of a crooner as time passed but retained a bluesy tinge until his death, evidenced in "Muddy Water" from his final session (COLUMBIA, 1947). Back in Fort Worth, his career on hold, he suffered a fatal heart attack at forty-one. —*Kevin Coffey*

## The Reinsmen

Anchored by Dick Goodman (vocal, guitar, bass), Don Richardson (vocal, guitar, bass, banjo), and Jerry Compton (vocal, guitar, steel guitar), the Reinsmen have been one of America's most enduring and appealing western singing groups.

It was the magnetism of the music written by western music legends—Bob Nolan, Tim Spencer, Stan Jones, MARTY ROBBINS, and others—that inspired the Reinsmen to portray the romance of the West in song. Goodman and Richardson were products of the Wagonmasters, a popular musical group at Knotts Berry Farm in Buena Park, California, for a number of years. In 1962 Jerry Compton joined Goodman and Richardson to form the Reinsmen. Bob Wagoner (vocal, guitar), known for his artistic paintings of the West; noted performer Max "Doc" Denning (vocal, fiddle, guitar); fiddler Harvey Walker; and guitarist/vocalist Johnny Blankenship joined the group at various times.

The Reinsmen have appeared in, and furnished musical backgrounds for motion pictures, made countless appearances with western movie and singing star REX ALLEN, performed at the White House, and recorded several albums. —*Ken Griffis*

## Herb Remington
b. Mishawaka, Indiana, June 9, 1926

A kingpin of postwar WESTERN SWING steel guitar, Herbert Leroy Remington is best known for his stint with BOB WILLS & His Texas Playboys from 1946 to 1950. One of the first important swing steel players born outside the Southwest, he grounded his style in HAWAIIAN MUSIC, a debt still audible in his playing and an approach that kept him eating during western swing's lean years.

Remington knew little country music when he joined RAY WHITLEY's western swing band in California upon leaving military service in 1946, but he soon auditioned successfully for Wills. Though inexperienced, he sounded remarkably assured and mature when he recorded with Wills in September of that year. With the Playboys he produced classic solos on sides such as "Fat Boy Rag" (1946) and his signature tune, "Boot Heel Drag" (1949), and created sophisticated string ensembles with guitarist ELDON SHAMBLIN and mandolinist TINY MOORE. Leaving Wills, Remington worked briefly with HANK PENNY, recording his classic "Remington Ride" in 1950. Remington then joined DICKIE AND LAURA LEE McBRIDE's Ranch Hands in Houston. A busy session player, Remington recorded countless sides with artists such as FLOYD TILLMAN and later toured the nation with his own Beachcombers. During the 1990s and beyond he co-led Playboys II, a Wills-revival group, with JOHNNY GIMBLE, also appearing with Clyde Brewer's Original River Road Boys. Remington has marketed his own line of non–pedal steel guitars since 1986. —*Kevin Coffey*

## George Reneau
b. Jefferson County, Tennessee, 1901; d. December 1933

Known as the Blind Musician of the Smoky Mountains, George Reneau was one of the few traditional musicians to make the transition from wandering street minstrel to recording artist. He was one of the earliest country recording artists, making his first sides in April 1924 and his last in June 1927. For a short time Reneau's discs rivaled those of FIDDLIN' JOHN CARSON, HENRY WHITTER, and Charlie Oaks in popularity.

Born in the foothills of the Smokies, Reneau was apparently blind from birth. He moved to Knoxville as a teenager and learned to play guitar from a niece. By the early 1920s he had become a fixture on city street corners and at the train station, where he performed for tips. Gus Nennsteil, a local furniture dealer and talent scout for Vocalion records, heard him and arranged a New York recording trip.

At first Vocalion preferred Reneau's guitar and mouth harp playing to his vocals, and label executives didn't let Reneau sing on his own records; instead, he backed young studio singer Gene Austin (who would soon became a national star with his recording of "My Blue Heaven"). Reneau's early hits, including "Blue Ridge Blues," "Susie Ann," and "Lonesome Road Blues," featured Austin on vocals. By February 1925 Reneau began handling vocal duties himself, enjoying success with "The Prisoner's Song," "Woman's Suffrage," and "Wild Bill Jones." In 1927 Reneau teamed with Lester McFarland (of MAC & BOB) for a series of duets, with certain sides issued under the names the Gentry Brothers, the Smoky Mountain Twins, the Halliday Brothers, the Collins Brothers, the Cramer Brothers, and the Lonesome Pine Twins. Over the next five years these sides were released on various labels, including Banner, CHALLENGE, CONQUEROR, Oriole, and Paramount.

The Great Depression forced Reneau to return to street singing, and in December 1933 he died of pneumonia at age thirty-two.
—*Charles Wolfe*

## Renfro Valley Barn Dance
established in Cincinnati, Ohio, October 9, 1937

The *Renfro Valley Barn Dance* was heard Saturday nights, mainly in the Midwest and South, for a twenty-year period beginning October 9, 1937. Created by Kentuckian JOHN LAIR (1894–1985),

it was carried at times on the NBC Blue, CBS, and Mutual Networks. Mainly, however, the show's wide audience resulted from access provided by the far nighttime reach of Cincinnati's WLW and, after 1941, Louisville's WHAS.

On November 4, 1939, after stints first in the Cincinnati Music Hall and later in Dayton's Memorial Auditorium, the show moved to a real barn in Lair's native Renfro Valley, fifty miles south of Lexington, Kentucky. The barn was the centerpiece of a simulated turn-of-the-century village Lair eventually assembled with old and newly built structures. He told listeners they could come to Renfro Valley for a "glimpse of something of the pioneer days in Kentucky not cataloged in musty museums" and have "clean fun on Saturday night we won't be ashamed of on Sunday." The founding partners for the venture were Lair, singer RED FOLEY, and comedian Whitey Ford (THE DUKE OF PADUCAH).

Seeking distinctiveness for his program, Lair recruited most of the cast from Kentucky and points south and styled the performers and their music as "home folks" rather than "hillbilly." With these "makers of music and distributors of mirth"—who also included a few tabloid and BLACKFACE MINSTREL show veterans—Lair crafted a format that initially aired more comedy than WSM's GRAND OLE OPRY and music more rural in flavor than that of WLS's *NATIONAL BARN DANCE*, on which Lair had earlier performed with his CUMBERLAND RIDGE RUNNERS. Comedy, both musical and spoken, was meted out by the likes of HOMER & JETHRO, fiddler Slim Miller, the Duke of Paducah, Margaret Lillie (A'nt Idy), and Gene "Honey Gal" Cobb.

Over the years, many important country singers and instrumentalists appeared on the show. Lair gave equal time to traditional performers such as Lily May Ledford's COON CREEK GIRLS and then-current artists such as Red Foley, the Range Riders, and the Holden Brothers. Gospel music became a regular feature after 1939, with the Crusaders and, later, other quartets. At that time,

*The big barn in
Renfro Valley, Kentucky*

Lair also began distancing the program from the cowboy-western image, no longer allowing western attire onstage and renaming the Range Riders the Mountain Rangers.

The *Renfro Valley Barn Dance* left the air in 1957 because its sponsors opted for television advertising. However, it continued as an important stage attraction. Beginning in 1989, Lair's successor, Renfro Valley Entertainment, Inc., headed by Warren Rosenthal, rebuilt and expanded the original facility. Several weekly performances and special events, March through December, continue to draw visitors from near and far. —*Harry S. Rice*

## Reno & Smiley

Donald Wesley Reno b. Spartanburg, South Carolina, February 21, 1926; d. October 16, 1984
Arthur Lee "Red" Smiley b. Marshall, North Carolina, May 17, 1924; d. January 2, 1972

Don Reno and Red Smiley formed one of the most innovative acts in the early days of BLUEGRASS music. The core of their sound was a bluesy duet featuring the rich baritone lead vocals of guitarist Red Smiley and the soaring tenor harmonies of banjoist Don Reno, augmented by Reno's jazzy banjo work.

They first met in 1950 as members of a band called TOMMY MAGNESS & His Tennessee Buddies. While with Magness, they made their first recordings for the Cincinnati-based Federal label, a KING RECORDS subsidiary. Impressed with their talents, label owner SYD NATHAN soon arranged a recording session for Reno and Smiley under their own names. In January 1952 a marathon sixteen-song session launched the classic Reno & Smiley sound. Relying exclusively on Reno's original songs, the session produced the first of many hits for the duo, including the perennial favorite "I'm Using My Bible for a Road Map."

Reno & Smiley scored well with radio hits and record sales but were unable to maintain a reliable touring band. Reno soon found himself working in Charlotte, North Carolina, with ARTHUR "GUITAR BOOGIE" SMITH & His Crackerjacks. While with Smith, Reno helped polish and record "Feuding Banjos," a familiar instrumental that was later retitled "Dueling Banjos" and showcased in the 1972 movie *Deliverance*.

Although not working the road together, Reno & Smiley continued to record and release material for King. Response to their recordings mounted, and in May 1955 Reno & Smiley organized the classic lineup of their Tennessee Cut-Ups, including fiddler Mack Magaha and bassist John Palmer. They were soon appearing on the OLD DOMINION BARN DANCE on Richmond, Virginia's WRVA, a powerful AM station that beamed their sound up and down the East Coast. In 1957 the group settled in Roanoke, Virginia, and secured a daily television program called *Top of the Morning*.

The glory years of Reno & Smiley reached from 1955 to 1964. During this time they recorded prolifically for King, notching hits such as "I Know You're Married, but I Love You Still," "Don't Let Your Sweet Love Die," and "Please Remember That I Love You."

In the fall of 1964 the two musicians terminated their long-standing partnership. Smiley remained in Roanoke with the *Top of the Morning* show, and Reno moved to Nashville. In the late 1960s, a series of Reno & Smiley reunions led to Smiley's joining Don Reno and his new partner, BILL HARRELL. Several memorable recordings followed, capturing the classic sound of earlier Reno & Smiley duets. January 1972 marked the death of Red Smiley, a diabetic who lived most of his life with one lung

*Reno & Smiley: Don Reno (left) and Red Smiley*

(the result of a war injury). Don Reno died in October 1984 of complications from a circulatory problem, and subsequently his sons, Ronnie, Don Wayne, and Dale, already experienced professionals, formed their own bluegrass act. Reno & Smiley were elected to the IBMA Hall of Fame in 1992. —*Gary B. Reid*

## Republic Records (*see* Gene Autry, Tennessee/Republic Records)

## Restless Heart

John Dittrich b. Batavia, New York, April 7, 1951
Paul Gregg b. Altus, Oklahoma, December 3, 1954
Dave Innis b. Bartlesville, Oklahoma, April 9, 1959
Greg Jennings b. Nicoma Park, Oklahoma, October 2, 1954
Larry Stewart b. Paducah, Kentucky, March 2, 1959

Since the mid-1980s, Restless Heart has pursued a light COUNTRY-ROCK approach highlighting a silky-smooth harmonic blend.

Consisting of former session musicians, Restless Heart organized in 1983 to help producer-songwriter TIM DuBOIS make demo recordings of songs that explored the territory between country and pop. Keyboard player Dave Innis had written the Pointer Sisters hit "Dare Me," while guitarist Greg Jennings had played on several DAN SEALS hits.

The band jelled well enough to garner an RCA recording contract. Just before making their first album, original lead singer Verlon Thompson left, replaced by Larry Stewart. The group found acceptance with the 1985 release of their eponymous debut album. Their second single, "I Want Everyone to Cry," began a string of thirteen straight Top Ten hits through 1990, including six #1 records. Among these were "Why Does It Have to Be (Wrong or Right)," "Wheels," and "Bluest Eyes in Texas." "I'll Still Be Loving You" became a wedding classic and a Top Forty crossover hit.

In 1992 vocalist Stewart departed for a solo career. Nevertheless, the four-man Restless Heart came up with "When She Cries," a massive crossover hit, featuring drummer John Dittrich on lead vocals. Around this same time, Innis was dismissed.

Operating as a trio, the group released the 1994 album *Matters of the Heart*, which was largely ignored. The threesome then took a year off to evaluate their prospects. The original lineup, minus Innis, re-formed in late 1997 and again signed with RCA, but commercial results were slim. In the new century, Innis rejoined, and in 2004 the group had a #29 country single with "Feel My Way to You," from its Koch Records album *Still Restless*. —*Tom Roland*

## Reunion of Professional Entertainers (*see* ROPE)

## Jimmie Revard
b. Pawhuska, Oklahoma, November 26, 1909; d. April 12, 1991

Leader of one of the most popular pre-war WESTERN SWING bands, the Oklahoma Playboys, James Osage Revard vied with Buster Coward's THE TUNE WRANGLERS for supremacy on the competitive 1930s San Antonio scene. Revard was a top BLUEBIRD country act during the years 1936–38, scoring hits with "Holding the Sack" (1936) and "Tulsa Waltz" (1937).

Revard came from a long line of fiddlers. He began violin lessons at age twelve but eventually played mostly bass and guitar with his own bands. Formed in about 1935, the Oklahoma Playboys originally included ADOLPH HOFNER on guitar and Emil Hofner on steel, soon joined by fiddler Ben McKay and two defectors from the Tune Wranglers, guitarist Curley Williams (not the Georgia Peach Pickers bandleader) and jazz pianist Eddie Whitley. Revard secured a Bluebird contract in 1936, and his first sessions were dominated by Whitley's piano and bluesy vocals. Whitley left soon after, eventually replaced by another Tune Wrangler, pianist George Timberlake, while vocals chores were divided among Revard, Williams, and Adolph Hofner.

Revard established local popularity on San Antonio's KTSA. After an ill-fated stay in the Midwest during the winter of 1937–38, he returned to San Antonio, broadcasting on 50,000-watt WOAI. By 1938 Revard had replaced McKay with the excellent fiddler-vocalist Leon Seago; Revard began featuring himself on clarinet and added drummer Edmond Franke, thus solidifying the Oklahoma Playboys as one of the era's most sophisticated country dance bands. Tiring of the grind, Revard disbanded in 1939 (though he recorded again in 1940) and became a San Antonio policeman. After the war, he led bands on a part-time basis, recording for the Everstate label in 1950. In the 1980s, encouraged by new interest in his music, he issued a single on Sarg Records in 1982. —*Kevin Coffey*

## Allen Reynolds
b. North Little Rock, Arkansas, August 18, 1938

Although Allen Reynolds has made significant contributions to the careers of DON WILLIAMS, KATHY MATTEA, and CRYSTAL GAYLE, he is likely best known for having produced all of GARTH BROOKS's albums except for his pop departure, *Garth Brooks . . . In the Life of Chris Gaines*. When starting Brooks's first album, Reynolds convinced the Oklahoman to sing in his natural voice, instead of the bellowing, soaring style he had been using. The intimate, accessible tone heard on "The Dance" and "Friends in Low Places" set Brooks off on his landmark career.

Reynolds is also a successful songwriter, penning such hits as "We Should Be Together," "Ready for the Times to Get Better," and "Five O'Clock World," which was a hit for the pop group the Vogues in the 1960s and for HAL KETCHUM in the 1990s. WAYLON JENNINGS, JOHNNY RUSSELL, Don Williams, COLLIN RAYE, the Cowboy Junkies, and JAMEY JOHNSON have all recorded Reynolds's compositions.

Reynolds began writing with DICKEY LEE while the two attended Rhodes College in Memphis, and became friends with SUN RECORDS engineer-producer JACK CLEMENT. Reynolds and Lee moved to Beaumont, Texas, where Clement had opened Gulf Coast Recording Studios, and the two wrote "I Saw Linda Yesterday," a Top Fifteen hit for Lee.

The duo moved back to Memphis in 1964 and signed with Screen Gems Publishing Company in Nashville. With producer Stan Kesler they started their own Memphis production and publishing company and developed a staff that included writers BOB McDILL and PAUL CRAFT.

In 1970 Reynolds moved to Nashville and was hired by Clement to manage and produce for JMI Records. Reynolds produced two albums for Don Williams before Clement closed the label in 1975. Reynolds then became an independent producer and purchased Jack's Tracks Recording Studio. Besides producing additional Williams albums, Reynolds began working with Crystal Gayle. She earned her first Top Ten with the Reynolds-penned "Wrong Road Again." Over the next eight years he produced ten albums for Gayle, including five gold and two platinum successes; these albums yielded nineteen additional Top Ten hits.

Kathy Mattea had made little headway in country music before she teamed with Reynolds in 1986. He overhauled her sound, taking her from heavily produced pop-country to

*Allen Reynolds*

understated acoustic-country. "Love at the Five and Dime," Mattea's first single with Reynolds as producer, hit the Top Ten.

Reynolds has also produced or coproduced EMMYLOU HARRIS, Hal Ketchum, the CACTUS BROTHERS, THE O'KANES, and JOHNNY RODRIGUEZ, among others.

A longtime music publisher, Reynolds and his colleagues sold their company, Forerunner Music, to Universal Music Publishing Group in 2000. That same year, Reynolds was elected to the NASHVILLE SONGWRITERS HALL OF FAME. —Beverly Keel

## Michael Rhodes
b. West Monroe, Louisiana, September 16, 1953

A successful studio and touring bassist and frequent ACM award winner, Michael Wayne Rhodes's typically huge sound, funky and melodic lines, and strong rhythmic sense have made him one of Nashville's most called-upon musicians.

Rhodes started playing professionally in Louisiana bands at age fourteen, taking on country, R&B, CAJUN—"whatever paid," as he recalled in 1995. He mastered various musical styles in AUSTIN, TEXAS, where he moved in the early 1970s; in Memphis, where he worked in the mid-1970s with CHARLIE RICH; and in Nashville, where he moved in 1978 and played in the acclaimed local funk band the Nerve.

Rhodes's session career began as a demo musician for Nashville's TREE PUBLISHING COMPANY. Session bassist-guitarist Tommy Cogbill mentored Rhodes, and keyboardist-producer BARRY BECKETT was another key influence. Rhodes has worked on the road and/or recorded with a multitude of stars, including J. J. Cale, DOLLY PARTON, RODNEY CROWELL, ROSANNE CASH, REBA MCENTIRE, and DIXIE CHICKS. Rhodes's signature work includes Cash's *King's Record Shop* (1987), HANK WILLIAMS JR.'s *Born to Boogie* (1987), and Crowell's *Diamonds and Dirt* (1988). In 1997 Rhodes joined Crowell, STEUART SMITH, and Vince Santoro in the Cicadas. Into the 2000s he has contributed to hits by the likes of BROOKS & DUNN, GRETCHEN WILSON, KENNY CHESNEY, and TOBY KEITH. He was also bassist for the landmark album *Last of the Breed* (LOST HIGHWAY, 2007), which featured WILLIE NELSON, MERLE HAGGARD, and RAY PRICE. —Thomas Goldsmith

## Speck Rhodes
b. West Plains, Missouri, July 16, 1915; d. March 19, 2000

Gilbert "Speck" Rhodes was one of country music's most endearing comedians, with a musical-vaudeville career dating to the Great Depression. He was forty-four when he joined television's syndicated PORTER WAGONER *Show* in 1960, performing as the program's rube comedian during its lengthy run.

Rhodes's parents moved to Arkansas when he was five years old. Speck played old-fashioned five-string banjo, and by 1931 he, his two brothers, and his sister were performing on the local town square and making five or six dollars at a time. As a touring act, they covered more than thirty states between 1933 and 1937.

Rhodes bought a bass fiddle in 1936, and by 1939 he was working on radio in Poplar Bluff, Missouri. He began to try "clowning"—copying some MEDICINE SHOW techniques—and in 1941 he adopted his famous checkered-suit costume. By 1947 the Rhodes family was performing on Memphis radio and, later, on television.

When Rhodes was invited to join the *Porter Wagoner Show*, he updated some of his earlier Memphis scripts and developed his imaginary telephone character, Sadie. In this role he also sang "Sweet Fern" and other numbers. His appearance in the 1984 film *Rhinestone*, starring DOLLY PARTON and Sylvester Stallone, marked a long rise from picking cotton for fifty cents a day and singing on sidewalks for pocket change. —Steve Eng

## RIAA
established in New York, New York, 1952

The Recording Industry Association of America is a nonprofit organization that tracks record sales and acts as a government liaison for companies that create and distribute recorded music. Membership includes some 1,600 record companies and distributors, with the four largest members being EMI Group, SONY MUSIC ENTERTAINMENT, Universal Music Group, and Warner Music Group.

Based in Washington, D.C., for many years, RIAA has set technical standards for recorded media, mounted defenses against censorship of recorded music and related record labeling, participated in copyright negotiations, fought music piracy, and assisted the FBI in catching music counterfeiters.

But the organization's highest-profile work involves its issuance of gold, platinum, and multiplatinum awards for singles and albums, certifying the achievement of significant sales levels. Six years after the agency's founding, the RIAA instituted its certification policies to provide a factual, measurable basis for the multitude of gold albums that record labels were handing out in the 1950s.

Originally, gold records represented $1 million earned in wholesale album sales or 1 million singles sold. In 1975 the album criterion was altered, requiring sales of 500,000 copies. In 1989, singles followed suit, with a half-million in sales resulting in gold status. In 1976, the platinum category was added, recognizing sales of 1 million singles or albums. Multiplatinum categories later came into existence: double-platinum for 2 million albums, triple-platinum for 3 million, and so on. In 2004, RIAA began formally tracking digital music sales, including ringtones. Certifications for digital sales mirror those of hard-copy sales: 500,000 for gold, 1 million for platinum, etc.

Among country artists, the first album to be certified gold was TENNESSEE ERNIE FORD's *Hymns* (certified February 20, 1959), and the first gold single was JIMMY DEAN's "Big Bad John" (certified December 14, 1961). Country's first certified platinum album was the various artists collection *Wanted! The Outlaws* (certified November 24, 1976). —Tom Roland

## Bill Rice (*see* Jerry Foster and Bill Rice)

## Tandy Rice
b. Franklin, Tennessee, August 16, 1938

Tandy C. Rice Jr. is a longtime music industry leader based in Nashville. A 1961 graduate of The Citadel in Charleston, South Carolina, with degrees in business and English, Rice served in the U.S. Air Force before starting work as a Nashville publicist in 1963. Eventually he recruited stations for Show Biz Inc.'s syndicated country television series, most notably the *Porter Wagoner Show*.

In 1971 Rice bought Show Biz's booking agency, Top Billing, Inc., which represented Wagoner, DOLLY PARTON, and comedian JERRY CLOWER. By 1978 Rice was handling at least eighteen acts, including TOM T. HALL, JIM ED BROWN, Helen Cornelius, and JEANNIE C. RILEY. For many of his clients, Rice acted as manager as well as agent. A past president of CMA, Rice remains active as president and chief executive officer of Top Billing and as a member of numerous professional and charitable organizations. —*Steve Eng*

## Tony Rice
b. Danville, Virginia, June 8, 1951

One of the most influential guitarists in BLUEGRASS and related acoustical styles, David Anthony Rice grew up in California. His entire family played bluegrass, and he also looked to DOC WATSON and the late CLARENCE WHITE for inspiration.

After playing in bands with his brothers and later with banjoist Bobby Atkins, Rice replaced Dan Crary in THE BLUEGRASS ALLIANCE, based in Louisville, in 1970. For a year Rice worked with SAM BUSH, Courtney Johnson, Lonnie Peerce, and Harry "Ebo Walker" Shelor—three-quarters of the band that later would become NEW GRASS REVIVAL.

Next, Rice joined J. D. CROWE & the New South for four years, initially with his brother Larry Rice and Bobby Slone. In 1974 RICKY SKAGGS replaced Larry; DOBRO player JERRY DOUGLAS joined the following April. Though short-lived, the resulting five-piece configuration became one of the most admired bluegrass bands of all time. Rice, Skaggs, and Douglas left at the end of August 1975.

Rice then spent four years with the DAVID GRISMAN Quartet, experimenting with everything from classical to jazz and combining these elements into what Grisman called "dawg" music. In 1979 Rice established the Tony Rice Unit—known for his own jazz-infused "spacegrass"—and continued producing projects for himself and others. With Crowe, Bobby Hicks, DOYLE LAWSON, and Todd Phillips, he recorded *The Bluegrass Album* (Rounder, 1981), a tribute to the music of the 1950s. Five sequels followed, the last in 1996; Douglas began participating with Volume 3.

Rice's fluid, highly ornamented guitar work has made him arguably the dominant bluegrass guitarist of his era. Prior to suffering vocal-cord damage in the 1990s, he was also a gifted and much-imitated singer, as exemplified by the Tony Rice Unit's *Manzanita* (Rounder, 1979) and the solo album *Church Street Blues* (Sugar Hill, 1983). Since 1990 Rice has recorded albums with his three brothers; with guitarist Norman Bake; with brother Larry, CHRIS HILLMAN, and HERB PEDERSEN; and with PETER ROWAN.

In 2007 Rice toured with ALISON KRAUSS & UNION STATION; Krauss has long praised him as a primary influence. Also in 2007, he won his sixth IBMA award as Instrumental Performer of the Year, adding to previous IBMA honors in the Instrumental Group and Instrumental Album categories. —*Frank and Marty Godbey*

## The Rice Brothers
Hoke Rice b. near Gainesville, Georgia, January 8, 1909; d. May 26, 1974
Paul Rice b. near Gainesville, Georgia, July 23, 1919; d. January 22, 1988

Hoke and Paul Rice were steeped in OLD-TIME MUSIC and STRING-BAND traditions of the Southeast, but when they decided to turn professional they sought to overcome the hillbilly image then used by many country acts. Hoke studied guitar under a classical

musician, and by the late 1920s he had settled in Atlanta, where he was a respected musician, admired by local hillbilly and jazz musicians with whom he worked on area radio stations.

Paul and Hoke later became one of the leading regional BROTHER DUET teams. They hired additional musicians, including horn players, and set about developing a hot, syncopated sound that featured pop-oriented material. They broadcast on radio throughout the Southeast before moving to KWKH in Shreveport, Louisiana, where their career peaked just before the brothers were drafted for military duty in World War II.

While working in Shreveport, Paul sold a song to JIMMIE DAVIS and musician Charles Mitchell for thirty-five dollars. The song, which Paul claimed to have written a couple of years earlier in Atlanta (evidence suggests that he, too, had bought the song), was "You Are My Sunshine." Prior to selling the song to Davis, the Rice Brothers recorded it for DECCA RECORDS, a label for which they ultimately made more than fifty sides.

After the war Hoke took a full-time job as a salesman. Paul continued working as a bass player, mainly in Atlanta, until his retirement from the music business in about 1960. —*Wayne W. Daniel*

## Charlie Rich
b. Forrest City, Arkansas, December 14, 1932; d. July 25, 1995

It's probably no exaggeration to say that Charlie Rich was the most eclectic musician ever to be called country. His natural métier was probably supper-club jazz. It's certainly the style with which he began his professional career and the one to which he periodically reverted. His success, though, came first with rock & roll, then—fleetingly—with white R&B, and finally with country-pop.

While serving in the U.S. Air Force, Rich played on and off base in a group called the Velvetones, a name suggesting their style. Back in Arkansas, Rich tried farming, while doubling as a supper-club pianist in Memphis. He signed with SUN RECORDS in 1957,

*Charlie Rich*

first as a songwriter and session pianist and then as a performer. He wrote several songs for JOHNNY CASH, JERRY LEE LEWIS, and other Sun artists and made his first record for Sun's Phillips International imprint in August 1958; the third, cut in October 1959, was "Lonely Weekends," a Presleyish rocker that peaked just outside the pop Top Twenty.

Rich recorded a wide variety of tracks for Phillips, including perhaps his most outstanding song, "Who Will the Next Fool Be?" Nothing charted, in part because his music was impossible to pigeonhole. In 1963 he signed with RCA's reactivated Groove Records in Nashville, cutting "Big Boss Man" and several bluesy country records ("There Won't Be Anymore," "I Don't See Me in Your Eyes Anymore") that were later overdubbed and successfully reissued. Then, in 1965, he went with Smash/MERCURY RECORDS and scored another Top Thirty pop hit with "Mohair Sam," but once again he couldn't find a follow-up. In 1966 he moved on to Hi Records, where he cut an odd mixture of country and Memphis R&B, with no success at all.

In December 1967 Rich signed with EPIC RECORDS in Nashville, working under the direction of BILLY SHERRILL. There were five commercially arid years when Rich seemed to be Sherrill's personal indulgence. Then Rich broke through with "I Take It on Home" and "Behind Closed Doors," the latter a giant pop, country, and international hit in 1973. He was CMA's 1973 Male Vocalist of the Year and 1974 Entertainer of the Year. Rich stayed with Epic until 1978, though he seemed to sleepwalk through increasingly overblown arrangements. He even appeared uncomfortable with success itself and occasionally exhibited bizarre behavior, such as setting fire to the envelope indicating that JOHN DENVER had won the Entertainer of the Year award on the nationally televised 1975 CMA Awards. Nevertheless, Rich and Sherrill defined crossover country, working the remunerative middle ground between country and easy listening. Rich's #1 country hits included "The Most Beautiful Girl," "A Very Special Love Song," "I Love My Friend," and "Rollin' with the Flow."

Rich's chart success faded quickly after he left Epic. Subsequent affiliations with United Artists and ELEKTRA produced only minor hits, which ended altogether in 1981. Rich then went into semiretirement in Memphis. In 1991 he made an impressive comeback album for Sire that, perhaps more than any other record, captured his sprawling genius. He died in 1995 from a blood clot in his lung. —Colin Escott

## Don Rich
b. Olympia, Washington, August 15, 1941; d. July 17, 1974

Donald Eugene Ulrich—best remembered as lead guitarist and harmony vocalist in BUCK OWENS's band the Buckaroos—began his musical career in 1958 as a sixteen-year-old fiddler playing gigs with Owens in the Seattle area. Together, Owens and Rich honed their partnership and vocal harmonies up and down the West Coast through the early 1960s as Owens's recording career at CAPITOL RECORDS was beginning.

Rich played a crucial role in Owens's band. Having learned to play lead electric guitar from Owens, Rich helped to develop and solidify the "Buck Owens Sound," a hard-edged, beat-driven HONKY-TONK style distinct from the smooth pop sounds of country music produced in Nashville at the time. Rich's incisive lead guitar playing in live performances and in most recording sessions from 1961 on enabled Owens to concentrate on his duties as vocalist, MC, and songwriter as well as on his burgeoning

business empire. Rich also wrote songs with Owens, including the classic "Waitin' in Your Welfare Line" (#1, 1966), on which NAT STUCKEY shared writing credit.

Twelve years Owens's junior, Rich became the star's erstwhile younger brother, best friend, and musical collaborator. Rich's life ended tragically in a 1974 motorcycle accident, an event that devastated Owens, who repeatedly explained that Rich's death was an important factor in his withdrawal from recording throughout most of the 1980s. —Mark Fenster

## Rich-R-Tone Records
established Johnson City, Tennessee, ca. 1946

One of the many regional independent labels to emerge after World War II, Rich-R-Tone was founded in about 1946 by Johnson City, Tennessee, businessman James Stanton. Using studios of radio stations in the Bristol–Kingsport–Johnson City area and having his discs pressed in Philadelphia, Stanton issued some 200 titles, generally featuring area artists who focused on grassroots music. Though many never rose much above their regional status, THE STANLEY BROTHERS and WILMA LEE AND STONEY COOPER, who made their first recordings for Rich-R-Tone, went on to national fame. Lesserknown but important acts such as the Bailey Brothers, the Church Brothers, and other BLUEGRASS bands were also on the roster, as were local favorites such as Buffalo Johnson. Stanton used a subsidiary label, Folk Star, for "custom" or "vanity press" recordings.

In the 1960s Stanton moved to Nashville, where he opened a studio on Church Street and enjoyed a successful business making custom recordings for bluegrass bands and gospel choirs. For a time he revived Rich-R-Tone as a bluegrass album label. Since Stanton's death the label has been managed by Fred Congdon on behalf of Stanton's heirs. —Charles Wolfe

## Ethel Park Richardson
b. Decherd, Tennessee, December 13, 1883; d. April 11, 1968

Ethel Park Richardson journeyed through the southern Appalachians riding a sway-backed horse and on foot, gathering material for her 1927 book American Mountain Songs and for a network radio career in which she would introduce country music to urban listeners.

Singing mountain songs on Chattanooga's WDOD in 1926, Richardson caught the attention of NBC Radio in New York, where she auditioned and landed her own program in 1927. She accompanied her singing with an autoharp and was the creatorwriter of a dozen different radio series. Writing, her first love, eclipsed her work as a performer.

Hillbilly Heart-Throbs, a weekly show in which Richardson dramatized country songs, began a five-year run on NBC in 1933. FRANK LUTHER, ZORA LAYMAN, CARSON ROBISON, TEX RITTER, TEXAS JIM ROBERTSON, and the Vass Family were among the show's regular talent. A later, recorded version of the series was syndicated throughout the 1940s.

In 1955 Richardson was the "folk-singing grandmother" who became the first contestant to win the top prize of $100,000 on NBC-TV's quiz program The Big Surprise. Her category was American folk music, prompting a reissue of her book, an offer for a guest shot on the GRAND OLE OPRY, and recognition for her pioneering efforts in presenting country music to a national audience. —Jonathan Guyot Smith

## J. P. Richardson (*see* The Big Bopper)

## Riders in the Sky

Douglas Bruce Green b. Great Lakes, Illinois, March 20, 1946
Frederick Owen LaBour b. Grand Rapids, Michigan, June 3, 1948
Paul Woodrow Chrisman b. Nashville, Tennessee, August 23, 1949
Joey Miskulin b. Chicago, Illinois, January 6, 1949

Since organizing in 1977, Riders in the Sky have played a major role in the renaissance of western music. Though the SONS OF THE PIONEERS were still active when Riders in the Sky took shape, western harmony singing seemed to be a dying art form. Inspired by the singing cowboys of vintage Hollywood films, the group's combination of skillfully blended harmonies, expert musicianship, and quick-witted humor brought a new vitality to the western genre.

The band formed at a Nashville night spot and included Douglas Green, Fred LaBour, and Bill Collins. Fiddler Paul "Woody" Chrisman replaced Collins in 1978, and each member acquired a colorful nickname: Green (guitar) became Ranger Doug, Idol of American Youth; LaBour (bass) became Too Slim; and Chrisman became Woody Paul, King of the Cowboy Fiddlers. The group took its name from the title of a Sons of the Pioneers reissue album.

In 1979 Riders made their first album for ROUNDER, followed by five albums for MCA, and then three albums with COLUMBIA before returning to Rounder in 1995. The act also recorded an album for Rhino and another for Rabbit Ears Radio (with ROY ROGERS). In 1997 Ranger Doug recorded his first solo album, *Songs of the Sage*, consisting entirely of his original songs in the classic western style, for the Warner Western label.

In addition, Riders in the Sky hosted *Tumbleweed Theater* on TNN (1983–86); had a Saturday morning children's show, *Riders in the Sky*, on CBS-TV (August 1991–August 1992); and starred in *Riders' Radio Theater* on public radio (1988–96). This last was taped in Nashville during its first season and thereafter in Cincinnati. Along the way Riders added Joey Miskulin ("The Cowpolka King") on accordion and joined the GRAND OLE OPRY (June 19, 1982). The group's broadcasting and recording achievements, together with tours that eventually embraced all fifty states and many foreign countries, led to induction into the Western Music Hall of Fame in 1993, the first contemporary act to receive this honor.

Riders in the Sky widened their fame via motion pictures, an XM Satellite Radio show, and the Internet, for which they wrote the theme song for the cartoon program *Thomas Timberwolf*. The act contributed "Woody's Roundup" to the hit animated film *Toy Story 2* (1999), and the album *Woody's Roundup* won a 2000 Grammy for Best Musical Album for Children. In 2002 the group won a second Grammy in this category for *Monsters, Inc: Scream Factory Favorites*, the companion album for the Pixar Animation–Disney movie *Monsters, Inc.* Subsequent albums have included *Public Cowboy #1: A Salute to the Music of Gene Autry* (2007) and a live album recorded with the Nashville Symphony (2009). —*Don Cusic*

## Billy Lee Riley

b. Pocahontas, Arkansas, October 5, 1933; d. August 2, 2009

SUN RECORDS issued only six Billy Lee Riley records, but those cuts made the singer one of ROCKABILLY's most revered artists.

Of Irish and Cherokee ancestry, Riley grew up in poverty in small towns in Arkansas and Mississippi. His father taught him harmonica, and at age nine he learned guitar from neighboring children on a primarily black plantation. In 1949 Riley joined the U.S. Army and performed HONKY-TONK MUSIC when off duty. Upon his discharge he relocated to Jonesboro, Arkansas, where he played in country bands.

Riley temporarily gave up music, moved to Memphis, and opened a restaurant with his brother-in-law. After the venture failed, Riley worked various jobs and joined Slim Wallace's Dixie Ramblers, an act including future engineer, producer, and songwriter JACK CLEMENT. Clement recorded Riley performing three numbers—including two originals, "Trouble Bound" and "Rock with Me, Baby"—that he sold to Sun Records in April 1956. At that point both Riley and Clement began long associations with Sun. To support his record, Riley formed a road band with Roland Janes (guitar) and J. M. Van Eaton (drums). The three men also became the house band at Sun, backing numerous rockabilly artists through the 1950s, most notably JERRY LEE LEWIS.

Riley's best-known recordings were "Flyin' Saucer Rock & Roll" and "Red Hot." He cut the former in December 1956 with Janes and Van Eaton (dubbed the Little Green Men by Sun owner

*Riders in the Sky: (from left) Joey Miskulin, "Ranger Doug" Green, "Woody Paul" Chrisman, and Fred "Too Slim" LaBour*

*Billy Lee Riley (center) and the Little Green Men*

Sam Phillips), augmented by Jerry Lee Lewis. "Red Hot" (1957) covered bluesman Billy "the Kid" Emerson's Sun original. Riley's sides epitomized classic rockabilly's raw energy and excitement, but just as "Red Hot" looked set to explode, Sun released Jerry Lee Lewis's crossover smash "Great Balls of Fire." With limited promotional resources, Phillips opted to give Lewis's record first priority, and Riley's disc languished. Yet even if Phillips had pushed "Red Hot" instead, it still may have stalled, for Riley may have proved too primal for national stardom.

Riley would later record under his own name and under various pseudonyms for a host of mostly small record companies, having ownership interest in the Rita and Mojo labels. In the early 1990s he emerged from a self-imposed semiretirement and released albums including *Blue Collar Blues* (HighTone Records, 1992) and *Hot Damn*! (Capricorn, 1997). *Hillbilly Rockin' Man* appeared on Reba Records in 2003. Though beset by health problems, he kept performing into 2009, when colon cancer took his life. —*Rob Bowman*

## Jeannie C. Riley
b. Anson, Texas, October 19, 1945

Jeannie C. Riley became an overnight sensation in 1968 on the strength of her #1 single "Harper Valley P.T.A."

Born Jeanne Carolyn Stephenson, she grew up in Anson, Texas, singing with the band of her uncle, Johnny Moore, and admiring country singers such as Connie Smith. She married auto mechanic Mickey Riley before moving to Nashville in 1966. There she worked as a demo singer and secretary for Jerry Chesnut's Passkey Music while Mickey ran a local Texaco service station.

Jeanne recorded Tom T. Hall's "Harper Valley P.T.A." for Shelby Singleton's Plantation Records on July 26, 1968. Singleton released it immediately, adding an "i" to her first name before printing labels. The tale of a single mother who turned the tables on a hypocritical small-town P.T.A. board, the record topped the *Billboard* country and pop charts, fueled by her appearance on Ed Sullivan's popular CBS network television show. The single won Riley a 1968 Grammy for Best Country Vocal.

Although "Harper Valley P.T.A." was her most enduring hit, Riley placed twenty-three more singles on the country charts between 1968 and 1973, among them "There Never Was a Time," "The Girl Most Likely," "Country Girl," and "Good Enough to Be Your Wife." But after leaving Plantation, subsequent moves to MGM, Mercury, and Warner Bros. failed to sustain her success. In the 1980s she turned her attention to her Three Fold Chord Gospel Ministries and to the career of her daughter, Kim Michelle Riley Coyle (who recorded as Riley Coyle). In 1981 Jeannie C. Riley published her autobiography, *From Harper Valley to the Mountaintop*, written with Jamie Buckingham. —*Don Rhodes*

## LeAnn Rimes
b. Jackson, Mississippi, August 28, 1982

With the 1996 release of Bill Mack's "Blue," thirteen-year-old prodigy Margaret LeAnn Rimes became an instant star. Since then, her powerful, full-throated vocals and youthful beauty have made her a prominent crossover act, but she has sometimes met with mixed reception from radio, record buyers, and critics.

*LeAnn Rimes*

Rimes won her first talent contest at age five and told her parents she wanted a show business career. The Rimes family moved from Jackson, Mississippi, to the Dallas area, where she appeared on the syndicated TV talent show *Star Search* and on Johnnie High's *Country Music Revue* stage show in Arlington, Texas.

At age eleven Rimes recorded her first album, *All That* (Nor Va Jak, 1994). In 1996 she signed with Curb Records in Nashville; that May her yodel-inflected rendition of "Blue" became her first *Billboard* country chart single. Though fans and the press hailed Rimes as a musical heir to Patsy Cline, some radio programmers judged the recording's style, steeped in The Nashville Sound, too dated, and "Blue" stalled at #10. Nevertheless, the *Blue* album went #1 and sold 3 million copies by year's end. The album's third single, "One Way Ticket (Because I Can)" (1996), became Rimes's first #1 country hit and went #26 pop.

In early 1997 Curb Records repackaged her *All That* cuts with her new recording of the pop standard "Unchained Melody" for *Unchained Melody: The Early Years*, which debuted at #1 on *Billboard*'s country and Hot 200 pop album charts. That September, Curb released *You Light Up My Life: Inspirational Songs*, consisting mostly of 1970s ballads. The album debuted simultaneously at #1 on the pop, country, and contemporary Christian album charts and quickly sold 4 million copies. Its first single, "How Do I Live," had only modest country success due to Trisha Yearwood's competing rendition, but Rimes's version hit #2 on *Billboard*'s cross-genre Hot 100 chart. Rimes won 1996 ACM awards for Single of the Year ("Blue") and Best Female Vocalist and also earned a 1996 Grammy in the Best New Artist category and CMA's 1997 Horizon Award. In 1998, sales of "How Do I Live" topped the 3 million mark.

Rimes's pop-oriented *Sittin' on Top of the World* (1998) and her country standards collection *LeAnn Rimes* (1999) each sold 1 million copies and generated Top Ten country singles, but some reviewers faulted her tendency to oversing and considered her delivery less than convincing.

In 2000 Rimes broke with her father, Wilbur C. Rimes, who had produced her early albums, as well as with her manager, who had dated LeAnn's mother, Belinda, for a time after LeAnn's parents had divorced. *I Need You* (2001), targeting the pop market, fared worse with critics, and sales declined by half. Rimes openly disavowed the album, alleging it was "unfinished." Signing a more favorable contract with Curb in 2001, she released the pop-oriented *Twisted Angel* (2002), followed by the contemporary country *This Woman* (2005), which included three Top Five country hits. The stylistically eclectic *Family* (2007), consisting of original songs, featured the Top Twenty country hit "Nothin' Better to Do" and the Grammy-nominated "What I Cannot Change." —*Marjie McGraw*

## Nolan "Cowboy Slim" Rinehart
b. near Gustine, Texas, March 11, 1911; d. October 28, 1948

Nolan Arthur Rinehart, often called the King of BORDER RADIO, was the most popular of the singing cowboys who worked stations along the Texas–Mexico border. After military service, during which he met JIMMIE RODGERS when Rodgers entertained troops at San Antonio's Fort Sam Houston, Rinehart began broadcasting in the early 1930s. His programs aired on KSKY–Dallas; on XEG–Monterrey, Mexico; and on a small 250-watt station in Brady, Texas, before he moved to the high-wattage border station XEPN in Eagle Pass, Texas/Piedras Negras, Mexico. After his initial appearances there, the station was deluged by mail from fans throughout XEPN's huge broadcast area. As his popularity grew, Rinehart syndicated his transcribed (recorded) programs on all the Mexican border stations and teamed with cowgirl singer PATSY MONTANA for a number of popular transcriptions. During his border radio years, Rinehart prospered by selling his SONG-BOOKS, which included numbers such as "Empty Saddles" and his theme song, "Roaming Cowboy." Unfortunately, he made no recordings for retail release. He went to Hollywood for a screen test but never appeared in any movies. Rinehart was killed in an automobile accident in Detroit in 1948 and was buried in Hobbs, New Mexico. —*Charlie Seemann*

## Ralph Rinzler
b. Passaic, New Jersey, July 20, 1934; d. July 2, 1994

Folklorist, promoter, and musician Ralph Rinzler played a vital role in preserving tradition-oriented country music and bringing it to new audiences. As a boy he was fascinated by a set of Library of Congress folk song recordings and later by Harry Smith's seminal 1951 record collection *The Anthology of American Folk Music*. At Swarthmore College (from which he graduated in 1956), Rinzler became part of the active campus folk scene, teaching himself mandolin, guitar, and banjo. During the late 1950s and early 1960s, he helped popularize BLUEGRASS and OLD-TIME MUSIC by performing and recording with THE GREENBRIAR BOYS and cofounding New York City's Friends of Old-Time Music, a group that staged concerts.

As a Folkways Records talent scout and producer, during a 1961 recording field trip to North Carolina, Rinzler discovered Arthel "DOC" WATSON, who subsequently became an influential flat-picking guitarist and traditional singer. Rinzler also revitalized the career of bluegrass pioneer BILL MONROE, documenting his accomplishments in a seminal 1963 *Sing Out!* magazine article and (while briefly serving as Monroe's manager) introducing him to the national folk music revival circuit.

From 1964 to 1967 Rinzler was a director of the prominent NEWPORT FOLK FESTIVAL, which showcased many tradition-minded country musicians. He helped country music promoter CARLTON HANEY organize Haney's landmark 1965 all-bluegrass festival in Fincastle, Virginia.

Rinzler went on to a distinguished career at the Smithsonian Institution in Washington, D.C. In 1967 he founded the Festival of American Folklife, an annual event from which evolved the Smithsonian's Center for Folklife Studies and Cultural Programs. He also facilitated the Smithsonian's 1987 acquisition of the important Folkways Records catalog and archives. —*Richard D. Smith*

## Tex Ritter
b. Panola County, Texas, January 12, 1905; d. January 2, 1974

The most well-versed western singer among Hollywood's singing cowboys was Tex Ritter. Born Woodward Maurice Ritter in Panola County, Texas (also the birthplace of JIM REEVES), Ritter was raised with a deep love of western music. Entering the University of Texas at Austin in 1922, he met J. Frank Dobie, Oscar J. Fox, and John Lomax—three of the most noted authorities on COWBOY MUSIC—who added to his knowledge. While in college Ritter had his own weekly radio program, singing cowboy songs on KPRC–Houston.

In 1928 Ritter went to New York, where he worked in a Broadway musical. Later he briefly studied law at Northwestern University in Illinois. Short of funds, he returned to New York, where he appeared in several more Broadway productions, including *Green Grow the Lilacs* (1931). (Rodgers and Hammerstein adapted the play for their 1943 musical *Oklahoma!*) Ritter also performed on several New York radio programs, and between 1932 and 1936 he recorded there for the AMERICAN RECORD COMPANY and DECCA.

*Tex Ritter*

By mid-decade, GENE AUTRY's successful Republic films led other studios to sign their own singing cowboys. Grand National's Edward Finney persuaded Ritter to move to Hollywood in 1936 and released Ritter's first starring film, *Song of the Gringo*, in November of that year.

Ritter was well suited to the role of singing cowboy. Unfortunately, most of his films were made for Grand National and Monogram, which were smaller than the majors and made their films on limited budgets. But even though his films never had the production values of those starring Autry or ROY ROGERS, Ritter still enjoyed considerable box office appeal.

In 1942, after a decade of recording, with little success, Ritter became one of the first artists signed by the newly formed CAPITOL RECORDS. He soon gained major hits with records such as "Jealous Heart," "Rye Whiskey," "I'm Wastin' My Tears on You," and "You Will Have to Pay." Ritter would record for Capitol for the rest of his life.

In 1952 Ritter was asked to sing the title song of the Gary Cooper–Grace Kelly western *High Noon*. The song served as a narrative element throughout the film and became Ritter's signature song. He went on to record a number of other western theme songs throughout the decade. Ritter was one of the first country artists to cut thematic albums, recording collections of cowboy songs, patriotic songs, hymns, and Mexican songs as well as country albums. In 1961 his rendition of "I Dreamed of a Hill-Billy Heaven" became a #5 hit and displayed his sure handling of recitations.

During two terms as CMA president (1963–66), Ritter spearheaded efforts to acquaint advertisers with country music's selling power and led CMA's fundraising efforts for the COUNTRY MUSIC HALL OF FAME AND MUSEUM.

In 1965 Ritter moved to Nashville. With GRANT TURNER (and later RALPH EMERY) he cohosted a late-night WSM country program and joined the GRAND OLE OPRY. In 1970 Ritter ran unsuccessfully for the Republican nomination to the U.S. Senate. His death on January 2, 1974, marked the passing of one of country music's most respected talents.

Ritter was elected to THE COUNTRY MUSIC HALL OF FAME in 1964. —*Laurence Zwisohn*

## The Riverside Rancho
established in Los Angeles, California, ca. 1942; closed 1959

During World War II, the Riverside Rancho, at 3213 Riverside Drive (near Griffith Park) in Los Angeles, California, became the standout among numerous country music nightclubs then proliferating in Southern California.

Owned by Kay and Lou DeRhoda and booked by West Coast promoter Marty Landau (beginning in March 1947), the Rancho featured a 10,000-square-foot dance floor, three bars, downstairs dressing facilities, an upstairs dining hall, and a large veranda. Starting in 1942, FOREMAN PHILLIPS, a prominent country music promoter, placed two of his numerous bandleaders, Bill "Happy" Perryman and SPADE COOLEY, at the Rancho; on their departure it featured TEX WILLIAMS's Western Caravan for some fifteen years. West Coast artists T. TEXAS TYLER, RAY WHITLEY, HANK PENNY, Dude Martin, JIMMY WAKELY, MERLE TRAVIS, WESLEY TUTTLE, and TEXAS JIM LEWIS made regular appearances there, as did BOB WILLS during and after his Hollywood residency. It was also the preferred Los Angeles venue for out-of-town country acts such as HANK WILLIAMS, ROY ACUFF, ERNEST TUBB, LEFTY FRIZZELL,

HANK SNOW, PEE WEE KING, WEBB PIERCE, and the MADDOX BROTHERS & ROSE. The club remained active until its demolition in 1959. —*Ken Griffis*

## Hargus "Pig" Robbins
b. Rhea County, Tennessee, January 18, 1938

Blinded in a knife accident at age three, Hargus Melvin "Pig" Robbins succeeded FLOYD CRAMER as the leading session pianist in Nashville, from the mid-1960s into the 1980s. Although he had classical piano training at the Tennessee School for the Blind from ages seven to fifteen, he built his style by listening to the keyboard work of Cramer, OWEN BRADLEY, MARVIN HUGHES, RAY CHARLES, and Papa John Gordy on records.

"I got [the nickname] 'Pig' at school," Robbins explained. "I had a supervisor who called me that because I used to sneak in through a fire escape and play when I wasn't supposed to and I'd get dirty as a pig."

His first big Nashville session yielded the 1959 GEORGE JONES hit "White Lightnin.'" Robbins's work on BOB DYLAN's *Blonde on Blonde* (1966) made the pianist in demand with pop and rock artists as well. He contributed distinctive touches to CHARLIE RICH's "Behind Closed Doors" and CRYSTAL GAYLE's "Don't It Make My Brown Eyes Blue." Robbins was CMA's Instrumentalist of the Year in 1976 and 2000, and ACM's top keyboard player in 1977. He won a Grammy in 1978 for Best Country Instrumental Performance.

Robbins embarked on a brief career as a solo instrumental artist in the late 1970s, recording the albums *Country Instrumentalist of the Year* (1977), *Pig in a Poke* (1978), and *Unbreakable Hearts* (1979). He remains an influential and active session player, working with artists including RANDY TRAVIS, ALAN JACKSON, DOLLY PARTON, PATTY LOVELESS, and MARTY STUART. —*Bob Millard*

## Marty Robbins
b. near Glendale, Arizona, September 26, 1925; d. December 8, 1982

A man of many talents, Martin David Robinson was a successful recording artist, stage performer, actor, author, songwriter, and stock car racer. Throughout his career he applied his supple baritone to a wide variety of musical styles, including country, western, ROCKABILLY, HAWAIIAN MUSIC, gospel, and pop. Indeed, his versatility made him a hit-making act for almost thirty years.

Robbins and his twin sister, Mamie, were born into a poverty-stricken family, and his childhood was difficult. He dropped out of school in his teens, served in the U.S. Navy during 1943–46, and began his musical career in 1947, soon landing his own radio and television programs on KPHO in Phoenix. On September 27, 1948, he married Marizona Baldwin; the couple had two children, Ronny and Janet.

The singer's break came in 1951. LITTLE JIMMY DICKENS guested on Robbins's TV show and encouraged his label to offer Robbins a recording contract—as did KPHO executive (and former WSM manager) HARRY STONE. Robbins signed with COLUMBIA RECORDS that year and remained with the label throughout his career, except for a stint on DECCA/MCA in 1972–74. Impressed by Robbins's talent, Stone also recommended

*Marty Robbins*

him to Nashville music publisher FRED ROSE, who flew to Phoenix to sign Robbins as a songwriter.

Robbins joined the GRAND OLE OPRY on January 19, 1953, and moved to Nashville. In 1965 he started performing on the latest segment of the program so that he could race at the Nashville Speedway earlier in the day. During the summer of 1968 he left a race before it ended in order to make his show, only to find that the Opry was running late and he might lose some of his stage time. That night, he not only performed for his assigned period, but also stayed beyond it. That act of defiance delighted the audience and became an enduring Opry tradition. Often he would gesture toward the stage manager to signal that he would sing one more song, only to repeat the process for more than an hour, thus cutting into ERNEST TUBB's *Midnite Jamboree*.

Robbins charted every year between 1952 and 1983, racking up ninety-four entries in *Billboard*'s country listings. Forty-seven of these recordings made the Top Ten, with sixteen reaching #1. In 1955 he hit with the rockabilly songs "That's All Right" and "Maybelline." In September 1956 his rendition of MELVIN ENDSLEY's "Singing the Blues" topped *Billboard*'s country chart and became a Top Twenty pop disc. (All told, from 1956 to 1970 Robbins notched twenty-four *Billboard* pop records, twenty of which were also country hits.) His crossover success continued with songs he recorded with the Ray Conniff Singers, aimed at the teen pop market. In April 1957 his self-written "A White Sport Coat (and a Pink Carnation)" became one of his biggest hits, reaching #1 country and #2 pop. Other late-1950s hits from these sessions included "Just Married," "The Story of My Life," and "The Hanging Tree." In 1957 he also released *Song of the Islands*, the first of several Hawaiian albums.

But the music and stories of the Old West fascinated Robbins even more strongly than Hawaiian sounds. His signature song, the self-penned "El Paso," was released in October 1959 and won Robbins his first Grammy. As a child, his grandfather "Texas Bob" Heckle told him stories of the Old West, and Robbins's most influential hero was GENE AUTRY. Robbins's album *Gunfighter Ballads and Trail Songs* became a hit the same year, and other western albums would follow. The one book he wrote was *The Small Man*, a paperback western novel.

As suggested by "A White Sport Coat" and "El Paso," Robbins excelled as a songwriter. Early on, his original hits included "I'll Go On Alone" (his first #1, 1952–53) and "I Couldn't Keep from Crying" (#5, 1953). In the 1960s and 1970s he cracked the Top Ten with his songs "Big Iron," "Don't Worry," "Devil Woman," "Begging to You," "Tonight Carmen," "My Woman, My Woman, My Wife," and "El Paso City." Eventually Robbins established his own music publishing company.

Onstage, Robbins was a genuine showman, not merely a singer, and his fans, who called themselves "Marty's Army," were remarkably supportive in return. Clearly reveling in performing, he loved to joke with the audience and mug for photos during his act.

In August 1969 Robbins suffered a heart attack, and on January 27, 1970, he underwent bypass surgery, which was still experimental at the time. The operation was successful, and he recovered quickly. In 1970 he received ACM's Man of the Decade Award, and in 1971 he received his second Grammy, for "My Woman, My Woman, My Wife."

Robbins was almost as passionate about stock car racing as he was about music. In the 1950s Robbins raced micro-midgets. By the 1960s he was racing modified stock cars at the Nashville Speedway, and in 1966 he entered his first NASCAR Grand National stock car race. Following his heart attack, he spent time off the track, but he resumed NASCAR racing in October 1970; he again withdrew briefly after suffering three wrecks in 1974 and 1975. He returned to the sport in 1977, participating in his final race on November 7, 1982, a month before his death.

Beginning in the 1950s, Robbins made more than a dozen films with western or country music themes. His TV series included the early 1950s Phoenix broadcast *Western Caravan* as well as three syndications: his self-produced *The Drifter* (1965), *The Marty Robbins Show* (1968–69), and *Marty Robbins Spotlight* (1977–78).

The last year of Robbins's life proved to be climactic. In May 1982 "Some Memories Just Won't Die" made the country Top Ten, and in October he received *Billboard*'s Artist Resurgence Award as the performer who had enjoyed the greatest career revival during the preceding year. On October 11, 1982, Robbins was inducted into THE COUNTRY MUSIC HALL OF FAME. He suffered a heart attack the following December 2 and died December 8, 1982, at age fifty-seven. —*Barbara Pruett*

## Fiddlin' Doc Roberts

b. Madison County, Kentucky, April 26, 1897; d. August 4, 1978

Dock Phil Roberts, better known as Fiddlin' Doc Roberts, was one of country music's pioneer recorded fiddlers. Roberts's neighbor, talent scout Dennis Taylor, arranged his first sessions (with singer Welby Toomey) for GENNETT in Richmond, Indiana, in October 1925, launching a prolific decade of record making for the musician. For three different companies, Roberts recorded more than eighty songs and backed other musicians on at least as many more. According to historian Charles Wolfe, only an aversion to travel (ruling out big-city radio and touring) made Roberts less famous than contemporaries FIDDLIN' ARTHUR SMITH and CLAYTON MCMICHEN. Roberts's fiddling style, as Wolfe has described it, featured a smooth, long-bow technique. A remarkable number of blues songs and tunes local to eastern Kentucky dominated Roberts's repertory.

Besides Welby Toomey, his recording partners included Dick Parman, Ted Chesnut, fiddler Asa Martin, and Roberts's young singing son, James Roberts. Always a popular fiddler for dances in his home area, Roberts was rediscovered by folklorists and other scholars in the 1960s and 1970s and performed frequently at Kentucky's Berea College during his last years. —*Ronnie Pugh*

## Kenny Roberts
b. Orange, Massachusetts, October 14, 1926

Kenny Roberts's spectacular yodeling prompted standing ovations during a fifty years in show business.

Born George Kingsbury, he grew up in Athol, Massachusetts, listening to the GRAND OLE OPRY, learning to yodel by studying the records of WILF CARTER and ELTON BRITT, and working in a part-time local band that included Yodeling Slim Clark. Roberts quit high school to join the fully professional Down Homers on a New Hampshire radio station in 1943. In 1944 the group joined WOWO's *Hoosier Hop* in Fort Wayne, Indiana, where they gained network exposure that led to making picture discs for VOGUE RECORDS early in 1946. Roberts went solo later that year. After a stint on *Uncle Dick Slack's Barn Dance* at KMOX–St. Louis, by mid-1948 he was working WLW–Cincinnati's televised *MIDWESTERN HAYRIDE* as well as his own daily TV show for children. Billed as the Jumping Cowboy, his acrobatics and youthful charm made him a hero to local schoolkids, while his singing attracted adult viewers. His Coral recordings of "I Never See Maggie Alone" and "Chocolate Ice Cream Cone" were Top Ten country hits in 1949 and 1950, respectively.

After 1950 Roberts worked TV stations in Ohio and Michigan, and made regular radio appearances on Wheeling's *WWVA JAMBOREE* from the early 1960s into the mid-1970s. He also recorded for other labels, including DOT, STARDAY, and KING. —*Jonathan Guyot Smith*

## Don Robertson
b. Beijing, China, December 5, 1922

Songwriter and pianist Don Robertson left an indelible mark on country music in pioneering the slip-note piano style. Born in China, where his father was a doctor, Robertson moved to the United States in 1927 at age five. He studied music at the University of Chicago and early in his career performed as a pop pianist in Chicago and then in Hollywood, where he worked sessions for CAPITOL RECORDS beginning in 1947. In 1956 he had a hit record of his own, an infectious novelty called "The Happy Whistler."

Though he wrote several pop hits starting in the 1950s (including "Hummingbird" for LES PAUL & MARY FORD), during his association with HILL AND RANGE music publishers Robertson wrote a number of major songs for country artists. These include "I Really Don't Want to Know" for EDDY ARNOLD in 1954, "I Don't

Hurt Anymore" for HANK SNOW in that same year, "You're Free to Go" for CARL SMITH in 1956, and "Ninety Miles an Hour Down a Dead End Street" for Snow in 1963.

More importantly, though, Robertson introduced the slip-note playing technique (in which the pianist slides up into a note from the one beneath) on the demo recording of his song "Please Help Me I'm Falling," which HANK LOCKLIN recorded in 1960, with FLOYD CRAMER playing the distinctive piano part in Robertson's style at the instruction of CHET ATKINS. After the record became a #1 country hit, Atkins encouraged Cramer to record piano instrumentals in the slip-note style, further popularizing Robertson's sound. —*Stacey Wolfe*

## Eck Robertson
b. Madison County, Arkansas, November 20, 1887; d. February 17, 1975

Considered by many historians to be the first southern musician to record what would later be considered country music, Alexander Campbell Robertson was a legendary Texas fiddler who helped to define the long-bow style still used by contest fiddlers today. In spite of a relatively slim recorded output, his work influenced several generations of musicians.

Eck Robertson grew up in the town of Hamlin in the Texas panhandle, where his father was a preacher and where he learned his first fiddle tunes from veterans such as Polk Harris and Matt Brown (credited with tunes such as "Ragtime Annie" and "Done Gone"—both of which Robertson would later record). Shortly after 1900, Robertson joined a traveling MEDICINE SHOW, and for the next few years he absorbed fiddle tunes and showmanship skills. After he married his childhood sweetheart, Jeanetta Levy, the pair continued to tour; as their children (eventually numbering ten) grew up, they, too, joined the troupe. In the off-season

*Eck Robertson*

Robertson worked as a piano tuner and frequented the many fiddling contests that dotted the Texas musical landscape.

Featured in a 1922 Fox Movietone newsreel, Robertson became interested in another emerging technology of the day: recordings. In 1922 he and a friend, Civil War veteran Henry Gilliland, attended a Confederate veterans' reunion in Richmond, Virginia. When Gilliland mentioned he had a friend in New York who worked for the Victor Talking Machine Company, the pair caught the next train and appeared in the Victor offices, dressed in western garb, to ask for an audition. The Victor bosses were impressed and promptly recorded ten numbers by the musicians—some as a duo, others solos by Robertson, still others by Robertson with a studio pianist. The high point was Robertson's solo reading of "Sallie Gooden," with its elaborate variations and improvisations—one of the acknowledged masterpieces of OLD-TIME MUSIC.

Robertson's recordings inspired a generation of other Texas fiddlers to record in the next few years: Red Steeley, Oscar Harper, W. B. Chenoweth, Prince Albert Hunt, and Samuel Morgan Peacock. Ironically, Robertson himself did not record again until almost the end of the 1920s fiddling craze: A 1929 session featured his family and yielded important recordings, such as "There's a Brown Skin Gal Down the Road Somewhere," "Brown Kelly Waltz," and "Brilliancy Medley." But after this he made no more commercial recordings. A series of radio transcriptions he made for Sellers in 1940 has never surfaced. For most of the 1940s and 1950s Robertson retreated from country music's mainstream, preferring to fiddle at local contests.

Like so many other stars of the 1920s, Robertson was rediscovered by musicians and fans during the 1960s folk revival; he made some festival appearances with THE NEW LOST CITY RAMBLERS and let Rambler John Cohen record some of his fiddle solos. (These were released years later as an LP called *Eck Robertson: Famous Cowboy Fiddler*.) In his last years Robertson was often interviewed by fiddling enthusiasts, and he was active in contests as late as the 1960s. —*Charles Wolfe*

## Texas Jim Robertson
b. Gastonia, North Carolina, February 27, 1914; d. November 11, 1966

James Battle Robertson was billed as a western singer, but his repertoire ranged from "Slipping Around" to "Home on the Range" to "The Old Rugged Cross." While publicity releases claimed he was from Texas, he started his radio career in the 1930s in Charlotte, North Carolina, in his native state. Later he broadcast over NBC from New York. The popular performer sang and acted in radio series as diverse as *Death Valley Days* and *Dick Tracy*, and he long enjoyed a vast radio audience for his strong baritone voice and open-chord guitar picking. He recorded for BLUEBIRD, MGM, and RCA, scoring three Top Ten RCA hits from 1946 to 1948. He also recorded for lesser-known labels and appeared on GEORGE HAMILTON IV's syndicated television shows. Robertson committed suicide in 1966. —*Guy Logsdon*

## Carson Robison
b. Oswego, Kansas, August 4, 1890; d. March 24, 1957

Between 1924 and 1956 Carson Jay Robison had a successful career as a country recording artist and as a tunesmith specializing in songs inspired by current events. Well-known Robison compositions include "Carry Me Back to the Lone Prairie," "Barnacle Bill

the Sailor," and "I'm Goin' Back to Whur I Come From." Robison also broadcast live on network radio, recorded radio programs, appeared in movie shorts, and published SONGBOOKS.

The son of a fiddler and dance caller, Robison was raised in Chetopa, Kansas. In addition to singing, whistling, and playing guitar, he worked on the railroad and in Oklahoma oil fields.

After performing on Kansas City radio station WDAF for about a year, he moved to New York. There he teamed with WENDELL HALL (with whom he had performed in the Midwest), playing guitar and whistling on Hall's records. Victor Records (predecessor to RCA VICTOR) soon signed Robison as a staff guitarist; in this role he backed artists and sang duets with Hall, Gene Austin, and BUELL KAZEE (as Sookie Hobbs).

In 1924 Robison became VERNON DALHART's guitar player. A gifted composer, Robison excelled at event songs such as "The Mississippi Flood." More than sixty of Robison's estimated 300 songs were recorded by Dalhart, with some, such as "My Blue Ridge Mountain Home," becoming big hits. Robison also penned songs for Dalhart under the pseudonyms Carlos B. McAfee ("The John T. Scopes Trial," "Wreck of the 1256") and Maggie Andrews, his mother's maiden name ("The Engineer's Child," "My Little Home in Tennessee").

Robison sang no vocal solos while working with Dalhart, but in mid-1926 Robison began harmonizing with him in duets, and later in trios including Adelyne Hood. In June 1926 Robison recorded two whistling solos, "Nola" and "Whistleitis," for four different labels, calling himself the Kansas Jayhawk. He won large audiences by whistling two notes in harmony at the same time.

Robison and Dalhart parted in June 1928, due chiefly to a disagreement on sharing royalties from Robison's compositions. Immediately Robison brought in FRANK LUTHER as his recording partner. Until April 1932 they sang almost 300 duets (chiefly Robison originals), released on many labels. Probably their best-known

*Carson Robison*

number was "Barnacle Bill the Sailor," which spawned two sequels. Their chief label credits were as Bud & Joe Billings or Billings & Robison, for Victor; the Carson Robison Trio, for many labels; and the Black Brothers, for OKeh. As with Dalhart, Robison sang few solos, with the exception of twenty recordings for the GENNETT label. Two of his most outstanding solos, which he recorded several times, were "Naw I Don't Wanta Be Rich" and "So I Joined the Navy." He also recorded an event song, "The Ohio Prison Fire," for COLUMBIA and made two topical Depression-era songs for the AMERICAN RECORD COMPANY/: "Prosperity Is Just Around Which Corner?" and "What Are You Squawkin' About?"

After his last session with Frank Luther, in April 1932, Robison formed a new act with John, Bill, and Pearl Mitchell, whom he billed as the Buckaroos in the United States, where they worked NBC radio shows. He also took them to England for a personal appearance tour that included a number of recording sessions, billing them overseas as the Pioneers. Dressed in cowboy costumes, they were an immediate hit. They later made two trips to England, in 1936 and 1939, recording both times for the Rex label. Robison also continued recording for RCA Victor. In 1936 he released ten sides on the MONTGOMERY WARD label (pressed by RCA Victor). During the years 1941–45 he wrote and recorded a number of wartime numbers, such as "1942 Turkey in the Straw" and "Hitler's Last Letter to Hirohito." He recorded a square dance album for Columbia in 1941 and another for RCA Victor in 1946.

Between 1947 and 1956 Robison made his final recordings for MGM, with his Pleasant Valley Boys, named for the New York area where he enjoyed his 140-acre ranch. His original "Life Gets Tee-Jus Don't It" was his best-known song from this period. Always trying to stay current, Robison titled one of his last recordings "Rockin' and Rollin' with Grandma." Robison was elected to the NASHVILLE SONGWRITERS HALL OF FAME in 1971. —Bob Olson

## Fabor Robison
b. Beebe, Arkansas, November 3, 1911; d. September 1986

Fabor Robison was one of the most influential and controversial independent record owners and talent scouts of the 1950s. Although some of his artists claimed that he shortchanged them on royalties, he played a crucial role in developing the early careers of JIM REEVES, JOHNNY HORTON, THE BROWNS, MITCHELL TOROK, and FLOYD CRAMER, among others. After a tour in the U.S. Army during World War II, Robison settled in California. There he worked for a time as a talent agent with clients such as Johnny Horton and, with druggist Sid Abbott, started ABBOTT RECORDS, primarily to record Horton. Robison also began scouting songs for the American Music publishing company, traveling the nation to find new singers and song material.

Robison soon discovered a hotbed of young talent on Shreveport, Louisiana's KWKH LOUISIANA HAYRIDE. He used KWKH studios for recording sessions and enlisted KWKH staff musicians as sidemen. Regular players included a young Floyd Cramer, steel guitarist JIMMY DAY, and fiddlers Big Red and Little Red Hayes. In 1953 they backed Jim Reeves on "Mexican Joe" and Mitchell Torok on "Caribbean"; both became #1 country records.

In 1953 Robison also started FABOR RECORDS, for which he recorded important sides by the Browns and Ginny Wright. He soon opened his own studio in Southern California, where he used West Coast instrumental greats such as SPEEDY WEST and Roy Lanham. Like most independent record owners, Robison ultimately saw most of his biggest finds move onto major labels.

In about 1959 Robison sold off his music publishing and some of his recording masters to Jamie/Guyden Records. In 1965 he left the music business and sold all remaining masters to the SHELBY SINGLETON Corporation. —Stacey Wolfe

## Rock 'n' Roll Trio (see Johnny Burnette & the Rock 'n' Roll Trio)

## Rockabilly

Rockabilly music was a transition between the HONKY-TONK and country boogie styles and what became rock & roll. Whereas country boogie was a cousin of honky-tonk, centering on a boogie-woogie beat, rockabilly added blues guitar, a heavier dose of R&B tunes, and the driving BLUEGRASS rhythms of BILL MONROE. Instrumentally, rockabilly was not a radical departure, relying as it did mostly on the instruments of honky-tonk: electric and acoustic guitars, string bass, piano, steel guitar, drums, and, on occasion, even fiddles, though many acts used only guitars and bass behind the vocalist. Rock & roll added formalized arrangements (as with BILL HALEY's music), while rockabilly's spontaneity, energy, and intensity often seemed about to career out of control.

No single artist can claim to have invented rockabilly. In the early 1950s various southern performers were evolving toward that sound. Near Jackson, Tennessee, CARL PERKINS and his band performed in bars, with Perkins singing uptempo numbers filled with his stinging blues guitar, boogie beats, and bluegrass rhythms. In Texas, Sid King & His Five Strings mixed honky-tonk with R&B. In Memphis in 1954, ELVIS PRESLEY and Memphis honky-tonk musicians Scotty Moore and Bill Black created a sparse sound featuring Presley's hypnotic country-blues vocals, Moore's CHET ATKINS–MERLE TRAVIS–influenced electric guitar, and Black's slapped bass. When Elvis became the breakthrough rockabilly artist with his 1954–55 recordings for SUN RECORDS, he proved to be the commercial catalyst for the rockabilly style. He soon attracted others to the label, including Perkins and JERRY LEE LEWIS, who adapted boogie-woogie piano to the new sound. Others had their own variations; though horns were seldom used, SONNY BURGESS (Sun Rockabilly) included a trumpet in his band, the Pacers.

Many major labels signed rockabilly artists, but since older producers rarely understood the music, they often tried too hard to control it, resulting in many failed recordings. A case in point is BUDDY HOLLY's commercially disappointing 1956 DECCA session in Nashville, though JOHNNY BURNETTE had greater artistic (if not commercial) success on Decca with the Rock 'n' Roll Trio, highlighting a wildly distorted, overamplified lead guitar. The music's influence spread through the mid-to-late 1950s. RICK NELSON, who admired Presley and Perkins, made authentic rockabilly music part of his parents' top-rated TV sitcom The Adventures of Ozzie and Harriet and recorded hit rockabilly singles for IMPERIAL. Both Gene Vincent and WANDA JACKSON cut explosive sides for CAPITOL. Nonetheless, many of the best and rawest rockabilly singles were primitive performances recorded by virtual unknowns on tiny regional labels. By the late-1950s rockabilly began to vanish nearly as quickly as it appeared, as its original practitioners matured into other, more well-defined musical styles.

Overseas, however, particularly in England, rockabilly reemerged in the-1970s, attracted younger fans, and inspired extensive European LP reissues from Sun Records and other labels.

The revival spread to the United States with the early 1980s popularity of the U.S. band Stray Cats. Since then U.S. rockabilly revival acts have continued to thrive. —*Rich Kienzle*

## Jesse Rodgers
b. Waynesboro, Mississippi, March 5, 1911; d. December 1973

Born in Mississippi but raised by a Texas uncle after his mother died, Jesse Otto Rodgers was influenced by his superstar cousin JIMMIE RODGERS and by singing cowboy film stars of the 1930s.

Borrowing from Jimmie's "blue yodel" style, Jesse began performing in a similar vein on Mexican BORDER RADIO stations XEPN and XERA, beginning about 1932. Signed to record for RCA VICTOR RECORDS' BLUEBIRD label soon after Jimmie's death, Jesse continued the tradition in selections such as "The Rambler's Yodel" and "Yodeling the Railroad Blues."

But Jesse also began to develop a cowboy image, reflected in early recordings such as "When the Texas Moon Is Shining" and "The Empty Cot." By 1938, as his cousin's influence waned, Jesse began spelling his name "Rogers," without the "d." As if to further establish his own identity, his 1946 SONGBOOK touted his birthplace as Claremore, Oklahoma, rather than Mississippi.

Jesse's biggest success, however, came after moving in 1944 to Philadelphia, where he became a mainstay for nearly two decades. Starring on WFIL's *Hayloft Hoedown* and cavorting in the 1950s on a children's TV show as Ranger Joe with his trained horse Topaz, he acquired a large regional following. Recordings for Sonora (1946–47), RCA (1948–51), and MGM (1952–54) helped preserve his national recognition. Emphysema forced his return to Texas's warmer climate in the early 1960s, where he lived in Houston during his final decade. —*Bob Pinson*

## Jimmie Rodgers
b. Meridian, Mississippi, September 8, 1897; d. May 26, 1933

James Charles Rodgers, known professionally as the Singing Brakeman and America's Blue Yodeler, was the first performer inducted into THE COUNTRY MUSIC HALL OF FAME. He was honored as the Father of Country Music, "the man who started it all." From the traditional melodies and folk music of his southern upbringing, early jazz, stage show yodeling, the work chants of railroad section crews, and, most importantly, African American blues, Rodgers developed a lasting musical style that made him immensely popular in his own time and has influenced generations of country artists. GENE AUTRY, ERNEST TUBB, HANK SNOW, LEFTY FRIZZELL, BILL MONROE, JOHNNY CASH, MERLE HAGGARD, TANYA TUCKER, and DOLLY PARTON are only a few among dozens of stars who have acknowledged Rodgers's impact on their careers.

Rodgers was the son of a railroad section foreman but was attracted to show business early on. At thirteen he won an amateur talent contest and ran away with a traveling MEDICINE SHOW. Stranded far from home, he was retrieved by his father and put to work on the railroad. For a dozen years or so, through World War I and into the 1920s, he rambled far and wide on "the high iron," working as callboy, flagman, baggage master, and brakeman, all the while polishing his musical skills and looking for a chance to become a professional entertainer.

After developing tuberculosis in 1924, Rodgers gave up railroading and began to devote his attention to his music, organizing amateur bands, touring with ragtag tent shows, playing on

street corners, and performing at any opportunity. Success eluded him until the summer of 1927. In Asheville, North Carolina, he wrangled a regular (but unpaid) spot on the local radio station, WWNC, and persuaded the Tenneva Ramblers, a STRINGBAND from BRISTOL, TENNESSEE-VIRGINIA, to join him as the Jimmie Rodgers Entertainers. When the radio program was abruptly canceled, they found work at a resort in the Blue Ridge Mountains. There they learned that RALPH PEER, an agent for the Victor Talking Machine Company (predecessor to RCA VICTOR), was making field recordings in Bristol, not far away. Rodgers loaded up the band, went to Bristol, and gained an audition with Peer. Before they could record, however, the group quarreled over billing and broke up. Deserted by the band, Rodgers persuaded Peer to let him record alone, accompanied only by his own guitar.

Prompted by the public's unusually strong response to Rodgers's first release ("Sleep, Baby, Sleep," paired with "The Soldier's Sweetheart"), Peer arranged for Rodgers to record again in November at Victor's home studios in Camden, New Jersey. From this session came the immortal "Blue Yodel (T for Texas)," Rodgers's first big hit. Within months he was on his way to national stardom, playing first-run theaters, broadcasting regularly from Washington, D.C., and signing for a vaudeville tour of major southern cities on the prestigious Loews Circuit.

In the ensuing five years the singer traveled to Victor's studios in numerous cities, including New York and Hollywood, eventually recording 110 titles, including such classics as "Waiting for a Train," "Daddy and Home," "In the Jailhouse Now," "Frankie and Johnny," "Treasures Untold," "My Old Pal," "T. B. Blues," "My Little Lady," "The One Rose," "My Blue-Eyed Jane," "Miss the Mississippi and You," and the series of twelve sequels to "Blue Yodel," for which he was most famous. In 1929 Rodgers appeared in a movie, *The Singing Brakeman*, a fifteen-minute short made in Camden by Columbia Pictures. He also worked with many other

*Jimmie Rodgers*

established performers of the time, touring in 1931 with Will Rogers (who jokingly referred to him as "my distant son") and recording with such country music greats as the CARTER FAMILY, CLAYTON MCMICHEN, and BILL BOYD and in at least one instance with a jazz star of national prominence, Louis Armstrong, who appears with him on "Blue Yodel No. 9." One of the first white stars to work with black musicians, Rodgers also recorded with the fine St. Louis bluesman Clifford Gibson.

Whether onstage or through film, radio, or recordings, Rodgers's awareness of his own mortality gave his performances an emotional immediacy that captivated audiences. He widened his appeal by adopting various personas, including workingman, rambling loner, cowboy, and lady-killing man-about-town.

Rodgers's career reached its high point from 1928 to 1932. By late 1932 the Depression was decimating record sales and theater attendance, and Rodgers's worsening tuberculosis frustrated his plans for movie projects and international tours. Through the spring of 1933 he tried, with little success, to book personal appearances. In May he went to New York to fulfill his contract with RCA Victor for twelve more recordings. It took him a week to finish them, resting between takes. Two days later, on May 26, he collapsed on the street and died a few hours later, in his room at the Hotel Taft, of a massive hemorrhage.

Rodgers's impact on country music can scarcely be exaggerated. At a time when "hillbilly music" consisted largely of OLD-TIME instrumentals and lugubrious vocalists who sounded much alike, Rodgers brought a distinctive, colorful personality and a rousing vocal style that created and defined the role of the singing star in country music. His records turned the public's attention away from rustic fiddles and disaster songs to popularize the free-swinging, born-to-lose blues tradition of cheatin' hearts and faded love, whiskey rivers and stoic endurance. Although Rodgers scrabbled for material throughout his career, his recorded repertoire was remarkably broad and diverse, ranging from love songs and risqué ditties to whimsical blues tunes and even gospel hymns. He wrote songs about railroaders and cowboys, cops and robbers, Daddy and Mother, and home—plaintive ballads with the nostalgic flavor of traditional music but invigorated by a distinctly original approach and punctuated by Rodgers's yodel and unorthodox guitar runs, which became his trademarks.

In *Meeting Jimmie Rodgers* (Oxford, 2009), author Barry Mazor shows how Rodgers's influence continues to affect rock & roll, western music, blues, jazz, and BLUEGRASS in addition to mainstream country music. —*Nolan Porterfield*

## Johnny Rodriguez
b. Sabinal, Texas, December 10, 1951

Juan Raoul Davis "Johnny" Rodriguez was the first mainstream country star with Hispanic roots. Born into a large, music-loving family in rural South Texas, he grew up hearing Spanish-language songs and various country styles, including COWBOY MUSIC and WESTERN SWING. In September 1971, while performing in Brackettville, Texas, Rodriguez was discovered by TOM T. HALL. In May 1972 Rodriguez joined Hall's band as a guitarist, though MERCURY RECORDS soon signed the young singer to a solo contract. By year's end Rodriguez's first single, "Pass Me By (If You're Only Passing Through)," had become a #9 *Billboard* chartmarker; in 1973–74 he had three straight #1 hits: "You Always Come Back (To Hurting Me)," "Ridin' My Thumb to Mexico," and "That's the Way Love Goes."

His Mercury years included six #1 country singles and other intriguing album tracks that showcased Rodriguez's eclectic musical personality. Not only did he interpret numerous country chestnuts—some, such as "Faded Love" and "Born to Lose," sung in both Spanish and English—but he also recorded original songs ("Ridin' My Thumb") and covered rock & roll and pop classics, including the Beatles' "Something" and THE EAGLES' "Desperado." After signing with EPIC RECORDS and producer BILLY SHERRILL in 1979, Rodriguez had several more hit singles through the mid-1980s.

Rodriguez has continued to record and tour despite his involvement in drug arrests and other headline-grabbing incidents. He remains a hero to Hispanic audiences because he has retained his ethnic identity while becoming a celebrity in mainstream American culture. —*Ted Olson*

## Frank Rogers
b. Florence, South Carolina, February 4, 1972

With production credits for albums by BRAD PAISLEY, DARIUS RUCKER, TRACE ADKINS, JOSH TURNER, and others, Frank Rogers became one of country music's most successful producers in the new century's first decade. Raised in Sumter, South Carolina, Rogers attended Nashville's Belmont University in hopes of finding his way into the music industry. There he befriended fellow student Paisley, and the two began writing songs together. When Paisley got a record deal, he insisted that Rogers produce his debut album. Paisley's stubbornness paid off, for the album launched an A-list career and Rogers became an in-demand music maker.

Rogers's productions have tended toward mainstream country's traditional side, though he has been willing to tailor soundscapes to various artists' desires. "I've tried not to have a 'Frank Rogers sound,'" he said in 2009, "because I always wanted the record to sound like the artist. I like the records where you hear two notes and instantly know the singer, not the ones where you instantly know the producer."

Rogers is co-owner of Sea Gayle Publishing (with Paisley and Chris DuBois) and has cowritten songs for Paisley, Rucker, Adkins, and others. —*Peter Cooper*

## Kenny Rogers
b. Houston, Texas, August 21, 1938

Kenneth Donald Rogers parlayed a distinctive, husky voice and laid-back sex appeal into durable superstardom. Between 1977 and 1987 Rogers logged twenty #1 country hits, many of which climbed the pop charts. During his lengthy career the international star has sold more than 50 million albums in the United States alone.

Rogers entered country music with a broad musical background. Growing up in public housing in Houston, he was exposed to R&B, pop, and jazz as well as country. His first professional group was a late-1950s vocal act called the Scholars, which had local hits in Houston. "That Crazy Feeling," a 1958 solo hit on Carlton Records, earned him an appearance on *American Bandstand*.

During the early 1960s Rogers played bass, and occasionally sang, in a Houston jazz trio. Membership in the New Christy Minstrels folk group spurred the founding of First Edition, in which Rogers and other former Minstrels mixed folk, rock, and country sounds. The new group went #5 pop in 1967 with MICKEY NEWBURY's psychedelic "Just Dropped In (To See What Condition

*Kenny Rogers*

My Condition Was In)" and gained several additional pop hits on Reprise Records.

After the group's breakup in 1974, producer-executive LARRY BUTLER signed Rogers to United Artists Records, on which he had modest hits until the stunning success of the mournfully catchy, Grammy-winning "Lucille" (#1 country, #5 pop) in 1977. For the next dozen years Rogers logged hit after hit, including "The Gambler" (1978)—penned by DON SCHLITZ— "She Believes in Me" (1979), and "Coward of the County" (1979). In 1980, on LIBERTY RECORDS, Rogers's #1 country hit "Lady"—a romantic ballad written by pop star Lionel Richie—ruled the pop charts for six weeks. Successful duets included "Every Time Two Fools Collide" (1978), with DOTTIE WEST, and the crossover smash "Don't Fall in Love With a Dreamer" (1980), with Kim Carnes. As the country-pop era reached a peak, Rogers piled up three Grammys, five CMA awards, and eight ACM awards, adding to his stature as one of country's first artists to sellout arena shows.

Already a veteran TV performer, Rogers gained further exposure through acting in a series of made-for-television movie treatments of "The Gambler." His hit "Love the World Away" was a theme song in the era-defining 1980 film URBAN COWBOY. The 1980s also saw hits on Liberty and RCA, including "Love Will Turn You Around" (1982), the Sheena Easton duet "We've Got Tonight" (1983), and the memorable DOLLY PARTON duet "Islands in the Stream" (1983)—all country #1s that made the pop charts. Rogers appeared front and center in the megastar collaboration "We Are the World" (1985), scoring additional chart-toppers such as "Crazy," "Real Love," and the sensual George Martin–produced "Morning Desire." But the solo hit "Tomb of the Unknown Love" (1986) and the RONNIE MILSAP duet "Make No Mistake, She's Mine" (1987) were Rogers's last #1 records until "Buy Me A Rose" (1999–2000), recorded with ALISON KRAUSS and BILLY DEAN.

Rogers's crossover approach began to work against him as pop took on a harder edge and younger country artists went back to the music's roots. Nevertheless, he invested in BRANSON, MISSOURI, ventures; published several well-received photography books; engaged in major philanthropic endeavors; and launched a chain of restaurants. Though his chart success slipped in the late 1980s and 1990s through stints with GIANT, ATLANTIC, Reprise, and Magnatone, "Buy Me A Rose" (on Dreamcatcher) gave him a boost at the outset of the twenty-first century. Since then he has continued to tour and has released hits collections and albums of new material, the latter including *Water & Bridges* (CAPITOL Nashville, 2006), which yielded the Top Twenty hit "I Can't Unlove You." —*Thomas Goldsmith*

## Roy Rogers
b. Cincinnati, Ohio, November 5, 1911; d. July 6, 1998

Roy Rogers earned the title King of the Cowboys by becoming the most popular western film star of his era. But before starring in his first motion picture, Rogers earned his place in THE COUNTRY MUSIC HALL OF FAME by founding the SONS OF THE PIONEERS.

Leonard Franklin Slye (Rogers's birth name) was raised on a farm in Duck Run, Ohio. In June 1930 the Slye family visited one of Roy's sisters in California. The warm weather and the hope of better job prospects led Rogers's family to move to Los Angeles. Still, the Depression made employment hard to find. Rogers drove a gravel truck and worked as a fruit picker in the central California farm camps that inspired novelist John Steinbeck's *The Grapes of Wrath*.

Rogers had grown up playing mandolin and calling square dances. When his sister encouraged him to appear on a local radio program featuring amateurs, he reluctantly gave it a try. A few days later he was asked to join a country music band, the Rocky Mountaineers, as singer and guitarist. Before long he convinced them to add another vocalist so that they could harmonize. Bob Nolan was hired; when he left, Tim Spencer replaced him. For two years Rogers sang with a variety of country acts, each less successful than the one before. Finally, late in the summer of 1933, he formed a group consisting of himself, Nolan, and Spencer. The Pioneer Trio, as they originally named themselves, perfected their harmonies, and Nolan and Spencer began writing the songs that would become the heart of their repertoire.

Los Angeles radio station KFWB hired the group and soon gave them their own program. The Pioneers' unique harmony and fine original songs—such as "Cool Water" and "Tumbling Tumbleweeds"—led to a series of radio transcriptions, a DECCA recording contract, and film appearances in westerns, including two with GENE AUTRY. During the years 1937–42 Rogers also recorded as a featured artist for Vocalion and DECCA. (Between 1946 and 1950 he would gain four Top Ten country hits on RCA VICTOR.)

In October 1937 Rogers learned that Republic Pictures was searching for a new singing cowboy. Although he didn't have an appointment, he managed to get into the studio and gain an audition. His screen test yielded a contract and the professional name Roy Rogers, which he later made his legal name.

When Gene Autry walked out on his contract, Rogers was given the leading role in *Under Western Stars*, originally scheduled to be Autry's next film. The picture's tremendous success marked the emergence of a new star. Athletic and handsome, by 1943 Rogers was the nation's top western box office attraction, a rank he retained until transitioning into television in 1951.

*Roy Rogers*

In 1944 DALE EVANS was cast as Rogers's leading lady in *The Cowboy and the Señorita*. The chemistry between them was apparent to studio executives and audiences. Over the next five years Evans was featured in Rogers's next nineteen films. A little more than a year after the death of his first wife, Rogers and Evans married, on New Year's Eve 1947. Four years later the couple began their television series, which quickly became a favorite with Sunday-night viewers.

Although Rogers enjoyed enormous popularity through the media of film, radio, television, and recordings as well as through nationwide personal appearances, he endured a series of tragedies. His first wife, Arlene, the mother of his first three children, died a week after the birth of their third child, Roy Jr., in 1946. Robin, the only child born to Rogers and Evans, suffered from Down syndrome and died shortly before her second birthday, in 1952. Rogers and Evans eventually adopted four children from different ethnic and social backgrounds, only to lose two of them tragically. Debbie, a Korean orphan they welcomed into their family, died in a church-bus accident. Their adopted son Sandy, who had suffered brain damage due to earlier physical abuse, died while serving in the U.S. Army.

Each of these losses took a tremendous toll on Rogers and Evans, but the couple's religious faith sustained them. Their positive outlook amid life's challenges only increased the public's regard for them.

To date, Rogers is the only person to be elected twice to the Country Music Hall of Fame: in 1980 as an original member of the Sons of the Pioneers, and in 1988 for his solo career achievements. To fans throughout the world, the King of the Cowboys was an authentic American hero. —*Laurence Zwisohn*

## Smokey Rogers

b. McMinnville, Tennessee, March 23, 1917; d. November 23, 1993

Singer-songwriter-banjoist Eugene "Smokey" Rogers was an important figure in the Southern California country music scene of the 1940s and early 1950s. He began his musical career in Detroit at age thirteen with Jack West & His Circle Star Cowboys and became an original member of TEXAS JIM LEWIS's Lone Star Cowboys in 1935.

By the early 1940s Rogers was working in SPADE COOLEY's band on the West Coast. He later left with other band members to form TEX WILLIAMS's Western Caravan, in which he served as Williams's bandleader. At this time Rogers also ran Smokey's Village Music Store in El Cajon, California. Rogers penned "Gone" for FERLIN HUSKY, a #1 country hit and #4 pop hit in 1957, and BOB WILLS popularized Rogers's "Spanish Fandango" on MGM RECORDS. Rogers's singing and banjo playing can be heard on his own recordings (some billed as Buck Rogers) for FOUR STAR, CAPITOL, Western Caravan (his own label), and STARDAY. He scored his only Top Ten hit as an artist in 1949 with his Capitol recording "A Little Bird Told Me." —*Steve Hathaway*

## Matt Rollings

b. Bridgeport, Connecticut, December 14, 1964

One of Nashville's most sought-after piano and keyboard players, Matthew C. Rollings has put his stamp on thousands of country recordings since 1985. Rollings is also an accomplished jazz musician, a hit songwriter (SUZY BOGGUSS's "Letting Go"), and a successful producer (MARY CHAPIN CARPENTER, KEITH URBAN).

Rollings began studying piano under jazz musician Alan Swain at age nine. Rollings made great strides on the instrument when his family moved in 1976 to Phoenix, where music was part of the public school curriculum. By his high school years he was playing jazz with the school band and was introduced to country music as part of a local HONKY-TONK ensemble.

In 1983 bandleader Billy Williams produced then-unknown LYLE LOVETT and hired Rollings to play piano on the session. With visions of jazz and New York City in his head, Rollings enrolled at the Berklee School of Music in Boston, but he also accepted invitations for studio work in Nashville. When the offers kept coming and prominent producer TONY BROWN called him for Lyle Lovett's MCA debut, Rollings moved to MUSIC CITY, where he has subsequently played on albums by hit makers including CLINT BLACK, MARK CHESNUTT, GEORGE STRAIT, VINCE GILL, and FAITH HILL.

As of 2011, Rollings has been named ACM's Keyboard Player of the Year ten times. —*Michael Hight*

## Linda Ronstadt

b. Tucson, Arizona, July 15, 1946

Linda Ronstadt is a renowned interpreter of rock, soul, operetta, cabaret, jazz, and Mexican mariachi music. But her folk-music roots have often led her to country. As a pioneer in the Southern California COUNTRY-ROCK movement of the late 1960s and early 1970s, her influence on country artists has been vast: WYNONNA, PATTY LOVELESS, KATHY MATTEA, TRISHA YEARWOOD, and many others cite Ronstadt as a major inspiration. In 1996 TERRI CLARK reworked Ronstadt's 1978 pop rocker "Poor, Poor Pitiful Me" into a #5 country hit.

*Linda Ronstadt*

Ronstadt began performing with her sister and brother on a Tucson television station. At eighteen she formed the Stone Poneys in Los Angeles with Bob Kimmel and Kenny Edwards. They signed with CAPITOL in 1966, and their version of Michael Nesmith's "Different Drum" climbed to #13 on the pop charts in 1967–68. In 1969 Ronstadt went solo with *Hand Sown . . . Home Grown*, an album fusing country and rock.

Ronstadt recorded her 1970 album *Silk Purse* in Nashville, playing the GRAND OLE OPRY and appearing on JOHNNY CASH's ABC Network television show. The album included "Long Long Time," her first solo hit. Back in California, Ronstadt hired a band that would become THE EAGLES and released two more country-rock albums.

With her 1974 album *Heart Like a Wheel*, she found major commercial success. Her revival of soul singer Betty Everett's "You're No Good" went to #1 on the pop charts, and her remake of HANK WILLIAMS's "I Can't Help It (If I'm Still in Love with You)" became a #2 country hit in 1975, winning a Grammy for Best Country Vocal Performance, Female.

Throughout the 1970s Ronstadt connected with both pop and country material. *Prisoner in Disguise* (1975) contained the country hit "Love Is a Rose," DOLLY PARTON's "I Will Always Love You," and a duet with EMMYLOU HARRIS on "The Sweetest Gift." For *Hasten Down the Wind* (1976) Ronstadt covered PATSY CLINE's "Crazy" and BUDDY HOLLY's "That'll Be the Day," while *Simple Dreams* (1977) showcased the CARTER FAMILY classic "I Never Will Marry." Ronstadt's reading of ROY ORBISON's "Blue Bayou" was a major pop and country smash that same year.

Ronstadt joined Harris and Parton on the landmark 1987 album *Trio*, which had an unmistakable country flavor. It sold more than 1 million copies, received a Grammy and a CMA award, and contained four Top Ten country hits.

Ronstadt has recorded two albums of traditional *Mariachi* music (1987's *Canciones de Mi Padre* and 1990's *Mas Canciones*); in 1992 she released another Spanish-language album, *Frenesi*, which drew on Cuban and South American music. All three albums won Grammys.

As she returned to country and folk influences, 1995's *Feels Like Home* featured several tracks with Harris initially intended for a Trio reunion. Finally scheduling time to record, the three stars released *Trio 2* in 1999. Ronstadt released more duets with Harris on 1999's *Western Wall: The Tucson Sessions*. Ronstadt and CAJUN specialist Ann Savoy (see MARK AND ANN SAVOY) billed

themselves as the Zozo Sisters on the 2006 album *Adieu False Heart,* which blended Cajun music, American pop standards, and contemporary folk-rock.

As of 2011, fifteen Ronstadt albums had reached the *Billboard* country charts, including four #1s. —*Mary A. Bufwack*

## Jim Rooney
b. Boston, Massachusetts, January 28, 1938

During his long career, Jim Rooney has left a lasting mark on folk and country music, advancing the careers of NANCI GRIFFITH, IRIS DEMENT, and JOHN PRINE along the way. Rooney was a fixture in Boston during the folk revival of the 1960s and played an integral role in its resurgence in the 1980s.

Rooney began performing on Boston radio as a teenager. While pursuing a master's degree in classical literature at Harvard, in 1960 he established an ongoing musical partnership with banjoist BILL KEITH. Managing Club 47, an important venue that booked the likes of Joan Baez and Tom Rush, Rooney was central to the Cambridge folk scene. From 1967 until 1969 Rooney served as talent coordinator and a director of the NEWPORT FOLK FESTIVAL. He also wrote *Bossmen: Bill Monroe & Muddy Waters* (1971), and cowrote *Baby Let Me Follow You Down: The Illustrated Story of the Cambridge Folk Years* (1979).

In 1970 Rooney moved to Woodstock, New York, where he managed Bearsville Sound Studios and welcomed such clients as the Band, Bonnie Raitt, and Van Morrison.

Relocating to Nashville in 1978, Rooney became associated with "COWBOY" JACK CLEMENT. Rooney began engineering and producing records, engineering the first albums of ALISON KRAUSS and Edgar Meyer. In addition, Rooney released his own recordings and played in Cowboy's Ragtime Band. Partnering with ALLEN REYNOLDS, Rooney produced HAL KETCHUM and established Forerunner Music, whose catalog boasted songs by PAT ALGER, Tony Arata, and others. (Universal Music Group bought the firm in 2000.)

Rooney is best known for producing singer-songwriters who are considered musically left of center, including Griffith, Prine, DeMent, ROBERT EARL KEEN, JERRY JEFF WALKER, TOWNES VAN ZANDT, and PETER ROWAN. Griffith won a Grammy in 1993 for the Rooney-produced *Other Voices, Other Rooms*. Rooney's production credits also include Tom Paxton's Grammy-nominated *Comedians & Angels* and Tom Rush's popular *What I Know*. In 2009 Rooney received the AMERICANA Music Association's Lifetime Achievement Award for his producing and engineering accomplishments. —*Beverly Keel*

## ROPE
established in Nashville, Tennessee, 1983

The Reunion of Professional Entertainers (ROPE) is a Nashville-based association created to promote communication among country music professionals and to care for fellow members in time of serious illness, death, or other distress.

Federally chartered in 1983 as a nonprofit organization, ROPE accepts for membership those who have worked in the music industry at least twenty-five years. Since its beginnings, membership has grown from seventy to some 700. GORDON TERRY, a founder and first president, helped initiate a trust fund and a death, health, and welfare insurance program.

An early mission of ROPE was to build a retirement center for seniors in need. Five-term ROPE president Mac Wiseman has served on a CMA steering committee exploring the possibility of making this dream a reality. During Wiseman's tenure a Friends of ROPE program was approved to allow fans and friends of entertainers to contribute as organizational boosters.

ROPE publishes a newsletter, holds quarterly social gatherings, conducts benefit concert fundraisers, sponsors annual Golden ROPE Awards, and offers an annual booth and show during the CMA Music Festival. —*Walt Trott*

## Fred Rose

b. Evansville, Indiana, August 24, 1898; d. December 1, 1954

A music publisher, songwriter, producer, and talent scout, Knowles Fred Rose was a principal figure in the rise of the Nashville music industry between 1942 and 1954.

Rose's parents separated soon after he was born, and he grew up with his mother and other relatives in St. Louis. There he supplemented the family income by singing for tips in local saloons. By 1917 he had moved to Chicago, where he played piano and sang in rough-and-tumble clubs and bars of the South Side. During the 1920s Rose made his name as a songwriter, authoring or coauthoring pop and jazz hits such as "Red Hot Mama," "Deed I Do," and "Honest and Truly." He also made piano rolls; broadcast on Chicago radio stations KYW, WLS, and WBBM; and recorded for the Brunswick label.

In 1933, having lost his Chicago radio job because of a drinking problem, Rose moved to Nashville to broadcast over WSM. Between 1933 and 1938 he divided his time mostly among Nashville, Chicago, and New York, performing on live radio shows and shopping his songs to music publishers. While continuing to

*Fred Rose*

write pop material, he began to work closely with The Vagabonds and the Delmore Brothers at WSM and wrote songs for cowboy singer Ray Whitley, then working in New York. In about 1935, in New York, Rose converted to Christian Science, a faith that would guide his personal and professional life from then on.

In 1936 he scored his first pop-western hit, "We'll Rest at the End of the Trail," recorded by Tex Ritter, the Sons of the Pioneers, and Bing Crosby. Partly as a result, Rose spent most of the years 1938–42 in Hollywood penning hits for Whitley, Gene Autry, and Roy Rogers.

In 1942 Rose joined Roy Acuff in founding Acuff-Rose Publications, Nashville's first major country publishing house. Rose continued to write or cowrite country standards such as "Wait for the Light to Shine," "Afraid," and "Blue Eyes Crying in the Rain" while serving as an expert editor, most notably for his protégé Hank Williams. Rose also made the company a solid base for aspiring songwriters such as Boudleaux and Felice Bryant. In addition, Rose served as MGM Records' unsalaried, Nashville-based A&R man. For this label he supervised sessions for Williams, The Louvin Brothers, Red Sovine, Bob Wills, and many other acts. Rose's greatest success was recruiting Williams for MGM, but he also acted as talent scout for other labels; for example, he steered both Martha Carson and the Louvin Brothers to contracts with Capitol, and Rosalie Allen to an RCA Victor deal. For all these efforts and for his tireless promotion of country music within the American music industry, Rose was elected to The Country Music Hall of Fame in 1961—the first year CMA bestowed this honor. —*John W. Rumble*

## Wesley Rose

b. Chicago, Illinois, February 11, 1918; d. April 26, 1990

Although not initially inclined toward country music, Wesley Herman Rose ascended through this field to become one of the world's top music-publishing executives. He received his degree in accounting from Chicago's Walton School of Commerce and was working as an accountant with Standard Oil Company when his father, Fred Rose, invited him to join the recently established Acuff-Rose Publications in 1945. The younger man accepted, on the condition that he become general manager, handling most of the firm's business functions. This freed the elder Rose, a talented songwriter and song editor, to work with songwriters on new material, scout new talent, produce artists for MGM Records, and assist producers at other labels.

Father and son made a good team, especially in promoting the songs and recordings of Hank Williams in the country market. The Roses also scored hit after hit with pop covers of Williams's songs, and Wesley continued to make the Williams catalog one of the most valuable in popular music after Fred Rose died in 1954.

By then Wesley had become a partner in BMI-affiliated Acuff-Rose, its ASCAP-affiliated companion firm Milene Music, and in Hickory Records. From 1955 he served as president of Acuff-Rose, Milene, Hickory, and, beginning in 1959, Acuff-Rose Artists Corporation. Continuing in his father's footsteps, Wesley also served as an independent producer for MGM, Warner Bros., and other labels. Although he contributed to the careers of The Everly Brothers, Roy Orbison, Sue Thompson, and other acts, his primary role was to promote songs penned by Acuff-Rose writers, including the Everlys, Orbison, Marty Robbins, Boudleaux and Felice Bryant, Don Gibson, John D.

*Wesley Rose*

LOUDERMILK, MICKEY NEWBURY, and EDDY RAVEN. "The object," Rose said, "is to bring your song to an artist that will make it believable to the public because the public picks the hits." By the time he and Acuff sold the Acuff-Rose catalogs to Gaylord Broadcasting (GAYLORD ENTERTAINMENT) in 1985, more than thirty songs he published had been performed on radio and TV more than 1 million times each.

Rose was extremely active in making Acuff-Rose a vital part of the music industry's organizational framework. Not only did he set up Acuff-Rose affiliates around the world and help to found the Country Music Association (CMA), he also served as the first Nashville publisher on the national boards of ASCAP and the Music Publishers Association. On the local scene he served on the boards of the Nashville Area Chamber of Commerce, First American Bank, Belmont College, and the Nashville Symphony. A 1967 recipient of Nashville's prestigious Metronome Award for contributions to the city's music industry, he was elected to THE COUNTRY MUSIC HALL OF FAME in 1986. —*John W. Rumble*

## Rounder Records
established in Somerville, Massachusetts, October 1970

As Michael F. Scully explains in *The Never-Ending Revival: Rounder Records and the Folk Alliance* (University of Illinois Press, 2008), Rounder Records is one of the most successful independent labels because it has balanced "romantic folk world idealism and commercial necessity," broadening the concept of folk music in the process. Rounder was founded as a "collective" in the Boston suburb of Somerville in 1970 by a group of OLD-TIME MUSIC aficionados, including two graduate students, Ken Irwin (b. New York, New York, May 23, 1944) and Marian Leighton-Levy (b. Harrington,

Maine, August 22, 1948), and political science professor Bill Nowlin (b. Boston, February 14, 1945). Irwin soon took charge of production; Leighton-Levy, publicity and promotion; and Nowlin, legal and financial matters. The trio became the label's owners, adding more staff as the enterprise grew.

Initially patterned after COUNTY RECORDS, Rounder began with two old-timey releases, a newsletter, and a mail-order service. It has since developed a diverse catalog of some 4,500 titles. BLUEGRASS acts have included Joe Val & the New England Bluegrass Boys, J. D. CROWE & the New South, the JOHNSON MOUNTAIN BOYS, TONY RICE & the Tony Rice Unit, and RHONDA VINCENT. Rounder released singer-fiddler ALISON KRAUSS's debut album in 1987, and her album *Now That I've Found You: A Collection* (1995) became the label's first million-seller. D. L. MENARD and RIDERS IN THE SKY have provided CAJUN and western sounds, respectively, and the label has also offered blues, blues rock, zydeco, contemporary folk, roots jazz, polka, Tex-Mex, and a variety of "world" musics.

Early on, Irwin, Leighton-Levy, and Nowlin organized Rounder Distribution, which by 1990 also represented some 500 other labels. By 1998, however, faced with the difficulties caused by consolidation in record retailing, Rounder struck a distribution deal with MERCURY-PolyGram (now part of Universal Music Group) to handle albums with projected sales of 7,500 units or more; independent distributors handle albums with lower sales expectations. John Virant became president and CEO in 1997. In 1998 he created Zoe Records to record cutting-edge rock acts. As of 2010 Rounder maintained facilities in Cambridge and in Burlington, Massachusetts.

In 2010 Rounder was purchased by the Concord Music Group, of Beverly Hills, California. —*Tom Ewing*

## Rouse Brothers
Earl B. Rouse b. November 1, 1911; death information unknown
Ervin Rouse b. Craven County, North Carolina, September 18, 1917;
    d. July 8, 1981
Gordon Rouse b. July 4, 1914; d. May 17, 1996

The Rouse Brothers came from a large musical family, but they were the children who left their mark on country music. Most important was Ervin Rouse, a fiddler and singer best known for his songs "Orange Blossom Special" and "Sweeter Than the Flowers." Something of a child prodigy, Ervin joined his brothers on the vaudeville circuit from 1928 to 1933. By 1939 he and brother Gordon were working in New York at THE VILLAGE BARN and writing songs for BOB MILLER's publishing company; Ervin even spent a few months as a singer for big band leader Glenn Miller.

As early as 1936 the brothers recorded for the AMERICAN RECORD CORPORATION, and in 1939 they began a relationship with BLUEBIRD. In the meantime, Ervin had written a fiddle tune called "South Florida Blues" and later renamed "Orange Blossom Special." Their 1939 Bluebird rendition was an early entry in a long line of recordings of the piece during succeeding decades. Indeed, the number became one of the most frequently played fiddle tunes in modern history.

Ervin Rouse also composed "Some Old Day" (a song they recorded in 1936), which eventually became a BLUEGRASS favorite. He also penned the mother song "Sweeter Than the Flowers," a 1948 hit for MOON MULLICAN. Later the brothers played large resort hotels in Miami. —*Charles Wolfe*

## Brent Rowan
b. Waxahachie, Texas, May 28, 1956

As one of the first Nashville studio guitarists to introduce electronic rack-mounted signal-processing gear, Brent Rowan helped to change the recorded sound of country music. Beginning in the mid-1980s his smooth guitar tones have advanced country's ongoing crossover to pop audiences, though his fresh approach also graced hits by country artists with more traditional stylistic leanings.

After touring for several years with gospel outfits and briefly with Grandpa Jones, Rowan cut his first master session, John Conlee's "Friday Night Blues" (1980)), at age twenty-three. Rowan's catchy guitar hook helped make it a #1 hit and launched one of Nashville's most successful studio careers. "The key to my job is interpretation of lyrics," he has said. "We're trying to create moods that help songs sell." A master of taste, restraint, and versatility, Rowan has done just that, contributing to hits by artists as varied as Reba McEntire, Mark Chesnutt, Shania Twain, Brooks & Dunn, Randy Travis, George Strait, Toby Keith, and Josh Turner. Even-tempered, hard-working, and reliably attuned to both performers and songs, the guitarist can also be heard on recordings by Chris LeDoux, Doug Stone, Tim McGraw, Tracy Lawrence, and Alabama.

Rowan was ACM's Guitarist of the Year for 1989 and has performed on numerous movie soundtracks. In the 2000s he has produced albums by hard-country singer Joe Nichols and blues-influenced country vocalist Julie Roberts, along with recording and coproducing several guitar albums of his own. —*Jon Sievert*

## Peter Rowan
b. Boston, Massachusetts, July 4, 1942

Peter Hamilton Rowan has long explored traditional, ethnic-based music of the United States and the world. Born into a musical family, he soon mastered the guitar and mandolin. In high school he performed in a regional rock & roll band, the Cupids.

In 1963 Rowan left Colgate University to pursue music full time, working folk and bluegrass clubs in the Boston area with Jim Rooney and banjo innovator Bill Keith, among others. From 1964 to 1967 Rowan was lead singer-guitarist for bluegrass progenitor Bill Monroe and helped win young, urban converts to the music's cause. Next, with mandolin virtuoso David Grisman, Rowan formed Earth Opera, whose drums and horns contrasted sharply with bluegrass. In 1969 Rowan joined SeaTrain, a San Francisco Bay Area band fusing folk, rock, and jazz. In 1973 he formed Old and in the Way with Grisman, Grateful Dead member Jerry Garcia, John Kahn, and fiddler extraordinaire Vassar Clements; in that year this group recorded a strong-selling, self-titled live album featuring Rowan's "Panama Red."

Since the mid-1970s the philosophical Rowan has continued to embrace many musical traditions—including bluegrass, blues, Native American, Celtic, Afro-Cuban, and Latin—recording solo and group albums with his brothers Christopher and Lorin, Tex-Mex accordion ace Flaco Jimenez, and Nashville Bluegrass Band, with whom he was a 1988 Grammy finalist for Best Bluegrass Album (*New Moon Rising*, Sugar Hill). In the mid-1980s Rowan lived in Nashville and wrote songs for country artists such as Ricky Skaggs and George Strait. Among Rowan's many albums, all showcasing his songs, are the multiethnic *Awake Me in a New World* (1993), *Dust Bowl Children* (1989)—a compilation reminiscent of Woody Guthrie—and *Bluegrass Boy* (1996), a tribute to Bill Monroe.

Since 2000 Rowan's albums have included *Reggaebilly* (2002); two with Tony Rice, *You Were There for Me* (2004) and *Quartet* (2007); and, as leader of the Peter Rowan Bluegrass Band, *Legacy* (2010). —*John W. Rumble*

## Billy Joe Royal
b. Valdosta, Georgia, April 3, 1942

Billy Joe Royal scored with the late-1960s pop hits "Down in the Boondocks," "I Knew You When," and "Cherry Hill Park" long before his foray into country music. In the late 1980s, however, he recorded country hits without substantially changing his sound.

Early on, Royal joined Ray Stevens, Joe South, and Jerry Reed on Atlanta's *Georgia Jubilee*. Working with diverse acts in Savannah, Georgia, further enhanced his versatility.

While Royal was playing a Cincinnati club, South pitched him an original song titled "Down in the Boondocks." Royal cut it in an Atlanta school building converted to a studio, using an empty septic tank for an echo chamber. Publisher Bill Lowery (The Lowery Music Group) took the demo to Columbia Records, which signed Royal and released the #9 single in 1965. Other pop chart-makers followed.

As his pop career faded, Royal sensed a country feel to his music, found "Burned Like a Rocket" in Nashville, and released the song on Atlantic Records. The #10 country hit (1985–86) ignited a string of fifteen country chart-makers, including the #2 hits "Tell It Like It Is" (1989) and "Till I Can't Take It Anymore" (1989–90). He continued to record independently into the 2000s. —*Gerry Wood*

## Royalties

Writers of country songs derive income mainly from two types of royalties: mechanical royalties from the sale of recordings; and performance royalties, which cover most broadcast and concert uses of songs.

Mechanical royalties are the fees paid by record companies for the rights to use songs on their recordings; they are based on a statutory rate set by Congress under the 1976 Copyright Act (which has been amended repeatedly in the digital age). From 1973 to 1993, this rate was adjusted by a Copyright Royalty Tribunal. Since that time, Congress has adjusted the rate, most recently (2006) to 9.1 cents for songs under five minutes in length (which practically all country songs are). This royalty covers retail sales through normal distribution channels; songwriters are often asked to accept a royalty below the statutory rate for songs licensed to budget-line or compilation albums, and they receive no royalties on promotional copies or store returns. Artists' royalties on record sales are a separate matter; these are set in the contracts artists sign with their record companies and are not subject to regulation.

Although Nashville-based Copyright Management Inc. (CMI) provides similar services, the New York–based Harry Fox Agency (HFA) is the company most music publishers in the United States use to issue mechanical licenses to record companies. Fox acts as the publisher's agent, not only issuing the licenses but collecting royalties and transferring those funds to the publisher. The publishing company then pays its songwriters, usually on a semiannual basis. For its work, the Harry Fox Agency keeps 4.5 percent of funds collected. HFA also issues synchronization (or "synch") licenses for publishers (see Music Publishing).

Performance royalties are paid to publishers and songwriters for broadcasts and other public performances (nightclubs, concerts, elevators) of copyrighted music. These royalties are set, monitored, and collected for publishers and writers via blanket license fees. Music users pay these fees through performing rights organizations (PROs). In the United States the three main PROs are ASCAP, BMI, and SESAC. Publishers affiliate with one of these organizations, which collect performance monies for copyrighted songs nationwide. (Most publishers have at least two companion firms, respectively affiliated with ASCAP and BMI.) Writers affiliate with one (and only one) PRO; when they do so, performance royalties for their songs come directly from the PRO and are not paid through the publisher.

Royalty amounts are based on complex radio/TV/Internet tracking procedures. The agencies pay performance royalties quarterly, usually a year behind actual performances. Interestingly, U.S. movies do not pay performance royalties—a partial explanation of why their in-perpetuity synch rights for songs are so costly.

Until the 1950s, country songwriters historically earned low or nonexistent royalties. Even when BMI came along in 1940 and aggressively recruited country songwriters as it competed with ASCAP, performance royalties stayed comparatively low for years because relatively few radio stations played country records or gave prime airtime to in-studio country talent. Moreover, until the 1950s, when BMI began paying writers directly, the organization typically paid performance royalties to publishers, many of which did not share performance royalties with writers. As for mechanical royalties, record companies winked at their producers' moonlighting as song publishers because it kept both salaries and royalty rates low; since the same people would usually get both, artists and writers were often cut out.

Several factors helped increase honesty in the publishing business and make royalties a more significant part of songwriters' income. One was direct confrontation by astute writers who realized they were being cheated of deserved earnings, especially on big crossover hits. Stories still circulate about legendary confrontations, such as when SLIM WILLET pulled a gun on Bill McCall of FOUR STAR RECORDS (and its companion publishing firm) and marched him to the bank for an overdue payment for royalties on Willet's self-penned 1952 hit "Don't Let the Stars Get in Your Eyes."

Another factor was simply the growth of competition. The concentration of so many publishers in Nashville (ACUFF-ROSE, TREE, CEDARWOOD, Moss-Rose) professionalized the country songwriting business. A new standard of honesty and fair play arose: If writers weren't treated well by a publisher, they could take their songs elsewhere.

Improved technology also played a part. The advent of electronic monitoring of retail sales and radio airplay made it easier to determine who owed what to whom.

Royalties and methods of protecting intellectual property are central to an ongoing debate about how to compensate songwriters and artists in the age of the Internet. Amid these challenges, the future undoubtedly will bring new laws for copyright protection and new formulas and means for devising and paying royalties. —Ronnie Pugh

*Darius Rucker*

artistic ties in 2008 when he signed with CAPITOL RECORDS and released *Learn to Live*, a successful solo country album that received RIAA platinum certification in August 2009.

In the 1990s Rucker and other members of Hootie & the Blowfish began visiting Nashville to write songs. In interviews, Rucker talked of his appreciation of country music and how the contemporary country duo FOSTER & LLOYD persuaded him to form a band and pursue music as a career. Rucker's first solo album, *Back to Then* (Hidden Beach, 2002), celebrated his R&B roots. But *Learn to Live* balanced contemporary and traditional influences, and thanks to three consecutive #1 singles—"Don't Think I Don't Think About It," "It Won't Be Like This for Long," and "Alright"—Rucker quickly established himself as the most successful black artist in country music since CHARLEY PRIDE. Rucker won CMA's 2009 New Artist award, and his "History in the Making" became a #3 country single in March 2010. His second country solo album, *Charleston, SC 1966,* was released in October 2010; its first single, "Come Back Song," reached #1 in early November. —*Michael McCall*

## Darius Rucker

Charleston, S.C., b. May 13, 1966

As lead singer of Hootie & the Blowfish, one of rock music's most popular bands in the 1990s, Darius Rucker often cited country music as a songwriting influence. He confirmed those

## Hal Rugg

b. New York, New York, July 21, 1936; d. August 9, 2005

Forever linked to the bracingly honest recordings of LORETTA LYNN, PEDAL STEEL GUITAR player Harald "Hal" Rugg parlayed an innovative and commercial style into an exemplary career as a top Nashville session player.

Rugg first recorded with GEORGE JONES in 1963. Work soon followed with the WILBURN BROTHERS and then with their protégé, Loretta Lynn, with whom he began recording under meticulous DECCA producer OWEN BRADLEY in 1965. Rugg's steel became a signature component of Lynn's sound, and he played on most of her albums through the early 1980s. Rugg recorded with many others and performed on television shows fronted by the Wilburns and THE STATLER BROTHERS as well as on the mid-1960s country showcase *That Good Ole Nashville Music*. He was a GRAND OLE OPRY house band member from 1963 to 1979.

Rugg was known for experimenting with his playing style and with the mechanics of the steel guitar itself. His sound showcased cleanly executed, fast-picked double- and triple-stop passages. Celebrated for his contributions to country hits, including Lynn's "Coal Miner's Daughter," THE OSBORNE BROTHERS' "Rocky Top," and K. D. LANG's "I'm Down to My Last Cigarette," Rugg was also an excellent jazz player. He was inducted into the Steel Guitar Hall of Fame in 1989. —*Elek Horvath and Robert Kramer*

## Johnny Russell
b. Sunflower County, Mississippi, January 23, 1940; d. July 3, 2001

Johnny Bright Russell was one of country music's biggest talents—not only in girth, but also in vocal style, songwriting, humor, and stage presence.

By the time twelve-year-old Russell's family moved to California, he was already considering a performing career. Influenced by ERNEST TUBB and LEFTY FRIZZELL, he recorded for the small Radio label in the late 1950s. CHET ATKINS heard Russell's version of his original song "In a Mansion Stands My Love" and showed it to JIM REEVES, whose rendition became the flip side of Reeves's million-selling 1960 crossover hit "He'll Have to Go."

During the early 1960s, Russell recorded for ABC Records, without success. Then, in 1963, BUCK OWENS hit with Russell's "Act Naturally" (cowritten with Voni Morrison), and the industry began taking notice. Russell moved to Nashville and signed with the WILBURN BROTHERS' publishing company, quickly securing cuts with the Wilburns, pop star Patti Page, LORETTA LYNN, and GEORGE HAMILTON IV; the Beatles covered "Act Naturally" in 1965.

Russell signed with RCA RECORDS in 1971. His first Top Twenty chartmaker, "Catfish John," came in 1973, and he had his biggest hit that same year with the blue-collar anthem "Rednecks, White Socks and Blue Ribbon Beer" (#4). Russell moved to MERCURY (1978–81) and 16th Avenue Records (1987). Joining the GRAND OLE OPRY in 1985, he also appeared regularly on *HEE HAW*.

Other Russell songwriting hits include "Making Plans" (PORTER WAGONER and DOLLY PARTON, 1980), "You'll Be Back (Every Night in My Dreams)" (THE STATLER BROTHERS, 1982), and "Let's Fall to Pieces Together" (GEORGE STRAIT, 1984). —*Don Roy*

## Leon Russell
b. Lawton, Oklahoma, April 2, 1942

Singer-pianist Leon Russell (birth name Claude Russell Bridges) gained recognition as musical director of Joe Cocker's 1970 Mad Dogs and Englishmen tour and as a star of George Harrison's 1971 Concert for Bangladesh. Nevertheless, Russell was raised in Oklahoma on HONKY-TONK and ROCKABILLY, and he periodically returned to those roots.

Russell was playing Tulsa nightclubs with David Gates and J. J. Cale at fourteen, touring with JERRY LEE LEWIS at eighteen, and, from age twenty-two, working Los Angeles recording sessions backing the Crystals, the Ronettes, the Righteous Brothers, and Tina Turner. He performed on THE BYRDS's "Mr. Tambourine Man"; cowrote, arranged, and played on most of Gary Lewis's hits; formed the Asylum Choir, a duo with Mark Benno, in 1968; and established Shelter Records with producer Denny Cordell in 1969.

In 1970 Russell released his self-titled debut solo album, including such enduring songs as "Delta Lady" and "A Song for You," both written for versatile vocalist Rita Coolidge. He followed with *Leon Russell and the Shelter People* (1971) and *Carney* (1972), both successful pop albums, and also penned hits for the Carpenters and for George Benson.

In 1973 Russell used a country persona for *Hank Wilson's Back, Vol. I*, featuring a cover photo of his back. Recorded with Nashville session players and Oklahoma pals, the album showcased raucous, rockabilly arrangements of country standards. His versions of FLATT & SCRUGGS's "Roll in My Sweet Baby's Arms" and HANK THOMPSON's "Six Pack to Go" became minor country hits. Russell married his backup singer Mary McCreary in 1974 and later recorded two albums with her. Russell and WILLIE NELSON toured together in 1978–79, and their 1979 double-album, *One for the Road*, yielded the #1 country hit "Heartbreak Hotel," a remake of the ELVIS PRESLEY classic.

In 1981 Russell teamed with the progressive-BLUEGRASS band NEW GRASS REVIVAL for a live album of country standards and rock oldies. He resurrected his Hank Wilson persona for another country album, 1984's *Vol. II*. Russell spent most of the late 1980s running his Paradise Video studio, but 1992's *Anything Can Happen*, coproduced by Bruce Hornsby for Virgin Records, heralded a fuller recording schedule. *Hank Wilson, Vol. III: Legend in My Time* appeared in 1998. Since then his albums have included 2001's *Rhythm & Bluegrass: Hank Wilson, Vol. IV*, recorded with New Grass Revival, and 2002's *Moonlight & Love Songs*, recorded with the Nashville Symphony Orchestra. *The Union*, a 2010 duet album with Elton John, reached #3 on the all-genre *Billboard* sales chart. In 2011, Russell was inducted into the Rock and Roll Hall of Fame and into the Songwriters Hall of Fame. —*Geoffrey Himes*

## The Ryman Auditorium
established May 12, 1892

Known worldwide as the Mother Church of Country Music, Nashville's Ryman Auditorium opened originally as the Union Gospel Tabernacle. It was built by Captain Thomas G. Ryman (1841–1904), the Nashville-based owner of a riverboat fleet, who was inspired by Methodist evangelist Sam Jones to build the red brick hall on Fifth Avenue, just north of Broadway. The building opened for religious services and other public events on May 12, 1892; in 1897 a second-floor gallery was added to accommodate a reunion of Confederate veterans. After Ryman died, the structure was renamed in his honor.

Early in the twentieth century, local citizens formed an association to oversee the building and to sponsor performances by New York's Metropolitan Opera, the Chicago Symphony, and similar ensembles that used the facility. Over the years, the building's magnificent acoustics showcased dozens of top classical and popular artists, including soprano Marian Anderson, tenor Enrico Caruso, cowboy idol GENE AUTRY, and Nashville's Fisk Jubilee Singers.

*Ryman Auditorium, 1960s*

The Ryman hosted country music as early as 1925, with local pickers entertaining for police benefit shows. The GRAND OLE OPRY broadcast at least once from the hall in 1942 but did not begin regular broadcasts there until June 5, 1943. At the time, the program was being staged at the Tennessee War Memorial Auditorium, but state authorities objected to fans sticking chewing gum under the seats. In desperation, WSM manager HARRY STONE persuaded longtime Ryman manager Lula Naff to rent the hall for Saturday-night Opry shows.

From the 1940s into the 1960s, the Ryman showcased country's evolving styles, from the HONKY-TONK MUSIC of ERNEST TUBB, who joined in 1943, to BLUEGRASS, which gelled within BILL MONROE's seminal band of 1945–1948, to THE NASHVILLE SOUND, voiced by smooth singers including JIM REEVES, FERLIN HUSKY, MARTY ROBBINS, and PATSY CLINE. During these same years, many other country greats made their Opry debuts there, including RED FOLEY, LITTLE JIMMY DICKENS, HANK WILLIAMS, KITTY WELLS, and DON GIBSON. Noncountry concerts continued as well, and record producers used the building for sessions by country stars and big bands led by Ray Anthony and Jan Garber. Opry founder GEORGE D. HAY routinely called the Ryman "The Grand Ole Opry House," but the Nashville-based National Life

and Accident Insurance Company—which owned WSM— officially endorsed this moniker after purchasing the building on September 12, 1963, for a reported $200,000.

In 1968, with crowds growing and estimated repair costs mounting, National Life and WSM executives announced plans to build a new Opry House as the centerpiece for an OPRYLAND theme park north of town. In 1971, a year before the park opened, these officials stated their intention to tear down the Ryman and use its bricks in a new Opryland chapel. Preservationists and entertainers nationwide protested, and the building stood. The Opry's last pre-move Ryman performance took place on Friday, March 15, 1974, followed by the Reverend Jimmy Snow's Grand Ole Gospel program, which concluded with regulars and guests singing the gospel standard "Will the Circle Be Unbroken." The following Saturday marked the first Opry broadcast from the new facility at Opryland east of downtown.

Although the Ryman remained a tourist destination, the facility lay virtually dormant as a concert hall for two decades, largely because it didn't meet city fire codes. Movie producers did use it to film scenes for *Nashville* (1975), *Coal Miner's Daughter* (1980), and *Sweet Dreams* (1985), and EMMYLOU HARRIS used the facility to record her critically acclaimed *At the Ryman* album (Reprise, 1992) between April 30 and May 2, 1991.

After Labor Day weekend in 1993 the building closed, and an $8.5 million renovation project was begun by GAYLORD ENTERTAINMENT, which had purchased Opryland and related properties in 1983. A new lobby was created, eventually featuring bronze statues of ROY ACUFF and MINNIE PEARL. On June 4, 1994, the hall officially reopened, with Garrison Keillor hosting a special radio broadcast of his long-running *A PRAIRIE HOME COMPANION* program before a packed house. That summer, stalwart Opry sponsor MARTHA WHITE FLOUR offered its first series of BLUEGRASS shows. Since then, the Ryman has witnessed numerous televised broadcasts, popular stage productions, including *Lost Highway* (on the life of Hank Williams) and *Always . . . Patsy Cline*, as well as concerts by country legend MERLE HAGGARD and rock stars BOB DYLAN and Bruce Springsteen. Beginning with one weekend in 1999, the Ryman began hosting Opry performances again, eventually expanding to a winter season of several months. The building has a current seating capacity of 2,362 and was designated a National Historic Landmark in 2001. —*John W. Rumble*

# The Talking Machine

## How Records Shaped Country Music

**COLIN ESCOTT**

I n December 1877 Thomas Edison filed a patent for what became records and record-playback equipment, and the following January he incorporated the Edison Speaking Phonograph Company (see EDISON RECORDS). A machine had never before talked. True, the telephone carried the human voice, but when the phonograph was unveiled, it was as if a machine had developed a soul. Its primary purpose, declared Edison, would be dictation, along with the teaching of elocution, preserving the last words of dying persons, and recording books for the blind. The fact that music wasn't mentioned meant that Edison was a visionary who didn't see very far. It was only after the novelty value of the talking machine wore off and technical advances improved its sound quality that some began thinking of it as a means of recording music.

Evidence now seems to be accumulating that Edison wasn't the first to record sound. A barely audible recording from 1860 by a French typesetter and inventor, Édouard-Léon Scott de Martinville, has surfaced. But for the record business to have anything more than novelty value, recordings had to be mass-produced, and that didn't happen until around 1900. Another twenty years would pass before record companies turned to country music. Some say that June 1922 recordings by two fiddle players, ECK ROBERTSON and Henry Gilliland, mark the beginning of the country record business, while others credit a 1921 disc cut by a country gospel quartet. The point, though, is that most other forms of music were represented on disc *before* country music was. In the early 1900s, top-of-the-line phonographs retailed for $200 (equivalent to $4,900 today) and records sold for around fifty cents (equivalent to $11.50 today), making the phonograph a toy for rich urbanites. Mass production eventually brought the phonograph within reach of all, and cheaper wind-up models became ideal for homes without electricity.

In 1921, record production topped 100 million units, but this number fell sharply thereafter as radio stations proliferated. The wider availability of record players, combined with the need to seek out new niche markets in the face of declining sales, sent record companies in search of blues and country performers (as well as those who played other forms of ethnic music) in the hinterlands. In a 1938 interview with Kyle Crichton from *Collier's*, A&R man RALPH PEER recalled his first Atlanta field session with FIDDLIN' JOHN CARSON some fifteen years earlier. Even allowing for exaggeration, it showed the pent-up demand for southern rural music. "We didn't even put a serial number on the record," Peer said, referring to "The Little Old Log Cabin in the Lane" b/w "The Old Hen Cackled and the Rooster's Going to Crow." "[We thought] that when the local dealer got his supply that would be the end of it. We sent him 1,000 records. . . . That night he called New York and ordered 5,000 more by express and 10,000 by freight. When the sales got up to 500,000 we were so ashamed we had Fiddlin' John come up to New York and do a rerecording." The field trip soon became a necessary part of an A&R man's job, and in 1927, Peer—formerly with OKEH, now with the Victor Talking Machine Company (later RCA VICTOR)— famously discovered JIMMIE RODGERS and the CARTER FAMILY in BRISTOL, TENNESSEE.

Part of the importance of country records from the 1920s is that they more or less tell us what the first A&R men found when they went in search of country music. "More or less" because some of the recorded performances were almost certainly more stilted than they would have been in an informal setting and were definitely edited for length and taste. The old British murder ballad "The Wexford Girl," for example, is at least fifteen verses long, and the reason for the murder is clear ("For the damsel came to me and said 'By you I am with child/I hope dear John you'll marry me for you have me defil'd'"). It was recorded frequently in the United States from 1924 onward as "The Knoxville Girl" or "The Waco Girl," usually with six verses, none of which so much as hint at the reason for the crime. Still, for all their drawbacks, the interwar recordings enable us to experience country music as a number of discrete regional musics that often had relatively little in common with one another. As late as 1944, COLUMBIA A&R man ART SATHERLEY told *The Saturday Evening Post*, "I would never think of hiring a Mississippi boy to play in a Texas band. Any Texan would know right off it was wrong." The irony of the record business is that it preserved these regional musics even as it was helping to destroy them.

Satherley was Columbia's "folk" A&R man, which meant that he recorded not only all the different styles that we would call early forms of country music but also blues, CAJUN, Mexican, and even Quebecois music. His circuit took him from his home in Los Angeles to Dallas, Tulsa, San Antonio, New Orleans, Shreveport, Chicago, and, beginning in 1947, Nashville. Yet, just fifteen years after he spoke to *The Saturday Evening Post*, several developments had overtaken Satherley's world. A country mainstream evolved from the many different kinds of folk and western music, and its ballooning sales distinguished it from all other folk-based musical forms. *Billboard* tacitly recognized as much when its charts dropped the term "folk music" in 1949, replacing it with a neologism, "country & western." It was entirely fitting that the "folk music" tag was dropped because country music no longer was folk music; it was a commercial discipline. And, as a country mainstream developed, it quickly became quite feasible for a Mississippi boy to play with a Texas band.

Yet another change overtook Satherley's world. The new country music business increasingly centered itself on Nashville. Field recordings became things of the past. As late as 1946, a poll of A&R men found that Chicago had the highest concentration of country musicians, and the A&R men considered it the hub of the business. Recordings were made there, and in Dallas, Cincinnati, Los Angeles, and other centers, but by the late 1950s RCA, Columbia, and DECCA were holding almost all of their country sessions in Nashville.

The development of a country mainstream went hand-in-hand with the rise of Nashville and the postwar growth of the country record business. "Country and western" embraced OLD-TIME fiddling and STRINGBAND MUSIC, WESTERN SWING, COWBOY MUSIC, ERNEST TUBB's HONKY-TONK, EDDY ARNOLD's country-pop, ROY ACUFF's hillbilly sounds, duet harmony, and sacred quartet singing. But in addition to all the different strains that went to make up country music, now there was a mainstream.

The fact that Nashville became country music's postwar business hub played a role in the growth of that mainstream. Because of the GRAND OLE OPRY, most of the major artists were together in one place, with a shared pool of session men and much of the country industry's infrastructure (music publishers, bookers, etc.) gathered around them. Records helped to forge a mainstream sound. They disseminated music more effectively than 50,000-watt radio stations or any amount of social migration. It was one thing to hear Roy Acuff on the Saturday-night Opry; it was quite another to have his records and learn their every nuance. Records were so efficient in spreading music that a younger performer such as Opry singer CARL SMITH, who came from Roy Acuff's hometown, had not only a little Acuff in his style but also a little Eddy Arnold, HANK WILLIAMS, and TOMMY DUNCAN. Smith carried drums, much like a western dance band, sang the occasional cowboy song, and cut gospel sides with the CARTER FAMILY. Records probably accounted for a large part of his musical education.

At the same time, records upped the ante for performers. It was no longer sufficient to be the best fiddler or singer for miles around; now there were discs providing tangible evidence of someone doing it better—often much better. Recordings were not only humbling but also a learning tool. They made it possible for ARTHUR "GUITAR BOOGIE" SMITH, ZEB AND ZEKE TURNER, and HANK GARLAND to grow up in rural South Carolina and to study Django Reinhardt and Eddie Lang. Records cross-pollinated musical genres with a speed that was unthinkable before their arrival.

Records eventually came to assume an economic importance as well. Early sales figures are often hard to come by, but it's probably safe to say that the best-selling country disc prior to World War II was VERNON DALHART's "Wreck of the Old 97" b/w "The Prisoner's Song," a twin-sided smash that sold just over 1 million copies. Jimmie Rodgers's first "Blue Yodel (T for Texas)" was his biggest hit, topping out at just over 500,000. Charles Wolfe's research reveals that the Carter Family's "Wildwood Flower" sold about 100,000 units, as did the DELMORE BROTHERS' "Brown's Ferry Blues," but these were anomalies for hillbilly music in the 1920s and 1930s. More typical were the sales of UNCLE JIMMY THOMPSON's first record, "Karo" b/w "Billy Wilson" for Columbia in 1926, which totaled just 9,000 copies, despite his presence on the Grand Ole Opry. And an unknown act in country's early days might sell very little at all.

For instance, the Delmores' first release, which came in 1931 in the depths of the Depression and two years before they joined the Opry, sold only 511 copies.

Such low sales figures made it difficult for most country performers to put much stock in record making as an income source prior to World War II. Moreover, payment for recording was often strictly in the form of a flat fee, usually ranging from $15 to $50 per recorded side. Royalties, when paid at all, typically amounted to one-half cent per side. At these rates, few country artists earned more than $100 for any release. "It never really bothered me that much that I didn't get anything for [my] records," Texas country singer FRANKIE MILLER said. "For one thing, I just wanted to have a record out. I would have paid them. And there wasn't any real money in records then. The money was in personal appearances, and having a record out—especially a hit record—boosted crowds and upped your asking price, but you didn't really expect to make anything off the records themselves."

Miller was talking about the early 1950s, just as the picture was changing. Earlier, the goal of most country artists had been to get to a major market, such as Dallas, Chicago, or Cincinnati, gain live radio exposure, and then work that market for years. In that world, records were, as Miller explained, little more than self-promotional tools. By the 1960s they became a viable source of income, especially after radio increasingly turned to playing records as opposed to airing live performances. A landmark decision by the U.S. Court of Appeals in 1940 ruled once and for all that radio stations could play records on the air for free, and pioneering country disc jockeys, such as NELSON KING at WLW in Cincinnati, did much to elevate the importance of the record.

In September 1947, *Billboard* reported that Ernest Tubb's royalties for the first six months of the year had exceeded $50,000. In February of the following year, the trade magazine reported that Eddy Arnold's 1947 sales had topped 2.7 million records, equating to more than $70,000 in royalties. Additionally, many top stars wrote or acquired a share in the songs they recorded, thereby compounding their earnings.

Most records were then sold to JUKEBOXES. By 1950 there were 400,000 jukeboxes serviced by 5,500 jukebox operators. The ops, as they were called in the music business, bought an average of 150 records a week, while the average consumer was still buying fewer than ten a year. Music publisher WESLEY ROSE stated that if one of Hank Williams's records sold 250,000 copies, the ops accounted for 150,000 of those sales. Poor distribution to rural areas partially explained this pattern, a problem that Ernest Tubb boldly aimed to solve when in 1947 he launched the Ernest Tubb Record Shop, which offered a mail-order service reaching all areas of the United States (and guaranteed to replace—free of charge—any records damaged in shipping). Meanwhile, record companies were trying harder to develop a network of branches and subdistributors that would get records to outlets where potential customers could find them.

More than ever before, both artists and A&R men focused their attention on the profits to be had from records. If you recorded, you were now competing with everyone in the marketplace. To do this, you had to stop thinking locally and start thinking nationally. To go coast to coast, you needed a mainstream sound. Artists who could only achieve local sales with regional styles were increasingly likely to get shown the door by the major record labels. *Billboard*'s introduction of popularity charts in 1944 increased competition for a small number of chart positions (only ten to fifteen, early on), and emphasized records that appealed to the broadest possible audience.

Country music, once based in the oral and mostly noncommercial traditions of folk music, was now a commodity, and records hastened its commodification. In rural settings, country music had been played on porches, at outdoor gatherings, or in small community centers. Suddenly, records made old songs into potentially lucrative copyrights; they turned musicians at the local barn dance into prospective recording stars; and they drew a line between performers and audiences. At one time it wasn't unthinkable for everyone to join in or feel part of the performance. That was no longer the case. What had once been a social experience was now a solitary one.

As country music became an integral part of the popular music mix, records came to determine touring schedules, positions on a showbill, and the prices artists could charge for personal appearances. It's now almost impossible to sustain a career without a recording contract. If a singer came to Nashville in 1946, it was with the goal of getting on the Grand Ole Opry. Today, even the record industry's well-publicized decline hasn't significantly dampened the enthusiasm of most new arrivals in Music City to land a record deal with one of the corporate giants on MUSIC ROW. Records still hold the key to everything.

Seventy-eights gave way to 45s and LPs, which have in turn been supplanted in succession by compact discs and digital downloads. Strangely, though, the country recording business remains locked in one curious anachronism: song length. From the beginning, pop and country 78s timed out at about three minutes, because that was all the discs would allow. Long-playing records were introduced in 1948, and they had a gradual effect on the way most forms of popular music were composed and played. It became possible for songs or suites of songs to last as long as twenty minutes per side. Adult popular music remained singles-driven into the 1950s; rock & roll was singles-driven until the mid- to late 1960s; but country music remained singles-driven into the era when singles as such had, temporarily, almost ceased to exist. "You just cut a little record and threw it out there" was the way JERRY KENNEDY, president of MERCURY RECORDS Nashville during the 1970s (and beyond), characterized the business. Kennedy had started producing in the early 1960s and regarded albums as a nuisance at first. "If you cut a hit, it was like a bummer," he said, "because you'd have to find songs enough for an album. The sales weren't there. Six, eight, nine thousand copies wasn't bad."

Even today, when a sale of 600,000, 800,000, or 900,000 albums isn't bad, the focus is still on assembling an album that contains at least two and ideally three, four, or more songs that can be "pulled" as singles for radio broadcast or digital downloading. More than twenty-five years after CDs came to market, bringing with them a maximum playing time of eighty minutes, country CDs are rarely longer than the old forty-minute LP time limit because the focus is still on singles-length songs.

By the time CDs were introduced in the early 1980s, recording itself had improved dramatically, and the nature of recording was beginning to challenge the notion of what constituted a recorded performance. Fiddlin' John Carson recorded into an acoustical horn, and the signal (or some of it, anyway) was encrypted onto a wax disc. Human hearing can pick up a range of ten octaves, from 16 to 16,000 cycles per second, or hertz (Hz). Acoustic recordings captured a range of roughly 164 Hz to 2 kHz (two kilohertz, or 2,000 cycles per second). Electrical recording, widely introduced in 1925, brought with it a range of 30 Hz to 8 kHz. Engineers at British Decca developed full-frequency-range recording during World War II to detect the difference between Allied and German submarine engines. At the same time, microphone technology improved to the point that sheer lung power was no longer a prerequisite for singers. Rudy Vallee and Bing Crosby were the first to perfect an intimate singing style. In country music, the Delmore Brothers were among the first to craft a style in which nuance replaced declamation and for which the microphone was essential. By 1950, artists such as the note-bending LEFTY FRIZZELL were exploiting the potential of ever-improving microphone technology.

Recordings were still made onto discs until the widespread introduction of audiotape in 1950. Discs meant that if a performance went off the rails, it was started afresh. Tape led inexorably to splicing, editing, and overdubbing. Multitrack tape was introduced in the mid-1950s, and by the mid-1990s primitive three-track tape had gradually evolved and expanded to four tracks to eight, sixteen, thirty-two, to sixty-four-track digital. Before multitrack, a record enshrined an ensemble performance. The singer sang; the band played. Everyone hoped that the best vocal performance wouldn't be marred by a flubbed note from the band, or vice versa. By the 1980s sixty or more tracks could be recorded separately, and a four-minute recording could be pieced together from them. There was no need for an ensemble performance as such. In the 1990s and into the new century, with the advance of digital recording through ProTools and other technologies, bad notes could be "repaired," and a flat vocal note or phrase could be brought up on key. Technical perfection is easily realizable. Singers and producers tend to emerge from a session with a "bed track" (usually the rhythmic skeleton of a song), a "scratch" (or guide) vocal, and weeks of additional recording ahead of them to add instrumental and vocal parts, mix them, and perfect the final product. The pooling of ideas during the session, once a prized feature of Nashville recordings, hasn't altogether disappeared, but it's rare for a singer and all the musicians to be in the studio at the same time and walk out with a finished recording.

While it's possible to draw a tortuous line from Fiddlin' John to today's country stars, it's tempting to see the earlier forms of country music as somehow purer and less commercial. But while records hastened the commercialism of country music, it was a development that didn't need much encouragement. In 1927, when Ralph Peer went to Bristol, Tennessee, and discovered the Carter Family and Jimmie Rodgers, he didn't get an overwhelming response when he first advertised for performers to audition. Then, as researcher Charles Wolfe discovered, Peer let it be known that featured performers got $100 a day and sidemen $25. Suddenly he was deluged with audition requests. And lo! the country record business was born.

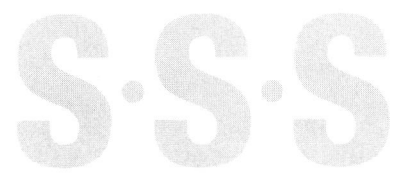

## Junior Samples

b. Cumming, Georgia, August 10, 1926; d. November 13, 1983

With only a third-grade education, rotund rural comic Junior Samples became a fixture in country fans' living rooms starting in 1969, as a regular in the colorful world of HEE HAW, a popular network and syndicated TV series. Obviously reading from cue cards, Alvin Samples Jr. would speak in a slow southern drawl, often stumbling on his lines for effect. His costume consisted of bibbed overalls, an open-necked shirt with rolled-up sleeves, and work boots. In a regularly scheduled skit, he would be featured with such cast members as GRANDPA JONES, KENNY PRICE, and an old hound dog—a stereotypical, shiftless hillbilly clan.

Earlier, during the summer of 1967, the nonmusical Samples had a novelty comedy record on the Chart label, "The World's Biggest Whopper" (featuring interviewer Jim Morrison), which garnered enough airplay to spend four weeks on *Billboard*'s country charts. Samples also teamed with comedian ARCHIE CAMPBELL for *Bull Session at Bull's Gap*, a 1968 Chart Records comedy album deriving its name from Campbell's hometown.

Samples's used-car salesman segment on *Hee Haw* always ended with his displaying a sign citing the fictional phone number BR549. The contemporary country band BR549 borrowed it for their group name. —*Walt Trott*

## Billy Sanford

b. Natchitoches, Louisiana, January 9, 1940

For more than thirty years, session guitarist William R. Sanford Jr. played on country hits such as "Easy Loving" (1971) and "He Stopped Loving Her Today" (1980), each a CMA Song of the Year two years successively. He also contributed to pop hits, including ROY ORBISON's "Oh, Pretty Woman" (1964) and Dave Loggins's "Please Come to Boston" (1974).

Self-taught, Sanford started performing as a teenager in Texas nightclubs and then landed a stint as a staff musician on Shreveport's *LOUISIANA HAYRIDE* from 1958 to 1959. Later he played bass in BOB LUMAN's ROCKABILLY road band before Luman invited him to record in Nashville in 1962. After relocating there in February 1964, Sanford joined Orbison's road band, the Candy Men, recording pop singles such as "Goodnight" and "You're My Girl."

Sanford also played on ELVIS PRESLEY's Graceland recordings in 1976 and on TV jingles. In addition, he supplied acoustic and electric guitar parts for KEITH WHITLEY's 1989 #1 hit "I'm No Stranger to the Rain." —*Walt Trott*

## Sarie and Sally

Edna "Sarie" Wilson b. July 15, 1896; d. June 27, 1994
Margaret "Sally" Waters b. Chattanooga, Tennessee, May 2, 1903;
    d. November 2, 1967

Sarie and Sally were two of the earliest professional comedians on the GRAND OLE OPRY, starring there between 1934 and 1939. The team portrayed two mountain women whose style and repartee anticipated the later comedy of MINNIE PEARL and caused many fans to see them as a female Lum & Abner. The creative force behind the team was Edna Wilson (Sarie). After forming the act in Florida, she and her younger sister, Margaret Waters, auditioned for WSM's daytime schedule in 1934 and landed a fifteen-minute show that was part rural soap opera, part vaudeville dialogue—but without music. In January 1935 the pair also began appearing on the Opry, drawing sacks of fan mail. Soon they were working the Opry nearly every week and touring with the Dixieliners, PEE WEE KING, and even a young ROY ACUFF. In 1939, after they left the program, they traveled to Hollywood to appear in *In Old Monterey* with GENE AUTRY. Margaret Waters's failing health caused the team to split up in 1941, though Edna Wilson continued to work as a solo act over WSB–Atlanta and WMC–Memphis (where she created a new character, "Aunt Bunie") before returning to Nashville and retiring. —*Charles Wolfe*

## Art Satherley

b. Bristol, England, October 19, 1889; d. February 10, 1986

"He was the recording genius for COLUMBIA RECORDS for a good number of years. . . . [H]e was a good judge of what the market needed." Such was the estimate by music business pioneer RALPH PEER of Arthur Edward "Uncle Art" Satherley, whose career had begun before Peer's did. Producer, talent scout, manufacturing supervisor, and salesman, Satherley easily ranks among early country music's half-dozen essential businessmen. Like Peer, he was equally as important to the recording of blues (then called "race music") before World War II as he was to the recording of country music (then known as "hillbilly").

An Episcopal minister's son born in Bristol, England, young Satherley shared turn-of-the-century Europe's fascination with the American West. In his middle twenties, he came to the United States and went to work grading lumber for the Wisconsin Chair Company in Port Washington, Wisconsin. When Thomas Edison purchased a subsidiary of Wisconsin Chair, Satherley spent a brief period as one of the inventor's secretaries. In 1918 Satherley joined Wisconsin Chair's new record label, Paramount, first in manufacturing, then as a salesman. By the mid-1920s, after earning

*Art Satherley*

a reputation as an expert in the infant hillbilly and race music fields, he was spending the bulk of his time scouting and recording talent.

Satherley left Paramount in 1929 for the AMERICAN RECORD CORPORATION (ARC); when the Columbia Broadcasting System bought ARC in 1938, he became country and race music A&R chief for the revived Columbia label. "What I was interested in," he would recall, "was the acceptance of the public. Does the public want it? Not what I want, or the artist wanted. Would the public want it?"

The leitmotif in Satherley's self-appraisals is a fierce pride in his empathy, despite his English rearing, with rural Americans. "I was brought up on the farm," he recalled. "I said my prayers on a sheepskin at night on a stone floor [under] a thatched roof. I have shucked wheat with my hands, and oats and barley. I have done much around the farmyard. So you see, I have understood country music from my early childhood days."

Country artists Satherley recorded include the PICKARD FAMILY, JOHN MCGHEE & FRANK WELLING, FLEMING & TOWNSEND, CARSON ROBISON, VERNON DALHART, the ALLEN BROTHERS, THE CALLAHAN BROTHERS, CLIFF & BILL CARLISLE, DOC ROBERTS, Asa Martin, AL DEXTER, ROY ACUFF (whom Satherley called a "a pure, unadulterated country American"), BILL MONROE, TEX RITTER, RED FOLEY, GEORGE MORGAN, SPADE COOLEY, TED DAFFAN, and JOHNNY BOND (whose records were Satherley's final productions). He also oversaw the recording of blues artists Ma Rainey, Blind Lemon Jefferson, Alberta Hunter, Ida Cox, Big Bill Broonzy, Josh White, Leroy Carr, and Memphis Minnie.

Satherley worked especially closely with GENE AUTRY and BOB WILLS. Largely responsible for Autry's recording success, he produced Autry's early hit "That Silver Haired Daddy of Mine" and promoted Autry's records through the vast distribution networks of ARC and Columbia. Satherley helped secure Autry's cowboy image in radio, and the executive's persistent lobbying in Hollywood helped launch the young singer in films. Satherley was

introduced to Wills in 1935 by his assistant, DON LAW (his eventual successor as Columbia's country A&R chief), and oversaw hundreds of Wills's recordings (he always took credit for naming the bandleader's signature tune, "San Antonio Rose"). Late in life, Wills called his departure from Satherley's stewardship—Wills left Columbia for MGM in October 1947—the worst decision of his career.

Satherley left Columbia in 1952, spent a long retirement primarily in Southern California, and died February 10, 1986. He was elected to THE COUNTRY MUSIC HALL OF FAME in 1971.

"I'm the only living man who's been through this business with his hands," Satherley said in the late 1970s, "running the factories, making the records, making the formulas, finding the material, seeing that the pressing's done, selling [the records], and finding the artists. Nearly fifty years at it. And always of no fixed abode, just traveling, finding country people to make these recordings. And now considered the daddy of it all. That's what they call me, the daddy of all recordings country: country black, country white."
—*Tony Scherman*

## Mark and Ann Savoy

Mark Savoy b. Eunice, Louisiana, October 1, 1941
Ann Allen Savoy b. St. Louis, Missouri, January 20, 1952

Mark and Ann Savoy, who were married in 1976, have been leaders in perpetuating traditional CAJUN music. Mark grew up in the heart of Cajun country and became an accomplished musician, playing fiddle and accordion, as well as Louisiana's most respected accordion maker. He has performed and recorded with many of Cajun music's greats, including Michael Doucet of BEAUSOLEIL, DEWEY BALFA and his brothers, and D. L. MENARD.

Ann, who grew up in Virginia, began playing guitar at age twelve and eventually pursued various kinds of folk music. She also studied French, which she later taught. After their marriage the Savoys became popular at dances and special events in Louisiana as well as ambassadors of traditional Cajun music on the folk music circuit. Ann produced and performed with LINDA RONSTADT on *Evangeline Made*, a 2002 various-artists Vanguard album of Cajun music, and collaborated with Ronstadt as the Zozo Sisters on the 2006 Vanguard release *Adieu False Heart*. In addition to her roles as musician and mother, Ann is a scholar of Cajun music, writing numerous articles and compiling and editing the book *Cajun Music: A Reflection of a People* (Bluebird Press, 1984). Today the Savoys operate an accordion factory and music store in Eunice and continue to record and perform locally, nationally, and internationally. —*Charlie Seemann*

## Sawyer Brown

Gregg Hubbard b. Orlando, Florida, October 4, 1960
Mark Miller b. Dayton, Ohio, October 25, 1958
Bobby Randall b. Midland, Michigan, September 16, 1952
Jim Scholten b. Bay City, Michigan, April 18, 1952
Joe Smyth b. Portland, Maine, September 6, 1957
Duncan Cameron b. Utica, New York, July 27, 1956
Shayne Hill b. Spearfish, South Dakota, March 21, 1970

Sawyer Brown has been well served by the artistic maturation process. When the band established itself nationally with the 1985 hit "Step That Step," it earned a reputation for playing "bubblegum country." Six years later, after the industry had all but left it behind, the group reemerged with considerably more depth and focus.

Revolving around lead singer Mark Miller and keyboard player Gregg (Hobie) Hubbard, who met at the University of Central Florida, the group coalesced after the duo moved to Nashville in 1981. Initially known as Savannah, the members took the name Sawyer Brown from a road in suburban Nashville.

In 1984 Sawyer Brown won the $100,000 first prize in the *Star Search* television series, leading to a contract with CURB RECORDS. Onstage, the band presented a wild, colorful show, with outlandish outfits and Miller's propensity for whirling and dancing. Buoyed by their youthful worldview and high-energy performances, they scored three straight Top Ten hits before the end of 1985. But radio and critics cooled on the band. The group managed only two more Top Ten records through 1991—"This Missin' You Heart of Mine" (1987–88) and a remake of GEORGE JONES's classic "The Race Is On" (1989)—though it remained one of country music's top-drawing live acts.

"The Walk" changed Sawyer Brown's reputation in 1991 with images of a sentimental-but-realistic father-son relationship that displayed an understanding of common-man issues the group had not previously addressed. Mixing blue-collar themes with the occasional boy-girl ditty, Sawyer Brown hit consistently in the early 1990s with such singles as "The Dirt Road," "Café on the Corner," "All These Years," and "Thank God for You." Ironically, the act's newfound seriousness emerged at a time when much of the industry became enamored with seminovelty records. Although the group's hits declined after 1997, it continued to chart into the 2000s.

Bobby Randall departed in February 1991 and was replaced by former Amazing Rhythm Aces member Duncan Cameron. In turn, Shayne Hill replaced Cameron in 2004. —*Tom Roland*

## Don Schlitz
b. Durham, North Carolina, August 29, 1952

Don Schlitz is one country music's most successful songwriters, with a host of #1 hits to his credit. The first of these was a career maker—KENNY ROGERS's "The Gambler"—and Schlitz's later chart-toppers have included THE JUDDS' "Rockin' with the Rhythm of the Rain" and MICHAEL JOHNSON's "Give Me Wings." Schlitz and frequent cowriter PAUL OVERSTREET provided RANDY TRAVIS with Travis's first #1 smash, "On the Other Hand," as well as Travis's later blockbuster "Forever and Ever, Amen." With these and other compositions Schlitz helped set the tone for country songwriting during the 1980s NEW TRADITIONALISM era and beyond.

After briefly attending Duke University, Schlitz moved to Nashville in 1973, taking a night-shift job as a computer operator at Vanderbilt University so that he could pitch his songs during the day. In 1978 Rogers recorded "The Gambler" (Schlitz had previously recorded his own version), and the Grammy-winning song changed Schlitz's life forever.

Subsequently, Schlitz penned hits for the NITTY GRITTY DIRT BAND, TANYA TUCKER, and the BELLAMY BROTHERS. "On the Other Hand" and "Forever and Ever, Amen" earned CMA and ACM Song of the Year awards, and the latter won a 1987 Grammy for Best Country Song. ASCAP named Schlitz the organization's Writer of the Year four times, from 1988 to 1991. His other 1980s credits include KEITH WHITLEY's "When You Say Nothing at All," Travis's "Deeper Than the Holler," and Tanya Tucker's "Strong Enough to Bend."

Schlitz's writing success continued into the 2000s with hits such as GARTH BROOKS's "Learning to Live Again," MARK CHESNUTT's "Almost Goodbye," LEE ANN WOMACK's "Why They

*Don Schlitz*

Call It Falling," and SARA EVANS's "Cheatin'." Cowriting sessions with MARY CHAPIN CARPENTER produced "I Feel Lucky," "He Thinks He'll Keep Her," and "I Take My Chances."

Schlitz released an album, *Dreamers Matinee*, on CAPITOL RECORDS in 1980. He also joined four other prominent songwriters on the RCA album *Signatures* in 1988. His *Live at the Bluebird Café* appeared on the American Originals label in 2001.

Schlitz was elected to the NASHVILLE SONGWRITERS HALL OF FAME in 1993. —*Beverly Keel*

## David Schnaufer
b. Hearne, Texas, September 28, 1952; d. August 23, 2006

A soft-spoken Texan, David Lynn Schnaufer devoted himself to bringing the Appalachian dulcimer, or mountain dulcimer, to larger audiences, becoming the instrument's most important figure since Kentucky folksinger Jean Ritchie. Schnaufer reawakened interest in one of America's most important folk instruments through his solo recordings, instructional tapes, award-winning videos, and workshops as well as through his extensive session work with JOHNNY CASH, EMMYLOU HARRIS, FAITH HILL, THE JUDDS, Cyndi Lauper, KATHY MATTEA, and LINDA RONSTADT.

Schnaufer lived as a wandering troubadour after taking up the dulcimer in AUSTIN, TEXAS, in 1973. His travels took him to Colorado, Washington, D.C., and West Virginia before he settled in Nashville in 1984. By this time he had won seven major competitions, including the National Championship title in Winfield, Kansas.

Schnaufer's solo albums earned him public attention and critical raves; the *Nashville Scene* said of him: "Years from now they'll remember Schnaufer as the man who did for the mountain dulcimer what LES PAUL did for the guitar." A founding member of the Cactus Brothers, Schnaufer performed with them until early

1994, when he returned to solo work. At the time of his death from cancer, he was an adjunct professor at the Blair School of Music of Vanderbilt University in Nashville, where he had taught since 1995. He donated his large collection of dulcimers and music boxes, with instruments dating from the early 1800s, to the Tennessee State Museum. —*John Lomax* III

## John Schneider
b. Mount Kisco, New York, April 8, 1960

John Richard Schneider came to prominence as Bo Duke, a rural hot-rodder and all-around hero on CBS-TV's popular *Dukes of Hazzard* series (January 26, 1979–July 26, 1985), which featured Tom Wopat as Bo's brother Luke Duke and WAYLON JENNINGS as unseen narrator and theme song singer.

Scotti Bros. Records capitalized on Schneider's popularity, starting with a Top Ten cover of ELVIS PRESLEY's "It's Now or Never" in 1981. But each release, including a remake of Presley's "Are You Lonesome Tonight," was worse than the last. Embarrassed with the lounge-Elvis role and wanting to be taken seriously as a country singer, Schneider came to Nashville, where JOHNNY CASH helped him hone his talents.

Between 1984 and 1987 Schneider established himself on MCA RECORDS as a country chart-maker, though he is still best identified as a television actor. His three-year run of hits included eight Top Tens and four #1 singles, the best known being 1984's "I've Been Around Enough to Know." As his chart performance slipped, Schneider went back to acting, screenwriting, and directing. —*Bob Millard*

## Thom Schuyler
b. Bethlehem, Pennsylvania, June 10, 1952

Thom Schuyler has been a solo artist, hit songwriter, member of a successful country group, and record company executive, but he is perhaps best known as the composer of "16th Avenue." A 1982 Top Ten hit for LACY J. DALTON, the song recounts the highs and lows of MUSIC ROW songwriters.

During the 1970s, Thomas James Schuyler spent years as an aspiring New York tunesmith and then came to Nashville in 1977 after hearing striking new sounds on country radio. Success came with lyrically sweet, folk-tinged hits such as "Love Will Turn You Around" (KENNY ROGERS, 1982), "I Don't Know Where to Start" (EDDIE RABBITT, 1982), and "I Fell in Love Again Last Night" (FORESTER SISTERS, 1985). *Brave Heart*, Schuyler's 1983 solo album on CAPITOL RECORDS, climbed to the middle reaches of the country album charts. In 1986 Schuyler joined songwriter friends Fred Knobloch and PAUL OVERSTREET in the trio S-K-O, which became S-K-B with Overstreet's replacement by Craig Bickhardt in 1987. After two albums the group disbanded, in 1989. Continuing to write hit songs, Schuyler also became involved with NSAI and CMA, where he rose to become president and chairman. From 1992 to 1994 he ran RCA RECORDS's Nashville division, and with former Nashville chief JOE GALANTE's returning from New York after heading the entire label (1990–94), Schuyler stayed on as vice president of Nashville A&R. While with RCA he re-signed WAYLON JENNINGS and advanced the careers of O'KANES veteran Jamie O'Hara, KENNY CHESNEY, SARA EVANS, LONESTAR, and MARTINA MCBRIDE.

Since leaving RCA in 1998, Schuyler has kept writing and performing, revamped a music publishing firm (2001–2005), served

part time as youth minister of his church, and recorded the occasional album, including 2009's *Prayer of a Desperate Man*, issued on his own TJS label.

Schuyler was elected to the NASHVILLE SONGWRITERS HALL OF FAME in 1996. —*Thomas Goldsmith*

## Ramblin' Tommy Scott
b. Stephens County, Georgia, June 24, 1917

Born Tommy Lee Scott, singer and showman Ramblin' Tommy Scott became a country music entertainer in the 1930s, when he gained experience in an old-fashioned MEDICINE SHOW. In succeeding decades he recorded for KING, BULLET, FOUR STAR, and other labels (though without hits) and was long one of the industry's busiest road performers.

A close associate of CLYDE MOODY and Curly Seckler, Scott became a television pioneer, in 1948, by filming fifty-two quarter-hour shows for syndication. He appeared briefly on the GRAND OLE OPRY as a ventriloquist with his dummy Luke McLuke. Early on, Scott showcased BLACKFACE comedy in his entourage, which sometimes featured cowboy stars such as Tim McCoy and Johnny Mack Brown. Scott toured from his base in Toccoa, Georgia, leading what he called America's Last Real Medicine Show into the mid-1990s. At that point he cut back his schedule to care for his ailing wife, Frankie, who died in 2004. —*Ronnie Pugh*

## Scottdale String Band

The popular Scottdale String Band emerged in the 1920s from the DeKalb County town of Scottdale, Georgia, east of Atlanta. An instrumental ensemble unique in instrumentation and with a more varied repertoire than that of other Georgia STRINGBANDS, its Atlanta recordings (for OKEH) sold quite well.

The group featured a banjo-mandolin as lead instrument (played by Belvie Freeman prior to 1927 and Charlie Simmons thereafter) and two guitars, played by Barney Pritchard (b. June 29, 1904; d. March 1963) and Marvin Head. Performances ranged from traditional folk tunes to jazz and blues pieces to HAWAIIAN or pop melodies to original material. Better-sellers included the traditional "Chinese Breakdown," originals such as "Scottdale Stomp" and "Stone Mountain Wobble," and a ragtime number, "Carbolic Rag."

The band journeyed to Grafton, Wisconsin, for a last recording session in 1932 for Paramount Records, but sales were practically nonexistent for the resulting two Depression-era releases. Appearances in the Atlanta area continued until the band's demise, in about 1940. —*Bob Pinson*

## Earl Scruggs & the Earl Scruggs Revue
Earl Scruggs b. Flint Hill, North Carolina, January 6, 1924
Randy Scruggs b. Nashville, Tennessee, August 3, 1953
Gary Scruggs b. Knoxville, Tennessee, May 18, 1949
Steve Scruggs b. Nashville, Tennessee, February 8, 1958; d. September 23, 1992
Jody Maphis b. August 18, 1954
Bob Wilson b. July 16, 1946

Eager to strengthen his appeal to America's emerging youth culture and frustrated by the musical inflexibility of his FLATT & SCRUGGS partner, LESTER FLATT, BLUEGRASS banjo pioneer Earl

Eugene Scruggs recruited sons Randy Scruggs and Gary Scruggs to form a rock-influenced ensemble in early 1969. The Earl Scruggs Revue initially featured Gary on lead vocals, bass, and harmonica; Randy on electric and acoustic guitar; Bob Wilson on piano; and Jody Maphis on drums. The group's repertoire mixed traditional songs and contemporary folk-rock covers with Earl's instrumental specialties.

During the early 1970s the band included Vassar Clements, a bluegrass fiddler with an affinity for blues, who joined Earl, Gary, and Randy Scruggs on the Nitty Gritty Dirt Band's 1972 homage to traditional country music, *Will the Circle Be Unbroken*. Bluegrass dobro veteran and blues singer Uncle Josh Graves came aboard in March 1972; by then Earl's youngest son, Steve, worked occasional dates and eventually replaced Wilson. Taylor Rhodes replaced Maphis in 1978.

Though never embraced by bluegrass or country music purists, the Revue found its niche as a live act playing to college-age audiences. The group recorded for Columbia throughout the decade and made frequent network television appearances. The act remained a major draw on campuses and in auditoriums as well as other venues until 1980, when persistent back problems forced Earl Scruggs's retirement from the road.

Scruggs is a member of The Country Music Hall of Fame (1985) and the IBMA Hall of Fame (1991). In 1989, he was awarded a National Heritage Fellowship, and three years later was honored with the National Medal of Arts. In addition to his 1968 Grammy while a member of Flatt & Scruggs, the banjo legend won three more Grammys between 1998 and 2004, including Best Country Instrumental Performance in 2001 for a new recording of "Foggy Mountain Breakdown," from the album *Earl Scruggs and Friends*, which included his sons Gary and Randy. The elder Scruggs was awarded a Grammy Lifetime Achievement Award in 2008.

His wife and longtime manager, Louise Scruggs, died February 2, 2006. —*Dave Samuelson*

## Randy Scruggs

b. Nashville, Tennessee, August 3, 1953

A son of bluegrass great Earl Scruggs, Randy Lynn Scruggs has firmly established his own imprint on contemporary country music. He earned CMA awards as producer of the 1989 Album of the Year, the Nitty Gritty Dirt Band's *Will the Circle Be Unbroken, Vol. II*, and Alison Krauss & Union Station's 1995 Single of the Year, "When You Say Nothing At All." His recordings of "Amazing Grace" (1989) and "A Soldier's Joy" (1998) won Grammys for Best Country Instrumental Performance. As a songwriter, Scruggs's credits include Earl Thomas Conley's "Angel in Disguise" and Deana Carter's "We Danced Anyway."

Introduced to the autoharp by Mother Maybelle Carter (Carter Family) at age six, Scruggs developed a fascination with that instrument, which led him to learn many of the early songs of the Carter Family and other traditional artists. At age nine he made his first guest appearance on the syndicated Flatt & Scruggs television program.

Taking up the guitar, Randy Scruggs spent his childhood summers touring with his father's band, and at age thirteen he played on his first recording. Later he formed the Scruggs Brothers with older brother Gary, releasing two albums on Vanguard Records. With younger brother Steve and father Earl they created the Earl Scruggs Revue.

Meanwhile, Randy continued to build his reputation as a top studio guitarist. In 1980 he opened Scruggs Sound Studio.

With more than one hundred original songs recorded by top country artists, Scruggs has also produced records by Moe Bandy, Bobby Bare, Earl Thomas Conley, Dean Dillon, Skip Ewing, Waylon Jennings, and Sawyer Brown. In 1998 Scruggs released a solo album, *Crown of Jewels*, on Reprise Records, featuring performances with guest artists ranging from Vince Gill, Travis Tritt, and Emmylou Harris to Iris DeMent, John Prine, and Bruce Hornsby. At this writing Scruggs held three CMA Musician of the Year Awards (1999, 2003, and 2006). —*Janet E. Williams*

## Dan Seals

b. McCamey, Texas, February 8, 1948; d. March 25, 2009

Sweet-voiced Dan Seals enjoyed hits with a rock band, in a pop duo, and as a solo country singer and duet artist, racking up gold records in the pop and country fields and earning two CMA awards. He also wrote or cowrote many of his major country hits (usually with Bob McDill).

Danny Wayland Seals grew up in the oil field country of West Texas, surrounded by music. His father, Wayland, was an amateur musician good enough to sit in with Bob Wills, Ernest Tubb, and Jim Reeves. Dan's older brother, Jim Seals, scored early-1970s pop hits with Dash Crofts in Seals & Crofts; a cousin, Johnny Duncan, tallied several hits on Columbia; while two other cousins, Troy Seals and Chuck Seals, are award-winning songwriters.

Following a minor pop hit with the act Southwest F.O.B. ("The Smell of Incense," 1968), Dan Seals and bandmate John Ford Coley moved to California to become England Dan & John Ford Coley. With producer Kyle Lehning they created six Top Forty pop hits between 1976 and 1979, best exemplified by the gentle rock of "I'd Really Like to See You Tonight" (#2, 1976).

When the pair split in 1979, Seals tried a pop solo career as England Dan and then became simply Dan Seals in 1980 with releases for Atlantic (1980) and MCA (1981). In 1983 he moved to Liberty, where he immediately began placing records on the country charts. Working with Kyle Lehning again to craft a country-pop sound, Seals issued hits such as "Everything That Glitters (Is Not Gold)"; "You Still Move Me"; and "Bop," CMA's 1986 Single of the Year.

Between 1985 and 1989 he posted nine consecutive #1 singles (on EMI America, Capitol, and Curb/Capitol), including "Meet Me in Montana," a duet with Marie Osmond that helped the singers become CMA's 1986 Vocal Duo of the Year. After "Love on Arrival" and "Good Times," both #1 hits in 1990, Seals fell out of favor with radio. Additional recordings for Warner Bros. and for independent labels failed to sell, though he continued to tour. He and brother Jim were collaborating on an album when he died from lymphoma. —*John Lomax III*

## Troy Seals

b. Bighill, Kentucky, November 16, 1938

Troy Harold Seals wrote numerous country hits in the 1970s and 1980s. He learned guitar in his teens, and after his family moved to Hamilton, Ohio, he began performing on a country radio show. During the late 1950s Troy Seals & the Earthquakes played rock & roll and backed headliners such as Conway Twitty, who became their mentor.

Seals married singer Jo Ann Campbell in 1962. They released pop singles as Jo Ann & Troy, but Seals soon entered the construction business in Indianapolis. In 1969 the couple moved to Nashville. Seals worked as a session guitarist and built Quadraphonic Studios for owners DAVID BRIGGS and Norbert Putnam, his eventual publishing partners.

Though he recorded for various labels, Seals never sold widely, but his songs did. Scoring his first #1 in 1974 with Twitty's "There's a Honky Tonk Angel (Who'll Take Me Back In)," Seals penned dozens of country hits, including "Lost in the Fifties Tonight (In the Still of the Night)," "Seven Spanish Angels," "When We Make Love," and "Maybe Your Baby's Got the Blues." He was inducted into the NASHVILLE SONGWRITERS HALL OF FAME in 1988.

Seals's extended family includes DAN SEALS, JOHNNY DUNCAN, and Brady Seals (of LITTLE TEXAS). —*Michael Gray*

## Jeannie Seely

b. Titusville, Pennsylvania, July 6, 1940

Strong-voiced singer Jeannie Seely is best known for her Grammy-winning 1966 hit "Don't Touch Me." A popular fixture on the GRAND OLE OPRY, she has remained an audience favorite, in large part due to her vibrant onstage personality.

Born Marilyn Jeanne Seely, she was raised in western Pennsylvania, where her father worked in steel mills and as a farmer. By age eleven she was singing on radio station WMGW in Meadville, Pennsylvania, and by sixteen on television in Erie.

Moving to Los Angeles in 1961, Seely worked in a bank while singing and writing songs. At the urging of songwriter HANK COCHRAN, she relocated to Nashville in 1965 and briefly joined PORTER WAGONER's syndicated television show. She signed with MONUMENT RECORDS, for whom she recorded "Don't Touch Me," written by Cochran (whom she later would marry and divorce). In 1967 Seely joined the Opry, challenging its conservative standards by wearing miniskirts. That year, "I'll Love You (More Than You Need)" became her second Top Ten hit.

Seely became a popular figure on television programs hosted by the WILBURN BROTHERS and by ERNEST TUBB, and in 1969 she formed a road show with JACK GREENE and signed with DECCA RECORDS. A duet with Greene, "Wish I Didn't Have to Miss You," reached #2 on the charts. Her last Top Ten hit, "Can I Sleep in Your Arms?" (written by Cochran), went to #6 in 1973 for MCA RECORDS. Seely's songs have been recorded by NORMA JEAN, RAY PRICE, CONNIE SMITH, DOTTIE WEST, FARON YOUNG, and R&B singer Irma Thomas. Seely has acted in musicals and stage plays, and she has had roles in two films, *Honeysuckle Rose* with WILLIE NELSON and *Changing Hearts* with Faye Dunaway. She also has compiled a book of witty epigrams, *Pieces of a Puzzled Mind* (1989). In 2002 she received IBMA's Recorded Event of the Year award for her duet with RALPH STANLEY on the album *Clinch Mountain Sweethearts*. She released her own BLUEGRASS album, *Life's Highway*, in 2003. —*Steve Eng*

## Seldom Scene

Known for blending innovation and tradition, the Seldom Scene became one of BLUEGRASS music's most highly regarded bands, despite performing part time for most of its early years.

Its mainstay was John Duffey (b. Washington, D.C., March 4, 1934; d. December 10, 1996), who had provided flamboyant mandolin and tenor vocal stylings for another inventive Washington, D.C.–area ensemble, THE COUNTRY GENTLEMEN, before concentrating on musical instrument repair. In mid-1971 Duffey participated in a jam session with banjo player and mathematician Ben Eldridge; DOBRO player and commercial artist Mike Auldridge (both former members of Cliff Waldron & the New Shades of Grass); cartographer and former Country Gentlemen bassist Tom Gray; and John Starling, an army surgeon and talented amateur singer-guitarist.

The quintet decided to form a band for fun. Country Gentlemen leader Charlie Waller quipped that they should be called the Seldom Seen, thus inspiring their name. Starting in November 1971 the new band drew large weekly audiences at Washington-area clubs, became bluegrass festival headliners, and developed a national following onstage and on disc.

The outspoken Duffey shunned overreliance on standard bluegrass songs, so the band drew material from folk music, rock, country, and the work of songwriter friends. Even on bluegrass classics, the Seldom Scene's fresh, energetic, and dramatic arrangements created enthralling, near-theatrical performances.

Despite personnel changes, the act has maintained its high standards. Gifted lead singers have included Starling, Phil Rosenthal, Lou Reid, Moondi Klein, and Dudley Connell (formerly of the JOHNSON MOUNTAIN BOYS). Although Duffey's death from a heart attack in 1996 dealt the lineup a severe blow, the band has continued to perform and record, releasing albums including *Scene It All* (2000) and *Scenechronized* (2007) on SUGAR HILL, the group's label since 1981. At this writing, personnel included Connell (guitar), Eldridge (banjo), Reid (mandolin), Fred Travers (dobro), and Ronnie Simpkins (bass). —*Richard D. Smith*

## Leon "Pappy" Selph

b. Houston, Texas, April 17, 1914; d. January 8, 1999

An accomplished fiddler, Leon Selph is best known for leading the Blue Ridge Playboys, one of the most popular and influential WESTERN SWING bands of the 1930s. Some of Selph's band members, including pianist MOON MULLICAN, singer-guitarist FLOYD TILLMAN, and songwriter TED DAFFAN, also became HONKY-TONK pioneers.

Leonidas Selph began playing fiddle at age five and performed with the Houston Youth Symphony (1929–1930). After he met SHELLY LEE ALLEY, a popular fiddler and accomplished songwriter, Alley taught Selph country fiddle, while Selph instructed Alley in classical execution. Eventually both led successful Houston-based western swing bands.

According to Selph, BOB WILLS first brought him to Fort Worth to play fiddle for Papa Sam Cunningham's Crystal Springs Ramblers in 1935. The gig was short-lived, but, along with observing MILTON BROWN & His Musical Brownies, it inspired Selph to start his own band. Sponsoring his new group on Houston's KXYZ was station owner Jesse Jones, the oil-and-real-estate magnate who would later become head of the Reconstruction Finance Corporation under President Franklin D. Roosevelt. Jones named Selph's band the Blue Ridge Playboys, after one of his properties, the Blue Ridge oil patch. Initially calling himself Smilin' Leon, Selph received the nickname Pappy after his first daughter was born, in 1939.

Like many Texas STRINGBANDS, the Blue Ridge Playboys patterned their rhythm after Milton Brown's band. During the late

1930s the Playboys played "battle dances" with their South Texas rivals, the Bar-X Cowboys and Cliff Bruner & His Texas Wanderers. The Blue Ridge Playboys often shared recording personnel with Shelly Lee Alley & His Alley Cats in sessions for the American Record Corporation and Decca before World War II.

In 1941 Jesse Jones hired Selph and some of his Playboys to campaign with then-congressman Lyndon B. Johnson in his race against governor W. Lee O'Daniel for a U.S. Senate seat. Johnson lost the controversial election.

World War II ended the Blue Ridge Playboys' career as Selph entered military service. After the war he worked for the local fire department, but he resumed his music career, remaining a familiar presence on the Texas music scene into his eighties. —*Cary Ginell*

## SESAC
established in New York, 1930

SESAC, Inc., originally the Society of European Stage Authors and Composers (now the acronym stands on its own), is a performance-rights licensing organization (PRO), with U.S. headquarters in Nashville and offices in New York, Atlanta, Miami, Los Angeles, and London. It was founded in 1930 by German immigrant Paul Heinecke, a music publisher, to represent various foreign publishers not already affiliated with ASCAP, then the nation's only PRO. Unlike ASCAP and BMI, SESAC was and is a for-profit corporation. It originally represented publishers exclusively and shared all collected mechanical, synchronization, and performing-rights revenues with affiliated publishers on a 50–50 percentage basis, after deduction of operating expenses. Since 1970 SESAC has also represented songwriters and now focuses on performance-rights licensing.

SESAC's early catalog consisted primarily of gospel songs (including many Stamps-Baxter, James D. Vaughan, and Albert E. Brumley classics), other religious music, and folk music. During the 1950s, SESAC expanded into pop by supplying radio stations with recordings of SESAC-licensed music performed by big bands and solo jazz artists. By 1960 the firm had some 320 affiliated publishers.

SESAC opened a Nashville office in 1964, and songwriters including Ted Harris ("Paper Mansions"), C. W. McCall ("Convoy"), K. T. Oslin ("80s Ladies"), and Susan Longacre ("Is There Life Out There") gradually put SESAC on the country music map. As of 2010, SESAC-affiliated songwriters active in the genre included Jim Lauderdale ("Twang"), Joe Nichols ("What's a Guy Gotta Do"), Lady Antebellum's Hillary Scott ("I Run to You"), Thom Shepherd and Steve Williams ("Redneck Yacht Club"), and Karen Taylor-Good ("How Can I Help You Say Goodbye").

Since 1970 SESAC has renewed its efforts in the Christian music field, helping to establish the Contemporary Christian radio format. Opening a Los Angeles office in 2000, the company has since expanded into television and film music.

For years a family business (passed down from founder Paul Heinecke to his daughter, Alice Prager), SESAC was purchased in 1992 by the New York–based team of Freddie Gershon, Stephen Swid, and Ira Smith. About 1–3 percent of all licensed U.S. music is now handled by SESAC, which represents about 10,000 writers and publishers and licenses some 200,000 copyrights. SESAC's ownership has always been based in New York, but the organization has been headquartered in Nashville since 1985. Pat Collins became president and COO in 2004. —*Ronnie Pugh*

## Whitey Shafer
b. Whitney, Texas, October 24, 1934

Sanger D. "Whitey" Shafer has written or cowritten some of the most important country songs of the post-1960 era. He hails from the same central Texas region that produced Willie Nelson, and Shafer's honky-tonk roots have served him well in providing material for George Strait ("Does Fort Worth Ever Cross Your Mind," "All My Ex's Live in Texas") and Keith Whitley ("I Never Go Around Mirrors," "I Wonder if You Think of Me"). Shafer is also known for his friendship with Lefty Frizzell, an association that resulted in their cowriting "I Never Go Around Mirrors" and "That's the Way Love Goes" (a #1 hit for Johnny Rodriguez in 1974 and for Merle Haggard in 1984).

Growing up in Whitney, the child of gospel singers, Shafer idolized Frizzell from the moment he heard the young star's first hit in 1950. "I heard that 'If You Got the Money, I Got the Time'—I knew I'd found me a hero," Shafer said. After high school he started singing in local honky-tonks, occasionally sharing the bandstand with young Willie Nelson. Shafer spent three years in the U.S. Army in California and then returned to Texas, where he held a variety of jobs, including raising turkeys. In 1967 he moved to Nashville and fell in with songwriters A. L. "Doodle" Owens and Dallas Frazier. Shafer signed with Blue Crest Music, Frazier's publisher, and had a short-lived record deal with RCA. George Jones cut some of Shafer's songs, and Frizzell recorded his "You, Babe" in 1972, leading to a songwriting partnership that lasted until Frizzell's death three years later. In the meantime, Shafer and Owens cowrote "I Just Started Hatin' Cheatin' Songs Today," the 1974 breakthrough record for Moe Bandy.

Eight years before Strait, Bandy also recorded "Does Fort Worth Ever Cross Your Mind," which Shafer wrote with his then-wife, Darlene. Ironically, "All My Ex's Live in Texas" was cowritten by Shafer's later wife, Lyndia. Both songs were nominated for CMA Song of the Year, for 1985 and 1987, respectively. Shafer was elected to the Nashville Songwriters Hall of Fame in 1989. Since 1990 his songs have been recorded by Kenny Chesney, Lee Ann Womack, and John Michael Montgomery. —*Daniel Cooper*

## Eldon Shamblin
b. Weatherford, Oklahoma, April 24, 1916; d. August 5, 1998

Of Bob Wills's myriad Texas Playboys, none had a greater impact on shaping western swing's sound than guitarist-arranger Eldon Shamblin. If not for the Depression, Shamblin might have been a welder in Weatherford, Oklahoma. Hard times drove him to perform in Oklahoma City beer joints in 1934. A short-lived solo spot on Oklahoma City radio station KFXR preceded Shamblin's joining the Tulsa-based Alabama Boys, who recorded for Decca in 1938 after Shamblin's two-year stint in the group.

On Tulsa's KTUL, Shamblin was a staff guitarist noted for his swing versions of popular classics. Bob Wills tuned in and hired Shamblin on November 8, 1937. By 1939 Shamblin was arranging for the Texas Playboys; Wills also entrusted him with extensive hiring and firing powers. The evolution of the Texas Playboys from a stringband to a horn-heavy big band was largely Shamblin's doing. The duos he worked out with steel guitarist Leon McAuliffe, most notably 1941's "Twin Guitar Special," swung tightly. In 1941 the jazz journal *Metronome* cited Shamblin's lead electric guitar work as "closer than any other white plectrist to getting the solidity and swing and steady flow of ideas of [electric jazz guitar pioneer] Charlie Christian."

After World War II, Shamblin shifted his emphasis from lead to rhythm in a scaled-down Playboys. Ever the pragmatist, he credited his fluid bass lines to the need to "cover for a bad bass man." (In 1974 *Rolling Stone* said he played "the world's best rhythm guitar.") Shamblin left the Playboys in the mid-1950s and, following stints in bands of McAuliffe and fiddler-singer HOYLE NIX, settled in Tulsa to tune pianos. MERLE HAGGARD recalled Shamblin to active duty, first for Haggard's Wills tribute album *A Tribute to the Best Damn Fiddle Player in the World* (recorded 1970) and then as a member of Haggard's road band, the Strangers. From the mid-1970s Shamblin was also a key figure in various Playboys reunion bands (principally the Original Texas Playboys, 1975–86) and played on ASLEEP AT THE WHEEL's 1994 *Tribute to the Music of Bob Wills & the Texas Playboys*. "Eldon," said Wheel boss Ray Benson, "is like Elvis to us." Failing health forced Shamblin to retire in 1996. —*Mark Humphrey*

## Tom Shapiro
b. Kansas City, Missouri, May 18, 1950

Tom Shapiro has written or cowritten more than twenty *Billboard* #1 country hits and dozens of Top Ten hits for artists including NEAL McCOY, TIM McGRAW, MONTGOMERY GENTRY, TANYA TUCKER, KEITH URBAN, and TRISHA YEARWOOD.

Shapiro began writing songs while attending college in France. After graduation, he taught briefly at the prestigious Berklee College of Music and founded his own music school before moving to Los Angeles to pursue songwriting. By the mid-1970s, Shapiro gained pop cuts by L.T.D., Smokey Robinson, and Sister Sledge. After meeting Nashville songwriter and producer Michael Garvin, Shapiro penned several country songs, one of which landed on GEORGE STRAIT's 1981 debut album, *Strait Country*.

Shapiro moved to Nashville on the momentum of "Never Give Up on a Good Thing," an international hit for George Benson in 1982. Shapiro signed with TREE PUBLISHING and began his long run of top country hits, including "Ain't Nothing About You" (BROOKS & DUNN), "I Miss My Friend" (DARRYL WORLEY), and "No Place That Far" (SARA EVANS), to name only a few.

As of 2011, Shapiro had been named BMI's Country Songwriter of the Year four times. He was inducted into the NASHVILLE SONGWRITERS HALL OF FAME in 2008. —*Jeremy Rush*

## Billy Joe Shaver
b. Corsicana, Texas, August 16, 1939

Most country listeners are familiar with Billy Joe Shaver's songs through versions by other performers. Singers ranging from JOHN ANDERSON to longtime Shaver pal WILLIE NELSON have recorded his compositions, as have the Allman Brothers, BOBBY BARE, JOHNNY CASH, BOB DYLAN, TOM T. HALL, WAYLON JENNINGS, KRIS KRISTOFFERSON, JERRY LEE LEWIS, PATTY LOVELESS, ELVIS PRESLEY, JOHNNY RODRIGUEZ, MARTY STUART, and many more. Most of Shaver's songs marry solid country rhythms with lyrics that voice plainspoken truths and use images that seem uniquely his; for example, "I'm Just an Old Chunk of Coal (But I'm Gonna Be a Diamond Someday)" is the title of a song Anderson turned into a sizable hit in 1981.

*Billy Joe Shaver*

In the late 1960s and early 1970s, Shaver was part of that era's great explosion of new Nashville songwriting, during which writers such as Kris Kristofferson and GUY CLARK came to the fore. But what attracted other composers to Shaver's material was its distinctive grounding—direct yet poetic, simultaneously self-effacing and boastful.

Shaver was raised in Corsicana, Texas, by his grandmother and later, in Waco, by his mother. A stint in the U.S. Navy led to a series of go-nowhere jobs, including one at a sawmill that cost him most of the index and middle fingers on his right hand. His late-1960s arrival in Nashville led to friendships and alliances with many stars of the day. Shaver had a part in writing all but one number on Waylon Jennings's landmark album *Honky Tonk Heroes* (1973), including "Black Rose," which contains the famous Shaver couplet "The devil made me do it the first time/The second time I done it on my own."

Shaver's recorded debut, *Old Five and Dimers Like Me*, appeared on MONUMENT later the same year. He enjoyed two minor hits in the 1970s ("Georgia on a Fast Train" in 1973 and "You Asked Me To" in 1978) and made two albums for Capricorn: the brilliant *When I Get My Wings* (1976) and *Gypsy Boy* (1977), which some considered weighed down by an all-star cast and misguided production decisions. But in part because his songwriting voice is usually stronger than his singing voice, Shaver had little commercial success as a recording artist at that time. His personal and professional life went into a tailspin until Anderson's "I'm Just an Old Chunk of Coal" reinvigorated his career.

Shaver returned to recording with three consistent albums for COLUMBIA in the 1980s, during which time his son, guitarist Eddy Shaver (1962–2000), gradually played a more assertive role in developing lead lines and rhythms as strong as his father's images and aphorisms. Their collaboration reached a peak with 1993's *Tramp on Your Street* (Praxis/Zoo), a spirited collection that astonished even longtime fans of the wily songwriter with its rock & roll punch and musical diversity. Albums for the Praxis/Zoo and Justice labels followed in 1995–96. Since 1998, albums for New West, Compadre, SUGAR HILL, and New World Entertainment have explored many aspects of Billy Joe Shaver's musical sensibilities. For the critically acclaimed 2007 gospel album *Everybody's Brother*—produced by John Carter Cash—he recorded duets with John Anderson, Johnny Cash, Kris Kristofferson, Bill Miller, Marty Stuart, and TANYA TUCKER.

In 1997 Shaver appeared with actor Robert Duvall in the film *The Apostle*. He was elected to the NASHVILLE SONGWRITERS HALL OF FAME in 2004. —*Jimmy Guterman*

## Dorothy Shay
b. Jacksonville, Florida, April 11, 1921; d. October 22, 1978

Known as the Park Avenue Hillbilly, Dorothy Shay developed a comedic act by singing humorous hick tunes while dressed in glamorous designer gowns.

Born Dorothy Nell Sims, she became a New York supper club attraction during World War II. Shay scored a smash hit on COLUMBIA in 1947 with "Feudin' and Fightin'" and followed it with dozens of similar hokum ditties. By 1951 she was earning $5,000 a night in clubs.

Shay relocated to Los Angeles and appeared in *Comin' Round the Mountain* (1951) with Abbott & Costello. She was a particular favorite of President Dwight D. Eisenhower's and performed at his 1953 inaugural ball. Shay resurfaced in the 1970s with a recurring role as a mountain spinster on the hit TV series *The Waltons*. —*Robert K. Oermann*

## Harold Shedd
b. Bremen, Alabama, November 8, 1931

Harold Shedd's risk taking and his search for innovative sounds made him one of the country music's top executives of the 1980s and early 1990s. Much of his acclaim revolved around his role as producer for the supergroup ALABAMA.

At the time he began this highly productive association, Shedd was better known for producing jingles for Shoney's, Bayer, and McDonald's, but he sensed a unique talent when he brought the harmony-laden, COUNTRY-ROCK band into his Music Mill Recording Studio in Nashville in 1979. Alabama emerged as a megaforce, melding southern-rock roots with a love of solid country.

One of twelve children born to a rural Alabama preacher-farmer and his wife, Shedd worked at numerous radio stations—he eventually owned WWCC in his hometown—gaining experienced that helped him find a long string of upbeat songs for his best-known act. "[W]e were not looking for any beer-drinking, cheating kinds of songs," he explained. "We were looking for positive things with positive messages."

Among his production touches, Shedd electronically altered the vocals on 1983's "The Closer You Get," came up with four different versions of 1984's "Roll On (Eighteen Wheeler)," and developed a drum sound on "She And I" (1986) that utilized reverse echo effects. In the eight years that Shedd produced the group, Alabama notched two dozen Top Ten hits, including twenty-one #1 singles.

But Alabama wasn't Shedd's only successful venture. In 1987 he introduced the world to forty-six-year-old K. T. OSLIN, and as the

head of MERCURY RECORDS' Nashville office from 1988 to 1994 he oversaw the careers of KATHY MATTEA, BILLY RAY CYRUS, SHANIA TWAIN, and TOBY KEITH.

Not all of Shedd's moves were as fruitful, however. He ran Mercury's sister label Polydor when it was opened in 1994, but two years later, after A&M took over Polydor, Shedd left just before the operation closed down, having failed to break any major new acts. With partners, Shedd later launched VFR Records, but the undercapitalized independent folded in 2002. —*Tom Roland*

## Blake Shelton
b. Ada, Oklahoma, June 18, 1976

In retrospect, Blake Tollison Shelton's confident vocals, rugged good looks, and down-to-earth charm made his rise to country stardom seem virtually inevitable. Under the sway of JOHN ANDERSON, CLINT BLACK, and other neo-traditionalists, Shelton wrote his first song at fifteen, while starting his performing career in Oklahoma clubs.

Two weeks after completing high school, in 1994, Shelton moved to Nashville, determined to secure a record deal. He struggled for several years, working day jobs and honing his songwriting skills, but his persistence paid off when WARNER BROS. released his self-titled debut album in 2001. Produced by veteran songwriter BOBBY BRADDOCK, *Blake Shelton* included his hit, "Ol' Red," and his first #1 single, "Austin."

On his next two albums, *The Dreamer* (2003) and *Blake Shelton's Barn & Grill* (2004), Shelton walked the line between his HONKY-TONK roots—displayed on his cover of Mary Gauthier's "I Drink"—and the contemporary Nashville songcraft of "The Baby" and "Some Beach" (both #1 hits). Additional successful albums and chart-topping singles followed ["Home" (2008), "She Wouldn't Be Gone" (2009), and "Hillbilly Bone" (2010)] as Shelton continued to forge his musical identity and establish his commercial presence. —*Mick Buck*

*Blake Shelton*

## Ricky Van Shelton
b. Grit, Virginia, January 12, 1952

During the late 1980s and early 1990s, Ricky Van Shelton parlayed his good looks and mellifluous voice into country music success. Born into a large family, Shelton was singing gospel tunes in public by age three. After a 1960s flirtation with British rock, a teenage Shelton converted to country when his older brother Ronnie offered him use of his car if Ricky would join him playing country and BLUEGRASS. For some fifteen years he worked late-night gigs, toiling by day as a pipe fitter and construction worker.

Shelton and his future wife, Bettye, moved to Nashville in late 1984. *Tennessean* newspaper columnist Jerry Thompson took on Shelton's management and landed him a COLUMBIA RECORDS deal that produced a debut single in 1986. The singer's on-the-money vocals during a first studio outing startled the experienced ears of producer STEVE BUCKINGHAM and MUSIC ROW session pros. Shelton's first album, 1987's *Wild-Eyed Dream*, combined hard country and ROCKABILLY stylings to produce hits: the rocking "Wild-Eyed Dream" and "Crime of Passion" and the aching country #1's "Somebody Lied," "Life Turned Her That Way," and "Don't We All Have the Right." A follow-up, 1988's *Loving Proof*, yielded the chart-topping "I'll Leave This World Loving You," "From a Jack to a King," and "Living Proof." At thirty-six, Shelton was now a full-fledged country star, touring constantly, stacking up five platinum and three gold albums, and winning major awards, including CMA's Horizon Award in 1988 and its male vocalist honor for 1989.

In 1990 "Statue of a Fool," "I've Cried My Last Tear for You," "I Meant Every Word He Said," and "Life's Little Ups and Downs," all Top Five singles from *RVS III*, continued his string of hits. *Backroads* (1992) scored with a rollicking title track, the DOLLY PARTON duet "Rockin' Years," and the sentimental "Keep It Between the Lines." But, as detailed in Bettye Shelton's 1995 book *She Stays* (cowritten with Andy Landis and Carol Gift Page), by 1991 the couple had severe marital problems aggravated by his infidelities and drinking. He had a soul-wrenching religious conversion in early 1992. That year also saw the renewal of Shelton's marriage; the start of a successful series of children's books; and a gospel release, *Don't Overlook Salvation*.

Shelton may have alienated some in the country music industry after a disagreement with director IRVING WAUGH over Shelton's role on the 1993 *CMA Awards Show* and some frank remarks about country radio consultants. Declining sales contributed further to his split with Columbia in 1996. In 1997 he released *Making Plans* on RVS, his own Walmart-distributed label. Later he signed with Audium; the label released *Fried Green Tomatoes* in 2000, but in 2006 he announced his decision to stop touring. —*Thomas Goldsmith*

## The Shelton Brothers
Bob Attlesey (Shelton) b. Reilly Springs, Texas, July 4, 1909; d. November 1986
Joe Attlesey (Shelton) b. Reilly Springs, Texas, January 27, 1911; d. December 26, 1980

The Shelton Brothers embodied fascinating changes in southwestern hillbilly music during the 1930s, when they transformed themselves from a traditional southeastern-styled vocal duo into a WESTERN SWING–influenced HONKY-TONK act. In addition to singing, Bob handled comedy, bass, jug, and ukulele, while Joe also sang and played mandolin and guitar.

Bob and Joe Attlesey—they later took their mother's maiden name for commercial purposes—formed the Lone Star Cowboys in Tyler, Texas, and performed over KGKB, in 1929, with guitarist LEON CHAPPELEAR. From the early 1930s the group worked on KWKH–Shreveport; in 1933 they recorded the classics "Just Because" and "Deep Elm Blues" for RCA VICTOR. They backed JIMMIE DAVIS in this same group of sessions.

Splitting from Chappelear, the brothers followed Davis to DECCA in 1935. By then they had relocated to New Orleans, where they broadcast on WWL and teamed with fiddler CURLY FOX. Soon they returned to Shreveport and, into the 1940s, they divided their time between KWKH and Dallas–Fort Worth stations WFAA and WBAP. Their group, the Sunshine Boys, became increasingly influenced by western swing as their Decca tenure continued through 1941; traditional tunes such as "Stay in the Wagon Yard" gave way to swing-flavored JUKEBOX fare such as "Parking Meter Blues." At various points the Sunshine Boys included such swing stalwarts as steel guitarist BOB DUNN and pianist MOON MULLICAN. From 1938, by which time younger brother Merle had joined the group on guitar, Joe Shelton amplified his mandolin and played in a jazzy style reminiscent of pioneering electric mandolinist Leo Raley (who appeared on the band's 1939 sessions, as did fiddler CLIFF BRUNER).

The Sheltons concentrated on show dates rather than dances, though they periodically maintained a top-notch, dance-oriented swing unit through the late 1940s and made sides for KING RECORDS before disbanding. From the mid-1940s, the brothers began to work separately. For Jimmie Davis, Joe worked bandleader stints that included Davis's successful 1943 gubernatorial campaign. Joe essentially retired from music after 1950, but Bob continued to perform as a comedian—always his stock-in-trade—through the 1970s. His work included appearances on the *Big D Jamboree* and the *Louisiana Hayride*. —*Kevin Coffey*

## Shenandoah
Ralph Ezell b. Union, Mississippi, June 26, 1953; d. November 30, 2007
Mike McGuire b. Haleyville, Alabama, December 28, 1958
Marty Raybon b. Greenville, Alabama, December 8, 1959
Jim Seales b. Hamilton, Alabama, March 20, 1954
Stan Thorn b. Kenosha, Wisconsin, March 16, 1959

One of several ALABAMA-inspired contemporary country bands to emerge in the late 1980s and early 1990s, Shenandoah initially formed in Muscle Shoals, Alabama, as the MGM Band. Drummer Mike McGuire, guitarist Jim Seales, and keyboardist Stan Thorn organized the group, and when their lead singer departed, they brought in Marty Raybon. Bass player Ralph Ezell was imported from a rival act.

McGuire invited record producers Rick Hall and Robert Byrne to hear the ensemble, and a record deal with COLUMBIA ensued, leading to the name Shenandoah. Between 1988 and 1990 the group established a presence with dense harmonies and a knack for strong melodies on such hit singles as "Mama Knows," "The Church on Cumberland Road," "Two Dozen Roses," "Next to You, Next to Me," and "Ghost in This House." But three other bands claimed rights to their name, and lawsuits forced them into bankruptcy.

Eventually Shenandoah paid off the other acts and gained permanent rights to the name. Subsequently the band notched such hits as "Rock My Baby"; "I Want to Be Loved Like That"; and a duet with ALISON KRAUSS, "Somewhere in the Vicinity of the Heart," which won CMA's Vocal Event of the Year award in 1995.

Thorn left to pursue jazz interests in 1995, Ezell departed in 1996, and the group disbanded in 1997. In 2000 McGuire and Seales reunited under the Shenandoah name with new members, and the act continues to tour. Raybon formed the Raybon Brothers with brother Tim, then went on to record BLUEGRASS albums as a solo act. —*Tom Roland*

## Jean Shepard
b. Pauls Valley, Oklahoma, November 21, 1933

During the 1950s few women managed to break through industry barriers to enjoy full-blown country careers. Even fewer did so singing forthright material in a hard-core HONKY-TONK style. But one who did was Jean Shepard, whose lively records set the stage for artists such as LORETTA LYNN and TAMMY WYNETTE in the following decade. Shepard continued to score Top Ten hits into the 1970s, and as of 2011 she remained a popular star of the GRAND OLE OPRY.

Born Ollie Imogene Shepard, she grew up in rural Oklahoma listening to both Nashville's Grand Ole Opry and BOB WILLS's radio broadcasts over KVOO–Tulsa. Just before the end of World War II her family moved to California, settling in Visalia. While in high school, Shepard and some friends formed the Melody Ranch Girls, with whom she sang and played upright bass. In 1952, acting on HANK THOMPSON's recommendation, KEN NELSON of CAPITOL RECORDS signed Shepard to the label.

Shepard's debut single, on which she was cobilled with steel guitar legend SPEEDY WEST, fared poorly. But her second single, recorded May 19, 1953, was a #1 smash. That record was "A Dear John Letter," to which FERLIN HUSKY contributed the recitation part. The duet crossed over to the pop Top Five and established both singers' careers. From that point forward, Shepard recorded one vibrant honky-tonk single after another, many featuring BILL WOODS's band out of BAKERSFIELD, which included guitarist BUCK OWENS.

In January 1955 Shepard was part of the cast that inaugurated the *Ozark Jubilee* telecast. But in November that year, coming off successive Top Five hits with "A Satisfied Mind" and "Beautiful Lies," she joined the Grand Ole Opry. The following month she recorded *Songs of a Love Affair*, which is said to have been the first concept album ever recorded by a female country singer.

During the late 1950s Shepard became involved romantically with fellow Opry star HAWKSHAW HAWKINS. On November 26, 1960, the two were married onstage in Wichita, Kansas. Tragically, Hawkins died in the same 1963 plane crash that killed singers PATSY CLINE and COWBOY COPAS. Devastated, Shepard gave up singing for several months. But by the close of the year she had returned to the Opry, and in early 1964 she scored a major comeback hit with "Second Fiddle (to an Old Guitar)." (Since 1968 Shepard has been married to BLUEGRASS musician Benny Birchfield, who was ROY ORBISON's road manager at the time of Orbison's death.)

Through the remainder of the 1960s Shepard enjoyed moderate success, both solo and in duets with RAY PILLOW. Many of her records continued to feature her spunky intolerance of male foibles. In 1973 she switched labels from Capitol to United Artists. She landed an immediate Top Five hit with BILL ANDERSON's "Slippin' Away," but it proved to be her last major chart-maker. Like many singers of her generation, she found radio airplay increasingly hard to come by. Her tenure with United Artists ended in 1977, and since then her infrequent recordings have been issued on a series of small, independent labels.

Shepard was elected to THE COUNTRY MUSIC HALL OF FAME in 2011. —*Daniel Cooper*

## T. G. Sheppard
b. Humbolt, Tennessee, July 20, 1944

T. G. Sheppard had a long run of chart success by finding a niche somewhere between 1970s-style HONKY-TONK and easy-listening pop crossover, scoring fourteen #1 hits between 1974 and 1986.

Born William Neal Browder, he began singing professionally in Memphis, recording as "Brian Stacy." He moved into record promotion, but when that gambit failed he worked as a background singer and relaunched himself as T. G. Sheppard in 1974 with a #1 hit, "Devil in the Bottle." During the period 1974–91 he recorded for Melodyland, Hitsville, WARNER BROS., ELEKTRA, COLUMBIA, and CURB/CAPITOL.

Sheppard's recorded repertoire embraced the wide-ranging eclecticism of contemporary country music in his era. In between honky-tonk–themed songs such as "Motels and Memories" and "Party Time," he covered pop hits from Neil Diamond, Harry Nilsson, the Turtles, and Elvin Bishop and turned in duets with Judy Collins and Clint Eastwood. Though his best-known record is probably SONNY THROCKMORTON's beautiful "Last Cheater's Waltz" (#1, 1979), Sheppard also hit #1 in 1982 with Gary Chapman's "Finally," a song that could be taken as a paean of gratitude either to a woman or to the Messiah.

Sheppard's sales and radio airplay with pop-flavored records survived into the mid-1980s, even as the URBAN COWBOY boom collapsed. His last chart hit came in 1988–89, just as a new generation of country stars was breaking through. Nevertheless, the continued success of artists who span country and pop proves the viability of Sheppard's musical approach. As of 2011 Sheppard continued to tour and record. —*Bob Millard*

## Billy Sherrill
b. Phil Campbell, Alabama, November 5, 1936

Perhaps the most influential producer in country music during the 1970s, Nashville-based Billy Norris Sherrill played a far-reaching role in shaping the genre's sound and direction. A partial listing of the artists he produced at EPIC and COLUMBIA RECORDS between the late 1960s and early 1990s conveys his commercial and aesthetic

*Jean Shepard*

*Billy Sherrill*

impact: GEORGE JONES, TAMMY WYNETTE, CHARLIE RICH, TANYA TUCKER, DAVID HOUSTON, BARBARA MANDRELL, JANIE FRICKE, JOHNNY PAYCHECK, JOHNNY RODRIGUEZ, and SHELBY LYNNE.

The son of an evangelist whom he often backed on piano at tent revivals, Sherrill apprenticed in Alabama R&B and rock bands before breaking into country music as a songwriter. One of his earliest Nashville assignments was as a producer-engineer for SUN RECORDS founder SAM PHILLIPS in a studio Phillips then operated in MUSIC CITY. Early on, Sherrill made several records of his own, sometimes playing all the instruments himself. In 1967 he released an album called *Classic Country*, credited to the Billy Sherrill Quintet.

Much of Sherrill's later influence on the country scene derived from his experience as an iconoclast who freely drew from pop, R&B, and rock influences in his country production style. As a youth in Alabama, he had favored R&B and disdained country music. When he belatedly came to the field, he was determined to do things his way.

When Epic hired Sherrill in 1963 he was initially relegated to handling unknowns and veterans no one else was interested in producing—often noncountry artists, such as the R&B act the Staple Singers and the rock band Barry & the Remains. Sherrill was enamored of rock producer Phil Spector's "Wall of Sound" approach and imbued many of his own records with a lush, full, multitracked sound. Frequently the result was unprecedented sales (sometimes in the form of country-to-pop crossover success), along with scorn from purist fans and certain critics.

Sherrill's detractors often grumbled that his lavish production style violated country music's basic tenets of rusticity. Yet Sherrill produced some of the most credible and traditionally faithful HONKY-TONK music recorded in Nashville in the 1970s and early 1980s, such as George Jones's "A Picture of Me (Without You)," "Bartender's Blues," and "He Stopped Loving Her Today."

Sherrill did not content himself with merely producing artists. For some, such as Tammy Wynette, he created entire musical personas and wrote or cowrote songs that enlarged on these images, such as "Stand By Your Man," "Your Good Girl's Gonna Go Bad," and "I Don't Wanna Play House."

In the case of Charlie Rich, Sherrill took a journeyman white R&B singer and reinvented him as a 1970s-style country-pop crooner. This strategy yielded massive crossover hits such as "Behind Closed Doors," "The Most Beautiful Girl in the World" (which Sherrill cowrote), and "A Very Special Love Song" (also a co-composition). "Almost Persuaded," another Sherrill classic, won Sherrill and cowriter Glenn Sutton a 1966 Grammy for Best Country & Western Song and helped push singer David Houston to country's front ranks.

By the mid-1970s Sherrill was vice president of A&R at Columbia/Epic Records (he would rise to the position of vice president and executive producer in 1980), and he began to get some heat for his reluctance to embrace the minimalism of the burgeoning OUTLAW movement. He is said to have resisted releasing WILLIE NELSON's *Red Headed Stranger*, an austere album completely devoid of the studio refinements and overdubs Sherrill loved but one that eventually sold more than 1 million copies and won numerous awards. Nevertheless, Sherrill ventured far enough beyond country's commercial mainstream to produce albums with such artists as RAY CHARLES and British rocker Elvis Costello.

Sherrill's sarcasm, reclusiveness, and egotism kept him from winning any popularity contests along MUSIC ROW. But the fiercely independent producer preferred to let his work speak for itself, and when it came to coaxing great music out of temperamental artists such as George Jones, DAVID ALLAN COE, and Johnny Paycheck, he succeeded brilliantly where others failed. Sherrill left Epic and Columbia Records in 1985 but continued for a time as an independent producer, working with Jones, among others, and occasionally developing new artists, such as Shelby Lynne. By the early 1990s Sherrill had more or less retired from the music business.

Sherrill was elected to THE COUNTRY MUSIC HALL OF FAME in 2010. —*Bob Allen*

## Steve Sholes

b. Washington, D.C., February 12, 1911; d. April 22, 1968

As a high-level recording executive, Stephen Henry Sholes helped to shepherd country music's commercial growth and publicize its cultural importance in the years following World War II. After his family moved near RCA VICTOR's Camden, New Jersey, plant, where his father worked, Sholes began his RCA career in 1929 as a messenger boy and worked part time for the firm while attending Rutgers University. In 1935 he joined RCA's radio department, but his experience playing saxophone and clarinet in regional dance bands soon landed him a sales clerk's position in the record department. Under senior executives ELI OBERSTEIN and, after 1939, FRANK WALKER, he assisted in producing pop, country, and ethnic acts, mostly in New York, Chicago, and Atlanta. During the war Sholes worked in the U.S. Army's V-disc operation, which made recordings for radio broadcast and for personal listening by soldiers.

In 1945 Sholes became head of both country and R&B recording for RCA, based out of New York. Over the next two decades he would sign or develop such country artists as CHET ATKINS, EDDY ARNOLD, THE BROWNS, HANK LOCKLIN, HOMER & JETHRO, HANK SNOW, JIM REEVES, and PEE WEE KING. At various points in his RCA career the producer also recorded jazz artists such as Jelly Roll Morton, Earl Hines, and Dizzy Gillespie. Along with producers for

*Steve Sholes*

other labels, Sholes strengthened Nashville as a music center by recording country talent there. After using a series of local studios (beginning in 1949), in 1957 he convinced RCA to sign a long-term lease on a studio on Seventeenth Avenue South, just two years after OWEN BRADLEY had opened Nashville's first MUSIC ROW studio a block away. Sholes's influence in this decision was greatly enhanced by his signing of ELVIS PRESLEY in 1955, a seminal event in the international rock & roll revolution. As Presley's sales skyrocketed and other Sholes-produced acts gained hits, the rising executive became RCA's pop singles manager in 1957, pop singles and albums manager in 1958, and West Coast manager in 1961. In this last role, Sholes moved to Los Angeles and supervised recording, administration, sales, and marketing. Sholes had installed Chet Atkins (his production assistant since 1952) to run the label's Nashville operation in 1957 but continued to supervise Presley's recordings there and in other cities. In 1963 Sholes became RCA RECORDS' vice president for pop A&R and returned to New York.

During the 1960s Sholes served on the boards of CMA and the COUNTRY MUSIC HALL OF FAME AND MUSEUM. He died only a year after the April 1967 opening of the museum, which he and fellow CMA leaders had worked hard to establish.

Sholes was elected to THE COUNTRY MUSIC HALL OF FAME in 1967. —*John W. Rumble*

## Jack Shook
b. Decatur, Illinois, September 11, 1910; d. September 23, 1986

A versatile, self-taught guitarist and singer who bridged boundaries between country and pop, Jack Shook played in clubs and on radio stations in the Midwest, Southeast, and Southwest before landing at WSM in 1933. First working solo as a pop act, he soon joined Napoleon "Nap" Bastien and Dee Simmons in a pop trio

that became a mainstay of WSM's programming into the late 1940s. (There were brief interruptions while Shook backed pop star Kate Smith on New York–originated CBS network shows in 1934 and served in the U. S. Marine Corps from 1943 to 1945.)

From 1935 until decade's end, Shook and his partners also played on the GRAND OLE OPRY as the Missouri Mountaineers, with Mack McGarr on mandolin and fiddle and Elbert McEwen succeeding Bobby Castlen on accordion. Specializing in harmony vocals and smooth western ballads, this aggregation helped add professionalism and country-pop sounds to an Opry roster that still featured many semiprofessional hoedown bands.

Beginning in 1939, Shook became part of the initial cadre of studio professionals who helped to create Nashville's recording industry, first by recording radio shows for syndication and then by playing on commercially released discs. In this capacity his pop sensibilities and distinctive rhythm playing—enhanced by a left-handed style in which he struck his guitar strings from treble to bass—helped to give a commercial edge to recordings by HANK WILLIAMS ("Lost Highway") and numerous others. As a vocalist, Shook sang on "Blues Stay Away from Me," a 1950 hit for the OWEN BRADLEY Quintet, and on eight sides of his own, made for DECCA's Coral label that same year.

Shook continued to work recording sessions into the early 1960s, but until his retirement, in 1982, he mostly played in WSM staff bands for programs such as *The Waking Crew* and *The Noon Show*. —*Charles Wolfe* and *John W. Rumble*

## Show Dog Records (*see* Toby Keith)

## Arnold Shultz
b. Ohio County, Kentucky, 1886; d. 1931

Influential black guitarist Arnold Shultz is widely regarded as a primary source of the thumb-style of guitar playing, also known as Travis picking. The son of a former slave, he came from a musical family and evidently traveled widely as a young man, working on riverboats that traveled the Green River, the Ohio, and the Mississippi. Shultz not only played with musicians among West-Central Kentucky's substantial African American population, but also with white musicians, such as banjoist Clarence Wilson, bandleader Forrest "Boots" Faught, and Pendleton Vandiver, BLUEGRASS pioneer BILL MONROE's famous "Uncle Pen." Monroe himself worked with Shultz as a young man, playing guitar behind Shultz's fiddle at local house parties. Between work in the area's coal mines, Shultz also performed solo or with others at storefronts, schoolhouses, taverns, and railroad crossings in the Green River area embracing Ohio, Muhlenberg, Butler, and McClean counties. A short, slightly pudgy man who liked to wear a big black hat, he could play guitar in a variety of styles and sometimes fretted the instrument with a knife or bottleneck in typical blues fashion.

Shultz is best known, however, for his seminal role in the evolution of thumb-style guitar. Scholar William Lightfoot has characterized Shultz's approach as "alternated bass under a syncopated melody, supported by rich, rhythmic chords and applied to a wide range of music." Central to Shultz's influence as a thumb-picker was white guitarist Kennedy Jones, who learned chords and picking techniques from the black musician. Jones, in turn, transmitted the thumb-style to white guitarist MOSE RAGER, who passed it along to other white guitarists, including Ike Everly (father of THE EVERLY BROTHERS) and MERLE TRAVIS.

Shultz himself evidently never recorded, but Travis's records and radio shows ultimately extended Shultz's influence to Chet Atkins, Jerry Reed, Lenny Breau, and a host of other thumb-style pickers who have made this technique an essential part of country music. Although official reports cite Shultz's cause of death as an organic "mitral lesion" of the heart, some still believe that jealous white musicians poisoned him with bad whiskey. —*John W. Rumble*

## Shel Silverstein

b. Chicago, Illinois, September 25, 1930; d. May 10, 1999

First known as a *Playboy* cartoonist and later as illustrator and author of witty children's books, Sheldon Allan Silverstein also became a celebrated country songwriter.

Musically, Silverstein was influenced by the folk music scenes centered around Chicago's Gate of Horn club and New York City's Bitter End. His 1961 album *Inside Folk Songs* included "The Unicorn" and "25 Minutes to Go," which became folk standards. Drawn to Nashville's songwriting circles, he penned Johnny Cash's mega-hit "A Boy Named Sue," Loretta Lynn's "One's on the Way," and "Queen of the Silver Dollar," Dave & Sugar's first chart record.

A chance meeting with the bar band Dr. Hook & the Medicine Show resulted in Silverstein's writing their breakthrough pop hits: "Sylvia's Mother" and "The Cover of Rolling Stone" (which led to the group's appearance on the cover of that magazine and also led to a spinoff country version by Buck Owens as "On the Cover of the Music City News").

Silverstein continued to write for other country artists, especially frequent cowriter Bobby Bare, and their collaboration on Bare's 1975 double album *Lullabies, Legends and Lies* set a benchmark in modern country songwriting. Silverstein's own albums include *Freakin' at the Freakers' Ball* in 1972 and *Drain My Brain* in 1980. His books include *A Light in the Attic* and *Where the Sidewalk Ends.* —*Chet Flippo*

*Shel Silverstein*

## Si Siman

b. Springfield, Missouri, January 17, 1921; d. December 16, 1994

Ely Earl Siman Jr. was the driving force in the emergence of Springfield, Missouri, as a country music center in the 1950s.

After service in the U.S. Navy during World War II, Siman began producing radio shows at KWTO–Springfield and serving as MC on road shows featuring KWTO talent. With partners Ralph Foster, Lester E. Cox, and John Mahaffey, he formed RadiOzark Enterprises to produce and distribute syndicated radio programs. In 1954 Siman recruited Grand Ole Opry star Red Foley to host a new barn dance from Springfield, the *Ozark Jubilee*, which aired on the ABC radio network and, from 1955 to 1960, on ABC-TV. Siman was instrumental in securing the show's network television slot. Crossroads Television Productions, organized by Siman and his partners, not only produced the *Jubilee* (sometimes airing as *Jubilee USA* and *Country Music Jubilee*) but also produced *The Eddy Arnold Show* for ABC-TV in 1956 and *Five Star Jubilee* for NBC-TV in 1961. The latter, featuring pop star Snooky Lanson and country singers Jimmy Wakely, Rex Allen, Tex Ritter, and Carl Smith, was one of the first country programs to be telecast in color.

All the while Siman was helping to land recording contracts for Chet Atkins, Porter Wagoner, and Brenda Lee; assisting in running the Top Talent booking operation he formed with his associates; and building the catalog of Earl Barton Music, a music-publishing firm he founded with Mahaffey in 1952. During the 1960s Siman managed Red Foley but increasingly turned his attention to publishing, eventually establishing several companion music firms with writers such as Jay Stevens ("Rocky") and Wayne Carson ("The Letter"). In 1987, anticipating retirement, Siman sold these catalogs. His son, Scott Siman, has been an entertainment lawyer, a Sony Music Nashville senior vice president, and an artist manager (Tim McGraw). —*John W. Rumble*

## Red Simpson

b. Higley, Arizona, March 6, 1934

Although he recorded truck driving songs in the 1960s and 1970s for Capitol Records, including the Bob Stanton–penned "I'm a Truck" (#4, 1971–72), Joe Cecil Simpson is best known as a successful songwriter. Buck Owens recorded some thirty-five Simpson songs, including "Gonna Have Love," "Sam's Place," and "The Kansas City Song" (all cowritten with Owens). Artists such as Merle Haggard, Roy Clark, Ferlin Husky, Connie Smith, and Del Reeves recorded dozens more.

Simpson and his family moved to the Bakersfield, California, area in 1937, settling in a small community known as Little Okie. A natural comedian and a versatile musician who mostly played guitar and piano, Simpson first supported himself performing in Bakersfield clubs. He eventually worked local television shows such as *Cousin Herb Henson's Trading Post* and toured with Buck Owens and Merle Haggard. Simpson signed with Capitol Records in 1965, and in December recorded the album *Roll, Truck, Roll.* In 1966 the title cut, written by Tommy Collins, became Simpson's first Top Forty country chart-maker. Mostly, however, Simpson was known around Bakersfield as "Suitcase" Simpson because he could always be found at clubs, radio stations, or TV stations, pitching his suitcase full of songs.

Junior Brown's 1993 cover of Simpson's "Highway Patrol" led to renewed interest in Simpson's music. In 1996 Brown and Simpson collaborated on the title track of Brown's album *Semi Crazy* and on a remake of "Nitro Express" for *Rig Rock Deluxe*, a multiartist compilation of truck-driving songs. —*Dale Vinicur*

## Shelby Singleton

b. Waskom, Texas, December 16, 1931; d. October 7, 2009

Rockabilly fans know Shelby Singleton as the man who purchased Sun Records of Memphis in July 1969. But long before that, Singleton established himself as a highly successful A&R man. As a Mercury Records executive in the early 1960s, he advanced the careers of such artists as George Jones, Roger Miller, Jerry Lee Lewis, and Faron Young. Later, as head of his own independent label conglomerate, he produced Jeannie C. Riley's "Harper Valley P.T.A." Active until his death on the fringes of the country music industry, Singleton was one of Music City's most colorful characters.

Born near the Texas–Louisiana border, Singleton was involved with the *Louisiana Hayride* in the 1950s and worked as a field promotion representative for Mercury/Starday during the labels' 1957–58 union. After the Mercury/Starday deal fell apart, Singleton continued fieldwork for Mercury. His promotion and sales expertise were all he brought with him when Mercury promoted him to the creative sector in Nashville in early 1961. As his wife, Margie Singleton (then a Mercury country artist), said at the time, "Sometimes he knocks the musicians out—he tells them to play something and there's no such thing." (The couple later divorced.).

Nevertheless, Singleton's commercial instincts proved acute, and within a year he was heading the A&R department in New York as well as Nashville. He split his time between the two cities, and, maverick that he was, he brought many of the label's pop and R&B artists, such as Clyde McPhatter, to Nashville to record, as well as producer-arranger Quincy Jones. (Nashville hotels were segregated, so the black artists and musicians with whom Singleton worked would often stay at his home.)

Singleton hired Shreveport guitarist Jerry Kennedy as his number-two man in the Nashville office and eventual successor. With Kennedy's assistance, Singleton oversaw records, including the crossover phenomenon "Walk On By" (Leroy Van Dyke) and the pop hits "Ahab the Arab" (Ray Stevens) and "Wooden Heart" (Joe Dowell) during his tenure with Mercury and its sister label, Smash Records.

In 1966 Singleton set up his independent Shelby Singleton Corporation at 3106 Belmont Boulevard in Nashville. By the end of the decade, the building (to which a studio was added in 1969) housed an array of Singleton-owned publishing businesses and record labels. Released on Plantation in 1968, Riley's "Harper Valley P.T.A." sold 1 million copies and, as Sun Records historian Colin Escott has speculated, probably enabled Singleton to purchase the Sun catalog. Singleton then flooded the market with low-budget LPs featuring the Sun recordings of Jerry Lee Lewis, Johnny Cash, and others.

In 1977, though, when Singleton issued some of Elvis Presley's Sun material, RCA sued him, eventually winning a $45,000 settlement. The whole episode had simply been one of Singleton's many entrepreneurial gambits—no more or less surprising than his having scored one of his empire's biggest hits with C Company's controversial "Battle Hymn of Lt. Calley" (a million-seller in 1971) or having turned out a tribute record to John Lennon just days after Lennon's murder.

With his brother and business partner John Singleton—now company CEO—Shelby continued to license Sun masters to other labels for rerelease while also licensing recordings to TV and movie producers and to Internet music providers. —*Daniel Cooper*

## Asher & Little Jimmie Sizemore

Asher Sizemore b. Manchester, Kentucky, June 6, 1906; d. November 24, 1975
Little Jimmie Sizemore b. Paintsville, Kentucky, January 29, 1928

Country music's premier child star of the 1930s was James L. Sizemore, or Little Jimmie, a Grand Ole Opry member at age five. Although he was talented, his success was largely due to his father, Asher Sizemore, a pleasant but undistinguished singer who was one country's most assiduous early businessmen.

Before pursuing music full time, Asher worked briefly as a bookkeeper for a coal-mining company in Pike County, Kentucky. In 1931, after his marriage to Odessa Foley and the birth of their first child, Jimmie, Asher landed a show on a Huntington, West Virginia, radio station, where he sang old-time songs and cowboy music. He later moved to WCKY–Cincinnati and WHAS–Louisville, by which time Jimmie was performing with him. By 1933 father and son were dividing their time between WSM's Grand Ole Opry and WHAS; Little Jimmie won fans with songs such as "The Booger Bear," "Little Feet," and "Has Anybody Seen My Kitty." In 1934 he recorded "Little Jimmie's Good-bye to Jimmie Rodgers," his best-selling record.

The duo prospered in the 1930s, due as much to Asher's promotional skills as to Little Jimmie's singing and enormous repertory. Besides their WHAS and WSM broadcasts, the Sizemores cut fifteen-minute transcriptions that were syndicated throughout the Midwest. Like their live shows, these recorded programs proved highly profitable because Asher used them to hawk songbooks; he was among the first—and the most successful—country performers to do so. Asher also placed songs he owned with other acts and invested in Indiana farmland.

In the late 1930s Jimmie's younger brother, Charles Edward, called Buddy Boy, joined the family act; sister Nancy Louise followed later, though neither child was as popular as Little Jimmie. The Sizemores briefly performed on the NBC Network, and then, after leaving the Opry in 1942, they worked mainly in the Midwest throughout the 1940s. The group appeared on KXEL–Waterloo, Iowa; WHO–Des Moines; KMOX–St. Louis; and WSB–Atlanta. By 1950 they were on WKLO–Louisville.

Jimmie and Buddy served in the Korean War, and Buddy was declared lost in action on November 2, 1950. Both Asher and Jimmie eventually moved to Arkansas; Asher settled in DeQueen, where he died in 1975. Jimmie served as an executive with KGMR–Jacksonville, Arkansas, until he moved to Muskogee, Oklahoma, and then to Florida and the Midwest. As of 2011 he was retired but still performing occasionally. —*W. K. McNeil*

## Ricky Skaggs

b. Cordell, Kentucky, July 18, 1954

From 1970 to 1980 Ricky Lee Skaggs was arguably the hottest young picker and singer in bluegrass, both as heir apparent to the reigning legends and as a leader of the progressive bluegrass movement. From 1981 to 1989 he adapted his sound enough to become a mainstream country star and scored twenty Top Ten country singles. Since 1990 he has become bluegrass music's leading ambassador, prominent as a TV host, concert attraction, and award-winning recording artist.

*Ricky Skaggs*

He grew up in the mountains of eastern Kentucky, where he heard his parents sing, listened to their bluegrass 78s, and soaked up country sounds from radio station WCKY–Cincinnati. Skaggs had been playing mandolin less than a year in 1959 when BILL MONROE invited the five-year-old boy onstage to sing THE OSBORNE BROTHERS' "Ruby." The youngster sang the same song on the FLATT & SCRUGGS television show two years later and eventually mastered fiddle and guitar as well. By 1969 Skaggs had met another young Kentuckian, KEITH WHITLEY, assembled a band called the East Kentucky Mountain Boys, and did note-perfect imitations of THE STANLEY BROTHERS. One night in 1970 Skaggs and Whitley went to see RALPH STANLEY in West Virginia, but when the headliner was late, the club owner asked the two teenagers to entertain the crowd.

Arriving in mid-set, Stanley liked what he heard and soon hired both of them; Skaggs stayed with the Clinch Mountain Boys through 1974. During that time Skaggs and Whitley recorded the album *Second Generation Bluegrass*, backed by Stanley and his band. Skaggs then worked outside of professional music in Washington, D.C., but before long he was playing with THE COUNTRY GENTLEMEN and then J. D. CROWE & the New South, both pioneering progressive bluegrass acts.

Next Skaggs formed his own group, Boone Creek, which included DOBRO player JERRY DOUGLAS, and recorded albums for ROUNDER (1977) and SUGAR HILL (1978). Skaggs also released solo collections for REBEL, Sugar Hill, and Rounder and recorded a duet album with guitarist TONY RICE.

In 1977 Skaggs replaced RODNEY CROWELL in EMMYLOU HARRIS's Hot Band and eventually helped her make the bluegrass-inspired *Roses in the Snow* (1980). In turn, Harris sang on Skaggs's *Sweet Temptation*, a 1979 solo effort that also featured Rice, Douglas, THE WHITES, and fellow Hot Band members TONY BROWN, EMORY GORDY, and ALBERT LEE. Both albums served as blueprints for Skaggs's first major-label project, *Waitin' for the Sun to Shine* (EPIC, 1981). The basic sound was still bluegrass, but the banjo had been eliminated; drums and electric bass had been added; and the vocal harmonies were sweet and full rather than mournful and lonesome.

The result was a fresh, unusual hybrid that appealed to broad audiences and produced four chart singles, including back-to-back #1s with "Crying My Heart Out Over You" and "I Don't Care." Just as the album was breaking in the summer of 1981, Skaggs married one of his harmony singers, Sharon White of the Whites. The Whites would continue to pursue their own career while contributing to many of Skaggs's studio recordings.

*Waitin' for the Sun to Shine* netted Skaggs two 1982 CMA Awards: the Horizon Award and Male Vocalist of the Year. In May 1982 he joined the GRAND OLE OPRY and soon celebrated with the album *Highways & Heartaches*; during 1982–83 it yielded three #1 singles: GUY CLARK's "Heartbroke," the JIM EANES number "I Wouldn't Change You if I Could," and Larry Cordle's "Highway 40 Blues."

*Don't Cheat in Our Hometown* (1983) also produced three chart-topping singles: the title tune, MEL TILLIS's "Honey (Open That Door)," and BILL MONROE's "Uncle Pen." In 1984 Skaggs released his fourth straight gold album, *Country Boy*, whose title track went #1. The 1985 concert album *Live in London* featured a guest appearance by Elvis Costello on "Don't Get Above Your Raising" and sent "Cajun Moon" to the top of the charts. In that same year Skaggs won CMA's Entertainer of the Year award, and "Wheel Hoss" (from *Country Boy*) received a Grammy for Best Country Instrumental.

Skaggs's chart performance slowed after 1985, though he scored six Top Tens between 1986 and 1989, including "Cajun Moon" and "Lovin' Only Me." He moved to ATLANTIC RECORDS for 1995's *Solid Ground* but found only limited success; he also alienated some fans by becoming increasingly outspoken about his Christian beliefs.

At the same time, however, Skaggs emerged as a leading advocate for tradition-based country sounds. He became the performing MC of a popular television program on TNN, taped live onstage at THE RYMAN AUDITORIUM. His weekly radio show, *Simple Life with Ricky Skaggs*, was heard on 400 radio stations in the United States and twenty-nine other countries. Beginning in 1991 he hosted the annual Ricky Skaggs Pickin' Party at Wolf Trap Farm Park in Virginia. There he presented such top bluegrass acts as Bill Monroe, Ralph Stanley, Tony Rice, Jerry Douglas, J. D. Crowe, DOC WATSON, ALISON KRAUSS, the SELDOM SCENE, and DEL McCOURY and jammed with them in intriguing combinations.

In 1997 Skaggs established his own label, Skaggs Family Records (distributed by Rounder), and released the straight-ahead bluegrass album *Bluegrass Rules!* This Grammy-winning collection took home IBMA Album of the Year honors and helped Skaggs and his band, Kentucky Thunder, win IBMA's 1998 Instrumental Group of the Year award (a prize they had won seven more times as of 2011). That success convinced Skaggs to retire his touring country band and stick with his drummer-less bluegrass ensemble. As of 2011 he had accumulated thirteen Grammy awards. Since 1997 Skaggs's label has released recordings by acts including the Del McCoury Band, the Whites, Blue Highway, Mountain Heart, and Cherryholmes, some of whom Skaggs has produced. (Earlier Skaggs produced DOLLY PARTON's 1990 COLUMBIA album *White Limozeen*.)

Skaggs proved the wisdom of his return to bluegrass with two more Grammy-winning albums—including tributes to bluegrass patriarchs and a 2007 duet album with multigenre singer-songwriter Bruce Hornsby—a 2000 tour with DIXIE CHICKS, a role as performing host of the 2002 PBS special *All Star Bluegrass Celebration*, and a featured role alongside EARL SCRUGGS and Doc Watson in the 2003 PBS special *The Three Pickers: Legends of American Music*. Ever creatively restless, Skaggs released a contemporary folk-pop album, *Mosaic*, in 2010. —*Geoffrey Himes*

## Skillet Lickers (*see* Gid Tanner)

## Jimmie Skinner
b. Blue Lick, Kentucky, April 27, 1909; d. October 28, 1979

James Skinner contributed several standard songs to the BLUEGRASS and country canons. In addition, for twenty-five years his Cincinnati record store provided fans with their favorite discs.

Natives of the rich musical area surrounding Berea, Kentucky, in 1925 Skinner's family moved to Ohio, where Jimmie performed locally until 1945. When his recordings for the Red Barn and Radio Artists labels began attracting wider attention, he moved up to CAPITOL, DECCA, and MERCURY. His original songs include "Doin' My Time" (FLATT & SCRUGGS), "You Don't Know My Mind" (JIMMY MARTIN), and "Let's Say Goodbye Like We Said Hello" (ERNEST TUBB). Ray Lunsford's electric mandolin dominated the instrumentation on Skinner's discs.

Although Skinner was a radio regular in such locales as Knoxville, Tennessee, and Huntington, West Virginia, Cincinnati remained his home base until 1974, when he moved to Nashville to further his writing. His Jimmie Skinner Music Center in Cincinnati was a major mail-order and retail outlet for a quarter-century starting in 1950. His biggest chart successes, such as "I Found My Girl in the U.S.A." and "Dark Hollow," came on Mercury between 1957 and 1960. Later releases appeared on smaller labels, such as STARDAY, Vetco, and RICH-R-TONE, some with bluegrass accompaniment. —*Ivan M. Tribe*

## Melvin Sloan Dancers
Ralph Sloan b. Wilson County, Tennessee, March 9, 1925; d. March 12, 1980
Melvin Sloan b. Wilson County, Tennessee, March 27, 1940

The Melvin Sloan Dancers were a SQUARE DANCING troupe that performed at the GRAND OLE OPRY from 1952 into the twenty-first century. Formed in about 1949 and named the Cedar Hill Square Dancers, they later were reorganized as the Tennessee Travelers. Performances at mid-state county fairs led to a guest spot on the Opry and eventually to membership. The troupe was later known as Ralph Sloan and the Tennessee Travelers, until the death of leader Ralph Sloan in 1980. His brother Melvin took over the act, which was then renamed the Melvin Sloan Dancers. The troupe performed on the Opry as late as 2001 but subsequently retired as management brought in younger dancers, now known as the Grand Ole Opry Square Dancers.

In addition to working the Opry, the Sloan ensemble performed locally on WLAC-TV's *Country Junction* TV show. The size of the group varied from seventeen to eight members; smaller units allowed them to demonstrate their skills in less spacious venues. In 1988 their Appalachian style of square dancing was officially named the Tennessee state dance. —*Stacey Wolfe*

## Ben Smathers & the Stoney Mountain Cloggers
Ben Smathers b. Hendersonville, North Carolina, May 17, 1928;
d. September 13, 1990

For thirty-two years Ben Ray Smathers led the popular Stoney Mountain Cloggers dance troupe at the GRAND OLE OPRY. Organized in the mid-1950s, the group first appeared on the show on September 13, 1958, and was immediately hired for the cast. Until they joined the program, CLOGGING, a cross between

European folk dancing, buck dancing, and SQUARE DANCING, flourished primarily in Dutch-Irish communities of the Carolinas.

Largely a family group, the Stoney Mountain Cloggers included at various points Ben's wife, Margaret, and their children Hal, Mickey, Candy, Debbie, and Sally. In 1961 the troupe appeared at CARNEGIE HALL with a Grand Ole Opry show featuring PATSY CLINE, JIM REEVES, BILL MONROE, GRANDPA JONES, MARTY ROBBINS, FARON YOUNG, and MINNIE PEARL. In 1981 the Stoney Mountain Cloggers returned, performing with MERLE HAGGARD and TAMMY WYNETTE. After the death of patriarch Ben Smathers on the thirty-second anniversary of his initial Opry appearance, the group continued until September 11, 1993, when they ended the act. —*Stacey Wolfe*

## Arthur "Guitar Boogie" Smith
b. Clinton, South Carolina, April 1, 1921

An inventive country musician with a flair for pop tunes, Arthur Smith parlayed his 1945 instrumental hit "Guitar Boogie" into a lengthy broadcasting and entrepreneurial career.

Raised in Kershaw, South Carolina, Smith played trumpet in his father's brass band, later forming a traditional jazz ensemble with his two brothers, Ralph and Sonny, and bassist Luke Tucker. By 1938 the Arthur Smith Quartet appeared daily on WSPA–Spartanburg. Frustrated by a lack of success, Smith embraced country music for a BLUEBIRD RECORDS session in 1938. As the Carolina Crackerjacks the group offered an appealing mix of country ballads, gospel quartets, and pop standards, usually spotlighting Smith on fiddle. Unlike most country bands, though, the Crackerjacks relied heavily on written charts.

When World War II broke up the band in 1943, Smith briefly worked at WBT–Charlotte before joining the U.S. Navy. Returning to Charlotte after the war, he played guitar with the Briarhoppers and CECIL CAMPBELL's Tennessee Ramblers. To wrap up a fall 1945 Campbell session for Super Disc, Smith quickly cut "Guitar Boogie," an acoustic guitar instrumental backed by Campbell's rhythm section. Credited to the Rambler Trio, it became an enormous regional hit, helped launch a wave of country boogie records, and established Smith as a recording artist. After signing with MGM in 1947, he recorded country songs, guitar instrumentals, and tenor banjo specialties with his Crackerjacks and made gospel numbers with the Crossroads Quartet. MGM's October 1948 reissue of "Guitar Boogie" rose to #8 on *Billboard*'s country chart. "Feuding Banjos," a 1955 call-and-response novelty featuring Smith's tenor banjo and DON RENO's five-string, became a BLUEGRASS standard. Renamed "Dueling Banjos," the tune was featured in Warner Bros.' 1972 movie *Deliverance* without crediting Smith; he eventually won a prolonged lawsuit over its use.

In 1951 Smith entered television with daily and weekly shows over WBT-TV; their popularity led him to promote country and gospel PACKAGE SHOWS throughout the South. In 1959 *The Arthur Smith Show* was syndicated to fourteen stations; by 1977 it was airing in sixty-eight markets across the United States. During the mid-1980s Smith largely retired from performing to concentrate on his business interests. —*Dave Samuelson*

## Arthur Q. Smith
b. Griffin, Georgia, December 11, 1909; d. March 21, 1963

During the 1940s and 1950s, the man known as Arthur Q. Smith would stand outside the studios at Knoxville radio station WNOX and peddle songs the way a flea market vendor would peddle hubcaps. For ten or twenty-five dollars a song, young country artists could buy all rights to some of the best songs of the era, including "Rainbow at Midnight," "If Teardrops Were Pennies," "Wedding Bells," and "I Wouldn't Change You If I Could." Customers included Roy Acuff, Bill Monroe, Maybelle Carter (Carter Family), Carl Smith, Carl Butler, Hank Williams, and Kitty Wells—and dozens of others not yet identified. Smith's name seldom if ever appeared on the song credits, though he kept private notebooks identifying who bought each song.

James Arthur Pritchett—Smith's real name—grew up in Harlan, Kentucky; in the 1940s he tried a singing career, recording for King and Deluxe. He signed as a songwriter with Acuff-Rose Publications, but the company let him go when he proved unproductive, and Pritchett returned to selling his songs independently. His drinking contributed to an unstable life, though several of his protégés, including Harlan Howard, went on to win recognition for him. —*Charles Wolfe*

## Cal Smith
b. Gans, Oklahoma, April 7, 1932

Born Calvin Grant Shofner, Cal Smith became a country star in the early 1970s. He grew up around San Jose, California, where he first sang in nightclubs in a style similar to Hank Thompson's. With Uncle Phil Philley's band, Smith sang for inmates at San Quentin Prison along with Johnny Cash and other artists in 1958. Smith's first recording, a 1960 effort for Plaid Records, was a prison ballad, "Eleven Long Years."

By then Smith was also a popular country music disc jockey with KEEN–San Jose, but he left the West Coast in December 1962 to join Ernest Tubb's Texas Troubadours as rhythm guitarist and frontman, a job he held until July 1968. Tubb boosted Smith's career with featured tracks on Texas Troubadours albums and with featured performances on the Grand Ole Opry and on Tubb's syndicated TV show. Smith signed with Kapp Records in 1966, later leaving Tubb's band to promote his recording of "Drinking Champagne," a Top Forty country disc. Smith's popularity built slowly until his breakthrough song on Decca/MCA, Bill Anderson's "The Lord Knows I'm Drinking" (#1, 1972–73). "Country Bumpkin" and "It's Time to Pay the Fiddler" (both 1974) also reached #1, the former earning CMA's Single of the Year Award.

From MCA Smith moved to the Soundwaves label. He charted his last single on Step One Records in 1986. —*Ronnie Pugh*

## Carl Smith
b. Maynardville, Tennessee, March 15, 1927; d. January 16, 2010

A second national country star from Maynardville, Tennessee— Roy Acuff being the first—Carl M. Smith was one of country music's most popular hit makers of the 1950s and 1960s. Combining custom-tailored stage clothes and a confident manner with a singing style influenced by Acuff and Hank Williams, Smith developed an updated yet hard-edged sound that earned him a wide and loyal following.

Smith grew up listening to the Grand Ole Opry and to daily country broadcasts on Knoxville radio stations. In 1944 sponsor Cas Walker, a local grocer, gave him his first radio work, on Knoxville's WROL. As singer, guitarist, and sometime bass player, Smith performed with Knoxville's Brewster Brothers after military service and then, between 1947 and 1949, moved many times among Knoxville; Asheville, North Carolina; and Augusta, Georgia. He was back at WROL, working in Archie Campbell's band, when Knoxville dobro player George "Speedy" Krise made a demo of Smith's singing and sent it to Troy Martin, Peer-Southern Music's Nashville representative and an able scout for Columbia Records producer Don Law. Impressed, Martin arranged an audition with WSM program director Jack Stapp. After WSM guest spots in March 1950, Stapp gave Smith a six-day-a-week morning show in May, and Opry appearances about every third week led to membership that year. Don Law signed Smith to Columbia on May 5, 1950; six days later Smith recorded his first Columbia sides in Nashville's Castle Studios.

A year passed before Smith's first hit, but then the hits came steadily—earnest love songs, principally, suitably framed by bandsman Johnny Sibert's crying steel guitar. "Let's Live a Little" was Smith's first; "Mr. Moon" and "If Teardrops Were Pennies" also made the Top Ten in 1951.

Grand Ole Opry friends boosted Smith's career. Hank Williams let Smith record his "Me and My Broken Heart" and "There's Nothing as Sweet as My Baby"; Ernest Tubb, with whom Smith toured early on, brought him Jack Henley's "(When You Feel Like You're in Love) Don't Just Stand There." In 1952 this song became Smith's second #1 hit, preceded by "Let Old Mother Nature Have Her Way," his best-selling single.

For the next few years, each of his recordings made the Top Twenty—sometimes both sides of a single release. Smith's rendition of The Louvin Brothers' "Are You Teasing Me" went to #1 in 1952, and its flip side, Boudleaux and Felice Bryant's "It's a Lovely, Lovely World," climbed to #5. This talented couple became reliable Smith song sources, supplying "Just Wait 'Til I Get You Alone" (1953), "Hey Joe!" (1953), and "Back Up Buddy" (1954).

*Carl Smith*

Amid a welter of behind-the-scenes politics, Smith left the Grand Ole Opry in late 1956 to take star billing on the PHILIP MORRIS COUNTRY MUSIC SHOW, a touring free show sponsored by the cigarette maker that ran some eighteen months in 1957 and 1958. The handsome Smith then made television a favored venue. He frequently guested on RED FOLEY's *Ozark Jubilee* (broadcast on ABC-TV as *Jubilee U.S.A.*), and in 1961 Smith was cohost of its follow-up series, *Five Star Jubilee*, also out of Springfield, Missouri. Between 1964 and 1969, Smith's regular TV exposure crossed the border into Canada as he hosted 190 episodes of *Carl Smith's Country Music Hall.*

Meanwhile, Smith placed at least one record on the country charts every year between 1951 and 1973, which was virtually his entire tenure with Columbia. Briefly coaxed back into recording in the late 1970s for HICKORY RECORDS, Smith gradually gave up music to live the life of a gentleman horse breeder on his estate near Franklin, Tennessee.

Twice married to country music performers, Smith and his first wife, JUNE CARTER (1952–56), were the parents of singing star CARLENE CARTER. From 1957 until her death in 2005, Smith was married to GOLDIE HILL, a DECCA recording artist and, at the time of their wedding, a costar on the Philip Morris Country Music Show.

Carl Smith was elected to THE COUNTRY MUSIC HALL OF FAME in 2003. —*Ronnie Pugh*

## Connie Smith
b. Elkhart, Indiana, August 14, 1941

In November 1964 the talk of Nashville's annual country music DJ CONVENTION was young Connie Smith, whose debut hit, "Once a Day," was among the hottest items on the DJs' playlists. A year before, Smith had been a small-town housewife in Ohio; now she was a breakout RCA artist with a country voice as powerful as any the seasoned jocks had ever heard. Though not as well known as contemporaries LORETTA LYNN and TAMMY WYNETTE, Smith has been cited as a favorite singer of everyone from GEORGE JONES to JUNIOR BROWN. DOLLY PARTON once said, "You know, there's really only three real female singers in the world: Streisand, Ronstadt, and Connie Smith. The rest of us are only pretending."

Born Constance June Meador, Smith grew up in West Virginia and Ohio in a family of fourteen children. Her parents were migrant farm workers, her father an abusive alcoholic. As a teenager Smith listened to both the GRAND OLE OPRY and pop radio, paying close attention to KITTY WELLS and JEAN SHEPARD on the former and to Sarah Vaughan and Nancy Wilson on the latter. Laid up in bed after a lawn mower accident when she was eighteen, Smith taught herself to play guitar. Though not serious about a music career, she sang at local square dances and Grange halls. For a time she performed in the traveling band of a man named Floyd Miller and then later with the cast of *Saturday Night Jamboree*, a live TV show carried on WSAZ in Huntington, West Virginia.

On August 4, 1963, Smith won a talent contest that preceded an Opry-troupe concert in Columbus, Ohio. First prize included the chance to sing on the Opry program. Opry headliner BILL ANDERSON took note of Smith's talent, and when the two met again at a New Year's Day concert in Canton, Ohio, he suggested that she consider coming to Nashville.

At Anderson's invitation, Smith flew to Nashville to sing on the March 28, 1964, edition of the ERNEST TUBB *Midnite Jamboree*. In May Anderson invited her back, this time to make a demo recording of four of his songs. Anderson pitched the tape to CHET

ATKINS, who signed Smith to RCA on June 24. On July 16, with BOB FERGUSON producing, she recorded Anderson's "Once a Day," her debut single. It eventually spent eight weeks at #1 and propelled her to Grand Ole Opry membership in 1965.

Smith never repeated the spectacular success of "Once a Day," but for the next few years she recorded a succession of albums and Top Ten singles of consistent quality and dramatic impact. As producer, Ferguson sometimes employed NASHVILLE SOUND techniques; Smith's most effective work, however, was usually with straight-ahead country backup highlighted by WELDON MYRICK's PEDAL STEEL GUITAR. Her material leaned heavily toward standard themes of lost love and heartache, as exemplified on Anderson's "Then and Only Then" (#4, 1965) and DALLAS FRAZIER's "Ain't Had No Lovin'" (#2, 1966). But as 1970 approached, Smith's song choices (such as "Ribbon of Darkness" and "The Last Letter") seemed to grow more darkly personal.

Never comfortable with the trappings of stardom, Smith was rapidly moving toward a spiritual crisis, and she eventually joined the Rev. Jimmie Snow's Evangel Temple congregation. In 1973, when she left RCA for COLUMBIA, her new contract specified that she would be allowed to record one gospel album per year along with two country LPs. By then she was retreating from the road and limelight anyway, devoting herself more to home and family. She recorded briefly for MONUMENT in the late 1970s and then disappeared from the charts until 1985, when her EPIC recording of "A Far Cry from You"—penned by STEVE EARLE—became her final *Billboard* chart-maker. Since then, Smith has returned to more active work on the road, in the studio, and at the Grand Ole Opry, where she remains an audience favorite. In 1998 she recorded a self-titled WARNER BROS. album of new material, produced by MARTY STUART, but it had little commercial impact. She and Stuart married on July 8, 1997. Smith released the album "Long Line of Heartaches" on Sugar Hill Records in August of 2011. —*Daniel Cooper*

*Connie Smith*

## Fiddlin' Arthur Smith
b. Bold Springs, Tennessee, April 10, 1898; d. February 28, 1971

Fiddlin' Arthur Smith was one of the most influential fiddlers in prewar country music. As a star of the GRAND OLE OPRY and a prolific recording artist (for BLUEBIRD RECORDS) he enjoyed wide exposure. As a composer he produced dozens of fiddle tunes as well as popular songs, such as "More Pretty Girls Than One." As a stylist he helped to popularize the "long bow" style featuring smooth bowing strokes instead of the older "jiggy bow" style using short, chopping strokes. This long-bow style has dominated modern contest and BLUEGRASS fiddling.

Hailing from Dickson County, in the hills west of Nashville, Smith absorbed some of the distinctive folk fiddle styles of the region before he began performing with his cousin Homer Smith at the Grand Ole Opry in 1929. After a few years, Opry managers teamed Fiddlin' Arthur Smith with SAM AND KIRK McGEE to form an all-star STRINGBAND called the Dixieliners (in deference to Smith's work on the Nashville, Chattanooga, & St. Louis Railroad, nicknamed the Dixie Line). The act was enormously popular on the air and on tour, but when Smith started to make records in 1935, he joined forces with the DELMORE BROTHERS. During the next five years he recorded some forty solo sides, including signature numbers such as "Blackberry Blossom," "Cheatham County Breakdown," and "Fiddler's Dream." The Delmores convinced him to record vocal numbers as well, and he turned out the enduring country favorites "Walking in My Sleep," "Beautiful Brown Eyes," and "Pig at Home in the Pen."

Leaving the Opry in 1938, Smith spent time with THE BAILES BROTHERS in West Virginia and then made his way to the West Coast, where he worked for singer JIMMY WAKELY in the 1940s. By this point Smith was introducing the fiddle classic "Orange Blossom Special" to audiences in Las Vegas and on the West Coast. He returned to Tennessee in the 1950s, intending to retire from music, but folklorist Mike Seeger persuaded him to reunite the Dixieliners for a pair of Folkways Records albums. Smith made numerous appearances during the folk revival and eventually cut an album for STARDAY RECORDS. Health problems caught up with him, and he died in 1971. —*Stacey Wolfe*

## Hal Smith
b. Fairview (Cullman County), Alabama, November 21, 1923; d. September 13, 2008

A founding partner of PAMPER MUSIC, James Harrell "Hal" Smith also worked by turns as a Nashville musician, artist manager, and television producer.

Smith left the family farm at age sixteen to become a fiddle player with Birmingham radio station WAPI. After receiving a medical discharge from the U.S. Army in 1943, Smith moved to Nashville, and over the years he toured as a sideman with ROY ACUFF, PEE WEE KING, EDDY ARNOLD, ERNEST TUBB, GEORGE MORGAN, and CARL SMITH. In 1948 Smith married guitar player VELMA WILLIAMS (SMITH), a former member of Acuff's troupe who went on to work Nashville recording sessions.

In 1954 Smith launched his career as an entertainment executive, as manager first for RAY PRICE and JIM REEVES and then for Carl Smith. Other artists Hal Smith managed included Ernest Tubb, JIMMY C. NEWMAN, and JACK GREENE. One of Smith's most prosperous ventures was Pamper Music, which published classics penned by HANK COCHRAN, WILLIE NELSON, and HARLAN HOWARD. Additional companies owned or operated by Smith included the talent agencies Curtis Artists Productions (established in late 1956) and Hal Smith Artists Productions, Hal Smith TV Programs, Cullman Records, and Boone Records. Among the syndicated television shows Smith produced were *The Ernest Tubb Show*, *Wills Family Inspirational Time*, *Country Music Carousel*, and *Skylite Cavalcade*. Significant business associates included talent agents Jimmy Key and Haze Jones as well as television programming personnel A. O. Stinson, Dave White, and Bill Brittain. Smith also owned Kentucky's RENFRO VALLEY BARN DANCE for a time in the late 1960s but sold most of his music properties in about 1969. —*Kent Henderson*

## Sammi Smith
b. Orange, California, August 5, 1943; d. February 12, 2005

Jewel Fay "Sammi" Smith was one of the leading female vocalists of the 1970s and one of the few women performers associated with that decade's OUTLAW phenomenon. Born in Southern California but raised throughout the Southwest, she began performing in nightclubs (primarily as a rock & roll singer) at age eleven. Smith moved to Nashville in 1967 and signed with COLUMBIA RECORDS. She also became friends with aspiring songwriter KRIS KRISTOFFERSON, who would provide her with her biggest hit.

Released early in 1971 on the independent Mega label, "Help Me Make It Through the Night" became a #1 country single and a Top Ten pop hit. It was a breakthrough recording in many ways, introducing an unprecedented level of sexual candor that was highlighted by Smith's husky voice and sensual reading of the lyrics. For the recording she won a 1971 Grammy for Best Country Vocal Performance, Female. In addition, it secured Kristofferson's status as Nashville's leading young songwriter on the crest of a new wave of creativity and experimentation.

Unfortunately for Smith, her commercial success peaked with this effort. Several subsequent releases on Mega generated solid to unspectacular sales, as did two of her compositions for other artists, "Cedartown, Georgia" (for WAYLON JENNINGS) and "Sand-Covered Angels" (for CONWAY TWITTY).

A brief stay in Texas from 1973 to 1975 raised Smith's profile as she appeared regularly with old friends WILLIE NELSON and Waylon Jennings. But a move to ELEKTRA RECORDS in 1975 and subsequent affiliations with three minor companies into the 1980s failed to revive Smith's career. Her talent usually exceeded her material as she searched for a sequel to one of country music's modern masterpieces. Smith died in 2005. —*Stephen R. Tucker*

## Velma Williams Smith
b. Logan County, Kentucky, July 27, 1924

Velma Elizabeth Williams Smith first gained recognition in 1942 when she became a member of ROY ACUFF's Smoky Mountain Boys and Girls. Performing with her sister, Mildred, as the Williams Sisters, Velma Williams played the bass and sang. Following the departure of Rachel Veach from the band, Williams was briefly billed with BASHFUL BROTHER OSWALD as Oswald and his Big Sister. Williams left Acuff's troupe in about 1948 and married HAL SMITH, who was then the fiddler for ERNEST TUBB. During THE NASHVILLE SOUND era, Williams's distinctive rhythm guitar style earned session work with many of CHET ATKINS's RCA acts, including JIM REEVES, DOTTIE WEST, and SKEETER DAVIS. —*Kent Henderson*

## Warren Smith
b. Humphreys County, Mississippi, prob. February 7, 1932; d. January 30, 1980

Although he scored several big country hits in the early 1960s, Warren Smith is better known today for his unsuccessful ROCKABILLY recordings for SUN RECORDS.

He grew up in Louise, Mississippi, and moved to West Memphis, Arkansas, in 1955. A local bandleader, Clyde Leoppard, brought him to Sun, and Smith recorded five singles for the label that veered precipitously between country music and rockabilly, the best-known probably being "Ubangi Stomp." Smith acquired the demeanor and mien of the rock & roll star; all he lacked were the hits. His Sun singles were later regarded as quintessential rockabilly.

Smith moved to California in 1959, cut three singles for WARNER BROS., and then recorded for LIBERTY (1960–64). "I Don't Believe I'll Fall in Love Today" and "Odds and Ends" were Top Ten country discs, utilizing the hillbilly shuffle that had been so successful for RAY PRICE and others. Smith's career quickly disintegrated, though. A serious automobile accident in 1965 and a jail term both stemmed from prescription drug abuse, and singles released on ever-smaller labels, such as Skill and Jubal, went nowhere. Smith moved to Texas in the mid-1960s and worked outside of music, although he toured Europe to some acclaim as a rockabilly in 1977 and 1978. He died of a heart attack preparing for his third overseas tour. —*Colin Escott*

## Smith's Sacred Singers

An informal collection of friends and neighbors from northeastern Georgia, Smith's Sacred Singers became one of the most popular gospel groups of the prewar era. Their 1926 debut single, "Pictures from Life's Other Side" b/w "Where We'll Never Grow Old," became the best-selling gospel record in COLUMBIA's 15000 series and one of the best-selling recordings of OLD-TIME MUSIC.

A devout Methodist and singing-school teacher, barber J. Frank Smith (1885–1937) was based in Braselton, Georgia, and rehearsed his quartet to sing from shape-note hymnals, usually with piano accompaniment. His original ensemble included the Rev. M. L. Thrasher on bass vocals; Clyde Smith (no relation), who played violin and sang baritone; Clarence Cronic (1902–1990), who sang tenor and played guitar; and Smith himself singing lead.

Amazed by the spectacular success of the first Smith's record, Columbia quickly scheduled more sessions for April 1927, and other hits followed: "Going Down the Valley," "Shouting on the Hills," "The Eastern Gate," and "He Will Set Your Fields on Fire." The act eventually made sixty-six sides for Columbia between 1926 and 1930 as well as an additional thirty-eight titles for BLUEBIRD during 1934–35, and the singers' popularity set off a small boom in gospel music with major record companies. Smith never tried to professionalize the group—they never toured or pursued extensive radio work—and personnel typically shifted from session to session. —*Charles Wolfe*

## Mike Snider
b. Gleason, Tennessee, May 30, 1960

Multi-instrumentalist William Michael Snider has taken the venerable country traditions of OLD-TIME banjo playing and downhome humor and carried them lovingly into contemporary times. He was one of the first stars created by TNN via guest spots on Ralph Emery's *Nashville Now* (more than a hundred appearances) and the syndicated *Hee Haw* series (he joined the cast in 1987). With his West Tennessee drawl, he initially seemed to be a bashful and simple country boy, but he quickly proved himself a shrewd and effective entertainer, mixing old-time tunes with humorous stories about his wife, "Sweetie" (Sabrina). He often generated twice the fan mail of famous guests.

At sixteen, Snider received his first banjo. After winning the Mid-South Banjo Championship, he became National Bluegrass Banjo Champion at twenty-three. On January 21, 1984, Snider made his first appearance on the GRAND OLE OPRY. A prouder moment came on June 2, 1990, when he was officially welcomed as a cast member by his comedy idol, MINNIE PEARL. Snider later added backup musicians, novelty songs ("If My Nose Was Runnin' Money"), and witty one-liners to his act. In 1989 he hosted TNN's *Fairs & Festivals* series and often played banquets and conventions. He was also a familiar face at OPRYLAND theme park prior to its closing.

The composer of original instrumental tunes, Snider markets his albums at personal appearances and via the Internet. Thanks to TV appearances, he says, these releases have sold respectably. —*Walt Trott*

## Glenn Snoddy
b. Shelbyville, Tennessee, May 4, 1922

Long esteemed for his expertise and quiet efficiency, Woodland Sound studio manager Glenn Snoddy contributed greatly to Nashville's reputation as a recording center. Early on he played trombone and piano but found his calling after World War II as an engineer, working first for Middle Tennessee radio stations and then for Nashville's BROWN RADIO PRODUCTIONS. There he engineered hundreds of transcriptions and live radio broadcasts as well as recording sessions for RCA acts such as JOHNNIE & JACK. He also worked sessions for the CASTLE RECORDING STUDIO. In 1955 Snoddy joined WSM's radio and television staff and spent five years broadcasting "everything from big bands to the GRAND OLE OPRY."

Snoddy focused on recording in 1960 when he became an engineer at OWEN BRADLEY's legendary Quonset Hut studio, recording JOHNNY CASH, MARTY ROBBINS, and others after COLUMBIA RECORDS purchased it in 1962. After a brief stint at the ACUFF-ROSE studio, in 1967 he established Woodland in a former movie theater in East Nashville and made it one of the city's most active and well-regarded recording facilities. Two years later Woodland expanded to become a 16,000-square-foot complex. California-based AVI purchased Woodland in 1980; Snoddy worked for the company into the late 1980s, when he retired. Through his tenure the technologically advanced studio hosted such landmark events as the sessions for the NITTY GRITTY DIRT BAND's 1971 *Will the Circle Be Unbroken* album as well as sessions by LEFTY FRIZZELL, the OAK RIDGE BOYS, TAMMY WYNETTE, and JOHN PRINE, along with artists from pop vocalists Andy Williams and BOBBY GOLDSBORO to soul singer Joe Simon and rock acts NEIL YOUNG, LINDA RONSTADT, and Kansas. —*Thomas Goldsmith*

## Hank Snow
b. Brooklyn, Nova Scotia, Canada, May 9, 1914; d. December 20, 1999

Following World War II, Canadian Clarence Eugene "Hank" Snow emerged as one of country music's most distinctive vocal stylists. He was a fine songwriter, a prolific recording artist, a solid

*Hank Snow*

guitarist, and a successful businessman who at various points owned a Nashville music school, a New York music publishing firm, and two radio stations. Snow never turned his back on the JIMMIE RODGERS style that first made him famous, but he also experimented with Latin rhythms, jazz, blues, HAWAIIAN MUSIC, recitations, and gospel songs.

The some 840 commercial recordings he made between 1936 and 1985 include Canadian folk songs, Rodgers-styled songs, hobo and railroad songs, COWBOY MUSIC, pop standards, and country classics penned by Nashville songwriters. Snow continually resurrected old songs for new audiences, even as he recorded newly written material. From 1949 to 1980 he placed eighty-five singles on *Billboard*'s country charts, and no one was surprised when he was elected to the NASHVILLE SONGWRITERS HALL OF FAME in 1978 and to THE COUNTRY MUSIC HALL OF FAME in 1979.

His had been a long, torturous road to Nashville; it began in the windswept village of Brooklyn in Nova Scotia. One of four children (he had three sisters), he was eight years old when his parents divorced. He was sent off to his paternal grandparents, but he repeatedly ran away and returned to his mother. When she remarried, a violent stepfather physically abused him. "I was treated by him . . . like a dog," Snow recalled. To escape, Snow went to sea as a teenager working on a fishing trawler in the treacherous North Atlantic, where he entertained the crew by singing and playing the harmonica. At home, he listened to records, first by VERNON DALHART and then by Jimmie Rodgers, newly signed to the Victor label (see RCA VICTOR).

Armed with a mail-order Timothy Eaton guitar, Snow began singing over CHNS in Halifax in 1933; he also met and married a local Dutch-Irish woman named Minnie Blanch Aalders. The young couple soon landed a paying radio job for the laxative company CRAZY WATER CRYSTALS, and Snow started billing himself as Hank the Yodeling Ranger after learning that Jimmie Rodgers had been made an honorary Texas Ranger.

In October 1936 Snow traveled to Montreal to make his first records for Canadian BLUEBIRD (an RCA VICTOR imprint): "Lonesome Blue Yodel" and "Prisoned Cowboy." All told, he made some ninety recordings for the label between 1936 and 1949, including hits such as "Blue Velvet Band," "Galveston Rose," and "My Blue River Rose." Though he became popular in Canada, few of his recordings were released in the United States. After abortive stays in Hollywood and West Virginia, Snow finally cracked the American market in 1948. An expert rider, he built a following on tour with his horse Pawnee. He was a modest success in Dallas on the *BIG D JAMBOREE* and enlisted GRAND OLE OPRY star ERNEST TUBB, a fellow Rodgers admirer, as an ally. Tubb liked Snow's work and began to lobby WSM executives on his behalf; they relented and invited Snow to join in 1950. He was introduced onstage by HANK WILLIAMS.

For a time it seemed that Snow's Opry tenure would be short. Though he had scored a Top Ten *Billboard* hit with 1949's "Marriage Vow," he seemed unable to catch fire with Opry audiences. Then came "I'm Moving On." A piece that Snow's producer had not even wanted to cut, this original song rode the country charts for forty-four weeks in 1950 and 1951, twenty-one of them at #1. Two more self-penned #1s followed: "The Golden Rocket" (1950–51) and "Rhumba Boogie" (1951). Into 1963 he typically enjoyed two or three Top Ten hits a year, including "Bluebird Island" (1951), an original song recorded with Anita Carter); "The Gold Rush Is Over" (1952); "(Now and Then, There's) A Fool Such as I" (1952–53); "I Don't Hurt Anymore" (1954); "Let Me Go, Lover!" (1954–55); "Conscience, I'm Guilty" (1956); and "I've Been Everywhere" (1962). Additionally, Snow became one of the first country singers to record theme, or concept, albums. He utilized his considerable skills as a lead guitarist to enhance his recordings, including a series of duets with CHET ATKINS.

Snow's chart success ebbed after 1968, though he did score a #1 country hit in 1974 with "Hello Love." Yet throughout his career Snow offered a tradition-based alternative to country-pop and to rock-influenced country sounds. He traveled widely (including visits to Korea and Vietnam) and continued as a fixture on the Opry. He notched a #1 hit in 1974 with "Hello Love," and in 1977 he recorded his 104th album for RCA, the aptly titled *Still Movin' On*. Founder of the Hank Snow Child Abuse Foundation, he published his autobiography, *The Hank Snow Story*, through the University of Illinois Press in 1994. By the late 1990s, health problems forced him to retire, and he died of heart failure in 1999. —*Charles Wolfe*

## Society of European Stage Authors and Composers (*see* SESAC)

## Leo Soileau
b. Ville Platte, Louisiana, January 19, 1904; d. August 2, 1980

Leo Soileau was one of CAJUN MUSIC's most innovative and important musicians. As a youngster, he became an accomplished traditional fiddler, learning from veterans such as DENNIS MCGEE. In 1928 Soileau joined accordionist Mayuse Lafleur to make the second commercial recording of Cajun music, "Basile Waltz," for Victor (later RCA Victor). The next year he and accordionist Moise Robin recorded for several labels. In November 1929 Soileau cut some outstanding OLD-TIME fiddle duets with his cousin Alius Soileau as the Soileau Couzens. At the same sessions he also recorded with accordionist Oscar "Slim" Doucet.

Soileau was one of the first performers to incorporate elements of mainstream country into Cajun music. In 1934 he formed a STRINGBAND, Leo Soileau & His Three Aces. The accordion was dropped from the lineup, and the new sound was Cajun country music. Soileau's Three Aces later became Four Aces and, in 1937 (the last year he recorded), Leo Soileau's Rhythm Boys. He remained active in Louisiana and southeastern Texas playing dances and radio shows until 1953. Later he worked in an oil refinery and as a janitor until he retired in 1968. —*Charlie Seemann*

## Songbooks

Songbooks were once central to country music's popularity and were basic ingredients of virtually every early country singer's professional career. Their origins were rooted in the broadside BALLADS and song folios hawked on British and American colonial streets in the seventeenth and eighteenth centuries. Early country entertainers were well aware of pocket songsters sold by BLACKFACE MINSTRELS, circus performers, and vaudevillians, just as they were familiar with colorfully illustrated sheet music and song folios that circulated widely in nineteenth-century and early-twentieth-century America. Most southerners likely encountered wandering folksingers, many of whom were blind, and who peddled their songsheets and "ballet" books in railroad stations and at county fairs, court days, public hangings, and other gatherings. At least two of these itinerant balladeers, Charlie Oaks and Dick Burnett, made the transition to commercial country music in the 1920s. Burnett, for example, was peddling a small printed booklet of songs at least fourteen years before he made his first recordings, in 1927.

Country singers sold their songbooks at public appearances and advertised them on their radio broadcasts. Published privately by radio stations and by such publishing houses as M. M. COLE in Chicago, early songbooks usually contained photographs of the musicians and their families, human interest stories, and the lyrics of the entertainers' most popular songs. The earliest of these picture-songbooks has not been determined, but BRADLEY KINCAID's booklet of 1928, *Favorite Mountain Ballads and Old Time Songs*, was one of the first and the most successful, demonstrating radio's powerful role in popularizing country music. Published by WLS–Chicago, the book went through six printings, sold more than 100,000 copies, and was the first of thirteen similar books issued by Kincaid into the late 1940s. Country entertainers produced a massive array of songbooks, and performers sometimes made more money from such sales than they did from recordings or personal appearances.

The songbook's popularity is explained, in part, by fans' desire to get as close as possible to entertainers' personal lives and by performers' awareness of a widespread hunger for homespun entertainment stressing family values. For example, ASHER SIZEMORE, a Kentucky singer who performed with his young son, LITTLE JIMMIE, on a string of radio stations from the early 1930s to the early 1950s, issued several songbooks with titles such as *Family Circle Songs* and *Hearth and Home Songs*. Exact sales figures are unknown, but the Sizemores claimed to have received 42,000 letters at WSM on a single day in January 1937. Songbook sales later declined with the fading of live country radio, but music publishers have continued to issue material performed by leading country artists.

In addition to using songbooks published by particular entertainers, fans and fledgling singers have learned songs from books issued by radio barn dances or by commercial publishers. The *Renfro Valley Bugle*, a newspaper, has typically printed old songs

that are in the public domain, while commercial firms have emphasized newly published material. For decades the most widely circulated commercial song magazine for fans was *Country Song Roundup*, first published in 1949 in Derby, Connecticut, and continuing into the early 2000s. —*Bill C. Malone*

## Jo-El Sonnier
b. Rayne, Louisiana, October 2, 1946

Although singer and accordionist Jo-El Sonnier is principally associated with CAJUN MUSIC, his eclectic repertoire extends to mainstream country, blues, rock, and Gulf Coast swamp-pop. He unites these styles with powerful, passionate vocals and a formidable upper-register range. Sonnier launched his career with traditional Cajun music. He began playing accordion at age four and two years later was a regular live performer on KSIG in Crowley, Louisiana. As a teenager Sonnier began recording prolifically for such regional labels as Swallow, Goldband, and Dupree, sometimes billed as the Cajun Valentino.

In the early 1970s Sonnier moved to Southern California, worked as a sideman with various bands, and then spent a six-year stint in Nashville, where he recorded for MERCURY. Several singles resulted, including "I've Been Around Enough to Know"; none did well, though a CD reissue reveals some strong material in his Mercury sessions. Sonnier also appeared on ASLEEP AT THE WHEEL's *Wheelin' and Dealin'* before leaving Music City in 1980.

Returning to Louisiana, Sonnier recorded *Cajun Life* for ROUNDER RECORDS, with accompanists including Michael Doucet. Unfortunately, the album appeared a few years before the early 1980s Cajun craze that popularized such bands as BEAUSOLEIL.

Back in California, Sonnier fronted a group called Friends, which included ex-Band keyboardist Garth Hudson as well as stellar guitarists ALBERT LEE and David Lindley. Ensuing critical acclaim led Sonnier to a deal with RCA in Nashville and the 1987 album *Come On Joe*, which yielded Top Ten country renditions of "No More One More Time" and "Tear Stained Letter" and a Top Forty country hit with Slim Harpo's bluesy swamp-pop classic "Raining in My Heart."

No charted singles followed on albums for RCA, CAPITOL, and LIBERTY in 1990, 1991, and 1992, but Sonnier's energetic performances have maintained his popularity in both country and Cajun circles. In 1994 he returned to Rounder, releasing the traditional set *Cajun Roots*, with backup musicians again including Michael Doucet. A similar album, *Cajun Pride* (1997), was nominated for a Grammy in the Traditional Folk category. Sonnier has also found success as a songwriter, session musician, and actor, with credits including director Peter Bogdanovich's film *Mask* (1987). Sonnier has continued to tour and release albums in the twenty-first century. —*Ben Sandmel*

## Sons of the Pioneers
Leonard Franklin Slye [Roy Rogers] b. Cincinnati, Ohio, November 5, 1911; d. July 6, 1998
Robert Clarence Nobles [Bob Nolan] b. New Brunswick, Canada, April 1, 1908; d. June 16, 1980
Lloyd Wilson Perryman b. Ruth, Arkansas, January 29, 1917; d. May 31, 1977
Vernon Tim Spencer b. Webb City, Missouri, July 13, 1908; d. April 26, 1974
Thomas Hubert "Hugh" Farr b. Llano, Texas, December 6, 1903; d. March 17, 1980
Karl Marx Farr b. Rochelle, Texas, April 25, 1909; d. September 20, 1961

America's premier western singing group was formed in 1933 by Leonard Franklin Slye—later known as ROY ROGERS—and was initially called the Pioneer Trio, consisting of Slye, Bob Nolan,

*Sons of the Pioneers: (from left) Karl Farr, brother Hugh Farr, Tim Spencer, Len Slye (a.k.a. Roy Rogers), and Bob Nolan with Gus Mack of the Beverly Hill Billies*

and Tim Spencer. By early 1934 the musical partners added expert fiddler Hugh Farr, and in mid-1935 guitarist Karl Farr, Hugh's brother, joined as well. Slye, Spencer, Nolan, and Hugh and Karl Farr are generally regarded as the act's original members.

As the Sons of the Pioneers, the men began a series of transcriptions (syndicated radio shows) for Standard Radio in late 1934, ushering in an exciting new musical genre that featured western themes, three-part close-harmony vocals, and impressive instrumental backup. (In addition, they may have been the first western group to feature three-part harmony yodeling.) Spread via radio syndication and local Los Angeles broadcasts, their songs and harmony were soon emulated by scores of country acts and western bands across the nation, and they have continued to set benchmarks into the twenty-first century.

Recordings widened the group's popularity. In 1934 the Pioneers were the third act signed by newly formed DECCA RECORDS, following pop vocalist Bing Crosby and cowboy singer-songwriter STUART HAMBLEN. The group recorded for the label into February 1937 before switching to the AMERICAN RECORD CORPORATION (ARC). New member Lloyd Perryman, an excellent tenor and vocal arranger, was on hand for the act's ARC sessions (October and December, 1937). Comedian–bass player Pat Brady also came aboard, and his second session (December 14, 1937) proved to be Rogers's final prewar recording date with the band.

Working separately and together, Bob Nolan and Tim Spencer turned out songs of exceptional quality. Indeed, the lyrics and melodies of classics such as "Tumbling Tumbleweeds," "Cool Water," "Blue Prairie," "Way Out There," "Happy Rovin' Cowboy," "Room Full of Roses," and "A Cowboy Has to Sing" were virtually unprecedented in western music. Many of their compositions were inspired by the Pioneers' participation in a large number of B-western movies, first in 1935 with Charles Starrett and then, from 1941, with Slye, who had left the group by early 1938 for movie roles as Roy Rogers.

Signing with RCA VICTOR in 1945, while Ken Carson, Perryman's wartime replacement, was still a member, the ensemble logged nine Top Ten hits through 1949, including "Stars and Stripes on Iwo Jima," "Cool Water," "Cigareetes, Whusky, and Wild, Wild Women," "Teardrops in My Heart," "Blue Shadows on the Trail" (with Rogers), and "Room Full of Roses." The Pioneers would remain with the label until 1969.

The early group stayed largely intact until 1949, when both Spencer and Nolan retired and were replaced by Ken Curtis and Tommy Doss. Upon Curtis's departure in 1952, Dale Warren joined and provided continuity until his death in 2008. Over the years, the band took on many incarnations as veterans left or passed away and new members took their places. Karl Farr died in 1961. Perryman passed away in 1977, three years after Spencer's death. Hugh Farr, who had retired in the late 1950s, died in 1980, as did Bob Nolan. Assisted by group founder Roy Rogers, the act notched its most recent *Billboard* chart record that year, "Ride Concrete Cowboy, Ride," from the movie *Smokey & The Bandit II*, starring Burt Reynolds and JERRY REED. Rogers's death in 1998 marked the passing of the last living original member.

Bob Nolan and Tim Spencer were elected to the NASHVILLE SONGWRITERS HALL OF FAME in 1971. In 1980 the original Sons of the Pioneers were elected to THE COUNTRY MUSIC HALL OF FAME. The Pioneers continued to perform regularly in BRANSON, MISSOURI, as of 2011. —*Ken Griffis*

## Sons of the San Joaquin

Joe Hannah b. Marshfield, Missouri, February 1, 1932
Jack Hannah b. Marshfield, Missouri, October 25, 1933
Lon Hannah b. Pasadena, California, April 10, 1956

A popular western music group, family trio Sons of the San Joaquin specializes in the harmony singing style popularized by the SONS OF THE PIONEERS. Brothers Jack and Joe Hannah sang

Pioneers numbers while growing up, and Joe's son Lon grew up listening to his father and uncle. Eventually Lon convinced them to form a trio.

Before pursuing music full time, the Hannahs worked as teachers and school counselors. They were invited to perform at the 1989 Cowboy Poetry Gathering in Elko, Nevada, where they were a huge hit. Later that year MICHAEL MARTIN MURPHEY used them as backup singers on his *Cowboy Songs* album, and their career took off. The act became a favorite at COWBOY MUSIC and poetry events throughout the West and issued two independent albums, *Bound for the Rio Grande* (1989) and *Great American Cowboy* (1991), before signing with Warner Western, which released two CDs showcasing the ensemble. *Gospel Trails* (1997), the group's first album for Western Jubilee Recording Company, featured a special appearance by DALE EVANS as lead vocalist on "In the Sweet By and By." Several albums for that label have followed, including 2005's *Way Out Yonder*. —*Charlie Seemann*

## Sony/ATV Tree (see Tree Publishing Company)

## Sony BMG (see Sony Music Entertainment)

## Sony Music Entertainment (Sony Music)

Sony Music Entertainment (or Sony Music) is a global record company owned by Sony Corporation of America. Its history began with the AMERICAN RECORD CORPORATION (ARC), founded in 1929 and bought by the Columbia Broadcasting System (CBS) in 1938. By this time, ARC had acquired both COLUMBIA RECORDS, launched in 1889, and OKEH RECORDS, established in 1918. Columbia became the leading CBS label, with subsidiary EPIC RECORDS organized in 1953. In 1961, CBS established CBS Records to release Columbia recordings outside the United States and Canada, and by 1968 the CBS Records Group included the Date and CBS Masterworks imprints as well as Columbia and Epic.

In that same year the CBS Records Group launched a joint venture with Sony, Inc., called CBS/Sony Records and renamed CBS/Sony Group, Inc., by the early 1980s. In 1988, CBS sold its half of the joint venture to Sony, which eventually retitled the label group as Sony Music Entertainment. In a joint venture with Bertelsmann AG's BMG label, Sony merged its music division with BMG to form Sony BMG in 2004, thus bringing BMG's ARISTA, BNA Entertainment, and RCA labels under the Sony BMG umbrella. Four years later Sony purchased Bertelsmann's interest in Sony BMG and applied the Sony Music Entertainment name to the labels complex. As of 2011, the company's Nashville division had strong-selling artists on its various imprints. Arista counted Ronnie Dunn, who went solo after the dissolution of BROOKS & DUNN, Brad Paisley and Carrie Underwood; BNA boasted KENNY CHESNEY and KELLIE PICKLER; Columbia's hit makers included MIRANDA LAMBERT; while RCA Nashville offered SARA EVANS. In May 2010 Gary Overton took the helm of Sony Music Nashville, the company's MUSIC CITY division. —*John W. Rumble*

## Joe South
b. Atlanta, Georgia, February 28, 1942

Although he may be best known in country circles as the author of LYNN ANDERSON's 1970 hit "I Never Promised You a Rose Garden," Joe South (born Joseph Souter) has had a colorful and varied career.

Raised in Atlanta, South entered the music business at age twelve with his own radio show on WYST. Nurtured by local impresario BILL LOWERY, South spent his teenage years working as a novice songwriter and recording artist (for the NRC label, 1958–60). In 1961 he took a stab at making it in Nashville, but he soon returned to Atlanta and hit his stride producing and writing chart records for the Tams ("Untie Me") and Billy Joe Royal ("Down in the Boondocks"). Additional session work as a guitarist for notables such as BOB DYLAN, Simon & Garfunkel, and Aretha Franklin as well as for EDDY ARNOLD and MARTY ROBBINS further raised his profile in the industry.

In the late 1960s Lowery landed South a deal with CAPITOL RECORDS, and South recorded his *Introspect* LP. Shortly after the album track "Games People Play" was released as a single in January 1969, South became a sensation, appearing on prime-time TV variety programs. The socially relevant lyrics and innovative production style of "Games" established the Joe South sound. Follow-ups "Walk a Mile in My Shoes" and "Don't It Make You Want to Go Home" placed high on both the pop and country charts. Soon his songs were covered by artists as diverse as Ed Ames, Deep Purple, JERRY LEE LEWIS, and Dizzy Gillespie. South released several more albums on Capitol, but following his brother Tommy's suicide in 1971 he retreated to the jungles of Hawaii. He returned in 1975 with one album on Island Records and has since been living in semiretirement in Atlanta. —*Ben Vaughn*

## Red Sovine
b. Charleston, West Virginia, July 17, 1918; d. April 4, 1980

Excelling in recitations, singer-songwriter-guitarist Woodrow Wilson "Red" Sovine scored most of his biggest hits with self-penned storytelling pieces, including "Little Rosa" (#5, 1956) and the trucking songs "Giddyup Go" (#1, 1965), "Phantom 309" (#9, 1967), and "Teddy Bear" (#1, 1976).

He started professionally with Jim Pike's Carolina Tarheels in 1935 on WCHS–Charleston, West Virginia. By 1947 Sovine had formed his Echo Valley Boys band, and they were making their mark on Wheeling's *WWVA JAMBOREE*. In 1949 he signed with MGM RECORDS and moved to Shreveport, where he worked the *LOUISIANA HAYRIDE* and hosted KWKH's daily *Johnnie Fair Syrup Show* after its previous host, HANK WILLIAMS, left for the GRAND OLE OPRY. Sovine joined the Opry in 1954.

On January 12, 1954, he made his first recordings for DECCA, with WEBB PIERCE singing harmony on Sovine's "My New Love Affair." "Missing You," a song Sovine wrote and recorded, was cut by Pierce and by JIM REEVES. Sovine's first chart single came in 1955 with "Are You Mine," a #14 duet with GOLDIE HILL; he followed it with the #1 hit "Why, Baby, Why," a duet with Webb Pierce. From 1956 through 1980, the year of his last chart record, Sovine recorded primarily for STARDAY and, later, Gusto Records, Starday's successor.

In 1963 Sovine heard struggling country singer CHARLEY PRIDE in Great Falls, Montana, and encouraged him to try his luck in Nashville. Sovine recommended him to CEDARWOOD, a music-publishing firm Pierce co-owned. Pierce introduced Pride to manager Jack Johnson, who landed him an RCA RECORDS contract. —*Walt Trott*

## Larry Sparks
b. Lebanon, Ohio, September 25, 1947

An important player of BLUEGRASS music's second generation, Larry Eugene Sparks has forged a deeply personal sound from blues, HONKY-TONK, and the traditional music of Appalachia. He is descended from Kentucky mountain folk who migrated north for work; his grandfather was a champion OLD-TIME fiddler from Jackson County, Kentucky. As a boy in southern Ohio, Sparks listened to WAYNE RANEY's country music radio programs on Cincinnati's WCKY and became a hot guitar picker on the local bluegrass scene.

The sixteen-year-old Sparks joined THE STANLEY BROTHERS as lead guitarist in 1964. In 1965, while with the Stanleys, Sparks recorded his first single, a cover of Carter Stanley's "It's Never Too Late," for Dayton's Jalyn label. After Carter's death in 1966, Sparks became lead singer for RALPH STANLEY, one of the leading traditionalist acts in bluegrass. In 1969 he started his own band, the Lonesome Ramblers, which celebrated its fortieth anniversary in 2009. The ever-changing aggregation has always featured Sparks's brooding vocals, blues-style guitar, and stubbornly traditional sound.

Early on, Sparks recorded for Pine Tree, Old Homestead, and STARDAY. His album *You Could Have Called* (King Bluegrass, 1976) boasted three-part fiddle back-up supplied by RICKY SKAGGS, DOBRO work by Tommy Boyd, and a title track penned for Sparks by R&B legend Charles Brown. In 1977 Sparks shifted to REBEL RECORDS; he remained there for nearly three decades. His 2005 Rebel album *40*, featuring many top bluegrass and country performers, won IBMA's Album and Vocal Event honors in 2005; Sparks was the organization's Male Vocalist of the Year two years running, in 2004–05. In 2007 he released *The Last Suit You Wear* on DEL MCCOURY's McCoury Music label.

Other career highlights include Sparks's masterful, low-key tribute album to HANK WILLIAMS and his renditions of such standards as "John Deere Tractor" and the gospel chestnut "Going Up Home (To Live in Green Pastures)."

Along with mentor Ralph Stanley, Sparks continues to carry the torch for hard-core traditionalist bluegrass. —*Eddie Dean*

## Billie Jo Spears
b. Beaumont, Texas, January 14, 1937

Billie Jo Spears is best known for her sexy 1975 #1 hit "Blanket on the Ground." Although she hasn't been on the U.S. country charts since 1984, she has enjoyed a considerable following in Great Britain since her first appearance at England's Wembley Festival in 1977.

Born Billie Jean Spears, she began singing professionally at age thirteen. In 1953, as Billie Jean Moore, she made her first recording, "Too Old for Toys, Too Young for Boys," for ABBOTT RECORDS and eventually performed the song on the LOUISIANA HAYRIDE.

In 1964 Spears moved to Nashville. Shortly afterward, A&R man Kelso Herston signed her to United Artists Records, and in 1966 she followed him to CAPITOL when he became head of that label's Nashville office. During her stint with Capitol from 1966 to

1972, Spears scored her first Top Ten country hit, "Mr. Walker, It's Over," but felt typecast by uptempo, humorous material.

After recovering from vocal cord problems, she returned to United Artists in 1974. LARRY BUTLER (who replaced Herston as label head) produced her fairly successful string of United Artists hits that ran through 1980. "Blanket on the Ground"—with backing vocals from the JORDANAIRES and PEDAL STEEL GUITAR from PETE DRAKE—became her trademark hit. Along with "Misty Blue" and "What I've Got in Mind," both Top Five recordings of 1976, it paved the way for her ACM Most Promising Female Vocalist award in 1976.

By the early 1980s, her records were becoming more popular in the United Kingdom than in the United States. She survived heart surgery in 1993 and has continued to tour, especially overseas. —*Don Rhodes*

## Buddy Spicher
b. Dubois, Pennsylvania, July 28, 1938

At the height of his career as a session fiddler, from the late 1960s through the 1970s, Buddy Spicher backed artists such as CHARLEY PRIDE ("Is Anybody Goin' to San Antone"), DOLLY PARTON ("Coat of Many Colors"), and GENE WATSON ("Love in the Hot Afternoon") on some of country's biggest hits. Later he did studio work with REBA MCENTIRE, GEORGE STRAIT, and GARTH BROOKS. His specialty was playing second fiddle (harmony) with fellow fiddlers, such as CHUBBY WISE and JOHNNY GIMBLE.

Norman Keith Spicher started playing at age thirteen and progressed to Wheeling's *WWVA JAMBOREE*. He first recorded at seventeen with Rusty & Doug (see DOUG KERSHAW) at WWVA for Admiral Records. At eighteen, he moved to Nashville at AUDREY WILLIAMS's invitation. Spicher was most visible on *The Wilburn Brothers Show*, but he was also a sideman for, at various times, HANK SNOW, RAY PRICE, FARON YOUNG, and THE OSBORNE BROTHERS. In addition, Spicher accompanied KITTY WELLS, PATSY CLINE, ROSE MADDOX, and LORETTA LYNN. Initially he lived at MOM UPCHURCH's boardinghouse, forming valued friendships with HANK GARLAND and SHORTY LAVENDER. "TOMMY JACKSON and DALE POTTER also helped me a lot in those early days," Spicher has said.

Spicher proved equally adept on pop or jazz recordings for Rosemary Clooney, Gary Burton, LINDA RONSTADT, and Henry Mancini. In the 1990s and beyond he has created his own studio, the Fiddle House, and continues to tour and record the occasional album. —*Walt Trott*

## Carl T. Sprague
b. near Houston, Texas, May 10, 1895; d. February 19, 1979

Known as the Original Singing Cowboy, Carl T. Sprague grew up working on a ranch near Alvin, Texas, and learned first-hand much of the COWBOY MUSIC he would later record. In 1915 he entered Texas A&M University, where he performed on the campus radio station. He left school for military service during World War I but returned to graduate in 1922.

In 1925, inspired by the success of fellow Texan VERNON DALHART, Sprague recorded ten songs for Victor (later RCA VICTOR), including Montana cowboy D. J. O'Malley's classic "When the Work's All Done This Fall," which sold an astonishing 900,000 copies. Sprague was not the first to record cowboy songs, for he was preceded by concert singer Bentley Ball, who cut "The Dying Cowboy" and "Jessie James" for COLUMBIA in 1919, and Charles Nabell, an obscure performer who made "The Great Roundup" and "Utah Carl" for OKEH RECORDS in 1924 and 1925, respectively. But Sprague was the first person known to come from an authentic ranching background who recorded cowboy material, and his popular "When the Work's All Done This Fall" helped ignite recording executives' interest in the commercial potential of cowboy songs. He made some thirty-three recordings for Victor in nine sessions between 1925 and 1927, including "Following the Cow Trail," "The Last Longhorn," "Is Your Saddle Good and Tight," and "The Cowman's Prayer."

Sprague came out of retirement to appear at a few folk festivals in the 1960s. In 1972, at age seventy-seven, he made his final recordings, an album for the German Folk Variety label titled *Carl T. Sprague: The First Popular Singing Cowboy.* —*Charlie Seemann*

## Square Dancing

Square dancing is an American dance form descended from European court and folk dances brought to the New World by colonial settlers. Steps and formations from English contra and Morris dances and French quadrilles and cotillions (as well as the French military drill) evolved into a dance that took hold chiefly in rural and isolated areas of the United States. Appalachian-style square dancing, sometimes called "Dix," was danced to the accompaniment of a single instrument, usually the fiddle. In areas where churches prohibited dancing and fiddle music, an unaccompanied form of rhythmic dance called "play parties" derived from square dancing.

Square dancing was introduced to a widespread audience in the 1920s, on country radio shows such as Chicago's WLS *NATIONAL BARN DANCE.* Curiosity about square dancing grew along with a public demand for instruction, and in 1939 Dr. Lloyd ("Pappy") Shaw's book *Cowboy Dances* further popularized this American dance form.

By the 1950s, teachers and callers were instructing hundreds of community groups in the rudiments of square dancing, which had also become a popular part of America's educational curriculum. Eventually, recorded music, specially metered for square dance, began replacing live bands at many gatherings.

As of 1965 there were approximately 30 million square dancers in the United States. By the 1990s, square dancing was bolstered by a resurging interest in country dancing in general. Currently there are thousands of square dance clubs around the world, their members competing for awards and traveling to dance festivals featuring nationally known callers. The square dance has been deemed the national dance of the United States.

Although innovation has played a role, most square dances are generally based on traditional configurations. Each square is made up of four couples; in each the woman stands to the man's right. The squares are directed by a caller, who sings or chants instructions (many of them rhyming) to the music—usually eight- or sixteen-bar Anglo-American folk tunes, country songs, or popular rock songs. Calls are arranged so that each man moves around the square, dancing with all four women, until he arrives "home" to his original partner. Traditional square dances include "Bird in the Cage," "The Virginia Reel" ("Sir Roger de Coverly"), "Take a Little Peek," "Solomon Levi," and "Marching Through Georgia."

Many early square dance callers were large-voiced hog farmers or auctioneers. Calling has become a unique art form consisting of approximately thirty basic commands, with more than 5,000 variations. Calls such as "allemande left," "promenade," "do-si-do," and "sashay" are borrowed directly from the French dance terms allemande, promenade, dos-à-dos, and chassez. Other calls, such as "ladies chain," "split the ring," and "grand right and left" are American originals.

Square dancing helped set the stage for the burgeoning popularity of other country dance forms, such as CLOGGING and LINE DANCING, although their respective roots can be traced to various sources. —*Patricia Hall*

## Joe Stampley
b. Springhill, Louisiana, June 6, 1943

Following a brief career as a regionally successful rock & roll artist, Joe Stampley turned to country music in the early 1970s. Teamed with producer NORRO WILSON and writers (frequently including himself) from AL GALLICO's publishing firm, Stampley released fifty-three chart singles between 1971 and 1989, on the DOT, ABC/Dot, EPIC, and Evergreen labels, plus nine duet singles with MOE BANDY, recorded for COLUMBIA between 1979 and 1985.

Through local promoter and *LOUISIANA HAYRIDE* performer MERLE KILGORE, Stampley signed with Los Angeles–based IMPERIAL RECORDS while in the tenth grade. He made four sides, and two were released. Later he recorded for Chess Records. Still in high school, Stampley joined a rock & roll band eventually named the Uniques, who recorded successfully for the Paula label in 1964 and hit with a Stampley-Kilgore original, "Not Too Long Ago." Another Uniques hit was a 1966 cover of New Orleans singer Art Neville's "All These Things," which Stampley later rerecorded for Dot Records, with great success.

Stampley's Gallico association began with "Not Too Long Ago," and it was Gallico who placed Stampley with Dot in 1970. Stampley's eighteen Top Ten country hits include "If You Touch Me (You've Got to Love Me)" (1972), "Soul Song" (1973), "Roll On Big Mama" (1975), and—with Bandy—"Just Good Ol' Boys" (1979), "Holding the Bag" (1979), and "Hey Joe (Hey Moe)" (1981). During the 1970s and early 1980s, these hits offered a hard-edged alternative to the era's prevailing country-pop trend.

Stampley has continued to record and tour. —*Todd Everett*

## Stamps-Baxter
established in Jacksonville, Texas, 1926

In the 1930s and 1940s, the Stamps-Baxter Music and Printing Company of Dallas, Texas, became the South's dominant gospel music enterprise. Home of leading religious songwriters—such as ALBERT E. BRUMLEY, Cleavant Derricks, W. Oliver Cooper, Vep Ellis, Eugene Bartlett, James B. Coats, and Luther G. Presley— the firm used aggressive promotional techniques that helped get the company's songs onto radio and records. Among the many Stamps-Baxter songs that have entered country and BLUE-GRASS repertoires are "Rank Stranger to Me," "Just a Little Talk with Jesus," "Precious Memories," "Farther Along," and "If We Never Meet Again."

Virgil Oliver (V. O.) Stamps and Jesse Randall (J. R.) Baxter Jr. founded the business in 1926. Songwriter-teacher Stamps (September 18, 1892–August 19, 1940), of Upshur County, Texas, began organizing singing schools in 1914. After starting his own publishing company in Jacksonville, Texas, in 1924, he issued the hugely successful collection *Harbor Bells*, with new editions released through the 1960s. In 1926 Stamps joined forces with singing-school teacher and prolific gospel songwriter Baxter (December 8, 1887–January 21, 1960), of Lebanon, Alabama. Advertising "new, snappy, and peppy" songs, the pair began a series of annual songbooks whose cumulative sales numbered in the millions.

Like JAMES D. VAUGHAN, the partners organized touring quartets, some of which included Stamps. But instead of starting their own record firm as Vaughan did, Stamps and Baxter helped place their ensembles on major labels. In 1927, one Stamps Quartet (featuring V. O.'s brother Frank) recorded "Give the World a Smile Each Day" for Victor (later RCA VICTOR), thereby creating a gospel classic and defining the type of happy, uptempo music the company would come to symbolize. The firm also established its own printing plant in Dallas, Stamps-Baxter's headquarters from 1929, and published custom gospel songbooks for country and gospel groups. "All-night singings" at the company's school of music helped inaugurate another gospel tradition, and a weekly radio program, "Singing Convention of the Air," further promoted sales of both shape-note and round-note songbooks.

When Stamps died in 1940, Baxter became the company's president. After Baxter's death in 1960, his widow, Clarice Howard "Ma" Baxter, ran the operation until its sale to the Zondervan conglomerate, a leading publisher of hymns, in 1974. —*Charles Wolfe*

## Ralph Stanley

b. Stratton, Virginia, February 25, 1927

When Carter Stanley's death in 1966 ended THE STANLEY BROTHERS' twenty-year professional career, Ralph Stanley reshaped the Clinch Mountain Boys to fit his personal approach to BLUEGRASS. In so doing, he became one of country music's strongest links to its roots in Appalachian folk music.

Pushed to the front of the band, he sang lead more frequently, his quavering vocals reflecting the lonesome modality common to the traditional music of western Virginia and eastern Kentucky. Instead of relying exclusively on Carter's songs, Ralph created a fresh repertoire of new and traditional pieces, using the Stanley Brothers' classic mid-1950s sound as a stylistic benchmark. He recruited young LARRY SPARKS as his lead vocalist and guitarist; seasoned LONESOME PINE FIDDLERS veterans Curly Ray Cline and Melvin Goins played fiddle and rhythm guitar, respectively. The Clinch Mountain Boys' clockwork rhythm underscored Cline's unadorned OLD-TIME fiddling, and virtually every performance featured one of Stanley's trademark clawhammer banjo specialties.

When Sparks and Goins left to start their own bands in 1970, Stanley assembled what many consider his finest ensemble, including Carter Stanley sound-alike Roy Lee Centers on guitar and former BILL MONROE sideman Jack Cooke on bass. Two eastern Kentucky teenagers, KEITH WHITLEY and RICKY SKAGGS, performed with the band during the 1971–73 festival seasons. During this period Stanley introduced a cappella gospel quartets to his shows; he also began his long affiliation with REBEL RECORDS.

Centers's death in May 1974 disrupted the band's momentum, even though Whitley seamlessly filled his position. After this point Stanley rarely broke new ground stylistically, although he continued to find new songs that fit his musical vision. When

Whitley left to join J. D. CROWE in November 1977, seventeen-year-old Charlie Sizemore replaced him. Sizemore's nine-year tenure sparked the band's return to form. During this period Stanley enjoyed some of his brightest moments onstage and on record. Stanley's son, Ralph Stanley II, assumed the lead singer-guitarist position in his father's band in 1995.

During the 1980s Stanley's contributions to American culture were acknowledged with a National Heritage Fellowship and an honorary doctorate from Lincoln Memorial University. In 1992 numerous bluegrass and country music greats paid homage to Stanley on *Saturday Night and Sunday Morning*, a two-CD set produced by Charles R. "Dick" Freeland. A second two-CD, multi-artist tribute collection, *Clinch Mountain Country*, appeared on REBEL RECORDS in 1998. Both sets won IBMA awards for Recorded Event of the Year. In 2000 Stanley joined the GRAND OLE OPRY.

Stanley's chilling rendition of "O Death" in the hit 2000 film *O BROTHER, WHERE ART THOU?* propelled him to new levels of fame, as did the song's inclusion on the movie's multiplatinum, Grammy-winning soundtrack album. He also performed the number in *Down From the Mountain* (2001), a documentary and concert film, and appeared on follow-up tours by this same name. "O Death" earned Stanley a 2001 Grammy for Best Male Country Vocal Performance.

Since then Stanley's albums have continued to win recognition. *Lost in the Lonesome Pines*, recorded with admirer JIM LAUDERDALE, garnered a 2002 Grammy for Best Bluegrass Album. The year 2006 witnessed Stanley's critically acclaimed *A Distant Land to Roam: Songs of the Carter Family* (COLUMBIA/DMZ). In that same year Stanley was featured in a special celebration of country music at the John F. Kennedy Center for the Performing Arts in Washington, D.C. Later in 2006 he received the National Medal of Arts, the nation's highest honor for artistic excellence. An autobiography, *Man of Constant Sorrow: My Life and Times,* cowritten with Eddie Dean, was published in 2009 by Gotham Books. Stanley has maintained an active touring schedule well into his eighties, often with his grandson Nathan Stanley sharing lead vocals. —*Dave Samuelson*

## Roba Stanley

b. Gwinnet County, Georgia, 1910; d. June 8, 1986

Though her career in country music lasted only months, Roba Stanley had the distinction of being one of the genre's first female vocal soloists to record. She grew up in Dacula, Georgia, the home of pioneering fiddler GID TANNER, and was the daughter of R. M. Stanley, a well-known local fiddler who often competed against Tanner, JOHN CARSON, and other early Georgia fiddlers. By age twelve, young Stanley was joining her father as they played for dances and political rallies and, beginning in 1924, over Atlanta radio station WSB. This led to a contract with OKEH RECORDS; later in 1924, at a temporary studio in Atlanta, Stanley recorded a version of the traditional British ballad "Devilish Mary," among other songs.

Though barely fourteen, Stanley had a clear, strong voice and a sense of tradition that gave her recordings a distinctive style. In 1925 OKeh had her back for more sessions, at which she cut "All Night Long" and "Single Life." Despite her professional potential, her entire output totaled only nine sides, and she was not interested in touring or following up with her music. In that year she met a young man from Florida and retired to marry him and begin a family. For decades she thought little about her early music until historians rediscovered her in the mid-1970s; newspaper feature writers had a field day, and Stanley eventually visited Nashville, where she was saluted from the stage of the GRAND OLE OPRY. —*Charles Wolfe*

## The Stanley Brothers

Carter Glen Stanley b. Stratton, Virginia, August 27, 1925; d. December 1, 1966
Ralph Edmond Stanley b. Stratton, Virginia, February 25, 1927

One of BLUEGRASS music's pioneering groups, the Stanley Brothers and their band, the Clinch Mountain Boys, combined elements from OLD-TIME MUSIC with the snappy, quick rhythms associated with BILL MONROE's 1945–48 Blue Grass Boys. Guitarist Carter Stanley's emotional lead vocals, complemented by his younger brother Ralph's soaring tenor, produced a distinctive, haunting duet.

The Stanleys formed their professional partnership in November 1946 after a month backing Roy Sykes over WNVA–Norton, Virginia. Recruiting Sykes's mandolin player, Pee Wee Lambert, and a local fiddler, the brothers briefly worked on WNVA before moving to the popular noonday *Farm and Fun Time* program over WCYB in BRISTOL, TENNESSEE-VIRGINIA. The station's powerful signal carried their music across a five-state area, helping make the band one of the region's most popular acts. By mid-1947 the brothers began recording for RICH-R-TONE, an independent label based in Johnson City, Tennessee. Their second release, "Little Glass of Wine," was a regional hit and resulted in a COLUMBIA RECORDS contract in late 1948. By then Ralph Stanley had abandoned his two-finger banjo style in favor of the three-finger roll popularized by EARL SCRUGGS (FLATT & SCRUGGS). A striking feature of the Stanley Brothers' Columbia recordings was a unique trio harmony structure featuring Carter Stanley's lead vocal, Ralph's tenor, and an even higher third part, or "high baritone," by Pee Wee Lambert. This voicing gave a lovely yet ghostly effect to songs such as "The Fields Have Turned Brown," "The Lonesome River," and "The White Dove," all penned by Carter.

From 1953 through 1958 the Stanley Brothers recorded for MERCURY RECORDS. The forty-five songs and instrumentals they made for the label are considered by many Stanley fans to be the group's finest. Generally, these recordings showed subtle refinements of the sound the Stanley's established on their Columbia records: tighter arrangements, more fluid rhythms, and higher vocal pitches, with Ralph's mountain tenor brought to the forefront.

From 1958 to 1965 the Stanley Brothers recorded primarily for KING RECORDS (though they also recorded in these years for the STARDAY, Blue Ridge, Rimrock, Wango, and Cabin Creek labels). In a span of eight years, King released a total of fifteen albums, making the act one of the most recorded bands in bluegrass. With King, the Stanleys recorded their only song to hit the country record charts, a comic novelty ditty called "How Far to Little Rock" (#17, 1960). During this period the duo also introduced lead guitar into their sound. Throughout the 1940s and 1950s, bluegrass bands had used the lead guitar mainly on sacred recordings, but the Stanleys were the first bluegrass band to give lead guitar consistent prominence in secular settings. The Stanleys' lead guitarists during their King years were Bill Napier, followed by George Shuffler.

During the 1960s, at the height of the folk boom, the Stanley Brothers often performed on college campuses and at folk festivals. Tragically, their twenty-year partnership ended on December 1, 1966, with the death of Carter Stanley at age forty-one.

Original songs made up a large percentage of the Stanley Brothers' repertoire. Carter Stanley composed more than a hundred songs during his lifetime, many of which have become bluegrass standards. His songs have been recorded by artists including PATTY LOVELESS, RICKY SKAGGS, JOHN CONLEE, and EMMYLOU HARRIS. Ralph Stanley continued with a highly successful solo career, and the Stanley Brothers' recordings remain a touchstone for bluegrass players and fans worldwide. —*Gary B. Reid*

## Jack Stapp

b. Nashville, Tennessee, December 8, 1912; d. December 20, 1980

As WSM's program director from 1939 to 1957 and founder of the enormously successful TREE PUBLISHING COMPANY, Jack Stapp was instrumental in Nashville's growth as a music center.

Jack Smiley Stapp was born in Nashville but moved with his family to Atlanta in 1923. At age fifteen he landed his first radio job at Atlanta's Winecoff Hotel, programming broadcasts that were piped into the hotel's rooms. Next, he studied at Georgia Tech and became involved with campus radio station, WGST, which ultimately became a commercial station; Stapp eventually became program manager. Later Stapp moved to CBS in New York, where he rose to the position of evening network manager.

In 1939 Stapp returned to Nashville to become program director for WSM. Over the years he produced many WSM shows fed to various networks, including *Sunday Down South, Hospitality Time, Mr. Smith Goes to Town, Riverboat Revels,* and the children's program *Wormwood Forest.* In October 1939 a thirty-minute portion of the GRAND OLE OPRY, the *Prince Albert Show,* sponsored by the R. J. Reynolds Tobacco Company, first aired over the NBC network. Stapp and station manager HARRY STONE worked with the New York–based William Esty Agency to secure this sponsorship, and Stapp rehearsed the program every Saturday morning.

Stapp was also a major decision maker in auditioning performers for the Opry. Along with Stone, he led the program's transition from a rural, STRINGBAND-focused show to one with broader audience appeal. During Stapp's WSM tenure the Opry added talent including RED FOLEY, LITTLE JIMMY DICKENS, HANK WILLIAMS, HANK SNOW, and CARL SMITH, among others.

*The Stanley Brothers: Ralph (left) and Carter*

*Jack Stapp*

During World War II Stapp enlisted in the army, studied psychological warfare in New York, and then moved on to London, where he helped broadcast Allied propaganda supporting the war effort. At war's end he returned to his WSM duties.

In 1951 Stapp and CBS-TV producer Lou Cowan, with whom he had served in London, formed Tree Publishing. Nevertheless, Stapp remained at WSM throughout the early 1950s and hired others to run the company's day-to-day activities. In July 1957 Stapp announced his pending resignation from WSM; he became program director for WKDA at the outset of 1958. This Nashville rock & roll station became #1 in the market. Stapp also continued as Tree's president, although he did not join the enterprise full time until 1964.

Stapp remained head of the company throughout its early growth, fueled by the acquisition of other publishing firms, including PAMPER MUSIC (1969), whose catalog held many valuable WILLIE NELSON, HANK COCHRAN, and HARLAN HOWARD songs. Meanwhile, in 1968 Stapp and WSM's IRVING WAUGH secured the *CMA Awards Show's* first network TV exposure.

In 1974 BUDDY KILLEN, Stapp's hand-picked second in command, became Tree's president and COO, with Stapp holding the titles of board chairman and CEO. (Killen acquired Stapp's interest on Stapp's death in 1980 and later sold the firm to Sony/ATV.)

Stapp was elected to THE COUNTRY MUSIC HALL OF FAME in 1989. —*Don Cusic*

## Buddy Starcher
b. near Ripley, West Virginia, March 16, 1906; d. November 2, 2001

The Boy from Down Home, as he was frequently billed, was born Oby Edgar Starcher, the oldest of eight children of Homer Francis and Leona Starcher. An expert builder, Homer was an excellent fiddler who taught Buddy chords on the banjo, probably to make sure he had an accompanist at dances. Buddy also learned guitar and was performing actively by age sixteen. In 1928 he left the coal

mines to make his living as a musician, first on WFBR–Baltimore. He then moved to WOBY–Charleston, West Virginia, but in 1932 was back in the Baltimore–Washington, D.C., area. That year he wrote "The Bonus Blues," about the "Bonus Army" of World War I veterans who marched on Washington seeking early payment of promised bonuses. The song's national success led to Starcher's appearance in a Pathé News film.

Next, Starcher broadcast on stations in several states, most notably WCHS–Charleston, West Virginia. There he hit with "Brown Eyes," a song he had introduced earlier in Baltimore. Starcher's later work took him from Iowa to Texas to Florida to Pennsylvania. In the 1940s he wrote two songs, "Sweet Thing" and "I'll Still Write Your Name in the Sand," that became country standards. In 1949 the latter song, recorded for FOUR STAR, became Starcher's first of two Top Ten hits. He also wrote "You'll Still Be in My Heart," whose melody HANK WILLIAMS used for "Cold, Cold Heart," as well as SLIM WHITMAN's first Top Ten record, "Love Song of the Waterfall" (1952). Starcher's biggest hit, however, as a songwriter and performer, came in 1966 with a recitation for the Boone label—"History Repeats Itself," which noted similarities and coincidences between the lives of Abraham Lincoln and John F. Kennedy. A #2 country hit, the record also made the pop Top Forty.

At this point Starcher left his Charleston, West Virginia, television show and relocated to Nashville. In 1968 he moved to Florida and then to Albany, New York, where he briefly retired. In the early 1970s he managed radio stations in Texas. He eventually returned to West Virginia, where he worked as a car salesman and appeared at festivals and country music parks. —*W. K. McNeil*

## Starday Records
established in Beaumont, Texas, June 1953

Starday Records went through several distinct phases. During the early to mid-1950s it was synonymous with East Texas HONKY-TONK MUSIC, particularly the records of GEORGE JONES, who started his recording career with the company. During the 1960s, it emphasized commercially marginal areas of country music, particularly, BLUEGRASS, OLD-TIME MUSIC, instrumentals, and older artists.

Launched in June 1953, by talent manager JACK STARNES (Star) and jukebox operator–record distributor HAROLD "PAPPY" DAILY (day), the label was an adjunct to both of their businesses and operated out of Starnes's base in Beaumont and Daily's in Houston. DON PIERCE joined in September and was made president, working out of Los Angeles. The company's first hit, ARLIE DUFF's "Y'All Come," arrived in late 1953. George Jones, discovered by Starnes, had become the label's biggest seller by 1956. Starnes, though, sold his share in 1955.

As of January 1957 Starday operated MERCURY RECORDS' country division under a joint imprint, Mercury-Starday. The arrangement fell apart in July 1958, and Pierce and Daily also parted ways at that time, dividing the Starday assets between them. Pierce kept the trademark and operated Starday out of Madison, Tennessee, with emphasis on promoting albums and using flashy covers to stimulate sales. He rebuilt the catalog with bluegrass and old-time music but also scored some significant mainstream country hits, such as RED SOVINE's "Giddyup Go," COWBOY COPAS's "Alabam," FRANKIE MILLER's "Blackland Farmer," and JOHNNY BOND's "10 Little Bottles." With the help of Martin Haerle (later the founder of CMH Records), Pierce aggressively marketed Starday product overseas and via mail order domestically.

Pierce acquired KING RECORDS and sold both companies to Lin Broadcasting of Nashville for $5 million in 1968. Lin sold them to Tennessee Recording and Publishing in 1971, and the masters (without the copyrights) were sold to GML in Nashville in 1975. GML revived the Starday trademark for new product and scored a #1 hit with Red Sovine's "Teddy Bear" in 1976. Since then, the Starday label has been used for reissues. —*Colin Escott*

## Jack and Neva Starnes
Jack Starnes Jr. birthplace and birth date unknown
Neva Starnes birthplace and birth date unknown

For a time in the early 1950s, Jack Starnes Jr. and his wife, Neva, were serious movers and shakers in the talent-rich Beaumont, Texas, country music scene. Jack Starnes came to prominence in early 1951 when he took over management of LEFTY FRIZZELL, at that moment the hottest property in country music. Neva Starnes managed a number of acts as well, including, briefly, prestardom RAY PRICE and, later, JEAN SHEPARD. Jack Starnes was also one of the original partners in STARDAY RECORDS, the label for which GEORGE JONES first recorded.

Before their management odyssey began, the Starneses owned a successful motel and restaurant complex in Voth, north of Beaumont. Looking to expand, Neva bought a Beaumont dance hall, and it was there that the couple met Frizzell. Jack Starnes signed Frizzell to a fifty–fifty management deal that soon went sour and resulted in a lawsuit in 1952. The lawsuit was settled out of court in June 1953, and within a matter of weeks, Starnes and HAROLD "PAPPY" DAILY launched Starday Records. Starnes did not remain with the label for long, and little was heard from him or Neva after the mid-1950s. However, their son Bill (who as a young man served time for bank robbery) went on to manage George Jones and TAMMY WYNETTE, among others. —*Daniel Cooper*

## The Statler Brothers
Harold Wilson Reid b. Augusta County, Virginia, August 21, 1939
Donald Sydney Reid b. Staunton, Virginia, June 5, 1945
Philip Elwood Balsley b. Staunton, Virginia, August 8, 1939
Lewis Calvin DeWitt b. Roanoke, Virginia, March 12, 1938; d. August 15, 1990
Lester James Fortune b. Williamsburg, Virginia, March 11, 1955

With a winning combination of musical skills, showmanship, professionalism, and business acumen, the Statler Brothers built a career that lasted almost half a century. For more than thirty years they maintained one of country music's top-grossing road shows and enjoyed great success as recording artists and television performers. All the while they helped extend country's venerable tradition of quartet singing, a tradition that reaches back to the genre's early roots in gospel music.

In the early 1960s, the group coalesced around the talents of four Virginians: Harold Reid, Phil Balsley, Lew DeWitt, and Harold's brother Don Reid. Harold Reid, DeWitt, Balsley, and Joe McDorman had worked in a Staunton, Virginia, high school group, the Four Star Quartet, making their first appearance in 1955. By 1961, when Harold reorganized the act as the Kingsmen, Harold's younger brother, Don, had replaced McDorman. The act featured country, pop, and gospel material but crafted their harmonies along the lines of influential white gospel quartets, such as the Statesmen and the Blackwood Brothers. To avoid confusion with a popular North Carolina–based gospel group also named the Kingsmen, they changed their name to the Statler Brothers (after Statler Tissues).

The year 1964 marked a turning point for the four young men. Early that year they joined JOHNNY CASH's road show. They would remain with Cash's troupe for more than eight years, and they were key members of his ABC network television show from 1969 to 1971.

A COLUMBIA RECORDS hit maker, Cash insisted that the label add the Statlers to its roster, and they made their first Columbia

*The Statler Brothers: (from left) Harold Reid, Phil Balsley, Don Reid, and Lew DeWitt*

session in April 1964. In March 1965 they cut DeWitt's composition "Flowers on the Wall," a #2 country hit that crossed over to #4 on the pop charts, won a 1965 Grammy for Best Contemporary Performance, Group, and helped the quartet garner another 1965 Grammy for Best New Country & Western Artist. But with the exception of two country Top Tens in 1967, they struggled to follow up on this success at Columbia.

As recording artists, the Statlers hit their stride after JERRY KENNEDY, head of MERCURY's country division, signed them in 1969. Throughout their long career with the label, Kennedy produced their recordings, even after leaving to form his own production company in 1984. The group's first Mercury single, "Bed of Rose's," became a Top Ten country single in 1970–71. Eleven more Top Ten records followed during the 1970s, many of them written by the Reid brothers. These included the nostalgic "Do You Remember These" and "The Class of '57," "I'll Go to My Grave Loving You," and the act's first chart-topping hit, 1978's "Do You Know You Are My Sunshine." They snagged another Grammy for "The Class of '57" and won CMA's Vocal Group of the Year Award six years running (1972–77) and again in 1979, 1980, and 1984.

The Statlers' third Mercury album, *Country Music Then and Now*, included their comic alter egos "Lester 'Roadhog' Moran & His Cadillac Cowboys," who parodied a fourth-rate hillbilly band from the waning days of live radio. An entire parody album followed, the hilarious *Lester "Roadhog" Moran & His Cadillac Cowboys: Alive at the Johnny Mack Brown High School* (1974). Subsequently "the Old Road Hog" was retired and, according to the Statlers' last report, was "recovering from an autopsy."

Never in robust health, Lew DeWitt contended with Crohn's disease, a disorder that sapped his energy and forced him to leave the group in 1982. (He died August 15, 1990.) His replacement, fellow Virginian Jimmy Fortune, joined on a permanent basis the same year. By now the Statlers were hitting on all cylinders, and during the 1980s they scored eighteen more Top Ten singles, including three #1 hits penned by Fortune: "Elizabeth" (1983–84), "My Only Love" (1984–85), and "Too Much on My Heart" (1985). Fortune also wrote the group's final Top Ten record, "More Than a Name on a Wall" (#6, 1989).

Though they recorded and did business in Nashville, the Statlers made Staunton their base of operations, and they continued to live there. In 1970 they staged their first Happy Birthday U.S.A. Fourth of July concert, parade, and community celebration. A powerful tourism draw, the event featured leading country artists as guest performers. It continued through 1995, with proceeds going to local charities.

From 1991 to 1997, a top-rated TNN television show widened the Statlers' fame as one of country music's most award-winning acts. This weekly Saturday-night program resembled a typical 1950s variety show—a strategy the group deliberately pursued to reach a wide, often-underserved audience. Although hit records eluded them, TV exposure supported their tours, and they consistently played to sellout crowds until they retired from the road in 2002.

Election to THE COUNTRY MUSIC HALL OF FAME in 2008 was a well-deserved ending for one of American music's greatest success stories. —*Colin Escott*

## Red Steagall
b. Gainesville, Texas, December 22, 1937

Russell Steagall, a longtime favorite among WESTERN SWING and COWBOY MUSIC fans, is a recording artist, songwriter, performer, producer, and, by act of the Texas legislature, official Cowboy Poet

of Texas. He discovered REBA McENTIRE singing the national anthem at the 1974 PRCA National Finals Rodeo in Oklahoma City and helped her land her first recording contract, with MERCURY RECORDS.

Stricken with polio at fifteen and left with diminished use of his left hand and arm, Steagall learned to play mandolin and guitar as part of his physical therapy. He earned an animal husbandry degree from West Texas State University and while there formed his band, the Coleman County Cowboys. Following graduation he worked as a soil chemistry analyst but continued his interest in music.

After RAY CHARLES recorded "Here We Go Again," penned by Steagall and Don Lanier, Steagall moved to California. He eventually became West Coast representative for Nashville publishing companies TREE and COMBINE, headed United Artists' West Coast office, and formed his own publishing company. As a songwriter he had cuts by some sixty artists by 1969. His best-known songs include "Miles and Miles of Texas" and "Lone Star Beer & Bob Wills Music."

Steagall signed with DOT RECORDS in 1969 and in 1970 moved to CAPITOL, where "Party Dolls & Wine" became the first of his twenty-three chart records. In 1976 he returned to ABC/Dot, and that year's "Lone Star Beer and Bob Wills Music," became a #11 country hit. In 1979 he switched to ELEKTRA, following with several albums for Warner Western.

Although he last charted in 1980, Steagall has continued to play the rodeo and western poetry circuit; publish cowboy poetry; host a syndicated radio show devoted to western music, poetry, and stories; host his own annual Cowboy Gathering and Western Swing Festival in Fort Worth; and record the occasional album. In April of 2003 he was officially inducted into the Hall of Great Westerners at the National Cowboy and Western Heritage Museum in Oklahoma City. Steagall was named 2006 Poet Laureate of the State of Texas during ceremonies at the State Capitol in AUSTIN in the spring of 2005. He is the first cowboy poet to be named poet laureate of his state. —*William P. Davis*

## Steve Stebbins
b. Chico, California, February 17, 1903; d. March 19, 1983

A former Los Angeles policeman who loved country music, Steve Stebbins got into the country talent business in the mid-1940s and wound up running the Americana Corporation. Throughout the 1950s, Americana was among the top booking agencies on the West Coast, its client list including, at various times, such stars as TENNESSEE ERNIE FORD, JOHNNY BOND, and LEFTY FRIZZELL.

Stebbins started Americana in the late 1940s as a partnership with Stuart "Buzz" Carlton and CLIFFIE STONE. Stebbins had met Stone during the war years when Stone had a popular morning radio show on KFVD. Recently retired from the police force, Stebbins had talked Stone into letting him book an appearance for him at a Ventura dance hall. Later, both were involved in *HOMETOWN JAMBOREE*, the country TV program hosted by Stone beginning in 1949, as well as in Americana. Stone got out of Americana to manage Tennessee Ernie Ford full time, and Carlton also stepped aside, leaving the company to Stebbins.

Though Stebbins, well liked by the artists, had a large stable, he was most closely associated with Frizzell. From late 1952 until about 1962 Stebbins played a role in Frizzell's career that was more than booking agent but less than manager. After Frizzell moved to Nashville, Stebbins never again handled such a high-profile artist, though he kept Americana active until his death. —*Daniel Cooper*

## Jeffrey Steele
b. Burbank, California, August 27, 1961

After achieving fame in the 1990s leading country band Boy Howdy, Jeffrey Steele wrote career-defining songs for numerous country acts.

Jeffrey A. LeVasseur began singing, playing piano and guitar, writing songs, and appearing professionally during his childhood. In his teens he divided his time between performing country music and hard rock in Southern California nightclubs. He adopted the surname Steele as a nod to his father, who cut metal for a living. In 1990 Steele formed Boy Howdy with Hugh Wright and brothers Larry and Cary Park. The band charted seven singles with CURB RECORDS, including the Top Five "She'd Give Anything." Steele moved to Nashville in 1994, disbanded Boy Howdy in 1996, and pursued songwriting, song publishing, record producing, and a solo recording career.

Steele has penned dozens of Top Ten hits, and his #1s include "What Hurts the Most," "My Wish," and "These Days," all by RASCAL FLATTS; MONTGOMERY GENTRY's "Something to Be Proud Of"; and TIM McGRAW's "The Cowboy in Me"; among others. NSAI named Steele its top writer in 2003, 2005, and 2006, and he was BMI's country songwriter of the year in 2003 and 2007.

Steele served as a judge on NBC's *Nashville Star* in 2008, and costarred on GAC's *The Hitmen of Music Row.* —*Michael Gray*

## Adam Steffey
b. Norfolk, Virginia, November 24, 1965

Mandolinist Adam Steffey is one of his generation's most respected instrumentalists. His grandfather, kin to the CARTER FAMILY, exposed him to BLUEGRASS and folk music during his teens in Kingsport, Tennessee, and bought him his first mandolin. Steffey's first professional group, the Boys in the Band, included guitarist-singer Tim Stafford. A stint with the Lonesome River Band preceded Steffey's enrolling in a bluegrass program at East Tennessee State University's (ETSU).There, he and Stafford formed Dusty Miller with bassist Barry Bales. All three joined ALISON KRAUSS (& UNION STATION) in the early 1990s.

Steffey collected five Grammy Awards with Krauss, including Best Country Instrumental for "Liza Jane." Leaving the band in 1998, he played with family gospel group the Isaacs for three years and then with bluegrass band Mountain Heart from 2001 to 2008. During those years he won six IBMA Mandolinist of the Year awards. He has played sessions with artists ranging from DOLLY PARTON and DIXIE CHICKS to the folk-influenced Michelle Shocked and jazz guitarist Bill Frisell. Steffey's first solo album, *Grateful* (Mountain Railroad, 2001), was followed by *One More for the Road* (SUGAR HILL, 2009). Today he plays in the Dan Tyminski Band and is a guest teacher at ETSU. —*Craig Havighurst*

## Keith Stegall
b. Wichita Falls, Texas, November 1, 1955

Best known for his production work with multiplatinum sensation ALAN JACKSON, Robert Keith Stegall has had considerable success as a songwriter and a producer. He also has been a recording artist with the CAPITOL, EPIC, and MERCURY labels as well as a Mercury A&R executive.

Stegall's father had played PEDAL STEEL GUITAR for JOHNNY HORTON, and Stegall learned piano, guitar, and drums by age fifteen. In high school he toured with a gospel band, the Cheerful Givers. He earned a B.A. in theology from Centenary College in Shreveport, Louisiana, his home until, on the advice of KRIS KRISTOFFERSON, he moved to Nashville in 1978.

In the early 1980s, Stegall found success as a songwriter with the hits "Sexy Eyes" (Dr. Hook), "We're in This Love Together" (Al Jarreau), "Lonely Nights" (MICKEY GILLEY), "Let's Get Over Them Together" (MOE BANDY and Becky Hobbs), and "Stranger Things Have Happened" (RONNIE MILSAP). Stegall also had cuts by Johnny Mathis, Helen Reddy, REBA McENTIRE, CHARLEY PRIDE, and others. In the 1990s and beyond, Stegall cowrote the #1 Alan Jackson hits "Don't Rock the Jukebox," "Love's Got a Hold on You," and "Dallas" along with "If I Could Make a Living" (CLAY WALKER), "Between an Old Memory and Me" (TRAVIS TRITT), "Love of My Life" (SAMMY KERSHAW), "I Do (Cherish You)" (Mark Wills), and "I Hate Everything" (GEORGE STRAIT).

Stegall's production work began in 1985, when he coproduced several songs for RANDY TRAVIS's debut WARNER BROS. album. One of these, "On the Other Hand," was named ACM's 1986 Single of the Year. In 1989 Stegall produced the demo recordings that landed Alan Jackson his ARISTA RECORDS contract. He has been retained for nearly every Jackson album since, and he has worked on projects with SHENANDOAH, TRACY BYRD, Jamie O'Neal, Clay Walker, and the ZAC BROWN BAND. —*Michael Hight*

## Step One Records
established in Nashville, Tennessee, February 1984; closed ca. 1998

Step One Records was one of the few independent country labels to achieve significant chart success during the years following the URBAN COWBOY boom. Although this Nashville label leaned heavily toward recording such veteran stars as RAY PRICE (1985–91), HANK THOMPSON (1987–88), and FARON YOUNG (1988–91), its most notable success was with a younger talent, CLINTON GREGORY (1989–93).

Step One was guided by songwriter-producer Ray Pennington, a MUSIC ROW veteran who had written and produced WAYLON JENNINGS's "I'm a Ramblin' Man," among other records. In 1984 Pennington was pondering retirement when singer Curtis Potter introduced him to Mel Holt, who became Pennington's partner in Step One. Potter and Ray Price became the label's first artists. Eventually Pennington experimented with younger singers, and in 1991 Clinton Gregory made a splash with "(If It Weren't for Country Music) I'd Go Crazy," which rose to #25 at a time when it was the only independent label release on *Billboard*'s country singles chart. Gregory later signed with a major label, MERCURY RECORDS, but Step One continued to defy the odds until shuttering in the late 1990s. —*Daniel Cooper*

## Ray Stevens
b. Clarkdale, Georgia, January 24, 1939

Ray Stevens may be known as the Clown Prince of Country Music for his novelty hits, but his list of talents is even more impressive: singer, songwriter, arranger, producer, music publisher, multi-instrumentalist, TV star, and real estate developer.

*Ray Stevens*

Born Harold Ray Ragsdale, Stevens began piano lessons at age six, and as his musical talents blossomed, so did his interest in many types of music. His family moved to Atlanta when Stevens was sixteen, and he began working as a DJ and performing in a small combo. Atlanta music publisher BILL LOWERY introduced him to the music business, got him signed to a small record label, and suggested he change his name.

While still studying music at Georgia State University, Stevens began recording for MERCURY RECORDS. His first self-composed chart-maker was "Jeremiah Peabody's Poly Unsaturated Quick Dissolving Fast Acting Pleasant Tasting Green and Purple Pills" (#35 pop, 1961), which heralded the string of novelty songs that would be his forte for the next three decades. He moved to Nashville in 1962, and in that decade he scored with off-the-wall compositions such as "Ahab the Arab" (#5 pop, 1962), "Harry the Hairy Ape" (#17 pop, 1963), and "Gitarzan" (#8 pop, 1969). When not recording himself, he worked recording sessions for various artists, singing harmony, arranging, and playing several different instruments.

In 1970 Stevens had the million-selling and Grammy-winning "Everything Is Beautiful" (#39 country, #1 pop) and hosted a summer replacement TV show for pop singer Andy Williams. Stevens's hilarious hits continued with "The Streak" (#3 country, #1 pop, 1974), "Shriner's Convention" (#7 country, 1980), and "Mississippi Squirrel Revival" (#20 country, 1984–85). Ironically, his biggest country hit was the straight (though unusually arranged) recording of "Misty" (#3 country, 1975), which also garnered him another Grammy.

From 1991 to 1993 Stevens operated an entertainment center in BRANSON, MISSOURI. At about this time he began selling video collections of his performances through enormously successful direct marketing TV campaigns. He has also continued releasing new recordings, including *Hum It* (1997), *Osama-Yo' Mama: The Album* (2002), *Laughter Is the Best Medicine* (2009), and *Sings Sinatra . . . Say What?* (2009).

Stevens was elected to the NASHVILLE SONGWRITERS HALL OF FAME in 1980. —*Don Roy*

## Gary Stewart

b. Letcher County, Kentucky, May 28, 1945; d. December 16, 2003

In the mid-1970s, when many country fans worried that loud, guitar-oriented COUNTRY-ROCK was threatening the art of HONKY-TONK singing, Gary Stewart offered them both in a single package. The tall, skinny singer-guitarist combined a rocking band with heart-baring hillbilly vocals as no one had, perhaps, since JERRY LEE LEWIS.

When Stewart's father was maimed in a mining accident, he moved his family to Fort Pierce, Florida. Gary played both rock and country in bar bands around town, where MEL TILLIS heard him and pointed him toward Nashville. Stewart recorded for Cory Records in 1964 and signed with Kapp in 1968, also writing hit songs for BILLY WALKER, JIM ED BROWN, and CAL SMITH.

Nevertheless, after seeing the Allman Brothers in 1971 Stewart went home determined to merge the new southern rock with his love of honky-tonk. Eventually RCA producer Roy Dea called Stewart back to MUSIC CITY, and they cut the Top Ten country hit "Drinkin' Thing," a barroom cry of desperation, with Stewart warbling in an over-the-top vibrato reminiscent of Lewis.

The singer soon followed with two smashes in the same vein, "Out of Hand" (#4) and "She's Actin' Single (I'm Drinkin' Doubles)" (#1). All three found a place on Stewart's 1975 debut album, *Out of Hand*. Cranked-up guitars and drums became even more prominent on subsequent albums, which produced Top Twenty singles including "Flat Natural Born Good-Timin' Man," "In Some Room Above the Street," "Your Place or Mine," and 1978's "Whiskey Trip," his last substantial chart-maker.

Stewart's albums were loud and wild by the standards of mid-1970s Nashville, but his live shows, featuring bluesy slide-guitar solos and wailing vocal improvisations, were even more so. This made him a favorite among younger audiences and rock critics

*Gary Stewart*

(*Rolling Stone* called him a "vintage country boy gone crazy"), but it made the Nashville establishment wary. Stewart's bacchanalian personal habits and indifferent attitude toward stardom also helped sink him.

Additional albums produced few hits, and by the mid-1980s Stewart's recording career seemed to be over; the singer went back to Fort Pierce and played bars in Florida and Texas. Marital problems and drug addiction, worsened by his son's suicide in 1988, kept him from recording. Then the unexpected happened: California's HighTone Records not only rereleased his greatest hits and early albums but also put Stewart back in the studio with Dea for three fine CDs issued between 1988 and 1993. Stewart kept touring honky-tonks, and he released *Live at Billy Bob's Texas* in 2003.

Nevertheless, Stewart became despondent after Mary Lou Stewart, his wife of many years, died in November 2003. On December 16 he was found dead in his home, from a self-inflicted gunshot wound. —*Geoffrey Himes*

## Redd Stewart
b. Ashland City, Tennessee, May 27, 1921; d. August 2, 2003

Henry Redd Stewart spent his formative years in Louisville, Kentucky, a city to which he returned after several years of working as a musician in other parts of the nation. The product of a musical family, he formed his own band when he was thirteen years old and began performing on local radio stations. While still in his teens, he went on the road as fiddle player with fellow Kentuckian Cousin Emmy. In 1937 he joined Pee Wee King's Golden West Cowboys, a move that took him to the stage of the Grand Ole Opry. When King's featured vocalist, Eddy Arnold, left the group, Stewart replaced him as lead singer.

While serving in the U.S. Army, Stewart wrote his first hit song, "Soldier's Last Letter," a World War II hit for Ernest Tubb in 1944. Stewart's most enduring compositions were the result of his longtime collaboration with Pee Wee King. The most famous song penned by this team is "Tennessee Waltz"—a 1948 hit for King, on which Stewart sang the lead vocal, and subsequently recorded by numerous artists. In 1950–51, it became a blockbuster crossover hit for pop star Patti Page. Other notable songs credited to King and Stewart include "Bonaparte's Retreat" and (cowritten with Chilton Price) "Slow Poke" and "You Belong to Me."

In 1947 Stewart and King moved back to Louisville, and for another decade *The Pee Wee King Show* was a regular feature on WAVE-TV. Stewart also appeared with King on King's TV shows broadcast from other cities, including an ABC network origination from Cleveland in 1955. After King's group disbanded, Stewart continued working solo, sitting in with Louisville bands and writing songs. Over the years, he cut his own records for the King, Starday, and Hickory labels. He had his own TV show at WBBM in Chicago for one season, 1956–57. —*Wayne W. Daniel*

## Wynn Stewart
b. Morrisville, Missouri, June 7, 1934; d. July 17, 1985

Though he never attained the career heights of Buck Owens or Merle Haggard, Wynnford Lindsey Stewart was, in terms of stylistic influence, nearly as important a purveyor of the postwar honky-tonk sound associated with the West Coast. He had a tremendous impact on Owens's style, and he wrote Haggard's first hit, "Sing a Sad Song." At the time, Haggard was playing bass with

Stewart, and when Haggard formed his own band, the Strangers, the nucleus of the band came from Stewart's group. As a singer, Stewart was so committed to hard, West Coast–style country that he once described his "darkest moment" as being "when some country artists recorded pop."

Stewart started playing guitar at age eight, and by the time he turned thirteen he had landed a radio spot on KWTO in Springfield, Missouri. A year later his family moved to Huntington Park, California, where Stewart formed a new band. He first recorded for the Intro label, and in 1956, on the recommendation of Skeets McDonald, he was signed to Capitol Records. He scored his first hit with "Waltz of the Angels" in that same year. In 1958 Stewart's "Above and Beyond," written by a young Harlan Howard, appeared on Jackpot, a subsidiary of the Challenge label. ("Above and Beyond" later became a #3 hit for Buck Owens.) Stewart recorded several lively duets with Jan Howard, Harlan's wife, and he had his first Top Ten record with his 1959 Challenge recording of "Wishful Thinking."

Throughout the 1950s Stewart employed top pickers, among them future Strangers Roy Nichols and Ralph Mooney. They, and Haggard, worked with Stewart at the Nashville Nevada Club, a Las Vegas nightspot Stewart opened in 1961. In 1964 Capitol executive Ken Nelson saw Stewart in Vegas and re-signed him to the label. Stewart had the only #1 hit of his career with the ballad "It's Such a Pretty World Today," released on Capitol in 1967.

Stewart left Capitol in 1972, and for the next thirteen years he was on the charts only sporadically. He died of a heart attack in 1985, unfortunately too soon for him to have enjoyed the acclaim his steadily rising historic profile later engendered. —*Daniel Cooper*

## Ocie Stockard
b. Crafton, Texas, May 11, 1909; d. April 23, 1988

A pioneer of western swing, Ocie Blanton Stockard was a charter member of Milton Brown & His Musical Brownies. During his career Stockard played tenor banjo, tenor guitar, and fiddle for a variety of western swing bands, including Bob Wills & his Texas Playboys and Tommy Duncan's Western All-Stars.

Stockard worked as a barber before moving to Fort Worth in 1928. His musical career began in 1929 when he became an original member of The Hi Flyers, one of Fort Worth's earliest stringbands. He also played dances with Bob Wills and Milton Brown at Fort Worth's Crystal Springs Dancing Pavilion. Stockard joined Brown's Musical Brownies in September 1932, playing tenor banjo on all of the band's recording sessions. Stockard provided the Musical Brownies with banjo rhythm inspired by New Orleans jazz bands. Additionally, he would take occasional improvisational solos and sing harmony. After Brown's death in 1936, Stockard worked for Milton's brother Derwood for a year before forming his own band, the Wanderers. Stockard's 1937 and 1941 recording sessions for Bluebird and OKeh are highly regarded by jazz fans. He recorded for King Records before joining Bob Wills in California in 1946. —*Cary Ginell*

## Dave Stogner
b. Gainesville, Texas, May 15, 1920; d. May 3, 1989

A western swing bandleader who experienced his greatest success when most of the genre's big names were struggling, Dave Stogner may have been the only bandleader of the 1950s to base his approach directly on the pioneering sound of MILTON BROWN's Musical Brownies.

Active in North Texas by his early teens, Stogner concentrated on fiddle but was proficient on a number of instruments. Galvanized by Brown's jazzy music, Stogner was leading his own band in Ardmore, Oklahoma, by 1937 and followed with stints in Oklahoma City and with the Sons of the West in Amarillo. He was in California by the early 1940s, starting his own band, the Western Rhythmairs, in 1944. Moving to the Fresno area after the war, he worked the San Joaquin Valley circuit and began recording for independent labels such as FOUR STAR and Morgan. Stogner appeared on Fresno television throughout the 1950s, but his fame did not spread beyond the area until JIMMY WAKELY helped him secure a DECCA recording contract in 1957. Stogner recorded a fine album featuring former BOB WILLS fiddler Joe Holley, who'd also been heavily influenced in his youth by the Musical Brownies and helped Stogner evoke the Brownies' spirit. Stogner's heyday was short-lived, and by the late 1960s he had disbanded his group. He reorganized it in the 1970s, however, performing and recording into the 1980s. —*Kevin Coffey*

## Cliffie Stone
b. Stockton, California, March 1, 1917; d. January 17, 1998

In a career that lasted more than six decades, Cliffie Stone wore a variety of hats. To the public he was a radio and TV personality, recording artist, comic straight man, MC, and bass player. Behind the scenes he was a record producer, talent scout, song publisher, and personal manager. In all these roles Stone was pivotal in the development of California's thriving postwar country music scene.

Clifford Gilpin Snyder moved with his family at age nine from Stockton to Burbank, then a hamlet outside Los Angeles.

*Cliffie Stone*

His father, Herman Snyder, raised dogs and was also the performer Herman the Hermit, nicknamed for his long hair and beard. Herman began working with pioneer Los Angeles country radio personality STUART HAMBLEN in the 1930s. In 1935, when Cliffie was eighteen, he also joined Hamblen, on the KFVD *Covered Wagon Jubilee*, as a bass player and comic known as Cliffie Stonehead. Hamblen hosted multiple daily shows on several stations and turned two of them over to Stone in the early 1940s. In 1944 Stone started a third program, *Dinner Bell Round-Up*, over KPAS (later KXLA) in Pasadena, featuring live music and comedy. He also freelanced as a bass player and ran his own record production company, Lariat Records.

Stone's work at Lariat landed him a job with CAPITOL RECORDS, in 1945, as assistant to country A&R man LEE GILLETTE. As a performer he played bass on Capitol country sessions with TEX RITTER and WESLEY TUTTLE and was instrumental in signing MERLE TRAVIS to the label. He and Travis cowrote Travis hits such as "Divorce Me C.O.D." (1946) and "So Round! So Firm! So Fully Packed!" (1947). Stone also had several Capitol hits: "Silver Stars, Purple Sage, Eyes of Blue" in 1947; "Peepin' Through the Keyhole (Watching Jole Blon)" in 1948; and "When My Blue Moon Turns to Gold Again," likewise in 1948.

As host of *Dinner Bell Round-Up*, Stone constantly sought new talent and added KXLA's morning disc jockey, TENNESSEE ERNIE FORD, to the cast as comic and vocalist in 1947. In 1948 the impresario founded a new Saturday-night stage and radio show: *HOMETOWN JAMBOREE*, produced at the American Legion Stadium in El Monte, California. The program debuted as a weekly TV broadcast in December 1949 over KCOP-TV in Pasadena. (In 1953 it moved to KTLA-TV, where it ran until its cancellation in 1959.) Along with Ford—the show's star—other regulars at various times included Herman the Hermit, Eddie Kirk, JOHNNY HORTON, Molly Bee, and FERLIN HUSKY.

When Ford was asked to perform in Las Vegas after his 1950 hit country and pop duet "I'll Never Be Free" with Kay Starr, Stone became his personal manager. In 1956, after Ford landed his prime-time NBC-TV variety series *The Ford Show*, Stone became producer, integrating Ford's down-home flair with the mainstream appeal that a network show required.

At the same time, Stone operated the West Coast music-publishing company CENTRAL SONGS along with Capitol producers Lee Gillette and KEN NELSON. After *The Ford Show* ended its prime-time run in 1961, Stone retired as Ford's manager but kept his hand in radio as a disc jockey and concentrated on Central Songs. The partners sold the enterprise to Capitol in 1969. In the 1970s Stone worked for ATV Music and later for GENE AUTRY's publishing firm. For his own label, Granite Records, he recorded TEX WILLIAMS and Molly Bee.

Stone was elected to THE COUNTRY MUSIC HALL OF FAME in 1989. After he retired, he continued to host occasional *Hometown Jamboree* reunion shows in Southern California. He died of a heart attack on January 17, 1998, at his Saugus, California, home. Stone's youngest son, Curtis, played bass with HIGHWAY 101 during that act's most successful years. —*Rich Kienzle*

## David Stone
b. Savannah, Georgia, October 27, 1901; d. August 31, 1995

David P. Stone was instrumental in the early growth of the GRAND OLE OPRY and in promoting country music in the upper Midwest. He grew up in Hamlet, North Carolina, where his father ran a

Coca-Cola bottling plant, and in Nashville, where his father later managed an engine repair and distribution company. After high school, David became assistant manager of Loew's Vendôme theater in Nashville and then took the manager's position of another Loew's house, in Memphis. Next he became roving relief manager for the Nashville-based Crescent Amusement Company, which operated theaters in Tennessee, Kentucky, and Alabama. As the radio boom of the 1920s gradually undercut vaudeville, on which theaters then relied so heavily, Stone took a job running the radio system of Nashville's Andrew Jackson Hotel, often announcing broadcasts fed from the hotel's ballroom to local station WLAC.

Stone progressed to an announcer's post at WLAC and to a similar position at Nashville's WSM, where his brother HARRY STONE was station manager. During the 1930s David not only served as a general staff announcer but also handled Grand Ole Opry broadcasts while running the Opry's booking department and traveling with Opry units on the road.

In 1940 Stone moved to KSTP in St. Paul, Minnesota, where he founded the long-running *Sunset Valley Barn Dance*. The program enjoyed TV exposure for a time, beginning in the 1950s, and spin-off broadcasts included both early-morning and noon-time radio and TV shows. *Hymn Time*, a Sunday-morning TV broadcast hosted by Stone, ran for more than 600 weeks until his retirement, in 1977. Prior to retiring Stone served for many years as KSTP's farm service director, and in this role he hosted special broadcasts from the Minnesota State Fair while also promoting the annual Farm Forum in Minneapolis–St. Paul. —*John W. Rumble*

## Doug Stone
b. Atlanta, Georgia, June 19, 1956

Health problems, including quadruple-bypass surgery in April 1992, have impaired Doug Stone's promise as a HONKY-TONK–influenced country singer. By that point Stone (born Douglas Jackson Brooks) had released seven Top Ten country singles—beginning with 1990's Grammy-nominated ballad "I'd Be Better Off (in a Pine Box)"—and three albums, all ultimately certified gold or platinum.

Stone's mother, singer Gail Menseer, taught him guitar, and at age seven he appeared on a bill with LORETTA LYNN. When his parents divorced, Stone moved with his father and two brothers to a mobile home in Newnan, Georgia, where his father trained him as a mechanic. The young musician formed a local band and eventually was discovered by his future manager, Phyllis Bennett. Nashville's BOB MONTGOMERY, A&R chief for COLUMBIA RECORDS, signed him to the company's EPIC label, changed his last name to Stone (reportedly to avoid confusion with GARTH BROOKS or Kix Brooks of BROOKS & DUNN), and produced "I'd Be Better Off (in a Pine Box)." Stone's later hits included the chart-topping "In a Different Light" and "A Jukebox with a Country Song."

Stone's chart performance slipped, however, after shifting to Columbia (1995) and ATLANTIC (1999). A stroke and another heart attack forced him to cut back touring in the mid-1990s. In 1999 and 2000, injuries from self-guided ultralight plane crashes slowed him further.

Stone has since recorded albums for Audium Entertainment and Lofton Creek Records, without commercial success. He also has battled other issues, including a 2005 sentence for contempt of court for failure to pay alimony and child support and a 2009 arrest for assaulting his twenty-two-year-old son. —*Todd Everett*

## Harry Stone
b. Jacksonville, Florida, February 14, 1898; d. October 8, 1968

Harry Leith Stone was one of the most important radio executives in the early history of country music. The son of a Coca-Cola bottling plant operator turned Nashville machinery distributor, he broke into radio at the dawn of the radio age. Stone gained his first experience as an amateur, when he and Jack DeWitt made broadcasts from the DeWitt home, with DeWitt serving as engineer and Stone as announcer. Next, Stone and DeWitt helped operate Nashville station WCBQ for the First Baptist Church and then ran WBAW for the Waldron Drug Company. In 1928 Stone signed with WSM as announcer and quickly became assistant manager; DeWitt assisted the station's engineering staff.

As station manager GEORGE D. HAY's failing health forced him to take frequent sick leaves, Stone replaced him in 1932 and set about putting WSM on firm commercial footing. He worked diligently to line up sponsors for a wide variety of pop, country, news, and educational shows. WSM's programming, much of it originated for NBC, continued to diversify after Stone hired JACK STAPP as program director in 1939.

Stone gained sponsors for the GRAND OLE OPRY and, with WSM librarian and Opry stage manager VITO PELLETTIERI, divided the show into the segmented format it retains. Assisted by his brother, WSM announcer and booking department manager DAVID STONE, Harry deliberately built a star system by hiring new professional talent, including PEE WEE KING, ROY ACUFF, BILL MONROE, and EDDY ARNOLD. Harry also helped convince the R. J. Reynolds Tobacco Company to underwrite a half-hour Opry segment carried by NBC, the *Prince Albert Show*, beginning in 1939.

*Harry Stone*

Harry Stone was well connected organizationally. He collaborated with Nashville's Chamber of Commerce in promoting tourism, chaired NBC's Station Planning and Advisory Committee, and worked with R. J. Reynolds to organize WSM's CAMEL CARAVAN tour in 1941–42.

By 1950, however, policy and personality clashes with WSM board chairman Edwin Craig and WSM president Jack DeWitt, who was placed over Stone in 1947, led to Stone's resignation. He moved on to manage stations in Texas and Arizona and filled a West Coast regional sales slot for ABC. From October 1958 to November 1959 he served as CMA's first executive director, but this organization, still in its infancy, lacked sufficient funds to implement his promotional ideas. From 1960 to 1968 he was advertising manager for *Tennessee* magazine, published by the Tennessee Electric Cooperative Association. —*John W. Rumble*

## Ernest V. Stoneman
b. Monarat, Virginia, May 25, 1893; d. June 14, 1968

Patriarch of a legendary musical family, Ernest Van "Pop" Stoneman helped establish country music's viability during its first wave of commercial success. Convinced he could play and sing better than other musicians who preceded him on disc, he journeyed to New York in 1924 to record for OKEH RECORDS. Early in 1925 he recorded his hit rendition of "The Titanic," a song memorializing the sensational 1912 ocean disaster. This became Stoneman's breakthrough number, and other sessions for OKeh soon followed. Accompanied by his own autoharp, harmonica, and guitar, the multi-instrumentalist and vocalist cut traditional songs ("John Hardy"), sentimental numbers ("Bury Me Beneath the Willow"), and event songs ("Wreck of the C&O").

Early on, Stoneman recorded solo for the EDISON label as the Blue Ridge Mountaineer, a name befitting his birth in the mountain community of Iron Ridge, near Monarat, Virginia. By August 1926 he began to enlist neighbors and kin in various combinations. His wife, Hattie; Kahle Brewer; and Eck Dunford played fiddle. Ernest's cousin George Stoneman played banjo, and Hattie's siblings Bolen and Irma Frost played banjo and organ, respectively. Hattie Stoneman, Edna Brewer, and Walter Mooney, among others, also assisted Ernest on vocals. For the Edison, GENNETT, OKeh, and Victor (see RCA VICTOR) labels, Pop and his musical cohorts recorded as Ernest Stoneman & His Dixie Mountaineers, amassing an extensive repertoire of sacred songs ("The Great Reaping Day"), tragic numbers ("The Fatal Wedding"), sentimental pieces ("Two Little Orphans"), and traditional tunes ("Old Joe Clark"). As Ernest Stoneman & the Blue Ridge Corn Shuckers, they also preserved rural comedy skits such as "Old Time Corn Shuckin'" and "Possum Trot School Exhibition."

Strong sales encouraged Victor Records producer RALPH PEER to set dates in BRISTOL, TENNESSEE-VIRGINIA, in 1927 to record Stoneman and other artists Stoneman recruited. The CARTER FAMILY and JIMMIE RODGERS, drawn by Peer's advertising, made their first recordings during those landmark sessions.

Stoneman prospered in the late 1920s as his recording income surpassed his earnings as a carpenter. During these flush times, he purchased home appliances to lighten the workload shared by his wife and daughters and generously loaned money to friends. But when the Great Depression set in, many of these loans went unpaid, and his record sales fell dramatically. In fact, Stoneman did not record between December 1929 and December 1933, and only six of the eighteen sides he made in 1934 were issued. His sessions of January 10, 1934, marked the end of his prewar recording career.

*Ernest V. Stoneman (center, on guitar)*
*with the Dixie Mountaineers*

In 1932, Ernest and Hattie Stoneman had moved with their nine children to the Washington, D.C., area, where Ernest found intermittent carpentry work. As hard times wore on and their family grew, the Stonemans knew poverty firsthand. At times they were forced to seek shelter in leaky, dilapidated houses, and more than once the children went to school hungry.

Prospects brightened with the improving economy of the World War II years, and after the conflict Pop began organizing a band featuring a number of his offspring, who eventually coalesced as THE STONEMAN FAMILY. During the 1960s, with Pop playing autoharp and singing, this group cut albums, worked folk festivals and clubs, and starred on their own syndicated TV series. Pop lived to see the Stoneman Family win CMA's 1967 Vocal Group of the Year award. Hattie Stoneman, who died on July 22, 1976, also witnessed this triumph.

Election to THE COUNTRY MUSIC HALL OF FAME in 2008 was a fitting honor for this remarkable musician. —*Ivan M. Tribe*

## The Stoneman Family

Pattie Inez "Patsy" Stoneman b. Galax, Virginia, May 27, 1925
Calvin Scott Stoneman b. Galax, Virginia, August 4, 1932; d. March 4, 1973
Donna LaVerne Stoneman b. Alexandria, Virginia, February 7, 1934
Oscar James Stoneman b. Washington, D.C., March 8, 1937; d. September 22, 2002
Veronica Loretta Stoneman b. Washington, D.C., May 5, 1938
Van Haden Stoneman b. Washington, D.C., December 31, 1940; d. June 3, 1995

The children of country music pioneer ERNEST V. STONEMAN forged a career for themselves with a style that fused an exciting blend of BLUEGRASS and country music. Although various Stoneman siblings were performing together by the late 1940s, the group grew out of a Washington, D.C., band called the Bluegrass Champs, which featured the fiddling talents of Scott Stoneman, sister Donna's mandolin work, brother Jim's bass, and the skills of nonfamily members. They emerged as winners on an *Arthur Godfrey's Talent Scouts* CBS-TV show in 1956. By 1961, following the addition of Van Stoneman on guitar, sister Veronica (Roni) on banjo, and Ernest "Pop" Stoneman as featured vocalist and autoharpist, the all-family group had set their sights on stardom.

The Stoneman Family cut a pair of albums for STARDAY in 1962 and 1963, with JACK CLEMENT as their manager. After moving briefly to Texas and then California, they recorded for the World Pacific label and worked at various clubs and Disneyland before finally coming to Nashville late in 1965. In MUSIC CITY they signed with MGM RECORDS and soon started their own syndicated television program, *Those Stonemans*, which ran into 1972. Their showmanship helped win them CMA's Vocal Group of the Year Award in 1967, but Pop's death the following year left a void. Older sister Patsy replaced him and exercised increasing leadership as time progressed.

The Stonemans moved to RCA in 1969 but had less success than they had on MGM. Although Roni's departure in 1971 and Donna's in 1972 took a toll on the group's audience appeal, Patsy, Jimmy, and Van carried on with the help of nonfamily sidemen. Donna later returned and Roni continued to work with them at times, but by the 1980s much of their momentum had ebbed. Roni established an independent image for some eighteen years (1973–1991) as a banjo picker and comedienne on the popular TV show HEE HAW. By the time of the biography, *The Stonemans*, appeared in 1993, increasing health problems for Jim and Van had rendered the group inactive. Roni continues to work as a solo act, Donna pursues evangelistic and gospel music endeavors, and Patsy also makes occasional appearances. —*Ivan M. Tribe*

## Carl Story

b. Lenoir, North Carolina, May 29, 1916; d. March 31, 1995

Although he recorded on major labels for a decade before using full BLUEGRASS instrumentation and never performed sacred music exclusively, Carl Moore Story is known as the Father of Bluegrass Gospel.

Story matured in the Carolina Piedmont and started his band the Rambling Mountaineers in the late 1930s. For the next three decades he maintained radio—and later television—bases in Knoxville, Charlotte, and Asheville, among other cities. Over these years Story's group included such key figures as Red Rector, Claude Boone, Harold Austin, Tater Tate, and the Brewster Brothers. Story himself favored the fiddle in earlier years, for a time performing with BILL MONROE at the GRAND OLE OPRY, though Story later switched to guitar.

Story's recording career began in 1947 with MERCURY RECORDS; he moved to COLUMBIA briefly (1953–55). Beginning in the late 1950s he recorded a series of bluegrass gospel albums for STARDAY and then recorded often for smaller companies. As the country music business changed, Story began working as a disc jockey through the week and taking a band out on weekends. In later years he resided in Greer, South Carolina; he remained active until the last months of his life. —*Ivan M. Tribe*

## George Strait

b. Poteet, Texas, May 18, 1952

George Strait sauntered onto the contemporary country scene in 1981 as a Texas traditionalist, a rarity amid the URBAN COWBOY phenomenon of the era. He went on to become one of the most successful, most enduring, and most influential recording artists in any field.

As of early 2011, Strait had achieved forty-four #1 *Billboard* country hits, more than any other artist. By then, he had earned thirteen multiplatinum, thirty-two platinum, and thirty-five gold album certifications from the RIAA. These certifications place him third among all musicians, behind ELVIS PRESLEY and The Beatles.

By this point, Strait also had won twenty-two CMA awards, including nine for Album of the Year, five for Male Vocalist of the Year, and two for Entertainer of the Year. He had compiled twenty ACM awards, among them Artist of the Decade, given to him in 2008.

Strait's influence can be seen as well as heard. His unadorned Texas rancher's look—cowboy hat, western shirt, and blue jeans—became the image of choice for a legion of young "hat acts" in the 1990s and beyond. His penchant for the WESTERN SWING and HONKY-TONK traditions of his native Texas helped revive both styles.

George Harvey Strait's parents divorced when he was still in grade school. Strait and his older brother, Buddy, were raised in Pearsall by their father, John Strait, a junior high school math teacher and rancher. The boys learned a cowboy's ways early on, helping out on the family's 2,000-acre spread. George didn't listen to much country music growing up; instead, he was inspired by the mid-1960s British Invasion rock groups and joined a number of garage bands in high school. He eloped after graduation with longtime sweetheart Norma and then signed up for a stint in the U.S. Army.

Stationed in Hawaii, Strait found his true calling: country music. In 1973 he auditioned and won the slot as singer in an army base

*George Strait*

country band and started absorbing the music of HANK WILLIAMS, GEORGE JONES, and MERLE HAGGARD. Haggard's tribute album to the legendary BOB WILLS, *Tribute to the Best Damn Fiddle Player in the World*, inclined Strait's ear toward western swing.

Back home, Strait enrolled at Southwest Texas State University to pursue a degree in agriculture, but he also set his sights on a music career. He hooked up with the Ace in the Hole band and began extensive regional gigging. The band also released singles on D RECORDS. Despite club success, several trips to Nashville failed to drum up interest in Strait as a major-label prospect.

Then Texas club owner and former record promotion man Erv Woolsey saw Strait with the Ace in the Hole band and liked what he heard. In 1981 Woolsey guided Strait to an MCA recording contract. Woolsey would remain Strait's behind-the-scenes advocate before eventually becoming his manager. When Strait arrived in Nashville, the urban cowboy movement was in full swing. His debut MCA album, *Strait Country*, yielded his first honky-tonk missive, 1981's "Unwound," which climbed to #6 on the *Billboard* charts and helped increase hardcore country's radio airplay.

As a vocalist, Strait proved a masterful interpreter. His Texas accent came through, but he avoided over-the-top twang and flashy fillips in favor of subtle phrasing. Through his love of Haggard, he developed both the evocative nuance of LEFTY FRIZZELL and the smooth shadings of crooners Bing Crosby and Perry Como.

Although his roots were in Texas dancehall music, Strait also had a way with pop-influenced numbers, such as "If You're Thinking You Want a Stranger (There's One Coming Home)" (#3, 1982) and the smooth ballad "Marina Del Rey" (#6, 1983). His #1 hits have

included his cover of the Bob Wills staple "Right or Wrong" (1983), the sly "All My Ex's Live in Texas" (1987), and his western swing treatment of "Am I Blue" (1987). Albums such as 1984's *Does Fort Worth Ever Cross Your Mind* emphasized Strait's roots in western swing and honky-tonk.

Personal tragedy struck in 1986 when Strait's thirteen-year-old daughter, Jenifer, was killed in a car accident. (Strait's only other child, George Jr., was born in 1981.) When Strait won that year's CMA Male Vocalist of the Year Award, he accepted it in Jenifer's memory.

By 1990 country's ranks had swelled with many young stars who dressed like Strait, but few were able to duplicate his keen blend of traditional and contemporary sounds. As evidence of his staying power, his blockbuster hit "Love Without End, Amen" topped the charts for five weeks that year.

Strait hit the big screen in 1992 with *Pure Country*, a film in which he played a disillusioned country star named Dusty Chandler. The soundtrack album became Strait's biggest seller to date, yielding the #1 hits "I Cross My Heart" and the album opener, "Heartland."

Although not a songwriter himself, Strait has relied on the cream of the tunesmith crop throughout the years, including stalwart WHITEY SHAFER and young blood DEAN DILLON. In more recent years Strait has leaned on the talents of singer-songwriter JIM LAUDERDALE, Aaron Barker, and Bruce Robison.

In 1995 Strait celebrated his fifteenth year as a recording artist by releasing the boxed-set career retrospective *Strait Out of the Box*, which flew out of stores in unprecedented numbers for a multialbum collection. The success of *Pure Country* and *Strait Out of the Box* catapulted the singer to another flurry of awards and top-selling albums that led him through the 1990s. In 1998 he kicked off the George Strait Country Music Festival, a multiartist nationwide stadium tour—a rarity in country music at the time.

Strait's winning streak continued into the new century. He occasionally experimented with new sounds, as heard on the hit singles "Run," "You'll Be There" (his first song to appear on the adult-contemporary charts), "River of Love," and "Living for the Night." At the same time, he continued his role as one of the few contemporary country stars to issue tradition-minded material, including the hits "Wrapped" and "Give It Away," the latter including a recitation. On his 2009 album *Twang*, Strait cowrote three songs on which his son Bubba shared writing credit; the album also featured his first recording in Spanish, on the traditional Mexican ballad "El Rey." Strait was elected to THE COUNTRY MUSIC HALL OF FAME in 2006. —*Chrissie Dickinson*

## Mel Street
b. Grundy, Virginia, October 21, 1933; d. October 21, 1978

A gifted hard-country singer, King Malachi "Mel" Street was steeped in the sounds of GEORGE JONES and other HONKY-TONK masters. Street enjoyed moderate chart success in the 1970s with singles such as "Borrowed Angel" (a Street original that became a Top Ten hit in 1972), "Lovin' on Back Streets" (the highest chart showing of his career, it hit #5 in early 1973), and "I Met a Friend of Yours Today" (#10, 1976). He seemed bound for greater stardom when he took his own life on October 21, 1978, on the morning of his forty-fifth birthday.

Street made his radio debut at age sixteen on a Bluefield, West Virginia, radio station. Later, in West Virginia; Ohio; and in Niagara Falls, New York; he worked in construction, as an auto body and fender man, and as an electrician. He played nightclubs in West Virginia and New York before getting his first significant musical break. This came in 1963 on *Country Jamboree*, a Saturday-night Bluefield TV offering on which he appeared regularly until the show's demise in 1968. Another TV program, *Country Showcase*, followed, eventually leading to Street's first record contract.

Street's earliest chart action—actually, the lion's share of his chart success between his chart debut in 1972 and his death six years later—came on various independent labels: Metromedia, Tandem, Royal American, and GRT.

Street shot himself just months after signing a major label deal with MERCURY. George Jones, who had admired Street's talent enough to write liner notes for one of his early albums, sang at his funeral. —*Bob Allen*

## Texas Bill Strength
b. Bessemer, Alabama, August 28, 1928; d. October 1, 1973

Singer and disc jockey William Thomas "Texas Bill" Strength spent years on the fringes of country stardom.

He grew up in Houston and began singing on area radio stations in his teens. Inspired by ERNEST TUBB and TEX RITTER, Strength first recorded for Houston's tiny Cireco label but joined FOUR STAR RECORDS by 1949. He worked at stations in St. Joseph, Missouri; Denver; and Birmingham before performing in 1950–51 for the CIO's *American Folk Songs* radio series and for CIO conventions nationwide. His theme song, "We Will Overcome," embodied the labor organization's zeal.

After a stint with Coral Records (1951–54), Strength signed with CAPITOL in 1955. During these years he worked on WEAS–Atlanta (1951–54) and KWEM–West Memphis (1954–55).

Late in 1955 Strength moved to Minneapolis–St. Paul, where he booked country talent into the popular Flame Supper Club, spun records as country DJ, and hosted TV kiddie shows. Briefly working California radio in Long Beach and BAKERSFIELD, Strength returned to Minnesota and recorded sporadically for SUN RECORDS, STARDAY, and several smaller labels in the 1960s and 1970s. Probably his best-remembered record (none charted) was his 1967 Starday parody "Hillbilly Hades." —*Ronnie Pugh*

## Stringband Music

Before the popularity of country vocalists such as JIMMIE RODGERS and the CARTER FAMILY, stringbands provided the most common form of rural country music. As the name implies, these ensembles comprised stringed instruments—fiddles, banjos, guitars, and sometimes a mandolin or autoharp.

The first stringbands consisted of fiddle-and-banjo duets. Early settlers in the American colonies brought the fiddle, and with it fiddle tunes, from the British Isles. The banjo, of African origin, became widespread by the mid-1800s. At about the turn of the twentieth century, rural musicians began to take up the guitar, adding to the stringband ensemble primarily for rhythmic accompaniment. The stringband tradition was well established by the 1920s, when the first country music recordings were made. Many bands adopted names intended to reflect their country roots: the SKILLET LICKERS, THE HILL BILLIES, EARL JOHNSON & His Dixie Clodhoppers. Repertoires of these groups included OLD-TIME fiddle tunes, folk songs, and popular nineteenth-century parlor songs, many of which had entered oral tradition.

Old-time stringband music remained popular through the 1930s but was eventually eclipsed by the advent of newer forms of country music, such as electrified WESTERN SWING and HONKY-TONK. During the mid-1940s BILL MONROE and banjo player EARL SCRUGGS pioneered a new kind of polished, high-energy stringband music eventually known as BLUEGRASS.

Enclaves of old-time stringband music still thrive. In mountain towns such as GALAX, VIRGINIA, and Mount Airy, North Carolina, many fine old-time fiddlers and banjo players still play for local dances and at banjo and fiddle contests, and many fans enjoy both stringband music and contemporary country styles. —*Charlie Seemann*

## Stringbean
b. Annville, Kentucky, June 17, 1916; d. November 10, 1973

Many country fans may remember David "Stringbean" Akeman only as he died—murdered with his wife at their remote Tennessee farm in 1973. But those who saw him perform in person or on *HEE HAW* realized that he was one of country music's most memorable comedians as well as a fine clawhammer banjo player and traditional singer. His distinctive striped shirt, low-belted pants, and funny duckwalk were as familiar as MINNIE PEARL's trademark straw hat. Signature one-liners ("Lord, I feel so unnecessary!") reflected his droll wit and deadpan humor.

Growing up in eastern Kentucky, Akeman worked in Civilian Conservation Corps camps during the Great Depression before receiving his first musical job, as well as his nickname, from country performer Asa Martin. After playing banjo for several bands around Lexington, he moved to Nashville in about 1942 and became BILL MONROE's first banjo player. Later in the 1940s he joined forces with fellow GRAND OLE OPRY member LEW CHILDRE for a duet act and became a protégé of UNCLE DAVE MACON. The older banjo player taught Stringbean many songs and even gave him one of his own banjos. By the time of Macon's death in

*Stringbean*

1952, Stringbean was working as an Opry soloist and adapting current songs to his clawhammer style.

Believing his appeal lay primarily in personal appearances, Stringbean postponed making his own records until 1960, when he began recording a series of extended-play discs and full-length albums for the STARDAY label. The first of these was *Old Time Banjo Pickin' and Singin'* (1960); the best-known and most reissued was *A Salute to Uncle Dave Macon* (1963). Later he recorded singles and albums for the Nugget and Cullman labels. Joining the cast of *Hee Haw* in 1969 rejuvenated his career, though producers typically featured his comedy more than his music. He often teamed with fellow banjoist-comedian GRANDPA JONES, a close friend and neighbor.

In 1973, the brutal murder of Stringbean and his wife, Estelle Stanfill Akeman, at their rustic, three-room dwelling shocked Nashville's music community. Two gunmen were waiting for Stringbean at home after a Saturday-night Opry performance in hopes of robbing him of cash rumored to be hidden there; they came away with a few guns and a chainsaw. Though the killers were caught and convicted, an important link with country music's tradition had been senselessly broken. In 1996, police discovered remnants of thousands of dollars stashed in the walls of the Akemans' cabin. —*Stacey Wolfe*

## Stripling Brothers

Charlie Melvin Stripling b. Pickens County, Alabama, August 8, 1896;
    d. January 19, 1966
Ira Lee Stripling b. Pickens County, Alabama, June 5, 1898; d. March 11, 1967

This powerful OLD-TIME fiddle-guitar duo from rural northwestern Alabama recorded forty-six sides for BRUNSWICK and DECCA between 1928 and 1936. Charlie Stripling had already established his reputation as a formidable contest fiddler when Brunswick set up a temporary recording studio in Birmingham. There, in 1928, A&R man JACK KAPP recorded the Striplings' virtuoso performance of "Lost Child." Its success led Brunswick to issue sixteen more Stripling numbers (breakdowns, rags, and waltzes) on the Vocalion label. In 1934 and 1936 Decca issued twenty-four additional Stripling sides, many of them "ragtime breakdowns" that Charlie Stripling composed for dancers who wanted to fox-trot and two-step. The Stripling Brothers are most admired today, however, for their masterful renditions of archaic fiddle tunes such as "Horseshoe Bend," "Big Eyed Rabbit," "Wolves Howling," and "Lost Child." Charlie Stripling's recording of this last is considered the source of the popular fiddle tune "Black Mountain Rag."

The Great Depression forced Ira, a storeowner, to end his musical career, but Charlie, a cotton farmer, continued to play through the 1950s at schoolhouse performances, square dances, and fiddlers' conventions across northwestern Alabama. When recordings by the Stripling Brothers were reissued by COUNTY RECORDS in 1971, their music gained another generation of fans. —*Joyce Cauthen*

## James Stroud

b. Shreveport, Louisiana, July 4, 1949

In the 1990s, veteran studio drummer James Stroud became one of country music's dominant producers, helping to shape the rock-influenced sounds that drove the genre to record-setting sales by mid-decade. His background in pop, rock & roll, and R&B helped him expand country's borders, and his drumming skills heightened his feel for the drum-and-bass-driven grooves essential to the youth-oriented direction country took in the 1990s and beyond. His production credits include hits by the likes of JOHN ANDERSON, the BELLAMY BROTHERS, CLINT BLACK, TRACY LAWRENCE, TIM MCGRAW, and DOUG STONE.

Stroud got his start by filling in for another drummer at the R&B-oriented Malaco Studios in Jackson, Mississippi. His role in Jean Knight's "Mr. Big Stuff" and King Floyd's "Groove Me" secured his standing as a session musician. Working in Jackson, Atlanta, and Los Angeles, Stroud played on such 1970s pop hits as the Pointer Sisters' "Yes We Can Can" and Melissa Manchester's "Midnight Blue."

EDDIE RABBITT's producer, David Malloy, called on Stroud to work on Rabbitt's *Horizon* album, which yielded the 1980–81 crossover smashes "Drivin' My Life Away" and "I Love a Rainy Night." Stroud moved to Nashville and became a busy session drummer, contributing to EDDY RAVEN's "I'm Gonna Get You," TANYA TUCKER's "Highway Robbery," and CONWAY TWITTY's "That's My Job."

Having produced Dorothy Moore's 1976 pop-soul hit "Misty Blue," Stroud also produced Fred Knobloch's 1980 minor pop-country success "Why Not Me." After working in the creative departments at MCA RECORDS and CAPITOL, in 1991 Stroud became president of GIANT RECORDS' newly opened Nashville office. There he supervised the careers of artists including CARLENE CARTER, Daryle Singletary, and CLAY WALKER while also producing non-Giant acts. (In addition, he had established Loud Recording Studio and his own publishing house).

Stroud left Giant in 1997 to head the Nashville offices of DREAMWORKS RECORDS, where he oversaw the advancement of TOBY KEITH, TRACY LAWRENCE, RANDY TRAVIS, and DARRYL WORLEY. Following Universal Music Group's purchase of Dream-Works—and DreamWorks' closure in late 2005—Stroud became

*James Stroud*

cochairman (with Luke Lewis) of UMG Nashville, home to superstars VINCE GILL, REBA MCENTIRE, GEORGE STRAIT, SUGARLAND, and TRISHA YEARWOOD. In early 2007 Stroud resigned to focus on producing BILLY CURRINGTON and other artists. In 2008 Stroud launched Stroudavarious Records in partnership with Ronnie Gilley Entertainment. In addition to Worley, by early 2011 the label's roster included singer Richie McDonald, formerly of LONESTAR, and the solo country recordings of Aaron Lewis, lead singer of the rock band Staind. —*Tom Roland*

## Henry Strzelecki
b. Birmingham, Alabama, August 8, 1939

In thirty years as one of Nashville's most in-demand bassists, Henry P. Strzelecki (pronounced Struh-lecki) performed on at least 500 Top Ten hits, more than 120 of which went #1. He's on ROY ORBISON's pop million-seller "Oh, Pretty Woman," CONWAY TWITTY's "Happy Birthday, Darlin'," and GEORGE JONES's "He Stopped Loving Her Today."

Strzelecki's idol, HANK GARLAND, recruited him for a 1956 DECCA RECORDS session for new singer Baker Knight, produced by OWEN BRADLEY. Meanwhile, with brother Larry and friends, Strzelecki formed the Four Flickers and recorded a Strzelecki original called "Long Tall Texan"; Strzelecki sang, and the record was issued under a pseudonym, Hank Wallis. Though it made no impression on the national charts, a cover by Murry Kellum was a #51 pop hit in 1963. (The Beach Boys and LYLE LOVETT also covered the song.)

In 1960 Strzelecki moved to Nashville, and CHET ATKINS hired him for an EDDY ARNOLD session. In the busy years that followed, Strzelecki backed Fats Domino, Gordon Lightfoot, Simon & Garfunkel, Perry Como, and BOB DYLAN, in addition to numerous country artists. After a mild stroke that impaired his hearing, the bassist retired in the late 1980s. —*Walt Trott*

## Marty Stuart
b. Philadelphia, Mississippi, September 30, 1958

As vigorously as any country performer, John Marty Stuart openly expresses his love for the genre's traditions and his loyalty to the artists who have made the music what it is. As a recording artist, he had achieved four gold albums and six Top Ten hits as of 2011. But he is valued beyond those chart numbers, both for his creative eclecticism (he's recorded BLUEGRASS, HONKY-TONK, COUNTRY-ROCK, gospel, AMERICANA, and a suite of Native American songs) and for his devotion to country music as an important expression of American culture.

Stuart has befriended and recorded with numerous contemporary and legendary figures; he owns an extensive collection of country music artifacts; he has published books and magazine articles of writing and photography about country musicians; he has served as president of the board of officers and trustees of the COUNTRY MUSIC HALL OF FAME AND MUSEUM; and, starting in 2008, he hosted an old-fashioned country TV series on the RFD cable network. His unbridled enthusiasm feeds his songwriting, his recordings, his concerts, and his TV appearances.

A top-notch guitarist and mandolinist and a songwriter with cuts by the likes of WYNONNA and GEORGE STRAIT, Stuart has played onstage or in the studio with JOHNNY CASH, BOB DYLAN, EMMYLOU HARRIS, WAYLON JENNINGS, WILLIE NELSON, the Staple

Singers, ERNEST TUBB, and NEIL YOUNG. He first toured at age twelve with Jerry and Tammy Sullivan, a gospel group. Bluegrass legend LESTER FLATT hired a thirteen-year-old Stuart as a mandolinist; they played together for six years until Flatt died in 1979. The youngster switched to electric guitar for a tour with VASSAR CLEMENTS's Hillbilly Jazz and then back to acoustic guitar to play with DOC WATSON and his son, Merle. For several years Stuart backed his biggest hero of all, Johnny Cash. Stuart was briefly married to Cash's daughter Cindy.

In 1977 Stuart released his debut solo album, *Marty, With a Little Help from My Friends,* on the bluegrass label Ridge Runner; then came 1982's *Busy Bee Café* on the larger SUGAR HILL label. In 1986 he signed with COLUMBIA RECORDS, but the ROCKABILLY-influenced album *Marty Stuart* didn't sell, and Columbia didn't release the follow-up, *Let There Be Country*, until 1992, after he had scored hits for MCA RECORDS.

Stuart's first MCA album, 1989's *Hillbilly Rock*, featured traditional country music with a rhythmic kick. The same approach fueled 1991's *Tempted*, which yielded two Top Ten singles: "Burn Me Down" and the title track. About this time, Stuart cowrote "The Whiskey Ain't Workin'" for a TRAVIS TRITT album. The two musicians became buddies, and Tritt asked Stuart to sing a duet vocal on the song, which went to #2 in 1991.

In 1992, the year Stuart joined the GRAND OLE OPRY, he and Tritt hit the road on their "No Hats Tour," an irreverent allusion to the male "hat acts" dominating Nashville at that time. In 1994 Stuart's album *Love and Luck* received a lackluster reception, and none of its songs appeared on the 1995 anthology *The Marty Party Hit Pack*. His 1996 album, *Honky Tonkin's What I Do Best,* included two Top Forty songs.

In 1997 Stuart married country singer CONNIE SMITH; in 1998 he produced her comeback album on WARNER BROS. RECORDS and cowrote eight of its ten songs. Not having a Top Ten hit since 1992, Stuart gambled with his 1999 album, the artistically ambitious

*Marty Stuart*

*The Pilgrim.* Although critically acclaimed, the songs received little airplay and sales were stagnant.

Stuart left MCA in 2000, returned to Columbia, and issued the 2003 album *Marty Stuart and the Fabulous Superlatives,* featuring guitarist Kenny Vaughan and drummer Harry Stinson. In 2005, he launched his own label, Superlatone Records, releasing a gospel collection (*Soul's Chapel*), a concept album honoring Native American culture (*Badlands: Ballads of the Lakota*), and a live album recorded at THE RYMAN AUDITORIUM. He also produced PORTER WAGONER's final album, *Wagonmaster,* and in 2010 he released *Ghost Train*, a tribute to RCA Studio B recorded in the historic MUSIC ROW landmark.

The popular *Marty Stuart Show* debuted on the RFD cable TV network in November 2008 and completed its second season in the summer of 2010. —*Geoffrey Himes*

## Eddie Stubbs (*see* Johnson Mountain Boys)

## Nat Stuckey
b. Cass County, Texas, December 17, 1933; d. August 24, 1988

Nathan Wright Stuckey II was a successful disc jockey, songwriter, and recording artist. He earned a degree in radio and TV from Arlington State College (Texas) and then worked as a DJ at KALT in Atlanta, Texas, before spending two years in the U.S. Army. After returning to KALT, he later joined KWKH–Shreveport, where he served as an announcer for the *LOUISIANA HAYRIDE.*

Stuckey's "Sweet Thang," on Paula Records, was a #4 country hit of 1966. Two years later his first RCA single, the risqué "Plastic Saddle," reached #9. He continued to record for RCA until 1976 but had only two other Top Ten recordings, "Sweet Thang and Cisco" in 1969 and "Take Time to Love Her," in 1973. In 1976 he switched to MCA but never had another major hit.

As a songwriter, however, Stuckey hit pay dirt with "Waitin' in Your Welfare Line," a #1 hit for BUCK OWENS in 1966, and "Pop-a-Top" (#3, 1967) by JIM ED BROWN. Additionally, "Sweet Thang" was a 1967 chart-maker for ERNEST TUBB and LORETTA LYNN. After Stuckey's recording career ended he made numerous commercials before his death, from lung cancer, on August 24, 1988. —*Don Cusic*

## Sugar Hill Records
established in Durham, North Carolina, 1978

Independent label Sugar Hill Records was founded in 1978 in Durham, North Carolina, by Barry Poss (b. Brantford, Ontario, Canada, September 7, 1945), who came to Durham in 1968 to study sociology at Duke University. Interested in OLD-TIME MUSIC, in 1975 he joined the staff of David Freeman's COUNTY RECORDS, then newly located in Floyd, Virginia. In 1978 Poss produced *Mountain Fiddler* by Senator Robert Byrd and *Texas Crapshooter* by fiddler Bobby Hicks. The latter album, which included electric instruments, was such a radical departure from County's traditional fare that Freeman saw a need for a new, distinct label and enlisted Poss to start it. Sugar Hill (named for an old-time tune) would operate in tandem with County, with both labels sharing warehousing.

Poss eventually gained full control of Sugar Hill and sold it in 1998 to the Welk Music Group. Poss remained president and became chairman in 2002. Sugar Hill moved from Durham to Nashville in 2007.

Early on, the label found success with RICKY SKAGGS's Boone Creek and his solo albums. These efforts led to Skaggs's EPIC albums and fueled Nashville's NEW TRADITIONALISM movement. Sugar Hill acts of the 1980s and '90s included GUY CLARK, CARL JACKSON, ROBERT EARL KEEN, NASHVILLE BLUEGRASS BAND, DOYLE LAWSON & QUICKSILVER, PETER ROWAN, the SELDOM SCENE, BILLY JOE SHAVER, TOWNES VAN ZANDT, and DOC WATSON. DOLLY PARTON released her first Sugar Hill album, *The Grass Is Blue*, in 1999.

By the 2000s Sugar Hill's roster was diversifying beyond BLUE-GRASS, country, and folk into the AMERICANA field. In addition to recordings by Parton, Clark, and bluegrass- or folk-based acts NICKEL CREEK, TIM O'BRIEN, ADAM STEFFEY, and BRYAN SUTTON, Sugar Hill has released albums by Sarah Jarosz, Black Prairie, and Donna the Buffalo.

Over the years, numerous Grammys and IBMA awards won by Sugar Hill artists have heightened the label's profile. Barry Poss received an Americana Music Association Lifetime Achievement Award in 2006. —*Tom Ewing*

## Sugarland
Jennifer Odessa Nettles, b. Douglas, Georgia, September 12, 1974
Kristian Merrill Bush, b. Knoxville, Tennessee, March 14, 1970
Kristen Alison Hall, b. Grosse Pointe, Michigan, October 26, 1964

Formed by three musicians from folk and rock backgrounds, Sugarland appeared in the 2000s as an unlikely country powerhouse. But their jangling melodies, high-energy live shows, and lead

*Sugarland: Jennifer Nettles and Kristian Bush*

singer's belting, soul-tinged voice gave Sugarland a COUNTRY-ROCK appeal that placed them just behind country stars CARRIE UNDERWOOD and TAYLOR SWIFT as crossover artists.

By 2003 lead vocalist Jennifer Nettles, Kristian Bush, and Kristen Hall met through the Atlanta rock scene and formed Sugarland. Bush had been half of the indie-rock duo Billy Pilgrim, Hall was already an established singer-songwriter, and Nettles had fronted several regionally successful bands. Their combined experience helped them navigate their skyrocketing career after their debut for MERCURY, *Twice the Speed of Life* (2004), went multiplatinum on the strength of three country Top Ten singles, two of which also made *Billboard*'s all-genre Hot 100 chart. Still, a grueling tour schedule and constant media attention took their toll, and in 2006 Kristen Hall abruptly left the band to return to songwriting. (A 2008 lawsuit against the band fueled speculation that she had been forced out because of her weight or open lesbianism.)

Hall had been Sugarland's songwriting force, but on *Enjoy the Ride* (2006) Nettles and Bush proved their own writing skills while scoring another multiplatinum success. The album's biggest hit, the Nettles original "Stay," broke the Top Forty on the Hot 100 chart and netted Grammys for Best Country Performance by a Duo or Group and Best Country Song.

To keep their sound fresh, the duo coproduced their third album, *Love on the Inside* (2008), and recorded it in Atlanta. The album's rootsier feel and spare production contrasted sharply with the pop sounds of many of their country contemporaries. Their fans embraced it nonetheless, giving the band three #1 singles and confirming their place among Nashville's hottest, and most reliable, hit makers. The 2010 album *The Incredible Machine* continued their crossover success, with lead-off single "Stuck Like Glue" reaching #2 on the country charts and #17 on the *Billboard* Hot 100. The album was certified platinum by the RIAA in early 2011. —*Diane Pecknold*

## Gene Sullivan (*see* Wiley & Gene)

## Sun Records
established in Memphis, Tennessee, February 1952

Whether it was JOHNNY CASH's lanky railroad rhythms or ELVIS PRESLEY's shotgun marriage of nearly every form of American music that preceded him, the cast of musicians and producers at Sun Records in Memphis reimagined what pop music could do. Their efforts in the 1950s have profoundly affected the course of popular culture ever since.

Sun was established in 1952 as an outgrowth of producer SAM PHILLIPS's Memphis Recording Service, at 706 Union Avenue. For several years the label's only employee was Phillips's secretary, Marion Keisker, whose own understanding of new talent made her an ideal associate. Phillips's brother Jud and JIM BULLEIT of Nashville were early investors in the label.

Sam Phillips cut his earliest blues recordings (e.g., of Bobby Bland, B. B. King, and Howlin' Wolf) at his Union Avenue studio but released them on leading independent labels, such as Chess and RPM. The first single to appear on the Sun label, Johnny London's "Drivin' Slow," was a bluesy instrumental. From 1952 to 1954 Sun released classic R&B records by Rufus Thomas, the Prisonaires, Little Junior's Blue Flames, and Little Milton.

In 1954 Sun released Earl Peterson's "Boogie Blues" and began its move into recording country music just as elemental as its blues catalog. Phillips's interest in mixing country and blues

produced Sun's greatest triumph. In early 1954 Sun released "My Kind of Carrying On," the lone single by Doug Poindexter, whose Starlite Wranglers included bassist Bill Black and guitarist Scotty Moore. Phillips introduced Black and Moore to Elvis Presley, whose 1954–55 Sun sessions yielded "That's All Right" (recorded July 5, 1954), a record many consider to have announced the arrival of rock & roll. The top tier of Sun's performers soon included Johnny Cash (1955–58), JERRY LEE LEWIS (1956–63), and CARL PERKINS (1954–58).

When the pop-music market turned away from Sun's hard-edged sound, the label still put out exciting records—Phillips's protégé JACK CLEMENT produced more and more sessions into 1959—but scored fewer hits. By 1960 all the label's major performers except Lewis had gone, and new discoveries, such as CHARLIE RICH (whose records appeared on the affiliated label Phillips International), were more successful artistically than commercially. What's more, crosstown independent-label rivals Hi and Satellite/Stax picked up on Sun's method—blending country and blues—in new, exciting ways. Phillips opened a second studio, at 639 Madison, in 1960, and soon thereafter bought a studio in Nashville, where BILLY SHERRILL served as his engineer. (Phillips later sold the Nashville facility to FRED FOSTER of MONUMENT RECORDS.)

In 1969 Phillips sold the Sun label and its catalog to Nashville-based recording executive SHELBY SINGLETON. Under Singleton, Sun occasionally launched releases by contemporary artists such as Orion (an Elvis impersonator) in the late 1970s and Jason D. Williams (a Jerry Lee Lewis impersonator) in the early 1990s. But most of Sun's many releases in the past quarter-century have been reissues of recordings from the label's 1950s heyday. Since the mid-1970s Sun has licensed much of its catalog to a wide variety of companies, while many of the label's most popular songs, such as "Whole Lotta Shakin' Goin' On," have been licensed for popular radio and television commercials, motion pictures, and Internet music providers. The Sun logo has also been licensed for an array of merchandise. Following Singleton's death on October 7, 2009, his brother and longtime business partner, John, has continued the Sun operation as CEO. —*Jimmy Guterman*

## Sunshine Sue
b. Kesauqua, Iowa, November 12, 1912; d. June 13, 1979

Sunshine Sue was the only female star to host a major radio barn dance program, serving for ten years as the guiding spirit of the OLD DOMINION BARN DANCE, broadcast from Richmond, Virginia, station WRVA.

Born Mary Arlene Higdon, she married musician John Workman, and the couple took their Rock Creek Rangers on the radio barn dance circuit in the 1930s. After stints at Louisville's WHAS, Chicago's WLS, Cincinnati's WLW, and other stations, they arrived at WRVA.

The *Old Dominion Barn Dance* began in Richmond in 1946 with Sunshine Sue at the helm. The show was heard nationally on CBS and traveled to Broadway as part of the 1954 musical *Hayride*. Virginia's governor dubbed Sunshine Sue the Queen of the Hillbillies, and she was also billed as the Sweetheart of the Southland.

Sue was an accordionist, singer, and homey MC. Always more of a personality than a great vocalist, she recorded little. DECCA issued "Blackberry Winter" (1954) and other sides, but her radio signatures were softly sentimental renditions of "You Are My Sunshine" and "My Mother's Mansions Are Higher Than Mine."

Highly organized, self-disciplined, and prim, Sue invested wisely and retired at age forty-five, for rock & roll and competition from television led WRVA to end the *Old Dominion Barn Dance*. She continued to make personal appearances until 1963, later returning only for a 1975 reunion show and record album. —*Robert K. Oermann*

## Suppertime Frolic

A freewheeling radio program that aired six evenings a week on WJJD–Chicago, *Suppertime Frolic* was an important force in popularizing country music throughout the upper Midwest from the 1930s into the 1950s. Though overshadowed in Chicago by the WLS *NATIONAL BARN DANCE*, the *Frolic* was significant enough to be hailed by *Billboard* magazine in 1944 as a "major country music program." The show had evolved by that point into a distinctive mixture of live performance and recorded music. The two-hour broadcast, heard every night except Sunday, was hosted by Randy Blake, a veteran WJJD air personality and pioneering country music disc jockey.

Although the music featured on *Suppertime Frolic* was more urbane (or at least less Appalachian) than that on some of its southern counterparts, the show's talent roster also boasted such traditionalists as KARL & HARTY (who joined the program in 1937 after leaving the crosstown rival *National Barn Dance*); banjo picker-singer COUSIN EMMY; the PICKARD FAMILY (led by Obed "Dad" Pickard, an early singing star on the GRAND OLE OPRY); Sally & Billy; and Uncle Henry's Original Kentucky Mountaineers. —*Jon Hartley Fox*

## Bryan Sutton
b. Asheville, North Carolina, October 16, 1973

Bryan Sutton is one of the new century's most complete acoustic guitarists. Raised in Asheville, North Carolina, Sutton idolized legendary North Carolina guitarist DOC WATSON. He played a variety of instruments growing up, and hiring on with RICKY SKAGGS in July of 1995 made him a utility player in a country band. As Skaggs and Kentucky Thunder turned to BLUEGRASS, Sutton focused on flat-picking.

With Skaggs spearheading a bluegrass revival, Sutton became widely admired for his speed, precision, and tone. When he left the band in early 1999, abundant session work awaited. He backed DIXIE CHICKS on several albums and tours, and he replaced an injured TONY RICE for the *Bluegrass Sessions* tour, solidifying his ties with BÉLA FLECK, JERRY DOUGLAS, and other newgrass pioneers. DOLLY PARTON called him for her career-turning *The Grass Is Blue* album. Along the way, Sutton has made a number of solo albums, starting with *Ready to Go* in 2000. A duet of "Whiskey Before Breakfast" with Doc Watson on Sutton's album *Not Too Far From The Tree* took the 2006 Grammy for best country instrumental performance, and as of 2010 Sutton had been named IBMA Guitarist of the Year five times. —*Craig Havighurst*

## Glenn Sutton
b. Hodge, Louisiana, September 28, 1937; d. April 17, 2007

As a songwriter and producer, Royce Glenn Sutton had a hand in creating several country classics. His song credits include the Grammy-winning "Almost Persuaded," cowritten with BILLY

SHERRILL and a #1 hit for DAVID HOUSTON; "What Made Milwaukee Famous (Has Made a Loser Out of Me)," a Top Ten hit for JERRY LEE LEWIS; and "Your Good Girl's Gonna Go Bad" and "I Don't Wanna Play House," both cowritten with Sherrill and hits for TAMMY WYNETTE. Sutton also produced the crossover hit "(I Never Promised You) a Rose Garden" for LYNN ANDERSON, to whom he was married from 1968 to 1977.

But Sutton was also famous for his colorful personality and his outrageous pranks. He would don a silver mask, blue body suit, and blue cape to show up at MUSIC ROW events as the mock superhero Angelman. He would also put on an old-man mask and perform comic, off-the-cuff songs as Bluewater Dave, who called himself "the world's oldest living entertainer."

Sutton was inducted into the NASHVILLE SONGWRITERS HALL OF FAME in 1999. —*Michael McCall*

## Billy Swan
b. Cape Girardeau, Missouri, May 12, 1942

A ROCKABILLY-styled singer, Billy Swan enjoyed his greatest success with his self-penned "I Can Help," a perky, organ-driven sensation that topped the country and pop charts in 1974.

Earlier, at age sixteen, Swan had written "Lover Please," a 1962 Top Ten pop hit for R&B singer Clyde McPhatter. Before moving to Nashville in 1963, Swan recorded with Mirt Mirley & the Rhythm Steppers in Memphis, where he also served as a gate guard at ELVIS PRESLEY's Graceland mansion. In Nashville Swan worked as a janitor at the COLUMBIA studio before turning the job over to buddy KRIS KRISTOFFERSON. Swan produced TONY JOE WHITE's first three MONUMENT albums, including White's biggest hit, "Polk Salad Annie," and played in bands with Kristofferson and KINKY FRIEDMAN before hitting on Monument with "I Can Help." Swan followed with several Top Twenty country singles on Monument and EPIC. In 1986 he and former EAGLES member Randy Meisner organized the band Black Tie and released the commercially disappointing album *When the Night Falls*. Other albums followed, but principally Swan continued as a road and studio musician. —*Jack Bernhardt*

## Sweethearts of the Rodeo
Janis Gill b. Manhattan Beach, California, November 28, 1955
Kristine Arnold b. Manhattan Beach, California, March 1, 1957

Sweethearts of the Rodeo enjoyed a brief run on the country charts between 1986 and 1991. Growing up in Los Angeles, sisters Janis and Kristine Oliver learned to trade lead and harmony vocals. In 1973 they began performing a mix of BLUEGRASS, WESTERN SWING, and COUNTRY-ROCK as Sweethearts of the Rodeo, a name lifted from THE BYRDS' landmark 1968 country-rock LP by this title. With help from EMMYLOU HARRIS, the duo became regulars on the West Coast bluegrass circuit. At a show date with PURE PRAIRIE LEAGUE, Janis and Kristine met their future husbands, respectively—VINCE GILL, then a member of Pure Prairie League, and Leonard Arnold of Blue Steel. Both couples wed in 1980, and by the end of 1984 both had moved to Nashville.

The next year, the Sweethearts won the national finals of the annual Wrangler Country Showdown and signed with COLUMBIA RECORDS. Their first two albums yielded seven Top Ten singles, including "Midnight Girl/Sunset Town" (1986) and "Chains of

Gold" (1987). Three of their songs were featured in the 1987 movie *Nadine*, starring Kim Basinger.

In 1993, with their chart run ended, they signed with Sugar Hill Records, and Janis Gill produced both *Rodeo Waltz* (1994) and *Beautiful Lies* (1996). For a time the singing partners, who had typically designed and sewn their own stagewear, operated an upscale boutique in Franklin, Tennessee. Janis and Vince Gill began divorce proceedings in 1997; each has since remarried, with Vince wedding singer Amy Grant. The Sweethearts still tour and record, and they have found acceptance among Americana, folk, and bluegrass audiences. —*Marjie McGraw*

## Taylor Swift
b. Wyomissing, Pennsylvania, December 13, 1989

On a scale unprecedented for a country artist, Taylor Alison Swift harnessed online social networks to build an enormous fan base in a short period during a transitional time for the music industry. In so doing, she greatly broadened country music's teenage audience while selling millions of albums since her 2006 debut. A prolific songwriter, her intimate love songs have resulted in substantial crossover chart success and appearances on MTV's *Total Request Live* and NBC's *Saturday Night Live* and acting on TV's *CSI: Crime Scene Investigation* and in the hit film *Valentine's Day*.

*Taylor Swift*

Inspired by LeAnn Rimes, six-year-old Taylor Swift set her sights on a country music career, and as a child she performed at karaoke bars and in a local children's musical-theater company. At age eleven she persuaded her parents to take her to Nashville, but garnering no interest from record labels she returned home and began composing songs and learning guitar.

At Swift's urging, her family relocated to Nashville in 2004; within six months, fourteen-year-old Swift became the youngest writer ever signed by Sony/ATV Music's Music City office. In August 2005 Swift created a MySpace page and began communicating directly with fans by blogging, regularly uploading new music, and adding behind-the-scenes video footage.

In 2006 Swift signed with Big Machine Records, which released her self-titled debut CD that October. Its wistful lead single, "Tim McGraw," reached #6 on the country charts. Buoyed by four more Top Ten country singles—including the #1 country hits "Our Song" and "Should've Said No" and the crossover hit "Teardrops on My Guitar"—*Taylor Swift* had sold more than 4 million copies in less than three years. Industry accolades followed, as Swift won CMA's Horizon Award in 2007 and gained honors as ACM's Top New Female Vocalist of 2007.

Swift's follow-up CD, *Fearless* (2008), debuted at #1 on the all-genre *Billboard* 200 and Top Country Albums charts and yielded the country hits "Love Story" (#1), "White Horse" (#2), "You Belong with Me" (#1), "Fifteen," (#7), and "Fearless" (#10). "Love Story" also topped *Billboard*'s Adult Contemporary chart.

In 2008–09 Swift took home a mountain of awards, including ACM's 2008 Album of the Year (*Fearless*); 2009 CMA Awards for Entertainer of the Year, Female Vocalist, Album (*Fearless*) and Music Video ("Love Story"); and 2009 Grammys for Album of the Year, Best Country Album, Best Country Song ("White Horse"), and Best Country Vocal Performance by a Female ("White Horse"). By 2010 *Fearless* had sold 6 million copies. Swift released her third album, *Speak Now*, in that same year. It sold more than 1 million units in its first week. —*Tina Wright*

## Swift Jewel Cowboys

Founded on April 8, 1933, in Houston, Texas, and disbanded in July 1942, in Memphis, Tennessee, the Swift Jewel Cowboys were named after Swift & Company's Jewel Oil and Shortening products. The original members included Don José Cortes on fiddle, Clifford Zebedee "Kokomo" Crocker on accordion and vocals, Elmer "Slim" Hall on guitar and vocals, and Calvin "Curly" Noland on string bass and vocals. Houston served as the group's home base until fall 1934, when Swift transferred their manager and mentor, Frank B. Collins, to Memphis. The band soon followed, first broadcasting over WMC on November 4 of that year.

In Memphis, the ensemble's sound evolved from cowboy toward a hot dance beat approaching Western Swing with the addition in early 1936 of Farris "Lefty" Ingram, who was proficient on sax, clarinet, and fiddle. By 1938, when jazz cornetist-pianist David "Pee Wee" Wamble had joined, the act's musical transition was nearing completion.

July 1939 witnessed the Cowboys' only recording activity, with three sessions held at the Gayoso Hotel in Memphis for Vocalion Records. Tunes such as "Memphis Blues," "Fan It," "Coney Island Washboard," and "Dill Pickle Rag"—the last featuring a guest participant, Jimmy Riddle, on harmonica—embodied the group's jazz repertoire. Riddle later gained recognition as one of Roy Acuff's

Smoky Mountain Boys. Another notable Cowboys alumnus was Wiley Walker, who later teamed with Gene Sullivan (WILEY & GENE) on several 1940s hits, including "When My Blue Moon Turns to Gold Again." A child mascot of the band, Bill Justis, eventually won fame for his 1957 crossover hit "Raunchy" and for subsequent record production and arranging achievements. —*Bob Pinson*

# Sylvia
b. Kokomo, Indiana, December 9, 1956

Through the early 1980s, Sylvia Kirby had a string of Top Ten country hits that included "Tumbleweed," "Drifter," and especially her 1982 crossover smash "Nobody." All were recorded in a light, airy style she called "prairie music."

She moved to Nashville in 1975. There she worked as a receptionist for producer-publisher TOM COLLINS, who helped her land a recording contract with RCA in 1979 and became her producer. By 1982 she already had four Top Ten records to her credit when "Nobody"—penned by the prolific songwriting team of Kye Fleming and Dennis Morgan—shot to #1 on the country charts and rose to #15 pop. Singing her 1983 hit "Snapshot," Sylvia also became one of the first country performers to be featured in a modern video clip.

After charting eleven Top Tens, she left RCA in 1988 and began appearing as Sylvia Hutton, writing and performing family-centered songs designed to encourage children. Several of her albums have appeared on the independent label Red Pony Records. —*Mary A. Bufwack*

# It All Begins with a Song

## A Brief History of Country Songwriting

## WALTER CARTER

It sounds so easy.

> I heard the wreck on the highway / But I didn't hear nobody pray
> Your cheatin' heart will tell on you
> You walk by and I fall to pieces
> If drinkin' don't kill me, her memory will
> I'm just an old chunk of coal / But I'm gonna be a diamond someday
> Timber, I'm falling in love*

The songs are so simple—especially the good ones. "Three chords and the truth." That's how HARLAN HOWARD, the dean of Nashville songwriters, with well over a thousand songs recorded in his forty-year career, described country music.

But it's not that easy. Howard himself, on the eve of his induction into THE COUNTRY MUSIC HALL OF FAME in 1997, compared songwriting to hitting a baseball. "Mickey Mantle hits .300," he said. "That's hard to do—three out of ten. And out of those hits is a certain percentage of singles, doubles, home runs. He's [in the Baseball] Hall of Fame, but seven out of ten times he didn't get on base. If I told you I have 3,000 unrecorded songs, you'd say, 'Boy, he wasted his life away.'"

CINDY WALKER, who, like Howard, had hits in five different decades and was inducted into the Country Music Hall of Fame in 1997, said she might write twenty songs or more to come up with a single good one. "Good songs are few and far between," she explained. "It's never easy. It's like digging a ditch. You've got to work at it."

Not only is songwriting hard, achieving success and recognition is even harder. The Country Music Hall of Fame is filled with record producers and music-publishing executives as well as recording stars, but not songwriters. The Hall of Fame was established in 1961, and it took thirty years before BOUDLEAUX and FELICE BRYANT were inducted, purely on the strength of their songwriting. Cindy Walker and Harlan Howard brought the grand total of "pure songwriters" (as Walker called them) in the Hall of Fame to four. BOBBY BRADDOCK, elected in 2011, added one more.

For country songwriters, competition is brutal. Out of the thousands of writers in Nashville, only a few hundred make a living at it. Only a few dozen make a good living. Yet in cities and towns all across America, there are folks setting an alarm clock an hour early or staying up after the kids are in bed to polish a few lines of rhyme, strum a chord on a guitar, and dream of songwriting success.

Wannabes may get some encouragement from NSAI (Nashville Songwriters Association International), but the overriding message from Nashville's music industry is "Don't give up your day job." That weeds out the undedicated—those who aren't willing to give up careers, families, and other responsibilities to move to Nashville, work menial jobs, stand in line for a ten-minute spot on a songwriters night, search for a compatible cowriter, and pray for a publisher who will take a phone call and listen to a song.

---

* From, in order: "The Wreck on the Highway" written by Dorsey Dixon, "Your Cheatin' Heart" by HANK WILLIAMS, "I Fall to Pieces" by HANK COCHRAN and Harlan Howard, "If Drinkin' Don't Kill Me (Her Memory Will)" by Harlan Sanders and Rick Beresford, "I'm Just an Old Chunk of Coal (But I'm Gonna Be a Diamond Someday)" by BILLY JOE SHAVER, "Timber, I'm Falling in Love" by Kostas.

Once they're in Nashville, songwriters face a new set of challenges: making the transition from hobbyist to professional, from writing by inspiration to writing by appointment; learning the craft without losing creativity; balancing originality with commercial flair; making contacts; and playing the politics of music publishing and recordings.

NSAI's motto is, "It all begins with a song." You'd think, by definition, that means it all begins with a songwriter, but it hasn't always been that way. Country music as a defined, commercial style of music has been around since the 1920s, but country songwriters—the "boys who make the noise on Sixteenth Avenue," as they were described in a 1982 hit—didn't become prevalent until the 1950s.

Many songwriters can recall a moment of enlightenment when they realized that someone actually wrote songs. Until that moment, they thought songs were somehow just always there. And for first-generation country performers, that's largely the way it was. There were plenty of traditional songs and fiddle tunes to fill up an evening's entertainment. Depending on how isolated a rural musician was, he might also know some popular tunes from the minstrel era, such as "Camptown Races" and "Dem Golden Slippers," which had entered folk tradition even though their authors were known.

There was little need for new country songs until the late 1920s, when an emerging country music industry produced the first country stars. Through records and radio, their music went out almost instantaneously to a wider audience than they might reach in a lifetime of touring, but national popularity was a beast that demanded constant feeding. They needed new material—and lots of it.

VERNON DALHART, who had the first million-selling country record, "The Prisoner's Song" b/w "Wreck of the Old '97" (1924–25), used his star status to secure a writer, CARSON ROBISON. Robison is often cited as the first professional country songwriter, but he was a product of the major songwriting center that existed at that time: New York's Tin Pan Alley. From 1924 to 1928 Robison supplied new, traditional-sounding country songs to Dalhart, until he tired of giving Dalhart half the writing credit and focused on his own career as a featured singer-songwriter.

In 1927 the CARTER FAMILY and JIMMIE RODGERS made their first recordings and were immediately pressed for more material. The pressure came from RALPH PEER, the Victor Talking Machine Company (see RCA VICTOR) talent scout who discovered them. Peer had already adopted the philosophy that artists needed original material so that it would be (1) new to the ears of record buyers and (2) copyrightable. Publishing royalties were thought to be so insignificant for the hillbilly and race music Peer recorded that Victor let Peer control publishing rights. The standard practice among record companies was either to insist on recording public domain songs or simply to buy songs for a flat fee, but Peer believed he could build loyalty and long-term relationships with his artists if he shared song royalties with them.

A.P. Carter and Jimmie Rodgers took Peer's bait and amassed catalogs that would strengthen the foundation of country music. Ironically, neither Carter nor Rodgers was as prolific as their catalogs suggest. They met the demand for material in other ways.

"As the Carters' recording career widened, there were more and more demands on A. P. to find songs from any sources possible, as they gradually ran out of well-known folk songs to record," wrote John Atkins in his contribution to *Stars of Country Music*. "He would often go off for a week at a time on 'song-hunting' trips, and he had, according to his family, an uncanny ability for finding new songs." These "finds" would range from traditional pieces to newly written material that he might have purchased. He would then rewrite, rearrange and "work up" these numbers for the Carter Family to perform and record.

As Nolan Porterfield explained in *Jimmie Rodgers: The Life and Times of America's Blue Yodeler*, Rodgers "often found himself scrambling to produce 'original' material to fill the demand. Although some 83 percent of the Blue Yodeler's recordings carry his name as composer or co-composer, he actually wrote very little of the material, and was always dependent on a variety of random sources—his sister-in-law [Elsie McWilliams], amateur composers, Tin Pan Alley hacks—for suitable songs."

Even as country music grew in popularity, songwriting followed the patterns set by Carter and Rodgers. With country music still emanating from many regional centers—wherever there was a "barn dance" or a "jamboree" radio show—a songwriter would have had to crisscross the country seeking artists, few of whom had the kind of popularity that would produce significant song royalties. With few professional songwriters, artists were often forced to adapt older material or to write their own songs. GENE AUTRY was based at Tulsa station KVOO in 1931 when he and Jimmy Long wrote Autry's first smash hit, "That Silver-Haired Daddy of Mine." When ROY ACUFF a performer on WNOX in Knoxville,

Tennessee, recorded his first signature song in 1936, he wrote extra verses to an existing version of "The Great Speckled Bird," which used the same melody A. P. Carter had appropriated for "I'm Thinking Tonight of My Blue Eyes." JIMMIE DAVIS, of Shreveport, Louisiana, had had some national success by 1940 when he and his steel guitarist Charles Mitchell bought "You Are My Sunshine" from writer Paul Rice and reworked it into Davis's ticket to the Louisiana governorship. ERNEST TUBB, singing on KGKO in Fort Worth, Texas, made his breakthrough with his original "Walking the Floor Over You," in 1941.

While the hillbilly side of country music remained too dispersed to make songwriting a viable profession, the rising popularity of singing-cowboy movies helped to create a songwriting center in Hollywood by the late 1930s. Although Hollywood would never have a publishing community as geographically centralized as New York's Tin Pan Alley or Nashville's MUSIC ROW, it was nevertheless a songwriters' town for country and western writers. In a classic Hollywood scenario, Texas-born Cindy Walker saw the name Crosby on a building on Sunset Boulevard, walked in with her guitar, talked her way into singing a song for Bing Crosby's brother, and wound up the next day on a movie set singing the song to Bing himself. Bing Crosby recorded that song, "Lone Star Trail," in December 1940.

Walker moved to Hollywood and lived there for thirteen years, making her living as a country and western songwriter. When BOB WILLS, the king of WESTERN SWING (who, like other seminal stars of country music, wrote many of his early hits himself), made a series of movies, he recorded thirty-nine of Walker's songs. Hollywood's recording studios attracted a wide variety of singers, including country stars. "All the artists used to come out to Hollywood to record—EDDY ARNOLD, Ernest Tubb, HANK SNOW," she said. "Whenever I heard they were coming, well, I'd get busy and start to write something." And with a flourishing live country music scene at venues such as THE RIVERSIDE RANCHO, the Palomino Ballroom, and the Venice Pier Ballroom, Walker said, "It was just a wonderful place for songwriters."

In fact, Hollywood in the early 1940s was the *best* place for a country songwriter. Even though many country artists still recorded in New York and Chicago, when asked what was going on in Nashville when she moved west, Cindy Walker replied, "I don't have the slightest idea." As far as country music was concerned, Nashville offered little in 1940 except for the GRAND OLE OPRY. No country publishers. No independent studios. No record companies.

Nashville's publishing void was its most serious drawback for a writer. Unless he had an affiliation with a New York, Chicago, or Hollywood publisher, he could get little help in placing songs with artists. Furthermore, ASCAP would not admit most writers of hillbilly music (or blues, folk, or jazz), so few country writers made royalties from radio airplay.

That all changed in 1940–41. First, leading broadcasters, in defiance of ASCAP's proposed 50 percent hike in its licensing fees, formed BMI in 1940 and immediately signed up writers who had been snubbed by ASCAP. Financial incentives for country songwriters increased markedly, because BMI eventually ensured that they would receive royalties from radio exposure of their works. (Until the late 1940s, BMI paid publishers, who, in theory, paid writers. By 1948, BMI was reimbursing publishers who paid half of their royalties to affiliated writers, and soon BMI began paying writers directly.)

Then, in 1942, Roy Acuff, to protect and develop the copyrights in his best-selling song folios, partnered with country and pop songwriter FRED ROSE to create ACUFF-ROSE PUBLICATIONS. That started the ball rolling in the Tennesssee capital. Songwriters—foremost among them HANK WILLIAMS, beginning in 1946—now had a Nashville home. Williams was not solely a songwriter, of course, but his music changed the world for country songwriters in three ways. First, he made country music more personal. In his writing and his singing—which were inseparable—Williams seemed to tear open his heart. When he sang "I'm so lonesome I could cry," he made Jimmie Rodgers's "T for Thelma, that gal that made a wreck out of me" or Ernest Tubb's "I'm walking the floor over you" sound like a party record. Second, Williams's songs, coupled with Fred Rose's vision, opened the lucrative pop market to country songwriters as never before, with such hits as "Cold, Cold Heart," recorded by Tony Bennett; "Jambalaya," by Jo Stafford; and "Your Cheatin' Heart," by Joni James. Third, William's songwriting, while setting standards that sometimes seem impossibly high, continues to inspire other Nashville tunesmiths.

To early songwriters trying to make a living in Nashville, however, Williams was not as important as singers such as Eddy Arnold or WEBB PIERCE—essentially nonwriting artists. A songwriter had little chance of getting a song recorded by Hank, since Hank could write his own, but a nonwriting artist was always in need of good material.

"I looked to the publishers," Arnold recalled. "I always got the best songs from the publishers." The problem was that for nearly a decade, for Nashville writers anyway, the city had only one major country publisher. A Chicago firm supplied Arnold's 1947 #1 hit "I'll Hold You in My Heart (Till I Can Hold You in My Arms)," written by HAL HORTON and Tommy Dilbeck. Steve Nelson and Bob Hilliard penned Arnold's 1948 hit "Bouquet of Roses" for a New York publisher. When publishing houses opened in Nashville, Arnold said, "I wouldn't wait for them to bring a song out to me. I'd just get in the car and go down to their office. 'Play me something.' I could say yes or no right there. I wanted to have a good rapport with the publishers."

It's impossible to say whether Nashville's growing songwriting community attracted more artists or whether the Opry's increasing talent pool attracted more writers, but by 1950 Nashville's burgeoning recording industry convinced Boudleaux and Felice Bryant to move there permanently. This husband-wife team involved the first great country tunesmiths who came to MUSIC CITY for the sole purpose of writing songs. By the end of the 1950s their songs "Bye Bye Love" and "Wake Up, Little Susie," both hits for THE EVERLY BROTHERS, had played a monumental role in building Nashville into a music center.

In the 1950s, Nashville finally became a songwriter's town. JACK STAPP, then program director for WSM, established TREE PUBLISHING in 1951. WSM booking department manager JIM DENNY and Webb Pierce started CEDARWOOD PUBLISHING in 1953. As the decade advanced, record companies opened Nashville offices (DECCA had been the first to do so, in 1947), and recording studios were built on what would become Music Row, following precedents set by the downtown CASTLE RECORDING STUDIO. Pop stars such as ELVIS PRESLEY and BRENDA LEE, as well many leading country stars, recorded hit after hit. By 1960 Nashville looked promising even to a successful West Coast country songwriter such as Harlan Howard. "I had a couple of hits—'Pick Me Up on Your Way Down' and 'Heartaches by the Number'—before '60," Howard recalled, "so when the publisher sent me a check for one hundred grand, I said 'Wow!' and moved here."

Like Hollywood in the 1940s, Nashville in 1960 was a wonderful place for songwriters, with the demand for material exceeding the supply of local song craftsmen. "At that time, all the Opry stars had record deals," Howard recalled. "All of a sudden these singers didn't write their own songs, even if they used to. People like Ernest Tubb and LEFTY FRIZZELL, they became superstars and didn't write like they used to. There came a need for writers, and if there's a need for writers, they'll be there. . . . It was easy back then," he added. "There were only eight of us: me, HANK COCHRAN, WILLIE NELSON, MEL TILLIS, Felice and Boudleaux, BILL ANDERSON, and ROGER MILLER."

Opportunities for country songwriters expanded in the late 1950s with the rise of folk music, which shared roots with country. Nashville's DANNY DILL and MARIJOHN WILKIN penned "The Long Black Veil" in 1959, and it was immediately embraced by the folk audience as a traditional song. BOBBY BARE crossed over to the pop charts with songs that were decidedly country, including the Danny Dill–Mel Tillis classic "Detroit City," which borrowed the line "I wanna go home" from the folk song "Sloop John B." Lefty Frizzell, who had first recorded "The Long Black Veil," edged onto the pop charts in 1964 with the story song "Saginaw, Michigan," authored by Bill Anderson and Don Wayne.

The success of Harlan Howard and his contemporaries in the early 1960s brought a new group of writers to Nashville in mid-decade, among them CURLY PUTMAN, DALLAS FRAZIER, and KRIS KRISTOFFERSON. In a replay of the Fred Rose–Hank Williams story, pop artists continued finding hits in Nashville publishing houses. Tom Jones gave a straightforward reading to Putman's old-time-sounding (but newly written) country tearjerker "Green, Green Grass of Home" in 1966–67. O. C. Smith, a black singer, scored a pop hit with Frazier's "Son of Hickory Holler's Tramp" in 1968 and followed with "Little Green Apples," composed by Nashville's Bobby Russell. And in 1969, the First Edition, led by future country superstar KENNY ROGERS, went #6 pop with "Ruby, Don't Take Your Love to Town," Mel Tillis's heartbreaking story of a disabled Vietnam veteran and his straying wife.

Still, despite country songwriters' ever-widening success, few outside the country music industry knew anything about "C. Putman" or "Howard-Cochran"—the names in small print under the song titles on record labels. In 1970, however, Kris Kristofferson changed that.

In one sense, Kristofferson extended the Hank Williams tradition of self-destruction. A hard drinker, he had given up a secure career (in the U.S. Army) and a promising one (as a West Point professor) and pretty well destroyed his first marriage to pursue his songwriting dream. Williams died at age twenty-nine; Kristofferson arrived in Nashville in 1965 at age twenty-nine, so you could say Kris picked up where Hank left off.

In one monumental year—1970—Kristofferson influenced country songwriting as no one ever has. "Help Me Make It Through the Night" and "For the Good Times," (recorded by SAMMI SMITH and RAY PRICE, respectively), were, in their most basic form, pleas for mercy sex. The subject was racy, but the lyrics were tender, intimate, and poetic in a way that made the songs more about love than about sex alone. Although the songs had classic, simple structures straight out of country tradition, the writer was anything but. Rather, Kristofferson was schooled in English literature at Oxford—a Rhodes scholar. There had been educated writers in country music before him (Bill Anderson, for instance, had a college degree); but after Kristofferson, formal education was no longer something a writer needed to hide.

In country's traditions of realism and honesty—which go back to Elizabethan murder ballads—Kristofferson also opened a disturbing new window on the songwriter's life with "Sunday Morning Coming Down," first cut by RAY STEVENS in 1969 but a hit for JOHNNY CASH in 1970. In this depressing confessional, Kristofferson again picked up where Hank left off. When he wrote "wishing, Lord, that I was stoned," he wasn't talking about booze. Although back pain led Hank to use morphine and chloral hydrate, a central nervous system depressant, he didn't sing about drugs the way Kris did.

People didn't want to glance in Kristofferson's window; they wanted to shine a spotlight through it. For the first time, the songwriter was the star. After Janis Joplin's posthumous 1971 pop hit "Me and Bobbie McGee," written by Kristofferson and his publisher, FRED FOSTER, Kristofferson became more famous than all but a handful of country artists. He didn't die young, as Williams did, but he might as well have. No sooner had he found success than he was gone. By 1973 he had moved to Hollywood to play Billy the Kid in a movie. And, like Hank before him, he left his ghost to haunt and inspire Music Row songwriters.

Nashville immediately felt Kristofferson's influence. Songwriters poured into town, from college kids who loved the poetry of his lyrics to Vietnam veterans who related to his rejection of his military career. The deluge of writers created a new phenomenon in Nashville nightclubs: Writers Night. It started in late 1971 at the newly opened Exit/In, a small club located a block from the Vanderbilt campus, so named because the entrance was in the back. At the Exit/In's Writers Night, singers counted for nothing—unless they were also able songwriters. A typical night might include Jimmy Buffett singing the country song parody "Why Don't We Get Drunk (And Screw)," John Hiatt singing "Sure as I'm Sittin' Here" (Three Dog Night made it a pop hit), Mac Gayden playing his soul music hit "She Shot a Hole in My Soul," and RODNEY CROWELL, newly arrived in town and taking a night off from washing dishes across the street at T.G.I. Friday's restaurant.

The increasing awareness of songwriters in the 1970s provided the perfect setting for Willie Nelson's rise to superstardom as an artist. A legendary figure in the songwriting community for such standards as "Crazy" and "Hello Walls," Nelson had been unable to muster a Top Ten record of his own since 1962. With his 1975 album *Red Headed Stranger*, he not only established himself as a singer—he also focused attention on the songwriter's life. It wasn't the songs (most of which, ironically, he did not write) so much as the production—so sparse that the collection was criticized within the record industry as being nothing more than a demo, or songwriter's work tape, the most basic, original form of a song. But to many writers, there was no better way to present a song, with nothing to focus on but the song itself.

The country song industry had grown from one publisher in 1942 to hundreds in the 1970s, many of them housed in former homes in a six-block area around Sixteenth Avenue South. Recording executive JIMMY BOWEN would describe it as a "horizontal Brill Building," referring to the building that was long the center of New York pop publishing. This was the songwriter's Nashville that THOM SCHUYLER captured when he wrote "God bless the boys who make the noise on Sixteenth Avenue," a 1982 hit for LACY J. DALTON.

As country's audience expanded in the 1980s and beyond, the profile of a typical country writer broadened to the point that there was no longer a single prototype. At one end of the spectrum is the traditional country success story of MAX D. BARNES ("Chiseled in Stone"), a former truck driver who waited until his kids were grown before moving to Nashville to try his hand at songwriting, or DEAN DILLON ("Unwound"), an East Tennessee native who portrayed Hank Williams in an OPRYLAND USA show and then temporarily seemed hell-bent on following Hank's unstable lifestyle. At the other end is BOB DIPIERO ("American Made"), who played guitar in rock bands while earning a degree in music from Ohio's Youngstown State University, or Roger Cook ("Talking in Your Sleep"), who came to Nashville after a successful career as a pop writer and producer in England.

BOB McDILL, one of Nashville's most successful songwriters, represents both ends of the spectrum. He grew up in Texas and landed in Music City after an aborted singing career in Memphis. He followed in the footsteps of Kris Kristofferson and Tom T. Hall as a writer with a deep foundation in literature, as expressed in McDill's line "Those Williams boys, they still mean a lot to me—Hank and Tennessee" (from "Good Ole Boys Like Me"). And he is equally at home with the decidedly nonliterary crowd he celebrated (with cowriters Waylon Holyfield and Chuck Neese) in the Johnny Russell hit "Red Necks, White Socks and Blue Ribbon Beer."

Similarly, the prototypical country song evolved into numerous types. The most obvious change came in response to the booming popularity of country dance clubs. To an unprecedented degree, the beat was as important as the lyric. "It's got a good beat and you can dance to it"—the famous phrase from the perennial teen dance show *American Bandstand*—now applied to country music.

Country dance songs may have received the most consistent exposure, but songwriters by no means switched over to a diet of "lite" music. Country writers Frank Myers and Gary Baker created the love ballad "I Swear," a country smash by JOHN MICHAEL MONTGOMERY that, when recorded by All 4-One, became one of the biggest pop and urban contemporary hits of the 1990s. And in the tradition of "There Stands the Glass" and "Ruby, Don't Take Your Love to Town," country tunesmiths took the lead in writing sensitively and honestly about troubling social issues, as in "Where've You Been" (by Jon Vezner and Don Henry), about Alzheimer's disease, and "She Thinks His Name Was John" (by Sandy Knox and Steve Rosen), about AIDS.

As always, artists who can write their own songs have had an advantage over the competition, as exemplified by the three superstars most responsible for the country music boom in the 1990s. GARTH BROOKS had a hand in penning his first three hits; after that he wrote about half of them. ALAN JACKSON cowrote nine out of his first ten. Except for remakes of older hits, CLINT BLACK wrote or cowrote virtually every song he ever recorded.

Songwriters followed the country music industry in becoming more businesslike in their approach to their craft. The intensity of competition and the demand from publishers for a consistent flow of new songs forced many songwriters into daily office routines. Unfortunately, going in to "work" every day can have a stifling effect on creativity, and the great majority of Nashville writers found that the only way to maintain an infusion of fresh ideas was through collaboration. Cowriting became a way of life in Nashville in the 1990s, with writers typically filling their calendars with appointments, whether they had a reserve of ideas or not. For volume and variety, cowriting was the fastest and easiest way to churn out material. Gary Burr, for example, wrote his first country hits, "Love's Been a Little Bit Hard on Me" in 1982 and "Make My Life With You" in 1985, by himself. But in 1994, when four artists simultaneously released singles of his songs, three of those songs were cowritten—with three different partners. The best advertisement for cowriting in 1996 was Mark D. Sanders, who had ten hit songs that year (five of them reaching #1), created with a total of ten different cowriters.

Even though Internet downloading and MP3 file sharing has reduced CD sales since the mid-1990s, in some ways the world has never been better for country songwriters. The mechanical royalty rate, which did not change from 1909 to 1976, tripled in the last quarter of the twentieth century, and in the Internet age record companies and publishers have strived to expand revenue streams, including telephone ringtones and licensing songs for TV and film use. Singer-songwriters have also been able to market their music directly to consumers via their own websites, thus cutting out publishing and recording company middlemen. With more and more investment at stake in a country record, producers and artists began looking for the best songs, period, and it became harder to demand a piece of the publishing or a partial writer's share of a song in exchange for recording it.

Not every industry change worked to the songwriter's advantage, however. ASCAP and BMI quit giving advances to songwriters and publishers. Some publishers began recouping the cost of demo sessions from writers' royalties. Additionally, publishers for a time forced some songwriters into agreements that lengthened the publisher's hold on a copyright but shortened the length of the copyright for the writer and his or her heirs. Recently, though, it hs become easier for writers and heirs to get copyrights back from music publishers.

In the early 2000s, Nashville retained its reputation as the songwriter's town, but at a cost, particularly from the point of view of aspiring newcomers to the field. Well into the 1970s a writer could walk in the front door of a publishing company with a demo or even just a guitar (as in the Hank Williams biopic, *Your Cheatin' Heart*), and someone would listen to his songs. A few years later, a writer would have to make an appointment or leave a tape. By the 1980s, receptionists at some publishing companies were turning writers away at the door, claiming that the company wasn't accepting new material. One publisher even had an unlisted phone number. In the 1990s, as was accurately portrayed in the 1993 film *The Thing Called Love*, songwriters wanting to play on a writers night at one of Nashville's leading "listening rooms" had to wait in line outside the nightclub, fill out an application, and then audition for the chance to play a few songs for free.

For something that continues to sound so easy, country songwriting seems to have gotten more difficult through the years. But ultimately, writers don't really care about the current mechanical royalty rate or the current "standard" publisher's contract. They don't even care whether the odds against them are a thousand to one or a million to one. They write for the same reason country songwriters have always written—out of a desire to express a simple truth in a new way, to tell an entertaining story, to touch listeners' emotions or move their feet on a dance floor, and, of course, to give a singer something to sing.

For country songwriters, public recognition may come and go, but singers will always need a good song. As Eddy Arnold pointed out, "An artist is only as strong as his songs. I don't care how hot he is, he's got to have a good song."

# The South and Country Music

## BILL C. MALONE

It may seem foolhardy to attribute a southern identity to country music when we note the music's strength everywhere in the United States and throughout the world. Music, of course, has thrived in every region of rural America, and fiddlers, STRINGBANDS, and balladeers could be heard in New England, in the Midwest, and on the West Coast long before the commercialization of grass-roots styles began in the 1920s. Fiddlers abounded from Nova Scotia to California, and it is instructive to note that a Yankee fiddler, Mellie Dunham of Maine, was a finalist in Henry Ford's nationally sponsored fiddle talent contest in 1926. When commercialization did come, the Sears, Roebuck radio station in Chicago, WLS (World's Largest Store), became one of the pioneers of barn dance–style programming, a format rapidly adopted by other stations in the Midwest and Southeast. Since that time, country entertainers have found enthusiastic receptions at state fairs and other personal appearances across America.

Nevertheless, the music has always had a special relationship with the South. Beginning with ECK ROBERTSON and Henry Gilliland's recordings for the Victor Talking Machine Company (see RCA VICTOR) in 1922 and, more crucially, with those made by FIDDLIN' JOHN CARSON for OKEH in 1923, the preponderance of early professional country entertainers came from eleven states of the former Confederacy or from the bordering states of Kentucky, West Virginia, Missouri, and Oklahoma.

Although performers now come from Canada and even Australia, the majority of country musicians still come from that region running from Virginia to Texas, described by sociologist Richard Peterson as "the fertile crescent of country music." In that area one still finds the greatest concentration of all-country radio stations. Most of the genre's "influentials," or style setters, such as UNCLE DAVE MACON, JIMMIE RODGERS, the CARTER FAMILY, BOB WILLS, GENE AUTRY, BILL MONROE, EARL SCRUGGS, HANK WILLIAMS, ELVIS PRESLEY, and a host of others, have come from the South. Hearing these musicians, listeners and critics could not be blamed for assuming that what they were experiencing was a southern phenomenon. Furthermore, the hillbilly image that was attached to the music in its commercial infancy conditioned listeners to link the music not only to the South but also to a stereotypically rural version of southernness. Many listeners judge the authenticity of country singers by the degree to which their sounds seem to reflect a southern working-class origin, while those who try to burlesque or make fun of country music usually affect what they think is a southern twang.

It might be correct to argue, as some have done, that early recording expeditions would have found comparable rural talent in other parts of the United States if they had chosen to travel there. But, like Cecil Sharp, John Lomax, and other folk music collectors who came before them, RALPH PEER, FRANK WALKER, and other pioneering talent scouts of the 1920s went south expecting to find a musical land and a musical people. By the time country music became a staple of the recording and radio industries in the 1920s, Americans were preconditioned to think of the South and its music in stereotypical ways. Those perceptions that did so much to inspire folk song collectors and A&R men to scour the region also influenced the ways in which the music was interpreted. STEPHEN FOSTER, BLACKFACE MINSTRELSY, and Tin Pan Alley songwriters had fashioned a musical vision of a placid, romantic South filled with banjo-strumming "darkies" that was hard to extricate from the popular mind.

The music of the South's plain white folk, on the other hand, was either ignored or denigrated, or it was perceived as an archaic form of Elizabethan culture preserved in the Appalachians. Plain white people, as a whole, were not ignored, but visions of sharecropping, poverty, racism, religious fundamentalism, ignorance, and pellagra prevented a clear or compassionate understanding of their culture. Could such people make music? Early hillbilly musicians labored under the burdens imposed by these preconceptions. A few musicians bitterly resisted negative stereotypes, but, like early African American entertainers who had to deal with demeaning images, most country entertainers tried to adapt to the various perceptions that clung to their art and profession. Some musicians deliberately assumed the parts of awkward hillbillies or shy country boys or girls. A few, in fact, projected exaggerated hayseed personas, especially in their humor, which, ironically, came as often from the "rube comedy" of the minstrel or vaudeville stage as from rural culture. Generally, though, musicians tried to build positive images within the often-embarrassing parameters that defined their music. Over time, many of them have adopted the persona of the cowboy.

Although the powerful role played by mythmaking in country music history should not be discounted, the music's relationship with the South has been based on more than myth. Not only has country music sounded southern—because of the performers' dialects, vocal inflections, and phrasing—but also its lyric content and tone have reflected southern regional origins. The folk South from which country music evolved, however, should not be viewed as a pristine ethnic or racial culture. The musical South was neither Celtic, Anglo-Saxon, nor Elizabethan (to use only a few of the descriptive terms that still obscure an understanding of the region and its music), nor was it overwhelmingly isolated and rural. The South that nurtured country music has been racially and ethnically diverse, and it has vacillated between tradition and modernity. Country music has been a socially conservative phenomenon, but it could not have developed without the support of radio, recording, and other examples of urban media. The music has always embodied the tensions and contradictions felt by the culture that gave it birth—a rural, working-class South that has been persistently transformed by modernity and industrial change.

Two phenomena that have contributed most to country music's distinctiveness—African American culture and evangelical Protestant Christianity—best illustrate the music's roots in southern soil. While white and black working-class southerners have lived in uneasy proximity, they have borrowed musical ideas from each other since the beginnings of southern history. African American influences are felt and heard in songs shared by the two cultures as well as in the beat and rhythms of many of country music's most distinctive styles. The country entertainers who have gained fame as innovators and who have taken the music into new and boundary-breaking areas of experimentation have tended to be those who have fused African American and white rural traditions in powerful ways: Jimmie Rodgers, Bob Wills, MERLE TRAVIS, Bill Monroe, Hank Williams, and Elvis Presley.

Just as the blues-tinged melodies and syncopated rhythms of the African American tradition insinuated themselves into the music of fiddlers and other country musicians, country's evangelical Protestant religious heritage provided a body of cherished songs, influential performance styles, and a persistent reminder of mortality and ultimate judgment for transgressions committed in this world. The conflict between hedonism and moral inhibition has fueled tensions that have made country music fascinating, just as it provided a basis for the intense singing of such great vocalists as Hank Williams, ROSE MADDOX, and GEORGE JONES.

Socioeconomic forces that have transformed the rural South in the decades since the Civil War have also colored country music lyrics. With its panorama of songs about railroads, coal mining, textile work, trucking, migration, and the decline of agriculture, country music has documented the industrialization of the South and the transformation of its rural folk into blue-collar workers. Nostalgic evocations of place, Mama and the old hometown, and the country church reveal a dislocated people who have been uprooted from those scenes and symbols of childhood security and who consequently sense the fragility of all relationships. Songs about ramblers, bad men, and boastful lovers may recall the deeds of real people, but just as often they appeal to listeners whose lives of toil, social isolation, and poverty have never permitted much more than the thrill of vicarious enjoyment.

Although the country music industry continues to reach for mainstream acceptance by striving to be all things to all people, the music's southernness still manifests itself in a variety of ways. Songs about the South or about southern places (both real and imagined) actually seem to have increased in the past thirty years or so, and, unlike most earlier song about Dixie, these recent compositions have tended to be written by native southerners. Just as they did during the days of Stephen Foster and his Tin Pan Alley descendants, songs of the South often find commercial resonance among listeners who cannot claim a southern origin. Country music's popularity north of the Mason-Dixon Line may in fact be a facet of what social critic John Egerton has called the "Southernization of the North." Hits such as

HANK WILLIAMS JR.'s "Dixie on my Mind," the BELLAMY BROTHERS' "You Ain't Just Whistling Dixie," SHENANDOAH's "Sunday in the South," Buddy Jewell's "Sweet Southern Comfort," and even ALAN JACKSON's "Small Town Southern Man" may suggest nothing more than the old, undying fascination with a romantic South, but their attraction probably has been enhanced by the mood of social and political conservatism that began to envelop the United States after 1968. "Dixie on My Mind," for example, does more than cater to southerners' chauvinistic pride; with its contempt for New York, it may also appeal to those who equate big-city "liberalism" with many of the nation's social ills. On the other hand, the popularity of such songs as THE OSBORNE BROTHERS' "Rocky Top" and the WAYLON JENNINGS–WILLIE NELSON hit "Luckenbach, Texas (Back to the Basics of Love)," which praise the virtues of mythical communities, suggests the presence of a pervasive and nonideological hunger for the down-home rootedness and quiet stability that seems to be slipping from the grasp of most Americans. When country singers and songwriters express nostalgia for the South and the alleged virtues of small-town life, listeners everywhere may feel a longing for a domestic security they never had.

Country songs are by no means the exclusive products of southern writers, but, as a body, contemporary songs still exhibit a preoccupation with themes that, according to sociologist John Shelton Reed, are more strongly embraced by Southerners than by other Americans: a sense of place, spirituality, and the acceptance of violence as an appropriate solution for both private and public problems. These traits, Reed argues, indicate the existence of an "enduring South." Songs such as "Carolina, I Knew You," "Lubbock in My Rear View Mirror," "Why Me, Lord," "Sunday in the South," "The Coward of the County," "A Country Boy Can Survive," and "Sweet Southern Comfort" might be viewed as the musical illustrations of these persistent southern characteristics. The extensive acceptance of these songs and of country music in general suggests further that the gap between "southern" and "national" views has narrowed significantly since the 1960s.

In stressing the South's importance in shaping country music's style and content, we must not forget that the music has also done much to fashion or reaffirm public perceptions of the South and its people. Whether viewed as a land of placid domestic stability, populated by warm and gentle spirits, or as an exotic region filled with eccentric and violently impulsive individuals, the publicly perceived South has been, in large part, a musical creation. The outlines of an intriguing and musical South were first drawn by other music makers at least a century and a half ago, but country singers and songwriters have preserved and revitalized that tradition with songs that both document and mythologize the region. Country music often merely reinforces myths concerning the South, as do songs such as "A Country Boy Can Survive" and "Amos Moses," but, in songs including "Ode to Billy Joe," "Coat of Many Colors," "Sunday in the South," "Mud on the Tires," and "Good Directions," the music also captures the texture of the everyday life of average people in a way that no Tin Pan Alley writer was ever able to do. And in hit songs such as "California Cotton Fields" (penned by DALLAS FRAZIER), "The Roots of My Raising" (written by TOMMY COLLINS), and his own "Hungry Eyes," native Californian MERLE HAGGARD has lovingly and sensitively recalled the experiences of growing up in a family of southerners transplanted from Depression-era Oklahoma to the West Coast. Whether wedded to older ideas of fantasy and myth or committed to a realistic depiction of people and places, these songs continue to epitomize the historic relationship between the South and country music.

## Joe Talbot
b. Nashville, Tennessee, March 25, 1927; d. March 24, 2000

Joseph Hale Talbot, six feet, seven inches tall and salty of tongue, became a Nashville music industry icon. Inspired as a preschooler by the train whistle on a recording of "The Wreck of the Old 97," Talbot learned to play the steel guitar and served as one of HANK SNOW's Rainbow Ranch Boys during the singer's peak years (1950–54). Meanwhile, Talbot earned a Vanderbilt University law degree in 1952, at the insistence of his accountant father. But even with these credentials, he allowed, most of his efforts failed until he turned forty; prior to that age his experiences included three years of practicing law; traveling as a salesman for Rickenbacker guitars; and working at radio stations, music publishing companies, and record plants. Then, in the mid-1960s, two of his ventures began to pay off. The first was music publishing, a field in which he and partner Ted Harris started Harbot Music in 1965. (Talbot later became sole owner.) Dr. Russell T. Birmingham and Randall Yearwood encouraged Talbot in his second successful venture—record pressing. Soon Talbot and his partners owned two pressing plants: Precision Record Pressing, Inc., and United Record Pressing, Inc.

Talbot's business acumen and winsome personality soon made him a fixture on the boards of the Country Music Association (CMA) and the COUNTRY MUSIC HALL OF FAME AND MUSEUM; he became a lifetime director of the former and served as board chairman for both. Between 1967 and 1971 he managed the Nashville office of SESAC. Talbot eventually sold his pressing plants, concentrating on his Talbot Music Group until his death. Today his daughter Jana continues this enterprise. —*Ronnie Pugh*

## James Talley
b. Tulsa, Oklahoma, November 9, 1943

In the mid-1970s former social worker and carpenter James Talley recorded four critically acclaimed albums issued on CAPITOL RECORDS. Although Talley was marketed as a country singer, he was influenced by folk music and the blues as well as by country music, and he held his primary musical heroes—WOODY GUTHRIE, B. B. King, and BOB WILLS—in equally high regard. Each of Talley's Capitol albums contained original songs that wedded socially concerned lyrics to simple melodies; master instrumentalists such as JOHNNY GIMBLE, UNCLE JOSH GRAVES, and CHARLIE MCCOY provided accompaniment. Talley's music was serious, idiosyncratic, and often political—qualities that in the mid-1970s typically doomed a recording artist to little or no airplay on mainstream country radio. Nevertheless, he reached an enthusiastic, if small, audience.

Talley dealt himself a severe blow by leaving Capitol when he still owed the label three new albums. The label then deleted his four albums from its catalog, and other labels steered clear of him. Disillusioned, Talley went into the real estate business in Nashville in 1983. Beginning in 1989 Germany's Bear Family Records released several new Talley albums and reissued his earlier Capitol sides. Since 2000 Talley has released additional albums on his own Cimarron label. —*Ted Olson*

## Gid Tanner
b. Thomas Bridge, Georgia, June 6, 1885; d. May 13, 1960

OLD-TIME fiddler James Gideon Tanner made his living as a chicken farmer in northern Georgia, but in the world of country music he will be remembered as the patriarch of one of the most popular and influential STRINGBANDS of the 1920s: the SKILLET LICKERS. By the time he made his first recordings, in 1924, he was already renowned as a perennial favorite at Atlanta's celebrated fiddlers' conventions.

Showman first and fiddler second, Tanner regaled crowds with his singing and humorous antics. His prodigious recorded output from 1924 to 1941 reveals a fiddler of modest abilities (he played banjo on his last recordings) but a fine singer and entertainer. Tanner recorded mostly traditional folk songs and fiddle tunes of the nineteenth century or earlier. Though his earliest recordings were solos or duets with RILEY PUCKETT, his most successful discs were those recorded with the Skillet Lickers, a wild, exuberant ensemble whose personnel on COLUMBIA sides generally consisted of Tanner, Puckett, CLAYTON MCMICHEN, and Fate Norris. Tanner and the Skillet Lickers' best-selling discs were made in 1934 for RCA VICTOR, at which time Tanner's son, Gordon, played fiddle. Such favorites as "Back Up and Push" and "Down Yonder" (the latter reportedly selling more than 1 million copies) stayed in print for more than two decades. —*Norm Cohen*

## Barry & Holly Tashian
Barry Tashian b. Oak Park, Illinois, August 5, 1945
Holly P. Kimball Tashian b. New York, New York, January 8, 1946

A husband-wife acoustic duet, Nashville-based singer-songwriters Barry & Holly Tashian have performed on the GRAND OLE OPRY and *A PRAIRIE HOME COMPANION* and at numerous venues in the United States and abroad. Holly's song "Home" was twice nominated for a BLUEGRASS Grammy. Three of their songs hit #1 on the British country charts in 1992, and the title cut for their popular 1995 album *Straw into Gold* reached #11 on the *Gavin Report*'s AMERICANA chart. The Tashians cite THE EVERLY

BROTHERS, THE LOUVIN BROTHERS, and JIM & JESSE as musical influences.

Holly grew up in Westport, Connecticut, studying violin and piano and singing madrigals. She began singing country music as a harmony vocalist with the Outskirts (1976–80), a regional all-female band until Barry joined as drummer and vocalist.

Barry, who also grew up in Westport, began guitar at age eight and gravitated to sounds of rockers CARL PERKINS, Bo Diddley, and Little Richard. As a Boston University student (1963–64) he formed the Remains, a short-lived but highly acclaimed rock group, and then moved to the West Coast in 1967 to work with GRAM PARSONS and join the original Flying Burrito Brothers. Barry recorded with Parsons and EMMYLOU HARRIS on *GP* (1972) and was a guitarist and vocalist in Harris's Hot Band from 1980 to 1989.

Since 1989 the Tashians have recorded a number of albums with producer JIM ROONEY, including *Long Story Short* (Rock-A-Lot, 2008). As a session musician, Barry has also contributed to albums by Charlie Louvin, NANCI GRIFFITH, IRIS DEMENT, SUZY BOGGUSS, and Delia Bell. —*Cecelia Tichi*

## Tut Taylor
b. Milledgeville, Georgia, November 20, 1923

DOBRO virtuoso Robert Arthur "Tut" Taylor emerged from the BLUEGRASS ranks in the 1960s to become a respected session player and featured artist. A multi-instrumentalist, he took up the dobro after hearing ROY ACUFF's famed dobro player BASHFUL BROTHER OSWALD. Unlike most musicians, however, Taylor plays the instrument with a flat pick.

During the 1950s and 1960s Taylor hosted bluegrass jam sessions at Nashville's annual DJ CONVENTION and became a prominent trader and collector of vintage instruments. In 1964 he recorded *Twelve String Dobro* (World Pacific), to which GLEN CAMPBELL, CHRIS HILLMAN, and BILL KEITH contributed. Also in 1964, Taylor joined forces with CLARENCE and ROLAND WHITE, Billy Ray Lathum, and Victor Gaskin for the World Pacific release *Dobro Country*. Subsequent Taylor albums (on various labels) featured VASSAR CLEMENTS, Norman Blake, and SAM BUSH.

In 1970, in Nashville, Taylor, George Gruhn, and Randy Wood established GTR Instruments, forerunner of Nashville's famous Gruhn Guitars instrument store. With Wood and singer-guitarist Grant Boatright, Taylor opened the city's Old Time Pickin' Parlor, a music venue and instrument-building and -repair shop. Taylor left GTR to form a band with JOHN HARTFORD, Clements, and Blake, recording the 1971 Hartford album *Aereo-Plain* and touring widely. Taylor also recorded with LEON RUSSELL (*Hank Wilson's Back*, 1973).

Tut Taylor Music, his next venture, made stringed instruments under the Tennessee brand and built Ode instruments for Baldwin, which had acquired the Ode Banjo Company. (Taylor's son Mark continues to make and market custom instruments.) By 1978 the elder Taylor opened a tourist-oriented crafts and dulcimer business in Pigeon Forge, Tennessee, and then toured arts and crafts fairs before settling in 1992 in Maryville, Tennessee, his base for many years.

In addition, Taylor produced his own albums and collections by Bashful Brother Oswald and by Norman Blake. Together with Douglas, he produced and performed on the multiartist, Grammy-winning *The Great Dobro Sessions* (SUGAR HILL, 1994), which

also won IBMA honors for Instrumental Album and Recorded Event of the Year.

In 2010 Douglas and other dobro greats saluted him with the compilation *Southern Filibuster: A Tribute to Tut Taylor* (Koch/Entertainment One Music). As of 2011 Taylor was living in the mountains of western North Carolina. He has continued to record and to perform at conferences, festivals, and nearby venues. —*Frank and Marty Godbey*

## Tee Tot (Rufus Payne)
birthplace and birth date unknown; d. 1939

Rufus Payne was an itinerant black STRINGBAND musician whose existence is all but undocumented. Researcher Alice Harp places his birth in Lowndes Co., Alabama, circa 1884. In 1935 and 1936 Payne, who probably lived in Greenville, Alabama, at the time, gave guitar lessons to a teenaged HANK WILLIAMS, and such fame as he has rests on that accomplishment.

Payne led a group of musicians who performed on the sidewalks of small towns around Greenville. Williams summed up his influence in these terms: "I learned to play the git-tar from an old colored man. . . . He played in a colored street band. . . . I was shinin' shoes, sellin' newspapers, and followin' this old man around to get him to teach me to play the guitar. I'd give him fifteen cents, or whatever I could get hold of for the lesson." —*Colin Escott*

## Tennessee/Republic Records
established in Nashville, Tennessee, 1949; ended 1956

Record distributors Alan Bubis and William Beasley, in partnership with Bubis's cousin Reynold Bubis and Howard Allison, founded Tennessee Records in 1949 and released the label's first single in January 1950. The Nashville-based company had its own studio and publishing firm. Though Tennessee's only chart hit was DEL WOOD's "Down Yonder" (#12, 1951), its roster included Helen Carter (CARTER SISTERS), GRANT TURNER, RANDY HUGHES, and Kirk McGee (SAM AND KIRK McGEE). As Bubis and Beasley were shuttering Tennessee Records in late 1952, possibly due to conflict with the musicians' union, their Republic label was already in full swing. The two labels shared many of the same acts—including R&B singer Christine Kittrell—though Republic, active into 1956, recorded pop artists, including Pat Boone. —*Don Roy*

## Tenneva Ramblers
James "Jack" Grant b. Bristol, Tennessee, July 25, 1903; d. March 29, 1968
Claude Grant b. Bristol, Tennessee, April 17, 1906; d. October 1975
Jack Pierce b. Smyth County, Virginia, 1908; d. March 1950

Although the Tenneva Ramblers constituted one of the better STRINGBANDS of the 1920s, their fame derives largely from the brief time (May–August 1927) they were billed as the JIMMIE RODGERS Entertainers, accompanying the Father of Country Music.

Coining their name from the Tennessee-Virginia border that bisects their hometown, the group originated in the early 1920s with guitarist and lead vocalist Claude Grant, his brother Jack on mandolin, and fiddler Jack Pierce. They began by playing square dances and school auditoriums with a repertoire of folk songs, HAWAIIAN melodies, and current pop tunes. In 1927 they met Jimmie Rodgers in Johnson City, Tennessee, and agreed to join him on his continuing radio show at WWNC in Asheville, North Carolina. Soon they learned that RALPH PEER was holding auditions in Bristol for the Victor Talking Machine Company (predecessor to RCA VICTOR); but in a disagreement over how their names should appear on disc, the Grant brothers and Pierce left Rodgers before they could record together.

As the Tenneva Ramblers once more, they enlisted the services of banjoist Claude Slagle, and on August 4, prior to Rodgers's solo session that afternoon, the group made three sides for Victor. They recorded six more numbers for the label in February 1928, and, at their final session in October of that year, four sides for COLUMBIA.

As the Ramblers' popularity waned during the Depression, Jack Pierce left to join a Hopkinsville, Kentucky, band known as the Oklahoma Cowboys. The Grant brothers toured locally throughout the 1930s, sometimes joined by Smoky Davis, a BLACKFACE comedian. Pierce returned to the group briefly in the late-1940s, but soon after his death in 1950 the act no longer appeared professionally. —Nolan Porterfield

## Tent Shows

Tent shows belong to a grand tradition of touring shows, embracing circuses, BLACKFACE MINSTRELSY, MEDICINE SHOWS, and dramatic shows—the common denominators being variety and bringing entertainment within reach of rural and small-town audiences as well as urban ones. Although not confined exclusively to the GRAND OLE OPRY (e.g., the RENFRO VALLEY BARN DANCE also launched tent shows during the early 1940s), Opry tent shows were the most numerous and visible in the country music industry. Evidently the first was assembled about 1941 and headed by the blackface comedy team JAMUP AND HONEY. Also along for this tour was ROY ACUFF, then coming into his own as an Opry star. Soon Acuff was fronting his own unit, and BILL MONROE quickly did the same. Considering the large potential profits, this was hardly surprising; Acuff and Monroe estimated their incomes during 1942 and 1943, respectively, at $200,000 or more, most of which came from show dates.

By 1945 the Opry was fielding several tent units each season, which ran from spring to early fall. Routes were concentrated mainly in the Southeast, then country music's principal stronghold. Most tent show schedules consisted of one- or two-day stops in small towns, often of 5,000 or fewer inhabitants, for this is where most Southerners lived until well after World War II and where many families were slow to buy TV sets. Low admission prices—usually no more than a dollar or so—made tent shows accessible to a large public. Monroe, Acuff, and other troupe leaders played especially hard to their audiences' hunger for comedy and often featured band members who did pantomimes and burlesque routines as well as musical numbers. Monroe even pressed his tent unit into service as a baseball team that challenged local athletes.

The Opry continued to send out tent shows into the late-1950s, even into New England. But by then the growing popularity of television and touring rock & roll acts had cut into country artists' gate receipts, and Opry stars, like their counterparts elsewhere, were banding together in PACKAGE SHOWS focusing on urban auditoriums. —John W. Rumble

## Al Terry
b. Kaplan, Louisiana, January 14, 1922; d. November 23, 1985

Allison Joseph Theriot Jr. was among the first musicians of CAJUN ancestry to succeed in both country and ROCKABILLY. As a teenager he learned to play guitar and formed a band called the Drifting Cowboys, at about the same time HANK WILLIAMS began using the name. The group performed live on KVOL in Lafayette, Louisiana, where Terry also worked as an announcer.

Terry's recording career began in 1946, when he cut "I'll Be Glad When I'm Free" b/w "If You Want a Broken Heart" for Gold Star. Al and brother Bob Terry toured with Hank Williams in the fall of 1952. In 1954 Al released the original "Good Deal, Lucille"—complete with rockabilly/Cajun swagger and some French lyrics—for HICKORY RECORDS; accompanists included Bob on lap steel and guitarist CHET ATKINS. The record's Top Ten country success led to an appearance on the LOUISIANA HAYRIDE (cobilled with ELVIS PRESLEY) and tours with RED FOLEY, RAY PRICE, and MARTY ROBBINS. The song also did well for MOON MULLICAN and CARL SMITH.

Through the late 1960s Terry recorded for various labels. There were no more hits, but he remained quite popular in Louisiana, appearing on radio and television and running a nightclub in Lafayette. —Ben Sandmel

## Gordon Terry
b. Decatur, Alabama, October 7, 1931; d. April 9, 2006

Fiddler Gordon Terry once appeared destined for major stardom—the strikingly handsome and versatile entertainer was an actor and musician, fluent in playing BLUEGRASS, modern country, WESTERN SWING, and ROCKABILLY music. Though he never reached the heights many predicted for him, his achievements earned him a reputation as a highly respected country performer and Nashville recording session musician.

After apprenticing in his father's band, Terry became fiddler for BILL MONROE's Blue Grass Boys in late 1950. Drafted into the army in 1952, he worked with FARON YOUNG's Special Services band, the Circle A Wranglers, and he kept working with Young after their 1954 discharge.

Terry launched his singing career in 1956, recording for COLUMBIA, Cadence, and RCA VICTOR; he also appeared in three Republic westerns and the Sky King network television series. He moved to Los Angeles in 1958 and toured with the JOHNNY CASH show for four years. Before leaving California, Terry joined guitarist CLARENCE WHITE in backing Eric Weissberg and Marshall Brickman on their groundbreaking progressive bluegrass set New Dimensions in Banjo and Bluegrass; WARNER BROS. later used most of its tracks to complete the Deliverance motion picture soundtrack album.

Returning to Alabama in 1963, Terry operated Terrytown, a music and amusement complex in Loretta, Tennessee, until 1966. He continued to act, appearing in such cult favorite B-pictures as Girl from Tobacco Row. In 1970, under contract to CAPITOL, he recorded his only charted single, "The Ballad of J. C.," a novelty about Johnny Cash. Terry played fiddle on MERLE HAGGARD's 1970 BOB WILLS salute, A Tribute to the Best Damned Fiddle Player in the World, and later toured with Haggard's band the Strangers. He died in April 2006, following a struggle with emphysema and diabetes that had sidelined him for many years. —Dave Samuelson

# Texas Top Hands

Founded in 1945, the Texas Top Hands are a San Antonio–based WESTERN SWING band that still retains a loyal dancehall following. Over the years the group has recorded for Savoy, Everstate, TNT, and other labels, while backing RED RIVER DAVE McENERY on numerous recordings for Continental. The group's original lineup included Walter Kleypas (piano, accordion, leader), Clarence "Sleepy" Short (fiddle), W. W. "Rusty" Locke (steel guitar, leader), Harrell "Curley" Williams (guitar, fiddle), and George "Knee Hi" Holley (bass).

The Top Hands originated in 1941 as the Texas Tumbleweeds. By the time the band coalesced into the Texas Top Hands, at radio WOAI in 1945, Kleypas was its de facto leader. Under Kleypas the band enjoyed its most successful years: moving to KABC, the Top Hands recorded prolifically, appeared in several films with McEnery, and enjoyed a major regional hit with "Bandera Waltz." Subsequent bandleaders were steel guitarist Rusty Locke and Adams, who held the band's reins from 1955 to 1979. Since that time the band has been led by vocalist-guitarist Ray Sczepanik, who joined in 1967. —*Kevin Coffey*

# Texas Tornados (*see* Freddy Fender)

# IIIrd Tyme Out

Formed in 1991, quintet IIIrd Tyme Out became the decade's leading BLUEGRASS vocal group, earning seven consecutive IBMA Vocal Group of the Year awards between 1994 and 2000 for a sound built around strong harmonies and the expressive, high-pitched lead singing of three-time IBMA Male Vocalist of the Year Russell Moore. The group coalesced when guitarist Moore, bassist Ray Deaton, and fiddler Mike Hartgrove left DOYLE LAWSON's band, Quicksilver, to join with Lawson's first banjo player, the influential Terry Baucom, and mandolinist Alan Bibey.

IIIrd Tyme Out's self-titled REBEL RECORDS debut (1991) and follow-up, *Puttin' New Roots Down* (1992), established a popular and widely imitated modern bluegrass style the group has maintained through changes in personnel and label affiliations. Though best known for impeccable, rich harmonies (including many quartet arrangements), these have always been underpinned by instrumental virtuosity and a distinctively heavy rhythmic drive, applied to a repertoire that adds WESTERN SWING, R&B, and older country material to mainstream bluegrass songs. Reflecting the most constant and notable element in their sound, the band renamed itself Russell Moore & IIIrd Tyme Out in 2008. Besides Moore, at this writing members include Wayne Benson (mandolin), Steve Dilling (banjo), Justen Haynes (fiddle), and Edgar Loudermilk (bass). —*Jon Weisberger*

# B. J. Thomas
b. Hugo, Oklahoma, August 7, 1942

Billy Joe Thomas began his recording career as a pop singer rendering a country standard; later he moved into country and gospel.

Thomas grew up in Rosenberg, Texas, near Houston. He recorded HANK WILLIAMS's "I'm So Lonesome I Could Cry" at Huey Meaux's Houston studio. Released on Scepter Records in 1966, it became a Top Ten pop hit. Thomas was less successful with another Hank Williams song, "I Can't Help It (If I'm Still in Love With You)" (1967).

Next came a string of pop hits, including "Billy and Sue," "The Eyes of a New York Woman," and "Hooked on a Feeling." His biggest pop record was "Raindrops Keep Fallin' on My Head" (1969), the Academy Award–winning theme song for the movie *Butch Cassidy and the Sundance Kid*.

In 1975 Thomas had his first country hit on the ABC label with "(Hey Won't You Play) Another Somebody Done Somebody Wrong Song." Produced by CHIPS MOMAN, the record went to #1 on both the country and pop charts and won a 1975 Grammy for Best Country Song. A series of personal problems beset the singer, who emerged as a born-again Christian in 1976 and began recording successfully for the Christian label Myrrh. He received five Grammys for his gospel recordings, one each year between 1977 and 1981.

In 1978 Thomas returned to country music, first for MCA and then for COLUMBIA and its subsidiary Cleveland International, where he had two #1 country hits in 1983: "Whatever Happened to Old Fashioned Love" (Cleveland International) and "New Looks from an Old Lover" (Columbia). In 1981 Thomas joined the GRAND OLE OPRY.

Thomas continues to enjoy a dedicated, though smaller, fan base. His single "You Call That a Mountain," title track for a Kardina Records album, became a minor chart record in 2000. —*Don Cusic*

# Ernest Thompson
b. Forsyth County, North Carolina, 1892; d. 1961

Born Ernest Errott Thompson, this blind street singer was one of the earliest country singers to record commercially, cutting thirty-four sides for COLUMBIA in 1924. He had an unusually high-pitched voice, reportedly the result of a childhood accident in which his clothing caught fire and gave him a "scorched throat and voice box." Although born with perfect vision, Thompson lost his sight progressively over a ten-year period (possibly due to a sawmill accident). At the North Carolina State School for the Blind he learned piano tuning and broom making but was more interested in music, eventually learning enough to play as a one-man band.

Thompson frequently performed at dances and schools and on the streets until the late 1940s. Generally he accompanied himself on guitar or harmonica, although he was proficient on several stringed instruments. He had a large repertoire of traditional BALLADS, hymns, pop songs, and instrumental numbers. Thompson usually worked alone, but he sometimes joined a STRINGBAND including his sister, Agnes, and a niece, Connie Faw Sides. Like many street singers he worked a specific area, and in his case he covered a rather large one: Forsyth, Surry, and Stokes Counties in North Carolina and bordering counties in southern Virginia.

From April to September 1924 Thompson went to New York for recording sessions. His first two releases, "Are You from Dixie," a pop song from 1915, and "Wreck of the Southern Old 97," a ballad about a 1903 train wreck, both became standards. (HENRY WHITTER recorded the latter song four months earlier, but the two versions were not identical.) Thompson's repertoire also included the 1896 Gussie Davis sentimental classic

"The Baggage Coach Ahead," the Horatio R. Palmer hymn "Yield Not to Temptation," and the comical 1919 Prohibition protest song "How Are You Going to Wet Your Whistle (When the Whole Darn World Goes Dry)." Connie Sides went along on Thompson's second recording session and sang on a few numbers, thereby becoming one of the first country female vocalists on disc.—*W. K. McNeil*

## Hank Thompson

b. Waco, Texas, September 3, 1925; d. November 6, 2007

Few country music artists can claim the longevity and track record of Hank Thompson. Between 1948 and 1974 he scored twenty-eight Top Ten hits, with another nineteen in the Top Twenty, and continued to chart into the 1980s. Many of these, including "Green Light," "Whoa Sailor," and "Waiting in the Lobby of Your Heart," he penned himself, thus securing his place in country music's venerable singer-songwriter tradition. Along the way Thompson created a potent blend of HONKY-TONK and WESTERN SWING that long provided continuity amid country's experimentation with rock and pop sounds.

Like many country artists, Henry William Thompson took an early interest in music, enthralled by cowboy movie idol GENE AUTRY. With a Christmas present from his parents, a four-dollar, secondhand guitar, he was on his way. By the time he finished high school he was broadcasting over radio station WACO as Hank the Hired Hand, sponsored by a local flour company.

After graduating, Thompson enlisted in the U.S. Navy. While stationed in San Diego, he persuaded his superiors to let him play area clubs, and after putting out to sea he entertained his shipmates as well. He kept on broadcasting, too, over a network of small

*Hank Thompson*

stations organized by American military personnel in the South Pacific. While in service he took advantage of training programs and, after leaving the military, studied electrical engineering at Southern Methodist University, the University of Texas, and Princeton University—making him one of country music's better-educated stars.

Although he pondered an engineering career, radio work and his first hit record, "Whoa Sailor," kept him on a show business track. Assisted by prominent DJ HAL HORTON of the 50,000-watt KRLD in Dallas, this Globe Records release became a minor regional success. Thompson also recorded four sides with the Blue Bonnet label before TEX RITTER, then a prominent act on CAPITOL RECORDS, helped him gain a contract with this larger, major label. During 1948–49 Thompson notched hits such as "Humpty Dumpty Heart" (based on the children's nursery rhyme), "Green Light," and a remake of "Whoa Sailor."

During the 1950s Thompson's songwriting talents, booming baritone, precise diction, and powerful combination of western swing and honky-tonk helped him continue his string of hits. The year 1952 brought his first #1 disc, "The Wild Side of Life," which inspired the hit that launched KITTY WELLS's career: "It Wasn't God Who Made Honky-Tonk Angels." Subsequent 1950s Thompson chart-makers included "Waiting in the Lobby of Your Heart," "Rub-A-Dub-Dub," "Yesterday's Girl," "Wake Up, Irene," "Honky Tonk Girl," "Most of All," "The Blackboard of My Heart," and "Squaws Along the Yukon," all Top Ten records.

During these years Thompson also made inroads into television, hosting a variety show on WKY-TV in Oklahoma City from 1954 to 1957. In addition, he was one of the earliest country performers to entertain in Las Vegas showrooms, and he recorded one of country's first live albums, *Live at the Golden Nugget*, there in 1960. Meanwhile, using his engineering knowledge, he built top-flight sound and lighting systems that heightened his drawing power at the more than 250 show dates he typically played each year. Thanks to his musical and technical leadership, his Brazos Valley Boys were *Billboard*'s top-ranked band from 1953 to 1965.

Into the 1960s and beyond, Thompson's easy manner made him a welcome guest on network TV variety shows, as did a dynamic stage presence magnified by his size (he stood six feet, two inches tall); a rough-hewn, handsome appearance; and custom-made western outfits. But following "A Six Pack to Go" (#10, 1960) and "Oklahoma Hills" (#7, 1961), he didn't make the Top Ten again until 1968's "On Tap, in the Can, or in the Bottle" and "Smoky the Bar," both recorded early in his association with DOT RECORDS, which he began after a brief stay at WARNER BROS. Although two more Top Ten hits came in 1974, the 1970s belonged to country pop, and Thompson's chart success dwindled to the point that he pared down his road schedule and spent more time hunting or tending to his various real estate, broadcasting, and music publishing interests.

In the 1980s, however, as hard-edged country enjoyed renewed popularity, Thompson hit the road again in earnest, playing dates in Europe, Africa, Asia, and South America as well as in the United States. He also kept recording, and he signed with Nashville's STEP ONE RECORDS in 1987. In 1997 CURB RECORDS released *Hank Thompson and Friends*, a critically acclaimed collection of duets pairing Thompson with BROOKS & DUNN, VINCE GILL, GEORGE JONES, LYLE LOVETT, TANYA TUCKER, and Kitty Wells, among others. Thompson's hard-core honky-tonk–western swing sound—marked by a strong rhythm section of piano, bass, guitar, and drums; lead and fill parts supplied by twin fiddles, electric guitar, and steel; frequent shifts from 2/4 to 4/4 time; and above all his magnetic vocals—has continued to influence country acts such as GEORGE STRAIT, DWIGHT YOAKAM, and ASLEEP AT THE WHEEL.

Hank Thompson was elected to THE COUNTRY MUSIC HALL OF FAME in 1989. He performed throughout the world until just before his death from lung cancer in November 2007. —*John W. Rumble*

## Uncle Jimmy Thompson
b. Smith County, Tennessee, 1848; d. February 17, 1931

Though Uncle Jimmy Thompson had one of the shorter careers in country music—from 1925 until 1931—he had one of the most potent. His defining moment came on November 28, 1925, when he played an informal program of fiddle tunes on the newly opened Nashville station WSM, a broadcast that led to the founding of the GRAND OLE OPRY. Cantankerous, hard-drinking, white-bearded, and loquacious, he was a press agent's dream, and the famous pictures of him seated before the microphone with Opry founder GEORGE D. HAY are among the most iconic in country music history. Behind the legend, though, was a fine musician who represented a long tradition of American fiddling.

Jesse Donald Thompson was born in Smith County, Tennessee, in 1848. Shortly before the Civil War, his family moved to Texas. There he developed his fiddling style, adopting long-bow techniques favored in Texas and learning tunes such as "Flying Clouds" from fiddlers whose styles dated from earlier decades. As a young man he traveled widely, eventually marrying and settling back in Smith County and temporarily taking up farming. Restless, he moved his family back to Texas, where he won a 1907 national championship fiddling contest. By 1912 he had returned to Tennessee again, and after his first wife died he married a Wilson County woman named "Aunt" Ella Manners. By now he was well known as a fiddler, and he traveled the area in a homemade camper, playing for tips while Aunt Ella buck-danced.

Thompson gained his WSM debut through his niece, Eva Thompson Jones, a staff pianist for the station. A few weeks after this initial appearance, he was asked to become a founding member of and regular performer on the *WSM Barn Dance*, soon renamed the Grand Ole Opry. His fame spread even farther when he became involved with Henry Ford's national fiddling contests in early 1926

*Uncle Jimmy Thompson*

and exchanged taunts with Maine's champion fiddler Mellie Dunham. As the Opry became more structured, Thompson spent less and less time on it. By 1928 he made just two appearances a year, partly due to his unreliability and drinking and partly because he could earn more money doing personal appearances. He did make a handful of records: a splendid rendition of "Billy Wilson" b/w "Karo" for COLUMBIA in 1926 and a version of "Flying Clouds," replete with dialog, for Vocalion in 1930. These recordings only hint at Thompson's huge repertoire that he claimed to include more than a thousand tunes. —*Charles Wolfe*

## Thrasher Family

This 1920s gospel group was headed by the Rev. M. L. Thrasher, a Congregationalist minister from Braselton, Georgia. Thrasher began his recording career by preaching and singing bass on some of the best-selling records by SMITH'S SACRED SINGERS, led by J. Frank Smith, but by mid-1927 he had dropped out, believing he could do better with his own group. Thrasher recruited some of the original members of Smith's group, among them singer-guitarist Clarence Cronic, and started his band a few months later, billed as M. L. Thrasher and his Gospel Singers. Thrasher began a run of some twenty-six COLUMBIA sides, including his best-seller, "When the Roll Is Called Up Yonder" b/w "What Shall We Do with Mother."

In later years he recorded an additional six titles with members of his family as the Thrasher Family. By 1931 his recording career was effectively over, and Rev. Thrasher returned to his original vocation as a preacher. —*Charles Wolfe*

## The Three Little Maids
Eva Alaine Overstake b. Decatur, Illinois, July 23, 1918; d. November 17, 1951
Evelyn Overstake b. Decatur, Illinois, December 20, 1913; d. April 15, 2002
Lucille Overstake b. Decatur, Illinois, January 13, 1915; d. December 16, 1978

One of the *NATIONAL BARN DANCE*'s most beloved acts during the early 1930s, the Three Little Maids infused vintage BALLADS and sentimental songs with sprightly three-part harmonies. Influenced by the Brox Sisters, a popular recording trio of the mid-1920s, their sound was rooted in Evelyn Overstake's soft, low alto vocals and complemented by Eva Overstake's yodels and Lucille Overstake's deft guitar work.

The daughters of two Salvation Army workers, the Overstake Sisters began harmonizing at school functions and mission meetings in Decatur, Illinois. This led to radio appearances over WJBL–Decatur and other central Illinois stations; WLS brought them to Chicago in late summer 1931. Renamed the Three Little Maids, the sisters sang on the local broadcasts and NBC network feeds of the *National Barn Dance*; they also appeared on WLS's daily *Round-Up* and *Dinnerbell* programs. Like many *Barn Dance* acts, the Maids signed with the AMERICAN RECORD CORPORATION; they cut four titles in April 1933, all issued on Sears, Roebuck's CONQUEROR RECORDS.

On August 9, 1933, Eva married CUMBERLAND RIDGE RUNNERS singer-bassist RED FOLEY, whose wife had died in childbirth earlier that year. The Overstakes continued performing and recorded four more titles for BLUEBIRD that December. Eva's pregnancy ended the act in early 1934.

Evelyn maintained a solo career on WLS through 1942; her younger sisters sang occasionally at midwestern farm meetings until spring 1935, when Lucille moved to Memphis. Eva then formed the Play Party Girls with Jean Davis and toured that summer with the Cumberland Ridge Runners. Lucille later performed as Jenny Lou Carson; Eva had a brief solo career as Judy Martin. —*Dave Samuelson*

## Sonny Throckmorton
b. Carlsbad, New Mexico, April 2, 1941

Every country songwriter dreams about having the hot streak Sonny Throckmorton had from 1976 to 1980. Signed for a second stretch to country music powerhouse Tree Publishing (he had lost his original deal due to a lack of hits), the affable Texan penned such hits as "I'm Knee Deep in Loving You" for Dave & Sugar, "If We're Not Back in Love by Monday" and "The Way I Am" for Merle Haggard, and "Middle Age Crazy" for Jerry Lee Lewis. Throckmorton also wrote "I Wish I Was Eighteen Again" for Lewis and for George Burns, "It's a Cheatin' Situation" for Moe Bandy, "Temporarily Yours" for Jeanne Pruett, and "Trying to Love Two Women" for the Oak Ridge Boys.

The son of a Pentecostal preacher, James Fron Throckmorton bounced between San Francisco and Los Angeles before moving to Nashville in 1964 at the urging of steel guitarist–producer–music publisher Pete Drake. Throckmorton claimed his first major country success in 1966 with "How Long Has It Been," a #6 hit for Bobby Lewis. The song's title proved to be prophetic, however. Throckmorton hit a dry spell and went to Texas in 1975 for a few months. When he returned to Nashville, his luck changed dramatically.

In addition to writing songs, Throckmorton recorded for Starcrest, Mercury, and MCA with modest success. A double-sided single of "Smooth Sailin'" b/w "Last Cheater's Waltz" went to #47 on *Billboard*'s country charts in 1979. However, both songs were major hits for T. G. Sheppard, for whom "Last Cheater's Waltz" reached #1. Throckmorton continued to score hits in the 1980s with his writing. His credits during that decade include The Judds' "Why Not Me," Mel McDaniel's "Stand Up," and George Strait's "The Cowboy Rides Away."

NSAI named Throckmorton Songwriter of the Year in 1978, 1979, and 1980, and he shared honors with others as BMI Songwriter of the Year in 1980. He was inducted into the Nashville Songwriters Hall of Fame in 1987.

In 1988 he moved to Brownwood, Texas, to care for his now-deceased father. He continues to live there, writing songs and performing occasionally. —*Jay Orr*

## Mel Tillis
b. Pahokee, Florida, August 8, 1932

Lonnie Melvin Tillis, who is gifted with a robust country baritone, parlayed his success as a respected Nashville songwriter in the 1950s and 1960s into a substantial recording career that flourished in the 1970s and early 1980s. Tillis is also famous for his chronic stutter—the result of a childhood case of malaria—a liability he used to enhance his affable, down-home stage persona. (He even titled his 1984 autobiography *Stutterin' Boy*.)

Tillis briefly attended the University of Florida, served in the U.S. Air Force, and worked on the railroad before coming to Nashville in 1957. One of his first big successes came that year when Webb Pierce's version of Tillis's "I'm Tired" went to #3 on

*Mel Tillis*

the country charts. "Detroit City," one of his most famous compositions (cowritten with Danny Dill), was a Top Ten country hit and a Top Twenty pop hit for Bobby Bare in 1963. In 1969 Kenny Rogers & the First Edition had a #6 pop hit and a #39 country single with Tillis's "Ruby, Don't Take Your Love to Town." Other early Tillis-penned hits include "Tupelo County Jail" (cocredited to and recorded by Webb Pierce), "Heart Over Mind" (Ray Price), and "Snakes Crawl at Night" (Charley Pride).

Tillis launched his own recording career with Columbia in the late 1950s. In 1963 he and Webb Pierce had a modestly successful duet single, "How Come Your Dog Don't Bite Nobody but Me." Tillis moved on to Kapp Records in the mid-1960s and later to MGM Records at about the turn of the decade. But it was not until the 1970s that he became a significant player in the charts, on MGM and, later, MCA. Some of his #1 hits—which stylistically ran the gamut from honky-tonk to light country-pop—include "I Ain't Never," "Good Woman Blues," "Heart Healer," "Coca Cola Cowboy," and "Southern Rains." He won CMA's Entertainer of the Year Award in 1976 and was inducted into the Nashville Songwriters Hall of Fame in that same year. In 1979 he signed with Elektra Records, and in the early 1980s he recorded for MCA, and briefly for RCA.

Tillis has occasionally ventured into feature films, mostly of the lightweight comedy/action variety. His motion picture credits include *W.W. and the Dixie Dancekings* (1975, with Burt Reynolds), *Smokey and the Bandit II* (1980, also with Reynolds), *Murder in Music City* (a 1979 made-for-TV movie), *Cannonball Run* (1982), *Cannonball Run II* (1984), and *Uphill All the Way* (1989, with Roy Clark).

Though his recording career began to wane by the mid-1980s, Tillis, a shrewd businessman, had by then segued into various business ventures, including management of his extensive music-publishing concerns and his theater in Branson, Missouri, where he frequently performs.

In 2007 his daughter PAM TILLIS, herself a GRAND OLE OPRY member, inducted her father into the show's cast. Later that year, he was elected to THE COUNTRY MUSIC HALL OF FAME. —*Bob Allen*

## Pam Tillis
b. Plant City, Florida, July 24, 1957

Pam Tillis has distinguished herself as a vocal stylist by pairing contemporary country lyrics with traditional country vocals while also becoming one of the few female country singers to write and solely produce her own albums.

The oldest of country star MEL TILLIS's five children, Pam often allowed that she loved his success but resented the absences that his tour schedule demanded. A trained classical pianist and self-taught guitarist, she performed her first solo gig at Nashville's Exit/In as a teenager. At sixteen, her face was injured in a car accident, resulting in many years of surgical reconstruction. When she recovered, she enrolled in the University of Tennessee and formed her first band, presenting jug band tunes with a COUNTRY-ROCK edge.

In 1976 Tillis briefly returned to Nashville to write songs and work in her father's publishing company but soon headed to San Francisco to perform jazz and rock with her band Freelight and sell Avon cosmetics to supplement her income. After two years she became a Nashville session singer and songwriter, penning songs recorded by CONWAY TWITTY, HIGHWAY 101, JUICE NEWTON, and Chaka Khan.

Tillis signed with WARNER BROS. RECORDS and released the pop-rock album *Above and Beyond the Doll of Cutey* (1983). After five low-level country chart entries, she left the label for a staff writing job with TREE PUBLISHING. During the next few years she changed her focus from pop to contemporary country.

A 1989 move to ARISTA RECORDS brought the soulful soprano hit singles and a string of gold and platinum albums. Her Arista debut, *Put Yourself in My Place* (1991), yielded her first

Top Five country single, "Don't Tell Me What to Do" (1990–91) as well as the #3 hit "Maybe It Was Memphis" (1991–92). *Sweetheart's Dance* netted Tillis her first #1, "Mi Vida Loca (My Crazy Life)" (1994–95) while becoming her first platinum album. In 1994 CMA named her Female Vocalist of the Year. *All of This Love*, her first effort as a solo producer, contained more hits, including "Deep Down" and "The River and the Highway" (1995–96).

"All the Good Ones are Gone" and "Land of the Living," both in 1997, proved to be her last Top Tens of the 1990s. Subsequent recordings, while artistically strong, have had relatively little commercial impact. Nevertheless, she joined the GRAND OLE OPRY in 2000, saluted her father's songs on her album *It's All Relative* (Lucky Dog), and released the album *Rhinestoned* in 2007 on her own Stellar Cat label, all while continuing to tour. —*Marjie McGraw*

## Floyd Tillman
b. Ryan, Oklahoma, December 8, 1914; d. August 22, 2003

During the 1930s and 1940s, singer-songwriter Floyd Tillman contributed to the rise of WESTERN SWING and HONKY-TONK while penning country music standards, some of which were among the genre's earliest crossover hits. WILLIE NELSON dubbed him the Original Outlaw for his ability to transcend musical stereotypes and stylistic boundaries.

The son of a sharecropper, Tillman grew up in the cotton mill town of Post, Texas. As a young man he worked as a Western Union telegraph operator while playing mandolin with his brothers at local dances. In about 1934 he began singing as well, forging a distinctive style that has influenced numerous singers, Willie Nelson being the best known. As jazz singers did, he freely interpreted meter and melody, often coming in ahead of or behind the beat; likewise, he often slurred words and bent notes. Later he mastered the resonator guitar, eventually playing jazzy solos on an electrified model; he played lead electric guitar for ADOLPH HOFNER, a western swing bandleader based in San Antonio. There, listening to other musicians as well as recordings, Tillman absorbed the sounds and styles of numerous pop, jazz, blues, and country artists.

Tillman's songwriting, singing, and guitar-playing skills led to jobs with Houston pop bandleader Mack Clark and western swing groups fronted by LEON "PAPPY" SELPH and CLIFF BRUNER. Personnel changed frequently in those days, and Tillman worked with many top musicians in these bands, including steel guitarist TED DAFFAN and singer-pianist MOON MULLICAN.

Tillman recorded as a featured vocalist with Selph's Blue Ridge Playboys in 1939; later that same year, DECCA recorded him as a solo performer. Though his early recordings mainly sought to provide danceable rhythms, songs such as "Daisy May," recorded in 1940, reveal his trademark half-singing, half-speaking vocals.

By now Tillman had scored his first big songwriting hit, "It Makes No Difference Now," cut by Cliff Bruner in 1938 and pop star Bing Crosby in 1940. Tillman himself recorded the 1944 multimarket hit "Each Night at Nine," which appealed to Americans separated from loved ones by military service during World War II. During the conflict Tillman served as a radio operator, and being stationed near Houston allowed him to keep recording. After war's end his radio and club work reinforced Houston's role as a country music center.

Tillman continued to write prolifically and hit the bull's-eye again with "I Love You So Much It Hurts," a love song eventually recorded by RED FOLEY, Andy Williams, and Vic Damone.

*Pam Tillis*

*Floyd Tillman*

Tillman's own COLUMBIA rendition became a #5 country hit in 1948. He demonstrated his versatility with "Slippin' Around," possibly country music's most recognized cheating song, which CAPITOL artists JIMMY WAKELY and Margaret Whiting took to #1 on the country and pop charts in 1949. Tillman's reading of the song became a Top Five country disc that same year. His recording of "I Gotta Have My Baby Back," another original, reached #4 in 1950.

At the peak of his career the independent-minded musician decided to retire from grinding road work. In truth, however, Tillman never quit music altogether. Until his death, he continued to record occasionally and to make infrequent TV appearances. He also kept writing, eventually counting more than 1,000 songs to his credit. An estimated 50 million recordings have featured his tunes.

Tillman was elected to the NASHVILLE SONGWRITERS HALL OF FAME in 1970 and to THE COUNTRY MUSIC HALL OF FAME in 1984. —*John W. Rumble*

## Aaron Tippin
b. Pensacola, Florida, July 3, 1958

Beginning in the 1990s, Aaron Tippin's in-your-face delivery and blue-collar pride made him popular with country purists.

Raised in the hills of South Carolina, he initially worked as a private pilot for corporate executives. He competed unsuccessfully on TNN: THE NASHVILLE NETWORK's *You Can Be a Star* in 1986 and then moved to Nashville in 1987, working as a pipe welder, heavy equipment operator, and truck driver while honing his songwriting skills. He also lifted weights and competed in bodybuilding contests.

Tippin was signed as a writer by ACUFF-ROSE PUBLICATIONS, and his tunes were recorded by artists including CHARLEY PRIDE

and DAVID BALL. When RCA signed Tippin as a singer, many of his peers were emulating GEORGE STRAIT, but he reached back to the emotional whine of HANK WILLIAMS and WEBB PIERCE.

From 1990 to 1993, Tippin's Top Ten hits included "You've Got to Stand For Something" (1991), "There Ain't Nothing Wrong With the Radio" (1992), "My Blue Angel" (1993), and "Working Man's Ph.D." (1993). Four consecutive albums were million-sellers. Fans wore hard hats and overalls to his shows, relishing his highly physical performances, working-class values, and patriotism. He was the first singer to entertain troops during the Persian Gulf War crisis of 1990.

After a slump in 1994–95 Tippin hit #1 with "That's as Close as I'll Get to Loving You" (1995–96). His album *Tool Box* led to a tool belt as stage attire and a tie-in with Channelock Tools. Slipping sales prompted a move to LYRIC STREET RECORDS, where he returned to Top Ten with "For You I Will" (1998–99), from *What This Country Needs*, and the #1 hit "Kiss This" (2000), from the hit album *People Like Us*. Following the September 11, 2001, terrorist attacks on the United States, Tippin's "Where the Stars and Stripes and the Eagle Fly" climbed to #2 country and into the pop Top 20.

Once again, his singles flagged, and forming Nippit Records in partnership with Rust Nashville in 2006 proved unsuccessful. Signing with the Country Crossing label in 2008, he released *In Overdrive*, a cover album of trucking songs, in 2009. —*Robert K. Oermann*

## TNN: The Nashville Network
established in Nashville, Tennessee, March 7, 1983

The Nashville Network found a niche on cable television by focusing on country music and the country lifestyle, exploring these themes through talk shows, music videos, live concerts, game shows, sports, and dance programs. The network's success helped fuel a country music resurgence in the 1980s and 1990s by providing national exposure for the genre's performers and their music videos.

In the early years, eighteen hours of programming each day was produced by The Nashville Network and several outside production companies. The network's cornerstone program, *Nashville Now*, featured veteran broadcaster RALPH EMERY as host; the talk show highlighted interviews and performances by country music artists five nights a week in prime-time evening hours. Other prominent shows were hosted by BILL ANDERSON, BOBBY BARE, CROOK & CHASE, actress Florence Henderson, and David Holt.

TNN's significant milestones included: in September 1985, live, exclusive coverage of the first Farm Aid concert; in April 1986, the creation of TNN Motor Sports and TNN Outdoors, which added racing events (including NASCAR), fishing, hunting, and other outdoor sports to the programming lineup; and in June 1990, the launch of fan-voted TNN Music City News Awards.

Initially owned by WSM, Inc., a subsidiary of the National Life and Accident Insurance Company, TNN became the property of the GAYLORD ENTERTAINMENT COMPANY after Gaylord bought WSM, the GRAND OLE OPRY, OPRYLAND USA, and other former National Life/WSM entertainment properties. Westinghouse-CBS bought TNN in 1995 and sold it to Viacom in 1997, which made it part of its many music-centered cable networks, including MTV and VH1.

In 1998, Viacom dropped The Nashville Network name and went solely with TNN. In 2000, TNN dropped country programming altogether and marketed itself as TNN: The National Network.

In 2003, highlighting wrestling and other male-oriented programming, the former TNN became Spike TV. —*Bob Paxman*

## Tootsie's Orchid Lounge
established March 1960

Located at 422 Broadway in Nashville, directly across the alley from THE RYMAN AUDITORIUM, Tootsie's Orchid Lounge may be the world's most famous country music bar. With its close proximity to the GRAND OLE OPRY, Tootsie's provided an informal gathering place for singers, musicians, and, most famously, struggling songwriters. WILLIE NELSON pitched the song "Hello Walls" to FARON YOUNG while inside Tootsie's, and ROGER MILLER wrote his career breakthrough hit, "Dang Me," by imagining himself at the famous Nashville hangout.

Known as Mom's Place when run by Louise Hackler, the bar was purchased by entertainers Jeff Bess and Hattie Louise "Tootsie" Bess in March 1960. Hailing from Hohenwald, Tennessee, she and her husband operated a series of nightclubs during the 1950s. The Besses divorced shortly after buying the bar, and Tootsie became sole proprietress and den mother to the ne'er-do-wells who congregated there. (She called them her "funky young 'uns.") Famous for her good heart, Bess kept a cigar box of unpaid tabs that totaled hundreds of dollars. Kind as she was, she was tough on troublemakers. She utilized a hat pin to motivate those who were too casual about leaving their barstool at closing time—an eviction tool in honor of which CHARLEY PRIDE gave her a jeweled version.

Tootsie's was hit hard when the Grand Ole Opry moved to OPRYLAND in 1974. "They ran off and left me, I didn't go off and leave them," Bess said at the time. As business fell off, her health also deteriorated, and she died February 18, 1978. Since then, Tootsie's Orchid Lounge has changed hands numerous times and has been the subject of various legal battles. Steve Smith bought the bar in 1992 and eventually expanded it to include Tootsie's locations at the Nashville International Airport and Panama City, Florida. Smith launched Tootsie's Records, an independent label, in 2003.

Though it has always been a popular stop for tourists, its fate has been tied to the commercial vicissitudes of Nashville's Lower Broadway district. When that district underwent a revival in the early to mid-1990s, Tootsie's became a flash point for an underground, roots-oriented country music scene. TERRI CLARK, Greg Garing, and some members of BR 549 (before that band was fully formed) performed at Tootsie's en route to signing record deals. —*Daniel Cooper*

## Mitchell Torok
b. Houston, Texas, October 28, 1929

Mitchell Torok is best remembered as the composer of "Mexican Joe," the song that launched JIM REEVES toward stardom, though Torok also found modest success as a recording artist. The son of Hungarian immigrants, he became interested in country music while growing up in Houston. After high school, Torok flirted briefly with a music career before graduating from Stephen F. Austin State College in Nacogdoches, Texas.

In 1953 Torok met ABBOTT RECORDS owner FABOR ROBISON and played "Mexican Joe" for him. Robison produced the Jim Reeves recording, and it became a #1 country song for nine weeks in 1953. In that same year Torok wrote and recorded "Caribbean."

It, too, reached #1 on the country charts, and a new recording of it became a #27 pop hit in 1959.

During the 1950s Torok was a LOUISIANA HAYRIDE regular and had a #9 country hit with "Hootchy Kootchy Henry (From Hawaii)" (1954) as well as a #25 pop record, "Pledge of Love" (1957). In 1956 his song "When Mexico Gave Up the Rumba," released on BRUNSWICK in England, became a #6 pop hit there. Torok recorded for various labels through the years, including DECCA, MERCURY, CAPITOL, RCA, and Reprise. His songs have been recorded by artists ranging from HANK SNOW to Dean Martin and have included Vernon Oxford's #17 country hit "Redneck! (The Redneck National Anthem)." —*Don Roy*

## Town Hall Party
established in Compton, California, ca. 1952; ended 1960

One of Southern California's most popular country music television programs, Bill Wagnon's *Town Hall Party* began as a KFI radio broadcast in 1951 and first hit the small screen either in late 1952 or early 1953. The show lasted until 1960.

Broadcast live from Compton, California, every Saturday night on Los Angeles station KTTV, channel eleven, the three-hour program was emceed by Jay Stewart, who later appeared on the long-running TV game show *Let's Make a Deal*. Each *Town Hall Party* segment had its own sponsor (a furniture company, Rheingold Beer, Chevrolet), and the show featured a cast of thirty-two, whose ranks included the COLLINS KIDS, JOHNNY BOND, JOE & ROSE LEE MAPHIS, Les "Carrot Top" Anderson, SKEETS McDONALD, and MERLE TRAVIS. Wagnon also booked an average of ten guest performers each week; among those who appeared were EDDIE DEAN, the MADDOX BROTHERS & ROSE, LEFTY FRIZZELL, and JOHNNY CASH. The show helped launch the careers of California-based talent such as FREDDIE HART and BUCK OWENS.

Audiences at the 3,000-capacity Town Hall were not seated, allowing them to crowd around the bandstand, and Wagnon also ran dances there every Friday night. By the mid-1950s the program was being filmed for overseas broadcast by Armed Forces Television Service. Screen Gems, a Columbia pictures subsidiary, shot thirty-nine half-hour episodes of a show titled *Western Ranch Party*, hosted by TEX RITTER, which used much the same cast and aired in syndication for several years beginning in 1957. —*Jonny Whiteside*

## Merle Travis
b. Rosewood, Kentucky, November 29, 1917; d. October 20, 1983

The multitalented Merle Travis was an innovative guitarist, agile songwriter, distinctive vocalist, creative guitar designer, gifted cartoonist, and author. He profoundly influenced several generations of performers—from CHET ATKINS to Merle's biological son, entertainer Thom Bresh, and hit makers including MARTY STUART.

Merle Robert Travis, son of farmer Rob Travis and his wife, Etta, grew up in the heart of western Kentucky's coal country. When Rob Travis took a job at a nearby mine in 1925, the family moved to a coal company–owned farm near Ebenezer, Kentucky. At age twelve Merle became obsessed with learning the area's unique guitar finger-picking style, which involved playing syncopated accompaniment on the bass strings with the right thumb

Town Hall Party *cast*

while simultaneously playing lead on the treble strings with the index finger. To learn the style, Merle followed coal miners Ike Everly and MOSE RAGER as the two played local parties and dances.

After graduating from high school and serving in the federally sponsored Civilian Conservation Corps program in 1936, Travis

moved to Evansville, Indiana, where he worked with two local bands. In 1937 fiddler CLAYTON McMICHEN hired Travis as one of his Georgia Wildcats. Soon Travis joined the Drifting Pioneers, a Chicago-area gospel quartet that moved to WLW in Cincinnati, joining the radio station's *Boone County Jamboree* when it began in 1938. (The show later became the MIDWESTERN HAYRIDE.) Travis remained at WLW after the group dissolved, and worked with the DELMORE BROTHERS and GRANDPA JONES. In 1943 SYD NATHAN recorded Travis and Jones as the "Sheppard Brothers," the first artists for his Cincinnati-based KING RECORDS.

Travis moved to California in March 1944 and played radio and recording sessions. He also recorded solo material, under his own name and pseudonyms, for various small labels. Signed to CAPITOL as a singer in the spring of 1946, his first single, "Cincinnati Lou," b/w "No Vacancy," became his first hit. Following that he reached #1 with "Divorce Me C.O.D.," which remained at that position for fourteen weeks in 1947. It was one of many songs Travis cowrote with CLIFFIE STONE, at the time an assistant A&R man at Capitol. Other song successes included 1947's "So Round, So Firm, So Fully Packed" (also a #1 hit for fourteen weeks). The Travis–Stone composition "Smoke! Smoke! Smoke! (That Cigarette)" became a huge hit for TEX WILLIAMS, spending sixteen weeks atop the country charts in that same year.

Appreciating the sound of solid-body electric steel guitars, Travis designed an electric Spanish solid-body guitar; in 1948 he had it built by Paul Bigsby, a California pattern maker and steel guitar builder. The guitar may have inspired Travis's friend Leo Fender to design what was to become the legendary Fender Telecaster electric guitar.

After a brief stay in Richmond, Virginia, in 1949, Travis spent the 1950s in and around California, appearing on local TV, recording, and touring. As a guitar-picking soldier in the classic 1953 World War II film *From Here to Eternity*—starring Montgomery

*Merle Travis*

Clift, Burt Lancaster, Frank Sinatra, and Deborah Kerr—Travis sang "Re-Enlistment Blues," which was used as the movie's leitmotif. In 1955, TENNESSEE ERNIE FORD's recording of "Sixteen Tons," an imaginative coal-mining tune Travis had written in 1946, became a multimillion-seller. Travis had recorded this song using acoustic guitar, along with two other folk-flavored originals and a few traditional songs, on the 78-rpm album *Folk Songs of the Hills*, which had drawn little attention at the time. With Ford, "Sixteen Tons" became an American standard and renewed interest in Travis.

Travis and his third wife, Bettie, moved to Nashville in 1968. In 1973 he joined his friend and musical disciple Chet Atkins to record the album *The Atkins-Travis Traveling Show*, which won a Grammy in 1974 for Best Country Instrumental Performance. Inducted into THE COUNTRY MUSIC HALL OF FAME in 1977, Travis spent his later years living in Eastern Oklahoma with his fourth wife, Dorothy, ex-wife of HANK THOMPSON, and often wrote superb memoirs of his career for music magazines. In 1979 he started recording for the Los Angeles–based, tradition-oriented country label CMH. His 1981 album *Travis Pickin'* received a Grammy nomination. On October 19, 1983, he suffered a massive coronary; he died in an Oklahoma hospital the next morning. His ashes were later interred in Ebenezer, Kentucky, under the Merle Travis monument, which had been dedicated in 1956 to honor the singer-songwriter and his success with "Sixteen Tons." —*Rich Kienzle*

# Randy Travis
b. Marshville, North Carolina, May 4, 1959

Randy Bruce Traywick eventually became the de facto leader of a handful of tradition-minded artists who dramatically changed the course of country music's evolution beginning in 1986. Singers including RICKY SKAGGS, GEORGE STRAIT, REBA MCENTIRE, JOHN ANDERSON, and EMMYLOU HARRIS had already plowed the

*Randy Travis*

first furrows of hard-country's regeneration, but Travis's understated baritone twang and square-jawed sex appeal built on their achievements while endearing him both to hard-country loyalists and to millions of fans beyond country's core boundaries. In addition, the image he projected inspired a raft of good-looking young male stars, who continued to fuel country's sales explosion of the late 1980s and early 1990s.

Born into a family who loved country music, Randy Traywick started playing and singing at home in tiny Marshville, North Carolina. From the recordings that his guitar-playing father bought, he absorbed the music of HANK WILLIAMS, LEFTY FRIZZELL, and similar singers. The teenager began playing square dances and clubs with brother Ricky, but from age eleven to age eighteen Randy abused drugs and alcohol and had run-ins with the law over speeding, burglary, and other infractions.

On the brink of doing significant jail time, Travis was saved by the intercession of Elizabeth "Lib" Hatcher, then manager of the Country Palace Nightclub in Charlotte, where he had been performing. Hatcher took him in, let authorities know he'd be looked after, and planned his career. Travis honed his singing and entertaining skills at the club, and he made his recording debut as Randy Traywick on the independent Paula label in 1978, reaching #91 on *Billboard*'s country chart in early 1979 with "She's My Woman."

Travis and Hatcher moved to Nashville in 1981. Known for a time as Randy Ray, Travis put in time singing and cooking hamburgers at the Nashville Palace, managed by Hatcher and located just minutes from the GRAND OLE OPRY's back door. He recorded an independent live album at the club and established friendships with Opry stalwarts JIMMY DICKENS and JOHNNY RUSSELL but drew scant attention from MUSIC ROW executives then attuned to country-pop sounds. Even WARNER BROS., which eventually signed him, turned him down twice. Finally, Warner A&R executive Martha Sharp—who heard in Travis someone who could win hard-country audiences—put Travis with producer KYLE LEHNING. Lehning's knack for supporting Travis's Lefty Frizzell–tinged vocals with excellent studio musicians complemented Sharp's keen song-spotting sense and helped make Travis a success. The first of his Warner singles, the DON SCHLITZ–PAUL OVERSTREET true-love anthem "On the Other Hand," only reached #67 in late 1985, but began its climb to #1 in April 1986 after the plaintive, steel-driven "1982" had become Travis's first Top Ten earlier in that same year. Strong fan and radio response convinced the label to release the landmark album *Storms of Life* in 1986, the year Travis joined the Grand Ole Opry. Fueled by hit singles including "On the Other Hand," "1982," and "Diggin' Up Bones," the #1 album sold 3 million copies. Its successor, *Always and Forever* (1987), stayed at #1 for forty-three weeks on its way to selling 5 million copies and winning CMA's 1987 Album of the Year award. It contained Travis's first hit as a writer, "I Told You So," as well as a major career song, "Forever and Ever, Amen," a bouncy Overstreet-Schlitz tune that became CMA's 1987 Single of the Year. Through the late 1980s Travis notched #1 albums with *Old 8x10* (1988) and *No Holdin' Back* (1989) and recorded a string of #1 singles, including "Honky Tonk Moon," "Deeper than the Holler," and "Is It Still Over?" Meanwhile, Travis won dozens of awards, including ACM honors in the New Male Vocalist, Album, Single, and Top Male Vocalist categories; CMA's Horizon Award (1986) and Male Vocalist of the Year award (1987, 1988); and Grammys for Best Country Vocal Performance, Male, in 1987 and 1988.

As his fame grew, Travis found his personal life, particularly his relationship with Hatcher, becoming grist for the media and the gossip mills. In May 1990, after years of describing their relationship as one based on business and friendship, Travis and Hatcher married in Hawaii. That year also saw the release of the platinum-selling *Heroes and Friends*, which included the GEORGE JONES duet "A Few Ole Country Boys." Even as the spotlight shifted to GARTH BROOKS, Travis continued to make some of the era's most memorable music, such as a remake of Brook Benton's "It's Just a Matter of Time" (1989), "Hard Rock Bottom of Your Heart" (1990), the blue-collar anthem "Better Class of Losers" (1991), "If I Didn't Have You" (1992), "Before You Kill Us All" (1994), and his self-penned "The Box" (1995).

Beginning in 1992 Travis drastically cut down his road schedule. Increasingly he devoted time to acting in feature or televised movies that numbered more than thirty as of 2010, including the TV movies *Frank and Jesse*, *Edie & Pen*, *A Dead Man's Revenge*, *Texas*, and *A Holiday to Remember* and the feature films *The Legend of O. B. Taggert*, *At Risk*, *Maverick*, *The Rainmaker*, and *Black Dog*. He has also appeared in the TV series *Matlock* and *Touched By an Angel*.

With his album sales declining, Travis switched to DREAM-WORKS RECORDS Nashville. His 1998 album *You and You Alone* contained three Top Ten singles, though it did not herald a lasting return to the upper reaches of the charts. *Inspirational Journey* (2000) and the Grammy-winning *Rise and Shine* (2002), both on Word/Warner Bros./CURB RECORDS, proved his growing acceptance among gospel music fans. The latter featured the career-boosting hit "Three Wooden Crosses" (2002–03); his first #1 country single since 1994, it became CMA's 2003 Single of the Year. Several inspirational albums followed, and even though 2008's *Around the Bend* was Travis's first secular country album of the decade, it still won Travis his eighth Dove Award from the Gospel Music Association. In 2009 Travis and CARRIE UNDERWOOD won a Grammy for Best Country Collaboration with Vocals for their reinterpretation of Travis's earlier hit "I Told You So."

Travis was honored with a star in the Hollywood Walk of Fame in 2004. —*Thomas Goldsmith*

# Tree Publishing Company

established in New York, New York, and Nashville, Tennessee, 1951

Tree Publishing Company, long one of Nashville's major independent country music-publishing firms, was formed in 1951 by JACK STAPP, then program director at WSM, and Lou Cowan, a CBS network broadcasting executive later responsible for successful TV game shows such as *The $64,000 Question* and *Break the Bank*. Administrative offices were originally in New York; Stapp was in charge of finding songs and songwriters in Nashville.

The company's name came from Polly Spiegel Cowan, wife of Lou Cowan and heiress to the Spiegel catalog fortune, who had drawn a tree on the back of her menu in a restaurant as Stapp and Cowan discussed the future firm. (The company would later be known as Tree International and today is known as Sony/ATV Tree Music Publishing.)

Tree existed mostly on paper until 1953, when Stapp, busy with his WSM responsibilities, hired local bass player BUDDY KILLEN to recruit songwriters and build the company's catalog. In 1956 ELVIS PRESLEY, in his first RCA session, recorded the Tree copyright "Heartbreak Hotel," thus providing the firm with an infusion of cash and a heightened profile. At this point Tree's headquarters shifted to offices in the Cumberland Lodge Building in downtown Nashville.

Also in 1956, Lou Cowan became president of CBS Television and had to divest himself of his stake in Tree. Stapp purchased the interests of Cowan and third partner Harry Fleishman in 1957 and gave 30 percent to Killen and another 10 percent to Joyce Bush, Stapp's longtime secretary.

Stapp left WSM in 1958 to become program director of Nashville rock & roll radio station WKDA, while Killen continued to handle Tree's day-to-day activities. In 1963 the publishing house marked its first million-dollar year, and Stapp exited WKDA in 1964 to assume full-time duties at Tree.

After "Heartbreak Hotel," the company's next major success came with ROGER MILLER, who began writing Tree hits including "Billy Bayou" and "Home" (both for JIM REEVES) in 1958 and who became a superstar when he wrote and recorded such hits as "Dang Me," "Chug-a-Lug," and "King of the Road" during 1964–65. In 1965 Tree further benefited from CURLY PUTMAN's "Green Green Grass of Home," which became a country and pop standard. Welsh pop singer Tom Jones made it an international hit in 1966–67. Putman also contributed the 1967 DAVID HOUSTON–TAMMY WYNETTE classic "My Elusive Dreams" (penned with BILLY SHERRILL) and TANYA TUCKER's 1973 hit "Blood Red and Goin' Down." Over the years other outstanding writers have deepened Tree's catalog, including SONNY THROCKMORTON, BOBBY BRADDOCK, RED LANE, BROOKS & DUNN and their producer DON COOK, DEAN DILLON, TOM SHAPIRO, John Scott Sherrill, Casey Beathard, and TAYLOR SWIFT.

In May 1969 Tree purchased PAMPER MUSIC, owned by HAL SMITH and RAY PRICE, for $1.6 million. Pamper controlled many hit songs written by WILLIE NELSON, HANK COCHRAN, and HARLAN HOWARD, such as "Crazy," "Hello Walls," "Make the World Go Away," "Pick Me Up on Your Way Down," and "Funny How Time Slips Away." The purchase doubled Tree's size—making it Nashville's largest independent publisher—and began an era in which Tree would grow by catalog acquisitions as well as by developing its own writers. The company eventually acquired the publishing firms of DOLLY PARTON, CONWAY TWITTY, JIM ED NORMAN, BUCK OWENS, MERLE HAGGARD, JIM REEVES, NAT STUCKEY, and JERRY CHESNUT—in all, more than fifty catalogs.

Tree moved into a newly purchased building on MUSIC ROW at 905 Sixteenth Avenue South in 1964. Eight years later the firm bought a building at 8 Music Square West.

In 1964 Tree expanded into the record business—and the field of rhythm and blues—with the formation of Dial Records. Originally created for singer Joe Tex, the label hit with recordings of "Hold What You've Got," "Skinny Legs and All," and "I Gotcha" during the late 1960s and early '70s.

In 1974 Joyce Bush, one of Tree's owners, succumbed to cancer; Stapp's administrative assistant, DONNA HILLEY, replaced her, and Killen received Bush's stock in the company. In this same year Stapp assumed the role of CEO and board chairman, with Killen becoming president and COO.

On December 20, 1980, Jack Stapp died at age sixty-seven. Under the terms of an agreement he and Killen had made, Killen purchased Stapp's interest and became sole owner. The following year Donna Hilley became Killen's executive assistant, and in 1978 she was named executive vice president and COO.

On January 10, 1989, Sony's music-publishing division bought Tree from Buddy Killen for $40 million. Killen remained head of the company but stepped down by year's end. Hilley stayed on as senior vice president and COO. She became president and CEO in 1994.

The firm marked another milestone in 1995 when Sony formed a fifty–fifty partnership with ATV Publishing, then controlled by pop superstar Michael Jackson. Sony/ATV further strengthened its position as a Music Row powerhouse by purchasing Little Big Town Music and Tom Shapiro Music in 1998. The acquisition of the lucrative ACUFF-ROSE catalogs followed in 2002.

Hilley announced her retirement in December 2005. Troy Tomlinson succeeded her as the company's top Nashville executive in January 2006. —*Don Cusic*

## Buck Trent
b. Spartanburg, South Carolina, February 17, 1938

An expert banjo player and longtime PORTER WAGONER band member, Charles Wilburn "Buck" Trent became a well-known performer in his own right after appearing on the *Porter Wagoner Show* and HEE HAW and recording with *Hee Haw* cohost ROY CLARK.

Trent grew up in the textile town of Arcadia Mills, near Spartanburg. His first love was HAWAIIAN steel guitar; he then switched to five-string banjo. By age eleven he was performing on Spartanburg radio stations WSPA and WORD; later he appeared on WLOS-TV in Asheville, North Carolina. He also played on California's *TOWN HALL PARTY* television show, but in 1959 he moved to Nashville. At MOM UPCHURCH's rooming home, HANK SNOW's steel guitar player Howard White encouraged Trent to place a special steel bar beneath his banjo strings. It added a distinctive ring to the sound and inspired Trent to have his instrument electrified.

Trent had already cut two albums when he joined Porter Wagoner's band, the Wagonmasters, in 1962. He traveled (and appeared on TV) with Wagoner until 1973. Trent contributed to many hits recorded for RCA, such as Wagoner's "The Cold Hard Facts of Life" (#2, 1967) and DOLLY PARTON's "Mule Skinner Blues (Blue Yodel #8)" (#3, 1970). Trent also performed in the 1966 film *Nashville Rebel*.

For their work together, Trent and Roy Clark won CMA's Instrumental Group of the Year award in 1975 and 1976. In 1990 Trent began performing regularly in BRANSON, MISSOURI. —*Steve Eng*

## Rick Trevino
b. Houston, Texas, May 16, 1971

When Rick Trevino's "Just Enough Rope" garnered significant country radio airplay in 1993, he became the first nationally recognized country singer of Hispanic descent since JOHNNY RODRIGUEZ and FREDDY FENDER emerged in the 1970s.

Ricardo Trevino Jr. was born in Houston's East End, where his father had played with a popular Tejano band. The family moved to a predominantly Anglo neighborhood in AUSTIN when Rick was five, and he grew up studying classical piano and listening to pop and country music. He began performing solo and singing with country cover bands after high school and was signed by COLUMBIA producer STEVE BUCKINGHAM.

Over Trevino's objections, his first album, 1993's *Dos Mundos* ("Two Worlds"), consisted of country songs sung in Spanish and was promoted to the Tejano market. "Just Enough Rope" appeared in English, Spanish, and bilingual versions. The last might have helped listeners identify Trevino on the playing field of sound-alike hat acts, but he insisted he was not "crossing over" to country: "I am a country singer who happens to have a Hispanic background." A single from his 1995 self-titled English debut album,

the ballad "She Can't Say I Didn't Cry," went to the Top Five, and the album eventually was certified gold. Next, *Looking for the Light* (1995) produced a #6 single, "Bobbie Ann Mason." *Learning as You Go* (1996) yielded the #2 title track and the #1 hit "Running Out of Reasons." Both of the latter two albums had companion Spanish-language versions.

In the late 1990s, Trevino contributed to Los Super Seven's self-titled, Grammy-winning, Spanish-language album (RCA, 1998) and to that group's 2001 Legacy/Columbia album *Canto* ("I Sing"). In that same year he released the Spanish-language *Mi Son* ("My Song") on Vanguard. An English-language album, *In My Dreams*, followed on WARNER BROS. in 2003, and *Whole Town Blue* appeared on the same label in 2011. —*Rick Mitchell*

## Travis Tritt
b. Marietta, Georgia, February 9, 1963

In the early 1990s, Travis Tritt's bluesy amalgam of hard-core country and southern rock made him arguably the most significant COUNTRY-ROCK vocal stylist since HANK WILLIAMS JR.

Early on, James Travis Tritt sang solos in the First Assembly of God's children's choir in Marietta. By age eight he had taught himself to play guitar and by fourteen had written his first song. Because his family discouraged him from pursuing a musical career, Tritt worked at a variety of blue-collar jobs, but he quit in 1981 and started singing at Atlanta-area nightclubs.

In 1982 Tritt met Danny Davenport, a rock radio promoter for WARNER BROS. RECORDS, who also owned a small recording studio. Davenport helped Tritt work on demo recordings and introduced him to Warner's Nashville division. In 1988, after showcasing in Atlanta for label executives, Tritt joined the Nashville division's artist roster. The following year he signed a management contract with Ken Kragen, KENNY ROGERS's manager.

Initially signed to a singles-only recording contract, Tritt shot to stardom with the March 1990 release of his debut album, *Country Club*. The title cut became his first Top Ten single, and "Help Me Hold On" became his first #1. Tritt's next three albums, *It's All About to Change*, *T-R-O-U-B-L-E*, and *Ten Feet Tall and Bulletproof*, delivered a string of Top Ten hits, including "Here's a

*Travis Tritt*

Quarter (Call Someone Who Cares)" (1991) and "Anymore" (1991), both self-penned. "The Whiskey Ain't Workin'," a rowdy 1991 duet with MARTY STUART, earned the performers a 1992 Grammy and led to their successful 1992 "No Hats" tour and 1996 "Double Trouble" tour.

Tritt's autobiography, *Ten Feet Tall and Bulletproof,* was published in 1994. The following year he expanded his career to include acting, eventually appearing in the TV movie *Rio Diablo*, the HBO series *Tales from the Crypt*, and feature films *The Cowboy Way* (1994), *Sgt. Bilko* (1996*)*, and *Blues Brothers 2000* (1998). He also performed on the movie soundtracks of *My Cousin Vinny* (1992), *Honeymoon in Vegas* (1992), and *The Cowboy Way* (1994).

Tritt has received numerous awards, including CMA's 1991 Horizon Award, 1992 Vocal Event Award (with Marty Stuart), and a share of the 1994 Album of the Year Award for recording "Take It Easy" for *Common Thread: The Songs of the Eagles*. On February 29, 1992, he was inducted into the cast of the GRAND OLE OPRY.

Shifting to COLUMBIA RECORDS, Tritt released *Down the Road I Go* in 2000. The album yielded the #1 hit "The Best of Intentions" (2000) and three additional Top Tens during 2000–02. *Strong Enough* (2002) and *My Honky Tonk History* (2004), however, were less successful, and Tritt moved on to Category 5 Records, which released *The Storm* in August 2007. The following December Tritt sued the label for failure to pay royalties and misrepresenting the company's assets. Late in 2008 Tritt and Marty Stuart reunited for a national concert tour. —*Marjie McGraw*

## Ernest Tubb
b. near Crisp, Texas, February 9, 1914; d. September 6, 1984

HONKY-TONK singer-songwriter, movie actor, record retailer, and GRAND OLE OPRY star, Ernest Dale Tubb was among history's most influential country performers. Throughout his illustrious fifty-year career he gave numerous younger stars invaluable broadcast and concert exposure.

The youngest of five children in a sharecropper's family, Ernest Tubb was born on a cotton farm near Crisp, Texas (thirty-five miles southeast of Dallas), and spent his youth farming in various parts of the state. A fan of early movie cowboys Buck Jones and Tom Mix, Tubb first heard the recordings of JIMMIE RODGERS in 1928 and became a huge fan of the Singing Brakeman. In his spare time, Tubb learned to sing, yodel, and play guitar, much like Rodgers did, and shortly after the star's death in 1933, the nineteen-year-old Tubb first sang on radio in San Antonio, the city of Rodgers's final residence. Tubb's singing paid little or nothing, so he supported himself by digging ditches for the WPA and later clerking in a local drugstore.

In 1936, now married and still enthralled by Rodgers's music, Tubb phoned Rodgers's widow, Carrie, to ask for an autographed photo. A friendship developed as Mrs. Rodgers listened to Tubb's radio shows and offered professional advice. Impressed by Tubb's friendly personality and heartfelt singing, Mrs. Rodgers did much to assist him. She helped him buy clothes, find songs, land a contract with her late husband's label (RCA VICTOR, by then releasing all country product on its BLUEBIRD imprint), and make a regional tour of movie theaters to promote his recordings.

His first records—which were done in the Rodgers vein—and the tour proved unsuccessful. Between 1937 and 1940 Tubb worked for radio stations and at day jobs in several Texas cities

*Ernest Tubb*

(Midland, San Angelo, and Corpus Christi). A 1939 tonsillectomy in San Angelo lowered his voice and effectively eliminated the Rodgers-style yodel and hence the Rodgers song repertory. As a result, Tubb became a more energetic and effective songwriter. In 1940 he got a second chance with a major record label, for DAVE KAPP at DECCA agreed to record him during Houston sessions that spring. Of the four songs he cut on April 4, "Blue Eyed Elaine" and its flip side, "I'll Get Along Somehow," became his first successful disc.

Tubb moved to Fort Worth's KGKO during December 1940, and for the first time he became a full-time musician. The following June, Universal Mills, makers of Gold Chain Flour, became his radio sponsor/employer and launched the singer in his role as the Gold Chain Troubadour. As such, he toured Texas grocery and feed stores and sang on town squares, where such future stars as CHARLIE WALKER and HANK THOMPSON first heard him. On the strength of his sixth Decca release and all-time biggest hit, "Walking the Floor Over You" (1941), Tubb sang in two Columbia western movies made in 1942, *Fighting Buckaroo* and *Riding West*. He also appeared on package shows with fellow headliners including BOB WILLS and ROY ACUFF in cities such as Little Rock, Memphis, and Shreveport.

Playing in Birmingham during December 1942, Tubb established a relationship with Nashville talent agent and manager J. L. FRANK, who helped him secure Grand Ole Opry guest spots and other personal appearances during January 1943. In February 1943 Tubb joined the Opry cast; he remained one of its major stars for the rest of his career. At Frank's behest, Tubb sold SONGBOOKS via WSM broadcasts, hired his first band, the Texas Troubadours, and continued his film work (he made *Jamboree* for Republic in 1944 and *Hollywood Barndance* for an independent studio in 1947), in addition to ambitious touring. Tubb then was considered one of country music's major acts, regularly climbing the *Billboard* country charts with "Soldier's Last Letter" (1944),

"Tomorrow Never Comes" (1945), "It's Been So Long Darling" (1945), "Rainbow at Midnight" (1946), and "Filipino Baby" (1946). His style—a spare, personalized brand of honky-tonk music featuring an electric lead guitar playing straight melody—made him distinctive, recognizable, and, during his heyday, often imitated.

In May 1947 Tubb opened the Ernest Tubb Record Shop at 720 Commerce Street in downtown Nashville, the first major all-country record store. Over the next year, his *Midnite Jamboree* show emerged, staged at the store before a live audience immediately after the Grand Ole Opry and carried over WSM. Regularly showcasing deserving young hopefuls and their latest record releases, the program continues today as WSM's second-longest continuous broadcast.

Beneficiary of Mrs. Rodgers's assistance early in his career, Tubb did all he could to help others: taking artists on tour with him, putting in a good word with Opry management or record producers, exposing talent on the *Midnight Jamboree*, hiring performers for his Texas Troubadours, and offering words of advice. Boosting major acts in these and other ways established his reputation as one of country's most generous, selfless personalities. Hank Williams, Hank Snow, Carl Smith, Charlie Walker, Justin Tubb (his first child), Patsy Cline, the Wilburn Brothers, Johnny Cash, Stonewall Jackson, Skeeter Davis, George Hamilton IV, Loretta Lynn, Jack Greene, and Cal Smith all owed Tubb various degrees of thanks.

In September 1947, Tubb became the first artist to bring a Grand Ole Opry show to Carnegie Hall. In keeping with Decca's penchant for recording and promoting duo acts, he became a prolific duet artist over the years, recording with the Andrews Sisters (1949), Red Foley (1949–53), the Wilburn Brothers (1957), and Loretta Lynn (1964–69).

While his own career was on an upswing in the early and middle 1960s, honors and accolades came his way, including election to The Country Music Hall of Fame in 1965, the same year he received a gold record for "Walking the Floor Over You." Tubb hosted a syndicated TV show out of Nashville between 1965 and 1968, with Willie Nelson costarring in early episodes.

No artist toured as much for as long as Ernest Tubb, who worked 150 to 200 shows each year between the early 1960s (when he first turned his Texas Troubadours into a dance band and started playing the nightclub circuit) and 1982, at which time a long-standing battle with emphysema forced him to quit. No artist was more devoted to his fans, and no fans were more loyal: Ernest Tubb had one national fan club with a single president (Norma Winton Barthel) for its entire existence between 1944 and its deactivation in the early 1990s, a few years after Tubb's death in September 1984. —*Ronnie Pugh*

## Justin Tubb
b. San Antonio, Texas, August 20, 1935; d. January 24, 1998

Many consider singer-songwriter Justin Wayne Tubb, eldest son of Ernest Tubb, one of country music's most underrated talents. Though mindful of his legacy, the smooth-voiced performer tried hard not to walk in his father's shadow.

Early on, Justin Tubb attended the University of Texas at Austin, where he majored in broadcast journalism. He once hoped to be a sports announcer, but by 1953 he was a DJ at WHIN in Gallatin, Tennessee.

At age nine Tubb made his Grand Ole Opry debut and at twenty became one of the show's youngest members. For his

father, he wrote "My Mother Must Have Been a Girl Like You" (1951), which sold some 250,000 copies thanks to a hit flip side, "Somebody's Stolen My Honey."

Justin Tubb burst onto the national scene with a 1954 hit, "Lookin' Back to See," recorded with Decca Records label mate Goldie Hill. In 1955 he broke the country Top Ten with Marvin Rainwater's composition "I've Gotta Go Get My Baby"; he then hit a career slump.

Songwriting skills helped him make a comeback. Tubb ballads for other artists included the early 1960s hits "Big Fool of the Year" (George Jones), "Lonesome 7-7203" (Hawkshaw Hawkins), "Imagine That" (Patsy Cline), "Keeping Up with the Joneses" (Faron Young & Margie Singleton), "Love Is No Excuse" (Dottie West & Jim Reeves), "Walkin' Talkin' Cryin' Barely Beatin' Broken Heart" (first for Johnny Wright, later Highway 101), and "Be Glad" (Del Reeves).

In 1963 Tubb wrote and recorded the #6 country hit "Take a Letter, Miss Gray," which put him back on the charts. For his father he also wrote "Be Better to Your Baby." He managed WSM's *Midnite Jamboree*; founded FOR E.T., a nonprofit agency to promote research on emphysema; and worked on behalf of the American Lung Association of Tennessee. —*Walt Trott*

## Tanya Tucker
b. Seminole, Texas, October 10, 1958

After her 1972 smash hit "Delta Dawn" made her a star at age thirteen, Tanya Denise Tucker soon became one of country music's most popular singers. By her thirty-sixth birthday, an age at which many country artists are just becoming established, she had already scored more than fifty chart singles, including (besides "Delta Dawn") such enduring favorites as "San Antonio Stroll" (#1, 1974), "Strong Enough to Bend" (#1, 1988), and "Down to My Last Teardrop" (#2, 1991). Her instantly recognizable husky voice, her extraordinary success, her upbringing in the media spotlight, and her wild "Texas Tornado" persona made

*Tanya Tucker*

Tucker not only a superstar but also a full-blown tabloid-magnet household name.

The daughter of Beau and Juanita Tucker, Tanya was born in the West Texas town of Seminole. Working a variety of jobs, Beau Tucker moved his family around the Southwest while Tanya was young. The Tuckers settled for a time in Willcox, Arizona, and then later moved to Phoenix. At age six Tanya shocked and impressed her father by showing off her precocious vocal prowess in the house one day. With Beau's approval she started talking her way onto local shows headlined by visiting country stars.

When she was nine years old, her father made some primitive, living room recordings of Tanya singing and took the tapes to Nashville, but no one was interested in his talented daughter. In Phoenix she appeared on a children's TV program, and when the Tuckers moved to Utah she landed a brief spot alongside Robert Redford in the movie *Jeremiah Johnson* (1972). Soon Beau Tucker moved the family to Henderson, Nevada, to be close to the Las Vegas entertainment industry. He and Tanya made a studio demo tape and gave a copy to actress and songwriter Dolores Fuller; in turn, Fuller helped bring Tanya to the attention of BILLY SHERRILL, the A&R chief of EPIC/COLUMBIA RECORDS in Nashville, and he signed her.

On March 17, 1972, at her first Columbia session, Tucker recorded "Delta Dawn," with Sherrill producing. The record charted in May, and in July the thirteen-year-old sensation debuted on the GRAND OLE OPRY. For the next two and a half years she and Sherrill collaborated on a series of brilliantly layered, melodramatic singles that capitalized on her uncanny ability to handle adult material. "What's Your Mama's Name" (1973) was her first #1 record, followed by "Blood Red and Goin' Down" (1973) and the controversial "Would You Lay with Me (In a Field of Stone)" (1974). By then the press was portraying her as a pubescent hillbilly sex goddess, an image that *Rolling Stone* intensified by putting her on the cover of the magazine's September 26, 1974, issue. Within a month Beau Tucker swung a million-dollar deal for her with MCA RECORDS.

Tanya's seven-year tenure on MCA yielded the #1 hits "Lizzie and the Rainman" (1975), "San Antonio Stroll" (1975), and "Here's Some Love" (1976). In 1978, hoping to expand her audience, she recorded the notorious *T.N.T.* album in Los Angeles. The material was more 1970s rock than country, and the album jacket featured Tanya in cheesecake poses. Soon she started dating GLEN CAMPBELL, twenty-two years her senior. The two recorded duets and announced their engagement in the press, but their turbulent relationship fell apart short of the altar, and the tabloids had a field day following their breakup.

Tucker's career nearly fell apart at the same time. In 1982 she recorded *Changes*, evidently the first mainstream country album to appear on the ARISTA label. The album, one of Tucker's best, sold poorly, and securing another record deal took three more years. Nashville producer JERRY CRUTCHFIELD, who had worked with Tucker on several of her MCA albums, took her to CAPITOL RECORDS, which released *Girls Like Me* in 1986. The collection yielded four Top Ten hits.

With her career back in full swing, the tabloid press resumed its interest in Tucker. She gave them plenty to work with. In 1988 she checked into the Betty Ford clinic, and on July 5, 1989, her first child, Presley Tanita Tucker, was born out of wedlock. On October 2, 1991, the day of that year's *CMA Awards* show, Tucker, still unmarried, gave birth to her second child, Beau Grayson Tucker. Tanya was in the hospital, watching the program on TV, when it was announced that she had been voted the 1991 Female

Vocalist of the Year. After nearly twenty years in the business, it was the first time she had been so honored. Her autobiography, *Nickel Dreams: My Life* (written with Patsi Bale Cox), was published in 1997, the same year that Tucker's album *Complicated* was released.

In 1998 she left Capitol, openly claiming that label executives were promoting GARTH BROOKS's recordings at the expense of her own. Her next album, *Tanya*, appeared on her own imprint in 2002. Her stormy relationship with one-time fiancé Jerry Laseter (with whom she had her third child, in 1999) continued for several more years, further heightening her tempestuous public image. In 2009, three years after her father's death, Tanya released the Saguaro Road album *My Turn*, an album of country classics he had loved. —*Daniel Cooper*

## The Tune Wranglers

One of the wildest and most infectious WESTERN SWING bands, the Tune Wranglers were formed by guitarist Buster Coward and fiddler Tom Dickey in 1934. Claiming to be real cowboys, the band was also one of the first western swing groups to wear western attire.

The Wranglers broadcast on San Antonio's 50,000-watt WOAI and constantly toured central Texas. By the time they made their first BLUEBIRD recordings, in February 1936, they had added jazz pianist Eddie Whitley and tenor banjoist and vocalist Red Brown; Brown's risqué renditions of tunes such as "Red's Tight Like That" dominated the first sessions, though it was Coward's "Texas Sand" that became a hit and eventually a country standard.

Subsequent sessions featured the freewheeling electric steel guitar of Eddie Duncan, also an able crooner, but the band grew more sophisticated as time progressed. Tom Dickey left to form his own band in June 1937. Later sessions combined COWBOY MUSIC with pop and jazz tunes. Important additions included twins Beal (sax and clarinet) and Neal Ruff (tenor banjo), and fiddler-vocalist Leon Seago. Remaining popular on radio, on disc, and onstage, the Tune Wranglers scored another hit with "Hawaiian Honeymoon" in 1939. In that year Coward took the Tune Wranglers to Fort Worth's KFJZ and the new Texas State Network, but he evidently disbanded his group in 1940. —*Kevin Coffey*

## Nathan Turk

b. Torshaw, Poland, May 10, 1895; d. October 21, 1988

The beautiful and lavishly embroidered western-wear designs of Nathan Turk became the signature stagewear of the MADDOX BROTHERS & ROSE, resulting in the group's billing as "the most colorful hillbilly band in the land." From the 1930s to the 1970s, Turk's ready-to-wear and custom western designs became favorites of celluloid cowboys, country artists, and their fans.

At age ten, Nathan Teig began apprenticing with a tailor in Warsaw, Poland. Eight years later he immigrated to America, and in 1923 he and his wife, Bessie, opened a shop at 13711 Ventura Boulevard in Van Nuys, California; in the late 1940s the shop moved to a larger space next door at 13715, where the store remained until 1977. Among Turk's clients were cowboy stars GENE AUTRY and ROY ROGERS as well as numerous B-western leading men. In the 1940s Turk began designing for SPADE COOLEY, HANK THOMPSON, ERNEST TUBB, and HANK SNOW. He began a relationship with the Maddoxes that lasted until the group disbanded in 1956. The Maddox Family's spectacular Turk outfits dazzled with an array of rich hues and eye-catching flowers, hearts, or other organic embroidery designs; many of Rose Maddox's colorful suits featured the flower for which she was named.

Turk's exquisitely well-made designs combined western elements, such as fringe, embroidery, and arrowhead-bordered "smile pockets," with tailored men's and women's suit styles. The reportedly polite, soft-spoken tailor often designed embroidery motifs inspired by Slavic folk art. Turk commissioned much of the delicate, custom embroidery work to a local woman named Viola Grae (who later worked for NUDIE THE RODEO TAILOR before starting her own shop); Turk's wife, Bessie, perfected the crescent-shaped smile pocket detailed with stitched arrowheads; and his son-in-law, Irwin Simon, did the rhinestone work. Turk's ready-to-wear business made handsome cowboy shirts and suits for men and women. Turk also designed elaborate outfits for riders in Pasadena's Rose Bowl parade.

By the late 1940s Simon helped him run the shop, which featured both ready-to-wear items and custom tailoring. Due to failing health, Nathan Turk retired in 1977, though he continued to do some custom work the following year. After his death his family closed the business, but his designs live on in the closets of vintage-western-wear enthusiasts as well as in various museums. —*Holly George-Warren*

## Grant Turner
b. Baird, Texas, May 17, 1912; d. October 19, 1991

Jesse Granderson "Grant" Turner, known as the Voice of the GRAND OLE OPRY, served on that show's announcing staff for forty-seven years and became a broadcasting icon to performers, announcers, and fans nationwide. In 1981 he became the first announcer/disc jockey to be elected to THE COUNTRY MUSIC HALL OF FAME.

*Grant Turner*

Growing up in Baird, Texas, near Abilene, Turner was the son of a banker and the grandson of a rancher. While in high school, he performed on Abilene's KFYO as Ike and His Guitar in 1928 and first announced for that station in that same year. Majoring in journalism at college, Turner worked for Texas and Louisiana newspapers during the 1930s, but he returned to radio announcing in 1940 at KFRO in Longview, Texas. In Sherman he held his last Texas radio job and then moved to Knoxville, Tennessee, in 1942.

Turner joined the WSM announcing staff on June 6, 1944, the day the Allies invaded Europe in World War II. At first he handled early-morning programs, but soon he added Saturday night Grand Ole Opry duties. In the late 1940s Turner gained what he called the "big prize" when he became announcer for the *Prince Albert Show*, the Opry's R. J. Reynolds–sponsored, half-hour NBC network segment; eventually this broadcast reached some 10 million listeners weekly via more than 170 stations. Later he hosted WSM's *Mr. DJ, USA* program, featuring guest DJs from around the nation, and in the mid-1950s he became the third regular announcer for ERNEST TUBB's WSM *Midnite Jamboree*, a job Turner held until 1977.

Turner's recordings were few and forgettable: four duets with Helen Carter (CARTER SISTERS) for the Nashville-based TENNESSEE and REPUBLIC labels in 1951–52 and four solo numbers for Chart Records in 1964–65. Turner also made spoken-word LPs, including one personal Opry memoir in 1980 for CVS Records.

For years the genial Turner hosted the *Grand Ole Opry Warmup Show*—spinning records and taking requests on the Opry House stage—and worked Friday- and Saturday-night Opry performances, besides summer matinees, until the night before he died. Known for his careful diction, ingratiating personality, and professionalism, in 1975 Turner was one of three original members elected to the Country Disc Jockey Hall of Fame, established by the Country Music Disc Jockey Hall of Fame Foundation in 1974. —*Ronnie Pugh*

## Josh Turner
b. Hannah, South Carolina, November 20, 1977

Joshua Otis "Josh" Turner was largely unknown when he stepped onto the GRAND OLE OPRY stage in December 2001. In a deep, resonant, unmistakably country voice, he sang "Long Black Train," a tradition-minded song he wrote while attending Nashville's Belmont University, and the audience gave him two standing ovations. In one stroke, Turner launched a career that brought a roots-based flavor to country radio. "Long Black Train" soon became a country gospel standard.

Turner grew up in rural South Carolina, influenced by quartets he heard in church and the music of JOHNNY CASH, THE STANLEY BROTHERS, and RANDY TRAVIS. After college, Turner signed with MCA Nashville in 2001 and two years later released *Long Black Train*, whose title cut went to #13 on the *Billboard* charts and helped the album gain platinum status. His sophomore album, 2006's *Your Man*, which eventually went double-platinum, gave him back-to-back #1 hits with the title track and "Would You Go with Me." Turner joined the Grand Ole Opry in October 2007, the same year "Firecracker," from his album *Everything is Fine*, peaked at #2 and the album was certified gold. In 2008 he starred as gospel singer George Beverly Shea in the film *Billy: The Early Years*, based on the life of the Reverend Billy Graham. In 2010 he released his album *Haywire*. —*Michael Manning*

*Josh Turner*

## Zeb and Zeke Turner

Zeb Turner b. Lynchburg, Virginia, June 23, 1915; d. January 10, 1978
Zeke Turner b. Lynchburg, Virginia, June 18, 1923; d. April 13, 2003

Zeke and Zeb Turner were influential country instrumentalists. Zeke, born James Grishaw, was an electric guitar specialist who became one of country music's first studio musicians; older brother Zeb, born William Edward Grishaw, was a guitarist, songwriter, and singer who recorded for KING RECORDS and smaller labels. Both grew up listening to local blues musicians and to pop/jazz guitarists such as George Barnes and Coco Heimal. By 1938 William had adopted the name Zeb Turner and recorded his first solo, "Guitar Fantasy," with a band called the Hi Neighbor Boys.

After jobs on the West Coast and at Renfro Valley, Kentucky, Zeb came to Nashville in 1944 to play with WALLY FOWLER's band. In 1946 he recorded "Zeb's Mountain Boogie," the first release on the city's new BULLET label and one of the nation's early boogie hits. Brother Zeke joined RED FOLEY's band and became one of Nashville's first session players. In 1947 he began working HANK WILLIAMS sessions ("Move It On Over" and "Honky Tonkin'"), on which he popularized the dead-string technique, muting the guitar strings with the heel of his right hand and turning his amp volume down to create percussive effects.

After the brothers cut a handful of sides together (including "Guitar Reel" for Bullet), Zeke moved to Cincinnati, where he worked sessions for King and other labels and contributed the signature guitar riff that opens the DELMORE BROTHERS' #1 rendition of "Blues Stay Away From Me" (1949–50). Zeb spent several years in the Washington, D.C., area, where he played clubs and performed with JIMMY DEAN. Zeb also published songs through ACUFF-ROSE and cowrote the 1947 EDDY ARNOLD chart-topper "It's a Sin" with FRED ROSE. Eventually relocating to Canada, Zeb remained active through the 1960s. Zeke had dropped out of music by the 1970s. —*Charles Wolfe*

## Wesley Tuttle

b. Lamar, Colorado, December 13, 1917; d. September 29, 2003

Wesley Tuttle played an important though largely overlooked role in developing and popularizing West Coast country music. A presence on California radio beginning in 1933, the San Fernando–based singer-yodeler turned professional after he met CLIFFIE STONE and joined STUART HAMBLEN's troupe.

Despite the fact that he had accidentally lost three fingers in a mishap at his father's Pacoima butcher shop, Tuttle was an accomplished guitarist and yodeled so well that Walt Disney hired him for the *Snow White and the Seven Dwarfs* soundtrack's "Silly Song." Tuttle broadcast steadily, performed with the SONS OF THE PIONEERS for a time, and in 1938 had Leo Fender build him one of the earliest left-handed electric guitars. Tuttle left California in 1940 to work at Cincinnati station WLW, where he met MERLE TRAVIS and encouraged Travis to head west.

By 1942 Tuttle was back in San Fernando, specializing in a smooth western croon and concentrating more on love songs than HONKY-TONK or WESTERN SWING. Landing a contract with CAPITOL RECORDS, he quickly recorded two strong sellers: "With Tears in My Eyes" (#1, 1945) and "Detour" (#3, 1946). The label fitted him with a custom-made latex glove to camouflage his damaged hand and sent him on the road with label mate TEX RITTER. A dedicated, hardworking entertainer, Tuttle also led the house band at the Painted Post, a San Fernando Valley nightclub on Ventura Boulevard in North Hollywood (today Studio City). By the early 1950s he had become a fixture on Southern California television via regular appearances on KTTV's Saturday night *TOWN HALL PARTY* (he also handled directing duties) and, with his wife, Marilyn, on KTLA's five-day-a-week *Foreman Phillips Show*.

Tuttle left Capitol in 1949 for a brief stint on Coral; he then returned to Capitol and recorded some extraordinary topical ballads ("Heartsick Soldier on Heartbreak Ridge," "They Locked God Outside the Iron Curtain"). In 1957 he retired from country music to become an ordained minister, after which he and Marilyn Tuttle recorded a number of spiritual albums. —*Jonny Whiteside*

## Shania Twain

b. Windsor, Ontario, Canada, August 28, 1965

After a tentative start, Shania Twain erupted onto the country music scene to become an international star; her unprecedented sales and multimedia success helped signal a new era for female country singers. The groundbreaking pop-country sound she crafted with producer-husband Robert John "Mutt" Lange proved original and influential, crossing over to the pop market as she became the first female artist in any genre to have each of three separate albums sell more than 10 million copies. Along the way, she brought a new sensuality and freedom to the image of female artists in country music.

Born Eileen Regina Edwards, she was raised in the mining town of Timmins, Ontario. Her father deserted the family when she was two. Mother Sharon married Ojibway Indian Jerry Twain, who raised her, and Shania adopted her Ojibway name in his honor.

Twain began singing around her hometown at age eight and was writing songs by age ten. By her teens she was a veteran of Canadian country TV shows. When she wasn't singing, she and her stepfather toiled as reforestation workers in northern Canadian logging camps.

After Twain's mother and stepfather were killed in a car accident in 1987—they were hit head-on by a logging truck—she

*Shania Twain*

raised her younger siblings on her own, supporting them by singing at a resort. She came to Nashville with a tape in 1991 and was signed by MERCURY RECORDS.

In 1993 she filmed a flashy video for "What Made You Say That" in Miami Beach and then worked with actors Charles Durning and Sean Penn on a clip for "Dance with the One That Brought You." Both songs were on her debut CD, which sold in modest numbers but caught Lange's attention. The producer of Foreigner, AC/DC, the Cars, Billy Ocean, Def Leppard, and Bryan Adams, Lange was an avid country fan. He called Mercury to get Twain's number, and came to Fan Fair (now the CMA MUSIC FESTIVAL) in June 1993 to meet her. They married on December 21, 1993. A native of South Africa, Lange stayed in the background throughout Twain's rise to stardom, preferring not to be photographed or interviewed.

When they began work on *The Woman in Me*, Lange insisted they use only original songs written by Twain—something Mercury Records executives hadn't allowed on her debut. He cowrote with her and provided background harmonies.

"Whose Bed Have Your Boots Been Under" began Twain's march to stardom. The CD went on to yield seven hit singles, including the bright, danceable "Any Man of Mine," her first #1. Three more #1 hits followed, and the album won a 1995 Grammy for Best Country Album. *The Woman in Me* also was cited as ACM's 1995 Album of the Year, the same year for which Twain was named ACM's Top New Female Vocalist.

In 1996 Jon Landau, known for his long association with Bruce Springsteen, became Twain's manager. Her album *Come on Over* appeared in the fall of 1997. Twain eventually released eleven singles from the album, three of which went #1; five more reached the Top Ten. The album eventually sold more than twenty million units and was responsible for four Grammy Awards over two years.

Going against conventional wisdom, Twain didn't perform live or tour widely until 1998, when she staged her first tour as a headliner. Most country artists are expected to perform concerts across America to support the release of an album, but Twain waited

until she had enough material to do a full show. Her subsequent concert tours, like her albums, proved to be top-sellers.

Twain changed management from Landau to a veteran rock company, Q Prime, before issuing her next album. With 2002's *Up!*, Twain and Lange created "country mixes" and "pop mixes" and issued the two as a double-disc set. Country radio didn't respond kindly to the move. Only three singles went Top Ten, with no #1s. But fans did respond, and *Up!* has since sold more than 11 million copies.

A *Greatest Hits* album followed in 2004, with one single, "Party for Two," cracking the Top Ten. Afterward, Twain retreated, focusing on raising her son, Eja Lange, born August 12, 2001, and residing primarily on mountainside retreats in Switzerland and New Zealand. In May 2007, Twain announced she was writing songs and taking time for serious reflection. On May 15, 2008, she filed for divorce from Lange. She was a guest judge on *American Idol* in 2010. The reality show, *Why Not? with Shania Twain* debuted on the Oprah Winfrey Network (OWN) in 2011. —*Robert K. Oermann*

## Conway Twitty
b. Friars Point, Mississippi, September 1, 1933; d. June 5, 1993

During his lifetime, Conway Twitty had more #1 records than any country artist had then achieved, his stardom having endured through five decades of changing musical fashions. He was also one of country music's most diverse stylists and a major songwriting talent: Eleven of his #1 hits were self-penned.

Twitty was born Harold Lloyd Jenkins, the son of a Mississippi ferryboat captain. Taught guitar by his grandfather and a neighborhood blues singer, Twitty broadcast over radio station KFFA in Helena, Arkansas, at age twelve. A talented baseball player, he was

*Conway Twitty*

scouted by the Philadelphia Phillies and then drafted for military service during the Korean War. Upon his discharge, he heard ELVIS PRESLEY's music and headed to SUN RECORDS in Memphis. Twitty's Sun sides were imitative of Presley and were not issued, but label mate ROY ORBISON's recording of Twitty's song "Rockhouse" was released.

Twitty then signed with Mercury as a ROCKABILLY performer and combined the names of Conway, Arkansas, and Twitty, Texas, to create his new professional moniker. Moving to MGM, he struck pay dirt with 1958's million-selling "It's Only Make Believe." This solidified his status as a teen idol, as did his appearances in *Platinum High School*, *College Confidential* (both 1960), and other teen movies. The "Conrad Birdie" character in the 1960 Broadway musical *Bye Bye Birdie* parodied Twitty.

Twitty wrote country songs throughout this period and yearned to return to that genre as a performer. Songwriter HARLAN HOWARD took Twitty's "Walk Me to the Door" to COLUMBIA country star RAY PRICE, and urged DECCA's OWEN BRADLEY to sign Twitty in 1965. Initially, country DJs were skeptical of the former pop star. But in 1968 he finally broke into the country Top Ten with "The Image of Me."

Twitty's follow-up single, "Next in Line," became the first of his forty #1 *Billboard* country hits. His intensely emotional singing and passion-filled lyrics energized such career-building records as "Hello Darlin'" (1970), "Fifteen Years Ago" (1970), "How Much More Can She Stand (And Still Stand By Me)" (1971), the steamy "You've Never Been This Far Before" (1973), "There's a Honky Tonk Angel" (1974), and "Linda on My Mind" (1975). Many of these embodied his trademark formula combining infidelity with guilt. Twitty and LORETTA LYNN won a Grammy and four CMA awards for a series of classic duets, including "After the Fire Is Gone" (1971), "Louisiana Woman, Mississippi Man" (1973), and "Feelin's" (1975).

Twitty's concerts, with their crowds of fervent female fans, often resembled religious revivals, leading JERRY CLOWER to dub him "The High Priest of Country Music." Holding to a dramatic, minimalist style, for years Twitty did not speak onstage, do interviews, attend music-business parties, appear on TV shows, or perform encores.

In the late 1970s Twitty began experimenting, adding elements of rock ("Boogie Grass Band"), soul ("Don't Take It Away"), and OUTLAW sounds ("Play Guitar Play"). He also began producing his own albums and adopted a curly new hairdo in place of his previous pompadour and sideburns. Hits such as "I'd Love to Lay You Down" (1980) and "Tight Fittin' Jeans" (1981) also signified a more contemporary sound and a more open, less guilt-ridden sexuality.

Twitty switched from MCA (his label after it absorbed Decca) to WARNER/ELEKTRA in 1981 and recorded country versions of the pop hits "Slow Hand," "The Rose," and "Three Times a Lady." Other early 1980s hits included "I Don't Know a Thing About Love (The Moon Song)," penned by Harlan Howard. Twitty opened his $3 million Twitty City tourism complex in Nashville in 1981 and inaugurated annual "Country Explosion" concerts to kick off Fan Fair (later called the CMA MUSIC FESTIVAL). He also invested in the Nashville Sounds minor-league baseball team and the United Talent booking agency.

VINCE GILL, KATHY MATTEA, NAOMI JUDD, and REBA MCENTIRE were among the many acts whose early careers Twitty boosted. His concern for songwriters and their work led to Twitty's billing as "the best friend a song ever had."

Rejoining MCA by 1987, Twitty issued some of his most creative singles to date—"That's My Job," "Goodbye Time," "She's Got a Single

Thing in Mind," and the controversial "Saturday Night Special." He quit smoking and gained new vocal power, made music videos, and began to do interviews and TV appearances. His authorized biography appeared in 1986.

As the 1990s dawned, Twitty was back in the Top Ten with "Crazy in Love" and "I Couldn't See You Leavin'." His last recording session was a duet with Sam Moore, formerly of the hit-making soul duo Sam & Dave, on "Rainy Night in Georgia," included in *Rhythm Country & Blues*, a multiartist collection released by MCA in 1994. Twitty died suddenly of a stomach aneurysm en route from a show in BRANSON, MISSOURI, to Nashville's 1993 Fan Fair celebration. Before his death, however, he had recorded an album coincidentally titled *Final Touches*. He was inducted into THE COUNTRY MUSIC HALL OF FAME in 1999. —*Robert K. Oermann*

## T. Texas Tyler
b. Mena, Arkansas, June 20, 1916; d. January 23, 1972

David Luke Myrick, known professionally as T. Texas Tyler, "the Man with a Million Friends," scored his biggest hit in 1948 with the sentimental recitation "Deck of Cards." Tyler's almost archaic, trumpet-filigreed recitations were steeped in Anglo-Celtic tradition but nonetheless represented country music's vast commercial potential. On the strength of "Deck of Cards," Tyler appeared at New York's CARNEGIE HALL on April 25, 1948, thus becoming one of the earlier country acts to do so.

Raised in Philadelphia, Tyler appeared on the *Major Bowes Amateur Hour* network radio talent show at age fourteen and then graduated to radio work in West Virginia and Indiana and on Shreveport, Louisiana's KWKH in 1942. While in West Virginia and Indiana, he nurtured the early career of LITTLE JIMMY DICKENS.

*T. Texas Tyler*

Discharged after a year in the army in 1946, Tyler signed with struggling Pasadena, California, independent FOUR STAR RECORDS as the label's first country artist. (Tyler's subsequent success would later attract both MADDOX BROTHERS & ROSE and WEBB PIERCE to the company.) Tyler had another major hit in 1948 with "Dad Gave My Dog Away," after the style of RED FOLEY's sentimental "Old Shep." Tyler's 1949 Los Angeles television show *Range Round Up* was a local favorite, and he had a number of other successful records, including "Filipino Baby" (1946), "Bumming Around" (1953), and "Courting in the Rain" (1954). Unfortunately, Tyler had serious drug and alcohol problems. In the mid-1950s, while on a brief tour with HANK SNOW, Tyler was arrested in San Antonio, Texas, for possession of marijuana, and his career never recovered.

In the 1960s STARDAY RECORDS' DON PIERCE (who had promoted Tyler's discs at Four Star years earlier) did an album with Tyler, mostly remakes of past triumphs. Late in life, Tyler turned to a career in the ministry. —*Jonny Whiteside*

# Ian Tyson
b. Victoria, British Columbia, Canada, September 25, 1933

Ian Tyson has had two virtually separate musical careers. First, he was half of the 1960s folk duo Ian & Sylvia; then, from the mid-1980s, he became a pioneer of new western music, or COWBOY MUSIC. His cowboy songs were among the first new songs in that genre for a generation and served as a catalyst in the renaissance of cowboy culture.

Tyson grew up on Vancouver Island, the grandson of a British shipping magnate. After art school he moved to Toronto, and he met Sylvia Fricker in 1959. The two musicians went to New York in 1961 and were taken on by BOB DYLAN's manager, Albert Grossman. They recorded seven albums for Vanguard Records (1961–67), including original songs, such as "Four Strong Winds," "Someday Soon," and "You Were on My Mind." Ian & Sylvia also helped to introduce the music of singer-songwriter Gordon Lightfoot. After two albums for MGM RECORDS the pair cut a COUNTRY-ROCK record for Ampex, submerging their own identity into that of the band Great Speckled Bird.

Ian and Sylvia drifted apart personally and professionally in the early 1970s. Tyson hosted a mainstream country television program (*Nashville North*, subsequently *The Ian Tyson Show*, on the CTV network in Canada, 1969–75) and recorded a country album for A&M Canada before temporarily retiring in 1977. Moving to Alberta to work on a ranch, he didn't record again until 1983, when he began cutting a series of cowboy culture albums, first for COLUMBIA RECORDS of Canada and then for his own Eastern Slope Records, licensed to Stony Plain (Canada) and Vanguard (United States). The third, *Cowboyography*, which reached gold-record status in Canada, is generally considered one of the best in contemporary cowboy music.

A championship cutting horse rider, Tyson has continued to tour, write, record, and run his ranch near Calgary, in addition to participating in cowboy celebration events. His work is a powerful evocation of cowboy life in the era of the satellite dish. —*Colin Escott*

# From Schoolhouses to Arenas

A History of Country Music Touring

**RONNIE PUGH**

From the time country music became a profession, a performer's income, be it little or much, has always come principally from touring: taking one's music in person to paying customers. Early on, there weren't many other ways to make money. Record making was almost a novelty, and radio, though a major entertainment medium and a sometime source of modest talent fees, proved most valuable for exposure and advertising show dates. Most radio stations had limited reach, and once radio artists had "played out" an area's best venues, they had to move to another station and build a brand new following.

Today the industry is larger, and an artist has more potential sources of income. The country divisions of major record labels are powers within a multibillion-dollar industry. National and international media—broadcast, print, and Internet—are filled with the faces, the music, and the news of a growing number of young country stars. Most established country singers own a song-publishing venture or two; there are huge sums to be made via product endorsements; and some artists even have best-selling autobiographies. But for all that, touring typically remains the largest and most important slice of this financially rewarding pie. It means survival and vital exposure for newer or midlevel acts, and big dollars for superstars such as KENNY CHESNEY, who sold more than 1 million tickets in 2009 and enjoyed the year's highest-grossing country music tour, taking in $71.1 million, according to trade magazine *Pollstar*. The essence of country touring is still what MARTY ROBBINS once described as the modern equivalent to the James boys in the Old West—ride into town, take the money, and ride out. But since the 1920s the road itself has changed, and so have the venues, those places where traveling performers have found their fans.

A few early country music personalities were showmen of the old school, who knew the entertainment business from its pre-electronic era, when it consisted almost entirely of live performing. One such act was OTTO GRAY and his cowboy orchestra; his few 1920s recordings were negligible, but he played lucrative vaudeville circuits for years and often received press notices in prominent entertainment trade papers including *Billboard* and *Variety*. UNCLE DAVE MACON worked vaudeville shows mostly as a solo act, with an acceptance in southern theaters unheard of for most of his country colleagues. When he gave up hauling freight by wagons for full-time musicianship, his many contacts came in handy. To book a tour, he'd just write letters to a few of his old friends and line up a supporting act or two to drive him around and share the profits.

Some early country stars (JIMMIE RODGERS, GENE AUTRY, and ROY ACUFF among them) learned their craft with itinerant showmen who barnstormed the country on flatbed trucks to put on minstrel or MEDICINE SHOWS and comedy revues. With the dawn of radio in the 1920s, rural music became a business; at the same time, the automobile and the open road first captured America's fancy, and since most bands were small and their instruments few, cars were the preferred means of touring. Except over the worst of winter's roads, cars could generally take a hillbilly entourage anywhere it needed to go within a reasonable time. Trains, though a favorite subject of country songs, simply didn't run to most remote hamlets, where many country shows were staged in schoolhouses lit with kerosene lanterns.

For all its privacy and convenience, touring by car could be crowded, rushed, and dangerous. Aggravated by bad roads and bad tires, tempers sometimes flared in such close quarters, often over such mundane matters as where to eat or where to bed down. In the Southwest and California, most country bands were larger, used more instruments, and carried amplifiers and public address systems. Terrain and settlement patterns in those states meant greater distances between show dates but safer (straighter and flatter) highways. Hence it was in Texas and Oklahoma during the 1930s that country music's first tour buses (and even some airplanes) were used by WESTERN SWING bands to cover their vast dancehall circuits—BOB WILLS, MILTON BROWN (in 1936 country music's first major car wreck fatality), the LIGHT CRUST DOUGHBOYS, and others.

The latter groups all enjoyed established, home-base radio jobs, typical for the most successful touring artists. But radio spots and sponsors did not always come easily, and most acts moved from station to station, working first one territory and then another, plugging show dates on the air. Station management sometimes set up artist service bureaus to help with booking and promotion (for a per-show fee). Stations with the most popular radio barn dances—Chicago's WLS and Nashville's WSM—kept booking departments for years, though all hands soon discovered that radio spots alone provided insufficient advertising. Advance men using show posters, handbills, and local radio and newspaper ads soon took up on-site promotion.

Early managers, promoters, and bookers were a mixed lot of honest, dishonest, and indifferent men; but in quest of profits, each made important contributions to the growth of country music's tour business. Larry Sunbrock promoted all-country shows built around the ever-popular fiddle contest (CURLY FOX, Red Herron, CLAYTON MCMICHEN, or whomever against his regular, Natchee the Indian). Yet Sunbrock was notorious for advertising acts he hadn't booked and then feigning innocence and bewilderment before local officials and crowds when these performers didn't appear.

OSCAR DAVIS also helped bring country shows into big-city auditoriums. A Rhode Island native whose promotion background included theater revues and dance marathons, Davis was convinced by hillbilly radio musician "Happy" Hal Burns to promote multiartist hillbilly shows beginning in the early 1940s, and their big Sunday "National Championship Hillbilly Jamborees" in such cities as Memphis, Birmingham, Little Rock, Dallas, and Nashville were usually packed. At first they used spacious, good-weather sites such as ballparks or fairgrounds because many auditorium managers viewed hillbilly artists as unreliable drunks and resented country fans who spat on walls and stuck chewing gum underneath seats. But in nine shows during the summer of 1941, using Roy Acuff, the HOOSIER HOT SHOTS, ERNEST TUBB, and other stars, Davis's shows made $180,000—the kind of money that changed venue bosses' minds. After the war, Davis, the flamboyant "Baron" known for his white-on-black newspaper ads and fast-talking radio spiels ("Don't You Dare Miss It!"), regularly booked Ernest Tubb and MINNIE PEARL into 5,000-seat venues, such as Detroit's Masonic Auditorium, and into CARNEGIE HALL in September 1947.

With civilian tires and cars out of production during wartime, the traveling TENT SHOW caught on at WSM, pioneered there by blackface comics JAMUP AND HONEY in about 1940. "From the first of April to Labor Day we weren't in Nashville," recalled David Wilds, son of Lee Davis "Honey" Wilds. "We lived on the road in a forty-foot house trailer that was towed behind a Pontiac four-door. Anywhere from eight to ten trucks moved the whole thing around." By war's end WSM was fielding several tent shows at the same time, featuring the station's growing stable of country talent. Meanwhile, the RENFRO VALLEY BARN DANCE was offering tent shows of its own.

First opening in the Northeast and Midwest in the 1930s and proliferating in the 1940s were popular open-air parks, including Sunset Park in West Grove, Pennsylvania, and Buck Lake Ranch in Angola, Indiana, which became regular stopping points for countless country acts over the next twenty-plus years. These were precursors to the weekend-long BLUEGRASS festivals that proliferated after the mid-1960s.

Nationwide talent agencies soon began to handle country acts: Jolly Joyce, General Artists Corporation, American Corporation, MCA (Music Corporation of America, which booked its first big Bob Wills tour in November 1944), and William Morris (which booked Ernest Tubb for a 1947 theater tour). A growing number of personal managers, agents, bookers, promoters, traveling advance men, and charter pilots—all usually clustered around major radio stations—further reflected country artists' increasing business sophistication. Joining established agents was a newer crop of professionals, such as Frankie More, Gabe Tucker, HAL SMITH, and RANDY HUGHES, many of whom were musicians who loved the music and knew the problems of the road firsthand. A. V. BAMFORD, booking Nashville entertainers, became famous for the huge geographic sweep of his tours. COLONEL TOM PARKER, a former carney advance man from Florida who had helped J. L. FRANK and Oscar Davis promote country shows, signed in succession three choice managerial plums—EDDY ARNOLD, HANK SNOW, and ELVIS PRESLEY. Across the nation, promoters brought acts into their territories and/or developed local talent into national stars. Chief among these promoters were CONNIE B. GAY (Washington, D.C.), HAL HORTON (Dallas), JIM DENNY (Nashville), Cracker Jim Brooker (Miami), TILLMAN FRANKS (Shreveport), SI SIMAN (Springfield), and Ken Ritter (Beaumont and Houston).

Performers themselves hardly had time to sort out this burgeoning new business, but they tried. Back in town for weekend broadcasts after a hard week of touring, artists exchanged information on the best venues, booking agencies, and road conditions. There was still an air of fun, informality, and cooperation about it all, but that was about to change.

In the mid-1950s came rock & roll, which posed a serious challenge to country music's survival. Moreover, television was keeping many Americans away from the concert box office. For many country artists, the tour business was hard hit, and one response was the PACKAGE SHOW, akin to older tent shows. The hope was that more names on the marquee would draw more customers. This approach had been used earlier with various traveling "caravans": mixed country-pop entourages such as R. J. Reynolds's CAMEL CARAVAN out of WSM in 1941–42 and Dudley LeBlanc's 1951 HADACOL CARAVAN, and one of the earliest all-country tours, 1954's RCA VICTOR Country Caravan. Mindful of these precedents—and a simultaneous competing free show—the PHILIP MORRIS COUNTRY SHOW (1957–58)—WSM used the all-Opry package concept from 1957 until good times came again in the early 1960s. In that decade and beyond, corporate sponsors of single- and multiartist tours have included MARTHA WHITE FLOUR, Marlboro, Fruit of the Loom, Kraft, Ford Trucks, Chevy Trucks, J. C. Penney, Resistol Hats, and Wrangler Jeans.

After 1956 the interstate highway system greatly facilitated touring, and newly customized tour buses, which could transport an entire show in safety and comfort, soon became the preferred mode of travel for individual acts as well. PEE WEE KING, Ernest Tubb, HANK THOMPSON, Marty Robbins, and FLATT & SCRUGGS were among the first to use such buses. Nearly all of the touring stars of the 1960s and 1970s had buses featuring some or all of the comforts of home: bunk beds, refrigerators, card tables, bathrooms, sound systems, hot plates (later microwave ovens), and costume closets. By the 1980s these custom-made travel coaches sold for $300,000 to $350,000, but they could be leased when not in use by the owner and resold five or six years (and maybe 600,000 miles) later, often for a small profit. Fading by then were memories of country music's highway fatalities (Milton Brown, JOHNNY HORTON, Ira Louvin) and many near-deaths (T. TOMMY CUTRER, BILL MONROE, Earl Scruggs, Roy Acuff).

While their bands traveled by car or bus, some stars personally preferred (and in some cases needed) the speed and convenience of the private plane. Minnie Pearl's husband, Henry Cannon, was one pioneer in flying stars such as his wife and Hank Williams to show dates. Hank Thompson and LEON MCAULIFFE were early pilots; LEFTY FRIZZELL owned a plane at his peak; and ROY DRUSKY bought a plane after his first few hits a decade later. Earl Scruggs flew his own plane, as did talent agent Randy Hughes and singer JIM REEVES. Hughes crashed in March 1963, killing himself and his better-known passengers: PATSY CLINE, COWBOY COPAS, and HAWKSHAW HAWKINS; Reeves, headstrong and newly licensed at the time, died with his pianist, Dean Manuel, in 1964, unwisely trying (as Hughes had) to get home through bad weather. In 1980 CHARLEY PRIDE's plane landed safely in Dallas after a midair collision in which the other plane was not so lucky. And in 1991 most of REBA MCENTIRE's band perished when their flight struck a mountain moments after takeoff from the San Diego airport. Though major stars such as McEntire frequently use Learjets, the 1963–64 air tragedies for a time cemented the dominance of the custom tour bus, a status strengthened by completed interstate highways and a boom in quality motel construction.

Several trends, pronounced since about 1980, have transformed the world of country touring, which today involves more artists and more dollars than ever before. Travel is safer, the businessmen are generally more honest, and the whole process is highly organized, with little left to chance or improvisation. Road books, which detail a tour day by day, minute by minute, are the artist's bible. An increasing number of talent agencies, tour managers (the plotters and mappers), and road managers (together with on-site personnel and traveling advance men) also symbolize touring's growing professionalization. There are even travel agents who specialize in arranging tours, from creating road books to selecting hotel room locations for the convenience of a large entourage. For many of today's top country stars, tours resemble those of their rock counterparts.

With routine transoceanic flights increasing since the 1960s—a far cry from Gene Autry's 1939 triumphal ocean liner tour of Ireland, England, and Danzig (days before Hitler invaded)—country performers now play to worldwide audiences. GRAND OLE OPRY acts visited the Panama Canal Zone in

1942 and traveled to U.S. military bases in Germany in 1949. Country entertainers first toured active war zones in Korea between 1951 and 1953 (GRANDPA JONES, ELTON BRITT, CAROLINA COTTON, Ernest Tubb, Hank Snow) and later visited Vietnam. In more peaceful times, some U.S. country singers have found almost greater (or more lasting) fame abroad than at home. Jim Reeves toured South Africa twice, making a movie there on one trip. In the mid-1970s, ROY CLARK and TENNESSEE ERNIE FORD brought country stage shows to the Soviet Union. SLIM WHITMAN and GEORGE HAMILTON IV remain British favorites, and numerous country entertainers have large followings in Continental Europe. In 1997 LEANN RIMES toured Australia, land of a thriving indigenous country music scene since the days of Jimmie Rodgers and the nation where KEITH URBAN began his career.

Whether in the United States or overseas, the onstage product has changed markedly in recent years. Concept tours have become popular—songwriter tours, tours to promote specific albums—and concert mechanics are considerably more complex. By the 1990s, many artists were performing in larger arenas—ALAN JACKSON, BROOKS & DUNN, GARTH BROOKS, and others—using huge screens to bring music videos to the concert experience. Others, following an approach used by BARBARA MANDRELL and Reba McEntire, employed strobe lights, smoke, and choreography. A box-office blockbuster, Brooks drew attention with rock-styled acrobatics. In the new century, arena shows have become even more theatrical. Early in the 2000s, the Brooks & Dunn Neon Circus Tour included circus performers, magicians, and comedians. By 2010 artists such as BRAD PAISLEY were customizing concert screen footage and other visual effects to accompany each song.

To mount such spectacles is no mean feat. In 1997, for example, exemplifying the trend of pairing major stars, Brooks & Dunn and Reba McEntire joined forces for an eighty-five-city tour that required twenty trucks and nine buses to transport the forty tons of equipment and the hundred-person crew. The tour hired seventy-five to a hundred additional personnel on a show-by-show basis in each city along the route. From 1997 into the twenty-first century, GEORGE STRAIT's Country Music Festival took package tours of top-drawing artists (Alan Jackson, TIM MCGRAW and FAITH HILL, Kenny Chesney) into some twenty stadiums per year in a similarly complex production. From 2003 to 2011, amid a downturn in the music industry, Kenny Chesney regularly headlined multiartist stadium concerts when few performers in any genre risked such ventures.

None of this mounting prosperity and professionalization means that risk has been eliminated from touring. Some promoters still lose money, and after a few years the majority of artists lose some or all of their box-office appeal.

Although change has generally brought previously unheard of prosperity, much has been lost. Artist–fan contact is not as close as it was in smaller venues, and working the road, if not as dangerous for the artist, has lost much of its spontaneity. The growing impersonality and slickness of the concert experience may be one reason why Nashville's annual CMA MUSIC FESTIVAL (originally called Fan Fair) has grown so tremendously from its 1972 inception. At shows in their home areas, fans don't generally get the sort of up-close-and-personal experiences they do at this festival. Early each June, offering autograph sessions, meet-and-greet events, and many musical performances, the gathering brings to Nashville thousands of country's most dedicated fans, who see most of the stars as informally and intimately as all fans once did near home.

Any way you choose to measure it, country stars have come a long way from the schoolhouses and kerosene lamps of the 1920s and 1930s.

## Carrie Underwood

b. Muskogee, Oklahoma, March 10, 1983

Carrie Marie Underwood rose to stardom after winning the 2005 season of TV's *American Idol* and quickly emerged as one of country music's most popular and acclaimed artists. Within four years of prevailing on the Fox Broadcasting Company's talent competition, Underwood had sold more 10 million albums, charted ten Top Ten hits, including eight #1s, had won four Grammy awards—including three successive trophies for Best Female Country Vocal Performance—and was named ACM's Entertainer of the Year for 2008 and 2009.

Raised on a farm near Checotah, Oklahoma, Underwood performed regularly in church, at school, in local talent shows, and at regional festivals throughout her childhood and teens. After high school, she enrolled in Northeastern State University in Tahlequah, Oklahoma, and planned a career in broadcast journalism. Her friends, however, encouraged her to try out for Fox's hit reality show.

During her senior year, Underwood traveled to St. Louis to audition for *American Idol*'s sixth season, and her rendition of "I Can't Make You Love Me" earned her a ticket to Hollywood. As the *Idol* season unfurled, Underwood emerged as a frontrunner and her powerful performance of Heart's "Alone" during Top 11 week compelled judge Simon Cowell to predict, "Not only will you win this show, you will sell more records than any other previous *Idol* winner." Although her performances ranged across multiple music genres, per *Idol*'s format, Underwood unabashedly declared her preference for country.

After she was crowned the winner during *American Idol*'s May 25, 2005, finale, Underwood's debut single, "Inside Your Heaven," was released. While it went to #1 on *Billboard*'s all-genre Hot 100 chart, the song barely registered with country radio, peaking at #52. Underwood's next single, however, made an impression: "Jesus, Take the Wheel," from her ARISTA Nashville debut CD, *Some Hearts*, spent six weeks at #1 on *Billboard*'s country chart. Released in November 2005, the album delivered two additional #1 country hits—"Before He Cheats" and "Wasted"— and the #2 hit "Don't Forget to Remember Me." It is the best-selling *American Idol* album to date, selling 7 million copies in the United States alone.

In 2006, Underwood received numerous awards, including ACM's Top New Female Vocalist and Single Record of the Year honors (for her 2005 success) and CMA's Horizon and Female Vocalist of the Year awards. She also found time to finish her degree and tour with both KENNY CHESNEY and BRAD PAISLEY. *Carnival Ride*, Underwood's 2007 sophomore effort, featured four songs she cowrote, including the #1 hits "So Small," "Last Name," and "All-American Girl." She supported the album, which also contained the #1 single "Just a Dream" and a #2 remake of RANDY TRAVIS's "I Told You So," with a successful headlining tour.

From 2007 to 2011, Underwood continued to be lauded by critics, peers, and fans. She joined the GRAND OLE OPRY on May 10, 2008, and won three more CMA Awards and eight additional ACM trophies, including recognition as Entertainer of the Year for 2008 and 2009.

In 2009, she released her third album, *Play On*. It debuted at #1 on the all-genre *Billboard* 200, and as of March 2011, had sold more than 2 million units. She won a 2008 Grammy for Best Female Country Vocal Performance for "Last Name" and a 2009 Grammy for Best Country Collaboration with Vocal for "I Told You So," a duet with Randy Travis. —*Tina Wright*

*Carrie Underwood*

## Universal Music Group (see Decca Records, MCA Records)

## Universal Records South
established 2002

Veteran Nashville recording kingpins TONY BROWN and TIM DuBois established Universal Records South in January 2002 as a joint venture with New York–based Universal Records. The new company had its own publicity and promotion departments and received marketing and sales support from Universal. Universal South's initial acts were Allison Moorer, Dean Miller, Holly Lamar, and Bering Strait. None had lasting success on the label. Soon, however, label powerhouse JOE NICHOLS went gold, and in 2004 a Cherry Bombs reunion album and a multiartist LOUVIN BROTHERS tribute album raised the firm's profile. PHIL VASSAR and Shooter Jennings joined the label in 2005, the same year that initiated a series of critically acclaimed MARTY STUART albums issued on his own affiliated Superlatone imprint. In 2006 Brown and DuBois sold their interest to Universal, which recruited Nashville recording executive MARK WRIGHT as president. Later signings included the Eli Young Band. TOBY KEITH's Show Dog label merged with Universal Records South in January 2010, with Wright remaining as president. —*John W. Rumble*

## Delia "Mom" Upchurch
b. Gainesboro, Tennessee, August 10, 1891; d. September 1, 1976

For more than twenty years after World War II, Delia "Mom" Upchurch operated an East Nashville rooming house for struggling country musicians. The list of those who stayed in her home at 620 Boscobel Street reads like a street-level hall of fame for the early years of Nashville's country music industry—from rising stars CARL SMITH and FARON YOUNG, to famous session musicians LLOYD GREEN and BUDDY SPICHER, to legendary songwriters HANK COCHRAN and ROGER MILLER. Like Tootsie Bess and a handful of others, Upchurch came to be regarded as a den mother to the whole community. "They were coming into town with no money, no jobs, and no friends," she said. "They needed someone to give them a place to stay and sort of look after them until they got started. Someone to give them a home." For most rooms Upchurch charged less than ten dollars per week, and she would only rent to country performers. "They don't mix too good with people in other livelihoods," she explained. "And I just like good old hillbilly music."

Upchurch's first roomers were members of PEE WEE KING's Golden West Cowboys. They moved out, however, after her husband, Louis K. Upchurch, died on October 5, 1947. She spent nearly a year coming to terms with his death and then began taking in musicians anew. By the 1950s her home was so well known as a pickers' crash pad that when musicians needed a sideman for an upcoming session or tour they would call Mom's to see who was available. "Mom knew how long you were going to be out on tour, and if someone showed up while you were on the road, she had a habit of renting your bed out to them," recalled musician Howard White. Upchurch maintained her rooming home into the late 1960s, by which time she was nearly eighty years old. —*Daniel Cooper*

## Keith Urban
b. Whangarei, New Zealand, October 26, 1967

Keith Urban overcame false starts and personal setbacks to become the most enduring American country star to emerge from Australia. He did so by bringing rock energy and a spirited guitar style to contemporary country music.

Urban initially signed with EMI Australia and, in 1991, released a successful self-titled debut album in his home country. In 1992 he moved to Nashville, working briefly in the road band for BROOKS & DUNN and appearing as a guitarist in the ALAN JACKSON video "Mercury Blues."

In the mid-1990s, he formed The Ranch, a popular Nashville club band. The trio signed with CAPITOL RECORDS and released a self-titled album that found little success. Later, Urban would describe his first seven years in America as a period of increasing drug use that led him to enter a rehab facility in 1998. Afterward, he went solo and released his debut album, *Keith Urban,* on Capitol in 1999. It included his first #1 hit, "But for the Grace of God," cowritten with Charlotte Caffey and Jane Wiedlin of the Go-Gos. ACM named him Top New Male Vocalist of 2000, and he won CMA's 2001 Horizon Award.

His second album, 2002's *Golden Road,* found him working with producer DANN HUFF to create a distinctive sound built around cascading chords on his guitar buoyed by sunny melodies and upbeat rhythms. The singles "Somebody Like You" and "Who Wouldn't Want to Be Me" set his signature sound in place, with both reaching #1 on the charts. The album sold 3 million copies, topped by 2004's *Be Here,* which sold 4 million and became his first #1 on *Billboard*'s country album chart. It included the

*Keith Urban*

energetic #1 hits "Days Go By" and "Better Life," balanced by the RODNEY CROWELL ballad "Making Memories of Us," another #1, and "Tonight I Wanna Cry," a #2 single. He was named CMA Male Vocalist of the Year in 2005.

Urban married Australian actress Nicole Kidman on June 25, 2006, and on October 19 admitted himself into the Betty Ford Clinic in California after relapsing into drug abuse. His fourth album, *Love, Pain, & the Whole Crazy Thing*, was released in November 2006. It debuted at #1 on *Billboard*'s country album charts and #3 on the all-genre *Billboard* 200 listing. The collection featured four Top Ten hits—including "Once in a Lifetime" and "Stupid Boy"—but was his first not to include a #1 single. Urban returned to the top of the singles charts with a revised version of his previously released "You Look Good in My Shirt," from the 2007 compilation *Greatest Hits: 18 Kids*. "Sweet Thing," his first single from his 2009 album *Defying Gravity*, went to #1, as did "Start a Band," recorded with BRAD PAISLEY, who wrote the song.

As of spring 2011, Urban had received four Grammy awards, all for Best Male Country Vocal Performance: for "You'll Think of Me" (2005), "Stupid Boy" (2007), "Sweet Thing" (2009), and "'Til Summer Comes Around" (2010). He had also won six CMA Awards.

His album *Get Closer* appeared in November 2010, with the initial single, "Put You in a Song," becoming a #2 country hit. —*Michael McCall*

## Urban Cowboy

The term "urban cowboy" first gained currency in the summer of 1980 with the release of the Paramount Pictures film *Urban Cowboy*, starring John Travolta and Debra Winger. The movie that gave a brief country music boom (1980–82) a name was inspired by a nonfiction article in *Esquire* by Aaron Latham ("The Ballad of the Urban Cowboy," September 12, 1978), and it was shot in 1979 at GILLEY's nightclub in Pasadena, Texas. The film became the surprise smash hit of 1980, boosting the careers of MICKEY GILLEY and JOHNNY LEE while making country music a major national fad. Basically an oil-patch-and-trailer-park love story, directed by James Bridges from a screenplay Bridges wrote with Aaron Latham, *Urban Cowboy* put a cowboy hat and a Lone Star beer stamp on an American postdisco singles scene that was desperate for a new identity.

The double-LP soundtrack album on ASYLUM/Full Moon Records featured country-tinged rock artists such as THE EAGLES, LINDA RONSTADT, and Bonnie Raitt alongside Gilley and Lee. It also featured CHARLIE DANIELS, who appeared in the movie, performing his stirring "The Devil Went Down to Georgia." The album gave Lee his first #1 country hit—as well as a #5 pop hit—with the movie theme "Lookin' for Love (In All the Wrong Places)." The soundtrack quickly passed the million-sales mark, and Lee's *Lookin' for Love* album went gold. Country music got a huge sales boost, with gross sales for 1980 rising nearly 24 percent over 1979.

Boots, blue jeans, and cowboy garb became the look of the day as dance clubs switched overnight from disco to the cotton-eyed Joe. The demand for mechanical bulls was so great that manufacturers couldn't keep up with orders. Most importantly for the art form, country music suddenly had access to adult contemporary (AC) radio.

Perhaps it was the last throes of THE NASHVILLE SOUND, but Nashville became so enamored of pop-crossover records that, temporarily, it largely abandoned its southern, rural, working-class

Urban Cowboy *movie poster*

roots and promoted a class of AC-ready recording acts typified by JANIE FRICKE, SYLVIA, RAZZY BAILEY, EARL THOMAS CONLEY, T. G. SHEPPARD, and other rising stars of that era. All of them had #1 radio hits. Sylvia and Fricke enjoyed a brief flash of gold and platinum record sales, but urban cowboy crossover music devolved into a hybrid misfire, neither good pop nor good country, ultimately failing to satisfy either country or adult contemporary fans.

In1983 the bubble burst, with country records sales falling back to previous levels, but it took Nashville a few years to understand that such artists as GEORGE STRAIT, RICKY SKAGGS, and RANDY TRAVIS, leaders of the NEW TRADITIONALISM movement, would be country music's salvation. In January 1985 *Variety* ran the front-page headline "Country Music Sales Turn Sour" and declared "The Urban Cowboy is definitely buried in boot hill." —*Bob Millard*

## The Vagabonds
Herald Goodman b. August 8, 1900; d. March 6, 1974
Dean Upson b. November 12, 1900; d. October 1975
Curtis "Curt" Poulton b. Dulaney, West Virginia, 1907; d. ca. 1957

The Vagabonds were active in country music only five years (1929–34), but this smooth-singing vocal trio had a major impact on the GRAND OLE OPRY and its fans. One of the first full-time professional groups to appear on the show, they were also one of the first to publish their own SONGBOOKS and issue their own recordings. In addition, though guitarist Curt Poulton was born in Dulaney, West Virginia, they were one of the Opry's first non-southern groups, having risen to fame in the Midwest.

The trio was formed in 1927 by recent Otterbein College graduates—Dean Upson, brother Paul Upson, and friend Robert Dugan—in Chicago, where they appeared on WLS as a pop and novelty act called the Three Hired Men. Soon they changed their name to the Vagabonds and made their first records with Charley Straight's orchestra. By 1929 the group had replaced Paul Upson and Dugan with Poulton and Herald Goodman and had moved to KMOX–St. Louis. Organizing their own radio production company, the men broadened their repertoire to include more folk and OLD-TIME songs and thus were able to tailor a greater variety of shows for local and network sponsors. WSM manager HARRY STONE hired them in August 1931 for both pop and country programs, including the Grand Ole Opry.

Unlike many Opry regulars, the Vagabonds were WSM staff musicians, and they developed their own songwriting and publicity. The pop-influenced act scored a huge hit with "When It's Lamp-Lighting Time in the Valley" and issued the songbook *Old Cabin Songs of the Fiddle and Bow*, which they sold by mail and reprinted six times within months to meet demand.

In January 1933 the Vagabonds made a series of custom recordings they sold under their Old Cabin label. Next they recorded for RCA VICTOR's BLUEBIRD imprint; most of their thirty-two sides were either originals or current Tin Pan Alley pieces. Due to personal and professional disputes, they split in 1934, after a move to Schenectady, New York. Goodman came back to Nashville temporarily and worked the Opry with a newly formed band before moving to Tulsa, Oklahoma, to start KVOO's *Saddle Mountain Roundup* barn dance in 1939. Upson briefly helmed WSM's booking department in the mid-1940s and then became commercial manager for Shreveport's station KWKH, where he helped to found the LOUISIANA HAYRIDE. Poulton returned to WSM for several years, making Opry appearances as a soloist and later with the DELMORE BROTHERS. He spent his last years in Missouri, working in a camera shop. —*Charles Wolfe*

## Valory Music (*see* Big Machine Records)

## Leroy Van Dyke
b. Spring Fork, Missouri, October 4, 1929

Smooth-singing Leroy Van Dyke had only three Top Ten country records: his #9 1957 DOT smash, "The Auctioneer" (a song he cowrote about his uncle), his MERCURY rendition of KENDALL HAYES's blockbuster cheating song "Walk On By" (#1, 1961–62), and his Mercury hit "If a Woman Answers (Hang Up the Phone)" (#3, 1962). Nevertheless, these crossover hits launched Van Dyke's lengthy career.

The son of livestock breeder Frank Van Dyke and mother Irene, Leroy graduated from the University of Missouri, where he studied journalism and animal husbandry, later attending livestock auctioneering school in Decatur, Illinois.

Following army service during the Korean War, Van Dyke spent three years on the OZARK JUBILEE and appeared on Arthur Godfrey's CBS-TV shows. From Dot (1956–58) Van Dyke moved to Mercury (1961–65), where he had most of his chart success.

Darkly handsome, he helped usher in a new era of sophisticated country entertainers. Perfecting his stage show, he was among the first entertainers to perform in tuxedos at posh nightspots such as Las Vegas showrooms.

But the 1960s also brought challenges. In February 1966 his five-year-old son, Ray Leroy, fell through thin ice near his Nashville home and drowned. Although Van Dyke starred in the movie *What Am I Bid?* (1967), the low-budget project failed to generate further film offers. He continued to reach the lower rungs of the country charts through 1977 on WARNER BROS., Kapp, DECCA, ABC, and ABC/Dot, but additional hits eluded him. Eventually he returned to Missouri, where his ranch near Sedalia serves as home base for extensive touring. —*Walt Trott*

## Townes Van Zandt
b. Fort Worth, Texas, March 7, 1944; d. January 1, 1997

An enigmatic, mysterious, compelling troubadour, John Townes Van Zandt personified the term "cult figure" and was a modern link to the wandering minstrel tradition embodied by WOODY GUTHRIE and Ramblin' Jack Elliott. Born into a well-to-do Texas oil family, Van Zandt spent several weeks during his teenage years in a mental hospital, diagnosed as a manic depressive with schizophrenic tendencies. For much of his life he lived at no fixed address, preferring the road. Influenced by Lightning Hopkins, HANK WILLIAMS, and BOB DYLAN, Van Zandt began performing in Texas folk clubs in the mid-1960s. MICKEY NEWBURY brought him to Nashville to make his first album, *For the Sake of the Song*, in 1968.

Van Zandt's commercial success was limited, partly due to inconsistent management and personal problems. Because his work appeared on small labels, his recordings lacked focused promotion and widespread distribution. But his reputation among other songwriters is immense. He has been cited as a major influence by GUY CLARK, STEVE EARLE, NANCI GRIFFITH, LYLE LOVETT, RODNEY CROWELL, ROBERT EARL KEEN, the Cowboy Junkies, HAL KETCHUM, and countless others. *Billboard* magazine referred to Van Zandt as "the Van Gogh of lyrics," a songwriter whose vibrant poetic imagery recalls that of the finest expressionist painters.

His best-known songs include "Pancho & Lefty" (recorded by MERLE HAGGARD & WILLIE NELSON), "If I Needed You" (DON WILLIAMS & EMMYLOU HARRIS), and "Be Here to Love Me" (Norah Jones).

Van Zandt released fifteen albums in his lifetime, the last, 1995's *No Deeper Blue*, recorded in Ireland. He died of a heart attack at home in Mt. Juliet, Tennessee, while recuperating from surgery. Posthumous releases, tribute albums—most notably Steve Earle's *Townes* (2009)—several biographies, and a 2004 feature film, *Be Here to Love Me*, have reflected continuing interest in his life and music, as have covers of his songs by Robert Plant and ALISON KRAUSS, among other artists. —*John Lomax III*

## Phil Vassar
b. Lynchburg, Virginia, May 28, 1964

A self-defined "piano player in a guitar town," Nashville-based singer-songwriter Phil Vassar is responsible for a run of catchy, upbeat country hits influenced more by his idol, rock tunesmith Billy Joel, than by HONKY-TONK tradition.

The son of a Virginia factory worker, Vassar moved to Nashville in 1987, where he spent the next decade performing in local clubs. After getting a song recorded by pop crooner Engelbert

Humperdinck in 1996, Vassar landed a writing deal with EMI. In 1998 ALAN JACKSON, JO DEE MESSINA, and TIM MCGRAW scored hits with songs written or cowritten by Vassar. He was named ASCAP Songwriter of the Year in 1999.

Vassar's self-titled debut album, released on ARISTA in 2000, gave rise to four Top Ten hits, including "Carlene" and "Just Another Day in Paradise," his first #1 single. These and subsequent hits "American Child" (2002), "In a Real Love" (2004), and "Last Day of My Life" (2006) were repackaged with Vassar's versions of best-sellers he penned for other artists on *Greatest Hits Vol. 1* in 2006. Vassar's 2008 release *Prayer of a Common Man*, recorded for UNIVERSAL RECORDS SOUTH, found this rocker-at-heart tempering his buoyant sound with a more reflective approach. *Traveling Circus* (2009), also for Universal South, returned to an upbeat style. —*Mick Buck*

## James D. Vaughan
b. Giles County, Tennessee, December 14, 1864; d. February 9, 1941

James David Vaughan was a pioneering gospel songwriter and publisher who had a major impact on early country music. Between 1900 and 1930 he emerged as the nation's most successful publisher of paperback, shape-note gospel SONGBOOKS. Centering his efforts in his native South, he also popularized gospel quartets, radio, and recordings as promotional vehicles for his music.

Shortly after the Civil War, southern gospel music began to emerge from a central location in the Shenandoah Valley of Virginia, under the aegis of the Reubush-Kieffer Company. One of its leading teachers and composers, E. T. Hildebrand, took on young Vaughan as an apprentice and schooled him in songwriting and in running music schools. After an abortive stay in Texas, where he operated his own music schools, Vaughan returned to Tennessee, settling in Lawrenceburg in 1902.

In 1900, however, he had already issued his own song collection, *Gospel Chimes*, and its success guaranteed a series of sequels. By 1909 he had sold some 30,000 songbooks in one year, and by 1910 this figure doubled. He soon organized workers from his Lawrenceburg office to travel as quartets, singing numbers from the new books for local churches. This technique worked so well that many churches began to appreciate the quartets as much as the songs, and by the 1930s some quartets were breaking away to tour independently. Two of the best-known were the Speer Family and the John Daniel Quartet, the latter finding fame on the GRAND OLE OPRY.

Vaughan quartets recorded for major labels such as Victor (later RCA VICTOR) and Paramount, but Vaughan also started his own company, Vaughan Records. In 1922 it became perhaps the first southern-based record firm. In addition, he founded one of the earliest radio stations in Tennessee, WOAN, to broadcast his music.

Vaughan's various music schools were training grounds for important country musicians, including the DELMORE BROTHERS and SAM AND KIRK MCGEE. By the 1930s his songs were widely heard on radio and records. "I Need the Prayers of Those I Love" was a hit for the Delmores and for other duets. The MONROE BROTHERS learned "What Would You Give in Exchange?"—their signature hit—directly from a Vaughan book, while the CARTER FAMILY adapted various Vaughan numbers, including "No Depression in Heaven."

During his 1920s heyday, Vaughan published two new collections each year and promoted them with related recordings. The Depression, as well as increasing competition from newer outfits such as STAMPS-BAXTER, cut into his sales, and Vaughan's death in 1941 robbed the company of its leader. But his tradition survived, and Vaughan songbooks are still being published by the Church of God Publishing Company in Cleveland, Tennessee. —*Charles Wolfe*

## Victor Talking Machine Company (*see* RCA Victor Records)

## Videos (*see* Music Videos)

## The Village Barn
established in New York, New York, October 1929

For more than twenty years, the Village Barn offered club-hopping New Yorkers a curious taste of rural American culture, as seen through a big-city lens. Located at 52 West Eighth Street in Manhattan's Greenwich Village, the 250-seat nightspot sported a farmyard decor, complete with a live, caged rooster. Its floor show mixed western singers, country performers, novelty acts, vaudeville hoofers, and low comics with ballroom dance bands. Between sets, audiences participated in square dances, hobby horse and sack races, and musical chairs games.

Opened by Meyer Horowitz in October 1929, the Village Barn was a springboard for diverse young talent, including hillbilly comedians Anne, Zeke, and JUDY CANOVA; novelty jazz composer Raymond Scott; and pop vocalist Helen O'Connell. Established country or western performers who played there included Zeke Manners, PATSY MONTANA, THE PRAIRIE RAMBLERS, ROSALIE ALLEN, ESMERELDY, RED RIVER DAVE, TEXAS JIM ROBERTSON, CAPTAIN STUBBY & THE BUCCANEERS, and comedian RED INGLE. On May 28, 1948, the Village Barn launched a self-titled weekly remote broadcast that NBC fed to its television affiliates on the East Coast and eventually the Midwest. The show, which ran for two years, inspired a 1949 low-budget feature film, also called *Village Barn*. On March 25, 1953, Horowitz replaced the club's rustic entertainment with a Gay Nineties revue. —*Dave Samuelson*

## Rhonda Vincent
b. Kirksville, Missouri, July 13, 1962

Rhonda Vincent's combination of hard-core, energetic BLUEGRASS with country-friendly ballads has earned her multiple IBMA awards as well as a high profile among mainstream country fans.

She began her career at age five, playing a snare drum and singing in her family's band, the Sally Mountain Show. She soon switched to mandolin (adding guitar and fiddle in later years) and took an increasingly prominent role in the group, which recorded for the Vincents' own label and regional labels throughout the 1970s and 1980s. In 1985 Rhonda competed on TNN's *You Can Be a Star* and began working for GRAND OLE OPRY member JIM ED BROWN. She launched her solo career in the early 1990s by releasing three solo REBEL RECORDS albums including both bluegrass and country instrumentation. A 1992 signing with GIANT RECORDS yielded two strong albums that tempered modern country production with bluegrass-leaning songs and harmonies.

*Rhonda Vincent*

Vincent returned to bluegrass in 1998 when she formed her band, the Rage (originally the Raje), and cohosted IBMA's awards show. In 1999 she signed with ROUNDER RECORDS, and her label debut, aptly titled *Back Home Again*, was an unqualified success, earning her the first of seven consecutive IBMA Female Vocalist of the Year awards in 2000 and the organization's prized Entertainer of the Year trophy the following year. A succession of equally successful CDs followed, as Vincent weathered numerous changes in band personnel. Along the way, she developed a musical and business formula that combined intensive touring; a MARTHA WHITE endorsement; highly polished country ballads and videos; and hard-charging, traditional bluegrass patterned after favorites including JIMMY MARTIN and THE OSBORNE BROTHERS. This blend has made her one of bluegrass's most popular and successful artists.

Vincent left the Rounder label in February 2010. She released the album *Taken* in September of that year, on her own label, Upper Management. *—Jon Weisberger*

## VOA (*see* The Voice of America)

## Vogue Records
established in Detroit, Michigan, 1945; ended 1947

Vogue Records was founded by Tom Saffady, a twenty-nine-year-old Detroit industrialist. Saffady's goal was to invent an eye-catching unbreakable and unwarpable record. After years of research, he introduced a picture disc featuring an aluminum core on which the picture was placed, sealed with a clear-vinyl coating, and then impressed with recorded grooves. Vogue located its plant near downtown Detroit while maintaining studios in both Detroit and Chicago. General manager Al Lynas arranged sessions, talent, and distribution, while A&R chief Seymour Simons selected talent and songs.

The first Vogue releases went on sale in May 1946 for $1.05 each, when standard records were selling at fifty cents each. Each disc had multicolored illustrations to represent the song title. Out of the company's sixty-six total releases of mostly popular tunes, six discs contained country music. Veteran performers LULU BELLE & SCOTTY made three records, and PATSY MONTANA recorded one. The remaining two discs contained songs by the Downhomers, Nancy Lee & the Hilltoppers, and Judy & Jen. Unfortunately, the label was not successful, and by August 1947 the company had entered bankruptcy. The files and recording masters were later destroyed, although the records themselves still exist in the hands of collectors and in the archives of the COUNTRY MUSIC HALL OF FAME AND MUSEUM. *—Don Roy*

## The Voice of America

The Voice of America (VOA), an international broadcast service funded by the United States government, claims an achievement similar to that of Chicago's WLS from 1924 to 1960 and to that of WSM since 1925: It has brought country music to audiences who have never heard it before. While those radio stations made the music available at the national level, VOA has been a major force in country's overseas popularity. With its mandate to "tell the world about America," VOA broadcasts to an audience of some 125 million listeners over shortwave transmissions as well as AM and FM radio. It also broadcasts by satellite and is available through the Internet, widening its reach via affiliate and contract agreements with radio and TV stations and cable networks.

As of 2011, the network continued to broadcast a weekly program, *Country Hits USA*, initiated in 1984 by former VOA music director Judy Massa, who hosted the show until her retirement in 2001. The program often features interviews with stars and live broadcasts from important country music events. *—Barbara Pruett*

# "The Fightin' Side of Me"

## The Politics of Country Music

## CHRIS WILLMAN

Of the many ways country music is not like polite dinner conversation, foremost among them may be how discussions of politics and religion are not only tolerated but welcomed. If the music is at its best when it is honest about the way people are thinking, living, and loving, then walling off the economy, war, and pressing social issues would constitute an unreasonable restriction of creative trade. Country has often stood out as the form of popular music most willing to confront concerns or controversies of the day. As CHELY WRIGHT said, "The thing that keeps country rearing its head above water, or creates those moments where we're the #1 kind of music, is the fact that it's a Polaroid of what's going on in our nation."

Of course, there's another way to look at country's willingness to tackle tough issues. This view assumes that country's audience is monolithic, especially in terms of religious or patriotic issues that might divide a rock or pop fan base. As DIXIE CHICKS famously discovered, though country music might be a big philosophical tent, the bulk of the audience often crowds toward one end of that tent in times of deep national division, punishing artists who come down on the "wrong" side of partisanship. Even so, renegade voices are heard loud and clear, if sometimes by smaller niche audiences, such as AMERICANA fans.

By the outset of the twenty-first century, certain stereotypes had been established: mainstream country music was a GOP hotbed, with Americana offering a safe but less profitable haven for left-leaners. There's truth in those assumptions, but accepting them at face value ignores complexities built over a contentious century. Through the mid-1960s, at least, the heart of the country music audience—as found in the South and rural states outside the region—might have been considered the very heart of the Democratic Party. A shift was well under way during the Vietnam years, as MERLE HAGGARD became more famous for rabble-rousing songs like "Okie from Muskogee" and "Fightin' Side of Me" than his poetic evocations of poverty, and Hag became a symbol, perhaps unintentionally, of the anti-antiwar movement. By the George H. W. Bush years, if a major country singer went out to stump for a candidate, that contender almost certainly would be a Republican.

At the same time, artists such as TIM MCGRAW, pondered running for governor of Tennessee as a Democrat in the 2000s, have resisted the tides of the moment. JOHNNY CASH's odd mix of social conservatism and liberalism marked him as a sort of third-way star, and the same was true of Haggard, who ultimately came to be thought of as a bit of a hippie himself. There were moments, albeit rare ones, when country fans saw the lion lie down with the lamb. Conservative TRAVIS TRITT initiated a "let's talk" duet with liberal John Mellencamp. And TOBY KEITH, who'd been accused of warmongering with "Courtesy of the Red, White, and Blue (The Angry American)," often happily partnered with buddy WILLIE NELSON, whose antiwar stance hardly seemed to cost him a fan, even though his advocacy for peace, pot, and Dennis Kucinich might have been considered to the left of ostracized Dixie Chicks lead singer Natalie Maines. In the end, most fans might care less about whether artists have the right country politics than that they have the right country attitude—which is to say, both fiercely independent and a little bit polite.

War has been a recurring topical theme in country music, whether the songs ponder the need for conflict or describe its human cost. All the way back in 1914, hillbilly trailblazer FIDDLIN' JOHN CARSON scored a hit with a World War I–themed song, but it had nothing to do with putting a boot in anyone's rear end. Rather, in "I'm Glad My Wife's in Europe" the narrator expressed his thankfulness for the Great War, as it prevented his vacationing spouse from returning from overseas. Soon, however, Fiddlin' John moved on to the more sober "Dixie Division," which lauded southern troops headed to the front. Still, it took World War II to produce the kind of go-get-'em material that later came to be associated with Toby Keith. DENVER DARLING specialized in songs on the order of "Cowards Over Pearl Harbor," while CARSON ROBISON enjoyed an even longer run of topical hits, including the provocatively titled "We're Gonna Have to Slap the Dirty Little Jap (And Uncle Sam's the Guy Who Can Do It)" and "Get Your Gun and Come Along (We're Fixin' to Kill a Skunk)." "Smoke on the Water," a #1 *Billboard* hit for RED FOLEY and, shortly afterward, for BOB WILLS, promised that America would make "a graveyard of Japan."

Anticommunism and the atom bomb became equally rich sources of material in the 1950s. A character named "Joe"—that would be Joe Stalin—was frequently addressed in contemporary recordings, such as ROY ACUFF's threatening "Advice to Joe" and HANK WILLIAMS's "No, No, Joe." ELTON BRITT, who had a World War II smash with "There's a Star-Spangled Banner Waving Somewhere," kept the flag aloft with "The Red We Want Is the Red We've Got in the Old Red, White and Blue." LULU BELLE & SCOTTY didn't have to be subpoenaed by the other notorious Joe of the era, Joseph McCarthy, to testify proudly, "I'm No Communist."

Contrary to country's sometimes-war-thirsty image, a hopeful strain of peace-mongering emerged during the Korean War and the Cold War, too. In "Old Man Atom," THE SONS OF THE PIONEERS pleaded for international cooperation to avoid a nuclear holocaust. JIMMY DEAN's "Dear Ivan" was a musical letter to a Russian farmer stating that peace could be achieved if it were up to the little men on both sides, not their nations' leaders. Somewhat bravely at the time, Cactus Pryor's "Point of Order" even spoofed the McCarthy hearings.

On the economics side, Depression-era hillbilly songs leaned toward "How Can a Poor Man Stand Such Times and Live," a 1929 recording that continued to be covered eighty years later by the likes of Bruce Springsteen. While most country fans might have been presumed to be pro–New Deal, the conservative-minded Roy Acuff recorded "Old Age Pension Check" in 1939, spoofing the idea of deferred retirement money as pie in the sky. By the 1960s, you could find attitudes toward government assistance as polarized as those in Merle Haggard's rueful "They're Tearing the Labor Camps Down" and Guy Drake's angrily satirical "Welfare Cadillac." Actually, you didn't need to venture beyond the Haggard canon to find polarization, for Hag was also delivering lines such as "I ain't never been on welfare—that's one place I won't be" in his 1969 classic "Workin' Man Blues." Antigovernment sentiments were still popping up in the 2000s, when Ray Scott sang, "There's a whole lot of able bodied takers out there in that welfare line/But you can bet old Uncle Sam ain't wipin' this boy's behind." Though it didn't sell, BOBBY BARE devoted an entire concept album to Americans on the bottom rung and in danger of falling still further: 1975's *Hard Time Hungrys*, a recessionary song cycle penned by SHEL SILVERSTEIN.

Women's rights occasionally proved itself a hot topic, starting with Blind Alfred Reed's decidedly nonprogressive "Why Do You Bob Your Hair, Girls?" (1927). As late as the 1970s, JOHNNY PAYCHECK could get away with openly deriding career women in "All-American Man." At the same time, country's tradition of tolerance stretches from the CARTER FAMILY's "There'll Be No Distinction There," which envisioned an inclusive afterlife, through GARTH BROOKS's "We Shall Be Free," whose call for individuals to love whomever they choose seemed to accept gay relationships.

Country artists have long endorsed political candidates—and occasionally run for office themselves. W. LEE "PAPPY" O'DANIEL, who had written "On to Victory Mr. Roosevelt" for the LIGHT CRUST DOUGHBOYS, switched parties (and positions on FDR) and became Texas governor in 1938 and then a senator in 1941. In 1948 Roy Acuff unsuccessfully ran for Tennessee governor on the Republican ticket. Singer and public official JIMMIE DAVIS successfully used the theme song "You Are My Sunshine" in two campaigns for the Louisiana governorship, in 1943 and again in 1959. SAMMY KERSHAW was not so lucky in his 2007 bid to become Louisiana's lieutenant governor, and fans still wonder if Tim McGraw's plans to run for the Louisiana statehouse as a Democrat when he's older are a put-on or a promise. More recently, John Rich of BIG & RICH and HANK WILLIAMS JR. have hinted at running for office, both on conservative platforms.

GRAND OLE OPRY star UNCLE DAVE MACON seems to have started country's tradition of musical endorsements with "Governor Al Smith" (1928), which, perhaps curiously for a Protestant performer, supported a New York Catholic running for president (as a Democrat), though they both opposed

Prohibition. JIMMIE OSBORNE's "A Tribute to Robert A. Taft" (1953) lauded a conservative Republican senator. The last time anyone had a modest chart hit with an endorsement song, much less an endorsement for a Democrat, was LAWTON WILLIAMS's "Everything's OK on the LBJ" in 1964.

Nevertheless, country songs increasingly popped up in campaign rallies. TAMMY WYNETTE serenaded George Wallace with "Stand by Your Man" in his 1982 race for the governorship. Ross Perot legendarily used PATSY CLINE's "Crazy" to respond to critics who considered his 1992 presidential expectations downright nutty. Toby Keith, although he then publicly identified himself as a conservative Democrat, played George W. Bush's election eve rally in 2004. BROOKS & DUNN also stumped for the younger Bush, and their "Only in America" became a rallying song for Republicans at the time. In an ironic twist, Barack Obama selected the song to follow his acceptance speech at the 2008 Democratic convention—greatly pleasing DON COOK, one of the song's cowriters, who had cofounded the Nashville-based Music Row Democrats and hadn't been thrilled with the GOP's use of the tune.

In some ways, Richard Nixon was the first "country music president," inviting stars like Haggard, Cash, and LORETTA LYNN to perform at the White House. In 1974, Nixon endeared himself to country fans by appearing at the opening of the Grand Ole Opry House at OPRYLAND, even playing a bit of piano. Jimmy Carter had Willie Nelson to the White House but more famously identified himself with rock artists. The senior George Bush may have been the first true country fan in the Oval Office, even if his tastes tended more toward country-pop than anything twangy. "I find myself more relaxed with Reba coming over the airwaves," he wrote in a widely published pro-country essay in 1990. "Country music hits all the right chords—like caring for your family, remembering the good times, and keeping faith in God."

How did country come to be so identified with Republican candidates in the 1990s and 2000s? Longtime Nashville record executive JOE GALANTE holds the politicians, not the stars responsible, blaming Democrats for distancing themselves from singers and audiences whom many denigrated as hicks. "It's amazing to me, from a political standpoint, how many of the senators and representatives that are Democrats don't reach out for country acts," Galante said in 2004. "They reach out for the rock acts or hip-hop acts or movie stars. . . . The politicians want to be aligned with Barbra Streisand, as opposed to being involved with Brooks & Dunn." In certain union-heavy areas, he believed, you'd still find as many Democrats as Republicans at a typical country show.

But there was little doubt that a definite split had occurred in the country audience, and most observers would trace it to the Vietnam years, even though a massive change in party affiliation in the southern states didn't fully take hold until the Reagan era. For anyone worried that returning vets were being spat on by counterculturalists, literally or—in rock & roll—figuratively, country provided a safe harbor for patriotism. Future leftist KRIS KRISTOFFERSON had his first songwriting success with the 1966 DAVE DUDLEY hit "Vietnam Blues," about a veteran disgusted by a rally held by Ho Chi Minh sympathizers. Future liberal activist BOBBY BRADDOCK cowrote Autry Inman's "Ballad of Two Brothers," a Goofus and Gallant–style look at a responsible boy who proudly goes off to Vietnam and a lazy hippie brother who insists that "this God and country bit just isn't my bag." In 1966 STONEWALL JACKSON derided antiwar protesters in "The Minute Men (Are Turning in Their Graves)" and in 1970 ERNEST TUBB defended the war by recording "It's America (Love It or Leave It)." One of country's most revered writers, HARLAN HOWARD, was stirred to write and record a concept album titled *To the Silent Majority, With Love* (1971), which included the draft-dodger-baiting lyrics "They're needin' you boy, and you're sittin' in your coffeehouse/Whatcha gonna do when your woman begs you save her from a mouse?" The quintessential recording of its kind, however, was Merle Haggard's "The Fightin' Side of Me," arguably the biggest antiprotester protest song of all time and a #1 hit in 1970.

But country was too diverse not to explore the human toll of war. Loretta Lynn's "Dear Uncle Sam" (#4, 1966) begged America to bring the boys (or at least her boy) home. The WILBURN BROTHERS' "Little Johnny from Down the Street" was almost gothically realistic, progressing from middle-American innocence to the horror of combat, as was ARLENE HARDEN's chartmaking recording of "Congratulations (You Sure Made a Man Out of Him)," as bitter and searing a song as was ever written about post-traumatic stress disorder. Or maybe that claim really belongs to TOM T. HALL's composition "Mama Bake a Pie (Daddy Kill a Chicken)"—recorded by George Kent—in which a returning vet says: "Thank you sir and yes sir, it was worth it for the ol' red white and blue/And since I won't be walking I suppose I'll save some money buying shoes."

In the 1970s the OUTLAW movement threatened to bring left and right together again, as symbolized in the peaceful coexistence of diverse audiences at Willie Nelson's Fourth of July picnics and cross-cultural anthems such as Bobby Bare's "Redneck Hippie Romance." Early in country's evolution, little or no distinction was made between hillbilly music and Woody Guthrie's brand of folk, and in the 1970s it looked as though the cultural twain again might meet, with a mainstream country artist like Hall appealing to all sides with a song as cheerfully cynical as "Watergate Blues." But division over Reagan-era politics and the advent of the URBAN COWBOY circumvented that unity.

The blowup that shook the world, and not just country music, occurred in 2003 when Natalie Maines told a London audience that she and her Dixie Chicks partners were ashamed to share their home state with President George W. Bush—just as the United States was preparing to invade Iraq. At the time, the trio, whose last two albums had both sold over 10 million copies, had the #1 CD in the country. Ironically, they were also topping the country singles chart with the Vietnam-themed "Travelin' Soldier," which its writer, Bruce Robison, later described as "the fastest-descending #1 country single in the history of the *Billboard* charts."

Reaction was swift and severe, with most country stations immediately dropping Dixie Chicks from their playlists and a handful even holding record-smashing rallies. Toby Keith lit a match to the feud he already had going with Maines, putting up a doctored slide of the group with Saddam Hussein on his overhead concert screen. Comedian Larry the Cable Guy spoke for a small but vocal portion of the country audience when he angrily wrote on his blog: "How dare this first hippo of country music go to a country whose support we're trying to get for a possible war and then attack our President in that country?" Ultimately, Dixie Chicks decided they'd rather switch than fight, moving on to a more rock-oriented sound and fan base and winning multiple Grammys in 2007 for "Not Ready to Make Nice," a swipe at their attackers.

Some began to wonder if country music and liberalism were compatible in such a heated environment. But writer-editor Martha Hume wondered if the real problem was that "to the fans, [Dixie Chicks'] statements came out of left field. Willie and Merle can sing antiwar songs or anything they want and even audience members who are voting for Bush will say, 'They're good men, they can do it.' . . . My feeling is that it's because [Dixie Chicks'] politics are not otherwise reflected in their work, and with Cash and those guys, their politics were, so when you hear what they're saying, it's consistent with the character they've put out there."

Highly rated Fox News talk show host Sean Hannity felt confident to claim country as an essentially conservative genre. "The values that we talk about on my show are very similar to the values they sing about in their country songs," he said. "There's a common theme of God, faith, family, and love of country." But as the invasion of Iraq dragged on and the nation wearied of the conflict, songs about the troops began to fade from the country charts, and light-hearted anthems celebrating the South or small-town life began to replace deeply felt, aggressively patriotic fare. Country's left flank became more outspoken, with former mainstream stars recording more politically charged material, albeit for a smaller, heavily Americana audience. Steve Earle's "Rich Man's War" and "Condi Condi" (both 2004) and Rodney Crowell's "The Outsider" (2005) gave voice to country's loyal opposition. Within country's mainstream, though, "Courtesy of the Red, White and Blue" was giving way to "Redneck Woman."

Given country's history of addressing the issues of the day, it's inevitable that the pendulum will continue swinging back to topicality. Maybe it's always there, even when no banners are being waved. Says Kristofferson: "Everything is political. It just sounds worse if you *call* it political. I mean, we're talking about life and death and the things that matter."

## Porter Wagoner
b. Howell County, Missouri, August 12, 1927; d. October 28, 2007

Noted for his onstage jokes, blond pompadour, rhinestone-studded stage wardrobe, and partnership with DOLLY PARTON, Porter Wagoner became one of country music's elder statesmen in the 1990s. His eighty-one chart records included several country standards, and his television performing since 1955 culminated in his cohosting TNN's *Opry Backstage* for nearly a decade, starting in 1992. In the wake of ROY ACUFF's death in November 1992, he became the unofficial spokesman for the GRAND OLE OPRY.

Wagoner was born in the Ozark Mountains of Missouri, a region steeped in ancient English balladry. A farm boy, he moved with his family to West Plains, where he married in 1946. He formed the Blue Ridge Boys band and by 1950 was singing over local radio (KWPM) out of a butcher shop where he cut meat.

Wagoner's big break came when Springfield, Missouri, radio station KWTO hired him in 1951. He signed with RCA RECORDS in 1952, but because his early records didn't sell well, he committed himself to a hard-traveling career of playing schoolhouses for gate proceeds. His act was billed as the Porter Wagoner Trio, with Don Warden on steel guitar and Herschel "Speedy" Haworth on rhythm guitar.

Wagoner's "Trademark," cowritten with Gary Walker, went to #2 for CARL SMITH in 1953, and Wagoner's hits penned by other writers, such as "Company's Comin'" (#7, 1954–55) and "A Satisfied Mind" (#1, 1955) kept him on RCA. Wagoner was an early mainstay on the *OZARK JUBILEE* ABC television show (1955–1956), but he moved to Nashville with his wife and three children in 1956 and joined the Grand Ole Opry the following year.

In 1960 Wagoner was invited by the Chattanooga Medicine Company to front a syndicated television show. Immediately he broadened his act, adding comedian SPECK RHODES, singer NORMA JEAN, and eventually BUCK TRENT (banjo), Mack Magaha (fiddle), and George McCormick (guitar). Featuring celebrities such as TEX RITTER and COWBOY COPAS, plus newcomers such as WILLIE NELSON and WAYLON JENNINGS, the program ran an impressive two decades, ending in 1981.

As his TV show's reach expanded into nearly one hundred markets, with over 3 million viewers, Wagoner recorded a succession of hits that included "Misery Loves Company" (#1, 1962), "I've Enjoyed As Much of This As I Can Stand" (#7, 1962–63), "Sorrow on the Rocks" (#5, 1964), "Green, Green Grass of Home" (#4, 1965), "Skid Row Joe" (#3, 1965–66), "The Cold Hard Facts of Life" (#2, 1967), and "The Carroll County Accident" (#2, 1968–69). Unlike some of his colleagues, he utilized but never pandered to THE NASHVILLE SOUND, and he never traded his flashy rhinestone suits for tuxedos. The versatile performer also

won three Grammys for sacred recordings with the Blackwood Brothers (1966, 1967, 1969).

In 1967 Dolly Parton replaced Norma Jean in the show's cast and began recording duets with Wagoner, including fourteen Top Ten hits and one #1, "Please Don't Stop Loving Me" (1974). Wagoner was their de facto producer-arranger on thirteen duet albums, and he also supervised Parton's RCA solo output during this same period. While she eventually outshone Wagoner on the charts, he nevertheless prospered from his tireless efforts in building her career. Although Parton's departure from the show in mid-decade led to angry words and legal action, the two eventually resolved their differences.

Wagoner's post-Parton career upheld his innovative, persistently upbeat persona. He brought James Brown to the Grand Ole Opry, produced R&B sessions for Joe Simon, appeared in the Clint Eastwood film *Honkytonk Man* (1982), and served as an Opryland tourist ambassador in the 1990s. A mainstay of the Opry until his death, he was honored in May 2007 for his fifty years as a member. In collaboration with MARTY STUART, Wagoner recorded a final album, *Wagonmaster*, which drew rave

*Porter Wagoner*

reviews and feature articles in the *New York Times* and AMERICANA music magazine *No Depression*. In July, he opened for the White Stripes at Madison Square Garden. Porter Wagoner was elected to THE COUNTRY MUSIC HALL OF FAME in 2002. —*Steve Eng*

## Jimmy Wakely
b. Mineola, Arkansas, February 16, 1914; d. September 23, 1982

At the height of his career in the 1940s and 1950s, James Clarence Wakely was one of country music's most prominent West Coast performers, with starring roles in movies and on network radio and TV, in addition to an impressive array of crossover hits.

He grew up in Oklahoma and began his professional career in 1937 when he began playing piano with Merle Salathiel (later known as Merle Lindsay) and his Barnyard Boys; he also had a fifteen-minute morning radio show on KTOK–Oklahoma City. In the summer of 1937 he traveled with a MEDICINE SHOW led by Little Doc Roberts. Wakely soon began performing on Oklahoma City's WKY with a trio called the Bell Boys and eventually reorganized them as the Jimmy Wakely Trio.

In the 1940s Wakely and his musical partners JOHNNY BOND and DICK REINHART (who replaced Scotty Harrell) were regulars on GENE AUTRY's *Melody Ranch* show on CBS network radio. Simultaneously, Wakely began recording for DECCA RECORDS and embarked on a film career, eventually starring in twenty-eight movies and appearing in seventy. His biggest hits came on CAPITOL RECORDS, where he helped introduce cheating songs to country music with his chart-topping 1948 hit "One Has My Name, the Other Has My Heart" and "Slipping Around" (a duet with pop singer Margaret Whiting), which went #1 country and #2 pop in 1949. Between 1948 and 1951 he notched twenty-two country chart hits, eight of which crossed over to the pop charts.

In the 1950s and 1960s Wakely appeared on a number of country music television shows, including his own self-titled program and ABC-TV's *Five Star Jubilee* (1961), produced in Springfield, Missouri. He continued to perform on a limited basis during the 1970s, often with his children Johnny and Linda Lee. He died in Mission Hills, California, in 1982. —*Charlie Seemann*

## Bill Walker
b. Sydney, New South Wales, Australia, April 28, 1937

Arranger-conductor William Alfred Walker popularized written arrangements in Nashville studios during the 1960s and 1970s. Studio musicians and vocalists had relied mostly on "head" arrangements, but Walker—educated at the Sydney Conservatory—wrote precise, elegant arrangements that further stylized the lush NASHVILLE SOUND.

Before arriving in MUSIC CITY, Walker worked for RCA VICTOR's South African franchise and produced one of JIM REEVES's 1963 Johannesburg sessions. Consequently Reeves invited Walker to work for him in Nashville, but, sadly, he arrived on the weekend of Reeves's fatal plane crash in 1964. EDDY ARNOLD sought out Walker instead, and through 1968 Walker helped fashion Arnold's uptown, career-rejuvenating style. By the late 1960s Walker was one of Nashville's busiest arranger-conductors.

In the 1970s Walker produced numerous country acts for his Con Brio label and he did the arrangement on DONNA FARGO's

DOT smash "The Happiest Girl in the Whole U.S.A."—1972's CMA Song of the Year. Other hits featuring Walker's arranging and conducting include Eddy Arnold's "Make the World Go Away" (1965), JOHNNY CASH's "Sunday Morning Coming Down" (1970), ROY CLARK's "Come Live with Me" (1973), and GEORGE JONES's Grammy-winning "He Stopped Loving her Today" (1980)—also CMA's 1980 Single of the Year. In 1968 Walker joined Cash's ABC-TV show as music director, and subsequently his name appeared on dozens of Nashville television productions, including THE STATLER BROTHERS' TNN show. As of 2011, Walker was still active. —*Michael Streissguth*

## Billy Walker
b. Ralls, Texas, January 14, 1929; d. May 21, 2006

In a very real sense, the career of Billy Marvin Walker epitomized changes that affected country music over a thirty-year period. Starting out with Texas HONKY-TONK, he dabbled in rock & roll and then went to Nashville just as the NASHVILLE SOUND was a term on everyone's lips. Along the way, Walker both made and witnessed history. He was at HANK WILLIAMS's last show and at ELVIS PRESLEY's first major public appearance. He sat waiting to record while BUDDY HOLLY was finishing a session in Clovis, New Mexico, and narrowly missed boarding the plane on which PATSY CLINE, COWBOY COPAS, and HAWKSHAW HAWKINS died.

Walker was inspired by GENE AUTRY to take up music. After getting out of school in 1947, the young singer worked various day jobs before fronting for COLUMBIA artist Jimmy Lawson in 1948. He joined the *BIG D JAMBOREE* in Dallas (where he was billed as the Traveling Texan and performed in a Lone Ranger mask) and worked in Waco for HANK THOMPSON, who got him his first contract, with CAPITOL RECORDS, in 1949. Eighteen months later, Walker switched to Columbia. Several early Columbia records, particularly "Anything Your Heart Desires"

*Billy Walker*

and the cover version of "Mexican Joe," sold well without charting. His first charted hit was "Thank You for Calling" in 1954.

Walker joined Shreveport's LOUISIANA HAYRIDE in 1952 and shifted to the OZARK JUBILEE in Springfield, Missouri, in 1954. He flirted with rock & roll before returning to Texas in November 1958 to work the country bar circuit. In 1959 he moved to Nashville to join the GRAND OLE OPRY. Walker's original version of "Funny How Time Slips Away" (1961) stalled at #23, but the follow-up, "Charlie's Shoes," became his first and only #1 hit, in April 1962. At this point he came into his own, and he continued to chart steadily into the late 1980s.

Walker's records clearly reflected changing times and production values. He recorded western-influenced songs such as "Cross the Brazos at Waco" and "Matamoros," country versions of pop songs such as "Ramona," and even tried some of the self-consciously poetic songs that were in vogue in the early 1970s. He left Columbia in 1965, joined MONUMENT, and then went with MGM in 1970. From that point, he was on RCA (1974–77) and then several smaller labels. His last chart records were on his Tall Texan label, in 1988.

Along with two backup musicians, Walker and his wife, Bettie, died in a motor vehicle accident in Alabama on May 21, 2006. —Colin Escott

## Charlie Walker
b. Copeville, Texas, November 2, 1926; d. September 12, 2008

Charles Levi Walker came from the cotton fields of Collin County, Texas, to become one of country music's most popular disc jockeys and then one of its best shuffle-beat HONKY-TONK singers. A singer-guitarist with BILL BOYD's Cowboy Ramblers in Dallas from 1943 to 1944, Walker also worked daily remote radio broadcasts fed from Sellers Studio to stations in Corpus Christi and other Texas outlets. With the Eighth Army Signal Corps in the Tokyo occupation forces, he broadcast country music to fellow soldiers in Asia. Discharged in 1947, Walker and his band the Texas Ramblers performed in and around Corpus Christi for several years.

Moving to San Antonio in 1951, Walker became KMAC's country disc jockey and built an enormous listenership with great records and colorful antics. His sign-on was "This is ol' poke salad, cotton-picking, boll-pulling, corn-shucking, snuff-dipping Charlie Walker." On DECCA RECORDS (1954–56), after a short previous stint with IMPERIAL, Walker had a regional hit, "Tell Her Lies and Feed Her Candy," and his first charted record, "Only You, Only You" (1956). PAPPY DAILY then signed Walker to MERCURY, but it was an opportunity with COLUMBIA RECORDS (thanks to RAY PRICE) that made possible Walker's first big hit, the HARLAN HOWARD–penned "Pick Me Up on Your Way Down" (1958), which helped introduce the infectious shuffle beat to country music.

Walker remained San Antonio's top country DJ while building his own touring and recording career with a few widely spaced honky-tonk hits: "Who Will Buy the Wine" (1960), "Wild as a Wildcat" (1965), and "Don't Squeeze My Sharmon" (1967). The last enabled Walker to join the GRAND OLE OPRY, where he remained a staunch exponent of honky-tonk and WESTERN SWING styles until his death. Walker portrayed HAWKSHAW HAWKINS in the 1985 film biography of PATSY CLINE, Sweet Dreams. —Ronnie Pugh

## Cindy Walker
b. Mart, Texas, July 20, 1918; d. September 12, 2008

One of country music's finest songwriters, Cindy Walker became a charter member of the NASHVILLE SONGWRITERS HALL OF FAME in 1970 and was elected to THE COUNTRY MUSIC HALL OF FAME in 1997. Renowned for tailoring songs for diverse stylists, her Top Ten hits spanned half a century and include such country standards as "Cherokee Maiden" and "You Don't Know Me."

Walker's grandfather F. P. Eiland was a hymn writer of note ("Hold to God's Unchanging Hand"), and her mother, Oree, was an accomplished pianist. After appearing in Texas stage shows, Walker traveled to Hollywood. She successfully pitched tunes to Bing Crosby, landed a 1941 DECCA contract, filmed Soundie musical shorts, and scored a Top Ten hit with "When My Blue Moon Turns to Gold Again" in 1944.

Walker had a star's looks but set aside her performing career to focus on composing. Autry popularized her "Blue Canadian Rockies," AL DEXTER sang "Triflin' Gal," and the Ames Brothers did "China Doll." One of her regular customers was BOB WILLS, for whom she wrote more than fifty numbers, including "Cherokee Maiden," "Bubbles in My Beer," and "You're From Texas." ERNEST TUBB also relied on her, recording "Warm Red Wine," "Two Glasses Joe," and "Hey Mr. Bluebird," among other songs.

In 1954 Walker returned to Texas and thereafter divided her time between her home in Mexia and Nashville. Her 1950s classics include EDDY ARNOLD's "Take Me in Your Arms and Hold Me" and "You Don't Know Me," HANK SNOW's "The Gold Rush Is Over" and "The Next Voice You Hear," WEBB PIERCE's "I Don't Care," and JIM REEVES's "Anna Marie."

In the 1960s ROY ORBISON's "Dream Baby (How Long Must I Dream)," Reeves's "Distant Drums," Jerry Wallace's "In the Misty Moonlight," JACK GREENE's "You Are My Treasure,"

Cindy Walker

Sonny James's "Heaven Says Hello," and Stonewall Jackson's "Leona" all became sizable Walker songwriting hits.

Glen Campbell, Ricky Skaggs, Ray Charles, Lacy J. Dalton, Riders in the Sky, Mickey Gilley, and Merle Haggard are among those who kept her songwriting legacy alive in subsequent decades. Ill health and the death of her accompanist mother in 1991 slowed Walker, but Willie Nelson's album *You Don't Know Me: The Songs of Cindy Walker* (Lost Highway, 2006) reminded the industry of her achievements. Walker willed her song royalties to the Country Music Hall of Fame and Museum. —*Robert K. Oermann*

## Clay Walker
b. Beaumont, Texas, August 19, 1969

After Mark Chesnutt and Tracy Byrd, Earnest Clayton Walker was the third new singer to emerge from the fertile Beaumont, Texas, country scene in as many years when he debuted on Giant Records in 1993. His career started with quick radio success as his first two singles, "What's It to You" and "Live Until I Die," both hit #1.

Walker grew up in a musical family on an eighty-acre spread in southeastern Texas informally called "Walkerville" and attended high school in nearby Vidor, where he played basketball with Tracy Byrd.

Walker began performing professionally at sixteen. He briefly worked as his own manager, agent, music director, and accountant, and he studied business in college, with an eye toward becoming his own lawyer as well. Among the venues he played regularly were Beaumont's Neon Armadillo and George Jones's Jones Country theme park.

Walker's first two albums, both of which sold more than 1 million copies, yielded five chart-topping singles, including "Dreaming with My Eyes Open," "If I Could Make a Living," and "This Woman and This Man." During 1993–95 he was the most successful artist on Giant's roster and helped give the young label a significant presence in country music. Subsequent hits included "Who Needs You Baby" (#2, 1995) and "Hypnotize the Moon" (#2, 1996), the title track from his third platinum album. In 1996 he revealed his recent diagnosis of multiple sclerosis, maintaining that the disease was not then a hindrance to his career.

Since Giant folded in 2001, Walker has released albums on Warner Bros., RCA, and Curb. —*Brian Mansfield*

## Frank Walker
b. Fly Summit, New York, October 24, 1889; d. October 15, 1963

For all that Frank B. Walker accomplished as a music executive, his reputation rests primarily on two signings, Bessie Smith and Hank Williams. It might be fairer, though, to see him as one of the industry's last generalists who knew every facet of the business.

After finishing his education in upstate New York, Walker worked in banking in Albany and New York City until 1916. He went into the U.S. Navy that year and remained there until February 1, 1919. A navy officer found him a job at Columbia Records, where Walker learned record manufacturing. Then he borrowed $60,000 to buy a controlling interest in the Central Concert Company of Detroit, which booked Enrico Caruso and others. Walker stayed until 1921, when he sold his share and went back to Columbia as an A&R man.

*Frank Walker*

One of his first assignments was to make field recordings. He traveled throughout the South and later said he would ride horses deep into the woods in search of performers someone had told him about. He would often sell records on his junkets by renting a storefront for a day. Among the country artists he discovered were Riley Puckett, Gid Tanner, Charlie Poole, and Clarence "Tom" Ashley. Early in his Columbia career, Walker was instrumental in signing pioneer blues singer Bessie Smith. The precise circumstances are unclear, but apparently he sent composer and arranger Clarence Williams to Philadelphia to bring her to New York in February 1923.

Rising to the position of vice president at Columbia, Walker created the 14000-D blues series and the 15000-D hillbilly series. Shortly before he left, he made the newly purchased OKeh Records into a low-priced imprint. He brought the same philosophy of lower pricing on blues and country music to RCA Victor when he headed the company's Bluebird Records subsidiary, listing his product at thirty-five cents instead of the regular price of seventy-five cents when Bluebird began issuing 78-rpm discs in March 1933. This enabled him to keep sales buoyant throughout the Depression. By the late 1930s he held the rank of vice president within RCA.

During World War II Walker headed the government's V-Disc program of troop entertainment and rejoined RCA immediately afterward. Loew's, Inc., recruited him in August 1945 to start a record division for MGM. The label's official launch was in March 1947. By then Walker had arranged for a former munitions plant in Bloomfield, New Jersey, to be converted into a pressing plant, and he personally supervised every aspect of the company, including artist signings, manufacturing, and distribution.

MGM Records remained a marginal enterprise throughout the years that Walker remained president, but he will be remembered chiefly for taking a chance on Hank Williams after other major labels had turned him down. Walker remained head of MGM Records until 1956; stayed on as a consultant to and vice president of Loew's, Inc., until his death; and helped to create the Recording Industry Association of America (RIAA) in 1952. —*Colin Escott*

## Jerry Jeff Walker

b. Oneonta, New York, March 16, 1942

Perhaps more than any artist besides WILLIE NELSON, Jerry Jeff Walker personified the loose, COUNTRY-ROCK hybrid sound and lifestyle of 1970s AUSTIN, TEXAS. The author of "Mr. Bojangles," Walker and his appealingly gruff voice represented everything that was carefree, boozy, and musically alive about Austin's "progressive country." His 1973 album *Viva! Terlingua*, recorded in a dance hall in Luckenbach, Texas, set the era's tone with its mixture of country soul balladry (especially on GUY CLARK's "Desperados Waiting for the Train") and party anthems such as Ray Wylie Hubbard's "Up Against the Wall, Red Neck." As Walker once told a reporter, "I wanted our records to sound like we were having a grand time at a party thrown for a bunch of our best friends— which, I guess, is exactly what it was."

Born Ronald Clyde Crosby in Oneonta, New York, Walker learned banjo, ukulele, and guitar. Still in his teens, he hitchhiked to Florida and then to New Orleans, where he sang for tips on the street. He eventually gravitated to New York City's Greenwich Village folk scene. In 1966 he joined a progressive rock group, Circus Maximus (originally the Lost Sea Dreamers), but he left the group after its first Vanguard album, having already written "Mr. Bojangles," inspired by a character he had met in a jail cell in New Orleans. Walker sang it one night over an influential live radio program on WBAI–New York, and the song became an instant local hit. He signed with ATLANTIC RECORDS, and in 1968 his album *Mr. Bojangles* appeared on the Atlantic subsidiary Atco. In 1970–71 the song was a major pop hit for the NITTY GRITTY DIRT BAND.

Walker recorded two more albums for Atco and one for Vanguard before moving to Austin in 1971. In 1972 DECCA released an eponymous Walker album featuring two cuts penned by Guy Clark, including the FM radio hit "L.A. Freeway." Next came *Viva! Terlingua*, on which Walker was backed by the Lost Gonzo Band. The album included their "London Homesick Blues," a Gary P. Nunn composition, which became the famous theme song for *AUSTIN CITY LIMITS*.

Into the early 1980s Walker released a series of albums of erratic but intermittently fine quality. Meanwhile, he also established a reputation for drunken onstage behavior that sometimes overwhelmed interest in his music. In 1985, determined to turn his life and career around, he sobered up and started his own label, Tried & True Music, helmed by his wife, Susan. By 2010, several albums had appeared on the imprint, including *Viva Luckenbach!*—recorded in 1993 in the same dance hall where he had cut *Viva! Terlingua*—*Gonzo Stew* (2001), *Jerry Jeff Jazz* (2003), and the online collection *Moon Child* (2009). —*Daniel Cooper*

## Lawrence Walker

b. Duson, Louisiana, September 1, 1907; d. August 15, 1968

Lawrence Walker led a favorite CAJUN dance-hall band from the mid-1940s until his death in 1968. He popularized many Cajun classics—for example, "Chère Alice" (La Louisiane, 1960s)—and

wrote some of the most lyrical of Cajun songs, including "Yeaux Noir," "The Unlucky Waltz" (both on La Louisiane, 1960s), and "Reno Waltz" (Khoury, early 1950s). His band's smooth, well-paced, danceable sound was central to its popularity in various Louisiana communities.

Walker's father, Allen Walker, a popular local fiddler, exposed his son to Cajun music at an early age. Though Lawrence was not a "full-bred" Cajun, he spoke Cajun French well. His brother, Elton, played the guitar. When the family moved to Orange, Texas, in 1915, the three formed the Walker Brothers and made two recordings in Dallas in 1929, "La Breakdown la Louisiane" and "La Vie Malheureuse."

The family later returned to Louisiana, and Lawrence Walker and his family band continued to play local dances. In 1935 he recorded several songs on the BLUEBIRD label. Six featured Walker on accordion backed by two unknown guitarists, and two showcased Tony Alleman on vocals and Lawrence Walker on violin.

In 1936 Walker appeared at the National Folk Festival in Dallas, Texas, with Aldus "Pop Eye" Broussard and Sidney Broussard on fiddle, Junior Broussard on guitar, Norris Mire on guitar, and Evelyn Broussard on triangle and vocals. Joining them was Elemore Sonnier, a solo vocalist from Scott, Louisiana. These were the first appearances that brought Cajun music to the public's attention on a national level.

The post–World War II years were a high point in Walker's musical career. His band played at all of Louisiana's popular clubs, such as the OST Club in Rayne, the Jolly Rogers Club in Forked Island, the Welcome Club in Crowley, and the Bon Temps Rouler Club in Lafayette. He recorded his most beloved songs in the 1950s and 1960s on the Khoury, La Louisiane, and Swallow labels. His perfectionism and wide choice of material made these recordings a strong and unique contribution to the annals of Cajun music. Walker died of a heart attack in 1968. —*Ann Allen Savoy*

## Wayne Walker

b. Quapaw, Oklahoma, December 13, 1925; d. January 2, 1979

Raised in Kilgore, Texas, country music singer-songwriter Wayne Paul Walker played the *LOUISIANA HAYRIDE* and recorded for record labels including DECCA, COLUMBIA, Ric, ABC-Paramount, Everest, and Chess. Though he didn't hit on disc, his prolific songwriting established his show business success.

Walker signed with JIM DENNY's CEDARWOOD PUBLISHING COMPANY shortly after it opened in 1953. Along with WEBB PIERCE, DANNY DILL, JOHN D. LOUDERMILK, MEL TILLIS, and MARIJOHN WILKIN, Walker made Cedarwood one of Nashville's legendary publishers. Walker wrote or cowrote songs that provided hits for top artists during the 1950s and 1960s, including some that later proved to be hits for other stars: "I've Got a New Heartache" (RAY PRICE, 1956; RICKY SKAGGS, 1986), "Are You Sincere" (Andy Williams, 1957; ELVIS PRESLEY, 1979), "Holiday for Love" (Webb Pierce, 1957), "Burning Memories" (Ray Price, 1964; Mel Tillis, 1977), "Leavin' on Your Mind" (PATSY CLINE, 1963), "Little Boy Sad" (JOHNNY BURNETTE, 1961; BILL PHILLIPS, 1969), "Cut Across Shorty" (CARL SMITH, 1960; NAT STUCKEY, 1969), and "All the Time" (KITTY WELLS, 1959; JACK GREENE, 1967).

Walker was married for fifteen years (1958–73) to Violet Elaine "Scooter Bill" Tubb, the eldest daughter of ERNEST TUBB. Walker was elected into the NASHVILLE SONGWRITERS HALL OF FAME in 1975. —*Don Roy*

## Wiley Walker (see Wiley & Gene)

## Jo Walker-Meador
b. Orlinda, Tennessee, February 16, 1924

As executive director of the Country Music Association (CMA) from 1962 to 1991, Jo Walker-Meador played an influential role in the music's remarkable growth during those years. One year before she took the helm, full-time country radio stations numbered fewer than one hundred nationwide. By 1995 this number exceeded 2,300.

Born Edith Josephine Denning, she was educated at Peabody College in Nashville and Lambuth College in Jackson, Tennessee. When industry leaders organized CMA in 1958, they hired Walker-Meador as office manager to handle bookkeeping, typing, and general office duties, while former WSM manager HARRY STONE served as executive director. In 1959 she organized a banquet that was to become an annual event and awards program. After Stone's departure, Walker-Meador stayed on and soon assumed his role. Under her direction, the staff eventually grew to more than twenty employees.

CMA prospered under Walker-Meador's gracious and skillful leadership. Among the organization's well-known programs adopted during her tenure were a national fundraising drive to build the COUNTRY MUSIC HALL OF FAME AND MUSEUM (CMA had created THE COUNTRY MUSIC HALL OF FAME in 1961) and

*Jo Walker-Meador*

CMA's annual awards show, begun in 1967 and televised nationally for the first time in 1968. Fan Fair, an annual gathering of fans and performers now known as the CMA MUSIC FESTIVAL, was inaugurated in 1972. Thanks to the efforts of Walker-Meador and others, CMA has grown from approximately 200 members to a membership of more than 7,000 individuals and organizations. Today it is the most important music trade organization on the Nashville music scene and among the most active in the world. Walker-Meador has remained involved in events on MUSIC ROW since her retirement in 1991. She was elected to the Country Music Hall of Fame in 1995. —*Mary A. Bufwack*

## Jerry Wallace
b. Guilford, Missouri, December 15, 1928; d. May 5, 2008

Aptly nicknamed Mr. Smooth, Jerry Leon Wallace credited Nat "King" Cole as his primary influence and made eleven chart-making pop records for CHALLENGE RECORDS (1958–65) before entering the country rankings. Today, many listeners consider some of these pop releases, including "Shutters and Boards" and the million-selling "Primrose Lane," to be country recordings.

"In the Misty Moonlight" (1964), written by CINDY WALKER, was a special favorite with country audiences. Although it failed to chart country, it garnered Wallace several GRAND OLE OPRY guest shots.

The 1965 MERCURY release "Life's Gone and Slipped Away" was the first of his thirty-five country chart singles. He was a consistent chart presence for some fifteen years, recording for Mercury (1965–66), LIBERTY (1967–70), DECCA (1971–72), MCA (1973), MGM (1975), and several smaller labels afterward. His most notable release during these years was 1972's "If You Leave Me Tonight I'll Cry." Included in the soundtrack for a *Night Gallery* TV series episode titled "The Tune in Dan's Cafe," the Decca single topped the country charts and became a #38 pop disc. "Do You Know What It's Like to Be Lonesome," released later that year, earned him a 1973 CMA nomination as Male Vocalist of the Year. Wallace notched his last chart record in 1980, but during the 1980s and 1990s he continued to perform in nightclubs. —*William P. Davis*

## Don Walser
b. Brownfield, Texas, September 14, 1934; d. September 20, 2006

Donald Ray Walser was a country traditionalist from West Texas with a penchant for COWBOY MUSIC, WESTERN SWING, and yodel tunes. Among his early yodeling influences he preferred the material of ELTON BRITT to that of SLIM WHITMAN, and he began writing his own songs for yodel-worthy material. Raised in Lamesa, Texas, near Lubbock, he started performing in bands when he was fifteen and wrote his signature song, "Rolling Stone from Texas," when he was eighteen. Walser's first recording of it, under the name of his Texas Plainsman band, was released in July 1963 on the tiny Plainsman label. Thirty-one years later, the song became the title cut of his first nationally distributed album, coproduced by ASLEEP AT THE WHEEL's Ray Benson for the AUSTIN-based Watermelon label.

During the interim, music had been a sideline for Walser, who continued to write and perform while serving for decades in the Texas National Guard. Upon his retirement at age sixty, he found a receptive audience for the music of his Pure Texas Band among older country traditionalists and younger fans alike, though his style was considered anachronistic by contemporary country standards.

In 2000 Walser received a prestigious National Heritage Award from the National Endowment for the Arts and performed at the Kennedy Center for the Performing Arts in Washington, D.C. He retired in 2003 and died in 2006 of complications resulting from diabetes. —*Don McLeese*

## Steve Wariner
b. Noblesville, Indiana, December 25, 1954

As an instrumentalist, recording artist, and songwriter, Steven Noel Wariner has been a dependably rewarding talent for more than forty years.

By age ten Wariner was absorbing the music of HANK WILLIAMS, BUCK OWENS, and GEORGE JONES while playing bass in his father's country band on regional radio and television. Soon Wariner fronted his own band and began writing his own songs. Discovered by DOTTIE WEST at age seventeen, he toured with her, BOB LUMAN, and musical idol CHET ATKINS before landing an RCA contract with Atkins's help in 1976. The label released Wariner's pop-country singles for two years before issuing his self-titled debut album. His first #1 hit came in 1981 with "All Roads Lead to You." Chart-makers such as "Kansas City Lights" brought comparisons to major Wariner influence GLEN CAMPBELL. The hot picking of "Midnight Fire" (1983) and the hard-country remake of Bob Luman's "Lonely Women Make Good Lovers" (1983–84) broadened Wariner's appeal.

Moving in 1984 to MCA RECORDS, where he worked with producer-executive TONY BROWN, Wariner recast his image for a new country era. Harder-edged sounds and careful song selection

yielded a run of Top Ten hits, many cowritten by Wariner. These include the wistful "Some Fools Never Learn" (1985), "You Can Dream of Me" (1985–86), the BLUEGRASS-influenced "Life's Highway" (1986), "Small Town Girl" (1987), the rocking "Lynda" (1987), and "I Got Dreams" (1989)—all #1 records.

Collaborations with Nicolette Larson ("That's How You Know When Love's Right," 1986) and with Glen Campbell ("The Hand That Rocks the Cradle," 1987) produced other Top Tens. Along with VINCE GILL and RICKY SKAGGS, Wariner shared in a Grammy and a CMA Vocal Event of the Year Award for his instrumental and vocal contributions to MARK O'CONNOR's hot album *Mark O'Connor and the New Nashville Cats* (1991).

Shifting to ARISTA RECORDS in 1991 resulted in more hits, including the BILL ANDERSON–penned "The Tips of My Fingers" (#3, 1992). Wariner's 1996 instrumental album *No More Mr. Nice Guy*, showcasing Gill, O'Connor, Atkins, and rocker Richie Sambora, demonstrated Wariner's mastery of diverse musical styles. Wariner joined the GRAND OLE OPRY in May 1996.

Next, he signed with CAPITOL on the strength of songwriting hits including "Longneck Bottle" (GARTH BROOKS) and "Nothing but the Tail Lights" (CLINT BLACK). Wariner's "Holes in the Floor of Heaven" climbed to #2 and became CMA's 1998 Single of the Year. During 1998–2000 he notched three more Top Five records: the chart-topping "What If I Said," with Anita Cochran; "I'm Already Taken"; and "Been There," with Clint Black. Instrumental collaborations with ASLEEP AT THE WHEEL (1999) and BRAD PAISLEY (2008) led to additional Grammys. Wariner's "Producer's Medley," from his 2009 album honoring Chet Atkins, won another Grammy for Best Country Instrumental Performance. Meanwhile, Wariner continued to pen hit songs such as KEITH URBAN's "Where the Blacktop Ends" (#3, 2001). Since 2003 he has recorded for his own label, Selectone Records. —*Thomas Goldsmith*

## Warner Bros./Reprise Records
established in Hollywood, California, 1958

One of the last major labels to arrive in Nashville, Warner Bros./Reprise Records steadily grew until, by the mid-1980s, it ranked with the city's most successful record firms.

Warner Bros. Records, founded in Los Angeles in 1958, began as a division of the Warner Bros. movie studio. The label gained status and respect after acquiring Reprise Records from Frank Sinatra in 1963.

Although the company's country music output began with BOB LUMAN's hit "Let's Think about Living" in 1960, Warner Bros. did not open a Nashville office until 1975, when Englishman Andy Wickham was sent to oversee the operation, with NORRO WILSON as A&R director. EMMYLOU HARRIS provided the label's next major country success, although she was signed to Warner's pop roster by the Los Angeles office.

The Nashville branch grew gradually under Wickham, Wilson, and FRANK JONES, who ran the Nashville office from 1980 to 1983. The label's biggest stars in the 1970s were HANK WILLIAMS JR. (1977–78, 1983–91), JOHN ANDERSON (1977–87), T. G. SHEPPARD (1977–85), and the BELLAMY BROTHERS (1976–83).

Warner Bros. absorbed ELEKTRA RECORDS in 1983; JIMMY BOWEN headed the combined labels in Nashville for a year. One of Bowen's appointees, JIM ED NORMAN, succeeded him and settled into a twenty-year run, expanding the office to include Christian, western, and jazz music.

*Steve Wariner*

In the 1980s Warner Bros. struck pay dirt with CRYSTAL GAYLE (1983–89) while also launching the careers of two remarkable stylists: RANDY TRAVIS (1985–97) and DWIGHT YOAKAM (1986–2002). In the 1990s TRAVIS TRITT, LITTLE TEXAS, and FAITH HILL were among the company's more successful artists. In the 2000s that list included BLAKE SHELTON, BIG & RICH, the Wreckers, and James Otto.

Meanwhile, the Nashville division reached beyond country music, enjoying significant sales from a cappella sextet Take 6, banjo virtuoso BÉLA FLECK, and comedian JEFF FOXWORTHY. In 1992 the company created the relatively short-lived Warner Western imprint, presenting cowboy artists such as the SONS OF THE SAN JOAQUIN and MICHAEL MARTIN MURPHEY.

After Norman's departure, veteran record executive Bill Bennett headed the Nashville office from 2004 to 2009. In September 2009, John Esposito was named president of the newly revamped Warner Music Nashville, comprising Warner Bros. Nashville, ATLANTIC Nashville, and Word Entertainment. —*John Lomax III*

## Country Music in Washington, D.C.

The nation's capital has long been a country music stronghold and a starting point for country artists. By the 1920s, rural Americans seeking jobs—especially those from southern Appalachia—increasingly swelled the music's audiences in Washington, D.C. In 1927 JIMMIE RODGERS began working area venues; he started broadcasting live on radio station WTFF the following year. ERNEST V. STONEMAN brought his large family to town in the early 1930s, and after World War II he organized a band with his children, some of whom later formed the Bluegrass Champs. By the early 1950s live shows, country bars, and radio programs abounded in Washington and its environs. In 1946 CONNIE B. GAY began producing country radio programs; he patented the name "Town and Country" and moved into local and syndicated television by 1954. An aggressive promoter, he also staged country shows in many area venues, including Constitution Hall. Gay helped to organize the Country Music Association (CMA) in 1958 and served as its first president. He was elected to THE COUNTRY MUSIC HALL OF FAME in 1980.

Some of country's most successful singers of the 1950s launched their careers on Gay's radio and TV programs. JIMMY DEAN served in the U.S. Air Force near Washington and stayed after his 1948 discharge. Within a few years Gay made him the star of *Town and Country Time* on WMAL-TV, which led to a network show on CBS-TV. ROY CLARK joined Dean's WMAL show briefly in 1954. PATSY CLINE, discovered by Gay in 1954, became a regular on the program until late 1957. GEORGE HAMILTON IV came to D.C. from North Carolina after scoring a pop hit with "A Rose and a Baby Ruth" in 1956. Gay became his manager, and the singer appeared on Jimmy Dean's local and national television programs in addition to a short-lived network show of his own. Singer-guitarist BILLY GRAMMER also worked in the area in the late 1940s, eventually joining Dean's shows before organizing his own band.

During the early 1960s, CHARLIE DANIELS made Washington his home when he played in a rock & roll group named the Rockets, but the city's country scene was changing. Gay retired, Hamilton and Cline moved to Nashville, and Dean graduated to a self-titled ABC-TV series (1963–66). Racial tensions hurt the city's nighttime business, even as suburbs grew. Venues such as the Shamrock (in Georgetown since 1953) closed or, like country performers, followed their patrons to new locations.

In the early 1970s, however, EMMYLOU HARRIS began her career in local clubs. MARY CHAPIN CARPENTER, CLEVE FRANCIS, and JETT WILLIAMS likewise gained early performing experience in the area. BLUEGRASS has always been popular in metropolitan Washington, and the THE COUNTRY GENTLEMEN and the SELDOM SCENE formed there in 1957 and 1971, respectively. In the late 1970s and 1980s, the JOHNSON MOUNTAIN BOYS helped keep the area's bluegrass flame burning brightly. Fifty-thousand-watt station WMZQ-FM continues as a leading country radio outlet, while the John F. Kennedy Center for the Performing Arts staged a multiday 2006 festival celebrating country music's contributions to American culture. —*Barbara Pruett*

## Dale Watson
b. Birmingham, Alabama, October 7, 1962

Since settling in AUSTIN, TEXAS, in 1993, Kenneth Dale Watson has become an accomplished purveyor of lean, hard-driving HONKY-TONK MUSIC. Watson spent fifteen years playing roadhouses and bars throughout Texas and the South before releasing his debut album, *Cheatin' Heart Attack* (HighTone), in 1995. His musical apprenticeship began much earlier when, as a boy, he rode along as his truck-driving father sang in the truck stops and cafés of rural West Tennessee.

The younger Watson first made his mark as a performer after moving in 1988 to Los Angeles, where he became a fixture on the *Western Beat Barn Dance*. He then spent a year in Nashville, working as a songwriter and lead guitarist, but his tattoos, pompadour, and maverick spirit never quite agreed with MUSIC CITY. After briefly returning to California, Watson arrived in Austin, where he has made his mark. Sometimes reminiscent of MERLE HAGGARD, at others of JOHNNY PAYCHECK, Watson's heartrending baritone is an ideal instrument for his plainspoken original songs—real-life tales of work, family, liquor, and heartache. As a list these subjects may read like clichés, but in album after album Watson renders them with vividness and conviction. —*Bill Friskics-Warren*

## Doc Watson
b. Deep Gap, North Carolina, March 2, 1923

Though he has never had a hit single or a gold record award, Arthel Lane "Doc" Watson has nevertheless been an enormously influential performer. His clean, precise, and lightning-fast flat-picking technique on the acoustic guitar has been emulated by innumerable players. As a singer, he has popularized vintage country tunes for many fans of folk music and BLUEGRASS.

Born in the Appalachian town of Deep Gap, North Carolina, Watson was the sixth of nine children of General Dixon and Annie Watson. Young Arthel lost his sight to illness around age one. Encouraged by his loving and musical family, however, he soon graduated from harmonica to banjo and finally to guitar. Besides the CARTER FAMILY, other early musical influences were JIMMIE RODGERS, the DELMORE BROTHERS, Don Reno (RENO & SMILEY), and RILEY PUCKETT.

After a few frustrating years at the School for the Blind in Raleigh, North Carolina, Watson became a professional musician, first busking at taxi stands and eventually joining the dance band of Jack Williams, a local piano player. During his stint with that band (roughly 1953–62), Watson played a Gibson LES PAUL electric guitar. At age nineteen he was still known by his birth name, until

*Doc Watson*

an appearance in Lenoir, North Carolina. When someone couldn't pronounce his name, a girl in the audience shouted, "Call him Doc!" The nickname stuck.

His career took a major turn in 1960 when Watson met Smithsonian Institution folklorist RALPH RINZLER at a festival near Union Grove, North Carolina. Rinzler was playing with THE GREENBRIAR BOYS, and Watson, now on acoustic guitar, was rhythm guitarist for OLD-TIME recording artist CLARENCE "TOM" ASHLEY. As the folk music craze surged in the early 1960s, Rinzler booked Ashley's band in New York City. That successful concert led to a booking at the Ash Grove in Los Angeles. There Ashley caught laryngitis, forcing Watson to become lead singer and group spokesman—roles he would continue. Eventually Watson began being booked as a solo act and soon had gigs coast to coast, teaming occasionally with BILL MONROE, a teenaged CLARENCE WHITE, and many others, along the way making an incalculable impression on an entire generation of flat-pickers.

Watson recorded for Folkways Records in 1962 and 1963 before moving to Vanguard Records in 1964. Subsequent label affiliations included United Artists, Verve, Poppy, and Flying Fish. Since the early 1990s his releases have appeared primarily on SUGAR HILL RECORDS. Among Watson's recorded works are two standout collaborations: *Strictly Instrumental* (COLUMBIA, 1967) with FLATT & SCRUGGS and *Will the Circle Be Unbroken* (United Artists, 1972) with the NITTY GRITTY DIRT BAND and many all-star guests, including Maybelle Carter (CARTER FAMILY), ROY ACUFF, and MERLE TRAVIS. Watson has won Grammys for his albums *Then and Now* (1973), *Two Days in November* (1974), *Riding the Midnight Train* (1986), *On Praying Ground* (1990), and *Legacy* (2002). As of 2011 he had twice won Grammys for Best Country Instrumental Performance, in 1979 and 2006.

For some twenty years, Watson's son, Eddy Merle Watson (b. Deep Gap, North Carolina, February 8, 1949; d. October 23, 1985), joined him onstage and on recordings. Merle quickly developed his own personal, bluesy, signature style—compatible with but distinct from his father's—on banjo and both fingerstyle and slide guitar. Their partnership ended in 1985, when Merle died in a tractor accident at his North Carolina farm. After that, Doc Watson's primary accompanists were Merle's son, Richard Watson; Jack Lawrence; and David Holt.

Watson was elected to the IBMA Hall of Fame in 2000. He received the prestigious National Medal of Arts in 1997 and the Grammy Lifetime Achievement Award in 2004. As of

early 2011, he has continued to tour on a limited basis and hosted MERLEFEST, the annual North Carolina music festival named in his son's honor. *—Don Rhodes*

## Gene Watson
b. Palestine, Texas, October 11, 1943

Long before country music's 1980s NEW TRADITIONALISM movement, some singers had been adhering steadfastly to a no-frills, hard-country approach. Since Gary Gene Watson entered the Top Ten in 1975 with "Love in the Hot Afternoon," a sultry song of passion set in New Orleans, he has been one of country music's greatest voices and song stylists. His tenor voice is smooth and expressive and, as best displayed in his signature song, "Farewell Party," it can soar with intensity and conviction.

Watson came to CAPITOL RECORDS in 1975 after a long and hard apprenticeship in Houston honky-tonks and a succession of small regional labels. He worked as an automobile body specialist by day and sang country music at night. "Love in the Hot Afternoon," initially released on the Resco label in 1974, freed him from day labor (but not from his love for automobiles), and he recorded a series of Top Ten Capitol hits that included "Paper Rosie," "Nothing Sure Looked Good on You," and "Farewell Party," followed by additional Top Tens for MCA ("Fourteen Carat Mind," "Got No Reason Now for Going Home") and EPIC ("Memories to Burn") before slipping off the charts in the early 1990s.

The only factors in Watson's career that have changed in the past thirty years are his record labels and his personal grooming style. In the early 1980s a beard and frizzy, permed hair replaced his earlier clean-shaven look and straight, swept-back black hair, but his recordings on MCA (1981–85), Epic (1985–87), WARNER BROS. (1988–91), Broadland (1993), and STEP ONE (1993–97) continued to offer the best in bedrock country music. Highlights of his releases since 2000 include *Gene Watson . . . Then & Now* (Koch, 2005) and *In a Perfect World* (Shanachie, 2007), the latter also featuring vocals by artists including JOE NICHOLS, LEE ANN WOMACK, MARK CHESNUTT, CONNIE SMITH, and RHONDA VINCENT. *—Bill C. Malone*

## Irving Waugh
b. Danville, Virginia, December 8, 1912; d. April 17, 2007

Between 1947 and 1992, radio and television executive Irving Cambridge Waugh Jr. played important roles at Nashville station WSM and with the *CMA Awards* TV show. He grew up in Norfolk, Virginia, and during high school he worked his way around the South Pacific on tramp freighters. Later he attended a division of the College of William and Mary, followed by a stint with the Provincetown Players theatrical company in New York. While working odd jobs there during the late 1930s, he gained early radio exposure on the CBS network program *March of Time*, a dramatization of news of the week. He also worked briefly in Atlanta with a Federal Theater Project company.

After serving as a radio announcer in Norfolk, Roanoke, Nashville, and Cleveland, Waugh joined WSM's announcing staff in 1941. His first experience with country music came in handling early-morning country broadcasts. During World War II he served as a special NBC correspondent in the Pacific Theater.

Waugh returned to WSM's commercial department in 1947, became commercial manager the next year, and in 1948 helped to organize the GRAND OLE OPRY's Friday night show. He was promoted to commercial manager for WSM's radio and TV operations in 1950 and to general manager of WSM-TV in 1957. In 1958 he rose to vice president of WSM, Inc., embracing both radio and TV interests, and in 1968 he became president. In this capacity he was instrumental in the planning and building of the OPRYLAND theme park, which opened in 1972.

Together with music-publishing executive JACK STAPP, Waugh helped to sell the *CMA Awards* show to NBC-TV in 1968. Although Waugh retired from WSM in 1978, through 1992 he remained executive producer of this program. —*John W. Rumble*

## The Weaver Brothers & Elviry

June Petrie "Elviry" Weaver b. Chicago, Illinois, June 23, 1891; d. November 1977
Leon "Abner" Weaver b. Ozark, Missouri, April 18, 1886; d. December 1962
Frank "Cicero" Weaver b. Ozark, Missouri, February 2, 1891; d. October 1967

Leon "Abner" Weaver liked to bill himself as vaudeville's first rube; he began portraying his hillbilly character in about 1902 in MEDI-CINE SHOWS. He brought brother Frank, billed as "Cicero," into the act, and then the pair joined June Petrie—"Elviry"—in 1913. With Petrie as frontwoman, the Weaver Brothers & Elviry rose to headlining status as a $5,000-a-week attraction on the RKO vaudeville circuit after World War I.

Abner and Elviry were married ca. 1916–24; Elviry married brother Cicero in 1928. Daughters, in-laws, cousins, and other kin were incorporated into a nineteen-member troupe called the Home Folks.

Abner played mandolin, guitar, and fiddle and is believed to have originated the musical handsaw. Cicero, who never spoke in the act, also played the saw and patented a number of novelty instruments, including a spinning banjo and a one-man-band apparatus. Elviry sang and played piano, ukulele, or mandolin. Her humorous poker-faced delivery and the brothers' shenanigans attracted Hollywood attention. The Weavers appeared in thirteen films from 1937 to 1944, including *GRAND OLE OPRY* (1940).

In the late 1940s the Weaver Brothers and Elviry starred on radio station KWTO in Springfield, Missouri. The act ended with Abner's death in 1962. —*Robert K. Oermann*

## Gillian Welch

b. New York, New York, October 2, 1967

Gillian Howard Welch's disarmingly spare songs evoke Appalachian music and culture, and many country and BLUEGRASS performers have recorded her hauntingly imagistic compositions. Yet Welch didn't grow up in the South. She moved to Los Angeles at age three, with parents who adopted her at birth. Early on, she played in rock bands before becoming obsessed with OLD-TIME mountain songs and bluegrass music.

As she has worked as a duo with singer-guitarist David Rawlings, the disparity between Welch's urban background and rural sound drew the ire of some music critics, yet was lavishly praised by many others. She won a 2001 Grammy for her contributions to the multiplatinum-selling soundtrack to the hit film *O BROTHER, WHERE ART THOU?*

Welch grew up in an entertainment household. Her adoptive parents, Ken and Mitzie Welch, performed comedy and music, once appearing on *The Tonight Show*; they also wrote music for television's *The Carol Burnett Show*. Gillian attended college in Santa Cruz, California, before enrolling in Boston's Berklee College of Music, where she studied songwriting and met Rawlings. In 1992 the duo moved to Nashville, captivating clubgoers with their close-harmony singing and delicately flat-picked guitars.

Welch recorded her debut album, *Revival*, for the Almo Sounds label with producer T Bone Burnett, whose vintage equipment and recording techniques captured the intimacy and passion of her live duo performances with Rawlings. Welch started her own label, Acony Records, for her second album, 1998's *Hell Among the Yearlings*. Also produced by Burnett, it explored the same spare, haunting sounds and dark themes as had her debut.

At Burnett's invitation, Welch became involved in recording the soundtrack for *O Brother Where Art Thou?* In addition to singing a duet with ALISON KRAUSS on gospel standard "I'll Fly Away," she sang in a trio with Krauss and EMMYLOU HARRIS on "Didn't Leave Nobody but the Baby." Welch also appeared on a live concert DVD featuring songs from the film and performed as part of the Down from the Mountain tour series, which showcased songs from the movie.

For Welch's next album, 2001's *Time (The Revelator)*, Rawlings joined Burnett as coproducer, and they expanded the duo's acoustic sound a bit without losing its primitive feel. Rawlings took over production on 2003's *Soul Journey*, which added drums, bass, and organ to some of the recordings.

Welch's songs have been covered by Ryan Adams, Joan Baez, Jimmy Buffett, Solomon Burke, Dailey & Vincent, Emmylou Harris, Alison Krauss, MIRANDA LAMBERT, LAURIE LEWIS, and KATHY MATTEA as well as by Allison Moorer, NASHVILLE BLUEGRASS BAND, TIM O'BRIEN, and TRISHA YEARWOOD. A frequent guest on others' recordings, she has collaborated on disc

*Gillian Welch*

with the Chieftains, GUY CLARK, RODNEY CROWELL, NANCI GRIFFITH, Norah Jones, ROBERT EARL KEEN, Mark Knopfler, and RALPH STANLEY. —*Bill Friskics-Warren*

## Kitty Wells
b. Nashville, Tennessee, August 30, 1919

Kitty Wells was a thirty-three-year-old wife and mother when her 1952 recording of "It Wasn't God Who Made Honky Tonk Angels" suddenly made her a star. Other female country singers of her day were trying their hands at hard-living, HONKY-TONK sounds, but it was the intense, piercing style of Kitty Wells, with her gospel-touched vocals and tearful restraint, that resonated with country audiences and broke industry barriers for women.

Born Muriel Ellen Deason in Nashville, her country roots ran deep: Her father and uncle were country musicians, and her mother was a gospel singer. In 1934, amid the Great Depression, Wells dropped out of school to work at the Washington Manufacturing Company, where she earned nine dollars a week ironing shirts. With her two sisters and a cousin, she also broadcast on radio as the Deason Sisters.

On October 30, 1937, Wells married Johnnie Wright, and with Wright's sister Louise they performed as Johnnie Wright and the Harmony Girls. In 1939 Wright and Jack Anglin formed the duo JOHNNIE & JACK. Wells was the "girl singer" with Johnnie & Jack on radio programs and show dates as they performed throughout the South in the early 1940s, and Wright began referring to his wife as "Kitty Wells," a name taken from a nineteenth-century tune the PICKARD FAMILY had recorded in 1930.

During World War II, Anglin served in the army and Wright worked at a DuPont chemical factory north of Nashville. After the war Johnnie and Jack reunited, and, with Wells, helped inaugurate the *LOUISIANA HAYRIDE* on KWKH in Shreveport, in 1948. As "Rag Doll," Wells also spun records and sold quilting supplies.

Wells's recordings for RCA in 1949 and 1950 found no success, but Johnnie & Jack's "Poison Love" took them back to the GRAND OLE OPRY in 1952. (They had worked a brief Opry stint in 1947–48.) At this time Wells was persuaded to record an answer song to "The Wild Side of Life," a 1952 HANK THOMPSON hit that featured the line "I didn't know God made honky-tonk angels."

Thinking primarily of the $125 recording session payment, Wells arrived at Nashville's CASTLE RECORDING STUDIO on May 3, 1952, to cut "It Wasn't God Who Made Honky Tonk Angels" for DECCA RECORDS. The #1 country single took off during the summer and sold more than 800,000 copies in its initial release.

The song's sentiments are similar to 1894's "She Is More to Be Pitied Than Censured," with its premise that deceitful men are responsible for fallen women. Cautious NBC executives asked that Wells refrain from performing her breakthrough song on the GRAND OLE OPRY's network segment and change the words "trustful wife" to "trusting wife," but on non-network portions—as on radio stations and stage shows nationwide—fans couldn't get enough of it.

Subsequent records followed this pattern of deep emotion and restrained hurt expressed from a woman's point of view. Other Wells honky-tonk ballads include the classics "Release Me," "Making Believe," and "I Can't Stop Loving You." Songs such as "Your Wild Life's Gonna Get You Down," "A Woman Half My Age," "Broken Marriage Vows," "I Heard the Jukebox Play," "Cheatin's a Sin," "Mommy for a Day," and "Will Your Lawyer Talk to God?" explored contemporary themes and modern problems. On Wells's records, sorrowful men and women acted out their emotional dramas through her plaintive vocals accompanied by a crying steel guitar.

Onstage, Wells was unpretentious, proper, and even old-fashioned in her gingham dresses with full skirts, rickrack, and puffed sleeves. Her private life was family-oriented and without controversy, crisis, or scandal. But in her songs Wells could be the rejected woman or the barroom sinner—worldly wise, a victim of her own passion, even morally weak.

As the top female country star of her generation she accumulated thirty-five *Billboard* Top Ten records and eighty-one charted singles, the last coming in 1979. She starred in her own syndicated TV show in 1968. Her three children with Wright—daughters Ruby and Carol Sue and son Bobby—all became part of the Kitty Wells–Johnnie Wright Family Show, which continued to tour throughout 2000, when Wells and Wright announced their retirement and gave their final performance, on New Year's Eve.

Wells was elected to THE COUNTRY MUSIC HALL OF FAME in 1976 and was nominated for a 1989 Grammy for her "Honky-Tonk Angels Medley" with K. D. LANG, LORETTA LYNN, and BRENDA LEE. In 1991 Wells received a Grammy Lifetime Achievement Award, along with BOB DYLAN, Marian Anderson, and John Lennon. She was the first female country singer to receive the honor and only the third country performer overall, following ROY ACUFF and HANK WILLIAMS.

Ultimately, Wells's great achievement was disproving the accepted country music wisdom of her time, which held that women couldn't sell records or headline shows. Her success led record companies to welcome other female artists and to experiment with new themes and images for women, thereby changing country music forever. —*Mary A. Bufwack*

*Kitty Wells*

# E. W. "Bud" Wendell
b. Akron, Ohio, August 17, 1927

As manager of the GRAND OLE OPRY and later president and CEO of the companies that have owned the Opry and OPRYLAND, Bud Wendell significantly advanced the growth of country music in the 1970s, 1980s, and 1990s.

After graduating from Wooster College in Ohio with a degree in economics, Wendell started with the National Life and Accident Insurance Company (then the parent company of WSM and the Opry) in 1950 as a door-to-door insurance salesman in Hamilton, Ohio. After several transfers, he moved to the home office in Nashville in 1962. He became an assistant to John H. "Jack" DeWitt, WSM's president and was named the Opry's manager in April 1968.

In this role, Wendell got off to a shaky start when his very first show was canceled due to the assassination of civil rights leader Martin Luther King Jr., but Wendell soon established himself as an executive who saw country music's potential. He smoothed over rifts between the Opry and the country music industry and developed a close relationship with Nashville's business community.

Wendell became vice president of WSM and general manager of the Grand Ole Opry and Opryland theme park in 1974, just as the Opry was being moved from the aging RYMAN AUDITORIUM to the present Opryland grounds. He became president and CEO of WSM in 1978 and chairman in 1980. The Gaylord Broadcasting Company acquired National Life's entertainment interests in 1983, and Wendell was named president and CEO of GAYLORD ENTERTAINMENT in 1991.

The controversial move of the Opry, along with the opening of Opryland (1972) and the development of the Opryland Hotel, had been the visions of IRVING WAUGH (whom Wendell had succeeded as CEO of WSM), but Wendell took Waugh's plan many steps farther. Under Wendell's leadership, Gaylord or its predecessors launched TNN: THE NASHVILLE NETWORK in 1983, acquired Country Music Television (CMT) in 1991, launched CMT Europe in 1992, expanded the Opryland Hotel into a leading Nashville convention facility, and established the Opryland Music Group (which acquired the massive ACUFF-ROSE publishing catalogs). In addition, Wendell oversaw Gaylord's renovation of the Ryman Auditorium and the opening of the Wildhorse Saloon dance club, which helped revive a declining downtown Nashville.

In 1994 Gaylord honored Wendell with the opening of the E. W. Wendell Building, which houses all of Gaylord Entertainment's corporate departments. Wendell retired from Gaylord in 1997 and was elected to THE COUNTRY MUSIC HALL OF FAME in 1998. During many years as board chairman of the COUNTRY MUSIC HALL OF FAME AND MUSEUM, he oversaw the opening of the museum's new facility in downtown Nashville in 2001. —*Walter Carter*

# Dottie West
b. McMinnville, Tennessee, October 11, 1932; d. September 4, 1991

Country music stylist Dottie West enjoyed one of the longest hitmaking careers of any woman of her generation. Known for her 1964 Grammy-winning recording "Here Comes My Baby," she was a country pioneer with advertising jingles (including Coca-Cola's famous "Country Sunshine" campaign of the 1970s), and she recorded successful duets with JIM REEVES, DON GIBSON, JIMMY DEAN, and KENNY ROGERS.

Born Dorothy Marie Marsh, she grew up in a large, impoverished family. Her father sexually abused her and was imprisoned. She worked her way through college and married steel guitarist

E. W. "Bud" Wendell

Dottie West

Bill West in 1953. When he took a job in Cleveland, Ohio, Dottie landed a singing slot on that city's *Landmark Jamboree* TV show as half of the Kay-Dots duo with Kathy Dee (Kathy Dearth, 1933–68).

On weekends the Wests would drive to Nashville to cultivate music industry contacts. Dottie successfully auditioned for STARDAY in 1959, but little came of the affiliation. In 1961 the couple moved to MUSIC CITY. West signed with ATLANTIC, but fared no better than she had at Starday.

She continued to write songs, however, and Jim Reeves had a hit with her composition "Is This Me?" in 1963. He brought her to the attention of RCA's CHET ATKINS, who signed her and produced her self-penned "Here Comes My Baby," a Top Ten country hit. It earned West GRAND OLE OPRY membership and the first Grammy ever won by a female country artist. She had other Top Ten singles with "Would You Hold It Against Me" (1966) and "Paper Mansions" (1967) as well as hit duets with Reeves ("Love Is No Excuse," 1964) and Don Gibson ("Rings of Gold," 1969).

PATSY CLINE served as her mentor, and West, in turn, befriended other performers and writers, boosting the careers of Larry Gatlin, JEANNIE SEELY, and STEVE WARINER.

West composed twelve Coca-Cola jingles, including the Clio Award–winning "Country Sunshine," which became a 1973 Top Ten hit. She moved to United Artists in 1976 and later scored a pair of #1 hits with "A Lesson in Leavin'" (1980) and "Are You Happy Baby?" (1980–81). A string of hit duets with Kenny Rogers included "Every Time Two Fools Collide" (1978) and "What Are We Doin' in Love" (1981), which also became a Top Twenty pop disc.

Along the way, West shed her gingham, sweetheart image and emerged as a glamorous, sexy star with a $50,000 wardrobe and a glitzy stage show. After she and Bill West divorced, she married two younger husbands in succession and lived extravagantly.

Bad investments and a lull in West's career in the late 1980s led to bankruptcy in 1990. She died a year later, of injuries from a Nashville car crash. A TV movie of her life aired in 1995.

Daughter Shelly West became a country star, recording several hits, including duets with DAVID FRIZZELL, in the early 1980s. —*Robert K. Oermann*

## Speedy West & Jimmy Bryant

Wesley Webb West b. Springfield, Missouri, January 25, 1924; d. November 15, 2003

Ivy Bryant b. Pavo, Georgia, March 5, 1925; d. September 22, 1980

PEDAL STEEL GUITAR pioneer Speedy West and electric guitarist Jimmy Bryant recorded some of the most spirited instrumental duets in country music history. Their versatility and drive were manifest on thirty-five singles and five albums as well as countless West Coast sessions for artists ranging from TENNESSEE ERNIE FORD to Frank Sinatra. The freshness of their playing combined speed and technique with a jazz-like improvisational daring. West was especially known for his zany "crash bar" effects, which created not only the sound of the chord but also the sound of the strings crashing against the bar.

West and Bryant were standouts among midwestern and southern migrant musicians active in post–World War II Los Angeles. They met (ca. 1947) when playing down the street from one another in competing bars. CLIFFIE STONE teamed them on his *HOMETOWN JAMBOREE* radio and television programs, billed them as the "Flaming Guitars," and recommended them to CAPITOL

*Speedy West & Jimmy Bryant*

RECORDS. The duo first recorded together backing Tennessee Ernie Ford and Kay Starr on 1950's "I'll Never Be Free" b/w "Ain't Nobody's Business but My Own." The dynamic interplay of West's Bigsby pedal steel (one of the first) and Bryant's electric guitar gave the twin-sided hit an exciting sound, one Capitol would use on hundreds of country and pop sessions during the 1950s.

West and Bryant spent eleven years on the *Hometown Jamboree* and recorded prolifically as an act into October 1956. They maintained successful separate careers, albeit not always as performers: Bryant was a songwriter best remembered for WAYLON JENNINGS's 1968 hit "Only Daddy That'll Walk the Line"; West, whose session work included LORETTA LYNN's 1960 Zero label debut, became the manager of the Fender Distribution Center in Tulsa, Oklahoma. Steel player and producer PETE DRAKE reunited them to record for his First Generation label (the album *For the Last Time* was ultimately issued in 1990 by STEP ONE RECORDS). In 1975 they performed for the first time in years at Nashville's annual Fan Fair (today's CMA MUSIC FESTIVAL).

Once billed as the "Fastest Guitar in the Country," Bryant died in 1980, the year West was inducted into the Steel Guitar Hall of Fame. In 1981 a debilitating stroke ended West's playing, but the fun and fury of the 1950s West-Bryant recordings will always mirror the vitality and experimental spirit of the postwar West Coast country scene. —*Mark Humphrey*

## Western Swing

Western swing is a style of country music that reached its zenith during the era of big band swing. Like the music of the big bands, western swing was originally intended for dancing. In fact, the term "western swing" was initially used to distinguish the swing music of pop dance orchestras from the music of western dance bands.

BOB WILLS, the nation's best known western swing bandleader, combined fiddles, guitars, banjos, piano, bass, and drums with reeds and brass to play a stylistic hybrid that smoothly integrated elements of big band swing, OLD-TIME fiddling, Dixieland jazz, blues, and Mexican music. According to LEON MCAULIFFE, a member of Wills's bands and leader of his own band after World War II, musicians defined this eclectic mixture as simply "a fiddle band that played dance music."

The seeds of western swing were sown in Fort Worth, Texas, when Bob Wills and singer MILTON BROWN began performing together on radio and at dance clubs. Beginning in the summer of 1930, Wills and Brown, joined by guitarist Herman Arnspiger, started broadcasting over Fort Worth's WBAP as the Aladdin Laddies and eventually, joined by Brown's brother Derwood on second guitar, as the popular LIGHT CRUST DOUGHBOYS. Two years later Brown left to front his own band, the highly influential though short-lived Musical Brownies, and the following year Wills left to lead his enormously influential Texas Playboys.

Based in the Dallas–Fort Worth area during the 1930s, Milton Brown & His Musical Brownies, Bill Boyd (see BILL AND JIM BOYD), and other pioneering western swing bands spread the music's regional popularity through successful recordings and radio shows. The maturation of the genre and national recognition came between 1934 and 1942, when Wills based his Texas Playboys band in Tulsa, Oklahoma, broadcasting daily over KVOO and recording for COLUMBIA RECORDS. The national sales of such later Wills hits as "San Antonio Rose" (1944), "Texas Playboy Rag" (1945), and "Stay a Little Longer" (1946) symbolized the music's commercial appeal. In the 1940s and 1950s western swing became a truly national phenomenon, as Bob Wills's brother JOHNNIE LEE WILLS, Leon McAuliffe, and HANK THOMPSON led popular western swing bands in the Southwest and as bandleaders such as HANK PENNY and PAUL HOWARD brought western swing to fans in the Southeast. Meanwhile, SPADE COOLEY challenged Bob Wills for the title King of Western Swing in packed ballrooms across Southern California.

With the rise of television after 1950, Americans no longer went to dances by the thousands, and both big dance orchestras and western swing bands went into decline or broke up for good. Only a few outfits could draw crowds large enough to keep large dance bands—which were expensive for bandleaders to pay and transport—on the road. By the mid-1960s, the era of western swing was history.

In the early 1970s, however, there was a revival, sparked in part by MERLE HAGGARD's 1970 tribute album to Bob Wills (*A Tribute to the Best Damn Fiddle Player in the World*) and by the success of Wills's last recording session (captured on the Grammy-winning album *For the Last Time*) in 1973. In addition, a new generation of fans and musicians discovered western swing through contemporary musicians such as WILLIE NELSON, ASLEEP AT THE WHEEL, and GEORGE STRAIT. Though today only Asleep at the Wheel and a few regional groups can be considered genuine western swing bands, many country artists continue to perform occasionally in the western swing style, while evergreen western swing classics such as "San Antonio Rose," "Right or Wrong," "Stay a Little Longer," and "Faded Love" continue to be revived on record and in live performance. —*Charles R. Townsend*

## Billy Edd Wheeler
b. Whitesville, West Virginia, December 9, 1932

Although he has received critical acclaim for his recordings, Billy Edward "Edd" Wheeler is still primarily regarded as a songwriter. His songs have won numerous ASCAP awards, sold more than forty-five million copies, and have been recorded by artists as varied as ELVIS PRESLEY, Judy Collins, TEX RITTER, CONWAY TWITTY, Nancy Sinatra, MERLE HAGGARD, and KENNY ROGERS. A graduate of Warren Wilson and Berea Colleges, he also attended Yale Drama School. At various times he has been an editor, music business executive, navy pilot, fund-raiser, and an instructor at Berea College.

In the late 1950s Wheeler started appearing on such programs as *Today*, *The Merv Griffin Show*, and Wheeling, West Virginia's *WWVA Jamboree*. In 1959 he started recording for the Monitor label, but moved to United Artists, Kapp, and RCA. He had some success with the LPs *The Wheeler Man* (1963), *Town and Country* (1965), and *Nashville Zodiac* (1969), the latter gaining the greatest critical respect. Still, his royalties have come mainly from recordings of his songs by others, the notable exception being "Ode to the Little Brown Shack Out Back," his most successful single, which reached #3 on *Billboard*'s country charts in 1964 while also denting the pop charts.

His first major songwriting success was "Reverend Mister Black," with which the Kingston Trio had a Top Ten hit in 1963. JOHNNY CASH and June Carter (CARTER SISTERS) had a crossover hit in 1967 with Wheeler's "Jackson," and Kenny Rogers scored in 1979–80 with his "Coward of the County."

Wheeler has also published novels, folk plays, and several collections of folk humor. —*W. K. McNeil*

## Onie Wheeler
b. Senath, Missouri, November 10, 1921; d. May 26, 1984

Sometimes an artist will carve a niche for himself, with an obvious debt to no one, yet influencing few. Onie Daniel Wheeler was like that; he had a quirky style, blending his harmonica and strangely inflected vocals, but he never achieved much recognition. He worked alongside FLATT & SCRUGGS, ROY ACUFF, ELVIS PRESLEY, HANK SNOW, and GEORGE JONES, but stubbornness, lack of commercial appeal, and bad luck dogged Wheeler's career.

Wheeler worked on the family farm until entering military service. After his discharge he attempted a career in country music, working live radio in Missouri, Arkansas, and Michigan. In August 1953 he signed with COLUMBIA RECORDS in Nashville, and his first Columbia session included two of his best-known songs, "Run 'Em Off" and "Mother Prays Loud in Her Sleep." Flatt & Scruggs recorded the latter the day after Wheeler's session, and LEFTY FRIZZELL covered "Run 'Em Off." Starting in 1955, Wheeler toured with Elvis Presley and other SUN RECORDS artists. He also tried recording ROCKABILLY for Columbia and Sun, but without much conviction.

For the remainder of his career Wheeler flitted in and out of the music business. He recorded for many labels and scored a minor hit in 1973 with "John's Been Shucking My Corn" on Royal American Records. He was operated on for an aneurysm in January 1984 and started work again a few months later, but he collapsed and died onstage at the GRAND OLE OPRY House during Jimmie Snow's *Grand Ole Gospel* radio show. —*Colin Escott*

## Bryan White
b. Lawton, Oklahoma, February 17, 1974

When the country music industry began seeking a younger demographic in the 1990s, Bryan S. White proved that teen appeal doesn't negate musical substance. Although White has attracted his share of screaming adolescent female fans, he also won the respect of his primary influences, STEVE WARINER and GLEN CAMPBELL.

White began playing drums at age five, and was seventeen when he switched to guitar and began writing songs. A year later he moved to Nashville and secured a staff writer's job at Glen Campbell Music, also signing with ASYLUM RECORDS, in 1993. White's self-titled debut album in 1994 was slow to attract attention, but its third single, "Someone Else's Star," went #1, as did the follow-up, "Rebecca Lynn."

White's second album, *Between Now and Forever*, was released in 1996; it provided additional hits, including two more #1s, "Sittin' on Go" and his self-penned "So Much for Pretending." White won 1995's ACM New Male Vocalist honor and, the following year, CMA's Horizon Award.

His third album, *The Right Place*, yielded only one major hit, "Love Is the Right Place" (#4, 1997). By 1999, Asylum Records shut down shortly after the release of White's fourth album, the ironically named *How Lucky I Am*. A subsequent Christmas collection and later albums generated no hits.

As a songwriter, White also enjoyed hits with other artists, including SAWYER BROWN'S "I Don't Believe in Goodbye" and DIAMOND RIO'S "Imagine That." After a ten-year recording break, he released *Dustbowl Dreams* in 2009. —*Calvin Gilbert*

## Clarence and Roland White
Clarence White b. Lewiston, Maine, June 7, 1944; d. July 15, 1973
Roland White b. Madawaska, Maine, April 23, 1938

With his brother Clarence, Roland White influenced the evolution of BLUEGRASS, beginning in the late 1950s. In addition, Clarence was an important figure in the creation of COUNTRY-ROCK.

Of French-Canadian ancestry, the LeBlanc family, who later changed their name to White, relocated from their native Maine to Southern California in 1954. Father Eric White played guitar, tenor banjo, and harmonica. Eventually a family band featured brothers Eric on tenor banjo, Roland on mandolin (and sometimes on banjo), guitarist Clarence, and sister Joanne on bass. Early on, the group performed contemporary country music, but by the mid-1950s they focused on bluegrass. As the Country Boys, the Whites won a talent contest hosted by broadcaster Carl "Squeakin' Deacon" Moore on Pasadena radio station KXLA. Regular appearances on *TOWN HALL PARTY* and *HOMETOWN JAMBOREE* soon followed.

Over the next few years Eric and Joanne dropped out, replaced by Billy Ray Lathum (banjo), Leroy Mack (DOBRO), and Roger Bush (bass). The group made two appearances on CBS-TV's popular *THE ANDY GRIFFITH SHOW* in 1961. In 1962 the band changed its name to the Kentucky Colonels and released its first album, *New Sounds of Bluegrass America* (Briar).

Clarence's guitar work took on a more prominent role in the band. After seeing guitarist DOC WATSON at the Ash Grove nightclub in L.A., Clarence began to test new possibilities for the instrument in bluegrass. At the time, the guitar was considered primarily a rhythm instrument, and few musicians—save for DON RENO, Watson, and EARL SCRUGGS—had bothered to explore its

potential for soloing. In 1964 the group recorded the seminal instrumental album *Appalachian Swing!* for World Pacific Records. Fiddlers Bobby Slone and Scott Stoneman also did hitches with the group in the 1960s.

By the mid-1960s Clarence's interest shifted to the electric guitar. His work on THE BYRDS' "Time Between" in 1966 introduced the now-popular String Bender to rock and country fans. Developed by White and Byrds band member Gene Parsons, the device was a mechanism applied to the B string of the guitar. When activated (by pulling down on the neck), it bent the string, thereby simulating the crying sound of a PEDAL STEEL GUITAR. Two years later Clarence became a full-time Byrd, remaining until the group's dissolution in February 1973. Until his death that same year (he was hit by a drunk driver while loading equipment into a car), he was a highly sought-after session musician who recorded with LINDA RONSTADT, RICK NELSON, and THE EVERLY BROTHERS.

Meanwhile, elder brother Roland continued to nurture his passion for bluegrass. After the Colonels disbanded, he went on to work with bluegrass legends BILL MONROE and LESTER FLATT. In 1973 he joined THE COUNTRY GAZETTE, where he remained until 1987, when he joined NASHVILLE BLUEGRASS BAND. Since December 2000 he has fronted the Roland White Band. The group's album *Jelly on My Tofu* (Copper Creek, 2003) was nominated for a Grammy. —*Chris Skinker*

## Lari White
b. Dunedin, Florida, May 13, 1965

In 1996 RCA RECORDS dropped the talented Lari White, after two albums that sold 500,000 units each. The move reflected Nashville labels' tremendous promotional costs, which frequently require millions in sales to recoup.

White began performing at age four with her parents. Despite losing the little finger of her left hand in an accident at age one, she began playing piano and performed throughout the Gulf Coast in her teens. After studying voice at the University of Miami, White moved to Nashville at age twenty-three. She won TNN's *You Can Be a Star* contest in 1988, began getting cuts as a songwriter, and became a back-up singer for RODNEY CROWELL in 1992.

Signed to RCA, she displayed her bluesy, gospel-tinged country style on piano-driven numbers such as "Lead Me Not," the title cut of her 1993 debut album. Her first Top Ten hit was 1994's "That's My Baby." Despite two more Top Tens in 1994–95, RCA decided to drop her. White moved to LYRIC STREET RECORDS (1997–98) for *Stepping Stone* (1998), but her self-produced indie album *Green Eyed Soul*, reflecting her blend of soul, "Southern Americana," and jazz, didn't appear until 2004. *My First Affair*, likewise issued on the Skinny White Girl label, followed in 2007. White also has gained credits in films and on Broadway. —*Clark Parsons*

## Martha White (*see* Martha White Flour, under M)

## Tony Joe White
b. Oak Grove, Louisiana, July 23, 1943

Tony Joe White's spare, southern style of music made him equally at home on the pop charts, in country songwriting circles, and as a European rock idol. Known as the Swamp Fox, he wrote the soul classic "Rainy Night in Georgia" and had a pop hit in 1969 with "Polk Salad Annie." HANK WILLIAMS JR., GEORGE JONES, RAY CHARLES, JERRY REED, and WAYLON JENNINGS have all recorded his tunes.

As a Louisiana teenager White gravitated to his older brother's blues records. He began performing regionally and then came to Nashville in 1967. There he landed a staff songwriting job with COMBINE MUSIC and a MONUMENT RECORDS contract, with BILLY SWAN as his producer.

White's "Soul Francisco" became a hit in France in 1968 (leading to his European popularity); then "Polk Salad Annie," a 1969 pop hit, climbed to #8. Pop chart-makers "Roosevelt and Ira Lee" and "Save Your Sugar for Me" followed in 1969–70.

White's "Rainy Night in Georgia" became a pop and R&B hit for Brook Benton in 1970 and received country exposure as a 1993 CONWAY TWITTY–Sam Moore duet, the last song Twitty ever recorded. White also penned ELVIS PRESLEY's "I've Got a Thing About You, Baby" (#39, 1974) and Tina Turner's 1990 hit "Steamy Windows."

White recorded albums for Monument (1968–70), WARNER BROS. (1971–73), 20th Century (1976), Casablanca (1980), and COLUMBIA (1983). After a lull he began recording more frequently in the 1990s. In the new century his albums have included *One Hot July* (Hip-O, 2000); *The Beginning* (on his own Swamp Records, 2001); *The Heroines* (Sanctuary, 2004), featuring duets with JESSI COLTER, SHELBY LYNNE, EMMYLOU HARRIS, and LUCINDA WILLIAMS; and *Uncovered* (Swamp, 2006), whose guests and contributors included WAYLON JENNINGS. —*Robert K. Oermann*

## The Whites

Sharon White b. Wichita Falls, Texas, December 17, 1953
Cheryl White b. Wichita Falls, Texas, January 27, 1955
Buck White b. Oklahoma, December 13, 1930

The Whites' captivating family harmony, dominated by female voices, began attracting listeners when Sharon and Cheryl White were young teenagers. Emerging from BLUEGRASS into the country mainstream in 1981, they became associated with country's NEW TRADITIONALISM movement through their own work and through affiliations with EMMYLOU HARRIS and RICKY SKAGGS.

Father Buck White's music reflects his Oklahoma and Texas roots. An accomplished HONKY-TONK pianist and bluegrass mandolinist, his style also incorporates WESTERN SWING, gospel, Mexican music, and blues. Early on he performed on radio with swing bands and bluegrass groups and even played electric piano for a rock & roll band. In 1962, while Buck worked as a pipefitter in Arkansas, he and his wife, Pat, formed the Down Home Folks with another couple. In 1966 Sharon, then thirteen, joined on guitar, while Cheryl, age eleven, played bass. (By the mid-1980s, the band often included third daughter Rosie on percussion and guitar.) The group initially performed at bluegrass festivals, and in 1971 the Whites moved to Nashville to pursue music full time. Pat White retired from music in 1973 and died in 2002.

The act first recorded as Buck White & the Down Home Folks on COUNTY RECORDS in 1972, and the 1980 SUGAR HILL album *More Pretty Girls Than One* captured their maturing harmony. After Emmylou Harris heard them in 1975, the Whites provided vocals on her "Blue Kentucky Girl" (1979) and joined her for a time on tour. Sharon married Skaggs, Harris's bandleader at the time, in 1982.

The Whites first charted with "Send Me the Pillow You Dream On" on CAPITOL in 1981. Skaggs began producing them in 1982, and Top Ten hits such as "You Put the Blue in Me" (ELEKTRA, 1982) and "Pins and Needles" (MCA, 1984) followed. Sharon White and Skaggs also recorded successfully, winning CMA's 1987 Vocal Duo of the Year award. The Whites joined the GRAND OLE OPRY in 1984.

The group made the gospel album *Doing It by the Book* for New Canaan Records in 1988 and recorded the secular *Give a Little Back* for STEP ONE RECORDS in 1996. They appeared in the hit film *O BROTHER, WHERE ART THOU?* (2000) and on its multi-platinum soundtrack album as well as on the related documentary *Down from the Mountain*, its companion album, and associated tours. In 2007 Skaggs and the Whites released *Salt of the Earth* on Skaggs Family Records, winning a Dove Award in 2008. —*Mary A. Bufwack*

## Whitey & Hogan

Roy "Whitey" Grant b. Shelby, North Carolina, April 7, 1916; d. September 17, 2010
Arval Albert Hogan b. Robbinsville, Carolina, July 24, 1911; d. September 12, 2003

Based in Charlotte, North Carolina, Whitey & Hogan were a popular harmony team from the late-1930s to the mid-1950s. Hogan was the son of a western North Carolina lumberman; Whitey was a farm boy. The pair met in about 1936 while working at a Gastonia, North Carolina, textile mill. Discovering their mutual love of music, they assembled a repertoire of hymns, folk songs, contemporary love songs, and novelty numbers, all rendered in the era's duet harmony style and backed by Whitey's guitar and Hogan's mandolin.

In about 1938 they began broadcasting on WSPA in Spartanburg, South Carolina; they then shifted to WGNC–Gastonia in 1939. At this point Charlotte record distributor Vann Sills recruited them for a DECCA recording session in New York. Shortly after World War II they recorded several sides for the New York–based Sonora label, but mostly they remained radio performers.

In 1941 the duo moved to WBT–Charlotte and worked on the daily *Briarhopper Time* show. Whitey & Hogan also worked regional CBS network programs, such as the *Dixie Jamboree*, *Carolina Hayride*, and *Carolina Calling*. Early in the 1950s, local Charlotte TV shows broadened the team's exposure. In mid-decade, with demand for their style fading, the partners became Charlotte mail carriers and bought homes next door to each other. Beginning in the 1970s, the duet found a new generation of fans at BLUEGRASS and OLD-TIME MUSIC festivals. Active into the 1990s, Whitey & Hogan made occasional appearances until failing health sidelined Hogan early in the 2000s. —*John W. Rumble*

## Keith Whitley

b. Sandy Hook, Kentucky, July 1, 1955; d. May 9, 1989

Hard-country singer Jessie Keith Whitley was just beginning to hit his stride when he died at his Goodlettsville, Tennessee, home on May 9, 1989, of alcohol poisoning. He was just thirty-three years old, but he left a powerful musical legacy, influencing many young country singers. A writer of talent and depth, Whitley penned songs that ranged from soulful gospel ("Great High Mountain") to humorous ("I Want My Rib Back").

Steeped in the HONKY-TONK sounds of LEFTY FRIZZELL and GEORGE JONES and the BLUEGRASS stylings of THE STANLEY BROTHERS, Whitley brought a vocal maturity and sensibility to country music far beyond his years. Like his heroes Frizzell, Jones, and Carter Stanley, he struggled with alcoholism for most of his adult life.

By age eight Whitley appeared on singer BUDDY STARCHER'S television show in Charleston, West Virginia, and was working on local radio shows with his elder brother, Dwight. A few years later Whitley met another child prodigy, RICKY SKAGGS (from nearby Cordell), at a talent show. Both were contestants, but neither took home first prize. The two became friends and soon formed the East Kentucky Mountain Boys.

In 1970 Whitley and Skaggs were asked to fill in at a nightclub for RALPH STANLEY, who was late for the show date due to bus trouble. As Stanley later recounted the story, "I walked in and they were doing the Stanley Brothers better than the Stanleys." Although they were still in high school, Ralph hired the two teenagers virtually on the spot. Whitley played guitar and handled some of the vocals, while Skaggs was featured on mandolin and vocals. The pair performed in Stanley's Clinch Mountain Boys throughout the next two summer festival seasons and recorded a pair of albums—*Tribute to the Stanley Brothers* (Jalyn, 1971) and *Second Generation Bluegrass* (REBEL, 1971).

Whitley left Stanley's outfit in 1972 and joined forces with mandolin player Jimmy Gaudreau and banjoist CARL JACKSON in the Country Store (also dubbed New Tradition). In 1974 Whitley returned to the Clinch Mountain Boys for a second hitch. This time he assumed the role of lead vocalist, replacing Roy Lee Centers, who was fatally shot in May of that year. Whitley worked with Stanley until 1978, when he joined J. D. CROWE's New South. While with Crowe, Whitley recorded a handful of albums, including *Live in Japan* (1979) and *Somewhere Between* (1982).

Although successful in bluegrass, Whitley had wider aspirations. In 1984 he moved to Nashville just as the back-to-basics NEW TRADITIONALISM movement was gaining momentum. By September Whitley landed a contract with RCA RECORDS and

had a single on the country charts, "Turn Me to Love," featuring PATTY LOVELESS on background vocals.

Whitley's fourth single, "Miami, My Amy," was his first to crack the country Top Twenty, and his next three singles all made the Top Ten. In 1988 he hit #1 with the romantic ballads "Don't Close Your Eyes" and "When You Say Nothing at All." Whitley's introspective, soul-searching recordings of "I'm No Stranger to the Rain" and "I Wonder Do You Think of Me" also topped the charts, in 1989. The former was named the CMA's Single of the Year. Several posthumous hits followed, including "It Ain't Nothin'" and a duet with his wife, LORRIE MORGAN, whom he married in 1986, "'Til a Tear Becomes a Rose." The recording, on which Morgan's vocals were overdubbed onto an existing Whitley track, won CMA's Vocal Event of the Year award in 1990. —*Chris Skinker*

## Ray Whitley
b. Atlanta, Georgia, December 5, 1901; d. February 21, 1979

Raymond Otis Whitley was a noted singer, songwriter, and western film star. Not unlike Hollywood actor Randolph Scott, the Georgia-born, Alabama-raised Whitley was the same profoundly decent, unassuming gentleman whether onscreen or off.

After he appeared on New York City's *WHN Barn Dance* in the mid-1930s, Whitley's baritone voice, bluesy yodeling, considerable charm, and rugged good looks made him a natural for the burgeoning singing-cowboy film genre. Beginning in 1936, Whitley starred in sixteen singing-cowboy shorts for RKO and appeared in some sixty features. His film career ended after a role in the 1956 epic *Giant*.

In addition, he managed the SONS OF THE PIONEERS in their early years, led a WESTERN SWING band, toured relentlessly, recorded for a number of labels (DECCA, OKEH, and others), and aided the Gibson Guitar Company in developing its J-200 deluxe guitar in 1938. Soon GENE AUTRY, TEX RITTER, and JIMMY WAKELY featured the jumbo rosewood instrument onscreen, making it the sine qua non of the singing cowboy. Later artists who favored it include THE EVERLY BROTHERS and EMMYLOU HARRIS.

An open and generous man, Whitley and his wife, Kay, befriended FRED ROSE in the late 1930s, and while Rose was living with the Whitleys the two men collaborated on several successful songs, all popularized by Autry: "Lonely River," "I Hang My Head and Cry," and "Ages and Ages Ago." Whitley himself wrote one of western music's most enduring pieces, "Back in the Saddle Again," which became Autry's theme song.

With the decline of the singing cowboy and the rise of rock, Ray Whitley quietly phased out of film and music. Rediscovered during the 1970s, he charmed his old fans and a new generation with rope and whip tricks and his still-strong voice. He died of diabetic shock while on a fishing trip in Baja California, Mexico. —*Douglas B. Green*

## Slim Whitman
b. Tampa, Florida, January 20, 1924

Known for his sky-high falsetto flourishes on sentimental pop songs such as "Indian Love Call" and "Secret Love," Otis Dewey Whitman Jr. also played an early role in popularizing country music overseas.

Slim Whitman grew up around Tampa. During World War II he enlisted in the U.S. Navy, and while onboard ship he found a

*Keith Whitley*

*Slim Whitman*

guitar and strung the instrument upside down to accommodate his left-handed playing style. After his discharge he played minor-league baseball for a time and then decided to pursue a musical career. In 1948 he began working nightclubs and radio stations in the Tampa area. In that year, on a recommendation by COLONEL TOM PARKER, he was signed to RCA RECORDS. He joined the LOUISIANA HAYRIDE in 1950.

In late 1951 Whitman signed with IMPERIAL RECORDS (eventually absorbed by United Artists and then by CAPITOL RECORDS), for which he would record for eighteen years. Whitman's first release, "Love Song of the Waterfall," reached #10 on the country charts. His second single, "Indian Love Call" (first popularized by Jeanette MacDonald and Nelson Eddy in the 1936 film *Rose Marie*), became a million-seller, peaking at #2 country and #9 pop in 1951. During the next three years Whitman's singles charted consistently. His success spread overseas to England with the 1954 release of "Rose-Marie," title song from the film of the same name. A #4 country hit in the United States, the record went to #1 in England.

At about the time Slim Whitman joined the GRAND OLE OPRY in 1955, he found his American career on a downslide. Nevertheless, his British popularity remained strong. After a chart-making disc in 1961, he returned to the U.S. country charts in 1964 and remained through 1974.

In 1979 the Whitman LP *All My Best* was offered through a telemarketing campaign and reportedly sold in the millions. Its success led to Whitman's signing with Cleveland International Records, for which he recorded several moderate hit singles and additional telemarketed albums in the early 1980s. During the 1990s and beyond, he recorded occasionally and toured successfully, especially in Europe and Australia. Since 1977, when his rendition of "Love Song of the Waterfall" was included in the hit film *Close Encounters of the Third Kind*, his recordings have been used in additional movie soundtracks. —*Don Roy*

## Henry Whitter
b. Grayson County, Virginia, April 6, 1892; d. November 17, 1941

One of the first rural folk musicians to make commercial recordings, William Henry Whitter was born near Fries, Virginia, and began playing musical instruments while working in textile mills. Dissatisfied with his mill job, Whitter turned to music as the road to a better life, singing and playing his guitar and harmonica in and around Fries. In 1923, possibly in March, Whitter journeyed to New York to visit the General Phonograph Corporation for a recording audition. A more successful session, in December, resulted in his first release: "Lonesome Road Blues"/"The Wreck on the Southern Old 97" (OKEH 40015). It was this recording of "Wreck" that VERNON DALHART later heard, revised, and recorded in 1924 for the Victor Talking Machine Company (later RCA VICTOR), coupled with "The Prisoner's Song"—a disc that became country music's first million-selling hit. Whitter recorded with a number of artists between 1924 and 1930, but his most successful partnership was with blind fiddler Gilliam Banmon "G. B." Grayson (b. Ashe County, North Carolina, November 11, 1888; d. August 16, 1930). Together they recorded some forty selections—a collection that influenced not only other southeastern musicians during the 1930s but also early BLUEGRASS musicians in the 1950s and urban folk song revival singers in the 1960s and 1970s. The duo's recordings ended with Grayson's death in a 1930 automobile accident.

Solo, Whitter's performances were rather lackluster. He was an uninteresting singer with only passable guitar backup and acceptable harmonica work. But with Grayson, something had clicked, and the results were outstanding: beautiful, archaic singing and fiddling on Grayson's part, with guitar accompaniment ranging from adequate to very good. Nearly all of the Grayson & Whitter duets have been reissued on LP or CD, but hardly any of Whitter's nearly five dozen solo pieces have been brought out. Whitter's importance rests on his recording of "Old 97," historically one of the most significant in early country music, and in his bringing G. B. Grayson before the microphone, thereby creating one of the finest country music acts to record in the prewar years. —*Norm Cohen*

## Little Roy Wiggins
b. Nashville, Tennessee, June 27, 1926; d. August 3, 1999

Ivan Leroy "Little Roy" Wiggins, the diminutive steel guitar wizard, was best known for his many years with singer EDDY ARNOLD. Inspired by the playing of the GRAND OLE OPRY's Bert Hutcherson, Wiggins first took steel guitar lessons at age six from Nashville's Robert E. Martin. At thirteen Wiggins got a job with the Opry's PAUL HOWARD; two years he later replaced Clell Summey (who left for World War II military service) as steel guitarist with PEE WEE KING's Golden West Cowboys. Wiggins was lured away in 1943 when Arnold left King's band to start his own, the Tennessee Plowboys. With his distinctive "ting-a-ling" cry supporting Arnold's smooth vocals, Wiggins provided a key component of Arnold's highly successful sound during the superstar's initial rise to fame.

Beginning in the late 1950s Wiggins made instrumental records for DOT RECORDS, STARDAY RECORDS, and such labels as Midland, Diplomat, Empire Sound, American Sound, Stoneway, and O'Brien. As Arnold trimmed steel guitar from his recordings and added strings, Wiggins joined Arnold's partner and accountant, Charles Mosley, in the insurance and real estate business in Brentwood, Tennessee. Another business boon came his way when Vox Instruments chose Wiggins to endorse its products and also to find other country pickers to do the same.

Leaving Arnold's employ in about 1968, Wiggins opened a music store at 427 Broadway near THE RYMAN AUDITORIUM, Little Roy Wiggins's Music City. At this point he returned to the Grand Ole Opry to play behind THE WILLIS BROTHERS, GEORGE MORGAN, ERNIE ASHWORTH, and other acts, also touring with Morgan. After the Opry's 1974 move from the Ryman to the OPRYLAND USA complex, Wiggins closed his music store, and in the 1980s he left to perform for tourists in Pigeon Forge, Tennessee. —*Ronnie Pugh*

## Wilburn Brothers
Virgil Doyle Wilburn b. Hardy, Arkansas, July 7, 1930; d. October 16, 1982
Thurman Theodore Wilburn b. Hardy, Arkansas, November 30, 1931; d. November 24, 2003

One of country music's smoothest duet harmony acts, Doyle and Teddy Wilburn also set an important example as astute businessmen. They first performed publicly on Christmas Eve 1937, on a Thayer, Missouri, street corner with older siblings Lester, Leslie, and Geraldine. In 1940 ROY ACUFF sponsored the Wilburn Family's GRAND OLE OPRY debut, though child labor laws barred their membership. The group later recorded briefly for FOUR STAR.

The four brothers performed on KWKH in Shreveport, Louisiana, beginning in about 1948; by 1951 Doyle and Teddy had been drafted for the Korean War. The Wilburns had already invited a relatively unknown WEBB PIERCE to guest on their radio show, leading to Pierce's career-launching *LOUISIANA HAYRIDE* stint, and eventually Doyle and Teddy played guitar and bass, respectively, on Pierce's first DECCA session. Following military discharge, the duo toured with Pierce, by now an Opry star. In 1954 Teddy and Doyle signed with Decca and joined the Opry in 1956 as full-fledged members.

*The Wilburn Brothers: Teddy and Doyle*

During the late 1950s and 1960s the Wilburns recorded hits including "I'm So in Love With You," "Trouble's Back in Town," and "Roll, Muddy River" and displayed songwriting talents with hits such as "Somebody's Back in Town." Their harmonies also enhanced others' recordings, notably Pierce's "In the Jailhouse Now" and ERNEST TUBB's "Hey, Mr. Bluebird."

The brothers' business achievements included their Sure-Fire music-publishing firm and the Wil-Helm Talent Agency, the latter founded with steel guitar player Don Helms. While Sure-Fire published early songs by LORETTA LYNN—whose Decca contract the Wilburns negotiated—Wil-Helm booked the likes of JEAN SHEPARD; THE OSBORNE BROTHERS, who covered many Wilburn Brothers hits; and SONNY JAMES. In 1963 the Wilburns launched their successful syndicated TV show, which ran into the early 1970s and provided Lynn and others with invaluable early exposure.

Soon independently wealthy, Teddy studied acting in Hollywood. Doyle was wed briefly to singer Margie Bowes. The brothers continued touring until Doyle's death from cancer in 1982. Teddy then performed occasionally and focused on his business interests until illness sidelined him. He died in 2003 of congestive heart failure after suffering from Parkinson's disease. In 2011, the Wilburn family was still operating Sure-Fire Music as an independent publisher. —*Walt Trott*

## Wiley & Gene
Wiley Walker b. Laurel Hill, Florida, November 17, 1911; d. May 17, 1966
Gene Sullivan b. Carbon Hill, Alabama, November 6, 1914; d. October 24, 1984

Unlike many duet harmony teams, which often based their acoustic, sentimental styles on mandolin and guitar, Wiley & Gene projected an overall sound and ambience suggesting the emerging HONKY-TONK trend of the 1940s. Although their recordings, such as "Live and Let Live" and "I Want to Live and Love," showed up nationwide in honky-tonks, on JUKEBOXES, and in the performances of other musicians, the duo avoided the dancehall circuit. Instead, they were fixtures on Texas and Oklahoma radio stations, particularly in Oklahoma City.

Walker was a singer, buck dancer, and fiddler who traveled for several years with the Harley Sadler Tent Show. There he met entertainer LEW CHILDRE, and the two performed as the Alabama Boys on WWL–New Orleans and on other southern radio stations. While working with THE SHELTON BROTHERS in Louisiana, Walker began singing duets with Sullivan, a singer, guitarist, and comedian who sometimes recited humorous poetry, including "Sleeping at the Foot of the Bed" (later a hit for LITTLE JIMMY DICKENS). Sullivan played with several Texas country swing bands and wrote most of the classic songs he and Walker recorded. Wiley & Gene launched their popular duet act on Fort Worth's KFJZ and the Texas State Network in 1939 and reached the pinnacle of their career during the war years, when hits such as "When My Blue Moon Turns to Gold Again" mirrored emotions felt by many Americans. Wiley & Gene recorded for COLUMBIA during 1939–47 and again in 1950. Sullivan recorded solo for Columbia in 1951 and 1957. —*Bill C. Malone*

## Marijohn Wilkin
b. Kemp, Texas, July 14, 1920; d. October 28, 2006

During the NASHVILLE SOUND era, few women were deeply involved in the country industry in any area other than singing. One was Marijohn Wilkin, one of the most successful

*Marijohn Wilkin*

first-generation Music Row songwriters. Wilkin cowrote such classic tunes as "The Long Black Veil," "Waterloo," "Cut Across Shorty," and, many years later, the gospel standard "One Day at a Time." She also worked as a song plugger and lead-sheet writer for Cedarwood Publishing, and in 1964 she started Buckhorn Music, Kris Kristofferson's publishing base when he arrived in Nashville.

Born Marijohn Melson, she grew up in Sanger, Texas, and learned to play piano at an early age. In college she sang with the Hardin-Simmons University Cowboy Band, a traveling troupe that performed at Franklin D. Roosevelt's third inauguration. Eventually landing in Tulsa, she became a schoolteacher and started writing songs. In 1955, when her eight-year-old musician son, John Buck "Bucky" Wilkin, was discovered by a representative of the *Ozark Jubilee*, she and her family moved to Springfield, Missouri. Guitarist Bucky backed Brenda Lee for a time while his mother sang with Red Foley's road show. Foley and others recorded her songs, and in 1958, when Nashville booking agent Lucky Moeller heard Wilkin at a Springfield piano bar, he convinced her to move to Nashville.

In Music City Wilkin initially worked at another piano bar but soon quit to accept a fifty-dollar-a-week job with Cedarwood, where she was part of an all-star stable of writers, including, among others, John D. Loudermilk, Danny Dill, Wayne Walker, and Mel Tillis. She also recorded two albums, one a collection of Civil War songs that appeared on Columbia in 1961. After Cedarwood chief Jim Denny died, Wilkin left the company to start Buckhorn Music in partnership with Nashville arranger and saxophonist Bill Justis.

Ironically, Buckhorn's first success was the surf-era rock & roll hit "G.T.O.," which Bucky Wilkin wrote and recorded in 1964 under the name of Ronny & the Daytonas. At about that time Kristofferson moved to town and contacted Wilkin, having heard of her through mutual acquaintances while he was in the

U.S. Army. Wilkin signed him. Among the songs Kristofferson wrote during his tenure at Buckhorn was "For the Good Times," a #1 hit for Ray Price in 1970.

For all her success, Wilkin grew suicidally depressed during this period, and she embarked on a long, spiritual journey overseas in 1968. She began to write "One Day at a Time" as a prayer, and in 1973 Kristofferson helped her finish the song. Recorded first by Marilyn Sellars, the song became a gospel standard and a hit for Cristy Lane.

During the 1970s Wilkin recorded several gospel albums before easing from the limelight. She made headlines anew in 1995 when her "I Just Don't Understand," cowritten with Kent Westberry, appeared on the Beatles' *Live at the BBC* collection. She also found success with Seventeenth Avenue Music, another publishing company she co-owned, which published songs recorded by LeAnn Rimes. A founder of NSAI, she was elected to the Nashville Songwriters Hall of Fame in 1975. —*Daniel Cooper*

## Slim Willet
b. Victor, Texas, December 1, 1919; d. July 1, 1966

Winston Lee Moore, better known as Slim Willet, is probably best remembered as the writer of "Don't Let the Stars Get in Your Eyes." He adopted his pseudonym while working as student manager of the radio station at Hardin-Simmons University in Abilene, Texas. After graduation in 1949 he joined Abilene radio station KRBC. In 1950 his recording career began with "I'm a Tool Pusher from Snyder," released on the Dallas-based Star Talent label. "Don't Let the Stars Get in Your Eyes," issued on Four Star Records in 1952, proved so popular that four different performers (including Willet) had versions in *Billboard*'s Top Ten country jukebox, radio, and record sales charts at the same time. Perry Como made it a #1 pop record. Although he never had another hit of this magnitude, Willet remained active professionally. For a time he spelled his name backwards and established a rock & roll alter ego, Telli W. Mils, the Fat Cat. In addition to his own publishing company and advertising agency, he established the Edmoral and Winston labels to release his recordings and those by performers such as Hoyle Nix, Dean Beard, Jimmy Seals, Darrell Rhodes, and Curtis Potter. Willet was also a pioneer in live television, with a show on Abilene's KRBC-TV featuring new talent such as Larry Gatlin, and in 1962 Willet helped to establish Abilene's KCAD, one of Texas's earliest full-time country radio stations. —*Joe W. Specht*

## Audrey Williams
b. Enon Community, Alabama, February 28, 1923; d. November 4, 1975

As the wife of Hank Williams, the mother of Hank Williams Jr., and a force behind both men's rise to stardom, Audrey Mae Sheppard Williams's contributions to the history of country music could easily stand on these facts alone. However, throughout the 1950s and 1960s she established herself as one of Nashville's first female music entrepreneurs, with her own publishing company, booking agency, record label, all-girl band, and movie production company.

She met Hank Williams at a medicine show in the summer of 1943 and married him in December 1944. Audrey's young daughter, Lycrecia, from an earlier marriage, was raised by Hank as his own; their son, Randall Hank Williams, was born in 1949.

Audrey was an integral part of Hank's early career, handling his bookings, collecting money at the door, playing stand-up bass, and singing backup with his band. But theirs was a tempestuous union, marked by a divorce (May 26, 1948), a divorce annulment (August 9, 1949), and a final divorce (April 3, 1952). The anguish in Hank's greatest songs ("Cold, Cold Heart," "I Can't Help It If I'm Still in Love with You," "Your Cheatin' Heart") bears testimony to their rocky relationship.

In the 1950s Audrey recorded briefly for both DECCA and MGM herself (she had previously recorded a few MGM duets with Hank). After Hank died on January 1, 1953, Audrey struggled with guilt and sorrow, and she died of alcoholism. They are buried side by side in Montgomery, Alabama. —*Dale Vinicur*

## Curley Williams & His Georgia Peach Pickers
Doc "Curley" Williams b. near Cairo, Georgia, June 3, 1914; d. September 5, 1970

Curley Williams is principally remembered for writing "Half As Much." Though he recorded the song for COLUMBIA RECORDS in 1951, it became a national hit when HANK WILLIAMS released his version the following year, followed by Rosemary Clooney's pop rendition. But in his day, Curley Williams was a popular bandleader, starring briefly on the GRAND OLE OPRY (1942–45) and recording forty-four sides during his 1945–52 stint with Columbia.

Born Doc Williams, he grew up on a South Georgia farm listening to his father's fiddling. After forming his first band, Doc Williams & His Santa Fe Trail Riders, in 1940, Williams appeared on several small-town Georgia radio stations. In December 1942 the group—renamed Curley Williams & the Georgia Peach Pickers—made its Grand Ole Opry debut. The band consisted of Williams on fiddle; his brothers Sanford and Joseph on bass and guitar, respectively; steel guitarist Boots Harris; pianist Joe Pope; and Jimmy Selph, guitarist and vocalist.

In 1945 Williams left the Opry for the West Coast, where his band appeared at major dance halls and in a movie, *Riders of the Lone Star* (1947), featuring Charles Starrett. Williams later appeared on radio stations in Louisiana, Tennessee, and Alabama. In 1954 he had his own TV show on WSFA in Montgomery, Alabama. Subsequently he operated a Montgomery nightclub called The Spur—for which his band provided music—until his death. —*Wayne W. Daniel*

## Doc & Chickie Williams
Andrew John Smik Jr. b. Cleveland, Ohio, June 26, 1914; d. January 31, 2011
Jessie Wanda Crupe b. Bethany, West Virginia, February 13, 1919; d. November 18, 2007

Incorporating East European ethnic sounds into their style, Doc & Chickie Williams were stalwarts of traditional country music in the American Northeast and eastern Canada for more than a half-century. Andy Smik grew up in the coal-mining country of Pennsylvania and gained early radio experience in Cleveland and Pittsburgh—where he adopted the stage name Doc Williams—before joining the *WWVA JAMBOREE* in Wheeling, West Virginia, in May 1937. He was associated with the *Jamboree* off and on for decades thereafter. Williams married Jessie Wanda "Chickie" Crupe in 1939, but Chickie did not become a regular in her husband's band, the Border Riders, until 1946. The act carved out a distinctive sound highlighted by Doc's brother Cy on fiddle and

Marion Martin on accordion. Doc started his own Wheeling Records in 1947, and the company's initial release, Chickie's rendition of "Beyond the Sunset," was quickly covered by the major labels.

Although they never enjoyed national stardom, the duo gained loyal fans in rural areas extending from Ohio to Newfoundland. They recorded numerous singles and albums on the Wheeling label both individually and together. By the late 1970s they began to curtail extensive touring, but they remained semiactive into the late 1990s. —*Ivan M. Tribe*

## Don Williams
b. Floydada, Texas, May 27, 1939

Known as country music's "Gentle Giant" for his warm baritone and laid-back ways, Don Williams was a major country hit maker and international ambassador. Scoring at least one major hit every year between 1974 and 1991, he had an impressive fifty-six chart records. Forty-five of these made the Top Ten, with seventeen reaching #1. In 1978 he was CMA Male Vocalist of the Year, and his recording of "Tulsa Time" was ACM Single of the Year. In 1980, readers of London's *Country Music People* magazine named him Artist of the Decade.

Williams learned guitar from his mother and performed in various country, folk, and rock & roll bands as a teenager; he found success in the 1960s as a member of folk-pop trio the Pozo-Seco Singers. The group had six pop chart–making records during 1966–67, the best known being the hauntingly nostalgic "Time." The act broke up in 1969, and Williams tried several nonmusical jobs before traveling to Nashville to make another stab at music.

There "COWBOY" JACK CLEMENT signed the lanky Texan to his Jack Music publishing company as a writer. Working with Clement

*Don Williams*

and songwriter-producer ALLEN REYNOLDS, then new to Nashville, Williams recorded publisher's demo recordings. When other artists proved reluctant to record his songs, the three men decided that Williams should record them himself.

*Don Williams, Volume One*, his first album, appeared in 1972 on Clement's JMI Records. It contained several chart singles, including Williams's self-penned "The Shelter of Your Eyes (#14, 1972) and BOB McDILL's "Come Early Morning" (#12, 1973) and "Amanda" (#33, 1973). *Don Williams, Volume Two* featured Williams's own "Atta Way to Go" (#13, 1973–74) and Reynolds's "We Should Be Together" (1974), the singer's first Top Five hit. Recordings such as these established his style, noted for its mellow yet masculine vocals and often-pensive song material.

In 1974 Williams scored his first chart-topping record, "I Wouldn't Want to Live If You Didn't Love Me." It launched a string of fifteen straight Top Ten hits, among them "You're My Best Friend," "Some Broken Hearts Never Mend," "Say It Again," and "It Must Be Love." The singer's winning streak also included the Williams originals "Lay Down Beside Me" and "Love Me Over Again."

During the 1980s and early 1990s, top-tier songwriters supplied Williams with first-rate material, most notably McDill's literary and evocative "Good Ole Boys Like Me." "I Believe in You," "I Wouldn't Be a Man," and "Then It's Love" were also hits of this era. Williams's success helped establish Allen Reynolds not only as a songwriter but also as a producer who would later guide talents such as CRYSTAL GAYLE and GARTH BROOKS. Williams eventually coproduced his own albums with GARTH FUNDIS, likewise destined for success with a wide range of artists.

As of 2010 the prolific Williams had released more than thirty-five albums. *The Best of Don Williams, Volume II* and *The Best of Don Williams, Volume III* have been certified gold, and *I Believe in You* has been certified platinum. His video collection *Don Williams Live* has attained gold status. After switching from JMI to ABC-DOT (1974–78), Williams moved in succession to MCA (1979–85), CAPITOL (1985–89), and RCA (1989–92). Later releases appeared on American Harvest, GIANT, RMG, and Intersound/ Compendia. Williams was one of the first country artists to make a music video, 1973's "Come Early Morning."

From the outset, country radio embraced Williams, while onstage he steadily built a large and loyal fan base. In addition to his domestic audience, he won fans worldwide, selling records in the British Isles, Europe, Latin America, and Australia. He is one of the few country stars to tour in Africa; his DVD *Into Africa* draws on his performances on that continent.

Among country's major acts, Don Williams is perhaps the least enamored of his success. Avoiding music industry parties, he gave few interviews and deliberately limited his tour schedule so that he could spend time on his Tennessee farm with his family. Following a worldwide farewell tour in 2006, he has made this his top priority. Williams was elected to THE COUNTRY MUSIC HALL OF FAME in 2010. —*John Lomax III*

## Hank Williams

b. Mount Olive, Alabama, September 17, 1923; d. January 1, 1953

Hank Williams's legend has long overtaken the rather frail, moody man who spawned it. Almost single-handedly, Williams set the agenda for contemporary country songcraft, and whether onstage, on recordings, on radio, or on television, he riveted audiences as few performers have before or since. But his appeal lies as much in the myth that even now surrounds his short life. Though many artists have surpassed him in record sales, his is the standard by which success is measured in country music on virtually every level, even self-destruction.

Hiram Williams (misspelled "Hiriam" on his birth certificate) came from a rural background. His parents were probably strawberry farmers when he was born, although his father, Lon, later worked for logging companies around Georgiana in South Alabama. Hank was born with a spinal deformity, spina bifida, which would later plague him. An ailing Lon entered a Veterans Administration hospital in 1930, and Hank rarely saw him until the early 1940s. Hank's mother, Lillie, moved the family to Greenville and then, in 1937, to Montgomery, Alabama, where she ran a boarding house. Already pursuing music by the mid-1930s, Hank formed the first of his DRIFTING COWBOYS bands around 1938.

He spent the war years shuttling between Montgomery, where he played music, and Mobile, where he worked in the shipyards. In December 1944 he married Audrey Mae Sheppard, and, after the war, he reformed the Drifting Cowboys and became Montgomery's leading hillbilly performer. Drinking impeded his progress, as did a musical style that some considered anachronistic.

In 1946 Nashville music publisher FRED ROSE invited Williams to supply songs for MOLLY O'DAY and recorded him for Sterling Records that December. Public response to those records enabled Rose to place the singer with MGM RECORDS, and his first MGM release, "Move It on Over," hit in the fall of 1947. Eventually Rose secured an opening for his protégé on the relatively new *LOUISIANA HAYRIDE* in Shreveport, beginning in August 1948.

There Williams began performing "Lovesick Blues," a 1920s show tune he had learned from either REX GRIFFIN or EMMETT MILLER. Enthusiastic audience reaction encouraged him to record it after the 1948 musicians' union strike against the record companies ended. It reached #1 in May 1949 and stayed there

*Hank Williams*

sixteen weeks. The success of "Lovesick Blues" and its follow-up, another nonoriginal, called "Wedding Bells," convinced Grand Ole Opry officials to make Williams a member, despite misgivings about his reliability.

The rising young star moved to Nashville in June 1949 and swiftly became one of the biggest names in country music. Increasingly he decided to stand or fall with his own songs, and, after the success of his "Long Gone Lonesome Blues" in the spring of 1950, virtually all of his hits were original compositions.

At the January 1950 session that produced "Long Gone Lonesome Blues," Williams began recording a series of narrations and "talking blues" issued under the pseudonym Luke the Drifter. Most had strong moral messages, making them unsuitable for the jukebox trade, which accounted for more than half of his record sales. There was never any serious attempt to hide Luke the Drifter's identity; it was simply a ploy to keep jukebox distributors from ordering unsuitable records.

The peak years of Hank Williams's career were 1950 and 1951. He was one of country music's most successful touring acts, and, assisted by Fred Rose, his producer, and his band—especially steel guitarist Don Helms—he perfected an identifiable, commercial sound. Every one of his records charted, except for those issued as Luke the Drifter and his religious duets with Audrey. His songs, which had matured greatly since the demos he had submitted to Rose for Molly O'Day, began finding a wider audience than his own recordings of them ever could. Starting with "Honky Tonkin'" in 1949, his material had been covered by pop artists, but it was not until Tony Bennett covered "Cold, Cold Heart" in 1951 that Williams began to be recognized as an important popular songwriter. From that point artists rushed to reinterpret his songs for the pop market. Guy Mitchell, for instance, recorded "I Can't Help It (If I'm Still in Love with You)," and the duo of Frankie Laine and Jo Stafford took "Hey, Good Lookin'" into the pop Top Twenty.

Williams had long wrestled with his drinking problem, but career pressures, marital problems, and crippling spinal pain multiplied his binges during 1951. An unsuccessful spinal operation in December led to a dependence on painkillers. He disbanded his group, and when he started performing again in March 1952 it was with pickup bands. Audrey had ordered him out of the family home shortly after he returned from the hospital, and he moved into a house with Ray Price.

As 1952 wore on, Williams appeared to care less and less about his career. His appearances dwindled, and by June he had stopped work altogether. In August the Grand Ole Opry fired him for missing show dates, and he moved back to Montgomery. Fred Rose negotiated his return to the *Louisiana Hayride* as of September. In October he married Billie Jean Jones Eshliman, a young woman from Shreveport whom he had met in Nashville when she came there with Faron Young. By this point, another girlfriend, Bobbie Jett, was pregnant with his child.

Williams worked in Shreveport from September to December 1952. Most of his bookings were in smaller venues, and his drunkenness was now a serious problem compounded by medication prescribed by a bogus doctor, Toby Marshall. Through it all, however, the artist never seemed to falter in the studio. Even as he played small halls in East Texas, his recording of "Jambalaya" was #1. If anything, his hits increased in magnitude as his bookings diminished.

Just before Christmas 1952 Williams took a leave of absence from the *Hayride* and went to Montgomery to rest. On December 30 he left for two bookings in Charleston, West Virginia, and Canton, Ohio, but died en route. He may have died on December 31, 1952,

in the back seat of his chauffeured Cadillac, but he was pronounced dead early on January 1, 1953, in Oak Hill, West Virginia.

Along with Jimmie Rodgers and Fred Rose, Williams was elected to The Country Music Hall of Fame in 1961. In 2010 he was posthumously awarded a special Pulitzer Prize for his songwriting craftsmanship and his role in making country music a powerful component of American culture. Into the twenty-first century, dozens of artists in many genres have continued to record his songs, and his brief, troubled, but enormously productive life remains a touchstone for veteran and aspiring artists alike. —*Colin Escott*

## Hank Williams Jr.
b. Shreveport, Louisiana, May 26, 1949

For part of his career, Randall Hank Williams wrestled with the knowledge that his lineage had given him his start. He came to realize that to be taken seriously he needed something uniquely his own, and by combining his love for southern rock with his honky-tonk pedigree, he eventually succeeded in establishing his own identity. His success has been such that there are many who only think of Hank Williams as the father of Hank Jr.

Hank Jr. has reinterpreted his father's songs consistently since his first recording sessions, but it has been more interesting to chart the changing way he has handled the emotional baggage of being Hank Williams Jr. That burden has been made more difficult by the fact that Hank Jr. never really knew his father; he was only three when Hank Williams died. (It was Hank Sr. who gave Hank Jr. the nickname Bocephus, reportedly after a ventriloquist's dummy owned by comedian Rod Brasfield.)

Hank Jr. grew up in Nashville. He made his stage debut at age eight, his Grand Ole Opry debut at eleven, and his recording

*Hank Williams Jr.*

debut at fourteen. His career was orchestrated by his mother, Audrey, who saw in Hank Jr. an opportunity to sustain the legend in which she had such a huge financial and personal stake. She signed him with his father's label, MGM RECORDS, and billed him as Hank Williams Jr. The first promotional appearance was scheduled for Canton, Ohio, the town where Hank Sr. was to have performed the day he was pronounced dead.

Fans came in droves to see Hank's son, but they didn't buy the records. Also, by recording from an early age, all of Hank Jr.'s growth as an artist has been done in public. He was manipulated by producers who were mostly trying to get a facsimile of Hank Sr. to double their money—hence a series of records as Luke the Drifter Jr. and albums such as *Songs My Father Left Me*, *The Legend of Hank Williams in Story and Song*, and an album of father–son duets.

Hank Jr. started to assert his independence in the early 1970s. The albums *Living Proof* and *Bocephus* saw him slowly siding with southern rock acts such as the MARSHALL TUCKER BAND and the Allman Brothers. The first clear summation of this direction came with the *Hank Williams Jr. and Friends* album. Its release coincided with what was almost his death, though; he fell from a mountain in Montana on August 8, 1975, and was seriously injured. His face was severely damaged, and he could not perform again until May 1976.

The singles drawn from . . . *And Friends* didn't do well, and Hank Jr. left MGM in 1976 to join ELEKTRA RECORDS in partnership with CURB RECORDS, until WARNER BROS. phased out Elektra's country division in 1983, at which time Williams's albums were released by Warner/Curb. Radio finally responded to his music when he reexamined his honky-tonk roots on "Family Tradition" (a record produced by JIMMY BOWEN, as were all Hank Jr.'s albums from 1980 to 1985). That song did much to establish the image that Hank Jr. wanted for himself, an image he intensified on his next hit, "Whiskey Bent and Hell Bound." He was now the party man living on borrowed time; he was the outlaw, albeit one with a private income. Many of his records were swaggering and self-referential, and they had a character that was unique to Hank Jr. He found a new audience with hits such as "Dixie on My Mind," "All My Rowdy Friends (Are Coming Over Tonight)"—which took CMA's 1985 Music Video of the Year honors—"This Ain't Dallas," "Gonna Go Huntin' Tonight," and "Born to Boogie," the title cut for CMA's 1988 Album of the Year. Hank Jr. now ranked alongside Lynyrd Skynyrd among fans of southern rock, and his music was in fact much closer to rock than to the sounds of the OUTLAW country acts with whom he identified himself in song and in person.

Occasionally Hank Jr. would reveal his deep musicianship; he can play many instruments, including lead guitar and piano, and he has as thorough a knowledge of American roots music as anyone in the business. "Ain't Misbehavin'," a novel slant on the old Fats Waller tune, displayed that knowledge and surprised Hank Jr. by reaching #1 on the country charts. In general, though, he has written his own songs to showcase his party animal persona. His autobiography, *Living Proof*, completed soon after the accident and subsequently filmed for television in 1983 (with former *Waltons* TV star Richard Thomas playing Hank Jr.), showed his reflective, vulnerable side, but he has only occasionally let that seep into his music. "My fans don't want to hear about family values," he told interviewer Jimmy Guterman. "They want to rock." Williams's 1980s rise to stardom culminated in his being named Entertainer of the Year by both the Academy of Country Music (ACM), for the years 1986, 1987, and 1988, and the Country

Music Association (CMA), in 1987 and 1988. Williams reached a new career milestone when he retooled his song "All My Rowdy Friends (Are Coming Over Tonight)" into an Emmy-winning theme song for *Monday Night Football*. The opening line of its chorus ("Are you ready for some football?") has become a familiar American catchphrase. By 1995, he had left Warner Bros. to record solely for Curb Records, an association that ended in March 2010. By his fifties, he began receiving career honors, such as a *CMT Giants* tribute special and a BMI Icon Award, which credited his enduring success and the influence he has had on younger generations of country rockers. —*Colin Escott*

## Hank Williams III
b. Houston, Texas, December 12, 1972

Shelton Williams adopted the stage name Hank Williams III in 1996 when he switched from punk rock to a raging combination of HONKY-TONK, swing, and hard rock. The grandson of HANK WILLIAMS and the first child of HANK WILLIAMS JR. and his second wife, Gwen, Hank III began playing drums and guitar on stage with his father at age twelve. By high school, the Nashville resident shifted to punk rock, touring regionally with the bands Buzzkill and Bedwetter.

In 1996, pressured by a court order to make child support payments, Hank III began performing country songs in BRANSON, MISSOURI. That year, he recorded an album, *Three Hanks: Men with Broken Hearts*, which merged his voice in a trio including his grandfather and father.

From 1999 to 2006, Hank III released three albums of honky-tonk and rock on CURB RECORDS, gaining a passionate underground

*Hank Williams III*

following. His fourth and fifth albums, 2008's *Damn Right, Rebel Proud* and 2010's *Rebel Within,* appeared on a Curb subsidiary, Sidewalk Records. After years of fighting with Curb, Williams secured the 2009 release of a self-titled album by Williams's rock band, Assjack. Williams left Curb in 2010.

Outspoken and controversial, he continues the Williams tradition of writing autobiographical songs while, like his father, striving to combine honky-tonk with the rock music he favored growing up. —*Michael McCall*

## Jett Williams
b. Montgomery, Alabama, January 6, 1953

Singer-songwriter Jett Williams was born five days after her father, HANK WILLIAMS, died. Her stage name is a tribute to her parents, Bobbie Webb Jett and Hank Williams.

After giving birth, Bobbie Jett granted legal custody of her daughter to Hank's mother, Lillybelle "Lillie" Stone, who adopted the baby. Stone died two years later. Jett was given up for adoption and became a ward of the state of Alabama until February 1956, when she was adopted by Wayne and Louise Deupree; they changed her name from Cathy Yvonne Stone to Cathy Louise Deupree, and she was raised by them. Jett received a degree from the University of Alabama in 1975 and began a career as a recreational therapist.

Jett was told she was possibly Hank Williams's daughter on her twenty-first birthday, in 1974, because she was to receive money from Lillie Stone's estate. A prebirth notarized agreement signed by Hank Williams and Bobbie Jett acknowledged Hank as her father, yet she went through legal action from 1984 to 1992 to receive recognition and her share of her father's estate. The legal proceedings culminated in a 1989 Alabama Supreme Court ruling upholding a state court decree that she was "entitled to receive her proportionate share of any proceeds of the estate of her natural father, Hank Williams."

On June 4, 1989, she made her professional debut as a singer. In August of that year she joined with two members of her father's DRIFTING COWBOYS, Don Helms and Jerry Rivers, and formed Jett Williams & the Drifting Cowboys Band. She made her GRAND OLE OPRY debut in a guest appearance on New Year's Eve 1993, the evening of the forty-first anniversary of her father's death.

Jett married her attorney, F. Keith Adkinson, on September 28, 1986, and the couple reside on a farm in Tennessee. Jett's book, *Ain't Nothin' as Sweet as My Baby: The Story of Hank Williams' Lost Daughter* (1990), became a best-seller. —*Barbara Pruett*

## Jody Williams
b. Nashville, Tennessee, November 1, 1955

Born to a family known for boosting country music's fortunes, BMI executive Joseph Driver Williams is a highly respected "song man" who has worked in MUSIC PUBLISHING for all of his professional life. His grandfather, uncle, and father for many years ran the MARTHA WHITE FLOUR COMPANY, longtime sponsor of FLATT & SCRUGGS and the GRAND OLE OPRY. After studying advertising at the University of Denver, he went to work for BMI in 1976. Subsequently he moved to Hat Band Music, Screen-Gems Music, and TREE PUBLISHING COMPANY. He became head of the Nashville office for Dick James Music in 1986 and then returned to BMI in 1987. He left BMI again in 1995 to become president of

the Nashville division of MCA Music Publishing, and under his leadership the company was ASCAP Country Music Publisher of the Year in 1997. In 1999 he formed Jody Williams Music, a joint publishing venture with Sony/ATV Tree, where he discovered, developed, and published JOSH TURNER and published Liz Rose, who cowrote hits with TAYLOR SWIFT. Williams was appointed BMI vice president, writer/publisher relations, Nashville, in May 2006. —*Jay Orr*

## Lawton Williams
b. Troy, Tennessee, July 24, 1922; d. July 26, 2007

Lawton Williams was already a seasoned singer-songwriter when his song "Fraulein" became a mammoth hit for BOBBY HELMS in 1957.

The son of a Tennessee fiddler, Williams began his musical career around Detroit in 1940. He became a military policeman during World War II, and by 1943 he was stationed near Houston. There he bonded with FLOYD TILLMAN, who taught him the rudiments of songwriting. CLIFF BRUNER and LAURA LEE MCBRIDE cut Williams's earliest recorded compositions. Williams appeared regularly on Houston's KTRH and Corpus Christi's KEYS before returning to Michigan in 1947, where he made his first recordings for the Sultan and Fortune labels and broadcast on WKMH–Dearborn. Returning to Texas by 1950, he became a DJ at Fort Worth's KCNC. An association with HANK LOCKLIN yielded Locklin's FOUR STAR recording of Williams's "Paper Face" and won Williams a contract with that label. He would subsequently record for Coral and IMPERIAL before Locklin hit with his "Geisha Girl" on RCA and Helms released "Fraulein" on DECCA, both in 1957. From that point Williams was chiefly a songwriter and churned out additional classics—notably "Farewell Party" (1962), a 1979 hit for GENE WATSON—though he continued to perform and recorded for RCA, MERCURY, and other labels. Williams retired from performing in 1970, but he continued to write, and for a time he co-owned a publishing company with JIM REEVES's widow, Mary. —*Kevin Coffey*

## Lucinda Williams
b. Lake Charles, Louisiana, January 26, 1953

As a songwriter, Lucinda Williams occasionally reached the country music charts, most notably with MARY CHAPIN CARPENTER's version of "Passionate Kisses" and PATTY LOVELESS's 1990 hit "The Night's Too Long." But Williams built a broader reputation as a performer and recording artist whose original songs drew on country, rock, blues, and folk to create her own distinctive style, thereby placing herself among the maverick artists who helped create a template for what became known as AMERICANA music.

Daughter of poet Miller Williams, the singer-songwriter moved through the South and Mexico while growing up, as her father took different university posts. She began performing in Mexico City and AUSTIN, TEXAS, before releasing her debut album, *Ramblin'*, in 1978 on the Smithsonian/Folkways label. Moving to Los Angeles in the early 1980s, she released her breakthrough, self-titled album on Rough Trade Records in 1988.

Williams won a Grammy for Best Country Song of 1993 for "Passionate Kisses," and another Grammy for 1998's Best Contemporary Folk Recording for her album *Car Wheels on a Gravel Road*. After living in Nashville in the 1990s, she moved back to Los Angeles, where her music took on a hard-edged sound on such albums as 2003's *World Without Tears* and 2008's *Little Honey*. —*Michael McCall*

## Tex Williams
b. Ramsey, Illinois, August 23, 1917; d. October 11, 1985

Sollie Paul "Tex" Williams took a well-known traditional style known as the "talking blues," used by everyone from CHRIS BOUCHILLON and WOODY GUTHRIE to the GRAND OLE OPRY's ROBERT LUNN and pop singer Phil Harris, and forever made it a part of WESTERN SWING. Williams grew up in rural Illinois, where his father, a local blacksmith, played OLD-TIME fiddle tunes. A victim of polio, Williams got his start playing guitar and singing over local radio. He went on to perform around Illinois and then in Washington State and California with various groups.

In 1942 he moved to Los Angeles and joined SPADE COOLEY's western swing band as bass player and vocalist; there Venice Pier Ballroom operator FOREMAN PHILLIPS named him "Tex." Williams's smooth singing on Cooley's 1944 OKeh hit "Shame on You" landed Williams a CAPITOL recording contract in 1946. That June, after a growing estrangement, Cooley fired Williams, who took most of Cooley's band with him and regrouped as the Western Caravan. Although Williams scored with "California Polka" in 1946, he needed another hit to keep his contract, and MERLE TRAVIS wrote the talking blues "Smoke! Smoke! Smoke! (That Cigarette)" specifically for him. Released in the spring of 1947, Williams's record soon topped the country and pop charts.

The talking blues became Williams's trademark, and most of his other hit singles followed that style, including "That's What I Like About the West," "Never Trust a Woman," "Suspicion," "Who? Me?," "Talking Boogie," and CARSON ROBISON's "Life Gets

Tee-Jus, Don't It." Unfortunately, these songs eventually stereotyped Williams, obscuring his gifts as a singer. His record sales declined, and he and Capitol parted ways in 1951. Stints with RCA (1952–53) and DECCA (1953–58) proved unproductive.

After disbanding the Caravan in 1957, Williams kept touring and ran a California nightclub until 1965. He recorded LPs for Capitol, LIBERTY, Boone, and other labels, with little success. Though he worked extensively in Nevada and overseas throughout the 1970s and early 1980s, his health declined, and he died in 1985. —*Rich Kienzle*

## Foy Willing
b. Bosque County, Texas, 1915; d. June 24, 1978

Leader of the popular second-tier western vocal group the Riders of the Purple Sage—who took their name from a Zane Grey novel—Foy Willing (born Willingham) began performing as a teen-ager around Waco, Texas. His first instrument was the harmonica, but he became a proficient guitarist and steel guitarist as well.

By 1933 Willing worked a New York radio show for CRAZY WATER CRYSTALS. He returned to Texas in 1935. By decade's end he had joined a cowboy group, Lew Preston & the Men of the Range, at Fort Worth's KFJZ, flagship of the Texas State Network (TSN). Heart problems interrupted his tenure with the band, which moved to Oklahoma City when TSN faltered in 1940, but Willing made his recording debut at the group's 1940–41 OKeh sessions.

Willing relocated to California and in 1943 formed the Riders of the Purple Sage with Al Sloey and EDDIE DEAN's brother, Jimmie, appearing on the HOLLYWOOD BARN DANCE, recording for CAPITOL, and notching a #3 hit with "Texas Blues" in 1944. Willing subsequently recorded for COLUMBIA, DECCA, and Majestic and gained four more Top Twenty hits between 1946 and 1949. The band remained popular on radio and in western films (backing, among others, ROY ROGERS) until Willing disbanded the group in 1952. Willing performed and recorded occasionally over the next quarter-century, making western-film festival appearances until shortly before his death. —*Kevin Coffey*

## Kelly Willis
b. Lawton, Oklahoma, October 1, 1968

A talented singer-songwriter with a sweet vibrato voice, Kelly Willis relocated from Virginia to AUSTIN, TEXAS, with her husband-to-be, drummer Mas Palermo, formed the band Radio Ranch, and began winning recognition in the 1980s. MCA Nashville executive TONY BROWN caught the group's 1989 show at Austin's South by Southwest music festival and signed them to the label.

*Well-Traveled Love* (1990) and *Bang Bang* (1991) featured Willis's distinctively honest, big-voiced delivery and the group's electrified, rock-tinged, Austin-style HONKY-TONK backing. Despite critical praise, neither album sold well, and in 1993 Willis recorded for MCA without her band. Willis and Palermo divorced, and her songwriting continued to shine, but her third album also failed to sell, and the label soon dropped her. Along the way she appeared as an earnest folksinger in the Tim Robbins film *Bob Roberts* (1993).

Later marrying songwriter Bruce Robison, Willis signed with A&M Records in 1996. In that year she released an independent, four-song EP (*Fading Fast*) to radio, but limited demand led to a

*Tex Williams*

Texas-only retail release. The record did give her entrée to the AMERICANA field, an opportunity she has since developed.

Later albums include the Rykodisc collections *What I Deserve* (1998) and *Translated from Love* (2007). —*Clark Parsons*

## The Willis Brothers

James Ulysses Harrod Lyn "Guy" Willis b. Alex, Arkansas, July 5, 1915; d. April 13, 1981
Charles Ray Clayton "Skeeter" Willis b. Coalton, Oklahoma, December 20, 1917; d. January 28, 1976
John Victor "Vic" Willis b. Schulter, Oklahoma, May 31, 1922; d. January 15, 1995

In four decades together, the Willis Brothers cut hit records, worked the GRAND OLE OPRY, and helped make country music history. They were the first musicians to accompany HANK WILLIAMS on disc (1946), and, backing EDDY ARNOLD, they were in the first presentation of Opry stars at Constitution Hall in WASHINGTON, D.C. (1947). Their western-style show took them around the world and onto national radio and television.

Brothers Guy (guitar), Skeeter (fiddle), and Vic (accordion) Willis began performing professionally in 1932 as the Oklahoma Wranglers. Following wartime military service they reunited in 1946, adding bass player Chuck "the Indian" Wright, around whom swirled much good-natured onstage hilarity until his retirement in 1960.

In June 1946 they debuted on the Opry and on WSM's Mutual Network *Checkerboard Jamboree* broadcasts, sponsored by Purina and starring Eddy Arnold and ERNEST TUBB. On December 11, 1946, FRED ROSE recorded four sides by the Wranglers for the Sterling label. Following their session, they accompanied new-comer Hank Williams on his first four recordings, also for Sterling. The group's historic Constitution Hall performance followed the next year. In late 1948 Arnold asked the Wranglers to join his roadshow, where they remained until 1957; they also worked with Arnold in two 1949 western movies, *Feudin' Rhythm* and *Hoedown*. The act ended the 1950s as regulars on the OZARK JUBILEE and the MIDWESTERN HAYRIDE and on Chattanooga and Birmingham TV stations. By now renamed the Willis Brothers, the band returned to Nashville and the Opry in 1960. Although they recorded for MERCURY, Coral, RCA VICTOR, and CMH Records, their success came largely on STARDAY, which they joined that year. Their biggest-selling singles were "Give Me 40 Acres (To Turn This Rig Around)" (1964) and "Bob" (1967).

After Guy died in 1981, Vic formed the Vic Willis Trio and made Opry appearances until his death. He served thirteen years as secretary-treasurer of Nashville's AFM chapter, helmed the AFM's southern conference, and pioneered the creation of the Musicians' Relief Fund. Willis's production company, Custom Jingles, serviced national accounts including beverage companies, banks, and musical instrument manufacturers. —*Paul W. Soelberg*

## Billy Jack Wills

b. Hall County, Texas, February 26, 1926; d. March 2, 1991

WESTERN SWING bandleader, musician, vocalist, and songwriter Billy Jack Wills was the youngest brother of BOB WILLS. Overshadowed much of his career by his older brothers, Billy Jack nevertheless left a legacy of songs and music that attest to his talent. He played bass and drums for brother JOHNNIE LEE WILLS's

band in the early 1940s and, after World War II, for Bob Wills & His Texas Playboys. With the Playboys he contributed superb vocals and compositions on MGM recordings such as "Rock-A-Bye Baby Blues," "Cadillac in Model 'A,'" and "King Without a Queen." But best known are his lyrics to the classic ballads "Faded Love" and "Lilly Dale." In 1949 Billy Jack and TINY MOORE formed a group based at Wills Point Ballroom near Sacramento, California. Until it disbanded in 1954, this progressive western swing outfit experimented with jump blues and the emerging rhythm & blues sound, incorporating a 4/4 beat instead of Bob Wills's usual 2/4 time. With Tiny Moore's tight arrangements and jazzy electric mandolin and Vance Terry's hot steel guitar, Wills and his band members made some superb transcription recordings, which were commercially released on the Western label in the early 1980s. The act also recorded for FOUR STAR and MGM Records. —*Steve Hathaway*

## Bob Wills

b. Kosse, Texas, March 6, 1905; d. May 13, 1975

As bandleader, showman, fiddler, singer, and songwriter, James Robert Wills remains the most famous exponent of WESTERN SWING, which synthesized ragtime, traditional fiddling, New Orleans jazz, blues, Mexican numbers, and big band swing. Wills blended these components into an infectious dance music that was wildly popular in the Southwest and on the West Coast from the 1930s into the 1950s. He achieved his greatest success with his Texas Playboys band while based at KVOO in Tulsa, Oklahoma, between 1934 and 1942 and, later, on the West Coast. Many of his compositions, such as "Faded Love," "Maiden's Prayer," "Take Me Back to Tulsa," and "San Antonio Rose," became country and pop standards.

Wills grew up in a family of fiddle players and in an area famous for African American musicians, including Scott Joplin,

*Bob Wills*

Victoria Spivey, and Blind Lemon Jefferson. From his family, young Jim Rob Wills (as he was then called) learned to play frontier fiddle music; his father had defeated ECK ROBERTSON in fiddle contests on more than one occasion. At age ten Bob Wills played fiddle for his first ranch dance. From African American neighbors and migrant workers he learned blues and jazz, and in his late teens he once rode fifty miles on horseback to see blues legend Bessie Smith.

Wills left the family farm at age seventeen and drifted from job to job across Texas, working in construction and selling insurance during separate stops in Amarillo; preaching in Knox County; barbering in Roy, New Mexico, and in Turkey, Texas; and laboring on several farms in various parts of the state. Whenever possible, he played ranch dances and performed with MEDICINE SHOWS.

In November 1929, after teaming with guitarist Herman Arnspiger, Wills made his first recordings for the BRUNSWICK label, "Gulf Coast Blues" and "Wills Breakdown"; they were never issued and are now presumed lost. In 1930 singer MILTON BROWN and his guitar-playing brother Derwood joined Wills and Arnspiger. In due course they became the Aladdin Lamp Company's "Aladdin Laddies" on WBAP–Fort Worth, and tenor banjoist Sleepy Johnson joined them for dances at the local Crystal Springs pavilion. The five-piece STRINGBAND produced the first glimmerings of what would be called western swing a decade later. In late 1930 W. Lee "PAPPY" O'DANIEL hired the band to promote Burrus Mill's Light Crust Flour on radio, first at tiny KFJZ and soon at WBAP, where the LIGHT CRUST DOUGHBOYS became a favorite.

After the Browns left in September 1932 to form their own outfit, Wills soon exited the Doughboys as well. Taking with him vocalist TOMMY DUNCAN (who had replaced Milton Brown as a Doughboy), Wills formed his own Playboys band and tried Waco for three months before heading to Oklahoma City in early 1934. After a short stint there, Wills and his five musicians arrived in Tulsa on February 9 after being offered a regular KVOO program on a trial basis. A daily 12:30 p.m. spot, sponsored first by CRAZY WATER CRYSTALS and soon after by General Mills, launched Wills as the most popular act in the Southwest. Adding brass, reeds, and drums, he developed a band that by 1940 numbered sixteen members, among them such outstanding players as steel guitarist LEON MCAULIFFE, guitarist ELDON SHAMBLIN, and fiddler JESSE ASHLOCK. The versatile group could play anything from fiddle breakdowns to George Gershwin compositions. On disc, Bob Wills & His Texas Playboys enjoyed their widest acceptance from 1935 to 1947 while recording for the Vocalion, OKeh, AMERICAN RECORD CORPORATION (ARC), and COLUMBIA labels. These recordings sold in the hundreds of thousands, with "San Antonio Rose" probably selling in the millions. On the strength of his radio and recording fame, Wills began making musical westerns in Hollywood in 1940.

A December 1942 induction into the army broke up the Texas Playboys, but on Wills's discharge in 1943 he relocated to Southern California and re-formed the group. There he enjoyed his greatest financial success. Huge crowds at his dances and strong-selling recordings made him one of the nation's highest-paid bandleaders.

After the war Wills gave up most of the ensemble's brass and reeds and relied more on fiddles, guitars, steel guitars, and mandolins. The shift helped him maintain a substantial following into the late 1940s, even as the age of the big bands was fading. Unfortunately for Wills, his accomplished singer Tommy Duncan left the Texas Playboys in 1948 to form his own unit. After leaving Columbia

Records in 1947, Wills recorded for a series of labels: MGM (1947–54), DECCA (1955–57), LIBERTY (1960–63), Longhorn (1964), and Kapp (1965–69).

With the resurging interest in western swing in the late 1950s, Wills returned to Tulsa. The band quickly added a saxophone section and a superb new vocalist, LEON RAUSCH. When the act's bookings concentrated in Las Vegas, Wills moved the group there in late 1959. Tommy Duncan returned briefly (1960–62). By 1967 Wills had disbanded the Texas Playboys. Although he still toured and performed, he did so with house bands and one lone employee, vocalist Gene "Tag" Lambert, who doubled as his driver.

In October 1968 Wills was elected to THE COUNTRY MUSIC HALL OF FAME, but the following May he suffered a stroke that ended his live-performing days. In December 1973 he recorded his final album, *For the Last Time* (United Artists). Other strokes followed, but he held on until May 13, 1975, when pneumonia took his life. Bob Wills & His Texas Playboys were elected to the Rock and Roll Hall of Fame in 1999 in the early influence category. —*Charles R. Townsend*

## Johnnie Lee Wills
b. Jewett, Texas, September 2, 1912; d. October 25, 1984

Diehard BOB WILLS fans tend to look on Johnnie Lee, his younger brother, as the Wills who stayed home in Tulsa and ran a farm club band for Bob's Texas Playboys after they moved to the West Coast. Johnnie Lee indeed started as a tenor banjo player in Bob's mid-1930s band, but he soon emerged as an important WESTERN SWING bandleader in his own right—a longtime fixture on the Tulsa music scene who scored a number of national hits in the 1940s.

The second of four Wills brothers, Johnnie Lee was especially influenced by their father, Uncle John Wills. After touring with Bob for six years, Johnnie Lee started his own band in 1940 and quickly obtained a DECCA recording contract. This resulted in the 1941 hit "Milk Cow Blues," whose arrangement influenced dozens of later versions. Working from their base at KVOO, Johnnie Lee Wills & His Boys featured musicians such as Guy "Cotton" Thompson (fiddle, vocals), Millard Kelso (piano), Lester "Junior" Barnard (electric guitar), and singer LEON HUFF. The band's eclectic repertoire ranged from OLD-TIME fiddle breakdowns to modern country songs. In 1949 Wills signed with the independent label BULLET RECORDS; in 1950 he gained huge novelty hits with "Rag Mop" and "Peter Cotton Tail."

In later years Wills tried his luck with RCA VICTOR, and in the 1960s he made a couple of LPs on the Sims label. By the mid-1960s, though, he broke up his band and operated a successful western wear store and a local rodeo, the Tulsa Stampede. He made a comeback of sorts in the 1970s, when his splendid Flying Fish album *Reunion* (1978) provided a testament to the many excellent sidemen who had passed through his band. —*Charles Wolfe*

## Luke Wills
b. Hall County, Texas, September 10, 1920; d. October 21, 2000

WESTERN SWING bandleader, musician, and vocalist Luther J. Wills was the next-to-youngest brother of BOB WILLS. Luke began his musical career much like his older brothers, accompanying their father, Uncle John Wills, at dances. The first band Luke worked in was his older brother JOHNNIE LEE WILLS's first aggregation, the Rhythmaires, in 1938. Luke played bass, rhythm guitar, or banjo and contributed occasional vocals for his older brothers' bands until Bob's Texas Playboys disbanded in the mid-1960s. Luke's best-known vocal was "Little Star of Heaven." He also appeared in several B-western films with the Texas Playboys. In 1946 he formed his own unit, originally called the Texas Playboys Number 2. Based in Fresno, California, as was Bob Wills, they played the central and northern California areas when Bob Wills & His Texas Playboys were on tour elsewhere. Renamed Luke Wills' Rhythm Busters, Luke's outfit recorded for KING and RCA VICTOR RECORDS. These recordings featured such stellar sidemen as Junior Barnard, Joe Holley, Bobby Bruce, and Cotton Thompson. The band dissolved in 1948. Luke Wills started another short-lived band in 1950, in Oklahoma City. Though he typically limited himself to vocal asides with bands he fronted, both groups were first-rate. —*Steve Hathaway*

## Gretchen Wilson
b. Pocahontas, Illinois, June 26, 1973

Gretchen Wilson became an instant phenomenon with her 2004 debut single, "Redneck Woman." Both the song, a spirited anthem of individuality and working-class pride, and its brash, independent singer offered a counterpoint to the bevy of glamorous female contemporaries populating the country charts. Cowritten by Wilson and John Rich (of BIG & RICH), "Redneck Woman," topped *Billboard*'s Hot Country Singles chart. Her debut album, *Here for the Party*, went to #1, sold more than 5 million copies, and delivered the Top Ten singles "When I Think about Cheatin'," "Homewrecker," and the title cut.

Wilson's humble roots and regional authenticity evoked comparisons with LORETTA LYNN, and she quickly garnered a slew of

*Gretchen Wilson*

awards, including CMA's 2004 Horizon and Female Vocalist of the Year honors, a 2005 Grammy for Best Country Female Vocal Performance, and 2004 ACM kudos for Best New Female Artist and Top Female Vocalist.

Born to a teenage mother and absentee father, Wilson grew up in an Illinois trailer park and was bartending by age fourteen. At fifteen, she dropped out of school in Miami, where her mother and stepfather had moved, and returned to Illinois, where she managed a bar and sang for tips. Later, she led cover bands and moved to Nashville in 1996.

While bartending in Printers' Alley, Wilson met MuzikMafia cofounder Rich and joined the fledgling cooperative. She pitched herself to record labels, but without success until she had an epiphany while songwriting. Realizing she wasn't "the Barbie-doll type," Wilson decided to celebrate her roots. The result was "Redneck Woman," and SONY MUSIC's Epic label soon signed her.

Wilson's follow-up albums *All Jacked Up* (2005) and *One of the Boys* (2007) each peaked at #1 but failed to recapture the radio airplay and critical success of her debut CD. Her sales declined, and she and Sony parted ways in 2009. Wilson created her own label, Redneck Records, for her fourth album, *I Got Your Country Right Here* (2010). —*Tina Wright*

## Norro Wilson
b. Scottsville, Kentucky, April 4, 1938

Norris D. "Norro" Wilson has been involved in the music business since 1956, whether as a performer, songwriter, producer, A&R executive, or publisher. During his long Nashville tenure he has penned hits for GEORGE JONES, TAMMY WYNETTE, CHARLIE RICH, and CHARLEY PRIDE while producing artists including CHET ATKINS, KEITH WHITLEY, JOHN ANDERSON, MICKEY GILLEY, SAMMY KERSHAW, KENNY CHESNEY, and SARA EVANS.

While in high school, Wilson and three friends formed a barbershop quartet and won a local Kentucky contest. Frequent family trips to Nashville for all-night gospel singings led to a gig as tenor for the Southlanders Quartet. Wilson toured with that group until 1960 and then toured with future publishing magnate Don Gant in a duo. In 1967 Wilson began a fourteen-year stint as a songplugger with AL GALLICO Music. By 1970 Wilson was writing songs for Gallico and receiving the first of many BMI airplay awards (for the Tammy Wynette hit "I'll See Him Through").

Wilson kept connecting as a songwriter, scoring such #1 hits as "The Most Beautiful Girl" (1973) and "A Very Special Love Song" (1974), both recorded by Charlie Rich; "He Loves Me All the Way" (1970) and "Another Lonely Song" (1973–74) for Tammy Wynette; "The Grand Tour" (1974) and "The Door" (1974–75) for George Jones; and Charley Pride's "Never Been So Loved (in All My Life)" (1981) and "Night Games" (1983).

Although Wilson had minor hits as a recording artist—his biggest record was the Top Twenty "Do It to Someone You Love" (MERCURY, 1970)—he gave up performing in 1977, two years after settling into an A&R position with WARNER BROS RECORDS.

Wilson moved to RCA's A&R department in 1982 and then became CEO for Merit Music in 1987. When Merit was sold in 1990, he started Norro Productions and quickly landed Sammy Kershaw as a client. Wilson and BUDDY CANNON produced albums for artists such as George Jones and Kenny Chesney, and together they formed Bud Ro Productions in 1998. Since then Wilson has produced successful albums for Chely Wright, Sara Evans, and JOHN MICHAEL MONTGOMERY, in addition to top-selling albums for Chesney. Wilson was elected to the NASHVILLE SONGWRITERS HALL OF FAME in 1996. —*Michael Hight*

## Chubby Wise
b. Lake City, Florida, October 2, 1915; d. January 6, 1996

For more than a half century, Robert Russell Wise built a reputation as one of country music's best fiddlers. He began honing his skills as a youth, although he first learned the guitar. By his early twenties, Wise had become a regular performer on the Jacksonville, Florida, club scene and an associate of Ervin Rouse, from whom he apparently learned the fiddle classic "Orange Blossom Special." In 1938 Wise joined a WESTERN SWING band, the Jubilee Hillbillies, and came to Nashville in the mid-1940s to work with BILL MONROE at the GRAND OLE OPRY and on the road.

His main years with Monroe's Blue Grass Boys (1946–48) —including fiddling on all of Monroe's seminal COLUMBIA releases (1945–49)—helped make Wise a legend on his instrument. He also made recordings with CLYDE MOODY, including "Shenandoah Waltz," on which he and Moody share composer credit. In February 1948 Wise and Moody went to Arlington, Virginia, to perform on shows produced by CONNIE B. GAY at WARL. By 1949, however, Wise rejoined Monroe's band. In 1950 Wise left again and fiddled briefly with THE YORK BROTHERS and FLATT & SCRUGGS, and for Connie B. Gay. In 1954 he began a sixteen-year tenure with HANK SNOW's Rainbow Ranch Boys. In addition to many of Snow's RCA VICTOR sessions, Wise recorded with Snow's band for STARDAY, recorded an instrumental album on his own, and backed such performers as HYLO BROWN and MAC WISEMAN in the studio.

In 1970 Wise left Snow and went solo as a freelance fiddler. Having gained recognition through a recording of "Maiden's Prayer" for the Houston-based Stoneway label, the veteran musician earned a living as a guest fiddler at Texas dances. Through the 1970s Wise cut a string of albums for Stoneway and appeared at numerous BLUEGRASS festivals. In 1984 he returned to Florida with some intention of retiring but remained active. Into the 1990s, Wise maintained a solid schedule of bookings and recorded two CDs for Pinecastle before his death from heart failure. —*Ivan M. Tribe*

## Craig Wiseman
b. Selma, Alabama, August 4, 1963

Craig Wiseman's mastery of modern country song craft has placed him among the genre's most rewarded songwriters of the 1990s and 2000s. Raised in Hattiesburg, Mississippi, Craig Michael Wiseman lost his father, a pilot whose plane went unrecovered, at age eleven. Wiseman found solace in music and soon began writing songs and playing drums. He performed in bar bands around Hattiesburg before moving to Nashville in 1985. His first songwriting success came in 1989 when ROY ORBISON recorded "The Only One" for his final studio album.

Wiseman scored his first #1 hit in 1994 with "If the Good Die Young," recorded by TRACY LAWRENCE. Wiseman's songs consistently have appeared on the charts ever since. He supplied TIM MCGRAW with "Everywhere," "The Cowboy in Me," "Where the Green Grass Grows," and the 2004 blockbuster "Live Like You Were Dying," which won CMA Song of the Year, ACM Song of the Year, and a Grammy for Best Country Song. Wiseman wrote KENNY CHESNEY's "She's Got It All," "The Good Stuff," "Young,"

and "Summertime"; BROOKS & DUNN's "Believe"; and many other hits. Wiseman was named ASCAP's top country songwriter in 2003, 2005, and 2007. He starred in the GAC series *The Hitmen of Music Row*. —*Michael Gray*

## Mac Wiseman
b. Crimora, Virginia, May 23, 1925

As a popular BLUEGRASS vocalist noted for his gentlemanly manner and clear tenor voice, Malcolm B. "Mac" Wiseman is perhaps best known for such DOT recordings as "Shackles and Chains," "Jimmie Brown the Newsboy," "I'll Be All Smiles Tonight," "I Wonder How the Old Folks Are at Home," "'Tis Sweet to Be Remembered," and "Love Letters in the Sand." In the 1950s and beyond, these and other songs established his reputation as "The Voice with a Heart." But the versatile singer has played many roles in country music, including stints as a sideman with FLATT & SCRUGGS and BILL MONROE, as Dot's country A&R director on the West Coast and in Nashville (1957–61), as CMA's founding secretary (1958), as manager of the *WWVA JAMBOREE* (1966–70), and as host of his own annual bluegrass festival at Renfro Valley, Kentucky (1970–83).

Wiseman grew up in Virginia's Shenandoah Valley and made his first public performances in the late 1930s, while still in high school, singing at WSVA in Harrisonburg, Virginia. A teenage bout with polio left him with a limp, but the National Foundation for Polio offered him a scholarship that helped him enter the Conservatory of Music in Dayton, Virginia. There he studied piano, music theory, and radio broadcasting.

Wiseman returned briefly to WSVA before joining MOLLY O'DAY in Knoxville, Tennessee, in 1946 as a featured vocalist and upright bass player on her radio show. He played bass on her first recordings for COLUMBIA RECORDS in 1946.

Wiseman left O'Day's group in 1947 and performed that spring over WCYB in Bristol, Virginia. The next year, Lester Flatt also joined the station, starting a friendship that led to Wiseman's becoming one of the original members of Flatt & Scruggs's Foggy Mountain Boys in 1948 and to three early-1970s albums pairing Flatt and Wiseman—*Lester 'N' Mac, On the Southbound*, and *Over the Hills to the Poorhouse*—all for RCA RECORDS.

In between, Wiseman was briefly a member of Bill Monroe's Blue Grass Boys (1949) and a longtime recording artist for Dot Records (1951–63). At various points his Country Boys band included such stellar musicians as Eddie Adcock and Scott Stoneman. Wiseman also starred on the *OLD DOMINION BARN DANCE* in Richmond, Virginia (1953–56). From the mid-1960s he has been a favorite on the bluegrass festival circuit. He has served as an officer of Nashville's chapter of the AFM and has also served as a board member for ROPE.

In addition to his Dot and RCA output, Wiseman has recorded for CAPITOL, MGM, Churchill, and CMH. A highlight among albums released since 2000 is his 2007 collection *Standard Songs for Average People*, recorded with singer-songwriter JOHN PRINE for Prine's Oh Boy label.

Wiseman was elected to the IBMA Hall of Fame in 1993. Widely respected as a balladeer and folksong interpreter, he continues to influence younger musicians in his role as a bluegrass elder statesman. —*Don Rhodes*

## WLS (see *National Barn Dance*)

## Da Costa Woltz (*see* Da Costa Woltz's Southern Broadcasters, under D)

## Lee Ann Womack
b. Jacksonville, Texas, August 19, 1966

Lee Ann Womack emerged as a rare tradition-leaning artist amid the contemporary country boom of the 1990s. Although she occasionally recorded pop-influenced material—such as 2000's massive crossover hit "I Hope You Dance"—Womack continually has sung effectively about familiar themes, such as cheating and drinking, while emphasizing steel guitars and fiddles in many of her arrangements.

The daughter of a Texas disc jockey, Womack interned at MCA RECORDS while studying at Nashville's Belmont University. She later signed with DECCA RECORDS, an MCA subsidiary, in 1996. Her first single, "Never Again, Again," released in 1997, drew the attention of traditionalists and critics. Her second single, "The Fool," reached *Billboard*'s Top Five, and ACM named Womack its Top New Female Vocalist for 1997. When Decca closed, Womack was moved to the larger MCA Nashville.

Her second album, 1998's *Some Things I Know,* featured two #2 singles, "A Little Past Little Rock" and "I'll Think of a Reason Later." *I Hope You Dance* (2000) made her a national star, with the Grammy Award–winning title song becoming her first #1 country hit and reaching #14 on *Billboard*'s all-genre Hot 100 chart. She was CMA's 2001 Female Vocalist of the Year.

*Something Worth Leaving Behind* (2002) displayed even stronger pop influences but was received poorly by critics and didn't sell well. That same year, Womack joined WILLIE NELSON on a duet hit, "Mendocino County Line," which snagged a Grammy for Best Country Collaboration with Vocals.

*Lee Ann Womack*

Womack returned to a more traditional sound on 2005's *There's More Where That Came From,* which yielded the hit "I May Hate Myself in the Morning." These earned her 2005 CMA honors for Album and Single of the Year, respectively. *Call Me Crazy* (2008), including the song "Last Call," followed a similar approach. Both albums found Womack fashioning a mature sound that blended traditional and contemporary elements in fresh ways. —*Michael McCall*

## Del Wood
b. Nashville, Tennessee, February 22, 1920; d. October 3, 1989

From 1953 to 1989 Del Wood was a fixture at the GRAND OLE OPRY, playing rollicking ragtime piano instrumentals. She was also one of the few female instrumentalists to win fame in country music.

Polly Adelaide Hendricks began playing piano at age five and gained early experience demonstrating songs in the sheet music sections of Nashville department stores. She had been a staff pianist at Bowling Green, Kentucky, station WLBJ when she made her career record for the Nashville-based TENNESSEE label. "Mine All Mine" was a potential A side, and L. Wolfe Gilbert's minstrel tune "Down Yonder" (popularized in 1921 by Ernest Hare & Billy Jones and again by GID TANNER in the middle 1930s) was the flip side. As it happened, the latter, played in Wood's trademark ragtime style, hit first on the pop charts, on August 24, 1951, peaking at #6, and then became a #5 country single. Selling an estimated 3 million copies, the hit made Wood the first female instrumentalist to enjoy a million-seller. Her gender-neutral stage name—a shortening of her married name, Adelaide Hazelwood—may have helped her avoid the prejudice that many male radio programmers displayed against distaff artists.

Wood joined WSM's Grand Ole Opry on November 13, 1953. Recording more than sixty singles and twenty-five albums for major labels—RCA, DECCA, MERCURY, and COLUMBIA—she earned the sobriquets Queen of Ragtime Piano and Queen of the Ivories. The first female board member of Nashville's chapter of the AFM, she was also a board member of AFTRA's Nashville chapter and the fraternal organization ROPE. She made a cameo appearance performing in DOLLY PARTON's 1984 film *Rhinestone.* JERRY LEE LEWIS has credited Wood's piano style as an influence. Wood remained a member of the Opry until the end of her life. —*Walt Trott*

## Smokey Wood (*see* The Modern Mountaineers)

## Bill Woods
b. Denison, Texas, May 12, 1924; d. April 30, 2000

Known as the father of the BAKERSFIELD sound, Bill Woods moved from Texas to California with his family at age sixteen. As a musician he toured with BOB WILLS & His Texas Playboys and then with TOMMY DUNCAN after Duncan left Wills's band. Woods also toured with JIMMIE DAVIS. In 1950 Woods began a stint as the leader of the Orange Blossom Playboys, the house band at the Blackboard, a club that would become one of Bakersfield's major honky-tonks. There, Woods hired BUCK OWENS and, later, MERLE HAGGARD as band members, playing an important role in the careers of both stars. Woods increased his influence on the local country scene as a disc jockey on radio station KERN. He recorded for Modern Records in 1949, and in the 1950s he recorded for a variety of small labels, some of which he owned. He was also active as a West Coast session musician, often backing such artists as JEAN SHEPARD in the studio. Woods was a regular on Bakersfield's KERO-TV show *Cousin Herb Henson's Trading Post*, which began on September 26, 1953. Woods later recorded for CAPITOL and remained active in Bakersfield country music for a number of years, managing several acts and producing TV shows. —*Don Cusic*

## Sheb Wooley
b. Erick, Oklahoma, April 10, 1921; d. September 16, 2003

Shelby F. Wooley was equally well known as an actor and as a recording artist. His most famous musical creations were humorous: "The Purple People Eater" (#1 pop, 1958) and "That's My Pa" (#1 country, 1962). Wooley's humorous alter ego, Ben Colder, first hit the charts with "Almost Persuaded, Number 2" (#6, 1966). In 1968 Ben Colder won CMA's Comedian of the Year Award.

As a youngster in Oklahoma, Wooley learned to ride horses and worked in a few rodeos. That experience served him well in Hollywood, where he made more than sixty films, many of them westerns, beginning with *Rocky Mountain* (1950) and including the award-winning *High Noon* (1954). He also appeared in *Giant* (1955) and *Hoosiers* (1986). He costarred as Pete Nolan in the popular *Rawhide* network TV series.

As an artist Wooley recorded for BULLET RECORDS (1946) and the Bluebonnet label (1947). He signed with MGM RECORDS in 1948, remaining until 1973. As a songwriter Wooley penned "Too Young to Tango," a Top Ten country single for teenager Sunshine Ruby (#4, 1953), and "Are You Satisfied," a pop success (#11, 1956) for RUSTY DRAPER. Wooley also wrote the *HEE HAW* theme.

Wooley remained active into the 1990s through his recordings (some of them marketed on TV and the Internet), occasional film work, and personal appearances. —*Walt Trott*

## Glenn Worf
b. Dayton, Ohio, January 24, 1954

Top-tier bassist Glenn Worf began playing the instrument at age thirteen after a memorable family vacation to Texas, where he saw a musical group and felt the bass guitar rumbling in his stomach. After earning a degree in music from the University of Wisconsin–Eau Claire, he breezed through an endless array of lounges in a number of rock, blues, and country bands. In one group that played original material, he discovered the joy of creating his own parts, so in 1979 he decided to try his luck on the Nashville session scene.

After many all-night club gigs and countless demo sessions, Worf eventually landed a master session gig for FOSTER & LLOYD's first album, in 1987. When he was hired to play on Kevin Welch's debut album, producers in town discovered an edginess in Worf's playing that got him hired for recordings by BROOKS & DUNN, GEORGE JONES, WILLIE NELSON, GEORGE STRAIT, FAITH HILL, and TOBY KEITH, among many more.

In addition, Worf recorded two albums as part of the BlueBloods, for which he wrote a number of songs with Mike Henderson, leader of this blues band. Worf has also appeared and recorded frequently with stellar rock guitarist Mark Knopfler.

As of 2011, Worf had won ACM's Bass Player of the Year award thirteen times. —*Michael Hight*

## Darryl Worley
b. Pyburn, Tennessee, October 31, 1964

In the wake of the terrorist attacks of September 11, 2001, Darryl Wade Worley's patriotic anthem "Have You Forgotten?" voiced support for the George W. Bush administration's "War on Terror." Cowritten by Worley and Wynn Varble after traveling with the USO to Afghanistan, the song remained at #1 on the country charts for seven weeks in 2003, crossing over to the pop charts as well.

"Have You Forgotten?" wasn't Worley's first taste of success, though. As a singer-songwriter in the NEW TRADITIONALISM country mold, Worley signed with DREAMWORKS RECORDS in 1999 and released a debut album, *Hard Rain Don't Last*, that yielded three Top Twenty songs. A second album, *I Miss My Friend*, topped the country album charts, and the title track became Worley's first #1 hit. After radio embraced "Have You Forgotten?" DreamWorks quickly issued a new album by the same title, which also reached #1 and included songs from his previous albums. Worley's 2004 self-titled album featured his third #1 hit, "Awful Beautiful Life."

With the closing of DreamWorks in 2005, Worley went on to record *Here and Now* (2006) for 903 Music and *Sounds Like Life* (2009) for JAMES STROUD's Stroudivarious label. —*Scott Anderson*

## Paul Worley
b. Nashville, Tennessee, February 16, 1950

Paul N. Worley started in country music as a session guitarist, but over time he asserted himself as a top record producer and music executive especially adept at developing talent. Worley has had a hand in producing successful albums by a score of country stars, including BIG & RICH, the DESERT ROSE BAND, DIXIE CHICKS, SARA EVANS, LADY ANTEBELLUM, MARTINA MCBRIDE, the NITTY GRITTY DIRT BAND, COLLIN RAYE, and PAM TILLIS.

Encouraged by his parents, Worley learned guitar at age thirteen, and while studying philosophy at Vanderbilt University he gave guitar lessons at a nearby music store. After graduation Worley toured as a member of Just Friends, a rock band briefly signed to COLUMBIA RECORDS.

By the mid-1970s Worley became an in-demand session guitarist, playing on recordings by JOHN ANDERSON, GLEN CAMPBELL, REBA MCENTIRE, MICHAEL MARTIN MURPHEY, ANNE MURRAY, EDDY RAVEN, and HANK WILLIAMS JR. In 1981 Worley had his first hit as a producer, GARY MORRIS's "Headed for a Heartache." From there Worley evolved into one of country music's most productive producers; his hits included HIGHWAY 101's "Somewhere Tonight," Pam Tillis's "Don't Tell Me What To Do," Martina McBride's "Independence Day," Collin Raye's "Little Rock," Dixie Chicks' "There's Your Trouble," Sara Evans's "Born to Fly," Cyndi Thomson's "What I Really Meant to Say," Big & Rich's "Save a Horse (Ride a Cowboy)," The Wreckers' "Leave the Pieces," and Lady Antebellum's "Need You Now."

Besides producing, Worley has worked in several executive posts. In 1989 he became vice president of creative services at SONY/TREE PUBLISHING, where he specialized in developing songwriter-artists, helping to advance the careers of BROOKS &

DUNN and TRAVIS TRITT, among others. In late 1993 Worley moved to SONY MUSIC's Nashville record division as executive vice president for the COLUMBIA and EPIC labels, where he nurtured the careers of MARY CHAPIN CARPENTER, PATTY LOVELESS, Collin Raye, and RICK TREVINO. In 2002 he assumed the role of chief creative officer at WARNER BROS., where he signed Big & Rich, Cowboy Troy, James Otto, The Wreckers, and others. In 2004 Worley founded Skyline Music Publishing with several partners. —*Clark Parsons*

## Mark Wright
b. Fayetteville, Arkansas, September 21, 1957

Since the 1980s Mark Wright has been a leading force in country music as a songwriter, producer, and record label executive.

The son of a Baptist minister of music, Wright began getting songs recorded while still a music business student at Nashville's Belmont University. His cowriting credits include STEVE WARINER's "Why Goodbye," VERN GOSDIN's and GEORGE STRAIT's "Today My World Slipped Away," the MICKEY GILLEY/CHARLY McCLAIN duet "Paradise Tonight," ALABAMA's "Take a Little Trip," and the OAK RIDGE BOYS' "Lucky Moon." Wright also penned KENNY ROGERS's "I Prefer the Moonlight," EARL THOMAS CONLEY's "Nobody Falls Like a Fool," EDDIE RABBITT's "Repetitive Regret," and MARK CHESNUTT's "Blame It on Texas," "Your Love Is a Miracle," and "Goin' Through the Big D."

After joining RCA RECORDS in 1984 as an A&R manager, Wright established himself in the recording studio as coproducer of CLINT BLACK's multiplatinum debut album, *Killin' Time* (1989). In the early 1990s, as an independent producer, he began an association with MCA RECORDS, shaping hits for GARY ALLAN, Mark Chesnutt, and LEE ANN WOMACK, including Womack's Grammy-winning "I Hope You Dance."

In 1994 Wright became senior vice president of DECCA RECORDS, after Universal Music Group revived the label. When UMG folded Decca back into MCA RECORDS in 1999, Wright was promoted to the position of MCA executive vice president; in this role he signed and began producing JOSH TURNER. In June 2003 Wright was hired as executive vice president of SONY MUSIC, where he signed GRETCHEN WILSON and produced her first two albums. In 2006 he became president of UNIVERSAL RECORDS SOUTH; he remained the top executive after December 2009, when the label merged with Show Dog Records to become Show Dog–Universal. —*Brian Mansfield*

## WSM
established in Nashville, Tennessee, October 5, 1925

Nashville radio station WSM has long played a significant role in country music history and in American radio broadcasting. From the mid-1930s into the 1950s, the station originated many programs for various national networks, and in the 1940s WSM employees provided the technology and expertise that, along with the station's large pool of musical talent, nurtured the city's recording industry. Moreover, WSM executives such as JACK STAPP and JIM DENNY went on to head prominent music enterprises. As its early sobriquet, "The Air Castle of the South," suggests, the station has been a southern institution, and its far-reaching signal has made it a powerful presence in the lives of generations of listeners across much of the United States.

WSM was not the first commercial radio station in Nashville. This honor goes to WDAD, which operated out of a local radio-parts store and signed on a month before WSM did. WSM had its formal grand opening on Monday, October 5, 1925; its call letters stood for "We Shield Millions," motto of the station's owners, the National Life and Accident Insurance Company. National Life executive Edwin Craig, son of National Life cofounder C. A. Craig, pressured the National Life board to establish a radio station, and a state-of-the-art studio was installed on the fifth floor of the newly completed National Life headquarters at Seventh Avenue North and Union Street in downtown Nashville.

Although clearly intended to boost sales of National Life insurance policies, most early programming was aimed at Nashville's upper- and middle-class listeners and their counterparts elsewhere. On the inaugural program there was not a note of the country or folk music that would become so closely associated with the station. On November 9, 1925, however, GEORGE D. HAY became radio director of the station and quickly started the show soon known as the GRAND OLE OPRY.

WSM began broadcasting at 1,000 watts of power—then stronger than 85 percent of U.S. stations. In those days of uncluttered airwaves, radio signals could carry for hundreds of miles, and WSM started receiving letters from as far away as Iowa and Puerto Rico. One of the station's early favorites was a dance band led by Francis Craig, also of the National Life Craigs; it would remain a fixture on WSM for the next three decades and in 1947 would enjoy a huge national hit with "Near You," recorded in a WSM studio.

By 1927, with its power increased to 5,000 watts, WSM had affiliated with the newly organized NBC network, bringing many network productions to the station's broadcast area; only on Saturday nights did WSM preempt network fare for its barn dance show. (The exception was the wildly popular *Amos and Andy* series, for which the station interrupted the Opry broadcast for

*Radio station WSM's tower, 1930s*

thirty minutes.) By 1933 WSM had organized a booking service for its increasing number of professional entertainers, some of whom worked daytime country and pop programs as station staff as well as working the Opry. VITO PELLETTIERI came aboard as music librarian to build up WSM's music files and keep track of performing rights licensing. By 1934 the station secured one of forty federal "clear channel" licenses, which meant that no other station in the country could broadcast at 650 kilocycles. The station's superb technology, symbolized by its giant new free-standing tower (which, after its 1932 completion, became the nation's tallest, and a favorite of tourist postcards), allowed "remote" broadcasts of network quality. Meanwhile, building on precedents set by HARRY STONE, who became general manager in 1932, additional executives, including Harry's brother DAVID STONE and, from 1939, Jack Stapp, helped recruit additional stars who could attract new sponsors.

WSM began regular network program originations in 1935, and by the end of World War II the station was becoming a major supplier of shows to NBC, Mutual, and CBS and to networks assembled by particular sponsors. One of the best of these last was The Lion Oil Company's *Sunday Down South*, a musical variety show built around the excellent big band of Beasley Smith—essentially the station's studio orchestra for years. Running into the 1950s, the program eventually had a cast of sixty and served as a springboard for nationally known pop vocalists Kitty Kallen and Snooky Lanson. Other WSM programs helped launch pop singers Dinah Shore and Phil Harris and operatic tenor James Melton.

When WSM celebrated its silver anniversary in 1950, it was a huge operation, with as many as 200 professional entertainers on the payroll (sixty-six of whom were on the Opry). Its writing staff was churning out dozens of scripts, and WSM was sending seventeen weekly programs to the networks, including children's shows, such as *Wormwood Forest* (cowritten by Tom Tichenor), and southern-flavored variety shows, such as *Riverboat Revels*.

At the same time, though, National Life recognized the monumental changes radio faced and established WSM-TV in 1950. Television was making traditional radio programming obsolete, and radio was becoming home to a new type of entertainer: the disc jockey. Therefore, in 1952 WSM sponsored the nation's first annual country DJ CONVENTION as part of the radio station's birthday anniversary festivities, attended by about a hundred DJs. During the next two decades, recorded music replaced live performers, and the Opry became WSM's last major live show. In 1968 WSM-FM made its debut on a permanent basis, and in 1972, in conjunction with CMA, WSM-AM decided to establish Fan Fair (now the CMA MUSIC FESTIVAL) to accommodate the increasing hordes of fans who were attending the country music trade show that had grown up around the station's birthday celebration.

A decade later, WSM's association with country music grew stronger still when, together with the Associated Press, it created the Music Country Radio Network via satellite. By 1982 National Life sold WSM-TV (renamed WSMV) to Gillette Broadcasting. In that same year, the Texas-based American General Insurance Company purchased National Life and its entertainment properties (WSM radio, OPRYLAND, the Grand Ole Opry, and Opryland Productions). In 1983 the Oklahoma-based GAYLORD Broadcasting Company acquired the latter operations, together with TNN: THE NASHVILLE NETWORK (recently evolved from Opryland Productions), further signaling the end of WSM's local ownership. In October 1997 WSM ended its long affiliation with NBC,

signing with the ABC radio network. The giant Cumulus group bought WSM-FM in 2003.

In September 1979, WSM-AM adopted an all-country format, and today the station features both classic and current country hits, along with a sprinkling of recordings by AMERICANA artists. (WSM-FM, stressing current hits, has been all-country since 1983.) In its terrestrial and online broadcasts, WSM-AM continues to carry the Grand Ole Opry's various weekday and weekend broadcasts as well as the long-running MIDNITE JAMBOREE and, since 2009, *Music City Roots*, a program featuring country and Americana acts and broadcast live from Nashville's Loveless Barn.

Sirius Satellite Radio began carrying WSM programs in 2002 but stopped simulcasting them in September 2006. In October 2007, rival XM Satellite radio started broadcasting "encore" (or delayed) Opry performances. As of 2011, the merged SiriusXM operation was featuring live Friday and Saturday Opry shows. —*Charles Wolfe*

## Roy Wunsch
b. St. Louis, Missouri, June 23, 1945

During the 1980s and 1990s marketing expert Roy Wunsch helmed the Nashville division of the CBS/Sony Records joint venture and, later, Imprint Records. Wunsch began his music career with a summer job at CBS Records' St. Louis Distribution Center and rapidly advanced through the label's local and regional marketing departments. In 1975 he was promoted to national promotion and sales manager for EPIC RECORDS' Nashville division. He was named vice president of marketing in 1981, second in command of the Nashville division in 1985, and senior vice president and general manager of Nashville operations in 1988, shortly after the Japanese firm SONY MUSIC ENTERTAINMENT acquired CBS Records (including the COLUMBIA and Epic labels). In 1990 Wunsch became the Nashville division's first-ever president, a position he held until 1993. Among the artists signed during his Sony years were JOE DIFFIE, COLLIN RAYE, PATTY LOVELESS, DOUG STONE, and RICK TREVINO.

In July 1995, with High Five Entertainment founder Bud Schaetzle, Wunsch cofounded Imprint Records (originally named Veritas Music Entertainment). Wunsch served as chairman and CEO, while Schaetzle served as president. Imprint artists included Al Anderson, Charlie Major, Gretchen Peters, Ryan Reynolds, Jeff Wood, and Bob Woodruff. The label ceased releasing product in June 1997 and is now defunct. —*Marjie McGraw*

## WWVA Jamboree (Jamboree U.S.A.)
established in Wheeling, West Virginia, January 7, 1933

Under a variety of names—most recently *Jamboree U.S.A.*—the live-audience country music show from radio station WWVA in Wheeling, West Virginia, had a record for longevity second only to the GRAND OLE OPRY. Local musicians appeared on the station from the time it went on the air in 1926, but the *Jamboree* as a stage program dates from January 7, 1933, at the Capitol Theater in downtown Wheeling. Soon the broadcast site moved to the Wheeling Market Auditorium.

Early stars included the trio of Cap, Andy, & Flip; Silver Yodelin' Bill Jones; the Tweedy Brothers; COUSIN EMMY; GRANDPA JONES; and, from 1937, DOC WILLIAMS and Big Slim the Lone

WWVA Jamboree *cast*

Cowboy (Harry McAuliffe). George Smith, WWVA's program director, was the guiding force in making the *Jamboree* a venerated institution. During its peak years, WWVA was one of several stations owned by Storer Broadcasting. On October 8, 1942, WWVA became a 50,000-watt outlet, helping to increase the *Jamboree*'s popularity in the Northeast and in eastern Canada.

From December 12, 1942, to July 13, 1946, wartime conditions forced the station to curtail the live-audience show, although the *Jamboree* continued as a studio program. It reopened to fans in the Virginia Theater and over the next decade reached its peak in terms of overall influence. New stars, such as HAWKSHAW HAWKINS, WILMA LEE & STONEY COOPER, Roy Scott, and Lee Moore, who also gained renown as the station's all-night DJ, took their places beside veterans, such as Williams and Big Slim. The program also showcased several popular female performers, including CHICKIE WILLIAMS, Betty Cody (LONE PINE & BETTY CODY), Milly Wayne, and Bonnie Baldwin, as well as popular rustic comics, typified by Hiram Hayseed (W. H. Godwin) and Crazy Elmer (Anthony Slater). For a time in the mid-1950s, a portion of the *Jamboree* was carried by the CBS network.

The spread of TV ownership and the rock & roll surge diminished the program's prestige, but the show survived even after the demise of the Virginia Theater in 1962. The *Jamboree* moved to the Rex Theater (1962–66) and to the Wheeling Island Exhibition Center (1966–69) before returning in 1969 to its original home, the Capitol Theater (renamed Capitol Music Hall). It continued to thrive under the name *Jamboree U.S.A.* until December 2005.

Although the 1969 move probably helped the *Jamboree* avoid the fate of most live radio barn dances, some of its older traditions and spontaneity seem to have suffered. Increasingly, guest stars from Nashville became central attractions, and *Jamboree* regulars such as Darnell Miller and Junior Norman were relegated to the status of opening acts. Since 2005, a show using the name "Wheeling Jamboree" has been staged for live audiences in various locales around the city but not always for radio broadcast. —*Ivan M. Tribe*

## Tammy Wynette
b. Itawamba County, Mississippi, May 5, 1942; d. April 6, 1998

In the late-1960s and early 1970s a trio of unique, creative women dominated the ranks of female country stars: LORETTA LYNN, DOLLY PARTON, and Tammy Wynette. As stylists and songwriters, they each voiced women's perspectives with an autobiographical slant that made their lives as much an object of audience interest as their music.

Like Lynn and Parton, Wynette grew up in a hardscrabble household in the rural South, but she had big-city dreams. Born Virginia Wynette Pugh, she was raised by her cotton-farming grandparents. Her father, William Hollice Pugh, died of a brain tumor when she was less than a year old; he left her a recording of himself and a musical legacy, having tried (unsuccessfully) to escape sharecropping through professional singing. Her mother, Mildred, left to work in a Memphis defense plant during World War II.

Wynette picked cotton, played her father's instruments, took music lessons, and absorbed the music of gospel quartets who crisscrossed Mississippi and Alabama during the late-1940s and early 1950s. With two friends she performed on a local gospel radio show as Wynette, Linda, and Imogene.

Wynette married Euple Byrd a month before finishing high school in 1959. They had two children, and, with no steady employment, Byrd moved the family from place to place. Wynette went to beauticians' school and even did a stint as a Memphis barmaid and singer. Divorced in 1965, at age twenty-three, she was by then the mother of three, working at a Birmingham beauty salon, singing on a local TV show, living in government housing, and making forty-five dollars a week. But several trips to Nashville and a brief tour with PORTER WAGONER fueled her ambitions for a musical career, and she moved to MUSIC CITY in 1966.

That year, she walked into the office of EPIC RECORDS producer BILLY SHERRILL to pitch songs. Two weeks later her name was changed to Tammy Wynette, and Sherrill was recording her for the label. He would cowrite many of her songs with

*Tammy Wynette*

collaborators including GLENN SUTTON, NORRO WILSON, and Wynette herself.

Wynette's first single, the JOHNNY PAYCHECK–Bobby Austin composition "Apartment #9" (1966–67), earned decent airplay but failed to ignite as a hit. But her next release, "Your Good Girl's Gonna Go Bad" (1967)—the story of a woman who promises to join her man in his own philandering game—reached the Top Ten. Her first #1, a 1967 duet with DAVID HOUSTON titled "My Elusive Dreams," soon followed, and her first solo #1, "I Don't Wanna Play House" (1967), won her a Grammy. With her classic "D-I-V-O-R-C-E," (1968), Wynette continued to explore the complicated feelings of women and children faced with a family breakup.

Sherrill and Wynette cowrote her signature tune, "Stand By Your Man" (1968), a #1 country smash that also climbed to #19 on the pop charts. As the women's liberation movement gathered force, Wynette's song, recommending forgiveness of wayward men, hit the airwaves. A statement of womanly domestic strength, the record nevertheless drew harsh criticism in some quarters (her critics tended to overlook rocker Janis Joplin's singing of allowing men to take her heart if it made them feel good) but also led to the first of Wynette's three consecutive CMA Female Vocalist of the Year awards (1968–70). "Stand By Your Man" was also featured in the 1970 film *Five Easy Pieces*, starring Jack Nicholson.

Wynette cowrote her next two hits, "Singing My Song" and "The Ways to Love a Man." But no matter who wrote the songs she recorded, they made a seamless presentation befitting the "Heroine of Heartbreak." Her gripping, teardrop-in-every-note vocal style seemed to weep with emotion, while her songs elaborated on the theme that suffering ennobles a woman.

Wynette's marriage to singer-songwriter Don Chapel in 1967 was beset by professional jealousy. In 1968 country star GEORGE JONES witnessed a fight between the Chapels, and at Jones's urging Wynette and her daughters drove away with him. Wynette and Jones married on February 16, 1969, and Wynette's fourth daughter, Georgette, was born in 1970.

Nicknamed the "President and First Lady of Country Music," Jones and Wynette recorded a string of hit duets that seemed to reflect their volatile relationship, which resulted in their divorcing in 1975. Their classic recordings included "Take Me," "We're Gonna Hold On," and "Golden Ring." Wynette married Nashville businessman Michael Tomlin in 1976, but the marriage lasted only six weeks. In 1978 she married songwriter-producer

GEORGE RICHEY, a presence in her life for many years. Her 1979 autobiography and a 1981 TV movie based on her life chronicled her frequent illnesses, often-tumultuous relationships, and other hardships—including a violent abduction, a death threat, and a public bankruptcy case.

By the end of the 1980s Wynette had scored twenty #1 singles and sold some 30 million records. Her surprising 1992 collaboration with the British duo KLF—which yielded the international dance-pop hit "Justified and Ancient"—capped a decade of collaborative projects that reached beyond the country field. In 1995 she joined Jones again to record *One* (MCA), an album produced by TONY BROWN and Norro Wilson.

Wynette strove to be professional, dignified, and ladylike while coping with major challenges. Yet her cosmopolitan style had a country-grit soul. Assertively working-class and womanly, Wynette expressed the difficulties facing working women: raising children, holding down a job, and filling domestic roles. Her "steel magnolia" image allowed her to succeed within a male-dominated environment in which prejudices against women were still strong. If her songs and her marital problems made her seem to be the victim, she was also the survivor. Her professional and personal lives were indistinguishably interwoven, revealing her partially realized dreams and painful experiences.

Wynette died of a blood clot at age fifty-five and was mourned by the industry and her fans during a nationally televised memorial service broadcast from THE RYMAN AUDITORIUM on April 9, 1998. Appearing at the ceremonies were, among others, RANDY TRAVIS, the OAK RIDGE BOYS, Dolly Parton, MERLE HAGGARD, WYNONNA, and LORRIE MORGAN. Later that year Wynette won election to THE COUNTRY MUSIC HALL OF FAME. —*Mary A. Bufwack*

# Wynonna
b. Ashland, Kentucky, May 30, 1964

Wynonna Judd, who came to be billed by her first name, parlayed an award-winning career as a member of THE JUDDS, a duo with her mother Naomi, into a successful solo career.

*Wynonna*

Born Christina Claire Ciminella, Wynonna was raised in adventurous transience, living with her mother in California, Kentucky, and eventually Tennessee. By age thirteen Wynonna was recording demos in California; by seventeen, guided by her mother's musical tastes and ambition, the two were signed to RCA RECORDS as the Judds. Stardom soon followed.

When illness forced Naomi to quit the duo in 1991, a solo career was thrust on Wynonna. Emerging a year later on a new label, CURB/MCA, she redefined her music, influenced by the bluesy, West Coast sound of Bonnie Raitt and Lowell George. She quickly returned to the top of the charts, scoring three consecutive #1 singles with "She Is His Only Need," "I Saw the Light," and "No One Else on Earth."

The Judds' record sales had begun to lag, but Wynonna's self-titled solo album debut returned her to the top of the charts, eventually shipping 5 million units. Her 1993 release, *Tell Me Why*, included five Top Ten singles and sold a million copies, as did her third album, 1996's *Revelations*. It included "To Be Loved by You," her last #1 as of 2011.

As her record sales slipped, Wynonna released albums less frequently in the 2000s. As of 2010, Curb had continued to issue her albums, including 2005's *Her Story: Scenes from a Lifetime*, a two-part CD/DVD.

A frequent guest on *Oprah* and other daytime talk shows, Wynonna also maintained the Judds' tradition of drawing tabloid headlines, from an out-of-wedlock pregnancy to battles with her weight to controversies involving successive divorces from two husbands. Judd published a best-selling autobiography, *Coming Home to Myself,* in 2006. In 2011, she and her mother starred on the Oprah Winfrey Network (OWN) reality series *The Judds*, chronicling an eighteen-city reunion tour. —*Bob Millard*

# Twenty Years of Change

## Music's Digital Transformation

## DAVID M. ROSS

Like an idyllic backwoods fishing hole surrendering to the parking lots of progress, country music has evolved dramatically since the heady days of 1991. Back then, Garth Brooks and fellow hat acts Brooks & Dunn, Clint Black, Alan Jackson, and George Strait drove the format's album sales to its highest peaks of prosperity. In the ensuing years, change has swept through every nook and cranny of the music industry, affecting how music is created, recorded, marketed, delivered, and exposed. The balance of power among labels, managers, artists, songwriters, publishers, talent agents, and others in 2010 would be virtually unrecognizable to executives fulfilling those roles in the early 1990s. So what caused these changes? What forces were at play? Arguably, the sharpest lens through which to view this massive restructuring is technology, and the first such game-changing event was the creation of an improved method to measure sales.

## A NEW SALES YARDSTICK

SoundScan emerged on May 25, 1991, and turned the album charts on their ear. *Billboard* began using the new system, which tabulated sales based on bar-code readers from nationwide accounts, to create the industry's most accurate album charts. (RIAA, by contrast, measures albums shipped, not sold.) In the process, country music gained new respect. According to *MusicRow* magazine, country artists reaped massive gains the first week *Billboard* used the new system. "Country acts had thirty-five albums in the Top 200, up from eleven the previous week," the trade publication noted. "Garth Brooks, Dolly Parton, Clint Black, and Reba McEntire all moved into the Top Forty. Travis Tritt's *Country Club* rose eighty-two positions. *Billboard*'s old method of tabulation asked retailers to give a ranked listing of best-sellers, listings which many believed could be manipulated...." As MCA Nashville President Bruce Hinton told *MusicRow* at the time, "It's been self-evident to us in Nashville how well country music is doing, but the national charts, especially the *Billboard* Top 200, haven't necessarily reflected that in the past. All the SoundScan chart is doing is reflecting what we already know to be true." Hinton was right: the Nashville music machine was on fire. Several months later newcomer Garth Brooks would celebrate the sale of over 6 million units with his first two CDs. During 1992, the first full year of SoundScan data, the country music format sold 80.3 million albums. Little did anyone realize at the time that it would be a high-water mark the format would not duplicate, at least through 2010.

**COUNTRY ALBUM SALES**

| Year | Units (millions) | Year | Units (millions) |
|------|------------------|------|------------------|
| 1992 | 80.3 | 2004 | 78.0 |
| 1995 | 76.0 | 2006 | 74.9 |
| 1996 | 66.9 | 2007 | 62.7 |
| 1998 | 72.3 | 2008 | 47.7 |
| 2000 | 67.1 | 2009 | 46.1 |
| 2002 | 76.9 | 2010 | 43.7 |

*Source:* Nielsen SoundScan, a division of The Nielsen Company.

Today Nielsen SoundScan, a division of the Nielsen Company, continues to deliver the most accurate picture of nationwide album sales, both CDs and digital downloads. SoundScan also counts individual digital download single-song sales. Looking back to the early 1990s, the importance of the new data stream cannot be overstated. Suddenly it gave media gatekeepers—tour agents, managers, and labels—a verifiable way to measure the popularity of an artist as a function of sales. Moreover, it became possible to segment those sales geographically. Suffice it to say the data gave marketers new tools with which to focus their efforts, maximize sales, and work more cost-effectively.

## CD Leads the Way

The adoption of the compact disc (CD) mostly took place during the 1980s. At the time, audiophiles, fans, and the recording industry debated the merits of the new music-delivery system. It was a fair discussion. Was the music warmer on vinyl? Did the CD alter musical harmonics? What about pops and clicks? One element most everyone missed, however, was that the digital 1s and 0s embedded on the CD could speak to computers. That single fact likely ensured the CD's triumph over analog and to some degree made the quality debate irrelevant. In retrospect, the CD was a baby step toward the information highway, because just over the horizon was a tsunami that would marry digital technology to something called the Internet. The power this new online world would exert over society and the music industry would be transformative.

## Napster and the MP3 file

As the music industry's 1990s prosperity ran out of steam in the new century, leaders realized a new future was fast approaching. Unfortunately, the music industry's leadership was unprepared for how fast change would take place. Two events of acute historical significance were the development and adoption of the MP3 musical file format and the rise and fall of Napster. During the late 1990s, music fans' love affair with MP3s intensified as use of the Internet grew. By late 1997, MP3s featuring independent artists could be obtained free at mp3.com. Moreover, MP3 files were small, making it possible for fans to share music created from CDs. In the face of this widespread copyright infringement, which reduced CD sales, record companies branded file sharing as "music piracy."

The MP3 file was perhaps the first shot fired in what has become a copyright war between the music industry and its consumers. The new files allowed consumers to share perfect digital copies of songs over the Internet without buying them. Sharing songs was clearly a violation of copyright (piracy), but instead of finding a way to embrace the technology and form a new business model around it, the industry responded with litigation. Unfortunately, the genie was out of the bottle, and no argument would convince consumers to stop using the newfound freedoms of file sharing and the Internet.

Music file–sharing program Napster emerged from June 1999 to July 2001. It began in founder Shawn Fanning's dorm room at Northeastern University in Boston and without warning turned the music world upside down. Suddenly friends and strangers could share a seemingly unlimited menu of MP3 files without cost or controls. An added appeal was that Napster fans could find songs that were difficult to obtain or out of print. The service was ultimately shut down by court order, but it ignited a spark of innovation that spurred more advanced and decentralized peer-to-peer systems.

In an article titled "The Day Napster Died," Brad King expressed Napster's importance (Wired. com, 5/15/02):

> Once the darling of the technology world with 80 million registered users, the revolutionary software allowed people to use the Internet to do what they had done for years in neighborhoods, schoolyards, and concert venues: they swapped music. Within months of its release, Napster was the Internet's killer app. Napster and its founder held the promise of everything the new medium of the Internet encompassed: youth, radical change, and the free exchange of information. But youthful exuberance would soon give way to reality as the music industry placed a bull's-eye squarely on Napster. Ironically, that litigation propelled file trading to further astronomical heights. Open-source developers, long the defenders of free speech in the digital world, set about developing alternatives to Napster in case the record industry successfully shut down the rogue service.

It was a classic example of an opportunity missed. Napster had aggregated more than 80 million active music users into a single network—a marketer's dream. Could the record labels have worked with Napster to try to monetize the service with a monthly subscription fee? One would think so. But labels were accustomed to exerting a great deal more control over the distribution of music, and Napster abruptly threatened to dilute that dominance. Labels weren't ready to consider an alternative strategy. Hindsight shows it was an uninformed choice. Today, peer-to-peer file sharing (piracy) continues to be rampant, and the power of the record label to control its destiny and that of its content has been greatly eroded.

## DEMOCRATIZING THE MUSIC, 2002–2010

The new millennium arrived, the labels litigated Napster out of existence, and for a short period executives wearing blinders believed the natural order of the industry had been restored. But the digital revolution was relentless, integrating itself so thoroughly into our everyday lives that sweeping change became inevitable.

### Recording Music

During the 1980s and 1990s record labels had been the hub of the wheel. They advanced large sums of money needed for recording, distribution, publicity, and marketing to a select group of artists and were successful in launching new artists about 10–15 percent of the time. That wouldn't make for a good major league batting average, but each superstar generated such enormous label profits that a low success rate was more than adequate. Several years into the new century, recording software such as Apple's Garage Band™ and ProTools™ became available at minimal cost. Suddenly acts that never dreamt of having the money to make professional-sounding recordings found they could do so at home using a laptop computer and some affordable gear. A major barrier to entry had been lowered, weakening label control.

### Distribution

As more and more unknown artists began recording at home, new websites appeared to help distribute their music. The economics of the business were completely different for these struggling new musicians. They had no large advance to recoup and instead were willing to give away music in the hopes of gaining fans. As the decade continued, digital distribution grew, at the expense of physical distribution. iTunes created an online revenue source for labels, but individual digital track sales were unable to offset the staggering revenue declines from physical album sales. Record labels were the victims of a quadruple whammy: sales of physical product began dropping significantly; stores responded by shrinking shelf space; competition from video games, DVDs, and digital piracy forced labels to lower CD prices; and overall distribution expenses rose. Ultimately profit margins suffered. The cushiony business model had hiccupped, forcing labels to cut expenses, contract, and begin a massive exile of experienced executives.

### Transforming the Independents

As in earlier times, independent labels existed during the 1980s and 1990s, but they had frequently lacked the expertise to compete against major labels for airplay and shelf space. Often the best they could hope for was to get an artist signed to a major label. But suddenly the streets were full of former major-label experts who created small companies that could be hired by indie artists to help shepherd careers through all aspects of the industry. With access to top-level executive talent, small labels had a greatly improved chance to go head-to-head with the majors.

### Revenue Streams

When asked about studying an industry, analysts often echo the dictum "follow the money," and the record business is no exception. Much of the change can be seen accurately through the perspective of revenue streams. For decades, the typical record label's business model was based on earning substantial profits from record sales. Successful artists didn't gain proportionate rewards from record sales, but the popularity and fame created from the label's massive investment allowed artists to earn substantial income from touring, songwriting, product endorsements, and merchandise sales. As a result almost everyone was content. As record sales plummeted, labels noticed that touring revenue and other artist streams (merchandise, endorsements, etc.) remained strong. Labels argued, "We are making you a star, without us you wouldn't be able to sell tickets. Our revenue has shrunk; we want some of yours." Thus, the 360 deal was created, a contract that gave the labels rights to portions of additional revenue streams beyond record sales. As might be expected, the concept was not universally embraced, especially by superstar artists with little reason to surrender revenues. As the decade moved on, labels grew weaker and continued to consolidate.

## The Brand Manager

As a direct result of the change in revenue-stream economics discussed earlier, artist managers became more empowered. Especially in the case of superstars, the manager who partnered with the artist in all revenue streams had the ability and leverage to bargain and negotiate for all kinds of goods and services. The star artist didn't need a label to provide investment capital. As the 2000s were closing, this revenue stream fight was continuing.

## Exposing the Music

The early 1990s saw country music marketing become more sophisticated. Previously it was simple— put the albums in the stores, create a wall poster, job done. But with the rise of the business-minded, multiplatinum-selling Garth Brooks and the popular class-of-'89, tradition-oriented hat acts, labels realized they could reach higher. Today marketing departments are much like those in any major corporation, plotting campaigns to create awareness across all available channels. Country radio, which has approximately 2,000 radio stations nationwide, has been, and remains, the primary means of reaching country consumers and exposing new music. Music video networks (CMT and GAC), social networking, touring, YouTube, and other means have all become important components in the sales process, but there is still not one example of a country artist breaking without strong radio support. Recent CMA research confirms radio's importance but notes that as country consumers become more technology-savvy, the balance among marketing channels will change.

## The Promotion Team

Securing radio exposure is the task of radio-promotion teams. These teams generally comprise a national "captain" and regional members assigned to persuade stations in specific geographical regions to add records to their playlists. Due to the high cost of salaries, travel, and entertainment expenses, top promotion teams were once owned exclusively by record labels. Today, in the wake of consolidation, there are experienced independent street teams available for hire on a record-by-record basis. In the country format, however, aggressively seeking radio airplay on mainstream national stations remains cost prohibitive, available only to high rollers willing to place hundreds of thousands of dollars at risk.

## LOOKING TO THE FUTURE

As of 2010, the worldwide music industry had been unable to solve the challenges of the Internet, piracy, and digital downloading. According to NPD Research Group, the percentage of paid (legal) CD and digital download sales compared with total music consumption was "accelerating in the wrong direction." The RIAA agrees, showing U.S. retail sound-recording industry sales falling from $14.58 billion in 1999 to $6.85 billion in 2010—a drop of 53 percent in eleven years.

One model, suggested by this writer in *Music Row* in 2003—The Digital Manifesto—would make the Internet service provider (ISP) the consumer toll booth, charging every Internet subscriber a small monthly fee for a blanket source license allowing legal open streaming and downloading of all music.

Under this mandatory-access-fee scenario, everything online is paid for in advance, ending piracy and changing new technology from villain to friend. If, say, 150 million U.S. Internet subscribers paid $6.50 per month each, this would generate some $11.7 billion annually, drastically increasing the net retail size of today's music industry in just one year. There could also be a small tax on blank media and advertising revenues from websites that use music. Fees from the collected revenue pool could be distributed based on a digital survey of downloaded files. Movies, books, and other intellectual property could also be compensated under such a system.

Unfortunately, a Digital Manifesto–based solution appeared still distant on the horizon in 2011 and much of the industry remained dazed and confused. However, society's adoption of new technology continues to race like arrows toward a techno-target. Mobile devices, cloud computing, location-based marketing, and Internet availability in automobiles are all adding to the industry's complexity. Mobile devices, already powerful and sophisticated, are leading consumers to adopt an on-demand lifestyle— content when they want it, how they want it, and on whatever size screen they want to view it. These devices already sync your location to the world around you and are ushering in myriad new marketing and media opportunities.

Cloud computing is a concept that places content on massive centralized servers instead of saving it on the user's hard drive, thus making it available to the user wherever there is an Internet connection. The cloud could make downloading music obsolete. If a consumer can access a song at a desktop computer, on a mobile device, or in the car, then why download it and waste time making copies? Internet radio in automobiles will also change the radio equation. Companies such as Rhapsody and Spotify are early explorers in this direction, but as yet they do not seem to have sustainable business models.

Traditionally, the financial barrier for owning a terrestrial radio station has been astronomical— FCC licensing, transmitters, towers, and other equipment typically cost millions of dollars. In the Internet radio model, one need only a low-cost Internet address and space on a server. A proliferation of small stations will greatly increase the supply of advertising inventory, pushing down rates, complicating the fight for survival of the terrestrial signals, and upending the balance of power inside the industry.

While it's anyone's guess as to exactly how the music industry may evolve over the next twenty years, music will continue to be an essential way of enriching our lives, especially country music, whose songs tell stories that resonate with the human condition. Although the industry must struggle with business models, profit margins, and discovering new talent, for fans it's as simple as pushing a button and enjoying the result. Industry leaders will continue to face challenges in coping with new means of producing, marketing, and consuming recorded music. But over the preceding century, music executives have dealt with many changes in media and related technology in serving diverse audiences, and they will surely continue to do so.

# X·Y·Z

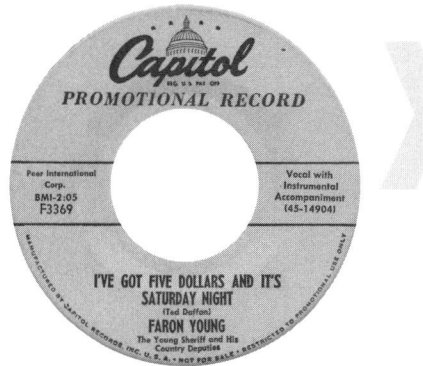

## X Stations (*see* Border Radio)

## Trisha Yearwood
b. Monticello, Georgia, September 19, 1964

One of country music's strongest vocalists, Patricia Lynn "Trisha" Yearwood broke barriers with her first releases and became one of several women who redefined the genre's sound and lyrical themes in the 1990s. In 1991, her single "She's in Love with the Boy" was the first debut song by a female to reach #1 in eighteen years. She also became the first female country singer to have a debut album sell a million copies in its first year.

Daughter of a banker and a teacher, Yearwood grew up in the small community of Monticello, Georgia, as an avid fan of Elvis Presley and Linda Ronstadt. Following high school, Yearwood attended Nashville's Belmont University, where she majored in music business.

Before landing her recording contract with MCA Records, Yearwood sang demos and worked as a receptionist for MTM Records (see MTM Music Group). While doing session work, she met two men who shared an unusual first name: Garth Fundis, who would produce several of her albums, and Garth Brooks, who promised that if he made it in the music business, he'd help her any way he could. True to his word, Brooks invited Yearwood to open his first headlining tour; she later sang on his albums, and in 2005 the two stars married. It was her third marriage and his second.

After her successful debut, Yearwood created two ballad-heavy albums, *Hearts in Armor* and *The Song Remembers When*, that drew

critical praise and maintained her platinum status. In 1993 Yearwood was the subject of *Get Hot or Go Home*, a biography written by Lisa Gubernick. In addition, Yearwood was featured in "The Song Remembers When," a one-hour special for the Disney Channel. That same year she made her movie debut, portraying herself in *The Thing Called Love*, directed by Peter Bogdanovich.

In 1994 she shared CMA's Album of the Year honors for her contribution to *Common Thread: The Songs of the Eagles*. Her albums took on a more uptempo, rocking country feel with *Thinkin' About You* (1994) and *Everybody Knows* (1995), which included the #1 hits "XXX's and OOO's (An American Girl)" and "Believe Me Baby (I Lied)." She won her first Grammy in 1995 for Best Country Collaboration with Vocals for a duet with Aaron Neville on Patsy Cline's "I Fall to Pieces."

Yearwood's recording of "How Do I Live" from the movie soundtrack *Con Air* won 1997 Female Vocalist of the Year honors from CMA and a Grammy for Best Country Female Vocal Performance. She also shared a Grammy that year with duet partner Garth Brooks for "In Another's Eyes." In 1998 she returned as CMA Female Vocalist of the Year and released her sixth album, *Where Your Road Leads*, the first she made with producer Tony Brown. Yearwood joined the Grand Ole Opry in 1999.

Yearwood's albums from 2000–05—*Real Live Woman*, *Inside Out*, and *Jasper County*—dipped in sales and airplay but still went gold. They were her last albums for MCA. She moved to Big Machine Records for her 2007 release, *Heaven, Heartache and the Power of Love*.

From 1997 to 2002, Yearwood had a recurring role in the TV series *JAG*. As of 2011, she had released two cookbooks.
—*Janet E. Williams*

## Dwight Yoakam
b. Pikeville, Kentucky, October 23, 1956

Dwight Yoakam stands as one of the most significant country artists of the 1980s and 1990s, despite (or perhaps because of) his stubbornly distancing himself from Nashville. Although his flashy appearance and defiant attitude first drew attention to him, it's his talents as a songwriter and honky-tonk singer that have continued to resonate over time.

Yoakam was born in rural Kentucky and raised in Ohio. He grew up on the Beatles and The Byrds but got the hillbilly music bug from his parents and from attending church. After a short period in Nashville in 1977, he moved in 1978 to California, where Gram Parsons and Emmylou Harris had created an alternative to Nashville formulas and where Merle Haggard and Buck Owens kept Bakersfield traditions alive. In Los

*Trisha Yearwood*

*Dwight Yoakam*

Angeles Yoakam connected with guitarist and producer PETE ANDERSON; together they fashioned a unique sound, one steeped in 1950s hard-country but broadened with the ambitious melodies and harmonies of 1960s rock.

Yoakam began raising his profile while opening for L.A. roots-rock acts the Blasters, Los Lobos, and X. A 1984 six-song EP, *Guitars, Cadillacs, Etc.*, on the tiny Oak label, led to a contract with Reprise Records. Reprise reissued the EP's songs with four new ones, recasting it as *Guitars, Cadillacs, Etc., Etc.* in 1986. The album slowly pushed to the top of the country charts and eventually sold 2 million units.

Yoakam's next two studio albums—1987's *Hillbilly Deluxe* and 1988's *Buenos Noches from a Lonely Room*—established his style and commercial strengths, as both went platinum. After a hits compilation, he released 1990's *If There Was a Way*, another million-seller. *This Time* (1993) included "Ain't That Lonely Yet," which won the 1994 Grammy for Best Male Country Vocal Performance. The album sold 3 million copies, his most successful release to date.

In 1995 Yoakam recorded his first concert album, *Dwight Live*, as well as the musically ambitious *Gone*. Both albums went gold; from there his sales slipped further, although critical acclaim remained high for such collections as 1997's *Under the Covers*, which interpreted earlier hits by acts from the Rolling Stones to ROY ORBISON, and 1998's *A Long Way from Home*.

By the mid-1990s, Yoakam started pursuing an interest in acting. His first film roles came in 1994's *Red Rock West* and cable TV's *Roswell*, but he more fully demonstrated his considerable acting skills in Billy Bob Thornton's 1996 film *Slingblade*. He has appeared in more than fifteen films since, including a recurring role in the *Crank* series. He wrote, directed, and acted (with

Thornton and Luke Askew) in 2000's *South of Heaven, West of Hell.*

Yoakam's recording output slowed in the 2000s, and he filled time with acoustic versions of his hits, cover albums (including a 2007 collection of Buck Owens songs on *Dwight Sings Buck*), hits compilations, and a couple of albums of originals released on Audium Records and New West Records.

Unlike his L.A. roots-rock contemporaries and fellow 1986 rookies STEVE EARLE and LYLE LOVETT, Yoakam flourished on the country charts; his twangy tenor was simply too spellbinding for country radio to ignore. Moreover, the prime strength of Yoakam's songwriting is his music more than his lyrics, and country radio warmed to the hook-laden, COUNTRY-ROCK guitars of his records. In addition, Yoakam clearly aligned himself with an enduring tradition—the Bakersfield sound of Owens and Haggard—that has repeatedly proven its commercial appeal. —*Geoffrey Himes*

## The York Brothers
George York b. Louisa, Kentucky, February 10, 1910; d. July 1974
Leslie York b. Louisa, Kentucky, August 23, 1917; d. February 21, 1984

The York Brothers bridged the gap between the older style of harmony duets and more modern country sounds. Natives of eastern Kentucky, the Yorks first worked as a team at WPAY in Portsmouth, Ohio. This led to a contract with the DECCA label, for which they cut six songs in 1941. Later they moved to Detroit, where they recorded "Hamtramck Mama" for Universal. Shortly afterward, they entered military service.

After World War II the York Brothers recorded for the Nashville independent BULLET RECORDS and appeared on the GRAND OLE OPRY. In 1947 they began a decade of recording for KING RECORDS, often making country versions of rhythm & blues songs. In 1950 the brothers returned to Detroit and then permanently relocated to the Dallas–Fort Worth area. They continued in music for several more years and issued several records on their own York label. As time passed, George apparently experienced voice problems, prompting Leslie to handle more of their vocals. —*Ivan M. Tribe*

## Chip Young
b. Atlanta, Georgia, May 19, 1938

Chip Young (Jerry Marvin Stembridge) came of age in the late 1950s playing guitar in Atlanta with JERRY REED, JOE SOUTH, and RAY STEVENS. Young toured with South and gravitated to THE LOWERY MUSIC GROUP, where he wrote songs and engineered recordings and publishing demos. Following an army stint (1961–63), he moved to Nashville in 1963 to back Reed on tour. Before long, Young became a studio guitarist behind ELVIS PRESLEY, Ann-Margret, EDDY ARNOLD, and GEORGE JONES. Signing as a writer with Bill Justis's Tuneville Music, Young helped Justis build a studio and began producing sessions. Young also recorded instrumentals as a Bell Records artist.

In 1968 he bought a farm near Murfreesboro, Tennessee, and built his own studio, Young 'Un Sound. There he produced recordings by Reed, BILLY SWAN, and DELBERT MCCLINTON while recording others ranging from country/pop singer Jimmy Buffett to pop balladeer Johnny Mathis. By 1978 Young moved his operation to a studio on Seventeenth Avenue South in Nashville, where he produced Larry Gatlin (of THE GATLIN BROTHERS), and recorded others, including REBA MCENTIRE, JOHNNY RODRIGUEZ, THE STATLER BROTHERS, and TOM T. HALL.

After selling his studio in 1987, Young remained in demand as a session guitarist until health problems forced him to retire in 1990. He continued to produce, working with acts such as Deryl Dodd. In 2000 he released *Having Thumb Fun with My Friends*, an album of guitar duets with other pickers, including CHET ATKINS, GRADY MARTIN, and Scotty Moore. —*John W. Rumble*

## Faron Young
b. Shreveport, Louisiana, February 25, 1932; d. December 10, 1996

From the early 1950s through the mid-1970s, Faron Young was among the top stars and most colorful personalities in all of country music. Signature hits such as "If You Ain't Lovin' (You Ain't Livin')" and "Live Fast, Love Hard, Die Young" marked him as a HONKY-TONK man in both sound and personal style, while other chart-topping singles, such as "Hello Walls" and "It's Four in the Morning," displayed his versatility as a vocalist. A music industry entrepreneur, he invested in MUSIC ROW real estate, and in the 1960s he published the influential trade paper *Music City News*. Though his career did not lack controversy, Young's voluble, outgoing personality was well received, and the entire community was as shocked as it was saddened when he died of a self-inflicted gunshot wound at age sixty-four.

Born in Shreveport and raised on a farm outside of town, Young, as a teenager, was more interested in pop music than in country. But that changed when his high school football coach, who moonlighted in a country band, started Young singing at the local Optimist Club and in nursing homes. Young then met WEBB PIERCE and began working with him in clubs and on KWKH. By 1951 Young was appearing on the station's feature program, the *LOUISIANA HAYRIDE*.

Though he recorded in Shreveport, Young's first sides appeared on Philadelphia's Gotham label. But by February 1952 he had been signed to CAPITOL RECORDS, for which he would record for the next ten years. His first Capitol single appeared that spring, and soon thereafter he moved to Nashville. He recorded his first chart hit, "Goin' Steady," in October 1952, but his career got sidetracked when he was drafted the following month. While in the U.S. Army, he performed on recruitment programs and continued to record. He was discharged in November 1954, just as "If You Ain't Lovin'" was hitting the charts.

From 1954 to 1962 Young cut a slew of HONKY-TONK classics for Capitol, including the first hit version of DON GIBSON's "Sweet Dreams." Most famous was "Hello Walls," a crossover smash for Young in 1961. It was written by WILLIE NELSON, who pitched the song to Young at TOOTSIE'S ORCHID LOUNGE.

In 1963 Young switched from Capitol to MERCURY RECORDS. Though initially his Mercury catalog drifted through various bland NASHVILLE SOUND stylings, by the end of the decade he had recaptured much of his hard-country fire with hits such as "Wine Me Up." Released in 1971, the waltz-time ballad "It's Four in the Morning" was one of Young's finest records and his last #1 hit. By the mid-1970s his records were becoming overshadowed by his salty and sometimes unstable persona. For example, he made headlines in 1972 when he spanked a little girl who was in the audience at a concert in Clarksburg, West Virginia.

*Faron Young*

Young switched labels again in 1979, signing with MCA. The association lasted only two years, and little was heard from Young until the Nashville independent STEP ONE picked him up in 1988. He recorded for Step One into the early 1990s (including a charming, if not particularly exciting, duet album with RAY PRICE), and then he withdrew from public view. Though young country acts such as BR549 were putting his music before a whole new audience in the mid-1990s, Young apparently believed the industry had turned its back on him. That and despondency over his deteriorating health were cited as possible reasons why Young shot himself on December 9, 1996. He died in Nashville the following day.

Young was elected to THE COUNTRY MUSIC HALL OF FAME in 2000. —*Daniel Cooper*

## Kyle Young
b. Hattiesburg, Mississippi, March 26, 1953

Kyle Young worked numerous jobs within the COUNTRY MUSIC HALL OF FAME AND MUSEUM prior to becoming director in 1999. Young then led the organization through a period of unprecedented growth as the museum expanded into a larger building in downtown Nashville and its annual operating budget grew from $1 million to more than $13 million.

Young began working at the museum in 1976, taking a summer job after graduating with an English literature degree from Kenyon College. That fall, Young launched the museum's education department. He became editor of the *Journal of Country Music,* the museum's in-house magazine, in 1977 and revamped it from a purely academic publication to a broader one that featured the work of some of America's best writers, journalists, and historians.

In 1985 Young became the driving force behind the creation of CMF Records, which focused on quality historical reissues. He also established the museum's first creative partnerships with major record labels and book publishers, leading to ongoing series of albums, books, DVDs, and other historical materials.

Young was named acting director of the museum in 1998 when his predecessor, BILL IVEY, left to head the National Endowment for the Arts. The museum's board of directors confirmed Young as director in February 1999. As the museum's chief executive, his first major task was the funding and construction of the museum's new home in downtown Nashville, which tripled its exhibition and office space. Construction of the new museum, opened in May 2001, came in on time and under the allotted $37 million budget. The museum's move and its advances in exhibitions, publications, school programs, and public programs have proven highly successful, despite travel industry challenges brought on by the September 11, 2001, terrorist attacks on the United States, fluctuating gas prices, and other problems affecting the national economy. At press time, Young was spearheading the museum's expansion, which would more than double its size by 2013. —*Michael McCall*

## Neil Young
b. Toronto, Ontario, Canada, November 12, 1945

Though best known as a rock singer-songwriter, Neil Percival Young has continually interacted with country music and with Nashville. In the mid-1960s, as a member of Buffalo Springfield, he helped create a sound that became known as COUNTRY-ROCK. With Crosby, Stills, Nash, and Young, he recorded country-inspired tracks ("Teach Your Children") for their multimillion-selling album *Déjà Vu* (1970). And Young's songs have been recorded by numerous country artists, including EMMYLOU HARRIS, MARTY STUART, WAYLON JENNINGS, and DOLLY PARTON.

His own recordings closely identify Young with country music. Beginning with his self-titled debut album for Reprise in 1969, he has often blended PEDAL STEEL GUITAR, country rhythms, and rural imagery with distorted, noisy electric guitars. Follow-up albums, including *Everybody Knows This Is Nowhere* and *After the Gold Rush*, had country overtones; *Gold Rush* even included a cover of DON GIBSON's "Oh, Lonesome Me."

In February 1971 Young was invited to Nashville as a guest on JOHNNY CASH's ABC television program, along with pop stars James Taylor and LINDA RONSTADT. Young booked time at Nashville's Woodland Sound Studios and recruited local musicians (including Ben Keith and KENNY BUTTREY) as well as Taylor and Ronstadt. The resulting album, *Harvest*, proved to be one of Young's most successful recordings and yielded his only #1 single, "Heart of Gold."

In 1978 he released *Comes a Time*, also recorded in Nashville. In addition to Ben Keith, by then a mainstay in Young's outfit, Young enlisted multi-instrumentalist Anthony Crawford, CAJUN fiddler Rufus Thibodeaux, and BLUEGRASS guitarist Grant Boatright for the million-selling album. Young's composition "Lotta Love" provided country-rock singer Nicolette Larsen with her commercial breakthrough later in the same year.

In the early 1980s Young tapped into country music again when forming the International Harvesters. Keith, Crawford, and Thibodeaux returned, and Young added legendary Nashville session pianist PIG ROBBINS and songwriter–bass player Joe Allen. The group played on Young's debut for Geffen Records, *Old Ways*, a throwback to THE NASHVILLE SOUND. In July 1985, Young took the Harvesters to Live Aid in Philadelphia, thus being MUSIC CITY's sole representation at the historic concert benefitting Ethiopian famine victims. On September 22, 1985, Young joined Willie Nelson and John Mellencamp in launching the first Farm Aid benefit, in Champaign, Illinois.

Young's 1992 album, *Harvest Moon,* found him returning to Nashville and employing the musicians used on *Harvest* twenty years earlier. The album won a 1994 Juno Award (for Canadian artists) for Album of the Year. *Prairie Moon*, released in 1995, followed the same pattern, using Nashville musicians who had previously performed with Young. The album's concert premiere at Nashville's RYMAN AUDITORIUM was documented in Jonathan Demme's 2006 film *Neil Young: Heart of Gold*. In it, Young tells of a Martin D-28 he has owned for more than thirty years that once was owned by HANK WILLIAMS. He also addresses a 2005 brain aneurysm that nearly took his life.

Young was inducted into the Rock and Roll Hall of Fame in 1995 and again, as a member of Buffalo Springfield, in 1997. —*Chris Skinker*

## Reggie Young
b. Caruthersville, Missouri, December 12, 1936

Master guitarist Reggie Grimes Young Jr. contributed to the rise of Memphis ROCKABILLY in the mid-1950s, the flourishing of CHIPS MOMAN's enormously productive American Studio in Memphis during the 1960s, and the expansion of the Nashville recording scene in the 1970s and beyond. Young started playing guitar in 1951, learning from his father. Influenced by the music of CHET ATKINS and Django Reinhardt, Young played in regional WESTERN SWING and country bands, recorded with Memphis rockabilly bands, and worked with country star JOHNNY HORTON out of Shreveport, Louisiana, before returning to Memphis in 1959 to help form the Bill Black Combo, much in demand for road shows and for Royal Recording studio sessions. After a stint in the U.S. Army (1960–62), Young rejoined the Black unit, which opened for the Beatles on their historic 1964 American tour.

In about 1965 Young began working almost exclusively as a studio player, soon becoming part of American Studio's famous rhythm section. Over the next seven years he played on some 400 chart-making discs recorded in Memphis by artists ranging from ELVIS PRESLEY and soul singer Wilson Pickett to pop stars Dusty Springfield and Neil Diamond.

As Memphis recording activity slackened, Young moved briefly to Atlanta (1972) and later in the year to Nashville. Immediately he became a "first call" guitarist, whose lead and rhythm parts contributed to such hits as Dobie Gray's pop smash "Drift Away," WAYLON JENNINGS's "Luckenbach, Texas," and WILLIE NELSON's "Always on My Mind." Young's stylings have also graced recordings by artists as diverse as Jimmy Buffett, rock star Joe Cocker, jazz innovator Herbie Mann, multimarket singer B. J. THOMAS, and country greats HANK WILLIAMS JR., CONWAY

Twitty, Reba McEntire, Merle Haggard, and George Strait. In the 2000s, Young periodically toured Europe as a member of the Memphis Boys, consisting of top studio musicians associated with Memphis recordings. He continues to play the occasional session, and he has cut instrumental tracks with his wife, Jennifer, a cellist. —*John W. Rumble*

## Steve Young

b. near Newnan, Georgia, July 12, 1942

Steve Young played key roles in the evolution of two historical movements in country music: country-rock and Outlaw country. Young's first solo album, *Rock, Salt & Nails*, released in 1969 by A&M Records, was one of a handful of late-1960s albums that synthesized the stylistic elements and emotional concerns of country music with those of 1960s rock. By the early 1970s this musical blend—often called country-rock—had become mainstream.

Young's long-standing personal and artistic nonconformity was also an inspiration to Outlaws such as Waylon Jennings and Willie Nelson. Jennings once stated that Young "has no earthly idea how great he is." Young himself recorded two of the most enduring Outlaw albums: *Honky Tonk Man* (Mountain Railroad, 1975) and *Renegade Picker* (RCA, 1976).

Raised in rural and urban settings in Georgia, Alabama, and Texas, Young grew up listening to both amateur and professional country musicians. Accordingly, he has always performed an eclectic mix of songs—powerful interpretations of traditional and contemporary songs alongside compelling original compositions in a wide range of styles. Although his own recordings have never sold widely or received much airplay, other musicians have recognized his talents as a songwriter (e.g., Jennings covered Young's "Lonesome, On'ry, and Mean," and The Eagles recorded Young's best-known composition, "Seven Bridges Road"); a vocalist

(Jennings once asserted that "Young is the second greatest country music singer—to George Jones, of course"); and as a guitar virtuoso. —*Ted Olson*

## Zac Brown Band

Coy Bowles, b. Thomaston, Georgia, February 20, 1979
Zac Brown, b. Dahlonega, Georgia, July 31, 1978
Clay Cook, b. Snellville, Georgia, April 20, 1978
Jimmy De Martini, b. Marietta, Georgia, August 3, 1976
Chris Fryar, b. Gardenville, Alabama, November 22, 1970
John Driskell Hopkins, b. Gainesville, Georgia, May 3, 1971

After building a large following as a live act, the Zac Brown Band burst onto the country music charts in 2008 with a series of top hits. Singer, songwriter, and guitarist Zac Brown formed his namesake group in 2002. From the start, the Atlanta-based ensemble presented breezy country songs peppered with extended hot instrumentals that made them a popular club attraction.

Between 2004 and 2007, the band released three studio albums and a live collection on its own Home Grown Records. The last of the studio recordings, *The Foundation*, was coproduced by Nashville's Keith Stegall and picked up for national distribution in 2008 by Live Nation Records. When that label folded, Atlantic Records signed the group and rereleased *The Foundation*.

The band's first single, "Chicken Fried," reached #1 on the country charts in late 2008. It was followed by two more #1 hits, "Toes" and "Highway 20 Ride," and the #2 hit "Whatever It Is." The Zac Brown Band was named ACM's 2008 Top New Vocal Duo or Group, and won a 2009 Grammy in the all-genre Best New Artist category. The group issued a double-CD/DVD set, *Pass the Jar*, in early 2010, followed by the studio album *You Get What You Give* in September of that year. The Country Music Association (CMA) tapped the Zac Brown Band for its 2010 Best New Artist honor,

*Zac Brown Band: (from left) Chris Fryar, Jimmy De Martini, Clay Cook, Zac Brown, Coy Bowles, and John Driskell Hopkins*

and the Recording Academy awarded a Grammy to the act and collaborator Alan Jackson for "As She's Walking Away," 2010's Best Country Collaboration with Vocals. —*Michael McCall*

## Joe Zinkan
b. Indianapolis, Indiana, December 16, 1918; d. January 15, 2003

Acoustic stand-up bassist Joseph Scudder Zinkan first recorded with the DELMORE BROTHERS for BLUEBIRD RECORDS in September 1938 in Rock Hill, South Carolina. He performed with PEE WEE KING's Golden West Cowboys and then joined ROY ACUFF's Smoky Mountain Boys in 1943. Working with Acuff into the late-1950s, Zinkan played on Acuff's 1947 recording of "Wabash Cannonball." Although Zinkan generally played bass, on occasion he also sang harmony and played rhythm guitar at sessions. He toured with KITTY WELLS and JOHNNIE & JACK from 1956 to 1959, contributing to many of their records, and wrote the duo's "Camel Walk Stroll." He also recorded with LITTLE JIMMY DICKENS, MARTY ROBBINS, and TAMMY WYNETTE. He retired from music in 1980. —*Walt Trott*

# APPENDICES

## Country Music's All-Time Best-Selling Albums

Certified by the Recording Industry Association of America, Inc. (RIAA), as of April 2010

**20 million units and above sold in the United States**
Garth Brooks, *Double Live* (Capitol, 1998), 21 million sold
Eagles, *Their Greatest Hits 1971–1975* (Elektra, 1976), 29 million sold
Shania Twain, *Come on Over* (Mercury, 1997), 20 million sold

**10 million to 19 million units sold**
Garth Brooks, *Garth Brooks* (Capitol, 1989), 10 million sold
Garth Brooks, *No Fences* (Capitol, 1990), 17 million sold
Garth Brooks, *Ropin' the Wind* (Capitol, 1991), 14 million sold
Garth Brooks, *Sevens* (Capitol, 1997), 10 million sold
Garth Brooks, *The Hits* (Liberty, 1994), 10 million sold
Patsy Cline, *Greatest Hits* (MCA, 1967), 10 million sold
Dixie Chicks, *Fly* (Monument, 1999), 10 million sold
Dixie Chicks, *Wide Open Spaces* (Monument, 1998), 12 million sold
Eagles, *Greatest Hits Volume 2* (Asylum, 1982), 11 million sold
Eagles, *Hotel California* (Asylum, 1976), 16 million sold
Kenny Rogers, *Greatest Hits* (Liberty, 1988), 12 million sold
Shania Twain, *The Woman in Me* (Mercury, 1995), 12 million sold
Shania Twain, *Up!* (Mercury, 2002), 11 million sold

**9 million units sold**
Garth Brooks, *The Chase* (Liberty, 1992)
Billy Ray Cyrus, *Some Gave All* (Mercury, 1992)
John Denver, *Greatest Hits* (RCA, 1973)
Elvis Presley, *Elvis' Christmas Album* (Reissue) (RCA Camden, 1970)

**8 million units sold**
Garth Brooks, *In Pieces* (Liberty, 1993)
Eagles, *Hell Freezes Over* (Geffen, 1994)
Faith Hill, *Breathe* (Warner Bros., 1999)
Soundtrack, *O Brother, Where Art Thou?* (Lost Highway, 2000)
George Strait, *Strait Out of the Box* (MCA, 1995)

**7 million units sold**
Garth Brooks, *Fresh Horses* (Capitol, 1995)
Jimmy Buffett, *Songs You Know by Heart* (MCA, 1985)
Eagles, *Live* (Asylum, 1980)
Eagles, *Long Road Out of Eden* (Lost Highway/Eagles Recording
   Company II, 2007)
Eagles, *The Long Run* (Asylum, 1979)
Linda Ronstadt, *Greatest Hits* (Asylum, 1977)
George Strait, *50 #1's* (MCA, 2004)
Carrie Underwood, *Some Hearts* (Arista, 2005)

**6 million units sold**
Brooks & Dunn, *Brand New Man* (Arista, 1991)
Dixie Chicks, *Home* (Open Wide/Monument, 2002)
Faith Hill, *Faith* (Warner Bros., 1998)
Alan Jackson, *A Lot About Livin' (And a Little 'bout Love)* (Arista, 1992)
Alan Jackson, *Greatest Hits Collection* (Arista, 1995)
Alan Jackson, *Greatest Hits, Volume II* (Arista, 2003)
Tim McGraw, *Greatest Hits* (Curb, 2000)
Tim McGraw, *Not a Moment Too Soon* (Curb, 1994)
Elvis Presley, *Elvis' Golden Records* (RCA, 1957)
LeAnn Rimes, *Blue* (Curb, 1996)
George Strait, *Pure Country* (Soundtrack) (MCA, 1992)
Taylor Swift, *Fearless* (Big Machine, 2008)

**5 million units sold**
Alabama, *For the Record: 41 Number One Hits* (RCA, 1998)
Alabama, *Greatest Hits* (RCA, 1986)
Alabama, *Mountain Music* (RCA, 1982)
Brooks & Dunn, *Hard Workin' Man* (Arista, 1993)
Garth Brooks, *Scarecrow* (Capitol, 1999)
Garth Brooks, *The Ultimate Hits* (Pearl, 2007)
Deana Carter, *Did I Shave My Legs for This?* (Capitol, 1996)
Eagles, *The Very Best of the Eagles* (Warner Bros., 2003)
Vince Gill, *I Still Believe in You* (MCA, 1992)
Waylon Jennings, *Greatest Hits* (RCA, 1979)
Wynonna Judd, *Wynonna* (Curb, 1992)
Reba McEntire, *Greatest Hits, Volume II* (MCA, 1993)
Willie Nelson, *Stardust* (Columbia, 1978)
Elvis Presley, *Aloha from Hawaii: Via Satellite* (RCA, 1973)
Elvis Presley, *Elvis: 30 #1 Hits* (RCA, 2002)
Rascal Flatts, *Feels Like Today* (Lyric Street, 2004)
Kenny Rogers, *The Gambler* (United Artists, 1978)
Randy Travis, *Always & Forever* (Warner Bros., 1987)
Hank Williams, Jr., *Greatest Hits* (Curb, 1982)
Gretchen Wilson, *Here for the Party* (Epic, 2004)

**4 million units sold**
Alabama, *Feels So Right* (RCA, 1981)
Alabama, *Roll On* (RCA, 1984)
Alabama, *The Closer You Get* (RCA, 1983)
Brooks & Dunn, *Greatest Hits* (Arista, 1997)
Mary Chapin Carpenter, *Come On, Come On* (Columbia, 1992)
Kenny Chesney, *Greatest Hits* (BNA, 2000)
Kenny Chesney, *No Shoes, No Shirt, No Problems* (BNA, 2002)
Kenny Chesney, *When the Sun Goes Down* (BNA, 2004)
Charlie Daniels Band, *A Decade of Hits* (Epic, 1983)
Eagles, *One of These Nights* (Asylum, 1975)
Vince Gill, *When Love Finds You* (MCA, 1994)
Faith Hill, *It Matters to Me* (Warner Bros., 1995)
Alan Jackson, *Don't Rock the Jukebox* (Arista, 1994)
Alan Jackson, *Drive* (Arista, 2002)
Alan Jackson, *Who I Am* (Arista, 1994)
Toby Keith, *Shock'n Y'all* (DreamWorks, 2003)
Toby Keith, *Unleashed* (DreamWorks, 2002)
Kris Kristofferson and Barbra Streisand, *A Star Is Born* (Soundtrack)
   (Columbia, 1976)
Reba McEntire, *For My Broken Heart* (MCA, 1991)
Tim McGraw, *Everywhere* (Curb, 1997)
Tim McGraw, *Live Like You Were Dying* (Curb, 2004)
John Michael Montgomery, *John Michael Montgomery* (Atlantic, 1995)
John Michael Montgomery, *Kickin' It Up* (Atlantic, 1994)
Anne Murray, *Greatest Hits* (Capitol, 1980)
Willie Nelson, *Always on My Mind* (Columbia, 1982)
Willie Nelson, *Willie & Family Live* (Columbia, 1978)
Willie Nelson, *Willie Nelson's Greatest Hits (& Some That Will Be)*
   (Columbia, 1981)
Elvis Presley, *The Top Ten Hits* (RCA, 1987)
Rascal Flatts, *Me and My Gang* (Lyric Street, 2006)
Charlie Rich, *Behind Closed Doors* (Epic, 1973)
LeAnn Rimes, *You Light Up My Life: Inspirational Songs* (Curb, 1997)
Kenny Rogers, *20 Greatest Hits* (Liberty, 1983)

**4 million units sold** (*continued*)
Kenny Rogers, *Ten Years of Gold* (United Artists, 1977)
Soundtrack, *Coyote Ugly* (Curb, 2000)
George Strait, *Greatest Hits* (MCA, 1985)
Taylor Swift, *Taylor Swift* (Big Machine, 2006)
Shania Twain, *Greatest Hits* (Mercury, 2004)
Keith Urban, *Be Here* (Capitol, 2004)
Various Artists, *Take Me Home Country Roads* (Reader's Digest Music, 1976)
Trisha Yearwood, *Songbook: A Collection* (MCA, 1997)

**3 million units sold**
Big & Rich, *Horse of a Different Color* (Warner Bros., 2004)
Clint Black, *Killin' Time* (RCA, 1989)
Clint Black, *Put Yourself in My Shoes* (RCA, 1990)
Brooks & Dunn, *Waitin' on Sundown* (Arista, 1994)
Garth Brooks, *Beyond the Season* (Liberty, 1992)
Garth Brooks, *The Garth Brooks Collection* (Liberty, 1994)
Garth Brooks, *The Lost Sessions* (Pearl, 2005)
Johnny Cash, *Johnny Cash at Folsom Prison* (Columbia, 1968)
Johnny Cash, *Johnny Cash at San Quentin* (Columbia, 1969)
Kenny Chesney, *The Road and the Radio* (BNA, 2005)
Charlie Daniels Band, *Million Mile Reflection* (Epic, 1978)
John Denver, *An Evening with John Denver* (RCA, 1975)
John Denver, *Back Home Again* (RCA, 1974)
Jeff Foxworthy, *Games Rednecks Play* (Warner Bros., 1995)
Jeff Foxworthy, *You Might be a Redneck If . . .* (Warner Bros., 1993)
Vince Gill, *Souvenirs* (MCA, 1995)
Faith Hill, *Take Me as I Am* (Warner Bros., 1993)
Alan Jackson, *Everything I Love* (Arista, 1996)
Toby Keith, *Greatest Hits 2* (DreamWorks, 2004)
Lonestar, *Lonely Grill* (BNA, 1999)
Reba McEntire, *Greatest Hits* (MCA, 1987)
Reba McEntire, *It's Your Call* (MCA, 1992)
Reba McEntire, *Read My Mind* (MCA, 1994)
Reba McEntire, *Rumor Has It* (MCA, 1990)
Tim McGraw, *A Place in the Sun* (Curb, 1999)
Tim McGraw, *All I Want* (Curb, 1995)
Tim McGraw, *Set This Circus Down* (Curb, 2001)
Tim McGraw, *Tim McGraw and the Dancehall Doctors* (Curb, 2002)
Martina McBride, *Evolution* (RCA, 1997)
Martina McBride, *Greatest Hits* (RCA, 2001)
John Michael Montgomery, *Life's a Dance* (Atlantic, 1992)
Elvis Presley, *Blue Hawaii* (RCA, 1961)
Elvis Presley, *Elvis as Recorded at Madison Square Garden* (RCA, 1972)
Elvis Presley, *Elvis' Christmas Album (Original)* (RCA, 1957)
Elvis Presley, *Elvis in Concert* (RCA, 1977)
Elvis Presley, *The Number One Hits* (RCA, 1987)
Elvis Presley, *The Wonderful World of Christmas* (RCA, 1971)
Elvis Presley, *You'll Never Walk Alone* (RCA, 1971)
Rascal Flatts, *Melt* (Lyric Street, 2002)
Kenny Rogers, *Kenny* (Capitol, 1979)
Linda Ronstadt, *Simple Dreams* (Asylum, 1977)
Statler Brothers, *The Best of the Statler Brothers* (Mercury, 1975)
George Strait, *Blue Clear Sky* (MCA, 1996)
George Strait, *Carryin' Your Love with Me* (MCA, 1997)
George Strait, *Greatest Hits Volume Two* (MCA, 1987)
Sugarland, *Enjoy the Ride* (Mercury, 2006)
Sugarland, *Twice the Speed of Life* (Mercury, 2004)
Randy Travis, *Storms of Life* (Warner Bros., 1986)
Travis Tritt, *It's All About to Change* (Warner Bros., 1991)
Carrie Underwood, *Carnival Ride* (Arista, 2007)
Keith Urban, *Golden Road* (Capitol, 2002)
Various Artists, *Common Thread: The Songs of the Eagles* (Giant, 1993)
Lee Ann Womack, *I Hope You Dance* (MCA, 2000)
Dwight Yoakam, *This Time* (Reprise, 1993)

**2 million units sold**
Trace Adkins, *Songs About Me* (Capitol, 2005)
Alabama, *40 Hour Week* (RCA, 1985)
Alabama, *Alabama Christmas* (RCA, 1985)
Alabama, *Greatest Hits, Volume III* (RCA, 1994)
Alabama, *My Home's in Alabama* (RCA, 1980)
John Anderson, *Seminole Wind* (BNA, 1992)
Eddy Arnold, *Welcome to My World* (RCA, 1971)
Clint Black, *Greatest Hits* (RCA, 1996)
Blackhawk, *Blackhawk* (Arista, 1994)
Brooks & Dunn, *Borderline* (Arista, 1996)
Brooks & Dunn, *If You See Her* (Arista, 1998)
Garth Brooks, *In . . . the Life of Chris Gaines* (Capitol, 1999)
Zac Brown Band, *The Foundation* (Homegrown/Atlantic, 2008)
Tracy Byrd, *No Ordinary Man* (MCA, 1994)

Glen Campbell, *Wichita Lineman* (Capitol, 1968)
Mary Chapin Carpenter, *Stones in the Road* (Columbia, 1994)
Johnny Cash, *16 Biggest Hits* (Columbia/Legacy, 1999)
Johnny Cash, *Johnny Cash's Greatest Hits* (Columbia, 1967)
Johnny Cash, *The Legend of Johnny Cash* (Mercury, 2005)
Kenny Chesney, *Everywhere We Go* (BNA, 1999)
Confederate Railroad, *Confederate Railroad* (Atlantic, 1992)
Charlie Daniels Band, *Super Hits* (Epic, 1994)
John Denver, *Greatest Hits, Volume 2* (RCA, 1983)
John Denver, *Rocky Mountain Christmas* (RCA, 1975)
John Denver, *Rocky Mountain High* (RCA, 1972)
John Denver, *Windsong* (RCA, 1975)
Dixie Chicks, *Taking the Long Way* (Columbia, 2006)
Eagles, *Desperado* (Asylum, 1973)
Eagles, *On the Border* (Asylum, 1974)
Sara Evans, *Born to Fly* (RCA, 2000)
Vince Gill, *Let There Be Peace on Earth* (MCA, 1993)
Vince Gill, *Pocket Full of Gold* (MCA, 1991)
Vince Gill, *When I Call Your Name* (MCA, 1989)
Billy Gilman, *One Voice* (Epic, 2000)
Faith Hill, *Cry* (Warner Bros., 2002)
Faith Hill, *Fireflies* (Warner Bros., 2005)
Alan Jackson, *Here in the Real World* (Arista, 1990)
Waylon Jennings and Willie Nelson, *Waylon & Willie* (RCA, 1978)
Waylon Jennings, Willie Nelson, Jessi Colter, and Tompall Glaser, *Wanted! The Outlaws* (RCA, 1976)
George Jones, *Super Hits* (Epic, 1987)
The Judds, *Greatest Hits* (RCA/Curb, 1988)
The Judds, *Why Not Me* (RCA/Curb, 1984)
Toby Keith, *Greatest Hits, Volume 1* (Mercury, 1998)
Toby Keith, *Pull My Chain* (DreamWorks, 2001)
Kentucky Headhunters, *Pickin' on Nashville* (Mercury, 1989)
Alison Krauss & Union Station, *Live* (Rounder, 2002)
Alison Krauss, *Now That I've Found You: A Collection* (Rounder, 1995)
Lady Antebellum, *Need You Now* (Capitol, 2010)
Tracy Lawrence, *Alibis* (Atlantic, 1993)
Tracy Lawrence, *Time Marches On* (Atlantic, 1996)
Little Texas, *Big Time* (Warner Bros., 1993)
Mindy McCready, *Ten Thousand Angels* (BNA, 1996)
Reba McEntire, *Merry Christmas to You* (MCA, 1987)
Reba McEntire, *Reba #1's* (MCA, 2005)
Reba McEntire, *What If It's You* (MCA, 1996)
Tim McGraw, *Greatest Hits Vol. 2—Reflected* (Curb, 2006)
Martina McBride, *Martina* (RCA, 2003)
Jo Dee Messina, *I'm Alright* (Curb, 1998)
Ronnie Milsap, *Greatest Hits* (RCA, 1980)
Lorrie Morgan, *Greatest Hits* (BNA, 1995)
Anne Murray, *Christmas Wishes* (Capitol, 1981)
Willie Nelson, *Red Headed Stranger* (Columbia, 1975)
Willie Nelson, *Super Hits* (Columbia, 1994)
Willie Nelson & Family, *Honeysuckle Rose (Soundtrack)* (Columbia, 1980)
Olivia Newton-John, *Greatest Hits* (MCA, 1977)
Oak Ridge Boys, *Fancy Free* (MCA, 1981)
Brad Paisley, *Mud on the Tires* (Arista, 2003)
Brad Paisley, *Time Well Wasted* (Arista, 2005)
Elvis Presley, *50 Years 50 Hits* (RCA, 1976)
Elvis Presley, *A Legendary Performer, Volume 1* (RCA, 1973)
Elvis Presley, *A Legendary Performer, Volume 2* (RCA, 1976)
Elvis Presley, *Amazing Grace: His Greatest Sacred Performances* (RCA, 1994)
Elvis Presley, *Burning Love and Hits from His Movies, Volume 2* (RCA, 1972)
Elvis Presley, *How Great Thou Art* (RCA, 1966)
Elvis Presley, *It's Christmas Time* (RCA, 1999)
Elvis Presley, *Moody Blue* (RCA, 1977)
Elvis Presley, *Pure Gold* (RCA, 1975)
Elvis Presley, *The Elvis Presley Story* (RCA, 1977)
Elvis Presley, *The King of Rock 'n' Roll: The Complete 50's Masters* (RCA, 1992)
Elvis Presley, *50 Worldwide Gold Award Hits, Volume 1, Parts 1 & 2* (RCA, 1990)
Rascal Flatts, *Rascal Flatts* (Lyric Street, 2000)
Rascal Flatts, *Still Feels Good* (Lyric Street, 2007)
LeAnn Rimes, *Unchained Melody: The Early Years* (Curb, 1997)
Kenny Rogers, *Christmas* (Liberty, 1981)
Kenny Rogers, *Eyes That See in the Dark* (RCA, 1983)
Kenny Rogers and Dolly Parton, *Once Upon a Christmas* (RCA, 1984)
Linda Ronstadt, *Heart Like a Wheel* (Capitol, 1974)
Linda Ronstadt, *Living in the U.S.A.* (Asylum, 1978)
George Strait, *Easy Come, Easy Go* (MCA, 1993)
George Strait, *Latest Greatest Straitest Hits* (MCA, 2000)
George Strait, *Lead On* (MCA, 1994)
George Strait, *Merry Christmas Strait to You* (MCA, 1986)
George Strait, *Ocean Front Property* (MCA, 1987)
George Strait, *One Step at a Time* (MCA, 1998)

**2 million units sold** (continued)

Sugarland, *Love on the Inside* (Mercury, 2008)
The Tractors, *The Tractors* (Arista, 1994)
Randy Travis, *No Holdin' Back* (Warner Bros., 1989)
Randy Travis, *Old 8 x 10* (Warner Bros., 1988)
Travis Tritt, *Country Club* (Warner Bros., 1990)
Travis Tritt, *Ten Feet Tall and Bulletproof* (Warner Bros., 1994)
Travis Tritt, *T-R-O-U-B-L-E* (Warner Bros., 1992)
Josh Turner, *Your Man* (MCA, 2006)
Trisha Yearwood, *Trisha Yearwood* (MCA, 1991)
Dwight Yoakam, *Guitars, Cadillacs, Etc., Etc.* (Reprise, 1986)

**1 million units sold**

Trace Adkins, *Comin' on Strong* (Capitol, 2003)
Trace Adkins, *Dreamin' Out Loud* (Capitol, 1996)
Trace Adkins, *Greatest Hits, Vol. 1* (Capitol, 2003)
Alabama, *Alabama Live* (RCA, 1988)
Alabama, *American Pride* (RCA, 1992)
Alabama, *Cheap Seats* (RCA, 1993)
Alabama, *Dancin' on the Boulevard* (RCA, 1997)
Alabama, *Greatest Hits Volume II* (RCA, 1991)
Alabama, *In Pictures* (RCA, 1995)
Alabama, *Just Us* (RCA, 1987)
Alabama, *Pass It on Down* (RCA, 1990)
Alabama, *Southern Star* (RCA, 1989)
Alabama, *The Touch* (RCA, 1986)
Jason Aldean, *Jason Aldean* (Broken Bow, 2005)
Jason Aldean, *Wide Open* (Broken Bow, 2009)
Gary Allan, *Alright Guy* (MCA, 2001)
Gary Allan, *See if I Care* (MCA, 2003)
Gary Allan, *Smoke Rings in the Dark* (MCA, 1999)
Lynn Anderson, *Rose Garden* (Columbia, 1970)
Rodney Atkins, *If You're Going Through Hell* (Curb, 2006)
David Ball, *Thinkin' Problem* (Warner Bros., 1994)
Dierks Bentley, *Dierks Bentley* (Capitol, 2003)
Dierks Bentley, *Modern Day Drifter* (Capitol, 2005)
John Berry, *John Berry* (Liberty, 1993)
Big & Rich, *Comin' to Your City* (Warner Bros., 2005)
Clint Black, *No Time to Kill* (RCA, 1993)
Clint Black, *Nothin' but the Taillights* (RCA, 1997)
Clint Black, *One Emotion* (RCA, 1994)
Clint Black, *The Hard Way* (RCA, 1992)
Suzy Bogguss, *Aces* (Liberty, 1991)
Brooks & Dunn, *Greatest Hits, Vol. II* (Arista, 2004)
Brooks & Dunn, *Hillbilly Deluxe* (Arista, 2005)
Brooks & Dunn, *Red Dirt Road* (Arista, 2003)
Brooks & Dunn, *Steers & Stripes* (Arista, 2001)
Garth Brooks, *Garth Brooks & the Magic of Christmas* (Capitol, 1989)
Jimmy Buffett, *Changes in Latitudes, Changes in Attitudes* (ABC, 1977)
Jimmy Buffett, *Son of a Son of a Sailor* (ABC, 1978)
Glen Campbell, *By the Time I Get to Phoenix* (Capitol, 1967)
Glen Campbell, *Galveston* (Capitol, 1969)
Glen Campbell, *Gentle on My Mind* (Capitol, 1967)
Glen Campbell, *Greatest Hits* (Capitol, 1971)
Mary Chapin Carpenter, *Shooting Straight in the Dark* (Columbia, 1990)
Johnny Cash, *American IV: The Man Comes Around* (American/Lost Highway, 2002)
Johnny Cash, *Super Hits* (Columbia, 1994)
Johnny Cash, *The Essential Johnny Cash* (Columbia, 2002)
Johnny Cash, *A Johnny Cash Portrait/His Greatest Hits, Vol. 2* (Columbia, 1971) (Reissued 1976 as *The Johnny Cash Collection/His Greatest Hits, Vol. 2*)
Kenny Chesney, *Be As You Are* (BNA, 2005)
Kenny Chesney, *I Will Stand* (BNA, 1997)
Kenny Chesney, *Just Who I Am: Poets & Pirates* (BNA, 2007)
Kenny Chesney, *Me and You* (BNA, 1996)
Mark Chesnutt, *Almost Goodbye* (MCA, 1993)
Mark Chesnutt, *Greatest Hits* (Decca, 1996)
Mark Chesnutt, *Longnecks and Short Stories* (MCA, 1992)
Mark Chesnutt, *Too Cold at Home* (MCA, 1990)
Terri Clark, *How I Feel* (Mercury, 1998)
Terri Clark, *Just the Same* (Mercury, 1996)
Terri Clark, *Terri Clark* (Mercury, 1995)
Patsy Cline, *Heartaches* (MCA, 1985)
Patsy Cline, *Patsy Cline Sings Songs of Love* (MCA, 1995)
Patsy Cline, *Patsy Cline Story* (MCA, 1963)
Patsy Cline, *The Patsy Cline Collection* (MCA, 1991)
David Allan Coe, *Greatest Hits* (Columbia, 1978)
Confederate Railroad, *Notorious* (Atlantic, 1994)
Billy Currington, *Doin' Somethin' Right* (Mercury, 2005)
Billy Ray Cyrus, *It Won't Be the Last* (Mercury, 1993)
Charlie Daniels Band, *Fire on the Mountain* (Kama Sutra, 1974)

Charlie Daniels Band, *Full Moon* (Epic, 1980)
Charlie Daniels Band, *Simple Man* (Epic, 1989)
Mac Davis, *Baby, Don't Get Hooked on Me* (Columbia, 1972)
Mac Davis, *Stop and Smell the Roses* (Columbia, 1974)
John Denver, *I Want to Live* (RCA, 1971)
John Denver, *Poems, Prayers, & Promises* (RCA, 1971)
John Denver, *Rocky Mountain Collection* (RCA, 1996)
John Denver, *Rocky Mountain High: The Best of John Denver* (Madacy, 1998)
John Denver, *Spirit* (RCA, 1976)
John Denver, *The Very Best of John Denver* (Heartland, 1994)
John Denver & the Muppets, *A Christmas Together* (RCA, 1988)
Diamond Rio, *Diamond Rio* (Arista, 1991)
Diamond Rio, *Greatest Hits* (Arista, 1997)
Diamond Rio, *Love a Little Stronger* (Arista, 1994)
Joe Diffie, *Honky Tonk Attitude* (Epic, 1993)
Joe Diffie, *Third Rock from the Sun* (Epic, 1994)
Eagles, *Eagles* (Asylum, 1972)
Eagles, *Selected Works: 1972–1999* (Elektra, 2000)
Sara Evans, *Real Fine Place* (RCA, 2005)
Sara Evans, *Restless* (RCA, 2003)
Jeff Foxworthy, *Crank It Up: The Music Album* (Warner Bros., 1996)
Larry Gatlin, *Straight Ahead* (Columbia, 1979)
Crystal Gayle, *We Must Believe in Magic* (United Artists, 1977)
Crystal Gayle, *When I Dream* (United Artists, 1978)
Vince Gill, *Best of Vince Gill* (RCA, 1989)
Vince Gill, *Breath of Heaven* (MCA, 1998)
Vince Gill, *High Lonesome Sound* (MCA, 1996)
Vince Gill, *The Key* (MCA, 1998)
Vince Gill, *These Days* (MCA, 2006)
Lee Greenwood, *American Patriot* (Capitol, 1992)
Lee Greenwood, *Greatest Hits* (MCA, 1985)
Merle Haggard, *His Epic Hits–The First Eleven: To Be Continued* (Epic, 1984)
Merle Haggard, *Okie from Muskogee* (Capitol, 1969)
Merle Haggard, *The Best of the Best of Merle Haggard* (Capitol, 1972)
Merle Haggard & Willie Nelson, *Pancho & Lefty* (Epic, 1982)
The Highwaymen, *The Highwaymen* (Columbia, 1985)
Johnny Horton, *Johnny Horton's Greatest Hits* (Columbia, 1961)
Alan Jackson, *Good Time* (Arista, 2008)
Alan Jackson, *High Mileage* (Arista, 1998)
Alan Jackson, *Honky Tonk Christmas* (Arista, 1993)
Alan Jackson, *Precious Memories* (Arista, 2006)
Alan Jackson, *Under the Influence* (Arista, 1999)
Alan Jackson, *What I Do* (Arista, 2004)
Alan Jackson, *When Somebody Loves You* (Arista, 2000)
Waylon Jennings, *Ol' Waylon* (RCA, 1977)
George Jones, *I Am What I Am* (Epic, 1980)
Wynonna Judd, *Revelations* (Curb, 1996)
Wynonna Judd, *Tell Me Why* (Curb, 1993)
The Judds, *Christmas Time with the Judds* (Curb, 1987)
The Judds, *Heartland* (Curb, 1987)
The Judds, *Love Can Build a Bridge* (Curb, 1990)
The Judds, *Rockin' with the Rhythm* (Curb, 1985)
Toby Keith, *Blue Moon* (Mercury, 1996)
Toby Keith, *Boomtown* (Mercury, 1994)
Toby Keith, *Honky Tonk U* (DreamWorks, 2005)
Toby Keith, *How Do You Like Me Now?!* (DreamWorks, 1999)
Toby Keith, *Toby Keith* (Mercury, 1993)
Toby Keith, *Toby Keith: 35 Biggest Hits* (Show Dog, 2008)
Toby Keith, *White Trash with Money* (Show Dog, 2006)
Sammy Kershaw, *Don't Go Near the Water* (Polydor, 1991)
Sammy Kershaw, *Haunted Heart* (Mercury, 1993)
Sammy Kershaw, *Labor of Love* (Mercury, 1997)
Robert Plant and Alison Krauss, *Raising Sand* (Rounder, 2007)
Lady Antebellum, *Lady Antebellum* (Capitol, 2008)
Miranda Lambert, *Kerosene* (Epic, 2005)
Tracy Lawrence, *I See It Now* (Atlantic, 1994)
Tracy Lawrence, *Sticks and Stones* (Atlantic, 1991)
Chris LeDoux, *20 Greatest Hits* (Capitol, 1999)
Little Texas, *Kick a Little* (Warner Bros., 1994)
Lonestar, *From Here to There: Greatest Hits* (BNA, 2003)
Lonestar, *I'm Already There* (BNA, 2001)
Patty Loveless, *Honky Tonk Angel* (MCA, 1988)
Patty Loveless, *Only What I Feel* (Epic, 1993)
Patty Loveless, *The Trouble with the Truth* (Epic, 1996)
Patty Loveless, *When Fallen Angels Fly* (Epic, 1994)
Kathy Mattea, *A Collection of Hits* (Mercury, 1990)
The Mavericks, *What a Crying Shame* (MCA, 1994)
Lila McCann, *Lila* (Elektra, 1997)
Neal McCoy, *Greatest Hits* (Atlantic, 1997)
Neal McCoy, *No Doubt About It* (Atlantic, 1994)
Neal McCoy, *You Gotta Love That* (Atlantic, 1995)

**1 million units sold** (continued)
Reba McEntire, *If You See Him* (MCA, 1998)
Reba McEntire, *Reba* (MCA, 1988)
Reba McEntire, *Reba Duets* (MCA, 2007)
Reba McEntire, *Reba McEntire Live* (MCA, 1989)
Reba McEntire, *Room to Breathe* (MCA, 2003)
Reba McEntire, *So Good Together* (MCA, 1999)
Reba McEntire, *Starting Over* (MCA, 1995)
Reba McEntire, *Sweet Sixteen* (MCA, 1989)
Reba McEntire, *The Last One to Know* (MCA, 1987)
Reba McEntire, *Whoever's in New England* (MCA, 1986)
Tim McGraw, *Let It Go* (Curb, 2007)
Martina McBride, *Emotion* (RCA, 1999)
Martina McBride, *The Way That I Am* (RCA, 1993)
Martina McBride, *Timeless* (RCA, 2005)
Martina McBride, *White Christmas* (RCA, 1998)
Martina McBride, *Wild Angels* (RCA, 1995)
Jo Dee Messina, *Burn* (Curb, 2000)
Ronnie Milsap, *Greatest Hits Volume 2* (RCA, 1985)
Montgomery Gentry, *My Town* (Columbia, 2002)
Montgomery Gentry, *Tattoos & Scars* (Columbia, 1999)
Montgomery Gentry, *You Do Your Thing* (Columbia, 2004)
John Michael Montgomery, *Greatest Hits* (Atlantic, 1997)
John Michael Montgomery, *What I Do the Best* (Atlantic, 1996)
Lorrie Morgan, *Leave the Light On* (BNA, 1989)
Lorrie Morgan, *Something in Red* (BNA, 1991)
Lorrie Morgan, *Watch Me* (BNA, 1992)
Anne Murray, *Let's Keep It That Way* (Capitol, 1978)
Anne Murray, *New Kind of Feeling* (Capitol, 1979)
Anne Murray, *The Best So Far* (Capitol, 1994)
Anne Murray, *What a Wonderful World: 26 Inspirational Classics*
   (Sparrow, 1999)
Willie Nelson, *16 Biggest Hits* (Legacy/Columbia, 1998)
Willie Nelson, *City of New Orleans* (Columbia, 1984)
Willie Nelson, *Half Nelson* (Columbia, 1985)
Willie Nelson, *Pretty Paper* (Columbia, 1979)
Willie Nelson, *Somewhere Over the Rainbow* (Columbia, 1981)
Willie Nelson, *The Sound in Your Mind* (Columbia, 1976)
Willie Nelson, *Willie Nelson Sings Kristofferson* (Columbia, 1979)
Willie Nelson, *Without a Song* (Columbia, 1983)
Juice Newton, *Juice* (Capitol, 1981)
Joe Nichols, *Man with a Memory* (Universal South, 2002)
Nitty Gritty Dirt Band, *20 Years of Dirt: The Best of The Nitty Gritty Dirt*
   *Band* (Warner Bros., 1986)
Nitty Gritty Dirt Band, *Will the Circle Be Unbroken* (United Artists, 1972)
Nitty Gritty Dirt Band, *Will the Circle Be Unbroken: Volume Two*
   (MCA, 1989)
Oak Ridge Boys, *Greatest Hits* (MC, 1980)
Oak Ridge Boys, *Greatest Hits 2* (MCA, 1984)
Roy Orbison, *All Time Greatest Hits of Roy Orbison* (Columbia, 1989)
Roy Orbison, *Mystery Girl* (Virgin, 1989)
K.T. Oslin, *80's Ladies* (RCA, 1987)
K.T. Oslin, *This Woman* (RCA, 1988)
Brad Paisley, *5th Gear* (Arista, 2007)
Brad Paisley, *Part II* (Arista, 2001)
Brad Paisley, *Who Needs Pictures* (Arista, 1999)
Dolly Parton, *Eagle When She Flies* (Columbia, 1991)
Dolly Parton, *Greatest Hits* (RCA, 1982)
Dolly Parton, *Here You Come Again* (RCA, 1977)
Dolly Parton, *Slow Dancing with the Moon* (Columbia, 1993)
Dolly Parton, Linda Ronstadt, and Emmylou Harris, *Trio*
   (Warner Bros., 1987)
Johnny Paycheck, *Take This Job and Shove It* (Epic, 1978)
Elvis Presley, *2nd to None* (BMG Heritage, 2003)
Elvis Presley, *Almost in Love* (RCA, 1970)
Elvis Presley, *Double Dynamite* (RCA, 1975)
Elvis Presley, *Elvis Aron Presley* (RCA, 1980)
Elvis Presley, *Elvis' Golden Records, Volume 2* (RCA, 1959)
Elvis Presley, *Elvis' Golden Records, Volume 3* (RCA, 1963)
Elvis Presley, *Elvis Sings Hits from His Movies, Volume 1* (RCA, 1972)
Elvis Presley, *Elvis (NBC-TV Special)* (RCA, 1968)
Elvis Presley, *Elvis! His Greatest Hits* (Reader's Digest Music, 1983)
Elvis Presley, *Flaming Star* (RCA, 1969)
Elvis Presley, *Frankie & Johnny* (RCA, 1966)
Elvis Presley, *From Nashville to Memphis* (RCA, 1993)
Elvis Presley, *G.I. Blues* (RCA, 1960)
Elvis Presley, *He Touched Me* (RCA, 1972)
Elvis Presley, *His Hand in Mine* (RCA, 1960)
Elvis Presley, *If Every Day Was Like Christmas* (RCA, 1994)
Elvis Presley, *Let's Be Friends* (RCA, 1970)
Elvis Presley, *On Stage February, 1970* (RCA, 1970)

Elvis Presley, *Separate Ways* (RCA, 1973)
Elvis Presley, *Welcome to My World* (RCA, 1977)
Ray Price, *For the Good Times* (Columbia, 1970)
Eddie Rabbit, *Horizon* (Elektra, 1980)
Rascal Flatts, *Unstoppable* (Lyric Street, 2009)
Collin Raye, *All I Can Be* (Epic, 1991)
Collin Raye, *Extremes* (Epic, 1994)
Collin Raye, *I Think About You* (Epic, 1995)
Collin Raye, *In This Life* (Epic, 1992)
Collin Raye, *The Best of Collin Raye: Direct Hits* (Epic, 1997)
Jim Reeves, *The Unforgettable Jim Reeves* (Reader's Digest Music, 1976)
LeAnn Rimes, *Greatest Hits* (Curb, 2003)
LeAnn Rimes, *LeAnn Rimes* (Curb, 1999)
LeAnn Rimes, *Sittin' on Top of the World* (Curb, 1998)
Marty Robbins, *Gunfighter Ballads and Trail Songs* (Columbia, 1959)
Kenny Rogers, *20 Great Years* (Reprise, 1990)
Kenny Rogers, *Daytime Friends* (United Artists, 1977)
Kenny Rogers, *Duets (With Kim Carnes, Dottie West, & Sheena Easton)*
   (Capitol, 1984)
Kenny Rogers, *Gideon* (United Artists, 1980)
Kenny Rogers, *Kenny Rogers* (United Artists, 1976)
Kenny Rogers, *Love Will Turn You Around* (Liberty, 1982)
Kenny Rogers, *Share Your Love* (Liberty, 1981)
Kenny Rogers, *She Rides Wild Horses* (DreamCatcher/Navarre, 1999)
Kenny Rogers, *We've Got Tonight* (Liberty, 1983)
Kenny Rogers, *What About Me* (RCA, 1984)
Kenny Rogers & Dottie West, *Classics* (United Artists, 1979)
Kenny Rogers & the First Edition, *Kenny Rogers & the First Edition: Greatest*
   *Hits* (Reprise, 1971)
Linda Ronstadt, *Greatest Hits Volume Two* (Asylum, 1980)
Linda Ronstadt, *Hasten Down the Wind* (Asylum, 1976)
Linda Ronstadt, *Prisoner in Disguise* (Asylum, 1975)
Darius Rucker, *Learn to Live* (Capitol, 2008)
Dan Seals, *The Best Of* (Capitol, 1987)
SHeDAISY, *The Whole Shebang* (Lyric Street, 1999)
Ricky Skaggs, *Highways & Heartaches* (Epic, 1982)
Soundtrack, *8 Seconds* (MCA, 1994)
Soundtrack, *Honeymoon in Vegas* (Epic, 1992)
Soundtrack, *Urban Cowboy* (Asylum, 1980)
Soundtrack, *Walk the Line* (Wind-Up Records, 2005)
Statler Brothers, *Christmas Card* (Mercury, 1978)
Ray Stevens, *Greatest Hits* (MCA, 1987)
Ray Stevens, *He Thinks He's Ray Stevens* (MCA, 1984)
Doug Stone, *Doug Stone* (Epic, 1990)
Doug Stone, *I Thought It Was You* (Epic, 1991)
George Stait, *#7* (MCA, 1986)
George Strait, *20th Century Masters: The Millennium Collection*
   (MCA, 2002)
George Strait, *Always Never the Same* (MCA, 1999)
George Strait, *Beyond the Blue Neon* (MCA, 1989)
George Strait, *Chill of an Early Fall* (MCA, 1991)
George Strait, *Does Fort Worth Ever Cross Your Mind* (MCA, 1984)
George Strait, *Fresh Cut Christmas* (Hallmark, 2006)
George Strait, *Holding My Own* (MCA, 1992)
George Strait, *Honkytonkville* (MCA, 2003)
George Strait, *If You Ain't Lovin' (You Ain't Livin')* (MCA, 1988)
George Strait, *It Just Comes Natural* (MCA, 2006)
George Strait, *Livin' It Up* (MCA, 1990)
George Strait, *Right or Wrong* (MCA, 1983)
George Strait, *Something Special* (MCA, 1985)
George Strait, *Somewhere Down in Texas* (MCA, 2005)
George Strait, *Strait Country* (MCA, 1981)
George Strait, *Strait from the Heart* (MCA, 1982)
George Strait, *Ten Strait Hits* (MCA, 1991)
George Strait, *The Road Less Traveled* (MCA, 2001)
George Strait, *Troubadour* (MCA, 2008)
Pam Tillis, *Greatest Hits* (Arista, 1997)
Pam Tillis, *Homeward Looking Angel* (Arista, 1992)
Pam Tillis, *Sweetheart's Dance* (Arista, 1994)
Aaron Tippin, *Read Between the Lines* (RCA, 1992)
Randy Travis, *Greatest Hits, Volume Two* (Warner Bros., 1992)
Randy Travis, *Greatest Hits, Volume One* (Warner Bros., 1992)
Randy Travis, *Heroes and Friends* (Warner Bros., 1990)
Randy Travis, *High Lonesome* (Warner Bros., 1991)
Travis Tritt, *Down the Road I Go* (Columbia, 2000)
Travis Tritt, *Greatest Hits: From the Beginning* (Warner Bros., 1995)
Travis Tritt, *The Restless Kind* (Warner Bros., 1996)
Tanya Tucker, *Can't Run from Yourself* (Liberty, 1992)
Tanya Tucker, *Greatest Hits 1990–1992* (Liberty, 1993)
Tanya Tucker, *Greatest Hits* (Columbia, 1975)
Tanya Tucker, *What Do I Do with Me* (Capitol, 1991)

**1 million units sold** (continued)

Josh Turner, *Long Black Train* (MCA, 2003)
Shania Twain, *Shania Twain* (Mercury, 1993)
Conway Twitty, *The Very Best of Conway Twitty* (MCA, 1978)
Carrie Underwood, *Play On* (Arista, 2009)
Keith Urban, *Keith Urban* (Capitol, 1999)
Keith Urban, *Love, Pain & the Whole Crazy Thing* (Capitol, 2006)
Ricky Van Shelton, *Backroads* (Columbia, 1991)
Ricky Van Shelton, *Greatest Hits Plus* (Columbia, 1992)
Ricky Van Shelton, *Loving Proof* (Columbia, 1988)
Ricky Van Shelton, *RVS III* (Columbia, 1990)
Ricky Van Shelton, *Wild-Eyed Dream* (Columbia, 1987)
Various Artists, *30 Years of No. 1 Country Hits* (Reader's Digest Music, 1987)
Various Artists, *Academy of Country Music's The 101 Greatest Country Hits* (K-Tel, 1995)
Various Artists, *Amazing Grace: A Country Salute to Gospel* (Sparrow, 1995)
Various Artists, *Totally Country* (BNA, 2002)
Various Artists, *Tumbling Tumbleweeds* (Reader's Digest, 1980)
Clay Walker, *Clay Walker* (Giant, 1993)
Clay Walker, *Hypnotize the Moon* (Giant, 1995)
Clay Walker, *If I Could Make a Living* (Giant, 1994)
Clay Walker, *Rumor Has It* (Giant, 1997)
Bryan White, *Between Now and Forever* (Elektra, 1996)
Bryan White, *Bryan White* (Asylum, 1994)
Keith Whitley, *Greatest Hits* (RCA, 1990)
Don Williams, *I Believe in You* (MCA, 1980)
Hank Williams, *24 of Hank Williams' Greatest Hits* (MGM, 1971)
Hank Williams, *40 Greatest Hits* (Mercury, 1978)
Hank Williams, *Greatest Hits* (MGM, 1961)
Hank Williams, *Very Best of Hank Williams* (Mercury, 2006)
Hank Williams, Jr., *Born to Boogie* (Curb, 1987)
Hank Williams, Jr., *Greatest Hits III* (Curb, 1989)
Hank Williams, Jr., *Greatest Hits Volume 2* (Curb, 1985)
Hank Williams, Jr., *Hank Live* (Curb, 1987)
Hank Williams, Jr., *Major Moves* (Curb, 1984)
Hank Williams, Jr., *The Pressure is On* (Curb, 1981)
Hank Williams, Jr., *Whiskey Bent and Hell Bound* (Warner Bros./Curb, 1981)
Mark Wills, *Wish You Were Here* (Mercury, 1998)
Gretchen Wilson, *All Jacked Up* (Epic, 2005)
Lee Ann Womack, *Lee Ann Womack* (Decca, 1997)
Tammy Wynette, *Tammy's Greatest Hits* (Epic, 1969)
Trisha Yearwood, *Hearts in Armor* (MCA, 1992)
Trisha Yearwood, *The Song Remembers When* (MCA, 1993)
Trisha Yearwood, *Thinkin' About You* (MCA, 1995)
Trisha Yearwood, *Where Your Road Leads* (MCA, 1998)
Dwight Yoakam, *Buenas Noches from a Lonely Room* (Reprise, 1988)
Dwight Yoakam, *Hillbilly Deluxe* (Reprise, 1987)
Dwight Yoakam, *If There Was a Way* (Reprise, 1990)
Dwight Yoakam, *Just Lookin' for a Hit* (Reprise, 1989)

**500,000 units sold**

Trace Adkins, *American Man, Greatest Hits Vol. 2* (Capitol, 2007)
Trace Adkins, *Big Time* (Capitol, 1997)
Trace Adkins, *Chrome* (Capitol, 2001)
Trace Adkins, *Dangerous Man* (Capitol, 2006)
Alabama, *Super Hits* (RCA, 1996)
Alabama, *Twentieth Century* (RCA, 1999)
Jason Aldean, *Relentless* (Broken Bow, 2007)
Gary Allan, *Greatest Hits* (MCA, 2007)
Gary Allan, *Living Hard* (MCA, 2007)
Gary Allan, *Tough All Over* (MCA, 2005)
Gary Allan, *Used Heart for Sale* (MCA, 1996)
John Anderson, *Greatest Hits* (Warner Bros., 1984)
John Anderson, *Solid Ground* (RCA, 1993)
John Anderson, *Wild & Blue* (Warner Bros., 1982)
Keith Anderson, *Three Chord Country and American Rock & Roll* (Arista, 2005)
Lynn Anderson, *Greatest Hits* (Columbia, 1973)
Jessica Andrews, *Who I Am* (DreamWorks, 2001)
Eddy Arnold, *My World* (RCA, 1965)
Eddy Arnold, *The Best of Eddy Arnold* (RCA, 1967)
The Bellamy Brothers, *Greatest Hits* (Warner Bros./Curb, 1982)
Dierks Bentley, *Long Trip Alone* (Capitol, 2006)
John Berry, *Faces* (Capitol, 1996)
John Berry, *Standing on the Edge* (Capitol, 1995)
Big & Rich, *Between Raising Hell and Amazing Grace* (Warner Bros., 2007)
Clint Black, *D'lectrified* (RCA, 1999)
Blackhawk, *Strong Enough* (Arista, 1995)
Suzy Bogguss, *Greatest Hits* (Capitol, 1994)
Suzy Bogguss, *Something Up My Sleeve* (Capitol, 1993)
Suzy Bogguss, *Voices in the Wind* (Liberty, 1992)

Paul Brandt, *Calm Before the Storm* (Reprise, 1996)
Brooks & Dunn, *Tight Rope* (Arista, 1999)
Jimmy Buffett, *Take the Weather with You* (RCA, 2006)
Jimmy Buffett, *Volcano* (MCA, 1979)
Jimmy Buffett, *You Had to Be There* (ABC, 1978)
Tracy Byrd, *Big Love* (MCA, 1996)
Tracy Byrd, *Keepers: Greatest Hits* (MCA, 1999)
Tracy Byrd, *Love Lessons* (MCA, 1995)
Tracy Byrd, *Tracy Byrd* (MCA, 1993)
Chris Cagle, *Chris Cagle* (Capitol, 2003)
Chris Cagle, *Play It Loud* (Capitol, 2000)
Glen Campbell, *Live* (Capitol, 1969)
Glen Campbell, *Hey Little One* (Capitol, 1968)
Glen Campbell, *Rhinestone Cowboy* (Capitol, 1975)
Glen Campbell, *Southern Nights* (Capitol, 1977)
Glen Campbell, *That Christmas Feeling* (Capitol, 1968)
Glen Campbell, *Try a Little Kindness* (Capitol, 1970)
Mary Chapin Carpenter, *A Place in the World* (Columbia, 1996)
Mary Chapin Carpenter, *Party Doll and Other Favorites* (Columbia, 1999)
Mary Chapin Carpenter, *State of the Heart* (Columbia, 1989)
Rodney Carrington, *Greatest Hits* (Capitol, 2004)
Rodney Carrington, *Morning Wood* (Capitol, 2000)
Deana Carter, *Everything's Gonna Be Alright* (Capitol, 1998)
Johnny Cash, *American V: A Hundred Highways* (Lost Highway, 2006)
Johnny Cash, *Hello, I'm Johnny Cash* (Columbia, 1970)
Johnny Cash, *I Walk the Line* (Columbia, 1964)
Johnny Cash, *Ring of Fire* (Columbia, 1963)
Johnny Cash, *The Johnny Cash Show* (Columbia, 1970)
Johnny Cash, *The Legend* (Columbia, 2005)
Johnny Cash, *The World of Johnny Cash* (Columbia, 1970)
Johnny Cash, *Unearthed* (American/Lost Highway, 2003)
Rosanne Cash, *Greatest Hits 1979–1989* (Columbia, 1989)
Rosanne Cash, *King's Record Shop* (Columbia, 1987)
Rosanne Cash, *Seven Year Ache* (Columbia, 1981)
Ray Charles, *Modern Sounds in Country & Western Music* (ABC, 1962)
Ray Charles, *Modern Sounds in Country & Western Music, Vol. 2* (ABC, 1962)
Kenny Chesney, *All I Need to Know* (BNA, 1995)
Kenny Chesney, *All I Want for Christmas Is a Real Good Tan* (BNA, 2003)
Kenny Chesney, *Live Those Songs Again* (BNA, 2006)
Mark Chesnutt, *What a Way to Live* (Decca, 1994)
Terri Clark, *Greatest Hits 1994–2004* (Mercury, 2004)
Patsy Cline, *Sweet Dreams* (Soundtrack) (MCA, 1985)
Patsy Cline/Jim Reeves, *Remembering* (MCA, 1988)
Jerry Clower, *From Yazoo City (Mississippi Talkin')* (MCA, 1971)
Jerry Clower, *Greatest Hits* (MCA, 1979)
Jerry Clower, *Mouth of the Mississippi* (Decca, 1972)
David Allan Coe, *17 Greatest Hits* (Columbia, 1985)
David Allan Coe, *For the Record: The First Ten Years* (Columbia, 1985)
David Allan Coe, *Super Hits* (Columbia, 1993)
John Conlee, *John Conlee's Greatest Hits* (MCA, 1983)
Earl Thomas Conley, *Greatest Hits* (RCA, 1988)
Rodney Crowell, *Diamonds & Dirt* (Columbia, 1988)
Billy Currington, *Little Bit of Everything* (Mercury, 2008)
Billy Ray Cyrus, *Storm in the Heartland* (Mercury, 1994)
Charlie Daniels Band, *Midnight Wind* (Epic, 1977)
Charlie Daniels Band, *Saddle Tramp* (Epic, 1976)
Charlie Daniels Band, *Windows* (Epic, 1981)
Mac Davis, *All the Love in the World* (Columbia, 1975)
Mac Davis, *Greatest Hits* (Columbia, 1979)
Mac Davis, *It's Hard to Be Humble* (Casablanca, 1980)
Billy Dean, *Billy Dean* (Liberty, 1991)
Billy Dean, *Fire in the Dark* (Liberty, 1992)
Billy Dean, *Greatest Hits* (Capitol, 1994)
Billy Dean, *Young Man* (Liberty, 1990)
John Denver, *Aerie* (RCA, 1971)
John Denver, *Farewell Andromeda* (RCA, 1973)
John Denver, *John Denver* (RCA, 1978)
John Denver, *Greatest Hits, Volume 3* (RCA, 1984)
John Denver, *Seasons of the Heart* (RCA, 1982)
John Denver, *Some Days Are Diamonds* (RCA, 1981)
John Denver, *The Wildlife Concert* (Legacy/Columbia, 1995)
Diamond Rio, *Close to the Edge* (Arista, 1992)
Diamond Rio, *Completely* (Arista, 2002)
Diamond Rio, *IV* (Arista, 1996)
Diamond Rio, *One More Day* (Arista, 2001)
Diamond Rio, *Unbelievable* (Arista, 1998)
Joe Diffie, *Life's So Funny* (Epic, 1995)
Joe Diffie, *Regular Joe* (Epic, 1992)
Dixie Chicks, *Top of the World: Live* (Columbia, 2003)
Bob Dylan, *Nashville Skyline* (Columbia, 1969)

**500,000 units sold** (*continued*)
Steve Earle, *Copperhead Road* (MCA, 1988)
Steve Earle, *Guitar Town* (MCA, 1986)
Sara Evans, *No Place That Far* (RCA, 1998)
The Everly Brothers, *The Very Best of the Everly Brothers*
  (Warner Bros., 1964)
Exile, *Greatest Hits* (Epic, 1986)
Donna Fargo, *The Happiest Girl in the Whole U.S.A.* (Dot, 1972)
Freddy Fender, *Before the Next Teardrop Falls* (Dot, 1975)
Tennessee Ernie Ford, *Hymns* (Capitol, 1956)
Tennessee Ernie Ford, *Nearer the Cross* (Capitol, 1957)
Tennessee Ernie Ford, *Spirituals* (Capitol, 1957)
Tennessee Ernie Ford, *Star Carol* (Capitol, 1956)
Jeff Foxworthy, *Greatest Bits* (Warner Bros., 1999)
Jeff Foxworthy, *Totally Committed* (Warner Bros., 1998)
Larry Gatlin, *Greatest Hits* (Columbia, 1980)
Crystal Gayle, *Classic Crystal* (United Artists, 1979)
Crystal Gayle, *Crystal Gayle's Greatest Hits* (Columbia, 1983)
Crystal Gayle, *Miss the Mississippi* (Columbia, 1979)
Crystal Gayle, *These Days* (Columbia, 1980)
Bobbie Gentry, *Ode to Billy Joe* (Capitol, 1967)
Bobbie Gentry and Glen Campbell, *Bobbie Gentry and Glen Campbell*
  (Capitol, 1968)
Vince Gill, *I Never Knew Lonely* (RCA, 1992)
Vince Gill, *Let's Make Sure We Kiss Goodbye* (MCA, 2000)
Mickey Gilley, *Biggest Hits* (Epic, 1982)
Mickey Gilley, *Encore* (Epic, 1980)
Billy Gilman, *Classic Christmas* (Epic, 2000)
Billy Gilman, *Dare to Dream* (Epic, 2001)
Bobby Goldsboro, *Honey* (United Artists, 1968)
Vern Gosdin, *10 Years of Greatest Hits* (Columbia, 1990)
Vern Gosdin, *Chiseled in Stone* (Columbia, 1987)
Vern Gosdin, *Super Hits* (Columbia, 1993)
Pat Green, *Wave on Wave* (Universal Records, 2003)
Lee Greenwood, *Inside Out* (MCA, 1981)
Lee Greenwood, *Somebody's Gonna Love You* (MCA, 1983)
Lee Greenwood, *You've Got a Good Love Comin'* (MCA, 1984)
Merle Haggard, *16 Biggest Hits* (Legacy/Epic, 1998)
Merle Haggard, *Big City* (Epic, 1981)
Merle Haggard, *For the Record* (BNA, 1999)
Merle Haggard, *Super Hits, Volume Two* (Epic, 1994)
Merle Haggard, *The Fightin' Side of Me* (Capitol, 1970)
Tom T. Hall, *Greatest Hits Vol. 2* (Mercury, 1975)
Emmylou Harris, *Blue Kentucky Girl* (Warner Bros., 1979)
Emmylou Harris, *Elite Hotel* (Reprise, 1975)
Emmylou Harris, *Evangeline* (Warner Bros., 1981)
Emmylou Harris, *Luxury Liner* (Warner Bros., 1977)
Emmylou Harris, *Pieces of the Sky* (Reprise, 1975)
Emmylou Harris, *Profile: Best of Emmylou Harris* (Warner Bros., 1978)
Emmylou Harris, *Quarter Moon in a Ten Cent Town* (Warner Bros., 1978)
Emmylou Harris, *Roses in the Snow* (Warner Bros., 1980)
Freddie Hart, *Easy Loving* (Capitol, 1971)
Wade Hayes, *Old Enough to Know* (Columbia, 1994)
Wade Hayes, *On a Good Night* (Columbia, 1996)
Ty Herndon, *Livin' in a Moment* (Epic, 1996)
Ty Herndon, *What Mattered Most* (Epic, 1995)
Highway 101, *Highway 101* (Warner Bros., 1987)
Faith Hill, *Joy to the World* (Warner Bros., 2008)
Steve Holy, *Blue Moon* (Curb, 2000)
Alan Jackson, *Let It Be Christmas* (Arista, 2002)
Alan Jackson, *Like Red on a Rose* (Arista, 2006)
Waylon Jennings, *Are You Ready for the Country* (RCA, 1976)
Waylon Jennings, *Dreaming My Dreams* (RCA, 1975)
Waylon Jennings, *I've Always Been Crazy* (RCA, 1978)
Waylon Jennings, *Music Man* (RCA, 1982)
Waylon Jennings, *Waylon Live* (RCA, 1976)
Waylon Jennings, *What Goes Around* (RCA, 1979)
Waylon Jennings & Jessi Colter, *Leather and Lace* (RCA, 1981)
Waylon Jennings & Willie Nelson, *WWII* (RCA, 1982)
Jamey Johnson, *That Lonesome Song* (Mercury, 2008)
George Jones, *16 Biggest Hits* (Legacy/Epic, 1998)
George Jones, *50 Years of Hits* (Bandit, 2004)
George Jones, *Anniversary: Ten Years of Hits* (Epic, 1982)
George Jones, *Cold Hard Truth* (Elektra, 1999)
George Jones, *High Tech Redneck* (MCA, 1993)
George Jones, *Still the Same Ole Me* (Epic, 1981)
George Jones, *Walls Can Fall* (MCA, 1992)
George Jones, *Wine Colored Roses* (Epic, 1986)
George Jones & Tammy Wynette, *Greatest Hits* (Epic, 1977)
Cledus T. Judd, *I Stoled This Record* (Razor & Tie, 1996)
Wynonna Judd, *The Other Side* (MCA/Curb, 1997)
The Judds, *Collector's Series* (RCA, 1990)

The Judds, *Greatest Hits Volume Two* (RCA/Curb, 1991)
The Judds, *Number One Hits* (RCA/Curb, 1994)
The Judds, *Rivers of Time* (RCA/Curb, 1989)
The Judds, *Wynonna & Naomi* (RCA/Curb, 1984)
Toby Keith, *20th Century Masters: The Best of Toby Keith* (Mercury, 2003)
Toby Keith, *Big Dog Daddy* (Show Dog, 2007)
Toby Keith, *Dream Walkin'* (Mercury, 1997)
Toby Keith, *That Don't Make Me a Bad Guy* (Show Dog, 2008)
The Kendalls, *Heaven's Just a Sin Away* (Churchill, 1977)
Kentucky Headhunters, *Electric Barnyard* (Mercury, 1991)
Sammy Kershaw, *Feeling Good Train* (Mercury, 1994)
Sammy Kershaw, *Politics, Religion and Her* (Mercury, 1996)
Sammy Kershaw, *The Hits: Chapter I* (Mercury, 1995)
Hal Ketchum, *Past the Point of Rescue* (Curb, 1991)
The Kinleys, *Just Between You and Me* (Epic, 1997)
Alison Krauss, *A Hundred Miles or More: A Collection* (Rounder, 2007)
Alison Krauss, *Forget About It* (Rounder, 1999)
Alison Krauss & Union Station, *Lonely Runs Both Ways* (Rounder, 2004)
Alison Krauss & Union Station, *New Favorite* (Rounder, 2001)
Alison Krauss & Union Station, *So Long, So Wrong* (Rounder, 1997)
Kris Kristofferson, *Jesus Was a Capricorn* (Monument, 1972)
Kris Kristofferson, *Me and Bobby McGee* (Monument, 1971)
Kris Kristofferson, *Songs of Kristofferson* (Columbia, 1988)
Kris Kristofferson, *The Silver Tongued Devil and I* (Monument, 1971)
Kris Kristofferson and Rita Coolidge, *Full Moon* (A&M, 1973)
Miranda Lambert, *Crazy Ex-Girlfriend* (Columbia, 2007)
Miranda Lambert, *Revolution* (Columbia, 2009)
k. d. lang, *Shadowland* (Sire, 1988)
k. d. lang & the Reclines, *Absolute Torch and Twang* (Sire, 1989)
Tracy Lawrence, *The Best of Tracy Lawrence* (Atlantic, 1998)
Tracy Lawrence, *The Coast Is Clear* (Atlantic, 1997)
Chris LeDoux, *Best Of* (Capitol, 1997)
Chris LeDoux, *Whatcha Gonna Do with a Cowboy* (Liberty, 1992)
Johnny Lee, *Lookin' for Love* (Full Moon, 1980)
Little Big Town, *The Road to Here* (Equity, 2005)
Little Texas, *First Time for Everything* (Warner Bros., 1992)
Little Texas, *Greatest Hits* (Warner Bros., 1995)
Lonestar, *Crazy Nights* (BNA, 1997)
Lonestar, *Let's Be Us Again* (BNA, 2004)
Lonestar, *Lonestar* (BNA, 1995)
Patty Loveless, *Classics* (Epic, 1999)
Patty Loveless, *Greatest Hits* (MCA, 1993)
Patty Loveless, *Long Stretch of Lonesome* (Epic, 1997)
Patty Loveless, *On Down the Line* (MCA, 1990)
Lyle Lovett, *I Love Everybody* (MCA, 1994)
Lyle Lovett, *Joshua Judges Ruth* (Curb, 1992)
Lyle Lovett, *Lyle Lovett and His Large Band* (Curb, 1989)
Lyle Lovett, *Pontiac* (Curb, 1987)
Lyle Lovett, *Step Inside This House* (MCA, 1998)
Lyle Lovett, *The Road to Ensenada* (Curb, 1996)
Loretta Lynn, *Coal Miner's Daughter* (MCA, 1980)
Loretta Lynn, *Don't Come Home a Drinkin'* (Decca, 1967)
Loretta Lynn, *Greatest Hits Volume II* (MCA, 1974)
Loretta Lynn, *Greatest Hits* (Decca, 1968)
Barbara Mandrell, *Live* (MCA, 1981)
Barbara Mandrell, *The Best of Barbara Mandrell* (ABC, 1979)
Kathy Mattea, *Lonesome Standard Time* (Mercury, 1992)
Kathy Mattea, *Time Passes By* (Mercury, 1991)
Kathy Mattea, *Untasted Honey* (Mercury, 1987)
Kathy Mattea, *Walking Away a Winner* (Mercury, 1994)
Kathy Mattea, *Willow in the Wind* (Mercury, 1989)
The Mavericks, *Music for All Occasions* (MCA, 1995)
McBride & the Ride, *Sacred Ground* (MCA, 1992)
C.W. McCall, *Black Bear Road* (MGM, 1975)
Neal McCoy, *Neal McCoy* (Atlantic, 1996)
Mindy McCready, *If I Don't Stay the Night* (BNA, 1997)
Reba McEntire, *Best of Reba McEntire* (Mercury, 1985)
Reba McEntire, *Greatest Hits Vol. III: I'm a Survivor* (MCA, 2001)
Reba McEntire, *Have I Got a Deal for You* (MCA, 1985)
Reba McEntire, *Keep on Loving You* (Valory, 2009)
Reba McEntire, *Love Revival* (Hallmark, 2008)
Reba McEntire, *My Kind of Country* (MCA, 1984)
Reba McEntire, *The Secret of Giving: A Christmas Collection* (MCA, 1999)
Reba McEntire, *What Am I Gonna Do About You* (MCA, 1986)
Tim McGraw, *Southern Voice* (Curb, 2009)
Martina McBride, *My Heart* (Hallmark, 2005)
Martina McBride, *Waking Up Laughing* (RCA, 2007)
Jo Dee Messina, *Delicious Surprise* (Curb, 2005)
Jo Dee Messina, *Greatest Hits* (Curb, 2003)
Jo Dee Messina, *Jo Dee Messina* (Curb, 1996)
Roger Miller, *Dang Me* (Smash, 1992)
Roger Miller, *Golden Hits* (Smash, 1965)

**500,000 units sold** (continued)

Roger Miller, *Return of Roger Miller* (Smash, 1965)
Ronnie Milsap, *40 #1 Hits* (Capitol, 2000)
Ronnie Milsap, *It Was Almost Like a Song* (RCA, 1977)
Ronnie Milsap, *Lost in the Fifties* (RCA, 1986)
Ronnie Milsap, *Only One Love in My Life* (RCA, 1978)
Ronnie Milsap, *Ronnie Milsap Live* (RCA, 1976)
Ronnie Milsap, *There's No Gettin' Over Me* (RCA, 1981)
Montgomery Gentry, *Carrying On* (Columbia, 2001)
Montgomery Gentry, *Greatest Hits: Something to Be Proud Of* (Columbia, 2005)
John Michael Montgomery, *Brand New Me* (Atlantic, 2000)
John Michael Montgomery, *Leave a Mark* (Warner Bros., 1998)
Craig Morgan, *My Kind of Livin'* (Broken Bow, 2005)
Lorrie Morgan, *Greater Need* (BNA, 1996)
Lorrie Morgan, *Shakin' Things Up* (BNA, 1997)
Lorrie Morgan, *War Paint* (BNA, 1994)
Gary Morris, *Why Lady Why* (Warner Bros., 1983)
Michael Martin Murphey, *Blue Sky–Night Thunder* (Epic, 1975)
Michael Martin Murphey, *Cowboy Songs* (Warner Bros., 1990)
David Lee Murphy, *Out with a Bang* (MCA, 1994)
Anne Murray, *A Little Good News* (Capitol, 1983)
Anne Murray, *Country* (Capitol, 1974)
Anne Murray, *Country Croonin'* (Straightway, 2002)
Anne Murray, *Heart over Mind* (Capitol, 1984)
Anne Murray, *I'll Always Love You* (Capitol, 1979)
Anne Murray, *Snowbird* (Capitol, 1970)
Anne Murray, *Something to Talk About* (Capitol, 1986)
Anne Murray, *The Very Best of Anne Murray* (Heartland, 1991)
Anne Murray, *Where Do You Go When You Dream* (Capitol, 1981)
Willie Nelson, *Electric Horseman* (Soundtrack) (Columbia, 1979)
Willie Nelson, *Take It to the Limit* (Columbia, 1987)
Willie Nelson, *The Essential Willie Nelson* (Columbia, 2003)
Willie Nelson, *The Troublemaker* (Columbia, 1976)
Willie Nelson and Leon Russell, *One for the Road* (Columbia, 1979)
Willie Nelson and Ray Price, *San Antonio Rose* (Columbia, 1980)
Juice Newton, *Juice Newton's: Greatest Hits* (Capitol, 1987)
Juice Newton, *Quiet Lies* (Capitol, 1982)
Olivia Newton-John, *Clearly Love* (MCA, 1975)
Olivia Newton-John, *Come on Over* (MCA, 1976)
Olivia Newton-John, *Don't Stop Believin'* (MCA, 1976)
Olivia Newton-John, *Have You Never Been Mellow* (MCA, 1975)
Olivia Newton-John, *If You Love Me, Let Me Know* (MCA, 1974)
Olivia Newton-John, *Let Me Be There* (MCA, 1973)
Joe Nichols, *III* (Universal South, 2005)
Nickel Creek, *Nickel Creek* (Sugar Hill Records, 2000)
Nickel Creek, *This Side* (Sugar Hill Records, 2002)
Nitty Gritty Dirt Band, *More Great Dirt: The Best of Vol. II* (Warner Bros., 1989)
Oak Ridge Boys, *American Made* (MCA, 1983)
Oak Ridge Boys, *Bobbie Sue* (MCA, 1982)
Oak Ridge Boys, *Christmas* (MCA, 1985)
Oak Ridge Boys, *20th Century Masters–The Millennium Collection: The Best Of . . .* (MCA, 2000)
Oak Ridge Boys, *Deliver* (MCA, 1985)
Roy Orbison, *16 Biggest Hits* (Monument/Legacy, 1999)
Roy Orbison, *In Dreams: Greatest Hits* (Virgin, 1987)
Roy Orbison, *Roy Orbison's Greatest Hits* (Monument, 1976)
Roy Orbison, *Super Hits* (Columbia, 1995)
K.T. Oslin, *Love in a Small Town* (RCA, 1990)
Buck Owens, *Best of Buck Owens* (Capitol, 1964)
Dolly Parton, *9 to 5 and Odd Jobs* (RCA, 1980)
Dolly Parton, *Great Balls of Fire* (RCA, 1979)
Dolly Parton, *Heartbreaker* (RCA, 1978)
Dolly Parton, *Home for Christmas* (Columbia, 1990)
Dolly Parton, *The Best of Dolly Parton* (RCA, 1975)
Dolly Parton, *White Limozeen* (Columbia, 1989)
Dolly Parton, Tammy Wynette, and Loretta Lynn, *Honky Tonk Angels* (Columbia, 1993)
Dolly Parton, Linda Ronstadt, and Emmylou Harris, *Trio II* (Elektra, 1999)
Johnny Paycheck, *Greatest Hits Vol. II* (Epic, 1974)
Michael Peterson, *Michael Peterson* (Reprise, 1997)
Kellie Pickler, *Small Town Girl* (BNA, 2006)
Elvis Presley, *A Legendary Performer, Volume 3* (RCA, 1978)
Elvis Presley, *Blue Christmas* (RCA, 1992)
Elvis Presley, *C'mon Everybody* (RCA, 1971)
Elvis Presley, *Elvis* (RCA, 1956)
Elvis Presley, *Elvis: That's the Way It Is* (RCA, 1970)
Elvis Presley, *Elvis Country* (RCA, 1971)
Elvis Presley, *Elvis' Golden Records, Volume 4* (RCA, 1968)
Elvis Presley, *Elvis' Golden Records, Volume 5* (RCA, 1984)

Elvis Presley, *Elvis in Person at the International Hotel Las Vegas Nevada* (RCA, 1969)
Elvis Presley, *Elvis Is Back!* (RCA, 1960)
Elvis Presley, *Elvis Now* (RCA, 1972)
Elvis Presley, *Elvis Presley* (RCA, 1956)
Elvis Presley, *Elvis Presley Gospel Treasury* (Time Life Music, 1996)
Elvis Presley, *From Elvis in Memphis* (RCA, 1969)
Elvis Presley, *From Elvis Presley Boulevard, Memphis, Tennessee* (RCA, 1976)
Elvis Presley, *From Memphis to Vegas* (RCA, 1969)
Elvis Presley, *Girl Happy* (RCA, 1965)
Elvis Presley, *Girls! Girls! Girls!* (RCA, 1962)
Elvis Presley, *He Walks Beside Me: Favorite Songs of Faith and Inspiration* (RCA, 1978)
Elvis Presley, *Heart & Soul* (RCA, 1995)
Elvis Presley, *I Got Lucky* (RCA, 1971)
Elvis Presley, *King Creole* (RCA, 1958)
Elvis Presley, *Love Me Tender* (RCA, 1987)
Elvis Presley, *Loving You* (RCA, 1957)
Elvis Presley, *Memories of Christmas* (RCA, 1982)
Elvis Presley, *Our Memories of Elvis* (RCA, 1979)
Elvis Presley, *Platinum: A Life in Music* (RCA, 1997)
Elvis Presley, *Recorded Live on Stage in Memphis* (RCA, 1974)
Elvis Presley, *Roustabout* (RCA, 1964)
Elvis Presley, *Something for Everybody* (RCA, 1961)
Elvis Presley, *The Complete Sun Sessions* (RCA, 1987)
Elvis Presley, *The Legend Lives On* (Readers Digest, 1986)
Elvis Presley, *The Rock 'n' Roll Era* (BMG, 1988)
Elvis Presley, *This Is Elvis* (RCA, 1981)
Elvis Presley, *Ultimate Gospel* (BMG Heritage, 2004)
Elvis Presley, *Walk a Mile in My Shoes: The Essential 70's Masters* (RCA, 1995)
Ray Price, *All-Time Greatest Hits* (Columbia, 1972)
Ray Price, *Greatest Hits* (Columbia, 1986)
Charley Pride, *Charley Pride in Person* (RCA, 1969)
Charley Pride, *Charley Pride Sings Heart Songs* (RCA, 1971)
Charley Pride, *Charley Pride's 10th Album* (RCA, 1970)
Charley Pride, *Country* (RCA, 1966)
Charley Pride, *Did You Think to Pray* (RCA, 1971)
Charley Pride, *From Me to You* (RCA, 1971)
Charley Pride, *Just Plain Charley* (RCA, 1970)
Charley Pride, *The Best of Charley Pride* (RCA, 1969)
Charley Pride, *The Best of Charley Pride, Vol. 2* (RCA, 1972)
Charley Pride, *The Country Way* (RCA, 1967)
Charley Pride, *The Sensational Charley Pride* (RCA, 1969)
John Prine, *The Best of John Prine* (Atlantic, 1976)
Pure Prairie League, *Bustin' Out* (RCA, 1973)
Eddie Rabbitt, *Step by Step* (Elektra, 1981)
Eddie Rabbitt, *The Best of Eddie Rabbitt* (Elektra, 1979)
Boots Randolph, *Boots with Strings* (Monument, 1966)
Boots Randolph, *Yakety Sax* (Monument, 1960)
Collin Raye, *The Walls Came Down* (Epic, 1998)
Jim Reeves, *Distant Drums* (RCA, 1966)
Jim Reeves, *The Best of Jim Reeves* (RCA, 1964)
Jim Reeves, *The Legendary Jim Reeves* (RCA, 1988)
Restless Heart, *Big Dreams in a Small Town* (RCA, 1988)
Restless Heart, *Big Iron Horses* (RCA, 1992)
Restless Heart, *Fast Movin' Train* (RCA, 1990)
Restless Heart, *Wheels* (RCA, 1986)
Charlie Rich, *There Won't Be Anymore* (RCA, 1974)
Charlie Rich, *Very Special Love Songs* (Epic, 1974)
Ricochet, *Ricochet* (Columbia, 1996)
Jeannie C. Riley, *Harper Valley P.T.A.* (Plantation, 1968)
LeAnn Rimes, *I Need You* (Curb, 2001)
LeAnn Rimes, *This Woman* (Curb, 2005)
LeAnn Rimes, *Twisted Angel* (Curb, 2002)
Marty Robbins, *All-Time Greatest Hits* (Columbia, 1972)
Marty Robbins, *Biggest Hits* (Columbia, 1987)
Marty Robbins, *Greatest Hits, Vol. III* (Columbia, 1971)
Marty Robbins, *Marty's Greatest Hits* (Columbia, 1962)
Marty Robbins, *Super Hits* (Columbia/Legacy, 1995)
Julie Roberts, *Julie Roberts* (Mercury, 2004)
Kenny Rogers, *21 Number Ones* (Capitol, 2006)
Kenny Rogers, *42 Ultimate Hits* (Capitol, 2004)
Kenny Rogers, *Best of Kenny Rogers* (Capitol, 1982)
Kenny Rogers, *Christmas in America* (Reprise, 1989)
Kenny Rogers, *Greatest Country Hits* (Curb, 1990)
Kenny Rogers, *Greatest Hits* (RCA, 1980)
Kenny Rogers, *Heart of the Matter* (RCA, 1985)
Kenny Rogers, *Love Is What We Make It* (Capitol, 1985)
Kenny Rogers, *Love or Something Like It* (United Artists, 1978)
Kenny Rogers, *Something Inside So Strong* (Reprise, 1989)
Kenny Rogers, *The Gift* (Magnatone, 1996)

**500,000 units sold** (continued)

Kenny Rogers and Dottie West, *Every Time Two Fools Collide* (Capitol, 1978)
Linda Ronstadt, *A Retrospective* (Capitol, 1977)
Linda Ronstadt, *Don't Cry Now* (Asylum, 1973)
Linda Ronstadt, *Get Closer* (Asylum, 1982)
Billy Joe Royal, *The Royal Treatment* (Atlantic, 1987)
SSgt. Barry Sadler, *Ballads of the Green Berets* (RCA, 1966)
Sawyer Brown, *Greatest Hits 1990–1995* (Curb, 1995)
Sawyer Brown, *Outskirts of Town* (Curb, 1993)
Sawyer Brown, *The Dirt Road* (Curb, 1992)
Dan Seals, *Won't Be Blue Anymore* (EMI, 1985)
Kevin Sharp, *Measure of a Man* (Asylum, 1996)
SHeDAISY, *Sweet Right Here* (Lyric Street, 2004)
Blake Shelton, *Blake Shelton* (Giant, 2001)
Blake Shelton, *Blake Shelton's Barn and Grill* (Warner Bros., 2004)
Blake Shelton, *Pure BS* (Warner Bros., 2007)
Blake Shelton, *The Dreamer* (Warner Bros., 2003)
Shenandoah, *Super Hits* (Legacy/Columbia, 1994)
Shenandoah, *The Extra Mile* (Columbia, 1990)
Shenandoah, *The Road Not Taken* (Columbia, 1989)
Ricky Skaggs, *Country Boy* (Epic, 1984)
Ricky Skaggs, *Don't Cheat in Our Home Town* (Epic, 1983)
Ricky Skaggs, *Live in London* (Epic, 1985)
Ricky Skaggs, *Waitin' for the Sun to Shine* (Epic, 1981)
Soundtrack, *Coal Miner's Daughter* (MCA, 1980)
Soundtrack, *Dueling Banjos/Deliverance* (Warner Bros., 1973)
Soundtrack, *Maverick* (Atlantic, 1994)
Statler Brothers, *10th Anniversary* (Mercury, 1983)
Statler Brothers, *Atlanta Blue* (Mercury, 1984)
Statler Brothers, *Entertainers . . . On and Off the Record* (Mercury, 1978)
Statler Brothers, *Gospel Favorites* (Polygram, 1992)
Statler Brothers, *Holy Bible: New Testament* (Mercury, 1975)
Statler Brothers, *Holy Bible: Old Testament* (Mercury, 1975)
Statler Brothers, *Partners in Rhyme* (Mercury, 1987)
Statler Brothers, *The Best of The Statler Brothers Rides Again, Volume II* (Mercury, 1975)
Statler Brothers, *The Originals* (Mercury, 1979)
Statler Brothers, *Today* (Mercury, 1983)
Ray Stevens, *His All-Time Greatest Comic Hits* (Curb, 1990)
Ray Stevens, *Greatest Hits Volume 2* (MCA, 1987)
Ray Stevens, *I Have Returned* (MCA, 1985)
Doug Stone, *From the Heart* (Epic, 1992)
Doug Stone, *Greatest Hits* (Epic, 1994)
Doug Stone, *More Love* (Epic, 1993)
George Strait, *22 More Hits* (MCA, 2007)
George Strait, *For the Last Time: Live from the Astrodome* (MCA, 2003)
George Strait, *George Strait* (MCA, 2000)
George Strait, *Merry Christmas Wherever You Are* (MCA, 1999)
George Strait, *Twang* (MCA, 2009)
Marty Stuart, *Hillbilly Rock* (MCA, 1989)
Marty Stuart, *Tempted* (MCA, 1991)
Marty Stuart, *The Marty Party Hit Pack* (MCA, 1995)
Marty Stuart, *This One's Gonna Hurt You* (MCA, 1992)
Doug Supernaw, *Red and Rio Grande* (RCA, 1993)
Sylvia, *Just Sylvia* (RCA, 1983)
Cyndi Thomson, *My World* (Capitol, 2001)
Pam Tillis, *All of This Love* (Arista, 1995)
Pam Tillis, *Put Yourself in My Place* (Arista, 1991)
Aaron Tippin, *Call of the Wild* (RCA, 1993)
Aaron Tippin, *Lookin' Back at Myself* (RCA, 1994)
Aaron Tippin, *People Like Us* (Lyric Street, 2000)
Aaron Tippin, *Tool Box* (RCA, 1995)
Aaron Tippin, *You've Got to Stand for Something* (RCA, 1991)
Randy Travis, *An Old Time Christmas* (Warner Bros., 1989)
Randy Travis, *Rise and Shine* (Word, 2002)
Randy Travis, *This Is Me* (Warner Bros., 1994)
Randy Travis, *Worship and Faith* (Word, 2003)
Rick Trevino, *Rick Trevino* (Columbia, 1994)
Trick Pony, *Trick Pony* (Warner Bros., 2001)
Tanya Tucker, *Greatest Hits* (Liberty, 1989)
Tanya Tucker, *Love Me Like You Used To* (Liberty, 1987)
Tanya Tucker, *Soon* (Liberty, 1993)
Tanya Tucker, *Strong Enough to Bend* (Liberty, 1988)
Tanya Tucker, *Tennessee Woman* (Liberty, 1990)
Tanya Tucker, *TNT* (MCA, 1978)
Tanya Tucker, *What's Your Mama's Name?* (Columbia, 1973)
Tanya Tucker, *Would You Lay with Me* (Columbia, 1974)
Josh Turner, *Everything Is Fine* (MCA, 2007)
Conway Twitty, *Greatest Hits Vol. I* (Decca, 1972)

Conway Twitty, *Greatest Hits Vol. II* (MCA, 1976)
Conway Twitty, *Hello Darlin'* (Decca, 1970)
Conway Twitty, *Number Ones* (MCA, 1982)
Conway Twitty, *The Very Best of Conway Twitty* (MCA, 1978)
Conway Twitty, *You've Never Been This Far Before* (MCA, 1973)
Conway Twitty and Loretta Lynn, *Lead Me On* (Decca, 1971)
Conway Twitty and Loretta Lynn, *The Very Best Of* (MCA, 1979)
Conway Twitty and Loretta Lynn, *We Only Make Believe* (MCA, 1971)
Keith Urban, *Defying Gravity* (Capitol, 2009)
Keith Urban, *Greatest Hits* (Capitol, 2007)
Ricky Van Shelton, *A Bridge I Didn't Burn* (Columbia, 1993)
Ricky Van Shelton, *Don't Overlook Salvation* (Columbia, 1992)
Ricky Van Shelton, *Ricky Van Shelton Sings Christmas* (Columbia, 1989)
Ricky Van Shelton, *Super Hits* (Legacy/Columbia, 1995)
Van Zant, *Get Right with the Man* (Columbia, 2006)
Various Artists, *19 Hot Country Requests, Volume 1* (Epic, 1985)
Various Artists, *A Country Christmas with the Stars of Branson* (Unison, 1997)
Various Artists, *A Country Christmas with the Stars of Nashville* (Unison, 1997)
Various Artists, *Classic Country 1950–1959* (Time Life Music, 2001)
Various Artists, *Classic Country 1965–1969* (Time Life Music, 2001)
Various Artists, *Country Love* (Warner Special Products, 1995)
Various Artists, *Down from the Mountain* (Lost Highway, 2001)
Various Artists, *Keith Whitley: A Tribute Album* (RCA, 1994)
Various Artists, *Rhythm, Country & Blues* (MCA, 1994)
Various Artists, *Skynyrd Frynds* (MCA, 1994)
Various Artists, *Totally Country, Vol. 4* (BNA, 2005)
Various Artists, *Ultimate Country Party 1998* (Arista, 1998)
Phil Vassar, *Phil Vassar* (Arista, 2000)
Clay Walker, *Greatest Hits* (Giant, 1998)
Clay Walker, *Live, Laugh, Love* (Giant, 1999)
Jerry Jeff Walker, *Viva Terlingua* (MCA, 1973)
Steve Wariner, *Burnin' the Roadhouse Down* (Capitol, 1998)
Steve Wariner, *I Am Ready* (Arista, 1991)
Steve Wariner, *Two Teardrops* (Capitol, 1999)
Bryan White, *The Right Place* (Elektra, 1997)
Lari White, *Wishes* (RCA, 1994)
Keith Whitley, *Don't Close Your Eyes* (RCA, 1988)
Keith Whitley, *I Wonder Do You Think of Me* (RCA, 1989)
Keith Whitley, *Super Hits* (RCA, 1995)
The Wilkinsons, *Nothing but Love* (Giant, 1998)
Don Williams, *Best of Don Williams Volume II* (MCA, 1979)
Don Williams, *Best of Don Williams, Volume III* (MCA, 1984)
Hank Williams, *20 of Hank Williams' Greatest Hits* (Mercury, 1998)
Hank Williams Jr., *America (The Way I See It)* (Curb, 1990)
Hank Williams Jr., *Family Tradition* (Elektra/Curb, 1979)
Hank Williams Jr., *Five-O* (Curb, 1985)
Hank Williams Jr., *Habits Old and New* (Curb, 1980)
Hank Williams Jr., *High Notes* (Curb, 1982)
Hank Williams Jr., *Lone Wolf* (Curb, 1990)
Hank Williams Jr., *Man of Steel* (Curb, 1983)
Hank Williams Jr., *Maverick* (Curb, 1992)
Hank Williams Jr., *Montana Cafe* (Curb, 1986)
Hank Williams Jr., *Pure Hank* (Curb, 1991)
Hank Williams Jr., *Rowdy* (Curb, 1981)
Hank Williams Jr., *Strong Stuff* (Warner Bros./Curb, 1983)
Hank Williams Jr., *That's How They Do It in Dixie: The Essential Collection* (Curb, 2006)
Hank Williams Jr., *Wild Streak* (Curb, 1988)
Hank Williams Jr., *Your Cheatin' Heart* (Soundtrack) (MGM, 1964)
Lucinda Williams, *Car Wheels on a Gravel Road* (Mercury, 1998)
Mark Wills, *Permanently* (Mercury, 2000)
Lee Ann Womack, *Greatest Hits* (MCA, 2004)
Lee Ann Womack, *Some Things I Know* (Decca, 1998)
Lee Ann Womack, *There's More Where That Came From* (MCA, 2005)
Darryl Worley, *Have You Forgotten?* (DreamWorks, 2003)
The Wreckers, *Stand Still, Look Pretty* (Maverick, 2006)
Chely Wright, *Single White Female* (MCA, 1999)
Tammy Wynette, *Greatest Hits, Volume II* (Epic, 1971)
Trisha Yearwood, *Everybody Knows* (MCA, 1996)
Trisha Yearwood, *Inside Out* (MCA, 2001)
Trisha Yearwood, *Jasper County* (MCA, 2005)
Trisha Yearwood, *Real Live Woman* (MCA, 2000)
Trisha Yearwood, *The Sweetest Gift* (MCA, 1994)
Dwight Yoakam, *Dwight Live* (Reprise, 1995)
Dwight Yoakam, *Dwight Yoakam: The Very Best Of* (Rhino, 2004)
Dwight Yoakam, *Gone* (Reprise, 1995)
Dwight Yoakam, *Last Chance for a Thousand Years* (Warner Bros., 1999)

# American Society of Composers, Authors and Publishers (ASCAP)
# Most Performed Country Song of the Year Awards

(Year reflects previous year's performance)

| Year | Song | Writers | Publisher (at time of award) |
|------|------|---------|------------------------------|
| 1982 | "(There's) No Getting Over Me" | Tom Brasfield–Walt Aldridge | Rick Hall Music |
| 1983 | "Love Will Turn You Around" | Kenny Rogers–Even Stevens*–David Malloy*–Thom Schuyler* | Lion's Mate Music, DebDave Music, Briarpatch Music |
| 1984 | "We've Got Tonight" | Bob Seger | Gear Publishing Co. |
| 1985 | "To All the Girls I've Loved Before" | Hal David–Albert Hammond | April Music, Casa David |
| 1986 | "Lost in the Fifties Tonight (In the Still of the Night)" | Fred Parris*–Mike Reid–Troy Seals | Lodge Hall Music, Two-Sons Music, WB Music Corp. |
| 1987 | "Now and Forever (You and Me)" | Randy Goodrum–Jim Vallance*–David Foster* | California Phase Music, Tom Collins Music Corp., Lodge Hall Music, MCA Music |
| 1988 | "I'll Still Be Loving You" | Pat Bunch*–Mary Ann Kennedy*–Pam Rose*–Todd Cerney | Chriswald Music, Hopi-Sound Music, MCA Music |
| 1989 | "Too Gone, Too Long" | Gene Pistilli | Almo Music, High Falutin Music |
| 1990 | "What's Going on in Your World" | Red Stegall*–David Chamberlain–Royce Porter | Ha-Deb Music, Milene Music |
| 1991 | "Friends in Low Places" | Earl Bud Lee–Dewayne Blackwell* | Chancey Tunes—Music Ridge Music |
| 1992 | "Don't Rock the Jukebox" | Roger Murrah*–Keith Stegall*–Alan Jackson | Mattie Ruth Musick, Seventh Son Music |
| 1993 | "When She Cries" | Marc Beeson–Sonny LeMaire* | EMI April Music |
| 1994 | "Chattahoochee" | Alan Jackson–Jim McBride | Mattie Ruth Musick, Seventh Son Music, Sony/Cross Keys Music Publishing |
| 1995 | "I Swear" | Gary B. Baker–Frank Myers | Rick Hall Music, Morganactive Songs Inc. |
| 1996 | "I Can Love You Like That" | Steve Diamond*–Maribeth Derry–Jennifer Kimball | Criterion Music Corp., Friends & Angels Music, Full Keel Music, Second Wave Music |
| 1997 | "No News" | Phil Barnhart*–Sam Hogin*–Mark D. Sanders | MCA Music Publishing, Starstruck Writers Group |
| 1998 | "One Night at a Time" | Roger Cook*–Eddie Kilgallon–Earl Bud Lee | EMI Music Publishing, Hipp Row Music & Island Bound Music, Life's a Pitch Music, Neon Sky Music, Sony/ATV Cross Keys |
| 1999 | "Bye Bye" (tie) | Phil Vassar | EMI Music Publishing, Phil Vassar Music Almo Music Corp., Anwa Music, BNC Songs |
|      | "This Kiss" | Annie Roboff–Beth Nielsen Chapman | Almo Music Corp., Anwa Music, BNC Songs |
| 2000 | "How Forever Feels" (tie) | Tony Mullins–Wendell Mobley* | Warner/Chappell Music Group |
|      | Write This Down | Dana Hunt–Kent Robbins* | Neon Sky Music |
| 2001 | "I Hope You Dance" (tie) | Mark D. Sanders–Tia Sellers* | Soda Creek Songs, Universal Music Publishing Group |
|      | The Way You Love Me | Keith Follesé–Michael Dulaney | Airstream Dreams Music, Coyote House Music, Famous Music, Follazoo Crew Music, Scott and Soda, Warner/Chappell Music Group |
| 2002 | "Ain't Nothin' 'Bout You" (tie) | Rivers Rutherford–Tom Shapiro | Memphisto Music, Universal Music Publishing Group |
|      | "I'm Already There" | Gary Baker–Richie McDonald*–Frank Myers | Josh Nick Music, Swear By It Music, Zomba Enterprises |
| 2003 | "The Good Stuff" | Craig Wiseman–Jim Collins* | BMG Songs, Mrs. Lumpkin's Poodle Music |
| 2004 | "It's Five O'Clock Somewhere" | Jim "Moose" Brown–Don Rollins* | Sea Gayle Music |
| 2005 | "Live Like You Were Dying" | Craig Wiseman–Tim Nichols* | Big Loud Shirt Industries |
| 2006 | "Jesus, Take the Wheel" | Brett James–Hillary Lindsey–Gordie Sampson | Cornman Music, Dimensional Music Publishing No Such Music, Passing Stranger Music, Raylene Music, Songs of Combustion Music, Sony/ATV Music Publishing, Windswept Music |
| 2007 | "Before He Cheats" (tie) | Josh Kear–Chris Tompkins | Big Loud Shirt Industries, Mighty Under Dog Music, Sony/ATV Music Publishing |
|      | "If You're Going Through Hell (Before the Devil Even Knows)" | Dave Berg–Annie Tate*–Sam Tate* | BergBrain Music, Cal IV Entertainment |
| 2008 | "Good Directions" | Luke Bryan*–Rachel Thibodeau | Castle Street Music, Dan Hodges Music |
| 2009 | "You're Gonna Miss This" | Ashley Gorley–Lee Thomas Miller* | Songs of Combustion Music, Bug Music, Windswept Music |
| 2010 | "Need You Now" | Dave Haywood*–Josh Kear–Charles Kelley* Hillary Scott* | Big Yellow Dog Music, Darth Buddha |

*Writer and publisher share not licensed through ASCAP

## Country's Share of the U.S. Recorded-Music Market

| Year | Gross Country Sales (millions) | Country Portion of Dollars Spent on Recorded Music |
|------|-------------------------------|---------------------------------------------------|
| 1973 | $150.2 | 10.5% |
| 1974 | $255.2 | 11.6% |
| 1975 | $276.1 | 11.7% |
| 1976 | $331.2 | 12.1% |
| 1977 | $451.6 | 12.4% |
| 1978 | $426.5 | 10.2% |
| 1979 | $437.5 | 9.0% |
| 1980 | $526.5 | 12.0% |
| 1981 | $529.3 | 15.0% |
| 1982 | $538.8 | 15.0% |
| 1983 | $496.0 | 13.0% |
| 1984 | $393.3 | 10.0% |
| 1985 | $438.8 | 10.0% |
| 1986 | $415.6 | 10.0% |
| 1987 | $528.9 | 9.5% |
| 1988 | $425.3 | 6.8% |
| 1989 | $447.4 | 6.8% |
| 1990 | $663.6 | 8.8% |
| 1991 | $1,002.8 | 12.8% |
| 1992 | $1,570.2 | 17.4% |
| 1993 | $1,878.7 | 18.7% |
| 1994 | $1,967.1 | 16.3% |
| 1995 | $2,056.6 | 16.7% |
| 1996 | $1,837.5 | 14.7% |
| 1997 | $1,762.1 | 14.4% |
| 1998 | $1,931.7 | 14.1% |
| 1999 | $1,575.1 | 10.8% |
| 2000 | $1,532.6 | 10.7% |
| 2001 | $1,442.8 | 10.5% |
| 2002 | $1,349.7 | 10.7% |
| 2003 | $1,232.9 | 10.4% |
| 2004 | $1,604.9 | 13.0% |
| 2005 | $1,537.1 | 12.5% |
| 2006 | $1,528.6 | 13.0% |
| 2007 | $1,192.8 | 11.5% |
| 2008* | $1,009.1 | 11.9% |

*Last year for which RIAA has determined genre percentages
(Source: RIAA Annual Reports)

## Full-time Country Radio Stations in the United States

| Year | Full-time Country Stations | Percentage of All U.S. Stations |
|------|---------------------------|--------------------------------|
| 1961 | 81 | 1.7% |
| 1963 | 97 | 1.9% |
| 1965 | 208 | 3.8% |
| 1969 | 606 | 9.0% |
| 1971 | 525 | 7.8% |
| 1972 | 633 | 8.6% |
| 1973 | 764 | 10.2% |
| 1974 | 856 | 11.0% |
| 1975 | 1,116 | 13.9% |
| 1977 | 1,140 | 13.6% |
| 1978 | 1,150 | 13.4% |
| 1979 | 1,434 | 16.4% |
| 1980 | 1,534 | 17.2% |
| 1981 | 1,785 | 19.6% |
| 1982 | 2,114 | 23.1% |
| 1983 | 2,266 | 24.3% |
| 1984 | 2,265 | 23.5% |
| 1985 | 2,289 | 23.2% |
| 1986 | 2,275 | 22.6% |
| 1987 | 2,212 | 21.6% |
| 1988 | 2,169 | 20.7% |
| 1989 | 2,086 | 19.6% |
| 1990 | 2,108 | 19.5% |
| 1991 | 2,140 | 19.4% |
| 1992 | 2,203 | 19.5% |
| 1993 | 2,402 | 20.8% |
| 1994 | 2,427 | 20.7% |
| 1995 | 2,346 | 19.5% |
| 1996 | 2,321 | 19.1% |
| 1997 | 2,505 | 20.1% |
| 1998 | 2,382 | 18.8% |
| 1999 | 2,320 | 18.0% |
| 2000 | 2,284 | 17.2% |
| 2001 | 2,200 | 16.3% |
| 2002 | 2,142 | 15.9% |
| 2003 | 2,100 | 15.1% |
| 2004 | 2,060 | 14.8% |
| 2005 | 2,030 | 14.3% |
| 2006 | 2,046 | 14.2% |
| 2007 | 2,046 | 14.0% |
| 2008 | 2,037 | 13.4% |
| 2009 | 2,009 | 12.9% |
| 2010 | 2,002 | 12.6% |

(Sources: RIAA Consumer Profile; CMA Country Radio Book; Inside Radio/ M Street Corp.; Arbitron)

# BMI's Most Performed Country Song of the Year Awards

(The Robert J. Burton Award)

| Year | Song | Writers | Publisher (at time of award) |
|------|------|---------|------------------------------|
| 1967 | "Almost Persuaded" | Glenn Sutton–Billy Sherrill | Al Gallico Music Corp. |
| 1968 | "Release Me" | Eddie Miller–W. S. Stevenson | Four Star Music Co. |
| 1969 | "Gentle on My Mind" | John Hartford | Glaser Publications |
| 1970 | "Gentle on My Mind" | John Hartford | Glaser Publications |
| 1971 | "(I Never Promised You a) Rose Garden" | Joe South | Lowery Music Co. |
| 1972 | "Help Me Make It Through the Night" | Kris Kristofferson | Combine Music Corp. |
| 1973 | "The Happiest Girl in the Whole U.S.A." | Donna Fargo | Algee Music Corp., Prima-Donna Music Corp. |
| 1974 | "Let Me Be There" | John Rostill | Al Gallico Music Corp. |
| 1975 | "If You Love Me (Let Me Know)" | John Rostill | Al Gallico Music Corp. |
| 1976 | "When Will I Be Loved" | Phil Everly | Acuff-Rose Publications |
| 1977 | "Misty Blue" | Bob Montgomery | Talmont Music |
| 1978 | "Here You Come Again" | Barry Mann–Cynthia Weil | Screen Gems-EMI Music, Summerhill Songs |
| 1979 | "Talkin' in Your Sleep" | Roger Cook–Bobby Wood | Chriswood Music, Roger Cook Music |
| 1980 | "Suspicions" | David Malloy–Randy McCormick–Eddie Rabbitt–Even Stevens | Briarpatch Music, DebDave Music |
| 1981 | "9 to 5" | Dolly Parton | Fox Fanfare Music, Inc., Velvet Apple Music |
| 1982 | "Elvira" | Dallas Frazier | Acuff-Rose Publications |
| 1983 | "Nobody" | Kye Fleming–Dennis Morgan | Tom Collins Music Corp. |
| 1984 | "Islands in the Stream" | Barry Gibb–Maurice Gibb–Robin Gibb | Gibb Brothers Music |
| 1985 | "Mama He's Crazy" | Kenny O'Dell | Kenny O'Dell Music |
| 1986 | "Don't Call It Love" | Dean Pitchford–Tom Snow | Careers Music, Pzazz Music, Snow Music |
| 1987 | "Hold On" | Rosanne Cash | Atlantic Music Corp., Chelcait Music |
| 1988 | "To Know Him Is to Love Him" | Phil Spector | Mother Bertha Music |
| 1989 | "Fallin' Again" | Greg Fowler–Teddy Gentry–Randy Owen | Maypop Music |
| 1990 | "Cathy's Clown" | Don Everly | Acuff-Rose Music |
| 1991 | "Hard Rock Bottom of Your Heart" | Hugh Prestwood | Careers-BMG Music Publishing |
| 1992 | "She's in Love with the Boy" | John Ims | Rites of Passage Music, Warner/Elektra/Asylum Music |
| 1993 | "Achy Breaky Heart" | Don Von Tress | Millhouse Music |
| 1994 | "Blame It on Your Heart" | Harlan Howard–Kostas | Harlan Howard Songs, Seven Angels Music, Songs of PolyGram International |
| 1995 | "Wink" | Bob DiPiero–Tom Shapiro | American Made Music, Diamond Struck Music, Little Big Town Music, Hamstein Cumberland Music, Mike Curb Music |
| 1996 | "I Can Love You Like That" | Steve Diamond–Jennifer Kimball–Maribeth Derry* | Diamond Cuts |
| 1997 | "Nobody Knows" | Dohn DuBosé–Joe Rich | D'Jonsongs, EMI-Blackwood Music, Hitco Music, Joe Shade Music |
| 1998 | "It's Your Love" | Stephony Smith | EMI–Blackwood Music, Inc. |
| 1999 | "You're Still the One" | Shania Twain–Robert John "Mutt" Lange* | Loon Echo, Inc., Universal-Songs of Polygram International, Inc. |
| 2000 | "Amazed" | Marv Green–Chris Lindsey–Aimee Mayo | Careers-BMG Music Publishing Inc., Golden Wheat Music, Silverkiss Music, Songs of Nashville DreamWorks, Warner- Tamerlane Publishing Corp. |
| 2001 | "I Hope You Dance" | Tia Sillers–Mark D. Sanders* | Choice Is Tragic Music, Ensign Music |
| 2002 | "I'm Already There" | Richie McDonald–Frank Myers*–Gary Baker* | Sony/ATV Tree |
| 2003 | "Landslide" | Stevie Nicks | Welsh Witch Music |
| 2004 | "Forever and For Always" | Shania Twain–Robert John "Mutt" Lange* | Loon Echo Inc., Universal-Songs of Polygram International, Inc. |
| 2005 | "Live Like You Were Dying" | Tim Nichols–Craig Wiseman* | Nichols Worth Music, Warner-Tamerlane Publishing Corp. |
| 2006 | "As Good As I Once Was" | Toby Keith–Scotty Emerick | Big Yellow Dog Music, Florida Cracker Music, Sony/ATV Tree, Tokeco Tunes |
| 2007 | "What Hurts the Most" | Jeffrey Steele–Steve Robson* | Gottahaveable Music, Bug Music/Songs of Windswept |
| 2008 | "Teardrops on My Guitar" | Taylor Swift–Liz Rose* | Sony/ATV Tree, Taylor Swift Music |
| 2009 | "Love Story" | Taylor Swift | Sony/ATV Tree, Taylor Swift Music |
| 2010 | "You Belong with Me" | Taylor Swift–Liz Rose* | Sony/ATV Tree, Taylor Swift Music, Wagnerville Music |

* Writer and publisher share not licensed through BMI

# Grand Ole Opry Members and the Dates They Joined the Show's Cast

Trace Adkins (August 23, 2003)
Bill Anderson (July 15, 1961)
Dierks Bentley (October 1, 2005)
Clint Black (January 10, 1991)
Garth Brooks (October 6, 1990)
Jim Ed Brown (August 12, 1963)
Roy Clark (August 22, 1987)
Terri Clark (June 12, 2004)
John Conlee (February 7, 1981)
Charlie Daniels (January 19, 2008)
Diamond Rio—Gene Johnson, Jimmy Olander, Brian Prout, Marty Roe, Dan Truman & Dana Williams (April 18, 1998)
Little Jimmy Dickens (September 25, 1948; rejoined 1975)
Joe Diffie (November 27, 1993)
The Gatlins—Larry, Steve & Rudy (December 25, 1976)
Vince Gill (August 10, 1991)
Jack Greene (December 23, 1967)
Tom T. Hall (January 1, 1971; rejoined 1980)
George Hamilton IV (February 6, 1960)
Emmylou Harris (January 25, 1992)
Jan Howard (March 27, 1971)
Alan Jackson (June 7, 1991)
Stonewall Jackson (November 10, 1956; rejoined 1969)
George Jones (August 4, 1956; rejoined January 4, 1969)
Hal Ketchum (January 22, 1994)
Alison Krauss (July 3, 1993)
Patty Loveless (June 11, 1988)
Loretta Lynn (September 25, 1962)
Barbara Mandrell (July 29, 1972)
Martina McBride (November 30, 1995)
Del McCoury (October 25, 2003)
Reba McEntire (January 17, 1986)
Jesse McReynolds (March 7, 1964)
Ronnie Milsap (February 6, 1976)

Montgomery Gentry—Troy Gentry & Eddie Montgomery (June 23, 2009)
Craig Morgan (October 25, 2008)
Lorrie Morgan (June 9, 1984)
Jimmy C. Newman (August 4, 1956)
Oak Ridge Boys—Duane Allen, Joe Bonsall, William Lee Golden, Richard Sterban (August 6, 2011)
Bobby Osborne (August 8, 1964)
Brad Paisley (February 17, 2001)
Dolly Parton (January 4, 1969)
Stu Phillips (June 1, 1967)
Ray Pillow (April 30, 1966)
Charley Pride (May 1, 1993)
Jeanne Pruett (July 21, 1973)
Rascal Flatts—Jay DeMarcus, Gary LeVox & Joe Don Rooney (October 8, 2011)
Riders in the Sky—Doug Green, Fred Labour, Joey Miskulin & Woody Paul (June 19, 1982)
Jeannie Seely (September 16, 1967)
Blake Shelton (October 23, 2010)
Ricky Van Shelton (June 10, 1988)
Jean Shepard (November 21, 1955)
Ricky Skaggs (May 15, 1982)
Connie Smith (September 18, 1965)
Mike Snider (June 2, 1990)
Ralph Stanley (January 15, 2000)
Marty Stuart (November 28, 1992)
Mel Tillis (June 9, 2007)
Pam Tillis (August 26, 2000)
Randy Travis (December 20, 1986)
Travis Tritt (February 29, 1992)
Josh Turner (October 27, 2007)
Carrie Underwood (May 10, 2008)
Steve Wariner (May 11, 1996)
The Whites—Buck, Cheryl & Sharon (March 2, 1984)
Trisha Yearwood (March 13, 1999)

# Country Music Hall of Fame Members and Their Years of Election

**1961**
Jimmie Rodgers, Fred Rose, Hank Williams

**1962**
Roy Acuff

**1963**
Elections held, but no one candidate had
enough votes

**1964**
Tex Ritter

**1965**
Ernest Tubb

**1966**
Eddy Arnold, James R. Denny, George D. Hay,
Uncle Dave Macon

**1967**
Red Foley, J. L. Frank, Jim Reeves,
Stephen H. Sholes

**1968**
Bob Wills

**1969**
Gene Autry

**1970**
Bill Monroe, Original Carter Family

**1971**
Arthur Edward Satherley

**1972**
Jimmie Davis

**1973**
Chet Atkins, Patsy Cline

**1974**
Owen Bradley, Frank "Pee Wee" King

**1975**
Minnie Pearl

**1976**
Paul Cohen, Kitty Wells

**1977**
Merle Travis

**1978**
Grandpa Jones

**1979**
Hubert Long, Hank Snow

**1980**
Johnny Cash, Connie B. Gay, Original Sons of
the Pioneers

**1981**
Vernon Dalhart, Grant Turner

**1982**
Lefty Frizzell, Roy Horton, Marty Robbins

**1983**
Little Jimmy Dickens

**1984**
Ralph Peer, Floyd Tillman

**1985**
Lester Flatt & Earl Scruggs

**1986**
The Duke of Paducah (Whitey Ford),
Wesley Rose

**1987**
Rod Brasfield

**1988**
Loretta Lynn, Roy Rogers

**1989**
Jack Stapp, Cliffie Stone, Hank Thompson

**1990**
Tennessee Ernie Ford

**1991**
Boudleaux & Felice Bryant

**1992**
George Jones, Frances Preston

**1993**
Willie Nelson

**1994**
Merle Haggard

**1995**
Roger Miller, Jo Walker-Meador

**1996**
Patsy Montana, Buck Owens, Ray Price

**1997**
Harlan Howard, Brenda Lee, Cindy Walker

**1998**
George Morgan, Elvis Presley, E.W. "Bud"
Wendell, Tammy Wynette

**1999**
Johnny Bond, Dolly Parton, Conway Twitty

**2000**
Charley Pride, Faron Young

**2001**
Bill Anderson, The Delmore Brothers, The Everly
Brothers, Don Gibson, Homer & Jethro, The
Jordanaires, Don Law, The Louvin Brothers,
Ken Nelson, Sam Phillips, Webb Pierce

**2002**
Bill Carlisle, Porter Wagoner

**2003**
Floyd Cramer, Carl Smith

**2004**
Jim Foglesong, Kris Kristofferson

**2005**
Alabama, DeFord Bailey, Glen Campbell

**2006**
Harold Bradley, Sonny James, George Strait

**2007**
Ralph Emery, Vince Gill, Mel Tillis

**2008**
Tom T. Hall, Emmylou Harris, The Statler
Brothers, Ernest V. "Pop" Stoneman

**2009**
Roy Clark, Barbara Mandrell, Charlie McCoy

**2010**
Jimmy Dean, Ferlin Husky, Billy Sherrill,
Don Williams

**2011**
Bobby Braddock, Reba McEntire,
Jean Shepard

# Nashville Songwriters Hall of Fame Members

(Administered by the Nashville Songwriters Foundation)

**1970**
Gene Autry, Johnny Bond, Albert Brumley, A. P. Carter, Ted Daffan, Vernon Dalhart, Rex Griffin, Stuart Hamblen, Pee Wee King, Vic McAlpin, Bob Miller, Leon Payne, Jimmie Rodgers, Fred Rose, Redd Stewart, Floyd Tillman, Merle Travis, Ernest Tubb, Cindy Walker, Hank Williams, Bob Wills

**1971**
Smiley Burnette, Jenny Lou Carson, Wilf Carter, Zeke Clements, Jimmie Davis, Alton & Rabon Delmore, Al Dexter, Vaughan Horton, Bradley Kincaid, Bill Monroe, Bob Nolan, Tex Owens, Tex Ritter, Carson J. Robison, Tim Spencer, Gene Sullivan, Jimmy Wakely, Wiley Walker, Scotty Wiseman

**1972**
Boudleaux & Felice Bryant, Lefty Frizzell, Jack Rhodes, Don Robertson

**1973**
Jack Clement, Don Gibson, Harlan Howard, Roger Miller, Steve Nelson & Ed Nelson Jr., Willie Nelson

**1974**
Hank Cochran

**1975**
Bill Anderson, Danny Dill, Eddie Miller, Marty Robbins, Wayne Walker, Marijohn Wilkin

**1976**
Carl Belew, Dallas Frazier, John D. Loudermilk, Moon Mullican, Curly Putman, Mel Tillis

**1977**
Johnny Cash, Woody Guthrie, Merle Haggard, Kris Kristofferson

**1978**
Joe Allison, Tom T. Hall, Hank Snow, Don Wayne

**1979**
Rev. Thomas A. Dorsey, Charles & Ira Louvin, Elsie McWilliams, Joe South

**1980**
Huddie "Leadbelly" Ledbetter, Mickey Newbury, Ben Peters, Ray Stevens

**1981**
Bobby Braddock, Ray Whitley

**1982**
Chuck Berry, William J. "Billy" Hill

**1983**
W. C. Handy, Loretta Lynn, Beasley Smith

**1984**
Hal David, Billy Sherrill

**1985**
Bob McDill, Carl Perkins

**1986**
Otis Blackwell, Dolly Parton

**1987**
Roy Orbison, Sonny Throckmorton

**1988**
Hoagy Carmichael, Troy Seals

**1989**
Rory Michael Bourke, Maggie Cavender, Sanger D. "Whitey" Shafer

**1990**
Sue Brewer, Ted Harris, Jimmy Webb

**1991**
Charlie Black, Sonny Curtis

**1992**
Max D. Barnes, Wayland Holyfield

**1993**
Red Lane, Don Schlitz, Conway Twitty

**1994**
Jerry Foster & Bill Rice, Buddy Holly, Richard Leigh, Bobby Russell

**1995**
Waylon Jennings, Dickey Lee, Dave Loggins

**1996**
Jerry Chesnut, Kenny O'Dell, Buck Owens, Norro Wilson

**1997**
Wayne Carson, Roger Cook, Hank Thompson

**1998**
Merle Kilgore, Eddie Rabbitt, Kent Robbins

**1999**
Tommy Collins, Wayne Kemp, A.L. "Doodle" Owens, Glenn Sutton

**2000**
Mac Davis, Randy Goodrum, Allen Reynolds, Billy Edd Wheeler

**2001**
Don Everly, Phil Everly, Dennis Linde, Johnny Russell

**2002**
Dean Dillon, Bob Dylan, Shel Silverstein

**2003**
Hal Blair, Rodney Crowell, Paul Overstreet, John Prine

**2004**
Guy Clark, Freddie Hart, Dennis Morgan, Billy Joe Shaver

**2005**
Gary Burr, Vince Gill, Roger Murrah, Jerry Reed, Mike Reid

**2006**
Jimmy Buffett, Hugh Prestwood, Jim Weatherly

**2007**
Bob DiPiero, Mac MacAnally, Lester Flatt and Earl Scruggs, Dottie Rambo, Hank Williams Jr.

**2008**
Matraca Berg, John Hiatt, Tom Shapiro

**2009**
Kye Fleming, Mark D. Sanders, Tammy Wynette

**2010**
Pat Alger, Steve Cropper, Paul Davis, Stephen Foster

# Grammy Awards Related to Country Music

(Years shown are years recordings were eligible, except for Hall of Fame, Lifetime Achievement, and Trustees Awards, which reflect years awards were given.)

**1958**

Best Country & Western Performance: "Tom Dooley"—The Kingston Trio (Capitol)

**1959**

Best Country & Western Performance: "The Battle of New Orleans"—Johnny Horton (Columbia)

Song of the Year: "The Battle of New Orleans" (Jimmy Driftwood)

Best Folk Performance: *The Kingston Trio at Large*—The Kingston Trio (Capitol)

Best Comedy Performance—Musical: "The Battle of Kookamonga"—Homer & Jethro (RCA)

**1960**

Best Country & Western Performance: "El Paso"—Marty Robbins (Columbia)

**1961**

Best Country & Western Recording: "Big Bad John"—Jimmy Dean (Columbia)

**1962**

Best Country & Western Recording: "Funny Way of Laughin'"—Burl Ives (Decca)

Best Rhythm & Blues Recording: "I Can't Stop Loving You"—Ray Charles (ABC-Paramount)

**1963**

Best Country & Western Recording: "Detroit City"—Bobby Bare (RCA)

Best Rhythm & Blues Recording: "Busted"—Ray Charles (ABC-Paramount)

Best Instrumental Arrangement: "I Can't Stop Loving You"—Count Basie; Arranger: Quincy Jones (Reprise)

**1964**

Best Country & Western Album: *Dang Me/Chug-a-Lug*—Roger Miller (Smash)

Best Country & Western Single: "Dang Me"—Roger Miller (Smash)

Best Country & Western Song: "Dang Me" (Roger Miller)

Best Country & Western Vocal Performance, Male: "Dang Me"—Roger Miller (Smash)

Best Country & Western Vocal Performance, Female: "Here Comes My Baby"—Dottie West (RCA)

Best New Country & Western Artist: Roger Miller (Smash)

Best Gospel or Other Religious Recording (Musical): *Great Gospel Songs*—Tennessee Ernie Ford (Capitol)

**1965**

Best Country & Western Album: *The Return of Roger Miller*—Roger Miller (Smash)

Best Country & Western Single: "King of the Road"—Roger Miller (Smash)

Best Country & Western Song: "King of the Road" (Roger Miller)

Best Country & Western Vocal Performance, Male: "King of the Road"—Roger Miller (Smash)

Best Country & Western Vocal Performance, Female: "Queen of the House"—Jody Miller (Capitol)

Best New Country & Western Artist: The Statler Brothers (Columbia)

Best Performance by a Vocal Group: *We Dig Mancini*—Anita Kerr Singers (RCA)

Best Contemporary (R&R) Single: "King of the Road"—Roger Miller (Smash)

Best Contemporary (R&R) Vocal Performance, Male: "King of the Road"—Roger Miller (Smash)

Best Contemporary (R&R) Performance Group (Vocal or Instrumental): "Flowers on the Wall"—The Statler Brothers (Columbia)

Best Gospel or Other Religious Recording (Musical): *Southland Favorites*—George Beverly Shea and the Anita Kerr Singers (RCA)

**1966**

Best Country & Western Recording: "Almost Persuaded"—David Houston (Epic)

Best Country & Western Song: "Almost Persuaded" (Billy Sherrill–Glenn Sutton)

Best Country & Western Vocal Performance, Male: "Almost Persuaded"—David Houston (Epic)

Best Country & Western Vocal Performance, Female: "Don't Touch Me"—Jeannie Seely (Monument)

Best Performance by a Vocal Group: "A Man and a Woman"—Anita Kerr Singers (Warner Bros.)

Best Sacred Recording (Musical): *Grand Ole Gospel*—Porter Wagoner and the Blackwood Brothers (RCA)

Best Rhythm & Blues Solo Vocal Performance, Male or Female: "Crying Time"—Ray Charles (ABC-Paramount)

Best Rhythm & Blues Recording: "Crying Time"—Ray Charles (ABC-Paramount)

Best Album Cover, Photography: *Confessions of a Broken Man*—Porter Wagoner; Art Direction: Robert Jones; Photographer: Les Leverett (RCA)

**1967**

Best Country & Western Recording: "Gentle on My Mind"—Glen Campbell (Capitol)

Best Country & Western Song: "Gentle on My Mind" (John Hartford)

Best Country & Western Solo Vocal Performance, Female: "I Don't Wanna Play House"—Tammy Wynette (Epic)

Best Country & Western Solo Vocal Performance, Male: "Gentle on My Mind"—Glen Campbell (Capitol)

Best Country & Western Performance, Duet, Trio, or Group (Vocal or Instrumental): "Jackson"—Johnny Cash & June Carter (Columbia)

Best Vocal Performance, Female: "Ode to Billie Joe"—Bobbie Gentry (Capitol)

Best Vocal Performance, Male: "By the Time I Get to Phoenix"—Glen Campbell (Capitol)

Best Contemporary Female Solo Vocal Performance: "Ode to Billie Joe"—Bobbie Gentry (Capitol)

Best Contemporary Male Solo Vocal Performance: "By the Time I Get to Phoenix"—Glen Campbell (Capitol)

Best New Artist: Bobbie Gentry (Capitol)

Best Sacred Performance: *How Great Thou Art*—Elvis Presley (RCA)

Best Gospel Performance: *More Grand Old Gospel*—Porter Wagoner and the Blackwood Brothers (RCA)

Best Folk Performance: "Gentle on My Mind"—John Hartford (RCA)

Best Instrumental Performance: *Chet Atkins Picks the Best*—Chet Atkins (RCA)

Best Arrangement Accompanying Vocalist(s) or Instrumentalist(s): "Ode to Billie Joe"—Bobbie Gentry; arranger: Jimmie Haskell (Capitol)

Best Album Notes: *Suburban Attitudes in Country Verse*—John D. Loudermilk (RCA)

**1968**

Best Country Vocal Performance, Female: "Harper Valley P.T.A."—Jeannie C. Riley (Plantation)

Best Country Vocal Performance, Male: "Folsom Prison Blues"—Johnny Cash (Columbia)

Best Country & Western Performance, Duet, Trio or Group (Vocal or Instrumental): "Foggy Mountain Breakdown"—Flatt & Scruggs (Columbia)

Best Country Song: "Little Green Apples" (Bobby Russell)

Album of the Year: *By the Time I Get to Phoenix*—Glen Campbell (Capitol)

Song of the Year: "Little Green Apples" (Bobby Russell)

Best Engineered Recording: "Wichita Lineman"—Glen Campbell; engineers: Joe Polito & Hugh Davies (Capitol)

Best Album Notes: *Johnny Cash at Folsom Prison*; annotator: Johnny Cash (Columbia)

**1969**

Best Country Vocal Performance, Female: *Stand By Your Man*—Tammy Wynette (Epic)

Best Country Vocal Performance, Male: "A Boy Named Sue"—Johnny Cash (Columbia)

Best Country Song: "A Boy Named Sue" (Shel Silverstein)

Best Country Performance by a Duo or Group: "MacArthur Park"—Waylon Jennings and the Kimberleys (RCA)

Best Country Instrumental Performance: *The Nashville Brass Featuring Danny Davis Play More Nashville Sounds*—Danny Davis & the Nashville Brass (RCA)

**1969** (*continued*)
Song of the Year: "Games People Play" (Joe South)
Best Contemporary Song: "Games People Play" (Joe South)
Best Gospel Performance: *In Gospel Country*—Porter Wagoner & the Blackwood Brothers (RCA)
Best Album Notes: *Nashville Skyline*—Bob Dylan; annotator: Johnny Cash (Columbia)

**1970**
Best Country Vocal Performance, Female: "Rose Garden"—Lynn Anderson (Columbia)
Best Country Vocal Performance, Male: "For the Good Times"—Ray Price (Columbia)
Best Country Vocal Performance by a Duo or Group: "If I Were a Carpenter"—Johnny Cash & June Carter (Columbia)
Best Country Instrumental Performance: *Me and Jerry*—Chet Atkins and Jerry Reed (RCA)
Best Country Song: "My Woman, My Woman, My Wife" (Marty Robbins)
Best Contemporary Vocal Performance, Male: "Everything Is Beautiful"—Ray Stevens (Barnaby)
Best Gospel Performance (Other Than Soul Gospel): "Talk About the Good Times"—Oak Ridge Boys (Heartwarming)

**1971**
Best Country Vocal Performance, Female: "Help Me Make It Through the Night"—Sammi Smith (Mega)
Best Country Vocal Performance, Male: "When You're Hot, You're Hot"—Jerry Reed (RCA)
Best Country Vocal Performance by a Duo or Group: "After the Fire Is Gone"—Conway Twitty and Loretta Lynn (Decca)
Best Country Instrumental Performance: "Snowbird"—Chet Atkins (RCA)
Best Country Song: "Help Me Make It Through the Night" (Kris Kristofferson)
Best Sacred Performance: "Did You Think to Pray"—Charley Pride (RCA)
Best Gospel Performance (Other Than Soul Gospel): "Let Me Live"—Charley Pride (RCA)
Lifetime Achievement Award: Elvis Presley

**1972**
Best Country Vocal Performance, Female: "Happiest Girl in the Whole U.S.A."—Donna Fargo (Dot)
Best Country Vocal Performance, Male: *Charley Pride Sings Heart Songs*—Charley Pride (RCA)
Best Country Vocal Performance by a Duo or Group: "Class of '57"—The Statler Brothers (Mercury)
Best Country Instrumental Performance: *The Real McCoy*—Charlie McCoy (Monument)
Best Country Song: "Kiss an Angel Good Mornin'" (Ben Peters)
Best Inspirational Performance: "He Touched Me"—Elvis Presley (RCA)
Best Album Notes: *Tom T. Hall's Greatest Hits*, Annotator: Tom T. Hall (Mercury)

**1973**
Best Country Vocal Performance, Female: "Let Me Be There"—Olivia Newton-John (MCA)
Best Country Vocal Performance, Male: "Behind Closed Doors"—Charlie Rich (Epic/Columbia)
Best Country Vocal Performance by a Duo or Group: "From the Bottle to the Bottom"—Kris Kristofferson and Rita Coolidge (A & M)
Best Country Instrumental Performance: "Dueling Banjos"—Eric Weissberg and Steve Mandell (Warner Bros.)
Best Country Song: "Behind Closed Doors" (Kenny O'Dell)
Best Ethnic or Traditional Recording: *Then and Now*—Doc Watson (United Artists)

**1974**
Best Country Vocal Performance, Female: "Love Song"—Anne Murray (Capitol)
Best Country Vocal Performance, Male: "Please Don't Tell Me How the Story Ends"—Ronnie Milsap (RCA)
Best Country Vocal Performance by a Duo or Group: "Fairytale"—The Pointer Sisters (Blue Thumb)
Best Country Song: "A Very Special Love Song" (Norro Wilson–Billy Sherrill)
Best Country Instrumental Performance: *The Atkins-Travis Traveling Show*—Chet Atkins and Merle Travis (RCA)
Best Traditional or Ethnic Recording: *Two Days in November*—Doc and Merle Watson (United Artists)
Best Gospel Performance: "The Baptism of Jesse Taylor"—Oak Ridge Boys (Columbia)
Best Inspirational Performance: "How Great Thou Art"—Elvis Presley (RCA)
Record of the Year: "I Honestly Love You"—Olivia Newton-John (MCA)

Best Pop Vocal Performance, Female: "I Honestly Love You"—Olivia Newton-John (MCA)
Best Album Notes: *For the Last Time*—Bob Wills; annotator: Charles R. Townsend (United Artists)

**1975**
Best Country Vocal Performance, Female: "I Can't Help It (If I'm Still in Love with You)"—Linda Ronstadt (Capitol)
Best Country Vocal Performance, Male: "Blue Eyes Crying in the Rain"—Willie Nelson (Columbia)
Best Country Vocal Performance by a Duo or Group: "Lover Please"—Kris Kristofferson and Rita Coolidge (Monument)
Best Country Instrumental Performance: "The Entertainer"—Chet Atkins (RCA)
Best Country Song: "(Hey Won't You Play) Another Somebody Done Somebody Wrong Song" (Chips Moman–Larry Butler)
Best Arrangement Accompanying Vocalists: "Misty"—Ray Stevens; arranger: Ray Stevens (Barnaby)

**1976**
Best Country Vocal Performance, Female: *Elite Hotel*—Emmylou Harris (Reprise)
Best Country Vocal Performance, Male: "(I'm a) Stand by My Woman Man"—Ronnie Milsap (RCA)
Best Country Vocal Performance by a Duo or Group: "The End Is Not in Sight (The Cowboy Tune)"—Amazing Rhythm Aces (ABC)
Best Country Instrumental Performance: *Chester and Lester*—Chet Atkins and Les Paul (RCA)
Best Country Song: "Broken Lady" (Larry Gatlin)
Best Pop Vocal Performance, Female: *Hasten Down the Wind*—Linda Ronstadt (Asylum)
Best Ethnic or Traditional Recording: *Mark Twang*—John Hartford (Flying Fish)
Best Gospel Performance: "Where the Soul Never Dies"—Oak Ridge Boys (Columbia)

**1977**
Record of the Year: *Hotel California*—Eagles; Producer: Bill Szymczyk
Best Country Vocal Performance, Female: "Don't It Make My Brown Eyes Blue"—Crystal Gayle (United Artists)
Best Country Vocal Performance, Male: "Lucille"—Kenny Rogers (United Artists)
Best Country Vocal Performance by a Duo or Group: "Heaven's Just a Sin Away"—The Kendalls (Ovation)
Best Country Instrumental Performance: *Country Instrumentalist of the Year*—Hargus "Pig" Robbins (Elektra)
Best Country Song: "Don't It Make My Brown Eyes Blue" (Richard Leigh)
Best Gospel Performance, Traditional: "Just a Little Talk with Jesus"—Oak Ridge Boys (Rockland Road)
Best Inspirational Performance: *Home Where I Belong*—B. J. Thomas (Myrrh/Word)
Best Album Package: *Simple Dreams*—Linda Ronstadt; Art Director: John Kosh (Asylum)

**1978**
Best Country Vocal Performance, Female: *Here You Come Again*—Dolly Parton (RCA)
Best Country Vocal Performance, Male: "Georgia on My Mind"—Willie Nelson (Columbia)
Best Country Vocal Performance by a Duo or Group: "Mammas, Don't Let Your Babies Grow Up to Be Cowboys"—Waylon Jennings and Willie Nelson (RCA)
Best Country Instrumentalist Performance: "One O'clock Jump"—Asleep at the Wheel (Capitol)
Best Country Song: "The Gambler" (Don Schlitz)
Best Pop Vocal Performance, Female: "You Needed Me"—Anne Murray (Capitol)
Best Inspirational Performance: *Happy Man*—B. J. Thomas (Myrrh)

**1979**
Best Country Vocal Performance, Female: *Blue Kentucky Girl*—Emmylou Harris (Warner Bros.)
Best Country Vocal Performance, Male: "The Gambler"—Kenny Rogers (United Artists)
Best Country Vocal Performance by a Duo or Group: "The Devil Went Down to Georgia"—Charlie Daniels Band (Epic)
Best Country Instrumentalist Performance: "Big Sandy/Leather Britches"—Doc and Merle Watson (United Artists)
Best Country Song: "You Decorated My Life" (Debbie Hupp–Bob Morrison)
Best Rock Vocal Performance by a Duo or Group: "Heartache Tonight"—Eagles (Asylum)

**1979** (continued)

Best Inspirational Performance: *You Gave Me Love (When Nobody Gave Me a Prayer)*—B. J. Thomas (Myrrh)

Producer of the Year (Non-Classical): Larry Butler

**1980**

Best Country Vocal Performance, Female: "Could I Have This Dance"— Anne Murray (Capitol)

Best Country Vocal Performance, Male: "He Stopped Loving Her Today"— George Jones (Epic)

Best Country Vocal Performance by a Duo or Group: "That Lovin' You Feelin' Again"—Roy Orbison & Emmylou Harris (Warner Bros.)

Best Country Instrumentalist Performance: "Orange Blossom Special/ Hoedown"—Gilley's Urban Cowboy Band (Full Moon/Asylum)

Best Country Song: "On the Road Again" (Willie Nelson)

**1981**

Best Country Vocal Performance, Female: "9 to 5"—Dolly Parton (RCA)

Best Country Vocal Performance, Male: "(There's) No Gettin' Over Me"—Ronnie Milsap (RCA)

Best Country Vocal Performance by a Duo or Group: "Elvira"—Oak Ridge Boys (MCA)

Best Country Instrumental Performance: "After All These Years"—Chet Atkins (RCA)

Best Country Song: "9 to 5" (Dolly Parton)

Best Inspirational Performance: *Amazing Grace*—B. J. Thomas (Myrrh/Word)

Best Recording for Children: *Sesame Country*—The Muppets, Glen Campbell, Crystal Gayle, Loretta Lynn, Tanya Tucker; creator: Jim Henson; album producer: Dennis Scott (Sesame Street)

**1982**

Best Country Vocal Performance, Female: "Break It to Me Gently"—Juice Newton (Capitol)

Best Country Vocal Performance, Male: "Always on My Mind"—Willie Nelson (Columbia)

Best Country Vocal Performance by a Duo or Group: *Mountain Music*— Alabama (RCA)

Best Country Song: "Always on My Mind" (Johnny Christopher–Mark James–Wayne Carson)

Best Country Instrumental Performance: "Alabama Jubilee"—Roy Clark (Churchill)

Song of the Year: "Always on My Mind" (Johnny Christopher–Mark James–Wayne Carson)

Best Inspirational Performance: *He Set My Life to Music*—Barbara Mandrell (Songbird/MCA)

**1983**

Best Country Vocal Performance, Female: "A Little Good News"—Anne Murray (Capitol)

Best Country Vocal Performance, Male: "I.O.U."—Lee Greenwood (MCA)

Best Country Vocal Performance by a Duo or Group: *The Closer You Get…* Alabama (RCA)

Best Country Instrumental Performance: "Fireball"—The New South: Ricky Skaggs, Jerry Douglas, Tony Rice, J. D. Crowe, Todd Phillips (Sugar Hill)

Best Country Song: "Stranger in My House" (Mike Reid)

Best Soul Gospel Performance by a Duo or Group: "I'm So Glad I'm Standing Here Today"—Bobby Jones with Barbara Mandrell (Myrrh/ Word)

Hall of Fame Award: "Your Cheating Heart"—Hank Williams (MGM, 1953)

**1984**

Best Country Vocal Performance, Female: "In My Dreams"—Emmylou Harris (Warner Bros.)

Best Country Vocal Performance, Male: "That's the Way Love Goes"—Merle Haggard (Epic/CBS)

Best Country Vocal Performance by a Duo or Group: "Mama He's Crazy"—The Judds (RCA)

Best Country Instrumental Performance: "Wheel Hoss"—Ricky Skaggs (Columbia)

Best Country Song: "City of New Orleans" (Steve Goodman)

Best Ethnic or Traditional Folk Recording: *Elizabeth Cotten Live!*—Elizabeth Cotten (Arhoolie)

**1985**

Best Country Vocal Performance, Female: "I Don't Know Why You Don't Want Me"—Rosanne Cash (CBS)

Best Country Vocal Performance, Male: "Lost in the Fifties Tonight (in the Still of the Night)"—Ronnie Milsap (RCA)

Best Country Performance, Duo or Group with Vocal: *Why Not Me*—The Judds (RCA)

Best Country Instrumental Performance: "Cosmic Square Dance"—Chet Atkins & Mark Knopfler (Columbia/CBS)

Best Country Song: "Highwayman" (Jimmy L. Webb)

Hall of Fame Award: "Blue Yodel (T for Texas)"—Jimmie Rodgers (Victor, 1928)

**1986**

Best Country Vocal Performance, Female: "Whoever's in New England"— Reba McEntire (MCA)

Best Country Vocal Performance, Male: "Lost in the Fifties Tonight (in the Still of the Night)"—Ronnie Milsap (RCA)

Best Country Performance, Duo or Group with Vocal: "Grandpa (Tell Me 'Bout the Good Old Days)"—The Judds (RCA)

Best Country Instrumental Performance (Orchestra, Group, or Soloist): "Raisin' the Dickens"—Ricky Skaggs (Epic)

Best Country Song: "Grandpa (Tell Me 'Bout the Good Old Days)" (Jamie O'Hara)

Best Traditional Folk Recording: *Riding the Midnight Train*—Doc Watson (Sugar Hill)

Best Contemporary Folk Album: *Tribute to Steve Goodman*—Various Artists (Red Pajamas)

Best Mexican/American Performance: *Ay Te Dejo en San Antonio*—Flaco Jiminez (Arhoolie)

Best Spoken Word or Nonmusical Recording: *Interviews from "The Class of '55" Recording Sessions*—Carl Perkins, Jerry Lee Lewis, Roy Orbison, Johnny Cash, Sam Phillips, Rick Nelson, and Chips Moman (America Record Corp.)

Hall of Fame Awards: "Blue Suede Shoes"—Carl Perkins (Sun, 1956); "Cool Water"—Sons of the Pioneers (Decca, 1941)

**1987**

Best Country Vocal Performance, Female: "80's Ladies"—K. T. Oslin (RCA)

Best Country Vocal Performance, Male: *Always and Forever*—Randy Travis (Warner Bros.)

Best Country Performance, Duo or Group with Vocal: *Trio*—Emmylou Harris, Dolly Parton, Linda Ronstadt (Warner Bros.)

Best Country Vocal Performance, Duet: "Make No Mistake, She's Mine"— Ronnie Milsap and Kenny Rogers (RCA)

Best Country Instrumental Performance (Orchestra, Group or Soloist): "String of Pars"—Asleep at the Wheel (Epic)

Best Country Song: "Forever and Ever, Amen" (Don Schlitz–Paul Overstreet)

Best Album Package: *King's Record Shop*—Rosanne Cash; art director: Bill Johnson (Columbia)

Lifetime Achievement Award: Roy Acuff, Hank Williams, Ray Charles

**1988**

Best Country Vocal Performance, Female: "Hold Me"—K. T. Oslin (RCA)

Best Country Vocal Performance, Male: *Old 8 x 10*—Randy Travis (Warner Bros.)

Best Country Performance, Duo or Group with Vocal: "Give a Little Love"—The Judds (RCA)

Best Country Instrumental Performance (Orchestra, Group or Soloist): "Sugarfoot Rag"—Asleep at the Wheel (Epic)

Best Country Vocal Collaboration: "Crying"—Roy Orbison and k. d. lang (Virgin)

Best Country Song: "Hold Me" (K. T. Oslin)

Best Bluegrass Recording (Vocal or Instrumental): *Southern Flavor*—Bill Monroe (MCA)

Best Traditional Folk Recording: *Folkways: A Vision Shared—A Tribute to Woody Guthrie & Leadbelly*—Various Artists; producers: Don DeVito, Joe McEwen, Harold Leventhal, Ralph Rinzler (Columbia)

Best Mexican/American Performance: *Canciónes de Mi Padre*—Linda Ronstadt (Elektra)

Best Album Package: *Tired of the Runnin'*—The O'Kanes; art director: Bill Johnson

Hall of Fame Award: "Hound Dog"—Elvis Presley (RCA, 1956)

**1989**

Best Country Vocal Performance, Female: *Absolute Torch and Twang*—k. d. lang (Sire)

Best Country Vocal Performance, Male: *Lyle Lovett and His Large Band*—Lyle Lovett (MCA)

Best Country Performance, Duo or Group with Vocal: *Will the Circle Be Unbroken, Volume II*—The Nitty Gritty Dirt Band (Universal)

Best Country Instrumental Performance: "Amazing Grace"—Randy Scruggs (Universal)

Best Country Vocal Collaboration: "There's a Tear in My Beer"—Hank Williams and Hank Williams Jr. (Curb)

Best Country Song: "After All This Time" (Rodney Crowell)

**1989** (*continued*)

Best Bluegrass Recording: "The Valley Road"—Bruce Hornsby and the Nitty Gritty Dirt Band (Universal)

Song of the Year: "Wind Beneath My Wings" (Larry Henley–Jeff Silbar)

Hall of Fame Award: "This Land Is Your Land"—Woody Guthrie (Asch, 1947)

**1990**

Best Country Vocal Performance, Female: "Where've You Been"—Kathy Mattea (Mercury)

Best Country Vocal Performance, Male: "When I Call Your Name"—Vince Gill (MCA)

Best Country Performance, Duo or Group with Vocal: *Pickin' on Nashville*—The Kentucky HeadHunters (Mercury)

Best Country Instrumental Performance: "So Soft, Your Goodbye"—Chet Atkins and Mark Knopfler (Columbia)

Best Country Vocal Collaboration: "Poor Boy Blues"—Chet Atkins and Mark Knopfler (Columbia)

Best Country Song: "Where've You Been" (Jon Vezner–Don Henry)

Best Bluegrass Recording: *I've Got That Old Feeling*—Alison Krauss (Rounder)

Best Traditional Folk Recording: *On Praying Ground*—Doc Watson (Sugar Hill)

Best Mexican/American Performance: "Soy de San Luis"—Texas Tornados (Reprise)

Best Pop Vocal Performance, Male: "Oh, Pretty Woman" (track from *A Black & White Night Live*)—Roy Orbison (Virgin)

Best Mexican/American Performance: "Soy de San Luis"—Texas Tornados (Reprise)

Grammy Legend Award: Willie Nelson

**1991**

Best Country Vocal Performance, Female: "Down at the Twist and Shout"—Mary Chapin Carpenter (Columbia)

Best Country Vocal Performance, Male: *Ropin' the Wind*—Garth Brooks (Capitol)

Best Country Performance, Duo or Group with Vocal: "Love Can Build a Bridge"—The Judds (Curb/RCA)

Best Country Instrumental Performance: *The New Nashville Cats*—Mark O'Connor, with Steve Wariner, Ricky Skaggs and Vince Gill (Warner Bros.)

Best Country Vocal Collaboration: "Restless"—Steve Wariner, Ricky Skaggs, and Vince Gill, from Mark O'Connor's *The New Nashville Cats* (Warner Bros.)

Best Country Song: "Love Can Build a Bridge" (Naomi Judd–John Jarvis–Paul Overstreet)

Best Bluegrass Album: *Spring Training*—Carl Jackson and John Starling (& the Nash Ramblers) (Sugar Hill)

Best Contemporary Folk Album: *The Missing Years*—John Prine (Oh Boy)

Lifetime Achievement Award: Kitty Wells, Bob Dylan

Grammy Legend Award: Johnny Cash

Trustees Award: Sam Phillips

**1992**

Best Country Vocal Performance, Female: "I Feel Lucky"—Mary Chapin Carpenter (Columbia)

Best Country Vocal Performance, Male: *I Still Believe in You*—Vince Gill (MCA)

Best Country Performance, Duo or Group with Vocal: *At the Ryman*—Emmylou Harris & the Nash Ramblers (Reprise)

Best Country Instrumental Performance: *Sneakin' Around*—Chet Atkins & Jerry Reed (Columbia)

Best Country Vocal Collaboration: "The Whiskey Ain't Workin'"—Travis Tritt and Marty Stuart (Warner Bros.)

Best Country Song: "I Still Believe in You" (Vince Gill–John Barlow Jarvis)

Best Bluegrass Album: *Every Time You Say Goodbye*—Alison Krauss & Union Station (Rounder)

Best Traditional Folk Album: *An Irish Evening at the Grand Opera House, Belfast*—The Chieftains (RCA)

Best Contemporary Folk Album: *Another Country*—The Chieftains (RCA)

Best Mexican/American Performance: *Mas Canciones*—Linda Ronstadt (Elektra)

Hall of Fame Award: "Crazy"—Patsy Cline (Decca, 1961)

Trustees Award: Thomas A. Dorsey

**1993**

Best Country Vocal Performance, Female: "Passionate Kisses"—Mary Chapin Carpenter (Columbia)

Best Country Vocal Performance, Male: "Ain't That Lonely Yet"—Dwight Yoakam (Reprise)

Best Country Performance, Duo or Group with Vocal: "Hard Workin' Man"—Brooks & Dunn (Arista)

Best Country Instrumental Performance: "Red Wing"—Asleep at the Wheel featuring Eldon Shamblin, Johnny Gimble, Chet Atkins, Vince Gill, Marty Stuart, and Reuben "Lucky Oceans" Gosfield (Liberty)

Best Country Vocal Collaboration: "Does He Love You"—Reba McEntire and Linda Davis (MCA)

Best Country Song: "Passionate Kisses" (Lucinda Williams)

Best Bluegrass Album: *Waitin' for the Hard Times to Go*—The Nashville Bluegrass Band (Sugar Hill)

Best Southern Gospel, Country Gospel, or Bluegrass Gospel Album: *Good News*—Kathy Mattea (Mercury)

Lifetime Achievement Award: Chet Atkins, Bill Monroe, Pete Seeger

**1994**

Best Female Country Vocal Performance: "Shut Up and Kiss Me"—Mary Chapin Carpenter (Columbia)

Best Male Country Vocal Performance: "When Love Finds You"—Vince Gill (MCA)

Best Country Performance, Duo or Group with Vocal: "Blues for Dixie" (track from *A Tribute to the Music of Bob Wills & the Texas Playboys*)—Asleep at the Wheel with Lyle Lovett (Liberty)

Best Country Instrumental Performance: "Young Thing"—Chet Atkins (Columbia)

Best Country Vocal Collaboration: "I Fall to Pieces"—Aaron Neville and Trisha Yearwood (MCA)

Best Country Album: *Stones in the Road*—Mary Chapin Carpenter (Columbia)

Best Country Song: "I Swear" (Gary Baker–Frank J. Meyers)

Best Bluegrass Album: *The Great Dobro Sessions*—Various Artists (Sugar Hill)

Best Pop Vocal Collaboration: "Funny How Time Slips Away"—Al Green and Lyle Lovett (MCA)

Best Southern Gospel, Country Gospel, or Bluegrass Gospel Album: *I Know Who Holds Tomorrow*—Alison Krauss & the Cox Family (Rounder)

Best Contemporary Folk Album: *American Recordings*—Johnny Cash (American)

Best Recording Package: *Tribute to the Music of Bob Wills & the Texas Playboys*—Asleep at the Wheel; art director: Buddy Jackson (Liberty)

Best Pop Performance by a Duo or Group with Vocal: "I Swear"—All-4-One (Blitz/Atlantic)

Producer of the Year: Don Was

**1995**

Best Female Country Vocal Performance: "Baby, Now That I've Found You"—Alison Krauss (Rounder)

Best Male Country Vocal Performance: "Go Rest High on That Mountain"—Vince Gill (MCA)

Best Country Performance, Duo or Group with Vocal: "Here Comes the Rain"—The Mavericks (MCA)

Best Country Instrumental Performance: "Hightower"—Asleep at the Wheel featuring Béla Fleck and Johnny Gimble (Capitol)

Best Country Vocal Collaboration: "Somewhere in the Vicinity of the Heart"—Shenandoah and Alison Krauss (Capitol)

Best Country Song: "Go Rest High on That Mountain" (Vince Gill)

Best Country Album: *The Woman in Me*—Shania Twain (Mercury)

Best Bluegrass Album: *Unleashed*—The Nashville Bluegrass Band (Sugar Hill)

Best Contemporary Folk Album: *Wrecking Ball*—Emmylou Harris (Asylum/Elektra)

Lifetime Achievement Award: Patsy Cline

**1996**

Best New Artist: LeAnn Rimes (Curb)

Best Female Country Vocal Performance: "Blue"—LeAnn Rimes (Curb)

Best Male Country Vocal Performance: "Worlds Apart"—Vince Gill (MCA)

Best Country Performance by a Duo or Group with Vocal: "My Maria"—Brooks & Dunn (Arista)

Best Country Instrumental Performance: "Jam Man"—Chet Atkins (Columbia)

Best Country Vocal Collaboration: "High Lonesome Sound"—Vince Gill featuring Alison Krauss & Union Station (MCA)

Best Country Song: "Blue" (Bill Mack)

Best Country Album: *The Road to Ensenada*—Lyle Lovett (Curb/MCA)

Best Bluegrass Album: *True Life Blues: The Songs of Bill Monroe*—Various Artists (Sugar Hill)

Best Pop Instrumental Performance: "Sinister Minister," from *Live Art*—Béla Fleck & the Flecktones (Warner Bros.)

**1997**

Best Female Country Vocal Performance: "How Do I Live"—Trisha Yearwood (MCA)

Best Male Country Vocal Performance: "Pretty Little Adriana"—Vince Gill (MCA)

Best Country Performance by a Duo or Group with Vocal: "Looking In the Eyes of Love"—Alison Krauss & Union Station (Rounder)

**1997** (*continued*)

Best Country Instrumental Performance: "Little Liza Jane"—Alison Kraus & Union Station

Best Country Vocal Collaboration: "In Another's Eyes"—Trisha Yearwood and Garth Brooks

Best Country Song: "Butterfly Kisses" (Bob Carlisle–Randy Thomas)

Best Country Album: *Unchained*—Johnny Cash (American Recordings)

Best Bluegrass Album: *So Long So Wrong*—Alison Krauss & Union Station

Lifetime Achievement Award: The Everly Brothers

### 1998

Best Female Country Vocal Performance: "You're Still the One"—Shania Twain (Mercury Nashville)

Best Male Country Vocal Performance: "If You Ever Have Forever in Mind"—Vince Gill (MCA Nashville)

Best Country Performance by a Duo or Group with Vocal: "There's Your Trouble"—Dixie Chicks (Monument)

Best Country Instrumental Performance: "A Soldier's Joy"—Randy Scruggs and Vince Gill (Reprise)

Best Country Vocal Collaboration: "Same Old Train"—Clint Black, Joe Diffie, Merle Haggard, Emmylou Harris, Alison Krauss, Patty Loveless, Earl Scruggs, Ricky Skaggs, Marty Stuart, Pam Tillis, Randy Travis, Travis Tritt, Dwight Yoakam (Columbia Nashville)

Best Country Song: "You're Still the One" (Robert John "Mutt" Lange–Shania Twain)

Best Country Album: *Wide Open Spaces*—Dixie Chicks (Monument)

Best Bluegrass Album: *Bluegrass Rules!*—Ricky Skaggs & Kentucky Thunder (Skaggs Family)

Best Southern, Country, or Bluegrass Gospel Album: *The Apostle*—Soundtrack/Various Artists (Sparrow/Rising Tide)

Best Contemporary Folk Album: *Car Wheels on a Gravel Road*—Lucinda Williams (Mercury)

Best Boxed Recording Package: *The Complete Hank Williams*—Hank Williams (Mercury Nashville)

Best Historical Album: *The Complete Hank Williams*—Hank Williams (Mercury Nashville)

Hall of Fame Award: "Blue Moon of Kentucky"—Bill Monroe (Columbia, 1946), "Bye Bye Love"—The Everly Brothers (Cadence, 1957), "Can the Circle Be Unbroken (Bye and Bye)"—Carter Family (Banner, 1935), "Coal Miner's Daughter"—Loretta Lynn (Decca, 1970), *Dust Bowl Ballads, Vols. 1 & 2*—Woody Guthrie (RCA Victor, 1940), "El Paso"—Marty Robbins (Columbia, 1959), "Great Balls of Fire"—Jerry Lee Lewis (Sun, 1957), "Help Me Make It Through the Night"—Sammi Smith (Mega, 1970), "I Walk the Line"—Johnny Cash (Sun, 1956), "It Wasn't God Who Made Honky Tonk Angels"—Kitty Wells (Decca, 1952), "The Little Old Log Cabin in the Lane"—Fiddlin' John Carson (OKeh, 1923), "Mr. Tambourine Man"—The Byrds (Columbia, 1965), "The Prisoner's Song"—Vernon Dalhart (Victor, 1925), "The Tennessee Waltz"—Patti Page (Mercury, 1950), "That'll Be The Day"—The Crickets (Brunswick, 1957), "Wabash Cannon Ball"—Roy Acuff (Columbia, 1947), "Walking the Floor Over You"—Ernest Tubb (Decca, 1941)

Lifetime Achievement Award: Roy Orbison

Trustees Award: Frances Preston

### 1999

Best Female Country Vocal Performance: "Man! I Feel Like a Woman!"—Shania Twain (Mercury)

Best Male Country Vocal Performance: "Choices"—George Jones (Asylum)

Best Country Performance by a Duo or Group with Vocal: "Ready to Run"—Dixie Chicks (Monument)

Best Country Instrumental Performance: "Bob's Breakdown"—Asleep at the Wheel featuring Tommy Allsup, Floyd Domino, Larry Franklin, Vince Gill, and Steve Wariner (DreamWorks Nashville)

Best Country Vocal Collaboration: "After the Gold Rush"—Emmylou Harris, Linda Ronstadt, Dolly Parton (Asylum)

Best Country Song: "Come on Over" (Robert John "Mutt" Lange–Shania Twain)

Best Country Album: *Fly*—Dixie Chicks (Monument)

Best Bluegrass Album: *Ancient Tones*—Ricky Skaggs & Kentucky Thunder (Skaggs Family)

Best Southern, Country, or Bluegrass Gospel Album: *Kennedy Center Homecoming*—Bill & Gloria Gaither & Their Homecoming Friends (Spring House)

Best Traditional Folk Album: *Press On*—June Carter Cash (Risk/Small Hairy Dog)

Best Recording Package: *Ride With Bob*—Asleep at the Wheel (DreamWorks Nashville)

Hall of Fame Award: "Behind Closed Doors"—Charlie Rich (Epic, 1973), *Blonde on Blonde*—Bob Dylan (Columbia, 1966), "Crazy Arms"—Ray Price (Columbia, 1956) "Dang Me"—Roger Miller (Smash, 1961), "Eight Miles

High"—The Byrds (Columbia, 1966), "He'll Have to Go"—Jim Reeves (RCA Victor, 1959), "Hello Darlin'"—Conway Twitty (Decca, 1970), "If You've Got the Money, I've Got the Time"—Lefty Frizzell (Columbia, 1950), "I've Got a Tiger by the Tail"—Buck Owens (Capitol, 1965), "Mama Tried"—Merle Haggard (Capitol, 1968), "Make the World Go Away"—Eddy Arnold (RCA Victor, 1965), "Ode to Billie Joe"—Bobbie Gentry (Capitol, 1967), "Oh, Pretty Woman"—Roy Orbison (Monument, 1964), "Only the Lonely (Know How I Feel)"—Roy Orbison (Monument, 1960), "Peggy Sue"—Buddy Holly (Coral, 1957), "Ring of Fire"—Johnny Cash (Columbia, 1963), "She Thinks I Still Care"—George Jones (United Artists, 1962), "Stand By Your Man"—Tammy Wynette (Epic, 1968), "Summertime Blues"—Eddie Cochran (Liberty, 1958), "Suspicious Minds"—Elvis Presley (RCA Victor, 1969), "Whole Lotta Shakin' Goin' On"—Jerry Lee Lewis (Sun, 1957), "The Wild Side of Life"—Hank Thompson & His Brazos Valley Boys (Capitol, 1952), "Wildwood Flower"—The Carter Family (Victor, 1928)

Lifetime Achievement Award: Johnny Cash

### 2000

Best New Artist: Shelby Lynne

Best Female Country Vocal Performance: "Breathe"—Faith Hill (Warner Bros.)

Best Male Country Vocal Performance: "Solitary Man"—Johnny Cash (American/Columbia)

Best Country Performance by a Duo or Group with Vocal: "Cherokee Maiden"—Asleep at the Wheel (DreamWorks Nashville)

Best Country Instrumental Performance: "Leaving Cottondale"—Alison Brown and Béla Fleck (Compass)

Best Country Vocal Collaboration: "Let's Make Love"—Faith Hill and Tim McGraw (Warner Bros.)

Best Country Song: "I Hope You Dance" (Mark D. Sanders–Tia Sellers)

Best Country Album: *Breathe*—Faith Hill (Warner Bros.)

Best Bluegrass Album: *The Grass Is Blue*—Dolly Parton (Sugar Hill)

Best Southern, Country, or Bluegrass Gospel Album: *Soldier of the Cross*—Ricky Skaggs & Kentucky Thunder (Skaggs Family)

Best Traditional Folk Album: *Public Domain: Songs from the Wild Land*—Dave Alvin (HighTone)

Best Contemporary Folk Album: *Red Dirt Girl*—Emmylou Harris (Nonesuch)

Best Classical Crossover Album: *Appalachian Journey*—Yo-Yo Ma, Edgar Meyer, Mark O'Connor (Sony Classical)

Hall of Fame Award: *Desperado*—The Eagles (Asylum, 1973), "Hello Walls"—Faron Young (Capitol 1961), "I'm Moving On"—Hank Snow (RCA Victor, 1950), "Pistol Packin' Mama"—Al Dexter (OKeh, 1943), *Sweetheart of the Rodeo*—The Byrds (Columbia, 1968), "Wichita Lineman"—Glen Campbell (Capitol, 1968)

Lifetime Achievement Award: Woody Guthrie, Willie Nelson

### 2001

Album of the Year: *O Brother, Where Art Thou?*—Soundtrack/Various Artists (Lost Highway)

Best Female Rock Vocal Performance: "Get Right with God"—Lucinda Williams (Lost Highway)

Best Female Country Vocal Performance: "Shine"—Dolly Parton (Sugar Hill/Blue Eye)

Best Male Country Vocal Performance: "O Death"—Ralph Stanley (Lost Highway)

Best Country Performance by a Duo or Group with Vocal: "The Lucky One"—Alison Krauss & Union Station (Rounder)

Best Country Instrumental Performance: "Foggy Mountain Breakdown"—Earl Scruggs, Glen Duncan, Randy Scruggs, Steve Martin, Vince Gill, Marty Stuart, Gary Scruggs, Albert Lee, Paul Shaffer, Jerry Douglas, Leon Russell (MCA Nashville)

Best Country Vocal Collaboration: "I Am a Man of Constant Sorrow"—Dan Tyminski, Harley Allen, Pat Enright (The Soggy Bottom Boys) (Lost Highway)

Best Country Song: "The Lucky One" (Robert Lee Castleman)

Best Country Album: *Timeless* (Hank Williams tribute)—Various Artists (Lost Highway)

Best Bluegrass Album: *New Favorite*—Alison Krauss & Union Station (Rounder)

Best Traditional Folk Album: *Down from the Mountain*—Various Artists (Lost Highway)

Best Compilation Soundtrack Album for a Motion Picture, Television or Other Visual Media: *O Brother, Where Art Thou?*—Various Artists (Lost Highway)

Producer of the Year, Non-Classical: T Bone Burnett

Hall of Fame Award: "Foggy Mountain Breakdown"—Flatt & Scruggs (Mercury, 1950), "Hey, Good Lookin'"—Hank Williams (MGM, 1951), "I Can't Stop Loving You"—Ray Charles (ABC-Paramount, 1962), "I Fall to Pieces"—Patsy Cline (Decca, 1961), "Turn! Turn! (To Everything There Is a Season)"—The Byrds (Columbia 1965)

## 2002

Best Female Country Vocal Performance: "Cry"—Faith Hill (Warner Bros.)

Best Male Country Vocal Performance: "Give My Love to Rose"—Johnny Cash (American/Lost Highway)

Best Country Performance by a Duo or Group with Vocal: "Long Time Gone"—Dixie Chicks (Open Wide/Monument/Columbia)

Best Country Instrumental Performance: "Lil' Jack Slade"—Dixie Chicks (Open Wide/Monument/Columbia)

Best Country Vocal Collaboration: "Mendocino County Line"—Willie Nelson and Lee Ann Womack (Lost Highway)

Best Country Song: "Where Were You (When the World Stopped Turning)" (Alan Jackson)

Best Country Album: *Home*—Dixie Chicks (Open Wide/Monument/Columbia)

Best Bluegrass Album: *Lost in the Lonesome Pines*—Jim Lauderdale, Ralph Stanley & The Clinch Mountain Boys (Dualtone)

Best Southern, Country, or Bluegrass Gospel Album: *We Called Him Mr. Gospel Music: The James Blackwood Tribute Album*—The Jordanaires, Larry Ford & The Light Crust Doughboys (Art Greenhaw)

Best Traditional Folk Album: *Legacy*—Doc Watson & David Holt (High Windy)

Best Contemporary Folk Album: *This Side*—Nickel Creek (Sugar Hill)

Best Musical Album for Children: *Monsters, Inc.-Scream Factory Favorites*—Riders in the Sky (Walt Disney)

Best Recording Package: *Home*—Dixie Chicks (Open Wide/Monument/Columbia)

Hall of Fame Award: "Battle of New Orleans"—Johnny Horton (Columbia, 1959), "Crying"—Roy Orbison (Monument,1961), "Don't Be Cruel"—Elvis Presley (RCA, 1956), "Goodnight Irene"—Huddie "Leadbelly" Ledbetter (Library of Congress, 1936), "Jambalaya (On the Bayou)"—Hank Williams (MGM, 1952), "Me and Bobby McGee"—Janis Joplin (Columbia, 1971), "The Midnight Special"—Huddie "Leadbelly" Ledbetter with the Golden Gate Quartet (RCA Victor, 1940), "Mr. Tambourine Man"—Bob Dylan (Columbia, 1965), *Red Headed Stranger*—Willie Nelson (Columbia, 1975), "Tumbling Tumbleweeds"—Sons of the Pioneers (Decca, 1934)

## 2003

Best Female Country Vocal Performance: "Keep on the Sunny Side"—June Carter Cash (Dualtone Music Group)

Best Male Country Vocal Performance: "Next Big Thing"—Vince Gill (MCA Nashville)

Best Country Performance by a Duo or Group with Vocal: "A Simple Life"—Ricky Skaggs & Kentucky Thunder (Skaggs Family Records)

Best Country Instrumental Performance: "Cluck Old Hen"—Alison Krauss & Union Station (Rounder Records)

Best Country Vocal Collaboration: "How's the World Treating You"—James Taylor and Alison Krauss (Universal South)

Best Country Song: "It's Five O' Clock Somewhere" (Jim Brown–Don Rollins)

Best Country Album: *Livin', Lovin', Losin': Songs of the Louvin Brothers*—Various Artists (Universal South)

Best Bluegrass Album: *Live*—Alison Krauss & Union Station (Rounder Records)

Best Southern, Country, or Bluegrass Gospel Album: *Rise and Shine*—Randy Travis (Word Records)

Best Traditional Folk Album: *Wildwood Flower*—June Carter Cash (Dualtone Music Group)

Best Short Form Music Video: "Hurt"—Johnny Cash (American Recordings/Lost Highway Records)

## 2004

Best Female Country Vocal Performance: "Redneck Woman"—Gretchen Wilson (Epic Records)

Best Male Country Vocal Performance: "Live Like You Were Dying"—Tim McGraw (Curb Records)

Best Country Performance by a Duo or Group with Vocal: "Top of the World"—Dixie Chicks (Columbia)

Best Country Instrumental Performance: "Earl's Breakdown"—Nitty Gritty Dirt Band featuring Earl Scruggs, Randy Scruggs, Vassar Clements, and Jerry Douglas (Capitol Records Nashville)

Best Country Vocal Collaboration: "Portland Oregon"—Loretta Lynn & Jack White (Interscope Records)

Best Country Song: "Live Like You Were Dying" (Tim Nichols–Craig Wiseman)

Best Country Album: *Van Lear Rose*—Loretta Lynn (Interscope Records)

Best Bluegrass Album: *Brand New Strings*—Ricky Skaggs & Kentucky Thunder (Skaggs Family Records)

Best Southern, Country, or Bluegrass Gospel Album: *Worship & Faith*—Randy Travis (Word Records)

Best Traditional Folk Album: *Beautiful Dreamer: The Songs of Stephen Foster*—Various Artists (American Roots Publishing)

Best Contemporary Folk Album: *The Revolution Starts . . . Now*—Steve Earle (Artemis Records/E-Squared)

Lifetime Achievement Award: Doc Watson

## 2005

Best Female Country Vocal Performance: "The Connection"—Emmylou Harris

Best Male Country Vocal Performance: "You'll Think of Me"—Keith Urban

Best Country Performance by a Duo or Group with Vocal: "Restless"—Alison Krauss & Union Station

Best Country Instrumental Performance: "Unionhouse Branch"—Alison Krauss & Union Station

Best Country Vocal Collaboration: "Like We Never Loved at All"—Faith Hill and Tim McGraw

Best Country Song: "Bless the Broken Road" (Bobby Boyd –Jeff Hanna–Marcus Hummon)

Best Country Album: *Lonely Runs Both Ways*—Alison Krauss & Union Station

Best Bluegrass Album: *The Company We Keep*—The Del McCoury Band

Best Traditional Folk Album: *Fiddler's Green*—Tim O'Brien

Best Contemporary Folk Album: *Fair & Square*—John Prine

Best Boxed or Special Limited Edition Package: *The Legend*—Johnny Cash

Lifetime Achievement Award: Eddy Arnold, The Carter Family, Jerry Lee Lewis

## 2006

Record of the Year: "Not Ready to Make Nice"—Dixie Chicks

Album of the Year: *Taking the Long Way*—Dixie Chicks

Song of the Year: "Not Ready to Make Nice"—Dixie Chicks

Best New Artist: Carrie Underwood

Best Female Country Vocal Performance: "Jesus, Take the Wheel"—Carrie Underwood

Best Male Country Vocal Performance: "The Reason Why"—Vince Gill

Best Country Performance by a Duo or Group with Vocal: "Not Ready to Make Nice"—Dixie Chicks

Best Country Instrumental Performance: "Whiskey Before Breakfast"—Bryan Sutton and Doc Watson

Best Country Vocal Collaboration: "Who Says You Can't Go Home"—Bon Jovi and Jennifer Nettles

Best Country Song: "Jesus, Take the Wheel" (Brett James–Gordie Sampson–Hillary Lindsey)

Best Country Album: *Taking the Long Way*—Dixie Chicks

Best Bluegrass Album: *Instrumentals*—Ricky Skaggs & Kentucky Thunder

Best Southern, Country, or Bluegrass Gospel Album: *Glory Train*—Randy Travis

Best Traditional Folk Album: *We Shall Overcome: The Seeger Sessions*—Bruce Springsteen

Best Compilation Soundtrack Album for Motion Picture, Television or Other Visual Media: *Walk the Line*—Joaquin Phoenix & Various Artists

Lifetime Achievement Award: Merle Haggard

Trustees Award: Owen Bradley

## 2007

Best Pop Collaboration with Vocals: "Gone Gone Gone (Done Moved On)"—Robert Plant and Alison Krauss

Best Female Country Vocal Performance: "Before He Cheats"—Carrie Underwood

Best Male Country Vocal Performance: "Stupid Boy"—Keith Urban

Best Country Performance by a Duo or Group with Vocal: "How Long"—Eagles

Best Country Instrumental Performance: "Throttleneck"—Brad Paisley

Best Country Vocal Collaboration: "Lost Highway"—Willie Nelson and Ray Price

Best Country Song: "Before He Cheats" (Chris Tompkins–Joshua Kear)

Best Country Album: *These Days*—Vince Gill

Best Bluegrass Album: *The Bluegrass Diaries*—Jim Lauderdale

Best Southern, Country, or Bluegrass Gospel Album: *Salt of the Earth*—Ricky Skaggs & The Whites

Best Traditional Folk Album: *Dirt Farmer*—Levon Helm

Best Contemporary Folk/Americana Album: *Washington Square Serenade*—Steve Earle

Best Historical Album: *The Live Wire: Woody Guthrie in Performance 1949*—Woody Guthrie

Best Short Form Music Video: "God's Gonna Cut You Down"—Johnny Cash

Lifetime Achievement Award: Bob Wills

## 2008

Record of the Year: "Please Read the Letter"—Robert Plant & Alison Krauss

Album of the Year: *Raising Sand*—Robert Plant & Alison Krauss

**2008** (*continued*)

Best Pop Collaboration with Vocals: "Rich Woman"—Robert Plant and Alison Krauss

Best Pop Instrumental Performance: "I Dreamed There Was No War"—Eagles

Best Pop Instrumental Album: *Jingle All the Way*—Béla Fleck & the Flecktones

Best Female Country Vocal Performance: "Last Name"—Carrie Underwood

Best Male Country Vocal Performance: "Letter to Me"—Brad Paisley

Best Country Performance by a Duo or Group with Vocal(s): "Stay"—Sugarland

Best Country Instrumental Performance: "Cluster Pluck"—Albert Lee, Brad Paisley, Brent Mason, James Burton, John Jorgenson, Redd Volkaert, Steve Wariner, Vince Gill

Best Country Vocal Collaboration: "Killing the Blues"—Robert Plant and Alison Krauss

Best Country Song: "Stay" (Jennifer Nettles)

Best Country Album: *Troubadour*—George Strait

Best Bluegrass Album: *Honoring the Fathers of Bluegrass: Tribute to 1946 and 1947*—Ricky Skaggs & Kentucky Thunder

Best Contemporary Folk/Americana Album: *Raising Sand*—Robert Plant and Alison Krauss

Best Zydeco or Cajun Music Album: *Live at the 2008 New Orleans Jazz & Heritage Festival*—BeauSoleil & Michael Doucet

Best Historical Album: *Art of Field Recording Volume I: Fifty Years of Traditional American Music Documented by Art Rosenbaum*—Various Artists

Hall of Fame Award: "Always on My Mind"—Willie Nelson (Columbia, 1982)

Lifetime Achievement Award: Earl Scruggs

**2009**

Album of the Year: *Fearless*—Taylor Swift

Best New Artist: Zac Brown Band

Best Pop Instrumental Performance: "Throw Down Your Heart"—Béla Fleck

Best Female Country Vocal Performance: "White Horse"—Taylor Swift

Best Male Country Vocal Performance: "Sweet Thing"—Keith Urban

Best Country Performance by a Duo or Group with Vocal: "I Run to You"—Lady Antebellum

Best Country Instrumental Performance: "Producer's Medley"—Steve Wariner

Best Country Vocal Collaboration: "I Told You So"—Carrie Underwood and Randy Travis

Best Country Song: "White Horse" (Liz Rose and Taylor Swift)

Best Country Album: *Fearless*—Taylor Swift

Best Americana Album: *Electric Dirt*—Levon Helm

Best Bluegrass Album: *The Crow: New Songs for the Five-String Banjo*—Steve Martin

Best Traditional Folk Album: *High Wide & Handsome: The Charlie Poole Project*—Loudon Wainwright III

Best Contemporary Folk Album: *Townes*—Steve Earle

Lifetime Achievement Award: Gene Autry, Brenda Lee

**2010**

Record of the Year: "Need You Now"—Lady Antebellum (Capitol Nashville)

Best Female Country Vocal Performance: "'The House that Built Me"—Miranda Lambert (Columbia Nashville)

Best Male Country Vocal Performance: "'Til Summer Comes Around"—Keith Urban

Best Country Performance by a Duo or Group with Vocals: "Need You Now"—Lady Antebellum (Capitol Nashville)

Best Country Vocal Collaboration: "As She's Walking Away"—Zac Brown Band & Alan Jackson

Best Country Instrumental Performance: "Hummingbyrd"—Marty Stuart (Sugar Hill)

Best Country Song: "Need You Now" (Dave Haywood–Josh Kear–Charles Kelley–Hillary Scott)

Best Country Album: *Need You Now*—Lady Antebellum

Best Southern, Country, or Bluegrass Gospel Album: *The Reason*—Diamond Rio

Best Bluegrass Album: *Mountain Soul II*—Patty Loveless (Saguaro Road)

Best Traditional Folk Album: *Genuine Negro Jig*—Carolina Chocolate Drops (Nonesuch)

Lifetime Achievement Award: Loretta Lynn

Trustees Award: Harold Bradley

**2011**

Lifetime Achievement Award: The Kingston Trio, Dolly Parton

# Country Music Association (CMA) Awards

## Entertainer
1967 Eddy Arnold
1968 Glen Campbell
1969 Johnny Cash
1970 Merle Haggard
1971 Charley Pride
1972 Loretta Lynn
1973 Roy Clark
1974 Charlie Rich
1975 John Denver
1976 Mel Tillis
1977 Ronnie Milsap
1978 Dolly Parton
1979 Willie Nelson
1980 Barbara Mandrell
1981 Barbara Mandrell
1982 Alabama
1983 Alabama
1984 Alabama
1985 Ricky Skaggs
1986 Reba McEntire
1987 Hank Williams Jr.
1988 Hank Williams Jr.
1989 George Strait
1990 George Strait
1991 Garth Brooks
1992 Garth Brooks
1993 Vince Gill
1994 Vince Gill
1995 Alan Jackson
1996 Brooks & Dunn
1997 Garth Brooks
1998 Garth Brooks
1999 Shania Twain
2000 Dixie Chicks
2001 Tim McGraw
2002 Alan Jackson
2003 Alan Jackson
2004 Kenny Chesney
2005 Keith Urban
2006 Kenny Chesney
2007 Kenny Chesney
2008 Kenny Chesney
2009 Taylor Swift
2010 Brad Paisley

## Female Vocalist
1967 Loretta Lynn
1968 Tammy Wynette
1969 Tammy Wynette
1970 Tammy Wynette
1971 Lynn Anderson
1972 Loretta Lynn
1973 Loretta Lynn
1974 Olivia Newton-John
1975 Dolly Parton
1976 Dolly Parton
1977 Crystal Gayle
1978 Crystal Gayle
1979 Barbara Mandrell
1980 Emmylou Harris
1981 Barbara Mandrell
1982 Janie Fricke
1983 Janie Fricke
1984 Reba McEntire
1985 Reba McEntire
1986 Reba McEntire
1987 Reba McEntire
1988 K. T. Oslin
1989 Kathy Mattea
1990 Kathy Mattea
1991 Tanya Tucker
1992 Mary Chapin Carpenter
1993 Mary Chapin Carpenter
1994 Pam Tillis
1995 Alison Krauss
1996 Patty Loveless

1997 Trisha Yearwood
1998 Trisha Yearwood
1999 Martina McBride
2000 Faith Hill
2001 Lee Ann Womack
2002 Martina McBride
2003 Martina McBride
2004 Martina McBride
2005 Gretchen Wilson
2006 Carrie Underwood
2007 Carrie Underwood
2008 Carrie Underwood
2009 Taylor Swift
2010 Miranda Lambert

## Male Vocalist
1967 Jack Greene
1968 Glen Campbell
1969 Johnny Cash
1970 Merle Haggard
1971 Charley Pride
1972 Charley Pride
1973 Charlie Rich
1974 Ronnie Milsap
1975 Waylon Jennings
1976 Ronnie Milsap
1977 Ronnie Milsap
1978 Don Williams
1979 Kenny Rogers
1980 George Jones
1981 George Jones
1982 Ricky Skaggs
1983 Lee Greenwood
1984 Lee Greenwood
1985 George Strait
1986 George Strait
1987 Randy Travis
1988 Randy Travis
1989 Ricky Van Shelton
1990 Clint Black
1991 Vince Gill
1992 Vince Gill
1993 Vince Gill
1994 Vince Gill
1995 Vince Gill
1996 George Strait
1997 George Strait
1998 George Strait
1999 Tim McGraw
2000 Tim McGraw
2001 Toby Keith
2002 Alan Jackson
2003 Alan Jackson
2004 Keith Urban
2005 Keith Urban
2006 Keith Urban
2007 Brad Paisley
2008 Brad Paisley
2009 Brad Paisley
2010 Blake Shelton

## Musician
(changed from Instrumentalist of the Year in 1988)
1967 Chet Atkins
1968 Chet Atkins
1969 Chet Atkins
1970 Jerry Reed
1971 Jerry Reed
1972 Charlie McCoy
1973 Charlie McCoy
1974 Don Rich
1975 Johnny Gimble
1976 Hargus "Pig" Robbins
1977 Roy Clark
1978 Roy Clark
1979 Charlie Daniels

1980 Roy Clark
1981 Chet Atkins
1982 Chet Atkins
1983 Chet Atkins
1984 Chet Atkins
1985 Chet Atkins
1986 Johnny Gimble
1987 Johnny Gimble
1988 Chet Atkins
1989 Johnny Gimble
1990 Johnny Gimble
1991 Mark O'Connor
1992 Mark O'Connor
1993 Mark O'Connor
1994 Mark O'Connor
1995 Mark O'Connor
1996 Mark O'Connor
1997 Brent Mason
1998 Brent Mason
1999 Randy Scruggs
2000 Hargus "Pig" Robbins
2001 Dann Huff
2002 Jerry Douglas
2003 Randy Scruggs
2004 Dann Huff
2005 Jerry Douglas
2006 Randy Scruggs
2007 Jerry Douglas
2008 Mac McAnally
2009 Mac McAnally
2010 Mac McAnally

## Vocal Group
1967 Stoneman Family
1968 Porter Wagoner & Dolly Parton
1969 Johnny Cash & June Carter
1970 Glaser Brothers
1971 Osborne Brothers
1972 Statler Brothers
1973 Statler Brothers
1974 Statler Brothers
1975 Statler Brothers
1976 Statler Brothers
1977 Statler Brothers
1978 Oak Ridge Boys
1979 Statler Brothers
1980 Statler Brothers
1981 Alabama
1982 Alabama
1983 Alabama
1984 Statler Brothers
1985 The Judds
1986 The Judds
1987 The Judds
1988 Highway 101
1989 Highway 101
1990 Kentucky Headhunters
1991 Kentucky Headhunters
1992 Diamond Rio
1993 Diamond Rio
1994 Diamond Rio
1995 Mavericks
1996 Mavericks
1997 Diamond Rio
1998 Dixie Chicks
1999 Dixie Chicks
2000 Dixie Chicks
2001 Lonestar
2002 Dixie Chicks
2003 Rascal Flatts
2004 Rascal Flatts
2005 Rascal Flatts
2006 Rascal Flatts
2007 Rascal Flatts
2008 Rascal Flatts
2009 Lady Antebellum
2010 Lady Antebellum

## Vocal Duo

1970 Porter Wagoner & Dolly Parton
1971 Porter Wagoner & Dolly Parton
1972 Conway Twitty & Loretta Lynn
1973 Conway Twitty & Loretta Lynn
1974 Conway Twitty & Loretta Lynn
1975 Conway Twitty & Loretta Lynn
1976 Waylon Jennings & Willie Nelson
1977 Jim Ed Brown & Helen Cornelius
1978 Kenny Rogers & Dottie West
1979 Kenny Rogers & Dottie West
1980 Moe Bandy & Joe Stampley
1981 David Frizzell & Shelly West
1982 David Frizzell & Shelly West
1983 Merle Haggard & Willie Nelson
1984 Willie Nelson & Julio Iglesias
1985 Anne Murray & Dave Loggins
1986 Dan Seals & Marie Osmond
1987 Ricky Skaggs & Sharon White
1988 The Judds
1989 The Judds
1990 The Judds
1991 The Judds
1992 Brooks & Dunn
1993 Brooks & Dunn
1994 Brooks & Dunn
1995 Brooks & Dunn
1996 Brooks & Dunn
1997 Brooks & Dunn
1998 Brooks & Dunn
1999 Brooks & Dunn
2000 Montgomery Gentry
2001 Brooks & Dunn
2002 Brooks & Dunn
2003 Brooks & Dunn
2004 Brooks & Dunn
2005 Brooks & Dunn
2006 Brooks & Dunn
2007 Sugarland
2008 Sugarland
2009 Sugarland
2010 Sugarland

## Instrumental Group

(discontinued in 1987)
1967 Buckaroos
1968 Buckaroos
1969 Danny Davis & the Nashville Brass
1970 Danny Davis & the Nashville Brass
1971 Danny Davis & the Nashville Brass
1972 Danny Davis & the Nashville Brass
1973 Danny Davis & the Nashville Brass
1974 Danny Davis & the Nashville Brass
1975 Roy Clark & Buck Trent
1976 Roy Clark & Buck Trent
1977 Original Texas Playboys
1978 Oak Ridge Boys Band
1979 Charlie Daniels Band
1980 Charlie Daniels Band
1981 Alabama
1982 Alabama
1983 Ricky Skaggs Band
1984 Ricky Skaggs Band
1985 Ricky Skaggs Band
1986 Oak Ridge Boys Band

## Vocal Event

1988 *Trio*—Emmylou Harris, Dolly Parton & Linda Ronstadt (Warner Bros.)
1989 "There's a Tear in My Beer"—Hank Williams and Hank Williams Jr. (Curb)
1990 "Til a Tear Becomes a Rose"—Lorrie Morgan and Keith Whitley (RCA)
1991 "Restless"—Mark O'Connor & the New Nashville Cats (featuring Vince Gill, Ricky Skaggs, and Steve Wariner) (Warner Bros.)
1992 "This One's Gonna Hurt You (for a Long, Long Time)"—Marty Stuart and Travis Tritt (Warner Bros.)

1993 "I Don't Need Your Rocking Chair"—George Jones with Vince Gill, Mark Chesnutt, Garth Brooks, Travis Tritt, Joe Diffie, Alan Jackson, Pam Tillis, T. Graham Brown, Patty Loveless, and Clint Black (MCA)
1994 "Does He Love You"—Linda Davis and Reba McEntire (MCA)
1995 "Somewhere in the Vicinity of the Heart"—Shenandoah and Alison Krauss (Liberty)
1996 "I Will Always Love You"—Dolly Parton and Vince Gill (Columbia)
1997 "It's Your Love"—Tim McGraw and Faith Hill (Curb)
1998 "You Don't Seem to Miss Me"—Patty Loveless and George Jones (Epic)
1999 "My Kind of Woman/My Kind of Man"—Vince Gill and Patty Loveless (MCA Nashville)
2000 "Murder on Music Row"—Alan Jackson and George Strait (MCA Nashville)
2001 "Too Country"—Brad Paisley, Buck Owens, George Jones, and Bill Anderson (Arista Nashville)
2002 "Mendocino County Line"—Lee Ann Womack and Willie Nelson (Lost Highway)
2003 "It's Five O'Clock Somewhere"—Alan Jackson and Jimmy Buffett (Arista Nashville)
2004 "Whiskey Lullaby"—Brad Paisley and Alison Krauss (Arista Nashville)
2005 "Good News/Bad News"—George Strait and Lee Ann Womack (MCA)
2006 "When I Get Where I'm Going"—Brad Paisley and Dolly Parton (Arista)
2007 "Find Out Who Your Friends Are"—Tracy Lawrence, Tim McGraw, and Kenny Chesney (Rocky Comfort Records)
2008 "Gone Gone Gone (Done Moved On)"—Robert Plant and Alison Krauss (Rounder)
2009 "Start a Band"—Brad Paisley and Keith Urban (Arista Nashville)
2010 "Hillbilly Bone"—Blake Shelton featuring Trace Adkins (Warner Bros.)

## Single of the Year

1967 "There Goes My Everything"—Jack Greene (Decca)
1968 "Harper Valley P.T.A."—Jeannie C. Riley (Plantation)
1969 "A Boy Named Sue"—Johnny Cash (Columbia)
1970 "Okie from Muskogee"—Merle Haggard (Capitol)
1971 "Help Me Make It Through the Night"—Sammi Smith (Mega)
1972 "The Happiest Girl in the Whole U.S.A."—Donna Fargo (Dot)
1973 "Behind Closed Doors"—Charlie Rich (Epic)
1974 "Country Bumpkin"—Cal Smith (MCA)
1975 "Before the Next Teardrop Falls"—Freddy Fender (ABC-Dot)
1976 "Good Hearted Woman"—Waylon Jennings & Willie Nelson (RCA)
1977 "Lucille"—Kenny Rogers (United Artists)
1978 "Heaven's Just a Sin Away"—The Kendalls (Ovation)
1979 "The Devil Went Down to Georgia"—Charlie Daniels Band (Epic)
1980 "He Stopped Loving Her Today"—George Jones (Epic)
1981 "Elvira"—Oak Ridge Boys (MCA)
1982 "Always on My Mind"—Willie Nelson (Columbia)
1983 "Swingin'"—John Anderson (Warner Bros.)

1984 "A Little Good News"—Anne Murray (Capitol)
1985 "Why Not Me"—Judds (RCA/Curb)
1986 "Bop"—Dan Seals (EMI America)
1987 "Forever and Ever, Amen"—Randy Travis (Warner Bros.)
1988 "Eighteen Wheels and a Dozen Roses"—Kathy Mattea (PolyGram)
1989 "I'm No Stranger to the Rain"—Keith Whitley (RCA)
1990 "When I Call Your Name"—Vince Gill (MCA Nashville)
1991 "Friends in Low Places"—Garth Brooks (Capitol Nashville)
1992 "Achy Breaky Heart"—Billy Ray Cyrus (Mercury Nashville)
1993 "Chattahoochee"—Alan Jackson (Arista Nashville)
1994 "I Swear"—John Michael Montgomery (Atlantic)
1995 "When You Say Nothing at All"—Alison Krauss & Union Station (BNA)
1996 "Check Yes or No"—George Strait (MCA Nashville)
1997 "Strawberry Wine"—Deana Carter (Capitol Nashville)
1998 "Holes in the Floor of Heaven"—Steve Wariner (Capitol Nashville)
1999 "Wide Open Spaces"—Dixie Chicks (Monument)
2000 "I Hope You Dance"—Lee Ann Womack with Sons of the Desert (MCA Nashville)
2001 "I Am a Man of Constant Sorrow"—Soggy Bottom Boys (Lost Highway)
2002 "Where Were You (When the World Stopped Turning)"—Alan Jackson (Arista Nashville)
2003 "Hurt"—Johnny Cash (Lost Highway)
2004 "Live Like You Were Dying"—Tim McGraw (Curb)
2005 "I May Hate Myself in the Morning"—Lee Ann Womack (MCA Nashville)
2006 "Believe"—Brooks & Dunn (Arista Nashville)
2007 "Before He Cheats"—Carrie Underwood (19 Recordings/Arista Nashville)
2008 "I Saw God Today"—George Strait (MCA Nashville)
2009 "I Run to You"—Lady Antebellum (Capitol Nashville)
2010 "Need You Now"—Lady Antebellum (Capitol Nashville)

## Song of the Year

1967 "There Goes My Everything" (Dallas Frazier)
1968 "Honey" (Bobby Russell)
1969 "Carroll County Accident" (Bob Ferguson)
1970 "Sunday Morning Coming Down" (Kris Kristofferson)
1971 "Easy Loving" (Freddie Hart)
1972 "Easy Loving" (Freddie Hart)
1973 "Behind Closed Doors" (Kenny O'Dell)
1974 "Country Bumpkin" (Don Wayne)
1975 "Back Home Again" (John Denver)
1976 "Rhinestone Cowboy" (Larry Weiss)
1977 "Lucille" (Roger Bowling–Hal Bynum)
1978 "Don't It Make My Brown Eyes Blue" (Richard Leigh)
1979 "The Gambler" (Don Schlitz)
1980 "He Stopped Loving Her Today" (Bobby Braddock–Curly Putman)
1981 "He Stopped Loving Her Today" (Bobby Braddock–Curly Putman)
1982 "Always on My Mind" (Wayne Carson–Johnny Christopher–Mark James)
1983 "Always on My Mind" (Wayne Carson–Johnny Christopher–Mark James)

**Song of the Year** (continued)

1984 "Wind Beneath My Wings" (Larry Henley–Jeff Silbar)
1985 "God Bless the U.S.A." (Lee Greenwood)
1986 "On the Other Hand" (Paul Overstreet–Don Schlitz)
1987 "Forever and Ever, Amen" (Paul Overstreet–Don Schlitz)
1988 "80's Ladies" (K. T. Oslin)
1989 "Chiseled in Stone" (Max D. Barnes–Vern Gosdin)
1990 "Where've You Been" (Don Henry–Jon Vezner)
1991 "When I Call Your Name" (Tim DuBois–Vince Gill)
1992 "Look at Us" (Max D. Barnes–Vince Gill)
1993 "I Still Believe in You" (Vince Gill–John Barlow Jarvis)
1994 "Chattahoochee" (Alan Jackson–Jim McBride)
1995 "Independence Day" (Gretchen Peters)
1996 "Go Rest High on That Mountain" (Vince Gill)
1997 "Strawberry Wine" (Matraca Berg–Gary Harrison)
1998 "Holes in the Floor of Heaven" (Steve Wariner–Billy Kirsch)
1999 "This Kiss" (Robin Lerner–Annie Roboff–Beth Nielson Chapman)
2000 "I Hope You Dance" (Tia Sellers–Mark D. Sanders)
2001 "Murder on Music Row" (Larry Cordle–Larry Shell)
2002 "Where Were You (When the World Stopped Turning)" (Alan Jackson)
2003 "Three Wooden Crosses" (Doug Johnson–Kim Williams)
2004 "Live Like You Were Dying" (Tim Nichols–Craig Wiseman)
2005 "Whiskey Lullaby" (Bill Anderson–Jon Randall)
2006 "Believe" (Craig Wiseman–Ronnie Dunn)
2007 "Give It Away" (Bill Anderson–Buddy Cannon–Jamey Johnson)
2008 "Stay" (Jennifer Nettles)
2009 "In Color" (Jamey Johnson–Lee Thomas Miller–James Otto)
2010 "The House that Built Me" (Tom Douglas–Allen Shamblin)

**Album of the Year**

1967 *There Goes My Everything*—Jack Greene (Decca)
1968 *Johnny Cash at Folsom Prison*—Johnny Cash (Columbia)
1969 *Johnny Cash at San Quentin*—Johnny Cash (Columbia)
1970 *Okie from Muskogee*—Merle Haggard (Capitol)
1971 *I Won't Mention It Again*—Ray Price (Columbia)
1972 *Let Me Tell You About a Song*—Merle Haggard (Capitol)
1973 *Behind Closed Doors*—Charlie Rich (Epic)
1974 *Very Special Love Songs*—Charlie Rich (Epic)
1975 *A Legend in My Time*—Ronnie Milsap (RCA)
1976 *Wanted! The Outlaws*—Waylon Jennings, Willie Nelson, Jessi Colter, Tompall Glaser (RCA)
1977 *Ronnie Milsap Live*—Ronnie Milsap (RCA)
1978 *It Was Almost Like a Song*—Ronnie Milsap (RCA)
1979 *The Gambler*—Kenny Rogers (United Artists)
1980 *Coal Miner's Daughter*—Soundtrack (MCA)
1981 *I Believe in You*—Don Williams (MCA)

1982 *Always on My Mind*—Willie Nelson (Columbia)
1983 *The Closer You Get...*—Alabama (RCA)
1984 *A Little Good News*—Anne Murray (Capitol)
1985 *Does Fort Worth Ever Cross Your Mind*—George Strait (MCA)
1986 *Lost in the Fifties Tonight*—Ronnie Milsap (RCA)
1987 *Always and Forever*—Randy Travis (Warner Bros.)
1988 *Born to Boogie*—Hank Williams Jr. (Warner Bros./Curb)
1989 *Will the Circle Be Unbroken, Volume II*—Nitty Gritty Dirt Band (Universal)
1990 *Pickin' on Nashville*—Kentucky HeadHunters (Mercury Nashville)
1991 *No Fences*—Garth Brooks (Capitol Nashville)
1992 *Ropin' the Wind*—Garth Brooks (Liberty)
1993 *I Still Believe in You*—Vince Gill (MCA Nashville)
1994 *Common Thread: The Songs of the Eagles*—Various Artists (Giant)
1995 *When Fallen Angels Fly*—Patty Loveless (Epic)
1996 *Blue Clear Sky*—George Strait (MCA Nashville)
1997 *Carrying Your Love with Me*—George Strait (MCA Nashville)
1998 *Everywhere*—Tim McGraw (Curb)
1999 *A Place in the Sun*—Tim McGraw (Curb)
2000 *Fly*—Dixie Chicks (Monument)
2001 *O Brother, Where Art Thou?*—Soundtrack/Various Artists (Lost Highway)
2002 *Drive*—Alan Jackson (Arista Nashville)
2003 *American IV: The Man Comes Around*—Johnny Cash (Lost Highway)
2004 *When the Sun Goes Down*—Kenny Chesney (BNA)
2005 *There's More Where That Came From*—Lee Ann Womack (MCA Nashville)
2006 *Time Well Wasted*—Brad Paisley (Arista Nashville)
2007 *It Just Comes Natural*—George Strait (MCA Nashville)
2008 *Troubadour*—George Strait (MCA Nashville)
2009 *Fearless*—Taylor Swift (Big Machine)
2010 *Revolution*—Miranda Lambert (Columbia Nashville)

**Music Video of the Year**

(initiated in 1985; not awarded in 1988)

1985 "All My Rowdy Friends Are Comin' Over Tonight"—Hank Williams Jr.; directed by John Goodhue (Warner Bros./Curb)
1986 "Who's Gonna Fill Their Shoes"—George Jones; directed by Marc Ball (Epic)
1987 "My Name Is Bocephus"—Hank Williams Jr.; directed by Bill Fishman and Preacher Ewing (Warner Bros./Curb)
1989 "There's a Tear in My Beer"—Hank Williams and Hank Williams Jr.; directed by Ethan Russell (Warner Bros./Curb)
1990 "The Dance"—Garth Brooks; directed by John Lloyd Miller (Capitol Nashville)
1991 "The Thunder Rolls"—Garth Brooks; directed by Bud Schaetzle (Capitol Nashville)
1992 "Midnight in Montgomery"—Alan Jackson; directed by Jim Shea (Arista Nashville)
1993 "Chattahoochee"—Alan Jackson; directed by Martin Kahan (Arista Nashville)
1994 "Independence Day"—Martina McBride; directed by Robert Deaton & George J. Flanigen IV (RCA)
1995 "Baby Likes to Rock It"—Tractors; directed by Michael Salomon (Arista Nashville)

1996 "My Wife Thinks You're Dead"—Junior Brown; directed by Michael McNamara (Curb)
1997 "455 Rocket"—Kathy Mattea; directed by Steven Goldmann (Mercury Nashville)
1998 "This Kiss"—Faith Hill; directed by Steven Goldmann (Warner Brothers)
1999 "Wide Open Spaces"—Dixie Chicks; directed by Thom Oliphant (Monument)
2000 "Goodbye Earl"—Dixie Chicks; directed by Evan Bernard (Monument)
2001 "Born to Fly"—Sara Evans; directed by Peter Zavadil (RCA)
2002 "I'm Gonna Miss Her (The Fishin' Song)"—Brad Paisley; directed by Peter Zavadil (Arista Nashville)
2003 "Hurt"—Johnny Cash; directed by Mark Romanek (Lost Highway)
2004 "Whiskey Lullaby"—Brad Paisley and Alison Krauss; directed by Rick Schroder (Arista Nashville)
2005 "As Good as I Once Was"—Toby Keith; directed by Michael Salomon (DreamWorks Nashville)
2006 "Believe"—Brooks & Dunn; directed by Robert Deaton and George J. Flanigen IV (Arista Nashville)
2007 "Online"—Brad Paisley; directed by Jason Alexander (Arista Nashville)
2008 "Waitin' On a Woman"—Brad Paisley featuring Andy Griffith; directed by Jim Shea and Peter Tilden (Arista Nashville)
2009 "Love Story"—Taylor Swift; directed by Trey Fanjoy (Big Machine)
2010 "The House that Built Me"—Miranda Lambert; directed by Trey Fanjoy (Columbia Nashville)

**Comedian**

(discontinued in 1971)

1967 Don Bowman
1968 Ben Colder
1969 Archie Campbell
1970 Roy Clark

**Horizon Award**

1981 Terri Gibbs
1982 Ricky Skaggs
1983 John Anderson
1984 Judds
1985 Sawyer Brown
1986 Randy Travis
1987 Holly Dunn
1988 Ricky Van Shelton
1989 Clint Black
1990 Garth Brooks
1991 Travis Tritt
1992 Suzy Bogguss
1993 Mark Chesnutt
1994 John Michael Montgomery
1995 Alison Krauss
1996 Bryan White
1997 LeAnn Rimes
1998 Dixie Chicks
1999 Jo Dee Messina
2000 Brad Paisley
2001 Keith Urban
2002 Rascal Flatts
2003 Joe Nichols
2004 Gretchen Wilson
2005 Dierks Bentley
2006 Carrie Underwood
2007 Taylor Swift

**New Artist**

(Started in 2008 in lieu of Horizon Award)

2008 Lady Antebellum
2009 Darius Rucker
2010 Zac Brown Band

# Academy of Country Music (ACM) Awards

## Entertainer

1970 Merle Haggard
1971 Freddie Hart
1972 Roy Clark
1973 Roy Clark
1974 Mac Davis
1975 Loretta Lynn
1976 Mickey Gilley
1977 Dolly Parton
1978 Kenny Rogers
1979 Willie Nelson
1980 Barbara Mandrell
1981 Alabama
1982 Alabama
1983 Alabama
1984 Alabama
1985 Alabama
1986 Hank Williams Jr.
1987 Hank Williams Jr.
1988 Hank Williams Jr.
1989 George Strait
1990 Garth Brooks
1991 Garth Brooks
1992 Garth Brooks
1993 Garth Brooks
1994 Reba McEntire
1995 Brooks & Dunn
1996 Brooks & Dunn
1997 Garth Brooks
1998 Garth Brooks
1999 Shania Twain
2000 Dixie Chicks
2001 Brooks & Dunn
2002 Toby Keith
2003 Toby Keith
2004 Kenny Chesney
2005 Kenny Chesney
2006 Kenny Chesney
2007 Kenny Chesney
2008 Carrie Underwood
2009 Carrie Underwood
2010 Taylor Swift

## Female Vocalist

1965 Bonnie Owens
1966 Bonnie Guitar
1967 Lynn Anderson
1968 Cathie Taylor
1969 Tammy Wynette
1970 Lynn Anderson
1971 Loretta Lynn
1972 Donna Fargo
1973 Loretta Lynn
1974 Loretta Lynn
1975 Loretta Lynn
1976 Crystal Gayle
1977 Crystal Gayle
1978 Barbara Mandrell
1979 Crystal Gayle
1980 Dolly Parton
1981 Barbara Mandrell
1982 Sylvia
1983 Janie Fricke
1984 Reba McEntire
1985 Reba McEntire
1986 Reba McEntire
1987 Reba McEntire
1988 K. T. Oslin
1989 Kathy Mattea
1990 Reba McEntire
1991 Reba McEntire
1992 Mary Chapin Carpenter
1993 Wynonna
1994 Reba McEntire
1995 Patty Loveless
1996 Patty Loveless
1997 Trisha Yearwood
1998 Faith Hill

1999 Faith Hill
2000 Faith Hill
2001 Martina McBride
2002 Martina McBride
2003 Martina McBride
2004 Gretchen Wilson
2005 Sara Evans
2006 Carrie Underwood
2007 Carrie Underwood
2008 Carrie Underwood
2009 Miranda Lambert
2010 Miranda Lambert

## Male Vocalist

1965 Buck Owens
1966 Merle Haggard
1967 Glen Campbell
1968 Glen Campbell
1969 Merle Haggard
1970 Merle Haggard
1971 Freddie Hart
1972 Merle Haggard
1973 Charlie Rich
1974 Merle Haggard
1975 Conway Twitty
1976 Mickey Gilley
1977 Kenny Rogers
1978 Kenny Rogers
1979 Larry Gatlin
1980 George Jones
1981 Merle Haggard
1982 Ronnie Milsap
1983 Lee Greenwood
1984 George Strait
1985 George Strait
1986 Randy Travis
1987 Randy Travis
1988 George Strait
1989 Clint Black
1990 Garth Brooks
1991 Garth Brooks
1992 Vince Gill
1993 Vince Gill
1994 Alan Jackson
1995 Alan Jackson
1996 George Strait
1997 George Strait
1998 Tim McGraw
1999 Tim McGraw
2000 Toby Keith
2001 Alan Jackson
2002 Kenny Chesney
2003 Toby Keith
2004 Keith Urban
2005 Keith Urban
2006 Brad Paisley
2007 Brad Paisley
2008 Brad Paisley
2009 Brad Paisley
2010 Brad Paisley

## Vocal Group

(no awards given for 1968, 1971, 1974–76, and 1979–80)
1967 Sons of the Pioneers
1969 Kimberlys
1970 Kimberlys
1972 Statler Brothers
1973 Brush Arbor
1977 Statler Brothers
1978 Oak Ridge Boys
1981 Alabama
1982 Alabama
1983 Alabama
1984 Alabama
1985 Alabama
1986 Forester Sisters
1987 Highway 101

1988 Highway 101
1989 Restless Heart
1990 Shenandoah
1991 Diamond Rio
1992 Diamond Rio
1993 Little Texas
1994 Mavericks
1995 Mavericks
1996 Sawyer Brown
1998 Dixie Chicks**
1999 Dixie Chicks**
2000 Dixie Chicks
2001 Lonestar
2002 Rascal Flatts
2003 Rascal Flatts
2004 Rascal Flatts
2005 Rascal Flatts
2006 Rascal Flatts
2007 Rascal Flatts
2008 Rascal Flatts
2009 Lady Antebellum
2010 Lady Antebellum

**In this year the award was presented as Top Vocal Duo/Group*

## Vocal Duo

(called Vocal Duet from 1980 to 1996)
(no awards given for 1969–70, 1972–73, 1977–78)
1965 Merle Haggard and Bonnie Owens
1966 Merle Haggard and Bonnie Owens
1967 Merle Haggard and Bonnie Owens
1968 Merle Haggard and Bonnie Owens, Johnny & Jonie Mosby (tie)
1971 Loretta Lynn and Conway Twitty
1974 Loretta Lynn and Conway Twitty
1975 Loretta Lynn and Conway Twitty
1976 Loretta Lynn and Conway Twitty
1979 Moe Bandy and Joe Stampley
1980 Moe Bandy and Joe Stampley
1981 David Frizzell and Shelly West
1982 David Frizzell and Shelly West
1983 Dolly Parton and Kenny Rogers
1984 The Judds
1985 The Judds
1986 The Judds
1987 The Judds
1988 The Judds
1989 The Judds
1990 The Judds
1991 Brooks & Dunn
1992 Brooks & Dunn
1993 Brooks & Dunn
1994 Brooks & Dunn
1995 Brooks & Dunn
1996 Brooks & Dunn
1997 Brooks & Dunn**
2000 Brooks & Dunn
2001 Brooks & Dunn
2002 Brooks & Dunn
2003 Brooks & Dunn
2004 Brooks & Dunn
2005 Brooks & Dunn
2006 Brooks & Dunn
2007 Brooks & Dunn
2008 Sugarland
2009 Brooks & Dunn
2010 Sugarland

**In this year the award was presented as Top Vocal Duo/Group*

## Single Record

1967 "Gentle on My Mind"—Glen Campbell (Capitol)
1968 "Little Green Apples"—Roger Miller (Smash)

**Single Record** (continued)

1969 "Okie from Muskogee"—Merle Haggard (Capitol)
1970 "For the Good Times"—Ray Price (Columbia)
1971 "Easy Loving"—Freddie Hart (Capitol)
1972 "The Happiest Girl in the Whole U.S.A."—Donna Fargo (Dot)
1973 "Behind Closed Doors"—Charlie Rich (Epic)
1974 "Country Bumpkin"—Cal Smith (MCA)
1975 "Rhinestone Cowboy"—Glen Campbell (Capitol)
1976 "Bring It on Home"—Mickey Gilley (Playboy)
1977 "Lucille"—Kenny Rogers (United Artists)
1978 "Tulsa Time"—Don Williams (ABC)
1979 "All the Gold in California"—Larry Gatlin & the Gatlin Brothers (Columbia)
1980 "He Stopped Loving Her Today"—George Jones (Epic)
1981 "Elvira"—Oak Ridge Boys (MCA)
1982 "Always on My Mind"—Willie Nelson (Columbia)
1983 "Islands in the Stream"—Kenny Rogers & Dolly Parton (RCA)
1984 "To All the Girls I've Loved Before"—Willie Nelson and Julio Iglesias (Columbia)
1985 "Highwayman"—Willie Nelson, Waylon Jennings, Kris Kristofferson, and Johnny Cash (Columbia)
1986 "On the Other Hand"—Randy Travis (Warner Bros.)
1987 "Forever and Ever, Amen"—Randy Travis (Warner Bros.)
1988 "Eighteen Wheels and a Dozen Roses"—Kathy Mattea (PolyGram)
1989 "Better Man"—Clint Black (RCA)
1990 "Friends in Low Places"—Garth Brooks (Capitol)
1991 "Don't Rock the Jukebox"—Alan Jackson (Arista)
1992 "Boot Scootin' Boogie"—Brooks & Dunn (Arista)
1993 "Chattahoochee"—Alan Jackson (Arista)
1994 "I Swear"—John Michael Montgomery (Arista)
1995 "Check Yes or No"—George Strait (MCA)
1996 "Blue"—LeAnn Rimes (Curb)
1997 "It's Your Love"—Tim McGraw & Faith Hill (Curb)
1998 "This Kiss"—Faith Hill (Warner Bros.)
1999 "Amazed"—Lonestar (BNA)
2000 "I Hope You Dance"—Lee Ann Womack (Decca)
2001 "Where Were You (When the World Stopped Turning)"—Alan Jackson (Arista)
2002 "The Good Stuff"—Kenny Chesney (BNA)
2003 "It's Five O'Clock Somewhere"—Alan Jackson and Jimmy Buffett (Arista)
2004 "Live Like You Were Dying"—Tim McGraw (Curb)
2005 "Jesus, Take the Wheel"—Carrie Underwood (Arista)
2006 "Give It Away"—George Strait (MCA)
2007 "Stay"—Sugarland (Mercury)
2008 "You're Gonna Miss This"—Trace Adkins (Capitol)
2009 "Need You Now"—Lady Antebellum (Capitol)
2010 "The House that Built Me"—Miranda Lambert (Columbia Nashville)

**Song (Songwriter)**

1966 "Apartment #9" (Bobby Austin–Johnny Paycheck)
1967 "It's Such a Pretty World Today" (Dale Noe)

1968 "Wichita Lineman" (Jimmy Webb)
1969 "Okie from Muskogee" (Merle Haggard–Roy Edward Burris)
1970 "For the Good Times" (Kris Kristofferson)
1971 "Easy Loving" (Freddie Hart)
1972 "The Happiest Girl in the Whole U.S.A." (Donna Fargo)
1973 "Behind Closed Doors" (Kenny O'Dell)
1974 "Country Bumpkin" (Don Wayne)
1975 "Rhinestone Cowboy" (Larry Weiss)
1976 "Don't the Girls All Get Prettier at Closing Time" (Baker Knight)
1977 "Lucille" (Roger Bowling–Hal Bynum)
1978 "You Needed Me" (Randy Goodrum)
1979 "It's a Cheatin' Situation" (Sonny Throckmorton–Curly Putman)
1980 "He Stopped Loving Her Today" (Bobby Braddock–Curly Putman)
1981 "You're the Reason God Made Oklahoma" (Sandy Pinkard–Larry Collins)
1982 "Are the Good Times Really Over" (Merle Haggard)
1983 "The Wind Beneath My Wings" (Larry Henley–Jeff Silbar)
1984 "Why Not Me" (Harlan Howard–Sonny Throckmorton–Brent Maher)
1985 "Lost in the Fifties (In the Still of the Night)" (Mike Reid–Troy Seals–Fred Parris)
1986 "On the Other Hand" (Don Schlitz–Paul Overstreet)
1987 "Forever and Ever, Amen" (Don Schlitz–Paul Overstreet)
1988 "Eighteen Wheels and a Dozen Roses" (Paul Nelson–Gene Nelson)
1989 "Where've You Been" (Jon Vezner–Don Henry)
1990 "The Dance" (Tony Arata)
1991 "Somewhere in My Broken Heart" (Billy Dean–Richard Leigh)
1992 "I Still Believe in You" (John Barlow Jarvis–Vince Gill)
1993 "I Love the Way You Love Me" (Victoria Shaw–Chuck Cannon)
1994 "I Swear" (Gary B. Baker–Frank Myers)
1995 "The Keeper of the Stars" (Karen Staley–Dickey Lee–Danny Mayo)
1996 "Blue" (Bill Mack)
1997 "It's Your Love" (Stephony Smith)
1998 "Holes in the Floor of Heaven" (Steve Wariner–Billy Kirsch)
1999 "Amazed" (Aimee Mayo–Chris Lindsey–Marv Green)
2000 "I Hope You Dance" (Mark D. Sanders–Tia Sillers)
2001 "Where Were You (When the World Stopped Turning)" (Alan Jackson)
2002 "I'm Movin' On" (D. Vincent Williams–Phillip White)
2003 "Three Wooden Crosses" (Doug Johnson–Kim Williams)
2004 "Live Like You Were Dying" (Craig Wiseman–Tim Nichols)
2005 "Believe" (Craig Wiseman–Ronnie Dunn)
2006 "Give It Away" (Bill Anderson–Buddy Cannon–Jamey Johnson)
2007 "Stay" (Jennifer Nettles)
2008 "In Color" (Jamey Johnson–Lee Thomas Miller–James Otto)
2009 "Need You Now" (Dave Haywood–Josh Kear–Charles Kelley–Hillary Scott)
2010 "The House That Built Me" (Tom Douglas–Allen Shamblin)

**Album**

1967 *Gentle on My Mind*—Glen Campbell (Capitol)
1968 *Glen Campbell & Bobbie Gentry*—Glen Campbell & Bobbie Gentry (Capitol)

1969 *Okie from Muskogee*—Merle Haggard (Capitol)
1970 *For the Good Times*—Ray Price (Columbia)
1971 *Easy Loving*—Freddie Hart (Capitol)
1972 *Happiest Girl in the Whole U.S.A.*—Donna Fargo (Dot)
1973 *Behind Closed Doors*—Charlie Rich (Epic)
1974 *Back Home Again*—John Denver (RCA)
1975 *Feelins'*—Conway Twitty and Loretta Lynn (MCA)
1976 *Gilley's Smokin'*—Mickey Gilley (Playboy)
1977 *Kenny Rogers*—Kenny Rogers (United Artists)
1978 *Y'all Come Back Saloon*—Oak Ridge Boys (MCA)
1979 *Straight Ahead*—Larry Gatlin & the Gatlin Brothers (Columbia)
1980 *Urban Cowboy*—Soundtrack (Asylum)
1981 *Feels So Right*—Alabama (RCA)
1982 *Always on My Mind*—Willie Nelson (CBS)
1983 *The Closer You Get*—Alabama (RCA)
1984 *Roll On*—Alabama (RCA)
1985 *Does Forth Worth Ever Cross Your Mind*—George Strait (MCA)
1986 *Storms of Life*—Randy Travis (Warner Bros.)
1987 *Trio*—Dolly Parton, Emmylou Harris, and Linda Ronstadt (Warner Bros.)
1988 *This Woman*—K. T. Oslin (RCA)
1989 *Killin' Time*—Clint Black (RCA)
1990 *No Fences*—Garth Brooks (Capitol)
1991 *Don't Rock the Jukebox*—Alan Jackson (Arista)
1992 *Brand New Man*—Brooks & Dunn (Arista)
1993 *A Lot About Livin' (And a Little 'Bout Love)*—Alan Jackson (Arista)
1994 *Not a Moment Too Soon*—Tim McGraw (Curb)
1995 *The Woman in Me*—Shania Twain (Mercury)
1996 *Blue Clear Sky*—George Strait (MCA)
1997 *Carrying Your Love with Me*—George Strait (MCA)
1998 *Wide Open Spaces*—Dixie Chicks (Monument)
1999 *Fly*—Dixie Chicks (Monument)
2000 *How Do You Like Me Now?!*—Toby Keith (DreamWorks)
2001 *O Brother, Where Art Thou?*—Soundtrack (Mercury)
2002 *Drive*—Alan Jackson (Arista Nashville)
2003 *Shock'n Y'all*—Toby Keith (DreamWorks)
2004 *Be Here*—Keith Urban (Capitol Nashville)
2005 *Time Well Wasted*—Brad Paisley (Arista Nashville)
2006 *Some Hearts*—Carrie Underwood (19 Recordings/Arista)
2007 *Crazy Ex-Girlfriend*—Miranda Lambert (Columbia Nashville)
2008 *Fearless*—Taylor Swift (Big Machine)
2009 *Revolution*—Miranda Lambert (Columbia Nashville)
2010 *Need You Now*—Lady Antebellum (Capitol Nashville)

**Video**

1984 "All My Rowdy Friends Are Coming Over Tonight"—Hank Williams Jr.
1985 "Who's Gonna Fill Their Shoes"—George Jones
1986 "Whoever's in New England"—Reba McEntire
1987 "80's Ladies"—K. T. Oslin
1988 "Young Country"—Hank Williams Jr.
1989 "There's a Tear in My Beer"—Hank Williams and Hank Williams Jr.
1990 "The Dance"—Garth Brooks
1991 "Is There Life Out There"—Reba McEntire
1992 "Two Sparrows in a Hurricane"—Tanya Tucker

## Video (continued)

1993 "We Shall Be Free"—Garth Brooks
1994 "The Red Strokes"—Garth Brooks
1995 "The Car"—Jeff Carson
1996 "I Think About You"—Collin Raye
1997 "It's Your Love"—Faith Hill and Tim McGraw
1998 "This Kiss"—Faith Hill
1999 "Breathe"—Faith Hill
2000 "Goodbye Earl"—Dixie Chicks
2001 "Only in America"—Brooks & Dunn
2002 "Drive (For Daddy Gene)"—Alan Jackson
2003 "Beer for My Horses"—Toby Keith and Willie Nelson
2004 "Whiskey Lullaby"—Alison Krauss and Brad Paisley
2005 "When I Get Where I'm Going"—Brad Paisley and Dolly Parton
2006 "Before He Cheats"—Carrie Underwood
2007 "Online"—Brad Paisley
2008 "Waitin' on a Woman"—Brad Paisley
2009 "White Liar"—Miranda Lambert
2010 "The House that Built Me"—Miranda Lambert

## New Female Vocalist (Most Promising)

1965 Kay Adams
1966 Cathie Taylor
1967 Bobbie Gentry
1968 Cheryl Poole
1969 Donna Fargo
1970 Sammi Smith
1971 Barbara Mandrell
1972 Tanya Tucker
1973 Olivia Newton-John
1974 Linda Ronstadt
1975 Crystal Gayle
1976 Billie Jo Spears
1977 Debby Boone
1978 Christy Lane
1979 Lacy J. Dalton
1980 Terri Gibbs
1981 Juice Newton
1982 Karen Brooks
1983 Gus Hardin
1984 Nicolette Larson
1985 Judy Rodman
1986 Holly Dunn
1987 K. T. Oslin
1988 Suzy Bogguss
1989 Mary Chapin Carpenter
1990 Shelby Lynne
1991 Trisha Yearwood
1992 Michelle Wright
1993 Faith Hill
1994 Chely Wright
1995 Shania Twain
1996 LeAnn Rimes
1997 Lee Ann Womack
1998 Jo Dee Messina
1999 Jessica Andrews
2000 Jamie O'Neal
2001 Carolyn Dawn Johnson
2002 Kellie Coffey
2003 (no award given)
2004 (no award given)
2005 Carrie Underwood
2006 Miranda Lambert
2007 Taylor Swift
2008 Julianne Hough
2009 (no award given)
2010 (no award given)

## New Male Vocalist (Most Promising)

1965 Merle Haggard
1966 Billy Mize
1967 Jerry Inman
1968 Ray Sanders
1969 Freddy Weller
1970 Buddy Alan
1971 Tony Booth
1972 Johnny Rodriguez
1973 Dorsey Burnette
1974 Mickey Gilley
1975 Freddy Fender
1976 Moe Bandy
1977 Eddie Rabbitt
1978 John Conlee
1979 R. C. Bannon
1980 Johnny Lee
1981 Ricky Skaggs
1982 Michael Martin Murphey
1983 Jim Glaser
1984 Vince Gill
1985 Randy Travis
1986 Dwight Yoakam
1987 Ricky Van Shelton
1988 Rodney Crowell
1989 Clint Black
1990 Alan Jackson
1991 Billy Dean
1992 Tracy Lawrence
1993 John Michael Montgomery
1994 Tim McGraw
1995 Bryan White
1996 Trace Adkins
1997 Kenny Chesney
1998 Mark Wills
1999 Brad Paisley
2000 Keith Urban
2001 Phil Vassar
2002 Joe Nichols
2003 (no award given)
2004 (no award given)
2005 Jason Aldean
2006 Rodney Atkins
2007 Jack Ingram
2008 Jake Owen
2009 (no award given)
2010 (no award given)

## New Vocal Duo/Group

1989 Kentucky HeadHunters
1990 Pirates of the Mississippi
1991 Brooks & Dunn
1992 Confederate Railroad
1993 Gibson/Miller Band
1994 The Mavericks
1995 Lonestar
1996 Ricochet
1997 The Kinleys
1998 Dixie Chicks
1999 Montgomery Gentry
2000 Rascal Flatts
2001 Trick Pony
2002 Emerson Drive
2003 (no award given)
2004 (no award given)
2005 Sugarland
2006 Little Big Town
2007 Lady Antebellum
2008 Zac Brown Band
2009 Gloriana*
2010 The Band Perry

*A separate category for Top New Vocal Duo in 2009

## New Vocal Duo

2009 Joey + Rory

## New Solo Vocalist

2009 Luke Bryan
2010 Eric Church

## New Artist

2003 Dierks Bentley
2004 Gretchen Wilson
2008 Julianne Hough
2009 Luke Bryan
2010 The Band Perry

## Vocal Event

1997 "It's Your Love"—Faith Hill and Tim McGraw

1998 "Just to Hear You Say You Love Me"—Faith Hill and Tim McGraw
1999 "When I Said I Do"—Clint Black and Lisa Hartman Black
2000 "I Hope You Dance"—Lee Ann Womack and Sons of the Desert
2001 "I Am a Man of Constant Sorrow"—Soggy Bottom Boys
2002 "Mendocino County Line"—Lee Ann Womack and Willie Nelson
2003 "It's Five O'Clock Somewhere"—Alan Jackson and Jimmy Buffett
2004 "Whiskey Lullaby"—Alison Krauss and Brad Paisley
2005 "When I Get Where I'm Going"—Brad Paisley and Dolly Parton
2006 "Building Bridges"—Brooks & Dunn, Sheryl Crow, Vince Gill
2007 "Find Out Who Your Friends Are"—Tim McGraw, Kenny Chesney, Tracy Lawrence
2008 "Start a Band"—Brad Paisley and Keith Urban
2009 "Hillbilly Bone"—Blake Shelton and Trace Adkins
2010 "As She's Walking Away"—Zac Brown Band featuring Alan Jackson

## Artist of the Decade

1960–69 Marty Robbins
1970–79 Loretta Lynn
1980–89 Alabama
1990–99 Garth Brooks
2000–09 George Strait

## The Home Depot Humanitarian Award

2001 Reba McEntire
2002 Lonestar
2003 Martina McBride
2004 Neal McCoy
2005 Vince Gill
2006 Brooks & Dunn
2007 Rascal Flatts
2008 LeAnn Rimes
2009 Montgomery Gentry
2010 (no award given)

## Fiddle

1965 Billy Armstrong
1966 Billy Armstrong
1967 Billy Armstrong
1968 Billy Armstrong
1969 Billy Armstrong
1970 Billy Armstrong
1971 Billy Armstrong
1972 Billy Armstrong
1973 Billy Armstrong
1974 Billy Armstrong
1975 Billy Armstrong
1976 Billy Armstrong
1977 Billy Armstrong
1978 Johnny Gimble
1979 Johnny Gimble
1980 Johnny Gimble
1981 Johnny Gimble
1982 Johnny Gimble
1983 Johnny Gimble
1984 Johnny Gimble
1985 Johnny Gimble
1986 Mark O'Connor
1987 Johnny Gimble
1988 Mark O'Connor
1989 Mark O'Connor
1990 Mark O'Connor
1991 Mark O'Connor
1992 Mark O'Connor
1993 Mark O'Connor
1994 Mark O'Connor
1995 Rob Hajacos
1996 Stuart Duncan
1997 Larry Franklin
1998 Stuart Duncan
1999 Stuart Duncan

**Fiddle** (*continued*)

2000 Mark O'Connor
2001 Stuart Duncan
2002 Larry Franklin
2003 Aubrey Haynie
2004 Stuart Duncan
2005 Jonathan Yudkin
2006 Aubrey Haynie
2007 Stuart Duncan
2008 Aubrey Haynie
2009 Stuart Duncan
2010 Aubrey Haynie

**Steel Guitar**

1965 Red Rhodes
1966 Ralph Mooney, Tom Brumley (tie)
1967 Red Rhodes
1968 Red Rhodes
1969 Buddy Emmons
1970 Jay Dee Maness
1971 Jay Dee Maness
1972 Buddy Emmons
1973 Red Rhodes
1974 Jay Dee Maness
1975 Jay Dee Maness
1976 Jay Dee Maness
1977 Buddy Emmons
1978 Buddy Emmons
1979 Buddy Emmons
1980 Jay Dee Maness, Buddy Emmons (tie)
1981 Buddy Emmons
1982 Jay Dee Maness
1983 Jay Dee Maness
1984 Buddy Emmons
1985 Buddy Emmons
1986 Jay Dee Maness
1987 Jay Dee Maness
1988 Jay Dee Maness
1989 Jay Dee Maness
1990 Jay Dee Maness
1991 Paul Franklin
1992 Jay Dee Maness
1993 Jay Dee Maness
1994 Paul Franklin
1995 Paul Franklin
1996 Paul Franklin
1997 Paul Franklin
1998 Paul Franklin
1999 Jay Dee Maness
2000 Paul Franklin
2001 Paul Franklin
2002 Jay Dee Maness
2003 Paul Franklin
2004 Dan Dugmore
2005 Paul Franklin
2006 Michael Johnson
2007 Lloyd Green
2008 Dan Dugmore
2009 Paul Franklin
2010 Dan Dugmore

**Keyboard**

1965 Billy Liebert
1966 Billy Liebert
1967 Earl Ball
1968 Earl Ball
1969 Floyd Cramer
1970 Floyd Cramer
1971 Floyd Cramer
1972 Floyd Cramer
1973 Floyd Cramer
1974 Floyd Cramer
1975 Jerry Lee Lewis
1976 Hargus "Pig" Robbins
1977 Hargus "Pig" Robbins
1978 Jimmy Pruett
1979 Hargus "Pig" Robbins
1980 Hargus "Pig" Robbins
1981 Hargus "Pig" Robbins
1982 Hargus "Pig" Robbins
1983 Floyd Cramer
1984 Hargus "Pig" Robbins

1985 Glen D. Hardin
1986 John Hobbs
1987 John Hobbs, Ronnie Milsap (tie)
1988 John Hobbs
1989 Skip Edwards
1990 John Hobbs
1991 Matt Rollings
1992 Matt Rollings
1993 Matt Rollings
1994 Matt Rollings
1995 Matt Rollings
1996 Matt Rollings
1997 Matt Rollings
1998 Matt Rollings
1999 Hargus "Pig" Robbins/John Hobbs
2000 John Hobbs
2001 John Hobbs
2002 Matt Rollings
2003 John Hobbs
2004 Steve Nathan
2005 Mike Rojas
2006 John Hobbs
2007 Matt Rollings
2008 Gordon Mote
2009 Michael Rojas
2010 Gordon Mote

**Bass**

1965 Bob Morris
1966 Bob Morris
1967 Red Wooten
1968 Red Wooten
1969 Billy Graham
1970 Doyle Holly, Billy Graham (tie)
1971 Larry Booth
1972 Larry Booth
1973 Larry Booth
1974 Billy Graham
1975 Billy Graham
1976 Curtis Stone
1977 Larry Booth
1978 Rod Culpepper
1979 Billy Graham
1980 Curtis Stone
1981 Curtis Stone, Joe Osborn (tie)
1982 Red Wooten
1983 Joe Osborn
1984 Joe Osborn
1985 Joe Osborn
1986 Emory Gordy Jr.
1987 Emory Gordy Jr., David Hungate (tie)
1988 Curtis Stone
1989 Michael Rhodes
1990 Bill Bryson
1991 Roy Huskey Jr.
1992 Glenn Worf
1993 Glenn Worf
1994 Glenn Worf
1995 Glenn Worf
1996 Glenn Worf
1997 Glenn Worf
1998 Glenn Worf
1999 Glenn Worf
2000 Michael Rhodes
2001 Michael Rhodes
2002 Glenn Worf
2003 Michael Rhodes
2004 Glenn Worf
2005 Michael Rhodes
2006 Glenn Worf
2007 Michael Rhodes
2008 Glenn Worf
2009 Michael Rhodes
2010 Glenn Worf

**Guitar**

1965 Phil Baugh
1966 Jimmy Bryant
1967 Jimmy Bryant
1968 Jimmy Bryant
1969 Al Bruno, Jerry Inman (tie)
1970 Al Bruno

1971 Al Bruno
1972 Al Bruno
1973 Al Bruno
1974 Al Bruno
1975 Jerry Inman (rhythm), Russ Hansen (lead)
1976 Danny Michaels
1977 Roy Clark
1978 James Burton
1979 Al Bruno
1980 Al Bruno
1981 James Burton
1982 Al Bruno
1983 Reggie Young
1984 James Burton
1985 James Burton
1986 Chet Atkins
1987 Chet Atkins
1988 Al Bruno
1989 Brent Rowan
1990 John Jorgenson
1991 John Jorgenson
1992 John Jorgenson
1993 Brent Mason
1994 Brent Mason
1995 Brent Mason
1996 Brent Mason
1997 Brent Mason
1998 Brent Mason
1999 Brent Mason
2000 Brent Mason
2001 Jimmy Olander
2002 John Willis
2003 Brent Rowan
2004 Brent Mason
2005 Pat Buchanan
2006 Brent Mason
2007 Dann Huff
2008 Tom Bukovac
2009 Brent Mason
2010 Tom Bukovac

**Drums**

1965 Muddy Berry
1966 Jerry Wiggins
1967 Pee Wee Adams
1968 Jerry Wiggins
1969 Jerry Wiggins
1970 Archie Francis
1971 Jerry Wiggins
1972 Jerry Wiggins
1973 Jerry Wiggins
1974 Jerry Wiggins
1975 Archie Francis
1976 Archie Francis
1977 Archie Francis, George Manz (tie)
1978 Archie Francis
1979 Archie Francis
1980 Archie Francis
1981 Buddy Harman
1982 Archie Francis
1983 Archie Francis
1984 Larrie Londin
1985 Archie Francis
1986 Larrie Londin
1987 Archie Francis
1988 Steve Duncan
1989 Steve Duncan
1990 Steve Duncan
1991 Eddie Bayers
1992 Eddie Bayers
1993 Eddie Bayers
1994 Eddie Bayers
1995 Eddie Bayers
1996 Eddie Bayers
1997 Eddie Bayers
1998 Eddie Bayers
1999 Eddie Bayers
2000 Eddie Bayers
2001 Eddie Bayers
2002 Lonnie Wilson
2003 Eddie Bayers

**Drums** (*continued*)
2004 Lonnie Wilson
2005 Shannon Forest
2006 Eddie Bayers
2007 Shannon Forest
2008 Greg Morrow
2009 Shannon Forest
2010 Eddie Bayers

**Specialty Instrument**
1969 John Hartford, banjo
1977 Charlie McCoy, harmonica
1978 Charlie McCoy, harmonica
1979 Charlie McCoy, harmonica
1980 Charlie McCoy, harmonica
1981 Charlie McCoy, harmonica
1982 James Burton, dobro
1983 Charlie McCoy, harmonica
1984 Ricky Skaggs, mandolin
1985 James Burton, dobro
1986 James Burton, dobro
1987 Ricky Skaggs, mandolin; Jerry Douglas, dobro
1988 Charlie McCoy, harmonica
1989 Jerry Douglas, dobro
1990 Jerry Douglas, dobro
1991 Jerry Douglas, dobro
1992 Jerry Douglas, dobro
1993 Terry McMillan, percussion & harmonica
1994 Terry McMillan, percussion & harmonica
1995 Terry McMillan, percussion & harmonica
1996 Terry McMillan, percussion, harmonica, & cowbells
1997 Jerry Douglas, dobro
1998 Jerry Douglas, dobro
1999 Jerry Douglas, dobro
2000 Jerry Douglas, dobro
2001 Jerry Douglas, dobro
2002 Mark Casstevens
2003 Kirk "Jelly Roll" Johnson
2004 Randy Scruggs
2005 Bryan Sutton
2006 Stuart Duncan
2007 Eric Darken
2008 Eric Darken/Kirk "Jelly Roll" Johnson (tie)
2009 Randy Scruggs
2010 Bryan Sutton

**Touring Band**
(award given from 1965 to 1990)
1965 Buck Owens & the Buckaroos
1966 Buck Owens & the Buckaroos
1967 Buck Owens & the Buckaroos
1968 Buck Owens & the Buckaroos
1969 Merle Haggard & the Strangers
1970 Merle Haggard & the Strangers
1971 Merle Haggard & the Strangers
1972 Merle Haggard & the Strangers
1973 Brush Arbor
1974 Merle Haggard & the Strangers
1975 Merle Haggard & the Strangers
1976 Mickey Gilley & the Red Rose Express
1977 Asleep at the Wheel, Sons of the Pioneers (tie)
1978 Original Texas Playboys
1979 Charlie Daniels Band
1980 Charlie Daniels Band
1981 Merle Haggard & the Strangers
1982 Ricky Skaggs Band
1983 Ricky Skaggs Band
1984 Ricky Skaggs Band
1985 Ricky Skaggs Band
1986 Ricky Skaggs Band
1987 Merle Haggard & the Strangers
1988 Desert Rose Band
1989 Desert Rose Band
1990 Desert Rose Band

**Nontouring Band**
(award given from 1970 to 1990)
1970 Tony Booth Band

1971 Tony Booth Band
1972 Tony Booth Band
1973 Ronnie Truhett & the Sound Company
1974 Palomino Riders
1975 Jerry Inman & the Palomino Riders
1976 Possum Holler
1977 Palomino Riders
1978 Rebel Playboys
1979 Midnight Riders
1980 Palomino Riders
1981 Desperados
1982 Desperados
1983 Billy Mize & the Tennesseans
1984 Billy Mize & the Tennesseans
1985 Nashville Now Band
1986 Nashville Now Band
1987 Nashville Now Band
1988 Nashville Now Band
1989 Nashville Now Band
1990 Boy Howdy

**Individual Awards**
(not awarded every year; awards not given after 1996)
1965 *Billboard*, publication; Central Songs, publisher; Jack McFadden, talent manager; Roger Miller, songwriter and Man of the Year; Billy Mize, TV personality; Ken Nelson, producer/A&R man
1966 Central Songs, publisher; Dean Martin, Man of the Year; Jack McFadden, talent manager; Billy Mize, TV personality; Ken Nelson, producer/A&R man
1967 Joey Bishop, Man of the Year; Freeway Music, publisher; Billy Mize, TV personality
1968 Glen Campbell, TV personality; Nudie, Director's Award; Tom Smothers, Man of the Year
1969 John Aylesworth, Man of the Year; Johnny Cash, TV personality; Roy Clark, comedy act; Frank Peppiatt, Man of the Year
1970 *Billboard*, publication; Johnny Cash, TV personality; Hugh Cherry, Man of the Year; Roy Clark, comedy act
1971 Glen Campbell, TV personality; Roy Clark, comedy act; Walter Knott, Man of the Year
1972 Roy Clark, TV personality; Lawrence Welk, Man of the Year
1977 Johnny Paycheck, career achievement
1980 George Burns, special achievement
1983 Elvis Presley, Golden Hat Award for contributions to the country music industry
1986 Carl Perkins, career achievement
1993 John Anderson, career achievement; Bill Blanchard—Mr. Bill Presents (Phoenix, Arizona), Talent Buyer & Promoter of the Year
1994 George Moffett (Zanesville, Ohio), Talent Buyer & Promoter of the Year
1995 Jeff Foxworthy, Special Achievement Award; George Moffett (Zanesville, Ohio), Talent Buyer & Promoter of the Year
1996 Bob Romeo (Omaha, Nebraska), Talent Buyer & Promoter of the Year

**Pioneer Award**
1968 Uncle Art Satherley
1969 Bob Wills
1970 Patsy Montana, Tex Ritter
1971 Stuart Hamblen, Bob Nolan, Tex Williams
1972 Gene Autry, Cliffie Stone
1973 Hank Williams
1974 Johnny Bond, Tennessee Ernie Ford, Merle Travis
1975 Roy Rogers
1976 Owen Bradley
1977 Sons of the Pioneers
1978 Eddie Dean
1979 Patti Page
1980 Ernest Tubb

1981 Leo Fender
1982 Chet Atkins
1983 Eddy Arnold
1984 Roy Acuff
1985 Kitty Wells
1986 Minnie Pearl
1987 Roger Miller
1988 Buck Owens
1990 Johnny Cash
1991 Willie Nelson
1992 George Jones
1993 Charley Pride
1994 Loretta Lynn
1995 Merle Haggard
1996 Roy Clark
1997 Charlie Daniels
1998 Glen Campbell
1999 Tammy Wynette
2000 Barbara Mandrell
2001 Ronnie Milsap
2002 Alabama
2003 Ray Price
2004 Chris LeDoux
2005 Little Jimmie Dickens, Bill Monroe, Kris Kristofferson, Earl Scruggs
2006 Waylon Jennings, Harlan Howard, Dolly Parton, Don Williams
2007 Brenda Lee, Oak Ridge Boys, Conway Twitty, Porter Wagoner
2008 Hank Williams Jr., Jerry Reed, Kenny Rogers, Randy Travis
2009 Mel Tillis, Marty Robbins
2010 Garth Brooks, Larry Gatlin & the Gatlin Brothers

**Jim Reeves Memorial Award**
(not awarded every year)
1969 Joe Allison
1970 Bill Boyd
1971 Roy Rogers
1972 Thurston Moore
1973 Sam Lovullo
1974 Merv Griffin
1975 Dinah Shore
1976 Roy Clark
1977 Jim Halsey
1978 Joe Cates
1979 Bill Ward
1980 Ken Kragen
1981 Al Gallico
1982 Jo Walker-Meador
1994 Garth Brooks
1996 Bob Saporiti
2004 Charlie Nagatani
2005 Louise Scruggs
2006 Buck Owens

**Jim Reeves International Award**
(award name changed)
2007 Dick Clark
2008 Dolly Parton
2009 Keith Urban
2010 Taylor Swift

**Tex Ritter Award (for motion picture soundtrack)**
(not awarded every year)
1979 *Electric Horseman*
1980 *Coal Miner's Daughter*
1981 *Any Which Way You Can*
1982 *The Best Little Whorehouse in Texas*
1983 *Tender Mercies*
1984 *Songwriter*
1985 *Sweet Dreams*
1992 *Pure Country*
2001 *O Brother, Where Art Thou?*
2005 *Walk the Line*
2008 *Beer for My Horses*
2009 *Crazy Heart*
2010 *Country Strong*

# International Bluegrass Music Association (IBMA) Awards

## Hall of Fame Inductees
1991 Lester Flatt, Earl Scruggs, Bill Monroe
1992 The Stanley Brothers, Reno & Smiley
1993 Jim & Jesse McReynolds, Mac Wiseman
1994 The Osborne Brothers
1995 Jimmy Martin
1996 Peter V. Kuykendall, The Country Gentlemen
1997 Josh Graves
1998 Carlton Haney, Chubby Wise
1999 Kenny Baker
2000 Lance LeRoy, Arthel "Doc" Watson
2001 The Carter Family
2002 The Lilly Brothers & Don Stover, David Freeman
2003 J. D. Crowe
2004 Bill Vernon, Curly Seckler
2005 Benny Martin, Red Allen
2006 Syd Nathan, The Lewis Family
2007 Howard Watts (Cedric Rainwater), Carl Story
2008 Charles K. Wolfe, Bill Clifton
2009 The Lonesome Pine Fiddlers, The Dillards
2010 John Hartford, Louise Scruggs

## Entertainer of the Year
1990 Hot Rize
1991 Alison Krauss & Union Station
1992 Nashville Bluegrass Band
1993 Nashville Bluegrass Band
1994 The Del McCoury Band
1995 Alison Krauss & Union Station
1996 The Del McCoury Band
1997 The Del McCoury Band
1998 The Del McCoury Band
1999 The Del McCoury Band
2000 The Del McCoury Band
2001 Rhonda Vincent & the Rage
2002 The Del McCoury Band
2003 The Del McCoury Band
2004 The Del McCoury Band
2005 Cherryholmes
2006 The Grascals
2007 The Grascals
2008 Dailey & Vincent
2009 Dailey & Vincent
2010 Dailey & Vincent

## Vocal Group of the Year
1990 Nashville Bluegrass Band
1991 Nashville Bluegrass Band
1992 Nashville Bluegrass Band
1993 Nashville Bluegrass Band
1994 IIIrd Tyme Out
1995 IIIrd Tyme Out
1996 IIIrd Tyme Out
1997 IIIrd Tyme Out
1998 IIIrd Tyme Out
1999 IIIrd Tyme Out
2000 IIIrd Tyme Out
2001 Doyle Lawson & Quicksilver
2002 Doyle Lawson & Quicksilver
2003 Doyle Lawson & Quicksilver
2004 Doyle Lawson & Quicksilver
2005 Doyle Lawson & Quicksilver
2006 Doyle Lawson & Quicksilver
2007 Doyle Lawson & Quicksilver
2008 Dailey & Vincent
2009 Dailey & Vincent
2010 Dailey & Vincent

## Instrumental Group of the Year
1990 The Bluegrass Album Band
1991 The Tony Rice Unit
1992 California
1993 California
1994 California
1995 The Tony Rice Unit
1996 The Del McCoury Band
1997 The Del McCoury Band
1998 Ricky Skaggs & Kentucky Thunder
1999 Ricky Skaggs & Kentucky Thunder
2000 Ricky Skaggs & Kentucky Thunder
2001 Nickel Creek
2002 Ricky Skaggs & Kentucky Thunder
2003 Ricky Skaggs & Kentucky Thunder
2004 Ricky Skaggs & Kentucky Thunder
2005 Ricky Skaggs & Kentucky Thunder
2006 Ricky Skaggs & Kentucky Thunder
2007 Michael Cleveland & Flamekeeper featuring Audie Blaylock
2008 Michael Cleveland & Flamekeeper
2009 Michael Cleveland & Flamekeeper
2010 Michael Cleveland & Flamekeeper

## Female Vocalist of the Year
1990 Alison Krauss
1991 Alison Krauss
1992 Laurie Lewis
1993 Alison Krauss
1994 Laurie Lewis
1995 Alison Krauss
1996 Lynn Morris
1997 Claire Lynch
1998 Lynn Morris
1999 Lynn Morris
2000 Rhonda Vincent
2001 Rhonda Vincent
2002 Rhonda Vincent
2003 Rhonda Vincent
2004 Rhonda Vincent
2005 Rhonda Vincent
2006 Rhonda Vincent
2007 Dale Ann Bradley
2008 Dale Ann Bradley
2009 Dale Ann Bradley
2010 Claire Lynch

## Male Vocalist of the Year
1990 Del McCoury
1991 Del McCoury
1992 Del McCoury
1993 Tim O'Brien
1994 Russell Moore
1995 Ronnie Bowman
1996 Del McCoury
1997 Russell Moore
1998 Ronnie Bowman
1999 Ronnie Bowman
2000 Dudley Connell
2001 Dan Tyminski
2002 Dan Tyminski
2003 Dan Tyminski
2004 Larry Sparks
2005 Larry Sparks
2006 Tim O'Brien
2007 Bradley Walker
2008 Jamie Dailey
2009 Dan Tyminski
2010 Russell Moore

## Song of the Year
1990 "Little Mountain Church" (Jim Rushing—Carl Jackson)
1991 "Colleen Malone" (Pete Goble—Leroy Drumm)
1992 "Blue Train" (Dave Allen)
1993 "Lonesome Standard Time" (Larry Cordle—Jim Rushing)
1994 "Who Will Watch the Home Place" (Kate Long)
1995 "Cold Virginia Night" (Timmy Massey)
1996 "Mama's Hand" (Hazel Dickens)
1997 "High Lonesome Sound" (Vince Gill)

1998 "Lonesome Old Home" (Ed Hamilton)
1999 "Three Rusty Nails" (Ronnie Bowman—Terry Campbell—Jerry Nettuno)
2000 "Murder on Music Row" (Larry Cordle—Larry Shell)
2001 "I Am a Man of Constant Sorrow" (Dick Burnett; arr. Carter Stanley)
2002 "1952 Vincent Black Lightning" (Richard John Thompson)
2003 "Blue Train (of the Heartbreak Line)" (John D. Loudermilk)
2004 "Kentucky Borderline" (Rhonda Vincent—Terry Herd)
2005 "Me and John and Paul" (Harley Allen)
2006 "Look Down That Lonesome Road" (Tim O'Brien)
2007 "Fork in the Road" (Chris Jones—John Pennell)
2008 "Through the Window of a Train" (Tim Stafford—Steve Gulley)
2009 "Don't Throw Mama's Flowers Away" (Chris Stuart—Ivan Rosenberg)
2010 "Ring the Bell" (Chet O'Keefe)

## Album of the Year
1990 *At the Old Schoolhouse*—The Johnson Mountain Boys (Rounder)
1991 *I've Got That Old Feeling*—Alison Krauss & Union Station (Rounder)
1992 *Carrying the Tradition*—The Lonesome River Band (Rebel)
1993 *Every Time You Say Goodbye*—Alison Krauss & Union Station (Rounder)
1994 *A Deeper Shade of Blue*—Del McCoury (Rounder)
1995 *Cold Virginia Night*—Ronnie Bowman (Rebel)
1996 *It's a Long, Long Road*—Blue Highway (Rebel)
1997 *True Life Blues: The Songs of Bill Monroe*—Sam Bush, Vassar Clements, Mike Compton, Jerry Douglas, Stuart Duncan, Pat Enright, Greg Garing, Richard Greene, David Grier, David Grisman, John Hartford, Bobby Hicks, Kathy Kallick, Laurie Lewis, Mike Marshall, Del McCoury, Ronnie McCoury, Jim Nunally, Scott Nygaard, Mollie O'Brien, Tim O'Brien, Alan O'Bryant, Herb Pedersen, Todd Phillips, John Reischman, Peter Rowan, Craig Smith, Chris Thile, Tony Trischka, Roland White (Sugar Hill)
1998 *Bluegrass Rules!*—Ricky Skaggs & Kentucky Thunder (Rounder/Skaggs Family)
1999 *Clinch Mountain Country*—Ralph Stanley & Friends (Rebel)
2000 *The Grass Is Blue*—Dolly Parton (Sugar Hill)
2001 *O Brother, Where Art Thou?* soundtrack—Norman Blake, James Carter & the Prisoners, The Cox Family, Fairfield Four, Emmylou Harris, John Hartford, Chris Thomas King, Alison Krauss, Harry McClintock, The Peasall Sisters, The Soggy Bottom Boys, Ralph Stanley, The Stanley Brothers, Gillian Welch, The Whites (Mercury/Lost Highway)
2002 *Down from the Mountain*—Fairfield Four, John Hartford, Alison Krauss & Union Station, Dan Tyminski, The Cox Family, Gillian Welch, David Rawlings, The Whites, Chris Thomas King with Colin Linden, Emmylou Harris (Lost Highway)
2003 *Alison Krauss & Union Station Live*—Alison Krauss & Union Station (Rounder)
2004 *It's Just the Night*—The Del McCoury Band (McCoury Music)

## Album of the Year (continued)

2005 *40*—Larry Sparks (Rebel)
2006 *Celebration of Life: Musicians Against Childhood Cancer*— Various Artists (Skaggs Family)
2007 (tie) *Fork in the Road*—The Infamous Stringdusters (Sugar Hill)
 *Lefty's Old Guitar*—J.D. Crowe & the New South (Rounder)
2008 *Dailey & Vincent*—Dailey & Vincent (Rounder)
2009 *Wheels*—Dan Tyminski (Rounder)
2010 *Dailey & Vincent Sing the Statler Brothers*—Dailey & Vincent (Cracker Barrel/Rounder)

## Instrumental Recorded Performance of the Year
(formally Instrumental Album of the Year)

1990 *The Masters*—Eddie Adcock, Kenny Baker, Josh Graves, and Jesse McReynolds; (CMH)
1991 *Norman Blake & Tony Rice 2*—Norman Blake and Tony Rice (Rounder)
1992 *Slide Rule*—Jerry Douglas (Sugar Hill)
1993 *Stuart Duncan*—Stuart Duncan (Rounder)
1994 *Skip, Hop & Wobble*—Douglas, Barenberg, and Meyer (Sugar Hill)
1995 *The Great Dobro Sessions*—Mike Auldridge, Curtis Burch, Jerry Douglas, Josh Graves, Rob Ickes, Oswald Kirby, Stacy Phillips, Tut Taylor, Sally Van Meter, Gene Wooten (Sugar Hill)
1996 *Ronnie & Rob McCoury*—Ronnie and Rob McCoury (Rounder)
1997 *Bluegrass Instrumentals, Volume 6*—The Bluegrass Album Band (Rounder)
1998 *Fiddle Patch*—Bobby Hicks (Rounder)
1999 *Bound to Ride*—Jim Mills (Sugar Hill)
2000 *Bluegrass Mandolin Extravaganza*—David Grisman, Ronnie McCoury, Sam Bush, Frank Wakefield, Bobby Osborne, Jesse McReynolds, Ricky Skaggs, Buck White (Acoustic Disc)
2001 *Knee Deep in Bluegrass: The AcuTab Sessions*—Barry Bales, Butch Baldassari, Terry Baucom, Wayne Benson, Alan Bibey, Ronnie Bowman, Rob Ickes, Jason Moore, Joe Mullins, Alan Munde, Mark Newton, Alan O'Bryant, Sammy Shelor, Kenny Smith, Tim Stafford, Adam Steffey, Ron Stewart, Tony Trischka, Dan Tyminski, Scott Vestal, Pete Wernick (Rebel Records)
2002 *Flame Keeper*—Michael Cleveland (Rounder)
2003 *The Bluegrass Fiddle Album*—Aubrey Haynie (Sugar Hill)
2004 *Live at the Ragged Edge*—Tom Adams and Michael Cleveland (Rounder)
2005 *Slide Effects*—Phil Leadbetter (Pinecastle)
2006 *Let 'Er Go Boys*—Michael Cleveland (Rounder)
2007 *Double Banjo Bluegrass Spectacular*—Tony Trischka (Rounder)
2008 *Sound of the Slide Guitar*—Andy Hall (Sugar Hill)
2009 *"Jerusalem Ridge"*—Michael Cleveland & Flamekeeper (Rounder)
2010 *"Durang's Hornpipe"*—Adam Steffey (Sugar Hill)

## Recorded Event of the Year

1990 *Classic Country Gents Reunion*—John Duffey, Charlie Waller, Eddie Adcock, Tom Gray (Sugar Hill)
1991 *Families of Tradition*—Don Parmley, David Parmley, Del McCoury, Ronnie McCoury (BGC)

1992 *Slide Rule*—Jerry Douglas (Sugar Hill)
1993 *Saturday Night & Sunday Morning*—Ralph Stanley and special guests (Freeland)
1994 *A Touch of the Past*—Larry Perkins & Friends (Pinecastle)
1995 *The Great Dobro Sessions*—Mike Auldridge, Curtis Burch, Jerry Douglas, Josh Graves, Rob Ickes, Oswald Kirby, Stacy Phillips, Tut Taylor, Sally Van Meter, Gene Wooten (Sugar Hill)
1996 *Bluegrass '95*—Scott Vestal, Aubrey Haynie, Adam Steffey, Wayne Benson, Barry Bales, Clay Jones (Pinecastle)
1997 *True Life Blues: The Songs of Bill Monroe*—Sam Bush, Vassar Clements, Mike Compton, Jerry Douglas, Stuart Duncan, Pat Enright, Greg Garing, Richard Greene, David Grier, David Grisman, John Hartford, Bobby Hicks, Kathy Kallick, Laurie Lewis, Mike Marshall, Del McCoury, Ronnie McCoury, Jim Nunally, Scott Nygaard, Mollie O'Brien, Tim O'Brien, Alan O'Bryant, Herb Pedersen, Todd Phillips, John Reischman, Peter Rowan, Craig Smith, Chris Thile, Tony Trischka, Roland White (Sugar Hill)
1998 *Longview*—Longview (Rounder)
1999 *Clinch Mountain Country*—Ralph Stanley & Friends (Rebel)
2000 *Bluegrass Mandolin Extravaganza*—David Grisman, Ronnie McCoury, Sam Bush, Frank Wakefield, Bobby Osborne, Jesse McReynolds, Ricky Skaggs, Buck White (Acoustic Disc)
2001 *Follow Me Back to the Fold: A Tribute to Women in Bluegrass*—Mark Newton with Gloria Belle, Dale Ann Bradley, Louisa Branscomb, Gene Britt, Kathy Chiavola, Kim & Barb Fox, Sally Jones, Laurie Lewis, Claire Lynch, Lynn Morris, Missy Raines, Kristin Scott, Valerie Smith, Rhonda Vincent, Sharon and Cheryl White (Rebel)
2002 *Clinch Mountain Sweethearts*—Ralph Stanley & Friends: Iris DeMent, Pam Tillis, Patty Mitchell, Gillian Welch, Dolly Parton, Maria Muldaur, Sara Evans, Joan Baez, Kristi Stanley, Gail Davies, Chely Wright, Melba Montgomery, Jeannie Seely, Lucinda Williams, Valerie Smith (Rebel)
2003 *Will The Circle Be Unbroken Vol. III*—Nitty Gritty Dirt Band, Matraca Berg, Sam Bush, June Carter Cash, Johnny Cash, Vassar Clements, Iris DeMent, Rodney Dillard, Jerry Douglas, Glen Duncan, Vince Gill, Josh Graves, Jamie Hanna, Emmylou Harris, Taj Mahal, Jimmy Martin, Del McCoury, Robbie McCoury, Ronnie McCoury, Jonathan McEuen, Nashville Bluegrass Band, Willie Nelson, Tom Petty, Tony Rice, Earl Scruggs, Randy Scruggs, Ricky Skaggs, Doc Watson, Richard Watson, Glenn Worf, Dwight Yoakam (Capitol)
2004 *Livin', Lovin', Losin': Songs of the Louvin Brothers*—Joe Nichols, Rhonda Vincent, Emmylou Harris, Rodney Crowell, James Taylor, Alison Krauss, Vince Gill, Terri Clark, Merle Haggard, Carl Jackson, Ronnie Dunn, Rebecca Lynn Howard, Glen Campbell, Leslie Satcher, Kathy Louvin, Pamela Brown Hayes, Linda Ronstadt, Patty Loveless, Jon Randall, Harley Allen, Dierks Bentley, Larry Cordle, Jerry Salley, Dolly Parton, Sonya Isaacs, Marty Stuart, Del McCoury, Pam

Tillis, Johnny Cash, the Jordanaires (Universal South)
2005 *40*—Larry Sparks (Rebel)
2006 *Back to the Well*—The Daughters of Bluegrass featuring Lorraine Jordan, Gena Britt, Julie Elkins, Becky Buller, Vickie Simmons, Frances Mooney, Mindy Rakestraw, Jeanette Williams, Beth Lawrence, Angela Oudean, Michelle Nixon, Donica Christensen, Dale Ann Bradley, Heather Berry, Megan McCormick, Valerie Smith, Louisa Branscomb, Dixie Hall (Blue Circle)
2007 *Double Banjo Bluegrass Spectacular*—Tony Trischka with Earl Scruggs, Kenny Ingram, Tom Adams, Béla Fleck, Noam Pikelny, Alison Brown, Scott Vestal, Steve Martin, Bill Emerson (2007)
2008 *Everett Lilly & Everybody and Their Brother*—Everett Lilly, Bea Lilly, Charles Lilly, Daniel Lilly, Mark Lilly, Marty Stuart, Rhonda Vincent, Billy Walker, Ronnie McCoury, Rob McCoury, David Ball, Charlie Cushman, Larry Stephenson, Joe Spivey, Eddie Stubbs, Jason Carter, Dickey Lee, Freddie Weller, Mike Bub, Rad Lewis, Andy May, Darrin Vincent, Marcia Campbell, Clay Rigdon, Eric Blankenship, Bill Wolfenbarger (Swift River)
2009 *"Proud to Be a Daughter of Bluegrass"*—Daughters of Bluegrass featuring Dale Ann Bradley, Heather Berry, Lisa Martin, Gloria Belle, Sierra Hull, Rhonda Vincent, Lisa Ray, Linda Lay, Sally Jones, Jeanie Stanley, Carol Lee Cooper, Sonya Isaacs, Becky Isaacs Bowman, Michelle Nixon, Jeanette Williams, Sophie Haislip, Louise Tomberlain, Mindy Rakestraw, Lizzy Long, Frances Mooney, Lorraine Jordan, Annette Kelley, Lilly Lieux, Dixie Hall, Judi Marshall, Melissa Lawrence, Beth Lawrence, Rebecca Frazier, Donica Christensen, Lisa Manning, Jenni Lyn Gardner (Blue Circle)
2010 *"Give This Message to Your Heart,"* Larry Stephenson featuring Dailey & Vincent (Whysper Dream)

## Gospel Recorded Performance of the Year

1995 *One Beautiful Day*—Front Range (Sugar Hill)
1996 *There's A Light Guiding Me*—Doyle Lawson & Quicksilver (Sugar Hill)
1997 *"God Moves in a Windstorm"*—Blue Highway (Rebel)
1998 *Stanley Gospel Tradition: Songs About Our Savior*—Tim Austin, Barry Bales, Ronnie Bowman, Aubrey Haynie, James King, Dwight McCall, Dale Perry, Don Rigsby, James Alan Shelton, Junior Sisk, Charlie Sizemore, Craig Smith, Scottie Sparks, Adam Steffey, Ernie Thacker, Dan Tyminski (Doobie Shea)
1999 *"Three Rusty Nails"*—Ronnie Bowman (Sugar Hill)
2000 *Winding Through Life*—Doyle Lawson & Quicksilver (Sugar Hill)
2001 *"I'll Fly Away"*—Alison Krauss & Gillian Welch (Mercury/Lost Highway)
2002 *The Journey*—Mountain Heart (Doobie Shea)
2003 *"The Hand Made Cross"*—Doyle Lawson & Quicksilver (Sugar Hill)
2004 *Wondrous Love*—Blue Highway (Rounder)
2005 *"Praise His Name"*—Doyle Lawson & Quicksilver (Crossroads)
2006 *He Lives in Me*—Doyle Lawson & Quicksilver (Horizon)

## Gospel Recorded Performance of the Year
(*continued*)
2007 "He Lives in Me"—Doyle Lawson &
 Quicksilver (Horizon)
2008 "By the Mark"—Dailey & Vincent
 (Rounder)
2009 "On the Other Side"—Dailey & Vincent
 (Rounder)
2010 "Ring the Bell"—the Gibson Brothers

## Emerging Artist of the Year
1994 Lou Reid, Terry Baucom & Carolina
1995 Parmley, Vestal, & Continental Divide
1996 Blue Highway
1997 The James King Band
1998 The Gibson Brothers
1999 Mountain Heart
2000 Nickel Creek
2001 Karl Shiflett & the Big Country Show
2002 The Chapmans
2003 Kenny & Amanda Smith
2004 King Wilkie
2005 The Grascals
2006 Steep Canyon Rangers
2007 The Infamous Stringdusters
2008 Dailey & Vincent
2009 The SteelDrivers
2010 Josh Williams

## Instrumental Performers of the Year
### Banjo
1990 Béla Fleck
1991 Alison Brown
1992 Tom Adams
1993 Tom Adams
1994 J. D. Crowe
1995 Sammy Shelor
1996 Scott Vestal
1997 Sammy Shelor
1998 Sammy Shelor
1999 Jim Mills
2000 Jim Mills
2001 Jim Mills
2002 Tom Adams
2003 Jim Mills
2004 J. D. Crowe
2005 Jim Mills
2006 Jim Mills
2007 Tony Trischka
2008 Kristin Scott-Benson
2009 Kristin Scott-Benson
2010 Kristin Scott-Benson

### Guitar
1990 Tony Rice
1991 Tony Rice
1992 David Grier
1993 David Grier
1994 Tony Rice
1995 David Grier
1996 Tony Rice
1997 Tony Rice
1998 Kenny Smith
1999 Kenny Smith
2000 Bryan Sutton
2001 Jim Hurst
2002 Jim Hurst
2003 Bryan Sutton
2004 Bryan Sutton
2005 Bryan Sutton
2006 Bryan Sutton
2007 Tony Rice
2008 Josh Williams
2009 Josh Williams
2010 Josh Williams

### Fiddle
1990 Stuart Duncan
1991 Stuart Duncan
1992 Stuart Duncan
1993 Stuart Duncan
1994 Stuart Duncan
1995 Stuart Duncan
1996 Stuart Duncan
1997 Jason Carter
1998 Jason Carter
1999 Randy Howard
2000 Ronnie Stewart
2001 Michael Cleveland
2002 Michael Cleveland
2003 Jason Carter
2004 Michael Cleveland
2005 Stuart Duncan
2006 Michael Cleveland
2007 Michael Cleveland
2008 Michael Cleveland
2009 Michael Cleveland
2010 Michael Cleveland

### Bass
1990 Roy Huskey Jr.
1991 Roy Huskey Jr.
1992 Roy Huskey Jr.
1993 Roy Huskey Jr.
1994 Mark Schatz
1995 Mark Schatz
1996 Mike Bub
1997 Mike Bub
1998 Missy Raines
1999 Missy Raines
2000 Missy Raines
2001 Missy Raines
2002 Mike Bub
2003 Mike Bub
2004 Missy Raines
2005 Mike Bub
2006 Missy Raines
2007 Missy Raines
2008 Barry Bales
2009 Marshall Wilborn
2010 Marshall Wilborn

### Dobro
1990 Jerry Douglas
1991 Jerry Douglas
1992 Jerry Douglas
1993 Jerry Douglas
1994 Jerry Douglas
1995 Jerry Douglas
1996 Rob Ickes
1997 Rob Ickes
1998 Rob Ickes
1999 Rob Ickes
2000 Rob Ickes
2001 Jerry Douglas
2002 Jerry Douglas
2003 Rob Ickes
2004 Rob Ickes
2005 Phil Leadbetter
2006 Rob Ickes
2007 Rob Ickes
2008 Rob Ickes
2009 Rob Ickes
2010 Rob Ickes

### Mandolin
1990 Sam Bush
1991 Sam Bush
1992 Sam Bush
1993 Ronnie McCoury
1994 Ronnie McCoury
1995 Ronnie McCoury
1996 Ronnie McCoury
1997 Ronnie McCoury
1998 Ronnie McCoury
1999 Ronnie McCoury
2000 Ronnie McCoury
2001 Chris Thile
2002 Adam Steffey
2003 Adam Steffey
2004 Adam Steffey
2005 Adam Steffey
2006 Adam Steffey
2007 Sam Bush
2008 Adam Steffey
2009 Jesse Brock
2010 Adam Steffey

## Bluegrass Event of the Year
1999 The 28th Walnut Valley Festival &
 National Flatpicking Championship;
 Winfield, Kansas; Bob Redford,
 producer
2000 The 34th Annual Bill Monroe Bean
 Blossom Bluegrass Festival; Bean
 Blossom, Indiana; Dwight Dillman,
 producer
2001 Huck Finn's Country & Bluegrass Jubilee
 2001; Victorville, California; Don V.
 Tucker, producer
2002 Down from the Mountain; multi-city
 tour; produced by T Bone Burnett,
 the Coen Brothers, and Immortal
 Entertainment
2003 European World of Bluegrass;
 Voorthuizen, The Netherlands; produced
 by the European Bluegrass Music
 Association
2004 California Bluegrass Association 28th
 Annual Fathers Day Bluegrass Festival;
 Grass Valley, California
2005 Wintergrass; Tacoma, Washington
2006 The Joe Val Bluegrass Festival;
 Framingham, Massachusetts; produced
 by the Boston Bluegrass Union;
 Framingham, Massachusetts
2007 33rd Festival of the Bluegrass; Lexington,
 Kentucky; produced by Bob & Jean
 Cornett, Lexington, Kentucky
2008 29th Annual Thomas Point Beach
 Bluegrass Festival; Brunswick, Maine;
 produced by Pati Crooker, Brunswick,
 Maine
2009 2008 Grey Fox Bluegrass Festival;
 Oak Hill, New York; produced by
 Mary Doub, Oak Hill, New York
2010 14th Annual Podunk Bluegrass Music
 Festival; East Hartford, Connecticut

## Distinguished Achievement Award Recipients
1986 Albert E. Brumley, Ray Davis, Bill
 Monroe, Ruby Baker Moody, Cuzin' Isaac
 Page, Dr. Neil V. Rosenberg
1987 Dewitt "Snuffy" Jenkins, Bill Jones,
 Don Owens, Ralph Rinzler,
 Charlie Waller
1988 John Duffey, Tom Henderson, Peter V.
 Kuykendall, Ola Belle Reed, Earl Scruggs,
 Bill Vernon
1989 Lester Flatt, David Freeman, Kathy
 Kaplan, Robert Larkin, Dr. Bill C.
 Malone
1990 Carlton Haney, Wade Mainer, Joe Stuart,
 Dr. Charles Wolfe
1991 Ralph Epperson, Don Stover, The Blue
 Sky Boys (Bill & Earl Bolick)
1992 The Louvin Brothers (Charlie & Ira), Bill
 Clifton, Lloyd Loar, Burkett "Uncle Josh"
 Graves
1993 Curly Ray Cline, Hazel Dickens, Jim
 Eanes, Charles Richard Freeland
1994 Wilma Lee Cooper, Lance LeRoy,
 Ken Irwin, Johnnie Wright &
 Jack Anglin
1995 Rose Maddox, Mike Seeger, Joe Val,
 Toshio & Saburo Watanabe
1996 Curly Seckler, George Shuffler, The
 Martha White Flour Company,
 G.B. Grayson

**Distinguished Achievement Award Recipients**
(*continued*)

1997 Mary Tyler Doub, Vern Williams & Ray Park, Kenny Baker, Benny Martin

1998 Ed Ferris, Barry Poss, Gary Henderson, Bob & Jean Cornett

1999 The Martin Guitar Company, Lee Moore, Carl Pagter, Gloria Belle

2000 The Stoneman Family, Paul Mullins, Rienk Janssen, WSM's Grand Ole Opry

2001 The Coen Brothers & T Bone Burnett, Alice Gerrard, The Gibson Company, John Hartford, Les Leverett

2002 Janette Carter, Pete Goble, The Lewis Family, Judith McCulloh, Tom Riggs

2003 Jack Cooke, Terry Lickona, Bob Turbanic, Fiddlin' Arthur Smith, The Station Inn

2004 Art Stamper, Kirk & Becky Brandenberger, Moses "Mo" Asch, Tom T. & Dixie Hall, Jimmie Skinner

2005 Margie & Enoch Sullivan, Joe Clayton, Craig Ferguson, The Dopyera Brothers, Terry Woodward

2006 Fred Bartenstein, The Boys From Indiana, Bill Grant, Ronnie Reno, The Whites

2007 Mike Auldridge, *The Bluegrass Breakdown*, Marko Cermak, Warren Hellman, Happy & Jane Traum

2008 Bill Harrell, *The Banjo Newsletter*, Art Menius, Joe Carr, Alan Munde

2009 Hylo Brown, Pati Crooker, Jody Rainwater, Dick Spottswood, Joe Wilson. Adam Steffey

2010 Benjamin "Tex" Logan, Sherry Boyd, Lynn Morris, Richard Weize, Pete Wernick

# Contributors

**Jonita Aadland**
Fiddle Player and Stage Show Producer

**Thomas A. Adler**
Folklorist and Journalist

**Bob Allen**
Author, *George Jones: The Saga of an American Singer*

**Scott Anderson**
Former Curatorial Assistant, Country Music Hall of Fame and Museum

**Fred Bartenstein**
Bluegrass Music Historian

**LeAnn Bennett**
Former Director of Special Projects, Country Music Hall of Fame and Museum

**Jack Bernhardt**
Anthropologist; Country Music Correspondent, Raleigh *News and Observer*

**Stephen L. Betts**
Deputy Editor, *The Boot*/AOL Music

**Rob Bowman**
Author, *Soulsville USA: The Story of Stax Records*; 1996 Grammy winner, Best Liner Notes

**Mick Buck**
Curator of Collections, Country Music Hall of Fame and Museum

**Mary A. Bufwack**
Coauthor, *Finding Her Voice: Women in Country Music, 1800–2000*

**Walter Carter**
Author, *The Songwriter's Guide to Collaboration* and other books; Historian, Gibson Guitar Company

**Joyce Cauthen**
Author, *With Fiddle and Well-Rosined Bow: A History of Old-Time Fiddling in Alabama*

**Dale Cockrell**
Author, *Demons of Disorder: Early Blackface Minstrels and Their World* and other books

**Kevin Coffey**
Journalist and Recording Annotator

**Norm Cohen**
Author, *Long Steel Rail: The Railroad in American Folksong*, and Recording Annotator

**Daniel Cooper**
Author, *Lefty Frizzell: The Honky-Tonk Life of Country Music's Greatest Singer*

**Peter Cooper**
Musician and Music Reporter, *The Tennessean*

**Al Cunniff**
Author, *Waylon Jennings*

**Don Cusic**
Professor of Music Business, Belmont University, and Author

**Wayne Daniel**
Author, *Pickin' on Peachtree: A History of Country Music in Atlanta, Georgia*

**Fred Danker**
Professor Emeritus, American Studies, University of Massachusetts, Boston

**William P. Davis**
Former Deputy Director of Collections and Research, Country Music Foundation

**Eddie Dean**
Coauthor, with Ralph Stanley, *Man of Constant Sorrow: My Life and Times* and other books

**Warren Denney**
Creative Director, Country Music Hall of Fame and Museum

**Bryan Di Salvatore**
Author and Journalist

**Chrissie Dickinson**
Writer; Former Editor, *The Journal of Country Music*

**Steve Eng**
Author, *A Satisfied Mind: The Country Music Life of Porter Wagoner* and other books

**Colin Escott**
Author, *Hank Williams: The Biography* and other books

**Dennis Milton Estes**
Former Country Disc Jockey

**Marilyn Estes**
Freelance Writer

**Bill Evans**
Bluegrass Musician and Teacher

**Todd Everett**
Author and Music Journalist

**Tom Ewing**
Former Blue Grass Boy and Editor, *The Bill Monroe Reader*

**Mark Fenster**
Professor, University of Florida, and Author

**Kim Field**
Author, *Harmonicas, Harps, and Heavy Breathers*

**Chet Flippo**
Author, *Your Cheatin' Heart: A Biography of Hank Williams* and other books

**Ben Fong-Torres**
Journalist and Author, *Hickory Wind: The Life and Times of Gram Parsons* and other books

**Gene Fowler**
Author, *Border Radio* and other books

**Jon Hartley Fox**
Author, *King of the Queen City: The Story of King Records*

**Bill Friskics-Warren**
Music Journalist and Coauthor, *Heartaches by the Number: Country Music's 500 Greatest Singles*

**Holly George-Warren**
Author, *Public Cowboy No. 1: The Life and Times of Gene Autry* and other books

**Calvin Gilbert**
Managing Editor, CMT.com/CMT News at CMT: Country Music Television

**Cary Ginell**
Author, *Milton Brown and the Founding of Western Swing*

**Frank Godbey**
Bluegrass Musician and Journalist

**Marty Godbey**
Author and Journalist

**Thomas Goldsmith**
Editor, *The Bluegrass Reader*; former Music Writer and City Editor, *The Tennessean*

**John Gouge**
Special Projects Coordinator, Country Music Hall of Fame and Museum

**Michael Gray**
Museum Editor, Country Music Hall of Fame and Museum; 2004 Grammy Winner, Best Historical Album

**Archie Green**
Author, *Only a Miner: Studies in Recorded Coal-Mining Songs* and other books

**Douglas B. Green**
Founding Member, Riders in the Sky; Author, *Singing in the Saddle: The History of the Singing Cowboy*

**Sid Griffin**
Author, *Shelter from the Storm: Bob Dylan's Rolling Thunder Years* and other books

**Ken Griffis**
Author and Music Historian

**Jimmy Guterman**
Author, *12 Days on the Road* and other books

**Patricia Hall**
Author and Folklore Consultant

**Wade Hall**
Author, *Hell-Bent for Music: The Life of Pee Wee King*

**Steve Hathaway**
Music Researcher and Radio Programmer, westernswing.com

**Craig Havighurst**
Author, *Air Castle of the South: WSM and the Making of Music City*; former Music Writer, *The Tennessean*

**Kent Henderson**
Music Historian

**Michael Hight**
Music Journalist/Publisher

**Geoffrey Himes**
Music Journalist

**Fred Hoeptner**
Music Writer

**Elek Horvath**
Registrar, Country Music Hall of Fame and Museum, and Coauthor, *Hatch Show Print: The History of a Great American Poster Shop*

**Mark Humphrey**
Music Journalist

**Bill Ivey**
Director, Mike Curb Center for Art, Enterprise, and Public Policy, Vanderbilt University

**Loyal Jones**
Author, *Country Music Humorists and Comedians* and other books

**Margaret Jones**
Author, *Patsy: The Life and Times of Patsy Cline*

**Beverly Keel**
Professor of Recording Industry, Middle Tennessee State University, and Music Journalist

**Rich Kienzle**
Author, *Southwest Shuffle: Pioneers of Honky Tonk, Western Swing, and Country Jazz*; Recording Annotator and Producer

**Paul Kingsbury**
Editor-in-Chief, first edition, *The Encyclopedia of Country Music*; Former Deputy Director of Special Projects, Country Music Hall of Fame and Museum

**Burt Korall**
Author, *Drummin' Men: The Heartbeat of Jazz*

**Robert Kramer**
Country Music Hall of Fame and Museum, American Federation of Musicians Local #257, Pedal Steel Guitarist

**William E. Lightfoot**
Professor Emeritus, Department of English, Appalachian State University

**John Lilly**
Editor, *Goldenseal: West Virginia Traditional Life*

**Pete Loesch**
Record Collector and Recording Annotator

**Guy Logsdon**
Author, *"The Whorehouse Bells Were Ringing" and Other Songs Cowboys Sing*

**John Lomax III**
Author, *Nashville: Music City USA*; Columnist, *Country Update* and *Country Music People*

**Bill C. Malone**
Author, *Country Music U.S.A.* and other books

**Michael Manning**
Digital Marketing Coordinator, Country Music Hall of Fame and Museum

**Brian Mansfield**
Nashville Correspondent, *USA Today*; writer/producer, *America's Opry Weekend*

**Greil Marcus**
Author, *Mystery Train: Images of America in Rock 'n' Roll Music* and other books

**Barry Mazor**
Author, *Meeting Jimmie Rodgers: How America's Original Roots Music Hero Changed the Pop Sounds of a Century*

**Michael McCall**
Writer/Editor, Country Music Hall of Fame and Museum, and Music Journalist

**Brad McCuen**
Former Executive, RCA Records

**Marjie McGraw**
Music Journalist and Author, *The Great American Country Music Trivia Book* and other books

**Don McLeese**
Music Journalist and Associate Professor of Journalism, University of Iowa

**W. K. McNeil**
Author, *Southern Folk Ballads* and other books

**Bob Millard**
Author, *The Judds: A Biography* and other books

**Rick Mitchell**
Co-author, with Johnny Bush, *Whiskey River (Take My Mind): The True Story of Texas Honky Tonk*

**Toru Mitsui**
Author, *The Story of "You Are My Sunshine"* and other books

**Tom Morgan**
Musician and Journalist

**David C. Morton**
Coauthor, *DeFord Bailey: A Black Star in Early Country Music*

**Robert K. Oermann**
Music Journalist and Coauthor, *Finding Her Voice: Women in Country Music, 1800–2000*

**Bob Olson**
Record Collector and Discographer

**Ted Olson**
Author, *Blue Ridge Folklife*; Editor, *Journal of Appalachian Studies*

**Jay Orr**
Vice President for Museum Programs, Country Music Hall of Fame and Museum

**Clark Parsons**
Director, Berlin School of Creative Leadership, Berlin, Germany; Former Editor, *Nashville Life*

**Bob Paxman**
Entertainment Journalist; Senior Writer, *Country Weekly* magazine

**Diane Pecknold**
Author, *The Selling Sound: The Rise of the Country Music Industry*

**Bob Pinson**
Former Senior Researcher, Country Music Foundation

**Nolan Porterfield**
Author, *Jimmie Rodgers: The Life and Times of America's Blue Yodeler*

**Barbara Pruett**
Author, *Marty Robbins: Fast Cars and Country Music*

**Ronnie Pugh**
Author, *Ernest Tubb: The Texas Troubadour*

**Gary B. Reid**
Bluegrass Music Historian and Producer

**Don Rhodes**
Music Journalist

**Harry S. Rice**
Sound Archivist, Hutchins Library, Berea College, Berea, Kentucky

**Jim Ridley**
Editor, *Nashville Scene*

**Tom Roland**
Music Journalist and Owner, Rolandnote.com, the Ultimate Country Music Database

**David Romtvedt**
Poet Laureate of Wyoming and Author, *Powder River Breaks: A Cowboy's Introduction to American Poetry* and other books

**Kinney Rorrer**
Author, *Rambling Blues: The Life and Songs of Charlie Poole*

**Neil V. Rosenberg**
Author, *Bluegrass: A History* and other books

**David Ross**
CEO, *Music Row* magazine

**Don Roy**
Music Historian and Recording Annotator

**John W. Rumble**
Senior Historian, Country Music Hall of Fame and Museum

**Jeremy Rush**
Former Media Relations Manager, Country Music Hall of Fame and Museum

**Tony Russell**
Author, *Country Music Records: A Discography, 1921–1942*

**Dave Samuelson**
Music Historian and Recording Annotator

**Ben Sandmel**
Drummer, Hackberry Ramblers, and Folklore Researcher

**Walter V. Saunders**
Columnist, *Bluegrass Unlimited Magazine*

**Ann Allen Savoy**
Compiler and Editor, *Cajun Music: A Reflection of a People*

**Tony Scherman**
Author, *Backbeat: Earl Palmer's Story*

**Mark Schone**
Former Senior Contributing Writer, *SPIN* magazine; Managing Editor, ABC News Investigative Unit

**Charlie Seemann**
Director, Western Folklife Center, Elko, Utah

**Jon Sievert**
Author, *Concert Photography: How to Shoot and Sell Music-Business Photographs*

**Chris Skinker**
Music Journalist and Recording Annotator

**Jonathan Guyot Smith**
Music Historian and Recording Annotator

**Richard D. Smith**
Author, *Can't You Year Me Callin': The Life of Bill Monroe, Father of Bluegrass*

**Willie Smyth**
Director, Folk Arts Program, Washington State
Arts Commission

**Paul W. Soelberg**
Freelance Writer

**Joe W. Specht**
Music Historian and Collection Manager,
Grady McWhiney Research Foundation,
Abilene, Texas

**Dick Spottswood**
Author, *Ethnic Music on Records*

**Michael Streissguth**
Author, *Eddy Arnold: Pioneer of the Nashville
Sound* and other books

**Eddie Stubbs**
Announcer, WSM and the Grand Ole Opry, and
Fiddle Player

**Cecelia Tichi**
Author, *High Lonesome: The American Culture
of Country Music* and other books

**Jim Bob Tinsley**
Author, *He Was Singin' This Song*

**Charles R. Townsend**
Author, *San Antonio Rose: The Life and Music of
Bob Wills*

**Ivan M. Tribe**
Author, *Mountain Jamboree: Country Music in
West Virginia* and other books

**Walt Trott**
Former Editor, *The Nashville Musician* and
Author, *Sister Sunshine: Martha Carson* and
other books

**Stephen R. Tucker**
Historian and Journalist

**Ben Vaughn**
Recording Artist and Record Producer

**Dale Vinicur**
Coauthor, *Still in Love with You: The Story of
Hank and Audrey Williams*

**Paul F. Wells**
Former Director, Center for Popular Music,
Middle Tennessee State University

**Jon Weisberger**
Journalist and Bluegrass Musician

**Jonny Whiteside**
Author, *Ramblin' Rose: The Life and Career of
Rose Maddox*

**Gene Wiggins**
Author, *Fiddlin' Georgia Crazy: Fiddlin' John
Carson, His Real World, and the World of
His Songs*

**Janet E. Williams**
Author and Music Journalist

**Chris Willman**
Author, *Rednecks & Bluenecks: The Politics
of Country Music*

**Charles R. Wolfe**
Author, *The Devil's Box: Masters of Southern
Fiddling* and other books

**Stacey Wolfe**
Instructor, Middle Tennessee State
University

**Gerry Wood**
Former Editor in Chief, *Billboard* magazine

**Tina Wright**
Director of Media Relations, Country Music
Hall of Fame and Museum, and Author

**Marshall Wyatt**
Producer and Annotator, Old Hat Records

**Laurence Zwisohn**
Author, *Loretta Lynn's World of Music*